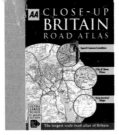

C000099640

Atlas conter

Map pages south	inside front cover

Route planning	**2–23**
Route planner	2–7
Useful motoring websites	8
Speed cameras	9–17
Avoiding congestion	18–23

Atlas symbols	**1**

Road maps	**2–609**

Britain at 1:100,000 scale

2–475, 480–503, 510–515, 526–529, 538–541, 554–561

Isles of Scilly 1:150,000 scale	3
Channel Islands 1:150,000 scale	34–35
Isle of Man 1:190,000 scale	322
Islay & Jura 1:150,000 scale	476–479
Mull, Tiree & Coll 1:150,000 scale	504–505, 516–518
Scottish Highlands 1:150,000 scale	
	506–509, 518–525, 531–537, 546–553, 562–589
Sky & Small Isles 1:150,000 scale	530, 542–545
Western Isles 1:150,000 scale	590–599
Orkney & Shetland Islands 1:150,000 scale	600–609

Ferry Ports				**11–561**	
Aberdeen Harbour	561	Heysham Harbour	350	Port of Southampton	36
Calais/Coquelles		Holyhead Harbour	302	Port of Tyne	407
Terminal	83	Hull Port	349	Rosyth Harbour	489
Dover Port	83	Newhaven Harbour	56	Stranraer Ferry Port	414
Fishguard Harbour	150	Plymouth Ferry Port	11	Swansea Harbour	103
Folkestone Terminal	82	Poole Harbour	35	Weymouth Harbour	33
Harwich Int. Port	177	Portsmouth Harbour	37		

Restricted junctions	**610–611**

Central London	**612–624**
Central London 1:10,000 scale	612–619

Central London street index	620–624

Town and airport plans	**625–651**
Aberdeen	625
Aberystwyth	204
Bath	625
Birmingham	627
Birmingham Airport	651
Blackpool	336
Bournemouth	626
Bradford	626
Brighton	55
Bristol	628
Brixham	13
Cambridge	629
Cardiff	628
Cheltenham	630
Coventry	630
Derby	631
Dover	631
Dundee	515
Durham	632
Edinburgh	633
Gatwick Airport	650
Glasgow	634
Glasgow Airport	651
Heathrow Airport	650
Inverness	632
Kingston upon Hull	635
Lancaster	350
Leeds	636
Leeds Bradford	
Airport	651
Leicester	635
Liverpool	637
Llandudno	306
London Central	612–619
Luton Airport	650
Manchester	638
Manchester Airport	651
Middlesbrough	397
Milton Keynes	639
Newcastle	
upon Tyne	640
Newquay	6
Norwich	641
Nottingham	641
Oxford	642
Paignton	21
Plymouth	10
Portsmouth	643
St Andrews	503
Scarborough	375
Sheffield	645
Southend-on-Sea	123
Southampton	644
Stansted Airport	650
Stockton-on-Tees	645
Stoke-on-Trent	
(Hanley)	646
Stratford-upon-Avon	646
Sunderland	407
Swansea	647
Swindon	647
Torquay	21
Tunbridge Wells	648
Wolverhampton	648
Worcester	649
York	649

Gazetteer of map entries & Distance chart	**652–728**
Using the National Grid	652
County, administrative area map	653
Recreation and leisure index	654–668
City, town and village index	669–727
Distance chart	728

Map pages north	inside back cover

1st edition October 2006

© Automobile Association Developments Limited 2006

Ordnance Survey This product includes mapping data licensed from Ordnance Survey® with the permission of the Controller of Her Majesty's Stationery Office. © Crown copyright 2006. All rights reserved. Licence number 399221.

© Crown copyright 2006. Permit No. 60029.

All rights reserved. No part of this publication may be reproduced, stored in a retrieval system, or transmitted in any form or by any means – electronic, mechanical, photocopying, recording or otherwise – unless the permission of the publisher has been given beforehand.

Published by AA Publishing (a trading name of Automobile Association Developments Limited, whose registered office is Fanum House, Basing View, Basingstoke, Hampshire RG21 4EA, UK. Registered number 1878835).

Mapping produced by the Mapping Services Department of The Automobile Association (A02720b).

ISBN-10: 0 7495 4985 8
ISBN-13: 978 0 7495 4985 5

A CIP catalogue record for this book is available from The British Library.

Printed in Portugal by Grafiasa Industria Grafica SA, Porto.

The contents of this atlas are believed to be correct at the time of the latest revision, it will not contain any subsequent amended, new or temporary information including diversions and traffic control or enforcement systems. The publishers cannot be held responsible or liable for any loss or damage occasioned to any person acting or refraining from action as a result of any use or reliance on material in this atlas, nor for any errors, omissions or changes in such material. This does not affect your statutory rights. The publishers would welcome information to correct any errors or omissions and to keep this atlas up to date. Please write to the Atlas Editor, AA Publishing, The Automobile Association, Fanum House, Basing View, Basingstoke, Hampshire RG21 4EA, UK. **E-mail: roadatlasfeedback@theaa.com**

A&E hospitals derived from data supplied by Johnsons.

Petrol station information supplied by Johnsons.

Information on National Parks in England provided by The Countryside Agency.

Information on National Nature Reserves in England provided by English Nature.

Information on National Parks, National Scenic Areas and National Nature Reserves in Scotland provided by Scottish Natural Heritage.

Information on National Parks and National Nature Reserves in Wales provided by The Countryside Council for Wales.

Information on Forest Parks provided by the Forestry Commission.

The RSPB sites shown are a selection chosen by the Royal Society for the Protection of Birds.

National Trust properties shown are a selection of those open to the public as indicated in the handbooks of the National Trust and the National Trust for Scotland.

National Cycle Network information supplied by Sustrans Limited www.sustrans.org.uk 0845 113 0065.

Marina information supplied courtesy of Noble Marine (Insurance Brokers) Ltd. www.noblemarine.co.uk

Crematoria data provided by The Cremation Society of Great Britain.

Information on fixed speed camera locations provided by Origin technologies.

Central London mapping in this atlas produced by the Mapping Services Department of The Automobile Association. Schools address data provided by Education Direct. One-way street data provided by © Tele Atlas N.V. The Post Office is a registered trademark of Post Office Ltd in the UK and other countries. The boundary of the London Congestion Charging Zone supplied by Transport for London.

Channel Islands update information supplied by David Moran.

Tram and Metro system logos used by kind permission of Nottingham Express Transit, Midland Metro, Metrolink (Manchester), Tyne & Wear Metro and Subway (Glasgow).

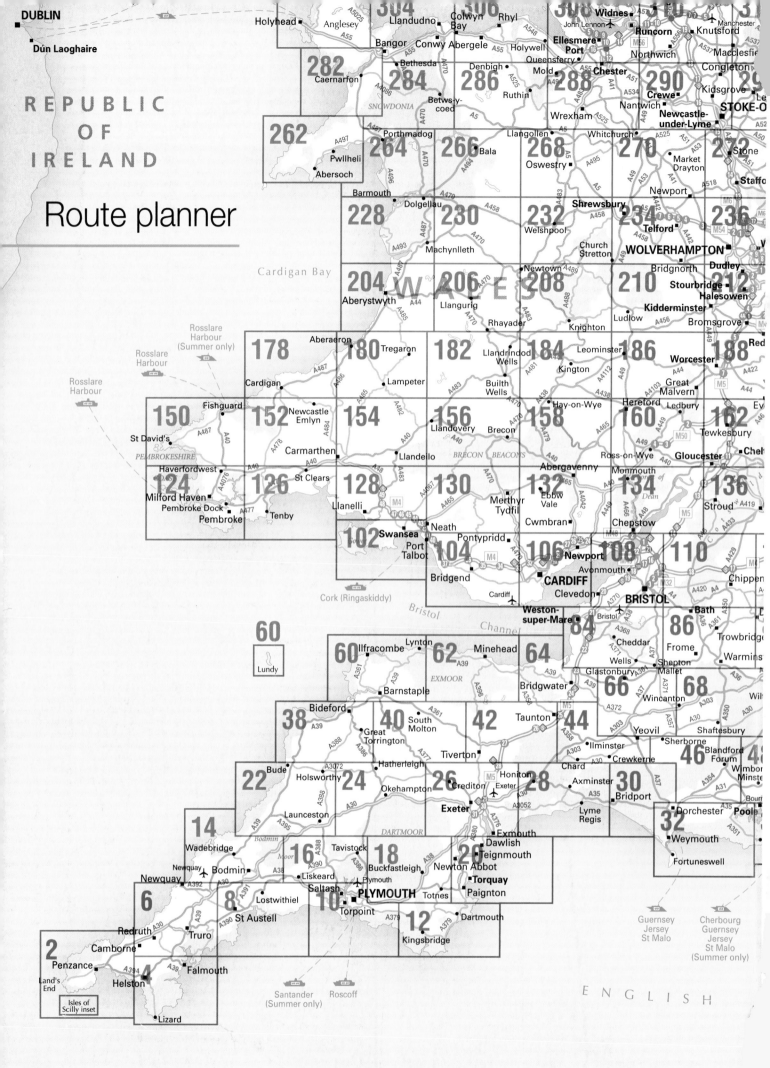

Route planner

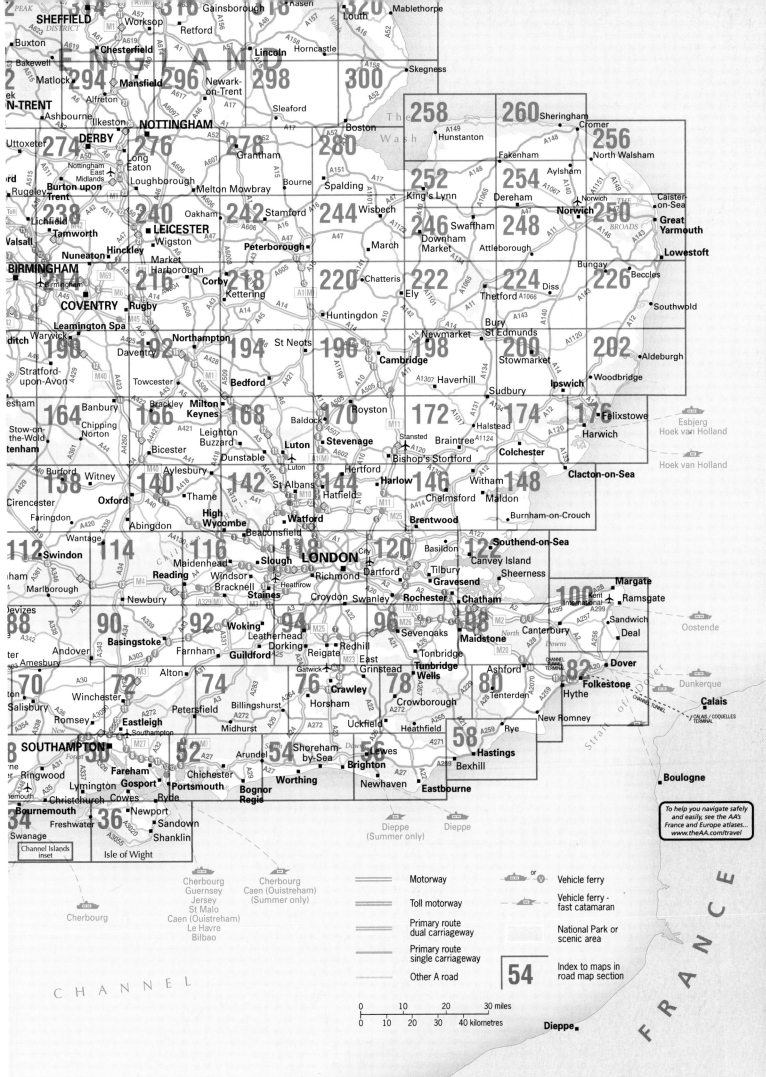

Motorway

Toll motorway

Primary route
dual carriageway

Primary route
single carriageway

Other A road

Vehicle ferry

Vehicle ferry -
fast catamaran

National Park or
scenic area

54 Index to maps in
road map section

To help you navigate safely
and easily, see the AA's
France and Europe atlases...
www.theAA.com/travel

0   10   20   30 miles
0 10 20 30 40 kilometres

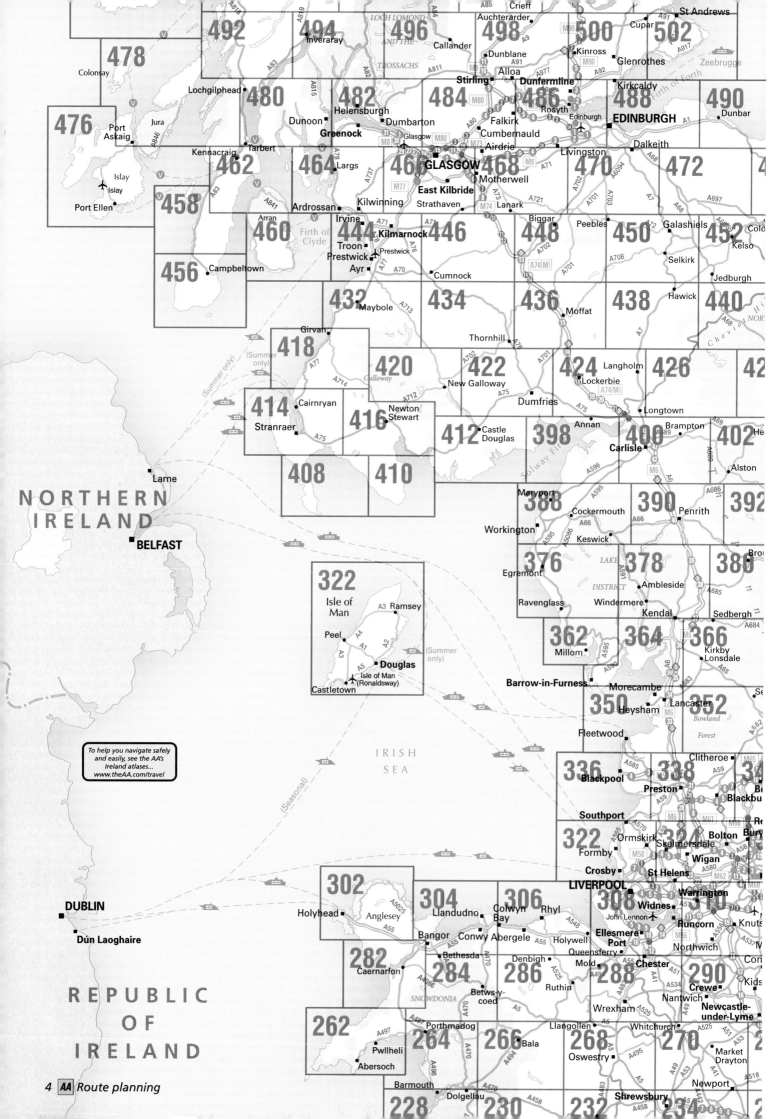

492 494 496 498 500 502

478

480 482 484 486 488 490

476

462 464 466 468 470 472

458

460 444 446 448 450 452

456

432 434 436 438 440

418 420 422 424 426 42

414 416 412 398 400 402

408 410 388 390 392

376 378 380

362 364 366

350 352

336 338 34

NORTHERN
IRELAND

BELFAST

322
Isle of
Man

322
324

302 304 306 308 310

DUBLIN

282 284 286 288 290

REPUBLIC
OF
IRELAND

262 264 266 268 270

228 230 232 234

To help you navigate safely
and easily, see the AA's
Ireland atlases...
www.theAA.com/travel

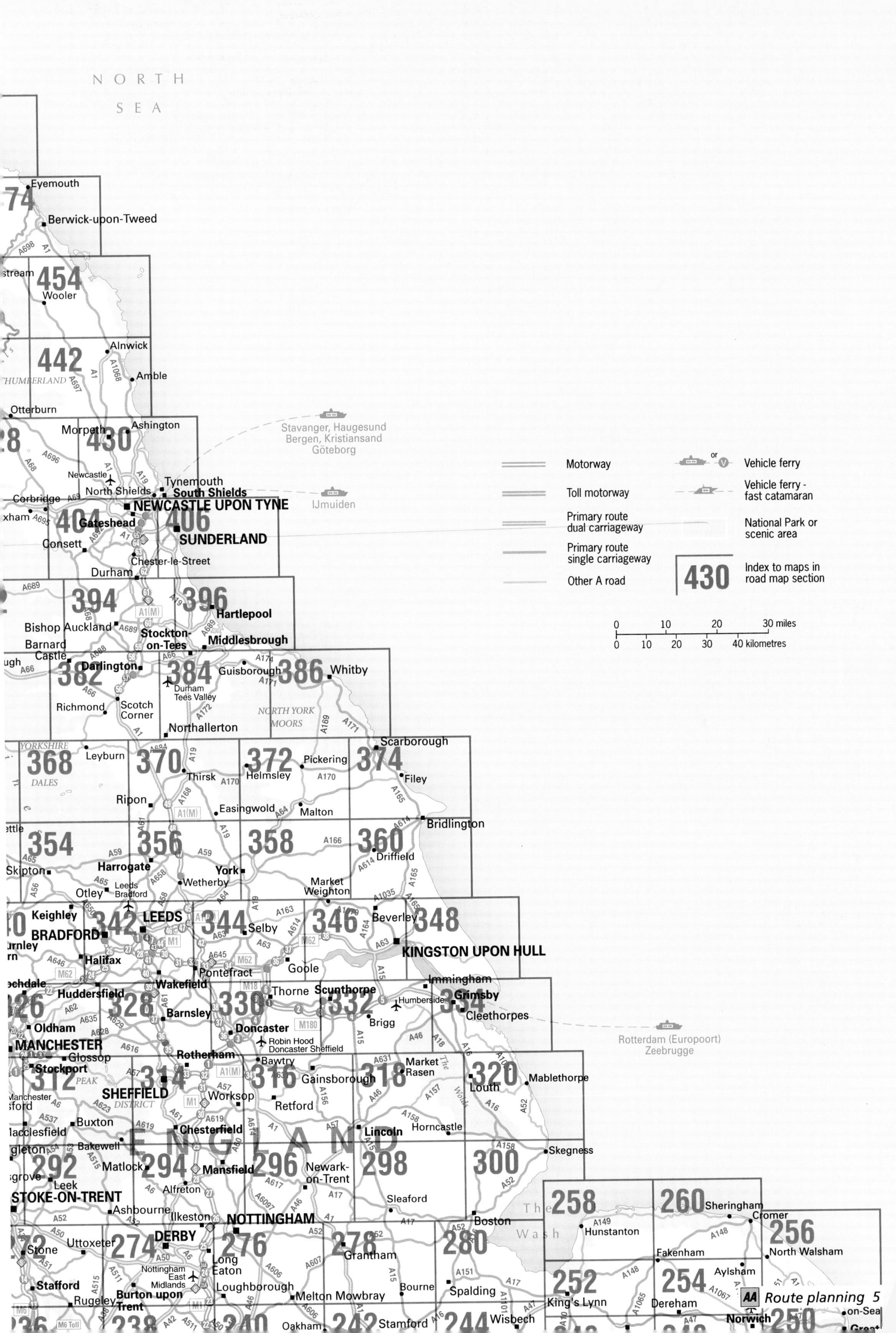

NORTH SEA

Legend

Motorway		Vehicle ferry	
Toll motorway		Vehicle ferry - fast catamaran	
Primary route dual carriageway		National Park or scenic area	
Primary route single carriageway			
Other A road		**430** Index to maps in road map section	

Scale:
0   10   20   30 miles
0   10   20   30   40 kilometres

Place names and map index numbers:

Eyemouth
Berwick-upon-Tweed
74
Coldstream
Wooler
454
A698
A697
A1
Alnwick
Amble
442
NORTHUMBERLAND
A697
A1
A1068
Otterburn
A696
Morpeth
Ashington
430
Newcastle
North Shields
Tynemouth
South Shields
Corbridge
A69
A19
NEWCASTLE UPON TYNE
Hexham
A695
404
Gateshead
406
SUNDERLAND
Consett
Chester-le-Street
Durham
A689
394
396
Bishop Auckland
A689
A1(M)
Hartlepool
Barnard Castle
Stockton-on-Tees
Middlesbrough
A66
A174
362
Darlington
A66
384
Guisborough
A171
386
Whitby
Richmond
Scotch Corner
Durham Tees Valley
A172
NORTH YORK MOORS
A169
A171
Northallerton
A1
YORKSHIRE DALES
Leyburn
A684
A19
368
370
Thirsk
A168
A170
372
Helmsley
A170
Pickering
374
Scarborough
Filey
Ripon
A65
A1(M)
Easingwold
A64
Malton
A165
Bridlington
Settle
354
356
A59
358
A166
360
Driffield
A614
A164
A165
Skipton
A65
Harrogate
A658
York
Market Weighton
Otley
Leeds Bradford
Wetherby
A64
A1035
Keighley
342
LEEDS
344
Selby
A163
346
Beverley
348
BRADFORD
A64
A614
A63
A164
Burnley
A646
Halifax
Pontefract
M62
Goole
A63
KINGSTON UPON HULL
Rochdale
M62
Huddersfield
Wakefield
M18
Thorne
Scunthorpe
Immingham
Humberside
326
328
Barnsley
330
A645
M180
Brigg
332
Grimsby
334
Cleethorpes
Oldham
A635
A628
Doncaster
Robin Hood Doncaster Sheffield
A46
A18
MANCHESTER
Glossop
A616
Baywtry
A15
A631
Market Rasen
A16
Rotterdam (Europoort) Zeebrugge
Stockport
PEAK
314
A1(M)
316
Gainsborough
A156
A46
A157
Louth
A16
Mablethorpe
312
SHEFFIELD
DISTRICT
A57
Worksop
Retford
A158
Horncastle
A52
Manchester
A6
M1
294
Mansfield
296
Newark-on-Trent
298
300
Skegness
Buxton
A619
Chesterfield
A619
Lincoln
A158
Macclesfield
Bakewell
A515
A6
ENGLAND
Matlock
A617
Sleaford
A52
Congleton
292
294
Mansfield
296
298
The Wash
258
Hunstanton
260
Sheringham
Leek
Alfreton
A6067
A46
A15
A149
Cromer
STOKE-ON-TRENT
Ashbourne
Ilkeston
NOTTINGHAM
Boston
A148
256
North Walsham
A52
272
Uttoxeter
274
DERBY
276
Long Eaton
278
Grantham
A52
280
A151
Bourne
Spalding
Fakenham
A148
Aylsham
A1067
254
Dereham
Stone
Nottingham East Midlands
Loughborough
Melton Mowbray
A606
A15
A17
King's Lynn
A10
A47
252
A148
Wisbech
Stafford
A511
Burton upon Trent
A42
M1
Oakham
Stamford
A47
244
Norwich
250
Rugeley
M6 Toll
238
240
242

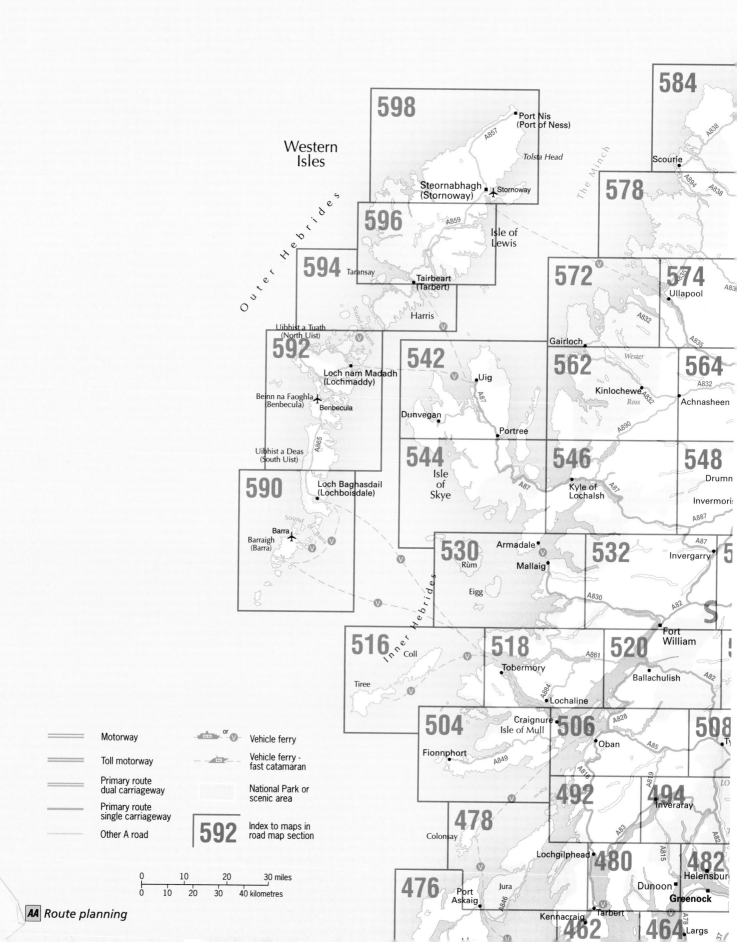

598

Western
Isles

Outer Hebrides

584

Scourie

A838

A857

Port Nis
(Port of Ness)

Tolsta Head

The Minch

578

A894

A838

Steornabhagh
(Stornoway) ■ Stornoway

596

A859

Isle of
Lewis

594

Taransay

572

574

Ullapool

A835

A832

Tairbeart
(Tairbert)

Harris

Gairloch

Wester

562

Kinlochewe

564

A832

A832

Ross

Achnasheen

Uibhist a Tuath
(North Uist)

Sound of Harris

592

Loch nam Madadh
(Lochmaddy)

542

Uig

546

Kyle of
Lochalsh

A87

548

Drumn

Invermoris

Beinn na Faoghla
(Benbecula)

Benbecula

Dunvegan

Portree

A890

A887

A865

Uibhist a Deas
(South Uist)

544

Isle
of
Skye

A87

590

Loch Baghasdail
(Lochboisdale)

530

Rùm

Armadale

Mallaig

532

Invergarry

A87

Sound of Barra

Barra

Barraigh
(Barra)

Eigg

A830

A82

S

516

Coll

518

A861

520

Fort
William

Inner Hebrides

Tobermory

A884

Ballachulish

A82

Tiree

Lochaline

504

Fionnphort

Craignure
Isle of Mull

506

A828

508

Ty

A849

Oban

A85

A816

492

494

Inveraray

478

Colonsay

A819

LO

A83

Lochgilphead

480

482

Helensburg

476

Jura

Dunoon ■

Greenock

A815

Port
Askaig

A846

Kennacraig ● Tarbert

462

464

Largs

A78

A78

| Motorway |
| Toll motorway |
| Primary route dual carriageway |
| Primary route single carriageway |
| Other A road |

or ⓥ Vehicle ferry

Vehicle ferry -
fast catamaran

National Park or
scenic area

592 Index to maps in
road map section

0   10   20   30 miles
0 10 20 30 40 kilometres

AA *Route planning*

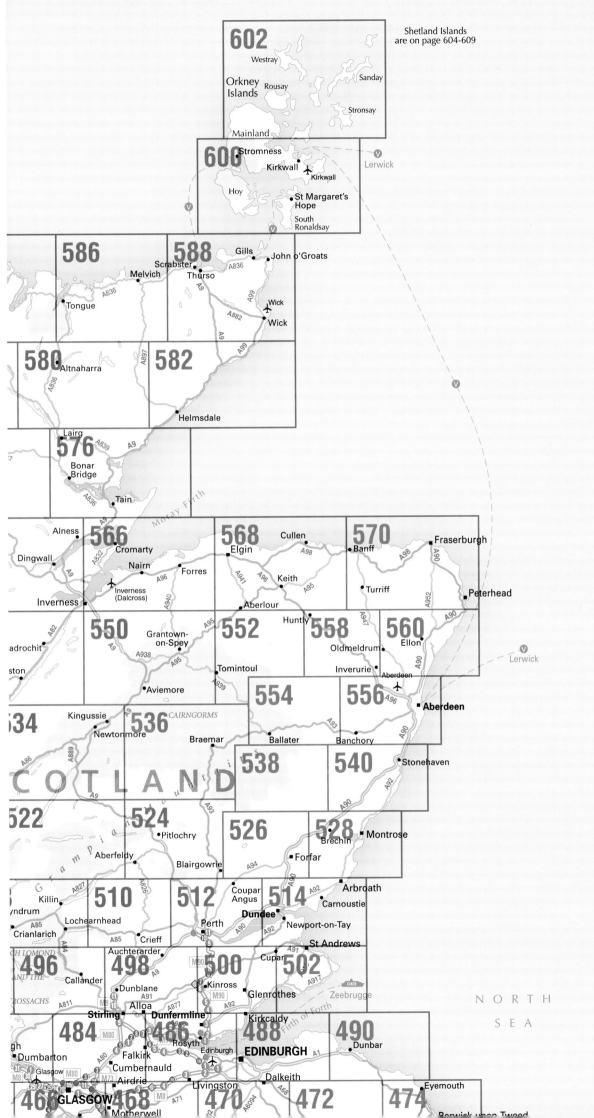

602

Westray

Orkney
Islands

Rousay

Sanday

Stronsay

Mainland

Shetland Islands
are on page 604-609

600

Stromness

Kirkwall

Kirkwall ✈

Hoy

St Margaret's
Hope

South
Ronaldsay

Lerwick Ⓥ

586

588

Gills

John o'Groats

Scrabster

A836

Melvich

Thurso

A9

Wick ✈

Tongue

A836

A882

Wick

580

Altnaharra

582

A897

A99

A836

Helmsdale

A9

Lairg

A9

576

A839

Bonar
Bridge

A836

Tain

Ⓥ

Moray Firth

Alness

566

Cullen

570

Fraserburgh

Dingwall

A832

Cromarty

Elgin

A98

Banff

A98

A90

Nairn

Forres

A96

A941

A96

Keith

A95

Turriff

A952

Peterhead

Inverness (Dalcross) ✈

A940

Aberlour

A947

A90

Inverness

A82

550

Grantown-
on-Spey

A95

552

Huntly

558

560

Ellon

adrochit

A9

A938

Tomintoul

Oldmeldrum

A90

ston

Aviemore

A939

Inverurie

Aberdeen

Lerwick Ⓥ

554

556

A96

Kingussie

536

CAIRNGORMS

Aberdeen ✈

Aberdeen

534

Newtonmore

A889

A86

Braemar

Ballater

Banchory

A93

A90

C O T L A N D

A9

538

540

Stonehaven

522

524

526

528

A92

A92

Montrose

Pitlochry

A93

Brechin

Aberfeldy

A827

Forfar

A90

Blairgowrie

A94

510

A826

Coupar
Angus

514

A92

Arbroath

Killin

yndrum

A85

Lochearnhead

512

Carnoustie

Crianlarich

A85

Crieff

Perth

Dundee

Newport-on-Tay

A90

A92

CH LOMOND

496

498

A9

500

Cupar

502

St Andrews

A91

Auchterarder

M90

A917

Callander

Dunblane

Kinross

M90

Zeebrugge

ROSSACHS

A811

Alloa

A91

Glenrothes

Firth of Forth

Stirling

A977

A92

N O R T H

Dunfermline

Kirkcaldy

S E A

484

M80

486

488

490

gh

Rosyth

EDINBURGH

A1

Dunbar

Dumbarton

M80

Falkirk

Edinburgh ✈

Glasgow

M80

Cumbernauld

M73

Dalkeith

A68

Airdrie

Livingston

Eyemouth

466

GLASGOW

468

M8

470

A71

472

A6094

474

Motherwell

A71

Berwick upon Tweed

Useful motoring websites

A vast amount of information can be found on the internet, with thousands of websites originating in Britain. Those listed here are a good place to start.

www.theaa.com
The AA's website provides advice and information on planning your route, buying a car and avoiding breakdowns. You can also find details of all AA recommended hotels online, research Britain's pubs and restaurants, golf courses and campsites, and much more.

● Road Safety

www.thinkroadsafety.gov.uk
Compendium of road safety in the UK.

www.aatrust.com
Road safety information.

www.childcarseats.org.uk
ROSPA child car seat advice.

www.srsc.org.uk
Scottish Road Safety Campaign.

www.euroncap.com
The European New Car Assessment Programme crash-tests cars and rates them for safety.

● Safety Camera Advance Warnings

Fixed, mobile and red light cameras in England.

www.dft.gov.uk/stellent/groups/ dft_rdsafety/documents/division homepage/032517.hcsp
Department for Transport Safety Camera location data in the UK.

www.safecam.org.uk
Avon and Somerset Safety Camera Partnership.

www.drivesafely.org
Bedfordshire and Luton Casualty Reduction Partnership.

www.cambssafetycameras.co.uk
Cambridgeshire Safety Camera Partnership.

www.cheshiresafecam.org.uk
Cheshire Safety Camera Partnership.

www.clevelandsafetycameras.co.uk
Cleveland Safety Camera Partnership.

www.cumbriasafetycameras.org
Cumbria Safety Cameras.

www.slowitdown.co.uk
Derbyshire Safety Camera Partnership.

www.dcsafetycameras.org
Devon and Cornwall Safety Camera Partnership.

www.dorsetsafetycameras.org.uk
Dorset Safety Camera Partnership.

www.durham.police.uk/durhamc/ central_deps/operations/scu.php
Durham Constabulary Speed Camera Unit.

www.essexsafetycameras.co.uk
Essex Safety Camera Partnership.

www.glossafetycameras.org.uk
Gloucestershire Safety Camera Partnership.

www.drivesafe.org.uk
Greater Manchester Casualty Reduction Partnership.

www.safetycamera.org.uk
Hampshire and Isle of Wight Safety Camera Partnership.

www.hertsdirect.org/roadtrans/ rsu/driving/safetycameras
Hertfordshire Safety Camera Partnership.

www.humbersidesafety cameras.com
Humberside Safety Camera Partnership.

www.kentandmedwaysafety cameras.org.uk
Kent and Medway Safety Camera Partnership.

www.safe2travel.co.uk
Lancashire Partnership for Road Safety.

www.speedorsafety.com
Leicester, Leicestershire and Rutland Safety Camera Scheme.

www.lincssafetycamera.com
Lincolnshire Road Safety Partnership.

www.lscp.org.uk
London Safety Camera Partnership.

www.no-excuses.org.uk
Merseyside Road Safety Camera Partnership.

www.norfolk-safety-camera.org.uk
Norfolk Safety Camera Partnership.

www.northants.police.uk
Road Policing/Safety Camera Locations (Northamptonshire Safety Camera Partnership).

www.safespeedforlife.com
Northumbria Safety Camera Partnership.

www.streettactics.co.uk
Nottinghamshire Safety Camera Partnership.

www.safetycamera.org
South Yorkshire Safety Camera Partnership.

www.staffordshire.gov.uk/camera lifesavers
Staffordshire Casualty Reduction Partnership.

www.suffolksafecam.com
Suffolk Safety Camera Partnership.

www.surrey-safecam.org
Surrey Safety Camera Partnership.

www.sussexsafetycameras.gov.uk
Sussex Safety Camera Partnership.

www.saferroads.org
Thames Valley Safer Roads Partnership.

www.smilecamera.co.uk
Warwickshire Casualty Reduction Partnership.

www.speedaware.org.uk
West Mercia Safety Camera Partnership.

www.wmsafetycameras.co.uk
West Midlands Casualty Reduction Partnership.

www.safetycameraswestyorkshire. co.uk
West Yorkshire Casualty Reduction Partnership.

www.safetycameras-wiltshire- swindon.co.uk
Wiltshire and Swindon Safety Camera Partnership.

Fixed, mobile and red light cameras in Scotland

www.centralscotland.police.uk/ safercentral/tundra.php
Central Scotland Police (Road Policing/ Camera Locations).

www.dgcommunity.net/safety camerapartnership
Dumfries and Galloway Safety Camera Partnership.

www.fifesafetycameras.org
Fife Safety Camera Partnership.

www.lbsafetycameras.co.uk
Lothian and Borders Safety Camera Partnership.

www.nescamp.co.uk
North East (Scotland) Safety Camera Scheme.

www.northern.police.uk
Northern (Scotland) Safety Camera Partnership.

www.camerascutcrashes.com
Strathclyde Safety Camera Partnership.

www.safetayside.co.uk
Tayside Safety Camera Partnership.

Fixed, mobile and red light cameras in Wales

www.checkyourspeed.org.uk
Mid and South Wales Safety Camera Partnership.

www.arrivealive.org.uk
North Wales Road Casualty Reduction Partnership.

● General Motoring

www.highways.gov.uk
The official website of the government's Highways Agency; provides traffic news plus information about roadworks and local road conditions within England. For Scotland and Wales go to:
www.trafficscotland.org
www.traffic-wales.com

www.highwaycode.gov.uk
Are you up-to-date? Read or search the full content of The Highway Code.

www.dvla.gov.uk
All you need to know about driving licences and vehicle taxation, plus all the official forms to download.

www.direct.gov.uk
Government information and service covering all areas, including motoring.

www.ukmot.com
Read what the MOT test covers or find your nearest test centre.

www.vcacarfueldata.org.uk
Official database of new car fuel consumption and emissions data.

● Channel Tunnel

www.eurotunnel.com
Passenger shuttle (car and coach) services between Folkestone and Calais

● Timetables

www.transportdirect.info
Plan UK journeys by plane, train or automobile.

www.traveline.org.uk
National and local timetables for bus, coach and rail services.

● Ferries

www.sailanddrive.com
Ferry information service. Links to the websites of all major ferry companies operating within the UK and to Ireland and continental Europe.

● Weather Forecasts

www.metoffice.com
The official weather service with detailed forecasts.

● National Parks

www.anpa.gov.uk
The Association of National Park Authorities site, with complete listings and descriptions for all UK National Parks plus news and events. Links to individual park sites.

● News

www.bbc.co.uk
Up-to-the-minute news, weather, and sport.

www.bbc.co.uk/travelnews
See up-to-date travel information at a local level for roads and public transport.

www.smmt.co.uk
The latest news and views from the motor industry.

Acknowledgements

The Route planning section of this atlas was edited, designed and produced by AA Publishing.
© Automobile Association Developments Limited 2006
Crown copyright material (road signs) is reproduced under licence from the Controller of HMSO and the Driving Standards Agency. Crown copyright material (mobile speed cameras) is reproduced with the permission of the Controller of HMSO and the Queen's Printer for Scotland (licence number C02W0005858).

The publishers wish to acknowledge and thank the following for their contribution to the 'Route planning' section of this atlas.
AA Motoring Trust, ITIS, Safety Camera Partnerships.

Traffic congestion 20 ©

Road safety and fixed speed cameras

First, the advice you would expect from the AA **– breaking the speed limit is illegal and can cost lives.**

Keeping to the speed limit is not always easy and it only takes one momentary lapse of concentration to break the law. The AA Motoring Trust estimate that in 2005 more than 3 million drivers in the UK were fined for doing just that and that 26% of all households in Britain have received a speeding ticket.

Most fixed speed cameras are installed at accident 'black spots' where four or more fatal or serious road collisions have occurred over the previous three years. It is the policy of both the police and the Department for Transport to make the location of cameras as well known as possible. By showing speed camera locations in this atlas the AA is identifying the places where extra care should be taken while driving. Speeding is illegal and dangerous and you MUST keep within the speed limit at all times.

Gatso™

Truvelo™

SPECS™

Traffipax™

There are currently more than 3,000 fixed speed cameras in Britain. The map on this page gives an overview of where speed cameras occur in Britain and the road mapping in this atlas identifies their on-the-road locations.

Traffic signs giving orders

National speed limit applies

Speed limits can vary depending on the type of road and your vehicle. See *The Highway Code* rule 103.

30

Maximum speed

Area in which cameras are used to enforce traffic regulations

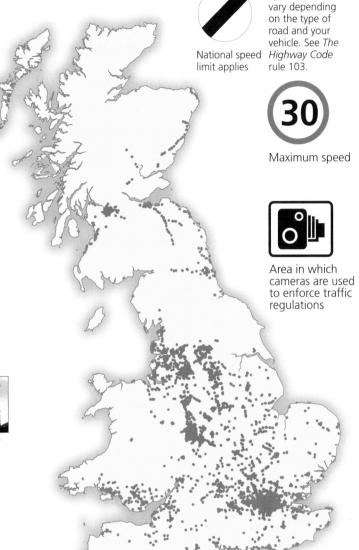

Camera locations – read this before you use the atlas

1 The speed camera locations were correct at the time of finalising the information to go to press.

2 Camera locations are approximate due to limitations in the scale of road mapping used in this atlas.

3 In towns and urban areas speed camera locations are shown only on roads that appear on the road maps in this atlas.

4 Where two or more cameras occur close together a special symbol is used to indicate multiple cameras on the same stretch of road.

5 Our symbols do not indicate the direction in which speed cameras point.

6 On the mapping we symbolise more than 3,000 fixed camera locations. Mobile laser device locations cannot be shown.

 This symbol is used on the mapping to identify **individual** camera locations

 This symbol is used on the mapping to identify **multiple** cameras on the same stretch of road

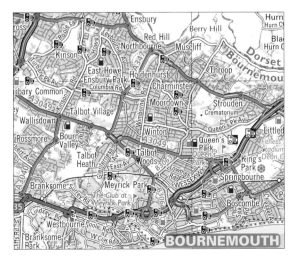

SEE ANY DANGER AHEAD?

DON'T WORRY, THIS WILL

Apart from the corner looming up fast, just over the brow of the hill is an accident black spot and speed camera and you're heading straight towards them. But how could you possibly know?

pogo GPS-based driver safety systems provide alerts for accident blackspots and all fixed speed cameras.

Use one and you'll be able to concentrate on other road users and the road ahead, rather than worrying about accident black spots and speed cameras.

VX Racing

pogo is official sponsor of the Vauxhall VX Racing Team, BTCC Champions 2001-2004

from only £249.95

 All fixed cameras

 Speed limit (on alert)

 Accident blackspots

 Schools

 Congestion charge zone

0870 205 3000   sales@mypogo.co.uk   www.mypogo.co.uk

get protected   pogo

Road safety and mobile speed cameras

Breaking the speed limit is illegal and can cost lives. The AA advises drivers to follow the legal speed limit at all times.

Both the AA Motoring Trust and the Government believe that speed cameras should be operated within a transparent system. By providing information relating to road safety and speed hotspots, the AA believes that the driver is better placed to be aware of speed limits and can ensure adherence to them, thus making the roads safer for all users. For this reason the AA has compiled a list of more than 3,000 regularly policed mobile camera sites, based on official Department for Transport and regional Safety Camera Partnership sources.

The police also deploy mobile cameras at "exceptional sites", at new sites and also at roadworks where temporary speed limits apply. Due to the nature and purpose of mobile speed control devices the list cannot be exhaustive or completely accurate all of the time and **we advise drivers to always follow the signed speed limits**.

Britain's speed camera regions

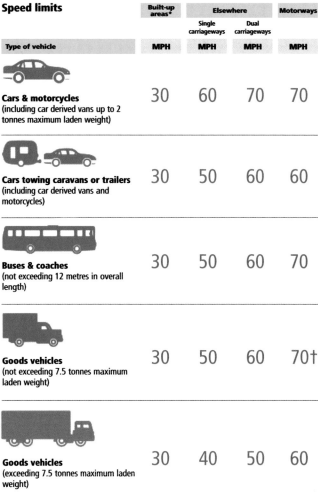

Speed limits

Type of vehicle	Built-up areas*	Elsewhere		Motorways
		Single carriageways	Dual carriageways	
	MPH	MPH	MPH	MPH
Cars & motorcycles (including car derived vans up to 2 tonnes maximum laden weight)	30	60	70	70
Cars towing caravans or trailers (including car derived vans and motorcycles)	30	50	60	60
Buses & coaches (not exceeding 12 metres in overall length)	30	50	60	70
Goods vehicles (not exceeding 7.5 tonnes maximum laden weight)	30	50	60	70†
Goods vehicles (exceeding 7.5 tonnes maximum laden weight)	30	40	50	60

These are the national speed limits and apply to all roads unless signs show otherwise.
*The 30mph limit applies to all traffic on all roads in England and Wales (only class C and unclassified roads in Scotland) with street lighting unless signs show otherwise.
†60 if articulated or towing a trailer

Region-by-region list of mobile camera sites

Road number	Location	Speed limit (mph)
England		
Avon and Somerset		
M32	Bristol Stadium	60
A4	Anchor Rd, Bristol	30
A4	Keynsham Bypass (at A4175 jct, Durley Hill)	50
A4	Newbridge Rd, Bath	30
A4	Portway, Bristol (near Sea Mills)	50
A4	Portway, Bristol (near A4176 Bridge Valley Rd)	30
A4	Totterdown Bridge, Bristol	30
A30	Cricket St Thomas	50
A30	East Chinnock	30
A30	Roundham	40
A30	Sherborne Rd, Yeovil	30
A30	Hospital Roundabout, Yeovil	40
A37	Wells Rd, Bristol (near St John's La)	30
A37	Chilthorne Domer (eastbound)	60
A37	Emborough	50
A37	Fosse Way (north of Podimore Roundabout)	60
A37	Gurney Slade (northbound)	30
A37	Lydford, near Hornblotton	60
A37	Lydford	40
A37	Shepton Mallet	30
A37	Wells Rd, Bristol (near A4174 Airport Rd)	30
A38	Aztec West, Patchway (near Bradley Stoke Way)	40
A38	Bridgwater Rd, Bedminster Down, Bristol	40
A38	Churchill to Lower Langford	40
A38	Cross	40
A38	Bedminster Down Rd/West St, Bristol	30
A38	Bedminster Down Rd, Bristol (near Bishopsworth Rd)	40
A38	Cheltenham Rd/Gloucester Rd, Bristol (near Cranbrook Rd)	30
A38	East Reach/Toneway, Taunton	30
A38	Gloucester Rd, Patchway (near Highwood Rd)	40
A38	Gloucester Rd North, Patchway (near B4057 Gypsy Patch La)	40
A38	Redhill	50
A38	Stokes Croft, Bristol	30
A38	Bathpool	30
A38	Gloucester Rd, Bristol (near B4052 Ashley Down Rd)	30
A38	Heatherton Grange, Bradford-on-Tone	50
A38	North Petherton	30/40
A38	Pawlett (southbound)	50
A38	Rooks Bridge (eastbound)	30
A38	Taunton Rd, Bridgwater	30
A38	Wellington Rd, Taunton	30
A38	West Huntspill (northbound)	30
A39	Ashcott	30
A39	Bilbrook	30
A39	Chewton Mendip	30
A39	Coxley	40
A39	Green Ore (southbound)	50
A39	Walton	30
A39	Bath Rd, Horsey	40
A39	Bath Rd, Bridgwater	30
A39	North Broadway, Bridgwater (near A38, Taunton Rd)	30
A39	Quantock Rd, Bridgwater	30
A39	North Broadway/Broadway/Monmouth St, Bridgwater	30
A46	Tormarton	60
A46	Dunkirk	50
A46	North of Nailsworth	40
A46	Shurdington	30
A303	Buckland St Mary	50
A303	Downhead (near Ilchester)	50
A303/A358	Southfields Roundabout	60
A303/A3088	Cartgate Roundabout	70
A357	Templecombe	30
A358	Ashill	60
A358	Donyatt	30
A358	Greenway Rd, Taunton	30
A358	Henlade	40
A358	Hornsbury Mill	40
A358	Pen Elm (3km west of Taunton)(southbound)	40
A358	Priorswood Rd, Taunton	30
A358	Staplegrove Rd, Taunton	30
A359	Mudford (northbound)	30
A361	Doulting	30
A361	Durston	40
A361	Frome Bypass	60
A361	Othery	30
A361	Pilton	30
A361	West Pennard	30
A362	Terry Hill (near A366 jct)	40
A367	Green Park Rd, Bath	30
A367	Wells Rd, Radstock	30
A367	Bear Flat, Bath	30
A369	Abbots Leigh	40
A369	Martcombe Rd, Easton-in-Gordano	60
A370	Beach Rd, Weston-super-Mare	30
A370	Cleeve Village	30

Road number	Location	Speed limit (mph)
A370	Station Rd/Bristol Rd, Congresbury	30
A370	Flax Bourton (near B3130)	30
A370	Long Ashton Bypass, Bristol end	40
A370	Herluin Way, Weston-super-Mare (near Winterstoke Rd)	50
A370	Somerset Ave, Weston-super-Mare (M5 to A371)	50
A370	Winterstoke Rd, Weston-super-Mare	30
A371	Draycott	30
A371	Priestleigh (southbound)	40
A371	Sidcot La, Winscombe (near A38)	30
A372	Aller	30
A378	Curry Rivel	30
A378	Wrantage	40
A403	Avonmouth Docks	40
A420	Church Rd, Redfield, Bristol	30
A420	Clouds Hill Rd/Bell Hill Rd, St George, Bristol	30
A420	High St/London Rd, Warmley, Bristol	30
A420	Lawrence Hill, Bristol	30
A420	Old Market, Bristol (near Temple Way/Bond St)	30
A420	Two Mile Hill Rd/Regent St, Kingswood, Bristol	30
A420	Wick/Tog Hill	60
A432	Kendleshire	40
A432	Badminton Rd, Bristol (near A4174 Avon Ring Rd)	40
A432	Fishponds Rd, Bristol (near B4048 Lodge Causeway)	30
A432	Fishponds Rd, Bristol (at B4469 Muller Rd)	30
A432	Fishponds Rd, Bristol (near B4469 Royate Hill)	30
A432	Stapleton Rd, Bristol (near A4320 Easton Way)	30
A432	Station Rd/B4059 Stover Rd, Yate	30
A3027	North St/East St, Taunton	30
A3029	Avon Bridge, Bristol	40
A3039	Devonshire Rd, Weston-super-Mare	30
A3088	Lysander Rd, Yeovil	30
A3259	Monkton Heathfield	30
A4018	Black Boy Hill/Whiteladies Rd, Bristol	30
A4018	Catbrain (near Cribbs Causeway)	40
A4018	Cribbs Causeway (at jct 17 M5)	30
A4018	Falcondale Rd, Westbury-on-Trym, Bristol	30
A4018	Park Row/Perry Rd, Bristol	30
A4018	Passage Rd, Bristol (near B4057 Crow La)	40
A4018	Westbury Rd, Bristol (near B4054 North View)	30
A4018	Whiteladies Rd into Queens Rd, Bristol	30
A4044	Temple Way, Bristol	30
A4162	Sylvan Way/Dingle Rd/Canford La, Bristol	30
A4174	Avon Ring Rd (near M32 jct 1)	50
A4174	Avon Ring Rd, Bromley Heath (east of Overndale Rd)	50
A4174	Filton Rd/Avon Ring Rd (near Coldharbour La)	50
A4174	Hartcliffe Way, Bristol	40
A4174	Hengrove Way/Airport Rd, Bristol (near Creswicke Rd)	40
A4174	Station Rd, Filton (near Great Stoke Way)	40
A4320	St Philips Causeway, Bristol (near A4 Bath Rd)	30
B3124	Walton Rd, Clevedon	30
B3130	Stockway North/Chapel Ave, Nailsea	30
B3130	Wraxall	30/40
B3133	Central Way, Clevedon	30
B3139	Chilcompton	30
B3139	Mark Causeway	30/40
B3140	Coast Rd, Berrow	30
B3141	East Huntspill	30
B3151	Compton Dundon	30
B3151	Ilchester	30
B3151	Somerton Rd, Street	30
B3153	Keinton Mandeville	30
B3170	Shoreditch Rd, Taunton	30
B3440	Locking Rd, Weston-super-Mare	30
B3440	Locking Rd/Regent St/Alexandra Pde, Weston-super-Mare	30
B4054	Avonmouth Rd, Bristol	30
B4054	Linden Rd, Westbury Park, Bristol	30
B4054	Shirehampton Rd, Sea Mills, Bristol	30
B4056	Southmead Rd, Bristol	30
B4057	Gypsy Patch La, Stoke Gifford (near Hatchet Rd)	30
B4057	Winterbourne Rd, Great Stoke (near B4427)	50
B4058	Frenchay Park Rd, Bristol	30
B4058	Winterbourne Hill/High St, Winterbourne	30
B4059	Goose Green Way, Yate	30
B4060	Station Rd/Bowling Hill/Rounceval St, Yate/Chipping Sodbury	30
B4061	Bristol Rd, Thornbury	30
B4465	Staplehill Rd/High St, Fishponds, Bristol	30
B4465	Broad St, Mangotsfield, Bristol	30
-	Bradley Stoke, Little Stoke La	30
-	Bristol, Bishport Ave, Hartcliffe	30
-	Bristol, Broadwalk, Knowle	30
-	Bristol, Hawkfield Rd, Hartcliffe (near A4174 Hengrove Way)	30
-	Bristol, Kingsway, St George	30
-	Bristol, Long Cross, Lawrence Weston	30
-	Bristol, Northumbria Dr, Westbury Park	30
-	Bristol, Redcliffe Way	30
-	Bristol, Stoke Hill/Stoke Rd, Clifton (near Saville Rd)	30
-	Bristol, Sturminster Rd, Stockwood	30
-	Bristol, Whitchurch La (near Dundry Rd)	30
-	Bristol, Whitchurch La/Hareclive Rd, Bishopsworth	30
-	Taunton, Cheddon Rd	30
-	Taunton, Chestnut Dr	30
-	Taunton, Lisieux Way	30
-	Taunton, Trull Rd	30
-	Watergore, Harp Rd (near Over Stratton)	50
-	Yeovil, Combe St	30

Bedfordshire and Luton

Road number	Location	Speed limit (mph)
A5	Battlesden	60
A5	Hockliffe	40
A5	Kensworth (near B4540)	60
A6	High St, Clapham (near Highbury Grove)	30
A6	High St, Clapham (near Mount Pleasant Rd)	30
A6	New Bedford Rd, Luton (near Alexandra Ave)	30
A6	New Bedford Rd, Luton (near Brook St)	30
A6	Pulloxhill	60
A6	Silsoe	60
A6	Silsoe (near Gravenhurst turn)	60
A421	Aspley Guise	60
A421	Brogborough	50
A428	Bromham Rd, Bedford	30
A428	Goldington Rd, Bedford	30
A505	Leighton Buzzard Bypass (near Grovebury Rd)	60
A505	Park Viaduct, Luton	30
A505	Tilsworth	60
A507	Shefford Bypass	60
A603	Cardington Rd, Bedford (near Mareth Rd)	30
A603	Cardington Rd, Bedford (near Lovell Rd)	30
A603	Willington	40
A1081	Airport Way, Capability Green, Luton	70
A1081	Airport Way, Gipsy Lane, Luton	60
A4146	Billington Rd, Leighton Buzzard	30
A5120	Ampthill Rd, Flitwick	30
A5120	Dunstable Rd, Flitwick	30
A5120	Bedford Rd, Houghton Regis	40
A5120	Station Rd, Toddington	30
A5134	High St, Kempston	30
B530	Houghton Conquest	60
B531	Bedford Rd, Kempston (Bunyan Rd to Beatrice Rd)	30
B1040	Potton Rd, Biggleswade	30
-	Bedford, Park Ave	30
-	Bedford, Roff Ave	30
-	Bromham, Stagsden Rd	30
-	Cranfield, High St	30
-	Luton, Crawley Green Rd (near Devon Rd)	30
-	Luton, Crawley Green Rd (near Leygreen Cl)	30
-	Luton, Dunstable Rd (near Beechwood Rd)	30
-	Luton, Leagrave High St (near Emerald Rd)	30
-	Luton, Leagrave High St (near Pastures Way)	30
-	Luton, Waller Ave (near Chester Ave)	30
-	Luton, Waller Ave (near Chiltern Gdns)	30
-	Luton, Whitehorse Vale	30

Cambridgeshire

Road number	Location	Speed limit (mph)
A1	Little Paxton to Southoe (northbound)	NSL
A1	South of Carpenter's Lodge Roundabout (B1081, south of Stamford)(northbound)	NSL
A14	Bottisham (westbound)	NSL
A14	Bythorn/Molesworth (eastbound)	NSL
A14	Ellington (eastbound)	NSL
A14	Fen Ditton	NSL
A14	Girton to jct 31 (A1307) (westbound)	NSL
A14	East of jct 35 (A1303) (westbound)	NSL
A14	North-east of jct 36 (A11) (eastbound)	NSL
A14	2km west of A1 to Brampton Hut Roundabout (eastbound)	NSL
A14	Jct 16 to 17 (eastbound)	NSL
A14	Jct 18 to 19 (westbound)	NSL
A14	Jct 23 (Spittals Interchange) (eastbound)	NSL
A15	London Rd, Peterborough (New Rd to Rivergate)	30
A15	Paston Pkwy, Peterborough (northbound)	NSL
A47	Soke Pkwy, Peterborough (eastbound)	NSL
A47	Thorney Toll (and to west)	NSL
A141	Clews Corner	NSL
A141	At B1040 jct, south of Warboys (southbound)	NSL
A141	Wimblington/Doddington Bypass	NSL
A142	Soham Bypass (southbound)	NSL
A142	Witchford Bypass (eastbound)	NSL
A605	Kings Dyke (west of Whittlesey)	40
A1073	Masons Bridge/Steam House Farm (north of Eye) (northbound)	NSL
A1123	Bluntisham, at Hedgerows Nursery	NSL
A1123	Houghton Hill, St Ives, east of B1090 (eastbound)	40
A1123	Wilburton bends to east of village	40
A1307	Bartlow Crossroads (dual carriageway)	NSL
A1307	Hills Rd, Cambridge (Gonville Pl to Worts' Cswy)(southbound)	30
A1307	Linton Bypass (westbound)	NSL
B645	Tilbrook bends	40

Cheshire

Road number	Location	Speed limit (mph)
A50	Knutsford Rd, Grappenhall, Warrington (B5157 Heath Field Park to Cliff La)	30
A50	Manchester Rd/Toft Rd, Knutsford (Woodvale Rd to Garden Rd)	30
A50	Long La, Warrington (Fisher Ave to Longfield Rd)	30
A54	Kelsall Rd, Ashton	60
A56	Camsley La, Lymm (Deans La to M6 overbridge)	40
A57	New Manchester Rd, Paddington, Warrington (Larkfield Ave to Greymist Ave)	40
A523	London Rd, Poynton (South Park Dr to Clifford Rd)	30
A532	West St, Crewe (Marshfield Ave to Peel St)	30
A533	Booth La, Middlewich	40
A533	Northwich Rd, Runcorn (Chester Rd to Rivington Rd)	30
A537	Buxton Rd, near Wildboarclough (100m north-west of Buxton Old Rd to 100m west of A54)	50
A5019	Mill St, Crewe	30
A5032	Chester Rd, Whitby, Ellesmere Port (A5117 to 130m south of Dunkirk La)	30
A5034	Mereside Rd, Mere	60
A5104	Hough Green, Chester (Cliveden Rd to Curzon Park)	30
B5071	Gresty Rd, Crewe (South St to 500m south of Davenport Ave)	30
B5078	Sandbach Rd North, Alsager (The Avenue to Leicester Ave)	30
B5082	Middlewich Rd, Northwich (East Ave to Pullman Dr)	30
B5132	Overpool Rd, Ellesmere Port (Sutton Way to Netherpool Rd)	30
B5463	Station Rd, Little Sutton	30
B5470	Rainow Rd, Macclesfield (Fence Ave to Well La)	30
-	Burtonwood, Lumber La (Green La to Melrose Ave)	30
-	Ellesmere Port, Overpool Rd (Wycliffe Rd to Fairview Rd)	30
-	Runcorn, Astmoor Rd (Lister Rd to Chadwick Rd)	40
-	Runcorn, Boston Ave (Morval Cres to Heath Rd)	30
-	Runcorn, Clifton Rd (Greenway Rd to Beaufort Close)	30
-	Runcorn, Halton Rd (Daresbury Expressway overbridge to Boston Ave)	30
-	Runcorn, Heath Rd (Halton Rd to Boston Ave)	30
-	Runcorn, Warrington Rd (Manor Park to Eastgate Rd)	30
-	Warrington, Battersby La, Howley (A49 roundabout to A574 March House La)	30
-	Warrington, Harpers Rd, Fearnhead (Pasture La to Freshfield Dr)	30
-	Warrington, Lovely La, Whitecross (Monks St to Clap Gates Rd)	30
-	Widnes, Birchfield Rd (Pit La to Rose View Ave)	30
-	Widnes, Hough Green Rd (Liverpool Rd to Arley Dr)	30
-	Widnes, Prescot Rd, Hough Green (Hough Green Rd to borough boundary)	30
-	Wilmslow, Hough La (northern end)	30
-	Winsford, Bradford La (either side of School Rd)	40
-	Winsford, St John's Dr/Woodford La (Brunner Pl to Grove Cl)	30

Cleveland

Road number	Location	Speed limit (mph)
A135	Yarm Rd, Eaglescliffe	30
A171	Charltons (near Margrove Park)	50
A171	Ormesby Bank, Ormesby	30
A172	Marton Rd, Middlesbrough (Longlands to St Lukes)	30
A172	Marton Rd, Middlesbrough (St Lukes to Marton crossroads)	40
A172	Dixons Bank, Nunthorpe (Guisborough Rd to Captain Cook's Cres)	40
A174	Carlin How	30
A177	From Savacentre to county boundary, Stockton-on-Tees	50/60
A178	Coronation Drive, Hartlepool	40/30
A178	The Front, Seaton Carew	30
A179	Easington Rd/Powlett Rd, Hartlepool	30/40/50
A689	Stockton Rd, Hartlepool (from Sappers Corner)	50/40
A1027	Bishopton Ave, Stockton-on-Tees	40
A1032	Acklam Rd, Brookfield (Blue Bell to Crematorium)	40
A1032	Acklam Rd, Linthorpe	30
A1042	Kirkleatham La, Redcar	30/40
A1085	High St, Marske-by-the-Sea	30
A1130	Acklam Rd, Thornaby-on-Tees	30
A1130	Mandale Rd, Acklam	30
B1269	Redcar La, Redcar	30
B1274	Junction Rd, Stockton-on-Tees	30
B1276	Seaton La, Hartlepool	30
B1276	Station La, Seaton Carew	30
B1380	High St, Eston	30
B1380	Ladgate La, Marton (Marton crossroads to Ormesby Rd)	40
B1380	Normanby Rd, Ormesby	30
-	Acklam, Trimdon Ave	30
-	Billingham, Thames Rd	30
-	Billingham, White House Rd	30
-	Dormanstown, Broadway	30
-	Eston, Church La	30
-	Eston, Normanby Rd	30
-	Hartlepool, Catcote Rd	30
-	Hartlepool, Owton Manor La	30
-	Hartlepool, Oxford Rd	30
-	Hartlepool, Raby Rd	30
-	Hartlepool, Throston Grange La	30
-	Hartlepool, Winterbottom Ave	30
-	Hartlepool, Wynyard Rd	30
-	Marske, Redcar Rd	30
-	Normanby, Bankfields Rd	30
-	Normanby, Flatts La	30
-	Park End, Ormesby Rd	30
-	Redcar, Greenstones Rd	30
-	Redcar, West Dyke Rd	30
-	Stanghow, Stanghow Rd	30
-	Stockton-on-Tees, Bishopton Rd West	30
-	Stockton-on-Tees, Darlington La	30
-	Stockton-on-Tees, Harrowgate La	30
-	Thornaby-on-Tees, Cunningham Ave	30
-	Thornaby-on-Tees, Thornaby Rd	30

Cumbria

Road number	Location	Speed limit (mph)
M6	Jct 36 to 40	NSL
A6	London Rd, Carlisle	30
A6	Milnthorpe Rd, Kendal	30
A6	Shap Rd, Kendal	30
A6	Scotland Rd, Penrith	30
A6	Garnett Bridge north to Hollowgate	60
A6	Thiefside (south of High Hesket)	60
A7	Westlinton crossroads	60
A65	Burton Rd/Lound Rd, Kendal	30
A65	Devil's Bridge, Kirby Lonsdale	40
A65	Hollin Hall to Hornsbarrow, Kirkby Lonsdale	60
A66	Brough Hill, Warcop	60
A66	Brigham/Broughton to Bridgefoot	60
A66	Crackenthorpe	60
A66	Dubwath/Bassenthwaite Lake	60
A66	Sandford road ends	60
A66	Troutbeck/Mungrisdale	60
A69	Aglionby (west of Warwick, single carr)	60
A69	Scarrow Hill (near Lanercost)	60
A74	Floriston (Todhills to River Esk)	70
A590	Bouth road ends	60
A590	Heaves Hotel/Levens/Gilpin Bridge	70
A590	Haverthwaite/Backbarrow	60
A590	Newland, Ulverston	60
A592	Rayrigg Rd, Bowness	30/40
A595	Greenhill Hotel, Red Dial	60
A595	Loop Rd, Whitehaven	40
A595	West Woodside/Curthwaite jct	60
A595	Wigton Rd, Carlisle	30
A595	Wreaks End, Broughton-in-Furness	60
A596	Micklethwaite	60
A683	Cautley to Middleton	60
A685	Appleby Rd, Kendal	30
A686	Edenhall to Gilderdale Forest	60
A5087	Ulverston	30
B5277	Lindale Rd, Grange-over-Sands	30
B5299	Dalston Rd, Carlisle	40
-	Barrow-in-Furness, Abbey Rd	30
-	Barrow-in-Furness, Michelson Rd	30
-	Carlisle, Blackwell Rd/Durdar Rd	30

Derbyshire

Road number	Location	Speed limit (mph)
A6	Allestree, Derby	30
A6	Bakewell	30
A6	Belper	30
A6	London Rd, Derby	30
A6	Taddington to Buxton	50
A52	Ashbourne Rd, Derby	30
A52	Main Rd, Brailsford	30
A52	Mackworth, Derby	40
A53	St John's Rd, Buxton	30
A61	Main Rd, Shirland	30
A511	Station Rd, Hatton	30
A514	Derby Rd, Chellaston	30
A514	Swadlincote to Hartshorne	40
A514	Swadlincote	30
A514	Ticknall	30
A608	Smalley	30
A609	Kilburn Rd, Belper	30
A609	Kilburn Rd to Horsley Woodhouse	30
A616	Clowne	30
A616	Cresswell	30
A617	Bramley Vale	40
A617	Glapwell to Pleasley	60
A618	Rotherham Rd, Killamarsh	30
A623	Stoney Middleton	30
A626	Marple Rd, Chisworth	30
A632	Bolsover (west)	30
A632	Langwith Rd, Bolsover	30
A632	Matlock	30
A632	Chesterfield Rd, Matlock	40
A5111	Raynesway, Derby (near West Service Rd)	n/a
A5132	Twyford Rd, Willington	40
A5250	Burton Rd, Derby	30
A5250	Burton Rd, Littleover, Derby	30
A6005	Draycott to Breaston	30
A6005	Draycott Rd, Borrowash	40
A6005	Nottingham Rd, Borrowash	30
A6007	Codnor to Heanor	30
A6016	Primrose La, Glossop	30
A6175	Holmewood	30
A6187	Sheffield Rd, Hathersage	30
A6187	Hope	30
B5008	Burton Rd, Repton	40
B5010	London Rd, Shardlow	30
B5036	Cromford Hill, Cromford	30
B5353	Park Rd, Newhall, Swadlincote	n/a
B5353	Union Rd/High St, Swadlincote	n/a
B6013	Far Laund, Belper	40
B6019	Alfreton Rd, Pinxton	30
B6051	Newbold Rd, Chesterfield	30
B6051	Newbold Rd, Newbold, Chesterfield	n/a
B6052	Whittington, Chesterfield	n/a
B6053	Eckington Rd, Staveley	30
B6057	Chesterfield Rd, Dronfield	n/a
B6062	Chinley	30
B6158	Green La, Coal Aston	30
B6179	Little Eaton	30
B6179	Lower Kilburn	40
B6179	Lower Kilburn to Little Eaton	50
B6179	Ripley to Marehay	30
B6419	Shuttlewood Rd, Shuttlewood	30
-	Bolsover, Mansfield Rd, Hillstown	30
-	Bolsover, Portland Ave	30
-	Borrowash, Victoria Ave	30
-	Brimington, Troughbrook Rd, Hollingwood	30
-	Charlesworth, Long La	30
-	Chesterfield, Ashgate Rd	30
-	Chesterfield, Boythorpe Rd	30
-	Chesterfield, Brockwell La	30
-	Chesterfield, Hawksley Ave	30
-	Chesterfield, Linacre Rd	30
-	Chesterfield, Old Rd	30
-	Chesterfield, Pennine Way	30
-	Chesterfield, Whitecotes La	30
-	Denby, Loscoe-Denby La	30
-	Denby, Street La	30
-	Derby, Acorn Way	40
-	Derby, Blagreaves La	30
-	Derby, Haven Baulk La, Littleover	30
-	Derby, Kedleston Rd	30
-	Derby, Ladybank Rd	30
-	Derby, Sinfin La	30
-	Derby, Stenson Rd	30
-	Derby, Stenson Rd, Stenson Fields	40
-	Derby, Wood Rd, Chaddesden	30
-	Derby, Wragley Way	30
-	Draycott, Sawley Rd	30
-	Ilkeston, Corporation Rd	30
-	Ilkeston, Quarry Hill Rd	30
-	Langley Mill, Cromford Rd	30
-	Langley Mill, Upper Dunstead Rd	30
-	Long Eaton, Draycott Rd, Sawley	30
-	New Whittington, Handley Rd	30
-	Old Brampton, Ashgate Rd	30
-	Pleasley, Newboundmill La	30
-	Ripley, Peasehill Rd	30
-	Ripley, Steam Mill La	30
-	Risley, Bostock's La	30
-	Shirland, Park La	30
-	Swadlincote, Church Ave	30
-	Swadlincote, Common Rd, Church Gresley	30
-	Swadlincote, Hearthcote Rd	30
-	Swadlincote, Midland Rd	30
-	Swadlincote, Sandcliffe Rd	30
-	Swanwick, Sleetmoor La	30

Devon and Cornwall

Road number	Location	Speed limit (mph)
A30	Chiverton Cross (A390/A3075 jct)	60
A30	Highgate	70
A30	Highgate Hill (A392 jct)	70
A30	Monkton	40
A30	Sowton	40
A30	Temple	60
A38	Lee Mill	70
A38	Near Lower Clicker (B3251 jct, south-east of Liskeard)	70
A38	Deep Lane jct, Plympton	70
A38	Smithaleigh (4km west of Ivybridge)	70
A38	Smithaleigh (overbridge) (4km west of Ivybridge)	70
A38	Wrangaton-Bittaford straight	70
A39	Barras Moor (near Perranarworthal)	60
A39	Perranarworthal	40
A39	Valley Truckle, Camelford	30
A361	Ashford	50
A361	Eastern Ave, Barnstaple	30
A361	Knowle	40
A361	Knowle (Westerland)	30
A361	Wrafton	30
A374	Plymouth Rd, Plymouth	40
A374	Antony Rd, Torpoint	30
A376	Ebford	30
A376	Exeter Rd, Exmouth	30
A377	Copplestone	30
A377	Western Rd, Crediton	30
A377	Alphington Rd, Exeter	30
A379	Brixton	30
A379	Dartmouth Rd, Paignton	30
A379	The Strand, Starcross	30
A379	Teignmouth Rd, Teignmouth	30
A379	Babbacombe Rd, Torquay	30
A379	Yealmpton	30
A380	Newton Rd, Kingskerswell	40
A381	East St, Newton Abbot	30
A385	Totnes Rd, Collaton St Mary	30
A385	Ashburton Rd, Totnes	30
A386	Chub Tor (2km south of Yelverton)	60
A386	Outland Rd, Plymouth	30
A386	Roborough Down, Plymouth	60
A386	Tavistock Rd, Plymouth	40
A388	Kelly Bray (north of Callington)	30
A390	Penstraze (1.5km east of A39)	60
A390	Sticker Bypass	60
A394	Kenneggy Downs (near Praa Sands)	40
A396	Rewe	30
A396	Exeter Rd, Stoke Canon	30
A3015	Topsham Rd, Exeter	30
A3047	Trevenson Rd, Pool, Camborne	30
A3047	Tuckingmill, Camborne	30
A3058	Trewoon	30
A3064	St Budeaux Bypass, Plymouth	30
A3074	Carbis Bay, St Ives	30
A3075	Rosecliston, near Newquay	60
B3165	Crewkerne Rd, Raymonds Hill (near A35)	30
B3174	Barrack Rd, Ottery St Mary	30
B3183	Heavitree Rd, Exeter	30
B3183	New North Rd, Exeter	30
B3212	Dunsford Rd, Exeter	30
B3212	Pinhoe Rd, Exeter	30
B3213	Wrangaton village	30
B3233	Bickington Rd, Barnstaple	30
B3250	North Hill, Plymouth	30
B3284	Liskey, Perranporth	30/60
B3344	Station Hill, Chudleigh	30
B3396	Milehouse Rd, Plymouth	30
B3416	Glen Rd, Plympton	30
B3432	Novorossisk Rd, Plymouth	40
-	Avonwick village	30
-	Castle-an-Dinas, (4km east of St Columb Major)	60
-	Exeter, Buddle La	30
-	Exeter, Exwick La	30
-	Fraddon village	30
-	Ivybridge, Exeter Rd	30
-	Paignton, Colley End Rd	30
-	Paignton, Preston Down Rd	30
-	Plymouth, Beacon Park Rd	30
-	Plymouth, Church Hill, Eggbuckland	30
-	Plymouth, Devonport Rd, Stoke	30
-	Plymouth, Eggbuckland Rd	30
-	Plymouth, Glen Rd	30
-	Plymouth, Grenville Rd, St Judes	30
-	Plymouth, Haye Rd, Elburton	30
-	Plymouth, Honicknowle La	30
-	Plymouth, Lipson Rd	30
-	Plymouth, Mannamead Rd	30
-	Plymouth, Molesworth Rd	30
-	Plymouth, North Prospect Rd	30
-	Plymouth, Pomphlett Rd	30
-	Plymouth, Shakespeare Rd, Honicknowle	30
-	Plymouth, Southway Dr	30
-	Plymouth, St Levan Rd	30
-	Plymouth, Tamerton Foliot Rd	30
-	Plymouth, Union St	30
-	Plymouth, Weston Park Rd	30
-	Plymouth, Wolseley Rd	30
-	Saltash, Callington Rd	30

Dorset

Road number	Location	Speed limit (mph)
A30	Babylon Hill (1.5km east of Yeovil)	70
A30	Long Cross, Shaftesbury	40
A31	East of Boundary La Roundabout, St Leonards	70
A35	Sea Rd South, Bridport	50
A35	Christchurch Bypass	70
A35	Lyndhurst Rd, Christchurch	60
A35	Friary Press, west of Dorchester	60
A35	Kingston Russell	60
A35	Baker's Arms Roundabout, Lytchett Minster, to roundabout with A350	70
A35	Organford	70
A35	Upton Rd, Poole	60
A35	Near Sherford/Slepe	60
A35	Vinney Cross (near Uploders)	60
A35	Whiteway Cross (2.5km west of Kingston Russell)	60
A35	Woodbury Cross (1.5km east of Bere Regis)	60
A37	Staggs Folly (near Chalmington)	60
A37	Long Ash La, Frampton	60
A37	Wardon Hill (near Frome St Quintin)	60
A37	Holywell Cross, Holywell	60
A338	Spur Rd (north of Hurn)	70
A338	Wessex Way, Cooper Dean, Bournemouth	50
A348	Ringwood Rd, Bear Cross, Bournemouth	40
A349	Gravel Hill, Poole	60
A350	Holes Bay Rd, Poole	50
A350	Poole Rd, Poole	60
A350	Shaston Rd, Stourpaine	30
A350	Upton Country Park to A35 jct	70
A352	Dorchester Rd, Wool	30
A354	Dorchester Rd, Ridgeway Hill (3km south of A35)	60
A354	Dorchester Rd (Manor Roundabout to Weymouth Hospital)	30
A354	Dorchester Rd, Redlands, Weymouth	40
A354	Buxton Rd, Weymouth	30
A354	Dorchester Rd, Upwey	30
B3065	Pinecliff Rd, Poole	30
B3065	The Avenue, Poole	30
B3073	Christchurch Rd, West Parley	30
B3073	Oakley Hill, Wimborne Minster	30
B3074	Higher Blandford Rd, Broadstone, Poole	30
B3082	Blandford Rd (near Badbury Rings)	60
B3092	Colesbrook, Gillingham	40
B3157	Chickerell Rd, Weymouth	30
B3157	Portesham	30
B3157	Lanehouse Rocks Rd, Weymouth	30
B3157	Limekiln Hill, West Bexington	50
B3369	Sandbanks Rd, Poole	30
B3369	Shore Rd, Poole	30
-	Blandford Forum, Salisbury Rd	30
-	Bournemouth, Branksome Wood Rd	30
-	Bournemouth, Carbery Ave	30
-	Bournemouth, Littledown Ave	30

Road number	Location	Speed limit (mph)
-	Bournemouth, Petersfield Rd	30
-	Bournemouth, Southbourne Overcliff Dr	30
-	Ferndown, Wimborne Rd West, Stapehill	40
-	Poole, Herbert Ave	30
-	Poole, Old Wareham Rd	30
-	Portland, Weston Rd	30
-	Upton, Poole Rd	30
-	Weymouth, Dorchester Rd	30

Durham Constabulary area

Road number	Location	Speed limit (mph)
A66	Bowes Moor/Galley Bank/Greta Bridge	n/a
A67	Conniscliffe, Darlington	n/a
A167	North Lodge, Chester-le-Street	n/a
A167	North Rd, Darlington	n/a
A167	Whitesmocks and Tollhouse Rd, Durham	n/a
A690	Low Willington up to West Rd, Crook	n/a
A690	West Rainton, Durham	n/a
A1086	Horden south to county boundary	n/a
B6280	Yarm Rd, Darlington	n/a
B6168	Annfield Plain (A692 to A693)	n/a
B6282	Etherley, Bishop Auckland	n/a
B6284	Ediscum Garth, Bishop Auckland	n/a
B6288	Spennymoor to A167 Croxdale	n/a
-	Darlington, McMullen Rd	n/a
-	Durham, Finchale Rd	n/a
-	Peterlee, Essington Way	n/a

Essex

Road number	Location	Speed limit (mph)
A12	Overbridge, near Kelvedon interchange	70
A13	High St, Hadleigh (towards London)	30
A13	London Rd, Leigh-on-Sea	30
A13	North Shoebury	n/a
A13	Bournes Green Chase, Southend-on-Sea	n/a
A13	Southchurch Blvd, Southend-on-Sea	n/a
A112	Sewardstone Rd, Waltham Abbey	n/a
A113	High Rd, Chigwell	30
A120	Harwich Rd, (Wix Arch Cottages to Cansey La, Goose Green)	n/a
A120	Horsley Cross (south-west to Park Rd)	n/a
A121	Goldings Hill, Loughton (at Monkchester Cl)	30
A121	High Rd, Loughton	n/a
A121	Farm Hill Rd, Waltham Abbey	n/a
A126	London Rd, Grays	30
A126	Montreal Rd, Tilbury	30
A126	London Rd, West Thurrock	30
A128	High St, Chipping Ongar	n/a
A128	Brentwood Rd, Ingrave/Herongate	30
A129	Crays Hill, Basildon	30
A129	Southend Rd, Billericay	n/a
A129	London Rd, Rayleigh	30
A129	London Rd, Wickford	30
A129	Southend Rd, Wickford	n/a
A130	Long Rd, Canvey Island	30
A133	Canvey Way, South Benfleet	n/a
A133	Clacton Rd, Elmstead Market	30
A133	Colchester Rd, (near Weeley)	n/a
A134	Nayland Rd, Great Horkesley	40
A137	Wignall St, Lawford	30
A414	Malden Rd, Danbury	n/a
A1016	Waterhouse La, Chelmsford	30
A1017	Swan St, Sible Hedingham	30
A1023	London Rd, Brentwood	30
A1023	Shenfield Rd, Brentwood	30
A1025	Second Ave, Harlow	40
A1025	Third Ave, Harlow	40
A1060	Lower Rd, Little Hallingbury	n/a
A1090	London Rd, Purfleet	30
A1090	Tank Hill Rd, Purfleet	30
A1124	Lexden Rd, Colchester	30
A1158	Southbourne Grove, Westcliff-on-Sea	30
A1168	Rectory La, Loughton	30
A1169	Southern Way, Harlow	40
A1232	Ipswich Rd, Colchester	n/a
A1235	Cranes Farm Rd, Basildon (at Honywood Rd)	40
B170	Chigwell Rise, Chigwell	n/a
B170	Roding La, Loughton	n/a
B172	Coppice Row, Theydon Bois	n/a
B173	Lambourne Rd, Chigwell	n/a
B184	Snow Hill, Great Easton	40
B186	South Rd, South Ockendon	n/a
B1002	Ingatestone High St, Ingatestone	30
B1007	Laindon Rd, Billericay (near School Rd)	30
B1007	Stock Rd, Billericay	30
B1007	Galleywood Rd, Chelmsford	30
B1007	Stock Rd, Chelmsford	40
B1008	Broomfield Rd, Chelmsford	30
B1013	Main Rd, Hawkwell	30
B1013	Southend Rd, Hockley/Hawkwell	30
B1013	High Rd, Rayleigh	30
B1013	Hockley Rd, Rayleigh	30
B1014	Benfleet Rd, South Benfleet	30
B1018	The Street, Latchingdon	30
B1018	The Causeway, Maldon	30
B1019	Maldon Rd, Hatfield Peveral	30
B1021	Church Rd, Burnham-on-Crouch	n/a
B1022	Maldon Rd, Colchester	30
B1022	Shrub End Rd, Colchester	30
B1022	Maldon Rd, Heckfordbridge	30
B1022	Colchester Rd, Maldon	30
B1022	Maldon Rd, Tiptree Heath	30
B1027	St Osyth Rd, Alresford	40
B1027	St John's Rd, Clacton-on-Sea	30
B1027	Valley Rd/Old Rd, Clacton-on-Sea	30
B1027	Pump Hill, St Osyth	30
B1027	Brightlingsea Rd, (near Wivenhoe)	40
B1028	Colchester Rd, Wivenhoe	30
B1028	The Avenue, Wivenhoe	30
B1033	Frinton Rd, Kirby Cross	30
B1256	Coggeshall Rd, Braintree	n/a
B1335	Stifford Rd, South Ockendon	40
B1352	Main Rd, Harwich	n/a
B1383	London Rd, Newport	30
B1383	Cambridge Rd, Stansted Mountfitchet	n/a
B1389	Colchester Rd, Witham	30
B1389	Hatfield Rd, Witham	30
B1393	High Rd, Epping	30
B1393	Palmers Hill, Epping	30
B1441	London Rd, Clacton-on-Sea	30
B1441	Clacton Rd, Weeley Heath	n/a
B1442	Thorpe Rd, Clacton-on-Sea	30
B1464	London Rd, Bowers Gifford	30
-	Aveley, Purfleet Rd	30
-	Aveley, Romford Rd	n/a
-	Basildon, Ashlyns	30
-	Basildon, Sandon Rd, Barstable	30
-	Basildon, Clayhill Rd	30
-	Basildon, Felmores	30
-	Basildon, High Rd, Langdon Hills	30
-	Basildon, Durham Rd, Laindon	30
-	Basildon, Nightingales, Laindon	30
-	Basildon, Wash Rd, Laindon	30
-	Basildon, Rectory Rd, Pitsea	30
-	Basildon, Vange Hill Dr	30
-	Basildon, Whitmore Way	30
-	Basildon, Wickford Ave	30
-	Billericay, Mountnessing Rd	30
-	Braintree, Coldnailhurst Ave (Alexander Rd towards Church La)	30
-	Brentwood, Chelmsford Rd	30
-	Brentwood, Eagle Way (Clive Rd to Warley Rd)	30
-	Buckhurst Hill, Buckhurst Way/Albert Rd	30
-	Canvey Island, Dovervelt Rd	30
-	Canvey Island, Link Rd	30
-	Canvey Island, Thorney Bay Rd	30
-	Chadwell St Mary, Brentwood Rd	n/a
-	Chadwell St Mary, Linford Rd	30
-	Chadwell St Mary, Riverview	30
-	Chelmsford, Baddow Rd	30
-	Chelmsford, Chignall Rd	30
-	Chelmsford, Copperfield Rd	30
-	Chelmsford, Longstomps Ave	30
-	Chelmsford, New Bowers Way, Springfield	30
-	Clacton-on-Sea, Burrs Rd	30
-	Clacton-on-Sea, Kings Parade	30
-	Clacton-on-Sea, Marine Parade East,	30
-	Clacton-on-Sea, St Osyth Rd, Rush Green	n/a
-	Colchester, Abbot's Rd	30
-	Colchester, Avon Way	30
-	Colchester, Bromley Rd	30
-	Colchester, Old Heath Rd	30
-	Daws Heath, Daws Heath Rd	30
-	Eastwood, Green La (at Kendal Way)	30
-	Eastwood, Western Approaches (at Rockall)	30
-	Grays, Blackshots La	30
-	Grays, Lodge La	30
-	Harlow, Abercrombie Way (towards Southern Way)	40
-	Harlow, Howard Way	40
-	Hullbridge, Coventry Hill	30
-	Leigh-on-Sea, Belton Way East (Marine Parade to Belton Gdns)	30
-	Leigh-on-Sea, Belton Way West	30
-	Leigh-on-Sea, Blenheim Chase	30
-	Leigh-on-Sea, Grand Parade/Cliff Parade	30
-	Leigh-on-Sea, Hadleigh Rd	30
-	Leigh-on-Sea, Highlands Blvd	30
-	Leigh-on-Sea, Manchester Dr	30
-	Leigh-on-Sea, Mountdale Gdns	30
-	Leigh-on-Sea, Western Rd	30
-	Loughton, Alderton Hill	30
-	Loughton, Loughton Way	30
-	Loughton, Valley Hill	n/a
-	Maldon, Fambridge Rd	30
-	Maldon, Holloway Rd	30
-	Maldon, Mundon Rd	30
-	Prittlewell, Kenilworth Gdns	30
-	Prittlewell, Prittlewell Chase	30
-	Rayleigh, Bull La	30
-	Rayleigh, Downhall Rd	n/a
-	Rayleigh, Trinity Rd (near Church Rd)	30
-	Rochford, Ashingdon Rd	30
-	Rochford, Rectory Rd	30
-	Shoeburyness, Ness Rd	30
-	Southend-on-Sea, Bournemouth Park Rd	n/a
-	Southend-on-Sea, Hamstel Rd	30
-	Southend-on-Sea, Lifstan Way	30
-	Southend-on-Sea, Western Esplanade	30
-	Southend-on-Sea, Woodgrange Dr (at Sandringham Rd)	30
-	South Woodham Ferrers, Hullbridge Rd	30
-	South Woodham Ferrers, Inchbonnie Rd	30
-	Stanford le Hope, London Rd	30
-	Stanford le Hope, Southend Rd, Corringham	30
-	Stanford le Hope, Springhouse Rd, Corringham	30
-	Theydon Bois, Piercing Hill	n/a
-	Thorpe Bay, Barnstable Rd	30
-	Thorpe Bay, Thorpe Hall Ave	30
-	Waltham Abbey, Paternoster Hill	n/a
-	Westcliff-on-Sea, Chalkwell Ave	30
-	Westcliff-on-Sea, Kings Rd	30
-	Wickford, Radwinter Ave	30
-	Witham, Powers Hall End	30
-	Witham, Rickstones Rd	30

Gloucestershire

Road number	Location	Speed limit (mph)
A38	Twigworth	40
A40	Andoversford	60
A40	The Barringtons	60
A40	Gloucester Rd, St Marks, Cheltenham	40
A40	Churcham	50
A40	Farmington	60
A40	Hampnett	60
A40	Hazleton	60
A40	Northleach	60
A40	Whittington/Andoversford	60
A46	Ashchurch	30
A46	North of Nailsworth	40
A417	Burford Junction (Cirencester)	70
A417	Dartley Bottom (north-west of Cirencester)	70
A417	Gloucester Rd, Corse	40
A417	Lechlade on Thames	40
A417	Maisemore	30
A417	North of Hartpury	40
A419	Oldends La to Stonehouse Court, Stonehouse	40
A429	South-west of Bourton-on-the-Water	60
A429	Fossebridge	40
A430	Hempstead Bypass, Gloucester	40
A435	Colesbourne	60
A436	Near jct with B4068	60
A4013	Princess Elizabeth Way, Arle, Cheltenham	30
A4013	Princess Elizabeth Way, Hester's Way, Cheltenham	30
A4019	Uckington	50
A4136	Brierley	40
A4136	Harrow Hill (near Drybrook)	40
A4136	Little London	40
A4151	Steam Mills, Cinderford	40
A4173	Near St Peter's School, Tuffley, Gloucester	30
B4008	Bristol Rd, Olympus Park area, Quedgeley	30
B4008	Bristol Rd, Hardwicke (south of Tesco roundabout)	40
B4008	Gloucester Rd, Stonehouse	30
B4060	Wooton-under-Edge/Kingswood (at school)	30
B4215	South-east of Rudford	50
B4215	South of Newent Bypass	50
B4221	Kilcot Village	40
B4221	Picklenash School, Newent	30
B4228	Old Station Way, Coleford	30
B4228	Perrygrove, south of Coleford	40
B4633	Gloucester Rd, Cheltenham (south-west of St Georges Rd)	30
-	Cheltenham, St Georges Rd	30
-	Cheltenham, Swindon La	30
-	Cheltenham, Wyman's Lane	30
-	Cirencester, Chesterton La	30
-	Gloucester, Abbeymead Ave	30
-	Gloucester, Barrow Hill, Churchdown	30
-	Minchinhampton Common	40
-	Siddington	30
-	Tewkesbury, Gloucester Rd	40

Greater Manchester

Road number	Location	Speed limit (mph)
A6	Buxton Rd, Hazel Grove	30
A6	Buxton Rd, High Lane	30
A6	Stockport Rd, Manchester	30
A6	Wellington Rd North, Stockport	30
A34	Kingsway, Cheadle	40
A34	Birchfields Rd, Rusholme, Manchester	30
A34	Kingsway, Manchester	40
A49	Wigan Rd, Standish	30
A49	Warrington Rd, Marus Bridge, Wigan	30
A56	Jubilee Way, Bury	30
A56	Manchester Rd, Bury	30
A56	Walmersley Rd, Bury	30
A56	Bury New Rd, Manchester	30
A56	Chester Rd, Old Trafford (at White City Way)	30
A56	Bury New Rd, Prestwich	30
A56	Whalley Rd, Shuttleworth	30
A57	Liverpool Rd, Eccles	30
A57	Manchester Rd, Hyde	30
A57	Mottram Rd, Hyde	30
A57	Hyde Rd/Manchester Rd, Manchester	30
A58	Lily La, Bamfurlong, Abram	30
A58	Liverpool Rd, Ashton-In-Makerfield	30
A58	Wigan Rd, Bolton	40
A58	Angouleme Way, Bury	30
A58	Bolton Rd, Bury	30
A58	Rochdale Rd, Bury	30
A58	Bury and Bolton Rd, Radcliffe	30
A58	Halifax Rd, Rochdale	30
A62	Oldham Rd, Failsworth	30
A62	Oldham Rd, Manchester	30
A62	Oldham Way, Oldham	50
A560	Shaftesbury Avenue,Timperley, Altrincham	40
A560	Crookilley Way, Stockport	50
A571	Pemberton Rd, Winstanley, Wigan	30
A571	Victoria St, Wigan	30
A572	Chaddock La, Astley, Tyldesley	30
A572	Newton Rd, Lowton (near Leigh)	30
A573	Wigan Rd, Golborne	30
A574	Warrington Rd, Leigh	30
A575	Walkden Rd, Worsley	30
A579	Atherleigh Way, Leigh	50
A580	East Lancashire Rd, Leigh	70
A580	East Lancashire Rd, Swinton/Worsley	50
A626	Marple Rd, Offerton, Stockport	30
A627	Chadderton Way, Chadderton	40
A635	Ashton Old Rd, Manchester	30
A635	Mancunian Way, Manchester	40
A635/A6018	Stamford St, Stalybridge	30
A662	Ashton New Rd, Manchester	30
A663	Broadway, Failsworth	40
A664	Rochdale Rd, Manchester	30
A664	Manchester Rd, Castleton, Rochdale	30
A665	Bury Old Rd, Prestwich	30
A665	Cheetham Hill Rd, Manchester	30
A665	New Rd, Radcliffe	30
A665	Higher La, Whitefield	30
A665	Radcliffe New Rd, Whitefield	30
A666	Blackburn Rd, Bolton	30
A666	St Peter's Way, Bolton	50
A666	Manchester Rd, Swinton	30
A667	Ringley Rd West, Whitefield	30
A670	Mossley Rd, Ashton-under-Lyne	30
A673	Chorley New Rd, Bolton	40
A676	Bolton Rd, Hawkshaw	30
A676	Bolton Rd West, Holcombe Brook, Ramsbottom	30
A676	Stubbins La, Ramsbottom	30
A680	Edenfield Rd, Rochdale	30
A5014	Talbot Rd, Stretford	30
A5079	Slade La, Levenshulme, Manchester	30
A5103	Princess Pkwy (near M60 jct 5)	50
A5103	Princess Rd, Manchester	30
A5106	Chorley Rd, Standish	30
A5143	Bridge La, Bramhall	30
A5143	Jacksons La, Hazel Grove	30
A5145	Edge La, Stretford	30
A5181	Mosley Rd, Trafford Park	30
A5209	Crow Orchard Rd, Shevington Moor	30
A5209	Almond Brook Rd, Standish	30
A6010	Alan Turing Way, Manchester	30
A6010	Pottery La, Manchester	30
A6017	Ashton Rd, Bredbury, Stockport	40
A6033	Todmorden Rd, Littleborough	30
A6044	Hilton La, Prestwich	30
A6044	Sheepfoot La, Prestwich	30
A6045	Manchester Rd, Heywood	30
A6045	Heywood Old Rd, Middleton	30
A6046	Hollin La, Middleton	30
A6053	Dumers La, Radcliffe	30
A6104	Victoria Ave, Blackley, Manchester	30
A6144	Warburton La, Partington	30
A6144	Harboro Rd, Sale	30
A6144	Old Hall Rd, Sale Moor	30
A6145	Hulton La, Bolton	30
B5158	Lostock Rd, Urmston	30
B5160	Park Rd, Bowdon	30
B5165	Park Rd, Timperley, Altrincham	30
B5166	Ashton La, Ashton upon Mersey	30
B5166	Styal Rd, Heald Green, Gatley	30
B5206	Upholland Rd, Billinge	30
B5213	Church Rd, Urmston	30
B5217	Seymour Grove, Old Trafford	30
B5218	Upper Chorlton Rd, Chorlton cum Hardy	30
B5237	Bickershaw La, Bickershaw, Abram	30
B5239	Bolton Rd, Aspull	30
B5239	Haigh Rd, Aspull	30
B5239	Dicconson La, Cooper Turning, Bolton	30
B5375	Miles La, Shevington	30
B5397	Dane Rd, Sale	30
B6101	Strines Rd, Marple	30
B6167	Gorton Rd, Reddish	30
B6177	Stamford Rd, Mossley	30
B6194	Broad La, Rochdale	30
B6196	Ainsworth Rd, Bury	30
B6196	Church St, Ainsworth, Bury	30
B6196	Cockey Moor Rd, Ainsworth, Bury	30
B6196	Hardy Mill Rd, Bolton	30
B6199	Plodder La, Farnworth	30
B6213	Bury Rd, Tottington	30
B6213	Turton Rd, Tottington	30
B6214	Brandlesholme Rd, Bury	30
B6214	Helmshore Rd, Holcombe, Ramsbottom	30
B6214	Longsight Rd, Holcombe Brook, Ramsbottom	30
B6215	Brandlesholme Rd, Greenmount, Ramsbottom	30
B6222	Bury Rd, Rochdale	30
B6225	Milnrow Rd, Littleborough	30
B6225	Wildhouse La, Milnrow	60
B6226	Chorley Old Rd, Bolton	30/50
B6292	Ainsworth Rd, Radcliffe	30
B6292	Starling Rd, Radcliffe	30
B6377	Shawclough Rd, Rochdale	30
-	Aspull, Scot La	30
-	Bolton, Stitch-Mi-La	30
-	Bury, Croft La, Hollins	30
-	Bury, Radcliffe Rd	30
-	Bury, Walshaw Rd	30
-	Cheadle, Birdhall La	30
-	Cheadle, Councillor La	30
-	Cheadle, Schools Hill	30
-	Cheadle Hulme, Carr Wood Rd	30
-	Hazel Grove, Chester Rd	30
-	Heywood, Bury Old Rd	30
-	Heywood, Queens Park Rd	30
-	Horwich, Lever Park Ave	30
-	Leigh, Queensway	30
-	Manchester, Blackley New Rd, Crumpsall	30
-	Manchester, Hazelbottom/Waterloo St, Cheetham Hill	30
-	Mellor, Longhurst La	30
-	Pendlebury, Langley Rd	30
-	Radcliffe, Stand La	30
-	Rochdale, Bagslate Moor Rd	30
-	Rochdale, Caldershaw Rd	30
-	Rochdale, Smithybridge Rd, Smithy Bridge	30
-	Romiley, Sandy La	30
-	Sale, Glebelands Rd	30
-	Sale, Hope Rd	30
-	Sale, Norris Rd	30
-	Salford, Belvedere Rd	30
-	Stockport, Dialstone La, Offerton	30
-	Stockport, Harrytown, Bredbury	30
-	Stretford, Kings Rd	30
-	Trafford Park, Westinghouse Rd	30
-	Westhoughton, The Hoskers	30

Hampshire and the Isle of Wight

Road number	Location	Speed limit (mph)
A27	Portchester to Titchfield	30/40
A27	Parkgate to A3024	30/40
A30	Blackwater	30/40
A33	Riseley to Basingstoke	50
A33	Western end of flyover (M271) to Mayflower Roundabout, Southampton	50
A325	Farnborough/Aldershot, Hawley La to Cranmore La	30/40/60/70
A325	Whitehill to county boundary near Farnham	30/40/60
A334	Wickham, A32 to B2177	n/a
A335	Eastleigh	30/40
A337	Lymington Rd/Christchurch Rd, New Milton	30/40
A337	Pennington, Lymington to Balmerlawn, Brockenhurst	30/40/50/60
A338	Fordingbridge to county boundary	40/60
A338	Ringwood to Ibsley	40/60
A340	Pamber End to Tadley	30/60
A2047	Fratton Rd, Portsmouth	30
A3020	Blackwater (IOW)	n/a
A3020	Blackwater Rd, Newport (IOW)	40
A3021	York Ave, East Cowes (IOW)	30
A3024	A27 to city centre, Southampton	30/40
A3054	Binstead Hill, Binstead (IOW)	30
A3054	Fairlee Rd, Newport (IOW)	30/40
A3054	High St/Lushington Hill, Wootton Bridge (IOW)	30/40
A3055	High St/New Rd, Brading (IOW)	30
A3056	Blackwater (IOW)	n/a
B2177	A334 to Winchester Rd, Bishop's Waltham	n/a
B3037	Fair Oak to Eastleigh	30/40
B3055	Brockenhurst to A35	30/40
B3321	Adelaide Gr/Victoria Gr, East Cowes (IOW)	30
B3395	Sandown to Yaverland (IOW)	30
-	Basingstoke, Tobago Close	30
-	Newport, Staplers Rd/Long La (IOW)	30
-	Portsmouth, Clarence Esplanade/Esplanade	30

Hertfordshire

Road number	Location	Speed limit (mph)
A41	North Western Ave, Watford (near East Dr)	40
A119	North Rd, Hertford (at St Josephs School)	30
A411	London Rd, Bushey (150m west of Merry Hill Rd)	30
A411	Hempstead Rd, Watford (at Glen Way)	30
A414	St Albans Rd, Hemel Hempstead (near Rant Meadow)	40
A414	Hertingfordbury Rd, Hertford (west of Valeside)	40
A505	Cambridge Rd, Hitchin (100m south-west of Queenswood Dr)	30
A600	Bedford Rd, Hitchin (at Times Close)	30
A600	Bedford Rd, Hitchin (75m south of north jct of Wellingham Ave)	30
A602	Stevenage Rd, Hitchin	40
A602	Broadhall Way, Stevenage (A1072 to 200m east of Broadwater Cres)	40
A602	Monkswood Way, Stevenage (100m north of Broadhall Way)	40
A1000	Barnet Rd, Ganwick Corner, Potters Bar (at Wagon Rd)	40
A1057	Hatfield Rd, St Albans (near Beechwood Ave)	30
A1057	St Albans Rd West, Hatfield (near Poplar Ave)	40
A1170	High Rd Wormley, Wormley	30
A4125	Sandy La, Northwood (180m south of Batchworth La)	40
A4125	Eastbury Rd, Watford	30
A4251	London Rd, Bourne End (near Lauries Cl)	30
A5183	Frogmore, Park Street (south of St Albans)	30
A6141	London Rd, Baldock (at Hillcrest)	30
A6141	Letchworth Gate, Letchworth (250m north-west of Baldock La)	60
B156	Goffs La, Broxbourne (at Goffs School)	30
B176	High St, Cheshunt (near Warwick Dr)	30
B197	North Rd, Stevenage (south of Rectory La)	30
B487	Redbourn La, Hatching Green, Harpenden (at Oakfield Rd)	30
B487	Queensway, Hemel Hempstead (near Highfield La)	40
B488	Icknield Way, Tring (at Little Tring Rd)	40
B556	Mutton La, Potters Bar (near Albermarle Ave)	30
B1502	Stanstead Rd, Hertford (east of Foxholes Ave)	30
B5378	Allum La, Borehamwood (at Lodge Ave)	30
B5378	Shenleybury, Shenley (150m either side of Shenleybury cottages)	40
-	Cheshunt, Hammondstreet Rd (Peakes La to Hammond Close)	30
-	Hoddesdon, Essex Rd (at Pindar Rd)	30
-	Letchworth, Pixmore Way (50m east of Shott La)	30
-	Royston, Old North Rd (York Way to Orchard Rd)	30
-	South Oxhey, Hayling Rd (Gosforth La to Arbroath Green)	30
-	St Albans, Sandpit La (at Gurney Court Rd)	30
-	Stevenage, Clovelly Way (Scarborough Ave to Eastbourne Ave)	30
-	Watford, Radlett Rd	30
-	Watford, Tolpits La (at Scammell Cl)	30
-	Watford, Whippendell Rd	30
-	Welwyn Garden City, Heronswood Rd (south of Linces Way)	30
-	Welwyn Garden City, Howlands (at garages at entrance to hospice)	30

Humberside

Road number	Location	Speed limit (mph)
M180	West of River Trent	70
A16	Louth Rd, Grimsby	30
A18	Barton Street, Central (north-east Lincs)	60
A18	Barton Street, North (north-east Lincs)	60
A18	Barton Street, South (north-east Lincs)	60
A18	Doncaster Rd, Scunthorpe	40
A18	Queensway, Scunthorpe	40
A18	Wrawby	30
A46	Clee Rd, Cleethorpes	30
A46	Laceby Rd, Grimsby	30
A46	Weelsby Rd, Grimsby	30
A46	Laceby Bypass	70
A63	Castle St, Kingston upon Hull	40
A63	Daltry Street Flyover, Kingston upon Hull	40
A63	Melton	50
A159	Ashby Rd, Scunthorpe	30
A159	Messingham Rd, Scunthorpe	30
A161	Belton	30
A163	Holme upon Spalding Moor	30
A164	Leconfield	30
A165	Beeford	30
A165	Kingsgate, Bridlington	30
A165	Coniston	40
A165	Freetown Way, Kingston upon Hull	30
A165	Holderness Rd, Kingston upon Hull	40
A165	Skirlaugh	30
A180	Great Coates junction	70
A614	Airmyn Rd, Goole	30
A614	Holme upon Spalding Moor	40
A614	Thorpe Rd, Howden	30
A614	Middleton on the Wolds	30
A614	Shiptonthorpe (north of roundabout)	60
A614	Shiptonthorpe (south of the village)	60
A1031	Tetney Rd, Humberston	30
A1033	Thomas Clarkson Way, Kingston upon Hull	40
A1033	Main St, Thorngumbald	30
A1033	Withernsea	30
A1035	Hull Bridge Rd, Beverley	30
A1038	Quay Rd/St John's St, Bridlington	30
A1077	Barton-upon-Humber	30
A1079	Barmby Moor	50
A1079	Beverley Rd, Kingston upon Hull (Desmond Ave to Riverdale Rd)	30
A1079	Beverley Rd, Kingston upon Hull (Sutton Rd to Mizzen Rd)	40
A1079	Bishop Burton	30
A1084	Bigby High Rd, Brigg	30
A1105	Anlaby Rd, Kingston upon Hull	30
A1105	Boothferry Rd, Kingston upon Hull	40
A1136	Cromwell Rd, Grimsby	30
A1136	Great Coates Rd, Grimsby	30
A1174	Dunswell	30
A1174	Woodmansey	30
A1243	Louth Rd, Grimsby	30
B1203	Waltham Rd, Grimsby	30
B1206	Wold Rd, Barrow-upon-Humber	30
B1207	High St, Broughton	30
B1230	Gilberdyke	40
B1230	Newport	40
B1231	Anlaby Rd, Kingston upon Hull	30
B1232	Beverley Rd, Hessle	30
B1237	Leads Rd, Kingston upon Hull	30
B1237	Saltshouse Rd, Kingston upon Hull	30
B1238	Main Rd, Bilton, Kingston upon Hull	30
B1240	Station Rd, Preston	30
B1242	Rolston Rd, Hornsea	30
B1398	Greetwell	40
B1501	Grange La South, Ashby, Scunthorpe	30
-	Belton, Westgate Rd	30
-	East Halton, College Rd	30
-	Grimsby, Cromwell Rd	30
-	Hessle, Beverley Rd	30
-	Immingham, Pelham Rd	30
-	Kingston upon Hull, Bricknell Ave	30
-	Kingston upon Hull, Bude Rd	30
-	Kingston upon Hull, Greenwood Ave	30
-	Kingston upon Hull, Hall Rd	30

Road number	Location	Speed limit (mph)
-	Kingston upon Hull, John Newton Way	30
-	Kingston upon Hull, Marfleet La	30
-	Kingston upon Hull, Marfleet Ave	30
-	Kingston upon Hull, Priory Rd	30
-	Kingston upon Hull, Spring Bank West	40
-	Kingston upon Hull, Wawne Rd	30
-	Scunthorpe, Ashby Rd	30
-	Scunthorpe, Cambridge Ave	30
-	Scunthorpe, Cottage Beck Rd	30
-	Scunthorpe, Doncaster Rd	40
-	Scunthorpe, Luneburg Way	30
-	Scunthorpe, Moorwell Rd, Yaddlethorpe	30
-	Scunthorpe, Rowland Rd	30
-	South Killingholme, Top Rd	30

Kent and Medway

Road number	Location	Speed limit (mph)
A2	Dunkirk to Upper Harbledown (eastbound)	70
A2	Guston (A256 to A258)	60
A2	London Rd, Rochester (opposite Lancelot Ave)	40
A2	Lydden (Wick La to Lydden Hill, coastbound)	70
A20	London Rd, Addington (Trottiscliffe Rd to Ryarsh Rd)	50
A20	Dover Rd/Archcliffe Rd, Aycliffe, Dover (eastbound approach to Western Heights roundabout)	70/40
A20	London Rd, Ditton (Bell La to Teapot La)	40
A21	Key's Green (Kipping's Cross to Beech La)	60
A21	Sevenoaks Bypass, Hubbard's Hill (southbound, Didben La to Morleys roundabout)	70
A21	Sevenoaks Bypass (northbound, Dibden La to Cold Arbor Rd)	70
A21	Castle Hill, Tonbridge	60
A25	Seal Rd, Sevenoaks (near Mill Pond)	30
A26	Maidstone Rd, Hadlow (Great Elms to Lonewood Way)	40
A28	Ashford Rd, Bethersden (near Kiln La)	40
A224	Tubs Hill, Sevenoaks (The Drive to Morewood Close)	30
A225	Sevenoaks Rd, Otford (Warham Rd to Old Otford Rd)	30
A226	Chalk, Gravesend	50
A226	Higham	40
A226	Shorne	50
A227	Culverstone Green	40
A227	Istead Rise	40
A227	Meopham Green	30
A228	Ratcliffe Highway, Chattenden	40
A229	Hartley Rd/Angley Rd, Cranbrook (Turnden Rd to High St)	40
A229	Bluebell Hill, Maidstone (Tyland La to Chatham Rd)	50
A229	Loose Rd, Loose, Maidstone (Linton Rd to Lancet La)	40/30
A229	City Way, Rochester	30
A249	South Street (Chalky Rd to Rumstead La)	70
A249	Chestnut Street (northbound, near slip rd to A2 Key St roundabout)	70
A256	Betteshanger	70
A256	London Rd, Dover	30
A256	Haine Rd, Haine (Manston Rd to Spratling St)	40
A256	Tilmanstone	70
A258	Dover Rd, Ringwould (north of Church La)	50
A259	Guldeford La (south-west of Brookland)	60
A259	High St, New Romney (near West St)	30
A259	St Mary's Bay (near Jefferstone La)	40
A262	High St, Biddenden	30
A268	Queen St, Stohurst	30
A289	Medway Tunnel, Chatham (near Vanguard Way)	50
A290	Blean	30
A291	Canterbury Rd, Herne (Lower Herne Rd to A299)	30
A292	Mace La, Ashford (Wellesley Rd to Mill Court)	30
A299	Canterbury Road West, Cliffsend	30
A2033	Dover Rd, Folkestone (Wear Bay Rd to Southern Way)	30
A2990	Thanet Way, Swalecliffe, Whitstable (east of Chestfield roundabout)	60
B258	Barn End La, Wilmington, Dartford	30
B2015	Maidstone Rd, Nettlestead Green (near Station Rd)	40
B2017	Badsell Rd, Five Oak Green (Whetstead Rd to Capel Grange Farm)	30
B2067	Woodchurch Rd, Tenterden	30
B2071	Littlestone Rd, New Romney (Warren Rd to Marine Parade)	30
B2097	Maidstone Rd, Rochester (Horwood Close to Valley View)	30
B2205	Mill Way, Sittingbourne (Tribune Dr to Cooks La)	30
-	Bromley Green, Ashford Rd (at Sugar Loaf Crossroads)	60
-	Chatham, Street End Rd	30
-	Chatham, Walderslade Rd (Snodhurst Ave to Chestnut Ave)	30
-	Cobham, Sole St (near Scratton Fields)	30
-	Gillingham, Beechings Way (Bradbourne Ave to Beechings Green)	30
-	Hartley, Ash Rd	30
-	Herne Bay, Mickleburgh Hill	30
-	Longfield, Hartley Rd/Ash Rd	30
-	Maidstone, Rough Common Rd, Rough Common	30
-	Margate, Shottendane Rd	30
-	New Ash Green, Ash Rd	30
-	Rainham, Maidstone Rd (Drury Dr to Thames Rd)	30
-	Teynham, Lower Rd (Station Rd to New Cottages)	30

Lancashire

Road number	Location	Speed limit (mph)
A6	Bolton Rd, Chorley	30
A6	Bay Horse Rd, Galgate	60
A6	Garstang Rd, Broughton (north of M55)	40
A6	Garstang Rd, Fulwood, Preston (north of Blackpool Rd)	30
A6	Garstang Rd, Fulwood, Preston (south of M55)	30
A6	Greaves Rd, Lancaster	30
A6	Scotforth Rd, Bailrigg, Lancaster (near Burrow La)	50
A6	North Rd, Preston	30
A6	Ringway, Preston	30
A56	Albert Rd, Colne	30
A56	Burnley Rd, Colne	30
A56	Leeds Rd, Nelson	30
A59	Gisburn Rd, Gisburn	60
A59	Liverpool Rd, Hutton	50
A59	New Hall La, Preston	30
A65	Cowan Bridge	40
A570	Southport Rd, Scarisbrick (at Brook House Farm)	40
A581	Southport Rd, Ulnes Walton	40
A583	Church St, Blackpool	30
A583	Whitegate Dr, Blackpool (near Waterloo Rd)	30
A584	Promenade, Blackpool	30
A584	Lytham Rd, Warton	30
A584	West/Central Beach, Lytham	30
A587	East/North Park Dr, Blackpool	30
A587	Fleetwood Rd, Blackpool	30
A587	Rossall Rd, Cleveleys	30
A588	Head Dyke La, Preesall/Pilling	60
A588	Lancaster Rd, Cockerham (at Gulf La)	60
A666	Blackburn Rd, Darwen	30
A666	Bolton Rd, Darwen (near Cross St)	30
A666	Duckworth St, Darwen	30
A671	Whalley Rd, Read	30
A674	Preston Old Rd, Cherry Tree, Blackburn	30
A675	Belmont Rd (north of Belmont village)	50
A675	Belmont Rd (south of Belmont village)	50
A675	Bolton Rd, Abbey Village, Chorley (Dole La to Calf Hey Bridge)	60
A680	Rochdale Rd, Edenfield	40
A682	Burnley Rd, Crawshawbooth	40
A682	Colne Rd, Brierfield	30
A682	Gisburn Rd, Gisburn	60
A682	Gisburn Rd, Barrowford (near Moorcock Inn)	60
A682	Long Preston Rd, north of Gisburn	60
A683	Morecambe Rd, Lancaster	30
A5073	Waterloo Rd, Blackpool	30
A5085	Blackpool Rd, Lane Ends, Preston	30
A5209	Course La/Ash Brow, Newburgh	30
A6068	Barrowford Rd, Barrowford	50
A6114	Casterton Ave, Burnley	30
A6177	Grane Rd, Haslingden (west of Holcombe Rd)	50
A6177	Haslingden Rd/Elton Rd, Blackburn	50
B5192	Preston St, Kirkham	30
B5251	Pall Mall, Chorley	30
B5254	Leyland Rd, Penwortham, Preston (Talbot Rd to A59)	30
B5254	Leyland Rd/Watkin La, Lostock Hall	30
B5256	Turpin Green La, Leyland	30
B5266	Newton Dr, Blackpool (near Church St)	30
B5269	Whittingham La, Goosnargh	40
B6231	Union Rd, Oswaldtwistle	30
-	Belmont, Egerton Rd	60
-	Blackburn, East Park Rd	30
-	Blackburn, Whalley Old Rd (west of railway bridge)	30
-	Blackpool, Dickson Rd (Queen St to Pleasant St)	30
-	Briercliffe, Burnley Rd	30
-	Darwen, Lower Eccleshill Rd	30
-	Nelson, Netherfield Rd	30
-	Preston, Lytham Rd	30
-	Preston, St George's Rd	30
-	St Annes, Church Rd/Albany Rd (near High School)	30

Leicester, Leicestershire and Rutland

Road number	Location	Speed limit (mph)
A1	Empingham	70
A1	Stretton	70
A5	B4455 towards Wibtoft	n/a
A5	Watling St (south of A426)	60
A5	Watling St, Hinckley (M69 to A47)	50
A5	Watling St, Hinckley (B578 to M69)	60
A5	Watling St, Sharnford (Highcross to B4114)	70
A6	Abbey La, Leicester	40
A6	Derby Rd, Loughborough	30
A6	Glen Rd/Harborough Rd, Oadby	40
A6	London Rd, Leicester (at Knighton Drive)	30
A6	Loughborough Rd, Birstall	40
A47	Billesdon Bypass	50
A47	Glaston Rd, Morcott	50
A47	Hinckley Rd, Earl Shilton	30
A47	Hinckley Rd, Leicester	30
A47	Humberstone Rd, Leicester	30
A47	Peterborough Rd, Barrowden	60
A47	Uppingham Rd, Bisbrooke	60
A47	Uppingham Rd, Houghton on the Hill	40
A47	Uppingham Rd, Skeffington	50
A47	Uppingham Rd, Tugby	50
A50	Groby Rd, Leicester	40
A50	Groby Rd/Leicester Rd, Glenfield, Leicester	30
A50	Woodgate, Leicester	30
A50	Hemington/Lockington	70
A426	Leicester Rd, Lutterworth	60
A426	Leicester Rd, Glen Parva, Leicester	40
A426	Lutterworth Rd, Dunton Bassett	50
A426	Lutterworth Rd, Whetstone	50
A444	Atherstone Rd, Fenny Drayton	60
A444	Main St, Twycross village	30
A444	Norton Juxta Twycross	60
A447	Hinckley Rd, Cadeby	60
A447	Wash La, Ravenstone	40
A512	Ashby Rd, Loughborough	30
A512	Ashby Rd Central, Shepshed	40
A563	Colchester Rd, Leicester	30
A563	Attlee Way, Leicester	30
A563	Hungarton Blvd, Leicester	30
A563	Krefeld Way, Leicester	40
A563	New Parks Way, Leicester	30
A563	Glenhills Way, Leicester	30
A594	St Georges Way, Leicester	30
A606	Broughton	60
A606	Stamford Rd, Barnsdale (east of Oakham)	60
A606	Stamford Rd, Tinwell (west of A1)	60
A607	Melton Rd, Leicester	30
A607	Melton Rd, Waltham/Croxton Kerrial	60
A607	Melton Rd, Waltham on the Wolds	60
A607	Newark Rd, Thurmaston, Leicester	70
A607	Norman Way, Melton Mowbray	30
A4304	Lubbenham Hill, Market Harborough	40
A5199	Bull Head St, Wigston	30
A5199	Leicester Rd, Wigston	30
A5199	Welford Rd, Leicester	30
A5460	Narborough Rd, Leicester	40
A6004	Alan Moss Rd, Loughborough	30
A6030	Wakerley Rd/Broad Ave, Leicester	30
A6121	Stamford Rd, Ketton	30
B568	Victoria Park Rd, Leicester	30
B581	Broughton Way, Broughton Astley	30
B582	Little Glen Rd, Blaby	30
B590	Rugby Rd, Hinckley	30
B591	Loughborough Rd, Charley (3km south-east of Shepshed)	60
B676	Saxby Rd, Freeby	60
B4114	Leicester Rd/King Edward Ave, Enderby/Narborough	40
B4114	Sharnford	30
B4666	Coventry Rd, Hinckley	30
B5003	Ashby Rd, Norris Hill (west of Ashby-de-la-Zouch)	40
B5010	London Rd, Shardlow	30
B5350	Forest Rd, Loughborough	30
B5350	Nanpantan Rd, Loughborough	30
B5366	Saffron La, Leicester	30
B6416	East Park Rd, Leicester	30
-	Barrow-upon-Soar, Sileby Rd	30
-	Blaby, Lutterworth Rd	30
-	Broughton Astley, Station Rd	30
-	Hinckley, Brookside, Burbage	n/a
-	Ibstock, Leicester Rd	30
-	Leicester, Fosse Rd South	30
-	Shepshed, Leicester Rd	30
-	Woodhouse Eaves, Maplewell Rd	n/a

Lincolnshire

Road number	Location	Speed limit (mph)
A15	Ashby Lodge	60
A15	Aswarby	60
A15	B1191 to Dunsby Hollow	60
A16	Burwell	40
A16	Tytton La, Boston	60
A16	North Thoresby	60
A17	Fleet Hargate	60
A17	Hoffleet Stow (near B1181)	60
A17	Moulton Common (south of B1357)	60
A52	Bridge End	60
A52	West of Swaton	60
A52	Ropsley	60
A153	Billinghay	40
A153	Tattershall	50
A158	Scremby to Candlesby	60
A631	Dale Bridge near West Rasen	n/a
A631	Hemswell Cliff	60
B1188	Branston	30
B1188	Canwick (at Highfield House)	60
B1188	Potterhanworth (near B1178)	60

London

Road number	Location	Speed limit (mph)
M11	Chigwell	n/a
M25	West Drayton	n/a
M25	Colnbrook	n/a
M25	Spelthorne Borough (jcts 13-14)	n/a
M25	Wraysbury	n/a
M25	Runnymede	n/a
M25	Egham	n/a
M25	Byfleet	n/a
A1	Upper St, Islington	n/a
A1	Holloway Rd, Upper Holloway	n/a
A2	Old Kent Rd	n/a
A3	Kennington Park Rd, Kennington	n/a
A3	Clapham Rd, South Lambeth	n/a
A3	Kingston Rd, Roehampton	n/a
A3	Kingston Bypass	n/a
A4	Great West Rd, Chiswick/Brentford/Hounslow	n/a
A5	Edgware Rd, Cricklewood	n/a
A5	The Broadway, West Hendon	n/a
A10	Great Cambridge Rd, Edmonton	n/a
A10	Stamford Hill, Stoke Newington	n/a
A11	Bow Rd, Bow	n/a
A11	Mile End Rd, Stepney	n/a
A12	Eastern Ave, Romford	n/a
A13	Alfred's Way, Barking	n/a
A13	Ripple Rd, Barking/Dagenham	n/a
A20	Lewisham Way, New Cross	n/a
A20	Lee High Rd, Lewisham	n/a
A20	Sidcup Rd, Eltham/New Eltham	n/a
A20	Sidcup Bypass, Sidcup	n/a
A21	Bromley Rd, Catford	n/a
A21	Bromley Rd, Downham	n/a
A22	Godstone Rd, Purley/Kenley	n/a
A23	Brixton Rd, Brixton	n/a
A23	Brixton Hill, Brixton	n/a
A23	Streatham High Road, Streatham	n/a
A23	Thornton Rd, Croydon	n/a
A24	High St Colliers Wood, Tooting	n/a
A40	Westway, Paddington/Shepherd's Bush	n/a
A40	Western Ave, Perivale	n/a
A40	Western Ave, Greenford	n/a
A40	Western Ave, Northolt	n/a
A40	Western Ave, Ruislip	n/a
A102	Homerton High St, Hackney	n/a
A107	Cambridge Heath Rd, Bethnal Green	n/a
A107	Upper Clapton Rd, Clapton	n/a
A107	Clapton Common, Stamford Hill	n/a
A109	Bounds Green Rd, Bowes Park	n/a
A109	Oakleigh Rd South, Friern Barnet	n/a
A110	Enfield Rd, Enfield	n/a
A112	Chingford Rd, Walthamstow	n/a
A112	Hoe St, Walthamstow	n/a
A118	Romford Rd, Forest Gate	n/a
A124	Barking Rd, East Ham	n/a
A124	Barking Rd, Plaistow	n/a
A200	Creek Rd, Greenwich	n/a
A202	Camberwell New Rd, Camberwell	n/a
A202	Vauxhall Bridge Rd, Westminster	n/a
A205	Brownhill Rd, Catford	n/a
A205	Stanstead Rd, Catford	n/a
A205	Upper Richmond Rd, Putney/Roehampton	n/a
A205	Mortlake/East Sheen	n/a
A206	Woolwich Church St, Woolwich	n/a
A206	Beresford St, Woolwich	n/a
A206	Woolwich Rd, Belvedere	n/a
A206	Erith Rd, Belvedere	n/a
A207	Bellegrove Rd, Welling	n/a
A207	Great Western Rd, Westbourne Park	n/a
A208	Court Rd, Eltham	n/a
A208/A205	Well Hall Rd, Eltham	n/a
A212	Westwood Hill, Sydenham	n/a
A213	Croydon Rd, Penge	n/a
A214	Elmers End Rd, Beckenham	n/a
A214	Trinity Rd, Wandsworth	n/a
A215	Denmark Hill, Camberwell	n/a
A215	Beulah Hill, Upper Norwood	n/a
A217	London Rd, Mitcham	n/a
A217	Garratt La, Wandsworth	n/a
A219	Fulham Palace Rd, Fulham	n/a
A219	Scrubs La, Willesden	n/a
A221	Penhill Rd, Blackfen	n/a
A222	Long La, Addiscombe	n/a
A222	Bromley Rd, Beckenham	n/a
A224	Sevenoaks Way, St Paul's Cray	n/a
A232	Cheam Rd, Sutton	n/a
A233	Main Rd, Biggin Hill	n/a
A234	Beckenham Rd, Beckenham/Penge	n/a
A234	Crystal Palace Park Rd, Sydenham	n/a
A239	Central Rd, Morden	n/a
A240	Kingston Rd, Tolworth/Stoneleigh	n/a
A298	Bushey Rd, Raynes Park	n/a
A307	Kew Rd, Kew	n/a
A307	Richmond Rd, Kingston upon Thames	n/a
A312	Harlington Rd West, Feltham	n/a
A312	Uxbridge Rd, Hampton	n/a
A312	Near Southall	n/a
A315	High St, Brentford	n/a
A315	Kensington Rd, Kensington	n/a
A402	Holland Park Ave, Notting Hill	n/a
A404	Hillside, Harlesden	n/a
A404	Watford Rd, Wembley	n/a
A404	Watford Rd, Harrow	n/a
A406	Barking Relief Rd, Barking	n/a
A406	Southend Rd (North Circular), Walthamstow/South Woodford	n/a
A406	North Circular Rd, Finchley	n/a
A406	North Circular Rd, Dollis Hill	n/a
A406	North Circular Rd, Neasden/Stonebridge	n/a
A408	Cowley Rd, Uxbridge	n/a
A408	Cowley Rd, Cowley	n/a
A408	High Rd, Cowley	n/a
A408	Stockley Rd, West Drayton	n/a
A410	Uxbridge Rd, Harrow Weald	n/a
A410	Fryent Way, Kingsbury	n/a
A501	Euston Rd	n/a
A503	Seven Sisters Rd, Finsbury Park/South Tottenham	n/a
A1010	Fore St, Edmonton	n/a
A1020	Royal Docks Rd, Beckton	n/a
A1020	Royal Albert Way	n/a
A1112	Rainham Rd, North Dagenham	n/a
A1153	Porters Ave, Becontree	n/a
A1199	Woodford Rd, South Woodford	n/a
A1206	Manchester Rd, Isle of Dogs	n/a
A1206	Westferry Rd, Poplar/Isle of Dogs	n/a
A1400	Woodford Ave, Gants Hill	n/a
A2043	Kingston Rd, Kingston upon Thames	n/a
A2043	Cheam Common Rd, North Cheam	n/a
A2043	Malden Rd, Cheam	n/a
A2206	Southwark Park Rd, Bermondsey	n/a
A2212	Burnt Ash La, Plaistow, Bromley	n/a
A2215	Peckham Rye	n/a
A3205	Battersea Park Rd, Battersea	n/a
A3212	Chelsea Embankment, Chelsea	n/a
A3212	Millbank, Westminster	n/a
A3216	Sloane St, Belgravia	n/a
A3220	Latchmere Rd, Battersea	n/a
A4000	Horn La, Acton	n/a
A4006	Kenton Rd, Kenton	n/a
A4006	Kingsbury Rd, Kingsbury	n/a
A4020	Uxbridge Rd, Shepherd's Bush	n/a
A4020	Uxbridge Rd, Southall	n/a
A4020	Uxbridge Rd, Hayes	n/a
A4090	Alexandra Ave, South Harrow	n/a
A4127	Greenford Rd, Greenford	n/a
A4127	Greenford Rd, Southall	n/a
A4140	Honeypot La, Queensbury	n/a
A4180	Ruislip Rd, Yeading	n/a
B155	Belmont Rd, Harringay	n/a
B160	Larkshall Rd, Chingford	n/a
B178	Ballards Rd, Dagenham	n/a
B205	Salter Rd, Rotherhithe	n/a
B213	Abbey Rd, Abbey Wood	n/a
B213	Lower Rd, Belvedere	n/a
B214	Albany Rd, Walworth	n/a
B218	Brockley Rd, Brockley/Crofton Park	n/a
B221	Kings Ave, Clapham Park	n/a
B238	Peckham Rye	n/a
B266	Brigstock Rd, Thornton Heath	n/a
B272	Beddington La, Croydon	n/a
B272	Foresters Dr, South Beddington	n/a
B278	Green La, Morden	n/a
B279	Tudor Dr, Morden Park	n/a
B282	West Barnes La, Raynes Park	n/a
B286	Martin Way, Morden	n/a
B302	Royal Hospital Rd, Chelsea	n/a
B358	Sixth Cross Rd, Strawberry Hill	n/a
B415	Kensington Park Rd, Notting Hill	n/a
B450	Ladbroke Gr, Notting Hill	n/a
B472	Joel St, Northwood Hills/Eastcote	n/a
B483	Park Rd, Uxbridge	n/a
B1421	Ockendon Rd, Upminster	n/a
B1459	Chase Cross Rd, Collier Row	n/a
B2030	Coulsdon Rd, Coulsdon	n/a
-	Balham, Atkins Rd	n/a
-	Beckenham, Wickham Way, Beckenham	n/a
-	Bedfont, Hatton Rd	n/a
-	Bexleyheath, Pickford La	n/a
-	Brixton, Herne Hill Rd	n/a
-	Coulsdon, Portnalls Rd	n/a
-	Cricklewood, Crest Rd	n/a
-	East Wickham, King Harolds Way	n/a
-	Eltham, Glenesk Rd	n/a
-	Eltham, Rochester Way	n/a
-	Grove Park/Lee, Burnt Ash Hill	n/a
-	Hainault, Manford Way	n/a
-	Hanworth, Castle Way	n/a
-	Harefield, Church Hill	n/a
-	Harrow, Harrow View	n/a
-	Harrow, Porlock Ave	n/a
-	Hayes, Kingshill Ave	n/a
-	Herne Hill, Sunray Ave	n/a
-	Honor Oak, Brenchley Gdns	n/a
-	Hornchurch, Parkstone Ave	n/a
-	Hornchurch, Wingletye La	n/a
-	Kenton, Woodcock Hill	n/a
-	Morden Park, Hillcross Ave	n/a
-	North Kensington, Barlby Rd	n/a
-	North Kensington, Chesterton Rd	n/a
-	North Kensington, Latimer Rd	n/a
-	North Kensington, St Helen's Gardens	n/a
-	Old Malden, Manor Dr North	n/a
-	Peckham Rye	n/a
-	Peckham, Linden Gr	n/a
-	Romford, Brentwood Rd	n/a
-	Sidcup, Faraday Ave	n/a
-	South Ruislip/Eastcote, Field End Rd	n/a
-	Southall, Lady Margaret Rd	n/a
-	St Helier, Morden, Middleton Rd	n/a
-	Upminster, Hall La	n/a
-	Upminster, Ingrebourne Gdns	n/a
-	West Dulwich, Alleyn Park	n/a
-	West Kensington, Holland Villas Rd	n/a
-	Wimbledon, Ridgeway Pl	n/a
-	Wood Green, White Hart La	n/a

Merseyside

The introduction of mobile safety cameras is under consideration.

Norfolk

Road number	Location	Speed limit (mph)
A10	Stow Bardolph	60
A10	Tottenhill/Watlington	60
A11	Attleborough Bypass	60
A11	Ketteringham	70
A11	Roudham Heath (A1075/B1111)	70
A11	Thetford (A134 roundabout)/Croxton	60
A11	Wymondham/Besthorpe	70
A12	Hopton on Sea	70
A17	Terrington St Clement	60
A47	East Winch	60
A47	Emneth	60
A47	Honingham/Easton	60
A47	Lingwood/Acle	50
A47	Mautby/Halvergate	60
A47	Narborough	60
A47	Postwick	70
A47	Pullover Roundabout, King's Lynn	70
A47	Scarning	60
A47	Swaffham/Sporle	60
A47	Terrington St John	70
A47	Tuddenham	70
A47	Wendling/Fransham	60
A47	West Bilney	60
A140	Aylsham	60
A140	Dickleburgh Moor	60
A140	Erpingham	60
A140	Harford Bridge, Norwich	30
A140	Newton Flotman/Stoke Holy Cross/Swainsthorpe	60
A140	Long Stratton/Tivetshall St Mary	60
A140	Roughton	40
A140	Saxlingham Thorpe	60
A140	Scole Bypass	70
A140	St Faiths	60
A143	Belton/St Olaves	60
A143	Billingford/Brockdish	60
A143	Haddiscoe (bends)	30
A146	Hales	60
A148	South Wootton, King's Lynn	40
A148	Bodham	60
A148	Fakenham Bypass	60
A148	Pretty Corner (near A1082/Sheringham)	60
A148	Thursford/B1354	50
A149	Caister Bypass	70
A149	Catfield/Potter Heigham	40
A149	Catfield	60
A149	Hunstanton	30
A149	Kings Lynn (A10/A47 to B1145)	60
A149	Knights Hill, King's Lynn	60
A149	Crossdale Street to Thorpe Market	60
A149	Sandringham	60
A149	Wayford Bridge East (west of Stalham)	50
A149	Wayford Bridge West/Smallburgh	50
A1065	Hempton	50
A1065	Hilborough	60
A1065	South Acre	60
A1065	Weeting	60
A1066	Roydon & Diss	30
A1066	Rushford	60
A1066	Mundford Rd, Thetford	40
A1066	South Lopham	60
A1067	Bawdeswell	50
A1067	Morton/Attlebridge	60
A1075	East Wretham (heath)	60
A1122	Swaffham/Beachamwell	60
A1151	Rackheath/Wroxham	60
B1108	Earlham Rd, Norwich	30
B1110	Beetley/Hoe	60
B1113	Wreningham/Ashwellthorpe	50
B1149	Horsford Woods (north of Horsford)	60
B1150	Scottow	50
B1150	Westwick	50
B1152	Bastwick/Billockby	60
B1332	Ditchingham	50
-	Caistor, Ormesby Rd	30
-	Dereham, Swanton Rd	30
-	Drayton/Thorpe Marriot, Reepham Rd	60
-	Norwich, Gurney Rd	30
-	Norwich, Plumstead Rd/Rd East	30
-	Wymondham (A11) to B1113 (Wreningham/Bracon Ash)	50

Northamptonshire

Road number	Location	Speed limit (mph)
A5	DIRFT to county boundary	n/a
A5/A428	DIRFT Logistic Park triangle (M1, jct 18)	n/a
A5	Long Buckby/Watford/Kilsby	n/a
A6	Burton Latimer Bypass	n/a
A14	Polwell Lane overbridge	n/a
A43	Duddington/Collyweston/Easton on the Hill	n/a
A43	Kettering	n/a
A43	Little Cransley (near Broughton)	n/a
A45	High St, Flore	n/a
A361	Daventry Rd, Kilsby	n/a
A361	Welton	n/a
A422	Brackley Bypass	n/a
A427	Oakley Rd, Corby	n/a
A427	Weldon Rd, Corby	n/a
A428	East Haddon	n/a
A428	Bedford Rd, Little Houghton	n/a
A428	Brafield on the Green	n/a
A428	Harlestone Rd, Northampton	n/a
A508	Broad St, Northampton	n/a
A508	Cattle Market Rd, Northampton	n/a
A508	Harborough Rd, Northampton	n/a
A508	Stoke Bruerne to Yardley Gobion	n/a
A509	Kettering Rd, Isham	n/a
A605	Barnwell	n/a
A605	Oundle Bypass	n/a
A605	Oundle to Warmington	n/a
A605	Thorpe Waterville	n/a
A4500	Ecton Brook	n/a
A5076	Mere Way, Northampton	n/a
A5095	Kingsley Rd/Kingsthorpe Gr, Northampton	n/a
A5095	St Andrew's Rd, Northampton	n/a
A5193	Harrowden Rd, Wellingborough	n/a
A5193	London Rd, Wellingborough	n/a

Road number	Location	Speed limit (mph)
A6003	Kettering to Great Oakley	n/a
A6014	Oakley Rd, Corby	n/a
A6116	Brigstock	n/a
A6116	Steel Rd, Corby	n/a
B569	Station Rd, Irchester	n/a
B569	Wollaston Rd, Irchester	n/a
B576	Desborough	n/a
B576	Rothwell	n/a
B4525	A43 to A422	n/a
B5385	Main St, Watford	n/a

Northumbria

Road number	Location	Speed limit (mph)
A1	Berwick Bypass at Dunns jct	60
A68	Colt Crag (reservoir)	60
A69	Haltwhistle Bypass	60
A69	Nafferton (near B6309) (eastbound)	70
A69	Two Mile Cottage, Hexham	70
A167	Stamfordham Rd, Newcastle	30
A182	Houghton Rd, Houghton-le-Spring	30
A183	Chester Rd/Broadway, Sunderland	30
A186	City Rd, Newcastle (at Beamish House)	30
A186	West Rd, Denton Burn, Newcastle (at Turret Rd)	40
A186	Westgate Rd, Newcastle (at Elswick Row)	30
A189	Haddricks Mill Rd, South Gosforth	30
A189	High Pitt, Cramlington	70
A189	Spine Rd, Cramlington	70
A191	Whitley Rd, Longbenton	30
A193	Church Bank, Wallsend	30
A194	Newcastle Rd, Simonside	40
A196	Blackclose Bank, Ashington	30
A690	Durham Rd, Houghton-le-Spring (at Stony Gate)	50
A690	Durham Rd, Sunderland	30
A694	At Winlaton Mill, Rowlands Gill	40
A694	Station Rd, Rowlands Gill	30
A695	Crawcrook Bypass	60
A695	Prudhoe	40
A696	Belsay village	30
A696	Blaxter Cottages, Otterburn	60
A696	Kirkwhelpington	60
A696	Otterburn Monkridge	60
A697	Heighley Gate, Morpeth	60
A697	Wooperton	60
A1018	Ryhope Rd, Sunderland (at Irene Ave)	30
A1058	Jesmond Rd, Newcastle (at Akenside Terr)	30
A1068	Amble Industrial Estate	30
A1147	Gordon Terr, Stakeford	30
A1171	Dudley La, Cramlington	30
A1290	Kier Hardie Way, Sunderland	30
A1300	Prince Edward Rd, Harton/Cleadon Park	30
A6085	Lemington Rd, Lemington, Newcastle	40
A6127	Durham Rd, Barley Mow, Birtley	30
B1288	Leam Lane, Gateshead (at A195)	40
B1296	Sheriffs Hwy, Gateshead (at QE Hospital)	30
B1296	Sheriffs Hwy, Gateshead (at Split Crow Rd)	30
B1298	New Rd, Boldon Colliery	30
B1301	Dean Rd, South Shields	30
B1301	Laygate, South Shields (at Eglesfield Rd)	30
B1316	Lynn Rd, North Shields	30
B1318	Bridge St, Seaton Burn	30
B1426	Sunderland Rd, Felling	30
B1505	Great Lime Rd, West Moor, Longbenton	30
B6315	Hookergate La, High Spen	30
B6317	Main Rd, Ryton	30
B6317	Whickham Highway, Whickham	30
B6318	Military Rd, Whitchester (east of Harlow Hill)	60
B6318	Military Rd, Whittington Fell (west of A68)	60
B6324	Stamfordham Rd, Westerhope, Newcastle (A1 to Walbottle Rd)	40
B6918	Woolsington Village	30
-	Ashington, Station Rd	30
-	Blaydon, Shibdon Bank	30
-	Boldon Colliery, Hedworth La/ Abingdon Way	40
-	Crawcrook, Greenside Rd	30
-	Dinnington, Dinnington Rd (north of Brunton La)	60
-	Felling, Watermill La	30
-	Gateshead, Askew Rd West	30
-	Harton, Harton La	30
-	Hebburn, Campbell Park Rd	30
-	Longbenton, Coach La	30
-	Newcastle, West Denton Way (east of Hawksley)	40
-	New Silksworth, Silksworth Rd at Rutland Ave	30
-	North Shields, Norham Rd	30
-	South Shields, Nevison Ave, Whiteleas	30
-	Sunderland, North Hylton Rd at Castletown Way, Southwick	40
-	Sunderland, North Moor La, Farringdon,	40
-	Sunderland, Springwell Rd	30
-	Sunderland, Warwick Ter	30
-	Wallsend, Battle Hill Dr	30
-	Whickham, Fellside Rd	30

North Yorkshire

There is currently no safety camera partnership.

Nottinghamshire

Road number	Location	Speed limit (mph)
A52	Clifton Blvd, Nottingham	40
A52	Grantham Rd, Radcliffe on Trent	40
A52	Derby Rd, Nottingham	30
A60	Doncaster Rd, Carlton in Lindrick	30
A60	Cuckney/Market Warsop	30
A60	Nottingham (south)	30
A60	Ravenshead	50
A609	Ilkeston Rd/Wollaton Rd/Russel Dr/Trowell Rd, Nottingham	30
A611	Derby Rd, Annesley	30
A611	Hucknall Rd, Nottingham	30
A612	Nottingham Rd, Southwell (Halloughton to Westgate)	30
A614	Ollerton Rd/Burnt Stump, Arnold, Nottingham	60
A616	Ollerton Rd, Caunton	60
A617	Chesterfield Rd South, Mansfield	30
A620	Welham Rd, Retford	30
A631	Beckingham Bypass	60
A631	West of Beckingham	60
A631	Flood Plain Rd, east of Gainsborough	60
A6005	Castle Blvd/Abbey Bridge/Beeston Rd/University Blvd, Nottingham	30
A6008	Canal St, Nottingham	30
A6130	Gregory Blvd, Nottingham	30
A6130	Radford Blvd/Lenton Blvd, Nottingham	30
A6200	Derby Rd, Nottingham	30
B679	Wilford La, West Bridgford	30
B682	Sherwood Rise/Nottingham Rd/Vernon Rd, Nottingham	30
B6004	Strelley Rd/Broxtowe La, Broxtowe	30
B6004	Oxclose La, Arnold, Nottingham	40
B6010	Nottingham Rd, Giltbrook, Eastwood	30
B6040	Retford Rd, Worksop	30
B6033	Bath La/Ravensdale Rd, Mansfield	30
B6166	Lincoln Rd/Northgate, Newark	40
B6326	London Rd, Newark	30
-	Hucknall, Nottingham Rd/ Portland Rd/Annesley Rd	30
-	Newark, Hawton La, Balderton	30
-	Nottingham, Beechdale Rd	30
-	Nottingham, Bestwood Park Drive West	30
-	Nottingham, Ridge Way/Top Valley Drive	30
-	Nottingham, Wigman Rd	30
-	Rainworth, Kirklington Rd	30

South Yorkshire

Road number	Location	Speed limit (mph)
A18	Carr House Rd/Leger Way, Doncaster	40
A18	Epworth Rd (Slay Pits to Tudworth) (near Hatfield Woodhouse)	NSL
A57	Sheffield Rd/ Worksop Rd, Aston	40/60
A57	Mosborough Parkway, Sheffield	NSL
A57	Worksop Rd, Aston/Todwick	60
A60	Doncaster Rd, Tickhill	NSL
A60	Worksop Rd, Tickhill	30/60
A61	Park Rd, Cutting Edge, Barnsley	30
A61	Chesterfield Rd/Chesterfield Rd South, Sheffield	30/40
A61	Halifax Rd, Sheffield	30/40
A61	Penistone Rd, Sheffield	30
A614	Selby Rd, Thorne	NSL
A618	Mansfield Rd, Wales Bar, Wales	40
A628	Dodworth	40/60
A628	Cundy Cross to Shafton Two Gates, Barnsley	30/40
A628	Barnsley Rd, Penistone	40
A629	New Wortley Rd, Rotherham	40
A629	Hallwood Rd/Burncross Rd, Burncross, Chapeltown	30
A629	Wortley Rd/Upper Wortley Rd, Rotherham	30/40
A629	Wortley	NSL
A630	Balby Flyover to Hill Top, Doncaster	30/40/60
A630	Centenary Way, Rotherham	40/50
A630	Doncaster Rd, Dalton/Thrybergh	30/40/60
A630	Wheatley Hall Rd, Doncaster	40
A631	Bawtry Rd/Rotherham Rd, Hellaby/Maltby	30/40
A631	Bawtry Rd, Brinsworth, Rotherham	40
A631	Bawtry Rd, Wickersley/Brecks	40
A631	West Bawtry Rd, Rotherham	50
A633	Rotherham Rd, Athersley South, Barnsley	30
A633	Rotherham Rd, Monk Bretton, Barnsley	40
A633	Barnsley Rd, Wombwell	30/40
A633	Sandygate, Wath upon Dearne	30
A635	Doncaster Rd/Saltersbrook Rd, Barnsley	30/40/60
A638	Bawtry Rd, Doncaster	40
A638	Great North Rd/York Rd, Doncaster	40/50
A6022	Swinton	30
A6101	Rivelin Valley Rd, Sheffield	40
A6102	Manchester Rd/Langsett Rd, Hillsborough/Deepcar	30/40
A6109	Meadow Bank Rd, Rotherham	40
A6123	Herringthorpe Valley Rd, Rotherham	40
A6135	Ecclesfield Rd/Chapeltown Rd, Ecclesfield/Chapeltown	40
B6059	Kiveton Park/Wales	30/40
B6089	Greasbrough Rd/Greasbrough St, Thorn Hill/Greasbrough	40
B6096	Wombwell to Snape Hill	30
B6097	Doncaster Rd, Wath upon Dearne	30/60
B6100	Ardsley Rd/Hunningley La, Barnsley	30
B6411	Houghton Rd, Thurnscoe	30
B6463	Stripe Rd, Tickhill	NSL
-	Armthorpe, Hatfield La/Mill St	30
-	Armthorpe, Nutwell La	30
-	Barnsley, Pogmoor Rd	30
-	Bolton Upon Dearne, Dearne Rd	30
-	Doncaster, Melton Rd/ Sprotbrough Rd	30
-	Doncaster, Thorne Rd, Wheatley	30
-	Doncaster, Urban Rd	30
-	Finningley, Hurst La	40/60
-	Grimethorpe, Brierley Rd	30
-	New Edlington/Warmsworth, Broomhouse La/Springwell La	30/60
-	Rawmarsh, Haugh Rd	30/40
-	Rawmarsh, Kilnhurst Rd	30
-	Rotherham, Fenton Rd	30/60
-	Stainforth, Station Rd	30
-	Wath upon Dearne, Barnsley Rd	40

Staffordshire

Road number	Location	Speed limit (mph)
A5	From M6 jct 12 to A460/A4601	50
A5	South Cannock, A460/A4601 to A34, Churchbridge	50/30
A5	South Cannock, from A34 (Churchbridge) to B4154 (Turf Pub island)	60/70/60/30
A5	Brownhills, from Hanney Hay/ Barracks La island to A461	60/70/60
A5	From A461 to A5127/A5148	70
A5	From A5127/A5148 to A38	60
A5	From A38 to Hints La, Tamworth	50/40
A34	Talke, from A500 to A5011	30/60
A34	Newcastle-under-Lyme to Talke, from B5369 to A500	40/70
A34	Newcastle-under-Lyme (north), from B5369 to B5368	40
A34	Newcastle-under-Lyme (south), from Barracks Rd (A527) to Stoke City roundabout (signed)	40
A34	Trent Vale, from A500 to London Rd Bowling Club	30/40
A34	Stone Rd, Hanford, from A5035 to A500	40/30
A34	Stone	50
A34	North of Stafford, from A513 to Lloyds island/Eccleshall Rd, Stone (B5026)	40/30
A34	From A5013 to A518, Stafford	30
A34	Queensway, Stafford	40
A34	Stafford (south), from A449 to Acton Hill Rd	30/40
A34	Cannock (north), from north of Holly La to A34/B5012 roundabout	30
A34	Cannock (south), through Great Wyrley from A5 to Jones La	30
A34	Cannock (south), from Jones La to county boundary	30/50/30
A38	From London Rd, Lichfield (A5206) to A5121, Burton upon Trent	70
A38	From Weeford island (A38) to Bassetts Pole island	70
A50	Kidsgrove, from city boundary to Oldcott Dr	30
A50	Victoria Rd, Fenton, Stoke-on-Trent, from Leek Rd to City Rd	30
A51	Weston, from New Rd to 500m north-east of Sandy La	60/40/50
A51	Pasturefields, from south of Amerton La to south of Hoomill La	50
A51	Rugeley (north), from Bower La to jct with A460/B5013	40/30
A51	Rugeley (south), from jct with A460/B5013 to Brereton island (A513)	30/40
A51	From Armitage La, Rugeley to A515 near Lichfield	60
A51	From A5127 (Birmingham Rd) to Heath Rd, Lichfield	30/40/60
A51	Tamworth Rd/Dosthill Rd, Tamworth, from south of Peelers Way to Ascot Dr	30
A52	Stoke-on-Trent (east), from A5272 to A522	30/40
A53	Blackshaw Moor (north of Leek)	50
A53	Longsden, from Dunwood La jct to Wallbridge Dr, Leek	60/40/30
A53	Leek New Rd, Endon, from Nursery Ave to Dunwood La jct	40/30/40/60
A53	Leek New Rd, from A5272 (Hanley Rd) to B5051 at Endon	30/40
A444	Stanton Rd, Burton on Trent, from St Peters Bridge to Derbyshire boundary	30
A449	Stafford (south) from A34 to Gravel La	30
A449	Penkridge, from Lynehill La to half mile north of Goodstation La	40
A449	Gailey, from Rodbaston Dr to Station Dr	60/70
A449	Coven, from Station Dr (Four Ashes) to M54	70/40
A449	Stourton	60/50/40
A449	Stourton to county boundary	40
A454	Trescott, from Brantley La to Shop La	50
A458	From Six Ashes Rd, Six Ashes to Morfe La, Gilberts Cross	40/50
A460	Sandy La/ Hednesford Rd, from A51 to south of Stile Cop Rd, Rugeley	30
A460/A4601	Wolverhampton Rd, Cannock from Saredon Rd to Longford island	40/30
A511	Burton upon Trent (north), from Anslow La to A5121	40/30
A511	Burton upon Trent (south), from A5121 to Derbyshire boundary	30
A518	Weston to Uttoxeter	60
A518	Stafford, from M6 to Bridge St	30
A518	Stafford, from Riverway to Blackheath La	30/40
A519	Woodseaves, from Moss La to Lodge La	30
A519	Clayton Rd, Newcastle-under-Lyme, from A53 to roundabout at Northwood La	40
A520	Weston Rd, Longton, from A50 north to city boundary	30
A520	Sandon Rd, Stoke-on-Trent, from Grange Rd to A50	30
A522	Beamhurst (near Uttoxeter), from Fole La to Grange Rd	50/40
A4601/A460	Wolverhampton Rd, Cannock, from Longford island toward jct 11 to Saredon Rd	30/40
A4601	Cannock, from A34 (Walsall Rd) to Longford island	30
A4601	Old Hednesford Rd, from A5190 (Lichfield Rd) to A460 (Eastern Way)	30
A5005	Lightwood Rd, Stoke-on-Trent, from A520 to A50	40/30
A5013	Eccleshall Rd, Stafford, from A34 to M6	30
A5035	From A34 (Trentham) to A50 (Longton)	30
A5121	Burton upon Trent, from B5108, Branston to Borough Rd	50/40/30
A5121	Burton upon Trent, from Byrkley St, Horninglow, to Hillfield La, Stretton	30/40
A5127	Lichfield, from Upper St John St to Burton Rd	30
A5189	Burton upon Trent, from Wellington Rd (A5121) to Stapenhill Rd (A444)	30/40
A5190	Cannock Rd, Burntwood, from Attwood Rd to Stockhay La	30
A5190	Cannock, from Five Ways island to Hednesford Rd	30/40/60
A5272	Dividy Rd from A52 to B5039	30
B5027	Stone Rd, Uttoxeter from Byrds La to Springfield Rd	30
B5044	Silverdale, Newcastle-under-Lyme, from Sneyd Terrace to B5368	30
B5051	Stoke-on-Trent, from Sneyd Hill to Brown Edge	30
B5066	From B5027 to Hall La, Hilderstone	30
B5066	Sandon Rd, Sandon, from A51 to Salt La	60
B5066	Sandon Rd, Stafford, from A513 to Marston Rd	30
B5080	Pennine Way, Tamworth, from B5000 to Pennymoor Rd	30/40
B5404	Tamworth, from Sutton Rd to A4091	40/30
B5404	Watling St, Tamworth, from A51 to A5	30
B5500	Audley, from Barthomley Rd to Park La	30
B5500	Bignall End (near Audley) from Boon Hill Rd to Alsager La	30/40
-	Burntwood, Church Rd from Rugeley Rd to Farewell La	30
-	Burton upon Trent, Rosliston Rd, from A5189 to county boundary	30
-	Burton upon Trent, Violet Way/ Beaufort Rd, from A444 to A511	30
-	Cannock, Pye Green Rd, from A34 (Stafford Rd) to Brindley Rd	30
-	Cheadle Rd, from Uttoxeter Rd to Quabbs La	30
-	Crackley, Cedar Rd, from Crackley Bank to B5500 (Audley Rd)	30
-	Cresswell, Sandon Rd, from Saverley Green Rd to Uttoxeter Rd	40
-	Hednesford, Rawnsley Rd, from A460 to Littleworth Rd	30
-	Stoke-on-Trent, Oxford Rd/Chell Heath Rd, from A527 to B5051	30

Suffolk

Road number	Location	Speed limit (mph)
A11	Barton Mills	50
A11	Chalk Hall, Elveden	NSL
A11	Elveden	NSL
A11	Elveden crossroads	40
A11	Worlington	NSL
A12	Blythburgh	40
A12	Kelsale	NSL
A12	Little Glemham	30
A12	Little Glemham, (north)	50
A12	Lound	NSL
A12	Marlesford	40
A12	Melton	40
A12	Saxmundham	NSL
A14	Exning	NSL
A14	Newmarket	NSL
A14	Rougham	NSL
A134	Barnham	40
A134	Little Welnetham	30
A134	Long Melford	NSL
A134	Nowton	40
A137	Brantham	30
A140	Thwaite	50
A140	Wetheringsett	40
A143	Bury St Edmunds	30
A143	Chedburgh	30
A143	Stanton	40
A143	Stanton Bypass	40
A143	Highpoint Prison, Stradishall	40
A144	Ilketshall St Lawrence	NSL
A146	Barnby Bends	NSL
A154	Trinity Ave, Felixstowe	40
A1065	Eriswell	40
A1065	Mildenhall	NSL
A1065	North of RAF Lakenheath	NSL
A1071	Boxford	40
A1071	Lady La, Hadleigh	NSL
A1088	Honington	30
A1092	Cavendish	30
A1092	Clare	30
A1092	Skates Hill, Glemsford	40
A1101	Flempton	30
A1101	Mildenhall	30
A1101	Shippea Hill	50
A1117	Saltwater Way, Lowestoft	30
A1120	Stonham Aspal	30
A1156	Nacton	40
A1156	Norwich Rd, Ipswich	30
A1214	London Rd, Ipswich	40
A1302	Bury St Edmunds	30
A1304	Golf Club, Newmarket	NSL
A1307	Haverhill	40
B1078	Barking	30
B1078	Needham Market	30
B1106	Fornham St Martin	30
B1113	Bramford	40
B1115	Chilton	40
B1384	Carlton Colville	30
B1385	Corton	30
B1438	Melton Hill, Woodbridge	30
B1506	Kentford	40
B1506	Moulton	NSL
-	Felixstowe, Grange Farm Ave	30
-	Felixstowe, High Rd	30
-	Ipswich, Ellenbrook Rd	30
-	Ipswich, Foxhall Rd, St Clements	30
-	Ipswich, Landseer Rd	30
-	Ipswich, Nacton Rd	30
-	Ipswich, Ropes Dr, Kesgrave	30

Surrey

Road number	Location	Speed limit (mph)
A31	Hogs Back, Guildford (central section)	60
A31	Hogs Back, Guildford (eastern section)	60
A308	Staines Bypass, Staines	50
-	Staines, Kingston Rd	30

Sussex

Road number	Location	Speed limit (mph)
A24	Broadwater Rd, Worthing (near Cecilian Ave)	30
A27	Hammerpot, Angmering (north side)	70
A27	Firle Straight, Firle	60
A27	Upper Brighton Rd, Lancing (near Grand Ave)	40
A27	Holmbush, Shoreham	70
A29	Westergate St, Aldingbourne (at Elmcroft Pl)	30
A29	Westergate St, Aldingbourne (at Hook La)	30
A29	Shripney Rd, Bognor Regis (northbound)	40
A259	Hotham Way, Bognor Regis	30
A259	Main Rd, Fishbourne	30
A259	Marine Dr, Saltdean	30
A270	Old Shoreham Rd, Hove (at Amherst Cres)	30
A271	North Trade Rd, Battle	30
A272	Midhurst Rd, Tillington	40
A280	Patching	40
A281	Guildford Rd, Horsham	30
A283	Northchapel	30
A283	Lower St, Pulborough	30
A285	Station Rd, Petworth	30
A2032	Littlehampton Rd, Worthing (near Little Gables)	30
A2038	Hangleton Rd, Hove (at Nevill Rd)	30
A2270	Eastbourne Rd, Willingdon	40
A2280	Lottbridge Drove, Eastbourne	40
B2093	The Ridge, Hastings	30
B2100	Crowborough Hill, Crowborough	30
B2104	Ersham Rd, Hailsham	30
B2111	Lewes Rd, Lindfield, Haywards Heath	30
B2138	Lower St, Fittleworth	30
B2166	Aldwick Rd, Bognor	30
-	Bognor Regis, Chalcraft La	30
-	Brighton, Carden Ave, (at Carden Cl)	30
-	Brighton, Falmer Rd, Woodingdean	30
-	Crawley, Gatwick Rd (near Hazlewick Flyover)	30
-	Crawley, Gossops Dr	30
-	Crawley, Manor Royal (at Faraday Rd)	30
-	Heathfield, Hailsham Rd	30
-	Horsham, Pondtail Rd (at Haybarn Dr)	30
-	Horsham, Pondtail Rd (at Pondtail Cl)	30
-	Hove, New Church Rd (at Wish Rd)	30
-	Hove, Shirley Dr (at Onslow Rd)	30
-	Hove, Shirley Dr (at Shirley Rd)	30
-	Worthing, The Boulevard	30

Thames Valley

Road number	Location	Speed limit (mph)
A4	Bath Rd, Beenham	60
A4	Bath Rd, Burnham	50
A4	Bath Rd, Hungerford	60
A4	Bath Rd, Kintbury	60
A4	Bath Rd, Speen, Newbury	60
A4	Bath Rd, Tilehurst, Reading	40
A4	Berkeley Ave, Reading	30
A4	London Rd, Earley	40
A4	London Rd, Slough	40
A4	Sussex Pl, Slough	30
A5	Bletchley	70
A5	Wolverton	70
A30	London Rd, Sunningdale	30
A34	Kennington	70
A34	Radley	70
A40	Cassington	60
A40	Forest Hill	70
A40	Oxford Rd, Denham	30
A40	West Wycombe Rd, High Wycombe	30
A41	Buckland	70
A41	Gatehouse Rd, Aylesbury	30
A41	Tring Rd, Aylesbury	30
A44	Over Kiddington	50
A44	London Rd, Chipping Norton	40
A308	Braywick Rd, Maidenhead	40
A322	Bagshot Rd, Bracknell	40
A329	Kings Rd, Reading	30
A329	London Rd, Wokingham	30
A329	Vastern Rd, Reading	30
A329	Wokingham Rd, Reading	30
A330	Brockenhurst Rd, Sunninghill	40
A338	Hungerford	50
A361	Burford Rd, Chipping Norton	30
A361	Little Faringdon	60
A404	Marlow Bypass, Little Marlow	70
A404	Marlow Hill, High Wycombe	30
A412	North Orbital Rd, Denham	40
A413	Buckingham Rd, Aylesbury	30
A413	Gravel Hill, Chalfont St Peter	30
A413	Hardwick	60
A413	Swanbourne	60
A413	Walton St, Aylesbury	30
A413	Weedon	60
A413	Wendover Rd, Aylesbury	30
A413	Wendover Bypass, Wendover	60
A417	Charlton Rd, Wantage	30
A417	Faringdon Rd, Stanford in the Vale	30
A418	Oxford Rd, Tiddington	30
A420	Headington Rd, Oxford	30
A420	London Rd, Oxford	30
A421	Standing Way, Woughton on the Green, Milton Keynes	70
A421	Tingewick Bypass, Tingewick	70
A421	Wavendon	60
A422	Newport Rd, Hardmead	60
A422	Radclive/Chackmore	50
A422	Stratford Rd, Buckingham	30
A422	Stratford Rd, Wroxton	60
A509	Emberton Bypass	60
A509	Newport Pagnell	70
A4010	Aylesbury Rd, Monks Risborough	30
A4010	New Rd, High Wycombe	30
A4074	Dorchester	60
A4074	Nuneham Courteney	50
A4095	Bampton Rd, Curbridge	40
A4095	Witney Rd, Freeland	40
A4130	Nuffield	60
A4130	Remenham Hill	40
A4155	Castle Hill, Reading	30
A4155	Shiplake	30
A4157	Oakfield Rd, Aylesbury	30
A4183	Oxford Rd, Abingdon	30
A4260	Banbury Rd, Rousham	60
A4260	Banbury Rd, Shipton-on-Cherwell	50
A4260	Oxford Rd, Kidlington	50
A4260	Steeple Aston	60
B480	Watlington Rd, Blackbird Leys, Oxford	30
B3349	Barkham Rd, Barkham	30
B3430	Nine Mile Ride, Bracknell	50
B4009	Ewelme	50
B4011	Bicester Rd, Long Crendon	30
B4011	Piddington	60
B4017	Drayton Rd, Abingdon	30
B4034	Buckingham Rd, Bletchley	30
B4494	Leckhampstead	60
B4495	Church Cowley Rd, Oxford	30
B4495	Windmill Rd, Oxford	30
-	Bracknell, Opladen Way	30
-	Great Missenden, Rignall Rd	30
-	High Wycombe, Sawpit Hill, Hazlemere	30
-	High Wycombe, Holmers Farm Way	30
-	Maidenhead, Greenways Dr	30
-	Milton Keynes, Avebury Blvd	30
-	Milton Keynes, Midsummer Blvd	30
-	Milton Keynes, Silbury Blvd	30
-	Reading, Park La	30
-	Slough, Cippenham La	30
-	Slough, Buckingham Ave	30
-	Slough, Parlaunt Rd	30
-	Witney, Corn St	30

Warwickshire

Road number	Location	Speed limit (mph)
A5	Grendon to Atherstone	50
A5	Clifton Fisheries, near Churchover	60
A46	Stratford northern Bypass, near Snitterfield	60
A46	Kenilworth Bypass at Stoneleigh	70
A47	The Long Shoot, Nuneaton	40
A423	Banbury Rd, near Fenny Compton	60
A423	Southam Rd, Ladbroke	60
A423	Coventry Rd, Marton village	30
A423	Oxford Rd, south of Marton	60
A425	Radford Rd, Radford Semele	40
A426	Rugby Rd, near Stockton	60
A428	Rugby Rd, Binley Woods	30
A428	Church Lawford	40
A428	Long Lawford	40
A429	Ettington Rd, south of Wellesbourne	60
A435	Birmingham Rd, Mappleborough Green	40
A435	The Boot, Mappleborough Green, Redditch	40
A439	Near Fishermans Car Park, Stratford-upon-Avon	50
A439	Near Hampton Lucy turn, 3km north-east of Stratford-upon-Avon	50
A452	Greys Mallory, near Bishop's Tachbrook	60
A452	Europa Way, Royal Leamington Spa	60
A3400	Shipston Rd, Alderminster	40
A3400	London Rd, Little Wolford	60
A3400	Stratford Rd, north of Henley in Arden	40
A3400	Birmingham Rd, Pathlow	50
A4189	Warwick Rd, Henley-in-Arden	30
A4189	Henley Rd, Lower Norton	60
B4089	Arden Rd, Alcester	30
B4100	Near jct with B4455 (near Warwick Services)	60
B4100	Banbury Rd, south of Gaydon	60

Road number	Location	Speed limit (mph)
B4101	Broad La, Tanworth in Arden	40
B4102	Arbury Rd, Nuneaton	30
B4112	Ansley Rd, Nuneaton	40
B4113	Coventry Rd, Nuneaton	30
B4114	Lutterworth Rd, Burton Hastings	60
B4114	Coleshill Rd, Church End	60
B4114	Coleshill Rd, Ansley Common (near Chapel End)	30
B4455	Fosse Way, south of Princethorpe	60
-	Coleshill, Station Rd	30
-	Nuneaton, Donnithorne Ave	30
-	Rugby, Clifton Rd/Vicarage Hill	30
-	Warwick, Primrose Hill	30

West Mercia

Road number	Location	Speed limit (mph)
A5	Aston	NSL
A5	Moreton Bridge (1.5km south of Chirk)	NSL
A5	West Felton	NSL
A40	Pencraig	50
A41	Albrighton Bypass	40/60
A41	Chetwynd	NSL
A41	Prees Heath	NSL
A41	Ternhill	40
A41	Whitchurch Bypass	NSL
A44	Bromyard Rd, Worcester	30
A44	Wickhamford	40
A46	Cheltenham Rd, Beckford	50
A46	Evesham Bypass	NSL
A49	Ashton	NSL
A49	Dorrington	NSL
A49	Harewood End	40
A417	Parkway (south of Ledbury)	40
A442	Crudgington	40
A456	Blakedown	30
A456	Newnham Bridge	30
A458	Morville	40
A458	Much Wenlock	30
A458	The Mount, Shrewsbury	30
A465	Allensmore	NSL
A483	Pant	30
A491	Sandy La (west of M5, jct 4)	NSL
A491	Stourbridge Rd (south-east of Hagley)	50
A4103	Lumber La to Lugg Bridge (north-east of Hereford)	NSL
A4103	Newtown Cross	40
A4103	Ridgeway Cross	NSL
A4103	Stifford's Bridge to Storridge	50
A4104	Drake St, Welland	30
A4104	Marlbank Rd, Welland	30
A4110	Three Elms Rd, Hereford	30
A5064	London Rd, Shrewsbury	30
B4096	Old Birmingham Rd, Marlbrook	30
B4211	Church St, Great Malvern	30
B4349	Clehonger	NSL
B4373	Castlefields Way, Telford	40
B4373	Wrockwardine Wood Way, Oakengates, Telford	40
B4386	Mytton Oak Rd, Shrewsbury	30
B4638	Woodgreen Dr, Worcester	30
B5060	Castle Farm Way, St George's, Telford	40
B5061	Holyhead Rd, Snedshill, Telford	30
B5062	Sundorne Rd Shrewsbury	30
B5069	Gobowen Rd, Oswestry/Gobowen	30
-	Hereford, Yazor Rd	30
-	Newport, Wellington Rd	30
-	Redditch, Birchfield Dr	30
-	Redditch, Coldfield Dr	40
-	Redditch, Studley Rd	30
-	Shrewsbury, Longden Rd (rural)	30
-	Shrewsbury, Monkmoor Rd	30
-	Telford, Britannia Way, Hadley	30
-	Telford, Hollinsgate, Hollinswood	30
-	Telford, Stafford Park 1	40
-	Telford, Trench Rd	30

West Midlands

Road number	Location	Speed limit (mph)
A41	Warwick Rd	30
A452	Collector Rd, Castle Bromwich/ Kingshurst	50
A4034	Birchfield La, Oldbury/Blackheath	40
A4036	Pedmore Rd, Dudley	40
A4040	Bromford La, Gravelly Hill/Ward End	30
A4123	Birmingham New Rd, Wolverhampton/Dudley (northbound)	40
A4600	Ansty Rd, Coventry	40
B425	Lode La, Solihull	30
B4114	Washwood Heath Rd, Washwood Heath	30
B4121	Barnes Hill, Selly Oak	40
B4121	Shenley La, Selly Oak	40
B4135	Cranford St/Heath St, Smethwick	30
-	Solihull, Widney Manor Rd	40
-	Wolverhampton, The Droveway	30

West Yorkshire

Road number	Location	Speed limit (mph)
A58	Easterley Rd, Leeds	n/a
A61	Scott Hall Rd, Leeds	n/a
A64	York Rd, Leeds	n/a
A65	Otley Rd, Guiseley	n/a
A65	Kirkstall Rd, Leeds	n/a
A65	Rawdon Rd, Rawdon (near Yeadon)	n/a
A629	Halifax Rd, Cullingworth	n/a
A629	Elland Bypass	n/a
A629	Keighley Rd, Ogden (near Halifax)	n/a
A629	Ovenden Rd, Halifax	n/a
A629	Skircoat Rd/Huddersfield Rd, Halifax	n/a
A636	Denby Dale Rd, Wakefield	n/a
A638	Dewsbury Rd, Wakefield	n/a
A638	Ossett Bypass	n/a
A642	Horbury Rd, Wakefield	n/a
A643	Morley	n/a
A646	Halifax Rd, Todmorden	n/a
A647	Great Horton Rd, Bradford	n/a
A647	Stanningley Bypass	n/a
A652	Bradford Rd, Batley	n/a
A657	Calverley	n/a
A657	Leeds Rd, Shipley	n/a
A657	Town St, Rodley	n/a
A660	Far Headingley, Leeds	n/a
A6036	Bradford Rd, Northowram	n/a
A6120	Ring Road Farsley, Farsley (near Pudsey)	n/a
A6186	Asdale Rd, Durkar (near Wakefield)	n/a
B6144	Haworth Rd, Daisy Hill, Morley	n/a
B6145	Thornton Rd, Thornton	n/a
B6154	Waterloo Rd, Pudsey	n/a
B6154	Tong Rd, Wortley	n/a
B6269	Cottingley Cliffe Rd, Cottingley (near Shipley)	n/a
B6273	Wakefield Rd, Kinsley	n/a
B6380	Beacon Rd, Bradford	n/a
-	Bradford, Gain La	n/a

Road number	Location	Speed limit (mph)
-	Bradford, Moore Ave	n/a
-	Huddersfield, Long La, Dalton	n/a
-	Leeds, Broad La, Sandford	n/a
-	Middleton, Middleton Ring Road	n/a

Wiltshire and Swindon

Road number	Location	Speed limit (mph)
M4	Approx 6.9km east of jct 15	70
M4	Jct 15	70
M4	Approx 1.8km west of jct 15	70
M4	Approx 3km east of jct 16	70
M4	Approx 8.4km west of jct 16	70
M4	Approx 3.1km east of jct 17	70
M4	Approx 8.3km east of jct 17	70
A4	Froxfield	40
A4	West Overton	60
A30	Fovant	40
A30	The Pheasant	60
A36	Brickworth (near A27 jct)	60
A36	Hanging Langford	60
A36	Knook	50
A36	South of Whaddon	60
A36	Wilton Rd, Salisbury	30
A36	Stapleford to Steeple Langford	60
A303	Chicklade	50
A303	West of Winterbourne Stoke	60
A303	Willoughby Hedge (1.5km west of A350)	60
A338	Boscombe	40
A338	Near Little Woodbury (1.5km south of Salisbury)	30
A338	Near Southgrove Copse (1.5km south of Burbage)	60
A342	Andover Rd, Ludgershall	30
A342	Chirton to Charlton	60
A342	Lydeway	50
A346	Chiseldon Firs	60
A346	Whitefield (5km south of M4)	60
A350	Heywood	60
A350	Pretty Chimneys	70
A354	Coombe Bissett	40
A360/A344	Airmans Corner	60
A361	Devizes to Beckhampton	60
A361	Inglesham	60
A361	Near jct with B3101, west of Devizes	70
A361	Southwick	30
A361	Frome Rd, Trowbridge	30
A363	Trowbridge Rd, Bradford-on-Avon	30
A363	Trowle Common	40
A363	Woodmarsh, North Bradley	30
A419	Near Covingham, Swindon	70
A419	Cricklade	70
A419	near Broad Blunsdon	70
A420	Giddeahall to Ford	60
A3026	Tidworth Rd, Ludgershall	40
A3028	Larkhill Rd, Durrington	40
A3102	Lyneham	30
A3102	Oxford Rd, Calne	30
A3102	Sandridge Rd, Melksham	30
A3102	Wootton Bassett	30
A4259	Near Coate, Swindon	50
A4259	Queens Dr, Swindon (at Rushton Rd)	40
A4361	Broad Hinton	60
A4361	Swindon Rd, Wroughton	30
A4361	Uffcott crossroads	60
B390	Maddington Farm, west of Shrewton	60
B3098	Bratton	30
B3105	Hill St/Marsh St, Hilperton	30
B3106	Hammond Way, Hilperton	30
B3107	Holt Rd, Bradford-on-Avon	30
B4006	Marlborough Rd, Swindon	40
B4006	Swindon Rd, Stratton St Margaret	30
B4006	Whitworth Rd, Swindon	30
B4040	Leigh	50
B4041	Station Rd, Wootton Bassett	30
B4143	Bridge End Rd, Swindon	30
B4192	Liddington	50
B4289	Great Western Way, Swindon (near Bruce St Bridges)	40
B4553	Tewkesbury Way, Swindon	40
B4587	Akers Way, Swindon	30
-	Corsham, Park La	30
-	Swindon, Ermin St	30
-	Swindon, Moredon Rd	30
-	Swindon, Merlin Way	30
-	Trowbridge, Wiltshire Dr	30

SCOTLAND

Central Scotland

A safety camera partnership will be launched mid 2006

Road number	Location	Speed limit (mph)
M9	At M876	n/a
M9	Cadger's Brae (near jct 5)	n/a
M9	Near jct 10	n/a
M80	At River Carron	n/a
M876	Near A9	n/a
A9	Dunblane	n/a
A82	Crianlarich	n/a
A706	Bo'ness	n/a
A809	Sauchie	n/a
A907	Cambus	n/a
A908	Devonside	n/a
A993	Dean Rd, Bo'ness	n/a

Dumfries and Galloway

Road number	Location	Speed limit (mph)
A74(M)	Multiple sites	70
A7	Langholm	60
A75	Multiple sites	60
A76	Closeburn to Thornhill	60
A76	Glasgow Rd, Dumfries	30
A77	Balyett (south of Innermessan)	60
A77	Cairnryan	30
A77	Whiteleys (2.5km south of Stranraer)	60
A701	Moffat	30
A701	St Ann's	60
A709	Burnside (1.5km east of Lochmaben)	60
A711	Beeswing	50
A711	Kirkcudbright	30
A716	Stoneykirk	60
A718	Craichmore (1km north of B798)	60
B721	Eastriggs	30

Fife

Road number	Location	Speed limit (mph)
A91	Deer Centre to Stratheden (Hospital) jct	n/a
A91	Guardbridge to St Andrews	n/a
A92	Cadham (Glenrothes) to New Inn (near A912/A914 jct)	n/a
A92	Cardenden overbridge to A910 jct	n/a
A92	Cowdenbeath to Lochgelly	n/a
A92	Freuchie to Annsmuir (south of A91 jct)	n/a
A92	A91 jct to 1.5km north of Fernie	n/a
A92	Rathillet (south) to Easter Kinnear (1km south-west of B946)	n/a
A823	St Margaret Dr, Dunfermline	n/a
A823	Queensferry Rd, Dunfermline	n/a
A907	Halbeath Rd, Dunfermline	n/a
A911	Glenrothes to Leslie	n/a
A911	Glenrothes to Milton of Balgonie	n/a
A914	Forgan (near A92) to St Michaels (A919 jct)	n/a
A914	Kettlebridge	n/a
A914	Pitlessie to Cupar	n/a
A915	Checkbar jct (Kirkcaldy) to B930 jct	n/a
A921	Esplanade, Kirkcaldy	n/a
A921	High St/The Path, Kirkcaldy	n/a
A921	Rosslyn St, Kirkcaldy	n/a
A921	St Clair St, Kirkcaldy	n/a
A955	Methilhaven Rd, Buckhaven	n/a
A955	Methilhaven Rd, Methil	n/a
A977	Fere Gait, Kincardine	n/a
A985	Culross (west) to Valleyfield	n/a
A985	Admiralty Rd, Rosyth	n/a
A985	Waulkmill (east of Crombie) to Brankholm (Rosyth)	n/a
B914	Redcraigs to Greenknowes (east of A823)	n/a
B920	Crosshill to Ballingry	n/a
B933	Glenlyon Rd, Leven	n/a
B942	East of Colinsburgh	n/a
B980	Castlandhill Rd, Rosyth	n/a
B981	Broad St, Cowdenbeath	n/a
B981	Dunnikier Way, Kirkcaldy	n/a
B9157	Orrock to Kirkcaldy	n/a
B9157	White Lodge jct to Croftgary	n/a
-	Dunfermline, Townhill Rd	n/a
-	Glenrothes, Formonthills Rd	n/a
-	Glenrothes, Woodside Rd	n/a
-	Glenrothes, Woodside Way	n/a
-	Kirkcaldy, Hendry Rd	n/a

Lothian and Borders

Road number	Location	Speed limit (mph)
A7	Crookston (near B6368)	60
A7	Galashiels, Buckholmside to Bowland	NSL
A7	Hawick	30
A7	Stow to Bowland	30
A8	Ratho Station, Edinburgh	40
A68	Jedburgh	30
A68	Soutra Hill	NSL
A70	Balerno (Bridge Rd to Stewart Rd)	30
A71	Breich	30
A71	Polbeth	30
A72	Castlecraig (near Blyth Bridge)	NSL
A72	Innerleithen Rd, Peebles	30
A72	Holylee (near Walkerburn)	NSL
A90	Burnshot flyover to Cammo Rd, Cramond Bridge, Edinburgh (southbound)	40
A697	Greenlaw and southern approach	30
A697	Ploughlands to Hatchednize (either side of B6461)	NSL
A697	Orange La (at B6461)	NSL
A697/8	Coldstream	30
A698	Ashybank (3km east of A6088)	NSL
A698	Near Crailing	NSL
A699	Maxton village	40
A701	Blyth Bridge to Cowdenburn (1km north-east of Lamancha)	NSL
A701	Rachan Mill, Broughton to A72	30
A702	Bruntsfield Pl, Edinburgh (Thorneybauk to Merchiston Pl)	30
A702	Comiston Rd, Edinburgh (Oxgangs Rd to Buckstone Dr)	40
A702	Dolphinton north to Medwyn Mains	NSL
A703	Eddleston and approaches	30
A703	Leadburn south to Shiplaw	NSL
A703	Edinburgh Rd, Peebles	30
A703	Peebles north to Milkieston	30
A705	Longridge Rd, Whitburn to East Whitburn	30
A706	Whitburn (at Cairnie Pl)	30
A720	City Bypass, east of Gogar roundabout, Edinburgh	50
A899	South of Deer Park roundabout (M8 jct 3) Livingston	50
A899	From Lizzie Bryce roundabout to Almond interchange, Livingston	50
A901	Lower Granton Rd, Edinburgh (Granton Sq to Trinity Rd)	30
A6091	Melrose Bypass	NSL
A6105	Gordon and approaches	30
B701	Frogston Rd West, Edinburgh (Mounthooly Loan to Mortonhall Gate)	40/60
B6374	Galashiels, Station Bridge to Lowood Bridge	30
B7069	West Main St, Whitburn	30
-	Edinburgh, Muirhouse Parkway	30
-	Edinburgh, West Approach Rd, from Morrison St link to Dundee St	40
-	Edinburgh, West Granton Rd	30

North East Scotland

Road number	Location	Speed limit (mph)
A90	Mid Stocket Rd to Whitestripes Ave roundabout, Aberdeen	40
A90	Newtonhill to South Damhead, Kincorth, Aberdeen	70
A90	South Damhead to Mid Stocket Rd, Aberdeen	40
A90	Fraserburgh to B9032 jct	60
A90	South of Leys (near Ellon) to Blackhills (near Longhaven)	60
A90	Upper Criggie (3km south-west of A92 jct) to Mill of Barnes (2.5km south-west of A937 jct)	70
A90	North Rd, Peterhead (A982) to 1km south-east of Crimond	60
A92	Johnshaven to Inverbervie	60
A92	Kinneff, north to Mill of Uras	60
A93	Aboyne	30
A93	Banchory, east from caravan site	40
A93	Banchory, west from church	30
A93	Cambus O'May to Dinnet	60
A93	Dinnet to Aboyne	60
A93	Kincardine O'Neil, south-east to Haugh of Sluie	60
A95	Cornhill	30
A95	Keith to Davoch of Grange	60
A96	Great Northern Rd, Aberdeen	30
A96	Haudagain Roundabout to Chapel of Stoneywood, Aberdeen	30
A96	B9002 jct to A920 at Kirkton of Culsalmond	60
A96	Mosstodloch to Lhanbryde (east)	60
A96	Fochabers to Forgie	60
A98	Banff	30
A98	Mill of Tynet to Barhill Rd jct, Buckie	60
A98	From Carnoch Farm Rd, Buckie to Cullen	60
A98	Fochabers to Mill of Tynet	60
A941	Elgin to Lossiemouth	60
A941	Elgin to Rothes	60
A944	Westburn Rd, Aberdeen	30
A947	Fyvie to Tulloch	60
A947	Whiterashes to Newmacher	60
A948	Ellon to Auchnagatt	60
A952	New Leeds to A90	60
A956	King St, Aberdeen	30
A956	Wellington Rd, Aberdeen	40
A978	St Machar Dr, Aberdeen	30
B9040	Silver Sands Caravan Park, Lossiemouth to B9012 jct	60
B9077	Great Southern Rd, Aberdeen	30
B9089	Kinloss north-east to Roseisle Maltings crossroads	60
-	Aberdeen, Beach Blvd	30
-	Aberdeen, Springhill Rd	30
-	Aberdeen, West Tullos Rd	40

Northern Scotland

Road number	Location	Speed limit (mph)
A9	Cuaich, north-east of Dalwhinnie	n/a
A9	Near Dalwhinnie	n/a
A9	North of Dalwhinnie jct	n/a
A9	Daviot	n/a
A9	Caulmaillie Farm, near Golspie	n/a
A9	South of The Mound (Loch Fleet near Golspie)	n/a
A9	Altnasleanach, near Inverness	n/a
A9	North Kessock jct	n/a
A9	Near Fearn jct, south of Tain	n/a
A82	North of Temple Pier, Drumnadrochit	n/a
A82	Near Kings House Hotel, Glencoe	n/a
A82	Invergarry Power Station	n/a
A82	Alltsigh Youth Hostel, north of Invermoriston	n/a
A82	Near White Corries, Rannoch Moor	n/a
A87	West of Bun Loyn jct (A887)	n/a
A95	Drumuillie, near Boat of Garten	n/a
A95	North of Cromdale	n/a
A95	Congash Farm, near Speybridge, Grantown-on-Spey	n/a
A96	Auldearn Bypass, western jct	n/a
A96	Auldearn Bypass, eastern jct	n/a
A96	West of Allanfearn jct (near Culloden)	n/a
A96	Gollanfield	n/a
A99	Hempriggs, south of Wick	n/a
A834	Near Fodderty Bridge, west of Dingwall	n/a
A834	Strathpeffer Rd, Dingwall	n/a
A835	Inverlael straight, south of Ullapool	n/a
A939	Ferness to Grantown-on-Spey	n/a
B9006	Sunnyside, Culloden	n/a

Strathclyde

Road number	Location	Speed limit (mph)
M74	Jct 11 (Happendon), northbound	70
M74	Jct 13 (Abington), northbound	70
A70	East Tarelgin (approx 5km west of Ochiltree)	n/a
A73	Carlisle Rd, Airdrie	n/a
A76	near Lime Rd, New Cumnock	n/a
A78	Main Rd, Fairlie	n/a
A82	Bridge of Orchy	n/a
A82	Dumbarton Rd, Milton	n/a
A85	5.5km west of Tyndrum	n/a
A89	Forrest St, Airdrie	n/a
A89	Glasgow Rd, Bargeddie, Coatbridge	n/a
A706	South of Forth	n/a
A730	Blairbeth Rd, Rutherglen	n/a
A730	Glasgow Rd, Rutherglen	n/a
A730	Mill St, Rutherglen	n/a
A737	New St/Kilwinning Rd, Dalry	n/a
A749	East Kilbride Rd, (Cathkin Rd (B759) to Cairnmuir Rd)	n/a
A761	Glasgow Rd, Paisley near Newtyle Rd	n/a
A807	Balmore Rd, Bardowie	n/a
A809/A810	Drymen Rd/Duntocher Rd, Bearsden	n/a
A814	Cardross Rd, Dumbarton	n/a
A814	Glasgow Rd, Clydebank	n/a
A815	near Ardkinglas (near A83 jct)	n/a
B749	Craigend Rd, Troon	n/a
B768	Burnhill St, Rutherglen	n/a
B803	Coatbridge Rd, Glenmavis	n/a
B814	Duntocher Rd, Clydebank (Singer Rd to Overton Rd)	n/a
B8048	Waterside Rd, Kirkintilloch	n/a
-	Barrhead, Aurs Rd	n/a
-	Bishopbriggs, Woodhill Rd	n/a
-	Coatbridge, Townhead Rd	n/a
-	East Kilbride, Maxwellton Rd at Kirkoswald	n/a
-	Johnstone, Beith Rd	n/a
-	Neilston, Kingston Rd	n/a
-	Newton Mearns, Mearns Rd	n/a

Tayside

Road number	Location	Speed limit (mph)
A9	Near Inveralmond Industrial Est, Perth	70
A9	Tibbermore jct	70
A9	Broom of Dalreoch (B9141) to Upper Cairnie (B934)	70
A9	Near Balnansteuartach (approx 1.5 miles west of Blair Atholl)	60
A90	Quilkoe jct (B9128) to Finavon	70
A90	Forfar Rd, Dundee (near Fountainbleau Dr)	40
A90	Kingsway, Dundee	50
A90	Strathmartine Rd roundabout to Swallow roundabout, Dundee	50
A90	M90 jct 11 to Inchyra	70
A90	West of Longforgan village	70
A91	Milnathort to Devon Bridge	60
A92	Arbroath to Montrose	60
A92	East Dock St, Dundee	40
A92	Greendykes Rd, Dundee (Arbroath Rd to Craigie Ave)	30
A93	Guildtown to Blairgowrie	60
A93	Old Scone to Guildtown	60
A94	Scone to Coupar Angus	60
A822	Crieff to Braco	60
A923	Blairgowrie to Tullybaccart (Sidlaw Hills)	60
A933	Colliston northwards to Redford	60
A935	Brechin to Montrose	60
A972	Kingsway East, Dundee (to Pitairlie Rd)	40
A977	Kinross to Crook of Devon	60
B961	Drumgeith Rd, Dundee	30
B996	Kinross to Kelty	60
-	Dundee, Broughty Ferry Rd	30
-	Dundee, Charleston Dr	30
-	Dundee, Laird St	30
-	Dundee, Old Glamis Rd	30
-	Dundee, Perth Rd	30
-	Dundee, Strathmartine Rd	30

WALES

Mid and South Wales

Road number	Location	Speed limit (mph)
M4	3km east of jct 24, Llanmartin overbridge	70
M4	Approx 5km east of jct 32, Cherry Orchard overbridge	70
M4	1km east of jct 32, Rhiwbina Hill overbridge	70
M4	1.1km east of jct 33, Llantrisant Rd overbridge	70
M4	2km east of jct 35 (overbridge)	70
M4	Jct 36 overbridge	70
M4	1.5km east of jct 37 (overbridge)	70
M4	Toll Plaza	50
A40	From 1.2km east to 100m west of Bancyfelin jct	70
A40	Buckland Hall, near Bwlch	60
A40	Johnstown (Carmarthen west)	70
A40	Opposite Llangattock Lodge (southeast of Abergavenny)	70
A40	Llanhamlach	60
A40	Llansantffraed	60
A40	Mitchel Troy	70
A40	Rhosmaen (B4302 jct to national speed limit)	40
A40	Scethrog	60
A40	Trecastle	40
A40	White Mill	60
A44	Forest Bends (5km south-east of Llandegley)	60
A44	Gwystre	60
A44	Llanbadarn Fawr, Aberystwyth	30
A44	Llanfihangel-nant-Melan	60
A44	Sweet Lamb (west of Llangurig)	60
A48	M4 jct 49 north to Bristol House layby	70
A48	From 1.8km west to 300m east of Foelgastell jct	70
A48	From 1.5km west to 300m east of Llanddarog jct	70
A48	From 700m east to 2.2km west of Nant-y-caws jct	70
A48	Dinas Baglan, Baglan	30
A48	Bonvilston	40
A48	Browcastle (2km south-east of Bridgend)	40
A48	Castleton	50
A48	Cowbridge Bypass	70
A48	Cross Hands to Cwmgwili	40
A48	Cwmgwili, (Pontarddulais Rd jct to Bristol House layby)	70
A48	Langstone	40
A48	Clasemont Rd, Morriston, Swansea	30
A48	Berryhill, Newport	50
A48	Parkwall (north-east of Caldicot)	60
A48	Bolgoed Rd, Pontarddulais	30
A48	Carmarthen Rd, Pontarddulais	30
A48	Fforest Rd, Fforest, Pontarddulais	30
A48	Margam Rd, Port Talbot (at Rhanallt St)	30
A48	Peniel Green Rd, Llansamlet, Swansea (near Station Rd outside TOTAL Garage)	30
A48	St Nicholas	30
A438	Three Cocks	40
A449	Near Coldra (near Cats Ash overbridge)	70
A449	Llandenny	70
A449	Llantrisant (south of Usk)	70
A458	Cefn Bridge	60
A458	Llanfair Caereinion (Neuadd Bridge)	60
A458	Trewern	40
A465	Near Clydach	50
A465	Llanfoist near Abergavenny	60
A465	West of Llanfoist, near B4246 jct	60
A465	Pandy	40/50
A465	Triley Mill (near Llantilio Pertholey)	60
A466	High Beech Roundabout to Old Hospital, Chepstow	40
A466	Llandogo	30
A466	Dixton Rd, Monmouth	30
A466	Hereford Rd, Monmouth	30
A466	Redbrook Rd, Monmouth	30
A466	St Arvans	30
A466	Tintern	30
A467	Abertillery	30
A467	Blaina	40
A467	Danygraig, Risca	70
A467	Warm Turn	30
A468	Machen village	30
A468	Caerphilly Rd, Rhiwderyn	30
A469	Lower Rhymney Valley Relief Rd	70
A469	Tir-y-Birth, north of Hengoed	30
A470	Abercynon (southbound)	70
A470	Aberfan (overbridge)	70
A470	Aberduhonw (2km east of Builth Wells)	60
A470	Near Alltmawr (south of Builth Wells)	60
A470	Beacons Reservoir (near A4059 jct)	60
A470	Ysgiog (4km south of Builth Wells)	60
A470	Overbridge north of Cilfynydd	70
A470	Storey Arms (Brecon to Merthyr Tydfil, 2km north of A4059)	60
A470	Erwood	30
A470	Erwood (south)	60
A470	Llandinam to Caersws jct	40
A470	Llandinam village	40
A470	Llanidloes to Llandinam	60
A470	Llyswen	30
A470	Manor Way, Cardiff	40
A470	Newbridge to Rhayader	60
A470	Newbridge on Wye	30
A470	North Rd, Cardiff	30
A470	Rhydyfelin (overbridge, Dynea Rd)	70
A470	Near Taffs Well	70
A472	Hafodyrynys Hill, Crumlin	30
A472	Hafodyrynys	30
A472	Maesycwmmer	30
A472	Monkswood	60
A472	Little Mill, Pontypool	30
A472	Usk Bridge to Old Saw Mill	30
A472/A4042	Pontymoel Gyratory (elevated section)	50
A473/A4063	Bridgend Inner Bypass	30
A473	Bridgend Rd, Llanharan	30
A473	Bryntirion Hill, Bridgend	30
A473	Main Rd, Church Village	30
A473	Penybont Rd, Pencoed	30
A474	Glanaman	30
A474	Glanffrwd Estate jct to 40mph speed limit, Garnant	30
A474	Graig Rd, Alltwen	40
A474	Commercial St, Rhydyfro	30
A474	Heol Wallasey jct, Ammanford to NSL, Portamman	30
A474	Heol-Y-Gors, Cwmgors	60
A474	Penywern Rd, Neath	30
A475	Pentrebach, Lampeter	40
A475	Lampeter (central)	30
A475	Llanwnnen	40
A476	Carmel north to NSL, Temple Bar	30
A476	Cross Hands Roundabout to the Phoenix Inn, Gorslas	30

Road number	Location	Speed limit (mph)
A476	Erw Non jct to Clos Rebecca jct, Llannon	30
A476	Heol Bryngwilli, south of Cross Hands (mobile near static)	30
A476	Llannon Rd/Bethania Rd, Upper Tumble	30
A476	Stag & Pheasant, south of Carmel	40
A476	The Gate, Gorslas	40
A476	Ffairfach	30
A476	Thomas Arms, Llanelli to NSL, Swiss Valley	30
A477	Cosheston	40
A477	Llanddowror	30
A478	Clunderwen	30
A478	Llandissilio	30
A478	Pentlepoir	30
A479	Bronllys	30
A482	Cwmann (south)	30
A482	Cwmann (north)	30
A482	Lampeter (central)	30
A482	Lampeter Rd, Aberaeron	30
A482	Llanwrda	n/a
A483	near Abbeycwmhir jct	60
A483	Carmarthen Rd, Fforest Fach	30
A483	Garthmyl	60
A483	Midway Bends, Llandrindod Wells to Crossgates	60
A483	NSL to Llandeilo Bridge, Ffairfach	30
A483	North of Crossgates	60
A483	Refail Garage, Garthmyl	50
A483	Rhosmaen St, Llandeilo (King St to Bypass roundabout)	30
A483	Tycroes to Villiers jct, Ammanford	30
A483	Carmarthen Rd, Cwmdu, Swansea	40
A483	Fabian Way, Swansea (western end)	30
A484	Bronwydd	40
A484	Burry Port (all of the 30mph area)	30
A484	Cenarth	30
A484	Cwmffrwd (first bend on entering from the north)	40
A484	Cynwyl Elfed	30
A484	Danybanc jct to St Illtyds Rise jct, Pembrey	30
A484	North of Pembrey	60
A484	Pentrecagel	40
A484	Rhos	30
A484	Sandy Rd, Llanelli (Wauneos Rd to Denham Ave)	30
A484	Saron (outside school)	40
A484	Saron	40
A484	Trostre Roundabout to Berwick Roundabout, Llanelli	60
A484	From B4309 jct to NSL, Idole	40
A484	From 80m west of New Rd jct east to NSL, Newcastle Emlyn	30
A485	Alltwalis	40
A485	From A482 jct to NSL, Cwmann	30
A485	Llanllwni	40
A485	Llanybydder (north)	30
A485	Llanybydder (south)	30
A485	Peniel	40
A487	Bow St	30
A487	Aberaeron (central)	30
A487	Aberystwyth (central)	30
A487	Eglwyswrw	30
A487	Furnace	40
A487	Llanrhystud (southern approach)	40
A487	Llanarth	30
A487	Llanfarian	30
A487	Newgale	30
A487	Newport	30
A487	Penglais Hill/Waunfawr, Aberystwyth	40
A487	Penparc	40
A487	Rhydyfelin	40
A487	Rhyd-y pennau	30
A487	Tal-y-bont	30
A489	Caersws jct to Penstrowed	60
A489	Glanmule (at garage)	60
A489	Penstrowed to Newtown	60
A489	West of Hafren College, Newtown	40
A4042	Llanover	60
A4042	Mamhilad	70
A4043	Cwmavon Rd, Abersychan	40
A4043	St Lukes Rd, Pontnewynydd, Pontypool	30
A4046	College Rd, Ebbw Vale	30
A4046	Ebbw Vale (near Tesco)	40
A4046	Waunllwyd	30
A4047	Beaufort Hill/Hing St, Brynmawr	30
A4048	Argoed	30
A4048	Blackwood (Sunnybank)	30
A4048	Hollybush	30
A4048	Blackwood Rd, Pontllanfraith	30
A4048	Cwmfelinfach village	30
A4049	Bryn Rd, Pontllanfraith	30
A4050	Jenner Rd, Barry	30
A4051	Cwmbran Dr, Cwmbran	60
A4054	Cardiff Rd, Merthyr Vale	30
A4054	Cardiff Rd, Upper Boat	30
A4054	Cilfynydd Rd, Cilfynydd	30
A4054	Edwardsville (near Treharris)	30
A4054	Cardiff Rd, Mt Pleasant (south of Merthyr Vale)	30
A4054	Oxford St, Nantgarw	30
A4054	Pentrebach Rd, Pontypridd	30
A4055	Gladstone Rd, Barry	30
A4058	The Broadway, Pontypridd	30
A4058	Hopkinstown Rd, Hopkinstown, Pontypridd	30
A4059	New Rd, Mountain Ash	30
A4061	Cemetery Rd, Ogmore Vale	30
A4063	Maesteg Rd/Bridgend Rd, Pont-Rhyd-y-cyff, Maesteg	30
A4063	Bridgend Rd, Pen-y-fai	30
A4063	Sarn Bypass near jct with Bryncoch Rd	50
A4066	Broadway	40
A4066	Llanmiloe	40
A4066	Marsh Rd, Pendine	30
A4067	Abercraf	60
A4067	Crai	60
A4067	Mumbles Rd, Swansea (Sketty La to St Helens Sports Ground)	40
A4068	Bethel Rd, Cwmtwrch (near Ystalyfera)	30
A4068	Heol Gleien, Cwmtwrch (near Ystalyfera)	30
A4069	Station Rd, Brynamman (county bdy to Remploy factory)	30
A4069	Brynamman Rd, south of Brynamman	30
A4069	Broad St, Llandovery (A40 south to NSL)	30
A4069	Llangadog (south)	30
A4069	Llangadog (east)	30
A4069	Station Rd, Llangadog (north)	30
A4075	Carew	30
A4075	Pembroke	30
A4076	Johnston	30
A4076	Steynton	30
A4093	Gilfach Rd, Hendreforgan, Gilfach Goch	30
A4093	Glynogwr (approx 2.5km east of A4061)	30
A4102	Goatmill Rd, Merthyr Tydfil	30
A4106	Newton Nottage Rd, Porthcawl	30
A4106	Bridgend Rd, Porthcawl	40
A4106	The Porthway, Porthcawl	n/a
A4107	High St, Abergwynfi	30
A4109	Main Rd, Aberdulais	n/a
A4109	Dulais Rd, south of Seven Sisters	30
A4109	Glynneath	30
A4109	Main Rd, Crynant	30
A4118	near Swansea Airport	60
A4119	Mwyndy Cross, Llantrisant	50
A4120	Aberystwyth	30
A4138	From the 30mph limit at Hendy to the B4297, Talyclun	40
A4138	Loughor Bridge to 40mph limit, Hendy	30
A4139	Pembroke	30
A4139	Pembroke Dock	30
A4139	Tenby	30
A4216	Cockett Rd, Cockett, Swansea	30
A4221	Caehopkin	60
A4222	Abertin Rd, Cowbridge	30
A4222	Primrose Hill, Cowbridge	30
A4222	Maendy	30
A4222	Cowbridge Rd, Pontyclun	30
A4226	Five Mile La, Barry	40
A4226	Five Mile La, Moulton	40
A4233	Ferndale (at Highfield)	30
A4233	Oakland Terr, Ferndale	30
A4233	The Parade, Ferndale	30
B4181	Coity Rd, Bridgend	30
B4181	Coychurch Rd, Bridgend	30
B4223	Gelli Rd, Gelli (Rhondda)	30
B4223	Maindy Rd/Pen-Twyn Rd, Ton Pentre (Rhondda)	30
B4235	Gwernesney, near Usk	60
B4236	Ponthir Rd, Caerleon	30
B4236	Llanfrechfa	30
B4236	Carleon Rd, Ponthir	30
B4237	Cardiff Rd, Belle Vue, Newport	30
B4237	Chepstow Rd, Newport (near Aberthaw Rd)	30
B4237	Chepstow Rd, Newport (near Royal Oak Hill)	40
B4237	Wharf Rd, Newport	30
B4239	Lighthouse Rd, Maes-glas, Newport	30
B4242	Pont-Nêdd-Fèchan	40
B4245	Caldicot Bypass	30
B4245	Leechpool (near Caldicot)	60
B4245	Magor Rd, west of Llanmartin	30
B4245	Magor (west)	30
B4245	Undy	30
B4245	Caldicot Rd, Rogiet	30
B4245	West of Rogiet (at Green Farm bend)	40
B4246	Foundry Rd, Abersychan	30
B4246	Varteg Rd, Abersychan	30
B4246	New Rd, Garndiffaith	30
B4248	Garn Rd, Blaenavon	40
B4251	Kendon Hill, Oakdale	30
B4254	Church Rd, Gelligaer	40
B4254	Pengam Rd, Penpedairheol (near Gelligaer)	30
B4254	Gelligaer Rd, Trelewis	30
B4257	Wellington Way, Rhymney	30
B4262	Heol Isaf, Radyr, Cardiff	30
B4265	Llantwit Major Bypass	50
B4265	St Brides Major	30
B4265	St Brides Rd, Wick	30
B4267	Leckwith Rd, Cardiff	30
B4267	South Rd, Sully	30
B4273	New Rd, Ynysybwl	30
B4275	Abercynon Rd, Abercynon	30
B4275	Park View Ter, Abercwmboi	30
B4275	Miskin Rd, Mountain Ash	30
B4275	Penrhiwceiber Rd, Penrhiwceiber	30
B4278	Dinas Rd, Dinas (near Tonypandy)	30
B4278	Gilfach Rd, Tonyrefail	30
B4278	Penrhiw-fer Rd, Tonyrefail	30
B4281	Cefn Rd, Cefn Criwber	30
B4281	High St, Kenfig Hill, Pyle	30
B4282	Bridgend Rd and Castle St, Maesteg (centre of 2.15km section)	30
B4282	Measteg Rd, Bryn	30
B4283	Heol Fach, North Connelly, Pyle	30
B4290	Burrows Rd, /Pen-yr-Heol, Skewen, Neath	30
B4290	New Rd, Jersey Marine	30
B4291	Birchgrove Grove, Birchgrove	30
B4293	Devauden	30
B4295	Cwmbach Rd, Cockett, Swansea	30
B4295	Gowerton to Penclawdd	40
B4295	New Rd, Crofty	30
B4295	Penclawdd to Llanrhidian	60
B4296	Goetre Fawr Rd, Killay, Swansea	30
B4296	Grovesend	30
B4296	Pentre Rd, Waungron	30
B4297	Capel Hendre (Nant yr Arw jct to the Parc Hendre jct)	30
B4297	Cleviston Park to Park La, Llangennech	30
B4297	Fforest	30
B4297	Llanedi (north of Pontarddulais)	30
B4297	Llwynhendy (Capel Soar to the Police Station)	30
B4297	Loughor Bridge Roundabout to Station Rd, Bynea	40
B4301	Bronwydd	30
B4302	Talley	30
B4303	Dafen Roundabout to Felinfoel Roundabout, Llanelli	30
B4304	Copperworks Roadbridge to Morfa Roundabout, Llanelli	40
B4304	Lower Trostre Rd Roundabout to Trostre Rd Roundabout, Llanelli	30
B4306	Heol Y Banc, Bancffosfelen	30
B4306	Llangendeirne	30
B4306	Llanon Rd, Pontyberem	30
B4308	Penmynnydd (east of Trimsaran)	40
B4309	Five Roads	30
B4310	Heol Caegwyn, Drefach	30
B4310	Station Rd, Nantgaredig	40
B4312	Johnstown, Carmarthen (from The Square south to NSL)	30
B4312	Llangain	30
B4312	St Clears Rd, Johnstown, Carmarthen	30
B4314	Pendine	30
B4314	Narberth	30
B4317	Carway (east)	30
B4317	Carway (west)	30
B4317	Heol Capel Ifan, Pontyberem	30
B4317	Myrtle Hill, Ponthenry	30
B4317	Station Rd, Pontyberem	30
B4320	Hundleton	30
B4322	Pembroke Rd, Pembroke Dock	40
B4325	Neyland	30
B4328	Trevaughan, Whitland	30
B4333	Aber-arad, Newcastle Emlyn	30
B4333	Cynwyl Elfed (north)	30
B4333	Hermon	40
B4336	Llanfihangel-ar-Arth	30
B4336	Pontwelly, Llandysul	30
B4436	Northway, Bishopston	40
B4337	Llanybydder	30
B4337	Talsarn	40
B4347	Newcastle (near Monmouth)	30
B4350	Glasbury to Hay-on-Wye	60
B4436	Pennard Rd, Kittle (near Bishopston)	40
B4459	Llanfihangel-ar-Arth (south)	30
B4459	Pencader	30
B4459	Pencader (south)	40
B4478	Letchworth Rd, Ebbw Vale	30
B4486	Steelworks Rd, Ebbw Vale	30
B4487	Newport Rd, Cardiff	30
B4488	Pencisely Rd, Cardiff	30
B4489	Llangyfelach Rd, Treboeth, Swansea	30
B4489	Swansea Rd, Llangyfelach, Swansea	30
B4511	Bedwellty Rd, Aberbargoed (at Coedymoeth Rd)	30
B4511	Penylan Rd, Argoed	30
B4521	Hereford Rd, Abergavenny	30
B4524	Corntown	30
B4556	Cae'r bryn, near Ammanford	30
B4556	Norton Rd, Penygroes	30
B4556	Penygroes Rd, Blaenau (east of Cae'r bryn)	30
B4556	Penygroes Rd, Gorslas	30
B4560	Llangynidr Rd, Beaufort, Ebbw Vale	30
B4591	Cromwell Rd, Risca	30
B4591	Pontymister, Risca (at Welsh Oak pub)	30
B4591	High Cross, Newport (near jct 27)	30
B4591	Risca Rd, Pontymister, Risca (opposite power station)	30
B4595	Brynteg Hill, Beddau	30
B4596	Caerleon Rd, Newport (south of M4)	30
B4596	Caerleon Rd, Newport (east of Beaufort Rd)	30
B4598	Horse and Jockey (near Abergavenny)	60
B4598	Llancayo	60
B4598	Porthycarne St, Usk	30
B4599	Ystradgynlais	30
B4603	Clydach Rd, Ynystawe	30
B4603	Pontardawe Rd, Clydach	30
B4622	Broadlands Link Rd, near Bridgend	30
B4623	Mountain Rd, Caerphilly	30
-	Abergwili (Ambulance Station to the Bypass roundabout)	30
-	Abertillery, Gwern-Berthi Rd	30
-	Ammanford, New Rd/ Pantyffynnon Rd	30
-	Ammanford, Dyffryn Rd, Saron	30
-	Ammanford, Saron (at Saron School)	30
-	Ammanford, Saron Rd (at Saron Church)	30
-	Barry, Barry Rd	30
-	Barry, Buttrills Rd	30
-	Barry, Holton Rd	30
-	Beddau, Gwaunmiskin Rd	30
-	Betws, Betws Rd (near Ammanford)	30
-	Betws, Maesquarre Rd	30
-	Blaenavon, Upper Coedcae Rd	30
-	Bridgend, Brackla Way, Brackla	30
-	Bridgend, Heol-y-Nant, Cefn Glas	30
-	Bridgend, Llangewydd Rd, Cefn Glas	30
-	Bridgend, Merlin Cres, Cefn Glas	30
-	Bridgend Industrial Estate, Kingsway	30
-	Bridgend Industrial Estate, North Rd	30
-	Bridgend Industrial Estate, South Rd	30
-	Bridgend Industrial Estate, Western Ave	30
-	Bridgend, Pen-Y-Cae La	30
-	Briton Ferry, Old Rd	30
-	Brynna, Brynna Rd	30
-	Caerleon, Usk Rd	30
-	Caerleon to Usk road (Apple Tree Farm, north of Garth)	60
-	Caldicot, Chepstow Rd	30
-	Cardiff, Colchester Ave, Penylan	30
-	Cardiff, Cyncoed Rd	30
-	Cardiff, Maes-y-Coed Rd, Heath	30
-	Cardiff, Circle Way, Llanedeyrn	30
-	Cardiff, Excalibur Dr, Thornhill	30
-	Cardiff, Heol y Deri, Rhiwbina	30
-	Cardiff, Rhiwbina Hill	30
-	Cardiff, Rhyd-y-Penau Rd	30
-	Cardiff, Lake Rd East, Roath	30
-	Cardiff, Lake Rd West, Roath	30
-	Cardiff, Wentloog Ave, Rumney	30
-	Cardiff, St Fagans Rd	30
-	Cardigan (north)	30
-	Carmarthen, Lime Grove Ave/ Fountain Head Terrace	30
-	Cefn Criwber	30
-	Cefneithin (west of Gorslas)	30
-	Church Village, Church Rd, Ton-teg	30
-	Church Village, Pen-yr-Eglwys	n/a
-	Church Village, Station Rd	30
-	Clydach, Vardre Rd	30
-	Coity, Heol Spencer	30
-	Cwmbran, Avondale Rd	30
-	Cwmbran, Greenforge Way	30
-	Cwmbran, Henllys Way	30
-	Cwmbran, Llanfrechfa Way	30
-	Cwmbran, Maendy Way	30
-	Cwmbran, Chapel St, Pontnewydd	30
-	Cwmbran, Thornhill Rd	30
-	Cwmbran, Ty Canol Way	30
-	Cwmbran, Ty Gwyn Way/ Greenmeadow Way	30
-	Cwmgwili	30
-	Cwmgwili, Thornhill Rd	30
-	Deri, New Rd	30
-	Dinas Powys, Pen-y-Turnpike Rd	30
-	Drefach, Heol Blaenhirwaun	30
-	Drefach, Heol Caegwyn	30
-	Ebbw Vale, Cwmgovilon, Beaufort	30
-	Ebbw Vale, Gwaun Helyg Rd, Willowtown	30
-	Ebbw Vale, Newchurch Rd	30
-	Ebbw Vale, Reservoir Rd, Rassau	30
-	Fochriw, Olgivie Ter	30
-	Foelgastell (west of Gorslas)	30
-	Forden	30
-	Gelli, (Rhondda), Gelli Industrial Estate	30
-	Gilwern, Cae Meldon (aka Ty Mawr La)	30
-	Gorseinon, Frampton Rd	30
-	Haverfordwest, Merlin's Bridge	30
-	Haverfordwest, New Rd/ Uzmaston Rd	30
-	Llanbradach	30
-	Llandysul (central)	30
-	Llanelli, Denham Ave	30
-	Llanelli, Heol Goffa (A476 to A484)	30
-	Llanharan, Brynna Rd	30
-	Llantrisant, Cross Inn Rd	30
-	Llantwit Major, Llanmaes Rd	30
-	Maesteg, Heol-Ty-Gwyn	30
-	Maesteg, Heol Ty With	30
-	Merthyr Tydfil, Brecon Rd	30
-	Merthyr Tydfil, High St, Cefn-coed-y-cymmer	30
-	Merthyr Tydfil, Vaynor Rd, Cefn-coed-y-cymmer	30
-	Merthyr Tydfil, High St, Dowlais	30
-	Merthyr Tydfil, Goetre La	30
-	Merthyr Tydfil, Gurnos Rd	30
-	Merthyr Tydfil, Heol-Tai-Mawr, Gellideg	30
-	Merthyr Tydfil, Swansea Rd, Gellideg	30
-	Merthyr Tydfil, Heolgerrig Rd	30
-	Merthyr Tydfil, Pant Rd	30
-	Merthyr Tydfil, High St, Pen-y-Darren	30
-	Merthyr Tydfil, Plymouth St	30
-	Merthyr Tydfil, The Walk	30
-	Merthyr Tydfil, Rocky Rd	30
-	Milford Haven, Priory Rd	30
-	Milford Haven, St Lawrence Hill	30
-	Mountain Ash, Llanwonno Rd	30
-	Nant-y-caws (from Heol Login along Nant-y-caws Hill)(east of Carmarthen)	60
-	Nash, West Nash Rd	30
-	Neath, Crymlyn Rd, Skewen	30
-	Newport, Allt-Yr-Yn Ave	30
-	Newport, Corporation Rd	30
-	Newport, Rowan Way, Malpas	30
-	New Quay (central)	30
-	New Tredegar, White Rose Way	30
-	Newbridge, Park Rd	30
-	Pencoed, Felindre Rd	30
-	Pendine (outside school)	30
-	South of Pentrecagel (near Newcastle Emlyn)	40
-	Pontypool, Greenhill/Sunnybank Rd, Griffithstown	30
-	Pontypool, Station Rd, Griffithstown	30
-	Pontypool, Plas y Coed Rd, Pontnewynydd	30
-	Pontypool, Riverside	30
-	Pontypool, Usk Rd	30
-	Porthcawl, Fulmar Rd	30
-	Port Talbot, Village Rd, Sandfields	30
-	Pyle, Fairfield, North Cornelly	30
-	Rhymney, Llys Joseph Parry (near Farmers Arms)	30
-	Risca, Holly Rd	30
-	Risca, Waun Fawr Park Rd	30
-	Rogerstone, Pontymason La	30
-	Sarn, Heol-Yr, Ysgol, Ynyswdre	30
-	St Athan, Cowbridge Rd	30
-	St Mellons, Willowbrook Dr	30
-	Steynton, Thornton Rd	40
-	Sully (near Barry), Hayes Rd	30
-	Swansea, Llethri Rd, Felinfoel	30
-	Swansea, Pentregethin Rd Farm Shop	30
-	Swansea, Mynydd Garnllwyd Rd/ Caemawr Rd/Parry Rd/ Vicarage Rd (Heol Ddu to Clasemont Rd) Morriston	30
-	Swansea, Rhyd-y-Dafaid Dr, Derwen Fawr	30
-	Tiers Cross	60
-	Tredegar, Vale Terrace	30
-	Upper Boat, (near Pontypridd), Tonteg Rd	30
-	Usk Bridge to Llanbadoc	30
-	Usk, Usk to Raglan road (at Coldharbour)	60
-	Whitland, Market St	30
-	Whitland, North Rd	30
-	Whitland (east), Spring Gardens	30
-	Whitland (west)	30

North Wales

Road number	Location	Speed limit (mph)
A5	Bangor to Llandygai	30/40
A5	Froncysyllte to Betws-y-Coed (seasonal)	30/40/60
A5	London Rd, Holyhead	30
A5	Menai Bridge to Gwalchmai	30/40/60
A5/A5025	Holyhead to Llanfachraeth	20/30/40/60
A458	Cwm-Cewydd east to county boundary (seasonal)	60
A470	Dolgellau (A496 to east of A494)	40/60
A470	Llansanffraid Glan Conwy to Betws-y-Coed	30/60
A470	Llandudno to A55, jct 19	30/40/60
A470	Mallwyd to A487 (seasonal)	30/40/60
A470	North of Rhiwbrifdir to Congl-y-wal, Blaenau Ffestiniog	30/40/60
A483/A5	Ruabon to Chirk	60
A487	Caernarfon to Dolbenmaen	30/40/50/60
A487	Pantperthog to A470 (seasonal)	30/40/60
A487	Penmorfa to Gellilydan	30/40/60
A494	Bala to Glan-yr-afon	40/60
A494	Llyn Tegid (Bala Lake)	30
A494	Ruthin to Corwen (seasonal)	30/40/60
A494	Ruthin to Llanferres	40/60
A496	Harlech to Llanbedr	30/40/60
A499	Pwllheli to Penrhos	30/40/60
A525	Llanfair Dyffryn Clwyd to Llandegla (near B5430)	30/40/60
A525	Ruthin to Denbigh	40/60
A525	St Asaph to Trefnant	30/40/60
A525	Vale Rd/Rhuddlan Rd, Rhyl	30
A525	Wrexham to Minera	30/60
A525	Wrexham to Redbrook	30/40/60
A534	Holt Rd, Wrexham	30
A539	Mill St, Llangollen	30/60
A539	Trevor to Erbistock (A528 jct)	30/40/60
A541	Caergwrle to Wrexham	30/40/60/70
A541	Mold to Caergwrle	30/40/60/70
A541	Mold Rd, Wrexham	30
A541	Trefnant to Bodfari	30/40/60
A542	Horseshoe Pass (seasonal)	60
A543	Denbigh to Pentrefoelas (seasonal)	30/60
A545	Menai Bridge to Beaumaris	30/40/60
A547	Colwyn Bay to Old Colwyn	30/40/50
A547	Prestatyn to Rhuddlan	30/40/60
A548	Dundonald Ave, Abergele	30
A548	Gronant to Flint (Oakenholt)	30/40/50/60/70
A548	Rhyl to Prestatyn	30/40
A548	Abergele to Kinmel Bay	30/40
A549	Mynydd Isa to Buckley	30/60
A550	Hawarden	30
A4080	Brynsiencyn to Rhosneigr (seasonal)	30/40/60
A4086	Cwm-y-Glo to Llanrug	30/40/60
A4086	Llanberis (seasonal)	30/40/60
A4212	Bala	30/60
A4212	Trawsfynydd to Llyn Celyn	60
A4244	Cwm-y-Glo to B4547	60
A5025	Amlwch to Menai Bridge	30/40/50/60
A5025/A5	Llanfachraeth to Holyhead	20/30/40/60
A5104	Coed-Talon to Leeswood (A541 to B5101)	30
A5104	Coed-Talon to A494 (seasonal)	30/40
A5119	Flint to Mold	30/50/60
A5152	Chester Rd, Wrexham	30
A5152	Rhostyllen	30/40
A5154	Victoria Rd, Holyhead	30
B4501	Denbigh to Cerrigydrudion (seasonal)	30/40/60
B4545	Kingsland to Valley (via Trearddur Bay)	30/40
B5105	Ruthin to Cerrigydrudion (seasonal)	30/40/60
B5108	Brynteg to Benllech	30/60
B5109	Llangefni towards Bodffordd	30
B5113	Kings Rd/Kings Dr, Colwyn Bay	30
B5115	Llandudno Promenade to Penrhyn Bay	30/40
B5115	Llandudno Rd, Llandrillo-yn-Rhos	30
B5118	Rhyl Promenade, Rhyl	30
B5120	Pendyffryn Rd, Prestatyn	30
B5125	Hawarden	30
B5129	Kelsterton to Saltney Ferry	30/60
B5420	Menai Bridge (Four Crosses to Menai Bridge Sq)	30
B5425	Wrexham to Llay	30/60
B5445	Rossett	30
B5605	Johnstown to Ruabon	30/40/60
-	Holyhead, Prince of Wales Rd	30
-	Penrhyn Bay to Rhos Point (coast road)	30
-	Kinmel Bay, St Asaph Ave	30/60

Key to listing

- Motorway
- Primary route
- Other A road
- B road
- Minor road

Avoiding congestion trouble spots

These **'jam busting'** maps pinpoint locations where traffic jams regularly occur and help you plan a route to avoid them. Only motorways and major A-roads are included but you can use the main-map pages in this atlas to plot a detailed route around potential trouble spots.

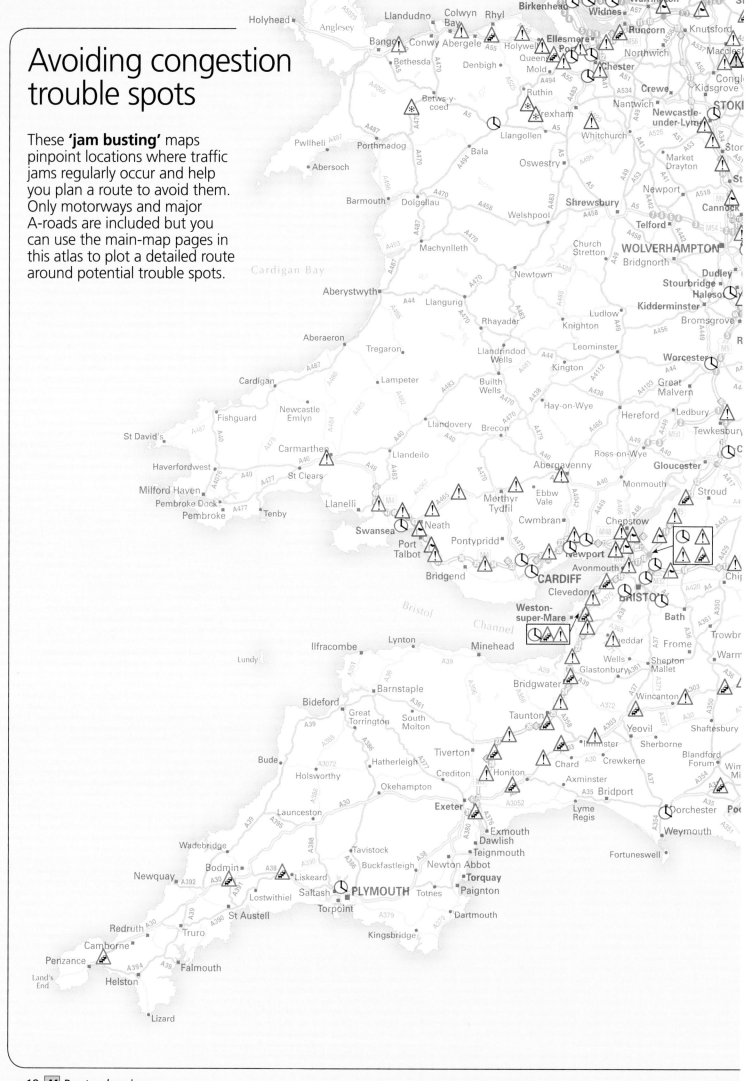

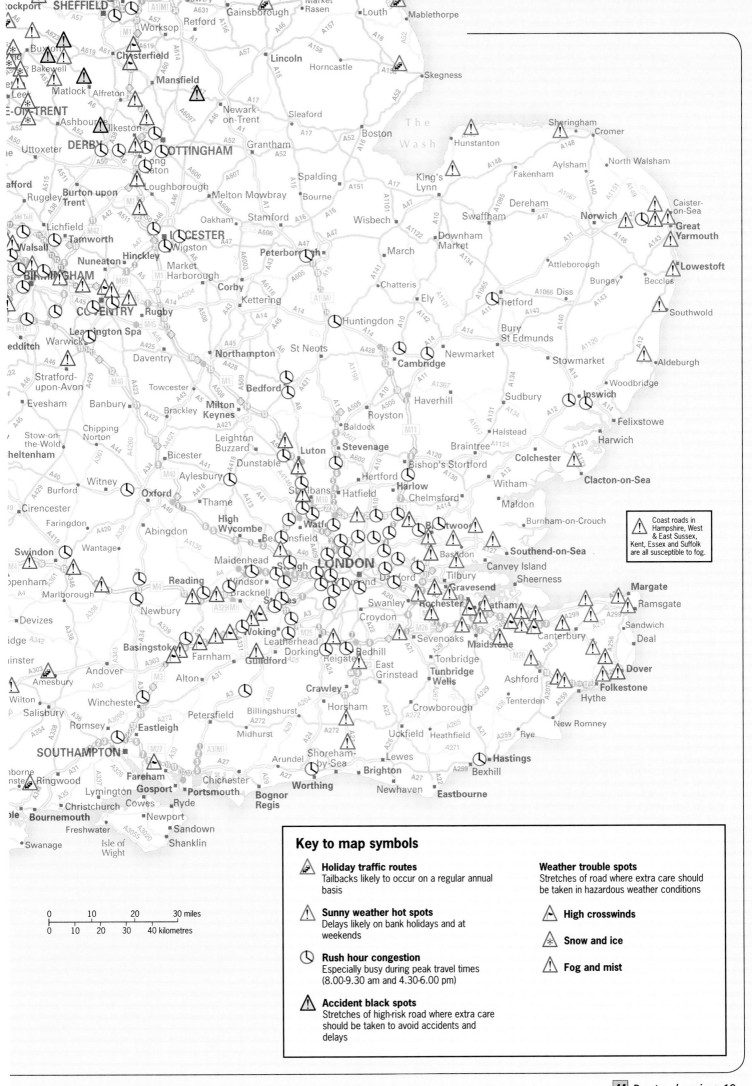

Key to map symbols

Holiday traffic routes
Tailbacks likely to occur on a regular annual basis

Sunny weather hot spots
Delays likely on bank holidays and at weekends

Rush hour congestion
Especially busy during peak travel times (8.00-9.30 am and 4.30-6.00 pm)

Accident black spots
Stretches of high-risk road where extra care should be taken to avoid accidents and delays

Weather trouble spots
Stretches of road where extra care should be taken in hazardous weather conditions

High crosswinds

Snow and ice

Fog and mist

Coast roads in Hampshire, West & East Sussex, Kent, Essex and Suffolk are all susceptible to fog.

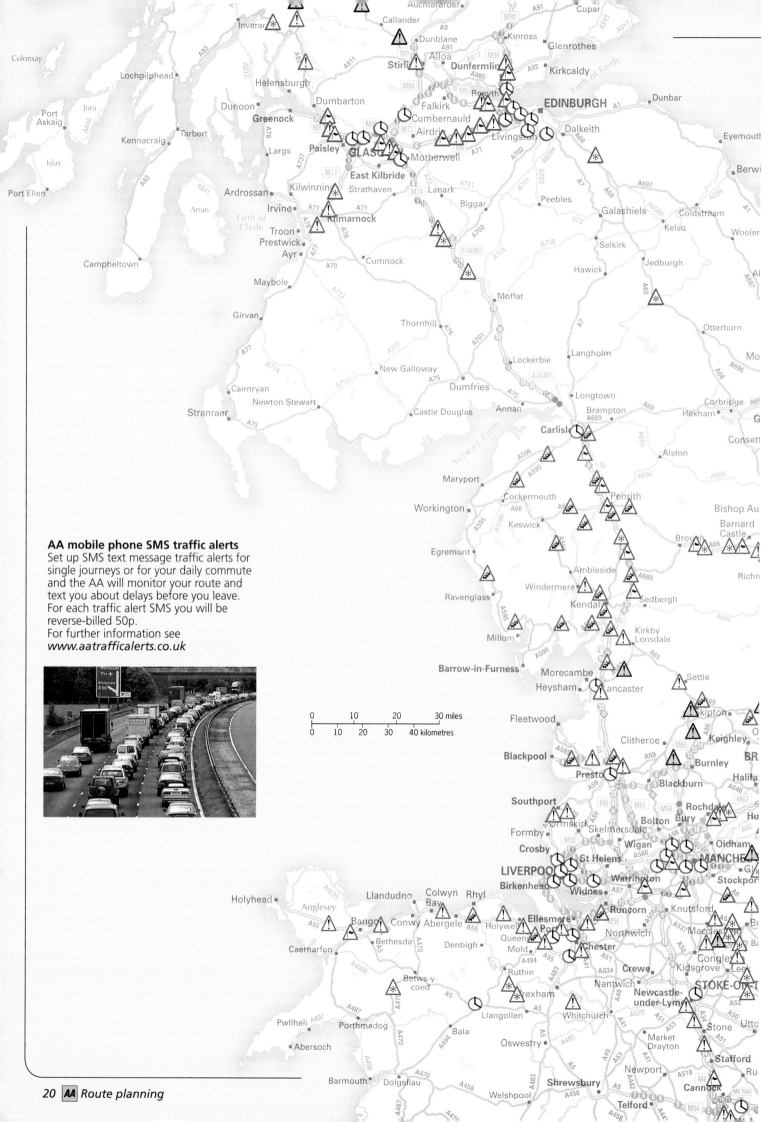

AA mobile phone SMS traffic alerts
Set up SMS text message traffic alerts for
single journeys or for your daily commute
and the AA will monitor your route and
text you about delays before you leave.
For each traffic alert SMS you will be
reverse-billed 50p.
For further information see
www.aatrafficalerts.co.uk

Avoiding congestion trouble spots

Planning to avoid delay

Before setting off on a journey, especially at weekends or on bank holidays, find out if there are any major events, such as music festivals, race meetings or other sporting fixtures taking place along your route and plan a revised route to avoid any hold-ups. At a more local level, events such as car boot sales can also be avoided. Congestion often occurs on routes to such attractions as theme parks, seaside resorts, retail parks and shopping centres. Roadworks can also cause delay but with prior knowledge can be avoided, see *www.theaa.com/travelwatch/travel_news.jsp*

'Jam buster' websites

To help you plan to avoid trouble spots a number of websites provide up-to-the-minute information on traffic flow, accidents, roadworks and other restrictions which may cause delays.

www.theaa.com/travelwatch/travel_news.jps
www.bbc.co.uk/travelnews
www.highways.gov.uk/trafficinfo for England
www.trafficscotland.org for Scotland
www.traffic-wales.com for Wales
trafficalerts.tfl.gov.uk/pinpointlite/main.php for London

Key to map symbols

Holiday traffic routes
Tailbacks likely to occur on a regular annual basis

Sunny weather hot spots
Delays likely on bank holidays and at weekends

Rush hour congestion
Especially busy during peak travel times (8.00-9.30 am and 4.30-6.00 pm)

Accident black spots
Stretches of high-risk road where extra care should be taken to avoid accidents and delays

Weather trouble spots
Stretches of road where extra care should be taken in hazardous weather conditions

High crosswinds

Snow and ice

Fog and mist

AA traffic news hot line

Beat the hold-ups by getting advance notice of congestion, accidents and road works, before you set out and during your journey. Call the AA's traffic and weather information line on 09003 401 100 or 401 100 from your mobile. Lines open 24 hours a day, 365 days a year (calls cost a minimum of 60p per minute - mobile rates vary). The service offers live traffic reports on specific motorways or A-roads of your choice, the latest traffic information for any region in the UK and regional five-day weather forecasts.

Local radio traffic reports

BBC local radio stations broadcast traffic reports throughout the day. Frequencies can be searched on most car radios and are listed at *www.bbc.co.uk/radio*

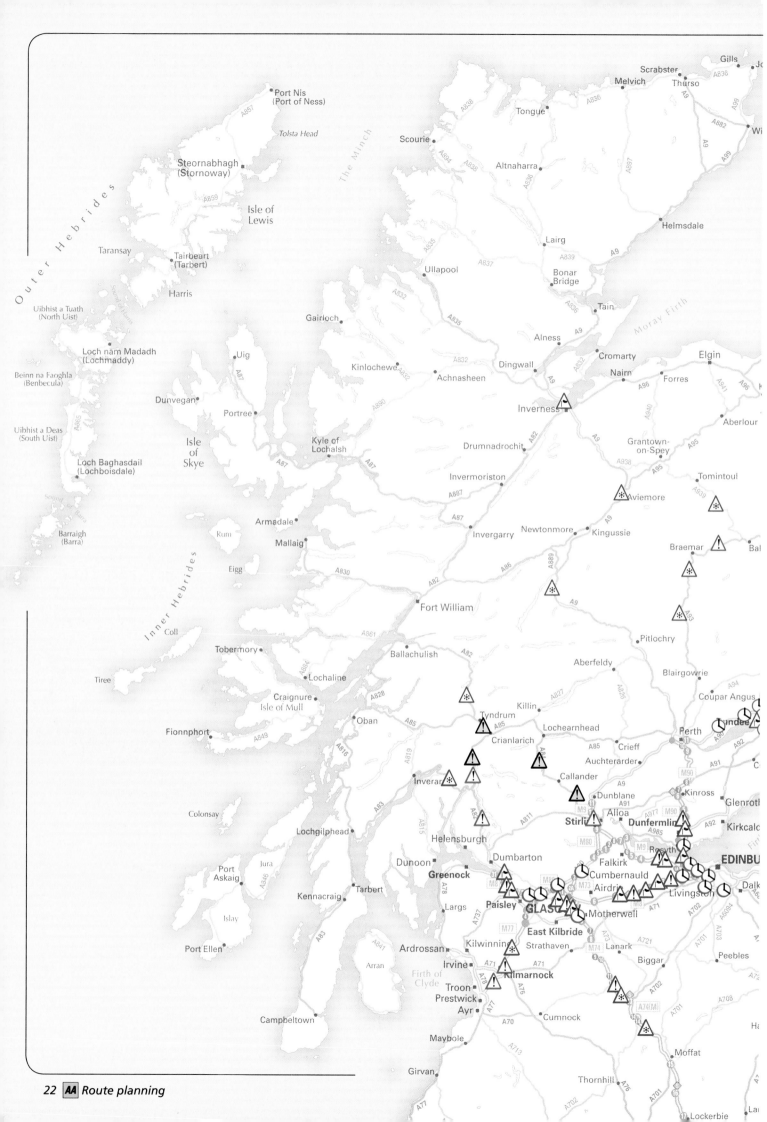

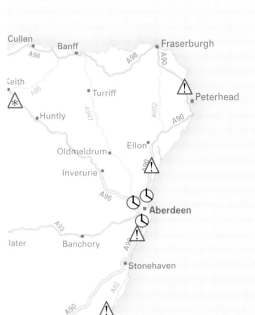
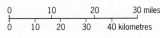

Avoiding congestion trouble spots

Month by month tips

January
Roads are most congested upon the return to work after the Christmas and New Year holiday. Expect a particularly heavy rush hour in the morning. Even small amounts of snow increase congestion as drivers slow down. The highest number of calls received in one day by the AA Roadwatch traffic line was over 97,000 when snow unexpectedly closed the M11 on 30 January 2003.

February
Mid-month, typically, the Friday afternoon at the start of half term is likely to be the busiest day. Between 4.00 pm and 7.00 pm on the following Sunday is likely to be busy as drivers return from weekend breaks.

March
Always the quietest month of the year on British roads. March calls to the traffic line only reach two thirds of those received in the busiest month of the year, July.

April
The combination of the Easter bank holiday and the Easter school holiday always causes problems with the Easter getaway. Motorway links around the airports always take the brunt of the congestion.

May
The Friday leading up to the bank holiday at the end of May is likely to be a busy day to travel as is between 11.00 am and 3.00 pm on the following Saturday which tends to suffer every year.

June
As fairer weather arrives weekend congestion takes a sudden upturn.

July
Always the busiest month of the year as the schools break up and more journeys are made around the country. Commuters fare better as annual holidays impact to reduce the number of rush hour journeys made.

August
The last bank holiday of the year before Christmas is in August and many take one of the last chances of the year for a warm UK getaway. Weekend congestion reaches its peak during this month.

September
As the schools go back, overall congestion decreases, although this spells bad news for commuters as rush hour congestion significantly increases.

October
Half term falls in October which creates a particularly busy Friday afternoon in the latter part of the month. Whilst temperatures often remain warm, gales and rain start to arrive which tend to cause extreme congestion.

November
Weather is the enemy of the November driver. Gales and rain continue in November and then fogs and frosts start. The end of British Summer Time in October adds to the problems as drivers struggle to cope with dark, cold and wet driving conditions.

December
The Friday of the last full working week before Christmas is usually the busiest day to travel as commuters finish early.

Key to map symbols

 Holiday traffic routes
Tailbacks likely to occur on a regular annual basis

 Sunny weather hot spots
Delays likely on bank holidays and at weekends

 Rush hour congestion
Especially busy during peak travel times (8.00-9.30 am and 4.30-6.00 pm)

 Accident black spots
Stretches of high-risk road where extra care should be taken to avoid accidents and delays

Weather trouble spots
Stretches of road where extra care should be taken in hazardous weather conditions

 High crosswinds

 Snow and ice

 Fog and mist

Atlas symbols

Motoring information

M4 Motorway	Primary route numbered junction: full access, restricted access	Roundabout
Motorway numbered junction: full access, restricted access	A25 Other A road: dual, single carriageway	Road under construction
Under construction	B382 B road: dual, single carriageway	Distance in miles between symbols
TOLL Toll motorway with toll station	Minor road: more than 4 metres wide, less than 4 metres wide	Road in tunnel
BATH Primary route destination	Narrow road with passing places (Scotland)	Vehicle ferry
Service area: motorway, primary route	Other road, drive or track: public, private access	Vehicle ferry - fast catamaran
Primary route: dual, single carriageway	Toll road, steep gradient (arrows point downhill)	Airport, airfield, heliport

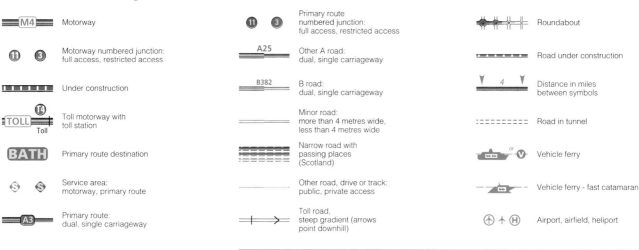

Recreation and leisure Before visiting check opening times, to avoid disappointment.

Sandy beach, heritage coast	C&CC site Camping & Caravanning Club site (AA approved)	Bird collection
National Park boundary	Sun Inn PH AA recommended pub (selected for good food, character & comfort)	Bird reserve (RSPB)
Scenic area	Abbey, cathedral or priory	Castle
Woodland	Abbey, cathedral or priory in ruins	Cave
Heritage railway	Agricultural showground	Country park
Tarka Trail National Cycle Network (Sustrans)	Air show venue	Farm or animal centre
Pennine Way Selection of national trails	Ancient monument	Garden
Hadrian's Wall Ancient wall	Aquarium	Hill-fort
AA approved campsite	Aqueduct or viaduct	Historic house
AA approved caravan site	Arboretum	Industrial attraction
AA approved caravan & campsite	Battle site	Marina

Town and airport plans Refer to the recreation and leisure legend, above, for a complete list of symbols.

M8 Motorway	B road: dual, single carriageway	Road under construction
Primary route: dual, single carriageway	Minor road: dual, single carriageway	Road in tunnel
Other A road: dual, single carriageway	Other road, drive or track: (access may be restricted)	Track or footpath

Central London plan (see pages 612 - 619)

Central London Congestion Charging Zone boundary, including the western extension (operational from February 2007)	Charge-free routes through the Charging Zone	Theatre, Cinema

Speed camera site
(fixed location)

Section of road
with two or more
fixed speed cameras

City, town, village
or other built-up area

24-hour Accident &
Emergency hospital

628 459 Height in metres:
peak, pass

Park & Ride (at least
6 days per week)

Ford, level crossing

24-hour petrol station

Petrol station, LPG station

Railway line, in tunnel

Railway, DLR station

Underground station

London underground station

Tramway

Borders
Cumbria National boundary

Devon
Cornwall County or unitary
authority boundary

4 Page on which
map continues

10 National Grid reference

Miles ½ 1
Km 1 1:100,000 scale bar

Miles ½ 1
Km 1 2 1:150,000 scale bar

Monument

Museum or gallery

National Nature Reserve:
England, Scotland, Wales

Local nature reserve

NTS National Trust for
Scotland property

NT National Trust property

Picnic site

Roman remains

Steam railway

Theme park

Tourist Information Centre
all year, seasonal

Viewpoint

Vineyard

Visitor or heritage centre

Windmill

World Heritage Site (UNESCO)

Zoo or wildlife collection

Other place of interest

Boxed symbols indicate
in-town attractions

AA golf course

Athletics

County cricket

Football

Horse racing

Ice hockey

Motorsport

Rugby Union

Rugby League

Ski slope:
natural, artificial

Speedway

Tennis

Arena (indoor)

Stadium

Pedestrians only road

One-way street, car park

Park & Ride (at least
6 days per week)

Building of interest

24-hour Accident &
Emergency hospital

6 3 Junction numbers

Church/chapel

Public toilet

Toilet with facilities
for the less able

AA inspected restaurant

Public Library

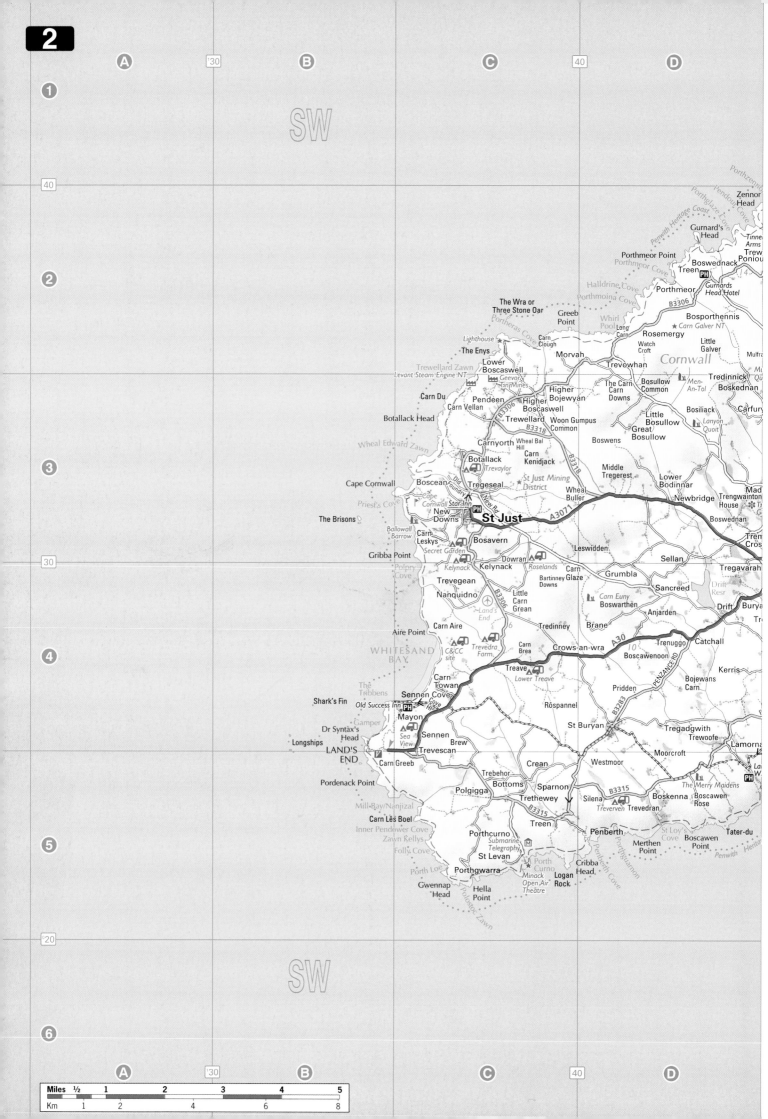

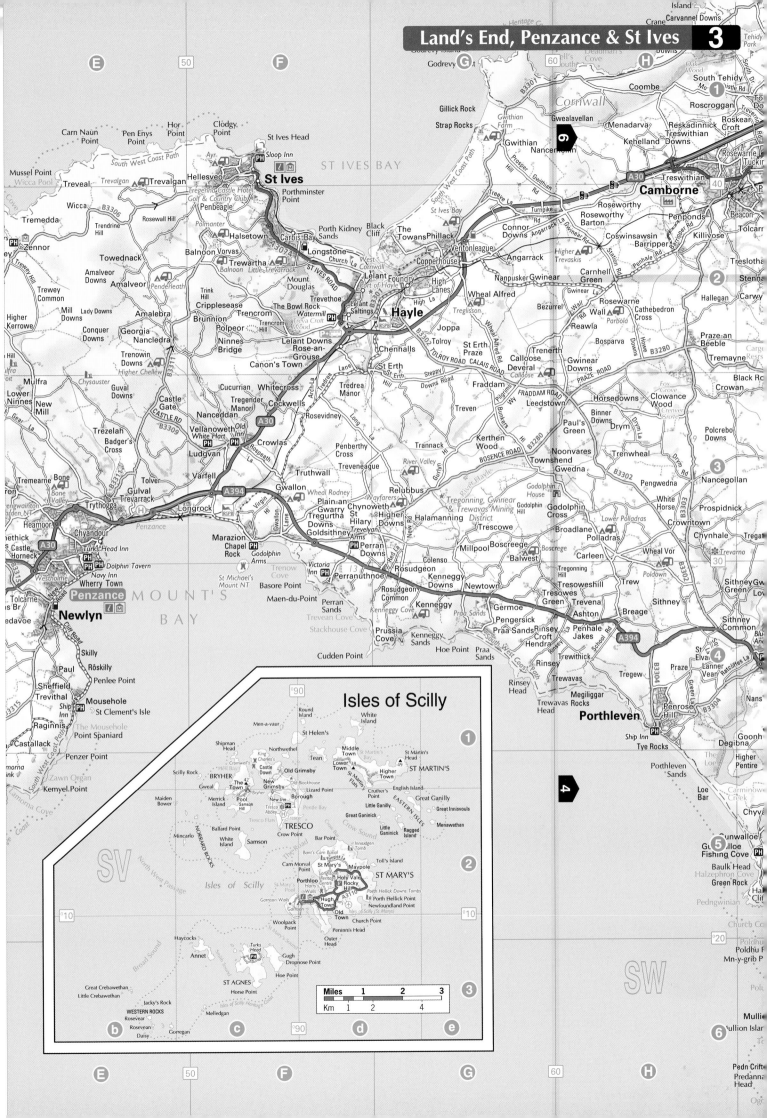

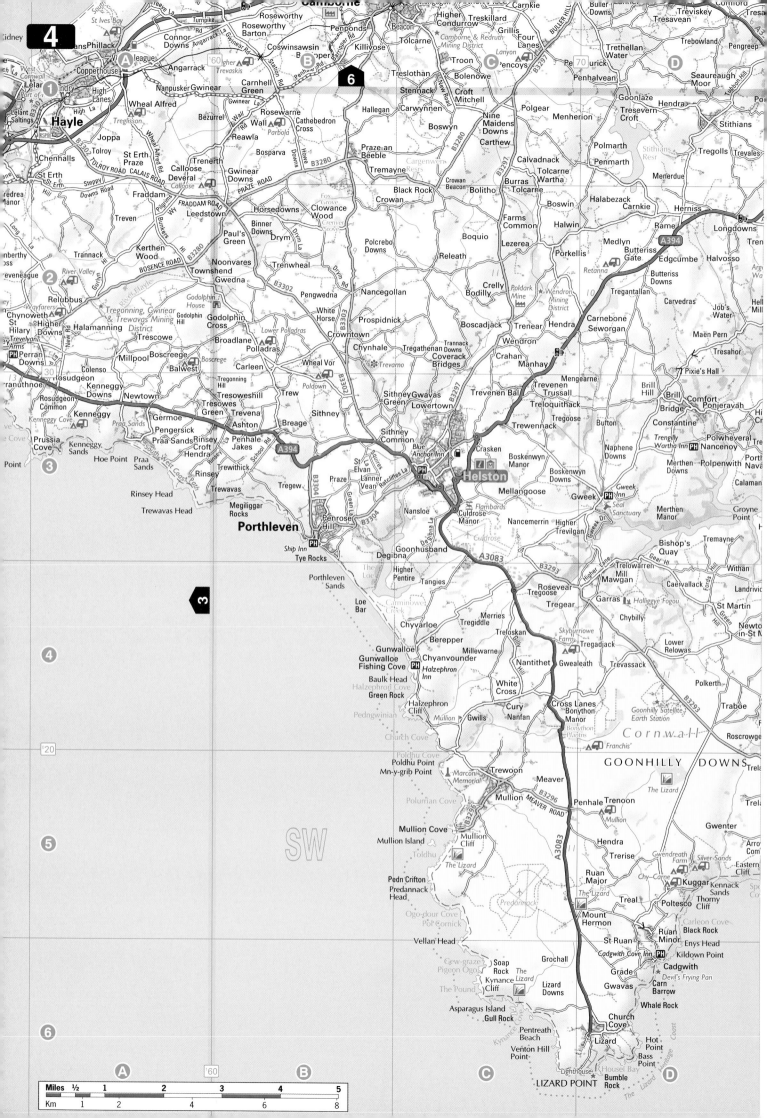

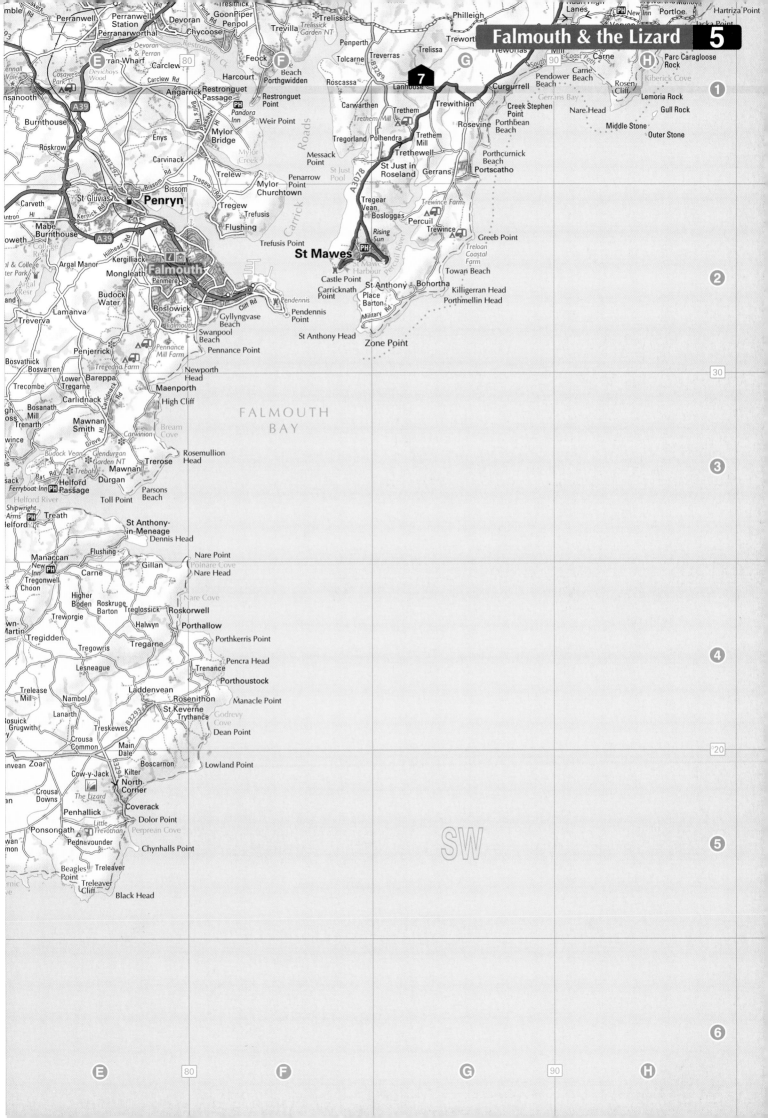

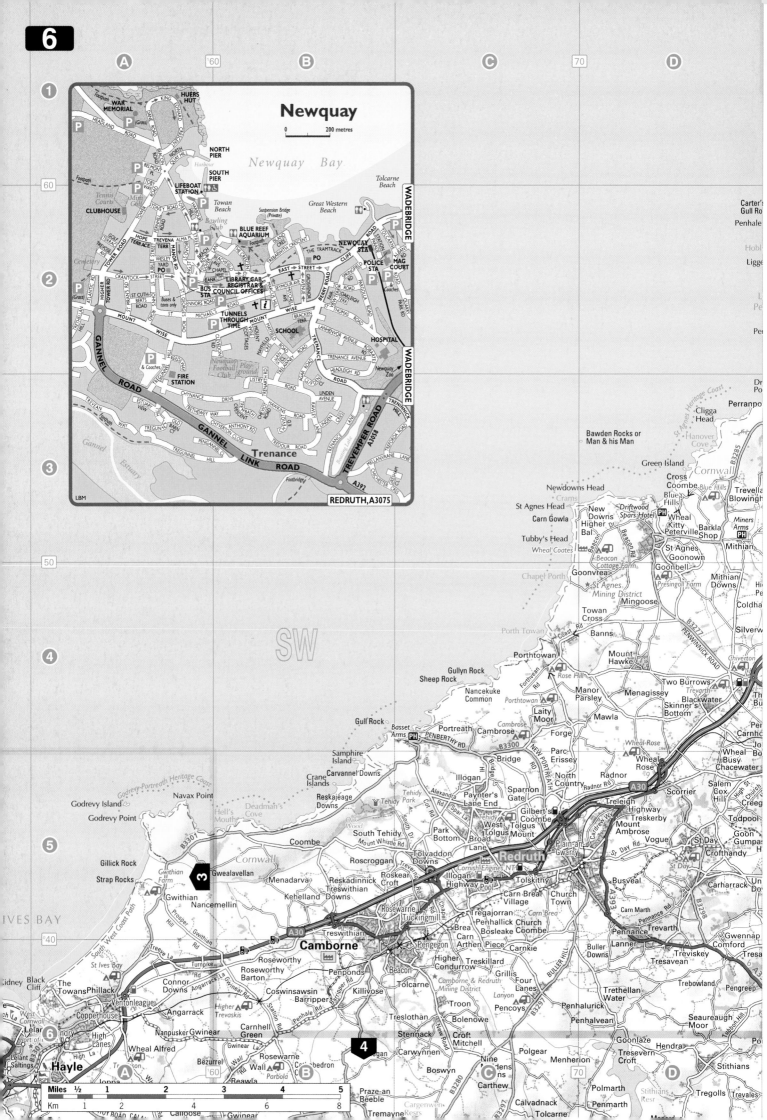

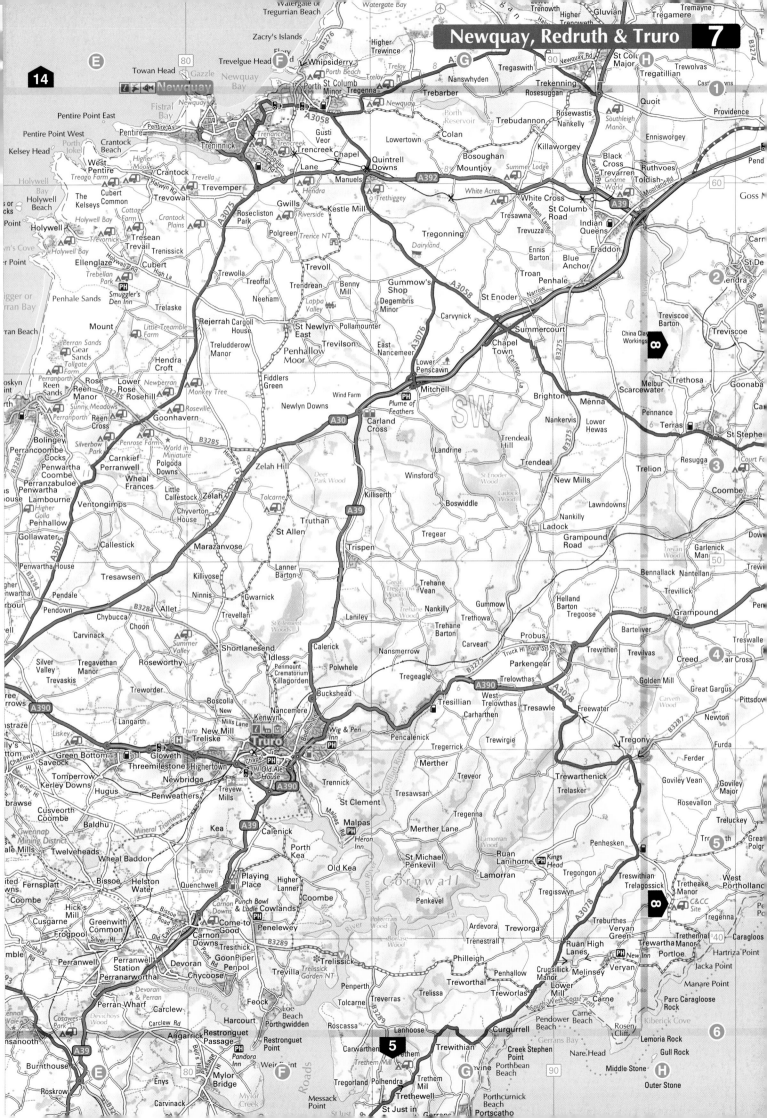

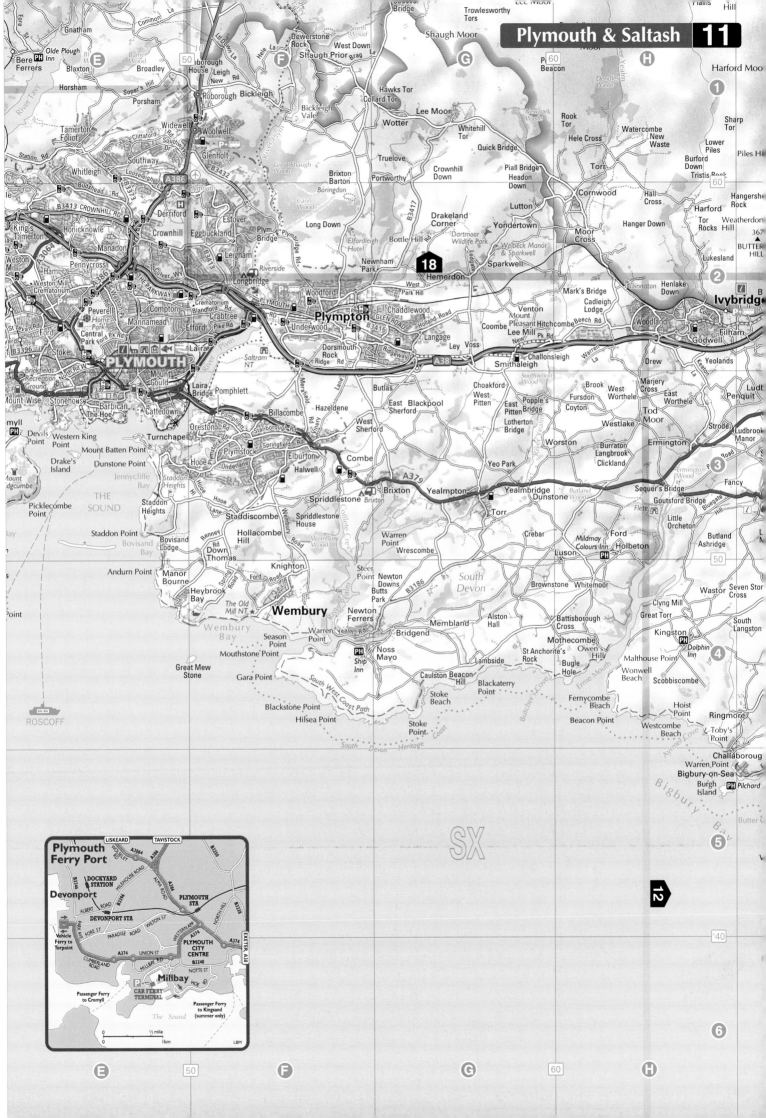

Brixham

20

Brixham

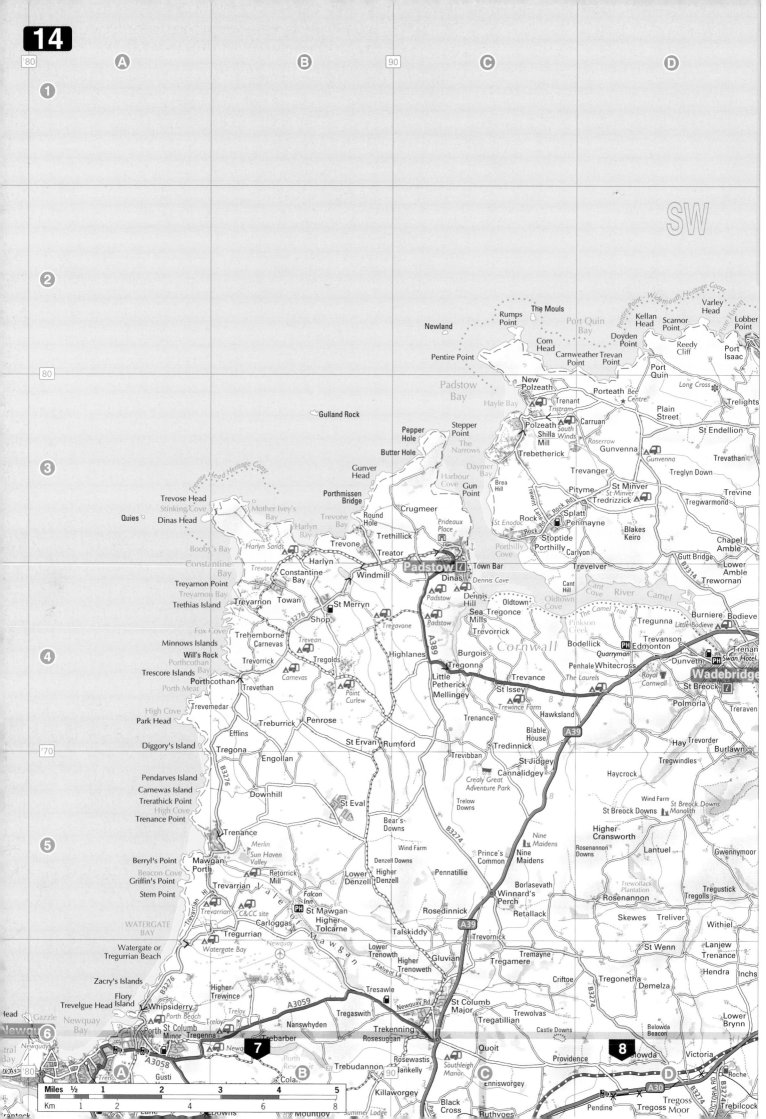

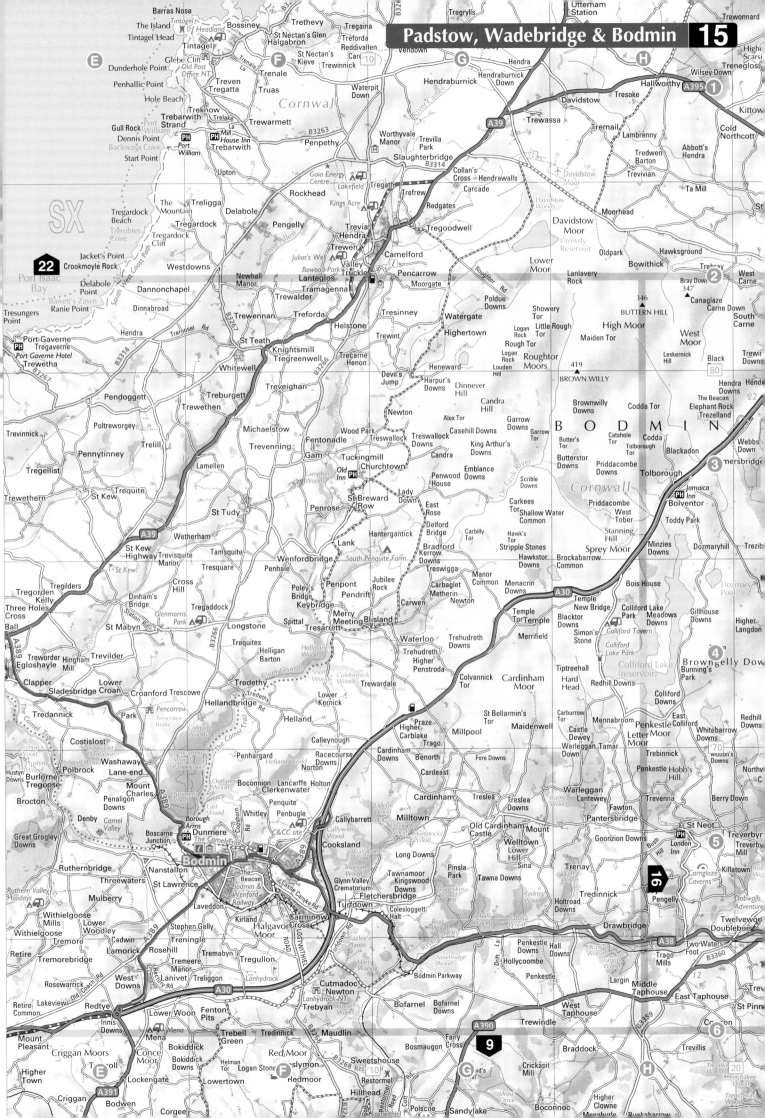

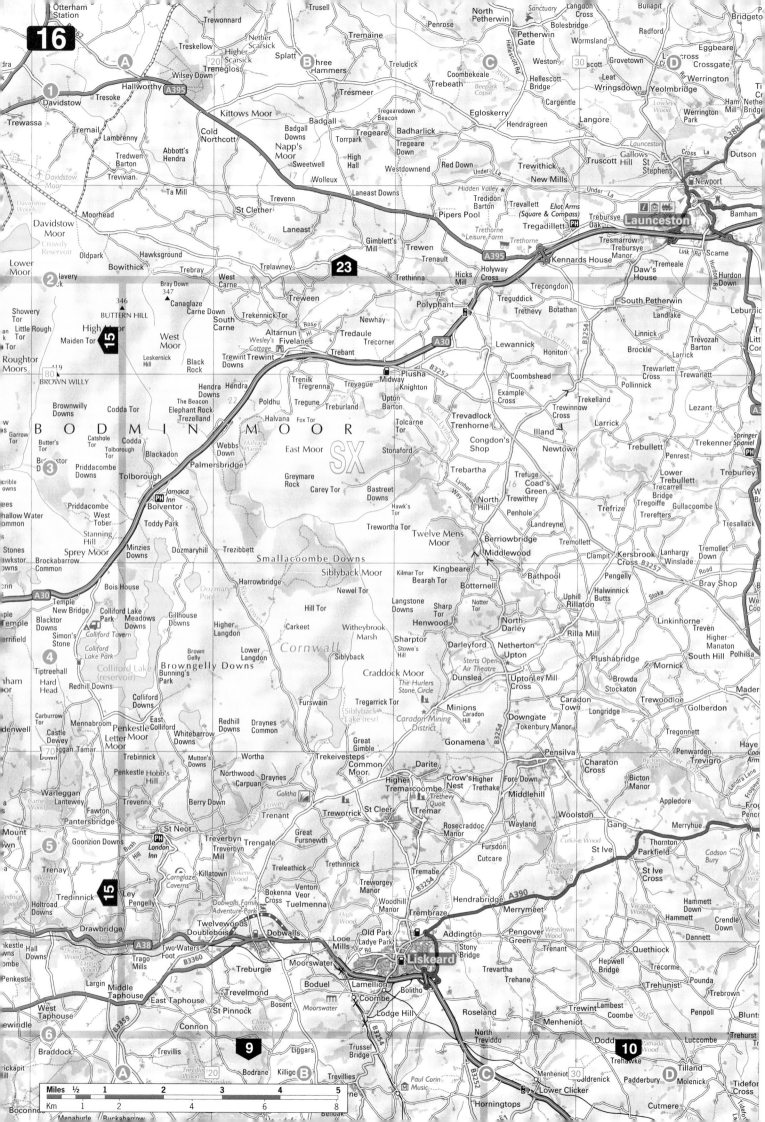

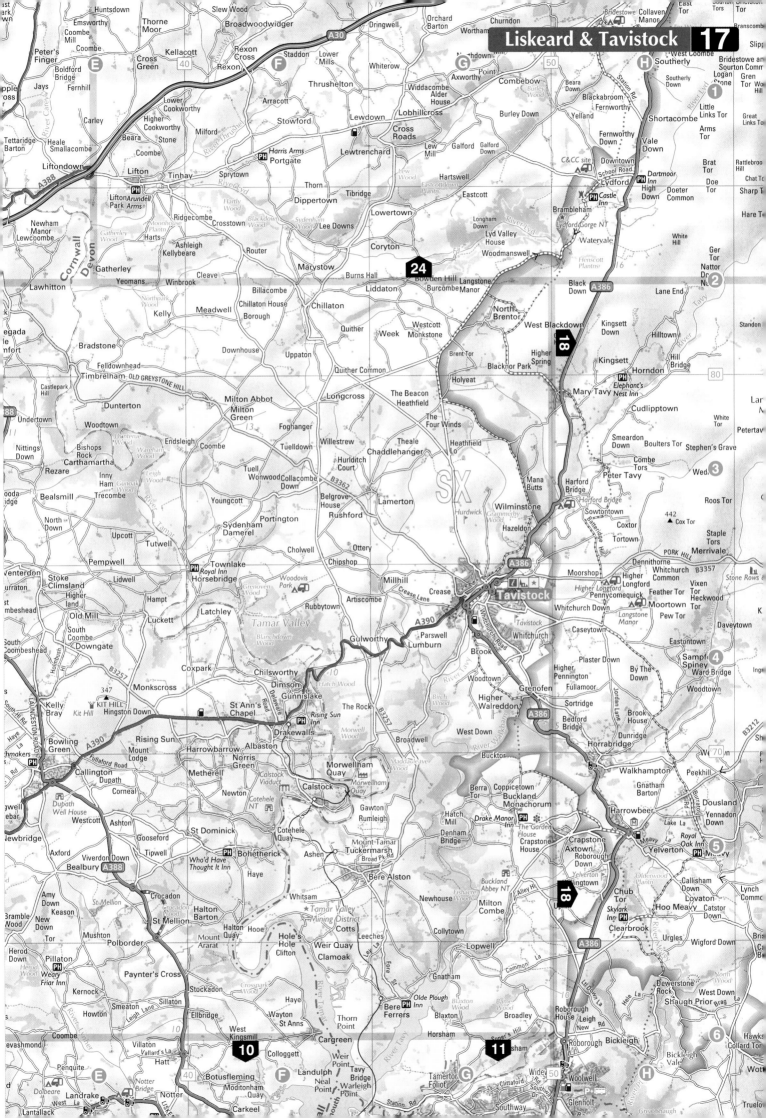

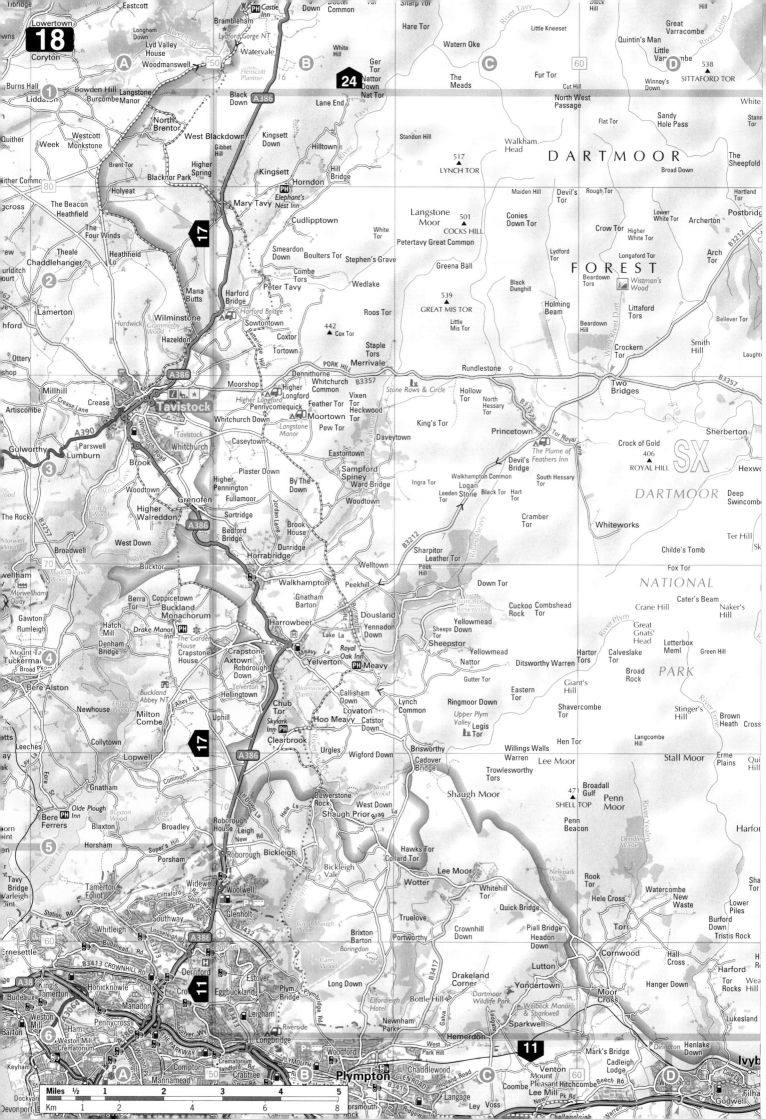

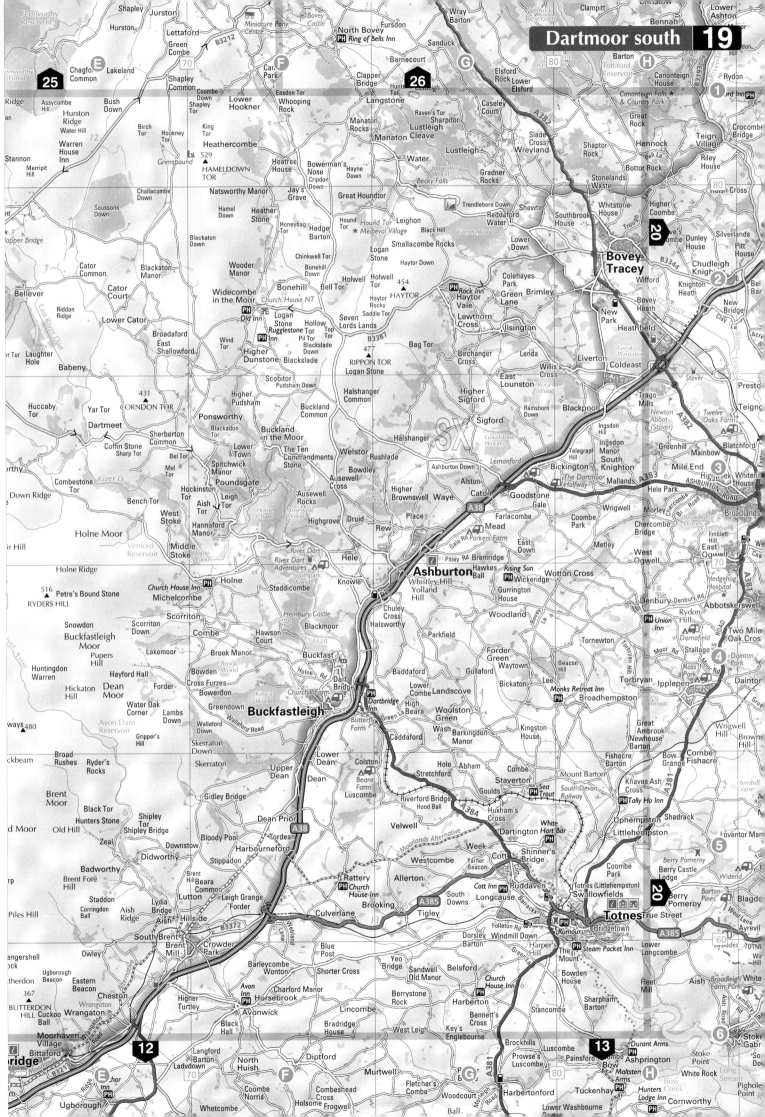

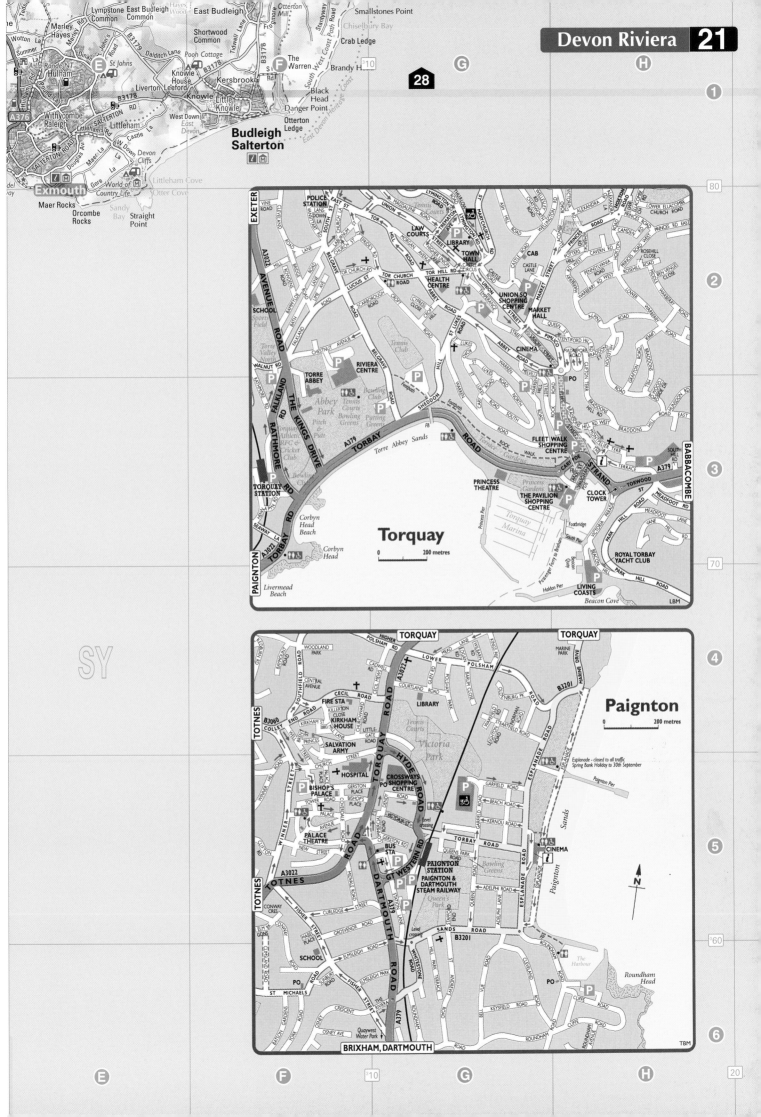

Torquay

0   200 metres

Paignton

0   200 metres

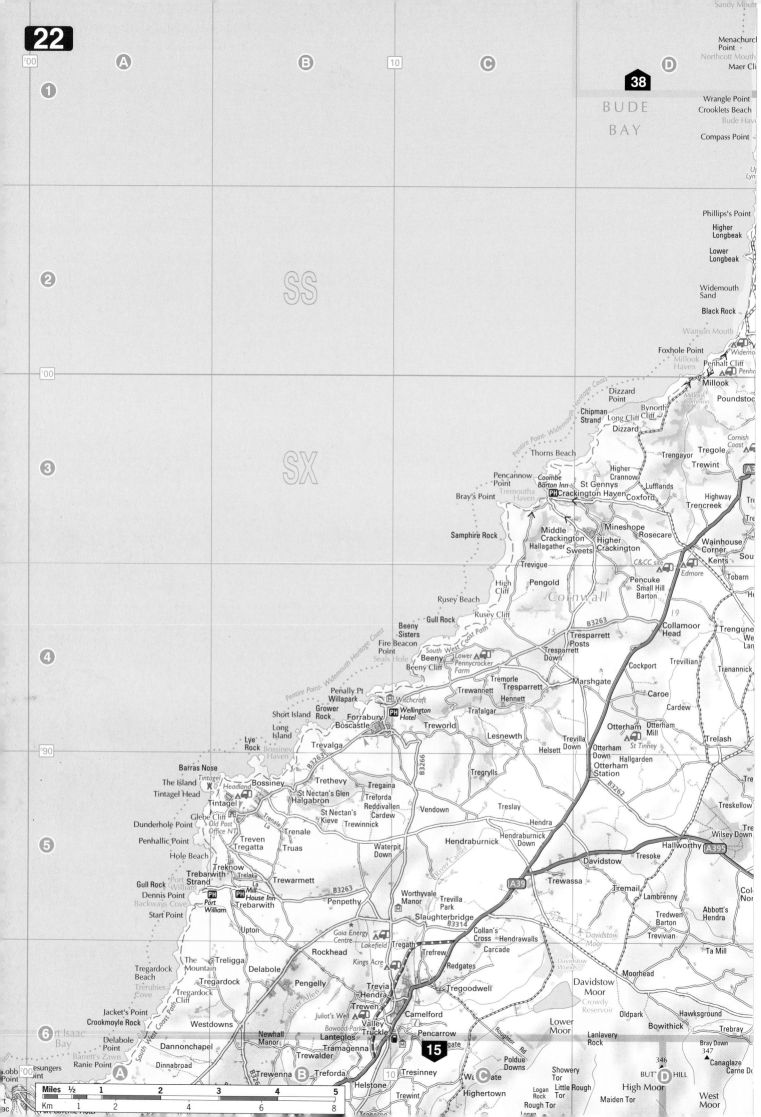

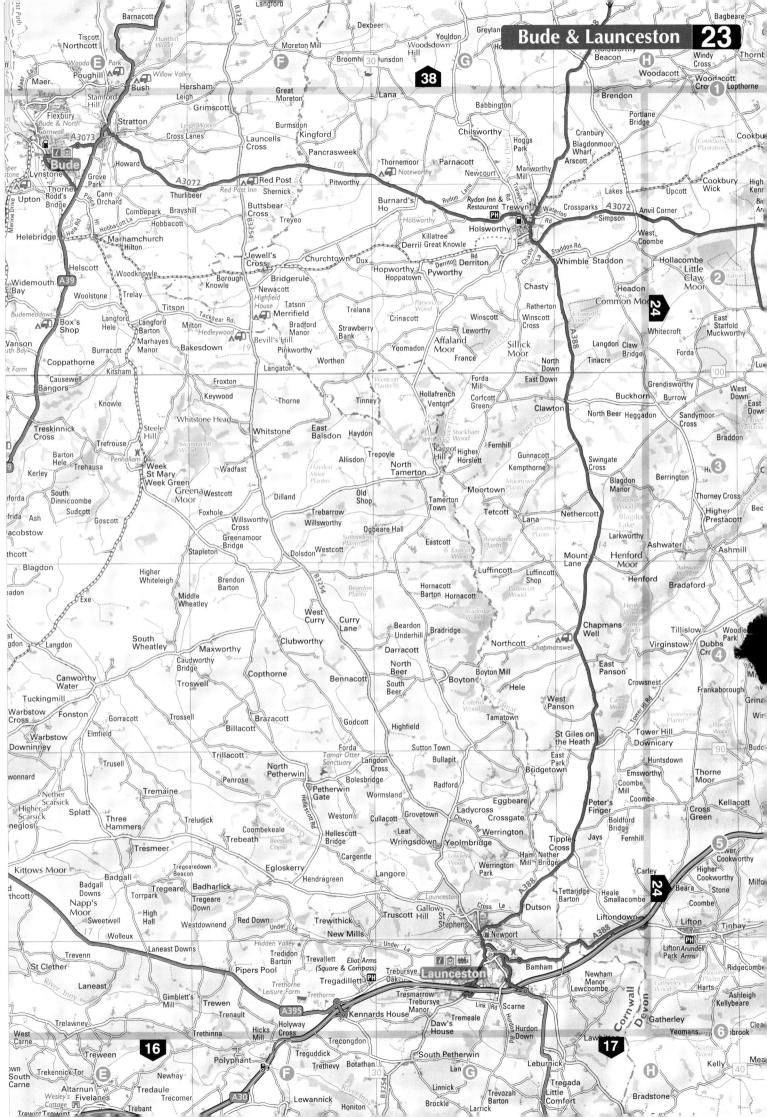

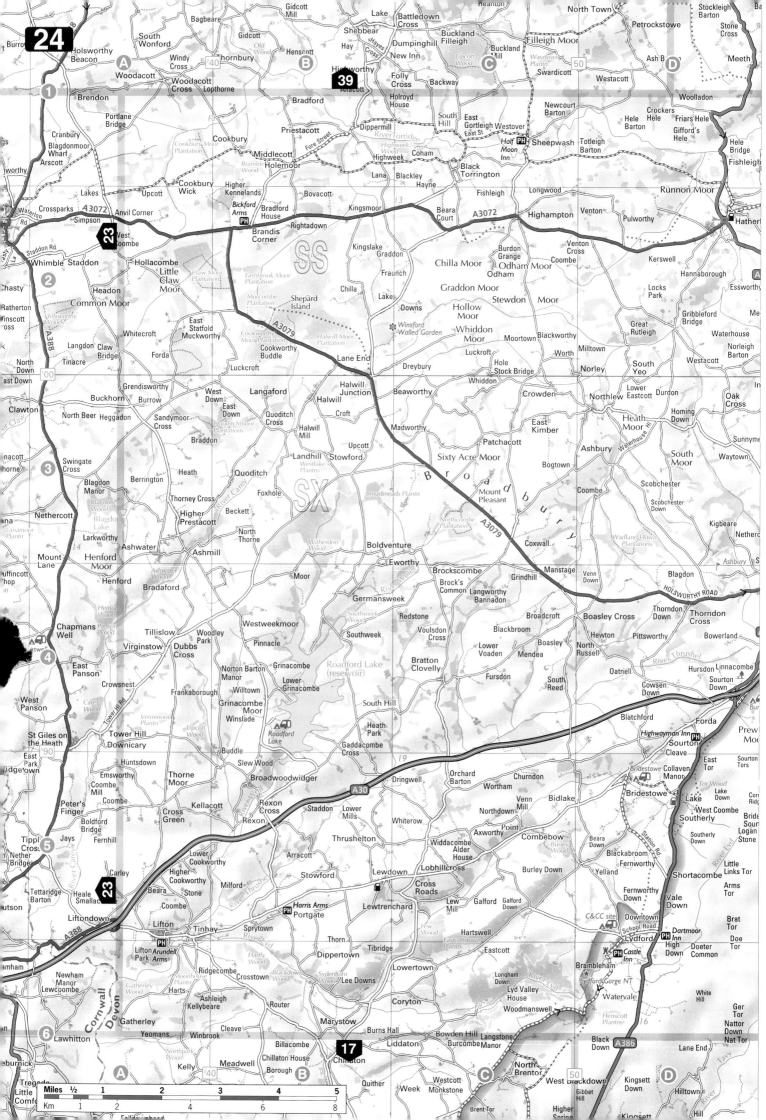

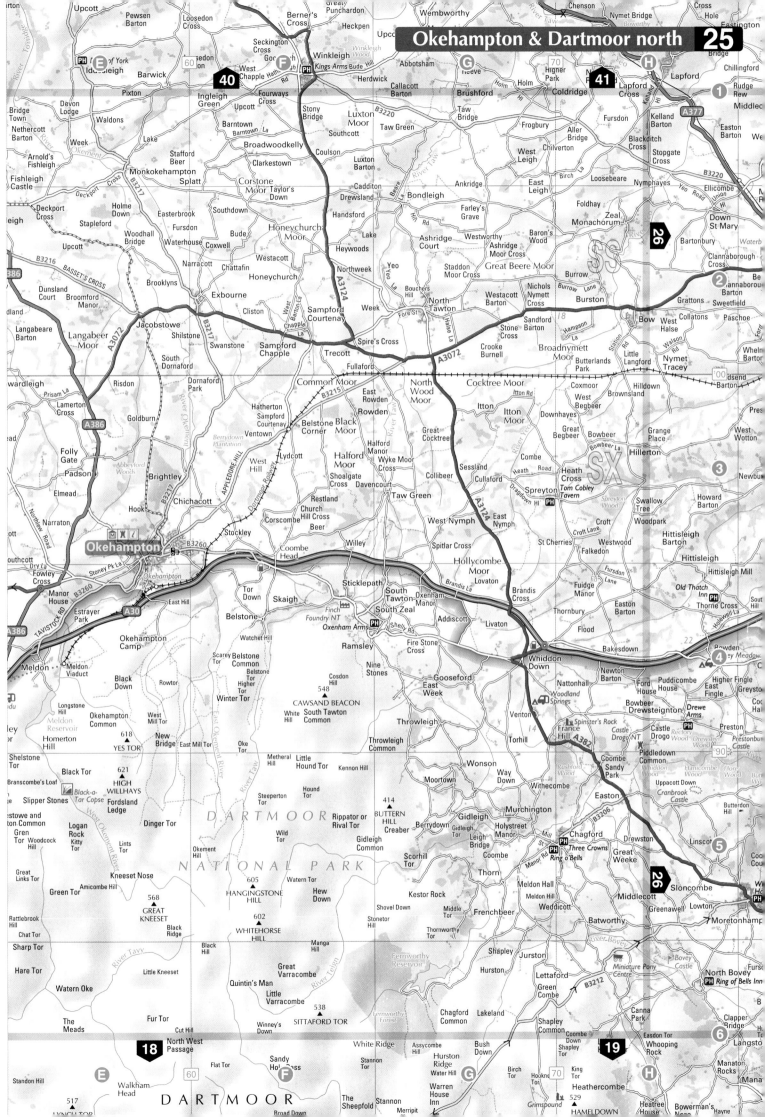

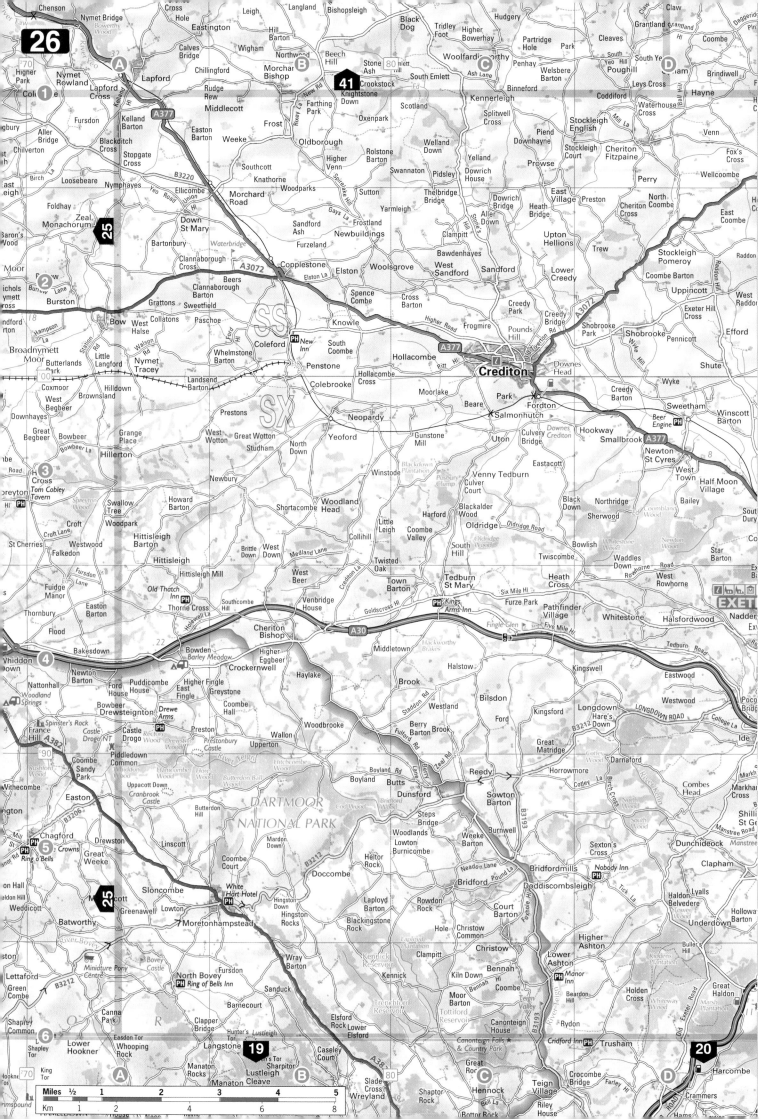

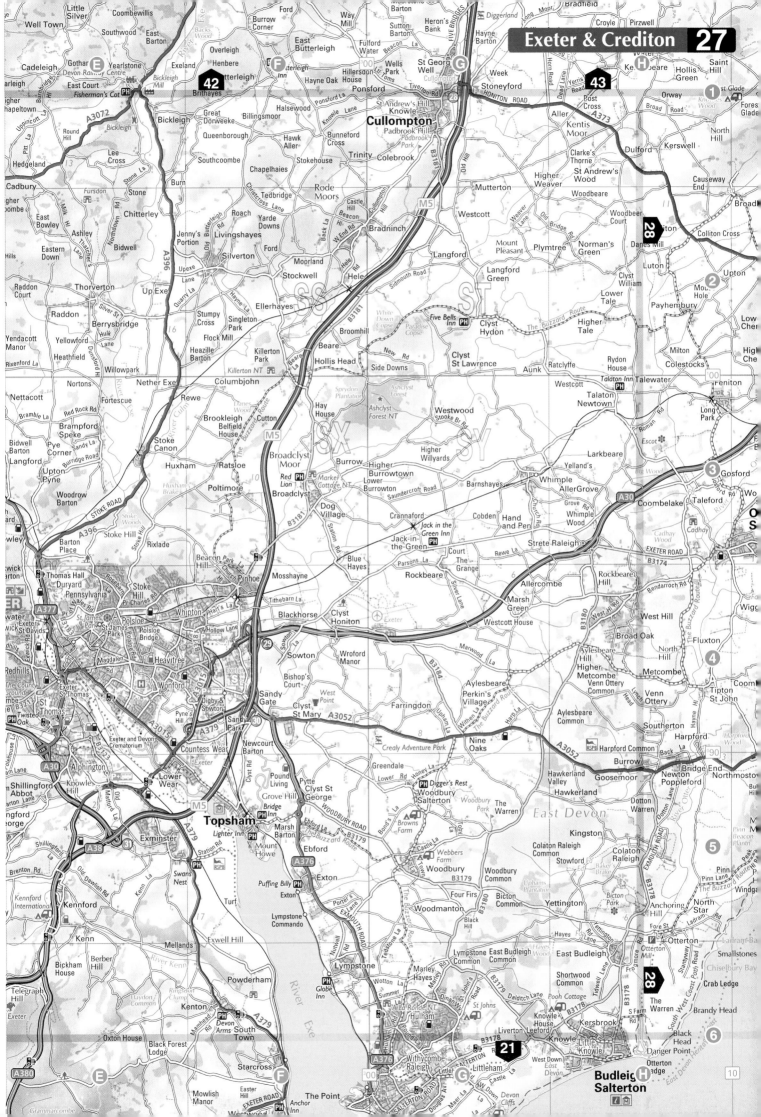

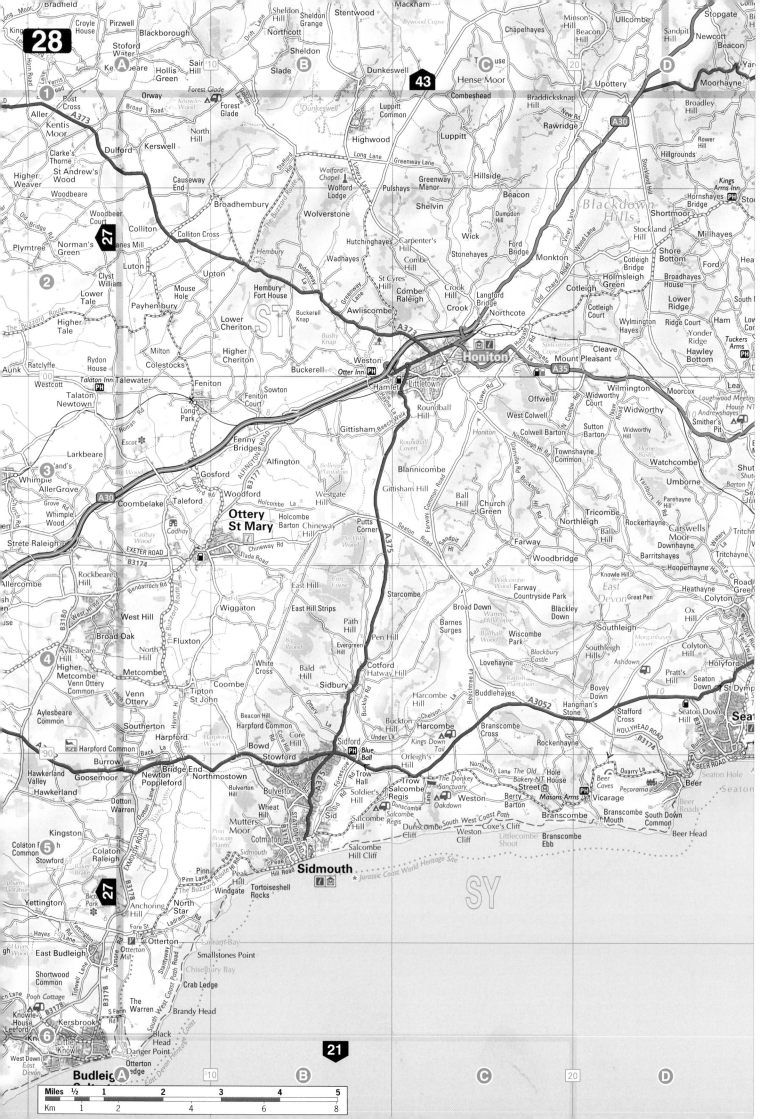

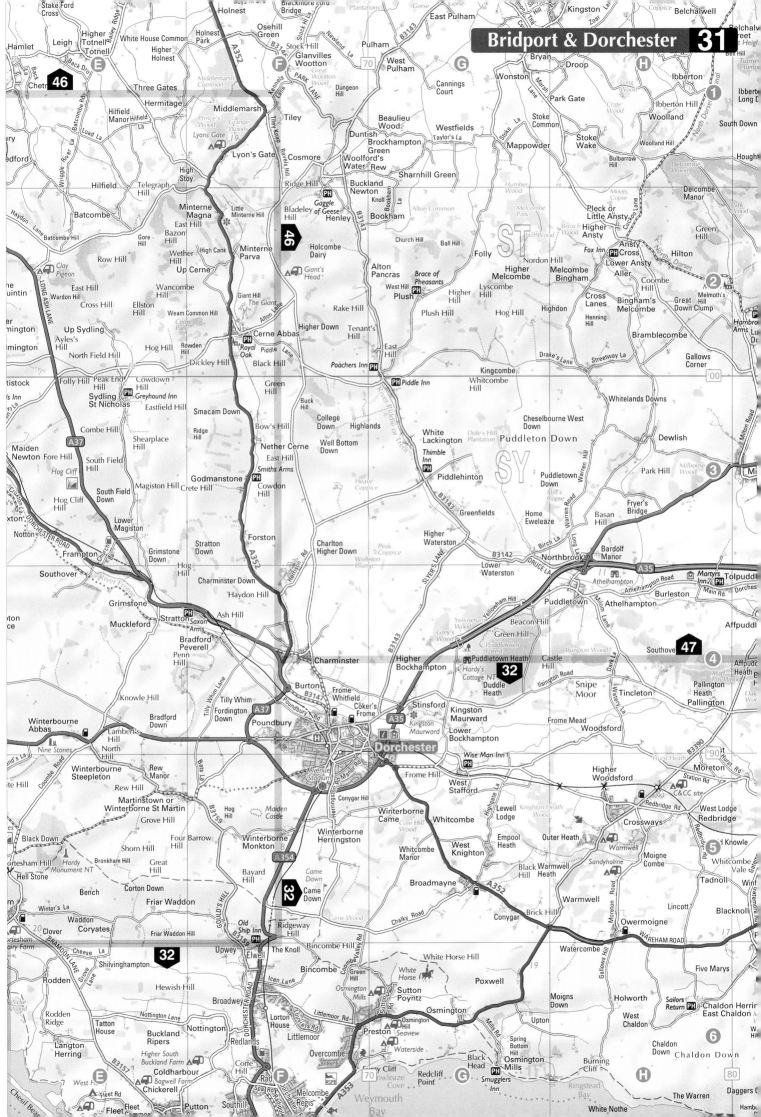

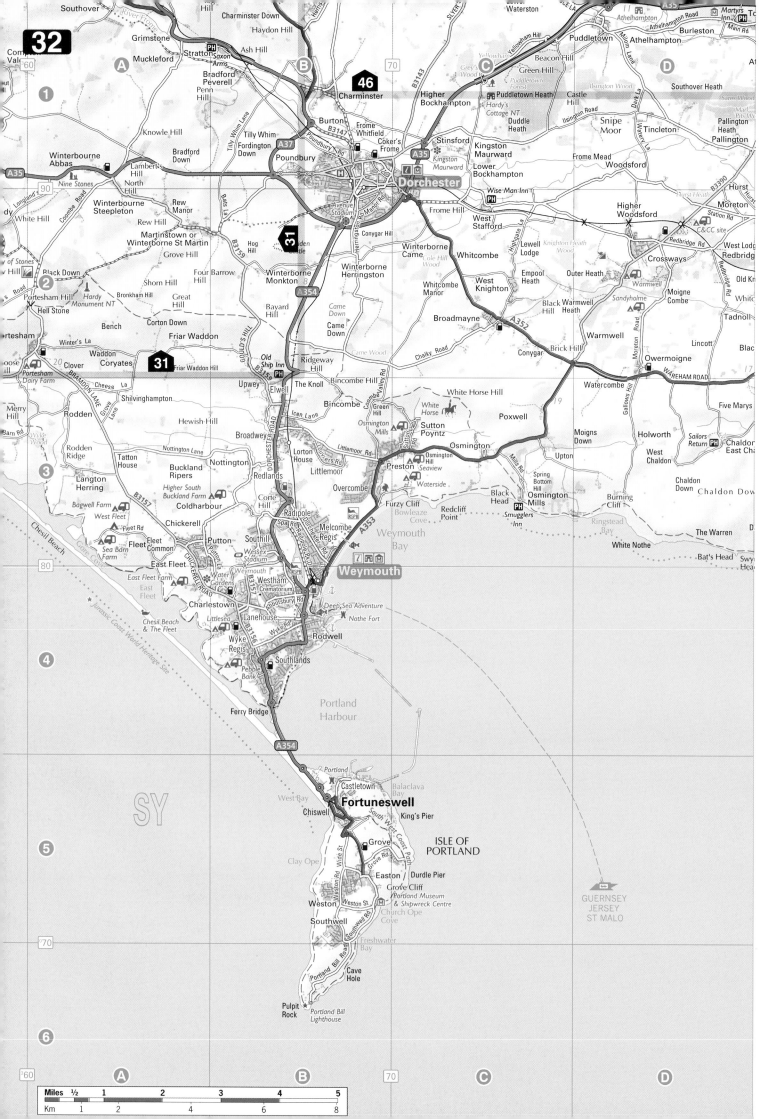

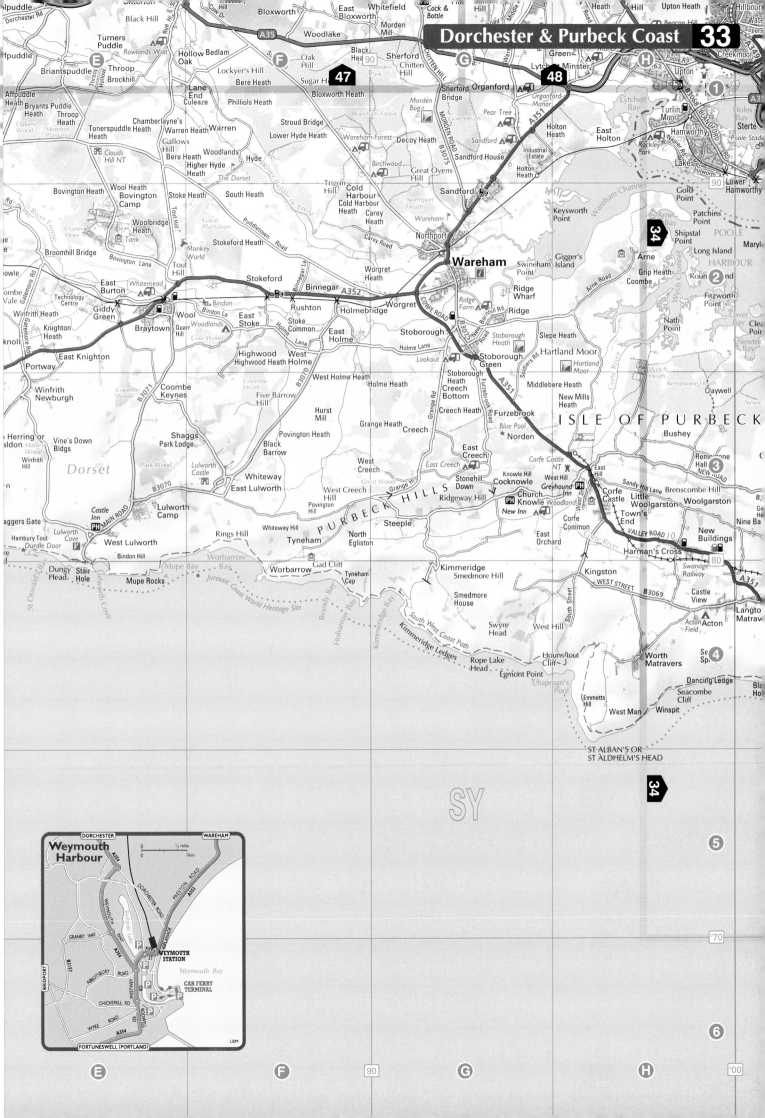

Poole Harbour

DORCHESTER, RINGWOOD

Holes Bay

POOLE STATION

HARBOUR OFFICE

POOLE QUAY BOAT HAVEN

Poole Harbour

CAR FERRY DEPARTURES

FREIGHT FERRY TERMINAL

PASSENGER FERRY TERMINAL

0 — 400 yards
0 — 500 metres
LBM

THE NEEDLES

Jersey

Miles 1 2
Km 1 2

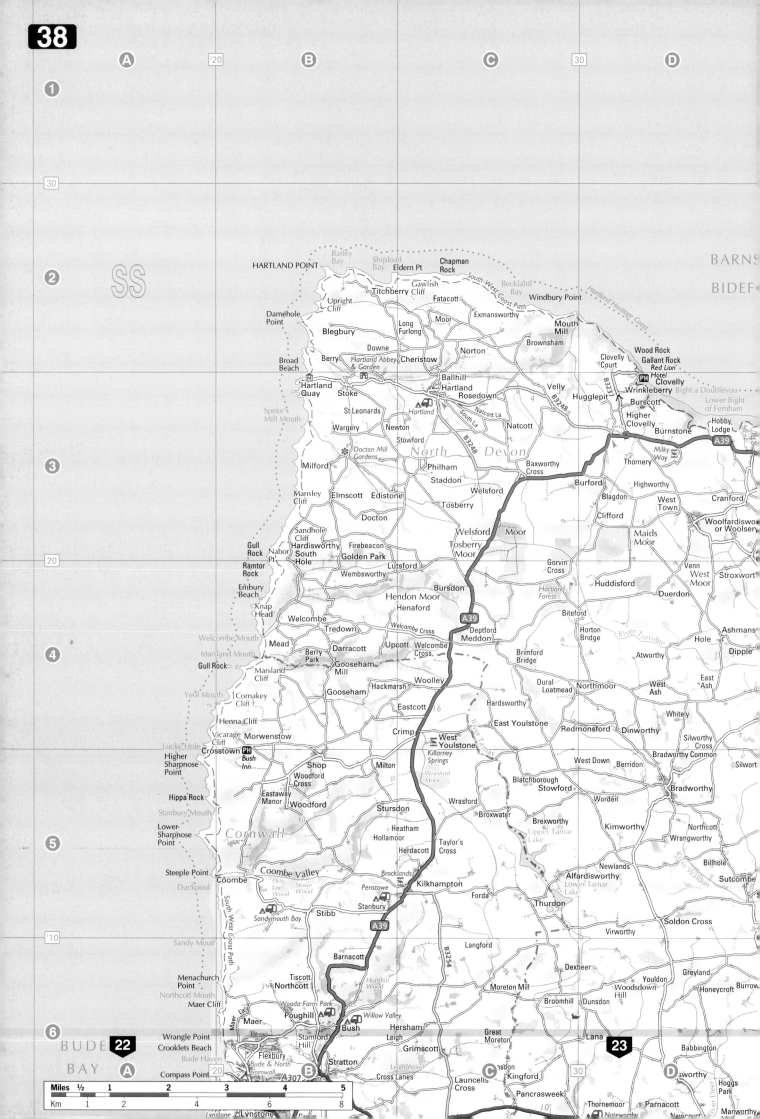

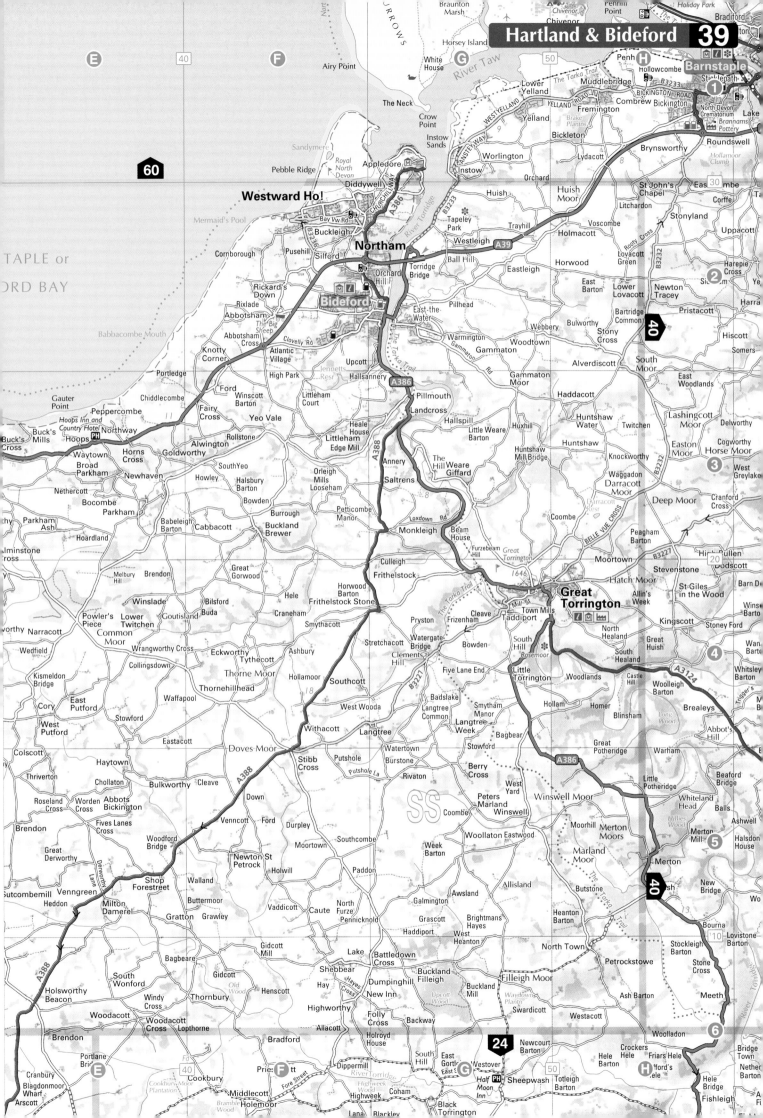

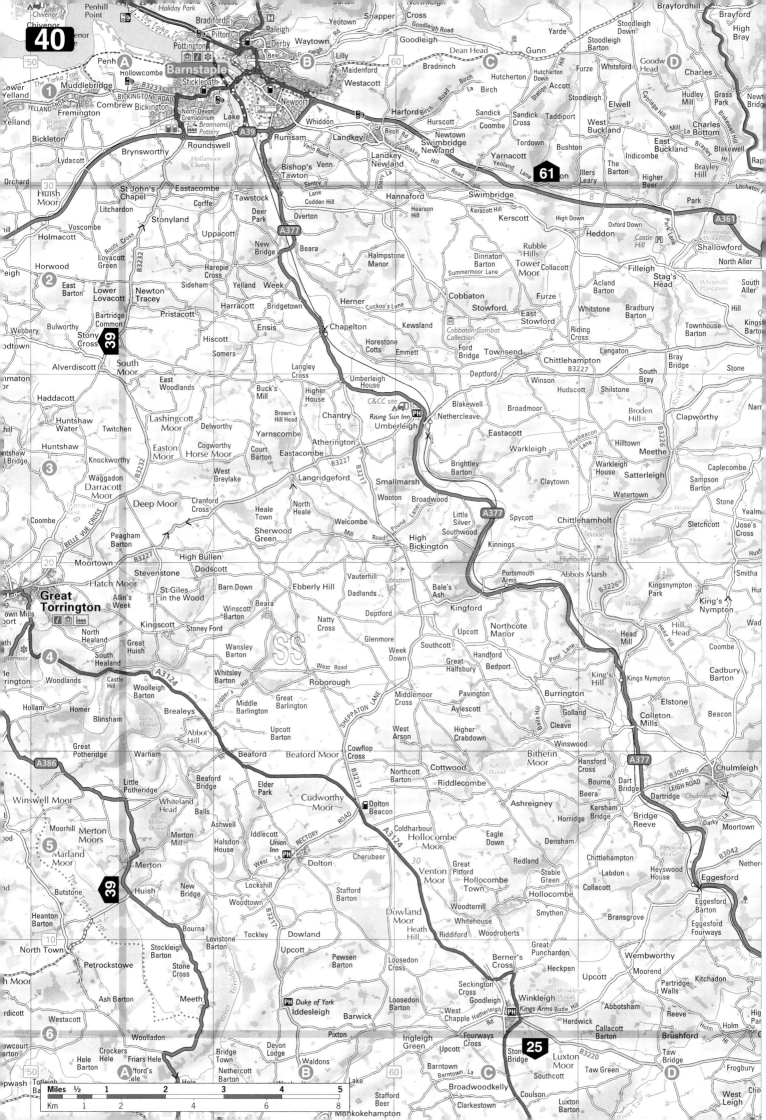

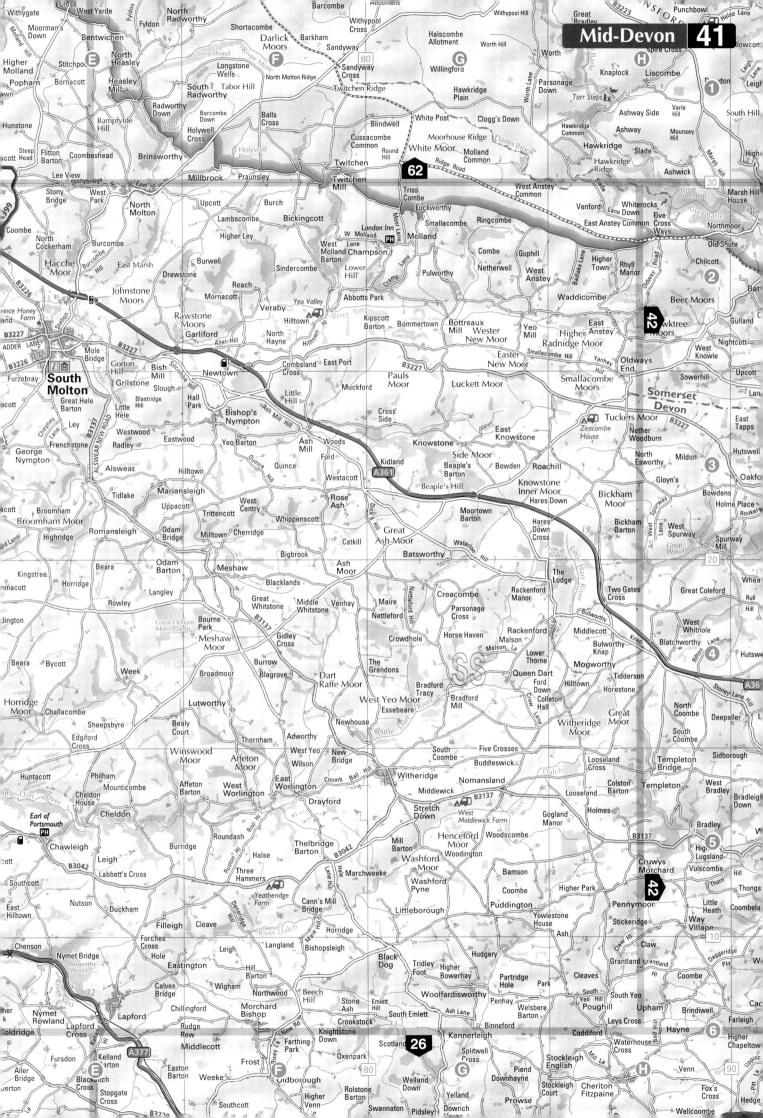

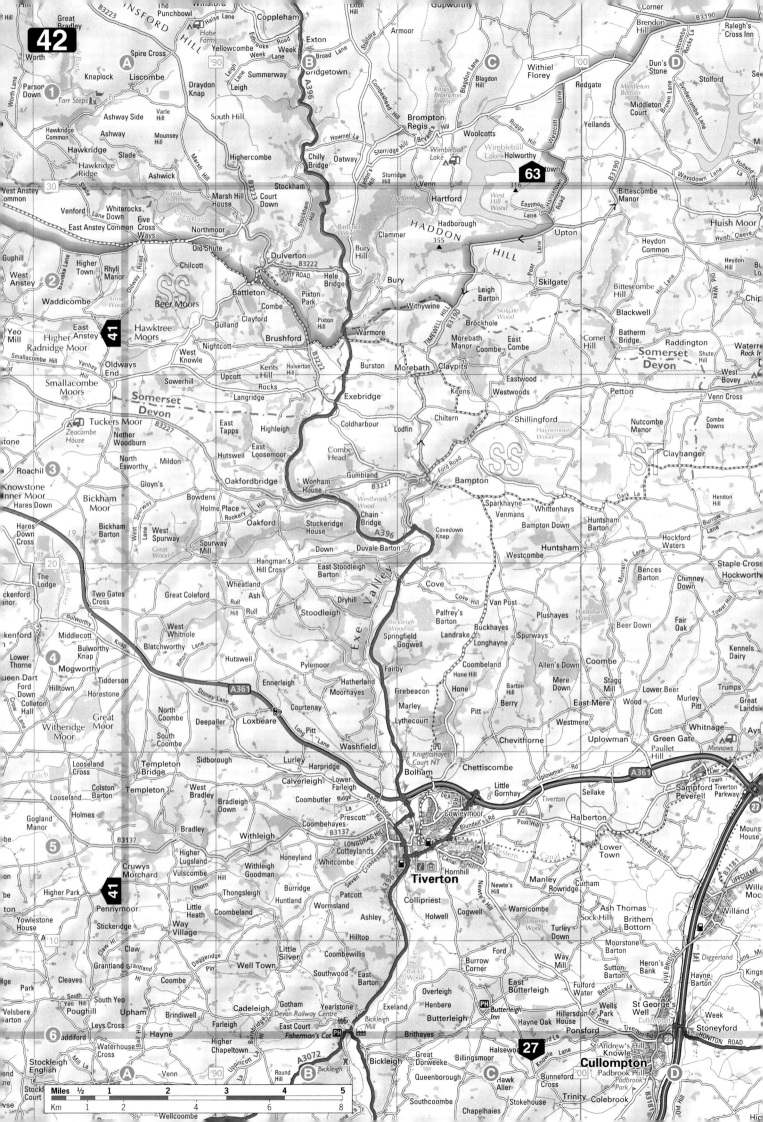

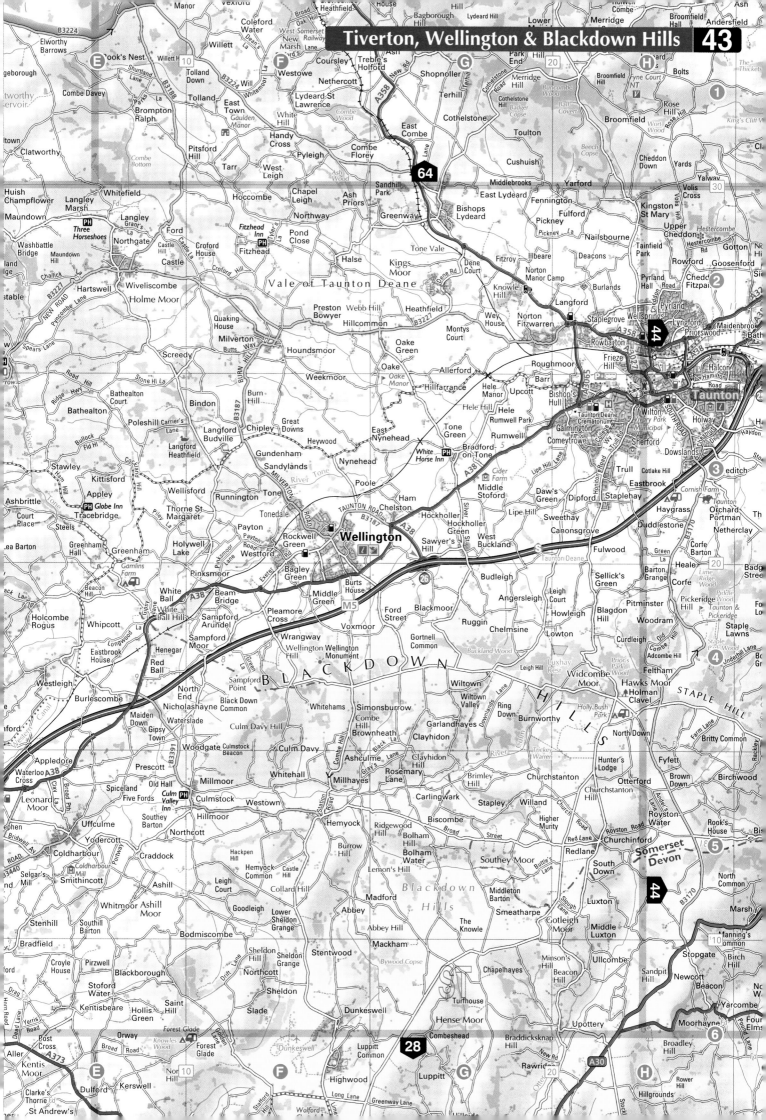

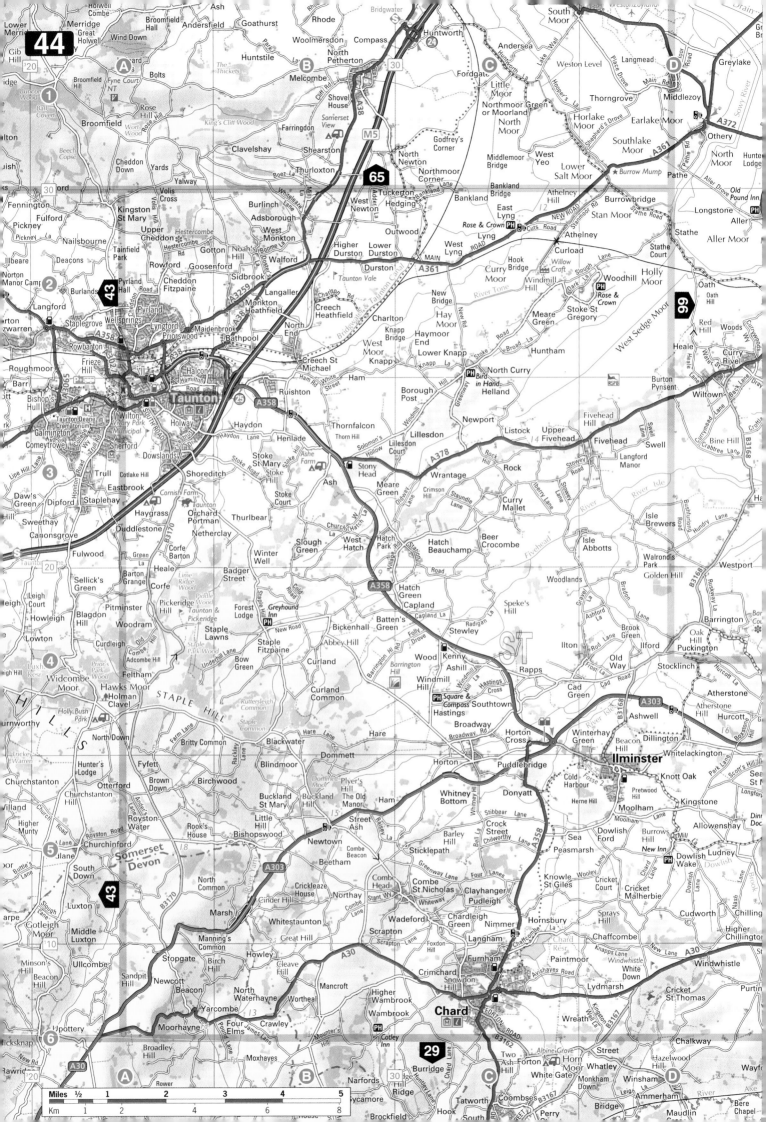

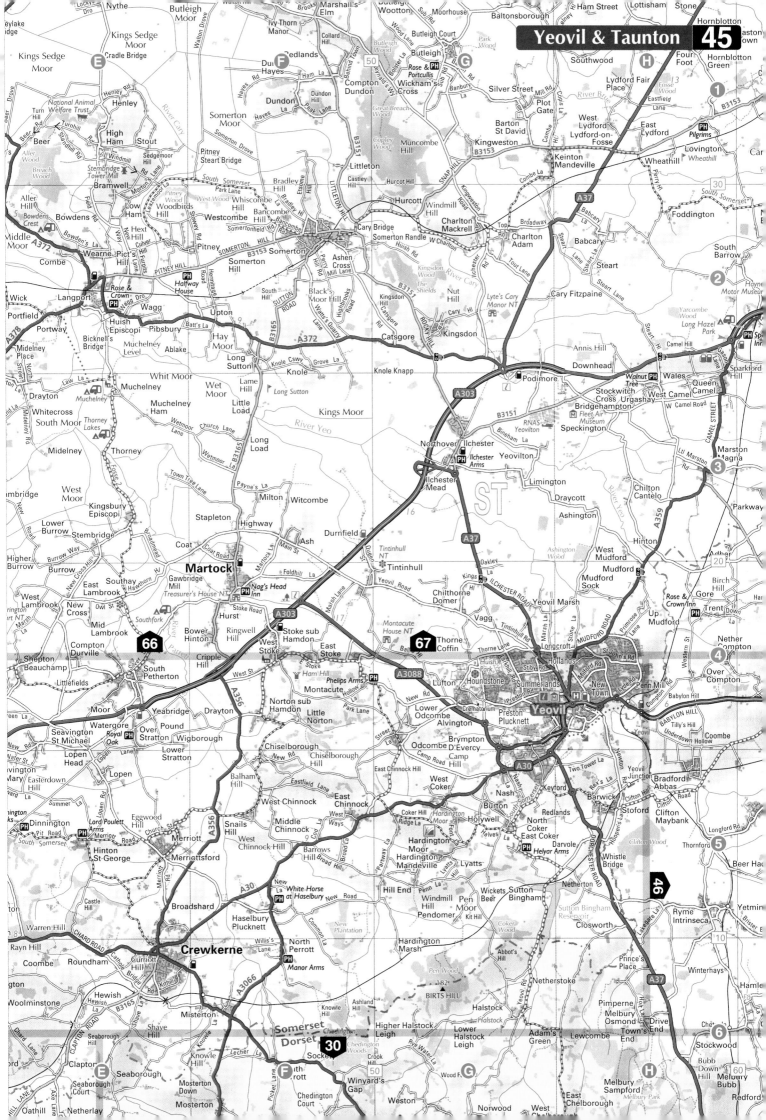

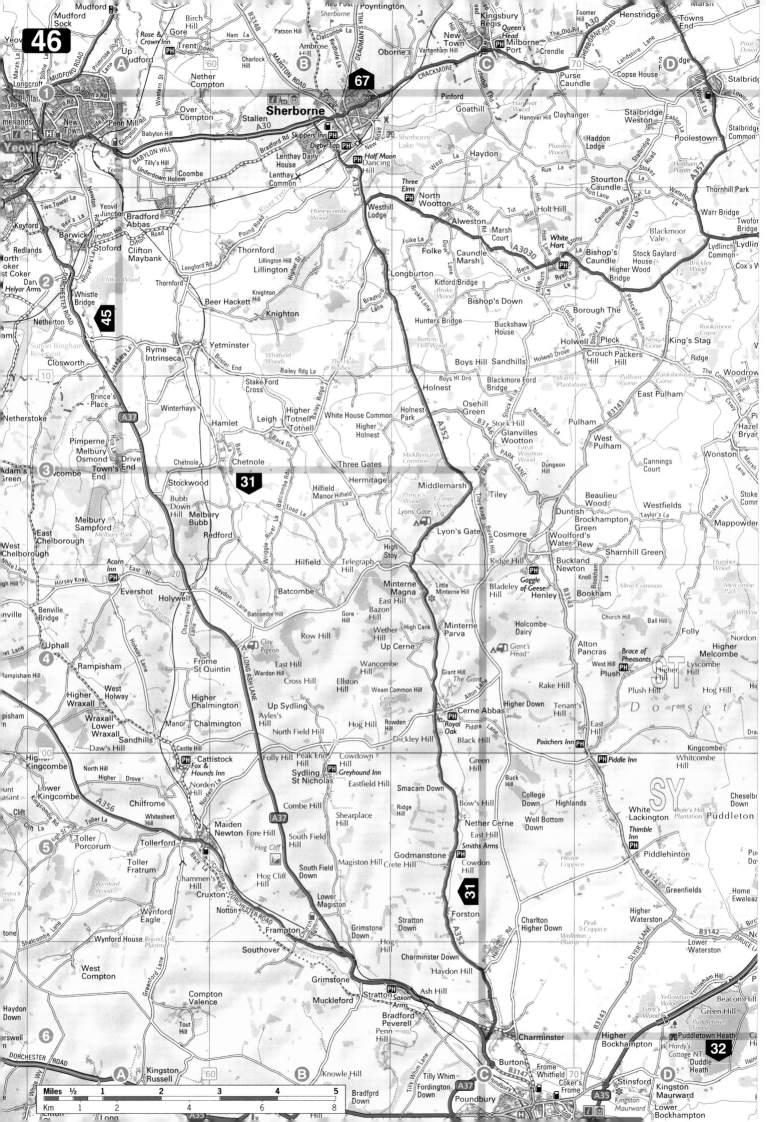

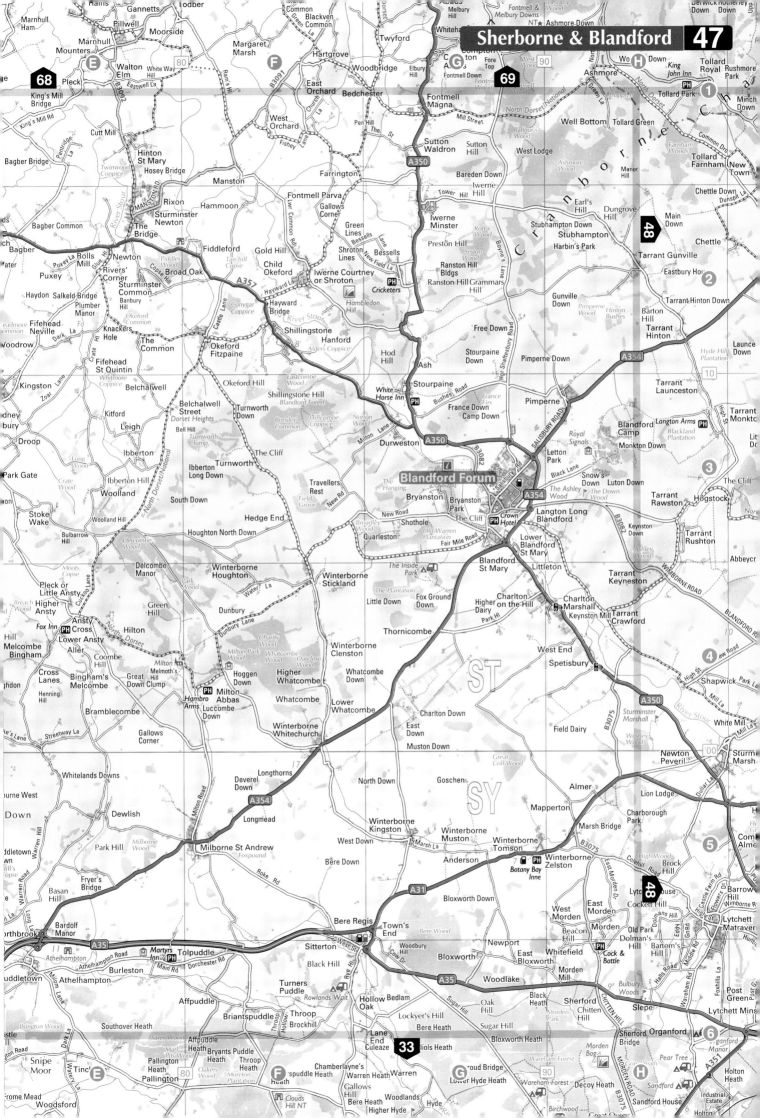

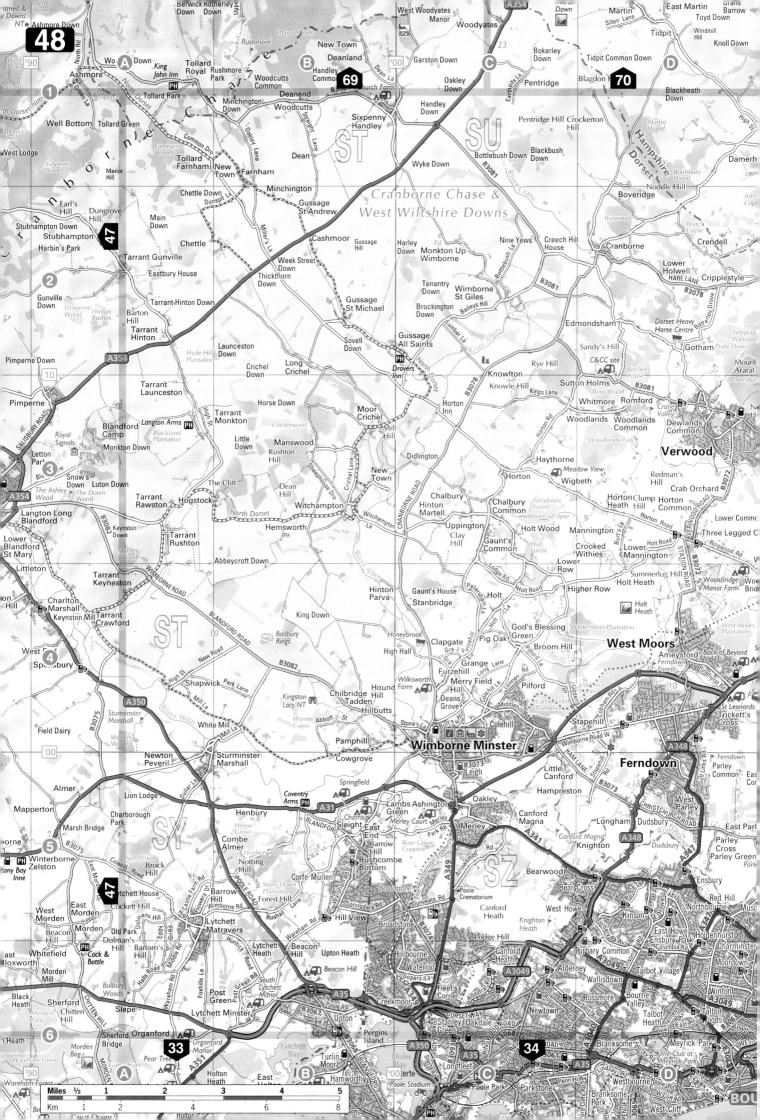

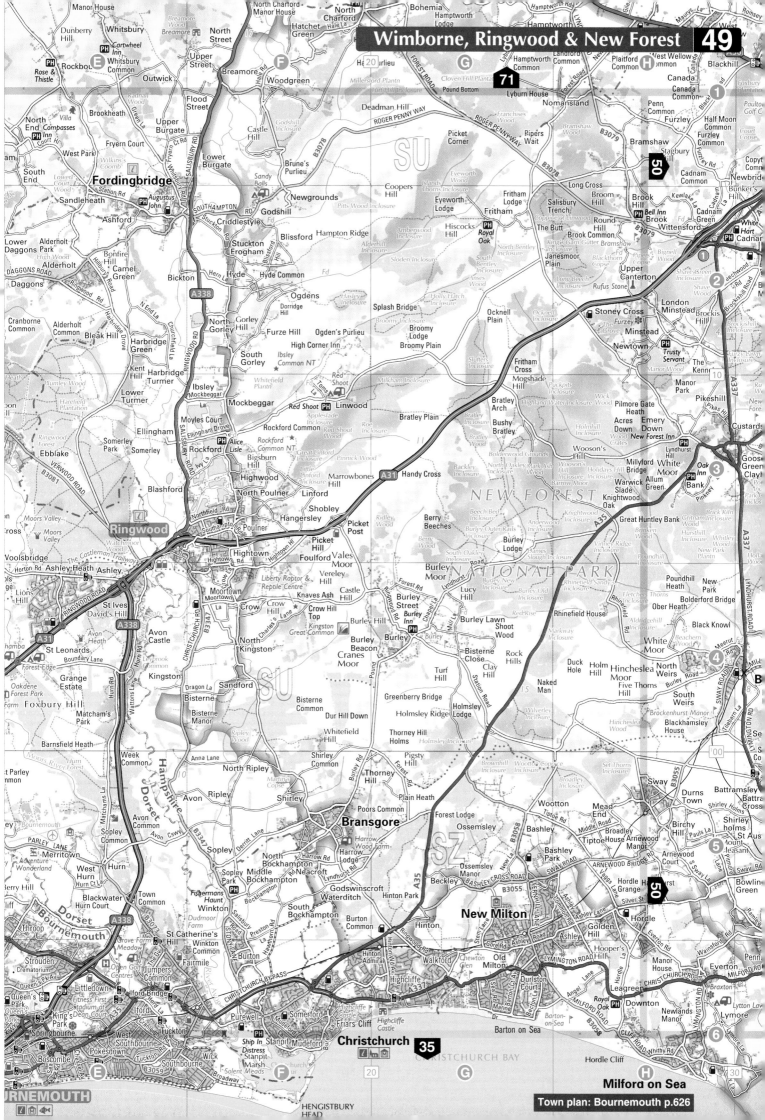

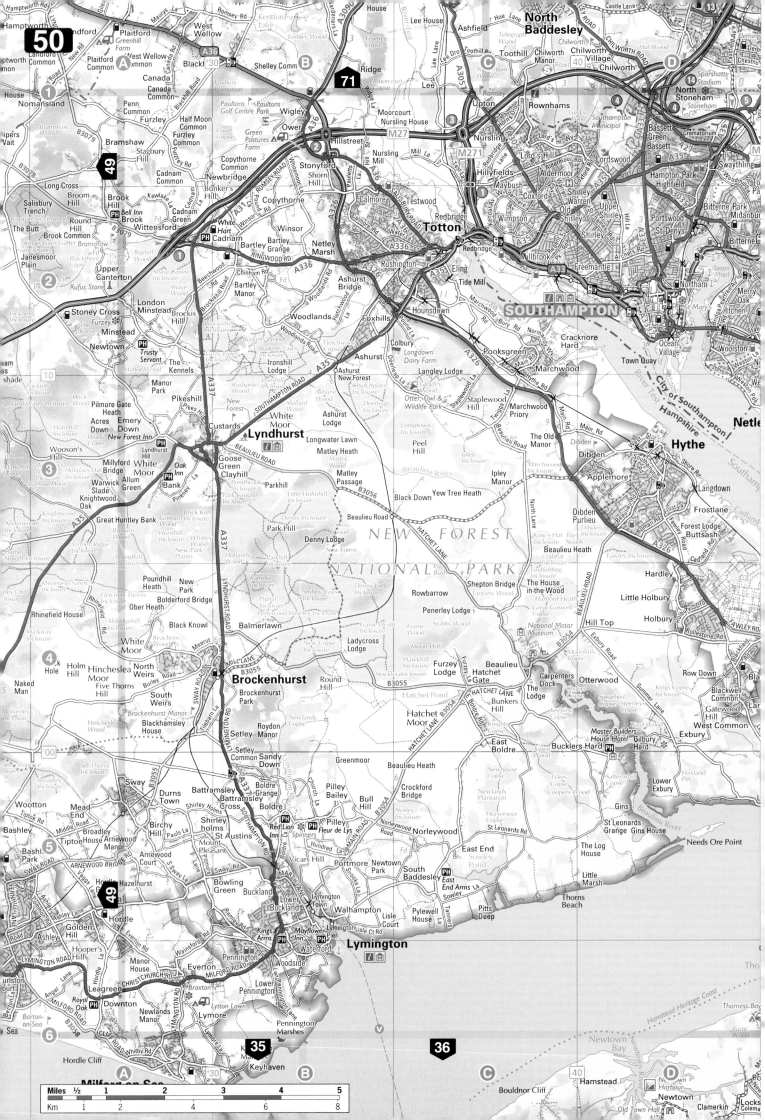

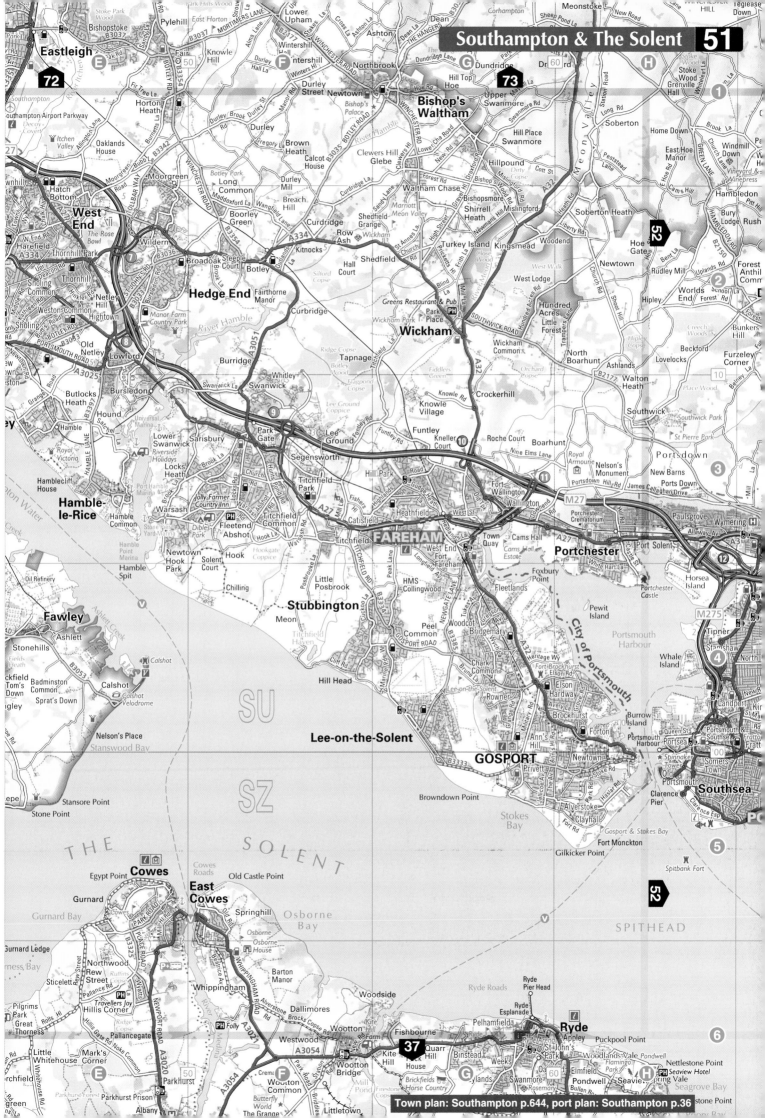

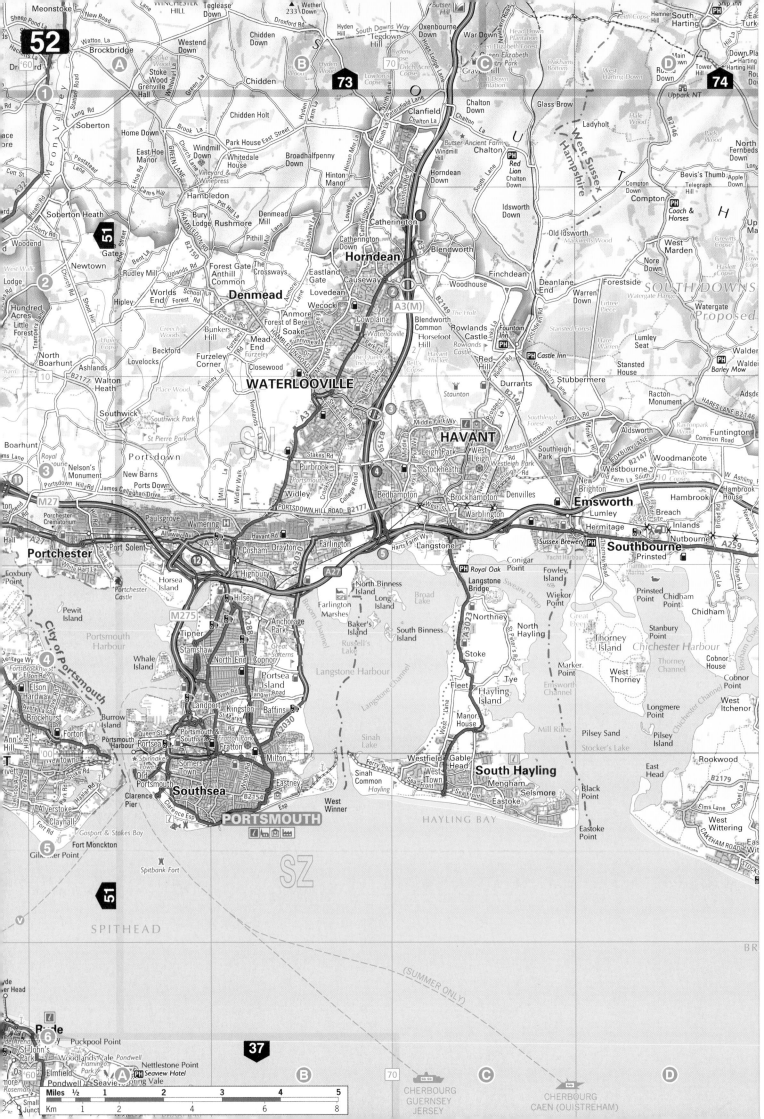

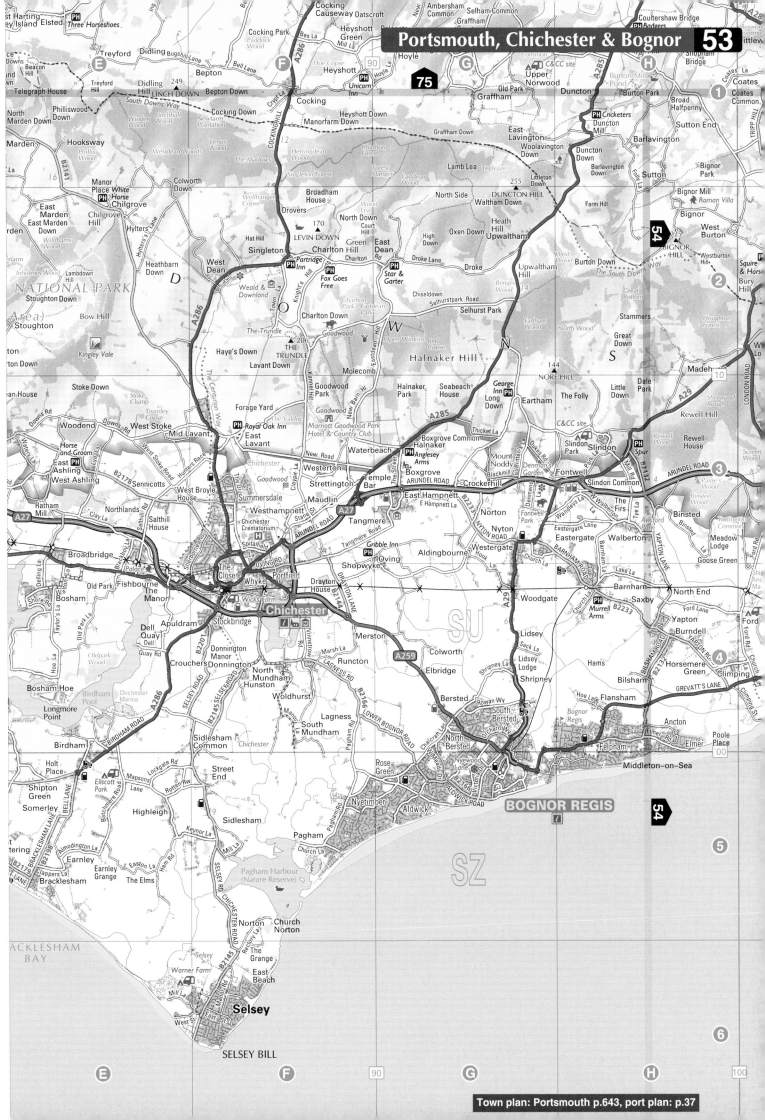

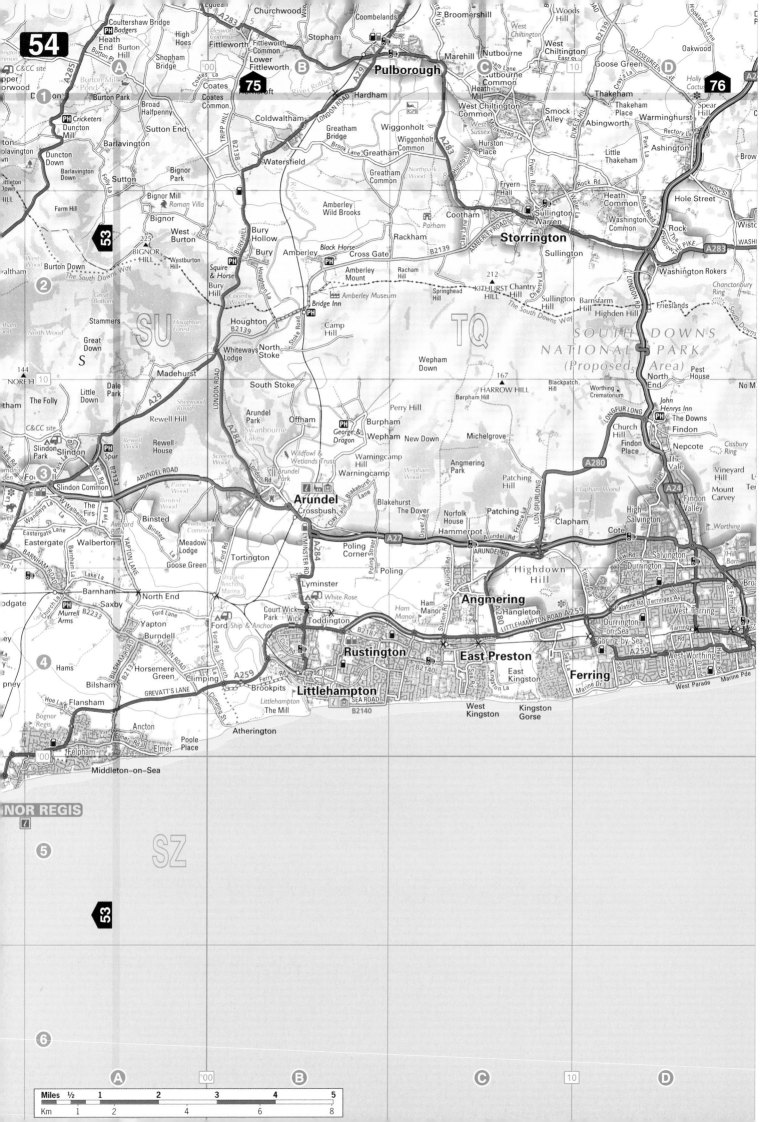

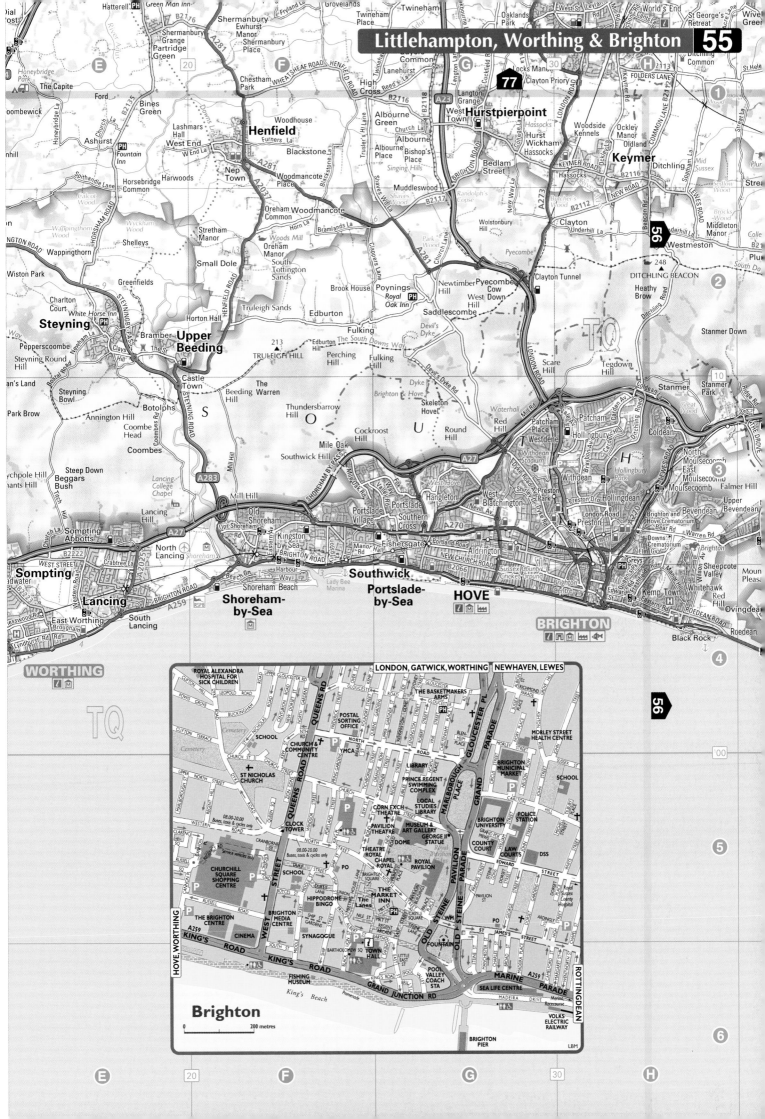

Brighton

0   200 metres

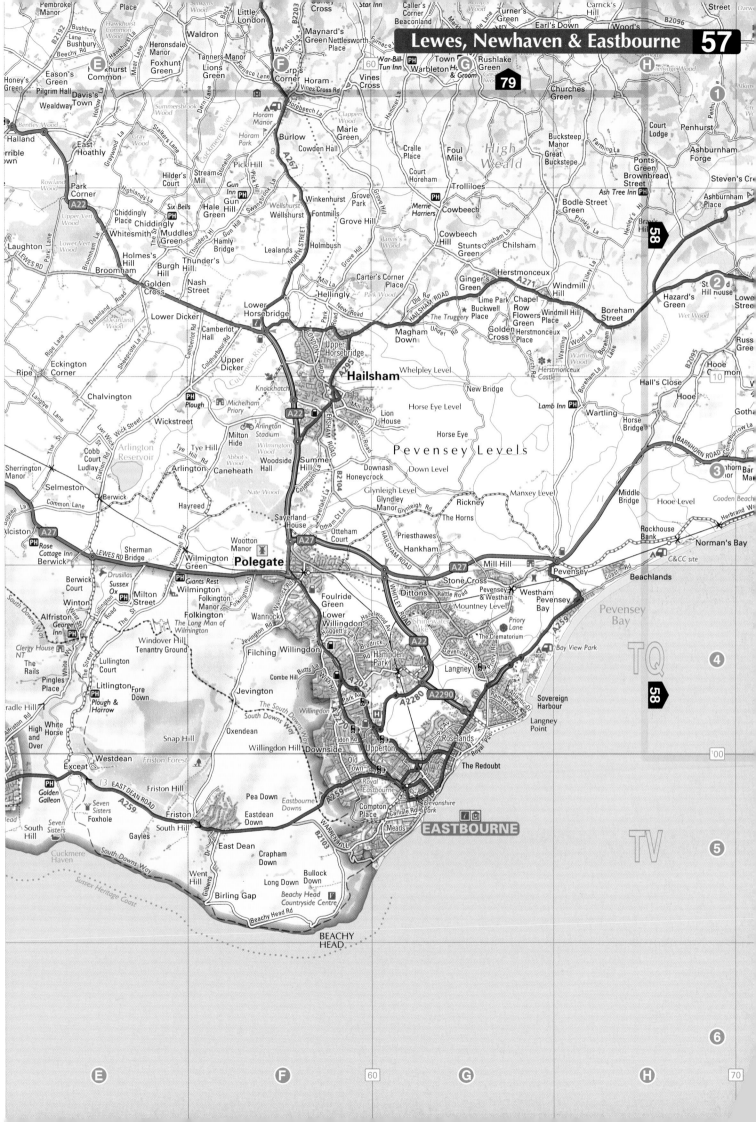

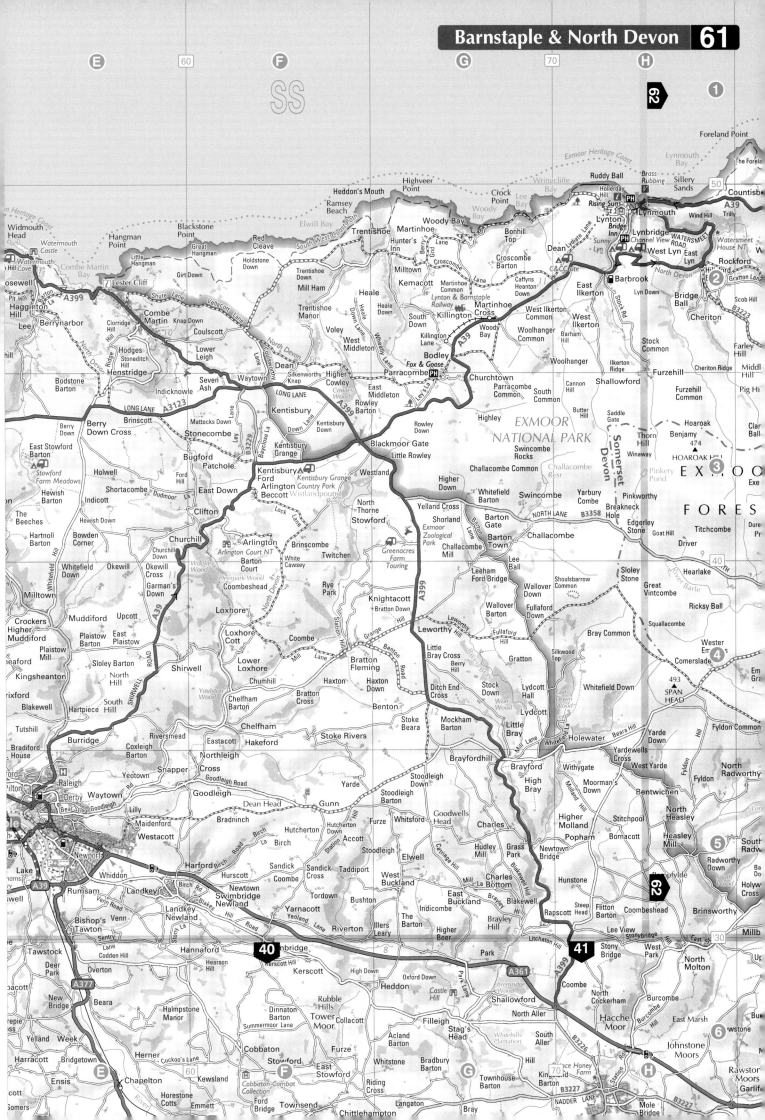

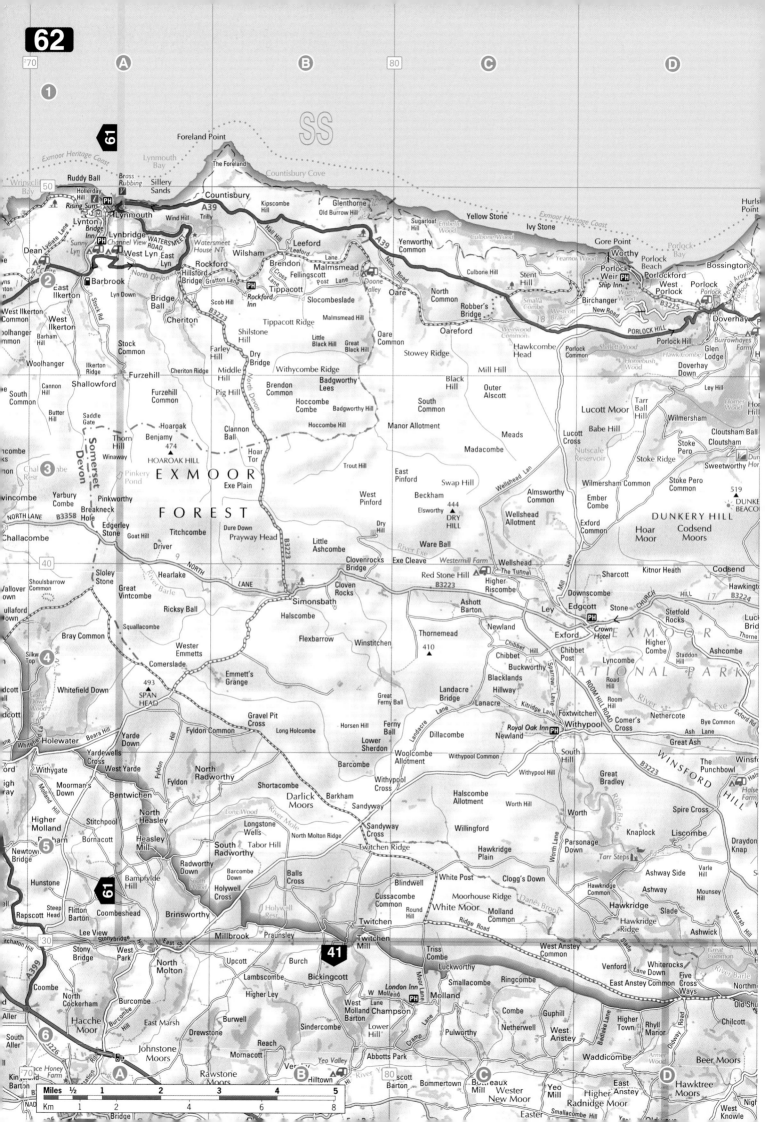

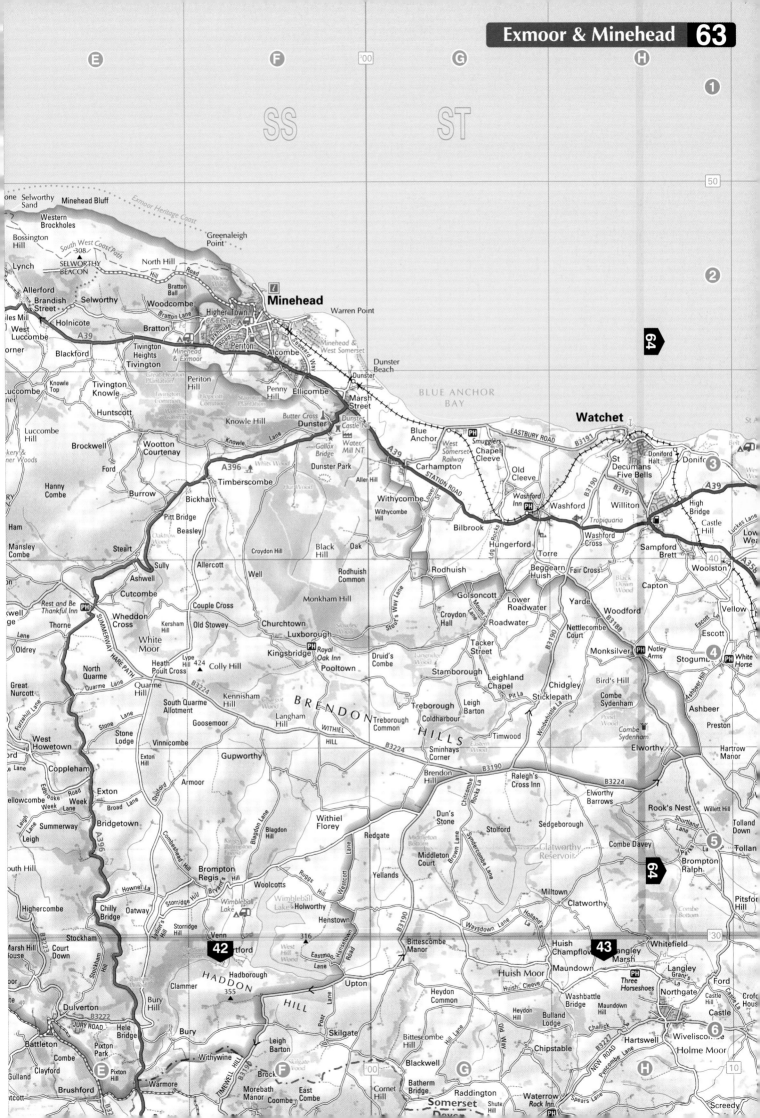

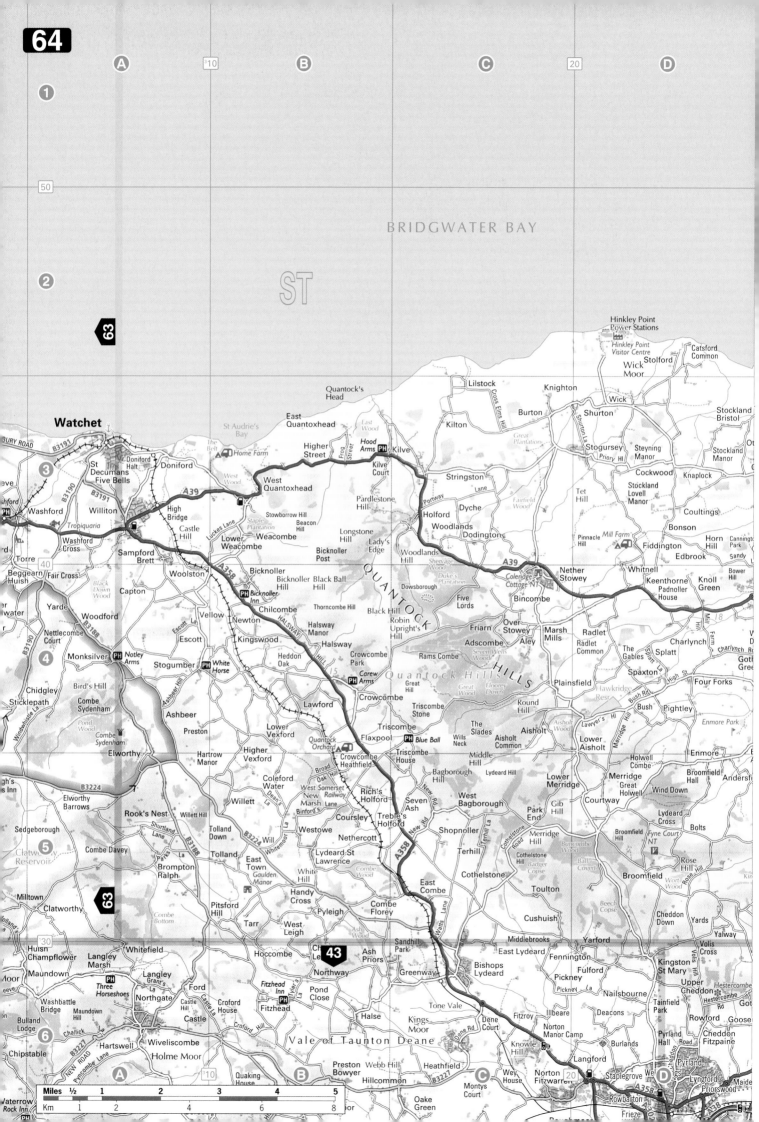

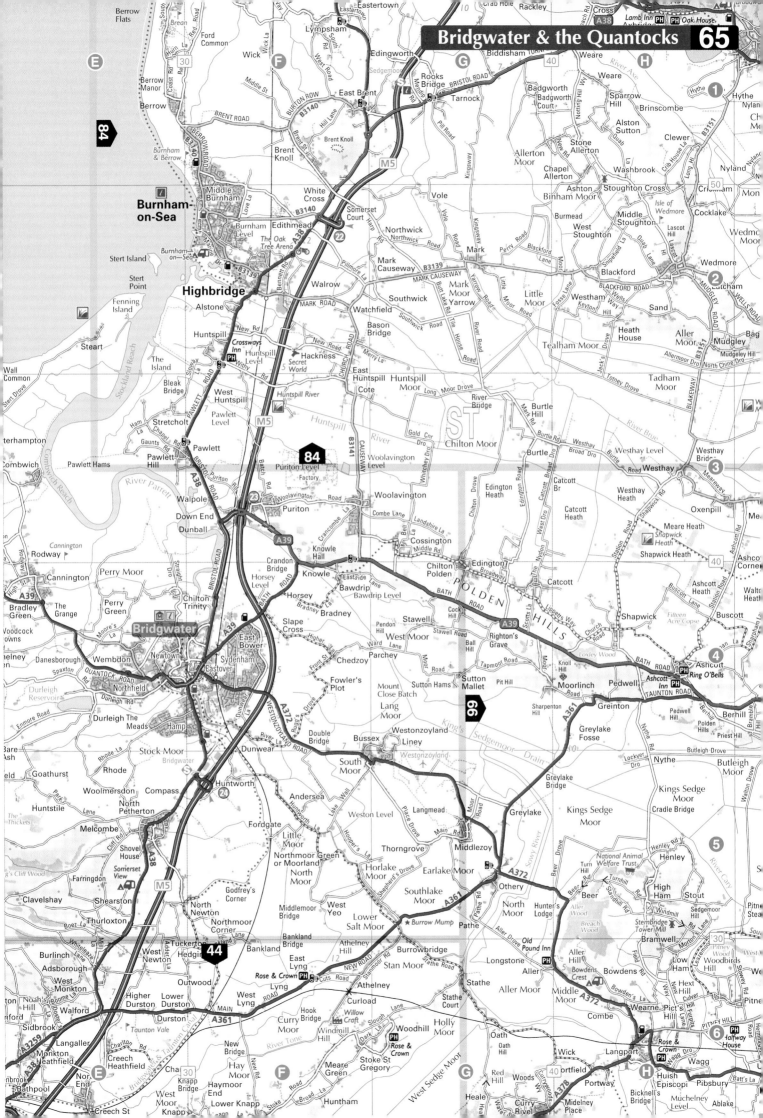

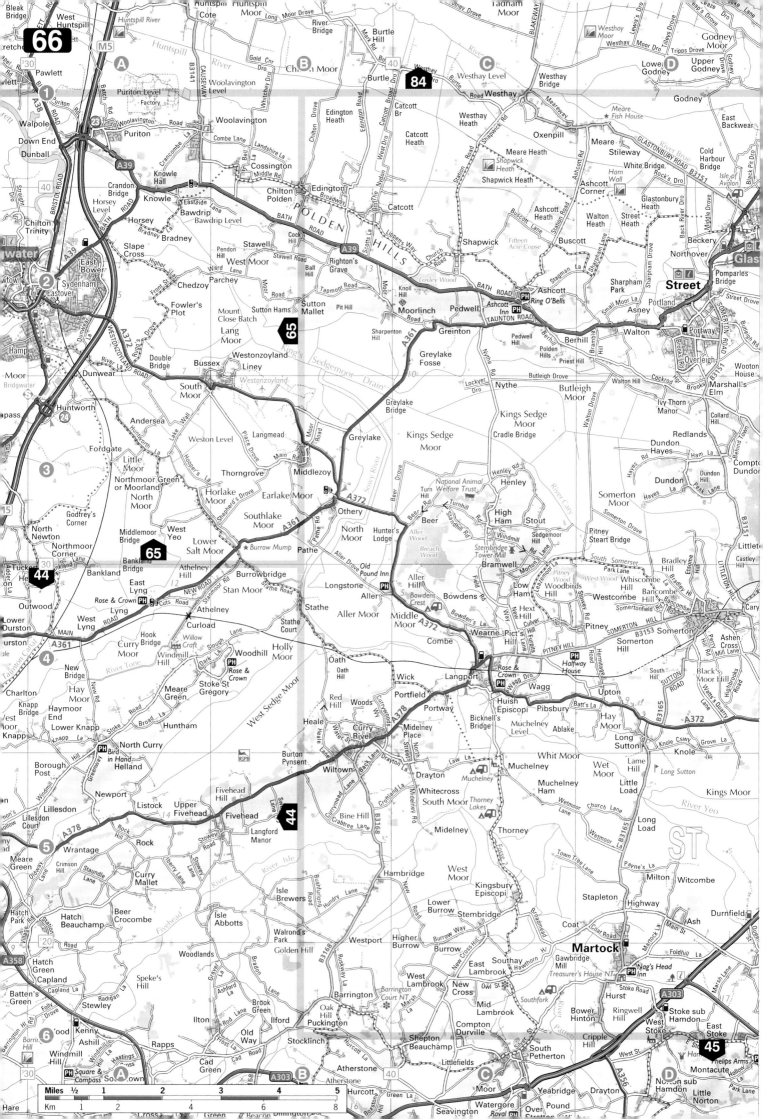

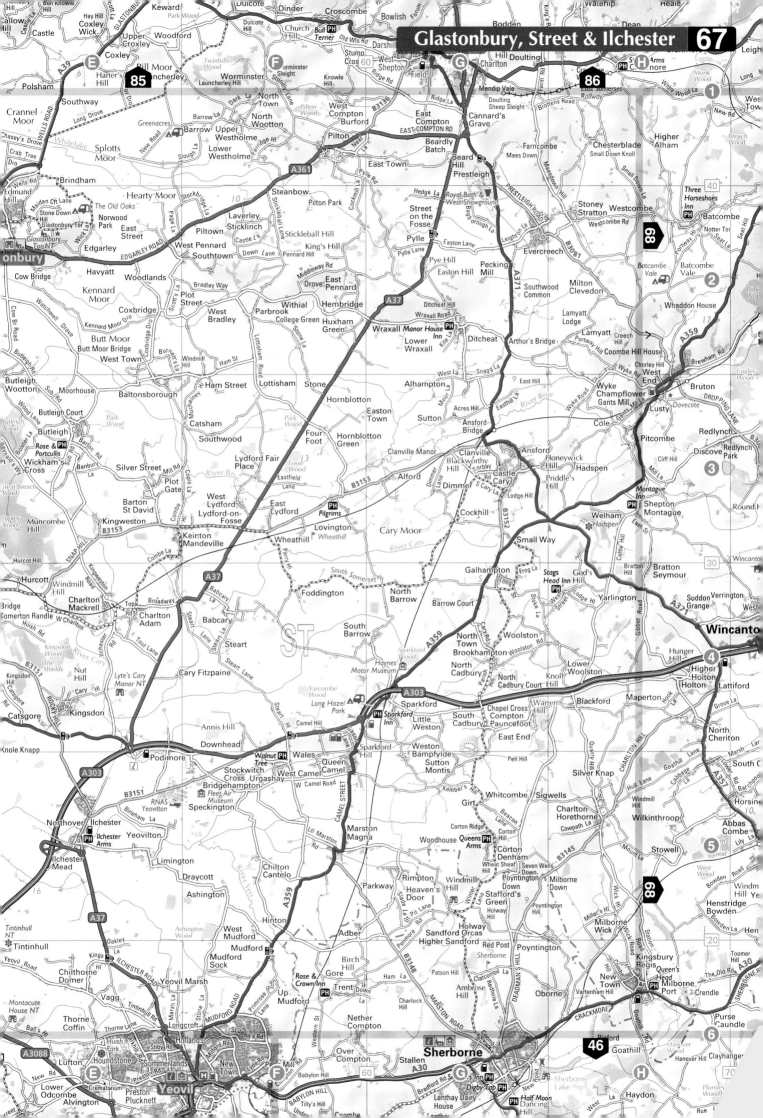

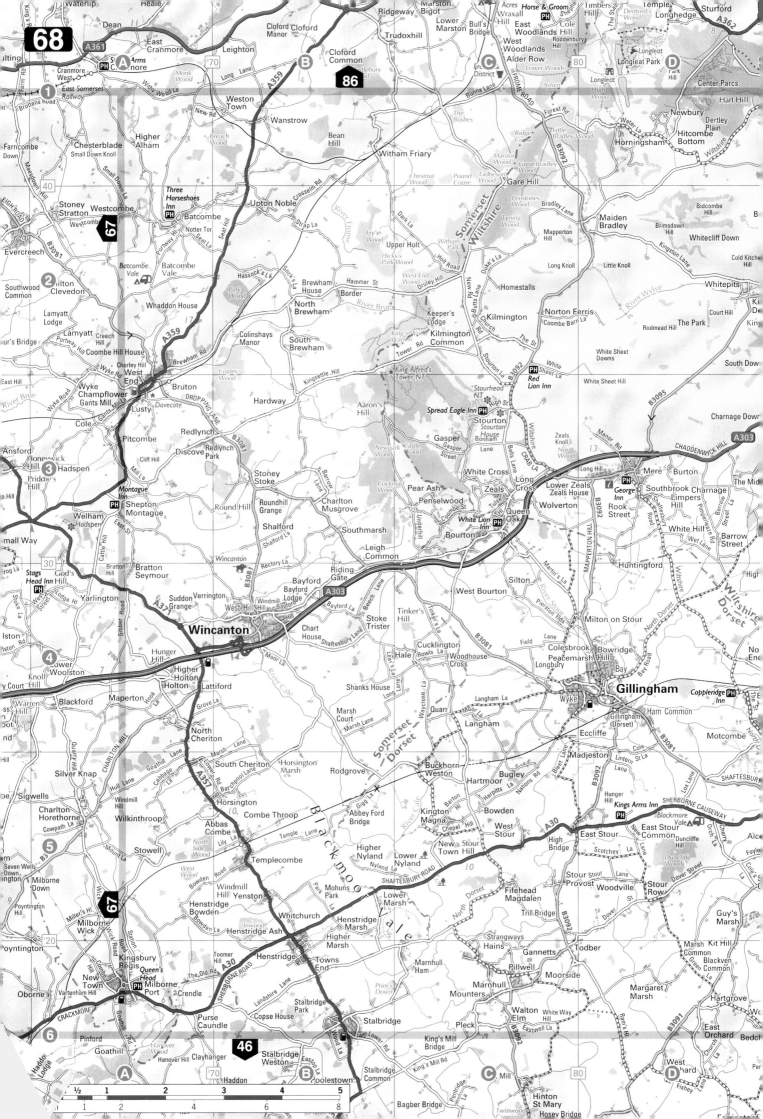

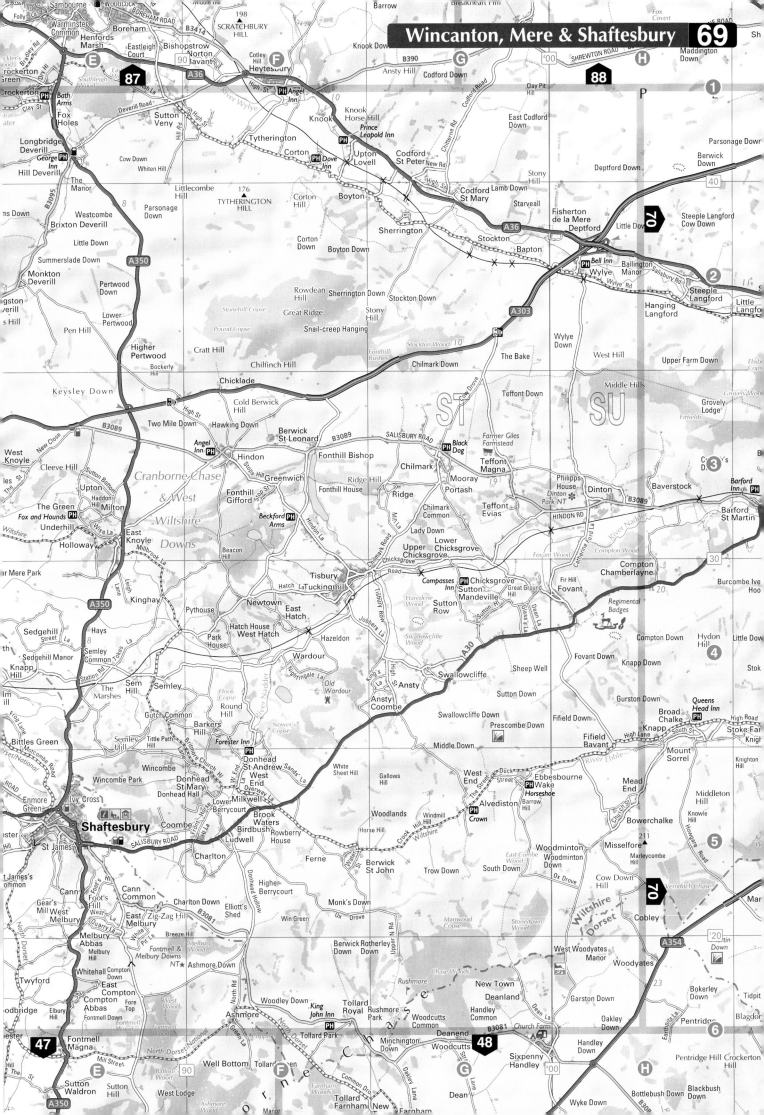

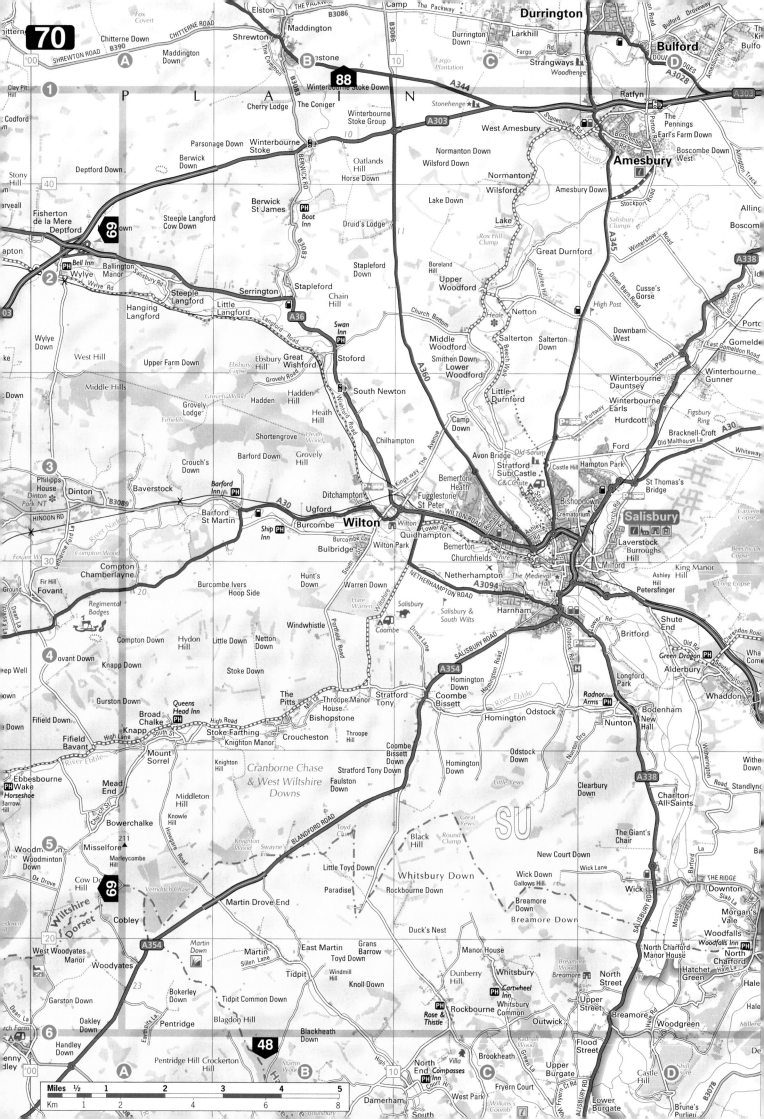

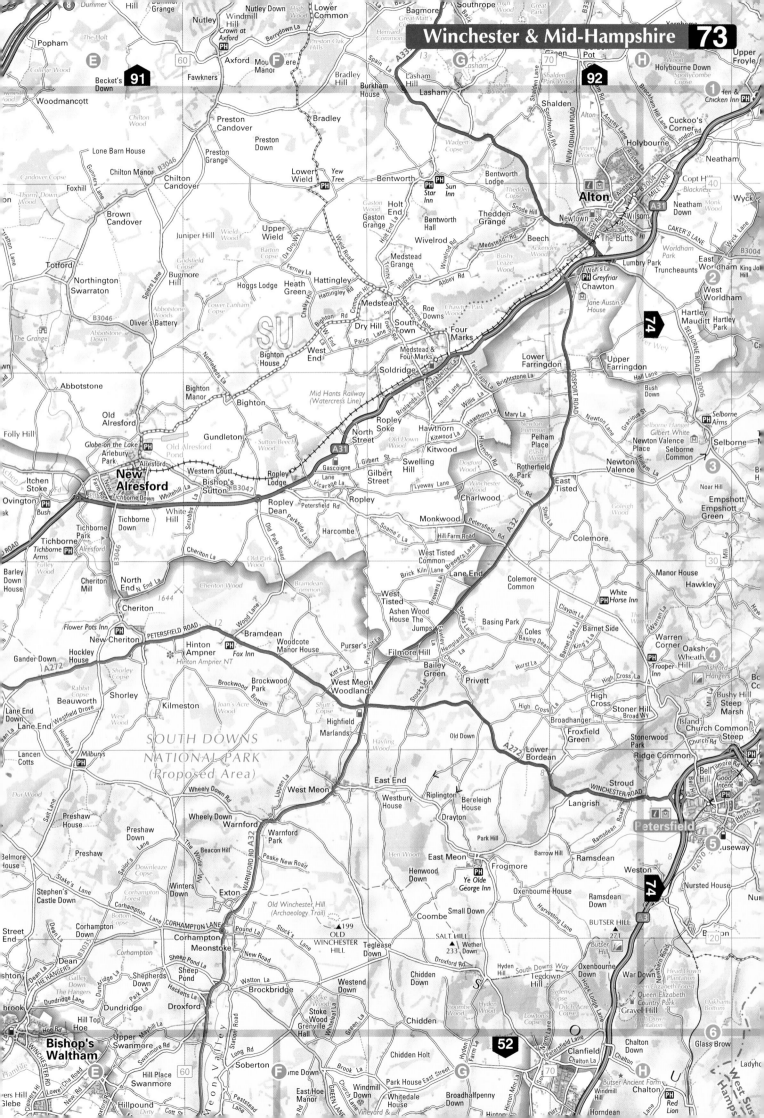

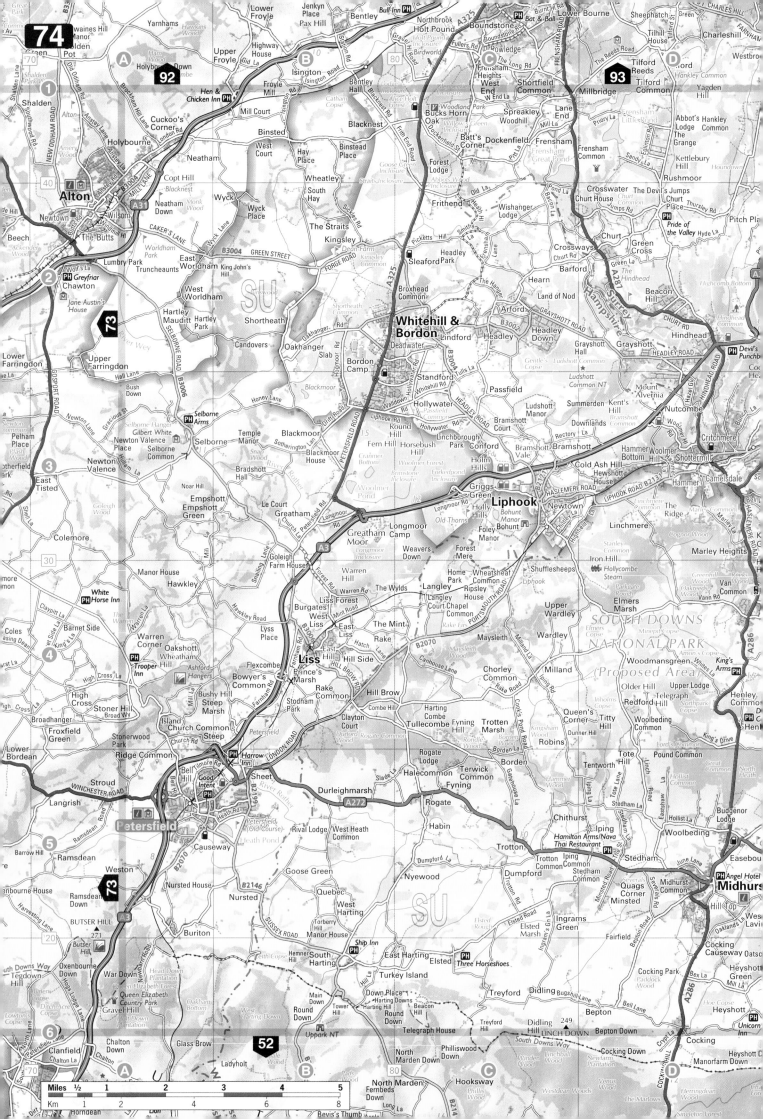

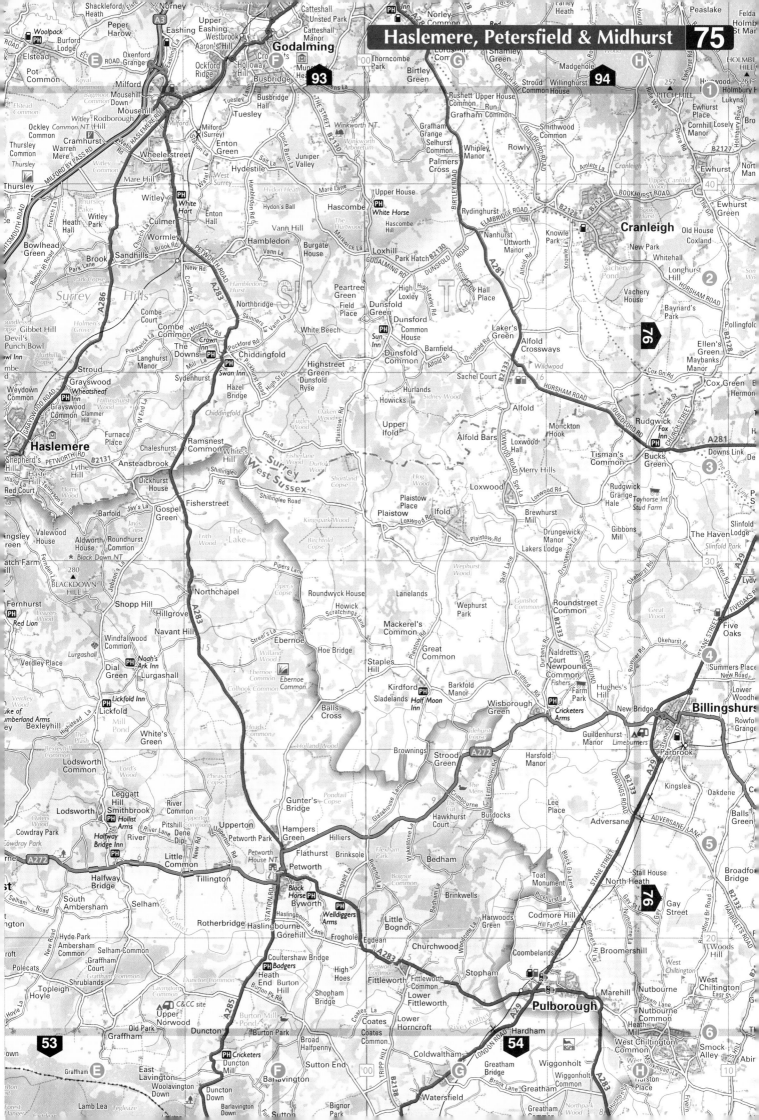

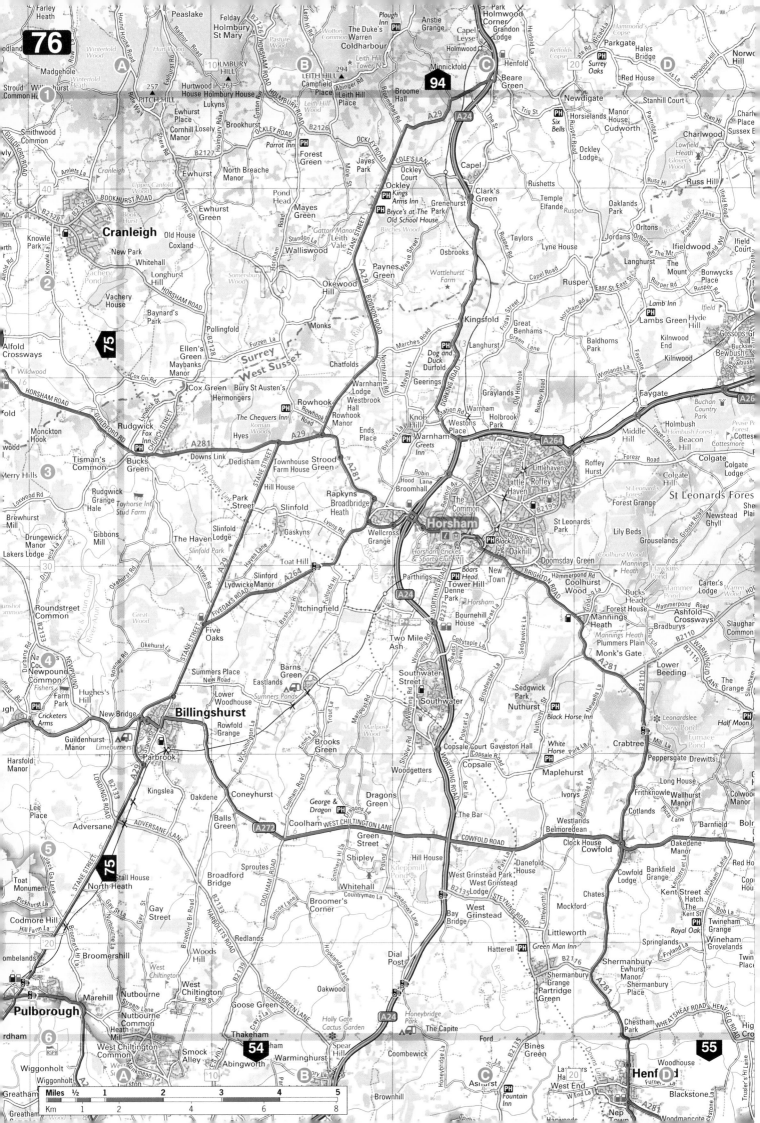

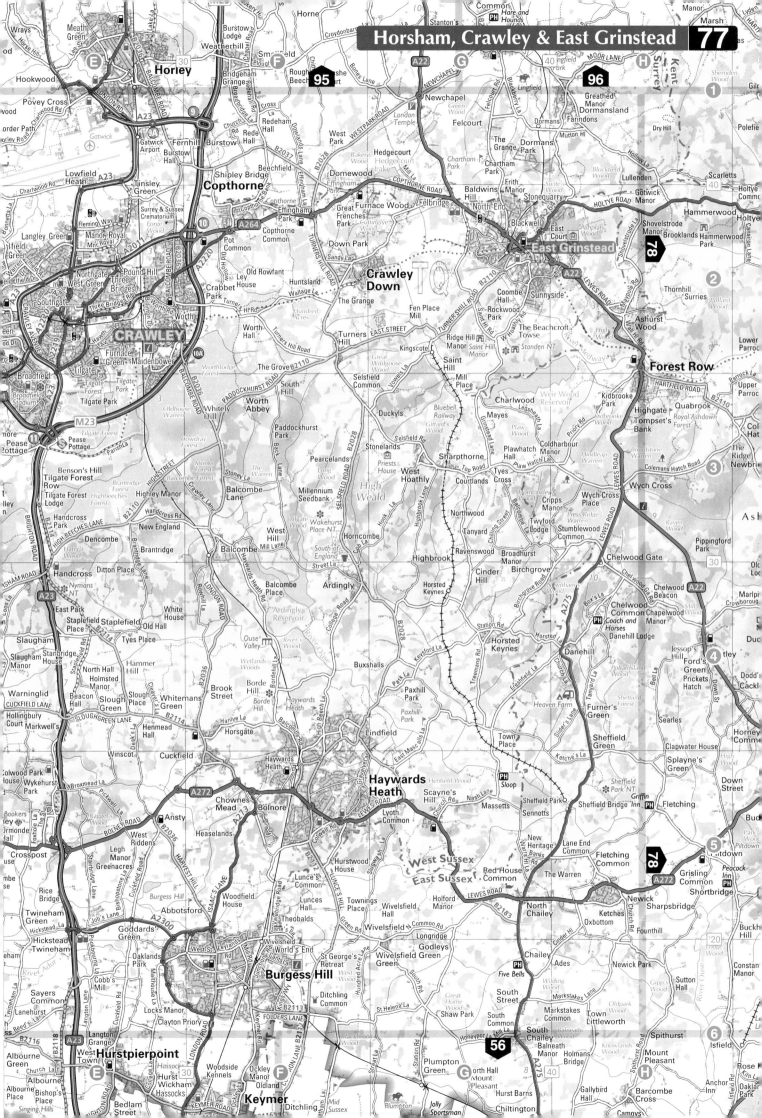

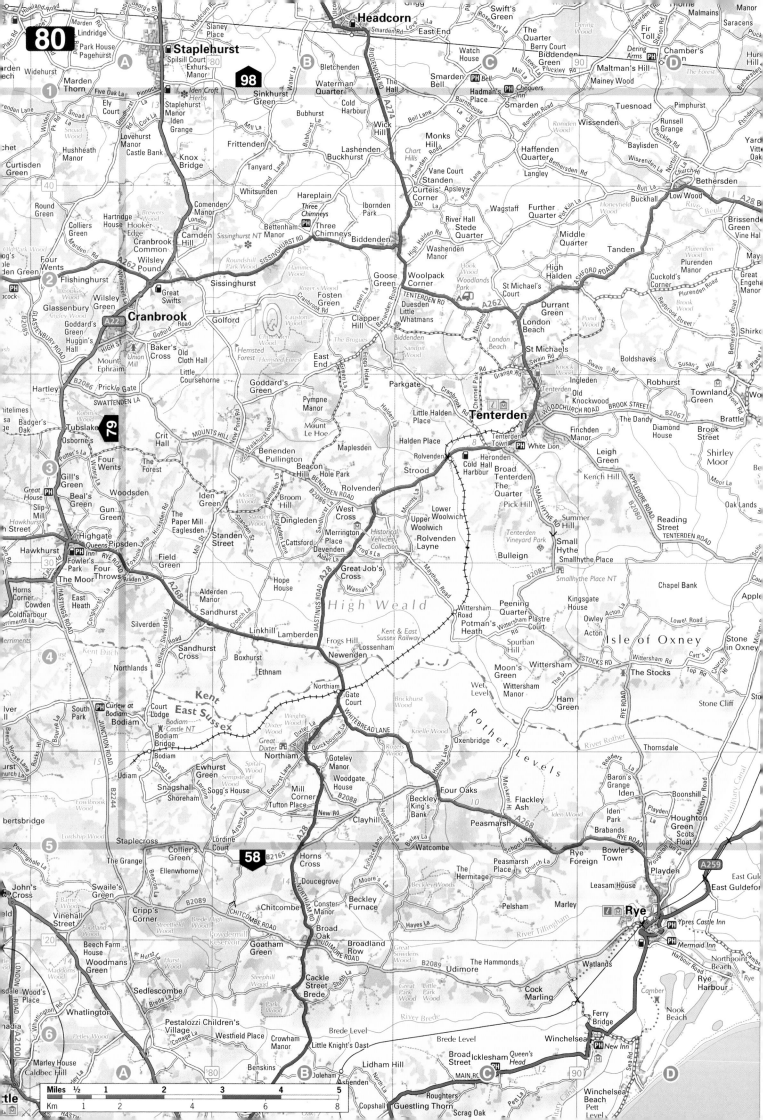

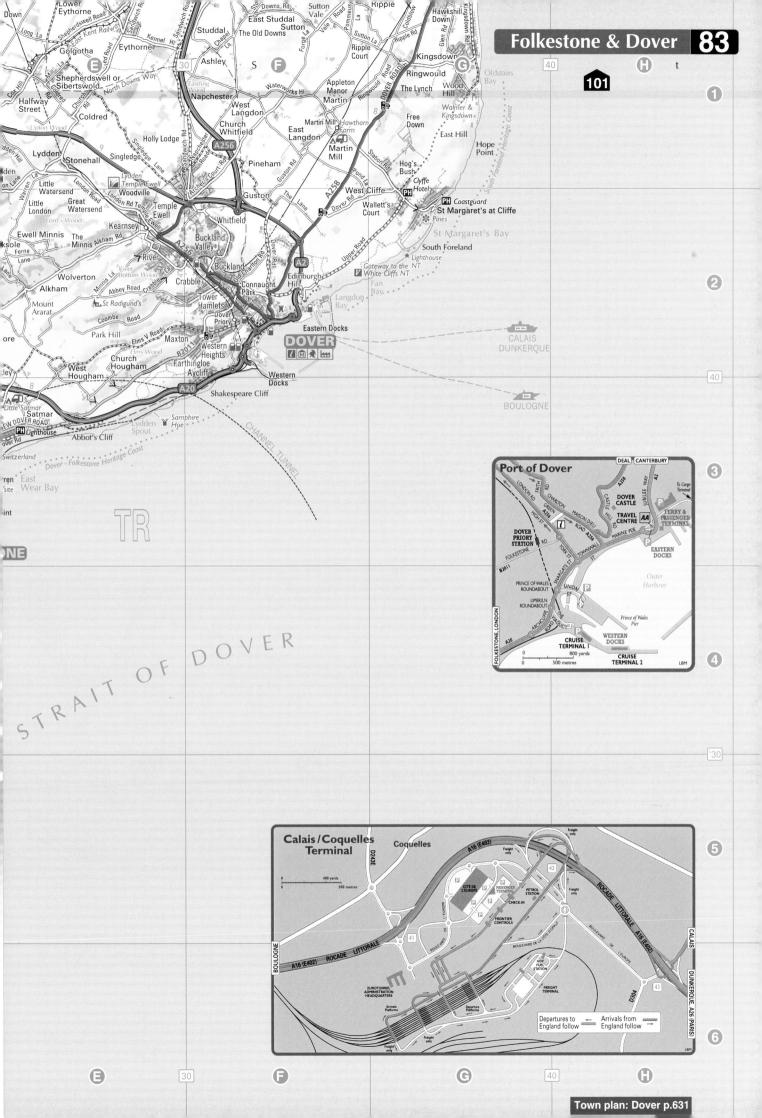

101

1

Lower Eythorne
Down
Long La
Golgotha
Mile
E
Shepherdswell or Sibertswold
Halfway Street
Coldred
Lydden
Stonehall
Little Watersend
Little London
Great Watersend
Lord's Wood
Ewell Minnis
ksole
ferne
Lane
Wolverton
Alkham
The Minnis
Mount Ararat
Kearnsey
St Radigund's
Coombe Road
Park Hill
West Hougham
Church Hougham
Maxton
Elms V Road
Farthingloe
Aycliff

East Kent Railway
Shepherdswell Road
East Kent Railway
Sandwich Rd
Kennel Hl
Eythorne
Ashley
30
Napchester
Church Rd
Holly Lodge
Woodville
Lydden Temple Ewell
London Rd
Temple Ewell
River
Buckland Valley
Buckland
Crabble
Abbey Road
Tower Hamlets
Dover Priory
B2011
Western Heights

Downs Rd
Studdal
Chapel La
East Studdal
Sutton
The Old Downs
Sutton Vale
Ripple
Forge La
Vale Rd
Sutton La
Ripple Rd
Ripple Court
S
F
Waterworks Hl
West Langdon
Church Whitfield
East Langdon
Pineham
Guston Rd
Guston
The Lane
Whitfield
A256
Sandwich Road
Napchester Road
Archer's Court Rd
Singledge Lane
A258
Dover Rd
West Cliffe
Wallett's Court
Appleton Manor
Martin
Hawthorn Farm
Martin Mill
Station Rd
Pond La
Upper Road
Coldblow
Kingsdown
Ringwould
The Lynch
Hog's Bush
Clyffe Hotel
PH Coastguard
St Margaret's at Cliffe
Pines
South Foreland
Lighthouse
PH
Hawkshill Down
Glen Rd
Kingsdown Rd
Ringwould
Wood Hill
Free Down
East Hill
Hope Point
Oldstairs Bay
Walmer & Kingsdown
South Foreland Heritage Coast
40
G
H
t
2
St Margaret's Bay
V Gateway to the NT
White Cliffs NT
Fan Bay
Buckland
Connaught Park
Edinburgh Hill
Eastern Docks
DOVER
Western Docks
Langdon Bay
CALAIS DUNKERQUE
A20
Shakespeare Cliff
B2011
Samphire Hoe
Lydden Spout
Abbot's Cliff
PH Lighthouse
Satmar
Little Satmar
NEW DOVER ROAD
over Rd
Switzerland
ren
site
int
East Wear Bay
Dover - Folkestone Heritage Coast
CHANNEL TUNNEL
BOULOGNE
40
'30

TR

ONE

S T R A I T   O F   D O V E R

Port of Dover

DEAL · CANTERBURY
LONDON RD
FRITH RD
CHARLTON GREEN
A256
MASON DIEU
A256
CASTLE HILL
JUBILEE WAY
A2
To Cargo Terminal
DOVER CASTLE
TRAVEL CENTRE
AA
FERRY & PASSENGER TERMINAL
P
P
DOVER PRIORY STATION
HIGH ST
A256
YORK ST
TOWNWALL ST
MARINE PDE
EASTERN DOCKS
FOLKESTONE RD
SNARGATE ST
UNION ST
P
Outer Harbour
B2011
PRINCE OF WALES ROUNDABOUT
LIMEKILN ROUNDABOUT
THE VIADUCT
ARCLIFFE RD
A20
FOLKESTONE, LONDON
CRUISE TERMINAL 1
P
WESTERN DOCKS
Prince of Wales Pier
CRUISE TERMINAL 2
0   800 yards
0   500 metres
LBM
3
4

Calais / Coquelles Terminal

Coquelles
A16 (E402)
D43E
Freight only
Freight only
ROCADE LITTORALE A16 (E402)
CITÉ DE L'EUROPE
PASSENGER TERMINAL
PETROL STATION
CHECK-IN
42
Freight only
BOULEVARD DE L'EUROPE
CALAIS
BOULOGNE
A16 (E402)
ROCADE LITTORALE
41
FRONTIER CONTROLS
BOULEVARD DE LA COTE D'OPALE
HGV FUEL STATION
43
D304
DUNKERQUE, A26 (PARIS)
EUROTUNNEL ADMINISTRATION HEADQUARTERS
Arrivals Platforms
Departure Platforms
FREIGHT TERMINAL
Freight only
Freight only
0   400 yards
0   500 metres
Departures to England follow →   Arrivals from England follow →
LBM
5
6

E   30   F   G   40   H

Town plan: Dover p.631

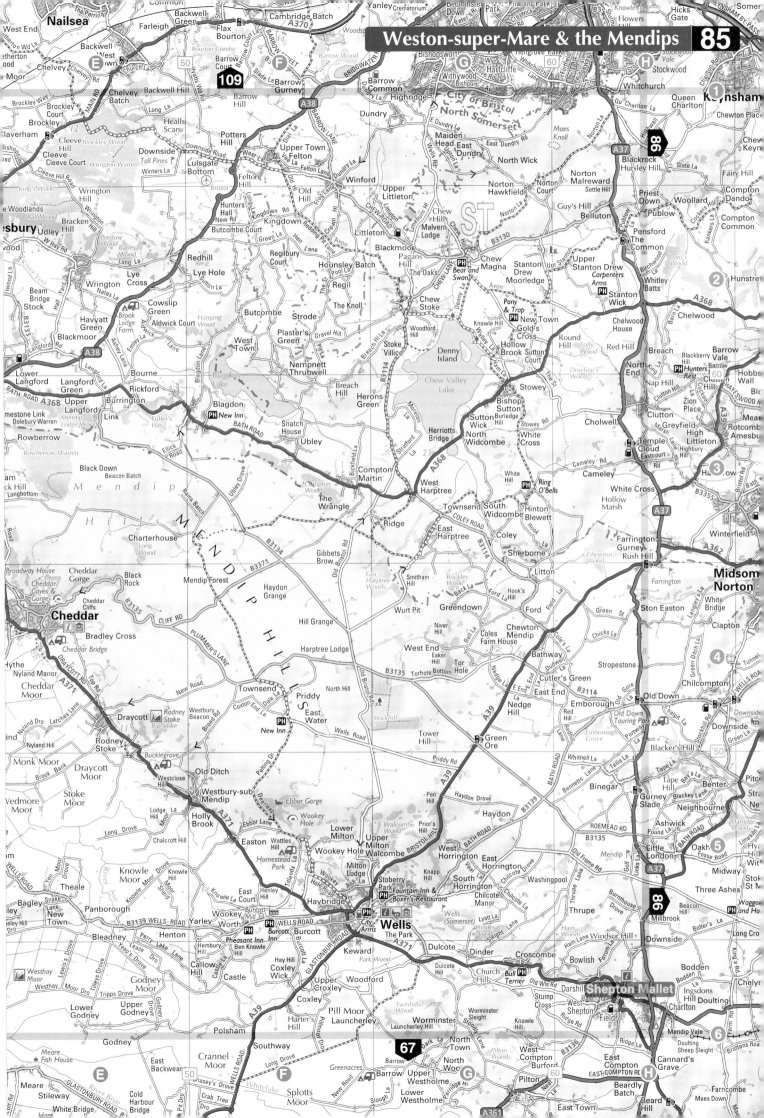

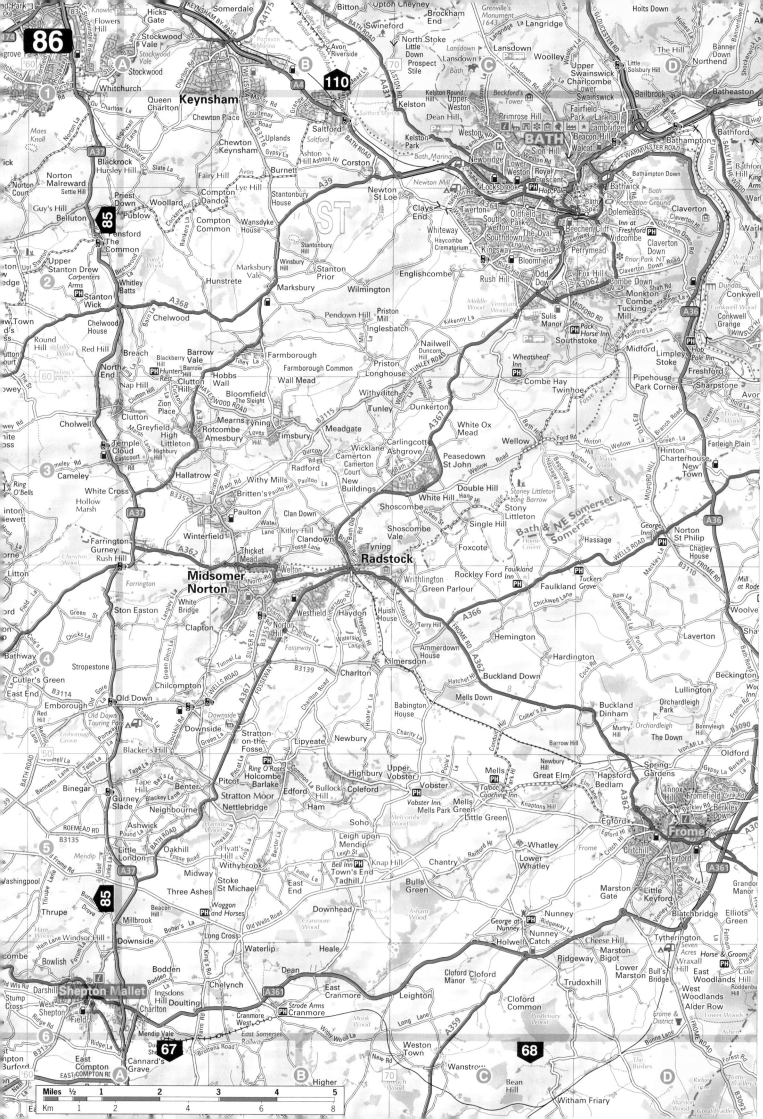

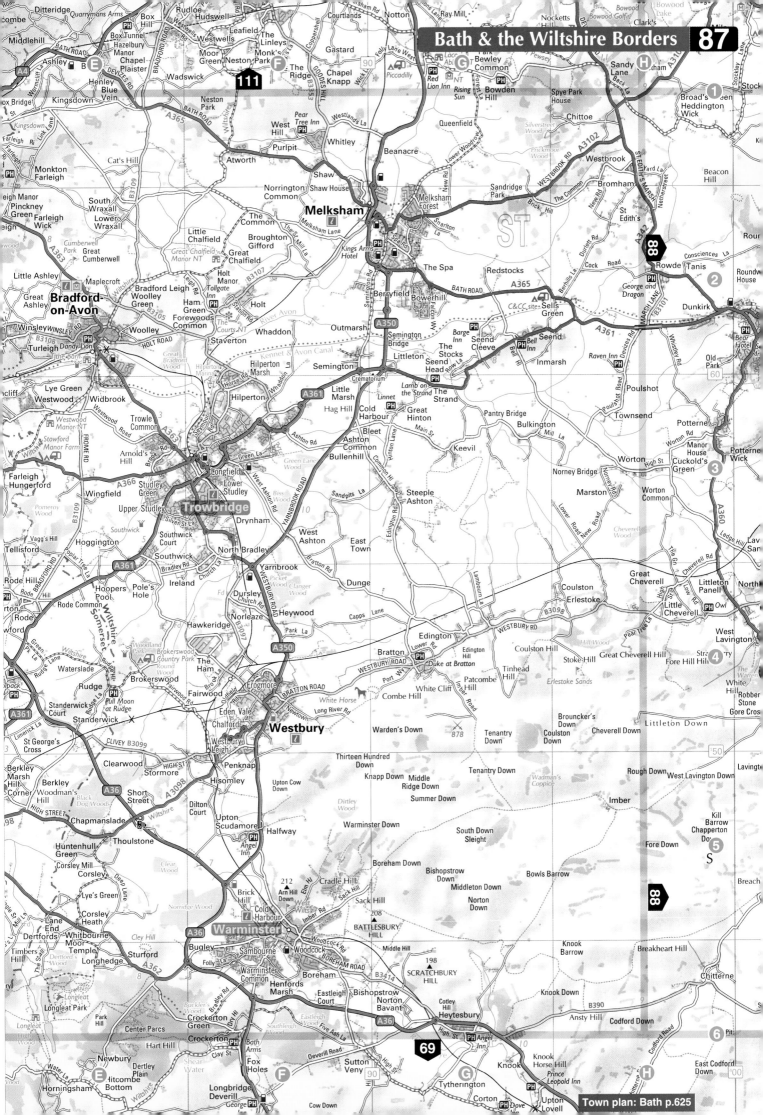

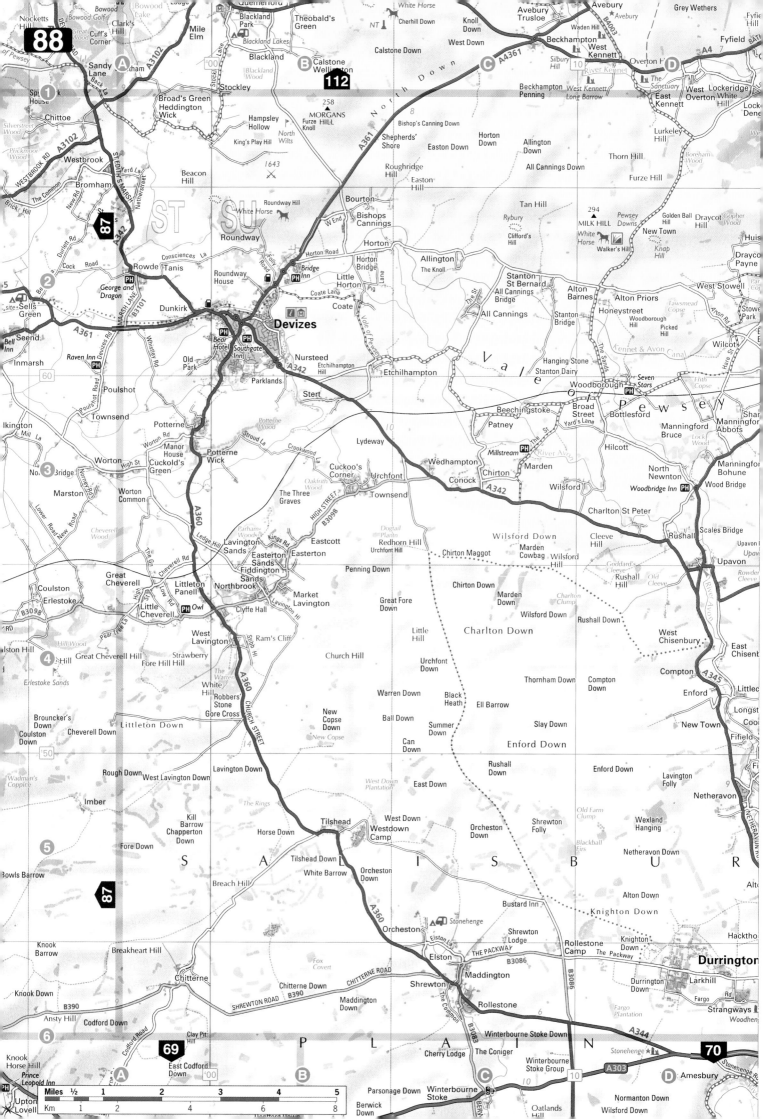

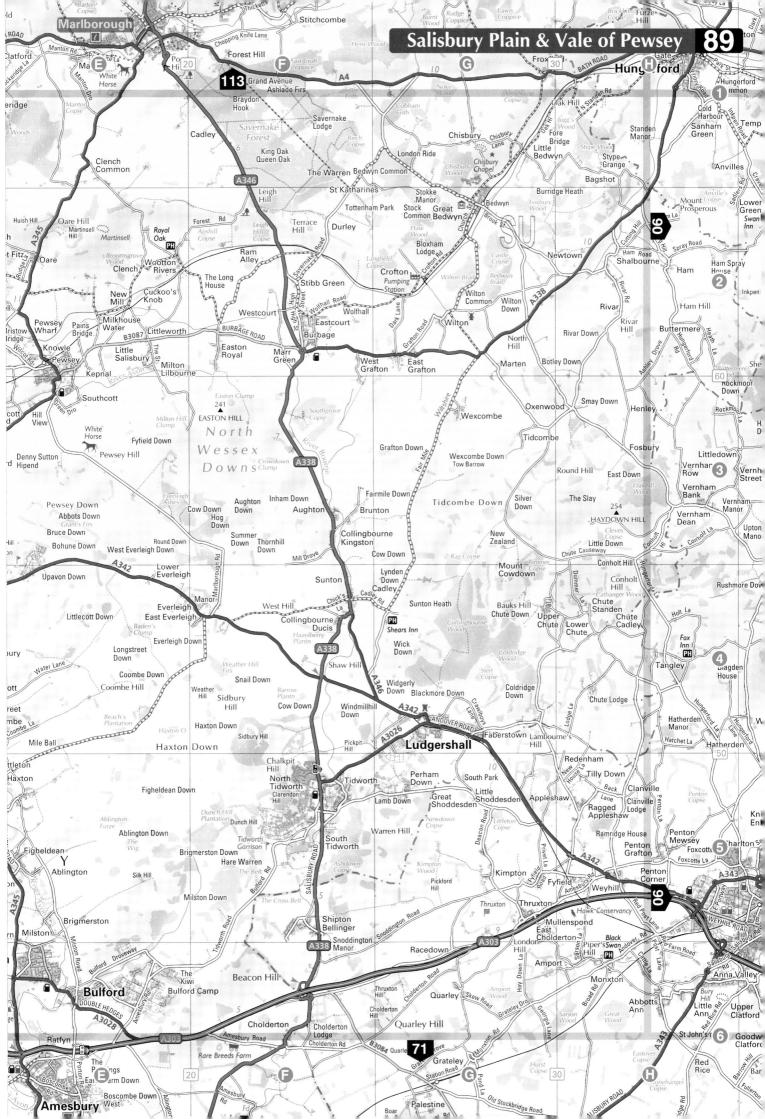

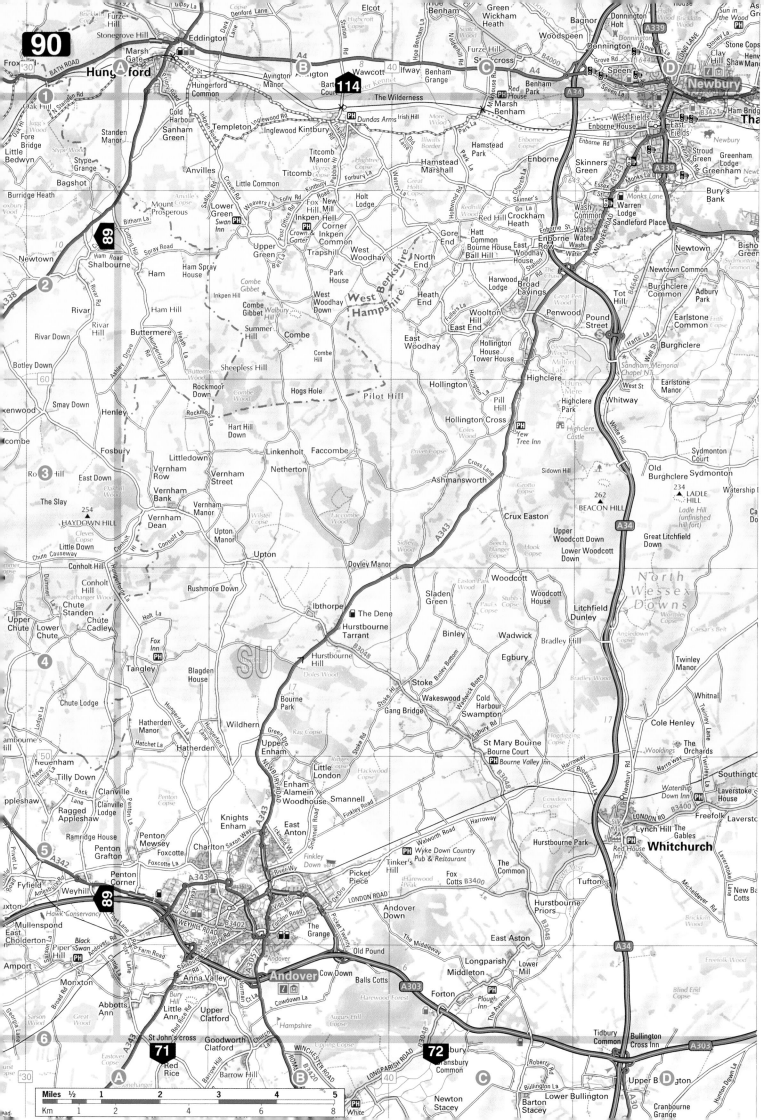

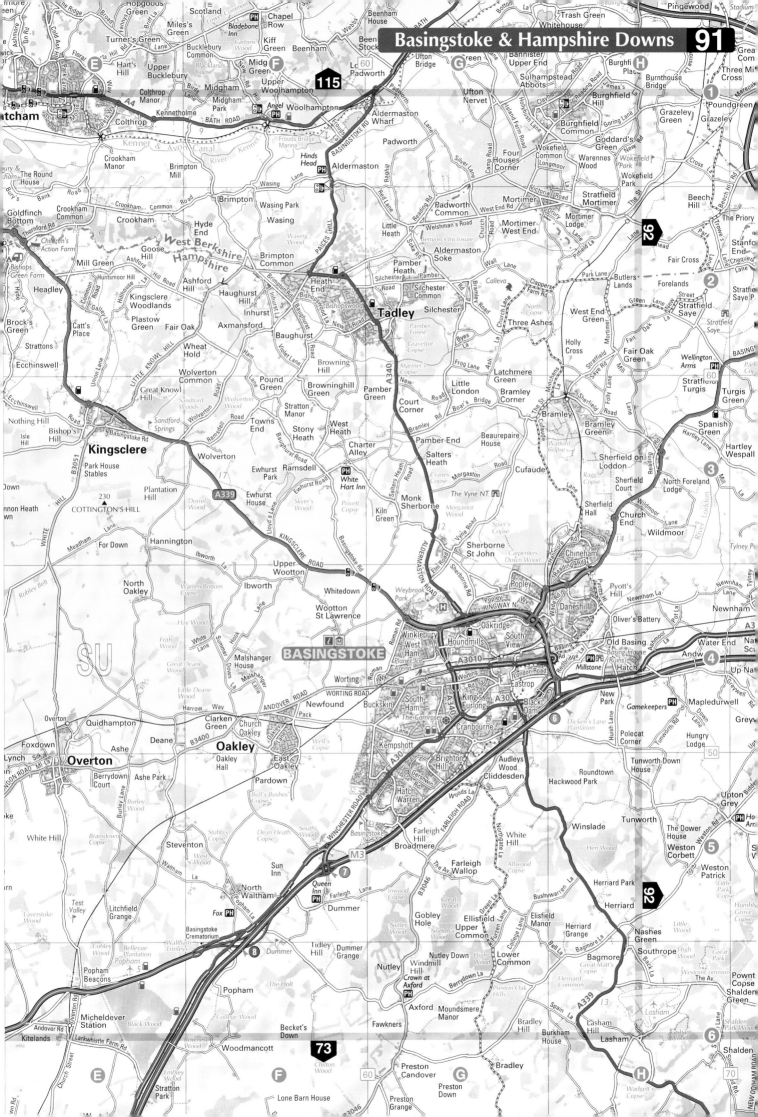

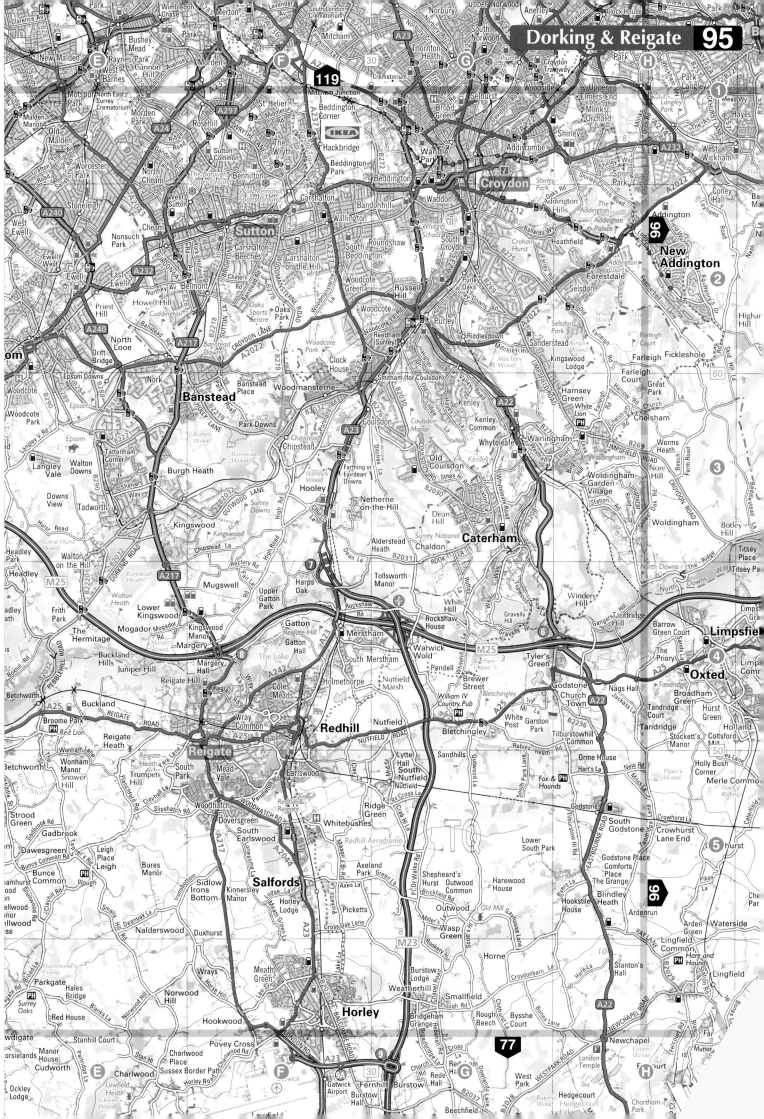

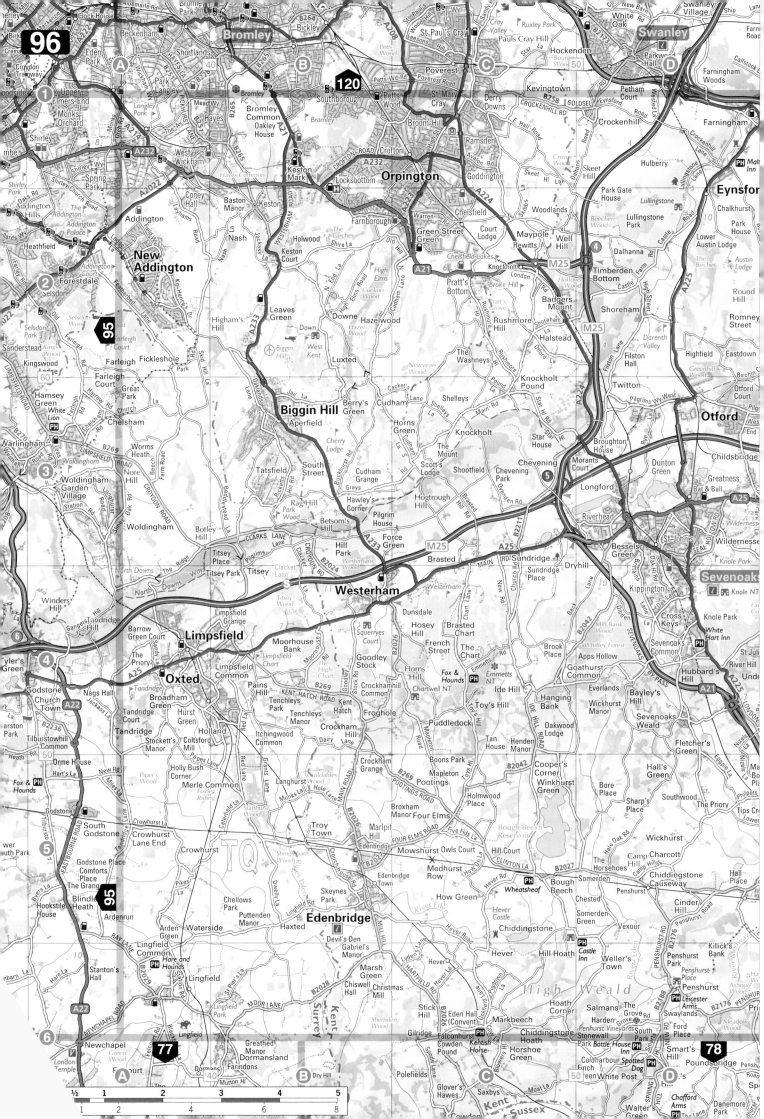

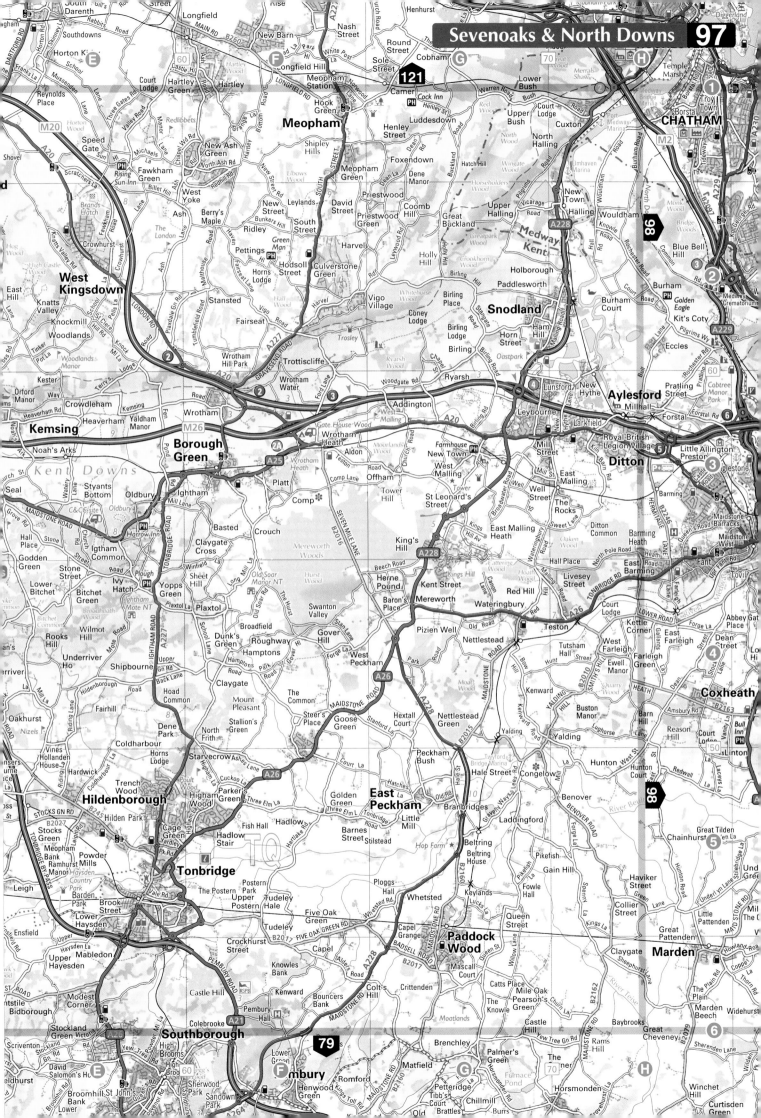

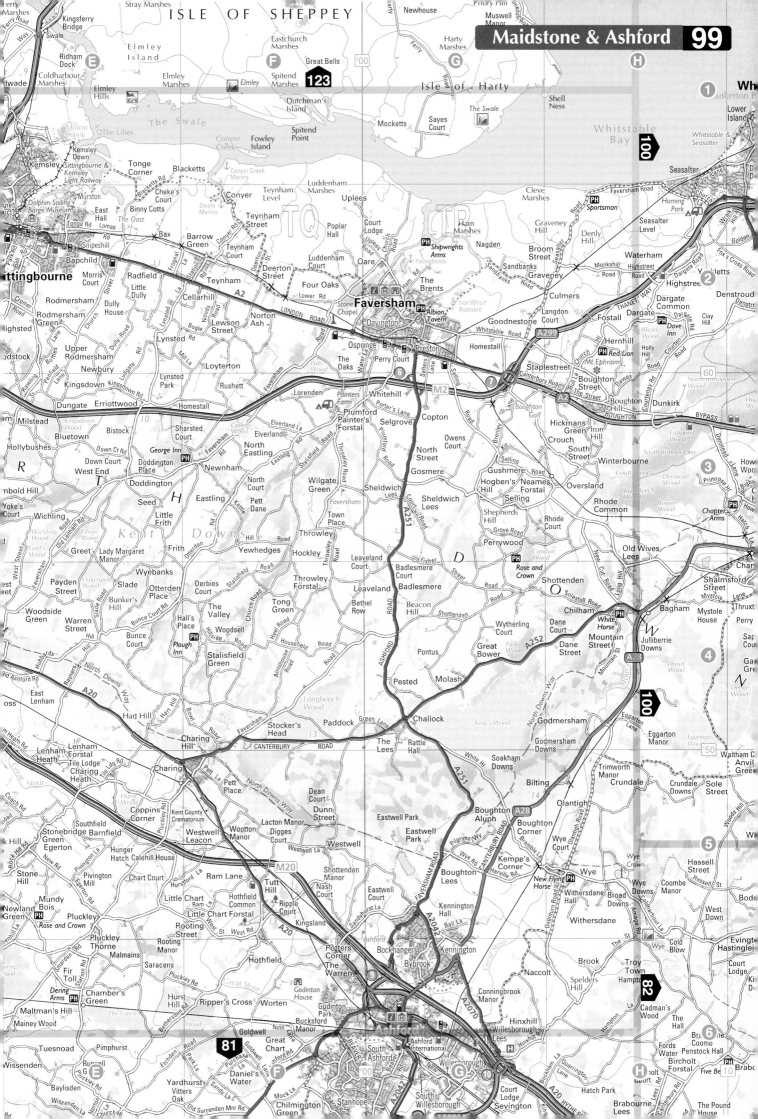

Town plan: Swansea p.647

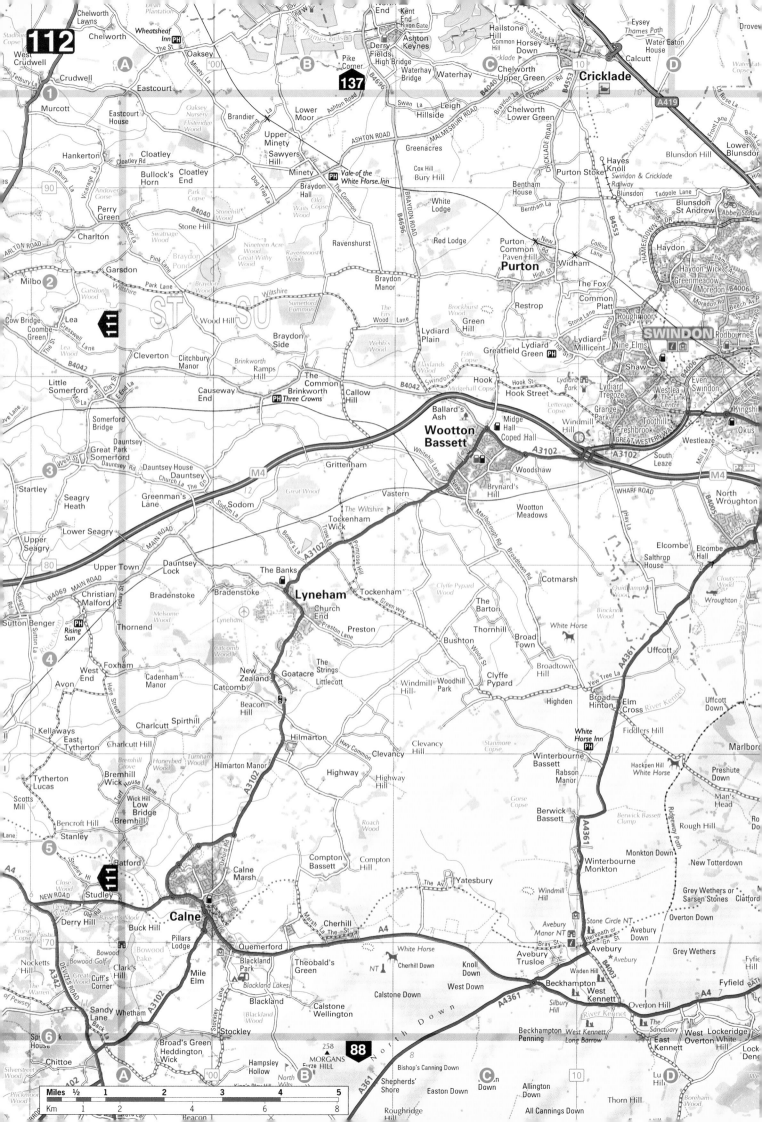

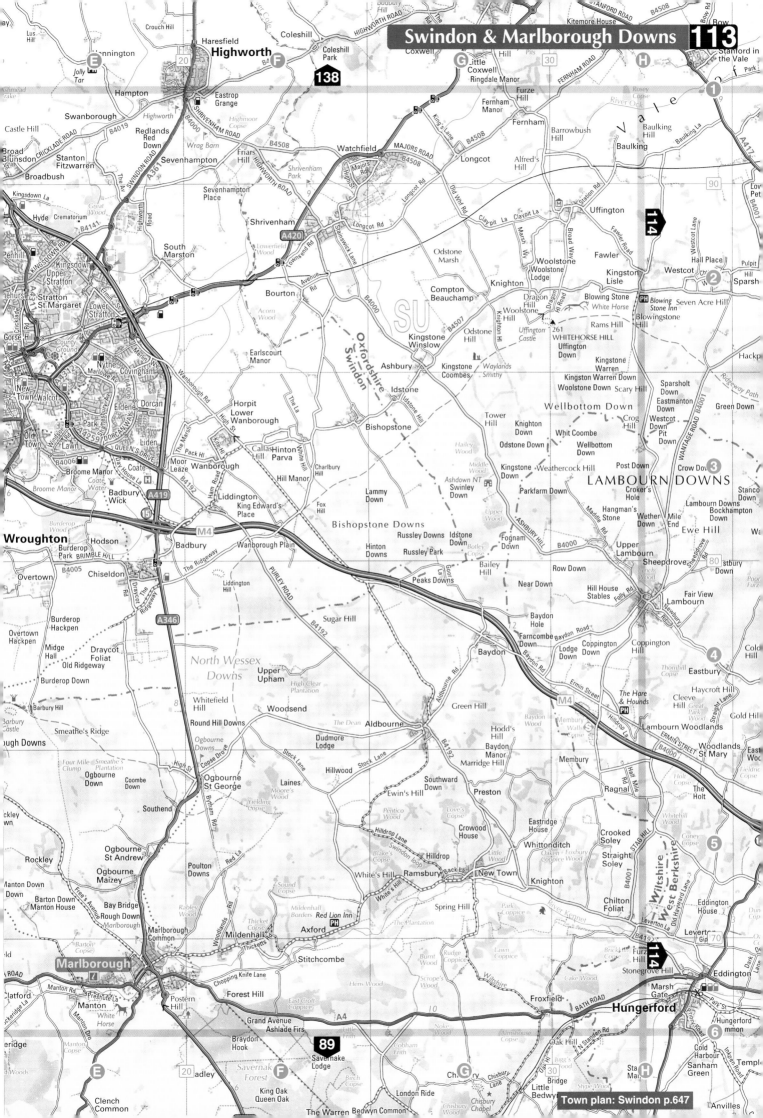

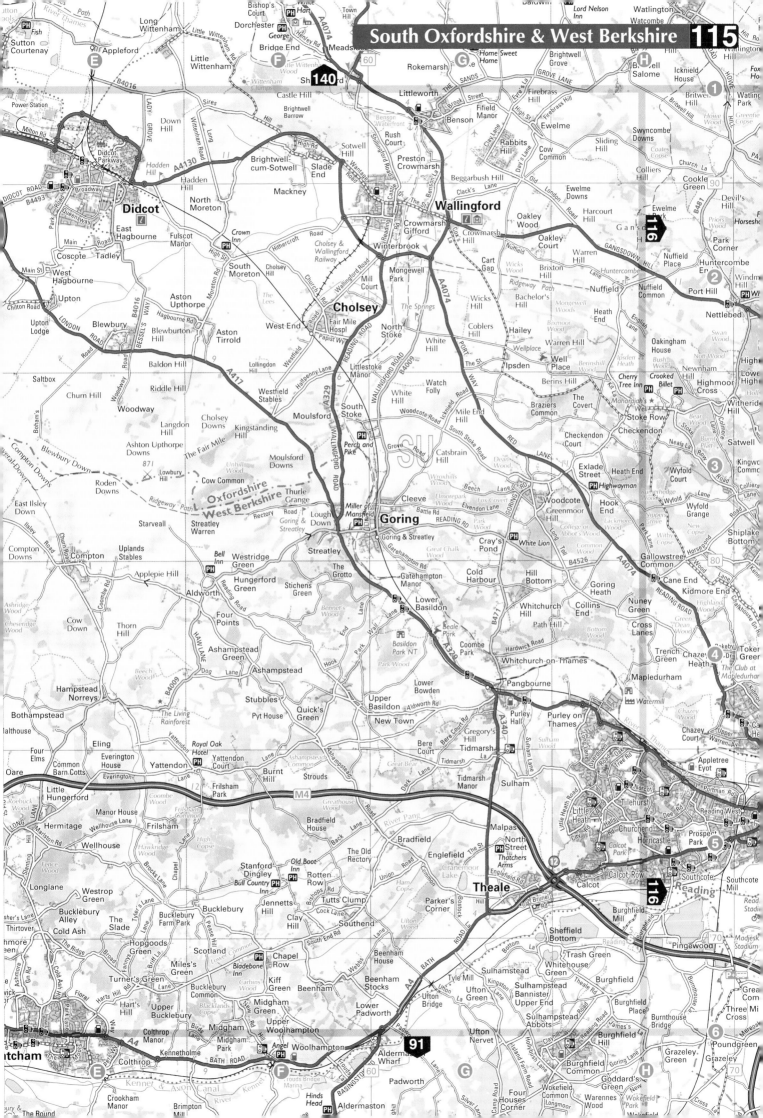

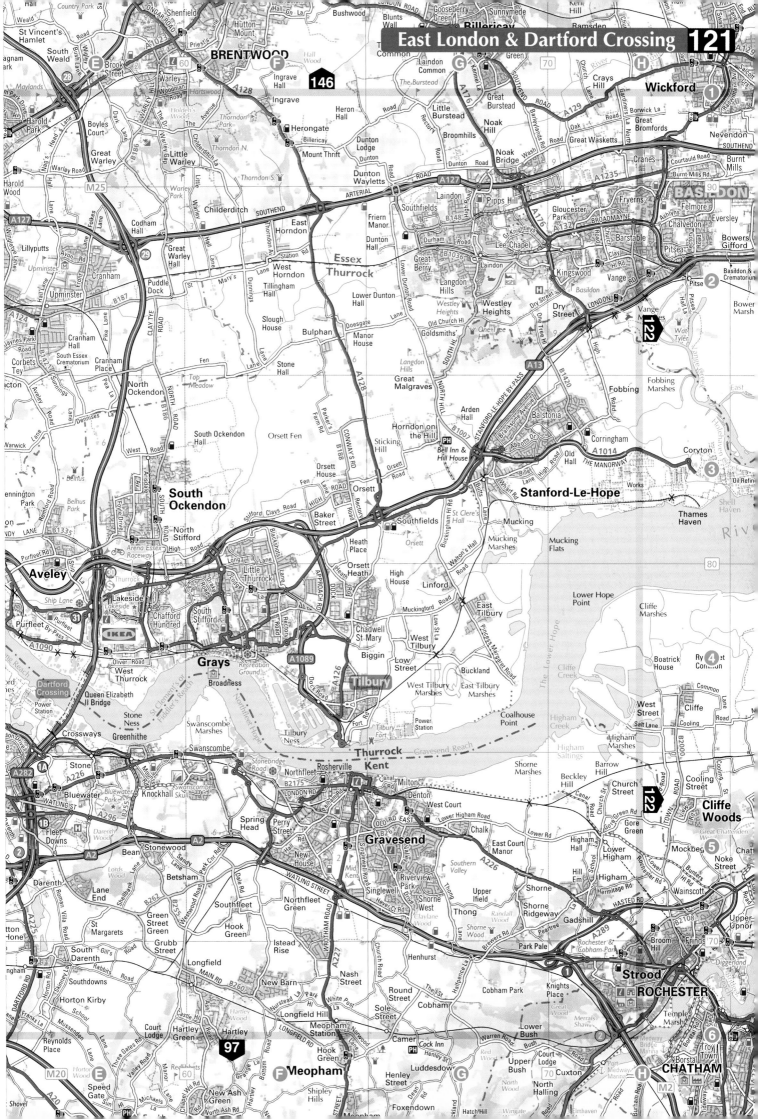

ST BRIDES BAY

150

PEMBROKESHIRE COAST
NATIONAL PARK

Rickets H

Madoc's

Druids

Sett
Bla

Sl

Bro

Stack Rocks
Howney
Stone
Ticklas
Point
Swan Inn & Resta
Borough Head
Lit
Ha

The S

Mill Haven

Warey Haven

Halfway
Rock

St Brides Haven

Talbenny

Re

The Nab Head

Tower Point

St Brides

Windmill
Park

South
Hill

Hasguard
Cross

Garland Stone

Pigstone Bay

Pig Stone

Skomer Head

SKOMER
ISLAND
Gorse Hill

The Wick

Shag
Rock

Midland
Isle

Mew
Stone

Marloes and Dale Heritage Coast

Wooltack
Point

Martin's Haven

Deadman's
Bay

Musselwick
Sands

Orlandon

Winterton

Marloes

B4327

Slatemill
Bridge

Hasgu

Broad Sound

Rainy Rock

Pembrokeshire Coast Path

Marloes Court

Gateholm
Stack

Gateholm
Island

Marloes
Sands

Bicton

St
Ishmael's

Sand
Have

Hooper's Point

Red
Cliff

Townsend

Musselwick

Lindsway
Bay

Little Bay
Point

SKOKHOLM
ISLAND

Mad Bay

Long Nose
Quarry Point

The Head

The Stack

Long Point

Hog Bay

Frank's
Point

Marloes and Dale Heritage Coast

Great Castle Head

Westdale Bay

Castle VV

Dale

Dale Roads

Watch
House
Point

Great
Head

Long Point

Long Point

Welshman's Bay

Little Castle
Point

Frenchman's Bay

Kete

Mill Bay

Dale Point

Castlebeach
Bay

Watwick Point

Watwick Bay

West Blockhouse
Point

Thorn Island

West Angle
Bay

St Ann's Head

Rat Island

Sheep Island

Castles Bay

Parsonsquarry Bay

West

Guttl

SM

SR

ROSSLARE HARBOUR

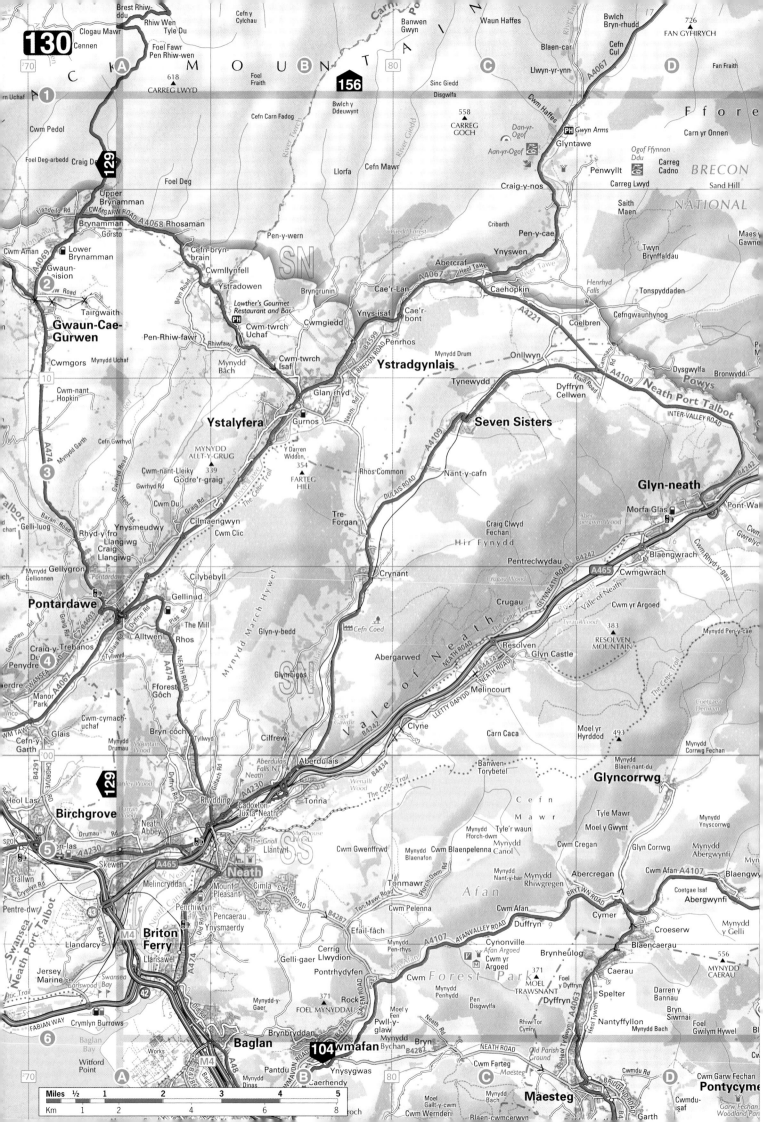

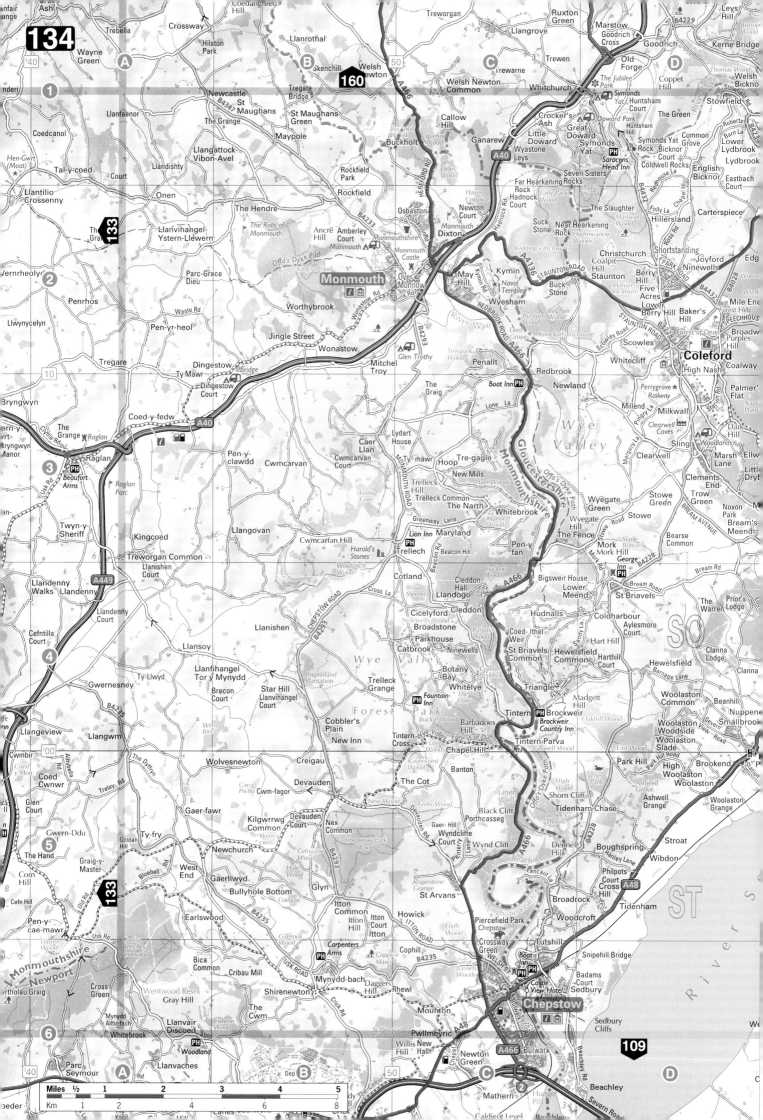

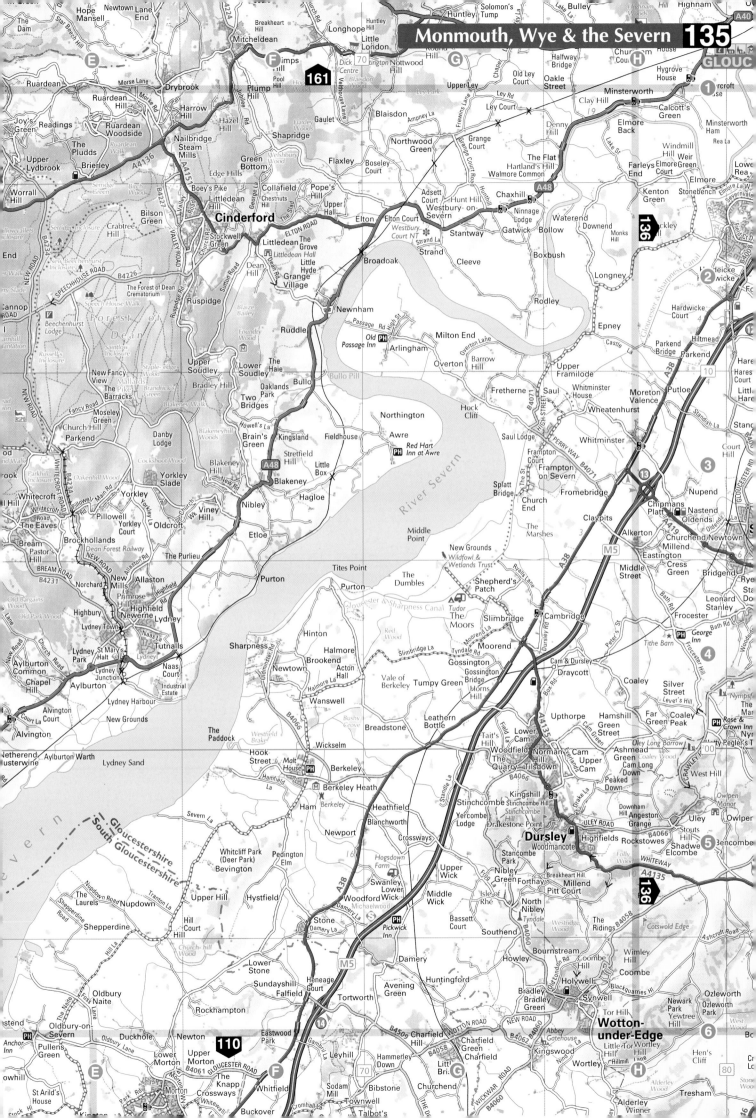

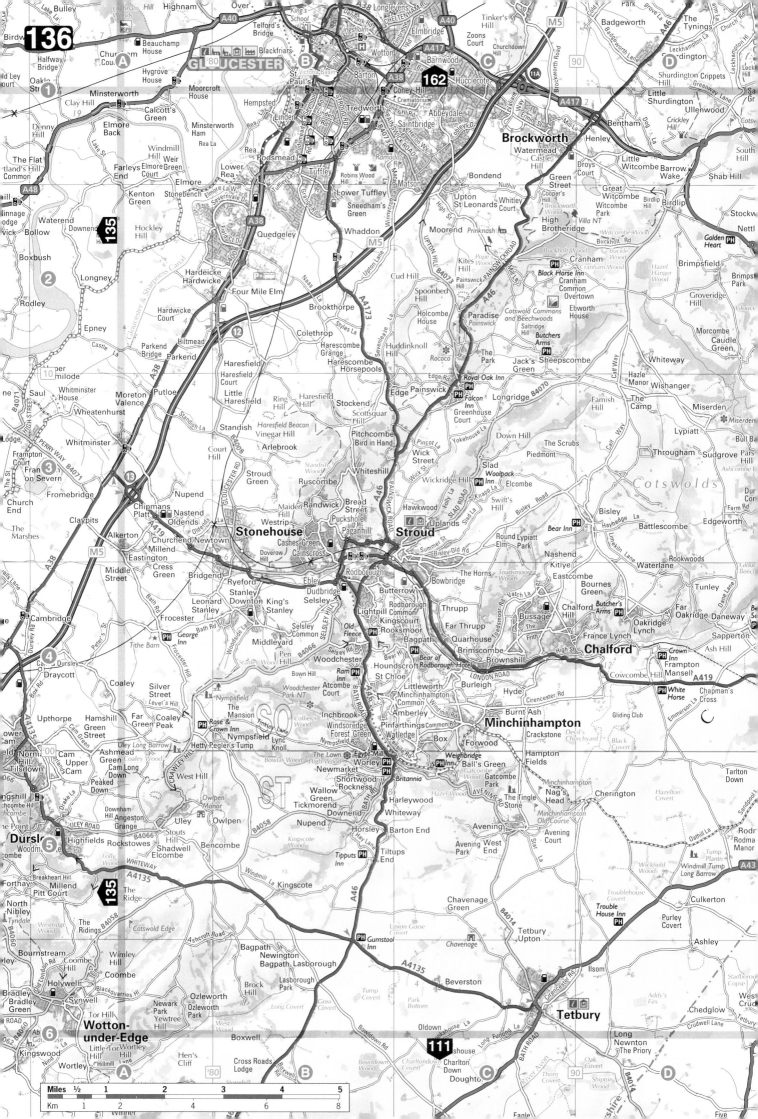

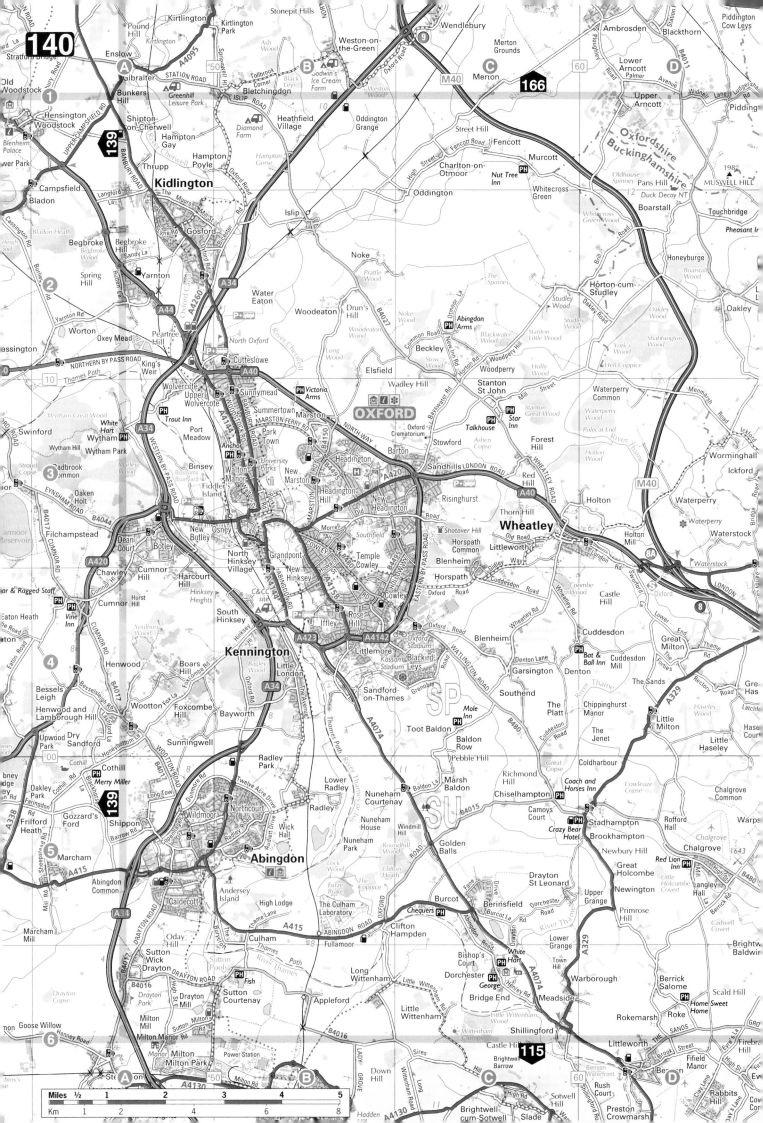

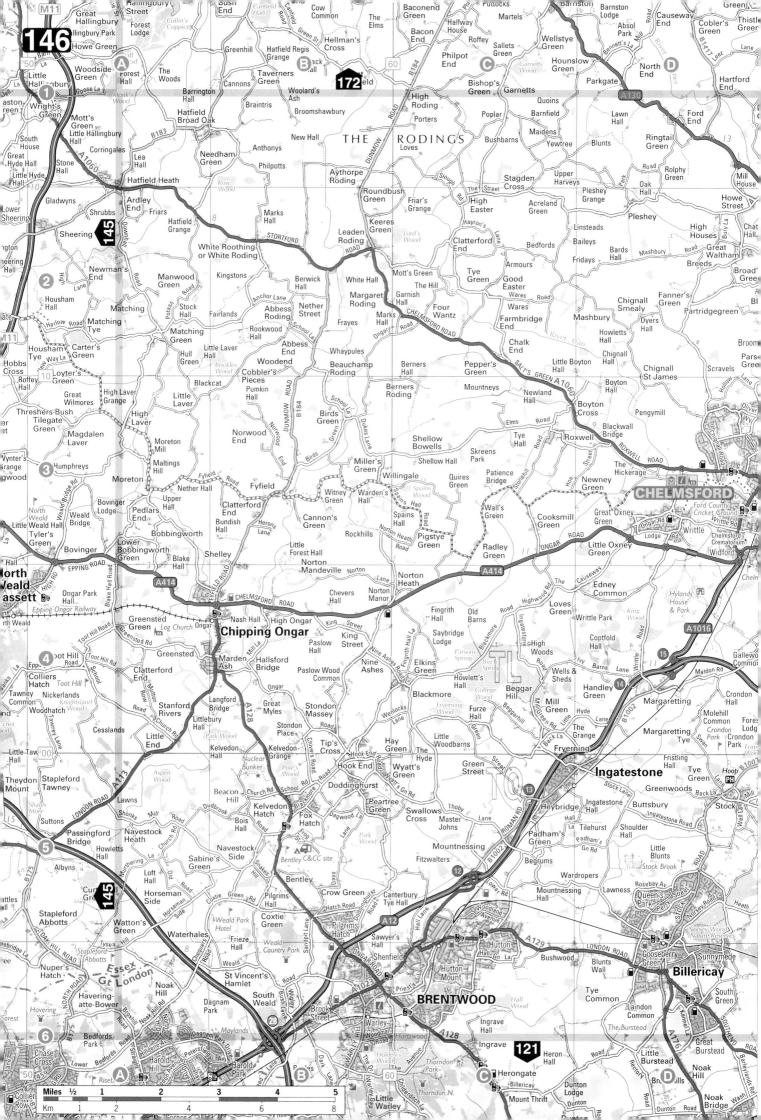

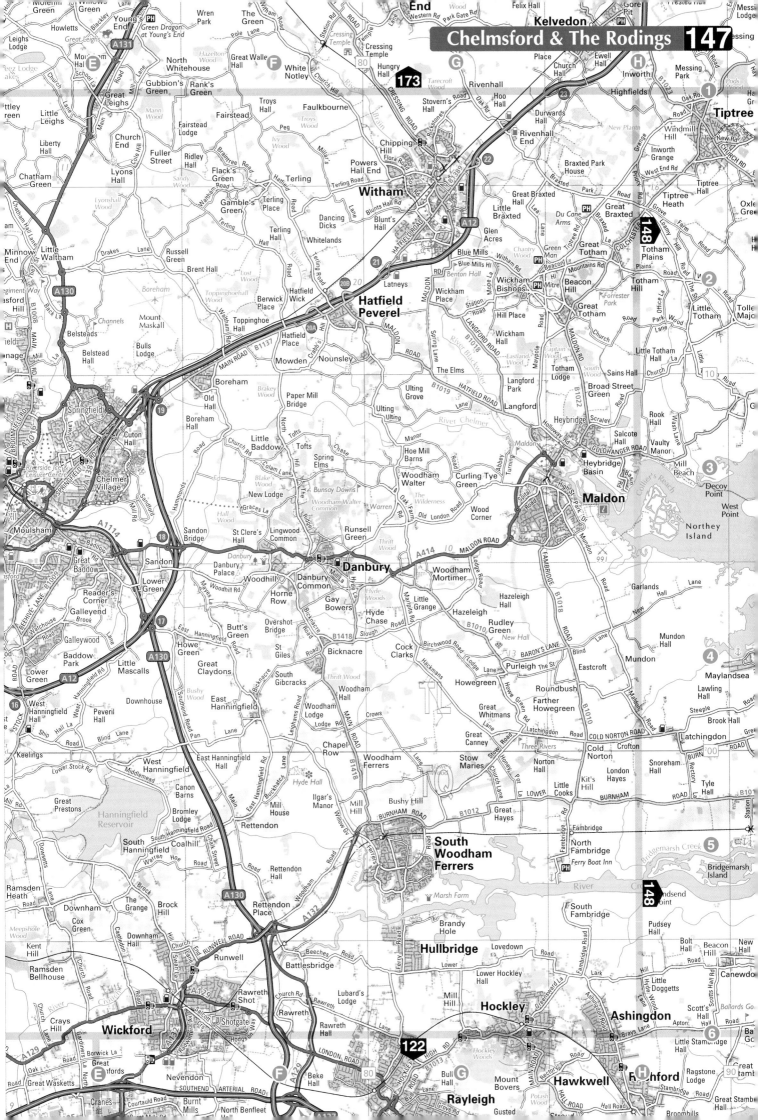

Frinton

The Lodge Green
Row Heath
South Heath
Milton Wood
Maldon Wood
Highbirch
Rectory Lane
Hollybush Hill
Eastmarsh Point
Frowick
Riddles Wood
St Osyth Heath
Hartley Wood
High Grove
Long Grove

Great Holland
Little
Clacton Lodge
Great Holland Green
bury's Old House
Pond House
Holland Gap
Sandy Point
Chevaux de frise Point
Holland Haven

Aldboro Point
River Colne
Alresford Creek
BRIGHTLINGSEA ROAD
COLCHESTER ROAD
Dead La
Dial Rd

E CHURCH
Morses
Brightlingsea
175

176

H

1

Pewit Island
Rat Island
Ivy House
Hurst Green
Regent Rd
Mill St
B1029
B1027
Clay
St Osyth

Bovill's Hall
Bocking's Elm
A133
LONDON RD
THORPE ROAD
Burrsville Park
Great Clacton
VALLEY RD
B1441
Corse La
20

G
B14

Westmarsh Point
Cindery Island
St Osyth Stone Point
Point Clear
Colne Estuary
Mersea Stone
St John's Road
Earls Hall
Coppins
Rd
Coles Lane
B1027
Oxford Rd
HOLLAND
FRINTON ROAD
B1027
Holland-on-Sea

2

East Mersea
Cudmore Grove
Sandy Point
Mill Dam Lake
Beach Rd
St Osyth Creek
Daltes La
Rush Green
Leas Rd
West Rd
Clacton
Golf Links

Mersea Flats
St Osyth Marsh
Seawick
Jaywick
CLACTON-ON-SEA
i

Lee-over-Sands
St Osyth Beach
Colne Point

10
200

TM

3

4

TR

5

6

E   10   F   G   20   H

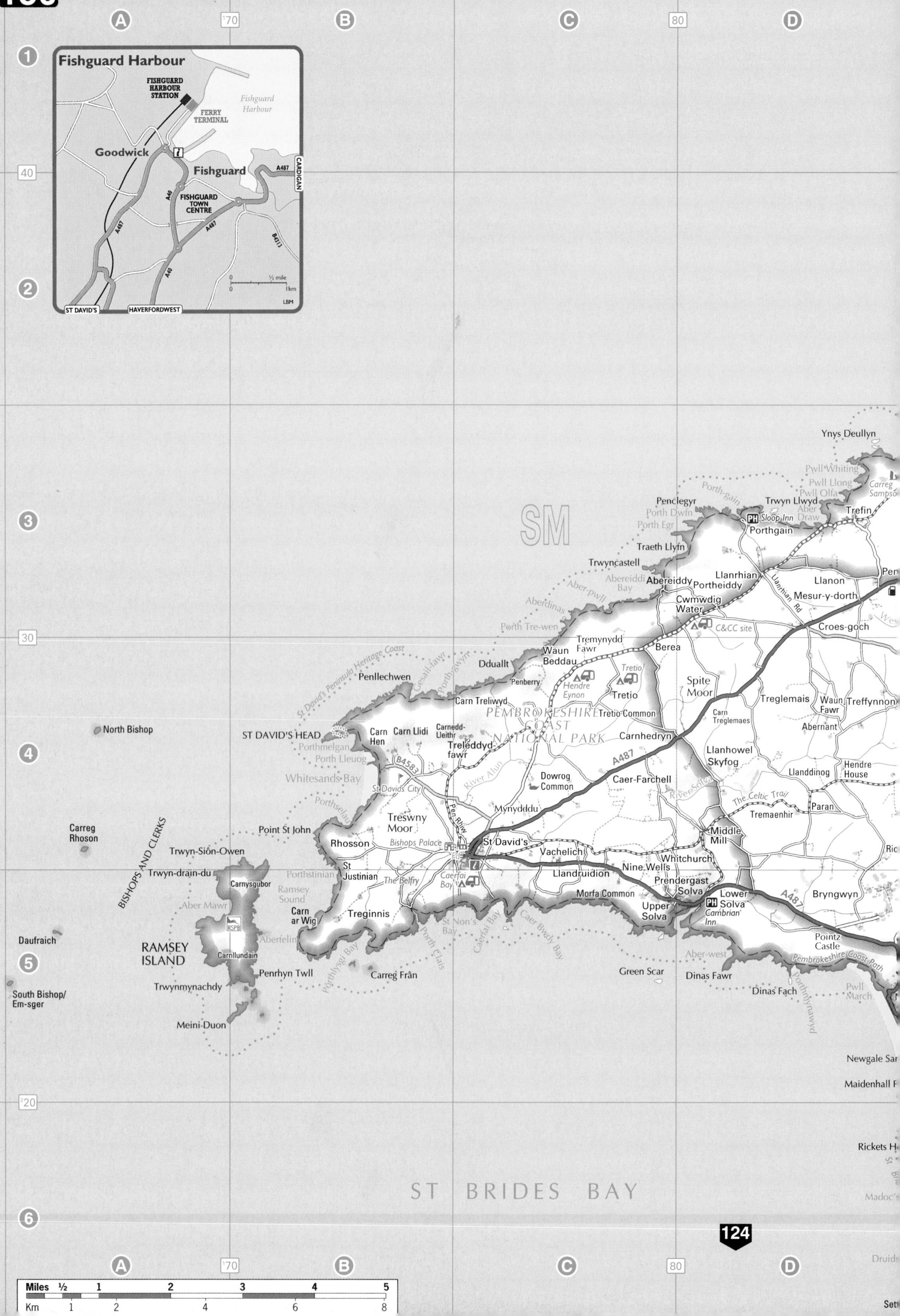

A · 70 · B · C · 80 · D

1

Fishguard Harbour

FISHGUARD
HARBOUR
STATION

FERRY
TERMINAL

*Fishguard
Harbour*

Goodwick

40

A487

CARDIGAN

Fishguard

A40

FISHGUARD
TOWN
CENTRE

A487

B4313

2

0   ½ mile
0   1km

ST DAVID'S   HAVERFORDWEST

LBM

3

Ynys Deullyn

Pwll Whiting

Pwll Llong
Pwll Olfa   Carreg
Sampso

Penclegyr   *Porth-gain*   **Trwyn Llwyd**   **Trefin**
Porth Dwfn   *Aber*
Porth Egr   PH *Sloop Inn*   *Draw*
                Porthgain

SM

Traeth Llyn

Trwyncastell   Llanon   **Pen**
Abereiddi   **Llanrhian**
Aber-pwll   *Bay*   **Abereiddy Portheiddy**   Llanrhian Rd   *Mesur-y-dorth*
Aberdinas   **Cwmwdig**
Water   *We*
Porth Tre-wen   ▲▢ C&CC site   **Croes-goch**

30

St David's Peninsula Heritage Coast   **Waun**   **Tremynydd**   **Berea**
Lecali-fawr   **Beddau**   **Fawr**
Penllechwen   *Porthtawyr*   *Hendre*   ▲▢   *Tretio*   **Spite**   **Treglemais**   **Waun** **Treffynnon**
Dduallt   *Eynon*   ▲▢   **Tretio**   **Moor**   **Fawr**
Penberry   **Tretio Common**   Carn   **Abernant**
Carn Treliwyd   *Treglemaes*
PEMBROKESHIRE   **Carnhedryn**   **Treglemais**
Carn **Carn Llidi**   *Carnedd-*   **COAST**   **Llanhowel**   **Llanddinog**   **Hendre**
Hen   *Lleithr*   **NATIONAL PARK**   **Skyfog**   **House**
ST DAVID'S HEAD   **Treleddyd-**
Porthmelgan   **fawr**   B458   **Caer-Farchell**   *River Solva*   *The Celtic Trail*
Porth Lleuog   *River Alun*   **Dowrog**   **Tremaenhir**   **Paran**
4   *Whitesands Bay*   *St David's City*   ▲   **Common**

North Bishop

Porthselau

Mynyddu

Carreg   **Point St John**   **Treswny**   *Pen Rhiw*   **Middle**   **Ric**
Rhoson   **Moor**   *Bishops Palace*   **St David's**   **Mill**
Trwyn-Siôn-Owen   **Rhosson**   ℹ   **Vachelich**   **Whitchurch**
BISHOPS AND CLERKS   **St**   **Nine Wells**   **Bryngwyn**
Trwyn-drain-du   *Porthstinian*   **Justinian**   **Llandruidion**   **Prendergast**
Carnysgubor   *The Belfry*   *Caerfai*   **Morfa Common**   **Solva**   A487
Ramsey   *Bay*   ▲▢   **Upper**   **Lower**   PH
Aber Mawr   *Sound*   **Llandruidion**   **Solva**   **Solva**   *Pointz*
RSPB   **Carn ar Wig**   *Porthlysgi Bay*   **Morfa Common**   *Cambrian*   **Castle**
Daufraich   *Aberfelin*   **Treginnis**   *St Non's*   *Inn*   *Pembrokeshire Coast Path*
RAMSEY   *Bay*   *Caer Bwdy Bay*   *Aber-west*
ISLAND   **Carnllundain**   *Porth Clais*   **Green Scar**   **Dinas Fawr**   *Pwll*
Penrhyn Twll   *Porthlysgi Bay*   *March*
South Bishop/   **Trwynmynachdy**   **Carreg Frân**   **Dinas Fach**
Em-sger   *Pembrokeshire Coast Path*

Meini-Duon

Newgale Sar

Maidenhall F

20

Rickets H

ST BRIDES BAY

6

A · 70 · B · C · 80 · D

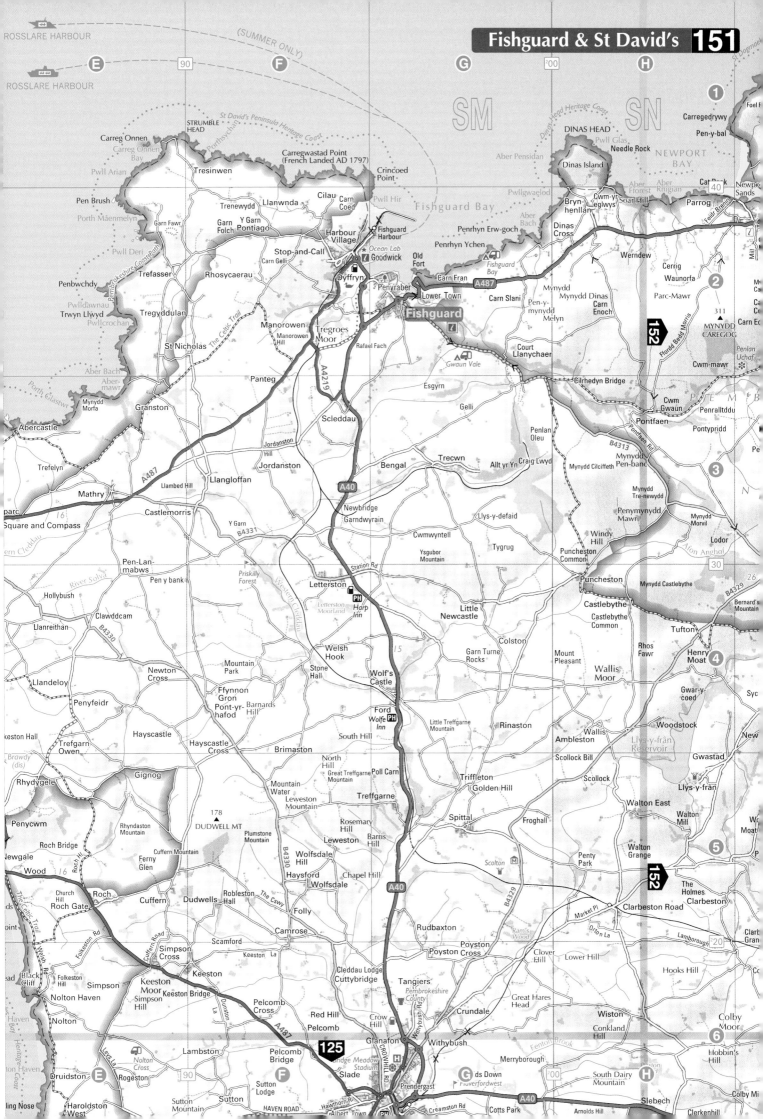

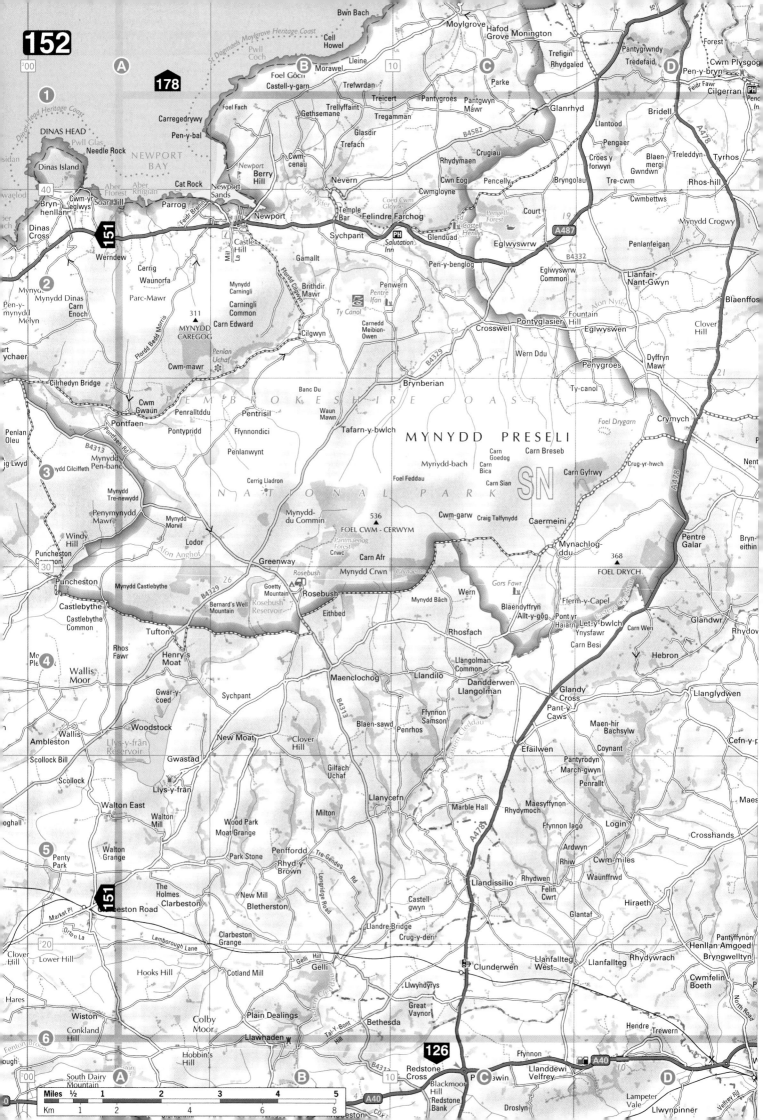

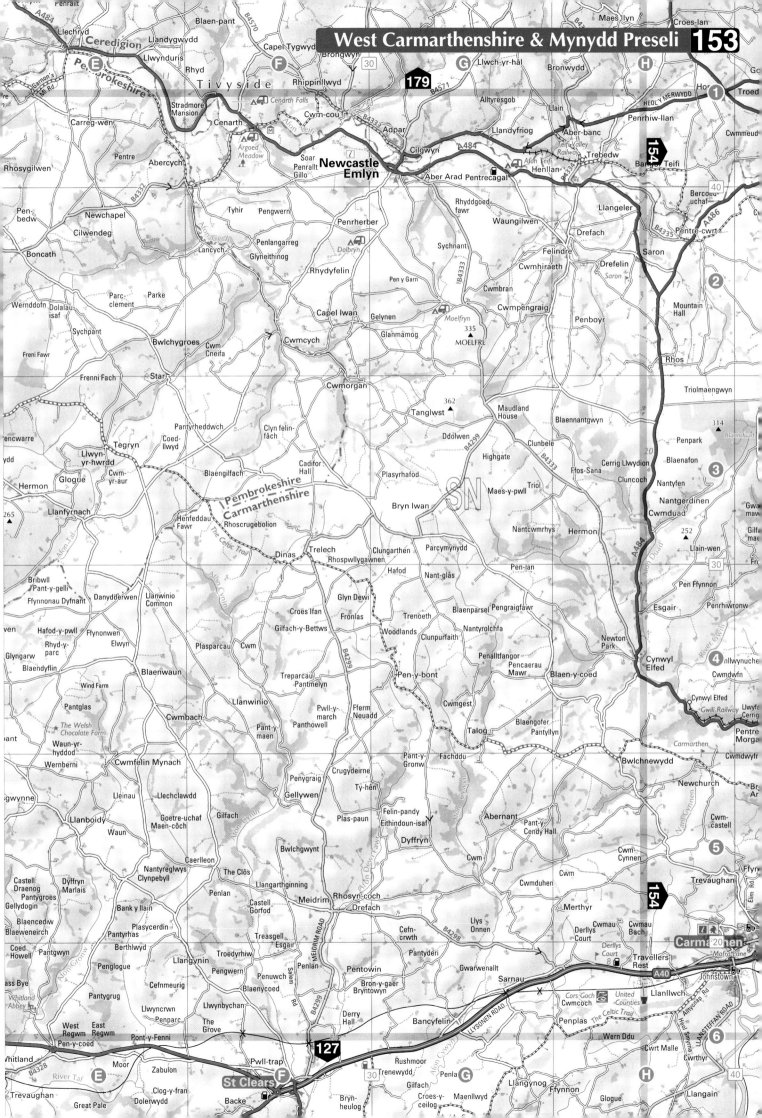

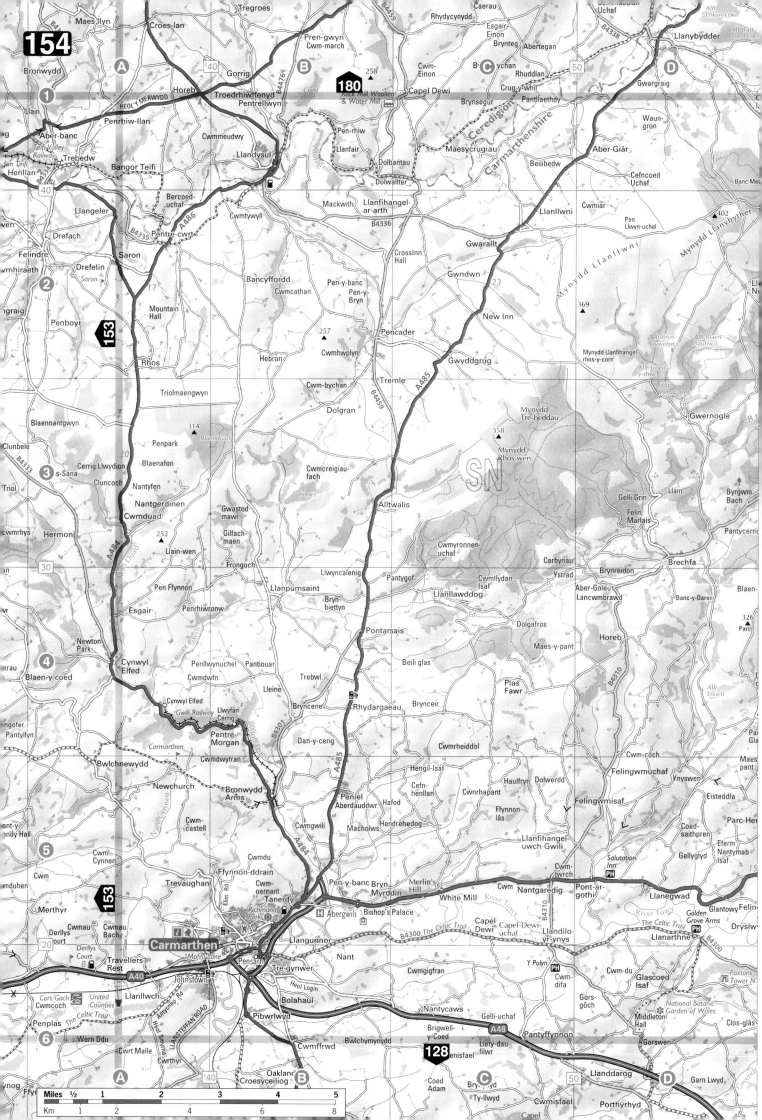

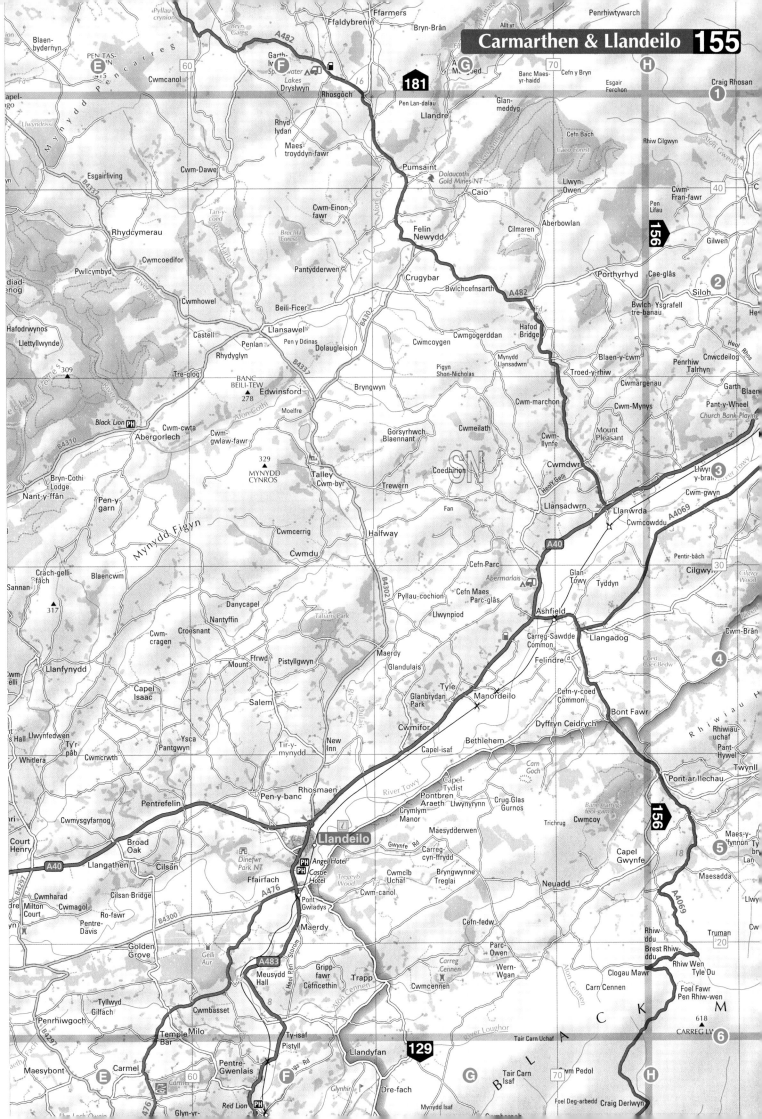

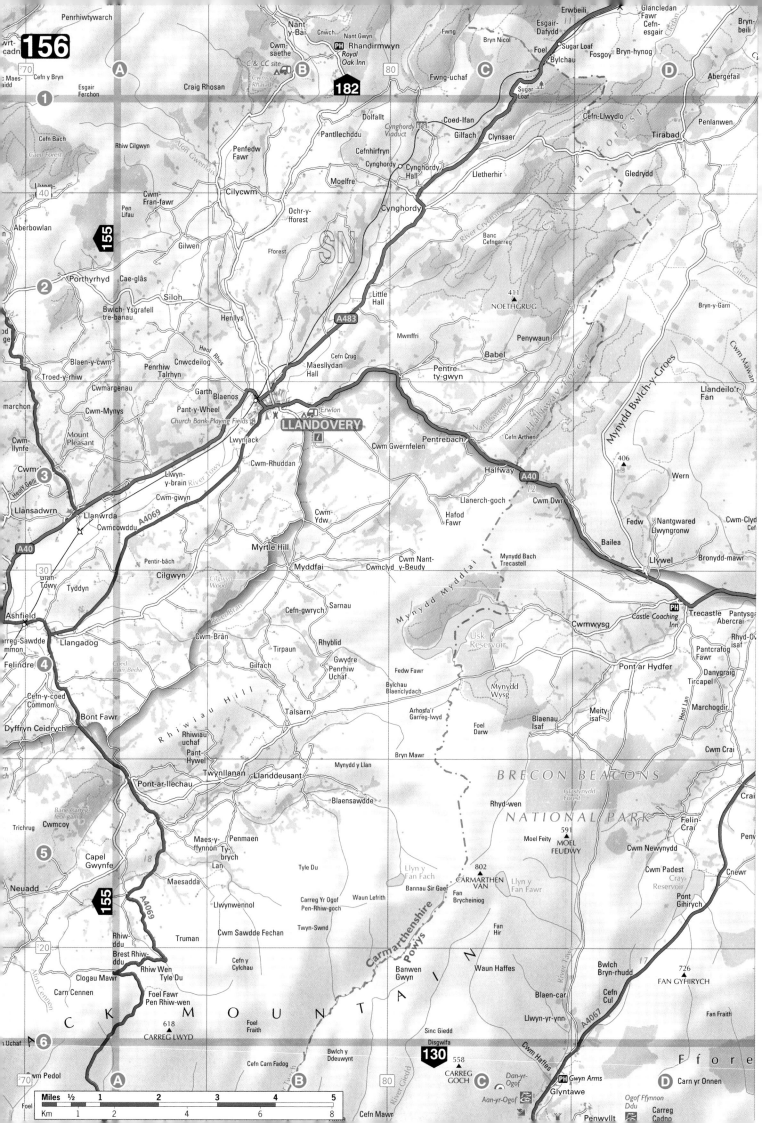

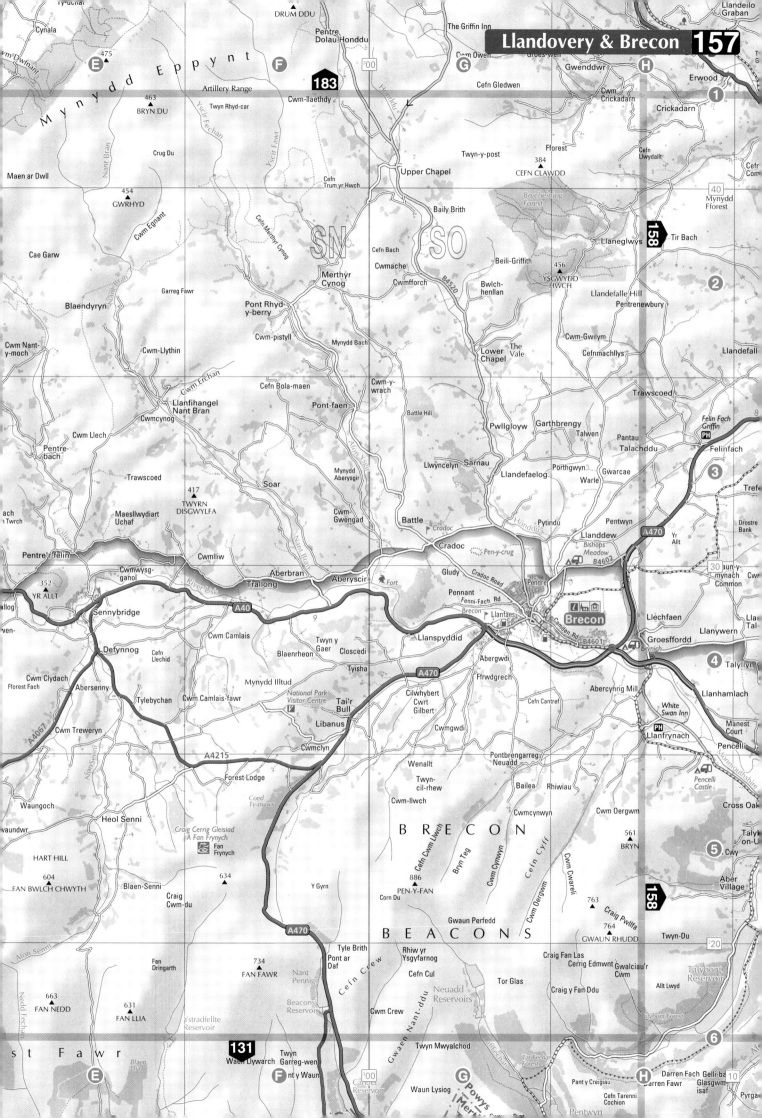

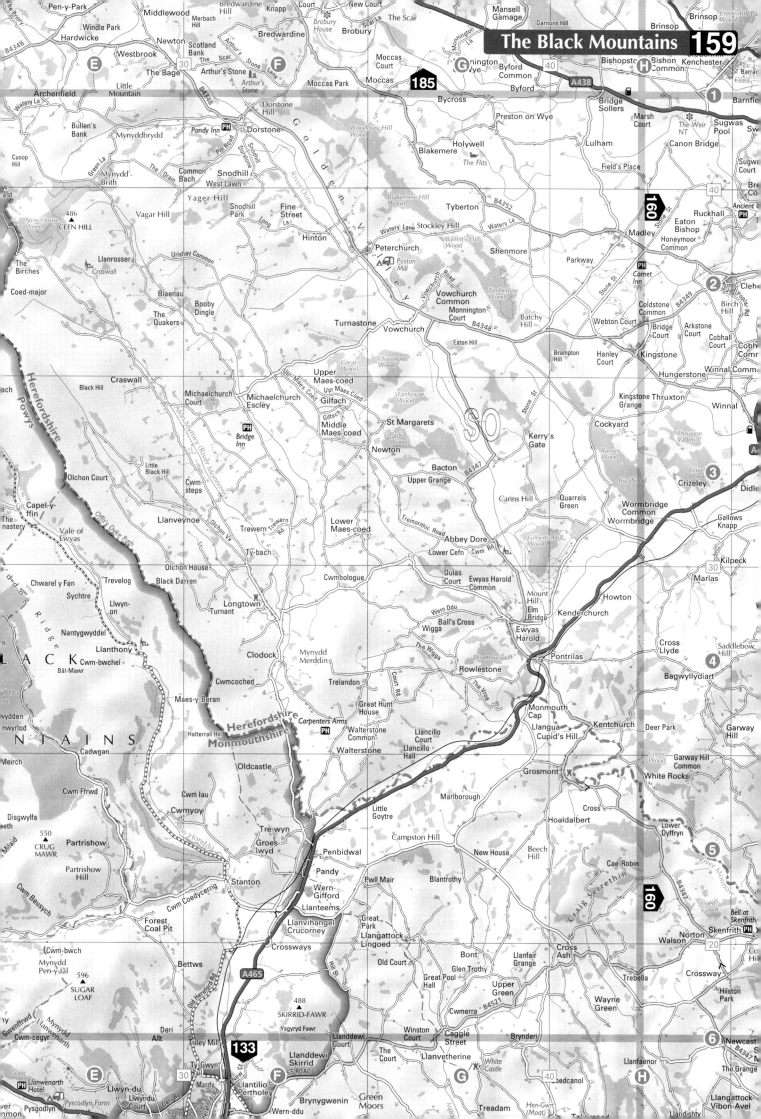

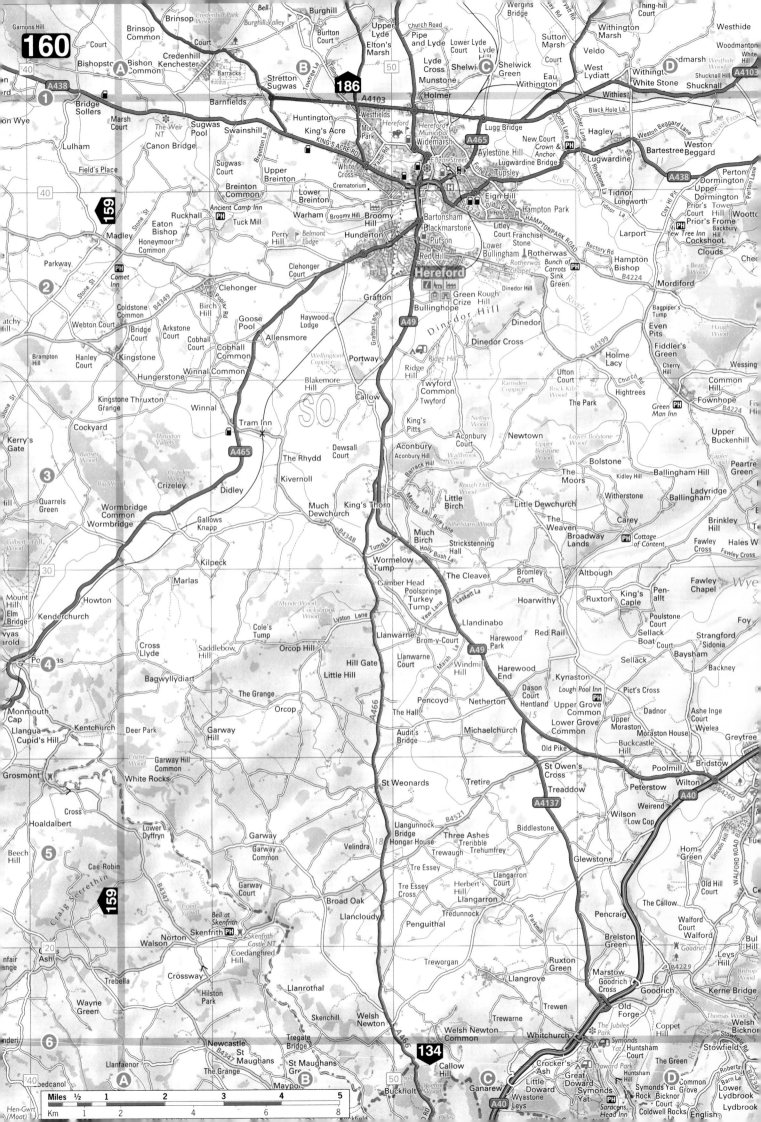

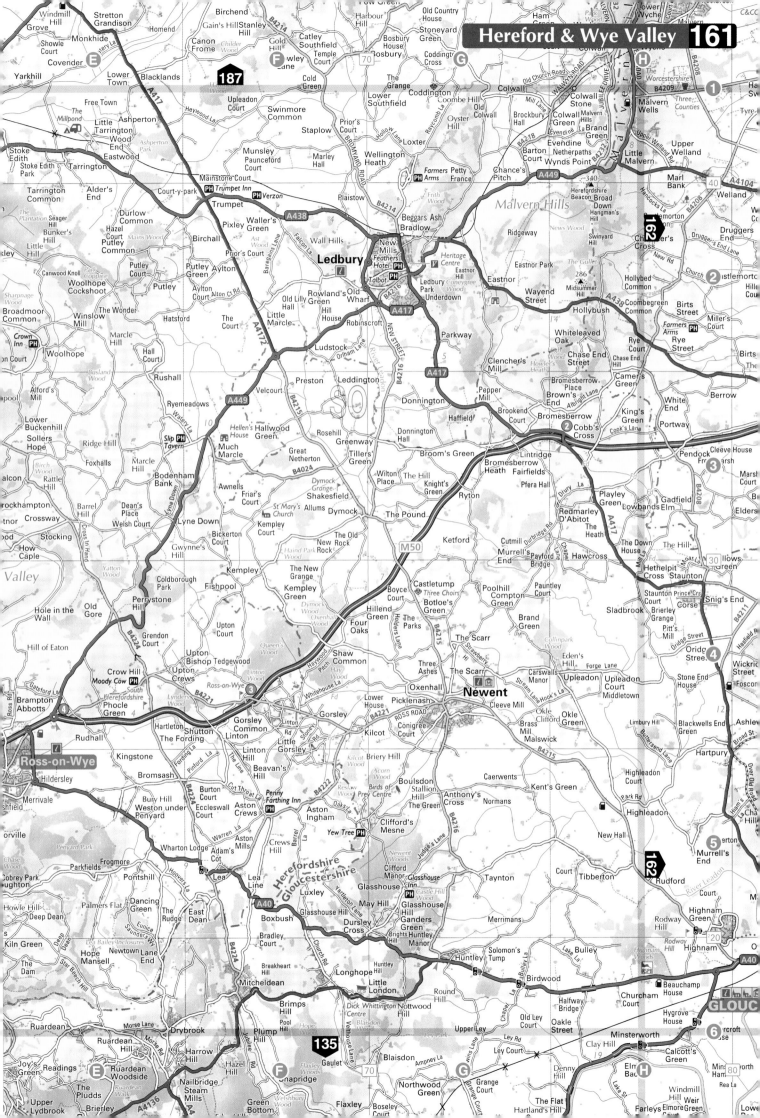

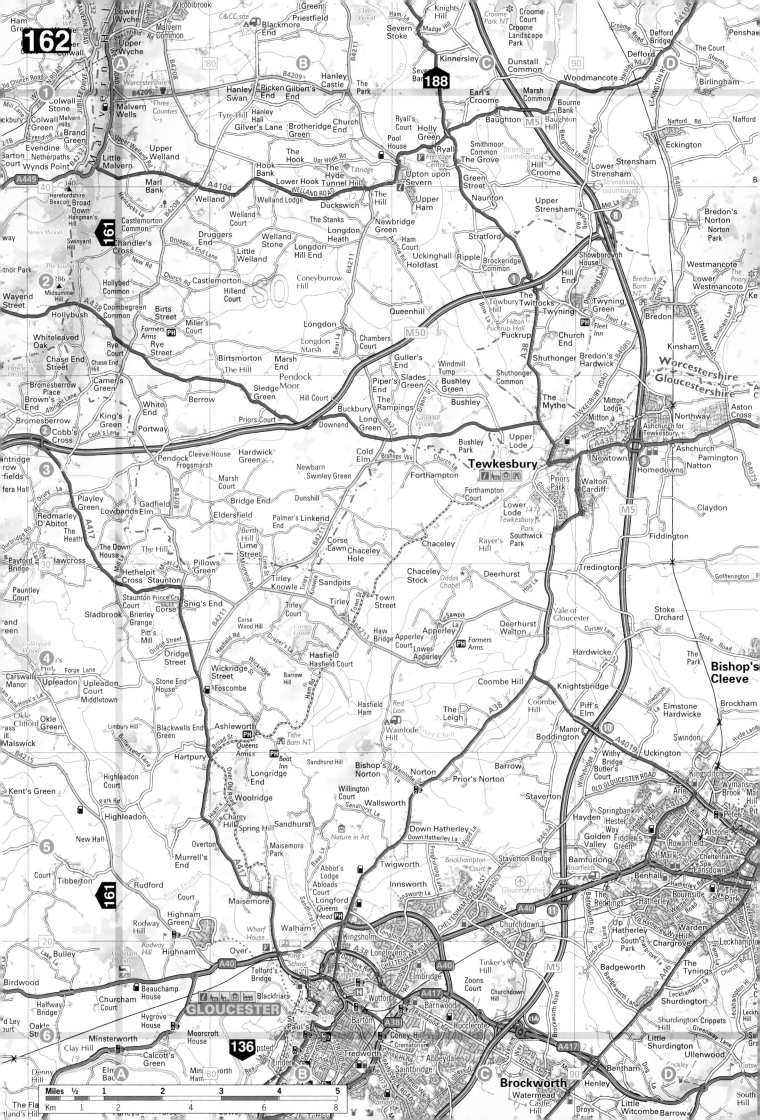

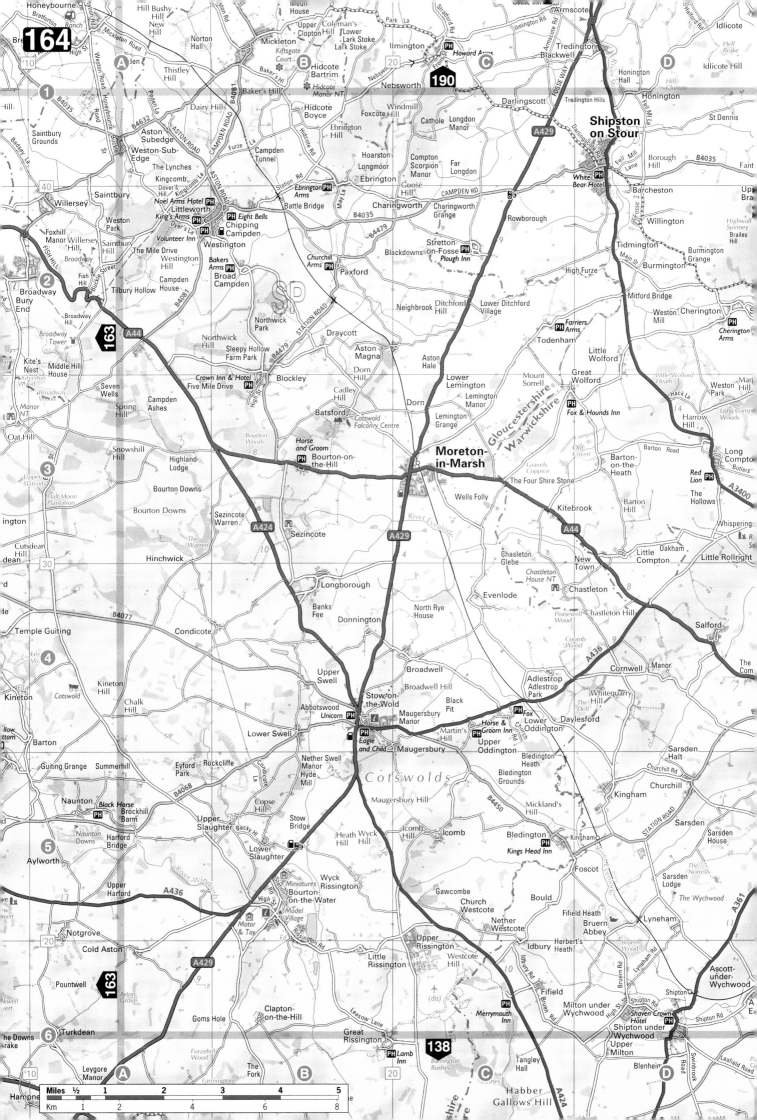

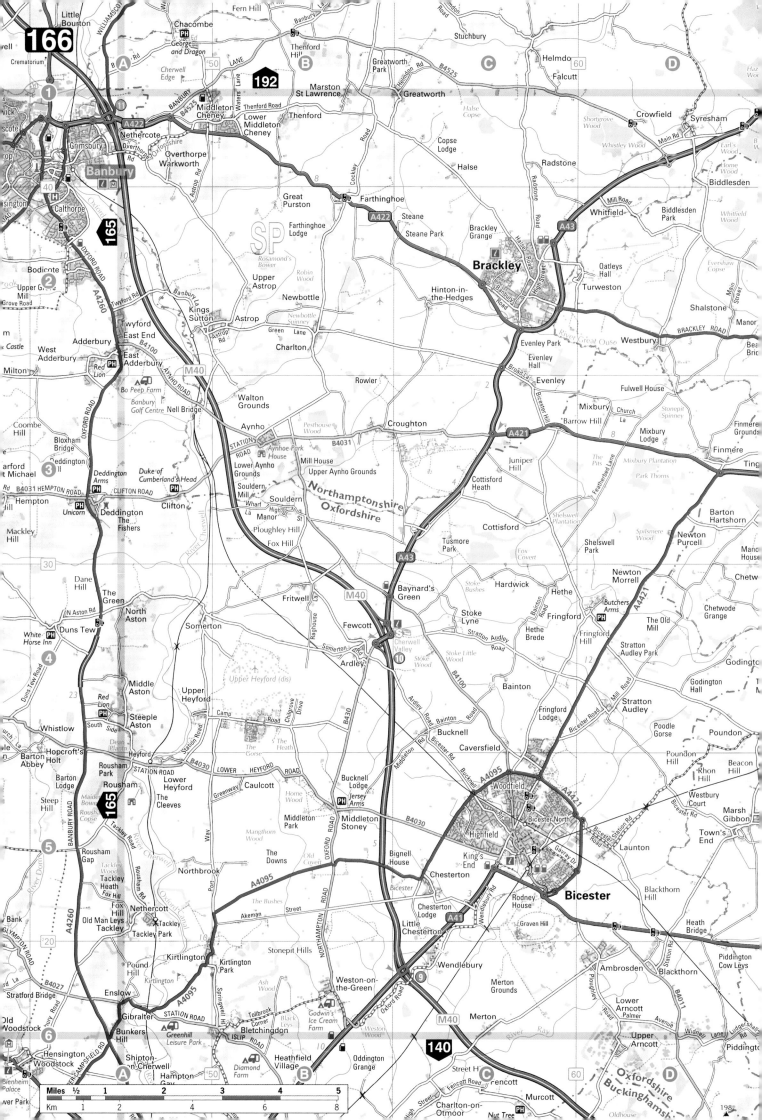

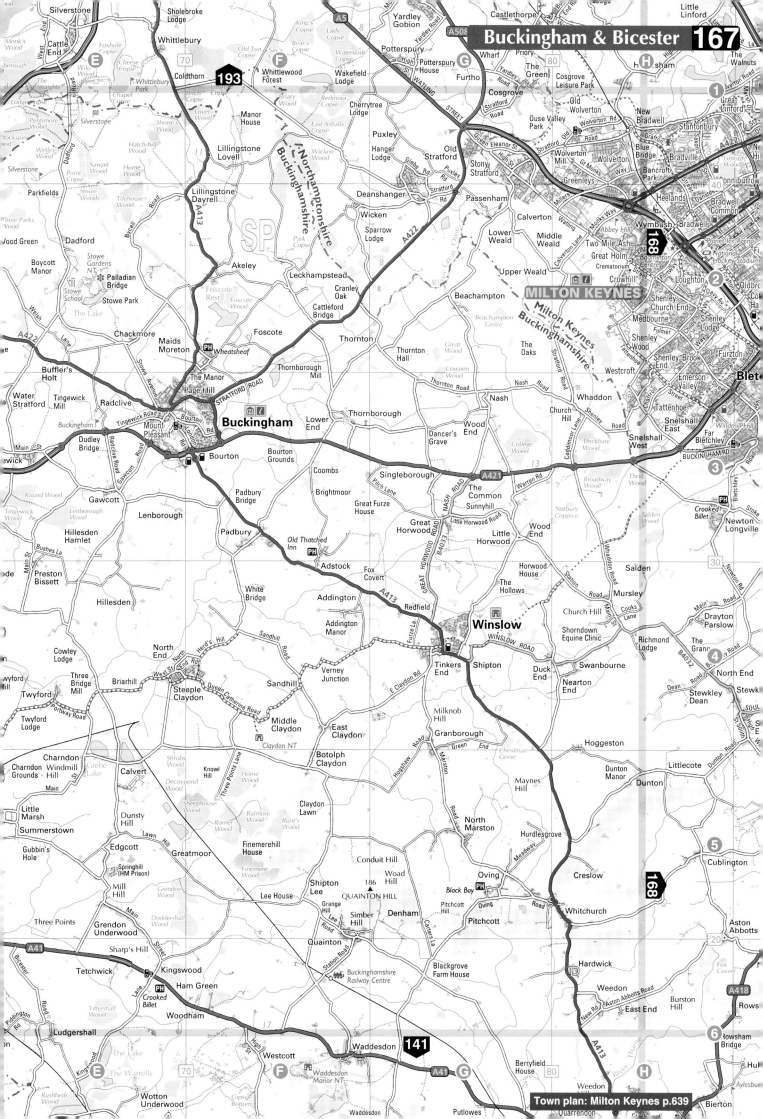

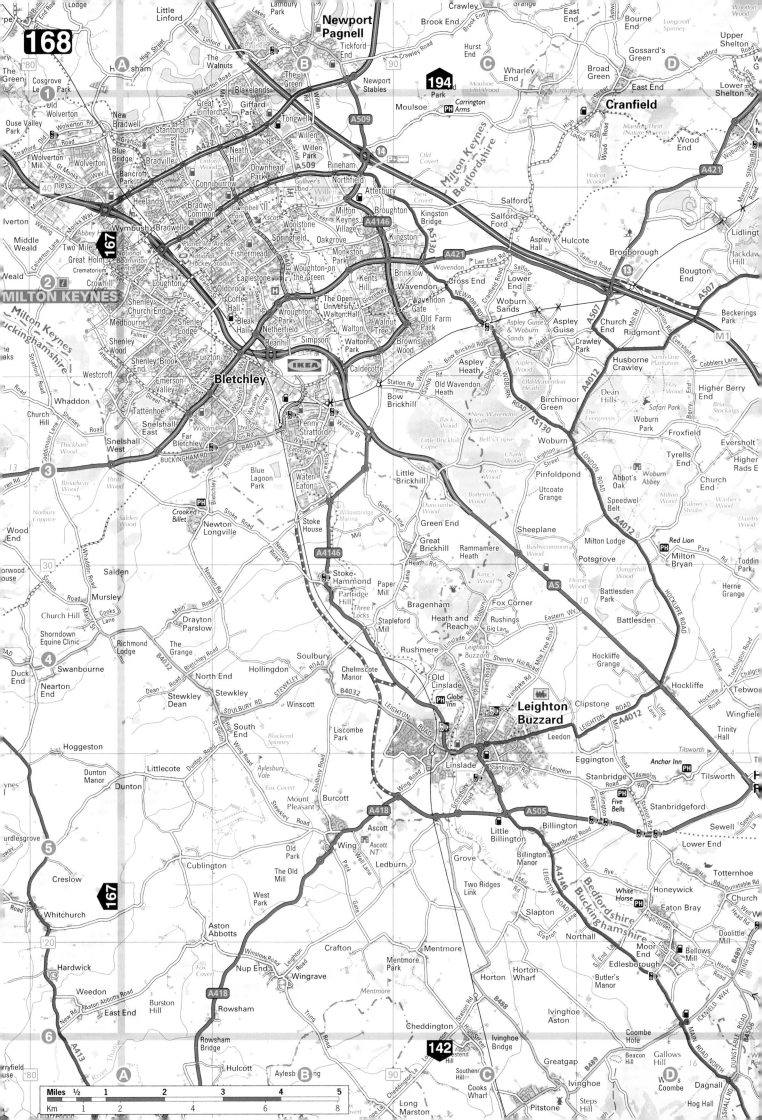

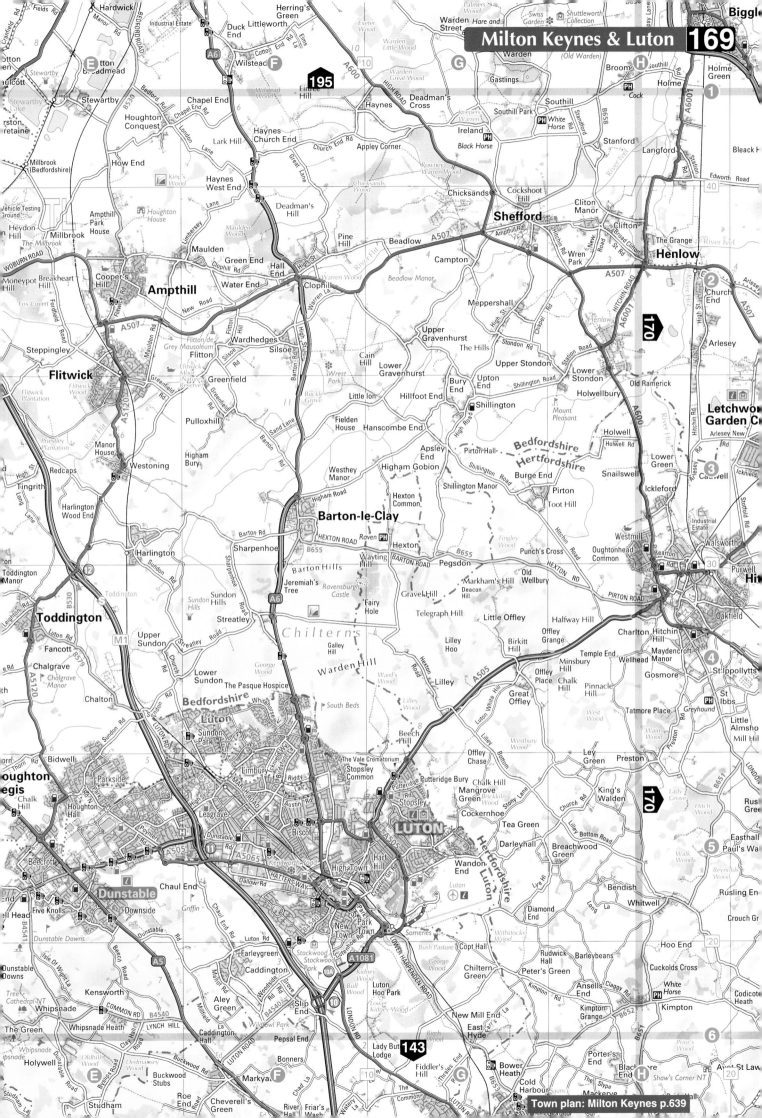

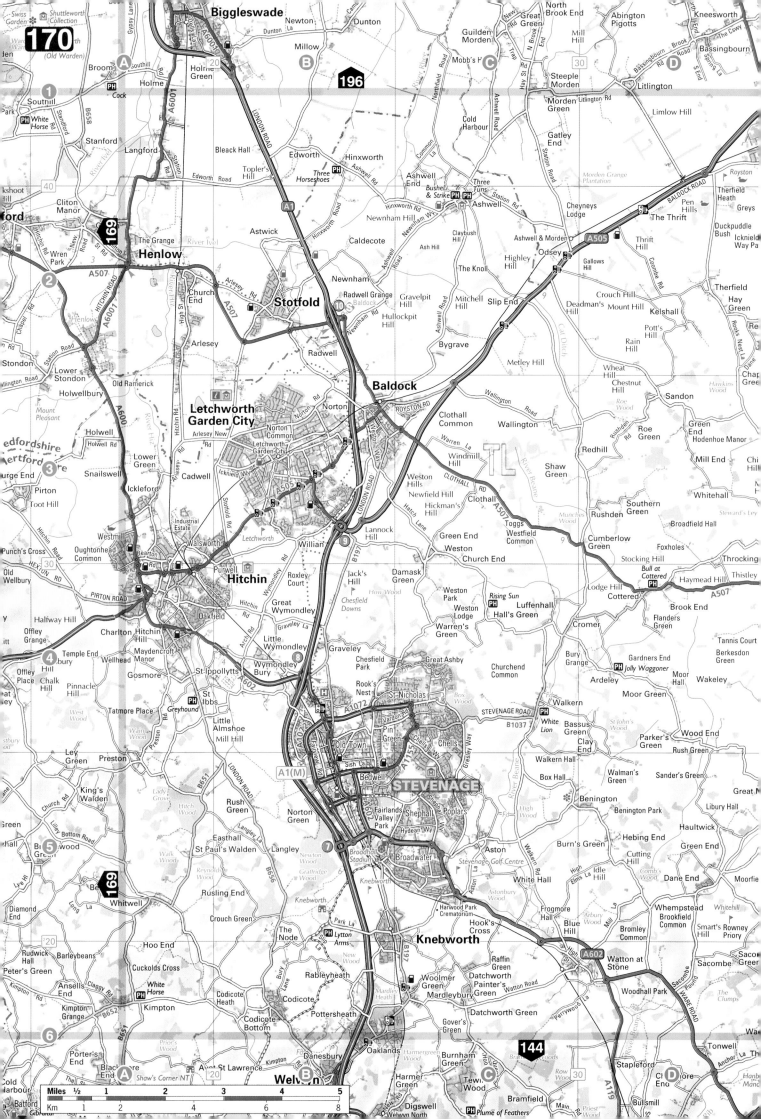

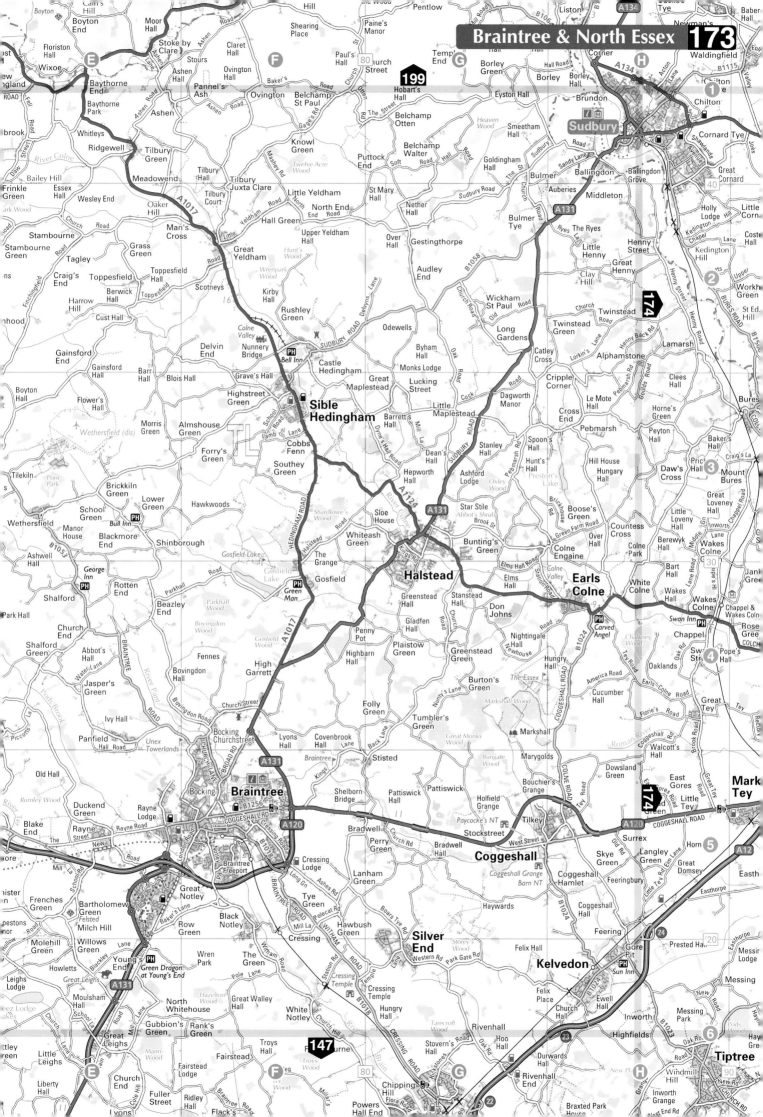

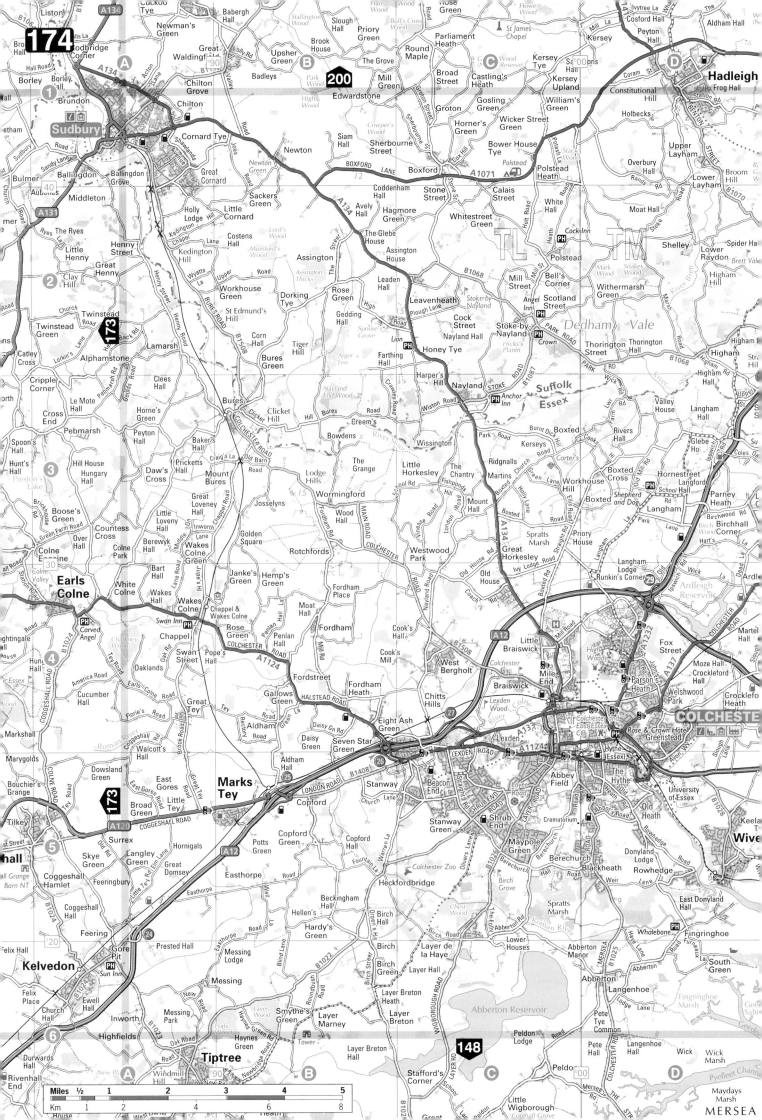

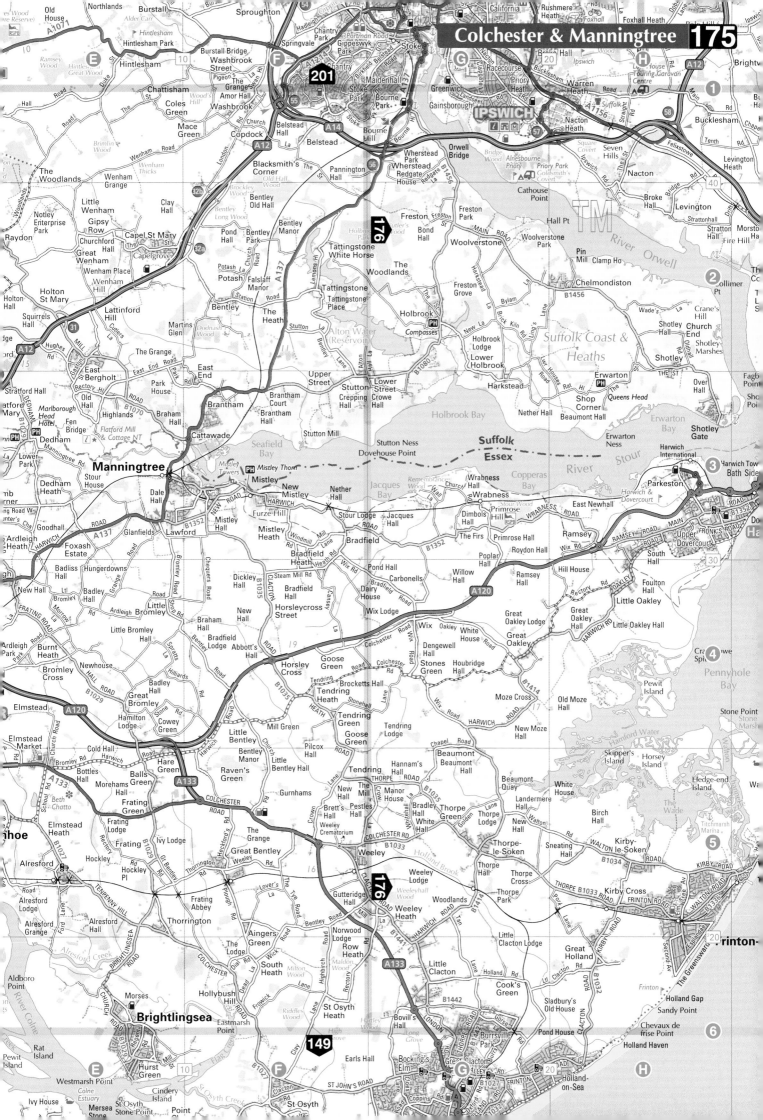

Stonner
Point
Pettistree
Hall
Street
Hollesley   Road
Box Hall
(HM Young
Offender
Institution)
Oxford
E
Ipswich
Road
Brightwell
Newbourne
White
Hall
Mill Rd
Newbourne Rd
Shottisham
The
Lodge
Shottisham
Lodge
Bushy
Lane
Oxley
Marshes
North Weir Point
G
40
H
202
1
Bucklesham
Hall
Hemley
Hall
30
Shottisham
Hall
WOODBRIDGE
F
Alderton
Rd
Shingle
Street
Kembroke
Hall
Chapel Rd
Kirton Lodge
Ramshott
Lodge
ROAD
B1083
HOLLESLEY BAY
40
ington
ath
7
Nursery
Wood
Ramsholt
Alderton
Suffolk Coastal Trimley Rd
Manor
Ho
Park Lane
Kirton Lodge
Peyton
Hall
Alderton
House
The
Grove
Bawdsey
40
Morston
Hall
e Hill
Innocence
Lane
A14
Kirton
Falkenham
Sink
Falkenham
Lower
Falkenham
Bawdsey
Hall
East La
Suffolk Heritage Coast
2
Thorpe
Common
59
Back Rd
Back La
Trimley
St Martin
Capel
Hall La
THE STREET
Road
Bawdsey Manor
Trimley
Lower
Street
Grimston Lane
High Rd
Grimston
Hall
Trimley
St Mary
Capel
Hall
Gulpher
Felixstowe
Ferry
Ferry
Woodbridge
Haven
Trimley
Marshes
A154
Road
PORT OF
Walton
Colneis Rd
Old
Felixstowe
Felixstowe
Ferry
Clickett
Hill
61
FELIXSTOWE RD
High
High Rd E
Fagbury
Point
Peewit
Felixstowe *i*
3
Shotley
Point
A154
The Port of
Felixstowe
Sea Rd
TM
Harwich
Harbour
Tower Hill
Landguard Fort
M
The
Redoubt
ch Town
ath Side
Landguard
Point
B1352
ROAD
Harwich *i*
Dovercourt
hole
y
HOEK VAN HOLLAND
4
e Point
Stone
Marsh
HOEK VAN HOLLAND
ESBJERG
Walton
Hall
Hall Lane
5
**Walton on
the Naze**

Harwich International Port

River Stour
0 ½ mile
0 1 km
HARWICH
INTERNATIONAL PORT STATION
(PASSENGER FERRY TERMINAL)
CAR FERRY
TERMINAL
P
P
EAST DOCK RD
INTERNATIONAL
FREIGHT
ENTRANCE
P
WEST DOCK RD
PETROL
STATION
Parkeston
i
A120
PATRICKS
JUNCTION
HARWICH
A120
20
PARKESTON
ROUNDABOUT
ST NICHOLAS
ROUNDABOUT
PARKESTON ROAD
Premier
Travel Inn
IPSWICH COLCHESTER
A120
DOVERCOURT BYPASS
MAIN ROAD
B1352
MAIN ROAD
B1414
FRONKS ROAD
B1352
6
LBM

nton-on-Sea

E
30
F
G
40
H

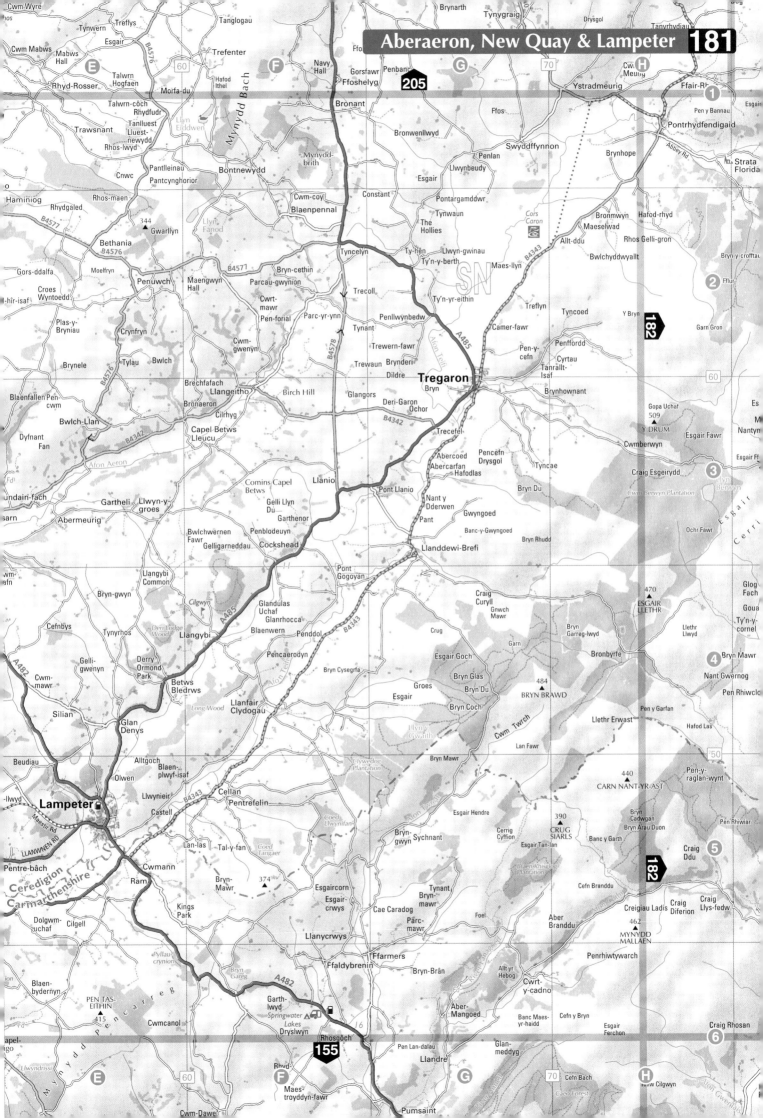

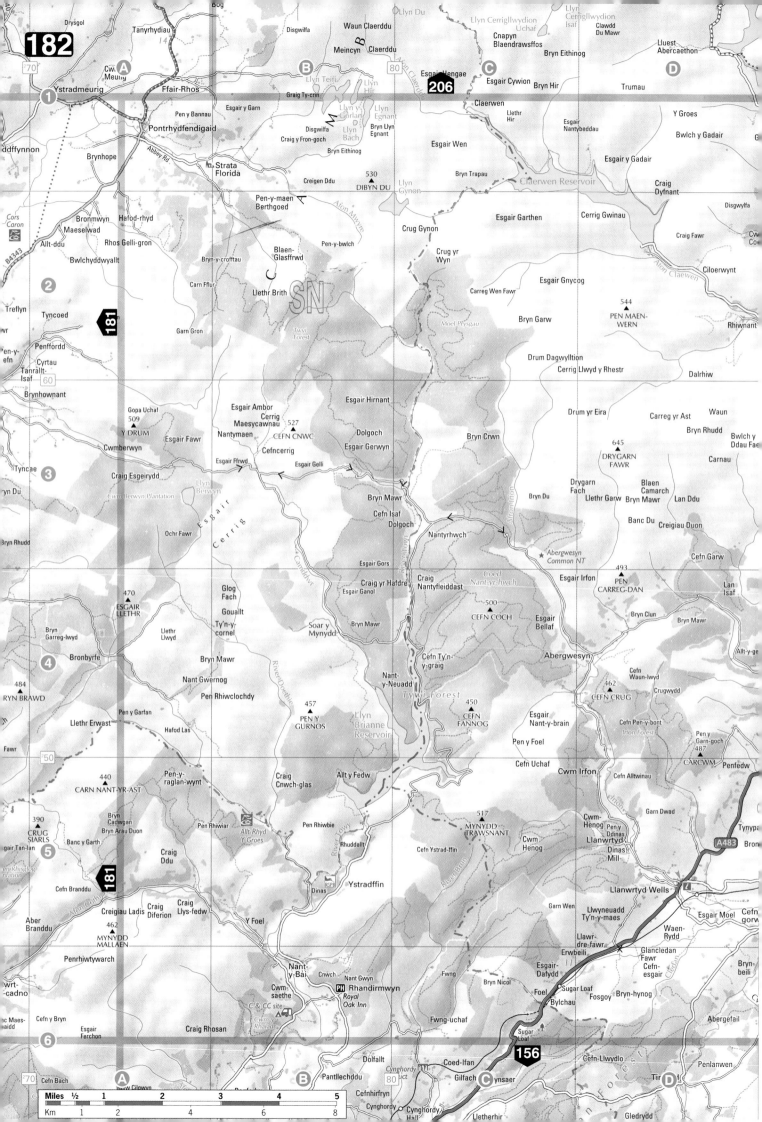

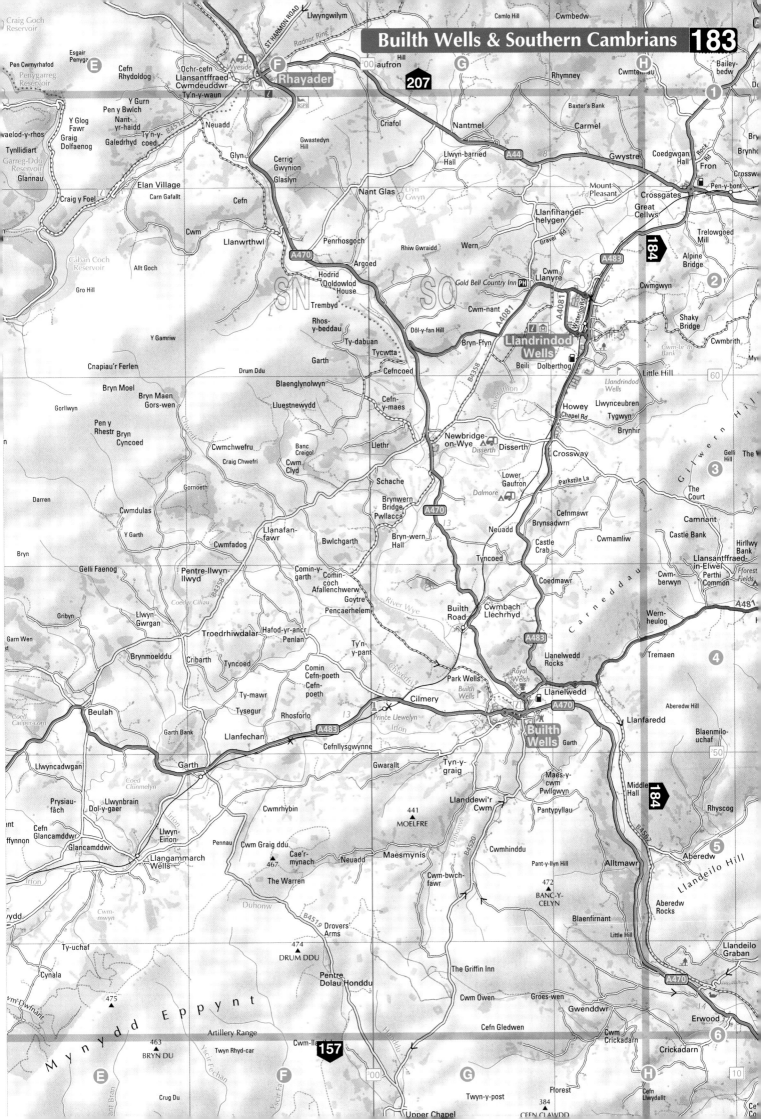

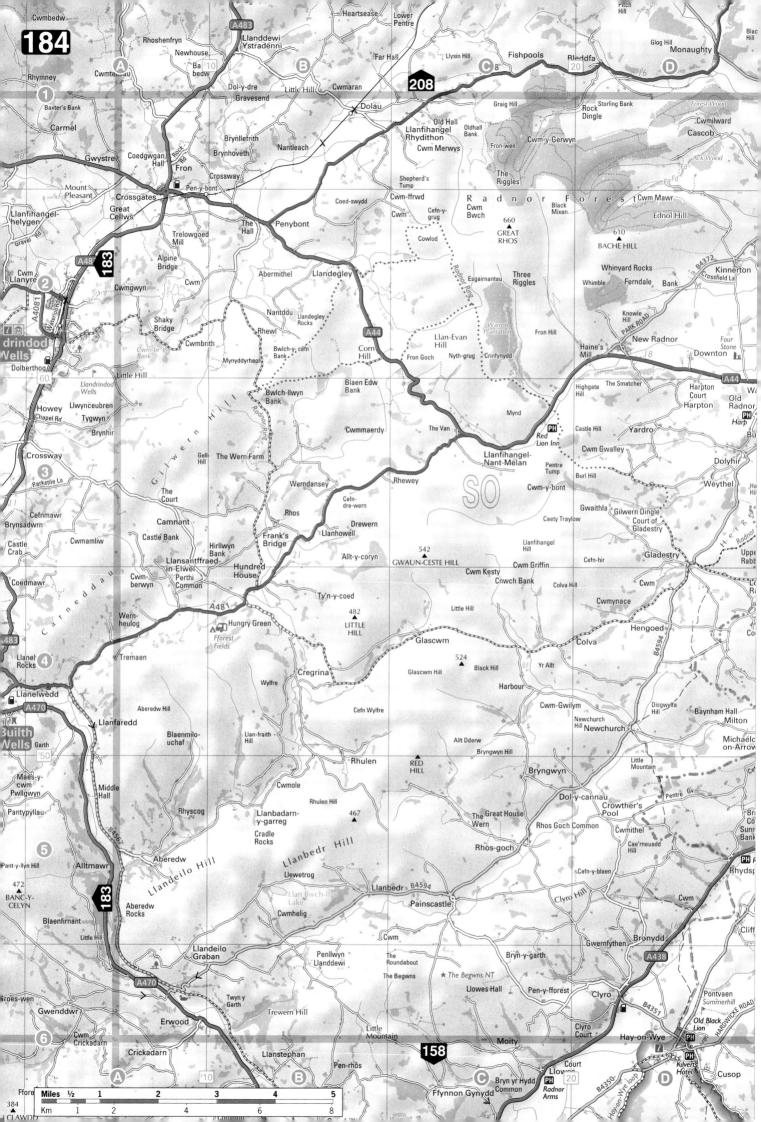

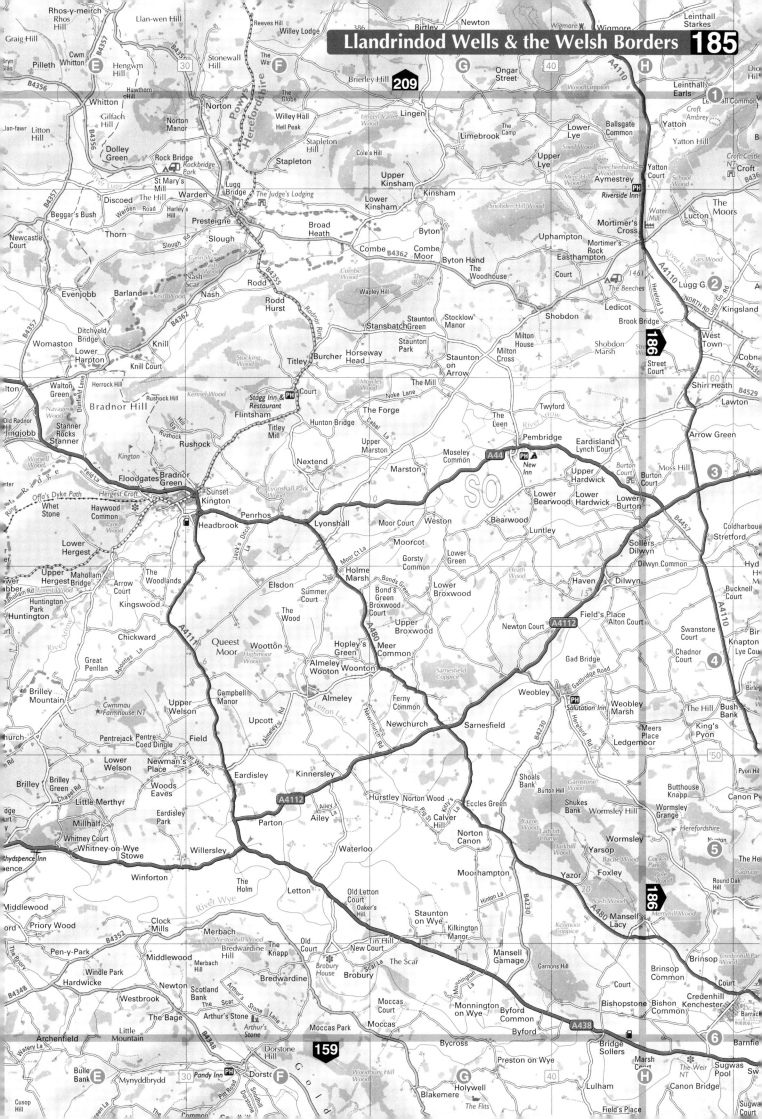

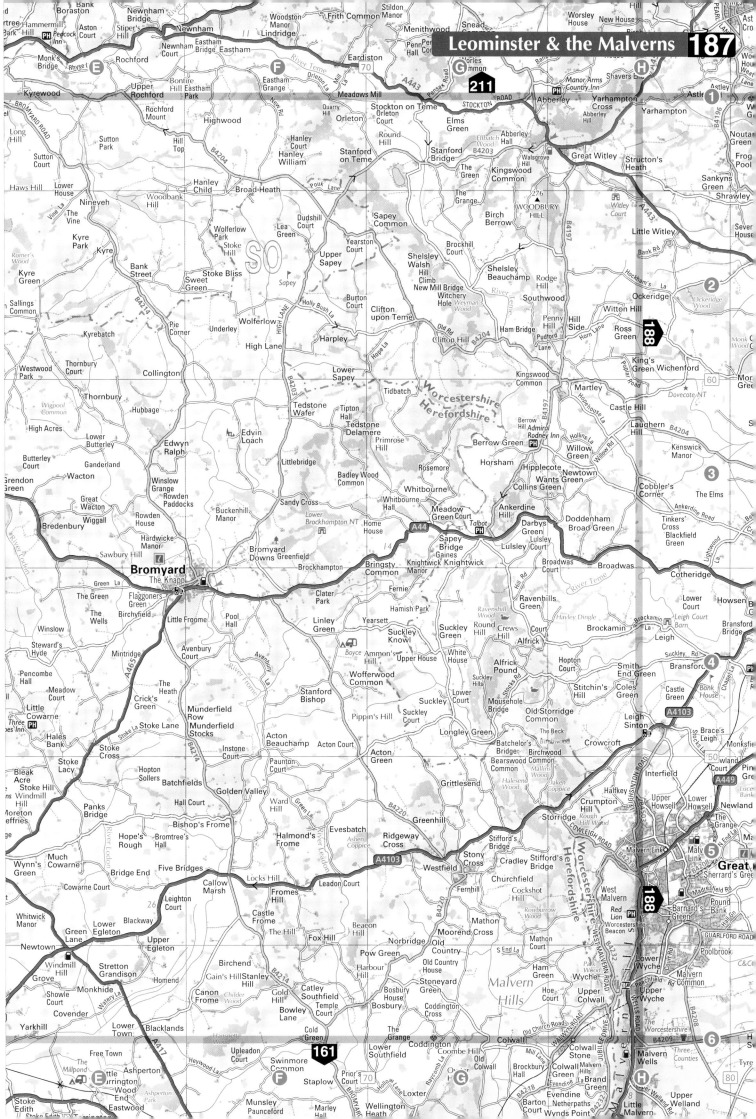

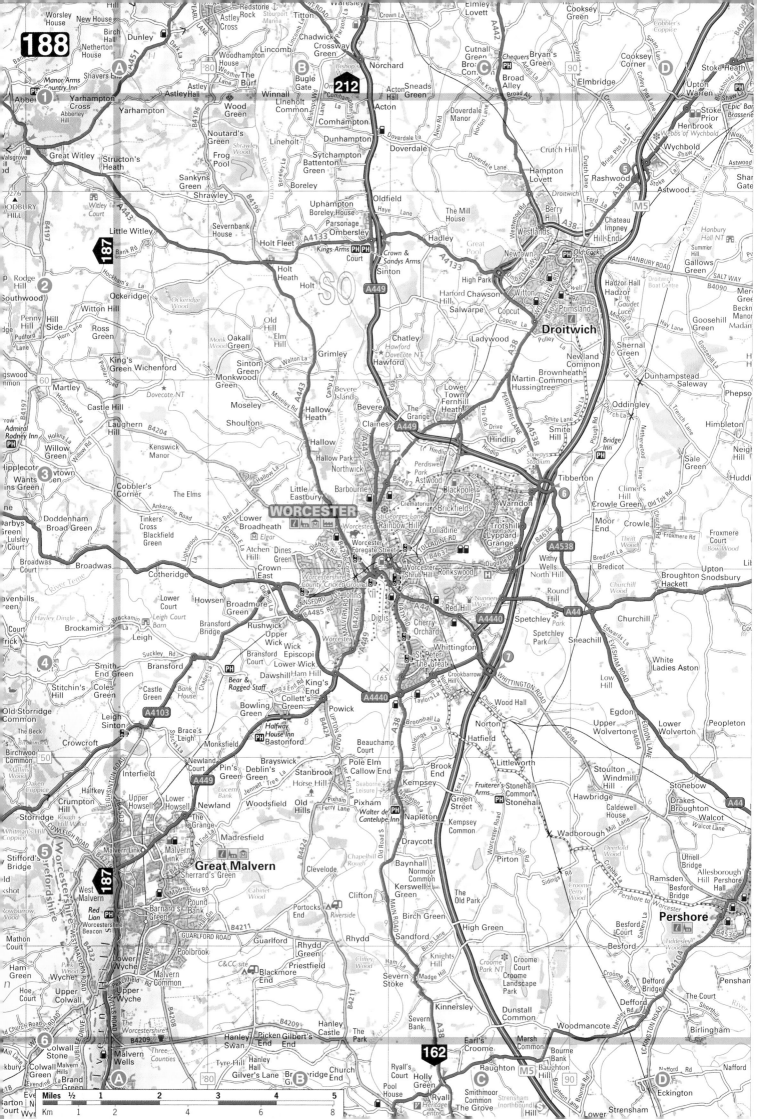

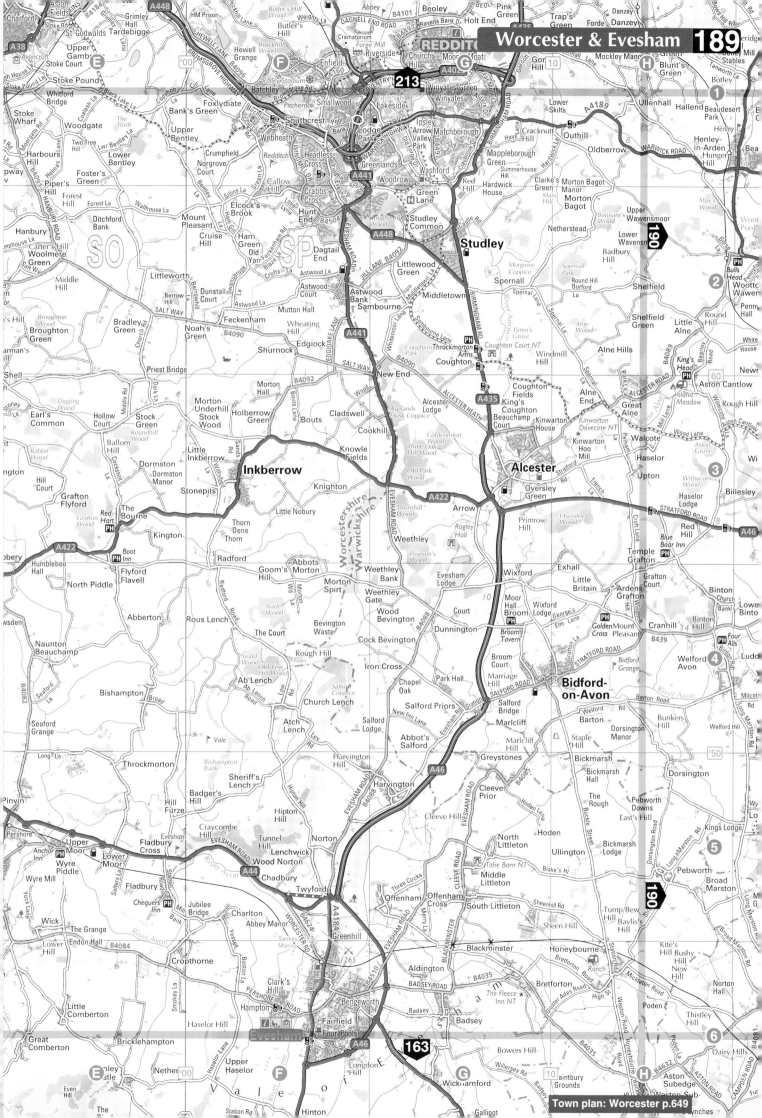

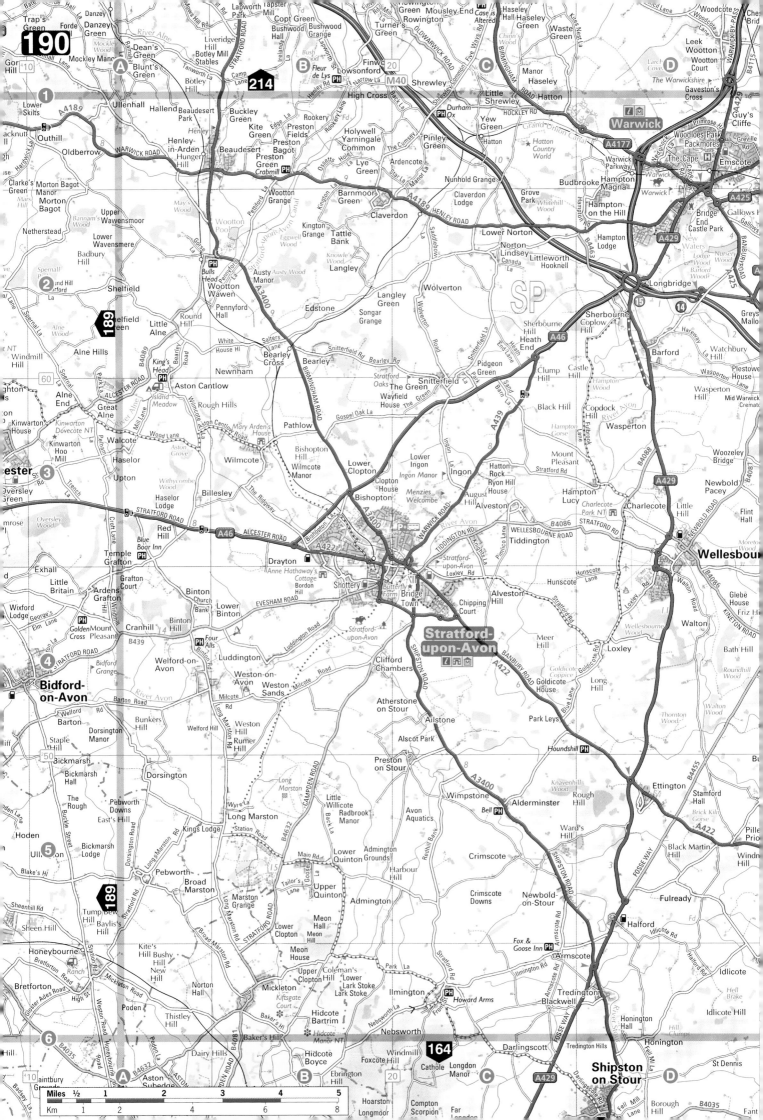

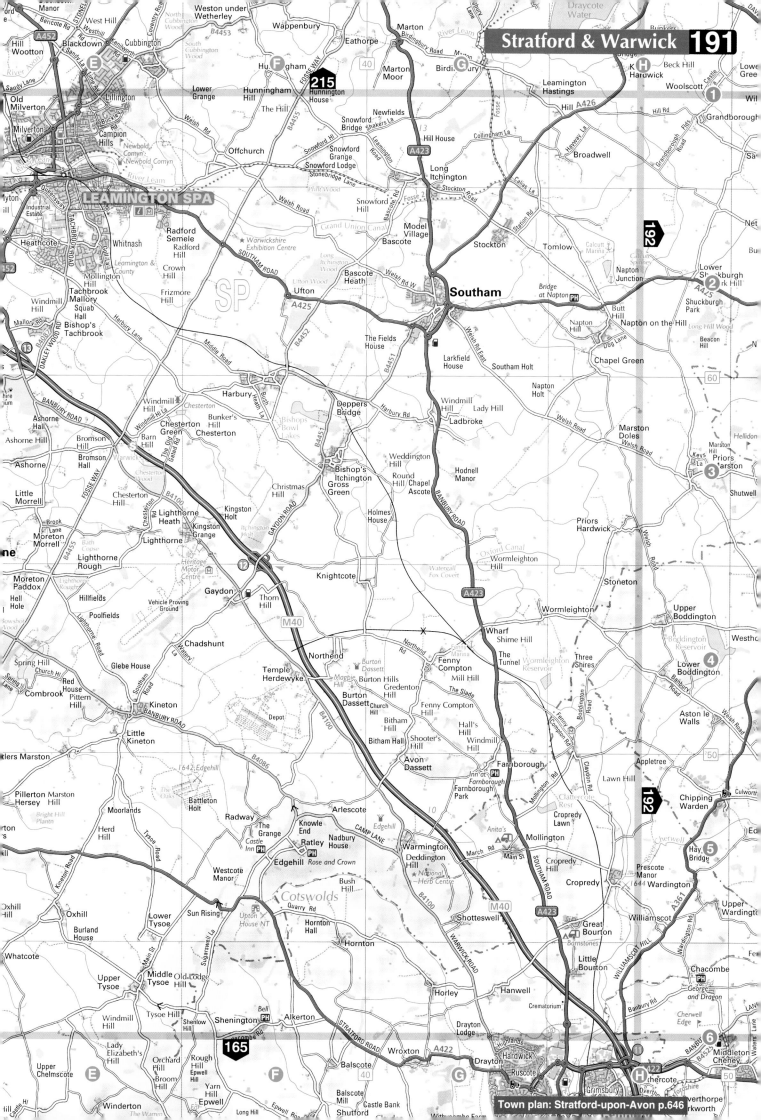

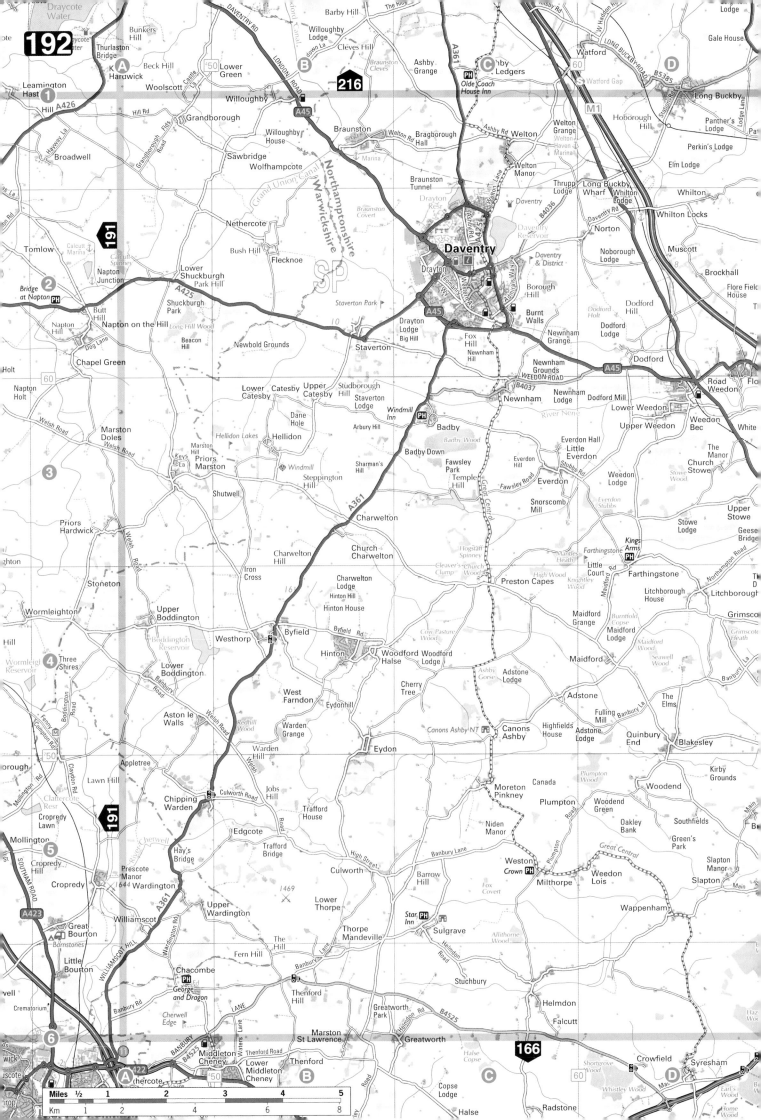

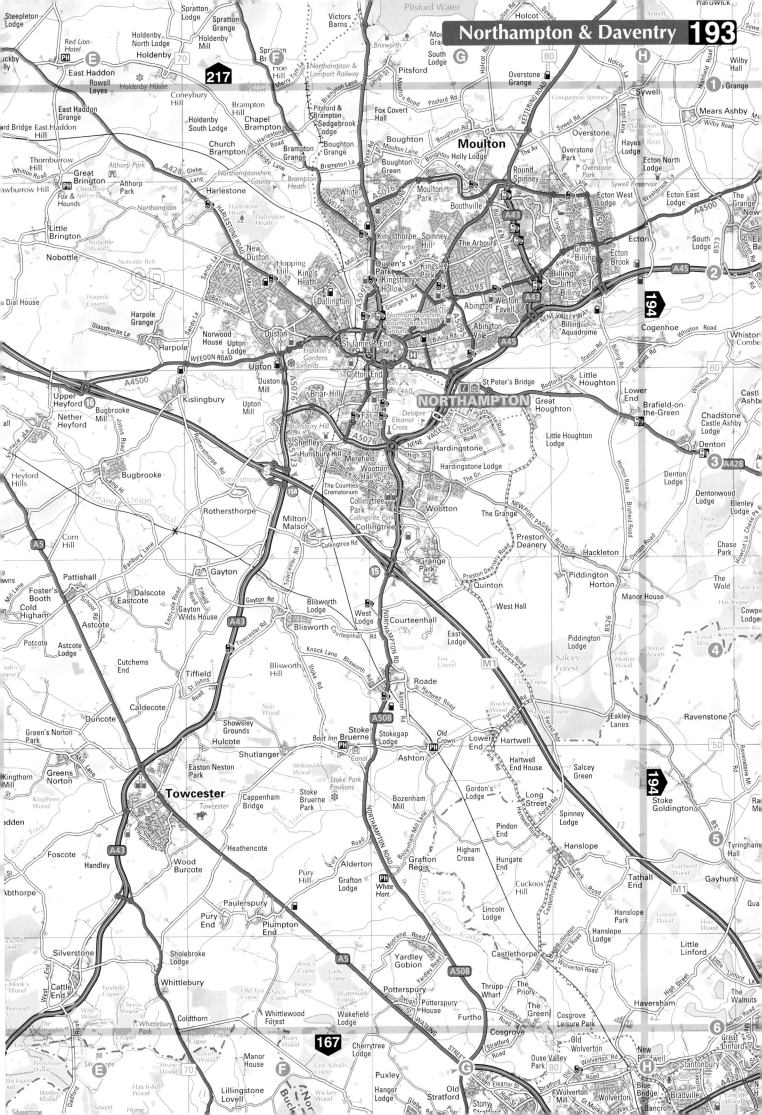

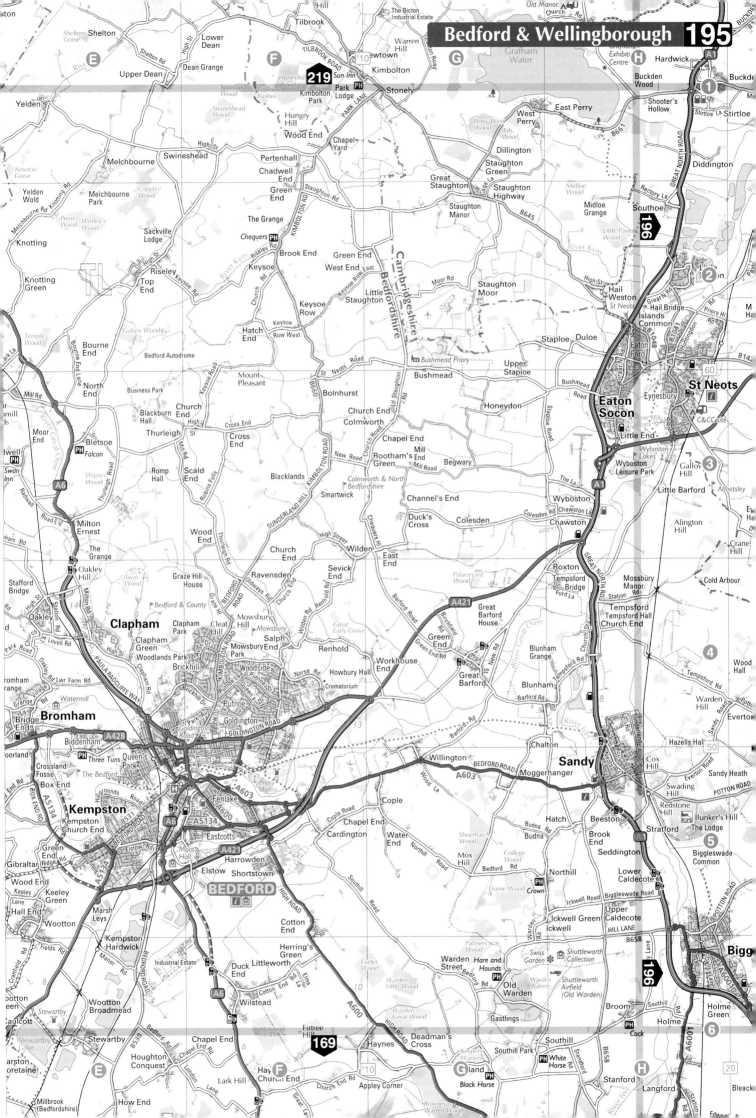

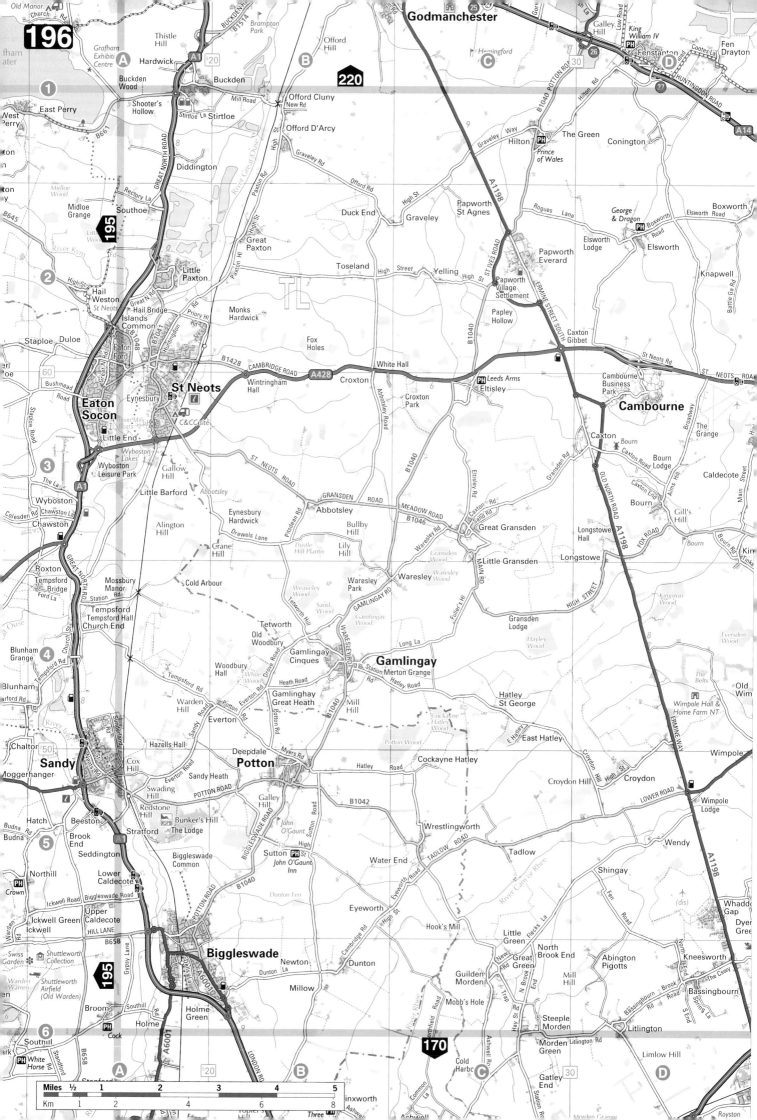

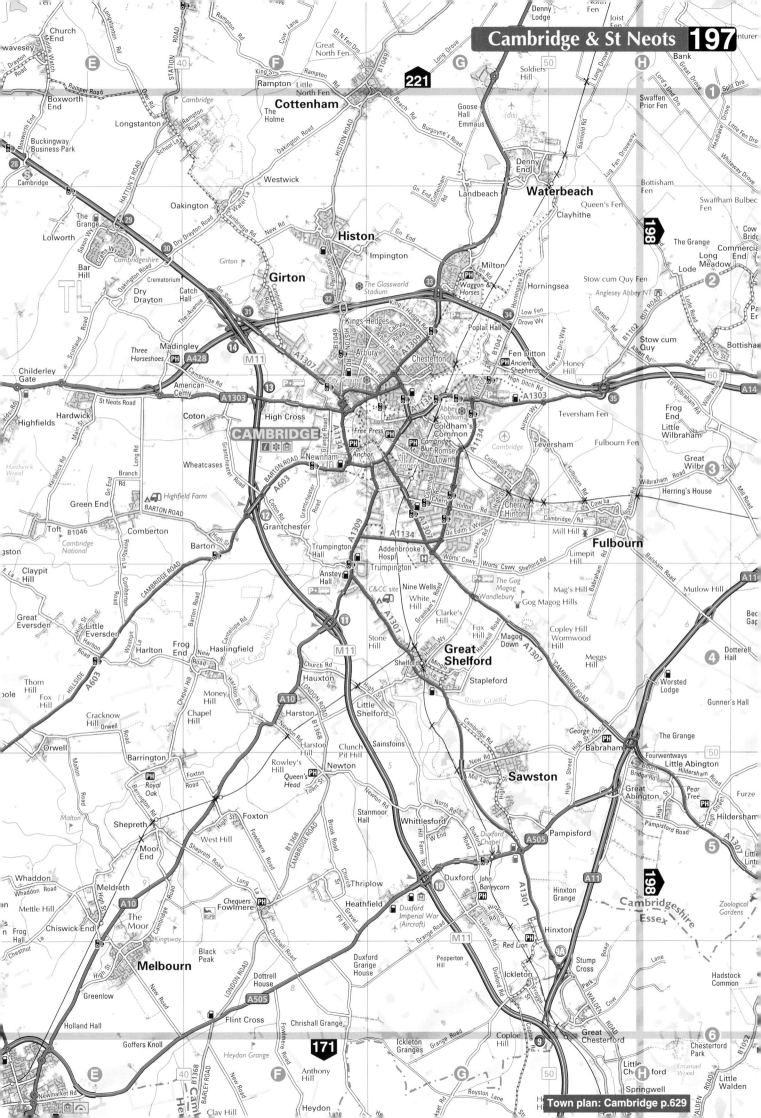

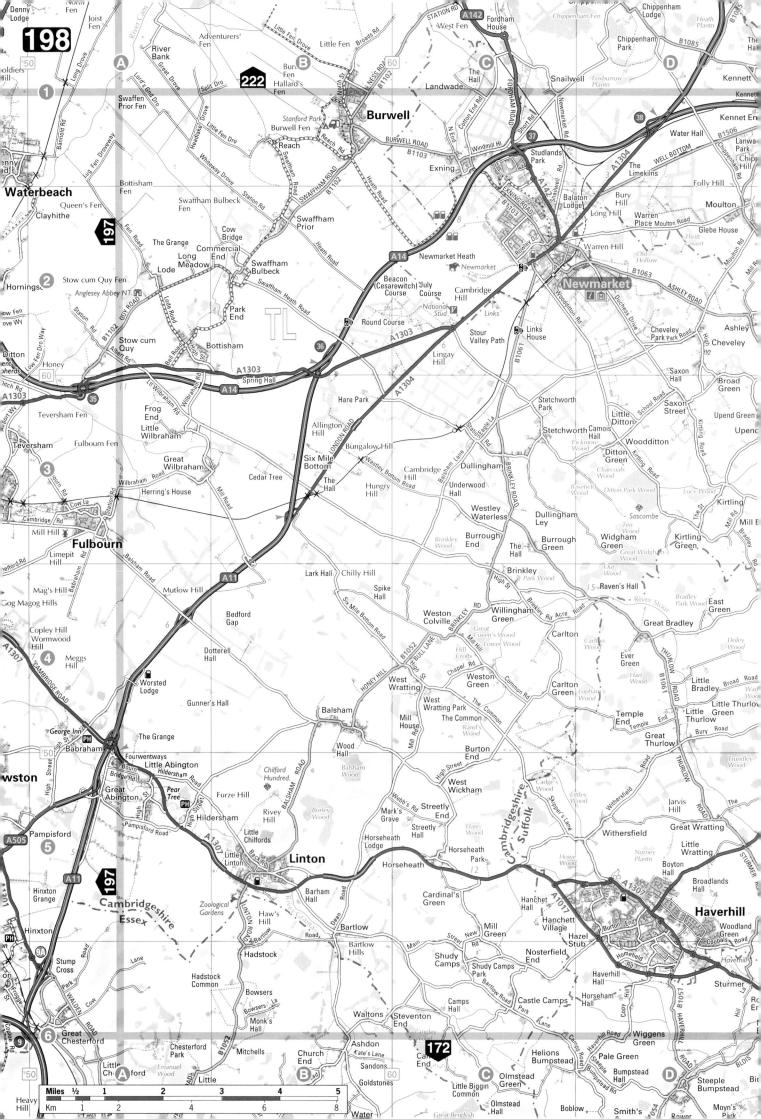

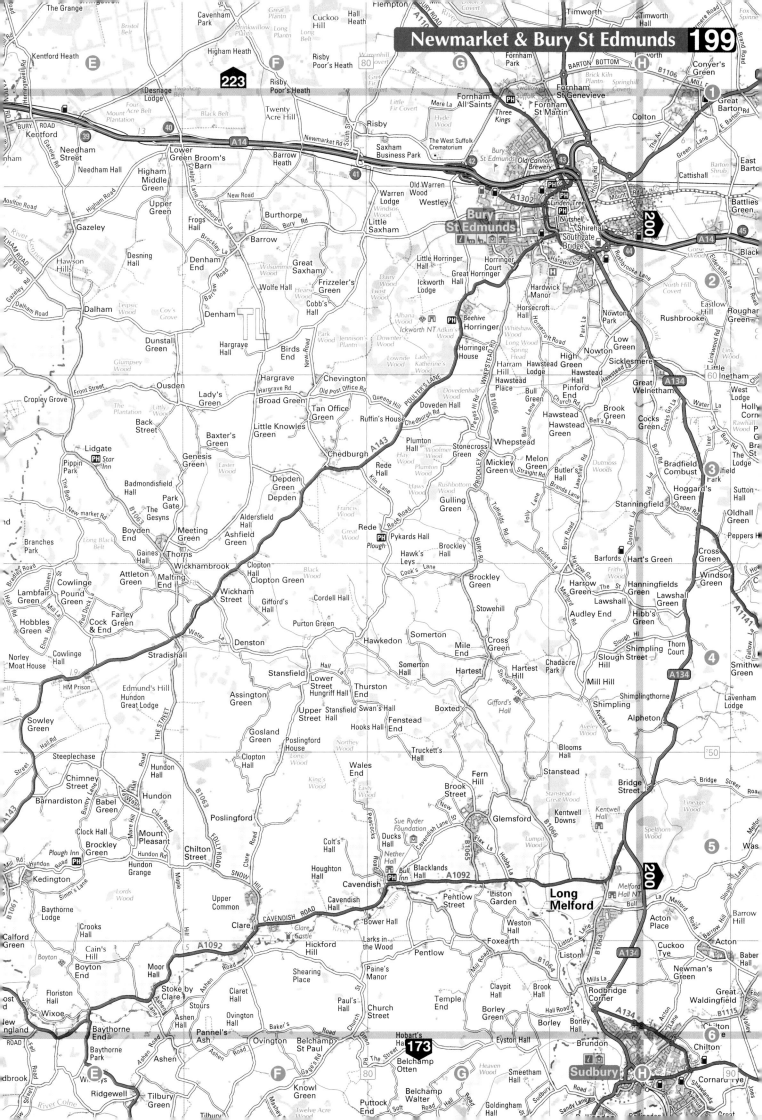

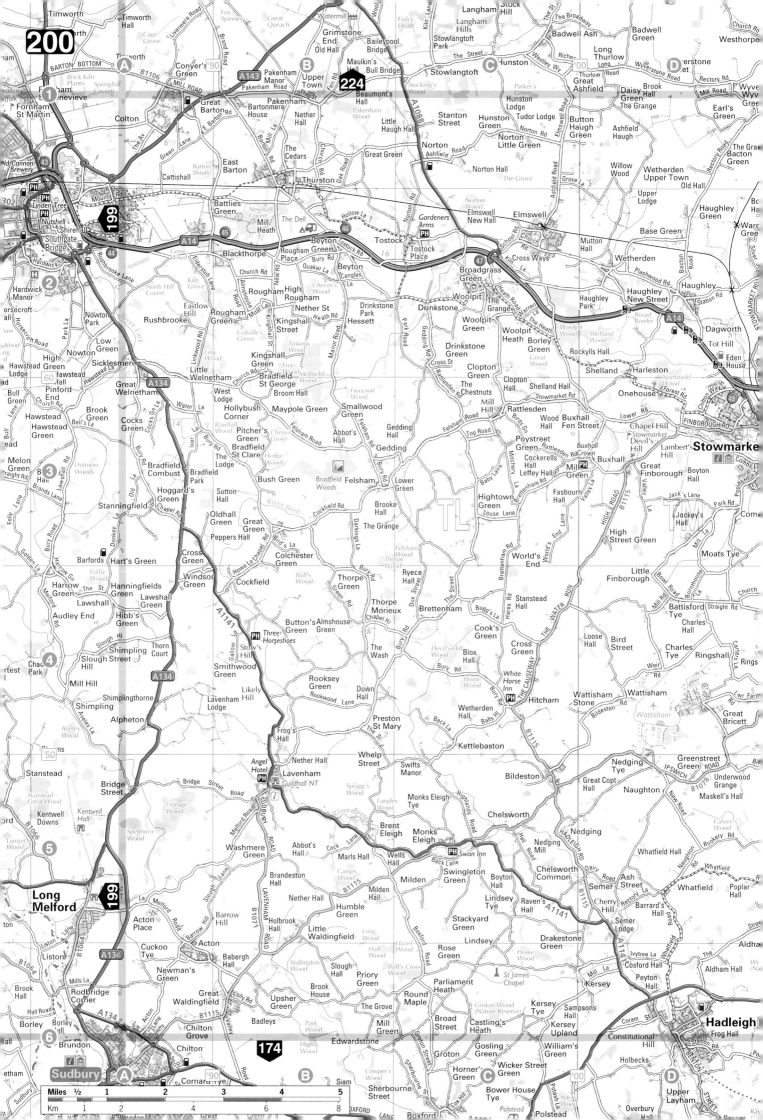

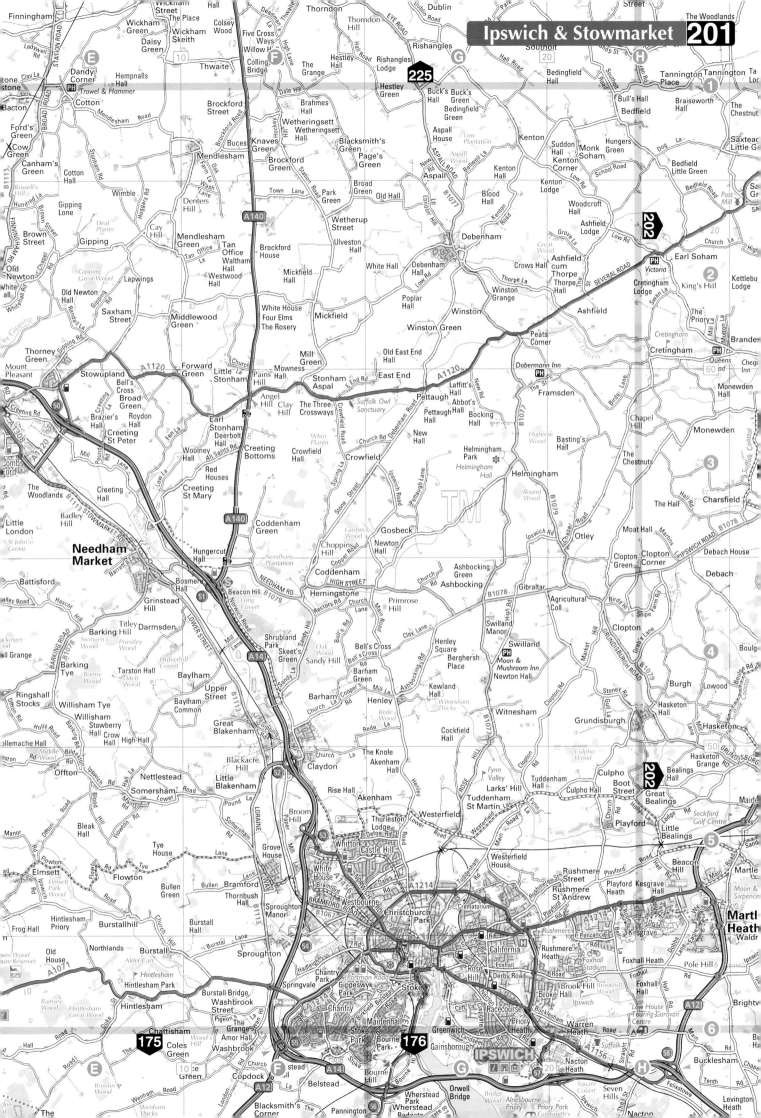

227

50 G H

1

Dunwich Road
Dunwich Cliffs
The Grange
Westleton Rd
Yoxford Rd
Mount Pleasant
Dunwich Cliffs
Middle Moor
Middleton
Fenstreet Rd
Westleton Crown
Mill Rd
Dunwich Heath
Minsmere
Scottshall Coverts
RSPB
Minsmere Cliffs
Scott's Hall
Vault Hill
Coney Hill
The Warren

Fordley Hall
Fordley Rd
East Green
Theberton
Theberton Woods
Moat Rd
Onner's La
Minsmere Level
Eastbridge
The Grove
The Sluice
Minsmere Haven

Pretty Road
Harrow Lane
Clay Hills
Cakes & Ale
Leiston
Ash Wood
Goose Hill
Kenton Hills

Knodishall Green
Brickle's Wood
Valley Rd
Leiston Common
Power Station

Saxmundham Road
Leiston
Sizewell

Knodishall
Coldfair Green
Parrot and Punchbowl
Aldringham
Ness House

B1121
Knodishall Common
Bull's Hall
School Rd
Billeaford Hall
Thorpeness
Thorpe Ness
Dolphin Inn
Friston
Mill Rd
Snape Road
Aldeburgh Rd
B1353
North Warren
RSPB
Thorpeness
The Meare

Ham Road
B1069
A1094
Aldeburgh Road
The Priory
Decoy Wood
Hazelwood Hall
Hazelwood Common
South Warren
Black Heath Wood
Red House
Great Wood
Leiston Road B1122
Thorpe Rd
The Haven

Snape Warren
Black Heath
Ham Creek
Cliff Plantation
Aldeburgh
Round Hill
Mill Inn
Saxmundham Road

Long Reach
Barber's Point
Aldeburgh
Fort Green
ALDEBURGH BAY

Cliff Reach
Iken Marshes
Yarn Hill
Redlands Covert
Aldeburgh Marshes
Slaughden
Iken
Sandy La

Heath
High Street
Cowton
Lambert's La
Fazeboons
Sudbourne Great Wood
Captain's Wood
Ferry Road
Sudbourne Marshes

School Road
The Firs
Sudbourne Beach
Sudbourne
Sudbourne Beach

The Birches
B1084
Watling Wood
Snape Road
River Alde
Lantern Marshes

Sudbourne Park
Hospital Rd
Town Marshes
Raydon Hall
Radio Station

Crown and Castle
Orford
King's Marshes
Gedgrave Hall
Jolly Sailor Inn
ORFORD NESS

Gedgrave Marshes
Orfordness-Havergate
RSPB
Havergate Island
Beach

Dove Point

TM

50

60

50

BAY

Aberystwyth

0   200 metres

North Beach

Cardigan Bay

South Beach

CINEMA & CONFERENCE CENTRE

BOAT LANDING STAGE

MUSEUM & ℹ️

ROYAL PIER

LIBRARY

UNIVERSITY OLD COLLEGE

COAST GUARD

CLOCK TOWER

WAR MEMORIAL

CASTLE RUINS

THEATRE

MKT HALL

SOUTH

TOWN HALL

QUEEN SQ

A487

NORTHGATE ST

MACHYNLLETH

THESPIAN ST

GREAT DARKGATE ST

NORTH PARADE

TERRACE RD

ALEXANDRA ROAD

CAB

SAL'Y ARMY

PO

ABERYSTWYTH STATION

GOVERNMENT OFFICES

VALE OF RHEIDOL STATION

BRIDGE STREET

MILL STREET

TREFECHAN ROAD

Pont Trefechan

Marina

GREEN GARDENS

RIVERSIDE TERRACE

GLYNDWR ROAD

ABERYSTWYTH FOOTBALL CLUB

POLICE STATION

FIRE STATION

LIFEBOAT STATION

PLAS YR AFON

CARDIGAN

LBM

Bowling Greens

Tennis Courts

SN

Brynbala

Moelcerni

Sarn Gynfelyn

Wallog

Rhoscellan

Ocean View

Clarach Bay

Aberystwyth

ℹ️ Aberystwyth

Trefechan The Bar

Park Avenue

Penparcau

Aberystwyth & District

Rhyd

Bryn-Eithyn Hall

Llanfarian

Cwm-ceirw

Chancery

ANTARON AVENUE

Blaenplwyf

Rhodmad

A487

Berth-Rhys

Cefngraigwen

Tynbwlch

16

Aelybryn

Blaencarrog

Ty-newydd

Maenelin

Llanddeiniol

Bryngwyn

Tregynan

Cnwc y Barcud

Tycam

Llanrhystud

Cwm Wyre

Tynwern

Treflys

Morfa

Penrhos

Esgair

B4576

Ty-Newydd

Cwm Mabws

Mabws Hall

Talwrn Hogfaen

Maesfron

Rhyd-Rosser

Llansantffraed

Talwrn-côch

Rhydfudr

Llanon

Cwm Peris

Tanlluest Lluest-newydd

B4337

Rhos-lwyd

Tryal-Bach

Cnwc

Miles   ½   1   2   3   4   5

Km   1   2   4   6   8

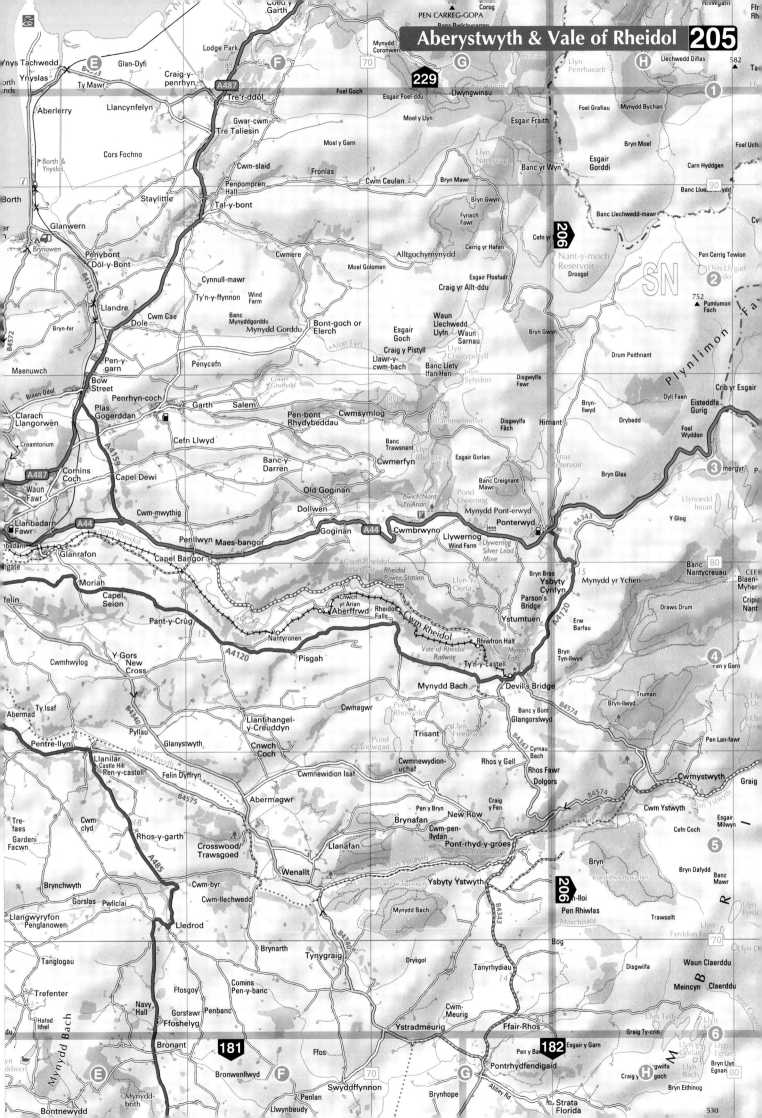

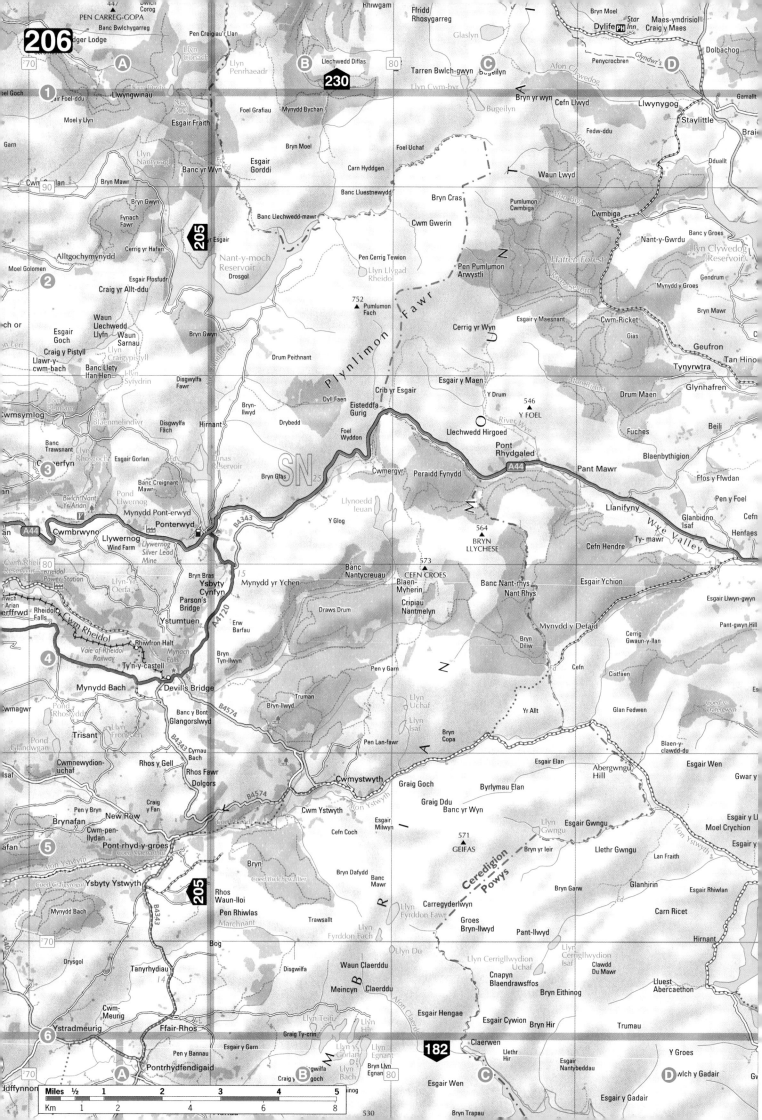

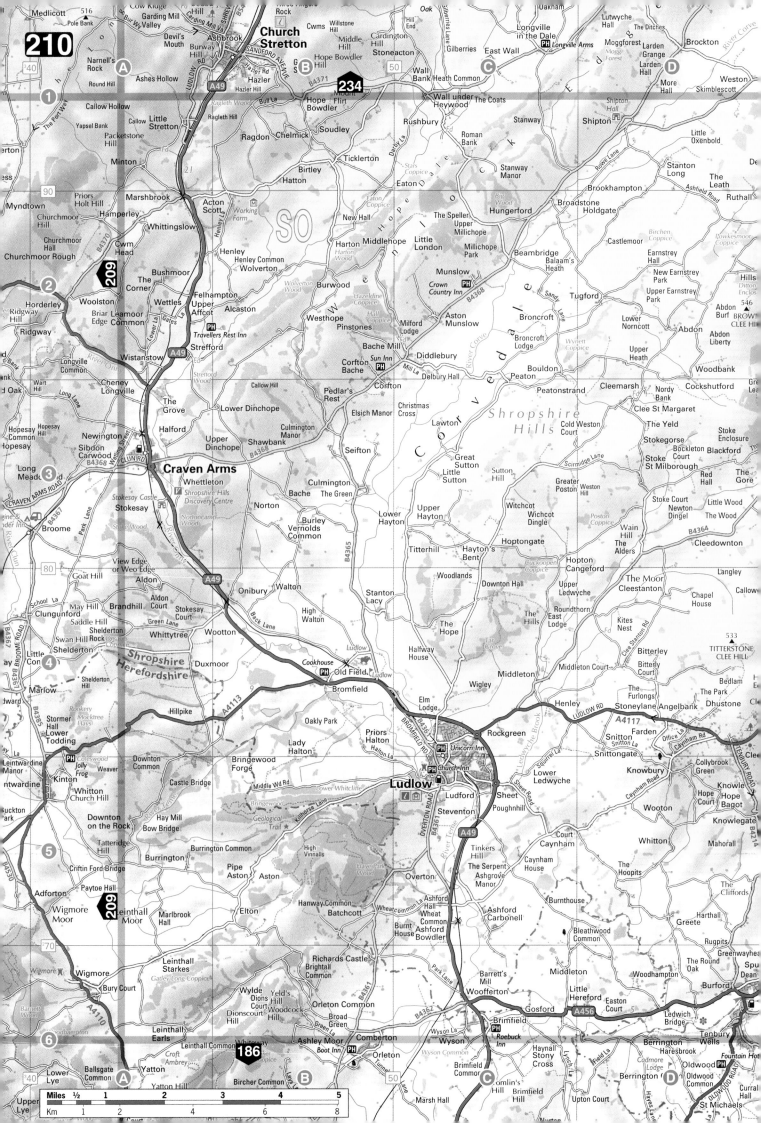

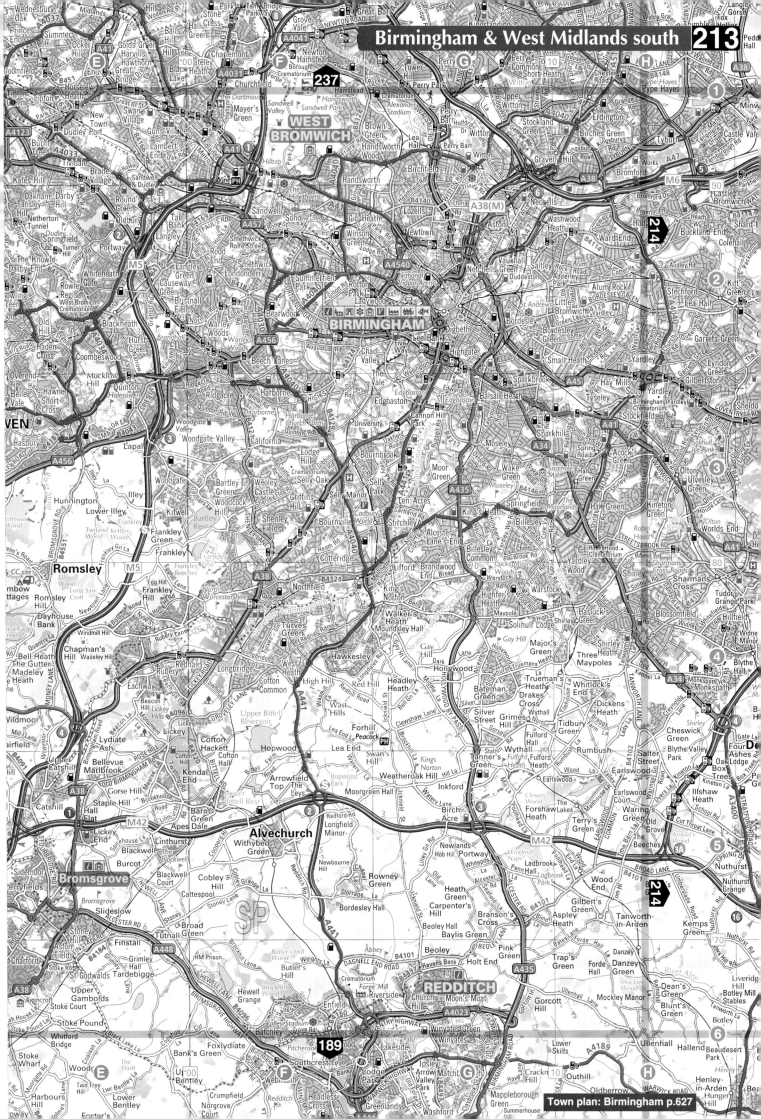

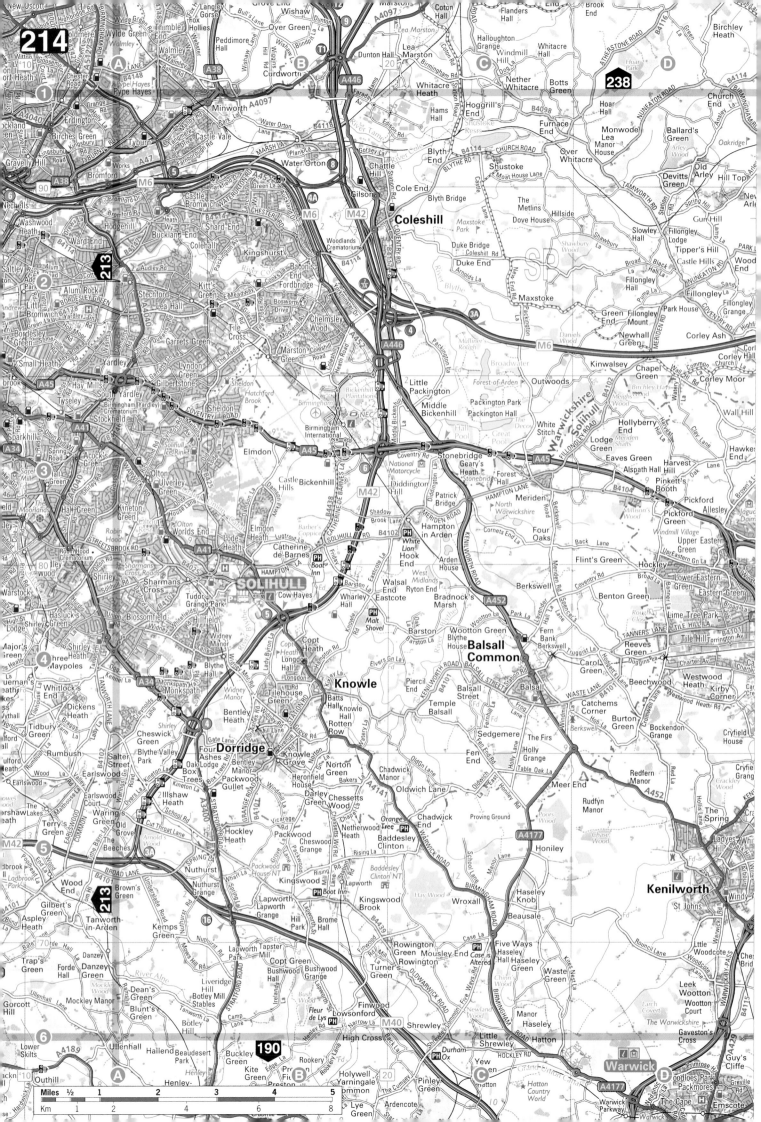

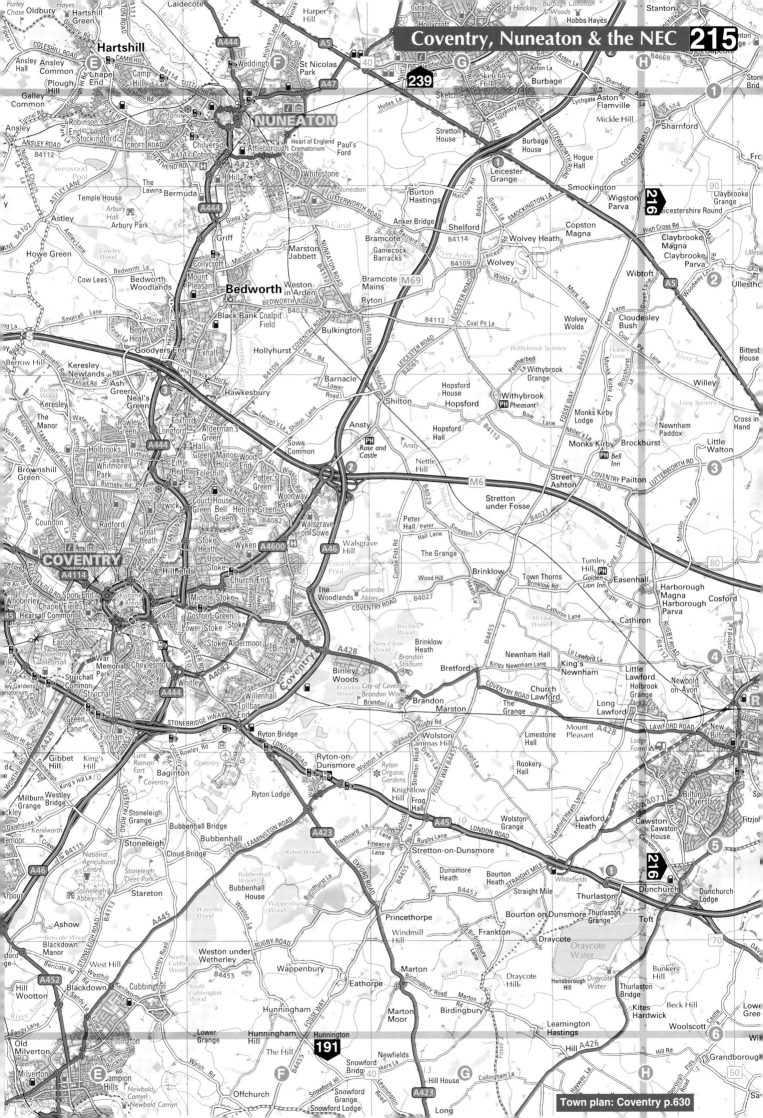

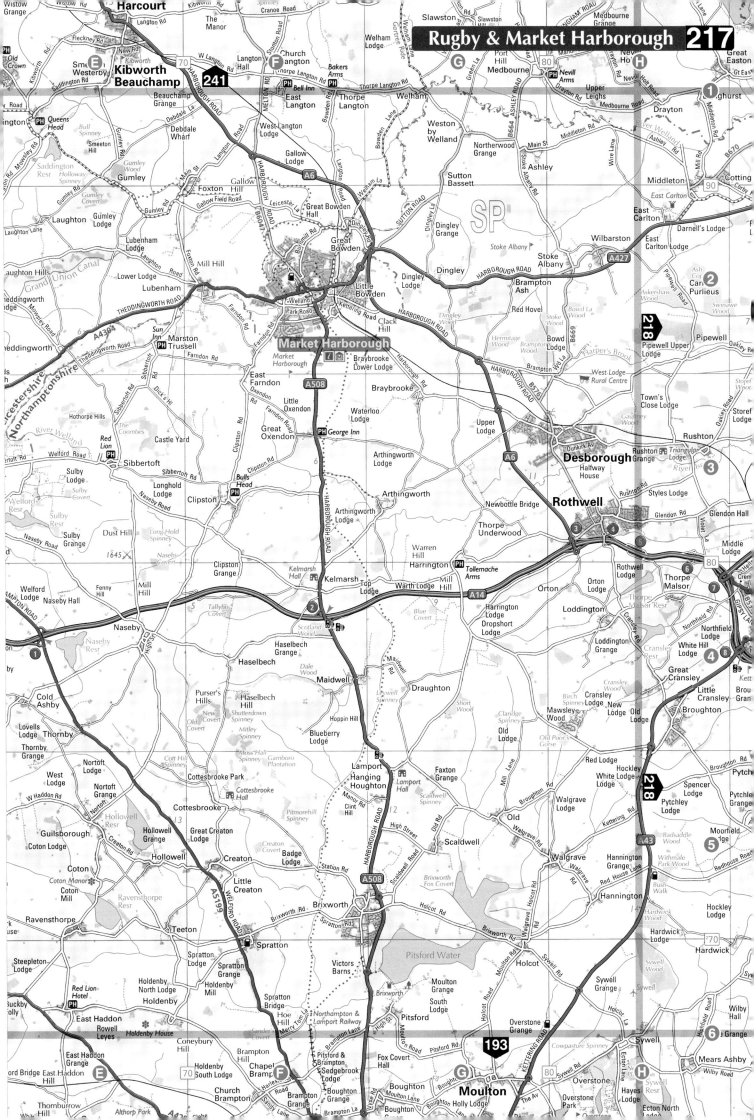

243

195

220

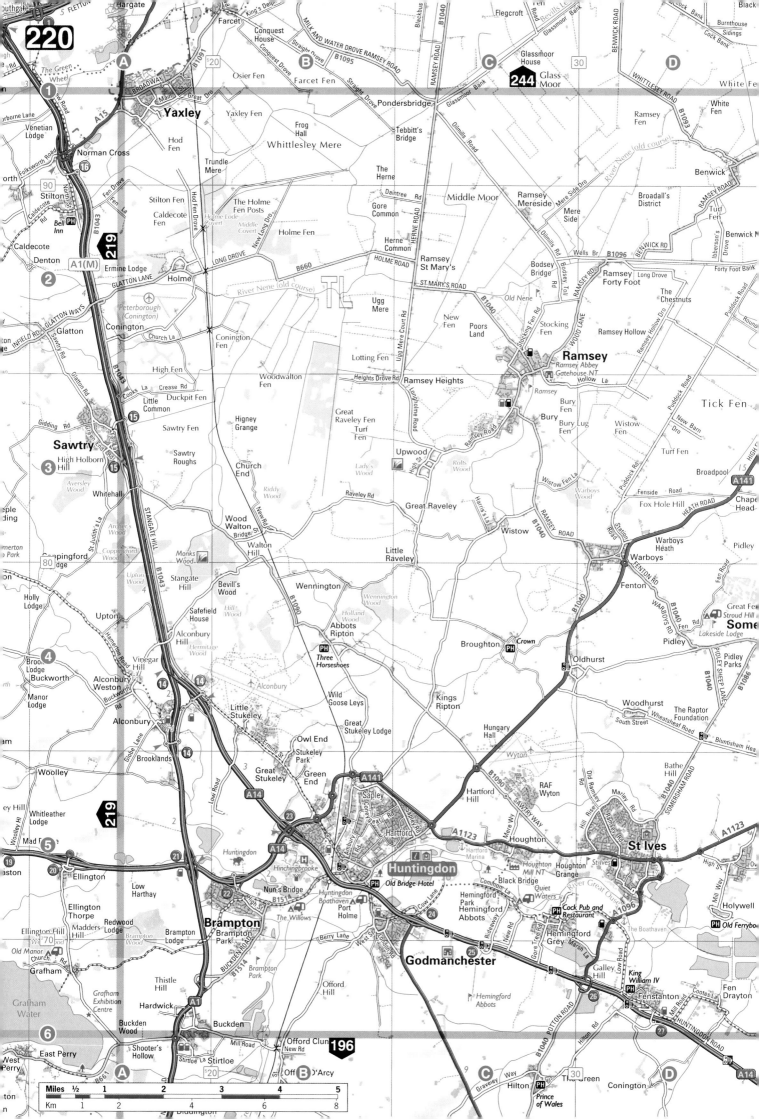

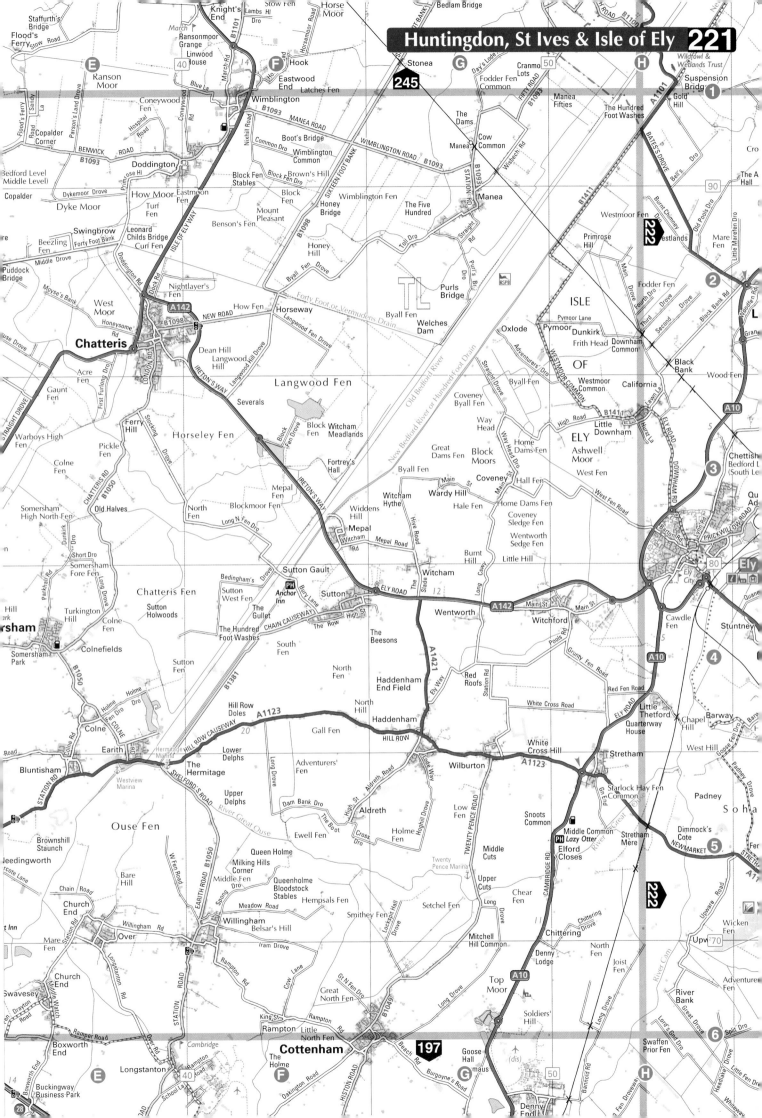

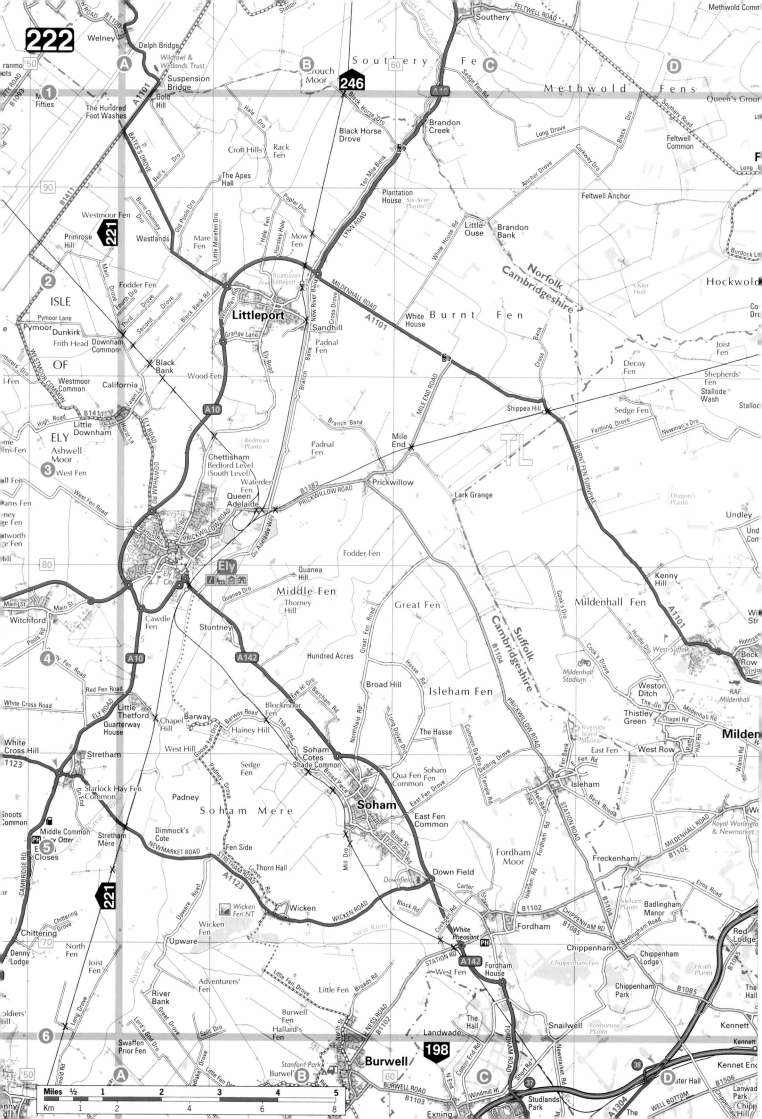

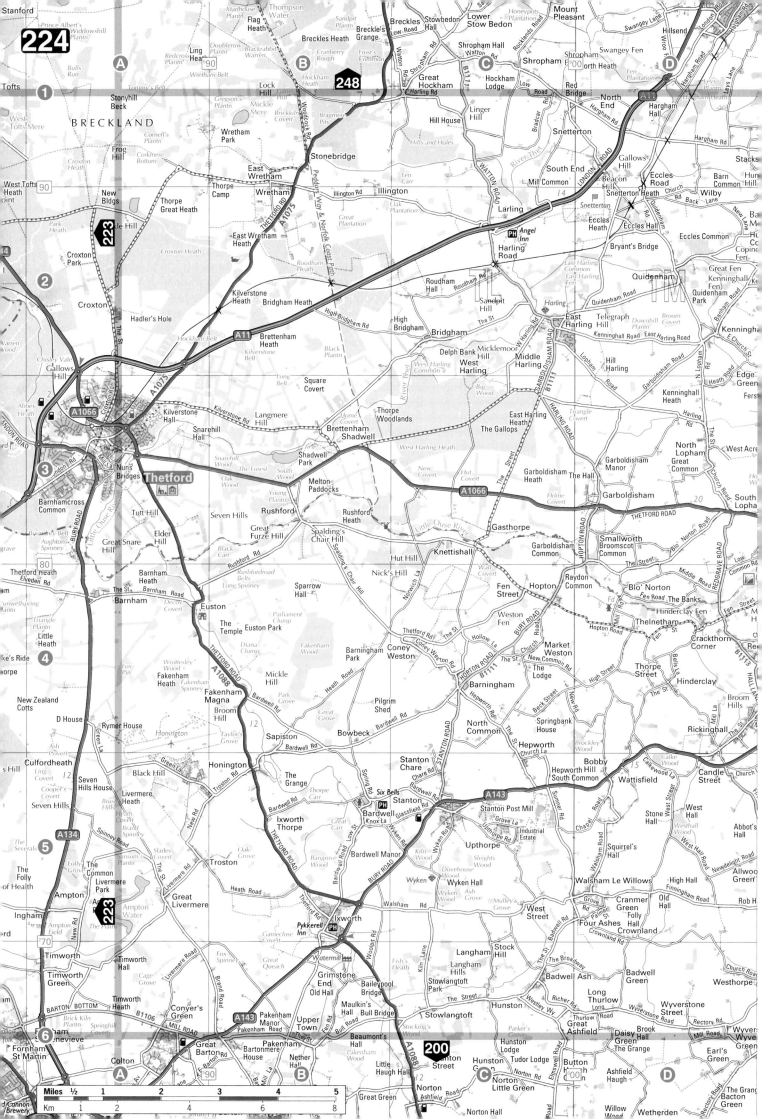

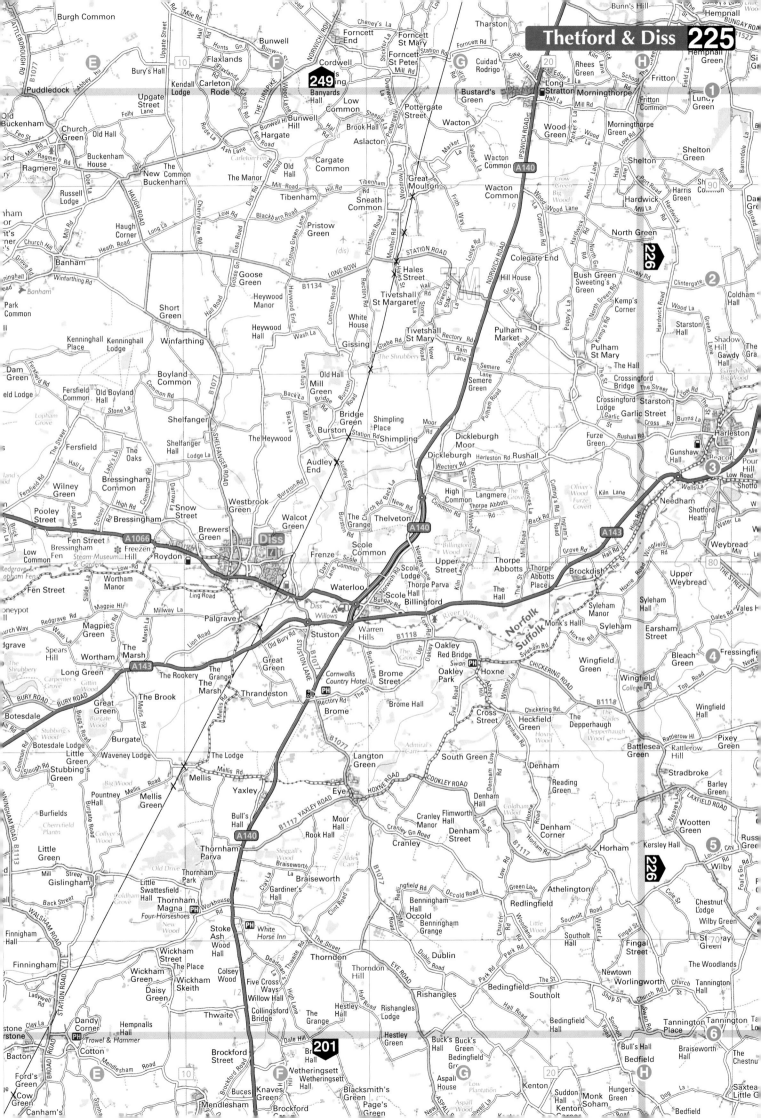

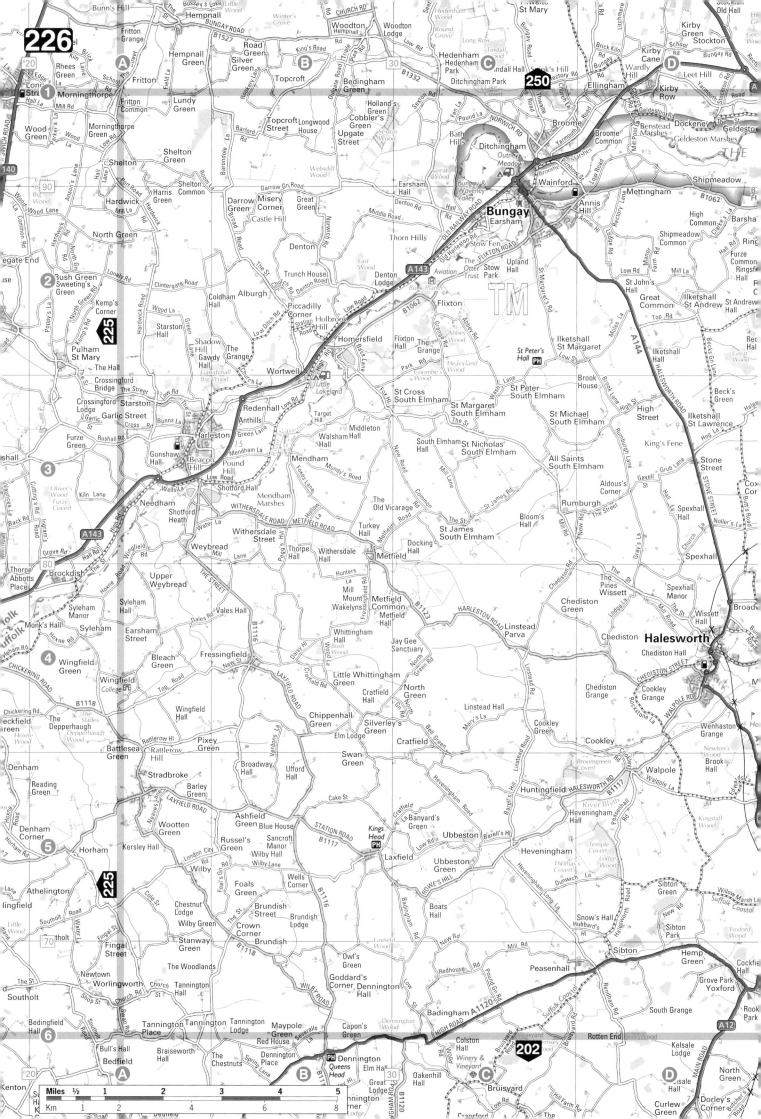

Trawsdir

264

A B C D

40 50

1

Penrhyn

Barmouth
Bay

2

C A R D I G A N

10

B A Y

3

G

Hend

Llwy

Figr
Oer

Llangelynnin

Rhoslefain

Bwlch

Llanfendigaid

Castell

Clos-bâch

Nantycynog

Talybont

Tonfanau

Tal y
gareg

Aber
Dysynni

SH

Broad Water

Ynysymaengwyn

Ffordd
Gwalia

Ffordd
Rhos

Bryn-
y-mor

Pendre

Tywyn Wharf

Tywi

Es
Ha

SN

Neptune Hall

264

204

A B C D

40 50

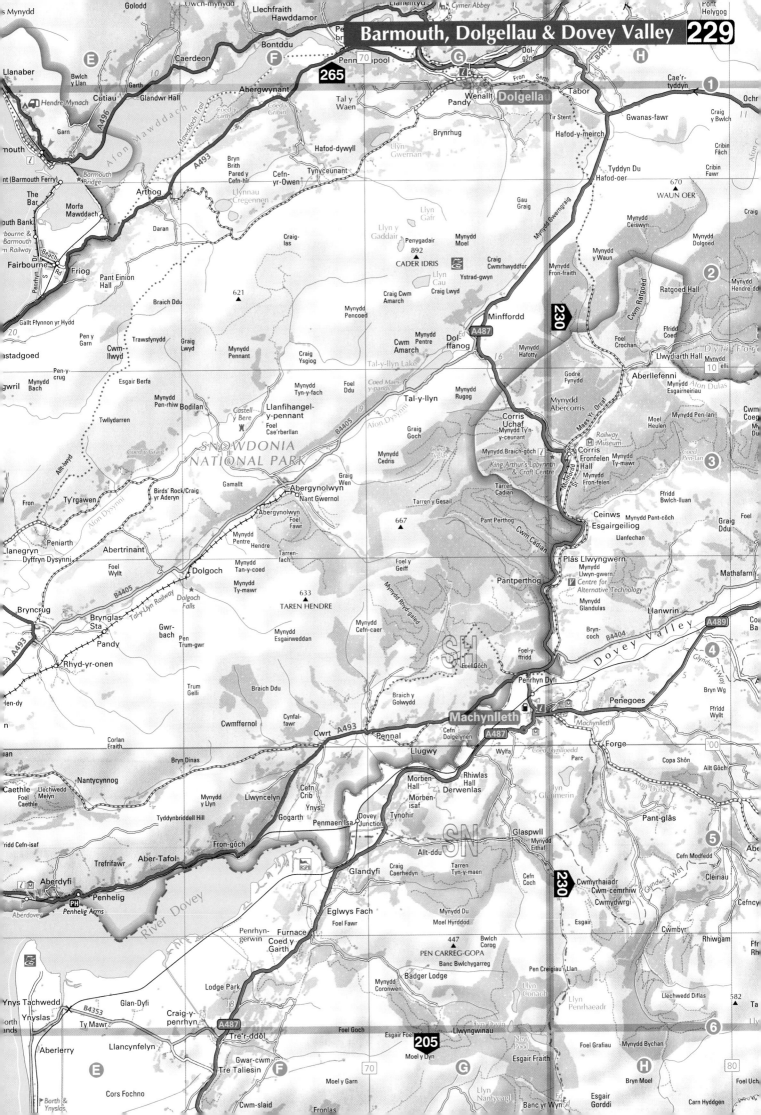

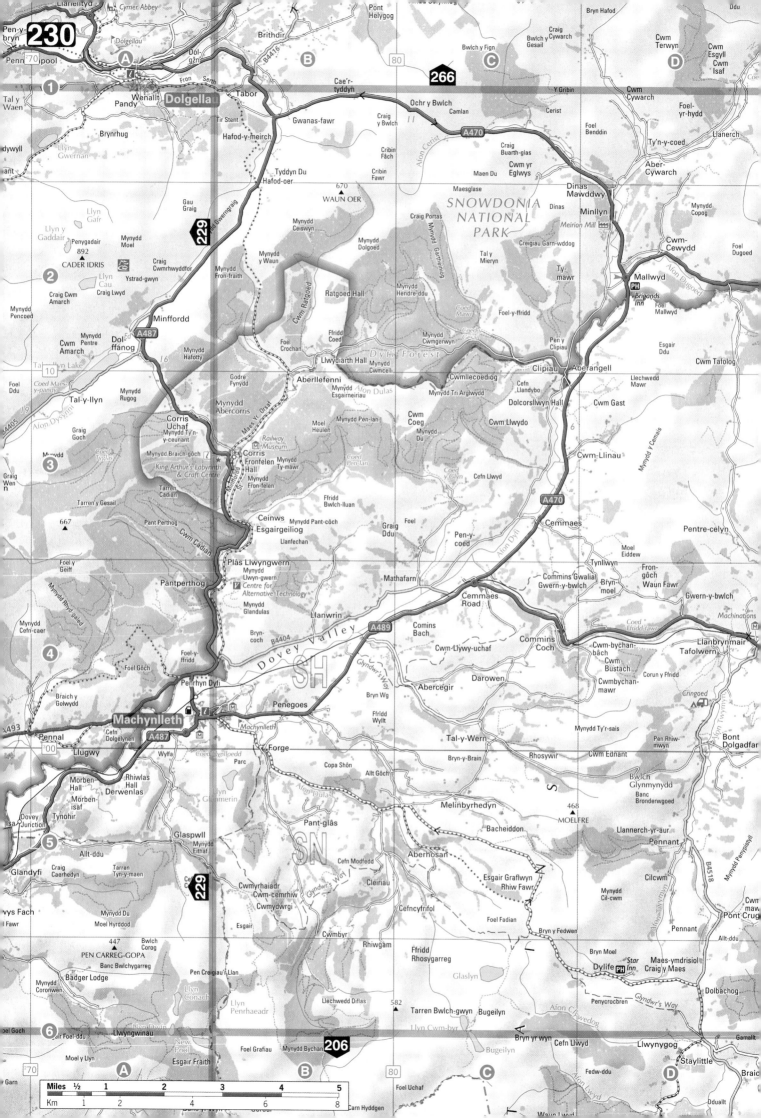

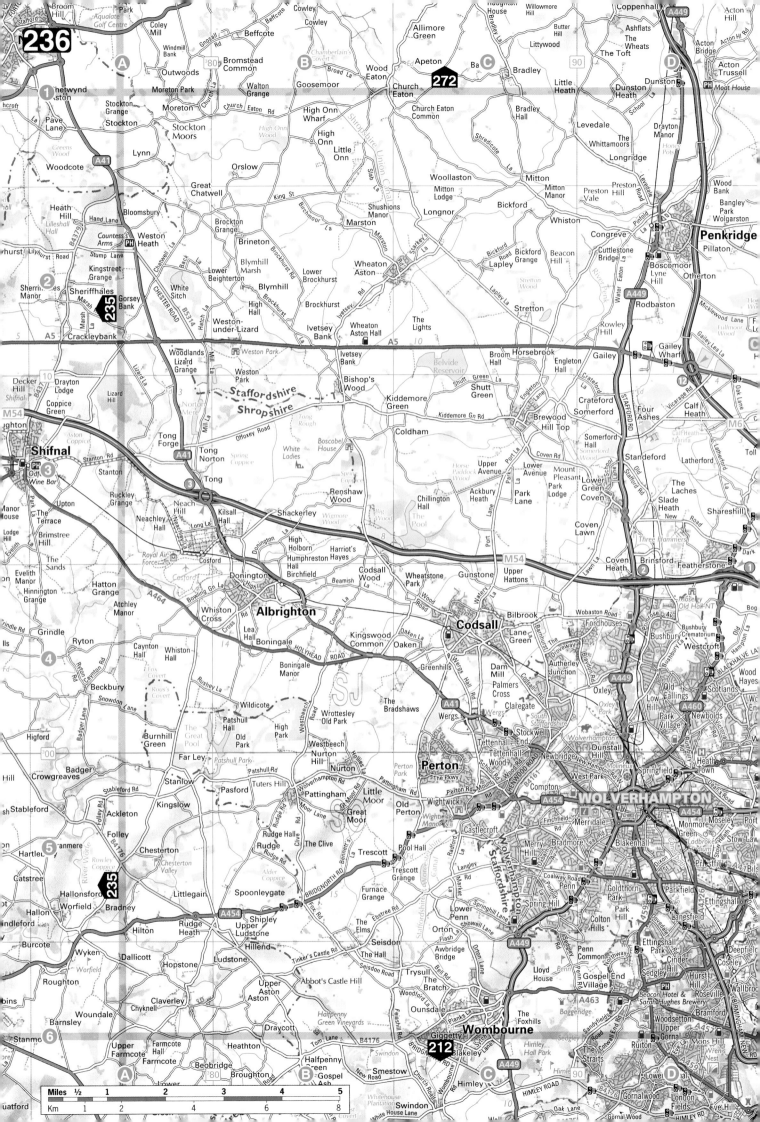

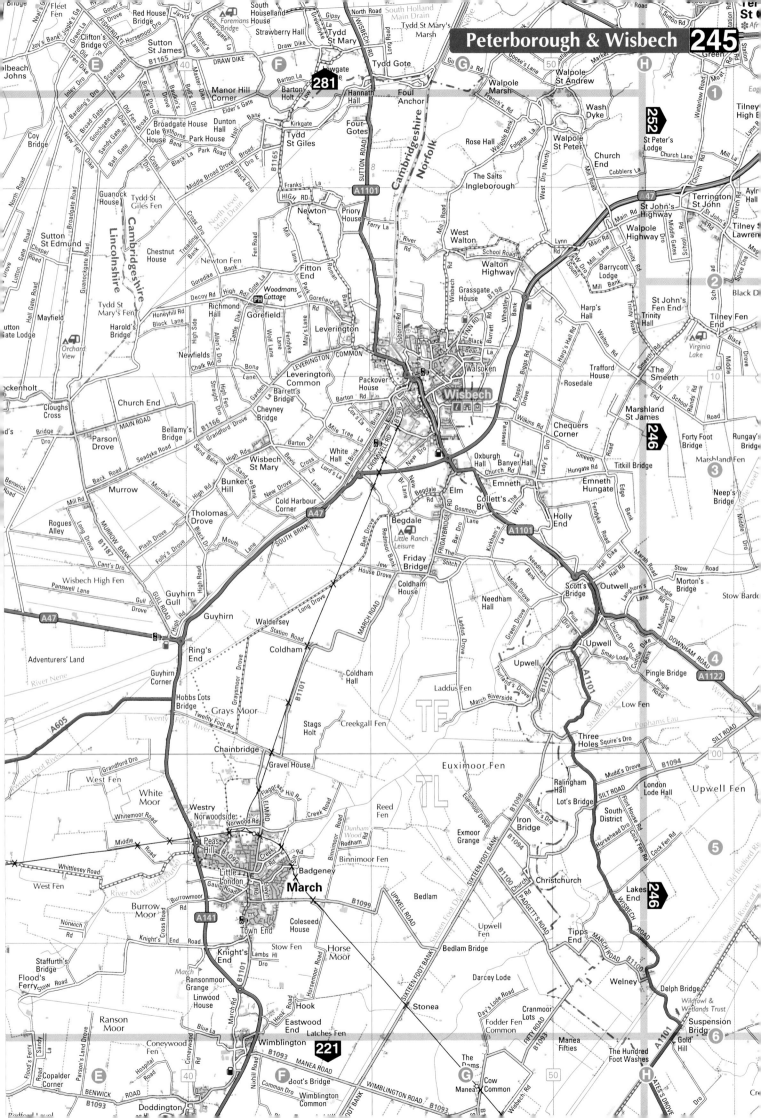

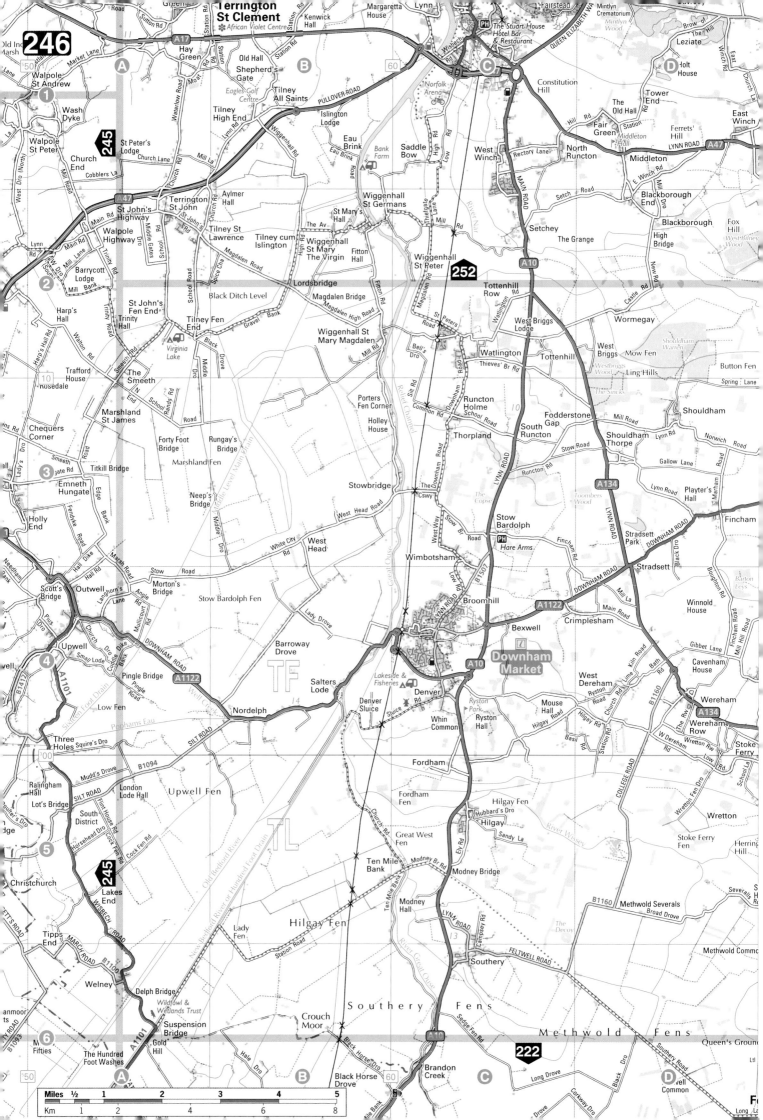

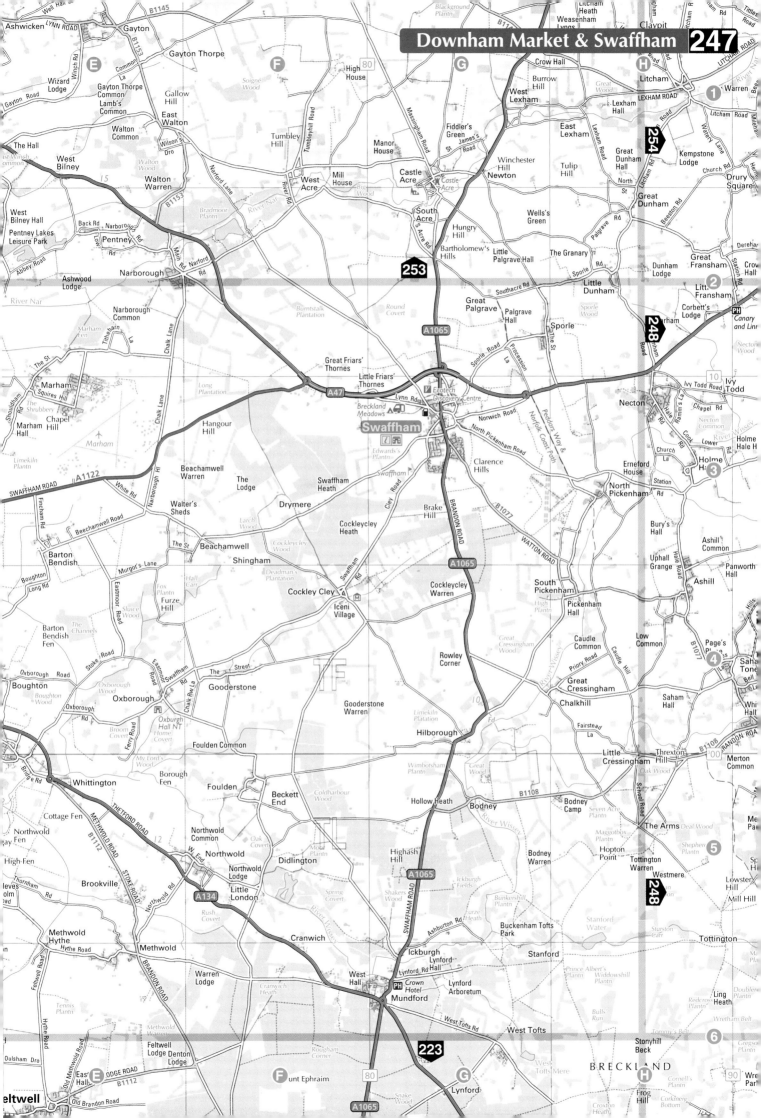

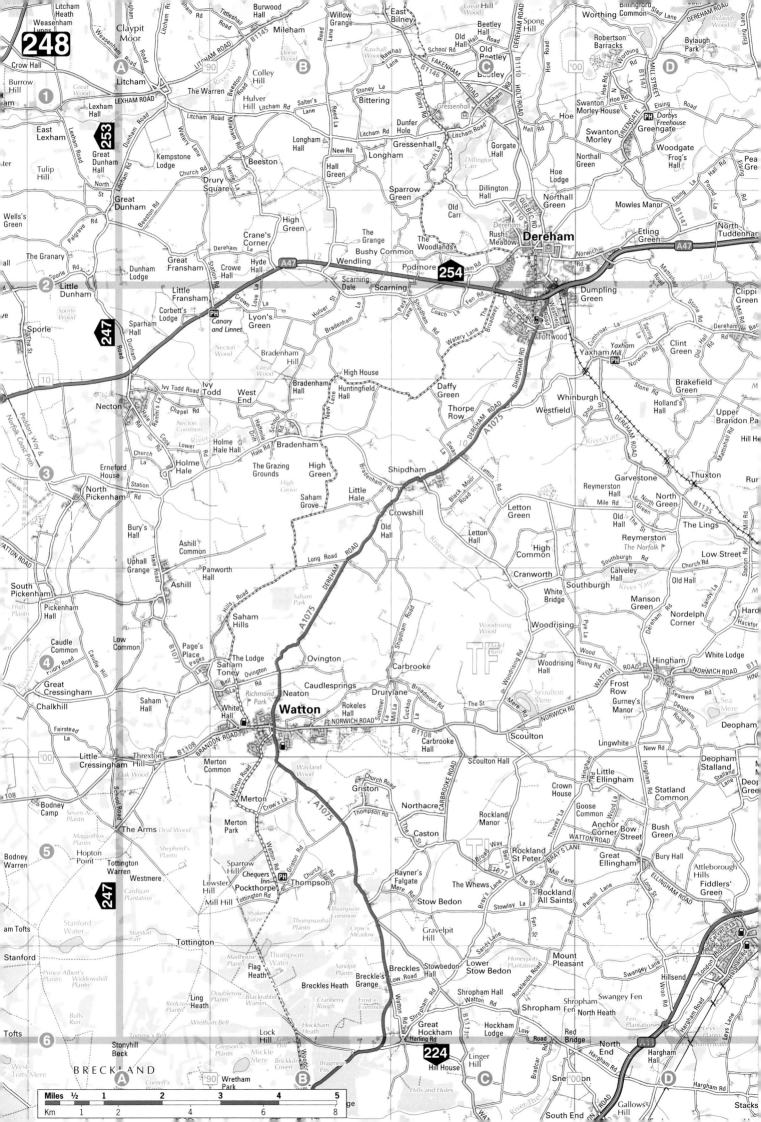

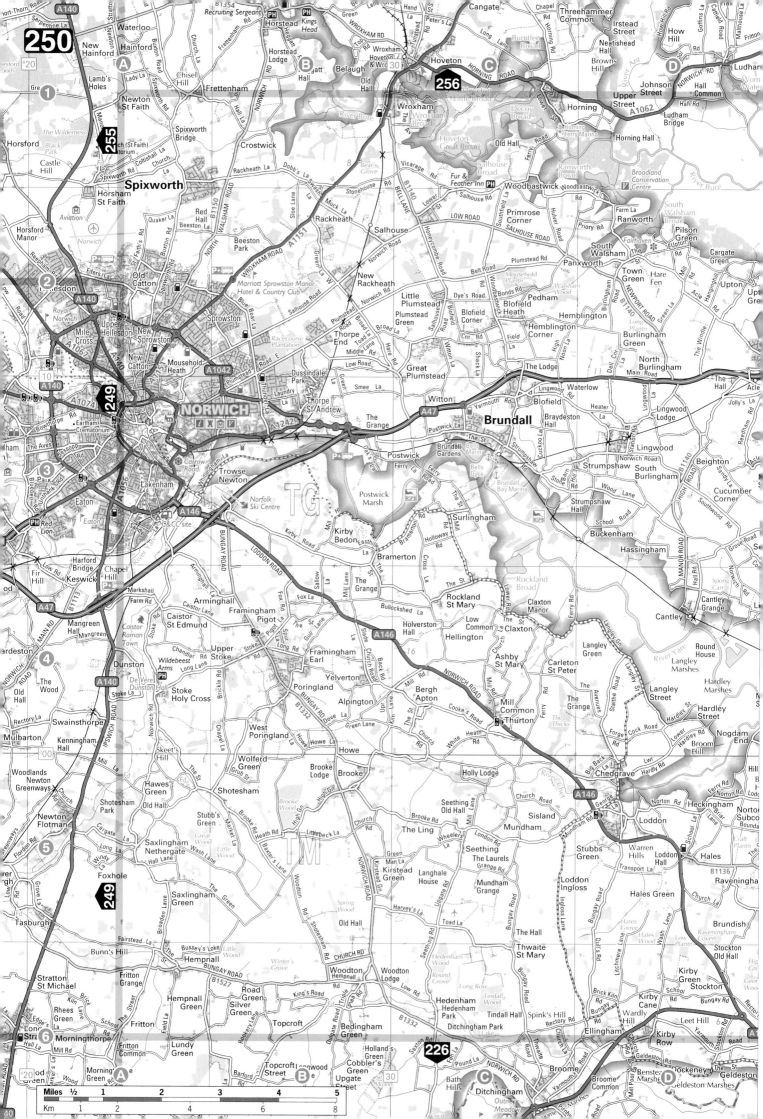

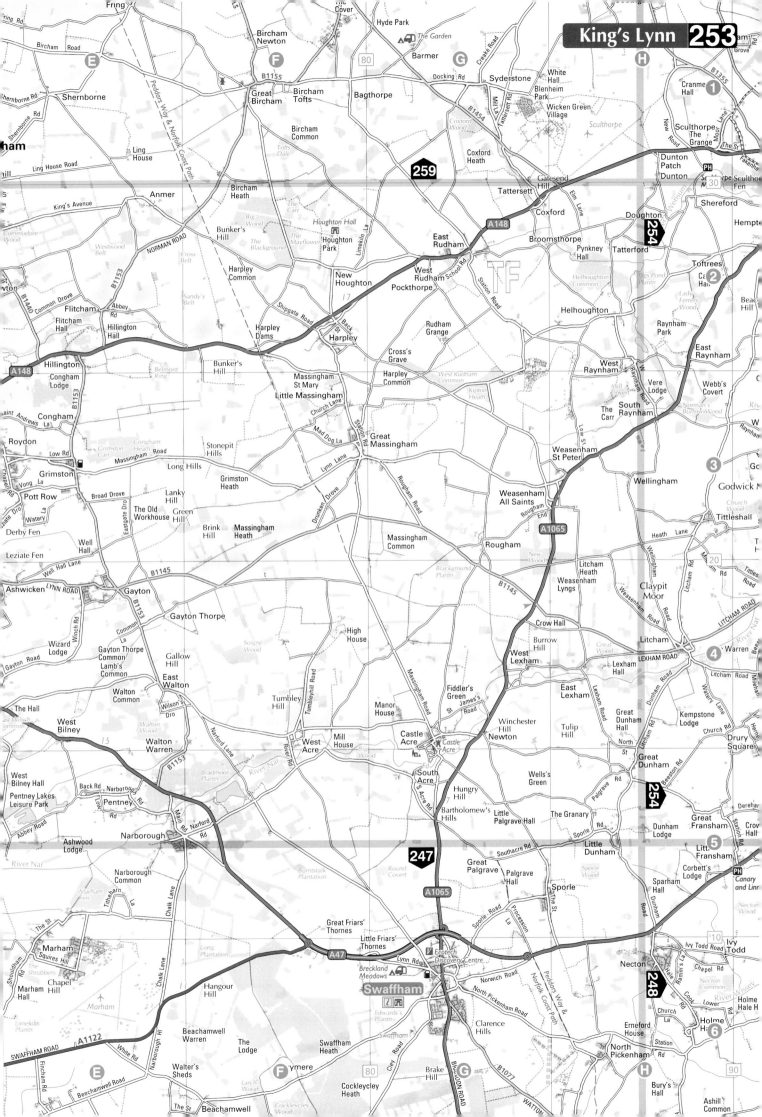

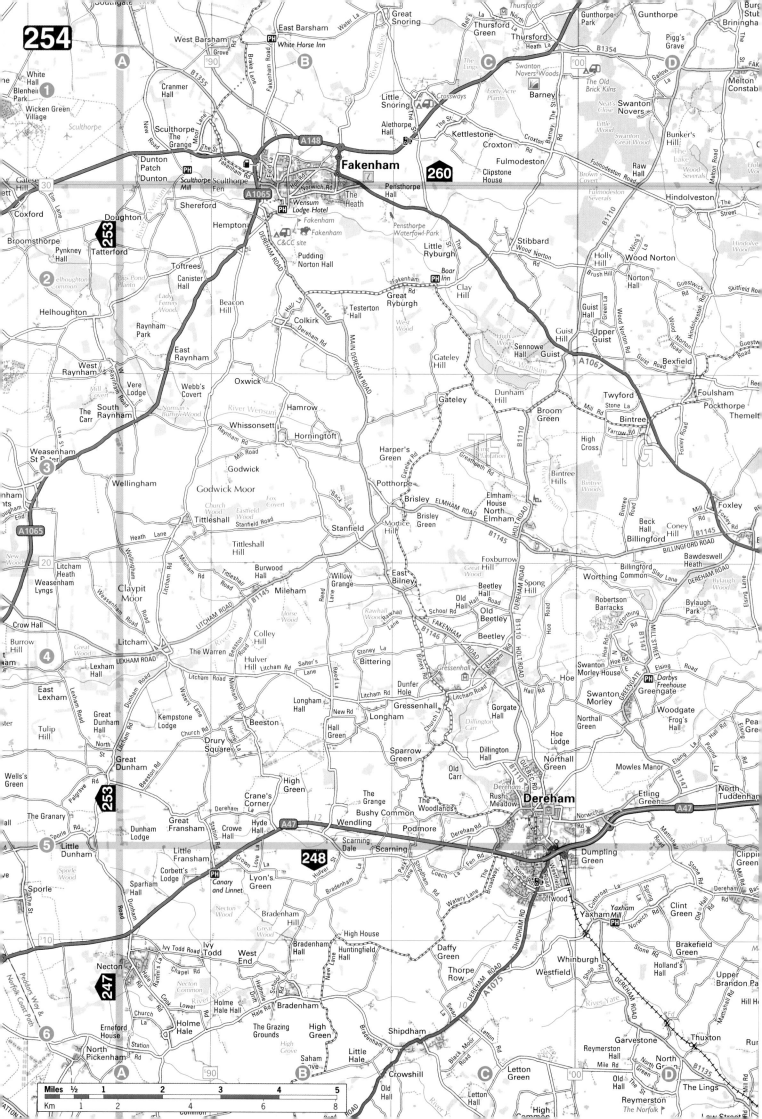

N O R T H   S E A

Eccles on Sea
North Gap
sh
Beach Road
ate
Hempstead
Hempstead
Heath
Hempstead Marshes
Sea Palling
Stalham Rd
Waxham Road
Rd
The Hall
Manor House
Randall's Mill
Great Moss Fen
Waxham
Marram Hills
Hickling Rd
Lambrigg Mill
Norfolk Coast
Sea Palling Rd
Brograve Level
Hickling
Eastfield Road
Stalham Rd
Hickling Green
Horsey Corner
Horsey
The Hall
PH Nelson Head
Stubb
Hickling Heath
Hill Common
Stubb Road
Horsey Mill
Bramble Hill
Catfield Common
Hickling Broad
Stubb Mill
Horsey Mere
Horsey Windpump NT
Hundred Stream
Winterton Ness
THE BROADS
Eelfleet Wall
Somerton Holmes
Winterton Ness
Swim Coots
Heigham Sound
Sound Plantation
Winterton Dunes
Decoy Wood
Back La
Green Lane
Church La
Heigham Holmes
Martham Broad
East Somerton
Fishermans Return
'20
Market Rd
Marsh Rd
Potter Heigham
High's Mill
Damgate
Ferrygate La
Somerton Road
West Somerton
PH
Winterton-on-Sea
Fritton
Lane
Cess
Mustard Hyrn
Cess Rd
Blood Hills
Collis Lane
Hemsby Rd
Bridge Rd
Repps Level
Bastwick
Martham
Hemsby Road
Martham Rd
Repps
HIGH ROAD
MILL RD
Repps Road
Common Rd
Beach Rd
Hemsby
Newport
251
Repps Rd
Chu
Back Lane
Orme's Broad
50
Dowe Hill
Scratby
Sand Cliffs
Thurne
Church Rd
Ashby Hall
Heath Rd
A149
Rollesby
Scratby Hall
Beach Rd
152
MAY

A   B   60   C   D

50

1

50

2

3

THE WASH

TF

St Edmund's Point

Hunstanton Park

Hunstanton

Redgate
Hill

Ringstead
Downs

Ringstead Road

40

Stubborn
Sand

Heacham
Harbour

Norfolk
Lavender

Station Rd

Heacham

Ken Hill
Wood

Ken Hill

Rose &
Crown
PH

Snettisham

Park
Farm

Beach   Road

Shepherd's
Port

Ingoldisthorpe

Wolferton
Creek

The
Decoy

Life
Wood

Dersing

Dodd

30

252

Dersingham
Wood

Dersingham Bog

281

Wolferton

Sandringha

Crab's
Hole

C&CC site

Wolferton
Wood

Babingle   D

Lynnroad
Plantation

Vincent
Hills

Wooton
Marsh

Marsh Road

Miles	½	1	2	3	4	5
Km	1	2	4	6	8	

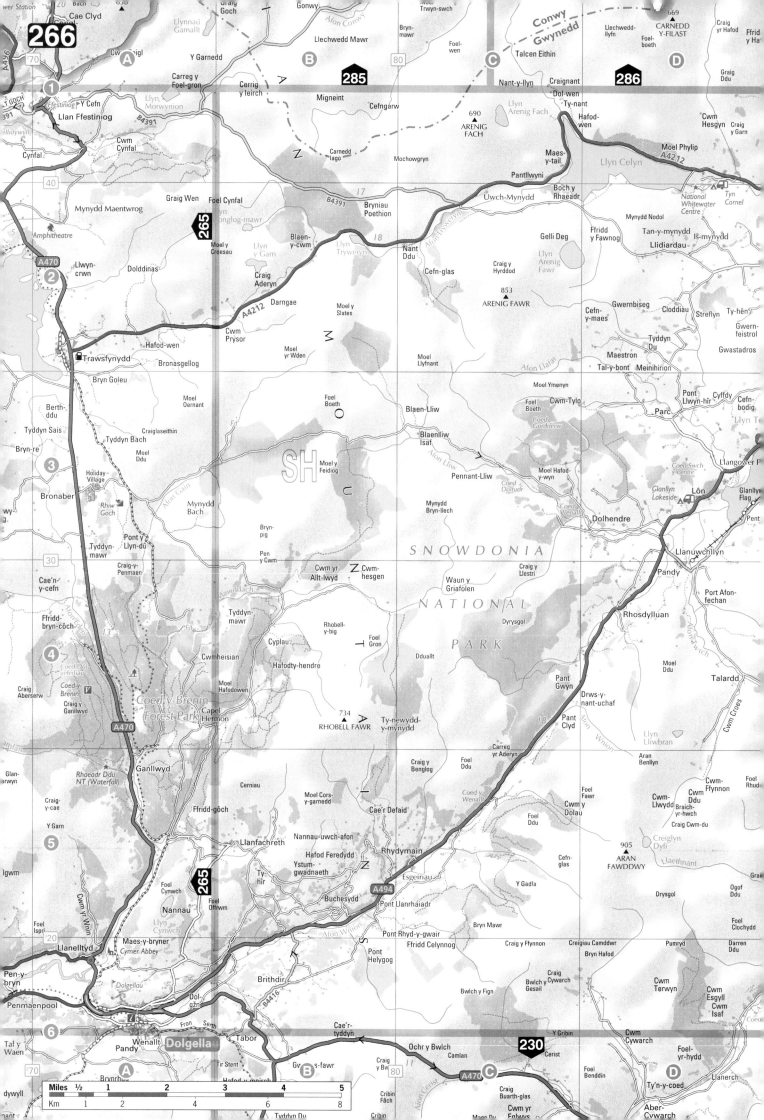

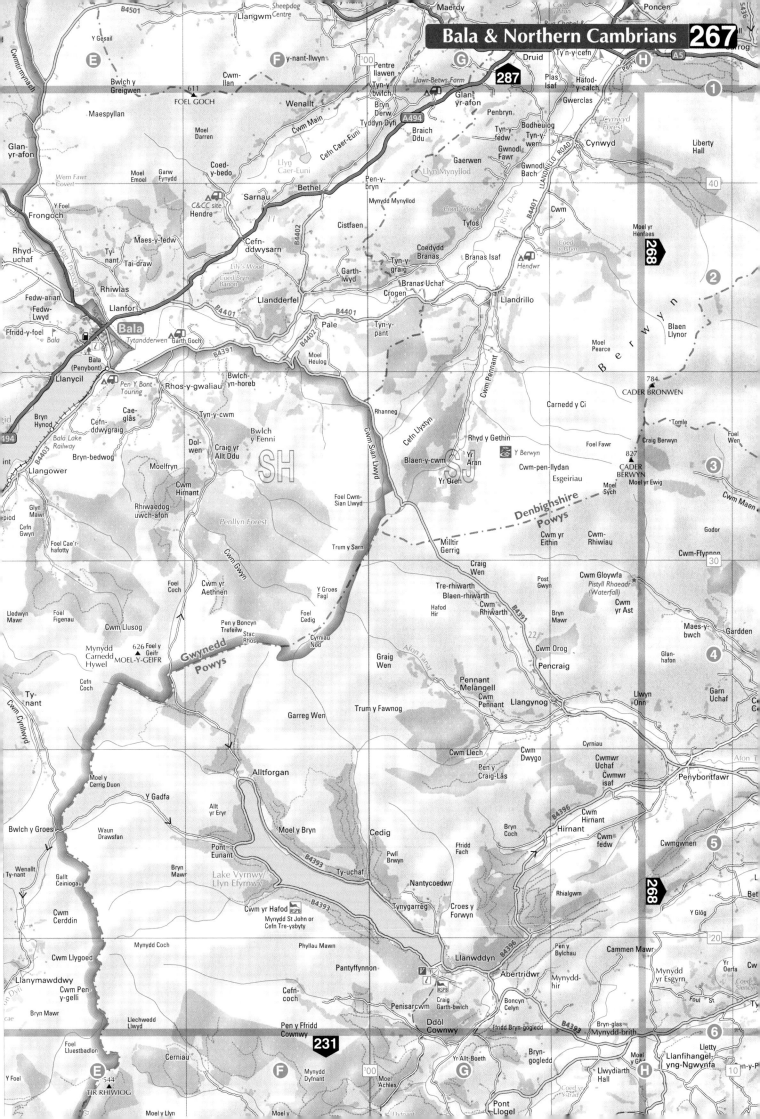

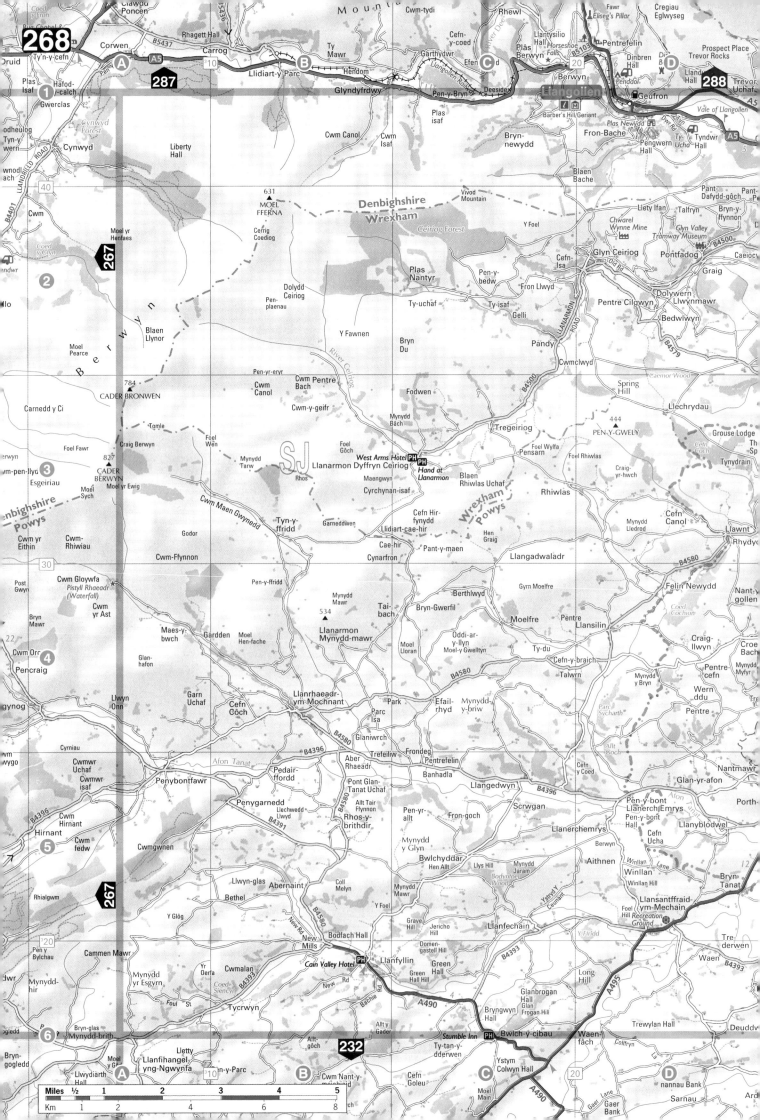

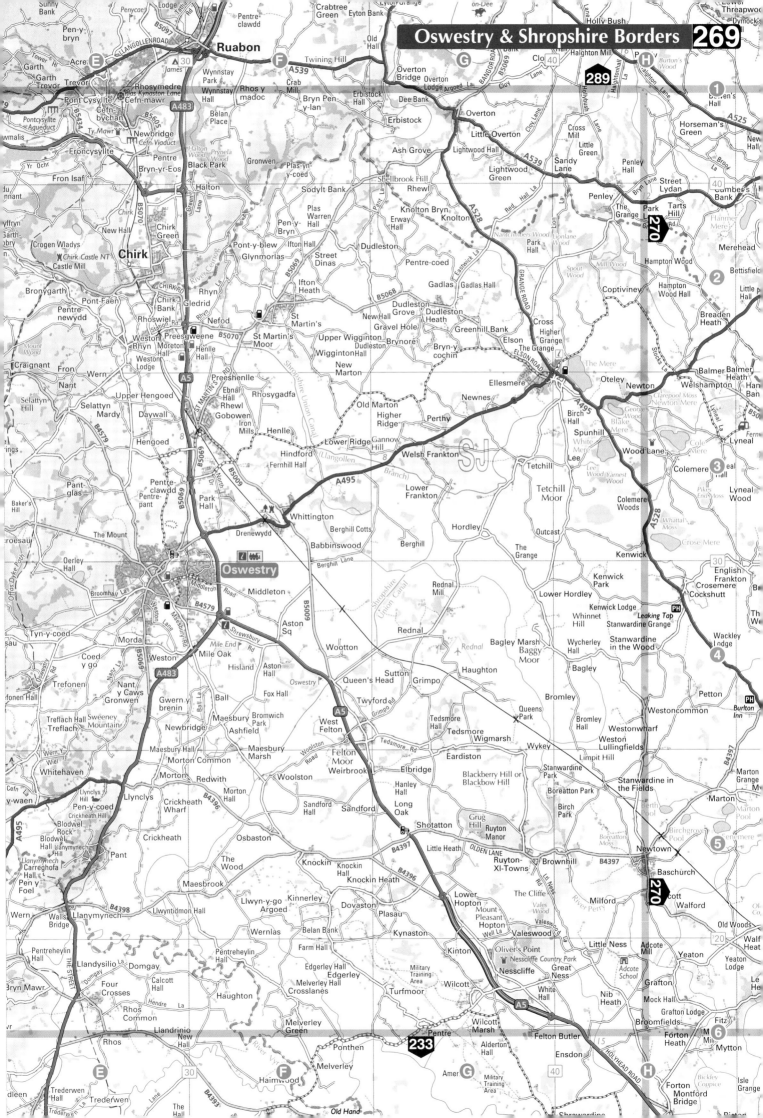

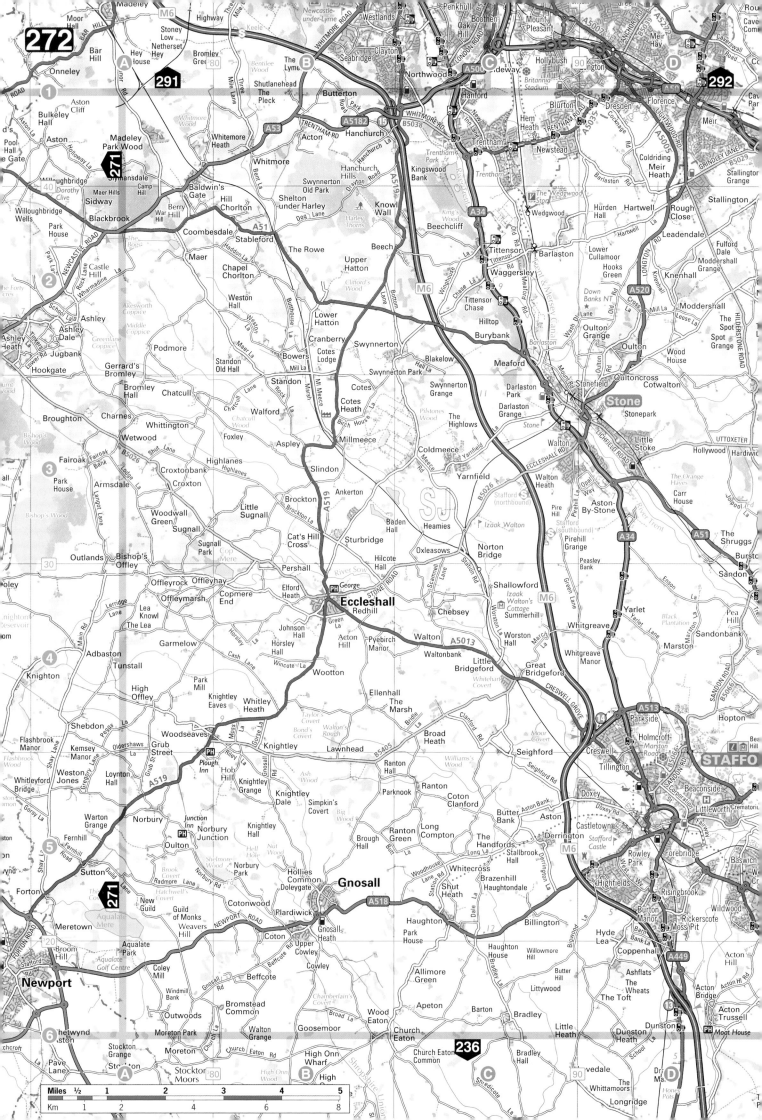

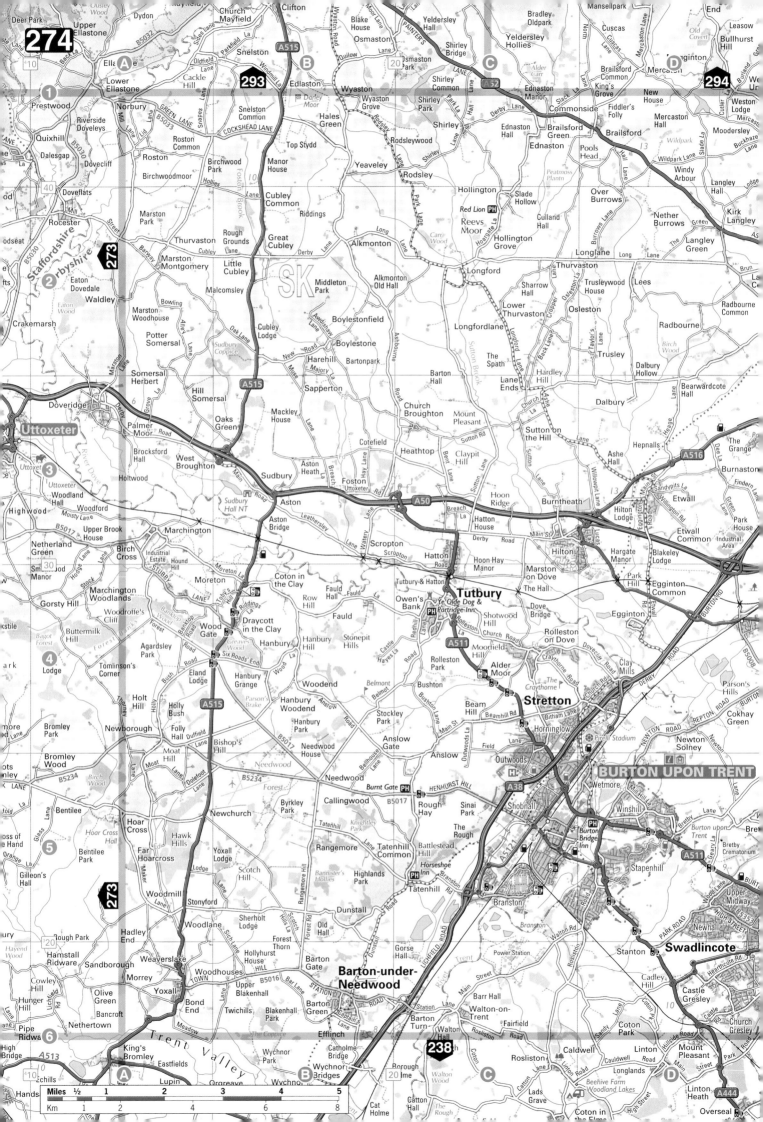

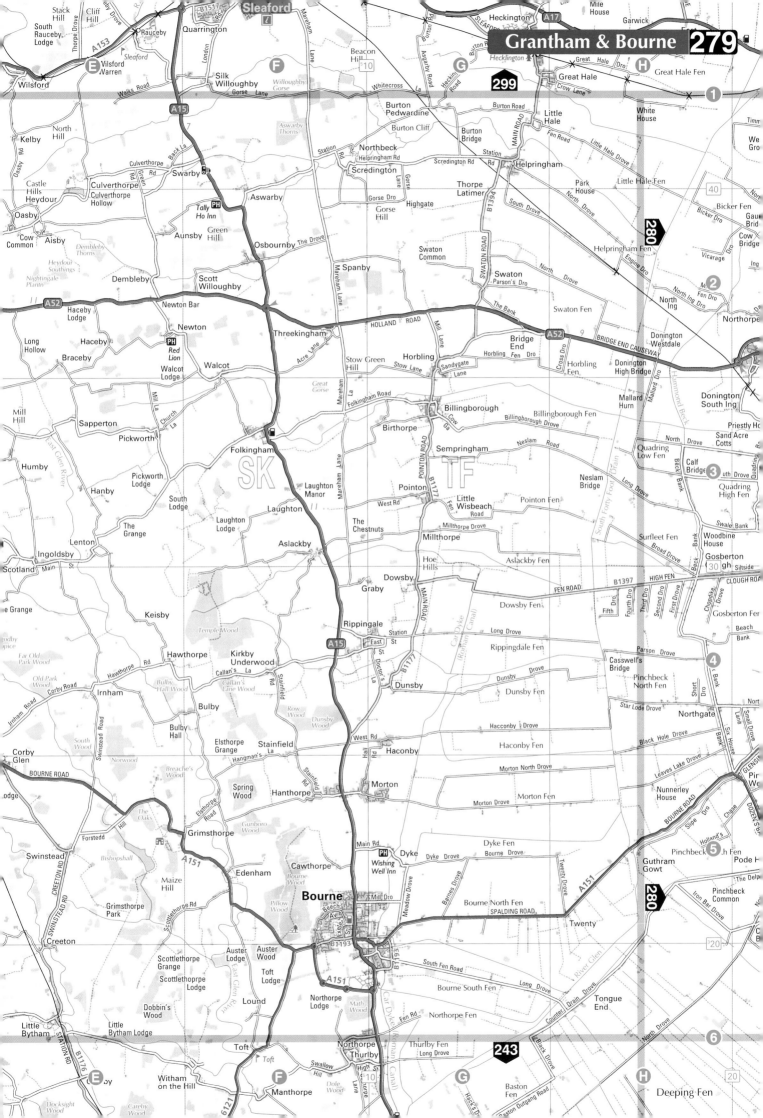

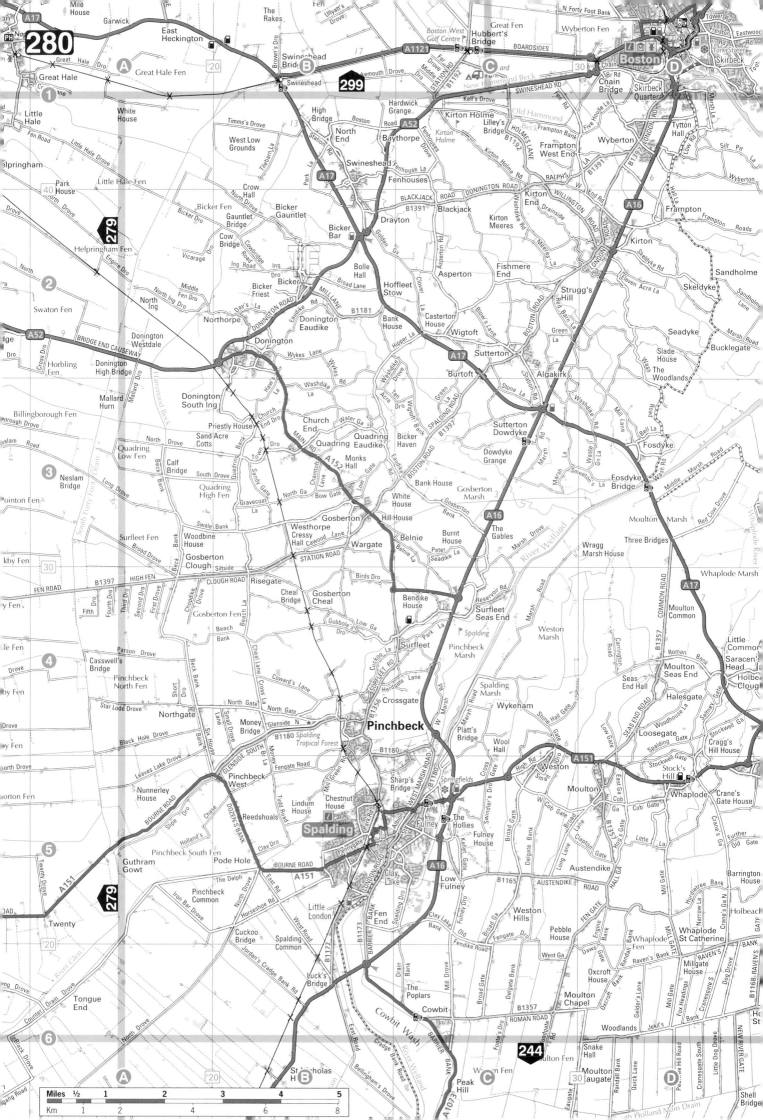

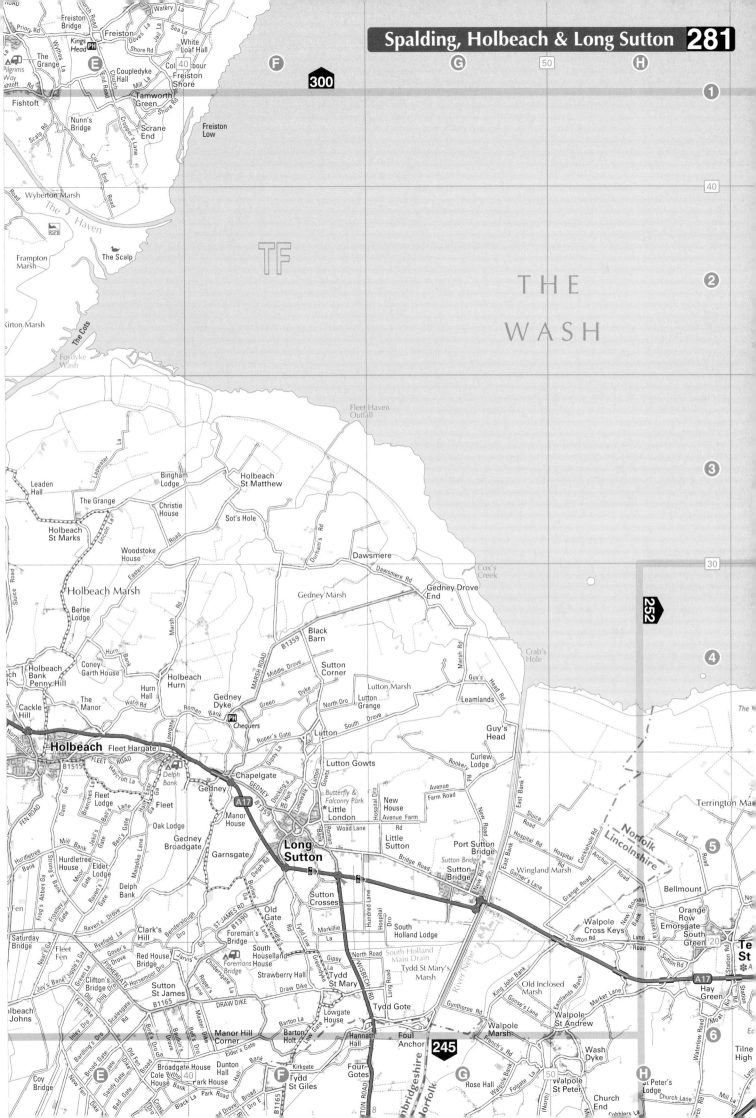

THE
WASH

TF

Priory Rd
Freiston
Church Road
Watery La
Dove's La
Sea La
Jail La
White Loaf Hall
Kings Head **PH**
Wythes La
Shore Rd
Col 40 bour
Freiston Shore
300

The Grange
Couchdyke Hall
Coupledyke Hall
End Road
Church La
Mill La
Tamworth Green
Freiston Low

Fishtoft
Nunn's Bridge
Scalp Rd
Cropper's Lane
Cut End
Road
Scrane End
Shore Rd

Freiston
Bridge

Wyberton Marsh

The Haven

RSPB
Frampton Marsh
The Scalp

Kirton Marsh

The Cats
Fosdyke Wash

Fleet Haven Outfall

Leaden Hall
Lawwater La
Bingham Lodge
Holbeach St Matthew

The Grange
Christie House
Sot's Hole
Durham's Rd

Holbeach St Marks
Lincoln La
Woodstoke House

Eastern

Holbeach Marsh
Sluice Road
Bertie Lodge

Dawsmere
Dawsmere Rd
Gedney Drove End

Cox's Creek

252

Crab's Hole

Gedney Marsh

Black Barn
Sutton Corner

Holbeach Bank Penny Hill
Coney Garth House
Hurn Bank
Holbeach Hurn
Hurn Hall
Hurn Rd
Gedney Dyke
Green Bank
Roman

Middle Drove
North Dro
Lutton Marsh
Lutton Grange

Guy's Head Rd
Leamlands

Cackle Hill
The Manor
PH
Chequers
Lutton
South Drove
Roper's Gate
Lutton Gowts

Guy's Head
Curlew Lodge
Rookery Rd

Holbeach Fleet Hargate
FLEET ROAD
B1515
Delph Bank
7
Chapelgate
Gedney
Docking's
Lutton Gowts
Little London
Butterfly & Falconry Park

Avenue
Farm Road
East Bank
Sluice Road

Fleet Lodge
Branches La
Half East
Fleet
Oak Lodge
A17 B1359
Manor House
Roman
Wood Lane
New House
Avenue Farm
Little Sutton

Port Sutton Bridge
Hospital Rd
East Bank
Wingland Marsh
Garner's Lane

Cockerell Rd
Anchor

Norfolk
Lincolnshire

Terrington Ma

Gedney Broadgate
Garnsgate
Long Sutton
Sutton Crosses

Delph Rd
Burdikes
Bridge Road
Sutton Bridge

Grange Road
New Roman Bank
Sutton Rd

Bellmount

Walpole Cross Keys

Orange Row
Emorsgate
South Green

Saturday Bridge
Fleet Fen
Clark's Hill
Foreman's Bridge
Old Gate
South Housellend House
Strawberry Hall
Tydd St Mary
Tydd St Mary's Marsh

South Holland Lodge
River Nene

King John Bank
Goose's Lane
Old Inclosed Marsh
Eastlands Bank
Market Lane

A17

Te St

Hay Green

Clifton's Bridge
Sutton St James
B1165
Foremans Bridge
Draw Dike
DRAW DIKE
Tydd Gote
Hannath Hall

South Holland Main Drain
Gipsy Road
Long Dro
Walpole Marsh
Walpole St Andrew

Walpole St Peter
Wash Dyke

Station Rd

Tilne High

Manor Hill Corner
Barton Holt
Kirkgate
Four Gotes

E
F Tydd St Giles
G
Foul Anchor
245
Rose Hall
Walpole Bank
Church End
H St Peter's Lodge
Church Lane
Mill La

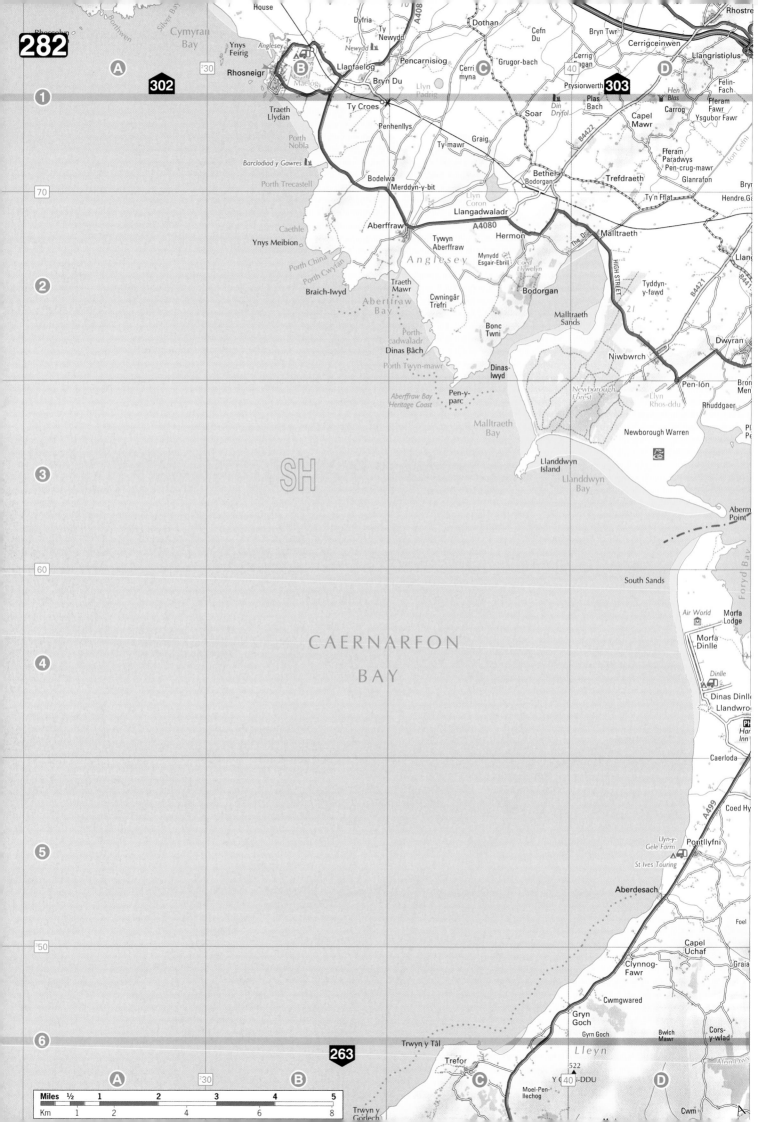

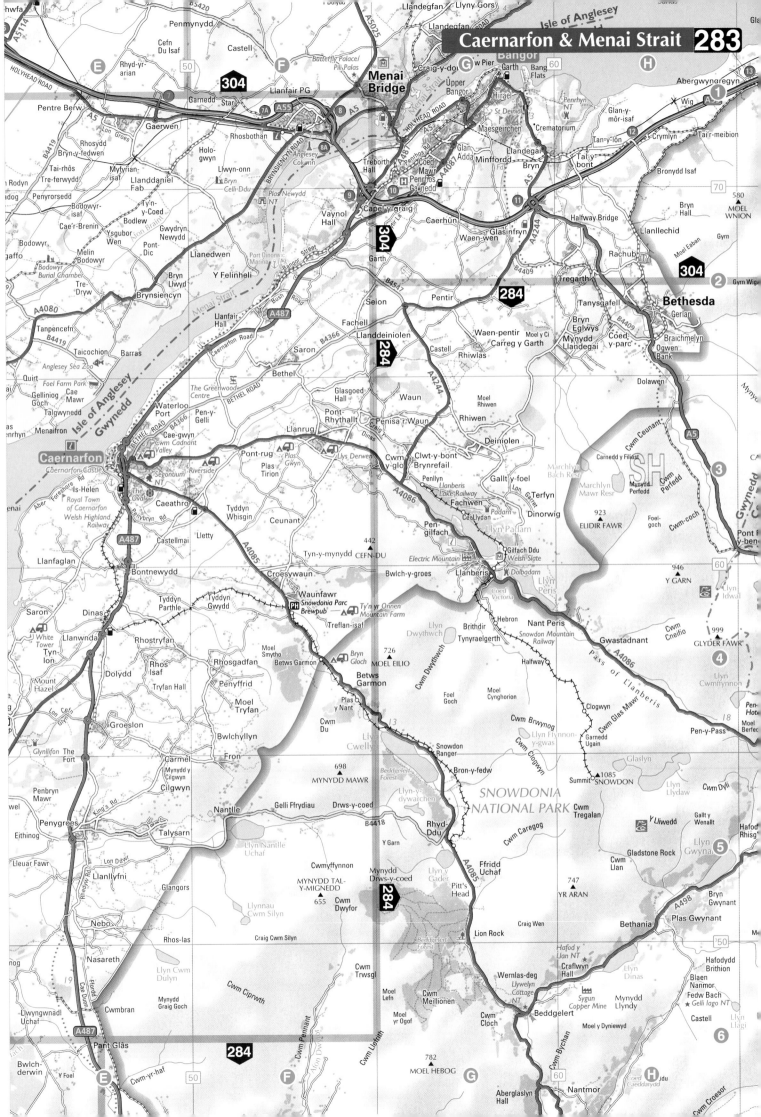

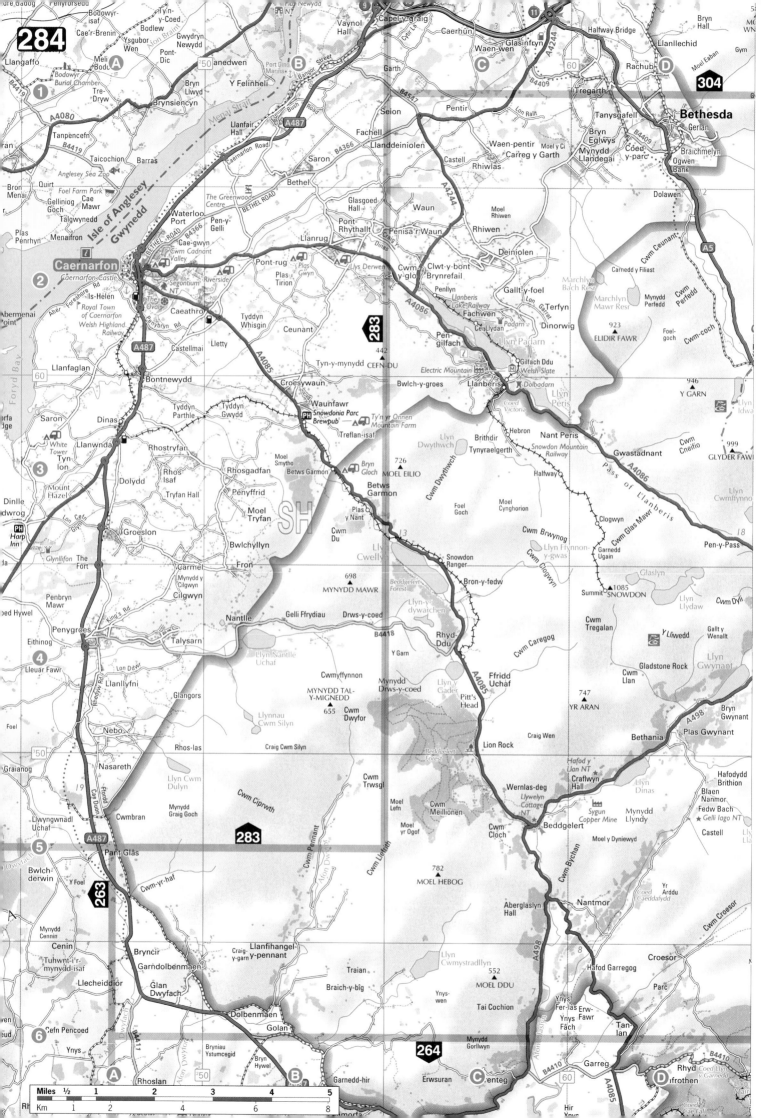

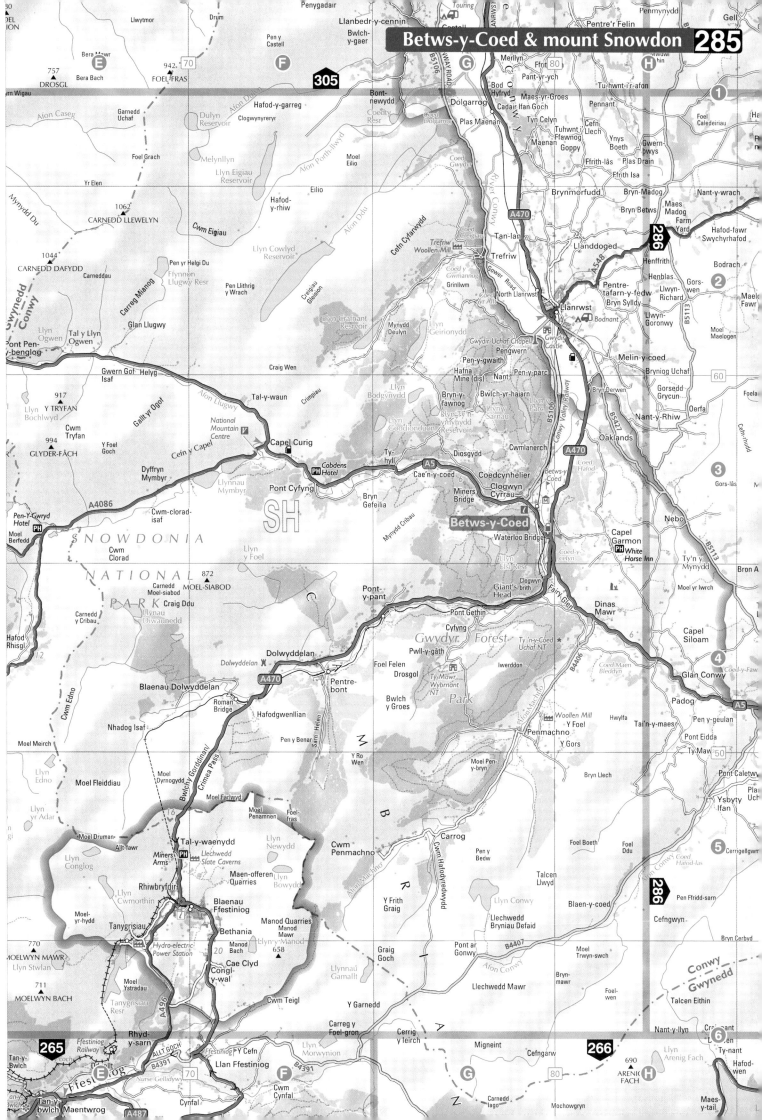

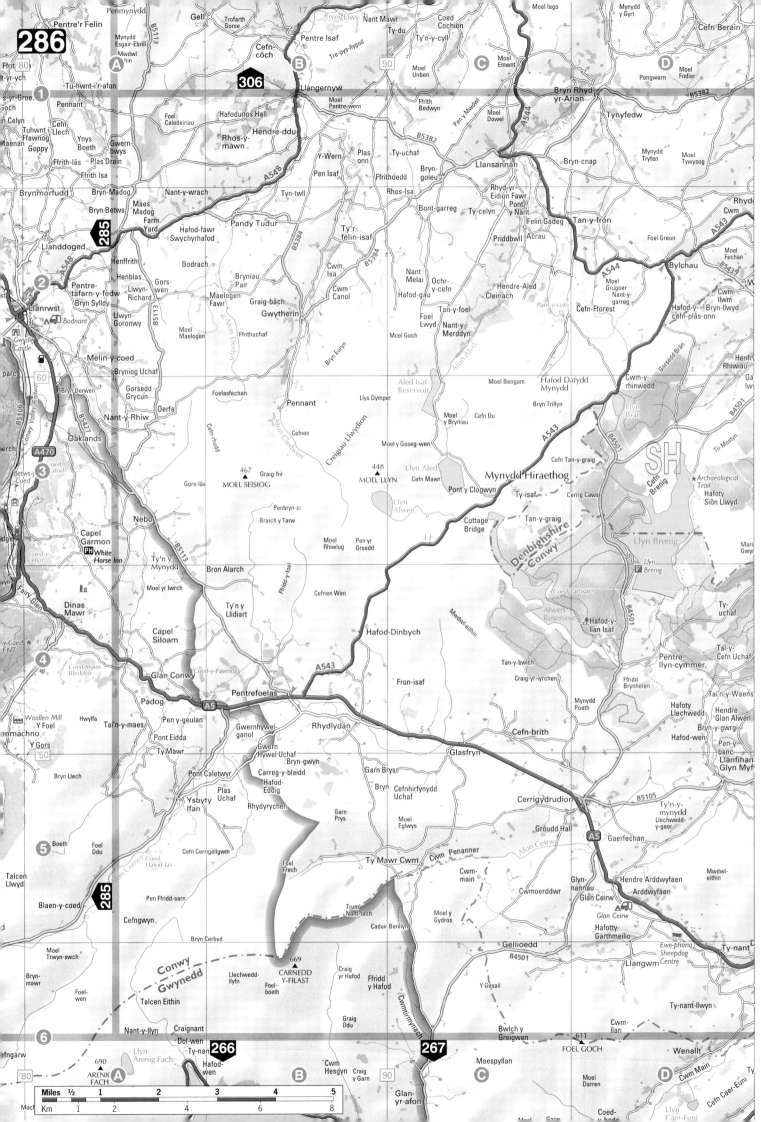

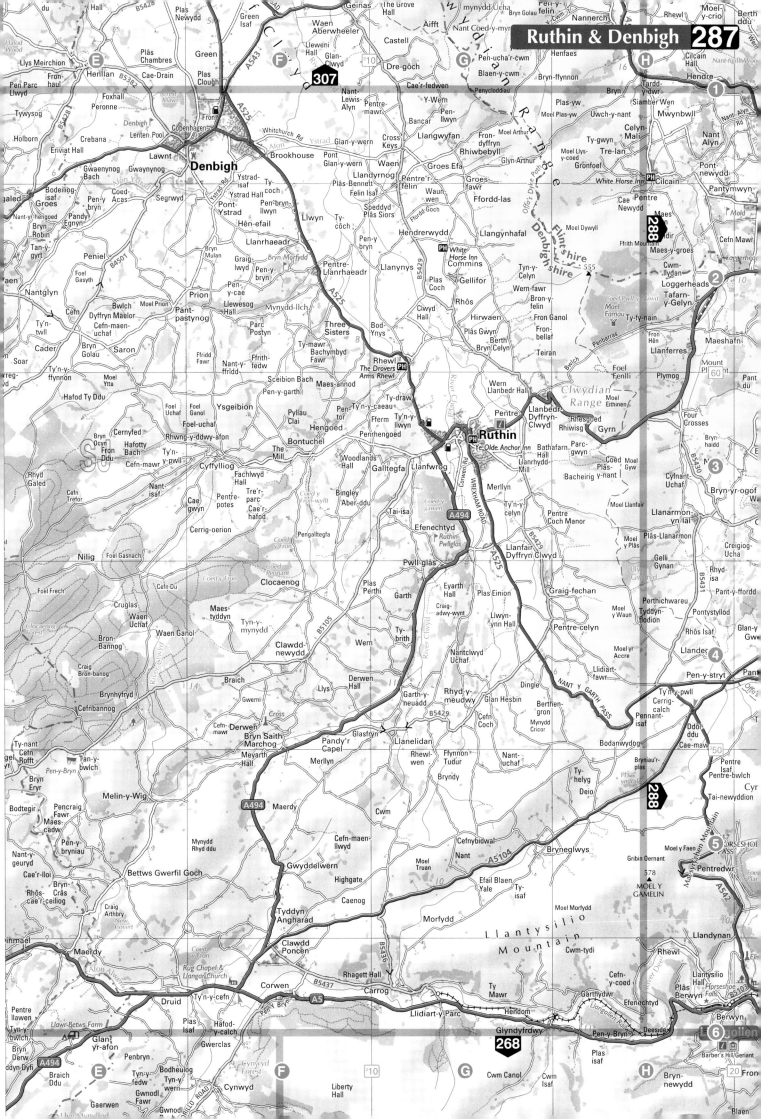

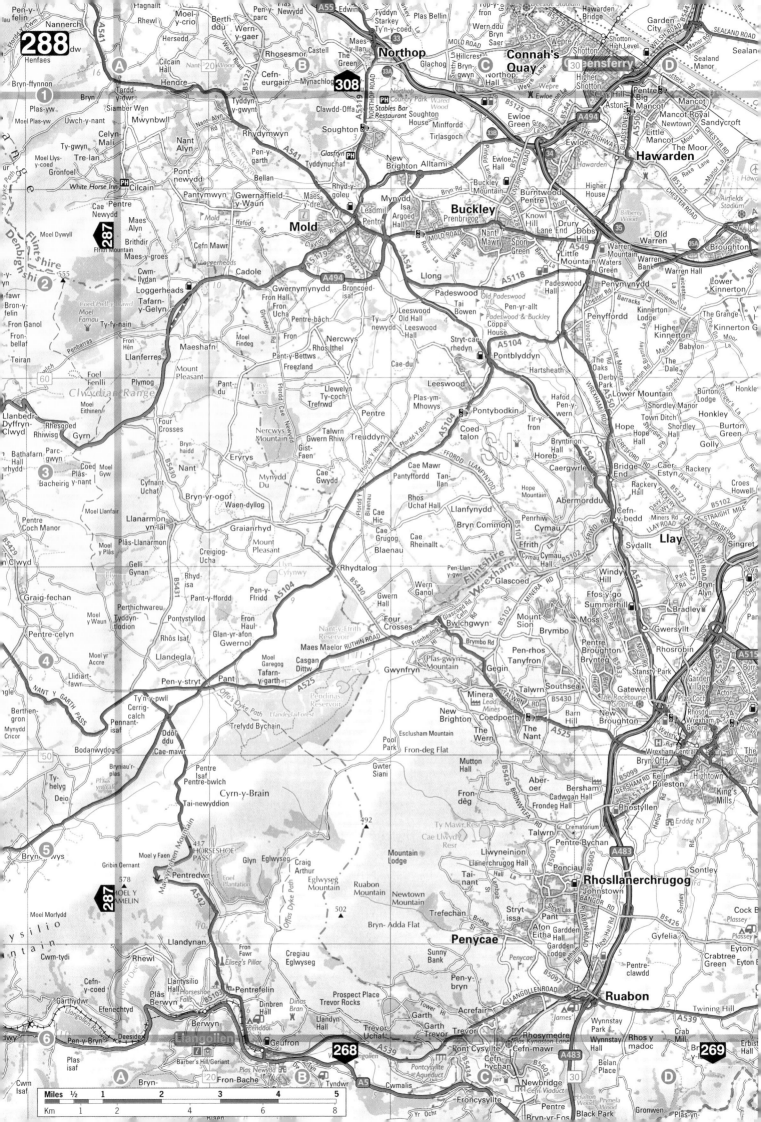

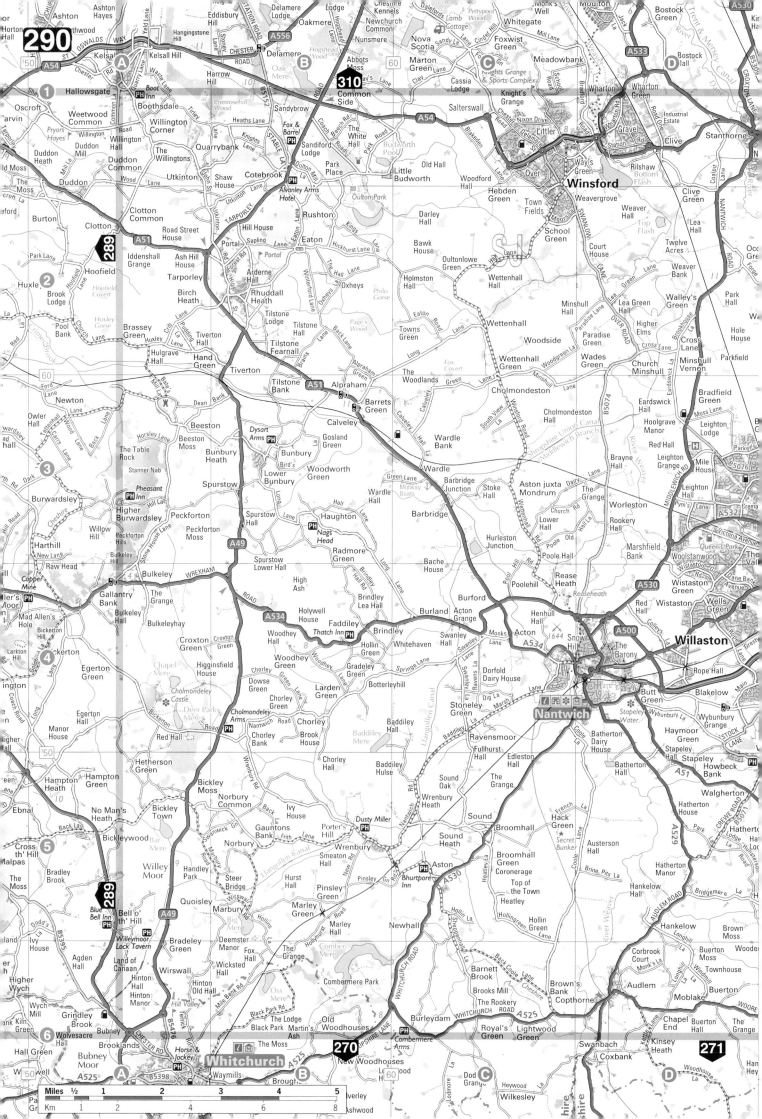

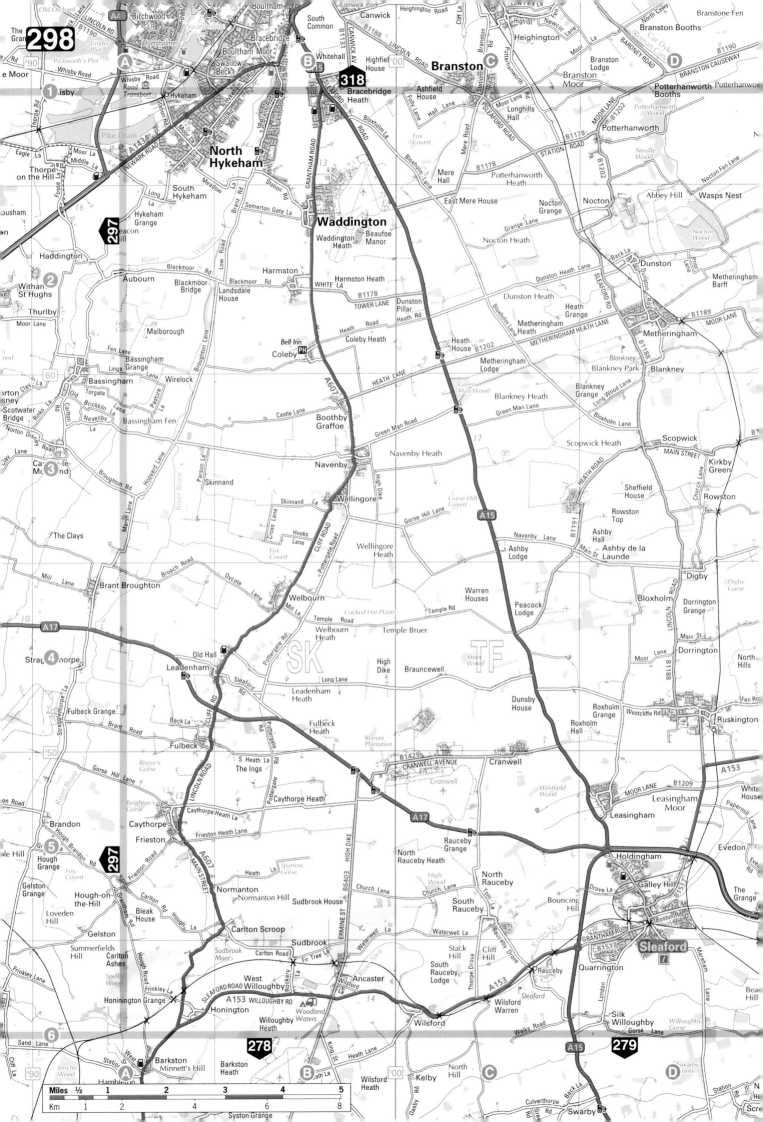

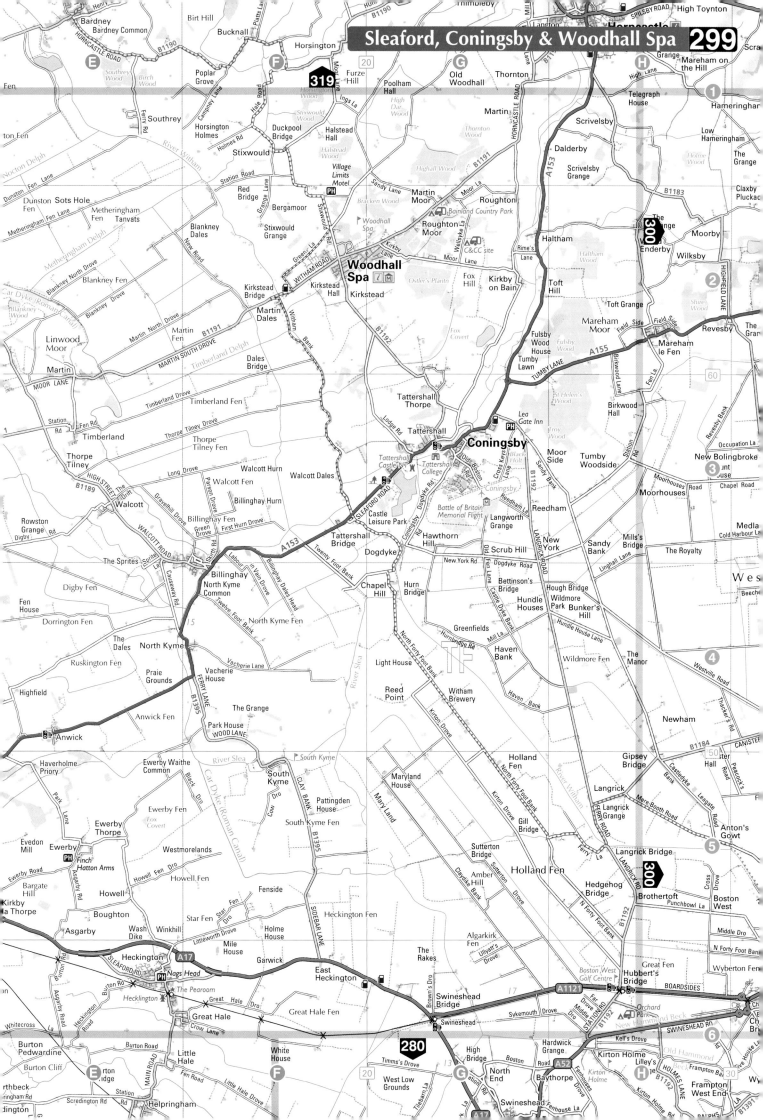

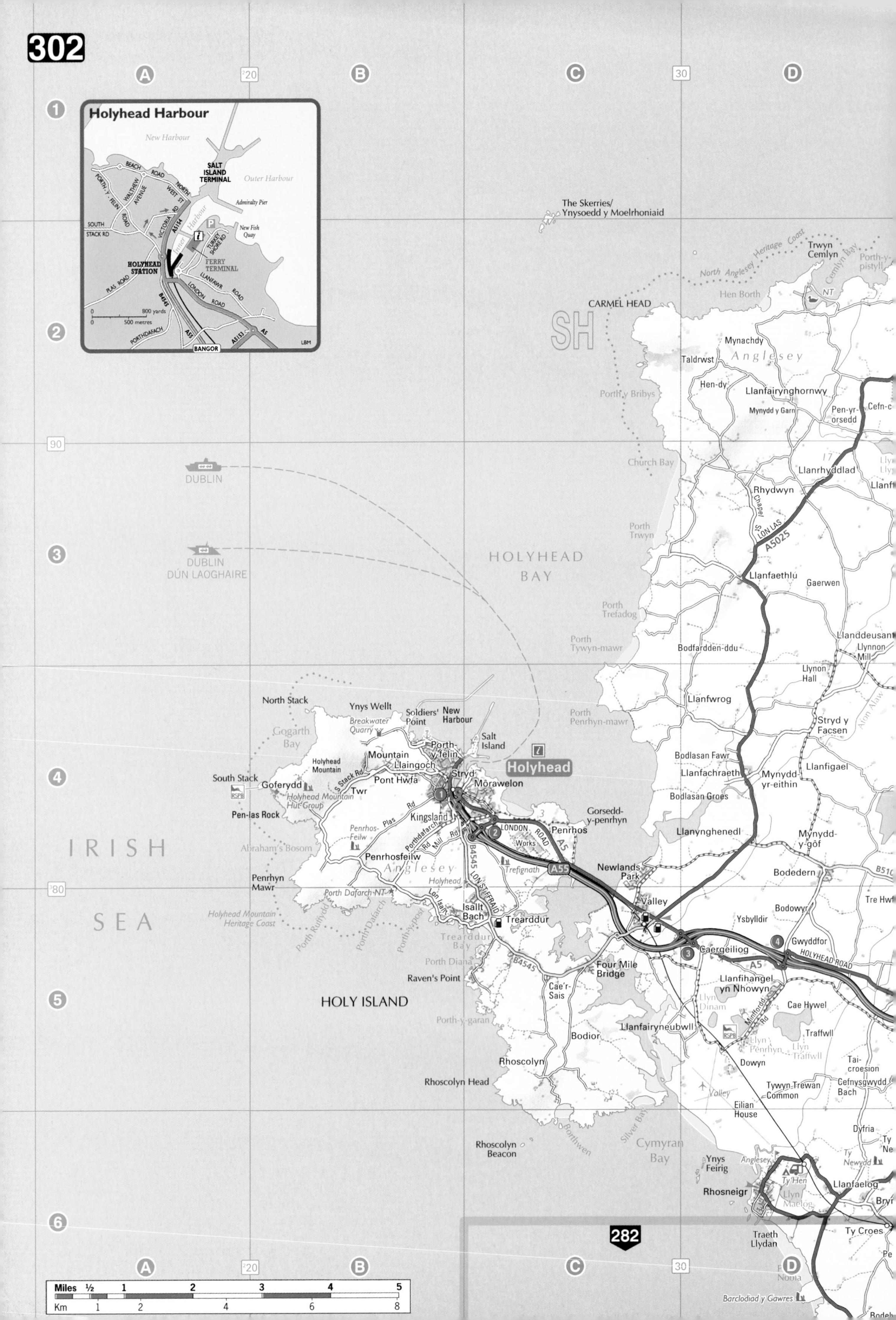

Holyhead Harbour

New Harbour

SALT ISLAND TERMINAL

Outer Harbour

BEACH ROAD

WALTHEW AVENUE

NORTH

WEST ST

Admiralty Pier

PORTH-Y-FELIN

SOUTH STACK RD

VICTORIA RD

A5154

P

New Fish Quay

TURKEY SHORE RD

FERRY TERMINAL

HOLYHEAD STATION

LLANFAWR ROAD

LONDON ROAD

PLAS ROAD

B4545

PORTHDAFACH

A55

A5153

A5

BANGOR

LBM

0   800 yards
0   500 metres

The Skerries/
Ynysoedd y Moelrhoniaid

CARMEL HEAD

North Anglesey Heritage Coast

Trwyn Cemlyn

Porth-y-pistyll

NT

SH

Hen Borth

Mynachdy

Anglesey

Taldrwst

Hen-dy

Llanfairynghornwy

Mynydd y Garn

Pen-yr-orsedd

Cefn-c

Porth y Bribys

Church Bay

Rhydwyn

Llanrhyddlad

17

Lly
Lly

Llanf

Chapel

LÔN LAS

A5025

HOLYHEAD
BAY

Porth
Trwyn

Llanfaethlu

Gaerwen

Porth
Trefadog

Bodfardden-ddu

Llanddeusan

Llynnon
Mill

Porth
Tywyn-mawr

Llanfwrog

Llynon
Hall

DUBLIN

Stryd y
Facsen

DUBLIN
DÚN LAOGHAIRE

Porth
Penrhyn-mawr

Bodlasan Fawr

Llanfachraeth

Mynydd-
yr-eithin

Llanfigael

North Stack

Ynys Wellt

Soldiers'
Point

New
Harbour

Bodlasan Groes

Porth
Penrhyn-mawr

Breakwater
Quarry

Salt
Island

Llanynghenedl

Mynydd-
y-gof

Gogarth
Bay

Mountain

Porth-
y-felin

Holyhead

B510

Holyhead
Mountain

Llaingoch

Stryd

Holyhead

Gorsedd-
y-penrhyn

South Stack

RSPB

Goferydd

Pont Hwfa

Môrawelon

Bodedern

Tre Hw

Twr

S Stack Rd

Holyhead Mountain
Hut Group

Plas Rd

Kingsland

Penrhos

LONDON ROAD

3

Pen-las Rock

Penrhos-
Feilw

Works

A5

Bodowyr

Ysbylldir

IRISH

Porthdafarch

Mill Rd

Trefignath

Newlands
Park

Penrhosfeilw

Anglesey

A55

Valley

Gwyddfor

Penrhyn
Mawr

Holyhead

LÔN ISFERAD

4

Caergeiliog

A5

HOLYHEAD ROAD

SEA

Porth Dafarch NT

Isallt
Bach

Trearddur

3

B4545

Llanfihangel
yn Nhowyn

Holyhead Mountain
Heritage Coast

Lôn Isallt

Cae Hywel

Porth Ruthin

Porth Dafarch

Four Mile
Bridge

Llyn
Dinam

Porth-y-post

Trearddur
Bay

B4545

Cae'r-
Sais

Llanfairneubwll

Traffwll

Raven's Point

Porth Diana

Llyn
Penrhyn

Tai-
croesion

Llyn
Traffwll

Porth-y-garan

HOLY ISLAND

Bodior

Dowyn

Cefnysgwydd
Bach

Rhoscolyn

RSPB

Tywyn-Trewan
Common

Valley

Eilian
House

Dyfria

Ty
Ne

Rhoscolyn Head

Porthwen

Silver Bay

Cymyran
Bay

Ynys
Feirig

Anglesey

Ty Hen

Ty
Newydd

Llanfaelog

Bryr

Rhoscolyn
Beacon

Rhosneigr

Llyn
Maelog

282

Traeth
Llydan

Ty Croes

Pe

Barclodiad y Gawres

Bodeb

Miles ½   1   2   3   4   5

Km   1   2   4   6   8

SH

306

E · 70 · F · G · 80 · H

1

90

2

Puffin Island

Great Orme Heritage Coast
Great Orme's Head
Marine Dr
Cable Car
Penmynydd
Pen-trwyn
Trwynygogarth
Gogarth
Great Orme
Maes-y-facrell
Llandudno Bay
or Ormes Bay
Little Ormes Head
Creigiau Rhiwledyn
3
Llandudno
North Wales
Llandudno (Maesdu)
A546
COLWYN ROAD
B5115
Penrhyn Bay
Rhôs Point
Colwyn Bay Cricket
Penrhyn side
Rhôs-on-
Conwy Sands
Maesdu Rd
Bryn Maelgwyn
Queens Head
Glanwydden
Dinarth Hall
Llandrillo-yn-Rhôs
Cwm Howard
Coed Isaf
Glôddaeth La
Llanrhos
Llangwstenin Hall
Deganwy
Bryn Pydew
Pabo
Esgyryn
Crematorium
Mochdre
Tywyn
A470
Mari Hall
Llandudno
Junction
Glyn

CONWY
BAY

Penmaen-bach Point
Conwy
Deganwy
Pen-y-Bryn
Mynydd
4
Penmaen-bach
Conwy Mountain
A547
Brynrhys
Bryn-y-maen
Pendyffryn Hall
Sychnant Pass
Conwy Castle
Conwy
Benarth Hall
Glan Conwy
B5113
Dwygyfylchi
Sychnant Pass Rd
Gyffin
A55
Penmaenmawr
Foel Lûs
Capelulo
Penmaenan
Bangor Road
Garizim
Penmaenan
Llechwedd
Llechan Ucha
Hafodty
Iolyn Hill Park
Llansanffraid Glan Conwy
Pentrefelin
Llanfairfechan
Bryn Derwydd
Moelfre
Plas Tirion
Henryd
Nant-y-cywarch
Deunant
Glan-y-môr Elias
Aber Rd
Nant-y-pandy
Groes Inn
Merchlyn
Croesau
Erw Goch
Cefn Du
Nant-y-felin
Llanfairfechan
Garnedd-wen
Gwern Borter
Bryncwm
Bodnant NT
5
Gorddinog
Garreg Fawr
Graig
Brymbo
Moel Gyffylog
Chwlordd
Gwyllt Rd
Foel Lwyd
610
Coed Mawr Hall
Ty'n-y-groes
Fron Gynnen
Nant
Foel-ganol
TAL-Y-FAN
Rowen
Ty Ucha
Eglwysbach
Coed Pant-glas
Aber Waterfall
Llyn Anafon
Drosgl
Bwlch y Ddeufaen
SNOWDONIA
NATIONAL PARK
White Hart
Caerhûn
Tanrallt
Penmynydd
Pentre'r Felin
Gell
Penygadair
Tynterfyn Touring
Bera Mawr
Llwytmor
Drum
Llanbedr-y-cennin
Castell
Dyto
Mynydd Esgair-Ebrill
Pen y Castell
Bwlch-y-gaer
Tal-y-Bont
Merllyn
Ffrith Lon
Mwdwl Eithin
757
942
Bera Bach
FOEL-FRAS
DROSGL
Bod Hyfryd
Pant-yr-ych
Tu-hwnt-i'r-afon
6
Wigau
Garnedd Uchaf
285
Hafod-y-garreg
Bont-newydd
Dôlgarrog
Maes-yr-Groes
Tyn Celyn
Pennant
Foel Caledeiriau
Foel Grach
Clogwynyreryr
Coedty Resr
Plas Maenan
Cefn
Ynys Boeth
Dulyn Reservoir
Coed Dôlgarrog
Maenan
Gwern
Melynllyn
Moel Eilio
Coed Gwydyr

E · 70 · F · G · 80 · H

Llandudno

0   200 metres

THE GREAT ORME TRAMWAY STATION
TABERNACLE
MARKET HALL
LLANDUDNO MUSEUM
GLODDAETH ST
DEGANWY
HOME FRONT EXPERIENCE
TOWN HALL
LLANDUDNO ARCHIVES & RECORD OFFICE
LIFEBOAT STATION
VICTORIA SHOPPING CENTRE
CAB
ORIEL MOSTYN ART GALLERY
LIBRARY
ALICE IN WONDERLAND CENTRE
PO
TRINITY SQUARE
POLICE STA
LLANDUDNO STATION
MAGISTRATES COURT
CLINIC
SCHOOL
Playing Fields
Recreation Ground
SCH
Coaches
LLANDUDNO FC
SCHOOL
FIRE STATION
SUPERSTORE
SUPERSTORE
CONWAY ROAD
TUDOR CRESCENT
SWIMMING POOL
NORTH WALES THEATRE & CONFERENCE CENTRE
Area under development
MOSTYN BROADWAY
MOSTYN CRES
NEVILL CRES
PENRHYN CRES
SAILING CLUB
BANDSTAND
North Shore
THE PROMENADE
Llandudno Bay
ST GEORGE'S CRESCENT
GLAN Y MOR PDE
SOUTH PARADE
MOSTYN CHAMPNEYS RETAIL PARK
TEN PIN BOWLING
SCHOOL
Playing Fields

BETWS-Y-COED, CONWY

SH

305

Llandudno Bay
Ormes Bay

Little Ormes Head
Creigiau Rhiwledyn
Penrhyn Bay
Rhos Point
Colwyn Bay Cricket Club
Rhôs-on-Sea
Penrhynside
Queens Head
Bryn Maelgwyn
Glanwydden
Dinarth Hall
Llandrillo-yn-Rhôs
Bryn Pydew
Crematorium
Llangwstenin Hall
Colwyn Bay
West Prom
Prom
Old Prom
Colwyn Bay
Bron-Y-Wendon
Abergele Roads
Kinmel Bay
Ty-mawr
Towyn
Llanddulas
TOWYN ROAD
Ty Mawr
Belgrano
Pensarn
River Gele
Plâs Llwyd
Glan-y-gors
Ty'n-y-llyn
Kinmel Park
Llandudno Junction
Pabo
Esgyryn
Mochdre
Pen-y-Bryn
Old Colwyn
Old Hwy
Old Colwyn
Pentre-uchaf
Mynydd Marian
Llysfaen
Terfyn
Bryn Dulas
Cefn yr Ogof
Rhyd-y-foel
RHUDDLAN ROAD
Tan-y-gopa
St Asaph Rd
Gofer
Abergele
St George's Rd
St George
Kinmel Arms
Kinmel Park
Kinmel Hall
Dolwyd
Mynydd
Glyn
Glan Conwy
Bryn-rhys
Llansanffraid Glan Conwy
Pentrefelin
Ffridd y Mynydd
Bryn-y-maen
Llanelian yn-Rhôs
Isallt Rd
Pen-y-corddyn-mawr
Tyddyn-uchaf
Nant Fawr
Ffynhonnau
Ysgeirallt
Sirior Bach
Tan-y-mynydd
Moelfre
Nant Meifod
Nant-y-cywarch
Deunant
Erw Goch
Mynydd Llanelian
Coed Bryndansi
Ffernant
Cefn Castell
Dolwen
Moelfre Isaf
Tyn-y-bedw
Pen-y-gribin
Pont-y-Ddôl
Bodysgallen Isa
Bodnant NT
Croesau
Fron Gynnen
Dawn
Baron Hill
Ty-mawr
Coed Bryn-mawr
DOLWEN ROAD
Dolwen
Betws-yn-Rhos
Hunters' Hamlet
Peniarthy Bach
Moelfre Uchaf
Mynydd Bodrochwyn
Mynydd-dir
Pen-y-Coed
Plâs-uchaf-Resr
Hawk & Buckle Inn
Graig
Brymbo
Rhandir
Chwefford
Cefn Du
Tai Codau Mawr
Mynydd Glyn-Lws
Wheatsheaf Inn
Roberts
Mynydd Bodran
Fron Fawr
Tal-y-bryn
305
Eglwysbach
Trofarth
Wenallt
River Elwy
Llanfair Talhaiarn
Llannefydd
Dolwen Resr
Penmynydd
Pentre'r Felin
Mynydd Esgair-Ebrill
Mwdwl Eithin
Gell
Trofarth Gorse
Ysgubor-newydd
Moel Iago
Mynydd y Gyrt
Cefn Berain
Pennant
Cefn Llech
Tu-hwnt-i'r-afon
Pentre Isaf
River Elwy
Nant Mawr
Ty-du
Ty'n-y-cyll
Coed Cochion
Moel Emwnt
Pengwern
Moel Fodiar
Tyn Celyn
Llangernyw
Moel Pentre-wern
Hendre-ddu
Rhôs-y
Plas-onn
Ty-uchaf
Pen Isaf
Pen y Mwdwl
Moel Dowel
Bryn Rhyd-yr-Arian
Tynyfedw
Mynydd Tryfan
Moel Tywysog
Llansannan
Bryn-cnap
286

308

1

Red
Rocks

2

We
Kir

308

River Dee

3

SJ

Point
of Ayr

Wild
Road

The Warren

Presthaven Sands

Prestatyn

Beach
Rd E

y-Efrith

Tyn-y-Morfa

Talacre

RSPB

90

80

PH

Nant Hall

Gronant Rd

Gronant

Gwespyr

Tanlan
Banks

Station Rd

Rhyl

Rhyl Coast Road

A548

Prestatyn

Flordd'sa

Glasdir

Ffynnongroyw

Rhyl

i

B5118

Teilia

Llanasa Road

Picton

Picton
Rd

23

A548

DYSERTH

Rhydorddwy
Fawr

St Meliden

Gwaenysgor

Llanasa

Rhewl-
fawr

Pen-y-
ffordd

Mostyn Quay

Belle
Vue

B5119

ROAD

Meliden

Glan-
yr-afon

Garth

Mostyn

ke

Derwen

A547

Allt
Graig

Tan-yr-allt

Gop Hill

Axton

Trelogan

Rhewl-Mostyn

Glan-y-don

80

Cwybr

Pentre
La Pen-y-
ffordd

Long
Acre

Bryniau

Mia Hall

Berthengam

Pentre-
ffynnon Hall

Tre-Mostyn

Llannerch-y-mor

Ynys

3

Dyserth

Trelawnyd

Marian

Walwen

Mynydd Mostyn

Maes Pennant

The
Marsh

Rhuddlan

Rhuddlan

A5151

Ochr-
y-foel

Henfryn
Hall

Sarn

Bryn-
coch

Mertyn
Downing

Hafod-llwyn

Ty-
Coch

Moel Hiraddug

Pen-y-
Cefn-Isaf

Graig-
Arthur

Tre
Abbot

12 Glol

Gelli

Downing

Pentre
Mertyn
Hall

Stokyn
Hall

Greenfield

The
Moor

H

A525

Criccin

Plas
Is Llan

Marian Frith

Plâs-
mawr

Plas
Captain

Whitford

Garreg

Tan-yr-
allt

Golch
Carmel

Bryn Celyn
Holway

Holywell

4

A5026

Pengwern

St Asaph Road

B5429

Cwm

Marian Cwm

Bryn
Glas

Pwllhalog

Llyn
Helyg

Per-ffordd-llân

Saith ffynnon

St Winefride's
Well

Pen-y-
maes

Bodelwyddan

Pentre

Ddwylig

Cyffredin

Ty
Celyn
Fron

Penisa r

Pant Glas

A5151

Lloc

Carmel
Road

Mwdwl-
eithin

26

Plas-
coch

Pen-y-
Bryn

Pen-y-
Palmant

Plas
yn Cwm
Hall

Brynllithrig
Hall

Pen-y-
mynydd

Penisar
Mynydd

Pant y Wacco

Gorsedd

Monastery
Rd

Pen-y-
Ball Top

Smithy
Gate

Bodelwyddan

Faenol-
Broper

27

The Roe

27A

Fachwen

Rhyllon

Rhuallt

29

Ty-
ali

Bryngwyn
Bach

Pant-y-dulath

30

Ffordd
Las

Llwybr-hir

31

Ffrith y Garreg Wen

Pen-y-cefn

Pantasaph

Naid-y-march

Calcoed

Ffordd
Calcoed

Ffordd
Holywell

Brynford
Calcot
Hall

Pwll
clai

Milwr

Pwll

A55

A5026

coed

H

GLASCOED ROAD

PH

Plough Inn

St Asaph

28

A55

Moel
Maenefa

Waen Hilin

Aelwyd-
uchaf

Plâs
Cerrig

Pant

Caerwys
Hall

Truly

Babell

Black
Lion
PH

Ffordd Babell

Prysau

Brynford

308

Dolphin

Llong

32

A5026

Groesffordd
Marli

Cefn
Meiriadog

Bryn
Asaph

B5381

Eryl
Hall

Glan-
Clwyd

Waen
Goleugoed

Wern Ddu

Tremeirchion

Bryngwyn
Hall

Pant
Glas

Croes-
wian

Ffrith

Ivy
House

Waen

Mynydd
Ilan

5

Pentre Halkyn

Pen-Uchar
Plwyf

Ty'n-y-
ffordd

Llannerch
Hall

UPPER DENBIGH RD

Castell

Hafod-
y-coed

Cefn Du

Ty-newydd

Caerwys

Maes-
mynan

B5122

Britannia Inn

PH

Pwll-melyn

Bwlch

Glascoed
Fawr

Wigfair

A525

Llannerch
Park

Ddolibod

Clwydian
Range

Graig

Afon-
wen

A541

Lixwm

Walwen

Halkyn
Windmill

Mountain

Ty'n-
y-coed

Glanllyn

Hafod-
y-Green

Perthewig

Sodom

Candy Mill

Ddol

Ysceifiog

Fron-
haul

Ffordd
y Graig

Rhes-
y-cae

Catch

Bont-
newydd

River Elwy

Trefnant

Berth
Bach

BODFARI

Vale of
Clwyd

Ty-isaf

Bryn yr
Eithin

Waen-
dymarch

Bryn
Rug

Halkyn
Mountain

Garneddwen

Graig

Trefant

Ty'n Lôn

Bodfari

A541

Coed-
mynydd-isaf

Fron-
haul

Ffagnallt

Pentre-
du

Galltfaenan
Hall

B5428

Plas
Newydd

Green
Isaf

Waen
Aberwheeler

Geinas

The Grove
Hall

Moel y Parc

Coed-y-
mynydd-Ucha

Pen-y-
felin

Bryn Golau

Nannerch

Rhewl

Moel-
y-crio

Berth-
ddu

Hafod
Wood

Llys Meirchion

Plâs
Chambres

Lleweni
Hall

Aifft

Nant Coed-y-mynydd

Hafod-
y-cwm

Nant-y-
cwm

Penbedw

Cilcain
Hall

Llys
Meirchion

Fron-
haul

Cae-Drain

Green

Glan-
Clwyd

Castell

Pen-ucha'r-cwm

Henfaes

Pen Parc
Llwyd

Henllan

B5382

Plas
Clough

Dre-gôch

Blaen-y-cwm

Bryn-ffynnon

16

Hendre

6

70

20

Tywysog

Fron

Foxhall
Peronne

Cae-
Mawr

287

Cae'r-fedwen

Bancar

Pen-
llwyn

Penycloddiau

Plas-yw

Moel Arthur

Uwch-y-nant

Cel
Mali

Mwynbwll

Holborn

E

Denbigh

Lenten
Pool

Copenhagen

A525

Fron

F

Wh ch Rd Ystrad

A5 10

Glan-y-wern

Cross
Keys

Nant-
Lewis-
Alyn

Pentre-
mawr

Llangwyfan

G

Fron-
dyfyrn

Rhiwbebyll

Moel Plas-yw

Glyn-Arthur

H

Tardd-
y-dwr

Siamber Wen

Moel Llys-
y-coed

Ty-gwyn

Tre-lan

Nant Alyn

Crebana

Eriviat Hall

Lawnt

Brookhouse

Pont
Glan-y-wern

Waen

Groes Efa

Gronfoel

Pont

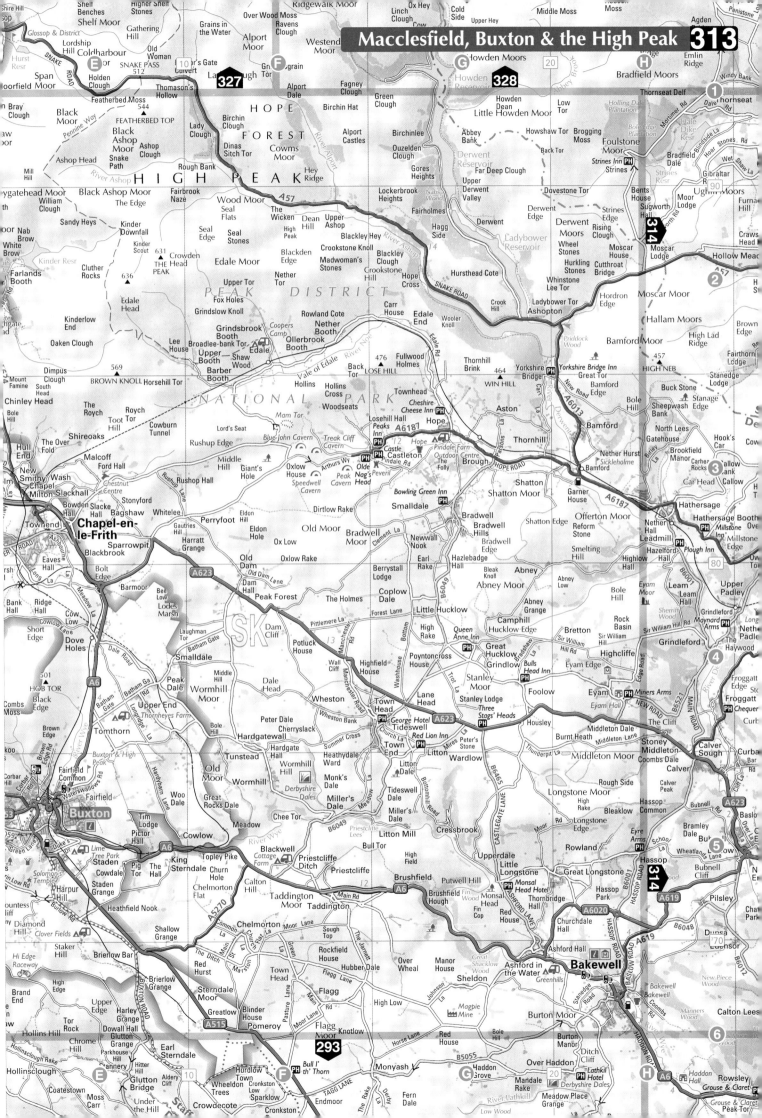

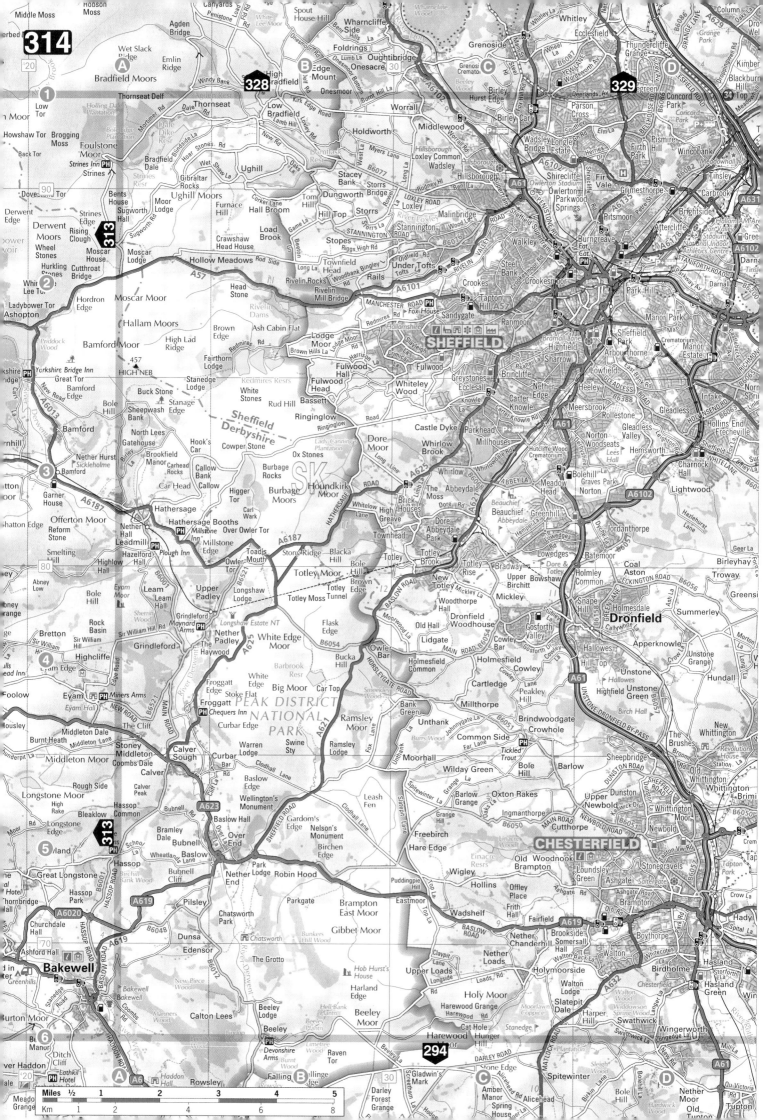

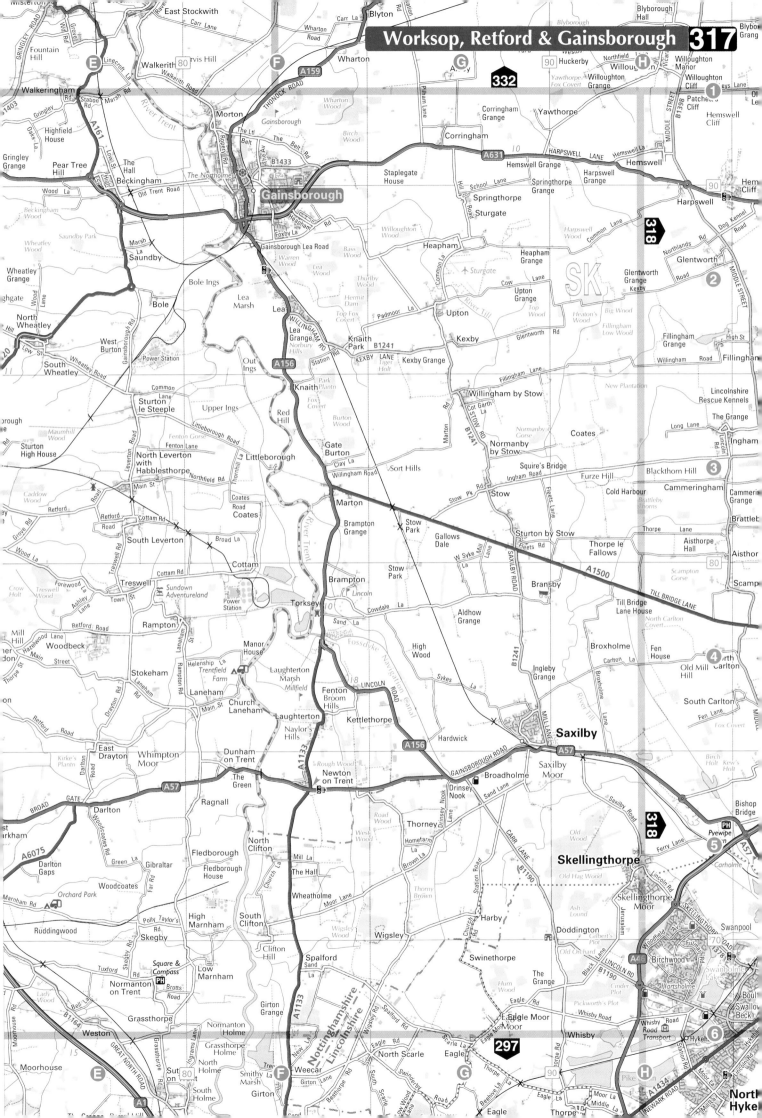

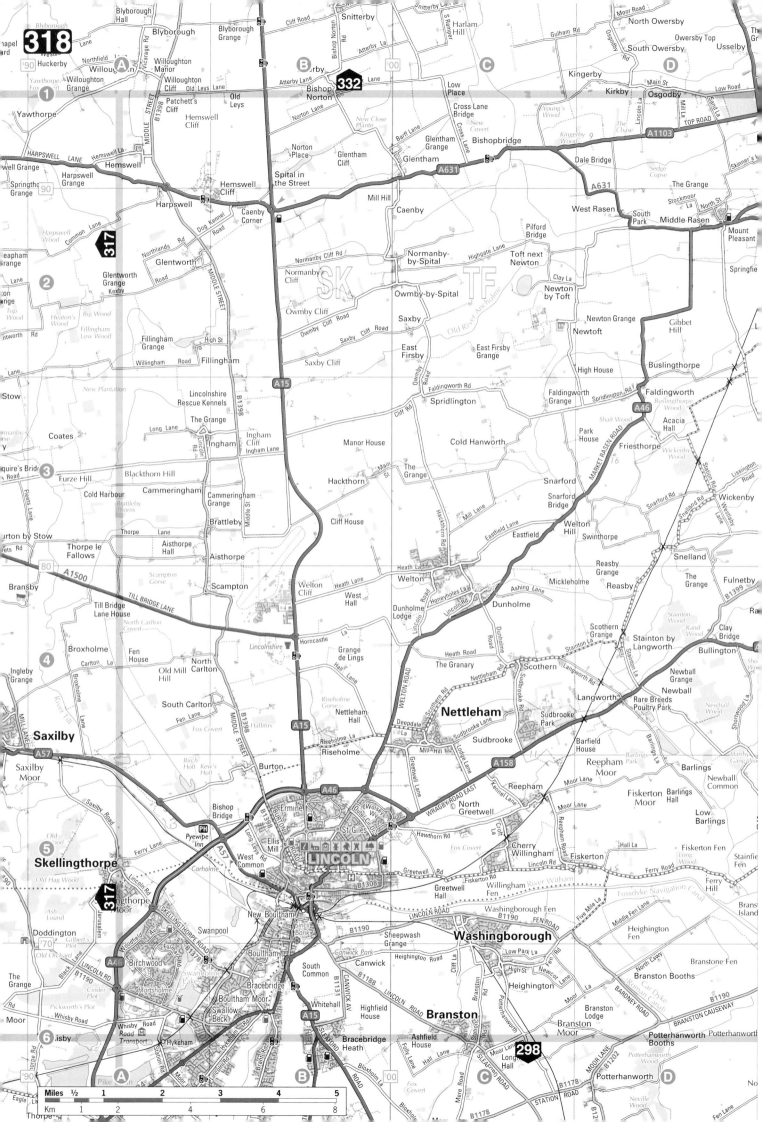

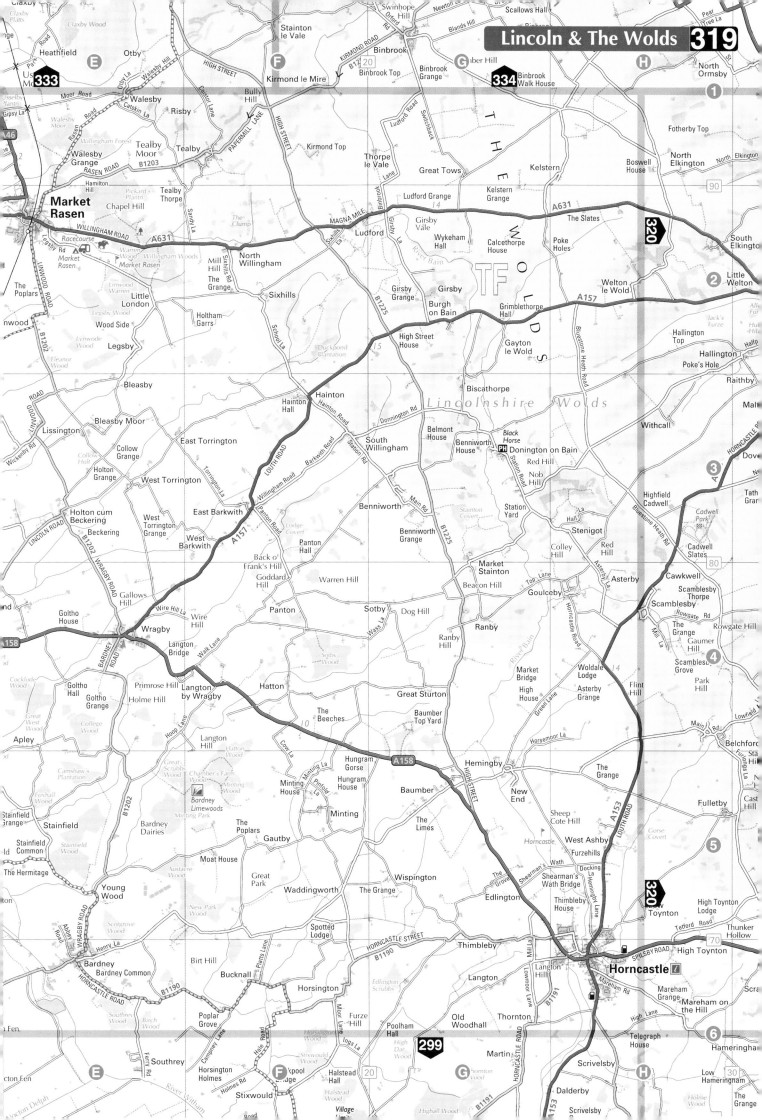

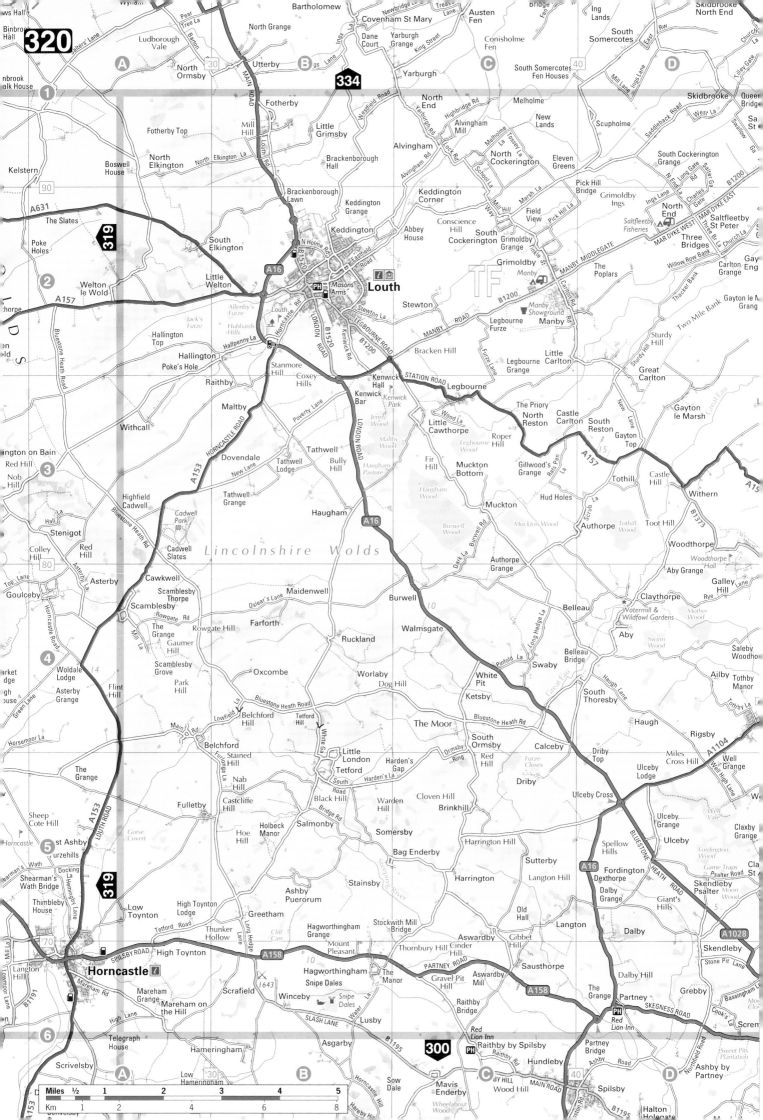

Toby's Hill
Saltfleet
Saltfleet Haven
E **335** **F**
Saltfleetby Theddlethorpe

fleetby ement
Rimac

fleetby range
Theddlethorpe St Helen
A1031
Theddlethorpe All Saints
marsh
Will Row
High Gate
Will Row
Rotten Row
Stain Hill
Stain Lane
Meers Bank
Meers Bridge
Kent Avenue
North End
Golden Sands
Quebec Rd
Golf Rd
Mablethorpe Hall
Seacroft Rd
Mablethorpe
C&CC site
Seaholme Rd
Kirkstead
Mile Lane
Bamber's Bridge
North Rd
North Street
Trusthorpe
Trusthorpe Hall
Main

onglands
Strubby Grange
A1104
Earl's Bridge
West Bank
Thorpe Hall
Axletree Hurn
Strubby
Maltby le Marsh
A52
Sutton on Sea
Sandilands

Beesby
Mill Hill
Beesby Grange
Hagnaby
Rossa Rd
Ings Rd
Sutton Ings
Crabtree La
ALFORD ROAD
HUTTOFT ROAD
Sandilands
A1104
Washdyke Bridge
A1111
Hannah
Saleby
Mill Lane
Markby
Cob Hill
Lane
Sea Lane
Saleby Manor
Sutton ROAD
Crawcroft Lane
The Grange
Roman
Huttoft Bank
Snape Hill
Mill Lane
Asserby Turn
Asserby
Huttoft Bank
ouse
Thoresthorpe
Bilsby
Alford Rd
Jolly Common La
Huttoft The Manor Rectory Rd
A52
Anderby Creek
M
Alford
THURLBY ROAD
The Grange
B1449
18
Rd
Anderby
Thurlby
Farlesthorpe Rd
Bilsby Field
LONG LANE
Alford Rd
Wolla Bank
B1196
Farlesthorpe Fen
Mumby
Chapel Six Marshes
Well Turn
Farlesthorpe
Mill Hill
Washdyke La
Mickleberry Hill
Ember Lane
Stonie's La
Authorpe Row
Wigg La
Chapel Point
Mawthorpe
Bonthorpe
Cumberworth Rd
Cumberworth
Helsey
Sea La
Ancaster Av
Chapel St Leonards
Bonthorpe Road
Cumberworth Ings
Listoft
Listoft La
Sea Rd
Hogsthorpe
xby Andrew
Willoughby
Hoplands Wood
Mill La
Sloothby
High La
Slackholme End
Trunch Lane
Shadoxx Walk
Willoughby Row Wood
Hogsbeck House
Sloothby
S Ings La
B1196
Thwaite Hall
Hasthorpe
Habertoft
Red Gowt
Orby Rd
Addlethorpe
Rectory Rd
Anchor Lane
Ingoldmells
Fantasy Island
Sea La
Ingoldmells Point
Welton High Wood
Mill Lane
Candlesby Hill
Welton le Marsh
Boothby Hall
Boothby Grange
Orby Marsh
Marsh Lane
Marsh Rd
Chapel La
Mill Road
Bolton's La
Roman Bank
A52
Holiday Village
301
The Grange
B1196
Candlesby
Gunby
STATION ROAD
Orby
Faulkers Lane
Heron's Mead
Teapot Hall
Ashington End
Hide's La
Skegness (Ingoldmells) Aerodrome
Seathorne
Winthorpe
E **50** **F**
G **60** **H**
Hunger Hill
The Grange
Gunby Lane
Orby
Willow Lodge
Younger's Lane
Common La
Ingoldr
Mill Hill
Chalk
Church

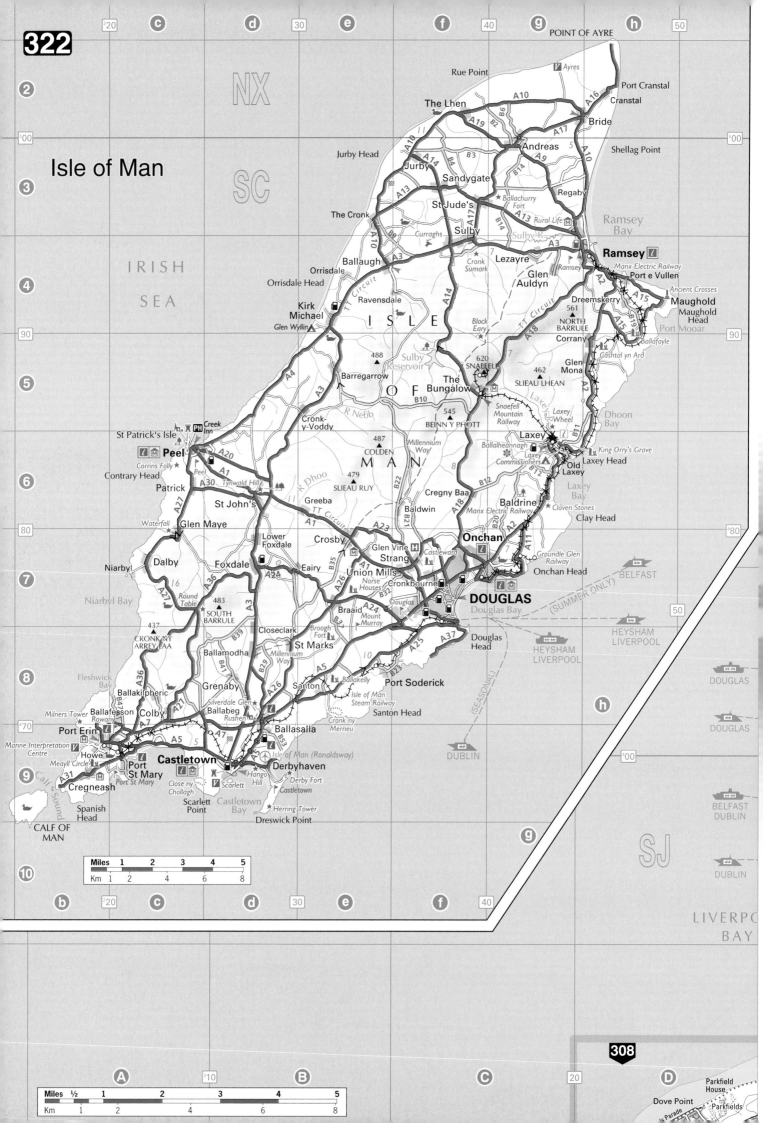

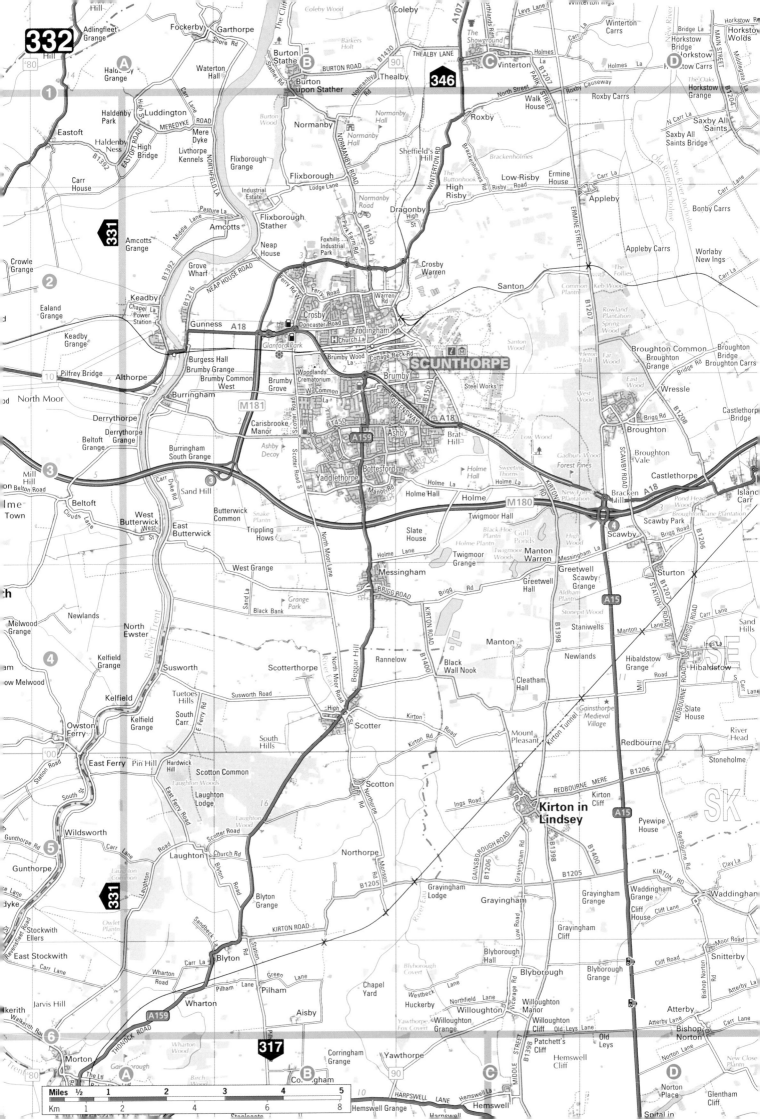

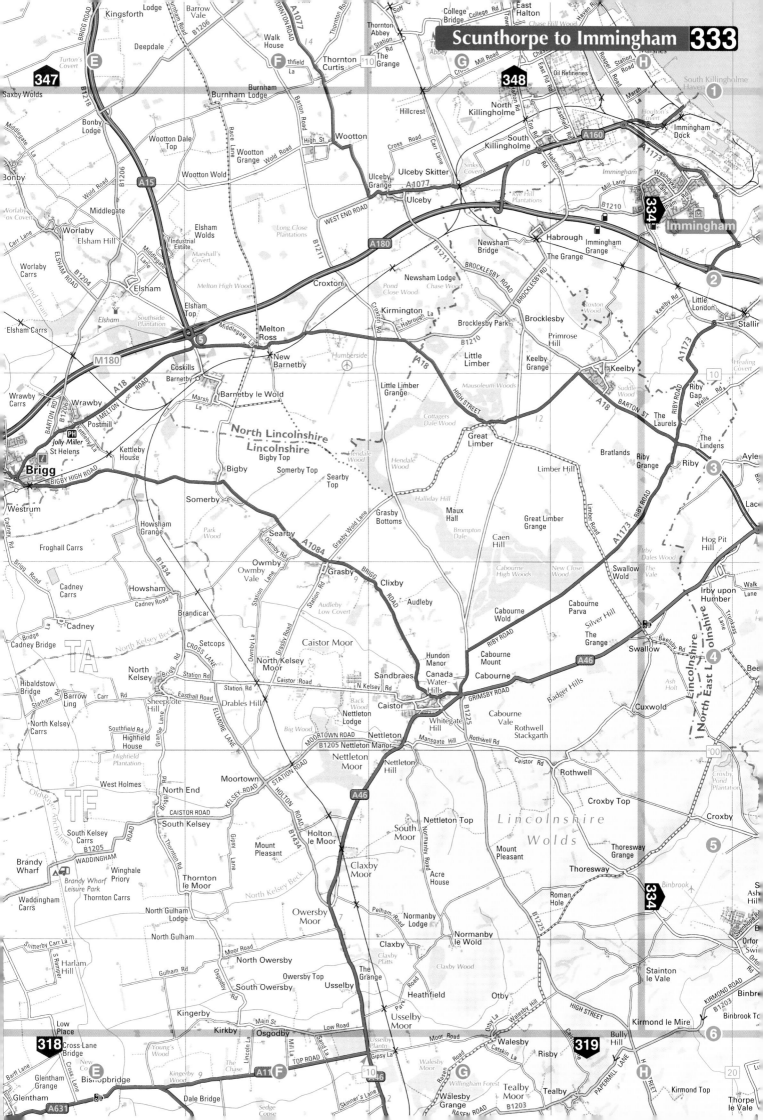

Port plan: Hull p.349

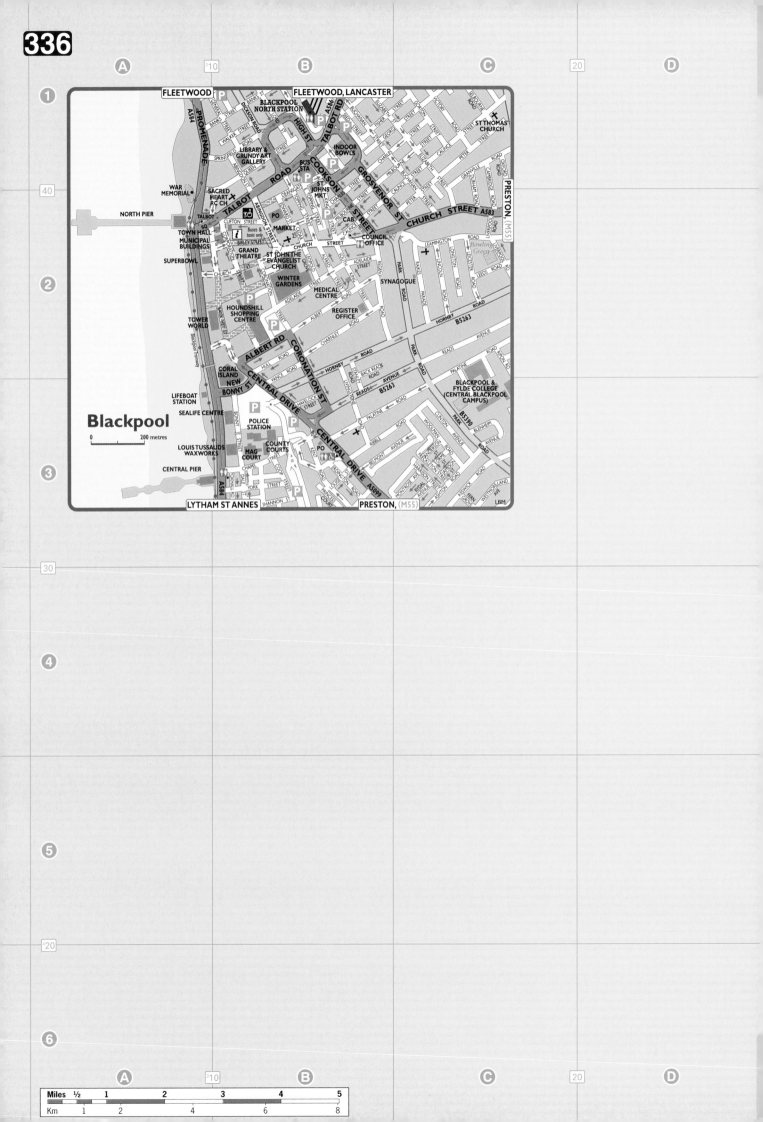

Blackpool

0   200 metres

Miles ½   1   2   3   4   5
Km   1   2   4   6   8

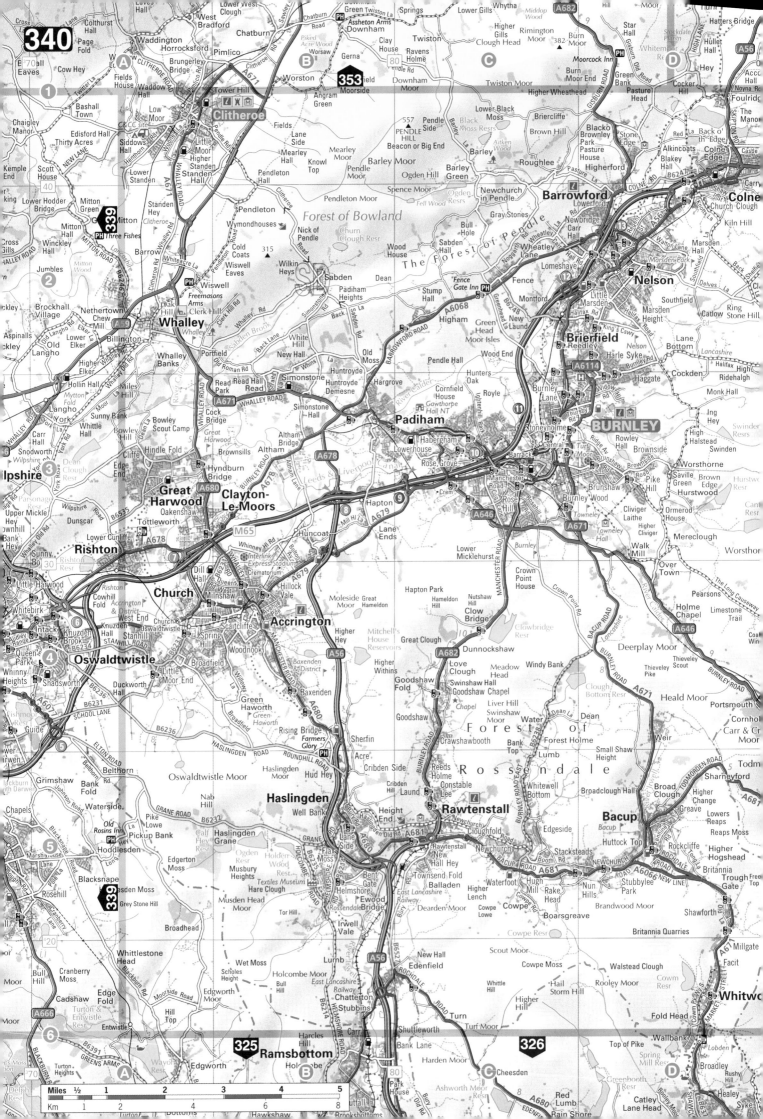

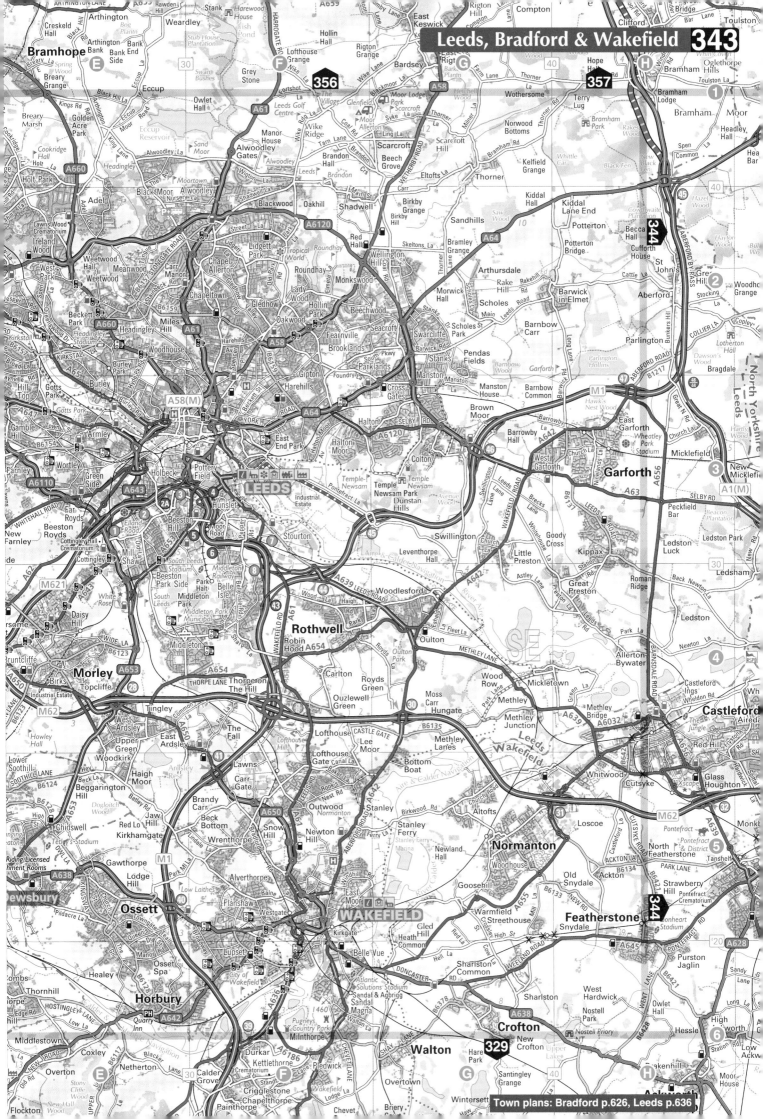

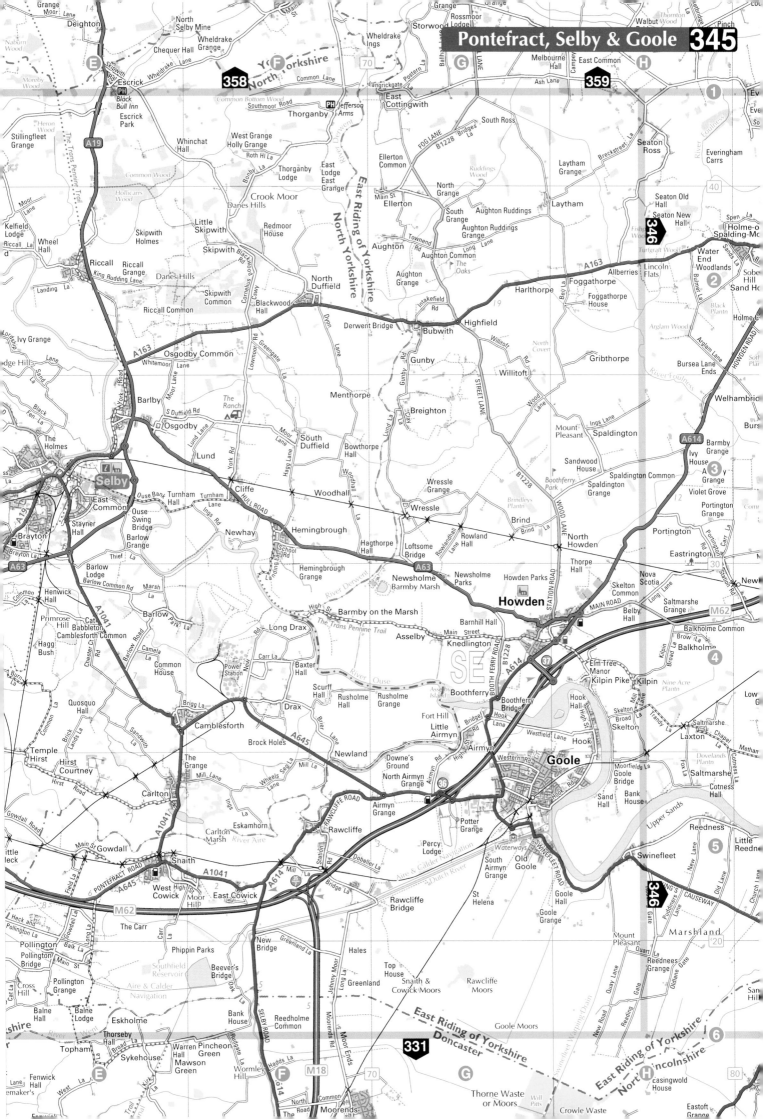

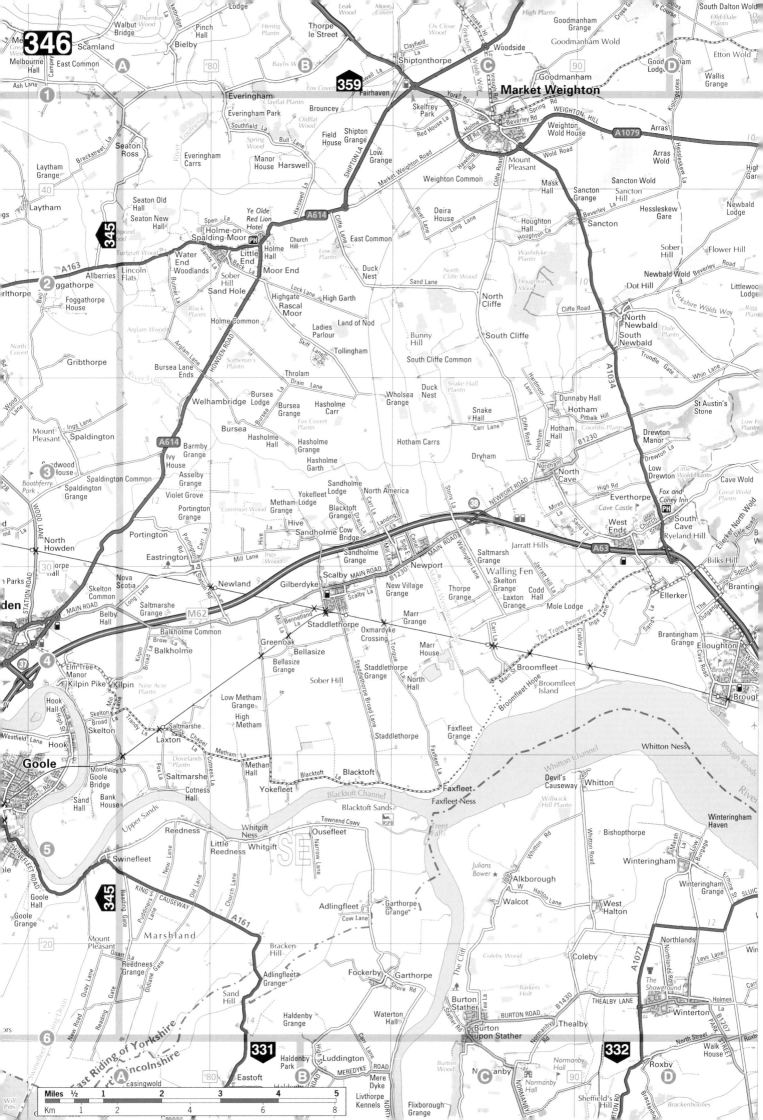

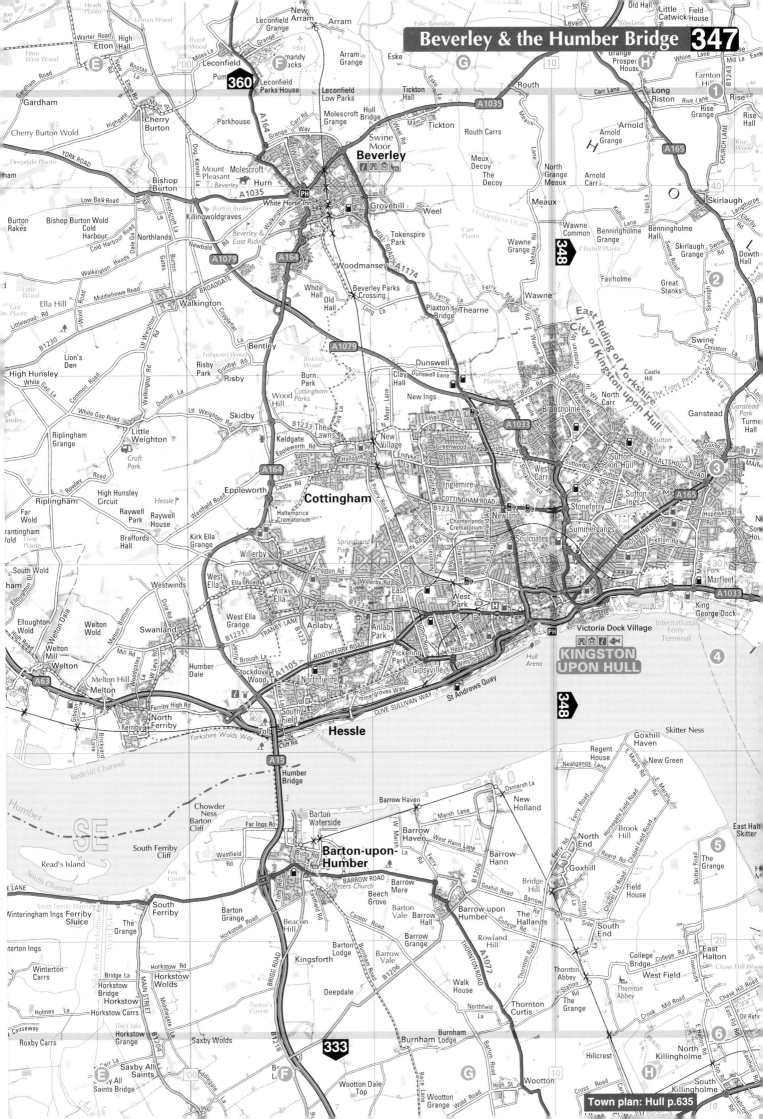

Town plan: Hull p.635

361

E 30 F G 40 H

1

40

TA

Hull Port

YORK
BRIDLINGTON
SUTTON ROAD
B1217 SALTHOUSE ROAD
B1238
BRIDLINGTON
A1033
A1165
B1217
INGS ROAD
A1165
CLOUGH RD
HOLDERNESS ROAD
MAYBURY ROAD
MARFLEET LANE
MT PLEASANT
A1165
A1033
SOUTHCOATES LANE
HEDON ROAD
A1033
A1033
HEDON
A1033
KINGSTON UPON HULL CITY CENTRE
A1033
HEDON ROAD
King George Dock
P
A63
GARRISON
CAR FERRY TERMINAL
P
P
LEEDS

0   1 mile
0   1km
River Humber
LBM

2

Thorpe Garth
Newton Rd
East Newton
Crossmere Hill
rough
Wood

17

Beacon Hill

Fitling
ALDBROUGH RD
Garton
Grimston
Rd
ambleton

Bracken Hill

tling Hall
Primrose Hill
Willow Toft
Fox Covert
pe
The Elms
Tower Rd
Hilston
Hogsea Lane
Pastures La
Owstwick
Furze Road
The Furze
Seaside La
Tunstall
The Grange
New Road
B1242
ALDBROUGH ROAD
Rostun Road
Burton
Pidsea
Burton Rd
North End
PILMAR LANE
Prospect Hill
Carr Rd
Roos
Renish
The Elms
Thirtle Br La
Waxholme

30

Halsham Grange
The Bog
Fox Covert
Rimswell
Rimswell Valley
Owthorne

Withernsea

B1362
NORTH RD
West End
Bunker's Hill
Batty's Corner
Tower Road
Rimswell Lodge
HULL ROAD
Withernsea

4

Halsham Old Hall
East End
Chantry La
Little Newsome
Little England Hill
Great England Hill
Withernsea

eyingham
Southside
North End Rd
Frodingham Hall
Red House

S

Burgany Hall
Weldon's Plantation
Crofts La
A1033
Hollym
Holmpton Road

16
Fields Cl
Station Rd
Whinhill La
Arables Lane
Bydales La
Winestead
Hollym North
Leys Rd
Withernsea Rd

Ottringham
The Poplars
White Hall
Mile House
HOLLYM ROAD

Westlands Plantation
Ottringham Grange
Winestead Grange
Enholmes Hall
Eastfield House
Holmpton Rd
Wakefield Lane
Patrington Rd
School La
Holmpton

5

Sunk Island Road
Patrington
WELWICK ROAD
Beacon Hill
Northfield Lane
Rysome Lane
Balk Hill
Out Newton

Patrington Haven
Haverfield House
Welwick
Dimlington Warmer
La

Patrington Rd
Row Lane
SKEFFLING RD
B1445
Weeton

20

Brick Road
Outstray Rd
Newlands
Stray Road
Skeffling
HULL ROAD
Easington
Winsetts

Sunk Island
Village Rd
Channel Road
Old Hall Rd
Eastfield Rd
Firtholme Road

Creek
East Bank Rd
The Old Hall

6

Patrington Channel

335

Long Bank Bridge
Easington Rd
Kilnsea Grange
Spurn Heritage Coast
Kilnsea

E 30 Hawkin's t F G 40 H

Town plan: Hull p.635

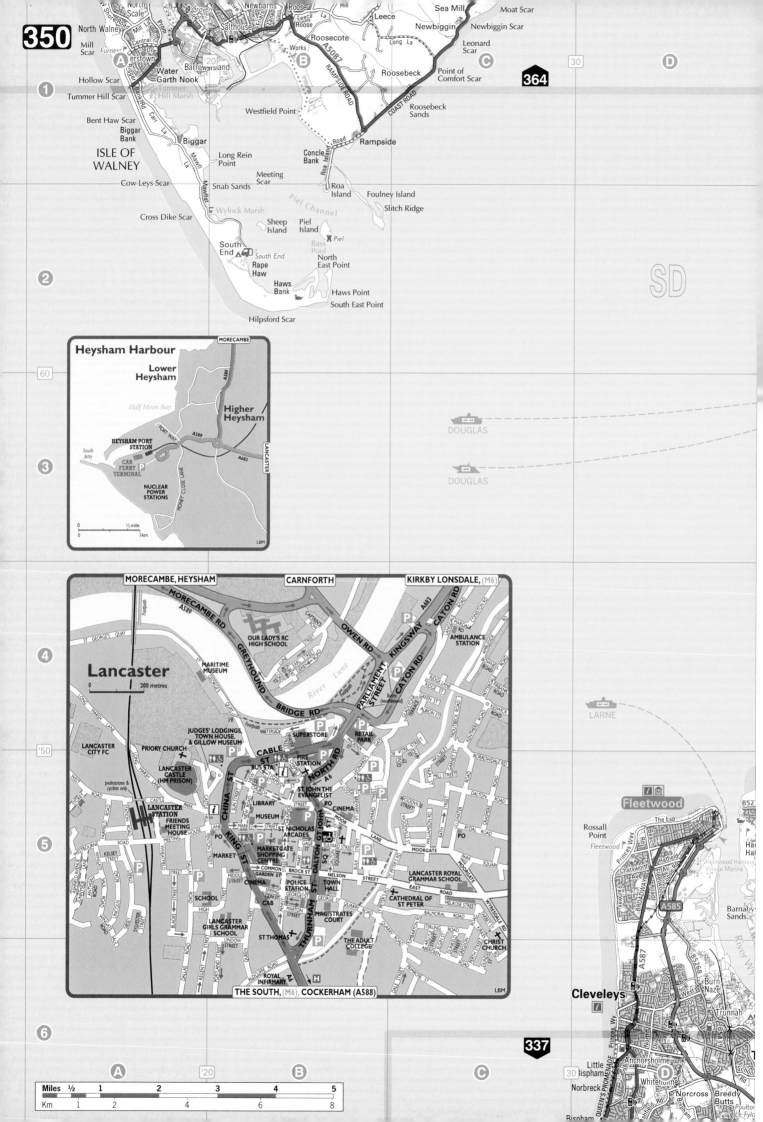

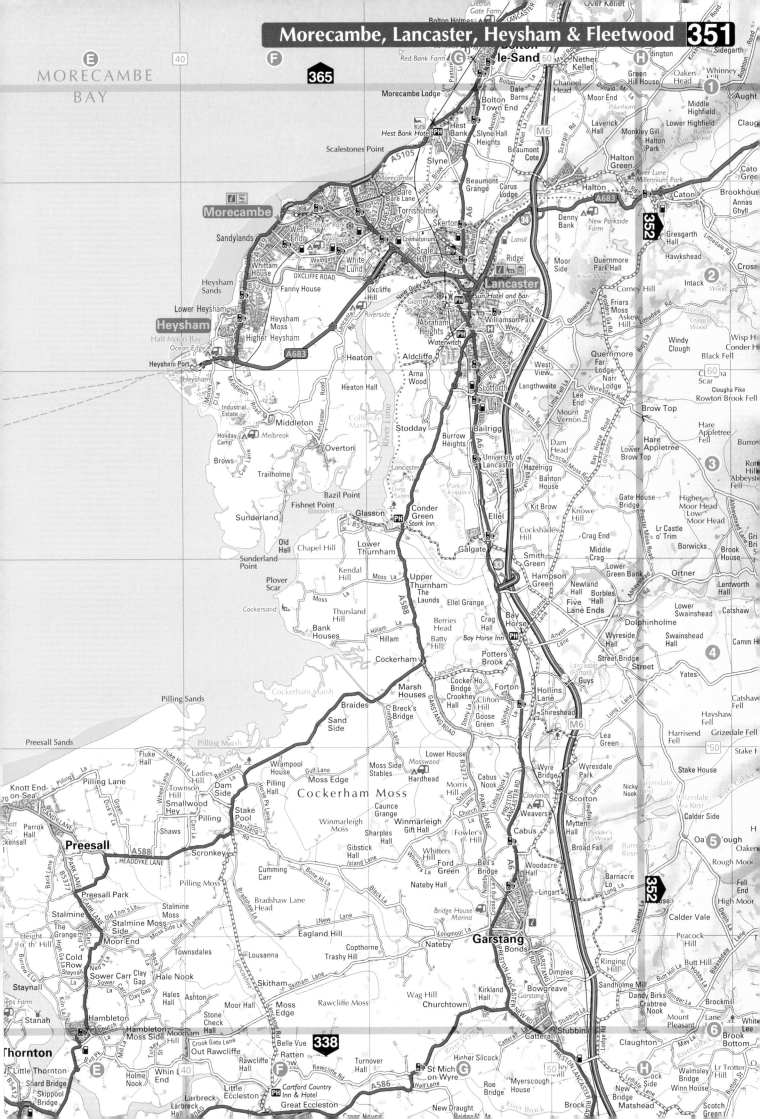

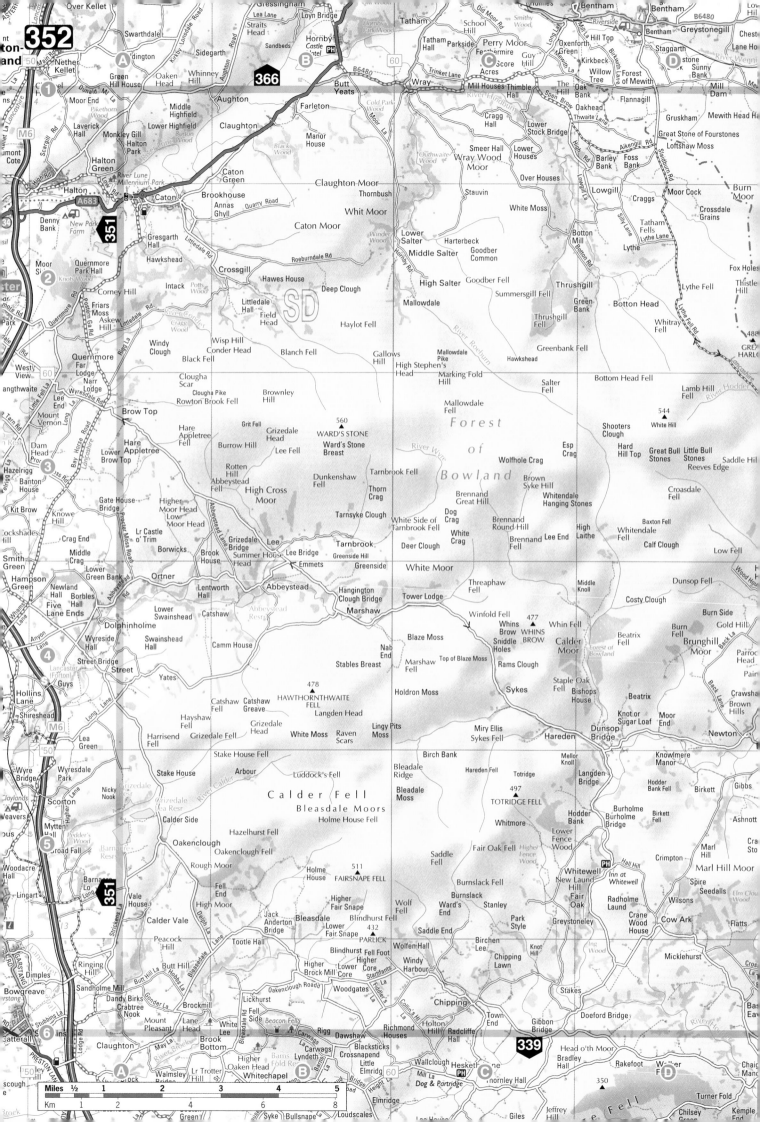

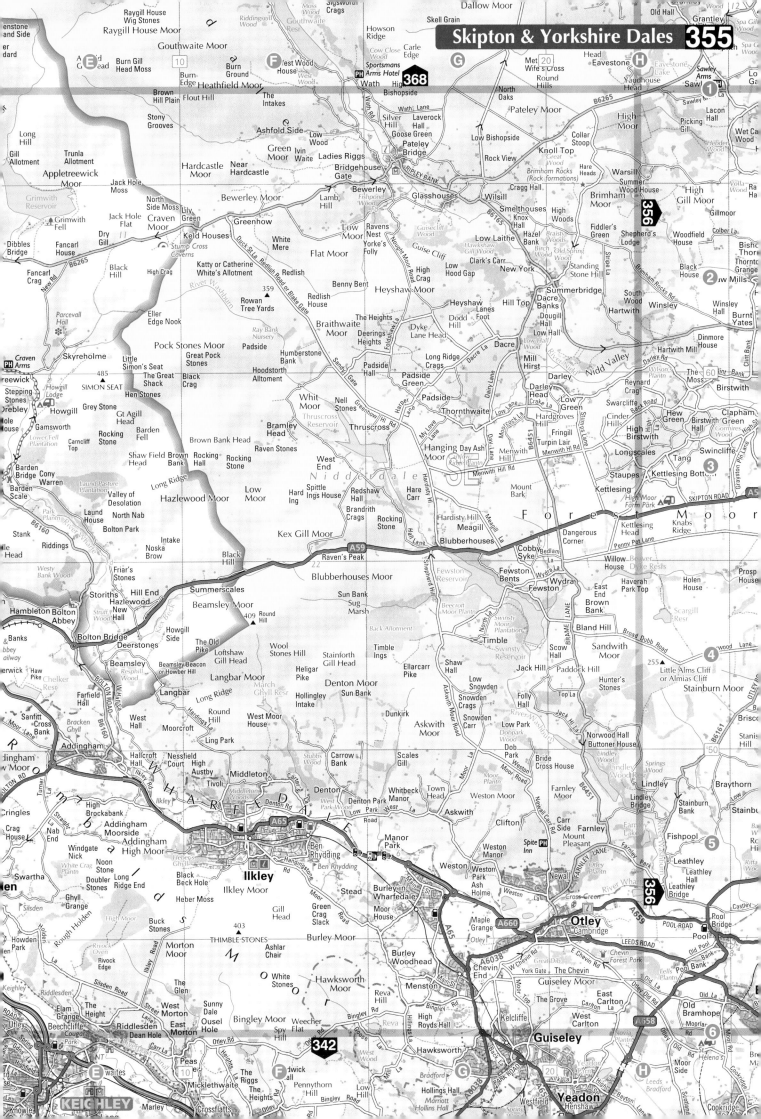

SE

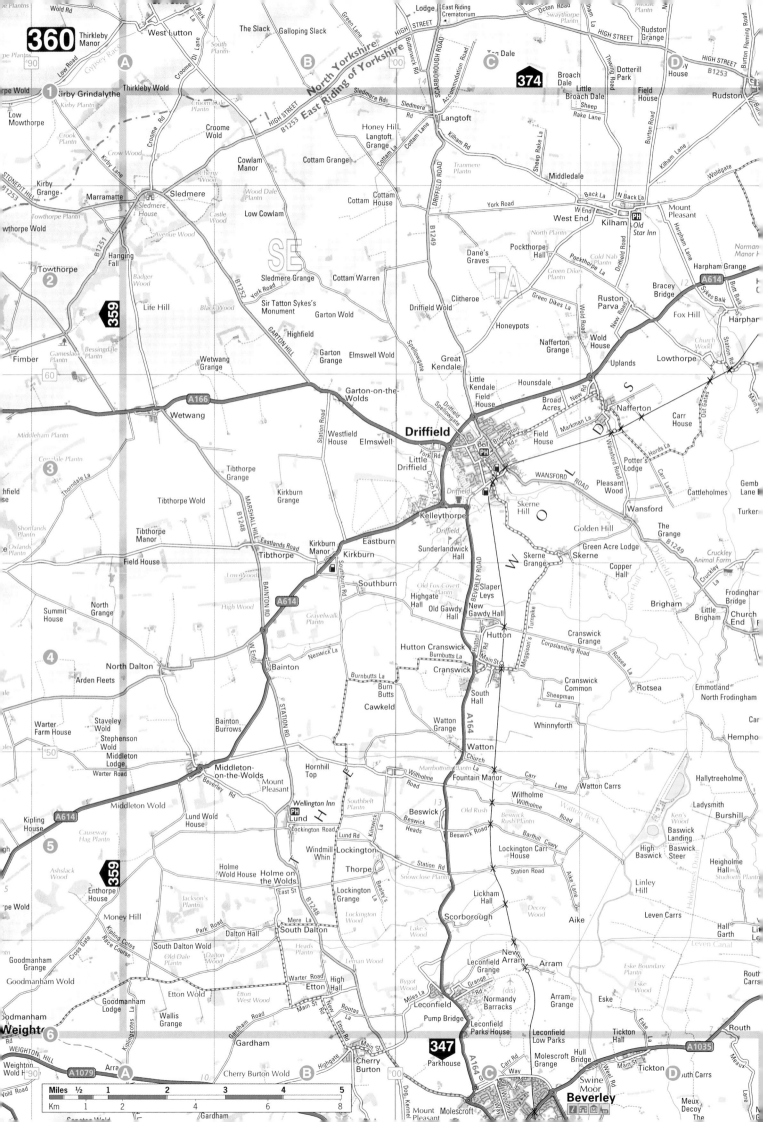

BRIDLINGTON BAY

TA

375

348

Bridlington
Bridlington Harbour
The Spa
Hilderthorpe
West Hill
Bessingby
Carnaby
Old Town
Boynton
Sewerby
Sewerby Hall
Marton Gate
Bondville Miniature Village
Flamborough Head
Beacon Hill
Highcliffe Manor
North Sands
South Sands

Thorpe Hall
North Wood
West Lawn Wood
Carr Plantn
Sands Wood
Hallowkiln Wood
High Wood
Fish Ponds Wood
Pits Plantn
Woldgate
Church Lane
Temple Lane

Thornholme
Haisthorpe
Back La
Burton Agnes
Horse Carr Lane
Thornholme Moor
Harpham Moor
Burtoncarr House
Gransmoor Wood
Carnaby Moor
North Kingsfield
South Kingsfield
Low Stonehills
High Stonehills
Fraisthorpe
Fraisthorpe Sands

Barmston
Barmston Sands
Barmston La

Gransmoor
Gransmoor Lodge
Great Kelk
Park House
Kelk Lane
Gransmoor Rd
Lissett
Ulrome Grange
Ulrome
Ulrome Sands
East End
Sand Lane
Gembling
Beeford Grange
Lisset Bridge
Allison Lane
Ulrome West End
Manor House
Mill Farm
Skipsea
Mill La
Foston on the Wolds
East Redcarr Plantn
Dringhoe
Beeford Road
Skipsea Brough
Hornsea Rd
Skipsea Sands

Upton
Main Street
B1249
Beeford
Beverley Road
Dunnington Grange
Dunnington
Dunnington Lane
Low Bonwick
High Bonwick
High Skirlington
Skipsea Grange
Skipsea Low Skirlington
Low Skirlington
Atwick Sands

North Dingham
Frodingham Grange
Highthorns
Moor Grange
Billings Hill
Warleycross Hill
Dunnington
North End
Atwick
Atwick Road
Cliff Rd
North Cliff

Mount Ephraim
Nunkeeling
Lord Mayor's Whins
Catfoss Road
Arram Hall
Little Arram
Northfield House
Bewholme
Bewholme Lane
Seaton Rd

Lane House
Aldermen's Gorse
Frodingham Rd
Pasturefield House
Harsell
Catfoss Grange
Seaton Hold
Bassymoor
Seaton Grange
Honeysuckle Farm
Brockholme
North Cliff
Hornsea
South Cliff
Hornsea Burton

Barff House
Hainsworth Park
Dacre
Brandesburton
New Rd
Seaton
Breamer La
B1244
Hornsea Mere
Low Wood
Southorpe
Southorpe Grange
Rolston
Rolston Sands

Leven
Catwick Grange
Catwick Lane
Wassand Hall
Wassand Balk
Sigglesthorne
Hornsea
Mappleton
Mappleton Sands
Broom Hill
Mappleton Road

Leven Grange
Old Hall
Little Catwick
Field House
Cobble Hall
The Hall
Sigglesthorne Grange
Goxhill
Bowlams Fox Covert
Huddlecross Plantn
Catwick Lane
Rise
Rise Grange
Rise Hall
Mill House
Eastfield La
Little Hatfield
Great Hatfield
Hatfield Grange
Mount Pleasant
Great Cowden
Cowden Sands

Riston Grange
Prospect House
Farnton Hill
Whins Lane
Mill La
B1243
Hull Rd
Hornsea Rd
Withernick Grange
Westlands
Beverley Rd
North End
Withernwick
Great Cowden
Garthends La
B1242
Cow Magna

Long Riston
Arnold
Arnold Grange
Rise Lane
Ruddens
Whitedale
Gt Hatfield Road
Main Road
Cowden Parva
Whitehill
Aldbrough

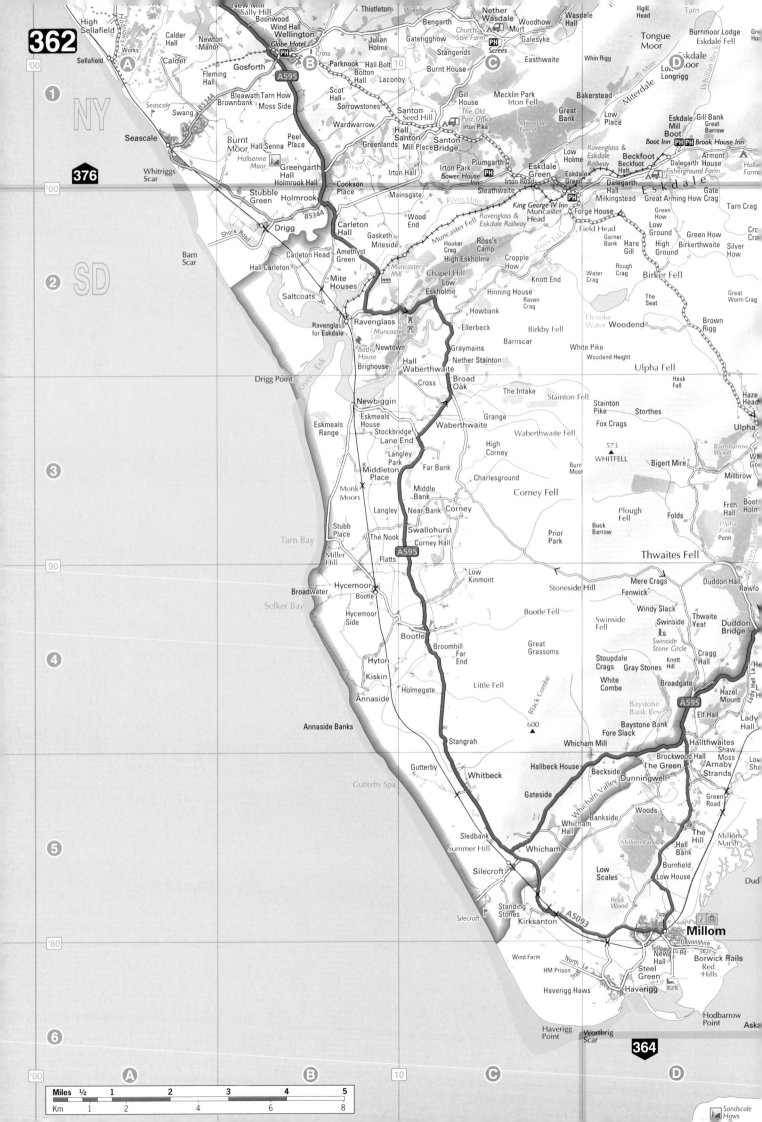

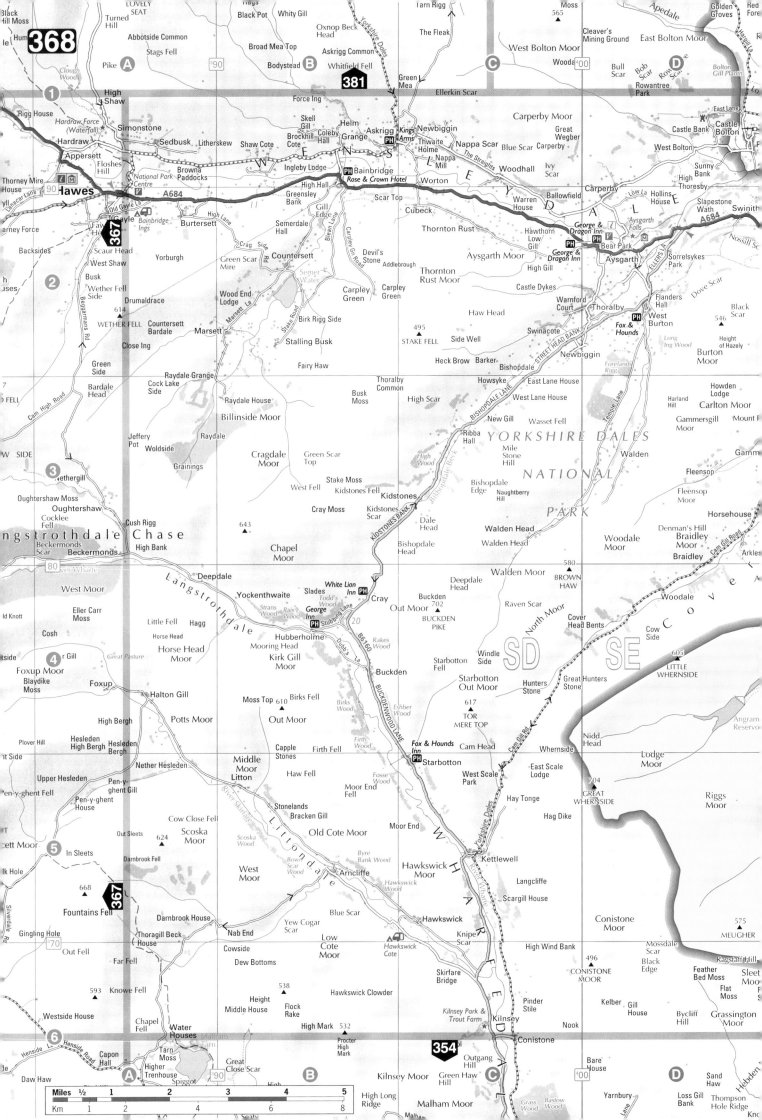

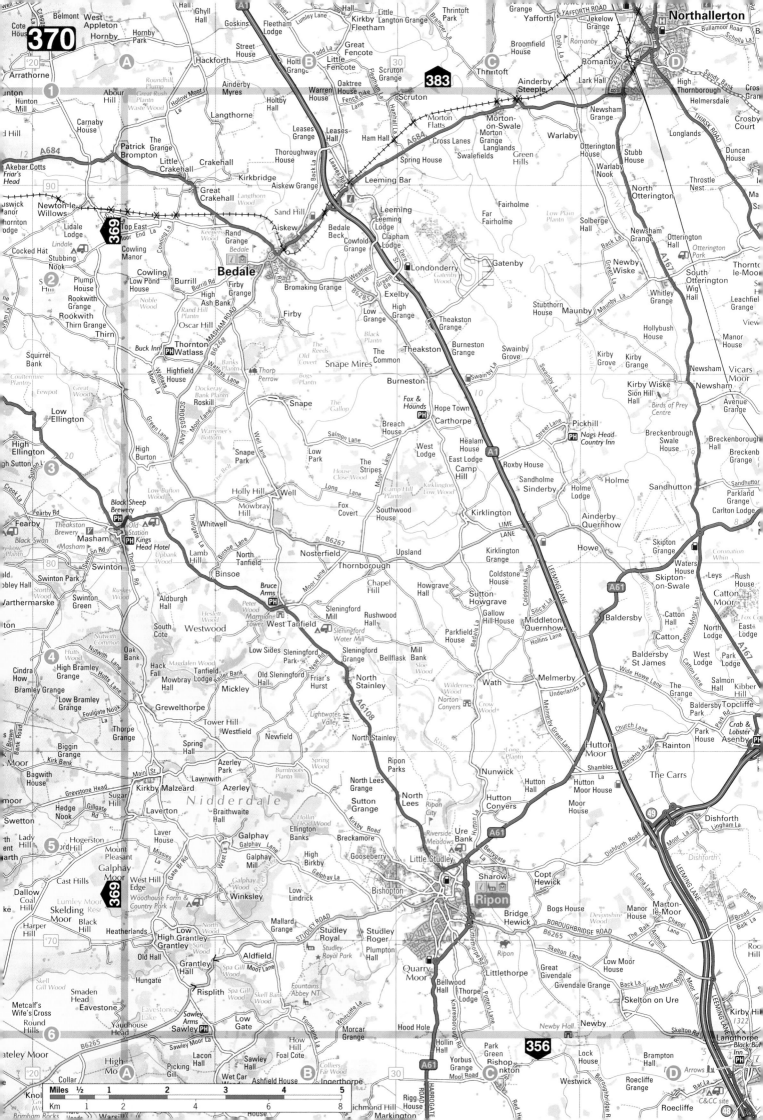

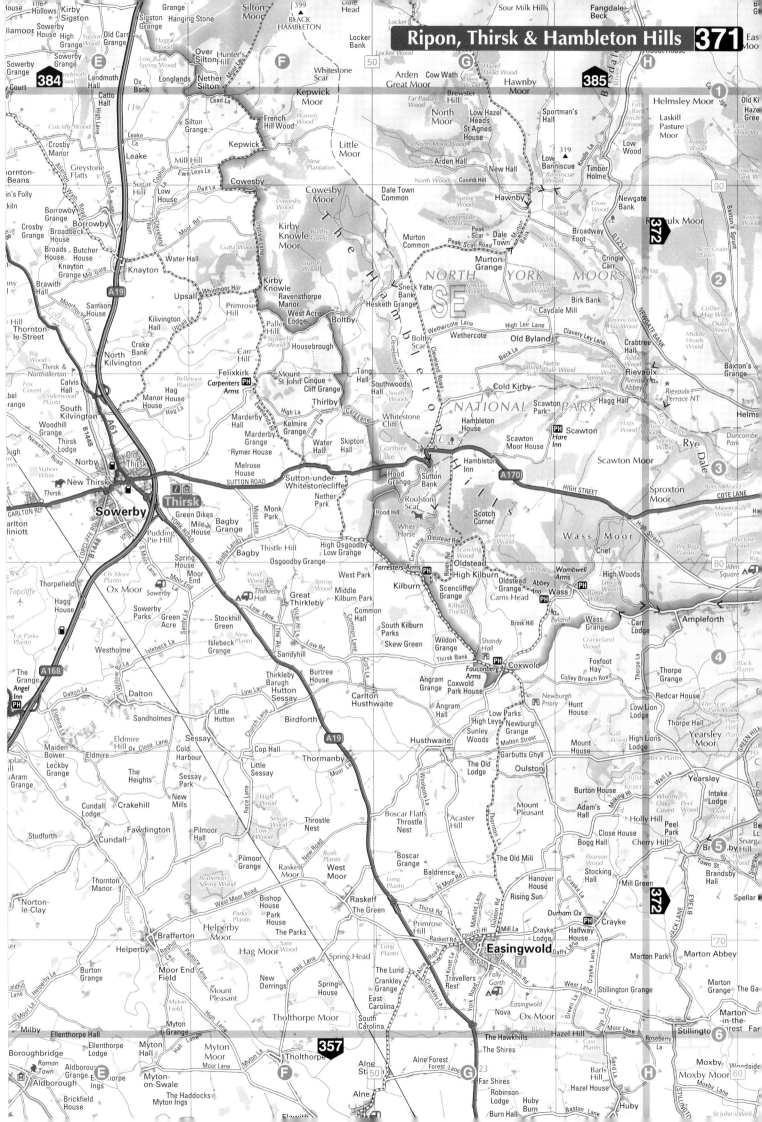

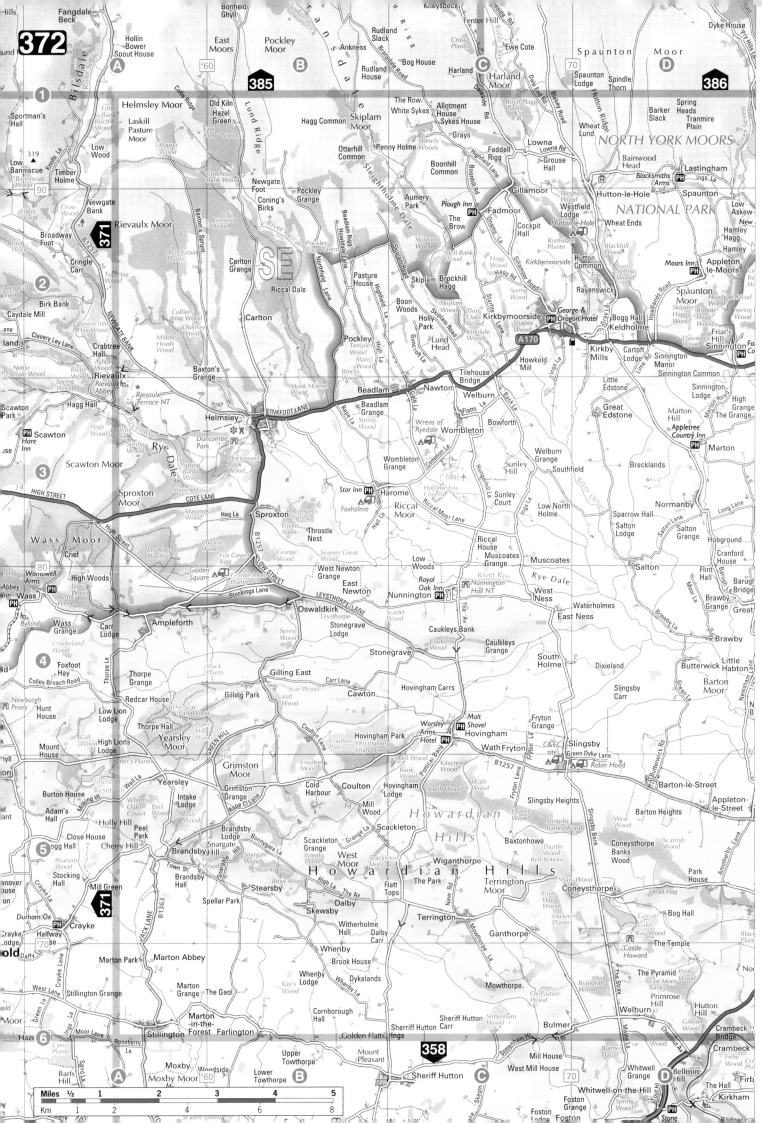

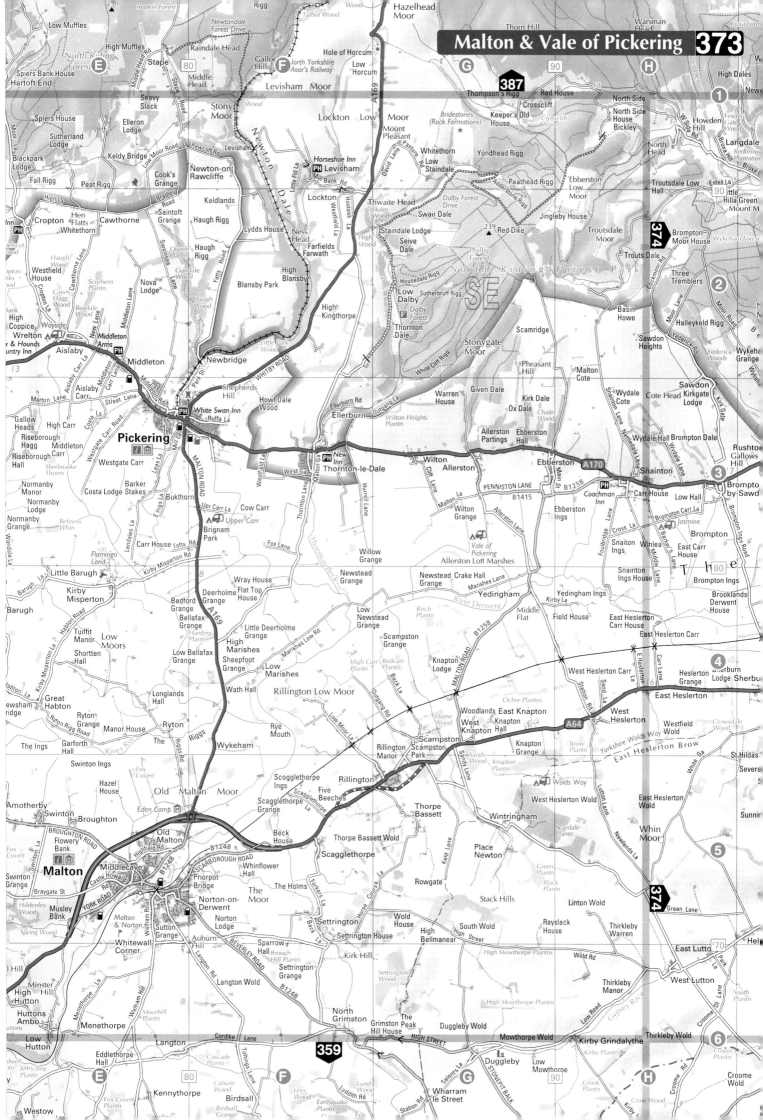

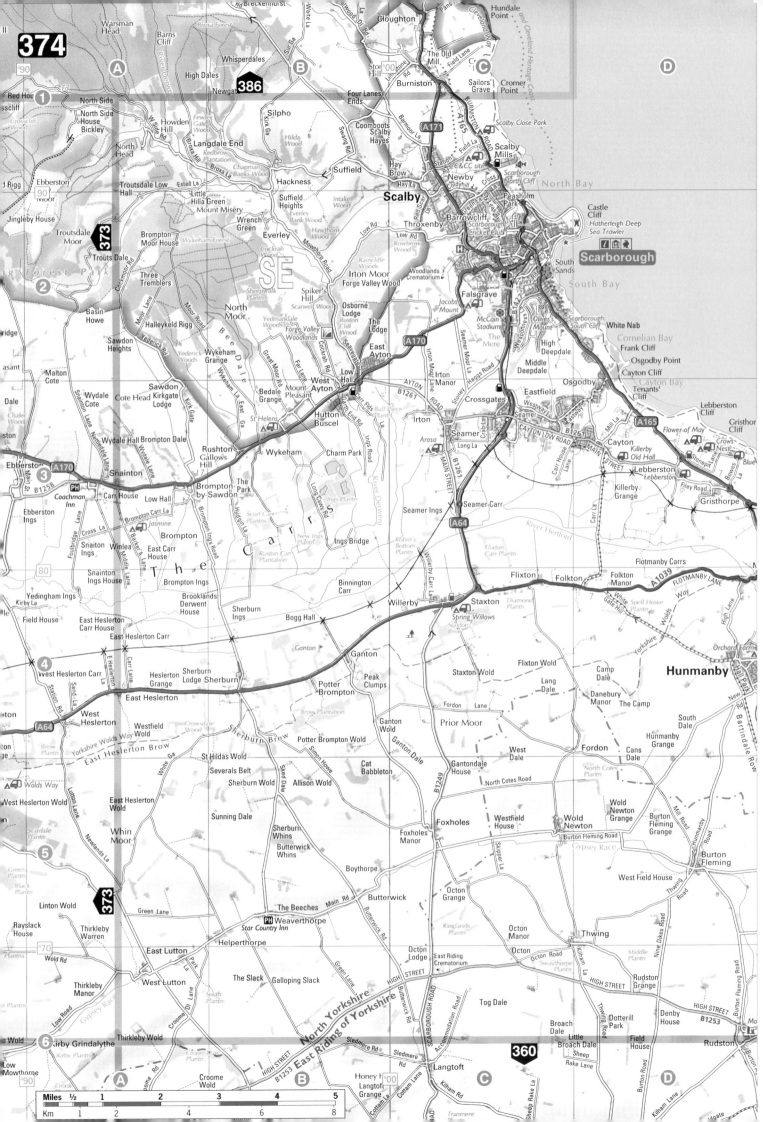

290

A

B

00

C

D

Tanyard Bay

Bleachgreen

Redness
Point

Bransty

Quality
Corner

School

Moresby
Parks

Sandsclose
Weddicar
Rig

Routon
Syke

Arlecdon
Rowrah

Low
Leys

Beck
Hollins

Inglenook

Knock Murton

Victoria
Brow

Scilly
Bank

Murton Fell

Harras

Acrewalls

Millyeat

Heather
Lea

Arlecdon
Hill

Leys

Kelton
Head

Keltonfell
Top

Keltonfell

Whitehaven

Harras Road

New
Monkwray

Bleak
House

388

Winder

Croa

Waterfront

PH

A595

Moresby Rd

Wreah

Weddicar
Hall

Frizington

Salter Hall

Stockhow
Hall

Croftfoot

Corkickle
Recreation
Ground

Hensingham

Keekle

Troughton
House

Frizington
Hall

Rheda

Frizington
Parks

Ennerdale
Bridge

Beck

Kells

Woodhouse

Low
Road

Meadow Road

B5295

Threapthwaite

Parkside

High
Longmoor
Waterside

Birk
Moss

Crag Farm
House

Angler
Crag

Saltom Bay

H

Keekle
Grove

**Cleator
MOOR**

Hazel
Holme

River Ehen

Swinside

Fellend

Heckbarley

Grike

Crag Fell

Works

Mirehouse

Birks Rd

Wath Brow

Headley
Resr

Low
Cock How

Cathow

Blakeley
Moss

Black Pots

Hannah
Moor

Sandwith

Hadrian's Coast to Coast

Moor
Row

Cleator

Flat
Fell

Scaly
Moss

Blakeley Raise

Whoap

North
Head

Mirehouse Rd

Ehen
Hall

Dent

Dalzell Rd

Standing
Stones
Lagget

Lankrigg
Moss

Sandwith
Newtown

Low
Walton

Bigrigg

Woodend

Long Barrow

Latterbarrow
Moss

533
▲
LANK RIGG

St Bees Head Heritage Coast

High
Walton

Southam

Row
Foot

Cow
Field

Lowther
Park

Latter Barrow

Kinniside Common

St Bees
Head

RSPB

Rottington

B5345

St Bees Road

Pallaflat

Briscoe

Moss
Dalts

Wilton

Farthwaite

Town Bank
Tongue How

Boat How

South Head

Seacote
Park

Watson
Hill

Gillfoot

St Helena

Black
Moss

Brackenthwaite

How
Hills

Bleak

Worm Gill

St
Bees

Egremont

Lynnwood

Florence
Mine

Oxenriggs

Great
Wood

10

South Head

St Bees

Out Rigg

Whitehow
Head

Haile
Hall

Cold
Fell

Side End

Scalderskew
Wood

S

Coulderton

Catgill
Hall

Carleton
Head

Winscales

Head of Haile

Thornhill

Haile

Cod Lane

Middletown

Low
Mill

B5345

Town
End

Strudda
Bank

Wheel Fell

Stords

Stone Pike

Nethertown

Sheepfields

Prior Scales

Ponsonby Fell

Middle
Ehenside

Beckermet

Mill

Blackbeck

Calder
Bridge

Laverock
How

Scargreen

Lowcray

Blengdale

Blengdale Fo

Braystones

Middlebank

Greenmoor
Side

Sellafield
Visitor
Centre

Ponsonby

Bleng Fell

River Ehen

Yottenfews

Ponsonby
Old Hall

Betwe
Guard
Thistleton

NX

NY

High
Sellafield

New Mill
Sally Hill

Calder
Hall

Works

Calder

Newton
Manor

Boonwood

Wind Hall

Wellington

Julian
Holme

Globe Hotel

Cross

Parknook

Hall Bolto

4

Sellafield

Gosforth

PH

A595

Bolton
Hall

Laco

Fleming
Hall

Scot
Hall

Sorrowstones

Bleawath
Brownbank

Tarn How
Moss Side

Wardwarrow

Seascale

Seascale

B5344

Swang

Burnt
Moor

Hall Senna

Peel
Place

Greenlands

00

Hallsenna
Moor

Greengarth
Hall

River Irt

Irt

M

Whitriggs
Scar

Holmrook Hall

Cookson
Place

Stubble
Green

Holmrook

Gasketh
Mitesid

SC

SD

Barn
Scar

Shore Road

B5344

Drigg

Carleton
Hall

5

Hall Carleton

Carleton Head

Amethyst
Green

13

Saltcoats

Mite
Houses

M

Ravenglass
for Eskdale

Ravenglass

Muncas

Bath
House

Newto

Brighouse

Drigg Point

River Esk

Newbiggin

Eskmeals
Range

Eskmeals
House

Stockb

La
Pa

6

362

Monk
Moors

Middleto
Place

Langley

Stubb
Place

The Noo

290

A

B

00

C

D

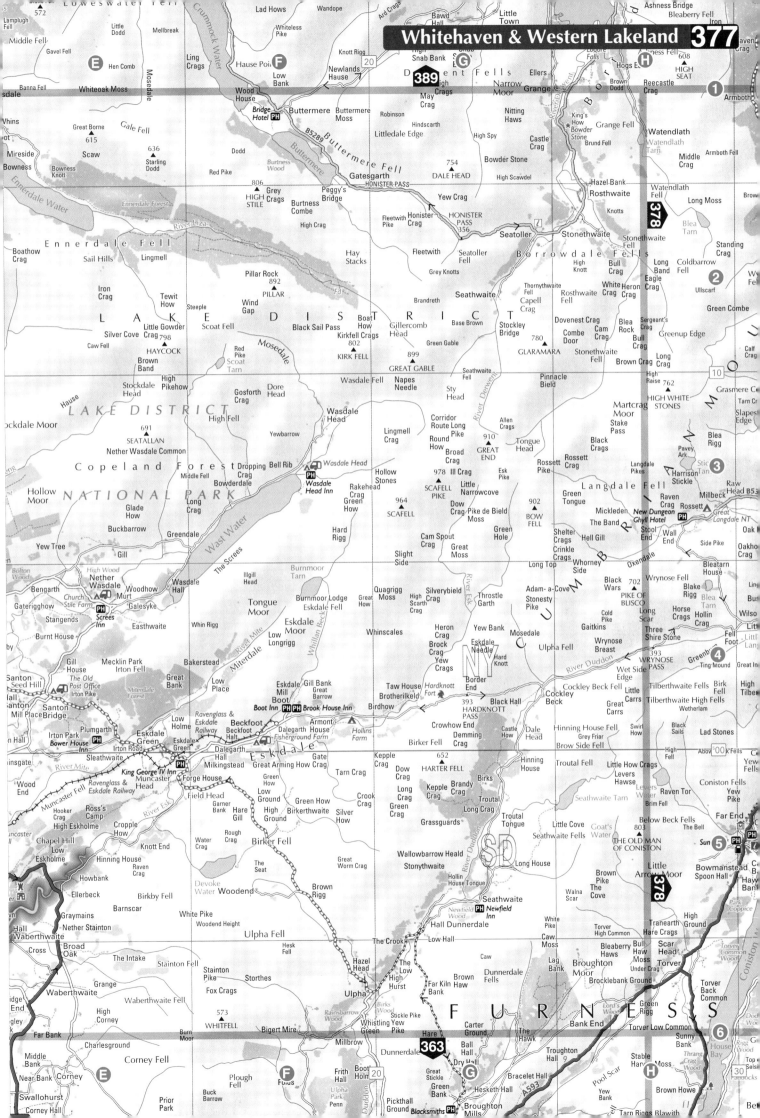

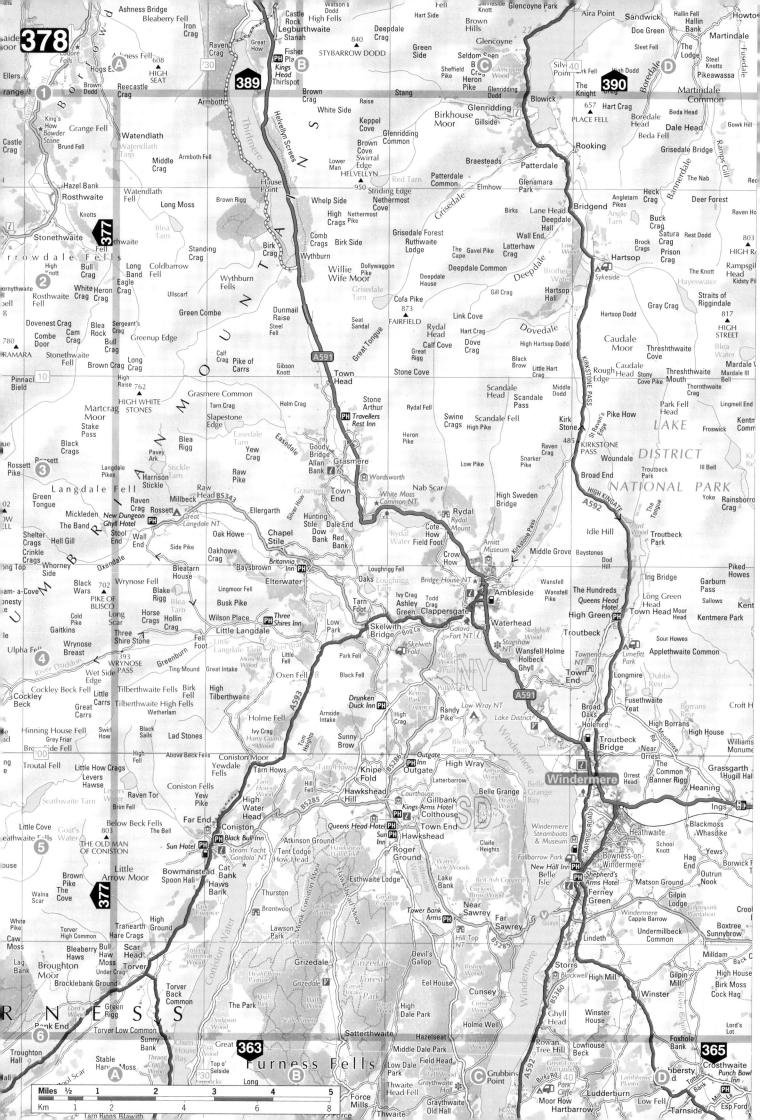

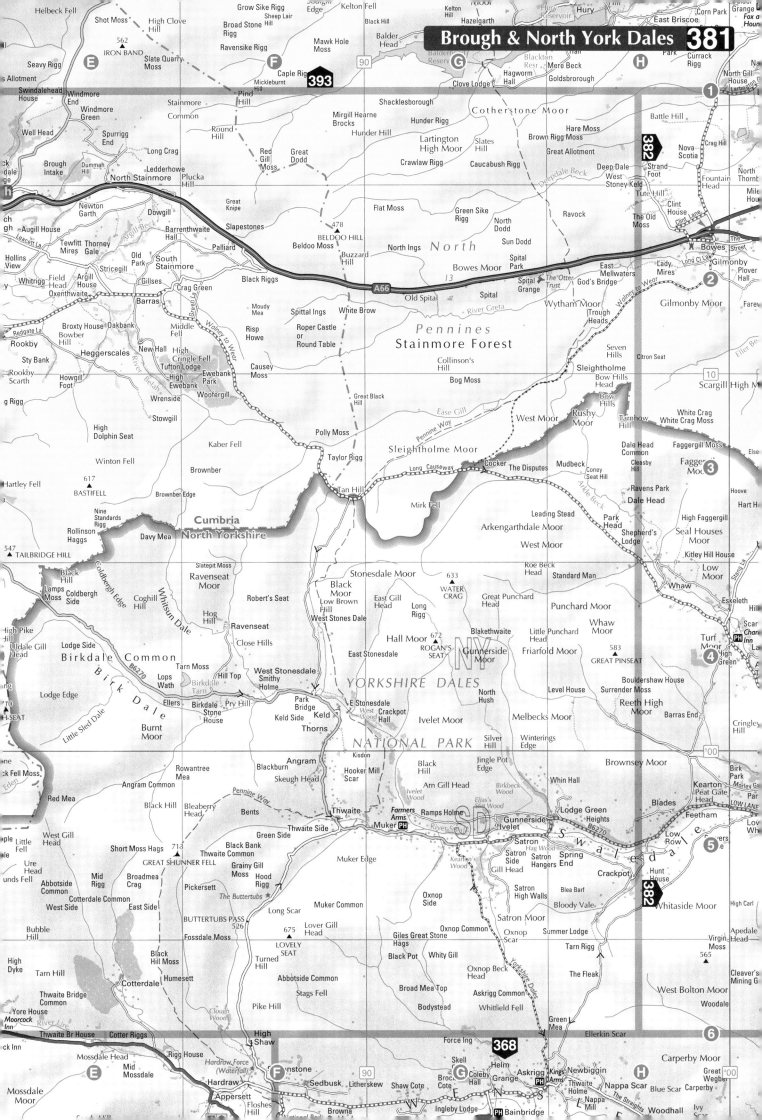

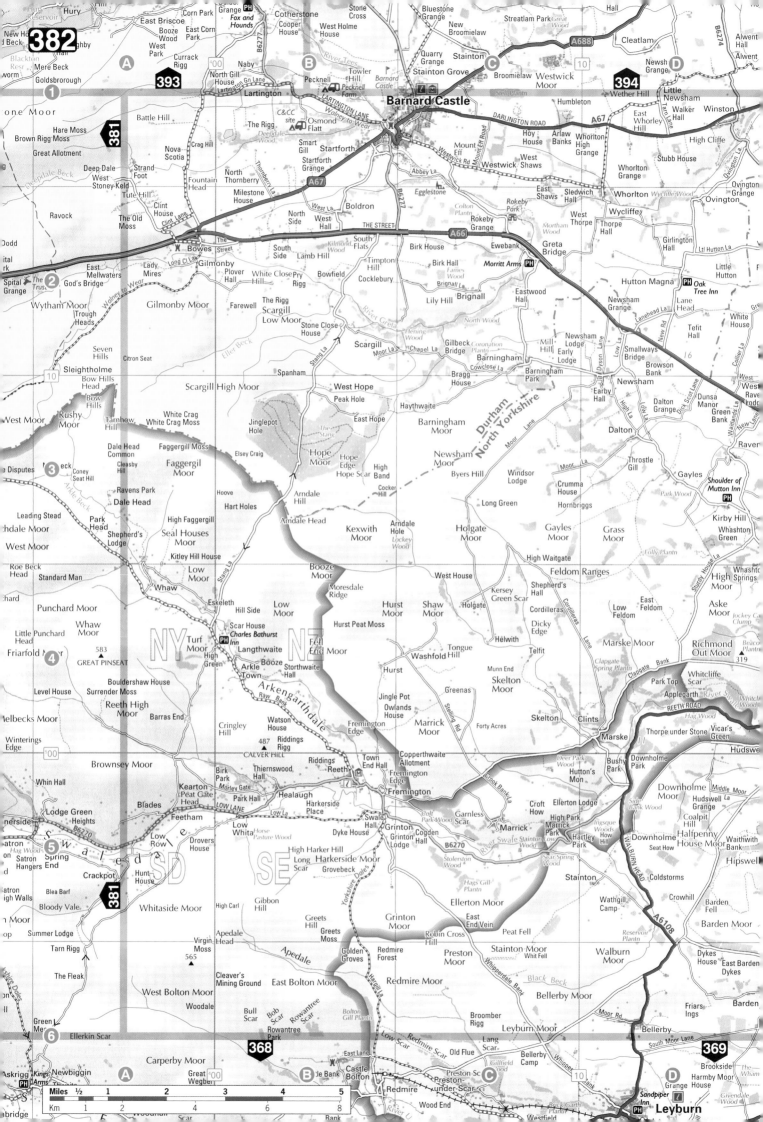

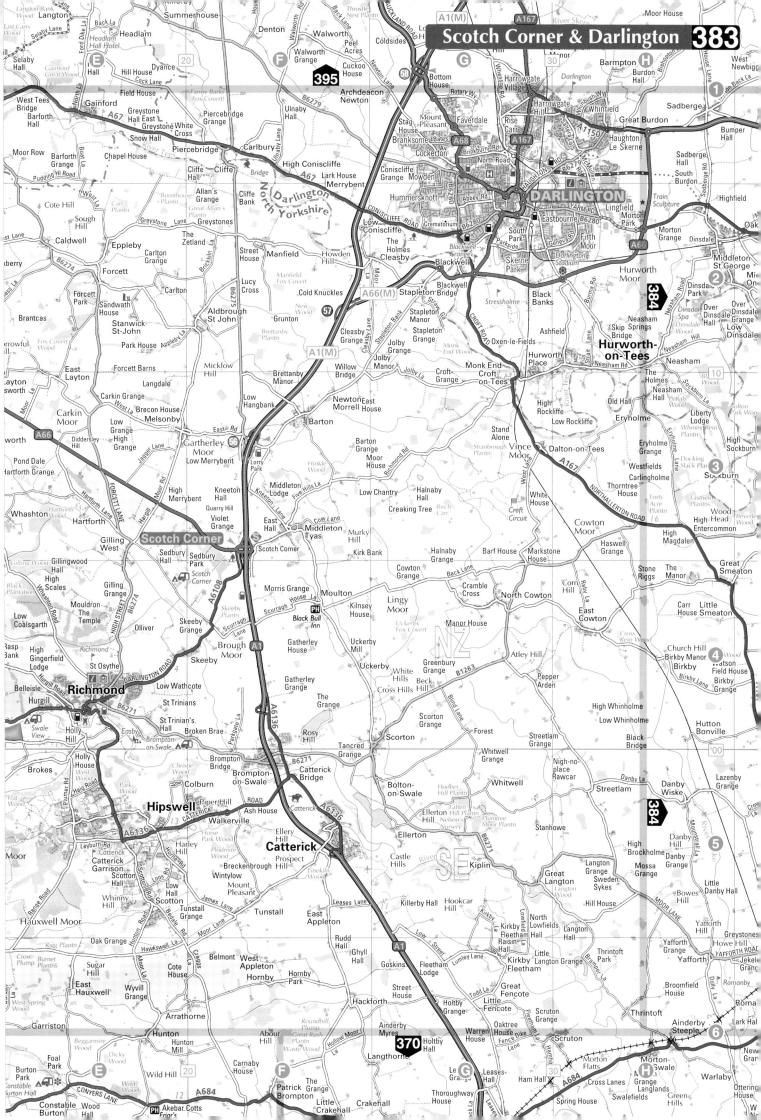

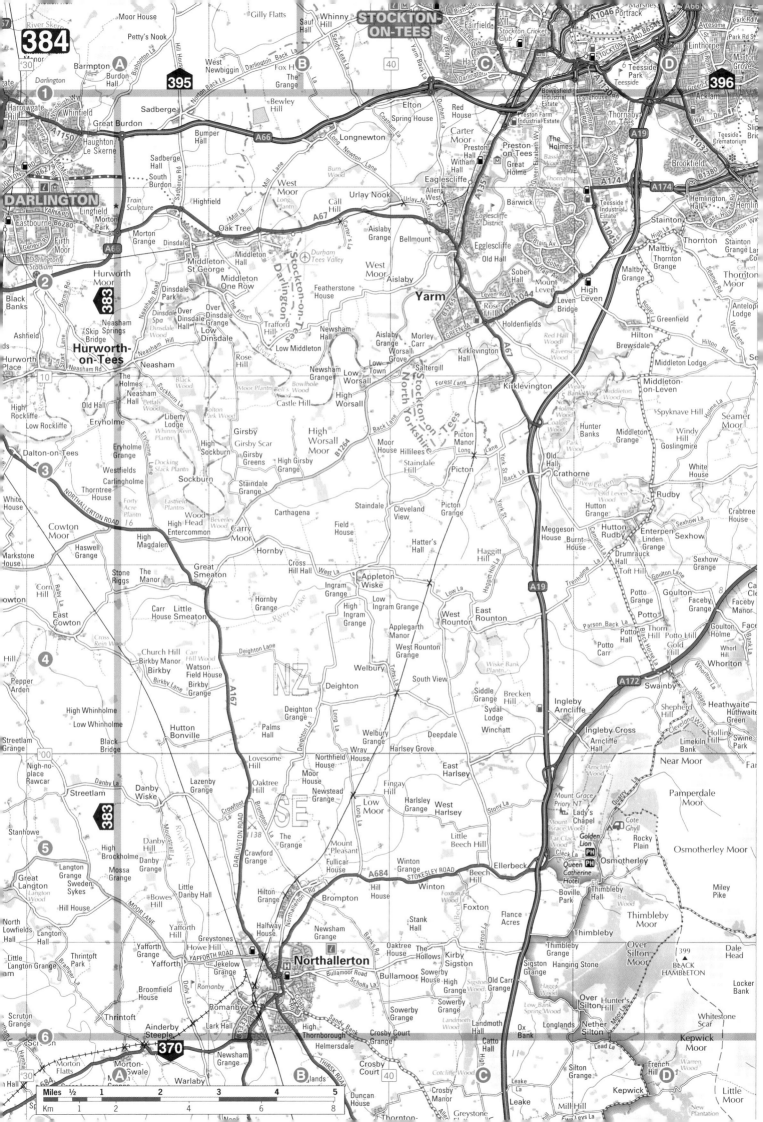

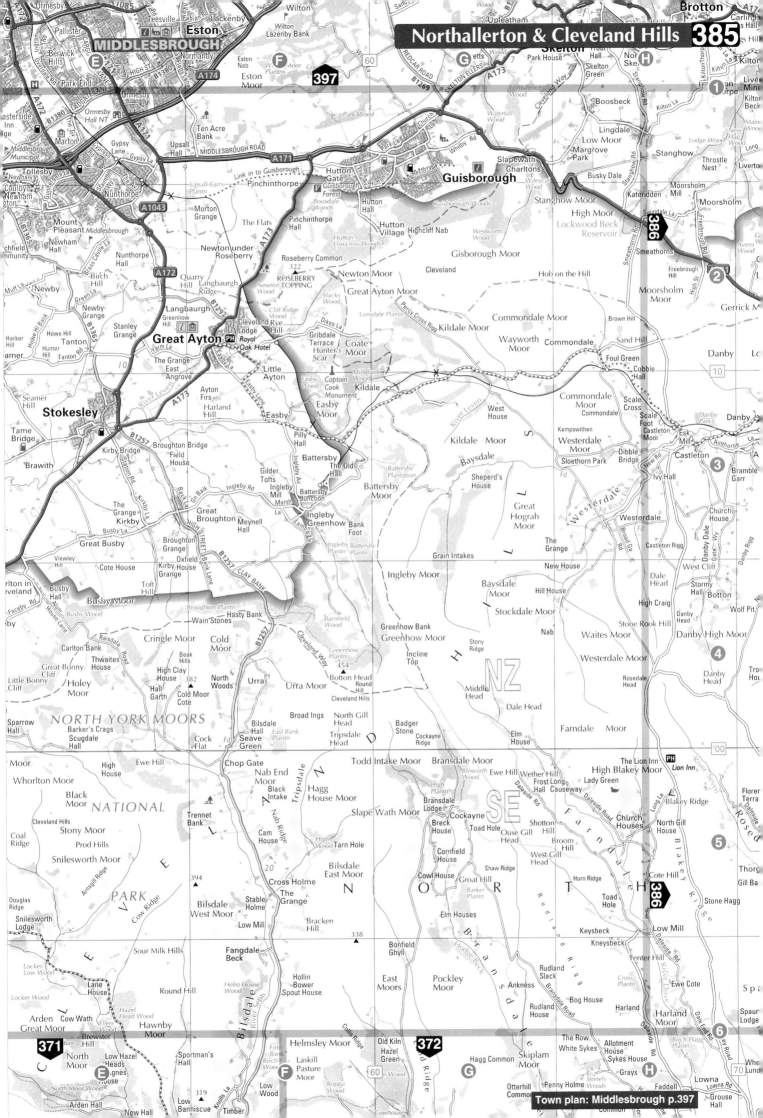

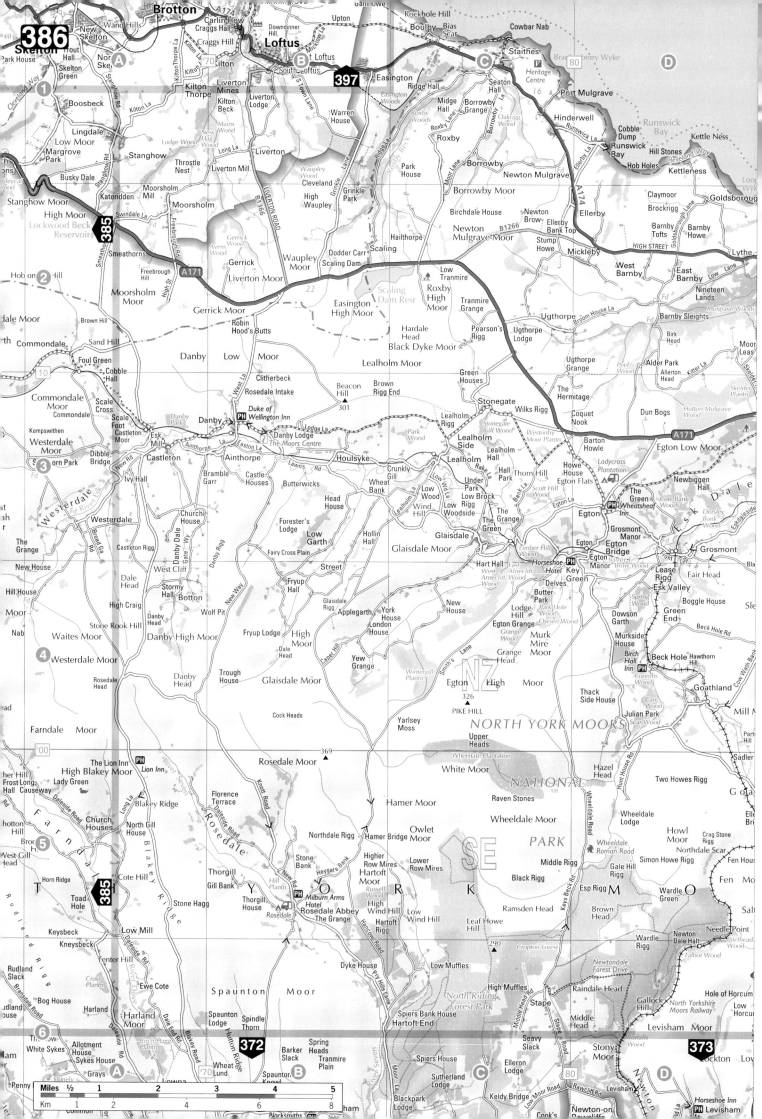

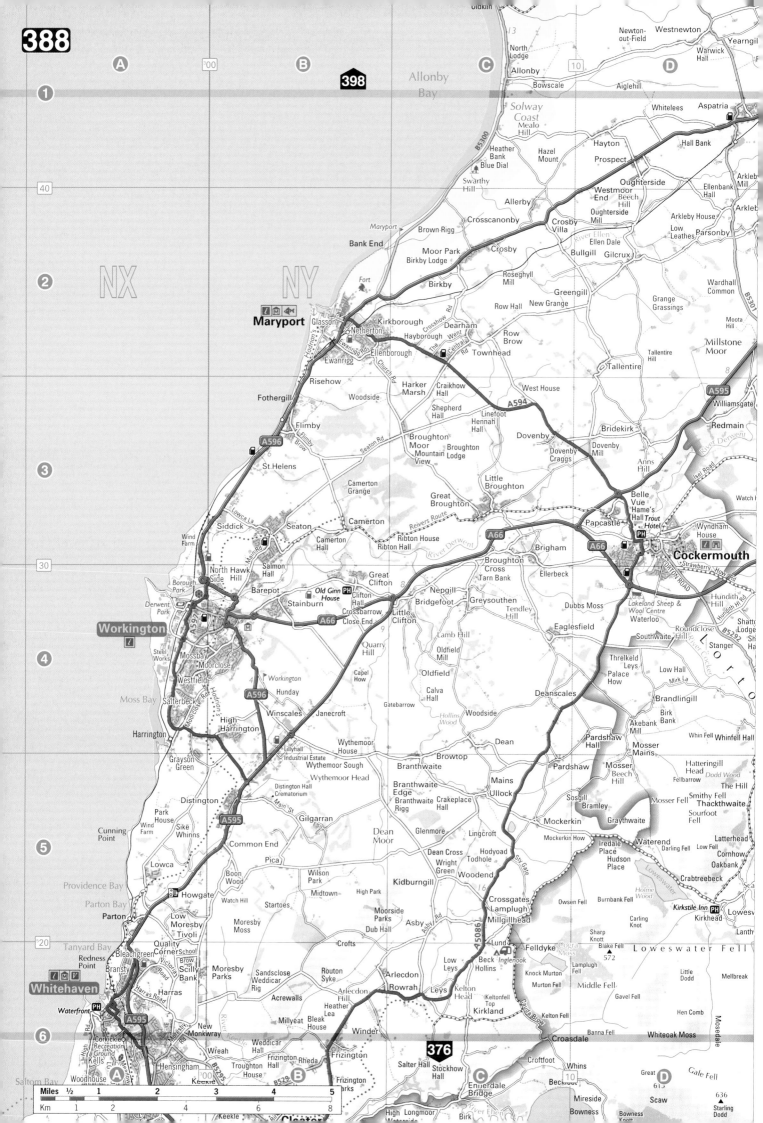

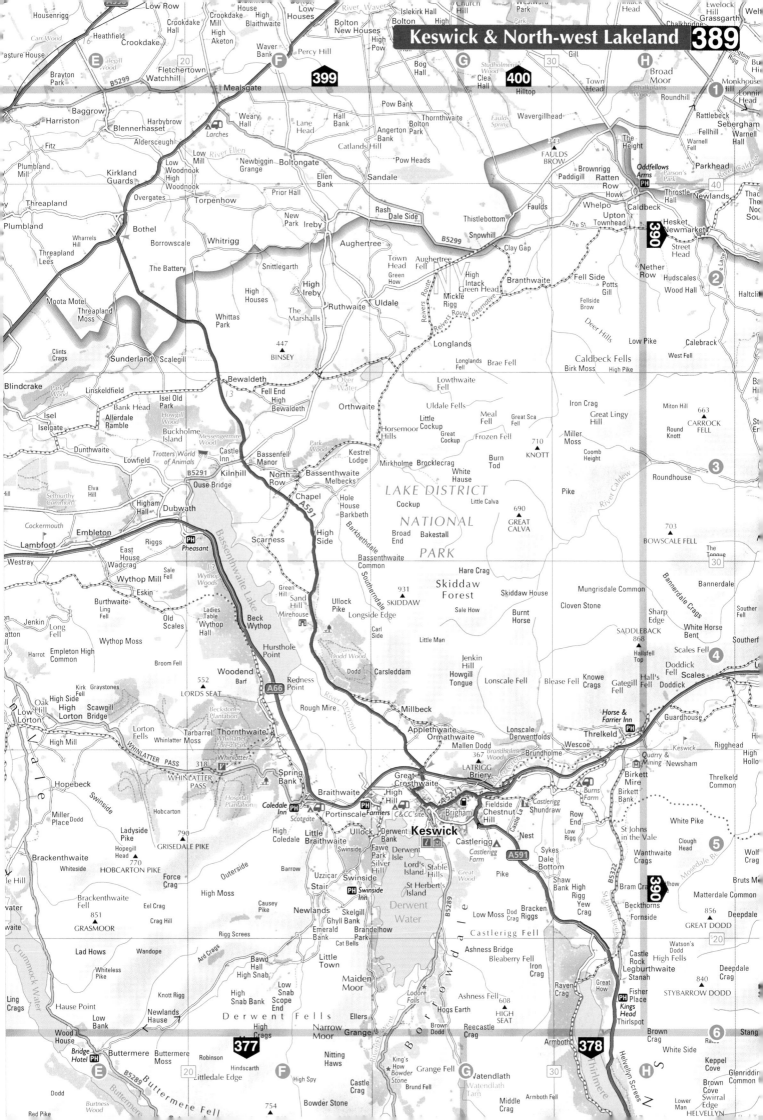

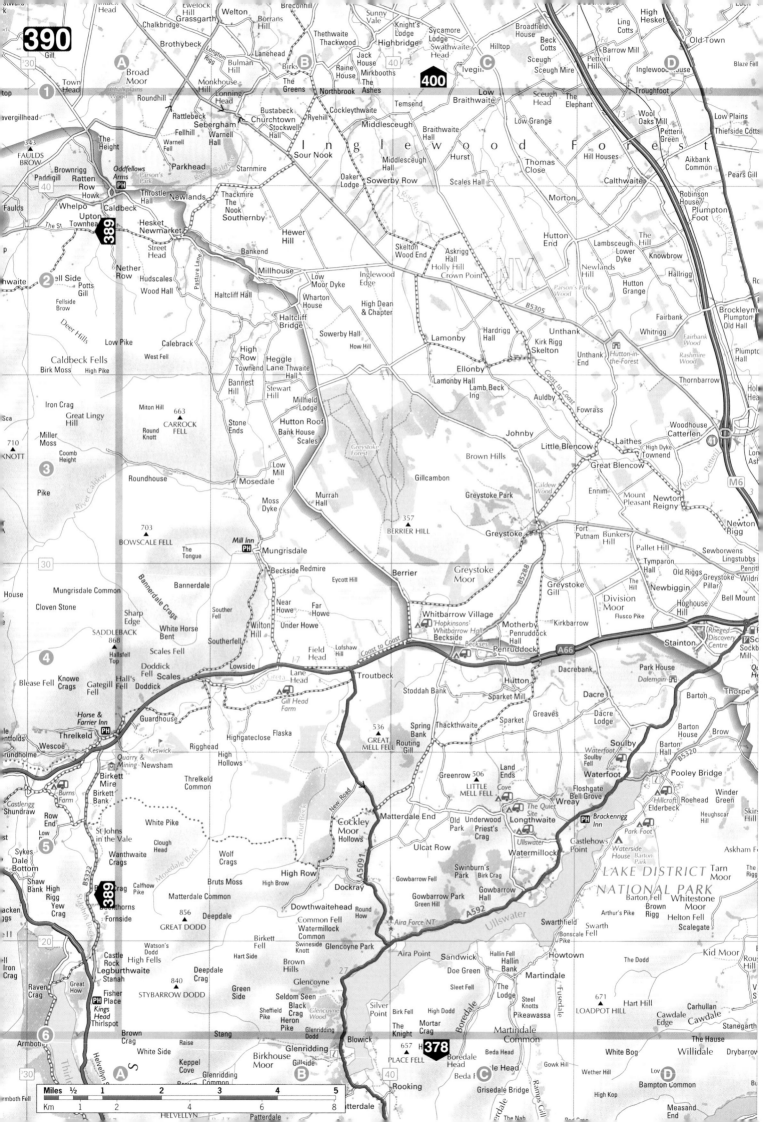

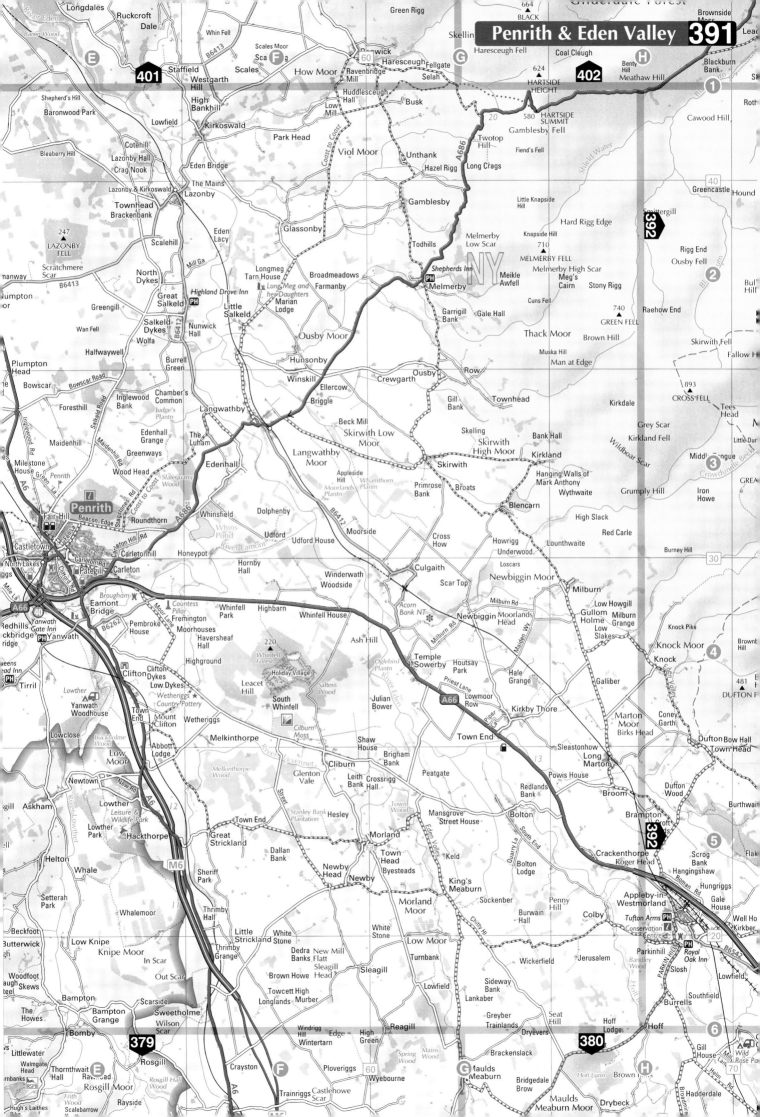

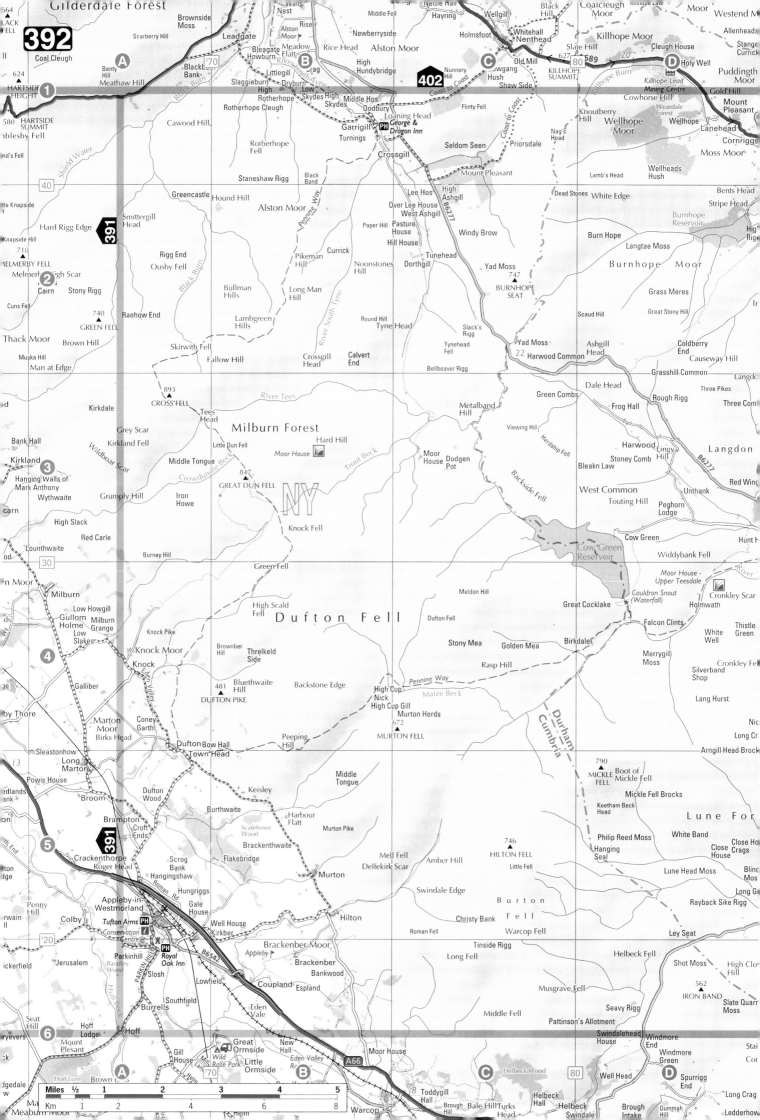

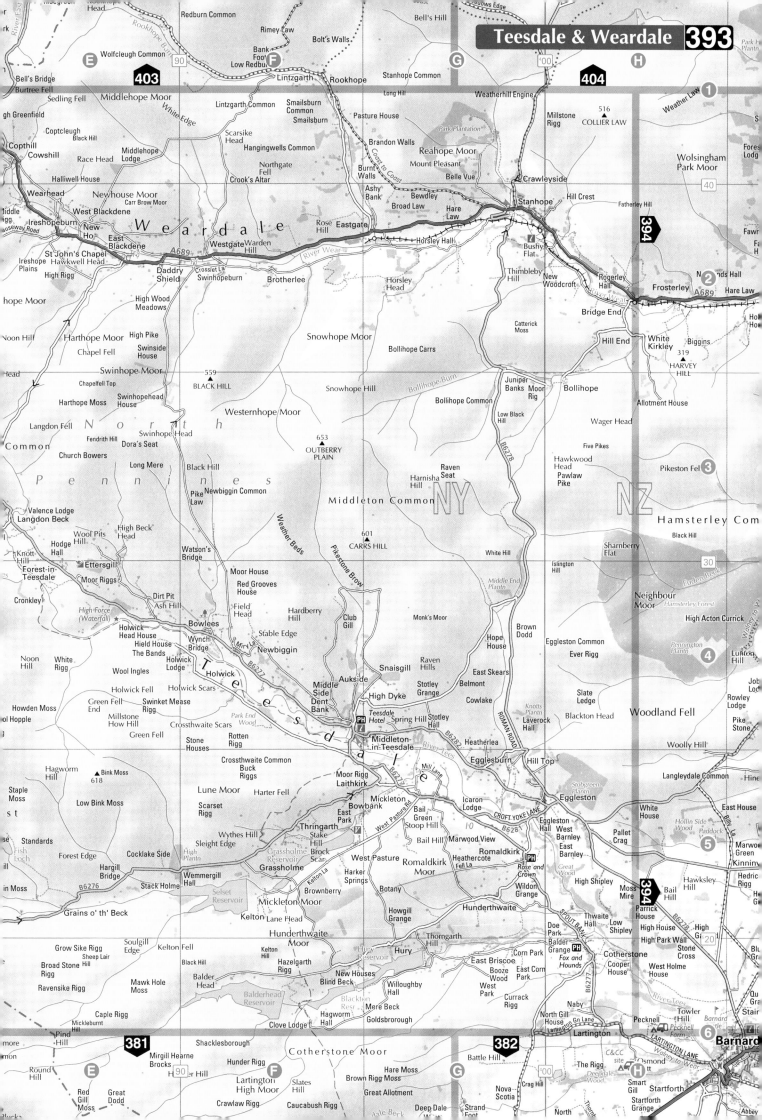

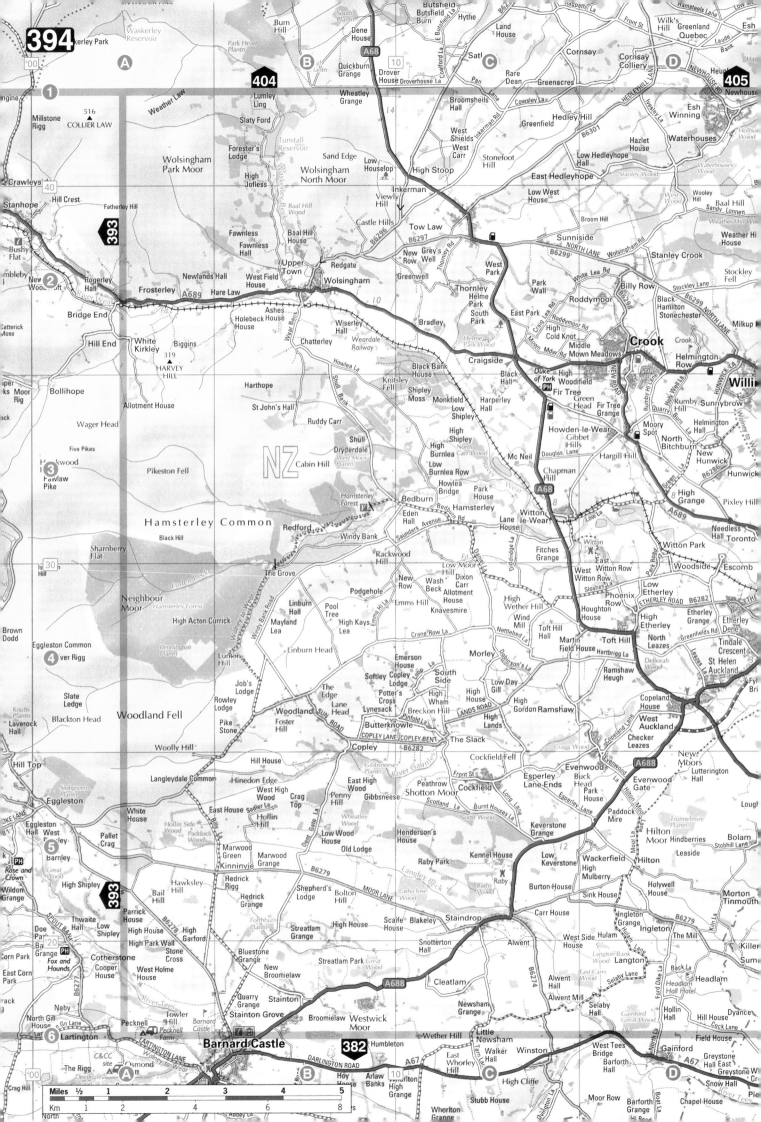

Middlesbrough

0   200 metres

MIDDLESBROUGH STATION

STOKESLEY

385   386

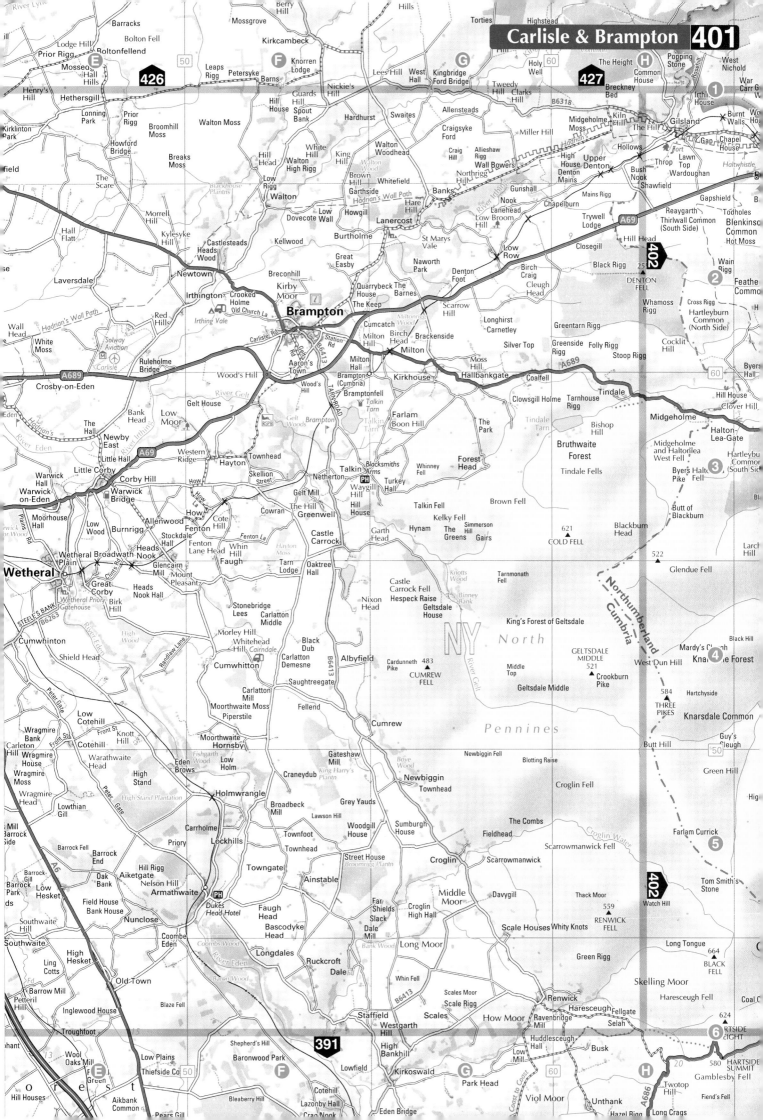

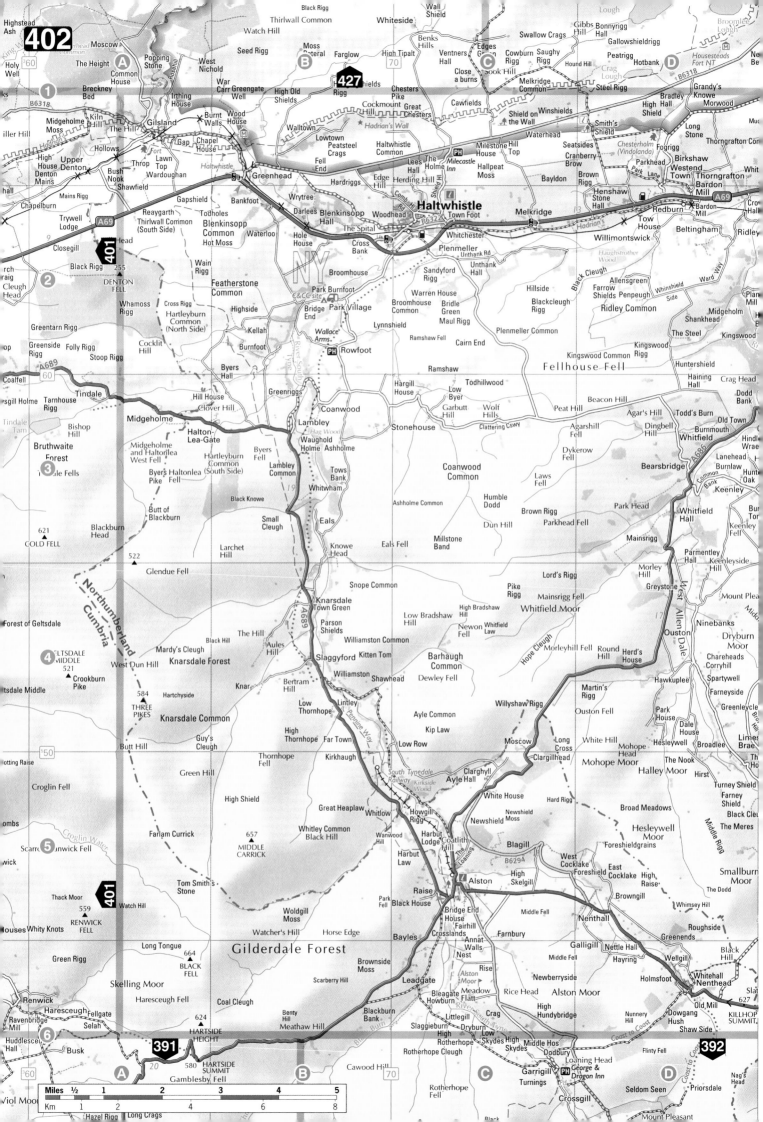

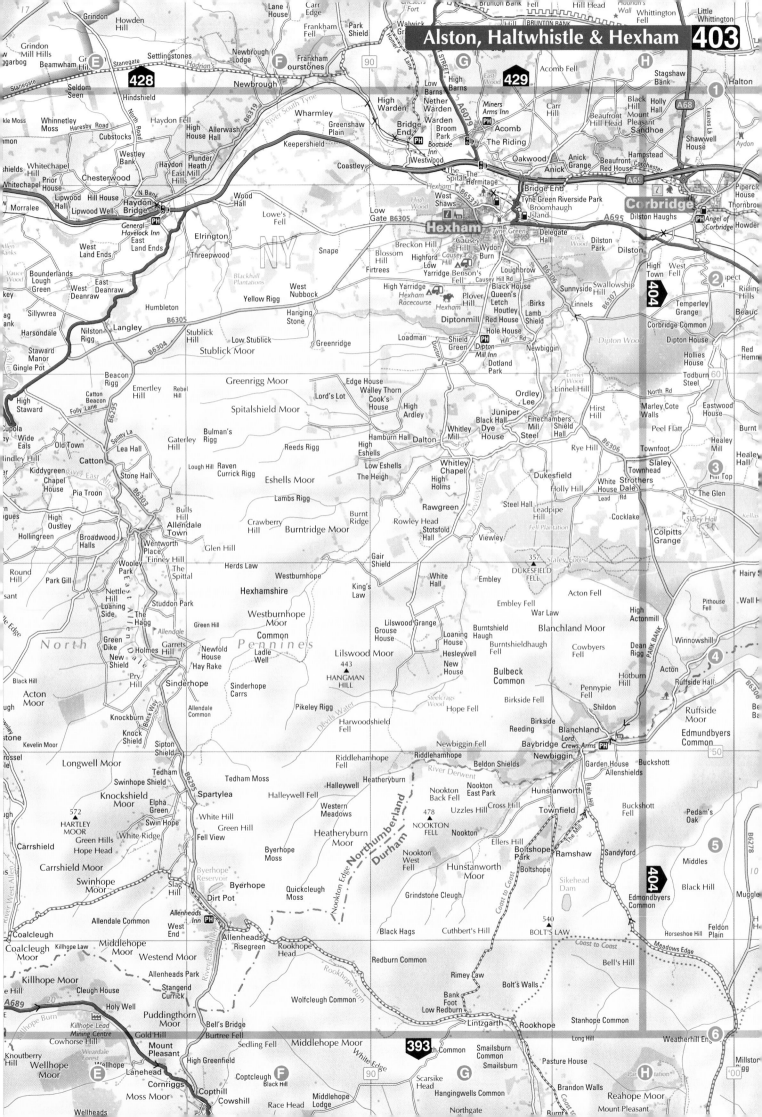

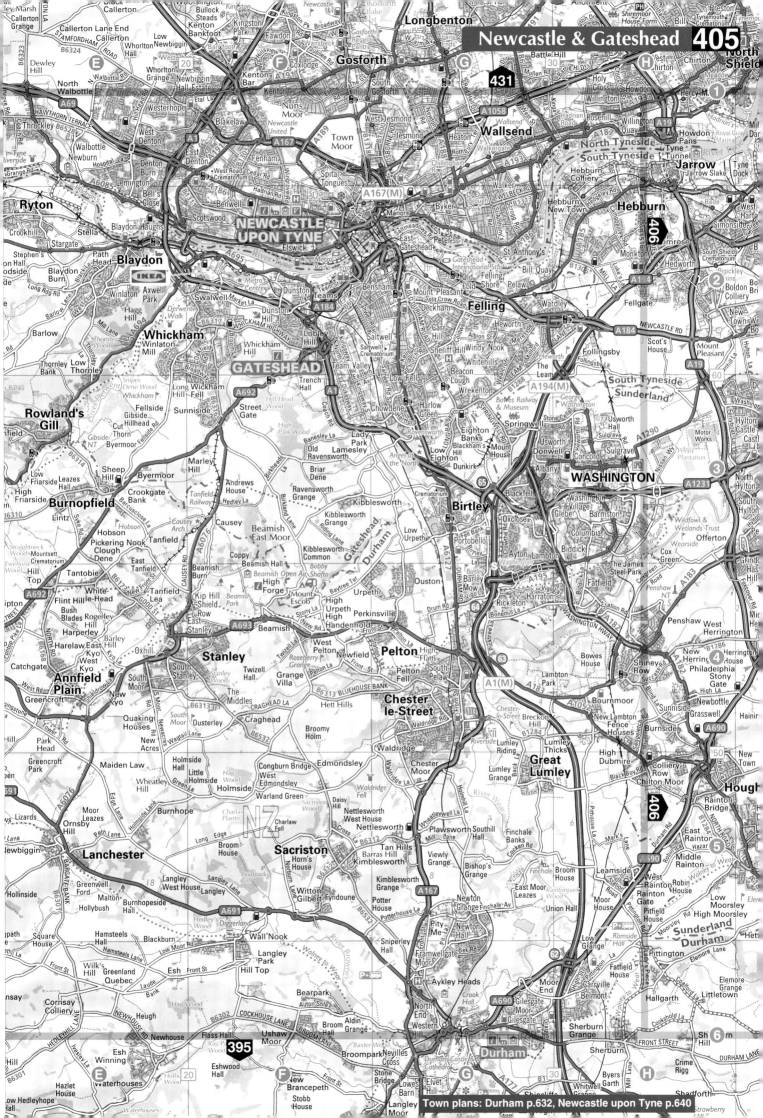

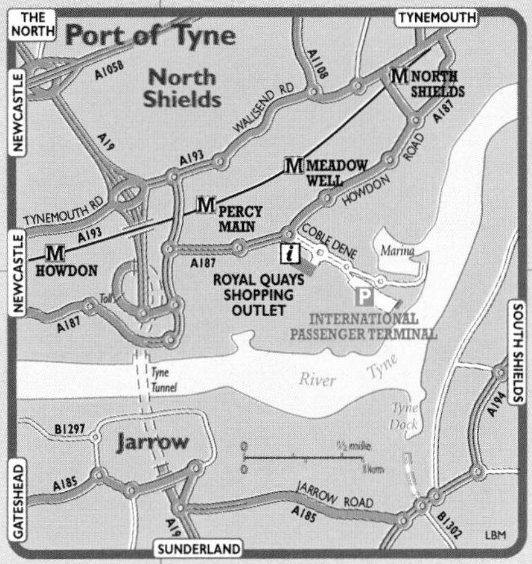

E F 60 G H

1

THE NORTH
Port of Tyne
North Shields
NEWCASTLE
WALLSEND RD
A108
TYNEMOUTH
A1058
A19
A193
M MEADOW WELL
M NORTH SHIELDS
A187
NEWCASTLE
TYNEMOUTH RD
A193
M PERCY MAIN
HOWDON
ROAD
M HOWDON
A187
COBLE DENE
Marina
A187
ROYAL QUAYS SHOPPING OUTLET
P
INTERNATIONAL PASSENGER TERMINAL
SOUTH SHIELDS
A194

Tyne Tunnel
River *Tyne*
Tyne Dock

2
B1297
Jarrow
½ mile
1 km
GATESHEAD
A185
A185
JARROW ROAD
B1302
A19
LBM
SUNDERLAND

60

3

GATESHEAD, NEWCASTLE   FP   **SOUTH SHIELDS**   *Wear*
Sunderland   *River*
4
A1231
TRIMDON STREET
0   200 metres
Wearmouth Bridge
UNIVERSITY OF SUNDERLAND
LOW
RUSSELL STREET
HIGH STREET EAST
A1018
CATHOLIC CHURCH OF ST MARY
M Metro station
Area under development
WEST WEAR STREET
CINEMA
P
WILLIAM ST WEST
ST MARYS WAY
P
LIVINGSTONE ROAD
POL STA
MAG COURT
JOB CENTRE PLUS
INLAND REVENUE OFFICE
EMPIRE THEATRE
HIGH STREET WEST
ST THOMAS STREET
CORK
DRURY LANE
50
SILKSWORTH ROW
FIRE STATION
ST MICHAELS
CROWTREE LEISURE CENTRE
BRIDGES SHOPPING CENTRE
M
i SUNDERLAND STATION
ATHENAEUM ST
HOLMESIDE
LIBRARY & ARTS CENTRE
BOROUGH RD
PO
HUDSON STREET
A1018
BROUGHAM
BLANDFORD
UNIVERSITY OF SUNDERLAND
UNIVERSITY OF SUNDERLAND
ST MICHAELS WAY
THE MARKET
MUSEUM & WINTER GARDENS
MEDICAL CENTRE
P
SCHOOL
5
CHESTER-LE-STREET
UNIVERSITY OF SUNDERLAND
CHESTER ROAD
UOS
UOS
UOS
ROYALTY THEATRE
M University
PRIESTMAN
VINE PLACE
TRANSPORT INTERCHANGE
WAR MEMORIAL
P
Mowbray Gardens
CIVIC CENTRE
B1219
A183
SOUTH HILL CRES
WESTERN HILL
NEW DURHAM RD
TUNSTALL TERRACE
COWAN TERR
Park Lane M
STOCKTON ROAD
UNIVERSITY OF SUNDERLAND
PARK ROAD
A1231
PEEL STREET
BURN PARK ROAD
DURHAM ROAD
TUNSTALL ROAD
THORNHILL TERRACE
ARGYLE
BELVEDERE ROAD
B1522
SCHOOL
6
A690
SCHOOL
THORNHOLME
TEESSIDE (A19)
LBM
DURHAM

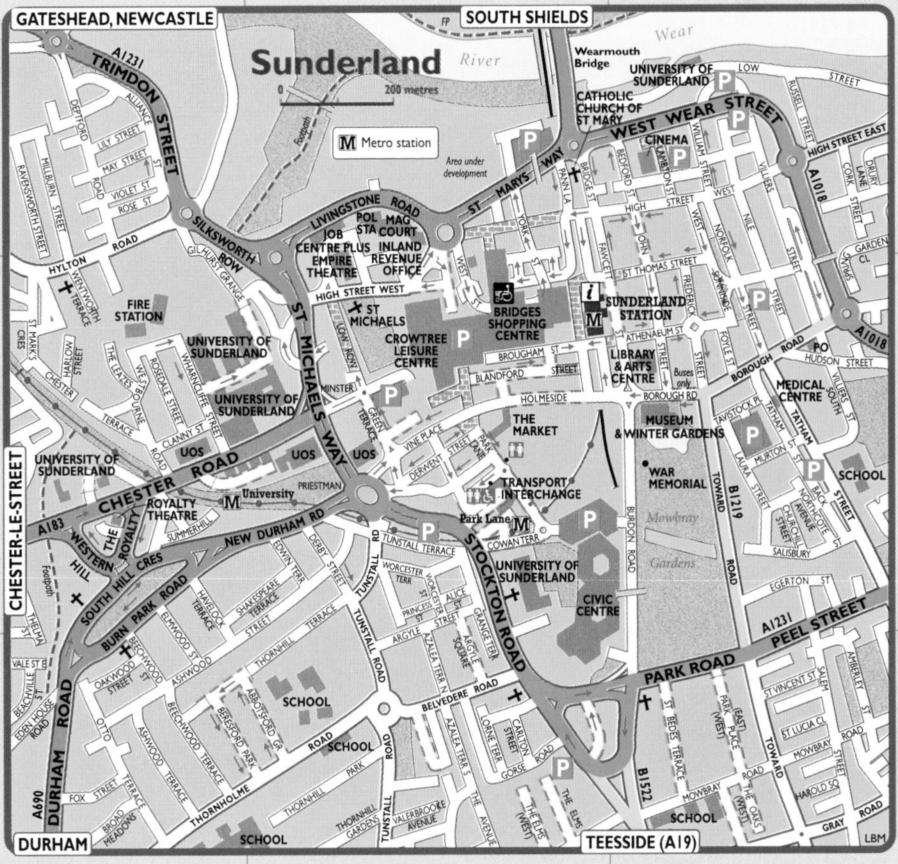

E F 60 G H 70

70

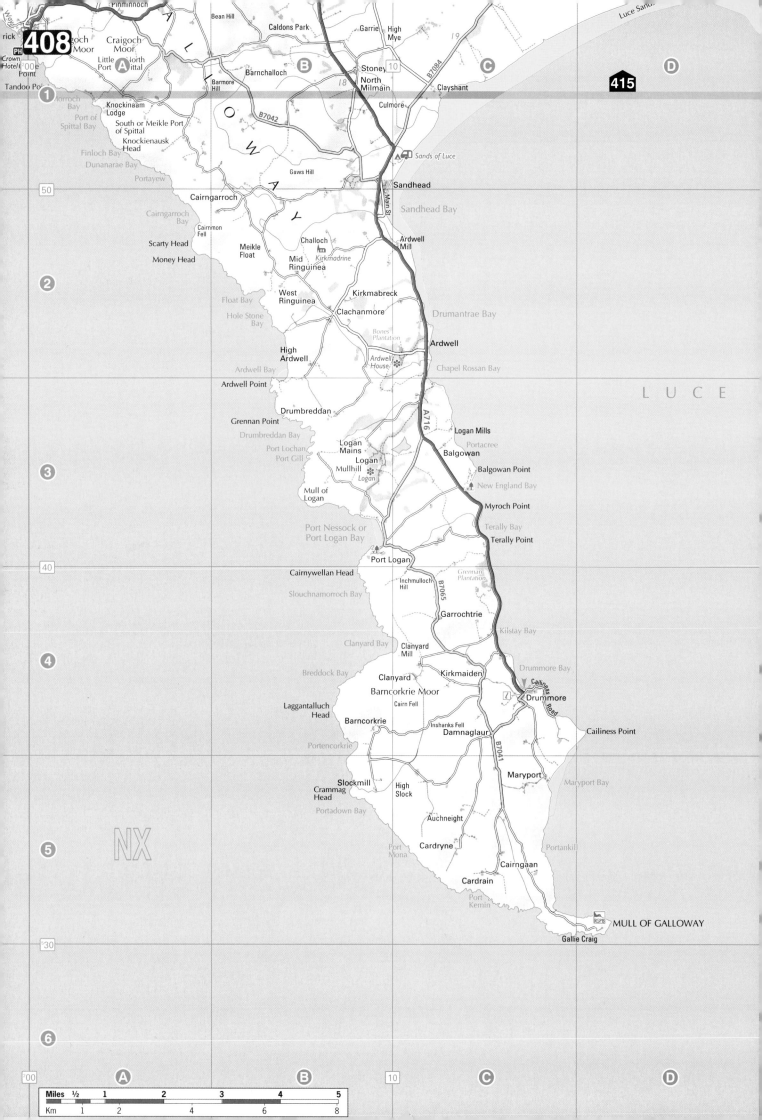

Milton
Stairhaven
Whitefield
Culroy
Culquhasen
E
Laigh Sinniness
Auchenmalg
Mull of Sinniness
Cock Inn
Craig Lodge
Auchenmalg Bay

Black Loch
Castle Loch
F
Gargrie Moor
Craignarget Hill
Drumblair Moor
Garheugh Fell
Culshabbin
Kirwar Plantation

Mochrum Loch
416
B7005
Glenling Moss
Mochrum Fell
High Moor
Low Moor
Chapel Finian (ruin).
Changue Fell
Airylick
Bennan Hill
Elrig Loch
G
White Dyke
Flow of Airriequhillart
Flow of Drumnescat
Loch Head
Barr Hill
Elrig
Corhulloch Hill
Druchtag Motte

Dounan Moor
Crouse Moor
H
Airriequhillart
Airlies
Gledmein
South Clutag
1
Barver
Sheep Park
Capenoch
Small Muir
Barrachan
Culgarie
Kirkland of Longcastle
Low Carseduchan
2
Boreland of Longcastle
Cairnfield
Stone

Garheugh Port
Corwall Port
Chippermore Port
Chippermore Point
Changue
Changue Port
Milton Fell
Airyolland
Kings Green
Milton Point
Barr Point
Killantrae
Mochrum
Meikle Killantrae
Low Drumskeog
Clone Point
Airyhassen
Balcraig Moor
Drummodie
Drummodie Moss
Drumtroddan
Drumtrodden Cup & Ring
Drumtrodden Standing Stones
Auchness Moss

410
A747

Port William
B7085
Monreith Mains
King's Loop
White Loch of Myrton
'Wrens Egg' Standing Stones
Big Balcraig
Fell of Barhullion
Blairbuy
Barsalloch Fort
Barsalloch Point
Port Whapple
Monreith Bay
Monreith
Larrock
Craigdhu
Garrarie
40
Front Bay
Point of Lag
St Medan
Back Bay
The Alt
Cairndoon Bank
Low Craiglemine
Point of Cairndoon
Carleton Port
4 Fell of Carleton

BAY

Little Scares
SCARES
Big Scare

410

NX
5

30

E
F
30
G
H
40

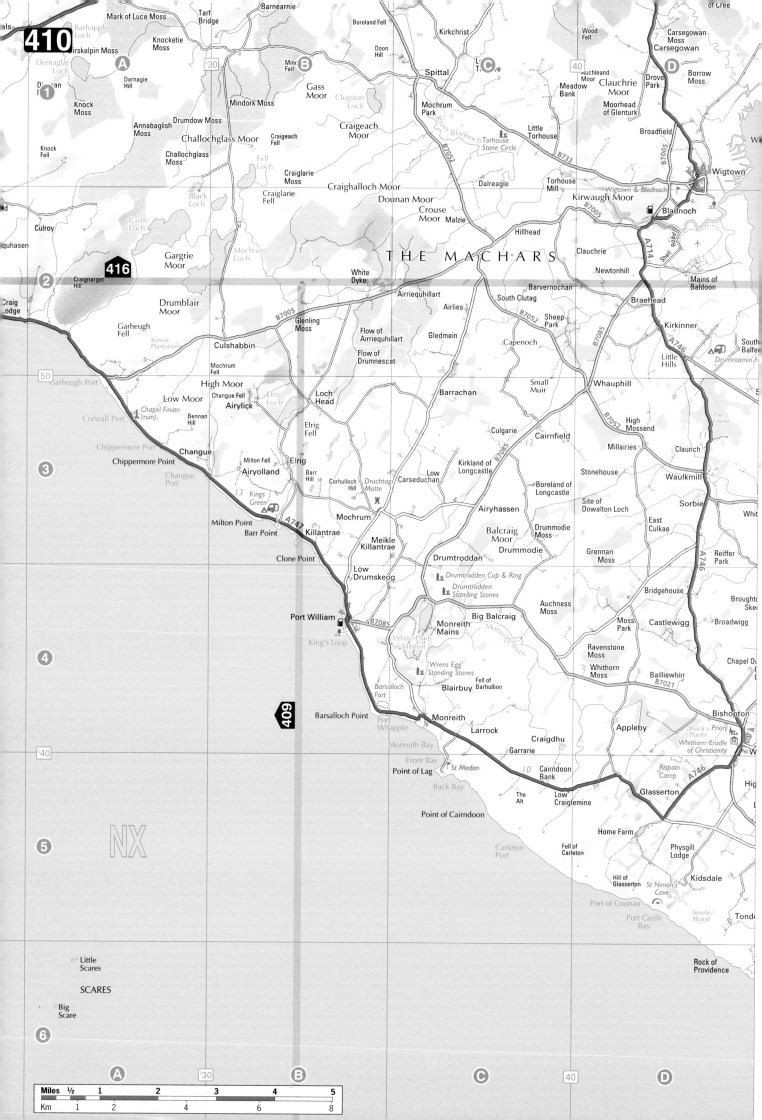

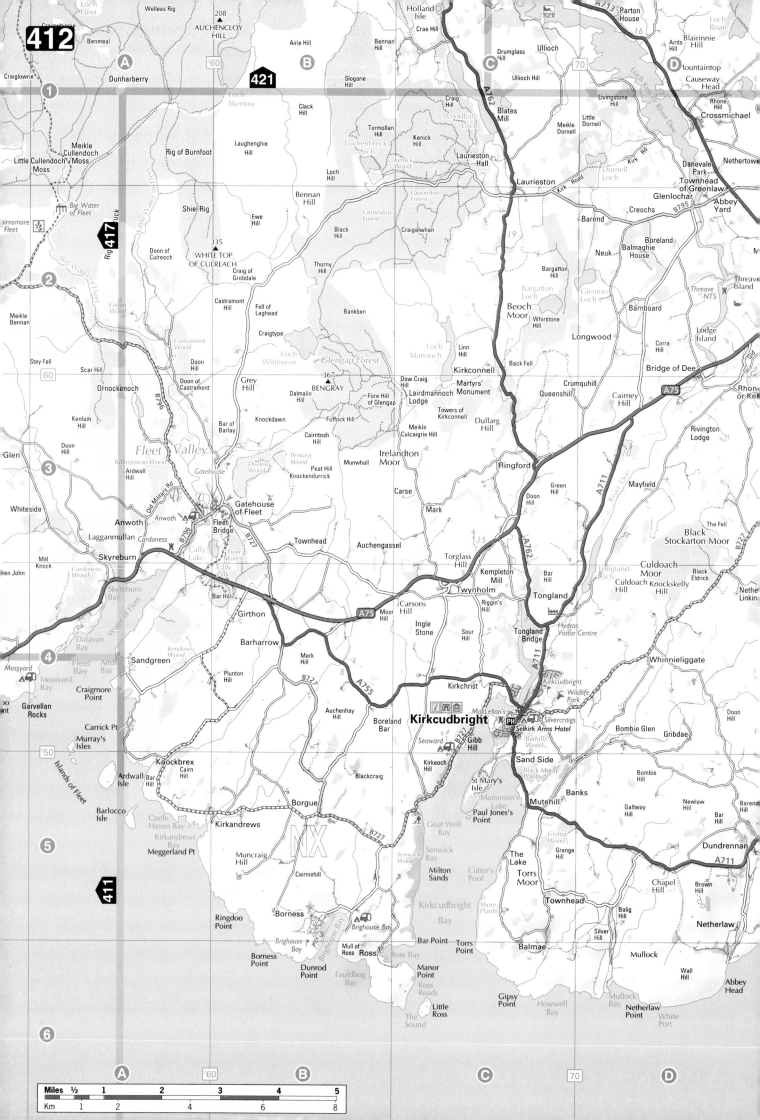

Stranraer Ferry Port

Loch Ryan

CAR FERRY TERMINAL

STRANRAER STATION

GARRICK HOSPITAL H

KIRKCOLM
B731
A718
GIRVAN
NEWTON STEWART
A77
A75
A77

0 ½ mile
0 1km

DRUMMORE

LBM

A
'90
B
(SUMMER ONLY)
LARNE
C
'200
D
418

LARNE

BELFAST

BELFAST

70

3

4

5

6

1

2

NW

NORTH CHANNEL

Curra
Brackness
Hole
Bur
Foo

Boak Port
Milleur Point
Finnarts Point

Port Leen
Stronach Hill
Heighton
Garry Point
Finnarts Bay

Corsewall Point
North Park
Culbee Moss
Portencalzie
Lady Bay

Barnhills
North Cairn
Cairnbowie Hill
Jamieson's Point

Braid Port
Blair More Hill
B738

Port Gavillan
Portnaughan Bay
North Cairn
South Cairn
B738
Balgown Moss
Loch Connell
Kirkcolm
The Scar
A718

Dounan Bay
T
H
E
Ervie
Marslauch
The Wig
Marian Port

Salt Pan Bay
Knockbennan Hill
Little Glengyre
Milton
Loch

Portobello
R
H
Barbeth
Balwherrie
B798

Strool Bay
Tor of Craigoch
Soleburn

Slouchnawen Bay
B738
Knocknain
Garchrie Moss
B7043
Leswalt
B798
A718

Port Beg
Galdenoch Moor
Half Mark
NX
Smithy Hill
Stranraer

Salt Pans Bay
Larbrax Moor
B738
Z
Z
Glenstockadale

Cranberry Pt
Springbank
Castle of St Jo
Gallow

60

Broadsea Bay
Dindinnie Resr
Upland Way
Southern
Knock and Maize
Crailloch Hill

Knockgour
Broad Moor
Knockglass

Portslogan
O
F

Knock Bay
Killantringan Bay
Craigslave Moorcroft
Craigenlee Fell
F

Black Head
Upper Dinvin
181
CAIRN PAT

Portamaggie
Southern Upland Way
Pinminnoch Burn
Spittal

Portavaddie
Dunskey Glen
Enoch
G
Pinminnoch

Port Kale Port Mora
A77

Portpatrick
Craigoch Park Moor
Craigoch Moor
A
L
L

PH
Crown Hotel
Castle Point
Little or North Port of Spittal

Tandoo Point

Morroch Bay
Knockinaam Lodge
Port of Spittal Bay
South or Meikle Port Spittal

Finloch Bay
Knockienausk Head
Dunanarae Bay

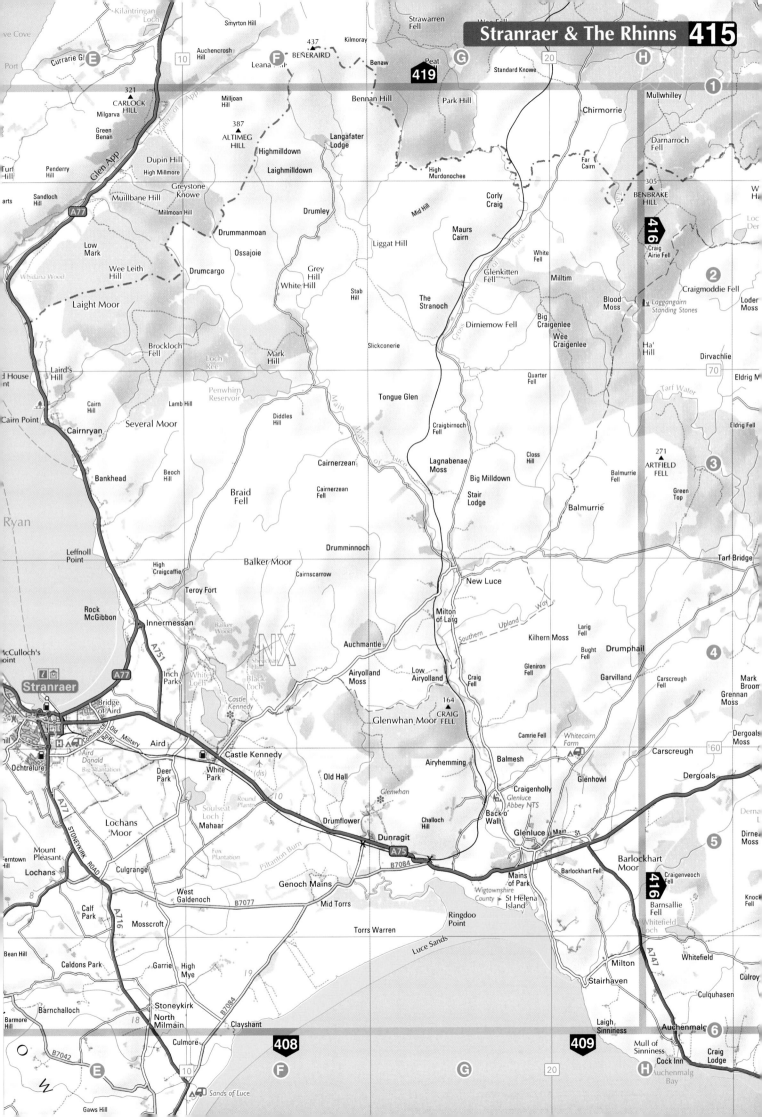

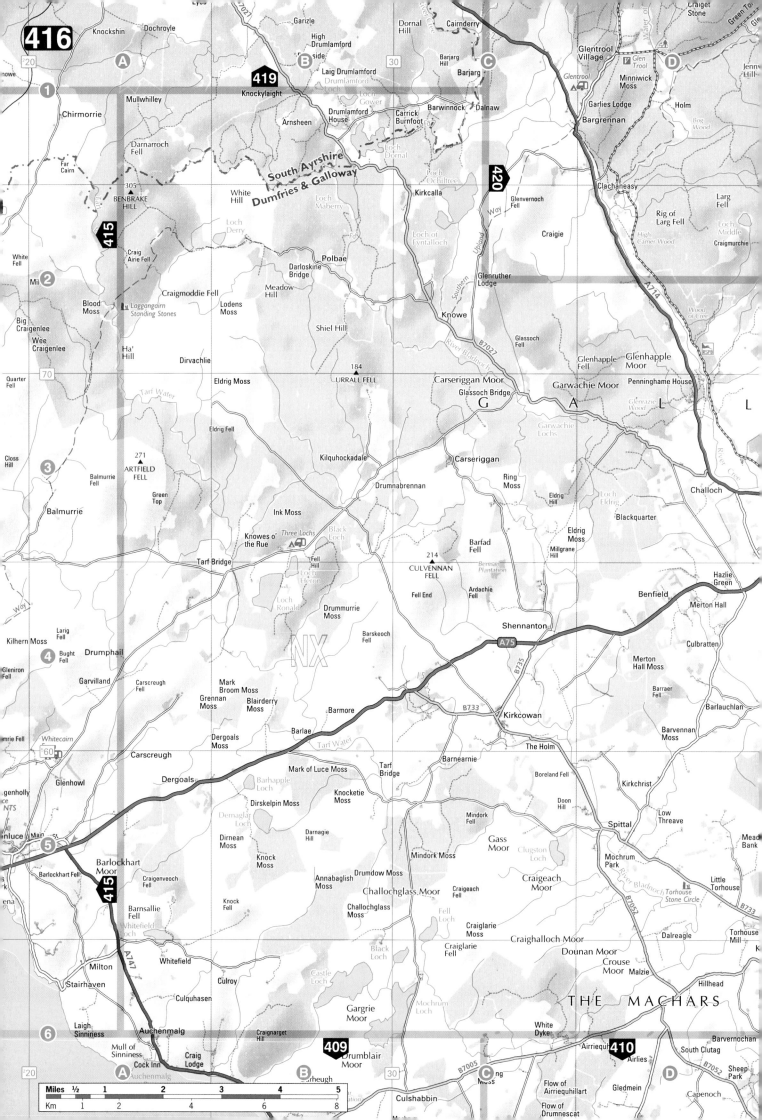

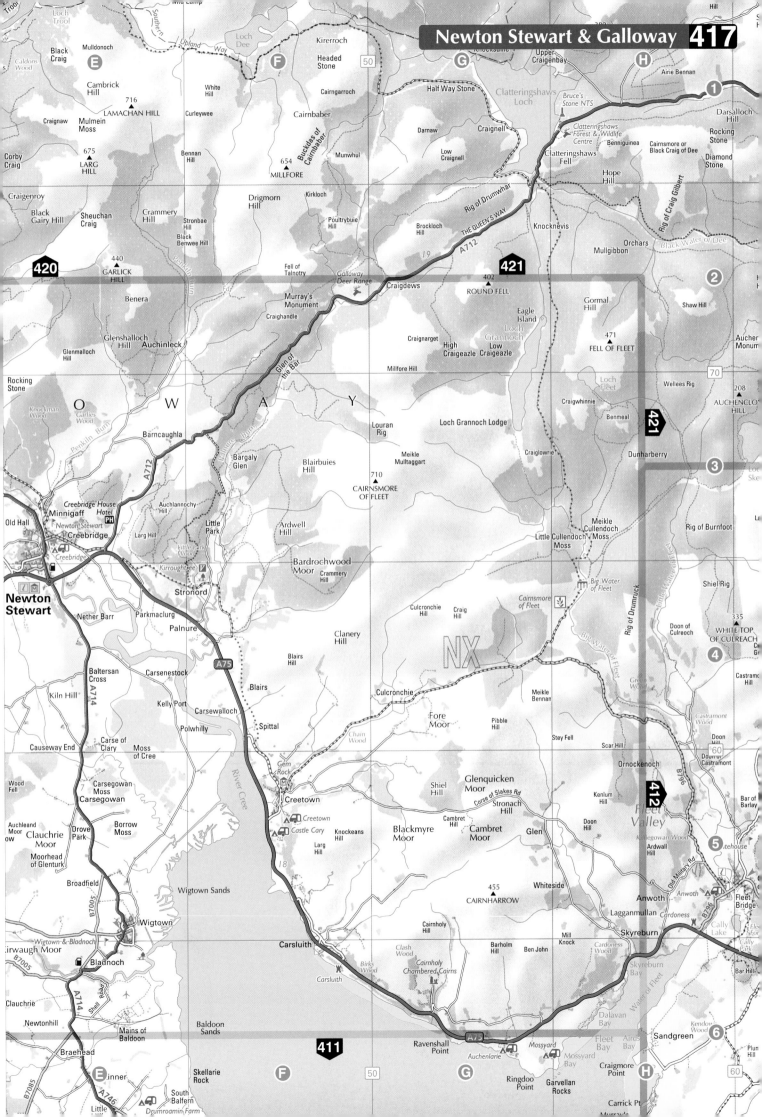

Loch Trool
Loch Dee
Loch Ken

Southern Upland Way
THE QUEEN'S WAY

Caldons Wood
Black Craig
Mulldonoch
Cambrick Hill
716 LAMACHAN HILL
Craignaw
Mulmein Moss
Corby Craig
675 LARG HILL
Black Gairy Hill
Sheuchan Craig
Crammery Hill
Stronbae Hill
Black Benwee Hill

White Hill
Curleywee
Bennan Hill
654 MILLFORE
Bucktas of Cairnbaber
Drigmorn Hill
Kirkloch
Poultrybuie Hill

Wild Lump
Kirerroch
Headed Stone
Cairngarroch
Cairnbaber
Munwhul

50
Knocksunie
Upper Craigenbay
Airie Bennan
Darsalloch Hill
Rocking Stone
Diamond Stone
Half Way Stone
Bruce's Stone NTS
Clatteringshaws Loch
Darnaw
Craignell
Low Craignell
Clatteringshaws Forest & Wildlife Centre
Clatteringshaws Fell
Benniguinea
Cairnsmore or Black Craig of Dee
Hope Hill
Rig of Drumwhar
Brockloch Hill
Knocknevis
Orchars
Mullgibbon
Black Water of Dee
Rig of Craig Gilbert

420
440 GARLICK HILL
Benera
Glenshalloch Hill
Glenmalloch Hill
Auchinleck
Penkiln Burn
Fell of Talnotry
Galloway Deer Range
Murray's Monument
Craighandle
Glen of the Bar
Craigdews
19 A712
402 ROUND FELL
421
Eagle Island
Loch Grannoch
Gormal Hill
471 FELL OF FLEET
Shaw Hill
70
Aucher Monum
Craigwhinnie
Benmeal
Wellees Rig
208 AUCHENCLO HILL

O W A Y

Barncaughla
Penkiln Burn
Bargaly Glen
Blairbuies Hill
High Craigeazle
Low Craigeazle
Millfore Hill
Louran Rig
Meikle Mulltaggart
Loch Grannoch Lodge
Craiglowrie
Dunharberry
421
3

Garlies Wood
Knockman Wood
Rocking Stone
Creebridge House Hotel
Minnigaff
Newton Stewart
Creebridge
Old Hall
Auchlannochy Hill
Little Park
Larg Hill
Little Park Wood
Kirroughtree
Stronord
710 CAIRNSMORE OF FLEET
Ardwell Hill
Bardrochwood Moor
Crammery Hill
Meikle Cullendoch Moss
Little Cullendoch Moss
Rig of Burnfoot
Shiel Rig

Newton Stewart
Nether Barr
Parkmaclurg
Palnure
Balneith
A712
Big Water of Fleet
Cairnsmore of Fleet
Culcronchie Hill
Craig Hill
Culcronchie
Clanery Hill
Blairs Hill
NX
Meikle Bennan
335
Doon of Culreoch
WHITE TOP OF CULREACH
4
Rig of Drumruck
Castramon Wood
Little Water of Fleet

Baltersan Cross
Kiln Hill
Carsenestock
A714
Kelly Port
Carsewalloch
Blairs
Spittal
Fore Moor
Pibble Hill
Stey Fell
Scar Hill
Ornockenoch
Doon of Castramont
60
B796
Doon Hill
Castramont Hill

Causeway End
Carse of Clary
Moss of Cree
Polwhilly
Chain Wood
Culcronchie
Shiel Hill
Glenquicken Moor
Corse of Slakes Rd
Stronach Hill
Kenlum Hill
Doon Hill
Fleet Valley
412
Bar of Barlay

Wood Fell
Carsegowan Moss
Carsegowan
Drove Park
Borrow Moss
Clauchrie Moor
Moorhead of Glenturk
River Cree
Gem Rock
Creetown
Castle Cary
Larg Hill
Knockeans Hill
Blackmyre Moor
Cambret Hill
Cambret Moor
Glen
Ardwall Hill
Killiegowan Wood
Old Military Rd
Cally Lake
5
itehouse

Auchleand Moor
Broadfield
B7005
18
Wigtown Sands
Creetown
455 CAIRNHARROW
Whiteside
Anwoth
Lagganmullan
Cardoness
Skyreburn
Cally Park
Bar Hill

-irwaugh Moor
Wigtown
Bladnoch
B7005
Cairnholy Hill
Barholm Hill
Ben John
Mill Knock
Cardoness Wood
Skyreburn Bay
Fleet Bay
Airds Bay

Clauchrie
Newtonhill
Braehead
A714
Shell Road
Mains of Baldoon
Baldoon Sands
Skellarie Rock
Carsluith
Carsluith
Birks Wood
Clash Wood
Cairnholy Chambered Cairns
Cairnholy
A75
Ravenshall Point
Auchenlarie
Mossyard
Mossyard Point
Craigmore Point
Sandgreen
Kendow Wood
6
60
Plun Bay

B7085
-inner
A746
South Balfern
Drumroamin Farm
411
Skellarie Rock
50
Ringdoo Point
Garvellan Rocks
Dalavan Bay
Carrick Pt
Murray's

E   F   G   H

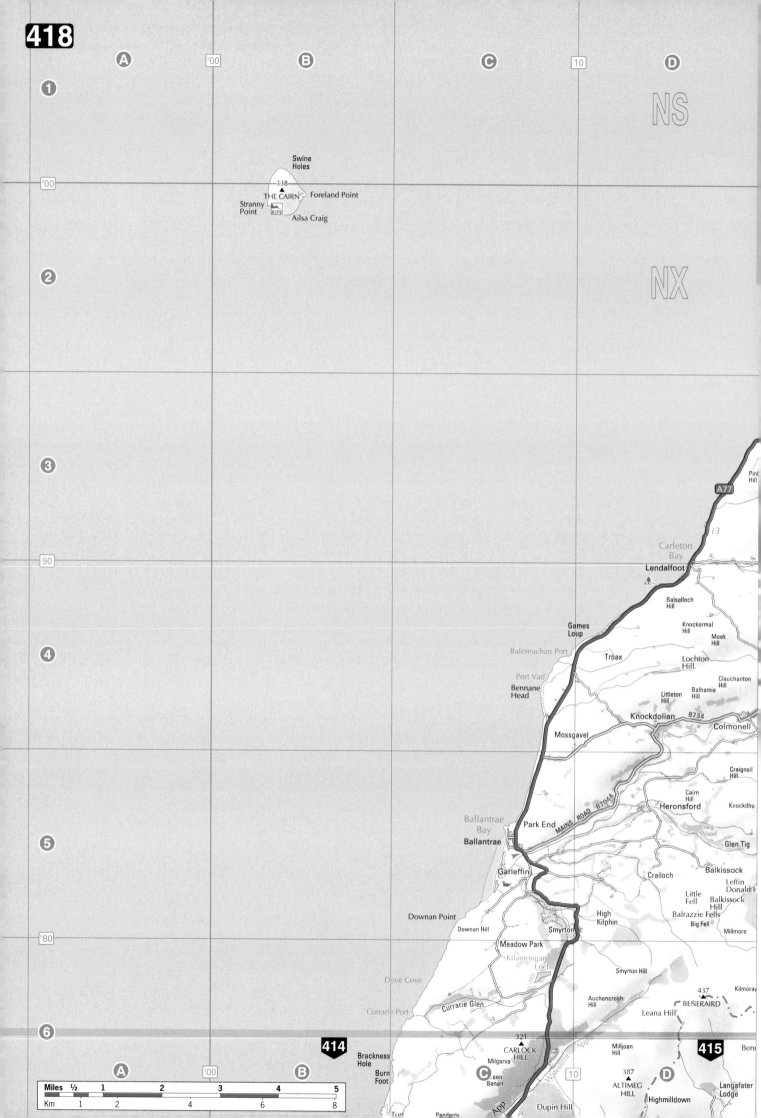

NS

NX

Swine
Holes

338
THE CAIRN ▲   Foreland Point
Stranny
Point   RSPB
          Ailsa Craig

A77

Pint
Hill

13

Carleton
Bay

Lendalfoot

Balsalloch
Hill

Knockormal
Hill

Games
Loup   Moak
                                        Hill
Balcreuchan Port
                   Tröax   Lochton
Port Vad   Hill
                                        Clauchanton
Bennane   Hill
Head   Littleton   Balhamie
                        Hill   Hill

                Knockdolian   B734
                                            Colmonell

        Mossgavel

                                        Craigneil
                                        Hill

                            Cairn
                            Hill
                                Heronsford   Knockdhu

Ballantrae   MAINS ROAD B7044
Bay   Park End
                                            Glen Tig

Ballantrae
                                        Balkissock
Garleffin
                            Crailoch   Leffin
                                          Donald F
                                Little   Balkissock
                                Fell   Hill
Downan Point   Balrazzie Fells
                                            Big Fell   Millmore
            Downan Hill   High
Meadow Park   Kilphin

Kilantringan
Loch   Smyrton
                                Smyrton Hill

Dove Cove
                                            437
                                Auchencrosh   ▲
Currarie Port   Hill   BENERAIRD
            Currarie Glen   Leana Hill   Kilmoray

414

Brackness
Hole   321
            Milgarva   ▲   Milljoan
Burn   CARLOCK   Hill
Foot   HILL

415   Ben

.een
Benan

                                387
                                ▲
                            ALTIMEG   Highmilldown
                            HILL

App   Dupin Hill

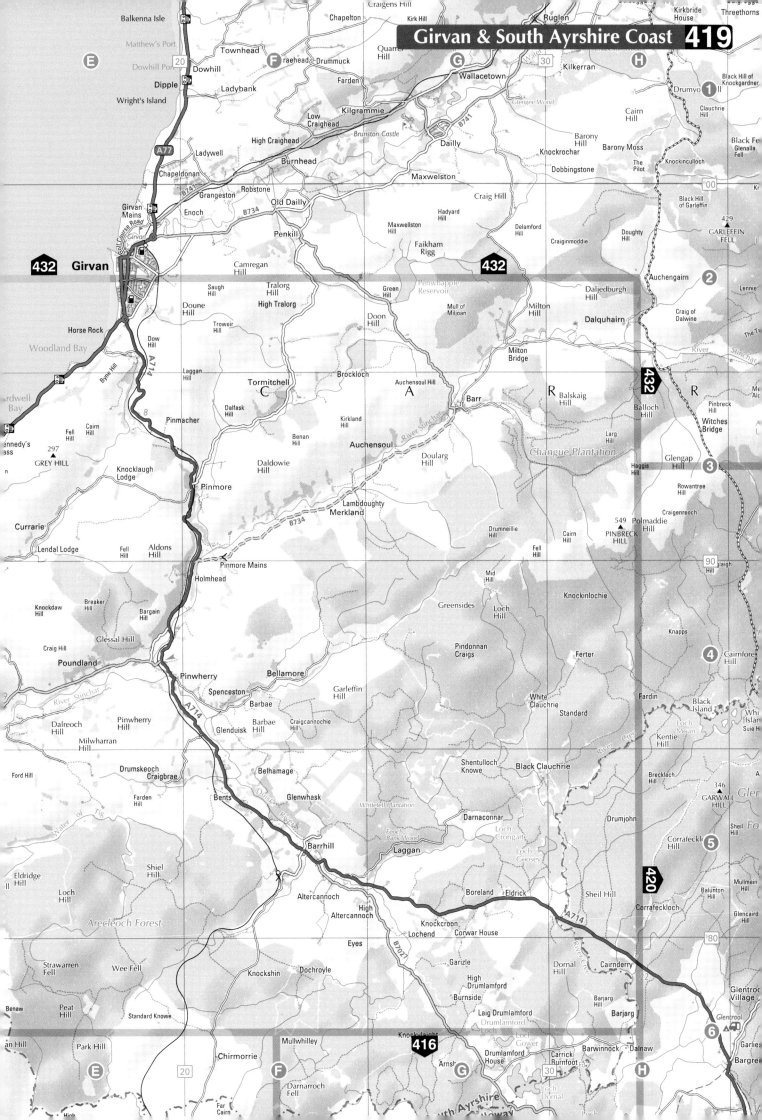

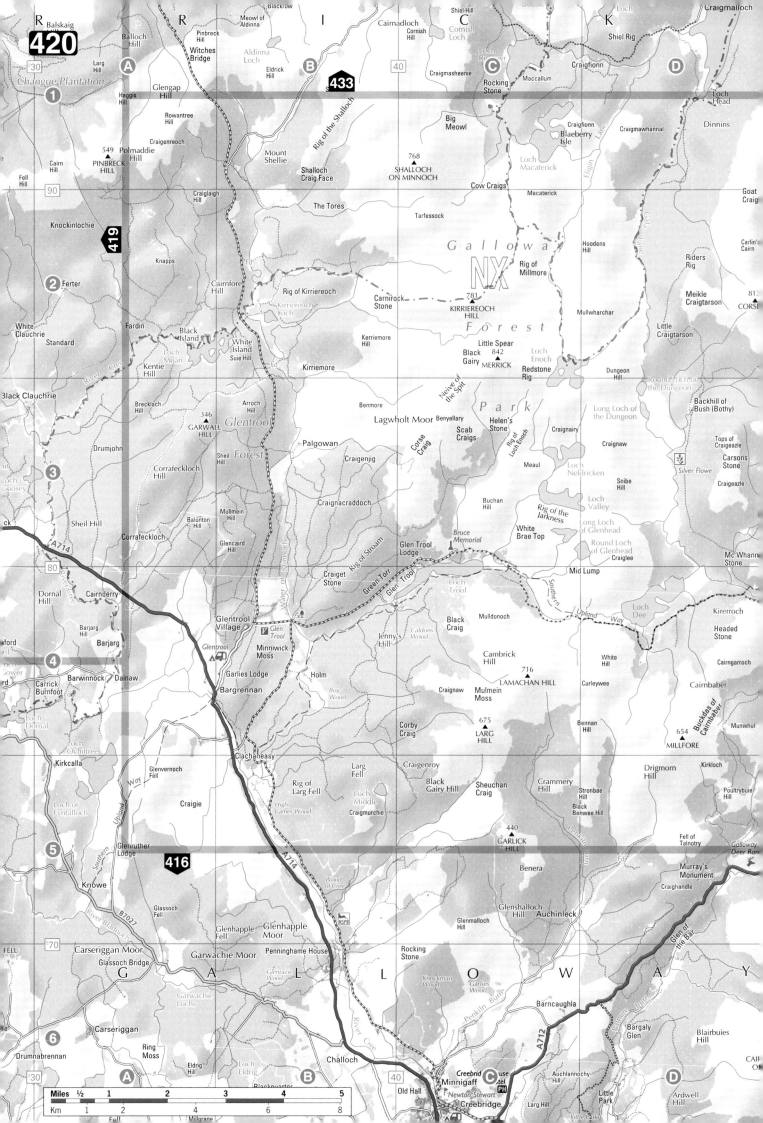

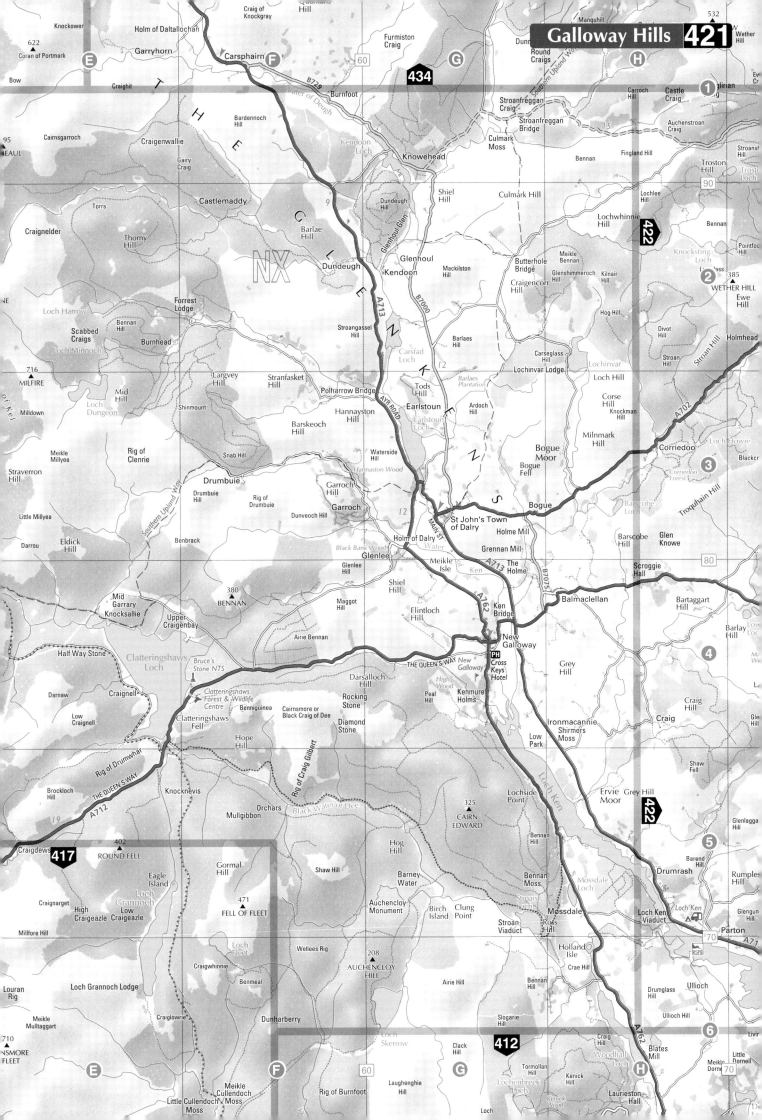

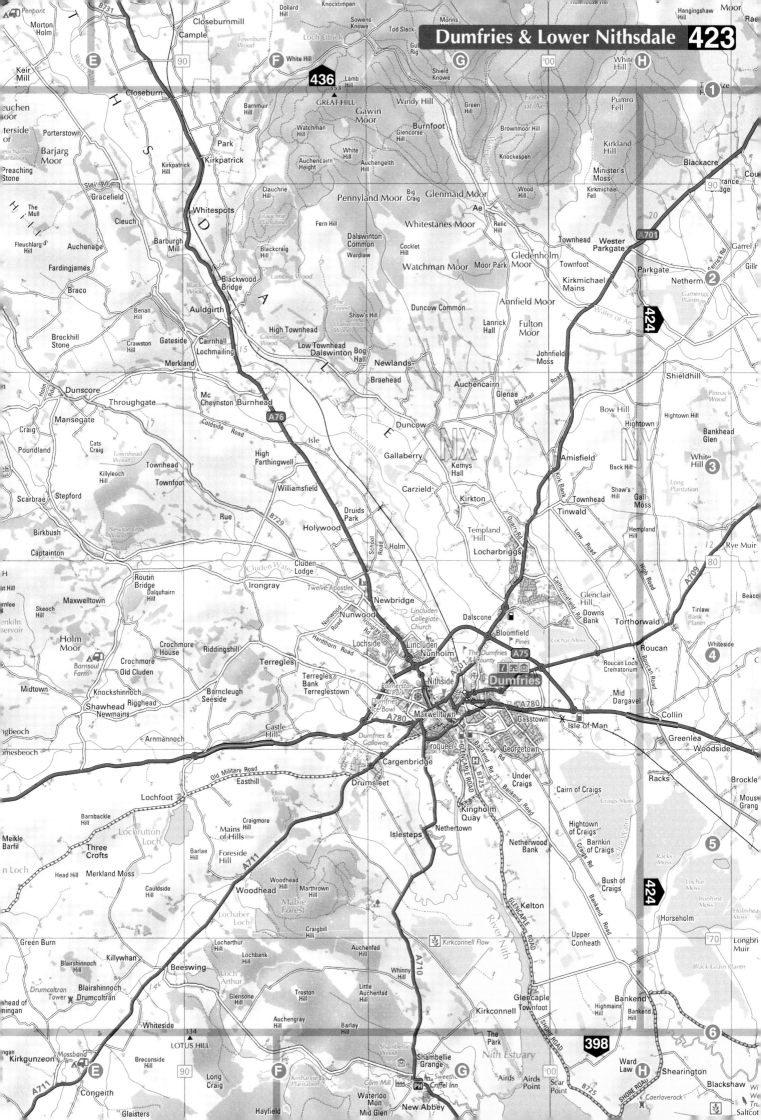

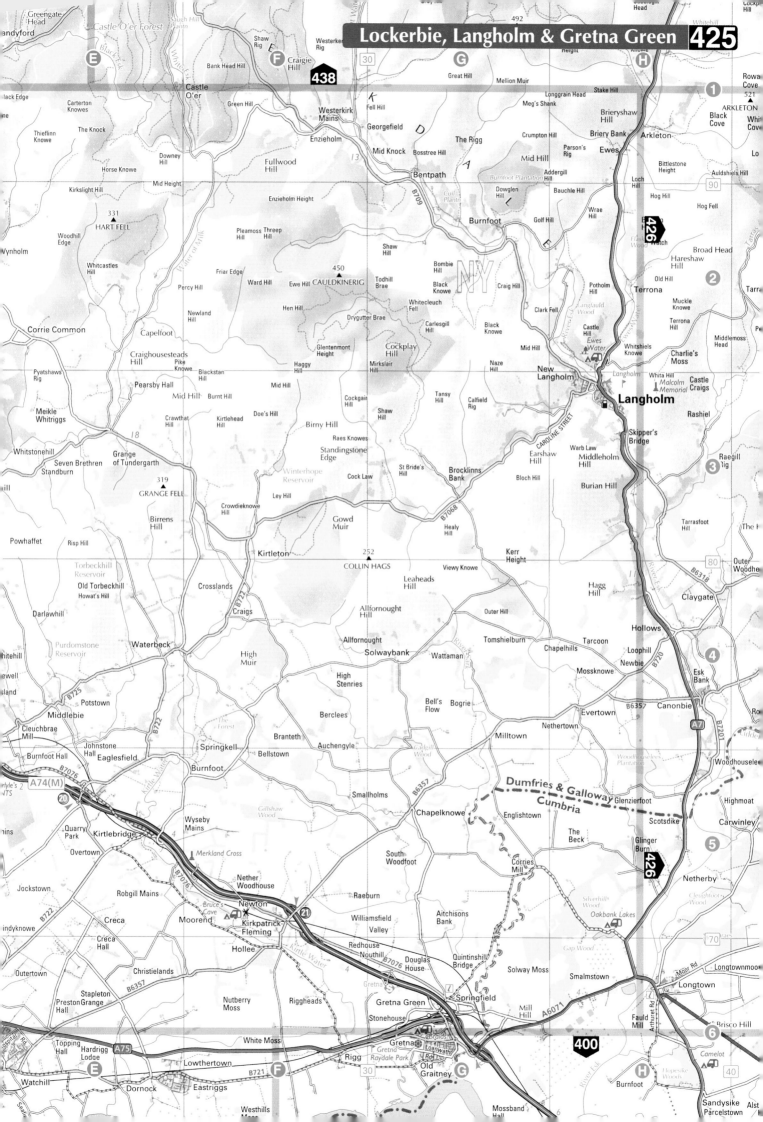

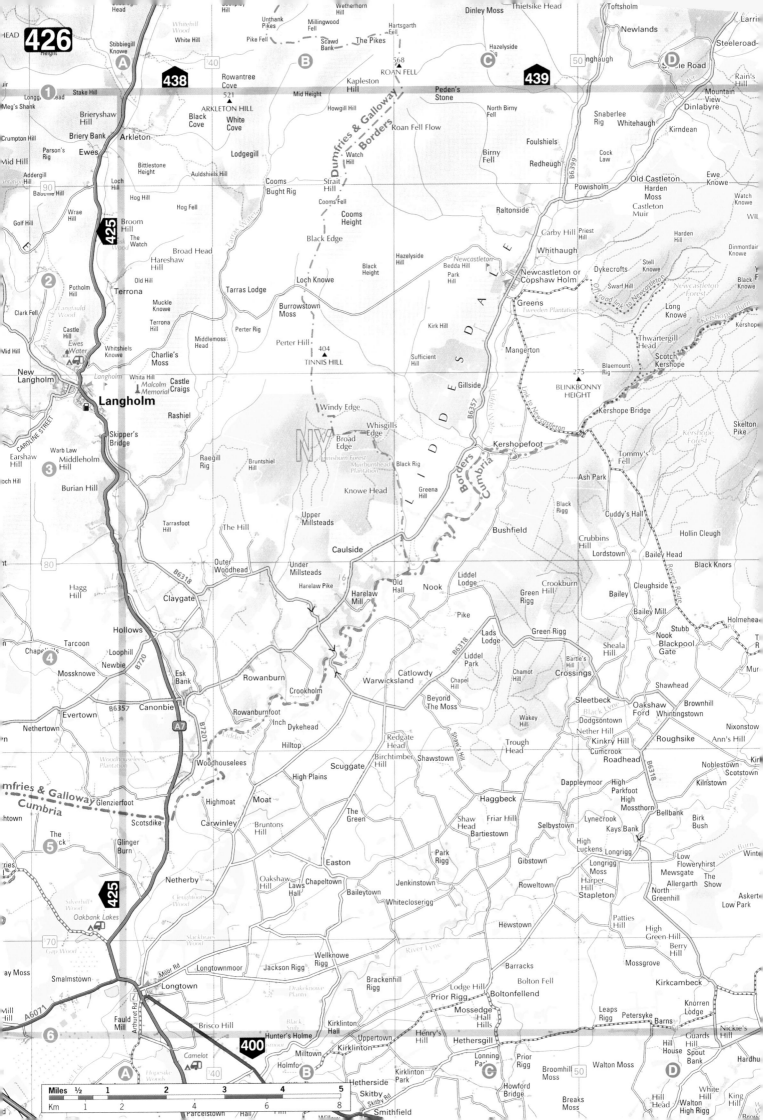

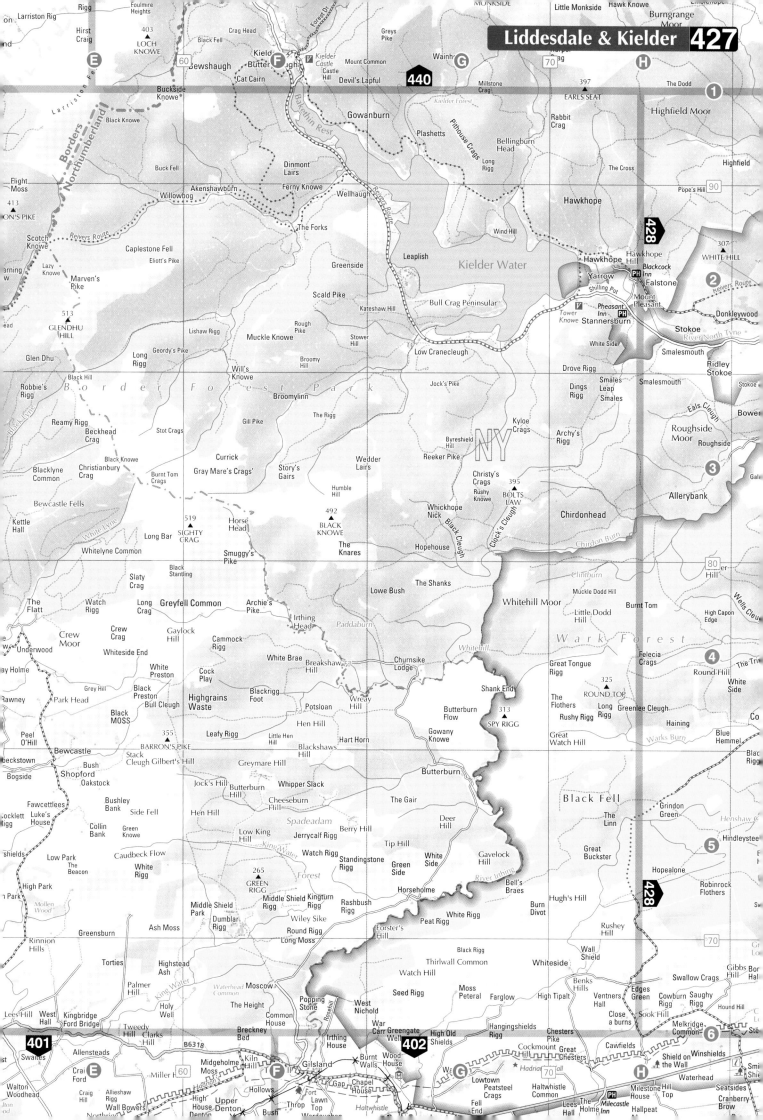

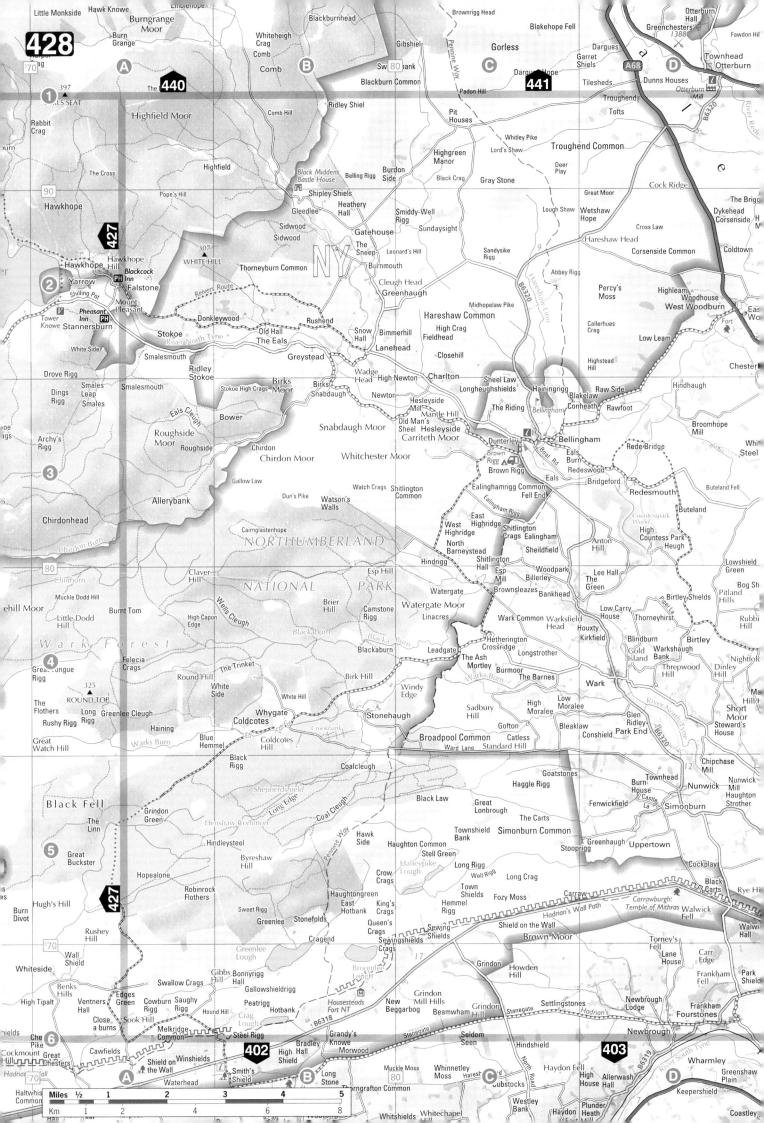

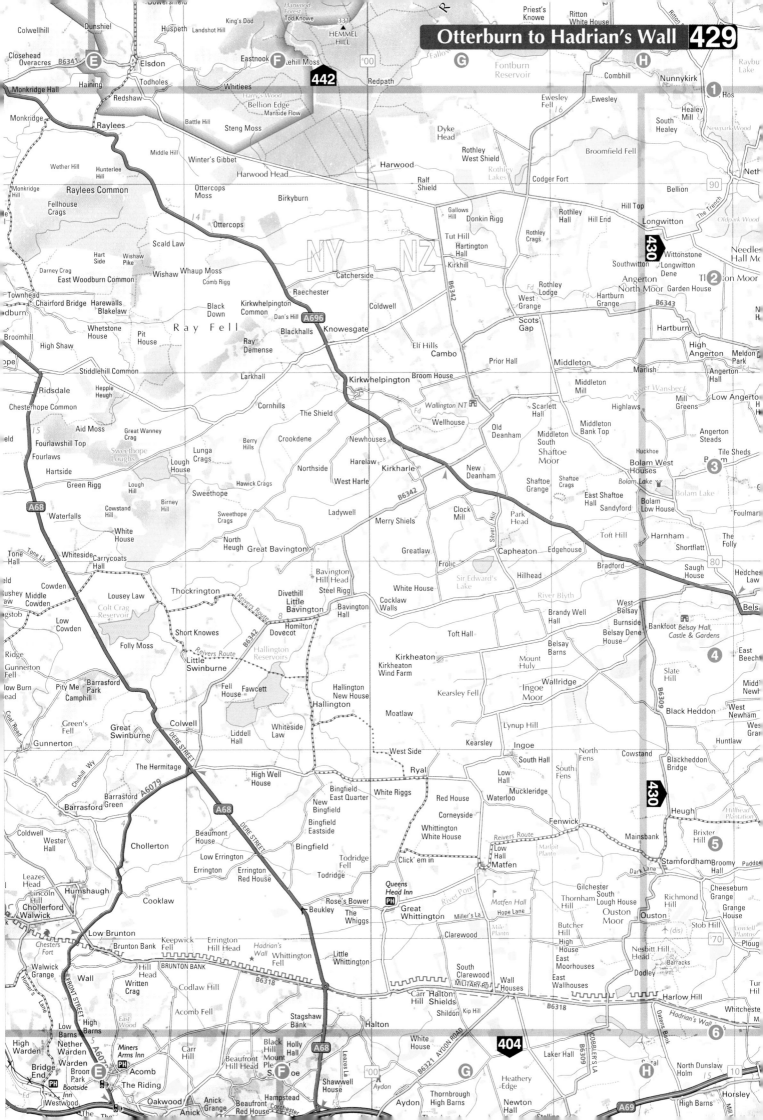

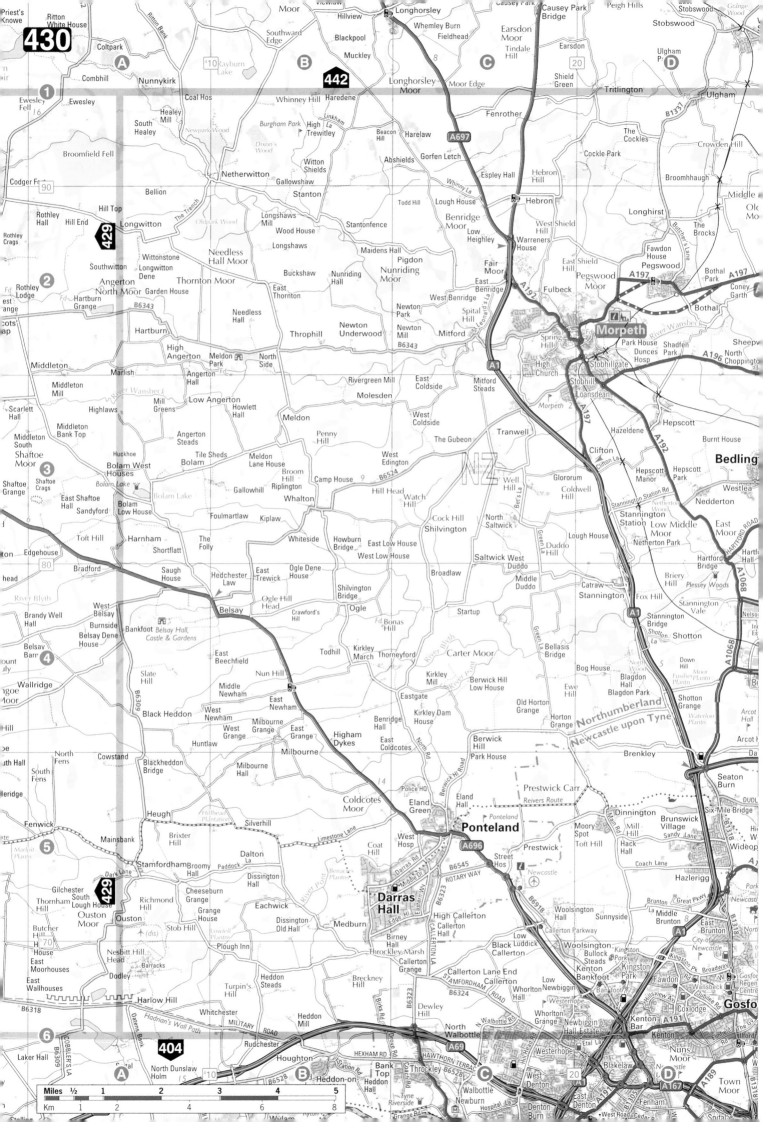

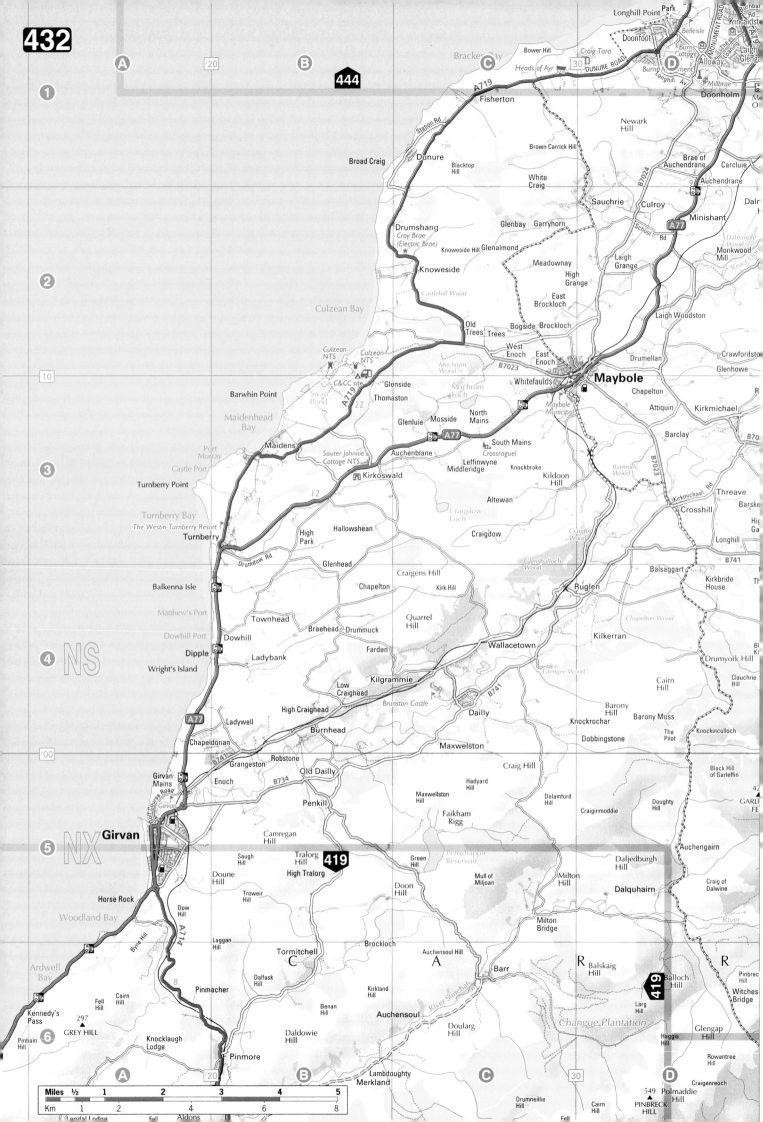

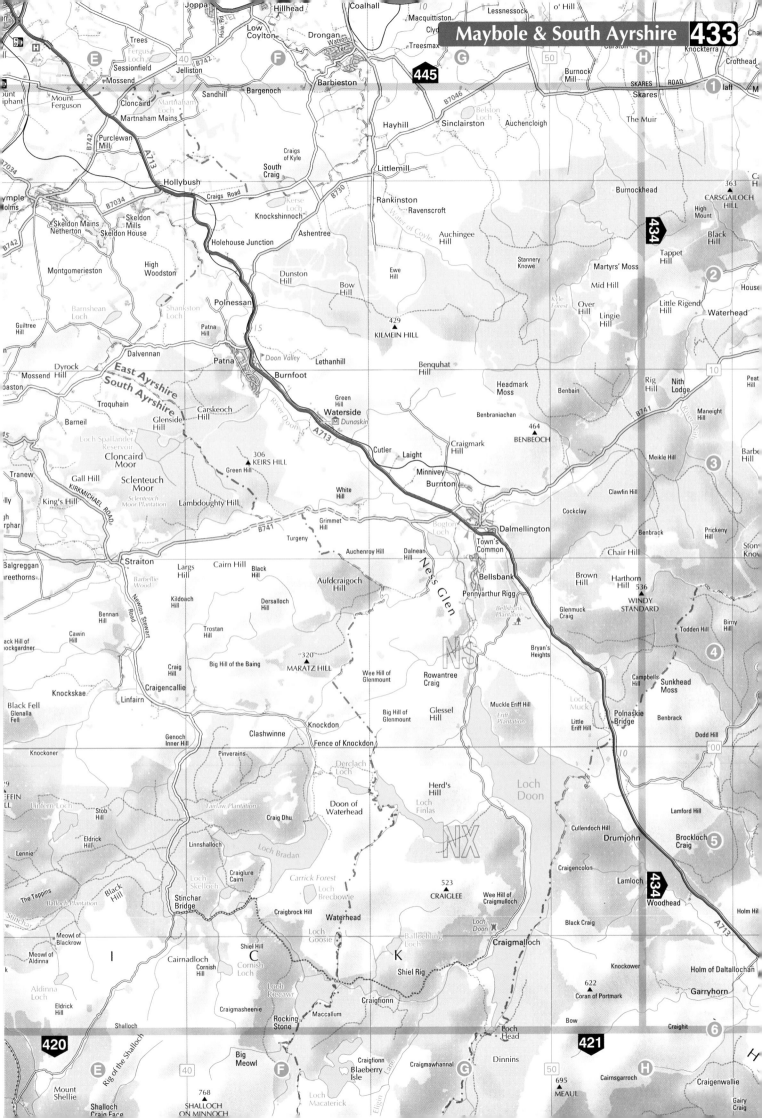

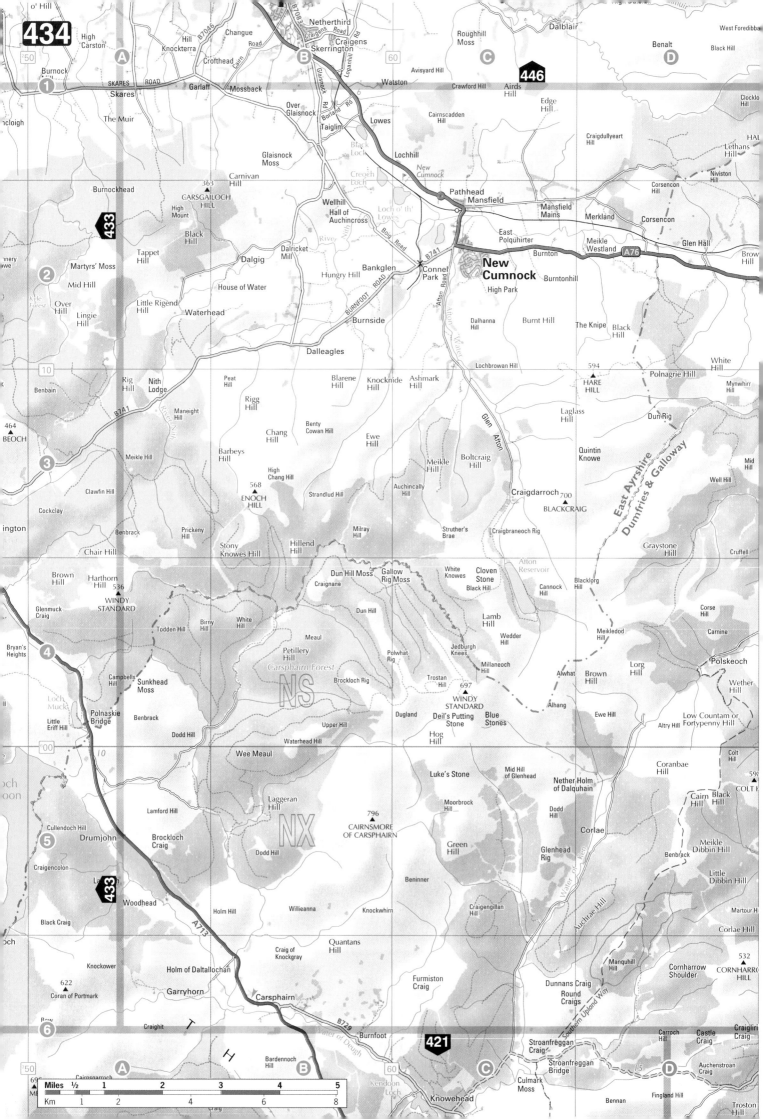

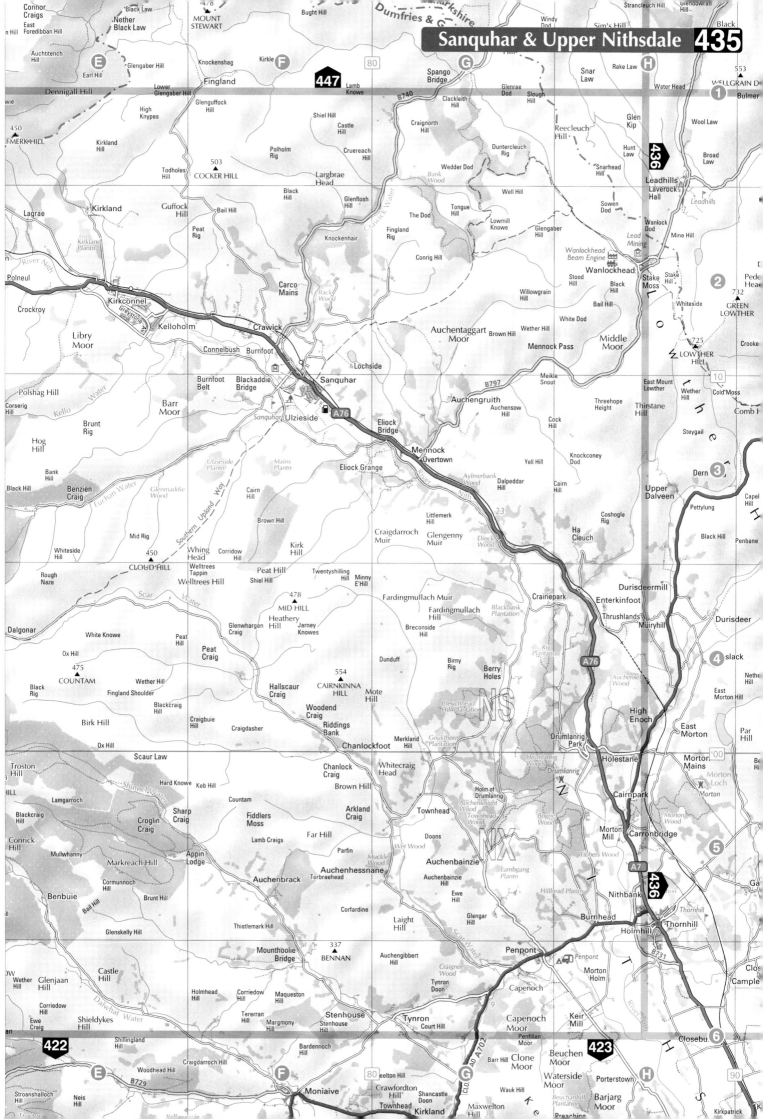

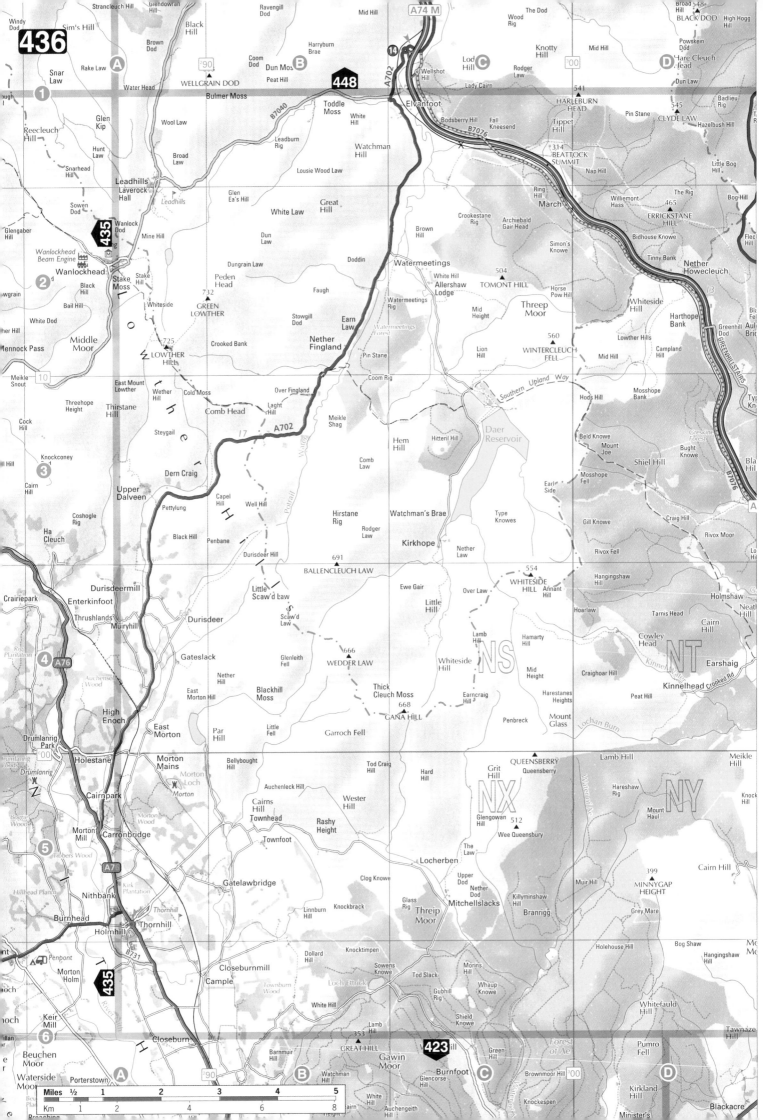

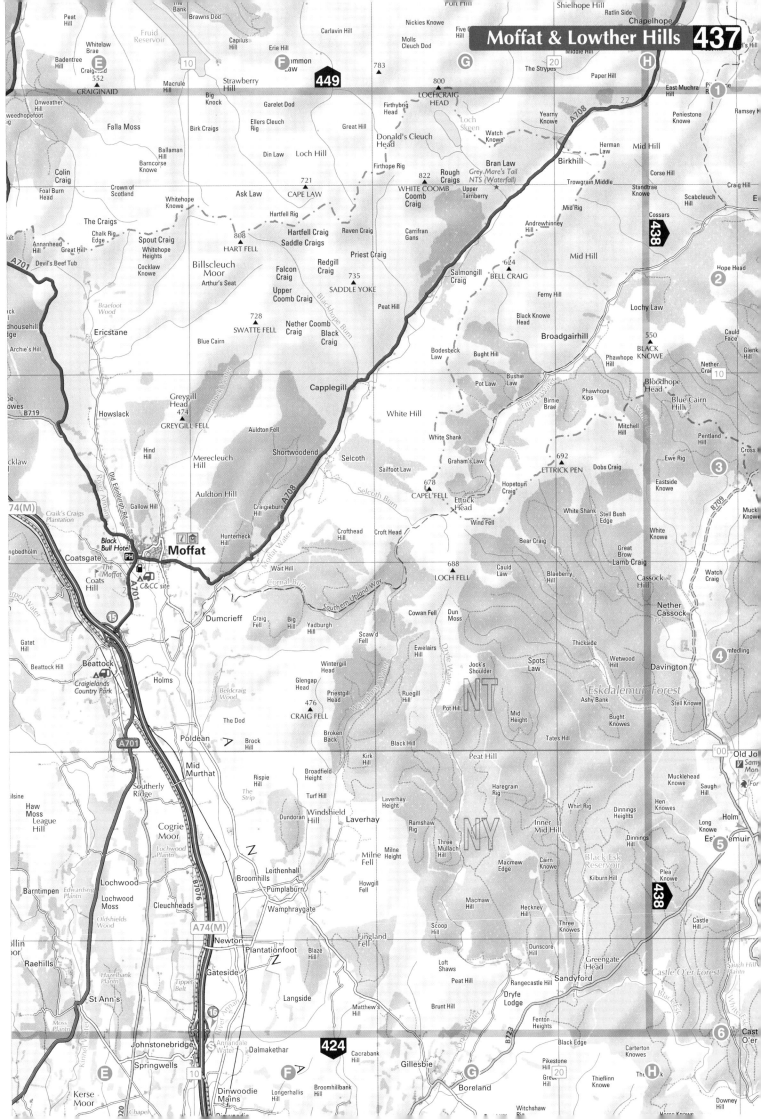

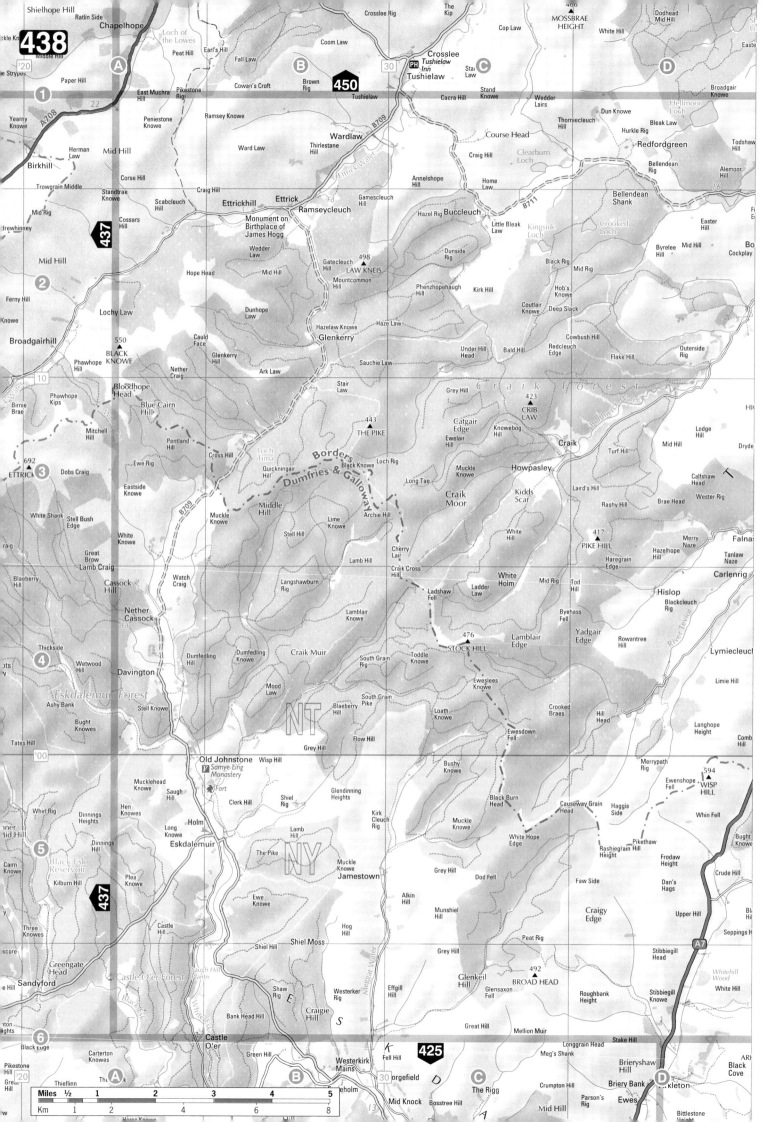

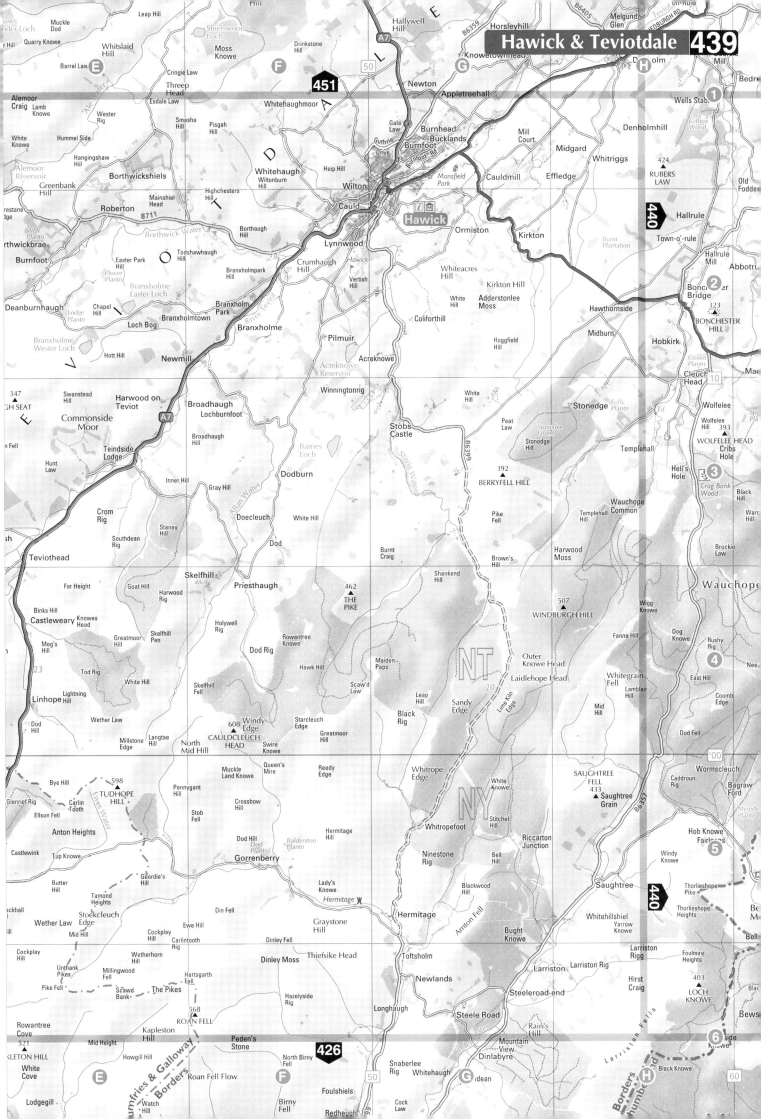

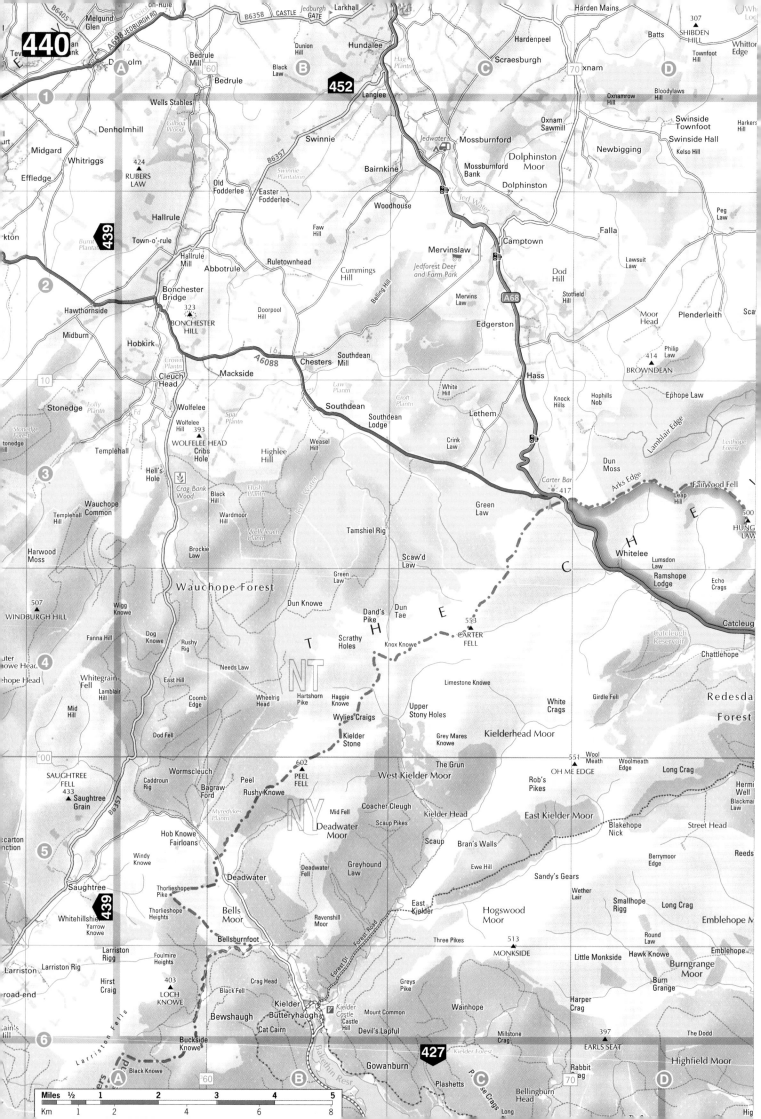

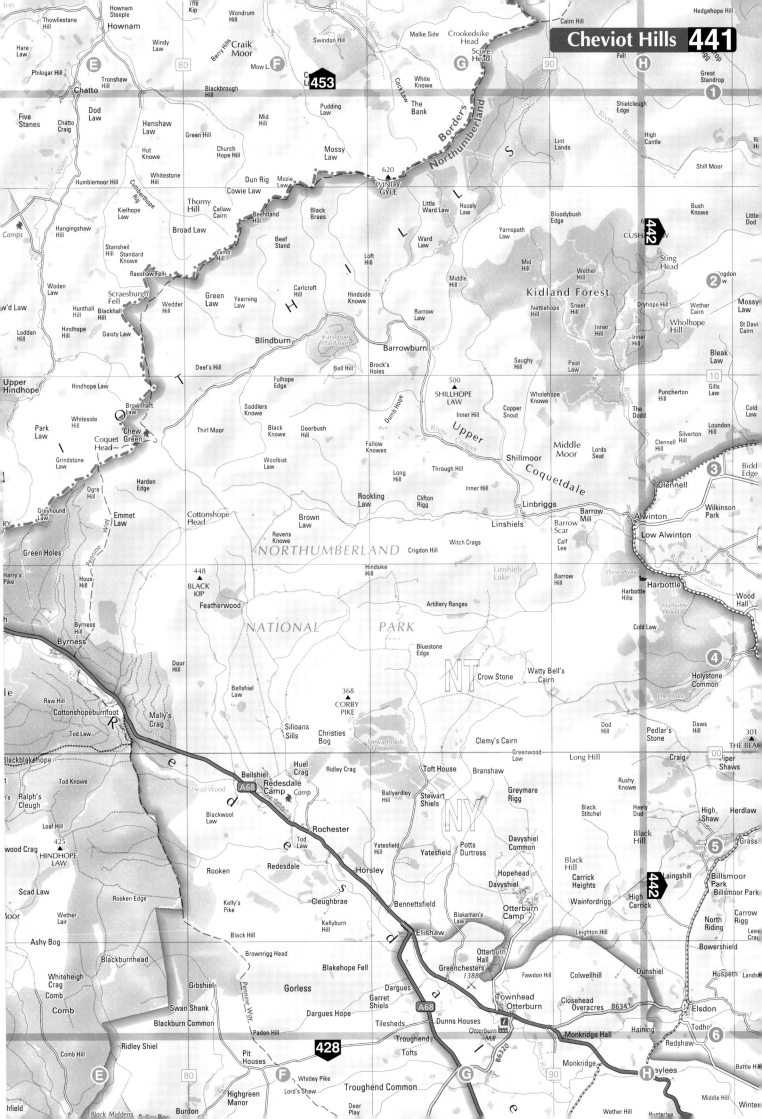

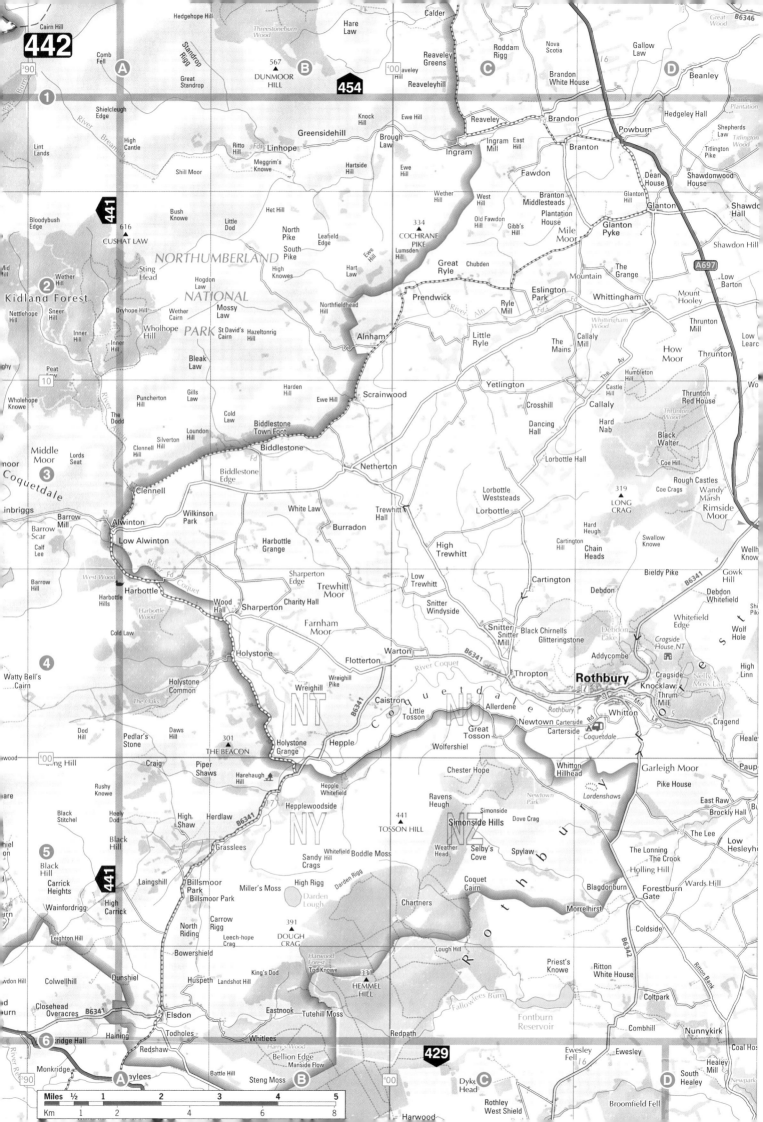

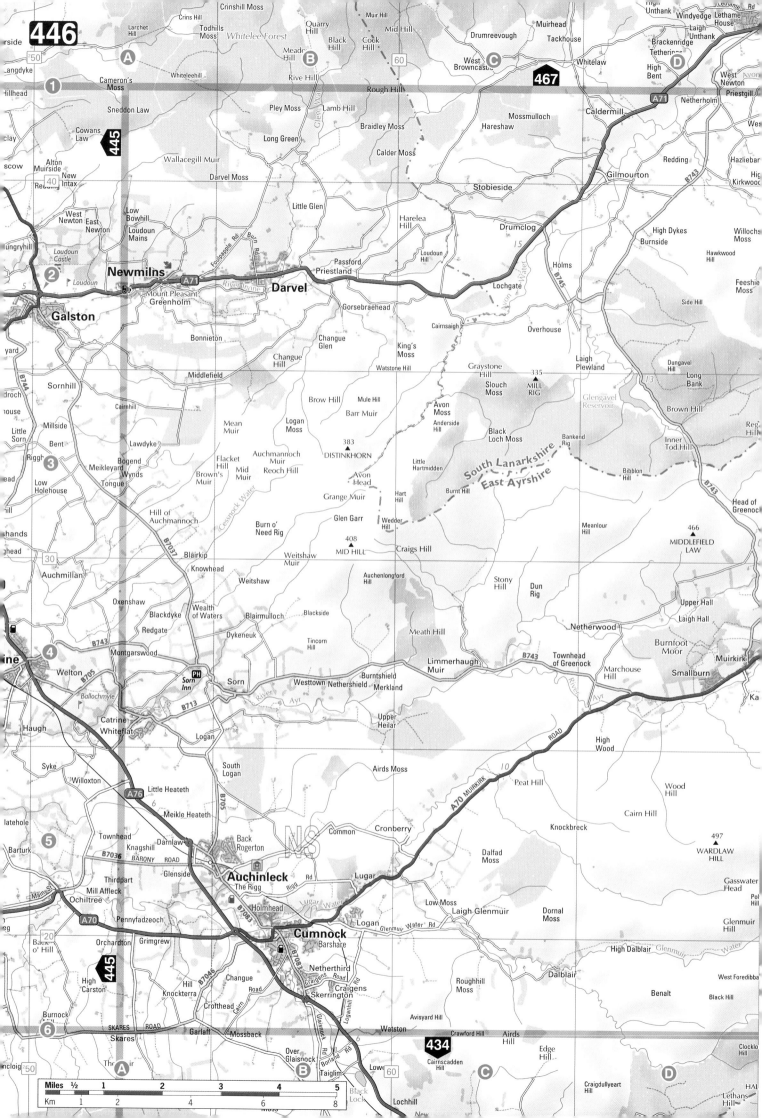

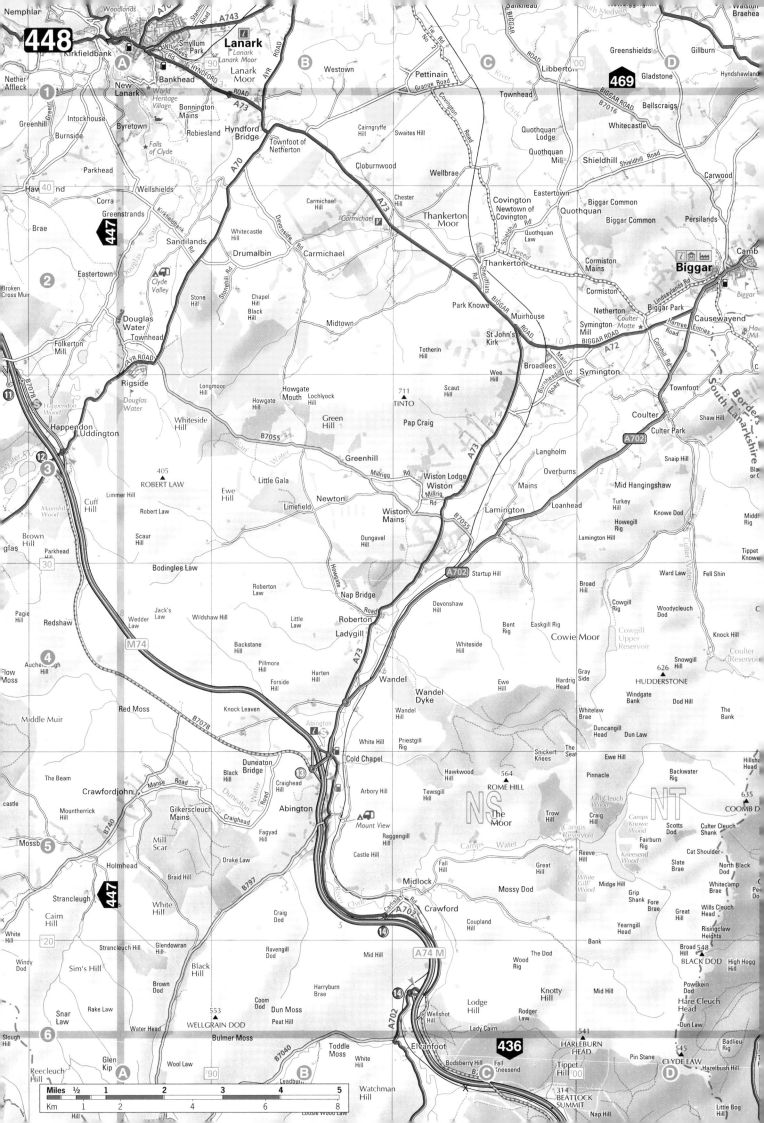

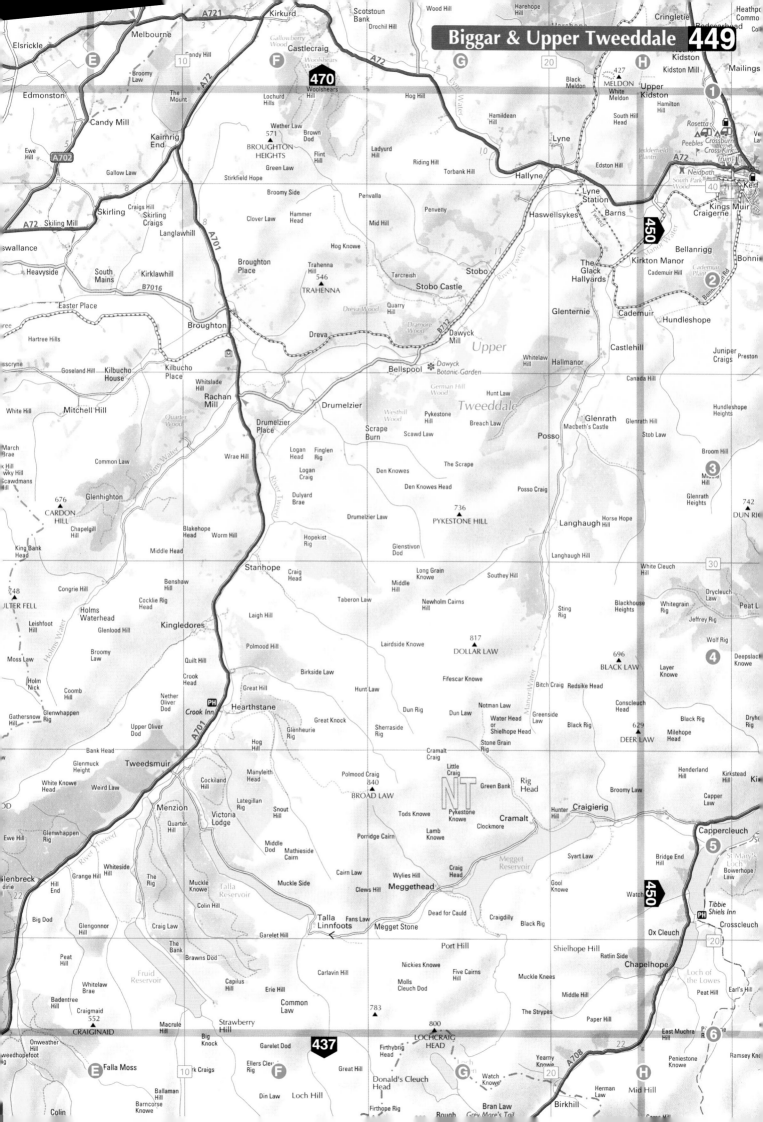

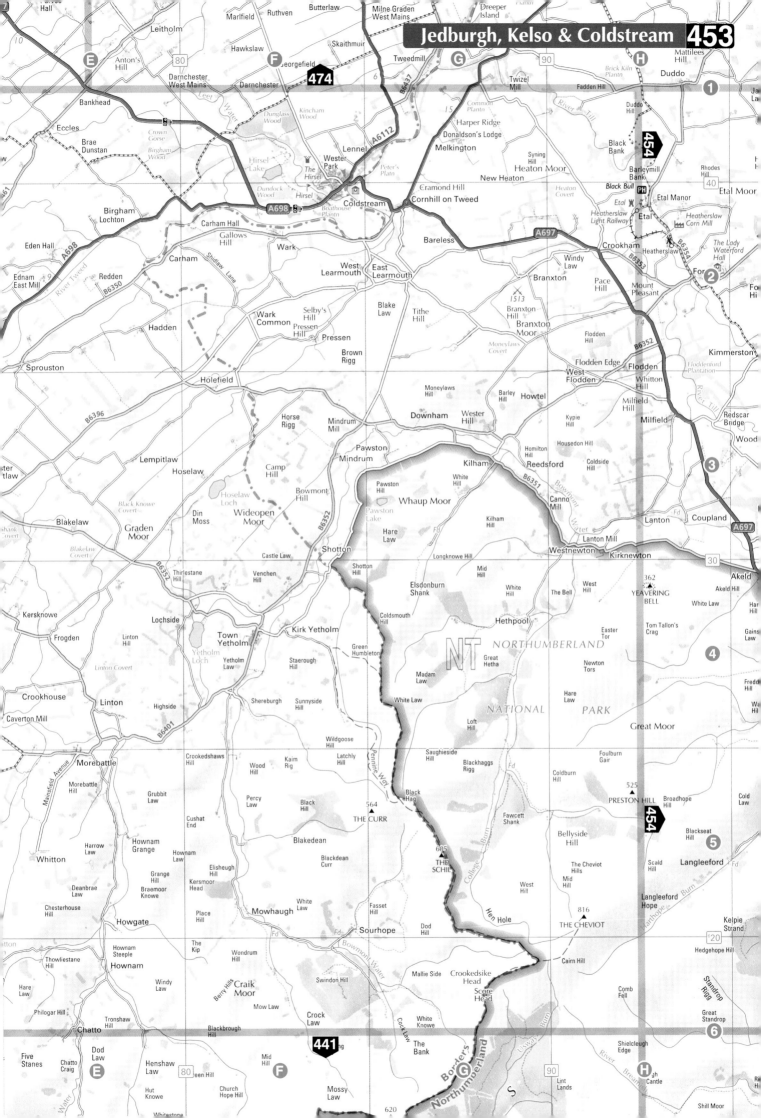

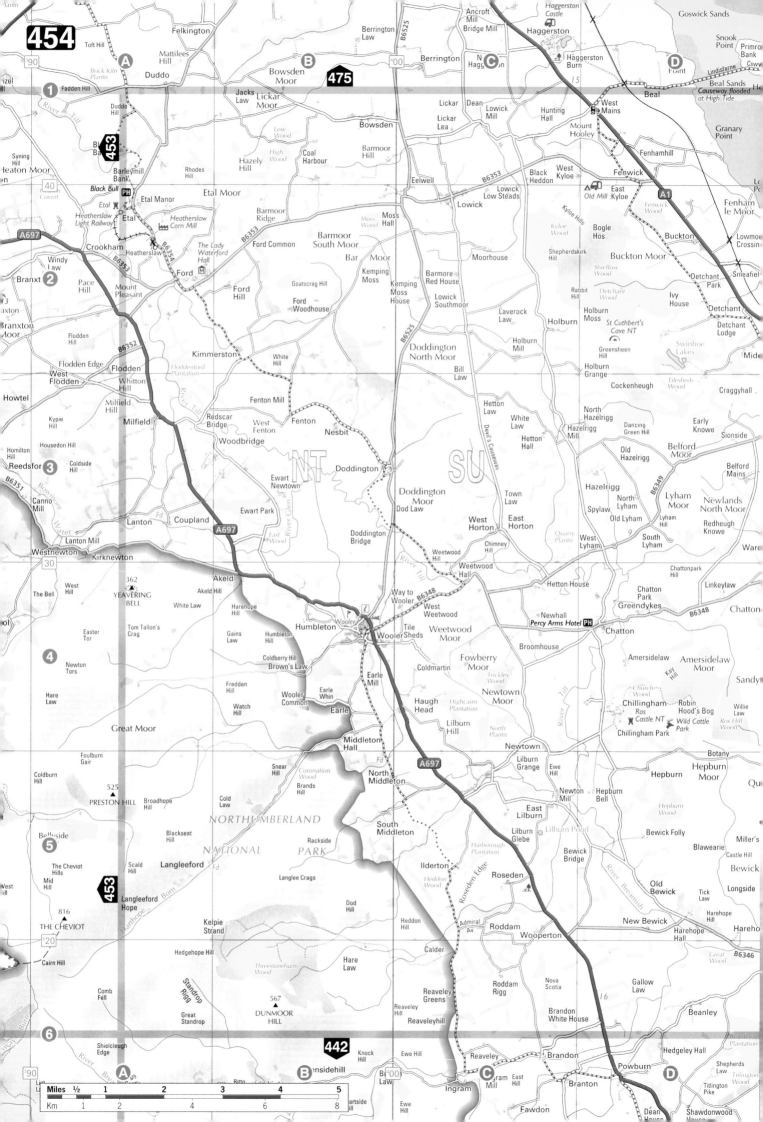

Ⓐ

Ⓑ

458

60

Ⓒ

Ⓓ

① ② ③ ④ ⑤ ⑥

Port na Croise
Cnocan Gean
Port Corbert
Tangy Loch
Tangy Lodge
Tangy
Port nam Marbh
Skeroblin
Skero
Cnoc a' Choire
Ranachan Hill
Kilchenzie
Darlochan
Craigs
A83
Machrihanish Bay
Dhurrie
Campbeltown
Machrihanish
Aros Moss
East Backs
Machrihanish Water
Can
Machrihanish
Bleachfield
Leac Bhuidhe
Drumlemble
B843
Ste
Ballygroggan
Killypole Loch
Skerry Fell Fad
Killypole
Knocknaha
Tirfergus Hill
Earadale Point
Beinn na Faire
Creag nan Cuilean
385
THE SLATE
Killellan Park
Black Hill
Coniglen Water
446
CNOC MOY
Killellan Lodge
10
Cnoc nan Gabhar
Rubha Dùin Bhàin
Cnocan Biorach
Dùn Bàn
Achnaslishaig Hill
Port na h-Olainn
Cnoc Reamhar
Cnoc na Grèine
Cnoc Odhar
Conie Glen
Rubh 'a' Mharaiche
Sliabh a' Bhiorain
Glen Remuil
Glen Breakevie
Remuil Hill
Amod Hill
Knoc
A'Chruach
Cnoc na Feudalach
Corr nan Long
Cnocan Lin
Corr Bhàn
North Carrine
Strone Glen
Lephenstrath Bridge
Cnoc Mòr
10
Glemanuilt Glen
Strone Water
Southe
428
Beinn Bhreac
BEINN NA LICE
Glenmanuilt Hill
B842
South Point
Torr Mòr
Torr Dubh
Carskiey
Duna
Rubha na Lice
Beinn a' Theine
Carskey Bay
Keil Point
Dunaverty Bay
Brunerican Bay
Rubha nan Scarlan
Port Mean
MULL OF KINTYRE
Sròn Uamha
Borgadalemore Point

NR

Ⓐ

Ⓑ

60

Ⓒ

Ⓓ

Miles	½	1	2	3	4	5
Km	1	2	4	6	8	

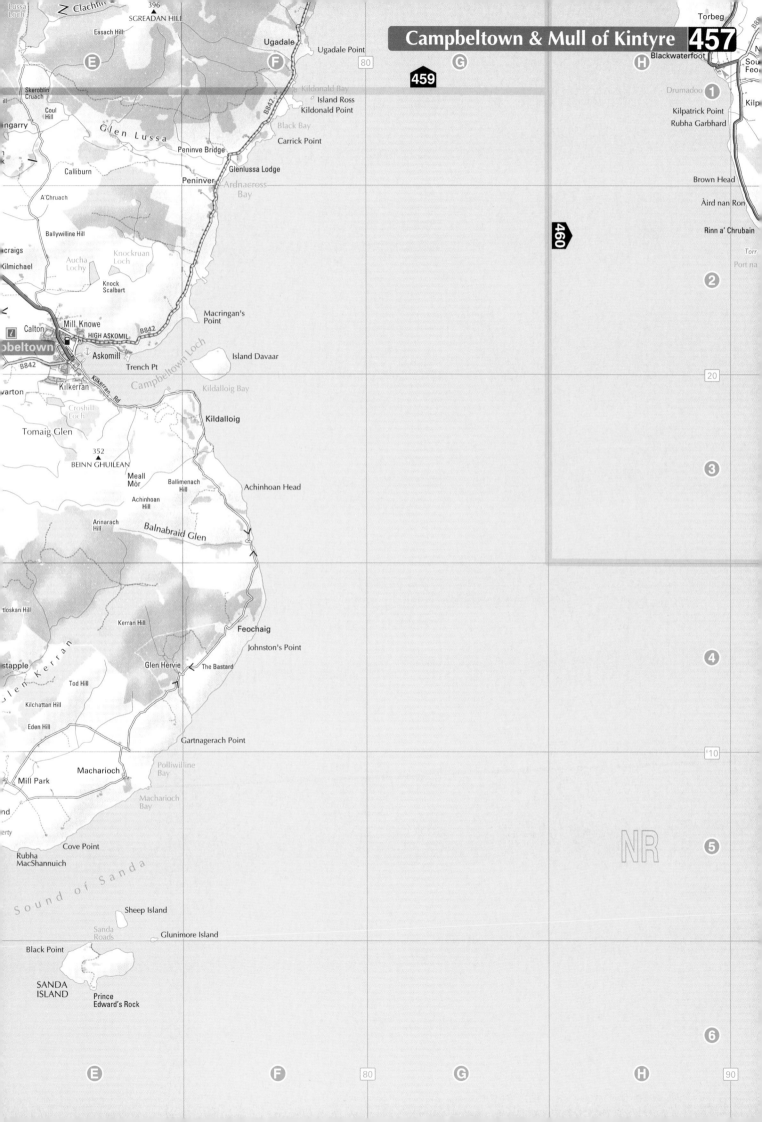

Lussa Loch

Clachan

SGREADAN HILL

Easach Hill

Ugadale

Ugadale Point

Torbeg

Blackwaterfoot

459

Kildonald Bay

Island Ross

Kildonald Point

Drumadoo

Skeroblin Cruach

Coul Hill

Black Bay

Carrick Point

Kilpatrick Point

Rubha Garbhard

ingarry

Glen Lussa

Peninve Bridge

Glenlussa Lodge

Brown Head

Calliburn

Peninver

Ardnacross Bay

Àird nan Ron

A'Chruach

Rinn a' Chrubain

Ballywilline Hill

Torr

craigs

Knockruan Loch

Port na

Aucha Lochy

Kilmichael

Knock Scalbart

460

Macringan's Point

Calton

Mill Knowe

HIGH ASKOMIL

B842

beltown

Askomill

Island Davaar

Trench Pt

Kilkerran Rd

Campbeltown Loch

Kildalloig Bay

Kilkerran

varton

Croshill Loch

Kildalloig

Tomaig Glen

352

BEINN GHUILEAN

Meall Mòr

Ballimenach Hill

Achinhoan Head

Achinhoan Hill

Arinarach Hill

Balnabraid Glen

tloskan Hill

Kerran Hill

Glen Kerran

Feochaig

Johnston's Point

stapple

Glen Hervie

The Bastard

Tod Hill

Kilchattan Hill

Eden Hill

Gartnagerach Point

Macharioch

Polliwilline Bay

Mill Park

Macharioch Bay

NR

Cove Point

Rubha MacShannuich

Sound of Sanda

Sheep Island

Sanda Roads

Glunimore Island

Black Point

SANDA ISLAND

Prince Edward's Rock

Ⓐ   Ⓑ   60   Ⓒ   Ⓓ

477

❶

50

477

Bàgh na
Dòirlinne
Sgeir Fhiacail
Eilean Garbh
Port Mòr
Cnoc nan
Gobhar
Rubh' a' Chairn Bhain

West Tarbert
Bay
East Tarbert
Bay

Port Bàn
Tarbert
Rubh' an Stearnail

Creag
Bhàn
Druimyean Bay
Port an Dùin

Cnoc Loisgte

Isle of Gigha
Ardminish Point
Rhunahaorine
Point

**ISLE OF
GIGHA**
Port nam
Faochag

Meall a'
Ghlamaidh
Carraig Mhòr

Ardminish
Ardminish
Bay

❷
Caolas Craro
Eilean a'Chùil
Craro Island
Achamore
Port a' Gharaidh
Port an Sgiathain

Rubha
Dubh
Leim
Eilean na h-Uilinn

Gròb Bàgh
Gigalum Island

Slocan Lèim
Sgeir an Ròin

462

Sound of Gigha

Port na Seralaic
Pòrt na Cille

CARA ISLAND

Mull of Cara

❸

K

Beacha
Red Cove
Beachmena
Cnoc
North Bea
South Beach

40
Muasdale
Sgeir Mhòr
Cruach
Muasdale

❹
Glenacardoch Point
Belloch
A83
Barr Glen
Glenbarr
Barr Water
Port a' Bhorrain
MacAlister
Clan
Cnoc

NR

Bellochantuy Bay
Cleongart

❺
Port nan Clachan
Bellochantuy

Killocraw
Cnoc Buidhe

30
Port Cròm
Cnocan Gean

Tangy
Loch
Port na Croise

Port Corbett

❻
Tangy
Lodge
Tangy
Skeroblin

456
Port nam Marbh
Skerob

50   Ⓐ   Ⓑ   60   Ⓒ   Ⓓ

Cnoc a'
Choire

Miles	½	1	2	3	4	5
Km	1	2	4	6	8	

A83

E

Creag Loisgte Talatoll

Loch Ciaran

Achaidh Ghlais

Lochan a'Chreimh

Seallaidh Bhig

Fuar Larach

Loch Romain

Rubha na h-Airde Bàine

Eascairt Point

F

Loch an Eilein Beag

Loch an Eilein Mor

80

Cru Bhreac

G

Creag Mhòr

H

Cnoc Donn

Ballochroy

Ballochroy Glen

Cruach na Seilcheig

Creag Eanaiche

Loch a'Ghatha

Crossaig Glen

Port Alasdair Ruaidh

Argyll and Bute
North Ayrshire

1

Sròn Albannach

Loch Garasdale

Crossaig

Port nan Gamhna

50

Cnoc nan Iteag

247 CRUACH MHIC GOUGAIN

Cnoc a'Bhraidein

Cnoc Laoighscan

Port a' Mhiadair

Rhunahaorine

264 CNOC-AN T-SAMHLAIDH

Cnoc na Buaile Salaich

Cnoc Dubh

Rubha Riabhach

Catac

Catacol Bay

Cnoc Airigh Luachraich

Gleann Laoigh

Loch nam Breac

Cour

Rubha Airigh Bheirg

2

Loch a'Mhuilinn

Cour Island

Rubha Glas

Meall Bhig

Beinn Bhreac

Cnoc Iaruinn

Thundergay

38

Loch an Fhraoich

Loch Tana

Rubha Dearg-uillt

Rubha Bàn

Meall Biorach

Loch Ulagadale

Cnoc Reamhar

Cnoc Rèilereidhe

Cnoc Dubh

Meall Donn

Loch Dirigadale

Cnoc nan Craobh

Lorgie Hill

Cruach Ruadh

Garrachcroit Bàgh

Pirnmill

17

Beinn E

ayinloan

Braids

Deucheran Hill

Cruach na Casaich

Cnoc Donn

Grogport

Sgeir Bhuidhe

Port Raoin Mhòir

Whitefarland

Ceann Reamhar

5 BEINN BHARRAIN

Cnoc Odhar Auchaluskin

Cruach Mhic-an t-Saoir

Cnoc Reamhar

462

Whitefarland Point

3

Coire nam Buabhall

ch Odhar

354 CRUACH NAN GABHAR

Brackley

Eilean Grianain

hmore

Teanchoisin Glen

Meall Buidhe

Kirnashie Hill

nore

Cnoc na Seilg

Lag Kilmichael

Imachar Point

Imachar

40

Cnoc an t-Seilich

Diollaid Mhòr

39

Cnoc nan Gabhar

Port na Cùile

Balliekine

Cnoc a' Choire Beag

Arnicle

Beinn Bhreac

Cnoc Donn

Carradale

Carradale

Port Righ

Cnoc Donn

Rubha Airigh Dhughaill

Meall Donn

Bridgend

Carradale Bay

B879

Carradale House

High Dougarie

Dougarie Point

4

Dougarie Lodge

Blary Hill

Waterfoot

Carradale Bay

Auchencar

454 BEINN AN TUIRC

Cnoc Breac

Dippen Bay

Torrisdale Bay

Carradale Point

Cnoc a' Choire Mhòr

Cnoc Eoghainn

B842

c Reamhar

Cnoc a' Mhadaidh

Cnocmalavilach

Greenhill

Cnocan Cuallaich

329

Braid Hill

408 BÒRD MÒR

Cnoc na Caillich

Rubha nan Sgarbh

Auchagallon

Auchagallon S

460

Machrie Bay

Machrie

Collusca

Meall Buidhe

Saddell Glen

Saddell

Machrie Bay

Cnoc nan Agh

Bord a Dubh

A'Chruach

Cnocan a' Bhuachaill

Pluck Point

NR

Tormore

5

Moss Farm Stone Circ

Clachfin Glen

396 SGREADAN HILL

Saddell Bay

Torr Righ Mòr

Lussa Loch

Easach Hill

Ugadale

Ugadale Point

Drumadoon Point

Shiskine

30

Torbeg

Drumadoon Point

Blackwaterfoot

Skeroblin Cruach

Kildonald Bay

Island Ross Kildonald Point

457

Drumadoo

6

ingarry

Coul Hill

Glen Lussa

B842

ack Bay

Carrick Point

80

G

Kilpatrick Point

Rubha Garbhard

Kilp

Peninve Bridge

Gienlussa Lodge

Callibur

90

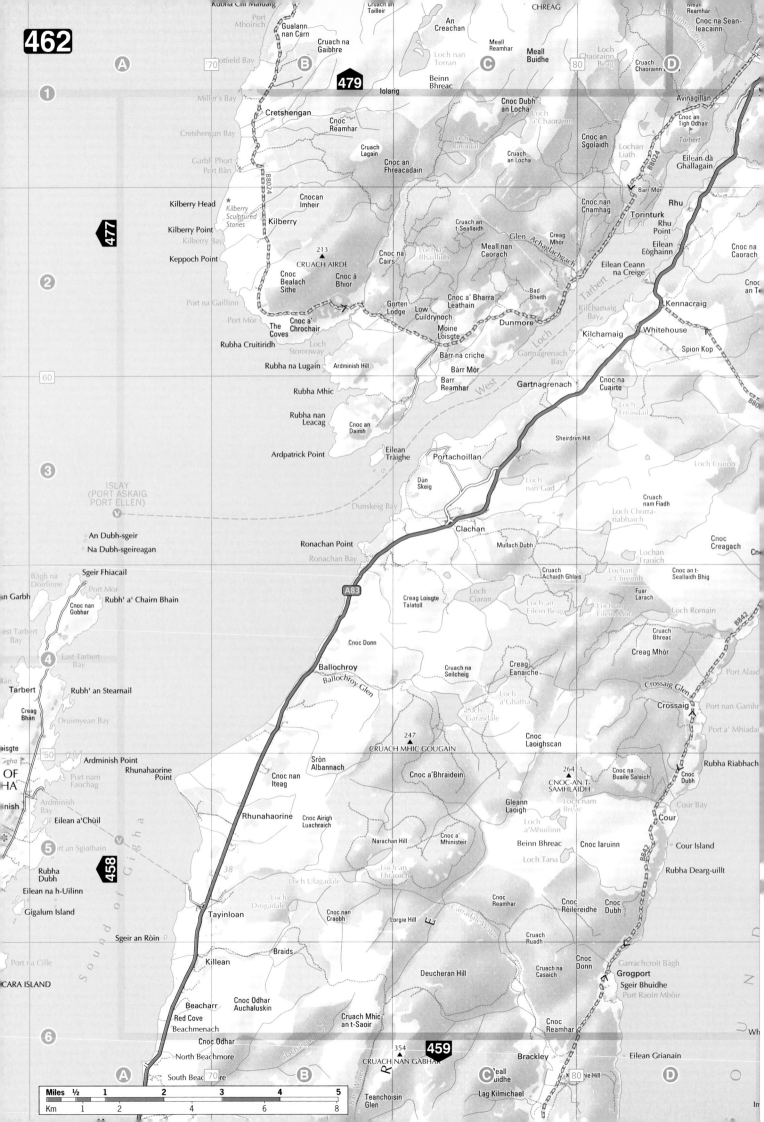

267

Kilbride Hill

KAMES HILL

Edinb

Rubha Bhadan

Lub na Laoenaige

Portavadie

Cnoc na
Cruime

South Wood
of Lenihuline

Clackrobae

Craig

Tarbert

East Loch Tarbert

Eilean Buidhe

Port a'
Mhadaidh

Colachla

Clate
Point

Eenan Hill

St 1 nac

Victoria Hotel

Tairbeart

PH

A8017

Mealdarroch
Point

90

Eilean a' Chomhraig

Port Leathan

Rubha Stillaig

480

Cnoc
Mòr

G

CNOC NA
CARRAIGE

Craig
Lodge

Carry
Point

H

Port Glas

Kildavanan

B875

West
arbert

Cnoc Mòr

Cnoc
Breac

E

Asgog
Bay

Cnocan
a'Chorra

Blindman's
Bay

Kildavanan Point

Ettrick Bay

B

Bàrr nan Cnoc

Cnoc nan
Caorach

Cnoc
Glas

Rubha Clach an
Tràghaidh

Eilean
Aoidhe

Sgat Mòr

Sgat Beag

Kilbride Bay/
Bàgh Osde

Ardlámont
Bay

Watch
Hill

Cnoc a'
Bholainn-airigh

Cnoc
Buidhe

Cnoc na
Faire

Camas na Ban-tighearna

Rubha na Peileig

464

343

CRUACH AN
T SORCHAIN

Rubha nan
Caorach

Ardlamont
Point

Rubha an Amair

2

Straad

bair

Cnoc
Breac

422

Rubha Lagganroaig

Fionn-Phort

(WINTER ONLY)

St Ninian's
Point

CNOC A' BHAILE-SHOIS

Carn Chaluim

Cruach na
Machrach

Guallann
Mhòr

Rubha Grianain

Camas na
Ceardaich

St Ninian's
Bay

Kilmory
Hill

Cnoc an Lochain

Meall
Donn

Sgolaig

Croit
Bàgh

Sallan Port

A84

60

Loc
Qu

Cruach na
Caol-bheinn

Cnoc nan
Gabhar

Cnoc na
Mèine

Cnoc Ceann
Tamhuis

Rubha Leathan

INCHMARNOCK

Carrick
Point

Tarmore
Hill

Cnoc na
Sgratha

Sgeir Bhuidhe

Glenreasdell
Mains

Cnoc Mòine
Raibeirt

Port a'
Chruidhe

Port na h-Aille

Ardscalpsie Po

Cnoc an
t-Suidhe

Skipness

Skipness River

Skipness

Chapel

3

Cnoc an
t-Sabhail

Cnoc na
h-Eireige

Chapel

Skipness
Point

Scalps
Bay

Claonaig

Cnoc na
Faire

B8001

Skipness
Bay

Cnoc
Creagain

Sgeir na Luing

Claonaig
Bay

c Dubh

(SUMMER ONLY)

S O U N D   O F   B U T E

Rubha na h-
Airde Bàine

Argyll and Bute

Port Fada

North Ayrshire

Eascairt Point

NR

NS

air Ruaidh

Rubha
Creagan
Dubha

Cock of Arran

4

Newton Point

Newton

Cnoc nan
Sgrath

Torr
Meadhonach

Coillemore Point

Lòch
Ranza

The Lodge

Millstone
Point

A841

Lochranza

Lochranza Golf

50

Catacol

Isle of Arran Distillery

Glen

Catacol Bay

Torr Nead
an Eoin

Fionn Bhealach

Chalmadale

Fairhaven

Glen

Meall nan Leac
Sleamhuinn

Meall Mòr

Clachan

Rubha
Airigh
Bheirg

Catacol

Rubha Glas

Meall
nan Damh

Beinn Bhiorach

Cnocan
Donna

Creag
Ghlas

8

A841

5

Thundergay

Meall
Bhig

North   Arran

464

Rubha Bàn

Coire Fhionn
Lochan

Glen Sannox

Sannox Bay

Meall Biorach

Beinn Bhreac

Carn Mòr

Corrie

Sannox

Meall Donn

Beinn Tarsuinn

834

Coire
na Ciche

Pirnmill

Beinn Bhreac

CAISTEAL ABHAIL

Cir Mh—r

Dearg
Choirein

Corrie

Loch
Tanna

Glen

Mullach Buidhe

Cnoc Breac
Gamhainn

460

Lorsa

6

tefarland Point

715

E

Whitefarland

BEINN BHARRAIN

90

F

874

GOATFELL

00

Rubha
Salach

Port nam
Balach

Ceann Reamhar

Coire nam
Buabha

Beinn Tarsuinn

G

Beinn a'
Chliabhain

Meall Breac

H

achar Point

Imachar

Cnoc Breac

Maol
Donn

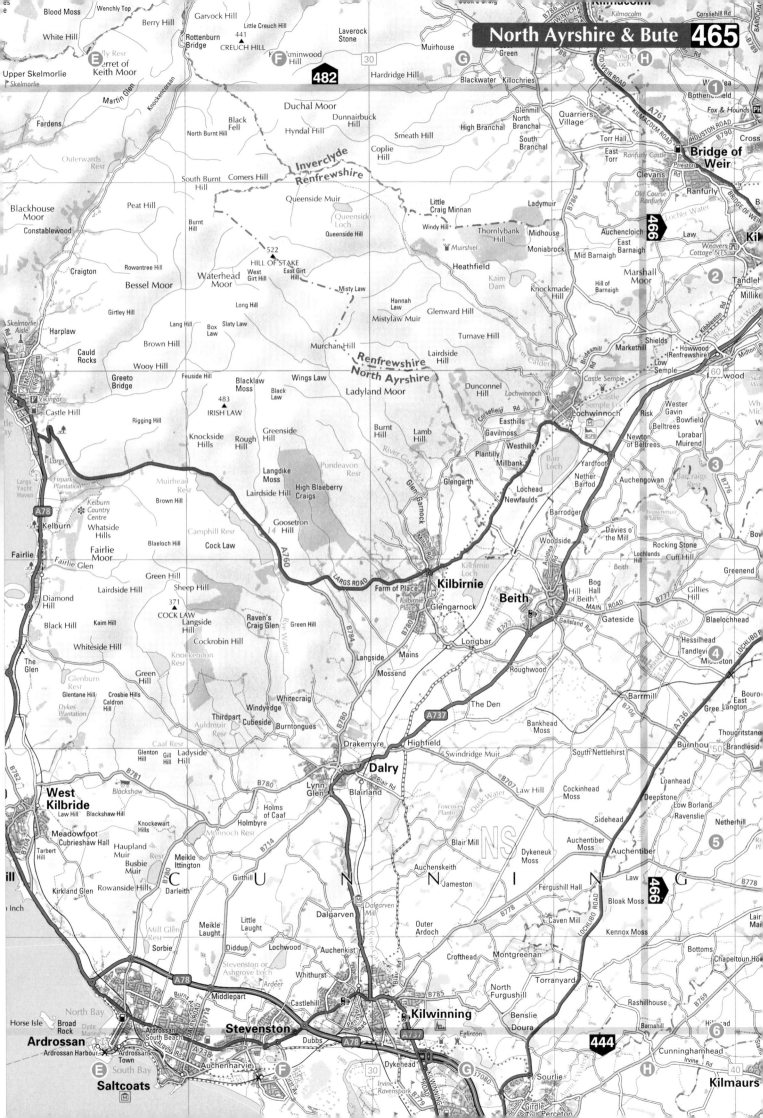

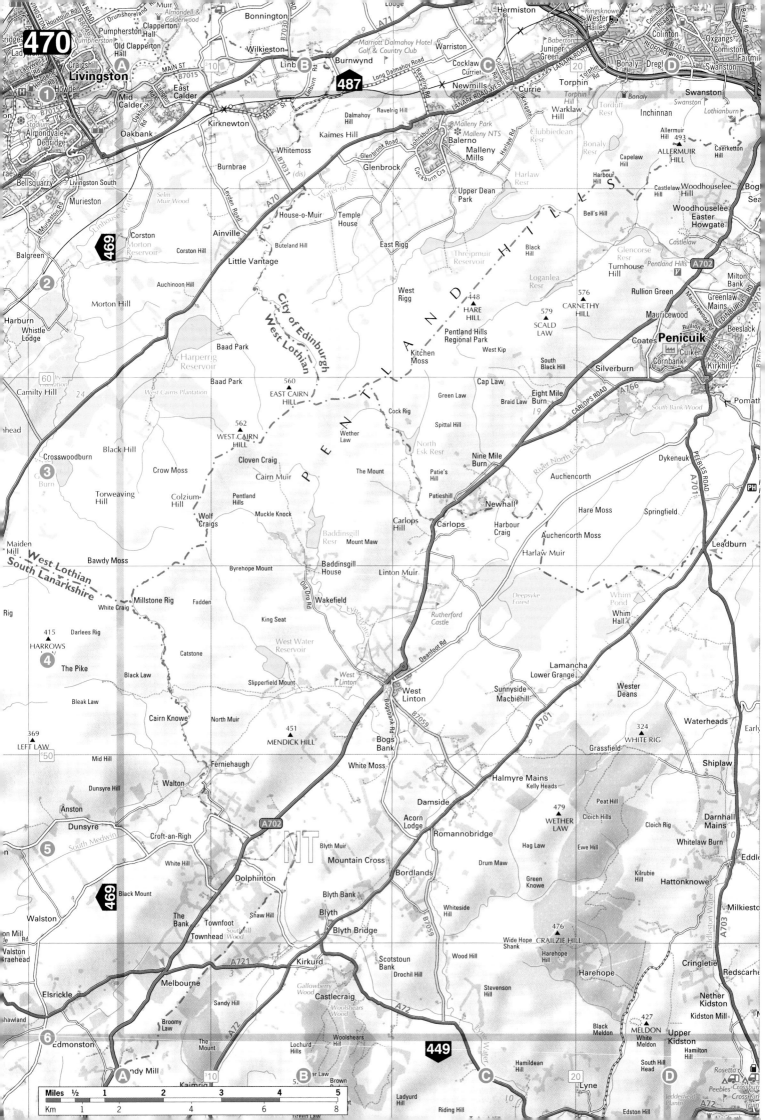

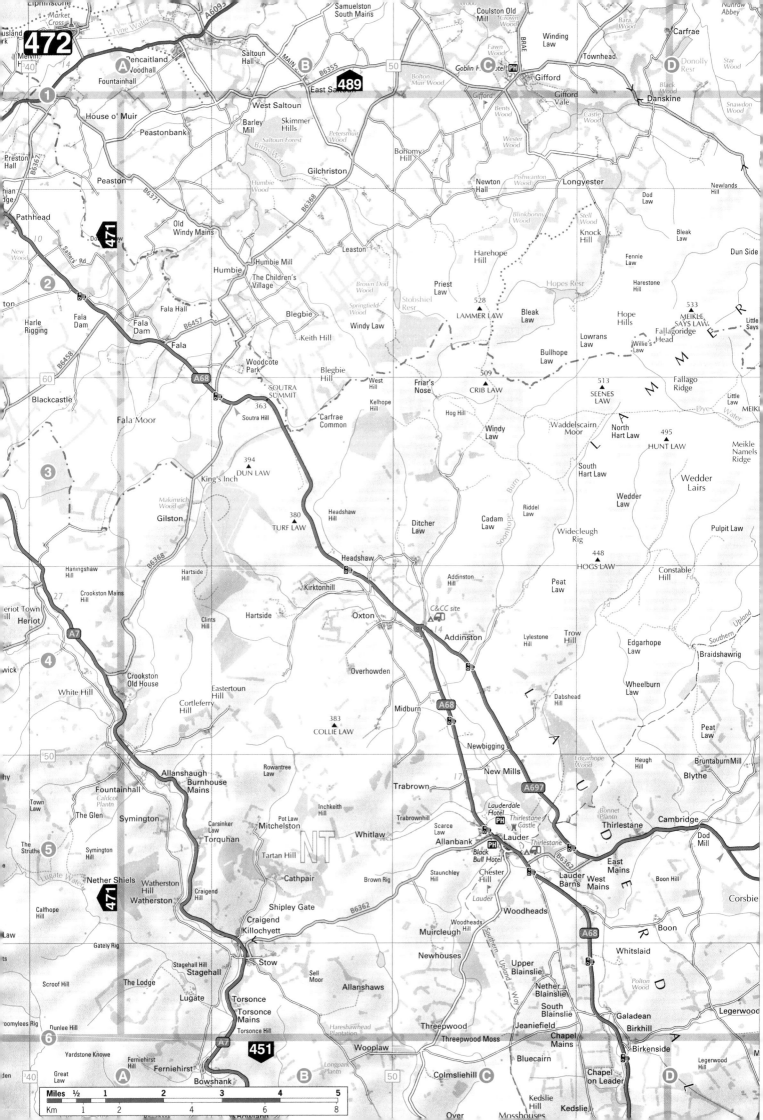

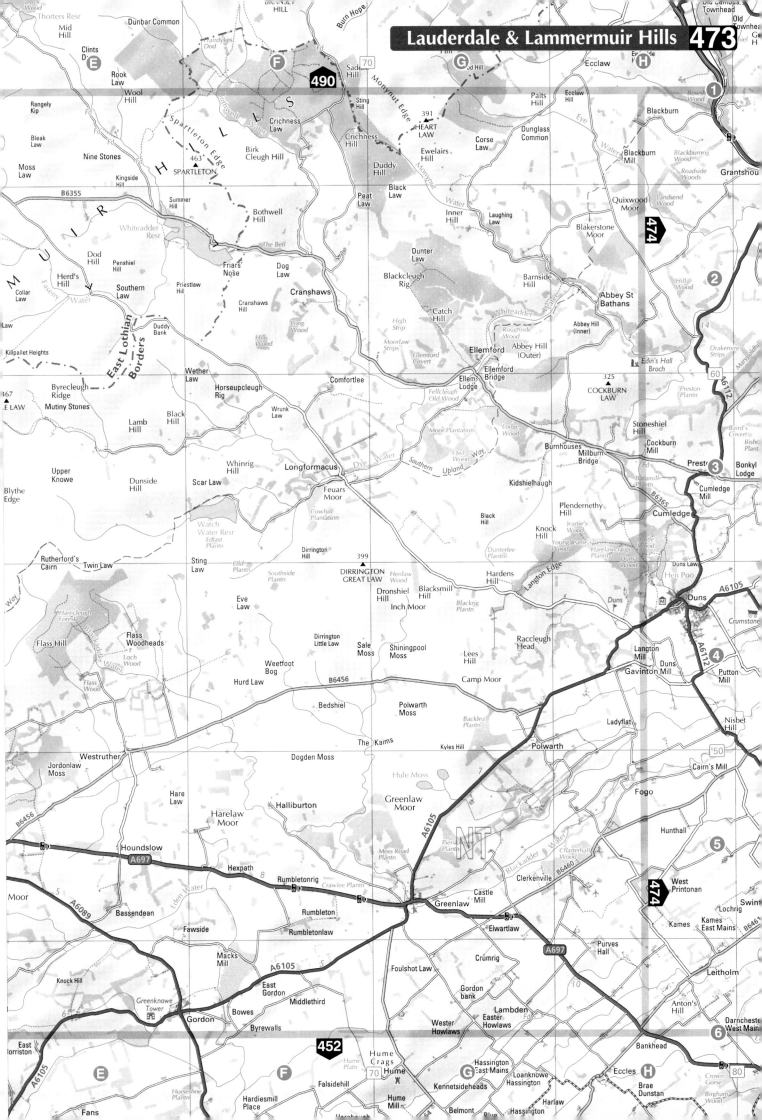

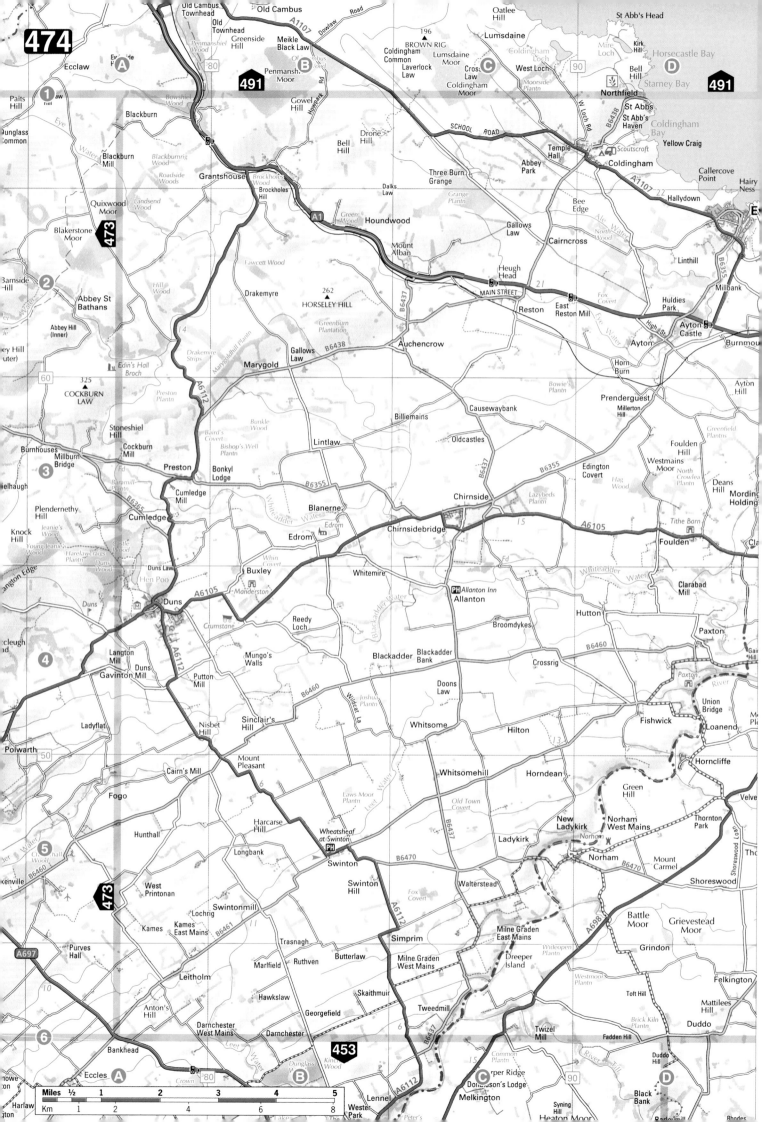

E   F   G   H

HOLY ISLAND

emouth
Eyemouth
Scout Point
Horse Head
Fancove Head
Breeches Rock
Burnmouth Hill
Ross   Ross Point
Chester Hill
Hilton Bay
Lamberton Moor   Lamberton Beach
Lamberton
Witches' Knowe
Marshall Meadows
Marshall Meadows Bay
St John's Haven
North Northumberland Heritage Coast

NT   NU

Brow of The Hill
Baldersbury Hill
DUNS ROAD
Highfields   Brotherston's Hole
Magdalene Fields
Sharper's Head
Ladies Skerrs
New Mills
Fairney Flat
Royal Border Bridge
Berwick-upon-Tweed
Barracks
Town Ramparts   Meadow Haven
B6461
Shielfield Park Stadium
Tweedmouth   Sandstell Pt
Spittal
Ord House Country Park
East Ord
Prior Park
Springhill La
Cow Rd
Bear's Head
Huds Head
Ord Mains
Redshin Cove
A698
Tweedmouthmoor
Ewe Hill
Murton
Unthank Moor
Scremerston
Allerdean Mill
Scremerston Hill
A1
Northumberland Coast
Shoreswood Hall
Shoresdean
West Allerdean
Allerdean Greens
Nabhill
Cheswick
Cheswick Sands
North Northumberland Heritage Coast
Berwick-upon-Tweed (Goswick)
Ancroft Northmoor
Allerdean Grange
Cheswick Buildings
Windmill Hill
B6525
Ancroft   East Ancroft
Goswick
Goswick Sands
Snipe Pt   Coves Haven   Keel Head
Emmanuel Head
Berrington Law
Ancroft Mill   Bridge Mill
Haggerston Castle
Haggerston
Snook Point   Primrose Bank
HOLY ISLAND
Bowsden Moor
Berrington
New Haggerston
Haggerston Burn
Beal Point
Lindisfarne Cswy
Chare Ends
Jacks Law
Lickar Moor
454
Lickar Dean
Lowick Mill
Hunting Hall
West Mains
Beal Sands
Causeway flooded at High Tide
Holy Island Sands
Beal
455
Lindisfarne Priory
Lindisfarne NT
Castle Point
Hole Mouth
Low Wood
Bowsde
Lickar Lea
Mount Hooley
Granary Point
Guile Point
Barmoor Hill
Hazely Hill
High Wood
Coal Harbour
Fenhamhill
Burrows Hole

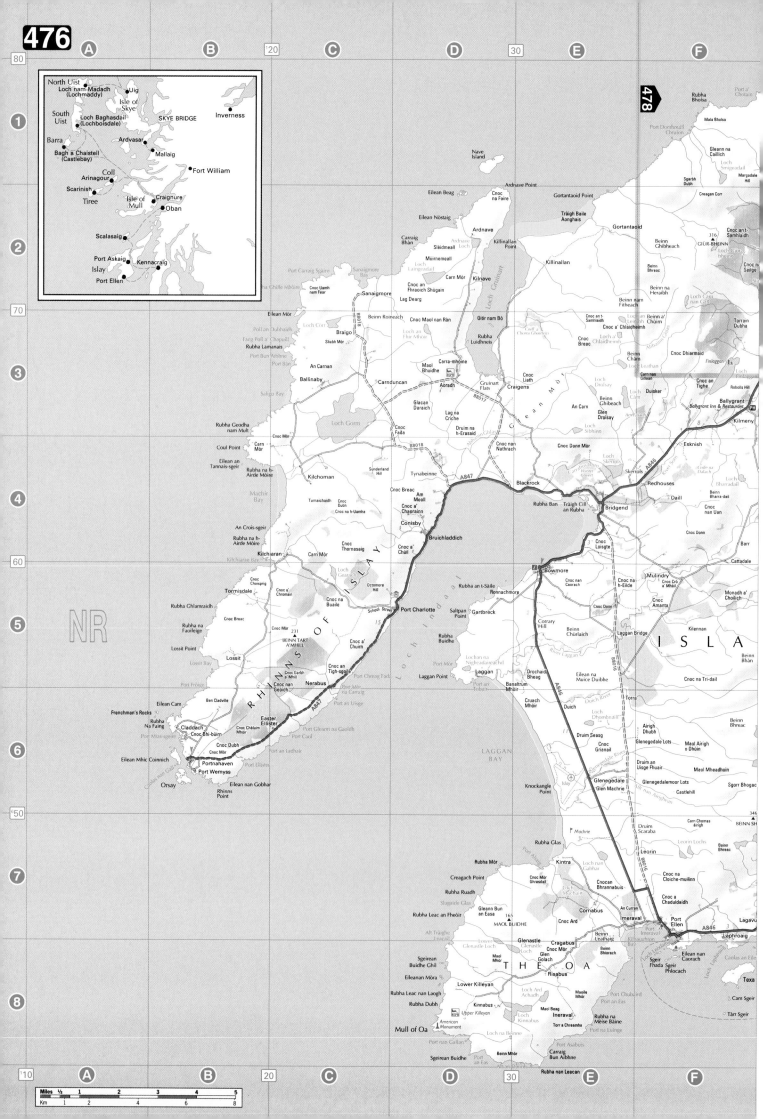

Jura Forest
Paps of Jura
Jura
SOUND OF JURA
Sound of Gigha
NR
478
479
462
458
PORT ASKAIG – KENNACRAIG
PORT ELLEN – KENNACRAIG
Eileanan Gleann Righ
Aird Reamhar
Loch Tarbert
Rubh' a' Chrois-aoinidh
Eilean Ard
Eilean Dubh a' Chumhainn Mhòr
Creag Làthaich
Tarbert
Rubha nan Crann
Creag nam Fiadh Mòr
Cnoc an-Ime
Lagg
Lagg Bay
Cnoc an Doire Dharaich
Port Doir' a' Chrorain
Cnoc nam Binneag
Am Bog-àirigh
Port an Aoinidh Uir
Ardmenish
Crom Dhoire
Lowlandman's Bay
Knockrome
Ardfernal
Rubha Bhride
Rubh Leanachais
Eilean Bhride
Cnoc na h-Iolaire
Leargybreck
Loch na Mile
Jura Forest
Cnoc Tigh Mhic Fhionnlaidh
Pladda
Eilean nan Coinein
Eilean Diomhain
SMALL ISLES
Keils
Sgeirean Buidhe
Craighouse
Eilean nan Gabhar
Rubha Laimhrige
Rubha na Caillich
Crackaig Hill
Port na Birlinne
Liath Sgeir
Port nan Clàdan
Rubha na Tràille
Rubha Uamh an Tuill
Poll a' Cheò
Brosdale Island
Am Fraoch Eilean
Cabrach
Cnoc na Mòine
Cnoc Reamhar
An Leargan
342 BRAT BHEINN
Na Minnean
Beinn na Doire Lèithe
Daimh-sgeir
Feolin Ferry
Caol Ila
Port Askaig
Keills
Beinn na Cille
Bunnahabhain
Rubha a' Mhill
Rubha Bhachlaig
Rubha Bàrr nan Gobag
Rubha Aoineadh an Reithe
Rubh' Àird na Sgitheich
Sliabh Àird na Sgitheich
Lang Aoineadh
Blàr Buidhe
Sgriob na Caillich
Cnocbreac
Lochan Gleann Astaile
Whitefarland Bay
Aonach-bheinn
Abhainn Gleann Iubharnadeal
560 GLASS BHEINN
529 DUBHA BHEINN
734 BEINN A' CHAOLAIS
784 BEINN AN OIR
757 BEINN SHIANTAIDH
506 SCRINADLE
398 BEINN TARSUINN
Glen Batrick
Beinn Bhreac
Cnoc na h-Uamha
Corra Bheinn
Cnoc an Oir
Càthar an Leargain Bhric
Gleann an t-Siob
Cnuic Charrach
Creag a' Chreamha Mòr
Doire Dubh
Loch Lesgamail
Corran River
A846
Rubh'a Mhàil
Cnoc na Faire
363 SGARBH BREAC
Cnoc na Piobaireachd
Cnoc na Croise
Cnoc Reamhar
Cnoc an t-Slèibh
Am Meall
Lossit Lodge
Rubha Bhoraraic
Rubh' an t-Salinn
Glas Eilean
Rubha nan Earachan
266 BEINNE DUBH
Sleivemore
Glen Logan
Storakaig
Beinn Bhreac
Rubha' a' Chladaich
Maol a' Bharra
429 SGÒRR NAM FAOILEANN
Mc Arthur's Head
Carraig an Ràtha
471 GLAS BHEINN
Maol nan Gobhar
Proaig
Rubha Biorach
Carraig Mhòr
Rubha Liath
Cnoc Bann nan Sgàilein
490 BEINN BHEIGEIR
Diollaid nam Fiadh
Ardtalla
Sgeir Liath
Eilean Liath
454 BEINN URARAIDH
Srath Bhata
Trudernish Point
Rubh' a' Mhullaich Bhàin
Kintour
Kildalton Cross
Ardmore
Ardmore Point
Port na Cille
Cnoc a' Chùirn
Sgeir nam Ban
Eilean Craobhach
Eilean a' Chùirn
Rubha na Muir-làin
Eilean Mhic Mhaolmhoire
Poll a' Chreoig
Eilean Bhride
Garbh-sgeir Mhòr
Ceann nan Sgeirean
Rubha na Gainmhich
Eilean Imersay
Eilean an t-Sluic
Corr Sgeir
Sgeir a' Chlachain
Ardbeg
Meall Ard
Lagavulin Bay
Carn Mòr
Claggain Bay
Rubha na Cille
Carraig an Daimh
Dubh Sgeir
Liath Eilean
New Danna
ISLAND OF DANNA
Eilean nan Uan
Eilean a' Chapuill
Sgeir Dhonncha
Corr Eilean
Eilean Ghamhna
Eilean Puirt Lèithe
Eilean Mòr
St Cormac's Chapel
Eilean nan Leac
Dubh Sgeir
Eilean a' Chapuill
Kilmory Bay
Carraig na h-Acairseid
Eilean Naomhachd
Glas Eilean
Point of Knap
Kilberry Head
Kilberry Sculpture Stones
Kilberry Point
Kilberry Bay
Keppoch Point
Port na Gaillinn
Cretshengan Bay
An Dubh-sgeir
Na Dubh-sgeireagan
Sgeir Fhiacail
Bàgh na Dòirlinne
Eilean Garbh
Cnoc nan Gobhar
Rubh' a' Chairn Bhain
West Tarbert Bay
East Tarbert Bay
Tarbert
Rubh' an Stearnail
Creag Bhàn
Druimyeon Bay
Port an Dùin
Cnoc Loisgte
Isle of Gigha
ISLE OF GIGHA
Ardminish Point
Rhunahaorine Point
Carraig Mhòr
Ardminish
Ardminish Bay
Eilean a' Chùil
Craro Island
Achamore
Port a' Gharaidh
Port an Sgiathain
Rubha Dubh
Leim
Eilean na h-Uilinn
Cigalum Island
Slocan Lèim
Sgeir an Ròin
Port na Cille
CARA ISLAND
Mull of Cara
Tayinloan
Killean
Beacharr
Red Cove
Beachmenach
North Beachmore
South Beachmore
Muasdale
Glenacardoch Point
Arnicle
Bellochantuy
G
H
J
K
L
M
1
2
3
4
5
6
7
8
50
60
70
80

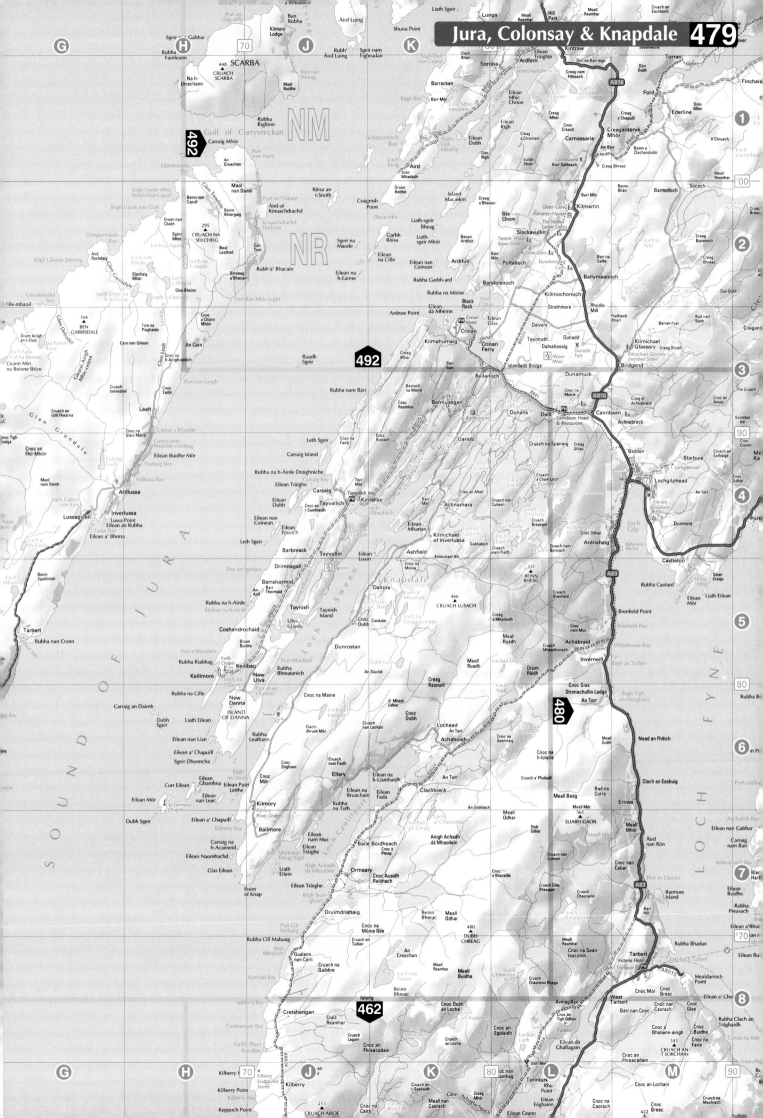

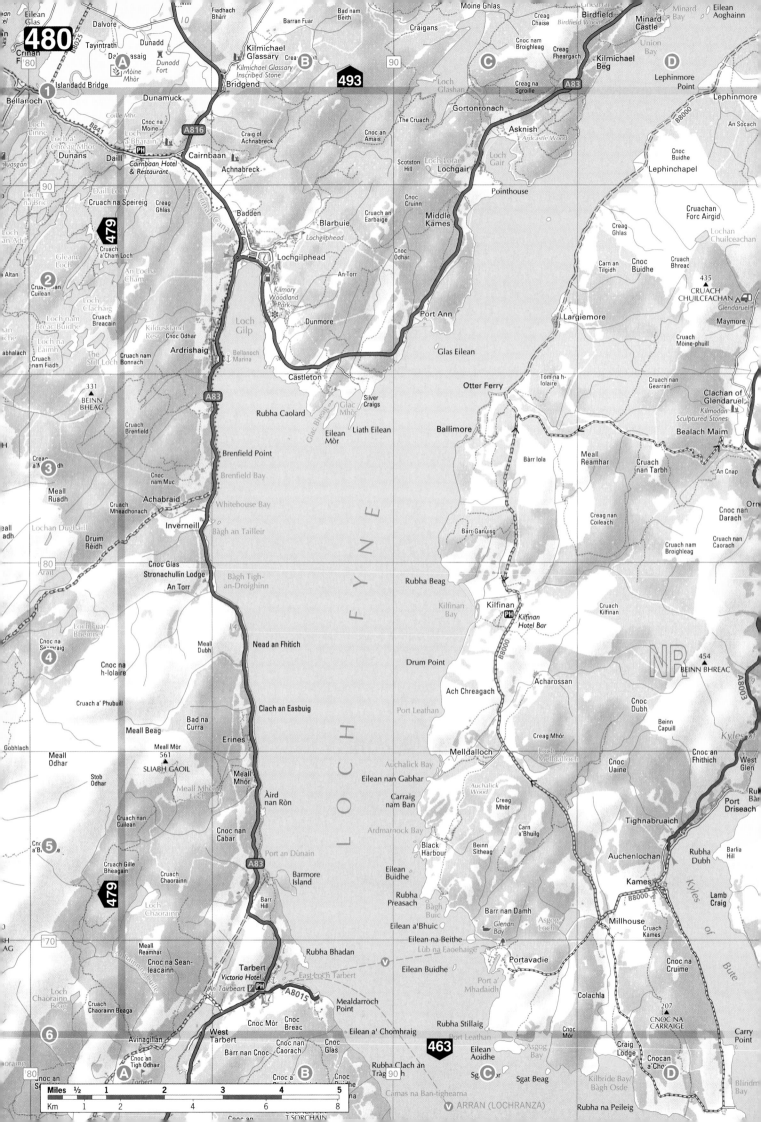

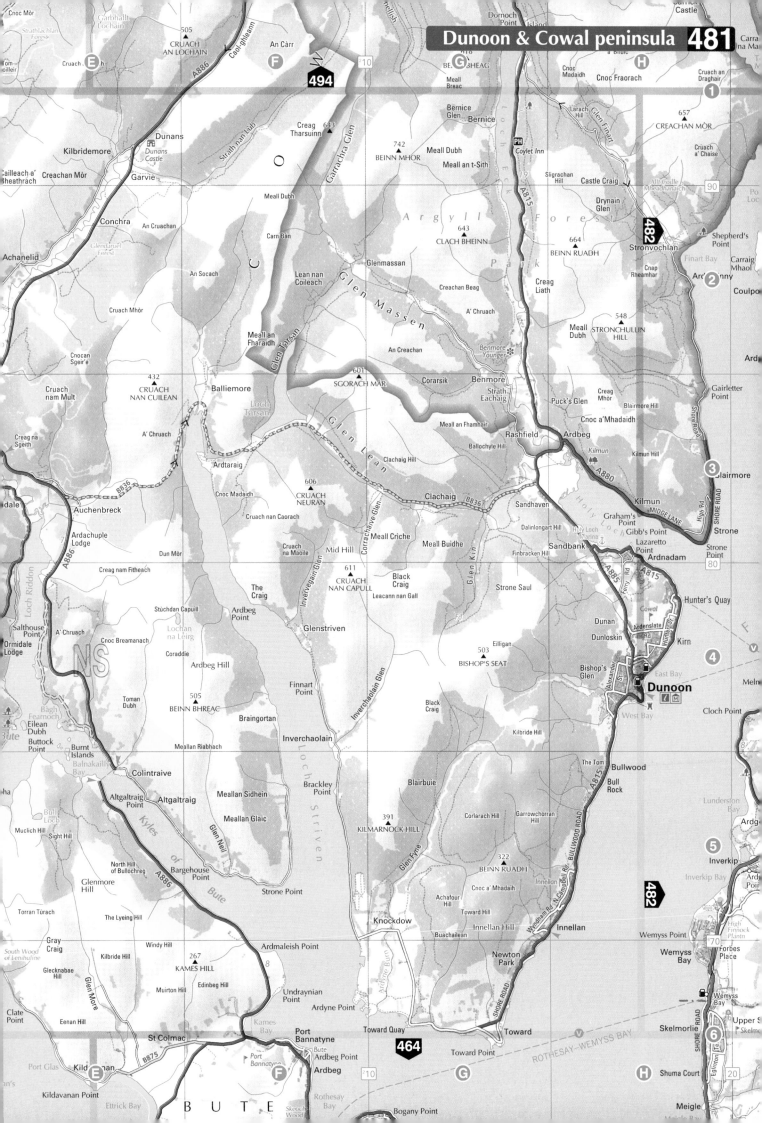

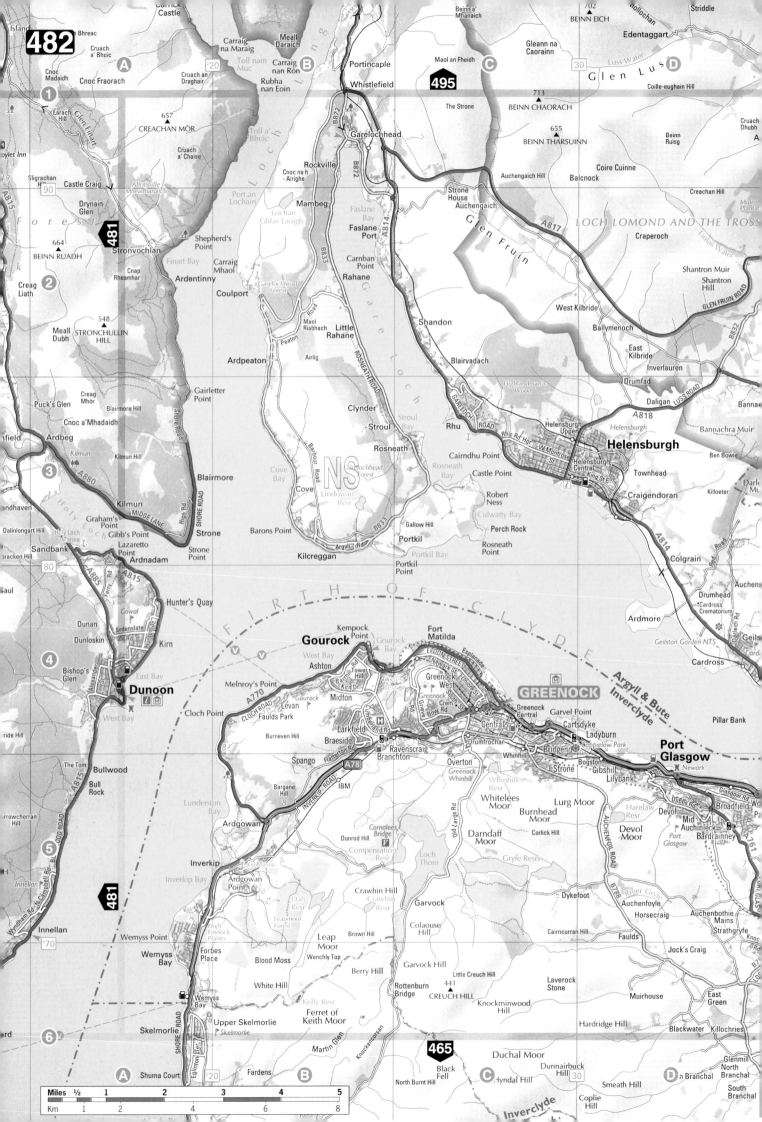

STIRLING 498

Tullibody

Alloa

Town plan: Glasgow p.634

Rosyth Harbour

DUNFERMLINE
A823(M)
PERTH
M90
ROSYTH STATION
2
A921
INVERKEITHING STATION
B980
Rosyth
KINCARDINE BRIDGE
A985
HM NAVAL BASE
ROSYTH EUROPARC
CAR FERRY TERMINAL
Inverkeithing
B981
River Forth
NORTH QUEENSFERRY STATION
A90
EDINBURGH
LBM
0   ½ mile
0   1 km

F I R T H   O F   F O R T H

490

Craigleith

Brigs of Fidra
Lamb
Longskelly Rocks
Longskelly Point
Broad Sands
Cowton Rocks West Links
Scottish Seabird
Milsey Bay
Leckmoram Ness
Canty Bay
Gin Head
Tantallon
Auldhame
Eldbotle Wood
West Links
Yellow Craig Plantn
Ware Rd
North Berwick Bay
East Links
The Glen
Glen
A198
Meadowhead's Tantallon
Blackdykes
West Links
Broad Wood
Duncan's Plantn
Dirleton Castle NTS
North Berwick
187
NORTH BERWICK LAW
Whitekirk
The Honourable Company of Edinburgh Golfers
Dirleton
Station Rd
B1347
White.
3
Gullane Bay
Gullane Point
Gullane
Saltcoats
B1345
Balgone Barns
Kingston
Sheriff Hall
East Craig
Whitekirk
Gullane Links
West Fenton
Fenton Barns
Old Stonelaws
Whitekirk Bridge
Gullane Sands
Gala Law
Luffness Links
East Fenton
Congalton Mains
Brownrigg
Craigmoor Wood
Binning Wood
Aberlady Bay
Luffness New
Park Hills
Oak Wood
80
Aberlady Point
Prora
Craigelaw Point
Kilspindie
Aberlady
Drem
B1377
West Fortune
East Fortune
Fortoun Bank
Tyningham
Craigielaw
A6137
Motor M
(dis)
B1347
Preston Mill & Phantassie Doocot NTS
B1407
Gosford Sands
Aberlady
Museum of Flight
Poffer Burn
Markle
Preston
Gosford Bay
Ballencrieff
Chesters
Kilduff Hill
Drovers Inn
4
tassie
Spittal
Camptoun
Athelstaneford
East Linton
A199
B1377
B1343
Pencraig Wood
Hairy Craig
Traprain
zie and eton
Seton Sands
LINKS ROAD
Longniddry
Bangly Hill
Hopetown Monument
Garleton Hills
Abbey Mains
PENCRAIG BRAE
Tyne
Brae Heads Loan
Luggate Burn
Seton Sands
Seton Mains
A6137
Amisfield Mains
Sandy's Mill
Hailes
Traprain Law
Collegiate Church
Huntington
St Martin's Kirk (ruin)
A1
Standingstone
Seton
B6363
Elvingston
Letham House
Lauderdale Aisle St Mary's Church
Haddington
West Bearford
Coldale
Meadowmill
A1
Gladsmuir
Birk Hedges
Clerkington
Mitchell Hall
490
5
Tranent
A199
Macmerry West Bank
Penston
Liberty Hall
Lamblair Wood
Lennoxlove Mains
Renton Hall
Mainshill
Whitelaw Hill
BLINDWELL BRAE
Garvald Grange
New Winton
Cuddie Wood
Lennoxlove
B6369
Colstoun Wood
Morham Bank
Garvald
North Elphinstone
B6371
New Town
Samuelston
Begbie Wood
Weird's Wood
Beech Hill
Sled Hill
70
South Elphinstone
B6355
A6093
Bolton
Clacherdean Wood
Nun Abbey
Market Cross
Samuelston South Mains
Coulston Old Mill
Bara Wood
Carfrae
Ormiston
Tyne Water
Crown Wood
Winding Law
Townhead
Star Wood
vin
Pencaitland Woodhall
Saltoun Hall
MAIN ST
Goblin Ha' Hotel
PH
Gifford
Black Wood
Donolly Resr
Fountainhall
House o' Muir
Peastonbank
West Saltoun
Barley Mill
Skimmer Hills
East Saltoun
B6355
472
Petersmuir Wood
Gifford
Gifford Vale
Danskine
Snawdon
6
Bohomy Hill
Saltoun Forest
Bents Wood
Castle Wood
Wester Wood
Birns Water
60
Gilchriston
Pishwanton

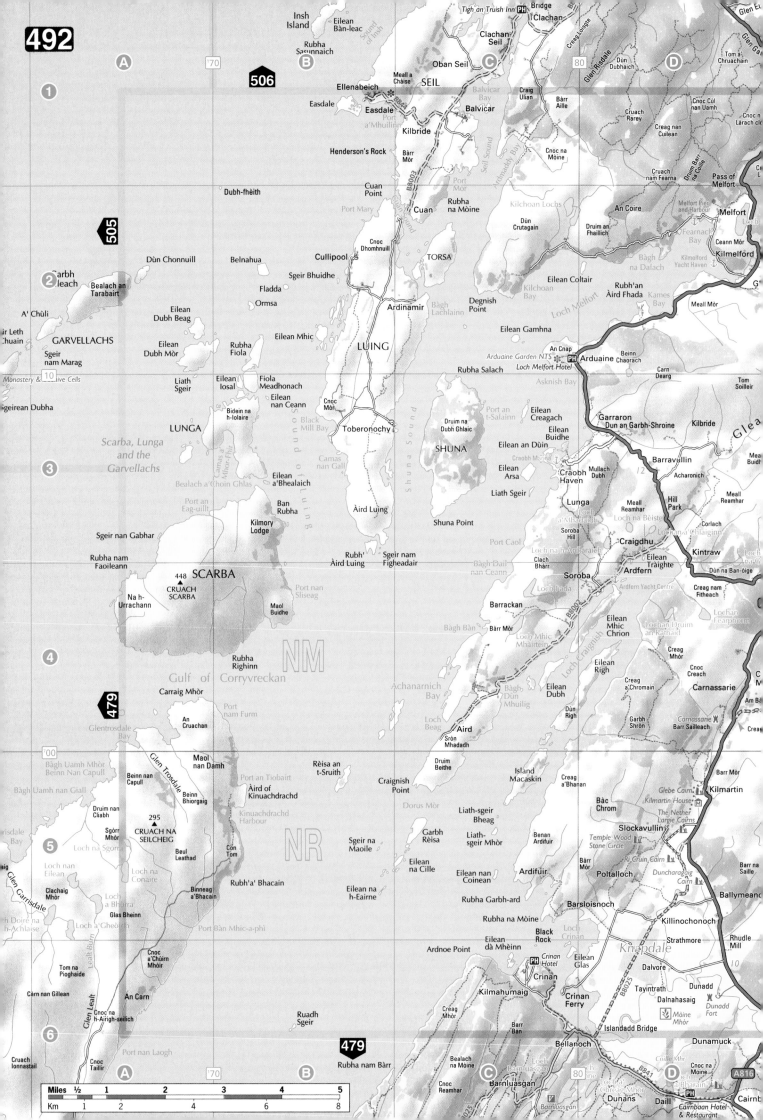

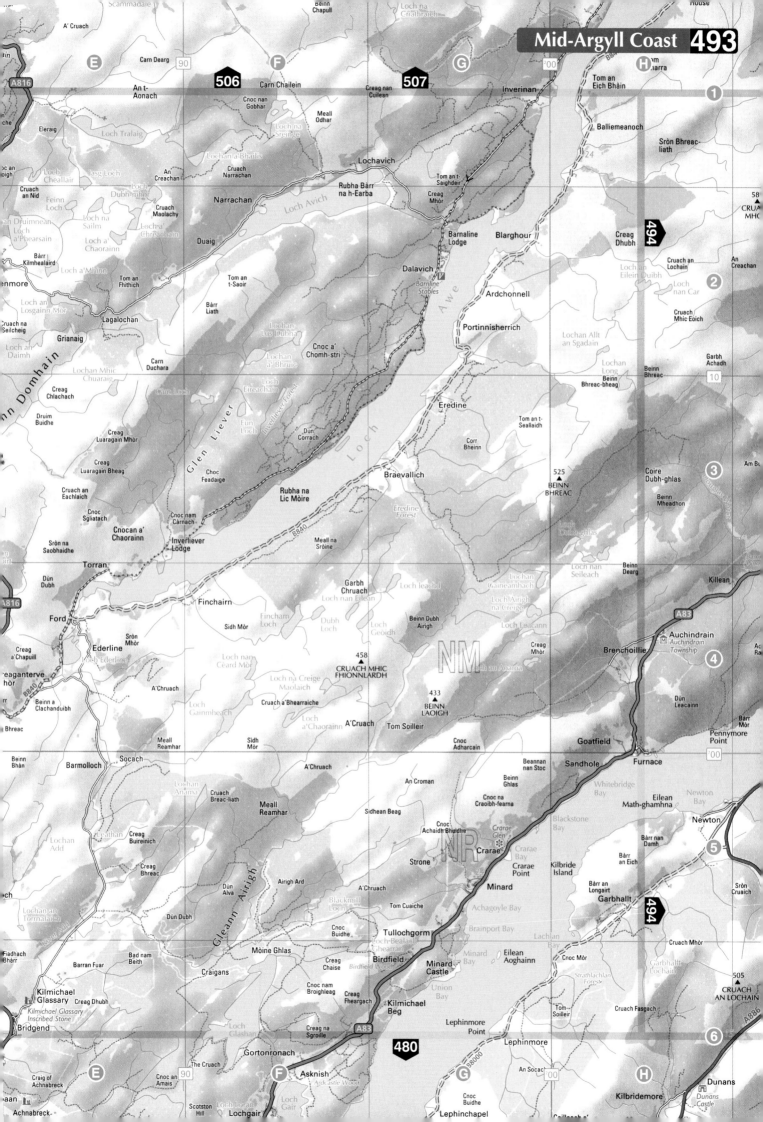

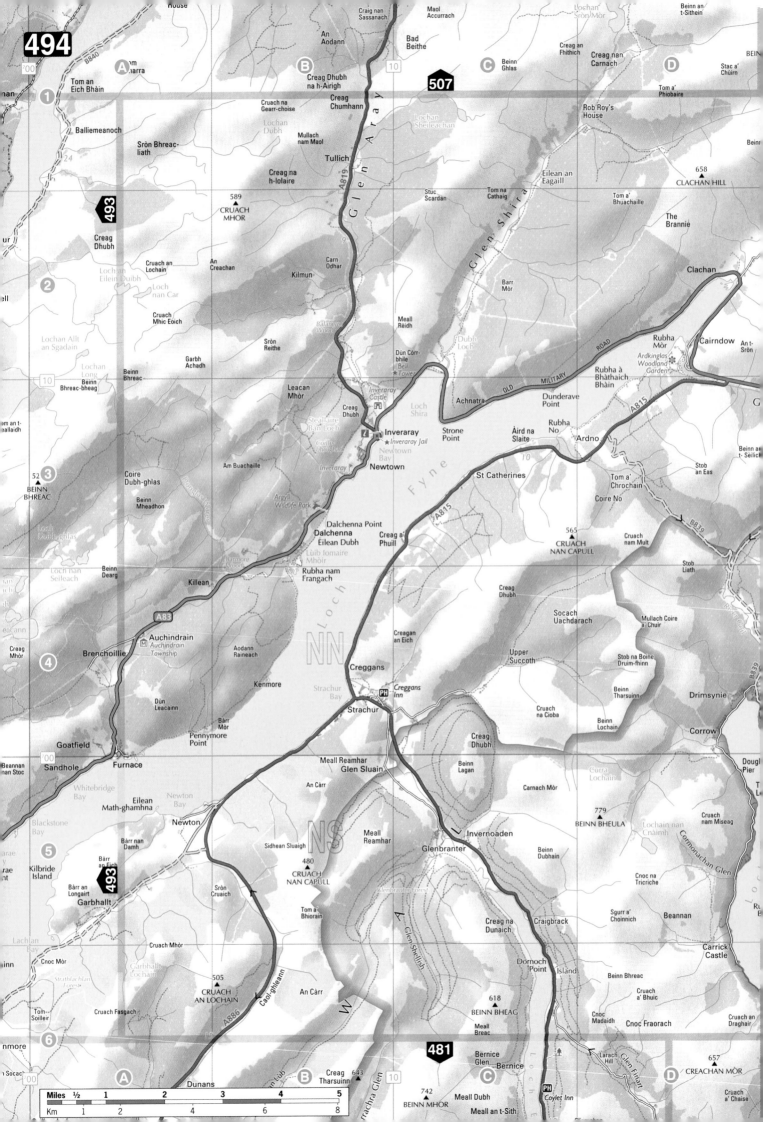

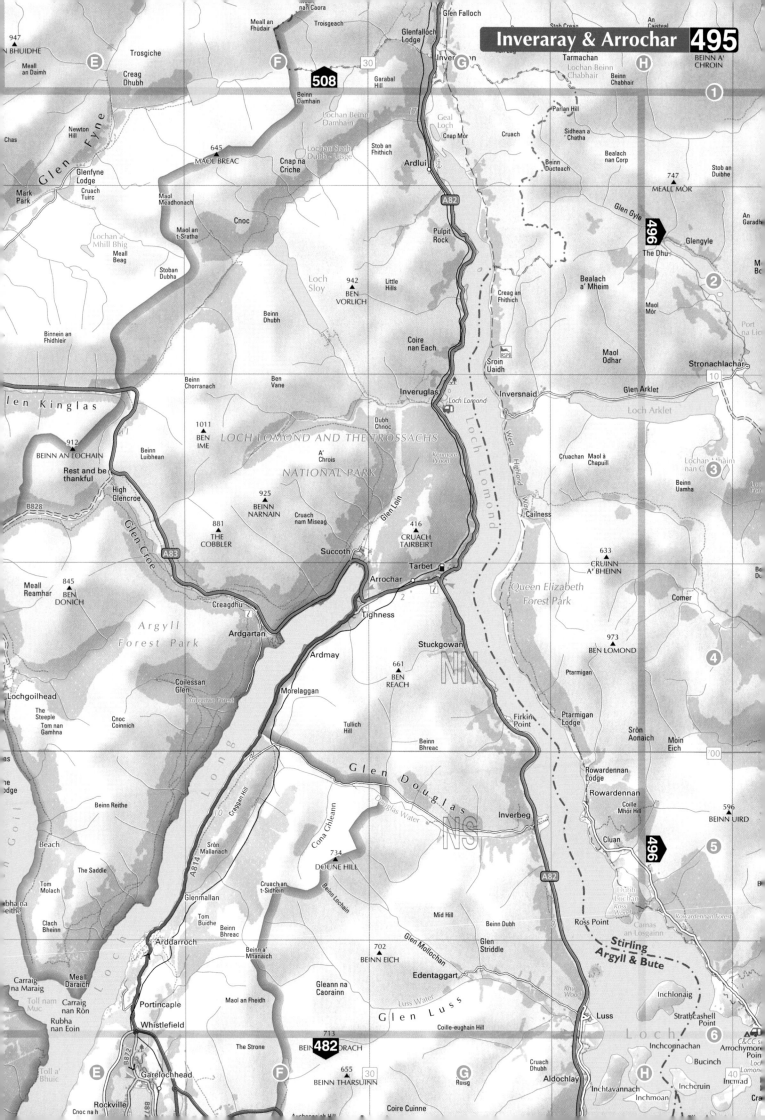

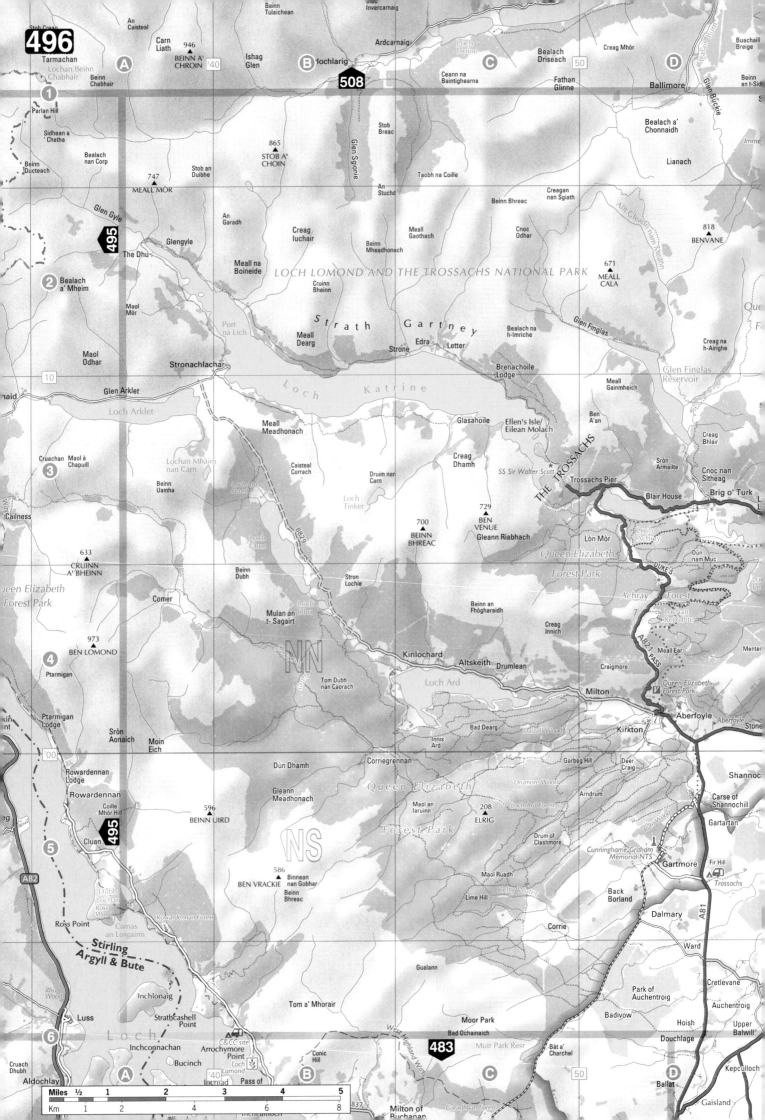

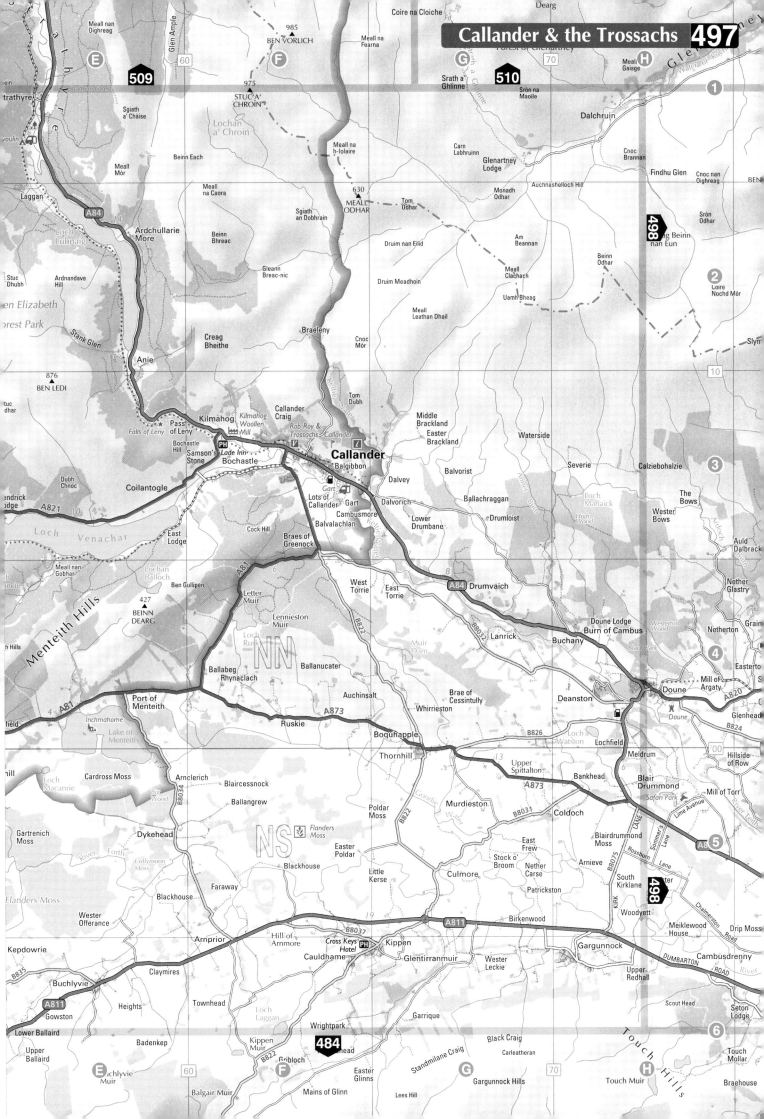

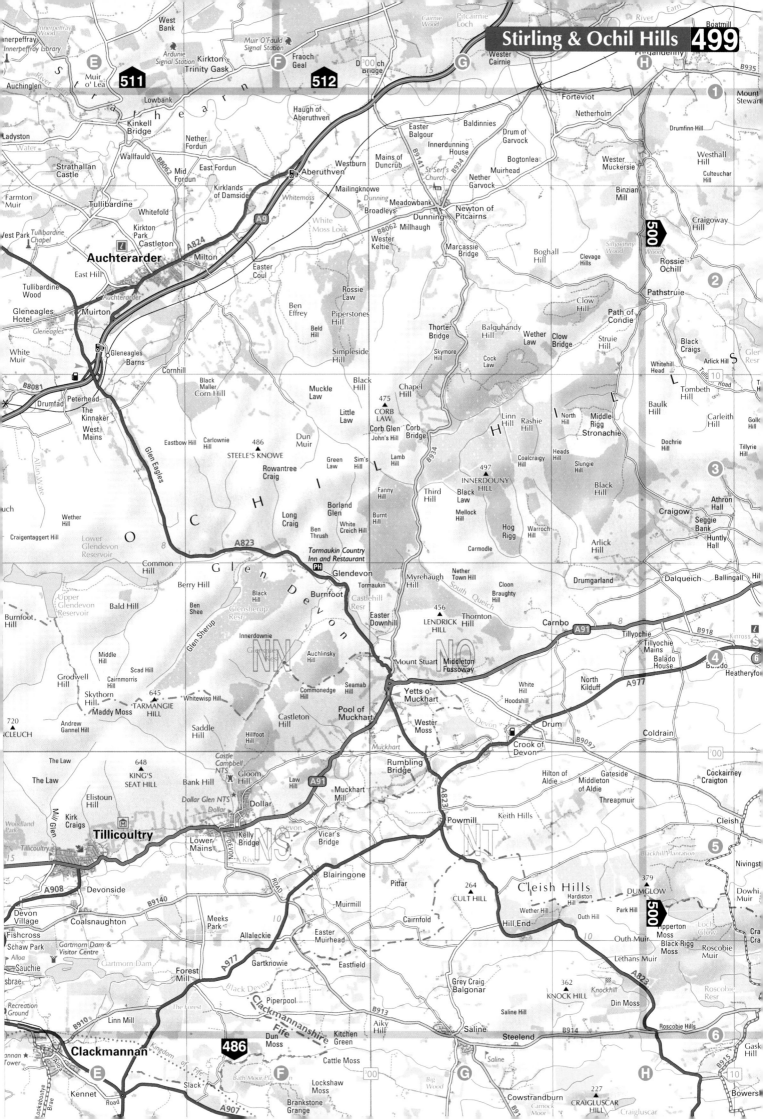

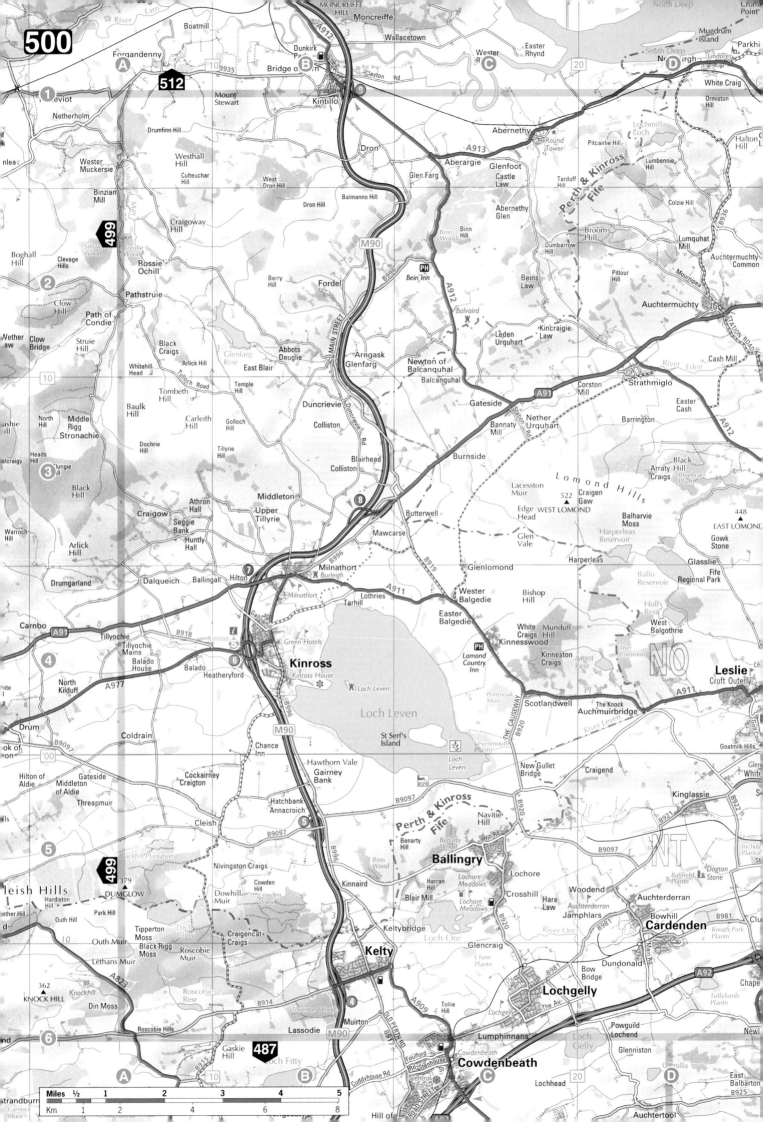

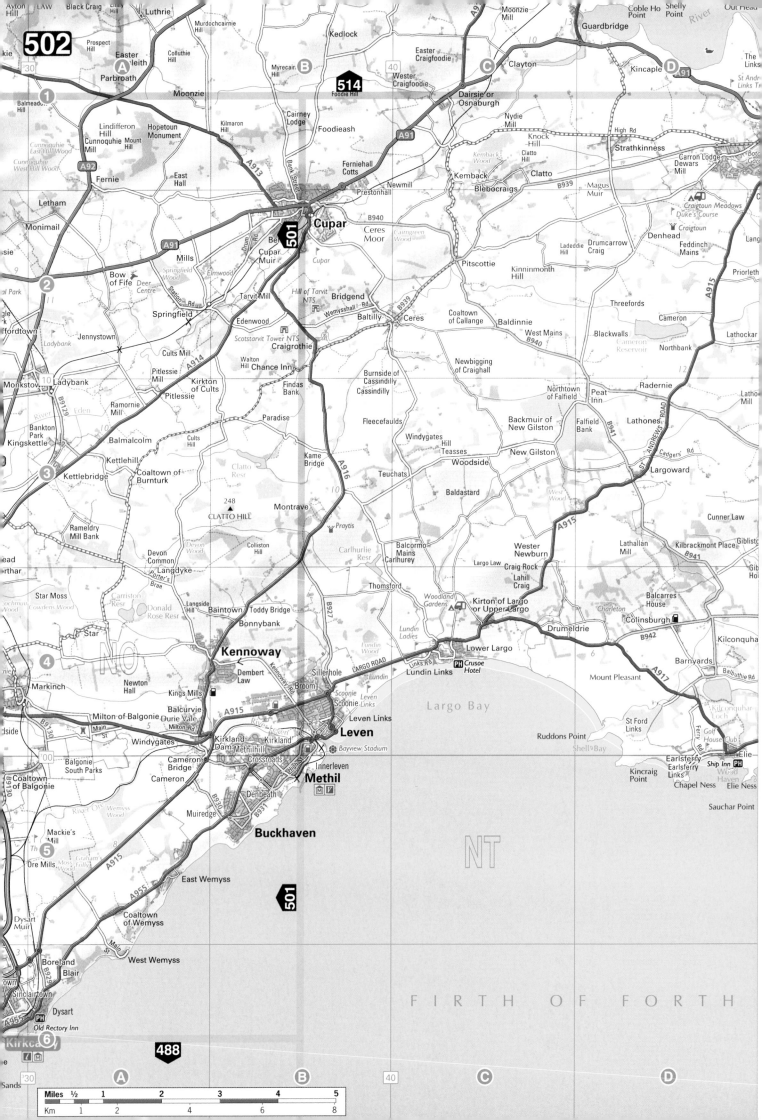

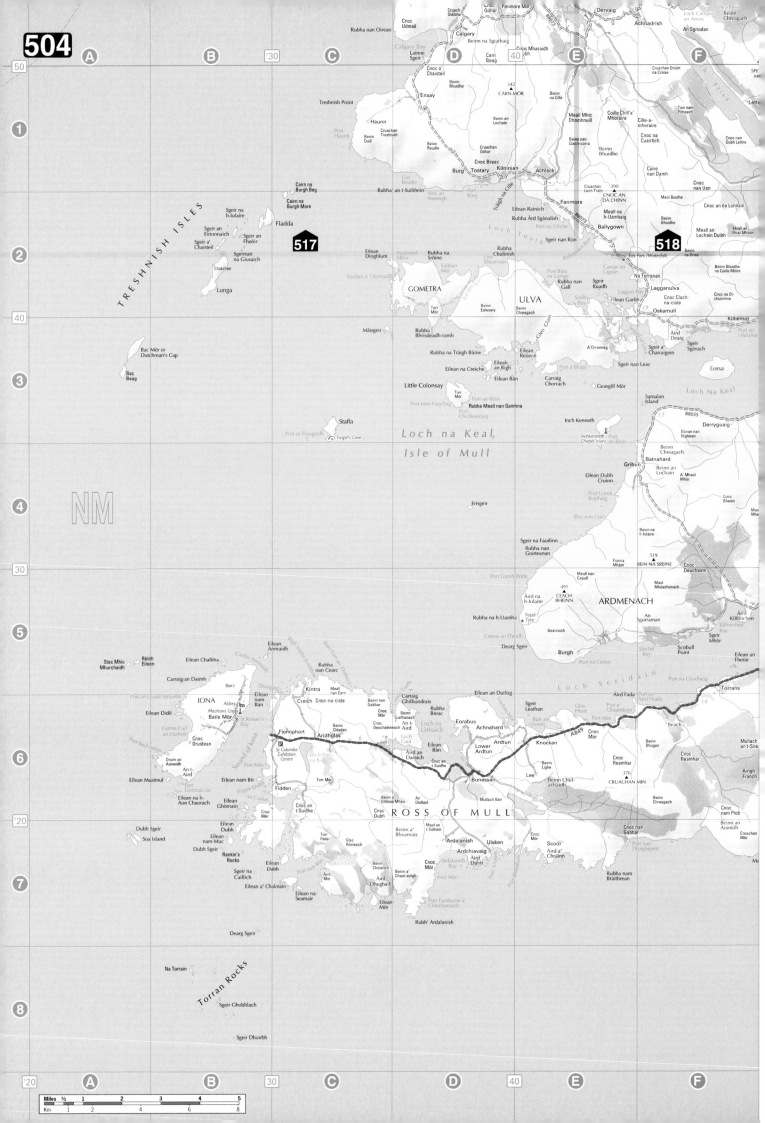

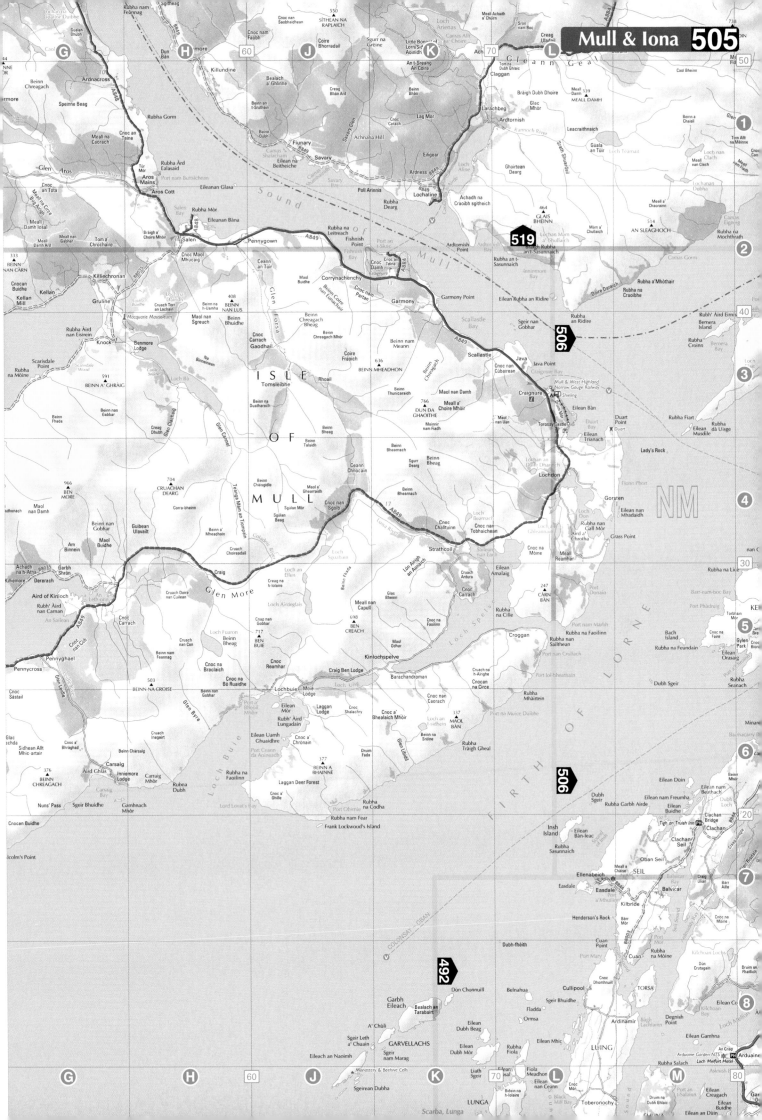

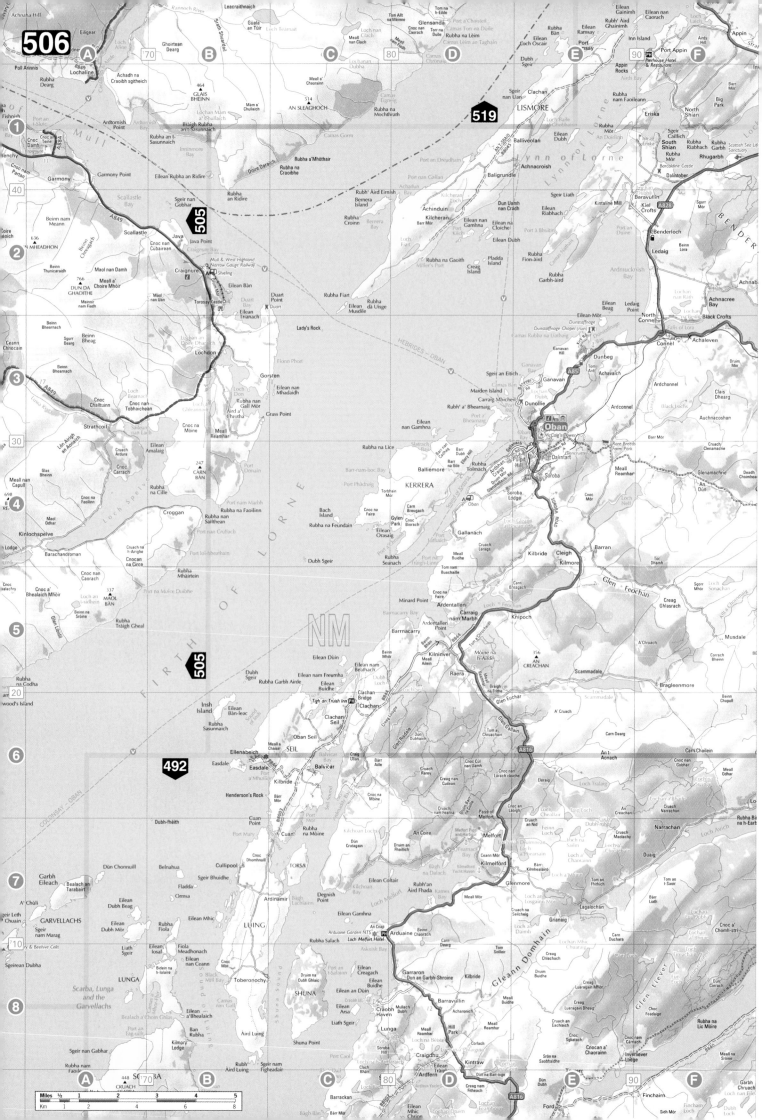

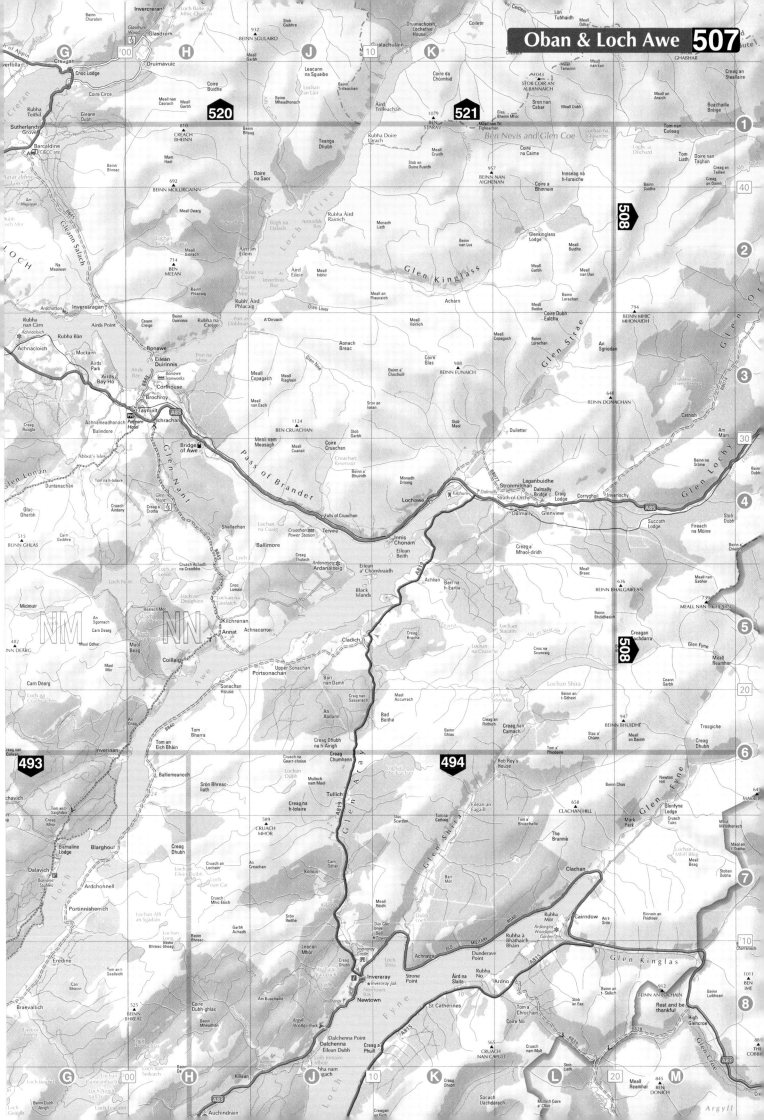

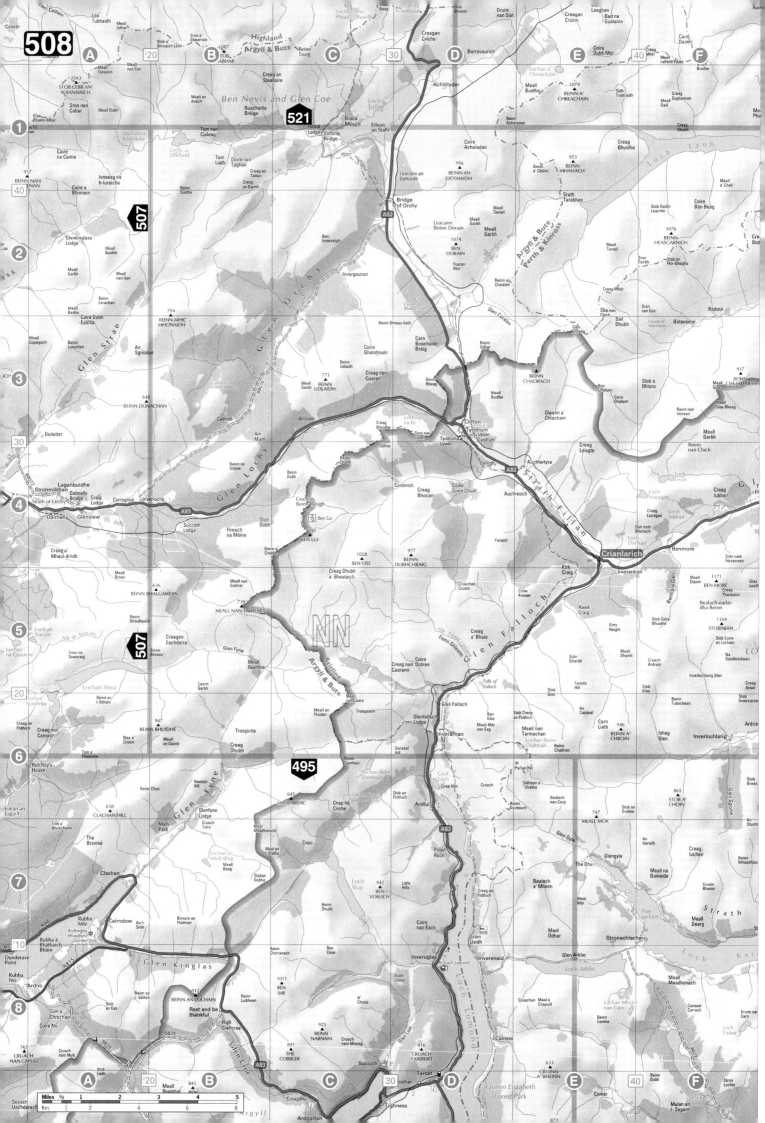

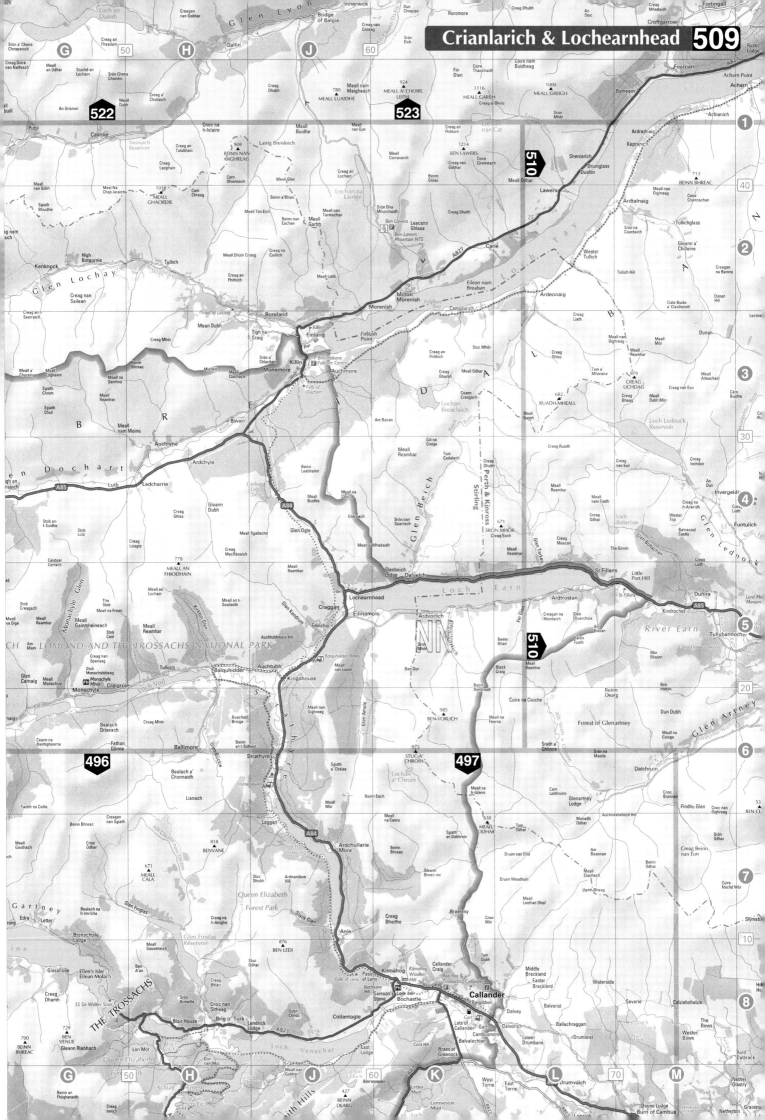

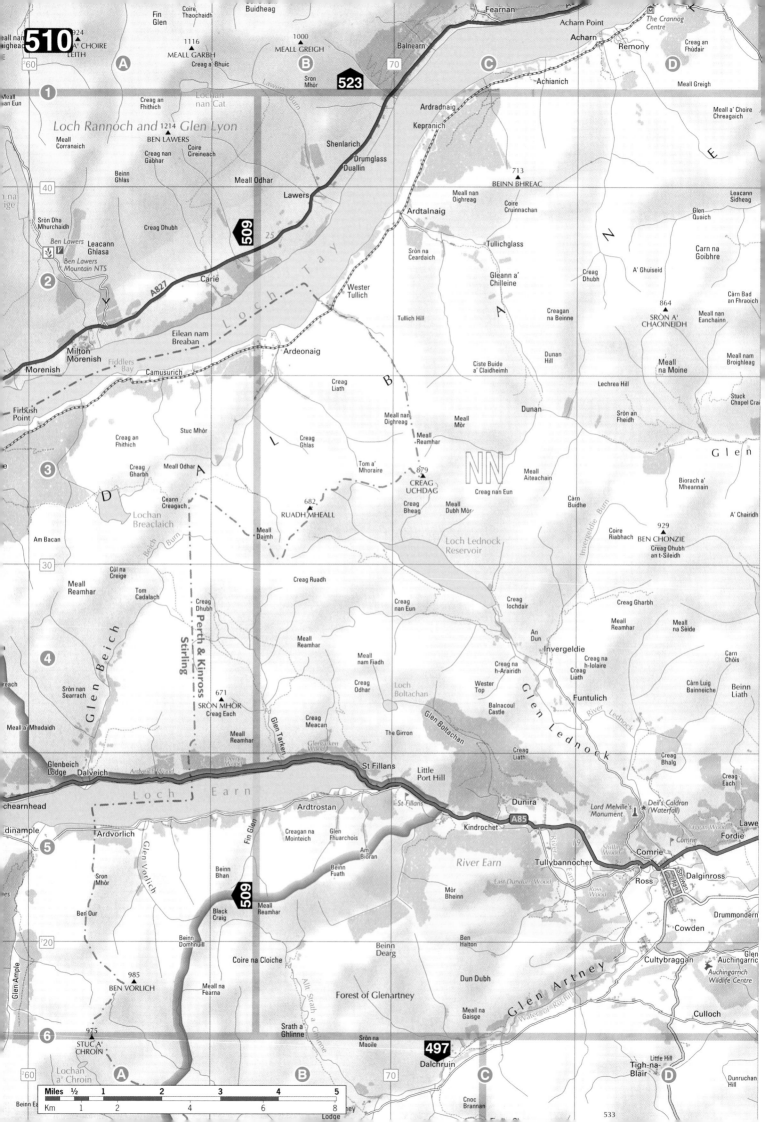

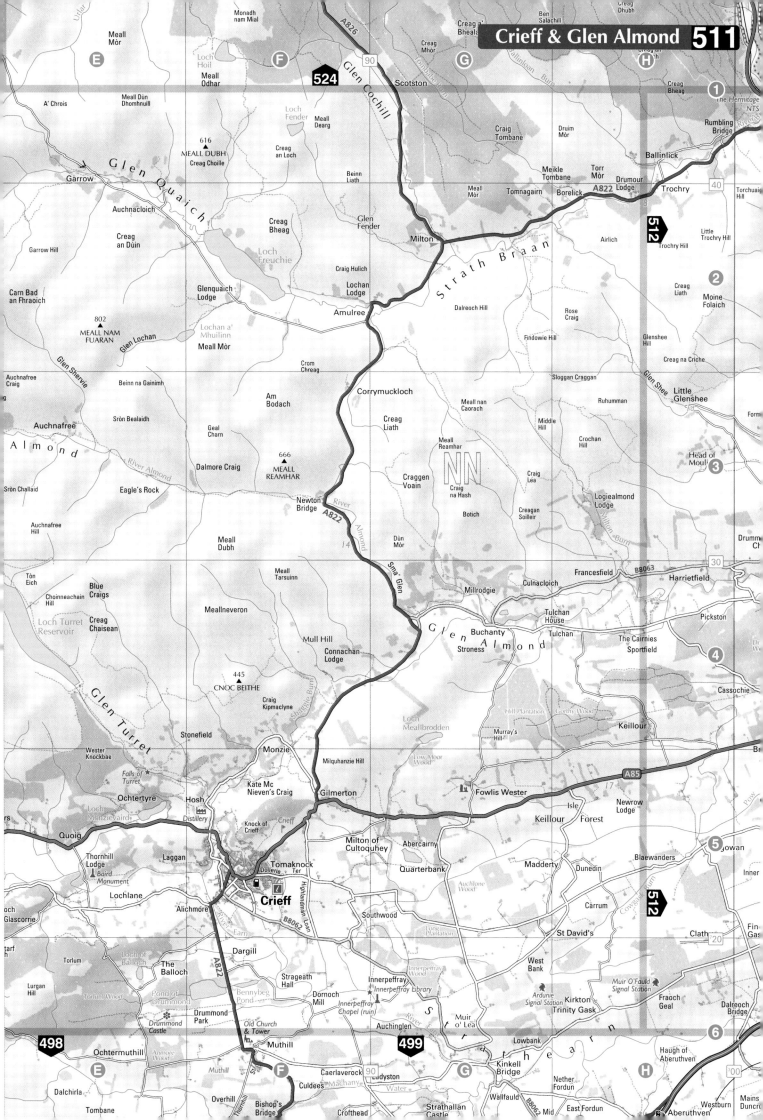

524
512
498
499

E F G H

1 2 3 4 5 6

A826
A822
A85
B8062
B8063
B8062

Crieff

Glen Cochill
Glen Quaich
Glen Almond
Glen Turret
Glen Shervie
Glen Lochan
Glen Fender
Glen Shee
Strath Braan
Sma' Glen
Strathearn

Place names (top row / Glen Cochill area):
Meall Mòr, Monadh nam Mial, Creag Dhubh, Ben Salachill, Creag a' Bheala, Creag an Dubh, Creag Mhòr, Creag an Loch
Loch Hoil, Meall Odhar, Scotston, Ballinloan Burn, Creag Bheag, The Hermitage NTS, Rumbling Bridge, Ballinlick
A' Chrois, Meall Dùn Dhomhnuill, Loch Fender, Meall Dearg, Craig Tombane, Druim Mòr, Creag Bheag
616 MEALL DUBH, Creag Choille, Creag an Loch, Meikle Tombane, Torr Mòr, Drumour Lodge, Trochry, Torchuai Hill
Garrow, Auchnacloich, Beinn Liath, Meall Mòr, Tomnagairn, Borelick, A822, Little Trochry Hill
Garrow Hill, Creag an Dùin, Glen Fender, Milton, Airlich, Trochry Hill
Carn Bad an Fhraoich, Glenquaich Lodge, Craig Hulich, Dalreoch Hill, Rose Craig, Creag Liath, Moine Folaich
Loch Freuchie, Lochan Lodge, Amulree, Findowie Hill, Glenshee Hill, Creag na Criche
802 MEALL NAM FUARAN, Lochan a' Mhuilinn, Meall Mòr, Crom Chreag, Meall nan Caorach, Middle Hill, Sloggan Craggan, Little Glenshee
Auchnafree Craig, Beinn na Gainimh, Sròn Bealaidh, Am Bodach, Geal Charn, Corrymuckloch, Creag Liath, Meall Reamhar, Ruhumman, Crochan Hill
Auchnafree, Dalmore Craig, 666 MEALL REAMHAR, Craggen Voain, Craig na Hash, Craig Lea, Logiealmond Lodge, Head of Moul
Sròn Challaid, Eagle's Rock, Newton Bridge, Botich, Creagan Soilleir, Drumm
Auchnafree Hill, Meall Dubh, Dùn Mòr, Francesfield, B8063, Harrietfield
Tòn Eich, Blue Craigs, Choinneachain Hill, Meall Tarsuinn, Millrodgie, Culnacloich, Tulchan House, Pickston
Loch Turret Reservoir, Creag Chaisean, Meallneveron, Glen Almond, Buchanty, Tulchan, The Cairnies, Sportfield
Mull Hill, Stroness, Keillour, Cassochie
Connachan Lodge, 445 CNOC BEITHE, Loch Meallbrodden, Hill Plantation, Gorthy Wood, Murray's Hill
Craig Kipmaclyne, Stonefield, Shaggie Burn, Keillour
Wester Knockbae, Monzie, Milquhanzie Hill, Low Moor Wood, Fowlis Wester, Keillour Forest, Newrow Lodge
Falls of Turret, Ochtertyre, Kate Mc Nieven's Craig, Gilmerton, Isle, Keillour
Hosh, Distillery, Knock of Crieff, Quoig, Loch Monzievaird
Thornhill Lodge, Laggan, Milton of Cultoquhey, Abercairny, Maddertly, Dunedin, Blaewanders, Gowan
Baird Monument, Tomaknock, Dollerie Ter, Quarterbank, Auchlone Wood, Carrum, Inner
Lochlane, Alichmore, Crieff, Highlandman Loan, Southwood, West Bank, St David's, Clath
Loch Glascorrie, Dargill, Long Plantation, Madderty, Kirkton, Trinity Gask, Fin Gas
Torlum Wood, Torlum, The Balloch, Bennybeg Pond, Strageath Hall, Dornoch Mill, Innerpeffray Wood, Ardunie Signal Station, Fraoch Geal, Dalreoch Bridge
Lurgan Hill, Pond of Drummond, Old Church & Tower, Innerpeffray, Innerpeffray Library, Muir o' Lea, Muir O'Fauld Signal Station, Kinkell Bridge
Dalchirla, Drummond Castle, Drummond Park, Muthill, Auchinglen, Innerpeffray Chapel (ruin), Lowbank, Haugh of Aberuthven
Tombane, Ochtermuthill, Annore Wood, Bishop's Bridge, Caerlaverock, Ledyston, Machany Water, Nether Fordun, Westburn, Mains Duncr
Overhill, Culdees, Crofthead, Strathallan Castle, Wallfauld, East Fordun, Aberuthven

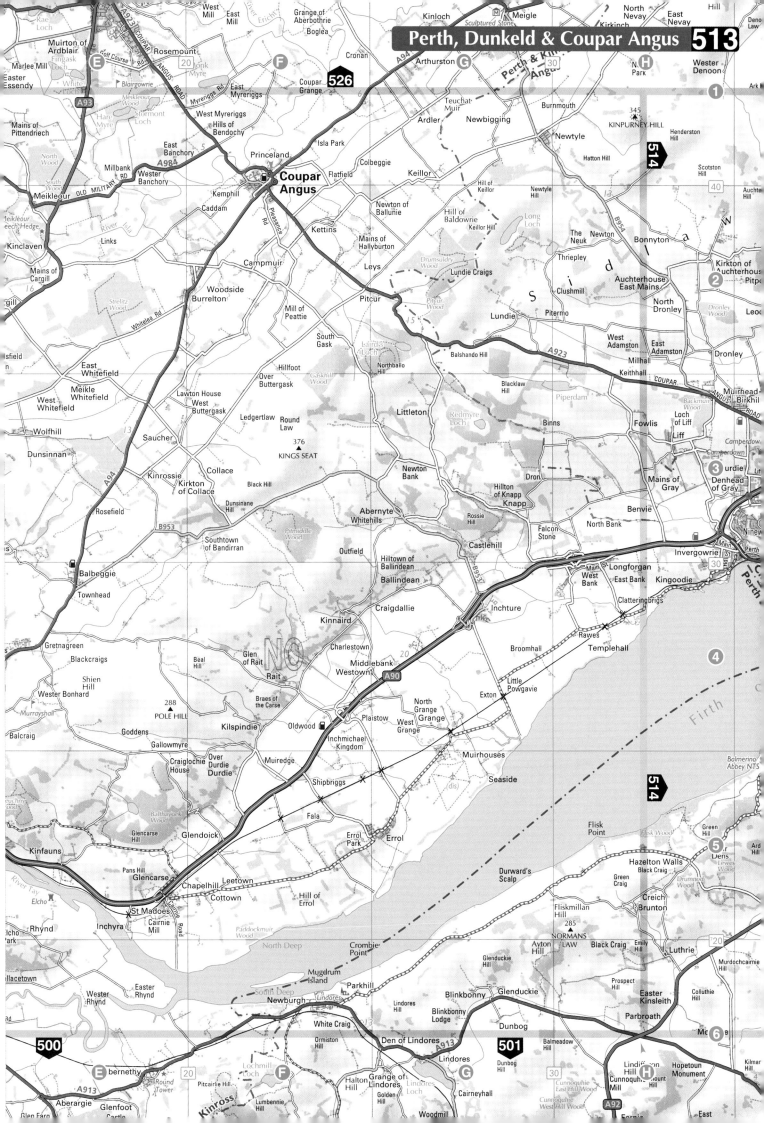

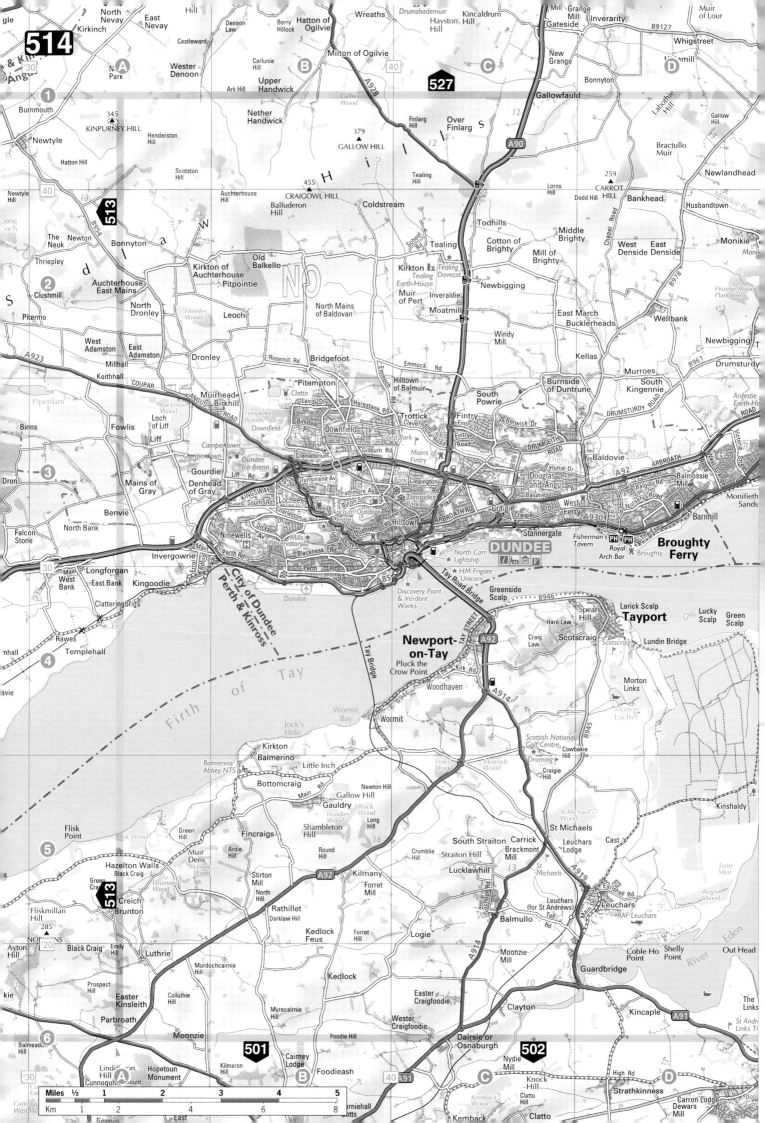

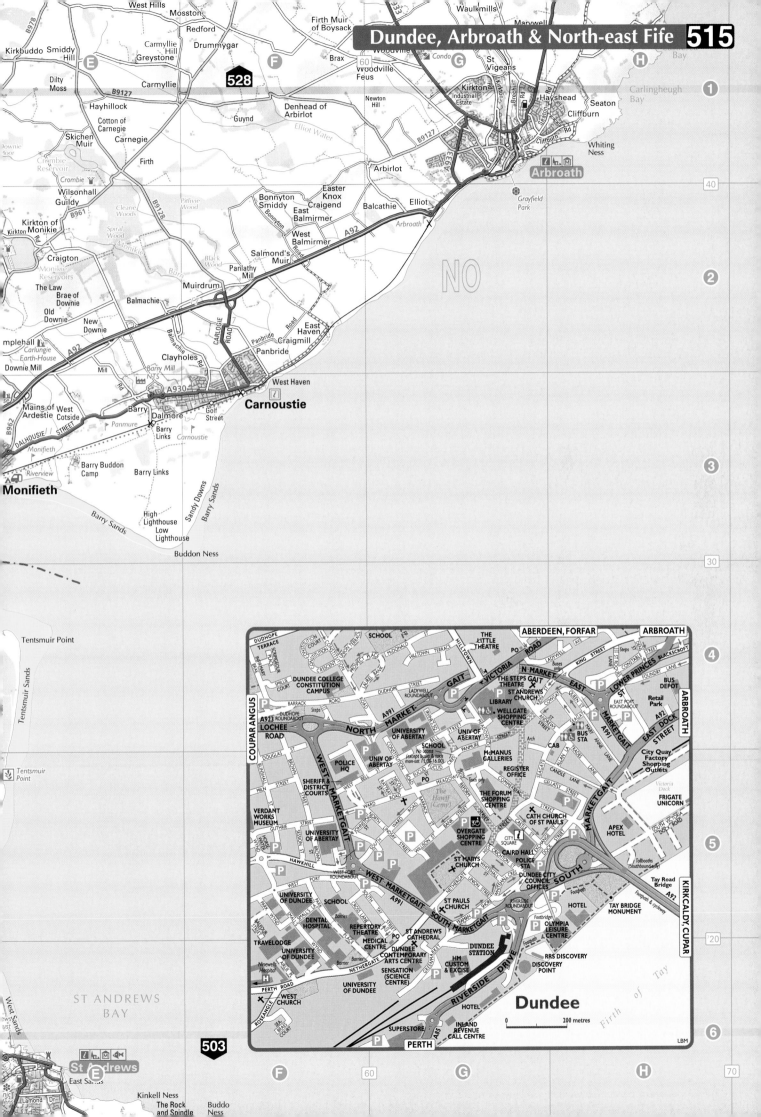

Arbroath

Carnoustie

Monifieth

Dundee

St Andrews

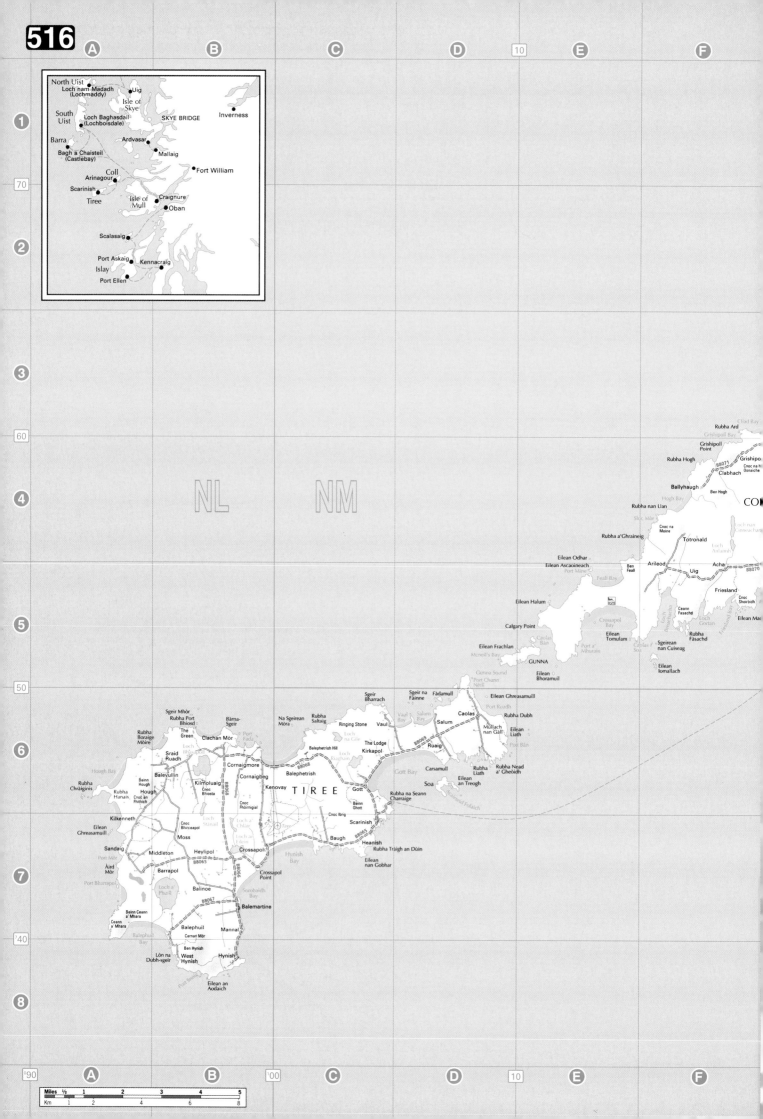

Inset map

North Uist
Loch nam Madadh (Lochmaddy)
Uig
Isle of Skye
Inverness
SKYE BRIDGE
South Uist
Loch Baghasdail (Lochboisdale)
Ardvasar
Barra
Mallaig
Bagh a Chaisteil (Castlebay)
Fort William
Coll
Arinagour
Scarinish
Craignure
Tiree
Isle of Mull
Oban
Scalasaig
Port Askaig
Kennacraig
Islay
Port Ellen

Main map

NL   NM

Rubha Ard
Cliad Bay
Grishipoll Bay
Grishipoll Point
Rubha Hogh
Grishipo
B8071
Cnoc na h'
Osnaiche
Clabhach
Ballyhaugh
Ben Hogh
Hogh Bay
Rubha nan Uan
CO
Rubha a'Ghraineig
Cnoc na Moine
Totronald
Loch nan Cinneachan
Eilean Odhar
Eilean Ascaoineach
Port Mine
Ben Feall
Arileod
Uig
Acha
B8070
Friesland
Cnoc Shorbidh
Feall Bay
Eilean Halum
Loch Breacachadh
Loch Anlaimh
Ceann Fasachd
Calgary Point
Crossapol Bay
Eilean Tomulam
Rubha Fàsachd
Eilean Mac
Eilean Frachlan
Caolas Bàn
Port a' Mhurain
Sgeirean nan Cuiseag
Mcneil's Bay
GUNNA
Eilean Bhoramuil
Eilean Iomallach
Gunna Sound
Port Chunn Nèill
Sgeir Bharrach
Sgeir na Fàinne
Fàdamull
Eilean Ghreasamuill
Port Ruadh
Sgeir Mhòr
Rubha Port Bhiosd
Bàrna-Sgeir
Na Sgeirean Mòra
Rubha Saltaig
Ringing Stone
Vaul
Vaul Bay
Salum Bay
Salum
Caolas
Rubha Dubh
The Green
Port Fada
Mullach nan Gall
Eilean Liath
Rubha Boraige Mòire
Clachan Mòr
Balephetrish Hill
Loch Bhasapol
The Lodge
Kirkapol
B8069
Ruaig
Poll Bàn
Sraid Ruadh
Cornaigmore
Balephetrish
Loch Riaghain
Carsamull
Rubha Liath
Rubha Nead a' Gheòidh
Hough Bay
Balevullin
Kilmoluaig
B8068
Cornaigbeg
Gott Bay
Soa
Eilean an Treogh
Beinn Hough
Cnoc Bhiosta
Kenovay
TIREE
Gott
Moorland Folaich
Rubha Chràiginis
Rubha Hanais
Hough
Cnoc an Fhithich
Cnoc Fhòirnigial
Beinn Ghott
Rubha na Seann Charraige
Kilkenneth
Cnoc Bhrrceapol
Loch Stanail
Loch a' Bhaic
Cnoc Ibrig
Scarinish
B8065
Eilean Ghreasamuill
Sandaig
Moss
Loch an Eilein
Tiree
Baugh
Heanish
Middleton
Heylipol
Crossapol
Rubha Tràigh an Dùin
Àird Mòr
Port Mòr
B8065
B8066
Crossapol Point
Eilean nan Gobhar
Barrapol
Hynish Bay
Loch a' Phuill
Balinoe
Sorobaidh Bay
Port Bharrapol
B8067
Balemartine
Beinn Ceann a' Mhara
Ceann a' Mhara
Balephuil
Carnan Mòr
Mannal
Balephuil Bay
Ben Hynish
West Hynish
Hynish
Lòn na Dubh-sgeir
Eilean an Aodaich
Port Snèois

Miles ½ 1 2 3 4 5
Km 1 2 4 6 8

530

518

518

504

G   H   30   J

NM

TRESHNISH ISLES

Highland
Argyll & Bute

OBAN

COLL OBAN

BAGH A CHAISTEIL
(CASTLEBAY)
LOCH BAGHASDAIL
(LOCHBOISDALE)

Rubha Mòr
Eilean Mòr
Acairseid Mhòr
Eilean nan Uan
Druim nan Carn
Rubha Sgor-innis
Bousd
Sorisdale
B8072
Sorisdale Bay
Bàgh na Coille
Gallanach
Arnabost
Loch Fada
Meall na h-Iolaire
Meall nan Uan
Sloc na Gamhna
Eileanan na h-Aornan
Loch Ronard
Loch an t-Sàilein
Bàgh an Trailleich
The Lodge
Meall nam Muc
Eilean nam Muc
Arinagour
Eilean Ornsay
Rubha Bàn
Airne na Sgeire
Eilean na h-Eathar
Mòr

Point of Ardnamurchan
Eilean Carrach
Portuairk
Sgurr nam Meann
Sanna Point
Sanna Bay
Sgeir Ghobhlach
Sgeir Horsgate
Sanna
Rubha an Dùin Bhàin
Rubha Carrach
Meall Eigin-aig
Meall Buidhe Mòr
Fascadale Bay
Port Kilchoan
Fascadale
Meall Clach an Daraich
Meall an Fhir-eòin
Meall Sanna
Achnaha
Meall Meadhoin
Beinn na h-Imeilte
Bruighlean
Achosnich
Beinn Bhuidhe
Creag an Airgid
Meall an Fhreiceadain
Meall an Tarmachain
Port Mòr
Loch Grigadale
Beinn na h-Imeilte
Loch Caorach
Beinn nan Òrd
Druim Reidh-dhalach
342
BEINN NA SEILG
Glebe Hill
Meal Chrò Bheinn
Glas Bheinn
Eilean nan Seachd Seisrichean
An Acairseid
Beinn nan Codhan
Dubh Chreag
Druim nan Gearr Leacainn
Ormsaigmore
Ormsaigbeg
Kilchoan
Mingary
Kilchoan Bay
Rubhan a' chall
Rubha Àird an Iasgaich
Rubha Àird an Iasgaich
Mingary Pier
436
MEALL N

Eilean an Fhuarain
Some Point
Cuan Mòr
Laorin Bay
Glengorm Castle
Port Chill Bhraonainn
Cnoc a' Chait
Ardmore Bay
Ardmore Point
Rubha na Sealbhaig
Bloody Bay
Quinish Point
Dun Ban
Loch Mingary
An Inbhire
Meall an Inbhire
An Speireachan
Druim na Sròine-cruime
Tobermory
Tobermory / Stror
Ledaig
Eile na
Rubha an Àird
Port
Caliach Point
Port na Caillich
Port Langamull
Poll Athach
Cnoc Leathan
Beinn nan Dearcag
Glen Gorm
Sgùlan Breac
'S AIRDE BEINN
292
Coire Sgamadail
Meall Doire nan Damh
Cnoc Cappullac
Langamull
Port nam Partan
Rubha nan Oirean
Cruach Sleibhe
Cnoc Odhar
Penmore Mill
An Torr
Loch an Torr
Dervaig
Achnadrish
An Sgriodan
Beinn Chreagach
Meall Doire nan Damh
5
Cnoc Udmail
Calgary
Beinn na Sgiathaig
Crois Mharaidh Dhubh
Loch Carnain an Amais
50
SPERNE MòR
Calgary Bay
Lainne Sgeir
Carn Beag
Cnoc a' Chaisteil
342
CÀRN MÒR
Cruachan Druim na Croise
Tom nam Fitheach
Lettermore
Treshnish Point
Ensay
Beinn Bhuidhe
Beinn na Cille
Coille Chill a' Mhoraire
Cille-a-mhoraire
Ch
Haunn
Beinn an Lochain
Meall Mhic Dhomhnuill
Cnoc na Cuairtich
Cnoc nan Dubh Leitire
Port Haunn
Beinn Duill
Cruachan Treshnish
Cruachan Odhar
Beinn Reudle
Cruachan Odhar
Beinn nan Clach-corra
Beinn Bhuidhe
Coire nan Damh
Cnoc nan Uan
6
Cnoc Breac
Burg
Tostary
Kilninian
Achleck
518
Lòn Reudle
Cairn na Burgh Beg
Cairn na Burgh More
Rubha an t-Suibhein
Sloc na Neheogh
Burg
Tràigh na Cille
Cruachan Loch Tràth
390
CNOC AN DÀ CHINN
Maol Buidhe
Cnoc an da Lunnain
Fanmore
Eilean Rainich
Meall na h-Uamhaig
Beinn Bhuidhe
Meall an Lochain Duibh
Meall an Fhlar Mhàm
Dan
Sgeir na h-Iolaire
Sgeir an Eirionnaich
Sgeir a' Chaisteil
Fladda
Sgeir an Fheòir
Sgeirean na Giusaich
Cruachan
Rubha Àrd Sgànalish
Port na Crìche
Ballygown
Eilean Dioghlum
Acairseid Mhòr
Rubha na Sròine
Sàilean Mòr
Rubha Chulinish
Sgeir nan Ròn
Loch Tuath
Eas Fors (Waterfall)
Camas an Lagain
Beinn na Drise
Beinn Bhuidhe na Coille Mòire
7
BEINN NAN CÀRN
Lunga
Lochan a' Churraidh
Lòn Bhreacuil
Port Bàta na Luinge
Na Torranan
Rubha nan Gall
Sgeir Ruadh
Sgeir nan Ròn
Lagganulva
Eilean Garbh
Cnoc Clach-na-cuimhne
Cnoc na Di-chuimhne
Cnocan Buidhe
Kellan Mill
GOMETRA
Torr Mòr
Beinn Eolasary
Beinn Chreagach
ULVA
Beinn na-ciste
Soriby Bay
Oskamull
Àird Dearg
Killiemor
40
Màisgeir
Rubha Bhrisdeadh-ramh
A'Chrannag
Sgeir a' Charraigein
Sgeir Sgòrach
Port an t-Salainn
Bac Mòr or Dutchman's Cap
Rubha na Tràigh Bàine
Eilean Reilean
Eilean na Creiche
Eilean an Rìgh
Carraig Chorrach
Geasgill Mòr
Eorsa
Loch Na Keal
bha ine
Bac Beag
Little Colonsay
Torr Mòr
Eilean Bàn
Port an Ròin
Rubha Meall nan Gamhna
Samalan Island
8
Loch na Keal, Isle of Mull
Inch Kenneth
Derryguaig
B8035
Port nam Faochag
Port Chicheamaig
Inchkenneth Chapel
Port na Ròin
Dùnan nan Nighean
Staffa
Port an Eisgaidh
Fingal's Cave
Gribun
Balnahard
Beinn Chreagach
Beinn an Lochain
A' Mhaol Mhòr
Eilean Dubh Cruinn
Port Tràin
G   H   30   J   K   40   L   M   50

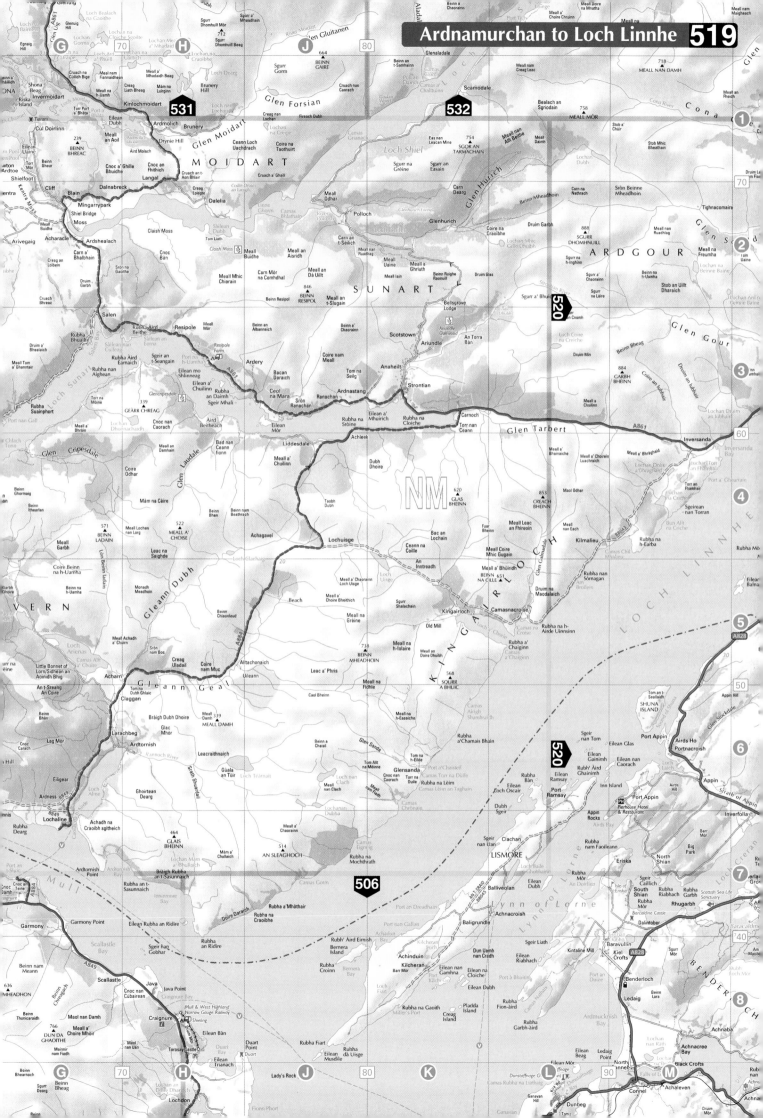

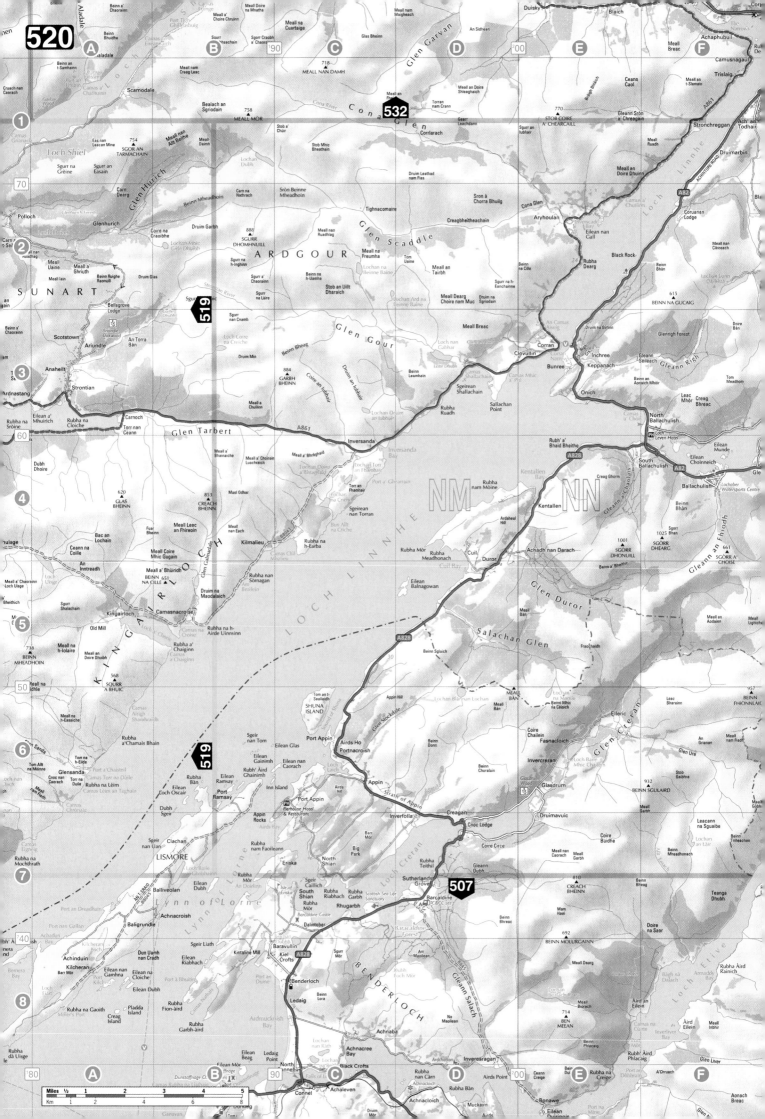

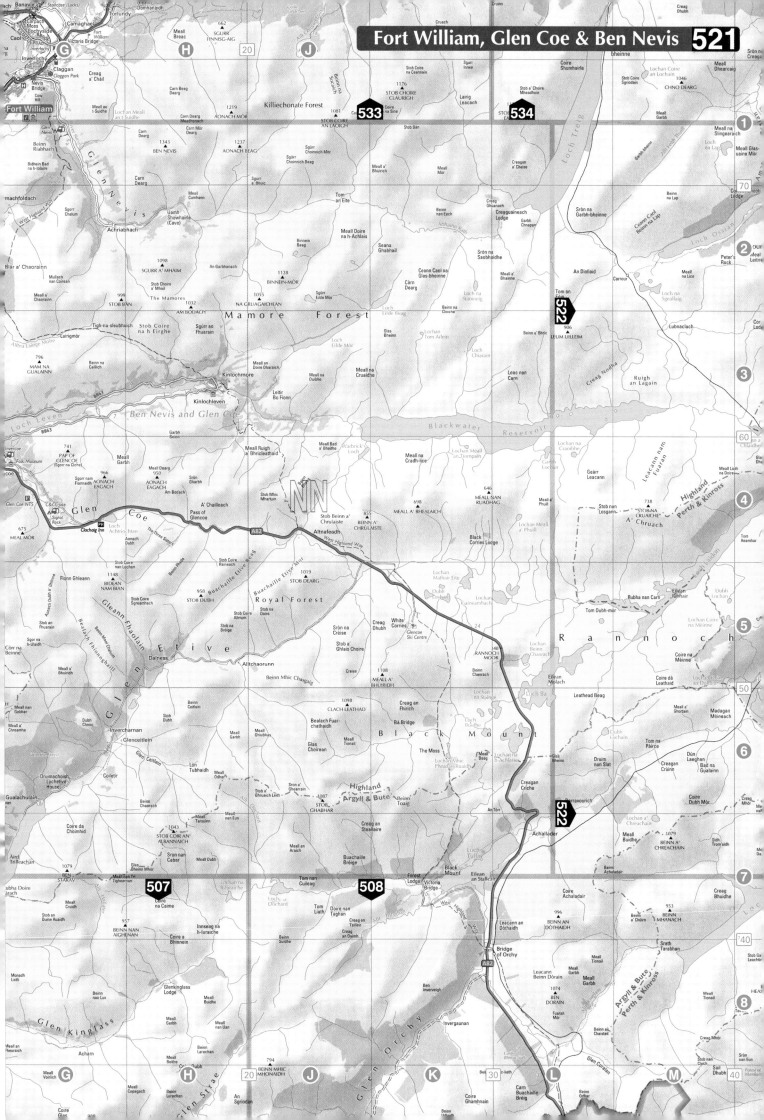

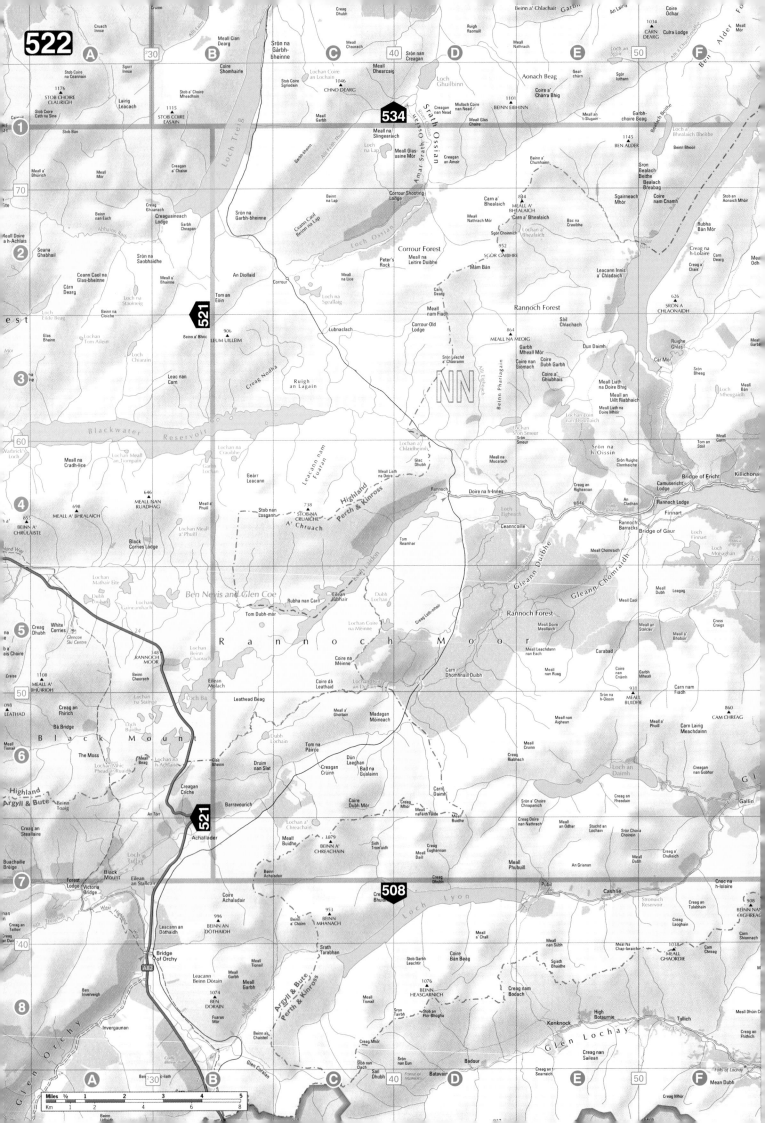

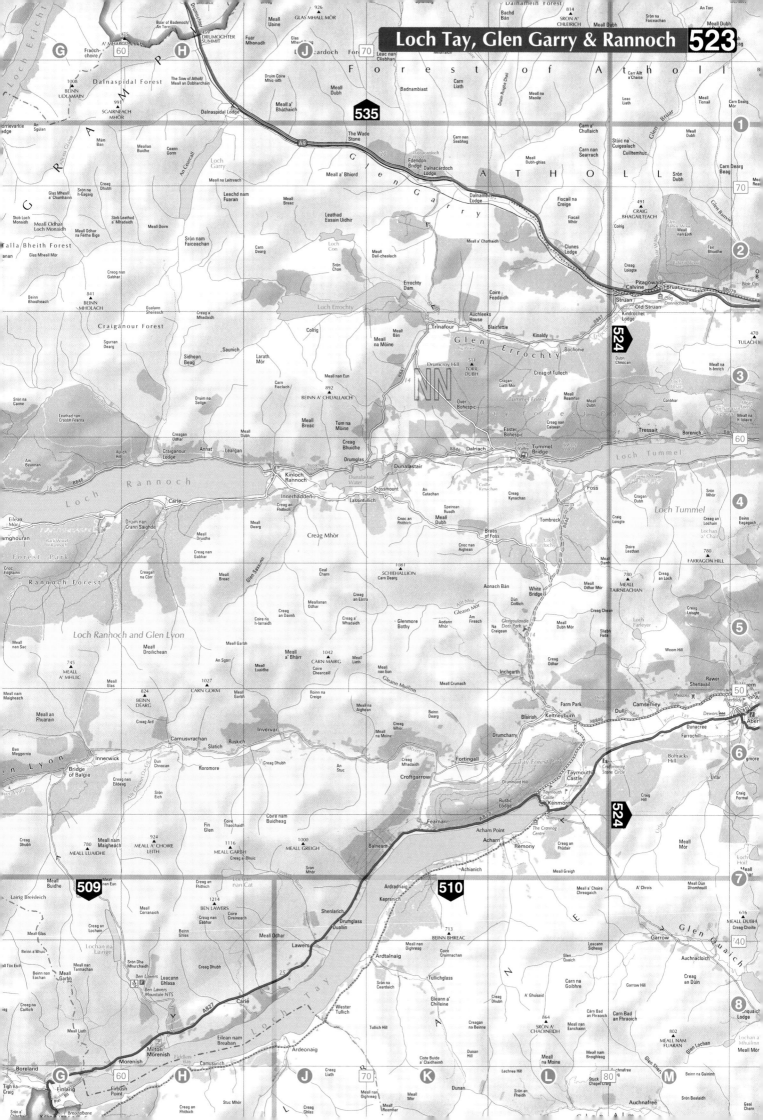

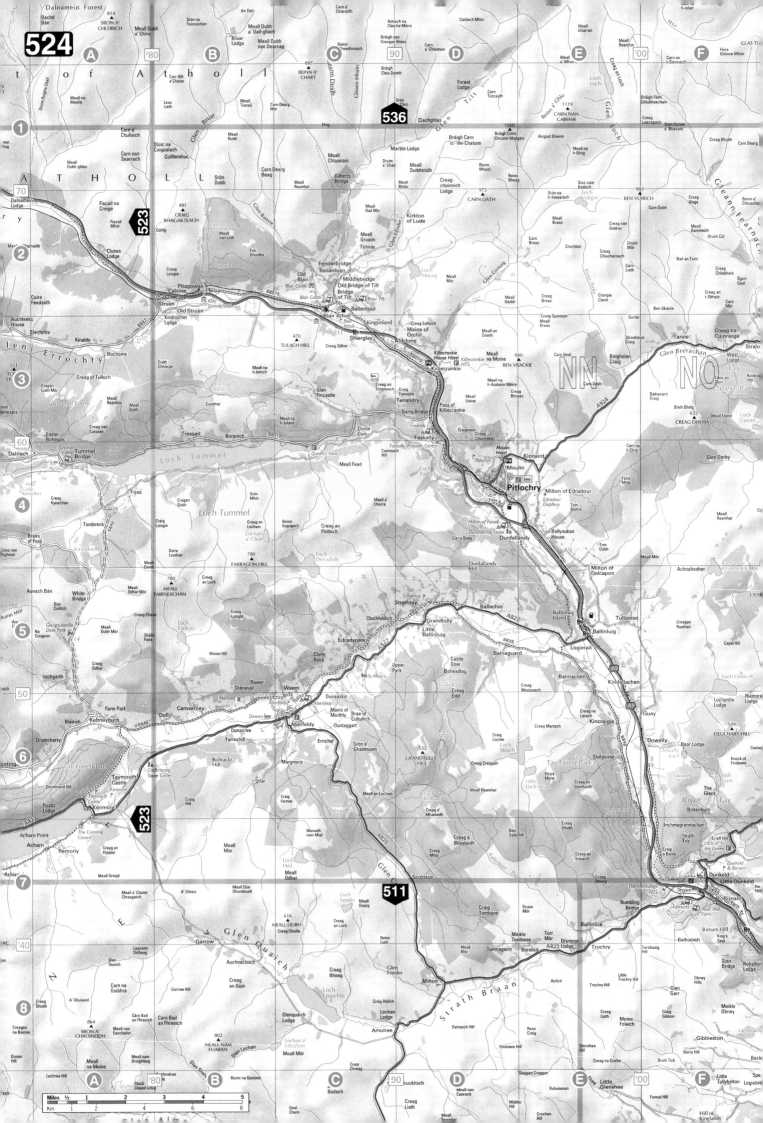

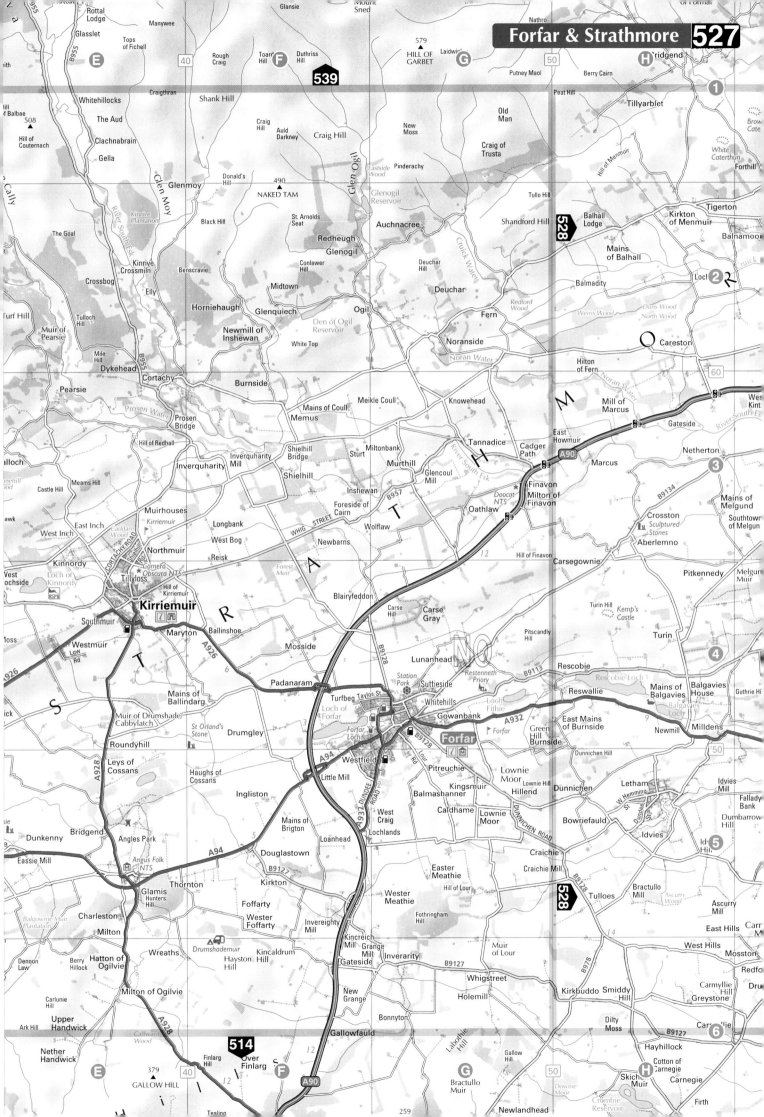

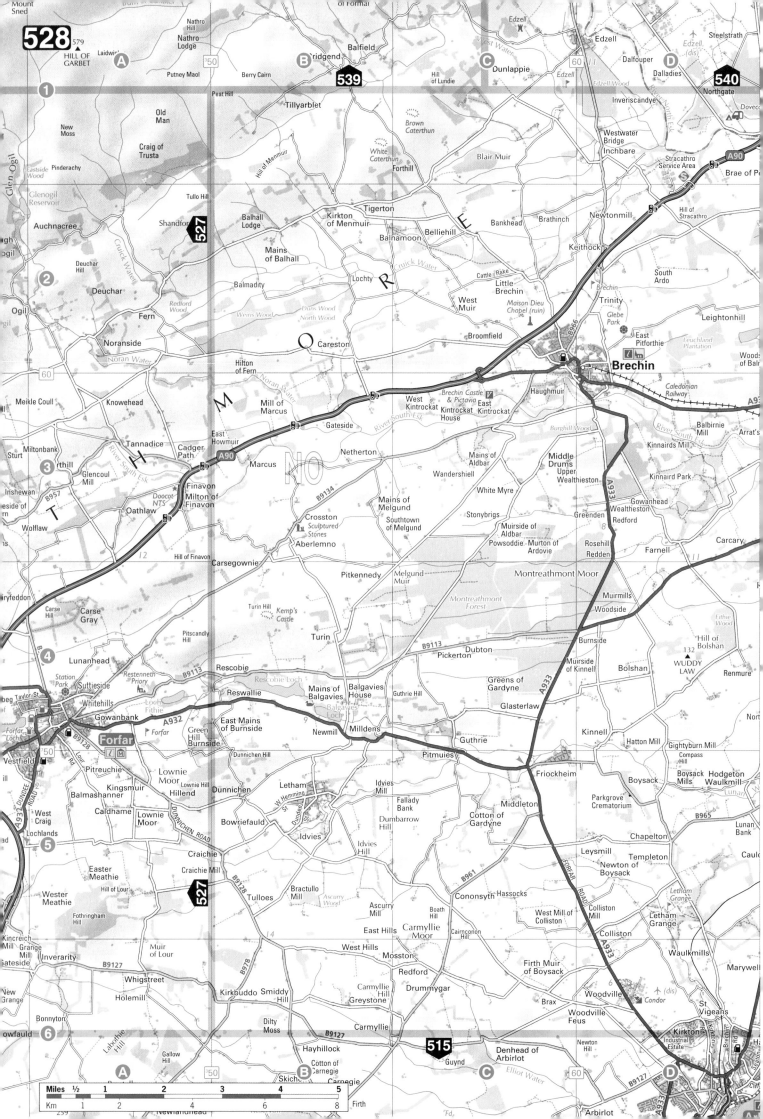

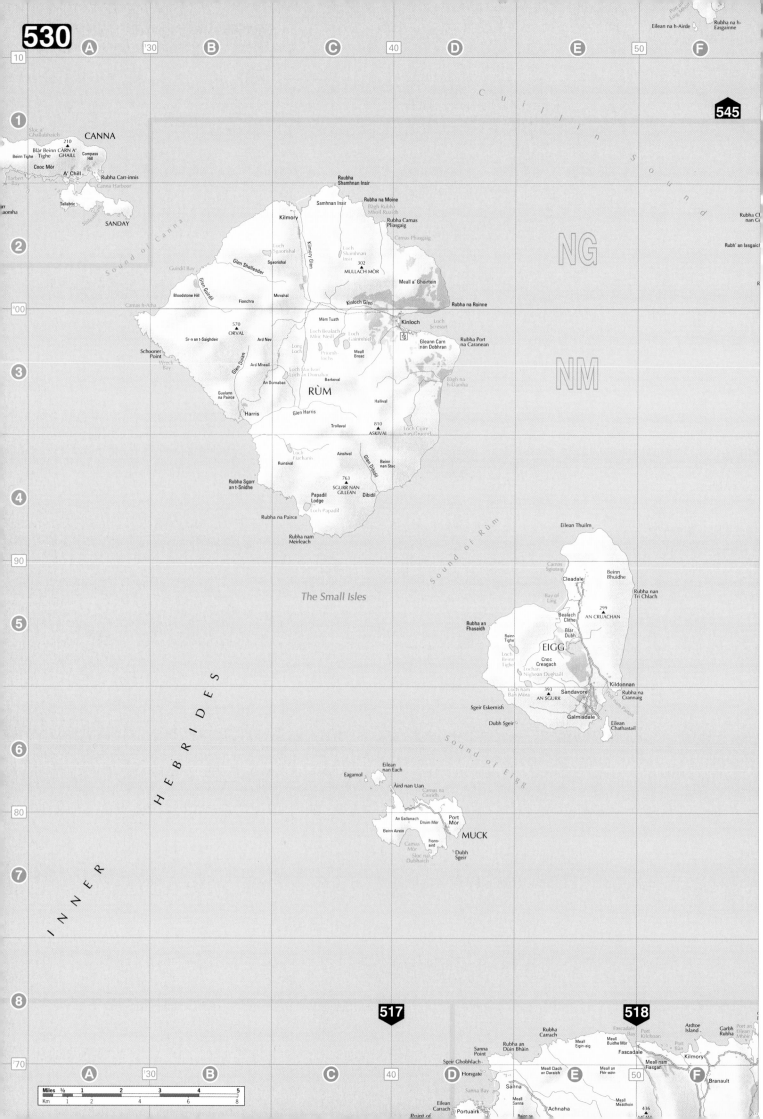

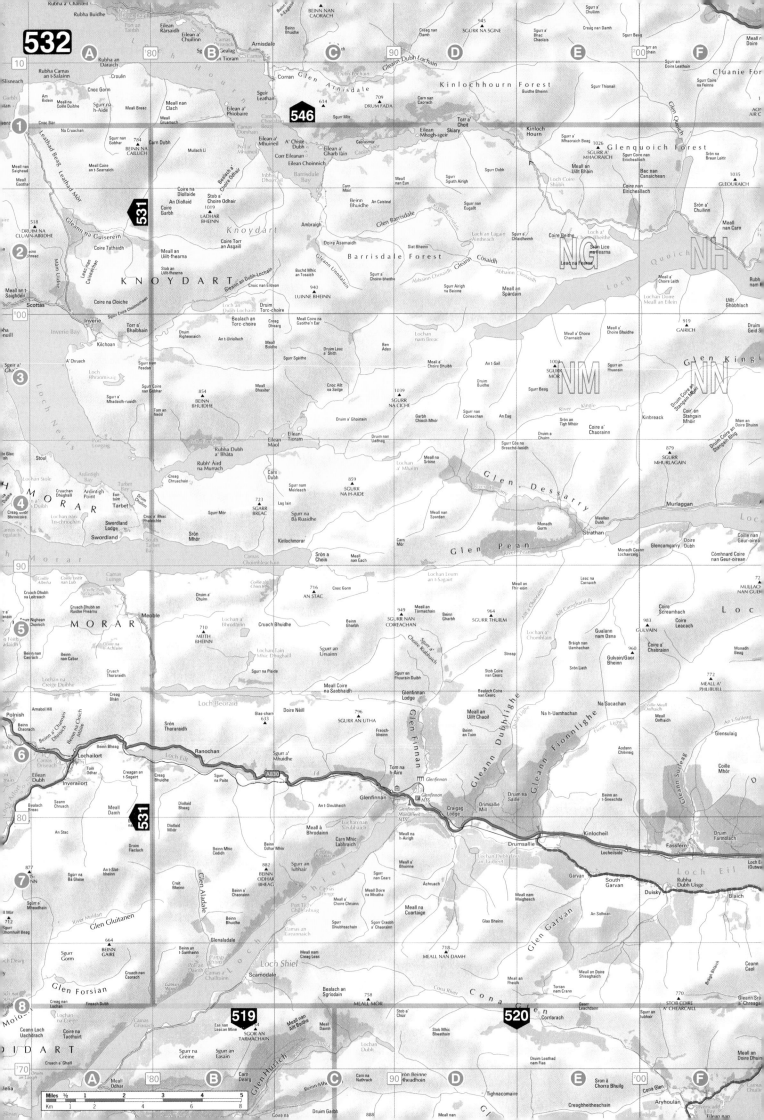

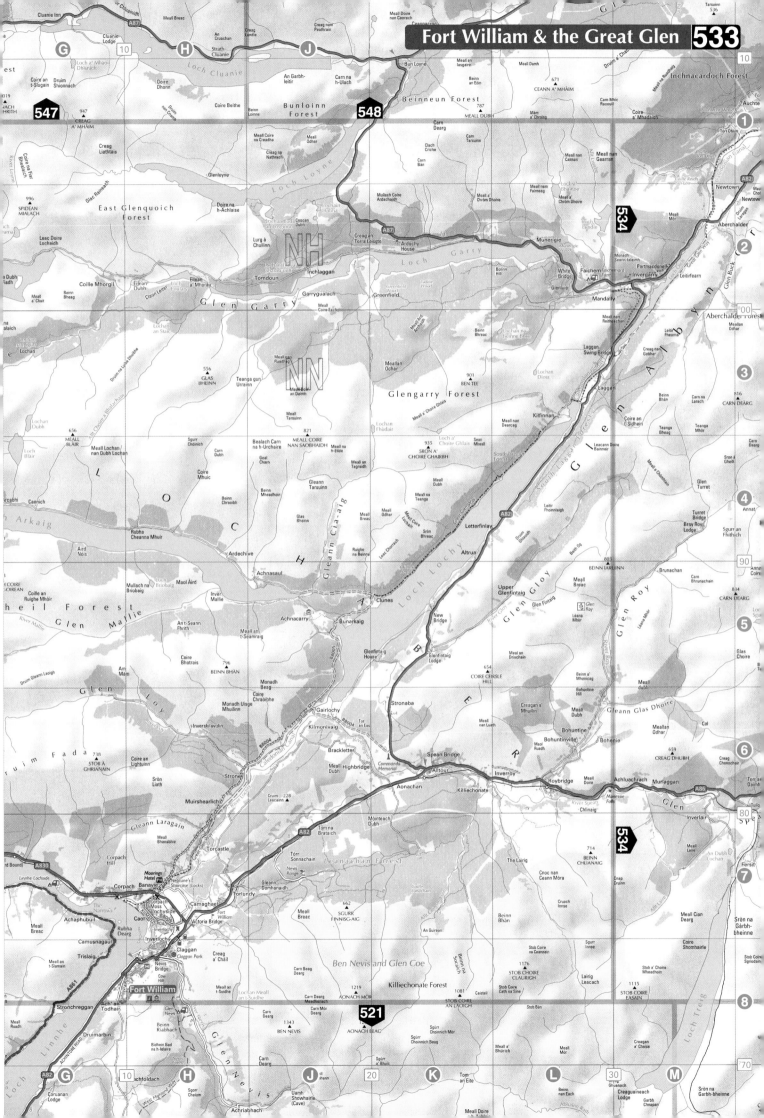

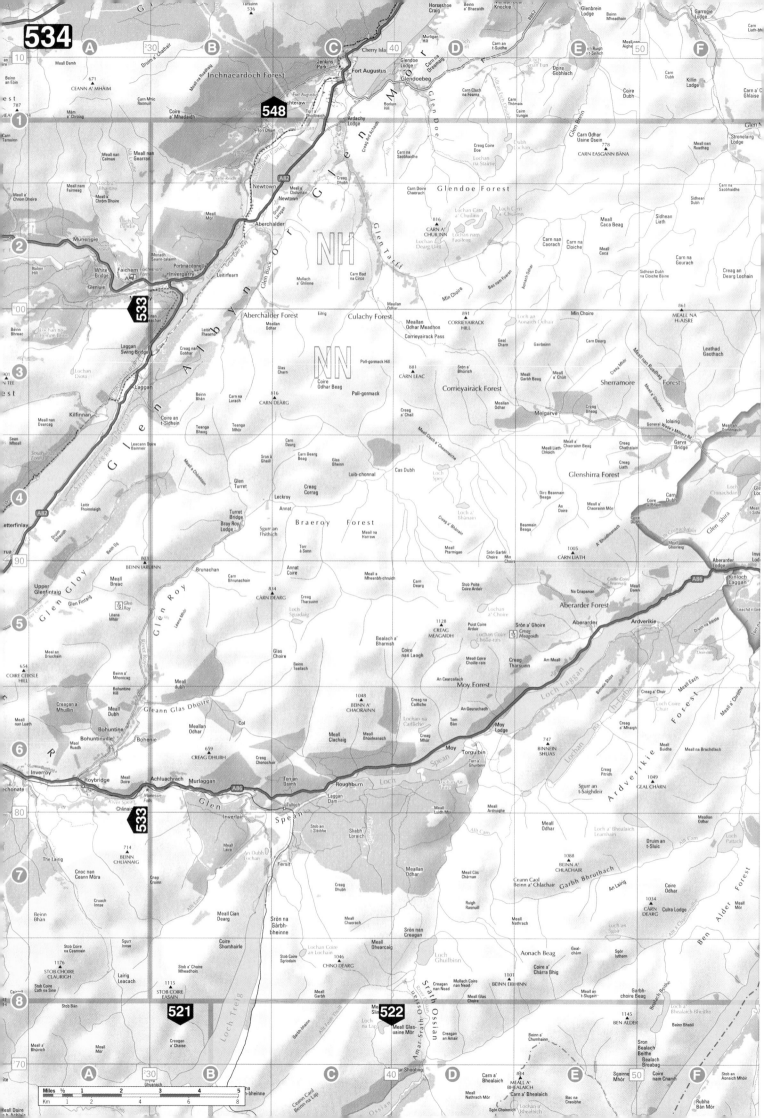

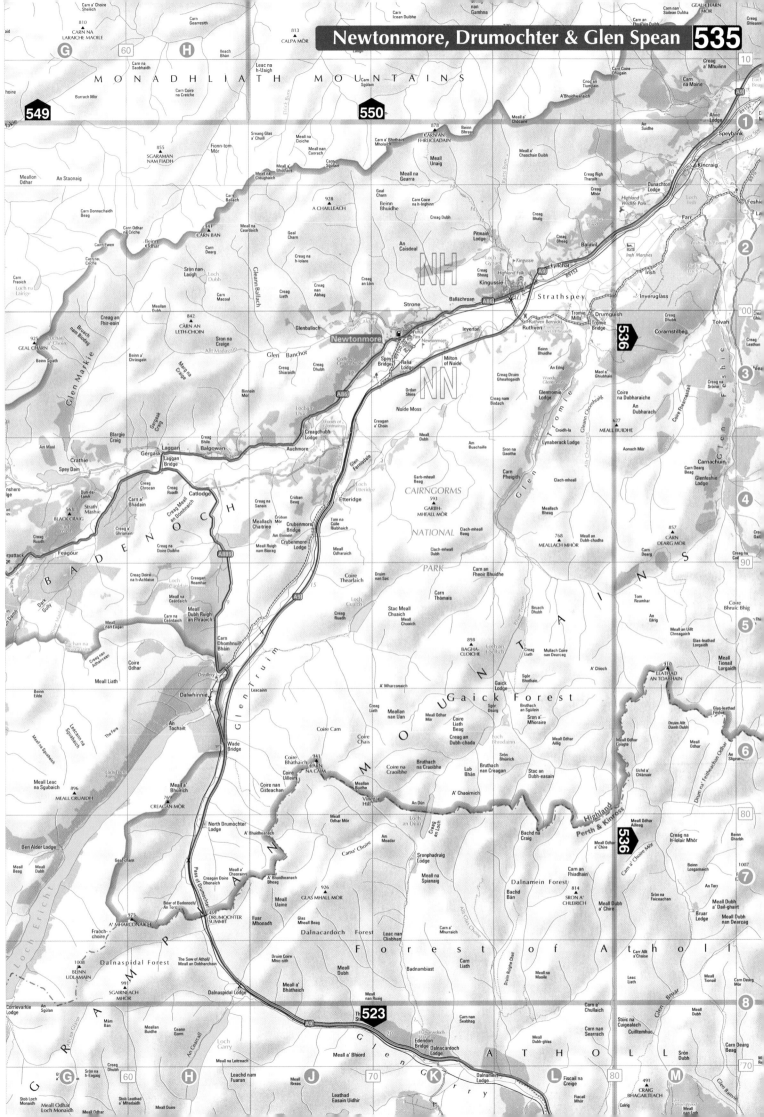

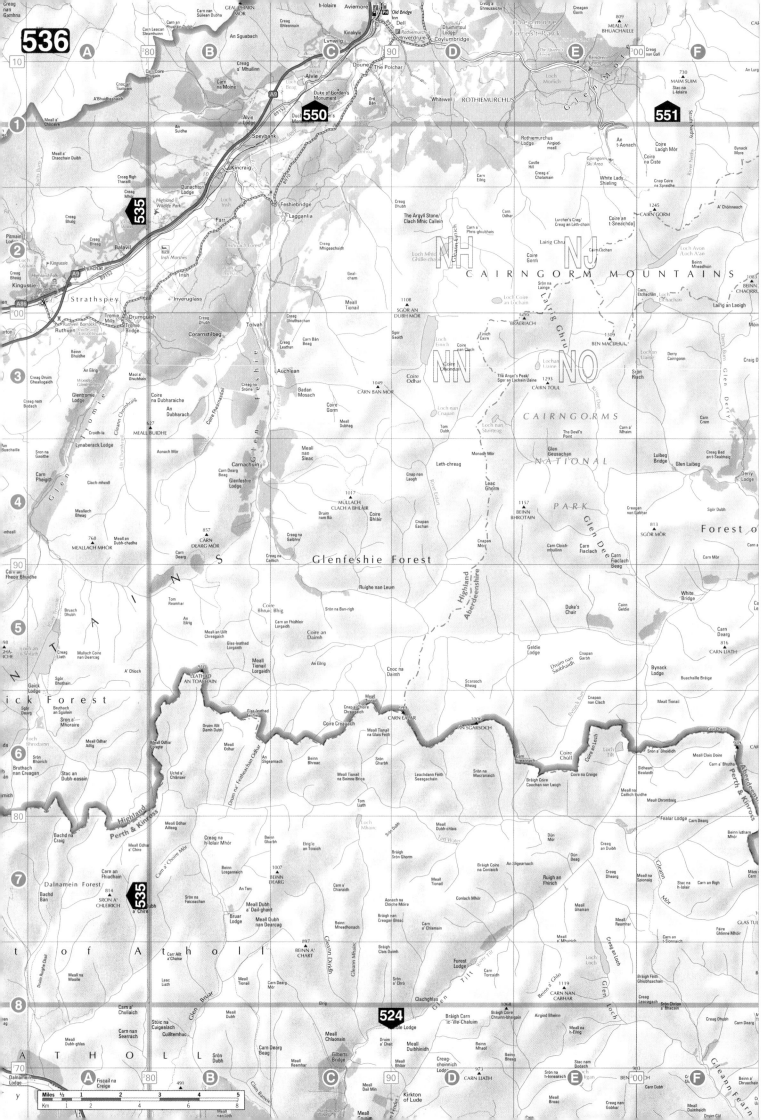

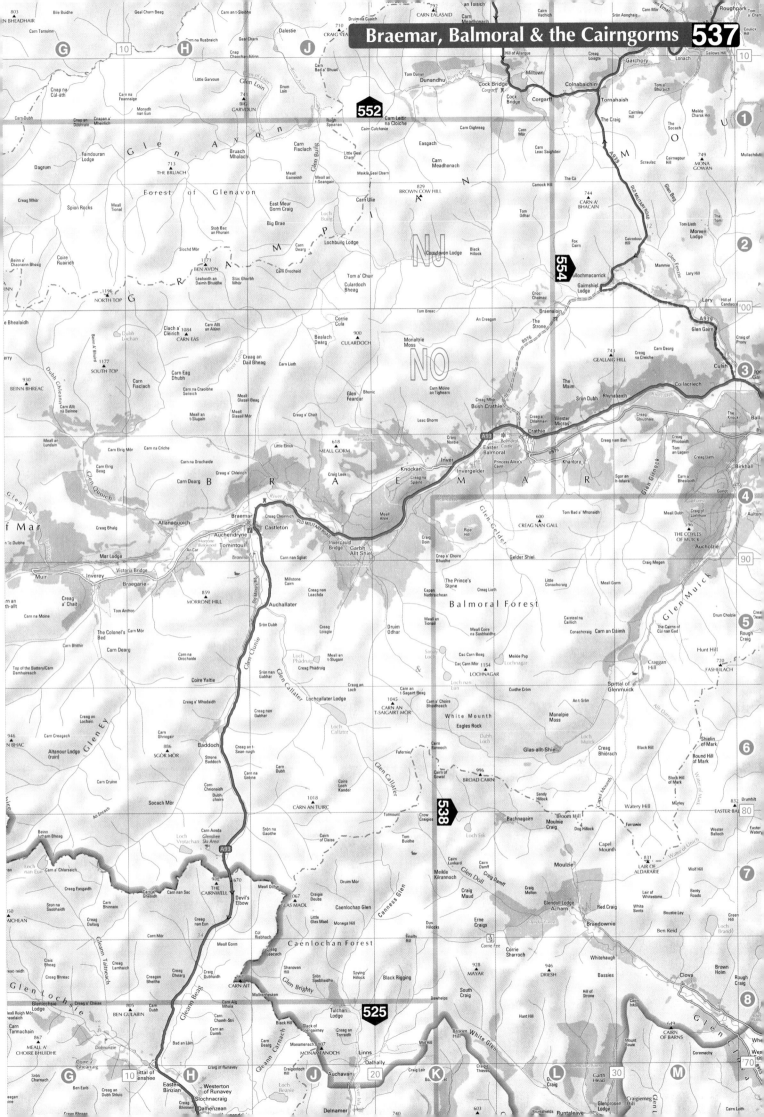

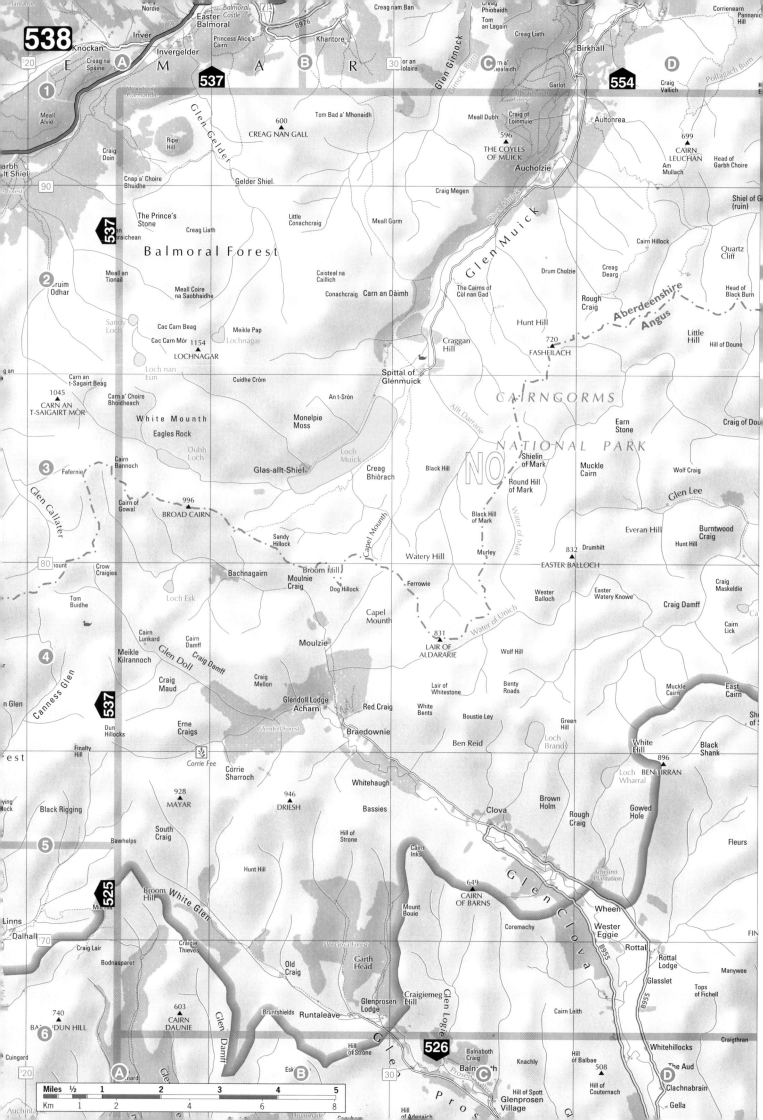

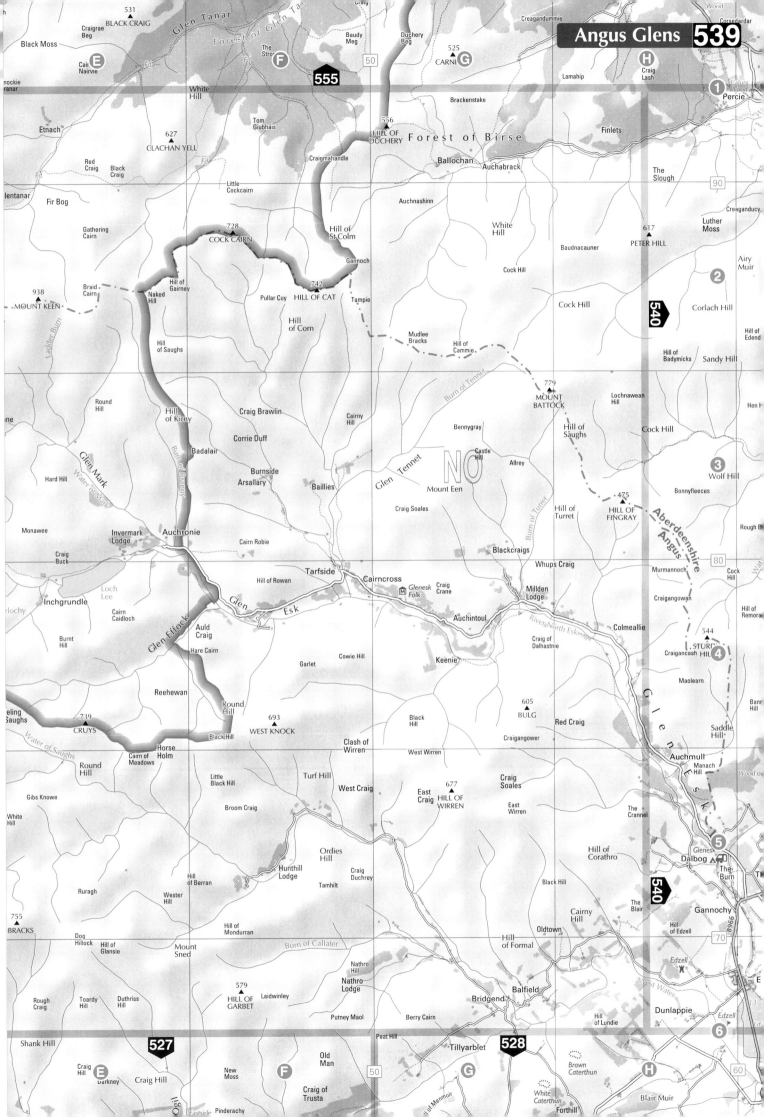

Wood

Corsedardar

Creagandummie

E Cai Nairvie
nockie
ranar

Black Moss

Craigrae Beg

531 **BLACK CRAIG**

Glen Tanar

Forest of Glen Tanar

Craig

Baudy Meg

Duchery Beg

50

525 **CARN** **G**

Lamahip

H Craig Lash

1 Percie

Etnach

The Stro **F**

White Hill

555 **555**

556 **HILL OF DUCHERY**

Forest of Birse

Ballochan

Auchabrack

Brackenstake

Finlets

The Slough

90

627 **CLACHAN YELL**

Craigmahandle

Auchnashinn

White Hill

Baudnacauner

617 **PETER HILL**

Luther Moss

Creaganducy

Red Craig

Black Craig

Little Cockcairn

Hill of St.Colm

Cock Hill

Airy Muir

2

entanar

Fir Bog

Fd

Gathering Cairn

728 **COCK CAIRN**

Gannoch

540 **540**

Corlach Hill

938 **MOUNT KEEN**

Braid Cairn

Naked Hill

Hill of Gairney

Pullar Cuy

742 **HILL OF CAT**

Tampie

Mudlee Bracks

Hill of Cammie

Hill of Badymicks

Sandy Hill

Hill of Edend

Ladder Burn

Hill of Saughs

Hill of Corn

779 **MOUNT BATTOCK**

Lochnawean Hill

Cock Hill

Hen H

Round Hill

Hill of Kirny

Craig Brawlin

Cairny Hill

Bennygray

Hill of Saughs

Cock Hill

3 Wolf Hill

Hard Hill

Burn of Branny

Badalair

Corrie Duff

Castle Hill

Allrey

Bonnyfleeces

475 **HILL OF FINGRAY**

Rough Br

Glen Mark

Water of Mark

Monawee

Burnside
Arsallary

Baillies

Glen Tennet

NO
Mount Een

Craig Soales

Hill of Turret

Burn of Turret

80

Murmannoch

Craigangowan

Cock Hill

Hill of Remora

Craig Buck

Invermark Lodge

Auchronie

Cairn Robie

Tarfside

Hill of Rowan

Cairncross

Glenesk Folk **M**

Craig Crane

Blackcraigs

Whups Craig

Millden Lodge

Auchintoul

River North Esk

Colmeallie

Craigangowan

544 **STURF HILL**

Loch Lee

Inchgrundle

Cairn Caidloch

Glen Effock

Auld Craig

Hare Cairn

Glen Esk

Cowie Hill

Garlet

Keenie

Craig of Dalhastnie

Craigancash

4

rlochy

Burnt Hill

Reehewan

605 **BULG**

Black Hill

Red Craig

Maolearn

Banr Hill

eling Saughs

739 **CRUYS**

Round Hill

Horse Holm

Black Hill

693 **WEST KNOCK**

Clash of Wirren

West Wirren

Craigangower

Saddle Hill

Auchmull

Manach Hill

Water of Saughs

Cairn of Meadows

Little Black Hill

Turf Hill

West Craig

East Craig

677 **HILL OF WIRREN**

Craig Soales

East Wirren

The Crannel

Glen Esk

Gibs Knowe

White Hill

Round Hill

Broom Craig

Ordies Hill

Hunthill Lodge

Craig Duchrey

Tamhilt

Hill of Corathro

Black Hill

5 Dalbog

Glenesk

The Burn

Ruragh

Hill of Berran

Wester Hill

755 **BRACKS**

Dog Hillock

Hill of Glansie

Mount Sned

Hill of Mondurran

Burn of Callater

Laidwinley

579 **HILL OF GARBET**

Nathro Hill

Nathro Lodge

Hill of Formal

Oldtown

Cairny Hill

The Blair

540 **540**

Hill of Edzell

Gannochy

Edzell

70

Rough Craig

Toardy Hill

Duthriss Hill

Putney Maol

Berry Cairn

Bridgend

Balfield

Balbog

Hill of Lundie

West Water

Dunlappie

Edzell

6

60

Shank Hill

Peat Hill

Tillyarblet

528 **528**

Brown Caterthun

H

Craig Hill

Darkney

Craig Hill

New Moss

Old Man

Craig of Trusta

527 **527** **E**

Pinderachy

50

F

Craig of Menmuir

G

White Caterthun

Forthill

Blair Muir

H

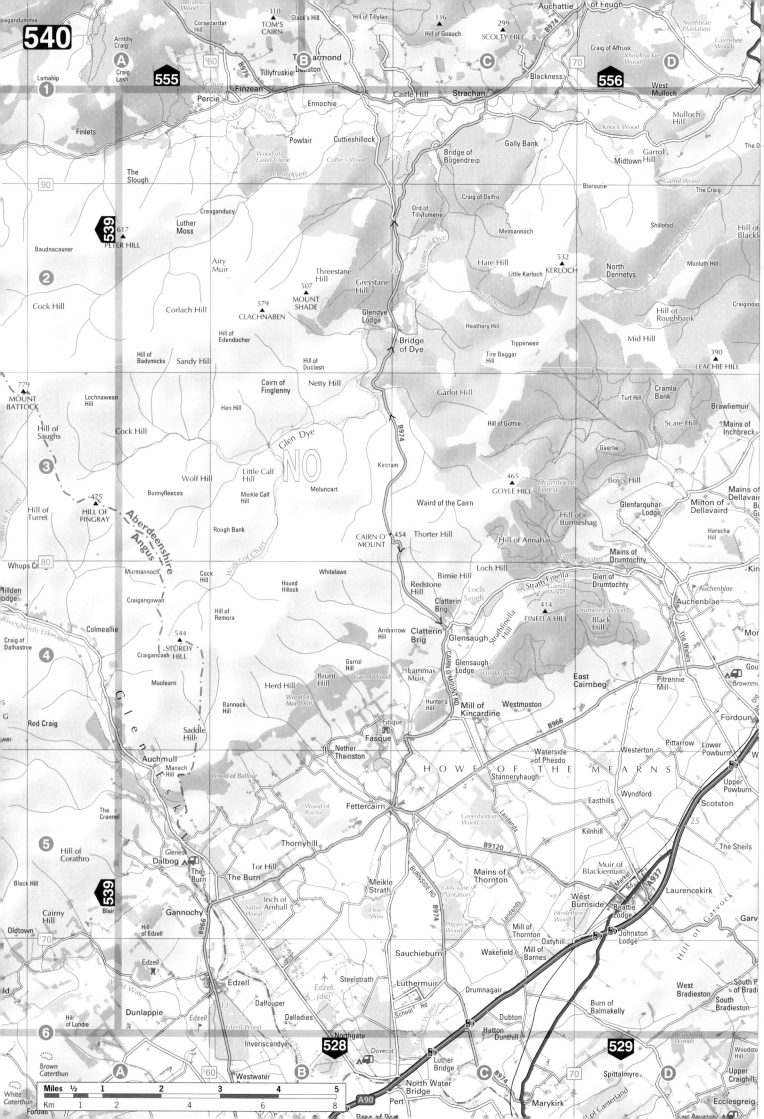

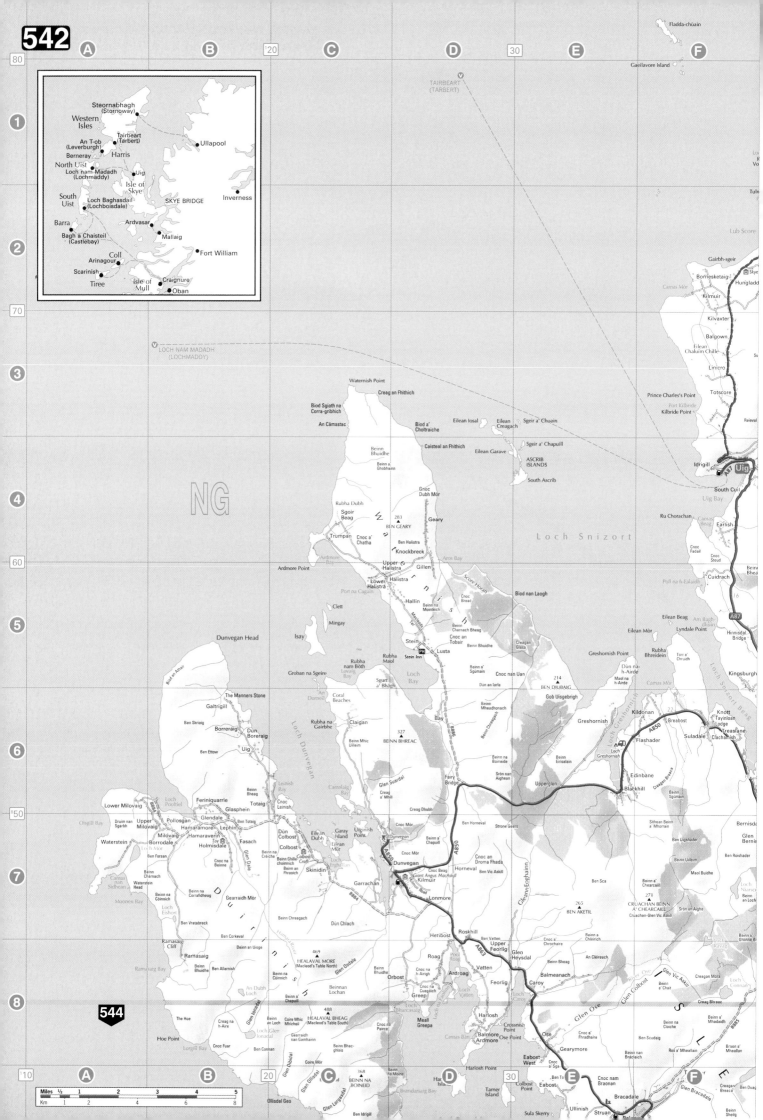

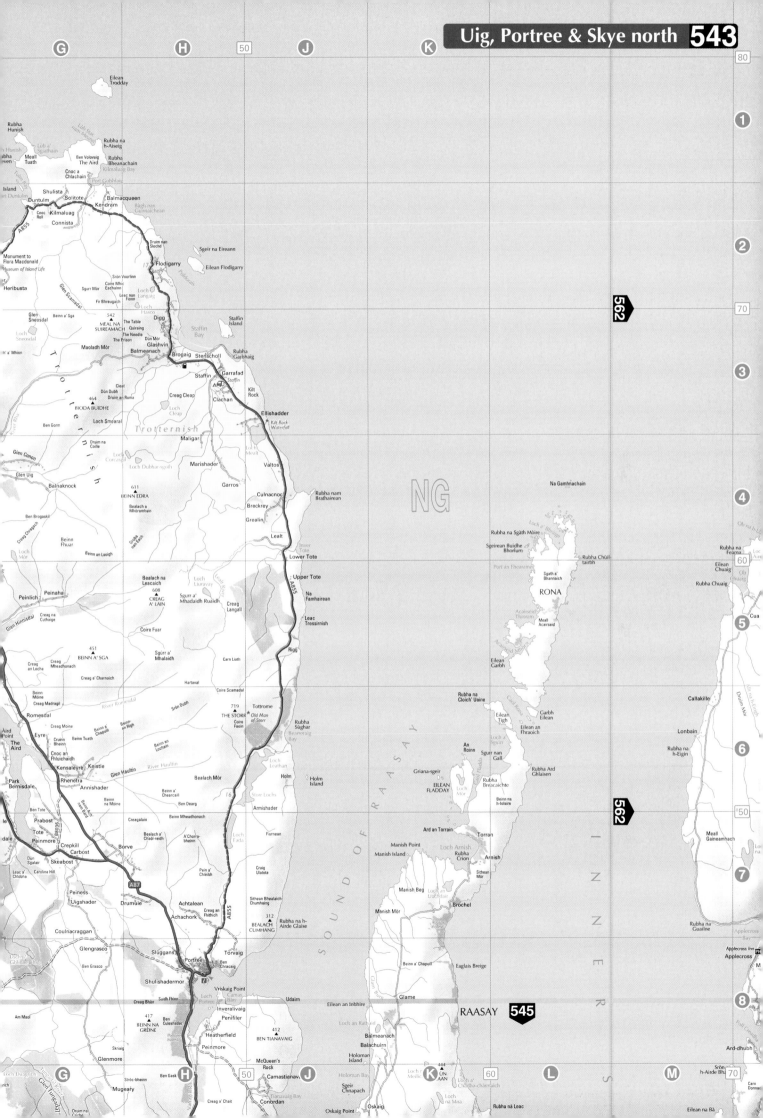

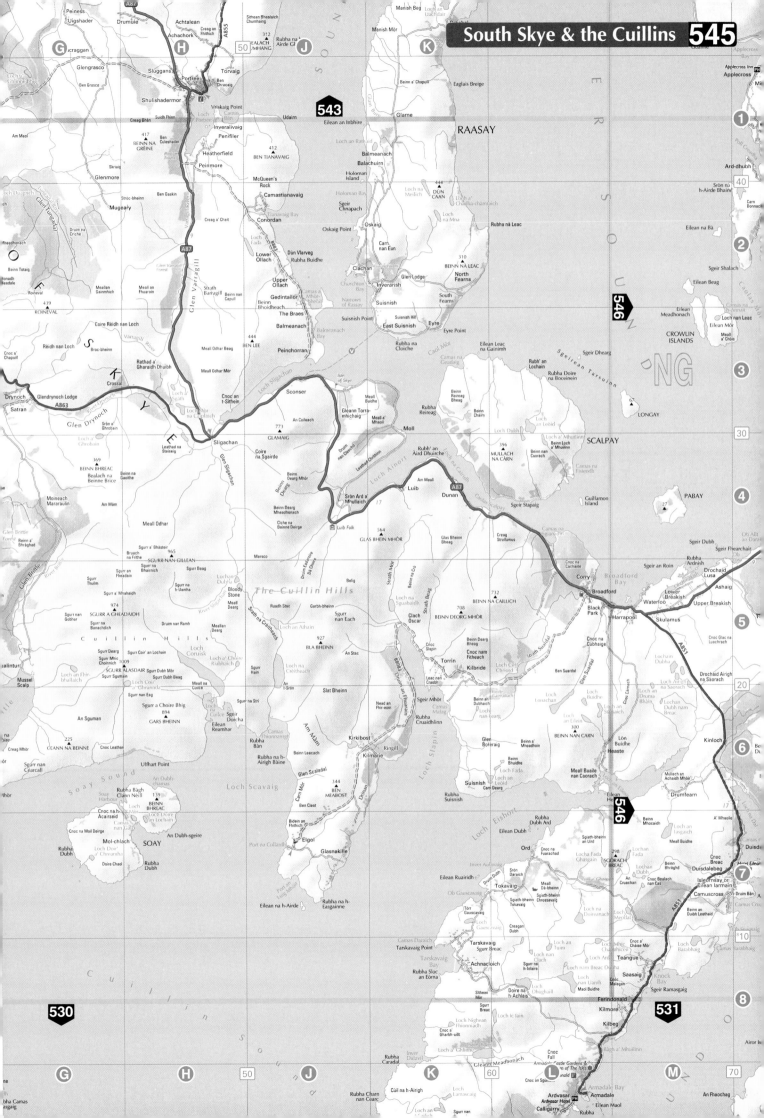

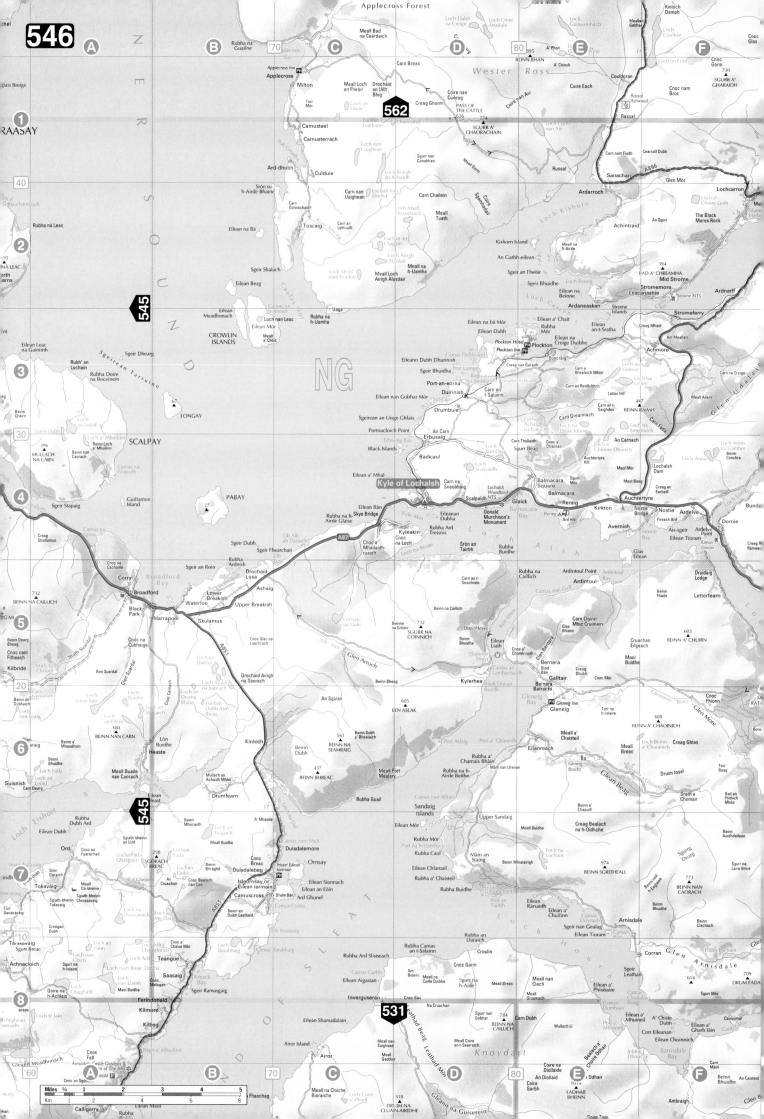

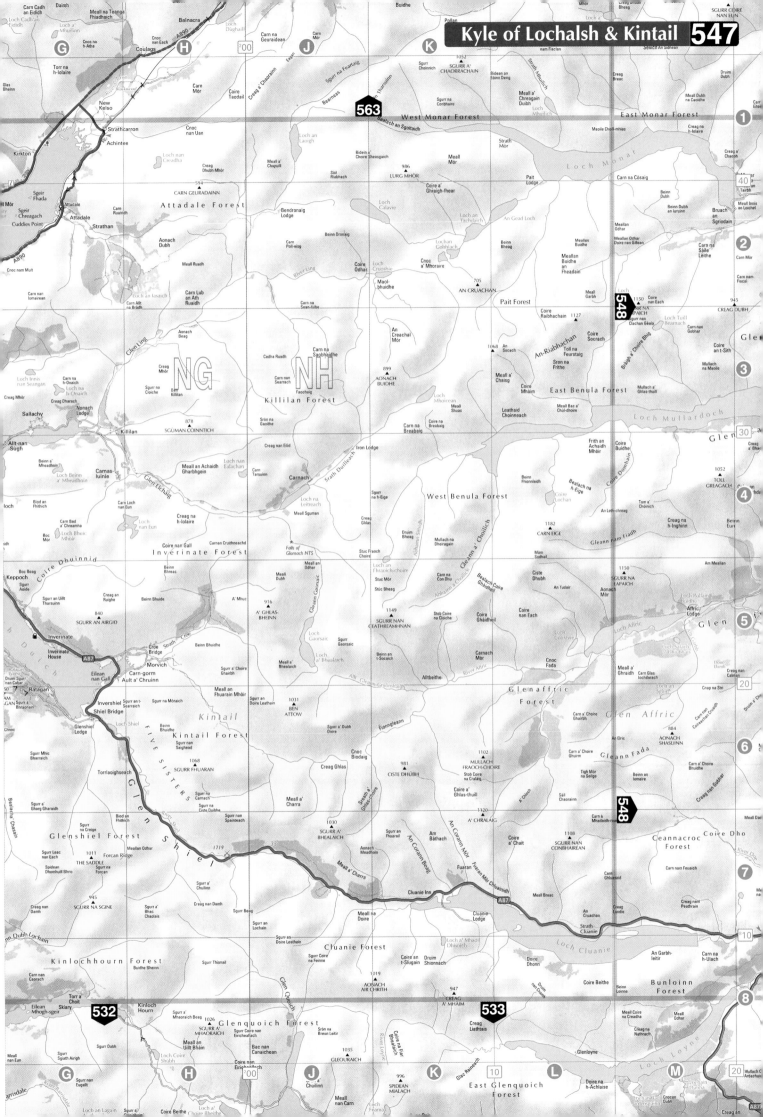

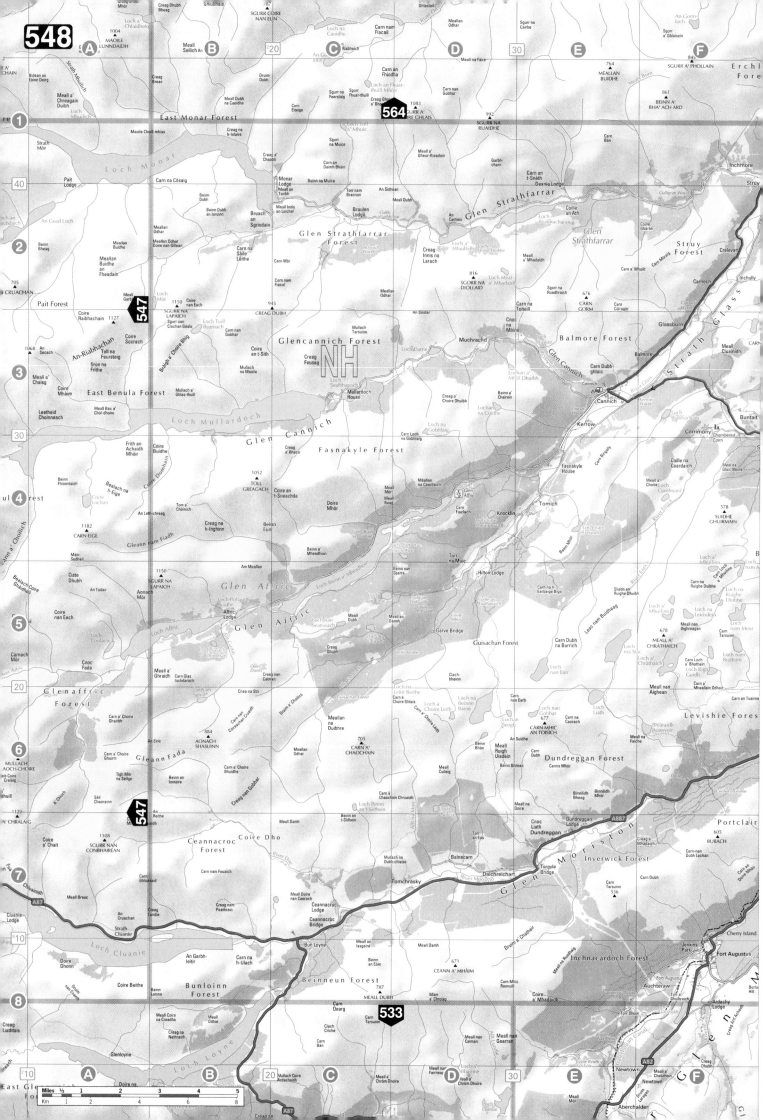

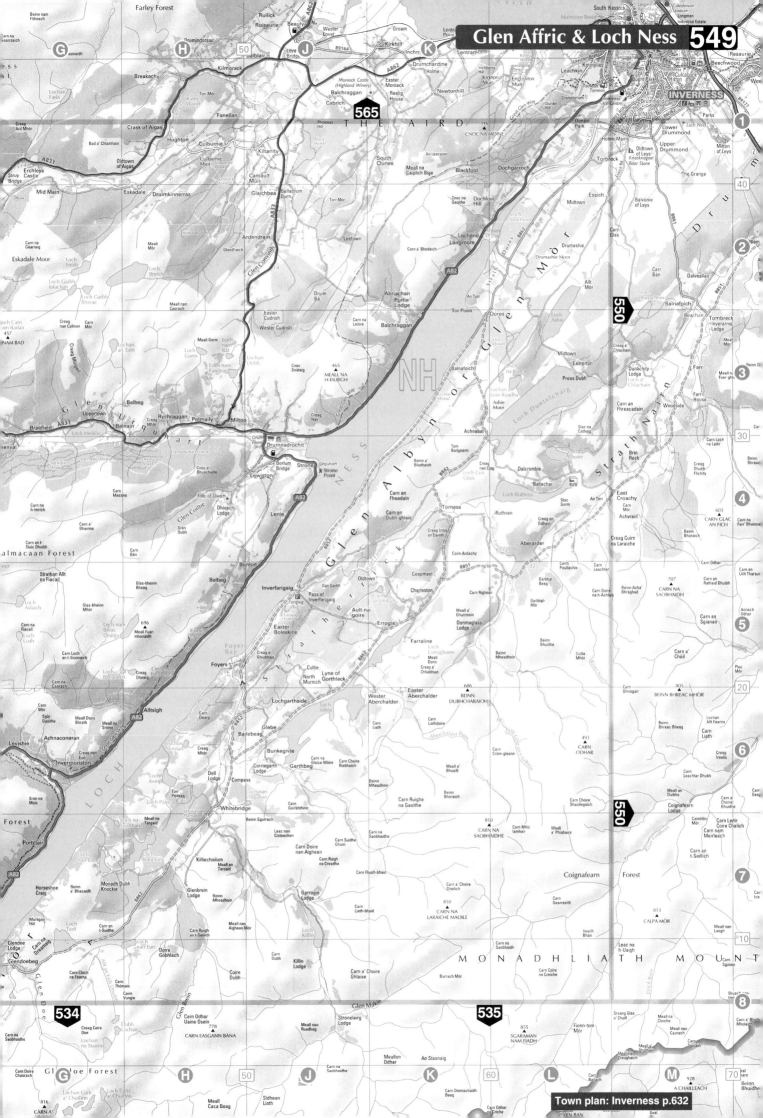

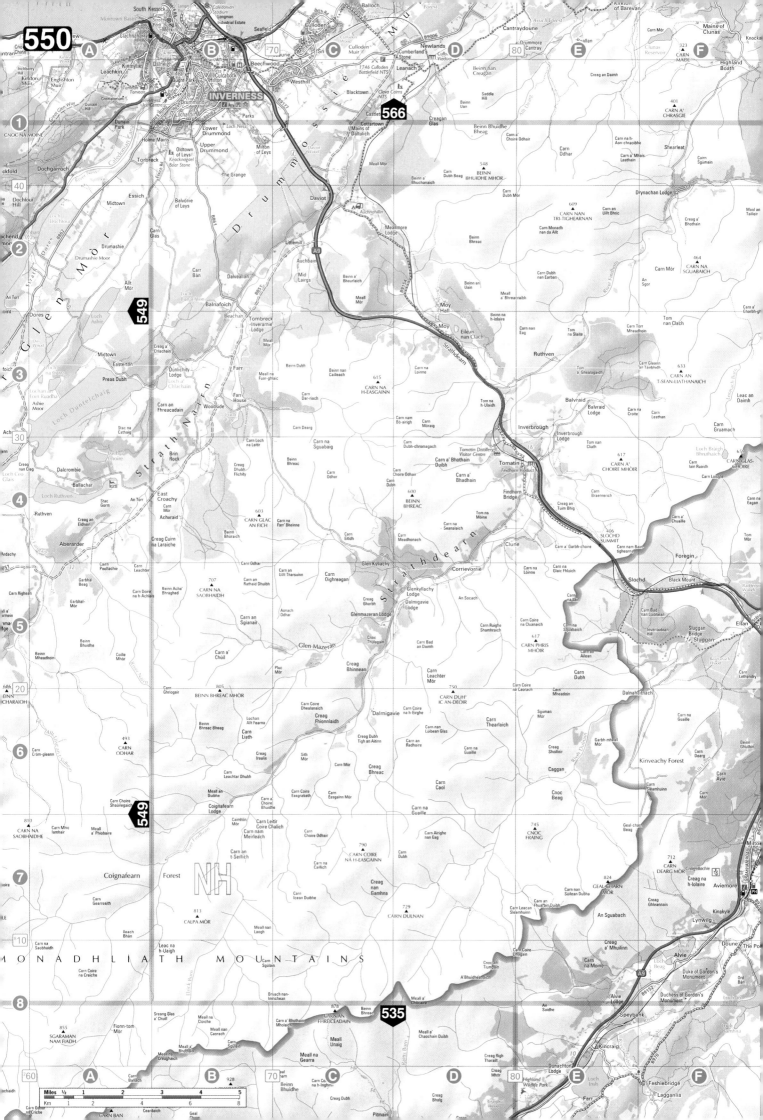

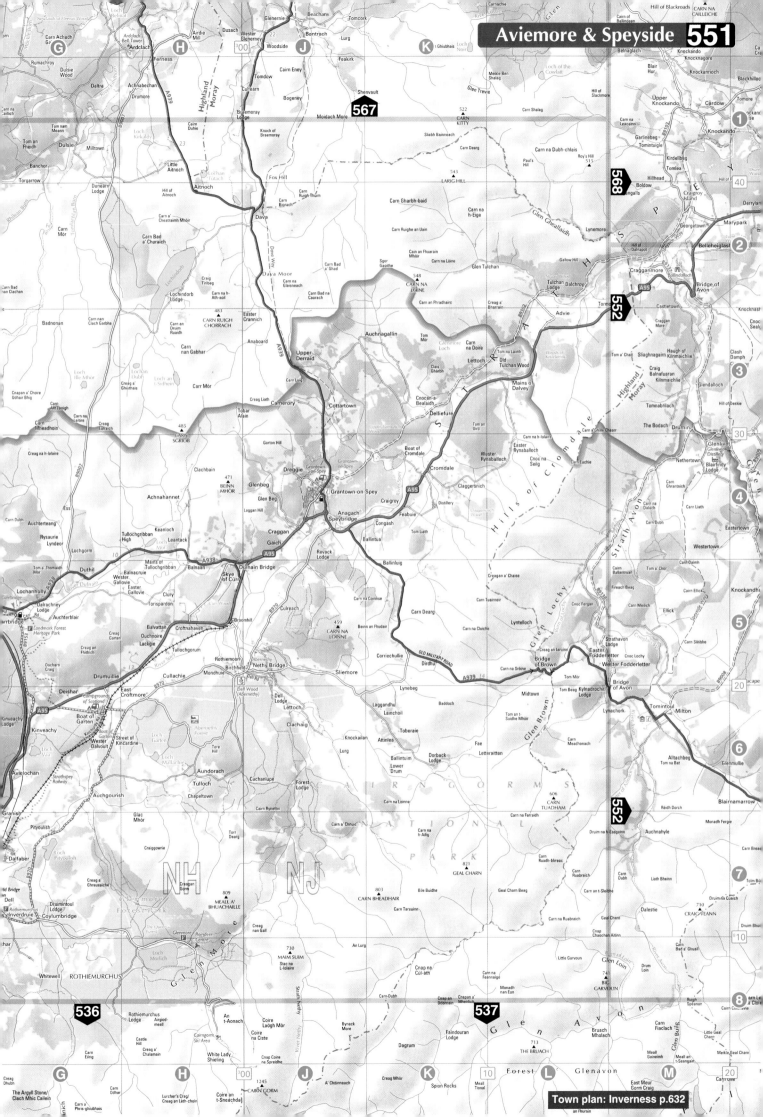

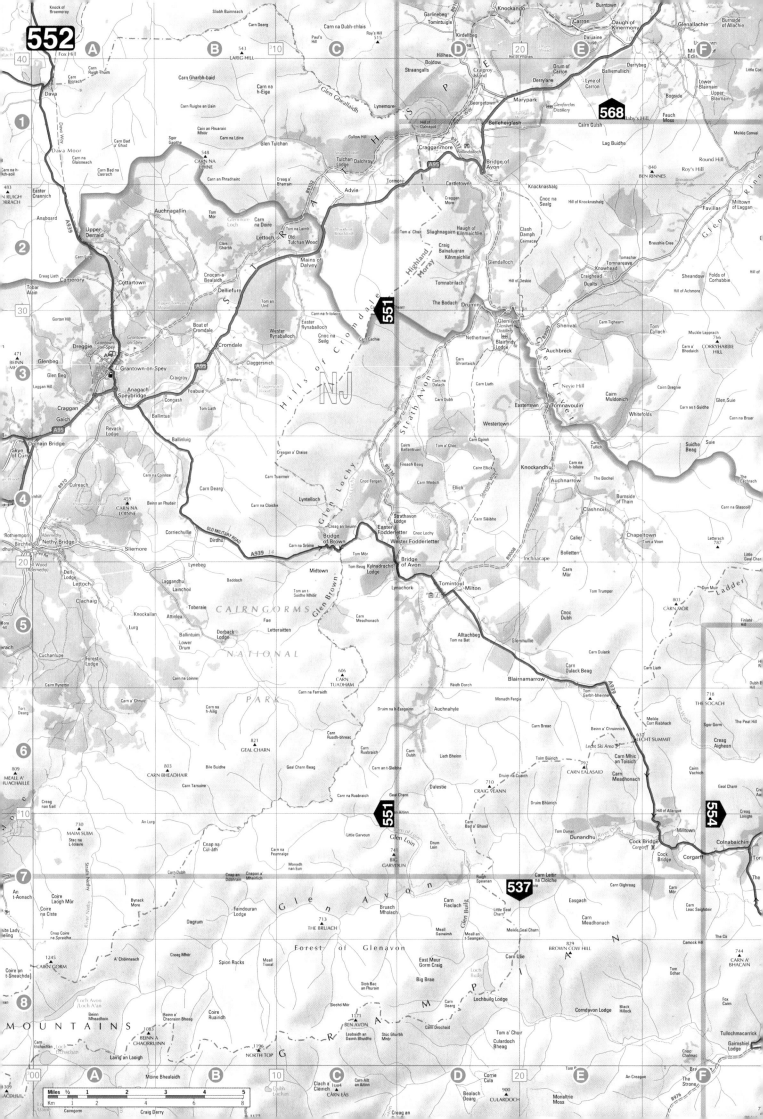

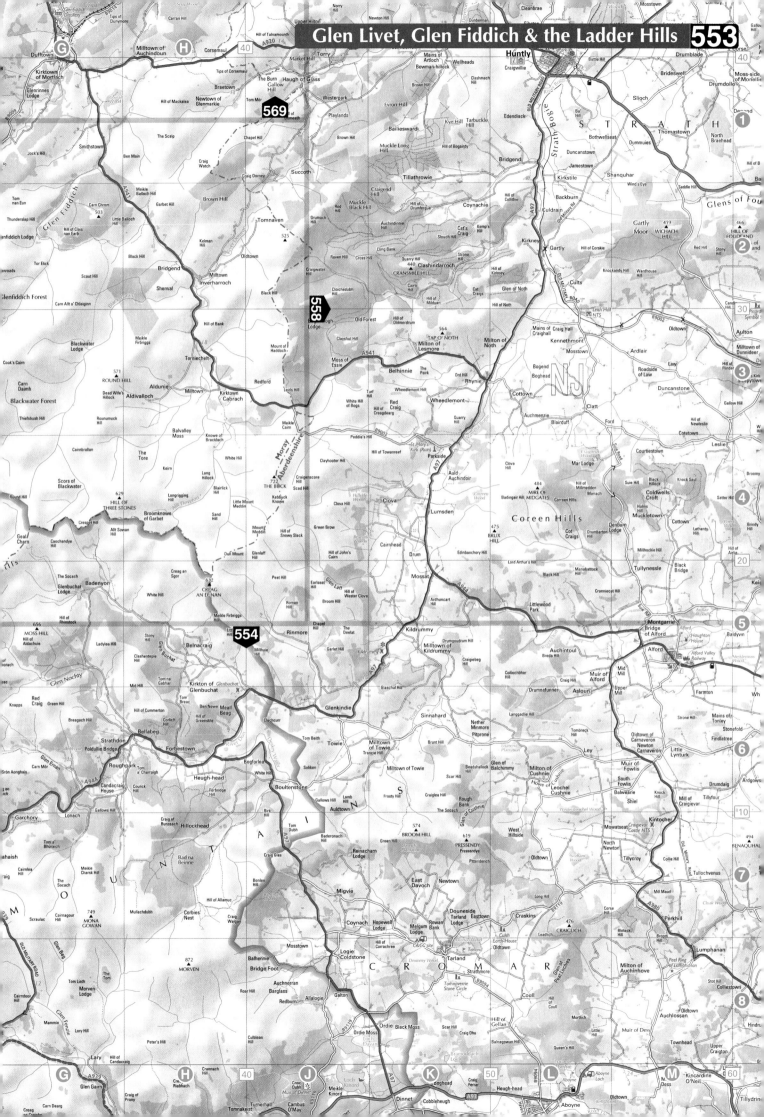

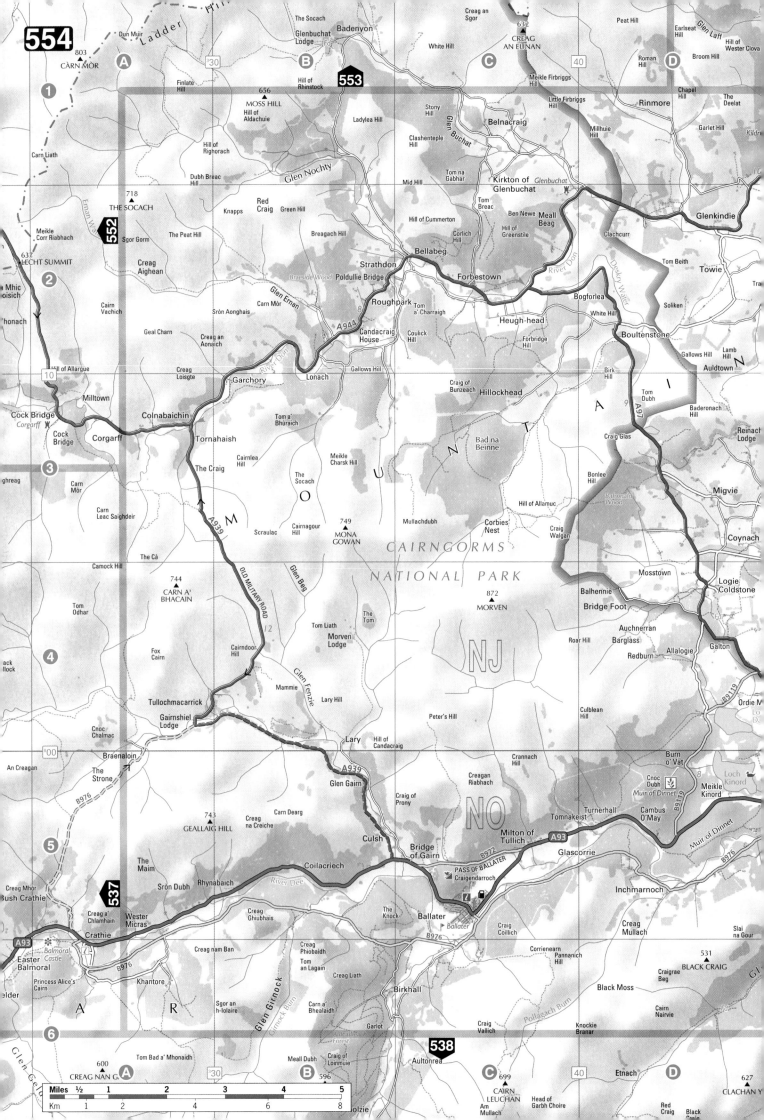

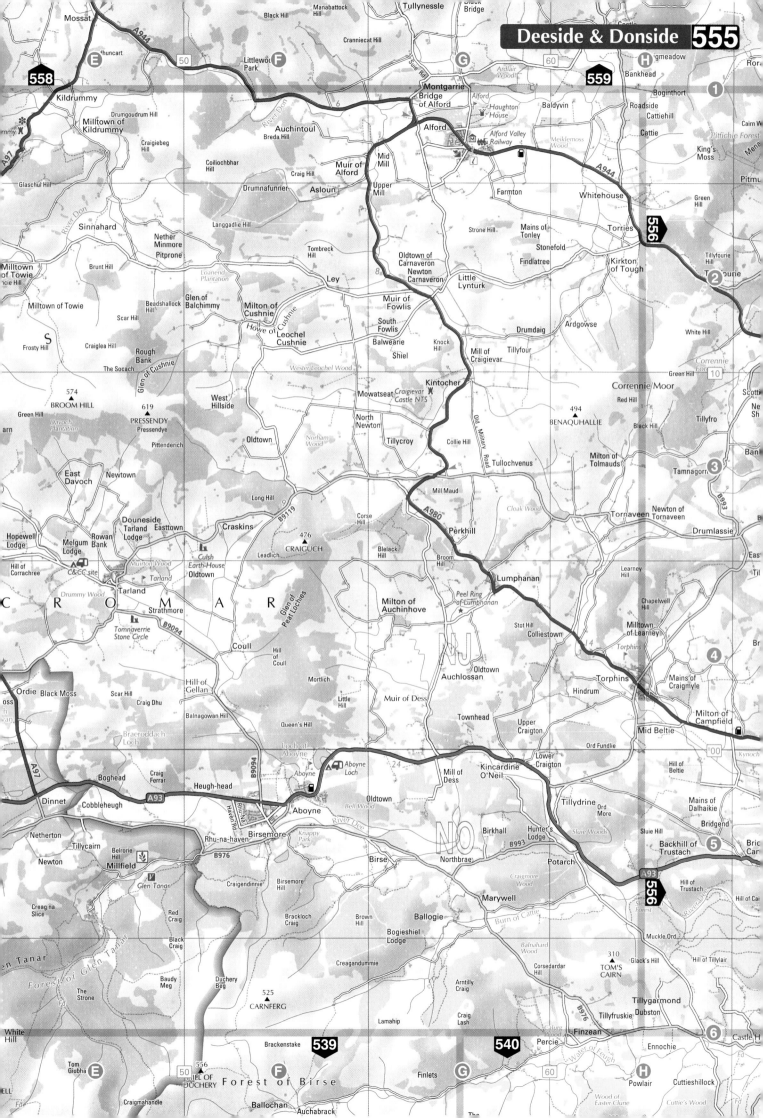

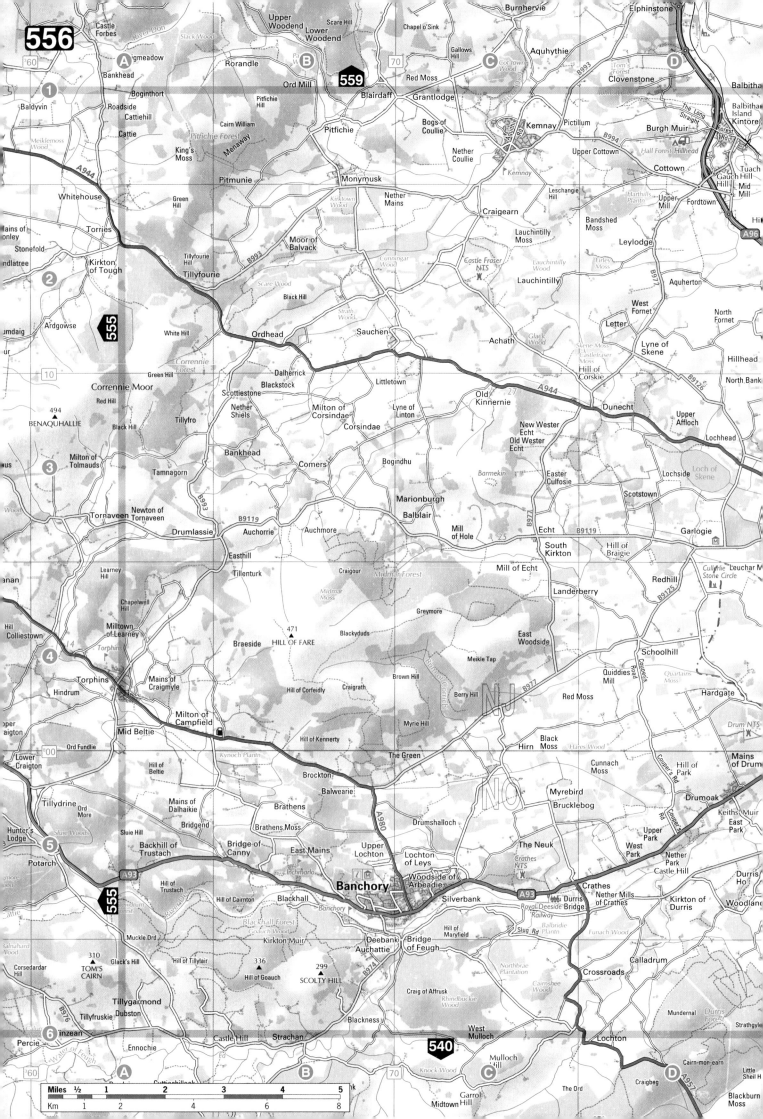

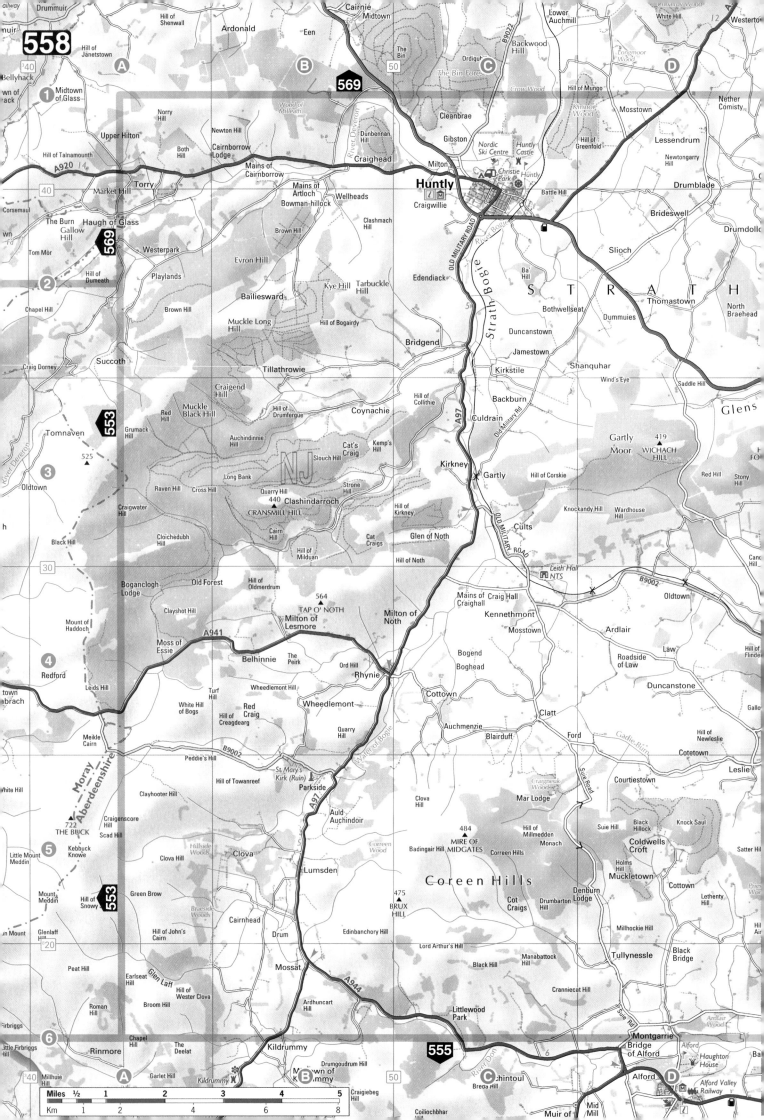

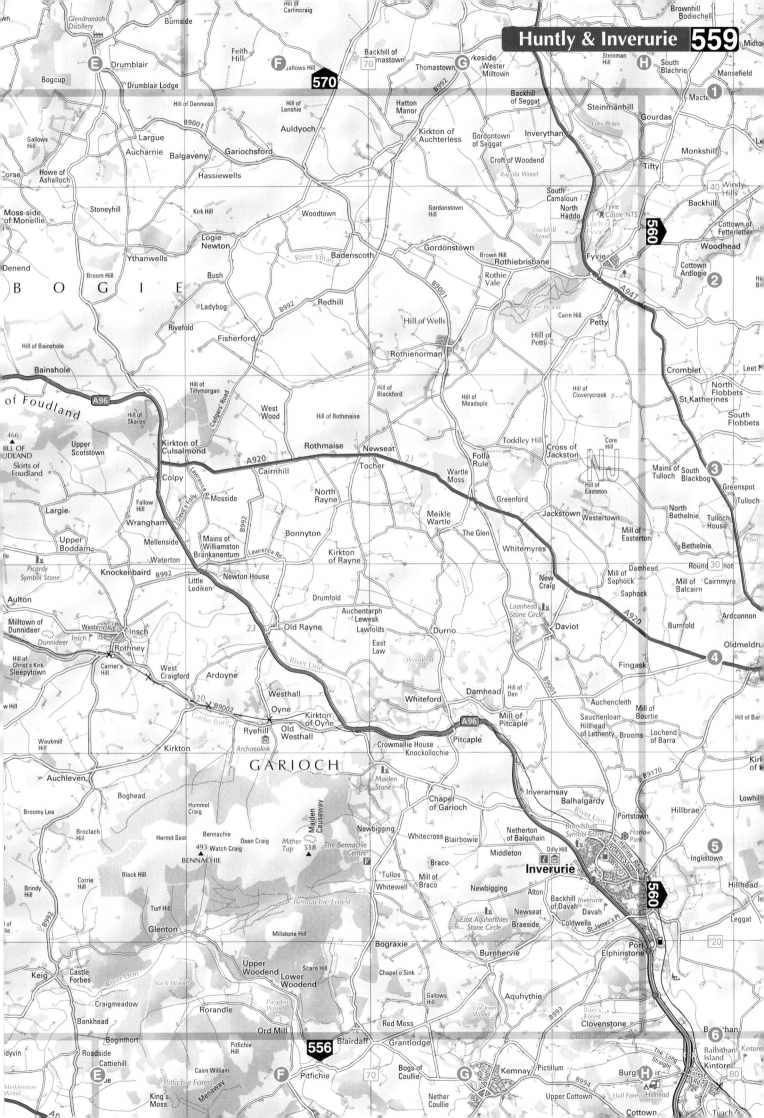

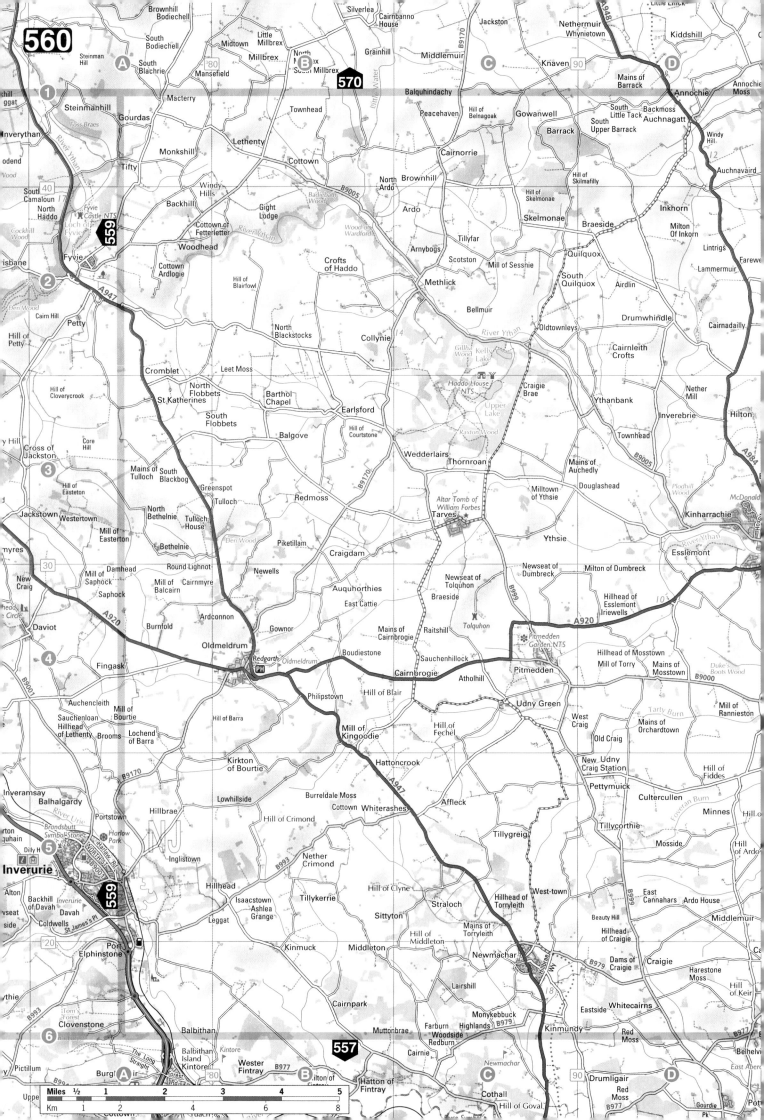

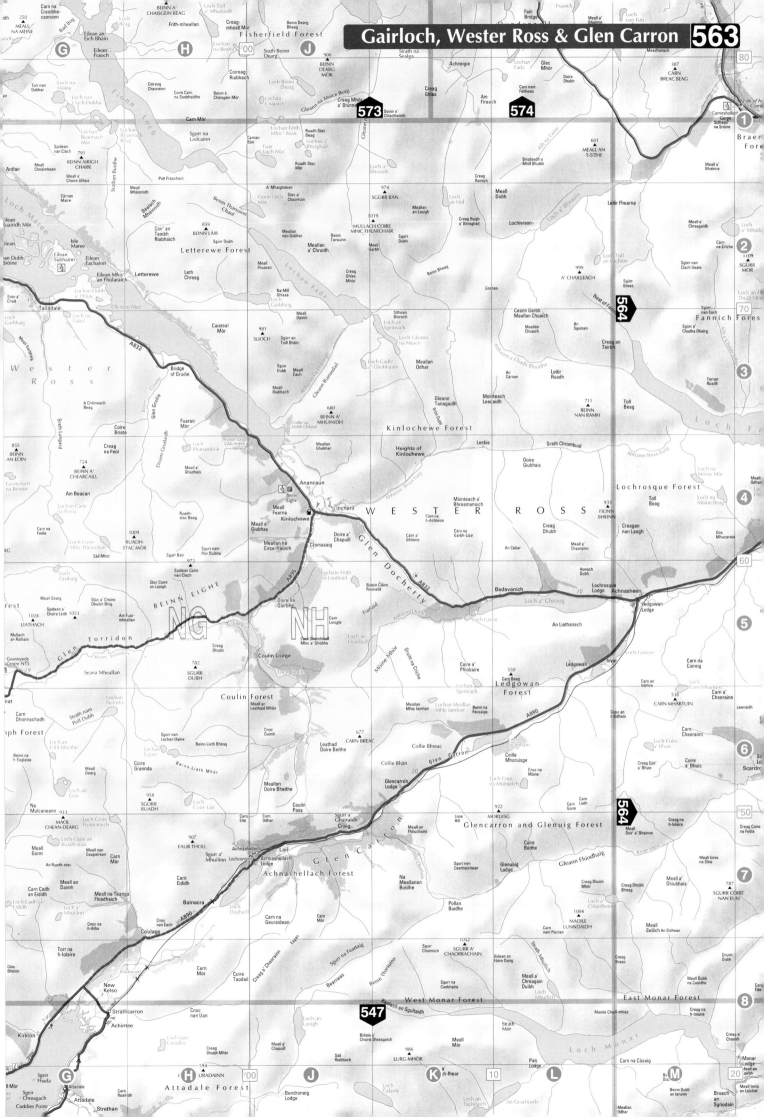

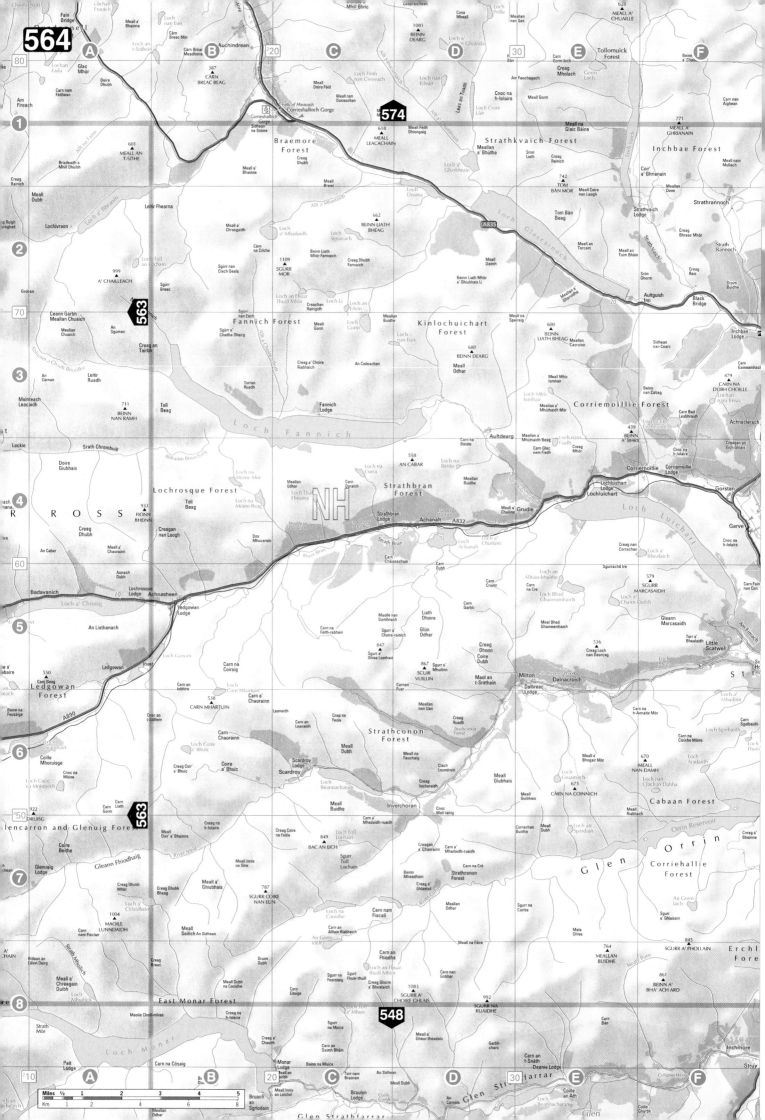

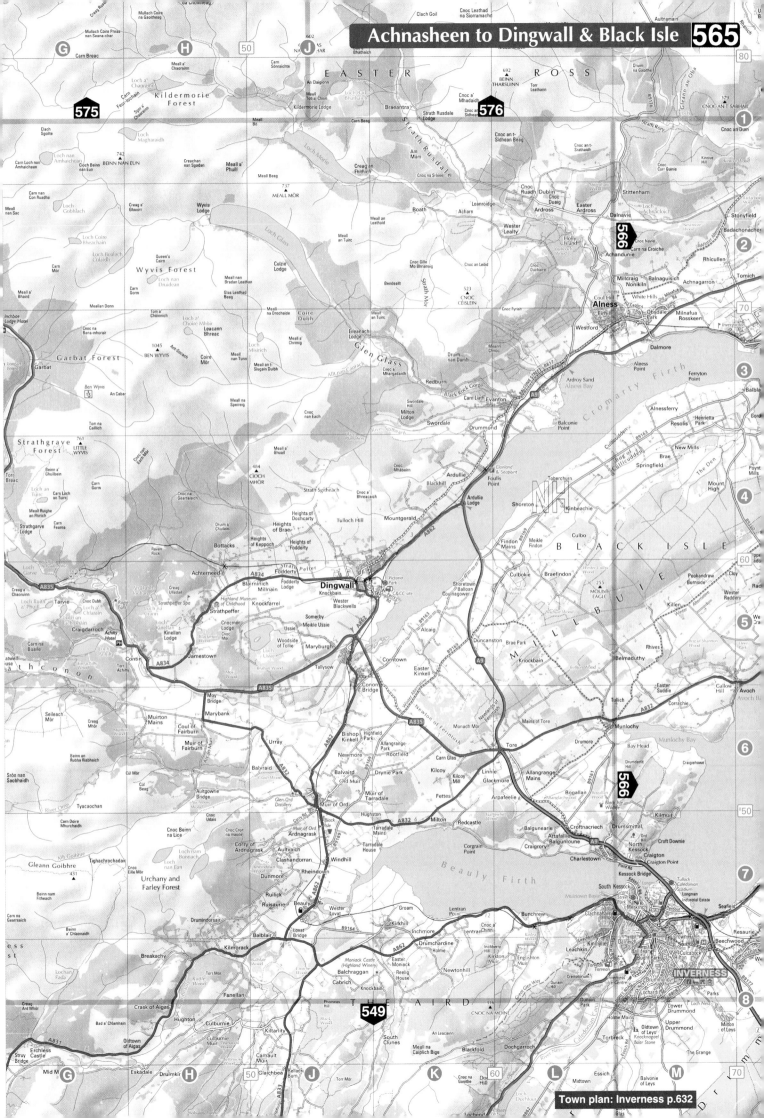

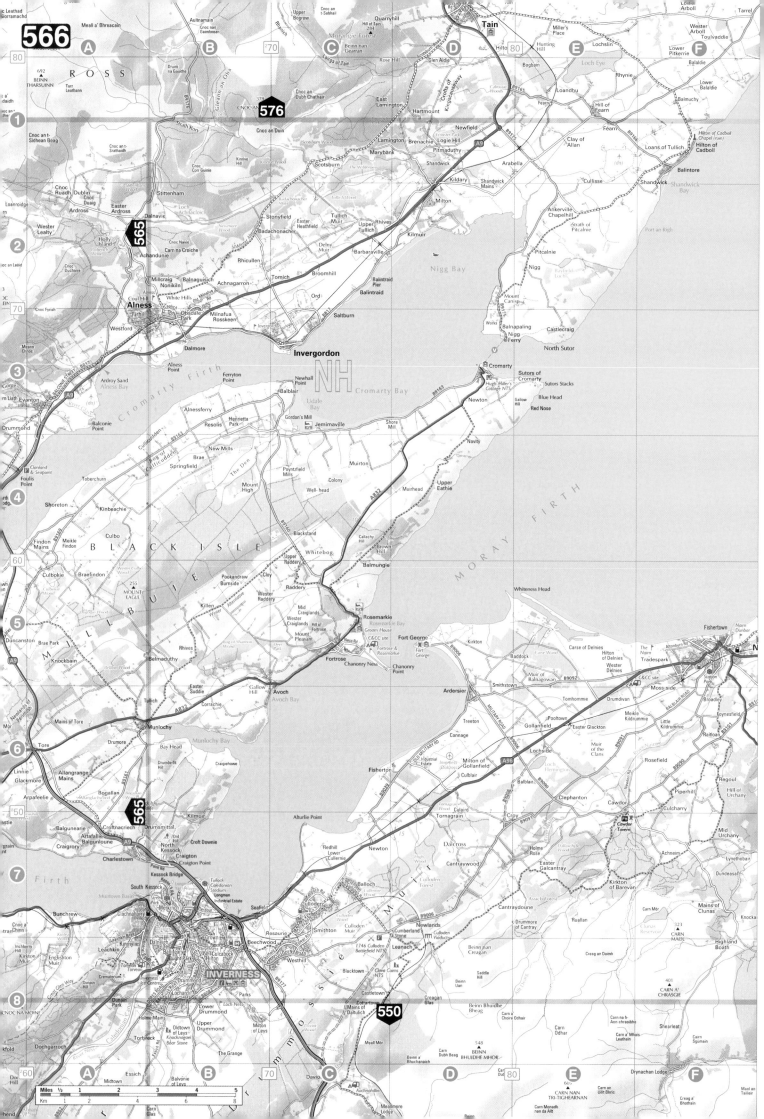

577

568

568

551

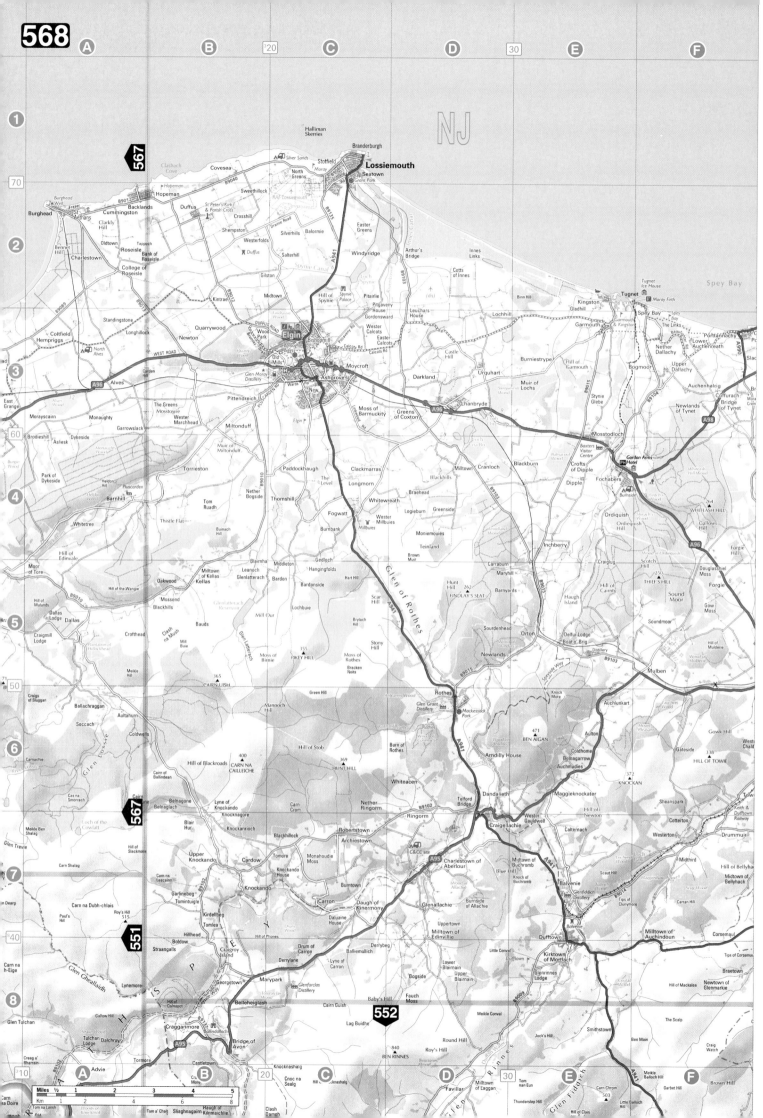

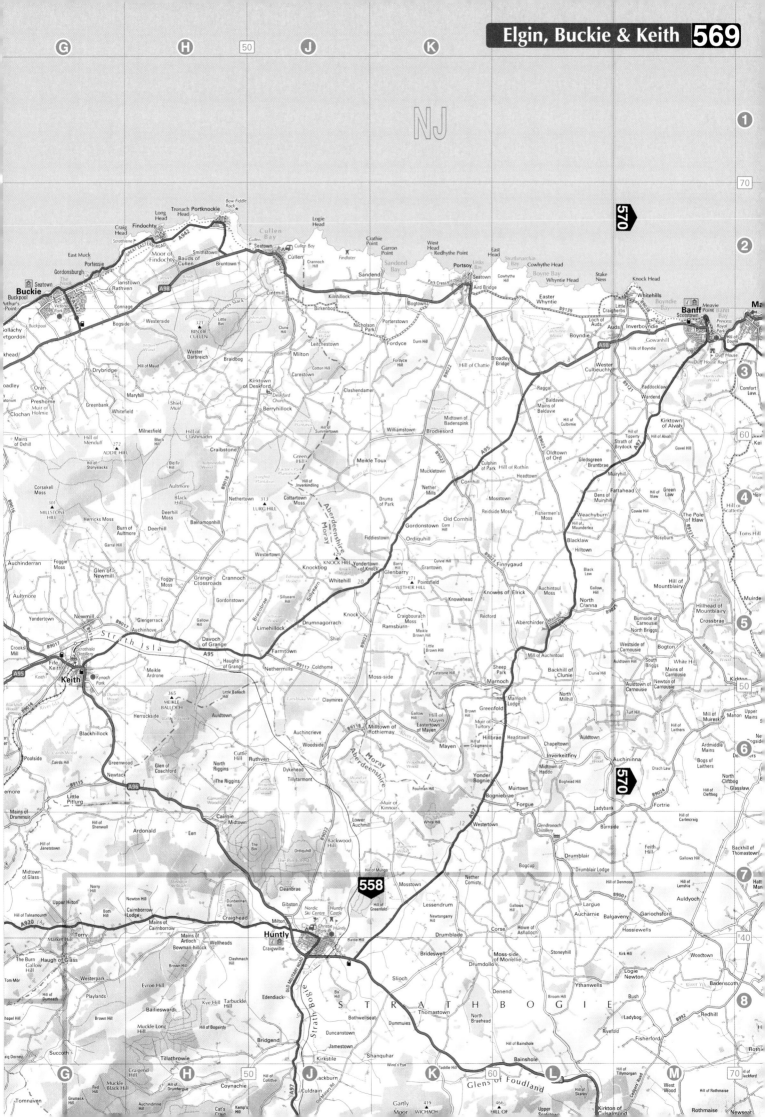

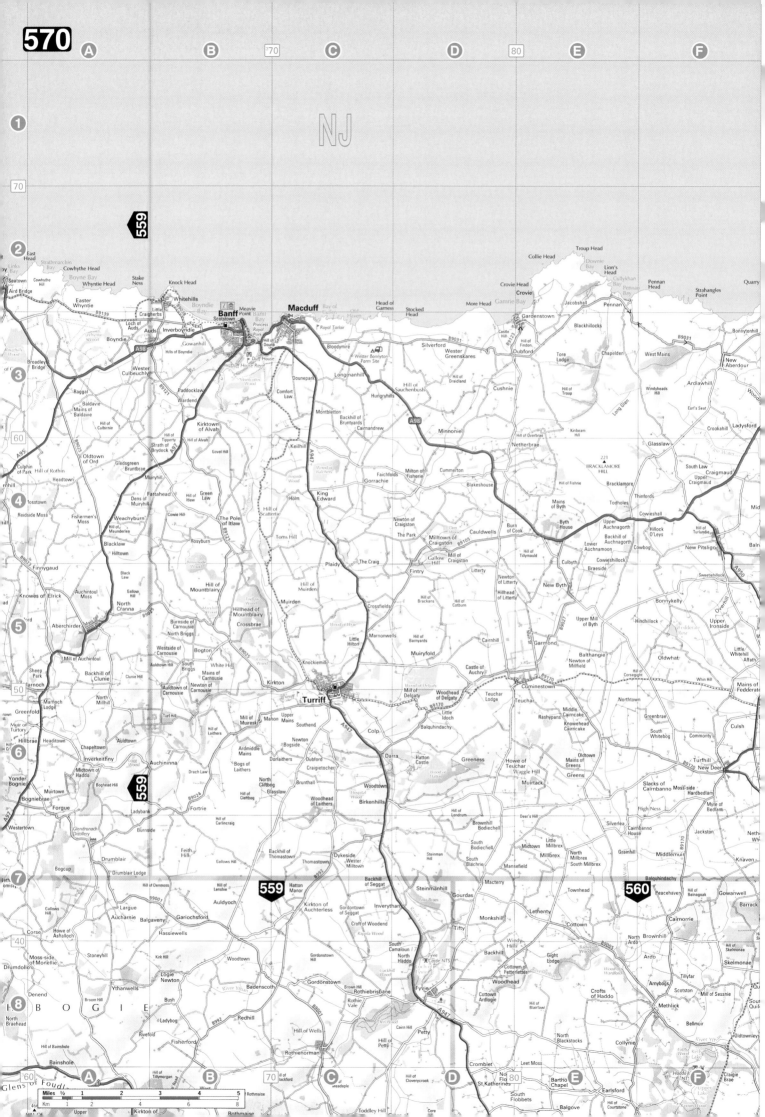

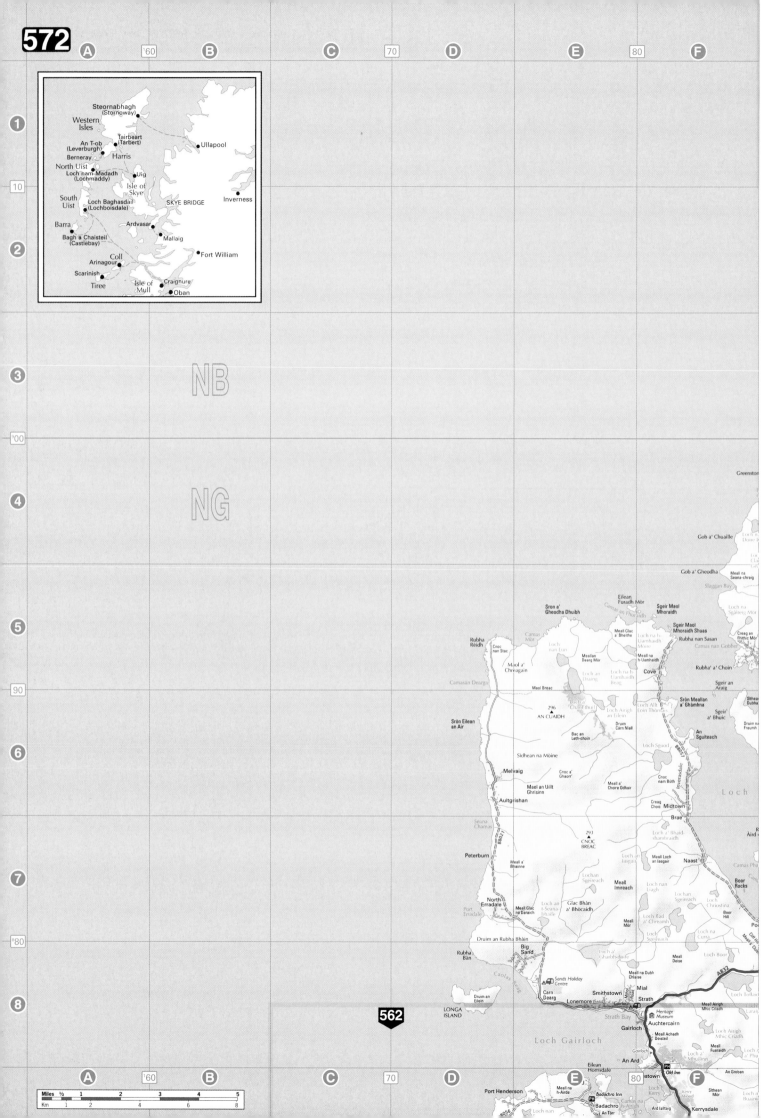

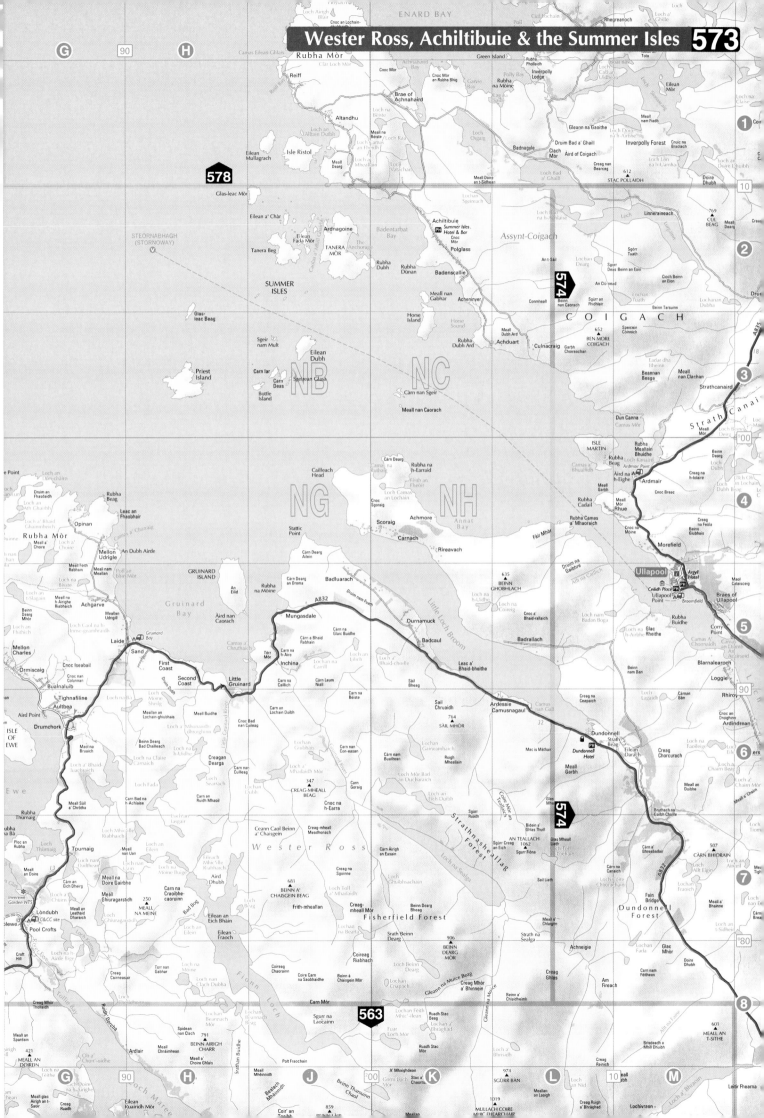

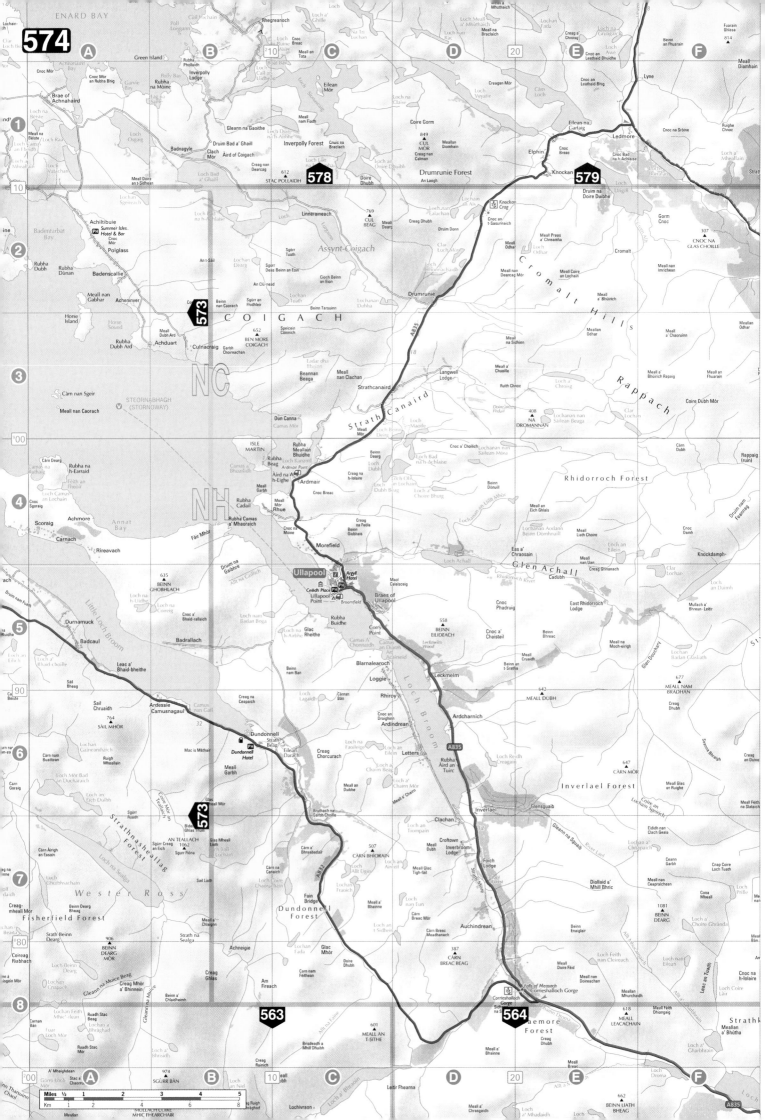

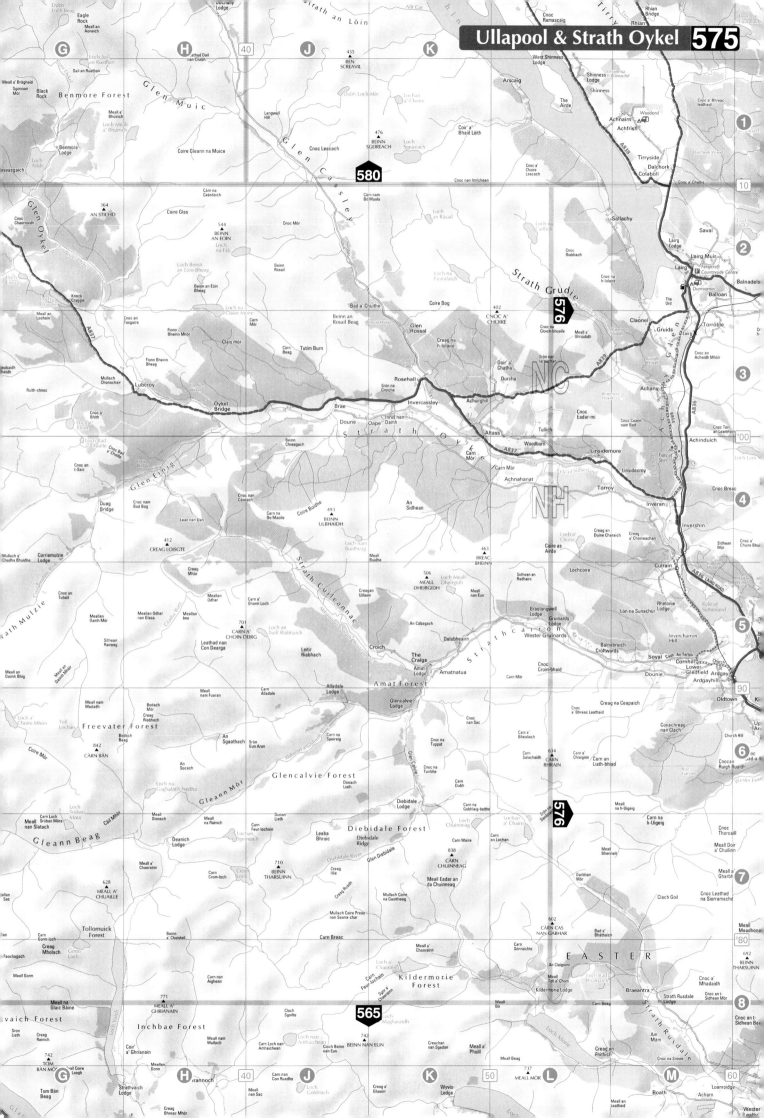

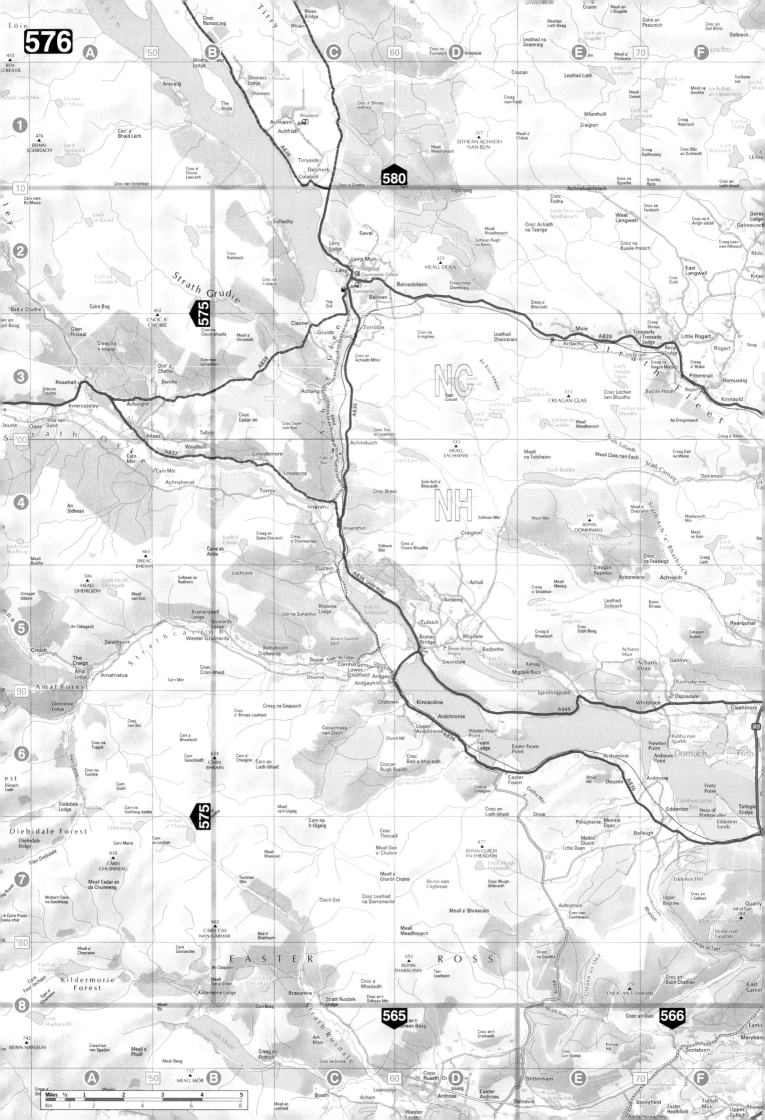

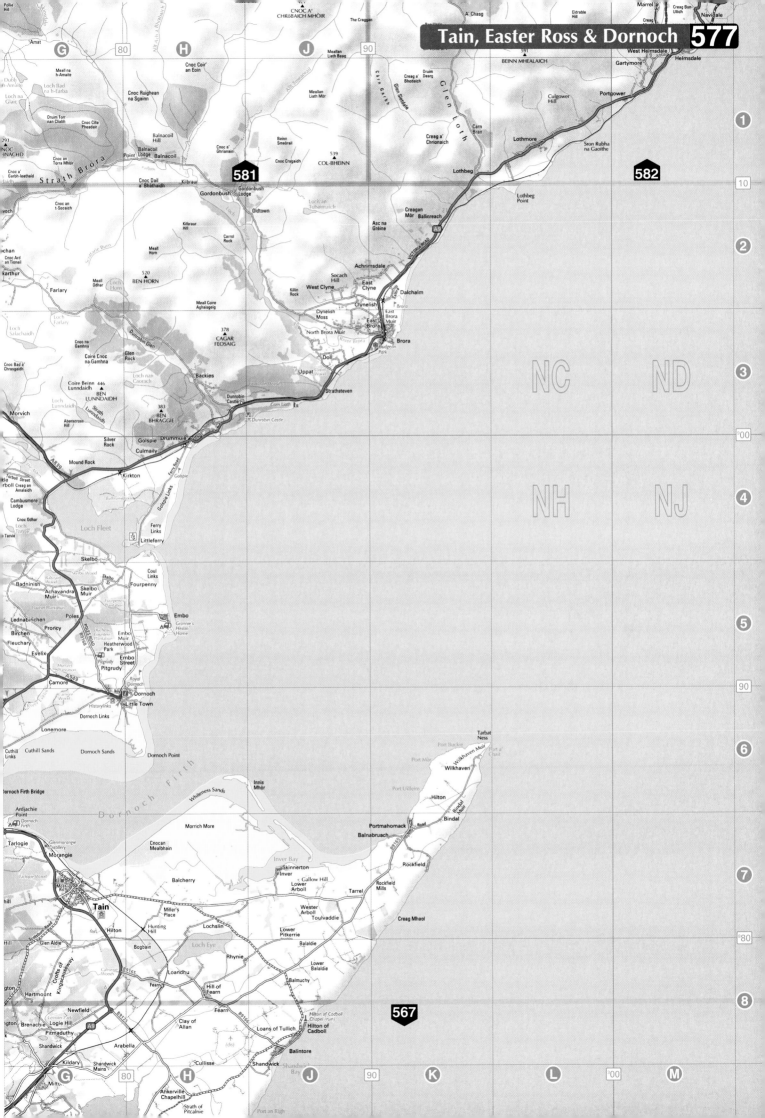

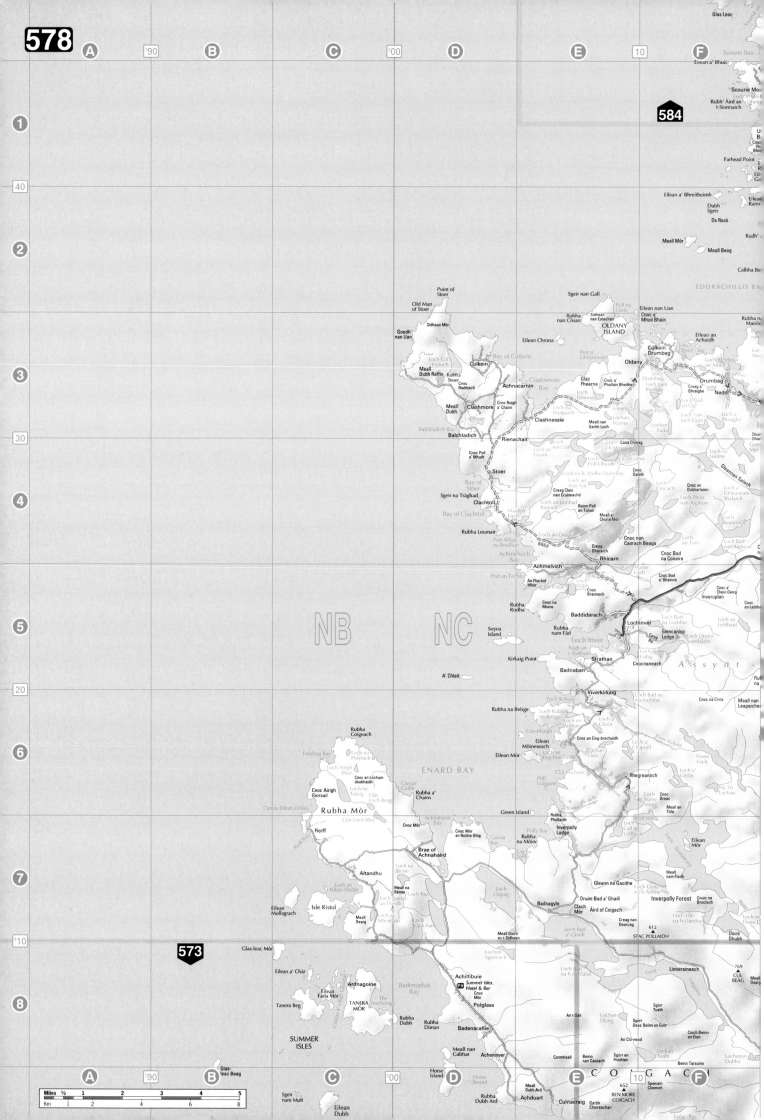

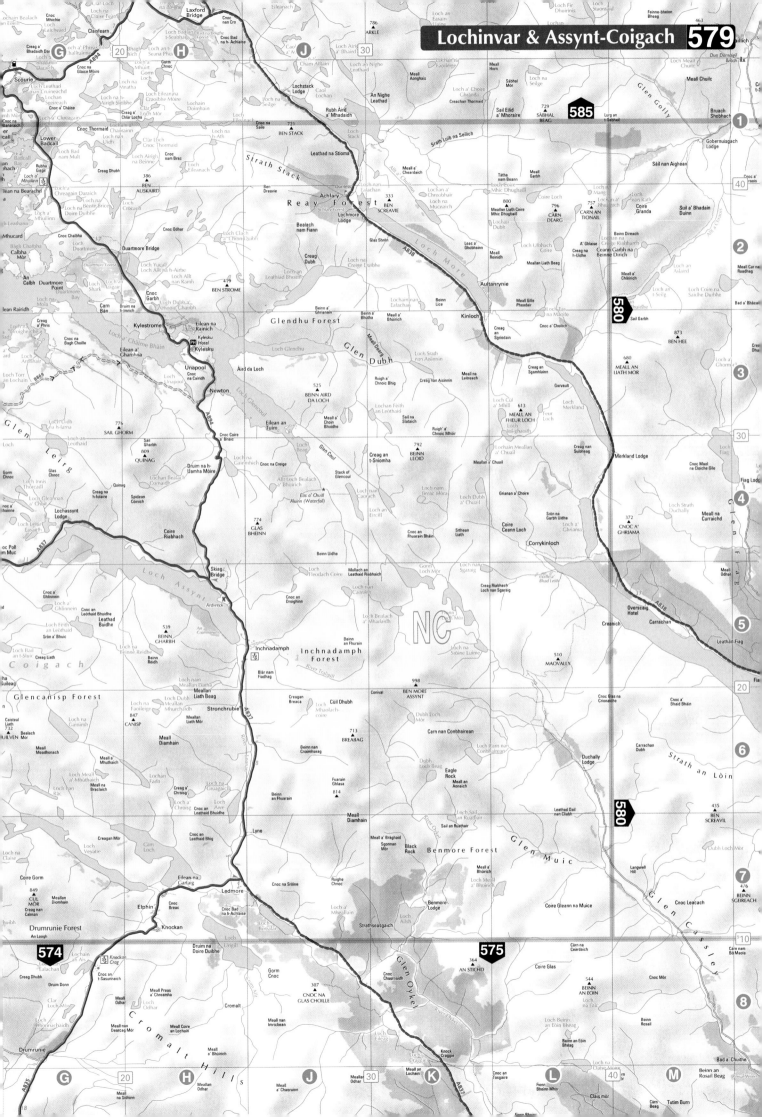

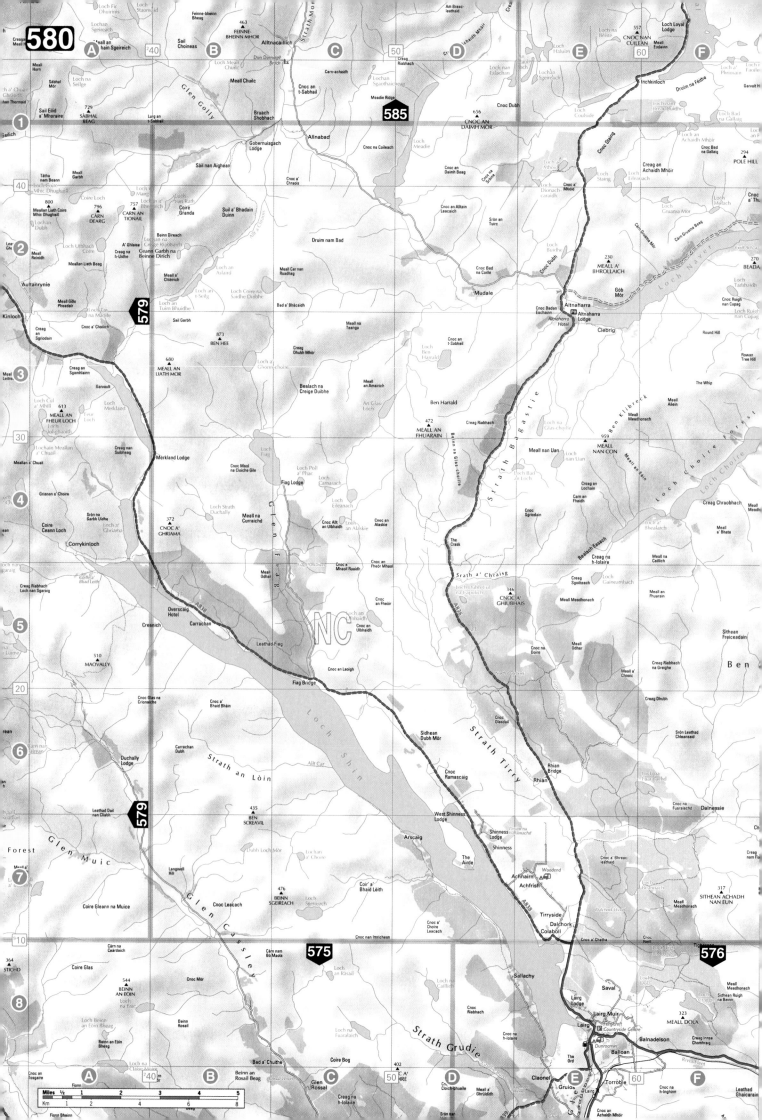

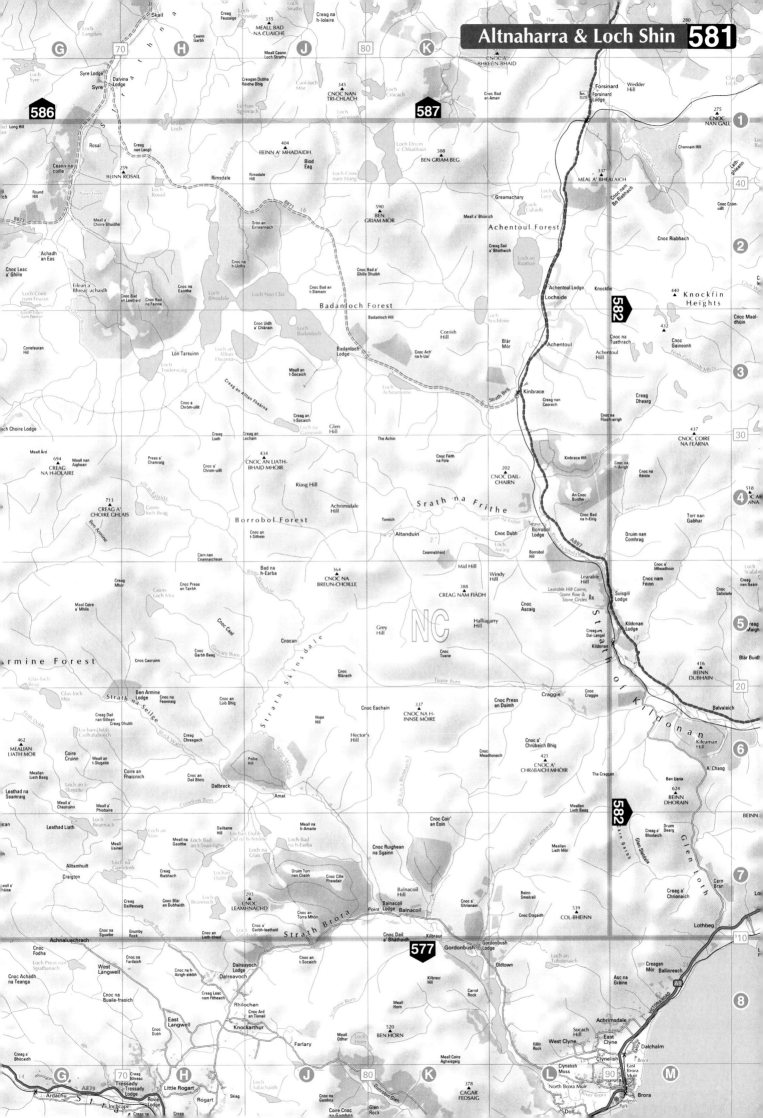

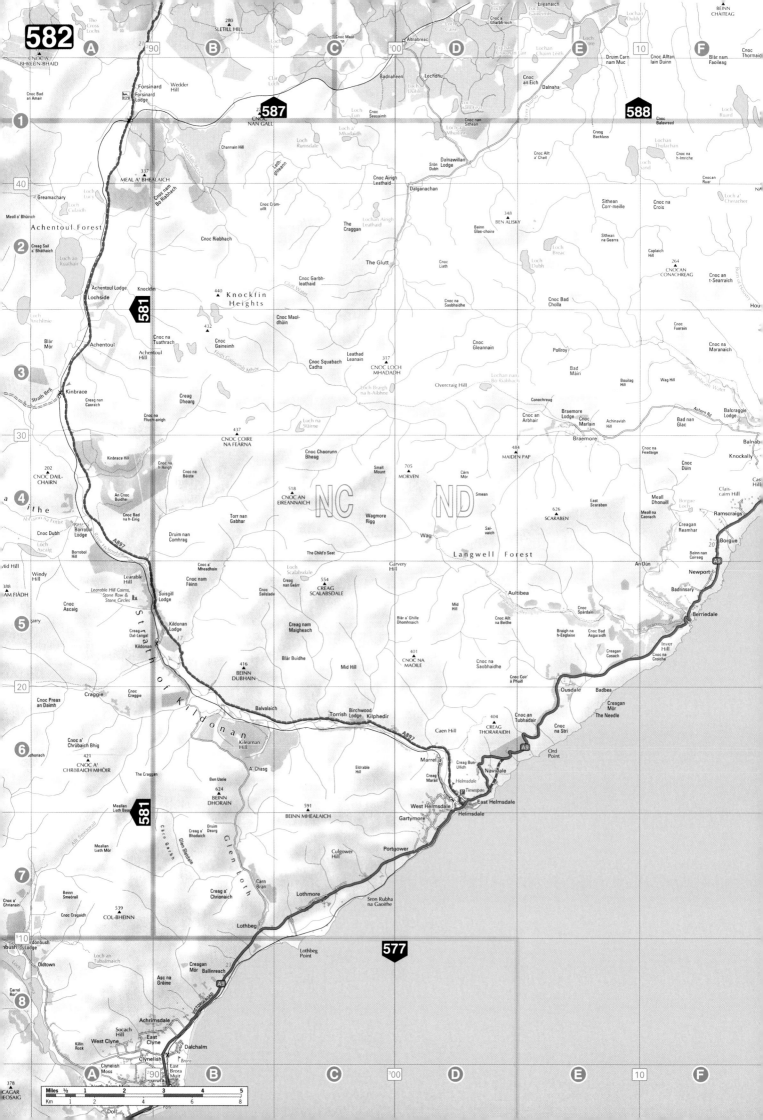

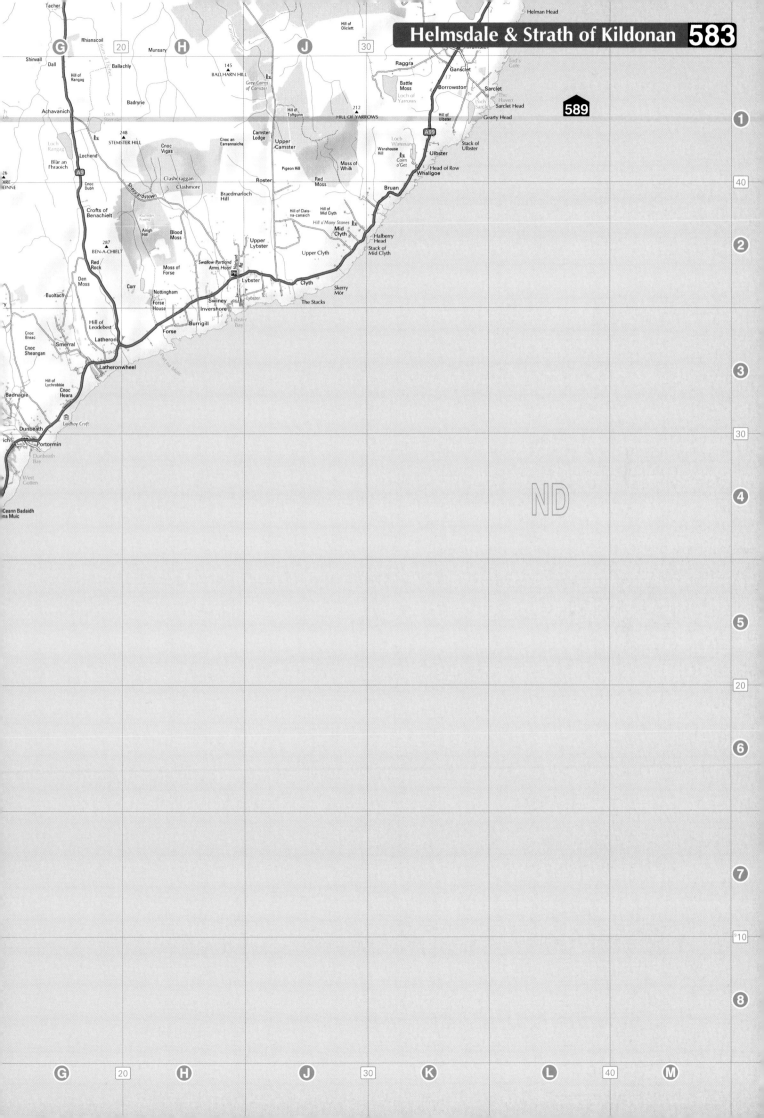

589

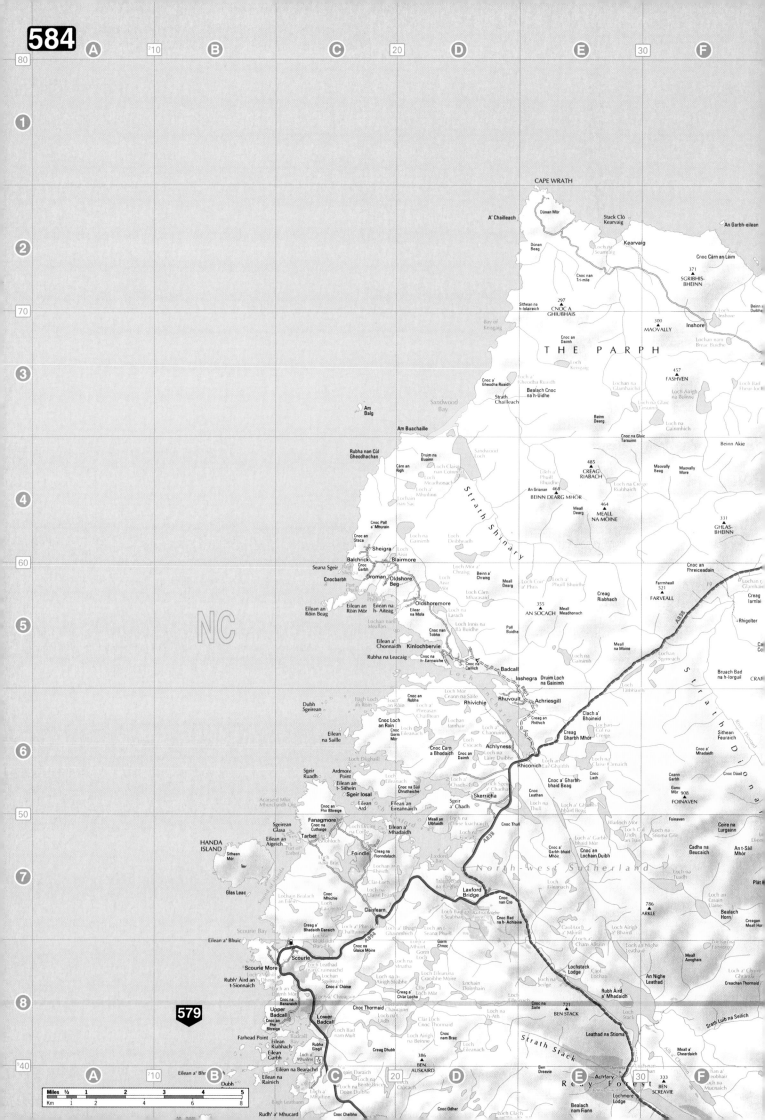

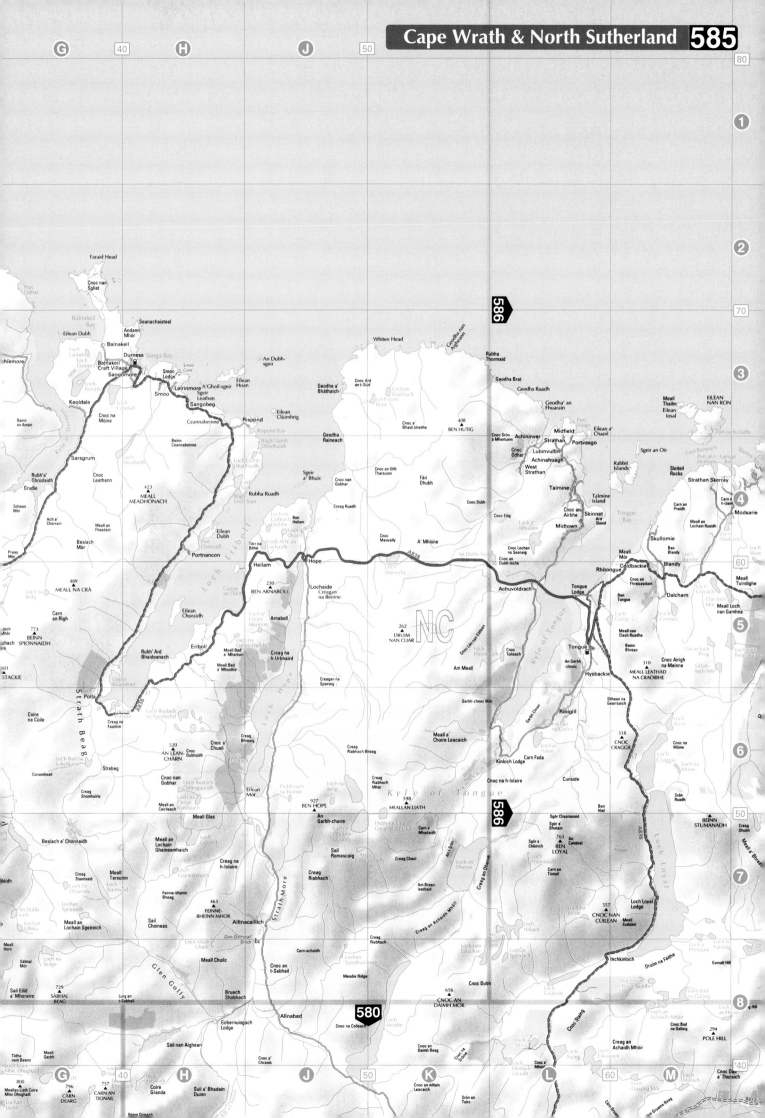

Faraid Head

Port Odhar

Balnakeil Bay

Eilean Dubh

Loch Lanlish
Loch Croispol

Durness
Sango Bay

Seanachaisteal

Aodann Mhòr

Balnakeil

Balnakeil Craft Village
Sangomore
Smoo Lodge
Smoo Cove

Leirinmore A'Ghoil-sgeir
Sgeir Leathan
Sangobeg

Keoldale

Cnoc na Mòine

Smoo

Ceannabeinne

An Dubh-sgeir

Eilean Hoan

Whiten Head

Geodha nan Aigheann

Rubha Thormaid

Eilean Clùimhrig

Geodha a' Bhàthaich

Geodha Raineach

Geodha Ruadh

Cnoc Ard an t-Siuil

Lochan Riabhach

Loch nam Breac

Cnoc a' Bhaid-bheithe

408 ▲ BEN HUTIG

Meall Thailm
Eilean Iosal

EILEAN NAN RON

Geodha' an Fhuarain

Geodha Brat

Rubha Ruadh

Cnoc Sròn à Mhartuinn

Cnoc Odhar

Achininver
Strathan
Lubinvullin
Achinahuagh
West Strathan
Talmine

Midfield
Portvasgo
Eilean a' Chaoil

Sgeir an Oir

Rabbit Islands

Sleiteil Rocks
Strathan Skerray

Carn an Fheidh

Carn n h-Uaimh
Modsarie

Meall an Lochain Ruaidh

Tongue Bay

Skinnet
Ard Skinid

Skullomie

Ben Blandy

Blandy

Meall Skerr

Beinn an Amair

Sarsgrum

Rubh' a' Ghrùdaidh
Grudie

Sithean Mòr

Ach a' Chorrain

Cnoc Leathann

423 ▲ MEALL MEADHONACH

Meall an Fheadain

Bealach Mòr

Preas Mòr

Eilean Dubh

Portnancon

Eilean Choraidh

Rubh' Ard Bhaideanach

Eriboll

Heilam

Hope

Lochside
Creagan na Beinne

Arnaboll

230 ▲ BEN ARNABOLL

Torr na Bathe

Loch Ach' an Lochaidh

Ben Heilam

Loch a' Choire

Cnoc na Cathair Dubhha

Rubha Ruadh

Sgeir a' Bhuic

Cnoc nan Gobhar

Creag Ruadh

Cnoc an Uillt Tharsuinn

Fàir Dhubh

A' Mhòine

Cnoc Maovally

A838

Cnoc Dubh

Cnoc Eilig

Loch a' Mhuilinn

Midtown

Cnoc an Airbhe

Talmine Island

Cnoc Lochan na Seanaig

Cnoc an Dubh-lochà

Achuvoldrach

Meall Mòr

Rhitongue

Coldbackie

Cnoc an Fhreiceadain

Dalcharn

Clàr-loch

Meall Loch nan Gamhna

MEALL NA CRÀ 489 ▲

Loch na Seilg

Carn an Righ

BEINN SPIONNAIDH 773 ▲

489 ▲ MEALL NA CRÀ

Loch Bad na h-Achlaise

Conamheall

Strabeg

520 ▲ AN LEAN-CHÀRN

Cnoc a' Chuail

Cnoc Dubhaidh

Loch Bealach Odhrsgaraidh

Eilean Mòr

Meall Bad a' Mhartuinn

Creag na h-Urbhaird

Creagan na Speireig

Creag Bhreaig

Creag Riabhach Bheag

Dubh-loch na Beinne

Loch na Seilg

262 ▲ DRUIM NAN CLIAR

NC

Cnoc Lòn nas Eilean

Am Meall

Cnoc Toiteach

An Garbh-chnoc

Tongue

Hysbackie

Ben Tongue

Loch Craigie

Loch Eireannaich

Tongue Lodge

Meall nan Clach Ruadha

Beinn Bhreac

310 ▲ Cnoc Airigh na Meinne

MEALL LEATHAD NA CRAOIBHE

Grian-loch Beag

Loch nan Breac Buidhe

Grian-loch Mòr

Garbh-chnoc Mòr

Garbh-chnoc

Ribigill

Lochan na Culce

Sithean na Gearrsaich

Loch Slaim

Cnoc na Mòine

Loch Craggie

318 ▲ CNOC CRAGGIE

Loch Craggie

Coire na Cùile

Polla

Creag na Faoilinn

Loch Bealach na Sgeulachd

Cnoc nan Gobhar

Meall an Ceirleach

Loch na Creige Riabhaich

Meall Glas

Kinloch Lodge

Meall a' Choire Leacaich

Carn Fada

Cunside

Cnoc na h-Iolaire

Sròn Ruadh

BEALACH A' CHONNAIDH

Bealach a' Chonnaidh

Creag Shomhairle

Ailtnacaillich

927 ▲ BEN HOPE

An Garbh-choire

598 ▲ MEALLAN LIATH

586

Sgòr Chaonasaid

Sgòr a' Bhatain

Sgòr a' Chlèirich

763 ▲ BEN LOYAL

An Caisteal

BEINN STUMANADH

Creag Dhubh

Meall a' Bhràta

Meall an Lochain Ghaineamhaich

Creag na h-Iolaire

Creag Riabhach

Sail Romascaig

An Commhoch

Creag Chaol

Ant Sgòr

Loch an Dherue

Creas an Dherue

Carn an Tionail

Loch Fhionnaich

Carn a' Mhadaidh

Am Breac-leathaid

Feinne-bheinn Bheag

463 ▲ FEINNE-BHEINN MHOR

Sail Choineas

Dun Dornadil Broch

Sail Eilid a' Mhoraire

729 ▲ SÀBHAL BEAG

Lurg an t-Sabhail

Meall Chuilc

Gobernuisgach Lodge

Sàil nan Aighean

Carn-achaidh

Lochan Sgiathaiginich

Creag Riabhach

Meadie Ridge

Cnoc an t-Sabhail

Allnabad

580

Loch Meadie

Cnoc na Coileach

Cnoc an Daimh Beag

656 ▲ CNOC AN DAIMH MOR

Loch Loyal

557 ▲ CNOC NAN CUILEAN

Loch Loyal Lodge

Meall Eudainn

Loch na Beiste

Loch Haluim

Inchkinloch

Druim na Fèithe

Garvalt Hill

Loch Coulside

Cnoc Staing

Loch Staing

294 ▲ POLE HILL

Creag an Achaidh Mhòir

Cnoc Bad na Gallaig

Tàtha nam Beann

Meall Garbh

Meallan Liath Coire Mhic Dhughaill

800

Loch-Coire Mhic Dhughaill

796 ▲ CÀRN DEARG

757 ▲ CARN AN TIONAIL

Coire Granda

Suil a' Bhadain Duinn

Cnoc an Alltain Leacaich

Sròn na Tuirc

Cnoc a' Mhòir

Loch Gruama Beag

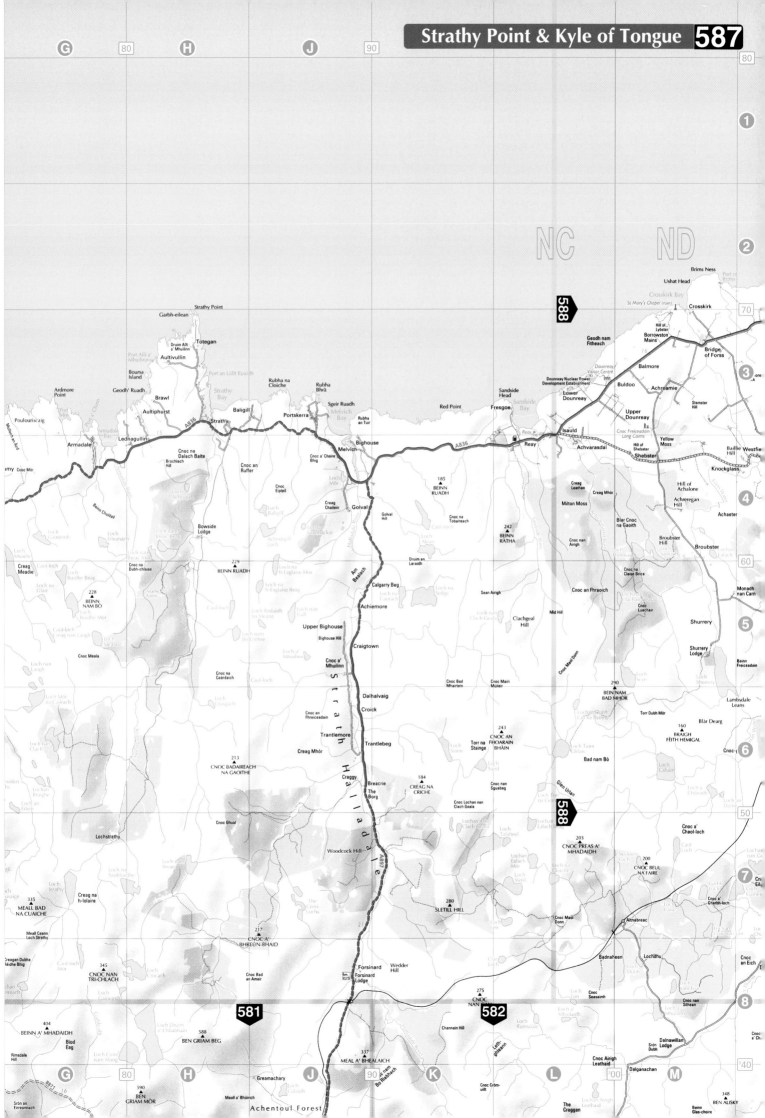

G 80 H J 90

NC ND

1

2

Brims Ness
Ushat Head Port o' Brims
Crosskirk Bay
St Mary's Chapel (ruin) Crosskirk 70

588

Hill of Lybster
Borrowston Mains Bridge of Forss 3
Geodh nam Fitheach
Dounreay Visitor Centre Balmore Achreamie
Dounreay Nuclear Power Buldoo Stemster Hill
Development Establishment
Lower Dounreay Upper Dounreay Baillie Westfield
Strathy Point
Garbh-eilean Cnoc Freiceadain Yellow Moss Hill
Druim Allt Totegan Sandside Long Cairns Achreregan
a' Mhuilinn Head Fresgoe Hill of Shebster Hill Achaeter
Port Allt Aultivullin Sandside Isauld Knockglass
a' Mhuilinn Boursa Island Strathy Red Point Bay Reay Achvarasdal 4
Geodh' Ruadh Bay Rubha na Cloiche Rubha Milton Moss Shebster
Ardmore Brawl Cloiche Bhrà Melvich Bay 185 Creag Leathan Creag Mhòr Hill of Achalone
Point Aultiphurst Sgeir Ruadh Rubha BEINN Blar Cnoc Broubster
Poulouriscaig Lednagullin A836 Baligill Portskerra an Tuir RUADH Milton Moss na Gaoith Hill
Armadale Strathy Melvich Cnoc na Tobaireach Cnoc nan Broubster 60
Armadale Bay Cnoc na Bighouse Airigh
Cnoc Mòr Dalach Baite Cnoc a' Choire Golval 242 Cnoc na Claise Brice
Brachlach Bhig BEINN Cnoc an Fhraoich
Hill Cnoc an Loch Golval RATHA Monadh
Ruffer Mòr Hill nan Carn
Cnoc Cnoc Sean Airigh Mid Hill Shurrery
Eipteil Chailein Caol-loch 290 5
Creag Meadie Cnoc na Loch na Druim an Loch na Clachgeal Shurrery
Caol-loch Dubh-chlaise h-Eaglaise Mòr Laraidh Seilge Hill Lodge
229 Loch na Calgarry Beg Beinn
BEINN RUADH h-Eaglaise Beag Achiemore Freiceadain
228 Cnoc Bad Cnoc Mairi BEINN NAM
BEINN Upper Bighouse Mhairtein Muilcir BAD MHÒR Lambsdale
NAM BÒ Bighouse Hill Torr Dubh Mòr Leans
Cnoc Meala Craigtown 160 Blàr Dearg
Cnoc a' BRAIGH
Cnoc na Mhuilinn FÈITH HEMIGAL 6
Ceàrdaich Dalhalvaig 243 Bad nam Bò
Cnoc an Croick CNOC AN
Fhreiceadain FHOARAIN Glen Urian
Trantlemore BHÀIN 203 Cnoc a'
Creag Mhòr Trantlebeg Torr na CNOC PREAS A' Chaol-loch
213 Stainge MHADAIDH
CNOC BADAIREACH Craggy 184 Cnoc nan 200
NA GAOITHE Breacrie CREAG NA Sguabag CNOC BEUL
Lochstrathy The Borg CRICHE NA FAIRE
Cnoc Ghual Lochan Lochan nan 7
Clach Geala
588 50
Woodcock Hill Cnoc a'
335 Gharbh-loch
MEALL BAD Altnabreac
NA CUAICHE A897 SLETILL HILL Cnoc Maol
Meall Ceann 280 Donn
Loch Strathy 217 Badanheen Lochdhu
CNOC A' Cnoc 8
345 BHREUN-BHAID an Eich
CNOC NAN
TRI-CHLACH Forsinard Wedder
Cnoc Bad Forsinard Hill Cnoc nan
an Amair Lodge Sithean

581 BEINN BEN GRIAM BEG **582** 275 Cnoc Airigh Dalnawillan 348
A' MHADAIDH 588 CNOC Leathaid Lodge BEN ALISKY
404 Biod 337 NAN Srón
Eag MEAL A' BHEALAICH Channain Hill Dubh
Rimsdale Dalganachan
Hill
Srón an 590 The
Eirreannach BEN Cnoc Cròm- Craggan
GRIAM MÒR Greamachary Bò Riabhach uillt Beinn
Meall a' Bhairich Achentoul Forest Glas-choire

G 80 H J 90 K L M 40

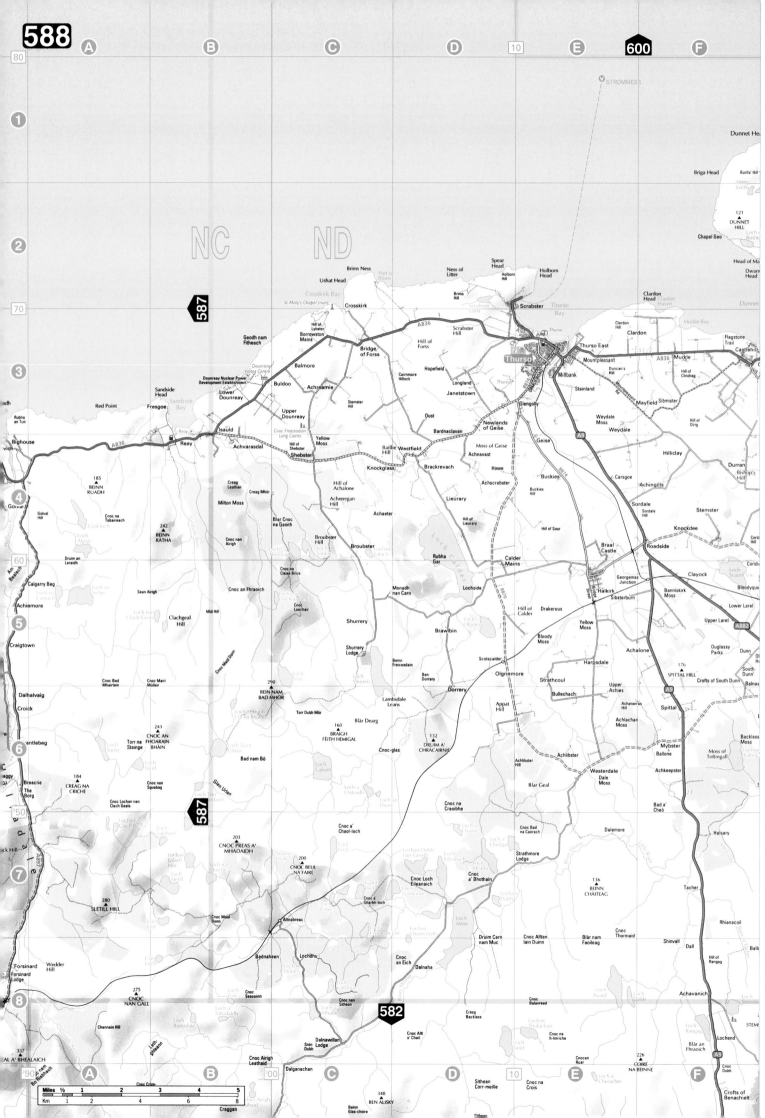

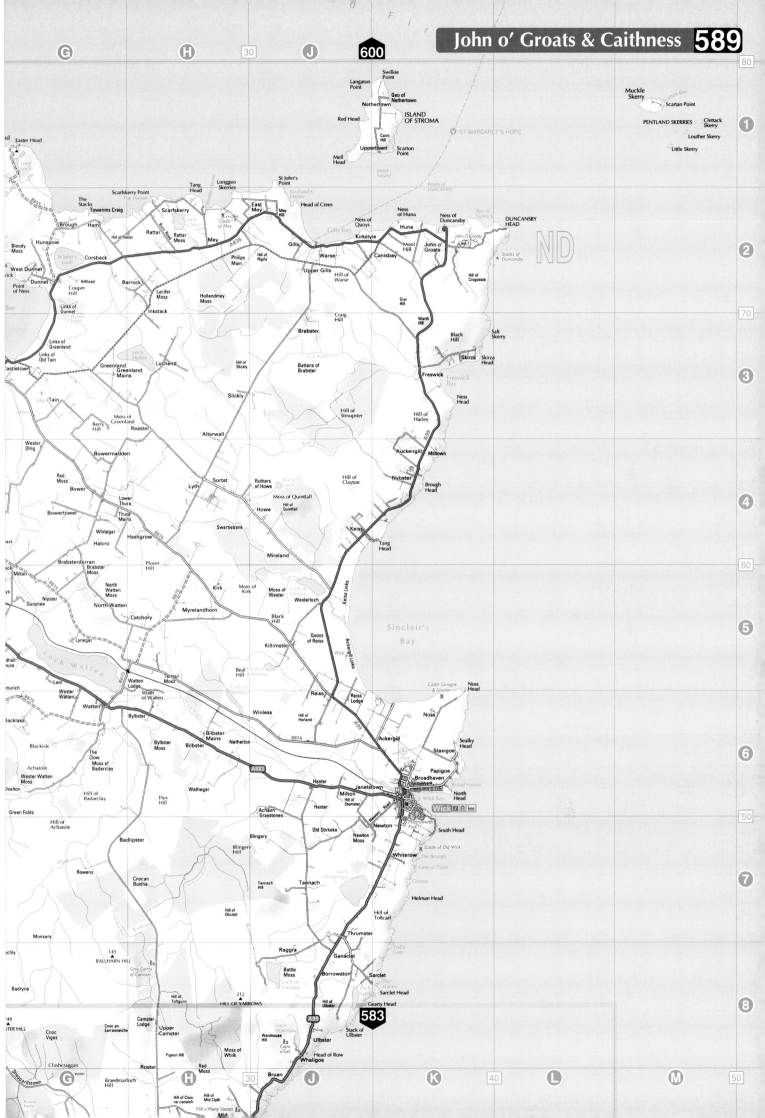

600

583

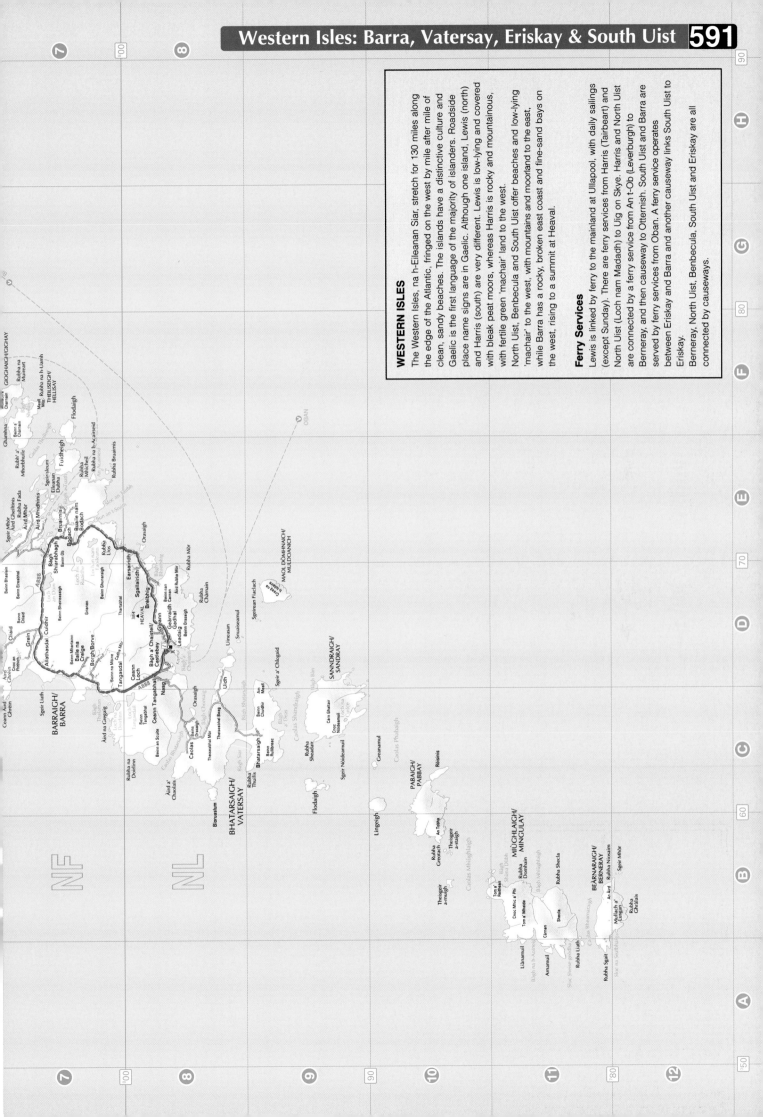

WESTERN ISLES

The Western Isles, na h-Eileanan Siar, stretch for 130 miles along the edge of the Atlantic, fringed on the west by mile after mile of clean, sandy beaches. The islands have a distinctive culture and Gaelic is the first language of the majority of islanders. Roadside place name signs are in Gaelic. Although one island, Lewis (north) and Harris (south) are very different. Lewis is low-lying and covered with bleak peat moors, whereas Harris is rocky and mountainous, with fertile green 'machair' land to the west. North Uist, Benbecula and South Uist offer beaches and low-lying 'machair' to the west, with mountains and moorland to the east, while Barra has a rocky, broken east coast and fine-sand bays on the west, rising to a summit at Heaval.

Ferry Services

Lewis is linked by ferry to the mainland at Ullapool, with daily sailings (except Sunday). There are ferry services from Harris (Tairbeart) and North Uist (Loch nam Madadh) to Uig on Skye. Harris and North Uist are connected by a ferry service from An t-Ob (Leverburgh) to Berneray, and then causeway to Otternish. South Uist and Barra are served by ferry services from Oban. A ferry service operates between Eriskay and Barra and another causeway links South Uist to Eriskay.

Berneray, North Uist, Benbecula, South Uist and Eriskay are all connected by causeways.

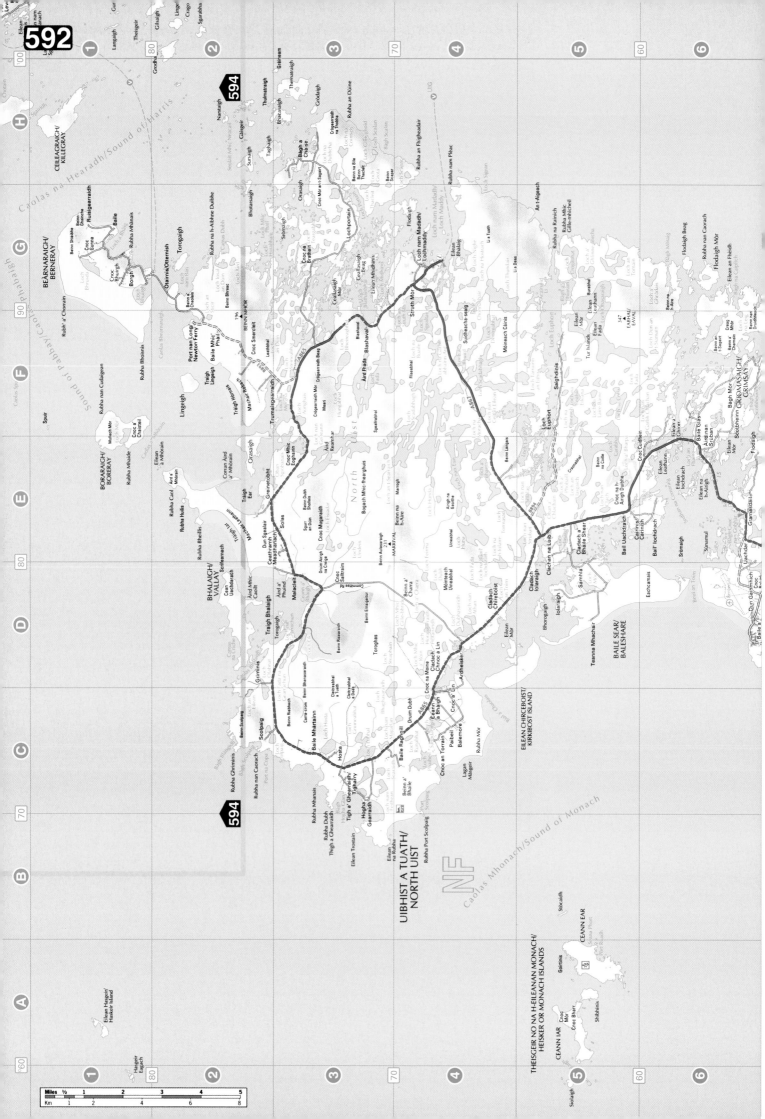

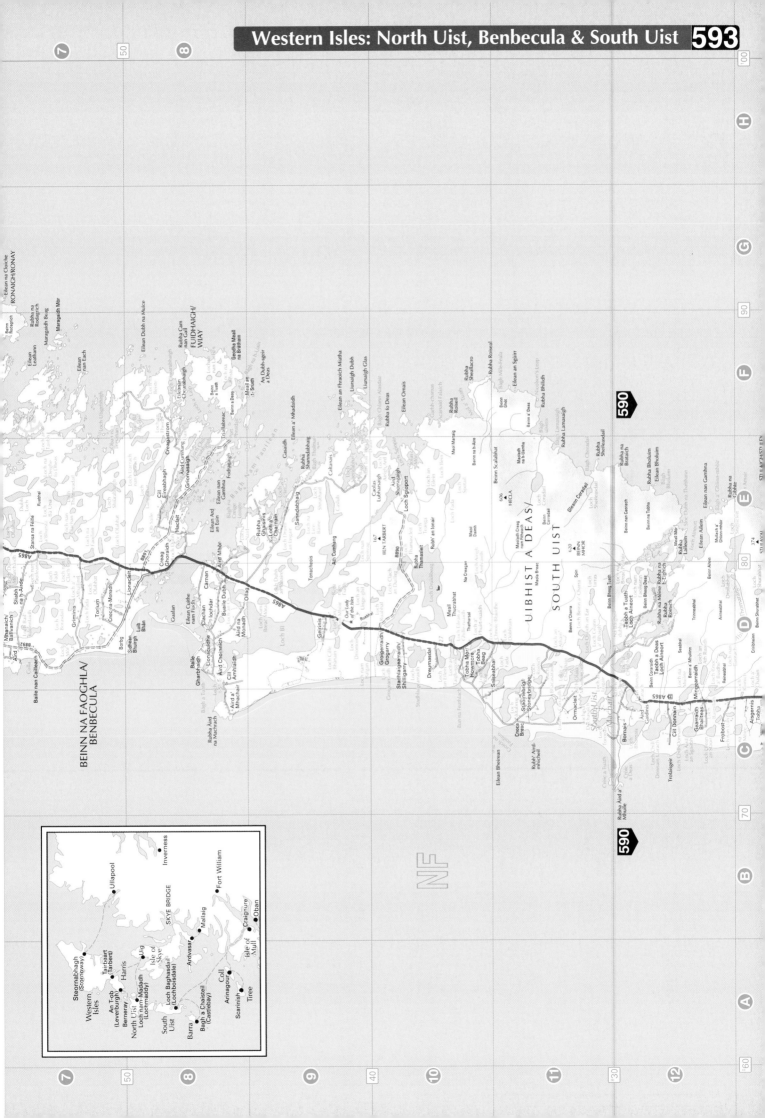

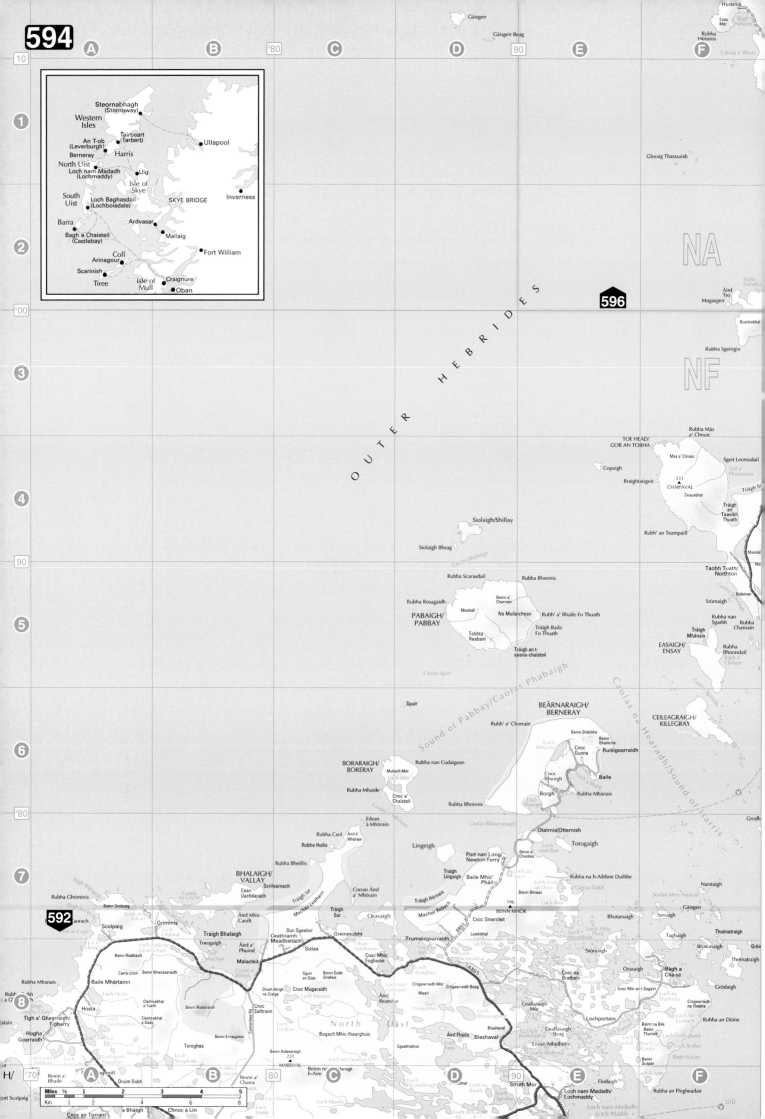

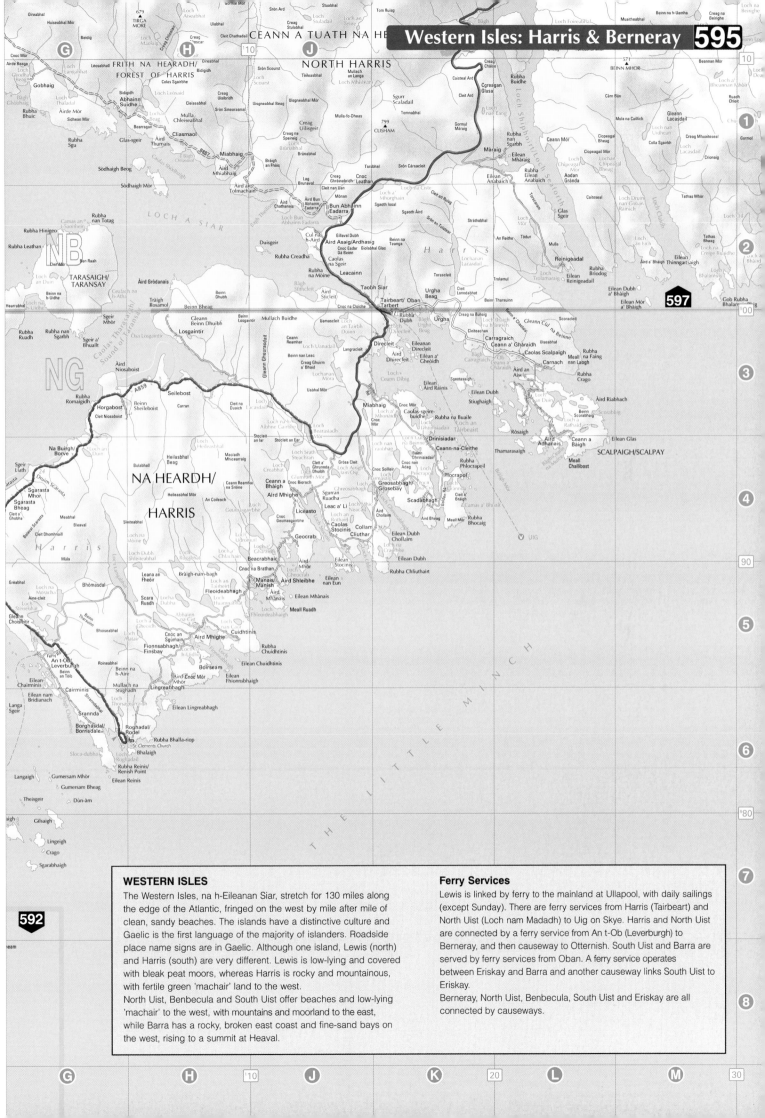

WESTERN ISLES

The Western Isles, na h-Eileanan Siar, stretch for 130 miles along the edge of the Atlantic, fringed on the west by mile after mile of clean, sandy beaches. The islands have a distinctive culture and Gaelic is the first language of the majority of islanders. Roadside place name signs are in Gaelic. Although one island, Lewis (north) and Harris (south) are very different. Lewis is low-lying and covered with bleak peat moors, whereas Harris is rocky and mountainous, with fertile green 'machair' land to the west.

North Uist, Benbecula and South Uist offer beaches and low-lying 'machair' to the west, with mountains and moorland to the east, while Barra has a rocky, broken east coast and fine-sand bays on the west, rising to a summit at Heaval.

Ferry Services

Lewis is linked by ferry to the mainland at Ullapool, with daily sailings (except Sunday). There are ferry services from Harris (Tairbeart) and North Uist (Loch nam Madadh) to Uig on Skye. Harris and North Uist are connected by a ferry service from An t-Ob (Leverburgh) to Berneray, and then causeway to Otternish. South Uist and Barra are served by ferry services from Oban. A ferry service operates between Eriskay and Barra and another causeway links South Uist to Eriskay.

Berneray, North Uist, Benbecula, South Uist and Eriskay are all connected by causeways.

WESTERN ISLES

The Western Isles, na h-Eileanan Siar, stretch for 130 miles along the edge of the Atlantic, fringed on the west by mile after mile of clean, sandy beaches. The islands have a distinctive culture and Gaelic is the first language of the majority of islanders. Roadside place name signs are in Gaelic. Although one island, Lewis (north) and Harris (south) are very different. Lewis is low-lying and covered with bleak peat moors, whereas Harris is rocky and mountainous, with fertile green 'machair' land to the west.

North Uist, Benbecula and South Uist offer beaches and low-lying 'machair' to the west, with mountains and moorland to the east, while Barra has a rocky, broken east coast and fine-sand bays on the west, rising to a summit at Heaval.

Ferry Services

Lewis is linked by ferry to the mainland at Ullapool, with daily sailings (except Sunday). There are ferry services from Harris (Tairbeart) and North Uist (Loch nam Madadh) to Uig on Skye. Harris and North Uist are connected by a ferry service from An t-Ob (Leverburgh) to Berneray, and then causeway to Otternish. South Uist and Barra are served by ferry services from Oban. A ferry service operates between Eriskay and Barra and another causeway links South Uist to Eriskay.

Berneray, North Uist, Benbecula, South Uist and Eriskay are all connected by causeways.

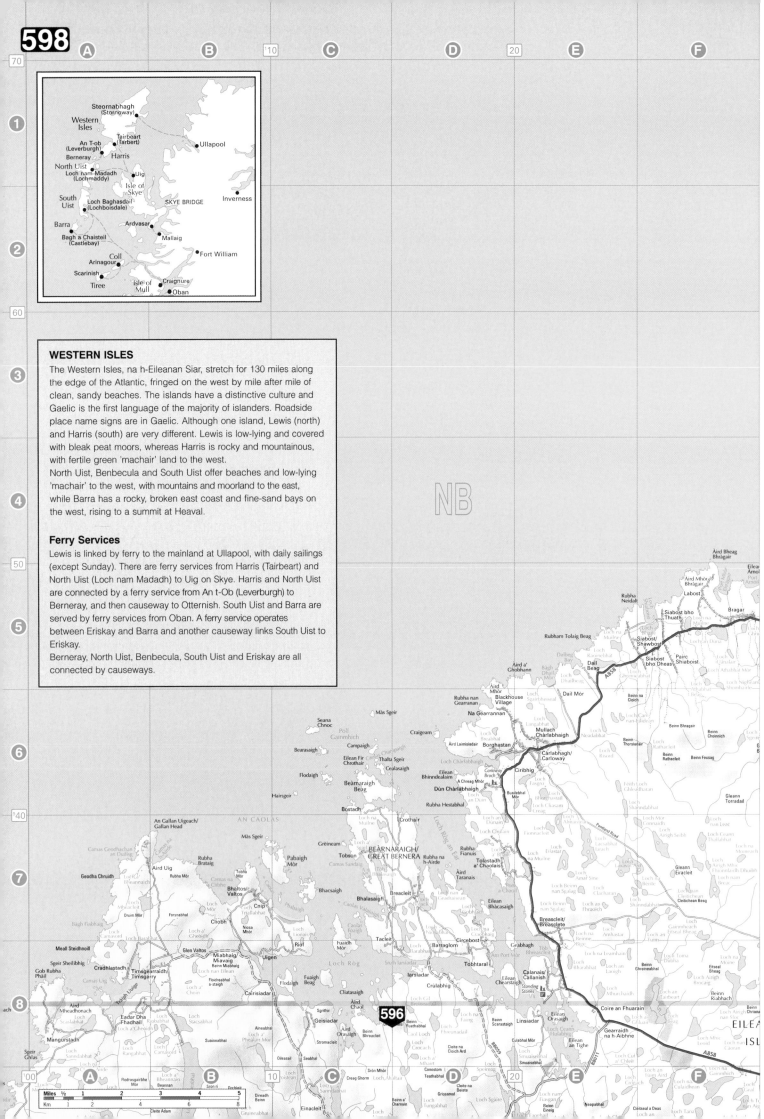

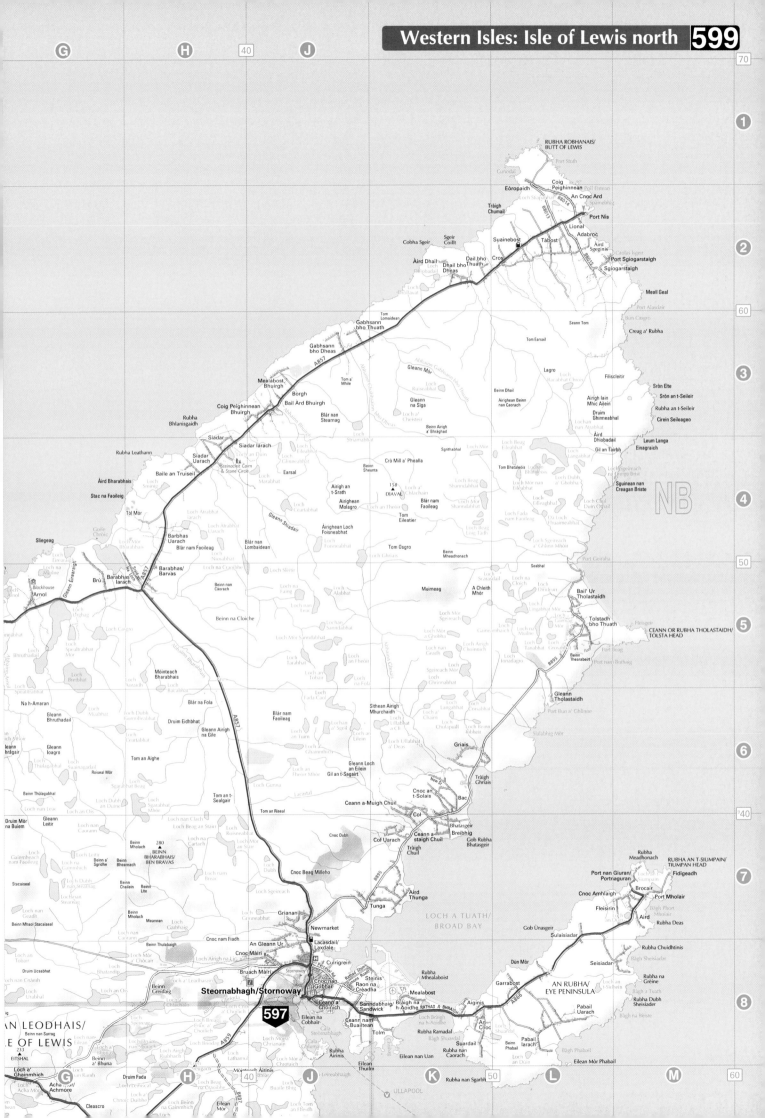

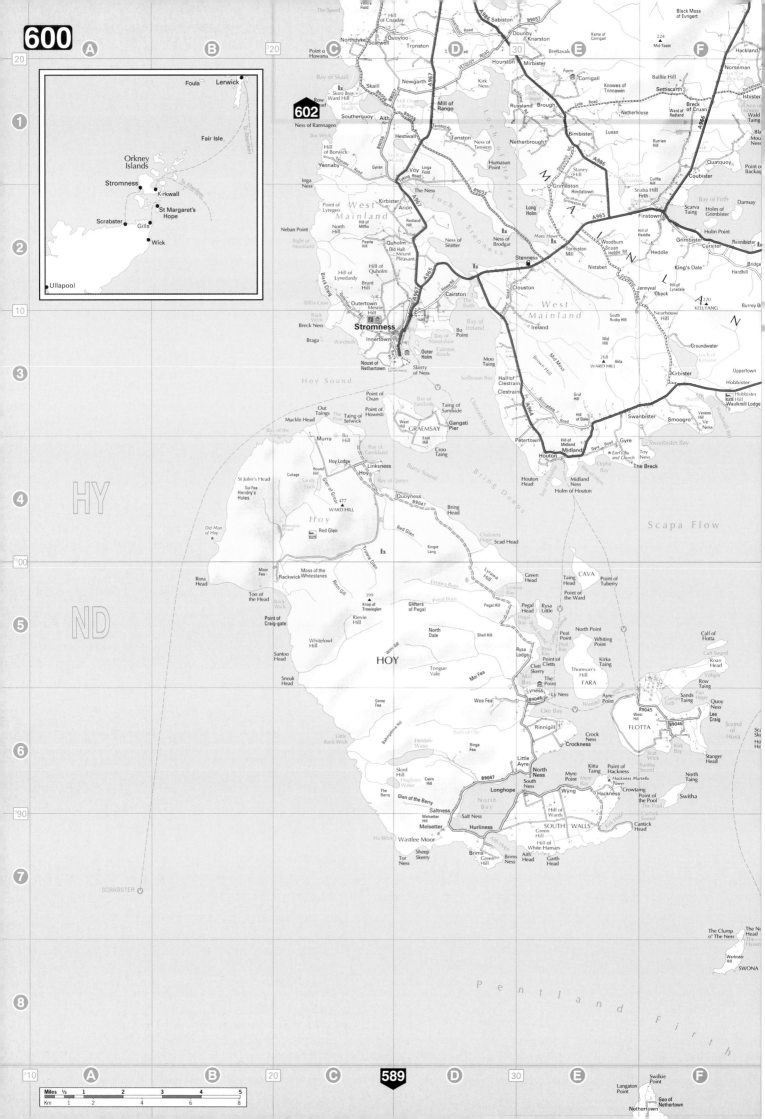

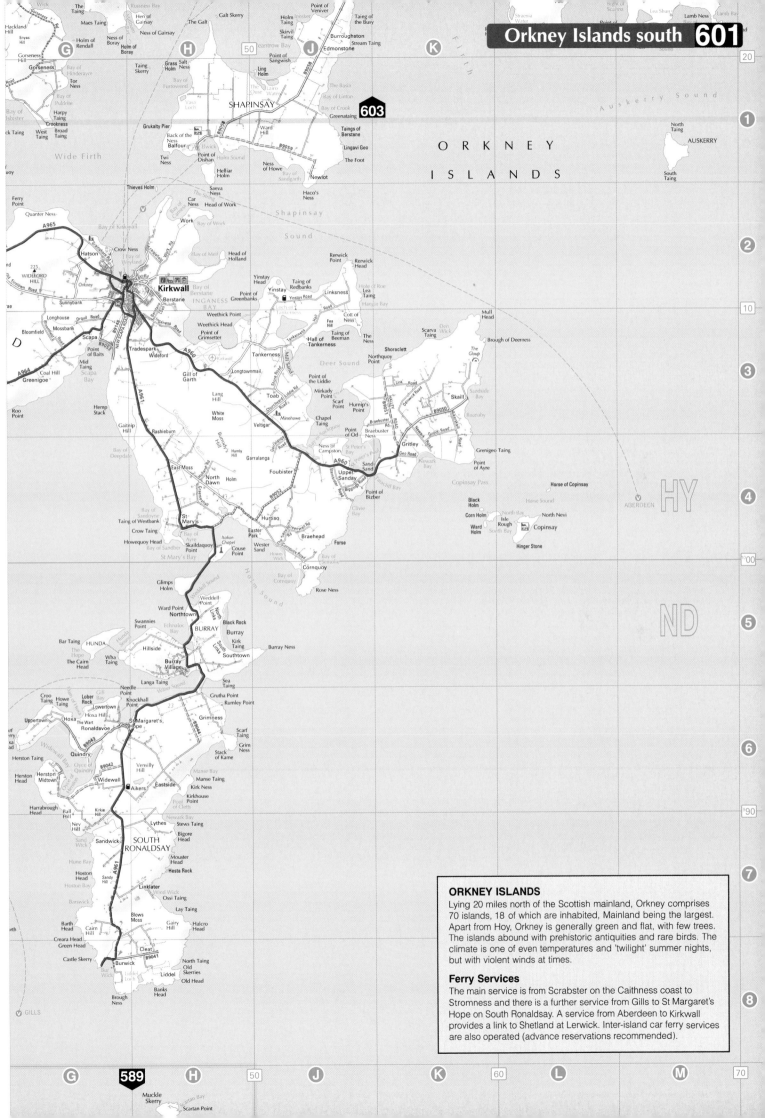

ORKNEY ISLANDS

Lying 20 miles north of the Scottish mainland, Orkney comprises 70 islands, 18 of which are inhabited, Mainland being the largest. Apart from Hoy, Orkney is generally green and flat, with few trees. The islands abound with prehistoric antiquities and rare birds. The climate is one of even temperatures and 'twilight' summer nights, but with violent winds at times.

Ferry Services

The main service is from Scrabster on the Caithness coast to Stromness and there is a further service from Gills to St Margaret's Hope on South Ronaldsay. A service from Aberdeen to Kirkwall provides a link to Shetland at Lerwick. Inter-island car ferry services are also operated (advance reservations recommended).

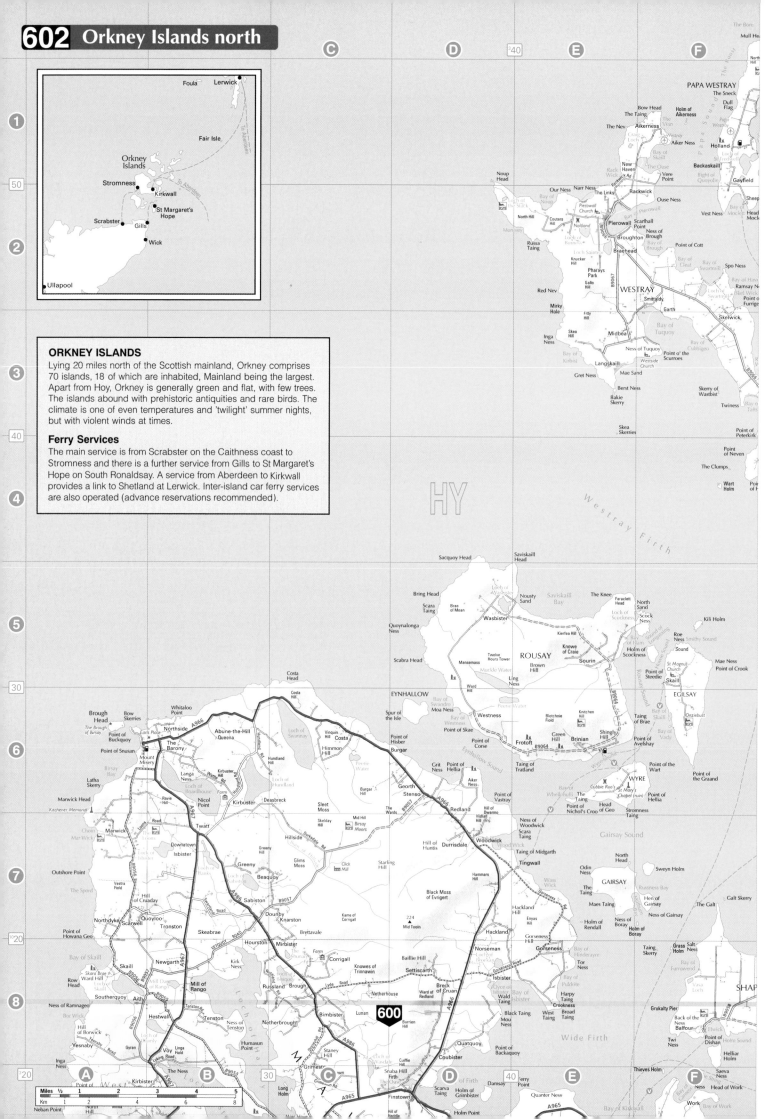

ORKNEY ISLANDS

Lying 20 miles north of the Scottish mainland, Orkney comprises 70 islands, 18 of which are inhabited, Mainland being the largest. Apart from Hoy, Orkney is generally green and flat, with few trees. The islands abound with prehistoric antiquities and rare birds. The climate is one of even temperatures and 'twilight' summer nights, but with violent winds at times.

Ferry Services

The main service is from Scrabster on the Caithness coast to Stromness and there is a further service from Gills to St Margaret's Hope on South Ronaldsay. A service from Aberdeen to Kirkwall provides a link to Shetland at Lerwick. Inter-island car ferry services are also operated (advance reservations recommended).

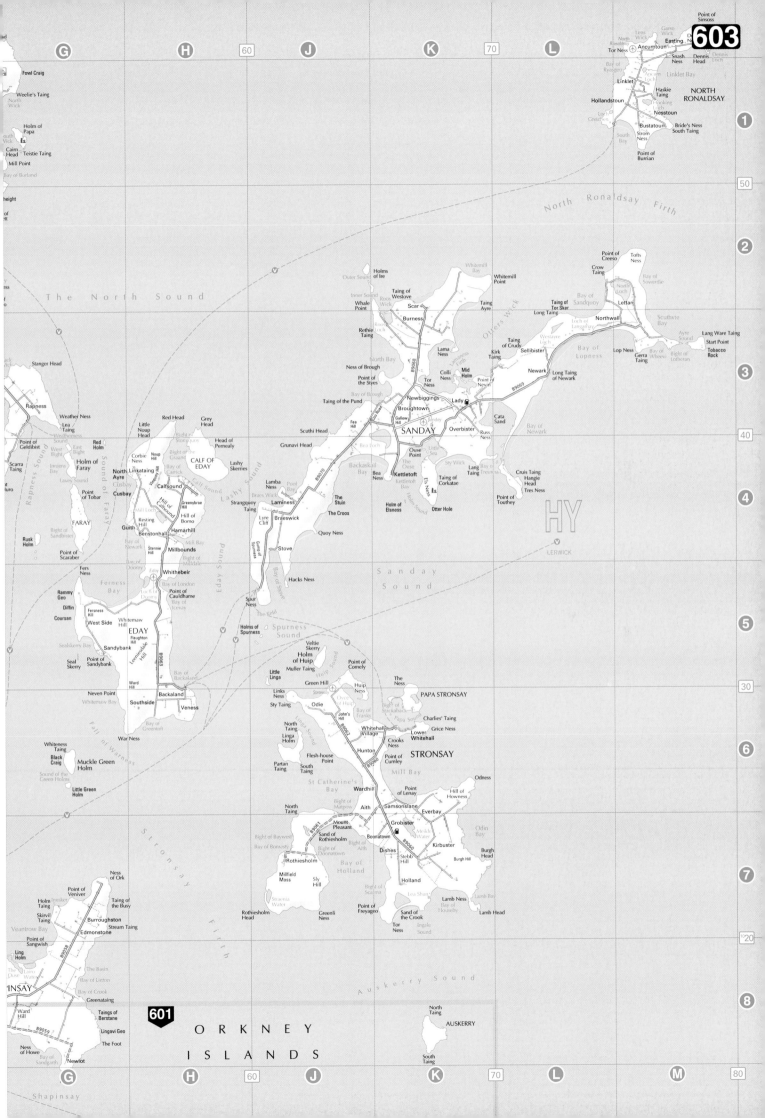

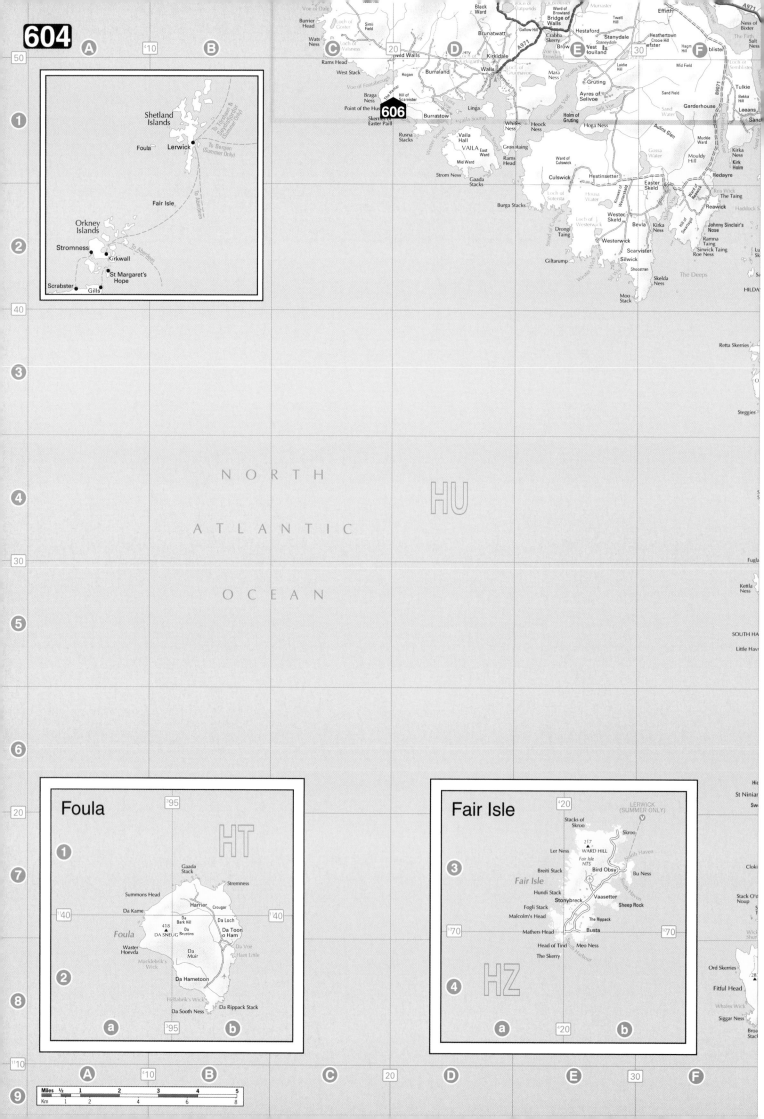

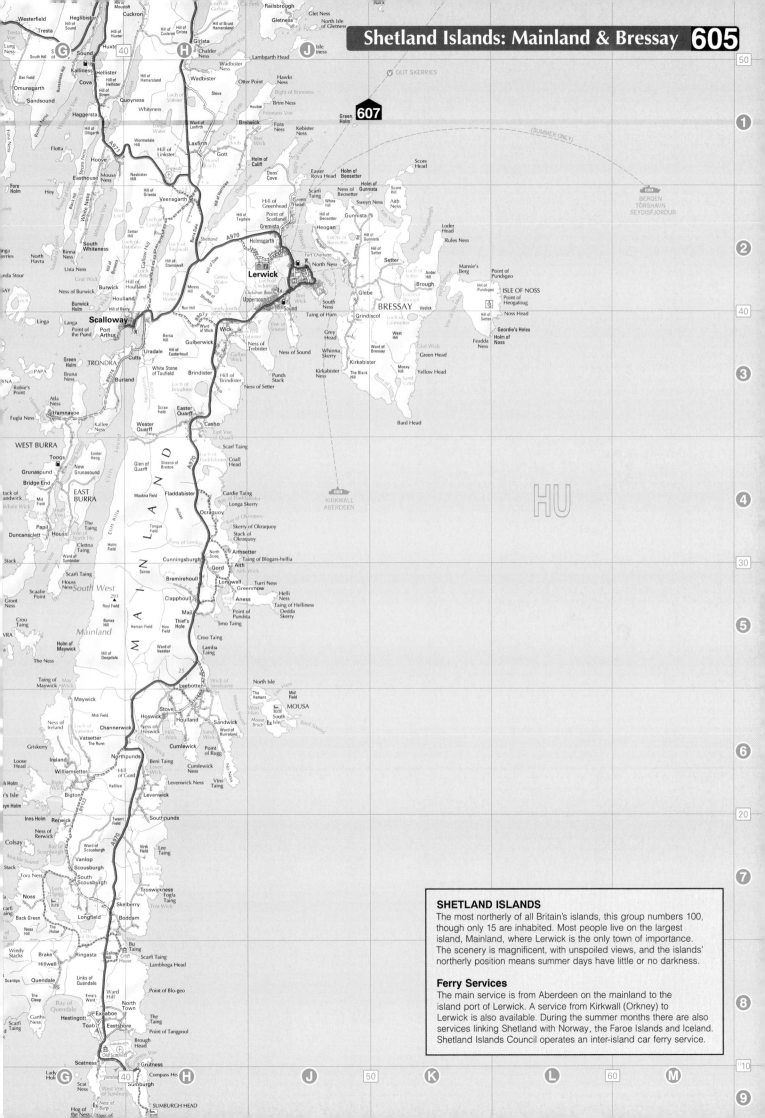

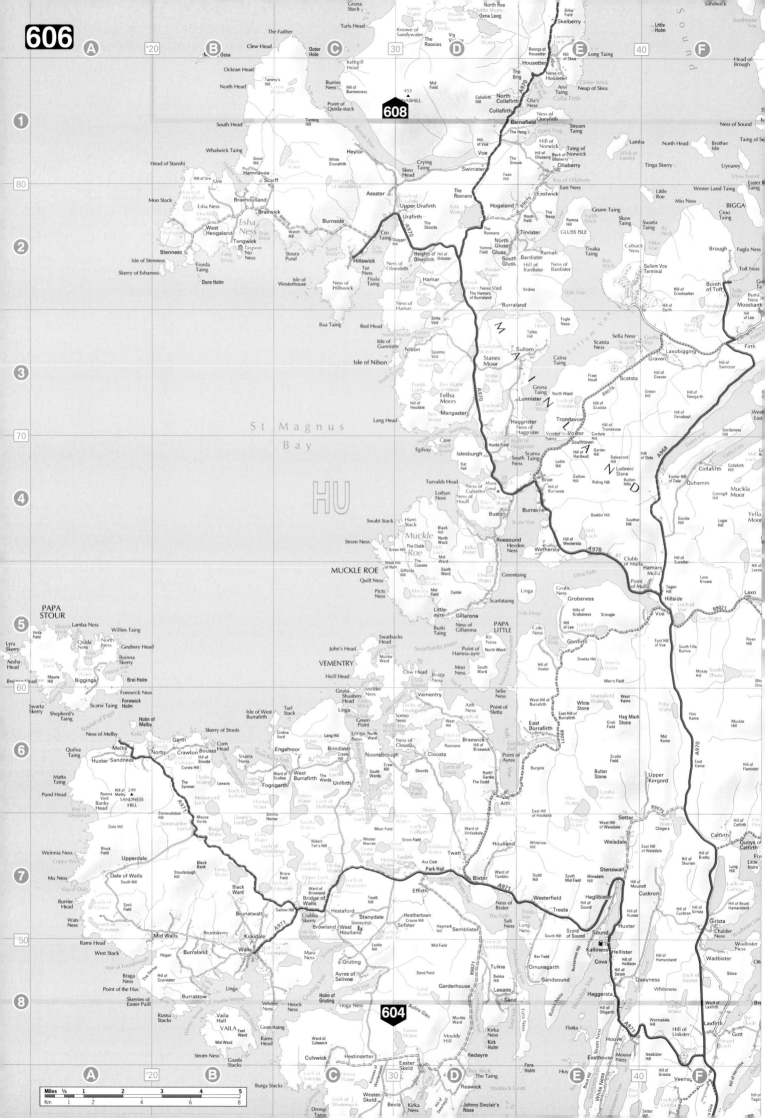

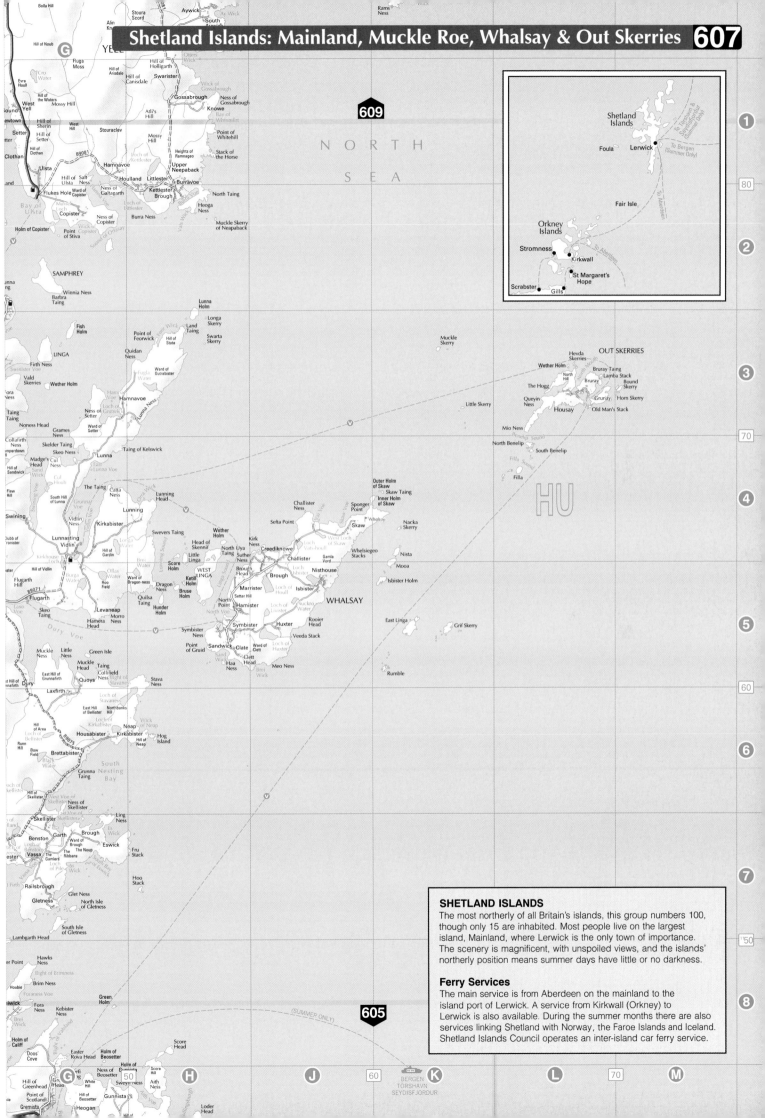

SHETLAND ISLANDS
The most northerly of all Britain's islands, this group numbers 100, though only 15 are inhabited. Most people live on the largest island, Mainland, where Lerwick is the only town of importance. The scenery is magnificent, with unspoiled views, and the islands' northerly position means summer days have little or no darkness.

Ferry Services
The main service is from Aberdeen on the mainland to the island port of Lerwick. A service from Kirkwall (Orkney) to Lerwick is also available. During the summer months there are also services linking Shetland with Norway, the Faroe Islands and Iceland. Shetland Islands Council operates an inter-island car ferry service.

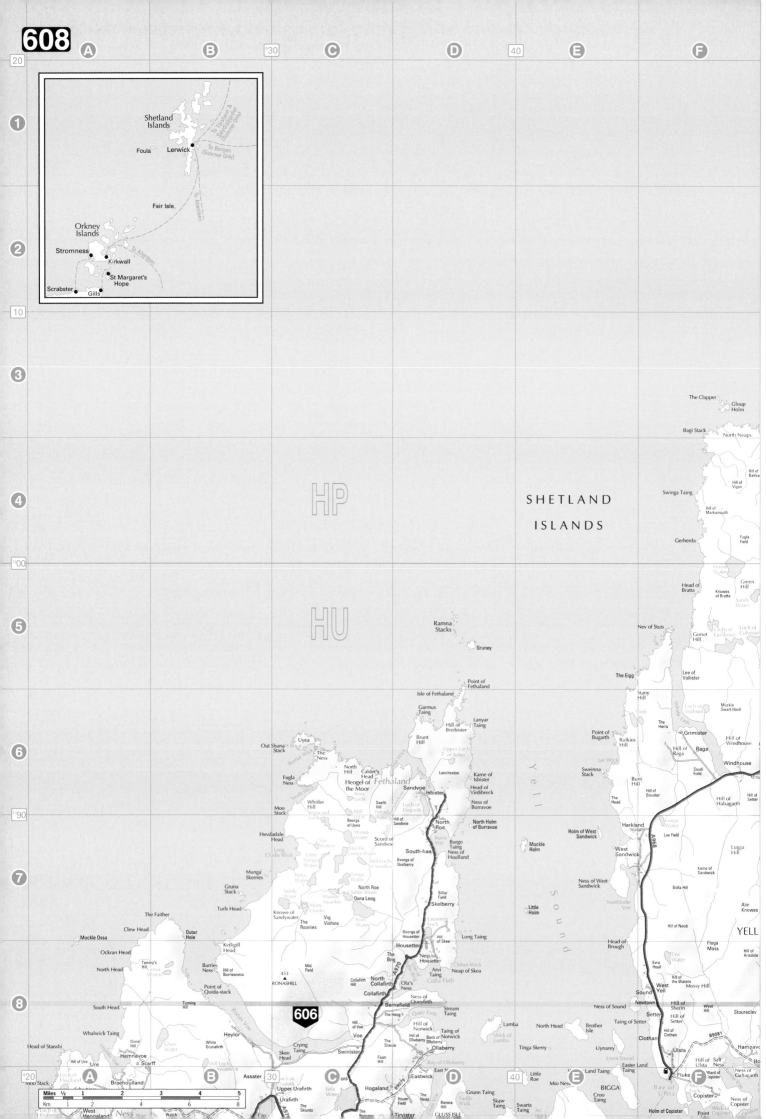

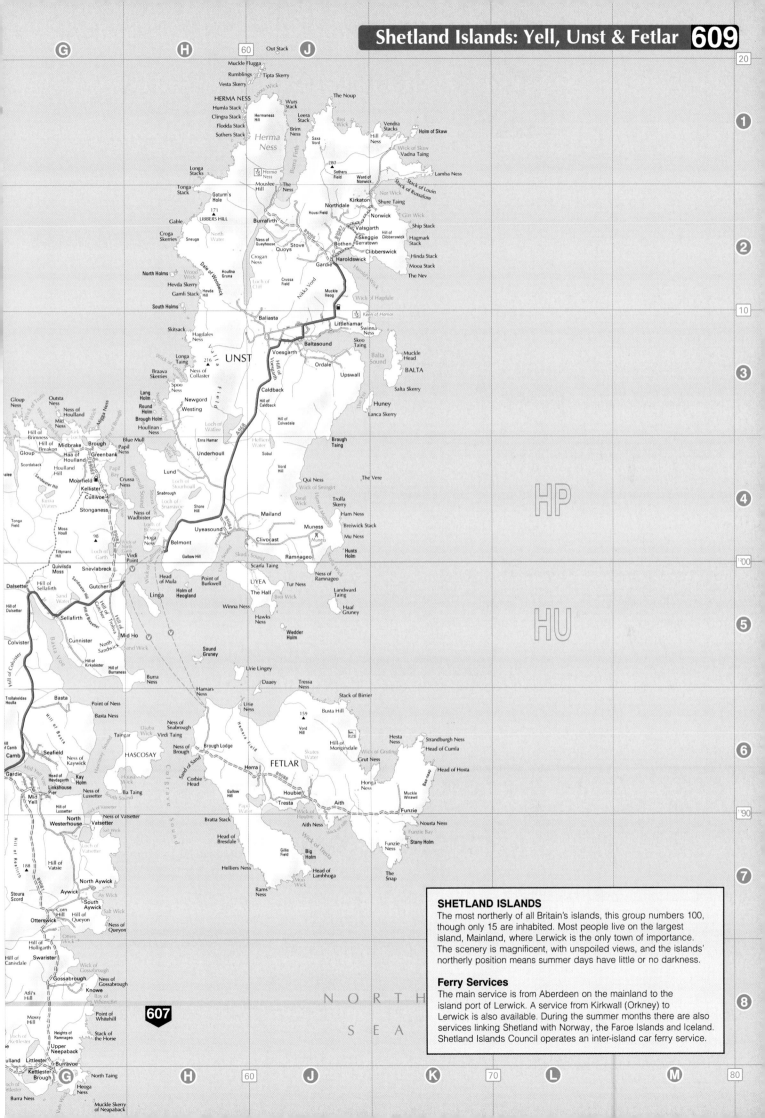

SHETLAND ISLANDS

The most northerly of all Britain's islands, this group numbers 100, though only 15 are inhabited. Most people live on the largest island, Mainland, where Lerwick is the only town of importance. The scenery is magnificent, with unspoiled views, and the islands' northerly position means summer days have little or no darkness.

Ferry Services

The main service is from Aberdeen on the mainland to the island port of Lerwick. A service from Kirkwall (Orkney) to Lerwick is also available. During the summer months there are also services linking Shetland with Norway, the Faroe Islands and Iceland. Shetland Islands Council operates an inter-island car ferry service.

Restricted junctions

Motorway and Primary Route junctions which have access or exit restrictions are shown thus ⬛3⬛ , ⬛R5⬛ on the map pages.

M1 London - Leeds

Junction	Northbound	Southbound
2	Access only from A1 (*northbound*)	Exit only to A1 (*southbound*)
4	Access only from A41 (*northbound*)	Exit only to A41 (*southbound*)
6A	Access only from M25 (no link from A405)	Exit only to M25 (no link from A405)
7	Access only from M10	Exit only to M10
17	Exit only to M45	Access only from M45
19	Exit only to northbound M6	Access only from M6
21A	Exit only to A46	Access only from A46
23A	Access only from A42	Exit only to A42
24A	Access only from A50	Exit only to A50
35A	Exit only to A616	Access only from A616
43	Exit only to M621	Access only from M621
48	Exit only to A1(M) (*northbound*)	Access only from A1(M) (*southbound*)

M2 Rochester - Faversham

Junction	Westbound	Eastbound
1	Exit only to A289 (*eastbound*)	Access only from A289 (*westbound*)

M3 Sunbury - Southampton

Junction	Southwestbound	Northeastbound
8	Exit only to A303	Access only from A303
10	Access only from Winchester & A31	Exit only to Winchester & A31
13	Access only to M27 (westbound) & A33	No restriction
14	Exit only to M27 (eastbound) & A33	Access only

M4 London - South Wales

Junction	Westbound	Eastbound
1	Access only from A4 (*westbound*)	Exit only to A4 (*eastbound*)
4A	No exit to A4 (*westbound*)	No restriction
21	Exit only to M48	Access only from M48
23	Access only from M48	Exit only to M48
25	Exit only to B4596	Access only from B4596
25A	Exit only to A4042	Access only from A4042
29	Exit only to A48(M)	Access only from A48(M)
38	Exit only to A48	No restriction
39	Access only from A48	No access/exit
42	Staggered junction; follow signs - exit only to A483	Staggered junction; follow signs - access only from A483

M5 Birmingham - Exeter

Junction	Southwestbound	Northeastbound
10	Exit only to A4019	Access only from A4019
11A	Exit only to A417 (*eastbound*)	Access only from A417 (*westbound*)
18A	Access only from M49	Exit only to M49
29	Access only from A30 (*westbound*)	No restriction

M6 Toll Motorway

Junction	Northbound	Southbound
T1	Access only	No access or exit
T2	No access or exit	Exit only
T3	Staggered junction; follow signs - access only from A38	Staggered junction; follow signs - no restriction
T5	Access only from A5127 (*southbound*)	Exit only to A5148 (*northbound*)
T7	Exit only	Access only
T8	Exit only	Access only

M6 Rugby - Carlisle

Junction	Northbound	Southbound
3A	Exit only	Access only
4	No access from M42 (*southbound*). No exit to M42 (*northbound*)	No access from M42 (*southbound*). No exit to M42
4A	Access only from M42 (*southbound*)	Exit only to M42

5	Exit only to A452	Access only from A452
10A	Exit only to M54	Access only from M54
11A	Access only	Exit only
20A (with M56)	No restriction	No access from M56 (*westbound*)
20	Access only from A50	No restriction
24	Access only from A58	Exit only to A58
25	Exit only	Access only
29	No direct access, use adjacent slip road to jct 29A	No direct exit, use adjacent slip road from jct 29A
29A	No direct exit, use adjacent slip road from jct 29	No direct access, use adjacent slip road to jct 29
30	Access only from M61	Exit only to M61
31A	Exit only	Access only

M8 Edinburgh - Bishopton

Junction	Westbound	Eastbound
8	No access from M73 (*southbound*) or from A8 (*eastbound*) & A89	No exit to M73 (*northbound*) or to A8 (*westbound*) & A89
9	Access only	Exit only
13	Access only from M80 (*southbound*)	Exit only to M80 (*northbound*)
14	Access only	Exit only
16	Exit only to A804	Access only from A879
17	Exit only to A82	No restriction
18	Access only from A82 (*eastbound*)	Exit only to A814
19	No access from A814 (westbound)	Exit only to A814 (*westbound*)
20	Exit only	Access only
21	Access only	Exit only to A8
22	Exit only to M77 (*southbound*)	Access only from M77 (*northbound*)
23	Exit only to B768	Access only from B768
25	No access or exit from or to A8	No access or exit from or to A8
25A	Exit only	Access only
28	Exit only	Access only
28A	Exit only to A737	Access only from A737

M9 Edinburgh - Dunblane

Junction	Northwestbound	Southeastbound
1A	Exit only to A8000	Access only from A8000
2	Access only	Exit only
3	Exit only	Access only
6	Access only from A904	Exit only to A905
8	Exit only to M876 (*southwestbound*)	Access only from M876 (*northeastbound*)

M10 St Albans - M1

Junction	Northwestbound	Southeastbound
with M1 (jct 7)	Exit only to M1 (*northbound*)	Access only from M1 (*southbound*)

M11 London - Cambridge

Junction	Northbound	Southbound
4	Access only from A406	Exit only to A406
5	Exit only to A1168	Access only from A1168
9	Exit only to A11	Access only from A11
13	Exit only to A1303	Access only from A1303
14	Exit only to A14 (*eastbound*)	Access only from A14

M20 Swanley - Folkestone

Junction	Southeastbound	Northwestbound
2	Staggered junction; follow signs - exit only to A227	Staggered junction; follow signs - access only from A227
3	Access only from M26 (*eastbound*)	Exit only to M26 (*westbound*)
5	For access follow signs - exit only to A20	Access only from A20
6	For exit follow signs	No restriction
11A	Exit only	Access only

M23 Hooley - Crawley

Junction	Southbound	Northbound
7	Access only from A23 (*southbound*)	Exit only to A23 (*northbound*)
10A	Exit only to B2036	Access only from B2036

M25 London Orbital Motorway

Junction	Clockwise	Anticlockwise
1B	No direct access, use slip road to Jct 2. Exit only to A296	Access only from A296. No exit - use jct 2
5	No exit to M26	No access from M26
19	Exit only to A41	Access only from A41
21	Access only from M1 (*southbound*). Exit only to M1 (*northbound*)	Access only from M1 (*southbound*). Exit only to M1 (*northbound*)
31	No exit (use slip road via jct 30)	For access follow signs

M26 Sevenoaks - Wrotham

Junction	Eastbound	Westbound
with M25 (jct 5)	Access only from anticlockwise M25 (*eastbound*)	Exit only to clockwise M25 (*westbound*)
with M20 (jct 3)	Exit only to M20 (*southeastbound*)	Access only from M20 (*northwestbound*)

M27 Cadnam - Portsmouth

Junction	Eastbound	Westbound
4	Staggered junction; follow signs - access only from M3 (*southbound*). Exit only to M3 (*northbound*)	Staggered junction; follow signs - access only from M3 (*southbound*). Exit only to M3 (*northbound*)
10	Access only from A32	Exit only to A32
12	Staggered junction; follow signs - access only from M275 (*northbound*)	Staggered junction; follow signs - exit only to M275 (*southbound*)

M40 London - Birmingham

Junction	Northwestbound	Southeastbound
3	Exit only to A40	Access only from A40
7	Exit only to A329	Access only from A329
8	Exit only to A40	Access only from A40
13	Exit only to A452	Access only from A452
14	Access only from A452	Exit only to A452
16	Access only from A3400	Exit only to A3400

M42 Bromsgrove - Measham

Junction	Northeastbound	Southwestbound
1	Access only from A38	Exit only to A38
7	Exit only to M6 (*northwestbound*)	Access only from M6 (*northwestbound*)
7A	Exit only to M6 (*southeastbound*)	No access or exit
8	Access only from M6 (*southeastbound*)	Exit only to M6 (*northwestbound*)

M45 Coventry - M1

Junction	Eastbound	Westbound
unnumbered (Dunchurch)	Exit only to A45 & B4429	Access only from A45 & B4429
with M1 (jct 17)	Exit only to M1 (*southbound*)	Access only from M1 (*northbound*)

M53 Mersey Tunnel - Chester

Junction	Southeastbound	Northwestbound
11	Access only from M56 (*westbound*). Exit only to M56 (*eastbound*)	Access only from M56 (*westbound*). Exit only to M56 (*eastbound*)

M54 Telford

Junction	Westbound	Eastbound
with M6 (jct 10A)	Access only from M6 (*northbound*)	Exit only to M6 (*southbound*)

M56 North Cheshire

Junction	Westbound	Eastbound
1	Access only from M60 (*westbound*)	Exit only to M60 (*eastbound*) & A34 (*northbound*)
2	Exit only to A560	Access only from A560
3	Access only from A5103	Exit only to A5103 & A560
4	Exit only	Access only
9	Exit to M6 (*southbound*) via A50 interchange	Access from M6 (*northbound*) via A50 interchange
15	Exit only to M53	Access only from M53

M57 Liverpool Outer Ring Road

Junction	Northwestbound	Southeastbound
3	Access only from A526	Exit only to A526
5	Access only from A580 (*westbound*)	Exit only to A580

M58 Liverpool - Wigan

Junction	Eastbound	Westbound
1	Access only	Exit Only

M60 Manchester Orbital

Junction	Clockwise	Anticlockwise
2	Access only from A560	Exit only to A560
3	No access from M56	Access only from A34 (*northbound*)
4	Access only from A34 (*northbound*). Exit only to M56	Access only from M56 (*eastbound*). Exit only to A34 (*southbound*)
5	Access and exit only from and to A5103 (*northbound*)	Access and exit only from and to A5103 (*southbound*)
7	No direct access, use slip road to jct 8. Exit only to A56	Access only from A56. No exit - use jct 8
14	Access from A580 (*eastbound*)	Exit only to A580 (*westbound*)
16	Access only from A666	Exit only to A666
20	Exit only to A664	Access only from A664
22	No restriction	Exit only to A62
25	Exit only to A6017	No restriction
26	No restriction	No access or exit
27	Access only from A626	Exit only to A626

M61 Manchester - Preston

Junction	Northwestbound	Southeastbound
3	No access or exit	Exit only to A666
with M6 (jct 30)	Exit only to M6 (*northbound*)	Access only from M6 (*southbound*)

M62 Liverpool - Kingston upon Hull

Junction	Eastbound	Westbound
23	Exit only to A640	Access only from A640

M65 Preston - Colne

Junction	Northeastbound	Southwestbound
1	Access and exit to M6 only	Access and exit to M6 only
9	Exit only to A679	Access only from A679
11	Access only	Exit only

M66 Bury

Junction	Southbound	Northbound
with A56	Access only from A56 (*southbound*)	Exit only to A56 (*northbound*)
1	Access only from A56	Exit only to A56

M67 Hyde Bypass

Junction	Eastbound	Westbound
1	Exit only to A6017	Access only from A6017
2	Access only	Exit only to A57
3	No restriction	Exit only to A627

M69 Coventry - Leicester

Junction	Northbound	Southbound
2	Access only from B4669	Exit only to B4669

M73 East of Glasgow

Junction	Northbound	Southbound
2	No access from or exit to A89. No access from M8 (*eastbound*).	No access from or exit to A89. No exit to M8 (*westbound*)
3	Exit only to A80 (*northeastbound*)	Access only from A80 (*southwestbound*)

M74 and A74(M) Glasgow - Gretna

Junction	Southbound	Northbound
2	Access only from A763	Exit only to A763
3	Exit only	Access only
7	Exit only to A72	Access only from A72
9	Exit only to B7078	No access or exit
10	Access only from B7078	No restrictions
11	Exit only to B7078	Access only from B7078
12	Access only from A70	Exit only to A70
18	Access only from B723	Exit only to B723
21	Exit only to B6357	Access only from B6357
with B7076	Access only	Exit only
Gretna Green	Exit only	Access only
with A75	Access only from A75	Exit only to A75
with A6071	Exit only to A74 (*southbound*)	Access only from A74 (*northbound*)

M77 South of Glasgow

Junction	Southbound	Northbound
with M8 (jct 22)	No access from M8 (*eastbound*)	No exit to M8 (*westbound*)
4	Exit only	Access only
with A77	Exit only to A77 (*southbound*)	Access only from A77 (*northbound*)

M80 Stepps Bypass

Junction	Northeastbound	Southwestbound
1	Access only	No restriction
3	Exit only	Access only

M80 Bonnybridge - Stirling

Junction	Northbound	Southbound
5	Exit only to M876 (*northeastbound*)	Access only from M876 (*southwestbound*)

M90 Forth Road Bridge - Perth

Junction	Northbound	Southbound
2A	Exit only to A92 (*eastbound*)	Access only from A92 (*westbound*)
7	Access only from A91	Exit only to A91
8	Exit only to A91	Access only from A91
10	No access from A912. No exit to A912 (*southbound*)	No access from A912 (*northbound*). No exit to A912

M180 Doncaster - Grimsby

Junction	Eastbound	Westbound
1	Exit only to A18	Access only from A18

M606 Bradford Spur

Junction	Northbound	Southbound
2	Exit only	No restriction

M621 Leeds - M1

Junction	Clockwise	Anticlockwise
2A	Access only	Exit only
4	Exit only	No restriction
5	Access only	Exit only
6	Exit only	Access only
with M1 (jct 43)	Exit only to M1 (*southbound*)	Access only from M1 (*northbound*)

M876 Bonnybridge - Kincardine Bridge

Junction	Northeastbound	Southwestbound
with M80 (jct 5)	Access only from M80 (*northbound*)	Exit only to M80 (*southbound*)
2	Exit only to A9	Access only from A9
with M9 (jct 8)	Exit only to M9 (*eastbound*)	Access only from M9 (*westbound*)

A1(M) South Mimms - Baldock

Junction	Northbound	Southbound
2	Exit only to A1001	Access only from A1001
3	No restriction	Exit only to A414
5	Access only	No access or exit

A1(M) East of Leeds

Junction	Northbound	Southbound
44	Access only from M1 (*northbound*)	Exit only to M1 (*southbound*)

A1(M) Scotch Corner - Newcastle upon Tyne

Junction	Northbound	Southbound
57	Exit only to A66(M) (*eastbound*)	Access only from A66(M) (*westbound*)
65	No access Exit only to A194(M) & A1 (*northbound*)	No exit Access only from A194(M) and A1 (*southbound*)

A3(M) Horndean - Havant

Junction	Southbound	Northbound
1	Exit only to A3	Access only from A3
4	Access only	Exit only

A48(M) Cardiff Spur

Junction	Westbound	Eastbound
29	Access only from M4 (*westbound*)	Exit only to M4 (*eastbound*)
29A	Exit only to A48 (*westbound*)	Access only from A48 (*eastbound*)

A66(M) Darlington Spur

Junction	Eastbound	Westbound
with A1(M) (jct 57)	Access only from A1(M) (*northbound*)	Exit only to A1(M) (*southbound*)

A194(M) Newcastle upon Tyne

Junction	Northbound	Southbound
with A1(M) (jct 65)	Access only from A1(M) (*northbound*)	Exit only to A1(M) (*southbound*)

A12 M25 - Ipswich

Junction	Northeastbound	Southwestbound
13	Access only from B1002	No restriction
14	Exit only	Access only
20A	Exit only to B1137	Access only from B1137
20B	Access only B1137	Exit only to B1137
21	No restriction	Access only from B1389
23	Exit only to B1024	Access only from B1024
24	Access only from B1024	Exit only from B1024
27	Exit only to A113	Access only from A113
unnumbered (with A120)	Exit only A120	Access only from A120
29	Access only from A120 and A1232	Exit only to A120 and A1232
unnumbered	Exit only	Access only

A14 M1 - Felixstowe

Junction	Eastbound	Westbound
With M1/M6 (jct19)	Access only from M6 and M1 (*southbound*)	Exit only to M6 and M1 (*northbound*)
4	Access only from B669	Exit only to B669
31	Access only from A428 & M11. Exit only to A1307	Exit only to A428 & M11. Access only from A1307
34	Exit only to B1047	Access only from B1047
unnumbered	No access from or exit to A1303	Access only from A1303
36	Access only from A11	Exit only to A11
38	Exit only to A11	Access only from A11
39	Access only from B1506	Exit only to B1506
49	Exit only to A1308	Access only from A1308
61	Exit only to A154	Access only from A154

A55 Holyhead - Chester

Junction	Eastbound	Westbound
8A	Access only from A5	Exit only to A5
23A	Exit only	Access only
24A	No access or exit	Exit only
33A	No access from or exit to B5126	Exit only to B5126
33B	Access only from A494	Exit only to A494
35A (west)	Exit only A5104	Access only from A5104
35B (east)	Access only from A5104	Exit only to A5104

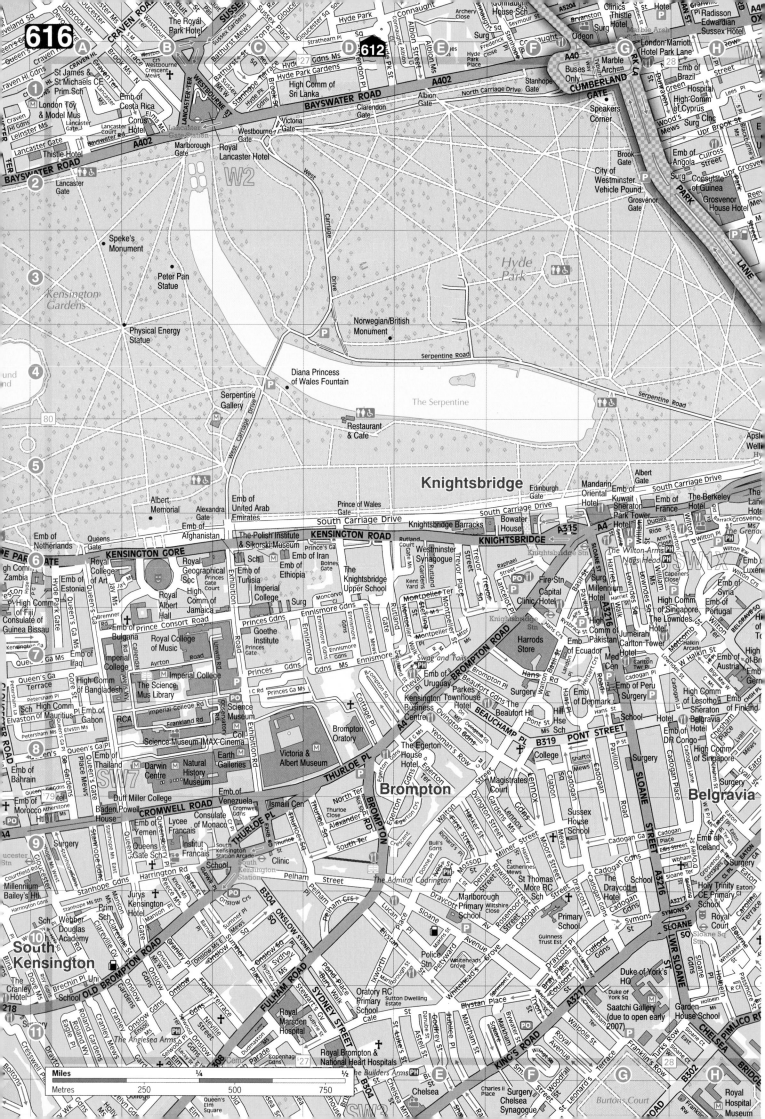

Central London street index

In the index, street names are listed in alphabetical order and written in full, but may be abbreviated on the map. Each entry is followed by its Postcode District and each street name is preceded by the page number and the grid reference to the square in which the name is found. Names are asterisked (*) in the index where there is insufficient space to show them on the map.

A

617 Q7 Abbey Orchard Street SW1P
619 Q7 Abbey Street SE1
619 P4 Abbots Lane SE1
617 K11 Abbots Manor SW1V
617 K11 Abbots Manor Estate SW1V
615 M10 Abchurch Lane EC4N
612 B5 Aberdeen Place NW8
619 N9 Aberdour Street SE1
619 R10 Abingdon Close SE1
618 A6 Abingdon Street SW1P
614 C3 Acton Street WC1X
612 A3 Ada Court NW8
617 J2 Adam's Row W1K
618 B2 Adam Street WC2R
614 H10 Addle Hill EC4V
615 K8 Addle Street EC2V
618 A2 Adelaide Street WC2N
613 Q7 Adeline Place WC1B
612 B6 Adpar Street W2
614 D1 Affleck Street N1
612 A2 Agar Street WC2N
614 G4 Agdon Street EC1V
617 N2 Air Street W1B
618 E4 Alaska Street SE1
617 M2 Albany Courtyard W1J
613 L2 Albany Street NW1
617 M2 Albemarle Street W1S
614 G5 Albemarle Way EC1M
618 H11 Alberta Estate SE17
618 H11 Alberta Street SE17
618 B11 Albert Embankment SE11
616 G5 Albert Gate SW1X
612 E10 Albion Close W2
612 E10 Albion Gate W2
612 E9 Albion Mews W2
614 G6 Albion Place EC1M
612 E9 Albion Street W2
614 B1 Albion Walk N1
615 J7 Albion Yard N1
619 P11 Aldbridge Street SE17
613 J8 Aldburgh Mews W1U
613 N1 Aldenham Street NW1
615 K8 Aldermanbury EC2V
615 K7 Aldermanbury Square EC2V
619 L7 Alderney Mews SE1
617 K10 Alderney Street SW1V
615 J6 Aldersgate Street EC1A
616 H3 Alford Street W1K
615 P9 Aldgate EC3M
615 R8 Aldgate Barrs * E1
615 Q9 Aldgate High Street EC3N
614 C9 Aldwych WC2B
616 D9 Alexander Place SW7
616 D9 Alexander Square SW3
616 B5 Alexandra Gate SW7
615 K1 Alford Place N1
613 P6 Alfred Mews W1T
613 P6 Alfred Place W1T
619 N8 Alice Street SE1
615 R1 Aligood Street E2
619 L2 Alhallows Lane EC4R
617 L8 Allington Street SW1E
612 D1 Allitsen Road NW8
612 D1 Allitson Road NW8
612 G5 Allsop Place NW1
613 L7 All Souls' Place W1B
619 R10 Alma Grove SE1
612 A2 Alma Square NW8
612 E4 Alpha Close NW1
619 N11 Alsace Road SE17
619 R8 Alscot Road SE16
619 Q9 Alscot Way SE1
619 N11 Alvey Street SE17
618 G11 Ambergate Street SE17
617 N8 Ambrosden Avenue SW1P
618 H11 Amelia Street SE17
614 H9 Amen Corner EC4M
614 H9 Amen Court EC4M
612 Q10 America Square EC3N
614 A2 America Street SE1
613 N1 Ampthill Estate NW1
613 N1 Ampthill Square NW1
614 C3 Ampton Street WC1X
614 E2 Amwell Street EC1R
615 K4 Anchor Yard EC1V
616 F11 Anderson Street SW3
613 Q8 Andrew Borde Street WC2H
615 R7 Angel Alley E1
615 M8 Angel Court EC2R
619 L2 Angel Passage EC4R
614 G1 Angel Square * EC1V
615 J8 Angel Street EC1A
615 P4 Anning Street EC2A
616 G6 Ann's Close SW1X
614 G9 Apothecary Street EC4V
617 N3 Apple Tree Yard SW1Y
615 N6 Appold Street EC2A
619 J9 Apsley Way * W1J
618 F4 Aquinas Street SE1
613 P10 Archery Close SE1
612 E9 Archery Close W2
617 J2 Archibald Mews W1J
619 J8 Arch Street SE1
615 N1 Arden Estate N1
614 B2 Argyle Square WC1H
614 A2 Argyle Street NW1
614 A3 Argyle Walk WC1H
613 M9 Argyll Street W1B
619 P6 Archie Street SE1
617 M3 Arlington Street W1J
614 F2 Arlington Way EC1R
614 B9 Arne Street WC2H
617 Q8 Arneway Street SW1P
615 Q3 Arnold Circus E2
619 R6 Arnold Street N1
619 M2 Arthur Street EC4R
615 P7 Artillery Lane EC2M
615 P7 Artillery Passage E1
617 P8 Artillery Row SW1P
615 P8 Artizan Street E1
614 D10 Arundel Street WC2R
612 D5 Ashbridge Street NW8
614 H3 Ashby Street EC1V
615 N2 Ashford Street N1
612 H6 Ashland Place W1U
617 M8 Ashley Place SW1P
612 D6 Ashmill Street NW8
615 N2 Aske Street N1
619 K11 Asolando Drive SE17
616 E11 Astell Street SW3
616 A9 Atherstone Mews SW7
617 Q10 Atterbury Street SW1P
614 E4 Attneave Street WC1X
617 J3 Audley Square W1K
613 L1 Augustus Street NW1
615 M8 Austin Friars EC2N
615 M8 Austin Friars Square EC2N
615 Q3 Austin Street E2

618 G9 Austral Street SE11
618 D11 Aveline Street SE11
614 H9 Ave Marie Lane EC4M
617 K10 Avery Farm Row SW1W
615 K10 Avery Row W1K
619 J7 Avonmouth Street SE1
612 H7 Aybrook Street W1U
614 G5 Aylesbury Street EC1R
616 K5 Ayres Street SE1
616 B7 Ayrton Road SW7

B

617 P3 Babmaes Street SW1Y
615 M3 Bache's Street N1
614 F5 Back Hill EC1R
619 Q9 Bacon Grove SE1
615 R4 Bacon Street E1
619 L5 Baden Place SE1
613 Q8 Bainbridge Street WC1A
615 K4 Baird Street EC1Y
617 H8 Bakers Mews W1U
615 Q2 Bakers Rents E2
614 E5 Baker's Row EC1R
612 G5 Baker Street NW1
614 E5 Baker's Yard EC1R
619 R10 Balaclava Road SE1
612 F4 Balcombe Street NW1
613 J9 Balderton Street W1K
614 E6 Baldwin's Gardens WC1X
615 L3 Baldwin Street EC1V
614 B1 Balfe Street N1
617 J3 Balfour Mews W1K
617 J2 Balfour Place W1K
615 L9 Balfour Street E1
617 J3 Baltic Street East EC1Y
617 J5 Baltic Street West EC1Y
614 A10 Banbury Court WC2E
619 K3 Bank End SE1
619 J2 Bankside SE1
617 N4 Banner Street EC1Y
614 B6 Barge Close NW1N
614 K5 Barge House Street SE1
617 L2 Barlow Place W1J
615 M9 Barlow Street SE17
618 B10 Barnaby Street SW7
613 N1 Barnby Street NW1
619 P5 Barnham Street SE1
615 R2 Baroness Road E2
618 F6 Baron's Place SE1
614 F1 Baron Street N1
613 J9 Barrett Street W1U
612 D1 Barrow Hill Estate NW8
612 D1 Barrow Hill Road NW8
614 B7 Barter Street WC1A
615 J7 Bartholomew Close EC1A
615 M8 Bartholomew Lane EC2R
615 K4 Bartholomew Square EC1V
619 L8 Bartholomew Street SE1
614 F8 Bartlett Court EC4A
617 R8 Barton Street SW1P
614 F7 Basil Street SW3
615 L8 Basinghall Avenue EC2V
615 L8 Basinghall Street EC2V
615 P2 Basing Place E2
614 H4 Bastwick Street EC1V
615 P4 Bateman Row EC2A
613 P9 Bateman Street W1D
615 N3 Bath Place N1
615 K3 Bath Street EC1V
619 J8 Bath Terrace SE1
612 C10 Bathurst Mews W2
612 C10 Bathurst Street W2
619 N4 Battle Bridge Lane SE1
613 R1 Battle Bridge Road NW1
617 P7 Bayley Street W1T
618 E7 Baylis Road SE1
616 D1 Bayswater Road W2
613 M10 Beak Street W1F
619 J3 Bear Gardens SE1
613 H3 Bear Lane SE1
613 Q10 Bear Street WC2H
616 E8 Beauchamp Place SW3
614 E7 Beauchamp Street EC1N
616 E7 Beaufort Gardens SW3
618 D10 Beaufoy Walk SE11
613 J6 Beaumont Mews W1U
614 N4 Beaumont Place W1T
613 J6 Beaumont Street W1U
619 L7 Becket Street SE1
619 M10 Beckway Street SE17
614 L4 Bedale Street SE1
613 Q7 Bedford Avenue W1T
614 A10 Bedfordbury WC2N
618 A2 Bedford Court WC2N
614 A6 Bedford Place WC1B
614 D6 Bedford Row WC1X
613 Q7 Bedford Square WC1B
614 A10 Bedford Street WC2E
614 Q5 Bedford Way WC1H
612 C5 Bedlow Close NW8
615 J6 Beech Street (Below) EC2Y
617 L8 Beeston Place SW1X
613 J7 Belgrave Mews South SW1X
616 H7 Belgrave Mews West SW1X
617 J8 Belgrave Place SW1X
617 M10 Belgrave Road SW1V
616 H7 Belgrave Square SW1X
614 A2 Belgrave Street SW1X
615 Q7 Bell Lane E1
612 D6 Bell Street NW1
619 K2 Bell Wharf Lane EC4R
614 E9 Bell Yard WC2A
619 P6 Bell Yard Mews SE1
615 P6 Belvedere Buildings SE1
618 C5 Belvedere Road SE1
612 E6 Bendall Mews NW1
614 G6 Benjamin Street EC1M
614 H10 Bennet's Hill EC4V
617 M3 Bennett Street SW1A
613 J8 Bentinck Mews W1U
613 J8 Bentinck Street W1U
612 G8 Berkeley Mews W1H
617 L2 Berkeley Square W1J
617 L2 Berkeley Street W1J
614 N4 Bermondsey Street SE1
614 A5 Bernard Street WC1N
613 N7 Berners Mews W1T
613 N8 Berners Place W1T
613 N7 Berners Street W1T
612 D4 Bernhardt Crescent NW8
618 H11 Berryfield Road SE17
614 H3 Berry Place EC1V
614 H5 Berry Street EC1V
613 N9 Berwick Street W1F
617 P11 Bessborough Street SW1V
615 R4 Bethnal Green Road E2
617 R8 Betterton Street WC2H
618 A9 Bevan Street N1
612 F7 Beverston Mews W1H
614 E1 Bevin Way N1
615 P8 Bevis Marks EC3A

612 G6 Bickenhall Street W1U
619 P6 Bickles Yard SE1
614 R3 Bidborough Street WC1H
615 P9 Billiter Square EC3M
615 P9 Billiter Street EC3M
612 H5 Bingham Place W1U
613 J10 Binney Street W1K
615 M9 Birchin Lane EC3V
617 N6 Birdcage Walk SW1H
613 J9 Bird Street W1U
614 B2 Birkenhead Street N1
612 A8 Bishop's Bridge Road W2
614 G8 Bishop's Court EC4M
615 P7 Bishopsgate EC2M
615 P6 Bishopsgate Arcade EC2M
618 F9 Bishops Terrace SE11
619 J6 Bittern Street SE1
615 N4 Blackall Street EC2A
615 R2 Blackbird Yard E2
612 H10 Blackburne's Mews W1K
618 G2 Blackfriars Bridge SE1
614 G9 Black Friars Lane EC4V
614 G10 Blackfriars Passage EC4V
618 G3 Blackfriars Road SE1
614 H10 Blackfriars Underpass EC4V
615 M8 Black Horse Court EC4M
615 F10 Blacklands Terrace SW3
615 R4 Blackmans Yard * E2
615 C10 Black Prince Road SE11
619 N5 Black Swan Yard SE1
612 E5 Blandford Square NW1
612 G8 Blandford Street W1U
614 F7 Bleeding Heart Yard EC1N
615 K9 Blenheim Street W1K
615 K1 Bletchley Street N1
615 A5 Blomfield Road W9
615 M7 Blomfield Street EC2M
615 L10 Bloomfield Place W1K
617 J11 Bloomfield Terrace SW1W
614 B7 Bloomsbury Place WC1A
614 B7 Bloomsbury Square WC1A
615 Q6 Bloomsbury Street WC1E
614 A7 Bloomsbury Way WC1A
617 P5 Blossom Street E1
617 M4 Blue Ball Yard SW1A
619 N7 Blue Lion Place SE1
612 D5 Boldero Place NW8
612 D6 Bolney Gate SW7
614 L5 Bolsover Street W1W
614 F9 Bolt Court EC4A
617 L3 Bolton Street W1J
617 P11 Bonaparte Mews SW1V
615 M5 Bonhill Street EC2A
615 J10 Booth Lane EC4V
615 N3 Boot Street N1
614 H1 Boreas Walk N1
619 K6 Borough High Street SE1
618 G7 Borough Road SE1
619 J6 Borough Square SE1
617 J9 Boscobel Place SW1W
612 C6 Boscobel Street W2
619 Q5 Boss Street SE1
612 B6 Boston Place NW1
614 B6 Boswell Court WC1N
614 B6 Boswell Street WC1N
619 N2 Botolph Alley EC3R
619 N2 Botolph Lane EC3R
618 G5 Boundary Row SE1
615 Q3 Boundary Street E2
613 P10 Bourchier Street W1D
617 L10 Bourdon Place W1K
615 L10 Bourdon Street W1K
613 M7 Bourlet Close W1T
614 E6 Bourne Estate * EC1N
616 H10 Bourne Street SW1W
612 C8 Bouverie Place W2
614 F9 Bouverie Street EC4Y
616 B9 Bow Churchyard EC4M
618 F11 Bowden Street SE11
615 G6 Bowland Yard SW1X
615 K5 Bow Lane EC4M
614 F5 Bowling Green Lane EC1R
619 L5 Bowling Green Place SE1
619 L6 Bowling Green Walk N1
614 B9 Bow Street WC2E
616 H6 Boyfield Street SE1
615 K5 Brackley Street EC2Y
618 F4 Brad Street SE1
615 R9 Braham Street E1
615 L6 Brandon Mews * EC2Y
619 K10 Brandon Street SE1
614 B1 Bravingtons Walk N1
612 F11 Bray Place SW3
615 K9 Bread Street EC4M
614 E8 Bream's Buildings EC4A
616 A11 Brechin Place SW7
616 A7 Bremner Road SW7
612 E8 Brendon Street W1H
617 L7 Bressenden Place SW1E
613 N10 Brewer Street W1B
614 H5 Brewery Square EC1V
619 Q4 Brewery Square SE1
614 G4 Brewhouse Yard EC1V
617 * EC4Y Brick Court
615 R3 Brick Lane E2
617 K4 Brick Street W1J
614 G9 Bride Court EC4V
614 G9 Bride Lane EC4Y
614 G1 Bridel Mews EC1V
619 Q7 Bridewain Street SE1
614 G9 Bridewell Place EC4V
612 L6 Bridford Mews W1G
612 D1 Bridgeman Street NW8
612 L9 Bridge Place SW1V
618 A6 Bridge Street SW1P
615 J6 Bridgewater Square EC2Y
615 J6 Bridgewater Street EC2Y
613 N1 Bridgeway Street NW1
613 N10 Bridle Lane W1F
613 Q1 Brill Place NW1
618 G6 Brinton Walk SE1
614 G6 Briset Street EC1M
614 C2 Britannia Street WC1X
615 L1 Britannia Walk N1
614 H4 Britton Street EC1M
615 K10 Broadbent Street W1K
615 B9 Broad Court WC2E
612 D6 Broadley Street NW8
612 E5 Broadley Terrace NW8
612 H7 Broadstone Place W1U
615 N7 Broad Street Avenue EC2M
615 M7 Broad Street Place EC2M
618 F3 Broadwall SE1
617 P7 Broadway SW1H
613 N10 Broadwick Street W1F
614 G5 Broad Yard EC1M
619 K7 Brockham Street SE1
619 R11 Brodie Street SE1
615 J10 Broken Wharf EC4V
616 F6 Brompton Arcade SW1X
616 E7 Brompton Place SW3
616 D9 Brompton Road SW3
616 D7 Brompton Square SW3

619 K11 Bronti Close SE17
618 F8 Brook Drive SE1
614 E6 Brooke's Market EC1N
614 E7 Brooke Street EC1N
616 G2 Brook Gate W2
612 A10 Brook Mews North W2
615 K10 Brook's Mews W1K
612 C10 Brook Street W2
613 J10 Brook Street W1K
612 J10 Brown Hart Gardens W1K
612 A5 Browning Close W9
613 J7 Browning Mews W1G
619 K11 Browning Street SE17
614 D4 Brownlow Mews WC1X
614 D7 Brownlow Street WC1R
612 F8 Brown Street W1H
615 Q7 Brune Street E1
619 P6 Brunswick Court SE1
612 G8 Brunswick Mews W1H
615 M3 Brunswick Place N1
614 B4 Brunswick Square WC1N
615 P6 Brushfield Street E1
617 L2 Bruton Lane W1J
617 L2 Bruton Place W1J
617 L2 Bruton Street W1J
612 F7 Bryanston Mews East W1H
612 F7 Bryanston Mews West W1H
612 F7 Bryanston Place W1H
612 F8 Bryanston Square W1H
612 F9 Bryanston Street W1H
617 R2 Brydges Place WC2N
617 M7 Buckingham Gate SW1E
617 M7 Buckingham Mews SW1E
617 K9 Buckingham Palace Road SW1V
617 M7 Buckingham Place SW1E
618 B2 Buckingham Street WC2N
615 M1 Buckland Street N1
615 L9 Bucklersbury EC4N
615 R8 Buckle Street E1
613 R8 Bucknall Street WC1A
615 L10 Budge Row EC4N
615 R10 Bulinca Street SW1P
617 L10 Bulleid Way SW1V
616 E9 Bull's Gardens SW3
613 J7 Bulstrode Place W1U
613 J8 Bulstrode Street W1U
615 L4 Bunhill Row EC1Y
615 H11 Bunhouse Place SW1W
619 L8 Burbage Close SE1
614 H9 Burgon Street EC4V
619 P6 Burgess Street SE1
619 P6 Burge Street SE1
619 M8 Burge Street SE1
619 K11 Burgon Street Hill EC4V
614 B10 Burleigh Street WC2E
617 M2 Burlington Arcade W1S
617 M2 Burlington Gardens W1S
619 R11 Burnell Walk SE1
614 D6 Burne Street NW1
619 R10 Burnham Close SE1
616 E11 Burnsall Street SW3
618 G3 Burrell Street SE1
618 G5 Burrows Mews SE1
614 N4 Bursar Street SE1
617 J10 Burton Mews SW1W
613 Q4 Burton Place WC1H
613 Q4 Burton Street WC1H
612 E8 Burwood Place W2
615 P8 Bury Court EC3A
614 A7 Bury Place WC1A
615 P9 Bury Street EC3A
617 M3 Bury Street SW1Y
615 D10 Bury Walk SW3
619 N8 Bushbaby Close SE1
615 L10 Bush Lane EC4R
619 R10 Bushwood Drive SE1
615 B9 Bute Street SW7
619 R5 Butlers & Colonial Wharf SE1
619 Q9 Buttermere Close SE1
615 M2 Buttesland Street N1
615 R5 Buxton Street E1
613 Q5 Byng Place WC1E
619 P2 Byward Street EC3R
616 F11 Bywater Street SW3
613 M7 Bywell Place W1W

C

612 D7 Cabbell Street NW1
615 R8 Cadbury Way SE16
615 R1 Cadell Close E2
615 R11 Cadet Drive SE1
616 G9 Cadogan Gardens SW3
616 G9 Cadogan Gate SW1X
616 H8 Cadogan Lane SW1X
616 G8 Cadogan Place SW1X
616 F8 Cadogan Square SW1X
616 F10 Cadogan Street SW3
615 K5 Cahill Street EC1Y
614 B1 Caledonia Street N1
616 D11 Cale Street SW3
615 P3 Calthorpe Street WC1X
615 Q5 Calvert Avenue E2
615 Q5 Calvin Street E1
613 Q9 Cambridge Circus W1D
613 K3 Cambridge Gate NW1
613 L3 Cambridge Gate Mews NW1
612 D8 Cambridge Square W2
612 L11 Cambridge Street SW1V
613 K3 Cambridge Terrace NW1
613 L3 Cambridge Terrace Mews NW1
615 Q4 Camlet Street E2
615 P8 Camomile Street EC3A
615 R9 Camperdown Street E1
615 M7 Candover Street W1W
615 J9 Cannon Street EC4M
619 Q8 Canon Murnane Road SE16
612 A6 Canon Row SW1A
616 H10 Canterbury Place SE17
619 J3 Canvey Street SE1
619 G6 Capeners Close SW1X
612 C4 Capland Street NW8
618 L6 Carburton Street W1W
618 E11 Cardigan Street SE11
615 M8 Cardinal Bourne Street SE1
613 N2 Cardington Street NW1
612 J8 Carey Lane EC2V
617 P10 Carey Place SW1P
614 D9 Carey Street WC2A
615 P9 Carlisle Avenue EC3N
615 D7 Carlisle Lane SE1
617 M8 Carlisle Place SW1P
613 P9 Carlisle Street W1F
617 J2 Carlos Place W1K
617 P4 Carlton Gardens SW1Y
617 P4 Carlton House Terrace SW1Y
617 P2 Carlton Street SW1Y
614 G7 Carlton Tower Place SW1X
614 F10 Carmelite Street EC4Y
613 M10 Carnaby Street W1B

615 P2 Caroline Gardens E2
616 H10 Caroline Terrace SW1W
615 K2 Carpenter Street W1K
617 K4 Carrington Street W1J
617 P6 Carteret Street SW1H
614 H9 Carter Lane EC4V
612 E7 Carthusian Street EC1M
618 B2 Carting Lane WC2R
613 Q7 Cartwright Gardens WC1H
615 R10 Cartwright Street EC3N
612 D3 Casey Close NW8
612 E5 Casey Close NW8
614 H10 Castle Baynard Street EC4V
612 G9 Castlebrook Close SE11
615 M9 Castle Court EC3V
617 M7 Castle Lane SW1E
612 F8 Castlereagh Street W1H
618 H3 Castle Yard SE1
619 M10 Catesby Street SE17
613 L3 Cathedral Street SE1
614 F4 Catherine Griffiths Court EC1R
617 M7 Catherine Place SW1E
614 C10 Catherine Street WC2B
615 P7 Catherine Wheel Alley EC3M
617 M4 Catherine Wheel Yard SW1A
612 E7 Cato Street W1H
614 C7 Catton Street WC1B
612 Q10 Causton Street SW1P
612 L6 Cavendish Avenue NW8
612 C2 Cavendish Close NW8
613 L6 Cavendish Mews North W1B
613 L7 Cavendish Mews South W1W
613 L8 Cavendish Place W1G
615 K8 Cavendish Square W1G
615 L1 Cavendish Street N1
617 N7 Caxton Street SW1H
619 P5 Cayenne Court SE1
615 L3 Cayton Street EC1V
613 R10 Cecil Court WC2H
615 D7 Centaur Street SE1
615 J2 Central Street EC1V
614 F2 Chadwell Street EC1R
617 P8 Chadwick Street SW1P
612 F5 Chagford Street NW1
613 Q2 Chalton Street NW1
615 R10 Chamber Street E1
615 R3 Chambord Street E2
618 G3 Chancel Street SE1
614 D7 Chancery Lane WC2A
615 Q4 Chance Street E2
618 A2 Chandos Place WC2N
613 L7 Chandos Street W1G
615 L5 Chapel Court SE1
613 K8 Chapel Place W1G
617 J7 Chapel Street SW1X
612 D7 Chapel Street W2
618 F5 Chaplin Close SE1
617 P10 Chapter Street SW1P
617 R3 Charing Cross WC2N
613 Q8 Charing Cross Road W1D
617 P3 Charles II Street SW1Y
612 C1 Charles Lane NW8
613 M3 Charles Place NW1
613 M3 Charles Square N1
613 M3 Charles Square Estate N1
617 K3 Charles Street W1J
615 K10 Charleston Street SE17
613 N6 Charlotte Mews W1T
613 N7 Charlotte Place W1T
615 N3 Charlotte Road N1
613 N7 Charlotte Street W1T
617 N10 Charlwood Place SW1V
617 N11 Charlwood Street SW1V
613 J5 Charterhouse Buildings EC1M
614 H6 Charterhouse Mews EC1M
614 F7 Charterhouse Street EC1N
615 M2 Chart Street N1
619 L9 Chatham Street SE17
619 R10 Chaucer Drive SE1
615 K9 Cheapside EC2V
616 H11 Chelsea Bridge Road SW1W
616 D11 Chelsea Manor Street SW3
616 G11 Cheltenham Terrace SW3
615 P5 Chenies Mews WC1E
613 P6 Chenies Street WC1E
615 L5 Chequer Street EC1Y
615 M1 Cherbury Street N1
614 F2 Cherry Tree Walk EC1Y
616 H8 Chesham Close SW1X
616 H8 Chesham Mews SW1X
616 H8 Chesham Place SW1X
616 H8 Chesham Street SW1X
613 J6 Chester Close SW1X
613 L2 Chester Close North NW1
613 L3 Chester Close South NW1
617 K2 Chesterfield Gardens W1J
617 K3 Chesterfield Hill W1J
617 K2 Chesterfield Street W1J
617 K8 Chester Gate NW1
617 K7 Chester Mews SW1X
613 K2 Chester Place NW1
613 J3 Chester Road NW1
617 K10 Chester Row SW1W
617 K8 Chester Square SW1W
617 K9 Chester Square Mews SW1W
617 J7 Chester Street SW1X
613 K2 Chester Terrace NW1
618 F10 Chester Way SE11
619 L7 Chettle Close SE1
616 E7 Cheval Place SW7
619 P6 Chicheley Street SE1
615 R7 Chicksand Street E1
612 H5 Chiltern Street W1U
615 R4 Chilton Street E2
612 A9 Chilworth Mews W2
612 A9 Chilworth Street W2
615 L6 Chiswell Street EC1Y
615 N6 Chitty Street W1T
615 N4 Christina Street EC2A
613 Q2 Christopher Place NW1
615 M5 Christopher Street EC2A
612 C5 Church Street W2
612 C5 Church Street Estate NW8
613 Q2 Churchway NW1
618 H8 Churchyard Row SE11
617 N10 Churton Place SW1V
617 N10 Churton Street SW1V
612 F6 Circus Mews W1H
615 M7 Circus Place EC2M
612 B3 Circus Road NW8
614 C11 Citadel Place SE11
614 H1 City Garden Row N1
614 G1 City Road N1
615 M5 City Road EC1Y
615 N7 City Walk SE1
616 F8 Clabon Mews SW1X
614 E1 Claremont Close N1
614 F1 Claremont Square N1
613 L3 Clarence Gardens NW1
612 G4 Clarence Gate NW1
613 R1 Clarence Passage NW1
613 L2 Clarence Terrace NW1
612 D5 Clarendon Close

612 A5 Clarendon Gardens W9
612 D10 Clarendon Gate W2
612 D10 Clarendon Mews W2
612 D10 Clarendon Place W2
617 L11 Clarendon Street SW1V
612 A4 Clarendon Terrace W9
616 A10 Clareville Grove SW7
616 A10 Clareville Street SW7
617 K3 Clarges Mews W1J
617 L3 Clarges Street W1J
613 J6 Clark Mews W1G
613 M1 Clarkson Row NW1
612 G7 Clay Street W1U
618 F11 Cleaver Square SE11
618 F11 Cleaver Street SE11
614 D9 Clements Inn WC2A
615 M10 Clement's Lane EC4N
619 K5 Clennam Street SE1
612 F8 Clenston Mews W1H
614 M4 Clere Place EC2A
615 M4 Clere Street EC2A
614 F4 Clerkenwell Close EC1R
614 G5 Clerkenwell Green EC1R
614 E5 Clerkenwell Road EC1R
613 M6 Cleveland Mews W1T
617 N3 Cleveland Place SW1Y
617 N4 Cleveland Row SW1A
615 L5 Cleveland Street NW1
612 A8 Cleveland Terrace W2
617 M2 Clifford Street W1S
612 C10 Clifton Place W2
612 A4 Clifton Road W9
615 N3 Clifton Street EC2A
619 L3 Clink Street SE1
613 M5 Clipstone Mews W1W
613 L6 Clipstone Street W1W
616 H9 Cliveden Place SW1W
615 K10 Cloak Lane EC4R
614 H7 Cloth Court EC1A
614 H7 Cloth Fair EC1A
615 P8 Clothier Street EC3A
615 J6 Clothier Street EC1A
615 Q4 Club Row E2
615 M1 Clunbury Street N1
619 N7 Cluny Estate SE1
619 N7 Cluny Place SE1
613 L10 Coach & Horses Yard W1S
615 Q8 Cobb Street E1
613 N3 Cobourg Street NW1
617 N9 Coburg Close SW1P
612 C1 Cochrane Mews NW8
612 C1 Cochrane Street NW8
612 Q3 Cockpur Court SW1Y
617 Q3 Cockspur Street SW1Y
615 K5 Code Street E1
618 F4 Coin Street SE1
615 N8 Colchester Street E1
614 E4 Coldbath Square EC1R
614 G1 Colebrooke Row N1
615 L8 Coleman Street EC2R
619 K6 Cole Street SE1
614 D5 Coley Street WC1X
615 R7 College East * E1
615 K10 College Hill EC4R
618 A7 College Mews SW1P
615 K10 College Street EC4R
614 C1 Collier Street N1
619 J6 Collinson Street SE1
619 J6 Collinson Walk SE1
618 G8 Colnbrook Street SE1
618 G4 Colombo Street SE1
614 A5 Colonnade WC1N
615 L4 Colosseum Terrace NW1
615 Q2 Columbia Road E2
613 N7 Colville Place W1T
617 K10 Colworth Grove SE17
615 Q5 Commercial Street E1
613 L3 Compton Close NW1
614 H4 Compton Passage EC1V
614 A4 Compton Place WC1H
614 G4 Compton Street EC1V
619 N10 Comus Place SE17
618 D4 Concert Hall Approach SE1
614 A10 Conduit Court WC2E
612 B9 Conduit Mews W2
612 B9 Conduit Passage W2
612 B9 Conduit Place W2
613 L10 Conduit Street W1S
619 N10 Congreve Street SE17
612 E9 Coniston Court W2
612 D9 Connaught Close W2
612 F10 Connaught Place W2
612 E9 Connaught Square W2
612 E9 Connaught Street W2
618 F5 Cons Street SE1
617 K5 Constitution Hill SW1A
619 K10 Content Street SE17
613 M6 Conway Mews W1T
613 M5 Conway Street W1T
614 H1 Coombs Street N1
618 F6 Cooper Close SE1
613 Q1 Coopers Lane NW1
615 Q10 Cooper's Row EC3N
616 C11 Copenhagen Gardens SW3
618 H5 Copperfield Street SE1
619 Q4 Copper Row SE1
615 M8 Copthall Avenue EC2R
613 R7 Coptic Street WC1A
618 F6 Coral Street SE1
613 R5 Coram Street WC1H
615 Q6 Corbet Place E1
617 M2 Cork St Mews W1S
617 M2 Cork Street W1S
612 D6 Corlett Street W2
615 M9 Cornhill EC3V
618 E14 Cornwall Road SE1
612 G5 Cornwall Terrace NW1
612 G5 Cornwall Terrace Mews NW1
615 N3 Coronet Street N1
614 F4 Corporation Row EC1R
615 M3 Corsham Street N1
614 B6 Cosmo Place WC1B
618 E7 Cosser Street SE1
612 E6 Cosway Street NW1
619 K10 Cotham Street SE17
617 L5 Cottage Place SW3
618 F7 Cottesloe Mews SE1
618 F11 Cottingham Street SE11
618 G10 Cotton Gardens Estate SE11
615 P2 Cotton's Gardens E2
616 F11 Coulson Street SW3
619 N3 Counter Street SE1
619 K8 County Street SE1
618 D11 Courtenay Street SE11
615 L2 Cousin Lane EC4R
614 B10 Covent Garden WC2E
614 B10 Covent Garden Piazza WC2E
617 P2 Coventry Street W1D
614 G6 Cowcross Street EC1M
617 R8 Cowley Street SW1P
615 M4 Cowper Street EC1Y
619 Q6 Coxson Way SE1
615 Q1 Crabtree Close E2
617 R3 Craig's Court SW1A
619 M10 Crail Row SE17
613 J7 Cramer Street W1U
619 J11 Crampton Street SE17
613 Q10 Cranbourn Street WC2H
614 F9 Crane Court EC4A
613 N1 Cranleigh Street NW1
614 A11 Cranley Gardens SW7
616 A11 Cranley Mews SW7
616 B10 Cranley Place SW7
615 M3 Cranwood Street EC1V
613 H2 Craven Hill W2
612 A10 Craven Hill Mews W2
612 A10 Craven Road W2
618 A3 Craven Street WC2N
612 A10 Craven Terrace W2

614 E5 Crawford Passage EC1R
612 E8 Crawford Place W1H
612 F7 Crawford Street W1H
615 P9 Creechurch Lane EC3A
615 P9 Creechurch Place EC3A
614 H9 Creed Lane EC4V
615 Q1 Cremer Street E2
615 Q10 Crescent EC3N
616 D9 Crescent Place SW3
615 J5 Crescent Row EC1Y
614 B2 Crestfield Street WC1H
619 L3 Crimscott Street SE1
615 J6 Cripplegate Street EC2Y
615 Q7 Crispin Street E1
614 B3 Cromer Street WC1H
612 B5 Crompton Street W2
616 C9 Cromwell Gardens SW7
616 B9 Cromwell Mews SW7
616 C9 Cromwell Place SW7
616 B9 Cromwell Road SW7
615 M1 Crondall Street N1
612 A12 Cropthorne Court NW8
619 L6 Crosby Row SE1
613 J7 Cross Keys Close W1U
619 M9 Crosslet Street SE17
615 Q10 Crosswall EC3N
614 B9 Crown Court WC2B
614 E10 Crown Office Row EC4Y
617 N4 Crown Passage SW1Y
615 N5 Crown Place EC2A
615 N5 Crucifix Lane SE1
614 E2 Cruickshank Street WC1X
615 P10 Crutched Friars EC3R
614 D3 Cubitt Street WC1X
616 G10 Culford Gardens SW3
615 N10 Cullum Street EC3M
612 H2 Culross Street W1K
612 D1 Culworth Street NW8
614 D2 Cumberland Gardens WC1X
612 F10 Cumberland Gate W2
613 L2 Cumberland Market NW1
613 K2 Cumberland Place NW1
617 L11 Cumberland Street SW1V
613 K1 Cumberland Terrace NW1
613 K1 Cumberland Terrace Mews NW1
614 D1 Cumming Street N1
617 J10 Cundy Street SW1W
612 B4 Cunningham Place NW8
617 Q11 Cureton Street SW1P
619 Q5 Curlew Street SE1
614 E8 Cursitor Street EC4A
615 P4 Curtain Road N1
615 P3 Curtain Road N1
619 Q9 Curtis Street SE1
619 Q9 Curtis Way SE1
617 J4 Curzon Place W1K
617 J4 Curzon Street W1J
612 B6 Cuthbert Street W2
615 P8 Cutlers Gardens Arcade E1
615 P8 Cutler Street EC3A
615 R4 Cygnet Street E1
614 D1 Cynthia Street N1
614 H4 Cyrus Street EC1V

D

617 P7 Dacre Street SW1H
614 H4 Dallington Square EC1V
614 H4 Dallington Street EC1V
614 C7 Dane Street WC1R
613 P10 Dansey Place W1D
613 Q9 Dante Road SE11
616 E11 Danube Street SW3
613 N9 D'Arblay Street W1F
617 P6 Dartmouth Street SW1H
619 M9 Darwin Street SE17
612 D6 Daventry Street NW1
618 G6 Davidge Street SE1
612 G6 David Mews W1U
613 K10 Davies Mews W1K
613 K10 Davies Street W1K
619 M11 Dawes Street SE17
615 R1 Dawson Street E2
619 J9 Deacon Way SE17
617 R8 Dean Bradley Street SW1P
617 J3 Deanery Mews W1K
617 J3 Deanery Street W1K
617 Q7 Dean Farrar Street SW1H
617 R9 Dean Ryle Street SW1P
617 M10 Dean's Buildings SE17
614 H9 Dean's Court EC4V
613 L8 Dean's Mews W1G
618 A8 Dean Stanley Street SW1P
613 P8 Dean Street W1F
617 Q7 Deans Yard SW1P
617 R8 Dean Trench Street SW1P
619 N7 Decima Street SE1
617 N10 Dell's Mews SW1V
618 H11 Delverton Road SE17
617 M11 Denbigh Place SW1V
617 N11 Denbigh Street SW1V
617 N2 Denman Street W1B
613 Q9 Denmark Street WC2H
612 A2 Denning Close NW8
618 F11 Denny Crescent SE11
618 F11 Denny Street SE11
616 E9 Denyer Street SW3
618 A5 Derby Gate SW1A
617 J4 Derby Street W1J
615 P4 Dereham Place EC2A
617 K9 Dering Street W1S
619 L8 Deverell Street SE1
614 E9 Devereux Court WC2R
613 K6 Devonshire Close W1G
613 K6 Devonshire Mews South W1G
613 J5 Devonshire Mews West W1G
613 J5 Devonshire Place W1G
613 J5 Devonshire Place Mews W1U
615 P7 Devonshire Row EC2M
613 P8 Devonshire Square EC2M
613 J6 Devonshire Street W1G
613 A2 Devonshire Terrace W2
613 J7 De Walden Street W1G
613 P8 Diadem Court W1D
613 L4 Diana Place NW1
614 G5 Dickens Mews * EC1M
619 K7 Dickens Square SE1
615 K3 Dingley Place EC1V
615 J3 Dingley Road EC1V
615 K5 Disney Place SE1
615 K5 Disney Street SE1
615 Q2 Diss Street E2
613 J10 Distaff Lane EC4V
618 E10 Distin Street SE11
619 R6 Dockhead SE1
618 F6 Dodson Street SE1
614 C6 Dolben Street SE1
614 C6 Dombey Street WC1N
614 J4 Domingo Street EC1V
615 M6 Dominion Street EC2M
614 D1 Donegal Street N1
616 E9 Donne Place SW3
618 E3 Doon Street SE1
613 P2 Doric Way NW1
614 E6 Dorrington Street EC1N
619 K5 Dorrit Street SE1
614 G9 Dorset Buildings EC4Y
612 F6 Dorset Close NW1
617 K7 Dorset Mews SW1X
614 G9 Dorset Rise EC4Y
612 E5 Dorset Square NW1
617 D7 Dorset Street W1U
614 C5 Doughty Mews WC1N
614 C5 Doughty Street WC1N
617 P10 Douglas Street SW1P
615 L9 Dove Court EC2R
617 L2 Dover Street W1J

615 L10 Dowgate Hill EC4R
617 R5 Downing Street SW1A
614 K4 Down Street W1J
617 K5 Down Street Mews W1J
619 J5 Doyce Street SE1
618 D10 Dragon Road SE11
614 C7 Drake Street WC1N
613 H9 Draper Estate SE1
616 E10 Draycott Avenue SW3
616 F10 Draycott Place SW3
616 F9 Draycott Terrace SW3
616 A11 Drayton Gardens SW10
619 Q5 Druid Street SE1
613 P5 Drummond Crescent NW1
617 Q11 Drummond Gate SW1V
613 M4 Drummond Street NW1
614 R8 Drum Street E1
614 B8 Drury Lane WC2H
616 B9 Dryden Street WC2E
615 P2 Drysdale Place E2
615 P3 Drysdale Street E2
615 R2 Ducal Street E2
613 L7 Duchess Mews W1G
613 L7 Duchess Street W1B
618 F3 Duchy Street SE1
613 P9 Duck Lane W1F
612 B7 Dudley Street W2
616 C11 Dudmaston Mews SW3
615 L5 Dufferin Avenue EC1Y
615 L5 Dufferin Street EC1Y
613 H9 Dufour's Place W1F
617 J5 Duke of Wellington Place SW1J
616 G11 Duke of York Square SW3
617 N3 Duke of York Street SW1Y
613 J8 Duke's Mews W1U
615 Q9 Duke's Place EC3A
613 Q3 Duke's Road NW1
613 J8 Duke Street W1H
619 M3 Duke Street Hill SE1
617 N3 Duke Street St James's W1J
613 J10 Duke's Yard W1K
617 R2 Duncannon Street WC2N
614 G1 Duncan Terrace N1
615 Q1 Dunloe Street E2
619 R8 Dunlop Place SE16
612 G10 Dunraven Street W1K
613 J6 Dunstable Mews W1G
615 N10 Dunster Court EC3M
619 M6 Dunsterville Way SE1
619 Q10 Dunton Road SE1
616 G6 Duplex Ride SW1X
618 B2 Durham House Street WC2N
612 G6 Durweston Mews W1U
614 E7 Dyer's Buildings EC4A
613 Q7 Dyott Street WC1B
615 M5 Dysart Street EC2A

E

614 G6 Eagle Court EC1M
616 A11 Eagle Street W10
614 C7 Eagle Street WC1R
613 Q9 Earlham Street WC2H
614 G2 Earlstoke Estate EC1V
614 G2 Earlstoke Street EC1V
615 N6 Earl Street EC2A
613 Q8 Earnshaw Street WC1A
612 A8 Eastbourne Mews W2
612 A8 Eastbourne Terrace W2
613 M8 Eastcastle Street W1W
615 M10 Eastcheap EC3M
614 F8 East Harding Street EC4A
614 E4 Easton Street WC1X
615 J6 East Passage EC1A
614 G7 East Poultry Avenue EC1M
615 M2 East Road N1
619 R2 East Smithfield E1W
619 K11 East Street SE17
615 R9 East Tenter Street E1
616 H9 Eaton Close SW1W
616 H9 Eaton Gate SW1W
618 L8 Eaton Lane SW1W
617 J8 Eaton Mews North SW1X
617 J9 Eaton Mews South SW1W
617 J9 Eaton Mews West SW1W
616 H8 Eaton Place SW1X
617 K7 Eaton Row SW1W
617 J9 Eaton Square SW1W
616 H9 Eaton Terrace SW1W
617 J9 Eaton Terrace Mews SW1X
615 L2 Ebenezer Street N1
615 Q4 Ebor Street E2
617 K11 Ebury Bridge SW1W
617 J9 Ebury Mews SW1W
617 K9 Ebury Mews East SW1W
617 K10 Ebury Square SW1W
617 J10 Ebury Street SW1W
617 J8 Eccleston Mews SW1X
617 K10 Eccleston Place SW1W
617 L10 Eccleston Square SW1V
617 L10 Eccleston Square Mews SW1V
617 J8 Eccleston Street SW1W
612 B5 Edgware Road W2
616 F5 Edinburgh Gate SW1X
613 L2 Edward Mews NW1
612 H9 Edwards Mews W1H
616 E9 Egerton Crescent SW3
616 D9 Egerton Gardens SW3
616 E8 Egerton Gardens Mews SW3
616 E8 Egerton Place SW3
616 E8 Egerton Terrace SW3
615 K9 Elba Place SE17
615 Q6 Elder Street E1
615 M7 Eldon Street EC2M
618 H9 Elephant & Castle SE1
619 J9 Elephant Road SE17
614 G1 Elia Mews N1
614 G1 Elia Street N1
619 N7 Elim Street SE1
617 K10 Elizabeth Bridge SW1W
612 A5 Elizabeth Close W9
617 J9 Elizabeth Street SW1W
618 H9 Elliott's Row SE11
616 G9 Ellis Street SW1X
616 B11 Elm Place SW7
612 B10 Elms Mews W2
614 D5 Elm Street WC1X
612 B2 Elm Tree Close NW8
612 B3 Elm Tree Road NW8
618 M10 Elsted Street SE17
616 A8 Elvaston Mews SW7
617 P9 Elverton Street SW1P
617 P9 Everton Street SW1P
617 P2 Ely Place EC1N
616 E11 Elystan Place SW3
613 D10 Elystan Street SW3
618 B3 Embankment Place WC2N
614 C6 Emerald Street WC1N
619 J3 Emerson Street SE1
618 N8 Emery Hill Street SW1P
618 F7 Emery Street SE1
619 L6 Empire Square SE1
614 H4 Enclave Court EC1V
618 R8 Endell Street WC2H
613 P4 Endsleigh Gardens WC1H
613 Q4 Endsleigh Place WC1H
613 Q4 Endsleigh Street WC1H
612 F6 Enford Street W1H
619 R7 Enid Street SE1
614 F3 Ennismore Gardens SW7
616 C7 Ennismore Gardens Mews SW7
616 D6 Ennismore Mews SW7
616 D6 Ennismore Street SW7
614 B11 Ensor Mews SW7
615 M5 Epworth Street EC2A
615 R3 Equity Square E2
617 Q10 Erasmus Street SW1P

615 K5 Errol Street EC1Y
614 E9 Essex Court * WC2R
614 E9 Essex Street WC2R
615 P10 Esterbrooke Street SW1P
618 E10 Ethelred Estate SE11
614 K10 Ethel Street SE17
613 M4 Euston Centre NW1
613 N3 Euston Road NW1
613 P3 Euston Square NW1
613 N4 Euston Street NW1
615 L1 Evelyn Walk N1
613 N1 Eversholt Street NW1
613 M3 Everton Buildings NW1
619 J4 Ewer Street SE1
617 Q2 Excel Court WC2H
615 N7 Exchange Arcade EC2M
615 N7 Exchange Court WC2N
615 P6 Exchange Square * EC2A
614 B10 Exeter Street WC2E
616 C6 Exhibition Road SW7
614 E4 Exmouth Market EC1R
614 N3 Exmouth Mews NW1
619 N10 Exton Street SE1
615 E4 Eyre Street Hill EC1R
615 E5 Ezra Street E2

F

615 L1 Fairbank Estate N1
615 P5 Fairchild Place EC2A
615 P5 Fairchild Street EC2A
616 E7 Fairholt Street SW7
619 P5 Fair Street SE1
615 P8 Falconberg Court W1D
618 H3 Falcon Close SE1
614 H1 Falcon Court N1
615 P1 Falkirk Street N1
619 K8 Falmouth Road SE1
615 J5 Fann Street EC1M
615 N2 Fanshaw Street N1
617 K2 Fareham Street W1F
617 K2 Farm Street W1J
614 H4 Farnham Place SE1
614 F5 Farringdon Lane EC1R
614 E4 Farringdon Road EC1X
614 G4 Farringdon Street EC1A
615 Q7 Fashion Street E1
615 L4 Featherstone Street EC1Y
615 N9 Fenchurch Avenue EC3M
615 P9 Fenchurch Buildings EC3M
615 P10 Fenchurch Place EC3M
615 N10 Fenchurch Street EC3M
619 P8 Fendall Street SE1
615 N5 Fenning Street SE1
614 E3 Fernsbury Street WC1X
614 F8 Fetter Lane EC4A
614 D7 Field Court WC1R
614 C2 Field Street WC1X
615 M9 Finch Lane EC3V
615 M7 Finsbury Avenue EC2M
615 M7 Finsbury Circus EC2M
614 F3 Finsbury Estate EC1R
615 N5 Finsbury Market EC2A
615 M6 Finsbury Pavement EC2A
615 M5 Finsbury Square EC2A
615 L6 Finsbury Street EC1Y
616 E7 First Street SW3
614 C7 Fisher Street WC1R
612 B5 Fisherton Street NW8
619 M2 Fish Street Hill EC3R
618 D9 Fitzalan Street SE11
612 H8 Fitzhardinge Street W1H
617 L3 Fitzmaurice Place W1J
613 M5 Fitzroy Mews W1W
613 M5 Fitzroy Square W1T
613 M5 Fitzroy Street NW1
613 Q3 Flaxman Terrace WC1H
614 G8 Fleet Place EC4M
614 C3 Fleet Square WC1X
614 F9 Fleet Street EC4A
615 P5 Fleur de Lis Street E1
619 P11 Flinton Street SE17
617 M10 Flint Street SE17
613 Q9 Flitcroft Street WC2H
614 B10 Floral Street WC2E
615 R7 Flower & Dean Walk E1
613 M7 Foley Street W1W
615 P6 Folgate Street E1
615 L7 Fore Street EC2Y
614 E8 Forset Street W1H
619 R10 Fort Road SE1
615 P7 Fort Street E1
619 R11 Fortune Place SE1
615 K5 Fortune Street EC1Y
618 C5 Forum Magnum Square SE1
615 J3 Foster Lane EC2V
613 M9 Foubert's Place W1B
618 B10 Foulis Terrace SW7
613 N4 Foundry Mews NW1
615 Q6 Fournier Street E1
614 H6 Fox & Knot Street EC1M
612 C5 Frampton Street NW8
617 N9 Francis Street SW1P
618 B8 Frankland Road SW7
616 G11 Franklins Row SW3
618 F8 Frazier Street SE1
615 L9 Frederick Close W1
615 L9 Frederick's Place EC2R
614 G12 Frederick's Row EC1V
614 C3 Frederick Street WC1X
616 H6 Frederic Mews SW1X
619 N11 Freemantle Street SE17
614 H3 French Place E2
618 H3 Friars Close * SE1
613 J10 Friday Street EC4V
614 G2 Friend Street EC1V
613 P9 Frith Street W1D
615 K6 Frobisher Crescent * EC2Y
615 R7 Frostic Walk E1
615 P7 Frying Pan Alley E1
616 C11 Fulham Road SW3
615 M2 Fullwood's Mews N1
614 D7 Fulwood Place WC1R
614 E8 Furnival Street EC4A
615 J10 Fye Foot Lane EC4V
617 P9 Fynes Street SW1P

G

618 E3 Gabriel's Wharf SE1
619 Q4 Gainsford Street SE1
619 J5 Gaitskell Way SE1
614 A7 Galen Place WC1A
615 K3 Galway Street EC1V
618 H4 Gambia Street SE1
613 M10 Ganton Street W1F
613 J6 Garbutt Place W1U
614 E10 Garden Court * WC2R
612 A2 Garden Road NW8
618 G8 Garden Row SE1
617 P11 Garden Terrace SW1V
615 N4 Garden Walk EC2A
615 J10 Gardners Lane EC4V
614 H2 Gard Street EC1V
615 K10 Garlick Hill EC4V
614 F3 Garnault Mews EC1R
614 F3 Garnault Place EC1R
615 J4 Garrett Street EC1Y
614 A10 Garrick Street WC2E
613 R10 Garrick Yard WC2N
619 Q6 Gascoigne Place E2
612 D5 Gateforth Street NW8
616 K3 Gatehouse Square SE1
616 E6 Gate Mews SW7

614 C8 Gate Street WC1V
618 H7 Gaunt Street SE1
617 M9 Gavel Street SE17
617 R8 Gayfere Street SW1P
618 H8 Gaywood Street SE1
619 Q7 Gedling Place SE1
613 J9 Gees Court W1U
615 J9 Gee Street EC1V
615 P1 Geffrye Estate N1
616 C9 George Mathers Road SE11
613 M3 George Mews NW1
612 F8 George Street W1H
617 M9 George Street EC3V
617 J10 George Yard W1K
615 R2 Georgina Gardens * E2
618 G8 Geraldine Street SE11
617 J9 Gerald Road SW1W
616 Q10 Gerrard Place W1D
617 P10 Gerrard Street W1D
615 F6 Gerridge Street SE1
615 R3 Gibraltar Walk E2
618 D10 Gibson Road SE11
614 A7 Gilbert Place WC1A
618 F9 Gilbert Road SE11
613 J9 Gilbert Street W1K
613 L7 Gildea Street W1B
617 L9 Gillingham Mews SW1V
617 M9 Gillingham Row SW1V
617 L10 Gillingham Street SW1V
612 A7 Gilpin Close W2
614 H8 Gilspur Street EC1A
613 G7 Gladstone Street SE1
618 H5 Glasshill Street SE1
617 N2 Glasshouse Street W1B
618 B11 Glasshouse Walk SE11
615 J5 Glasshouse Yard EC1A
616 B9 Glendower Place SW7
612 G5 Glentworth Street NW1
619 L6 Globe Street SE1
619 P2 Gloucester Court EC3R
612 A9 Gloucester Mews W2
612 F4 Gloucester Place NW1
612 G7 Gloucester Place Mews W1H
616 A9 Gloucester Road SW7
612 C9 Gloucester Square W2
617 M11 Gloucester Street SW1V
614 A9 Gloucester Terrace W2
614 F3 Gloucester Way EC1R
616 D6 Glynde Mews SW3
616 E11 Godfrey Street SW3
614 H9 Godliman Street EC4V
618 C3 Golden Jubilee Bridge SE1
615 J4 Golden Lane EC1Y
615 J5 Golden Lane Estate EC1Y
615 N10 Golden Square W1F
615 K8 Goldsmith Street EC2V
615 N7 Goodge Place W1T
615 N7 Goodge Street W1T
615 Q10 Goodman's Yard EC3N
619 R8 Goodwin Close SE16
613 R10 Goodwins Court WC2N
615 L10 Gophir Lane EC4R
613 Q4 Gordon Square WC1H
615 P4 Gordon Street WC1H
616 A7 Gore Street SW7
615 P8 Goring Street EC3A
615 Q2 Gorsuch Place E2
615 Q2 Gorsuch Street E2
613 L6 Gosfield Street W1W
613 Q8 Goslett Yard W1D
614 H3 Goswell Place EC1V
614 H2 Goswell Road EC1V
614 F8 Gough Square EC4A
614 D4 Gough Street WC1X
615 Q8 Goulston Street E1
613 Q7 Gower Mews WC1E
614 N4 Gower Place WC1H
613 P5 Gower Street WC1E
615 M10 Gracechurch Street EC3V
612 A1 Graces Mews * NW8
613 N7 Graduate Place SE1
613 M5 Grafton Mews W1T
613 P3 Grafton Place NW1
617 L2 Grafton Street W1J
613 M6 Grafton Way W1T
614 H1 Graham Street N1
616 H10 Graham Terrace SW1W
613 M1 Granby Terrace NW1
614 G6 Grand Avenue EC1M
615 J1 Grand Junction Wharf * N1
619 P8 Grange Road SE1
619 P7 Grange Walk SE1
619 P8 Grange Walk Mews SE1
619 Q8 Grange Yard SE1
617 K4 Grantham Place W1J
612 H9 Granville Place W1H
614 D3 Granville Square WC1X
614 A8 Grape Street WC2H
615 C11 Graphite Square SE11
615 Q8 Gravel Lane E1
614 B2 Gray's Inn Road N1
614 E6 Gray's Inn Square WC1R
618 G5 Gray Street SE1
613 J9 Gray's Yard W1U
613 M8 Great Castle Street W1B
613 F6 Great Central Street NW1
613 P8 Great Chapel Street W1F
617 R7 Great College Street SW1P
612 F8 Great Cumberland Mews W1H
612 F8 Great Cumberland Place W1H
615 L7 Great Dover Street SE1
615 N3 Great Eastern Street EC2A
617 Q6 Great George Street SW1H
619 J4 Great Guildford Street SE1
614 C6 Great James Street WC1N
613 M9 Great Marlborough Street W1F
619 M4 Great Maze Pond SE1
614 F8 Great New Street EC4A
614 B6 Great Ormond Street WC1N
614 D2 Great Percy Street WC1X
617 P8 Great Peter Street SW1P
613 L6 Great Portland Street W1W
615 N10 Great Pulteney Street W1F
614 B8 Great Queen Street WC2B
613 Q8 Great Russell Street W1T
615 N9 Great St Helen's EC3A
615 K10 Great St Thomas Apostle EC4V
617 R4 Great Scotland Yard SW1A
617 Q7 Great Smith Street SW1P
618 H4 Great Suffolk Street SE1
614 H5 Great Sutton Street EC1V
618 A3 Great Swan Alley EC2R
613 L6 Great Titchfield Street W1W
615 N10 Great Tower Street EC3R
615 K10 Great Trinity Lane EC4V
614 D7 Great Turnstile WC1V
615 M8 Great Winchester Street EC2N
613 P10 Great Windmill Street W1D
613 Q9 Greek Street W1D
614 G8 Green Arbour Court EC4M
612 D1 Greenberry Street NW8
617 N9 Greencoat Place SW1P
617 N8 Greencoat Row SW1P
618 E6 Greenham Close SE1
612 G6 Greenhill's Rents EC1M
615 P10 Green's Court W1F
612 G10 Green Terrace EC1R
615 F9 Green Walk SE1
615 N8 Green Yard WC1X
618 L5 Greenwell Street W1W
614 D4 Green Yard WC1X
618 F4 Greet Street SE1
612 D4 Grendon Street NW8
614 B5 Grenville Street WC1N
613 J8 Gresham Street EC2V
618 P7 Gresse Street W1T
617 P8 Greville Street EC1N
616 E6 Greycoat Place SW1P

617 P8 Greycoat Street SW1P
615 R6 Grey Eagle Street E1
619 P8 Grigg's Place SE1
615 R5 Grimsby Street E1
618 E6 Grindal Street SE1
615 L9 Grocers' Hall Court EC2R
617 J7 Groom Place SW1X
616 H9 Grosvenor Cottages SW1X
617 J6 Grosvenor Crescent SW1X
617 H6 Grosvenor Crescent Mews SW1X
617 L8 Grosvenor Gardens SW1W
617 L7 Grosvenor Gardens Mews East SW1W
617 K8 Grosvenor Gardens Mews North SW1W
616 G2 Grosvenor Gate W2
613 K10 Grosvenor Hill W1K
617 J5 Grosvenor Place SW1X
613 J10 Grosvenor Square W1K
613 J10 Grosvenor Street W1K
619 J5 Grotto Court SE1
612 H6 Grotto Passage W1U
612 B1 Grove End Road NW8
612 E3 Grove Gardens NW8
615 K9 Groveland Court EC4M
614 C5 Guilford Place WC1N
614 C5 Guilford Street WC1N
617 M10 Guildhouse Street SW1V
614 C5 Guilford Place WC1N
614 C5 Guilford Street WC1N
619 N8 Guinness Square SE17
616 F10 Guinness Trust Estate SW3
615 Q7 Gun Street E1
615 R7 Gunthorpe Street E1
616 D11 Guthrie Street SW3
615 J8 Gutter Lane EC2V
619 M5 Guy Street SE1

H

615 M2 Haberdasher Place N1
615 M2 Haberdasher Street N1
615 Q2 Hackney Road E2
615 R9 Half Moon Passage E1
617 L3 Half Moon Street W1J
616 H7 Halkin Arcade SW1X
616 H7 Halkin Mews SW1X
616 H7 Halkin Place SW1X
617 J6 Halkin Street SW1X
613 L6 Hallam Mews W1B
613 L6 Hallam Street W1W
612 A3 Hall Gate NW8
612 B5 Hall Place W2
612 A3 Hall Road NW8
614 H2 Hall Street EC1V
619 M10 Halpin Place SE17
616 F9 Halsey Street SW3
612 B3 Hamilton Close NW8
612 A2 Hamilton Gardens NW8
617 J4 Hamilton Place W1K
612 A3 Hamilton Terrace NW8
619 M6 Hamlet Way SE1
615 Q10 Hammett Street EC3N
613 Q1 Hampden Close NW1
612 F9 Hampden Gurney Street W1H
613 M1 Hampstead Road NW1
618 H10 Hampton Street SE17
613 P10 Ham Yard W1D
615 R6 Hanbury Street E1
614 D7 Hand Court WC1V
614 A4 Handel Street WC1N
616 M6 Henley Place SE1
614 B9 Hanover Place WC2E
613 L9 Hanover Square W1S
612 E9 Hanover Steps * W2
613 L9 Hanover Street W1S
612 F3 Hanover Terrace NW1
612 E3 Hanover Terrace Mews NW1
616 F7 Hans Crescent SW3
613 M6 Hanson Street W1W
616 F7 Hans Place SW1X
616 F7 Hans Road SW3
616 G8 Hans Street SW1X
613 P8 Hanway Place W1D
613 P8 Hanway Street W1T
612 C7 Harbet Road W2
612 E2 Harcourt Street W1H
614 D3 Hardwicke Mews WC1X
614 F3 Hardwick Street EC1R
619 N5 Hardwidge Street SE1
614 E9 Hare Court * EC4Y
615 P1 Hare Walk N1
612 E4 Harewood Avenue NW8
613 L9 Harewood Place W1S
612 E6 Harewood Row NW1
613 K7 Harley Place W1G
613 K5 Harley Street W1G
618 F8 Harmsworth Mews SE1
619 N2 Harp Cross Lane EC3R
619 K7 Harper Road SE1
614 C6 Harpur Street WC1N
616 G6 Harriet Street SW1X
616 G6 Harriet Walk SW1X
616 B9 Harrington Road SW7
613 M1 Harrington Street NW1
614 B3 Harrison Street WC1H
612 E8 Harrowby Street W1H
615 P8 Harrow Place E1
612 C7 Harrow Road Flyover W2
612 E6 Harrow Street NW1
615 P10 Hart Street EC3R
616 E9 Hasker Street SW3
615 R1 Hassard Street E2
613 R3 Hastings Street WC1H
619 P6 Hatchers Mews SE1
618 F3 Hatfields SE1
617 N10 Hatherley Street SW1P
614 H5 Hat & Mitre Court EC1M
614 F6 Hatton Garden EC1R
614 F5 Hatton Place EC1N
614 F5 Hatton Row NW8
612 C5 Hatton Street NW8
614 E6 Hatton Wall EC1N
613 K9 Haunch of Venison Yard W1K
614 F1 Haverstock Place N1
614 H1 Haverstock Street N1
615 Q10 Haydon Street EC3N
619 Q9 Haydon Walk E1
615 P2 Hayes Place NW1
613 L2 Hay Hill W1J
618 L9 Hayles Street SE11
617 P2 Haymarket SW1Y
614 H6 Hayne Street EC1A
619 N3 Hays Lane SE1
613 K3 Hay's Mews W1J
614 G5 Hayward's Place EC1R
619 Q3 Hazel Way SE1
617 J6 Headfort Place SW1X
619 M10 Hearn's Buildings SE17
615 P5 Hearn Street EC2A
614 C4 Heathcote Street WC1N
613 M2 Heddon Street W1S
618 G9 Hedger Street SE11
615 K4 Helmet Row EC1V
619 M9 Hemp Walk SE17
612 B4 Henderson Drive NW8
619 P10 Hendre Road SE1
615 P9 Heneage Lane EC3A
615 R6 Heneage Street E1
619 R9 Henley Drive SE16
614 B4 Henrietta Mews WC1N
613 K8 Henrietta Place W1G
614 B10 Henrietta Street WC2E
615 L9 Henshaw Street SE17
616 G9 Heralds Place SE11
614 F5 Herbal Hill EC1R
616 G7 Herbert Crescent SW1X

613 R4 Herbrand Street WC1N
618 D8 Hercules Road SE1
616 A10 Hereford Square SW7
614 E1 Hermes Street N1
612 B7 Hermitage Street W2
614 G2 Hermit Street EC1V
617 Q10 Herrick Street SW1P
617 K3 Hertford Street W1J
615 P5 Hewett Street EC2A
615 K9 Heygate Estate SE17
613 J10 Heygate Street SE17
617 P10 Hide Place SW1P
614 B8 High Holborn WC1V
613 J10 High Timber Street EC4V
614 C4 Hendrick Place SW7
612 E6 Highworth Street NW1
615 M10 Hillery Close SE17
612 A1 Hill Road NW8
613 M9 Hills Place W1F
617 K3 Hill Street W1J
614 F9 Hind Court EC4A
613 J8 Hinde Mews W1U
613 J8 Hinde Street W1U
617 K8 Hobart Place SW1W
615 Q3 Hocker Street E2
612 B6 Hogan Mews W2
616 H11 Holbein Mews SW1W
616 H10 Holbein Place SW1W
614 E7 Holborn EC1N
614 E7 Holborn Circus EC1N
614 C7 Holborn Place WC1V
614 C8 Holborn Viaduct EC1N
614 C2 Holford Mews * WC1X
614 E2 Holford Street WC1X
614 E1 Holford Yard * N1
612 H3 Holland Street SE1
613 N9 Hollen Street W1F
613 L8 Holles Street W1G
614 E5 Holmes Terrace SE1
614 D5 Holsworthy Square WC1X
618 G9 Holyoak Road SE11
614 N4 Holyrood Street SE1
615 P4 Holywell Lane EC2A
615 N5 Holywell Row EC2A
615 N1 Homefield Street N1
612 E7 Homer Row NW1
612 E7 Homer Street NW1
615 J4 Honduras Street EC1V
615 R7 Hopetown Street E1
617 R2 Hop Gardens WC2N
613 N9 Hopkins Street W1F
615 H3 Hoptons Gardens * SE1
618 H3 Hopton Street SE1
615 R1 Horatio Street E2
618 E9 Hornbeam Close SE11
617 P8 Horseferry Road SW1P
616 A4 Horse Guards Avenue SW1A
617 Q4 Horse Guards Road SW1A
619 Q5 Horselydown Lane SE1
614 G7 Hosier Lane EC1A
618 E11 Hotspur Street SE11
614 D9 Houghton Street WC2B
615 P8 Houndsditch EC3A
618 H10 Howell Walk SE17
617 N8 Howick Place SW1P
613 N6 Howland Mews East W1T
613 N6 Howland Street W1T
612 A6 Howley Place W2
613 N3 Hoxton Market N1
613 N3 Hoxton Square N1
615 P2 Hoxton Street E2
615 K10 Huggin Hill EC4V
613 L10 Hugh Mews SW1V
617 P9 Hugh Place SW1P
617 L10 Hugh Street SW1V
615 R6 Huguenot Place E1
613 J3 Hull Street EC1V
619 K6 Hulme Place SE1
619 Q11 Humphrey Street SE1
617 M8 Hunter Close SE1
614 B4 Hunter Street WC1N
614 N5 Huntley Street WC1E
619 N10 Huntsman Street SE17
612 F4 Huntsworth Mews NW1
614 F9 Hutton Street EC4Y
617 J5 Hyde Park Corner W1J
612 D9 Hyde Park Crescent W2
612 C10 Hyde Park Gardens W2
612 C10 Hyde Park Gardens Mews W2
616 A6 Hyde Park Gate SW7
616 A6 Hyde Park Gate Mews SW7
612 E10 Hyde Park Place W2
612 D9 Hyde Park Square W2
612 D10 Hyde Park Street W2

I

619 N2 Idol Lane EC3R
618 H11 Iliffe Street SE17
618 H11 Iliffe Yard SE17
616 B8 Imperial College Road SW7
615 Q9 India Street EC3N
613 N9 Ingestre Place W1F
614 E2 Inglebert Street EC1R
618 D9 Ingram Close SE11
612 H3 Inner Circle NW1
618 G3 Invicta Plaza SE1
615 L9 Ironmonger Lane EC2V
615 K3 Ironmonger Row EC1V
617 R2 Irving Street WC2H
615 K5 Isaac Way SE1
615 G4 Isabella Street SE1
616 E9 Ives Street SW3
612 F5 Ivor Place NW1
619 Q11 Ivy Church Lane SE1
616 D10 Ixworth Place SW3

J

619 R5 Jacob Street SE1
619 J8 Jacob's Well Mews W1U
619 R6 Jamaica Road SE1
614 B10 James Street WC2E
613 J9 James Street W1U
614 A6 Jay Mews SW7
617 M3 Jermyn Street SW1Y
615 D4 Jerome Crescent NW8
615 Q6 Jerome Street E1
615 P1 Jerrold Street N1
614 G5 Jerusalem Passage EC1R
615 Q9 Jewry Street EC3N
613 G4 Joan Street SE1
614 D6 Jockey's Fields WC1X
618 E6 Johanna Street SE1
618 B3 John Adam Street WC2N
614 A6 John Aird Court W2
614 G10 John Carpenter Street EC4Y
617 Q11 John Islip Street SW1P
619 L9 John Maurice Close SE17
613 L8 John Prince's Street W1G
614 D5 John's Mews WC1N
614 F9 Johnson's Court EC4A
614 D5 John Street WC1N
615 J6 John Trundle Highwalk * EC2Y
619 M4 Joiner Street SE1
614 C11 Jonathan Street SE11
614 F3 Joseph Trotter Close * EC1R
614 D4 Jubilee Gardens * SE1
618 E11 Jubilee Place SW3
614 A3 Judd Street WC1H
614 D8 Junction Mews W2
612 C8 Junction Place W2
618 D9 Juxon Street SE11

K

614 C9 Kean Street WC2B
614 Q10 Keats Close SE1
614 C9 Keeley Street WC2B
618 H7 Kell Street SE1
614 C9 Kemble Street WC2B
618 F10 Kempsford Road SE11
612 H7 Kendall Place W1U
612 E9 Kendal Steps * W2
612 E9 Kendal Street W2
612 B9 Kendrick Mews SW7
612 B10 Kendrick Place SW7
612 M10 Kennedy Walk SE17
615 K10 Kennett Wharf Lane EC4V
618 F11 Kennings Way SE11
618 F11 Kennington Lane SE11
618 G11 Kennington Park Road SE11
618 E8 Kennington Road SE11
612 H6 Kenrick Place W1U
614 A6 Kensington Gore SW7
616 D6 Kensington Road SW7
612 A4 Kent Passage NW1
612 E3 Kent Terrace NW1
616 E6 Kent Yard SW7
613 Q6 Keppel Street WC1E
619 Q8 Keyse Road SE1
614 B1 Keystone Crescent N1
615 R7 Keyworth Street SE1
619 K11 King and Queen Street SE17
617 R3 King Charles I Island WC2N
617 Q5 King Charles Street SW1A
615 J8 King Edward Street EC1A
618 F7 King Edward Walk SE1
615 J7 Kinghorn Street EC1A
618 H6 King James Street SE1
615 P4 King John Court EC2A
619 N11 Kinglake Estate SE17
618 P11 Kinglake Street SE17
613 N10 Kingly Court * W1B
613 M9 Kingly Street W1B
615 L8 King's Arms Yard EC2R
618 H5 King's Bench Street SE1
614 F10 King's Bench Walk * EC4Y
614 G10 Kingscote Street EC4Y
618 H5 King's Court SE1
614 B2 King's Cross Bridge N1
614 D2 King's Cross Road WC1X
615 P1 Kingsland Road E2
614 D5 King's Mews WC1N
613 J6 King's Place SE1
615 J3 King Square EC1V
614 F10 Kings Reach * EC4Y
618 B4 King's Road SW10
617 J8 King's Road SW1W
618 F11 King's Road SW3
617 M8 King's Scholars' Passage SW1P
615 K9 King Street EC2V
613 N4 King Street SW1Y
614 A10 King Street W2E
614 C9 Kingsway WC2B
614 F4 Kingsway Place EC1R
613 M2 King William Street EC4R
616 G6 Kinnerton Place North SW1X
616 G6 Kinnerton Place South SW1X
616 H6 Kinnerton Street SW1X
616 H6 Kinnerton Yard SW1X
619 M6 Kipling Estate SE1
619 M6 Kipling Street SE1
619 N5 Kirby Grove SE1
614 F6 Kirby Street EC1N
615 R3 Kirton Gardens E2
614 H9 Knightrider Court EC4V
614 J10 Knightrider Street EC4V
616 E6 Knightsbridge SW7
616 F6 Knightsbridge Green SW1X
618 G10 Knights Walk SE11
612 F6 Knox Street W1H

L

615 M6 Lackington Street EC2A
619 Q5 Lafone Street SE1
615 J6 Lambert Jones Mews * EC2Y
615 B9 Lambeth Bridge SW1P
618 C10 Lambeth High Street SE1
615 J10 Lambeth Hill EC4V
618 C8 Lambeth Palace Road SE1
618 E8 Lambeth Road SE1
618 D9 Lambeth Walk SE11
614 C6 Lamb's Conduit Passage WC1X
614 C5 Lamb's Conduit Street WC1N
614 L5 Lamb's Passage EC1Y
615 Q6 Lamb Street E1
619 N6 Lamb Walk SE1
618 G9 Lamlash Street SE11
612 A4 Lanark Place W9
615 K10 Lancashire Court W1K
612 A10 Lancaster Court W2
612 A2 Lancaster Gate W2
612 A10 Lancaster Mews W2
618 C1 Lancaster Place WC2E
618 G6 Lancaster Street SE1
612 B10 Lancaster Terrace W2
616 F6 Lancelot Place SW7
613 P3 Lancing Street NW1
616 F7 Landon Place SW1X
612 A1 Langford Place NW8
613 L7 Langham Place W1G
613 L7 Langham Street W1B
614 A10 Langley Court WC2E
614 A9 Langley Street WC2H
615 M8 Langthorn Court EC2R
614 D3 Langton Close WC1X
619 M7 Langton Place SE1
614 B5 Lansdowne Terrace WC1N
613 J5 Lant Street SE1
619 K10 Larcom Street SE17
615 M10 Larissa Street SE17
615 K7 Lauderdale Place * EC2Y
614 C11 Laud Street SE11
618 E6 Launcelot Street SE1
615 L10 Laurence Pountney Hill EC4R
615 L10 Laurence Pountney Lane EC4R
618 H4 Lavington Street SE1
614 C5 Lawrence Lane EC2V
614 M7 Law Street SE1
613 L4 Laxton Place NW1
614 E5 Laystall Street EC1R
614 A10 Lazenby Court WC2E
615 N9 Leadenhall Place EC3M
615 N9 Leadenhall Street EC3V
618 D5 Leake Street SE1
614 E6 Leather Lane EC1R
619 N6 Leathermarket Court SE1
619 N6 Leathermarket Street SE1
614 B11 Lecky Street SW7
614 C2 Leeke Street WC1X
612 H10 Lees Place W1K
613 Q10 Leicester Place WC2H
617 Q2 Leicester Square WC2H
613 Q10 Leicester Street W1D
613 R4 Leigh Street WC1H
615 R9 Leman Street E1
616 F8 Lennox Gardens SW1X
616 F9 Lennox Gardens Mews SW3
615 M4 Leonard Street EC2A
619 N9 Leroy Street SE1
615 M4 Leverett Street SW3
615 J3 Lever Street EC1V
613 N9 Lexington Street W1F
615 Q7 Leyden Street E1
618 H6 Library Street SE1

613 M1 Lidlington Place NW1
615 Q4 Ligonier Street E2
618 C10 Lilac Place SE11
612 D4 Lilestone Street NW8
617 N10 Lillington Gardens Estate SW1V
614 F6 Lily Place EC1N
614 C8 Limeburner Lane EC4M
615 N10 Lime Street EC3V
615 N9 Lime Street Passage EC3V
614 C8 Lincoln's Inn Fields WC2A
616 F10 Lincoln Street SW3
617 Q11 Lindsay Square SW1V
614 H6 Lindsey Street EC1M
612 F4 Linhope Street NW1
615 R6 Links Yard E1
617 J8 Lisle Street W1D
612 C4 Lisson Grove NW8
612 D6 Lisson Street NW8
617 Q10 Litchfield Street WC2H
613 L4 Little Albany Street NW1
613 M9 Little Argyll Street W1S
615 H7 Little Britain EC1A
617 K7 Little Chester Street SW1X
617 R7 Little Cloisters SW1P
617 R7 Little Deans Yard SW1P
619 K5 Little Dorrit Court SE1
613 L2 Little Edward Street NW1
614 E10 Little Essex Street WC2R
617 R6 Little George Street SW1P
613 M9 Little Marlborough Street W1B
613 Q10 Little Newport Street WC2H
614 F8 Little New Street EC4A
613 L8 Little Portland Street W1W
614 A7 Little Russell Street WC1A
617 M4 Little St James's Street SW1A
617 Q7 Little Smith Street SW1P
613 M7 Little Titchfield Street W1W
615 K10 Little Trinity Lane EC4V
614 C7 Little Turnstile WC1V
615 N7 Liverpool Street EC2M
615 K3 Lizard Street EC1V
614 E3 Lloyd Baker Street WC1X
612 P9 Lloyd's Avenue EC3M
614 E2 Lloyd Square WC1X
614 F3 Lloyd's Row EC1R
614 E2 Lloyd Street WC1X
612 M6 Lockyer Street SE1
615 R7 Lolesworth Close E1
618 D9 Lollard Street SE11
615 H5 Loman Street SE1
614 F9 Lombard Lane EC4Y
617 M9 Lombard Street EC3V
619 M2 London Bridge EC4R
619 M3 London Bridge Street SE1
619 M3 London Bridge Walk SE1
612 C9 London Mews W2
618 H7 London Road SE1
615 P10 London Street EC3M
612 B9 London Street W2
615 K7 London Wall EC2Y
615 M7 London Wall Buildings EC2M
614 A9 Long Acre WC2E
619 R10 Longfellow Way SE1
619 R9 Longfield Estate SE1
614 L4 Longford Street NW1
614 H6 Long Lane EC1A
617 M10 Longmoore Street SW1V
615 Q2 Long Street E2
618 G9 Longville Road SE11
619 P7 Long Walk SE1
614 C5 Long Yard WC1N
617 R8 Lord North Street SW1P
612 D3 Lords View NW8
612 E3 Lorenzo Street WC1X
615 L8 Lothbury EC2R
618 D11 Loughborough Street SE11
615 N10 Lovat Lane EC3M
617 K8 Love Lane EC2V
617 K8 Lower Belgrave Street SW1W
617 K7 Lower Grosvenor Place SW1W
613 N10 Lower James Street W1F
613 N10 Lower John Street W1F
618 E6 Lower Marsh SE1
615 G10 Lower Sloane Street SW1W
619 P2 Lower Thames Street EC3R
613 J8 Lowndes Close SW1X
613 M9 Lowndes Court W1B
616 G6 Lowndes Place SW1X
616 G6 Lowndes Square SW1X
616 G7 Lowndes Street SW1X
614 B3 Loxham Street WC1H
618 D10 Lucan Place SW3
614 H9 Ludgate Broadway EC4V
614 G9 Ludgate Circus EC4M
614 G9 Ludgate Hill EC4M
614 G9 Ludgate Square EC4V
615 J4 Ludlow Street EC1V
615 N4 Luke Street EC2A
613 J9 Lumley Street W1K
617 P11 Lupus Street SW1V
612 C5 Luton Street NW8
612 H5 Luxborough Street W1U
616 H8 Lyall Mews SW1X
616 H8 Lyall Mews West SW1X
616 H8 Lyall Street SW1X
617 K8 Lygon Place SW1W
619 R10 Lynton Estate SE1
619 R10 Lynton Road SE1
612 B5 Lyons Place NW8

M

613 Q3 Mabledon Place NW1
613 J2 Macclesfield Road EC1V
613 Q10 Macclesfield Street W1D
612 J5 MacFarren Place NW1
612 H2 Mackennal Street NW8
614 B8 Macklin Street WC2B
613 M2 Mackworth Street NW1
613 L10 Maddox Street W1K
619 P11 Madron Street SE1
619 R5 Magazine Gate * W2
619 N4 Magdalen Street SE1
619 R5 Maguire Street SE1
612 A6 Maida Avenue W2
612 A4 Maida Vale W9
619 K4 Maiden Lane SE1
614 B10 Maiden Lane WC2E
619 K4 Maidstone Buildings Mews SE1
616 E10 Makins Street SW3
613 Q6 Malet Street WC1E
612 E5 Mallory Street NW8
615 L4 Mallow Street EC1Y
614 G3 Malta Street EC1V
619 Q6 Maltby Street SE1
619 P5 Maltings Place SW6
614 D10 Maltravers Street WC2R
612 H7 Manchester Mews W1U
612 H7 Manchester Square W1H
612 H7 Manchester Street W1U
619 M6 Manciple Street SE1
612 P9 Mandela Way SE1
613 J8 Mandeville Place W1U
613 Q9 Manette Street W1D
614 G2 Manningford Close EC1V
611 J11 Manor Place SE17
615 K7 Mansell Street E1
613 K7 Mansfield Mews W1G
613 K7 Mansfield Street W1G
615 L9 Mansion House Place EC4N
612 A10 Manson Mews SW7
618 B10 Manson Place SW7

613 N6 Maple Place W1T
613 M6 Maple Street W1T
613 R3 Marble Quay E1W
612 M9 Marcia Road SE1
613 P10 Marcia Road SE1
613 M8 Margaret Street W1B
618 E3 Margaret Street W1X
618 G2 Marigold Alley SE1
617 K4 Market Mews W1J
613 M8 Market Place W1D
616 N7 Market Yard Mews SW3
616 F11 Markham Place SW3
616 F11 Markham Square SW3
616 E11 Markham Street SW3
615 P10 Mark Lane EC3R
615 N4 Mark Street EC2A
618 H10 Marlborough Close SE17
615 M10 Marlborough Court W1B
616 B2 Marlborough Gate W2
616 N4 Marlborough Road SW1A
616 D10 Marlborough Street SW3
619 R8 Marshall's Place SE16
613 N9 Marshall Street W1F
615 K5 Marshalsea Road SE1
617 Q9 Marsham Street SW1P
615 L4 Martha's Buildings EC1V
615 M4 Martin Lane EC4R
614 B9 Martlett Court WC2B
613 J7 Marylebone High Street W1U
613 J8 Marylebone Lane W1U
613 J6 Marylebone Mews W1G
613 N8 Marylebone Passage W1W
612 E6 Marylebone Road NW1
613 J7 Marylebone Street W1U
613 D10 Marylee Way SE11
613 L9 Mason's Arms Mews W1S
613 L9 Mason's Avenue EC2V
614 H2 Mason's Place * N1
619 M10 Mason Street SE17
613 J4 Masons Yard EC1V
617 N3 Masons Yard SW1Y
619 N10 Massinger Street SE17
613 R9 Mathews Yard WC2H
618 H6 Mathieson Court SE1
617 P9 Maunsel Street SW1P
614 K4 Mayall Court SE1
617 L3 Mayfair Place W1J
618 E7 Mays Court WC2N
619 J6 McCoid Way SE1
619 J8 Meadow Row SE1
618 E7 Mead Row SE1
615 P9 Meard Street W1F
614 C4 Mecklenburgh Place WC1N
614 C4 Mecklenburgh Square WC1N
614 C4 Mecklenburgh Street WC1N
617 P8 Medway Street SW1P
614 C10 Melbourne Place WC2B
612 F6 Melbury Terrace NW1
612 F6 Melcombe Place NW1
612 F6 Melcombe Street NW1
612 B3 Melina Place NW8
619 N5 Melior Place SE1
619 M5 Melior Street SE1
613 N3 Melton Street NW1
615 J5 Memel Street EC1Y
618 E5 Mepham Street SE1
613 R9 Mercer Street WC2H
614 E3 Meredith Street EC1R
614 C3 Merlin Street WC1X
619 L5 Mermaid Court SE1
619 L7 Merrick Square SE1
619 M11 Merrow Walk SE17
612 F8 Merton Terrace * W1H
617 K8 Mews North SW1W
619 N11 Mews South SW1W
619 R3 Mews Street E1W
615 G4 Meymott Street SE1
615 M1 Micawber Street N1
615 P7 Middlesex Street E1
615 J6 Middle Street EC1A
613 E9 Middle Temple Lane WC2R
613 M7 Middleton Buildings W1W
613 M7 Middleton Place W1W
619 M3 Middle Yard SE1
615 N5 Midford Place W1T
614 B3 Midhope Street WC1H
612 E6 Midland Road NW1
618 G6 Milcote Street SE1
614 E10 Milford Lane WC2R
615 K8 Milk Street EC2V
617 R11 Millbank SW1P
617 Q10 Millbank Estate SW1P
619 J2 Millennium Bridge SE1
619 Q5 Millennium Square SE1
619 J4 Miller Walk SE1
614 C5 Millman Mews WC1N
614 C5 Millman Place WC1N
614 C5 Millman Street WC1N
617 Q3 Millshott Close SW1Y
619 Q6 Millstream Road SE1
619 R6 Mill Street SE1
615 L10 Mill Street W1S
616 F9 Milner Street SW3
614 F3 Milroy Walk SE1
619 Q10 Milton Close SE1
615 L6 Milton Court EC2Y
615 L6 Milton Street EC2Y
615 N10 Mincing Lane EC3R
617 J9 Minera Mews SW1W
615 Q9 Minnow Walk SE17
615 Q9 Minories EC3N
615 N10 Minster Court EC3R
619 J5 Mint Street SE1
614 H3 Mitchell Street EC1V
618 F5 Mitre Road SE1
615 P9 Mitre Square EC3A
615 P9 Mitre Street EC3A
612 E7 Molyneux Street W1H
617 P8 Monck Street SW1P
616 D6 Moncorvo Close SW7
619 L5 Monkton Street SE11
615 K7 Monkwell Square EC2Y
619 R9 Monmouth Street WC2H
619 L3 Montague Close SE1
619 Q6 Montague Place WC1E
614 A7 Montague Street WC1A
613 R6 Montague Street WC1B
612 G8 Montagu Mansions W1U
612 G8 Montagu Mews North W1U
612 G8 Montagu Mews South W1H
612 G8 Montagu Mews West W1H
612 F7 Montagu Place W1H
612 G7 Montagu Row W1U
612 G7 Montagu Square W1H
612 G8 Montagu Street W1H
615 Q3 Montclare Street E2
616 E7 Montpelier Mews SW7
616 E7 Montpelier Place SW7
616 E7 Montpelier Square SW7
616 E6 Montpelier Street SW7
616 E7 Montpelier Terrace SW7
616 E7 Montpelier Walk SW7
614 C10 Montreal Place WC2B
619 M2 Montrose Place SW1X
619 M2 Monument Street EC3R
615 F9 Moore Street SW3
615 L7 Moorfields EC2M
615 L7 Moorfields Highwalk EC2Y
615 L8 Moorgate EC2M
615 L7 Moorgate EC2R
615 L7 Moor Lane EC2Y
615 Q9 Moor Street W1D
615 K3 Mora Street EC1V
619 N10 Morecambe Street SE17
614 H2 Moreland Street EC1V
619 N4 More London Place SE1
619 P4 More London Riverside SE1

617 N11 Moreton Place SW1V
617 N11 Moreton Street SW1V
617 N11 Moreton Terrace SW1V
617 N11 Moreton Terrace Mews South SW1V
619 N4 Morgans Lane SE1
618 F6 Morley Street SE1
619 N6 Morocco Street SE1
617 M8 Morpeth Terrace SW1P
618 F11 Morrells Yard SE11
613 L8 Mortimer Street W1B
618 L8 Morton Place SE1
613 P7 Morwell Street W1T
616 E9 Mossop Street SW3
616 H7 Motcomb Street SW1X
614 H3 Mount Mills EC1V
614 E5 Mount Pleasant WC1X
617 K2 Mount Row W1K
616 H2 Mount Street W1K
612 H7 Moxon Street W1U
612 D5 Mulready Street NW8
615 K8 Mumford Court EC2V
615 N2 Mundy Street N1
613 L3 Munster Square NW1
619 K9 Munton Road SE17
618 E6 Murphy Street SE1
615 L1 Murray Grove N1
619 P2 Muscovy Street EC3N
614 A7 Museum Street WC1A
614 F2 Myddelton Passage EC1R
614 F2 Myddelton Square EC1R
614 F3 Myddelton Street EC1R
614 E1 Mylne Street EC1R
615 N1 Myrtle Street N1
615 N1 Myrtle Walk N1

N
614 E3 Naoroji Street WC1X
615 K1 Napier Grove N1
613 L2 Nash Street NW1
613 M7 Nassau Street W1W
617 R7 Nathaniel Close E1
615 Q4 Navarre Street E2
615 Q2 Nazrul Street E2
614 A9 Neal Street WC2H
613 R9 Neal's Yard WC2H
617 M9 Neathouse Place SW1V
619 R7 Neckinger SE1
619 R7 Neckinger Estate SE16
619 R6 Neckinger Street SE1
614 H1 Nelson Place N1
618 G5 Nelson Square SE1
614 H1 Nelson Terrace EC1V
613 M3 Netley Street NW1
616 B11 Neville Street SW7
616 B11 Neville Terrace SW7
613 L9 New Bond Street W1K
614 C9 New Bridge Street EC4M
615 M7 New Broad Street EC2M
613 M9 Newburgh Street W1F
613 M10 New Burlington Mews W1S
613 M10 New Burlington Place W1S
613 M10 New Burlington Street W1S
618 D11 Newburn Street SE11
615 J7 Newbury Street EC1A
614 G8 Newcastle Close EC4M
612 C7 Newcastle Place W2
614 F5 Newcastle Row EC1R
613 J7 New Cavendish Street W1U
615 J9 New Change EC4M
614 H2 New Charles Street EC1V
615 L5 Newcomen Street SE1
613 Q9 New Compton Street WC2H
614 E10 New Court * WC2R
612 D1 Newcourt Street NW8
614 F8 New Fetter Lane EC4A
614 H8 Newgate Street EC1A
619 J3 New Globe Walk SE1
615 Q8 New Goulston Street E1
619 P6 Newham's Row SE1
618 H10 Newington Butts SE11
619 J7 Newington Causeway SE1
615 P4 New Inn Broadway EC2A
615 P4 New Inn Square EC2A
615 P4 New Inn Street EC2A
615 P4 New Inn Yard EC2A
619 K9 New Kent Road SE1
615 R2 Newling Estate E2
615 P10 New London Street EC3R
614 D7 Newman's Row WC2A
613 N7 Newman Street W1T
618 E7 Newnham Terrace SE1
615 N4 New North Place EC2A
615 M1 New North Road N1
614 C6 New North Street WC1N
615 Q8 New Oxford Street WC1A
613 Q10 Newport Court W1D
613 Q10 Newport Place W1D
614 C10 Newport Street SE11
612 G9 New Quebec Street W1H
613 R10 New Row WC2N
614 D8 New Square WC2A
614 F8 New Street EC1A
615 P7 New Street EC2M
614 F8 New Street Square EC4A
614 B8 Newton Street WC2B
615 L7 New Union Street EC2Y
615 M10 Nicholas Lane EC4N
618 G4 Nicholson Street SE1
618 F9 Nightingale Mews SE11
615 L2 Nile Street N1
615 J8 Noble Street EC2V
613 N9 Noel Street W1F
612 D8 Norfolk Crescent W2
612 C8 Norfolk Place W2
612 C9 Norfolk Row SE1
612 C9 Norfolk Square W2
612 C9 Norfolk Square Mews W2
615 J3 Norman Street EC1V
617 P2 Norris Street SW1Y
614 F4 Northampton Road EC1R
614 F4 Northampton Row EC1R
614 G3 Northampton Square EC1V
612 H10 North Audley Street W1K
612 D3 North Bank NW8
614 H5 Northburgh Street EC1V
612 E10 North Carriage Drive W2
613 P6 North Crescent W1T
614 C1 Northdown Street N1
613 M3 North Gower Street NW1
614 C6 Northington Street WC1N
614 D5 North Mews WC1N
612 E9 North Row W2
612 G10 North Row W1K
615 R9 North Tenter Street E1
616 P9 North Terrace SW3
615 P9 Northumberland Alley EC3N
618 A3 Northumberland Avenue WC2N
618 A3 Northumberland Street WC2N
612 B7 North Wharf Road W2
612 B4 Northwick Close NW8
612 B4 Northwick Terrace NW8
615 P5 Norton Folgate E1
614 E8 Norwich Street EC4A
614 A9 Nottingham Court WC2H
612 H5 Nottingham Place W1U
612 H6 Nottingham Street W1U
612 H5 Nottingham Terrace NW1
612 A1 Nugent Terrace NW8
619 L10 Nursery Row SE17
612 E8 Nutford Place W2

O
618 F9 Oakden Street SE11
618 E7 Oakey Lane SE1
614 H1 Oakley Crescent EC1V
615 R4 Oakley Yard * E2
612 C3 Oak Tree Road NW8
615 J8 Oat Lane EC2V
616 C7 Observatory Road SW7
612 J11 Occupation Road SE17
615 N7 Octagon Arcade EC2M
614 A9 Odhams Walk WC2H
613 M6 Ogle Street W1W
614 H9 Old Bailey EC4M
616 H5 Old Barrack Yard SW1X
617 M2 Old Bond Street W1S
615 N8 Old Broad Street EC2M
614 A11 Old Brompton Road SW7
616 E8 Old Buildings WC2A
613 M10 Old Burlington Street W1S
613 J6 Oldbury Place W1U
615 Q8 Old Castle Street E1
615 K8 Old Cavendish Street W1G
613 P10 Old Compton Street W1D
613 J10 Old Fish Street Hill EC4V
614 G8 Old Fleet Lane EC4M
614 B6 Old Gloucester Street WC1N
615 L9 Old Jewry EC2R
615 N9 Old Kent Road SE1
615 Q2 Old Market Square E2
612 E7 Old Marylebone Road NW1
614 F9 Old Mitre Court EC4Y
615 Q4 Old Nichol Street E2
614 C6 Old North Street WC1X
618 C9 Old Paradise Street SE11
617 J4 Old Park Lane W1J
617 P7 Old Pye Street SW1P
617 Q7 Old Quebec Street W1H
617 Q6 Old Queen Street SW1H
614 G9 Old Seacoal Lane EC4M
614 D8 Old Square WC2A
615 J4 Old Street EC1V
615 M4 Oliver's Yard EC1Y
619 K4 O'Meara Street SE1
614 B1 Omega Place N1
616 C10 Onslow Crescent SW7
616 B11 Onslow Gardens SW7
616 B10 Onslow Mews East SW7
616 B10 Onslow Mews West SW7
616 B10 Onslow Square SW7
614 F5 Onslow Street EC1M
618 H8 Ontario Street SE1
618 G11 Opal Street SE11
617 Q2 Orange Street WC2H
616 C11 Oratory Lane SW3
615 L10 Orb Street SE17
612 B5 Orchardson Street NW8
612 H9 Orchard Street W1H
614 C6 Orde Hall Street WC1N
618 G9 Orient Street SE11
614 B6 Ormond Close WC1N
612 J10 Ormonde Place SW1W
617 N3 Ormond Yard SW1Y
613 D11 Orsett Street SE11
617 P10 Osbert Street SW1V
615 R7 Osborn Street E1
613 L5 Osnaburgh Street NW1
613 L4 Osnaburgh Terrace NW1
612 H6 Ossington Buildings W1U
613 Q1 Ossulston Street NW1
618 H9 Oswin Street SE11
618 G11 Othello Close SE11
612 F4 Outer Circle NW1
615 P8 Outwich Street EC3A
616 E8 Ovington Gardens SW3
616 E8 Ovington Mews SW3
616 E8 Ovington Square SW3
616 E8 Ovington Street SW3
615 G2 Owen's Row EC1V
614 G1 Owen Street EC1V
617 P2 Oxendon Street W1D
615 L10 Oxford Court EC4N
612 D9 Oxford Square W2
612 H9 Oxford Street W1K
619 R11 Oxley Close SE1

P
615 R3 Padbury Court E2
612 B7 Paddington Green W2
612 H6 Paddington Street W1U
617 Q9 Page Street SW1P
619 N9 Page's Walk SE1
614 G2 Paget Street EC1V
614 D3 Pakenham Street WC1X
617 M7 Palace Place SW1E
617 M7 Palace Street SW1E
612 E4 Palgrave Gardens NW1
615 Q3 Palissy Street E2
617 P4 Pall Mall SW1Y
617 P3 Pall Mall East SW1Y
617 N4 Pall Mall Place SW1Y
617 P7 Palmer Street SW1H
615 K9 Pancras Lane EC4N
617 P2 Panton Street SW1Y
619 M9 Paragon Mews SE17
617 M7 Pardoner Street SE1
614 H4 Pardon Street EC1V
618 G3 Paris Garden SE1
616 F6 Park Close SW7
615 K5 Park Crescent W1B
613 L5 Park Crescent Mews East W1B
613 K5 Park Crescent Mews West W1G
614 B8 Parker Mews WC2B
614 B8 Parker Street WC2B
612 G10 Park Lane W1H
617 M4 Park Place SW1A
612 A6 Park Place Villas W2
612 E3 Park Road NW8
614 K4 Park Square East NW1
613 K5 Park Square Mews NW1
614 K4 Park Square West NW1
612 E10 Park Steps * W2
619 J3 Park Street SE1
613 H2 Park Street W1K
612 E8 Park West W2
612 E8 Park West Place W2
617 P6 Parliament Court E1
618 A5 Parliament Square SW1P
616 H10 Parliament Street SW1A
618 H9 Pastor Street SE1
617 J9 Paternoster Row EC4M
617 J9 Paternoster Square EC4M
615 N4 Paul Street E2
612 E3 Paveley Street NW8
616 G6 Pavilion Road SW1X
616 G8 Pavilion Street SW1X
614 F5 Peabody Estate * EC1R
615 K5 Peabody Estate * EC1Y
615 F3 Peabody Estate * SE1
617 J3 Peabody Estate * SE1
614 F5 Peabody Terrace * EC1R
615 H10 Peacock Street SE17
617 N4 Peacock Yard SE17
618 F7 Pearman Street SE1
618 E5 Pear Place SE1
614 F5 Pear Tree Court EC1R
614 H4 Peartree Street EC1V
617 Q6 Pecks Yard * E1
615 R5 Pedley Street E2
615 L3 Peerless Street EC1V
618 D10 Pelham Crescent SW7
616 D9 Pelham Place SW7
616 C9 Pelham Street SW7

615 Q2 Pelter Street E2
614 F8 Pemberton Row EC4A
614 J6 Pembroke Close SW1X
612 D6 Penfold Place W2
612 C5 Penfold Street NW8
619 P10 Penry Street SE1
614 E1 Penton Grove N1
618 H10 Penton Place SE17
614 D2 Penton Rise WC1X
614 C1 Pentonville Road N1
613 J5 Pepper Street SE1
615 P10 Pepys Street EC3N
614 G4 Percival Street EC1V
613 P7 Percy Mews W1T
613 P7 Percy Street W1T
617 P7 Perkin's Rents SW1P
619 K3 Perkins Square SE1
613 J10 Peter's Hill EC4V
617 P10 Peter Street W1F
613 L4 Peto Place NW1
615 P7 Petticoat Lane E1
615 Q8 Petticoat Square E1
615 Q8 Petticoat Tower * E1
617 N7 Petty France SW1H
619 P2 Petty Wales EC3R
618 E10 Petyward SW3
615 N10 Philpot Lane EC3M
617 K8 Phipp's Mews SW1W
615 N4 Phipp Street EC2A
613 D4 Phoenix Place WC1X
613 P2 Phoenix Road NW1
613 Q9 Phoenix Street WC2H
619 R6 Phoenix Wharf Road SE1
617 M3 Piccadilly W1J
617 M3 Piccadilly Arcade W1J
617 M2 Piccadilly Circus W1J
614 H2 Pickard Street EC1V
617 N4 Pickering Place SW1Y
615 J1 Pickfords Wharf * N1
617 J6 Pickwick Street SE1
613 J9 Picton Place W1H
619 L6 Pilgrimage Street SE1
614 G9 Pilgrim Street EC4V
615 K11 Pilton Place SE17
616 H11 Pimlico Road SW1W
615 N6 Pindar Street EC2A
617 M7 Pine Apple Court SW1E
614 E4 Pine Street EC1R
615 N1 Pitfield Street N1
617 J4 Pitt's Head Mews W1K
615 L5 Plantain Place SE1
615 N10 Plantation Lane EC3M
615 M4 Platina Street EC2A
619 J5 Playhouse Court SE1
615 G9 Playhouse Yard EC4V
615 K3 Pleydell Estate * EC1V
615 F8 Pleydell Street EC4Y
617 F9 Plough Place EC4A
615 P5 Plough Yard EC2A
614 F8 Plumtree Court EC4A
612 D5 Plympton Place NW8
612 D5 Plympton Street NW8
619 K8 Pocock Street SE1
613 N8 Poland Street W1F
613 L9 Pollen Street W1S
612 B4 Pollitt Drive NW8
618 F9 Polperro Mews SE11
619 P2 Polygon Road NW1
615 R8 Pomell Way E1
615 R8 Pomeroy Place E1
617 D10 Pond Place SW3
617 Q11 Ponsonby Place SW1P
617 Q11 Ponsonby Terrace SW1P
616 F8 Pont Street SW1X
616 F8 Pont Street Mews SW3
614 E5 Pooles Buildings WC1X
619 P6 Pope Street SE1
614 G9 Poppins Court EC4A
612 E9 Porchester Place W2
619 M5 Porlock Street SE1
615 K3 Porter Street SE1
612 G6 Porter Street W1U
612 A7 Porteus Road W2
613 N9 Portland Mews W1F
613 K9 Portland Place W1G
612 H8 Portman Close W1H
612 E5 Portman Gate NW8
612 H9 Portman Mews South W1H
612 G8 Portman Square W1H
612 H9 Portman Street W1H
612 G8 Portman Towers W1H
614 E6 Portpool Lane WC1X
612 E9 Portsea Mews W2
612 E9 Portsea Place W2
614 C8 Portsmouth Street WC2A
615 Q10 Portsoken Street EC3N
614 D9 Portugal Street WC2A
618 M8 Potier Street SE1
619 P4 Potters Fields * SE1
615 L9 Poultry EC2R
614 B5 Powis Place WC1N
612 C8 Praed Mews W2
612 C8 Praed Street W2
618 D9 Pratt Walk SE11
615 R10 Prescot Street E1
615 J2 President Street EC1V
615 N9 Preston Close SE1
615 K1 Prestwood Street N1
618 H4 Price's Street SE1
614 D2 Prideaux Place WC1X
618 F9 Primrose Hill EC4Y
615 N6 Primrose Street EC2A
612 E1 Prince Albert Road NW8
616 B7 Prince Consort Road SW7
615 R6 Princelet Street E1
616 D5 Prince of Wales Gate SW7
616 M3 Prince of Wales Passage NW1
613 M3 Prince Regent Mews NW1
617 N3 Princes Arcade W1J
616 C7 Princes Gardens SW7
616 C7 Prince's Gate SW7
616 D6 Prince's Gate SW7
616 B6 Prince's Gate Court SW7
616 C7 Princes Gate Mews SW7
612 C6 Princess Louise Close W2
618 H8 Princess Street SE1
615 L9 Prince's Street EC2R
615 L9 Prince's Street EC2R
614 C7 Princeton Street WC1R
614 E8 Printers Inn Court EC4A
615 P3 Printing House Yard E2
619 M8 Prioress Street SE1
619 P7 Priory Court * WC1R
614 C7 Procter Street WC1R
613 J10 Providence Court W1K
619 N5 Providence Square SE1
612 C2 Provost Estate N1
615 L1 Provost Street N1
615 H10 Pudding Lane EC3R
614 H10 Puddle Dock EC4V
615 Q6 Puma Court E1
614 E9 Pump Court * EC4Y
619 P7 Purbrook Street SE1

Q
617 N2 Quadrant Arcade W1B
615 Q5 Quaker Street * E1
614 E8 Quality Court EC4A
613 G9 Quebec Mews W1H
614 H9 Queen Anne Mews W1G
617 P6 Queen Anne's Gate SW1H
613 K8 Queen Anne Street W1G
619 P5 Queen Elizabeth Street SE1
615 K2 Queenhithe EC4V
614 J4 Queen Mother Gate W1J
616 B9 Queensberry Mews West SW7
616 B9 Queensberry Place SW7

616 B9 Queensberry Way SW7
616 A6 Queens Gate SW7
616 A6 Queen's Gate Mews SW7
616 A8 Queen's Gate Place SW7
616 A8 Queen's Gate Place Mews SW7
614 B5 Queen Square WC1N
615 K9 Queen Street EC4N
617 K3 Queen Street W1J
619 K2 Queen Street Place EC4R
614 N5 Queen's Yard W1T
614 G10 Queen Victoria Street EC4V
614 H1 Quick Street N1
619 J5 Quilp Street SE1

R
619 P7 Radcliffe Road SE1
612 C9 Radnor Mews W2
615 K3 Radnor Place W2
619 L3 Radnor Street EC1V
614 B1 Railway Approach SE1
612 D8 Railway Street N1
613 M9 Ramillies Place W1F
613 M9 Ramillies Street W1F
617 P11 Rampayne Street SW1V
618 C11 Randall Road SE11
614 C10 Randall Row SE11
612 A5 Randolph Mews W9
617 J11 Ranelagh Grove SW1W
619 Q9 Rangoon Street EC3N
612 D6 Ranston Street NW8
615 P2 Raphael Street SW7
613 P7 Rathbone Place W1T
613 N7 Rathbone Street W1T
615 R1 Ravenscroft Street E2
616 F9 Ravey Street EC2A
616 F9 Rawlings Street SW3
614 G2 Rawstorne Place EC1V
614 G2 Rawstorne Street EC1V
614 D6 Raymond Buildings * WC1R
614 F5 Ray Street EC1R
616 F9 Ray Street Bridge EC1R
615 Q4 Redchurch Street E2
615 K5 Redcross Way SE1
613 L1 Redhill Street NW1
614 F8 Red Lion Court EC4A
614 C7 Red Lion Square WC1N
614 C7 Red Lion Street WC1R
617 J3 Red Lion Yard W1K
617 M10 Red Place W1K
615 P2 Redvers Street N1
616 B9 Reece Mews SW7
618 F10 Reedworth Street SE11
617 K9 Reeves Mews W1K
619 R9 Regan Way N1
617 P9 Regency Place SW1P
617 Q10 Regency Street SW1P
616 B11 Regency Terrace SW7
613 R8 Regent Square WC1H
613 L8 Regent Street W1S
613 N3 Regnart Buildings NW1
616 E7 Relton Mews SW7
616 H1 Rembrandt Close SW1W
614 H1 Remington Street N1
614 C8 Remnant Street WC2B
618 E11 Renfrew Road SE11
618 G3 Rennie Street SE1
619 M8 Rephidim Street SE1
615 Q2 Retford Street N1
617 J3 Rex Place W1K
615 R4 Rhoda Street E2
613 M5 Richardson's Mews W1T
613 P9 Richard's Place SW3
614 C6 Richbell Place WC1N
613 P9 Richmond Buildings W1F
613 P9 Richmond Mews W1F
618 A5 Richmond Terrace SW1A
613 P6 Ridgmount Gardens WC1E
613 P6 Ridgmount Street WC1E
613 L7 Riding House Street W1B
619 Q7 Riley Road SE1
618 H5 Risborough Street SE1
616 E2 River Street EC1R
615 P3 Rivington Place EC2A
615 P3 Rivington Street EC2A
612 H8 Robert Adam Street W1H
612 A5 Robert Close W9
619 J10 Robert Dashwood Way SE17
616 H8 Roberts Mews SW1X
614 F4 Roberts Place EC1R
615 L3 Robert Street NW1
618 B2 Robert Street WC2N
615 Q3 Rochelle Street E2
617 N9 Rochester Row SW1P
617 P8 Rochester Street SW1P
619 L3 Rochester Walk SE1
617 J8 Rockingham Street SE1
614 H1 Rocliffe Street N1
612 G7 Rodmarton Street W1U
619 K9 Rodney Place SE1
619 K10 Rodney Road SE17
614 D5 Roger Street WC1N
614 A11 Roland Gardens SW7
616 A11 Roland Way SW7
614 E8 Rolls Buildings EC4A
615 R11 Rolls Road SE1
613 Q10 Romilly Street W1D
617 Q8 Romney Street SW1P
615 N10 Rood Lane EC3M
617 P6 Ropemaker Street EC2Y
619 P6 Roper Lane SE1
616 A10 Rosary Gardens SW7
615 K5 Roscoe Street EC1Y
619 J8 Rose Alley SE1
614 E5 Rosebery Avenue EC1R
614 E4 Rosebery Court EC1R
615 Q7 Rose Court SE1
617 N4 Rose & Crown Yard SW1Y
616 F10 Rosemoor Street SW3
614 A10 Rose Street WC2E
614 F4 Rosoman Place EC1R
614 F3 Rosoman Street EC1R
612 E5 Rossmore Close * NW8
612 E5 Rossmore Road NW8
618 G7 Rotary Street SE1
618 H4 Rotherham Walk * SE1
619 N7 Rothsay Street SE1
618 G3 Roupell Street SE1
619 Q11 Rowcross Street SE1
617 M2 Royal Arcade W1S
617 M2 Royal Avenue SW3
615 M9 Royal Court EC3V
618 D7 Royal Mint Place SE1
615 R10 Royal Mint Street EC3N
619 N6 Royal Oak Yard SE1
617 P3 Royal Opera Arcade SW1Y
618 D7 Royal Street SE1
615 N3 Rufus Street N1
614 C5 Rugby Street WC1N
615 P10 Rupert Court W1D
617 P2 Rupert Street W1D
618 H5 Rushworth Street SE1
615 N4 Russell Court SW1A
613 R5 Russell Square WC1B
615 B10 Russell Street WC2B
615 K9 Russia Row EC2V
617 P9 Rutherford Street SW1P
617 R6 Rutland Court SW7
616 E6 Rutland Gardens SW7
616 D6 Rutland Gate SW7
616 D6 Rutland Gate Mews SW7
616 D7 Rutland Mews South SW7

614 H6 Rutland Place EC1M
616 E7 Rutland Street SW7
617 M7 Ryder Street SW1Y
616 F7 Rysbrack Street SW3

S
617 M2 Sackville Street W1J
614 F6 Saffron Hill EC1N
614 F6 Saffron Street EC1M
614 C3 Sage Way WC1X
618 D9 Sail Street SE11
615 M4 St Agnes Well EC1Y
612 C6 St Alban's Mews W2
617 P2 St Alban's Street SW1Y
617 K7 St Alphage Garden EC2Y
615 K7 St Alphage Highwalk EC2Y
614 H10 St Andrew's Hill EC4V
613 K4 St Andrew's Place NW1
614 F7 St Andrew Street EC1N
617 P9 St Annes Court W1F
617 Q7 St Ann's Street SW1P
617 Q8 St Ann's Street SW1P
613 K10 St Anselm's Place W1K
617 J11 St Barnabas Street SW1W
615 Q8 St Botolph Street EC3A
614 G8 St Bride Street EC4A
616 F9 St Catherines Mews SW3
614 B2 St Chad's Place WC1X
614 B2 St Chad's Street WC1H
613 J9 St Christopher's Place W1U
615 Q9 St Clare Street EC3N
614 C9 St Clement's Lane WC2A
614 F6 St Cross Street EC1N
619 N2 St Dunstan's Hill EC3R
619 N2 St Dunstan's Lane EC3R
617 L10 St Georges Circus SE1
617 L10 St Georges Drive SW1V
612 E10 St George's Fields * W2
615 M10 St George's Lane EC3R
618 G8 St George's Road SE1
614 G8 St Georges's Court EC4M
617 P11 St George's Square SW1V
613 L10 St George Street W1S
615 K7 St Giles Churchyard * EC2Y
613 Q8 St Giles Court WC2H
615 Q8 St Giles High Street WC2H
613 Q9 St Giles Passage WC2
614 E3 St Helena Street WC1X
615 N8 St Helen's Place EC3N
615 N7 St James' Court * N1
617 N3 St James's Chambers * SW1Y
617 N7 St James's Court SW1E
613 M3 St James's Gardens * NW1
617 P2 St James's Market SW1Y
617 M4 St James's Place SW1A
617 P3 St James's Square SW1Y
617 M3 St James's Street SW1A
614 G4 St James Walk EC1R
615 M1 St John's Estate N1
615 Q5 St John's Estate N1
614 G5 St John's Lane EC1M
614 G5 St John's Place EC1M
614 G5 St John's Square EC1M
614 F1 St John Street EC1V
612 C1 St John's Wood High Street NW8
612 B4 St John's Wood Road NW8
619 R3 St Katharine's Way E1N
616 F11 St Leonards Terrace SW3
615 L4 St Luke's Estate * EC1V
615 K4 St Luke's Close EC1V
616 D11 St Luke's Street SW3
618 A6 St Margaret Street SW1P
615 R9 St Mark Street E1
617 R2 St Martin-in-the-Fields WC2H
613 R10 St Martins Court WC2H
613 R10 St Martin's Lane WC2N
615 J8 St Martin's Le Grand EC1A
617 R2 St Martin's Place WC2H
617 Q2 St Martin's Street WC2H
613 N2 St Mary At Hill EC3R
615 N9 St Mary Axe EC3A
619 R2 St Mary Graces Court * EC3N
618 F9 St Marys Gardens SE11
612 A6 St Mary's Mansions W2
612 B6 St Mary's Square W2
612 B6 St Mary's Terrace W2
618 F9 St Marys Walk SE11
617 P7 St Matthew Street SW1P
615 M9 St Michael's Alley EC3V
612 C8 St Michael's Street W2
615 L9 St Mildred's Court EC2R
618 C11 St Oswald's Place SE11
617 Q10 St Oswulf Street SW1P
614 H9 St Paul's Church Yard EC4V
619 Q7 St Saviour's Estate SE1
618 A5 St Stephens Parade SW1A
615 L10 St Swithin's Lane EC4N
619 M4 St Thomas Street SE1
613 J7 St Vincent Street W1U
618 C10 Salamanca Place SE11
618 C10 Salamanca Street SE11
612 D7 Sale Place W2
619 L9 Salisbury Close SE17
614 F9 Salisbury Court EC4Y
612 F6 Salisbury Place W1H
614 F9 Salisbury Square EC4Y
612 C5 Salisbury Street NW8
615 L10 Salters' Hall Court EC4N
612 D5 Samford Street NW8
618 D11 Sancroft Street SE11
619 K6 Sanctuary Street SE1
618 E5 Sandell Street SE1
619 L11 Sandford Row SE17
617 M2 Sandland Street WC1R
613 R3 Sandwich Street WC1H
615 P7 Sandy's Row E1
614 G4 Sans Walk EC1R
618 D9 Saperton Walk SE11
615 P2 Sarah Street E2
614 C9 Sardinia Street WC2A
618 E9 Saunders Street SE11
615 P10 Savage Gardens EC3N
613 M10 Savile Row W1S
618 B2 Savoy Court WC2R
618 C2 Savoy Hill WC2R
618 B2 Savoy Place WC2R
614 C10 Savoy Row WC2R
612 C2 Savoy Steps WC2R
614 C2 Savoy Street WC2R
612 C2 Savoy Way WC2R
615 J3 Sawyer Street SE1
617 M1 Scala Street W1T
613 N6 Scarborough Street E1
615 R1 Scawfell Street E2
615 Q4 Sclater Street E2
618 G4 Scoresby Street SE1
614 F3 Scotswood Street EC1R
612 B3 Scott Ellis Gardens NW8
618 D8 Scovell Crescent SE1
619 J6 Scovell Road SE1
615 N4 Scrutton Street EC2A
614 B3 Seaford Street WC1H
615 M9 Searles Road SE1
618 F11 Seaton Close SE11
614 H3 Sebastian Street EC1V
618 E4 Secker Street SE1
613 N11 Sedan Way SE17
616 H9 Sedding Street SW1X
614 C3 Seddon Street WC1X
615 C8 Sedley Place W1C
615 P10 Seething Lane EC3N
615 Q5 Sekforde Street EC1R
616 B11 Selwood Place SW7
616 B11 Selwood Terrace SW7
616 J10 Semley Place SW1W

614 F9 Serjeant's Inn EC4Y
614 D8 Serle Street WC2A
615 J9 Sermon Lane EC4V
616 E4 Serpentine Road W2
619 Q9 Setchell Estate SE1
619 Q9 Setchell Road SE1
619 Q9 Setchell Way SE1
613 R9 Seven Dials WC2H
615 R6 Seven Stars Yard E1
616 G6 Seville Street SW1X
614 H4 Seward Street EC1V
614 H4 Seymour Mews W1H
612 E7 Seymour Place W1H
612 E9 Seymour Street W2
615 R4 Shacklewell Street E2
612 Q4 Shad Thames SE1
613 P10 Shaftesbury Avenue WC2H
615 J7 Shaftesbury Place * EC2Y
615 K1 Shaftesbury Street N1
616 F8 Shafto Mews SW1X
619 P5 Shand Street SE1
617 P2 Shavers Place W1J
614 C9 Sheffield Street WC2A
612 A7 Sheldon Square W2
614 A9 Shelton Street WC2H
615 P1 Shenfield Street N1
615 K2 Shepherdess Place EC1V
615 K1 Shepherdess Walk N1
617 K4 Shepherd Market W1J
612 H10 Shepherds Place W1K
617 K4 Shepherd Street W1J
613 P9 Sheraton Street W1F
615 L10 Sherborne Lane EC4N
612 H6 Sherlock Mews W1U
612 F7 Sherwood Court W1H
613 N10 Sherwood Street W1D
612 E7 Shillibeer Place W1H
619 M5 Ship & Mermaid Row SE1
615 N10 Ship Tavern Passage EC3V
615 R2 Shipton Street E2
619 N4 Shipwright Yard SE1
614 F8 Shoe Lane EC4A
615 P3 Shoreditch High Street E1
615 Q10 Shorter Street E1
614 A9 Shorts Gardens WC2H
618 F5 Short Street SE1
612 E7 Shouldham Street W1H
612 D6 Shroton Street NW1
614 B7 Sicilian Avenue WC1A
612 G5 Siddons Lane NW1
613 D8 Sidford Place SE1
614 B3 Sidmouth Street WC1H
613 G1 Sidney Grove EC1V
615 L2 Silbury Street N1
618 H6 Silex Street SE1
615 K6 Silk Street EC2Y
613 M1 Silverdale NW1
613 N10 Silver Place W1F
619 L6 Silvester Street SE1
613 M3 Singer Street EC1V
615 L9 Sise Lane EC4N
616 H10 Skinner Place SW1W
615 K10 Skinners Lane EC4V
614 G3 Skinner Street EC1V
613 R10 Slingsby Place WC2E
612 E10 Sloane Avenue SW3
616 H11 Sloane Court East SW3
616 H11 Sloane Court West SW3
616 H10 Sloane Gardens SW1W
616 G10 Sloane Square SW1W
616 G6 Sloane Street SW1X
616 G9 Sloane Terrace SW1X
612 B9 Smallbrook Mews W2
614 B8 Smart's Place WC1V
614 C7 Smithfield Street EC1A
613 P10 Smith's Court W1D
617 R8 Smith Square SW1P
616 F11 Smith Street SW3
614 G4 Snow Hill EC1A
619 M5 Snowsfields SE1
613 P8 Soho Square W1D
613 P8 Soho Street W1D
612 D9 Somers Crescent W2
615 Q9 Somerset Street Little EC3N
619 L6 Southall Place SE1
614 E7 Southampton Buildings WC2A
614 B7 Southampton Place WC1A
614 A6 Southampton Row WC1B
614 B10 Southampton Street WC2E
617 J2 South Audley Street W1K
618 F2 South Bank SE1
616 D6 South Carriage Drive SW7
617 J9 South Eaton Place SW1W
616 C9 South Kensington Station Arcade SW7
613 K9 South Molton Lane W1K
613 K9 South Molton Street W1K
616 C11 South Parade SW3
615 M7 South Place EC2M
615 M7 South Place Mews EC2M
612 E10 South Rise * W2
614 E7 South Square WC1R
617 J3 South Street W1K
615 R10 South Tenter Street E1
616 D9 South Terrace SW7
619 K2 Southwark Bridge EC4R
619 K3 Southwark Bridge Road SE1
619 R9 Southwark Park Road SE16
618 H3 Southwark Street SE1
612 B8 South Wharf Road W2
612 C8 Southwick Mews W2
612 D9 Southwick Place W2
612 D8 Southwick Street W2
612 E9 Southwick Yard * W2
614 F2 Spafield Street EC1R
614 F2 Spa Green Estate * EC1R
613 J8 Spanish Place W1U
619 Q8 Spa Road SE16
617 N8 Spencer Place SW1P
614 G3 Spencer Street EC1V
617 N7 Spenser Street SW1E
615 P6 Spital Square E1
615 P6 Spital Yard E1
616 F11 Sprimont Place SW3
617 R3 Spring Gardens SW1A
612 G6 Spring Mews W1U
612 B9 Spring Street W2
619 L8 Spurgeon Street SE1
618 E5 Spur Road SE1
617 M6 Spur Road SW1A
612 B3 Squire Gardens NW8
618 E11 Stables Way SE11
617 N5 Stable Yard Road SW1A
613 Q9 Stacey Street WC2H
617 F7 Stackhouse Street SW1X
617 M7 Stafford Place SW1E
617 M3 Stafford Street W1S
617 M7 Stag Place SW1E
619 M4 Stainer Street SE1
615 K8 Staining Lane EC2V
612 E6 Stalbridge Street NW1
618 E3 Stamford Street SE1
615 Q1 Stamp Place E2
615 P3 Standard Place EC2A
619 N10 Stanford Place SE1
617 P10 Stanford Street SE1
616 A10 Stanhope Gardens SW7
617 J4 Stanhope Gate W1K
612 F10 Stanhope Gate W2
616 A9 Stanhope Mews East SW7
616 A10 Stanhope Mews South SW7
616 A9 Stanhope Mews West SW7
613 L2 Stanhope Parade NW1
612 F9 Stanhope Place W2
617 K4 Stanhope Row W1J
612 C10 Stanhope Terrace W2
613 R1 Stanley Passage N1
619 Q6 Stanworth Street SE1
614 E7 Staple Inn WC1V

619 M6 Staple Street SE1
613 N3 Starcross Street NW1
612 C8 Star Street W2
614 E8 Star Yard WC2A
612 H2 Station Approach * NW1
613 L5 Station Arcade * W1W
614 H9 Stationers Hall Court * EC4M
619 L10 Stead Street SE1
613 J10 Steedman Street SE17
613 L2 Steelyard Passage EC4R
613 P7 Stephen Mews W1T
613 N4 Stephenson Way NW1
613 P8 Stephen Street W1T
616 E6 Sterling Street SW7
619 L6 Sterry Street SE1
613 P7 Stevens Street SE1
615 P6 Steward Street E1
615 C11 Stewarts Grove SW3
615 J10 Stew Lane EC4V
617 N9 Stillington Street SW1P
614 D7 Stone Buildings WC2A
614 G8 Stonecutter Street EC4A
615 P8 Stone House Court EC3A
615 J6 Stones End Street SE1
615 P8 Stoney Lane EC3A
615 L3 Stoney Street SE1
613 P7 Store Street WC1E
615 Q6 Storeys Gate SW1H
618 D10 Stoughton Close SE11
612 F9 Stourcliffe Street W2
618 B2 Strand WC2R
615 K9 Stratford Place W1U
612 D10 Strathearn Place W2
617 L3 Stratton Street W1J
613 R8 Streatham Street WC1A
615 Q2 Strout's Place E2
617 P7 Strutton Ground SW1P
615 Q7 Strype Street E1
613 G6 Studio Place SW1X
614 B8 Stukeley Street WC2B
613 J6 Sturge Street SE1
615 K1 Sturt Street N1
614 H1 Sudeley Street N1
619 J6 Sudrey Street SE1
615 L10 Suffolk Lane EC4R
617 Q3 Suffolk Street SW1Y
618 F9 Sullivan Road SE11
614 E5 Summers Street EC1R
615 C10 Sumner Place SW7
616 C10 Sumner Place Mews SW7
619 J3 Sumner Street SE1
615 M6 Sun Street EC2A
618 G5 Surrey Row SE1
615 N11 Surrey Square SE17
614 D10 Surrey Street WC2R
617 P10 Surrey Terrace SE17
612 C9 Sussex Gardens W2
612 C10 Sussex Mews East W2
612 C10 Sussex Mews West W2
612 F4 Sussex Place NW1
612 C10 Sussex Square W2
617 L11 Sutherland Row SW1V
617 L11 Sutherland Street SW1V
616 D11 Sutton Dwelling Estate SW3
614 H5 Sutton Lane EC1V
613 P8 Sutton Row W1D
612 C5 Swain Street NW8
612 D4 Swain Street NW8
613 L9 Swallow Place W1S
617 N2 Swallow Street W1S
615 Q3 Swanfield Street E2
619 L2 Swan Lane EC4R
619 N8 Swan Mead SE1
619 R2 Swan Passage E1
617 K6 Swan Street SE1
619 K6 Sweeney Crescent SE1
614 C2 Swinton Place WC1X
614 C2 Swinton Street WC1X
615 J5 Sycamore Street EC1V
616 C10 Sydney Close SW7
616 C10 Sydney Mews SW7
616 C10 Sydney Place SW7
613 D11 Sydney Street SW3
615 N3 Symister Mews * N1
616 G10 Symons Street SW3

T

619 M6 Tabard Garden Estate SE1
619 L6 Tabard Street SE1
615 M5 Tabernacle Street EC2A
617 N10 Tachbrook Street SW1V
615 M10 Talbot Court EC3V
612 B9 Talbot Square W2
619 L4 Talbot Yard SE1
614 F10 Tallis Street EC4Y
614 B3 Tankerton Street WC1H
619 P6 Tanner Street SE1
618 E6 Tanswell Street SE1
615 K1 Taplow Street N1
619 J8 Tarn Street SE1
617 F2 Tarrant Place W1H
619 M10 Tatum Street SE17
612 F5 Taunton Mews NW1
612 F4 Taunton Place NW1
614 B10 Tavistock Court * WC2E
613 Q4 Tavistock Place WC1H
613 Q4 Tavistock Square WC1H
614 B10 Tavistock Street WC2E
613 P4 Taviton Street WC1H
618 F11 Tavy Close SE11
615 L8 Telegraph Street EC2R
614 E10 Temple Avenue EC4Y
614 E10 Temple Gardens * EC4Y
614 F9 Temple Lane EC4Y
614 D10 Temple Place WC2R
619 L5 Tennis Street SE1
613 L9 Tenterden Street W1S
615 Q7 Tenter Ground E1
617 L8 Terminus Street SW1V
619 P3 Thames Path EC3N
618 B8 Thames Path SW1P
613 R3 Thanet Street WC1H
613 J8 Thayer Street W1U
615 N7 The Arcade * EC2M
618 B3 The Arches * WC2N
614 H5 The Charterhouse * EC1M
618 F5 The Cut SE1
618 E4 Theed Street SE1
619 Q7 The Grange SE1
617 M3 The Mall SW1A
614 C6 Theobald's Road WC1X
614 L8 Theobald Street SE1
615 K7 The Postern * EC2Y
612 D8 The Quadrangle W2
619 P3 The Queens Walk EC3N
617 Q7 The Sanctuary SW1P
614 H1 Theseus Walk N1
612 D8 The Water Gardens W2
617 N8 Thirleby Road SW1P
618 G7 Thomas Doyle Street SE1
615 K2 Thoresby Street N1
617 P10 Thorndike Street SW1V
618 A9 Thorney Street SW1P
613 Q5 Thornhaugh Street WC1H
612 F6 Thornton Place W1H
619 K4 Thrale Street SE1
615 R7 Thrawl Street E1
615 M9 Threadneedle Street EC2R
615 K10 Three Kings Yard W1K
619 Q5 Three Oak Lane SE1
615 M8 Throgmorton Avenue EC2N
615 M8 Throgmorton Street EC2R
618 J11 Thrush Street SE17
615 D9 Thurloe Close SW7
616 C9 Thurloe Place SW7
616 C9 Thurloe Place Mews SW7
616 C9 Thurloe Square SW7

616 C9 Thurloe Street SW7
619 N11 Thurlow Walk SE17
617 J3 Tilney Street W1K
615 J4 Timber Street EC1V
618 B11 Tinworth Street SE11
615 M10 Tisdall Place SE17
612 E9 Titchborne Row W2
619 J7 Tiverton Street SE1
615 L8 Tokenhouse Yard EC2R
613 N4 Tolmer's Square NW1
614 G3 Tompion Street EC1V
614 E8 Took's Court EC4A
619 M3 Tooley Street SE1
614 E4 Topham Street EC1R
614 G1 Torrens Street EC1V
613 N6 Torrington Place W1T
613 Q5 Torrington Square WC1E
617 P6 Tothill Street SW1H
613 N5 Tottenham Court Road W1T
613 N6 Tottenham Mews W1T
613 N5 Tottenham Street W1W
619 J6 Toulmin Street SE1
619 Q3 Tower Bridge EC3N
619 Q3 Tower Bridge Approach EC3N
619 N8 Tower Bridge Road SE1
613 R9 Tower Court WC2H
619 R2 Tower Hill EC3N
619 P2 Tower Hill Terrace EC3R
619 P2 Tower Place EC3R
615 K10 Tower Royal EC4N
613 Q9 Tower Street WC2H
619 L11 Townley Street SE17
619 M10 Townsend Street SE17
615 Q7 Toynbee Street E1
617 Q3 Trafalgar Square WC2N
619 L11 Trafalgar Street SE17
612 E7 Transept Street NW1
617 K3 Trebeck Street W1J
612 D4 Tresham Crescent NW8
618 H4 Treveris Street SE1
616 E6 Trevor Place SW7
616 E6 Trevor Square SW7
616 E6 Trevor Street SW7
615 J10 Trig Lane EC4V
619 K7 Trinity Church Square SE1
619 P2 Trinity Square EC3N
619 K6 Trinity Street SE1
619 K6 Trio Place SE1
613 M4 Triton Square NW1
615 K9 Trump Street EC2V
619 J5 Trundle Street SE1
616 F11 Tryon Street SW3
614 F10 Tudor Street EC4Y
617 R8 Tufton Street SW1P
616 G11 Turks Row SW3
614 G8 Turnagain Lane EC4M
614 F5 Turnmill Street EC1M
617 L11 Turpentine Lane SW1V
619 K10 Turquand Street SE17
615 Q4 Turville Street E2
612 G10 Tyburn Way W1H
619 N6 Tyers Gate SE1
618 C11 Tyers Street SE11
619 R8 Tyne Street E1
614 E3 Tysoe Street EC1R

U

617 N10 Udall Street SW1P
618 F5 Ufford Street SE1
613 K5 Ulster Place W1K
615 N9 Undershaft EC3A
615 K2 Underwood Row N1
615 K2 Underwood Street N1
614 H4 Union Street N1
615 Q2 Union Walk E2
613 N5 University Street W1T
616 C7 Unwin Road SW7
612 A9 Upbrook Mews W2
619 P11 Upnor Way SE17
617 J7 Upper Belgrave Street SW1X
612 F9 Upper Berkeley Street W2
612 H10 Upper Brook Street W1K
616 H2 Upper Grosvenor Street W1K
618 E3 Upper Ground SE1
613 J5 Upper Harley Street NW1
613 N10 Upper John Street W1B
618 D7 Upper Marsh SE1
612 F6 Upper Montagu Street W1H
617 R9 Upper St Martin's Lane WC2H
617 M9 Upper Tachbrook Street SW1V
615 J10 Upper Thames Street EC4V
613 J6 Upper Wimpole Street W1G
613 Q3 Upper Woburn Place NW1

V

618 G5 Valentine Place SE1
617 N7 Vandon Street SW1H
615 N5 Vandy Street EC2A
613 M2 Varndell Street NW1
619 R8 Vauban Estate SE16
619 R8 Vauban Street SE16
615 Q2 Vaughan Estate * E2
617 M8 Vauxhall Bridge Road SW1V
618 D11 Vauxhall Street SE11
618 C11 Vauxhall Walk SE11
612 C5 Venables Street NW8
613 K9 Vere Street W1U
614 D2 Vernon Place WC1N
614 D2 Vernon Rise WC1X
614 D2 Vernon Square WC1X
614 E6 Verulam Street WC1X
615 L2 Vestry Street N1
617 L8 Victoria Arcade SW1V
618 B6 Victoria Embankment SW1A
618 B2 Victoria Embankment Gardens * WC2N
612 C10 Victoria Gate W2
617 L7 Victoria Square SW1W
617 L8 Victoria Street SW1V
617 K9 Victory Place SE17
617 M2 Vigo Street W1J
618 B3 Villiers Street WC2N
617 N9 Vincent Square SW1P
617 P9 Vincent Street SW1P
619 N5 Vinegar Yard SE1
614 E5 Vine Hill EC1R
619 P4 Vine Lane SE1
617 L8 Vine Street EC3N
617 N2 Vine Street W1J
614 F5 Vine Street Bridge EC1M
615 Q10 Vine Street Crescent EC3N
619 K5 Vine Yard SE1
614 E4 Vineyard Mews EC1R
614 E4 Vineyard Walk EC1R
618 D7 Virgil Street SE1
615 R2 Virginia Road E2
615 J5 Viscount Street EC1Y

W

619 L10 Wadding Street SE17
614 B3 Wakefield Mews WC1H
614 B4 Wakefield Street WC1H
614 G2 Wakley Street EC1V
615 L10 Walbrook EC4N
619 K10 Walcorde Avenue SE17
618 C9 Walcot Square SE11
617 N9 Walcott Street SW1P
613 P10 Walker's Court W1F

615 K7 Wallside * EC2Y
618 E9 Walnut Tree Walk SE11
616 F11 Walpole Street SW3
616 F7 Walton Place SW3
616 E9 Walton Street SW3
619 J9 Walworth Road SE17
615 K10 Wansey Street SE17
615 J4 Wardens Grove SE1
613 N9 Wardour Mews W1F
613 N8 Wardour Street W1F
614 H9 Wardrobe Place EC4V
614 E5 Warner Street EC1R
614 E5 Warner Yard EC1R
613 M5 Warren Mews W1W
613 M5 Warren Street W1T
614 D7 Warwick Court WC1V
617 P3 Warwick House Street SW1Y
614 H8 Warwick Lane EC4M
617 M10 Warwick Place North SW1V
617 M7 Warwick Row SW1E
614 H8 Warwick Square EC4M
617 M11 Warwick Square SW1V
617 M10 Warwick Square Mews SW1V
613 N10 Warwick Street W1B
617 L11 Warwick Way SW1V
615 K5 Warwick Yard EC1Y
615 G10 Watergate EC4Y
618 D2 Waterloo Bridge SE1
617 P3 Waterloo Place SW1Y
618 D3 Waterloo Road SE1
615 P2 Waterson Street E2
614 G10 Water Street WC2R
615 K9 Watling Court EC4M
615 J9 Watling Street EC4M
612 E7 Watson's Mews W1H
617 J3 Waverton Street W1K
619 P4 Weaver's Lane SE1
617 F6 Webber Row SE1
618 F5 Webber Street SE1
619 N8 Webb Street SE1
613 J10 Weighhouse Street W1K
613 Q2 Weirs Passage NW1
613 J7 Welbeck Street W1G
613 K8 Welbeck Way W1U
615 K9 Well Court EC4N
619 J5 Weller Street SE1
615 P3 Wellesley Place NW1
615 K2 Wellesley Terrace N1
612 C2 Wellington Place NW8
613 C1 Wellington Road NW8
615 R2 Wellington Row E2
616 F11 Wellington Square SW3
618 B10 Wellington Street WC2E
613 N7 Wells Mews W1T
613 C3 Wells Square WC1X
613 M7 Wells Street W1W
616 B7 Wells Way SW7
615 J1 Wenlock Road N1
615 K1 Wenlock Street N1
615 R7 Wentworth Street E1
613 N1 Werrington Street NW1
618 H10 Wesley Close SE17
613 J7 Wesley Street W1G
612 B10 Westbourne Crescent W2
612 B10 Westbourne Crescent Mews W2
612 C10 Westbourne Gate * W2
612 B10 Westbourne Street W2
612 A8 Westbourne Terrace W2
616 C5 West Carriage Drive W2
614 A8 West Central Street WC1A
616 H9 West Eaton Place SW1X
616 H9 West Eaton Place Mews SW1X
617 F8 West Halkin Street SW1X
614 F8 West Harding Street EC4A
614 L2 Westland Place EC1V
617 L10 West Mews SW1V
618 B6 Westminster Bridge SW1P
618 B6 Westminster Bridge Road SE1
613 J7 Westmoreland Street W1G
617 L11 Westmoreland Terrace SW1V
614 D2 Weston Rise WC1X
619 M5 Weston Street SE1
614 G7 West Poultry Avenue EC1M
612 E10 West Rise * W2
614 G7 West Smithfield EC1A
618 G8 West Square SE11
613 Q9 West Street WC2H
615 R9 West Tenter Street E1
617 M10 West Warwick Place SW1V
613 K6 Weymouth Mews W1G
613 J6 Weymouth Street W1G
615 J1 Wharf Road N1
614 D3 Wharton Street WC1X
613 J7 Wheatley Street W1G
615 Q6 Wheeler Lane E1
615 Q6 Wheler Street E1
615 C8 Whetstone Park WC2A
618 E4 Whichcote Street SE1
614 B3 Whidborne Street WC1H
614 G3 Whiskin Street EC1R
615 Q4 Whitby Street E1
613 P10 Whitcomb Street W1D
614 E5 White Bear Yard EC1R
615 R8 Whitechapel High Street E1
615 K4 Whitecross Street EC1Y
614 F9 Whitefriars Street EC4Y
618 A4 Whitehall SW1A
618 A4 Whitehall Court SW1A
618 A4 Whitehall Gardens SW1A
618 A4 Whitehall Place SW1A
618 F11 White Hart Street SE11
619 L4 White Hart Yard SE1
612 D5 Whitehaven Street NW8
616 E11 Whitehead's Grove SW3
614 J4 White Horse Street W1J
615 P8 White Kennett Street E1
615 N9 White Lion Court EC3V
614 H10 White Lion Hill EC4V
614 E1 White Lion Street N1
615 J6 White Lyon Court EC2Y
619 P5 White's Grounds SE1
619 P5 White's Grounds Estate SE1
615 Q7 White's Row E1
613 M5 Whitfield Place W1T
613 N6 Whitfield Street W1T
618 C9 Whitgift Street SE11
616 H10 Whittaker Street SW1W
615 N9 Whittington Avenue EC3V
618 F4 Whittlesey Street SE1
618 C11 Wickham Street SE11
614 C2 Wicklow Street WC1X
615 P7 Widegate Street E1
613 K8 Wigmore Place W1G
613 J8 Wigmore Street W1U
616 H9 Wilbraham Place SW1X
614 E3 Wild Court WC2B
615 N7 Wild's Rents SE1
614 B9 Wild Street WC2B
617 M7 Wilfred Street SW1E
615 R6 Wilkes Street E1
615 P1 Wilks Place N1
617 R2 William IV Street WC2N
612 G6 William Mews SW1X
613 M3 William Road NW1
612 G6 William Street SW1X
617 N9 Willow Place SW1P
615 N4 Willow Street EC2A
619 P9 Willow Walk SE1

616 K6 Wimpole Mews W1G
613 K7 Wimpole Street W1G
618 H10 Winchester Close SE1
619 L3 Winchester Square SE1
619 L11 Winchester Street SW1V
619 L3 Winchester Walk SE1
618 F9 Windmill Row SE11
618 F4 Windmill Walk SE1
615 K2 Windsor Terrace N1
614 F8 Wine Office Court EC4A
613 P10 Winnett Street W1D
612 B8 Winsland Mews W2
612 B8 Winsland Street W2
613 M8 Winsley Street W1W
613 R4 Winthrop Street E1
613 Q5 Woburn Square WC1H
613 Q3 Woburn Walk WC1H
618 H9 Wollaston Close SE17
615 R6 Wolseley Street SE1
614 G4 Woodbridge Street EC1R
615 R6 Woodseer Street E1
612 G10 Wood's Mews W1K
619 P8 Woods Place SE1
613 J7 Woodstock Mews W1G
615 K9 Woodstock Street W1K
615 K7 Wood Street EC2Y
613 R4 Woolf Mews WC1H
618 R4 Wootton Street SE1
619 Q10 Wordsworth Road SE1
618 C11 Worgan Street SE11
615 N8 Wormwood Street EC2M
615 N5 Worship Street EC2A
615 R6 Wren Street WC1X
614 D4 Wren Street WC1X
613 L3 Wybert Street NW1
614 G3 Wyclif Street EC1V
612 F7 Wyndham Mews W1H
612 F7 Wyndham Place W1H
612 F6 Wyndham Street W1H
618 D11 Wynyard Terrace SE11
614 G2 Wynyatt Street EC1V
612 F9 Wythburn Place W1H

Y

614 E3 Yardley Street WC1X
617 K4 Yarmouth Place W1J
616 E8 Yeoman's Row SW3
612 H4 York Bridge NW1
618 B2 York Buildings WC2N
613 J5 York Gate NW1
618 C5 York Road NW1
614 C7 Yorkshire Grey Yard WC1V
612 C6 York Street W1W
612 G6 York Street Chambers * W1U
613 J5 York Terrace East NW1
612 H5 York Terrace West NW1

Z

619 J3 Zoar Street SE1

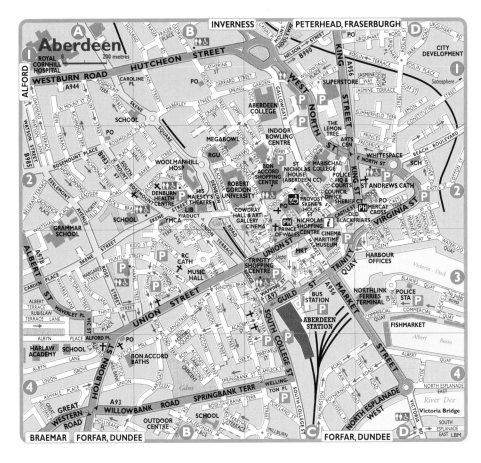

Aberdeen

Aberdeen is found on atlas page **557 G3**

C4	Affleck Street		A2	Kintore Place
A3	Albert Street		B3	Langstane Place
B4	Albury Road		C2	Little John Street
A4	Albyn Lane		C1	Loch Street
A4	Alford Place		B1	Maberley Street
C2	Back Wynd		D2	Marischal Street
D2	Beach Boulevard		C3	Market Street
C3	Belmont Street		C1	Mount Hooly Way
C2	Berry Street		A1	Mount Street
B2	Blackfriar Street		D4	North Esplanade West
D3	Blaikies Quay		D2	Park Street
B3	Bon Accord Street		C4	Portland Street
B3	Bon Accord Terrace		C2	Queen Street
C3	Bridge Street		D3	Regent Quay
C2	Broad Street		A2	Richmond Street
B4	Caledonian Place		A1	Richmond Terrace
D2	Castlegate		A3	Rose Street
B3	Chapel Street		A2	Rosemount Place
B1	Charlotte Street		B2	Rosemount Viaduct
D2	Commerce Street		C4	Russell Road
D3	Commercial Quay		B2	St Andrews Street
B3	Crimon Place		C1	St Clair Street
B2	Crooked Lane		C2	School Hill
B3	Crown Street		B3	Silver Street South
C3	Crown Terrace		B1	Skene Square
B3	Dee Street		A3	Skene Street
B2	Denburn Road		C3	South College Street
B3	Diamond Street		A2	South Mount Street
D2	East North Street		B2	Spa Street
A2	Esslemont Avenue		B1	Spring Garden
C3	Exchange Street		B4	Springbank Terrace
A1	Forbes Street		C3	Stirling Street
D2	Frederick Street		B3	Summer Street
C1	Gallowgate		C3	Trinity Quay
B1	George Street		A4	Union Glen
B2	Gilcomston Park		A4	Union Grove
C3	Guild Street		B3	Union Row
D2	Hanover Street		B3	Union Street
B4	Hardgate		B2	Union Terrace
A4	Holborn Street		D1	Urquhart Road
A3	Huntly Street		D4	Victoria Road
B1	Hutcheon Street		D2	Virginia Street
A2	Jack's Brae		C3	Wapping Street
D2	James Street		A3	Waverley Place
B2	John Street		C4	Wellington Place
B1	Jopps Lane		C1	West North Street
A4	Justice Mill Lane		A1	Westburn Road
C1	King Street		A4	Willowbank Road

Bath

Bath is found on atlas page **86 C2**

C3	Abbey Square		A3	Lower Bristol Road
B1	Alfred Street		A4	Lower Oldfield Park
B4	Ambury		C3	Manvers Street
C2	Argyle Street		A3	Midland Bridge Road
B3	Avon Street		B3	Mill Street
B2	Barton Street		B2	Milsom Street
B3	Bath Street		A2	Monmouth Place
C3	Beau Street		B2	Monmouth Street
B1	Bennett Street		B2	New Bond Street
C1	Bladud Buildings		A2	New King Street
B2	Bridewell Lane		C3	New Orchard Street
C2	Bridge Street		D3	North Parade Road
B4	Broad Quay		B4	Oak Street
C2	Broad Street		C3	Old Orchard Street
D3	Broadway		C3	Pierrepont Street
A1	Brock Street		B2	Princes Street
B2	Chapel Row		D2	Pulteney Road
B3	Charles Street		B2	Queen Square
A2	Charlotte Street		B2	Queen Square Place
C3	Cheap Street		B2	Queen Street
B1	Circus Mews		B2	Queens Parade Place
C4	Claverton Street		B2	Quiet Street
B3	Corn Street		C4	Railway Street
C4	Dorchester Street		A1	Royal Avenue
D2	Edward Street		A1	Royal Crescent
D3	Ferry Lane		B1	Russell Street
B1	Gay Street		C1	St John's Place
B1	George Street		B2	Saw Close
C2	Grand Parade		C3	South Parade
C2	Grange Grove		C4	Southgate Street
D2	Great Pulteney Street		C3	Stall Street
A2	Great Stanhope Street		D4	Sussex Place
A3	Green Park		D1	Sydney Place
B3	Green Park Road		B1	The Circus
B2	Green Street		C1	The Vineyards
C2	Grove Street		B2	Trim Street
D1	Henrietta Gardens		C2	Union Passage
D1	Henrietta Mews		C2	Union Street
C1	Henrietta Road		B2	Upper Borough Walls
C1	Henrietta Street		A2	Upper Bristol Road
C3	Henry Street		A1	Upper Church Street
A2	James Street West		C1	Walcot Street
B2	John Street		B4	Wells Road
B3	Kingsmead North		B3	Westgate Buildings
B3	Kingsmead Street		B3	Westgate Street
B1	Lansdown Road		A4	Westmoreland Road
A2	Little Stanhope Street		B2	Wood Street
B3	Lower Borough Walls		C3	York Street

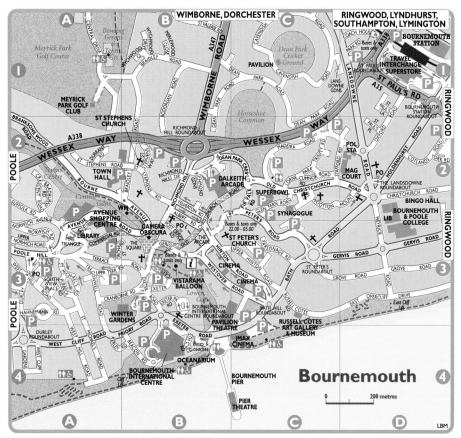

Bournemouth

Bournemouth is found on atlas page **34 C2**

B2	Albert Road	C3	Parsonage Road
A3	Avenue Lane	A3	Poole Hill
A3	Avenue Road	B3	Post Office Road
C3	Bath Road	B4	Priory Road
B4	Beacon Road	A3	Purbeck Road
B1	Bodorgan Road	B2	Richmond Gardens
A2	Bourne Avenue	B2	Richmond Hill
A2	Bradburne Road	B2	Richmond Hill Drive
B2	Braidley Road	C3	Russell Cotes Road
A2	Branksome Wood Road	A3	St Michael's Road
C1	Cavendish Road	D1	St Paul's Lane
A1	Central Drive	D2	St Paul's Place
D2	Christchurch Road	D1	St Paul's Road
D1	Coach House Place	C2	St Peter's Road
A3	Commercial Road	A2	St Stephens Road
C2	Cumnor Road	B2	St Stephens Way
D2	Cotlands Road	B1	St Valerie Road
A3	Cranborne Road	B4	South Cliff Road
A2	Crescent Road	A3	South View Place
B2	Dean Park Crescent	C2	Stafford Road
C1	Dean Park Road	A2	Suffolk Road
A3	Durley Road	A3	Terrace Road
A2	Durrant Road	B3	The Arcade
D3	East Overcliff Drive	B3	The Square
B3	Exeter Crescent	A3	The Triangle
B3	Exeter Park Road	A3	Tregonwell Road
B3	Exeter Road	C2	Trinity Road
C2	Fir Vale Road	C3	Upper Hinton Road
B3	Gervis Place	A3	Upper Norwich Road
D3	Gervis Road	A3	Upper Terrace Road
C2	Glen Fern Road	A2	Wessex Way
D3	Grove Road	A4	West Cliff Gardens
A3	Hahnemann Road	A4	West Cliff Road
B3	Hinton Road	A3	West Hill Road
D2	Holdenhurst Road	B3	Westover Road
A4	Kerley Road	B1	Wimborne Road
C1	Lansdowne Gardens	C2	Wootton Mount
D1	Lansdowne Road	B1	Wychwood Close
C2	Lorne Park Road	B1	Wychwood Drive
C2	Madeira Road	B2	Yelverton Road
B1	Merlewood Close	D2	York Road
D3	Meyrick Road		
A3	Norwich Avenue		
A3	Norwich Road		
B3	Old Christchurch Road		
A3	Orchard Street		
D2	Oxford Road		
D1	Park Road		

Bradford

Bradford is found on atlas page **342 C3**

B2	Bank Street	A1	Lumb Lane
D2	Barkerend Road	B4	Manchester Road
B2	Barry Street	B1	Manningham Lane
C2	Bolton Road	A4	Mannville Terrace
B3	Bridge Street	B1	Manor Row
C3	Broadway	C3	Market Street
D2	Burnett Street	A4	Morley Street
C2	Canal Road	B4	Neal Street
D1	Captain Street	C4	Nelson Street
A3	Carlton Street	B3	Norfolk Gardens
B3	Channing Way	C1	North Brook Street
D3	Chapel Street	B1	North Parade
C2	Charles Street	B1	Northgate
C2	Cheapside	D1	Otley Road
A4	Chester Street	D2	Peckover Street
C2	Church Bank	C2	Petergate
A4	Claremont	B2	Piccadilly
C4	Croft Street	B3	Princes Way
C2	Currer Street	A2	Providence Street
B2	Dale Street	B3	Quebec Street
A1	Darfield Street	B2	Rawson Place
B2	Darley Street	A2	Rawson Road
C3	Diamond Street	B2	Rawson Square
C3	Drake Street	C1	St Blaise Way
A1	Drewton Road	A2	St Thomas Road
D4	Dryden Street	B1	Salem Street
B2	Duke Street	B4	Senior Way
D3	East Parade	B4	Sharpe Street
D3	Ebenezer Street	D3	Shipley Airedale Road
A4	Edmund Street	A2	Simes Street
C4	Edward Street	C2	Stott Hill
C2	Forster Square	A2	Sunbridge Road
B2	Godwin Street	A3	Tetley Street
A2	Grattan Road	A3	Thornton Road
A3	Great Horton Road	A3	Tumbling Hill Street
C4	Guy Street	B3	Tyrrel Street
C3	Hall Ings	D2	Upper Parkgate
B1	Hamm Strasse	B2	Upper Piccadilly
C1	Holdsworth Street	C1	Valley Road
A1	Houghton Place	C3	Vicar Lane
A4	Howard Street	D4	Wakefield Road
B3	Ivegate	C2	Well Street
B2	James Street	D2	Wellington Street
B2	John Street	A2	Westgate
B2	Kirkgate	C1	Wharf Street
D3	Leeds Road	A1	White Abbey Road
B4	Little Horton Lane	A2	Wigan Street
C2	Lower Kirkgate	A4	Wilton Street

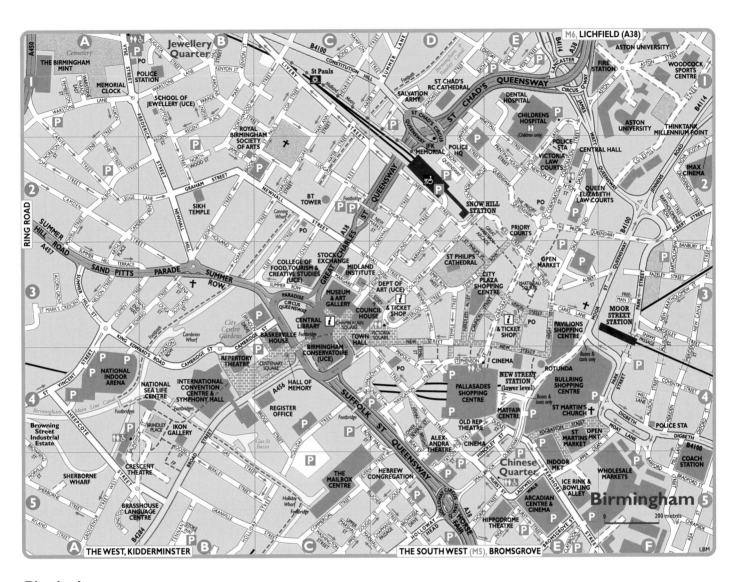

Birmingham

Birmingham is found on atlas page **213 G2**

A3	Acorn Grove	E3	Carrs Lane	B4	Gas Street
E3	Albert Street	A2	Carver Street	B2	George Street
A2	Albion Street	C4	Centenary Square	D5	Gough Street
F4	Allison Street	C3	Chamberlain Square	B2	Graham Street
A3	Arthur Place	D5	Chapmans Passage	B5	Granville Street
F1	Aston Street	B3	Charlotte Street	C3	Great Charles Street
B1	Augusta Street	F5	Cheapside		Queensway
F3	Banbury Street	D2	Church Street	E2	Great Western Arcade
F5	Barford Street	E5	Claybrook Street	F2	Grosvenor Street
F2	Bartholomew Row	A3	Clement Street	A5	Grosvenor Street West
F3	Bartholomew Street	F2	Coleshill Street	B1	Hall Street
D3	Barwick Street	E2	Colmore Circus	C1	Hampton Street
D1	Bath Street		Queensway	B3	Helena Street
D4	Beak Street	D3	Colmore Row	C1	Henrietta Street
D3	Bennetts Hill	C5	Commercial Street	E3	High Street
B5	Berkley Street	C1	Constitution Hill	D4	Hill Street
D5	Blucher Street	D2	Cornwall Street	D5	Hinckley Street
C1	Bond Street	E3	Corporation Street	B2	Holland Street
F3	Bordesley Street	F4	Coventry Street	B5	Holliday Street
F5	Bradford Street	C1	Cox Street	D5	Holloway Circus
C4	Bridge Street	E3	Dale End		Queensway
B3	Brindley Drive	E2	Dalton Street	D5	Holloway Head
B4	Brindley Place	F4	Digbeth	D5	Horse Fair
B5	Broad Street	E4	Dudley Street	E5	Hurst Street
E5	Bromsgrove Street	D3	Eden Place	E5	Inge Street
B2	Brook Street	E4	Edgbaston Street	B2	James Street
A4	Browning Street	D3	Edmund Street	E1	James Watt Queensway
D5	Brownsea Drive	A3	Edward Street	F2	Jennens Road
C4	Brunel Street	D5	Ellis Street	D4	John Bright Street
A4	Brunswick Street	A5	Essington Street	B1	Kenyon Street
E2	Bull Street	D4	Ethel Street	A3	King Edward's Road
B4	Cambridge Street	F3	Fazeley Street	B4	Kingston Row
A2	Camden Drive	C3	Fleet Street	E5	Ladywell Walk
A2	Camden Street	F2	Fox Street	E1	Lancaster Circus
D3	Cannon Street	B1	Frederick Street		Queensway
B1	Caroline Street	F3	Freeman Street	A2	Legge Lane

C3	Lionel Street	A1	Pemberton Street	A3	Summer Hill Terrace
C1	Livery Street	E5	Pershore Street	D1	Summer Lane
B3	Louisa Street	D4	Pinfold Street	B3	Summer Row
E1	Loveday Street	A2	Pope Street	C4	Swallow Street
D4	Lower Severn Street	A2	Powell Street	D3	Temple Row
C2	Ludgate Hill	E1	Price Street	D3	Temple Row West
C3	Margaret Street	E2	Printing House Street	D3	Temple Street
C5	Marshall Street	F5	Rea Street	A2	Tenby Street
E3	Martineau Square	B1	Regent Parade	A2	Tenby Street North
C1	Mary Ann Street	B1	Regent Place	B5	Tennant Street
B1	Mary Street	B2	Regent Street	E2	The Priory Queensway
F4	Meriden Street	C4	Royal Mail Street	D5	Thorpe Street
F5	Mill Lane	A5	Ryland Street	A3	Townsend Way
F4	Moat Lane	D1	St Chad's Circus	E3	Union Street
E3	Moor Street Queensway		Queensway	E5	Upper Dean Street
A2	Moreton Street	D1	St Chad's Queensway	C5	Upper Gough Street
A5	Morville Street	A3	St Mark's Crescent	C5	Upper Marshall Street
D4	Navigation Street	C2	St Paul's Square	E1	Vesey Street
D3	Needless Alley	D3	St Philips Place	D3	Victoria Square
A3	Nelson Street	A4	St Vincent Street	B1	Vittoria Street
F3	New Bartholomew Street	A3	Sand Pitts	A1	Vyse Street
F3	New Canal Street	B3	Scotland Street	A1	Warstone Lane
D2	New Market Street	C5	Severn Street	A1	Warstone Parade East
D3	New Street	D1	Shadwell Street	C5	Washington Street
B2	Newhall Hill	F3	Shaws Passage	C2	Water Street
C2	Newhall Street	A4	Sheepcote Street	D3	Waterloo Street
E2	Newton Street	A5	Sherborne Street	D1	Weaman Street
B2	Northwood Street	D5	Smallbrook Queensway	F4	Well Lane
F2	Nova Scotia Street	D2	Snow Hill Queensway	E2	Whittall Street
E2	Old Square	D5	Station Street		
B4	Oozel's Street	E2	Steelhouse Lane		
F4	Oxford Street	D4	Stephenson Street		
B3	Parade	B5	Stoke Way		
C3	Paradise Circus	C4	Suffolk Street Queensway		
	Queensway	A2	Summer Hill Road		
F4	Park Street	A3	Summer Hill Street		

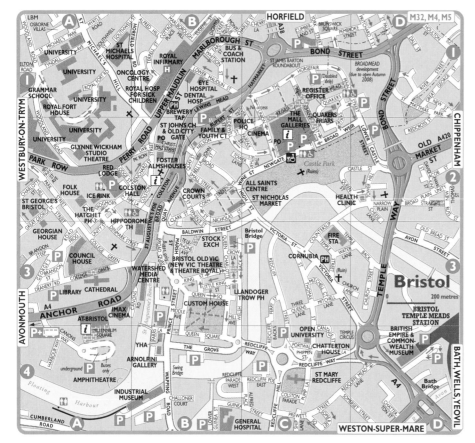

Bristol

Bristol is found on atlas page **109 G5**

A3	Anchor Road	A2	Park Row
B3	Baldwin Street	C1	Penn Street
C1	Barton Street	A2	Perry Road
C1	Bond Street	A2	Pipe Lane
A3	Brandon Street	C4	Portwall Lane
B2	Bridewell Street	B4	Prince Street
C1	Broad Mead	D1	Pritchard Street
B2	Broad Quay	C4	Pump Lane
B2	Broad Street	C1	Quakers Friars
C2	Broad Weir	B2	Quay Street
B3	Canons Road	B3	Queen Charlotte Street
A4	Canons Way	B4	Queen Square
D2	Castle Street	C3	Redcliff Street
C1	Charles Street	C4	Redcliffe Hill
B2	Christmas Steps	C4	Redcliffe Mead Lane
A3	College Green	C4	Redcliffe Parade East
B2	Colston Avenue	C4	Redcliffe Way
B2	Colston Street	D1	River Street
B2	Corn Street	A1	Royal Fort Road
C3	Counterslip	B2	Rupert Street
D1	Dale Street	B3	St Augustine's Parade
A3	Deanery Road	A3	St George's Road
A3	Denmark Street	D1	St Matthias Park
B1	Earl Street	A1	St Michael's Hill
C2	Fairfax Street	B2	St Nicholas Street
B4	Farrs Lane	D1	St Paul's Street
A2	Frogmore Street	B2	St Stephen's Street
A3	Great George Street	C3	St Thomas Street
B4	Guinea Street	C1	Silver Street
C1	Haymarket	B2	Small Street
C2	High Street	A1	Southwell Street
A2	Hill Street	C3	Temple Back
B1	Horfield Road	C3	Temple Street
B3	King Street	D3	Temple Way
B1	Lewins Mead	B1	Terrell Street
A2	Lodge Street	B4	The Grove
D2	Lower Castle Street	C1	The Horsefair
B1	Lower Maudlin Street	D2	Tower Hill
B2	Lower Park Row	B2	Trenchard Street
B1	Marlborough Street	A1	Tyndall Avenue
B3	Marsh Street	C1	Union Street
C1	Merchant Street	B1	Upper Maudlin Street
B1	Montague Street	C3	Victoria Street
D2	Narrow Plain	B4	Wapping Road
B2	Nelson Street	C3	Welsh Back
D1	Newfoundland Street	C2	Wine Street
C2	Newgate	A1	Woodland Road
D2	Old Market Street	C1	York Street

Cardiff

Cardiff is found on atlas page **106 C4**

D3	Adam Street	B4	Mill Lane
B3	Bakers Row	D2	Moira Place
C3	Barrack Lane	D2	Moira Terrace
B2	Boulevard de Nantes	B3	Morgan Arcade
C3	Bridge Street	B1	Museum Avenue
C4	Bute Street	B1	Museum Place
C3	Bute Terrace	D1	Newport Road
B4	Callaghan Square	C2	North Edward Street
B3	Caroline Street	A1	North Road
A3	Castle Street	D1	Oxford Lane
D4	Central Link	B1	Park Grove
B4	Central Square	B1	Park Lane
B2	Charles Street	B1	Park Place
B3	Church Street	B4	Penarth Road
C2	Churchill Way	A3	Quay Street
A1	City Hall Road	B2	Queen Street
D1	City Road	C1	Richmond Crescent
A1	College Road	C1	Richmond Road
B2	Crockherbtown Lane	B3	Royal Arcade
B4	Custom House Street	B1	St Andrew's Crescent
B2	Duke Street	C1	St Andrew's Lane
C2	Dumfries Place	B1	St Andrew's Place
C1	East Grove	B2	St John Street
D3	Ellen Street	B3	St Mary Street
D2	Fitzalan Place	C1	St Peter's Street
D2	Fitzalan Road	C1	Salisbury Road
A3	Fitzhamon Embankment	C3	Sandon Street
B3	Frederick Street	D4	Schooner Way
D1	Glossop Road	B1	Senghennydd Road
B3	Golate	C2	Station Terrace
B4	Great Western Lane	B2	Stuttgarter Strasse
B2	Greyfriars Place	C3	Taff Street
B2	Greyfriars Road	B2	The Friary
C3	Guildford Crescent	B3	The Hayes
C2	Guildford Street	C1	The Parade
B3	Hayes Bridge Road	B4	Tresillian Way
C4	Herbert Street	B3	Trinity Street
B3	High Street	D3	Tyndall Street
B3	Hill's Street	C1	West Grove
D2	Howard Gardens	A3	Westgate Street
D2	Howard Place	B3	Wharton Street
A1	King Edward VII Avenue	C2	Windsor Lane
B2	Kingsway	C2	Windsor Place
C2	Knox Road	D2	Windsor Road
C4	Lloyd George Avenue	A3	Womanby Street
D1	Longcross Street	B4	Wood Street
C3	Mary Ann Street	D1	Wordsworth Avenue
D2	Meteor Road	B3	Working Street

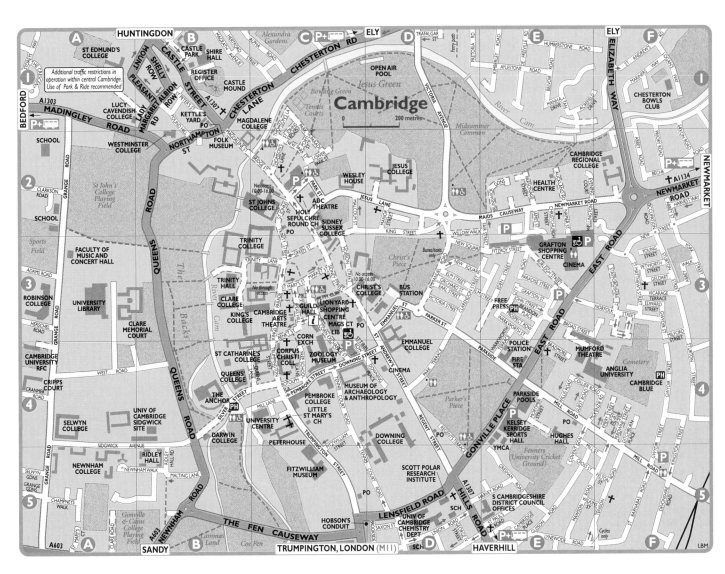

Cambridge

Cambridge is found on atlas page **197 F3**

F2	Abbey Road	F5	Devonshire Road	C3	Hobson Street	F3	New Street
F2	Abbey Street	F4	Ditchburn Place	E1	Humberstone Road	E2	Newmarket Road
F3	Abbey Walk	D4	Downing Place	E2	James Street	B5	Newnham Road
E1	Acrefield Drive	C4	Downing Street	C2	Jesus Lane	A5	Newnham Walk
A3	Adams Road	D3	Earl Street	E3	John Street	F3	Norfolk Street
B1	Albion Row	E4	East Road	E1	Kimberley Road	B2	Northampton Street
C1	Alpha Road	E3	Eden Street	D2	King Street	F2	Occupation Road
E2	Auckland Road	F3	Edward Street	C3	Kings Parade	D3	Orchard Street
E1	Aylestone Road	F1	Elizabeth Way	F5	Kingston Street	E3	Paradise Street
F2	Beche Road	D3	Elm Street	B1	Lady Margaret Road	C1	Park Parade
E1	Belvoir Road	F4	Emery Road	D5	Lensfield Road	C2	Park Street
C3	Bene't Street	F4	Emery Street	F1	Logan's Way	D4	Park Terrace
C4	Botolph Lane	D3	Emmanuel Road	C2	Lower Park Street	D3	Parker Street
E4	Bradmore Street	D3	Emmanuel Street	E5	Lynewode Road	E4	Parkside
E3	Brandon Place	E2	Evening Court	A1	Madingley Road	E2	Parsonage Street
C2	Bridge Street	E2	Fair Street	B2	Magdalene Street	C3	Peas Hill
E3	Broad Street	F5	Felton Street	B1	Magrath Avenue	C4	Pembroke Street
D5	Brookside	E3	Fitzroy Street	E2	Maids Causeway	F4	Perowne Street
E2	Brunswick Gardens	C4	Fitzwilliam Street	C2	Malcolm Street	C3	Petty Cury
E3	Burleigh Street	C4	Free School Lane	B5	Malting Lane	F3	Petworth Street
E5	Cambridge Place	F3	Geldart Street	E1	Manhattan Drive	C2	Portugal Street
B1	Castle Street	D5	George IV Street	D2	Manor Street	B1	Pound Hill
A5	Champneys Walk	E5	Glisson Road	F1	Mariners Way	D1	Pretoria Road
B1	Chesterton Lane	D5	Gonville Place	C3	Market Hill	F2	Priory Road
C1	Chesterton Road	E3	Grafton Street	C3	Market Street	E3	Prospect Row
E2	Christchurch Street	A5	Grange Gardens	E5	Mawson Road	C4	Queens Lane
E3	City Road	A5	Grange Road	E4	McKenzie Road	B4	Queens Road
A5	Clare Road	C3	Green Street	F3	Milford Street	D4	Regent Street
D3	Clarendon Street	E5	Gresham Road	C4	Mill Lane	D4	Regents Terrace
A2	Clarkson Road	E4	Guest Road	E4	Mill Road	B5	Ridley Hall Road
E4	Collier Road	F5	Gwydir Street	E5	Mill Street	D3	St Andrew's Street
C3	Corn Exchange Street	F2	Harvest Way	E4	Mortimer Street	F1	St Andrew's Road
E5	Covent Garden	D5	Harvey Road	B1	Mount Pleasant	F5	St Barnabas Road
A4	Cranmer Street	A3	Herschel Road	E2	Napier Street	C2	St Johns Road
E5	Cross Street	B1	Hertford Street	C2	New Park Street	C2	St Johns Street
E1	De Freiville Road	D5	Hills Road	D3	New Square	C3	St Mary's Street

F3	St Matthew's Street
E5	St Paul's Road
B1	St Peter's Street
C4	St Tibbs Row
F2	Saxon Road
D5	Saxon Street
A5	Selwyn Gardens
B1	Shelly Row
A4	Sidgwick Avenue
C3	Sidney Street
B4	Silver Street
F3	Staffordshire Street
A1	Storeys Way
F4	Sturton Street
F5	Tenison Road
C4	Tennis Court Road
A1	The Crescent
B5	The Fen Causeway
C1	Thomson's Lane
D1	Trafalgar Street
C3	Trinity Lane
C2	Trinity Street
C4	Trumpington Street
D5	Union Road
F3	Vicarage Terrace
D1	Victoria Avenue
D3	Victoria Street
E3	Warkworth Street
E4	Warkworth Terrace
E2	Wellington Street
A4	West Road
E5	Wilkins Street
E4	Willis Road
D2	Willow Walk
F3	York Street
F3	Young Street

University Colleges

C3	Christ's College
B3	Clare College
C4	Corpus Christi College
B4	Darwin College
D4	Downing College
D4	Emmanuel College
E4	Hughes Hall
D2	Jesus College
B3	King's College
A1	Lucy Cavendish College
B2	Magdalene College
A5	Newnham College
C4	Pembroke College
C4	Peterhouse
B4	Queen's College
B5	Ridley Hall
A3	Robinson College
C4	St Catharine's College
A1	St Edmund's College
C2	St John's College
A4	Selwyn College
C2	Sidney Sussex College
B3	Trinity College
B3	Trinity Hall
C2	Wesley House
B2	Westminster College

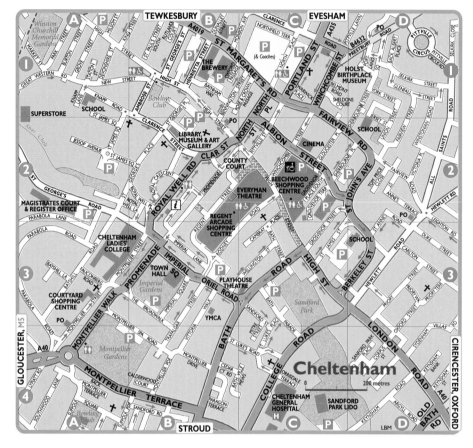

Cheltenham

Cheltenham is found on atlas page **163 E5**

C2	Albion Street	B3	Oriel Road
D2	All Saints Road	D3	Oxford Street
B1	Ambrose Street	A2	Parabola Lane
D1	Back Albert Place	A3	Parabola Road
C3	Bath Parade	A1	Park Street
B4	Bath Road	D1	Pittville Circus
C3	Bath Street	D1	Pittville Circus Road
B1	Baynham Way	D1	Pittville Lawn
A3	Bayshill Road	C2	Pittville Street
B1	Bennington Street	D1	Portland Square
D3	Berkeley Street	C1	Portland Street
A1	Burton Street	D1	Prestbury Road
C3	Cambray Place	D3	Priory Street
D3	Carlton Street	D3	Priory Terrace
C1	Clarence Road	D3	Priory Walk
B2	Clarence Street	B3	Promenade
C4	College Road	B3	Regent Street
A1	Devonshire Street	B3	Rodney Road
D3	Duke Street	B2	Royal Crescent
C2	Fairview Road	B2	Royal Well Place
D2	Fairview Street	B2	Royal Well Road
A3	Fauconberg Road	D3	St Anne's Road
D1	Glenfall Street	D2	St Anne's Terrace
C2	Gloucester Place	B2	St George's Place
A1	Great Western Road	A2	St George's Road
C2	Grosvenor Place South	B1	St George's Street
C3	Grosvenor Street	A2	St James Square
C2	Grosvenor Terrace	C3	St James Street
A1	Grove Street	D2	St John's Avenue
B1	Henrietta Street	C4	St Luke's Place
D3	Hewlett Road	C4	St Luke's Road
A1	High Street	B1	St Margaret's Road
B3	Imperial Lane	B1	St Paul's Street South
B3	Imperial Square	B4	Sandford Road
D4	Keynsham Road	C3	Sandford Street
A1	Knapp Road	D1	Selkirk Street
D4	London Road	C2	Sherbourne Place
B1	Monson Avenue	D1	Sherbourne Street
B4	Montpellier Drive	A4	Suffolk Square
B4	Montpellier Parade	D4	Sydenham Villas Road
A3	Montpellier Spa Road	B3	The Broadwalk
A3	Montpellier Street	B3	Trafalgar Street
A4	Montpellier Terrace	D2	Union Street
A4	Montpellier Walk	D2	Victoria Place
A1	New Street	B4	Vittoria Walk
C1	North Place	C3	Wellington Street
C2	North Street	C1	Winchcombe Street
C1	Northfield Terrace	D2	Winstonian Road

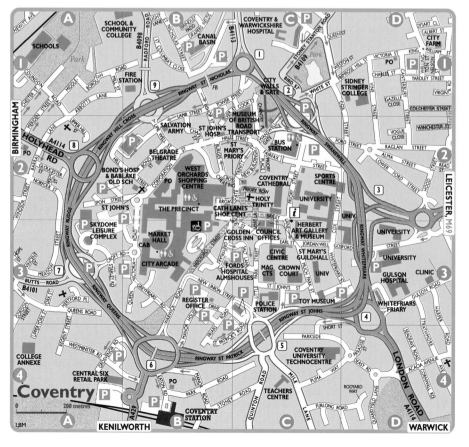

Coventry

Coventry is found on atlas page **215 E4**

A1	Abbotts Lane	A2	Meriden Street
D4	Acacia Avenue	A1	Middleborough Road
D2	Alma Street	C4	Mile Lane
A2	Barras Lane	C3	Much Park Street
C2	Bayley Lane	C2	New Buildings
C1	Bird Street	B3	New Union Street
B1	Bishop Street	A2	Norfolk Street
B2	Bond Street	B4	Park Road
B2	Broadgate	C4	Parkside
B2	Burges	D1	Primrose Hill Street
A3	Butts Road	C2	Priory Row
D1	Canterbury Street	C2	Priory Street
C2	Chantry Place	C4	Puma Way
B2	Chapel Street	D4	Quarryfield Lane
D1	Charles Street	B3	Queen Victoria Road
D1	Colchester Street	A3	Queens Road
C1	Cook Street	C4	Quinton Road
B2	Corporation Street	B1	Radford Road
A1	Coundon Road	D2	Raglan Street
D1	Cox Street	A4	Regent Street
A3	Croft Road	A2	Ringway Hill Cross
B2	Cross Cheaping	A3	Ringway Queens
C3	Earl Street	A3	Ringway Rudge
B4	Eaton Road	C3	Ringway St Johns
C2	Fairfax Street	B1	Ringway St Nicholas
D2	Ford Street	B4	Ringway St Patrick
B4	Friars Road	C2	Ringway Swanswell
D3	Gosford Street	D3	Ringway Whitefriars
B3	Greyfriars Lane	C3	St John's Street
B3	Greyfriars Road	B1	St Nicholas Street
A4	Grosvenor Road	B4	St Patrick's Road
D3	Gulson Road	C3	Salt Lane
B2	Hales Street	B1	Silver Street
C3	Hay Lane	A2	Spon Street
B3	Hertford Street	B4	Stoney Road
C3	High Street	C1	Stoney Stanton Road
A2	Hill Street	D4	Strathmore Avenue
A2	Holyhead Road	C2	Swanswell Gate
D2	Hood Street	B1	Tower Street
C3	Jordan Well	C2	Trinity Street
D1	King William Street	B2	Upper Well Street
B1	Lamb Street	D1	Victoria Street
C3	Little Park Street	D1	Vine Street
D4	London Road	B3	Warwick Road
D2	Lower Ford Street	A4	Westminster Road
B3	Manor House Drive	C1	White Street
B4	Manor Road	C3	Whitefriars Street
A3	Meadow Street	D1	Yardley Street

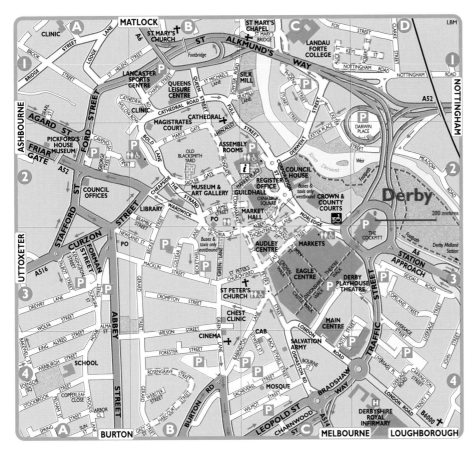

Derby

Derby is found on atlas page **275 F2**

A3	Abbey Street	C4	Leopold Street
A1	Agard Street	D4	Liversage Place
C2	Albert Street	D4	Liversage Road
C3	Albion Street	D3	Liversage Street
A3	Alma Street	A1	Lodge Lane
B2	Amen Alley	D4	London Road
B4	Babington Lane	B3	Macklin Street
C4	Back Sitwell Street	C2	Market Place
A4	Bakewell Street	D2	Meadow Road
B3	Becket Street	A4	Monk Street
B3	Becketwell Lane	C2	Morledge
B2	Bold Lane	A3	Newland Street
C4	Bradshaw Way	D1	Nottingham Road
B2	Bramble Street	B2	Old Blacksmith Yard
A1	Bridge Street	C4	Osmaston Road
A1	Brook Street	C2	Osnabrük Square
B4	Burton Road	C1	Phoenix Street
D4	Carrington Street	B1	Queen Street
C3	Castle Walk	B4	Sacheverel Street
B1	Cathedral Road	B2	Sadler Gate
A2	Cavendish Street	B1	St Alkmund's Way
B1	Chapel Street	A1	St Helens Street
C4	Charnwood Street	B2	St James Street
B2	Cheapside	C1	St Mary's Bridge
B3	Colyear Street	B2	St Mary's Gate
D3	Copeland Street	B1	St Michael's Lane
B2	Cornmarket	B3	St Peter's Churchyard
C2	Corporation Street	C3	St Peter's Street
C3	Crown Walk	D3	Siddals Road
A3	Curzon Street	C1	Silkmill Lane
D2	Darwin Place	C4	Sitwell Street
C2	Derwent Street	B1	Sowter Road
C3	Devonshire Walk	A3	Stafford Street
A3	Drewry Lane	D3	Station Approach
C3	East Street	A4	Stockbrook Street
C3	Exchange Street	C1	Stuart Street
C2	Exeter Place	A3	Talbot Street
C1	Exeter Street	D3	The Cockpitt
A2	Ford Street	B2	The Strand
B4	Forester Street	C3	Theatre Walk
A3	Forman Street	D4	Traffic Street
C1	Fox Street	D4	Trinity Street
A2	Friar Gate	B3	Victoria Street
B1	Full Street	B2	Wardwick
B3	Gerard Street	A4	Werburgh Street
B3	Green Lane	A1	Willow Row
B2	Irongate	C4	Wilmot Street
A4	King Alfred Street	B4	Wilson Street

Dover

Dover is found on atlas page **83 F2**

B3	Adrian Street	B2	Market Square
C2	Ashen Tree Lane	A3	Military Road
D2	Athol Terrace	B2	Mill Lane
B2	Bench Street	B3	New Bridge
B2	Biggin Street	B2	New Street
B2	Bowling Green Terrace	A2	Norman Street
B3	Cambridge Road	B1	Park Place
B3	Camden Crescent	B1	Park Street
B2	Cannon Street	B1	Pencester Road
C2	Canon's Gate Road	B2	Princes Street
C2	Castle Hill Road	A2	Priory Gate Road
B1	Castle Mount Road	A1	Priory Hill
B2	Castle Street	B2	Priory Road
A4	Channel View Road	B2	Priory Street
B1	Charlton Green	D2	Queen Elizabeth Road
B2	Church Street	B2	Queen Street
A2	Clarendon Place	B2	Queens Gardens
A2	Clarendon Road	C2	Russell Street
B2	Cowgate Hill	A2	St John's Road
A1	Crafford Street	A2	Saxon Street
B1	Dour Street	B3	Snargate Street
C2	Douro Place	B2	Stem Brook
A3	Drop Redoubt Road	C1	Taswell Close
B2	Durham Close	C1	Taswell Street
B2	Durham Hill	A1	Templar Street
D2	East Cliff	B1	The Paddock
A1	East Street	A4	The Viaduct
A1	Effingham Crescent	A1	Tower Hamlets Road
A2	Effingham Street	A1	Tower Street
A4	Elizabeth Street	C2	Townwall Street
A2	Folkestone Road	B3	Union Street
B1	Godwyne Close	C1	Victoria Park
B1	Godwyne Road	C2	Wellesley Road
B1	Harold Street	A1	Widred Road
C1	Heritage Gardens	A1	Wood Street
B1	Hewitt Road	C2	Woolcomber Street
A1	High Street	B2	Worthington Street
B2	King Street	B2	York Street
C1	Knights Road		
A3	Knights Templars		
B1	Ladywell		
B2	Lancaster Road		
C2	Laureston Place		
B1	Leyburne Road		
A4	Limekiln Street		
B1	Maison Dieu Road		
A2	Malvern Road		
B3	Marine Parade		

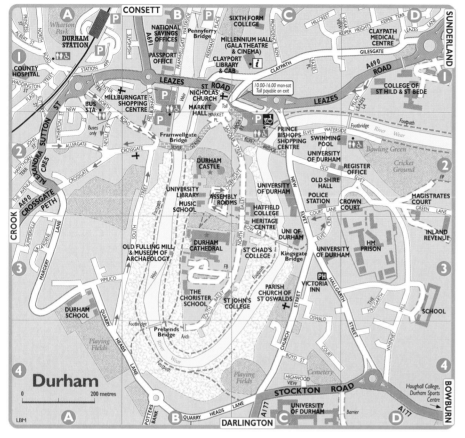

Durham

Durham is found on atlas page **395 F1**

A1	Albert Street	A3	Quarry Heads Lane
A2	Alexandra Crescent	B2	Saddler Street
A2	Allergate	B2	Silver Street
A2	Atherton Street	B3	South Bailey
C3	Bow Lane	B3	South Street
C4	Boyd Street	A1	Station Approach
A3	Briardene	C4	Stockton Road
C4	Church Street	A3	Summerville
C1	Claypath	A2	Sutton Street
C2	Court Lane	A1	Tenter Terrace
A2	Crossgate	A2	The Avenue
A2	Crossgate Peth	D3	The Hallgarth
C2	Elvet Bridge	A1	Waddington Street
C3	Elvet Crescent	D1	Wear View
C2	Elvet Waterside	D4	Whinney Hill
A1	Flass Street		
B1	Framwellgate Waterside		
B1	Freemans Place		
D1	Gilesgate		
D2	Green Lane		
C3	Hallgarth Street		
A2	Hawthorn Terrace		
B1	Highgate		
C2	High Street		
C4	Highwood View		
C1	Hillcrest		
A2	John Street		
D1	Keiper Heights		
D1	Keiper Terrace		
D1	Leazes Lane		
C1	Leazes Place		
B1	Leazes Road		
A3	Margery Lane		
B2	Market Place		
B1	Millburngate		
A2	Neville Street		
C2	New Elvet		
A1	New Street		
C3	North Bailey		
A1	North Road		
C2	Old Elvet		
C3	Oswald Court		
C2	Owengate		
D1	Pelaw Leazes Lane		
A3	Pimlico		
B4	Potters Bank		
A1	Princess Street		
C1	Providence Row		

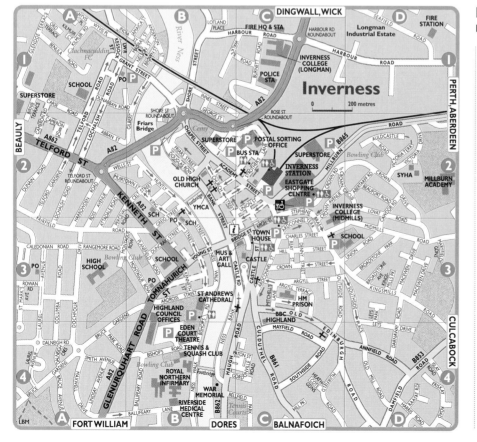

Inverness

Inverness is found on atlas page **566 B8**

D2	Abertarff Road	A4	Glenurquhart Road
B2	Academy Street	B1	Grant Street
B1	Anderson Street	B3	Greig Street
D4	Annfield Road	C1	Harbour Road
C3	Ardconnel Street	A2	Harrowden Road
C3	Ardconnel Terrace	B4	Haugh Road
B3	Ardross Street	C3	High Street
C3	Argyll Street	C3	Hill Street
C3	Argyll Terrace	B2	Huntley Street
A2	Attadale Road	A1	India Street
D2	Auldcastle Road	A2	Kenneth Street
B4	Ballifeary Lane	B2	King Street
B4	Ballifeary Road	D3	Kingsmills Road
B2	Bank Street	A3	Laurel Avenue
D2	Beaufort Road	D4	Leys Drive
A1	Benula Road	A2	Lochalsh Road
B4	Bishop's Road	D2	Lovat Road
C3	Bridge Street	A1	Lower Kessock Street
D3	Broadstone Park	D3	Macewen Drive
A4	Bruce Gardens	A4	Maxwell Drive
C1	Burnett Road	C4	Mayfield Road
A3	Caledonian Road	D3	Midmills Road
A2	Cameron Road	C2	Millburn Road
A1	Carse Road	B3	Montague Row
C3	Castle Road	C4	Muirfield Road
C3	Castle Street	A2	Muirtown Street
D2	Cawdor Road	B4	Ness Bank
B2	Celt Street	B4	Ness Walk
B2	Chapel Street	C3	Old Edinburgh Road
C3	Charles Street	D4	Old Mill Road
B2	Church Street	B3	Planefield Road
A3	Columba Road	A3	Rangemore Road
C2	Crown Avenue	D1	Seafield Road
C2	Crown Circus	B1	Shore Street
D2	Crown Drive	D3	Southside Place
C2	Crown Road	C4	Southside Road
C3	Crown Street	C2	Stephens Brae
C4	Culduthel Road	C2	Strother's Lane
A4	Dalneigh Road	A2	Telford Gardens
D4	Damfield Road	A2	Telford Road
D4	Darnaway Road	A2	Telford Street
A3	Dochfour Drive	B3	Tomnahurich Street
B2	Douglas Row	D3	Union Road
A2	Dunain Road	C2	Union Street
A3	Fairfield Road	D2	Victoria Drive
B2	Friars Street	B1	Walker Road
B2	Gilbert Street	A2	Wells Street
A1	Glendoe Terrace	B3	Young Street

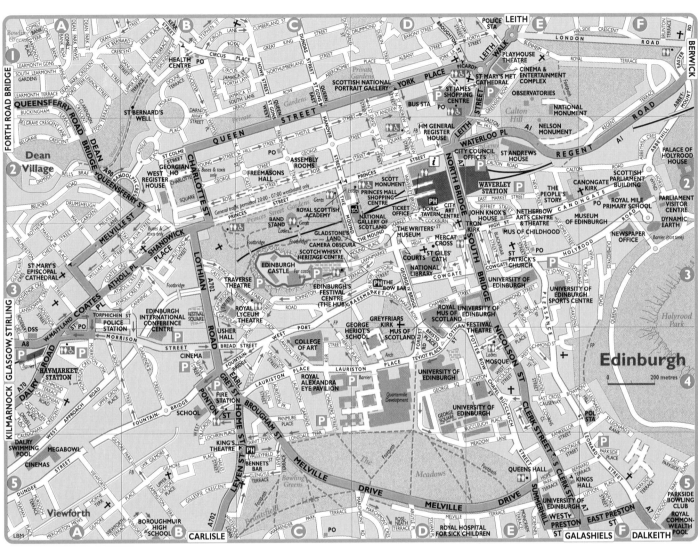

Edinburgh

Edinburgh is found on atlas page **488 B5**

F2	Abbeyhill	B3	Castle Terrace	E4	East Cross Causeway	B1	Jamaica Street North Lane	A4	Morrison Street	F5	St Leonard's Street
F2	Abbeyhill Crescent	C4	Chalmers Street	E2	East Market Street	C1	Jamaica Street South Lane	D3	Mound Place	E3	St Mary's Street
F1	Abbeymount	D3	Chambers Street	F5	East Preston Street	E2	Jeffrey Street	A5	Murdoch Terrace	B1	St Stephen Street
C1	Abercromby Place	E4	Chapel Street	A2	Eton Terrace	C3	Johnston Terrace	E2	New Street	B4	Semple Street
B2	Ainslie Place	B2	Charlotte Square	B3	Festival Square	C4	Keir Street	E4	Nicholson Street	B3	Shandwick Place
D1	Albany Street	A3	Chester Street Gardens	D4	Forrest Road	B1	Kerr Street	D2	North Bridge	E3	South Bridge
B3	Alva Street	B1	Circus Lane	E1	Forth Street	B3	King's Stables Road	C2	North Castle Street	E5	South Clerk Street
A1	Ann Street	B1	Circus Place	B4	Fountainbridge	C4	Lady Lawson Street	D1	North St Andrew Street	A1	South Learmonth Gardens
D5	Argyle Place	A1	Clarendon Crescent	C2	Frederick Street	A3	Lansdowne Crescent	D1	North St David Street	D2	South St Andrew Street
B3	Atholl Crescent	E4	Clerk Street	B4	Gardner's Crescent	C4	Lauriston Gardens	C1	Northumberland Street	D2	South St David Street
B3	Atholl Crescent Lane	A3	Coates Crescent	D3	George IV Bridge	C4	Lauriston Park	F5	Oxford Street	C4	Spital Street
A3	Atholl Place	A3	Coates Place	D4	George Square	C4	Lauriston Place	A3	Palmerston Street	B3	Stafford Street
D1	Barony Street	D2	Cockburn Street	B2	George Street	C4	Lauriston Street	C4	Panmure Place	E5	Summerhill
A2	Belford Road	A1	Comely Bank Avenue	B5	Gillespie Crescent	D3	Lawnmarket	F5	Parkside Terrace	C5	Tarvit Street
A2	Belgrave Crescent	D3	Cowgate	B5	Gilmore Park	B5	Leamington Terrace	E1	Picardy Place	D4	Teviot Place
A2	Belgrave Crescent Lane	E4	Crichton Street	A5	Gilmore Place	A1	Learmonth Terrace	E3	Pleasance	C2	The Mound
A2	Bells Brae	A4	Dalry Road	C4	Glen Street	E1	Leith Street	B4	Ponton Street	C2	Thistle Street
E5	Bernard Terrace	A2	Damside	C5	Glengyle Terrace	E1	Leith Walk	E4	Potter Row	A3	Torphichen Street
E3	Blackfriar Street	B1	Danube Street	B1	Gloucester Lane	A1	Lennox Street	C2	Princes Street	B1	Upper Dean Terrace
E4	Bowmont Place	B1	Darnaway Street	D3	Grassmarket	B1	Leslie Place	B2	Queen Street	B5	Upper Gilmore Place
B4	Bread Street	E4	Davie Street	C1	Great King Street	C5	Leven Street	C1	Queen Street	A4	Upper Grove Place
D4	Bristo Place	A2	Dean Bridge	E1	Greenside Row	C5	Leven Terrace		Gardens East / West	C5	Valleyfield Street
C4	Brougham Street	A1	Dean Park Crescent	B3	Grindlay Street	B5	Lochrin Place	F3	Queen's Drive	D3	Victoria Street
D1	Broughton Street	A1	Dean Park Mews	A3	Grosvenor Crescent	E1	London Road	A1	Queensferry Road	E3	Viewcraig Gardens
E4	Buccleuch Place	A1	Dean Park Street	A3	Grosvenor Street	C5	Lonsdale Terrace	A2	Queensferry Street	F3	Viewcraig Street
E4	Buccleuch Street	A1	Dean Street	A4	Grove Street	B3	Lothian Road	B2	Randolph Crescent	A5	Viewforth
A1	Buckingham Terrace	B1	Dean Terrace	C2	Hanover Street	D4	Lothian Street	E4	Rankeillor Street	A3	Walker Street
A4	Caledonian Crescent	A1	Doune Terrace	C4	Heriot Place	F5	Lutton Place	E2	Regent Road	C5	Warrender Park Terrace
A4	Caledonian Road	D1	Drummond Place	C1	Heriot Row	A3	Manor Place	F2	Regent Terrace	E2	Waterloo Place
E2	Calton Hill	E3	Drummond Street	D3	High Street	D5	Marchmont Crescent	B2	Rose Street	D2	Waverley Bridge
E2	Calton Road	A2	Drumsheugh	E4	Hill Place	D5	Marchmont Road	A3	Rothesay Place	A4	West Approach Road
B3	Cambridge Street	D1	Dublin Street	C2	Hill Street	D2	Market Street	E3	Roxburgh Place	D3	West Bow
D3	Candlemaker Row	F3	Dumbiedykes Road	F1	Hillside Crescent	C5	Meadow Lane	B1	Royal Circus	A4	West Maitland Street
B3	Canning Street	C1	Dundas Street	F5	Holyrood Park Road	D4	Melville Drive	F1	Royal Terrace	E4	West Nicholson Street
E2	Canongate	A5	Dundee Street	E3	Holyrood Road	A3	Melville Street	B3	Rutland Street	C4	West Port
C2	Castle Street	B4	Earl Grey Street	C4	Home Street	A2	Melville Street Lane	D2	St Andrew Square	E5	West Preston Street
				E5	Hope Park Terrace	D5	Melville Terrace	A1	St Bernard's Crescent	E4	West Richmond Street
				F2	Horse Wynd	E5	Montague Street	B2	St Colme Street	B4	West Tollcross
				E4	Howden Street	B1	Moray Place	E3	St John Street	A3	William Street
				C1	Howe Street	A4	Morrison Crescent	E3	St Johns Hill	D1	York Place
				B1	India Street	A4	Morrison Link	F4	St Leonard's Bank	B2	Young Street

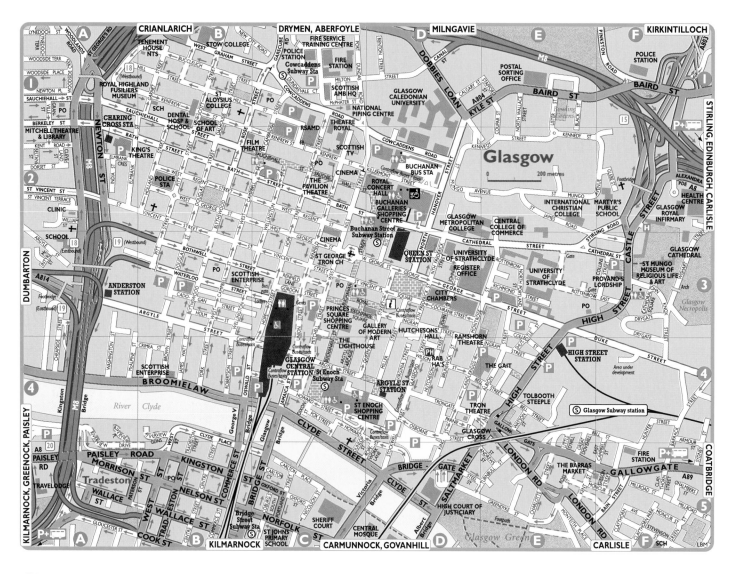

Glasgow

Glasgow is found on atlas page **467 E1**

E4 Albion Street
F2 Alexandra Parade
C4 Argyll Arcade
B3 Argyle Street
F4 Armour Street
F5 Bain Street
E1 Baird Street
F4 Barrack Street
B2 Bath Street
E4 Bell Street
A2 Beltane Street
A1 Berkeley Street
E1 Black Street
B3 Blythswood Street
B3 Bothwell Street
D5 Bridgegate
C5 Bridge Street
B4 Broomielaw
B4 Brown Street
D4 Brunswick Street
B1 Buccleuch Street
C4 Buchanan Street
B3 Cadogan Street
D1 Calgary Street
C2 Cambridge Street
D1 Canal Street
D4 Candleriggs
C5 Carlton Court
C5 Carlton Place
F3 Castle Street
F3 Cathedral Square
D3 Cathedral Street
B5 Centre Street
F5 Chambers Street
E5 Charlotte Street
A4 Cheapside Street

F5 Claythorn Avenue
F5 Claythorn Park
F5 Claythorn Street
A2 Cleveland Street
B4 Clyde Place
D5 Clyde Street
C5 Coburg Street
D3 Cochrane Street
E4 College Street
F3 Collins Street
B5 Commerce Street
B5 Cook Street
E1 Coupar Street
C1 Cowcaddens Road
B4 Crimea Street
C4 Dixon Street
D1 Dobbies Loan
A2 Dorset Street
B2 Douglas Street
F3 Drygate
F4 Duke Street
C1 Dundasvale Court
C5 Dunlop Street
F5 East Campbell Street
A2 Elmbank Crescent
A2 Elmbank Street
C4 Fox Street
E4 Gallowgate
B1 Garnet Street
C1 Garscube Road
D3 George Square
D3 George Street
F5 Gibson Street
D4 Glassford Street
F2 Glebe Street

A5 Gloucester Street
C3 Gordon Street
A1 Granville Street
E5 Great Dovehill
F5 Green Street
E5 Greendyke Street
E4 High Street
B1 Hill Street
B2 Holland Street
B3 Holm Street
C3 Hope Street
C4 Howard Street
F4 Hunter Street
D4 Hutcheson Street
A2 India Street
D3 Ingram Street
C4 Jamaica Street
B4 James Watt Street
F3 John Knox Street
D3 John Street
E2 Kennedy Street
A2 Kent Road
E5 Kent Street
D2 Killermont Street
D5 King Street
B5 Kingston Street
D1 Kyle Street
E1 Lister Street
E4 Little Dovehill
E5 London Road
A1 Lynedoch Street
A1 Lynedoch Terrace
A4 McAlpine Street
A3 McIntyre Street
C1 McPhater Street
D4 Miller Street

F5 Millroad Street
C1 Milton Street
C3 Mitchell Street
E5 Moncur Street
B2 Monteith Place
D3 Montrose Street
A5 Morrison Street
B5 Nelson Street
B1 New City Road
A1 Newton Place
C5 Nicholson Street
C5 Norfolk Street
D3 North Frederick Street
D3 North Hanover Street
E3 North Portland Street
E1 North Wallace Street
D4 Osborne Street
B4 Oswald Street
C5 Oxford Street
A5 Paisley Road
D4 Parnie Street
A5 Paterson Street
F1 Pinkston Road
B3 Pitt Street
C1 Port Dundas Road
C4 Queen Street
C3 Renfield Lane
C3 Renfield Street
B1 Renfrew Street
D1 Renton Street
E3 Richmond Street
A5 Riverview Drive
B4 Riverview Gardens
A4 Riverview Place
B4 Robertson Street
D5 Ropework Lane

B2 Rose Street
E5 Ross Street
E3 Rottenrow
E3 Rottenrow East
C3 Royal Exchange Square
E5 St Andrews Street
A1 St Georges Road
E2 St James Road
E2 St Mungo Avenue
C3 St Vincent Place
A2 St Vincent Street
A2 St Vincent Terrace
D5 Saltmarket
A1 Sauchiehall Street
B1 Scott Street
E4 Shuttle Street
D3 South Frederick Street
C5 South Portland Street
E1 Stafford Street
D5 Steel Street
F5 Stevenson Street
E3 Stirling Road
D5 Stockwell Street
F5 Sydney Street
B5 Tradeston Street
D4 Trongate
E5 Turnbull Street
C3 Union Street
D4 Virginia Street
A5 Wallace Street
A4 Washington Street
B3 Waterloo Street
E4 Watson Street
B3 Wellington Street
B3 West Campbell Street
B2 West George Street

B1 West Graham Street
C3 West Nile Street
B2 West Regent Street
B4 West Street
A2 William Street
D4 Wilson Street
F3 Wishart Street
A1 Woodlands Road
A1 Woodside Crescent
A1 Woodside Place
A1 Woodside Terrace
B4 York Street

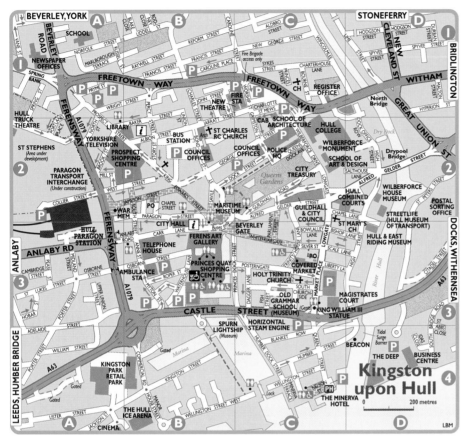

Kingston upon Hull

Kingston upon Hull is found on atlas page **347 G4**

A4	Adelaide Street	C3	Market Place
B2	Albion Street	A1	Marlborough Terrace
C2	Alfred Gelder Street	A3	Midland Street
A3	Anlaby Road	A2	Mill Street
B3	Anne Street	B3	Myton Street
B2	Baker Street	D1	New Cleveland Street
A1	Beverley Road	C1	New George Street
C3	Bishop Lane	A1	Norfolk Street
C4	Blanket Row	A3	Osborne Street
B2	Bond Street	B2	Paragon Street
C1	Bourne Street	C3	Parliament Street
C3	Bowlalley Lane	A3	Pease Street
A2	Brook Street	B1	Percy Street
B1	Caroline Place	A4	Porter Street
B1	Caroline Street	C3	Posterngate
B3	Carr Lane	C3	Princes Dock Street
B3	Castle Street	A1	Prospect Street
C2	Chapel Lane	C4	Queen Street
B1	Charles Street	C2	Queens Dock Avenue
C1	Charlotte Street Mews	B1	Raywell Street
C1	Charterhouse Lane	B1	Reform Street
D3	Citadel Street	B3	Roper Street
A2	Collier Street	A3	St Lukes Street
B4	Commercial Road	D2	St Peters Street
C3	Dagger Lane	B2	Savile Street
C2	Dock Street	C3	Scale Lane
A1	Ferensway	C3	Silver Street
C3	Fish Street	D4	South Bridge Road
A1	Freetown Way	C3	South Churchside
B2	George Street	B2	South Street
D2	Great Union Street	A1	Spring Bank
C2	Grimston Street	A1	Spring Street
C2	Guildhall Road	D1	Spyvee Street
D2	High Street	B2	Story Street
D1	Hodgson Street	C1	Sykes Street
C4	Humber Dock Street	C3	Trinity House Lane
C4	Humber Street	A3	Upper Union Street
D1	Hyperion Street	B3	Waterhouse Lane
B2	Jameson Street	C4	Wellington Street
B2	Jarratt Street	B4	Wellington Street West
B1	John Street	A2	West Street
B2	King Edward Street	C3	Whitefriargate
B4	Kingston Street	C2	Wilberforce Drive
C3	Liberty Lane	A4	William Street
D1	Lime Street	C1	Wincolmlee
A4	Lister Street	D1	Witham
C3	Lowgate	C1	Worship Street
B4	Manor House Street	A1	Wright Street

Leicester

Leicester is found on atlas page **240 C4**

C1	Abbey Street	C1	Mansfield Street
B2	Applegate	B2	Market Place
A2	Bath Lane	C3	Market Street
C1	Bedford Street South	C3	Marlborough Street
C3	Belvoir Street	A4	Mill Lane
C3	Bishop Street	C4	Mill Street
B4	Bonners Lane	B3	Millstone Lane
C3	Bowling Green Street	D4	Nelson Street
D3	Calais Hill	B3	Newarke Street
D3	Campbell Street	C4	Newtown Street
B4	Carlton Street	B3	Oxford Street
A3	Castle Street	B2	Peacock Lane
B1	Causeway Lane	C4	Pelham Street
C1	Charles Street	B3	Pocklingtons Walk
C3	Chatham Street	C4	Princess Road West
B1	Church Gate	C4	Regent Road
D2	Church Street	D4	Regent Street
C1	Clarence Street	C2	Rutland Street
C4	Crescent Street	A2	St Augustine Road
A1	Cumberland Street	D2	St George's Street
D4	De Montfort Street	D3	St George's Way
B4	Deacon Street	C1	St James Street
C3	Dover Street	D1	St Mathew's Way
B1	East Bond Street	A2	St Nicholas Circle
D3	East Street	B2	St Nicholas Place
C2	Every Street	B1	St Peter's Lane
B3	Friar Lane	C1	Sandiacre Street
C2	Gallowtree Gate	A1	Sanvey Gate
C2	Granby Street	B1	Short Street
B1	Gravel Street	B2	Silver Street
A1	Great Central Street	D3	South Albion Street
B2	Guildhall Lane	B3	Southgates
C2	Halford Street	A2	Talbot Lane
C1	Haymarket	B4	The Gateway
B2	High Street	A3	The Newarke
A1	Highcross Street	C4	Tower Street
C1	Hill Street	C4	Turner Street
C2	Horsefair Street	B3	Upper Brown Street
B2	Hotel Street	C4	Upper King Street
C2	Humberstone Gate	A2	Vaughan Way
D1	Humberstone Road	D4	Waterloo Way
B4	Infirmary Road	C3	Welford Road
B4	Jarrom Street	C3	Wellington Street
C3	King Street	C4	West Street
C1	Lee Street	D1	Wharf Street South
D4	London Road	D2	Wimbledon Street
B2	Loseby Lane	C2	Yeoman Street
C1	Lower Hill Street	B3	York Road

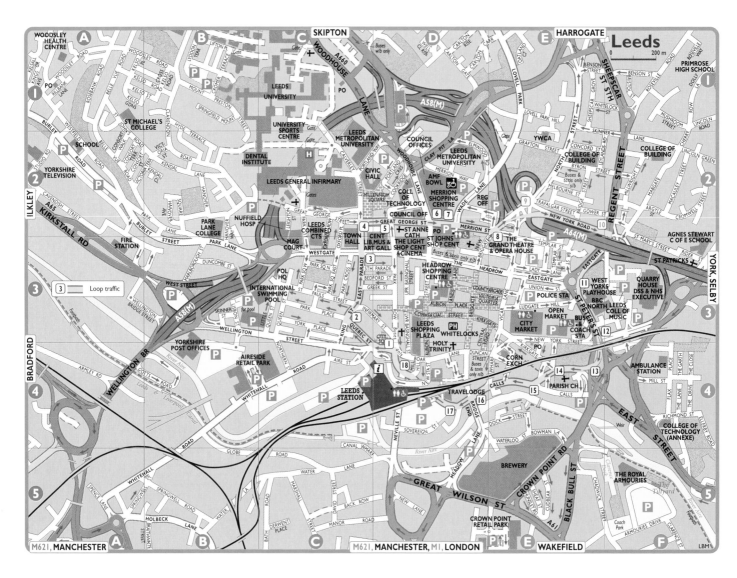

Leeds

Leeds is found on atlas page **343 E3**

C4 Aire Street	E2 Concord Street	C3 Infirmary Street	D4 Mill Hill	F3 St Mary's Street	B3 West Street
D3 Albion Place	A2 Consort Street	A1 Kelsall Grove	F4 Mill Street	C3 St Pauls Street	A1 Westfield Road
D4 Albion Street	A2 Consort Terrace	A1 Kelso Gardens	F2 Millwright Street	E3 St Peter's Street	C3 Westgate
F2 Argyle Street	A2 Consort Walk	A1 Kelso Place	B1 Mount Preston Street	E5 Sheaf Street	E4 Wharf Street
A4 Armley Road	D2 Cookridge Street	A1 Kelso Road	F1 Mushroom Street	E1 Sheepscar Grove	A5 Whitehall Road
F5 Armouries Drive	D3 County Arcade	A1 Kelso Street	D4 Neville Street	F1 Sheepscar Street South	E1 Whitelock Street
C5 Back Row	B1 Cromer Terrace	B2 Kendal Close	D5 New Lane	E1 Skinner Lane	C1 Woodhouse Lane
C5 Bath Road	F2 Cromwell Street	B2 Kendal Lane	D4 New Briggate	B3 Skinner Street	A1 Woodsley Road
C3 Bedford Street	B1 Cross Kelso Road	C3 King Street	D4 New Station Street	C3 South Parade	C3 York Place
A2 Belle Vue Road	E5 Crown Point Road	A1 Kings Avenue	E2 New York Road	D4 Sovereign Street	
E1 Benson Street	E5 Cudbear Street	D3 Kirkgate	E3 New York Street	A5 Spence Lane	
E5 Black Bull Street	C5 David Street	A2 Kirkstall Road	E2 North Street	B1 Springfield Mount	
D4 Boar Lane	C5 Derwent Place	E3 Lady Lane	C4 Northern Street	B5 Springwell Road	
E4 Bowman Lane	E4 Dock Street	D3 Lands Lane	E1 Oatland Court	A5 Springwell Street	
B5 Braithwaite Street	F1 Dolly Lane	C2 Leighton Street	C3 Oxford Place	A2 Studio Road	
D4 Bridge End	D4 Duncan Street	E2 Leylands Road	C3 Oxford Row	E3 Templar Place	
E3 Bridge Street	B3 Duncombe Street	B1 Lifton Place	C3 Park Cross Street	E3 Templar Street	
D3 Briggate	C3 East Parade	F2 Lincoln Green	B2 Park Lane	F4 The Close	
F1 Bristol Street	F4 East Street	F1 Lincoln Road	C3 Park Place	F4 The Drive	
A1 Burley Road	E3 Eastgate	B3 Lisbon Street	D3 Park Row	F4 The Garth	
A2 Burley Street	F4 Ellerby Road	C3 Little Queen Street	C3 Park Square East	D3 The Headrow	
E2 Byron Street	D2 Elmwood Road	E1 Lovell Park	C3 Park Square North	F4 The Lane	
E4 Calls	F4 Flax Place	E1 Lovell Park Hill	C3 Park Square West	E2 Trafalgar Street	
C2 Calverley Street	B5 Globe Road	D3 Lower Basinghall Street	C3 Park Street	E3 Union Street	
C4 Canal Wharf	B4 Gotts Road	E3 Ludgate Hill	D2 Portland Crescent	D3 Upper Basinghall Street	
D1 Carlton Carr	E2 Gower Street	B1 Lyddon Terrace	C2 Portland Way	E3 Vicar Lane	
D1 Carlton Gate	E2 Grafton Street	F2 Mabgate	C3 Quebec Street	E3 Victoria Quarter	
D1 Carlton Rise	C2 Great George Street	F2 Macauley Street	C3 Queen Street	B2 Victoria Street	
A2 Cavendish Street	D5 Great Wilson Street	C5 Manor Road	F2 Regent Street	A2 Victoria Terrace	
E3 Central Road	D3 Greek Street	B3 Marlborough Street	F4 Richmond Street	D2 Wade Lane	
E5 Chadwick Street	B2 Hanover Avenue	C5 Marshall Street	F3 Rider Street	B5 Water Lane	
F2 Cherry Row	B2 Hanover Square	D5 Meadow Lane	A1 Rillbank Lane	E4 Waterloo Street	
F5 Clarence Street	B2 Hanover Way	E2 Melbourne Street	A1 Rosebank Road	D1 Well Close Rise	
B2 Clarendon Road	B5 Holbeck Lane	D2 Merrion Street	F1 Roseville Road	A4 Wellington Bridge	
D2 Clay Pit Lane	E5 Hunslet Road	D2 Merrion Way	F1 Roseville Way	A3 Wellington Bridge Street	
D3 Commercial Street	B1 Hyde Terrace	D2 Millennium Square	A1 St John's Road	B3 Wellington Street	

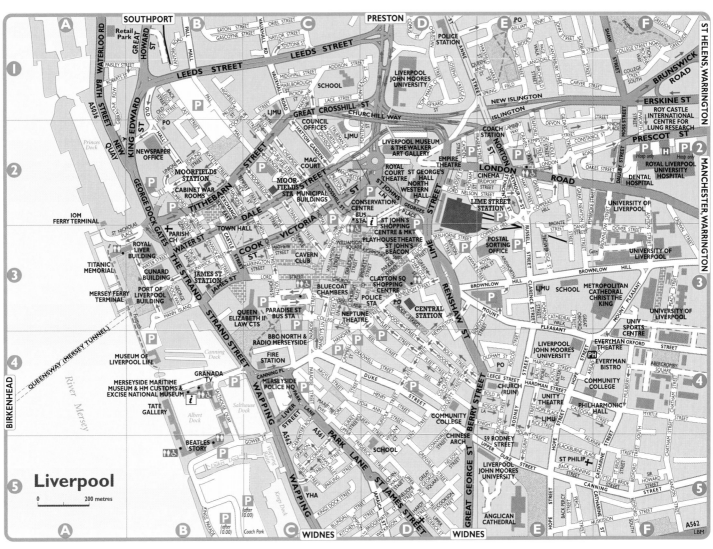

Liverpool

Liverpool is found on atlas page **308 D2**

F4	Abercromby Square
C1	Addison Street
E3	Ainsworth Street
C4	Argyle Street
E4	Arrad Street
F2	Ashton Street
E2	Audley Street
D3	Basnett Street
A1	Bath Street
F5	Bedford Street South
E3	Benson Street
D4	Berry Street
B2	Bixteth Street
E5	Blackburne Place
C5	Blundall Street
D3	Bold Street
D3	Bolton Street
E2	Bridport Street
E3	Bronte Street
E3	Brownlow Hill
F3	Brownlow Street
F1	Brunswick Road
B3	Brunswick Street
E4	Caledonia Street
D2	Camden Street
C4	Campbell Street
C4	Canning Place
F5	Canning Street
E1	Canterbury Street
C5	Carpenters Row
E1	Carver Street
B3	Castle Street
F5	Catharine Street
F4	Chatham Street
C2	Cheapside
D1	Christian Street

C3	Church Alley
C3	Church Street
C1	Churchill Way
E3	Clarence Street
B2	Cockspur Street
C3	College Lane
F1	College Street North
F1	College Street South
D4	Colquitt Street
E2	Constance Street
C3	Cook Street
D5	Cookson Street
E2	Copperas Hill
C5	Cornhill
D5	Cornwallis Street
B3	Covent Garden
E2	Craven Street
C2	Crosshill Street
F3	Crown Street
C2	Cunliffe Street
C2	Dale Street
E3	Dansie Street
F2	Daulby Street
E2	Devon Street
F3	Dover Street
B3	Drury Lane
D4	Duke Street
B1	East Street
C2	Eberle Street
B2	Edmund Street
D3	Elliot Street
F2	Epworth Street
F1	Erskine Street
B2	Exchange Street East
E5	Falkner Street
B3	Fenwick Street

D3	Fleet Street
D2	Fontenoy Street
E2	Fraser Street
B1	Gascoyne Street
B2	George Dock Gates
B3	George Dock Way
D1	Gerard Street
A1	Gibraltar Row
D4	Gilbert Street
E2	Gildart Street
E2	Gill Street
C1	Gladstone Street
C5	Gower Street
D4	Gradwell Street
D3	Great Charlotte Street
C1	Great Crosshill Street
D5	Great George Street
B1	Great Howard Street
E2	Great Newton Street
E3	Great Orford Street
E2	Greek Street
F1	Greenside
F1	Gregson Street
D5	Grenville Street
B2	Hackins Hey
C4	Hanover Street
E4	Hardman Street
E1	Harker Street
C3	Harrington Street
E2	Hart Street
C2	Hatton Garden
D3	Hawke Street
D4	Henry Street
B1	Highfield Street
E4	Hope Place
E3	Hope Street
D2	Hotham Street
C5	Hurst Street
F5	Huskisson Street
E1	Islington
D5	Jamaica Street

B3	James Street
E1	John Street
C2	Johnson Street
E2	Kempston Street
D4	Kent Street
B2	King Edward Street
C5	Kings Dock Street
B5	Kings Parade
C5	Kitchen Street
E4	Knight Street
C1	Lace Street
E1	Langsdale Street
E4	Leece Street
B1	Leeds Street
D3	Lime Street
C4	Liver Street
E2	London Road
D2	Lord Nelson Street
C3	Lord Street
D4	Lydia Ann Street
C2	Manchester Street
C4	Manesty's Lane
B3	Mann Island
C1	Marlborough Street
C1	Marybone
E4	Maryland Street
C2	Mathew Street
C1	Midghall Street
C2	Moorfields
F2	Moss Street
E3	Mount Pleasant
E5	Mount Street
F4	Mulberry Street
F4	Myrtle Street
C1	Naylor Street
D5	Nelson Street
E1	New Islington
A2	New Quay
D3	Newington
C3	North John Street
C2	North Street

E2	Norton Street
F2	Oakes Street
B1	Old Hall Street
B1	Old Leeds Street
E4	Oldham Street
F4	Oxford Street
A1	Paisley Street
B1	Pall Mall
C4	Paradise Street
C4	Park Lane
D3	Parker Street
F3	Peach Street
E2	Pembroke Street
C3	Peters Lane
E5	Pilgrim Street
E3	Pomona Street
F2	Prescot Street
C2	Preston Street
B1	Prussia Street
D2	Pudsey Street
D3	Raneleigh Street
D3	Renshaw Street
E4	Rice Street
C3	Richmond Street
A1	Roberts Street
E4	Rodney Street
E4	Roscoe Street
E3	Royal Mail Street
B2	Rumford Street
E3	Russell Street
D1	St Anne Street
D2	St Georges Place
D5	St James Street
D2	St Johns Lane
D1	St Josephs Crescent
E2	St Vincent Street
E1	Salisbury Street
B4	Salthouse Quay
F5	Sandon Street
C3	School Lane
D4	Seel Street

E2	Seymour Street
F1	Shaw Street
C5	Shaws Alley
C2	Sir Thomas Street
D3	Skelhorne Street
D4	Slater Street
C2	Smithfield Street
E1	Soho Street
C3	South John Street
C5	Sparling Street
E1	Springfield
E2	Stafford Street
C2	Stanley Street
B3	Strand Street
D4	Suffolk Street
C4	Surrey Street
C5	Tabley Street
C3	Tarleton Street
B2	Tempest Hey
C3	Temple Court
C2	Temple Street
B3	The Strand
B2	Tithebarn Street
D1	Tom Mann Close
E3	Trowbridge Street
C2	Trueman Street
B2	Union Street
E5	Upper Duke Street
C4	Upper Frederick Street
D5	Upper Pitt Street
C1	Vauxhall Road
C2	Vernon Street
C3	Victoria Street
E1	Wakefield Street
C4	Wapping
B3	Water Street
A1	Waterloo Road
C3	Whitechapel
C3	Williamson Street
D4	Wood Street
C4	York Street

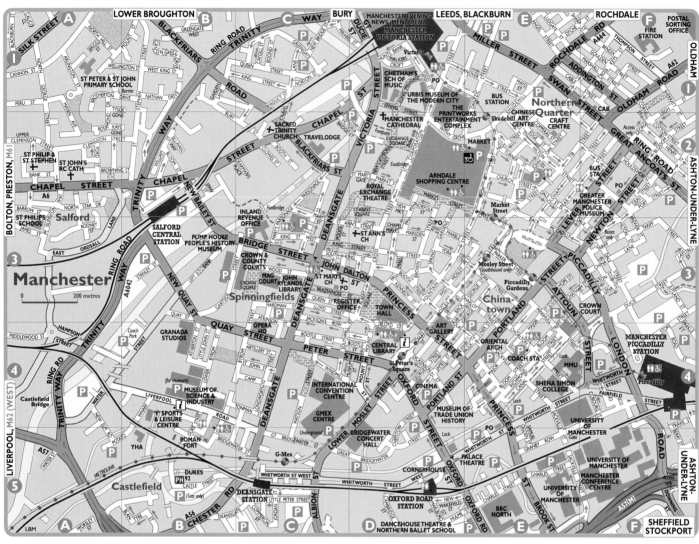

Manchester

Manchester is found on atlas page **326 B5**

E1	Addington Street	B2	Bury Street	F5	Downing Street	F3	Jutland Street	D5	New Wakefield Street	E5	Samuel Ogden Street
D3	Albert Square	C4	Byrom Street	F3	Ducie Street	A2	Kays Gardens	F3	Newton Street	E1	Sharp Street
C5	Albion Street	E1	Cable Street	B5	Duke Street	D3	Kennedy Street	D3	Nicholas Street	F1	Sherratt Street
E1	Angel Street	D5	Cambridge Street	E1	Dyche Street	C1	King Street	D2	Norfolk Street	E2	Shudehill
A1	Arlington Street	C4	Camp Street	A3	East Ordsall Lane	C3	King Street	A1	North George Street	A1	Silk Street
C4	Artillery Street	E4	Canal Street	E2	Edge Street	C3	King Street West	A1	North Hill Street	B2	Sillavan Way
B4	Atherton Street	A1	Cannon Street	D2	Exchange Square	F3	Laystall Street	A2	North Star Drive	C3	South King Street
C3	Atkinson Street	B1	Canon Green Drive	F4	Fairfield Street	B3	Left Bank	C1	Norton Street	C4	Southmill Street
E3	Aytoun Street	B5	Castle Street	F4	Faulkner Street	F3	Lena Street	E2	Oak Street	F4	Sparkle Street
E3	Back George Street	C1	Caygill Street	D1	Fennel Street	E3	Lever Street	F1	Oldham Road	B2	Spaw Street
E3	Back Piccadilly	A2	Chapel Street	A2	Ford Street	B4	Little John Street	E2	Oldham Street	E2	Spear Street
A2	Bank Street	D3	Chapel Walks	D3	Fountain Street	C5	Little Peter Street	E5	Oxford Road	D3	Spring Gardens
A2	Barrow Street	E5	Charles Street	B1	Garden Lane	B4	Liverpool Road	D4	Oxford Street	B3	Stanley Street
F1	Bendix Street	E3	Charlotte Street	B3	Gartside Street	C3	Lloyd Street	D3	Pall Mall	F4	Store Street
F5	Berry Street	E3	Chatham Street	F2	George Leigh Street	F4	London Road	E3	Parker Street	E1	Swan Street
A1	Blackburn Street	D5	Chepstow Street	D4	George Street	D1	Long Millgate	C2	Parsonage	F3	Tariff Street
B1	Blackfriars Road	B5	Chester Road	F1	Goulden Street	C4	Longworth Street	F3	Paton Street	F1	Thompson Street
C2	Blackfriars Street	F3	China Lane	E5	Granby Row	B4	Lower Byrom Street	A1	Peru Street	E2	Tib Street
B5	Blantyre Street	E4	Chorlton Street	C1	Gravel Lane	C5	Lower Mosley Street	C4	Peter Street	D1	Todd Street
B2	Bloom Street	E2	Church Street	F2	Great Ancoats Street	E4	Ludgate Street	E3	Piccadilly	C4	Tonman Street
E4	Bloom Street	A2	Cleminson Street	C5	Great Bridgewater Street	E4	Major Street	C3	Police Street	F4	Travis Street
F2	Blossom Street	C2	Clowes Street	D1	Great Ducie Street	D3	Marble Street	F2	Port Street	A4	Trinity Way
F4	Boad Street	F4	Cobourg Street	D5	Great Marlborough Street	D2	Market Street	E4	Portland Street	E2	Turner Street
C1	Boond Street	C5	Commercial Street	C1	Greengate	D3	Marsden Street	A5	Potato Wharf	A1	Tysoe Gardens
C2	Booth Street	E2	Copperas Street	B1	Greengate West	F1	Marshall Street	D3	Princess Street	A2	Upper Cleminson Street
D3	Booth Street	F1	Cornell Street	A4	Hampson Street	A1	Mayan Avenue	B4	Quay Street	C1	Viaduct Street
C4	Bootle Street	D2	Corporation Street	E1	Hanover Street	E1	Mayes Street	C1	Queen Street	C2	Victoria Bridge Street
C3	Brazennose Street	F2	Cotton Street	C3	Hardman Street	A4	Middlewood Street	C3	Queen Street	D2	Victoria Street
F3	Brewer Street	F1	Cross Keys Street	F2	Henry Street	E1	Miller Street	E4	Richmond Street	D1	Walkers Croft
C3	Bridge Street	D3	Cross Street	E2	High Street	E3	Minshull Street	E1	Rochdale Road	A4	Water Street
B5	Bridgewater Street	E2	Dale Street	E2	Hilton Street	C1	Mirabel Street	A3	Rodney Street	C4	Watson Street
A1	Briggs Street	E1	Dantzic Street	E3	Hope Street	D4	Mosley Street	A2	Rosamond Drive	B1	Wellington Street
E5	Brook Street	F2	Dean Street	F2	Houldsworth Street	B1	Mount Street	E4	Sackville Street	B1	West King Street
A1	Brotherton Drive	C4	Deansgate	D5	Hulme Street	D4	Mount Street	D2	St Ann's Square	D3	West Mosley Street
D3	Brown Street	C2	Dearman's Place	D1	Hunts Bank	D4	Museum Street	C3	St Ann's Street	E5	Whitworth Street
A2	Browning Street	D4	Dickenson Street	A2	Islington Way	B1	Nathan Drive	D4	St James Street	C5	Whitworth Street West
				A3	Jackson's Row	B2	New Bailey Street	C4	St John Street	B2	William Street
				C3	James Street	C1	New Bridge Street	C3	St Mary's Gate	C4	Windmill Street
				C3	John Dalton Street	A4	New Elm Road	C3	St Mary's Parsonage	D2	Withy Grove
				E2	John Street	D2	New Market	C2	St Mary's Street	C3	Wood Street
				C5	Jordan Street	B3	New Quay Street	B2	St Stephen Street	D3	York Street

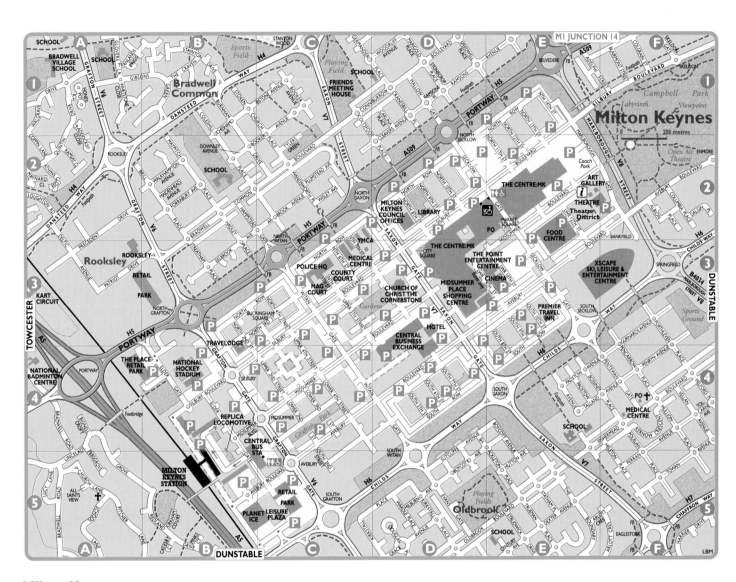

Milton Keynes

Milton Keynes is found on atlas page **168 A2**

E1	Adelphi Street	A2	Dansteed Way	E2	Lower 12th Street	C2	Plumstead Avenue	B1	The Craven
F2	Albion Place	A2	Deltic Avenue	A5	Lucy Lane	F4	Polruan Place	F4	Tolcarne Avenue
A5	All Saints View	E5	Dexter Avenue	B2	Maidenhead Avenue	F3	Porthleven Place	F5	Towan Avenue
C2	Arbrook Avenue	D5	Douglas Place	D1	Mallow Gate	A4	Portway	A1	Tranlands Brigg
E5	Arlott Crescent	B2	Downley Avenue	D1	Marigold Place	A3	Precedent Drive	E5	Trueman Place
A2	Athins Close	A5	Ebbsgrove	E2	Market Square	A2	Quintin Drive	C2	Tylers Green
C5	Avebury Boulevard	B3	Eelbrook Avenue	E2	Marlborough Gate	A2	Ramsay Close	C4	Upper 2nd Street
A4	Bignell Croft	B4	Elder Gate	E1	Marlborough Street	D1	Ramsons Avenue	C4	Upper 4th Street
F1	Blairmont Street	D5	Evans Gate	A2	Maynard Close	D1	Ramsons Place	C3	Upper 5th Street
B2	Booker Avenue	F4	Fishermead Boulevard	B2	Maypitch Place	B5	Redland Drive	F4	Vellan Avenue
E4	Bossiney Place	B2	Forrabury Avenue	B4	Midsummer Boulevard	D3	Saxon Gate	A1	Walgrave Drive
D5	Boycott Avenue	C1	Germander Place	D5	Milburn Avenue	C1	Saxon Street	B2	Walkhampton Avenue
B2	Bradwell Common	A1	Gibsons Green	F4	Mullion Place	E4	Saxon Street	C2	Wandsworth Place
	Boulevard	A1	Glovers Lane	B3	North 2nd Street	A5	School Lane	D5	Wardle Place
A5	Bradwell Road	D5	Grace Avenue	C3	North 3rd Street	D2	Secklow Gate	A1	Whetstone Close
B2	Brill Place	B4	Grafton Gate	C3	North 4th Street	D4	Shackleton Place	C2	Wisley Avenue
B3	Buckingham Square	A1	Grafton Street	C3	North 5th Street	B4	Silbury Boulevard	C3	Witan Gate
B1	Burnham Drive	F3	Gurnards Avenue	C3	North 6th Street	F1	Skeldon Gate	D1	Woodruff Avenue
D1	Caruna Place	B2	Hadley Place	C2	North 7th Street	C5	South 2nd Street		
B5	Catesby Court	B2	Hampstead Gate	D2	North 8th Street	D4	South 5th Street		
E5	Century Avenue	F5	Harrier Drive	D2	North 9th Street	D4	South 6th Street		
F5	Chaffron Way	F4	Helford Place	D2	North 10th Street	D4	South 7th Street		
B1	Chesham Avenue	F5	Helston Place	E2	North 11th Street	E3	South 8th Street		
D5	Childs Way	A1	Honey Pot Close	E1	North 12th Street	E3	South 9th Street		
A5	Church Lane	E5	Hutton Avenue	E1	North 13th Street	E3	South 10th Street		
D3	City Square	C1	Ibstone Avenue	E1	North 14th Street	D4	South Row		
D1	Cleavers Avenue	F4	Kernow Crescent	B3	North Row	D1	Speedwell Place		
B1	Coleshill Place	B5	Kirkham Court	D5	Oldbrook Boulevard	B1	Stainton Drive		
F1	Colgrain Street	C5	Kirkstall Place	E4	Padstow Avenue	E5	Statham Place		
C1	Coltsfoot Place	A5	Lincelade Grove	A3	Patriot Drive	B1	Stokenchurch Place		
F2	Columbia Place	A2	Loughton Road	F4	Pencarrow Place	D1	Stonecrop Place		
C1	Conniburrow Boulevard	C4	Lower 2nd Street	F4	Penryn Avenue	B3	Streatham Place		
A2	Coppin Lane	C4	Lower 3rd Street	F4	Pentewan Gate	E5	Strudwick Drive		
A1	Craddocks Close	C4	Lower 4th Street	F5	Perran Avenue	D5	Sutcliffe Avenue		
D1	Cranesbill Place	D3	Lower 9th Street	B5	Pinks Court	E4	Talland Avenue		
F2	Dalgin Place	E3	Lower 10th Street	A5	Pitcher Lane	E5	The Boundary		

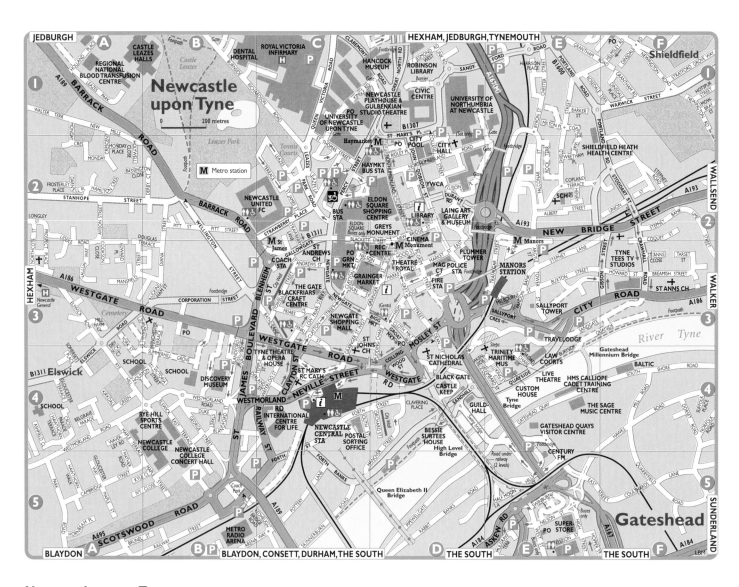

Newcastle upon Tyne

Newcastle upon Tyne is found on atlas page **405 F2**

D4 Akenside Hill	E1 Coppice Way	A5 Gloucester Way	C2 Leazes Park Road	D4 Orchard Street	A4 Somerset Place
E2 Albert Street	F2 Coquet Street	D3 Grainger Street	C2 Leazes Terrace	E3 Pandon Bank	F4 South Shore Road
B5 Arena Way	B3 Corporation Street	C3 Grainger Street West	A3 Liddle Road	A5 Park Road	C4 South Street
E3 Argyle Street	F5 Coulthards Lane	E1 Grantham Road	F2 Lime Street	C4 Peel Lane	A2 Stanhope Street
A4 Ashfield Close	F3 Crawhall Road	D1 Great North Road	D1 Link Road	C2 Percy Street	F2 Stepney Bank
E5 Askew Road	A4 Cross Parade	D3 Grey Street	E4 Lombard Street	D3 Pilgrim Street	E3 Stepney Lane
A2 Avison Street	A2 Darnell Place	D3 Groat Market	A2 Longley Street	D5 Pipewellgate	F2 Stepney Road
E1 Barker Street	D3 Dean Street	E5 Half Moon Lane	C3 Low Friar Street	B2 Pitt Street	F2 Stoddart Street
A1 Barrack Road	B3 Derby Court	A2 Hamilton Crescent	A3 Mansfield Street	E1 Portland Road	C3 Stowell Street
A2 Bassington Close	B3 Diana Street	D5 Hanover Street	B5 Maple Street	C5 Pottery Lane	F1 Stratford Grove Way
C3 Bath Lane	F1 Dinsdale Place	E1 Harrison Place	A4 Maple Terrace	A2 Prospect Place	C2 Strawberry Lane
A4 Belgrave Parade	F1 Dinsdale Road	F4 Hawks Road	D3 Market Street	D4 Pudding Chare	C2 Strawberry Place
D3 Bigg Market	F4 Dorset Road	A4 Hawthorn Terrace	D3 Market Street East	F5 Quarryfield Road	F4 Suffolk Place
C2 Blackett Street	B3 Douglas Terrace	A5 Hawthorn Walk	A5 Mather Road	E4 Quayside	B4 Summerhill Grove
B4 Blandford Square	A4 Drybeck Court	F1 Helmsley Road	E3 Melbourne Street	C1 Queen Victoria Road	B3 Summerhill Street
B4 Blandford Street	B4 Duke Street	E2 Henry Square	A3 Mill Farm Close	D5 Rabbit Banks Road	B4 Sunderland Street
C3 Blenheim Street	D2 Durant Road	D3 High Bridge	F4 Mill Road	B5 Railway Street	E5 Swinburne Street
F3 Breamish Street	E5 East Street	E5 High Street	E1 Milton Place	C5 Redheugh Bridge Road	F3 Tarset Street
E4 Broad Chare	A3 Edward Place	E5 Hills Street	A2 Monday Crescent	B1 Richardson Road	C4 Temple Street
A5 Brunel Street	C2 Eldon Square	A1 Holland Place	A2 Monday Place	D2 Ridley Place	D4 The Close
B3 Buckingham Street	D2 Ellison Place	A2 Holywell Close	D3 Mosley Street	E2 Rock Terrace	E3 Tower Street
B1 Burnside	E5 Ellison Street	D3 Hood Street	F1 Mowbray Street	E1 Rosedale Terrace	E3 Trafalgar Street
E4 Buryside	B4 Elswick East Terrace	E5 Hopper Street	E5 Mulgrave Terrace	A4 Rye Hill	F2 Union Street
E3 Buxton Street	A4 Elswick Road	A5 Hornbeam Place	C3 Nelson Street	A3 St Andrews Street	A3 Vallum Way
E1 Byron Street	A3 Elswick Row	F1 Hotspur Street	E5 Nelson Street (Gateshead)	F3 St Anns Close	B4 Victoria Street
A5 Cambridge Street	E2 Falconar Street	A4 Houston Street	C4 Neville Street	B4 St James Boulevard	A1 Walter Terrace
E1 Chester Street	C3 Fenckle Street	F3 Howard Street	D2 New Bridge Road	C2 St James Street	F1 Warwick Street
E3 City Road	C5 Forth Banks	A5 Ivy Close	E2 New Bridge Street	D1 St Mary's Place	C4 Waterloo Street
C1 Claremont Road	C4 Forth Street	D1 Jesmond Road West	A1 New Mills	C2 St Thomas Street	A4 Waverley Road
D4 Clavering Place	C3 Friars Street	D2 John Dobson Street	C3 Newgate	E3 Sallyport Crescent	B2 Wellington Street
C4 Clayton Street	A2 Frosterley Place	C1 King's Road	F1 Newington Road	E3 Sandgate	E5 West Street
D3 Cloth Market	C3 Gallowgate	E4 King Street	F4 Norfolk Road	D4 Sandhill	A3 Westgate Road
D2 College Street	E4 Gateshead Quay	A4 Kirkdale Green	A3 Northcote Street	D1 Sandyford Road	A4 Westmorland Road
D4 Collingwood Street	B4 George Street	A5 Kyle Close	D2 Northumberland Road	A5 Scotswood Road	B3 Winchester Terrace
A3 Cookson Close	F3 Gibson Street	C2 Leazes Lane	D2 Northumberland Street	E2 Shield Street	E2 Wretham Place
E2 Copland Terrace	A4 Gloucester Terrace	A1 Leazes Park	C3 Nun Street	C5 Skinnerburn Road	A3 York Street

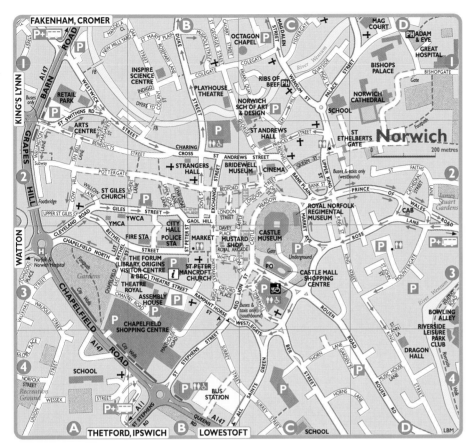

Norwich

Norwich is found on atlas page **250 A3**

C4	All Saints Green	C2	Opie Street
C2	Bank Plain	B3	Orford Place
C2	Bank Street	C1	Palace Street
A1	Barn Road	C1	Pigg Lane
B2	Bedford Street	A2	Pottergate
C4	Ber Street	D2	Prince of Wales Road
A3	Bethel Street	C2	Princes Street
D1	Bishopgate	C1	Quayside
B3	Brigg Street	C2	Queen Street
B1	Calvert Street	B4	Queens Road
C3	Castle Meadow	B3	Rampant Horse Street
C2	Castle Street	B3	Red Lion Street
D2	Cathedral Street	C2	Redwell Street
B3	Chantry Road	D3	Rose Lane
A3	Chapelfield East	B1	Rosemary Lane
A3	Chapelfield North	C3	Rouen Road
A3	Chapelfield Road	B3	Royal Arcade
B2	Charing Cross	B2	St Andrews Street
A3	Cleveland Road	D3	St Ann Lane
B1	Colegate	A2	St Benedicts Street
B1	Coslany Street	D2	St Faiths Lane
A2	Cow Hill	B1	St Georges Street
B3	Davey Place	D3	St John Street
B2	Dove Street	A2	St Margarets Street
B1	Duke Street	B1	St Marys Plain
C1	Elm Hill	B3	St Peter Street
B2	Exchange Street	B4	St Stephens Road
C1	Fishergate	B4	St Stephens Street
C1	Friars Quay	A1	St Swithins Road
B2	Gaol Hill	B4	Surrey Street
C4	Garden Street	A2	Ten Bell Lane
A2	Giles Street	B3	Theatre Street
A2	Grapes Hill	C4	Thorn Lane
B3	Haymarket	C3	Timberhill
C4	Horns Lane	A4	Union Street
C2	King Street	A3	Unthank Road
A3	Little Bethel Street	B2	Upper Goat Lane
B2	London Street	C2	Upper King Street
B2	Lower Goat Lane	A2	Upper St Giles Street
C1	Magdalen Street	A3	Vauxhall Street
B4	Malthouse Road	A3	Walpole Street
C2	Market Avenue	A2	Wellington Lane
D3	Mountergate	C1	Wensum Street
D4	Music House Lane	A4	Wessex Street
B1	Muspole Street	C3	Westlegate
A1	New Mills Yard	A1	Westwick Street
A4	Norfolk Street	B3	White Lion Street
B1	Oak Street	A2	Willow Lane

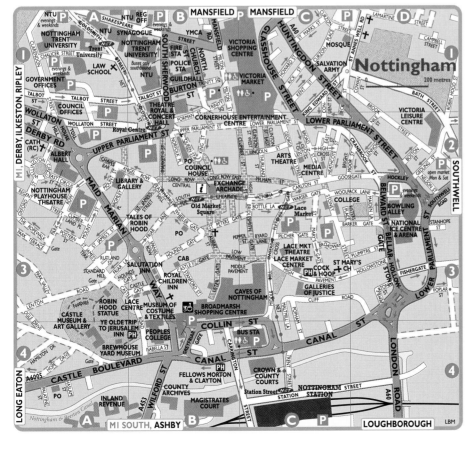

Nottingham

Nottingham is found on atlas page **276 C2**

B3	Albert Street	C1	Huntingdon Street
B2	Angel Row	C1	King Edward Street
C3	Barker Gate	B2	King Street
D1	Bath Street	D2	Lennox Street
B2	Beastmarket Hill	C2	Lincoln Street
C1	Beck Street	B3	Lister Gate
D3	Bellargate	D4	London Road
D2	Belward Street	B2	Long Row Central
C2	Bridlesmith Gate	B2	Long Row East
C2	Broad Street	B3	Low Pavement
A2	Bromley Place	C2	Lower Parliament Street
D1	Brook Street	A2	Maid Marion Way
B1	Burton Street	B1	Mansfield Road
B4	Canal Street	B2	Market Street
C2	Carlton Street	C3	Middle Hill
B4	Carrington Street	B1	Milton Street
A4	Castle Boulevard	A3	Mount Street
B3	Castle Gate	C2	Old Lenton Street
A3	Castle Road	A3	Park Row
A1	Chaucer Street	C2	Pelham Street
B2	Cheapside	D3	Pemberton Street
C3	Cliff Road	C3	Pilcher Gate
C2	Clinton Street East	D3	Plumptre Street
A1	Clarendon Street	B2	Queen Street
C2	Clumber Street	D1	St Annes Well Road
B4	Collin Street	A3	St James's Street
C1	Conuent Street	C1	St Marks Street
D2	Cranbrook Street	C2	St Mary's Gate
A2	Cumberland Place	B3	St Peters Gate
C1	Curzon Place	A1	Shakespeare Street
A2	Derby Road	B2	South Parade
A2	East Circus Street	B1	South Sherwood Street
C2	East Street	C4	Station Street
D3	Fishergate	C2	Stoney Street
C3	Fletcher Gate	A1	Talbot Street
B2	Forman Street	C2	Thurland Street
A3	Friar Lane	A2	Toll House Hill
D2	Gedling Street	C4	Trent Street
C2	George Street	B1	Trinity Square
C1	Glasshouse Street	A2	Upper Parliament Street
A1	Goldsmith Street	C2	Victoria Street
C2	Goosegate	C2	Warser Gate
B4	Greyfriar Gate	C3	Weekday Cross
C2	Heathcote Street	A2	Wellington Circus
C3	High Pavement	B2	Wheeler Gate
C2	High Street	B4	Wilford Street
D2	Hockley	A2	Wollaton Street
D3	Hollowstone	C2	Woolpack Lane

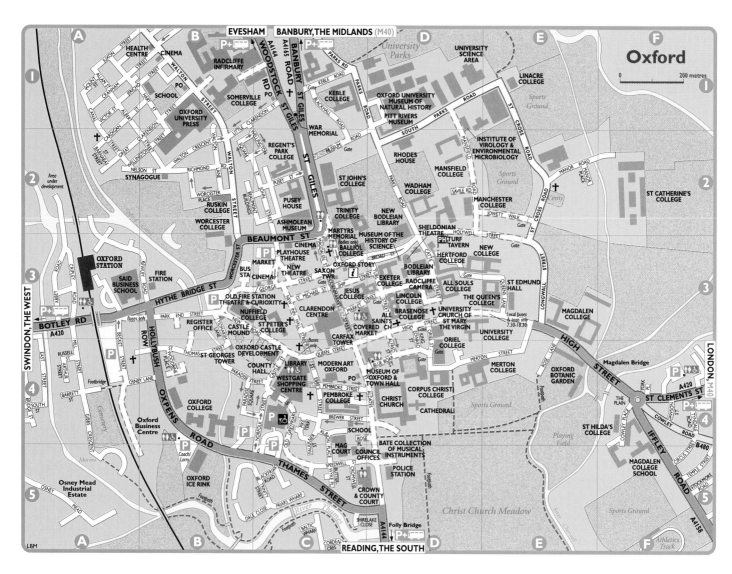

Oxford

Oxford is found on atlas page **140 B3**

A3	Abbey Road	C5	Faulkner Street
A1	Albert Street	C5	Friars Wharf
C4	Albion Place	C3	George Street
D4	Alfred Street	A4	Gibbs Crescent
A1	Allam Street	A2	Great Clarendon Street
A4	Arthur Street	B1	Hart Street
C5	Baltic Wharf	D3	High Street
C1	Banbury Road	B3	Hollybush Row
A4	Barrett Street	D2	Holywell Street
B2	Beaumont Buildings	B3	Hythe Bridge Street
C3	Beaumont Street	F4	Iffley Road
A3	Becket Street	A1	Jericho Street
C5	Blackfriars Road	E2	Jowett Walk
C1	Blackhall Road	A1	Juxon Street
D4	Blue Boar Street	C1	Keble Road
A3	Botley Road	D3	King Edward Street
F4	Boulter Street	B2	Little Clarendon Street
C4	Brewer Street	E3	Longwall Street
A4	Bridge Street	C3	Magdalen Street
D3	Broad Street	E2	Manor Place
C5	Butterwyke Place	E2	Manor Road
A1	Canal Street	D2	Mansfield Road
A2	Cardigan Street	C3	Market Street
C4	Castle Street	D4	Merton Street
D3	Catte Street	A4	Mill Street
F5	Circus Street	A1	Mount Street
C5	Cobden Crescent	C2	Museum Road
C3	Cornmarket Street	A2	Nelson Street
F4	Cowley Place	C3	New Inn Hall Street
F4	Cowley Road	B3	New Road
A1	Cranham Street	C4	Norfolk Street
A3	Cripley Road	C4	Old Greyfriars Street
C5	Cromwell Street	D3	Oriel Street
C5	Dale Close	A4	Osney Lane
F4	Dawson Street	A5	Osney Mead
A4	East Street	B4	Oxpens Road

B4	Paradise Square	F4	Tyndale Road
B4	Paradise Street	A1	Victor Street
B3	Park End Street	B2	Walton Crescent
C1	Parks Road	B2	Walton Lane
C4	Pembroke Street	B1	Walton Street
C4	Pike Terrace	C2	Wellington Square
C2	Pusey Street	A2	Wellington Street
C4	Queen Street	B4	Woodbine Place
E3	Queens Lane	C1	Woodstock Road
B3	Rewley Road	B2	Worcester Place
B2	Richmond Road	B3	Worcester Street
E4	Rose Lane	F4	York Place
C4	Rose Place		
A4	Russell Street		
D4	St Aldates		
A2	St Barnabas Street		
F4	St Clements Street		
E1	St Cross Road		
C4	St Ebbe's Street		
C1	St Giles		
C2	St John Street		
C3	St Michael Street		
B4	St Thomas Street		
D2	Savile Road		
C3	Ship Street		
C5	Shirelake Close		
D1	South Parks Road		
A4	South Street		
C5	Speedwell Street		
F5	Stockmore Road		
F5	Temple Street		
C5	Thames Street		
F4	The Plain		
B3	Tidmarsh Lane		
C5	Trinity Street		
D3	Turl Street		

University Colleges

D3	All Souls College
C3	Balliol College
D3	Brasenose College
D4	Christ Church College
D4	Corpus Christi College
D3	Exeter College
D3	Hertford College
C3	Jesus College
C1	Keble College
E1	Linacre College
D3	Lincoln College
E3	Magdalen College
D2	Manchester College
D2	Mansfield College
E4	Merton College
D3	New College
B3	Nuffield College
D4	Oriel College
C4	Pembroke College
E3	Queen's College
C2	Regent's Park College
B2	Ruskin College
F2	St Catherine's College
E3	St Edmund Hall
F4	St Hilda's College
C2	St John's College
C3	St Peter's College
B1	Somerville College
C2	Trinity College
D3	University College
D2	Wadham College
B2	Worcester College

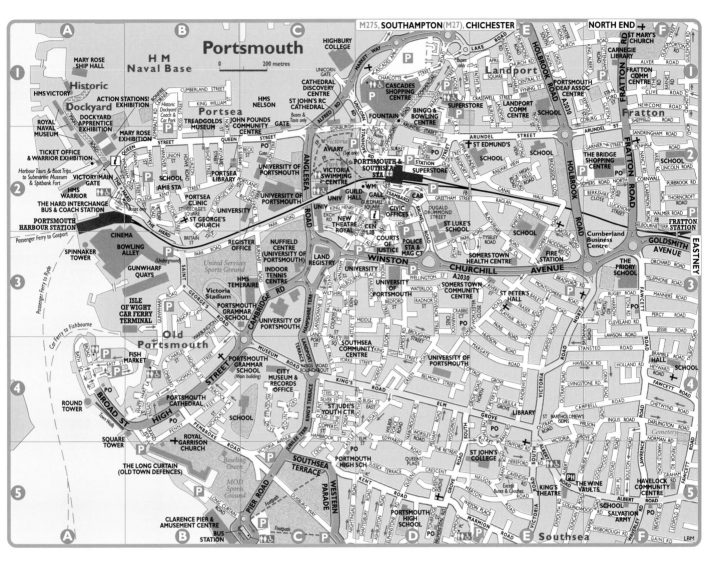

Portsmouth

Portsmouth is found on atlas page **52 A4**

B2	Admiralty Road	F4	Campbell Road	E5	Exmouth Road
E5	Albany Road	E2	Canal Walk	F3	Fawcett Road
E5	Albert Grove	E3	Carlisle Road	C4	Flint Street
E5	Albert Road	D1	Cascades Approach	E3	Fraser Road
D3	Alec Rose Lane	C4	Castle Road	F1	Fratton Road
E1	Alexandra Road	E5	Cavendish Road	F2	Garnier Street
C1	Alfred Road	E1	Charles Street	C4	Gold Street
F1	Alver Road	D1	Charlotte Street	F3	Goldsmith Avenue
C2	Angelsea Road	E5	Chelsea Road	F5	Goodwood Road
E1	April Square	F4	Chetwynd Road	D4	Great Southsea Street
F2	Ariel Road	E1	Church Road	D4	Green Road
B3	Armory Lane	F2	Claremont Road	D2	Greetham Street
E2	Arundel Street	F3	Cleveland Road	D3	Grosvenor Street
D5	Ashburton Road	F1	Clifton Street	E4	Grove Road North
C3	Astley Street	F1	Clive Road	D5	Grove Road South
B2	Aylward Street	F1	Coburg Street	D2	Guildhall Square
E3	Baileys Road	E5	Collingwood Road	D2	Guildhall Walk
A4	Bath Square	D2	Commercial Road	B3	Gunwharf Road
D4	Belmont Street	F2	Cornwall Road	C4	Hambrook Street
B2	Bishop Street	D4	Cottage Grove	C3	Hampshire Terrace
E2	Blackfriars Road	E2	Cottage View	B2	Hanover Street
C4	Blount Road	E1	Crasswell Street	F5	Harold Road
B1	Bonfire Corner	B1	Cross Street	B2	Havant Street
F5	Boulton Road	B1	Cumberland Street	E4	Havelock Road
F4	Bramble Road	B2	Curzon Howe Road	B2	Hawke Street
E2	Bridgeside Close	F4	Darlington Road	F4	Hereford Road
D2	Bridport Street	D2	Dugald Drummond Street	F4	Heyward Road
F3	Britannia Road	C5	Duisburg Way	B4	High Street
F3	Britannia Road North	E5	Duncan Road	B4	Highbury Street
A4	Broad Street	D2	Durham Street	E1	Holbrook Road
D3	Brougham Street	D3	Earlsdon Street	F4	Hudson Road
D1	Buck Street	A4	East Street	D3	Hyde Park Road
E1	Buriton Street	C2	Edinburgh Road	F4	Inglis Road
C3	Burnaby Road	D4	Eldon Street	D2	Isambard Brunel Road
B2	Butcher Street	D4	Elm Grove	D1	Jacobs Street
C3	Cambridge Road	D5	Elphinstone Road	F3	Jessie Road
				C4	Jubilee Terrace
				D5	Kent Road
				B2	Kent Street
				F1	King Albert Street
				B4	King Charles Street

C2	King Henry I Street	B4	Oyster Street	C5	Southsea Terrace
D4	King Street	E3	Pains Road	E5	Stafford Road
B1	King William Street	D5	Palmerston Road	D2	Stanhope Road
C4	King's Road	D1	Paradise Street	F4	Stansted Road
C4	King's Terrace	B3	Park Road	D2	Station Street
E1	Lake Road	C3	Park Street	C4	Stone Street
C3	Landport Street	B4	Peacock Lane	D2	Surrey Street
C4	Landport Terrace	D4	Pelham Road	D5	Sussex Road
C3	Lansdowne Street	B4	Pembroke Road	F3	Telephone Road
F5	Lawrence Road	F2	Penhale Road	D1	Temple Street
F3	Lawson Road	B4	Penny Street	A2	The Hard
C2	Lion Terrace	C5	Pier Road	D5	The Retreat
C4	Little Southsea Street	E3	Playfair Road	E4	The Thicket
E4	Livingstone Road	B2	Queen Street	D1	Unicorn Road
B4	Lombard Street	D5	Queens Crescent	E1	Union Place
B5	Long Curtain Road	D5	Queens Grove	D2	Upper Arundel Street
E1	Lords Street	D5	Queens Place	C5	Victoria Avenue
F4	Lorne Road	E2	Raglan Street	E4	Victoria Grove
F2	Lucknow Street	E2	Railway View	E4	Victoria Road North
A1	Main Road	F3	Rugby Road	E5	Victoria Road South
F3	Manners Road	E4	St Andrews Road	B2	Victory Road
E4	Margate Road	E4	St Davids Road	F2	Vivash Road
D1	Market Way	D4	St Edward's Road	F2	Walmer Road
E5	Marmion Road	E1	St Faith's Road	C3	Waltham Street
C3	Melbourne Place	B3	Saint George's Road	B3	Warblington Street
E5	Merton Road	B2	St George's Way	D3	Warwick Crescent
D3	Middle Street	D4	St James's Road	D3	Waterloo Street
E2	Milford Road	C2	St James's Street	F5	Waverley Road
E3	Montgomerie Road	B4	St Nicholas Street	D3	Wellington Street
C4	Museum Road	C3	St Paul's Road	C5	Western Parade
F2	Nancy Road	C4	St Paul's Street	B4	White Hart Lane
F5	Napier Road	E4	St Peter's Grove	B2	Wickham Street
E5	Nelson Road	B4	St Thomas's Street	D2	Willis Street
F1	Newcome Road	F2	Sandringham Road	F4	Wilson Grove
D1	Jacobs Street	F2	Selbourne Terrace	C3	Wiltshire Street
C5	Nightingale Road	D5	Shaftesbury Road	D3	Winston Churchill Avenue
D4	Norfolk Street	F1	Sheffield Road	F5	Wisborough Road
F4	Norman Road	C4	Silver Street	D4	Woodpath
B2	North Street	D2	Slindon Street	C4	Woodville Drive
F3	Orchard Road	E3	Somers Road	D4	Yarborough Road
E4	Outram Road	F2	Somers Road North	C4	Yorke Street
F5	Oxford Road				

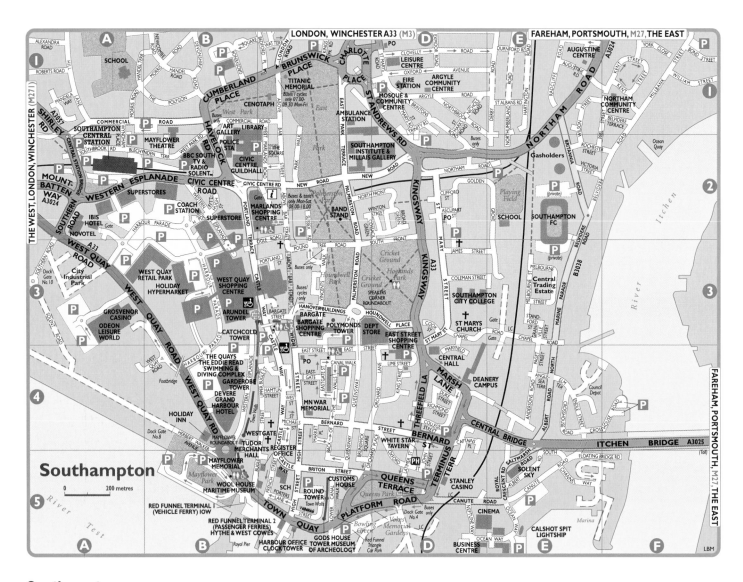

Southampton

Southampton is found on atlas page **50 D2**

C1	Above Bar Street
E4	Albert Road North
E5	Albert Road South
A1	Alexandra Road
E4	Andersons Road
E4	Anglesea Terrace
D1	Argyle Road
D2	Ascupart Street
E1	Augustine Road
C4	Back of the Walls
C3	Bargate Street
C1	Bedford Place
E2	Belvidere Road
F1	Belvidere Terrace
C4	Bernard Street
A2	Blechynden Terrace
F1	Bond Street
D1	Brintons Road
E2	Britannia Road
C5	Briton Street
D2	Broad Green
C1	Brunswick Place
C4	Brunswick Square
B5	Bugle Street
C4	Canal Walk
D5	Canute Road
D4	Captains Place
C3	Castle Way
D4	Central Bridge
A2	Central Station Bridge
E5	Channel Way
D3	Chapel Road
C1	Charlotte Place
B2	Civic Centre Road
D2	Clifford Street
D1	Clovelly Road

D3	Coleman Street
D4	College Street
A1	Commercial Road
D3	Cook Street
D2	Cossack Green
E4	Crosshouse Road
B1	Cumberland Place
E1	Derby Road
B1	Devonshire Road
D4	Duke Street
E1	Durnford Road
C1	East Park Terrace
C4	East Street
C4	Eastgate Street
E4	Elm Terrace
E4	Endle Street
D1	Exmoor Road
B2	Fitzhugh Street
E5	Floating Bridge Road
C5	French Street
E2	Golden Grove
E3	Granville Street
B1	Grosvenor Square
C4	Hamtun Street
B1	Handel Road
A1	Handel Terrace
C3	Hanover Buildings
A2	Harbour Parade
E1	Hartington Road
B2	Havelock Road
B4	Herbert Walker Avenue
C3	High Street
A1	Hill Lane
D3	Houndwell Place
F4	Itchen Bridge
D3	James Street

D5	John Street
F1	Kent Street
D4	King Street
C1	Kings Park Road
D2	Kingsway
D5	Latimer Street
D4	Lime Street
C1	London Road
C5	Lower Canal Walk
A1	Mandela Way
E3	Marine Parade
C4	Market Place
D4	Marsh Lane
D4	Maryfield
E3	Melbourne Street
F1	Millbank Street
A1	Morris Road
A2	Mountbatten Way
D5	Neptune Way
C2	New Road
B1	Newcombe Road
D1	Nichols Road
C2	North Front
D2	Northam Road
D1	Northbrook Road
E1	Northumberland Road
E5	Ocean Way
C2	Ogle Road
D4	Orchard Lane
C5	Orchard Place
D1	Oxford Avenue
D5	Oxford Street
E4	Paget Street
C2	Palmerston Road
C2	Park Walk
F1	Peel Street

C5	Platform Road
C5	Porters Lane
C3	Portland Street
B2	Portland Terrace
C3	Pound Tree Road
D5	Queens Terrace
C4	Queensway
E1	Radcliffe Road
D4	Richmond Street
A1	Roberts Road
E2	Rochester Street
E5	Royal Crescent Road
E1	St Albans Road
D1	St Andrews Road
D1	St Marks Road
D2	St Mary Street
D1	St Marys Road
C4	St Michaels Street
E5	Saltmarsh Road
A1	Shirley Road
A3	Solent Road
D3	South Front
A2	Southbrook Road
A2	Southern Road
E3	Standford Street
C2	Sussex Road
D5	Terminus Terrace
B1	The Polygon
C2	The Square
D4	Threefield Lane
C5	Town Quay
D1	Trinity Road
C4	Upper Bugle Street
E2	Victoria Street
C3	Vincents Walk
C1	Waterloo Terrace

C2	West Marlands Road
B2	West Park Road
A3	West Quay Road
C4	West Street
A2	Western Esplanade
F1	William Street
E1	Wilson Street
C5	Winkle Street
D2	Winton Street
A2	Wyndham Place
F1	York Close

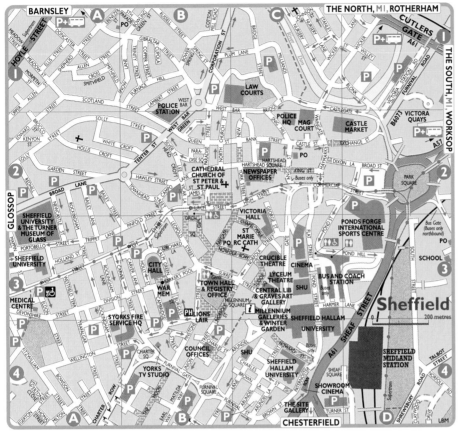

Sheffield

Sheffield is found on atlas page **314 D2**

A1	Allen Street	C2	King Street
C2	Angel Street	B1	Lambert Street
C4	Arundel Gate	B3	Leopold Street
C4	Arundel Street	A1	Meadow Street
A2	Bailey Lane	A4	Milton Street
B3	Balm Green	C2	New Street
C2	Bank Street	A2	Newcastle Street
B3	Barker's Pool	B3	Norfolk Row
D1	Blonk Street	C3	Norfolk Street
B1	Bower Spring	B2	North Church Street
C1	Bridge Street	C1	Nursery Street
A2	Broad Lane	B3	Orchard Square
D2	Broad Street	B2	Paradise Square
C4	Brown Street	B2	Paradise Street
B3	Burgess Street	D2	Park Square
B3	Cambridge Street	C4	Paternoster Row
B2	Campo Lane	B3	Pinfold Street
B3	Carver Street	B4	Pinstone Street
C2	Castle Street	B1	Plum Lane
C1	Castlegate	C3	Pond Street
C3	Chapel Walk	A3	Portobello Street
B4	Charles Street	B2	Queen Street
B4	Charter Square	A2	Rockingham Street
B2	Church Street	B1	Russell Street
C2	Commercial Street	B2	St James Street
B1	Corporation Street	A1	Scotland Street
A3	Devonshire Street	C4	Sheaf Square
A3	Division Street	A1	Shepherd Street
A1	Doncaster Street	C2	Snig Hill
A3	Eldon Street	B1	Snow Lane
D2	Exchange Street	A2	Solly Street
B4	Eyre Lane	D3	South Street
B3	Fargate	B1	Spring Street
A4	Fitzwilliam Street	C1	Stanley Street
C3	Flat Street	B3	Surrey Street
B1	Furnace Hill	B2	Townhead Street
D1	Furnival Road	A4	Trafalgar Street
B4	Furnival Street	A3	Trippet Lane
A2	Garden Street	C3	Tudor Square
C2	George Street	B4	Union Street
B1	Gibraltar Street	C2	Waingate
C3	Harmer Lane	A4	Wellington Street
B2	Hawley Street	B1	West Bar
C2	Haymarket	B2	West Bar Green
C2	High Street	A3	West Street
A2	Hollis Croft	D1	Wicker
B3	Holly Street	C1	Wicker Lane
A1	Hoyle Road	C2	York Street

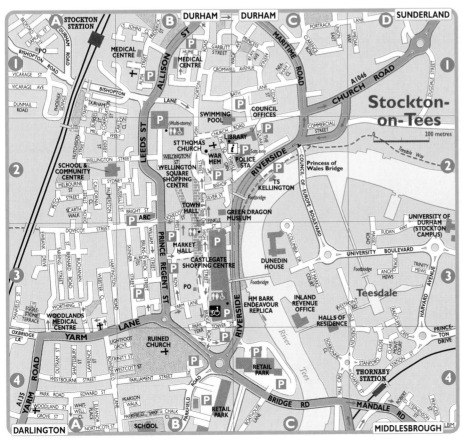

Stockton-on-Tees

Stockton-on-Tees is found on atlas page **396 B6**

B1	Allison Street	A2	Palmerston Street
B1	Alma Street	A4	Park Road
C1	Bath Lane	B3	Park Terrace
B2	Bishop Street	B4	Parkfield Road
A1	Bishopton Lane	B4	Parkfield Way
A1	Bishopton Road	B4	Parliament Street
C4	Boathouse Lane	A2	Petch Street
A4	Bowesfield Lane	A1	Phoenix Sidings
B3	Bridge Road	C1	Portrack Lane
B2	Bright Street	B3	Prince Regent Street
B3	Brunswick Street	C1	Princess Avenue
A3	Buchanan Street	D4	Princeton Drive
B4	Chalk Close	D3	Radcliffe Crescent
D4	Chapel Street	C3	Riverside
B2	Church Road	B2	Russell Street
D4	Claremont Court	C1	Ryan Avenue
C1	Clarence Row	A3	St Bernard Road
C3	Columbia Drive	B1	St Johns Close
C2	Commercial Street	C3	St Marks Court
A2	Corporation Street	A4	Shaftesbury Street
C2	Council of Europe Boulevard	B2	Silver Street
B1	Cromwell Avenue	B3	Skinner Street
A2	Derby Street	B2	Smith Street
A2	Dixon Street	A1	Stamp Street
A3	Dovecot Street	D4	Stanford Close
A1	Durham Road	D4	Station Street
A1	Durham Street	A2	Sydney Street
A4	Edward Street	A3	Tarring Street
A3	Ewbank Drive	B2	The Square
B3	Finkle Street	C2	Thistle Green
B1	Frederick Street	B3	Tower Street
D3	Fudan Way	C1	Union Street East
B1	Garbutt Street	D3	University Boulevard
A3	Hartington Road	A1	Vicarage Avenue
D3	Harvard Avenue	A1	Vicarage Street
B2	High Street	C1	Wade Avenue
B1	Hume Street	A3	Webster Close
A2	Hutchison Street	B2	Wellington Square
A4	Lawrence Street	A2	Wellington Street
B2	Leeds Street	B3	West Row
D4	Mandale Road	A4	Westbourne Street
C1	Maritime Road	C3	Westpoint Road
D3	Massey Road	B3	William Street
A2	Melbourne Street	A4	Woodland Street
A2	Mill Street West	A3	Worthing Street
B1	Norton Road	D3	Yale Crescent
A4	Outram Street	A4	Yarm Lane
A4	Oxbridge Lane	A4	Yarm Road

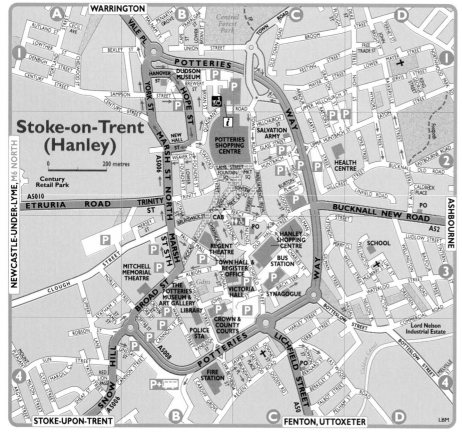

Stoke-on-Trent (Hanley)

Stoke-on-Trent (Hanley) is found on atlas page **292 A5**

B3	Albion Street	B2	Lower Foundry Street
B3	Bagnall Street	D1	Lower Mayer Street
D3	Balfour Street	C2	Market Lane
D1	Baskerville Street	C2	Market Square
C4	Berkeley Street	B2	Marsh Street North
B3	Bethesda Street	B3	Marsh Street South
C3	Birch Terrace	C1	Mayer Street
C3	Botteslow Street	C2	Meigh Street
B1	Brewery Street	A3	Morley Street
B3	Broad Street	D1	Mynors Street
C1	Broom Street	B2	New Hall Street
B3	Brunswick Street	C3	Old Hall Street
B1	Bryan Street	C1	Old Town Road
D2	Bucknall New Road	B3	Pall Mall
D2	Bucknall Old Road	C2	Parliament Row
C2	Burton Place	C2	Percy Street
B4	Cannon Street	B3	Piccadilly
A1	Century Street	D3	Picton Street
C3	Charles Street	A1	Portland Street
B3	Cheapside	B1	Potteries Way
A3	Clough Street	B2	Quadrant Road
A4	Clyde Street	B4	Raneleigh Street
D4	Commercial Road	C4	Regent Road
C4	Derby Street	A4	Robson Street
D3	Dresden Street	D2	St Ann Street
C4	Eastwood Road	D1	St John Street
D2	Eaton Street	A1	Sampson Street
A2	Etruria Road	A3	Slippery Lane
C1	Festing Street	A4	Snow Hill
B2	Foundry Street	B3	Stafford Street
B2	Fountain Square	A3	Statham Street
C2	Garth Street	A4	Sun Street
C3	Gilman Street	C4	Talbot Street
B2	Gitana Street	C2	Tontine Square
C2	Glass Street	C3	Tontine Street
C2	Goodson Street	C2	Town Road
C1	Grafton Street	B2	Trinity Street
B1	Hanover Street	B1	Union Street
C2	Hillchurch Street	C1	Upper Hillchurch Street
C2	Hillcrest Street	C2	Upper Huntbach Street
B1	Hope Street	B1	Vale Place
C2	Huntbach Street	B3	Warner Street
D1	Jervis Street	B2	Weaver Street
D1	John Bright Street	D3	Wellington Road
B3	John Street	D3	Wells Street
B2	Lamb Street	A4	Yates Street
C3	Lichfield Street	B1	York Street
B4	Lower Bethesda Street		

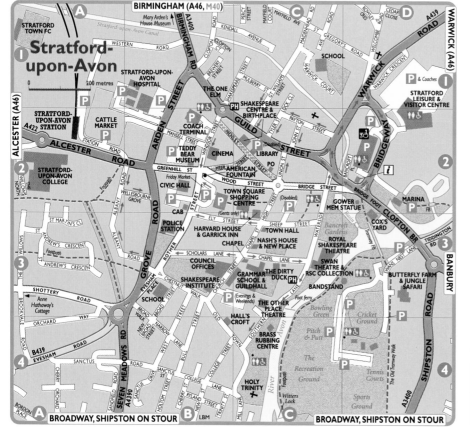

Stratford-upon-Avon

Stratford-upon-Avon is found on atlas page **190 C4**

A3	Albany Road	B4	New Broad Street
A2	Alcester Road	B4	New Street
B2	Arden Street	B3	Old Town
C1	Avenue Road	A4	Orchard Way
D2	Bancroft Place	C2	Payton Street
B1	Birmingham Road	C1	Percy Street
A4	Bordon Place	B3	Rother Street
B1	Brewery Street	D1	Rowley Crescent
D2	Bridge Foot	B4	Ryland Street
C2	Bridge Street	A3	St Andrew's Crescent
D2	Bridgeway	C1	St Gregory's Road
B3	Broad Street	A3	St Martin's Close
B3	Broad Walk	B4	Sanctus Drive
A3	Brookvale Road	A4	Sanctus Road
B4	Bull Street	B4	Sanctus Street
D1	Cedar Close	A4	Sandfield Road
C3	Chapel Lane	B3	Scholars Lane
C3	Chapel Street	A4	Seven Meadows Road
A4	Cherry Orchard	B1	Shakespeare Street
B4	Cherry Street	C3	Sheep Street
B3	Chestnut Walk	D4	Shipston Road
B3	Church Street	A3	Shottery Road
D3	Clopton Bridge	C4	Southern Lane
B1	Clopton Court	A2	Station Road
B1	Clopton Road	D3	Swans Nest Lane
B4	College Lane	A3	The Willows
B4	College Street	A2	The Willows North
B3	Ely Street	D3	Tiddington Road
B3	Evesham Place	B4	Trinity Street
A4	Evesham Road	C2	Tyler Street
C1	Great William's Street	C2	Union Street
B2	Greenhill Street	C1	Warwick Court
B3	Grove Road	D1	Warwick Crescent
C2	Guild Street	D1	Warwick Road
B2	Henley Street	C3	Waterside
C2	High Street	D1	Welcombe Road
B4	Holtom Street	B2	Wellesbourne Grove
C2	John Street	B4	West Street
B1	Kendall Avenue	A1	Western Road
C1	Lock Close	B2	Windsor Street
C1	Maidenhead Road	B2	Wood Street
B2	Mansell Street		
C1	Mayfield Avenue		
C1	Mayfield Court		
B2	Meer Street		
C4	Mill Lane		
C1	Mulberry Street		
B4	Narrow Lane		

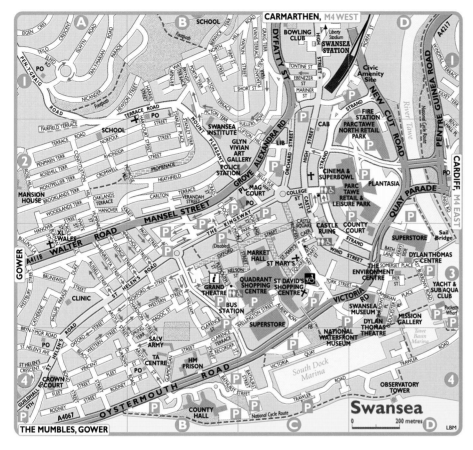

Swansea

Swansea is found on atlas page **103 G3**

C3 Albert Row	A1 Nicander Parade
C2 Alexandra Road	B3 Nicholl Street
A3 Argyle Street	A2 Norfolk Street
D3 Bath Lane	B1 North Hill
B4 Bathurst Street	C2 Orchard Street
A4 Beach Street	A4 Oxford Street
C2 Belle Vue Way	A4 Oystermouth Road
A4 Bond Street	B3 Page Street
A2 Brooklands Terrace	A1 Pen y Graig Road
A3 Brunswick Street	A2 Penmaen Terrace
B1 Brynsifi Terrace	D2 Pentre Guinea Road
A4 Burrows Road	A3 Phillips Parade
C3 Caer Street	B1 Picton Terrace
D3 Cambrian Place	D3 Pier Street
B2 Carlton Terrace	B3 Plymouth Street
C3 Castle Square	C2 Portland Street
C2 Castle Street	B1 Portia Terrace
A3 Catherine Street	B2 Primrose Hill
C2 Clifton Hill	C3 Princess Way
C2 College Street	B2 Promenade
A2 Constitution Hill	D2 Quay Parade
A2 Cromwell Street	A2 Rhondda Street
B2 Dock Union Street	B3 Richardson Street
A3 Duke Street	A4 Rodney Street
C1 Dyfatty Street	A2 Rosehill Terrace
D3 East Burrows Road	A3 Russell Street
A2 Fairfield Terrace	A3 St Helen's Road
A4 Fleet Street	C3 St Mary Street
C2 Fullers Row	C3 St Mary's Square
A3 George Street	D3 Somerset Place
B4 Glamorgan Street	B2 Stanley Place
D3 Gloucester Place	C2 Strand
C1 Graig Terrace	A1 Tan-y-Marian Road
C2 Grove Place	A2 Terrace Road
A3 Hanover Street	B3 The Kingsway
B2 Harcourt Street	C1 Tontine Street
B2 Heathfield	C4 Trawler Road
A3 Henrietta Street	C4 Victoria Quay
A1 Hewson Street	C3 Victoria Road
C1 High Street	A4 Vincent Street
A1 Islwyn Road	A3 Walter Road
B3 Madoc Street	C1 Watkin Street
B2 Mansel Street	C3 Wellington Street
B1 Milton Terrace	A4 Western Street
A2 Montpellier Terrace	B3 William Street
B2 Mount Pleasant	C3 Wind Street
B3 Nelson Street	A2 Woodlands Terrace
D1 New Cut Road	C3 York Street

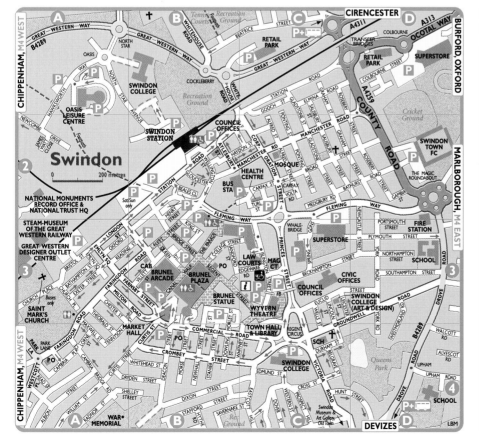

Swindon

Swindon is found on atlas page **113 E2**

C2 Alfred Street	B3 Havelock Street
B2 Aylesbury Street	A1 Hawksworth Way
A3 Bathampton Street	C2 Haydon Street
C2 Bathurst Road	B2 Henry Street
B2 Beales Close	C4 Hunt Street
C1 Beatrice Street	C3 Islington Street
C3 Beckhampton Street	A2 James Watt Close
C4 Belgrave Street	B3 King Street
B2 Bridge Street	C3 Leicester Street
A3 Bristol Street	C3 Lincoln Street
C2 Broad Street	A3 London Street
A4 Cambria Bridge Road	C2 Manchester Road
A4 Cambria Place	A4 Maxwell Street
B3 Canal Walk	A3 Milton Road
C2 Carfax Street	B3 Morley Street
A3 Chester Street	B4 Morse Street
A3 Church Place	D3 Newcastle Street
D1 Colbourne Street	A2 Newcombe Drive
B3 College Street	B4 Newhall Street
B4 Commercial Road	A1 North Star Avenue
C2 Corporation Street	D1 Ocotal Way
D1 County Road	A3 Oxford Street
B4 Crombey Street	A4 Park Lane
C4 Cross Street	D3 Plymouth Street
A4 Curtis Street	C2 Ponting Street
B4 Deacon Street	C3 Princes Street
B4 Dixon Street	B3 Queen Street
B4 Dowling Street	A3 Reading Street
D4 Drove Road	B3 Regent Street
B4 Dryden Street	C1 Rosebery Street
C4 Durham Street	C1 Salisbury Street
C4 Eastcott Hill	B3 Sandford Street
C3 Edgeware Road	D3 Southampton Street
C4 Edmund Street	B4 Stafford Street
C1 Elmina Road	B4 Stanier Street
A3 Emlyn Square	B2 Station Road
C3 Euclid Street	A4 Tennyson Street
A3 Exeter Street	B3 The Parade
A4 Faringdon Road	A3 Theobald Street
A3 Farnsby Street	C4 Victoria Road
B3 Fleet Street	B3 Villett Street
B2 Fleming Way	B2 Wellington Street
C1 Gladstone Street	C3 Wells Street
B2 Gloucester Street	A4 Westcott Place
C1 Gooch Street	B4 Whitehead Street
C1 Graham Street	B1 Whitehouse Road
A1 Great Western Way	C4 Whitney Street
C3 Groundwell Road	D3 York Road

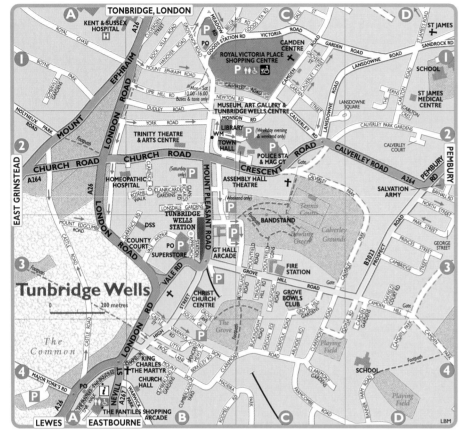

Tunbridge Wells

Tunbridge Wells is found on atlas page **78 D2**

C4	Arundel Road	B1	Lime Hill Road
D4	Banner Farm Road	B4	Little Mount Sion
D2	Bayhall Road	A2	London Road
B1	Belgrave Road	B2	Lonsdale Gardens
B4	Berkeley Road	B4	Madeira Park
A1	Boyne Park	A4	Major York's Road
C4	Buckingham Road	C3	Meadow Hill Road
C2	Calverley Park	B1	Meadow Road
D2	Calverley Park Gardens	A2	Molyneux Park Road
B1	Calverley Road	B2	Monson Road
C1	Calverley Street	A3	Mount Edgcumbe Road
D3	Cambridge Street	A2	Mount Ephraim
D3	Camden Gardens	B1	Mount Ephraim Road
D3	Camden Hill	B2	Mount Pleasant Road
D4	Camden Park	B4	Mount Sion
C1	Camden Road	C3	Mountfield Gardens
D2	Carlton Crescent	C3	Mountfield Road
D1	Carlton Road	A4	Nevill Street
A4	Castle Road	B1	Newton Road
B3	Castle Street	C4	Norfolk Road
B4	Chapel Place	D2	North Street
A2	Church Road	D3	Oakfield Court Road
B2	Clanricarde Gardens	D3	Park Street
B2	Clanricarde Road	D2	Pembury Road
C4	Claremont Gardens	C4	Poona Road
B4	Claremont Road	D3	Princes Street
B2	Clarence Road	D3	Prospect Road
C2	Crescent Road	B1	Rock Villa Road
B1	Culverden Street	B4	Rodmell Road
B4	Cumberland Gardens	B2	Rosehill Walk
B4	Cumberland Yard	A1	Royal Chase
B1	Dudley Road	D1	St James's Road
C4	Farmcombe Road	D1	Sandrock Road
B4	Frog Lane	A1	Somerville Gardens
C1	Garden Road	B3	South Grove
C1	Garden Street	B4	Spencer Mews
B1	Goods Station Road	B3	Station Approach
C4	Grecian Road	D1	Stone Street
B1	Grosvenor Road	B3	Sutherland Road
B3	Grove Avenue	D1	The Ferns
C3	Grove Hill Gardens	A4	The Pantiles Lower
C3	Grove Hill Road		Walk
C1	Grover Street	A4	The Pantiles
C3	Guildford Road	B3	Vale Avenue
B1	Hanover Road	B3	Vale Road
B4	High Street	C1	Victoria Road
C1	Lansdowne Road	B4	Warwick Road
C2	Lansdowne Square	B2	York Road

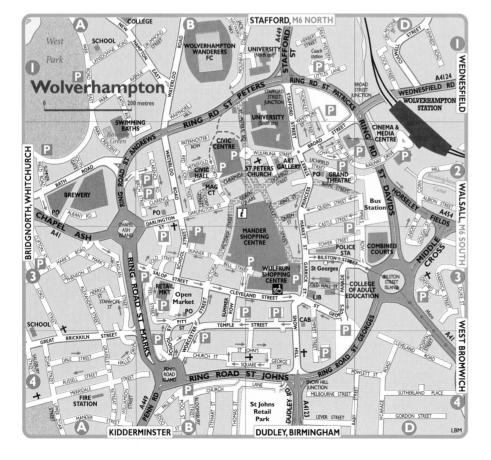

Wolverhampton

Wolverhampton is found on atlas page **236 D5**

A3	Alexandra Street	B3	Peel Street
A1	Bath Avenue	B4	Penn Road
A2	Bath Road	D2	Piper's Row
B3	Bell Street	B3	Pitt Street
C2	Berry Street	C2	Princess Street
C3	Bilston Street	C2	Queen Square
B2	Birch Street	C2	Queen Street
C2	Broad Street	C4	Raby Street
C2	Castle Street	A3	Raglan Street
A2	Chapel Ash	D2	Railway Drive
B2	Cheapside	B2	Red Lion Street
B4	Church Lane	A4	Retreat Street
B4	Church Street	A2	Ring Road St Andrews
B2	Clarence Road	D2	Ring Road St Davids
B2	Clarence Street	C4	Ring Road St Georges
D4	Cleveland Road	B4	Ring Road St Johns
B3	Cleveland Street	A3	Ring Road St Marks
D2	Corn Hill	C1	Ring Road St Patricks
B2	Corporation Street	B1	Ring Road St Peters
D1	Culwell Street	A4	Russell Street
A4	Dale Street	C3	St George's Parade
B2	Darlington Street	C4	St John's Square
C4	Dudley Road	A3	St Mark's Road
C2	Dudley Street	A3	St Mark's Street
B3	Fold Street	B1	St Peter's Square
C2	Fryer Street	B3	Salop Street
C3	Garrick Street	B4	School Street
A4	Graiseley Street	B3	Skinner Street
A4	Great Brickkiln Street	C3	Snow Hill
C1	Great Western Street	C1	Stafford Street
A4	Hallet Drive	A3	Stephenson Street
D2	Horseley Fields	B4	Stewart Street
C2	King Street	B3	Summer Row
C2	Lichfield Street	D4	Sutherland Place
C1	Littles Lane	C3	Tempest Street
C2	Long Street	B3	Temple Street
A3	Lord Street	B4	Thomas Street
C3	Market Street	C1	Thornley Street
A4	Merridale Street	C3	Tower Street
D3	Middle Cross	D4	Vicarage Road
B2	Mitrefold	B3	Victoria Street
B1	Molineux Street	B1	Waterloo Road
A1	New Hampton East	D1	Wednesfield Road
B2	North Street	B1	Whitmore Hill
C3	Old Hall Street	C1	Whitmore Street
A1	Park Avenue	B4	Worcester Street
A1	Park Road East	C2	Wulfruna Street
B2	Paternoster Row	A4	Zoar Street

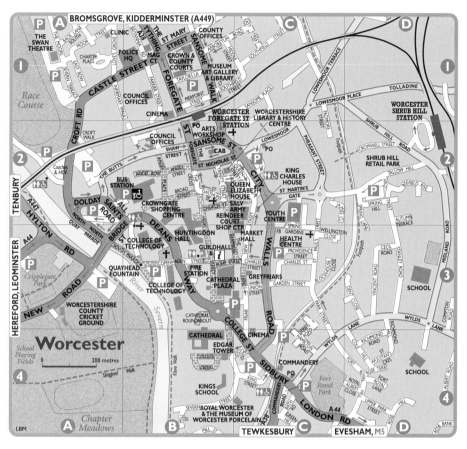

Worcester

Worcester is found on atlas page **188 B3**

A2	All Saints Road	A3	New Road
B2	Angel Place	C3	New Street
B2	Angel Row	A3	North Parade
B2	Angel Street	A2	North Quay
B1	Arboretum Road	C3	Park Street
C4	Bath Road	C2	Pheasant Street
A3	Bridge Street	B1	Pierpoint Street
B1	Britannia Road	C3	Providence Street
B2	Broad Street	B3	Pump Street
D2	Byfield Rise	C2	Queen Street
A1	Castle Street	D4	Richmond Hill
D3	Cecil Road	D4	Richmond Road
C3	Charles Street	D4	Rose Terrace
A1	Charter Place	C2	St James Close
B2	Church Street	C2	St Martin's Gate
C2	City Walls Road	B1	St Mary Street
D4	Cole Hill	B2	St Nicholas Street
B4	College Green	C3	St Paul's Street
B3	College Street	B2	St Swithuns Street
C4	Commandery Road	D4	St Wulstan's Crescent
B3	Copenhagen Street	C1	Sansome Place
A2	Croft Road	B2	Sansome Street
D2	Cromwell Street	B1	Sansome Walk
B3	Deans Way	B4	Severn Street
D3	Dent Close	A1	Severn Terrace
A2	Dolday	B2	Shaw Street
A1	Easy Row	D2	Shrub Hill Road
B1	Farrier Street	C4	Sidbury
B1	Foregate Street	A3	South Parade
D4	Fort Royal Hill	C1	Southfield Street
C3	Friar Street	C3	Spring Gardens
C3	Garden Street	D2	Spring Hill
C4	Green Hill	D2	Spring Lane
C4	Hamilton Road	D3	Stanley Road
B3	High Street	D2	Tallow Hill
D2	Hill Street	B1	Taylors Lane
A2	Hylton Road	A2	The Butts
A1	Infirmary Walk	B2	The Cross
C4	King Street	B2	The Foregate
B1	Little Southfield Street	C3	The Shambles
C4	London Road	B1	The Tything
A1	Love's Grove	D1	Tolladine
C2	Lowesmoor	B2	Trinity Street
C1	Lowesmoor Place	C3	Union Street
C1	Lowesmoor Terrace	D4	Upper Park Street
B1	Middle Street	D3	Vincent Road
D3	Midland Road	C3	Wellington Close
A1	Moor Street	C4	Wylds Lane

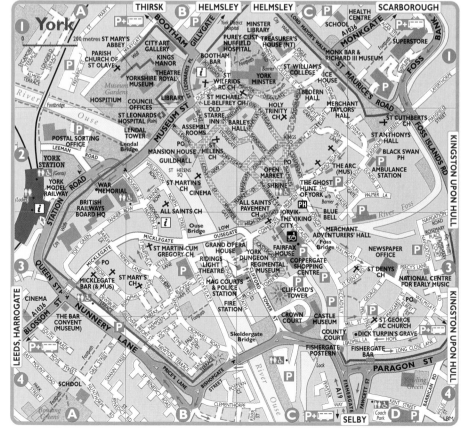

York

York is found on atlas page **358 A4**

C1	Aldwark	B3	Low Ousegate
B4	Baile Hill Terrace	C1	Low Petergate
A3	Barker Lane	D3	Margaret Street
C2	Bartle Garth	C2	Market Street
A3	Bishophill Junior	B1	Marygate
B3	Bishophill Senior	A3	Micklegate
B4	Bishopgate Street	D4	Mill Street
B2	Blake Street	C1	Minster Yard
A4	Blossom Street	C1	Monkgate
B1	Bootham	B2	Museum Street
B1	Bootham Row	D3	Navigation Road
C3	Castlegate	B4	Newton Terrace
C2	Church Street	B2	North Street
B4	Clementhorpe	A3	Nunnery Lane
C3	Clifford Street	A4	Nunthorpe Road
C1	College Street	C1	Ogleforth
C2	Colliergate	D4	Paragon Street
B2	Coney Street	C2	Parliament Street
C3	Coppergate	C2	Pavement
B4	Cromwell Road	D2	Peasholme Green
A4	Dale Street	D3	Peel Street
B2	Davygate	D3	Percy's Lane
C1	Deangate	C3	Piccadilly
B1	Duncombe Place	B4	Price's Lane
D4	Fawcett Street	A3	Priory Street
C2	Feasegate	A3	Queen Street
B3	Fetter Lane	B2	Rougier Street
D4	Fishergate	C2	St Andrewgate
D1	Foss Bank	C3	St Denys Road
D2	Foss Islands Road	B2	St Helens Square
C3	Fossgate	B1	St Leonards Place
A1	Frederic Street	B3	St Martins Lane
C2	Garden Place	C1	St Maurice's Road
B2	George Hudson Street	C2	St Saviourgate
D3	George Street	C2	Shambles
B1	Gillygate	B3	Skeldergate
C2	Goodramgate	C2	Spen Lane
C2	Grape Lane	A3	Station Road
C3	High Ousegate	B2	Stonegate
B1	High Petergate	A4	Swann Street
D4	Hope Street	C2	Swinegate
D4	Kent Street	A3	Tanner Row
C2	Kings Square	C2	The Stonebow
B3	Kings Staith	A3	Toft Green
D4	Leadmill Lane	C3	Tower Street
A2	Leeman Road	A3	Trinity Lane
B2	Lendal	B4	Victor Street
C1	Lord Mayor's Walk	C3	Walmgate

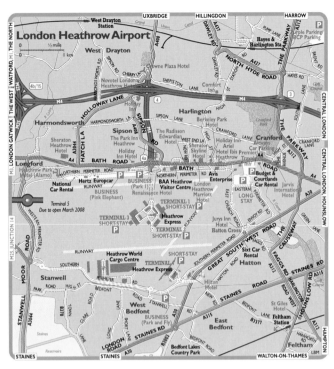

London Heathrow Airport – 16 miles west of London

Telephone: 0870 000 0123 or visit *www.heathrowairport.com*
Parking: short-stay, long-stay and business parking is available.
For charge details tel: 0870 000 1000
Public Transport: coach, bus, rail and London Underground.
There are several 4-star and 3-star hotels within easy reach of the airport.
Car hire facilities are available.

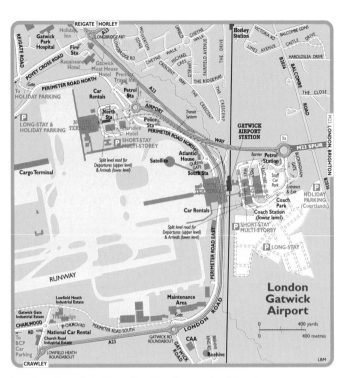

London Gatwick Airport – 35 miles south of London

Telephone: 0870 000 2468 or visit *www.gatwickairport.com*
Parking: short and long-stay parking is available at both the North and South terminals.
For charge details tel: 0870 000 1000
Public Transport: coach, bus and rail.
There are several 4-star and 3-star hotels within easy reach of the airport.
Car hire facilities are available.

London Stansted Airport – 36 miles north east of London

Telephone: 0870 000 0303 or visit *www.stanstedairport.com*
Parking: short, mid and long-stay open-air parking is available.
For charge details tel: 0870 000 1000
Public Transport: coach, bus and direct rail link to London on the Stansted Express.
There are several hotels within easy reach of the airport.
Car hire facilities are available.

London Luton Airport – 33 miles north of London

Telephone: 01582 405100 or visit *www.london-luton.co.uk*
Parking: short-term, mid-term and long-stay parking is available.
For charge details tel: 0870 606 7050
Public Transport: coach, bus and rail.
There are several hotels within easy reach of the airport.
Car hire facilities are available.

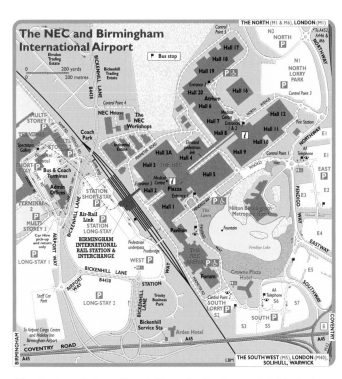

Birmingham International Airport – 8 miles east of Birmingham

Telephone: 0870 733 5511 or visit *www.bhx.co.uk*
Parking: short and long-stay parking is available. For charge details tel: 0870 733 5511
Public Transport: Air-Rail Link service operates every 2 minutes to and from Birmingham International Railway Station & Interchange.
There is one 3-star hotel adjacent to the airport and several 4 and 3-star hotels within easy reach of the airport. Car hire facilities are available.

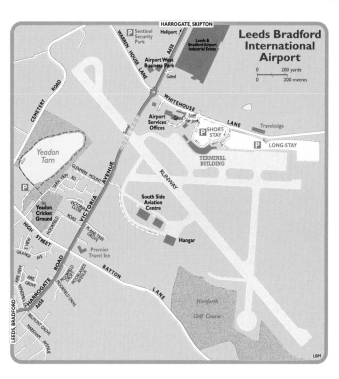

Leeds Bradford International Airport – 7 miles north east of Bradford and 9 miles north west of Leeds

Telephone: 0113 250 9696 or visit *www.lbia.co.uk*
Parking: short and long-stay parking is available. For charge details tel: 0113 250 9696
Public Transport: bus service operates every 30 minutes from Bradford, Leeds and Otley. There are several 4-star and 3-star hotels within easy reach of the airport.
Car hire facilities are available.

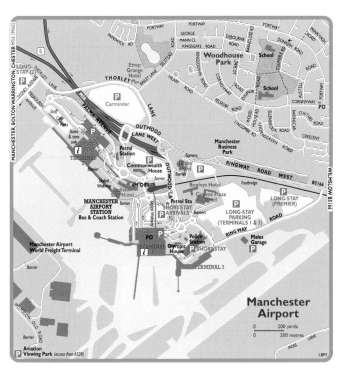

Manchester Airport – 10 miles south of Manchester

Telephone: 0161 489 3000 or visit *www.manchesterairport.co.uk*
Parking: short and long-stay parking is available.
For charge details tel: 0161 489 3723
Public Transport: bus, coach and rail.
There are several 4-star and 3-star hotels within easy reach of the airport.
Car hire facilities are available.

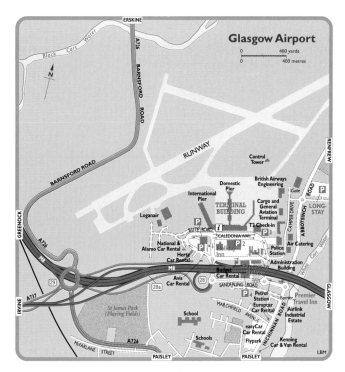

Glasgow Airport – 8 miles west of Glasgow

Telephone: 0870 040 0008 or visit *www.glasgowairport.com*
Parking: short and long-stay parking is available.
For charge details tel: 0870 000 1000
Public Transport: regular coach services operate direct to central Glasgow and Edinburgh.
There are several 3-star hotels within easy reach of the airport.
Car hire facilities are available.

Using the National Grid

With an Ordnance Survey National Grid reference you can pinpoint anywhere in the country using this atlas. The blue grid lines which divide the main-map pages into 5km squares for ease of indexing also match the National Grid. A National Grid reference gives two letters and some figures. This example shows how to find the summit of mount Snowdon using its 4-figure grid reference of **SH6154**.

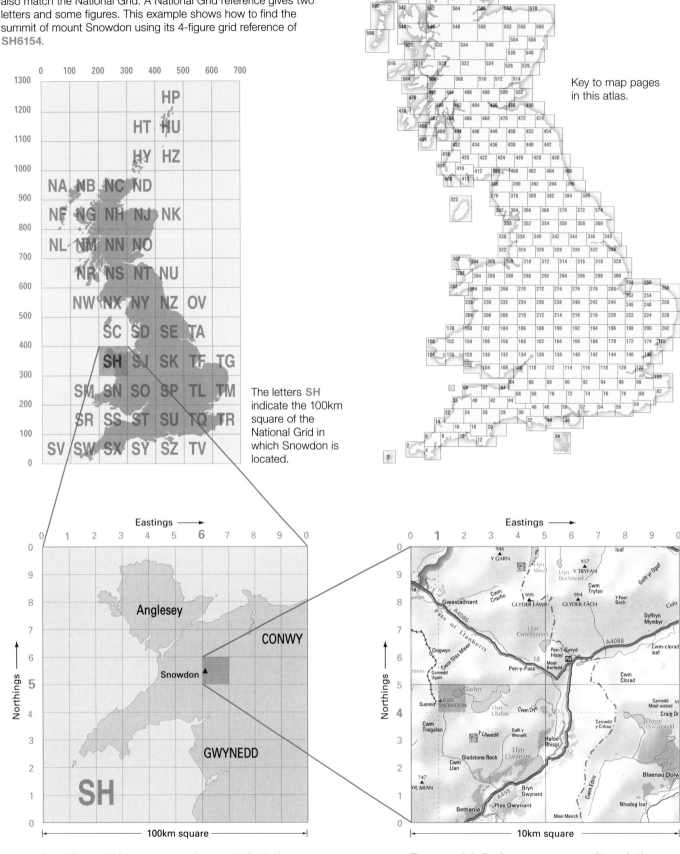

Key to map pages in this atlas.

The letters **SH** indicate the 100km square of the National Grid in which Snowdon is located.

In a 4-figure grid reference the first two figures (eastings) are read along the map from left to right, the second two (northings) up the map. The figures **6** and **5**, the first and third figures of the Snowdon reference, indicate the 10km square within the **SH** square, lying above (north) and right (east) of the intersection of the vertical (easting) line **6** and horizontal (northing) line **5**.

The summit is finally pinpointed by figures **1** and **4** which locate a 1km square within the 10km square. At road atlas mapping scales these grid lines are normally estimated by eye.

Gazetteer of map entries

Both sections of this gazetteer list entries appearing in the main-map section of the atlas in alphabetical order. The reference before each name gives the atlas page number and grid reference of the square in which the place appears. The map shows counties, unitary authorities and administrative areas, together with a list of the abbreviated name forms used in the gazetteer. The recreation and leisure index lists places of tourist interest including airports and airfields (shown in blue type), National Parks, main physical features, campsites, golf courses and cycle routes. The city, town and village index lists settlements.

Scotland

Abers	Aberdeenshire
Ag & B	Argyll & Bute
Angus	Angus
Border	Borders
C Aber	City of Aberdeen
C Dund	City of Dundee
C Edin	City of Edinburgh
C Glas	City of Glasgow
Clacks	Clackmannanshire (1)
D & G	Dumfries & Galloway
E Ayrs	East Ayrshire
E Duns	East Dunbartonshire (2)
E Loth	East Lothian
E Rens	East Renfrewshire (3)
Falk	Falkirk
Fife	Fife
Highld	Highland
Inver	Inverclyde (4)
Mdloth	Midlothian (5)
Moray	Moray
N Ayrs	North Ayrshire
N Lans	North Lanarkshire (6)
Ork	Orkney Islands
P & K	Perth & Kinross
Rens	Renfrewshire (7)
S Ayrs	South Ayrshire
Shet	Shetland Islands
S Lans	South Lanarkshire
Stirlg	Stirling
W Duns	West Dunbartonshire (8)
W Isls	Western Isles
W Loth	West Lothian

Wales

Blae G	Blaenau Gwent (9)
Brdgnd	Bridgend (10)
Caerph	Caerphilly (11)
Cardif	Cardiff
Carmth	Carmarthenshire
Cerdgn	Ceredigion
Conwy	Conwy
Denbgs	Denbighshire
Flints	Flintshire
Gwynd	Gwynedd
IoA	Isle of Anglesey
Mons	Monmouthshire
Myr Td	Merthyr Tydfil (12)
Neath	Neath Port Talbot (13)
Newpt	Newport (14)
Pembks	Pembrokeshire
Powys	Powys
Rhondd	Rhondda Cynon Taff (15)
Swans	Swansea
Torfn	Torfaen (16)
V Glam	Vale of Glamorgan (17)
Wrexhm	Wrexham

Channel Islands & Isle of Man

Guern	Guernsey
Jersey	Jersey
IoM	Isle of Man

England

BaNES	Bath & N E Somerset (18)
Barns	Barnsley (19)
Beds	Bedfordshire
Birm	Birmingham
Bl w D	Blackburn with Darwen (20)
Bmouth	Bournemouth
Bolton	Bolton (21)
Bpool	Blackpool
Brad	Bradford (22)
Br & H	Brighton and Hove (23)
Br For	Bracknell Forest (24)
Bristl	City of Bristol
Bucks	Buckinghamshire
Bury	Bury (25)
C Derb	City of Derby
C KuH	City of Kingston upon Hull
C Leic	City of Leicester
C Nott	City of Nottingham
C Pete	City of Peterborough
C Plym	City of Plymouth
C Port	City of Portsmouth
C Sotn	City of Southampton
C Stke	City of Stoke
Calder	Calderdale (26)
Cambs	Cambridgeshire
Ches	Cheshire
Cnwll	Cornwall
Covtry	Coventry
Cumb	Cumbria
Darltn	Darlington (27)
Derbys	Derbyshire
Devon	Devon
Donc	Doncaster (28)
Dorset	Dorset
Dudley	Dudley (29)
Dur	Durham
E R Yk	East Riding of Yorkshire
E Susx	East Sussex

Essex	Essex
Gatesd	Gateshead (30)
Gloucs	Gloucestershire
Gt Lon	Greater London
Halton	Halton (31)
Hants	Hampshire
Hartpl	Hartlepool (32)
Herefs	Herefordshire
Herts	Hertfordshire
IoS	Isles of Scilly
IoW	Isle of Wight
Kent	Kent
Kirk	Kirklees (33)
Knows	Knowsley (34)
Lancs	Lancashire
Leeds	Leeds
Leics	Leicestershire
Lincs	Lincolnshire
Lpool	Liverpool
Luton	Luton
M Keyn	Milton Keynes
Manch	Manchester
Medway	Medway
Middsb	Middlesbrough
NE Lin	North East Lincolnshire
N Linc	North Lincolnshire
N Som	North Somerset (35)
N Tyne	North Tyneside (36)
N u Ty	Newcastle upon Tyne
N York	North Yorkshire
Nhants	Northamptonshire
Norfk	Norfolk
Notts	Nottinghamshire
Nthumb	Northumberland
Oldham	Oldham (37)
Oxon	Oxfordshire
Poole	Poole
R & Cl	Redcar and Cleveland
Readg	Reading
Rochdl	Rochdale (38)
Rothm	Rotherham (39)
Rutlnd	Rutland
S Glos	South Gloucestershire (40)
S on T	Stockton-on-Tees (41)
S Tyne	South Tyneside (42)
Salfd	Salford (43)
Sandw	Sandwell (44)
Sefton	Sefton (45)
Sheff	Sheffield
Shrops	Shropshire
Slough	Slough (46)
Solhll	Solihull (47)
Somset	Somerset
St Hel	St Helens (48)
Staffs	Staffordshire
Sthend	Southend-on-Sea
Stockp	Stockport (49)
Suffk	Suffolk
Sundld	Sunderland
Surrey	Surrey
Swindn	Swindon
Tamesd	Tameside (50)
Thurr	Thurrock (51)
Torbay	Torbay
Traffd	Trafford (52)
W & M	Windsor & Maidenhead (53)
W Berk	West Berkshire
W Susx	West Sussex
Wakefd	Wakefield (54)
Warrtn	Warrington (55)
Warwks	Warwickshire
Wigan	Wigan (56)
Wilts	Wiltshire
Wirral	Wirral (57)
Wokham	Wokingham (58)
Wolves	Wolverhampton (59)
Worcs	Worcestershire
Wrekin	Telford and Wrekin (60)
Wsall	Walsall (61)
York	York

654 Leisure index: Abbeydale Golf Club - Ben Rhydding Golf Club

Recreation and leisure index

A

314 C3 **Abbeydale Golf Club** Sheff
324 A3 **Abbey Farm Caravan Park** Lancs
110 D1 **Abbey Gatehouse** Gloucs
167 H2 **Abbey Hill Golf Club** M Keyn
213 F6 **Abbey Hotel Golf & Country Club** Worcs
197 G3 **Abbey Stadium** Cambs
30 D5 **Abbotsbury Castle** Dorset
30 D6 **Abbotsbury Swannery** Dorset
451 G3 **Abbotsford** Border
196 A3 **Abbotsley Golf Hotel & Country Club** Cambs
131 G4 **Aberdare Golf Club** Rhondd
131 F4 **Aberdare Park** Rhondd
557 F2 **Aberdeen airport** C Aber
487 G3 **Aberdour Golf Club** Fife
229 E5 **Aberdovey Golf Club** Gwynd
130 B5 **Aberdulais Falls NT** Neath
263 G3 **Abererch Sands Holiday Centre** Gwynd
524 C6 **Aberfeldy Caravan Park** P & K
524 B6 **Aberfeldy Golf Club** P & K
496 D4 **Aberfoyle Golf Club** Stirlg
133 E1 **Abergavenny & Border Counties showground** Mons
306 C4 **Abergele Golf Club** Conwy
182 C3 **Abergwesyn Common NT** Powys
229 F3 **Abergynolwyn railway station** Gwynd
489 F4 **Aberlady Caravan Park** E Loth
155 G4 **Abermarlais Caravan Park** Carmth
551 J5 **Abernethy Golf Club** Highld
106 B2 **Aber railway station** Caerph
263 E5 **Abersoch Golf Club** Gwynd
304 B5 **Aber Waterfall** IoA
204 D4 **Aberystwyth & District showground** Cerdgn
204 D3 **Aberystwyth Golf Club** Cerdgn
448 B4 **Abington service area** S Lans
555 F5 **Aboyne Golf Club** Abers
555 F5 **Aboyne Loch Caravan Park** Abers
145 G5 **Abridge Golf & Country Club** Essex
339 H4 **Accrington & District Golf Club** Lancs
458 C2 **Achamore Gardens** Ag & B
507 G3 **Achnacloich Garden** Ag & B
563 H7 **Achnashellach railway station** Highld
250 D3 **Acle railway station** Norfk
391 G4 **Acorn Bank NT** Cumb
105 F6 **Acorn Camping & Caravan Site** V Glam
34 A5 **Acton Field Camping Site** Dorset
210 B2 **Acton Scott Historic Working Farm** Shrops
269 H6 **Adcote School** Shrops
213 G2 **Adderley Park railway station** Birm
95 H2 **Addington Court golf course** Gt Lon
95 H2 **Addington Palace Golf Club** Gt Lon
571 H6 **Aden Country Park** Abers
49 E5 **Adventure Wonderland** Dorset
81 F4 **Aeronautical museum** Kent
180 C2 **Aeron Coast Caravan Park** Cerdgn
130 C6 **Afan Argoed** Neath
130 C5 **Afan Forest Park** Neath
153 G1 **Afon Teifi Caravan & Camping Park** Cerdgn
252 B4 **African Violet Centre** Norfk
36 B3 **Afton Down NT & Compton Down NT** IoW
212 B4 **Aggborough Stadium** Worcs
451 E4 **Aikwood Tower** Border
323 G5 **Aintree racecourse** Sefton
390 C5 **Aira Force NT** Cumb
468 A3 **Airbles railway station** N Lans
297 F3 **Aircraft museum** Notts
415 E5 **Aird Donald Caravan Park** D & G
468 B1 **Airdrie Golf Club** N Lans
288 D2 **Airfields Stadium** Flints
118 C4 **Airlinks Golf Club** Gt Lon
282 D4 **Air World museum** Gwynd
27 G6 **A La Ronde NT** Devon
120 C5 **Albany Park railway station** Gt Lon
308 D2 **Albert Dock** Lpool
220 B4 **Alconbury airfield** Cambs
357 E1 **Aldborough Roman Town** N York
203 E3 **Aldeburgh Golf Club** Suffk
143 G5 **Aldenham Golf & Country Club** Herts
71 E4 **Alderbury Caravan & Camping Park** Wilts
311 G4 **Alderley Edge Golf Club** Ches
324 D6 **Alder Root Golf Club** Warrtn
357 F1 **Alders Caravan Park** N York
289 G3 **Aldersey Green Golf Club** Ches
357 F2 **Aldwark Manor Golf Club** N York
143 H2 **Aldwickbury Park Golf Club** Herts
213 G1 **Alexander Stadium** Birm
467 F1 **Alexandra Golf Club** C Glas
467 F1 **Alexandra Parade railway station** C Glas
291 E4 **Alexandra Stadium** Ches
555 G1 **Alford Golf Club** Abers
555 G1 **Alford Valley Railway** Abers
294 D3 **Alfreton Golf Club** Derbys
133 G3 **Alice Springs Golf Club** Mons
237 G6 **Alison Nicholas Golf Academy** Birm
557 H4 **Allan Park** C Aber
403 E4 **Allendale Golf Club** Nthumb
404 C4 **Allensford Caravan & Camping Park** Dur
384 C2 **Allens West railway station** S on T
359 E5 **Allerthorpe Park golf course** E R Yk
309 F2 **Allerton Park Golf Club** Lpool
275 E1 **Allestree Park golf course** C Derb
499 E6 **Alloa Golf Club** Clacks
486 A1 **Alloa Tower** Clacks
129 F4 **Allt-y-Graban golf course** Swans
487 E6 **Almondell & Calderwood Country Park** W Loth
469 G1 **Almond Valley Heritage Centre** W Loth
176 C1 **Alnesbourne Priory golf course** Suffk
565 L2 **Alness Golf Club** Highld
443 G2 **Alnmouth Golf Club** Nthumb
443 H2 **Alnmouth Village Golf Club** Nthumb
443 F2 **Alnwick Golf Club** Nthumb
29 F1 **Alpine Grove Touring Park** Somset
73 E3 **Alresford Golf Club** Hants
73 E3 **Alresford railway station** Hants
291 G4 **Alsager Golf & Country Club** Ches
12 C4 **Alston Farm Camping & Caravanning Site** Devon
402 C6 **Alston Moor Golf Club** Cumb
560 C3 **Altar Tomb of William Forbes** Abers
193 E1 **Althorp Park** Nhants
588 C7 **Altnabreac railway station** Highld
73 H1 **Alton Golf Club** Hants
293 E6 **Alton Towers** Staffs
311 F2 **Altrincham Golf Club** Traffd
498 D5 **Alva Golf Club** Clacks
343 F1 **Alwoodley Golf Club** Leeds
54 B2 **Amberley museum** W Susx
295 E6 **American Adventure** Derbys
273 E4 **Amerton Railway** Staffs
118 C5 **Amida golf course** Gt Lon
72 A5 **Ampfield Par Three Golf Club** Hants
137 F4 **Amphitheatre Roman site** Gloucs
265 G2 **Amphitheatre Roman site** Gwynd
158 B2 **Anchorage Caravan Park** Powys
514 B3 **Ancrum Outdoor Centre** C Dund
467 E1 **Anderston railway station** C Glas
310 C4 **Anderton Boat Lift** Ches
90 B6 **Andover Golf Club** Hants
28 D3 **Andrewshayes Caravan Park** Devon
323 G6 **Anfield** Lpool
405 G3 **Angel of the North** Gatesd
119 H1 **Angel Road railway station** Gt Lon
303 E4 **Anglesey** IoA
198 A2 **Anglesey Abbey NT** Cambs
302 D6 **Anglesey Golf Club** IoA
303 F5 **Anglesey showground** IoA
223 F5 **Anglo-Saxon Village Reconstruction** Suffk
527 E5 **Angus Folk museum NTS** Angus
114 B4 **Animal Retirement Centre** W Berk
191 G5 **Anita's Touring Caravan Park** Oxon
437 F4 **Annandale** D & G
424 C1 **Annandale Water service area** D & G
445 F2 **Annanhill Golf Club** E Ayrs
190 B4 **Anne Hathaway's Cottage** Warwks
503 F4 **Anstruther Golf Club** Fife
215 G3 **Ansty Golf Centre** Warwks
480 B6 **An Tairbeart Visitor Centre** Ag & B
485 G4 **Antonine Wall** Falk
10 D2 **Antony NT** Cnwll
310 C3 **Antrobus Golf Club** Ches
412 A3 **Anwoth Caravan Site** D & G
392 B6 **Appleby Golf Club** Cumb
81 E4 **Appledore railway station** Kent
37 E4 **Appuldurcombe Gardens Caravan & Camping Park** IoW
37 E4 **Appuldurcombe House** IoW
143 F4 **Apsley railway station** Herts
271 H6 **Aqualate Golf Centre** Staffs
398 B3 **Arbigland Gardens** D & G
293 G2 **Arbor Low Stone Circle** Derbys
515 G2 **Arbroath golf course** Angus
215 E2 **Arbury Hall** Warwks
559 F4 **Archaeolink museum** Abers
286 D3 **Archaeological Trail** Denbgs
430 D4 **Arcot Hall Golf Club** Nthumb
507 J4 **Ardanaiseig Garden** Ag & B
507 G2 **Ardchattan Priory** Ag & B
567 H7 **Ardclach Bell Tower** Highld
465 F6 **Ardeer Golf Club** N Ayrs
464 C2 **Ardencraig Gardens** Ag & B
515 E3 **Ardestie Earth-House** Angus
492 D4 **Ardfern Yacht Centre** Ag & B
494 D2 **Ardkinglas Woodland Garden** Ag & B
574 C4 **Ardmair Point Camping & Caravan Park** Highld
518 D2 **Ardnamurchan** Highld
444 B1 **Ardrossan Harbour railway station** N Ayrs
444 B1 **Ardrossan South Beach railway station** N Ayrs
444 B1 **Ardrossan Town railway station** N Ayrs
492 C2 **Arduaine Garden NTS** Ag & B
511 G6 **Ardunie Signal Station Roman site** P & K
579 H5 **Ardvreck Castle** Highld
408 C2 **Ardwell House** D & G
121 E3 **Arena Essex Raceway** Thurr
5 E2 **Argal & College Water Park** Cnwll
153 F1 **Argoed Meadow Caravan & Camping Site** Carmth
527 E5 **Argus Folk Castle NTS** Angus
467 E2 **Argyle Street railway station** C Glas
481 G2 **Argyll Forest Park** Ag & B
494 B3 **Argyll Wildlife Park** Ag & B
144 B5 **Arkley Golf Club** Gt Lon
310 D3 **Arley Hall** Ches
211 H4 **Arley railway station** Worcs
61 F3 **Arlington Court NT** Devon
57 F3 **Arlington Stadium** E Susx
531 H2 **Armadale Castle Gardens & Museum of The Isles** Highld
486 B6 **Armadale Stadium** W Loth
378 C3 **Armitt museum** Cumb
93 E4 **Army Golf Club** Hants
374 C3 **Arosa Caravan & Camping Park** N York
460 C2 **Arran** N Ayrs
308 C2 **Arrowe Park golf course** Wirral
234 A3 **Arscott Golf Club** Shrops
185 F6 **Arthur's Stone** Herefs
102 C3 **Arthur's Stone** Swans
54 B3 **Arundel Park** W Susx
117 F6 **Ascot racecourse** W & M
168 B5 **Ascott NT** Bucks
293 G6 **Ashbourne Golf Club** Derbys
128 B4 **Ashburnham Golf Club** Carmth
24 D3 **Ashbury Golf Hotel** Devon
326 C5 **Ashburys railway station** Manch
332 B3 **Ashby Decoy Golf Club** N Linc
162 D3 **Ashchurch for Tewkesbury railway station** Gloucs
27 G3 **Ashclyst Forest NT** Devon
28 D4 **Ashdown Caravan Park** Devon
113 G3 **Ashdown NT** Oxon
44 B3 **Ashe Farm Camping & Caravan Site** Somset
238 B5 **Ash End House** Warwks
379 E5 **Ashes Lane campsite** Cumb
100 B6 **Ashfield Farm campsite** Kent
484 B6 **Ashfield railway station** C Glas
484 B6 **Ashfield Stadium** C Glas
99 F6 **Ashford Golf Club** Kent
81 F1 **Ashford International railway station** Kent
118 B5 **Ashford Manor Golf Club** Surrey
81 E4 **Ashford to Lydd cycle route** Kent
162 B4 **Ashleworth Tithe Barn NT** Gloucs
93 E4 **Ash railway station** Surrey
142 D2 **Ashridge Estate NT** Herts
142 D2 **Ashridge Golf Club** Herts
109 F5 **Ashton Court** N Som
109 G5 **Ashton Gate** Bristl
324 D5 **Ashton-in-Makerfield Golf Club** St Hel
338 C3 **Ashton & Lea Golf Club** Lancs
325 H6 **Ashton on Mersey Golf Club** Traffd
327 E4 **Ashton-under-Lyne Golf Club** Tamesd
50 B2 **Ashurst New Forest railway station** Hants
171 F5 **Ash Valley Golf Club** Herts
170 C2 **Ashwell & Morden railway station** Herts
363 E6 **Askam railway station** Cumb
590 E3 **Askernish Golf Club** W Isls
168 C2 **Aspley Guise & Woburn Sands Golf Club** Beds
291 H2 **Astbury Golf Club** Ches
47 E6 **Athelhampton House** Dorset
239 E5 **Atherstone Golf Club** Warwks
524 C3 **Atholl Country Collection museum** P & K
343 F6 **Atlantic Solutions Stadium** Wakefd
547 G2 **Attadale railway station** Highld
234 C2 **Attingham Park NT** Shrops
460 B3 **Auchagallon Stone Circle** N Ayrs
540 D4 **Auchenblae golf course** Abers
485 F2 **Auchenbowie Caravan & Camping Site** Stirlg
411 F2 **Auchenlarie Holiday Park** D & G
494 A4 **Auchindrain Township museum** Ag & B
510 D6 **Auchingarrich Wildlife Centre** P & K
557 F3 **Auchmill golf course** C Aber
550 C2 **Auchnahillin Caravan & Camping Park** Highld
499 E2 **Auchterarder Golf Club** P & K
500 C5 **Auchterderran golf course** Fife
395 E3 **Auckland Castle** Dur
171 H2 **Audley End railway station** Essex
96 D2 **Austin Lodge Golf Club** Kent
112 C5 **Avebury Manor NT** Wilts
112 D6 **Avebury (UNESCO)** Wilts
32 B2 **Avenue Stadium** Dorset
255 H5 **Aviation museum (City of Norwich)** Norfk
226 C2 **Aviation museum (Norfolk & Suffolk)** Suffk
72 D3 **Avington Park** Hants
53 H3 **Avisford Park golf course** W Susx
213 E6 **Avoncroft museum** Worcs
85 G2 **Avon Cycleway** BaNES
108 D6 **Avon Cycleway** N Som
49 E4 **Avon Heath Country Park** Dorset
110 B6 **Avon Riverside railway station** BaNES
110 B6 **Avon Valley Railway** S Glos
110 D4 **Avon/Wiltshire link cycle route** S Glos
28 D5 **Axe Cliff Golf Club** Devon
404 B1 **Aydon Castle** Nthumb
142 B1 **Aylesbury Golf Centre** Bucks
141 G2 **Aylesbury Park Golf Club** Bucks
168 B5 **Aylesbury Vale Golf Club** Bucks
166 B3 **Aynhoe Park House** Nhants
3 F1 **Ayr Holiday Park** Cnwll
445 E5 **Ayr racecourse** S Ayrs

B

20 C4 **Babbacombe Model Village** Torbay
316 A4 **Babbage Way** Notts
487 G6 **Baberton Golf Club** C Edin
208 D1 **Bacheldre Watermill Touring & Camping Park** Powys
445 F4 **Bachelors' Club NTS** S Ayrs
309 F6 **Bache railway station** Ches
48 D4 **Back of Beyond Touring Park** Dorset
431 E5 **Backworth Golf Club** N Tyne
261 F4 **Baconsthorpe Castle** Norfk
340 D5 **Bacup Golf Club** Lancs
138 D6 **Badbury Hill** Oxon
48 B4 **Badbury Rings Hill Fort** Dorset
214 B5 **Baddesley Clinton NT** Warwks
116 B3 **Badgemore Park Golf Club** Oxon
328 C3 **Bagden Hall golf course** Kirk
236 C6 **Baggeridge Country Park & Local Nature Reserve** Staffs
32 A3 **Bagwell Farm Touring Park** Dorset
342 B1 **Baildon Golf Club** Brad
368 A2 **Bainbridge Ings Caravan & Camping Site** N York
299 G2 **Bainland Country Park** Lincs
314 A6 **Bakewell Golf Club** Derbys
313 H6 **Bakewell showground** Derbys
267 E2 **Bala Golf Club** Gwynd
267 E3 **Bala Lake Railway** Gwynd
267 E2 **Bala (Penybont) railway station** Gwynd
501 E4 **Balbirnie Park Golf Club** Fife
170 B2 **Baldock service area** Herts
322 g3 **Ballachurry Fort** IoM
322 h5 **Ballafoyle** IoM
322 e8 **Ballakelly** IoM
322 f6 **Ballalheannagh** IoM
148 A6 **Ballards Gore Golf & Country Club** Essex
554 C5 **Ballater Golf Club** Abers
552 D1 **Ballindalloch Castle** Moray
483 E3 **Balloch Castle** W Duns
445 H4 **Ballochmyle Golf Club** E Ayrs
2 C3 **Ballowall Barrow** Cnwll
561 E6 **Balmedie Country Park** Abers
514 B5 **Balmerino Abbey NTS** Fife
460 C3 **Balmichael Visitor Centre** N Ayrs
571 L6 **Balmoor Stadium** Abers
537 L4 **Balmoral Castle** Abers
484 B5 **Balmore Golf Club** E Duns
557 H3 **Balnagask golf course** C Aber
3 F2 **Balnoon campsite** Cnwll
509 J5 **Balquhidder Braes Holiday Park** Stirlg
500 C2 **Balvaird Castle** P & K
568 E7 **Balvenie Castle** Moray
455 F2 **Bamburgh Castle** Nthumb
455 F2 **Bamburgh Castle Golf Club** Nthumb
313 H3 **Bamford railway station** Derbys
166 A3 **Banbury Golf Centre** Oxon
556 B5 **Banchory Golf Club** Abers
353 H5 **Bancroft Mill** Lancs
289 E6 **Bangor-on-Dee racecourse** Wrexhm
225 E2 **Banham Zoo** Norfk
252 B4 **Bank Farm Caravan Park** Norfk
233 E2 **Bank Farm Caravan Park** Powys
323 F6 **Bank Hall railway station** Lpool
188 A4 **Bank House Hotel Golf & Country Club** Worcs
293 G4 **Bank Top Farm campsite** Derbys
485 F1 **Bannockburn 1314 battlefield NTS** Stirlg
95 F2 **Banstead Downs Golf Club** Surrey
3 d2 **Bant's Carn Burial** IoS
125 G5 **Barafundle Bay NT** Pembks
113 E4 **Barbury Castle** Wilts
506 F1 **Barcaldine Castle** Ag & B
265 E2 **Barcdy Touring Caravan & Camping Park** Gwynd
282 B1 **Barclodiad y Gawres** IoA
355 E3 **Barden Tower** N York
402 D2 **Bardon Mill railway station** Nthumb
364 C4 **Bardsea Leisure Park** Cumb
351 G2 **Bare Lane railway station** Lancs
132 B4 **Bargoed Golf Club** Caerph
171 E3 **Barkway Park Golf Club** Herts
272 C2 **Barlaston Golf Club** Staffs
26 A4 **Barley Meadow Caravan & Camping Park** Devon
413 F3 **Barlochan Caravan Park** D & G
556 C3 **Barmekin Hill Fort** Abers
98 A3 **Barming railway station** Kent
229 E1 **Barmouth Bridge** Gwynd
394 A6 **Barnard Castle Golf Club** Dur
120 C4 **Barnehurst golf course** Gt Lon
333 E3 **Barnetby railway station** N Linc
249 E3 **Barnham Broom Hotel & Golf Club** Norfk
467 F1 **Barnhill railway station** C Glas
493 G2 **Barnline Stables** Ag & B
479 K3 **Barnluasgan Visitor Centre** Ag & B
329 E2 **Barnsley Golf Club** Barns
423 E4 **Barnsoul Farm campsite** D & G
191 H6 **Barnstones Caravan & Camping Site** Oxon
219 E2 **Barnwell Country Park** Nhants
304 C4 **Baron Hill Golf Club** IoA
590 E6 **Barra airport** W Isls
475 F4 **Barracks (Berwick-upon-Tweed)** Nthumb
237 G5 **Barr Beacon** Wsall
466 C3 **Barrhead railway station** E Rens
66 B6 **Barrington Court NT** Somset
364 A5 **Barrow Golf Club** Cumb
347 G5 **Barrow Haven railway station** N Linc
315 E4 **Barrow Hill Railway Centre** Derbys
515 E3 **Barry Links railway station** Angus
515 E3 **Barry Mill NTS** Angus
410 B4 **Barsalloch Fort** D & G
466 D2 **Barshaw Golf Club** Rens
49 G6 **Barton-on-Sea Golf Club** Hants
20 A5 **Barton Pines campsite** Torbay
121 H2 **Basildon Golf Club** Essex
115 G4 **Basildon Park NT** W Berk
91 H4 **Basing House (Ruins)** Hants
91 F5 **Basingstoke Golf Club** Hants
308 A4 **Basingwerk Abbey** Flints
96 D3 **Bat & Ball railway station** Kent
143 G3 **Batchwood Hall Golf & Tennis Centre** Herts
68 A2 **Batcombe Vale Caravan & Camping Park** Somset
79 F5 **Bateman's NT** E Susx
486 C6 **Bathgate Golf Club** W Loth
86 D2 **Bath Golf Club** BaNES
376 D5 **Bath House (Ravenglass)** Cumb
86 C1 **Bath Marina & Caravan Park** BaNES
110 C6 **Bath racecourse** BaNES
86 D2 **Bath Spa railway station** BaNES
385 F3 **Battersby Junction railway station** N York
299 G3 **Battle of Britain Memorial Flight museum** Lincs
82 D3 **Battle of Britain museum** Kent
35 f5 **Battle of the Flowers** Jersey
249 F3 **Bawburgh Golf Club** Norfk
331 E5 **Bawtry Golf Club** Donc
340 B4 **Baxenden & District Golf Club** Lancs
568 E4 **Baxters Visitor Centre** Moray
13 F2 **Bayard's Cove Fort** Devon
79 F2 **Bayham Abbey** Kent
60 B4 **Bay View Farm Caravan & Camping Park** Devon
57 H4 **Bay View Park campsite** E Susx
502 B4 **Bayview Stadium** Fife
263 E5 **Beach View Caravan Park** Gwynd
57 F5 **Beachy Head** E Susx
57 F5 **Beachy Head Countryside Centre** E Susx
6 D3 **Beacon Cottage Farm Touring Park** Cnwll
324 C3 **Beacon Country Park** Lancs
352 B6 **Beacon Fell** Lancs
339 F2 **Beacon Fell View Holiday Park** Lancs
201 F4 **Beacon Hill service area** Suffk
48 B6 **Beacon Hill Touring Park** Dorset
324 C3 **Beacon Park Public Golf Centre** Lancs
270 C6 **Beaconsfield Farm Caravan Park** Shrops
117 G1 **Beaconsfield Golf Club** Bucks
169 G2 **Beadlow Manor Hotel & Golf & Country Club** Beds
115 G4 **Beale Park** W Berk
405 F4 **Beamish Open Air Museum** Dur
405 F4 **Beamish Park Golf Club** Dur
19 F5 **Beara Farm Caravan & Camping Site** Devon
484 A5 **Bearsden Golf Club** E Duns
98 B3 **Bearsted Golf Club** Kent
98 C4 **Bearsted vineyard** Kent
116 C6 **Bearwood Golf Club** Wokham
531 K6 **Beasdale railway station** Highld
436 C1 **Beattock Summit** S Lans
314 C3 **Beauchief golf course** Sheff
237 F2 **Beau Desert Golf Club** Staffs
50 B3 **Beaulieu Road railway station** Hants
304 D4 **Beaumaris Castle (UNESCO)** IoA
309 E3 **Bebington cycle route** Wirral
227 E1 **Beccles Golf Club** Suffk
120 A5 **Beckenham Hill railway station** Gt Lon
120 A5 **Beckenham Place Park golf course** Gt Lon
377 F4 **Beckfoot Halt railway station** Cumb
163 E2 **Beckford Silk** Worcs
86 C1 **Beckford's Tower museum** BaNES
390 C4 **Beckses Caravan Park** Cumb
19 G1 **Becky Falls** Devon
370 B2 **Bedale Golf Club** N York
242 B5 **Bede House** RutInd
195 E4 **Bedford & County Golf Club** Beds
194 D5 **Bedfordshire Golf Club** Beds
431 E3 **Bedlingtonshire Golf Club** Nthumb
89 G2 **Bedwyn railway station** Wilts
14 D3 **Bee Centre** Cnwll
135 E2 **Beechenhurst Lodge arboretum** Gloucs
486 D5 **Beecraigs Caravan & Camping Site** W Loth
486 D5 **Beecraigs Country Park** W Loth
240 D2 **Beedles Lake Golf Centre** Leics
238 D1 **Beehive Farm Woodland Lakes campsite** Derbys
28 D5 **Beer Caves** Devon
276 B2 **Beeston Fields Golf Club** Notts
276 B2 **Beeston Marina** Notts
593 D7 **Beinn na Faoghla** W Isls
465 H4 **Beith Golf Club** N Ayrs
117 F1 **Bekonscot Model Village** Bucks
163 F4 **Belas Knap** Gloucs
122 C2 **Belfairs golf course** Sthend
150 B5 **Belfry golf course** Pembks
490 C4 **Belhaven Bay Caravan & Camping Park** E Loth
121 E3 **Belhus Park golf course** Thurr
121 E3 **Belhus Park Heritage Trail** Gt Lon
480 B2 **Bellanoch Marina** Ag & B
444 D6 **Belleisle golf course** S Ayrs
307 E3 **Belle Vue** Denbgs
326 C5 **Belle Vue** Manch
467 F2 **Bellgrove railway station** C Glas
428 C3 **Bellingham Golf Club** Nthumb
250 C3 **Bells Dyke** Norfk
468 A3 **Bellshill Golf Club** N Lans
571 H2 **Bellslea Park** Abers
250 C3 **Bells Marina** Norfk
494 C2 **Bell Tower** Ag & B
274 B4 **Belmont golf course** Staffs
160 B2 **Belmont Lodge & Golf** Herefs
430 A4 **Belsay Hall, Castle & Gardens** Nthumb
278 C2 **Belton House NT** Lincs
278 C2 **Belton Park Golf Club** Lincs
277 H3 **Belvoir Castle** Leics
278 A3 **Belvoir Ride cycle route** Leics
37 G3 **Bembridge Windmill NT** IoW
264 D5 **Benar Beach Camping & Touring Park** Gwynd
580 F5 **Ben Armine Forest** Highld
593 D7 **Benbecula** W Isls
592 D6 **Benbecula airport** W Isls
357 G3 **Beningbrough Hall NT** N York
509 K2 **Ben Lawers Mountain NTS** P & K
481 G2 **Benmore Younger Botanic Garden** Ag & B
521 H1 **Ben Nevis** Highld
355 F5 **Ben Rhydding Golf Club** Brad

115 G1 Benson Waterfront Oxon
235 F4 Benthall Hall Shrops
366 B3 Bentham Golf Club N York
366 B6 Bentham railway station N York
146 B5 Bentley Golf Club Essex
56 D1 Bentley Wildfowl & Motor museum E Susx
147 G2 Benton Hall golf course Essex
202 C4 Bentwaters airfield (dis) Suffk
135 F5 Berkeley Castle Gloucs
143 E3 Berkhamsted Golf Club Herts
214 C4 Berkswell railway station Solhll
214 D4 Berkswell Windmill Solhll
251 E3 Berney Arms railway station Norfk
251 F4 Berney Arms Windmill Norfk
186 C2 Berrington Hall NT Herefs
20 A5 Berry Pomeroy Castle Devon
57 E2 Berwick railway station E Susx
475 G5 Berwick-upon-Tweed (Goswick) Golf Club Nthumb
323 G2 Bescar Lane railway station Lancs
237 F5 Bescot Stadium Wsall
237 F5 Bescot Stadium railway station Sandw
202 B4 Best Western Ufford Park Hotel Golf & Leisure Suffk
295 H5 Bestwood Country Park Notts
94 D4 Betchworth Park Golf Club Surrey
95 E4 Betchworth railway station Surrey
175 E5 Beth Chatto Gardens Essex
283 F4 Betws Garmon railway station Gwynd
285 G3 Betws-y-Coed Golf Club Conwy
227 F2 Beulah Hall Caravan Park Suffk
35 J6 Beuvelande Camp Site Jersey
347 F2 Beverley & East Riding Golf Club E R Yk
20 B6 Beverley Parks Caravan & Camping Park Torbay
347 F1 Beverley racecourse E R Yk
120 C5 Bexleyheath Golf Club Gt Lon
166 B5 Bicester Golf & Country Club Oxon
166 C5 Bicester North railway station Oxon
27 E1 Bickleigh Castle Devon
42 B6 Bickleigh Mill Devon
27 H5 Bicton Park Devon
80 C2 Biddenden vineyard Kent
292 A3 Biddulph Grange NT Staffs
189 H4 Bidford Grange Golf Club Warwks
308 C1 Bidston Golf Club Wirral
12 B3 Bigbury Golf Club Devon
448 D2 Biggar Golf Club S Lans
96 B2 Biggin Hill Gt Lon
364 D3 Bigland Hall Caravan Park Cumb
54 A2 Bignor Roman Villa W Susx
132 D3 Big Pit: National Coal Museum Torfn
417 H4 Big Water of Fleet D & G
396 B5 Billingham Beck Valley S on T
396 B5 Billingham Golf Club S on T
356 C3 Bilton Park campsite N York
334 A5 Binbrook airfield Lincs
33 F2 Bindon Abbey Dorset
342 A2 Bingley St Ives Golf Club Brad
171 H5 Birchanger Green service area Herts
237 F1 Birches Valley Forest Centre Staffs
174 C5 Birch Grove Golf Club Essex
314 D4 Birch Hall golf course Derbys
101 E2 Birchington-on-Sea railway station Kent
326 B3 Birch service area Rochdl
325 E6 Birchwood Golf Club Warrtn
120 C5 Birchwood Park golf course Gt Lon
33 G1 Birchwood Tourist Park campsite Dorset
117 E5 Bird Hills Golf Centre W & M
92 D6 Birdworld Hants
119 G6 Birkbeck railway station Gt Lon
308 D2 Birkenhead Central railway station Wirral
308 C1 Birkenhead North railway station Wirral
486 C4 Birkhill Claymine Falk
314 D3 Birley Wood Golf Club Derbys
214 B3 Birmingham airport Solhll
214 B3 Birmingham International railway station Solhll
240 C3 Birstall Golf Club C Leic
405 G4 Birtley Golf Club Gatesd
395 E3 Bishop Auckland Golf Club Dur
484 B5 Bishopbriggs Golf Club C Glas
91 E2 Bishops Green Farm campsite Hants
157 H3 Bishops Meadow Caravan Park Powys
51 G1 Bishop's Palace Hants
150 B4 Bishops Palace Pembks
171 H5 Bishop's Stortford Golf Club Herts
91 F2 Bishopswood golf course Hants
110 B5 Bitton railway station S Glos
339 G4 Blackburn Golf Club Bl w D
339 G5 Blackburn with Darwen service area Bl w D
28 C4 Blackbury Castle Devon
92 D3 Blackbushe Castle Bottom Hants
43 G4 Blackdown Hills Somset
75 E3 Black Down NT W Susx
36 D5 Blackgang Chine IoW
498 C2 Blackhall Camps Roman site P & K
405 G3 Blackham's Hill railway station Gatesd
468 C4 Blackhill NTS S Lans
119 H2 Blackhorse Road railway station Gt Lon
599 G5 Black Isle Highld
565 L4 Black Isle Highld
565 L6 Black Isle Wildlife Country Park Highld

112 B6 Blackland Lakes Holiday & Leisure Centre Wilts
326 C4 Blackley Golf Club Rochdl
129 E2 Black Lion Caravan & Camping Park Carmth
428 B1 Black Middens Bastle House Nthumb
74 B3 Blackmoor Golf Club Hants
68 B5 Blackmoor Vale Dorset
68 D5 Blackmore Vale Caravan & Camping Park Dorset
156 A6 Black Mountain Carmth
159 E4 Black Mountains Powys
74 A2 Blacknest Golf Club Hants
117 H3 Black Park Bucks
337 H3 Blackpool airport Lancs
337 F2 Blackpool Cricket Club Bpool
337 F2 Blackpool Model Village Bpool
337 E2 Blackpool North railway station Bpool
337 F2 Blackpool North Shore Golf Club Bpool
337 F2 Blackpool Park Golf Club Bpool
337 E3 Blackpool Pleasure Beach railway station Bpool
337 E3 Blackpool South railway station Bpool
465 E5 Blackshaw Farm Park N Ayrs
369 G3 Black Swan Holiday Park N York
383 G2 Blackwell Grange Golf Club Darltn
378 C6 Blackwell museum Cumb
132 C5 Blackwood Golf Club Caerph
524 C3 Blair Atholl Golf Club P & K
467 F3 Blairbeth Golf Club S Lans
524 C2 Blair Castle P & K
524 C2 Blair Castle Caravan Park P & K
498 A5 Blair Drummond Safari Park Stirlg
526 A6 Blairgowrie Golf Club P & K
109 G4 Blaise Hamlet NT Bristl
237 H4 Blake Street railway station Birm
298 D2 Blankney Golf Club Lincs
139 G1 Blenheim Palace Oxon
95 G4 Bletchingley Golf Club Surrey
255 G2 Blickling Hall NT Norfk
255 G2 Blists Hill Wrekin
322 f4 Block Eary IoM
237 E4 Bloxwich Golf Club Wsall
237 E4 Bloxwich North railway station Wsall
77 G3 Bluebell Railway W Susx
374 D3 Blue Dolphin Holiday Park N York
6 D3 Blue Hills Touring Park Cnwll
313 F3 Blue John Cavern Derbys
116 D5 Blue Mountain Golf Centre Br For
33 G3 Blue Pool Dorset
331 E2 Blue Water Marina Donc
121 E5 Bluewater Park Kent
334 C2 Blundell Park NE Lin
323 E5 Blundellsands & Crosby railway station Sefton
309 G1 Blundellsands Hill Golf Club St Hel
112 D2 Blunsdon railway station Wilts
273 E1 Blythe Bridge railway station Staffs
431 E4 Blyth Golf Club Nthumb
316 B2 Blyth service area Notts
222 B2 Boathaven Littleport Cambs
567 G5 Boath Doocot NTS Highld
551 G6 Boat of Garten Golf Club Highld
405 F4 Bobby Shafto Caravan Park Gatesd
94 D4 Bocketts Farm Park Surrey
307 E5 Bodelwyddan Castle Denbgs
212 B3 Bodenham Arboretum & Earth Centre Worcs
80 A4 Bodiam Castle NT E Susx
80 A5 Bodiam railway station E Susx
9 H3 Bodigga Cliff NT Cnwll
15 H3 Bodmin Moor Cnwll
15 G6 Bodmin Parkway railway station Cnwll
15 F5 Bodmin & Wenford Railway Cnwll
285 H2 Bodnant Caravan Park Conwy
305 H5 Bodnant NT Conwy
282 C1 Bodorgan railway station IoA
283 E2 Bodowyr Burial Chamber IoA
53 H4 Bognor Regis Golf Club W Susx
482 C5 Bogston railway station Inver
74 C3 Bohunt Manor Hants
430 A3 Bolam Lake Nthumb
12 B5 Bolberry House Farm Caravan & Camping Park Devon
237 G5 Boldmere golf course Birm
406 B2 Boldon Golf Club S Tyne
120 B3 Boleyn Ground Gt Lon
300 B2 Bolingbroke Castle Lincs
325 F3 Bolton Golf Club Bolton
325 F2 Bolton Old Links Golf Club Bolton
355 E4 Bolton Priory N York
325 E2 Bolton West service area Lancs
487 H6 Bonaly Country Park C Edin
576 D5 Bonar Bridge/Ardgay Golf Club Highld
507 H3 Bonawe Ironworks Ag & B
315 G4 Bondhay Golf & Fishing Club Derbys
375 F6 Bondville Miniature Village E R Yk
486 C4 Bo'ness & Kinneil Railway Falk
3 E3 Bone Valley Caravan & Camping Park Cnwll
466 D4 Bonnyton Golf Club E Rens
77 E5 Bookers vineyard W Susx
94 C3 Bookham railway station Surrey
358 A4 Bootham Crescent York
345 G3 Boothferry Park Golf Club E R Yk
323 G5 Bootle Golf Club Sefton
323 F5 Bootle New Strand railway station Sefton
323 F6 Bootle Oriel Road railway station Sefton
362 B4 Bootle railway station Cumb

165 H3 Bo Peep Farm Caravan Park Oxon
77 F4 Borde Hill W Susx
427 F3 Border Forest Park
452 D3 Border Union showground Border
147 E2 Boreham airfield Essex
18 B6 Boringdon Devon
568 C3 Borough Briggs Moray
388 A4 Borough Park Cumb
205 E1 Borth & Ynyslas Golf Club Cerdgn
15 E5 Boscarne Junction railway station Cnwll
236 B3 Boscobel House Shrops
3 G3 Boscrege Caravan & Camping Park Cnwll
140 A3 Bossoms Boatyard Oxon
300 B5 Boston Golf Club Lincs
299 H6 Boston West Golf Centre Lincs
239 F4 Bosworth 1485 battlefield Leics
239 F3 Bosworth Trail cycle route Leics
467 G3 Bothwell Castle Golf Club S Lans
467 H3 Bothwell (Southbound only) service area S Lans
51 F1 Botley Park Hotel Golf & Country Club Hants
99 G3 Boughton Golf Kent
218 C3 Boughton House Nhants
326 D3 Boundary Park Oldham
49 E5 Bournemouth airport Dorset
49 E5 Bournemouth Aviaton museum Dorset
196 D3 Bourn Mill Cambs
26 A6 Bovey Castle golf course Devon
33 E2 Bovington Tank museum Dorset
364 B5 Bow Bridge Cumb
19 H5 Bowden House Devon
66 C4 Bowdens Crest Caravan & Camping Park Somset
377 H1 Bowder Stone Cumb
326 D4 Bower Fold Tamesd
405 G3 Bowes Railway & Museum Sundld
569 H2 Bow Fiddle Rock Moray
451 E4 Bowhill House & Country Park Border
78 C3 Bowles Outdoor Centre & Dry Ski Slope E Susx
111 H6 Bowood Golf & Country Club Wilts
111 H6 Bowood House & Gardens Wilts
22 B6 Bowood Park golf course Cnwll
309 F1 Bowring Park Golf Club Knows
94 D4 Box Hill Surrey
143 E4 Boxmoor Golf Club Herts
187 F4 Boyce Caravan Park Herefs
122 B2 Boyce Hill Golf Club Essex
199 E6 Boyton vineyard Suffk
355 E4 Bracken Ghyll Golf Club Brad
308 D3 Brackenwood Golf Club Wirral
325 G4 Brackley Municipal Golf Club Salfd
342 C3 Bradford & Bingley Stadium Brad
342 C1 Bradford Golf Club Leeds
342 C3 Bradford Moor Golf Club Brad
87 E2 Bradford-on-Avon Tithe Barn Wilts
240 B2 Bradgate Park Leics
342 C5 Bradley Park golf course Kirk
498 D6 Braehead Golf Club Clacks
466 D1 Braehead Shopping Centre Rens
537 H4 Braemar Golf Club Abers
488 B6 Braid Hills golf course C Edin
400 B1 Braids Caravan Park D & G
165 E2 Brailes Golf Club Warwks
173 F5 Braintree Freeport railway station Essex
173 F5 Braintree Golf Club Essex
58 C4 Brakes Coppice Park E Susx
314 D2 Bramall Lane Sheff
312 A2 Bramall Park Golf Club Stockp
312 B3 Bramhall Golf Club Stockp
343 H1 Bramham Park Leeds
93 G5 Bramley Golf Club Surrey
401 F3 Brampton (Cumbria) railway station Cumb
401 F3 Brampton Golf Club Cumb
193 F2 Brampton Heath Golf Centre Nhants
220 B6 Brampton Park Golf Club Cambs
227 E3 Brampton railway station Suffk
49 H2 Bramshaw Golf Club Hants
395 E2 Brancepeth Castle Golf Club Dur
213 E2 Brandhall golf course Sandw
223 F2 Brandon Country Park Suffk
215 G4 Brandon Stadium Warwks
559 H5 Brandsbutt Symbol Stone Abers
97 E2 Brands Hatch Kent
333 E5 Brandy Wharf Leisure Park Lincs
512 D5 Branklyn NTS P & K
60 D5 Brannams Pottery Devon
259 F3 Branodunum NT Norfk
341 G2 Branshaw Golf Club Brad
274 C5 Branston Golf & Country Club Staffs
378 B5 Brantwood Cumb
62 A2 Brass Rubbing (Exmoor Centre) Devon
192 B1 Braunston Marina Nhants
151 E5 Brawdy airfield (dis) Pembks
50 A6 Braxton Gardens Hants
509 G3 Breadalbane Stirlg
509 J3 Breadalbane Folklore Centre Stirlg
302 B4 Breakwater Quarry IoA
56 C3 Breaky Bottom vineyard E Susx
70 D6 Breamore House Hants
84 A3 Brean Down Tropical Bird Garden Somset
84 A4 Brean Golf Club Somset
528 C3 Brechin Castle & Pictavia Angus
528 D2 Brechin Golf & Squash Club Angus
247 F3 Breckland Meadows Touring Park Norfk

157 G5 Brecon Beacons Powys
156 C5 Brecon Beacons National Park
157 F4 Brecon Beacons National Park Visitor Centre Powys
157 G4 Brecon Golf Club Powys
131 H2 Brecon Mountain Railway Powys
162 D2 Bredon Barn NT Worcs
275 F5 Breedon Priory Golf Centre Derbys
325 H2 Breightmet Golf Club Bury
63 F4 Brendon Hills Somset
118 C3 Brent Valley Golf Club Gt Lon
81 F4 Brenzett Aeronautical Museum Kent
174 D2 Brett Vale Golf Club Suffk
162 C5 Briarfields campsite Gloucs
144 D3 Brickendon Grange Golf Club Herts
37 F2 Brickfields Horse Country IoW
11 E3 Brickfields Recreation Ground C Plym
162 C5 Brickhampton Court Golf Club Gloucs
373 G1 Bridestones (Rock Formation) N York
24 D5 Bridestowe Caravan Park Devon
134 B2 Bridge Caravan Park & Camping Site Mons
498 C6 Bridgehaugh Park Stirlg
351 G5 Bridge House Marina & Caravan Park Lancs
378 C4 Bridge House NT Cumb
125 G1 Bridge Meadow Stadium Pembks
291 E6 Bridgemere Garden World Ches
498 B5 Bridge of Allan Golf Club Stirlg
383 F1 Bridge Roman site N York
235 G6 Bridgnorth Golf Club Shrops
65 E5 Bridgwater service area Somset
361 F2 Bridlington Golf Club E R Yk
361 F1 Bridlington Harbour Marina E R Yk
375 G6 Bridlington Links golf course E R Yk
30 B4 Bridport & West Dorset Golf Club Dorset
145 F2 Briggens House Hotel golf course Herts
412 B6 Brighouse Bay & Driving Range D & G
412 B5 Brighouse Bay Holiday Park D & G
55 G3 Brighton & Hove Golf Club Br & H
56 A3 Brighton racecourse Br & H
218 D2 Brigstock Country Park Nhants
292 C3 Brindley Mill Staffs
443 E5 Brinkburn Priory Nthumb
112 B2 Brinkworth golf course Wilts
85 F2 Bristol airport N Som
110 B6 Bristol & Bath/Avon Cycleway S Glos
109 F5 Bristol & Clifton Golf Club N Som
109 G5 Bristol Golf Club S Glos
109 H4 Bristol Parkway railway station S Glos
109 G5 Bristol Temple Meads railway station Bristl
488 B4 Britannia C Edin
292 A6 Britannia Stadium C Stke
22 C5 British Cycling museum Cnwll
104 B2 British Steel Port Talbot golf course Neath
397 E5 British Steel Redcar railway station R & Cl
11 F3 Brixton Caravan & Camping Park Devon
217 G6 Brixworth Country Park Nhants
138 D3 Brize Norton airport Oxon
77 E3 Broadfield Stadium W Susx
170 B5 Broadhall Stadium Herts
81 F2 Broad Hembury Holiday Park Kent
250 D1 Broadland Conservation Centre Norfk
71 H5 Broadlands Hants
20 A6 Broadleigh Farm campsite Devon
48 B5 Broadstone (Dorset) Golf Club Poole
93 G5 Broadwater Park Golf Club Surrey
163 H2 Broadway Golf Club Worcs
85 E4 Broadway House Holiday Caravan & Camping Park Somset
163 H2 Broadway Tower Worcs
485 E5 Broadwood Stadium N Lans
185 F6 Brobury House Herefs
50 A4 Brockenhurst Manor Golf Club Hants
82 B3 Brockhill Country Park Kent
38 C5 Brocklands Adventure Park Cnwll
240 D5 Brocks Hill Leics
273 E6 Brocton Hall Golf Club Staffs
461 E2 Brodick Castle NTS N Ayrs
461 E2 Brodick Golf Club N Ayrs
567 H5 Brodie Castle NTS Moray
330 B3 Brodsworth Welfare FC Donc
96 C2 Broke Hill Golf Club Kent
87 E4 Brokerswood Country Park Wilts
308 D3 Bromborough Golf Club Wirral
308 D3 Bromborough Rake railway station Wirral
120 B6 Bromley FC Gt Lon
96 B1 Bromley golf course Gt Lon
383 E4 Brompton-on-Swale Caravan & Camping Park N York
213 E5 Bromsgrove Golf Centre Worcs
158 C2 Bronllys Castle campsite Powys
306 B4 Bron-Y-Wendon Caravan Park Conwy
244 D3 Bronze Age Excavations C Pete
322 e8 Broogh Fort IoM
318 B4 Brookdale Golf Club Oldham
85 E2 Brook Lodge Farm Camping & Caravan Park N Som
337 G6 Brooklyn Park & Country Club Lancs
144 B4 Brookmans Park Golf Club Herts
113 E3 Broome Manor Golf Complex Swindn

100 D6 Broome Park Golf Club Kent
574 C5 Broomfield Holiday Park Highld
551 H5 Broomhill railway station Highld
471 F1 Broomieknowe Golf Club Mdloth
577 K2 Brora Golf Club Highld
391 E4 Brougham Castle Cumb
346 D4 Brough Golf Club E R Yk
405 G2 Brough Park N u Ty
165 G2 Broughton Castle Oxon
514 D3 Broughty Castle C Dund
528 C1 Brown Caterthun Angus
237 F3 Brownhills West railway station Staffs
540 D4 Brownmuir Caravan Park Abers
428 C3 Brown Rigg Caravan & Camping Park Nthumb
27 G5 Browns Farm Caravan Park Devon
485 G2 Brucefields Family Golfing Centre Stirlg
119 G1 Bruce Grove railway station Gt Lon
425 F5 Bruce's Cave Caravan & Camping Park D & G
250 C3 Brundall Bay Marina Norfk
250 C3 Brundall Gardens railway station Norfk
432 B4 Brunston Castle golf course S Ayrs
308 D2 Brunswick railway station Lpool
455 G4 Brunton airfield Nthumb
400 D3 Brunton Park Cumb
487 G4 Bruntsfield Links Golfing Society C Edin
3 C2 Bryher campsite IoS
263 E5 Bryn Bach Caravan & Camping Site Gwynd
132 B2 Bryn Bach Parc Blae G
283 F1 Bryn Celli Ddu IoA
105 E2 Bryngarw Country Park Brdgnd
283 F4 Bryn Gloch Caravan & Camping Park Gwynd
106 B5 Brynhill Golf Club V Glam
267 E3 Bryn Hynod railway station Gwynd
157 H4 Brynich Caravan Park Powys
132 B5 Bryn Meadows Golf & Country Hotel Caerph
287 F2 Bryn Morfydd Hotel Golf Club Denbgs
205 E2 Brynowen Holiday Park Cerdgn
207 E2 Bryn Tail Lead Mine Powys
483 G2 Buchanan Castle Golf Club Stirlg
76 D3 Buchan Country Park W Susx
19 F4 Buckfast Butterfly Farm Devon
167 E3 Buckingham Golf Club Bucks
118 A2 Buckinghamshire Golf Club Bucks
167 F6 Buckinghamshire Railway Centre Bucks
17 G5 Buckland Abbey NT Devon
85 E5 Bucklegrove Caravan & Camping Park Somset
569 G3 Buckpool Golf Club Moray
23 E2 Budemeadows Touring Holiday Park Cnwll
23 E1 Bude & North Cornwall Golf Club Cnwll
5 E3 Budock Vean Hotel on the River golf course Cnwll
235 E4 Buildwas Abbey Shrops
183 G4 Builth Wells Golf Club Powys
47 H6 Bulbury Woods Golf Club Dorset
303 F2 Bull Bay Golf Club IoA
295 G5 Bulwell Forest Golf Club C Nott
276 C1 Bulwell railway station C Nott
24 D4 Bundu Camping & Caravan Park Devon
226 C1 Bungay & Waveney Valley Golf Club Suffk
147 F3 Bunsay Downs Golf Club Essex
239 H6 Burbage Common & Woods Leics
85 F5 Burcott Mill Somset
256 A5 Bure Valley Railway Norfk
138 C2 Burford Golf Club Oxon
77 E5 Burgess Hill Golf Centre W Susx
430 B1 Burgham Park Golf & Leisure Club Nthumb
251 E4 Burgh Castle Marina Norfk
567 L3 Burghead Well Moray
186 B6 Burghill Valley Herefs
243 E3 Burghley House C Pete
243 E3 Burghley Park Golf Club C Pete
94 B2 Burhill Golf Club Surrey
500 B4 Burleigh Castle P & K
49 G4 Burley Golf Club Hants
343 E2 Burley Park railway station Leeds
359 F5 Burnby Hall E R Yk
117 F3 Burnham Beeches Bucks
117 F3 Burnham Beeches Golf Club Bucks
84 A4 Burnham & Berrow Golf Club Somset
148 B5 Burnham-on-Crouch Golf Club Essex
84 B5 Burnham-on-Sea Holiday Village Somset
340 C3 Burnley Barracks railway station Lancs
340 C3 Burnley Central railway station Lancs
340 C3 Burnley Golf Club Lancs
340 C3 Burnley Manchester Road railway station Lancs
444 D6 Burns Cottage museum S Ayrs
389 H5 Burns Farm Caravan Park Cumb
568 E4 Burnside Caravan Park Moray
467 F2 Burnside railway station S Lans
488 A2 Burntisland Golf House Club Fife
296 A4 Burntstump Country Park Notts
241 G2 Burrough Hill Leics
62 D2 Burrowhayes Farm Caravan & Camping Site Somset
65 G5 Burrow Mump Somset
324 A2 Burscough Junction railway station Lancs
291 H4 Burslem Golf Club C Stke

656 Leisure index: Burton Constable Hall - Commonwealth Indoor Stadium

348 C2 Burton Constable Hall E R Yk
348 C2 Burton Constable Holiday Park & Arboretum E R Yk
185 H3 Burton Court Herefs
191 F4 Burton Dassett Hills Country Park Warwks
365 H4 Burton-in-Kendal (Northbound Only) service area Lancs
274 D5 Burton upon Trent Golf Club Derbys
310 B1 Burtonwood service area Warrtn
326 B3 Bury Golf Club Bury
90 A6 Bury Hill Hants
199 G1 Bury St Edmunds Golf Club Suffk
270 D4 Bury Walls Shrops
138 C5 Buscot Park NT Oxon
143 G6 Bushey Golf & Country Club Herts
143 G5 Bushey Hall Golf Club Herts
144 D5 Bush Hill Park Golf Club Gt Lon
195 G2 Bushmead Priory Beds
94 B2 Bus museum Surrey
464 B1 Bute Ag & B
464 B1 Bute Golf Club Ag & B
237 H5 Butlers Lane railway station Birm
52 C1 Butser Ancient Farm Hants
304 B5 Butterfly Palace IoA
37 E2 Butterfly World IoW
295 E4 Butterley railway station Derbys
381 F5 Buttertubs Pass N York
215 E4 Butts Park Arena Covtry
313 E5 Buxton & High Peak Golf Club Derbys
256 A5 Buxton railway station Norfk
205 G3 Bwlch Nant Yr Arian Forest Visitor Centre Cerdgn
94 B2 Byfleet & New Haw railway station Surrey
371 H4 Byland Abbey N York
404 D3 Byreside Caravan Site Dur
20 A6 Byslades International Touring & Camping Park Devon

C

109 E5 Cadbury Camp N Som
213 F3 Cadbury World Birm
28 A3 Cadhay Devon
186 D1 Cadmore Lodge Hotel & Country Club Worcs
16 D5 Cadson Bury Cnwll
320 A3 Cadwell Park Lincs
234 B5 Caer Caradoc Shrops
150 B5 Caerfai Bay Caravan & Tent Park Pembks
398 C1 Caerlaverock Castle D & G
107 F1 Caerleon golf course Newpt
283 E3 Caernarfon Castle (UNESCO) Gwynd
106 C2 Caerphilly Golf Club Caerph
514 B3 Caird Park golf course C Dund
401 F4 Cairndale Caravan Park Cumb
536 E2 Cairngorm Mountains Highld
536 E1 Cairngorm Ski Area Highld
417 G6 Cairn Holy Chambered Cairns D & G
583 K1 Cairn o'Get Highld
540 C3 Cairn o'Mount Abers
417 G4 Cairnsmore of Fleet D & G
251 G2 Caister Castle Norfk
250 A4 Caistor Roman Town Norfk
512 C4 Caithness Glass P & K
203 E2 Cakes & Ale campsite Suffk
115 H5 Calcot Park Golf Club W Berk
191 H2 Calcutt Marina Warwks
251 F4 Caldecott Hall Golf & Leisure Norfk
467 G2 Calderbraes Golf Club C Glas
237 F5 Calderfields Golf Academy Wsall
467 G4 Calderglen S Lans
466 B4 Caldwell Golf Club E Rens
308 B3 Caldy Golf Club Wirral
528 D3 Caledonian Railway Angus
565 L7 Caley Marina Highld
236 D3 Calf Heath Marina Staffs
92 C1 California Chalet & Touring Park Wokham
92 C1 California Country Park Wokham
275 F5 Calke Abbey NT Derbys
497 F3 Callander Golf Club Stirlg
486 A4 Callendar Park Falk
91 G2 Calleva Roman site Hants
3 G3 Calloose Caravan & Camping Park Cnwll
51 E4 Calshot Castle Hants
51 E4 Calshot Velodrome Hants
17 F5 Calstock Viaduct Devon
342 C3 Calverley Golf Club Brad
59 F3 Camber Castle E Susx
93 E3 Camberley Heath Golf Club Surrey
6 C6 Camborne & Redruth Mining District (UNESCO) Cnwll
182 B2 Cambrian Mountains Cerdgn
197 G3 Cambridge airport Cambs
197 E1 Cambridge Golf Club Cambs
197 E3 Cambridge National golf course Cambs
197 E2 Cambridgeshire Moat House Golf Club Cambs
6 C4 Cambrose Touring Park Cnwll
135 H4 Cam & Dursley railway station Gloucs
32 B2 Came Down Golf Club Dorset
400 C1 Camelot Caravan Park Cumb
324 C1 Camelot Theme Park Lancs
15 E5 Camel Valley vineyard Cnwll
527 E4 Camera Obscura NTS Angus
483 E3 Cameron House Marina W Duns
168 B2 Campbell Park M Keyn
456 D2 Campbeltown airport Ag & B
514 B3 Camperdown Country Park C Dund
514 A3 Camperdown golf course C Dund
551 G6 Campgrounds of Scotland Highld
9 G3 Camping Caradon Touring Park Cnwll
441 F5 Camp Roman site Nthumb
484 B3 Campsie Fells Stirlg
484 C4 Campsie Golf Club E Duns
441 E2 Camps Roman site Border
51 G3 Cams Hall Estate Golf Club Hants
531 H5 Camusdarach campsite Highld
193 F5 Canal museum Nhants
236 D5 Canal path cycle route Wolves
48 C5 Canford Magna Golf Club Poole
487 E2 Canmore Golf Club Fife
548 E3 Cannich Caravan & Camping Park Highld
65 E3 Cannington golf course Somset
273 E6 Cannock Chase Staffs
237 F2 Cannock Chase museum Staffs
237 E2 Cannock Park golf course Staffs
328 D3 Cannon Hall museum Barns
192 C4 Canons Ashby NT Nhants
145 F2 Canons Brook Golf Club Essex
20 A1 Canonteign Falls & Country Park Devon
100 B4 Canterbury East railway station Kent
100 C4 Canterbury Golf Club Kent
100 B4 Canterbury West railway station Kent
380 B5 Cantley Spout (Waterfall) Cumb
234 C3 Cantlop Bridge Shrops
318 B6 Canwick Park Golf Club Lincs
2 C3 Cape Cornwall Golf & Country Club Cnwll
144 D5 Capel Manor Gardens Gt Lon
311 G5 Capesthorne Hall Ches
482 C4 Cappielow Park Inver
445 F2 Caprington Golf Club E Ayrs
16 C4 Caradon Mining District (UNESCO) Cnwll
254 B2 Caravan Club M.V.C. Site Norfk
105 H6 Cardiff airport V Glam
106 C4 Cardiff Athletic Stadium Cardif
106 C4 Cardiff Caravan Park Cardif
106 D3 Cardiff Gate service area Cardif
106 C3 Cardiff Golf Club Cardif
106 C4 Cardiff Queen Street railway station Cardif
106 A4 Cardiff West service area Cardif
178 D4 Cardigan Golf Club Cerdgn
178 D3 Cardigan Island Coastal Farm Park Cerdgn
412 A3 Cardoness Castle D & G
482 D4 Cardross Golf Club Ag & B
318 A5 Carholme Golf Club Lincs
365 E4 Cark & Cartmel railway station Cumb
401 E2 Carlisle airport Cumb
400 D3 Carlisle Golf Club Cumb
400 D4 Carlisle racecourse Cumb
202 D2 Carlton Park Caravan Park Suffk
468 C4 Carluke Golf Club S Lans
515 E2 Carlungie Earth-House Angus
119 F4 Carlyle's House NT Gt Lon
8 C3 Carlyon Bay Caravan & Camping Park Cnwll
8 D3 Carlyon Bay Hotel Golf Club Cnwll
154 A4 Carmarthen Golf Club Carmth
448 B2 Carmichael Visitor Centre S Lans
492 D4 Carnassarie Castle Ag & B
460 D4 Carn Ban N Ayrs
6 C5 Carn Brea Cnwll
2 D4 Carn Euny Cnwll
14 B4 Carnevas Holiday Park & Farm Cottages Cnwll
262 D3 Carn Fadrum Gwynd
2 D2 Carn Galver NT Cnwll
16 A5 Carnglaze Caverns Cnwll
155 G5 Carn Goch Carmth
577 J3 Carn Liath Highld
7 F5 Carnon Downs Caravan & Camping Park Cnwll
515 E3 Carnoustie Golf Links Angus
469 F5 Carnwath Golf Club S Lans
459 F4 Carradale Bay Caravan Park Ag & B
459 G4 Carradale Golf Club Ag & B
459 G4 Carradale House Ag & B
428 D5 Carrawburgh: Temple of Mithras Roman site Nthumb
551 G5 Carrbridge Golf Club Highld
155 G6 Carreg Cennen Castle Carmth
102 C5 Carreglwyd Camping & Caravan Park Swans
150 D3 Carreg Sampson Pembks
419 F3 Carrick S Ayrs
487 H5 Carrick Knowe golf course C Edin
250 A3 Carrow Road Norfk
294 A5 Carsington Fields Caravan Park Derbys
417 F6 Carsluith Castle D & G
139 E5 Carswell Golf & Country Club Oxon
440 C3 Carter Bar Border
174 C3 Carter's vineyard Essex
365 E4 Cartmel racecourse Cumb
379 F5 Carus Green & Driving Range Cumb
5 E3 Carwinion Gardens Cnwll
322 h5 Cashtal yn Ard IoM
106 B3 Castell Coch Cardif
158 C3 Castell Dinas Powys
152 C2 Castell Henllys Pembks
229 F3 Castell y Bere Gwynd
253 G4 Castle Acre Norfk
118 C3 Castle Bar Park railway station Gt Lon
499 F5 Castle Campbell NTS Clacks
417 F5 Castle Cary Holiday Park D & G
111 F4 Castle Coombe Circuit Wilts
35 d3 Castle Cornet Guern
413 E2 Castle Douglas Golf Club D & G
25 H4 Castle Drogo NT Devon
396 B4 Castle Eden Walkway S on T
556 C2 Castle Fraser NTS Abers
589 K6 Castle Girnigoe & Sinclair Highld
326 C2 Castle Hawk Golf Club Rochdl
40 D2 Castle Hill Devon
240 C3 Castle Hill Country Park C Leic
372 D5 Castle Howard N York
415 F4 Castle Kennedy D & G
470 D2 Castlelaw Mdloth
589 H2 Castle of Mey Highld
589 K7 Castle of Old Wick Highld
415 E4 Castle of St John D & G
330 D4 Castle Park Donc
413 G4 Castle Point Caravan Park D & G
122 B2 Castle Point Golf Club Essex
389 G5 Castlerigg Cumb
389 G5 Castlerigg Farm Camping & Caravan Site Cumb
237 F2 Castle Ring Staffs
465 H3 Castle Semple Rens
326 C2 Castleton (Greater Manchester) railway station Rochdl
385 H3 Castleton Moor railway station N York
322 d9 Castletown Golf Links IoM
322 f7 Castleward IoM
309 H3 Catalyst museum Halton
312 D5 Cat and Fiddle Ches
467 E3 Cathcart Castle Golf Club E Rens
467 F3 Cathkin Braes Golf Club S Lans
357 E3 Cattal railway station N York
383 E5 Catterick Golf Club N York
383 F5 Catterick racecourse N York
392 D4 Cauldron Snout (Waterfall) Cumb
9 G2 Causeland railway station Cnwll
142 A6 Causeway Stadium Bucks
405 F3 Causey Arch Dur
403 G2 Causey Hill Caravan Park Nthumb
346 D3 Cave Castle Hotel & Country Club E R Yk
312 D5 Cavendish Golf Club Derbys
484 C5 Cawder Golf Club E Duns
344 D2 Cawood Park campsite N York
596 E5 Ceann a Tuath na Hearadh W Isls
130 B4 Cefn Coed Colliery Museum Neath
269 E1 Cefn Viaduct Wrexhm
178 C4 Ceibwr Bay Pembks
284 C2 Cei Llydan railway station Gwynd
467 F2 Celtic Park C Glas
153 F1 Cenarth Falls Holiday Park Cerdgn
375 E4 Centenary Way Camping & Caravan Park N York
119 F5 Central London Golf Centre Gt Lon
487 G1 Central Park Fife
230 B4 Centre for Alternative Technology Powys
291 H5 Ceramica C Stke
145 E2 Chadwell Springs Golf Club Herts
169 E4 Chalgrave Manor Golf Club Beds
140 D5 Chalgrove airfield Oxon
60 D2 Chambercombe Manor Devon
548 F3 Chambered Cairn Highld
54 D2 Chanctonbury Ring W Susx
35 f6 Channel Islands Military Museum Jersey
147 E2 Channels Golf Club Essex
61 H2 Channel View campsite Devon
312 D3 Chapel-en-le-Frith Golf Club Derbys
23 G4 Chapmanswell Caravan Park Devon
174 A4 Chappel & Wakes Colne railway station Essex
119 G3 Charing Cross railway station Gt Lon
190 D3 Charlecote Park NT Warwks
56 D3 Charleston Farmhouse museum E Susx
8 C3 Charlestown (UNESCO) Cnwll
502 D4 Charleton golf course Fife
324 D1 Charnock Richard Golf Club Lancs
324 C2 Charnock Richard service area Lancs
240 B1 Charnwood Forest Golf Club Leics
48 B5 Charris Camping & Caravan Park Dorset
77 G1 Chartham Park golf course Surrey
80 C1 Chart Hills Golf Club Kent
142 C4 Chartridge Park Golf Club Bucks
96 C4 Chartwell NT Kent
237 F3 Chasetown railway station Staffs
237 F3 Chasewater Heaths railway station Staffs
237 F3 Chasewater Railway Staffs
325 H6 Chassen Road railway station Traffd
164 C4 Chastleton House NT Oxon
468 A4 Chatelherault Country Park S Lans
314 B5 Chatsworth Derbys
136 C5 Chavenage House Gloucs
311 H2 Cheadle Golf Club Stockp
85 E4 Cheddar Bridge Touring Park Somset
85 E4 Cheddar Caves & Gorge Somset
30 B1 Chedington Court Golf Club Dorset
146 D4 Chelmsford Golf Club Essex
96 C2 Chelsfield Lakes Golf Centre Gt Lon
163 E5 Cheltenham racecourse Gloucs
163 E4 Cheltenham racecourse railway station Gloucs
162 D5 Cheltenham Spa railway station Gloucs
134 C5 Chepstow racecourse Mons
404 C2 Cherryburn NT Nthumb
96 B3 Cherry Lodge Golf Club Gt Lon
93 E3 Cherrywood Road Hants
192 A6 Cherwell Edge Golf Club Nhants
166 C4 Cherwell Valley service area Oxon
170 B4 Chesfield Downs Golf Club Herts
142 D4 Chesham & Ley Hill Golf Club Bucks
308 D4 Cheshire Cycleway Ches
311 F3 Cheshire Cycleway Ches
144 D4 Cheshunt Park golf course Herts
32 A3 Chesil Beach Dorset
36 B3 Chessell Pottery IoW
94 D2 Chessington Golf Centre Gt Lon
94 D2 Chessington World of Adventures Surrey
314 D6 Chesterfield Golf Club Derbys
289 E2 Chester Golf Club Ches
402 D1 Chesterholm (Vindolanda) Roman site Nthumb
405 G4 Chester-le-Street Golf Club Dur
289 F1 Chester racecourse Ches
237 H6 Chester Road railway station Birm
309 G4 Chester service area Ches
429 E5 Chesters Fort Roman site Nthumb
489 G4 Chesters Hill Fort E Loth
289 E2 Chester Southerly Caravan Park Ches
291 G5 Chesterton Raceway Staffs
236 A5 Chesterton Valley Golf Club Shrops
191 E3 Chesterton Windmill Warwks
100 B2 Chestfield & Swalecliffe railway station Kent
100 B2 Chestfield (Whitstable) Golf Club Kent
313 E3 Chestnut Centre Derbys
46 A3 Chetnole railway station Dorset
37 F4 Cheverton Copse Holiday Park IoW
355 H6 Chevin Forest Park Leeds
294 C6 Chevin Golf Club Derbys
49 G6 Chewton Glen Hotel golf course Hants
218 D6 Chichele College Nhants
53 F3 Chichester airfield W Susx
53 F4 Chichester Golf Club W Susx
53 E4 Chichester Marina W Susx
75 F3 Chiddingfold golf course Surrey
114 D5 Chieveley service area W Berk
120 B1 Chigwell Golf Club Essex
91 E2 Children's Action Farm Hants
198 B5 Chilford Hundred vineyard Cambs
454 D4 Chillingham Wild Cattle Park Nthumb
142 B2 Chiltern Forest Golf Club Bucks
116 B2 Chiltern Hills Oxon
276 B2 Chilwell Manor Golf Club Notts
72 A6 Chilworth Golf Club Hants
10 D1 China Fleet Country Club Cnwll
339 E2 Chingle Hall Lancs
141 G4 Chinnor & Princes Risborough Railway Oxon
111 G4 Chippenham Golf Club Wilts
165 E4 Chipping Norton Golf Club Oxon
110 C3 Chipping Sodbury Golf Club S Glos
95 F3 Chipstead Golf Club Surrey
269 E2 Chirk Castle NT Wrexhm
269 E2 Chirk Golf Club Wrexhm
89 G1 Chisbury Chapel Wilts
120 B5 Chislehurst Golf Club Gt Lon
119 E4 Chiswick House Gt Lon
60 C5 Chivenor airfield Devon
60 D5 Chivenor Caravan Park Devon
6 D4 Chiverton Caravan & Touring Park Cnwll
93 G2 Chobham Golf Club Surrey
290 A4 Cholmondeley Castle Ches
115 F2 Cholsey & Wallingford Railway Oxon
324 D1 Chorley Golf Club Lancs
143 E5 Chorleywood Golf Club Herts
311 G1 Chorlton-cum-Hardy Golf Club Manch
558 C1 Christie Park Abers
351 F2 Christie Park Lancs
40 D5 Chulmleigh Golf Club Devon
156 B3 Church Bank Playing Fields Carmth
69 G6 Church Farm Caravan & Camping Park Dorset
19 F2 Church House NT Devon
212 C4 Churchill & Blakedown Golf Club Worcs
19 F4 Churchill Farm Campsite Devon
340 A4 Church & Oswaldtwistle railway station Lancs
118 B3 Church Road Gt Lon
377 E4 Church Stile Farm campsite Cumb
234 A5 Church Stretton Golf Club Shrops
292 C4 Churnet Valley Railway Staffs
13 F1 Churston Golf Club Torbay
13 F1 Churston railway station Torbay
268 D2 Chwarel Wynne Mine Wrexhm
4 D5 Chy-Carne Holiday Park Cnwll
3 E2 Chysauster Cnwll
43 G3 Cider Farm museum Somset
178 D5 Cilgerran Castle NT Pembks
181 F4 Cilgwyn Golf Club Cerdgn
137 F4 Cirencester Golf Club Gloucs
54 D3 Cissbury Ring W Susx
120 B3 City airport Gt Lon
276 C2 City Ground C Nott
197 G3 City Ground Cambs
215 F4 City of Coventry-Brandon Wood Golf Club Warwks
326 C5 City of Manchester Stadium Manch
430 D6 City of Newcastle Golf Club N u Ty
343 F6 City of Wakefield Golf Club Wakefd
469 G1 City Stadium W Loth
96 B4 Clacket Lane service area Surrey
486 B1 Clackmannan Tower Clacks
149 G2 Clacton Golf Club Essex
533 H8 Claggan Park Highld
519 H2 Claish Moss Highld
531 H2 Clan Donald Highld
524 B2 Clan Donnachaidh museum P & K
94 A4 Clandon Park NT Surrey
94 A4 Clandon railway station Surrey
94 A4 Clandon Regis Golf Club Surrey
565 K4 Clanland & Seapoint Highld
119 F4 Clapham Junction railway station Gt Lon
367 E6 Clapham (North Yorkshire) railway station N York
19 E2 Clapper Bridge Devon
119 G2 Clapton railway station Gt Lon
199 F5 Clare Castle Suffk
94 C2 Claremont NT Surrey
143 H3 Clarence Park Herts
421 F4 Clatteringshaws Forest & Wildlife Centre D & G
514 B3 Clatto Country Park C Dund
566 D8 Clava Cairns NTS Highld
167 F4 Claydon NT Bucks
351 G5 Claylands Caravan Park Lancs
31 E2 Clay Pigeon Caravan Park Dorset
289 E4 Clays Golf Centre Wrexhm
342 B3 Clayton Golf Club Brad
8 C2 Clay Trail: Bugle to Eden cycle route Cnwll
134 D3 Clearwell Caves Gloucs
342 C4 Cleckheaton & District Golf Club Brad
334 D3 Cleethorpes Golf Club NE Lin
63 G3 Cleeve Abbey Somset
163 E4 Cleeve Hill Golf Club Gloucs
211 F4 Cleobury Mortimer Golf Club Shrops
57 E4 Clergy House NT E Susx
108 D5 Clevedon Court NT N Som
108 D5 Clevedon Golf Club N Som
397 E4 Cleveland Golf Club R & Cl
371 G2 Cleveland Way N York
386 D1 Cleveland Way N York
87 E6 Cley Hill Wilts
118 C3 C & L Golf & Country Club Gt Lon
605 J2 Clickimin Broch Shet
602 C7 Click Mill Ork
468 A2 Cliftonhill Stadium N Lans
326 A4 Clifton railway station Salfd
251 E2 Clippesby Hall campsite Norfk
340 A2 Clitheroe Golf Club Lancs
117 F2 Cliveden NT Bucks
484 A4 Clober Golf Club E Duns
119 H6 Clock House railway station Gt Lon
284 D3 Clogwyn railway station Gwynd
33 E1 Clouds Hill NT Dorset
322 g6 Cloven Stones IoM
313 E5 Clover Fields Touring Caravan Park Derbys
316 B5 Clumber Park NT Notts
307 G6 Clwydian Range Denbgs
483 H5 Clydebank & District golf course W Duns
483 G5 Clydebank Municipal golf course W Duns
465 E6 Clyde Marina N Ayrs
448 A2 Clyde Valley Caravan Park S Lans
468 D6 Clyde Valley Woodlands S Lans
103 F3 Clyne Golf Club Swans
588 C3 Cnoc Freiceadain Long Cairns Highld
235 F4 Coalbrookdale Wrekin
235 F4 Coalport Wrekin
391 E3 Coast to Coast cycle route Cumb
400 C4 Coast to Coast cycle route Cumb
404 C4 Coast to Coast cycle route Dur
20 C3 Coast View Holiday Park Devon
468 A1 Coatbridge Sunnyside railway station N Lans
113 E3 Coate Water Country Park Swindn
40 C2 Cobbaton Combat Collection Devon
98 A3 Cobtree Manor Park golf course Kent
466 B2 Cochrane Castle Golf Club Rens
389 E3 Cockermouth Golf Club Cumb
351 F4 Cockersand Abbey Lancs
344 B2 Cocksford golf course N York
213 G4 Cocks Moors Woods Golf Club Birm
265 G4 Coed-y-Brenin Visitor Centre Gwynd
265 G4 Coed-y-Brenin Forest Park Gwynd
105 E3 Coed-Y-Mwstwr Golf Club Brdgnd
20 D2 Cofton Country Holiday Park Devon
173 G5 Coggeshall Grange Barn NT Essex
574 B3 Coigach Highld
542 C7 Colbost Croft museum Highld
126 D3 Colby Woodland Garden Pembks
174 C4 Colchester and East Essex Cricket Club Essex
174 C4 Colchester Golf Club Essex
174 C5 Colchester Zoo Essex
216 D4 Cold Ashby Golf Club Nhants
43 E5 Coldharbour Mill museum Devon
64 C4 Coleridge Cottage NT Somset
15 G5 Colesloggett Halt railway station Cnwll
13 G2 Coleton Fishacre NT Devon
162 D5 College Ground Gloucs
316 A4 College Pines golf course Notts
56 B2 College vineyard E Susx
491 E5 Collegiate Church Border
489 E4 Collegiate Church E Loth
15 H4 Colliford Lake Park Cnwll
15 H4 Colliford Tavern Campsite Cnwll
58 B5 Collington railway station E Susx
193 F3 Collingtree Park golf course Nhants
195 F3 Colmworth & North Bedfordshire golf course Beds
341 E1 Colne Golf Club Lancs
173 G4 Colne Valley Golf Club Essex
173 F2 Colne Valley Railway Essex
478 B3 Colonsay Golf Club Ag & B
413 G4 Colvend Golf Club D & G
468 B3 Colville Park Golf Club N Lans
276 D2 Colwick Country Park C Nott
306 A3 Colwyn Bay Cricket Club Conwy
90 B2 Combe Gibbet W Berk
139 G1 Combe railway station Oxon
64 A4 Combe Sydenham Hall & Country Park Somset
385 H3 Commondale railway station N York
326 C5 Commonwealth Indoor Stadium Manch

510 D5 Comrie Golf Club P & K
314 D1 Concord Park Golf Club Sheff
528 D6 Condor ski slope Angus
292 A2 Congleton Golf Club Ches
299 G3 Coningsby airfield Lincs
364 A0 Conishead Priory Cumb
239 E1 Conkers Discovery Centre Leics
292 D5 Consall railway station Staffs
404 D4 Consett & District Golf Club Dur
369 F1 Constable Burton Hall Caravan Park N York
308 D2 Conway Park railway station Wirral
305 G4 Conwy (Caernarvonshire) Golf Club Conwy
305 G4 Conwy Castle (UNESCO) Conwy
285 H3 Conwy Valley Railway Conwy
285 G3 Conwy Valley Railway museum Conwy
99 F1 Conyer Creek Marina Kent
58 A5 Cooden Beach Golf Club E Susx
58 B5 Cooden Beach railway station E Susx
343 E1 Cookridge Hall Golf Club Leeds
215 F4 Coombe Abbey Warwks
119 E5 Coombe Hill Golf Club Gt Lon
70 B4 Coombe Touring Park campsite Wilts
119 E5 Coombe Wood Golf Club Gt Lon
313 F2 Coopers Camp & Caravan Park Derbys
214 B4 Copt Heath Golf Club Solhll
77 F2 Copthorne Golf Club W Susx
442 D4 Coquetdale Caravan Park Nthumb
218 C1 Corby Public golf course Nhants
33 H3 Corfe Castle NT Dorset
552 F7 Corgarff Castle Abers
73 E6 Corhampton Golf Club Hants
466 D2 Corkerhill railway station C Glas
376 B1 Corkickle railway station Cumb
215 E2 Corley service area Warwks
482 B5 Cornalees Bridge Inver
22 D3 Cornish Coast Caravan & Camping Park Cnwll
6 C5 Cornish Engines NT Cnwll
44 A3 Cornish Farm Touring Park Somset
398 B1 Corn Mill D & G
558 C5 Correenhills Abers
538 A5 Corrie Fee Angus
463 H5 Corrie Golf Club N Ayrs
322 c6 Corrins Folly IoM
522 C2 Corrour railway station Highld
111 F5 Corsham Court Wilts
210 C3 Corvedale Shrops
7 E6 Cosawes Park campsite Cnwll
240 B6 Cosby Golf Club Leics
236 A4 Cosford airfield Shrops
236 A3 Cosford railway station Shrops
106 C6 Cosmeston Lakes & Medieval Village V Glam
249 G2 Costessey Park golf course Norfk
384 D5 Cote Ghyll Caravan & Camping Park N York
17 F5 Cotehele NT Cnwll
276 D2 Cotgrave Place Golf Club Notts
217 E5 Coton Manor Garden Nhants
136 A5 Cotswold Edge Golf Club Gloucs
164 B3 Cotswold Falconry Centre Gloucs
163 H4 Cotswold Farm Park Gloucs
136 D1 Cotswold Hills Golf Club Gloucs
164 B5 Cotswold Motor & Toy museum Gloucs
137 F3 Cotswolds
165 F5 Cotswold View Touring park Oxon
137 F5 Cotswold Water Park (Ashton Keynes Section) Wilts
138 B5 Cotswold Water Park (Fairford/Lechlade Section) Gloucs
163 E4 Cotswold Way Gloucs
110 C5 Cotswold Way S Glos
138 C3 Cotswold Wildlife Park Oxon
313 F5 Cottage Farm Caravan Park Derbys
7 E2 Cottage Farm Touring Park Cnwll
217 F5 Cottesbrooke Hall Nhants
242 C1 Cottesmore airfield Rutlnd
76 D3 Cottesmore Golf & Country Club W Susx
347 F3 Cottingham Parks Golf & Country Club E R Yk
343 E3 Cottingley railway station Leeds
105 H5 Cottrell Park Golf Club V Glam
341 H1 Cougar Park Brad
189 G2 Coughton Court NT Warwks
95 G3 Coulsdon Manor Hotel golf course Gt Lon
448 D2 Coulter Motte S Lans
211 G3 Country Park Halt railway station Shrops
563 G5 Countryside Centre museum NTS Highld
84 B1 Country View Caravan Park N Som
113 E2 County Ground Swindn
8 B3 Court Farm Holidays Cnwll
378 C3 Courthouse Cumb
141 K3 Courthouse NT Bucks
390 C5 Cove Caravan & Camping Park Cumb
215 F5 Coventry airport Warwks
215 E5 Coventry Golf Club Warwks
215 E4 Coventry Hearsall Golf Club Covtry
368 D4 Coverdale N York
481 F2 Cowal Ag & B
481 H4 Cowal Golf Club Ag & B
487 G1 Cowdenbeath Golf Club Fife
74 D5 Cowdray Park Golf Club W Susx
51 E5 Cowes Golf Club IoW
466 D2 Cowglen Golf Club C Glas

295 G3 Coxmoor Golf Club Notts
157 G3 Cradoc Golf Club Powys
440 A3 Crag Bank Wood Border
442 D4 Cragside House NT Nthumb
557 F2 Craibstone Golf Centre C Aber
157 E5 Craig Cerrig Gleisiad A Fan Frynych Powys
488 B4 Craigentinny golf course C Edin
512 D5 Craigie Hill Golf Club P & K
437 E4 Craigielands Country Park D & G
555 G3 Craigievar Castle NTS Abers
488 B5 Craigmillar Castle C Edin
488 B5 Craigmillar Park Golf Club C Edin
468 C5 Craignethan Castle S Lans
505 J2 Craignure Golf Club Ag & B
444 D2 Craig Tara Holiday Park S Ayrs
502 D2 Craigtoun Country Park Fife
502 D2 Craigtoun Meadows Holiday Park Fife
503 G3 Crail Golfing Society Fife
48 A1 Cranborne Chase Dorset
26 A5 Cranbrook Castle Devon
48 D3 Crane Valley Golf Club Dorset
194 C6 Cranfield airfield Beds
75 H1 Cranleigh Hall Golf & Leisure Club Surrey
86 B6 Cranmore West railway station Somset
7 E2 Crantock Plains Touring Park Cnwll
298 C3 Cranwell airfield Lincs
492 C3 Craobh Marina Ag & B
493 G5 Crarae Glen Ag & B
159 E2 Craswall Herefs
556 C5 Crathes Castle NTS Abers
119 E4 Craven Cottage Gt Lon
348 B3 Craven Park C KuH
364 A6 Craven Park Cumb
120 C6 Cray Valley Golf Club Gt Lon
259 H4 Creake Abbey Norfk
27 G4 Crealy Adventure Park Devon
14 C5 Crealy Great Adventure Park Cnwll
125 E2 Creampots Touring Caravan & Camping Park Pembks
417 E3 Creebridge Caravan Park D & G
417 F5 Creetown Caravan Park D & G
105 H3 Creigiau Golf Club Cardif
173 F6 Cressing Temple Essex
309 E3 Cressington railway station Lpool
315 G5 Creswell Crags Derbys
202 A2 Cretingham Golf Club Suffk
291 E4 Crewe Golf Club Ches
144 D4 Crews Hill Golf Club Gt Lon
264 C2 Criccieth Golf Club Gwynd
137 G6 Cricklade Hotel & Country Club Wilts
136 D1 Crickley Hill Gloucs
511 F5 Crieff Golf Club P & K
230 D4 Cringgred Caravan Park Powys
186 A1 Croft Ambrey Herefs
186 A1 Croft Castle NT Herefs
383 G3 Croft Circuit N York
8 C2 Croft Farm Holiday Park Cnwll
605 G8 Croft House museum Shet
523 L6 Croftmoraig Stone Circle P & K
119 H5 Crofton Park railway station Gt Lon
347 E3 Croft Park campsite E R Yk
95 G2 Croham Hurst Golf Club Gt Lon
515 E1 Crombie Country Park Angus
294 B3 Cromford Mill Derbys
294 C3 Cromford railway station Derbys
326 D3 Crompton & Royton Golf Club Oldham
3 C1 Cromwell's Castle IoS
146 D4 Crondon Park Golf Club Essex
322 f4 Cronk Sumark hill fort IoM
394 D2 Crook Golf Club Dur
405 G6 Crook Hall Dur
330 B5 Crookhill Park Municipal golf course Donc
466 D2 Crookston Castle NTS C Glas
188 C6 Croome Park NT Worcs
327 H2 Crosland Heath Golf Club Kirk
450 A1 Crossburn Caravan Park Border
355 H5 Cross Green Leeds
467 E2 Crosshill railway station C Glas
380 B5 Cross Keys Temperance Inn NT Cumb
432 C3 Crossraguel Abbey S Ayrs
260 C5 Crossways Caravan & Camping Park Norfk
119 G2 Crouch Hill railway station Gt Lon
78 B3 Crowborough Beacon Golf Club E Susx
374 D3 Crows Nest Caravan Park N York
484 D6 Crow Wood Golf Club N Lans
273 G2 Croxden Abbey Staffs
323 H6 Croxteth Hall Lpool
432 C2 Croy Brae (Electric Brae) S Ayrs
507 J4 Cruachan Power Station Ag & B
360 D4 Cruckley Animal Farm E R Yk
561 G2 Cruden Bay Golf Club Abers
158 D5 Crug Hywel hillfort Powys
474 B4 Crumstane Farm Park Border
602 E6 Cubbie Roo's Castle Ork
328 C2 Cuckoos Nest railway station Kirk
95 E2 Cuddington Golf Club Gt Lon
149 E1 Cudmore Grove Essex
339 E5 Cuerden Valley Lancs
545 G5 Cuillin Hills Highld
484 C2 Culcreuch Country Park Stirlg
4 C3 Culdrose airfield Cnwll
569 J2 Cullen Bay Holiday Park Moray
569 J2 Cullen Golf Club Moray
556 D4 Cullerlie Stone Circle Abers
566 C8 Culloden 1746 battlefield NTS Highld
566 D7 Culloden Viaduct Highld
566 C7 Culloden Visitor Centre NTS Highld

42 D6 Cullompton service area Devon
486 C2 Culross Palace NTS Fife
555 F3 Culsh Earth-House Abers
102 C5 Culver Hole Swans
432 B2 Culzean Castle NTS S Ayrs
87 E2 Cumberwell Park Golf Club Wilts
377 G4 Cumbrian Mountains Cumb
465 G5 Cunninghame N Ayrs
502 B2 Cupar Golf Club Fife
487 G6 Curriehill railway station C Edin
133 E6 Cwmbran Stadium Torfn
283 E3 Cwm Cadnant Valley campsite Gwynd
132 D6 Cwmcarn Forest Drive Caerph
132 D6 Cwmcarn Forest Drive campsite Caerph
126 A2 Cwm Deri vineyard Pembks
185 E4 Cwmmau Farmhouse NT Herefs
179 H2 Cwmtydu smugglers cove Cerdgn
265 G6 Cymer Abbey Gwynd
156 B1 Cynghordy railway station Carmth
156 C1 Cynghordy Viaduct Carmth
154 A4 Cynwyl Elfed railway station Carmth

D

361 E5 Dacre Lakeside Park E R Yk
120 C3 Dagenham Dock railway station Gt Lon
20 A4 Dainton Salt Golf Club Devon
7 G2 Dairyland Farm World Cnwll
326 D4 Daisy Nook Country Park Oldham
413 F2 Dalbeattie Golf Club D & G
373 G2 Dalby Forest N York
373 G2 Dalby Forest Drive N York
377 F4 Dalegarth railway station Cumb
79 F4 Dale Hill Hotel & Golf Club E Susx
390 D4 Dalemain Historic House & Gardens Cumb
465 F5 Dalgarven Mill museum N Ayrs
487 F3 Dalgety Bay railway station Fife
488 C6 Dalkeith Park Mdloth
567 J5 Dallas Dhu Distillery Moray
507 K4 Dalmally golf course Ag & B
487 G4 Dalmeny House C Edin
445 E5 Dalmilling Golf Club S Ayrs
183 G3 Dalmore Camping & Caravanning Park Powys
525 G1 Dalmunzie Golf Club P & K
483 E4 Dalreoch railway station W Duns
400 C4 Dalston Hall Caravan Park Cumb
60 C2 Damage Cliffs NT Devon
147 F3 Danbury Country Park Essex
400 C2 Dandy Dinmont Caravan & Camping Park Cumb
71 G2 Danebury Ring Hants
106 B4 Danescourt railway station Cardif
130 C1 Dan-yr-Ogof showcave Powys
213 H6 Danzey railway station Warwks
96 D2 Darenth Valley golf course Kent
274 B1 Darley Moor Derbys
395 G6 Darlington Golf Club Darltn
383 H2 Darlington Stadium Darltn
314 D2 Darnall railway station Sheff
120 D5 Dartford Golf Club Kent
13 F2 Dart Marina Devon
18 D1 Dartmoor Forest Devon
18 D3 Dartmoor National Park Devon
25 F3 Dartmoor Railway Devon
18 C6 Dartmoor Wildlife Park Devon
13 F2 Dartmouth Castle Devon
213 F1 Dartmouth Golf Club Sandw
18 C6 Dartmouth Golf & Country Club Devon
339 G5 Darwen Golf Club Bl w D
117 G4 Datchet Golf Club W & M
551 J2 Dava Way Highld
312 B3 Davenport Golf Club Ches
192 C2 Daventry Country Park Nhants
192 C2 Daventry & District Golf Club Nhants
22 D5 Davidstow Moor airfield Cnwll
325 G5 Davyhulme Park Golf Club Traffd
449 G2 Dawyck Botanic Garden Border
445 F2 Dean Castle E Ayrs
325 F3 Deane Golf Club Bolton
74 B2 Dean Farm Golf Club Hants
135 E3 Dean Forest Railway Gloucs
122 B5 Deangate Ridge Golf Club Medway
326 C4 Dean Lane railway station Manch
71 F4 Dean railway station Hants
324 C3 Dean Wood Golf Club Lancs
242 C6 Deene Park Nhants
338 D3 Deepdale Lancs
292 C4 Deep Hayes Country Park Staffs
571 H6 Deer Abbey Abers
13 F3 Deer Park Caravan & Camping Devon
486 D6 Deer Park Golf & Country Club W Loth
557 F4 Deeside Golf Club C Aber
268 C1 Deeside railway station Denbgs
308 C6 Deeside Stadium Flints
305 G4 Deganwy railway station Conwy
35 e1 Dehus Dolmen Guern
342 C6 Deighton railway station Kirk
510 D5 Deil's Caldron (Waterfall) P & K
310 B5 Delamere Forest Golf Club Ches
310 A5 Delamere Forest Park Ches
193 G3 Delapre Golf Centre Nhants
281 E5 Delph Bank Touring Caravan & Camping Park Lincs
94 D4 Denbies vineyard Surrey
287 E1 Denbigh Golf Club Denbgs
294 D5 Denby Potteries Derbys
117 H2 Denham Golf Club Bucks

53 G3 Denman's Garden W Susx
119 G4 Denmark Hill railway station Gt Lon
14 C4 Dennis Cove Camping Cnwll
221 G6 Denny Abbey Cambs
514 C3 Dens Park C Dund
326 D5 Denton Golf Club Manch
367 F2 Dent railway station Cumb
322 d9 Derby Fort IoM
201 G4 Derby Road railway station Suffk
275 G3 Derby service area Derbys
275 F2 Derbyshire County Cricket Ground C Derb
293 H1 Derbyshire Dales Derbys
254 C5 Dereham Golf Club Norfk
254 D5 Dereham towermill Norfk
326 D3 Derker railway station Oldham
153 H6 Derllys Court Golf Club Carmth
404 D3 Derwentcote Steel Furnace Dur
388 A4 Derwent Park Cumb
275 E2 Derwent Valley Mills (UNESCO) C Derb
405 E2 Derwent Walk Gatesd
389 G5 Derwent Water Cumb
569 J3 Deskford Church Moray
365 G6 Detron Gate Farm campsite Lancs
262 D5 Deucoch Touring Park Gwynd
278 C2 De Vere Belton Woods Hotel golf course Lincs
289 G4 De Vere Carden Park Hotel Golf Resort & Spa Ches
250 A4 De Vere Dunston Hall Hotel golf course Norfk
337 F2 De Vere Herons Reach golf course Bpool
312 A4 De Vere Mottram Hall golf course Ches
404 A3 De Vere Slaley Hall Hotel Golf Resort & Spa Nthumb
356 D1 Devil's Arrows N York
55 G2 Devil's Dyke W Susx
4 D6 Devil's Frying Pan Cnwll
21 E1 Devon Cliffs Holiday Park Devon
42 B6 Devon Railway Centre Devon
57 G5 Devonshire Park E Susx
7 E6 Devoran & Perran (UNESCO) Cnwll
524 B6 Dewars Distillery P & K
78 C4 Dewlands Manor golf course E Susx
342 D6 Dewsbury District Golf Club Kirk
109 E2 Dewstow Golf Club Mons
140 B1 Diamond Farm Caravan & Camping Park Oxon
50 C3 Dibden Golf Centre Hants
51 F3 Dibles Park campsite Hants
161 F6 Dick Whittington Centre Gloucs
115 E1 Didcot Parkway railway station Oxon
311 G1 Didsbury Golf Club Manch
27 F4 Digby & Sowton railway station Devon
42 D6 Diggerland Devon
405 F5 Diggerland Dur
122 B6 Diggerland Medway
292 C5 Dilhorne Park railway station Staffs
36 A3 Dimbola Lodge museum IoW
288 B6 Dinas Bran castle Denbgs
106 B5 Dinas Powis Golf Club V Glam
105 G1 Dinas Rhondda railway station Rhondd
282 C1 Din Dryfol IoA
155 F5 Dinefwr Park NT Carmth
106 C5 Dingle Road railway station V Glam
282 D4 Dinile Caravan Park Gwynd
303 G3 Din Lligwy IoA
11 H2 Dinnaton Golf Club Devon
255 F4 Dinosaur Adventure Park Norfk
37 G3 Dinosaur Isle IoW
384 A2 Dinsdale railway station Darltn
384 A2 Dinsdale Spa Golf Club Darltn
69 H3 Dinton Park NT Wilts
116 C5 Dinton Pastures Wokham
489 G3 Dirleton Castle NTS E Loth
514 C4 Discovery Point & Verdant Works C Dund
370 D5 Dishforth airfield N York
312 C3 Disley Golf Club Ches
183 G3 Disserth Caravan & Camping Park Powys
225 F4 Diss Golf Club Suffk
16 B5 Dobwalls Family Adventure Park Cnwll
366 B5 Docker Park Farm Lancs
10 D2 Dockyard railway station C Plym
38 B3 Docton Mill Gardens Devon
500 D5 Dogton Stone Fife
155 G1 Dolaucothi Gold Mines NT Roman site Carmth
284 C3 Dolbadarn Castle Gwynd
10 C1 Dolbeare Caravan and Camping Park Cnwll
153 F2 Dolbryn Camping & Caravanning Carmth
58 D3 Doleham railway station E Susx
232 C5 Dolforwyn Castle Powys
265 G6 Dolgellau Golf Club Gwynd
229 F4 Dolgoch Falls Gwynd
499 F5 Dollar Glen NTS Clacks
499 F5 Dollar Golf Club Clacks
297 E2 Dolls museum Notts
99 E2 Dolphin Sailing Barge museum Kent
285 F4 Dolwyddelan Castle Conwy
131 H2 Dol-y-gaer railway station Powys
331 E2 Doncaster North service area Donc
330 C4 Doncaster racecourse Donc
64 A3 Doniford Halt railway station Somset
239 G2 Donington Le Heath manor house Leics
275 G4 Donington Park Leics
275 G4 Donington Park Farmhouse Hotel Derbys
275 H5 Donington Park service area Leics
114 D6 Donnington Castle W Berk
114 D5 Donnington Valley W Berk
314 D2 Don Valley Stadium Sheff
527 G3 Doocot NTS Angus
62 B2 Doone Valley Holidays Devon
490 C4 Doonhill Homestead E Loth

433 F2 Doon Valley golf course E Ayrs
314 C3 Dore & Totley Golf Club Sheff
94 D4 Dorking Deepdene railway station Surrey
94 D5 Dorking Golf Club Surrey
94 D5 Dorking West railway station Surrey
77 G1 Dormans railway station Surrey
20 A4 Dornafield campsite Devon
117 F4 Dorney Court Bucks
577 G7 Dornoch Firth Caravan Park Highld
271 H2 Dorothy Clive Staffs
48 D2 Dorset Heavy Horse Centre Dorset
47 E3 Dorset Heights Golf Club Dorset
8 C3 Doubletrees Farm campsite Cnwll
322 f7 Douglas Golf Club IoM
484 B5 Douglas Park Golf Club E Duns
448 A5 Douglas Water Golf Club S Lans
498 A4 Doune Castle Stirlg
588 B3 Dounreay Visitor Centre Highld
528 D1 Dovecot Caravan Park Abers
83 F2 Dover Priory railway station Kent
229 F5 Dovey Junction railway station Powys
134 D1 Doward Park Camp Site Herefs
272 D2 Down Banks NT Staffs
26 C3 Downes Crediton Golf Club Devon
514 B3 Downfield Golf Club C Dund
222 C5 Downfield Windmill Cambs
96 B2 Down House Gt Lon
92 D1 Downshire Golf Complex Br For
86 B4 Downside Abbey Somset
55 F1 Downs Link cycle route Surrey
215 H6 Draycote Water Warwks
118 D3 Drayton Green railway station Gt Lon
238 B4 Drayton Manor Staffs
238 B4 Drayton Park Golf Club Staffs
140 A6 Drayton Park golf course Oxon
360 C3 Driffield Golf Club E R Yk
360 C3 Driffield showground E R Yk
94 B3 Drift Golf Club Surrey
188 D2 Droitwich Boat Centre Worcs
188 C2 Droitwich Golf & Country Club Worcs
410 B3 Druchtag Motte D & G
237 G4 Druids Heath Golf Club Wsall
369 G4 Druid's Temple N York
100 B3 Druidstone Wildlife Park Kent
556 B6 Drum Castle NTS Abers
423 E6 Drumcoltran Tower D & G
549 J4 Drum Farm Highld
482 C4 Drumfrochar railway station Inver
435 H5 Drumlanrig Castle D & G
488 D5 Drum Mohr Caravan Park E Loth
511 E6 Drummond Castle P & K
550 B2 Drummossie Muir Highld
535 H7 Drumochter Summit Highld
514 C5 Drumoig Hotel & golf course Fife
467 H1 Drumpellier Country Park N Lans
467 H1 Drumpellier Golf Club N Lans
410 D2 Drumroamin Farm Camping & Touring Site D & G
527 F6 Drumshademuir Caravan Park Angus
410 C4 Drumtrodden Cup & Ring D & G
410 C4 Drumtrodden Standing Stones D & G
443 H5 Druridge Bay Nthumb
57 E4 Drusillas E Susx
506 B2 Duart Castle Ag & B
213 G2 Duddeston railway station Birm
488 B5 Duddingston Golf Club C Edin
577 K3 Dudgeon Park Highld
213 F2 Dudley Golf Club Sandw
211 G2 Dudmaston NT Shrops
49 F5 Dudmoor Farm golf course Dorset
48 D5 Dudsbury Golf Club Bmouth
570 B3 Duff House Abers
570 B3 Duff House Royal Abers
568 D8 Dufftown Golf Club Moray
568 B2 Duffus Castle Moray
502 D2 Duke's golf course Fife
467 F1 Duke Street railway station C Glas
327 E5 Dukinfield Golf Club Tamesd
485 E4 Dullatur Golf Club N Lans
119 G5 Dulwich & Sydenham Hill Golf Club Gt Lon
483 E4 Dumbarton Central railway station W Duns
483 E5 Dumbarton East railway station W Duns
483 E4 Dumbarton Golf Club W Duns
423 F4 Dumfries & Galloway Golf Club D & G
423 G4 Dumfries Ice Bowl D & G
91 F6 Dummer Golf Club Hants
101 G2 Dumpton Park railway station Kent
492 D6 Dunadd Fort Ag & B
481 E1 Dunans Castle Ag & B
433 F3 Dunaskin museum E Ayrs
456 D5 Dunaverty Golf Club Ag & B
490 C4 Dunbar Golf Club E Loth
498 B4 Dunblane New Golf Club Stirlg
598 B3 Dun Carloway Broch W Isls
492 D5 Duncharagaig Cairn Ag & B
372 B3 Duncombe Park N York
546 E3 Duncraig railway station Highld
86 D2 Dundas Wilts
487 F4 Dundas Parks Golf Club C Edin
514 B4 Dundee airport C Dund
514 B3 Dundee Ice Arena C Dund
585 J8 Dun Dornaigil Broch Highld
524 D4 Dunfallandy Stone P & K
487 E2 Dunfermline Golf Club Fife

487 E2 **Dunfermline Town railway station** Fife
81 G6 **Dungeness** Kent
312 C4 **Dunge Valley Hidden Gardens & Hardy Plant Nursery** Ches
311 E2 **Dunham Forest Golf & Country Club** Traffd
311 E2 **Dunham Massey NT** Traffd
524 F7 **Dunkeld & Birnam Golf Club** P & K
28 B1 **Dunkeswell airfield** Devon
363 E6 **Dunnerholme Golf Club** Cumb
559 E4 **Dunnideer Fort** Abers
501 E6 **Dunnikier Park Golf Club** Fife
499 F2 **Dunning Golf Club** P & K
541 G3 **Dunnottar Castle** Abers
576 C2 **Dunroamin Caravan and Camping Park** Highld
577 J3 **Dunrobin Castle** Highld
577 H3 **Dunrobin Castle railway station** Highld
325 G2 **Dunscar Golf Club** Bolton
473 H4 **Duns Golf Club** Border
169 E5 **Dunstable Downs Golf Club** Beds
506 E3 **Dunstaffnage Castle** Ag & B
455 G5 **Dunstanburgh Castle Golf Club** Nthumb
455 H5 **Dunstanburgh Castle NT** Nthumb
63 F3 **Dunster Castle NT** Somset
63 F3 **Dunster railway station** Somset
542 C7 **Dunvegan Castle** Highld
71 G5 **Dunwood Manor Golf Club** Hants
17 E5 **Dupath Well House** Cnwll
395 F2 **Durham City Golf Club** Dur
395 G2 **Durham service area** Dur
384 B2 **Durham Tees Valley airport** S on T
34 B5 **Durlston Country Park & Marine Project** Dorset
579 J2 **Durness Golf Club** Highld
35 i6 **Durrell Wildlife Conservation Trust** Jersey
324 D2 **Duxbury Jubilee Park Golf Club** Lancs
197 G5 **Duxford Imperial War museum (Aircraft)** Cambs
557 F1 **Dyce Symbol Stones** C Aber
264 D5 **Dyffryn Ardudwy railway station** Gwynd
55 G3 **Dyke Golf Club** W Susx
81 H4 **Dymchurch Martello Tower Castle** Kent
161 F3 **Dymock Grange Golf Club** Gloucs
144 B5 **Dyrham Park Country Club** Herts
110 C4 **Dyrham Park NT** S Glos

E

487 G4 **Eagle Rock** C Edin
384 C2 **Eaglescliffe & District Golf Club** S on T
252 B4 **Eagles Golf Centre** Norfk
118 D3 **Ealing Golf Club** Gt Lon
600 E4 **Earl's Bu and Church** Ork
119 F4 **Earls Court** Gt Lon
602 B6 **Earls Place** Ork
103 H3 **Earlswood golf course** Neath
213 G5 **Earlswood (West Midlands) railway station** Warwks
315 E1 **Earth Arena** Rothm
330 B5 **Earth Centre** Donc
579 J4 **Eas a' Chual Aluinn (Waterfall)** Highld
383 E4 **Easby** N York
60 C2 **Easewell Farm Holiday Parc & Golf Club** Devon
504 E2 **Eas Fors (Waterfall)** Ag & B
371 G6 **Easingwold Golf Club** N York
527 E5 **Eassie** Angus
557 G1 **East Aberdeenshire Golf Centre** Abers
559 G5 **East Aquhorthies Stone Circle** Abers
92 D2 **East Berkshire Golf Club** Wokham
342 C4 **East Bierley Golf Club** Kirk
57 F5 **Eastbourne Downs Golf Club** E Susx
529 F1 **East Bowstrips Caravan Park** Abers
120 D2 **Eastbrookend Country Park** Gt Lon
218 A2 **East Carlton Country Park** Nhants
33 G3 **East Creech Camping & Caravan Park** Dorset
8 D3 **East Crinnis Camping & Caravan Park** Cnwll
21 E1 **East Devon Golf Club** Devon
487 F2 **East End Park** Fife
468 B1 **Easter Moffat Golf Club** N Lans
488 B5 **Easter Road** C Edin
576 B8 **Easter Ross** Highld
32 A4 **East Fleet Farm Touring Park** Dorset
309 E3 **Eastham Country Park** Wirral
337 G4 **Eastham Hall Caravan Site** Lancs
309 E3 **Eastham Lodge Golf Club** Wirral
308 D4 **Eastham Rake railway station** Wirral
171 E5 **East Herts Golf Club** Herts
72 D6 **East Horton Golf Centre** Hants
101 E6 **East Kent Railway** Kent
467 F3 **East Kilbride Golf Club** S Lans
340 C5 **East Lancashire Railway** Lancs
243 G5 **East of England showground** C Pete
202 B3 **Easton Farm Park** Suffk
466 D4 **East Renfrewshire Golf Club** E Rens
86 B6 **East Somerset Railway** Somset
78 B6 **East Sussex National** E Susx
466 D4 **Eastwood Golf Club** E Rens
289 G2 **Eaton Golf Club** Ches
249 H3 **Eaton Golf Club** Norfk
143 F6 **Ebury Way cycle route** Herts
324 B6 **Ecclescton Park Golf Club** St Hel
247 G3 **Ecotech Discovery Centre** Norfk
603 H5 **Eday airport** Ork
96 B5 **Edenbridge railway station** Kent
96 B5 **Edenbridge Town railway station** Kent
373 E5 **Eden Camp museum** N York

400 D3 **Eden golf course** Cumb
8 C3 **Eden Project** Cnwll
391 G5 **Eden Valley cycle route** Cumb
380 C1 **Eden Valley Railway** Cumb
160 C1 **Edgar Street** Herefs
213 G3 **Edgbaston** Birm
213 G3 **Edgbaston Golf Club** Birm
191 F5 **Edgehill 1642 battlefield** Warwks
191 G5 **Edgehill Country Park** Warwks
312 A2 **Edgeley Park** Stockp
487 F5 **Edinburgh airport** C Edin
488 C6 **Edinburgh Butterfly Farm** Mdloth
487 G5 **Edinburgh Park railway station** C Edin
473 H2 **Edin's Hall Broch** Border
144 D6 **Edmonton Green railway station** Gt Lon
22 D4 **Edmore Tourist Park** Cnwll
524 E4 **Edradour Distillery** P & K
474 B3 **Edrom church** Border
276 C2 **Edwalton Municipal** Notts
540 B6 **Edzell airfield (dis)** Abers
540 A6 **Edzell Castle** Angus
540 A6 **Edzell Golf Club** Angus
94 C4 **Effingham Golf Club** Surrey
94 B3 **Effingham Junction railway station** Surrey
77 F2 **Effingham Park Golf Club** Surrey
382 C1 **Egglestone** Dur
444 D1 **Eglinton Castle** N Ayrs
386 D3 **Egton railway station** N York
530 E5 **Eigg** Highld
546 F4 **Eilean Donan Castle** Highld
597 H1 **Eilean Leodhais** W Isls
264 C2 **Eisteddfa campsite** Gwynd
513 E5 **Elcho Castle** P & K
466 C2 **Elderslie Golf Club** Rens
284 C2 **Electric Mountain** Gwynd
406 B5 **Elemore golf course** Sundld
18 B6 **Elfordleigh Hotel Golf & Country Club** Devon
188 B3 **Elgar museum** Worcs
568 C3 **Elgin Golf Club** Moray
100 C6 **Elham Valley vineyard** Kent
35 h7 **Elizabeth Castle** Jersey
342 A5 **Elland Golf Club** Calder
343 E3 **Elland Road** Leeds
142 A3 **Ellesborough Golf Club** Bucks
325 G4 **Ellesmere Golf Club** Salfd
309 E4 **Ellesmere Port Golf Centre** Ches
53 E5 **Ellscott Park campsite** W Susx
97 H1 **Elmhaven Marina** Kent
501 E4 **Elmwood golf course** Fife
329 F5 **Elsecar Workshops** Rothm
333 E2 **Elsham Golf Club** N Linc
144 A5 **Elstree Golf & Country Club** Herts
120 B5 **Eltham Warren Golf Club** Gt Lon
243 G6 **Elton Furze Golf Club** Cambs
243 F6 **Elton Hall** Cambs
277 G2 **Elton & Orston railway station** Notts
222 A4 **Ely City Golf Club** Cambs
194 B4 **Emberton** M Keyn
354 D4 **Embsay & Bolton Abbey Steam Railway** N York
119 G2 **Emirates Stadium** Gt Lon
96 C4 **Emmetts NT** Kent
52 C3 **Emsworth Yacht Harbour** Hants
240 B5 **Enderby golf course** Leics
144 D5 **Enfield Chase railway station** Gt Lon
144 D5 **Enfield Golf Club** Gt Lon
209 G3 **Engine & Tender Inn campsite** Shrops
64 D4 **Enmore Park Golf Club** Somset
339 H6 **Entwistle railway station** Bl w D
212 B2 **Enville Golf Club** Staffs
145 F5 **Epping Forest** Essex
145 H4 **Epping Ongar Railway** Essex
95 E3 **Epsom Downs railway station** Surrey
95 E3 **Epsom Golf Club** Surrey
95 E3 **Epsom racecourse** Surrey
288 D5 **Erddig NT** Wrexhm
275 H2 **Erewash Valley golf course** Derbys
78 C3 **Eridge railway station** E Susx
87 G4 **Erlestoke Sands golf course** Wilts
483 F5 **Erskine Golf Club** Rens
156 B3 **Erwlon Caravan & Camping Park** Carmth
28 A3 **Escot Historic Gardens** Devon
377 E4 **Eskdale Green railway station** Cumb
484 B5 **Esporta Dougalston Golf Club** E Duns
453 H2 **Etal Castle** Nthumb
82 C2 **Etchinghill golf course** Kent
312 C1 **Etherow Country Park** Stockp
450 C5 **Ettrick Forest** Border
132 C2 **Eugene Cross Park** Blae G
60 C3 **Europa Park campsite** Devon
338 D6 **Euxton Balshaw Lane railway station** Lancs
189 E5 **Evesham Golf Club** Worcs
95 E2 **Ewell West railway station** Surrey
327 E5 **Ewen Fields** Tamesd
105 H4 **Ewenny Priory Church** V Glam
286 D6 **Ewe-phoria Sheepdog Centre** Conwy
425 H2 **Ewes Water Caravan & Camping Park** D & G
288 C1 **Ewloe Castle** Flints
339 G4 **Ewood Park** Bl w D
27 G4 **Exeter airport** Devon
27 F5 **Exeter Golf & Country Club** Devon
27 E6 **Exeter racecourse** Devon
27 E4 **Exeter St Davids railway station** Devon
27 E4 **Exeter St Thomas railway station** Devon
27 F4 **Exeter service area** Devon
62 A3 **Exmoor Forest** Somset
62 D4 **Exmoor National Park** Devon
61 G3 **Exmoor Zoological Park** Devon
27 F5 **Exton railway station** Devon
313 H4 **Eyam Hall** Derbys
314 A4 **Eyam Moor** Derbys
314 A4 **Eyam museum** Derbys
475 E2 **Eyemouth Golf Club** Border

F

533 L2 **Faichemard Farm Camping & Caravan Site** Highld
229 E2 **Fairbourne & Barmouth Steam Railway** Gwynd
326 C5 **Fairfield Golf & Sailing Club** Manch
138 A5 **Fairford** Gloucs
337 G4 **Fairhaven Golf Club** Lancs
250 D2 **Fairhaven woodland & water garden** Norfk
604 b3 **Fair Isle NTS** Shet
103 E3 **Fairwood Park Golf Club** Swans
254 B2 **Fakenham Golf Club** Norfk
254 B2 **Fakenham racecourse** Norfk
485 H3 **Falkirk Golf Club** Falk
486 A4 **Falkirk High railway station** Falk
486 B3 **Falkirk Stadium** Falk
485 H3 **Falkirk Tryst Golf Club** Falk
485 H4 **Falkirk Wheel** Falk
501 E3 **Falkland Golf Club** Fife
501 E3 **Falkland Palace NTS** Fife
378 C5 **Fallbarrow Park campsite** Cumb
448 A1 **Falls of Clyde** S Lans
507 J4 **Falls of Cruachan railway station** Ag & B
549 H4 **Falls of Divach** Highld
509 J3 **Falls of Dochart** Stirlg
508 D5 **Falls of Falloch** Stirlg
547 J4 **Falls of Glomach NTS** Highld
497 E3 **Falls of Leny** Stirlg
509 H2 **Falls of Lochay** Stirlg
574 E8 **Falls of Measach** Highld
576 C4 **Falls of Shin** Highld
511 E5 **Falls of Turret** P & K
5 E2 **Falmouth Golf Club** Cnwll
147 H5 **Fambridge railway station** Essex
358 D4 **Fangfoss Park campsite** E R Yk
321 E6 **Fantasy Island** Lincs
549 J5 **Farigaig visitor centre** Highld
95 H2 **Farleigh Court Golf Club** Surrey
72 B4 **Farley Mount Country Park** Hants
69 G3 **Farmer Giles Farmstead** Wilts
93 E4 **Farnborough** Hants
93 E3 **Farnborough North railway station** Hants
455 E3 **Farne Islands** Nthumb
93 E5 **Farnham Golf Club** Surrey
117 G3 **Farnham Park Golf Club** Bucks
92 D5 **Farnham Park golf course** Surrey
120 D6 **Farningham Road railway station** Kent
86 A4 **Farrington Golf & Country Club** Somset
192 D3 **Farthingstone Hotel** Nhants
524 D3 **Faskally Caravan Park** P & K
524 D4 **Faskally Wayside Centre** P & K
540 B4 **Fasque house** Abers
491 G5 **Fast Castle** Border
34 C3 **Fauxquets Valley Farm Camp Site** Guern
99 F2 **Faversham Golf Club** Kent
323 G5 **Fazakerley railway station** Lpool
577 H8 **Fearn railway station** Highld
261 G4 **Felbrigg Hall NT** Norfk
179 E3 **Felinwynt Rainforest & Butterfly Centre** Cerdgn
177 F2 **Felixstowe Ferry Golf Club** Suffk
365 E2 **Fell Foot Park NT** Cumb
173 E5 **Felsted vineyard** Essex
223 E1 **Feltwell Golf Club** Norfk
244 B2 **Fenland Cycle Trail** Lincs
197 G3 **Fenner's cricket & tennis ground** Cambs
191 G4 **Fenny Marina** Warwks
119 F2 **Fenton NT** Gt Lon
466 C3 **Fereneze Golf Club** E Rens
48 D4 **Ferndown Forest Golf Club** Dorset
48 D5 **Ferndown Golf Club** Dorset
270 B3 **Fernwood Caravan Park** Shrops
347 E4 **Ferriby railway station** E R Yk
344 B5 **Ferrybridge service area** Wakefd
576 C2 **Ferrycroft Countryside Centre** Highld
243 G5 **Ferry Meadows Country Park** C Pete
243 H5 **Ferry Meadows railway station** C Pete
265 G1 **Ffestiniog Golf Club** Gwynd
265 F1 **Ffestiniog Railway** Gwynd
184 B4 **Fforest Fields Caravan & Camping Park** Powys
310 B2 **Fiddlers Ferry Yacht Haven** Warrtn
295 G2 **Field Mill** Notts
501 E2 **Fife Animal Park** Fife
501 E6 **Fife Ice Arena** Fife
70 D3 **Figsbury Ring** Wilts
375 E3 **Filey Brigg Touring Caravan & Country Park** N York
375 E4 **Filey Golf Club** N York
109 H4 **Filton Abbey Wood railway station** S Glos
109 G4 **Filton Golf Club** Bristl
110 A3 **Filton Link cycle route** S Glos
405 G5 **Finchale** Dur
79 G2 **Finchcocks** Kent
25 F4 **Finch Foundry NT** Devon
119 E1 **Finchley Golf Club** Gt Lon
567 J4 **Findhorn Bay Holiday Park** Moray
550 E4 **Findhorn Viaduct** Highld
569 J2 **Findlater Castle** Abers
504 C3 **Fingal's Cave** Ag & B
369 G1 **Finghall railway station** N York
26 C4 **Fingle Glen Golf Hotel** Devon
90 B5 **Finkley Down** Hants
478 B8 **Finlaggan** Ag & B
483 E5 **Finlaystone Country Estate** Inver
484 B5 **Firhill Stadium** C Glas
56 D3 **Firle Place** E Susx
468 B3 **Fir Park** N Lans
486 A3 **Fir Park** Falk
375 F5 **Fir Tree Caravan Park** E R Yk
377 F4 **Fisherground Farm Campsite** Cumb
503 F4 **Fisheries museum** Fife
75 H4 **Fishers Farm Park** W Susx

151 G2 **Fishguard Bay Caravan & Camping Park** Pembks
151 G2 **Fishguard Harbour railway station** Pembks
339 E4 **Fishwick Hall Golf Club** Lancs
49 E6 **Fitness First Stadium at Dean Court** Bmouth
148 B2 **Five Lakes Resort golf course** Essex
213 G2 **Five Ways railway station** Birm
117 E2 **Flackwell Heath Golf Club** Bucks
244 B5 **Flag Fen Bronze Age Centre** C Pete
4 C3 **Flambards Experience** Cnwll
375 H5 **Flamborough Head** E R Yk
375 G5 **Flamborough Head Golf Club** E R Yk
373 E4 **Flamingo Land** N York
37 G2 **Flamingo Park** IoW
175 E3 **Flatford Mill & Cottage NT** Suffk
67 F5 **Fleet Air Arm museum** Somset
92 D3 **Fleet service area** Hants
350 D5 **Fleetwood Golf Club** Lancs
350 D5 **Fleetwood Harbour Village Marina** Lancs
72 B6 **Fleming Park Golf Club** Hants
223 G5 **Flempton Golf Club** Suffk
12 A2 **Flete Estate** Devon
308 B5 **Flint Golf Club** Flints
292 C4 **Flint Mill** Staffs
172 D5 **Flitch Way cycle route** Essex
325 H6 **Flixton Golf Club** Traffd
365 E5 **Flookburgh** Cumb
452 D3 **Floors Castle** Border
376 C2 **Florence Mine** Cumb
374 D3 **Flower of May Holiday Park** N York
152 D3 **Foel Drygarn** Pembks
283 E3 **Foel Farm Park** IoA
81 H2 **Folkestone racecourse** Kent
82 C3 **Folkestone West railway station** Kent
521 G4 **Folk museum** Highld
72 B3 **Folly Farm Touring Caravan Park** Hants
371 G6 **Folly Garth campsite** N York
69 E6 **Fontmell & Melbury Downs NT** Dorset
53 G3 **Fontwell Park racecourse** W Susx
147 E3 **Ford County Cricket Ground** Essex
29 G1 **Forde Abbey** Dorset
281 F6 **Foremans Bridge Caravan Park** Lincs
202 D5 **Forest campsite** Suffk
49 E4 **Forest Edge Touring Park** Dorset
43 E6 **Forest Glade Holiday Park** Devon
240 A3 **Forest Hill Golf Club** Leics
134 D2 **Forest Hills Golf Club** Gloucs
355 C3 **Forest Moor** N York
535 K8 **Forest of Atholl** P & K
135 E2 **Forest of Dean** Gloucs
134 D2 **Forest of Dean Golf Club & Bells Hotel** Gloucs
357 H3 **Forest of Galtres Golf Club** York
256 A1 **Forest Park Caravan Site** Norfk
358 B3 **Forest Park Golf Club** York
332 C3 **Forest Pines Golf Club** N Linc
527 G5 **Forfar Golf Club** Angus
527 G4 **Forfar Loch** Angus
213 F6 **Forge Mill Needle Museum** Worcs
323 E3 **Formby Golf Club** Sefton
323 F3 **Formby Hall Golf & Country Club** Sefton
323 E3 **Formby Ladies Golf Club** Sefton
567 K5 **Forres golf course** Moray
147 H2 **Forrester Park Golf Club** Essex
122 B6 **Fort Amherst** Medway
548 F8 **Fort Augustus Golf Club** Highld
51 G4 **Fort Brockhurst** Hants
605 J2 **Fort Charlotte** Shet
566 D5 **Fort George** Highld
34 a3 **Fort Grey Shipwreck Museum** Guern
498 C6 **Forthbank Stadium** Stirlg
485 E4 **Forth & Clyde Canal cycle route** N Lans
348 C4 **Fort Paul** E R Yk
35 i8 **Fort Regent** Jersey
566 C5 **Fortrose & Rosemarkie Golf Club** Highld
533 H7 **Fort William Golf Club** Highld
144 D3 **Forty Hall** Gt Lon
86 D2 **Fosse 2 cycle route** BaNES
240 C4 **Fosse 2 cycle route** C Leic
29 E3 **Fosse 2 cycle route** Devon
66 C5 **Fosse 2 cycle route** Somset
164 D2 **Fosse 2 cycle route** Warwks
191 G1 **Fosse 2 cycle route** Warwks
86 B4 **Fosseway golf course** Somset
504 E5 **Fossil Tree** Ag & B
474 D3 **Foulden Tithe Barn** Border
118 D4 **Fountain Leisure Centre** Gt Lon
370 B6 **Fountains Abbey NT** N York
452 C5 **Four Abbeys cycle route** Border
237 H5 **Four Oaks railway station** Birm
184 D2 **Four Stone** Powys
198 A5 **Fourwentways service area** Cambs
292 C6 **Foxfield Light Railway** Staffs
201 H6 **Foxhall Stadium** Suffk
93 H1 **Foxhills Resort & golf course** Surrey
372 B3 **Foxholme Caravan & Camping Park** N York
4 D4 **Franchis' Holiday Park** Cnwll
213 E3 **Frankley service area** Dudley
193 F2 **Franklin's Gardens** Nhants
79 E2 **Frant railway station** E Susx
571 J3 **Fraserburgh Golf Club** Abers
52 B4 **Fratton Park** C Port
36 B3 **Freshwater Bay Golf Club** IoW
30 B5 **Freshwater Beach Holiday Park** Dorset
139 G5 **Frilford Heath Golf Club** Oxon

176 D6 **Frinton Golf Club** Essex
251 F4 **Fritton Lake Countryworld** Norfk
136 A3 **Frocester Tithe Barn** Gloucs
309 H4 **Frodsham Golf Club** Ches
117 G4 **Frogmore House** W & M
86 D6 **Frome & District showground** Somset
86 D5 **Frome Golf Club** Somset
91 F1 **Frouds Bridge Marina** W Berk
358 B5 **Fulford Golf Club** York
213 G5 **Fulford Heath Golf Club** Worcs
342 D3 **Fulneck Golf Club** Leeds
118 C5 **Fulwell Goerf Club** Gt Lon
364 B5 **Furness** Cumb
364 D1 **Furness Fells** Cumb
364 A6 **Furness Golf Club** Cumb
27 E2 **Fursdon House** Devon
52 B2 **Furzeley golf course** Hants
49 H2 **Furzey Gardens** Hants
64 D5 **Fyne Court NT** Somset
201 G5 **Fynn Valley Golf Club** Suffk
559 H2 **Fyvie Castle NTS** Abers

G

22 B5 **Gaia Energy Centre** Cnwll
317 F1 **Gainsborough Golf Club** Lincs
317 F2 **Gainsborough Lea Road railway station** Lincs
332 D4 **Gainsthorpe Medieval Village** N Linc
572 E8 **Gairloch Caravan & Camping Park** Highld
562 D1 **Gairloch Golf Club** Highld
562 E1 **Gairloch Heritage museum** Highld
399 F1 **Galabank Caravan & Camping Group** D & G
451 F2 **Galashiels Golf Club** Border
378 C4 **Galava Fort NT Roman site** Cumb
353 G3 **Gallaber Park campsite** N York
416 C3 **Galloway** D & G
417 F2 **Galloway Deer Range** D & G
420 C2 **Galloway Forest Park** D & G
63 F3 **Gallox Bridge** Somset
13 F1 **Galmpton Touring Park** Torbay
328 B1 **Galpharm Stadium** Kirk
43 E4 **Gamlins Farm Caravan Park** Somset
348 B3 **Ganstead Park Golf Club** E R Yk
374 B4 **Ganton Golf Club** N York
304 D4 **Gaol & Courthouse museum** IoA
143 G4 **Gardens of the Rose** Herts
404 D3 **Garesfield Golf Club** Gatesd
343 G2 **Garforth Golf Club** Leeds
568 E3 **Garmouth & Kingston Golf Club** Moray
263 E3 **Garn Boduan** Gwynd
303 G4 **Garnedd Touring Park** IoA
3 C2 **Garrison Campsite** IoS
3 C2 **Garrison Walls** IoS
483 H6 **Garscadden railway station** C Glas
367 F1 **Garsdale railway station** Cumb
351 G6 **Garstang Country Hotel & Golf Club** Lancs
497 F3 **Gart Caravan Park** Stirlg
499 E6 **Gartmorn Dam & Visitor Centre** Clacks
241 G4 **Gartree Ride/Rutland Ride cycle route** Leics
104 D1 **Garw Fechan Woodland Park** Brdgnd
131 F2 **Garwnant Forest Centre** Rhondd
412 A3 **Gatehouse Golf Club** D & G
97 F3 **Gate House Wood Touring Park** Kent
405 G2 **Gateshead International Stadium** Gatesd
293 G5 **Gateway Caravan Park** Derbys
83 F2 **Gateway to the White Cliffs NT** Kent
324 C3 **Gathurst Golf Club** Wigan
311 G2 **Gatley Golf Club** Stockp
76 B2 **Gatton Manor Hotel Golf & Country Club** Surrey
77 E1 **Gatwick airport** W Susx
77 E1 **Gatwick airport railway station** W Susx
188 D2 **Gaudet Luce Golf Club** Worcs
64 B5 **Gaulden Manor** Somset
340 C3 **Gawthorpe Hall NT** Lancs
213 G4 **Gay Hill Golf Club** Worcs
234 C2 **Gay Meadow** Shrops
244 D2 **Gedney Hill golf course** Lincs
2 C3 **Geevor Tin Mines** Cnwll
482 D4 **Geilston Garden NTS** Ag & B
326 B2 **Gelder Wood Country Park** Rochdl
155 F6 **Gelli Aur country park** Carmth
284 D5 **Gelli Iago NT** Gwynd
417 F5 **Gem Rock museum** D & G
210 B5 **Geological Trail** Herefs
588 E5 **Georgemas Junction railway station** Highld
404 D1 **George Stephensons Birthplace NT** Nthumb
405 H3 **George Washington Golf & Country Club** Sundld
34 C4 **German Occupation Museum** Guern
34 C3 **German Underground Hospital** Guern
117 H2 **Gerrards Cross Golf Club** Bucks
354 A5 **Ghyll Golf Club** Lancs
542 D7 **Giant Angus MacAskill museum** Highld
351 G2 **Giant Axe** Lancs
46 C4 **Giant's Head Caravan & Camping Park** Dorset
405 E3 **Gibside NT** Gatesd
472 C1 **Gifford Golf Club** E Loth
199 G4 **Gifford's Hall vineyard** Suffk
326 B3 **Gigg Lane** Bury
74 A3 **Gilbert White museum** Hants
284 C2 **Gilfach Ddu railway station** Gwynd
132 C5 **Gilfach Fargoed railway station** Caerph
390 B4 **Gill Head Farm Caravan & Camping Park** Cumb
68 D4 **Gillingham (Dorset) railway station** Dorset

98 B1 Gillingham Golf Club Medway
484 B6 Gilshochill railway station C Glas
119 G5 Gipsy Hill railway station Gt Lon
197 F2 Girton Golf Club Cambs
432 A5 Girvan Golf Club S Ayrs
106 C6 Glamorganshire Golf Club V Glam
286 D5 Glan Ceirw Caravan Park Conwy
305 G4 Glan Conwy railway station Conwy
332 B2 Glanford Park N Linc
266 D3 Glanllyn Flag railway station Gwynd
266 D3 Glanllyn Lakeside Caravan & Camping Park Gwynd
232 C4 Glansevern Hall Powys
466 C1 Glasgow airport Rens
444 D2 Glasgow Golf Club N Ayrs
467 E1 Glasgow Queen Street railway station C Glas
351 F3 Glasson Basin Lancs
67 E2 Glastonbury Tor NT Somset
364 C5 Gleaston Watermill Cumb
492 D5 Glebe Cairn Ag & B
528 D2 Glebe Park Angus
483 E5 Gleddoch golf course Rens
534 C2 Glen Albyn (or Glen Mòr) Highld
485 G3 Glenbervie Golf Club Falk
554 C4 Glenbuchat Castle Abers
521 G4 Glen Coe NTS Highld
521 K5 Glencoe Ski Centre Highld
471 E2 Glencorse Golf Club Mdloth
519 H3 Glencripesdale Highld
506 E4 Glencruitten Golf Club Ag & B
542 B7 Glendale Toy museum
480 D2 Glenduruel Caravan Park Ag & B
569 L7 Glendronach Distillery Abers
5 E3 Glendurgan Garden NT Cnwll
499 E2 Gleneagles golf course P & K
499 E2 Gleneagles railway station P & K
413 F2 Glenearly Caravan Park D & G
546 E6 Glenelg Brochs Highld
540 A5 Glenesk Caravan Park Angus
539 G4 Glenesk Folk museum Angus
568 C8 Glenfarclas Distillery Moray
568 E7 Glenfiddich Distillery Moray
343 F1 Glenfield Caravan Park Leeds
532 D6 Glenfinnan Viaduct Highld
532 D6 Glenfinnan Visitor Centre NTS Highld
489 H2 Glen Golf Club E Loth
240 D5 Glen Gorse Golf Club Leics
523 L5 Glengoulandie Deer Park P & K
568 D6 Glen Grant Distillery Moray
466 C2 Gleniffer Braes Rens
552 D3 Glenlivet Distillery Moray
415 G5 Glenluce Abbey NTS D & G
577 G7 Glenmorangie Distillery Highld
568 B3 Glen Moray Distillery Moray
551 H7 Glenmore Highld
551 H8 Glen More Highld
551 H7 Glenmore Forest Park Highld
534 C2 Glen Mòr (or Glen Albyn) Highld
15 E4 Glenmorris Park campsite Cnwll
521 G1 Glen Nevis Caravan & Camping Park Highld
565 J6 Glen Ord Distillery Highld
500 D5 Glenrothes Golf Club Fife
501 E5 Glenrothes with Thornton railway station Fife
525 H3 Glen Shee P & K
537 H7 Glenshee Ski Area Abers
548 C2 Glen Strathfarrar Highld
555 E5 Glen Tanar Visitor Centre Abers
420 A4 Glentrool Holiday Park D & G
420 B4 Glen Trool Visitor Centre D & G
134 C2 Glen Trothy Caravan & Camping Park Mons
415 G5 Glenwhan Gardens D & G
322 d4 Glen Wyllin Campsite IoM
455 F3 Glororum Caravan Park Nthumb
327 G6 Glossop & District Golf Club Derbys
162 C5 Gloucestershire airport Gloucs
109 G4 Gloucestershire County Ground Bristl
163 F3 Gloucestershire Warwickshire Railway Gloucs
128 C3 Glyn Abbey Golf Club Carmth
207 G3 Glyndwr's Way Powys
230 D6 Glyndwr's Way Powys
129 F1 Glynhir Golf Club Carmth
120 C2 Glyn Hopkin Stadium Gt Lon
283 E4 Glynllifon country park Gwynd
131 E3 Glynneath Golf Club Powys
268 D2 Glyn Valley Tramway Museum Wrexhm
7 H1 Gnome World Caravan & Camping Site Cnwll
93 F3 Goal Farm Golf Club Surrey
99 F6 Godinton House Kent
4 B2 Godolphin House Cnwll
95 H5 Godstone railway station Surrey
166 B6 Godwin's Ice Cream Farm Caravan Park Oxon
488 B4 Goldenacre C Edin
30 A4 Golden Cap Caravan Park Dorset
60 C3 Golden Coast Holiday Village Devon
291 H4 Golden Hill golf course C Stke
20 D2 Golden Sands Holiday Park Devon
321 F2 Golden Sands Holiday Park Lincs
372 A4 Golden Square Touring Caravan Park N York
195 F4 Goldington Road Beds
502 D4 Golf House Club Fife
515 F3 Golf Street railway station Angus
577 H4 Golspie Golf Club Highld
323 G6 Goodison Park Lpool

160 D6 Goodrich Castle Herefs
53 F3 Goodwood Circuit W Susx
53 F3 Goodwood House W Susx
33 G4 Goodwood racecourse W Susx
4 D4 Goonhilly Satellite Earth Station Cnwll
358 A2 Goosewood Caravan Park N York
109 F4 Gordano service area N Som
144 D5 Gordon Hill railway station Gt Lon
115 F3 Goring & Streatley Golf Club W Berk
115 G3 Goring & Streatley railway station Oxon
251 G4 Gorleston Golf Club Norfk
152 G4 Gors Fawr Pembks
531 J5 Gorten Sands Caravan site Highld
173 F3 Gosfield Lake Golf Club Essex
430 D6 Gosforth Golf Club N u Ty
144 B2 Gosling Sports Park Herts
51 H5 Gosport & Stokes Bay Golf Club Hants
343 E3 Gotts Park Golf Club Leeds
482 B4 Gourock Golf Club Inver
102 C4 Gower Swans
103 E2 Gower Golf Club Swans
103 E3 Gower visitor centre Swans
240 E4 Grace Road C Leic
219 H6 Grafham Exhibition Centre Cambs
535 H7 Grampian Mountains P & K
275 D4 Grand Prix Collection museum Leics
488 A5 Grange Cricket Club C Edin
365 E4 Grange Fell Golf Club Cumb
486 B4 Grangemouth Golf Club Falk
365 F4 Grange-over-Sands Golf Club Cumb
332 B4 Grange Park Golf Club N Linc
329 F6 Grange Park Golf Club Rothm
324 B6 Grange Park Golf Club St Hel
577 H5 Grannie's Heilan' Hame Holiday Park Highld
278 B1 Grantham North service area Lincs
551 J4 Grantown-on-Spey Caravan Park Highld
551 J4 Grantown-on-Spey Golf Club Highld
568 C1 Grant Park Moray
566 B7 Grant Street Park Highld
235 G2 Granville country park Wrekin
315 E6 Grassmoor Golf Centre Derbys
515 G2 Grayfield Park Angus
365 E1 Graythwaite Hall Cumb
138 D6 Great Barn NT Oxon
237 F5 Great Barr Golf Club Wsall
192 C3 Great Central Cycle Ride Nhants
216 C2 Great Central Cycle Ride/Fosse 2 Braid cycle route Leics
240 C2 Great Central Railway Leics
276 C3 Great Central Railway (Nottingham) Notts
87 F2 Great Chalfield Manor NT Wilts
80 B4 Great Dixter House & Gardens E Susx
533 K4 Great Glen Way Highld
565 L8 Great Glen Way Highld
171 F6 Great Hadham Golf & Country Club Herts
340 A3 Great Harwood Golf Club Lancs
378 A3 Great Langdale NT campsite Cumb
173 E6 Great Leighs racecourse Essex
325 G3 Great Lever & Farnworth Golf Club Bolton
305 G3 Great Orme Country Park Conwy
128 C5 Great Pill Carmth
52 B4 Great Salterns Public Course C Port
39 G3 Great Torrington Golf Club Devon
251 G2 Great Yarmouth & Caister Golf Club Norfk
251 G2 Great Yarmouth racecourse Norfk
356 C4 Great Yorkshire showground N York
365 E3 Greaves Farm Caravan Park Cumb
264 C2 Greenacres campsite Gwynd
67 E1 Greenacres campsite Somset
400 D2 Green Acres Caravan Park Cumb
61 G3 Greenacres Farm Touring Caravan Park Devon
467 E3 Greenbank NTS E Rens
469 E2 Greenburn Golf Club W Loth
308 A4 Greenfield Valley Flints
340 B4 Green Haworth Golf Club Lancs
71 F6 Greenhill Farm Camping & Caravan Park Wilts
140 A1 Greenhill Leisure Park campsite Oxon
313 G6 Greenhills Holiday Park Derbys
500 B4 Green Hotels golf course P & K
473 E6 Greenknowe Tower Border
308 D2 Green Lane railway station Wirral
133 E5 Greenmeadow Community Farm Torfn
313 F5 Green Meadow Golf & Country Club Torfn
482 C4 Greenock Central railway station Inver
482 C4 Greenock Golf Club Inver
482 C5 Greenock Whinhill Golf Club Inver
50 B1 Green Pastures Farm campsite Hants
362 D5 Green Road railway station Cumb
329 E4 Greensprings Touring Park Barns
78 D5 Greenviews Caravan Park E Susx
292 A3 Greenway Bank Country Park Staffs
292 B4 Greenway Hall Golf Club Staffs
451 G3 Greenyards Border
242 C2 Greetham Valley Golf Club Rutlnd

254 C4 Gressenhall museum Norfk
400 B1 Gretna Golf Club D & G
425 F6 Gretna service area D & G
589 H8 Grey Cairns of Camster Highld
437 G2 Grey Mare's Tail NTS (Waterfall) D & G
116 B3 Greys Court NT Oxon
169 E5 Griffin Golf Club Beds
118 D4 Griffin Park Gt Lon
223 G1 Grimes Graves Norfk
334 C2 Grimsby Docks railway station NE Lin
334 B3 Grimsby Golf Club NE Lin
334 C3 Grimsby Town railway station NE Lin
143 G6 Grims Dyke Golf Club Herts
19 F1 Grimspound Devon
314 A4 Grindleford railway station Derbys
378 B6 Grizedale Cumb
363 D3 Grizedale Forest Park Cumb
566 C5 Groam House museum Highld
78 C2 Groombridge Place Gardens & Enchanted Forest E Susx
322 g7 Groundle Glen Railway IoM
294 A1 Grouse & Claret campsite Derbys
387 F4 Grouse Hill Caravan Park N York
49 E6 Grove Farm Meadow Holiday Caravan Park Dorset
573 H5 Gruinard Bay Caravan Park Highld
117 G6 Guards Polo Club W & M
34 c3 Guernsey airport Guern
95 G5 Guildford Cricket Club Surrey
200 B5 Guildhall NT Suffk
385 F2 Guisborough Forest R & Cl
489 F3 Gullane Golf Club E Loth
294 B3 Gulliver's Kingdom Derbys
168 B2 Gulliver's Land M Keyn
256 A3 Gunton railway station Norfk
14 D3 Gunvenna Caravan Park Cnwll
240 D6 Guthlaxton Trail cycle route Leics
151 G2 Gwaun Vale Touring Park Pembks
4 D5 Gwendreath Farm Holiday Park Cnwll
7 E5 Gwennap Mining District (UNESCO) Cnwll
133 G4 Gwent Rural Life museum Mons
154 A4 Gwili Railway Carmth
3 G1 Gwithian Farm campsite Cnwll
285 G2 Gwydir Castle Conwy
285 G4 Gwydyr Forest Park Conwy
385 E1 Gypsy Lane railway station R & Cl

H

212 A4 Habberley Golf Club Worcs
600 E6 Hackness Martello Tower Ork
141 F3 Haddenham & Thame Parkway railway station Bucks
115 E1 Hadden Hill Golf Club Oxon
489 G5 Haddington Golf Club E Loth
251 F5 Haddiscoe railway station Norfk
560 C2 Haddo House NTS Abers
294 A1 Haddon Hall Derbys
122 C2 Hadleigh Castle Essex
144 C5 Hadley Wood Golf Club Gt Lon
376 B1 Hadrian's Coast to Coast cycle route Cumb
376 C4 Hadrian's Cycleway Cumb
388 A4 Hadrian's Cycleway Cumb
399 G3 Hadrian's Cycleway Nthumb
404 B3 Hadrian's Cycleway Nthumb
401 E2 Hadrian's Wall Path Cumb
429 F6 Hadrian's Wall (UNESCO) Nthumb
67 H3 Hadspen Garden & Nursery Somset
180 D3 Hafod Brynog campsite Cerdgn
284 C5 Hafod y Llan NT Gwynd
475 F6 Haggerston Castle Nthumb
467 E2 Haggs Castle Golf Club C Glas
212 D3 Hagley Golf & Country Club Worcs
212 D3 Hagley Hall Worcs
323 G1 Haig Avenue Sefton
324 D3 Haigh Hall Golf Complex Wigan
163 G3 Hailes Abbey NT Gloucs
489 H4 Hailes Castle E Loth
145 G6 Hainault Forest (Country Park) Gt Lon
145 G6 Hainault Forest Golf Complex Gt Lon
361 E5 Hainsworth Park Golf Club E R Yk
122 C3 Halcon Marine Essex
213 E3 Halesowen Golf Club Dudley
226 D4 Halesworth Golf Club Suffk
236 B6 Halfpenny Green vineyard Staffs
284 C3 Halfway railway station Gwynd
342 A5 Halifax Bradley Hall Golf Club Calder
341 H3 Halifax Golf Club Calder
314 D2 Hallam AM Arena Sheff
314 B2 Hallamshire Golf Club Sheff
424 B3 Halleaths Caravan Site D & G
395 F5 Hall Garth & Country Club Hotel Darltn
94 B4 Hall Green railway station Birm
4 D4 Halliggye Fogou Cnwll
310 C2 Halliwell Jones Stadium Warrtn
365 H4 Hall More Caravan Park Cumb
314 D4 Hallowes Golf Club Derbys
120 D5 Hall Place Gt Lon
323 E4 Hall Road railway station Sefton
62 D5 Halse Farm Caravan & Camping Park Somset
45 G6 Halstock Golf Enterprises Dorset
309 H2 Halton Stadium Halton
402 A1 Haltwhistle golf course Nthumb
116 C3 Hambleden Mill Marina Bucks

51 E3 Hamble Point Marina Hants
51 E3 Hamble railway station Hants
219 G3 Hamerton Zoo Park Cambs
45 F4 Ham Hill Country Park Somset
118 D5 Ham House NT Gt Lon
467 H3 Hamilton Central railway station S Lans
468 A4 Hamilton Golf Club S Lans
467 H3 Hamilton (Northbound only) service area S Lans
325 F4 Hamilton Park Wigan
467 H3 Hamilton racecourse S Lans
308 D2 Hamilton Square railway station Wirral
467 H3 Hamilton West railway station S Lans
54 C4 Ham Manor Golf Club W Susx
467 E2 Hampden Park C Glas
90 B6 Hampshire Golf Club Hants
119 F2 Hampstead Golf Club Gt Lon
118 D6 Hampton Court Palace Gt Lon
118 D6 Hampton Court Palace Golf Club Gt Lon
35 h6 Hamptonne Country Life Jersey
71 E5 Hamptworth Golf & Country Club Wilts
213 F1 Hamstead railway station Birm
394 B3 Hamsterley Forest Dur
66 D1 Ham Wall Somset
139 G2 Hanborough railway station Oxon
188 D2 Hanbury Hall NT Worcs
213 F1 Handsworth Golf Club Birm
342 D5 Hanging Heaton Golf Club Kirk
322 d9 Hango Hill IoM
93 E6 Hankley Common Golf Club Surrey
213 F3 Harborne Church Farm Golf Club Birm
213 F3 Harborne Golf Club Birm
469 G2 Harburn Golf Club W Loth
377 G4 Hardknott Fort Roman site Cumb
377 G4 Hardknott Pass Cumb
367 H1 Hardraw Force (Waterfall) N York
395 G4 Hardwick Hall Dur
295 F2 Hardwick Hall NT Derbys
32 C1 Hardy's Cottage NT Dorset
312 A4 Hare Hill NT Ches
136 B3 Haresfield Beacon Gloucs
142 D5 Harewood Downs Golf Club Bucks
356 C6 Harewood House campsite Leeds
18 B2 Harford Bridge Holiday Park Devon
264 D3 Harlech Castle (UNESCO) Gwynd
116 D3 Harleyford Estate Bucks
116 D3 Harleyford Golf Club Bucks
224 C2 Harling vineyard Norfk
356 B4 Harlow Carr N York
145 G2 Harlow Mill railway station Herts
559 H5 Harlow Park Abers
145 F2 Harlow Town railway station Herts
14 B3 Harlyn Sands Holiday Park Cnwll
589 K7 Harmsworth Park Highld
134 B3 Harold's Stones Mons
143 G2 Harpenden Common Golf Club Herts
143 G2 Harpenden Golf Club Herts
242 C5 Harringworth Viaduct Nhants
595 H4 Harris W Isls
356 C3 Harrogate Golf Club N York
49 F5 Harrow Wood Farm Caravan Park Hants
3 d2 Harry's Walls IoS
325 E4 Hart Common Golf Club Bolton
220 C5 Hartford Marina Cambs
468 D2 Harthill service area N Lans
38 B3 Hartland Abbey & Garden Devon
38 C3 Hartland Caravan & Camping Park Devon
38 C4 Hartland Forest Golf Club Devon
396 C2 Hartlepool Golf Club Hartpl
396 D4 Hartlepool Power Station Visitor Centre Hartpl
92 C3 Hartley Wintney Golf Club Hants
448 D2 Hartree Mill Border
143 G6 Hartsbourne Golf & Country Club Herts
342 C5 Hartshead Moor service area Calder
239 E6 Hartshill Hayes Country Park Warwks
318 A6 Hartsholme Country Park Lincs
391 G1 Hartside Summit Cumb
121 F1 Hartswood Golf Club Essex
212 C5 Harvington Hall Worcs
176 D3 Harwich & Dovercourt Golf Club Essex
176 D3 Harwich International railway station Essex
176 D3 Harwich Town railway station Essex
325 H2 Harwood Golf Club (Bolton) Bolton
37 E3 Haseley Manor IoW
124 D2 Hasguard Cross Caravan Park Pembks
55 G1 Hassocks Golf Club W Susx
55 H1 Hassocks railway station W Susx
118 B2 Haste Hill golf course Gt Lon
214 B3 Hatchford Brook golf course Birm
94 B4 Hatchlands Park NT Surrey
172 A5 Hatfield Forest NT Essex
144 C3 Hatfield London Country Club Herts
144 B3 Hatfield Palace Herts
330 D2 Hatfield & Stainforth railway station Donc
374 D2 Hatherleigh Deep Sea Trawler N York
190 C1 Hatton Country World Warwks
190 C1 Hatton (Warwickshire) railway station Warwks
234 C1 Haughmond Abbey Shrops
555 G1 Haughton House Abers
301 F3 Havenhouse railway station Lincs
125 G1 Haverfordwest Golf Club Pembks
198 D6 Haverhill Golf Club Essex

145 H6 Havering Country Park Gt Lon
288 D2 Hawarden Golf Club Flints
188 B2 Hawford Dovecote NT Worcs
439 F2 Hawick Golf Club Border
89 H5 Hawk Conservancy Hants
466 C2 Hawkhead railway station Rens
79 G3 Hawkhurst Golf Club Kent
378 C5 Hawkshead Courthouse museum NT Cumb
270 D4 Hawkstone Park Shrops
368 B6 Hawkswick Cote Caravan Park N York
83 F1 Hawthorn Farm Caravan Park Kent
227 E5 Haw Wood Farm Caravan Park Suffk
324 D5 Haydock Park Golf Club Wigan
324 D5 Haydock Park racecourse St Hel
119 F5 Haydons Road railway station Gt Lon
118 B4 Hayes & Harlington railway station Gt Lon
108 C2 Hayley Stadium Newpt
52 B5 Hayling Golf Club Hants
52 C4 Hayling Island Hants
488 A5 Haymarket railway station C Edin
67 G4 Hayne Motor museum Somset
158 D1 Hay-on-Wye loop cycle route Powys
97 E5 Haysden Country Park Kent
484 C5 Hayston Golf Club E Duns
77 F4 Haywards Heath Golf Club W Susx
77 F5 Haywards Heath railway station W Susx
312 B2 Hazel Grove Golf Club Stockp
557 F3 Hazlehead golf course C Aber
142 B5 Hazlemere Golf Club Bucks
343 E1 Headingley Golf Club Leeds
343 E2 Headingley Stadium Leeds
394 D6 Headlam Hall Hotel golf course Dur
22 B5 Headland Caravan & Camping Park Cnwll
95 E4 Headley Common NT Surrey
342 A3 Headley Golf Club Brad
444 C6 Heads of Ayr S Ayrs
118 C1 Headstone Lane railway station Gt Lon
365 G5 Heald Brow NT Lancs
70 C2 Heale Garden & Plant Centre Wilts
454 A2 Heatherslaw Corn Mill Nthumb
453 H2 Heatherslaw Light Railway Nthumb
454 A2 Heatherslaw railway station Nthumb
36 A3 Heathfield Farm Camping IoW
106 C3 Heath High Level railway station Cardif
227 G2 Heathland Beach Caravan Park Suffk
106 C3 Heath Low Level railway station Cardif
118 B4 Heathpark Golf Club Gt Lon
118 B4 Heathrow airport Gt Lon
118 B5 Heathrow Terminal 4 railway station Gt Lon
118 B4 Heathrow Terminals 1, 2 & 3 railway station Gt Lon
326 B4 Heaton Hall Manch
311 H1 Heaton Moor Golf Club Stockp
326 B4 Heaton Park Golf Centre Manch
77 G4 Heaven Farm campsite E Susx
341 G4 Hebden Bridge Golf Club Calder
284 C3 Hebron railway station Gwynd
299 E6 Heckington windmill Lincs
20 A4 Hedgehog Hospital Devon
23 F2 Hedleywood Caravan & Camping Park Devon
294 B3 Heights of Abraham Derbys
482 C3 Helensburgh Central railway station Ag & B
482 C3 Helensburgh Golf Club Ag & B
482 C3 Helensburgh Upper railway station Ag & B
60 D2 Hele Valley Holiday Park Devon
8 C4 Heligan Woods campsite Cnwll
161 F3 Hellen's House Herefs
141 H5 Hell Fire Caves Bucks
142 A6 Hell Fire Club Bucks
192 B3 Hellidon Lakes Hotel & Country Club Nhants
201 G3 Helmingham Hall Suffk
582 D6 Helmsdale Golf Club Highld
309 G5 Helsby Golf Club Ches
19 F4 Hembury Castle Devon
28 B2 Hembury Fort Devon
220 C6 Hemingford Abbots golf course Cambs
80 B2 Hemsted Forest Golf Club Kent
282 D1 Hen Blas Park IoA
109 G4 Henbury Golf Club Bristl
119 E1 Hendon Golf Club Gt Lon
7 F2 Hendra Holiday Park Cnwll
150 C4 Hendre Eynon Camping & Caravan Site Pembks
229 E1 Hendre Mynach Touring Caravan & Camping Park Gwynd
267 G2 Hendwr Country Park campsite Denbgs
133 G1 Hen-Gwrt (Moat) Mons
232 B3 Heniarth Gate railway station Powys
116 C3 Henley Golf Club Oxon
190 A1 Henley Golf & Country Club Warwks
169 H2 Henlow airfield Beds
116 C3 Hennerton Golf Club Wokham
130 D2 Henrhyd Falls Powys
78 B2 Henry VIII Experience museum E Susx
344 D5 Hensall railway station N York
160 B1 Hereford racecourse Herefs
160 C1 Hereford Municipal golf course Herefs
186 A5 Herefordshire Golf Club Herefs

185 E3 Hergest Croft Herefs
191 F4 Heritage Motor Centre museum Warwks
342 D5 Heritage Road Kirk
439 F5 Hermitage Castle Border
221 E4 Hermitage Marina Cambs
100 C2 Hermitage Golf Club Kent
301 F1 Heron's Mead Fishing Lake & Touring Park Lincs
322 d9 Herring Tower IoM
57 G2 Herstmonceux Castle E Susx
34 B5 Herston Halt railway station Dorset
143 F2 Herts County showground Herts
347 E3 Hessle Golf Club E R Yk
44 A2 Hestercombe House Gardens Somset
118 C4 Heston service area Gt Lon
308 C3 Heswall Golf Club Wirral
96 C5 Hever Castle Golf Club Kent
96 C6 Hever railway station Kent
405 G2 Heworth Golf Club Gatesd
358 B4 Heworth Golf Club York
403 G2 Hexham Golf Club Nthumb
403 G2 Hexham racecourse Nthumb
403 G2 Hexham Racecourse Caravan Site Nthumb
171 F1 Heydon Grange golf course Cambs
166 A5 Heyford railway station Oxon
311 E4 Heyrose Golf Club Ches
351 F3 Heysham Golf Club Lancs
351 E2 Heysham Port railway station Lancs
117 F3 H F Marina Bucks
330 A3 Hickleton Golf Club Donc
190 B6 Hidcote Manor NT Gloucs
23 F6 Hidden Valley Discovery Park Cnwll
60 C3 Hidden Valley Park campsite Devon
313 E6 Hi Edge Raceway Derbys
100 C5 Higham Park Kent
145 F5 High Beech golf course Essex
78 D1 High Brooms railway station Kent
40 C3 Highbullen Hotel Golf & Country Club Devon
90 C3 Highclere Castle Hants
49 G6 Highcliffe Castle Dorset
49 F6 Highcliffe Castle Golf Club Dorset
96 B2 High Elms golf course Gt Lon
3 E2 Higher Chellew Holiday Park Cnwll
7 E3 Higher Golla Touring & Caravan Park Cnwll
18 B3 Higher Longford Caravan & Camping Park Devon
7 E1 Higher Moor campsite Cnwll
12 C5 Higher Rew Caravan & Camping Park Devon
31 E6 Higher South Buckland Farm campsite Dorset
6 B6 Higher Trevaskis Caravan Park Cnwll
13 F1 Higher Well Farm Holiday Park Devon
197 E3 Highfield Farm Touring Park Cambs
23 F2 Highfield House campsite Devon
393 E4 High Force (Waterfall) Dur
212 B4 Highgate Common Staffs
119 F2 Highgate Golf Club Gt Lon
535 L2 Highland Folk museum Highld
565 H5 Highland Museum of Childhood Highld
30 A4 Highlands End Farm Holiday Park Dorset
536 B2 Highland Wildlife Park Highld
311 E3 High Legh Park Golf Club Ches
223 G2 High Lodge Forest Centre Suffk
355 H3 High Moor Farm Park campsite N York
313 E1 High Peak Derbys
293 H3 High Peak Trail cycle route Derbys
70 D2 High Post Golf Club Wilts
101 F4 Highway Marina Kent
174 D4 High Woods Country Park Essex
58 B5 Highwoods Golf Club E Susx
113 E1 Highworth Golf Centre Swindn
54 D3 Hill Barn Golf Club W Susx
390 D5 Hillcroft Caravan & Camping Site Cumb
71 F5 Hill Farm Caravan Park Hants
484 B5 Hillfoot railway station E Duns
556 D1 Hillhead Caravan Park Abers
72 A5 Hillier arboretum Hants
118 C3 Hillingdon Cycle Circuit Gt Lon
118 B3 Hillingdon Golf Club Gt Lon
466 D1 Hillington East railway station C Glas
466 D2 Hillington West railway station C Glas
365 E1 Hill of Oaks & Blakeholme campsite Cumb
502 B2 Hill of Tarvit NTS Fife
583 J2 Hill o'Many Stanes Highld
314 C1 Hillsborough Sheff
314 C1 Hillsborough Golf Club Sheff
323 F2 Hillside Golf Club Sefton
378 F2 Hill Top NT Cumb
213 F1 Hilltop Public golf course Sandw
290 A6 Hill Valley Golf & Country Club Shrops
87 F2 Hilperton Marina Wilts
483 H4 Hilton Park Golf Club E Duns
237 E4 Hilton Park service area Staffs
162 C2 Hilton Puckrup Hall golf course Gloucs
212 C1 Himley Hall Park Staffs
212 C1 Himley Hall Park Staffs
220 B5 Hinchingbrooke Country Park Cambs
239 G6 Hinckley Golf Club Leics
325 E3 Hindley Hall Golf Club Wigan
64 D2 Hinkley Point Visitor Centre Somset
140 A4 Hinksey Heights Oxon
201 E6 Hintlesham Golf Club Suffk
49 F6 Hinton Admiral railway station Dorset

73 E4 Hinton Ampner NT Hants
453 F2 Hirsel Golf Club Border
80 B3 Historical Vehicles Collection Kent
396 D3 Historic Quay Hartpl
80 B3 Historic Vehicles Collection museum Kent
577 G6 Historylinks museum Highld
358 B4 Hiuntington Stadium York
514 C4 HM Frigate 'Unicorn' C Dund
273 H5 Hoar Cross Hall Health Spa Resort Staffs
314 B6 Hob Hurst's House Derbys
405 E3 Hobson Golf Club Dur
72 C4 Hockley Golf Club Hants
424 D5 Hoddom Castle Caravan Park D & G
271 E4 Hodnet Hall Gardens Shrops
93 H3 Hoebridge Golf Centre Surrey
339 F4 Hoghton Tower Lancs
135 G5 Hogsdown Farm Caravan & Camping Park Gloucs
217 E6 Holdenby House Nhants
348 B1 Holderness E R Yk
365 G4 Holgate's Caravan Park Cumb
364 A5 Holker Street Cumb
260 A3 Holkham Hall Norfk
447 G2 Holland Bush Golf Club S Lans
55 H3 Hollingbury Park Golf Club Br & H
326 D1 Hollingworth Lake Rochdl
326 D2 Hollingworth Lake Caravan Park Rochdl
377 F4 Hollins Farm Campsite Cumb
310 D4 Holly Bank Caravan Park Traffd
43 H4 Holly Bush Park campsite Somset
74 D4 Hollycombe Steam collection W Susx
76 B6 Holly Gate Cactus Garden W Susx
399 F4 Holm Cultram Abbey Cumb
259 E3 Holme Dunes Norfk
332 C3 Holme Hall Golf Club N Linc
327 G4 Holme Moss Derbys
366 A4 Holme Park Fell NT Cumb
94 D6 Holmwood railway station Surrey
23 G2 Holsworthy Golf Club Devon
261 E4 Holt Lowes Norfk
33 G1 Holton Heath railway station Dorset
78 B2 Holtye Golf Club E Susx
302 B4 Holyhead Golf Club IoA
302 B4 Holyhead Mountain Hut Group IoA
302 B4 Holy Island IoA
481 H3 Holy Loch Marina Ag & B
7 E2 Holywell Bay Golf Park Cnwll
7 E2 Holywell Bay Holiday Park Cnwll
307 H5 Holywell Golf Club Flints
358 A6 Home Farm Caravan & Camping N York
30 C5 Home Farm Caravan & Campsite Dorset
303 G4 Home Farm Caravan Park IoA
64 B3 Home Farm Holiday Centre Somset
81 E2 Homelands Bettergolf Centre Kent
11 E2 Home Park C Plym
85 F5 Homestead Park campsite Somset
100 A3 Homing Park campsite Kent
76 C6 Honeybridge Park campsite W Susx
48 C4 Honeybrook Farm Dorset
361 F5 Honeysuckle Farm E R Yk
377 G2 Honister Pass Cumb
28 C3 Honiton Golf Club Devon
235 F2 Hoo Farm Wrekin
29 F4 Hook Farm Caravan & Camping Park Devon
122 B5 Hoo Marina Medway
313 G3 Hoo campsite Derbys
568 B2 Hopeman Golf Club Moray
487 E4 Hopetoun House W Loth
97 G5 Hop Farm Kent
390 C4 Hopkinsons' Whitbarrow Hall Caravan Park Cumb
209 G4 Hoptonheath railway station Shrops
213 F5 Hopwood Park service area Worcs
57 F1 Horam Manor Touring Park E Susx
57 F1 Horam Park golf course E Susx
356 B4 Hornbeam Park railway station N York
319 G3 Horncastle Golf Club Lincs
120 D3 Hornchurch Country Park Gt Lon
250 C1 Horning Ferry Marina Norfk
361 G5 Hornsea Golf Club E R Yk
348 B2 Hornsea Rail Trail cycle route E R Yk
118 D3 Horsenden Hill Golf Club Gt Lon
288 A6 Horseshoe Falls Denbgs
288 A5 Horseshoe Pass Denbgs
257 F5 Horsey Windpump NT Norfk
342 D1 Horsforth Golf Club Leeds
76 C3 Horsham Cricket & Sports Club W Susx
76 C4 Horsham Golf W Susx
294 D6 Horsley Lodge Golf Club Derbys
94 B4 Horsley railway station Surrey
77 G4 Horsted Keynes railway station W Susx
110 D2 Horton Court NT S Glos
94 D2 Horton Park Golf & Country Club Surrey
325 E3 Horwich Parkway railway station Bolton
253 F2 Houghton Hall Norfk
169 E2 Houghton House Beds
406 B5 Houghton-Le-Spring Golf Club Sundld
71 G3 Houghton Lodge Hants
220 C5 Houghton Mill NT Cambs
324 C4 Houghwood Golf St Hel
326 C6 Houldsworth Golf Club Manch
19 F2 Hound Tor Medieval Village Devon
118 C5 Hounslow Heath golf course Gt Lon
529 E3 House of Dun NTS Angus
428 B6 Housesteads Fort museum NT Nthumb
256 B6 Hoveton & Wroxham railway station Norfk

372 B5 Howardian Hills N York
355 E3 Howgill Lodge campsite N York
443 H1 Howick Hall Nthumb
100 C4 Howletts Warwks
343 E4 Howley Hall Golf Club Leeds
466 A2 Howwood (Renfrewshire) railway station Rens
600 C5 Hoy Ork
308 B2 Hoylake Golf Club Wirral
342 B6 Huddersfield Golf Club Kirk
142 B5 Hughenden Manor NT Bucks
484 B6 Hughenden Stadium C Glas
566 D3 Hugh Miller's Cottage NTS Highld
45 G4 Huish Park Somset
347 G4 Hull Arena C KuH
347 G4 Hull Golf Club E R Yk
347 H4 Humber Bridge E R Yk
333 F2 Humberside airport N Linc
240 D3 Humberstone Heights Golf Club C Leic
326 A6 Humphrey Park railway station Traffd
397 G5 Hunley Hall Golf Club R & Cl
193 F3 Hunsbury Hill Nhants
258 D3 Hunstanton Golf Club Norfk
464 D4 Hunterston Power Station N Ayrs
115 H2 Huntercombe Golf Club Oxon
306 C5 Hunters Hamlet Caravan Park Conwy
220 B5 Huntingdon Boathaven & Caravan Park Cambs
220 B5 Huntingdon racecourse Cambs
558 C1 Huntly Castle Caravan Park Abers
558 C1 Huntly Golf Club Abers
17 G3 Hurdwick Golf Club Devon
116 D3 Hurley Riverside Park campsite Bucks
323 H2 Hurlston Hall Country Caravan Park Lancs
323 G2 Hurlston Hall Golf Club Lancs
35 H3 Hurst Castle Hants
93 F5 Hurtmore Golf Club Surrey
390 D2 Hutton-in-the-Forest Cumb
372 C2 Hutton-le-Hole Caravan Park N York
309 G1 Huyton & Prescot Golf Club Knows
147 F5 Hyde Hall Essex
326 D5 Hyde North railway station Tamesd
285 E6 Hydro-electric Power Station Gwynd
412 C4 Hydros Visitor Centre D & G
298 A1 Hykeham railway station Lincs
146 D4 Hylands House & Park Essex
399 E4 Hylton Caravan Park Cumb
406 B3 Hylton Castle Sundld
484 A6 Hyndland railway station C Glas
174 D4 Hythe (Essex) railway station Essex
82 C4 Hythe Imperial golf course Kent

482 B5 IBM railway station Inver
467 E2 Ibrox Stadium C Glas
49 F2 Ibsley Common NT Hants
199 G2 Ickworth NT Suffk
198 D3 Ickworth vineyard Cambs
199 G2 Ickworth vineyard Suffk
80 A1 Iden Croft Herbs Kent
76 D2 Ifield Golf & Country Club W Susx
97 E4 Ightham Mote NT Kent
293 F4 Ilam Park NT Staffs
120 B2 Ilford Golf Club Gt Lon
60 D2 Ilfracombe Golf Club Devon
355 E5 Ilkley Golf Club N York
496 D1 Immervoulin Caravan & Camping Park Stirlg
333 H1 Immingham Golf Club NE Lin
295 H3 Impact Arena Derbys
309 G4 Ince & Elton railway station Ches
324 D4 Ince railway station Wigan
487 G3 Inchcolm Abbey Fife
497 E4 Inchmahome Priory Stirlg
556 B5 Inchmarlo Golf Centre Abers
129 G4 Inco Golf Club Swans
273 E5 Ingestre Park Golf Club Staffs
367 F5 Ingleborough N York
388 C6 Inglenook Caravan Park Cumb
338 D3 Ingol Golf Club Lancs
190 C3 Ingon Manor Golf & Country Club Warwks
341 H2 Ingrow (West) railway station Brad
481 C5 Innellan golf course Ag & B
450 C2 Innerleithen Golf Club Border
511 F6 Innerpeffray Library P & K
3 d2 Innisidgen Tomb IoS
559 E4 Insch Golf Club Abers
340 B3 Interlink Express Stadium Lancs
571 J3 Inverallochy Golf Club Abers
494 B3 Inveraray Castle Ag & B
494 B3 Inveraray golf course Ag & B
494 B3 Inveraray jail Ag & B
521 G4 Invercoe Caravan & Camping Park Highld
488 C5 Inveresk Lodge NTS E Loth
573 G7 Inverewe Garden NTS Highld
566 B3 Invergordon Golf Club Highld
488 A4 Inverleith Ground C Edin
533 H7 Inverlochy Castle Highld
512 B1 Inver Mill Farm Caravan Park P & K
566 D6 Inverness (Dalcross) airport Highld
566 B8 Inverness Golf Club Highld
566 B8 Inverness Ice Centre Highld
559 H5 Inverurie Golf Club Abers
504 B6 Iona Ag & B
201 H6 Ipswich Golf Club Suffk
194 C1 Irchester Country Park Nhants
276 B2 Ireland Avenue Notts
235 F4 Ironbridge Gorge (UNESCO) Wrekin
235 F4 Iron Bridge museum Shrops
99 G2 Iron Wharf Boatyard Kent
132 D3 Ironworks Torfn
401 F2 Irthing Vale Holiday Park Cumb
377 E4 Irton Road railway station Cumb

444 D1 Irvine Golf Club N Ayrs
444 D1 Irvine Ravenspark Golf Club N Ayrs
190 A3 Island Meadow Caravan Park Warwks
476 F5 Islay Ag & B
476 E6 Islay airport Ag & B
463 F5 Isle of Arran Distillery N Ayrs
66 D1 Isle of Avalon Touring Caravan Park Somset
506 F1 Isle of Eriska golf course Ag & B
458 C2 Isle of Gigha Golf Club Ag & B
597 H1 Isle of Lewis W Isls
322 d9 Isle of Man (Ronaldsway) airport IoM
322 e8 Isle of Man Steam Railway IoM
505 J3 Isle of Mull Ag & B
33 H3 Isle of Purbeck Dorset
34 B4 Isle of Purbeck Golf Club Dorset
123 F6 Isle of Sheppey Kent
545 G6 Isle of Skye Highld
545 J3 Isle of Skye Golf Club Highld
84 D5 Isle of Wedmore Golf Club Somset
36 D3 Isle of Wight IoW
37 E5 Isle of Wight Glass IoW
37 F5 Isle of Wight Steam Railway IoW
3 d3 Isles of Scilly IoS
3 d2 Isles of Scilly (St Mary's) airport IoS
51 E1 Itchen Valley Hants
239 G3 Ivanhoe Trail cycle route Leics
117 H3 Iver Golf Club Bucks
272 C3 Izaak Walton Golf Club Staffs
272 C4 Izaak Walton's Cottage museum Staffs

J

291 G5 Jack Barker's Keele Golf Centre Staffs
365 G5 Jack Scout NT Lancs
374 C2 Jacobs Mount Caravan Park N York
214 D3 Jaguar Daimler Covtry
215 E3 Jaguar Daimler Heritage Centre museum Covtry
288 C6 James' Caravan Park Wrexhm
467 F3 James Hamilton Heritage Park S Lans
73 H2 Jane Austen's House & museum Hants
374 A3 Jasmine Caravan Park N York
452 B6 Jedburgh Golf Club Border
440 C2 Jedforest Deer and Farm Park Border
440 C1 Jedwater Caravan Park Border
35 g7 Jersey airport Jersey
35 g7 Jersey Lavender Farm Jersey
369 G2 Jervaulx Abbey N York
324 D3 JJB Stadium Wigan
311 F5 Jodrell Bank Ches
309 F3 John Lennon airport Lpool
490 B4 John Muir Country Park E Loth
116 D6 John Nike Leisuresport Complex Br For
196 B5 John O'Gaunt Golf Club Beds
589 K2 John O'Groats Caravan Site Highld
346 C5 Julian's Bower maze N Linc
22 B6 Juliot's Well Holiday Park Cnwll
325 G2 Jumbles Country Park Bolton
478 F5 Jura Ag & B
478 D6 Jura Forest Ag & B
29 G4 Jurassic Coast World Heritage Site (UNESCO) Dorset

K

450 B2 Kailzie Gardens Border
12 B5 Karrageen Caravan & Camping Park Devon
140 C4 Kassam Stadium Oxon
275 E1 Kedleston Hall NT Derbys
275 E1 Kedleston Park Golf Club Derbys
291 G6 Keele service area Staffs
355 G6 Keighley Golf Club Brad
341 H1 Keighley & Worth Valley Railway Brad
568 F6 Keith & Dufftown Railway Moray
569 G5 Keith Golf Club Moray
465 E3 Kelburn Country Centre N Ayrs
503 E3 Kellie Castle NTS Fife
261 F5 Kelling Heath Park railway station Norfk
217 F4 Kelmarsh Hall Nhants
452 D2 Kelso Golf Club Border
452 D2 Kelso racecourse Border
467 E1 Kelvin Hall International Sports Arena C Glas
2 C4 Kelynack Caravan & Camping Park Cnwll
556 C1 Kemnay Golf Club Abers
528 B4 Kemp's Castle Angus
118 C6 Kempton Park racecourse Surrey
35 f6 Kempt Tower Jersey
99 E1 Kemsley Down railway station Kent
379 F6 Kendal Golf Club Cumb
215 E5 Kenilworth Castle Highld Warwks
169 F5 Kenilworth Road Luton
95 G3 Kenley airfield Gt Lon
523 L6 Kenmore golf course P & K
185 L3 Kennall Vale (UNESCO) Cnwll
3 F4 Kenneggy Cove Holiday Park Cnwll
198 D1 Kennett railway station Cambs
27 E5 Kennford International Caravan Park Devon
119 F3 Kensington Palace Gt Lon
119 H5 Kent County Cricket Ground Gt Lon
98 C3 Kent County showground Kent
80 B4 Kent & East Sussex Railway Kent
119 H5 Kent House railway station Gt Lon

101 F2 Kent International airport Kent
61 F3 Kentisbury Grange Country Park Devon
199 H5 Kentwell Hall Suffk
320 B3 Kenwick Park Golf Club Lincs
119 F2 Kenwood House Gt Lon
227 G2 Kessingland Beach Holiday Park Suffk
390 A5 Keswick Golf Club Cumb
218 B4 Kettering Golf Club Nhants
118 D4 Kew Palace Gt Lon
10 D2 Keyham railway station C Plym
237 F2 Keys Park Staffs
241 E6 Kibworth Golf Club Leics
212 B4 Kidderminster Golf Club Worcs
440 B6 Kielder Castle Nthumb
440 C4 Kielderhead Nthumb
190 B6 Kiftsgate Court gardens Gloucs
462 B2 Kilberry Sculptured Stones Ag & B
465 G4 Kilbirnie Place Golf Club N Ayrs
507 K4 Kilchurn Castle Ag & B
581 L5 Kildonan railway station Highld
555 E1 Kildrummy Castle Abers
38 C4 Killarney Springs Cnwll
374 D3 Killerby Old Hall campsite N York
27 F2 Killerton NT Devon
403 E6 Killhope Lead Mining Centre Dur
402 D6 Killhope Summit Cumb
524 D3 Killiecrankie NTS P & K
9 G3 Killigarth Manor Holiday Centre Cnwll
509 J3 Killin Golf Club Stirlg
366 B1 Killington Lake (Southbound Only) service area Cumb
61 G2 Killington Lane railway station Devon
7 F5 Killiow Golf Club Cnwll
483 E6 Kilmacolm Golf Club Inver
497 F3 Kilmahog Woollen Mill Stirlg
444 D3 Kilmarnock (Barassie) Golf Club S Ayrs
492 D5 Kilmartin House museum Ag & B
492 D2 Kilmelford Yacht Haven Ag & B
493 E6 Kilmichael Glassary Inscribed Stone Ag & B
480 D3 Kilmodan Sculptured Stones Ag & B
480 B2 Kilmory Woodland Park Ag & B
481 H3 Kilmun arboretum Ag & B
126 C4 Kiln Park Holiday Centre Pembks
368 C6 Kilnsey Park & Trout Farm N York
359 F4 Kilnwick Percy Golf Club E R Yk
460 C4 Kilpatrick Dun N Ayrs
483 G5 Kilpatrick railway station W Duns
489 E3 Kilspindie Golf Club E Loth
485 E4 Kilsyth Lennox Golf Club N Lans
316 B3 Kilton Forest Golf Club Notts
543 J3 Kilt Rock Waterfall Highld
512 B1 Kilvrecht Campsite P & K
216 D3 Kilworth Springs Golf Club Leics
249 E4 Kimberley Park railway station Norfk
306 D4 Kimnel Park golf course Denbgs
230 B3 King Alfred's Tower NT Wilts
230 B3 King Arthur's Labyrinth & Craft Centre Gwynd
3 c1 King Charles's Castle IoS
486 B1 Kingdom of Fife Cycleway Clacks
93 H3 Kingfield Stadium Surrey
356 C2 Kingfisher Caravan Park N York
164 C5 Kingham railway station Gloucs
488 B2 Kinghorn Golf Club Fife
512 D5 King James VI Golf Club P & K
84 D4 King John's Hunting Lodge NT Somset
22 B6 Kings Acre campsite Cnwll
77 G2 Kingscote railway station W Susx
87 E1 Kingsdown Golf Club Wilts
28 C4 Kings Down Tail Caravan & Camping Park Devon
409 G2 Kings Green Caravan Site D & G
97 G4 Kings Hill Golf Club Kent
162 B6 Kingsholm Gloucs
487 H6 Kingsknowe Golf Club C Edin
292 D5 Kingsley & Froghall railway station Staffs
252 D3 King's Lynn Golf Club Norfk
297 E3 Kings Marina Notts
213 G5 Kings Norton Golf Club Worcs
40 D4 Kings Nympton railway station Devon
162 B6 King's School Gloucs
193 G2 Kingsthorpe Golf Club Nhants
347 G4 Kingston Communications Stadium C KuH
48 B4 Kingston Lacy NT Dorset
32 C1 Kingston Maurward Dorset
430 D6 Kingston Park N u Ty
30 D5 Kingston Russell stone circle Dorset
197 E6 Kingsway Golf Centre Cambs
95 F3 Kingswood Golf & Country Club Surrey
331 E2 Kings Wood golf course Donc
185 L3 Kington Golf Club Herefs
535 L2 Kingussie Golf Club Highld
560 A6 Kinkell Church Abers
486 C3 Kinneil House Falk
486 C3 Kinneil railway station Falk
512 D5 Kinnoull Forest P & K
500 B4 Kinross House P & K
500 A4 Kinross service area P & K
557 E1 Kintore golf course Abers
457 E2 Kintyre Ag & B
189 H3 Kinwarton Dovecote NT Warwks
482 B5 Kip Marina Inver
413 F3 Kippford Holiday Park D & G
602 B6 Kirbuster Farm museum Ork

242 C6 Kirby Hall Nhants
240 B4 Kirby Muxloe Golf Club Leics
370 D3 Kirby Wiske Birds of Prey Centre N York
366 C3 Kirkby Lonsdale Golf Club Cumb
372 C2 Kirkbymoorside Golf Club N York
488 B1 Kirkcaldy Golf Club Fife
412 C4 Kirkcudbright Golf Club D & G
338 B3 Kirkham & Wesham railway station Lancs
467 F3 Kirkhill Golf Club S Lans
467 F2 Kirkhill railway station S Lans
484 C5 Kirkintilloch Golf Club E Duns
328 C2 Kirklees Light Railway Kirk
424 B3 Kirkloch Caravan & Camping Site D & G
408 B2 Kirkmadrine church D & G
343 E2 Kirkstall Abbey Leeds
321 F3 Kirkstead Holiday Park Lincs
378 C3 Kirkstone Pass Cumb
601 H3 Kirkwall airport Ork
527 E3 Kirriemuir Golf Club Angus
417 F4 Kirroughtree D & G
166 A6 Kirtlington Golf Club Oxon
280 C1 Kirton Holme golf course Lincs
591 D8 Kisimul Castle W Isls
51 F6 Kite Hill Farm Caravan Park IoW
17 E4 Kit Hill Country Park Cnwll
88 D2 Knap Hill Wilts
356 D3 Knaresborough Golf Club N York
170 B5 Knebworth Golf Club Herts
170 B5 Knebworth House Herts
350 D6 Kneps Farm Holiday Park Lancs
209 E5 Knighton Golf Club Powys
48 C5 Knighton Heath Golf Club Poole
310 C6 Knights Grange Sports Complex & golf course Ches
42 C4 Knightshayes Court NT Devon
367 G6 Knight Stainforth Hall Caravan & Campsite N York
483 H6 Knightswood Golf Club C Glas
57 F3 Knockhatch Ski and Snowboard Centre E Susx
499 H6 Knockhill Racing Circuit Fife
96 C2 Knockholt railway station Gt Lon
550 B1 Knocknagael Boar Stone Highld
96 D4 Knole NT Kent
96 D3 Knole Park Golf Club Kent
350 D5 Knott End Golf Club Lancs
395 G3 Knotty Hill Golf Centre Dur
109 H6 Knowle Golf Club Bristl
324 B5 Knowsley Road St Hel
324 B6 Knowsley Safari Park Knows
531 L2 Knoydart Highld
208 D5 Knucklas Viaduct Powys
311 F4 Knutsford Golf Club Ches
311 E4 Knutsford service area Ches
569 G5 Kynoch Park Moray

L

35 d2 La Bailloterie Camping & Leisure Guern
111 G5 Lackham Countryside Centre Wilts
111 G6 Lacock Abbey NT Wilts
236 D5 Ladbroke Stadium Wolves
213 G5 Ladbrook Park Golf Club Warwks
292 C3 Ladderedge County Park Staffs
552 F5 Ladder Hills Abers
90 D3 Ladle Hill (unfinished hill fort) Hants
501 F2 Ladybank Golf Club Fife
55 F4 Lady Bee Marina W Susx
386 D3 Ladycross Plantation Caravan Park N York
20 D2 Lady's Mile Holiday Park Devon
416 A2 Laggangairn Standing Stones D & G
466 C2 Lagoon Leisure Centre Rens
34 C3 La Grande Mare Golf & Country Club Guern
583 G3 Laidhay Croft museum Highld
121 G2 Laindon railway station Essex
576 C3 Lairg railway station Highld
378 D3 Lake District National Park Cumb
378 C4 Lake District Visitor Centre Cumb
22 B6 Lakefield Caravan Park Cnwll
365 E5 Lakeland Leisure Park Cumb
365 E4 Lakeland Motor museum Cumb
388 D4 Lakeland Sheep & Wool Centre Cumb
365 H4 Lakeland Wildlife Oasis Cumb
291 E3 Lakemore Country Park Ches
223 E3 Lakenheath airfield Suffk
158 B4 Lakeside Caravan Park Powys
246 B4 Lakeside Caravan Park & Fisheries Norfk
104 C3 Lakeside golf course Neath
364 D2 Lakeside & Haverthwaite Railway Cumb
220 D4 Lakeside Lodge Golf Club Cambs
121 E4 Lakeside Shopping Centre Thurr
118 A6 Laleham Golf Club Surrey
35 g5 La Mare vineyard Jersey
310 C6 Lamb Cottage Caravan Park Ches
79 F2 Lamberhurst Golf Club Kent
461 A5 Lamlash Golf Club N Ayrs
472 D3 Lammermuir Hills Border
125 H4 Lamphey railway station Pembks
217 G5 Lamport Hall Nhants
469 E6 Lanark Golf Club S Lans
469 E6 Lanark Moor S Lans
340 D4 Lancashire Cycleway Lancs
351 F6 Lancashire Cycleway Lancs
351 H4 Lancaster (Forton) service area Lancs
351 G3 Lancaster Golf Club Lancs
55 E3 Lancing College Chapel W Susx

37 F4 Landguard Camping Park IoW
177 E3 Landguard Fort museum Suffk
551 G5 Landmark Forest Heritage Park Highld
2 B5 Land's End Cnwll
2 C4 Land's End airport Cnwll
401 E2 Lanercost Priory Cumb
121 G2 Langdon Hills Golf Club Thurr
425 H3 Langholm Golf Club D & G
103 E4 Langland Bay Golf Club Swans
96 A1 Langley Park Golf Club Gt Lon
18 B3 Langstone Manor Camping & Caravan Park Devon
15 F6 Lanhydrock Golf Club Cnwll
15 F6 Lanhydrock NT Cnwll
110 C6 Lansdown Golf Club BaNES
351 G2 Lansil Golf Club Lancs
6 C6 Lanyon Holiday Park Cnwll
2 D3 Lanyon Quoit Cnwll
7 F2 Lappa Valley Steam Railway Cnwll
214 B5 Lapworth railway station Warwks
389 F1 Larches Caravan Park Cumb
465 E3 Largs Golf Club N Ayrs
465 E3 Largs Yacht Haven N Ayrs
468 B4 Larkhall Golf Club S Lans
91 H6 Lasham airfield Hants
208 B1 Latham Park Powys
472 C4 Lauderdale D & G
489 G5 Lauderdale Aisle St Mary's Church E Loth
472 C5 Lauder golf course Border
127 G2 Laugharne Castle Carmth
23 G5 Launceston Golf Club Cnwll
487 H4 Lauriston Castle C Edin
78 B6 Lavender Line E Susx
117 F6 Lavender Park Golf Centre Br For
109 H5 Lawrence Hill railway station Bristl
322 g6 Laxey Commissioners Campsite IoM
322 g5 Laxey Wheel IoM
174 C3 Layer Road Essex
391 E2 Lazonby & Kirkoswald railway station Cumb
436 A2 Leadhills Golf Club S Lans
288 C4 Lead Mines (Minera) Wrexhm
435 H2 Lead Mining museum D & G
20 D2 Leadstone campsite Devon
238 C6 Lea Marston Hotel, Leisure Complex & golf course Warwks
191 E2 Leamington & County Golf Club Warwks
581 L5 Learable Hill Cairns, Stone Row & Stone Circles Highld
308 C1 Leasowe Golf Club Wirral
94 D3 Leatherhead Golf Club Surrey
374 D3 Lebberston Touring Park N York
552 E6 Lecht Ski Area Abers
552 E6 Lecht Summit Moray
71 H2 Leckford Golf Club Hants
106 C4 Leckwith Stadium Cardif
161 G2 Ledbury Heritage Centre Herefs
342 D1 Leeds Bradford airport Leeds
98 C4 Leeds Castle Kent
98 C4 Leeds Castle golf course Kent
343 F1 Leeds Golf Centre Leeds
343 F1 Leeds Golf Club Leeds
292 C4 Leek Golf Club Staffs
295 G5 Leen Valley Golf Centre Notts
51 G4 Lee-on-the-Solent Golf Club Hants
309 F2 Lee Park Golf Club Lpool
314 D3 Lees Hall Golf Club Sheff
145 E6 Lee Valley Camping & Caravan Park Gt Lon
145 E5 Lee Valley Campsite Essex
145 E3 Lee Valley Caravan Park Herts
120 A2 Lee Valley Cycle Circuit Gt Lon
119 H2 Lee Valley Ice Centre Gt Lon
145 E6 Lee Valley Leisure Gt Lon
145 E2 Lee Valley Marina Stanstead Abbotts Herts
145 E4 Lee Valley Park Essex
117 F5 Legoland Windsor W & M
241 E4 Leicester airfield Leics
240 C5 Leicester cycle route Leics
240 C5 Leicester Forest East service area Leics
240 C3 Leicester North railway station C Leic
240 D4 Leicester racecourse Leics
240 D5 Leicester Record Office museum Leics
188 A4 Leigh Court Barn Worcs
111 F4 Leigh Delamere service area Wilts
325 E5 Leigh Golf Club Warrtn
168 C4 Leighton Buzzard Golf Club Beds
365 G5 Leighton Hall Lancs
203 E2 Leiston Abbey Suffk
338 B6 Leisure Lakes Lancs
391 E5 Leisure & Wildlife Park Cumb
558 C4 Leith Hall NTS Abers
94 C6 Leith Hill Tower NT Surrey
3 F2 Lelant Saltings railway station Cnwll
19 G3 Lemonford Caravan Park Devon
35 g7 Le Moulin de Quetivel Jersey
489 G5 Lennoxlove House E Loth
484 D5 Lenzie Golf Club N Lans
186 C4 Leominster Golf Club Herefs
76 D2 Leonardslee lakes & gardens W Susx
500 D4 Leslie Golf Club Fife
35 f6 Les Mielles Golf & Country Club Jersey
170 B3 Letchworth Garden City railway station Herts
170 B3 Letchworth Golf Club Herts
528 D5 Lethan Grange Resort golf course Angus
467 F1 Lethamhill Golf Club C Glas
237 G3 Letocetum Baths NT Roman site Staffs
514 C5 Leuchars (for St Andrews) railway station Fife
2 C3 Levant Steam Engine NT Cnwll
502 B4 Leven Links golf course Fife
365 G2 Levens Hall Cumb
373 F1 Levisham railway station N York
56 C2 Lewes Golf Club E Susx

174 C4 Lexden Wood Golf Club Essex
339 E5 Leyland Golf Club Lancs
40 B4 Libbaton Golf Club Devon
488 B6 Liberton Golf Club C Edin
49 F4 Liberty Raptor & Reptile Centre Hants
237 H3 Lichfield City railway station Staffs
238 A3 Lichfield Trent Valley railway station Staffs
213 E4 Lickey Hills Golf Club Worcs
294 C2 Lickpenny Caravan Site Derbys
37 H3 Life Boat Station IoW
342 B4 Lightcliffe Golf Club Calder
370 B4 Lightwater Valley N York
235 G2 Lilleshall Abbey Wrekin
235 H2 Lilleshall Hall Golf Club Shrops
163 E6 Lilley Brook Golf Club Gloucs
75 H4 Limeburners campsite W Susx
378 D4 Limefitt Park campsite Cumb
313 E5 Lime Tree Park campsite Derbys
118 C3 Lime Trees Park Golf Club Gt Lon
96 B4 Limpsfield Chart Golf Club Surrey
423 G4 Lincluden Collegiate Church D & G
139 F4 Lincoln Farm Park campsite Oxon
317 F4 Lincoln Golf Club Lincs
300 B2 Lincolnshire Aviation Lincs
318 B4 Lincolnshire showground Lincs
334 D5 Lincolnshire Wolds Railway Lincs
369 H2 Lindale Holiday Park N York
443 F5 Linden Hall golf course Nthumb
455 E1 Lindisfarne NT Castle Nthumb
455 E1 Lindisfarne Priory Nthumb
513 F6 Lindores Abbey Fife
240 B2 Lingdale Golf Club Leics
96 B6 Lingfield Park Golf Club Surrey
96 A6 Lingfield racecourse Surrey
385 F1 Link in to Guisborough cycle route R & Cl
261 G3 Links Caravan Site Norfk
261 G3 Links Country Park Hotel & Golf Club Norfk
198 C2 Links Golf Club Cambs
529 F3 Links Park Stadium Angus
426 C3 Link to Newcastleton cycle route Border
486 C4 Linlithgow Golf Club W Loth
310 B5 Linmere visitor centre Ches
533 G7 Linnhe Lochside Holidays campsite Highld
467 E3 Linn Park C Glas
467 E3 Linn Park Golf Club C Glas
198 A5 Linton Zoological Gardens Cambs
487 E6 Linwater Caravan Park C Edin
344 A5 Lionheart Stadium Wakefd
35 h6 Lion Park Jersey
310 D4 Lion Salt Works Ches
74 C4 Liphook Golf Club W Susx
7 E4 Liskey Holiday Park Cnwll
106 C3 Lisvane & Thornhill railway station Cardif
237 G5 Little Aston Golf Club Staffs
14 D4 Little Bodieve Holiday Park Cnwll
143 E5 Little Chalfont Golf Club Bucks
13 E2 Little Cotton Caravan Park Devon
135 F2 Littledean Hall Gloucs
54 B4 Littlehampton Golf Club W Susx
76 C3 Littlehaven railway station W Susx
484 C6 Littlehill golf course C Glas
226 B3 Little Lakeland Caravan Park Norfk
211 H5 Little Lakes Golf & Country Club Worcs
291 G3 Little Moreton Hall NT Ches
245 G3 Little Ranch Leisure campsite Cambs
83 E3 Little Satmar Holiday Park Kent
32 A4 Littlesea Holiday Park Dorset
81 G4 Littlestone Golf Club Kent
82 D3 Little Switzerland Camping & Caravan Site Kent
7 E2 Little Treamble Farm Touring Park Cnwll
3 F2 Little Trevarrack Tourist Park Cnwll
5 E5 Little Trevothan Caravan & Camping Park Cnwll
308 D1 Liverpool Central railway station Lpool
309 E2 Liverpool Cricket Club Lpool
308 D1 Liverpool James Street railway station Wirral
309 E1 Liverpool Lime Street railway station Lpool
308 D1 Liverpool Moorfields railway station Lpool
323 G5 Liverpool Municipal Golf Club Sefton
119 G3 Liverpool St railway station Gt Lon
467 G3 Livingstone Centre museum NTS S Lans
486 D6 Livingston North railway station W Loth
469 H1 Livingston South railway station W Loth
406 B2 Lizard Lane Caravan & Camping Site Tyne
4 C6 Lizard Point Cnwll
391 F2 Llanbadarn railway station Cerdgn
284 C2 Llanberis Lake Railway Gwynd
208 C5 Llanbister Road railway station Powys
132 B5 Llancaiach Fawr Manor Caerph
106 B4 Llandaf railway station Cardif
265 E2 Llandecwyn railway station Gwynd
105 F5 Llandow Circuit V Glam
105 F5 Llandow Touring Caravan Park V Glam
183 H3 Llandrindod Wells Golf Club Powys
305 G3 Llandudno (Maesdu) Golf Club Conwy

105 G4 Llanerch V Glam
180 C2 Llanerchaeron NT Cerdgn
305 E5 Llanfairfechan Golf Club Conwy
129 E4 Llangennech railway station Carmth
287 H6 Llangollen Railway Denbgs
208 D5 Llangynllo railway station Powys
106 C3 Llanishen Golf Club Cardif
307 F5 Llannerch Park golf course Denbgs
127 H2 Llansteffan Castle Carmth
105 G3 Llantrisant & Pontyclun Golf Club Rhondd
108 C2 Llanwern Golf Club Newpt
269 E5 Llanymynech Golf Club Shrops
287 E6 Llawr-Betws Farm Caravan Park Gwynd
285 F5 Llechwedd Slate Caverns Gwynd
263 E3 Lleyn Peninsula Gwynd
154 B4 Llwyfan Cerrig railway station Carmth
264 B2 Llwyn-Bugeilydd Caravan & Camping Site Gwynd
286 D4 Llyn Brenig reservoir & visitor centre Conwy
129 E1 Llyn Llech Owain country park Carmth
282 D5 Llyn-y-Gele Farm & Caravan Park Gwynd
283 F3 Llys Derwen Caravan & Camping Site Gwynd
284 C5 Llywelyn Cottage NT Gwynd
205 G3 Llywernog Silver Lead Mine Cerdgn
559 G4 Loanhead Stone Circle Abers
60 C4 Lobb Fields Caravan & Camping Park Devon
326 C1 Lobden Golf Club Lancs
532 F5 Lochaber Highld
520 F4 Lochaber Watersports Centre Highld
546 D4 Lochalsh Woodland NTS Highld
563 H7 Lochcarron Golf Club Highld
433 G5 Loch Doon Castle E Ayrs
532 F7 Loch Eil Outward Bound railway station Highld
532 E7 Locheilside railway station Highld
500 C6 Lochgelly Golf Club Fife
480 B2 Lochgilphead golf course Ag & B
542 E6 Loch Greshornish Caravan Site Highld
422 A5 Loch Ken Holiday Park D & G
500 B4 Loch Leven Castle P & K
483 E2 Loch Lomond
483 E2 Loch Lomond Golf Club Ag & B
495 G3 Loch Lomond Holiday Park Ag & B
483 E3 Loch Lomond Marina W Duns
495 F3 Loch Lomond & The Trossachs National Park
424 B3 Lochmaben Golf Club D & G
549 J4 Loch Ness Highld
550 B1 Loch Ness golf course Highld
524 F7 Loch of the Lowes P & K
500 C5 Lochore Meadows Fife
500 C5 Lochore Meadows golf course Fife
463 F4 Lochranza Caravan & Camping Site N Ayrs
463 F4 Lochranza golf course N Ayrs
413 E2 Lochside Caravan & Camping Site D & G
465 G3 Lochwinnoch Golf Club Rens
424 C3 Lockerbie Golf Club D & G
215 H4 Lodge Farm campsite Warwks
389 G6 Lodore Falls Cumb
343 F4 Lofthouse Hill Golf Club Leeds
119 E3 Loftus Road Gt Lon
408 B3 Logan Botanic Garden D & G
146 A4 Log Church Essex
288 A2 Loggerheads Country Park Denbgs
567 J6 Logie Steading Moray
483 E5 Lomond Woods Holiday Park W Duns
120 A4 London Arena Gt Lon
80 C2 London Beach Hotel & Golf Club Kent
119 G3 London Bridge railway station Gt Lon
119 G3 London Fields railway station Gt Lon
144 A6 London Gateway service area Gt Lon
244 A5 London Road C Pete
55 H3 London Road (Brighton) railway station Br & H
119 E5 London Scottish Golf Club Gt Lon
77 G1 London Temple Surrey
109 F5 Long Ashton Golf Club N Som
397 F5 Longbeck railway station R & Cl
240 A1 Longcliffe Golf Club Leics
14 D3 Long Cross Victorian Gardens Cnwll
50 C2 Longdown Dairy Farm Hants
67 F4 Long Hazel Park campsite Somset
87 E6 Longleat Wilts
328 B1 Longley Park Golf Club Kirk
566 B7 Longman Yacht Haven Highld
190 B5 Long Marston (Shakespeare County Raceway) Warwks
391 F2 Long Meg and her Daughters Cumb
489 E4 Longniddry Golf Club E Loth
291 H5 Longport railway station C Stke
339 F2 Longridge Golf Club Lancs
314 B4 Longshaw Estate NT Derbys
3 d2 Longstone Heritage Centre IoS
455 C2 Longstone Lighthouse Nthumb
281 F5 Long Sutton Butterfly & Falconry Park Lincs
66 D5 Long Sutton golf course Somset
9 H2 Looe Golf Club Cnwll
93 E1 Look Out Discovery Centre Br For

33 G2 Lookout Holiday Park Dorset
442 D5 Lordenshaws Nthumb
119 F3 Lords Cricket Ground Gt Lon
388 D4 Lorton Vale Cumb
93 G5 Loseley Park Surrey
8 D1 Lostwithiel Hotel Golf & Country Club Cnwll
344 A2 Lotherton Hall Leeds
470 D1 Lothianburn Golf Club C Edin
445 H2 Loudoun Castle E Ayrs
445 H2 Loudoun Golf Club E Ayrs
276 B6 Loughborough Central railway station Leics
145 F5 Loughton Golf Club Essex
29 E3 Loughwood Meeting House NT Devon
320 B2 Louth Golf Club Lincs
187 F3 Lower Brockhampton NT Herefs
37 F4 Lower Hyde Holiday Park IoW
270 C3 Lower Lacon Caravan Park Shrops
22 C4 Lower Pennycrocker Farm Cnwll
4 B2 Lower Polladras Touring Park Cnwll
2 C4 Lower Treave Caravan & Camping Park Cnwll
326 B2 Lowes Park Golf Club Bury
76 D1 Lowfield Heath windmill Surrey
201 H6 Low House Touring Caravan Centre Suffk
343 E5 Low Laithes Golf Club Wakefd
361 F4 Low Skirlington Leisure Park E R Yk
367 E6 Lower Hill Caravan Park N York
436 A2 Lowther Hills D & G
391 E4 Lowther Holiday Park Cumb
378 C4 Low Wray NT campsite Cumb
334 D5 Ludborough railway station Lincs
210 B4 Ludlow Golf Club Shrops
210 B4 Ludlow racecourse Shrops
74 D2 Ludshott Common NT Hants
242 D4 Luffenham Heath Golf Club Rutlnd
489 F3 Luffness New Golf Club E Loth
545 J4 Luib Folk museum Highld
96 D2 Lullingstone Roman Villa Kent
33 F3 Lulworth Castle Dorset
33 E3 Lulworth Cove Dorset
502 B4 Lundin Golf Club Fife
502 C4 Lundin Ladies Golf Club Fife
215 E5 Lunt Roman Fort Roman site Warwks
75 E4 Lurgashall vineyard W Susx
19 G1 Lustleigh Devon
169 G5 Luton airport Luton
216 B3 Lutterworth Golf Club Leics
8 D2 Luxulyan Valley (UNESCO) Cnwll
583 J2 Lybster Golf Club Highld
81 G5 Lydd airport Kent
82 D1 Lydden Race Circuit Kent
81 F5 Lydd Golf Club Kent
24 D6 Lydford Gorge NT Devon
112 D3 Lydiard Park Swindn
135 E4 Lydney Golf Club Gloucs
135 E4 Lydney Junction railway station Gloucs
135 E4 Lydney Town railway station Gloucs
312 C3 Lyme Park NT Ches
29 F4 Lyme Regis Golf Club Dorset
50 B5 Lymington Pier railway station Hants
50 B5 Lymington Town railway station Hants
310 D2 Lymm Golf Club Warrtn
310 D3 Lymm service area Ches
27 F5 Lympstone Commando railway station Devon
112 B4 Lyneham airport Wilts
61 G2 Lynton & Barnstaple Railway Devon
31 F1 Lyons Gate Caravan & Camping Park Dorset
67 E4 Lyte's Cary Manor NT Somset
337 G4 Lytham Green Drive Golf Club Lancs
234 B3 Lyth Hill Shrops
50 A6 Lytton Lawn Touring Park Hants
218 D2 Lyveden New Bield NT Nhants

M

458 D4 MacAlister Clan visitor centre Ag & B
312 B5 Macclesfield Golf Club Ches
230 D4 Machinations museum Powys
460 B3 Machrie Bay golf course N Ayrs
476 E7 Machrie Hotel & Golf Links Ag & B
460 C3 Machrie Moor Stone Circles N Ayrs
456 D2 Machrihanish Golf Club Ag & B
230 B4 Machynlleth Golf Club Powys
568 D6 Mackessock Park Moray
412 C4 MacLellan's Castle D & G
116 B6 Madjeski Stadium Readg
264 D4 Maes Artro Centre museum Gwynd
600 E2 Maes Howe Ork
85 H1 Maes Knoll BaNES
104 C1 Maesteg Golf Club Neath
232 D3 Maes Y Dre Recreation Ground Powys
475 E4 Magdalene Fields Golf Club Nthumb
571 J2 Maggie's Hoosie Abers
315 E1 Magna Science Adventure Centre Sheff
191 F4 Magpie Hall Warwks
313 G6 Magpie Mine Derbys
92 D3 Maharajah's Well Oxon
116 A3 Maharajah's Well Oxon
31 F5 Maiden Castle Dorset
117 E3 Maidenhead Golf Club W & M
559 G5 Maiden Stone Abers
98 A3 Maidstone Barracks railway station Kent
98 B3 Maidstone East railway station Kent

98 C3 **Maidstone service area** Kent
98 A3 **Maidstone West railway station** Kent
293 E4 **Mainifold Trail cycle route** Staffs
600 E3 **Mainland** Ork
605 H5 **Mainland** Shet
514 C3 **Mains of Fintry Castle** C Dund
119 E6 **Malden Golf Club** Gt Lon
95 E1 **Malden Manor railway station** Gt Lon
147 G3 **Maldon Golf Club** Essex
354 A2 **Malham Cove** N York
291 F3 **Malkins Bank golf course** Ches
470 C1 **Malleny NTS** C Edin
470 C1 **Malleny Park** C Edin
239 G4 **Mallory Park** Leics
197 E5 **Malton golf course** Cambs
373 E5 **Malton & Norton Golf Club** N York
187 H5 **Malvern Link railway station** Worcs
546 F6 **Mam Ratagan** Highld
313 F3 **Mam Tor** Derbys
320 C2 **Manby Caravan Park** Lincs
320 C2 **Manby showground** Lincs
311 G3 **Manchester airport** Manch
311 E3 **Manchester Airport railway station** Manch
326 C3 **Manchester Golf Club** Rochdl
326 C5 **Manchester Indoor Tennis Centre** Manch
326 C5 **Manchester Velodrome** Manch
326 B5 **Manchester Victoria railway station** Salfd
474 B4 **Manderston Edwardian Country House** Border
221 G1 **Manea railway station** Cambs
110 B5 **Mangotsfield Golf Club** S Glos
110 B4 **Mangotsfield United FC** S Glos
76 D4 **Mannings Heath Golf Club** W Susx
76 D4 **Mannings Heath Hotel golf course** W Susx
261 F5 **Mannington Gardens** Norfk
126 B5 **Manorbier railway station** Pembks
20 B4 **Manor Farm campsite** Devon
261 G3 **Manor Farm Caravan & Campsite** Norfk
51 E2 **Manor Farm Country Park** Hants
29 G4 **Manor Farm Holiday Centre** Dorset
325 H4 **Manor Golf Club** Bolton
334 B3 **Manor Golf Club** NE Lin
273 F3 **Manor Golf Club** Staffs
126 B4 **Manor House Wildlife & Leisure Park** Pembks
215 F1 **Manor Park** Warwks
308 B2 **Manor Road railway station** Wirral
405 C2 **Manors railway station** N u Ty
289 G3 **Manor Wood Country Caravan Park** Ches
439 G1 **Mansfield Park** Border
101 F2 **Manston Caravan & Camping Park** Kent
27 E5 **Manstree vineyard** Devon
322 h4 **Manx Electric Railway** IoM
30 C3 **Mapperton Gardens** Dorset
310 D4 **Marbury Country Park** Ches
245 E6 **March Golf Club** Cambs
104 C2 **Margam Park** Neath
104 C2 **Margam Stones museum** Neath
322 b9 **Marine Interpretation Centre** IoM
60 a2 **Marisco Castle** Devon
120 A4 **Maritime Greenwich (UNESCO)** Gt Lon
27 F3 **Marker's Cottage NT** Devon
239 G4 **Market Bosworth** Leics
271 F3 **Market Drayton Golf Club** Shrops
217 F2 **Market Harborough Golf Club** Leics
294 A2 **Market House NT** Derbys
319 E2 **Market Rasen & District Golf Club** Lincs
319 E2 **Market Rasen racecourse** Lincs
326 C2 **Marland Park Golf Club** Rochdl
113 E5 **Marlborough Golf Club** Wilts
79 F2 **Marle Place** Kent
370 B4 **Marmion Tower** N York
312 B2 **Marple Golf Club** Stockp
275 F1 **Marriott Breadsall Priory Hotel & Country Club** Derbys
487 F6 **Marriott Dalmahoy Hotel Golf & Country Club** C Edin
214 C3 **Marriott Forest of Arden Golf & Country Club** Warwks
53 F3 **Marriott Goodwood Park Hotel & Country Club** W Susx
144 D1 **Marriott Hanbury Manor Golf & Country Club** Herts
342 C1 **Marriott Hollins Hall Hotel & Country Club** Brad
51 G2 **Marriott Meon Valley Hotel & Country Club** Hants
109 F1 **Marriott St Pierre Hotel & Country Club** Mons
250 B2 **Marriott Sprowston Manor Hotel & Country Club** Norfk
98 C4 **Marriott Tudor Park Hotel & Country Club** Kent
325 G4 **Marriott Worsley Park Hotel& Country Club** Salfd
340 D2 **Marsden Park golf course** Lancs
202 D2 **Marsh Farm Caravan Site** Suffk
147 G5 **Marsh Farm Country Park** Essex
272 D5 **Marston Road** Staffs
239 G5 **Marston's Stadium** Leics
83 F1 **Martin Mill railway station** Kent
89 E2 **Martinsell** Wilts
117 E6 **Martins Heron railway station** Br For
337 F3 **Marton Mere Holiday Village** Bpool
72 D5 **Marwell Zoological Park** Hants
60 D4 **Marwood Hill Gardens** Devon
190 B3 **Mary Arden's House** Warwks
120 A3 **Maryland railway station** Gt Lon
119 F3 **Marylebone (London) railway station** Gt Lon

388 B2 **Maryport Golf Club** Cumb
369 H3 **Masham Golf Club** N York
294 B3 **Masson Mills** Derbys
126 B3 **Masterland Farm Touring Caravan Park** Pembks
120 A2 **Matchroom Stadium** Gt Lon
429 C5 **Matfen Hall Country House Hotel & Golf Club** Nthumb
294 C3 **Matlock Golf Club** Derbys
294 B2 **Matlock Riverside railway station** Derbys
248 D3 **Mattishall golf course** Norfk
326 C6 **Mauldeth Road railway station** Manch
606 D4 **Mavis Grind** Shet
229 E1 **Mawddach Trail cycle route** Gwynd
214 C2 **Maxstoke Park Golf Club** Warwks
467 E2 **Maxwell Park railway station** C Glas
422 D2 **Maxwelton (Glencairn Castle)** D & G
432 C3 **Maybole Municipal Golf Club** S Ayrs
137 F3 **Mayfield Touring Park** Gloucs
146 B6 **Maylands Golf & Country Club** Gt Lon
275 H2 **Maywood golf course** Derbys
506 E3 **McCaig's Tower** Ag & B
374 C2 **McCain Stadium** N York
512 C4 **McDiarmid Park** P & K
560 D3 **McDonald Golf Club** Abers
488 B5 **Meadowbank Stadium** C Edin
314 D1 **Meadowhall** Sheff
314 D1 **Meadowhall railway station** Sheff
488 B6 **Meadowheads Mortonhall Caravan & Camping Park** C Edin
489 H3 **Meadowhead's Tantallon Caravan & Camping** E Loth
276 C2 **Meadow Lane** Notts
144 A5 **Meadow Park** Herts
48 C3 **Meadow View Caravan Park** Dorset
66 D1 **Meare Fish House** Somset
322 b9 **Meayll Circle** IoM
73 G2 **Medstead & Four Marks railway station** Hants
97 H1 **Medway Bridge Marina** Medway
122 B5 **Medway Pier Marina** Medway
98 C2 **Medway service area** Medway
488 A5 **Meggetland** C Edin
513 E2 **Meikleour Beech Hedge** P & K
230 D2 **Meirion Mill** Gwynd
351 F3 **Melbreak Caravan Park** Lancs
25 C4 **Meldon Viaduct railway station** Devon
199 H5 **Melford Hall NT** Suffk
492 D2 **Melfort Pier and Harbour** Ag & B
452 C2 **Mellerstain** Border
208 D1 **Mellington Hall Caravan Park** Powys
312 C2 **Mellor & Townscliffe Golf Club** Stockp
451 G3 **Melrose Golf Club** Border
327 H3 **Meltham Golf Club** Kirk
277 G5 **Melton Mowbray Golf Club** Leics
113 H4 **Membury service area** W Berk
571 H3 **Memsie Cairn** Abers
15 E6 **Mena Caravan & Camping Site** Cnwll
2 D3 **Men-An-Tol** Cnwll
326 B5 **MEN Arena** Manch
85 H5 **Mendip Golf Club** Somset
85 F4 **Mendip Hills** Somset
84 D2 **Mendip Spring Golf Club** N Som
86 A6 **Mendip Vale railway station** Somset
168 B6 **Mentmore Golf & Country Club** Bucks
524 B6 **Menzies Castle** P & K
190 C3 **Menzies Welcome Hotel golf course** Warwks
323 G1 **Meols Cop railway station** Sefton
488 A5 **Merchants of Edinburgh Golf Club** C Edin
311 E3 **Mere Golf & Country Club** Ches
334 C2 **Meridian Quay** NE Lin
48 B5 **Merley Court Touring Park** Poole
14 B5 **Merlin golf course** Cnwll
79 G4 **Merriments** E Susx
93 G4 **Merrist Wood Golf Club** Surrey
212 D2 **Merry Hill** Dudley
310 A2 **Mersey Valley Golf & Country Club** St Hel
131 G3 **Merthyr Tydfil Golf Club** Myr Td
452 B3 **Mertoun House Gardens** Border
405 F2 **Metro Centre** Gatesd
405 F2 **Metro Radio Arena** N u Ty
135 F5 **Michaelwood service area** Gloucs
57 F3 **Michelham Priory** E Susx
275 E3 **Mickleover Golf Club** C Derb
142 C4 **Mid Chiltern Villages cycle route** Bucks
189 G5 **Middle Littleton Tithe Barn NT** Worcs
385 E2 **Middlesbrough Golf Club** Middsb
385 E1 **Middlesbrough Municipal Golf Centre** Middsb
238 B5 **Middleton Hall** Warwks
252 D4 **Middleton Hall Golf Club** Norfk
343 E4 **Middleton Park Municipal Golf Club** Leeds
343 F4 **Middleton Railway** Leeds
71 G2 **Middle Wallop** Hants
387 G4 **Middlewood Farm Holiday Park** N York
73 F3 **Mid Hants Railway (Watercress Line)** Hants
143 H1 **Mid Herts golf course** Herts
121 F5 **Mid Kent Golf Club** Kent
215 F4 **Midland Air museum** Warwks
295 E4 **Midland Railway Centre** Derbys
248 D4 **Mid Norfolk Railway** Norfk
56 A1 **Mid Sussex Golf Club** E Susx
290 C3 **Midway Boats** Ches
344 B5 **Mid Yorkshire golf course** Wakefd
222 C4 **Mildenhall Stadium** Suffk

269 F4 **Mile End golf course** Shrops
75 E1 **Milford Golf Club** Surrey
125 E3 **Milford Haven Golf Club** Pembks
75 F1 **Milford (Surrey) railway station** Surrey
38 D3 **Milky Way Adventure Park** Devon
444 D6 **Millbrae** S Ayrs
169 E1 **Millbrook (Bedfordshire) railway station** Beds
568 C4 **Millbuies Country Park** Moray
322 f6 **Milenium Way** IoM
128 C5 **Millennium Coastal Park** Carmth
64 D3 **Mill Farm Caravan & Camping Park** Somset
361 F2 **Mill Farm Country Park** E R Yk
234 D3 **Mill Farm Holiday Park** Shrops
317 F4 **Millfield Golf Complex** Lincs
144 B2 **Mill Green Golf Club** Herts
144 B6 **Mill Hill Golf Club** Gt Lon
218 D4 **Mill Marina** Nhants
315 E1 **Millmoor** Rothm
464 D3 **Millport Golf Club** N Ayrs
117 F5 **Mill Ride Golf Club** Br For
326 C3 **Mills Hill railway station** Rochdl
514 B3 **Mills Observatory** C Dund
500 B4 **Milnathort Golf Club** P & K
322 b8 **Milners Tower** IoM
484 A4 **Milngavie Golf Club** E Duns
47 E4 **Milton Abbey** Dorset
114 D1 **Milton Manor House** Oxon
524 D4 **Milton of Fonab Caravan Site** P & K
2 C5 **Minack Open Air Theatre** Cnwll
136 C5 **Minchinhampton Golf Club** Gloucs
136 C5 **Minchinhampton Old Golf Course** Gloucs
222 D4 **Mindenhall Stadium** Suffk
63 E2 **Minehead & Exmoor Caravan & Camping Park** Somset
63 F2 **Minehead & West Somerset Golf Club** Somset
601 J3 **Minehowe** Ork
7 E5 **Mineral Tramways cycle route** Cnwll
518 D3 **Mingary Castle** Highld
25 H6 **Miniature Pony Centre** Devon
164 B5 **Miniatures museum** Gloucs
42 D4 **Minnows Touring Park** Devon
139 E2 **Minster Lovell Hall** Oxon
452 A5 **Minto Golf Club** Border
389 F4 **Mirehouse** Cumb
136 D3 **Miserden Park** Gloucs
175 F3 **Mistley Towers** Essex
119 F6 **Mitcham Golf Club** Gt Lon
95 F1 **Mitcham Junction railway station** Gt Lon
233 F5 **Mitchell's Fold Stone Circle** Shrops
559 F5 **Mither Tap** Abers
202 B4 **Moat Barn Touring Caravan Park** Suffk
97 G6 **Moatlands Golf Club** Kent
311 F3 **Mobberley railway station** Ches
287 H2 **Moel Famau Country Park** Denbgs
153 G2 **Moelfryn Caravan & Camping Site** Carmth
519 H1 **Moidart** Highld
288 A2 **Mold Golf Club** Flints
172 A3 **Mole Hall Wildlife Park** Essex
236 D5 **Molineux** Wolves
549 L8 **Monadhliath Mountains** Highld
126 C5 **Monastery** Pembks
533 L6 **Monessie Falls** Highld
565 K8 **Moniack Castle (Highland Winery)** Highld
515 E3 **Monifieth Golf Links** Angus
515 E2 **Monikie Country Park** Angus
329 F3 **Monk Bretton Priory** Barns
7 F3 **Monkey Tree Holiday Park** Cnwll
33 E2 **Monkey World** Dorset
56 C3 **Monk's House NT** E Susx
90 D2 **Monks Lane** Hants
29 F3 **Monkton Wyld Farm Caravan Park** Dorset
134 B2 **Monmouth Caravan Park** Mons
134 C2 **Monmouth Castle** Mons
134 C2 **Monmouth Golf Club** Mons
133 E2 **Monmouthshire Golf Club** Mons
67 E6 **Montacute House NT** Somset
35 j7 **Mont Orgueil** Jersey
529 F3 **Montrose Golf Links** Angus
202 B5 **Moon & Sixpence campsite** Suffk
343 F1 **Moor Allerton Golf Club** Leeds
358 A5 **Moor End Farm campsite** York
94 C2 **Moore Place Golf Club** Surrey
238 A5 **Moor Hall Golf Club** Birm
12 B1 **Moorlands Alternative cycle route** Cnwll
343 G1 **Moor Lodge Park campsite** Leeds
143 F6 **Moor Park Golf Club** Herts
343 F3 **Moor Road railway station** Leeds
325 H4 **Moorside railway station** Salfd
387 E3 **Moors to Sea 9 cycle route** N York
387 F3 **Moors to Sea 8 cycle route** N York
49 E3 **Moors Valley Country Park & Forest** Dorset
49 E3 **Moors Valley golf course** Dorset
16 B6 **Moorswater** Cnwll
343 H1 **Moortown Golf Club** Leeds
12 C2 **Moor View Touring Park** Devon
195 F5 **Moot Hall museum** Beds
568 C1 **Moray Firth** Moray
568 C1 **Moray Golf Club** Moray
351 G1 **Morecambe Golf Club** Lancs
308 C1 **Moreton (Merseyside) railway station** Wirral
154 B6 **Morfa Lane** Carmth
229 E2 **Morfa Mawddach railway station** Gwynd
131 G3 **Morlais Castle Golf Club** Myr Td
275 G1 **Morley Hayes golf course** Derbys

430 C3 **Morpeth Golf Club** Nthumb
129 G5 **Morriston Golf Club** Swans
60 C2 **Mortehoe & Woolacombe Golf Club** Devon
436 A5 **Morton Castle** D & G
488 B6 **Mortonhall Golf Club** C Edin
17 F5 **Morwellham Quay** Devon
213 G3 **Moseley Golf Club** Birm
236 D4 **Moseley Old Hall NT** Staffs
325 H3 **Moses Gate** Bolton
144 A2 **Mosquito Aircraft museum** Herts
413 G1 **Mossband Caravan Park** D & G
567 J5 **Mosset Park** Moray
460 C3 **Moss Farm Road Stone Circle** N Ayrs
311 F2 **Moss Lane** Traffd
323 H4 **Mossock Hall Golf Club** Lancs
312 B5 **Moss Rose** Ches
351 G5 **Mosswood Caravan Park** Lancs
411 F2 **Mossyard Caravan & Camping Park** D & G
98 B4 **Mote Cricket Club** Kent
413 F4 **Mote of Mark** D & G
71 G4 **Mottisfont Abbey NT** Hants
131 G4 **Mountain Ash Golf Club** Rhondd
106 B3 **Mountain Lakes & Castell Heights golf course** Rhondd
11 E3 **Mount Edgcumbe House & Country Park** Cnwll
485 E6 **Mount Ellen Golf Club** N Lans
99 H2 **Mt Ephraim gardens** Kent
384 C5 **Mount Grace Priory NT** N York
322 e7 **Mount Murray Hotel & Country Club** IoM
395 F1 **Mount Oswald Manor golf course** Dur
169 H3 **Mount Pleasant golf course** Beds
239 H1 **Mount St Bernard** Leics
12 D3 **Mounts Farm Touring Park** Devon
464 C3 **Mount Stuart** Ag & B
448 B5 **Mount View Caravan Park** S Lans
605 J6 **Mousa Broch** Shet
469 E5 **Mouse Valley Golf Club** S Lans
291 H3 **Mow Cop NT (folly)** Staffs
195 H4 **Mowsbury Golf Club** Beds
66 C5 **Muchelney Caravan & Camping Site** Somset
499 G4 **Muckhart Golf Club** Clacks
261 F3 **Muckleburgh Collection museum** Norfk
484 A4 **Mugdock Country Park** Stirlg
486 C4 **Muiravonside Country Park** W Loth
512 A6 **Muir O'Fauld Signal Station Roman site** P & K
565 J7 **Muir of Ord Golf Club** Highld
465 G2 **Muirshiel Country Park** Rens
3 E2 **Mulfra Quoit** Cnwll
4 C4 **Mullion Golf Club** Cnwll
4 D5 **Mullion Holiday Park** Cnwll
506 B2 **Mull & West Highland Narrow Gauge Railway** Ag & B
377 E5 **Muncaster** Cumb
376 D5 **Muncaster Mill** Cumb
256 B2 **Mundesley Golf Club** Norfk
609 J4 **Muness Castle** Shet
557 H2 **Murcar Golf Club** C Aber
264 D5 **Murmur-yr-Afon Touring Park** Gwynd
487 H5 **Murrayfield Golf Club** C Edin
488 A5 **Murrayfield Ice Rink** C Edin
488 A5 **Murrayfield Stadium** C Edin
513 E4 **Murrayshall Country House Hotel golf course** P & K
489 H4 **Museum of Flight** E Loth
127 E3 **Museum of Speed** Carmth
488 C5 **Musselburgh Golf Club** E Loth
488 D5 **Musselburgh racecourse** E Loth
119 F1 **Muswell Hill Golf Club** Gt Lon
498 D1 **Muthill Golf Club** P & K
178 D3 **Mwnt** Cerdgn
205 G4 **Mynach Falls** Cerdgn
488 A5 **Myreside** C Edin
489 F4 **Myreton Motor museum** E Loth
339 H3 **Mytton Fold Hotel & Golf Complex** Lancs

N

358 A6 **Naburn Lock Caravan Park** York
358 B5 **Naburn Marina** York
595 H4 **Na Heardh** W Isls
566 F5 **Nairn Dunbar Golf Club** Highld
229 F3 **Nant Gwernol railway station** Gwynd
205 F4 **Nantyronen railway station** Cerdgn
191 H2 **Napton Marina** Warwks
215 E5 **National Agricultural Centre showground** Warwks
66 C3 **National Animal Welfare Trust** Somset
168 A2 **National Badminton Centre** M Keyn
161 G5 **National Birds of Prey Centre** Gloucs
154 D6 **National Botanic Garden of Wales** Carmth
328 D1 **National Coal Mining Museum** Kirk
191 G5 **National Herb Centre** Warwks
168 A2 **National Hockey Stadium** M Keyn
276 C1 **National Ice Centre** C Nott
213 G2 **National Indoor Arena** Birm
106 C4 **National Indoor Athletics Centre** Cardif
314 D2 **National Indoor Athletics Centre** Sheff
238 B2 **National Memorial** Staffs
214 C3 **National Motorcycle museum** Solhll
50 C4 **National Motor museum** Hants
285 F3 **National Mountain Centre** Conwy
79 G3 **National Pinetum & Garden** Kent
93 F3 **National Shooting Centre** Surrey
240 C2 **National Space Centre** C Leic

119 G5 **National Sports Centre** Gt Lon
326 C5 **National Squash Centre** Manch
294 B3 **National Stone Centre** Derbys
198 C2 **National Stud** Suffk
103 G3 **National Water Front museum** Swans
276 D2 **National Watersports Centre** Notts
266 D2 **National Whitewater Centre** Gwynd
309 F2 **National Wildflower Centre** Lpool
162 B5 **Nature in Art museum** Gloucs
384 D1 **Natures World** Middsb
163 H5 **Naunton Downs Golf Club** Gloucs
134 C2 **Naval Temple** Mons
311 F2 **Navigation Road railway station** Traffd
145 F3 **Nazeing Golf Club** Essex
130 B5 **Neath Golf Club** Neath
214 B3 **NEC** Solhll
35 G4 **Needles Old Battery NT** IoW
262 D2 **Nefyn & District Golf Club** Gwynd
450 A1 **Neidpath Castle** Border
340 D2 **Nelson Golf Club** Lancs
218 D5 **Nene Park** Nhants
243 G5 **Nene Valley Railway** C Pete
533 H7 **Neptune's Staircase (Locks)** Highld
308 D4 **Ness Botanic Gardens** Ches
269 G6 **Nesscliffe Country Park** Shrops
451 G2 **Netherdale** Border
199 G5 **Nether Hall** Suffk
78 D2 **Nevill Golf Club** E Susx
533 J7 **Nevis Range Ski Centre** Highld
482 D5 **Newark Castle** Inver
297 E4 **Newark Castle railway station** Notts
297 F4 **Newark Golf Club** Notts
471 F1 **Newbattle Golf Club** Mdloth
431 F2 **Newbiggin Golf Club** Nthumb
191 E1 **Newbold Comyn Golf Club** Warwks
191 E1 **Newbold Comyn park** Warwks
468 B1 **New Broomfield Stadium** N Lans
561 F4 **Newburgh on Ythan Golf Club** Abers
371 G4 **Newburgh Priory** N York
405 F4 **Newburn Hall Motor museum** N u Ty
90 D1 **Newbury & Crookham Golf Club** W Berk
90 D1 **Newbury racecourse** W Berk
114 D5 **Newbury showground** W Berk
365 E2 **Newby Bridge railway station** Cumb
370 C6 **Newby Hall** N York
430 C5 **Newcastle airport** N u Ty
430 D5 **Newcastle racecourse** N u Ty
426 C2 **Newcastleton Golf Club** Border
291 G6 **Newcastle-Under-Lyme Golf Club** Staffs
405 F1 **Newcastle United Golf Club** N u Ty
334 C2 **New Clee railway station** NE Lin
434 C1 **New Cumnock Golf Club** E Ayrs
467 H3 **New Douglas Park** S Lans
50 B3 **New Forest Golf Club** Hants
50 C3 **New Forest National Park** Hants
421 G4 **New Galloway Golf Club** D & G
296 C4 **New Hall Farm Touring Park** Notts
147 G4 **New Hall vineyard** Essex
56 D4 **Newhaven Harbour railway station** E Susx
293 G3 **Newhaven Holiday Camping & Caravan Park** Derbys
326 D2 **New Hey railway station** Rochdl
366 C4 **New House Caravan Park** Lancs
468 B6 **New Lanark World Heritage Village (UNESCO)** S Lans
29 G4 **Newlands Caravan & Camping Park** Dorset
557 F1 **Newmachar Golf Club** Abers
198 C2 **Newmarket racecourse** Suffk
312 C2 **New Mills Golf Club** Derbys
312 C3 **New Mills Newtown railway station** Ches
326 B3 **New North Manchester Golf Club** Rochdl
126 A2 **New Park Farm campsite** Pembks
351 H2 **New Parkside Farm Caravan Park** Lancs
7 E3 **Newperran Holiday Park** Cnwll
37 E3 **Newport Golf Club** IoW
107 E2 **Newport Golf Club** Newpt
194 B6 **Newport Pagnell service area** M Keyn
152 B1 **Newport (Pemb) Golf Club** Pembks
107 F2 **Newport Stadium** Newpt
342 D3 **New Pudsey railway station** Leeds
14 B6 **Newquay airport** Cnwll
7 E1 **Newquay Golf Club** Cnwll
7 G1 **Newquay Holiday Park** Cnwll
119 G2 **New River Sports Stadium** Gt Lon
295 G4 **Newstead Abbey** Notts
20 B3 **Newton Abbot racecourse** Devon
20 A3 **Newton Abbot (Stover) Golf Club** Devon
386 D6 **Newtondale Forest Drive** N York
386 D5 **Newton Dale Halt railway station** N York
327 E5 **Newton for Hyde railway station** Tamesd
174 B1 **Newton Green Golf Club** Suffk
467 G2 **Newton (Lanarkshire) railway station** S Lans
86 C1 **Newton Mill campsite** BaNES
535 K3 **Newtonmore Golf Club** Highld
417 E3 **Newton Stewart Golf Club** D & G

93 H2 **New Zealand Golf Club** Surrey
369 F5 **Nidderdale** N York
487 E5 **Niddry Castle Golf Club** W Loth
294 A2 **Nine Ladies Stone Circle** Derbys
14 C5 **Nine Maidens Stone Circle** Cnwll
31 E4 **Nine Stones** Dorset
37 F4 **Ninham Country Holidays** IoW
106 C4 **Ninian Park** Cardif
106 C4 **Ninian Park railway station** Cardif
435 H5 **Nithsdale** D & G
97 L4 **Nizels golf course** Kent
109 E5 **Noah's Ark Zoo Farm** N Som
37 G3 **Nodes Point Holiday Park** IoW
35 g8 **Noirmont Command Bunker** Jersey
602 E2 **Noltland Castle** Ork
125 E1 **Nolton Cross Caravan Park** Pembks
135 E4 **Norchard railway station** Gloucs
558 C1 **Nordic Ski Centre** Abers
252 C1 **Norfolk Arena** Norfk
251 G2 **Norfolk Coast Cycleway** Norfk
257 E4 **Norfolk Coast Cycleway** Norfk
260 C4 **Norfolk Coast Cycleway** Norfk
258 D4 **Norfolk Lavender Garden** Norfk
261 G3 **Norfolk Shire Horse Centre** Norfk
250 B3 **Norfolk Ski Centre** Norfk
255 E4 **Norfolk Wildlife Park** Norfk
474 D5 **Norham Castle** Border
332 B1 **Normanby Hall** N Linc
332 B1 **Normanby Hall Golf Club** N Linc
332 B2 **Normanby Road** N Linc
361 E2 **Norman Manor House** E R Yk
343 F5 **Normanton Golf Club** Wakefd
567 L4 **North Alves Caravan Park** Moray
84 A3 **Northam Farm Caravan & Touring Park** Somset
193 E2 **Northampton Golf Club** Nhants
217 F6 **Northampton & Lamport Railway** Nhants
193 G2 **Northamptonshire County Cricket Ground** Nhants
193 F1 **Northamptonshire County Golf Club** Nhants
489 G2 **North Berwick Golf Club** E Loth
514 C3 **North Carr Lightship** C Dund
342 B2 **Northcliffe Golf Club** Brad
300 D2 **Northcote** Lincs
61 E2 **North Devon cycle route** Devon
48 B3 **North Dorset cycle route** Dorset
47 E3 **North Dorset cycle route/ National cycle route** Dorset
98 D3 **North Downs** Kent
95 H4 **North Downs Golf Club** Surrey
99 E4 **North Downs Way** Kent
93 G5 **North Downs Way** Surrey
119 G3 **North Dulwich railway station** Gt Lon
311 G1 **Northenden Golf Club** Manch
101 G2 **North Foreland Golf Club** Kent
92 D3 **North Hants Golf Club** Hants
596 E5 **North Harris** W Isls
80 B4 **Northiam railway station** E Susx
512 D5 **North Inch golf course** P & K
139 F1 **North Leigh Roman site** Oxon
285 G2 **North Llanrwst railway station** Conwy
144 C6 **North Middlesex Golf Club** Gt Lon
60 B2 **North Morte Farm Caravan & Camping Park** Devon
261 E3 **North Norfolk Railway** Norfk
118 B3 **Northolt airfield** Gt Lon
118 C2 **Northolt Park railway station** Gt Lon
308 B6 **Northop Country Park Golf Club** Flints
140 B2 **North Oxford Golf Club** Oxon
386 C6 **North Riding Forest Park** N York
383 G1 **North Road railway station** Darltn
603 M1 **North Ronaldsay airport** Ork
301 G2 **North Shore Hotel & Golf Club** Lincs
592 B4 **North Uist** W Isls
430 D5 **Northumberland Golf Club** N u Ty
428 B3 **Northumberland National Park** Nthumb
119 G1 **Northumberland Park railway station** Gt Lon
305 G3 **North Wales Golf Club** Conwy
238 D5 **North Warwickshire Cycleway** Warwks
214 C3 **North Warwickshire Golf Club** Solhll
145 G4 **North Weald airfield** Essex
145 H3 **North Weald Golf Club** Essex
145 G4 **North Weald railway station** Essex
88 B1 **North Wilts Golf Club** Wilts
118 B1 **Northwood Golf Club** Gt Lon
213 F4 **North Worcestershire golf course** Birm
386 C5 **North York Moors** N York
386 C4 **North York Moors National Park**
386 D6 **North Yorkshire Moors Railway** N York
237 F3 **Norton Canes service area** Staffs
370 C4 **Norton Conyers** N York
396 B5 **Norton golf course** S on T
237 F3 **Norton Lakeside railway station** Staffs
255 H1 **Norwich airport** Norfk
296 C2 **Norwood Park golf course** Notts
343 H6 **Nostell Priory NT** Wakefd
23 G1 **Noteworthy Caravan and Campsite** Devon
163 G5 **Notgrove long barrow** Gloucs

32 B4 **Nothe Fort** Dorset
10 C1 **Notter Bridge Caravan & Camping Park** Cnwll
276 D2 **Nottingham airfield** Notts
295 G5 **Nottingham City Golf Club** C Nott
275 H4 **Nottingham East Midlands airport** Leics
276 D2 **Nottingham racecourse** C Nott
297 F3 **Nottinghamshire showground** Notts
276 B2 **Nottingham Tennis Centre** C Nott
295 G3 **Notts Golf Club** Notts
146 B5 **Nuclear Bunker** Essex
215 F2 **Nuneaton Golf Club** Warwks
372 C4 **Nunnington Hall NT** N York
490 A5 **Nunraw Abbey** E Loth
37 F3 **Nunwell House and Gardens** IoW
95 G5 **Nutfield railway station** Surrey
53 G5 **Nyewood Lane** W Susx
77 E4 **Nymans NT** W Susx
136 A4 **Nympsfield long barrow** Gloucs

O

120 A3 **O2** Gt Lon
240 D4 **Oadby Golf Club** Leics
425 H5 **Oakbank Lakes campsite** Cumb
356 B3 **Oakdale Golf Club** N York
132 C5 **Oakdale golf course** Caerph
49 E4 **Oakdene Forest Park campsite** Dorset
28 C5 **Oakdown Touring & Holiday Home Park** Devon
43 G3 **Oake Manor Golf Club** Somset
235 F2 **Oakengates railway station** Wrekin
311 F2 **Oakfield Road ice rink** Traffd
242 B3 **Oakham School cricket ground** Rutlnd
365 E3 **Oak Head Caravan Park** Cumb
117 G1 **Oakland Park Golf Club** Bucks
395 F5 **Oakleaf Golf Complex** Dur
296 B4 **Oakmere Park golf course** Notts
92 D5 **Oak Park Golf Club** Hants
214 D1 **Oakridge golf course** Warwks
95 F2 **Oaks Sports Centre** Gt Lon
342 D4 **Oakwell Hall country park** Kirk
329 F3 **Oakwell Stadium** Barns
126 B2 **Oakwood Adventure & Leisure Park** Pembks
97 G2 **Oastpark golf course** Kent
506 D4 **Oban Caravan & Camping Park** Ag & B
351 E2 **Ocean Edge Leisure Park campsite** Lancs
151 F2 **Ocean Lab** Pembks
204 D3 **Ocean View Caravan Park** Cerdgn
485 H3 **Ochilview Park** Falk
162 C4 **Oddas Chapel** Gloucs
92 B5 **Odiham airfield** Hants
92 B4 **Odiham Castle** Hants
342 C4 **Odsall Stadium** Brad
209 E5 **Offa's Dyke Heritage Centre museum** Shrops
287 F3 **Offa's Dyke Path** Denbgs
288 B4 **Offa's Dyke Path** Denbgs
134 C3 **Offa's Dyke Path** Gloucs
185 E4 **Offa's Dyke Path** Herefs
209 E5 **Offa's Dyke Path** Powys
113 F4 **Ogbourne Downs Golf Club** Wilts
25 E4 **Okehampton Golf Club** Devon
37 F4 **Old Barn Touring Park** IoW
105 G5 **Old Beaupre Castle** V Glam
3 C1 **Old Blockhouse gun tower** IoS
97 F3 **Oldbury** Kent
187 F3 **Old Church** Herefs
498 D1 **Old Church & Tower** P & K
293 E6 **Old Churnet Railway Trail cycle route** Staffs
271 F3 **Old Colhurst Manor** Shrops
306 B4 **Old Colwyn Golf Club** Conwy
13 E4 **Old Cotmore Farm campsite** Devon
465 H2 **Old Course Ranfurly Golf Club** Rens
118 D4 **Old Deer Park** Gt Lon
85 H4 **Old Down Touring Park** Somset
144 B5 **Old Fold Manor Golf Club** Gt Lon
366 A5 **Old Hall Caravan Park** Lancs
397 E4 **Old Hall museum** R & Cl
327 E4 **Oldham Golf Club** Oldham
326 D4 **Oldham Mumps railway station** Oldham
240 D2 **Old Junction Boatyard** Leics
8 C2 **Old Kerrow Farm Holiday Park** Cnwll
81 G6 **Old Lighthouse (Dungeness)** Kent
600 B4 **Old Man of Hoy** Ork
543 J6 **Old Man of Storr** Highld
219 G6 **Old Manor Caravan Park** Cambs
560 B4 **Oldmeldrum Golf Club** Abers
454 D2 **Old Mill Caravan Site** Nthumb
95 G5 **Old Mill windmill** Surrey
220 C2 **Old Nene Golf & Country Club** Cambs
164 B5 **Old New Inn Model Village** Gloucs
288 C2 **Old Padeswood Golf Club** Flints
104 C1 **Old Parish Ground** Brdgnd
22 B5 **Old Post Office NT** Cnwll
365 G5 **Old Rectory** Lancs
331 H2 **Old Rectory** N Linc
158 C6 **Old Rectory Golf Club** Powys
323 G5 **Old Roan railway station** Sefton
70 C3 **Old Sarum Fort** Wilts
605 G8 **Old Scatness museum** Shet
37 E4 **Old Smithy & Gardens museum** IoW
97 F4 **Old Soar Manor NT** Kent
370 A3 **Old Station Caravan Park** N York
371 G3 **Oldstead White Horse** N York
74 C3 **Old Thorns Hotel Golf & Country Estate** Hants
100 C4 **Old Town Hall** Herts
36 C2 **Old Town Hall NT** IoW

498 B6 **Old Town Jail** Stirlg
557 H5 **Old Town or King's Links golf course** C Aber
326 B5 **Old Trafford cricket ground** Traffd
326 B5 **Old Trafford football ground** Traffd
69 F4 **Old Wardour Castle** Wilts
73 F5 **Old Winchester Hill (Archaeology Trail)** Hants
374 C2 **Oliver's Mount** N York
214 A3 **Olton Golf Club** Solhll
119 E4 **Olympia** Gt Lon
212 B6 **Ombersley Golf Club** Worcs
121 G2 **One Tree Hill** Thurr
146 A4 **Ongar railway station** Essex
291 F6 **Onneley Golf Club** Staffs
49 E6 **Open Golf Centres** Bmouth
374 D4 **Orchard Farm Holiday Village** N York
86 D4 **Orchardleigh Golf Club** Somset
299 H6 **Orchard Park campsite** Lincs
317 E5 **Orchard Park Touring Caravan & Camping Park** Notts
36 C3 **Orchards Holiday Caravan Park** IoW
413 F4 **Orchardton Tower** D & G
245 E2 **Orchard View Caravan & Camping Park** Lincs
475 E4 **Ord House Country Park campsite** Nthumb
58 D4 **Ore railway station** E Susx
33 G1 **Organford Manor campsite** Dorset
601 G2 **Orkney Golf Club** Ork
385 E1 **Ormesby Hall NT** R & Cl
295 E5 **Ormonde Fields Golf & Country Club** Derbys
324 A3 **Ormskirk Golf Club** Lancs
323 G5 **Orrell Park railway station** Lpool
121 G3 **Orsett Golf Club** Thurr
243 H5 **Orton Meadows Golf Centre** C Pete
243 H5 **Orton Mere railway station** C Pete
51 F5 **Osborne Golf Club** IoW
51 F6 **Osborne House** IoW
32 B3 **Osmington Mills Holidays** Dorset
118 C4 **Osterley Park NT** Gt Lon
269 F4 **Oswestry Golf Club** Shrops
355 G6 **Otley Golf Club** Leeds
441 G6 **Otterburn Mill** Nthumb
546 D5 **Otter Haven** Highld
370 D2 **Otterington Park campsite** N York
50 C3 **Otter & Owl Centre** Hants
28 A5 **Otterton Mill** Devon
251 G6 **Oulton Broad North railway station** Suffk
227 G1 **Oulton Broad South railway station** Suffk
343 G4 **Oulton Park golf course** Leeds
290 B2 **Oulton Park race circuit** Ches
219 E2 **Oundle Golf Club** Nhants
593 D9 **Our Lady of the Isles** W Isls
77 F4 **Ouse Valley Viaduct** W Susx
35 d2 **Outlands Village** Guern
327 G1 **Outlane Golf Club** Kirk
226 C1 **Outney Meadow Caravan Park** Suffk
12 C5 **Overbecks NT museum** Devon
193 H1 **Overstone Park golf course** Nhants
91 E4 **Overton railway station** Hants
314 C1 **Owlerton Stadium** Sheff
79 F2 **Owl House Gardens** Kent
136 A5 **Owlpen Manor** Gloucs
330 B2 **Owston Park golf course** Donc
247 E4 **Oxburgh Hall NT** Norfk
140 D4 **Oxford service area** Oxon
140 C4 **Oxford Stadium** Oxon
236 D4 **Oxley Park Golf Club** Wolves
234 B2 **Oxon Hall Touring Park** Shrops
102 C4 **Oxwich Castle** Swans

P

94 D3 **Pachesham Park Golf Centre** Surrey
214 B5 **Packwood House NT** Warwks
284 C3 **Padarn Country Park** Gwynd
27 G1 **Padbrook Park Golf Club** Devon
288 C2 **Padeswood & Buckley Golf Club** Flints
14 C4 **Padstow Holiday Park** Cnwll
14 C4 **Padstow Touring Park** Cnwll
13 F2 **Paignton and Dartmouth Steam Railway** Devon
20 B5 **Paignton Queen's Park railway station** Torbay
94 B2 **Painshill Park** Surrey
136 C2 **Painswick Golf Club** Gloucs
99 F3 **Painters Farm Caravan & Camping Site** Kent
329 E1 **Painthorpe House Golf & Country Club** Wakefd
466 C2 **Paisley Canal railway station** Rens
466 C2 **Paisley Gilmour Street railway station** Rens
466 C3 **Paisley Golf Club** Rens
466 C2 **Paisley St James railway station** Rens
485 F5 **Palacerigg Country Park** N Lans
485 F5 **Palacerigg Golf Club** N Lans
423 G4 **Palmerston Park** D & G
106 D1 **Pandy Park** Caerph
515 E3 **Panmure Golf Club** Angus
356 C4 **Pannal Golf Club** N York
144 C2 **Panshanger Golf & Squash Complex** Herts
126 D2 **Pantglas Farm Caravan Park** Pembks
602 D1 **Papa Westray airport** Ork
296 A4 **Papplewick Pumping Station** Notts
56 C4 **Paradise Park** E Susx
144 D3 **Paradise Wildlife Park** Herts
4 B1 **Parbola Holiday Park** Cnwll
132 B4 **Parc Cwm Darran** Caerph
355 E2 **Parcevall Hall** N York
107 E3 **Parc golf course** Newpt
54 C2 **Parham House and Gardens** W Susx
204 D3 **Park Avenue Stadium** Cerdgn
106 C3 **Park Cefn Onn** Cardif
365 E1 **Park Cliffe Camping & Caravan Estate** Cumb

19 G3 **Parkers Farm Holiday Park** Devon
366 B5 **Park Farm** Lancs
258 D5 **Park Farm** Norfk
390 D5 **Park Foot Caravan & Camping Park** Cumb
343 F4 **Park Halt railway station** Leeds
240 D1 **Park Hill Golf Club** Leics
430 D5 **Parklands golf course** N u Ty
326 A4 **Park Lane Stadium** Bury
122 C3 **Park Lane Stadium** Essex
422 D5 **Park of Brandedleys campsite** D & G
133 E4 **Park Road Stadium** Torfn
34 B2 **Parkstone Golf Club** Poole
143 G4 **Park Street railway station** Herts
120 C4 **Park View Road Stadium** Gt Lon
96 B3 **Park Wood Golf Club** Surrey
48 D5 **Parley golf course** Dorset
8 D3 **Par railway station** Cnwll
82 C1 **Parsonage Farm Rural Heritage Centre** Kent
109 G5 **Parson Street railway station** Bristl
79 G4 **Pashley Manor** E Susx
562 D8 **Pass of the Cattle** Highld
274 D3 **Pastures Golf Club** Derb
236 B5 **Patshull Park Hotel Golf & Country Club** Staffs
466 D3 **Patterton railway station** E Rens
9 H1 **Paul Corin Music museum** Cnwll
50 B1 **Paultons Golf Centre** Hants
50 B1 **Paultons Park** Hants
194 D3 **Pavenham Park golf course** Beds
102 B4 **Paviland** Swans
77 G4 **Paxhill Park Golf Club** W Susx
474 D4 **Paxton House** Border
154 D6 **Paxtons Tower NT** Carmth
173 G5 **Paycocke's NT** Essex
56 C4 **Peacehaven Golf Club** E Susx
313 F3 **Peak Cavern** Derbys
313 F2 **Peak District National Park**
294 B2 **Peak Railway** Derbys
33 G1 **Pear Tree Touring Park** Dorset
77 E3 **Pease Pottage service area** W Susx
32 B4 **Pebble Bank Caravan Park** Dorset
119 G4 **Peckham Rye railway station** Gt Lon
394 A6 **Pecknell Farm Caravan Park** Dur
28 D5 **Pecorama** Devon
62 D2 **Pedal Around Porlock cycle route** Somset
247 G3 **Peddars Way & Norfolk Coast Path** Norfk
259 E5 **Peddars Way & Norfolk Coast Path** Norfk
450 A1 **Peebles Golf Club** Border
555 G4 **Peel Ring of Lumphanan** Abers
177 E3 **Peewit Caravan Park** Suffk
324 D4 **Pemberton railway station** Wigan
128 B4 **Pembrey Circuit** Carmth
150 C4 **Pembrey Ski Slope** Carmth
124 C3 **Pembrokeshire Coast National Park** Pembks
178 C4 **Pembrokeshire Coast Path** Pembks
151 G6 **Pembrokeshire Coast Path** Pembks
151 G6 **Pembrokeshire County showground** Pembks
15 E4 **Pencarrow** Cnwll
158 A5 **Pencelli Castle Caravan & Camping Park** Powys
288 B6 **Penddol Caravan Park** Denbgs
5 F2 **Pendennis Castle** Cnwll
3 E2 **Penderleath Caravan & Camping Park** Cnwll
8 D3 **Penhale Caravan & Camping Park** Cnwll
23 E3 **Penhallam Castle** Cnwll
22 D2 **Penhalt Farm Holiday Park** Cnwll
96 D6 **Penhaven Touring Park** Cnwll
307 F4 **Penhurst vineyard** Kent
341 G2 **Penisar Mynydd Caravan Park** Denbgs
284 C2 **Penllyn railway station** Gwynd
285 G4 **Penmachno Woollen Mill** Conwy
305 F4 **Penmaenmawr Golf Club** Conwy
9 E3 **Penmarlam Caravan & Camping Park** Cnwll
5 E2 **Penmere railway station** Cnwll
304 D3 **Penmon Priory** IoA
5 E2 **Pennance Mill Farm Touring Park** Cnwll
102 D4 **Pennard Castle** Swans
102 D4 **Pennard Golf Club** Swans
263 G3 **Pennarth Fawr** Gwynd
236 C6 **Penn Golf Club** Staffs
453 G5 **Pennine Way** Border
341 E3 **Pennine Way** Calder
392 B2 **Pennine Way** Cumb
313 E1 **Pennine Way** Derbys
327 F3 **Pennine Way** Kirk
367 G3 **Pennine Way** N York
441 F6 **Pennine Way** Nthumb
325 E5 **Pennington Flash Country Park** Wigan
93 E2 **Pennyhill Park Hotel & Country Club** Surrey
12 B2 **Pennymoor Camping & Caravan Park** Devon
435 H6 **Penpont Caravan & Camping Park** D & G
302 B4 **Penrhos-Feilw standing stones** IoA
204 C6 **Penrhos Golf & Country Club** Cerdgn
304 D5 **Penrhyn Castle NT** Gwynd
228 D1 **Penrhyn Point (Barmouth Ferry) railway station** Gwynd
391 E3 **Penrith Golf Club** Cumb
390 D4 **Penrith North Lakes railway station** Cumb
7 E3 **Penrose Farm Touring Park** Cnwll
96 D6 **Penshurst Place and Gardens** Kent
99 G5 **Penshurst railway station** Kent
254 B2 **Penthorpe Waterfowl Park** Norfk

38 B5 **Penstowe Caravan & Camping Park** Cnwll
8 C4 **Pentewan Sands Holiday Park** Cnwll
470 B3 **Pentland Hills**
470 D2 **Pentland Hills Visitor Centre** Mdloth
118 A6 **Penton Hook Marina** Surrey
131 G4 **Pentre-Bach railway station** Myr Td
152 B2 **Pentre Ifan Burial Chamber** Pembks
266 D3 **Pentrepiod railway station** Gwynd
338 D4 **Penwortham Golf Club** Lancs
184 A2 **Pen-y-bont railway station** Powys
267 E3 **Pen Y Bont Touring & Camping Park** Gwynd
287 E5 **Pen-y-Bryn Farm** Denbgs
288 C6 **Penycae Golf Club** Wrexhm
157 G3 **Pen-y-crug campsite** Powys
132 C4 **Pen-y-fan-pond** Caerph
264 D2 **Pen-y-Mount railway station** Gwynd
3 E3 **Penzance heliport** Cnwll
311 E5 **Peover Golf Club** Ches
20 D2 **Peppermint Park campsite** Devon
188 C3 **Perdiswell Park golf course** Worcs
118 C3 **Perivale Park golf course** Gt Lon
7 E3 **Perranporth Camping & Touring Park** Cnwll
7 E3 **Perranporth Golf Club** Cnwll
7 E2 **Perran Sands Holiday Park** Cnwll
213 G1 **Perry Barr railway station** Birm
136 A4 **Perrygrove Railway** Gloucs
189 E5 **Pershore railway station** Worcs
512 D4 **Perth racecourse** P & K
512 C3 **Perthshire Visitor Centre** P & K
236 C5 **Perton Park Golf Club** Staffs
219 H2 **Peterborough (Conington) airport** Cambs
243 G5 **Peterborough Milton Golf Club** C Pete
243 G6 **Peterborough service area** Cambs
557 E5 **Peterc ulter golf course** C Aber
571 L6 **Peterhead Golf Club** Abers
56 C4 **Peter Leonard Marina** E Susx
74 B4 **Petersfield Golf Club (New Course)** Hants
74 B5 **Petersfield Golf Club (Old Course)** Hants
107 E3 **Peterstone Lakes Golf Club** Newpt
251 E4 **Pettitts Crafts & Animal Adventure Park** Norfk
75 F5 **Petworth House NT** W Susx
57 G4 **Pevensey & Westham railway station** E Susx
313 G3 **Peveril Castle** Derbys
315 E1 **Phoenix Golf Club** Rothm
559 E3 **Picardy Symbol Stone** Abers
111 G6 **Piccadilly Caravan Park** Wilts
125 H2 **Picton Castle** Pembks
350 B2 **Piel Castle** Cumb
602 E2 **Pierowall Church** Ork
357 H5 **Pike Hills Golf Club** York
179 G4 **Pilbach Holiday Park** Cerdgn
300 B6 **Pilgrims Way campsite** Lincs
304 B5 **Pili Palas** IoA
29 H2 **Pilsdon Pen** Dorset
78 B5 **Piltdown Golf Club** E Susx
98 C4 **Pine Lodge Touring Park** Kent
93 E3 **Pine Ridge Golf Club** Surrey
83 G2 **Pines Gardens** Kent
423 G4 **Pines Golf Centre** D & G
118 C1 **Pinner Hill Golf Club** Gt Lon
274 C1 **Pirelli Stadium** Staffs
267 H4 **Pistyll Rhaeadr (Waterfall)** Powys
189 F1 **Pitcheroak Golf Club** Worcs
577 G5 **Pitgrudy Caravan Park** Highld
524 D4 **Pitlochry golf course** P & K
560 C4 **Pitmedden Garden NTS** Abers
487 F2 **Pitreavie Golf Club** Fife
122 A2 **Pitsea railway station** Essex
193 F1 **Pitsford & Brampton railway station** Nhants
142 C1 **Pitstone Windmill** Bucks
557 G3 **Pittodrie Stadium** C Aber
102 B4 **Pitton Cross Caravan & Camping Park** Swans
20 C4 **Plainmoor** Torbay
468 B1 **Plains Country Park** N Lans
243 H4 **Planet Ice Arena** C Pete
91 G4 **Planet Ice Arena** Hants
168 A2 **Planet Ice Arena** M Keyn
283 F3 **Plas Gwyn Caravan Park** Gwynd
269 E1 **Plas Kynaston Lane** Wrexhm
268 D1 **Plas Newydd house and museum** Denbgs
283 F2 **Plas Newydd NT** IoA
288 D5 **Plassey Golf Club** Wrexhm
283 F4 **Plas y Nant railway station** Gwynd
262 C5 **Plas-Yn-Rhiw NT** Gwynd
339 F4 **Pleasington Golf Club** Lancs
334 D3 **Pleasure Island Theme Park** NE Lin
323 F1 **Pleasureland** Sefton
251 G5 **Pleasurewood Hills Theme Park** Suffk
430 D4 **Plessey Woods Country Park** Nthumb
56 B1 **Plumpton racecourse** E Susx
567 L5 **Pluscarden Abbey** Moray
18 B6 **Plymouth airport** C Plym
14 B4 **Point Curlew Chalet & Touring Park** Cnwll
10 A2 **Polborder House Caravan & Camping Park** Cnwll
4 C2 **Poldark Mine** Cnwll
4 B3 **Poldown Caravan Park** Cnwll
94 C4 **Polesdon Lacy NT** Surrey
469 E1 **Polkemmet Country Park** W Loth
469 E1 **Polkemmet Country Park golf course** W Loth
466 D2 **Pollok Country Park** C Glas
467 E2 **Pollok Golf Club** C Glas
3 F2 **Polmanter Tourist Park** Cnwll
486 B4 **Polmont Golf Club** Falk

9 G3 Polperro Model Village Cnwll
9 E3 Polruan Holidays-Camping & Caravanning Cnwll
27 E4 Polsloe Bridge railway station Devon
174 C1 Polstead Touring Park Suffk
37 G2 Pondwell Camp Site IoW
129 E3 Pont Abraham service area Carmth
129 H4 Pontardawe Golf Club Neath
269 E1 Pontcysyllte Aqueduct Wrexhm
344 B5 Pontefract Baghill railway station Wakefd
344 A5 Pontefract & District Golf Club Wakefd
344 A5 Pontefract racecourse Wakefd
344 A5 Pontefract Tanshelf railway station Wakefd
430 C5 Ponteland Golf Club Nthumb
155 F5 Pont Gwladys railway station Carmth
133 F3 Pont Kemys Caravan & Camping Park Mons
133 E5 Pontnewydd Golf Club Torfn
133 E4 Pontypool Golf Club Torfn
133 F4 Pontypool & New Inn railway station Torfn
106 A1 Pontypridd Golf Club Rhondd
27 G6 Pooh Cottage Holiday Park Devon
312 D5 Poole's Cavern Derbys
34 A2 Poole Stadium Poole
91 E6 Popham airfield Hants
178 D4 Poppit Sands Pembks
357 H4 Poppleton railway station York
9 F2 Porfell Animal Land Cnwll
62 D2 Porlock Caravan Park Somset
290 B2 Portal Golf & Country Club Ches
110 B6 Portavon Marina BaNES
464 B1 Port Bannatyne Golf Club Ag & B
51 H4 Portchester Castle Roman site Hants
283 F2 Port Dinorwic Marina Gwynd
143 H4 Porters Park Golf Club Herts
30 D5 Portesham Dairy Farm Campsite Dorset
482 D5 Port Glasgow Golf Club Inver
51 E3 Port Hamble Marina Hants
14 A6 Porth Beach Tourist Park Cnwll
302 B5 Porth Dafarch NT IoA
3 d2 Porth Hellick Downs Tombs IoS
264 C2 Porthmadog Golf Club Gwynd
264 D2 Porthmadog Harbour railway station Gwynd
8 C3 Porthpean Golf Club Cnwll
6 C4 Porthtowan Tourist Park Cnwll
32 B5 Portland Dorset
32 B6 Portland Bill Lighthouse Dorset
32 B5 Portland Castle Dorset
32 B5 Portland Museum & Shipwreck Centre Dorset
557 G5 Portlethen Golf Club Abers
81 H3 Port Lympne Wild Animal Park Kent
201 G6 Portman Road Suffk
97 H1 Port Medway Marina Medway
264 D2 Portmeirion Pottery Gwynd
488 B5 Portobello golf course C Edin
3 F2 Port of Hayle (UNESCO) Cnwll
414 C5 Portpatrick Golf Club D & G
322 C9 Port St Mary Golf Club IoM
40 C4 Portsmouth Arms railway station Devon
52 B3 Portsmouth golf course Hants
51 H4 Portsmouth Harbour railway station Hants
52 A4 Portsmouth & Southsea railway station C Port
52 A4 Port Solent Marina C Port
484 B6 Possilpark & Parkhouse railway station C Glas
202 B2 Post Mill Castle Suffk
194 D4 Postmill windmill Beds
159 G2 Poston Mill Caravan & Camping Park Herefs
144 B4 Potters Bar Golf Club Herts
337 F1 Poulton Le Fylde Golf Club Lancs
310 C1 Poulton Park golf course Warrtn
97 E5 Poult Wood Golf Centre Kent
8 D2 Powderham Castle Tourist Park Cnwll
81 G6 Power Station Visitor Centre Kent
399 E1 Powfoot Golf Club D & G
404 B4 Pow Hill Country Park Dur
232 D3 Powis Castle NT Powys
312 B3 Poynton showground Ches
3 G4 Praa Sands Golf Club Cnwll
502 B3 Praytis Country Park Fife
243 F5 Prebendal Manor House Nhants
4 C5 Predannack airfield Cnwll
270 C3 Prees railway station Shrops
308 D2 Prenton Golf Club Wirral
308 D2 Prenton Park Wirral
6 D4 Presingoll Farm Caravan & Camping Park Cnwll
307 F3 Prestatyn Golf Club Denbgs
312 A4 Prestbury Golf Club Ches
307 F3 Presthaven Sands campsite Denbgs
26 A4 Prestonbury Castle Devon
488 B5 Prestonfield Golf Club C Edin
338 D3 Preston Golf Club Lancs
488 D1 Prestongrange Heritage museum E Loth
338 D4 Preston Marina Lancs
490 A4 Preston Mill and Phantassie Doocot NTS E Loth
55 G3 Preston Park railway station Br & H
455 F4 Preston Pele Tower Nthumb
326 B4 Prestwich Golf Club Bury
445 E4 Prestwick airport S Ayrs
444 D4 Prestwick Golf Club S Ayrs

444 D4 Prestwick International Airport railway station S Ayrs
445 E5 Prestwick St Cuthbert Golf Club S Ayrs
444 D5 Prestwick St Nicholas Golf Club S Ayrs
444 D4 Prestwick Town railway station S Ayrs
14 C3 Prideaux Place Cnwll
275 F2 Pride Park Stadium C Derb
122 B6 Priestfield Stadium Medway
466 D3 Priesthill & Darnley railway station C Glas
77 G3 Priests House museum W Susx
375 E4 Primrose Valley Holiday Park N York
531 H6 Prince Charlie's Cairn Highld
101 F3 Prince's Golf Club Kent
304 C4 Princes golf course IoA
570 B3 Princess Royal Park Abers
136 C2 Prinknash Abbey Gloucs
86 D2 Prior Park NT BaNES
451 H3 Priorwood Garden NTS Border
365 E4 Priory Gatehouse NT Cumb
123 G5 Priory Hill campsite Kent
57 G4 Priory Lane Stadium E Susx
195 F5 Priory Marina Beds
176 C1 Priory Park campsite Suffk
151 E4 Priskilly Forest Golf Club Pembks
467 G1 Provan Hall NTS C Glas
404 C2 Prudhoe Castle Nthumb
404 D2 Prudhoe Golf Club Nthumb
289 H1 Pryors Hayes Golf Club Ches
343 F6 Pugneys Country Park Wakefd
142 A4 Pulpit Hill Bucks
487 E6 Pumpherston Golf Club W Loth
89 G2 Pumping Station Wilts
239 E6 Purley Chase Golf Club Warwks
95 G2 Purley Downs Golf Club Gt Lon
95 G2 Purley Oaks railway station Gt Lon
84 B3 Purn International Holiday Park N Som
93 F5 Puttenham Golf Club Surrey
263 F4 Pwllheli Golf Club Gwynd
55 G2 Pyecombe Golf Club W Susx
104 C4 Pyle & Kenfig Golf Club Brdgnd
237 H6 Pype Hayes Golf Club Birm
94 B3 Pyrford Basin (Marina) Surrey
94 A3 Pyrford Golf Club Surrey
133 E1 Pyscodlyn Farm Caravan & Camping Site Mons
218 B4 Pytchley Golf Lodge Nhants

Q

64 C4 Quantock Hills Somset
64 B4 Quantock Orchard Caravan Park Somset
311 G3 Quarry Bank Mill NT Ches
389 H5 Quarry & Mining museum Cumb
273 F1 Quarry Walk Park campsite Staffs
37 F4 Queen Bower Dairy Caravan Park IoW
73 H6 Queen Elizabeth Country Park Hants
496 C3 Queen Elizabeth Forest Park Stirlg
496 D4 Queen Elizabeth Forest Park Visitor Centre Stirlg
342 B4 Queensbury Golf Club Brad
566 D5 Queen's Own Highlanders Regimental museum Highld
49 E6 Queen's Park golf course Bmouth
290 D3 Queen's Park golf course Ches
119 E3 Queens Park (London) railway station Gt Lon
524 C4 Queen's View Visitor Centre P & K
186 C4 Queenswood Country Park Herefs
101 F2 Quex Caravan Park Kent
220 C5 Quiet Waters Caravan Park Cambs
41 E2 Quince Honey Farm Devon
240 C1 Quorn & Woodhouse railway station Leics

R

394 C5 Raby Castle Dur
319 E2 Racecourse Caravan Park Lincs
117 F4 Racecourse Yacht Basin Bucks
276 D2 Radcliffe (Nottinghamshire) railway station Notts
277 E2 Radcliffe-on-Trent Golf Club Notts
184 C2 Radnor Forest Powys
184 C2 Radnor Ring cycle route Powys
106 B3 Radyr Golf Club Cardif
567 K4 RAF Kinloss airfield Moray
514 D5 RAF Leuchars Fife
568 C2 RAF Lossiemouth airfield Moray
222 D4 RAF Mildenhall Suffk
119 E1 RAF museum Gt Lon
236 A3 RAF museum Shrops
105 G6 RAF St Athan Golf Club V Glam
298 B2 RAF Waddington Lincs
133 H3 Raglan Castle Mons
133 H3 Raglan Parc Golf Club Mons
189 G3 Ragley Hall Warwks
230 B3 Railway museum (Corris) Powys
98 C1 Rainham (Kent) railway station Medway
466 D2 Ralston Golf Club Rens
136 B1 Ramada Hotel & Resort Gloucester golf course Gloucs
296 A5 Ramsdale Park Golf Centre Notts
220 C2 Ramsey Abbey Gatehouse NT Cambs
220 C3 Ramsey Golf & Bowls Club Cambs
322 g4 Ramsey Golf & Bowls Club IoM
339 G3 Ramsgreave & Wilpshire railway station Lancs
405 H5 Ramside Hall Golf Club Dur
189 H6 Ranch Caravan Park Worcs

465 H1 Ranfurly Castle Golf Club Rens
522 C5 Rannoch Moor Highld
522 D4 Rannoch railway station P & K
37 E5 Rare Breeds and Waterfowl Park IoW
117 F2 Rare Breeds Centre Bucks
71 E1 Rare Breeds Farm (Cholderton) Wilts
506 E4 Rare Breeds Farm Park (Oban) Ag & B
487 F5 Ratho Park Golf Club C Edin
298 C6 Rauceby railway station Lincs
487 H5 Ravelston Golf Club C Edin
377 F4 Ravenglass & Eskdale Railway Cumb
376 D5 Ravenglass for Eskdale railway station Cumb
387 G4 Raven Hall Hotel golf course N York
120 A5 Ravensbourne railway station Gt Lon
169 F4 Ravensburgh Castle Herts
405 G3 Ravensworth Golf Club Gatesd
340 C2 Rawtenstall railway station Lancs
400 B1 Raydale Park D & G
116 B4 Reading Golf Club Readg
115 H6 Reading service area W Berk
116 B5 Reading Stadium Readg
116 A5 Reading West railway station Readg
290 C4 Reaseheath Golf Club Ches
587 L3 Reay Golf Club Highld
119 G2 Rectory Road railway station Gt Lon
365 G6 Red Bank Farm campsite Lancs
143 G2 Redbourn Golf Club Herts
50 C2 Redbridge railway station Hants
397 E4 Redcar Central railway station R & Cl
397 F5 Redcar East railway station R & Cl
397 F5 Redcar racecourse R & Cl
326 D6 Reddish Vale Golf Club Stockp
189 F1 Redditch Golf Club Worcs
95 F5 Redhill aerodrome Surrey
276 A4 Red Hill Marina Leics
95 F5 Redhill & Reigate Golf Club Surrey
124 D2 Redlands Caravan & Camping Park Pembks
97 E1 Redlibbets Golf Club Kent
162 C4 Red Lion Caravan Park Gloucs
269 G4 Rednal airfield Shrops
23 F2 Red Post Inn & Holiday Park Cnwll
49 F3 Red Shoot Camping Park Hants
325 E3 Reebok Stadium Bolton
95 G2 Reedham (Surrey) railway station Gt Lon
526 C4 Reekie Linn Falls Angus
325 F3 Regent Park golf course Bolton
69 H4 Regimental Badges Fovant chalk figure Wilts
146 D2 Regiment Way Golf Centre Essex
95 E5 Reigate Heath Golf Club Surrey
95 F4 Reigate Hill Golf Club Surrey
375 E4 Reighton Sands Holiday Park N York
551 H8 Reindeer Centre Highld
389 G2 Reivers cycle route Cumb
400 C3 Reivers cycle route Cumb
427 E2 Reivers cycle route Nthumb
429 G5 Reivers cycle route Nthumb
92 C1 REME museum Wokham
483 G6 Renfrew Golf Club Rens
315 E4 Renishaw Park Golf Club Derbys
546 E4 Reraig Caravan Site Highld
519 H3 Resipole Farm campsite Highld
527 G4 Restenneth Priory Angus
9 E1 Restormel Castle Cnwll
4 D2 Retanna Holiday Park Cnwll
316 C4 Retford (Gamston) airport Notts
316 C4 Retford Golf Club Notts
314 D4 Revolution House Derbys
265 G5 Rhaeadr Ddu NT (Waterfall) Gwynd
390 D4 Rheged Discovery Centre Cumb
205 G4 Rheidol Falls railway station Cerdgn
205 G4 Rheidol Power Station Cerdgn
476 C5 Rhinns of Islay Ag & B
205 G4 Rhiwfron Halt railway station Cerdgn
265 G3 Rhiw Goch Ski Centre Gwynd
131 G6 Rhondda Golf Club Rhondd
105 G1 Rhondda Heritage Park Rhondd
304 C4 Rhos Caravan Park IoA
307 E4 Rhuddlan Golf Club Denbgs
262 D5 Rhydolion campsite Gwynd
307 E3 Rhyl Golf Club Denbgs
367 F4 Ribblehead railway station N York
367 F4 Ribblehead Viaduct N York
353 G2 Ribblesdale N York
323 G5 Rice Lane railway station Lpool
101 F3 Richborough Roman site Kent
118 A4 Richings Park Golf Club Bucks
383 E4 Richmond Golf Club N York
154 B5 Richmond Park Carmth
248 B4 Richmond Park Golf Club Norfk
143 F6 Rickmansworth Public golf course Herts
215 E3 Ricoh Arena Covtry
492 D5 Ri Cruin Cairn Ag & B
355 E6 Riddlesden Golf Club Brad
95 G2 Riddlesdown railway station Gt Lon
33 G2 Ridge Farm Camping & Caravan Park Dorset
160 C2 Ridge Hill Caravan and Campsite Herefs
142 C2 Ridgeway Path Bucks
141 F5 Ridgeway Path Oxon
115 E3 Ridgeway Path W Berk
112 D5 Ridgeway Path Wilts
372 A3 Rievaulx Abbey N York
372 A3 Rievaulx Terrace NT N York
387 F3 Rigg Farm Caravan Park N York

353 G5 Rimington Caravan Park Lancs
311 F2 Ringway Golf Club Traffd
356 B2 Ripley Caravan Park N York
370 C5 Ripon City Golf Club N York
370 C6 Ripon racecourse N York
186 C3 Risbury Fort Herefs
120 D1 Risebridge golf course Gt Lon
339 H4 Rishton Golf Club Lancs
431 F6 Rising Sun Country Park N Tyne
410 D5 Rispain Camp D & G
309 E4 Rivacre Park Ches
293 G3 Rivendale Touring Caravan & Leisure Park Derbys
19 F3 River Dart Adventures campsite Devon
19 F3 River Dart Country Park Devon
351 H1 River Lune Millennium Park Lancs
195 H3 River Mill Boats (Marina) Cambs
116 C3 River & Rowing museum (Henley on Thames) Oxon
283 E3 Riverside Camping Gwynd
158 B6 Riverside Caravan & Camping Park Powys
358 B5 Riverside Caravan & Camping Park York
18 B6 Riverside Caravan Park C Plym
351 F2 Riverside Caravan Park Lancs
366 D6 Riverside Caravan Park N York
188 B5 Riverside Caravan Park Worcs
122 C6 Riverside Country Park Medway
405 G4 Riverside Cricket Ground Dur
7 F2 Riverside Holiday Park Cnwll
337 G6 Riverside Holiday Park Lancs
51 E3 Riverside Holidays campsite Hants
147 E3 Riverside Ice & Leisure Centre Essex
222 D4 Riverside Island Marina Suffk
138 C5 Riverside Lechlade Marina Gloucs
370 C5 Riverside Meadows Country Caravan Park N York
396 D5 Riverside Stadium Middsb
524 C2 River Tilt Caravan Park P & K
3 G3 River Valley Country Park Cnwll
8 C3 River Valley Holiday Park Cnwll
515 E3 Riverview Caravan Park Angus
129 E3 River View Touring Park Carmth
67 E5 RNAS Yeovilton Somset
24 B4 Roadford Lake campsite Devon
318 A6 Road Transport museum Lincs
306 C5 Roberts Caravan Park Conwy
450 C2 Robert Smail's Printing Works NTS Border
37 E3 Robin Hill Countryside Adventure Park IoW
372 D5 Robin Hood Caravan & Camping Park N York
331 E5 Robin Hood Doncaster Sheffield airport Donc
213 H3 Robin Hood Golf Club Solhll
497 F3 Rob Roy and Trossachs Visitor Centre Stirlg
326 C2 Rochdale Golf Club Rochdl
315 G2 Roche Abbey Rothm
8 B1 Roche railway station Cnwll
121 H6 Rochester & Cobham Park Golf Club Kent
122 D1 Rochford Hundred Golf Club Essex
185 E1 Rockbridge Park campsite Powys
49 F3 Rockford Common NT Hants
218 B1 Rockingham Castle Nhants
218 C1 Rockingham Circuit Nhants
218 B3 Rockingham Road Stadium Nhants
33 H1 Rockley Park campsite Poole
154 B1 Rock Mill Woollen & Water Mill Cerdgn
136 C2 Rococo Garden Gloucs
85 E4 Rodney Stoke Somset
162 A6 Rodway Hill golf course Gloucs
37 F3 Roebeck Camping & Caravan Park IoW
576 F3 Rogart railway station Highld
565 G5 Rogie Falls Highld
382 C2 Rokeby Park Dur
93 G4 Roker Park golf course Surrey
164 D3 Rollright Stones Oxon
80 C3 Rolvenden railway station Kent
285 F4 Roman Bridge railway station Conwy
384 A6 Romanby Golf & Country Club N York
424 D4 Roman Camp D & G
143 G3 Roman Theatre of Verulamium Herts
120 D2 Romford Golf Club Gt Lon
120 D2 Romford Ice Rink Gt Lon
312 B1 Romiley Golf Club Stockp
81 G4 Romney, Hythe & Dymchurch Railway Kent
81 F3 Romney Marsh Kent
81 G5 Romney Sands railway station Kent
81 G4 Romney Warren Golf Club Kent
50 C1 Romsey Golf Club Hants
227 G1 Rookery Park Golf Club Suffk
37 E4 Rookley Country Park IoW
364 B6 Roose railway station Cumb
122 D3 Roots Hall Stadium Sthend
454 D4 Ros Castle NT Nthumb
405 F4 Roseberry Grange Golf Club Dur
152 B4 Rosebush Caravan Park Pembks
386 B5 Rosedale Caravan & Camping Park N York

251 F4 Rose Farm Touring & Camping Park Norfk
312 B2 Rose Hill Marple railway station Stockp
6 C4 Rose Hill Touring Park Cnwll
2 C4 Roselands Caravan Park Cnwll
37 F2 Rosemary vineyard IoW
39 G4 Rosemoor Devon
14 D3 Roserrow Golf & Country Club Cnwll
450 A1 Rosetta Caravan & Camping Park Border
7 E3 Roseville Holiday Park Cnwll
340 B5 Rossendale Golf Club Lancs
323 F5 Rosset Park Sefton
504 D6 Ross of Mull Ag & B
161 F4 Ross-on-Wye Golf Club Herefs
20 A4 Ross Park campsite Devon
442 C5 Rothbury Forest Nthumb
442 C4 Rothbury Golf Club Nthumb
329 C6 Rotherham Central railway station Rothm
329 H5 Rotherham Golf Club Rothm
193 F3 Rotherthorpe service area Nhants
315 F3 Rother Valley Country Park Rothm
315 F3 Rother Valley Golf Centre Rothm
464 B2 Rothesay Golf Club Ag & B
568 D6 Rothes Golf Club Moray
551 G7 Rothiemurchus Visitor Centre Highld
240 C2 Rothley Park Golf Club Leics
261 H3 Roughton Road railway station Norfk
466 D3 Rouken Glen Park E Rens
343 F2 Roundhay Golf Club Leeds
322 c7 Round Table IoM
36 B4 Round the Island cycle route IoW
500 C1 Round Tower (Abernethy) P & K
35 d1 Rousse Tower (St Peter Port) Guern
464 D2 Routenburn Golf Club N Ayrs
322 b8 Rowany Golf Club IoM
52 C2 Rowlands Castle Golf Club Hants
47 F6 Rowlands Wait Touring Park Dorset
72 A6 Rownhams service area Hants
557 G2 Royal Aberdeen Golf Club C Aber
51 H3 Royal Armouries museum Hants
117 F6 Royal Ascot Golf Club W & M
78 A3 Royal Ashdown Forest Golf Club E Susx
67 G2 Royal Bath & West showground Somset
120 B5 Royal Blackheath Golf Club Gt Lon
118 D4 Royal Botanic Gardens of Kew (UNESCO) Gt Lon
487 G4 Royal Burgess Golfing Society of Edinburgh C Edin
101 G5 Royal Cinque Ports Golf Club Kent
14 D4 Royal Cornwall showground Cnwll
256 A1 Royal Cromer Golf Club Norfk
556 C5 Royal Deeside Railway Abers
577 H5 Royal Dornoch Golf Club Highld
57 F5 Royal Eastbourne Golf Club E Susx
145 E5 Royal Epping Forest Golf Club Gt Lon
35 d1 Royal Guernsey Golf Club Guern
487 F5 Royal Highland (Ingliston) showground C Edin
35 j7 Royal Jersey Golf Club Jersey
308 B2 Royal Liverpool Golf Club Wirral
93 F3 Royal Logistics Corps museum Surrey
337 F4 Royal Lytham & St Annes Golf Club Lancs
118 D4 Royal Mid-Surrey Golf Club Gt Lon
488 D5 Royal Musselburgh Golf Club E Loth
249 G2 Royal Norfolk showground Norfk
60 B5 Royal North Devon Golf Club Devon
249 H2 Royal Norwich Golf Club Norfk
488 B5 Royal Observatory C Edin
104 B4 Royal Porthcawl Golf Club Brdgnd
406 A1 Royal Quays Marina N Tyne
264 D3 Royal St Davids Golf Club Gwynd
101 F4 Royal St George's Golf Club Kent
47 H3 Royal Signals museum Dorset
570 C3 Royal Tarlair Golf Club Abers
283 E3 Royal Town of Caernarfon Golf Club Gwynd
444 D4 Royal Troon Golf Club S Ayrs
338 D6 Royal Umpire Caravan Park Lancs
51 E3 Royal Victoria Country Park Hants
183 G4 Royal Welsh showground Powys
259 F3 Royal West Norfolk Golf Club Norfk
119 E5 Royal Wimbledon Golf Club Gt Lon
72 C4 Royal Winchester Golf Club Hants
222 D5 Royal Worlington & Newmarket Golf Club Suffk
145 E2 Roydon Mill Leisure Park Herts
170 D1 Royston Golf Club Herts
35 j6 Rozel Camping Park Jersey
557 G3 Rubislaw Rugby Ground C Aber
356 C4 Rudding Holiday Park (Harrogate) N York
356 C4 Rudding Park Hotel golf course N York
276 C3 Ruddington Grange Golf Club C Nott
296 B2 Rufford Country Park Notts
324 B1 Rufford Old Hall NT Lancs
296 C1 Rufford Park Golf & Country Club Notts

216 B4 Rugby Golf Club Warwks
445 F2 Rugby Park E Ayrs
287 F6 Rug Chapel & Llangar Church Denbgs
273 F6 Rugeley Trent Valley railway station Staffs
118 B2 Ruislip Golf Club Gt Lon
530 C3 Rum Highld
355 E4 Rumbolds Moor Brad
310 B3 Runcorn East railway station Halton
309 H3 Runcorn Golf Club Halton
117 H5 Runcorn NT Surrey
322 g3 Rural Life Museum IoM
218 D6 Rushden Golf Club Nhants
322 d8 Rushen Abbey IoM
201 G5 Rushmere Golf Club Suffk
69 G6 Rushmore golf course Wilts
76 C2 Rusper golf course Surrey
470 C4 Rutherford Castle Golf Club Border
15 E5 Ruthern Valley Holidays Cnwll
287 G3 Ruthin-Pwllglas Golf Club Denbgs
535 L3 Ruthven Barracks Highld
242 C2 Rutland Caravan & Camping Rutlnd
242 D2 Rutland County Golf Club Rutlnd
243 E2 Rutland Open Air Theatre Rutlnd
242 B2 Rutland Railway Museum Rutlnd
241 E4 Rutland Ride cycle route Leics
242 C3 Rutland Water Circuit cycle route Rutlnd
120 C6 Ruxley Park Golf Centre Gt Lon
341 H5 Ryburn Golf Club Calder
88 C2 Rybury Camp Hill Fort Wilts
378 C3 Rydal Mount Cumb
51 G6 Ryde Arena IoW
51 G6 Ryde Esplanade railway station IoW
37 F2 Ryde Golf Club IoW
51 G6 Ryde Pier Head railway station IoW
326 C5 Ryder Brow railway station Manch
59 F3 Rye Golf Club E Susx
165 G2 Rye Hill Golf Club Oxon
145 E3 Rye House Stadium Herts
246 C4 Ryston Park Norfk
404 D1 Ryton Golf Club Gatesd
215 G5 Ryton Organic Gardens Warwks

S

243 F4 Sacrewell Farm & Country Centre C Pete
327 E3 Saddleworth Golf Club Oldham
327 E2 Saddleworth Moor Rochdl
171 H2 Saffron Walden Golf Club Essex
6 D4 St Agnes Mining District (UNESCO) Cnwll
143 G3 St Albans Abbey railway station Herts
213 G2 St Andrews Birm
503 E2 St Andrews Bay Golf Resort & Spa Fife
503 E1 St Andrews Botanic Gardens Fife
514 D6 St Andrews Links Trust golf course Fife
106 B5 St Andrews Major golf course V Glam
109 F4 St Andrews Road railway station Bristl
337 F3 St Annes Old Links golf course Lancs
337 F4 St Annes-on-the-Sea railway station Lancs
105 G6 St Athan airfield V Glam
101 F3 St Augustine's Cross Kent
101 F3 St Augustine's Golf Club Kent
8 B3 St Austell Golf Club Cnwll
376 B2 St Bees Golf Club Cumb
464 B4 St Blane's Church Ag & B
452 A3 St Boswells Golf Club Border
14 D5 St Breock Downs Monolith Cnwll
447 G3 St Bride's Church S Lans
487 G3 St Bridget's Kirk Fife
36 D5 St Catherine's Down NT IoW
36 D5 St Catherine's Lighthouse IoW
36 D5 St Catherine's Oratory IoW
35 i7 St Clement Golf & Sports Centre Jersey
595 H6 St Clements Church W Isls
121 G3 St Clere's Hall Golf Club Thurr
504 C6 St Columba Exhibition Centre Ag & B
454 D2 St Cuthbert's Cave NT Nthumb
263 G2 St Cybi's Well Gwynd
150 B4 St Davids City golf course Pembks
6 D5 St Day Holiday Park Cnwll
304 C5 St Deiniol Golf Club Gwynd
14 C3 St Enodoc Golf Club Cnwll
510 C5 St Fillans Golf Club P & K
94 B2 St George's Hill Golf Club Surrey
188 B3 St Georges Lane Worcs
208 B1 St Giles Golf Club Powys
342 D1 St Helena's Caravan Park Leeds
374 B3 St Helens Caravan Park N York
103 F3 St Helen's Cricket Club Swans
324 C6 St Helens Junction railway station St Hel
103 F3 St Helen's Rugby Ground Swans
77 G2 St Hill Manor W Susx
207 E2 St Idloes Golf Club Powys
3 G2 St Ives Bay Holiday Park Cnwll
220 D5 St Ives Golf Club Cambs
282 D5 St Ives Touring Caravan Park Gwynd
27 E4 St James Park Devon
405 F2 St James' Park N La Ty
27 E4 St James' Park railway station Devon
119 H2 St James Street railway station Gt Lon
27 G6 St Johns Caravan & Camping Park Devon
2 C3 St Just Mining District (UNESCO) Cnwll
15 E4 St Kew Golf course Cnwll
100 C4 St Lawrence Cricket Club Kent

48 D4 St Leonards Farm Caravan & Camping Park Dorset
58 D5 St Leonards Warrior Square railway station E Susx
602 F5 St Magnus Church Ork
202 C5 St Margaret's House campsite Suffk
100 C4 St Martin's Church (UNESCO) Kent
161 F3 St Mary's Church Gloucs
262 A6 St Mary's Church Gwynd
524 C5 St Mary's Church P & K
135 E4 St Mary's Halt railway station Gloucs
105 F3 St Mary's Hotel Golf & Country Club V Glam
431 G4 St Mary's Lighthouse N Tyne
50 D2 St Mary's stadium C Sotn
410 C5 St Medan Golf Club D & G
17 E5 St Mellion Hotel Golf & Country Club Cnwll
106 D3 St Mellons Golf Club Cardif
307 F3 St Melyd Golf Club Denbgs
309 G2 St Michael Jubilee Golf Club Halton
514 C5 St Michaels Golf Club Fife
3 F4 St Michael's Mount NT Cnwll
309 E2 St Michaels railway station Lpool
14 D3 St Minver Holiday Park Cnwll
466 C2 St Mirren Park Rens
195 H2 St Neots Golf Club Cambs
100 C2 St Nicholas Camping Site Kent
410 D5 St Ninian's Cave D & G
527 F4 St Orland's Stone Angus
347 F5 St Peters Church N Linc
35 d3 St Pierre Park Golf Club Guern
52 A3 St Pierre Park Golf Club Hants
83 E2 St Radigunds Abbey Kent
499 G2 St Serf's Church P & K
237 G1 St Thomas's Priory Golf Club Staffs
22 D4 St Tinney Farm Holidays Cnwll
488 B5 St Triduana's Chapel C Edin
308 A4 St Winefride's Well Flints
28 B5 Salcombe Regis Caravan & Camping Park Devon
311 G1 Sale Golf Club Traffd
326 B5 Salford Central railway station Salfd
326 B5 Salford Crescent railway station Salfd
486 D1 Saline Golf Club Fife
88 C5 Salisbury Plain Wilts
70 C4 Salisbury racecourse Wilts
70 C4 Salisbury & South Wilts Golf Club Wilts
101 G2 Salmestone Grange Kent
342 B2 Saltaire (UNESCO) Brad
397 G5 Saltburn by the Sea Golf Club R & Cl
397 G5 Saltburn railway station R & Cl
397 G5 Saltburn Smugglers Heritage Centre R & Cl
314 D5 Saltergate Stadium Derbys
320 D2 Saltfleetby Fisheries campsite Lincs
86 B1 Saltford Golf Club BaNES
86 B1 Saltford Marina BaNES
346 A4 Saltmarshe railway station E R Yk
11 F2 Saltram NT C Plym
338 C3 Salwick railway station Lancs
339 F3 Samlesbury aerodome Lancs
339 F3 Samlesbury Hall Lancs
25 F3 Sampford Courtenay railway station Devon
83 E3 Samphire Hoe country park Kent
438 B5 Samye Ling Monastery D & G
343 F6 Sandal & Agbrigg railway station Wakefd
603 K3 Sanday airport Ork
291 F2 Sandbach service area Ches
33 G1 Sandford Holiday Park Dorset
91 E3 Sandford Springs Golf Club Hants
90 D2 Sandham Memorial Chapel NT Hants
406 B1 Sandhaven Caravan & Camping Park S Tyne
329 G3 Sandhill Golf Club Barns
323 F6 Sandhills railway station Lpool
321 F4 Sandilands Golf Club Lincs
310 C5 Sandiway Golf Club Ches
82 B3 Sandling railway station Kent
92 C1 Sand Martins Golf Club Wokham
343 F1 Sand Moor Golf Club Leeds
94 C1 Sandown racecourse Surrey
9 G2 Sandplace railway station Ches
572 E8 Sands Holiday Centre Highld
365 G6 Sandside Caravan & Camping Park Lancs
408 C1 Sands of Luce Holiday Park D & G
213 E1 Sandwell & Dudley railway station Sandw
213 F1 Sandwell Park Golf Club Birm
213 F1 Sandwell Valley Country Park Sandw
101 F4 Sandwich Leisure Park Kent
49 F1 Sandy Balls Holiday Centre Hants
413 G3 Sandyhills Bay Leisure Park D & G
32 D2 Sandyholme Caravan Park Dorset
143 F6 Sandy Lodge Golf Club Herts
38 B5 Sandymouth Bay Holiday Park Cnwll
310 B2 Sankey for Penketh railway station Warrtn
189 F6 Sankey Marina Worcs
310 B1 Sankey Valley Country Park Warrtn
435 F3 Sanquhar Golf Club D & G
435 F2 Sanquhar Tolbooth museum D & G
194 D2 Santa Pod Raceway Beds
187 F2 Sapey Golf Club Herefs
105 H1 Sardis Road Rhondd
213 G3 Sarehole Mill museum Birm
105 E3 Sarn Park service area Brdgnd
153 H2 Saron golf course Carmth
198 D3 Sascombe vineyard Cambs
34 c2 Saumarez Park Museum NT Guern

126 C3 Saundersfoot railway station Pembks
289 E1 Saunders Honda Stadium Flints
141 H5 Saunderton railway station Bucks
60 B4 Saunton Golf Club Devon
35 d3 Sausmarez Manor Guern
117 G5 Savill Garden Surrey
254 C3 Saxon Cathedral Norfk
50 D2 Saxon Wharf C Sotn
377 G3 Scafell Pike Cumb
374 C1 Scalby Close Park campsite N York
374 C2 Scarborough Cricket Club N York
374 C1 Scarborough North Cliff Golf Club N York
374 C2 Scarborough South Cliff Golf Club N York
343 G1 Scarcroft Golf Club Leeds
344 B2 Scarthingwell Golf Club N York
606 E3 Scatsta airport Shet
467 F2 Science Centre C Glas
484 A6 Scitstoun Stadium C Glas
151 G5 Scolton Country Park Pembks
512 D4 Scone Palace P & K
502 B3 Scoonie golf course Fife
383 F4 Scotch Corner Caravan Park N York
383 F3 Scotch Corner service area N York
389 F5 Scotgate Holiday Park Cumb
503 F3 Scotland's Secret Bunker Fife
467 H3 Scotland's Theme Park (Motherwell) N Lans
79 F2 Scotney Castle NT Kent
588 D5 Scotscalder railway station Highld
514 D4 Scotscraig Golf Club Fife
501 G2 Scotstarvit Tower NTS Fife
483 H6 Scotstounhill railway station C Glas
501 F2 Scottish Deer Centre Fife
444 D2 Scottish Maritime museum N Ayrs
471 F2 Scottish Mining Museum Mdloth
514 C4 Scottish National Golf Centre Fife
498 C5 Scottish National Tennis Centre Stirlg
489 H2 Scottish Seabird Visitor Centre E Loth
145 E2 Scott's Grotto Herts
452 A3 Scott's View Border
474 D1 Scoutscroft Holiday Centre Border
240 D3 Scraptoft Golf Club Leics
251 F1 Scratby Hall Caravan Park Norfk
526 C6 Sculptured Stone museum P & K
528 B3 Sculptured Stones Angus
121 E4 Ship Lane Football Ground Thurr
259 H5 Sculthorpe airfield Norfk
32 A3 Sea Barn Farm campsite Dorset
188 B5 Seaborne Leisure Marina Worcs
376 B2 Seacote Park campsite Cumb
261 H3 Seacroft Camping Park Norfk
301 G2 Seacroft Golf Club Lincs
56 C4 Seaford Golf Club E Susx
56 D5 Seaford Head golf course E Susx
323 F5 Seaforth & Litherland railway station Sefton
406 C5 Seaham Golf Club Dur
455 G3 Seahouses Golf Club Nthumb
4 D3 Seal Sanctuary (Gweek) Cnwll
374 C3 Seamer railway station N York
566 B7 Seaport Marina Highld
258 D4 Searles Leisure Resort golf course Norfk
376 C4 Seascale Golf Club Cumb
396 D4 Seaton Carew Golf Club Hartpl
28 D4 Seaton Tramway Devon
2 C4 Sea View Holiday Park Cnwll
32 C3 Seaview Holiday Park Dorset
100 B2 Seaview Holiday Village Kent
8 B5 Sea View International Caravan & Camping Park Cnwll
412 C4 Seaward Caravan Park D & G
304 B2 Seawatch Centre IoA
20 D2 Seaway Touring Park Devon
202 A5 Seckford Golf Centre Suffk
138 A5 Second Chance Touring Park Wilts
290 C5 Secret Bunker (Nantwich) Ches
2 C3 Secret Garden Caravan & Camping Park Cnwll
84 B5 Secret World Wildlife Rescue Centre Somset
366 D1 Sedbergh Golf Club Cumb
395 G4 Sedgefield racecourse Dur
84 C4 Sedgemoor service area Somset
212 C1 Sedgley Golf Centre Staffs
58 C4 Sedlescombe Golf Club E Susx
237 H2 Seedy Mill Golf Club Staffs
283 E3 Segontium NT Roman site Gwynd
344 D4 Selby Golf Club N York
119 G6 Selhurst Park Gt Lon
451 F4 Selkirk Golf Club Border
376 C4 Sellafield railway station Cumb
376 C3 Sellafield Visitor Centre Cumb
95 G2 Selsdon Park Hotel golf course Gt Lon
53 F6 Selsey Golf Club W Susx
94 B3 Semaphore Tower Surrey
82 C3 Sene Valley Golf Club Kent
316 B2 Serlby Park golf course Notts
489 E4 Seton Sands Holiday Village E Loth
353 G1 Settle Golf Club N York
86 D6 Seven Acres Caravan & Camping Site Somset
57 E5 Seven Sisters Country Park E Susx
119 G2 Seven Sisters railway station Gt Lon
235 F3 Severn Gorge Park Wrekin
109 E2 Severn Tunnel Junction railway station Mons

211 H3 Seven Valley Country Park Shrops
212 A4 Severn Valley Railway Worcs
109 G2 Severn View service area S Glos
131 E3 Sgwd yr Eira (Waterfall) Rhondd
93 H5 Shalford Mill NT Surrey
48 D4 Shamba Holiday Park Dorset
371 G4 Shandy Hall N York
37 F4 Shanklin Chine historic gorge IoW
37 F4 Shanklin & Sandown Golf Club IoW
379 G2 Shap Summit Cumb
295 F2 Shardaroba Caravan Park Notts
275 H3 Shardlow Marina Caravan Park Derbys
214 A4 Sharmans Cross Roads Solhll
270 C5 Shawbury airfield Shrops
326 D3 Shaw & Crompton railway station Oldham
323 G2 Shaw Hall Caravan Park Lancs
339 E5 Shaw Hill Hotel Golf & Country Club Lancs
144 A1 Shaw's Corner NT Herts
202 B2 Shawsgate vineyard Suffk
356 C3 Shaws Trailer Park N York
58 D4 Shearbarn Holiday Park E Susx
123 E5 Sheerness Golf Club Kent
315 E2 Sheffield City airfield Sheff
77 H5 Sheffield Park NT E Susx
77 G5 Sheffield Park railway station E Susx
214 B3 Sheldon Country Park Birm
197 G4 Shelford railway station Cambs
143 F4 Shendish Manor Golf Club Herts
67 G6 Sherborne Golf Club Dorset
324 C6 Sherdley Park golf course St Hel
261 F3 Sheringham Golf Club Norfk
261 F3 Sheringham Park NT Norfk
296 A4 Sherwood Forest Notts
316 B6 Sherwood Forest Country Park Notts
296 A2 Sherwood Forest Golf Club Notts
296 B2 Sherwood Pines Forest Park Notts
605 H2 Shetland Golf Club Shet
342 B4 Shibden Hall Calder
475 E4 Shielfield Park Stadium Nthumb
506 B2 Shieling Holidays campsite Ag & B
235 G3 Shifnal Golf Club Shrops
54 B4 Ship & Anchor Marina W Susx
54 B4 Ship & Anchor Marina campsite W Susx
121 E4 Ship Lane Football Ground Thurr
295 E6 Shipley Country Park Derbys
342 B2 Shipley Golf Club Brad
222 C3 Shippea Hill railway station Cambs
163 F6 Shipton golf course Gloucs
210 D1 Shipton Hall Shrops
164 B2 Shipton railway station Oxon
109 F4 Shirehampton Park Golf Club Bristl
387 H5 Shire Horse Centre N York
294 D3 Shirland Golf Club Derbys
214 A4 Shirley Golf Club Solhll
95 G1 Shirley Park Golf Club Gt Lon
213 G4 Shirley railway station Solhll
460 B4 Shiskine Golf Club N Ayrs
120 B4 Shooters Hill Golf Club Gt Lon
55 E3 Shoreham airport W Susx
121 G5 Shorne Wood Country Park Kent
140 C3 Shotover Hill Country Park Oxon
308 D6 Shotton High Level railway station Flints
468 D2 Shotts Golf Club N Lans
234 B3 Shrewsbury Golf Club Shrops
312 B3 Shrigley Hall Hotel Golf & Country Club Ches
113 F1 Shrivenham Park Golf Club Oxon
210 A3 Shropshire Hills Discovery Centre Shrops
29 E4 Shrubbery Touring Park Devon
273 E5 Shugborough NT Staffs
29 E3 Shute Barton NT Devon
195 H6 Shuttleworth Airfield (Old Warden) Beds
195 H6 Shuttleworth Collection museum Beds
300 B4 Sibsey Trader Windmill Lincs
313 H3 Sickleholme Golf Club Derbys
120 C5 Sidcup Golf Club Gt Lon
514 A2 Sidlaw Hills P & K
28 B5 Sidmouth Golf Club Devon
112 C6 Silbury Hill earth mound Wilts
240 C1 Sileby Mill Boatyard Leics
362 C5 Silecroft Golf Club Cumb
329 E3 Silkstone Golf Club Barns
398 D4 Silloth on Solway Golf Club Cumb
355 E5 Silsden Golf Club Brad
7 E3 Silverbow Park campsite Cnwll
412 C4 Silvercraigs Caravan & Camping Site D & G
322 d8 Silverdale Glen IoM
365 G6 Silverdale Golf Club Lancs
487 G4 Silverknowes golf course C Edin
94 B2 Silvermere Golf Club Surrey
4 D5 Silver Sands Holiday Park Cnwll
568 C1 Silver Sands Leisure Park Moray
167 E3 Silverstone Bucks
167 E1 Silverstone golf course Bucks
144 D6 Silver Street railway station Gt Lon
318 B5 Sincil Bank football ground Lincs
275 F3 Sinfin golf course C Derb
483 G5 Singer railway station N Duns
55 G1 Singing Hills golf course W Susx

110 C5 Sir Bevil Grenville's Monument 1643 BaNES
80 B2 Sissinghurst NT Kent
99 E1 Sittingbourne & Kemsley Light Railway Kent
98 C2 Sittingbourne & Milton Regis Golf Club Kent
98 D2 Sittingbourne Viaduct railway station Kent
315 F1 Sitwell Park Golf Club Rothm
193 F2 Sixfields Nhants
276 D5 Six Hills Golf Club Leics
188 C3 Sixways Stadium Worcs
365 G2 Sizergh Castle NT Cumb
602 A8 Skara Brae neolithic village Ork
301 G1 Skegness (Ingoldmells) aerodrome Lincs
482 B6 Skelmorlie Golf Club N Ayrs
378 C4 Skelwith Fold Caravan Park Cumb
160 B5 Skenfrith Castle NT Mons
463 F3 Skipness Castle Ag & B
354 C4 Skipton Golf Club N York
4 C4 Skyburriowe Farm campsite Cnwll
215 E4 Skydome Arena Covtry
542 F2 Skye Museum of Island Life Highld
561 H2 Slains Castle Abers
471 E2 Slatebarns Caravan Club Site Mdloth
298 C6 Sleaford Golf Club Lincs
360 A2 Sledmere House E R Yk
370 B4 Sleningford Water Mill Caravan & Camping Park N York
76 A3 Slinfold Park Golf & Country Club W Susx
550 E4 Slioch Summit Highld
117 G4 Slough Ice Arena Slough
452 B3 Smailholm Tower Border
37 F2 Smallbrook Junction railway station IoW
37 F2 Smallbrook Stadium IoW
80 C4 Smallhythe Place NT Kent
213 F2 Smethwick Rolfe Street railway station Sandw
95 G3 Smitham (for Coulsdon) railway station Gt Lon
325 F2 Smithills Hall Bolton
585 H3 Smoo Cave Highld
322 g5 Snaefell Mountain Railway IoM
327 G6 Snake Pass Derbys
114 D5 Snelsmore Common W Berk
224 D2 Snetterton Race Circuit Norfk
239 G2 Snibston Discovery Park museum Leics
320 B6 Snipe Dales Country Park Lincs
284 D4 Snowdon Gwynd
266 C3 Snowdonia National Park
284 C3 Snowdon Mountain Railway Gwynd
284 C3 Snowdon Ranger railway station Gwynd
163 G3 Snowshill Manor NT Gloucs
35 E2 Solent Meads Golf Centre Bmouth
214 A3 Solihull Ice Rink Solhll
313 E5 Solomon's Temple Derbys
401 E2 Solway Aviation museum Cumb
169 G5 Someries Castle Beds
251 F5 Somerleyton Hall & Gardens Suffk
44 A2 Somerset County Ground Somset
444 D5 Somerset Park S Ayrs
65 E5 Somerset View Caravan Park Somset
116 C5 Sonning Golf Club Wokham
106 C4 Sophia Gardens Cricket Ground Cardif
432 B3 Souter Johnnie's Cottage NTS S Ayrs
406 C2 Souter Lighthouse NT S Tyne
51 E1 Southampton airport Hants
50 D1 Southampton Airport Parkway railway station Hants
50 D1 Southampton Municipal golf course Hants
169 F4 South Beds Golf Club Luton
119 G4 South Bermondsey railway station Gt Lon
342 C4 South Bradford Golf Club Brad
144 D5 Southbury railway station Gt Lon
125 E2 South Cockett Caravan & Camping Park Pembks
19 H5 South Devon Railway Devon
73 G6 South Downs Hants
52 D2 South Downs National Park (proposed area)
57 E5 South Downs Way E Susx
72 D4 South Downs Way Hants
53 E1 South Downs Way W Susx
122 C3 Southend airport Essex
350 B2 South End Caravan Park Cumb
122 D2 Southend East railway station Sthend
122 C3 Southend-on-Sea Cricket Club Sthend
122 D2 Southend Victoria railway station Sthend
104 D4 Southerndown Golf Club V Glam
398 B4 Southerness Golf Club D & G
398 B4 Southerness Holiday Village D & G
450 D3 Southern Upland Way Border
414 C5 Southern Upland Way D & G
436 C3 Southern Upland Way S Lans
121 G5 Southern Valley golf course Kent
347 E5 South Ferriby Marina N Linc
140 B3 Southfield Golf Club Oxon
66 C6 Southfork Caravan Park Somset
144 C6 Southgate Cricket Club Gt Lon
161 E4 South Herefordshire Golf Club Herefs
144 C6 South Herts Golf Club Gt Lon
118 D2 South Kenton railway station Gt Lon
299 F5 South Kyme Golf Club Lincs
364 B4 South Lakes Animal Park Cumb
37 E4 Southland Camping Park IoW
343 F4 South Leeds Golf Club Leeds
343 F4 South Leeds Stadium Leeds
7 H1 Southleigh Manor Tourist Park Cnwll

48 B6 **South Lytchett Manor Caravan Park** Dorset
144 B4 **South Mimms service area** Herts
405 E4 **South Moor Golf Club** Dur
81 E3 **South of England Rare Breeds Centre** Kent
77 F3 **South of England showground** W Susx
125 G4 **South Pembrokeshire Golf Club** Pembks
15 F4 **South Penquite Farm campsite** Cnwll
323 F2 **Southport & Ainsdale Golf Club** Sefton
337 F6 **Southport Municipal Golf Club** Sefton
337 G6 **Southport Old Links Golf Club** Sefton
406 B2 **South Shields Golf Club** S Tyne
45 G5 **South Somerset cycle route** Somset
66 D3 **South Somerset cycle route** Somset
236 C4 **South Staffordshire Golf Club** Wolves
402 B5 **South Tynedale Railway** Nthumb
593 D11 **South Uist** W Isls
400 D5 **Southwaite service area** Cumb
296 D4 **Southwell racecourse** Notts
3 E5 **South West Coast Path** Cnwll
7 G6 **South West Coast Path** Cnwll
15 E2 **South West Coast Path** Cnwll
11 F4 **South West Coast Path** Devon
38 C2 **South West Coast Path** Devon
29 G4 **South West Coast Path** Dorset
63 E2 **South West Coast Path** Somset
87 E3 **Southwick Country Park** Wilts
52 A3 **Southwick Park Naval Recreation Centre golf course** Hants
72 B4 **South Winchester Golf Club** Hants
14 C3 **South Winds Caravan & Camping Park** Cnwll
227 F4 **Southwold Golf Club** Suffk
92 D4 **Southwood golf course** Hants
472 B3 **Soutra Summit** Border
57 G4 **Sovereign Harbour Marina** E Susx
371 E4 **Sowerby Caravan Park** N York
280 C4 **Spalding Golf Club** Lincs
280 B4 **Spalding Tropical Forest** Lincs
72 B6 **Sparshatts Stadium** Hants
78 C2 **Spa Valley Railway** E Susx
93 H4 **Spectrum Leisure Centre** Surrey
313 F3 **Speedwell Cavern** Derbys
309 F3 **Speke Hall NT** Lpool
568 F3 **Spey Bay golf course** Moray
552 D1 **Speyside Way** Moray
52 A5 **Spinnaker Tower** C Port
50 B5 **Spinners Garden** Hants
25 H4 **Spinster's Rock** Devon
52 A5 **Spitbank Fort** C Port
101 F2 **Spitfire & Hurricane Memorial museum** Kent
326 C2 **Spotland Stadium** Rochdl
280 C5 **Springfields Gardens** Lincs
48 B5 **Springfield Touring Park** Dorset
347 F3 **Springhead Park Golf Club (Municipal)** E R Yk
213 H3 **Spring Road railway station** Birm
296 B5 **Springwater Golf Club** Notts
181 F6 **Springwater Lakes campsite** Carmth
374 C4 **Springwood Touring Caravan Park** N York
452 D3 **Springwood Caravan Park** Border
335 F1 **Spurn Heritage Coast** E R Yk
568 C2 **Spynie Palace** Moray
96 B4 **Squerryes Court** Kent
496 C3 **SS Sir Walter Scott** Stirlg
251 E3 **Stacey Arms Windpump** Norfk
589 L2 **Stacks of Duncansby** Highld
11 E3 **Staddon Heights Golf Club** C Plym
406 B3 **Stadium of Light** Sundld
543 H3 **Staffin Camping & Caravanning** Highld
272 D5 **Stafford Castle Golf Club** Staffs
272 C3 **Stafford (northbound) service area** Staffs
273 E4 **Staffordshire County showground** Staffs
238 A3 **Staffordshire Regiment museum** Staffs
272 C3 **Stafford (southbound) service area** Staffs
378 C4 **Stagshaw NT** Cumb
295 F1 **Stainsby Mill NT** Derbys
119 F4 **Stamford Bridge** Gt Lon
327 E4 **Stamford Golf Club** Tamesd
327 F2 **Standedge Experience visitor centre** Kirk
77 G2 **Standen NT** W Susx
326 A3 **Stand Golf Club** Bury
598 E8 **Standing Stones** W Isls
324 D3 **Standish Court Golf Club** Wigan
314 C6 **Stanedge Golf Club** Derbys
606 C7 **Staneydale Temple** Shet
216 C4 **Stanford Hall** Leics
198 B1 **Stanford Park campsite** Cambs
343 G5 **Stanley Ferry Marina** Wakefd
309 F4 **Stanlow & Thornton railway station** Ches
118 D1 **Stanmore Golf Club** Gt Lon
211 G1 **Stanmore Hall Touring Park** Shrops
172 A5 *Stansted airport* Essex
276 D3 **Stanton on the Wolds Golf Club** Notts
398 D4 **Stanwix Park Holiday Centre** Cumb
290 D4 **Stapeley Water Gardens** Ches
145 H6 **Stapleford Abbotts Golf Club** Essex
277 H6 **Stapleford Park golf course** Leics
109 H5 **Stapleton Road railway station** Bristl
488 B1 **Stark's Park** Fife
527 G4 **Station Park** Angus
566 F5 **Station Park** Highld
275 F5 **Staunton Harold NT** Leics

192 B2 **Staverton Park Golf Club** Nhants
225 E3 **Steam Museum & Gardens** Norfk
378 B5 **Steam Yacht 'Gondola' NT** Cumb
128 D4 **Stebonheath Park** Carmth
344 B3 **Steeton Hall Gatehouse** N York
354 D6 **Steeton & Silsden railway station** Brad
599 H4 **Steinacleit Cairn & Stone Circle** W Isls
66 C3 **Stembridge Tower Mill NT** Somset
16 C4 **Sterts Open-Air Theatre** Cnwll
170 C5 **Stevenage Golf Centre** Herts
195 E6 **Stewartby Lake Country Park** Beds
35 H3 **Stoats Farm campsite** IoW
146 D5 **Stinchcombe Hill Golf Club** Gloucs
498 B6 **Stirling Golf Club** Stirlg
485 F2 **Stirling service area** Stirlg
35 H3 **Stoats Farm campsite** IoW
146 D5 **Stock Brook Golf & Country Club** Essex
118 B3 **Stockley Park Golf Club** Gt Lon
312 B2 **Stockport Golf Club** Stockp
328 D5 **Stocksbridge & District Golf Club** Sheff
404 C3 **Stocksfield Golf Club** Nthumb
142 D2 **Stocks Hotel & Golf Club** Herts
328 B2 **Stocksmoor railway station** Kirk
396 B6 **Stockton Cricket Club** S on T
169 F6 **Stockwood museum** Luton
169 F6 **Stockwood Park Golf Club** Luton
110 A6 **Stockwood Vale Golf Club** BaNES
217 G2 **Stoke Albany golf course** Nhants
174 C2 **Stoke by Nayland Golf Club** Suffk
117 G3 **Stoke Park Golf Club** Bucks
193 F5 **Stoke Park Pavilions** Nhants
278 C4 **Stoke Rochford Golf Club** Lincs
278 C4 **Stoke Rochford Hall** Lincs
210 A3 **Stokesay Castle** Shrops
214 C3 **Stonebridge Golf Club** Solhll
121 F5 **Stonebridge Road football ground** Kent
112 D5 **Stone Circle NT** Wilts
79 F4 **Stonegate railway station** E Susx
272 C3 **Stone Golf Club** Staffs
50 D1 **Stoneham Golf Club** C Sotn
541 G2 **Stonehaven Golf Club** Abers
70 C1 **Stonehenge (UNESCO)** Wilts
88 C5 **Stonehenge Touring Park** Wilts
215 E5 **Stoneleigh Abbey** Warwks
215 E5 **Stoneleigh Deer Park Golf Club** Warwks
51 E3 **Stone Pier Yard Marina** Hants
18 C3 **Stone Rows & Circle** Devon
86 C3 **Stoney Littleton Long Barrow** BaNES
116 B2 **Stonor Park** Oxon
400 D3 **Stony Holme Municipal Golf Club** Cumb
112 D5 **Stonegate railway station** E Susx
68 C3 **Stourhead NT** Wilts
212 B6 **Stourport Marina** Worcs
68 C3 **Stourton House** Wilts
20 A2 **Stover Country Park** Devon
167 E2 **Stowe Gardens NT** Bucks
167 E2 **Stowe School Cricket Ground** Bucks
61 E3 **Stowford Farm Meadows campsite** Devon
87 E3 **Stowford Manor Farm campsite** Wilts
200 D3 **Stowmarket Golf Club** Suffk
256 C2 **Stow Mill windmill** Norfk
528 D1 **Stracathro service area** Angus
251 E3 **Stracey Arms Windpump** Norfk
128 C4 **Stradey Park** Carmth
414 D4 **Stranraer Golf Club** D & G
92 A2 **Stratfield Saye House** Hants
190 B3 **Stratford Oaks golf course** Warwks
190 C4 **Stratford-upon-Avon Butterfly Farm** Warwks
190 C4 **Stratford-upon-Avon Cricket Club** Warwks
190 C3 **Stratford-upon-Avon Golf Club** Warwks
190 B4 **Stratford-upon-Avon racecourse** Warwks
498 C3 **Strathallan** Stirlg
467 G5 **Strathaven Golf Club** S Lans
468 A3 **Strathclyde Country Park** N Lans
467 H3 **Strathclyde Country Park Camping & Caravan** N Lans
483 F5 **Strathclyde Homes Stadium** W Duns
467 H3 **Strathclyde Park Golf Club** S Lans
483 G2 **Strathendrick Golf Club** Stirlg
569 G5 **Strathisla Distillery** Moray
569 G2 **Strathlene Golf Club** Moray
526 B5 **Strathmore Golf Centre** P & K
565 H5 **Strathpeffer Spa Golf Club** Highld
551 L2 **Strathspey** Highld
551 G6 **Strathspey Railway** Highld
524 D5 **Strathtay Golf Club** P & K
395 G1 **Strawberry Hill Farm Camping & Caravan Park** Dur
118 D5 **Strawberry Hill Golf Club** Gt Lon
162 C1 **Strensham (northbound) service area** Worcs
162 D1 **Strensham (southbound) service area** Worcs
383 G2 **Stressholme Golf Club** Darltn
546 F2 **Strome Castle NTS** Highld
600 C3 **Stromness Golf Club** Ork
220 D4 **Stroud Hill Park campsite** Cambs
370 B6 **Studley Royal Park (UNESCO)** N York
140 C2 **Studley Wood Golf Club** Oxon
355 E2 **Stump Cross Caverns** N York

317 G2 *Sturgate airfield* Lincs
47 H4 **Sturminster Marshall Golf Course** Dorset
311 G3 **Styal Golf Club** Ches
311 G3 **Styal NT** Ches
2 C5 **Submarine Telegraphy museum** Cnwll
298 B6 **Sudbrook Moor Golf Club** Lincs
118 D3 **Sudbury Golf Club** Gt Lon
274 B3 **Sudbury Hall NT** Derbys
163 F4 **Sudeley Castle** Gloucs
567 K5 **Sueno's Stone** Moray
199 G5 **Sue Ryder Foundation museum** Suffk
227 F6 **Suffolk Coastal cycle route** Suffk
201 F3 **Suffolk Owl Sanctuary** Suffk
176 D1 **Suffolk showground** Suffk
227 G2 **Suffolk Wildlife Park** Suffk
182 C6 **Sugar Loaf railway station** Powys
605 G8 *Sumburgh airport* Shet
184 D6 **Summerhill golf course** Herefs
468 A1 **Summerlee Heritage Trust** N Lans
7 G1 **Summer Lodge Holiday Park** Cnwll
7 E4 **Summer Valley campsite** Cnwll
284 D4 **Summit railway station** Gwynd
76 B4 **Sumners Ponds Fishery & campsite** W Susx
519 K2 **Sunart** Highld
118 B6 **Sunbury Golf Centre** Surrey
169 F4 **Sundon Hills Country Park** Beds
317 E4 **Sundown Adventureland** Notts
120 B5 **Sundridge Park Golf Club** Gt Lon
445 E2 **Sundrum Castle Holiday Park** S Ayrs
14 B5 **Sun Haven Valley Holiday Park** Cnwll
93 G5 **Sunningdale Golf Club** W & M
93 F1 **Sunningdale Ladies Golf Club** Surrey
61 H2 **Sunny Lyn Holiday Park** Devon
7 E3 **Sunny Meadows Tourist Park** Cnwll
487 G5 **Suntrap Garden** C Edin
8 C4 **Sun Valley Holiday Park** Cnwll
94 D2 **Surbiton Golf Club** Surrey
95 F3 **Surrey Downs Golf Club** Surrey
95 G3 **Surrey National Golf Club** Surrey
55 G3 **Sussex County Cricket Ground** Br & H
281 G5 **Sutton Bridge Golf Club** Lincs
237 G5 **Sutton Coldfield Golf Club** Birm
95 F1 **Sutton Common railway station** Gt Lon
93 G3 **Sutton Green Golf Club** Surrey
310 A4 **Sutton Hall golf course** Ches
202 B5 **Sutton Hoo NT** Suffk
348 B3 **Sutton Park Golf Club** C KuH
358 A2 **Sutton Park House** N York
295 G3 **Sutton Parkway railway station** Notts
315 E6 **Sutton Scarsdale Hall** Derbys
247 G3 **Swaffham Golf Club** Norfk
381 H5 **Swaledale** N York
99 F2 **Swale Marina** Kent
123 E6 **Swale railway station** Kent
383 E4 **Swale View Caravan Park** N York
358 C5 **Swallow Hall golf course** York
223 G6 **Swallow Suffolk Hotel Golf & Country Club** Suffk
34 B5 **Swanage Coastal Park campsite** Dorset
34 A5 **Swanage Railway** Dorset
103 E3 *Swansea airport* Swans
103 H3 **Swansea Bay Golf Club** Neath
129 F5 **Swansea West service area** Swans
470 D1 **Swanston Golf Club** C Edin
295 E4 **Swanwick Junction railway station** Derbys
443 E4 **Swarland Hall golf course** Nthumb
479 J6 **Sween Castle** Ag & B
398 B1 **Sweetheart Abbey** D & G
78 B2 **Sweetwoods Park golf course** E Susx
112 D1 **Swindon & Cricklade Railway** Wilts
212 B1 **Swindon Golf Club** Staffs
112 C3 **Swindon loop cycle route** Wilts
299 G6 **Swineshead railway station** Lincs
93 F1 **Swinley Forest Golf Club** Br For
362 D4 **Swinside Stone Circle** Cumb
326 A4 **Swinton (Greater Manchester) railway station** Salfd
326 A4 **Swinton Park Golf Club** Salfd
116 C3 **Swiss Farm International Camping** Oxon
195 H6 **Swiss Garden** Beds
284 D5 **Sygun Copper Mine** Gwynd
378 D2 **Sykeside Camping Park** Cumb
232 C3 **Sylfaen Halt railway station** Powys
134 D1 **Symonds Yat Caravan & Camping Park** Herefs
118 D4 **Syon House** Gt Lon
118 D4 **Syon Lane railway station** Gt Lon
27 F3 *Sywell airfield* Nhants
194 A1 **Sywell Reservoir** Nhants

311 E4 **Tabley house** Ches
166 A5 **Tackley railway station** Oxon
165 F2 **Tadmarton Heath Golf Club** Oxon
577 G2 **Tain Golf Club** Highld
104 B2 **Talbot Athletic Ground** Neath
401 F3 **Talkin Tarn Country Park** Cumb
9 G3 **Talland Caravan Park** Cnwll
85 E1 **Tall Pines Golf Club** N Som
229 E4 **Tal-y-Llyn Railway** Gwynd
23 F5 **Tamar Otter Sanctuary** Cnwll

17 F5 **Tamar Valley Mining District (UNESCO)** Cnwll
237 F6 **Tame Bridge Parkway railway station** Sandw
238 C5 **Tame View Caravan Site** Warwks
238 C4 **Tamworth Municipal golf course** Warwks
238 C4 **Tamworth service area** Staffs
326 D3 **Tandle Hill** Oldham
96 A4 **Tandridge Golf Club** Surrey
405 F3 **Tanfield Railway** Dur
399 E4 **Tanglewood Caravan Park** Cumb
606 B2 **Tangwick museum** Shet
329 E5 **Tankersley Park Golf Club** Barns
514 C3 **Tannadice Park** C Dund
490 A2 **Tantallon Castle** E Loth
265 F1 **Tan-y-Bwlch railway station** Gwynd
265 F1 **Tan-y-Bwlch study centre** Gwynd
39 G2 **Tapeley Park** Devon
314 D5 **Tapton Park Golf Club** Derbys
462 D1 **Tarbert Golf Club** Ag & B
60 D5 **Tarka Holiday Park** Devon
555 E4 **Tarland Golf Club** Abers
62 D5 **Tarr Steps** Somset
95 E3 **Tattenham Corner railway station** Surrey
299 G3 **Tattershall Castle NT** Lincs
299 G3 **Tattershall College** Lincs
311 E3 **Tatton Park NT** Ches
43 G3 **Taunton Deane service area** Somset
44 A4 **Taunton & Pickeridge Golf Club** Somset
44 A3 **Taunton racecourse** Somset
44 B2 **Taunton Vale Golf Club** Somset
17 G4 **Tavistock Golf Club** Devon
523 G4 **Tay Forest Park** P & K
523 L6 **Taymouth Castle** P & K
514 C2 **Tealing Dovecot** Angus
514 C2 **Tealing Earth-House** Angus
379 G3 **Tebay Caravan Site** Cumb
379 H3 **Tebay service area** Cumb
393 F4 **Teesdale** Dur
396 C6 **Teesside Golf Club** S on T
312 B5 **Tegg's Nose Country Park** Ches
6 B5 **Tehidy Country Park** Cnwll
6 C5 **Tehidy Holiday Park** Cnwll
6 C5 **Tehidy Park Golf Club** Cnwll
153 H1 **Teifi Valley Railway** Cerdgn
20 C3 **Teignmouth Golf Club** Devon
26 C6 **Teign Valley Golf Club** Devon
235 G4 **Telford Golf & Country Club** Wrekin
235 F3 **Telford Ice Rink** Wrekin
235 G3 **Telford service area** Shrops
116 D3 **Temple Golf Club** W & M
116 D3 **Temple Marina** Bucks
343 F3 **Temple-Newsam Golf Club** Leeds
343 G3 **Temple Newsam house** Leeds
492 D5 **Temple Wood Stone Circle** Ag & B
58 C4 **Ten 66 Golf Club** E Susx
126 C4 **Tenby Golf Club** Pembks
9 G3 **Tencreek Holiday Park** Cnwll
80 C3 **Tenterden Golf Club** Kent
80 C3 **Tenterden Town railway station** Kent
80 C3 **Tenterden Vineyard Park** Kent
515 E5 **Tentsmuir Point campsite** Fife
91 E5 **Test Valley Golf Club** Hants
343 E5 **Tetley's Stadium** Kirk
334 D4 **Tetney Golf Club** Lincs
439 E2 **Teviotdale** Border
452 D4 **Teviot Water Gardens** Border
162 C3 **Tewkesbury Park Hotel Golf & Country Club** Gloucs
340 B5 **Textiles Museum** Lancs
116 B4 **Thames and Kennet Marina** Oxon
120 B4 **Thames Barrier** Gt Lon
94 C1 **Thames Ditton & Esher Golf Club** Surrey
118 D4 **Thames Path** Gt Lon
139 H3 **Thames Path** Oxon
140 B6 **Thames Path** Oxon
137 H6 **Thames Path** Wilts
120 C3 **Thamesview Golf Centre** Gt Lon
95 H2 **The Addington Golf Club** Gt Lon
369 H3 **Theakston Brewery** N York
119 E5 **The All England Lawn Tennis & Croquet Club** Gt Lon
526 C5 **The Alyth Golf Club** P & K
47 H3 **The Ashley Wood Golf Club** Dorset
239 F4 **The Battlefield Line** Leics
195 E5 **The Bedford Golf Club** Beds
185 H2 **The Beeches Touring Caravan Site** Herefs
184 C6 **The Begwns NT** Powys
455 E3 **The Belford Golf Club** Nthumb
559 F5 **The Bennachie Centre** Abers
93 E1 **The Berkshire Golf Club** Br For
39 F2 **The Big Sheep animal centre** Devon
213 E5 **The Blackwell Golf Club** Worcs
220 D5 **The Boathaven** Cambs
95 G3 **The Borough Sports Ground** Gt Lon
105 E3 **The Brewery Field** Brdgnd
251 F3 **The Broads** Norfk
602 A6 **The Brough of Birsay** Ork
142 A3 **The Bucks Goat Centre** Bucks
146 D6 **The Burstead Golf Club** Essex
326 D5 **The Butchers Arms** Tamesd
82 D2 **The Butterfly Centre** Kent
381 F5 **The Buttertubs** N York
27 F3 **The Buzzard cycle route** Devon
537 H7 **The Cairnwell** P & K
14 D4 **The Camel Trail cycle route** Cnwll
91 G4 **The Camrose** Hants
374 B3 **The Carrs** N York
48 C5 **The Castleman Trailway cycle route** Poole
108 C1 **The Celtic Manor Resort golf course** Newpt
128 A4 **The Celtic Trail cycle route** Carmth
125 F3 **The Celtic Trail cycle route** Pembks
131 F5 **The Celtic Trail cycle route** Rhondd
53 F2 **The Centurion Way cycle route** W Susx
237 E2 **The Chase Golf Club** Staffs

440 D3 **The Cheviot Hills** Border
309 F2 **The Childwall Golf Club** Lpool
116 A4 **The Club at Mapledurham golf course** Oxon
34 C2 **The Club at Meyrick Park golf course** Bmouth
26 D4 **The County Ground** Devon
87 F2 **The Courts NT** Wilts
523 L7 **The Crannog Centre museum** P & K
274 C4 **The Craythorne golf course** Staffs
19 H3 **The Dartmoor Halfway Caravan Park** Devon
200 B2 **The Dell Touring & Caravan Park** Suffk
119 H4 **The Den** Gt Lon
238 B5 **The De Vere Belfry golf course** Warwks
28 C5 **The Donkey Sanctuary** Devon
33 F1 **The Dorset Golf & Country Club** Dorset
75 G1 **The Downs Link cycle route** Surrey
56 C3 **The Dripping Pan** E Susx
423 G4 **The Dumfries & County Golf Club** D & G
37 G3 **The Duver NT** IoW
330 C4 **The Earth Stadium** Donc
145 G4 **The Epping golf course** Essex
173 G4 **The Essex Golf & Country Club** Essex
212 C4 **The Falconry Centre** Worcs
189 G6 **The Fleece Inn NT** Worcs
259 C5 **The Garden Caravan Site** Norfk
13 F2 **The Garden House** Devon
17 G5 **The Garden House** Devon
35 h6 **The German War Tunnels** Jersey
31 F2 **The Giant Cerne Abbas chalk figure** Dorset
197 F2 **The Glassworld Stadium** Cambs
421 F2 **The Glenkens** D & G
110 C5 **The Gloucestershire golf course** S Glos
601 K3 **The Gloup** Ork
130 B5 **The Gnoll** Neath
197 G4 **The Gog Magog Golf Club** Cambs
73 E2 **The Grange** Hants
233 G6 **The Green Caravan Park** Shrops
244 B4 **The Green Wheel cycle route** C Pete
283 F3 **The Greenwood Centre** Gwynd
143 F5 **The Grove golf course** Herts
371 F2 **The Hambleton Hills** N York
213 F1 **The Hawthorns** Sandw
116 B3 **The Herb Farm** Oxon
512 B1 **The Hermitage NTS** P & K
337 F6 **The Hesketh Golf Club** Sefton
74 D2 **The Hindhead Golf Club** Surrey
453 F1 **The Hirsel Country Park** Border
122 B6 **The Historic Dockyard Chatham** Medway
489 F3 **The Honourable Company of Edinburgh Golfers** E Loth
487 E4 **The House of the Binns NTS** W Loth
16 C4 **The Hurlers Stone Circle** Cnwll
47 G4 **The Inside Park campsite** Dorset
160 D6 **The Jubilee Park** Herefs
185 F2 **The Judge's Lodging** Herefs
334 D3 **The Jungle** NE Lin
344 A4 **The Jungle rugby ground** Wakefd
110 B4 **The Kendleshire golf course** S Glos
454 A2 **The Lady Waterford Hall museum** Nthumb
213 H5 **The Lakes (Warwickshire) railway station** Warwks
238 C4 **The Lamb Ground** Staffs
117 F2 **The Lambourne Club** Bucks
14 C4 **The Laurels Holiday Park** Cnwll
136 B5 **The Lawn** Gloucs
240 D4 **The Leicestershire Golf Club** C Leic
331 G2 **The Lincolnshire golf course** N Linc
112 D3 **The Link Centre** Swindn
35 g6 **The Living Legend** Jersey
115 E4 **The Living Rainforest** W Berk
97 E2 **The London Golf Club** Kent
57 E4 **The Long Man of Wilmington chalk figure** E Susx
8 B4 **The Lost Gardens of Heligan** Cnwll
416 D6 **The Machars** D & G
444 D2 **The Magnum Leisure Centre** N Ayrs
202 D3 **The Maltings** Suffk
111 E4 **The Manor House golf course** Wilts
70 C4 **The Medieval Hall** Wilts
109 G4 **The Memorial Stadium** Bristl
2 D5 **The Merry Maidens stone circle** Cnwll
119 E1 **The Metro Golf Centre** Gt Lon
169 E2 **The Millbrook Golf Club** Beds
161 E1 **The Millpond campsite** Herefs
20 D1 **The Model Railway** Devon
437 E4 **The Moffat Golf Club** D & G
10 A3 **The Monkey Sanctuary** Cnwll
213 H3 **The Moorlands** Birm
386 B3 **The Moors Centre** N York
566 F5 **The Nairn Golf Club** Highld
35 H3 **The Needles Park** IoW
492 D5 **The Nether Largie Cairns** Ag & B
103 G2 **The New Stadium** Swans
248 D3 **The Norfolk Golf & Country Club** Norfk
317 F1 **The Northolme** Lincs
476 E8 **The Oa** Ag & B
345 G2 **The Oaks Golf Club** E R Yk
84 B5 **The Oak Tree Arena** Somset
99 E2 **The Oast golf course** Kent
145 E4 **Theobalds Grove railway station** Herts
28 C5 **The Old Bakery NT museum** Devon
260 D5 **The Old Brick Kilns campsite** Norfk
60 D2 **The Old Corn Mill** Devon
67 E2 **The Old Oaks Touring Park** Somset
377 E4 **The Old Post Office Campsite** Cumb
233 F5 **The Old School Caravan Park** Shrops
56 C4 **The Old Shipyard** E Susx
237 E2 **The Otter Trust** Suffk

226 C2 The Otter Trust Suffk
119 G4 The Oval Gt Lon
283 E3 The Oval Gwynd
141 E4 The Oxfordshire Golf Club Oxon
584 E3 The Parph Highld
484 A6 The Pavilion C Glas
326 A5 The Pavilion Salfd
299 E6 The Pearoom craft centre Lincs
354 B5 The Pennines N York
188 D5 The Pershore to Worcester cycle route Worcs
486 A2 The Pineapple NTS Falk
288 D5 The Plassey Leisure Park campsite Wrexhm
110 C4 The Players golf course S Glos
18 C3 The Plume of Feathers Inn campsite Devon
375 F6 The Poplars Touring Park E R Yk
162 D2 The Priory Worcs
119 E4 The Queen's Club Gt Lon
390 C5 The Quiet Site campsite Cumb
288 D4 The Racecourse Ground Wrexhm
345 F3 The Ranch Caravan Park N York
120 C5 The Red House NT Gt Lon
177 E3 The Redoubt fort Essex
414 C3 The Rhinns of Galloway D & G
118 D5 The Richmond Golf Club Gt Lon
259 F4 The Rickels Caravan & Camping Park Norfk
98 C4 The Ridge Golf Club Kent
134 B2 The Rolls of Monmouth Golf Club Mons
51 E2 The Rose Bowl Hants
452 D4 The Roxburghe golf course Border
323 F2 The Royal Birkdale Golf Club Sefton
276 B4 The Rushcliffe Golf Club Notts
112 D6 The Sanctuary (Avebury) Wilts
342 A5 The Shay Stadium Calder
260 B4 The Shrine of Our Lady Norfk
235 G2 The Shropshire Golf Centre Wrekin
57 F4 The South Downs Way cycle route E Susx
53 H2 The South Downs Way cycle route W Susx
115 G2 The Springs Hotel & Golf Club Oxon
293 E5 The Star Caravan & Camping Park Staffs
131 G2 The Taff Trail cycle route Myr Td
106 A2 The Taff Trail cycle route Rhondd
39 G2 The Tarka Trail cycle route Devon
223 G2 Thetford Forest Park
223 G3 Thetford Forest Park Norfk
328 D4 The Trans Pennine Trail cycle route Barns
315 E4 The Trans Pennine Trail cycle route Derbys
330 D2 The Trans Pennine Trail cycle route Donc
348 B3 The Trans Pennine Trail cycle route E R Yk
323 F3 The Trans Pennine Trail cycle route Lancs
310 A2 The Trans Pennine Trail cycle route Warrtn
57 G2 The Truggers E Susx
53 F2 The Trundle W Susx
312 B4 The Tytherington Club Ches
120 B4 The Valley Gt Lon
100 D2 The Viking Coastal Trail cycle route Kent
343 F1 The Village golf course Leeds
91 G3 The Vyne NT Hants
118 C4 The Warren Gt Lon
214 D6 The Warwickshire golf course Warwks
272 C2 The Wedgwood Story C Stke
160 A1 The Weir NT Herefs
153 E4 The Welsh Chocolate Farm Carmth
485 F4 The Westerwood Hotel golf course N Lans
432 A3 The Westin Turnberry Resort golf course S Ayrs
464 D5 The West Kilbride Golf Club N Ayrs
119 E4 The Wetland Centre Gt Lon
220 B5 The Willows Caravan Park Cambs
112 B3 The Wiltshire Golf & Country Club Wilts
319 G2 The Wolds (Lincolnshire) Lincs
360 B5 The Wolds (Yorkshire) E R Yk
188 A6 The Worcestershire Golf Club Worcs
235 E3 The Wrekin Wrekin
164 D5 The Wychwood Golf Club Oxon
145 F4 Theydon Bois Golf Club Essex
371 F4 Thirkleby Hall Caravan Park N York
472 C5 Thirlestane Castle Border
472 C5 Thirlestane Castle Caravan & Camping Site Border
371 E2 Thirsk & Northallerton golf course N York
371 E3 Thirsk racecourse N York
424 D5 Thomas Carlyle's Birthplace museum NTS D & G
109 H2 Thorndon Golf Centre S Glos
121 F1 Thorndon North country park Essex
121 F1 Thorndon Park Golf Club Essex
121 F1 Thorndon South country park Essex
331 E2 Thorne Golf Club Donc
331 E2 Thorne North railway station Donc
331 E2 Thorne South railway station Donc
50 D6 Thorness Bay Holiday Park IoW
244 C3 Thorney Golf Centre C Pete
66 C5 Thorney Lakes Caravan Park Somset
118 A4 Thorney Park Golf Club Bucks
46 A2 Thornford railway station Dorset
52 D4 Thornham Marina W Susx
313 E4 Thornheyes Farm Campsite Derbys
436 A5 Thornhill Golf Club D & G
330 B2 Thornhurst Park Golf Club Donc

348 B6 Thornton Abbey N Linc
347 G6 Thornton Abbey railway station N Linc
501 F5 Thornton Golf Club Fife
276 D2 Thornton's Holt Camping Park Notts
361 E1 Thorpe Hall Caravan & Camping Site E R Yk
123 E2 Thorpe Hall Golf Club Cnwll
203 F2 Thorpeness Hotel & Golf Club Suffk
118 A6 Thorpe Park Surrey
334 D3 Thorpe Park Holiday Centre NE Lin
243 H5 Thorpe Wood golf course C Pete
370 B2 Thorp Perrow arboretum N York
412 D2 Threave Castle NTS D & G
413 E2 Threave Garden NTS D & G
161 G4 Three Choirs vineyard Gloucs
188 A6 Three Counties showground Worcs
236 D3 Three Hammers Short Course Staffs
416 B3 Three Lochs Holiday Park D & G
168 B4 Three Locks Golf Club Bucks
147 G4 Three Rivers Golf & Country Club Essex
324 D4 Three Sisters Wigan
251 F2 Thrigby Hall Norfk
89 G5 Thruxton Hants
330 A5 Thrybergh Country Park Rothm
12 B4 Thurlestone Golf Club Devon
121 E4 Thurrock service area Thurr
260 C5 Thursford museum Norfk
588 E3 Thurso Caravan & Camping Site Highld
588 D3 Thurso Golf Club Highld
490 D5 Thurston Manor Holiday Home Park E Loth
295 E3 Tibshelf service area Derbys
126 A4 Tide Mill Pembks
202 B5 Tidemill Yacht Harbour Suffk
89 F5 Tidworth Garrison Golf Club Wilts
141 F3 Tiggywinkles Bucks
121 G4 Tilbury Fort Thurr
77 E3 Tilgate Forest Golf Centre W Susx
77 E2 Tilgate Park W Susx
499 E5 Tillicoultry Golf Club Clacks
168 D4 Tilsworth Golf Centre Beds
162 B1 Tiltridge vineyard Worcs
582 D6 Timespan Highld
605 H1 Tingwall airport Shet
106 A5 Tinkinswood V Glam
314 D2 Tinsley Park Municipal Golf Club Sheff
22 A5 Tintagel Castle Cnwll
134 C4 Tintern Abbey Mons
67 E6 Tintinhull NT Somset
519 G1 Tioram Castle Highld
516 C6 Tiree Ag & B
516 C7 Tiree airport Ag & B
176 D5 Titchmarsh Nature Reserve Essex
42 A5 Tiverton Golf Club Devon
42 D5 Tiverton Parkway railway station Devon
518 D4 Tobermory Golf Club Ag & B
169 E4 Toddington service area Beds
341 E4 Todmorden Golf Club Calder
243 F1 Toft Hotel Golf Club Lincs
7 F3 Tolcarne Campsite Cnwll
357 G2 Tollerton Holiday Park N York
7 E2 Tollgate Farm Caravan & Camping Park Cnwll
560 C4 Tolquhon Castle Abers
550 D4 Tomatin Distillery Visitor Centre Highld
555 E4 Tomnaverrie Stone Circle Abers
145 H4 Toot Hill Golf Club Essex
371 E4 Topcliffe airfield N York
121 F3 Top Meadow golf course Gt Lon
416 D5 Torhouse Stone Circle D & G
505 L3 Torosay Castle railway station Ag & B
470 C1 Torphin Hill Golf Club C Edin
555 H4 Torphins Golf Club Abers
20 C4 Torquay Golf Club Torbay
460 C5 Torr a Chaisteal Fort N Ayrs
467 F4 Torrance House S Lans
460 D5 Torrylin Cairn N Ayrs
565 L8 Torvean Caravan Park Highld
565 L8 Torvean Golf Club Highld
451 F2 Torwoodlee Golf Club Border
19 H5 Totnes (Littlehempston) railway station Devon
193 F5 Towcester racecourse Nhants
427 H2 Tower Knowe visitor centre Nthumb
340 C3 Towneley Golf Club Lancs
340 D3 Towneley Hall museum Lancs
378 D4 Townend NT Cumb
475 F4 Town Ramparts Nthumb
76 A3 Toyhorse International Stud Farm W Susx
94 A3 Traditions golf course Surrey
325 H5 Trafford Centre Traffd
531 J5 Traigh golf course Highld
383 H2 Train Sculpture Darltn
294 C3 Tramway museum Derbys
490 A5 Traprain Law E Loth
264 D6 Trawsdir Touring & Camping Park Gwynd
7 E1 Treago Farm Caravan Site Cnwll
313 F3 Treak Cliff Cavern Derbys
66 D6 Treasurer's House NT Somset
5 E3 Trebah gardens Cnwll
7 E2 Trebellan Park campsite Cnwll
107 E2 Tredegar House Newpt
107 E2 Tredegar Park Golf Club Newpt
132 B3 Tredegar & Rhymney Golf Club Blae G
169 E2 Tree Cathedral arboretum NT Beds
126 B4 Trefalun campsite Pembks
158 B3 Trefeinon Open Farm Powys
302 C4 Trefignath IoA
126 C4 Trefloyne golf course Pembks
285 G2 Trefriw Woollen Mill Conwy
14 B4 Tregavone Touring Park Cnwll
5 E2 Tregedna Farm Touring Caravan & Tent Park Cnwll
3 F2 Tregenna Castle Hotel Golf & Country Club Cnwll
3 G2 Treglisson Camping & Caravan Park Cnwll
9 H2 Tregoad Park campsite Cnwll

3 G3 Tregonning, Gwinear & Trewavas Mining District (UNESCO) Cnwll
9 G3 Trelay Farmpark campsite Cnwll
8 B5 Trelispen Caravan & Camping Park Cnwll
7 F6 Trelissick Garden NT Cnwll
5 G2 Treloan Coastal Farm Holidays Cnwll
14 B6 Treloy Golf Club Cnwll
14 A6 Treloy Touring Park Cnwll
7 F1 Trenance Holiday Park Cnwll
8 B4 Trencreek Farm Country Holiday Park Cnwll
7 F1 Trencreek Holiday Park Cnwll
2 D3 Trengwainton Garden NT Cnwll
276 C2 Trent Bridge Notts
144 C5 Trent Country Park Gt Lon
317 F4 Trentfield Farm campsite Notts
272 C1 Trentham Golf Club C Stke
272 C1 Trentham Park Golf Club Staffs
276 A3 Trent Lock Golf Centre Derbys
144 C5 Trent Park Golf Club Gt Lon
263 F2 Tre'r Ceiri Gwynd
7 F2 Trerice NT Cnwll
3 C2 Tresco Abbey IoS
3 C2 Tresco heliport IoS
5 F1 Trethem Mill Touring Park Cnwll
16 C5 Trethevy Quoit Cnwll
7 G2 Trethiggey Touring Park Cnwll
23 F6 Trethorne Golf Club Cnwll
23 F6 Trethorne Leisure Farm Cnwll
150 C4 Tretio Caravan & Camping Park Pembks
158 C5 Tretower Court & Castle Powys
3 E1 Trevalgan Touring Park Cnwll
4 B2 Trevarno Cnwll
14 A5 Trevarrian Holiday Park Cnwll
6 D4 Trevarth Holiday Park Cnwll
2 C3 Trevaylor Caravan & Camping Park Cnwll
8 C5 Treveague Farm Caravan & Camping Site Cnwll
14 B4 Trevean Caravan & Camping Park Cnwll
2 C4 Trevedra Farm Caravan & Camping Site Cnwll
7 F1 Trevella Tourist Park Cnwll
8 B5 Treveor Farm Caravan & Camping Site Cnwll
2 D5 Treverven Touring Caravan & Camping Park Cnwll
7 E2 Trevornick Holiday Park Cnwll
14 B4 Trevose Golf Club Cnwll
8 C3 Trewhiddle Holiday Estate Cnwll
14 C4 Trewince Farm Holiday Park Cnwll
5 G2 Trewince Farm Touring Park Cnwll
218 A3 Triangular Lodge Nhants
92 D2 Trilakes Animal Park Hants
451 H3 Trimontium museum Border
14 C3 Tristram Caravan & Camping Park Cnwll
444 D3 Troon Municipal Golf Club S Ayrs
444 D3 Troon Yacht Haven S Ayrs
239 H4 Tropical Birdland Leics
343 F2 Tropical World Leeds
97 F2 Trosley Country Park Kent
496 D5 Trossachs Holiday Park Stirlg
389 F3 Trotters World of Animals Cumb
276 A1 Trowell service area Notts
7 E4 Truro Golf Club Cnwll
322 g4 TT Circuit IoM
135 G4 Tudor Caravan & Camping Gloucs
568 F2 Tugnet Ice House museum Moray
486 B2 Tulliallan Golf Club Fife
534 C6 Tulloch railway station Highld
566 B7 Tullock Caledonian Stadium Highld
523 L4 Tummel Valley Holiday Park P & K
78 D2 Tunbridge Wells Cricket Club Kent
78 D2 Tunbridge Wells Golf Club Kent
326 D2 Tunshill Golf Club Rochdl
340 D3 Turf Moor Lancs
145 E5 Turkey Street railway station Gt Lon
487 G5 Turnhouse Golf Club C Edin
570 C6 Turriff Golf Club Abers
325 G2 Turton Golf Club Bl w D
325 G1 Turton Tower Bl w D
535 K8 Turus Tim museum Highld
274 C4 Tutbury & Hatton railway station Derbys
448 C2 Tweed Cycleway S Lans
423 F4 Twelve Apostles D & G
20 A3 Twelve Oaks Farm Caravan Park Devon
221 G5 Twenty Pence Marina Cambs
118 D5 Twickenham Stoop Gt Lon
118 D5 Twickenham Stadium Gt Lon
60 C3 Twitchen Parc campsite Devon
101 F2 Two Chimneys Caravan Park Kent
256 B4 Two Mills Touring Park Norfk
239 E3 Twycross Zoo Leics
97 G5 Twyford Bridge Marina Kent
264 B1 Tyddyn Cethin Caravan Park Gwynd
303 G3 Tyddyn Isaf Caravan Park IoA
264 B1 Tyddyn Morthwyl Camping & Caravan Site Gwynd
106 C3 Ty Glas railway station Cardif
264 D3 Tygwyn railway station Gwynd
302 D6 Ty Hen campsite IoA
92 A3 Tylney Park Golf Club Hants
269 E1 Ty Mawr Country Park Wrexhm
306 D4 Ty Mawr Holiday Park Conwy
285 G4 Ty Mawr Wybrnant NT Conwy
266 D2 Tyn Cornel Camping & Caravan Park Gwynd
508 D3 Tyndrum Lower railway station Stirlg
488 A5 Tynecastle C Edin
403 G2 Tyne Green Nthumb
33 F3 Tyneham Village museum Dorset

431 F6 Tynemouth Golf Club N Tyne
405 E1 Tyne Riverside N u Ty
431 F5 Tyneside cycle route N Tyne
404 D2 Tyneside Golf Club Gatesd
302 D6 Ty Newydd IoA
304 B3 Ty Newydd Leisure Park IoA
303 G3 Ty'n Rhos Caravan Park IoA
305 G6 Tynterfyn Touring Caravan Park Conwy
109 F5 Tyntesfield NT N Som
322 d6 Tynwald Hill IoM
285 E4 Ty'n-y-Coed Uchaf NT Conwy
283 F4 Ty'n yr Onnen Mountain Farm Caravan & Camping Gwynd
94 D4 Tyrrells Wood Golf Club Surrey
267 E2 Tytandderwen Caravan Park Gwynd
268 D1 Ty-Ucha Caravan Park Denbgs
228 D4 Tywyn Wharf railway station Gwynd

U

113 G2 Uffington Castle Oxon
20 B2 Ugbrooke Park Devon
593 D11 Uibhist a Deas W Isls
592 B4 Uibhist a Tuath W Isls
136 A4 Uley Long Barrow Gloucs
216 B2 Ullenthorpe Garden Centre campsite Leics
216 B2 Ullesthorpe Golf Club Leics
390 C5 Ullswater Cumb
390 C5 Ullswater Caravan, Camping & Marine Park Cumb
364 C4 Ulverston Golf Club Cumb
34 B4 Ulwell Cottage Caravan Park Dorset
144 C5 Underhill Stadium Gt Lon
173 E4 Unex Towerlands Golf Club Essex
80 A2 Union Mill Kent
154 A6 United Counties showground Carmth
51 E3 Universal Marina Hants
140 B3 University Parks Oxon
213 F3 University railway station Birm
609 H3 Unst Shet
88 D3 Upavon Golf Club Wilts
98 C1 Upchurch River Valley Golf Centre Kent
487 E5 Uphall Golf Club W Loth
324 C4 Upholland railway station Lancs
121 E2 Upminster Golf Club Gt Lon
122 B5 Upnor Castle Medway
74 B6 Uppark NT W Susx
373 F3 Upper Carr Touring Park N York
166 B4 Upper Heyford airfield (dis) Oxon
22 D1 Upper Lynstone Caravan Park Cnwll
18 C4 Upper Plym Valley Devon
508 D3 Upper Tyndrum railway station Stirlg
309 F6 Upton-by-Chester Golf Club Ches
211 F1 Upton Cressett Hall Shrops
191 F5 Upton House NT Warwks
162 C1 Upton upon Severn Heritage Centre Worcs
549 J4 Urquhart Castle Highld
273 H3 Uttoxeter Golf Club Staffs
273 H3 Uttoxeter racecourse Staffs
118 B2 Uxbridge Cricket Ground Gt Lon
118 B2 Uxbridge golf course Gt Lon

V

189 F4 Vale Golf Club Worcs
105 G4 Vale Hotel Golf & Spa Resort V Glam
307 F5 Vale of Clwyd Denbgs
483 F3 Vale of Leven Golf Club W Duns
268 D1 Vale of Llangollen Golf Club Denbgs
88 D3 Vale of Pewsey Wilts
88 B2 Vale of Pewsey cycle route Wilts
373 G3 Vale of Pickering Caravan Park N York
205 G4 Vale of Rheidol Railway Cerdgn
139 F6 Vale of White Horse Oxon
291 H4 Vale Park C Stke
288 B6 Valle Crucis Abbey Denbgs
302 D5 Valley airfield IoA
117 G6 Valley Gardens Surrey
30 D5 Valley of Stones Dorset
213 F6 Valley Stadium Worcs
251 G3 Vauxhall Holiday Park Norfk
37 E5 Ventnor Botanic Gardens IoW
37 F5 Ventnor Down NT IoW
37 E5 Ventnor Golf Club IoW
551 F2 Venture Caravan Park Lancs
143 H3 Verulam Golf Club Herts
143 G5 Vicarage Road Herts
289 F1 Vicars Cross Golf Club Ches
162 B6 Victoria Basin Gloucs
119 F4 Victoria (London) railway station Gt Lon
396 D3 Victoria Park Hartpl
565 K5 Victoria Park Highld
569 G3 Victoria Park Moray
104 A2 Victoria Park Neath
308 D1 Victoria Park Wirral
451 F4 Victoria Park Caravan & Camping Park Border
310 D5 Victoria Stadium Ches
465 E3 Vikingar N Ayrs
101 G3 Viking Ship 'Hugin' Kent
213 G1 Villa Park Birm
246 A2 Virginia Lake Caravan Park Norfk
43 H3 Vivary Park Municipal golf course Somset
471 G2 Vogrie Country Park Mdloth
471 G2 Vogrie golf course Mdloth

W

141 F1 Waddesdon Manor NT Bucks
301 E3 Wainfleet railway station Lincs
329 E1 Wakefield Golf Club Wakefd
343 F5 Wakefield Kirkgate railway station Wakefd
343 F5 Wakefield Westgate railway station Wakefd
473 F5 Wakehurst Place NT W Susx
90 B2 Waibury Hill W Berk
148 D2 Waldegraves Holiday Park Essex

405 F5 Waldridge Fell Dur
202 B5 Waldringfield Golf Club Suffk
106 C4 Wales National Ice Rink Cardif
240 C4 Walkers Stadium C Leic
323 E6 Wallasey Golf Club Wirral
323 E6 Wallasey Grove Road railway station Wirral
323 E6 Wallasey Village railway station Wirral
429 G3 Wallington NT Nthumb
405 G1 Wallsend Golf Club N Tyne
83 G1 Walmer & Kingsdown Golf Club Kent
326 B2 Walmersley Golf Club Lancs
237 H6 Walmley Golf Club Birm
364 A5 Walney airfield Cumb
379 G6 Walney to Wear cycle route Cumb
381 F2 Walney to Wear cycle route Cumb
405 F2 Walney to Wear cycle route Dur
237 F5 Walsall Golf Club Wsall
260 B4 Walsingham railway station Norfk
334 C4 Waltham Windmill Golf Club NE Lin
334 C4 Waltham Windmill museum NE Lin
310 B3 Walton Hall Warrtn
95 E4 Walton Heath Golf Club Surrey
323 F5 Walton (Merseyside) railway station Sefton
93 F4 Wanborough railway station Surrey
197 G4 Wandlebury Country Park Cambs
95 F1 Wandle Trail cycle route Gt Lon
435 H2 Wanlockhead Beam Engine D & G
431 E2 Wansbeck Riverside Nthumb
243 F5 Wansford railway station Cambs
120 B2 Wanstead Golf Club Gt Lon
120 A2 Wanstead Park railway station Gt Lon
60 C2 Warcombe Farm Caravan & Camping Park Devon
33 F1 Wareham Forest Tourist Park Dorset
33 G2 Wareham Golf Club Dorset
455 E3 Waren Caravan Park Nthumb
260 B3 Warham St Mary railway station Nthumb
443 G3 Warkworth Castle & Hermitage Nthumb
121 E2 Warley Park Golf Club Essex
213 F2 Warley Woods Golf Club Sandw
95 F1 War Memorial Sports Ground Gt Lon
32 D2 Warmwell Country Touring Park Dorset
53 E6 Warner Farm Touring Park W Susx
76 C3 Warnham railway station W Susx
84 B3 Warren Farm Holiday Centre Somset
20 D2 Warren Golf Club Devon
147 G3 Warren Golf Club Essex
323 E6 Warren Golf Club Wirral
223 G3 Warren Lodge Norfk
310 B2 Warrington Bank Quay railway station Warrtn
310 C3 Warrington Golf Club Warrtn
338 B4 Warton airfield Lancs
190 D2 Warwick Golf Club Warwks
190 D1 Warwick Parkway railway station Warwks
190 D1 Warwick racecourse Warwks
191 E3 Warwick service area Warwks
191 F2 Warwickshire Exhibition Centre Warwks
377 F3 Wasdale Head National Trust campsite Cumb
405 G4 Washington service area Sundld
26 A2 Waterbridge golf course Devon
390 D5 Waterfoot Caravan Park Cumb
165 F3 Water Fowl Sanctuary & Children's Farm Oxon
32 A4 Water Gardens Dorset
14 A6 Watergate Bay Tourist Park Cnwll
55 G3 Waterhall Golf Club Br & H
323 F5 Waterloo (Merseyside) railway station Sefton
119 G4 Waterloo railway station Gt Lon
52 B2 Waterlooville Golf Club Hants
240 D2 Watermead Leics
320 D4 Watermill & Wildfowl Gardens Lincs
61 E2 Watermouth Castle Devon
61 E2 Watermouth Cove Holiday Park Devon
487 H5 Water of Leith C Edin
140 D3 Waterperry Gardens Oxon
42 D3 Waterrow Touring Park Somset
366 A3 Waters Edge Caravan Park Cumb
32 C3 Waterside Holiday Park Dorset
390 D5 Waterside House campsite Cumb
62 A2 Watersmeet NT Devon
140 D3 Waterstock golf course Oxon
345 G5 Waterways museum E R Yk
216 D6 Watford Gap service area Nhants
329 G5 Wath Golf Club Rothm
295 G5 Watnall Road Notts
200 C4 Wattisham airfield Suffk
76 C2 Wattlehurst Farm Surrey
122 A2 Wat Tyler Essex
106 B4 Waun-gron Park railway station Cardif
168 C2 Wavendon Golf Centre M Keyn
251 F6 Waveney River Centre Norfk
93 E5 Waverley Abbey Surrey
309 E1 Wavertree Technology Park railway station Lpool
3 F3 Wayfarers Caravan & Camping Park Cnwll
113 G2 Waylands Smithy Oxon
373 E2 Wayside Caravan Park N York
146 B6 Weald Country Park Essex
53 F2 Weald & Downland museum W Susx

98 C5 Weald of Kent golf course Kent
146 B5 Weald Park Hotel Golf & Country Club Essex
393 E2 Weardale Dur
394 B2 Weardale Railway Dur
406 A3 Wearside Golf Club Sundld
466 A2 Weavers Cottage NTS Rens
27 G5 Webbers Farm Caravan & Camping Park Devon
188 D1 Webbs of Wychbold Worcs
272 C2 Wedgwood railway station Staffs
356 B5 Weeton railway station N York
18 C6 Welbeck Manor & Sparkwell golf course Devon
240 C4 Welford Road Ground C Leic
218 B5 Wellingborough Golf Club Nhants
92 B2 Wellington Country Park Hants
92 D2 Wellingtonia Avenue campsite Wokham
71 G5 Wellow golf course Hants
126 C4 Well Park Caravan & Camping Site Pembks
115 G2 Wellplace Zoo Oxon
57 F2 Wellshurst Golf & Country Club E Susx
260 B3 Wells railway station Norfk
85 G5 Wells (Somerset) Golf Club Somset
260 B4 Wells & Walsingham Light Railway Norfk
264 D2 Welsh Highland Railway Gwynd
283 E3 Welsh Highland Railway Gwynd
106 B4 Welsh Life & Gardens Cardif
106 B4 Welsh Life museum Cardif
107 F2 Welsh National Cycling Centre Newpt
106 D4 Welsh National Tennis Centre Cardif
232 C3 Welshpool Golf Club Powys
232 B3 Welshpool & Llanfair Light Railway Powys
232 D3 Welshpool Raven Square railway station Powys
284 C2 Welsh Slate museum Gwynd
192 C1 Welton Haven Marina Nhants
144 B2 Welwyn Garden City Golf Club Herts
144 B1 Welwyn North railway station Herts
144 B2 Welwyn Viaduct Herts
118 D2 Wembley Arena & Conference Centre Gt Lon
118 D2 Wembley Stadium Gt Lon
4 C2 Wendron Mining District (UNESCO) Cnwll
369 F2 Wensleydale Railway N York
255 F5 Wensum Valley Hotel Golf & Country Club Norfk
117 G6 Wentworth golf course Surrey
106 B5 Wenvoe Castle Golf Club V Glam
102 C3 Weobley Castle Swans
308 C6 Wepre Country Park Flints
236 C4 Wergs Golf Club Staffs
133 F1 Wernddu Golf Centre Mons
326 D4 Werneth Golf Club Oldham
327 E6 Werneth Low Golf Club Tamesd
16 B2 Wesley's Cottage Cnwll
32 B3 Wessex Stadium Dorset
309 E2 West Allerton railway station Lpool
30 B4 West Bay Holiday Park Dorset
114 C4 West Berkshire golf course W Berk
342 C4 West Bowling Golf Club Brad
342 B3 West Bradford Golf Club Brad
135 G2 Westbury Court NT Gloucs
94 A2 West Byfleet Golf Club Surrey
76 A6 West Chiltington Golf Club W Susx
3 F2 West Cornwall Golf Club Cnwll
323 H6 West Derby Golf Club Lpool
84 B2 West End Farm campsite N Som
341 H4 West End Golf Club Calder
570 C3 Wester Bonnyton Farm campsite Abers
96 C4 Westerham Golf Club Kent
430 C6 Westerhope Golf Club N u Ty
62 C3 Westermill Farm campsite Somset
444 D2 Western Gailes Golf Club N Ayrs
240 B4 Western golf course C Leic
484 A5 Westerton railway station C Glas
145 E5 West Essex Golf Club Essex
32 A3 West Fleet Holiday Farm Dorset
101 F2 Westgate & Birchington Golf Club Kent
101 F1 Westgate-on-Sea railway station Kent
92 B3 West Green House NT Hants
143 F6 West Herts Golf Club Herts
521 G2 West Highland Way Highld
495 G3 West Highland Way Stirlg
496 B6 West Highland Way Stirlg
557 F3 Westhill Golf Club Abers
93 G3 West Hill Golf Club Surrey
3 E4 Westholme Cnwll
325 E3 Westhoughton Golf Club Bolton
55 G3 West Hove Golf Club Br & H
112 D6 West Kennett Long Barrow Wilts
96 B2 West Kent Golf Club Gt Lon
323 F4 West Lancashire Golf Club Sefton
338 B5 West Lancashire Light Railway Lancs
52 C3 Westleigh Park Hants
121 G2 Westley Heights country park Thurr
470 B4 West Linton Golf Club Border
217 H3 West Lodge Rural Centre Nhants
486 A4 West Lothian Golf Club Falk
97 G3 West Malling Golf Club Kent
118 C3 West Middlesex Golf Club Gt Lon
41 G5 West Middlewick Farm Caravan & Camping Site Devon
214 C4 West Midlands Golf Club Solhll
212 B4 West Midland Safari Park Worcs
132 C2 West Monmouthshire Golf Club Blae G
365 H3 Westmorland Cumb

111 E2 Westonbirt arboretum Gloucs
111 F2 Westonbirt golf course Gloucs
84 C2 Weston Gateway Caravan Site N Som
84 B2 Weston Milton railway station N Som
236 B2 Weston Park Staffs
255 F4 Weston Park Golf Club Norfk
84 B3 Weston-Super-Mare Golf Club N Som
142 A2 Weston Turville Golf Club Bucks
65 G5 Westonzoyland airfield Somset
27 F4 West Point showground Devon
602 F1 Westray airport Ork
261 G3 West Runton railway station Norfk
602 F3 Westside Church Ork
63 G3 West Somerset Railway Somset
222 D4 West Suffolk Golf Centre Suffk
75 F1 West Surrey Golf Club Surrey
54 C1 West Sussex Golf Club W Susx
95 E2 West Sutton railway station Gt Lon
221 E5 Westview Marina Cambs
87 F5 West Wilts Golf Club Wilts
292 C3 Westwood (Leek) golf course Staffs
87 E3 Westwood Manor NT Wilts
142 A6 West Wycombe Park NT Bucks
401 C4 Wetheral Priory Gatehouse Cumb
356 D5 Wetherby Golf Club Leeds
357 E5 Wetherby racecourse Leeds
356 C3 Wetherby Road N York
391 F4 Wetheriggs Country Pottery Cumb
173 E3 Wethersfield airfield Essex
128 D5 Wetlands & Wildfowl Trust Carmth
117 G3 Wexham Park Golf Club Bucks
91 G4 Weybrook Park Golf Club Hants
32 B4 Weymouth Golf Club Dorset
163 E5 Whaddon Road Gloucs
340 A2 Whalley Golf Club Lancs
607 J4 Whalsay Golf Club Shet
162 B6 Wharf House Gloucs
359 G2 Wharram Percy Deserted Medieval Village N York
211 H5 Wharton Park Golf Club Worcs
294 C4 Whatstandwell railway station Derbys
6 D3 Wheal Coates Mine Cnwll
8 C2 Wheal Martyn Heritage Centre Cnwll
3 F3 Wheal Rodney Holiday Park Cnwll
6 D4 Wheal Rose Caravan & Camping Park Cnwll
67 F3 Wheathill Golf Club Somset
330 D4 Wheatley Golf Club Donc
343 H3 Wheatley Park Stadium Leeds
386 D5 Wheeldale Roman Road Roman site N York
240 B5 Whetstone Golf Club Leics
405 E3 Whickham Golf Club Gatesd
482 C5 Whinhill railway station Inver
389 E4 Whinlatter Pass Cumb
389 F5 Whinlatter Visitor Centre Cumb
142 D1 Whipsnade Park golf course Bucks
143 E1 Whipsnade Zoo Beds
292 D5 Whiston Hall Golf Club Staffs
309 G1 Whiston railway station Knows
406 B2 Whitburn Golf Club S Tyne
387 E2 Whitby Golf Club N York
106 B3 Whitchurch (Cardiff) Golf Club Cardif
106 B3 Whitchurch (Cardiff) railway station Cardif
90 D5 Whitchurch Silk Mill Hants
7 G2 White Acres Holiday Park Cnwll
202 D2 Whitearch Touring Caravan Park Suffk
324 D2 White Bear Marina Lancs
415 H4 Whitecairn Farm Caravan Park D & G
133 G1 White Castle Mons
300 D5 White Cat Caravan & Camping Park Lincs
528 B1 White Caterthun Angus
37 G3 Whitecliff Bay Holiday Park IoW
326 A3 Whitefield Golf Club Bury
215 H5 Whitefields Golf Club Warwks
132 A6 Whitehall Golf Club Myr Td
119 G1 White Hart Lane Gt Lon
119 G1 White Hart Lane railway station Gt Lon
20 B6 Whitehill Country Park Devon
170 D5 Whitehill golf course Herts
88 D2 White Horse Alton Barnes chalk figure Wilts
112 C4 White Horse Broad Town chalk figure Wilts
32 C3 White Horse chalk figure Dorset
87 F4 White Horse chalk figure Wilts
112 B6 White Horse Cherhill chalk figure Wilts
88 B2 White Horse Devizes chalk figure Wilts
112 D5 White Horse Hackpen chalk figure Wilts
113 H2 White Horse Kingston Lisle chalk figure Oxon
113 E6 White Horse Malborough chalk figure Wilts
371 G3 White Horse Oldstead chalk figure N York
89 E3 White Horse Pewsey chalk figure Wilts
32 C3 White Horse Sutton Poyntz chalk figure Dorset
87 F4 White Horse Westbury chalk figure Wilts
490 A4 Whitekirk Golf & Country Club E Loth
236 B3 White Ladies Priory Shrops
141 H4 Whiteleaf Golf Club Bucks
33 E2 Whitemead Caravan Park Dorset
378 B3 White Moss Common NT Cumb
499 F2 Whitemoss golf course P & K

296 B3 White Post Modern Farm Centre Notts
343 E4 White Rose Leeds
54 B4 White Rose Touring Park W Susx
367 E5 White Scar Caves N York
283 E4 White Tower Caravan Park Gwynd
144 D5 Whitewebbs Park golf course Gt Lon
95 G2 Whitgift School Gt Lon
410 D4 Whithorn Cradle of Christianity museum D & G
461 B4 Whiting Bay Golf Club N Ayrs
153 E6 Whitland Abbey Carmth
431 F5 Whitley Bay Golf Club N Tyne
250 B3 Whitlingham Country Park Norfk
10 D3 Whitsand Bay Holiday Park Cnwll
10 B3 Whitsand Bay Hotel Golf & Country Club Cnwll
100 A2 Whitstable & Seasalter Golf Club Kent
326 D1 Whittaker Golf Club Rochdl
238 A3 Whittington Heath Golf Club Staffs
193 E6 Whittlebury Park Golf & Country Club Nhants
589 K6 Wick airport Highld
222 B5 Wicken Fen NT Cambs
589 J5 Wick Golf Club Highld
202 C3 Wickham Market railway station Suffk
51 F2 Wickham Park Golf Club Hants
51 F2 Wickham vineyard Hants
53 F4 Wicks Farm Holiday Park W Susx
218 B4 Wicksteed Park Nhants
20 B5 Widdicombe Farm Tourist Park Devon
22 D2 Widemouth Bay Caravan Park Cnwll
20 A5 Widend Touring Park Devon
309 H2 Widnes Golf Club Halton
214 B4 Widney Manor Golf Club Solhll
214 B4 Widney Manor railway station Solhll
324 D2 Wigan Golf Club Bolton
260 B4 Wighton railway station Norfk
236 C5 Wightwick Manor NT Wolves
209 H6 Wigmore Castle Herefs
417 E6 Wigtown & Bladnoch Golf Club D & G
415 G5 Wigtownshire County Golf Club D & G
251 F4 Wild Duck Holiday Park Norfk
96 D3 Wildernesse Golf Club Kent
98 B3 Wildlife Trust Tyland Barn Kent
398 D1 Wildlife & Wetlands Trust Centre D & G
380 C1 Wild Rose Park campsite Cumb
75 G2 Wildwood Country Club Surrey
100 C3 Wildwood Discovery Park Kent
48 C4 Wilksworth Farm Caravan Park Dorset
294 B3 Willersley Castle Derbys
239 F1 Willesley Park Golf Club Leics
467 E3 Williamwood Golf Club E Rens
325 G6 William Wroe Municipal golf course Traffd
57 F4 Willingdon Golf Club E Susx
323 E2 Willowbank Holiday Home & Touring Park Sefton
168 B3 Willowbridge Marina Bucks
44 C2 Willow Craft Somset
358 A3 Willow House Caravan Park York
116 C4 Willow Marina Oxon
276 A4 Willow Moorings Notts
225 F4 Willows Camping & Caravan Park Norflk
342 C5 Willow Valley Golf Club Calder
38 B6 Willow Valley Holiday Park Cnwll
311 G4 Wilmslow Golf Club Ches
339 G3 Wilpshire Golf Club Lancs
397 E6 Wilton Golf Club R & Cl
70 B3 Wilton House Wilts
87 E3 Wiltshire cycle route Somset
68 C3 Wiltshire cycle route Wilts
89 G3 Wiltshire cycle route Wilts
113 G6 Wiltshire cycle route Wilts
111 G6 Wiltshire cycle route/Vale of Pewsey cycle route Wilts
63 F5 Wimbleball Lake campsite Somset
119 E6 Wimbledon Chase railway station Gt Lon
119 E5 Wimbledon Common Golf Club Gt Lon
119 E5 Wimbledon Park Golf Club Gt Lon
119 F5 Wimbledon Stadium Gt Lon
196 D4 Wimpole Hall & Home Farm NT Cambs
68 B3 Wincanton racecourse Somset
163 F4 Winchcombe railway station Gloucs
188 A3 Winchenford Dovecote NT Worcs
72 D2 Winchester service area Hants
378 D5 Windermere Golf Club Cumb
378 C5 Windermere Quays Cumb
378 D5 Windermere Steamboats & museum Cumb
93 F2 Windlemere Golf Club Surrey
93 F2 Windlesham golf course Surrey
324 A1 Windmill Animal Farm Lancs
112 C5 Windmill Hill (Avebury) Wilts
168 A3 Windmill Hill Golf Centre M Keyn
136 D5 Windmill Tump Long Barrow Gloucs
214 D3 Windmill Village Hotel Golf & Leisure Club Covtry
192 B3 Windmill vineyard Nhants
117 F4 Windsor racecourse W & M
44 D6 Windwhistle Golf Club Somset
483 H5 Windyhill Golf Club E Duns
294 D4 Wingfield Manor Derbys
242 B4 Wing Maze Rutlnd
75 F1 Winkworth arboretum NT Surrey
116 C5 Winnersh Triangle railway station Wokham
24 B2 Winsford Walled Garden Devon
490 C4 Winterfield Golf Club E Loth
117 E2 Winter Hill Golf Club W & M

308 B3 Wirral Wirral
308 C2 Wirral Ladies Golf Club Wirral
468 B3 Wishaw Golf Club N Lans
238 B6 Wishaw golf course Birm
94 B3 Wisley Gardens Surrey
498 C5 Witches Craig Caravan & Camping Park Stirlg
55 G3 Withdean Stadium Br & H
349 F4 Withernsea Golf Club E R Yk
311 G1 Withington Golf Club Manch
75 E1 Witley Common NT Surrey
187 H2 Witley Court Worcs
139 E3 Witney Lakes golf course Oxon
243 E4 Wittering airfield Nhants
80 C4 Wittersham Road railway station Kent
394 D3 Witton Castle Dur
339 G4 Witton Country Park Bl w D
213 G1 Witton railway station Birm
77 F6 Wivelsfield railway station W Susx
168 B3 Woburn Abbey Beds
168 D3 Woburn Safari Park Beds
91 H1 Wokefield Park Golf Club W Berk
93 G3 Woking Golf Club Surrey
95 H3 Woldingham Golf Club Surrey
373 G5 Wolds Way Caravan & Camping N York
276 B2 Wollaton Hall C Nott
276 B2 Wollaton Park Golf Club C Nott
451 F5 Woll golf course Border
291 G5 Wolstanton Golf Club Staffs
261 G5 Wolterton Park Norfk
212 B1 Wolverhampton Business airport Staffs
236 D6 Wolverhampton racecourse Wolves
38 B6 Wooda Farm Park campsite Cnwll
315 F3 Woodall service area Rothm
202 C5 Woodbridge airport (dis) Suffk
202 B5 Woodbridge Golf Club Suffk
27 G5 Woodbury Park Hotel Golf & Country Club Devon
136 B4 Woodchester Park NT Gloucs
80 D2 Woodchurch Windmill Kent
366 C4 Woodclose Caravan Park Cumb
95 F2 Woodcote Park Golf Club Gt Lon
580 E7 Woodend Caravan & Camping Site Highld
29 G4 Wood Farm Caravan & Camping Park Dorset
145 E6 Woodford Golf Club Gt Lon
213 F3 Woodgate Valley Country Park Birm
120 B2 Woodgrange Park railway station Gt Lon
342 C2 Woodhall Hills Golf Club Leeds
299 F2 Woodhall Spa Golf Club Lincs
395 F4 Woodham Golf & Country Club Dur
328 B5 Woodhead Pass Barns
88 D6 Woodhenge Wilts
370 A5 Woodhouse Farm & Country Park N York
133 F4 Woodlake Park Golf & Country Club Mons
33 G3 Woodland Caravan & Camping Park Dorset
502 C4 Woodland Gardens Caravan & Camping Site Fife
256 B2 Woodland Leisure Park Norfk
74 C1 Woodland Park Hants
33 F2 Woodlands Camping Park Dorset
12 D2 Woodlands campsite Devon
180 D1 Woodlands Caravan Park Cerdgn
110 A3 Woodlands Golf & Country Club S Glos
13 E2 Woodlands Leisure Park Devon
97 E2 Woodlands Manor Golf Club Kent
311 E5 Woodlands Park campsite Ches
80 C2 Woodlands Park campsite Kent
25 G4 Woodland Springs Adult Touring Park Devon
134 D3 Woodlands View Camping & Caravan Park Gloucs
298 B6 Woodland Waters campsite Lincs
354 C2 Wood Nook Caravan Park N York
17 F4 Woodovis Park campsite Devon
126 C4 Wood Park Caravans Pembks
171 H5 Woodside Park Herts
328 B2 Woodsome Hall Golf Club Kirk
109 F6 Woodspring Golf & Country Club N Som
84 B3 Woodspring Park N Som
320 D3 Woodthorpe Hall Golf Club Lincs
61 G2 Woody Bay railway station Devon
85 F5 Wookey Hole Somset
60 C3 Woolacombe Bay Holiday Village Devon
60 C3 Woolacombe Sands Holiday Park Devon
90 D4 Wooldings vineyard Hants
454 B4 Wooler Golf Club Nthumb
328 D2 Woolley Edge service area Wakefd
329 E2 Woolley Park golf course Wakefd
48 D4 Woolsbridge Manor Farm Caravan Park Dorset
278 C5 Woolsthorpe Manor NT Lincs
145 F5 Woolston Manor Golf Club Essex
309 F2 Woolton Golf Club Lpool
188 B3 Worcester Foregate Street railway station Worcs
188 B4 Worcester Golf & Country Club Worcs
188 B3 Worcester racecourse Worcs
188 B4 Worcestershire County Cricket Ground Worcs
188 C4 Worcester Shrub Hill railway station Worcs
378 B3 Wordsworth museum Cumb
235 H6 Worfield golf course Shrops
388 B4 Workington Golf Club Cumb
316 B4 Worksop Golf Club Notts
74 A2 Worldham Park golf course Hants
7 E3 World in Miniature Cnwll
21 E1 World of Country Life museum Devon

137 H2 World of Mechanical Music museum Gloucs
84 B2 Worlebury Golf Club N Som
84 C2 Worle railway station N Som
93 G3 Worplesdon Golf Club Surrey
325 H5 Worsley Golf Club Salfd
256 B4 Worstead railway station Norfk
54 D3 Worthing Golf Club W Susx
329 E4 Wortley Golf Club Barns
113 F1 Wrag Barn Golf & Country Club Swindn
19 E6 Wrangaton (S Devon) Golf Club Devon
235 E3 Wrekin Golf Club Wrekin
410 C4 Wrens Egg' Standing Stones D & G
372 C3 Wrens of Ryedale Touring Park N York
169 F2 Wrest Park Gardens Beds
288 D4 Wrexham Central railway station Wrexhm
288 D4 Wrexham General railway station Wrexhm
289 E4 Wrexham Golf Club Wrexhm
97 F3 Wrotham Heath Golf Club Kent
112 D4 Wroughton Swindn
256 B6 Wroxham railway station Norfk
378 A4 Wrynose Pass Cumb
196 A3 Wyboston Lakes golf course Beds
117 F1 Wycombe Heights Golf Centre Bucks
99 H5 Wye Crown chalk figure Kent
207 F6 Wyeside Caravan & Camping Park Powys
134 C4 Wye Valley, Forest of Dean cycle route Mons
134 B4 Wye Valley Forest Park Mons
118 D4 Wyke Green Golf Club Gt Lon
224 C5 Wyken vineyard Suffk
237 H6 Wylde Green railway station Birm
249 F4 Wymondham Abbey railway station Norfk
396 B4 Wynyard Golf Club S on T
211 G5 Wyre Forest Worcs
212 B5 Wyre Forest Golf Club Worcs
213 G4 Wythall railway station Worcs
311 G2 Wythenshawe Hall Manch
220 C5 Wyton airfield Cambs

X

168 B2 Xscape sports complex M Keyn
466 D1 Xscape sports complex Rens
344 A5 Xscape sports complex Wakefd

Y

97 G4 Yalding railway station Kent
311 E6 Yatehouse Farm Caravan Park Ches
92 D3 Yateley Common Hants
110 C3 Yate railway station S Glos
41 F5 Yeatheridge Farm Caravan Park Devon
608 F7 Yell Shet
18 B4 Yelverton Golf Club Devon
41 F2 Yeo Valley Holiday Park Devon
45 H4 Yeovil Golf Club Somset
45 H5 Yeovil Junction railway station Somset
228 D4 Ynysymaengwyn Caravan Park Gwynd
358 B2 York Golf Club York
387 F3 York House Caravan Park N York
358 A5 York racecourse York
117 E3 York Road football ground W & M
358 C5 Yorkshire Air museum York
367 E2 Yorkshire Dales Cycleway Cumb
381 G6 Yorkshire Dales Cycleway N York
354 B5 Yorkshire Dales Lead Mining museum Lancs
367 F3 Yorkshire Dales National Park
354 D2 Yorkshire Dales National Park Centre (Grassington) N York
368 A2 Yorkshire Dales National Park Centre (Hawes) N York
354 A2 Yorkshire Dales National Park Centre (Malham) N York
366 D1 Yorkshire Dales National Park Centre (Sedbergh) Cumb
356 B2 Yorkshire Hussar Inn Holiday Caravan Park N York
358 B4 Yorkshire Museum of Farming York
328 D2 Yorkshire Sculpture Park Wakefd
347 F4 Yorkshire Wolds Way E R Yk
359 G3 Yorkshire Wolds Way E R Yk
373 H4 Yorkshire Wolds Way N York
300 B6 York Street football ground Lincs
358 B3 York Touring Caravan Site York
99 G2 Youngboats marina Kent
131 F5 Ystrad Rhondda railway station Rhondd
264 D2 Y Traeth Stadium Gwynd

Z

41 H3 Zeacombe House Caravan Park Devon

City, town and village index

A

93 G6 Aaron's Hill Surrey
68 A5 Abbas Combe Somset
187 F2 Abberley Worcs
174 D6 Abberton Essex
189 F4 Abberton Worcs
443 E2 Abberwick Nthumb
146 B2 Abbess End Essex
146 B2 Abbess Roding Essex
43 F5 Abbey Devon
207 H5 Abbey-cwm-hir Powys
136 C1 Abbeydale Gloucs
314 C3 Abbeydale Sheff
314 C3 Abbeydale Park Sheff
159 G3 Abbey Dore Herefs
174 C5 Abbey Field Essex
29 E3 Abbey Gate Devon
98 B3 Abbey Gate Kent
270 C3 Abbey Green Shrops
292 C3 Abbey Green Staffs
326 C5 Abbey Hey Manch
488 E3 Abbeyhill C Edin
44 B4 Abbey Hill Somset
292 B5 Abbey Hulton C Stke
94 A1 Abbey Mead Surrey
473 H2 Abbey St Bathans Border
352 B4 Abbeystead Lancs
399 F4 Abbey Town Cumb
339 F5 Abbey Village Lancs
120 C4 Abbey Wood Gt Lon
412 D2 Abbey Yard D & G
440 A2 Abbotrule Border
39 E5 Abbots Bickington Devon
273 G5 Abbots Bromley Staffs
30 D5 Abbotsbury Dorset
77 E5 Abbotsford W Susx
39 F2 Abbotsham Devon
20 A4 Abbotskerswell Devon
143 F4 Abbots Langley Herts
12 D3 Abbotsleigh Devon
109 F5 Abbots Leigh N Som
196 B3 Abbotsley Cambs
309 E6 Abbot's Meads Ches
189 F4 Abbots Morton Worcs
220 B4 Abbots Ripton Cambs
189 G4 Abbot's Salford Warwks
73 E3 Abbotstone Hants
71 H5 Abbotswood Hants
72 C3 Abbots Worthy Hants
89 H6 Abbotts Ann Hants
209 G4 Abcott Shrops
210 D2 Abdon Shrops
329 G5 Abdy Rothm
180 C5 Aber Cerdgn
180 B2 Aberaeron Cerdgn
131 G4 Aberaman Rhondd
230 C2 Aberangell Gwynd
153 G1 Aber Arad Carmth
534 E5 Aberarder Highld
549 L4 Aberarder Highld
500 C1 Aberargie P & K
180 C2 Aberarth Cerdgn
104 B1 Aberavon Neath
153 H1 Aber-banc Cerdgn
132 C4 Aberbargoed Caerph
232 B6 Aberbechan Powys
132 C4 Aberbeeg Caerph
157 F4 Aberbran Powys
131 G4 Abercanaid Myr Td
132 C6 Abercarn Caerph
151 E3 Abercastle Pembks
230 C4 Abercegir Powys
534 E2 Aberchalder Highld
569 L5 Aberchirder Abers
487 E4 Abercorn W Loth
130 C2 Abercraf Powys
130 C5 Abercregan Neath
503 E4 Abercrombie Fife
131 G5 Abercwmboi Rhondd
153 E1 Abercych Pembks
131 H5 Abercynon Rhondd
230 D1 Aber-Cywarch Gwynd
512 C6 Aberdalgie P & K
131 F4 Aberdare Rhondd
262 B5 Aberdaron Gwynd
557 G3 Aberdeen C Aber
282 D5 Aberdesach Gwynd
487 G3 Aberdour Fife
130 B5 Aberdulais Neath
229 E5 Aberdyfi Gwynd
184 A5 Aberedw Powys
150 C3 Abereiddy Pembks
263 G3 Abererch Gwynd
131 H4 Aberfan Myr Td
524 C6 Aberfeldy P & K
282 B2 Aberffraw IoA
205 F4 Aberffrwd Cerdgn
133 F3 Aberffrwd Mons
343 H2 Aberford Leeds
496 D4 Aberfoyle Stirlg
105 E3 Abergarw Brdgnd
130 B4 Abergarwed Neath
133 F2 Abergavenny Mons
306 C4 Abergele Conwy
154 D1 Aber-Giâr Carmth
155 E3 Abergorlech Carmth
182 C4 Abergwesyn Powys
154 B5 Abergwili Carmth
229 F1 Abergwynant Gwynd
130 D5 Abergwynfi Neath
304 D5 Abergwyngregyn Gwynd
229 F3 Abergynolwyn Gwynd
207 H1 Aberhafesp Powys
230 C5 Aberhosan Powys
104 D3 Aberkenfig Brdgnd
489 F4 Aberlady E Loth
528 B3 Aberlemno Angus
205 E1 Aberllefenni Gwynd
230 B3 Aberllynfi Powys
158 C2 Abermagwr Cerdgn
205 F5 Abermeurig Cerdgn
181 E3 Abermorddu Flints
288 C3 Abermule Powys
232 C6 Abernaint Powys
268 B5 Abernant Carmth
153 G5 Abernant Carmth
232 C5 Abernant Powys
131 G4 Abernant Rhondd
500 C1 Abernethy P & K
513 F3 Abernyte P & K
288 C5 Aber-oer Wrexhm
179 F3 Aberporth Cerdgn
263 E5 Abersoch Gwynd
133 E4 Abersychan Torfn
229 E5 Aber-Tafol Gwynd
105 G4 Aberthin V Glam
132 D4 Abertillery Blae G
106 B2 Abertridwr Caerph
267 G6 Abertridwr Powys
229 E3 Abertrinant Gwynd
132 B3 Abertysswg Caerph
499 F1 Aberuthven P & K
158 A5 Aber Village Powys
157 F4 Aberyscir Powys
204 D3 Aberystwyth Cerdgn
596 C6 Abhainn Suidhe W Isls
140 B5 Abingdon Oxon
94 B5 Abinger Common Surrey

94 B5 Abinger Hammer Surrey
193 G2 Abington Nhants
448 B5 Abington S Lans
196 D6 Abington Pigotts Cambs
193 G2 Abington Vale Nhants
54 D1 Abingworth W Susx
277 F5 Ab Kettleby Leics
189 F4 Ab Lench Worcs
137 H3 Ablington Gloucs
89 E5 Ablington Wilts
313 G4 Abney Derbys
555 F5 Aboyne Abers
351 G2 Abraham Heights Lancs
325 E4 Abram Wigan
549 K2 Abriachan Highld
145 G5 Abridge Essex
485 F4 Abronhill N Lans
51 F3 Abshot Hants
110 C5 Abson S Glos
192 D5 Abthorpe Nhants
602 B6 Abune-the-Hill Ork
320 D4 Aby Lincs
518 E1 Acarsaid Highld
358 A5 Acaster Malbis York
344 D1 Acaster Selby N York
340 B4 Accrington Lancs
516 F5 Acha Ag & B
480 A3 Achabraid Ag & B
543 H7 Achachork Highld
520 E4 Achadh nan Darach Highld
479 K6 Achahoish Ag & B
506 F3 Achaleven Ag & B
521 L7 Achallader Ag & B
588 E5 Achalone Highld
597 J2 Acha Mor W Isls
564 D4 Achanalt Highld
565 L2 Achandunie Highld
481 E2 Achanelid Ag & B
520 F1 Ach' an Todhair Highld
576 C3 Achany Highld
533 G7 Achaphubuil Highld
519 G2 Acharacle Highld
586 F6 Achargary Highld
538 B4 Acharn Angus
519 G5 Acharn Highld
523 K7 Acharn P & K
577 G5 Achath Abers
588 F8 Achavandra Muir Highld
128 B4 Achavanich Highld
573 L3 Achduart Highld
573 K2 Acheninver Highld
581 L3 Achentoul Highld
579 J2 Achfary Highld
580 E7 Achfrish Highld
573 G5 Achgarve Highld
584 F3 Achiemore Highld
587 J5 Achiemore Highld
544 D8 A' Chill Highld
573 K2 Achiltibuie Highld
586 C4 Achina Highld
586 C4 Achinahuagh Highld
576 C4 Achinduich Highld
506 D2 Achindunan Ag & B
586 C4 Achingills Highld
547 G1 Achininver Highld
546 E2 Achintee Highld
517 L6 Achintraid Highld
534 B6 Achleck Ag & B
584 D6 Achluachrach Highld
578 E5 Achlyness Highld
546 F3 Achmelvich Highld
573 K4 Achmore Highld
597 J2 Achmore W Isls
506 F2 Achnaba Ag & B
578 D3 Achnacarnin Highld
533 J5 Achnacarry Highld
507 G3 Achnacloich Ag & B
545 K8 Achnacloich Highld
549 G6 Achnaconeran Highld
506 F2 Achnacree Bay Ag & B
506 E1 Achnacroish Ag & B
518 B5 Achnadrish Ag & B
566 B2 Achnagarron Highld
518 C2 Achnaha Highld
575 L4 Achnahanat Highld
551 H4 Achnahannet Highld
504 D6 Achnahard Ag & B
580 D7 Achnairn Highld
576 E2 Achnaluachrach Highld
479 K4 Achnamara Ag & B
533 J5 Achnasaul Highld
563 L5 Achnasheen Highld
518 B2 Achosnich Highld
588 C3 Achreamie Highld
521 G2 Achriabhach Highld
584 E6 Achriesgill Highld
577 J2 Achrimsdale Highld
543 H7 Achtalean Highld
565 H5 Achterneed Highld
586 E4 Achtoty Highld
575 K3 Achuirghill Highld
219 E5 Achurch Nhants
586 C5 Achuvoldrach Highld
576 F5 Achvaich Highld
588 B4 Achvarasdal Highld
365 H3 Ackenthwaite Cumb
589 K6 Ackergill Highld
384 D1 Acklam Middsb
359 E2 Acklam N York
235 H5 Ackleton Shrops
443 G4 Acklington Nthumb
343 H5 Ackton Wakefd
329 G1 Ackworth Moor Top Wakefd
251 E2 Acle Norfk
213 H3 Acock's Green Birm
101 F2 Acol Kent
403 G1 Acomb Nthumb
357 H4 Acomb York
160 C3 Aconbury Herefs
340 B5 Acre Lancs
326 D3 Acre Oldham
288 C6 Acrefair Wrexhm
146 C2 Acreland Green Essex
291 G4 Acres Nook Staffs
290 C4 Acton Ches
34 A5 Acton Dorset
119 E3 Acton Gt Lon
209 F3 Acton Shrops
272 B1 Acton Staffs
200 A6 Acton Suffk
188 B1 Acton Worcs
288 D4 Acton Wrexhm
187 F4 Acton Beauchamp Herefs
310 B4 Acton Bridge Ches
234 C4 Acton Burnell Shrops
187 G4 Acton Green Herefs
234 C4 Acton Pigott Shrops
200 A5 Acton Place Suffk
270 C2 Acton Reynald Shrops
235 E5 Acton Round Shrops
210 A2 Acton Scott Shrops
272 D6 Acton Trussell Staffs
111 F3 Acton Turville S Glos
599 L2 Adabroc W Isls
469 G1 Adambrae W Loth
30 C1 Adam's Green Dorset
380 B5 Adamthwaite Cumb

271 H4 Adbaston Staffs
67 F5 Adber Dorset
276 D2 Adbolton Notts
165 H2 Adderbury Oxon
271 F2 Adderley Shrops
292 B5 Adderley Green C Stke
455 E3 Adderstone Nthumb
469 F2 Addiewell W Loth
355 E4 Addingham Brad
355 E5 Addingham Moorside Brad
167 F4 Addington Bucks
16 C5 Addington Cnwll
96 A2 Addington Gt Lon
97 G3 Addington Kent
472 C4 Addinston Border
95 G1 Addiscombe Gt Lon
25 G4 Addiscott Devon
94 A2 Addlestone Surrey
94 A1 Addlestonemoor Surrey
321 F6 Addlethorpe Lincs
343 E2 Adel Leeds
271 F6 Adeney Wrekin
143 F3 Adeyfield Herts
231 H4 Adfa Powys
209 H5 Adforton Herefs
37 F3 Adgestone IoW
100 D5 Adisham Kent
164 C4 Adlestrop Gloucs
346 B5 Adlingfleet E R Yk
312 B3 Adlington Ches
325 E2 Adlington Lancs
324 D2 Adlington Park Lancs
273 F5 Admaston Staffs
235 E2 Admaston Wrekin
190 B5 Admington Warwks
153 G2 Adpar Cerdgn
44 B2 Adsborough Somset
64 C4 Adscombe Somset
167 F4 Adstock Bucks
192 C4 Adstone Nhants
312 A2 Adswood Stockp
75 H5 Adversane W Susx
551 L3 Advie Highld
342 D4 Adwalton Leeds
141 E5 Adwell Oxon
330 B3 Adwick Le Street Donc
329 H4 Adwick upon Dearne Donc
571 G5 Adziel Abers
423 G2 Ae D & G
325 H2 Affetside Bury
560 C5 Affleck Abers
47 E6 Affpuddle Dorset
288 C3 Afon Eitha Wrexhm
307 G5 Afon-wen Flints
263 G3 Afon Wen Gwynd
36 B3 Afton IoW
239 G2 Agar Nook Leics
212 B4 Aggborough Worcs
369 E2 Agglethorpe N York
400 D3 Aglionby Cumb
307 G6 Aifft Denbgs
309 E2 Aigburth Lpool
599 K8 Aiginis W Isls
360 C5 Aike E R Yk
602 E1 Aikerness Ork
601 H6 Aikers Ork
401 E6 Aiketgate Cumb
399 H4 Aikton Cumb
320 D4 Ailby Lincs
185 F5 Ailey Herefs
190 C4 Ailstone Warwks
243 G5 Ailsworth C Pete
145 E4 Aimes Green Essex
370 D3 Ainderby Quernhow N York
384 A6 Ainderby Steeple N York
175 F5 Aingers Green Essex
323 F3 Ainsdale Lancs
323 E2 Ainsdale-on-Sea Sefton
401 F5 Ainstable Cumb
325 H3 Ainsworth Bury
386 B3 Ainthorpe N York
323 G5 Aintree Sefton
470 B2 Ainville W Loth
492 C4 Aird Ag & B
415 E4 Aird D & G
562 D2 Aird Highld
593 D7 Aird W Isls
599 M7 Aird W Isls
595 L4 Aird Adhanais W Isls
593 C8 Aird a' Mhachair W Isls
596 F5 Aird a' Mhulaidh W Isls
596 E7 Aird Asaig W Isls
593 D8 Aird Choinnich W Isls
599 K2 Aird Dhail W Isls
576 D5 Airdens Highld
591 E7 Aird Mhidhinis W Isls
595 H5 Aird Mhighe W Isls
595 J4 Aird Mhighe W Isls
591 E7 Aird Mhòr W Isls
593 D8 Aird Mhòr W Isls
592 E6 Aird na Monadh W Isls
593 D8 Aird na Sruban W Isls
505 G5 Aird of Kinloch Ag & B
531 G2 Aird of Sleat Highld
468 B1 Airdrie N Lans
468 B1 Airdriehill N Lans
590 E3 Aird Ruairidh W Isls
507 G3 Airds Bay Ho Ag & B
595 J5 Aird Shleibhe W Isls
520 C6 Airdsllo Ag & B
599 K7 Aird Thunga W Isls
586 E4 Airdtorrisdale Highld
598 B7 Aird Uig W Isls
344 B4 Airedale Wakefd
354 C5 Aire View N York
597 G4 Airidh a Bhruaich W Isls
526 D4 Airlie Angus
345 G4 Airmyn E R Yk
512 C2 Airntully P & K
531 K1 Airor Highld
486 A2 Airth Falk
498 C5 Airthrey Castle Stirlg
354 A3 Airton N York
410 C3 Airyhassen D & G
387 E3 Airy Hill N York
409 G2 Airylick D & G
409 G2 Airyolland D & G
279 G2 Aisby Lincs
332 B6 Aisby Lincs
590 E3 Aisgernis W Isls
19 E5 Aish Devon
20 A6 Aish Devon
64 C4 Aisholt Somset
370 B2 Aiskew N York
373 E2 Aislaby N York
387 E3 Aislaby N York
384 B2 Aislaby S on T
318 A3 Aisthorpe Lincs
602 A8 Aith Ork
603 J6 Aith Ork
605 H5 Aith Shet
606 D6 Aith Shet
609 J6 Aith Shet
268 D5 Aithnen Powys
605 H4 Aithsetter Shet
551 H2 Aitnoch Highld
454 A4 Akeld Nthumb
167 F2 Akeley Bucks
217 F4 Akenham Suffk
405 G3 Albany Sundld

17 F4 Albaston Cnwll
233 G2 Alberbury Shrops
125 F1 Albert Town Pembks
275 E6 Albert Village Leics
55 G1 Albourne W Susx
55 G1 Albourne Green W Susx
236 B4 Albrighton Shrops
270 B6 Albrighton Shrops
178 D4 Albro Castle Cerdgn
226 B2 Alburgh Norfk
171 F5 Albury Herts
94 B5 Albury Surrey
171 F5 Albury End Herts
94 B5 Albury Heath Surrey
401 F4 Albyfield Cumb
261 G5 Alby Hill Norfk
145 H5 Albyns Essex
565 K5 Alcaig Highld
210 B2 Alcaston Shrops
68 D5 Alcester Dorset
189 G3 Alcester Warwks
213 G3 Alcester Lane's End Birm
56 D3 Alciston E Susx
63 F2 Alcombe Somset
110 D6 Alcombe Wilts
219 H4 Alconbury Cambs
219 H4 Alconbury Weston Cambs
357 E1 Aldborough N York
120 C2 Aldborough Hatch Gt Lon
113 F4 Aldbourne Wilts
348 D2 Aldbrough E R Yk
383 F2 Aldbrough St John N York
142 D2 Aldbury Herts
351 G2 Aldcliffe Lancs
524 D3 Aldclune P & K
203 F3 Aldeburgh Suffk
251 F6 Aldeby Norfk
143 G5 Aldenham Herts
78 C4 Alderbrook E Susx
70 D4 Alderbury Wilts
295 E5 Aldercar Derbys
255 F4 Alderford Norfk
325 H4 Alder Forest Salfd
49 E2 Alderholt Dorset
110 D1 Alderley Gloucs
311 G4 Alderley Edge Ches
215 F3 Alderman's Green Covtry
91 F1 Aldermaston W Berk
91 F1 Aldermaston Soke W Berk
91 G1 Aldermaston Wharf W Berk
190 C5 Alderminster Warwks
50 C1 Aldermoor C Sotn
274 C4 Alder Moor Staffs
48 C6 Alderney Poole
86 D6 Alder Row Somset
120 B2 Aldersbrook Gt Lon
161 E2 Alder's End Herefs
289 G3 Aldersey Green Ches
237 H3 Aldershawe Staffs
92 D4 Aldershot Hants
163 F3 Alderton Gloucs
193 F5 Alderton Nhants
270 B5 Alderton Shrops
177 F1 Alderton Suffk
111 E3 Alderton Wilts
163 F3 Alderton Fields Gloucs
294 C4 Alderwasley Derbys
370 B6 Aldfield N York
289 F3 Aldford Ches
242 D4 Aldgate Rutlnd
174 B4 Aldham Essex
200 D6 Aldham Suffk
561 G1 Aldie Abers
53 G3 Aldingbourne W Susx
364 C5 Aldingham Cumb
81 G2 Aldington Kent
189 G6 Aldington Worcs
81 F2 Aldington Frith Kent
553 H3 Aldivalloch Moray
482 D1 Aldochlay Ag & B
210 A4 Aldon Shrops
399 E5 Aldoth Cumb
221 F5 Aldreth Cambs
237 G4 Aldridge Wsall
203 E2 Aldringham Suffk
55 G3 Aldrington Br & H
138 B2 Aldsworth Gloucs
553 H3 Aldunie Moray
294 A3 Aldwark Derbys
357 F2 Aldwark N York
329 G5 Aldwarke Rothm
53 G5 Aldwick W Susx
219 E3 Aldwincle Nhants
115 F4 Aldworth W Berk
208 D3 Ale Oak Shrops
483 E3 Alexandria Ag & B
64 C4 Aley Somset
169 F6 Aley Green Beds
38 C5 Alfardisworthy Devon
28 B3 Alfington Devon
75 G3 Alfold Surrey
75 G3 Alfold Bars W Susx
75 G2 Alfold Crossways Surrey
555 G1 Alford Abers
321 E4 Alford Lincs
66 F1 Alford Somset
212 D5 Alfred's Well Worcs
295 E3 Alfreton Derbys
187 G4 Alfrick Worcs
187 G4 Alfrick Pound Worcs
57 E4 Alfriston E Susx
280 C2 Algakirk Lincs
66 F1 Alhampton Somset
531 K7 Alisary Highld
346 C5 Alkborough N Linc
135 H3 Alkerton Gloucs
191 F6 Alkerton Oxon
83 F2 Alkham Kent
270 C2 Alkington Shrops
274 B2 Alkmonton Derbys
326 C4 Alkrington Garden Village Rochdl
13 E2 Allaleigh Devon
537 H4 Allanaquoich Abers
472 C5 Allanbank N Lans
468 C3 Allanbank N Lans
565 L6 Allangrange Mains Highld
472 A5 Allanshaugh Border
472 B6 Allanshaws Border
474 C4 Allanton Border
468 A4 Allanton N Lans
468 D3 Allanton S Lans
541 F5 Allardice Abers
135 E4 Allaston Gloucs
591 D7 Allathasdal W Isls
72 C5 Allbrook Hants
88 C2 All Cannings Wilts
403 E3 Allendale Town Nthumb
238 B5 Allen End Warwks
403 F5 Allenheads Nthumb
404 C4 Allen's Green Herts
145 G1 Allensmore Herefs
160 B2 Allensford Dur
275 F3 Allenton C Derb
401 E3 Allenwood Cumb
20 B4 Aller Devon
27 H1 Aller Devon
47 E4 Aller Dorset

66 B4 Aller Somset
388 C2 Allerby Cumb
27 G4 Allercombe Devon
43 G2 Allerford Somset
63 F2 Allerford Somset
27 H3 Aller Grove Devon
20 B4 Aller Park Devon
373 G3 Allerston N York
359 E5 Allerthorpe E R Yk
342 B3 Allerton Brad
19 G5 Allerton Devon
309 F2 Allerton Lpool
343 H4 Allerton Bywater Leeds
357 E3 Allerton Mauleverer N York
214 D3 Allesley Covtry
275 E2 Allestree C Derb
7 E4 Allet Cnwll
241 H4 Allexton Leics
292 C1 Allgreave Ches
122 C4 Allhallows Medway
122 C4 Allhallows-on-Sea Medway
562 E5 Alligin Shuas Highld
272 C6 Allimore Green Staffs
30 B4 Allington Dorset
98 A3 Allington Kent
278 B1 Allington Lincs
70 D2 Allington Lincs
88 C2 Allington Wilts
111 F4 Allington Wilts
111 F5 Allington Bar Wilts
365 E4 Allithwaite Cumb
580 C1 Allnabad Highld
498 D6 Alloa Clacks
398 D6 Allonby Cumb
311 E5 Allostock Ches
444 D6 Alloway S Ayrs
44 D5 Allowenshay Somset
29 E2 All Saints Devon
226 C3 All Saints South Elmham Suffk
235 G5 Allscott Shrops
235 E2 Allscott Wrekin
234 B5 All Stretton Shrops
129 E4 Allt Carmth
288 C1 Alltami Flints
521 H5 Alltchaorunn Highld
267 F5 Alltforgan Powys
183 H5 Alltmawr Powys
585 H7 Alltnacaillich Highld
547 G4 Allt-nan-Sùgh Highld
533 K6 Alltour Highld
549 H6 Alltsigh Highld
154 B3 Alltwalis Carmth
130 A4 Alltwen Neath
180 D5 Alltyblaca Cerdgn
107 E2 Allt-yr-yn Newpt
224 D5 Allwood Green Suffk
295 F4 Alma Notts
424 B4 Almagill D & G
185 F4 Almeley Herefs
185 F4 Almeley Wooton Herefs
47 H5 Almer Dorset
330 C3 Almholme Donc
271 G3 Almington Staffs
512 C4 Almondbank P & K
328 B1 Almondbury Kirk
109 G3 Almondsbury S Glos
469 G1 Almondvale W Loth
173 E3 Almshouse Green Essex
357 F1 Alne N York
189 H3 Alne End Warwks
189 H2 Alne Hills Warwks
565 L2 Alness Highld
566 B3 Alnessferry Highld
357 F1 Alne Station N York
442 B2 Alnham Nthumb
443 F2 Alnmouth Nthumb
443 F2 Alnwick Nthumb
118 D3 Alperton Gt Lon
173 H2 Alphamstone Essex
199 H4 Alpheton Suffk
27 E5 Alphington Devon
250 B4 Alpington Norfk
293 H2 Alport Derbys
233 E5 Alport Powys
290 B3 Alpraham Ches
175 E5 Alresford Essex
238 B2 Alrewas Staffs
291 F5 Alsager Ches
291 F5 Alsagers Bank Staffs
141 G4 Alscot Bucks
293 G3 Alsop en le Dale Derbys
402 C5 Alston Cumb
29 E2 Alston Devon
162 D5 Alstone Gloucs
163 E3 Alstone Gloucs
84 B5 Alstone Somset
293 F3 Alstonefield Staffs
84 D4 Alston Sutton Somset
41 E3 Alswear Devon
326 D4 Alt Oldham
578 C7 Altandhu Highld
581 K4 Altanduin Highld
16 B2 Altarnun Cnwll
575 K3 Altass Highld
160 D4 Altbough Herefs
557 H4 Altens C Aber
589 H3 Alterwall Highld
481 E5 Altgaltraig Ag & B
340 B3 Altham Lancs
326 D4 Alt Hill Tamesd
148 B5 Althorne Essex
331 H3 Althorpe N Linc
117 E4 Altmore W & M
521 J4 Altnafeadh Highld
580 C2 Altnaharra Highld
343 G5 Altofts Wakefd
294 D2 Alton Derbys
73 H2 Alton Hants
273 G1 Alton Staffs
88 D5 Alton Wilts
88 C2 Alton Barnes Wilts
445 F2 Altonhill E Ayrs
46 D4 Alton Pancras Dorset
88 D2 Alton Priors Wilts
311 F2 Altrincham Traffd
533 K4 Altrua Highld
496 C4 Altskeith Stirlg
213 H2 Alum Rock Birm
498 D5 Alva Clacks
309 G5 Alvanley Ches
275 F3 Alvaston C Derb
213 F5 Alvechurch Worcs
238 C4 Alvecote Warwks
69 G5 Alvediston Wilts
211 H3 Alveley Shrops
39 H2 Alverdiscott Devon
51 H5 Alverstoke Hants
37 F3 Alverstone IoW
343 F5 Alverthorpe Wakefd
277 G1 Alverton Notts
567 L4 Alves Moray
138 D4 Alvescot Oxon
110 A2 Alveston S Glos
190 C5 Alveston Warwks
190 D2 Alveston Down S Glos
190 C4 Alveston Hill Warwks
550 F8 Alvie Highld

670 City, town and village index: Alvingham - Auchallater

320 B1 Alvingham Lincs
135 E4 Alvington Gloucs
45 G4 Alvington Somset
243 G5 Alwalton Cambs
107 F2 Alway Newpt
46 C2 Alweston Dorset
39 F3 Alwington Devon
441 H3 Alwinton Nthumb
343 E2 Alwoodley Leeds
343 F1 Alwoodley Gates Leeds
526 B5 Alyth P & K
3 E2 Amalebra Cnwll
3 E2 Amalveor Cnwll
575 K5 Amatnatua Highld
590 F5 Am Baile W Isls
275 G3 Ambaston Derbys
294 C4 Ambergate Derbys
136 B4 Amberley Gloucs
186 C5 Amberley Herefs
54 B2 Amberley W Susx
443 H4 Amble Nthumb
212 C2 Amblecote Dudley
378 C4 Ambleside Cumb
151 H4 Ambleston Pembks
166 D6 Ambrosden Oxon
332 A2 Amcotts N Linc
116 D6 Amen Corner Br For
142 C5 Amersham Bucks
142 D5 Amersham Common Bucks
142 C5 Amersham Old Town Bucks
142 D5 Amersham on the Hill Bucks
273 E4 Amerton Staffs
86 A3 Amesbury BaNES
70 D1 Amesbury Wilts
48 D4 Ameysford Dorset
238 C4 Amington Staffs
423 H3 Amisfield D & G
303 F2 Amlwch IoA
303 G2 Amlwch Port IoA
129 F2 Ammanford Carmth
29 G1 Ammerham Somset
373 E5 Amotherby N York
72 B5 Ampfield Hants
372 A4 Ampleforth N York
137 G4 Ampney Crucis Gloucs
137 G4 Ampney St Mary Gloucs
137 G4 Ampney St Peter Gloucs
89 G6 Amport Hants
169 E2 Ampthill Beds
223 H5 Ampton Suffk
126 D3 Amroth Pembks
511 F2 Amulree P & K
143 H2 Amwell Herts
551 J4 Anagach Highld
519 K3 Anaheilt Highld
563 J4 Anancaun Highld
562 D1 An Ard Highld
298 B6 Ancaster Lincs
208 C3 Anchor Shrops
52 B4 Anchorage Park C Port
248 D5 Anchor Corner Norfk
337 F1 Anchorsholme Lancs
256 C5 Anchor Street Norfk
599 K8 An Cnoc W Isls
599 L2 An Cnoc Ard W Isls
326 B5 Ancoats Manch
475 F5 Ancroft Nthumb
475 E5 Ancroft Northmoor Nthumb
452 B5 Ancrum Border
54 A4 Ancton W Susx
601 M1 Ancumtoun Ork
321 F4 Anderby Lincs
321 G4 Anderby Creek Lincs
65 F5 Andersea Somset
64 D5 Andersfield Somset
47 G5 Anderson Dorset
310 C4 Anderton Ches
10 D3 Anderton Cnwll
325 E2 Anderton Lancs
324 C2 Andertons Mill Lancs
90 B6 Andover Hants
90 B5 Andover Down Hants
163 F6 Andoversford Gloucs
322 g3 Andreas IoM
92 A4 Andwell Hants
262 A5 Anelog Gwynd
119 G6 Anerley Gt Lon
605 H5 Aness Shet
323 G6 Anfield Lpool
3 G2 Angarrack Cnwll
5 E1 Angarrick Cnwll
210 D4 Angelbank Shrops
43 G4 Angersleigh Somset
399 G3 Angerton Cumb
125 E4 Angle Pembks
599 J8 An Gleann Ur W Isls
54 C4 Angmering W Susx
357 G5 Angram N York
381 F5 Angram N York
403 G1 Anick Nthumb
497 E2 Anie Stirlg
187 G3 Ankerdine Hill Worcs
566 E2 Ankerville Highld
347 F4 Anlaby E R Yk
347 F4 Anlaby Park C KuH
590 E4 An Leth Meadhanach W Isls
253 E2 Anmer Norfk
52 B2 Anmore Hants
399 F1 Annan D & G
362 B4 Annaside Cumb
507 H5 Annat Ag & B
562 F6 Annat Highld
90 A6 Anna Valley Hants
445 E5 Annbank S Ayrs
295 G4 Annesley Notts
295 F4 Annesley Woodhouse Notts
405 E4 Annfield Plain Dur
484 A6 Anniesland C Glas
543 G6 Annishader Highld
226 D2 Annis Hill Suffk
431 E5 Annitsford N Tyne
560 D1 Annochie Abers
234 B3 Annscroft Shrops
51 G4 Ann's Hill Hants
275 E6 Annwell Place Derbys
337 F4 Ansdell Lancs
169 H6 Ansells End Herts
67 G3 Ansford Somset
215 E1 Ansley Warwks
239 E6 Ansley Common Warwks
274 C5 Anslow Staffs
274 B4 Anslow Gate Staffs
75 E3 Ansteadbrook Surrey
171 F3 Anstey Herts
240 B3 Anstey Leics
315 G3 Anston Rothm
503 F4 Anstruther Easter Fife
503 E4 Anstruther Wester Fife
215 F3 Ansty Warwks
69 G4 Ansty Wilts
77 E5 Ansty W Susx
69 G4 Ansty Coombe Wilts
47 E4 Ansty Cross Dorset
52 B2 Anthill Common Hants
93 H2 Anthony's Surrey
161 G5 Anthony's Cross Gloucs
399 F3 Anthorn Cumb
256 A3 Antingham Norfk
595 G5 An t-Ob W Isls
300 A5 Anton's Gowt Lincs
486 A3 Antonshill Falk
10 D3 Antony Cnwll
10 D2 Antony Passage Cnwll
310 C4 Antrobus Ches
100 B6 Anvil Green Kent
90 A1 Anvilles W Berk
299 E4 Anwick Lincs
417 H5 Anwoth D & G
533 K6 Aonachan Highld
291 G5 Apedale Staffs
96 B3 Aperfield Gt Lon
213 E5 Apes Dale Worcs
243 E5 Apethorpe Nhants
272 C6 Apeton Staffs
319 E4 Apley Lincs
235 G5 Apley Forge Shrops
314 D4 Apperknowle Derbys
162 C4 Apperley Gloucs
404 C3 Apperley Dene Nthumb
367 H1 Appersett N York
520 C6 Appin Ag & B
410 D4 Appleby D & G
332 D2 Appleby N Linc
391 H5 Appleby-in-Westmorland Cumb
239 E3 Appleby Magna Leics
239 E3 Appleby Parva Leics
562 B8 Applecross Highld
43 E5 Appledore Devon
60 B5 Appledore Devon
80 D4 Appledore Kent
81 E3 Appledore Heath Kent
140 B6 Appleford Oxon
424 C3 Applegarthtown D & G
116 D3 Applehouse Hill W & M
50 D3 Applemore Hants
89 G5 Appleshaw Hants
389 G4 Applethwaite Cumb
309 H2 Appleton Halton
139 G4 Appleton Oxon
372 D2 Appleton-le-Moors N York
372 D5 Appleton-le-Street N York
310 C3 Appleton Park Warrtn
344 D1 Appleton Roebuck N York
310 C3 Appleton Thorn Warrtn
384 B4 Appleton Wiske N York
439 G1 Appletreehall Border
354 D3 Appletreewick N York
37 G2 Appley IoW
43 E3 Appley Somset
324 C3 Appley Bridge Lancs
37 F4 Apse Heath IoW
202 B2 Apsey Green Suffk
169 G3 Apsley End Beds
53 E4 Apuldram W Susx
235 F3 Aqueduct Wrekin
559 G6 Aquhythie Abers
566 D1 Arabella Highld
515 G1 Arbirlot Angus
92 C1 Arborfield Wokham
92 C1 Arborfield Cross Wokham
92 C1 Arborfield Garrison Wokham
314 D2 Arbourthorne Sheff
515 G1 Arbroath Angus
197 F2 Arbury Cambs
541 E4 Arbuthnott Abers
383 F1 Archdeacon Newton Darltn
159 E1 Archenfield Herefs
568 C7 Archiestown Moray
35 j6 Archirondel Jersey
291 F2 Arclid Ches
291 F2 Arclid Green Ches
576 E3 Ardachu Highld
504 D7 Ardalanish Ag & B
561 F2 Ardallie Abers
507 J5 Ardanaiseig Ag & B
546 E2 Ardaneaskan Highld
546 E2 Ardarroch Highld
464 B1 Ardbeg Ag & B
477 G7 Ardbeg Ag & B
481 H3 Ardbeg Ag & B
574 D6 Ardcharnich Highld
504 D7 Ardchiavaig Ag & B
493 G2 Ardchonnell Ag & B
576 D6 Ardchronie Highld
497 E2 Ardchullarie More Stirlg
509 H4 Ardchyle Stirlg
567 H7 Ardclach Highld
495 E6 Ardarroch Ag & B
546 B1 Ard-dhubh Highld
232 D1 Arddleen Powys
533 H4 Ardechive Highld
170 D4 Ardeley Herts
546 F4 Ardelve Highld
483 E3 Arden Ag & B
466 D3 Arden C Glas
549 H2 Ardendrain Highld
312 B1 Arden Park Stockp
189 H4 Ardens Grafton Warwks
506 D5 Ardentallen Ag & B
482 A2 Ardentinny Ag & B
510 B2 Ardeonaig Stirlg
566 D6 Ardersier Highld
519 J3 Ardery Highld
573 K6 Ardessie Highld
492 D4 Ardfern Ag & B
478 F7 Ardfernal Ag & B
495 F4 Ardgartan Ag & B
576 C5 Ardgay Highld
576 C5 Ardgayhill Highld
482 B5 Ardgowan Inver
592 D4 Ardheisker W Isls
562 D5 Ardheslaig Highld
492 C5 Ardifuir Ag & B
492 B2 Ardinamir Ag & B
574 C6 Ardindrean Highld
77 F4 Ardingly W Susx
114 C2 Ardington Oxon
114 C2 Ardington Wick Oxon
546 E5 Ardintoul Highld
558 D4 Ardlair Abers
570 F3 Ardlawhill Abers
174 D4 Ardleigh Essex
120 D2 Ardleigh Green Gt Lon
175 E3 Ardleigh Heath Essex
175 E4 Ardleigh Park Essex
513 G1 Ardler P & K
166 B4 Ardley Oxon
146 A2 Ardley End Essex
495 G1 Ardlui Ag & B
479 G4 Ardlussa Ag & B
574 C4 Ardmair Highld
495 F4 Ardmay Ag & B
478 F7 Ardmenish Ag & B
458 C2 Ardminish Ag & B
519 H1 Ardmolich Highld
477 H6 Ardmore Ag & B
482 D4 Ardmore Ag & B
544 D1 Ardmore Highld
576 F6 Ardmore Highld
518 D6 Ardnacross Ag & B
482 A3 Ardnadam Ag & B
573 J2 Ardnagoine Highld
565 J7 Ardnagrask Highld
546 F2 Ardnarff Highld
519 J3 Ardnastang Highld
476 D2 Ardnave Ag & B
494 C3 Ardno Ag & B
560 C2 Ardo Abers
483 E4 Ardoch Ag & B
512 C2 Ardoch P & K
569 H7 Ardonald Abers
559 F4 Ardoyne Abers
482 B2 Ardpeaton Ag & B
480 A2 Ardrishaig Ag & B
542 D8 Ardroag Highld
565 L2 Ardross Highld
444 B1 Ardrossan N Ayrs
519 G2 Ardshealach Highld
478 A3 Ardskenish Ag & B
329 F3 Ardsley Barns
518 E3 Ardslignish Highld
477 H6 Ardtalla Ag & B
510 C2 Ardtalnaig P & K
518 F1 Ardtoe Highld
519 H6 Ardtornish Highld
544 E3 Ardtreck Highld
510 B5 Ardtrostan P & K
504 D6 Ardtun Ag & B
492 D2 Arduaine Ag & B
565 K4 Ardullie Highld
576 E6 Ardvannie Highld
531 H2 Ardvasar Highld
534 E5 Ardverikie Highld
509 K5 Ardvorlich P & K
596 F5 Ardvourlie W Isls
408 C2 Ardwell D & G
326 C5 Ardwick Manch
531 H8 Arean Highld
212 A5 Areley Kings Worcs
74 C2 Arford Hants
132 C4 Argoed Caerph
209 E1 Argoed Powys
209 F3 Argoed Shrops
269 F5 Argoed Shrops
78 D4 Argos Hill E Susx
597 G4 Aribruach W Isls
504 C6 Aridhglas Ag & B
516 F5 Arileod Ag & B
562 C5 Arinacrinachd Highld
517 G4 Arinagour Ag & B
600 D2 Arion Ork
531 J5 Arisaig Highld
519 K3 Ariundle Highld
519 G2 Arivegaig Highld
356 D2 Arkendale N York
171 G3 Arkesden Essex
366 B5 Arkholme Lancs
388 D2 Arkleby Cumb
425 H1 Arkleton D & G
382 B4 Arkle Town N York
144 B5 Arkley Gt Lon
330 C3 Arksey Donc
315 E5 Arkwright Town Derbys
162 D5 Arle Gloucs
136 B3 Arlebrook Gloucs
388 B6 Arlecdon Cumb
191 F5 Arlescote Warwks
170 A2 Arlesey Beds
235 F2 Arleston Wrekin
310 D3 Arley Ches
310 D3 Arley Green Ches
135 G2 Arlingham Gloucs
61 F3 Arlington Devon
57 E3 Arlington E Susx
137 H3 Arlington Gloucs
61 F3 Arlington Beccott Devon
531 H2 Armadale Highld
587 G4 Armadale Highld
486 B6 Armadale W Loth
401 E5 Armathwaite Cumb
172 B4 Armigers Essex
250 A4 Arminghall Norfk
237 G1 Armitage Staffs
328 A2 Armitage Bridge Kirk
343 E3 Armley Leeds
190 C6 Armscote Warwks
271 H3 Armsdale Staffs
292 B5 Armshead Staffs
219 F2 Armston Nhants
330 D4 Armthorpe Donc
516 F3 Arnabost Ag & B
362 D5 Arnaby Cumb
368 B5 Arncliffe N York
503 E3 Arncroach Fife
568 D6 Arndilly House Moray
33 H2 Arne Dorset
216 D1 Arnesby Leics
500 B2 Arngask P & K
459 E4 Arnicle Ag & B
546 E7 Arnisdale Highld
543 K7 Arnish Highld
471 F2 Arniston Mdloth
599 G5 Arnol W Isls
348 B1 Arnold E R Yk
296 A5 Arnold Notts
109 H5 Arno's Vale Bristl
497 F6 Arnprior Stirlg
365 F4 Arnside Cumb
518 E7 Aros Cott Ag & B
518 E6 Aros Mains Ag & B
270 B2 Arowry Wrexhm
565 K6 Arpafeelie Highld
82 C3 Arpinge Kent
364 D3 Arrad Foot Cumb
360 C6 Arram E R Yk
383 E6 Arrathorne N York
37 E3 Arreton IoW
495 G4 Arrochar Ag & B
189 G3 Arrow Warwks
308 C2 Arrowe Hill Wirral
213 F5 Arrowfield Top Worcs
186 A3 Arrow Green Herefs
328 A3 Arrunden Kirk
580 D7 Arscaig Highld
234 A3 Arscott Shrops
565 L7 Artafallie Highld
311 E2 Arthill Ches
356 B6 Arthington Leeds
217 G3 Arthingworth Nhants
229 E2 Arthog Gwynd
561 E2 Arthrath Abers
343 G2 Arthursdale Leeds
526 C6 Arthurstone P & K
93 G5 Artington Surrey
561 F3 Artrochie Abers
54 B3 Arundel W Susx
520 E2 Aryhoulan Highld
388 C5 Asby Cumb
464 C2 Ascog Ag & B
117 F6 Ascot W & M
165 E3 Ascott Warwks
165 E6 Ascott d' Oyley Oxon
164 D6 Ascott Earl Oxon
164 D6 Ascott-under-Wychwood Oxon
526 D3 Ascreavie Angus
370 D4 Asenby N York
277 F6 Asfordby Leics
277 F6 Asfordby Hill Leics
299 E5 Asgarby Lincs
300 B1 Asgarby Lincs
13 E3 Ash Devon
30 B3 Ash Dorset
47 G2 Ash Dorset
97 E2 Ash Kent
101 E4 Ash Kent
44 B3 Ash Somset
66 D5 Ash Somset
93 E5 Ash Surrey
546 B5 Ashaig Highld
115 F4 Ashampstead W Berk
115 F4 Ashampstead Green W Berk
98 C4 Ashbank Kent
292 B5 Ash Bank Staffs
64 A4 Ashbeer Somset
201 G4 Ashbocking Suffk
293 G5 Ashbourne Derbys
43 F3 Ashbrittle Somset
234 A6 Ashbrook Shrops
58 A3 Ashburnham Forge E Susx
19 G4 Ashburton Devon
24 D3 Ashbury Devon
113 G2 Ashbury Oxon
332 B3 Ashby N Linc
300 D1 Ashby by Partney Lincs
334 C4 Ashby cum Fenby NE Lin
298 D3 Ashby de la Launde Lincs
239 E1 Ashby-de-la-Zouch Leics
241 F2 Ashby Folville Leics
334 B4 Ashby Hill NE Lin
216 C1 Ashby Magna Leics
216 B2 Ashby Parva Leics
320 B5 Ashby Puerorum Lincs
216 C6 Ashby St Ledgers Nhants
250 C4 Ashby St Mary Norfk
162 D3 Ashchurch Gloucs
20 C2 Ashcombe Devon
84 B2 Ashcombe Park N Som
66 C2 Ashcott Somset
66 D1 Ashcott Corner Somset
43 F5 Ashculme Devon
172 B1 Ashdon Essex
91 E4 Ashe Hants
148 C4 Asheldham Essex
173 E1 Ashen Essex
141 F2 Ashendon Bucks
142 C4 Asheridge Bucks
37 F3 Ashey IoW
380 C4 Ash Fell Cumb
479 K4 Ashfield Ag & B
155 G4 Ashfield Carmth
71 H6 Ashfield Hants
160 D5 Ashfield Herefs
269 F4 Ashfield Shrops
498 B4 Ashfield Stirlg
201 H2 Ashfield Suffk
201 H2 Ashfield cum Thorpe Suffk
199 F3 Ashfield Green Suffk
226 B5 Ashfield Green Suffk
271 G4 Ashfields Shrops
76 D4 Ashfold Crossways W Susx
355 F1 Ashfold Side N York
12 B3 Ashford Devon
60 D4 Ashford Devon
49 E2 Ashford Hants
81 F1 Ashford Kent
118 B5 Ashford Surrey
210 C5 Ashford Bowdler Shrops
210 C5 Ashford Carbonell Shrops
118 B5 Ashford Common Surrey
91 E2 Ashford Hill Hants
313 G6 Ashford in the Water Derbys
314 D5 Ashgate Derbys
468 B5 Ashgill S Lans
93 F5 Ash Green Surrey
215 E3 Ash Green Warwks
86 B3 Ashgrove BaNES
568 C3 Ashgrove Moray
269 G1 Ash Grove Wrexhm
20 C3 Ash Hill Devon
451 E2 Ashiestiel Border
43 E5 Ashill Devon
248 A4 Ashill Norfk
44 C4 Ashill Somset
147 H6 Ashingdon Essex
430 D2 Ashington Nthumb
48 C5 Ashington Poole
67 F5 Ashington Somset
54 D1 Ashington W Susx
301 F1 Ashington End Lincs
451 F5 Ashkirk Border
51 E4 Ashlett Hants
162 B4 Ashleworth Gloucs
198 D2 Ashley Cambs
311 F3 Ashley Ches
49 E4 Ashley Dorset
49 H5 Ashley Hants
72 A3 Ashley Hants
101 F6 Ashley Kent
217 G1 Ashley Nhants
271 H2 Ashley Staffs
111 E6 Ashley Wilts
136 D6 Ashley Wilts
271 H2 Ashley Dale Staffs
109 G4 Ashley Down Bristl
142 D3 Ashley Green Bucks
294 B4 Ashleyhay Derbys
49 E4 Ashley Heath Dorset
271 G2 Ashley Heath Staffs
311 F2 Ashley Heath Traffd
186 B1 Ashley Moor Herefs
94 C1 Ashley Park Surrey
270 D2 Ash Magna Shrops
256 C5 Ashmanhaugh Norfk
90 C3 Ashmansworth Hants
38 D4 Ashmansworthy Devon
135 H5 Ashmead Green Gloucs
24 A3 Ashmill Devon
41 F3 Ash Mill Devon
41 F4 Ash Moor Devon
69 F6 Ashmore Dorset
114 D6 Ashmore Green W Berk
237 E5 Ashmore Lake Wsall
237 E4 Ashmore Park Wolves
313 G2 Ashopton Derbys
191 E3 Ashorne Warwks
294 C2 Ashover Derbys
294 D2 Ashover Hay Derbys
215 E5 Ashow Warwks
270 D2 Ash Parva Shrops
161 E1 Ashperton Herefs
13 E1 Ashprington Devon
43 F2 Ash Priors Somset
40 C5 Ashreigney Devon
25 G2 Ashridge Court Devon
200 D5 Ash Street Suffk
94 D3 Ashtead Surrey
42 D5 Ash Thomas Devon
309 H6 Ashton Ches
4 B3 Ashton Cnwll
243 G3 Ashton C Pete
72 D6 Ashton Hants
186 C2 Ashton Herefs
482 B4 Ashton Inver
193 G5 Ashton Nhants
219 F2 Ashton Nhants
84 D5 Ashton Somset
87 F3 Ashton Common Wilts
109 G5 Ashton Gate Bristl
56 D2 Ashton Green E Susx
310 B4 Ashton Heath Ches
324 D5 Ashton-in-Makerfield Wigan
137 G6 Ashton Keynes Wilts
163 E2 Ashton under Hill Worcs
326 D5 Ashton-under-Lyne Tamesd
326 A6 Ashton Upon Mersey Traffd
109 G5 Ashton Vale Bristl
50 B2 Ashurst Hants
78 C2 Ashurst Kent
324 B3 Ashurst Lancs
55 E1 Ashurst W Susx
50 B2 Ashurst Bridge Hants
77 H2 Ashurst Wood W Susx
132 B2 Ashvale Blae G
93 E4 Ash Vale Surrey
24 A3 Ashwater Devon
20 B3 Ashwell Devon
170 C2 Ashwell Herts
242 B2 Ashwell Rutlnd
44 D4 Ashwell Somset
170 C1 Ashwell End Herts
249 F5 Ashwellthorpe Norfk
86 A5 Ashwick Somset
253 E4 Ashwicken Norfk
212 C2 Ashwood Staffs
362 D6 Askam in Furness Cumb
330 C2 Askern Donc
30 C4 Askerswell Dorset
297 F5 Askerton Hill Notts
141 H3 Askett Bucks
391 E5 Askham Cumb
316 D5 Askham Notts
357 H5 Askham Bryan York
357 G5 Askham Richard York
480 C1 Asknish Ag & B
457 E2 Askomill Ag & B
368 B1 Askrigg N York
355 G5 Askwith N York
279 F3 Aslackby Lincs
225 F1 Aslacton Norfk
277 F1 Aslockton Notts
555 F2 Asloun Abers
66 D2 Asney Somset
201 G1 Aspall Suffk
388 D1 Aspatria Cumb
171 E4 Aspenden Herts
280 C2 Asperton Lincs
276 B1 Aspley C Nott
272 B3 Aspley Staffs
168 C2 Aspley Guise Beds
168 C2 Aspley Heath Beds
213 G5 Aspley Heath Warwks
325 E3 Aspull Wigan
325 E5 Aspult Common Wigan
606 C2 Assater Shet
345 G4 Asselby E R Yk
321 E4 Asserby Lincs
321 E4 Asserby Turn Lincs
174 B2 Assington Suffk
199 F4 Assington Green Suffk
291 G2 Astbury Ches
193 E4 Astcote Nhants
319 H4 Asterby Lincs
233 G3 Asterley Shrops
209 G1 Asterton Shrops
138 D2 Asthall Oxon
139 E2 Asthall Leigh Oxon
311 G5 Astle Ches
270 C6 Astley Shrops
215 E2 Astley Warwks
325 G4 Astley Wigan
212 A6 Astley Worcs
235 G5 Astley Abbotts Shrops
325 G2 Astley Bridge Bolton
212 B6 Astley Cross Worcs
325 G5 Astley Green Wigan
310 A3 Astmoor Halton
213 G2 Aston Birm
290 C5 Aston Ches
310 B4 Aston Ches
274 B3 Aston Derbys
313 G3 Aston Derbys
288 D1 Aston Flints
210 B5 Aston Herefs
170 C5 Aston Herts
139 E4 Aston Oxon
186 B2 Aston Powys
209 E1 Aston Powys
315 F3 Aston Rothm
236 B6 Aston Shrops
270 C4 Aston Shrops
271 H1 Aston Staffs
272 C5 Aston Staffs
116 C3 Aston Wokham
235 E3 Aston Wrekin
168 A5 Aston Abbotts Bucks
211 E5 Aston Bank Worcs
211 E3 Aston Botterell Shrops
272 D3 Aston-By-Stone Staffs
190 A3 Aston Cantlow Warwks
142 B2 Aston Clinton Bucks
161 F5 Aston Crews Herefs
162 D3 Aston Cross Gloucs
235 F6 Aston Eyre Shrops
213 E6 Aston Fields Worcs
215 H1 Aston Flamville Leics
161 F5 Aston Ingham Herefs
290 C3 Aston juxta Mondrum Ches
192 A4 Aston le Walls Nhants
164 B2 Aston Magna Gloucs
210 C2 Aston Munslow Shrops
162 D3 Aston on Carrant Gloucs
209 G3 Aston on Clun Shrops
275 G4 Aston-on-Trent Derbys
233 F3 Aston Pigott Shrops
233 F3 Aston Rogers Shrops
141 F5 Aston Rowant Oxon
141 G3 Aston Sandford Bucks
163 F2 Aston Somerville Worcs
269 F4 Aston Sq Shrops
164 A1 Aston Subedge Gloucs
115 F2 Aston Tirrold Oxon
115 E2 Aston Upthorpe Oxon
166 B2 Astrop Nhants
142 B2 Astrope Herts
170 B2 Astwick Beds
295 E2 Astwith Derbys
194 D5 Astwood M Keyn
188 C3 Astwood Worcs
188 D2 Astwood Worcs
189 F2 Astwood Bank Worcs
279 F2 Aswarby Lincs
320 C5 Aswardby Lincs
234 C3 Atcham Shrops
189 F4 Atch Lench Worcs
47 E6 Athelhampton Dorset
225 G5 Athelington Suffk
44 C2 Athelney Somset
489 G4 Athelstaneford E Loth
36 D5 Atherfield Green IoW
40 B3 Atherington Devon
54 B4 Atherington W Susx
329 F3 Athersley South Barns
44 D4 Atherstone Somset
239 E5 Atherstone Warwks
190 B4 Atherstone on Stour Warwks
325 F4 Atherton Wigan
294 A5 Atlow Derbys
30 A3 Atrim Dorset
547 G2 Attadale Highld
276 B3 Attenborough Notts
168 B2 Atterbury M Keyn
332 D6 Atterby Lincs
314 D2 Attercliffe Sheff
235 E5 Atterley Shrops
239 E5 Atterton Leics
234 D3 Attingham Shrops
249 E5 Attleborough Norfk
215 F1 Attleborough Warwks
255 F4 Attlebridge Norfk
199 E4 Attleton Green Suffk
361 F4 Atwick E R Yk
87 F1 Atworth Wilts
186 B5 Auberrow Herefs
297 H2 Aubourn Lincs
460 B3 Auchagallon N Ayrs
537 J5 Auchallater Abers

559 E1 Aucharnie Abers
556 B6 Auchattie Abers
525 J2 Auchavan Angus
552 E3 Auchbreck Moray
466 C3 Auchenback E Rens
435 G5 Auchenbainzie D & G
540 D4 Auchenblae Abers
435 F4 Auchenbrack D & G
481 E3 Auchenbreck Ag & B
413 E4 Auchencairn D & G
423 G3 Auchencairn D & G
461 E4 Auchencairn N Ayrs
460 B2 Auchencar N Ayrs
483 F3 Auchencarroch W Duns
474 C2 Auchencrow Border
471 E2 Auchendinny Mdloth
537 H4 Auchendryne Abers
469 F4 Auchengray S Lans
435 G3 Auchengruith D & G
568 F3 Auchenhalrig Moray
444 C1 Auchenharvie N Ayrs
468 C6 Auchenheath S Lans
435 F5 Auchenhessnane D & G
461 E5 Auchenhew N Ayrs
480 D5 Auchenmalg D & G
416 A6 Auchenmade N Ayrs
419 F3 Auchensoul S Ayrs
467 G4 Auchentibber S Lans
465 H5 Auchentiber N Ayrs
551 C6 Auchgourish Highld
484 C6 Auchinairn C Glas
569 C5 Auchinderran Moray
494 A4 Auchindrain Ag & B
574 D7 Auchindrean Highld
569 L6 Auchininna Abers
417 E2 Auchinleck D & G
446 B5 Auchinleck E Ayrs
526 B3 Auchinleish Angus
484 D5 Auchinloch N Lans
467 G3 Auchinraith S Lans
484 D4 Auchinreoch E Duns
485 E4 Auchinstarry N Lans
555 F1 Auchintoul Abers
536 C3 Auchlean Highld
557 F5 Auchleuchries Abers
561 F2 Auchleuchries Abers
559 E5 Auchleven Abers
447 F2 Auchlochan S Lans
555 G4 Auchlossan Abers
557 F5 Auchlunies Abers
509 H4 Auchlyne Stirlg
561 E3 Auchmacoy Abers
445 J4 Auchmillan E Ayrs
529 E6 Auchmithie Angus
509 J3 Auchmore Stirlg
500 D4 Auchmuirbridge Fife
540 A5 Auchmull Angus
501 E4 Auchmuty Fife
527 G2 Auchnacree Angus
511 E3 Auchnafree P & K
551 K3 Auchnagallin Highld
560 D1 Auchnagatt Abers
552 E4 Auchnarrow Moray
538 C1 Aucholzie Abers
539 E3 Auchronie Angus
499 E2 Auchterarder P & K
548 F8 Auchteraw Highld
562 E1 Auchtercairn Highld
500 D5 Auchterderran Fife
513 H2 Auchterhouse Angus
500 D2 Auchtermuchty Fife
487 H1 Auchtertool Fife
546 E4 Auchtertyre Highld
509 J5 Auchtubh Stirlg
589 K4 Auckengill Highld
330 D4 Auckley Donc
326 D5 Audenshaw Tamesd
290 D6 Audlem Ches
291 F4 Audley Staffs
171 H2 Audley End Essex
173 G2 Audley End Essex
225 F3 Audley End Norfk
199 H4 Audley End Suffk
569 L3 Auds Abers
389 F2 Aughertree Cumb
345 G2 Aughton E R Yk
323 G4 Aughton Lancs
352 B1 Aughton Lancs
315 F2 Aughton Rothm
89 F3 Aughton Wilts
323 H3 Aughton Park Lancs
393 F4 Aukside Dur
411 E4 Auldbrck D & G
567 G5 Auldearn Highld
186 B4 Aulden Herefs
423 F2 Auldgirth D & G
490 A3 Auldhame E Loth
467 F4 Auldhouse S Lans
559 F1 Auldyoch Abers
547 G5 Ault a' Chruinn Highld
579 K2 Aultanrynie Highld
573 G6 Aultbea Highld
564 D3 Aultdearg Highld
572 D6 Aultgrishan Highld
295 F1 Ault Hucknall Derbys
582 D5 Aultiphurst Highld
587 H3 Aultivullin Highld
587 H3 Aultmore Highld
569 G5 Aultmore Moray
549 J5 Ault-na-goire Highld
559 E4 Aulton Abers
565 J7 Aultvaich Highld
243 E2 Aunby Lincs
551 H6 Aundorach Highld
27 G2 Aunk Devon
279 E2 Aunsby Lincs
560 B4 Auquharney Abers
109 G2 Aust S Glos
280 C5 Austendike Lincs
335 E6 Austen Fen Lincs
117 G2 Austenwood Bucks
331 E6 Austerfield Donc
327 E3 Austerlands Oldham
238 D3 Austrey Warwks
367 F6 Austwick N York
320 D3 Authorpe Lincs
321 F5 Authorpe Row Lincs
112 D6 Avebury Wilts
112 C6 Avebury Trusloe Wilts
121 E4 Aveley Thurr
136 C5 Avening Gloucs
135 G6 Avening Green S Glos
297 E4 Averham Notts
546 E4 Avernish Highld
120 B5 Avery Hill Gt Lon
12 B3 Aveton Gifford Devon
551 G6 Avielochan Highld
550 F7 Aviemore Highld
72 D3 Avington Hants
114 B6 Avington W Berk
566 C6 Avoch Highld
49 E5 Avon Hants
111 H4 Avon Wilts
486 A5 Avonbridge Falk
49 E4 Avon Castle Hants
86 D3 Avoncliff Wilts
191 G5 Avon Dassett Warwks
109 F4 Avonmouth Bristl
19 F6 Avonwick Devon
71 G5 Awbridge Hants
109 G2 Awkley S Glos
28 B2 Awliscombe Devon
135 G3 Awre Gloucs
295 F6 Awsworth Notts

84 D4 Axbridge Somset
91 G6 Axford Hants
113 F5 Axford Wilts
91 F2 Axmansford Hants
29 E3 Axminster Devon
29 E4 Axmouth Devon
307 F4 Axton Flints
18 B4 Axtown Devon
405 E2 Axwell Park Gatesd
83 F2 Aycliff Kent
395 F5 Aycliffe Village Dur
404 B3 Aydon Nthumb
405 G6 Aykley Heads Dur
135 E4 Aylburton Gloucs
135 E4 Aylburton Common Gloucs
402 C5 Ayle Nthumb
27 G4 Aylesbeare Devon
141 G2 Aylesbury Bucks
334 B3 Aylesby NE Lin
97 H3 Aylesford Kent
100 D5 Aylesham Kent
240 C1 Aylestone C Leic
160 C1 Aylestone Hill Herefs
240 C1 Aylestone Park C Leic
261 G2 Aylmerton Norfk
255 G2 Aylsham Norfk
161 F2 Aylton Herefs
163 G5 Aylworth Gloucs
185 H1 Aymestrey Herefs
166 B3 Aynho Nhants
144 B2 Ayot Green Herts
144 A1 Ayot St Lawrence Herts
144 B1 Ayot St Peter Herts
444 D5 Ayr S Ayrs
143 H2 Ayres End Herts
606 C8 Ayres of Selivoe Shet
406 B3 Ayres Quay Sundld
368 D2 Aysgarth N York
42 D4 Ayshford Devon
365 E3 Ayside Cumb
242 B4 Ayston Rutlnd
146 B1 Aythorpe Roding Essex
474 B2 Ayton Border
405 G3 Ayton Sundld
474 C2 Ayton Castle Border
609 G7 Aywick Shet
370 B5 Azerley N York

B

20 C4 Babbacombe Torbay
295 F6 Babbington Notts
269 F3 Babbinswood Shrops
145 E1 Babbs Green Herts
67 F4 Babcary Somset
156 C2 Babel Carmth
199 E5 Babel Green Suffk
307 G5 Babell Flints
19 E2 Babeny Devon
252 D2 Babingley Norfk
197 H4 Babraham Cambs
316 C3 Babworth Notts
599 K6 Bac W Isls
303 F4 Bachau IoA
210 B3 Bache Shrops
208 D1 Bacheldre Powys
58 D4 Bachelor's Bump E Susx
210 B2 Bache Mill Shrops
129 F4 Bach-y-gwreiddyn Swans
603 H6 Backaland Ork
602 F1 Backaskaill Ork
365 E3 Backbarrow Cumb
327 E6 Backbower Tamesd
541 F1 Backburn Abers
558 C3 Backburn Abers
127 F1 Backe Carmth
571 J5 Backfolds Abers
309 E5 Backford Ches
309 E5 Backford Cross Ches
560 A2 Backhill Abers
561 F2 Backhill Abers
571 G6 Backhill of Clackriach Abers
569 L5 Backhill of Clunie Abers
561 E1 Backhill of Fortrie Abers
556 A5 Backhill of Trustach Abers
577 H3 Backies Highld
567 L3 Backlands Moray
588 F6 Backlass Highld
502 C3 Backmuir of New Gilston Fife
531 H5 Back of Keppoch Highld
293 H2 Back o'th' Brook Staffs
446 B5 Back Rogerton E Ayrs
199 E3 Back Street Suffk
109 E6 Backwell N Som
109 E5 Backwell Common N Som
109 E6 Backwell Green N Som
431 F5 Backworth N Tyne
172 C6 Bacon End Essex
172 C6 Baconend Green Essex
214 B2 Bacon's End Solhll
261 F4 Baconsthorpe Norfk
159 G3 Bacton Herefs
256 C3 Bacton Norfk
201 E1 Bacton Suffk
256 C3 Bacton Green Norfk
200 D1 Bacton Green Suffk
340 D5 Bacup Lancs
566 B2 Badachonacher Highld
562 D2 Badachro Highld
563 L5 Badavanich Highld
113 E3 Badbury Swindn
113 E3 Badbury Wick Swindn
192 G3 Badby Nhants
584 D5 Badcall Highld
573 K5 Badcaul Highld
589 G7 Baddeley Edge C Stke
573 J5 Baddeley Green C Stke
214 B5 Baddesley Clinton Warwks
238 D5 Baddesley Ensor Warwks
578 E5 Baddidarrach Highld
537 H6 Baddoch Abers
147 E4 Baddow Park Essex
573 K2 Badenscallie Highld
559 F2 Badentoy Park Abers
557 F5 Badenyon Abers
553 G5 Badgall Cnwll
23 E5 Badgeney Cambs
245 F5 Badger Shrops
235 H5 Badger's Cross Cnwll
3 E3 Badger's Hill Worcs
189 H5 Badgers Mount Kent
96 C2 Badger Street Somset
44 B4 Badgeworth Gloucs
162 D6 Badgworth Somset
84 C4 Badharlick Cnwll
23 F5 Badicaul Highld
546 D4 Badingham Suffk
226 C6 Badlipster Highld
99 G4 Badluarach Highld
589 G2 Badminton S Glos
573 J5 Badnaban Highld
111 E3 Badnagie Highld
578 B3 Badninish Highld
583 G3 Badrallach Highld
577 G5 Badsey Worcs
573 L5 Badshalloch W Duns
189 G6 Badshot Lea Surrey
483 F2 Badsworth Wakefd
93 E5 Badwell Ash Suffk
341 H1 Badwell Green Suffk
200 D1 Badworthy Devon
224 C6

224 D6 Badwell Green Suffk
19 E5 Badworthy Devon
52 B4 Baffins C Port
47 E2 Bagber Dorset
371 F3 Bagby N York
371 F3 Bagby Grange N York
320 C5 Bag Enderby Lincs
137 F3 Bagendon Gloucs
211 F3 Bagginswood Shrops
389 E1 Baggrow Cumb
592 H3 Bàgh a Chàise W Isls
591 D8 Bàgh a' Chaisteil W Isls
100 A5 Bagham Kent
590 E4 Baghasdal W Isls
592 F6 Bàgh Mòr W Isls
591 D7 Bàgh Shiarabhagh W Isls
308 B4 Bagillt Flints
215 E5 Baginton Warwks
104 B1 Baglan Neath
342 D2 Bagley Leeds
269 H4 Bagley Shrops
85 E5 Bagley Somset
85 F4 Bagley Green Somset
269 G4 Bagley Marsh Shrops
91 H6 Bagmore Hants
292 B4 Bagnall Staffs
114 C6 Bagnor W Berk
136 B6 Bagpath Gloucs
136 C4 Bagpath Gloucs
313 E3 Bagshaw Derbys
93 F2 Bagshot Surrey
89 H1 Bagshot Wilts
93 F2 Bagshot Heath Surrey
326 C2 Bagslate Moor Rochdl
110 B2 Bagstone S Glos
259 F5 Bagthorpe Norfk
295 F4 Bagthorpe Notts
311 G2 Baguley Manch
37 E4 Bagwich IoW
239 G3 Bagworth Leics
160 A3 Bagwyllydiart Herefs
524 C2 Bailanloan P & K
599 J3 Bail Ard Bhuirgh W Isls
86 D1 Bailbrook BaNES
342 D2 Baildon Brad
342 B2 Baildon Green Brad
594 E6 Baile W Isls
597 H3 Baile Ailein W Isls
592 H4 Baile a' Mhanaich W Isls
599 H4 Baile an Truiseil W Isls
549 H6 Bailebeag Highld
479 J7 Baile Boidheach Ag & B
593 D8 Baile Gharbhaidh W Isls
592 E6 Baile Glas W Isls
592 E6 Baile Mhàrtainn W Isls
594 D7 Baile Mhic' Phàil W Isls
504 B6 Baile Mòr Ag & B
591 D7 Baile na Creige W Isls
593 C7 Baile na Cailleach W Isls
592 C4 Baile Raghnill W Isls
531 H8 Bailetonach Highld
73 G4 Bailey Green Hants
558 B2 Baileyward Abers
592 E6 Bail' Iochdrach W Isls
467 E2 Bailleston C Glas
351 G3 Bailrigg Lancs
592 E5 Bail Uachdraich W Isls
599 L5 Bail' Ur Tholastaidh W Isls
368 B1 Bainbridge N York
486 A3 Bainsford Falk
559 E2 Bainshole Abers
243 F3 Bainton C Pete
360 B4 Bainton E R Yk
166 C4 Bainton Oxon
501 F4 Baintown Fife
440 B1 Bairnkine Border
80 A3 Baker's Cross Kent
145 E1 Bakers End Herts
134 D2 Baker's Hill Gloucs
121 F3 Baker's Hill Gloucs
118 C4 Baker's Wood Bucks
23 E2 Bakesdown Cnwll
315 G4 Bakestone Moor Derbys
313 H6 Bakewell Derbys
267 E2 Bala Gwynd
545 J1 Balachuirn Highld
597 H3 Balallan W Isls
273 G3 Balance Hill Staffs
535 L2 Balavil Highld
549 H3 Balbeg Highld
549 H5 Balbeg Highld
513 H4 Balbeggie P & K
560 A6 Balbithan Abers
556 C5 Balblair Abers
565 J7 Balblair Highld
566 C3 Balblair Highld
503 E4 Balbuthie Fife
330 C4 Balby Donc
515 F2 Balcathie Angus
577 H7 Balcherry Highld
578 D3 Balchladich Highld
549 K3 Balchraggan Highld
565 J8 Balchraggan Highld
584 C4 Balchrick Highld
77 F3 Balcombe W Susx
77 F3 Balcombe Lane W Susx
503 G3 Balcomie Fife
501 F4 Balcurvie Fife
370 D4 Baldersby N York
370 D4 Baldersby St James N York
339 F3 Balderstone Lancs
326 D2 Balderstone Rochdl
289 E2 Balderton Ches
297 F3 Balderton Notts
7 E5 Baldhu Cnwll
326 A2 Baldingstone Bury
502 C2 Baldinnie Fife
170 B3 Baldock Herts
140 C4 Baldon Row Oxon
514 D3 Baldovie C Dund
322 g6 Baldrine IoM
58 D4 Baldslow E Susx
322 f6 Baldwin IoM
400 B4 Baldwinholme Cumb
272 A2 Baldwin's Gate Staffs
77 G2 Baldwins Hill W Susx
260 D4 Bale Norfk
516 B7 Balemartine Ag & B
592 C4 Balemore W Isls
516 C6 Balephetrish Ag & B
516 C6 Balephuil Ag & B
470 C1 Balerno C Edin
478 B3 Baleromindubh Ag & B
516 B6 Balevullin Ag & B
539 G6 Balfield Angus
601 H1 Balfour Ork
484 B2 Balfron Stirlg
483 H2 Balfron Station Stirlg
559 E1 Balgaveny Abers
528 B3 Balgavies House Angus
501 E4 Balgeddie Fife
499 G6 Balgonar Fife
560 B3 Balgove Abers
408 B3 Balgowan D & G
535 H4 Balgowan Highld
512 A5 Balgowan P & K
570 E5 Balgown Highld
544 E2 Balgown Highld
565 L7 Balgracie D & G
565 L7 Balgray Angus
565 J6 Balgreen Abers
492 C1 Balgy Highld
559 H5 Balhaldie Stirlg
119 F3 Balham Gt Lon

526 C5 Balhary P & K
609 J3 Baliasta Shet
587 H3 Baligill Highld
506 D1 Baligrundle Ag & B
479 J7 Balimore Ag & B
516 B7 Balinoe Ag & B
526 C3 Balintore Angus
566 F1 Balintore Highld
566 C2 Balintraid Highld
592 D6 Balivanich W Isls
526 D6 Balkeerie Angus
316 D3 Balk Field Notts
346 A4 Balkholme E R Yk
529 F4 Balkissock S Ayrs
418 D5 Balkissock S Ayrs
14 D4 Ball Cnwll
269 F4 Ball Shrops
322 d8 Ballabeg IoM
540 C5 Ballachulish Highld
340 C5 Balladen Lancs
322 c8 Ballafesson IoM
322 c8 Ballakilpheric IoM
322 d8 Ballamodha IoM
418 C5 Ballantrae S Ayrs
112 C3 Ballard's Ash Wilts
123 E1 Ballards Green Warwks
214 D1 Ballard's Green Warwks
322 d8 Ballasalla IoM
554 C5 Ballater Abers
322 e4 Ballaugh IoM
524 D5 Ballechin P & K
576 E7 Balleigh Highld
489 F4 Ballencrieff E Loth
486 C5 Ballencrieff Toll W Loth
524 C2 Ballentoul P & K
292 A4 Ball Green C Stke
292 C3 Ball Haye Green Staffs
38 C3 Ballhill Devon
90 C2 Ball Hill Hants
293 H4 Ballidon Derbys
460 B2 Balliekine N Ayrs
481 F3 Balliemore Ag & B
506 D4 Balliemore Ag & B
566 B8 Ballifeary Highld
480 C3 Ballimore Ag & B
507 J4 Ballimore Ag & B
509 H6 Ballimore Stirlg
476 C3 Ballinaby Ag & B
513 G4 Ballindean P & K
173 H1 Ballingdon Suffk
143 E2 Ballingdon Bottom Herts
173 H1 Ballingdon Grove Suffk
142 C4 Ballinger Bottom (South) Bucks
142 C4 Ballinger Bottom Bucks
142 C4 Ballinger Common Bucks
160 D3 Ballingham Herefs
160 D3 Ballingham Hill Herefs
500 C5 Ballingry Fife
512 A1 Ballinlick P & K
524 E5 Ballinluig P & K
525 H4 Ballintuim P & K
506 D1 Balliveolan Ag & B
576 C2 Balloan Highld
526 D3 Balloch Angus
566 C7 Balloch Highld
485 E5 Balloch N Lans
483 E3 Balloch W Duns
539 G1 Ballochan Abers
484 B2 Ballochearn Stirlg
464 B2 Ballochgoy Ag & B
462 B4 Ballochroy Ag & B
309 G2 Ball o' Ditton Halton
555 G5 Ballogie Abers
75 F4 Balls Cross W Susx
175 E5 Balls Green Essex
78 B2 Balls Green E Susx
136 C5 Ball's Green Gloucs
76 B5 Balls Green W Susx
237 E6 Balls Hill Sandw
518 B7 Ballygown Ag & B
476 F3 Ballygrant Ag & B
516 F4 Ballyhaugh Ag & B
492 D5 Ballymeanoch Ag & B
546 E4 Balmacara Highld
546 E4 Balmacara Square Highld
421 H4 Balmaclellan D & G
524 E5 Balmacneil P & K
543 G2 Balmacqueen Highld
412 C6 Balmae D & G
501 F3 Balmalcolm Fife
485 E4 Balmalloch N Lans
527 G5 Balmashanner Angus
542 E8 Balmeanach Highld
543 H3 Balmeanach Highld
545 J1 Balmeanach Highld
545 J3 Balmeanach Highld
540 E6 Balmedie Abers
270 A3 Balmer Shrops
270 A3 Balmer Heath Shrops
50 A1 Balmerlawn Hants
460 C3 Balmichael N Ayrs
451 F2 Balmoral Border
484 C5 Balmore E Duns
544 D1 Balmore Highld
588 C3 Balmore Highld
514 C5 Balmullo Fife
566 C5 Balmungie Highld
415 H3 Balmurrie D & G
526 D1 Balnaboth Abers
577 J7 Balnabruaich Highld
582 F4 Balnabruich Highld
581 K7 Balnacoil Highld
563 H7 Balnacra Highld
576 D2 Balnadelson Highld
550 B2 Balnafoich Highld
557 H4 Balnagask C Aber
540 D5 Balnaguard P & K
566 B2 Balnaguisich Highld
478 C2 Balnahard Ag & B
504 F4 Balnahard Ag & B
549 G3 Balnain Highld
585 G3 Balnakeil Highld
585 G3 Balnakeil Craft Village Highld
525 G3 Balnakilly P & K
543 G4 Balnaknock Highld
570 F4 Balnamoon Abers
528 B2 Balnamoon Angus
566 D3 Balnapaling Highld
344 D6 Balne N York
3 E2 Balnoon Cnwll
484 C6 Balornock C Glas
509 H5 Balquhidder Stirlg
213 G3 Balsall Solhll
213 G3 Balsall Common Solhll
214 C4 Balsall Heath Birm
165 F1 Balscote Oxon
198 B3 Balsham Cambs
121 G3 Balstonia Thurr
609 J3 Baltasound Shet
291 F5 Balterley Staffs
291 F4 Balterley Green Staffs
291 H4 Balterley Heath Staffs
570 E5 Balthangie Abers
570 E5 Balthayock P & K
502 B2 Baltilly Fife
67 E2 Baltonsborough Somset
565 J6 Balvaird Highld
565 J6 Balvaird Highld
568 E7 Balvenie Moray
492 C1 Balvicar Ag & B
559 H5 Balvraid Highld
550 E3 Balvraid Highld

565 J6 Balvraid Highld
3 G3 Balwest Cnwll
339 E4 Bamber Bridge Lancs
172 B5 Bamber's Green Essex
455 F2 Bamburgh Nthumb
526 B4 Bamff P & K
313 H3 Bamford Derbys
326 C2 Bamford Rochdl
162 C5 Bamfurlong Gloucs
324 D4 Bamfurlong Wigan
391 E6 Bampton Cumb
42 C5 Bampton Devon
139 E4 Bampton Oxon
391 E6 Bampton Grange Cumb
533 H7 Banavie Highld
165 H1 Banbury Oxon
128 C2 Bancffosfelen Carmth
556 B5 Banchory Abers
557 G4 Banchory-Devenick Abers
128 B2 Bancycapel Carmth
205 F3 Banc-y-Darren Cerdgn
153 G6 Bancyfelin Carmth
154 B2 Bancyffordd Carmth
95 F2 Bandonhill Gt Lon
364 C2 Bandrake Head Cumb
570 B3 Banff Abers
304 C3 Bangor Gwynd
289 E5 Bangor on Dee Wrexhm
23 E3 Bangors Cnwll
323 G3 Bangor's Green Lancs
153 H1 Bangor Teifi Cerdgn
225 E2 Banham Norfk
50 A3 Bank Hants
233 E2 Bank Powys
362 D4 Bank End Cumb
363 F3 Bank End Cumb
388 B2 Bank End Cumb
423 H6 Bankend D & G
339 H5 Bank Fold Bl w D
512 C2 Bankfoot P & K
434 B2 Bankglen E Ayrs
556 B3 Bankhead Abers
514 D2 Bankhead Angus
557 F3 Bankhead C Aber
485 E3 Bankhead Falk
468 D6 Bankhead S Lans
469 F6 Bankhead S Lans
465 G4 Bankhead Moss N Ayrs
339 G3 Bank Hey Bl w D
351 F4 Bank Houses Lancs
44 C2 Bankland Somset
326 B1 Bank Lane Bury
354 B4 Bank Newton N York
485 F4 Banknock Falk
401 G4 Banks Cumb
412 C5 Banks D & G
337 G5 Banks Lancs
189 E1 Bank's Green Worcs
209 F2 Bankshead Shrops
424 D3 Bankshill D & G
486 A3 Bankside Falk
187 E2 Bank Street Worcs
342 C2 Bank Top Brad
342 B5 Bank Top Calder
291 H4 Bank Top C Stke
324 C3 Bank Top Lancs
325 G2 Bank Top Lancs
404 D1 Bank Top N u Ty
237 G5 Banners Gate Birm
390 B3 Bannest Hill Cumb
255 H2 Banningham Norfk
172 D5 Bannister Green Essex
485 G1 Bannockburn Stirlg
6 D4 Banns Cnwll
95 E3 Banstead Surrey
485 H4 Bantaskin Falk
12 B4 Bantham Devon
485 F4 Banton N Lans
567 J7 Bantrach Moray
84 C3 Banwell N Som
226 C5 Banyard's Green Suffk
99 E2 Bapchild Kent
212 D2 Baptist End Dudley
69 G2 Bapton Wilts
599 H5 Barabhas W Isls
599 H5 Barabhas Iarach W Isls
531 H8 Baramore Highld
444 D3 Barassie S Ayrs
506 E2 Baravullin Ag & B
566 C2 Barbaraville Highld
486 B6 Barbauchlaw W Loth
313 F2 Barber Booth Derbys
365 E3 Barber Green Ches
338 C6 Barber's Moor Lancs
599 H4 Barbhas Uarach W Isls
11 E3 Barbican C Plym
445 F6 Barbieston S Ayrs
366 C3 Barbon Cumb
188 B3 Barbourne Worcs
479 J4 Barbreack Ag & B
290 C3 Barbridge Ches
61 H2 Barbrook Devon
216 B5 Barby Nhants
216 B5 Barby Nortoft Nhants
507 G1 Barcaldine Ag & B
9 G3 Barcelona Cnwll
164 D2 Barcheston Warwks
400 D2 Barclose Cumb
56 C2 Barcombe E Susx
56 C1 Barcombe Cross E Susx
341 G2 Barcroft Brad
382 D6 Barden N York
97 E5 Barden Park Kent
172 C5 Bardfield End Green Essex
172 D4 Bardfield Saling Essex
606 E2 Bardister Shet
319 E6 Bardney Lincs
239 H2 Bardon Leics
402 D2 Bardon Mill Nthumb
484 B5 Bardowie E Duns
79 F4 Bardown E Susx
482 D5 Bardrainney Inver
364 D5 Bardsea Cumb
356 D6 Bardsey Leeds
326 D4 Bardsley Oldham
224 B5 Bardwell Suffk
351 G2 Bare Lancs
64 D5 Bare Ash Somset
453 G2 Bareless Nthumb
413 G3 Barend D & G
72 C4 Bar End Hants
388 B4 Barepot Cumb
5 E3 Bareppa Cnwll
74 C2 Barford Hants
249 F3 Barford Norfk
190 D2 Barford Warwks
165 G5 Barford St John Oxon
70 A3 Barford St Martin Wilts
165 G5 Barford St Michael Oxon
101 E5 Barfrestone Kent
483 G5 Bargaran S Ayrs
294 D5 Bargate Derbys
467 G2 Bargeddie N Lans
132 B5 Bargoed Caerph
420 B4 Bargrennan D & G
219 G4 Barham Cambs
100 D6 Barham Kent
201 F4 Barham Suffk
412 B4 Barharrow D & G
197 E2 Bar Hill Cambs
291 F6 Bar Hill Staffs
243 F2 Barholm Lincs
240 D3 Barkby Leics
240 D3 Barkby Thorpe Leics

270 C4 Barkers Green Shrops
69 F4 Barkers Hill Wilts
277 G3 Barkestone-le-Vale Leics
92 C1 Barkham Wokham
120 B3 Barking Gt Lon
201 E4 Barking Suffk
120 B2 Barkingside Gt Lon
201 E4 Barking Tye Suffk
341 H6 Barkisland Calder
6 D3 Barkla Shop Cnwll
278 C1 Barkston Lincs
344 B2 Barkston Ash N York
171 E2 Barkway Herts
86 B5 Barlake Somset
467 G2 Barlanark C Glas
185 E2 Barland Powys
103 G4 Barland Common Swans
272 C2 Barlaston Staffs
53 H1 Barlavington W Susx
315 F4 Barlborough Derbys
345 E3 Barlby N York
239 G3 Barlestone Leics
171 F2 Barley Herts
340 C1 Barley Lancs
171 F4 Barleycroft End Herts
142 D2 Barley End Bucks
340 C1 Barley Green Lancs
405 G4 Barley Mow Gatesd
242 A3 Barleythorpe Rutlnd
123 E2 Barling Essex
318 D5 Barlings Lincs
314 C5 Barlow Derbys
405 E2 Barlow Gatesd
345 E4 Barlow N York
326 B6 Barlow Moor Manch
359 E5 Barmby Moor E R Yk
345 F4 Barmby on the Marsh E R Yk
259 G5 Barmer Norfk
97 H3 Barming Heath Kent
404 D2 Bar Moor Gatesd
228 D1 Barmouth Gwynd
395 G6 Barmpton Darltn
361 F3 Barmston E R Yk
405 H3 Barmston Sundld
484 C6 Barmulloch C Glas
227 F4 Barnaby Green Suffk
243 F4 Barnack C Pete
215 F3 Barnacle Warwks
606 D1 Barnafield Shet
382 B1 Barnard Castle Dur
139 G2 Barnard Gate Oxon
199 E5 Barnardiston Suffk
188 A5 Barnard's Green Worcs
107 F2 Barnardtown Newpt
343 G2 Barnbow Carr Leeds
330 A4 Barnburgh Donc
227 F2 Barnby Suffk
330 D3 Barnby Dun Donc
297 F4 Barnby in the Willows Notts
316 C3 Barnby Moor Notts
467 H4 Barncluith S Lans
408 B4 Barncorkrie D & G
10 D2 Barne Barton C Plym
120 C4 Barnehurst Gt Lon
119 E4 Barnes Gt Lon
120 D4 Barnes Cray Gt Lon
329 E5 Barnes Hall Sheff
97 F5 Barnes Street Kent
144 B5 Barnet Gt Lon
333 F3 Barnetby le Wold N Linc
144 B5 Barnet Gate Gt Lon
290 C6 Barnett Brook Ches
212 C4 Barnettbrook Worcs
260 C5 Barney Norfk
146 C1 Barnfield Essex
99 E5 Barnfield Kent
160 A1 Barnfields Herefs
292 C3 Barnfields Staffs
223 H4 Barnham Suffk
53 H4 Barnham W Susx
249 E3 Barnham Broom Norfk
529 E3 Barnhead Angus
514 D3 Barnhill C Dund
289 G4 Barnhill Ches
567 L5 Barnhill Moray
512 D5 Barnhill P & K
414 C2 Barnhills D & G
382 C2 Barningham Dur
224 C4 Barningham Suffk
261 F5 Barningham Green Norfk
479 K3 Barnluasgan Ag & B
190 B2 Barnmoor Green Warwks
334 B4 Barnoldby le Beck NE Lin
353 H5 Barnoldswick Lancs
366 D5 Barnoldswick N York
449 H2 Barns Border
242 B3 Barnsdale Rutlnd
76 B4 Barns Green W Susx
328 B3 Barnside Kirk
328 E3 Barnsley Barns
137 G3 Barnsley Gloucs
235 H6 Barnsley Shrops
101 E4 Barnsole Kent
60 D5 Barnstaple Devon
172 C6 Barnston Essex
308 C3 Barnston Wirral
277 F2 Barnstone Notts
213 F5 Barnt Green Worcs
487 G4 Barnton C Edin
310 C4 Barnton Ches
219 E3 Barnwell Nhants
162 C6 Barnwood Gloucs
502 D4 Barnyards Fife
186 B3 Barons' Cross Herefs
419 G3 Barr S Ayrs
43 G3 Barr Somset
410 C3 Barrachan D & G
467 G2 Barrachnie C Glas
560 C1 Barrack Abers
107 F2 Barrack Hill Newpt
598 D8 Barraglom W Isls
479 J5 Barrahormid Ag & B
506 E4 Barran Ag & B
516 B7 Barrapol Ag & B
381 E2 Barras Cumb
429 E5 Barrasford Nthumb
492 D3 Barravullin Ag & B
237 G2 Barr Common Wsall
322 e5 Barregarrow IoM
290 B3 Barrets Green Ches
466 D3 Barrhead E Rens
419 F5 Barrhill S Ayrs
197 E5 Barrington Cambs
66 B6 Barrington Somset
138 C2 Barrington Park Gloucs
6 B6 Barripper Cnwll
465 H4 Barrmill N Ayrs
506 D5 Barrnacarry Ag & B
589 G2 Barrock Highld
162 C5 Barrow Gloucs
340 A2 Barrow Lancs
329 F5 Barrow Rothm
242 B1 Barrow Rutlnd
235 F4 Barrow Shrops
67 F1 Barrow Somset
199 F2 Barrow Suffk
246 B4 Barroway Drove Norfk
325 F2 Barrow Bridge Bolton
441 G2 Barrowburn Nthumb
278 B2 Barrowby Lincs
374 C2 Barrowcliff N York
109 F6 Barrow Common N Som

242 D4 Barrowden Rutlnd
340 C2 Barrowford Lancs
99 F2 Barrow Green Kent
109 F6 Barrow Gurney N Som
347 G5 Barrow Hann N Linc
347 G5 Barrow Haven N Linc
315 E4 Barrow Hill Derbys
48 A5 Barrow Hill Dorset
81 G2 Barrowhill Kent
364 A5 Barrow-In-Furness Cumb
364 A6 Barrow Island Cumb
309 G6 Barrowmore Estate Ches
324 A4 Barrow Nook Lancs
290 D3 Barrows Green Ches
365 H2 Barrows Green Cumb
310 A2 Barrow's Green Halton
295 F4 Barrows Green Notts
68 D3 Barrow Street Wilts
347 G5 Barrow upon Humber N Linc
240 C1 Barrow upon Soar Leics
275 E4 Barrow upon Trent Derbys
86 A2 Barrow Vale BaNES
136 D1 Barrow Wake Gloucs
515 E3 Barry Angus
106 A6 Barry V Glam
106 B6 Barry Dock V Glam
106 B6 Barry Island V Glam
241 E2 Barsby Leics
226 D2 Barsham Suffk
446 B6 Barshare E Ayrs
492 C5 Barsloisnoch Ag & B
121 H2 Barstable Essex
214 C4 Barston Solhll
160 D7 Bartestree Herefs
560 B3 Barthol Chapel Abers
173 E5 Bartholomew Green Essex
291 F4 Barthomley Ches
50 B2 Bartley Hants
213 F3 Bartley Green Birm
198 B5 Bartlow Cambs
197 F3 Barton Cambs
289 F4 Barton Ches
162 B6 Barton Gloucs
163 H4 Barton Gloucs
37 E3 Barton IoW
323 F3 Barton Lancs
338 D2 Barton Lancs
84 C3 Barton N Som
383 F3 Barton N York
140 B3 Barton Oxon
20 C4 Barton Torbay
189 H4 Barton Warwks
165 G5 Barton Abbey Oxon
247 E3 Barton Bendish Norfk
161 C1 Barton Court Herefs
136 B5 Barton End Gloucs
61 G3 Barton Green Devon
274 B6 Barton Gate Staffs
274 B6 Barton Green Staffs
166 D3 Barton Hartshorn Bucks
109 H5 Barton Hill Bristl
358 B4 Barton Hill N York
276 B3 Barton in Fabis Notts
239 F3 Barton in the Beans Leics
169 F3 Barton-le-Clay Beds
372 D5 Barton-le-Street N York
358 D2 Barton-le-Willows N York
223 E5 Barton Mills Suffk
325 G5 Barton Moss Salfd
49 G6 Barton on Sea Hants
164 D3 Barton-on-the-Heath Warwks
67 E3 Barton St David Somset
218 B4 Barton Seagrave Nhants
160 C2 Bartonsham Herefs
72 B1 Barton Stacey Hants
61 G3 Barton Town Devon
256 D5 Barton Turf Norfk
274 C6 Barton Turn Staffs
274 B6 Barton-under-Needwood Staffs
347 F5 Barton-upon-Humber N Linc
325 H5 Barton upon Irwell Salfd
347 F5 Barton Waterside N Linc
329 E3 Barugh Barns
329 E3 Barugh Green Barns
599 H5 Barvas W Isls
222 A4 Barway Cambs
94 D2 Barwell Gt Lon
239 G5 Barwell Leics
40 B6 Barwick Devon
171 E6 Barwick Herts
45 H5 Barwick Somset
343 H2 Barwick in Elmet Leeds
270 A5 Baschurch Shrops
401 F5 Bascodyke Head Cumb
191 G2 Bascote Warwks
191 F2 Bascote Heath Warwks
200 D2 Base Green Suffk
169 G2 Basford Beds
291 H5 Basford Staffs
292 C4 Basford Green Staffs
352 D6 Bashall Eaves Lancs
49 G5 Bashley Hants
49 G5 Bashley Park Hants
122 A2 Basildon Essex
91 F4 Basingstoke Hants
314 A5 Baslow Derbys
84 B5 Bason Bridge Somset
107 E2 Bassaleg Newpt
389 F3 Bassenthwaite Cumb
50 D1 Bassett C Sotn
314 B3 Bassett Sheff
50 D1 Bassett Green C Sotn
196 D6 Bassingbourn Cambs
276 D2 Bassingfield Notts
297 H3 Bassingham Lincs
278 D4 Bassingthorpe Lincs
170 C4 Bassus Green Herts
609 G6 Basta Shet
97 F3 Basted Kent
243 G2 Baston Lincs
188 B4 Bastonford Worcs
257 E6 Bastwick Norfk
272 D5 Baswich Staffs
84 B3 Batch Somset
210 B5 Batchcott Shrops
187 F5 Batchfields Herefs
189 F1 Batchley Worcs
143 F6 Batchworth Herts
143 F6 Batchworth Heath Herts
31 E2 Batcombe Dorset
68 A2 Batcombe Somset
310 A4 Bate Heath Ches
213 G4 Bateman's Green Worcs
125 H4 Bateman's Hill Pembks
314 D3 Batemoor Sheff
143 G1 Batford Herts
86 C1 Bath BaNES
86 D1 Bathampton BaNES
43 E3 Bathealton Somset
110 D6 Batheaston BaNES
86 D1 Bathford BaNES
486 C6 Bathgate W Loth
297 E3 Bathley Notts
16 C4 Bathpool Cnwll
44 B2 Bathpool Somset
176 D3 Bath Side Essex
291 H2 Bath Vale Ches
486 B6 Bathville W Loth
43 F4 Bathway Somset
86 D2 Bathwick BaNES

143 H5 Batlers Green Herts
342 D5 Batley Kirk
342 D5 Batley Carr Kirk
164 B3 Batsford Gloucs
12 C5 Batson Devon
41 G3 Batsworthy Devon
44 B4 Batten's Green Somset
188 B1 Battenton Green Worcs
385 F3 Battersby N York
119 F4 Battersea Gt Lon
201 E4 Battisford Suffk
200 D4 Battisford Tye Suffk
58 B3 Battle E Susx
157 G3 Battle Powys
163 E5 Battledown Gloucs
39 G6 Battledown Cross Devon
467 E2 Battlefield Shrops
234 C1 Battlefield Shrops
431 E6 Battle Hill N Tyne
147 F6 Battlesbridge Essex
136 D3 Battlescombe Gloucs
168 D4 Battlesden Beds
225 H4 Battlesea Green Suffk
42 B3 Battleton Somset
200 B2 Battlies Green Suffk
239 G3 Battram Leics
50 A5 Battramsley Hants
50 B5 Battramsley Cross Hants
74 C1 Batt's Corner Hants
342 C5 Battyeford Kirk
25 H5 Batworthy Devon
569 H2 Bauds of Cullen Moray
516 C7 Baugh Ag & B
162 C1 Baughton Worcs
91 F2 Baughurst Hants
113 H1 Baulking Oxon
319 G5 Baumber Lincs
137 F4 Baunton Gloucs
70 A3 Baverstock Wilts
249 F3 Bawburgh Norfk
254 D3 Bawdeswell Norfk
65 F4 Bawdrip Somset
177 F1 Bawdsey Suffk
252 D4 Bawsey Norfk
330 D6 Bawtry Donc
340 B4 Baxenden Lancs
238 D5 Baxterley Warwks
199 F3 Baxter's Green Suffk
68 D4 Bay Dorset
542 D6 Bay Highld
72 D5 Baybridge Hants
403 G4 Baybridge Nthumb
364 C5 Baycliff Cumb
113 G4 Baydon Wilts
144 D3 Bayford Herts
68 B4 Bayford Somset
353 E5 Bay Gate Lancs
351 G4 Bay Horse Lancs
402 C5 Bayles Cumb
96 D4 Bayley's Hill Kent
201 E4 Baylham Suffk
213 G5 Baylis Green Worcs
166 C4 Baynard's Green Oxon
188 C5 Baynhall Worcs
160 D4 Baysham Herefs
234 B3 Bayston Hill Shrops
119 F3 Bayswater Gt Lon
199 E6 Baythorne End Essex
280 B1 Baythorpe Lincs
211 F5 Bayton Worcs
211 G5 Bayton Common Worcs
123 G5 Bay View Kent
140 B4 Bayworth Oxon
110 B5 Beach S Glos
167 G2 Beachampton Bucks
247 F3 Beachamwell Norfk
462 A6 Beacharr Ag & B
211 G5 Beach Hay Worcs
57 H4 Beachlands E Susx
109 G1 Beachley Gloucs
6 B6 Beacon Cnwll
28 C2 Beacon Devon
44 A6 Beacon Devon
78 D5 Beacon Down E Susx
174 C5 Beacon End Essex
86 C1 Beacon Hill BaNES
142 C6 Beacon Hill Bucks
364 B5 Beacon Hill Cumb
48 B6 Beacon Hill Dorset
147 H2 Beacon Hill Essex
80 B3 Beacon Hill Kent
297 F4 Beacon Hill Notts
430 D4 Beacon Hill Nthumb
202 A5 Beacon Hill Suffk
74 D2 Beacon Hill Surrey
405 G2 Beacon Lough Gatesd
141 G5 Beacon's Bottom Bucks
117 F1 Beaconsfield Bucks
272 C5 Beaconside Staffs
595 H4 Beacrabhaic W Isls
372 B3 Beadlam N York
169 G2 Beadlow Beds
455 G4 Beadnell Nthumb
40 B5 Beaford Devon
454 D1 Beal Nthumb
344 C4 Beal N York
480 D3 Bealach Maim Ag & B
17 E5 Bealbury Cnwll
79 H3 Beal's Green Kent
17 E3 Bealsmill Cnwll
210 C2 Beambridge Shrops
43 F4 Beam Bridge Somset
274 C4 Beam Hill Staffs
273 F2 Beamhurst Staffs
273 G2 Beamhurst Lane Staffs
30 B2 Beaminster Dorset
405 F4 Beamish Dur
142 C5 Beamond End Bucks
355 E4 Beamsley N York
121 E5 Bean Kent
87 G1 Beanacre Wilts
486 B4 Beancross Falk
168 B2 Beanhill M Keyn
454 D6 Beanley Nthumb
48 C5 Bear Cross Bmouth
67 G1 Beard Hill Somset
67 G1 Beardly Batch Somset
339 G4 Beardwood Bl w D
27 F2 Beare Devon
94 D6 Beare Green Surrey
190 B2 Bearley Warwks
190 B2 Bearley Cross Warwks
405 F6 Bearpark Dur
402 F6 Bearsbridge Nthumb
483 H5 Bearsden E Duns
98 B3 Bearsted Kent
271 G2 Bearstone Shrops
213 F2 Bearwood Birm
185 G3 Bearwood Herefs
48 G3 Bearwood Poole
437 E4 Beattock D & G
146 B2 Beauchamp Roding Essex
314 C3 Beauchief Sheff
404 B2 Beauclerc Nthumb
190 B1 Beaudesert Warwks
132 C2 Beaufort Blae G
50 C4 Beaulieu Hants
46 D3 Beaulieu Wood Dorset
565 J7 Beauly Highld
304 C4 Beaumaris IoA
400 B3 Beaumont Cumb

176 C5 Beaumont Essex
35 g7 Beaumont Jersey
117 G5 Beaumont W & M
395 F6 Beaumont Hill Darltn
240 C3 Beaumont Leys C Leic
176 C5 Beaumont Quay Essex
214 C5 Beausale Warwks
295 G5 Beauvale Notts
73 E4 Beauworth Hants
161 F5 Beavan's Hill Herefs
24 B3 Beaworthy Devon
173 E4 Beazley End Essex
309 E3 Bebington Wirral
431 E3 Bebside Nthumb
227 E2 Beccles Suffk
338 B5 Becconsall Lancs
364 C3 Beck Bottom Cumb
343 F5 Beck Bottom Wakefd
235 H4 Beckbury Shrops
120 A6 Beckenham Gt Lon
376 C3 Beckermet Cumb
367 H3 Beckermonds N York
66 D2 Beckery Somset
247 F5 Beckett End Norfk
377 F4 Beckfoot Cumb
379 H5 Beck Foot Cumb
398 D5 Beckfoot Cumb
163 E2 Beckford Worcs
112 C6 Beckhampton Wilts
365 F3 Beck Head Cumb
386 D4 Beck Hole N York
379 G5 Beck Houses Cumb
297 G4 Beckingham Lincs
317 E1 Beckingham Notts
86 D4 Beckington Somset
209 G4 Beckjay Shrops
80 C5 Beckley E Susx
49 G5 Beckley Hants
140 C2 Beckley Oxon
58 D2 Beckley Furnace E Susx
222 D4 Beck Row Suffk
363 E5 Beck Side Cumb
363 E5 Beck Side Cumb
366 C2 Beckside Cumb
120 B3 Beckton Gt Lon
356 B4 Beckwith N York
356 B4 Beckwithshaw N York
120 C2 Becontree Gt Lon
35 h6 Becquet Vincent Jersey
370 B2 Bedale N York
394 C3 Bedburn Dur
47 F1 Bedchester Dorset
105 G2 Beddau Rhondd
284 C5 Beddgelert Gwynd
56 C3 Beddingham E Susx
95 G1 Beddington Gt Lon
95 F1 Beddington Corner Gt Lon
201 H1 Bedfield Suffk
195 F5 Bedford Beds
325 F5 Bedford Wigan
119 E4 Bedford Park Gt Lon
79 G3 Bedgebury Cross Kent
142 A2 Bedgrove Bucks
75 G5 Bedham W Susx
52 B3 Bedhampton Hants
225 G6 Bedingfield Suffk
250 B6 Bedingham Green Norfk
356 B2 Bedlam N York
86 D5 Bedlam Somset
55 G1 Bedlam Street W Susx
171 H5 Bedlar's Green Essex
430 D3 Bedlington Nthumb
431 E3 Bedlington Station Nthumb
132 A4 Bedlinog Myr Td
109 H5 Bedminster Bristl
109 G6 Bedminster Down Bristl
143 H2 Bedmond Herts
273 E6 Bednall Staffs
237 E1 Bednall Head Staffs
452 B6 Bedrule Border
209 G4 Bedstone Shrops
106 C2 Bedwas Caerph
170 B5 Bedwell Herts
289 E5 Bedwell Wrexhm
132 C4 Bedwellty Caerph
132 B3 Bedwellty Pits Blae G
268 D2 Bedwlwyn Wrexhm
215 F2 Bedworth Warwks
215 E2 Bedworth Heath Warwks
215 E2 Bedworth Woodlands Warwks
241 E3 Beeby Leics
73 G2 Beech Hants
272 B2 Beech Staffs
272 C2 Beechcliff Staffs
355 E6 Beechcliffe Brad
86 C2 Beechen Cliff BaNES
92 A2 Beech Hill W Berk
324 D3 Beech Hill Wigan
88 C3 Beechingstoke Wilts
213 F2 Beech Lanes Birm
310 A4 Beechwood Halton
566 B8 Beechwood Highld
343 F2 Beechwood Leeds
107 F2 Beechwood Newpt
214 D4 Beechwood Solhll
169 E5 Beedon W Berk
114 D4 Beedon Hill W Berk
361 E4 Beeford E R Yk
314 B6 Beeley Derbys
334 D4 Beelsby NE Lin
115 F6 Beenham W Berk
116 A4 Beenham's Heath W & M
115 F6 Beenham Stocks W Berk
22 C4 Beeny Cnwll
28 D5 Beer Devon
66 C3 Beer Somset
44 C3 Beer Crocombe Somset
46 A2 Beer Hackett Dorset
13 E4 Beesands Devon
321 E3 Beesby Lincs
470 D2 Beeslack Mdloth
13 E4 Beeson Devon
195 H5 Beeston Beds
290 A3 Beeston Ches
254 B4 Beeston Norfk
276 B2 Beeston Notts
343 E3 Beeston Leeds
343 E3 Beeston Park Side Leeds
261 G3 Beeston Regis Norfk
343 E3 Beeston Royds Leeds
256 C5 Beeston St Lawrence Norfk
423 E6 Beeswing D & G
365 G4 Beetham Cumb
44 B5 Beetham Somset
254 C4 Beetley Norfk
106 D3 Began Cardif
139 H2 Begbroke Oxon
245 G3 Begdale Cambs
126 C3 Begelly Pembks
146 C4 Beggar Hill Essex
343 E5 Beggarington Hill Kirk
161 G2 Beggars Ash Herefs
55 E3 Beggars Bush W Susx
105 G6 Beggars Pound V Glam
63 G4 Beggearn Huish Somset
208 C3 Beguildy Powys
250 D3 Beighton Norfk
315 E3 Beighton Sheff

133 F2 Beili-glas Mons
597 L2 Beinn Casgro W Isls
465 G4 Beith N Ayrs
100 C4 Bekesbourne Kent
100 C4 Bekesbourne Hill Kent
400 C3 Belah Cumb
232 D4 Belan Powys
256 B6 Belaugh Norfk
71 H5 Belbins Hants
212 D4 Belbroughton Worcs
47 E3 Belchalwell Dorset
47 E3 Belchalwell Street Dorset
173 G1 Belchamp Otten Essex
173 F1 Belchamp St Paul Essex
173 G1 Belchamp Walter Essex
239 G3 Belcher's Bar Leics
320 A4 Belchford Lincs
571 J4 Belfatton Abers
326 D2 Belfield Rochdl
455 E3 Belford Nthumb
306 D4 Belgrave Conwy
289 E2 Belgrave Ches
240 C3 Belgrave C Leic
238 C4 Belgrave Staffs
490 C4 Belhaven E Loth
557 G1 Belhelvie Abers
558 B4 Belhinnie Abers
554 C2 Bellabeg Abers
466 D2 Bellahouston C Glas
419 F4 Bellamore S Ayrs
479 K3 Bellanoch Ag & B
450 A2 Bellanrigg Border
346 B4 Bellasize E R Yk
526 B3 Bellaty Angus
144 B4 Bell Bar Herts
501 G2 Bellbrae Fife
354 B3 Bell Busk N York
145 H4 Bell Common Essex
320 C4 Belleau Lincs
296 C3 Belle Eau Park Notts
329 F3 Belle Green Barns
552 D1 Belleheiglash Moray
343 F4 Belle Isle Leeds
212 D4 Bell End Worcs
382 D6 Bellerby N York
213 E3 Belle Vale Dudley
309 F2 Belle Vale Lpool
19 E2 Bellever Devon
388 D3 Belle Vue Cumb
400 C3 Belle Vue Cumb
330 C4 Belle Vue Donc
326 C5 Belle Vue Manch
234 B2 Belle Vue Shrops
343 F6 Belle Vue Wakefd
213 E5 Bellevue Worcs
445 F2 Bellfield E Ayrs
447 G2 Bellfield S Lans
93 G4 Bellfields Surrey
215 F3 Bell Green Covtry
119 H5 Bell Green Gt Lon
213 E4 Bell Heath Worcs
74 A5 Bell Hill Hants
528 C2 Belliehill Angus
142 C3 Bellingdon Bucks
119 H5 Bellingham Gt Lon
428 C3 Bellingham Nthumb
252 A3 Bellmount Norfk
458 D4 Belloch Ag & B
458 D5 Bellochantuy Ag & B
289 H5 Bell o' th' Hill Ches
433 G4 Bellsbank E Ayrs
405 E2 Bell's Close N u Ty
174 C2 Bell's Corner Suffk
468 A3 Bellshill N Lans
455 E3 Bellshill Nthumb
468 C3 Bellside N Lans
483 F4 Bellsmyre W Duns
449 G2 Bellspool Border
469 G1 Bellsquarry W Loth
79 E2 Bells Yew Green E Susx
85 H2 Belluton BaNES
487 F2 Bellyeoman Fife
566 B5 Belmaduthy Highld
243 E3 Belmesthorpe Rutlnd
325 F1 Belmont Bl w D
405 H6 Belmont Dur
58 D4 Belmont E Susx
95 E2 Belmont Gt Lon
118 D1 Belmont Gt Lon
114 B2 Belmont Oxon
444 D5 Belmont S Ayrs
609 H4 Belmont Shet
554 C1 Belnacraig Abers
280 C3 Belnie Lincs
8 B1 Belowda Cnwll
294 D5 Belper Derbys
294 C5 Belper Lane End Derbys
315 G4 Belph Derbys
430 B4 Belsay Nthumb
19 G6 Belsford Devon
143 E4 Belsize Herts
175 F1 Belstead Suffk
147 F2 Belsteads Essex
445 E5 Belston S Ayrs
25 F4 Belstone Devon
25 F3 Belstone Corner Devon
339 H5 Belthorn Bl w D
100 D2 Beltinge Kent
402 D2 Beltingham Nthumb
331 H3 Beltoft N Linc
275 G5 Belton Leics
278 C2 Belton Lincs
331 G3 Belton N Linc
251 F4 Belton Norfk
241 H4 Belton-in-Rutland Rutlnd
97 C3 Beltring Kent
120 C4 Belvedere Gt Lon
277 H3 Belvoir Leics
37 H3 Bembridge IoW
70 C3 Bemerton Wilts
70 C3 Bemerton Heath Wilts
375 F5 Bempton E R Yk
227 G3 Benacre Suffk
435 E5 Benbuie D & G
311 G2 Benchill Manch
136 A5 Bencombe Gloucs
506 F2 Benderloch Ag & B
169 H5 Bendish Herts
80 B3 Benenden Kent
416 D4 Benfield D & G
404 C4 Benfieldside Dur
151 G3 Bengal Pembks
256 B4 Bengate Norfk
144 D2 Bengeo Herts
189 F6 Bengeworth Worcs
163 E3 Bengrove Gloucs
162 D5 Benhall Gloucs
202 D2 Benhall Green Suffk
202 D2 Benhall Street Suffk
95 F1 Benhilton Gt Lon
541 F6 Benholm Abers
357 G3 Beningbrough N York
170 D5 Benington Herts
300 C5 Benington Lincs
300 C5 Benington Sea End Lincs
304 B3 Benllech IoA
481 G3 Benmore Ag & B
508 F4 Benmore Stirlg
23 F4 Bennacott Cnwll
26 C6 Bennah Devon
460 C5 Bennecarrigan N Ayrs
141 G5 Bennett End Bucks

143 F3 Bennetts End Herts
319 F3 Benniworth Lincs
97 H5 Benover Kent
355 F5 Ben Rhydding Brad
405 F2 Bensham Gatesd
465 G6 Benslie N Ayrs
115 G1 Benson Oxon
607 G7 Benston Shet
603 H4 Benstonhall Ork
86 A5 Benter Somset
171 G4 Bentfield Bury Essex
171 H4 Bentfield Green Essex
340 B5 Bent Gate Lancs
326 D2 Bentgate Rochdl
235 F4 Benthall Shrops
136 D1 Bentham Gloucs
557 K4 Benthoul C Aber
292 B5 Bentilee C Stke
125 G4 Bentlass Pembks
233 F4 Bentlawnt Shrops
330 C3 Bentley Donc
347 F2 Bentley E R Yk
146 B5 Bentley Essex
92 C6 Bentley Hants
175 F2 Bentley Suffk
238 D5 Bentley Warwks
237 E5 Bentley Wsall
238 D5 Bentley Common Warwks
144 B5 Bentley Heath Herts
214 B4 Bentley Heath Solhll
330 C4 Bentley Rise Donc
61 F4 Benton Devon
214 D4 Benton Green Solhll
425 G1 Bentpath D & G
469 F2 Bents W Loth
61 H5 Bentwichen Devon
73 G1 Bentworth Hants
513 H3 Benvie C Dund
30 C2 Benville Dorset
405 F2 Benwell N u Ty
220 D1 Benwick Cambs
212 A1 Beobridge Shrops
213 G6 Beoley Worcs
531 J4 Beoraidbeg Highld
74 D6 Bepton W Susx
171 G4 Berden Essex
150 C4 Berea Pembks
17 F5 Bere Alston Devon
174 C5 Berechurch Essex
17 G6 Bere Ferrers Devon
561 E2 Berefold Abers
4 C4 Berepper Cnwll
47 F5 Bere Regis Dorset
250 C4 Bergh Apton Norfk
117 F2 Berghers Hill Bucks
66 C2 Berhill Somset
140 C5 Berinsfield Oxon
135 F5 Berkeley Gloucs
135 F5 Berkeley Heath Gloucs
142 D3 Berkhamsted Herts
87 E5 Berkley Somset
86 D5 Berkley Down Somset
87 E5 Berkley Marsh Somset
214 C4 Berkswell Solhll
119 G4 Bermondsey Gt Lon
215 E2 Bermuda Warwks
143 H3 Bernards Heath Herts
546 E5 Bernera Highld
40 C6 Berner's Cross Devon
79 G3 Berner's Hill E Susx
146 B3 Berners Roding Essex
481 G1 Bernice Ag & B
542 F7 Bernisdale Highld
140 D6 Berrick Salome Oxon
582 F5 Berriedale Highld
390 C4 Berrier Cumb
232 C4 Berriew Powys
186 D1 Berrington Herefs
475 F6 Berrington Nthumb
234 C3 Berrington Shrops
186 D1 Berrington Green Herefs
16 C3 Berriowbridge Cnwll
84 A4 Berrow Somset
162 A3 Berrow Worcs
187 G3 Berrow Green Worcs
102 C4 Berry Swans
328 A2 Berry Brow Kirk
39 G5 Berry Cross Devon
61 E3 Berry Down Cross Devon
87 G2 Berryfield Wilts
348 D4 Berrygate Hill E R Yk
292 A5 Berry Hill C Stke
134 D2 Berry Hill Gloucs
152 B1 Berry Hill Pembks
188 C2 Berry Hill Worcs
569 J3 Berryhillock Moray
94 D1 Berrylands Gt Lon
328 D4 Berry Moor Barns
61 E2 Berrynarbor Devon
20 A5 Berry Pomeroy Devon
27 E2 Berrysbridge Devon
96 B3 Berry's Green Gt Lon
288 C5 Bersham Wrexhm
601 H2 Berstane Ork
53 G4 Bersted W Susx
308 B6 Berth-ddu Flints
307 G4 Berthengam Flints
57 E3 Berwick E Susx
81 H2 Berwick Kent
109 F3 Berwick S Glos
112 C5 Berwick Bassett Wilts
430 C4 Berwick Hill Nthumb
396 D6 Berwick Hills Middsb
70 B2 Berwick St James Wilts
69 F5 Berwick St John Wilts
69 F3 Berwick St Leonard Wilts
475 F4 Berwick-upon-Tweed Nthumb
234 C2 Berwick Wharf Shrops
288 A6 Berwyn Denbgs
277 H4 Bescaby Leics
323 G2 Bescar Lancs
237 F5 Bescot Wsall
270 D5 Besford Shrops
188 D6 Besford Worcs
330 D4 Bessacarr Donc
96 D3 Bessels Green Kent
139 H4 Bessels Leigh Oxon
326 B3 Besses o' th' Barn Bury
361 F1 Bessingby E R Yk
261 G4 Bessingham Norfk
79 E3 Best Beech Hill E Susx
249 E5 Besthorpe Norfk
297 F2 Besthorpe Notts
295 H5 Bestwood C Nott
295 H5 Bestwood Village Notts
360 C5 Beswick E R Yk
326 C5 Beswick Manch
234 A5 Betchcott Shrops
291 F2 Betchton Heath Ches
94 D5 Betchworth Surrey
181 E2 Bethania Cerdgn
284 A4 Bethania Gwynd
285 F5 Bethania Gwynd
10 B2 Bethany Cnwll
8 C3 Bethel Cnwll
267 F2 Bethel Gwynd
283 F2 Bethel Gwynd
282 C1 Bethel IoA
80 D1 Bethersden Kent
284 D1 Bethesda Gwynd
152 B6 Bethesda Pembks
155 G4 Bethlehem Carmth
119 G3 Bethnal Green Gt Lon

291 F5 Betley Staffs
291 E5 Betley Common Staffs
121 E5 Betsham Kent
101 F5 Betteshanger Kent
29 G2 Bettiscombe Dorset
270 B2 Bettisfield Wrexhm
233 F4 Betton Shrops
271 F2 Betton Shrops
234 C3 Betton Strange Shrops
104 D2 Bettws Brdgnd
159 H6 Bettws Mons
107 E1 Bettws Newpt
232 B5 Bettws Cedewain Powys
287 E5 Bettws Gwerfil Goch Denbgs
133 G3 Bettws Newydd Mons
208 D3 Bettws-y-crwyn Shrops
586 F4 Bettyhill Highld
129 F2 Betws Carmth
181 E4 Betws Bledrws Cerdgn
283 F4 Betws Garmon Gwynd
179 F4 Betws Ifan Cerdgn
285 G3 Betws-y-Coed Conwy
306 C5 Betws-yn-Rhos Conwy
179 F4 Beulah Cerdgn
183 E4 Beulah Powys
56 A3 Bevendean Br & H
316 D5 Bevercotes Notts
188 B3 Bevere Worcs
347 F1 Beverley E R Yk
136 C6 Beverston Gloucs
135 F5 Bevington Gloucs
604 E2 Bevla Shet
389 F3 Bewaldeth Cumb
76 D2 Bewbush W Susx
427 E5 Bewcastle Cumb
212 A4 Bewdley Worcs
355 F2 Bewerley N York
111 G6 Bewley Common Wilts
451 H4 Bewlie Border
451 G4 Bewlie Mains Border
310 B2 Bewsey Warrtn
254 D2 Bexfield Norfk
58 B5 Bexhill E Susx
120 C5 Bexley Gt Lon
120 C4 Bexleyheath Gt Lon
75 E4 Bexleyhill W Susx
98 D3 Bexon Kent
246 C4 Bexwell Norfk
200 B2 Beyton Suffk
200 B2 Beyton Green Suffk
598 C7 Bhalasaigh W Isls
598 B7 Bhaltos W Isls
591 C9 Bhatarsaigh W Isls
110 C1 Bibstone S Glos
137 H3 Bibury Gloucs
166 C5 Bicester Oxon
44 B4 Bickenhall Somset
214 B3 Bickenhill Solhll
280 B2 Bicker Lincs
280 B2 Bicker Bar Lincs
280 B2 Bicker Gauntlet Lincs
325 E4 Bickershaw Wigan
324 A4 Bickerstaffe Lancs
289 H4 Bickerton Ches
41 E2 Bickerton Devon
370 A4 Bickerton N York
357 E4 Bickerton Nthumb
236 C2 Bickford Staffs
63 E3 Bickham Somset
41 F2 Bickingcott Devon
19 G3 Bickington Devon
60 D5 Bickington Devon
18 B5 Bickleigh Devon
27 E1 Bickleigh Devon
60 D5 Bickleton Devon
120 B6 Bickley Gt Lon
211 E5 Bickley Worcs
290 A5 Bickley Moss Ches
290 A5 Bickley Town Ches
289 H5 Bickleywood Ches
189 H5 Bickmarsh Worcs
147 F4 Bicknacre Essex
64 B4 Bicknoller Somset
98 D3 Bicknor Kent
49 E2 Bickton Hants
186 B2 Bicton Herefs
124 D3 Bicton Pembks
209 E3 Bicton Shrops
234 A1 Bicton Shrops
234 A2 Bicton Heath Shrops
97 E6 Bidborough Kent
92 B5 Bidden Hants
80 B2 Biddenden Kent
98 D6 Biddenden Green Kent
195 E4 Biddenham Beds
111 F5 Biddestone Wilts
405 H3 Biddick Sundld
406 B2 Biddick Hall S Tyne
84 C4 Biddisham Somset
166 D1 Biddlesden Bucks
442 B3 Biddlestone Nthumb
291 H3 Biddulph Staffs
292 B3 Biddulph Moor Staffs
39 F2 Bideford Devon
189 H4 Bidford-on-Avon Warwks
24 C5 Bidlake Devon
308 C1 Bidston Wirral
308 C2 Bidston Hill Wirral
169 E5 Bidwell Beds
359 E6 Bielby E R Yk
557 F4 Bieldside C Aber
342 C3 Bierley Brad
37 E5 Bierley IoW
142 A1 Bierton Bucks
410 C4 Big Balcraig D & G
12 B3 Bigbury Devon
12 A4 Bigbury-on-Sea Devon
333 F3 Bigby Lincs
117 E3 Bigfrith W & M
350 A1 Biggar Brad
448 D2 Biggar S Lans
468 B2 Biggar Road N Lans
293 G3 Biggin Derbys
294 B5 Biggin Derbys
344 C3 Biggin N York
121 F4 Biggin Thurr
606 A5 Biggings Shet
96 B3 Biggin Hill Gt Lon
196 A6 Biggleswade Beds
587 J4 Bighouse Highld
73 F3 Bighton Hants
399 H4 Biglands Cumb
288 D1 Big Mancot Flints
291 G4 Bignall End Staffs
54 A2 Bignor W Susx
172 C5 Bigrigg Cumb
376 C2 Big Sand Highld
572 E8 Bigton Shet
605 G6 Bigton Shet
8 C1 Bilberry Cnwll
276 B1 Bilborough C Nott
63 G3 Bilbrook Somset
236 C4 Bilbrook Staffs
357 G5 Bilbrough N York
589 H6 Bilbster Highld
589 H6 Bilbster Mains Highld
316 B3 Bilby Notts
394 D5 Bildershaw Dur
200 C5 Bildeston Suffk
11 F3 Billacombe C Plym
23 F4 Billacott Cnwll
146 D6 Billericay Essex
241 F4 Billesdon Leics
213 G3 Billesley Birm

190 A3 Billesley Warwks
213 G3 Billesley Common Birm
193 H2 Billing Nhants
279 G3 Billingborough Lincs
324 C4 Billinge St Hel
225 G4 Billingford Norfk
254 D3 Billingford Norfk
396 C4 Billingham S on T
299 F4 Billinghay Lincs
329 G2 Billingley Barns
76 A4 Billingshurst W Susx
211 G3 Billingsley Shrops
168 C5 Billington Beds
339 H2 Billington Lancs
272 C5 Billington Staffs
251 E2 Billockby Norfk
405 G2 Bill Quay Gatesd
442 A5 Bilsmoor Park Nthumb
431 F6 Billy Mill N Tyne
394 D2 Billy Row Dur
270 B4 Bilmarsh Shrops
338 C1 Bilsborrow Lancs
321 E4 Bilsby Lincs
321 E4 Bilsby Field Lincs
26 C4 Bilsdon Devon
53 H4 Bilsham W Susx
81 F3 Bilsington Kent
135 E2 Bilson Green Gloucs
296 B2 Bilsthorpe Notts
296 B3 Bilsthorpe Moor Notts
471 E2 Bilston Mdloth
236 D5 Bilston Wolves
239 F3 Bilstone Leics
99 G5 Bilting Kent
348 C3 Bilton E R Yk
443 G2 Bilton Nthumb
356 C3 Bilton N York
216 A5 Bilton Warwks
357 F5 Bilton Haggs N York
357 F4 Bilton in Ainsty N York
600 E1 Bimbister Ork
334 B6 Binbrook Lincs
395 E3 Binchester Blocks Dur
32 B3 Bincombe Dorset
64 C4 Bincombe Somset
577 K7 Bindal Highld
43 F3 Bindon Highld
85 H5 Binegar Somset
55 E1 Bines Green W Susx
116 D5 Binfield Br For
116 B4 Binfield Heath Oxon
429 F5 Bingfield Nthumb
488 B5 Bingham C Edin
277 F1 Bingham Notts
47 E4 Bingham's Melcombe Dorset
342 B2 Bingley Brad
270 C6 Bings Heath Shrops
260 C4 Binham Norfk
215 F4 Binley Covtry
215 F4 Binley Hants
215 F4 Binley Woods Warwks
33 F2 Binnegar Dorset
485 H5 Binniehill Falk
95 G5 Binscombe Surrey
140 A3 Binsey Oxon
370 A4 Binsoe N York
37 F2 Binstead IoW
74 B1 Binsted Hants
54 A3 Binsted W Susx
190 A4 Binton Warwks
254 D3 Bintree Norfk
233 F4 Binweston Shrops
174 B6 Birch Essex
326 C3 Birch Rochdl
213 G5 Birch Acre Worcs
161 F2 Birchall Herefs
292 C4 Birchall Staffs
259 F5 Bircham Newton Norfk
259 F5 Bircham Tofts Norfk
212 B5 Birchan Coppice Worcs
171 H5 Birchanger Essex
187 G2 Birch Berrow Worcs
460 C4 Birchburn N Ayrs
273 H3 Birch Cross Staffs
78 C2 Birchden E Susx
577 G5 Birchen Highld
187 F6 Birchend Herefs
273 G2 Birchendale Staffs
186 B1 Bircher Herefs
213 H1 Birches Green Birm
292 A5 Birches Head C Stke
79 F3 Birchett's Green E Susx
213 G1 Birchfield Birm
174 B6 Birch Green Essex
144 C2 Birch Green Herts
324 B3 Birch Green Lancs
188 C5 Birch Green Worcs
106 C3 Birchgrove Cardif
129 H5 Birchgrove Swans
77 G4 Birchgrove W Susx
174 D3 Birchhall Corner Essex
290 A2 Birch Heath Ches
93 H1 Birch Hill Br For
29 F2 Birchill Devon
237 F5 Birchills Wsall
101 E2 Birchington Kent
238 D6 Birchley Heath Warwks
238 C4 Birchmoor Warwks
168 C3 Birchmoor Green Beds
81 G1 Bircholt Forstal Kent
294 A2 Birchover Derbys
312 D2 Birch Vale Derbys
144 B3 Birchwood Herts
318 A6 Birchwood Lincs
44 A5 Birchwood Somset
310 C1 Birchwood Warrtn
187 E4 Birchyfield Herefs
50 A5 Birchy Hill Hants
316 B1 Bircotes Notts
172 D1 Birdbrook Essex
69 F5 Birdbush Wilts
493 G6 Birdfield Ag & B
371 F4 Birdforth N York
53 E4 Birdham W Susx
314 D6 Birdholme Derbys
215 G6 Birdingbury Warwks
136 D2 Birdlip Gloucs
604 b3 Bird Obsy Shet
359 F1 Birdsall N York
328 C3 Birds Edge Kirk
199 F2 Birds End Suffk
146 B3 Birds Green Essex
211 H2 Birdsgreen Shrops
29 G2 Birdsmoorgate Dorset
484 C4 Birdston E Duns
200 D4 Bird Street Suffk
329 E4 Birdwell Barns
161 G6 Birdwood Gloucs
453 E2 Birgham Border
324 D1 Birkacre Lancs
388 C2 Birkby Cumb
342 B6 Birkby Kirk
384 A4 Birkby N York
323 F1 Birkdale Sefton
570 C6 Birkenhills Abers
342 D4 Birkenshaw Kirk
467 G2 Birkenshaw N Lans
468 B5 Birkenshaw S Lans
451 H1 Birkenside Border
389 H5 Birkett Mire Cumb
554 B6 Birkhall Abers
514 B3 Birkhill Angus

472 D6 Birkhill Border
437 H1 Birkhill D & G
278 D5 Birkholme Lincs
342 C5 Birkhouse Calder
344 C4 Birkin N York
366 C1 Birks Cumb
343 E4 Birks Leeds
402 D1 Birkshaw Nthumb
186 B4 Birley Herefs
314 C1 Birley Carr Sheff
329 E6 Birley Edge Sheff
314 D3 Birleyhay Derbys
97 G2 Birling Kent
443 H3 Birling Nthumb
57 F5 Birling Gap E Susx
188 D6 Birlingham Worcs
213 F2 Birmingham Birm
512 B1 Birnam P & K
561 E3 Birness Abers
467 F4 Birniehill S Lans
555 G5 Birse Abers
555 F5 Birsemore Abers
342 D4 Birstall Kirk
240 C3 Birstall Leics
356 A3 Birstwith N York
279 E3 Birthorpe Lincs
326 B2 Birtle Rochdl
405 G3 Birtley Gatesd
209 G6 Birtley Herefs
428 D4 Birtley Nthumb
210 B1 Birtley Shrops
93 H6 Birtley Green Surrey
162 B2 Birtsmorton Worcs
162 A2 Birts Street Worcs
319 G3 Bisbrooke Rutlnd
242 B5 Biscathorpe Lincs
43 G5 Biscombe Somset
169 F5 Biscot Luton
8 D3 Biscovey Cnwll
116 D2 Bisham W & M
189 E4 Bishampton Worcs
41 E2 Bish Mill Devon
186 A6 Bishon Common Herefs
395 E4 Bishop Auckland Dur
318 C1 Bishopbridge Lincs
484 B5 Bishopbriggs E Duns
347 E1 Bishop Burton E R Yk
70 C3 Bishopdown Wilts
565 J6 Bishop Kinkell Highld
395 G3 Bishop Middleham Dur
568 C3 Bishopmill Moray
356 C1 Bishop Monkton N York
332 D6 Bishop Norton Lincs
100 C5 Bishopsbourne Kent
88 B2 Bishops Cannings Wilts
209 F2 Bishop's Castle Shrops
46 D2 Bishop's Caundle Dorset
162 D4 Bishop's Cleeve Gloucs
46 C2 Bishop's Down Dorset
187 E5 Bishop's Frome Herefs
396 B5 Bishopsgarth S on T
117 G5 Bishopsgate Surrey
172 C6 Bishop's Green Essex
90 D2 Bishop's Green W Berk
43 G3 Bishop's Hull Somset
191 F3 Bishop's Itchington Warwks
43 G2 Bishops Lydeard Somset
162 B5 Bishop's Norton Gloucs
41 F3 Bishop's Nympton Devon
271 H3 Bishop's Offley Staffs
171 G5 Bishops Park Herts
4 D3 Bishop's Quay Cnwll
171 G6 Bishop's Stortford Herts
73 F3 Bishop's Sutton Hants
191 E2 Bishop's Tachbrook Warwks
61 E5 Bishop's Tawton Devon
20 C3 Bishopsteignton Devon
72 C6 Bishopstoke Hants
109 G4 Bishopston Bristl
103 E4 Bishopston Swans
141 H2 Bishopstone Bucks
56 D4 Bishopstone E Susx
185 H6 Bishopstone Herefs
100 D2 Bishopstone Kent
113 F3 Bishopstone Swindn
70 B4 Bishopstone Wilts
87 F6 Bishopstrow Wilts
85 G3 Bishop Sutton BaNES
51 G1 Bishop's Waltham Hants
44 B5 Bishopswood Somset
109 G6 Bishopsworth Bristl
356 B2 Bishop Thornton N York
358 A5 Bishopthorpe York
410 D4 Bishopton D & G
395 H5 Bishopton Darltn
370 B5 Bishopton N York
483 F5 Bishopton Rens
190 B3 Bishopton Warwks
406 B3 Bishopwearmouth Sundld
359 E3 Bishop Wilton E R Yk
107 F2 Bishpool Newpt
108 C2 Bishton Newpt
273 F5 Bishton Staffs
136 D3 Bisley Gloucs
93 G3 Bisley Surrey
93 F3 Bisley Camp Surrey
337 E1 Bispham Bpool
324 B2 Bispham Green Lancs
7 E5 Bissoe Cnwll
5 E2 Bissom Cnwll
49 E4 Bisterne Hants
49 E4 Bisterne Close Hants
97 E4 Bitchet Green Kent
278 D4 Bitchfield Lincs
60 D3 Bittadon Devon
12 B1 Bittaford Devon
254 B4 Bittering Norfk
210 D4 Bitterley Shrops
50 D2 Bitterne Sotn
50 D2 Bitterne Park C Sotn
238 B4 Bitteswell Leics
110 B6 Bitton S Glos
116 B2 Bix Oxon
606 D7 Bixter Shet
240 C5 Blaby Leics
424 A1 Blackacre D & G
474 B4 Blackadder Border
13 E2 Blackawton Devon
222 A2 Black Bank Cambs
215 F2 Black Banks Darltn
281 F4 Black Barn Lincs
376 C3 Blackbeck Cumb
43 E6 Blackborough Devon
252 D5 Blackborough Norfk
252 D5 Blackborough End Norfk
138 D4 Black Bourton Oxon
78 C5 Blackboys E Susx
294 C5 Blackbrook Derbys
313 E3 Blackbrook Derbys
271 H2 Blackbrook Staffs
324 C5 Blackbrook St Hel
94 D5 Blackbrook Surrey
557 G2 Blackburn Abers
339 F4 Blackburn Bl w D
568 E4 Blackburn Moray
329 F6 Blackburn Rothm
469 F1 Blackburn W Loth
430 C6 Black Callerton N u Ty
249 E5 Black Carr Norfk
471 H3 Blackcastle Mdloth

419 G5 Black Clauchrie S Ayrs
506 F3 Black Crofts Ag & B
7 H1 Black Cross Cnwll
91 G4 Black Dam Hants
311 F5 Blackden Heath Ches
139 G3 Blackditch Oxon
557 H2 Blackdog C Aber
41 G6 Black Dog Devon
29 G2 Blackdown Dorset
72 D5 Blackdown Hants
215 E6 Blackdown Warwks
399 E4 Blackdyke Cumb
490 A3 Blackdykes E Loth
329 F4 Blacker Hill Barns
99 E1 Blacketts Kent
405 G3 Blackfell Sundld
120 C5 Blackfen Gt Lon
50 D4 Blackfield Hants
549 K1 Blackfold Highld
400 C2 Blackford Cumb
424 C3 Blackford D & G
498 D3 Blackford D & G
210 D3 Blackford Shrops
63 E2 Blackford Somset
67 H4 Blackford Somset
84 D5 Blackford Somset
326 A3 Blackford Bridge Bury
275 E6 Blackfordby Leics
36 D5 Blackgang IoW
556 B5 Blackhall Abers
487 H5 Blackhall C Edin
466 C2 Blackhall Rens
396 C2 Blackhall Colliery Dur
404 D3 Blackhall Mill Gatesd
396 C2 Blackhall Rocks Dur
78 B2 Blackham E Susx
451 E2 Blackhaugh Border
174 D5 Blackheath Essex
120 A4 Blackheath Gt Lon
213 E2 Blackheath Sandw
227 E5 Blackheath Suffk
120 A4 Blackheath Park Gt Lon
430 A4 Black Heddon Nthumb
571 K4 Blackhill Abers
404 C4 Blackhill Dur
71 F6 Blackhill Hants
542 E6 Blackhill Highld
569 G6 Blackhillock Moray
103 E3 Blackhills Swans
27 F4 Blackhorse Devon
110 B4 Blackhorse S Glos
222 B1 Black Horse Drove Cambs
571 L6 Blackhouse Abers
598 D6 Blackhouse Village W Isls
140 C4 Blackland Leys Oxon
280 C2 Blackjack Lincs
237 E6 Black Lake Sandw
112 B6 Blackland Wilts
58 D4 Blacklands E Susx
187 E6 Blacklands Herefs
326 A3 Black Lane Bury
569 L4 Blacklaw Abers
338 C3 Blackleach Lancs
326 C4 Blackley Manch
525 H3 Blacklunans P & K
233 F5 Black Marsh Shrops
160 C2 Blackmarstone Herefs
105 E2 Blackmill Brdgnd
189 G6 Blackminster Worcs
85 G2 Blackmoor BaNES
74 B3 Blackmoor Hants
324 B2 Black Moor Lancs
343 E2 Blackmoor Leeds
85 E2 Blackmoor N Som
43 G4 Blackmoor Somset
325 F4 Blackmoor Wigan
327 G2 Blackmoorfoot Kirk
61 F3 Blackmoor Gate Devon
146 C4 Blackmore Essex
233 F3 Blackmore Shrops
173 E3 Blackmore End Essex
143 H1 Blackmore End Herts
188 B6 Blackmore End Worcs
521 K7 Black Mount Ag & B
487 E2 Black Muir Fife
78 C3 Blackness E Susx
487 E4 Blackness Falk
74 B1 Blacknest Hants
117 G6 Blacknest W & M
30 A3 Blackney Dorset
32 D2 Blacknoll Dorset
173 F5 Black Notley Essex
340 D1 Blacko Lancs
270 C2 Blackoe Shrops
545 L5 Black Park Highld
269 F1 Black Park Wrexhm
103 F3 Black Pill Swans
338 C2 Black Pole Lancs
188 C3 Blackpole Worcs
337 E2 Blackpool Bpool
11 G3 Blackpool Devon
13 F3 Blackpool Devon
19 H3 Blackpool Devon
126 B2 Blackpool Pembks
29 F3 Blackpool Corner Devon
426 D4 Blackpool Gate Cumb
468 D1 Blackridge W Loth
476 E4 Blackrock Ag & B
85 H1 Blackrock BaNES
56 A4 Black Rock Br & H
4 B2 Black Rock Cnwll
132 D2 Blackrock Mons
325 E2 Blackrod Bolton
398 C1 Blackshaw D & G
341 E4 Blackshaw Head Calder
292 C3 Blackshaw Moor Staffs
175 F1 Blacksmith's Corner Suffk
201 F1 Blacksmith's Green Suffk
339 H5 Blacksnape Bl w D
212 A5 Blackstone Worcs
55 F1 Blackstone W Susx
227 G2 Black Street Suffk
125 G3 Black Tar Pembks
166 D6 Blackthorn Oxon
200 B2 Blackthorpe Suffk
346 B5 Blacktoft E R Yk
557 F4 Blacktop C Aber
24 C1 Black Torrington Devon
106 D3 Blacktown Newpt
106 D1 Black Vein Caerph
294 B5 Blackwall Derbys
120 A3 Blackwall Gt Lon
6 D4 Blackwater Cnwll
49 E5 Blackwater Dorset
92 D2 Blackwater Hants
37 E3 Blackwater IoW
255 E3 Blackwater Norfk
44 B4 Blackwater Somset
460 B4 Blackwaterfoot N Ayrs
106 C4 Blackweir Cardif
400 D4 Blackwell Cumb
383 G2 Blackwell Darltn
295 E3 Blackwell Derbys
313 F5 Blackwell Derbys
42 D2 Blackwell Devon
190 C6 Blackwell Somset
213 E5 Blackwell Warwks
188 C3 Blackwell Worcs
77 G2 Blackwell W Susx
132 C5 Blackwood Caerph
437 G6 Blackwood D & G
468 B6 Blackwood S Lans
310 C1 Blackwood Warrtn
292 B3 Blackwood Hill Staffs
309 H6 Blacon Ches
82 C1 Bladbean Kent

382 A5 **Blades** N York
417 E6 **Bladnoch** D & G
139 G2 **Bladon** Oxon
179 E4 **Blaenannerch** Cerdgn
129 E4 **Blaenau** Carmth
288 B3 **Blaenau** Flints
285 E4 **Blaenau Dolwyddelan** Conwy
285 F5 **Blaenau Ffestiniog** Gwynd
132 D4 **Blaenau-Gwent** Blae G
133 E3 **Blaenavon** Torfn
179 H3 **Blaenbedw Fawr** Cerdgn
130 D6 **Blaencaerau** Neath
179 G3 **Blaencelyn** Cerdgn
131 F6 **Blaen Clydach** Rhondd
131 E5 **Blaencwm** Rhondd
157 E2 **Blaendyryn** Powys
152 D2 **Blaenffos** Pembks
130 D6 **Blaengarw** Brdgnd
130 D3 **Blaengwrach** Neath
130 D5 **Blaengwynfi** Neath
179 F5 **Blaen-pant** Cerdgn
181 F2 **Blaenpennal** Cerdgn
204 D4 **Blaenplwyf** Cerdgn
179 H4 **Blaenporth** Cerdgn
131 E5 **Blaenrhondda** Rhondd
153 E4 **Blaenwaun** Carmth
180 A4 **Blaen-waun** Cerdgn
153 G4 **Blaen-y-coed** Carmth
132 B2 **Blaen-y-cwm** Blae G
23 E4 **Blagdon** Cnwll
85 F3 **Blagdon** N Som
20 A5 **Blagdon** Torbay
43 H4 **Blagdon Hill** Somset
402 C5 **Blagill** Cumb
324 A3 **Blaguegate** Lancs
532 F7 **Blaich** Highld
132 D3 **Blaina** Blae G
519 G2 **Blain** Highld
501 F6 **Blair** Fife
524 C3 **Blair Atholl** P & K
461 E3 **Blairbeg** N Ayrs
486 C2 **Blairburn** Fife
410 C4 **Blairbuy** D & G
556 B1 **Blairdaff** Abers
497 H5 **Blair Drummond** Stirlg
525 J6 **Blairgowrie** P & K
486 D2 **Blairhall** Fife
467 H1 **Blairhill** N Lans
499 E6 **Blairingone** P & K
465 F5 **Blairland** N Ayrs
485 F5 **Blairlinn** N Lans
498 C5 **Blairlogie** Stirlg
482 A3 **Blairmore** Ag & B
584 C4 **Blairmore** Highld
552 D5 **Blairnamarrow** Moray
565 H5 **Blairninich** Highld
484 B4 **Blairskaith** E Duns
135 G1 **Blaisdon** Gloucs
109 F4 **Blaise Hamlet** Bristl
212 B4 **Blakebrook** Worcs
212 C4 **Blakedown** Worcs
173 E5 **Blake End** Essex
194 B6 **Blakelands** M Keyn
453 E3 **Blakelaw** Border
405 F1 **Blakelaw** N u Ty
212 C1 **Blakeley** Lancs
292 C5 **Blakeley Lane** Staffs
290 D4 **Blakelow** Ches
159 G1 **Blakemere** Herefs
237 F4 **Blakenall Heath** Wsall
135 F3 **Blakeney** Gloucs
260 D3 **Blakeney** Norfk
291 E5 **Blakenhall** Ches
236 D5 **Blakenhall** Wolves
212 B3 **Blakeshall** Worcs
192 D4 **Blakesley** Nhants
403 H4 **Blanchland** Nthumb
47 H3 **Blandford Camp** Dorset
47 G3 **Blandford Forum** Dorset
47 G4 **Blandford St Mary** Dorset
355 H4 **Bland Hill** N York
586 D5 **Blandy** Highld
484 A4 **Blanefield** Stirlg
474 B3 **Blanerne** Border
291 G5 **Blank Bank** Staffs
298 D2 **Blankney** Lincs
12 C4 **Blanksmill Bridge** Devon
28 C3 **Blannicombe** Devon
467 G3 **Blantyre** S Lans
521 G2 **Blàr a' Chaorainn** Highld
480 B2 **Blarbuie** Ag & B
493 G2 **Blarghour** Ag & B
520 F2 **Blarmachfoldach** Highld
574 F2 **Blarnalearoch** Highld
147 E2 **Blasford Hill** Essex
592 F3 **Blashaval** W Isls
49 E3 **Blashford** Hants
241 H5 **Blaston** Leics
86 D5 **Blatchbridge** Somset
242 C5 **Blatherwycke** Nhants
364 C2 **Blawith** Cumb
202 D3 **Blaxhall** Suffk
331 E4 **Blaxton** Donc
405 E2 **Blaydon** Gatesd
405 E2 **Blaydon Burn** Gatesd
405 E2 **Blaydon Haughs** Gatesd
388 A6 **Bleachgreen** Cumb
226 A4 **Bleach Green** Suffk
85 E5 **Bleadney** Somset
84 B3 **Bleadon** N Som
187 E5 **Bleak Acre** Herefs
168 B2 **Bleak Hall** M Keyn
327 F2 **Bleak Hey Nook** Oldham
49 E2 **Bleak Hill** Hants
100 B3 **Blean** Kent
319 E3 **Bleasby** Lincs
296 D5 **Bleasby** Notts
319 E3 **Bleasby Moor** Lincs
352 B5 **Bleasdale** Lancs
380 C2 **Bleatarn** Cumb
502 C2 **Blebocraigs** Fife
208 C6 **Bleddfa** Powys
164 C5 **Bledington** Gloucs
141 G4 **Bledlow** Bucks
141 G5 **Bledlow Ridge** Bucks
87 F3 **Bleet** Wilts
472 B2 **Blegbie** E Loth
38 B2 **Blegbury** Devon
391 G3 **Blencarn** Cumb
399 F5 **Blencogo** Cumb
52 C2 **Blenheim** Hants
295 G5 **Blenheim** Notts
140 C3 **Blenheim** Oxon
140 C4 **Blenheim** Oxon
402 B2 **Blennerhasset** Cumb
389 E1 **Blennerhasset** Cumb
166 B6 **Bletchingdon** Oxon
95 G4 **Bletchingley** Surrey
168 B3 **Bletchley** M Keyn
271 E3 **Bletchley** Shrops
152 B5 **Bletherston** Pembks
195 E3 **Bletsoe** Beds
115 E2 **Blewbury** Oxon
81 F2 **Bliby** Kent
255 G2 **Blickling** Norfk
296 A3 **Blidworth** Notts
296 A3 **Blidworth Bottoms** Notts
295 H4 **Blidworth Dale** Notts
441 E2 **Blindburn** Nthumb
389 E3 **Blindcrake** Cumb
95 H5 **Blindley Heath** Surrey
44 B5 **Blindmoor** Somset
513 G6 **Blinkbonny** Fife

15 F4 **Blisland** Cnwll
49 F2 **Blissford** Hants
211 G5 **Bliss Gate** Worcs
235 F4 **Blists Hill** Wrekin
193 F4 **Blisworth** Nhants
273 G5 **Blithbury** Staffs
399 E4 **Blitterlees** Cumb
164 B3 **Blockley** Gloucs
250 C3 **Blofield** Norfk
250 C2 **Blofield Heath** Norfk
224 D4 **Blo' Norton** Norfk
251 G5 **Bloodman's Corner** Suffk
86 B3 **Bloomfield** BaNES
86 C2 **Bloomfield** BaNES
236 D6 **Bloomfield** Sandw
119 F3 **Bloomsbury** Gt Lon
271 G3 **Blore** Staffs
293 F5 **Blore** Staffs
271 G3 **Bloreheath** Staffs
211 A4 **Blossomfield** Solhll
273 G5 **Blount's Green** Staffs
323 F1 **Blowick** Sefton
6 D3 **Blowinghouse** Cnwll
165 G2 **Bloxham** Oxon
298 D4 **Bloxholm** Lincs
237 E4 **Bloxwich** Wsall
47 G6 **Bloxworth** Dorset
355 G3 **Blubberhouses** N York
7 H2 **Blue Anchor** Cnwll
63 G3 **Blue Anchor** Somset
103 E3 **Blue Anchor** Swans
234 D2 **Bluebell** Shrops
98 A2 **Blue Bell Hill** Kent
451 G1 **Bluecairn** Border
170 C5 **Blue Hill** Herts
99 E3 **Bluetown** Kent
123 E4 **Blue Town** Kent
111 E6 **Blue Vein** Wilts
121 E5 **Bluewater** Kent
323 E5 **Blundellsands** Sefton
251 G5 **Blundeston** Suffk
212 B2 **Blundies** Staffs
195 G4 **Blunham** Beds
112 D2 **Blunsdon St Andrew** Swindn
212 C5 **Bluntington** Worcs
221 E5 **Bluntisham** Cambs
16 D6 **Blunts** Cnwll
214 A6 **Blunt's Green** Warwks
29 H3 **Bluntshay** Dorset
272 C1 **Blurton** C Stke
332 C6 **Blyborough** Lincs
227 E4 **Blyford** Suffk
236 B2 **Blymhill** Staffs
470 B5 **Blyth** Border
316 B2 **Blyth** Notts
431 F3 **Blyth** Nthumb
470 B5 **Blyth Bridge** Border
227 F4 **Blythburgh** Suffk
472 D5 **Blythe** Border
273 E1 **Blythe Marsh** Staffs
214 C1 **Blyth End** Warwks
483 G6 **Blythswood** Rens
332 B6 **Blyton** Lincs
503 F2 **Boarhills** Fife
51 G3 **Boarhunt** Hants
340 C5 **Boarsgreave** Lancs
78 C3 **Boarshead** E Susx
324 D3 **Boar's Head** Wigan
140 A4 **Boars Hill** Oxon
140 D2 **Boarstall** Bucks
24 D4 **Boasley Cross** Devon
565 K2 **Boath** Highld
551 G6 **Boat of Garten** Highld
98 D1 **Bobbing** Kent
212 B1 **Bobbington** Staffs
146 A3 **Bobbingworth** Essex
224 D5 **Bobby Hill** Suffk
9 F2 **Bocaddon** Cnwll
497 F3 **Bochastle** Stirlg
99 G6 **Bockhanger** Kent
173 F5 **Bocking** Essex
173 F4 **Bocking Churchstreet** Essex
149 G1 **Bocking's Elm** Essex
186 D2 **Bockleton** Worcs
116 D2 **Bockmer End** Bucks
39 E3 **Bocombe** Devon
9 E1 **Boconnoc** Cnwll
561 H1 **Boddam** Abers
605 M2 **Boddam** Shet
86 A6 **Bodden** Somset
529 F4 **Boddin** Angus
162 C4 **Boddington** Gloucs
302 D4 **Bodedern** IoA
14 C4 **Bodellick** Cnwll
8 D3 **Bodelva** Cnwll
307 E4 **Bodelwyddan** Denbgs
186 C4 **Bodenham** Herefs
70 D4 **Bodenham** Wilts
161 E3 **Bodenham Bank** Herefs
186 C4 **Bodenham Moor** Herefs
262 B6 **Bodermid** Gwynd
303 E2 **Bodewryd** IoA
307 F5 **Bodfari** Denbgs
303 F5 **Bodffordd** IoA
261 F3 **Bodham** Norfk
79 H4 **Bodiam** E Susx
165 G2 **Bodicote** Oxon
14 D4 **Bodieve** Cnwll
8 C2 **Bodiggo** Cnwll
4 C2 **Bodilly** Cnwll
9 E3 **Bodinnick** Cnwll
302 C5 **Bodior** IoA
57 H2 **Bodle Street Green** E Susx
61 G2 **Bodley** Devon
15 E5 **Bodmin** Cnwll
43 E5 **Bodmiscombe** Devon
247 G5 **Bodney** Norfk
282 C2 **Bodorgan** IoA
82 B1 **Bodsham** Kent
263 E3 **Boduan** Gwynd
16 B6 **Boduel** Cnwll
8 C1 **Bodwen** Cnwll
238 B5 **Bodymoor Heath** Warwks
15 G6 **Bofarnel** Cnwll
591 J2 **Bogach** W Isls
565 L6 **Bogallan** Highld
561 F2 **Bogbrae** Abers
295 F5 **Bogend** Notts
445 E3 **Bogend** S Ayrs
470 D2 **Boghall** Mdloth
486 C6 **Boghall** W Loth
447 F1 **Boghead** S Lans
568 B3 **Bogmoor** Moray
569 K6 **Bogniebrae** Abers
53 G5 **Bognor Regis** W Susx
559 G6 **Bograxie** Abers
470 B4 **Bogs Bank** Border
468 C4 **Bogside** N Lans
570 B5 **Bogton** Abers
24 C3 **Bogtown** Cnwll
421 G3 **Bogue** D & G
58 C4 **Bohemia** E Susx
71 E6 **Bohemia** Wilts
327 F1 **Bohemia Corner** IoW
362 C4 **Bohenie** Highld
323 F5 **Bohetherick** Cnwll
7 H5 **Bohortha** Cnwll
533 L6 **Bohuntine** Highld
533 L6 **Bohuntinville** Highld
595 H5 **Boirseam** W Isls
8 C1 **Bokiddick** Cnwll
154 B6 **Bolahaul** Carmth

394 D5 **Bolam** Dur
430 A3 **Bolam** Nthumb
429 H3 **Bolam West Houses** Nthumb
12 B5 **Bolberry** Devon
310 A2 **Bold Heath** St Hel
237 H6 **Boldmere** Birm
406 B2 **Boldon** S Tyne
406 A2 **Boldon Colliery** S Tyne
50 B5 **Boldre** Hants
382 B2 **Boldron** Dur
24 B3 **Boldventure** Devon
317 E2 **Bole** Notts
238 C4 **Bolehall** Staffs
314 C5 **Bole Hill** Derbys
315 E5 **Bolehill** Derbys
294 B3 **Bolehill** Sheff
314 C3 **Bolehill** Sheff
7 E3 **Bolenowe** Cnwll
451 F3 **Boleside** Border
237 H3 **Boley Park** Staffs
42 C5 **Bolham** Devon
43 G5 **Bolham** Notts
316 D3 **Bolham** Notts
43 G5 **Bolham Water** Devon
325 H2 **Bolholt** Bury
7 E3 **Bolingey** Cnwll
4 C2 **Bolitho** Cnwll
393 H3 **Bollihope** Dur
312 B4 **Bollington** Ches
312 B4 **Bollington Cross** Ches
135 G2 **Bollow** Gloucs
76 D5 **Bolney** W Susx
195 F3 **Bolnhurst** Beds
77 F5 **Bolnore** W Susx
528 D4 **Bolshan** Angus
315 F5 **Bolsover** Derbys
328 D5 **Bolsterstone** Sheff
160 D3 **Bolstone** Herefs
371 F2 **Boltby** N York
116 C1 **Bolter End** Bucks
325 G3 **Bolton** Bolton
342 C2 **Bolton** Brad
391 G5 **Bolton** Cumb
489 G5 **Bolton** E Loth
359 E4 **Bolton** E R Yk
443 E2 **Bolton** Nthumb
355 E4 **Bolton Abbey** N York
355 E4 **Bolton Bridge** N York
353 F5 **Bolton-by-Bowland** Lancs
426 C6 **Boltonfellend** Cumb
389 F1 **Bolton Green** Lancs
324 C1 **Bolton Green** Lancs
338 B3 **Bolton Houses** Lancs
365 G6 **Bolton-le-Sands** Lancs
399 G6 **Bolton Low Houses** Cumb
399 G6 **Bolton New Houses** Cumb
383 G5 **Bolton-on-Swale** N York
344 C1 **Bolton Percy** N York
351 G1 **Bolton Town End** Lancs
329 H4 **Bolton Upon Dearne** Barns
399 H6 **Bolton Wood Lane** Cumb
342 C2 **Bolton Woods** Brad
403 G5 **Boltshope Park** Dur
16 A3 **Bolventor** Cnwll
431 E3 **Bomarsund** Nthumb
379 F1 **Bomby** Cumb
270 B6 **Bomere Heath** Shrops
487 H6 **Bonaly** C Edin
576 D5 **Bonar Bridge** Highld
507 H3 **Bonawe** Ag & B
333 E1 **Bonby** N Linc
153 E2 **Boncath** Pembks
440 A2 **Bonchester Bridge** Border
37 F5 **Bonchurch** IoW
136 C1 **Bondend** Gloucs
274 A6 **Bond End** Staffs
25 G2 **Bondleigh** Devon
240 A3 **Bondman Hays** Leics
351 G6 **Bonds** Lancs
19 F2 **Bonehill** Devon
238 B4 **Bonehill** Staffs
468 C3 **Bo'ness** Falk
237 F2 **Boney Hay** Staffs
483 F4 **Bonhill** W Duns
236 B4 **Boningale** Shrops
452 B5 **Bonjedward** Border
468 C3 **Bonkle** N Lans
379 E5 **Bonning Gate** Cumb
450 B2 **Bonnington** Border
487 F6 **Bonnington** C Edin
81 F2 **Bonnington** Kent
501 G4 **Bonnybank** Fife
485 G3 **Bonnybridge** Falk
570 F5 **Bonnykelly** Abers
471 F2 **Bonnyrigg** Mdloth
559 F3 **Bonnyton** Abers
513 H2 **Bonnyton** Angus
529 E3 **Bonnyton** Angus
445 F2 **Bonnyton** E Ayrs
515 F2 **Bonnyton Smiddy** Angus
294 B3 **Bonsall** Derbys
64 D3 **Bonson** Somset
159 G6 **Bont** Mons
265 F6 **Bontddu** Gwynd
230 D4 **Bont Dolgadfan** Powys
155 H4 **Bont Fawr** Carmth
205 F2 **Bont-goch or Elerch** Cerdgn
321 E5 **Bonthorpe** Lincs
181 F1 **Bontnewydd** Cerdgn
307 E5 **Bont-newydd** Denbgs
283 E4 **Bontnewydd** Gwynd
287 F3 **Bontuchel** Denbgs
105 H5 **Bonvilston** V Glam
103 G3 **Bon-y-maen** Swans
60 D4 **Boode** Devon
116 D1 **Booker** Bucks
46 D4 **Bookham** Dorset
270 D4 **Booley** Shrops
270 D4 **Booleybank** Shrops
472 D5 **Boon** Border
603 K7 **Boonatown** Ork
291 K4 **Boon Hill** Staffs
51 F2 **Boorley Green** Hants
385 H1 **Boosbeck** R & Cl
173 H3 **Boose's Green** Essex
377 F4 **Boot** Cumb
341 G4 **Booth** Calder
273 F4 **Booth** Staffs
358 A4 **Bootham Stray** York
311 E2 **Booth Bank** Ches
354 B5 **Booth Bridge** N York
298 B3 **Boothby Graffoe** Lincs
278 D3 **Boothby Pagnell** Lincs
291 H6 **Boothen** C Stke
345 G4 **Boothferry** E R Yk
294 D5 **Boothgate** Derbys
312 B3 **Booth Green** Ches
606 F2 **Booth of Toft** Shet
342 D5 **Boothroyd** Kirk
290 A1 **Boothsdale** Ches
325 G4 **Boothstown** Salfd
342 A4 **Boothtown** Calder
193 G2 **Boothville** Nhants
327 F1 **Booth Wood** Calder
362 C4 **Bootle** Cumb
323 F5 **Bootle** Sefton
255 G1 **Boots Green** Norfk
311 F5 **Boot Street** Suffk
201 H5 **Booze** N York
382 B4 **Boquhan** Stirlg
484 A2 **Boquhan** Stirlg
497 G4 **Boquhapple** Stirlg
4 C2 **Boquio** Cnwll

211 E6 **Boraston** Shrops
211 E5 **Boraston Dale** Shrops
35 e2 **Bordeaux** Guern
98 D2 **Borden** Kent
74 C5 **Borden** W Susx
399 F4 **Border** Cumb
213 G2 **Bordesley** Birm
213 G2 **Bordesley Green** Birm
470 C5 **Bordlands** Border
354 B2 **Bordley** N York
74 B2 **Bordon Camp** Hants
147 F3 **Boreham** Essex
87 F6 **Boreham** Wilts
57 H2 **Boreham Street** E Susx
144 A5 **Borehamwood** Herts
424 D1 **Boreland** D & G
501 F6 **Boreland** Fife
509 J3 **Boreland** Stirlg
188 B1 **Boreley** Worcs
485 F1 **Borestone** Stirlg
594 E6 **Borgh** W Isls
599 J3 **Borgh** W Isls
595 G6 **Borghastan** W Isls
598 D6 **Borghastan** W Isls
586 E5 **Borgie** Highld
412 B5 **Borgue** D & G
582 F4 **Borgue** Highld
199 G6 **Borley** Essex
199 G6 **Borley Green** Essex
200 C2 **Borley Green** Suffk
590 E2 **Bornais** W Isls
542 F2 **Bornesketaig** Highld
412 B5 **Borness** D & G
3 c2 **Borough** IoS
356 D1 **Boroughbridge** N York
97 E3 **Borough Green** Kent
116 C4 **Borough Marsh** Wokham
238 C3 **Borough Park** Staffs
44 C3 **Borough Post** Somset
46 C2 **Borough, The** Dorset
288 D4 **Borras** Wrexhm
289 E4 **Borras Head** Wrexhm
542 B6 **Borreraig** Highld
595 G6 **Borrisdale** W Isls
542 B7 **Borrisdale** W Isls
275 G3 **Borrowash** Derbys
371 E2 **Borrowby** N York
386 C1 **Borrowby** N York
557 E6 **Borrowfield** Abers
589 J8 **Borrowston** Highld
486 C5 **Borrowstoun Mains** Falk
98 A1 **Borstal** Medway
205 E4 **Borth** Cerdgn
144 C5 **Borthwick** Mdloth
471 G3 **Borthwickbrae** Border
439 E1 **Borthwickshiels** Border
264 D2 **Borth-y-Gest** Gwynd
543 G7 **Borve** Highld
595 G6 **Borve** W Isls
595 G4 **Borve** W Isls
366 A5 **Borwick** Lancs
362 D6 **Borwick Rails** Cumb
2 C3 **Bosavern** Cnwll
187 G6 **Bosbury** Herefs
4 C2 **Boscadjack** Cnwll
22 B4 **Boscastle** Cnwll
2 D5 **Boscawen Point** Cnwll
2 C3 **Boscean** Cnwll
34 D2 **Boscombe** Bmouth
70 D2 **Boscombe** Wilts
236 D2 **Boscoomoor** Staffs
8 C3 **Boscoppa** Cnwll
3 G3 **Boscreege** Cnwll
53 E4 **Bosham** W Susx
53 E4 **Bosham Hoe** W Susx
125 G6 **Bosherston** Pembks
2 D3 **Boskednan** Cnwll
2 D5 **Boskenna** Cnwll
6 C5 **Bosleake** Cnwll
292 B1 **Bosley** Ches
5 E2 **Bosliowick** Cnwll
8 D1 **Boslymon** Cnwll
7 G1 **Bosoughan** Cnwll
2 D2 **Bosporthennis** Cnwll
358 D2 **Bossall** N York
22 B5 **Bossiney** Cnwll
100 C6 **Bossingham** Kent
71 G3 **Bossington** Hants
100 D4 **Bossington** Somset
62 D2 **Bossington** Somset
598 C6 **Bostadh** W Isls
310 D6 **Bostock Green** Ches
300 B6 **Boston** Lincs
300 D6 **Boston Long Hedges** Lincs
357 E5 **Boston Spa** Leeds
300 A5 **Boston West** Lincs
2 D2 **Boswednack** Cnwll
7 G3 **Boswin** Cnwll
4 C2 **Boswinger** Cnwll
8 B5 **Boswyn** Cnwll
2 C3 **Botallack** Cnwll
144 C5 **Botany Bay** Gt Lon
134 C4 **Botany Bay** Mons
400 D3 **Botcherby** Cumb
240 A4 **Botcheston** Leics
225 E4 **Botesdale** Suffk
430 D2 **Bothal** Nthumb
115 C4 **Bothampstead** W Berk
316 C3 **Bothamsall** Notts
389 E2 **Bothel** Cumb
609 J2 **Bothen** Shet
30 B4 **Bothenhampton** Dorset
467 G4 **Bothwell** S Lans
142 D4 **Botley** Bucks
51 F2 **Botley** Hants
140 A3 **Botley** Oxon
161 G4 **Botloe's Green** Gloucs
167 F5 **Botolph Claydon** Bucks
55 E5 **Botolphs** W Susx
565 H4 **Bottacks** Highld
16 C4 **Botternell** Cnwll
277 H2 **Bottesford** Leics
332 B3 **Bottesford** N Linc
198 A2 **Bottisham** Cambs
88 D3 **Bottlesford** Wilts
343 G5 **Bottom Boat** Wakefd
514 B5 **Bottomcraig** Fife
292 D4 **Bottom House** Staffs
341 H6 **Bottomley** Calder
338 C4 **Bottom of Hutton** Lancs
325 F2 **Bottom o' th' Moor** Bolton
98 D3 **Bottom Pond** Kent
2 C5 **Bottoms** Cnwll
386 A4 **Botton** N York
352 A2 **Botton Head** Lancs
41 G2 **Bottreaux Mill** Devon
238 C6 **Botts Green** Warwks
10 D1 **Botusfleming** Cnwll
262 D4 **Botwnnog** Gwynd
96 C5 **Bough Beech** Kent
158 B2 **Boughrood** Powys
158 B2 **Boughrood Brest** Powys
134 D3 **Boughspring** Gloucs
289 F1 **Boughton** Ches
318 C6 **Boughton** Lincs
193 G1 **Boughton** Nhants
247 E4 **Boughton** Norfk
316 C3 **Boughton** Notts
99 G5 **Boughton Aluph** Kent
99 G5 **Boughton Corner** Kent
98 B4 **Boughton Green** Kent
289 F1 **Boughton Heath** Ches

99 G5 **Boughton Lees** Kent
98 D5 **Boughton Malherbe** Kent
98 B4 **Boughton Monchelsea** Kent
99 H3 **Boughton Street** Kent
168 D2 **Bougton End** Beds
397 **Boulby** R & Cl
164 C5 **Bould** Oxon
341 G5 **Boulder Clough** Calder
36 B3 **Bouldnor** IoW
210 C2 **Bouldon** Shrops
443 H2 **Boulmer** Nthumb
161 G5 **Boulston** Pembks
125 G2 **Boulston** Pembks
554 D2 **Boultenstone** Abers
318 B6 **Boultham** Lincs
318 B6 **Boultham Moor** Lincs
275 E5 **Boulton** C Derb
275 F5 **Boulton Moor** C Derb
275 E6 **Boundary** Derbys
292 C6 **Boundary** Staffs
92 D6 **Boundary** Surrey
196 D3 **Bourn** Cambs
213 F3 **Bournbrook** Birm
279 F5 **Bourne** Lincs
85 E3 **Bourne** N Som
194 D6 **Bourne End** Beds
195 E2 **Bourne End** Beds
117 E2 **Bourne End** Bucks
34 C2 **Bournemouth** Bmouth
136 D4 **Bournes Green** Gloucs
123 G2 **Bournes Green** Sthend
212 D5 **Bournes Green** Worcs
237 G5 **Bourne Vale** Wsall
48 D6 **Bourne Valley** Poole
212 D5 **Bournheath** Worcs
405 H4 **Bournmoor** Dur
162 D5 **Bournside** Gloucs
135 G6 **Bournstream** Gloucs
213 F3 **Bournville** Birm
167 F3 **Bourton** Bucks
68 C3 **Bourton** Dorset
84 C2 **Bourton** N Som
113 F2 **Bourton** Oxon
234 D5 **Bourton** Shrops
88 B2 **Bourton** Wilts
215 G5 **Bourton on Dunsmore** Warwks
164 B3 **Bourton-on-the-Hill** Gloucs
164 B5 **Bourton-on-the-Water** Gloucs
444 D2 **Bourtreehill** N Ayrs
517 H3 **Bousd** Ag & B
606 B6 **Bousta** Shet
400 A3 **Boustead Hill** Cumb
364 D3 **Bouth** Cumb
369 F5 **Bouthwaite** N York
189 F3 **Bouts** Worcs
117 F4 **Boveney** Bucks
48 D2 **Boveridge** Dorset
105 F6 **Boverton** V Glam
19 H2 **Bovey Tracey** Devon
143 E4 **Bovingdon** Herts
116 D2 **Bovingdon Green** Bucks
143 E4 **Bovingdon Green** Herts
145 H3 **Bovinger** Essex
33 E2 **Bovington Camp** Dorset
400 B3 **Bow** Cumb
13 E1 **Bow** Devon
25 H2 **Bow** Devon
119 H3 **Bow** Gt Lon
139 E6 **Bow** Oxon
393 F5 **Bowbank** Dur
224 B4 **Bowbeck** Suffk
25 H4 **Bowbeer** Devon
168 B3 **Bow Brickhill** M Keyn
136 C4 **Bowbridge** Gloucs
234 A2 **Bowbrook** Shrops
329 G5 **Bow Broom** Rothm
395 F2 **Bowburn** Dur
36 D3 **Bowcombe** IoW
119 H3 **Bow Common** Gt Lon
28 B4 **Bowd** Devon
451 G3 **Bowden** Border
13 E3 **Bowden** Devon
68 C5 **Bowden** Dorset
87 C1 **Bowden Hill** Wilts
66 C4 **Bowdens** Somset
380 B4 **Bowderdale** Cumb
311 F2 **Bowdon** Traffd
589 G4 **Bower** Highld
428 B3 **Bower** Nthumb
109 G5 **Bower Ashton** Bristl
69 H5 **Bowerchalke** Wilts
143 G1 **Bower Heath** Herts
87 G2 **Bowerhill** Wilts
66 C6 **Bower Hinton** Somset
450 B5 **Bowerhope** Border
174 C1 **Bower House Tye** Suffk
589 G4 **Bowermadden** Highld
272 B2 **Bowers** Staffs
122 A2 **Bowers Gifford** Essex
487 E1 **Bowershall** Fife
589 G4 **Bowertower** Highld
382 A2 **Bowes** Dur
119 G1 **Bowes Park** Gt Lon
351 G6 **Bowgreave** Lancs
311 E2 **Bowgreen** Traffd
451 E4 **Bowhill** Border
500 D5 **Bowhill** Fife
468 D3 **Bowhousebog or Liquo** N Lans
309 F2 **Bowing Park** Knows
451 G5 **Bowismiln** Border
22 D6 **Bowithick** Cnwll
323 G4 **Bowker's Green** Lancs
451 F1 **Bowland** Border
365 F2 **Bowland Bridge** Cumb
111 G4 **Bowldown** Wilts
326 B3 **Bowlee** Rochdl
393 F4 **Bowlees** Dur
59 F2 **Bowler's Town** E Susx
186 C4 **Bowley** Herefs
187 F6 **Bowley Lane** Herefs
186 C4 **Bowley Town** Herefs
75 E2 **Bowlhead Green** Surrey
342 C3 **Bowling** Brad
483 G5 **Bowling** W Duns
92 C5 **Bowling Alley** Hants
289 E5 **Bowling Bank** Wrexhm
8 C2 **Bowling Green** Cnwll
17 E4 **Bowling Green** Cnwll
212 C2 **Bowling Green** Dudley
137 F4 **Bowling Green** Gloucs
50 B5 **Bowling Green** Hants
271 E4 **Bowling Green** Shrops
188 B4 **Bowling Green** Worcs
85 H6 **Bowlish** Somset
120 D5 **Bowmans** Kent
378 A5 **Bowmanstead** Cumb
476 E5 **Bowmore** Ag & B
399 G2 **Bowness-on-Solway** Cumb
378 D5 **Bowness-on-Windermere** Cumb
501 F2 **Bow of Fife** Fife
528 B5 **Bowridge Hill** Dorset
528 B5 **Bowriefauld** Angus
454 B1 **Bowsden** Nthumb
116 D4 **Bowsey Hill** Wokham
451 E1 **Bowshank** Border
379 F5 **Bowston** Cumb
205 E3 **Bow Street** Cerdgn
379 F5 **Bow Street** Norfk

City, town and village index: Bowthorpe - Broad Haven 675

249 G3 Bowthorpe Norfk
74 B4 Bowyer's Common Hants
136 C4 Box Gloucs
111 E6 Box Wilts
131 G2 Boxbush Gloucs
161 F5 Boxbush Gloucs
195 E5 Box End Beds
174 C1 Boxford Suffk
114 C5 Boxford W Berk
53 G3 Boxgrove W Susx
94 D4 Box Hill Surrey
111 E6 Box Hill Wilts
98 B3 Boxley Kent
143 E3 Boxmoor Herts
23 E2 Box's Shop Cnwll
174 C3 Boxted Essex
174 D3 Boxted Essex
199 G4 Boxted Suffk
174 D3 Boxted Cross Essex
214 A5 Box Trees Solhll
111 E1 Boxwell Gloucs
196 D2 Boxworth Cambs
197 E1 Boxworth End Cambs
411 E5 Boyach D & G
72 C5 Boyatt Wood Hants
199 E3 Boyden End Suffk
100 D2 Boyden Gate Kent
225 E3 Boyland Common Norfk
274 B2 Boylestone Derbys
274 B2 Boylestonfield Derbys
569 L3 Boyndie Abers
571 G3 Boyndlie Abers
117 E3 Boyn Hill W & M
375 E6 Boynton E R Yk
528 D5 Boysack Angus
46 C2 Boys Hill Dorset
105 G6 Boys Village V Glam
314 D5 Boythorpe Derbys
23 G4 Boyton Cnwll
202 D5 Boyton Suffk
69 F2 Boyton Wilts
146 D3 Boyton Cross Essex
172 C3 Boyton End Suffk
199 E6 Boyton End Suffk
194 C3 Bozeat Nhants
171 F4 Bozen Green Herts
322 e7 Braaid IoM
588 E4 Braal Castle Highld
202 B2 Brabling Green Suffk
81 H1 Brabourne Kent
81 G1 Brabourne Lees Kent
589 J3 Brabster Highld
589 G4 Brabsterdorran Highld
544 E2 Bracadale Highld
531 K4 Bracara Highld
243 F2 Braceborough Lincs
318 B6 Bracebridge Lincs
298 B1 Bracebridge Heath Lincs
279 E2 Braceby Lincs
353 H5 Bracewell Lancs
341 G2 Bracken Bank Brad
392 B6 Brackenber Cumb
367 G5 Brackenbottom N York
294 D3 Brackenfield Derbys
342 B6 Brackenhall Kirk
399 G5 Brackenlands Cumb
389 E5 Brackenthwaite Cumb
400 A5 Brackenthwaite Cumb
356 B4 Brackenthwaite N York
105 E4 Brackla (Bragle) Brdgnd
53 E5 Bracklesham W Susx
533 J6 Brackletter Highld
459 F3 Brackley Ag & B
166 C2 Brackley Nhants
117 E6 Bracknell Br For
588 D4 Brackrevach Highld
498 C3 Braco P & K
569 J5 Bracobrae Moray
331 G3 Bracon N Linc
249 G5 Bracon Ash Norfk
531 K4 Bracorina Highld
24 A4 Bradaford Devon
293 H4 Bradbourne Derbys
395 G4 Bradbury Dur
192 D5 Bradden Nhants
9 F1 Braddock Cnwll
292 A3 Braddocks Hay Staffs
292 A4 Bradeley C Stke
290 A6 Bradeley Green Ches
142 A5 Bradenham Bucks
248 B3 Bradenham Norfk
112 A4 Bradenstoke Wilts
112 B4 Bradenstoke Wilts
213 E1 Brades Village Sandw
43 E6 Bradfield Devon
175 F3 Bradfield Essex
256 B3 Bradfield Norfk
115 G5 Bradfield W Berk
200 A3 Bradfield Combust Suffk
290 D3 Bradfield Green Ches
175 F3 Bradfield Heath Essex
200 B3 Bradfield St Clare Suffk
200 B3 Bradfield St George Suffk
342 C3 Bradford Brad
15 G3 Bradford Cnwll
293 H2 Bradford Derbys
24 B1 Bradford Devon
326 C5 Bradford Manch
455 E3 Bradford Nthumb
46 A2 Bradford Abbas Dorset
87 E2 Bradford Leigh Wilts
87 E2 Bradford-on-Avon Wilts
43 G3 Bradford-on-Tone Somset
31 E4 Bradford Peverell Dorset
329 G6 Bradgate Rothm
60 D5 Bradiford Devon
37 G3 Brading IoW
293 H5 Bradley Derbys
135 G6 Bradley Gloucs
73 F1 Bradley Hants
342 C5 Bradley Kirk
334 B3 Bradley NE Lin
272 C6 Bradley Staffs
237 E5 Bradley Wolves
288 D4 Bradley Wrexhm
85 E4 Bradley Cross Somset
325 H3 Bradley Fold Bury
135 G6 Bradley Green Gloucs
65 E4 Bradley Green Somset
238 D4 Bradley Green Warwks
189 E2 Bradley Green Worcs
273 F1 Bradley in the Moors Staffs
312 B4 Bradley Mount Ches
109 H3 Bradley Stoke S Glos
161 G2 Bradlow Herefs
276 C3 Bradmore Notts
236 C5 Bradmore Wolves
235 H5 Bradney Shrops
65 F4 Bradney Somset
27 G2 Bradninch Devon
214 C4 Bradnock's Marsh Solhll
292 D3 Bradnop Staffs
185 E3 Bradnor Green Herefs
30 B4 Bradpole Dorset
325 G2 Bradshaw Bolton
342 A4 Bradshaw Calder
327 G2 Bradshaw Kirk
292 B3 Bradshaw Staffs
17 E2 Bradstone Devon
168 A1 Bradville M Keyn
291 E2 Bradwall Green Ches
314 C4 Bradway Sheff
313 G3 Bradwell Derbys
60 C3 Bradwell Devon
173 F5 Bradwell Essex
168 A2 Bradwell M Keyn
168 A2 Bradwell Common M Keyn
138 C3 Bradwell Grove Oxon
313 G3 Bradwell Hills Derbys
148 D3 Bradwell on Sea Essex
148 C3 Bradwell Waterside Essex
38 D5 Bradworthy Devon
566 B4 Brae Highld
572 F7 Brae Highld
575 J3 Brae Highld
606 E4 Brae Shet
576 C8 Braeantra Highld
538 B4 Braedownie Angus
485 F3 Braeface Falk
549 G3 Braefield Highld
565 L5 Braefindon Highld
537 G5 Braegarie Abers
512 B5 Braegrum P & K
410 D2 Braehead D & G
601 J4 Braehead Ork
602 E2 Braehead Ork
444 D5 Braehead S Ayrs
447 G3 Braehead S Lans
467 E3 Braehead S Lans
469 E4 Braehead S Lans
485 G1 Braehead Stirlg
529 E4 Braehead of Lunan Angus
606 B2 Braehoulland Shet
537 H4 Braemar Abers
582 E4 Braemore Highld
578 D7 Brae of Achnahaird Highld
528 D1 Brae of Pert Angus
487 G4 Braepark C Edin
560 D2 Braeside Abers
557 G4 Braeside C Aber
482 B4 Braeside Inver
526 C3 Braes of Coul Angus
574 C5 Braes of Ullapool Highld
603 J4 Braeswick Ork
493 G3 Braevallich Ag & B
606 B2 Braewick Shet
606 D6 Braewick Shet
395 F5 Brafferton Darltn
371 E5 Brafferton N York
194 A3 Brafield-on-the-Green Nhants
598 F5 Bragar W Isls
168 C4 Bragenham Bucks
506 F5 Brагleenmore Ag & B
284 D1 Braichmelyn Gwynd
206 D1 Braichyfedw Powys
351 F4 Braides Lancs
467 F2 Braidfauld C Glas
368 D3 Braidley N York
468 C5 Braidwood S Lans
599 K8 Bràigh na h-Aoidhe W Isls
476 C3 Braigo Ag & B
274 D1 Brailsford Derbys
274 C1 Brailsford Green Derbys
135 F3 Brain's Green Gloucs
173 F5 Braintree Essex
225 F5 Braiseworth Suffk
72 A4 Braishfield Hants
174 C4 Braiswick Essex
341 G1 Braithwaite Brad
389 F5 Braithwaite Cumb
330 D2 Braithwaite Donc
330 B6 Braithwell Donc
605 G8 Brake Shet
248 D3 Brakefield Green Norfk
329 G1 Brakenhill Wakefd
55 E2 Bramber W Susx
47 E4 Bramblecombe Dorset
72 C5 Brambridge Hants
276 B2 Bramcote Notts
215 F2 Bramcote Warwks
276 B2 Bramcote Hills Notts
215 F2 Bramcote Mains Warwks
73 F4 Bramdean Hants
250 B3 Bramerton Norfk
144 C1 Bramfield Herts
227 E5 Bramfield Suffk
236 D6 Bramford Dudley
201 F5 Bramford Suffk
312 A2 Bramhall Stockp
312 B2 Bramhall Moor Stockp
312 A2 Bramhall Park Stockp
357 E6 Bramham Leeds
356 B6 Bramhope Leeds
315 E4 Bramley Derbys
91 G3 Bramley Hants
342 D3 Bramley Leeds
330 A6 Bramley Rothm
93 G6 Bramley Surrey
91 G3 Bramley Corner Hants
91 H3 Bramley Green Hants
355 F3 Bramley Head N York
295 F1 Bramley Vale Derbys
100 D4 Bramling Kent
27 E3 Brampford Speke Devon
220 A5 Brampton Cambs
391 H5 Brampton Cumb
401 F2 Brampton Cumb
314 D5 Brampton Derbys
317 F4 Brampton Lincs
255 H3 Brampton Norfk
329 G4 Brampton Rothm
227 E3 Brampton Suffk
161 E4 Brampton Abbotts Herefs
217 G2 Brampton Ash Nhants
209 G5 Brampton Bryan Herefs
315 F2 Brampton en le Morthen Rothm
220 B5 Brampton Park Cambs
227 E3 Brampton Street Suffk
273 G3 Bramshall Staffs
49 H1 Bramshaw Hants
92 B2 Bramshill Hants
74 C3 Bramshott Hants
66 C4 Bramwell Somset
518 D2 Branault Highld
97 G5 Branbridges Kent
259 F3 Brancaster Norfk
259 F3 Brancaster Staithe Norfk
395 E2 Brancepeth Dur
404 C2 Branch End Nthumb
567 K6 Branchill Moray
482 B5 Branchton Inver
300 C5 Brand End Lincs
568 C1 Branderburgh Moray
361 E5 Brandesburton E R Yk
202 B2 Brandeston Suffk
161 G4 Brand Green Herefs
161 H1 Brand Green Herefs
209 H4 Brandhill Shrops
24 B2 Brandis Corner Devon
63 E2 Brandish Street Somset
255 F3 Brandiston Norfk
388 D4 Brandlingill Cumb
395 E2 Brandon Dur
297 H5 Brandon Lincs
442 C1 Brandon Nthumb
223 F2 Brandon Suffk
215 G4 Brandon Warwks
222 C2 Brandon Bank Norfk
222 C1 Brandon Creek Norfk
249 E3 Brandon Parva Norfk
372 A5 Brandsby N York
117 H4 Brands Hill Slough
270 B4 Brandwood Shrops
213 G4 Brandwood End Birm
343 F5 Brandy Carr Wakefd
147 G5 Brandy Hole Essex
333 E5 Brandy Wharf Lincs
2 D4 Brane Cnwll
172 D4 Bran End Essex
383 G1 Branksome Darltn
34 C2 Branksome Poole
34 C2 Branksome Park Poole
72 B1 Bransbury Hants
317 G4 Bransby Lincs
28 C5 Branscombe Devon
188 A4 Bransford Worcs
49 F5 Bransgore Hants
498 D6 Branshill Clacks
347 G3 Bransholme C KuH
213 G5 Branson's Cross Worcs
277 H4 Branston Leics
318 C6 Branston Lincs
274 C5 Branston Staffs
318 D6 Branston Booths Lincs
37 E4 Branstone IoW
388 A6 Bransty Cumb
297 H4 Brant Broughton Lincs
175 F3 Brantham Suffk
388 C5 Branthwaite Cumb
389 G2 Branthwaite Cumb
388 C5 Branthwaite Edge Cumb
346 D4 Brantingham E R Yk
330 D4 Branton Donc
442 C1 Branton Nthumb
357 E2 Branton Green N York
439 F2 Branxholme Border
453 G2 Branxton Nthumb
239 G4 Brascote Leics
290 A2 Brassey Green Ches
294 A4 Brassington Derbys
96 C3 Brasted Kent
96 C4 Brasted Chart Kent
556 B5 Brathens Abers
301 E2 Bratoft Lincs
80 D3 Brattle Kent
318 A3 Brattleby Lincs
63 E2 Bratton Somset
87 G4 Bratton Wilts
235 E2 Bratton Wrekin
24 C4 Bratton Clovelly Devon
61 F4 Bratton Fleming Devon
68 A4 Bratton Seymour Somset
171 E5 Braughing Herts
171 F5 Braughing Friars Herts
298 C4 Brauncewell Lincs
192 B1 Braunston Nhants
240 C4 Braunstone Leics
240 C4 Braunstone Town Leics
242 A3 Braunston-in-Rutland Rutlnd
60 C4 Braunton Devon
372 D4 Brawby N York
385 E3 Brawith N York
587 H3 Brawl Highld
588 D5 Brawlbin Highld
117 F4 Bray W & M
217 G3 Braybrooke Nhants
112 B2 Braydon Side Wilts
61 G5 Brayford Devon
61 G5 Brayfordhill Devon
16 D4 Bray Shop Cnwll
376 C3 Braystones Cumb
188 B5 Brayswick Worcs
356 A5 Braythorn N York
345 E3 Brayton N York
33 E2 Braytown Dorset
117 E4 Bray Wick W & M
117 E4 Braywoodside W & M
23 F4 Brazacott Cnwll
272 C5 Brazenhill Staffs
6 C5 Brea Cnwll
86 A2 Breach BaNES
98 C1 Breach Kent
52 D3 Breach W Susx
169 H5 Breachwood Green Herts
598 C7 Breacleit W Isls
270 A2 Breaden Heath Shrops
275 F2 Breadsall Derbys
275 F2 Breadsall Hilltop C Derb
135 G4 Breadstone Gloucs
136 B3 Bread Street Gloucs
4 B3 Breage Cnwll
565 H8 Breakachy Highld
40 A4 Brealeys Devon
135 E3 Bream Gloucs
70 D6 Breamore Hants
134 D3 Bream's Meend Gloucs
84 A3 Brean Somset
596 B2 Breanais W Isls
356 C2 Brearton N York
598 E7 Breascleit W Isls
598 E7 Breasclete W Isls
275 H3 Breaston Derbys
154 D3 Brechfa Carmth
528 D2 Brechin Angus
248 B6 Breckles Norfk
602 D8 Breck of Cruan Ork
543 J4 Breckrey Highld
315 F1 Brecks Rothm
157 H4 Brecon Powys
312 B1 Bredbury Stockp
312 B1 Bredbury Green Stockp
58 D3 Brede E Susx
187 E3 Bredenbury Herefs
202 B4 Bredfield Suffk
98 D3 Bredgar Kent
98 B2 Bredhurst Kent
162 D2 Bredon Worcs
162 D2 Bredon's Hardwick Worcs
162 D2 Bredon's Norton Worcs
185 F6 Bredwardine Herefs
275 G5 Breedon on the Hill Leics
146 D2 Breeds Essex
337 F1 Breedy Butts Lancs
599 K7 Breibhig W Isls
469 F2 Breich W Loth
325 G3 Breightmet Bolton
345 G3 Breighton E R Yk
160 B1 Breinton Common Herefs
605 H1 Breiwick Shet
160 D5 Brelston Green Herefs
111 H5 Bremhill Wilts
111 H5 Bremhill Wick Wilts
605 H5 Bremirehoull Shet
566 D1 Brenachie Highld
79 F1 Brenchley Kent
493 H4 Brenchoillie Ag & B
23 H1 Brendon Devon
39 E5 Brendon Devon
62 B2 Brendon Devon
596 B2 Brenish W Isls
430 D5 Brenkley N u Ty
9 G3 Brent Cnwll
200 B5 Brent Eleigh Suffk
118 D4 Brentford Gt Lon
277 G6 Brentingby Leics
84 B4 Brent Knoll Somset
19 E6 Brent Mill Devon
171 F3 Brent Pelham Herts
109 G4 Brentry Bristl
146 C6 Brentwood Essex
81 F4 Brenzett Kent
81 F4 Brenzett Green Kent
237 G1 Brereton Staffs
237 G1 Brereton Cross Staffs
291 F2 Brereton Green Ches
291 F2 Brereton Heath Ches
237 F1 Breretonhill Staffs
225 E3 Bressingham Norfk
225 E3 Bressingham Common Norfk
274 D5 Bretby Derbys
215 G4 Bretford Warwks
189 G6 Bretforton Worcs
379 G3 Bretherdale Head Cumb
338 C5 Bretherton Lancs
607 G6 Brettabister Shet
224 B3 Brettenham Norfk
200 C4 Brettenham Suffk
243 H4 Bretton C Pete
313 H4 Bretton Derbys
289 E2 Bretton Flints
2 C4 Brew Cnwll
172 B5 Brewer's End Essex
225 F3 Brewers Green Norfk
95 G4 Brewer Street Surrey
526 A2 Brewlands Bridge Angus
236 C3 Brewood Staffs
47 F6 Briantspuddle Dorset
193 F3 Briar Hill Nhants
172 B4 Brick End Essex
144 D3 Brickendon Herts
143 G4 Bricket Wood Herts
188 C3 Brickfields Worcs
195 E4 Brickhill Beds
93 G2 Brick Hill Surrey
171 G4 Brick House End Essex
291 F2 Brickhouses Ches
314 C3 Brick Houses Sheff
296 A3 Brick-kiln End Notts
173 E3 Brickkiln Green Essex
163 E1 Bricklehampton Worcs
322 g2 Bride IoM
388 D3 Bridekirk Cumb
152 D1 Bridell Pembks
24 D5 Bridestowe Devon
558 D2 Brideswell Abers
26 C5 Bridford Devon
26 C5 Bridfordmills Devon
4 D3 Bridge Cnwll
6 C5 Bridge Cnwll
100 C5 Bridge Kent
29 G1 Bridge Somset
62 A2 Bridge Ball Devon
195 E4 Bridge End Beds
400 C5 Bridge End Cumb
12 B3 Bridge End Devon
28 A5 Bridge End Devon
393 H2 Bridge End Dur
172 D3 Bridge End Essex
288 D3 Bridge End Flints
279 G2 Bridge End Lincs
403 G2 Bridge End Nthumb
140 C6 Bridge End Oxon
605 G4 Bridge End Shet
94 B3 Bridge End Surrey
190 D2 Bridge End Warwks
162 B3 Bridge End Worcs
187 E5 Bridge End Worcs
557 F2 Bridgefield C Aber
554 D4 Bridgefoot Abers
514 B2 Bridgefoot Angus
388 C4 Bridgefoot Cumb
171 G2 Bridge Green Essex
225 F3 Bridge Green Norfk
67 F5 Bridgehampton Somset
370 C5 Bridge Hewick N York
404 C4 Bridgehill Dur
312 D3 Bridgeholm Green Derbys
355 F1 Bridgehouse Gate N York
451 F3 Bridgelands Border
51 G4 Bridgemary Hants
291 E5 Bridgemere Ches
312 C3 Bridgemont Derbys
558 C2 Bridgend Abers
459 F4 Bridgend Ag & B
476 E4 Bridgend Ag & B
493 E6 Bridgend Ag & B
527 E5 Bridgend Angus
539 G6 Bridgend Angus
104 D3 Bridgend Brdgnd
178 D4 Bridgend Cerdgn
9 E2 Bridgend Cnwll
378 D2 Bridgend Cumb
11 G4 Bridgend Devon
502 B2 Bridgend Fife
136 A4 Bridgend Gloucs
482 C4 Bridgend Inver
553 H2 Bridgend Moray
484 D5 Bridgend N Lans
486 D4 Bridgend W Loth
526 C4 Bridgend of Lintrathen Angus
486 D3 Bridgeness Falk
555 G1 Bridge of Alford Abers
498 C5 Bridge of Allan Stirlg
552 D1 Bridge of Avon Moray
552 D4 Bridge of Avon Moray
507 H4 Bridge of Awe Ag & B
523 G6 Bridge of Balgie P & K
551 L5 Bridge of Brown Highld
525 H5 Bridge of Cally P & K
556 B5 Bridge of Canny Abers
526 C4 Bridge of Craigisla Angus
412 D2 Bridge of Dee D & G
557 G2 Bridge of Don C Aber
529 E3 Bridge of Dun Angus
540 C2 Bridge of Dye Abers
512 D6 Bridge of Earn P & K
522 F4 Bridge of Ericht P & K
556 C6 Bridge of Feugh Abers
588 C3 Bridge of Forss Highld
554 C5 Bridge of Gairn Abers
522 F4 Bridge of Gaur P & K
541 G1 Bridge of Muchalls Abers
508 D2 Bridge of Orchy Ag & B
524 C2 Bridge of Tilt P & K
568 F3 Bridge of Tynet Moray
606 C7 Bridge of Walls Shet
466 A1 Bridge of Weir Rens
40 D5 Bridge Reeve Devon
23 F2 Bridgerule Devon
8 C2 Bridges Cnwll
233 G5 Bridges Shrops
159 H1 Bridge Sollers Herefs
199 H5 Bridge Street Suffk
467 F2 Bridgeton C Glas
23 G5 Bridgetown Cnwll
19 H5 Bridgetown Devon
63 E5 Bridgetown Somset
190 C4 Bridge Town Warwks
309 G5 Bridge Trafford Ches
110 B5 Bridge Yate S Glos
224 C2 Bridgham Norfk
235 G6 Bridgnorth Shrops
237 E3 Bridgtown Staffs
65 E4 Bridgwater Somset
361 F1 Bridlington E R Yk
30 A4 Bridport Dorset
160 D5 Bridstow Herefs
340 C2 Brierfield Lancs
331 E2 Brierholme Carr Donc
329 G2 Brierley Barns
135 E1 Brierley Gloucs
186 B3 Brierley Herefs
212 D2 Brierley Hill Dudley
396 C4 Brierton Hartpl
389 G5 Briery Cumb
132 C3 Briery Hill Blae G
328 C1 Briestfield Kirk
366 C1 Briggflatts Cumb
333 E3 Brigg N Linc
256 C4 Briggate Norfk
387 E3 Briggswath N York
388 C3 Brigham Cumb
389 G5 Brigham Cumb
360 D4 Brigham E R Yk
342 B5 Brighouse Calder
36 C4 Brighstone IoW
294 B3 Brightgate Derbys
139 F4 Brighthampton Oxon
328 D6 Brightholmlee Sheff
25 E3 Brightley Devon
79 F5 Brightling E Susx
175 E6 Brightlingsea Essex
55 G4 Brighton Br & H
7 G3 Brighton Cnwll
91 G5 Brighton Hill Hants
323 E5 Brighton le Sands Sefton
486 B4 Brightons Falk
314 D2 Brightside Sheff
114 C4 Brightwalton W Berk
114 C4 Brightwalton Green W Berk
114 C4 Brightwalton Holt W Berk
202 B6 Brightwell Suffk
140 D6 Brightwell Baldwin Oxon
115 F1 Brightwell-cum-Sotwell Oxon
89 E5 Brigmerston Wilts
382 C2 Brignall Dur
496 D3 Brig o' Turk Stirlg
334 C4 Brigsley NE Lin
365 G2 Brigsteer Cumb
218 C2 Brigstock Nhants
141 E2 Brill Bucks
4 D3 Brill Cnwll
185 E5 Brilley Herefs
185 E4 Brilley Mountain Powys
151 F4 Brimaston Pembks
210 C6 Brimfield Herefs
315 E5 Brimington Derbys
315 E5 Brimington Common Derbys
19 G2 Brimley Devon
29 F2 Brimley Devon
136 D2 Brimpsfield Gloucs
161 F6 Brimps Hill Gloucs
91 F2 Brimpton W Berk
91 F2 Brimpton Common W Berk
600 D7 Brims Ork
136 C4 Brimscombe Gloucs
145 E5 Brimsdown Gt Lon
308 C3 Brimstage Wirral
314 C2 Brincliffe Sheff
345 G3 Brind E R Yk
67 E1 Brindham Somset
605 H3 Brindister Shet
606 C6 Brindister Shet
339 E5 Brindle Lancs
326 B4 Brindle Heath Salfd
290 B4 Brindley Ches
292 A4 Brindley Ford C Stke
314 C4 Brindwoodgate Derbys
236 B2 Brineton Staffs
210 B5 Bringewood Forge Herefs
218 A1 Bringhurst Leics
187 F3 Bringsty Common Herefs
219 F4 Brington Cambs
602 E6 Brinian Ork
260 D5 Briningham Norfk
320 C5 Brinkhill Lincs
198 C4 Brinkley Cambs
296 D4 Brinkley Notts
160 D3 Brinkley Hill Herefs
168 C2 Brinklow M Keyn
215 G4 Brinklow Warwks
112 B3 Brinkworth Wilts
312 B1 Brinnington Stockp
339 F5 Brinscall Lancs
84 D4 Brinscombe Somset
84 D2 Brinsea N Som
236 D4 Brinsford Staffs
295 F5 Brinsley Notts
186 A6 Brinsop Herefs
186 A6 Brinsop Common Herefs
315 E1 Brinsworth Rothm
62 A5 Brinsworthy Devon
260 D4 Brinton Norfk
400 D4 Brisco Cumb
376 C2 Briscoe Cumb
356 B4 Briscoerigg N York
254 C3 Brisley Norfk
109 H5 Brislington Bristl
80 D2 Brissenden Green Kent
213 E2 Bristnall Fields Sandw
109 G4 Bristol Bristl
261 E5 Briston Norfk
110 D2 Britain Bottom S Glos
340 D5 Britannia Lancs
70 D4 Britford Wilts
132 B4 Brithdir Caerph
179 G4 Brithdir Cerdgn
266 B6 Brithdir Gwynd
42 D5 Brithem Bottom Devon
132 D4 British Torfn
130 A5 Briton Ferry Neath
86 B3 Britten's BaNES
117 F3 Britwell Slough
141 E6 Britwell Salome Oxon
13 G1 Brixham Torbay
11 G3 Brixton Devon
119 G4 Brixton Gt Lon
69 E2 Brixton Deverill Wilts
217 F5 Brixworth Nhants
139 E3 Brize Norton Oxon
212 C6 Broad Alley Worcs
113 E1 Broad Blunsdon Swindn
327 E6 Broadbottom Tamesd
53 E3 Broadbridge W Susx
76 B3 Broadbridge Heath W Susx
113 E1 Broadbush Swindn
164 B2 Broad Campden Gloucs
70 A4 Broad Chalke Wilts
340 D5 Broad Clough Lancs
27 F3 Broadclyst Devon
144 A4 Broad Colney Herts
212 C6 Broad Common Worcs
482 D5 Broadfield Inver
340 A4 Broadfield Lancs
126 C4 Broadfield Pembks
326 B2 Broadfield Rochdl
338 D5 Broadfield Rochdl
77 E3 Broadfield W Susx
545 L5 Broadford Highld
79 G2 Broad Ford Kent
93 G5 Broadford Surrey
76 A5 Broadford Bridge W Susx
437 G2 Broadgairhill Border
72 B5 Broadgate Hants
200 C2 Broadgrass Green Suffk
194 D6 Broad Green Beds
198 D3 Broad Green Cambs
171 F2 Broad Green Essex
174 A5 Broad Green Essex
95 G1 Broad Green Gt Lon
309 F1 Broad Green Lpool
199 F3 Broad Green Suffk
201 E3 Broad Green Suffk
187 H3 Broad Green Worcs
213 E5 Broad Green Worcs
144 D3 Broadgreen Wood Herts
326 C2 Broadhalgh Rochdl
96 A4 Broadham Green Surrey
439 F3 Broadhaugh Border
589 K6 Broadhaven Highld
124 D2 Broad Haven Pembks

185 F2 Broad Heath Powys
272 C4 Broadheath Staffs
311 F2 Broadheath Traffd
187 F2 Broad Heath Worcs
28 B2 Broadhembury Devon
19 H4 Broadhempston Devon
222 B4 Broad Hill Cambs
112 D4 Broad Hinton Wilts
294 D5 Broadholm Derbys
317 G5 Broadholme Lincs
359 F4 Broad Ings E R Yk
58 D3 Broadland Row E Susx
20 A3 Broadlands Devon
4 B2 Broadlane Cnwll
6 C5 Broad Lane Cnwll
212 A2 Broad Lanes Shrops
127 H3 Broadlay Carmth
90 C2 Broad Layings Hants
326 C1 Broadley Lancs
568 F3 Broadley Moray
145 F3 Broadley Common Essex
190 A5 Broad Marston Worcs
32 C2 Broadmayne Dorset
451 E3 Broadmeadows Border
91 G5 Broadmere Hants
126 B3 Broadmoor Pembks
94 C5 Broadmoor Surrey
161 E2 Broadmoor Common Herefs
188 B4 Broadmore Green Worcs
155 E5 Broad Oak Carmth
377 E6 Broad Oak Cumb
27 H4 Broad Oak Devon
30 A3 Broadoak Dorset
47 E2 Broad Oak Dorset
58 D2 Broad Oak E Susx
79 E5 Broadoak E Susx
135 G2 Broadoak Gloucs
51 E2 Broadoak Hants
92 C4 Broad Oak Hants
160 B5 Broad Oak Herefs
81 F2 Broad Oak Kent
100 C3 Broad Oak Kent
212 A2 Broad Oak Shrops
234 B1 Broadoak Shrops
324 C5 Broad Oak St Hel
289 E3 Broad Oak Wrexhm
144 C2 Broadoak End Herts
325 H4 Broadoak Park Salfd
39 E3 Broad Parkham Devon
116 B3 Broadplat Oxon
134 C5 Broadrock Gloucs
13 F1 Broadsands Torbay
571 M4 Broadsea Abers
146 D2 Broad's Green Essex
88 A1 Broad's Green Wilts
45 E5 Broadshard Somset
101 H2 Broadstairs Kent
98 D5 Broadstone Kent
134 C4 Broadstone Mons
48 B5 Broadstone Poole
210 C2 Broadstone Shrops
59 E3 Broad Street E Susx
81 H1 Broad Street Kent
82 B2 Broad Street Kent
98 C3 Broad Street Kent
122 B5 Broad Street Medway
200 C6 Broad Street Suffk
88 C3 Broad Street Wilts
108 C3 Broadstreet Common Newpt
147 H3 Broad Street Green Essex
80 C3 Broad Tenterden Kent
112 C4 Broad Town Wilts
187 H3 Broadwas Worcs
170 C5 Broadwater Herts
54 D4 Broadwater W Susx
78 D2 Broadwater Down Kent
212 B4 Broadwaters Worcs
401 E3 Broadwath Cumb
127 G2 Broadway Carmth
128 A3 Broadway Carmth
125 E2 Broadway Pembks
44 C4 Broadway Somset
226 D4 Broadway Suffk
163 G2 Broadway Worcs
160 C3 Broadway Lands Herefs
134 D2 Broadwell Gloucs
164 C4 Broadwell Gloucs
138 D4 Broadwell Oxon
191 H1 Broadwell Warwks
31 F6 Broadwey Dorset
30 A2 Broadwindsor Dorset
25 F1 Broadwoodkelly Devon
24 B5 Broadwoodwidger Devon
185 F6 Brobury Herefs
599 M7 Brocair W Isls
543 K7 Brochel Highld
507 H3 Brochroy Ag & B
338 D1 Brock Lancs
187 H4 Brockamin Worcs
73 F6 Brockbridge Hants
225 H4 Brockdish Norfk
212 C5 Brockencote Worcs
50 B4 Brockenhurst Hants
447 G2 Brocketsbrae S Lans
29 E1 Brockfield Devon
201 F1 Brockford Green Suffk
201 F1 Brockford Street Suffk
192 D2 Brockhall Nhants
339 H2 Brockhall Village Lancs
94 D5 Brockham Surrey
110 C6 Brockham End BaNES
94 D5 Brockham Park Surrey
162 D4 Brockhampton Gloucs
163 F5 Brockhampton Gloucs
52 C3 Brockhampton Hants
160 D3 Brockhampton Herefs
46 C3 Brockhampton Green Dorset
450 D5 Brockhill Border
147 E5 Brock Hill Essex
328 A2 Brockholes Kirk
135 E3 Brockhollands Gloucs
294 C3 Brockhurst Derbys
51 G4 Brockhurst Hants
215 H3 Brockhurst Warwks
424 A5 Brocklehirst D & G
333 G2 Brocklesby Lincs
119 H5 Brockley Gt Lon
85 E1 Brockley N Som
223 G5 Brockley Corner Suffk
195 E6 Brockley Green Suffk
199 G4 Brockley Green Suffk
390 D2 Brockleymoor Cumb
186 C3 Brockmanton Herefs
212 D2 Brockmoor Dudley
24 C4 Brockscombe Devon
91 E2 Brock's Green Hants
249 F6 Brock's Watering Norfk
209 F2 Brockton Shrops
233 F4 Brockton Shrops
234 D6 Brockton Shrops
235 G4 Brockton Shrops
272 B3 Brockton Staffs
235 G1 Brockton Wrekin
134 C4 Brockweir Gloucs
63 E3 Brockwell Somset
136 C1 Brockworth Gloucs
15 E5 Brocton Cnwll
273 E6 Brocton Staffs
461 G2 Brodick N Ayrs
569 K3 Brodiesord Abers
330 B3 Brodsworth Donc

543 H3 Brogaig Highld
168 D2 Brogborough Beds
201 G6 Broke Hall Suffk
111 G2 Brokenborough Wilts
310 D5 Broken Cross Ches
312 A5 Broken Cross Ches
171 F5 Broken Green Herts
87 E4 Brokerswood Wilts
383 E5 Brokes N York
104 B2 Brokenry Neath
309 E3 Bromborough Wirral
308 D3 Bromborough Pool Wirral
211 E3 Bromdon Shrops
225 F4 Brome Suffk
161 G3 Bromesberrow Gloucs
161 G3 Bromesberrow Heath Gloucs
225 G4 Brome Street Suffk
202 B4 Bromeswell Suffk
399 F5 Bromfield Cumb
210 B4 Bromfield Shrops
213 H1 Bromford Birm
195 E4 Bromham Beds
87 H2 Bromham Wilts
329 E5 Bromley Barns
212 D2 Bromley Dudley
119 H3 Bromley Gt Lon
120 B6 Bromley Gt Lon
171 F5 Bromley Herts
235 G5 Bromley Shrops
269 G4 Bromley Shrops
96 B1 Bromley Common Gt Lon
325 G2 Bromley Cross Bolton
175 E4 Bromley Cross Essex
81 E2 Bromley Green Kent
272 A3 Bromley Hall Staffs
110 A4 Bromley Heath S Glos
120 A6 Bromley Park Gt Lon
273 H5 Bromley Wood Staffs
233 F4 Bromlow Shrops
119 F4 Brompton Gt Lon
122 B6 Brompton Medway
374 A3 Brompton N York
384 B5 Brompton N York
234 C3 Brompton Shrops
374 A3 Brompton-by-Sawdon N York
383 F5 Brompton-on-Swale N York
64 A5 Brompton Ralph Somset
63 F5 Brompton Regis Somset
161 E5 Bromsash Herefs
213 E5 Bromsberrow Worcs
272 B6 Bromstead Common Staffs
101 G2 Bromstone Kent
187 E4 Bromyard Herefs
187 F3 Bromyard Downs Herefs
265 G3 Bronaber Gwynd
181 F1 Bronant Cerdgn
210 C2 Broncroft Shrops
119 E3 Brondesbury Gt Lon
119 E3 Brondesbury Park Gt Lon
344 B4 Bronfield N York
400 B6 Broneirion Powys
397 G6 Brongest Cerdgn
179 F5 Brongwyn Cerdgn
270 B2 Bronington Wrexhm
158 B2 Bronllys Powys
179 G5 Bronwydd Cerdgn
154 B5 Bronwydd Arms Carmth
184 D3 Bronydd Powys
297 F3 Bronygarth Shrops
269 E2 Bronygarth Shrops
127 F3 Brook Carmth
17 G4 Brook Devon
26 C4 Brook Devon
50 A2 Brook Hants
71 G4 Brook Hants
36 B4 Brook IoW
99 H6 Brook Kent
75 E2 Brook Surrey
94 B5 Brook Surrey
312 C2 Brook Bottom Derbys
327 E4 Brook Bottom Oldham
338 D1 Brook Bottom Tamesd
250 B5 Brooke Norfk
242 A3 Brooke Rutlnd
334 B5 Brookenby Lincs
195 F2 Brook End Beds
195 H5 Brook End Beds
219 F5 Brook End Cambs
134 D5 Brookend Gloucs
135 F4 Brookend Gloucs
170 D4 Brook End Herts
194 C6 Brook End M Keyn
165 E5 Brookend Oxon
111 E3 Brook End Wilts
188 C5 Brook End Wilts
327 F5 Brookfield Derbys
339 E3 Brookfield Lancs
384 D1 Brookfield Middsb
466 B2 Brookfield Rens
342 B5 Brookfoot Calder
36 B4 Brookgreen IoW
199 H3 Brook Green Suffk
140 D5 Brookhampton Oxon
210 D2 Brookhampton Shrops
67 G4 Brookhampton Somset
49 H2 Brook Hill Hants
276 C3 Brook Hill Notts
339 G4 Brookhouse Bl w D
341 H4 Brookhouse Calder
312 B4 Brookhouse Ches
287 F1 Brookhouse Denbgs
352 A2 Brookhouse Lancs
315 G2 Brookhouse Rothm
291 G2 Brookhouse Green Ches
312 D2 Brookhouses Derbys
292 C6 Brookhouses Staffs
308 D3 Brookhurst Wirral
19 F5 Brooking Devon
81 E4 Brookland Kent
343 F2 Brooklands Leeds
270 C1 Brooklands Shrops
94 B2 Brooklands Surrey
311 F1 Brooklands Traffd
27 F3 Brookleigh Devon
144 B4 Brookmans Park Herts
54 B4 Brookpits W Susx
93 G2 Brook Place Surrey
211 E5 Brookrow Shrops
9 F1 Brooks Cnwll
232 B5 Brooks Powys
326 A1 Brooksbottoms Bury
241 E1 Brooksby Leics
101 E2 Brooks End Kent
76 B4 Brooks Green W Susx
117 F5 Brookside Br For
314 C5 Brookside Derbys
235 F3 Brookside Wrekin
146 B6 Brook Street Essex
80 D3 Brook Street Kent
97 E5 Brook Street Kent
199 G5 Brook Street W Susx
77 H4 Brook Street W Susx
136 B2 Brookthorpe Gloucs
310 A3 Brookvale Halton
247 E5 Brookville Norfk
290 C6 Brook Waters Wilts
69 F5 Brookwood Surrey
93 F3 Broom Beds
195 H6 Broom Cumb
29 F2 Broom Dorset
466 D3 Broom E Rens
501 G4 Broom Fife
126 C3 Broom Pembks

315 E1 Broom Rothm
189 G4 Broom Warwks
211 F5 Broombank Worcs
226 C1 Broome Norfk
209 H3 Broome Shrops
234 C5 Broome Shrops
212 D4 Broome Worcs
311 G2 Broomedge Warrtn
443 F2 Broome Park Nthumb
76 B5 Broomer's Corner W Susx
75 H6 Broomershill W Susx
400 B5 Broomfield Abers
146 D2 Broomfield Essex
98 C4 Broomfield Kent
100 C2 Broomfield Kent
64 D5 Broomfield Somset
111 F4 Broomfield Wilts
269 H6 Broomfields Shrops
346 C4 Broomfleet E R Yk
254 C3 Broom Green Norfk
290 C5 Broomhall Ches
93 G1 Broomhall W & M
290 C5 Broomhall Green Ches
57 E2 Broomham E Susx
404 B2 Broomhaugh Nthumb
451 F4 Broomhill Border
110 A4 Broomhill Bristl
110 A5 Broom Hill Bristl
309 G6 Broomhill Ches
48 C4 Broom Hill Dorset
404 D4 Broom Hill Dur
96 C1 Broom Hill Gt Lon
566 C2 Broomhill Highld
100 D4 Broomhill Kent
246 C4 Broomhill Norfk
295 G5 Broomhill Notts
443 G4 Broomhill Nthumb
202 B5 Broom Hill Worcs
212 D4 Broom Hill Worcs
78 D1 Broomhill Bank Kent
256 C3 Broomholm Norfk
467 G2 Broomhouse C Glas
444 D2 Broomlands N Ayrs
404 B2 Broomley Nthumb
395 E1 Broompark Dur
485 F1 Broomridge Stirlg
199 F1 Broom's Barn Suffk
161 G3 Broom's Green Gloucs
58 D4 Broomsgrove E Susx
253 G2 Broomsthorpe Norfk
99 G2 Broom Street Kent
160 B2 Broomy Hill Herefs
293 E5 Broomyshaw Staffs
577 K3 Brora Highld
235 F4 Broseley Shrops
125 G4 Brotherhill Pembks
162 B1 Brotheridge Green Worcs
393 F2 Brotherlee Dur
299 H5 Brothertoft Lincs
344 B4 Brotherton N York
400 B6 Brothybeck Cumb
397 G6 Brotton R & Cl
588 C4 Broubster Highld
380 D2 Brough Cumb
313 G3 Brough Derbys
346 D4 Brough E R Yk
589 G2 Brough Highld
297 F3 Brough Notts
602 C8 Brough Ork
605 K2 Brough Shet
606 F2 Brough Shet
607 G7 Brough Shet
607 H2 Brough Shet
607 J5 Brough Shet
609 G4 Brough Shet
270 D1 Broughall Shrops
380 D2 Broughton Sowerby Cumb
449 F2 Broughton Border
142 A2 Broughton Bucks
220 C4 Broughton Cambs
488 B5 Broughton C Edin
288 D2 Broughton Flints
71 G3 Broughton Hants
168 B2 Broughton M Keyn
218 A4 Broughton Nhants
332 D3 Broughton N Linc
354 B4 Broughton N York
373 E5 Broughton N York
602 E2 Broughton Ork
165 G2 Broughton Oxon
338 D3 Broughton Salfd
212 B1 Broughton Shrops
271 H3 Broughton Staffs
105 E5 Broughton V Glam
240 B6 Broughton Astley Leics
364 C3 Broughton Beck Cumb
332 D2 Broughton Common N Linc
388 C3 Broughton Cross Cumb
87 F2 Broughton Gifford Wilts
189 G2 Broughton Green Worcs
188 D4 Broughton Hackett Worcs
363 E4 Broughton in Furness Cumb
277 F5 Broughton Lodges Leics
363 E3 Broughton Mills Cumb
388 E3 Broughton Moor Cumb
326 B4 Broughton Park Salfd
138 C4 Broughton Poggs Oxon
603 K3 Broughtown Ork
355 H4 Broughty Ferry C Dund
365 E3 Brow Edge Cumb
400 A2 Browhouses D & G
606 C7 Browland Shet
57 H1 Brown Bank N York
73 E2 Brownbread Street E Susx
291 F2 Browncandover Hants
323 G2 Browneage Ches
292 B4 Brown Edge Staffs
324 B6 Brown Edge St Hel
289 G2 Brown Heath Ches
43 F4 Brownheath Devon
51 F1 Brown Heath Hants
270 B4 Brownheath Shrops
188 C2 Brownheath Common Worcs
560 C1 Brownhill Abers
339 G3 Brownhill Bl w D
269 G5 Brownhill Shrops
503 E1 Brownhills Fife
271 F2 Brownhills Shrops
237 G3 Brownhills Wsall
455 F5 Brownhills Shrops
91 F3 Brownieside Nthumb
289 G4 Browninghill Green Hants
291 G2 Brown Knowl Ches
288 D4 Brown Lees Ches
104 D3 Brownlow Ches
324 C4 Brownlow St Hel
325 F2 Brownlow Fold Bolton
291 G2 Brownlow Heath Ches
343 G3 Brown Moor Leeds
290 C6 Brown's Bank Ches
161 G3 Brown's End Gloucs
213 F1 Brown's Green Birm
136 C4 Brownshill Gloucs
215 E3 Brownshill Green Covtry
340 D3 Brownside Lancs
216 B4 Brownsover Warwks
12 B2 Brownston Devon
201 E2 Brown Street Suffk

168 C2 Browns Wood M Keyn
468 B2 Browsburn N Lans
388 C5 Browtop Cumb
352 A3 Brow Top Lancs
145 E3 Broxbourne Herts
490 C4 Broxburn E Loth
487 E5 Broxburn W Loth
443 G1 Broxfield Nthumb
317 H4 Broxholme Lincs
172 B4 Broxted Essex
289 G4 Broxton Ches
276 B1 Broxtowe C Nott
56 D2 Broyle Side E Susx
599 G5 Brù W Isls
599 H8 Bruach Màiri W Isls
583 K2 Bruairnis W Isls
524 B2 Bruan Highld
487 E2 Bruar P & K
483 E4 Brucefield Fife
310 C2 Brucehill W Duns
556 C5 Bruche Warrtn
289 F2 Bruera Ches
164 D5 Bruern Abbey Oxon
591 D8 Brùibhig W Isls
476 D4 Bruichladdich Ag & B
202 C1 Bruisyard Suffk
332 B3 Brumby N Linc
233 E3 Brunant Powys
606 B7 Brunatwatt Shet
293 F2 Brund Staffs
250 C3 Brundall Norfk
250 D5 Brundish Norfk
226 B6 Brundish Suffk
226 B5 Brundish Street Suffk
173 H1 Brundon Suffk
519 H1 Brunery Highld
3 F2 Brunnion Cnwll
340 D3 Brunshaw Lancs
488 C5 Brunstane C Edin
400 D3 Brunstock Cumb
430 D5 Brunswick Village N u Ty
342 D4 Bruntcliffe Leeds
216 C1 Bruntingthorpe Leics
513 H5 Brunton Fife
455 G5 Brunton Nthumb
89 F3 Brunton Wilts
311 H2 Bruntwood Hall Stockp
327 E5 Brushes Tamesd
313 G5 Brushfield Derbys
250 C4 Brushford Somset
42 B2 Brushford Somset
68 A3 Bruton Somset
471 F2 Bryans Mdloth
212 C6 Bryan's Green Worcs
47 G3 Bryanston Dorset
142 B4 Bryant's Bottom Bucks
424 D5 Brydekirk D & G
305 H5 Brymbo Conwy
288 C4 Brymbo Wrexhm
45 G4 Brympton D'Evercy Somset
132 C5 Bryn Caerph
128 D4 Bryn Carmth
310 C5 Bryn Ches
304 C5 Bryn Gwynd
104 C1 Bryn Neath
232 C4 Bryn Powys
131 E3 Bryn Rhondd
209 E2 Bryn Shrops
102 D3 Bryn Swans
324 D4 Bryn Wigan
205 G5 Brynafan Cerdgn
129 H2 Brynamman Carmth
106 C1 Brynawel Caerph
152 C3 Brynberian Pembks
130 B6 Brynbryddan Neath
265 E2 Bryn Bwbach Gwynd
308 A4 Bryncae Rhondd
104 D4 Bryn Celyn Flints
105 E3 Bryncethin Brdgnd
284 A6 Bryncir Gwynd
105 E3 Bryncoch Brdgnd
130 A4 Bryn-coch Neath
288 C3 Bryn Common Flints
262 C4 Bryncroes Gwynd
229 E4 Bryncrug Gwynd
232 C5 Brynderwen Gwynd
128 D3 Bryndu Carmth
302 D6 Bryn Du IoA
306 C4 Bryn Dulas Conwy
287 G5 Bryneglwys Denbgs
284 D1 Bryn Eglwys Gwynd
307 H5 Brynford Flints
324 D4 Bryn Gates Wigan
107 F1 Bryn Golau Rhondd
229 E4 Bryn Golau Gwynd
105 G2 Bryngwelltyn Carmth
152 D6 Bryngwran IoA
303 E5 Bryngwyn Cerdgn
179 F4 Bryngwyn Cerdgn
133 G3 Bryngwyn Mons
150 D5 Bryngwyn Pembks
184 C5 Bryngwyn Powys
151 H2 Bryn-henllan Pembks
130 C6 Brynheulog Brdgnd
179 G3 Brynhoffnant Cerdgn
307 F3 Bryniau Denbgs
338 B4 Bryning Lancs
132 D4 Brynithel Blae G
153 G3 Bryn Iwan Carmth
208 B2 Brynllywarch Powys
132 C2 Brynmawr Blae G
262 C4 Brynmawr Gwynd
268 D6 Bryn Mawr Gwynd
104 D2 Brynmenyn Brdgnd
103 F3 Brynmill Swans
285 F2 Brynmorfudd Conwy
154 B5 Bryn Myrddin Carmth
105 F3 Brynna Rhondd
105 F3 Brynnau Gwynion Rhondd
268 C1 Bryn-newydd Denbgs
288 D5 Bryn Offa Wrexhm
269 G5 Brynore Shrops
232 B4 Bryn-penarth Powys
269 F1 Bryn Pen-y-lan Wrexhm
305 G4 Bryn Pydew Conwy
284 C2 Brynrefail Gwynd
303 G3 Brynrefail IoA
286 C1 Bryn Rhyd-yr-Arian Conwy
305 H4 Bryn-rhys Conwy
105 H3 Brynsadler Rhondd
287 F4 Bryn Saith Marchog Denbgs
283 E2 Brynsiencyn IoA
60 D5 Brynsworthy Devon
268 D5 Bryn Tanat Powys
303 G4 Brynteg IoA
288 D4 Brynteg Wrexhm
104 D3 Bryntirion Brdgnd
106 B5 Brynwell V Glam
269 G2 Bryn-y-cochin Shrops
133 F1 Brynygwenin Mons
306 A4 Bryn-y-maen Conwy
228 D4 Bryn-y-mor Gwynd
269 E2 Bryn-y-Nant Wrexhm
288 A3 Bryn-yr-Eos Wrexhm
288 D5 Bryn-yr-ogof Denbgs
591 E7 Buaile Dubh W Isls
591 E7 Buaile nam Bodach W Isls
544 F5 Bualintur Highld
591 D8 Bualnaluib Highld
215 F5 Bubbenhall Warwks
12 B2 Bubwith Devon
201 E2 Bubwith Thurr

345 G2 Bubwith E R Yk
438 C2 Buccleuch Border
483 G2 Buchanan Smithy Stirlg
571 L6 Buchanhaven Abers
511 G4 Buchanty P & K
497 G4 Buchany Stirlg
484 B5 Buchley E Duns
497 E6 Buchlyvie Stirlg
400 A5 Buckabank Cumb
162 B3 Buckbury Worcs
220 B6 Buckden Cambs
368 B4 Buckden N York
250 D3 Buckenham Norfk
28 B2 Buckerell Devon
72 B5 Bucket Corner Hants
19 F4 Buckfast Devon
19 F4 Buckfastleigh Devon
30 B2 Buckham Dorset
501 G5 Buckhaven Fife
112 A5 Buck Hill Wilts
451 F2 Buckholm Border
134 B1 Buckholt Mons
23 H3 Buckhorn Devon
68 C5 Buckhorn Weston Dorset
80 B1 Buckhurst Kent
145 F5 Buckhurst Hill Essex
569 G2 Buckie Moray
588 E4 Buckies Highld
167 F3 Buckingham Bucks
142 B2 Buckland Bucks
12 B4 Buckland Devon
20 B3 Buckland Devon
163 G2 Buckland Gloucs
50 B5 Buckland Hants
171 E3 Buckland Herts
83 F2 Buckland Kent
139 E5 Buckland Oxon
95 E4 Buckland Surrey
39 F3 Buckland Brewer Devon
142 C3 Buckland Common Bucks
86 D4 Buckland Dinham Somset
86 C4 Buckland Down Somset
214 A2 Buckland End Birm
39 G6 Buckland Filleigh Devon
19 F3 Buckland in the Moor Devon
139 E5 Buckland Marsh Oxon
17 G5 Buckland Monachorum Devon
46 C3 Buckland Newton Dorset
31 E6 Buckland Ripers Dorset
439 G1 Bucklands Border
44 B5 Buckland St Mary Somset
83 F2 Buckland Valley Kent
142 B2 Bucklandwharf Bucks
115 F5 Bucklebury W Berk
115 E5 Bucklebury Alley W Berk
39 F2 Bucklegate Lincs
514 C2 Buckleheads Angus
50 C4 Bucklers Hard Hants
176 D1 Bucklesham Suffk
288 C2 Buckley Flints
326 D2 Buckley Rochdl
190 B1 Buckley Green Warwks
323 F5 Buckley Hill Sefton
311 E3 Bucklow Hill Ches
278 B5 Buckminster Leics
142 A4 Buckmoorend Bucks
292 B5 Bucknall C Stke
319 F6 Bucknall Lincs
166 C4 Bucknell Oxon
209 F5 Bucknell Shrops
309 H5 Buckoak Ches
110 B1 Buckover S Glos
212 C2 Buckpool Dudley
569 G2 Buckpool Moray
211 G5 Buckridge Worcs
557 F3 Bucksburn C Aber
38 D3 Buck's Cross Devon
76 A3 Bucks Green W Susx
143 F4 Bucks Hill Herts
74 C1 Bucks Horn Oak Hants
91 F4 Buckskin Hants
39 E3 Buck's Mills Devon
375 F5 Buckton E R Yk
209 G5 Buckton Herefs
454 D2 Buckton Nthumb
327 E4 Buckton Vale Tamesd
219 H4 Buckworth Cambs
190 C1 Budbrooke Warwks
316 B6 Budby Notts
291 E5 Buddileigh Staffs
23 E1 Bude Cnwll
10 B2 Budge's Shop Cnwll
455 F3 Budle Nthumb
43 G4 Budleigh Somset
21 F1 Budleigh Salterton Devon
78 B5 Budlett's Common E Susx
5 E2 Budock Water Cnwll
310 D4 Budworth Heath Ches
326 D2 Buersil Head Rochdl
290 D6 Buerton Ches
167 E3 Buffler's Holt Bucks
239 F3 Bufton Leics
193 E3 Bugbrooke Nhants
61 E3 Bugford Devon
487 G5 Bughtlin C Edin
291 H2 Buglawton Ches
8 C2 Bugle Cnwll
212 B6 Bugle Gate Worcs
68 C5 Bugley Dorset
87 F6 Bugley Wilts
359 E3 Bugthorpe E R Yk
171 F2 Building End Essex
235 E4 Buildwas Shrops
183 G4 Builth Road Powys
183 G4 Builth Wells Powys
142 C2 Bulbourne Herts
70 B3 Bulbridge Wilts
279 F4 Bulby Lincs
296 C6 Bulcote Notts
588 C3 Buldoo Highld
89 E6 Bulford Wilts
89 E6 Bulford Camp Wilts
290 A4 Bulkeley Ches
271 H1 Bulkeley Hall Shrops
215 F2 Bulkington Warwks
87 G3 Bulkington Wilts
39 E5 Bulkworthy Devon
384 B6 Bullamoor N York
294 C4 Bullbridge Derbys
117 E6 Bullbrook Br For
80 C3 Bullen's Green Kent
87 F3 Bullenhill Wilts
161 H6 Bulley Gloucs
388 C2 Bullgill Cumb
50 B5 Bull Hill Hants
294 B6 Bullhurst Hill Derbys
160 C2 Bullinghope Herefs
318 D4 Bullington Lincs
135 F3 Bullo Gloucs
39 E5 Bullworthy Devon
481 H5 Bulwood Ag & B
481 H5 Bulwood Ag & B
134 B5 Bulwhole Bottom Mons
173 G1 Bulmer Essex
355 E5 Bulmer N York
173 G2 Bulmer Tye Essex
573 Thurr Bulmer

City, town and village index: Bulstrode - Camelsdale 677

143 E4 Bulstrode Herts
233 F2 Bulthy Shrops
58 C5 Bulverhythe E Susx
28 B5 Bulverton Devon
109 F1 Bulwark Mons
295 G5 Bulwell C Nott
295 G5 Bulwell Forest C Nott
241 E5 Bulwick Leics
242 D6 Bulwick Nhants
145 E3 Bumble's Green Essex
596 E7 Bun Abhainn Eadarra W Isls
531 J5 Bunacaimb Highld
590 F5 Bun a'Mhuillin W Isls
533 J5 Bunarkaig Highld
518 E5 Bunavullin Ag & B
290 B3 Bunbury Ches
290 A3 Bunbury Heath Ches
95 E5 Bunce Common Surrey
565 L7 Bunchrew Highld
546 F4 Bundalloch Highld
504 D6 Bunessan Ag & B
226 C2 Bungay Suffk
549 J6 Bunkegivie Highld
245 F3 Bunker's Hill Cambs
299 H4 Bunker's Hill Lincs
249 G3 Bunker's Hill Norfk
165 H6 Bunkers Hill Oxon
312 B2 Bunkers Hill Stockp
251 G4 Bunker's Hill Suffk
549 H5 Bunloit Highld
478 C7 Bunnahabhain Ag & B
276 C4 Bunny Notts
276 C4 Bunny Hill Notts
520 E3 Bunree Highld
72 B5 Bunstead Hants
548 F3 Buntait Highld
171 E4 Buntingford Herts
173 G3 Bunting's Green Essex
249 F6 Bunwell Norfk
249 F5 Bunwell Bottom Norfk
225 F1 Bunwell Hill Norfk
312 D5 Burbage Derbys
239 G6 Burbage Leics
89 F2 Burbage Wilts
185 F2 Burcher Herefs
116 D3 Burchett's Green W & M
70 B3 Burcombe Wilts
140 C5 Burcot Oxon
213 E5 Burcot Worcs
235 G6 Burcote Shrops
142 A1 Burcott Bucks
168 B5 Burcott Bucks
85 F5 Burcott Somset
359 G2 Burdale N York
471 E1 Burdiehouse C Edin
406 B4 Burdon Sundld
106 B5 Burdonshill V Glam
165 F2 Burdrop Oxon
174 B3 Bures Suffk
174 B2 Bures Green Suffk
290 C4 Burford Ches
38 C3 Burford Devon
138 D2 Burford Oxon
210 D6 Burford Shrops
67 F1 Burford Somset
517 K6 Burg Ag & B
602 D6 Burgar Ork
225 E4 Burgate Suffk
74 B4 Burgates Hants
232 D2 Burgedin Powys
169 G3 Burge End Herts
77 F6 Burgess Hill W Susx
504 E5 Burgh Ag & B
202 A4 Burgh Suffk
400 B3 Burgh by Sands Cumb
251 F4 Burgh Castle Norfk
90 D2 Burghclere Hants
90 D2 Burghclere Common Hants
249 E6 Burgh Common Norfk
567 L3 Burghead Moray
115 H6 Burghfield W Berk
91 H1 Burghfield Common W Berk
91 H1 Burghfield Hill W Berk
95 E3 Burgh Heath Surrey
57 E2 Burgh Hill E Susx
79 G4 Burgh Hill E Susx
186 B6 Burghill Herefs
301 F1 Burgh le Marsh Lincs
556 D1 Burgh Muir Abers
255 H2 Burgh next Aylsham Norfk
319 G2 Burgh on Bain Lincs
251 F6 Burgh St Peter Norfk
260 D5 Burgh Stubbs Norfk
330 B2 Burghwallis Donc
14 C4 Burgois Cnwll
98 A2 Burham Kent
97 H2 Burham Court Kent
74 A5 Buriton Hants
290 C4 Burland Ches
605 G3 Burland Shet
14 D4 Burlawn Cnwll
136 C4 Burleigh Gloucs
43 E4 Burlescombe Devon
47 E6 Burleston Dorset
13 E3 Burlestone Devon
49 G4 Burley Hants
343 E3 Burley Leeds
242 B2 Burley Rutlnd
210 B3 Burley Shrops
49 F4 Burley Beacon Hants
290 C6 Burleydam Ches
186 D5 Burley Gate Herefs
355 G5 Burley in Wharfedale Brad
49 G4 Burley Lawn Hants
49 G4 Burley Street Hants
355 G6 Burley Woodhead Brad
44 B2 Burlinch Somset
250 D2 Burlingham Green Norfk
184 D3 Burlingjobb Powys
212 B5 Burlish Park Worcs
15 E5 Burlorne Tregoose Cnwll
57 F1 Burlow E Susx
270 B4 Burlton Shrops
186 C5 Burmarsh Herefs
81 G3 Burmarsh Kent
164 D2 Burmington Warwks
344 D4 Burn N York
326 C6 Burnage Manch
23 G2 Burnard's Ho Devon
274 D3 Burnaston Derbys
467 G3 Burnbank S Lans
356 B4 Burn Bridge N York
359 F5 Burnby E R Yk
329 E5 Burncross Sheff
54 A4 Burndell W Susx
325 G3 Burnden Bolton
326 D2 Burnedge Rochdl
379 F5 Burneside Cumb
603 K3 Burness Ork
370 B3 Burneston N York
86 B1 Burnett BaNES
439 E2 Burnfoot Border
439 G1 Burnfoot Border
423 G1 Burnfoot D & G
425 F5 Burnfoot D & G
425 G2 Burnfoot D & G
433 F3 Burnfoot E Ayrs
468 A1 Burnfoot N Lans
499 F4 Burnfoot P & K
314 D2 Burngreave Sheff
8 B3 Burngullow Cnwll
117 F3 Burnham Bucks
333 F1 Burnham N Linc
117 F3 Burnham Slough
259 G3 Burnham Deepdale Norfk
144 C1 Burnham Green Herts
259 G3 Burnham Market Norfk
259 G3 Burnham Norton Norfk
148 C5 Burnham-on-Crouch Essex
84 A5 Burnham-on-Sea Somset
259 G3 Burnham Overy Staithe Norfk
259 G3 Burnham Overy Town Norfk
259 H3 Burnham Thorpe Norfk
557 F6 Burnhead Abers
439 G1 Burnhead Border
423 F3 Burnhead D & G
435 H5 Burnhead D & G
432 B4 Burnhead S Ayrs
559 G6 Burnhervie Abers
236 A4 Burnhill Green Staffs
405 E5 Burnhope Dur
466 A4 Burnhouse N Ayrs
472 A5 Burnhouse Mains Border
14 D4 Burniere Cnwll
568 E3 Burniestrype Moray
387 H6 Burniston N York
327 H3 Burnlee Kirk
340 D3 Burnley Lancs
340 C3 Burnley Lane Lancs
340 C3 Burnley Wood Lancs
474 D2 Burnmouth Border
350 D6 Burn Naze Lancs
497 H4 Burn of Cambus Stirlg
405 E3 Burnopfield Dur
401 E3 Burnrigg Cumb
354 D2 Burnsall N York
170 C5 Burn's Green Herts
527 F3 Burnside Angus
527 G4 Burnside Angus
434 B2 Burnside E Ayrs
500 C3 Burnside P & K
512 B4 Burnside P & K
606 C2 Burnside Shet
406 A4 Burnside Sundld
487 E5 Burnside W Loth
514 C3 Burnside of Duntrune Angus
38 D3 Burnstone Devon
424 D4 Burnswark D & G
136 C4 Burnt Ash Gloucs
94 A4 Burntcommon Surrey
274 C3 Burntheath Derbys
175 E4 Burnt Heath Essex
115 F5 Burnt Hill W Berk
5 E1 Burnthouse Cnwll
488 A3 Burntisland Fife
122 A1 Burnt Mills Essex
78 C4 Burnt Oak E Susx
119 E1 Burnt Oak Gt Lon
433 G3 Burnton E Ayrs
213 E1 Burnt Tree Sandw
237 G3 Burntwood Staffs
237 G3 Burntwood Green Staffs
288 C2 Burntwood Pentre Flints
356 B2 Burnt Yates N York
43 G4 Burnworthy Somset
487 F6 Burnwynd C Edin
93 H4 Burpham Surrey
54 B3 Burpham W Susx
442 B3 Burradon Nthumb
431 E5 Burradon N Tyne
609 J2 Burrafirth Shet
606 B8 Burraland Shet
606 D2 Burraland Shet
4 C1 Burras Cnwll
606 B8 Burrastow Shet
10 D2 Burraton Cnwll
10 D2 Burraton Coombe Cnwll
606 E4 Burravoe Shet
607 H1 Burravoe Shet
601 H5 Burray Village Ork
392 A6 Burrells Cumb
513 F2 Burrelton P & K
29 F1 Burridge Devon
61 E4 Burridge Devon
51 F2 Burridge Hants
583 H3 Burrigill Highld
370 A2 Burrill N York
332 A3 Burringham N Linc
40 C4 Burrington Devon
210 A5 Burrington Herefs
85 E3 Burrington N Som
198 C3 Burrough End Cambs
198 C3 Burrough Green Cambs
241 G2 Burrough on the Hill Leics
116 D2 Burroughs Grove Bucks
603 G7 Burroughston Ork
27 F3 Burrow Devon
27 H5 Burrow Devon
63 E3 Burrow Somset
66 C6 Burrow Somset
44 D2 Burrowbridge Somset
93 G2 Burrowhill Surrey
94 B5 Burrows Cross Surrey
277 F1 Burrowsmoor Holt Notts
149 G1 Burrsville Park Essex
78 C2 Burrswood Kent
102 C3 Burry Swans
102 C3 Burry Green Swans
128 C4 Burry Port Carmth
38 D3 Burscott Devon
324 A2 Burscough Lancs
323 H2 Burscough Bridge Lancs
38 C4 Bursdon Devon
346 B3 Bursea E R Yk
360 D5 Burshill E R Yk
51 E3 Bursledon Hants
291 H5 Burslem C Stke
201 E6 Burstall Suffk
201 E5 Burstallhill Suffk
29 H2 Burstock Dorset
25 H2 Burston Devon
225 F3 Burston Norfk
272 D3 Burston Staffs
77 F1 Burstow Surrey
348 D4 Burstwick E R Yk
368 A2 Burtersett N York
401 F2 Burtholme Cumb
199 F2 Burthorpe Suffk
400 D5 Burthwaite Cumb
84 C6 Burtle Somset
84 C6 Burtle Hill Somset
280 C2 Burtoft Lincs
289 H2 Burton Ches
308 D5 Burton Ches
32 B1 Burton Dorset
49 F6 Burton Dorset
318 B5 Burton Lincs
455 F3 Burton Nthumb
125 G3 Burton Pembks
45 G5 Burton Somset
64 C3 Burton Somset
105 G6 Burton V Glam
68 D3 Burton Wilts
111 E4 Burton Wilts
289 E3 Burton Wrexhm
361 E2 Burton Agnes E R Yk
30 B4 Burton Bradstock Dorset
300 B5 Burton Corner Lincs
191 F4 Burton Dassett Warwks
198 C4 Burton End Cambs
198 C5 Burton End Cambs
172 A5 Burton End Essex
125 G3 Burton Ferry Pembks
374 D5 Burton Fleming E R Yk
214 D4 Burton Green Warwks
288 D3 Burton Green Wrexhm
215 G2 Burton Hastings Warwks
366 A4 Burton-in-Kendal Cumb
366 C5 Burton in Lonsdale N York
296 B6 Burton Joyce Notts
218 B5 Burton Latimer Nhants
241 G1 Burton Lazars Leics
278 D4 Burton-le-Coggles Lincs
356 C2 Burton Leonard N York
272 D5 Burton Manor Staffs
276 C5 Burton on the Wolds Leics
241 E5 Burton Overy Leics
279 G1 Burton Pedwardine Lincs
348 D3 Burton Pidsea E R Yk
344 B4 Burton Salmon N York
173 G4 Burton's Green Essex
346 C6 Burton Stather N Linc
346 C6 Burton upon Stather N Linc
274 D5 Burton upon Trent Staffs
234 D5 Burton Westwood Shrops
310 B1 Burtonwood Warrtn
289 H3 Burwardsley Ches
211 E2 Burwarton Shrops
79 F5 Burwash E Susx
79 E5 Burwash Common E Susx
79 F5 Burwash Weald E Susx
198 B1 Burwell Cambs
320 B4 Burwell Lincs
303 F2 Burwen IoA
601 G8 Burwick Ork
605 G2 Burwick Shet
210 B2 Burwood Shrops
94 B2 Burwood Park Surrey
326 A2 Bury Bury
220 C3 Bury Cambs
42 B2 Bury Somset
54 B2 Bury W Susx
2 D4 Buryas Br Cnwll
272 C2 Burybank Staffs
169 G3 Bury End Beds
194 D4 Bury End Beds
163 G2 Bury End Worcs
144 D4 Bury Green Herts
171 G5 Bury Green Herts
54 B2 Bury Hollow W Susx
199 G2 Bury St Edmunds Suffk
90 D2 Bury's Bank W Berk
359 E2 Burythorpe N York
445 E2 Busbiehill N Ayrs
93 G6 Busbridge Surrey
467 E3 Busby E Rens
512 B4 Busby P & K
138 C5 Buscot Oxon
66 C2 Buscott Somset
529 G1 Bush Abers
38 B6 Bush Cnwll
186 A4 Bush Bank Herefs
94 D5 Bushbury Surrey
236 D4 Bushbury Wolves
241 E4 Bushby Leics
537 K3 Bush Crathie Abers
172 B6 Bush End Essex
256 D4 Bush Estate Norfk
34 A4 Bushey Dorset
143 G5 Bushey Herts
139 E3 Bushey Ground Oxon
143 G6 Bushey Heath Herts
119 E6 Bushey Mead Gt Lon
426 C3 Bushfield Cumb
225 H2 Bush Green Norfk
248 D5 Bush Green Norfk
200 B3 Bush Green Suffk
144 D5 Bush Hill Park Gt Lon
162 C3 Bushley Worcs
162 C3 Bushley Green Worcs
195 G3 Bushmead Beds
210 A2 Bushmoor Shrops
112 C4 Bushton Wilts
254 B5 Bushy Common Norfk
391 G1 Busk Cumb
326 D3 Busk Oldham
318 D2 Buslingthorpe Lincs
136 C4 Bussage Gloucs
65 F4 Bussex Somset
604 b3 Busta Shet
606 D4 Busta Shet
172 C4 Bustard Green Essex
225 G1 Bustard's Green Norfk
603 M1 Bustatoun Ork
6 D5 Busveal Cnwll
256 C5 Butcher's Common Norfk
78 D4 Butcher's Cross E Susx
85 F2 Butcombe N Som
132 A3 Bute Town Caerph
106 C4 Butetown Cardif
233 H2 Butlane Head Shrops
67 E3 Butleigh Somset
67 E3 Butleigh Wootton Somset
270 D5 Butlersbank Shrops
142 A3 Butler's Cross Bucks
142 D6 Butlers Cross Bucks
295 G5 Butler's Hill Notts
190 D5 Butlers Marston Warwks
202 D4 Butley Suffk
202 D5 Butley High Corner Suffk
202 D5 Butley Low Corner Suffk
312 B4 Butley Town Ches
51 E3 Butlocks Heath Hants
272 C5 Butter Bank Staffs
427 G5 Butterburn Cumb
358 D3 Buttercrambe N York
4 D2 Butteriss Gate Cnwll
394 B4 Butterknowle Dur
42 C6 Butterleigh Devon
294 C2 Butterley Derbys
295 E4 Butterley Derbys
377 F1 Buttermere Cumb
90 A2 Buttermere Wilts
136 B4 Butterrow Gloucs
291 G4 Butters Green Staffs
525 G6 Butterstone P & K
272 B1 Butterton Staffs
293 E3 Butterton Staffs
390 D6 Butterwick Cumb
396 A3 Butterwick Dur
300 C6 Butterwick Lincs
372 D4 Butterwick N York
374 B5 Butterwick N York
440 B6 Butteryhaugh Nthumb
290 D4 Butt Green Ches
233 E3 Buttington Powys
291 G4 Butt Lane Staffs
211 G4 Buttonbridge Shrops
200 C1 Button Haugh Green Suffk
211 G4 Buttonoak Worcs
200 B4 Button's Green Suffk
26 B5 Butts Devon
50 D3 Buttsash Hants
23 F2 Buttsbear Cross Cnwll
146 D5 Buttsbury Essex
147 F4 Butt's Green Essex
171 G3 Butts Green Essex
71 F4 Butt's Green Hants
101 F5 Buttsole Kent
11 G4 Butts Park Devon
366 B6 Butt Yeats Lancs
200 D3 Buxhall Suffk
200 C3 Buxhall Fen Street Suffk
474 B4 Buxley Border
78 B5 Buxted E Susx
313 E5 Buxton Derbys
255 H3 Buxton Norfk
312 D3 Buxworth Derbys
308 A5 Bwlch Flints
228 D3 Bwlch Gwynd
158 C5 Bwlch Powys
263 H1 Bwlch-derwin Gwynd
288 C4 Bwlchgwyn Wrexhm
181 E3 Bwlch-Llan Cerdgn
153 H5 Bwlchnewydd Carmth
262 D5 Bwlchtocyn Gwynd
232 C1 Bwlch-y-cibau Powys
106 B3 Bwlch-y-cwm Cardif
268 C5 Bwlchyddar Powys
180 B5 Bwlch-y-fadfa Cerdgn
231 H5 Bwlch-y-ffridd Powys
231 G5 Bwlch y Garreg Powys
153 E2 Bwlchygroes Pembks
283 F4 Bwlchyllyn Gwynd
129 E5 Bwlchymynydd Carmth
208 D4 Bwlch-y-Plain Powys
207 G5 Bwlch-y-sarnau Powys
99 G6 Bybrook Kent
159 G1 Bycross Herefs
105 E3 Byeastwood Brdgnd
193 E4 Bye Green Bucks
403 F5 Byerhope Nthumb
405 E3 Byermoor Gatesd
395 E3 Byers Green Dur
192 B4 Byfield Nhants
94 B2 Byfleet Surrey
185 G6 Byford Herefs
185 G6 Byford Common Herefs
170 C2 Bygrave Herts
405 G2 Byker N u Ty
286 D2 Bylchau Conwy
311 E6 Byley Ches
128 D5 Bynea Carmth
370 D4 Byram N York
441 E4 Byrness Nthumb
219 F4 Bythorn Cambs
185 G2 Byton Herefs
185 G2 Byton Hand Herefs
404 B2 Bywell Nthumb
75 F5 Byworth W Susx

C

39 F3 Cabbacott Devon
117 E5 Cabbage Hill Br For
597 K3 Cabharstadh W Isls
209 F2 Cabin Shrops
333 G4 Cabourne Lincs
477 H4 Cabrach Ag & B
553 H3 Cabrach Moray
565 J8 Cabrich Highld
351 G5 Cabus Lancs
281 E4 Cackle Hill Lincs
58 A3 Cackle Street E Susx
58 D3 Cackle Street E Susx
78 B4 Cackle Street E Susx
27 E2 Cadbury Devon
42 D4 Cadbury Barton Devon
110 B5 Cadbury Heath S Glos
484 C5 Cadder E Duns
169 F6 Caddington Beds
451 F3 Caddonfoot Border
451 E2 Caddonlee Border
330 B4 Cadeby Donc
239 G4 Cadeby Leics
42 B6 Cadeleigh Devon
449 H2 Cademuir Border
287 E2 Cader Denbgs
79 E5 Cade Street E Susx
527 G3 Cadger Path Angus
44 C4 Cad Green Somset
4 D6 Cadgwith Cnwll
501 E4 Cadham Fife
311 E1 Cadishead Salfd
103 F2 Cadle Swans
338 D3 Cadley Lancs
89 F1 Cadley Wilts
89 F4 Cadley Wilts
116 C1 Cadmore End Bucks
50 B2 Cadnam Hants
333 E4 Cadney N Linc
270 B3 Cadney Bank Wrexhm
288 B2 Cadole Flints
106 B6 Cadoxton V Glam
130 B5 Cadoxton-Juxta-Neath Neath
339 H6 Cadshaw Bl w D
170 A3 Cadwell Herts
467 H4 Cadzow S Lans
283 E3 Caeathro Gwynd
285 F6 Cae Clyd Gwynd
130 C2 Caehopkin Powys
178 D4 Caemorgan Cerdgn
318 C2 Caenby Lincs
130 D6 Caerau Brdgnd
106 B4 Caerau Cardif
107 E2 Caerau Park Newpt
130 C2 Cae'r-bont Powys
129 E2 Cae'r-bryn Carmth
285 E6 Caerdeon Gwynd
288 D3 Caer-Estyn Wrexhm
150 C4 Caer-Farchell Pembks
302 D5 Caergeiliog IoA
288 C3 Caergwrle Flints
104 B1 Caerhendy Neath
304 C6 Caerhun Gwynd
130 B2 Cae'r-Lan Powys
107 F1 Caerleon Newpt
134 B3 Caer Llan Mons
105 F6 Caermead V Glam
152 C3 Caermeini Pembks
283 E3 Caernarfon Gwynd
106 C2 Caerphilly Caerph
207 G1 Caersws Powys
180 A3 Caerwedros Cerdgn
109 E1 Caerwent Mons
109 E2 Caerwent Brook Mons
307 G5 Caerwys Flints
229 E5 Caethle Gwynd
97 E5 Cage Green Kent
159 G6 Caggle Street Mons
304 D3 Caim IoA
136 B3 Cainscross Gloucs
155 G2 Caio Carmth
592 E5 Cairinis W Isls
598 B8 Cairisiadar W Isls
595 G6 Cairminis W Isls
480 A1 Cairnbaan Ag & B
560 C4 Cairnbrogie Abers
571 J2 Cairnbulg Abers
559 F4 Cairncross Angus
474 C2 Cairncross Border
494 D2 Cairndow Ag & B
571 J3 Cairness Abers
486 B4 Cairneyhill Fife
410 C3 Cairnfield D & G
408 C5 Cairngaan D & G
408 A2 Cairngarroch D & G
559 F3 Cairnhill Abers
468 B2 Cairnhill N Lans
569 H7 Cairnie Abers
560 D2 Cairnleith Crofts Abers
560 C1 Cairnorrie Abers
560 B6 Cairnpark Abers
435 H5 Cairnpark D & G
415 E3 Cairnryan D & G
600 D2 Cairston Ork
251 G2 Caister-on-Sea Norfk
333 G4 Caistor Lincs
250 A4 Caistor St Edmund Norfk
442 B4 Caistron Nthumb
212 C5 Cakebole Worcs
174 C2 Calais Street Suffk
598 E8 Calanais W Isls
597 L4 Calbost W Isls
36 C3 Calbourne IoW
320 C4 Calceby Lincs
307 H5 Calcoed Flints
137 G2 Calcot Gloucs
115 H5 Calcot W Berk
115 H5 Calcot Row W Berk
100 C3 Calcott Kent
234 A2 Calcott Shrops
136 A1 Calcott's Green Gloucs
356 C3 Calcutt N York
137 H6 Calcutt Wilts
609 J3 Caldback Shet
389 H2 Caldbeck Cumb
369 E2 Caldbergh N York
196 D3 Caldecote Cambs
219 G2 Caldecote Cambs
170 B2 Caldecote Herts
193 E4 Caldecote Nhants
239 E6 Caldecote Warwks
143 H6 Caldecote Hill Herts
140 A5 Caldecott Oxon
218 D6 Caldecott Rutlnd
242 B6 Caldecott Rutlnd
168 B2 Caldecotte M Keyn
376 C4 Calder Cumb
468 B2 Calderbank N Lans
376 C3 Calder Bridge Cumb
341 E6 Calderbrook Rochdl
485 G6 Caldercruix N Lans
329 E1 Calder Grove Wakefd
588 D4 Calder Mains Highld
446 D1 Caldermill S Lans
326 D1 Caldermoor Rochdl
309 E2 Calderstones Lpool
352 A5 Calder Vale Lancs
467 F3 Calderwood S Lans
527 G5 Caldhame Angus
109 E2 Caldicot Mons
237 F5 Caldmore Wsall
238 C1 Caldwell Derbys
383 E2 Caldwell N York
308 B2 Caldy Wirral
180 C4 Caledrhydiau Cerdgn
312 A2 Cale Green Stockp
7 F5 Calenick Cnwll
236 D3 Calf Heath Staffs
199 E5 Calford Green Suffk
603 H4 Calfsound Ork
517 K5 Calgary Ag & B
567 K5 Califer Moray
213 F3 California Birm
221 H3 California Cambs
486 B4 California Falk
251 G1 California Norfk
201 G6 California Suffk
12 C2 California Cross Devon
275 F5 Calke Derbys
556 D6 Calladrum Abers
562 B6 Callakille Highld
442 D3 Callaly Nthumb
497 F3 Callander Stirlg
310 B1 Callands Warrtn
598 E8 Callanish W Isls
235 E5 Callaughton Shrops
430 C6 Callerton N u Ty
430 C6 Callerton Lane End N u Ty
7 E3 Callestick Cnwll
531 H2 Calligarry Highld
17 E5 Callington Cnwll
274 B5 Callingwood Staffs
3 G2 Calloose Cnwll
294 B4 Callow Derbys
160 B3 Callow Herefs
188 B5 Callow End Worcs
134 C1 Callow Hill Herefs
85 F6 Callow Hill Somset
112 B3 Callow Hill Wilts
211 G5 Callow Hill Worcs
187 F5 Callow Marsh Herefs
50 B2 Calmore Hants
137 F3 Calmsden Gloucs
112 A5 Calne Wilts
112 B5 Calne Marsh Wilts
315 E5 Calow Derbys
315 E6 Calow Green Derbys
312 B5 Calrofold Ches
51 E4 Calshot Hants
17 F5 Calstock Cnwll
112 B6 Calstone Wellington Wilts
261 G5 Calthorpe Norfk
165 H2 Calthorpe Oxon
390 D1 Calthwaite Cumb
457 E2 Calton Ag & B
467 E2 Calton C Glas
354 B3 Calton N York
293 F4 Calton Staffs
314 A6 Calton Lees Derbys
4 C1 Calvadnack Cnwll
290 B3 Calveley Ches
314 A5 Calver Derbys
271 E2 Calverhall Shrops
185 G5 Calver Hill Herefs
42 B5 Calverleigh Devon
342 D2 Calverley Leeds
314 A4 Calver Sough Derbys
167 E5 Calvert Bucks
167 G2 Calverton M Keyn
296 B5 Calverton Notts
524 B2 Calvine P & K
399 E4 Calvo Cumb
135 H5 Cam Gloucs
533 H7 Camaghael Highld
547 G4 Camas-luinie Highld
519 L5 Camasnacroise Highld
545 J2 Camastianavaig Highld
549 J1 Camault Muir Highld
609 G6 Camb Shet
59 G3 Camber E Susx
93 E2 Camberley Surrey
119 G4 Camberwell Gt Lon
345 F4 Camblesforth N York
429 G2 Cambo Nthumb
431 E3 Cambois Nthumb
6 B6 Camborne Cnwll
196 D3 Cambourne Cambs
472 D5 Cambridge Border
197 F3 Cambridge Cambs
135 H4 Cambridge Gloucs
355 H5 Cambridge Leeds
109 F6 Cambridge Batch N Som
123 E3 Cambridge Town Sthend
6 C4 Cambrose Cnwll
498 D6 Cambus Clacks
485 F1 Cambusbarron Stirlg
498 A6 Cambusdrenny Stirlg
498 C6 Cambuskenneth Stirlg
467 F3 Cambuslang S Lans
468 C3 Cambusnethan N Lans
448 D2 Cambuswallace S Lans
80 A2 Camden Hill Kent
78 D2 Camden Park Kent
119 F3 Camden Town Gt Lon
85 H3 Cameley BaNES
22 C6 Camelford Cnwll
49 E2 Camel Green Dorset
485 H3 Camelon Falk
74 D3 Camelsdale W Susx

97 G1 Camer Kent
501 F5 Cameron Fife
501 F5 Cameron Bridge Fife
551 J3 Camerory Highld
161 H3 Camer's Green Worcs
86 B3 Camerton BaNES
388 D2 Camerton Cumb
348 D4 Camerton E R Yk
30 B3 Camesworth Dorset
522 F4 Camghouran P & K
557 F6 Cammachmore Abers
318 A3 Cammeringham Lincs
184 A3 Camnant Powys
484 A2 Camoquhill Stirlg
577 G5 Camore Highld
297 G4 Camp Lincs
464 C3 Campbelton N Ayrs
456 D2 Campbeltown Ag & B
141 E4 Camp Corner Oxon
431 E5 Camperdown N Tyne
313 G4 Camphill Derbys
309 F2 Camp Hill Lpool
370 C3 Camp Hill N York
126 C2 Camp Hill Pembks
239 E6 Camp Hill Warwks
191 E1 Campion Hills Warwks
436 A6 Cample D & G
513 F2 Campmuir P & K
330 B2 Campsall Donc
202 C3 Campsea Ashe Suffk
172 C1 Camps End Cambs
139 H2 Campsfield Oxon
198 C5 Camps Hall Cambs
251 G6 Camps Heath Suffk
169 G2 Campton Beds
489 G4 Camptoun E Loth
440 C2 Camptown Border
151 F5 Camrose Pembks
524 B6 Camserney P & K
546 B7 Camuscross Highld
533 G8 Camusnagaul Highld
573 L6 Camusnagaul Highld
546 C1 Camusteel Highld
546 C1 Camusterrach Highld
523 H6 Camusvrachan P & K
71 F6 Canada Hants
333 G4 Canada Lincs
58 B3 Canadia E Susx
364 C4 Canal Foot Cumb
301 E1 Candlesby Lincs
224 D5 Candle Street Suffk
449 E1 Candy Mill Border
116 A4 Cane End Oxon
57 F3 Caneheath E Susx
148 A6 Canewdon Essex
34 C3 Canford Cliffs Poole
48 C5 Canford Heath Poole
48 C6 Canford Heath Poole
48 C6 Canford Magna Poole
256 C6 Cangate Norfk
201 E1 Canham's Green Suffk
312 D5 Canholes Derbys
589 K2 Canisbay Highld
315 E1 Canklow Rothm
214 D4 Canley Covtry
69 E5 Cann Dorset
14 C5 Cannalidgey Cnwll
67 G1 Cannard's Grave Somset
69 E5 Cann Common Dorset
548 E3 Cannich Highld
65 E4 Cannington Somset
120 A3 Canning Town Gt Lon
236 D2 Cannock Staffs
237 F2 Cannock Wood Staffs
172 B6 Cannons Essex
146 B3 Cannon's Green Essex
134 D2 Cannop Gloucs
426 A4 Canonbie D & G
160 A1 Canon Bridge Herefs
187 F6 Canon Frome Herefs
186 A5 Canon Pyon Herefs
192 C4 Canons Ashby Nhants
43 G3 Canonsgrove Somset
118 D1 Canons Park Gt Lon
3 F2 Canon's Town Cnwll
100 C4 Canterbury Kent
330 D4 Cantley Donc
250 D4 Cantley Norfk
234 C3 Cantlop Shrops
106 C4 Canton Cardif
566 D7 Cantraydoune Highld
566 D7 Cantraywood Highld
366 C5 Cantsfield Lancs
122 B3 Canvey Island Essex
318 B6 Canwick Lincs
23 E4 Canworthy Water Cnwll
533 H7 Caol Highld
516 D6 Caolas Ag & B
591 C8 Caolas W Isls
595 L3 Caolas Scalpaigh W Isls
595 J4 Caolas Stocinis W Isls
478 C8 Caol Ila Ag & B
128 D4 Capel Carmth
97 F6 Capel Kent
158 B4 Capel Powys
76 C1 Capel Surrey
205 E3 Capel Bangor Cerdgn
181 F3 Capel Betws Lleucu Cerdgn
303 F4 Capel Coch IoA
79 G1 Capel Cross Kent
285 F3 Capel Curig Conwy
180 A5 Capel Cynon Cerdgn
154 C5 Capel Dewi Carmth
180 C6 Capel Dewi Cerdgn
205 E3 Capel Dewi Cerdgn
285 H3 Capel Garmon Conwy
202 D5 Capel Green Suffk
179 G4 Capel Gwnda Cerdgn
302 D5 Capel Gwyn IoA
155 H5 Capel Gwynfe Carmth
129 E2 Capel Hendre Carmth
155 E4 Capel Isaac Carmth
153 F2 Capel Iwan Carmth
82 D3 Capel-le-Ferne Kent
35 d2 Capelles Guern
106 A3 Capel Llanilltern Cardif
282 D1 Capel Mawr IoA
303 G5 Capel Parc IoA
202 D5 Capel St Andrew Suffk
175 E2 Capel St Mary Suffk
128 D2 Capel Seion Carmth
205 E4 Capel Seion Cerdgn
286 A4 Capel Siloam Conwy
179 F3 Capel Tygwydd Cerdgn
282 D5 Capel Uchaf Gwynd
305 F4 Capeluno Conwy
180 B3 Capel Vicar Cerdgn
159 E3 Capel-y-ffin Powys
283 F2 Capel-y-graig Gwynd
309 E5 Capenhurst Ches
366 A5 Capernwray Lancs
125 E3 Capeston Pembks
429 G3 Capheaton Nthumb
44 C4 Capland Somset
450 A5 Cappercleuch Border
437 F3 Capplegill D & G
98 B2 Capstone Medway
326 C2 Captain Fold Rochdl
13 E2 Capton Devon
64 A4 Capton Somset
512 C2 Caputh P & K
16 C4 Caradon Town Cnwll
3 F2 Carbis Bay Cnwll

176 C4 Carbonells Essex
543 G7 Carbost Highld
544 F3 Carbost Highld
485 F5 Carbrain N Lans
314 D2 Carbrook Sheff
248 C4 Carbrooke Norfk
316 B5 Carburton Notts
8 C3 Carcary Angus
7 E6 Carclew Cnwll
296 D6 Car Colston Notts
330 B2 Carcroft Donc
500 D5 Cardenden Fife
233 G2 Cardeston Shrops
400 B5 Cardew Cumb
400 B4 Cardewlees Cumb
106 D4 Cardiff Cardif
178 D4 Cardigan Cerdgn
198 C5 Cardinal's Green Cambs
195 F5 Cardington Beds
234 C5 Cardington Shrops
15 G5 Cardinham Cnwll
466 D2 Cardonald C Glas
568 B7 Cardow Moray
408 C3 Cardrain D & G
450 B2 Cardrona Border
482 D4 Cardross Ag & B
408 C5 Cardryne D & G
399 F3 Cardurnock Cumb
243 E1 Careby Lincs
528 B2 Careston Angus
241 F5 Care Village Leics
126 A4 Carew Pembks
126 A4 Carew Cheriton Pembks
126 A4 Carew Newton Pembks
160 D3 Carey Herefs
9 G3 Carey Park Cnwll
468 B3 Carfin N Lans
490 A6 Carfrae E Loth
2 D3 Carfury Cnwll
225 F1 Cargate Common Norfk
423 G5 Cargenbridge D & G
512 D2 Cargill P & K
400 C3 Cargo Cumb
396 D5 Cargo Fleet Middsb
10 D1 Cargreen Cnwll
453 E2 Carham Nthumb
63 G3 Carhampton Somset
6 D5 Carharrack Cnwll
509 K2 Carie P & K
523 H4 Carie P & K
592 E5 Carinish W Isls
36 D3 Carisbrooke IoW
365 E4 Cark Cumb
10 D1 Carkeel Cnwll
598 E6 Càrlabhagh W Isls
7 F3 Carland Cross Cnwll
383 F1 Carlbury Darltn
243 F2 Carlby Lincs
328 B4 Carlecotes Barns
4 B2 Carleen Cnwll
438 D4 Carlenrig Border
369 G5 Carlesmoor N York
376 C3 Carleton Cumb
391 E4 Carleton Cumb
400 D4 Carleton Cumb
337 F2 Carleton Lancs
344 B5 Carleton Wakefd
249 E3 Carleton Forehoe Norfk
376 D5 Carleton Hall Cumb
354 C5 Carleton-in-Craven N York
249 F6 Carleton Rode Norfk
250 C4 Carleton St Peter Norfk
406 B3 Carley Hill Sundld
5 E3 Carlidnack Cnwll
86 B3 Carlingcott BaNES
43 G5 Carlingwark Devon
397 G6 Carlin How R & Cl
400 D3 Carlisle Cumb
8 B3 Carloggas Cnwll
14 B5 Carloggas Cnwll
470 C3 Carlops Border
598 E6 Carloway W Isls
194 D3 Carlton Beds
198 C4 Carlton Cambs
329 F3 Carlton Leeds
343 F4 Carlton Leeds
239 F4 Carlton Leics
276 D1 Carlton Notts
345 E5 Carlton N York
369 E3 Carlton N York
372 B2 Carlton N York
396 A5 Carlton S on T
202 D2 Carlton Suffk
227 G1 Carlton Colville Suffk
241 E5 Carlton Curlieu Leics
198 C4 Carlton Green Cambs
371 F4 Carlton Husthwaite N York
384 D4 Carlton in Cleveland N York
316 A3 Carlton in Lindrick Notts
297 H3 Carlton-le-Moorland Lincs
370 D3 Carlton Miniott N York
297 E2 Carlton-on-Trent Notts
218 A2 Carlton Purlieus Nhants
298 B5 Carlton Scroop Lincs
8 C2 Carluddon Cnwll
468 D4 Carluke S Lans
14 D3 Carlyon Cnwll
8 D3 Carlyon Bay Cnwll
447 F4 Carmacoup S Lans
154 A6 Carmarthen Carmth
129 E1 Carmel Carmth
307 H4 Carmel Flints
283 E5 Carmel Gwynd
303 E4 Carmel IoA
183 H1 Carmel Powys
448 B2 Carmichael S Lans
15 F5 Carminow Cross Cnwll
541 F3 Carmont Abers
467 F3 Carmunnock C Glas
467 F2 Carmyle C Glas
528 B6 Carmyllie Angus
361 E1 Carnaby E R Yk
547 J4 Carnach Highld
573 K4 Carnach Highld
567 J7 Carnach Moray
595 L3 Carnach W Isls
536 B4 Carnachuin Highld
586 D6 Carnachy Highld
593 D8 Carnan W Isls
492 D4 Carn Arthen Cnwll
503 G3 Carnbee Fife
499 G4 Carnbo P & K
6 C5 Carn Brea Village Cnwll
468 A2 Carnbroe N Lans
476 B3 Carnduncan Ag & B
5 E4 Carne Cnwll
7 H6 Carne Cnwll
8 B2 Carne Cnwll
207 G1 Carnebone Cnwll
515 E1 Carnedd Powys
445 J2 Carnegie Angus
131 H6 Carnell S Ayrs
365 G5 Carnetown Rhondd
103 F3 Carnforth Lancs
107 C3 Carnglas Swans
547 H5 Carn-gorm Highld
150 C4 Carnhedryn Pembks
6 B6 Carnhell Green Cnwll
567 E3 Carnhot Cnwll
557 E3 Carnie Abers
4 D2 Carnkie Cnwll

6 C6 Carnkie Cnwll
7 E3 Carnkief Cnwll
231 F5 Carno Powys
486 D2 Carnock Fife
7 F5 Carnon Downs Cnwll
515 F3 Carnoustie Angus
8 C2 Carnsmerry Cnwll
2 C4 Carn Towan Cnwll
467 G6 Carntyne C Glas
466 D3 Carnwadric C Glas
469 F5 Carnwath S Lans
2 C3 Carnyorth Cnwll
22 D4 Caroe Cnwll
214 D4 Carol Green Solhll
542 E8 Caroy Highld
8 B3 Carpalla Cnwll
213 G5 Carpenter's Hill Worcs
368 D2 Carperby N York
368 B2 Carpley Green N York
326 A1 Carr Bury
315 G1 Carr Rothm
580 B5 Carrachan Highld
459 G4 Carradale Ag & B
595 K3 Carragraich W Isls
506 D5 Carraig nam Marbh Ag & B
365 G4 Carr Bank Cumb
550 F5 Carrbridge Highld
327 E4 Carrbrook Tamesd
323 G2 Carr Cross Lancs
35 h6 Carrefour Jersey
303 E3 Carreglefn IoA
153 E1 Carreg-wen Pembks
284 C1 Carreg y Garth Gwynd
343 F5 Carr Gate Wakefd
311 E2 Carr Green Traffd
405 G2 Carr Hill Gatesd
323 F4 Carr Houses Sefton
514 C5 Carrick Fife
494 D6 Carrick Castle Ag & B
486 D3 Carriden Falk
276 C1 Carrington C Nott
300 B4 Carrington Lincs
471 F2 Carrington Mdloth
325 G6 Carrington Traffd
285 G5 Carrog Conwy
287 F6 Carrog Denbgs
486 A3 Carron Falk
568 C7 Carron Moray
435 H5 Carronbridge D & G
485 E3 Carron Bridge N Lans
486 A3 Carronshore Falk
238 A4 Carroway Head Staffs
108 D1 Carrow Hill Mons
403 E5 Carrshield Nthumb
424 C5 Carrutherstown D & G
315 F6 Car Vale Derbys
405 H6 Carville Dur
479 J4 Carsaig Ag & B
505 G6 Carsaig Ag & B
416 A5 Carscreugh D & G
417 E5 Carsegowan D & G
528 B4 Carsegownie Angus
527 G4 Carse Gray Angus
416 C3 Carseriggan D & G
398 B3 Carsethorn D & G
95 F2 Carshalton Gt Lon
95 F2 Carshalton Beeches Gt Lon
95 F2 Carshalton on the Hill Gt Lon
294 A4 Carsington Derbys
456 D5 Carskiey Ag & B
417 F6 Carsluith D & G
434 B6 Carsphairn D & G
469 E5 Carstairs S Lans
469 F5 Carstairs Junction S Lans
139 E5 Carswell Marsh Oxon
93 H3 Cartbridge Surrey
451 E4 Carterhaugh Border
314 C3 Carter Knowle Sheff
71 F5 Carter's Clay Hants
145 H2 Carter's Green Essex
116 C6 Carter's Hill Wokham
134 D2 Carterspiece Gloucs
138 D3 Carterton Oxon
404 B4 Carterway Heads Nthumb
17 E3 Carthamartha Cnwll
4 C1 Carthew Cnwll
8 C2 Carthew Cnwll
370 C3 Carthorpe N York
442 C4 Cartington Nthumb
468 D5 Cartland S Lans
314 C4 Cartledge Derbys
365 E4 Cartmel Cumb
365 F2 Cartmel Fell Cumb
482 C4 Cartsdyke Inver
328 A3 Cartworth Kirk
172 B3 Carver Barracks Essex
7 G2 Carvynick Cnwll
128 C3 Carway Carmth
426 A5 Carwinley Cumb
4 C1 Carwynnen Cnwll
67 E4 Cary Fitzpaine Somset
423 G3 Carzield D & G
184 D1 Cascob Powys
136 B3 Cashes Green Gloucs
509 G1 Cashlie P & K
48 B2 Cashmoor Dorset
605 H3 Casho Shet
501 E4 Caskieberran Fife
137 F1 Cassey Compton Gloucs
139 G2 Cassington Oxon
395 G2 Cassop Dur
3 E4 Castallack Cnwll
34 C3 Castel Guern
305 G6 Castell Denbgs
307 G6 Castell IoA
304 B5 Castell IoA
180 B5 Castell Howell Cerdgn
133 E6 Castell-y-bwch Torfn
129 E2 Castell-y-rhingyll Carmth
366 C4 Casterton Cumb
29 F2 Castle Devon
43 E2 Castle Somset
85 F6 Castle Somset
253 G4 Castle Acre Norfk
194 B3 Castle Ashby Nhants
357 G5 Castlebay W Isls
368 D1 Castle Bolton N York
214 A2 Castle Bromwich Solhll
278 D6 Castle Bytham Lincs
151 H4 Castlebythe Pembks
232 C3 Castle Caereinion Powys
198 C6 Castle Camps Cambs
320 C3 Castle Carrock Cumb
401 F3 Castle Carrock Cumb
485 F4 Castlecary N Lans
67 G3 Castle Cary Somset
111 E4 Castle Combe Wilts
470 B6 Castlecraig Border
566 E3 Castlecraig Highld
236 D3 Castlecroft Wolves
275 H4 Castle Donington Leics
413 E2 Castle Douglas D & G
314 C3 Castle Dyke Sheff
138 B5 Castle Eaton Swindn
396 B2 Castle Eden Dur
243 G3 Castle End C Pete
570 D4 Castlefairn D & G
413 H3 Castlefields Halton
234 C2 Castle Fields Shrops
426 B3 Castle Frome Herefs
344 A4 Castle Gate Cnwll
3 E3 Castle Gate Cnwll
328 D4 Castle Green Barns
120 C3 Castle Green Gt Lon

209 F2 Castlegreen Shrops
93 G2 Castle Green Surrey
274 D6 Castle Gresley Derbys
466 C2 Castlehead Rens
173 F2 Castle Hedingham Essex
449 H2 Castlehill Border
78 A4 Castle Hill E Susx
588 F3 Castlehill Highld
97 G6 Castle Hill Kent
513 G3 Castlehill P & K
445 E5 Castle Hill S Ayrs
326 D6 Castle Hill Stockp
201 F5 Castle Hill Suffk
187 H3 Castle Hill Worcs
415 F5 Castle Kennedy D & G
421 F2 Castlemaddy D & G
125 F5 Castlemartin Pembks
467 F3 Castlemilk C Glas
424 C4 Castlemilk D & G
151 E3 Castlemorris Pembks
162 A2 Castlemorton Worcs
425 F1 Castle O'er D & G
309 H4 Castle Park Ches
389 F5 Castlerigg Cumb
252 D2 Castle Rising Norfk
404 C5 Castleside Dur
341 E4 Castle Street Calder
193 G6 Castlethorpe M Keyn
332 D3 Castlethorpe N Linc
537 J4 Castleton Abers
480 B3 Castleton Ag & B
526 D5 Castleton Angus
313 G3 Castleton Derbys
107 E3 Castleton Newpt
386 A3 Castleton N York
499 E2 Castleton P & K
326 C2 Castleton Rochdl
289 F4 Castletown Ches
391 E3 Castletown Cumb
32 B5 Castletown Dorset
588 F3 Castletown Highld
322 d9 Castletown IoM
272 C5 Castletown Staffs
406 B3 Castletown Sundld
55 E3 Castle Town W Susx
161 G4 Castletump Gloucs
105 E5 Castle-upon-Alun V Glam
214 A1 Castle Vale Birm
439 E4 Castleweary Border
410 D4 Castlewigg D & G
356 B5 Castley N York
200 C6 Castling's Heath Suffk
248 C5 Caston Norfk
243 G5 Castor C Pete
103 E4 Caswell Swans
463 F5 Catacol N Ayrs
378 B5 Cat Bank Cumb
109 G3 Catbrain S Glos
134 C4 Catbrook Mons
308 B5 Catch Flints
2 D4 Catchall Cnwll
214 D4 Catchems Corner Solhll
212 A4 Catchems End Worcs
405 E4 Catchgate Dur
589 H5 Catchory Highld
440 D4 Catcleugh Nthumb
315 E2 Catcliffe Rothm
112 B4 Catcomb Wilts
66 B2 Catcott Somset
95 G3 Caterham Surrey
192 B3 Catesby Nhants
256 D5 Catfield Norfk
606 F7 Catfirth Shet
120 A5 Catford Gt Lon
338 C2 Catforth Lancs
106 C4 Cathays Cardif
106 C4 Cathays Park Cardif
467 E2 Cathcart C Glas
158 B4 Cathedine Powys
214 B3 Catherine-de-Barnes Solhll
342 A4 Catherine Slack Brad
52 B2 Catherington Hants
29 G4 Catherston Leweston Dorset
211 F4 Catherton Shrops
328 C3 Cat Hill Barns
215 H4 Cathiron Warwks
366 C1 Catholes Cumb
472 B5 Cathpair Border
51 F3 Catisfield Hants
173 G2 Catley Cross Essex
326 C1 Catley Lane Head Rochdl
187 F6 Catley Southfield Herefs
535 H4 Catlodge Highld
426 C4 Catlowdy Cumb
171 G2 Catmere End Essex
114 C3 Catmore W Berk
19 G3 Caton Devon
352 A2 Caton Lancs
352 B1 Caton Green Lancs
19 E2 Cator Court Devon
445 H4 Catrine E Ayrs
108 C1 Cat's Ash Newpt
256 C5 Cat's Common Norfk
292 B4 Cats Edge Staffs
58 B4 Catsfield E Susx
58 B4 Catsfield Stream E Susx
67 E4 Catsgore Somset
67 F3 Catsham Somset
328 C4 Catshaw Barns
213 E5 Catshill Worcs
237 G4 Catshill Wsall
272 B3 Cat's Hill Cross Staffs
450 C4 Catslackburn Border
116 B2 Catslip Oxon
235 G5 Catstree Shrops
357 E4 Cattal N York
175 F3 Cattawade Suffk
11 E3 Cattedown C Plym
338 C1 Catteral Lancs
383 F5 Catterick N York
383 F5 Catterick Bridge N York
383 F5 Catterick Garrison N York
390 D3 Catterlen Cumb
541 G4 Catterline Abers
357 G5 Catterton N York
93 G6 Catteshall Surrey
216 B4 Catthorpe Leics
30 C3 Cattistock Dorset
403 E3 Catton Nthumb
370 D3 Catton N York
361 E5 Catwick E R Yk
219 F5 Catworth Cambs
136 D2 Caudle Green Gloucs
248 B4 Caudlesprings Norfk
194 D6 Caulcott Beds
140 B1 Caulcott Oxon
459 F2 Cauld Border
486 D4 Cauldcoats Holdings Falk
528 D3 Cauldcots Angus
497 F6 Cauldhame Stirlg
439 G1 Cauldmill Border
293 E3 Cauldon Staffs
293 E5 Cauldon Lowe Staffs
570 D4 Cauldwells Abers
413 H3 Caulkerbush D & G
426 B3 Caulside D & G
46 C2 Caundle Marsh Dorset
212 B3 Caunsall Worcs
296 D2 Caunton Notts

74 A5 Causeway Hants
364 D3 Causeway Cumb
365 G2 Causeway End Cumb
172 D6 Causeway End Essex
448 D2 Causeway End S Lans
112 A3 Causeway End Wilts
341 H3 Causeway Foot Calder
328 B2 Causeway Foot Kirk
213 E2 Causeway Green Sandw
498 B5 Causewayhead Stirlg
234 C5 Causewaywood Shrops
405 F3 Causey Dur
560 D6 Causeyend Abers
443 F6 Causey Park Bridge Nthumb
39 F5 Caute Devon
380 B5 Cautley Cumb
199 F5 Cavendish Suffk
275 G4 Cavendish Bridge Leics
223 F6 Cavenham Suffk
451 H4 Cavers Carre Border
166 C4 Caversfield Oxon
116 B4 Caversham Readg
116 B4 Caversham Heights Readg
292 C6 Caverswall Staffs
566 E6 Cawdor Highld
360 B4 Cawkeld E R Yk
320 A4 Cawkwell Lincs
344 D2 Cawood N York
255 F3 Cawsand Cnwll
210 C5 Cawston Norfk
298 A5 Cawston Warwks
296 C5 Cawthorne Barns
374 D3 Cawthorne N York
592 C4 Cawthorpe Lincs
595 J4 Cawton N York
595 L4 Caxton Cambs
597 L1 Caynham Shrops
590 F4 Caythorpe Lincs

255 F3 Cawston Norfk
215 H5 Cawston Warwks
328 D3 Cawthorne Barns
373 E2 Cawthorne N York
279 F5 Cawthorpe Lincs
372 B4 Cawton N York
196 D3 Caxton Cambs
210 C5 Caynham Shrops
298 A5 Caythorpe Lincs
296 C5 Caythorpe Notts
374 D3 Cayton N York
592 C4 Ceann a Bhàigh W Isls
595 J4 Ceann a Bhàigh W Isls
595 L4 Ceann a Bhàigh W Isls
597 L1 Ceann a' Chòinich W Isls
590 F4 Ceann a Deas Loch Baghasdail W Isls
595 K3 Ceann a' Ghàraidh W Isls
599 J6 Ceann a-Muigh Chuil W Isls
599 K7 Ceann a-staigh Chuil W Isls
590 F3 Ceann a Tuath Loch Baghasdail W Isls
591 D8 Ceann Loch W Isls
595 K4 Ceann-na-Cleithe W Isls
597 L1 Ceann nam Buailtean W Isls
597 H4 Ceann Shiphoirt W Isls
591 C8 Ceann Tangabhal W Isls
597 G4 Ceann Tarabhaigh W Isls
597 J4 Cearsiadair W Isls
592 D2 Ceathramh Meadhanach W Isls

267 G5 Cedig Powys
107 E2 Cefn Newpt
233 E2 Cefn Powys
306 D6 Cefn Berain Conwy
286 C4 Cefn-brith Conwy
130 A2 Cefn-bryn-brain Carmth
102 D3 Cefn-bychan Swans
269 E1 Cefn-bychan Wrexhm
128 D5 Cefncaeau Carmth
268 D3 Cefn Canol Powys
306 B6 Cefn-coch Conwy
231 H4 Cefn Coch Powys
268 B4 Cefn Coch Powys
131 G3 Cefn-coed-y-cymmer Myr Td
132 D3 Cefn-crib Torfn
104 D3 Cefn Cribwr Brdgnd
104 D3 Cefn Cross Brdgnd
267 F2 Cefn-ddwysarn Gwynd
209 E2 Cefn Einion Shrops
128 D2 Cefneithin Carmth
308 B6 Cefn-eurgain Flints
132 C5 Cefn Fforest Caerph
104 D3 Cefn Glas Brdgnd
132 B3 Cefn Golau Blae G
182 D5 Cefn-gorwydd Powys
132 B5 Cefn Hengoed Caerph
103 G2 Cefn-hengoed Swans
205 E3 Cefn Llwyd Cerdgn
269 E1 Cefn-mawr Wrexhm
131 G4 Cefnpennar Rhondd
131 E3 Cefn Rhigos Rhondd
288 D3 Cefn-y-bedd Flints
129 G4 Cefn-y-Garth Swans
152 D4 Cefn-y-pant Carmth
180 B3 Cei-bach Cerdgn
303 F3 Ceidio IoA
303 G5 Ceint IoA
230 B3 Ceinws Powys
181 F5 Cellan Cerdgn
503 F4 Cellardyke Fife
292 C5 Cellarhead Staffs
99 F2 Cellarhill Kent
287 H1 Celyn-Mali Flints
303 E2 Cemaes IoA
230 C3 Cemaes Powys
230 C4 Cemmaes Powys
230 C4 Cemmaes Road Powys
153 F1 Cenarth Carmth
263 H2 Cenin Gwynd
482 C4 Central Inver
519 J3 Ceol na Mara Highld
597 K3 Ceòs W Isls
502 C2 Ceres Fife
31 F2 Cerne Abbas Dorset
137 G5 Cerney Wick Gloucs
303 F6 Cerrigceinwen IoA
130 B6 Cerrig Llwydion Neath
303 C6 Cerrig-mân IoA
286 C5 Cerrigydrudion Conwy
257 E6 Cess Norfk
452 D5 Cessford Border
283 F3 Ceunant Gwynd
162 C3 Chaceley Gloucs
162 B3 Chaceley Hole Gloucs
162 C4 Chaceley Stock Gloucs
6 D5 Chacewater Cnwll
167 E2 Chackmore Bucks
192 A6 Chacombe Nhants
189 F5 Chadbury Worcs
326 C3 Chadderton Oldham
326 C3 Chadderton Fold Oldham
275 F2 Chaddesden C Derb
212 C5 Chaddesley Corbett Worcs
17 F3 Chaddlehanger Devon
11 G2 Chaddlewood C Plym
114 B4 Chaddleworth W Berk
312 B2 Chadkirk Stockp
165 G5 Chadlington Oxon
191 F4 Chadshunt Warwks
237 E2 Chadsmoor Staffs
194 A3 Chadstone Nhants
213 F2 Chad Valley Birm
277 G5 Chadwell Leics
195 F1 Chadwell End Beds
120 C2 Chadwell Heath Gt Lon
121 F4 Chadwell St Mary Thurr
212 B6 Chadwick Worcs
214 C5 Chadwick End Solhll
324 C5 Chadwick Green St Hel
44 D5 Chaffcombe Somset
121 E4 Chafford Hundred Thurr
25 H5 Chagford Devon

77 G6 Chailey E Susx
245 E4 Chainbridge Cambs
300 B6 Chain Bridge Lincs
98 A5 Chainhurst Kent
48 C3 Chalbury Dorset
48 C3 Chalbury Common Dorset
95 G3 Chaldon Surrey
32 D3 Chaldon Herring or East Chaldon Dorset
36 D5 Chale IoW
36 D5 Chale Green IoW
117 H1 Chalfont Common Bucks
117 G1 Chalfont Grove Bucks
142 D6 Chalfont St Giles Bucks
117 H1 Chalfont St Peter Bucks
136 D4 Chalford Gloucs
141 F4 Chalford Oxon
87 F4 Chalford Wilts
136 C4 Chalford Hill Gloucs
169 E4 Chalgrave Beds
140 D5 Chalgrove Oxon
121 G5 Chalk Kent
146 C2 Chalk End Essex
400 B5 Chalkfoot Cumb
247 H4 Chalkhill Norfk
116 B4 Chalkhouse Green Oxon
142 A3 Chalkshire Bucks
82 D2 Chalksole Kent
29 G1 Chalkway Somset
98 D2 Chalkwell Kent
122 C2 Chalkwell Sthend
12 A4 Challaborough Devon
61 G3 Challacombe Devon
607 J4 Challister Shet
416 D3 Challoch D & G
99 G4 Challock Kent
30 D2 Chalmington Dorset
169 E4 Chalton Beds
195 G5 Chalton Beds
52 C1 Chalton Hants
122 A2 Chalvedon Essex
117 G4 Chalvey Slough
57 E3 Chalvington E Susx
60 D2 Chambercombe Devon
99 E6 Chamber's Green Kent
486 D4 Champany Falk
29 G3 Champernhayes Marsh Dorset
41 F2 Champson Devon
501 G2 Chance Inn Fife
204 D4 Chancery Cerdgn
161 G1 Chance's Pitch Herefs
143 F5 Chandler's Cross Herts
161 H2 Chandler's Cross Worcs
72 B5 Chandler's Ford Hants
92 B3 Chandlers Green Hants
409 F2 Changue D & G
435 F4 Chanlockfoot D & G
195 G3 Channel's End Beds
605 G6 Channerwick Shet
40 B3 Chantry Devon
86 C5 Chantry Somset
201 F6 Chantry Suffk
7 F1 Chapel Cnwll
389 F3 Chapel Cumb
500 D6 Chapel Fife
343 F2 Chapel Allerton Leeds
84 C4 Chapel Allerton Somset
14 D3 Chapel Amble Cnwll
193 F1 Chapel Brampton Nhants
272 B2 Chapel Choriton Staffs
63 G3 Chapel Cleeve Somset
79 E5 Chapel Cross E Susx
169 F1 Chapel End Beds
195 F5 Chapel End Beds
195 G5 Chapel End Beds
219 G3 Chapel End Cambs
290 D6 Chapel End Ches
172 B4 Chapel End Essex
219 G3 Chapel End Nhants
239 E6 Chapel End Warwks
313 E3 Chapel-en-le-Frith Derbys
326 A3 Chapel Field Bury
256 D5 Chapel Field Norfk
215 E4 Chapel Fields Covtry
357 H4 Chapel Fields York
281 F5 Chapelgate Lincs
170 B3 Chapel Green Herts
191 H2 Chapel Green Warwks
214 D3 Chapel Green Warwks
214 D3 Chapel Green Warwks
116 D6 Chapel Green Wokham
344 D4 Chapel Haddlesey N York
468 E2 Chapelhall N Lans
220 D3 Chapel Head Cambs
561 G2 Chapel Hill Abers
566 E2 Chapelhill Highld
299 F4 Chapel Hill Lincs
134 C5 Chapel Hill Mons
135 E4 Chapel Hill Mons
512 B3 Chapelhill P & K
513 E5 Chapelhill P & K
449 H6 Chapelhope Border
324 B2 Chapel House Lancs
111 F6 Chapel Knapp Wilts
425 D6 Chapelknowe D & G
209 F4 Chapel Lawn Shrops
367 E4 Chapel-le-Dale N York
43 F2 Chapel Leigh Somset
451 G1 Chapel Mains Border
313 E3 Chapel Milton Derbys
132 D3 Chapel of Ease Caerph
559 G5 Chapel of Garioch Abers
557 F2 Chapel of Stoneywood C Aber
451 H1 Chapel on Leader Border
111 E6 Chapel Plaister Wilts
147 H4 Chapel Row Essex
57 G2 Chapel Row E Susx
115 F6 Chapel Row W Berk
339 G5 Chapels Bl w D
363 E5 Chapels Cumb
321 G5 Chapel St Leonards Lincs
378 B3 Chapel Stile Cumb
329 E1 Chapelthorpe Wakefd
557 F6 Chapelton Abers
528 D5 Chapelton Abers
40 B2 Chapelton Devon
467 G5 Chapelton S Lans
325 G1 Chapelton Bl w D
7 G2 Chapel Town Cnwll
343 F2 Chapeltown Leeds
552 E4 Chapeltown Moray
329 E5 Chapeltown Sheff
213 E4 Chapman's Hill Worcs
87 E5 Chapmanslade Wilts
79 E6 Chapman's Town E Susx
23 H4 Chapmans Well Devon
144 D1 Chapmore End Herts
174 A4 Chappel Essex
16 D5 Charaton Cross Cnwll
96 D5 Charcott Kent
44 C6 Chard Somset
29 F2 Chard Junction Somset
44 C5 Chardleigh Green Somset
29 F2 Chardstock Devon
110 C1 Charfield S Glos
110 C1 Charfield Green S Glos
110 C1 Charfield Hill S Glos
213 E6 Charford Worcs
162 D6 Chargrove Gloucs
99 E5 Charing Kent
99 E5 Charing Heath Kent
99 E4 Charing Hill Kent

164 B2 Charingworth Gloucs
165 F6 Charlbury Oxon
110 C6 Charlcombe BaNES
112 A4 Charlcutt Wilts
190 D3 Charlecote Warwks
237 F6 Charlemont Sandw
61 G5 Charles Devon
61 G5 Charles Bottom Devon
452 A4 Charlesfield Border
93 E6 Charleshill Surrey
527 E5 Charleston Angus
466 C2 Charleston Rens
571 J3 Charlestown Abers
342 C2 Charlestown Brad
557 G4 Charlestown C Aber
8 C3 Charlestown Cnwll
312 D1 Charlestown Derbys
32 A4 Charlestown Dorset
487 E3 Charlestown Fife
562 D2 Charlestown Highld
565 L7 Charlestown Highld
326 C4 Charlestown Manch
341 F4 Charlestown Manch
567 L3 Charlestown Moray
326 B5 Charlestown Salfd
568 D7 Charlestown of Aberlour Moray
200 D4 Charles Tye Suffk
327 F6 Charlesworth Derbys
120 B4 Charlton Gt Lon
90 A5 Charlton Hants
169 H4 Charlton Herts
166 B2 Charlton Nhants
428 C3 Charlton Nthumb
114 C2 Charlton Oxon
44 B2 Charlton Somset
86 B4 Charlton Somset
118 B6 Charlton Surrey
69 F5 Charlton Wilts
86 A6 Charlton Wilts
111 H2 Charlton Wilts
189 F5 Charlton Worcs
212 B5 Charlton Worcs
234 D2 Charlton Wrekin
53 F2 Charlton W Susx
163 F5 Charlton Abbots Gloucs
67 E4 Charlton Adam Somset
70 D5 Charlton-All-Saints Wilts
329 E5 Charltonbrook Sheff
67 H5 Charlton Horethorne Somset
163 E5 Charlton Kings Gloucs
67 E4 Charlton Mackrell Somset
47 H4 Charlton Marshall Dorset
68 B3 Charlton Musgrove Somset
140 C1 Charlton-on-Otmoor Oxon
47 G4 Charlton on the Hill Dorset
165 E5 Charlton Park Gloucs
385 G1 Charltons R & Cl
88 D3 Charlton St Peter Wilts
73 G3 Charlwood Hants
76 D1 Charlwood Surrey
77 G3 Charlwood Surrey
64 D4 Charlynch Somset
48 D6 Charminster Bmouth
32 B1 Charminster Dorset
29 G4 Charmouth Dorset
68 D3 Charnage Wilts
167 E5 Charndon Bucks
271 H3 Charnes Staffs
139 F6 Charney Bassett Oxon
324 C1 Charnock Green Lancs
314 D3 Charnock Hall Sheff
324 C1 Charnock Richard Lancs
202 A3 Charsfield Suffk
98 B4 Chart Corner Kent
91 F3 Charter Alley Hants
85 E3 Charterhouse Somset
485 F2 Chartershall Stirlg
139 E2 Charterville Allotments Oxon
100 B5 Chartham Kent
100 B4 Chartham Hatch Kent
98 B5 Chart Hill Kent
142 C4 Chartridge Bucks
98 B4 Chart Sutton Kent
116 C4 Charvil Wokham
192 B3 Charwelton Nhants
120 D1 Chase Cross Gt Lon
161 H2 Chase End Street Worcs
110 C2 Chase Hill Gloucs
237 F3 Chase Terrace Staffs
237 G3 Chasetown Staffs
164 C4 Chastleton Oxon
23 G2 Chasty Devon
353 F6 Chatburn Lancs
272 A3 Chatcull Staffs
234 B3 Chatford Shrops
106 D2 Chatham Caerph
98 A1 Chatham Medway
147 E1 Chatham Green Essex
342 B3 Chat Hill Brad
455 F4 Chathill Nthumb
188 C2 Chatley Worcs
122 B5 Chattenden Medway
171 G4 Chatter End Essex
221 E2 Chatteris Cambs
291 G4 Chatterley Staffs
118 B5 Chattern Hill Surrey
340 B6 Chatterton Lancs
175 E1 Chattisham Suffk
214 B1 Chattle Hill Warwks
453 E6 Chatto Border
454 D4 Chatton Nthumb
143 E3 Chaulden Herts
169 E5 Chaul End Beds
233 H2 Chavel Shrops
136 C5 Chavenage Green Gloucs
117 E6 Chavey Down Br For
41 E5 Chawleigh Devon
139 H4 Chawley Oxon
188 C2 Chawson Worcs
195 H3 Chawston Beds
73 H2 Chawton Hants
135 G2 Chaxhill Gloucs
116 A4 Chazey Heath Oxon
292 D6 Cheadle Staffs
311 H2 Cheadle Stockp
311 H2 Cheadle Heath Stockp
311 H2 Cheadle Hulme Stockp
292 D6 Cheadle Park Staffs
95 E2 Cheam Gt Lon
171 F3 Cheapside Herts
117 F6 Cheapside W & M
141 F2 Chearsley Bucks
272 C4 Chebsey Staffs
115 H3 Checkendon Oxon
291 E5 Checkley Ches
160 D2 Checkley Herefs
273 F2 Checkley Staffs
291 E5 Checkley Green Ches
199 F3 Chedburgh Suffk
85 E4 Cheddar Somset
168 C6 Cheddington Herts
292 C4 Cheddleton Staffs
292 C4 Cheddleton Heath Staffs
44 A2 Cheddon Fitzpaine Somset
136 D2 Chedglow Wilts
250 D5 Chedgrave Norfk
30 B1 Chedington Dorset
226 D4 Chediston Suffk
226 D4 Chediston Green Suffk
137 G2 Chedworth Gloucs

137 F2 Chedworth Laines Gloucs
65 F4 Chedzoy Somset
81 F2 Cheeseman's Green Kent
326 B4 Cheetam Hill Manch
60 D3 Cheglinch Devon
98 C4 Chegworth Kent
41 E5 Cheldon Devon
61 F4 Chelfham Devon
311 G4 Chelford Ches
275 F3 Chellaston C Derb
292 A4 Chell Heath C Stke
194 D3 Chellington Beds
170 C4 Chells Herts
211 G2 Chelmarsh Shrops
147 E3 Chelmer Village Essex
210 B1 Chelmick Shrops
176 D2 Chelmondiston Suffk
313 F5 Chelmorton Derbys
146 D3 Chelmsford Essex
43 G4 Chelmsine Somset
214 B2 Chelmsley Wood Solhll
119 F4 Chelsea Gt Lon
96 C2 Chelsfield Gt Lon
95 H3 Chelsham Surrey
43 G3 Chelston Somset
20 B5 Chelston Torbay
200 C5 Chelsworth Suffk
200 C5 Chelsworth Common Suffk
163 E5 Cheltenham Gloucs
218 D6 Chelveston Nhants
109 E6 Chelvey N Som
85 E1 Chelvey Batch N Som
86 A2 Chelwood BaNES
77 H4 Chelwood Common E Susx
77 H3 Chelwood Gate E Susx
137 E6 Chelworth Wilts
112 C1 Chelworth Lower Green Wilts
137 G6 Chelworth Upper Green Wilts
86 B6 Chelynch Somset
209 H3 Cheney Longville Shrops
3 G2 Chenhalls Cnwll
143 E5 Chenies Bucks
134 C6 Chepstow Mons
325 F3 Chequerbent Bolton
344 B5 Chequerfield Wakefd
245 H3 Chequers Corner Norfk
81 F2 Chequertree Kent
112 B5 Cherhill Wilts
136 D5 Cherington Gloucs
164 D2 Cherington Warwks
38 C2 Cheristow Devon
62 A2 Cheriton Devon
73 E4 Cheriton Hants
82 C3 Cheriton Kent
102 C3 Cheriton Swans
26 B4 Cheriton Bishop Devon
26 D1 Cheriton Fitzpaine Devon
125 G5 Cheriton or Stackpole Elidor Pembks
271 F6 Cherrington Wrekin
512 D5 Cherrybank P & K
347 E1 Cherry Burton E R Yk
172 B4 Cherry Green Essex
171 E4 Cherry Green Herts
197 G3 Cherry Hinton Cambs
234 B2 Cherry Orchard Shrops
188 C4 Cherry Orchard Worcs
339 F4 Cherry Tree Bl w D
312 C1 Cherry Tree Stockp
275 F2 Cherrytree Hill C Derb
318 C5 Cherry Willingham Lincs
94 A1 Chertsey Surrey
94 B1 Chertsey Meads Surrey
142 D4 Chesham Bucks
326 B2 Chesham Bury
142 D5 Chesham Bois Bucks
145 E4 Cheshunt Herts
98 D2 Chesley Kent
237 E3 Cheslyn Hay Staffs
214 B5 Chessetts Wood Warwks
94 D2 Chessington Gt Lon
142 D4 Chessmount Bucks
237 G2 Chestall Staffs
289 E1 Chester Flints
67 H1 Chesterblade Somset
314 C5 Chesterfield Derbys
237 G3 Chesterfield Staffs
198 A6 Chesterford Park Essex
471 G1 Chesterhill Mdloth
428 D2 Chesterhope Nthumb
451 G4 Chesterknowes Border
405 G4 Chester-le-Street Dur
405 G5 Chester Moor Dur
440 B2 Chesters Border
452 B5 Chesters Border
197 G2 Chesterton Cambs
243 G5 Chesterton Cambs
137 F4 Chesterton Gloucs
166 C5 Chesterton Oxon
236 A5 Chesterton Shrops
291 G5 Chesterton Staffs
191 F3 Chesterton Warwks
191 E3 Chesterton Green Warwks
403 E1 Chesterwood Nthumb
100 B2 Chestfield Kent
98 D2 Chestnut Hill Cumb
19 E6 Chestnut Street Kent
271 G4 Cheston Devon
271 G4 Cheswardine Shrops
235 G1 Cheswell Wrekin
475 F5 Cheswick Nthumb
475 F5 Cheswick West Gt Lon
100 D3 Chetsle Kent
100 D3 Cheslet Forstal Kent
32 B5 Chetnole Dorset
119 E4 Chetscombe Devon
197 E5 Chettiscombe Devon
222 A3 Chettisham Cambs
48 A2 Chettle Dorset
211 F1 Chetton Shrops
166 D4 Chetwode Bucks
271 H6 Chetwynd Aston Wrekin
198 D2 Cheveley Cambs
96 C3 Chevening Kent
143 F1 Cheverell's Green Herts
355 G6 Chevin End Brad
199 F3 Chevington Suffk
42 C4 Chevithorne Devon
85 G2 Chew Magna BaNES
325 F3 Chew Moor Bolton
85 G2 Chew Stoke BaNES
86 B1 Chewton Keynsham BaNES
85 G4 Chewton Mendip Somset
215 E4 Cheylesmore Covtry
25 E3 Chicacott Devon
194 C5 Chicheley M Keyn
53 F4 Chichester W Susx
48 F3 Chickerell Dorset
69 F3 Chicklade Wilts
172 B4 Chickney Essex
169 G4 Chicksands Beds
185 E4 Chickward Herefs
73 H2 Chidden Hants
75 F2 Chiddingfold Surrey
57 E2 Chiddingly E Susx
96 C5 Chiddingstone Kent
96 D5 Chiddingstone Causeway Kent
96 C6 Chiddingstone Hoath Kent
29 H4 Chideock Dorset
63 G4 Chidgley Somset

52 D4 Chidham W Susx
343 E5 Chidswell Kirk
114 D5 Chieveley W Berk
146 D2 Chignall St James Essex
146 D2 Chignall Smealy Essex
145 F6 Chigwell Essex
145 G6 Chigwell Row Essex
72 A2 Chilbolton Hants
72 B2 Chilbolton Down Hants
48 B4 Chilbridge Dorset
72 D4 Chilcomb Hants
30 C4 Chilcombe Dorset
64 B4 Chilcombe Somset
86 A4 Chilcompton Somset
238 D2 Chilcote Leics
121 F2 Childerditch Essex
197 E2 Childerley Gate Cambs
309 E4 Childer Thornton Ches
47 F2 Child Okeford Dorset
114 B2 Childrey Oxon
96 D3 Childsbridge Kent
119 E2 Child's Hill Gt Lon
163 G2 Childswickham Worcs
309 F2 Childwall Lpool
143 G2 Childwick Bury Herts
143 G2 Childwick Green Herts
30 D3 Chilfrome Dorset
53 E2 Chilgrove W Susx
99 H4 Chilham Kent
17 F2 Chillaton Devon
101 E5 Chillenden Kent
36 D4 Chillerton IoW
202 D4 Chillesford Suffk
454 D4 Chillingham Nthumb
12 D4 Chillington Devon
44 D5 Chillington Somset
79 F1 Chilmark Wilts
69 G3 Chilmark Wilts
81 E1 Chilmington Green Kent
57 G2 Chilsham E Susx
165 E6 Chilson Oxon
29 F2 Chilson Devon
29 F2 Chilson Common Somset
17 F4 Chilsworthy Cnwll
23 G1 Chilsworthy Devon
169 G6 Chiltern Green Beds
67 E6 Chilthorne Domer Somset
56 B1 Chiltington E Susx
141 E2 Chilton Bucks
395 F4 Chilton Dur
101 G3 Chilton Kent
114 D2 Chilton Oxon
174 A1 Chilton Suffk
73 E1 Chilton Candover Hants
67 F5 Chilton Cantelo Somset
113 H5 Chilton Foliat Wilts
200 A6 Chilton Grove Suffk
395 F3 Chilton Lane Dur
405 H5 Chilton Moor Sundld
65 G4 Chilton Polden Somset
199 F5 Chilton Street Suffk
65 E4 Chilton Trinity Somset
215 F1 Chilvers Coton Warwks
276 B2 Chilwell Notts
72 B6 Chilworth Hants
93 H5 Chilworth Surrey
72 A6 Chilworth Old Village Hants
139 E4 Chimney Oxon
139 E1 Chimney-end Oxon
199 E5 Chimney Street Suffk
91 H3 Chineham Hants
145 E6 Chingford Gt Lon
145 E6 Chingford Green Gt Lon
312 D3 Chinley Derbys
313 E3 Chinley Head Derbys
141 F4 Chinnor Oxon
43 F3 Chipley Somset
136 A3 Chipmans Platt Gloucs
271 G3 Chipnall Shrops
226 B4 Chippenhall Green Suffk
222 C6 Chippenham Cambs
111 G5 Chippenham Wilts
143 E4 Chipperfield Herts
171 E3 Chipping Herts
352 C6 Chipping Lancs
144 B5 Chipping Barnet Gt Lon
164 B2 Chipping Campden Gloucs
147 G1 Chipping Hill Essex
165 E4 Chipping Norton Oxon
146 B4 Chipping Ongar Essex
110 C3 Chipping Sodbury S Glos
192 A5 Chipping Warden Nhants
42 D2 Chipstable Somset
95 F3 Chipstead Surrey
233 E5 Chirbury Shrops
269 E2 Chirk Wrexhm
269 E2 Chirk Bank Shrops
269 E2 Chirk Green Wrexhm
415 H1 Chirmorrie S Ayrs
474 C3 Chirnside Border
474 B3 Chirnsidebridge Border
431 F6 Chirton N Tyne
88 C3 Chirton Wilts
116 D2 Chisbridge Cross Bucks
89 G1 Chisbury Wilts
45 F4 Chiselborough Somset
113 E4 Chiseldon Swindn
140 C5 Chiselhampton Oxon
341 G4 Chiserley Calder
120 B5 Chislehurst Gt Lon
120 B5 Chislehurst West Gt Lon
100 D3 Chislet Kent
100 D3 Chislet Forstal Kent
32 B5 Chiswell Dorset
119 E4 Chiswick Gt Lon
197 E5 Chiswick End Cambs
312 C1 Chisworth Derbys
58 D2 Chithurst W Susx
74 C5 Chittering Cambs
221 G5 Chitterley Devon
27 E2 Chitterne Wilts
88 A6 Chitterne Wilts
40 C3 Chittlehamholt Devon
40 C2 Chittlehampton Devon
87 H1 Chittoe Wilts
174 C4 Chitts Hills Essex
100 D3 Chitty Kent
60 C5 Chivelstone Devon
60 C5 Chivenor Devon
142 B3 Chivery Bucks
93 G2 Chobham Surrey
89 F6 Cholderton Wilts
142 C3 Cholesbury Bucks
429 E5 Chollerford Nthumb
429 E5 Chollerton Nthumb
290 C3 Cholmondeston Ches
115 F2 Cholsey Oxon
186 B3 Cholstrey Herefs
85 H3 Cholwell BaNES
385 F5 Chop Gate N York
431 E3 Choppington Nthumb
404 D3 Chopwell Gatesd
290 B4 Chorley Ches
324 D1 Chorley Lancs
211 F3 Chorley Shrops
237 G2 Chorley Staffs
74 C4 Chorley Common W Susx
143 E5 Chorleywood Herts
143 E5 Chorleywood Bottom Herts
143 E5 Chorleywood West Herts
291 E4 Choriton Ches

326 B6 Choriton-cum-Hardy Manch
289 G5 Choriton Lane Ches
209 G2 Choulton Shrops
405 G3 Chowdene Gatesd
289 G3 Chowley Ches
77 F5 Chownes Mead W Susx
171 F2 Chrishall Essex
245 E3 Christchurch Cambs
35 E2 Christchurch Dorset
134 D2 Christchurch Gloucs
107 F2 Christchurch Newpt
201 G5 Christchurch Park Suffk
201 G5 Christchurch Park Suffk
111 H4 Christian Malford Wilts
289 F1 Christleton Ches
141 F6 Christmas Common Oxon
84 C3 Christon N Som
455 F5 Christon Bank Nthumb
26 C6 Christow Devon
484 D5 Chryston N Lans
18 A4 Chub Tor Devon
78 B3 Chuck Hatch E Susx
20 B2 Chudleigh Devon
20 A2 Chudleigh Knighton Devon
40 D5 Chulmleigh Devon
312 D1 Chunal Derbys
340 A4 Church Lancs
161 H6 Churcham Gloucs
271 G6 Church Aston Wrekin
209 E4 Churchbank Shrops
193 F1 Church Brampton Nhants
9 G2 Churchbridge Cnwll
237 E3 Churchbridge Staffs
380 D2 Church Brough Cumb
274 C3 Church Broughton Derbys
192 B3 Church Charwelton Nhants
340 D2 Church Clough Lancs
74 A4 Church Common Hants
6 C5 Church Coombe Cnwll
4 D6 Church Cove Cnwll
92 D4 Church Crookham Hants
162 C5 Churchdown Gloucs
272 B6 Church Eaton Staffs
168 D2 Church End Beds
168 D3 Church End Beds
168 D5 Church End Beds
170 A2 Church End Beds
195 E3 Church End Beds
195 F3 Church End Beds
195 F4 Church End Beds
195 H4 Church End Beds
141 F3 Church End Bucks
142 C2 Church End Bucks
219 F5 Church End Cambs
220 B3 Church End Cambs
221 E5 Church End Cambs
221 E6 Church End Cambs
245 E3 Church End Cambs
215 F4 Church End Covtry
360 D4 Church End E R Yk
147 E1 Church End Essex
148 D6 Church End Essex
172 B1 Church End Essex
172 B4 Church End Essex
172 C5 Church End Essex
173 E4 Church End Essex
135 G3 Church End Gloucs
136 A3 Church End Gloucs
162 C2 Church End Gloucs
119 E3 Church End Gt Lon
91 H3 Church End Hants
119 E1 Church End Herts
143 E5 Church End Herts
143 F2 Church End Herts
170 C3 Church End Herts
171 F5 Church End Herts
280 B3 Church End Lincs
319 E5 Church End Lincs
335 F5 Church End Lincs
245 H1 Church End Norfk
139 F3 Church End Oxon
165 E3 Church End Oxon
115 H5 Church End Readg
91 H3 Church End Hants
176 D2 Church End Suffk
94 B3 Church End Surrey
214 D1 Church End Warwks
214 B4 Church End Wilts
162 B1 Church End Worcs
165 F4 Church End Worcs
79 E6 Churches Green E Susx
344 C2 Church Fenton N York
187 G5 Churchfield Herefs
237 F6 Churchfield Sandw
70 C3 Churchfields Wilts
144 D4 Churchgate Herts
145 G2 Churchgate Street Essex
28 C3 Church Green Devon
225 E1 Church Green Norfk
274 D6 Church Gresley Derbys
139 G2 Church Hanborough Oxon
431 E6 Church Hill Pembks
237 E6 Church Hill Sandw
213 G6 Church Hill Worcs
237 F2 Church Hill Worcs
385 H5 Church Houghton Kent
29 E2 Churchill Devon
61 E3 Churchill Devon
84 D3 Churchill N Som
164 D5 Churchill Oxon
188 D4 Churchill Worcs
212 C4 Churchill Worcs
84 D2 Churchill Green N Som
43 H5 Churchinford Somset
33 G3 Church Knowle Dorset
317 F4 Church Laneham Notts
241 F6 Church Langton Leics
215 G4 Church Lawford Warwks
291 G3 Church Lawton Ches
273 F2 Church Leigh Staffs
189 F4 Church Lench Worcs
293 G6 Church Mayfield Staffs
290 D2 Church Minshull Ches
209 G2 Churchmoor Rough Shrops
53 F5 Church Norton W Susx
91 F4 Church Oakley Hants
216 B3 Churchover Warwks
234 C5 Church Preen Shrops
234 A4 Church Pulverbatch Shrops
43 G5 Churchstanton Somset
233 E6 Churchstoke Shrops
12 C3 Churchstow Devon
192 D3 Church Stowe Nhants
199 F6 Church Street Essex
121 H5 Church Street Kent
234 B6 Church Stretton Shrops
126 C3 Churchton Pembks
6 C5 Church Town Cnwll
15 F3 Churchtown Cnwll
390 B1 Churchtown Cumb
294 B2 Churchtown Derbys
23 F2 Churchtown Devon
61 G3 Churchtown Devon
239 F1 Church Town Leics
331 G3 Churchtown N Linc
337 G6 Churchtown Sefton
351 G6 Churchtown Sefton
209 E2 Churchtown Shrops
63 F4 Church Town Somset
95 H4 Church Town Surrey

105 H2 Church Village Rhondd
315 H6 Church Warsop Notts
164 C5 Church Westcote Gloucs
83 F1 Church Whitfield Kent
275 G3 Church Wilne Derbys
75 G6 Churchwood W Susx
292 C4 Churnet Grange Staffs
20 B5 Churscombe Torbay
13 G1 Churston Ferrers Torbay
74 D2 Churt Surrey
289 F3 Churton Ches
89 H4 Chute Cadley Wilts
89 H4 Chute Standen Wilts
306 A5 Chwefforrdd Conwy
263 G3 Chwilog Gwynd
3 E3 Chyandour Cnwll
4 C4 Chyanvounder Cnwll
7 E6 Chycoose Cnwll
4 B2 Chynhale Cnwll
3 F3 Chynoweth Cnwll
4 C4 Chyvarloe Cnwll
134 C4 Cicelyford Mons
262 D6 Cilan Uchaf Gwynd
151 F2 Cilau Pembks
288 A2 Cilcain Flints
180 D2 Cilcennin Cerdgn
232 D4 Cilcewydd Powys
130 B4 Cilfrew Neath
106 A1 Cilfynydd Rhondd
178 D5 Cilgerran Pembks
156 A4 Cilgwyn Carmth
153 G1 Cilgwyn Cerdgn
283 E5 Cilgwyn Gwynd
180 D3 Ciliau-Aeron Cerdgn
593 D8 Cill Amhlaidh W Isls
590 E2 Cill Donnain W Isls
590 F5 Cille Bhrighde W Isls
593 E8 Cill Eireabhagh W Isls
590 E4 Cille Pheadair W Isls
130 A3 Cilmaengwyn Neath
183 G4 Cilmery Powys
155 E5 Cilsan Carmth
158 C1 Ciltwrch Powys
153 E2 Cilwendeg Pembks
130 A4 Cilybebyll Neath
156 B2 Cilycwm Carmth
263 E5 Cim Gwynd
130 B5 Cimla Neath
135 F2 Cinderford Gloucs
325 H3 Cinder Hill Bolton
295 G6 Cinderhill C Nott
294 D5 Cinderhill Derbys
96 D5 Cinder Hill Kent
236 D6 Cinder Hill Wolves
77 G4 Cinder Hill W Susx
310 C1 Cinnamon Brow Warrtn
117 F3 Cippenham Slough
178 C4 Cippyn Pembks
598 D8 Circebost W Isls
137 F4 Cirencester Gloucs
598 E6 Ciribhig W Isls
208 D2 City Powys
1 G4 City V Glam
303 G3 City Dulas IoA
516 F4 Clabhach Ag & B
481 G3 Clachaig Ag & B
551 J6 Clachaig Highld
462 C3 Clachan Ag & B
494 D2 Clachan Ag & B
506 C6 Clachan Ag & B
519 L7 Clachan Ag & B
543 H3 Clachan Highld
545 J2 Clachan Highld
574 D7 Clachan Highld
586 F4 Clachan Highld
593 D8 Clachan W Isls
516 B6 Clachan Mòr Ag & B
408 B2 Clachanmore D & G
592 D5 Clachan na Luib W Isls
484 C4 Clachan of Campsie E Duns
480 D3 Clachan of Glendaruel Ag & B
506 C6 Clachan-Seil Ag & B
479 K6 Clachbreck Ag & B
565 L7 Clachnaharry Highld
578 D4 Clachtoll Highld
486 B1 Clackmannan Clacks
568 C4 Clackmarras Moray
149 G2 Clacton-on-Sea Essex
461 E2 Cladach N Ayrs
592 E5 Cladach a' Bhaile Shear W Isls
592 D4 Cladach Chireboist W Isls
592 A4 Cladach Chnoc a Lin W Isls
592 D5 Cladach Iolaraigh W Isls
476 B6 Claddach Ag & B
507 J5 Cladich Ag & B
189 F3 Cladswell Worcs
519 G6 Claggan Highld
533 H8 Claggan Highld
542 C6 Claigan Highld
188 B3 Claines Worcs
584 C7 Claisfearn Highld
17 F6 Clamoak Devon
86 B3 Clandown BaNES
52 C1 Clanfield Hants
138 C4 Clanfield Oxon
141 H3 Clanking Bucks
89 H5 Clanville Hants
67 G3 Clanville Somset
111 G4 Clanville Wilts
408 B4 Clanyard D & G
463 E3 Claonaig Ag & B
576 C3 Claonel Highld
48 C4 Clapgate Dorset
171 F5 Clapgate Herts
195 E4 Clapham Beds
26 D5 Clapham Devon
119 F4 Clapham Gt Lon
367 E6 Clapham N York
54 C3 Clapham W Susx
195 E4 Clapham Green Beds
356 A3 Clapham Green N York
100 B3 Clapham Hill Kent
119 F5 Clapham Park Gt Lon
81 G2 Clap Hill Kent
15 E4 Clapper Cnwll
80 B2 Clapper Hill Kent
474 D3 Clappers Border
378 C4 Clappersgate Cumb
605 H5 Clapphoull Shet
29 H1 Clapton Somset
86 A4 Clapton Somset
114 B5 Clapton W Berk
109 H5 Clapton in Gordano N Som
164 B6 Clapton-on-the-Hill Gloucs
119 H2 Clapton Park Gt Lon
40 D3 Clapworthy Devon
205 E3 Clarach Cerdgn
404 C2 Clara Vale Gatesd
152 A5 Clarbeston Pembks
151 H5 Clarbeston Road Pembks
316 D3 Clarborough Notts
588 E3 Clardon Highld
141 E5 Clare Oxon
199 F5 Clare Suffk
413 E1 Clarebrand D & G
236 C4 Claregate Wolves
94 C2 Claremont Park Surrey
424 B6 Clarencefield D & G
84 B2 Clarence Park N Som
240 C4 Clarendon Park C Leic
125 F2 Clareston Pembks

451 H4 Clarilaw Border
91 F4 Clarken Green Hants
312 B4 Clark Green Ches
326 D3 Clarksfield Oldham
76 C2 Clark's Green Surrey
281 E5 Clark's Hill Lincs
189 F6 Clark's Hill Worcs
189 F6 Clark's Hill Worcs
467 E3 Clarkston E Rens
468 B1 Clarkston N Lans
129 E3 Clase Swans
565 J7 Clashandorran Highld
558 B3 Clashindarroch Abers
576 F6 Clashmore Highld
578 B2 Clashmore Highld
578 B3 Clashnessie Highld
552 E4 Clashnoir Moray
607 H5 Clate Shet
112 D6 Clatford Wilts
71 G2 Clatford Oakcuts Hants
512 A5 Clathy P & K
558 C4 Clatt Abers
231 F6 Clatter Powys
36 D3 Clatterford IoW
146 A4 Clatterford End Essex
146 B3 Clatterford End Essex
146 C2 Clatterford End Essex
540 C4 Clatterin' Brig Abers
502 C1 Clatto Fife
63 H5 Clatworthy Somset
461 E3 Clauchlands N Ayrs
338 D1 Claughton Lancs
352 B1 Claughton Lancs
308 D2 Claughton Wirral
65 E5 Clavelshay Somset
190 B2 Claverdon Warwks
84 D1 Claverham N Som
145 F4 Claverhambury Essex
171 G3 Clavering Essex
236 A6 Claverley Shrops
86 D2 Claverton BaNES
86 D2 Claverton Down BaNES
105 H4 Clawdd-côch V Glam
287 F4 Clawdd-newydd Denbgs
287 F6 Clawdd Poncen Denbgs
366 A4 Clawthorpe Cumb
23 G3 Clawton Devon
333 G6 Claxby Lincs
320 D5 Claxby St Andrew Lincs
250 C4 Claxton Norfk
358 C2 Claxton N York
216 A2 Claybrooke Magna Leics
216 A2 Claybrooke Parva Leics
227 F3 Clay Common Suffk
216 C4 Clay Coton Nhants
294 D2 Clay Cross Derbys
162 D3 Claydon Gloucs
201 F5 Claydon Suffk
170 C4 Clay End Herts
426 A4 Claygate D & G
97 F4 Claygate Kent
97 H6 Claygate Kent
94 D2 Claygate Surrey
97 F3 Claygate Cross Kent
120 B1 Clayhall Gt Lon
51 H5 Clayhall Hants
42 D3 Clayhanger Devon
44 C5 Clayhanger Somset
237 F4 Clayhanger Wsall
43 G4 Clayhidon Devon
109 H5 Clay Hill Bristl
80 B5 Clayhill E Susx
144 D5 Clayhall Gt Lon
50 B3 Clayhill Hants
115 F5 Clay Hill W Berk
197 H2 Clayhithe Cambs
515 E2 Clayholes Angus
280 B5 Clay Lake Lincs
484 A2 Clayland Stirlg
274 D4 Clay Mills Staffs
588 F5 Clayock Highld
566 E1 Clay of Allan Highld
197 E4 Claypit Hill Cambs
42 C2 Claypits Devon
135 H3 Claypits Gloucs
100 D4 Claypits Kent
223 E3 Claypits Suffk
297 F5 Claypole Lincs
86 C2 Clays End BaNES
320 D4 Claythorpe Lincs
329 H3 Clayton Donc
342 B3 Clayton Donc
514 C6 Clayton Fife
326 C5 Clayton Manch
291 G6 Clayton Staffs
55 H2 Clayton W Susx
339 E5 Clayton Brook Lancs
339 E5 Clayton Green Lancs
342 B3 Clayton Heights Brad
339 G3 Clayton Le Dale Lancs
339 E5 Clayton-le-moors Lancs
339 E5 Clayton-le-Woods Lancs
328 D2 Clayton West Kirk
316 D2 Clayworth Notts
530 E5 Cleadale Highld
406 B2 Cleadon S Tyne
406 B2 Cleadon Park S Tyne
18 B4 Clearbrook Devon
134 D3 Clearwell Gloucs
106 D2 Clearwell Newpt
87 E5 Clearwood Wilts
383 G2 Cleasby N York
601 H8 Cleat Ork
394 C6 Cleatlam Dur
376 C2 Cleator Cumb
376 C1 Cleator Moor Cumb
28 D2 Cleave Devon
580 E3 Clebrig Highld
342 C5 Cleckheaton Kirk
134 C4 Cleddon Mons
210 D3 Cleedownton Shrops
210 D5 Cleehill Shrops
468 B3 Cleekhimin N Lans
210 D3 Cleemarsh Shrops
210 D3 Clee St Margaret Shrops
334 D3 Cleethorpes NE Lin
211 E4 Cleeton St Mary Shrops
135 G2 Cleeve Gloucs
85 E1 Cleeve N Som
115 G3 Cleeve Oxon
163 E4 Cleeve Hill Gloucs
189 G5 Cleeve Prior Worcs
469 E6 Cleghorn S Lans
160 B2 Clehonger Herefs
506 F4 Cleigh Ag & B
500 A5 Cleish P & K
468 B3 Cleland N Lans
143 E1 Clement's End Beds
134 D3 Clements End Gloucs
120 D5 Clement Street Kent
109 H3 Clench Wilts
89 E1 Clench Common Wilts
161 G2 Clencher's Mill Herefs
252 B3 Clenchwarton Norfk
442 A3 Clennell Nthumb
212 D4 Clent Worcs
211 F4 Cleobury Mortimer Shrops
211 E3 Cleobury North Shrops
458 D5 Cleongart Ag & B
566 E6 Clephanton Highld
15 F5 Clerkenwater Cnwll
342 D5 Clerk Green Kirk
571 L6 Clerkhill Abers

451 G5 Clerklands Border
487 G6 Clermiston C Edin
600 D3 Clestrain Ork
440 A2 Cleuch Head Border
424 B5 Cleughbrae D & G
112 B5 Clevancy Wilts
465 H1 Clevans Rens
108 C5 Clevedon Bristl
165 F5 Cleveley Oxon
350 C6 Cleveleys Lancs
112 A2 Cleverton Wilts
84 D4 Clewer Somset
117 F4 Clewer Green W & M
117 F4 Clewer New Town W & M
117 F4 Clewer Village W & M
260 D3 Cley next the Sea Norfk
591 D7 Cliaid W Isls
596 D6 Cliasmaol W Isls
609 J2 Clibberswick Shet
391 F5 Cliburn Cumb
91 G5 Cliddesden Hants
312 D2 Cliff Derbys
519 G2 Cliff Highld
238 C5 Cliff Warwks
515 H1 Cliffburn Angus
340 A3 Cliffe Lancs
122 A4 Cliffe Medway
345 F3 Cliffe N York
383 F1 Cliffe N York
59 E4 Cliff End E Susx
122 A5 Cliffe Woods Medway
38 D3 Clifford Devon
184 D5 Clifford Herefs
357 E6 Clifford Leeds
190 B4 Clifford Chambers Warwks
161 G5 Clifford's Mesne Gloucs
101 F3 Cliffs End Kent
122 D2 Clifton Sthend
169 H2 Clifton Beds
109 G5 Clifton Bristl
342 C5 Clifton Calder
309 H4 Clifton Ches
276 C3 Clifton C Nott
391 E4 Clifton Cumb
293 G6 Clifton Derbys
61 F3 Clifton Donc
330 B5 Clifton Donc
338 C3 Clifton Nthumb
314 D3 Clifton Nthumb
395 G5 Clifton N York
132 C3 Clifton Oxon
447 F3 Clifton Rothm
325 H4 Clifton Salfd
508 D3 Clifton Stirlg
188 B5 Clifton Worcs
358 A4 Clifton York
238 D2 Clifton Campville Staffs
326 A4 Clifton Green Salfd
140 B5 Clifton Hampden Oxon
326 A4 Clifton Junction Salfd
46 A2 Clifton Maybank Dorset
358 A3 Clifton Moor York
194 C4 Clifton Reynes M Keyn
216 B4 Clifton upon Dunsmore Warwks
187 G2 Clifton upon Teme Worcs
101 G1 Cliftonville Kent
468 A2 Cliftonville N Lans
256 C2 Cliftonville Norfk
54 A4 Climping W Susx
324 C5 Clinkham Wood St Hel
356 B3 Clint N York
557 E2 Clinterty C Aber
248 D3 Clint Green Norfk
452 B3 Clintmains Border
382 C4 Clints N York
598 B7 Cliobh W Isls
230 C2 Clipiau Gwynd
251 E2 Clippesby Norfk
248 D2 Clippings Green Norfk
242 D1 Clipsham Rutlnd
217 F3 Clipston Nhants
276 D3 Clipston Notts
168 C4 Clipstone Beds
296 A2 Clipstone Notts
340 B1 Clitheroe Lancs
169 H2 Cliton Manor Beds
595 J4 Cliuthar W Isls
290 D1 Clive Ches
270 C5 Clive Shrops
290 D2 Clive Green Ches
58 D4 Clive Vale E Susx
609 J4 Clivocast Shet
333 G4 Clixby Lincs
112 A1 Cloatley Wilts
112 A1 Cloatley End Wilts
287 F4 Clocaenog Denbgs
569 G3 Clochan Moray
309 H1 Clock Face St Hel
160 B2 Clock House Gt Lon
185 E5 Clock Mills Herefs
232 D3 Cloddiau Powys
567 H4 Cloddymoss Moray
159 F4 Clodock Herefs
86 C6 Cloford Somset
86 C6 Cloford Common Somset
285 G3 Clogwyn Cyrrau Conwy
128 B2 Cloigyn Carmth
571 J7 Clola Abers
232 C2 Clolyn Powys
169 F2 Clophill Beds
219 F3 Clopton Nhants
201 H4 Clopton Suffk
202 A3 Clopton Corner Suffk
199 F4 Clopton Green Suffk
200 C3 Clopton Green Suffk
35 d1 Clos du Val Guern
423 E1 Closeburn D & G
436 B6 Closeburnmill D & G
322 d7 Closeclark IoM
395 E4 Close House N York
45 H5 Closworth Somset
170 C3 Clothall Herts
170 C3 Clothall Common Herts
607 G1 Clothan Shet
289 H2 Clotton Ches
290 A2 Clotton Common Ches
215 H2 Cloudesley Bush Warwks
160 D2 Clouds Herefs
292 B2 Cloud Side Staffs
327 G2 Clough Kirk
326 D3 Clough Oldham
326 D1 Clough Rochdl
405 E3 Clough Dene Dur
340 C5 Cloughfold Lancs
341 E5 Clough Foot Calder
291 G4 Clough Hall Staffs
341 H5 Clough Head Calder
327 G1 Cloughton N York
387 G6 Cloughton Newlands N York
606 D6 Clousta Shet
600 D2 Clouston Ork
558 B5 Clova Abers
538 C5 Clova Angus
38 D3 Clovelly Devon
451 E2 Clovenfords Border
559 H6 Clovenstone Abers
520 D3 Clovullin Highld
4 B2 Clowance Wood Cnwll
181 H5 Clows Top Worcs
211 G3 Cloy Wrexhm

289 E6 Cloy Wrexhm
323 G6 Clubmoor Lpool
23 F4 Clubworthy Cnwll
235 E2 Cluddley Wrekin
209 E3 Clun Shrops
209 G3 Clunbury Shrops
152 C6 Clunderwen Carmth
550 D4 Clune Highld
533 K5 Clunes Highld
209 H4 Clungunford Shrops
525 H7 Clunie P & K
509 F3 Clunton Shrops
500 D5 Cluny Fife
86 A3 Clutton BaNES
289 G4 Clutton Ches
86 A3 Clutton Hill BaNES
284 C2 Clwt-y-bont Gwynd
131 G3 Clwydyfagwyr Myr Td
132 D2 Clydach Mons
129 G4 Clydach Swans
132 G2 Clydach Terrace Blae G
131 F6 Clydach Vale Rhondd
483 G6 Clydebank W Duns
112 C4 Clyffe Pypard Wilts
482 B3 Clynder Ag & B
130 C4 Clyne Neath
577 J2 Clynelish Highld
282 D6 Clynnog-Fawr Gwynd
184 D6 Clyro Powys
27 F4 Clyst Honiton Devon
27 F4 Clyst Hydon Devon
27 F5 Clyst St George Devon
27 G2 Clyst St Lawrence Devon
27 F4 Clyst St Mary Devon
583 J2 Clyth Highld
133 G3 Clytha Mons
133 G3 Clytha Park Mons
598 B7 Cnip W Isls
592 B4 Cnoc a' Lin W Isls
599 L7 Cnoc Amhlaigh W Isls
592 C4 Cnoc an Torrain W Isls
599 K6 Cnoc an t-Solais W Isls
478 D7 Cnocbreac Ag & B
599 H8 Cnoc Màiri W Isls
599 J8 Cnoc nan Gobhar W Isls
565 L2 Cnoc Ruadh Highld
205 F5 Cnwch Coch Cerdgn
16 C3 Coad's Green Cnwll
314 D3 Coal Aston Derbys
395 G5 Coal Bank Darltn
132 C3 Coalbrookvale Blae G
447 F3 Coalburn S Lans
404 D2 Coalburns Gatesd
403 E5 Coalcleugh Nthumb
135 H4 Coaley Gloucs
136 A4 Coaley Peak Gloucs
557 E5 Coalford Abers
445 F6 Coalhall E Ayrs
147 E5 Coalhill Essex
235 F3 Coalmoor Wrekin
215 F2 Coalpit Field Warwks
110 B3 Coalpit Heath S Glos
291 G4 Coalpit Hill Staffs
237 F4 Coal Pool Wsall
499 E5 Coalsnaughton Clacks
501 E5 Coaltown of Balgonie Fife
501 F3 Coaltown of Burnturk Fife
501 F5 Coaltown of Wemyss Fife
239 G2 Coalville Leics
134 D2 Coalway Gloucs
402 B3 Coanwood Nthumb
66 C5 Coarsewell Devon
66 C5 Coat Somset
467 H2 Coatbridge N Lans
468 B2 Coatdyke N Lans
113 E3 Coate Swindn
88 B2 Coate Wilts
244 D5 Coates Cambs
137 E4 Coates Gloucs
354 A5 Coates Lancs
470 D2 Coates Mdloth
317 F3 Coates Notts
317 H3 Coates Notts
75 F6 Coates W Susx
397 E4 Coatham R & Cl
395 F6 Coatham Mundeville Darltn
437 E3 Coatsgate D & G
29 F4 Cobb Dorset
40 C2 Cobbaton Devon
187 H3 Cobbler's Corner Worcs
226 B1 Cobbler's Green Norfk
146 B2 Cobbler's Pieces Essex
134 B4 Cobbler's Plain Mons
310 C2 Cobbs Warrtn
161 H3 Cobb's Cross Gloucs
173 F3 Cobbs Fenn Essex
355 G3 Cobby Syke N York
137 E1 Coberley Gloucs
160 B2 Cobhall Common Herefs
121 G6 Cobham Kent
94 C2 Cobham Surrey
121 G6 Cobham Park Kent
251 E2 Cobholm Island Norfk
172 D6 Cobler's Green Essex
69 H5 Cobley Dorset
213 F5 Cobley Hill Worcs
186 B2 Cobnash Herefs
34 c2 Cobo Guern
292 A5 Cobridge C Stke
271 F2 Cobscot Shrops
199 E4 Cock & End Suffk
315 E5 Cock Alley Derbys
385 G5 Cockayne N York
196 C5 Cockayne Hatley Beds
288 D5 Cock Bank Wrexhm
189 F4 Cock Bevington Warwks
552 E7 Cock Bridge Abers
491 E5 Cockburnspath Border
147 G4 Cock Clarks Essex
340 D3 Cockden Lancs
488 D4 Cockenzie and Port Seton E Loth
338 C5 Cocker Bar Lancs
351 G4 Cockerham Lancs
388 D3 Cockermouth Cumb
169 G5 Cockernhoe Herts
342 D4 Cockersdale Leeds
383 G1 Cockerton Darltn
103 F3 Cockett Swans
394 C5 Cockfield Dur
200 B4 Cockfield Suffk
120 A4 Cockfosters Gt Lon
186 B1 Cock Gate Herefs
172 D6 Cock Green Essex
357 G3 Cock Hill N York
67 G3 Cockhill Somset
53 F1 Cocking W Susx
74 D6 Cocking Causeway W Susx
20 B5 Cockington Torbay
84 D5 Cocklake Somset
137 E2 Cockleford Gloucs
377 G4 Cockley Beck Cumb
247 H4 Cockley Cley Norfk
342 C6 Cockley Hill Kirk
59 E3 Cock Marling E Susx
33 G3 Cocknowle Dorset
116 C3 Cockpole Green Wokham
7 E3 Cocks Cnwll
199 H3 Cocks Green Suffk
181 F5 Cockshead Cerdgn
160 D2 Cockshoot Herefs
210 D3 Cockshutford Shrops
271 G3 Cockshutt Shrops

270 A4 Cockshutt Shrops
98 B4 Cock Street Kent
174 C2 Cock Street Suffk
260 C3 Cockthorpe Norfk
3 F3 Cockwells Cnwll
20 D1 Cockwood Devon
64 D3 Cockwood Somset
312 D4 Cockyard Derbys
159 H3 Cockyard Herefs
201 F4 Coddenham Suffk
201 F3 Coddenham Green Suffk
289 F3 Coddington Ches
161 G1 Coddington Herefs
297 F4 Coddington Notts
69 G2 Codford St Mary Wilts
69 G1 Codford St Peter Wilts
170 B6 Codicote Herts
170 B6 Codicote Bottom Herts
142 D4 Codmore Bucks
75 G5 Codmore Hill W Susx
295 E5 Codnor Derbys
295 E5 Codnor Breach Derbys
295 E4 Codnor Gate Derbys
295 E4 Codnor Park Derbys
110 C4 Codrington S Glos
236 C4 Codsall Staffs
236 B4 Codsall Wood Staffs
62 D4 Codsend Somset
132 D3 Coedcae Torfn
133 E3 Coedcae Torfn
133 H5 Coed Cwnwr Mons
285 G3 Coedcynhelier Conwy
105 G2 Coedely Rhondd
133 E6 Coed Eva Torfn
104 C3 Coed Hirwaun Neath
107 E3 Coedkernew Newpt
304 C5 Coed Mawr Gwynd
133 F2 Coed Morgan Mons
288 C4 Coedpoeth Wrexhm
288 C3 Coed-talon Flints
233 F2 Coedway Powys
179 G4 Coed-y-bryn Cerdgn
108 C1 Coed-y-caerau Newpt
134 A3 Coed-y-fedw Mons
229 F6 Coed y Garth Cerdgn
269 E4 Coed y go Gwynd
133 F5 Coed-y-paen Mons
284 D1 Coed-y-parc Gwynd
158 C5 Coed-yr-ynys Powys
264 D5 Coed Ystumgwern Gwynd
232 D3 Coed-y-wlad Powys
130 C2 Coelbren Powys
168 B2 Coffee Hall M Keyn
20 B4 Coffinswell Devon
20 D1 Cofton Devon
213 F4 Cofton Common Birm
213 F4 Cofton Hackett Worcs
106 C6 Cog V Glam
106 C5 Cogan V Glam
193 H2 Cogenhoe Nhants
139 F3 Cogges Oxon
173 G5 Coggeshall Essex
173 H5 Coggeshall Hamlet Essex
79 E4 Coggins Mill E Susx
599 L1 Coig Peighinnean W Isls
599 H3 Coig Peighinnean Bhuirgh W Isls
554 B5 Coilacriech Abers
497 E3 Coilantogle Stirlg
507 H5 Coillaig Ag & B
590 F5 Coilleag W Isls
533 G2 Coille Mhorgil Highld
544 F2 Coillore Highld
597 G1 Coire an Fhuarain W Isls
315 E3 Coisley Hill Sheff
105 E3 Coity Brdgnd
171 E2 Cokenach Herts
274 D4 Cokhay Green Derbys
599 K7 Col W Isls
580 F7 Colaboll Highld
7 G1 Colan Cnwll
27 H5 Colaton Raleigh Devon
542 C7 Colbost Highld
383 E5 Colburn N York
391 H5 Colby Cumb
322 c8 Colby IoM
261 H5 Colby Norfk
174 D3 Colchester Essex
200 B3 Colchester Green Suffk
106 B6 Colcot V Glam
115 E5 Cold Ash W Berk
217 E4 Cold Ashby Nhants
74 C3 Cold Ash Hill Hants
110 D5 Cold Ashton S Glos
163 H6 Cold Aston Gloucs
586 B6 Coldbackie Highld
120 C5 Coldblow Gt Lon
98 C3 Coldblow Kent
126 C2 Cold Blow Pembks
194 C4 Cold Brayfield M Keyn
158 C2 Coldbrook Powys
145 E1 Cold Christmas Herts
367 E5 Cold Cotes N York
56 A3 Coldean Br & H
19 H2 Coldeast Devon
293 F3 Coldeaton Derbys
162 B3 Cold Elm Worcs
341 F4 Colden Calder
72 C5 Colden Common Hants
203 E2 Coldfair Green Suffk
245 F4 Coldham Cambs
236 C3 Coldham Staffs
197 G3 Coldham's Common Cambs
318 C3 Cold Hanworth Lincs
6 D4 Cold Harbour Cnwll
43 E5 Coldharbour Devon
32 A3 Cold Harbour Dorset
33 F2 Cold Harbour Dorset
134 D4 Coldharbour Gloucs
120 D4 Cold Harbour Gt Lon
143 G1 Coldharbour Herts
97 E4 Coldharbour Kent
98 C3 Coldharbour Kent
98 D1 Cold Harbour Kent
278 D3 Cold Harbour Lincs
94 C6 Coldharbour Surrey
115 G4 Cold Harbour W & M
116 A3 Cold Harbour W & M
87 F3 Cold Harbour Wilts
87 F3 Coldharbour Wilts
271 E5 Cold Hatton Wrekin
271 E5 Cold Hatton Heath Wrekin
406 C5 Cold Hesledon Dur
329 F2 Cold Hiendley Wakefd
193 E4 Cold Higham Nhants
474 D2 Coldingham Border
126 C3 Cold Inn Pembks
272 C3 Cold Kirby N York
291 F2 Coldmeece Staffs
241 F3 Cold Moss Heath Ches
241 F3 Cold Newton Leics
22 D5 Cold Northcott Cnwll
147 H4 Cold Norton Essex
497 E3 Coldoch Stirlg
241 H2 Cold Overton Leics
108 C2 Coldra Newpt
500 A4 Coldrain P & K
83 E1 Coldred Kent
25 G1 Coldridge Devon
351 E6 Cold Row Lancs
514 B2 Coldstream Angus
453 F2 Coldstream Border
8 B2 Coldvreath Cnwll

54 B1 Coldwaltham W Susx
237 G2 Cold Well Staffs
561 H1 Coldwells Abers
558 D5 Coldwells Croft Abers
67 H3 Cole Somset
209 F2 Colebatch Shrops
27 G1 Colebrook Devon
26 B3 Colebrooke Devon
298 B2 Coleby Lincs
346 C6 Coleby N Linc
172 B2 Cole End Essex
214 C2 Cole End Warwks
26 B2 Coleford Devon
134 D2 Coleford Gloucs
86 B5 Coleford Somset
64 B5 Coleford Water Somset
225 G2 Colegate End Norfk
171 F3 Cole Green Herts
214 A2 Colehall Birm
90 D4 Cole Henley Hants
48 C4 Colehill Dorset
144 A2 Coleman Green Herts
78 B3 Coleman's Hatch E Susx
270 A3 Colemere Shrops
73 H3 Colemore Hants
235 G5 Colemore Green Shrops
275 F6 Coleorton Leics
239 G1 Coleorton Moor Leics
118 D5 Cole Park Gt Lon
111 E5 Colerne Wilts
137 E2 Colesbourne Gloucs
68 C4 Colesbrook Dorset
12 D3 Cole's Cross Devon
29 G2 Cole's Cross Dorset
195 G3 Colesden Beds
175 E1 Coles Green Suffk
202 B2 Cole's Green Suffk
187 H4 Coles Green Worcs
142 C5 Coleshill Bucks
138 C6 Coleshill Oxon
214 C2 Coleshill Warwks
95 F4 Coles Meads Surrey
28 A2 Colestocks Devon
136 B2 Colethrop Gloucs
85 G3 Coley BaNES
342 B4 Coley Calder
116 B5 Coley Readg
76 D3 Colgate W Susx
482 D3 Colgrain Ag & B
118 B3 Colham Green Gt Lon
119 E2 Coindale Gt Lon
502 D4 Colinsburgh Fife
487 H6 Colinton C Edin
481 E5 Colintraive Ag & B
254 B2 Colkirk Norfk
513 F3 Collace P & K
135 F2 Collafield Gloucs
606 H4 Collafirth Shet
608 C8 Collafirth Shet
595 J4 Collam W Isls
22 A1 Collamoor Head Cnwll
12 C5 Collaton Devon
20 B5 Collaton St Mary Torbay
467 F3 College Milton S Lans
567 L3 College of Roseisle Moray
93 E2 College Town Br For
444 D3 Collennan S Ayrs
501 E2 Collessie Fife
40 D4 Colleton Mills Devon
245 G3 Collett's Br Cambs
188 B4 Collett's Green Worcs
120 C1 Collier Row Gt Lon
58 C2 Collier's Green E Susx
145 H4 Colliers Hatch Essex
97 H5 Collier Street Kent
119 F5 Collier's Wood Gt Lon
406 A5 Colliery Row Sundld
561 F4 Collieston Abers
424 A4 Collin D & G
89 F4 Collingbourne Ducis Wilts
89 F3 Collingbourne Kingston Wilts
356 D5 Collingham Leeds
297 F2 Collingham Notts
187 E2 Collington Herefs
193 F3 Collingtree Nhants
193 F3 Collingtree Park Nhants
431 E4 Collingwood Nthumb
115 H4 Collins End Oxon
324 D6 Collins Green Warrtn
187 G3 Collins Green Worcs
42 C5 Collipriest Devon
528 C5 Colliston Angus
28 A2 Colliton Devon
28 A2 Colliton Cross Devon
215 F2 Collycroft Warwks
501 E4 Collydean Fife
326 B5 Collyhurst Manch
560 B2 Collynie Abers
242 D4 Collyweston Nhants
418 D4 Colmonell S Ayrs
451 G2 Colmslie Border
451 G1 Colmsliehill Border
195 F3 Colmworth Beds
554 A3 Colnabaichin Abers
117 H4 Colnbrook Slough
221 E4 Colne Cambs
340 D2 Colne Lancs
340 D1 Colne Edge Lancs
173 H3 Colne Engaine Essex
221 E4 Colnefields Cambs
249 G3 Colney Norfk
119 F1 Colney Hatch Gt Lon
137 G3 Coln Rogers Gloucs
138 A3 Coln St Aldwyns Gloucs
137 G3 Coln St Dennis Gloucs
570 C6 Colp Abers
404 A3 Colpitts Grange Nthumb
559 E3 Colpy Abers
39 E5 Colscott Devon
312 D6 Colshaw Staffs
369 F3 Colsterdale N York
278 C5 Colsterworth Lincs
19 G5 Colston Devon
484 B6 Colston E Duns
151 G4 Colston Pembks
277 F3 Colston Bassett Notts
116 C2 Colstrope Bucks
567 L4 Coltfield Moray
92 B4 Colt Hill Hants
378 C5 Colthouse Cumb
91 E1 Colthrop W Berk
256 B5 Coltishall Norfk
468 C3 Coltness N Lans
364 D2 Colton Cumb
343 G3 Colton Leeds
249 F3 Colton Norfk
357 G6 Colton N York
273 F5 Colton Staffs
199 H1 Colton Suffk
236 D5 Colton Hills Wolves
364 C5 Colt Park Cumb
110 C3 Colt's Green S Glos
97 F6 Colt's Hill Kent
599 K7 Col Uarach W Isls
405 H3 Columbia Sundld
27 F3 Columbjohn Devon
184 D4 Colva Powys
413 G4 Colvend D & G
609 G5 Colvister Shet
161 G1 Colwall Herefs
161 H1 Colwall Green Herefs
161 H1 Colwall Stone Herefs
35 H3 Colwell IoW

429 E4 Colwell Nthumb
273 F5 Colwich Staffs
276 D1 Colwick Notts
105 E4 Colwinston V Glam
53 G4 Colworth W Susx
194 D2 Colworth Ho Beds
306 B4 Colwyn Bay Conwy
29 E4 Colyford Devon
28 D4 Colyton Devon
441 E6 Comb Nthumb
11 F3 Combe Devon
12 C5 Combe Devon
19 F4 Combe Devon
79 E4 Combe E Susx
185 F2 Combe Herefs
139 G1 Combe Oxon
66 C4 Combe Somset
90 B2 Combe W Berk
48 B5 Combe Almer Dorset
24 C5 Combebow Devon
75 E2 Combe Common Surrey
86 D2 Combe Down BaNES
20 A5 Combe Fishacre Devon
64 B5 Combe Florey Somset
86 C3 Combe Hay Somset
20 C3 Combeinteignhead Devon
61 E2 Combe Martin Devon
185 G2 Combe Moor Herefs
20 C4 Combe Pafford Torbay
28 C2 Combe Raleigh Devon
310 C4 Comberbach Ches
238 B3 Comberford Staffs
197 E3 Comberton Cambs
186 B1 Comberton Herefs
212 B4 Comberton Worcs
44 C5 Combe St Nicholas Somset
68 B5 Combe Throop Somset
29 E4 Combpyne Devon
60 D5 Combrew Devon
273 G2 Combridge Staffs
191 E4 Combrook Warwks
312 D4 Combs Derbys
342 D6 Combs Kirk
200 D3 Combs Suffk
201 E3 Combs Ford Suffk
64 D3 Combwich Somset
556 B3 Comers Abers
6 D6 Come-to-Good Cnwll
43 G3 Comeytrowe Somset
6 D6 Comford Cnwll
4 D3 Comfort Cnwll
188 B1 Comhampton Worcs
205 E3 Comins Coch Cerdgn
488 A6 Comiston C Edin
234 B5 Comley Shrops
198 A2 Commercial End Cambs
287 G2 Commins Denbgs
230 C4 Commins Coch Powys
133 F6 Common Cefn-llwyn Mons
385 G2 Commondale N York
337 F3 Common Edge Lancs
388 B5 Common End Cumb
295 E2 Common End Derbys
160 D3 Common Hill Herefs
16 B5 Common Moor Cnwll
112 D2 Common Platt Wilts
290 B1 Common Side Ches
310 A5 Commonside Ches
274 C1 Commonside Derbys
295 E5 Common Side Derbys
314 C4 Common Side Derbys
295 F3 Commonside Notts
143 E4 Commonwood Herts
270 B4 Commonwood Shrops
289 E4 Commonwood Wrexhm
108 D2 Common-y-coed Mons
97 F3 Comp Kent
65 E5 Compass Somset
312 C1 Compstall Stockp
11 E2 Compton C Plym
293 G5 Compton Derbys
20 B5 Compton Devon
71 G4 Compton Hants
72 C4 Compton Hants
356 D6 Compton Leeds
93 E5 Compton Surrey
93 G5 Compton Surrey
115 E3 Compton W Berk
88 D4 Compton Wilts
212 B3 Compton Wolves
236 C5 Compton Wolves
52 D2 Compton W Susx
69 E6 Compton Abbas Dorset
137 G1 Compton Abdale Gloucs
112 B5 Compton Bassett Wilts
113 G2 Compton Beauchamp Oxon
84 C3 Compton Bishop Somset
69 H4 Compton Chamberlayne Wilts
86 A2 Compton Common BaNES
86 A2 Compton Dando BaNES
66 D3 Compton Dundon Somset
66 C6 Compton Durville Somset
72 C4 Compton End Hants
161 G2 Compton Green Gloucs
109 G3 Compton Greenfield S Glos
85 F3 Compton Martin BaNES
67 G4 Compton Pauncefoot Somset
30 D4 Compton Valence Dorset
486 D2 Comrie Fife
510 D5 Comrie P & K
330 A5 Conanby Rothm
481 E2 Conchra Ag & B
405 H3 Concord Sundld
314 D1 Concord Park Sheff
525 G7 Concraigie P & K
351 G3 Conder Green Lancs
163 E2 Conderton Worcs
164 A4 Condicote Gloucs
485 E5 Condorrat N Lans
234 B3 Condover Shrops
30 B4 Coneygar Dorset
96 A2 Coney Hall Gt Lon
136 B1 Coney Hill Gloucs
78 B5 Coneyhurst W Susx
372 C5 Coneysthorpe N York
356 D3 Coneythorpe N York
224 B4 Coney Weston Suffk
74 C3 Conford Hants
16 C3 Congdon's Shop Cnwll
413 G1 Congeith D & G
97 G5 Congelow Kent
239 F3 Congerstone Leics
253 E3 Congham Norfk
291 H2 Congleton Ches
292 A2 Congleton Edge Ches
285 F6 Congl-y-wal Gwynd
84 D2 Congresbury N Som
236 D3 Congreve Staffs
110 A5 Conham S Glos
567 H6 Conicavel Moray
299 G3 Coningsby Lincs
196 D1 Conington Cambs
219 H2 Conington Cambs
330 B5 Conisbrough Donc
476 D4 Conisby Ag & B
335 E5 Conisholme Lincs
378 B5 Coniston Cumb
348 C2 Coniston E R Yk
354 B4 Coniston Cold N York
354 C1 Conistone N York
86 D2 Conkwell Wilts

308 C6 Connah's Quay Flints
506 F3 Connel Ag & B
434 C2 Connel Park E Ayrs
168 A1 Conniburrow M Keyn
543 G2 Connista Highld
16 A6 Connon Cnwll
3 G2 Connor Downs Cnwll
88 C3 Conock Wilts
565 J6 Conon Bridge Highld
354 C5 Cononley N York
354 C5 Cononley Woodside N York
528 C5 Cononsyth Angus
545 J2 Conordan Highld
271 F6 Conquermoor Heath Wrekin
292 C5 Consall Staffs
404 C4 Consett Dur
369 G1 Constable Burton N York
340 C5 Constable Lee Lancs
4 D3 Constantine Cnwll
14 B4 Constantine Bay Cnwll
565 G5 Contin Highld
557 E4 Contlaw C Aber
305 G4 Conwy Conwy
99 F2 Conyer Kent
224 A6 Conyer's Green Suffk
58 B5 Cooden E Susx
24 B1 Cookbury Devon
24 A1 Cookbury Wick Devon
117 E3 Cookham W & M
117 E3 Cookham Dean W & M
117 E3 Cookham Rise W & M
189 F3 Cookhill Worcs
429 E5 Cooklaw Nthumb
226 D4 Cookley Suffk
212 B3 Cookley Worcs
116 A1 Cookley Green Oxon
557 F6 Cookney Abers
342 D1 Cookridge Leeds
56 C2 Cooksbridge E Susx
212 D6 Cooksey Corner Worcs
212 C6 Cooksey Green Worcs
176 C6 Cook's Green Essex
200 C4 Cook's Green Suffk
292 B6 Cookshill Staffs
15 F5 Cooksland Cnwll
146 C3 Cooksmill Green Essex
310 B5 Cooksongreen Ches
76 B5 Coolham W Susx
76 C4 Coolhurst Wood W Susx
122 B4 Cooling Medway
82 D3 Coolinge Kent
122 A5 Cooling Street Medway
142 A3 Coombe Bucks
6 B5 Coombe Cnwll
7 E5 Coombe Cnwll
7 F5 Coombe Cnwll
8 A3 Coombe Cnwll
16 B6 Coombe Cnwll
38 B5 Coombe Cnwll
20 C3 Coombe Devon
42 D4 Coombe Devon
28 B4 Coombe Devon
29 G3 Coombe Dorset
135 H6 Coombe Dorset
118 D5 Coombe Gt Lon
73 G5 Coombe Hants
101 E4 Coombe Kent
45 E6 Coombe Somset
69 E5 Coombe Wilts
88 D4 Coombe Wilts
70 C4 Coombe Bissett Wilts
109 F4 Coombe Dingle Bristl
162 C4 Coombe Hill Gloucs
33 E3 Coombe Keynes Dorset
27 H3 Coombelake Devon
55 E3 Coombes W Susx
272 A2 Coombesdale Staffs
213 E2 Coombeswood Dudley
97 G2 Coomb Hill Kent
110 C3 Coombs End S Glos
29 F1 Coombses Somset
145 G4 Coopersale Common Essex
96 C5 Cooper's Corner Kent
78 B5 Cooper's Green E Susx
144 A3 Cooper's Green Herts
169 E2 Cooper's Hill Beds
117 G5 Cooper's Hill Surrey
101 F4 Cooper Street Kent
325 E3 Cooper Turning Bolton
54 C2 Cootham W Susx
188 C2 Copcut Worcs
175 F1 Copdock Suffk
112 C3 Coped Hall Wilts
287 E1 Copenhagen Denbgs
174 B5 Copford Essex
174 B5 Copford Green Essex
356 C2 Copgrove N York
607 G2 Copister Shet
571 L6 Coplandhill Abers
195 G5 Cople Beds
342 A5 Copley Calder
394 B4 Copley Dur
327 E5 Copley Tamesd
342 D4 Copley Hill Kirk
313 C4 Coplow Dale Derbys
357 H5 Copmanthorpe York
272 B4 Copmere End Staffs
52 B4 Copnor C Port
338 B2 Copp Lancs
23 E2 Coppathorne Cnwll
291 E3 Coppenhall Ches
272 D6 Coppenhall Staffs
291 E3 Coppenhall Moss Ches
3 G2 Copperhouse Cnwll
326 D4 Coppice Oldham
211 G3 Coppicegate Shrops
219 H3 Coppingford Cambs
99 E5 Coppins Corner Kent
63 D3 Coppleham Somset
26 B2 Copplestone Devon
324 D2 Coppull Lancs
324 D2 Coppull Moor Lancs
76 C5 Copsale W Susx
119 E5 Copse Hill Gt Lon
339 G3 Copster Green Lancs
215 H2 Copston Magna Warwks
101 E4 Cop Street Kent
214 B6 Copt Green Warwks
145 F4 Copthall Green Essex
214 B4 Copt Heath Solhll
370 C5 Copt Hewick N York
393 E1 Copthill Dur
290 C6 Copthorne Cnwll
23 F4 Copthorne Cnwll
234 B2 Copthorne Shrops
77 F2 Copthorne W Susx
269 H2 Coptiviney Shrops
240 A2 Copt Oak Leics
99 G3 Copton Kent
260 B4 Copy's Green Norfk
50 B2 Copythorne Hants
536 B3 Corarnstilbeg Highld
121 E2 Corbets Tey Gt Lon
35 f7 Corbiere Jersey
403 H2 Corbridge Nthumb
315 E6 Corbriggs Derbys
218 B2 Corby Nhants
279 E4 Corby Glen Lincs
401 E3 Corby Hill Cumb
461 E3 Cordon N Ayrs
249 F6 Cordwell Norfk
211 E5 Coreley Shrops

117 F2 Cores End Bucks
44 A4 Corfe Somset
33 H3 Corfe Castle Dorset
48 B5 Corfe Mullen Dorset
507 H3 Corfhouse Ag & B
210 B3 Corfton Shrops
210 B2 Corfton Bache Shrops
552 F7 Corgarff Abers
8 C1 Corgee Cnwll
73 E6 Corhampton Hants
434 D5 Corlae D & G
104 B1 Corlannau Neath
214 D2 Corley Warwks
214 D2 Corley Ash Warwks
214 D3 Corley Moor Covtry
476 E7 Cornabus Ag & B
516 B6 Cornaigbeg Ag & B
516 B6 Cornaigmore Ag & B
174 A1 Cornard Tye Suffk
470 D2 Cornbank Mdloth
211 E4 Cornbrook Shrops
338 B2 Corner Row Lancs
186 D5 Cornett Herefs
362 C3 Corney Cumb
395 G3 Cornforth Dur
569 K4 Cornhill Abers
557 G3 Cornhill C Aber
292 A4 Cornhill C Stke
576 C5 Cornhill Highld
158 B1 Cornhill Powys
453 G2 Cornhill on Tweed Nthumb
340 D4 Cornholme Calder
172 D2 Cornish Hall End Essex
601 J5 Cornquoy Ork
392 D1 Cornriggs Dur
404 D6 Cornsay Dur
405 E6 Cornsay Colliery Dur
498 B5 Cornton Stirlg
565 K5 Corntown Highld
105 E4 Corntown V Glam
164 D4 Cornwell Oxon
18 D6 Cornwood Devon
13 E1 Cornworthy Devon
533 G7 Corpach Highld
255 F2 Corpusty Norfk
520 E3 Corran Highld
546 F8 Corran Highld
322 h5 Corrany IoM
463 H6 Corrie N Ayrs
425 E2 Corrie Common D & G
460 C5 Corriecravie N Ayrs
422 A3 Corriedoo D & G
564 E4 Corriemoillie Highld
550 D5 Corrievorrie Highld
602 C8 Corrigall Ork
548 F3 Corrimony Highld
317 G1 Corringham Lincs
121 H3 Corringham Thurr
230 B3 Corris Gwynd
229 G3 Corris Uchaf Gwynd
494 D4 Corrow Ag & B
545 L5 Corry Highld
525 H2 Corrydon P & K
579 L4 Corrykinloch Highld
511 F3 Corrymuckloch P & K
505 J2 Corrynachenchy Ag & B
565 H7 Corry of Ardnagrask Highld
589 G2 Corsback Highld
25 F3 Corscombe Devon
30 C1 Corscombe Dorset
558 D1 Corse Abers
162 A4 Corse Gloucs
162 B3 Corse Lawn Worcs
111 F6 Corsham Wilts
512 D5 Corsiehill P & K
556 B3 Corsindae Abers
87 E5 Corsley Wilts
87 E5 Corsley Heath Wilts
422 C4 Corsock D & G
86 B1 Corston BaNES
111 G3 Corston Wilts
487 H5 Corstorphine C Edin
527 E3 Cortachy Angus
251 G5 Corton Suffk
69 F1 Corton Wilts
67 G5 Corton Denham Somset
329 G5 Cortworth Rothm
287 F6 Corwen Denbgs
39 E4 Cory Devon
31 E5 Coryates Dorset
106 B3 Coryton Cardif
24 C6 Coryton Devon
29 E3 Coryton Devon
122 A3 Coryton Thurr
240 B5 Cosby Leics
115 E2 Coscote Oxon
236 D6 Coseley Dudley
216 A4 Cosford Warwks
167 G1 Cosgrove Nhants
52 B3 Cosham C Port
479 H5 Coshandrochaid Ag & B
125 G4 Cosheston Pembks
106 C6 Cosmeston V Glam
46 C3 Cosmore Dorset
276 A1 Cossall Notts
295 F6 Cossall Marsh Notts
240 D2 Cossington Leics
65 G3 Cossington Somset
602 C6 Costa Ork
249 G2 Costessey Norfk
249 G2 Costessey Park Norfk
316 A2 Costhorpe Notts
15 E4 Costislost Cnwll
276 C4 Costock Notts
278 B5 Coston Leics
249 E3 Coston Norfk
6 B6 Coswinsawsin Cnwll
139 F4 Cote Oxon
84 B6 Cote Somset
54 D3 Cote W Susx
290 B1 Cotebrook Ches
380 B4 Cotehill Cumb
401 E4 Cotehill Cumb
365 G2 Cotes Cumb
276 C5 Cotes Leics
272 B3 Cotes Staffs
216 B3 Cotesbach Leics
272 B3 Cotes Heath Staffs
295 E4 Cotes Park Derbys
28 B4 Cotford Devon
276 D2 Cotgrave Notts
557 F1 Cothal Abers
109 G5 Cotham Bristl
297 E5 Cotham Notts
64 C5 Cothelstone Somset
188 A4 Cotheridge Worcs
393 H6 Cotherstone Dur
139 H5 Cothill Oxon
134 C4 Cotland Mons
28 C2 Cotleigh Devon
295 F6 Cotmanhay Derbys
112 C4 Cotmarsh Wilts
28 B5 Cotmaton Devon
197 F3 Coton Cambs
270 C3 Coton Nhants
238 B4 Coton Shrops
272 B3 Coton Staffs
272 B5 Coton Staffs
273 E3 Coton Staffs
273 E3 Coton Staffs
272 C5 Coton Clanford Staffs
273 E3 Coton Hayes Staffs
234 B2 Coton Hill Shrops
273 E3 Coton Hill Staffs

274 B4 Coton in the Clay Staffs
238 C1 Coton in the Elms Derbys
274 D6 Coton Park Derbys
270 C2 Cotonwood Shrops
272 B5 Cotonwood Staffs
137 F5 Cotswold Community Wilts
19 G5 Cott Devon
338 D3 Cottam Lancs
317 F4 Cottam Notts
551 J3 Cottartown Highld
197 H1 Cottenham Cambs
119 E6 Cottenham Park Gt Lon
381 E6 Cotterdale N York
170 D4 Cottered Herts
315 H3 Cotterhill Woods Rothm
213 F3 Cotteridge Birm
219 E1 Cotterstock Nhants
217 E5 Cottesbrooke Nhants
242 C2 Cottesmore Rutlnd
42 B5 Cotteylands Devon
347 F3 Cottingham E R Yk
218 A1 Cottingham Nhants
342 B2 Cottingley Brad
166 C3 Cottisford Oxon
293 E5 Cotton Staffs
201 E1 Cotton Suffk
195 F5 Cotton End Beds
193 F3 Cotton End Nhants
514 C2 Cotton of Brighty Angus
528 C5 Cotton of Gardyne Angus
341 G5 Cotton Stones Calder
341 E2 Cotton Tree Lancs
72 A2 Cottonworth Hants
556 D1 Cottown Abers
558 C4 Cottown Abers
560 B1 Cottown Abers
513 F5 Cottown P & K
17 F5 Cotts Devon
40 C5 Cottwood Devon
235 E1 Cotwall Wrekin
272 D3 Cotwalton Staffs
600 F1 Coubister Ork
72 D3 Couch Green Hants
9 E2 Couch's Mill Cnwll
160 D5 Coughton Herefs
189 G2 Coughton Warwks
189 G3 Coughton Fields Warwks
563 H7 Coulags Highld
385 E2 Coulby Newham Middsb
376 B3 Coulderton Cumb
563 J5 Coulin Lodge Highld
555 F4 Coull Abers
543 G7 Coulnacraggan Highld
565 H6 Coul of Fairburn Highld
482 B2 Coulport Ag & B
95 F3 Coulsdon Gt Lon
87 H4 Coulston Wilts
448 D3 Coulter S Lans
64 D3 Coultings Somset
372 B5 Coulton N York
234 D4 Cound Shrops
234 D4 Coundlane Shrops
234 D4 Coundmoor Shrops
215 E3 Coundon Covtry
395 E4 Coundon Dur
395 E4 Coundongate Dur
395 E4 Coundon Grange Dur
143 E3 Counters End Herts
368 B2 Countersett N York
173 H3 Countess Cross Essex
27 E4 Countess Wear Devon
240 C5 Countesthorpe Leics
62 A2 Countisbury Devon
513 F1 Coupar Angus P & K
339 E4 Coup Green Lancs
392 B6 Coupland Cumb
454 A3 Coupland Nthumb
462 D5 Cour Ag & B
424 B1 Courance D & G
64 B5 Coursley Somset
81 G2 Court-at-Street Kent
26 C5 Court Barton Devon
104 D3 Court Colman Brdgnd
91 G3 Court Corner Hants
531 J3 Courteachan Highld
193 G4 Courteenhall Nhants
155 E5 Court Henry Carmth
309 F1 Court Hey Knows
215 F3 Court House Green Covtry
30 B4 Court Orchard Dorset
148 D6 Courtsend Essex
64 D5 Courtway Somset
488 D6 Cousland Mdloth
79 F3 Cousley Wood E Susx
606 E8 Cova Shet
482 B3 Cove Ag & B
491 E5 Cove Border
42 C4 Cove Devon
92 D3 Cove Hants
572 F5 Cove Highld
557 G4 Cove Bay C Aber
227 F4 Cove Bottom Suffk
227 G3 Covehithe Suffk
236 D3 Coven Staffs
187 E6 Covender Herefs
221 G3 Coveney Cambs
334 D6 Covenham St Bartholomew Lincs
334 D6 Covenham St Mary Lincs
236 D3 Coven Heath Staffs
236 C3 Coven Lawn Staffs
215 E4 Coventry Covtry
5 E5 Coverack Cnwll
4 C2 Coverack Bridges Cnwll
369 F2 Coverham N York
568 B1 Covesea Moray
113 E3 Covingham Swindn
219 F5 Covington Cambs
448 C2 Covington S Lans
366 C4 Cowan Bridge Lancs
352 D5 Cow Ark Lancs
57 G2 Cowbeech E Susx
57 G2 Cowbeech Hill E Susx
280 C6 Cowbit Lincs
300 B5 Cowbridge Lincs
105 F5 Cowbridge V Glam
342 B6 Cowcliffe Kirk
78 B1 Cowden Kent
510 D5 Cowden P & K
487 G1 Cowdenbeath Fife
379 E5 Cowen Head Cumb
294 C5 Cowers Lane Derbys
51 E5 Cowes IoW
371 F1 Cowesby N York
71 F5 Cowesfield Green Wilts
175 E4 Cowey Green Essex
76 D5 Cowfold W Susx
367 F2 Cowgill Cumb
201 E1 Cow Green Suffk
48 B5 Cowgrove Dorset
294 D5 Cowhill Derbys
339 E3 Cow Hill Lancs
109 G1 Cowhill S Glos
110 B5 Cowhorn Hill S Glos
541 G2 Cowie Abers
485 G2 Cowie Stirlg
467 F1 Cowlairs C Glas
7 F5 Cowlands Cnwll
139 E4 Cowleaze Corner Oxon
314 C4 Cowley Derbys
26 D3 Cowley Devon
137 E2 Cowley Gloucs
118 B3 Cowley Gt Lon

682 City, town and village index: Cowley - Cudliptown

140 B4 **Cowley** Oxon
42 C5 **Cowleymoor** Devon
118 B3 **Cowley Peachy** Gt Lon
324 D1 **Cowling** Lancs
354 C6 **Cowling** N York
370 A2 **Cowling** N York
199 E4 **Cowlinge** Suffk
313 E5 **Cowlow** Derbys
328 B1 **Cowmes** Kirk
340 C5 **Cowpe** Lancs
431 E3 **Cowpen** Nthumb
396 C5 **Cowpen Bewley** S on T
52 B2 **Cowplain** Hants
142 D2 **Cow Roast** Herts
393 E1 **Cowshill** Dur
85 E2 **Cowslip Green** N Som
486 D1 **Cowstrandburn** Fife
357 E4 **Cowthorpe** N York
209 G5 **Coxall** Herefs
271 F1 **Coxbank** Ches
294 D6 **Coxbench** Derbys
67 E2 **Coxbridge** Somset
226 D3 **Cox Common** Suffk
485 F1 **Coxet Hill** Stirlg
22 D3 **Coxford** Cnwll
50 C2 **Coxford** C Sotn
253 G2 **Coxford** Norfk
325 G2 **Cox Green** Bolton
212 A2 **Coxgreen** Staffs
76 A3 **Cox Green** Surrey
117 E4 **Cox Green** W & M
98 A4 **Coxheath** Kent
6 D5 **Cox Hill** Cnwll
395 G2 **Coxhoe** Dur
85 F6 **Coxley** Somset
328 D1 **Coxley** Wakefd
85 F6 **Coxley Wick** Somset
430 D6 **Coxlodge** N u Ty
295 G3 **Cox Moor** Notts
17 E4 **Coxpark** Cnwll
146 B5 **Coxtie Green** Essex
371 G4 **Coxwold** N York
105 E4 **Coychurch** Brdgnd
445 F5 **Coylton** S Ayrs
551 G7 **Coylumbridge** Highld
554 D3 **Coynach** Abers
558 B3 **Coynachie** Abers
104 D2 **Coytrahên** Brdgnd
77 F2 **Crabbet Park** W Susx
83 E2 **Crabble** Kent
189 F2 **Crabbs Cross** Worcs
171 F4 **Crabbs Green** Herts
255 E2 **Crabgate** Norfk
48 D3 **Crab Orchard** Dorset
11 F2 **Crabtree** C Plym
76 D4 **Crabtree** W Susx
288 D6 **Crabtree Green** Wrexhm
391 H5 **Crackenthorpe** Cumb
22 C3 **Crackington Haven** Cnwll
291 G4 **Crackley** Staffs
214 D5 **Crackley** Warwks
235 H2 **Crackleybank** Shrops
50 C2 **Cracknore Hard** Hants
381 H5 **Crackpot** N York
224 D4 **Crackthorn Corner** Suffk
354 C2 **Cracoe** N York
291 F5 **Cracow Moss** Staffs
43 E5 **Craddock** Devon
598 A8 **Cradhlastadh** W Isls
341 H2 **Cradle Edge** Brad
171 G5 **Cradle End** Herts
212 D3 **Cradley** Dudley
187 G5 **Cradley** Herefs
212 D2 **Cradley Heath** Sandw
157 G3 **Cradoc** Powys
10 C3 **Crafthole** Cnwll
168 B6 **Crafton** Bucks
476 E8 **Cragabus** Ag & B
365 G5 **Crag Bank** Lancs
365 G5 **Crag Foot** Lancs
551 J4 **Craggan** Highld
509 J5 **Craggan** Stirlg
552 D1 **Cragganmore** Moray
581 L6 **Craggie** Highld
341 G5 **Cragg Vale** Calder
405 F4 **Craghead** Dur
4 C2 **Crahan** Cnwll
156 D5 **Crai** Powys
569 H4 **Craibstone** Moray
527 G5 **Craichie** Angus
422 A4 **Craig** D & G
563 J7 **Craig** Highld
132 A5 **Craig Berthlwyd** Myr Td
129 G4 **Craig-cefn-parc** Swans
513 G4 **Craigdallie** P & K
560 B3 **Craigdam** Abers
434 C3 **Craigdarroch** E Ayrs
565 G5 **Craigdarroch** Highld
492 D3 **Craigdhu** Ag & B
410 C4 **Craigdhu** D & G
450 B5 **Craig Douglas** Border
556 C2 **Craigearn** Abers
568 D7 **Craigellachie** Moray
515 F2 **Craigend** Angus
472 B5 **Craigend** Border
467 G1 **Craigend** C Glas
512 D5 **Craigend** P & K
485 F2 **Craigend** Stirlg
482 D3 **Craigendoran** Ag & B
466 B1 **Craigends** Rens
476 D3 **Craigens** Ag & B
446 B6 **Craigens** E Ayrs
488 B4 **Craigentinny** C Edin
450 A2 **Craigerne** Border
557 E6 **Craiggie Cat** Abers
525 J6 **Craighall** P & K
483 G3 **Craighat** Stirlg
558 B1 **Craighead** Abers
477 J3 **Craighouse** Ag & B
560 D6 **Craigie** Abers
514 C3 **Craigie** C Dund
512 D5 **Craigie** P & K
525 H7 **Craigie** P & K
444 D5 **Craigie** S Ayrs
445 F3 **Craigie** S Ayrs
557 F3 **Craigiebuckler** C Aber
487 G4 **Craigiehall** C Edin
489 E4 **Craigielaw** E Loth
449 H5 **Craigierig** Border
487 H5 **Craigleith** C Edin
129 H3 **Craig Llangiwg** Neath
268 D4 **Craig-llwyn** Shrops
487 H5 **Craiglockhart** C Edin
433 G6 **Craigmalloch** E Ayrs
570 F4 **Craigmaud** Abers
515 F2 **Craigmill** Angus
498 C5 **Craigmill** Stirlg
488 B5 **Craigmillar** C Edin
464 C1 **Craigmore** Ag & B
269 E2 **Craignant** Wrexhm
468 B1 **Craigneuk** N Lans
468 B3 **Craigneuk** N Lans
505 L3 **Craignure** Ag & B
529 E2 **Craigo** Angus
500 A3 **Craigow** P & K
565 L7 **Craigrory** Highld
501 G2 **Craigrothie** Fife
509 G5 **Craigruie** Stirlg
173 E2 **Craig's End** Essex
451 H2 **Craigsford Mains** Border
487 E6 **Craigshill** W Loth
394 C2 **Craigside** Dur
515 E2 **Craigton** Angus
526 D4 **Craigton** Angus
557 E4 **Craigton** C Aber
466 D2 **Craigton** C Glas
566 B7 **Craigton** Highld
576 D4 **Craigton** Highld
587 J5 **Craigtown** Highld
304 C5 **Craig-y-don** IoA
129 H4 **Craig-y-Duke** Neath
130 C1 **Craig-y-nos** Powys
229 E6 **Craig-y-penrhyn** Cerdgn
106 C2 **Craig-y-Rhacca** Caerph
438 C3 **Craik** Border
503 G3 **Crail** Fife
452 C5 **Crailing** Border
452 D5 **Crailinghall** Border
370 A1 **Crakehall** N York
371 E5 **Crakehill** N York
273 G2 **Crakemarsh** Staffs
449 G5 **Cramalt** Border
358 D2 **Crambe** N York
358 D1 **Crambeck** N York
75 E1 **Cramhurst** Surrey
431 E4 **Cramlington** Nthumb
487 G4 **Cramond** C Edin
487 G4 **Cramond Bridge** C Edin
72 A5 **Crampmoor** Hants
311 E6 **Cranage** Ches
272 B2 **Cranberry** Staffs
48 D2 **Cranborne** Dorset
117 F5 **Cranbourne** Br For
91 G4 **Cranbourne** Hants
120 B2 **Cranbrook** Gt Lon
80 A2 **Cranbrook** Kent
80 A2 **Cranbrook Common** Kent
329 E4 **Crane Moor** Barns
121 H1 **Cranes** Essex
254 B5 **Crane's Corner** Norfk
168 D1 **Cranfield** Beds
38 D3 **Cranford** Devon
118 C4 **Cranford** Gt Lon
218 C4 **Cranford St Andrew** Nhants
218 C4 **Cranford St John** Nhants
136 C2 **Cranham** Gloucs
121 E2 **Cranham** Gt Lon
467 F1 **Cranhill** C Glas
190 A4 **Cranhill** Warwks
324 C5 **Crank** St Hel
325 E4 **Crankwood** Wigan
75 H2 **Cranleigh** Surrey
225 G5 **Cranley** Suffk
119 F2 **Cranley Gardens** Gt Lon
568 D4 **Cranloch** Moray
224 D5 **Cranmer Green** Suffk
36 B2 **Cranmore** IoW
86 B6 **Cranmore** Somset
569 H5 **Crannoch** Moray
241 G5 **Cranoe** Leics
202 C2 **Cransford** Suffk
473 F2 **Cranshaws** Border
322 h2 **Cranstal** IoM
360 C4 **Cranswick** E R Yk
7 E1 **Crantock** Cnwll
298 C5 **Cranwell** Lincs
247 F5 **Cranwich** Norfk
248 C4 **Cranworth** Norfk
492 C3 **Craobh Haven** Ag & B
18 B4 **Crapstone** Devon
493 G5 **Crarae** Ag & B
586 F4 **Crask** Highld
555 F3 **Craskins** Abers
549 H1 **Crask of Aigas** Highld
455 H6 **Craster** Nthumb
159 E3 **Craswall** Herefs
211 G2 **Crateford** Shrops
236 D3 **Crateford** Staffs
226 C4 **Cratfield** Suffk
556 D5 **Crathes** Abers
537 L3 **Crathie** Abers
535 G4 **Crathie** Highld
384 C3 **Crathorne** N York
210 A3 **Craven Arms** Shrops
404 D2 **Crawcrook** Gatesd
324 B4 **Crawford** Lancs
448 C5 **Crawford** S Lans
468 D5 **Crawforddyke** S Lans
447 H5 **Crawfordjohn** S Lans
435 F2 **Crawick** D & G
44 B6 **Crawley** Devon
72 B3 **Crawley** Hants
139 E2 **Crawley** Oxon
77 E2 **Crawley** W Susx
77 F2 **Crawley Down** W Susx
171 F2 **Crawley End** Essex
93 E3 **Crawley Hill** Surrey
393 G1 **Crawleyside** Dur
328 C2 **Crawshaw** Kirk
340 C4 **Crawshawbooth** Lancs
541 G4 **Crawton** Abers
606 B6 **Crawton** Shet
368 B4 **Cray** N York
525 H3 **Cray** P & K
120 D5 **Crayford** Gt Lon
371 H5 **Crayke** N York
260 D5 **Craymere Beck** Norfk
147 E6 **Crays Hill** Essex
115 G3 **Cray's Pond** Oxon
116 C3 **Crazies Hill** Wokham
41 G4 **Creacombe** Devon
520 D7 **Creagan** Ag & B
492 D4 **Creaganterve Mhòr** Ag & B
593 E8 **Creagastrom** W Isls
593 D8 **Creag Ghoraidh** W Isls
524 F3 **Creag na Cuinneige** P & K
270 C3 **Creamore Bank** Shrops
2 C5 **Crean** Cnwll
217 F5 **Creaton** Nhants
425 E5 **Creca** D & G
186 A6 **Credenhill** Herefs
26 C2 **Crediton** Devon
417 E3 **Creebridge** D & G
33 G3 **Creech** Dorset
33 G3 **Creech Bottom** Dorset
44 B2 **Creech Heathfield** Somset
44 B2 **Creech St Michael** Somset
8 A4 **Creed** Cnwll
607 J4 **Creediknowe** Shet
6 D5 **Creegbrawse** Cnwll
48 B6 **Creekmoor** Poole
120 C3 **Creekmouth** Gt Lon
148 B5 **Creeksea** Essex
201 F3 **Creeting Bottoms** Suffk
201 E3 **Creeting St Mary** Suffk
201 E3 **Creeting St Peter** Suffk
279 E5 **Creeton** Lincs
417 F5 **Creetown** D & G
494 B4 **Creggans** Ag & B
322 b9 **Cregneash** IoM
322 f6 **Cregny Baa** IoM
184 B4 **Cregrina** Powys
504 C6 **Creich** Ag & B
513 H5 **Creich** Fife
134 B5 **Creigau** Mons
273 G2 **Creighton** Staffs
106 A3 **Creigiau** Cardif
4 C2 **Crelly** Cnwll
10 D3 **Cremyll** Cnwll
48 D2 **Crendell** Dorset
543 G7 **Crepkill** Highld
167 H5 **Creslow** Bucks
234 D4 **Cressage** Shrops
313 G5 **Cressbrook** Derbys
126 B3 **Cresselly** Pembks
116 D1 **Cressex** Bucks
136 A4 **Cress Green** Gloucs
173 F5 **Cressing** Essex
443 H6 **Cresswell** Nthumb
273 E2 **Cresswell** Staffs
126 B3 **Cresswell Quay** Pembks
315 G5 **Creswell** Derbys
272 D5 **Creswell** Staffs
237 G2 **Creswell Green** Staffs
202 A2 **Cretingham** Suffk
462 B1 **Cretshengan** Ag & B
291 E4 **Crewe** Ches
289 F4 **Crewe-by-Farndon** Ches
391 G3 **Crewgarth** Cumb
233 F1 **Crewgreen** Powys
45 E6 **Crewkerne** Somset
144 D4 **Crews Hill** Gt Lon
109 H5 **Crew's Hole** Bristl
275 F3 **Crewton** C Derb
508 E4 **Crianlarich** Stirlg
109 G3 **Cribbs Causeway** S Glos
340 B5 **Cribden Side** Lancs
180 D4 **Cribyn** Cerdgn
264 B2 **Criccieth** Gwynd
294 D4 **Crich** Derbys
294 C4 **Crich Carr** Derbys
571 G7 **Crichie** Abers
471 G2 **Crichton** Mdloth
109 E1 **Crick** Mons
216 C5 **Crick** Nhants
158 A1 **Crickadarn** Powys
92 D3 **Cricket Hill** Hants
44 D5 **Cricket Malherbie** Somset
44 D6 **Cricket St Thomas** Somset
84 D5 **Crickham** Somset
269 E5 **Crickheath** Shrops
269 E5 **Crickheath Wharf** Shrops
158 D6 **Crickhowell** Powys
137 G6 **Cricklade** Wilts
119 E2 **Cricklewood** Gt Lon
271 F4 **Crickmery** Shrops
187 E4 **Crick's Green** Herefs
49 F2 **Criddlestyle** Hants
344 C5 **Cridling Stubbs** N York
36 D4 **Cridmore** IoW
511 F5 **Crieff** P & K
8 C1 **Criggan** Cnwll
233 E2 **Criggion** Powys
329 E1 **Crigglestone** Wakefd
326 C2 **Crimble** Rochdl
44 C6 **Crimchard** Somset
396 C2 **Crimdon Park** Dur
571 J4 **Crimond** Abers
571 J4 **Crimonmogate** Abers
38 B4 **Crimp** Cnwll
246 C4 **Crimplesham** Norfk
190 C5 **Crimscote** Warwks
492 C6 **Crinan** Ag & B
492 C6 **Crinan Ferry** Ag & B
107 F2 **Crindau** Newpt
468 C3 **Crindledyke** N Lans
249 G3 **Cringleford** Norfk
354 D5 **Cringles** Brad
470 D6 **Cringletie** Border
126 C2 **Crinow** Pembks
173 G3 **Cripple Corner** Essex
3 F2 **Cripplesease** Cnwll
48 D2 **Cripplestyle** Dorset
58 C2 **Cripp's Corner** E Susx
312 D3 **Crist** Derbys
71 F4 **Critchell's Green** Hants
86 D5 **Critchill** Somset
74 D3 **Critchmere** Surrey
80 A3 **Crit Hall** Kent
160 A3 **Crizeley** Herefs
15 E4 **Croanford** Cnwll
376 D1 **Croasdale** Cumb
96 D1 **Crockenhill** Kent
116 B2 **Crocker End** Oxon
51 G3 **Crockerhill** Hants
53 G3 **Crockerhill** W Susx
26 B4 **Crockernwell** Devon
61 E4 **Crockers** Devon
134 C1 **Crocker's Ash** Herefs
68 D1 **Crockerton** Wilts
87 E6 **Crockerton Green** Wilts
422 D5 **Crocketford** D & G
358 B5 **Crockey Hill** York
90 C2 **Crockham Heath** W Berk
96 B4 **Crockham Hill** Kent
97 F6 **Crockhurst Street** Kent
174 D4 **Crockleford Heath** Essex
600 E6 **Crockness** Ork
44 C5 **Crock Street** Somset
268 D4 **Croesau Bach** Shrops
130 D5 **Croeserw** Neath
150 D3 **Croes-goch** Pembks
133 F2 **Croes-Hywel** Mons
180 A6 **Croes-lan** Cerdgn
133 F3 **Croes Llanfair** Mons
284 D6 **Croesor** Gwynd
132 C5 **Croespenmaen** Caerph
307 G5 **Croes-wian** Flints
128 B1 **Croesyceiliog** Carmth
133 E5 **Croesyceiliog** Torfn
107 F1 **Croes-y-mwyalch** Torfn
133 F4 **Croes y pant** Mons
283 F4 **Croesywaun** Gwynd
24 B3 **Croft** Devon
186 B1 **Croft** Herefs
240 B5 **Croft** Leics
301 F2 **Croft** Lincs
325 E6 **Croft** Warrtn
483 G2 **Croftamie** Stirlg
467 E2 **Croftfoot** C Glas
523 K6 **Croftgarrow** P & K
6 D5 **Crofthandy** Cnwll
364 C4 **Croftlands** Cumb
469 E2 **Croftmalloch** W Loth
4 C1 **Croft Mitchell** Cnwll
565 L7 **Croftnacriech** Highld
400 B4 **Crofton** Cumb
96 B1 **Crofton** Gt Lon
343 G6 **Crofton** Wakefd
89 G2 **Crofton** Wilts
383 G3 **Croft-on-Tees** N York
500 D4 **Croft Outerly** Fife
325 H5 **Crofts Bank** Traffd
583 G2 **Crofts of Benachielt** Highld
568 E4 **Crofts of Dipple** Moray
560 B2 **Crofts of Haddo** Abers
577 G8 **Crofts of Kingscauseway** Highld
102 D2 **Crofty** Swans
505 L5 **Croggan** Ag & B
401 G5 **Croglin** Cumb
575 K5 **Croich** Highld
587 J6 **Croick** Highld
590 F3 **Crois Dùghaill** W Isls
566 D3 **Cromarty** Highld
487 E2 **Crombie** Fife
560 A2 **Cromblet** Abers
551 K4 **Cromdale** Highld
170 C4 **Cromer** Herts
261 H3 **Cromer** Norfk
144 A2 **Cromer-Hyde** Herts
294 B3 **Cromford** Derbys
110 B1 **Cromhall** S Glos
110 B2 **Cromhall Common** S Glos
597 L3 **Cromor** W Isls
327 E3 **Crompton Fold** Oldham
297 E2 **Cromwell** Notts
342 B5 **Cromwell Bottom** Calder
446 B5 **Cronberry** E Ayrs
92 C5 **Crondall** Hants
322 f7 **Cronkbourne** IoM
322 e5 **Cronk-y-Voddy** IoM
309 G2 **Cronton** Knows
379 E5 **Crook** Cumb
28 C2 **Crook** Devon
394 D2 **Crook** Dur
399 F6 **Crookdake** Cumb
324 D3 **Crooke** Wigan
445 G2 **Crookedholm** E Ayrs
113 H5 **Crooked Soley** Wilts
48 C3 **Crooked Withies** Dorset
314 C2 **Crookes** Sheff
314 C2 **Crookesmoor** Sheff
466 D3 **Crookfur** E Rens
405 E3 **Crookgate Bank** Dur
404 D4 **Crookhall** Dur
453 H2 **Crookham** Nthumb
91 E2 **Crookham** W Berk
92 C4 **Crookham Village** Hants
405 E2 **Crookhill** Gatesd
453 E4 **Crookhouse** Border
365 H3 **Crooklands** Cumb
499 G4 **Crook of Devon** P & K
424 C2 **Crookston** C Glas
191 H5 **Cropredy** Oxon
240 B2 **Cropston** Leics
189 E6 **Cropthorne** Worcs
373 E2 **Cropton** N York
277 E2 **Cropwell Bishop** Notts
277 E2 **Cropwell Butler** Notts
599 L2 **Cros** W Isls
597 K3 **Crosbost** W Isls
388 C2 **Crosby** Cumb
322 e7 **Crosby** IoM
332 B2 **Crosby** N Linc
323 E5 **Crosby** Sefton
370 D1 **Crosby Court** N York
380 C3 **Crosby Garrett** Cumb
401 E3 **Crosby-on-Eden** Cumb
379 H1 **Crosby Ravensworth** Cumb
388 C2 **Crosby Villa** Cumb
85 G6 **Croscombe** Somset
270 A4 **Crosemere** Shrops
327 H2 **Crosland Edge** Kirk
327 H2 **Crosland Hill** Kirk
327 H1 **Crosland Moor** Kirk
364 B5 **Croslands Park** Cumb
60 C4 **Cross** Devon
61 F5 **Cross** Devon
269 G2 **Cross** Shrops
84 D4 **Cross** Somset
464 D4 **Crossaig** Ag & B
545 H3 **Crossal** Highld
516 B7 **Crossapol** Ag & B
159 H6 **Cross Ash** Mons
98 B5 **Cross-at-Hand** Kent
211 H5 **Cross Bank** Worcs
570 B5 **Crossbrae** Abers
485 H5 **Crossburn** Falk
54 B3 **Crossbush** W Susx
388 C2 **Crosscanonby** Cumb
6 D3 **Cross Coombe** Cnwll
365 H2 **Crosscrake** Cumb
261 H4 **Crossdale Street** Norfk
195 F3 **Cross End** Beds
173 H3 **Cross End** Essex
168 C3 **Cross End** M Keyn
337 G5 **Crossens** Sefton
342 B1 **Crossflatts** Brad
487 E2 **Crossford** Fife
468 C5 **Crossford** S Lans
23 G5 **Crossgate** Cnwll
280 B4 **Crossgate** Lincs
272 D2 **Crossgate** Staffs
54 B2 **Cross Gate** W Susx
342 A2 **Cross Gates** Brad
388 C5 **Crossgates** Cumb
487 F2 **Crossgates** Fife
343 G3 **Cross Gates** Leeds
374 C3 **Crossgates** N York
183 H2 **Crossgates** Powys
392 B1 **Crossgill** Cumb
352 B2 **Crossgill** Lancs
24 A5 **Cross Green** Devon
234 B1 **Crossgreen** Shrops
235 E2 **Cross Green** Staffs
199 G4 **Cross Green** Suffk
200 A3 **Cross Green** Suffk
200 C4 **Cross Green** Suffk
129 E2 **Cross Hands** Carmth
152 D5 **Crosshands** Carmth
445 G3 **Crosshands** E Ayrs
445 G3 **Crosshands** E Ayrs
126 B2 **Cross Hands** Pembks
291 G5 **Cross Heath** Staffs
15 E4 **Cross Hill** Cnwll
295 E5 **Cross Hill** Derbys
445 G5 **Crosshill** E Ayrs
500 C5 **Crosshill** Fife
134 D5 **Cross Hill** Gloucs
432 D3 **Crosshill** S Ayrs
354 D6 **Cross Hills** N York
385 F5 **Cross Holme** N York
445 E2 **Crosshouse** E Ayrs
211 F1 **Cross Houses** Shrops
234 C3 **Cross Houses** Shrops
426 C4 **Crossings** Cumb
78 D5 **Cross in Hand** E Susx
127 F2 **Cross Inn** Carmth
180 A3 **Cross Inn** Cerdgn
180 D2 **Cross Inn** Cerdgn
105 H3 **Cross Inn** Rhondd
106 D1 **Crosskeys** Caerph
96 D4 **Cross Keys** Kent
111 F5 **Cross Keys** Wilts
588 C2 **Crosskirk** Highld
364 D2 **Crosslands** Cumb
290 D2 **Cross Lane** Ches
235 G5 **Cross Lane Head** Shrops
4 C4 **Cross Lanes** Cnwll
47 E4 **Cross Lanes** Dorset
357 G2 **Cross Lanes** N York
115 H4 **Cross Lanes** Oxon
269 F6 **Crosslanes** Shrops
289 E5 **Cross Lanes** Wrexhm
450 C6 **Crosslee** Border
466 B1 **Crosslee** Rens
160 A4 **Cross Llyde** Herefs
412 D1 **Crossmichael** D & G
466 D3 **Crossmill** E Rens
338 B2 **Crossmoor** Lancs
467 E2 **Crossmyloof** C Glas
158 A5 **Cross Oak** Powys
559 G3 **Cross of Jackston** Abers
294 B5 **Cross o'th hands** Derbys
289 G5 **Cross o' th' Hill** Ches
77 E5 **Crosspost** W Susx
556 D6 **Crossroads** Abers
24 C5 **Cross Roads** Devon
445 G3 **Crossroads** E Ayrs
501 G5 **Crossroads** Fife
225 G4 **Cross Street** Suffk
528 B3 **Crosston** Angus
311 F4 **Cross Town** Ches
38 A5 **Crosstown** Cnwll
105 G5 **Crosstown** V Glam
74 D2 **Crosswater** Surrey
161 E3 **Crossway** Herefs
160 A6 **Crossway** Mons
183 H3 **Crossway** Powys
134 C6 **Crossway Green** Mons
212 B6 **Crossway Green** Worcs
32 D2 **Crossways** Dorset
121 E4 **Crossways** Kent
159 F6 **Crossways** Mons
110 B1 **Crossways** S Glos
74 C2 **Crossways** Surrey
152 C2 **Crosswell** Pembks
205 F5 **Crosswood** Cerdgn
365 F1 **Crosthwaite** Cumb
338 C6 **Croston** Lancs
250 B1 **Crostwick** Norfk
256 C3 **Crostwight** Norfk
598 D7 **Crothair** W Isls
97 F3 **Crouch** Kent
99 H3 **Crouch** Kent
119 F2 **Crouch End** Gt Lon
53 E4 **Crouchers** W Susx
70 B4 **Croucheston** Wilts
46 D2 **Crouch Hill** Dorset
166 B3 **Croughton** Nhants
570 E2 **Crovie** Abers
49 F4 **Crow** Hants
4 B2 **Crowan** Cnwll
78 C3 **Crowborough** E Susx
292 B3 **Crowborough** Staffs
78 C3 **Crowborough Warren** E Susx
64 B4 **Crowcombe** Somset
187 H4 **Crowcroft** Worcs
293 F1 **Crowdecote** Derbys
327 G5 **Crowden** Derbys
24 C3 **Crowden** Devon
19 F6 **Crowder Park** Devon
72 C5 **Crowdhill** Hants
97 E3 **Crowdleham** Kent
387 G5 **Crowdon** N York
328 B4 **Crow Edge** Barns
141 F5 **Crowell** Oxon
141 G5 **Crowell Hill** Oxon
166 D1 **Crowfield** Nhants
201 F3 **Crowfield** Suffk
256 C5 **Crowgate Street** Norfk
235 H5 **Crowgreaves** Shrops
146 B5 **Crow Green** Essex
161 E4 **Crow Hill** Herefs
167 H2 **Crowhill** M Keyn
326 D5 **Crowhill** Tamesd
314 C4 **Crowhole** Derbys
58 C4 **Crowhurst** E Susx
96 A5 **Crowhurst** Surrey
96 A5 **Crowhurst Lane End** Surrey
244 B2 **Crowland** Lincs
3 F3 **Crowlas** Cnwll
331 G2 **Crowle** N Linc
188 D3 **Crowle** Worcs
188 D3 **Crowle Green** Worcs
331 G2 **Crowle Hill** N Linc
331 G2 **Crowle Park** N Linc
115 G2 **Crowmarsh Gifford** Oxon
566 B8 **Crown** Highld
226 B5 **Crown Corner** Suffk
188 B4 **Crown East** Worcs
141 G5 **Crownfield** Bucks
11 E2 **Crownhill** C Plym
240 D4 **Crown Hills** C Leic
224 D5 **Crownland** Suffk
93 G6 **Crownpits** Surrey
249 E4 **Crownthorpe** Norfk
4 B2 **Crowntown** Cnwll
93 E1 **Crown Wood** Br For
2 C4 **Crows-an-wra** Cnwll
172 D4 **Crow's Green** Essex
248 B3 **Crowshill** Norfk
116 B4 **Crowsley** Oxon
16 C5 **Crow's Nest** Cnwll
233 G4 **Crowsnest** Shrops
184 D5 **Crowther's Pool** Powys
92 D2 **Crowthorne** Br For
310 B5 **Crowton** Ches
309 H2 **Crow Wood** Halton
238 B2 **Croxall** Staffs
334 A5 **Croxby** Lincs
333 H5 **Croxby Top** Lincs
395 F2 **Croxdale** Dur
273 G2 **Croxden** Staffs
143 F5 **Croxley Green** Herts
323 H5 **Croxteth** Lpool
196 B3 **Croxton** Cambs
333 F2 **Croxton** N Linc
223 H2 **Croxton** Norfk
260 C5 **Croxton** Norfk
272 A3 **Croxton** Staffs
272 A3 **Croxtonbank** Staffs
290 A4 **Croxton Green** Ches
278 A4 **Croxton Kerrial** Leics
566 D7 **Croy** Highld
485 E4 **Croy** N Lans
60 B4 **Croyde** Devon
60 B4 **Croyde Bay** Devon
196 D5 **Croydon** Cambs
95 G2 **Croydon** Gt Lon
186 D5 **Crozen** Herefs
233 H3 **Cruckmeole** Shrops
234 A2 **Cruckton** Shrops
561 G2 **Cruden Bay** Abers
271 E6 **Crudgington** Wrekin
137 E6 **Crudwell** Wilts
208 C5 **Crug** Powys
130 C4 **Crugau** Neath
14 C3 **Crugmeer** Cnwll
155 G2 **Crugybar** Carmth
189 F2 **Cruise Hill** Worcs
598 D8 **Crùlabhig** W Isls
132 D5 **Crumlin** Caerph
9 G3 **Crumplehorn** Cnwll
326 B4 **Crumpsall** Manch
211 E4 **Crumpsbrook** Shrops
187 H5 **Crumpton Hill** Herefs
99 H5 **Crundale** Kent
151 G6 **Crundale** Pembks
41 H5 **Cruwys Morchard** Devon
90 C3 **Crux Easton** Hants
30 D3 **Cruxton** Dorset
128 C2 **Crwbin** Carmth
142 B5 **Cryers Hill** Bucks
152 D3 **Crymych** Pembks
130 B4 **Crynant** Neath
562 C5 **Cuaig** Highld
492 C2 **Cuan** Ag & B
215 E6 **Cubbington** Warwks
368 C2 **Cubeck** N York
7 E2 **Cubert** Cnwll
120 A4 **Cubitt Town** Gt Lon
328 C4 **Cubley** Barns
274 B2 **Cubley Common** Derbys
168 A5 **Cublington** Bucks
77 E5 **Cuckfield** W Susx
68 C4 **Cucklington** Somset
315 H5 **Cuckney** Notts
227 F3 **Cuckold's Green** Suffk
88 A3 **Cuckold's Green** Wilts
251 G5 **Cuckoo Green** Suffk
74 A1 **Cuckoo's Corner** Hants
88 B3 **Cuckoo's Corner** Wilts
89 E2 **Cuckoo's Knob** Wilts
200 A6 **Cuckoo Tye** Suffk
606 E7 **Cuckron** Shet
250 D3 **Cucumber Corner** Norfk
140 D4 **Cuddesdon** Oxon
141 F2 **Cuddington** Bucks
310 B5 **Cuddington** Ches
289 G5 **Cuddington Heath** Ches
338 C2 **Cuddy Hill** Lancs
96 B3 **Cudham** Gt Lon
18 B2 **Cudliptown** Devon

329 F3 **Cudworth** Barns
44 D5 **Cudworth** Somset
76 D1 **Cudworth** Surrey
329 F3 **Cudworth Common** Barns
339 E5 **Cuerden Green** Lancs
310 A2 **Cuerdley Cross** Warrtn
91 G3 **Cufaude** Hants
151 E5 **Cuffern** Pembks
144 D4 **Cuffley** Herts
568 F3 **Cuffurach** Moray
591 D7 **Cuidhir** W Isls
595 H5 **Cuidhtinis** W Isls
542 F5 **Cuidrach** Highld
470 D2 **Cuiken** Mdloth
520 D4 **Cuil** Highld
565 L4 **Culbo** Highld
565 L5 **Culbokie** Highld
549 H1 **Culburnie** Highld
566 B8 **Culcabock** Highld
566 F6 **Culcharry** Highld
325 F6 **Culcheth** Warrtn
519 G1 **Cùl Doirlinn** Highld
558 C3 **Culdrain** Abers
546 C1 **Culduie** Highld
223 G5 **Culford** Suffk
223 G5 **Culfordheath** Suffk
391 G4 **Culgaith** Cumb
140 B5 **Culham** Oxon
578 D3 **Culkein** Highld
578 F3 **Culkein Drumbeg** Highld
136 D5 **Culkerton** Gloucs
551 H5 **Cullachie** Highld
569 J2 **Cullen** Moray
431 G5 **Cullercoats** N Tyne
565 L4 **Cullicudden** Highld
341 H2 **Cullingworth** Brad
492 B2 **Cullipool** Ag & B
566 E1 **Cullisse** Highld
609 G4 **Cullivoe** Shet
510 D6 **Culloch** P & K
566 C7 **Culloden** Highld
27 F1 **Cullompton** Devon
577 H4 **Culmaily** Highld
43 F5 **Culm Davy** Devon
75 E2 **Culmer** Surrey
99 H2 **Culmers** Kent
210 B3 **Culmington** Shrops
497 G5 **Culmore** Stirlg
43 F5 **Culmstock** Devon
543 J4 **Culnacnoc** Highld
573 L3 **Culnacraig** Highld
201 H5 **Culpho** Suffk
576 C5 **Culrain** Highld
599 J8 **Cuirigrein** W Isls
486 C2 **Culross** Fife
432 D2 **Culroy** S Ayrs
411 E3 **Culscadden** D & G
554 B5 **Culsh** Abers
570 F6 **Culsh** Abers
409 G1 **Culshabbin** D & G
604 E1 **Culswick** Shet
560 D5 **Cultercullen** Abers
557 F4 **Cults** C Aber
558 C3 **Cults** C Aber
510 D6 **Cultybraggan** P & K
19 F5 **Culverlane** Devon
97 F2 **Culverstone Green** Kent
279 E1 **Culverthorpe** Lincs
192 B5 **Culworth** Nhants
170 D3 **Cumberlow Green** Herts
485 F5 **Cumbernauld** N Lans
485 E4 **Cumbernauld Village** N Lans
270 A2 **Cumber's Bank** Wrexhm
321 F5 **Cumberworth** Lincs
400 B5 **Cumdivock** Cumb
339 E2 **Cumeragh Village** Lancs
570 E5 **Cuminestown** Abers
474 A3 **Cumledge** Border
605 H6 **Cumlewick** Shet
400 C4 **Cummersdale** Cumb
399 E1 **Cummertrees** D & G
557 G3 **Cummings Park** C Aber
567 L3 **Cummingston** Moray
446 B6 **Cumnock** E Ayrs
139 H4 **Cumnor** Oxon
140 A4 **Cumnor Hill** Oxon
401 G4 **Cumrew** Cumb
401 E4 **Cumwhinton** Cumb
401 F4 **Cumwhitton** Cumb
371 E5 **Cundall** N York
329 E5 **Cundy Hos** Barns
445 E1 **Cunninghamhead** N Ayrs
605 H4 **Cunningsburgh** Shet
609 G5 **Cunnister** Shet
502 B2 **Cupar** Fife
501 G2 **Cupar Muir** Fife
71 H5 **Cupernham** Hants
143 F3 **Cupid Green** Herts
159 G4 **Cupid's Hill** Mons
314 B5 **Curbar** Derbys
238 A2 **Curborough** Staffs
51 F2 **Curbridge** Hants
139 E3 **Curbridge** Oxon
51 F2 **Curdridge** Hants
238 B6 **Curdworth** Warwks
7 G6 **Curgurrell** Cnwll
44 B4 **Curland** Somset
44 B4 **Curland Common** Somset
202 D1 **Curlew Green** Suffk
147 G3 **Curling Tye Green** Essex
44 C2 **Curload** Somset
419 E3 **Currarie** S Ayrs
114 D5 **Currian Vale** Cnwll
118 A1 **Curridge** W Berk
487 G6 **Currie** C Edin
400 D4 **Currock** Cumb
23 F4 **Curry Lane** Cnwll
44 C3 **Curry Mallet** Somset
66 B4 **Curry Rivel** Somset
600 F2 **Cursiter** Ork
80 C2 **Curteis' Corner** Kent
79 G1 **Curtisden Green** Kent
12 C2 **Curtisknowle** Devon
145 H5 **Curtismill Green** Essex
4 C4 **Cury** Cnwll
603 G4 **Cusbay** Ork
7 E5 **Cusgarne** Cnwll
570 D3 **Cushnie** Abers
64 C5 **Cushuish** Somset
158 D1 **Cusop** Herefs
50 A3 **Custards** Hants
7 E5 **Cusveorth Coombe** Cnwll
330 B4 **Cusworth** Donc
411 E6 **Cutcloy** D & G
63 E4 **Cutcombe** Somset
326 C2 **Cutgate** Rochdl
488 D5 **Cuthill** E Loth
229 E1 **Cutiau** Gwynd
172 B3 **Cutlers Green** Essex
85 G4 **Cutler's Green** Somset
15 F6 **Cutmadoc** Cnwll
10 B1 **Cutmere** Cnwll
212 C6 **Cutnall Green** Worcs
411 E5 **Cutreoch** D & G
163 G3 **Cutsdean** Gloucs
343 H5 **Cutsyke** Wakefd
140 B2 **Cutslowe** Oxon
314 C5 **Cutthorpe** Derbys
605 H3 **Cutts** Shet
151 F6 **Cuttybridge** Pembks
571 J5 **Cuttyhill** Abers
141 E5 **Cuxham** Oxon
97 H1 **Cuxton** Medway

333 H4 **Cuxwold** Lincs
132 C3 **Cwm** Blae G
307 F4 **Cwm** Denbgs
130 C6 **Cwm** Neath
209 E1 **Cwm** Powys
231 H5 **Cwm** Powys
209 F4 **Cwm** Shrops
104 B1 **Cwmafan** Neath
131 G5 **Cwmaman** Rhondd
181 E5 **Cwmann** Carmth
133 E3 **Cwmavon** Torfn
153 E4 **Cwmbach** Carmth
131 G4 **Cwmbach** Rhondd
158 C2 **Cwmbach** Rhondd
183 G4 **Cwmbach Llechrhyd** Powys
207 E3 **Cwmbelan** Powys
133 E6 **Cwmbran** Torfn
205 G3 **Cwmbrwyno** Cerdgn
128 B4 **Cwm Capel** Carmth
132 D6 **Cwmcarn** Caerph
134 B3 **Cwmcarvan** Mons
132 D3 **Cwm-celyn** Blae G
129 F3 **Cwmcerdinen** Swans
230 D2 **Cwm-Cewydd** Gwynd
179 G4 **Cwmcoednerth** Cerdgn
153 F1 **Cwm-Cou** Cerdgn
158 B6 **Cwmcrawnon** Powys
153 F2 **Cwmcych** Carmth
131 F4 **Cwmdare** Rhondd
132 C5 **Cwm Dows** Caerph
155 F3 **Cwmdu** Carmth
158 C5 **Cwmdu** Powys
103 F3 **Cwmdu** Swans
154 A3 **Cwmduad** Carmth
129 F4 **Cwm Dulais** Swans
155 G3 **Cwmdwr** Carmth
205 G3 **Cwmerfyn** Cerdgn
104 D2 **Cwmfelin** Brdgnd
132 D6 **Cwmfelin** Myr Td
106 C1 **Cwmfelin Boeth** Carmth
153 E5 **Cwmfelinfach** Caerph
128 B1 **Cwmfelin Mynach** Carmth
133 E4 **Cwm Ffrwd-oer** Torfn
133 E4 **Cwm-Fields** Torfn
132 C5 **Cwm Gelli** Caerph
130 B2 **Cwmgiedd** Powys
129 H2 **Cwmgors** Neath
129 E2 **Cwmgwili** Carmth
130 D4 **Cwmgwrach** Neath
103 F3 **Cwm Gwyn** Swans
209 H2 **Cwmhiraeth** Carmth
153 C2 **Cwmhiraeth** Carmth
131 E3 **Cwm-hwnt** Rhondd
155 G4 **Cwmifor** Carmth
182 C5 **Cwm Irfon** Powys
128 C1 **Cwmisfael** Carmth
230 C3 **Cwm-Llinau** Powys
130 A2 **Cwmllynfell** Neath
128 D2 **Cwm-mawr** Carmth
152 D5 **Cwm-miles** Carmth
132 C5 **Cwm Nant-gam** Mons
132 C5 **Cwmnantyrodyn** Caerph
153 F3 **Cwmorgan** Carmth
131 E5 **Cwmparc** Rhondd
153 G2 **Cwmpengraig** Carmth
285 F5 **Cwm Penmachno** Conwy
131 G4 **Cwmpennar** Rhondd
178 D5 **Cwm Plysgog** Pembks
158 C5 **Cwmrhos** Powys
129 G5 **Cwmrhydyceirw** Swans
180 C5 **Cwmsychbant** Cerdgn
132 C4 **Cwmsyfiog** Caerph
205 F3 **Cwmsymlog** Cerdgn
132 D3 **Cwmtillery** Blae G
130 B2 **Cwm-twrch Isaf** Powys
130 B2 **Cwm-twrch Uchaf** Powys
150 C3 **Cwmdwig Water** Pembks
156 C4 **Cwmwysg** Powys
284 C2 **Cwm-y-glo** Gwynd
133 E5 **Cwmynyscoy** Torfn
159 E5 **Cwmyoy** Mons
206 B5 **Cwmystwyth** Cerdgn
229 F4 **Cwrt** Gwynd
180 C5 **Cwrtnewydd** Cerdgn
181 G6 **Cwrt-y-cadno** Carmth
132 D1 **Cwrt Y gollen** Powys
287 F3 **Cyffylliog** Denbgs
232 B3 **Cyfronydd** Powys
288 C3 **Cymau** Flints
105 E3 **Cymdda** Brdgnd
130 D5 **Cymer** Neath
105 G1 **Cymmer** Rhondd
106 C3 **Cyncoed** Cardif
156 B2 **Cynghordy** Carmth
128 C3 **Cyneidre** Carmth
130 C6 **Cynonville** Neath
106 B4 **Cyntwell** Cardif
267 H1 **Cynwyd** Denbgs
154 A4 **Cynwyl Elfed** Carmth

D

20 B4 **Daccombe** Devon
390 D4 **Dacre** Cumb
355 G2 **Dacre** N York
355 G2 **Dacre Banks** N York
393 E2 **Daddry Shield** Dur
167 E2 **Dadford** Bucks
259 G5 **Dadlington** Leics
128 D4 **Dafen** Carmth
248 C3 **Daffy Green** Norfk
273 G3 **Dagdale** Staffs
120 C3 **Dagenham** Gt Lon
49 E2 **Daggons** Dorset
137 E3 **Daglingworth** Gloucs
142 D1 **Dagnall** Bucks
189 F2 **Dagtail End** Worcs
200 D2 **Dagworth** Suffk
604 b2 **Da Hametoon** Shet
598 E5 **Dail Beag** W Isls
599 K2 **Dail bho Thuath** W Isls
476 F4 **Daill** Ag & B
479 L3 **Daill** Ag & B
432 C4 **Dailly** S Ayrs
598 E6 **Dail Mòr** W Isls
20 A4 **Dainton** Devon
502 C1 **Dairsie or Osnaburgh** Fife
174 B4 **Daisy Green** Essex
200 D1 **Daisy Green** Suffk
224 D6 **Daisy Green** Suffk
225 E6 **Daisy Green** Suffk
325 E4 **Daisy Hill** Bolton
342 B3 **Daisy Hill** Brad
343 E4 **Daisy Hill** Leeds
326 D4 **Daisy Nook** Oldham
590 E3 **Dalabrog** W Isls
493 G2 **Dalavich** Ag & B
413 F2 **Dalbeattie** D & G
446 C6 **Dalblair** E Ayrs
540 A5 **Dalbog** Angus
274 D3 **Dalbury** Derbys
49 E2 **Dalby** IoM
320 D5 **Dalby** Lincs
372 B5 **Dalby** N York
577 K2 **Dalchalm** Highld
586 D5 **Dalcharn** Highld
494 B3 **Dalchenna** Ag & B
580 E7 **Dalchork** Highld
548 D7 **Dalchreichart** Highld
497 H1 **Dalchruin** P & K

299 H1 **Dalderby** Lincs
401 F6 **Dale** Cumb
327 E3 **Dale** Oldham
124 D3 **Dale** Pembks
275 G2 **Dale Abbey** Derbys
294 D2 **Dalebank** Derbys
389 G5 **Dale Bottom** Cumb
312 B4 **Dale Brow** Ches
293 H2 **Dale End** Derbys
354 C5 **Dale End** N York
378 D1 **Dale Head** Cumb
381 H3 **Dale Head** N York
79 G3 **Dale Hill** E Susx
519 H2 **Dalelia** Highld
275 G2 **Dale Moor** Derbys
606 A7 **Dale of Walls** Shet
325 H4 **Dales Brow** Salfd
291 H4 **Dales Green** Staffs
295 G2 **Dalestorth** Notts
551 G7 **Dalfaber** Highld
484 B2 **Dalfoil** Stirlg
465 F5 **Dalgarven** N Ayrs
487 G3 **Dalgety Bay** Fife
434 B2 **Dalgig** E Ayrs
510 D5 **Dalginross** P & K
524 E6 **Dalguise** P & K
525 J1 **Dalhally** Angus
587 J6 **Dalhalvaig** Highld
199 E2 **Dalham** Suffk
525 H2 **Dalhenzean** P & K
590 E3 **Daliburgh** W Isls
506 E4 **Dalintart** Ag & B
471 F1 **Dalkeith** Mdloth
310 B1 **Dallam** Warrtn
567 L6 **Dallas** Moray
434 B2 **Dalleagles** E Ayrs
235 H6 **Dallicott** Shrops
51 F6 **Dallimores** IoW
202 B3 **Dallinghoo** Suffk
79 F6 **Dallington** E Susx
193 F2 **Dallington** Nhants
369 G5 **Dallow** N York
507 L4 **Dalmally** Ag & B
467 F2 **Dalmarnock** C Glas
496 D5 **Dalmary** Stirlg
433 G3 **Dalmellington** E Ayrs
487 F4 **Dalmeny** C Edin
550 C6 **Dalmigavie** Highld
445 E5 **Dalmilling** S Ayrs
515 E3 **Dalmore** Angus
566 B3 **Dalmore** Highld
483 G5 **Dalmuir** W Duns
519 G2 **Dalnabreck** Highld
564 E5 **Dalnacroich** Highld
565 L2 **Dalnavie** Highld
566 B8 **Dalneigh** Highld
521 H5 **Dalness** Highld
580 F6 **Dalnessie** Highld
500 A4 **Dalqueich** P & K
419 H2 **Dalquhairn** S Ayrs
576 F2 **Dalreavoch** Highld
523 K4 **Dalriach** P & K
488 A5 **Dalry** C Edin
465 F5 **Dalry** N Ayrs
432 D2 **Dalrymple** E Ayrs
193 E4 **Dalscote** Nhants
468 B4 **Dalserf** S Lans
609 G5 **Dalsetter** Shet
485 E5 **Dalshannon** N Lans
400 C4 **Dalston** Cumb
119 G3 **Dalston** Gt Lon
423 F2 **Dalswinton** D & G
366 A4 **Dalton** Cumb
424 C5 **Dalton** D & G
328 B1 **Dalton** Kirk
324 B3 **Dalton** Lancs
403 G3 **Dalton** Nthumb
430 B5 **Dalton** Nthumb
371 E4 **Dalton** N York
382 D3 **Dalton** N York
329 H6 **Dalton** Rothm
467 G3 **Dalton** S Lans
364 B5 **Dalton-in-Furness** Cumb
406 C5 **Dalton-le-Dale** Dur
329 H6 **Dalton Magna** Rothm
383 G3 **Dalton-on-Tees** N York
329 H6 **Dalton Parva** Rothm
396 C3 **Dalton Piercy** Hartpl
479 K5 **Daltote** Ag & B
526 A1 **Dalvanie** Angus
509 K5 **Dalveich** Stirlg
535 H6 **Dalwhinnie** Highld
28 D2 **Dalwood** Devon
170 B4 **Damask Green** Herts
341 G2 **Damems** Brad
48 D1 **Damerham** Hants
135 G6 **Damery** Gloucs
251 E3 **Damgate** Norfk
257 F6 **Damgate** Norfk
225 E2 **Dam Green** Norfk
559 G4 **Damhead** Abers
342 A4 **Dam Mill** Staffs
471 E1 **Damhead Holdings** Mdloth
236 C4 **Dam Mill** Staffs
408 C4 **Damnaglaur** D & G
470 C5 **Damside** Border
351 F5 **Dam Side** Lancs
98 D2 **Danaway** Kent
147 F4 **Danbury** Essex
147 F4 **Danbury Common** Essex
386 A3 **Danby** N York
384 A5 **Danby Wiske** N York
105 H4 **Dan Caerlan** Rhondd
144 B5 **Dancers Hill** Herts
161 E5 **Dancing Green** Herefs
568 D6 **Dandaleith** Moray
152 C4 **Danderwen** Pembks
488 C6 **Danderhall** Mdloth
225 E6 **Dandy Corner** Suffk
312 C3 **Danebank** Ches
326 C5 **Dane Bank** Tamesd
292 C2 **Danebridge** Ches
170 D5 **Dane End** Herts
78 D3 **Danegate** E Susx
77 H4 **Danehill** E Susx
292 A2 **Dane in Shaw** Ches
249 E3 **Danemoor Green** Norfk
144 B1 **Danesbury** Herts
116 D2 **Danesfield** Bucks
211 G1 **Danesford** Shrops
91 H4 **Daneshill** Hants
295 E2 **Danesmoor** Derbys
312 B5 **Danes Moss** Ches
99 H4 **Dane Street** Kent
136 D4 **Daneway** Gloucs
324 C2 **Dangerous Corner** Wigan
325 E4 **Dangerous Corner** Wigan
81 E1 **Daniel's Water** Kent
15 E2 **Dannonchapel** Cnwll
472 D1 **Danskine** E Loth
348 D3 **Danthorpe** E R Yk
158 D2 **Dan-y-Capel** Powys
106 D1 **Danygraig** Caerph
213 H6 **Danzey Green** Warwks
273 F4 **Dapple Heath** Staffs
213 E2 **Darby End** Dudley
92 D2 **Darby Green** Hants
187 H3 **Darbys Green** Worcs
213 E2 **Darby's Hill** Sandw
325 G3 **Darcy Lever** Bolton
158 D6 **Dardy** Powys
121 E2 **Darenth** Kent
310 B3 **Daresbury** Halton
310 B3 **Daresbury Delph** Halton

329 G4 **Darfield** Barns
315 H4 **Darfoulds** Notts
99 H2 **Dargate** Kent
100 A3 **Dargate Common** Kent
511 F6 **Dargill** P & K
16 C5 **Darite** Cnwll
568 D3 **Darkland** Moray
289 E3 **Darland** Wrexhm
237 E5 **Darlaston** Wsall
237 E5 **Darlaston Green** Wsall
355 H3 **Darley** N York
235 F5 **Darley** Shrops
275 F2 **Darley Abbey** C Derb
294 B3 **Darley Bridge** Derbys
294 B2 **Darley Dale** Derbys
16 C4 **Darleyford** Cnwll
214 B5 **Darley Green** Solhll
169 G5 **Darleyhall** Herts
355 G3 **Darley Head** N York
294 B2 **Darley Hillside** Derbys
164 C1 **Darlingscott** Warwks
383 G2 **Darlington** Darltn
270 D3 **Darliston** Shrops
456 D2 **Darlochan** Ag & B
317 E5 **Darlton** Notts
201 E4 **Darmsden** Suffk
314 D2 **Darnall** Sheff
238 A3 **Darnford** Staffs
470 D5 **Darnhall Mains** Border
326 B2 **Darn Hill** Rochdl
451 G3 **Darnick** Border
230 C4 **Darowen** Powys
570 C6 **Darra** Abers
23 G4 **Darracott** Cnwll
38 B4 **Darracott** Devon
60 C4 **Darracott** Devon
430 B5 **Darras Hall** Nthumb
344 B5 **Darrington** Wakefd
226 B2 **Darrow Green** Norfk
227 E6 **Darsham** Suffk
85 H6 **Darshill** Somset
120 D5 **Dartford** Kent
121 E4 **Dartford Crossing** Thurr
19 G5 **Dartington** Devon
19 E3 **Dartmeet** Devon
13 F2 **Dartmouth** Devon
119 F2 **Dartmouth Park** Gt Lon
329 E2 **Darton** Barns
446 B2 **Darvel** E Ayrs
14 H5 **Darvillshill** Bucks
58 A3 **Darwell Hole** E Susx
339 G5 **Darwen** Bl w D
171 E4 **Dassels** Herts
117 G4 **Datchet** W & M
117 G4 **Datchet Common** W & M
170 C6 **Datchworth** Herts
170 C6 **Datchworth Green** Herts
325 G3 **Daubhill** Bolton
568 C7 **Daugh of Kinnermony** Moray
112 A3 **Dauntsey** Wilts
112 A4 **Dauntsey Lock** Wilts
551 J2 **Dava** Highld
310 C5 **Davenham** Ches
291 G1 **Davenport** Ches
312 A2 **Davenport** Stockp
311 F2 **Davenport Green** Traffd
311 G4 **Davenport Green** Traffd
192 C2 **Daventry** Nhants
487 H4 **Davidson's Mains** C Edin
22 D5 **Davidstow** Cnwll
97 F2 **David Street** Kent
207 G4 **David's Well** Powys
438 A4 **Davington** D & G
99 G2 **Davington** Kent
559 H4 **Daviot** Abers
550 C2 **Daviot** Highld
57 E1 **Davis's Town** E Susx
569 H5 **Davoch of Grange** Moray
325 H5 **Davyhulme** Traffd
356 B4 **Daw Cross** N York
406 C5 **Dawdon** Dur
237 F4 **Daw End** Wsall
95 E5 **Dawesgreen** Surrey
344 D2 **Dawker Hill** N York
235 F3 **Dawley** Wrekin
20 D2 **Dawlish** Devon
20 D2 **Dawlish Warren** Devon
306 B5 **Dawn** Conwy
174 A3 **Daw's Cross** Essex
43 G3 **Daw's Green** Somset
304 S **Daws Heath** Essex
23 G6 **Daw's House** Cnwll
188 B4 **Dawshill** Worcs
281 F3 **Dawsmere** Lincs
296 A5 **Daybrook** Notts
291 F3 **Day Green** Ches
273 E3 **Dayhills** Staffs
213 E4 **Dayhouse Bank** Worcs
164 C4 **Daylesford** Gloucs
269 E3 **Daywall** Shrops
307 G5 **Ddol** Flints
267 G6 **Ddôl Cownwy** Powys
144 A5 **Deacons Hill** Herts
169 G1 **Deadman's Cross** Beds
273 F2 **Deadman's Green** Staffs
74 B2 **Deadwater** Hants
440 B5 **Deadwater** Nthumb
10 C1 **Deaf Hill** Dur
48 A5 **Deal** Kent
488 A5 **Dean** C Edin
388 C4 **Dean** Cumb
19 F5 **Dean** Devon
61 E2 **Dean** Devon
48 B1 **Dean** Dorset
72 B3 **Dean** Hants
73 E6 **Dean** Hants
340 D4 **Dean** Lancs
165 E5 **Dean** Oxon
86 B6 **Dean** Somset
395 F3 **Dean Bank** Dur
439 E2 **Deanburnhaugh** Border
139 H3 **Dean Court** Oxon
60 C3 **Dean Cross** Devon
325 F3 **Deane** Bolton
91 E4 **Deane** Hants
48 B1 **Deanend** Dorset
328 D4 **Dean Head** Barns
69 G6 **Deanland** Dorset
466 D1 **Dean Park** Rens
19 F5 **Dean Prior** Devon
311 H3 **Dean Row** Ches
486 D6 **Deans** W Loth
98 D2 **Deans Bottom** Kent
388 C4 **Deanscales** Cumb
310 D2 **Deansgreen** Ches
214 A6 **Dean's Green** Warwks
167 F2 **Deanshanger** Nhants
510 A4 **Deanston** Stirlg
388 C4 **Dearham** Cumb
326 D1 **Dearnley** Rochdl
602 C6 **Deasbreck** Ork
202 A4 **Debach** Suffk
172 B3 **Debden** Essex
145 F2 **Debden Green** Essex
172 B3 **Debden Green** Essex
201 G2 **Debenham** Suffk
188 B5 **Deblin's Green** Worcs
486 D5 **Dechmont** W Loth

405 L2 **Deckham** Gatesd
165 H3 **Deddington** Oxon
175 E3 **Dedham** Essex
175 E3 **Dedham Heath** Essex
469 H1 **Dedridge** W Loth
117 F4 **Dedworth** W & M
556 B6 **Deebank** Abers
242 C6 **Deene** Nhants
218 D1 **Deenethorpe** Nhants
328 D5 **Deepcar** Sheff
327 F5 **Deepclough** Derbys
93 F3 **Deepcut** Surrey
196 B5 **Deepdale** Beds
367 E3 **Deepdale** Cumb
368 A4 **Deepdale** N York
94 D7 **Deepdene** Surrey
236 D6 **Deepfields** Dudley
243 G3 **Deeping Gate** C Pete
243 H3 **Deeping St James** Lincs
244 B1 **Deeping St Nicholas** Lincs
365 H3 **Deepthwaite** Cumb
109 E2 **Deepweir** Mons
569 H4 **Deerhill** Moray
162 C4 **Deerhurst** Gloucs
162 C4 **Deerhurst Walton** Gloucs
125 G2 **Deerland** Pembks
171 G3 **Deer's Green** Essex
355 E4 **Deerstones** N York
99 F2 **Deerton Street** Kent
188 D6 **Defford** Worcs
157 E4 **Defynnog** Powys
305 G4 **Deganwy** Conwy
105 G4 **Degar** Rhondd
4 B3 **Degibna** Cnwll
384 B4 **Deighton** N York
358 B6 **Deighton** York
284 C2 **Deiniolen** Gwynd
551 G6 **Deishar** Highld
22 B6 **Delabole** Cnwll
310 B6 **Delamere** Ches
561 E5 **Delfrigs** Abers
551 G7 **Dell** Highld
551 K3 **Delliefure** Highld
53 E4 **Dell Quay** W Susx
139 F2 **Delly End** Oxon
525 J2 **Delnamer** Angus
327 E3 **Delph** Oldham
404 D5 **Delves** Dur
512 D1 **Delvine** P & K
173 F2 **Delvin End** Essex
279 E2 **Dembleby** Lincs
14 D6 **Demelza** Cnwll
330 A5 **Denaby Main** Donc
501 C5 **Denbeath** Fife
287 F1 **Denbigh** Denbgs
19 H4 **Denbury** Devon
294 D5 **Denby** Derbys
294 D5 **Denby Bottles** Derbys
295 E5 **Denby Common** Derbys
328 C3 **Denby Dale** Kirk
114 B1 **Denchworth** Oxon
364 B5 **Dendron** Cumb
558 D2 **Denend** Abers
97 E4 **Dene Park** Kent
406 C5 **Deneside** Dur
218 D4 **Denford** Nhants
292 C4 **Denford** Staffs
148 C4 **Dengie** Essex
118 A2 **Denham** Bucks
167 G5 **Denham** Bucks
199 F2 **Denham** Suffk
225 G5 **Denham** Suffk
225 G5 **Denham Corner** Suffk
199 F2 **Denham End** Suffk
118 A2 **Denham Green** Bucks
225 G5 **Denham Street** Suffk
561 E3 **Denhead** Abers
571 H5 **Denhead** Abers
502 D2 **Denhead** Fife
515 F1 **Denhead of Arbirlot** Angus
514 A3 **Denhead of Gray** C Dund
451 H6 **Denholm** Border
341 H3 **Denholme** Brad
341 H3 **Denholme Gate** Brad
439 H1 **Denholmhill** Border
52 B2 **Denmead** Hants
557 G2 **Denmore** C Aber
202 B1 **Dennington** Suffk
202 B1 **Dennington Corner** Suffk
226 B6 **Dennington Hall** Suffk
467 F1 **Dennistoun** C Glas
485 G3 **Denny** Falk
78 D2 **Denny Bottom** Kent
197 G1 **Denny End** Cambs
485 E3 **Dennyloanhead** Falk
483 E4 **Dennystown** W Duns
501 E1 **Den of Lindores** Fife
327 E2 **Denshaw** Oldham
557 F5 **Denside** Abers
82 D2 **Densole** Kent
199 F4 **Denston** Suffk
273 G1 **Denstone** Staffs
100 A3 **Denstroude** Kent
367 E2 **Dent** Cumb
393 E2 **Dent Bank** Dur
219 H2 **Denton** Cambs
395 E6 **Denton** Darltn
56 D4 **Denton** E Susx
82 D1 **Denton** Kent
121 G5 **Denton** Kent
278 B3 **Denton** Lincs
194 A3 **Denton** Nhants
226 B2 **Denton** Norfk
355 F5 **Denton** N York
140 C4 **Denton** Oxon
326 D6 **Denton** Tamesd
405 E1 **Denton Burn** N u Ty
400 C3 **Denton Holme** Cumb
324 B5 **Denton's Green** St Hel
246 C4 **Denver** Norfk
52 C3 **Denvilles** Hants
443 G2 **Denwick** Nthumb
248 D4 **Deopham** Norfk
248 D5 **Deopham Green** Norfk
248 D5 **Deopham Stalland** Norfk
199 F3 **Depden** Suffk
199 F3 **Depden Green** Suffk
191 F3 **Deppers Bridge** Warwks
119 H4 **Deptford** Gt Lon
406 B3 **Deptford** Sundld
69 H2 **Deptford** Wilts
275 E2 **Derby** C Derb
61 E5 **Derby** Devon
322 d9 **Derbyhaven** IoM
324 C6 **Derbyshire Hill** St Hel
254 C5 **Dereham** Norfk
416 A5 **Dergoals** D & G
132 C3 **Deri** Caerph
11 E2 **Derriford** C Plym
23 G2 **Derril** Devon
100 C6 **Derringstone** Kent
210 D1 **Derrington** Shrops
272 C5 **Derrington** Staffs
23 G2 **Derriton** Devon
96 C1 **Derry Downs** Gt Lon
17 F5 **Derry Fields** Wilts
504 F3 **Derryguaig** Ag & B
111 H5 **Derry Hill** Wilts
331 H1 **Derrythorpe** N Linc
258 D5 **Dersingham** Norfk
87 E5 **Dertfords** Wilts
518 B5 **Dervaig** Ag & B
105 E3 **Derwen** Brdgnd
287 F4 **Derwen** Denbgs

229 G5 Derwenlas Powys
217 H3 Desborough Nhants
239 H4 Desford Leics
454 D2 Detchant Nthumb
98 B3 Detling Kent
527 G2 Deuchar Angus
268 D6 Deuddwr Powys
211 F2 Deuxhill Shrops
134 B5 Devauden Mons
3 G2 Deveral Cnwll
205 G4 Devil's Bridge Cerdgn
214 D1 Devitts Green Warwks
88 B2 Devizes Wilts
482 D5 Devol Inver
10 D2 Devonport C Plym
499 E5 Devonside Clacks
499 E5 Devon Village Clacks
7 E6 Devoran Cnwll
471 G2 Dewartown Mdloth
171 G3 Dewes Green Essex
48 D3 Dewlands Common Dorset
47 E5 Dewlish Dorset
342 D5 Dewsbury Kirk
38 C6 Dexbeer Devon
599 K2 Dhail bho Dheas W Isls
210 D4 Dhustone Shrops
75 E4 Dial Green W Susx
76 B6 Dial Post W Susx
30 B2 Dibberford Dorset
50 D3 Dibden Hants
50 C3 Dibden Purlieu Hants
213 H4 Dickens Heath Solhll
225 G3 Dickleburgh Norfk
225 G3 Dickleburgh Moor Norfk
300 D3 Dickon Hills Lincs
163 G3 Didbrook Gloucs
115 E2 Didcot Oxon
196 A1 Diddington Cambs
210 C2 Diddlebury Shrops
39 F2 Diddywell Devon
160 B3 Didley Herefs
74 C6 Didling W Susx
247 F5 Didlington Norfk
111 E2 Didmarton Gloucs
311 G1 Didsbury Manch
19 E5 Didworthy Devon
213 G2 Digbeth Birm
298 D4 Digby Lincs
543 H3 Digg Highld
327 F3 Diggle Oldham
188 B4 Diglis Worcs
324 B4 Digmoor Lancs
144 C1 Digswell Herts
144 B2 Digswell Park Herts
144 C1 Digswell Water Herts
180 C3 Dihewyd Cerdgn
256 C4 Dilham Norfk
292 C6 Dilhorne Staffs
340 A4 Dill Hall Lancs
195 G1 Dillington Cambs
44 D4 Dillington Somset
403 H2 Dilston Nthumb
185 H4 Dilwyn Herefs
186 A3 Dilwyn Common Herefs
105 F6 Dimlands V Glam
67 G3 Dimmer Somset
325 G1 Dimple Bolton
294 B2 Dimple Derbys
291 G5 Dimsdale Staffs
17 F4 Dimson Cnwll
153 H2 Dinas Carmth
14 C4 Dinas Cnwll
262 D3 Dinas Gwynd
264 B2 Dinas Gwynd
283 E4 Dinas Gwynd
151 H2 Dinas Cross Pembks
282 D4 Dinas Dinlle Gwynd
230 C2 Dinas Mawddwy Gwynd
285 G4 Dinas Mawr Conwy
106 B5 Dinas Powys V Glam
339 G2 Dinckley Lancs
85 G6 Dinder Somset
160 C2 Dinedor Herefs
160 C2 Dinedor Cross Herefs
188 B3 Dines Green Worcs
134 A2 Dingestow Mons
84 D3 Dinghurst N Som
309 E2 Dingle Lpool
80 B3 Dingleden Kent
451 G3 Dingleton Border
217 G2 Dingley Nhants
565 J5 Dingwall Highld
426 D1 Dinlabyre Border
286 D6 Dinmael Conwy
555 E5 Dinnet Abers
430 D5 Dinnington N u Ty
315 G2 Dinnington Rothm
45 E5 Dinnington Somset
284 C2 Dinorwig Gwynd
141 G2 Dinton Bucks
69 H3 Dinton Wilts
424 C1 Dinwoodie Mains D & G
38 D4 Dinworthy Devon
43 H3 Dipford Somset
92 B3 Dipley Hants
461 E5 Dippen N Ayrs
92 D5 Dippenhall Surrey
24 B6 Dippertown Devon
38 D4 Dipple Devon
568 E4 Dipple Moray
432 A4 Dipple S Ayrs
12 C1 Diptford Devon
404 D4 Dipton Dur
403 G2 Diptonmill Nthumb
595 K3 Direcleit W Isls
489 G3 Dirleton E Loth
525 G3 Dirnanean P & K
403 F5 Dirt Pot Nthumb
185 E2 Discoed Powys
68 A3 Discove Somset
275 H5 Diseworth Leics
603 K7 Dishes Ork
370 D5 Dishforth N York
276 B5 Dishley Leics
312 C3 Disley Ches
225 F3 Diss Norfk
183 E3 Disserth Powys
388 A5 Distington Cumb
70 B3 Ditchampton Wilts
67 G2 Ditcheat Somset
116 C1 Ditchfield Herefs
226 C1 Ditchingham Norfk
56 A1 Ditchling E Susx
234 C2 Ditherington Shrops
111 E6 Ditteridge Wilts
13 F2 Dittisham Devon
309 G2 Ditton Halton
97 H3 Ditton Kent
198 D3 Ditton Green Cambs
211 E2 Ditton Priors Shrops
57 G4 Dittons E Susx
163 E3 Dixton Gloucs
134 C2 Dixton Mons
22 D3 Dizzard Cnwll
327 E3 Dobcross Oldham
288 D2 Dobs Hill Flints
270 B3 Dobson's Bridge Shrops
16 B5 Dobwalls Cnwll
26 B5 Doccombe Devon
549 L1 Dochgarroch Highld
226 D1 Dockeney Norfk
74 C1 Dockenfield Surrey
366 B5 Docker Lancs
259 F4 Docking Norfk

186 D3 Docklow Herefs
390 B5 Dockray Cumb
341 G2 Dockroyd Brad
38 B3 Docton Devon
12 C4 Dodbrooke Devon
439 F3 Dodburn Border
187 H3 Doddenham Worcs
146 B5 Doddinghurst Essex
221 E1 Doddington Cambs
99 E3 Doddington Kent
317 H5 Doddington Lincs
454 B3 Doddington Nthumb
211 E4 Doddington Shrops
26 C5 Doddiscombsleigh Devon
258 D5 Dodford Nhants
10 B1 Doddycross Cnwll
192 D2 Dodford Nhants
212 D5 Dodford Worcs
110 C4 Dodington S Glos
64 C3 Dodington Somset
289 E2 Dodleston Ches
186 D6 Dodmarsh Herefs
40 A4 Dodscott Devon
273 H3 Dods Leigh Staffs
329 E3 Dodworth Barns
329 E3 Dodworth Bottom Barns
237 H5 Doe Bank Birm
310 A2 Doe Green Warrtn
294 D3 Doehole Derbys
295 F1 Doe Green Warrtn
294 D3 Doe Lea Derbys
325 F2 Doffcocker Bolton
323 C6 Dog & Gun Lpool
299 F3 Dogdyke Lincs
327 E3 Dog Hill Oldham
237 E2 Dogingtree Estate Staffs
92 C4 Dogmersfield Hants
244 A4 Dogsthorpe C Pete
27 F3 Dog Village Devon
231 H2 Dolanog Powys
184 B1 Dolau Powys
105 G3 Dolau Rhondd
284 B6 Dolbenmaen Gwynd
205 E2 Dole Cerdgn
86 D2 Dolemeads BaNES
271 G4 Doley Staffs
207 E4 Dolfach Powys
231 E4 Dol-fâch Powys
229 G2 Dol-ffanog Gwynd
208 B2 Dolfor Powys
285 G1 Dolgarrog Conwy
229 G1 Dolgellau Gwynd
180 B4 Dolgerdd Cerdgn
229 F4 Dolgoch Gwynd
154 B3 Dolgran Carmth
207 E5 Dolhelfa Powys
266 D3 Dolhendre Gwynd
577 J3 Doll Highld
499 F5 Dollar Clacks
185 E1 Dolley Green Powys
119 E2 Dollis Hill Gt Lon
205 F3 Dollwen Cerdgn
308 A5 Dolphinstone Ches
488 D5 Dolphinstone E Loth
351 H4 Dolphinholme Lancs
440 C1 Dolphinston Border
470 B5 Dolphinton Border
23 F3 Dolsdon Cnwll
40 B5 Dolton Devon
306 B5 Dolwen Conwy
231 F3 Dolwen Powys
305 H4 Dolwyd Conwy
285 F4 Dolwyddelan Conwy
205 G4 Dôl-y-Bont Cerdgn
184 C5 Dôl-y-cannau Powys
283 E4 Dolydd Gwynd
184 D3 Dolyhir Powys
232 A5 Dolymelinau Powys
268 D2 Dolywern Wrexhm
77 F1 Domewood Surrey
269 E6 Domgay Powys
44 B5 Dommett Somset
330 D4 Doncaster Donc
330 C4 Doncaster Carr Donc
310 B4 Dones Green Ches
69 F5 Donhead St Andrew Wilts
69 E5 Donhead St Mary Wilts
487 G4 Donibristle Fife
64 A3 Doniford Somset
280 D2 Donington Lincs
236 B4 Donington Shrops
280 B2 Donington Eaudike Lincs
239 G2 Donington le Heath Leics
319 G3 Donington on Bain Lincs
280 A3 Donington South Ing Lincs
239 F2 Donisthorpe Leics
173 G4 Don Johns Essex
81 H3 Donkey Street Kent
93 F2 Donkey Town Surrey
335 F3 Donna Nook Lincs
164 B4 Donnington Gloucs
161 G3 Donnington Herefs
234 D3 Donnington Shrops
114 D6 Donnington W Berk
235 G2 Donnington Wrekin
53 F4 Donnington W Susx
235 G2 Donnington Wood Wrekin
405 G3 Donwell Sundld
44 C5 Donyatt Somset
76 C3 Doomsday Green W Susx
444 D6 Doonfoot S Ayrs
432 D1 Doonholm S Ayrs
92 D5 Dora's Green Hants
113 E3 Dorcan Swindn
32 C1 Dorchester Dorset
140 C6 Dorchester Oxon
212 D5 Dordale Worcs
238 D4 Dordon Warwks
314 C3 Dore Sheff
549 L3 Dores Highld
94 D4 Dorking Surrey
174 B2 Dorking Tye Suffk
202 D1 Dorley's Corner Suffk
77 H1 Dormansland Surrey
77 G1 Dormans Park Surrey
397 E5 Dormanstown R & Cl
118 C3 Dormer's Wells Gt Lon
160 D1 Dormington Herefs
189 E3 Dormston Worcs
164 C3 Dorn Gloucs
117 F4 Dorney Bucks
546 F4 Dorney Reach Bucks
577 H6 Dornie Highld
399 G1 Dornoch D & G
588 D6 Dornock D & G
214 B4 Dorridge Solhll
298 D4 Dorrington Lincs
234 B4 Dorrington Shrops
190 A5 Dorsington Warwks
159 F1 Dorstone Herefs
141 E2 Dorton Bucks
235 F3 Doseley Wrekin
238 C4 Dosthill Staffs
303 E6 Dothan IoA
30 B3 Dottery Dorset
16 A5 Doublebois Cnwll
86 C3 Doughton Gloucs
111 F1 Doughton Gloucs
253 H2 Doulton Norfk
322 f7 Douglas IoM
447 G3 Douglas S Lans
514 C3 Douglas and Angus
527 F5 Douglastown Angus

448 A4 Douglas Water S Lans
447 G3 Douglas West S Lans
86 A6 Doulting Somset
602 B7 Dounby Ork
550 F8 Doune Highld
575 J3 Doune Highld
498 A4 Doune Stirlg
555 E3 Douneside Abers
576 C5 Dounie Highld
576 E6 Dounie Highld
465 G6 Doura N Ayrs
18 A4 Dousland Devon
269 F5 Dovaston Shrops
309 F1 Dovecot Lpool
466 D3 Dovecothall E Rens
295 H4 Dove Green Notts
313 E4 Dove Holes Derbys
388 C3 Dovenby Cumb
320 B3 Dovendale Lincs
308 B1 Dove Point Wirral
83 F2 Dover Kent
325 E4 Dover Wigan
177 E3 Dovercourt Essex
188 B1 Doverdale Worcs
62 D2 Doverhay Somset
273 H3 Doveridge Derbys
95 F5 Doversgreen Surrey
524 F6 Dowally P & K
467 E1 Dowanhill C Glas
338 B3 Dowbridge Lancs
163 E6 Dowdeswell Gloucs
251 G1 Dowe Hill Norfk
432 B4 Dowhill S Ayrs
132 A3 Dowlais Myr Td
131 H3 Dowlais Top Myr Td
40 B5 Dowland Devon
212 A4 Dowles Worcs
116 D6 Dowlesgreen Wokham
44 D5 Dowlish Ford Somset
44 D5 Dowlish Wake Somset
324 D4 Downall Green St Hel
137 H5 Down Ampney Gloucs
10 B3 Downderry Cnwll
96 B3 Downe Gt Lon
37 E3 Downend IoW
110 A4 Downend S Glos
136 B5 Downend S Glos
65 E3 Down End Somset
114 D4 Downend W Berk
222 C5 Down Field Cambs
514 B3 Downfield C Dund
16 C4 Downgate Cnwll
17 E4 Downgate Cnwll
400 A4 Down Hall Cumb
147 E5 Downham Essex
120 A5 Downham Gt Lon
353 F6 Downham Lancs
453 G3 Downham Nthumb
246 C4 Downham Market Norfk
162 C5 Down Hatherley Gloucs
67 F4 Downhead Somset
86 B5 Downhead Somset
168 M1 Downhead Park M Keyn
14 B5 Downhill Cnwll
406 B3 Downhill Sundld
323 G3 Downholland Cross Lancs
382 D5 Downholme N York
23 H4 Downicary Devon
557 G5 Downies Abers
307 H4 Downing Flints
23 E4 Downinney Cnwll
142 A5 Downley Bucks
77 E2 Down Park W Susx
106 B5 Downs V Glam
26 A2 Down St Mary Devon
169 E5 Downside Beds
57 F4 Downside E Susx
85 E1 Downside N Som
86 A4 Downside Somset
86 A6 Downside Somset
94 C3 Downside Surrey
565 K3 Downside Surrey
78 A5 Down Street E Susx
11 F3 Down Thomas Devon
49 H6 Downton Hants
184 D2 Downton Powys
234 C2 Downton Shrops
70 D5 Downton Wilts
209 H5 Downton on the Rock Herefs
279 G4 Dowsby Lincs
244 C4 Dowsdale Lincs
44 A3 Dowslands Somset
390 B5 Dowthwaitehead Cumb
272 D5 Doxey Staffs
406 B4 Doxford Park Sundld
110 C5 Doynton S Glos
255 G2 Drabblegate Norfk
106 D2 Draethen Caerph
468 B5 Draffan S Lans
364 C4 Dragley Beck Cumb
332 B2 Dragonby N Linc
76 B5 Dragons Green W Susx
29 F4 Dragon's Hill Dorset
315 E3 Drakehouse Sheff
18 C6 Drakeland Corner Devon
212 B3 Drakelow Worcs
561 E2 Drakemyre Abers
465 F4 Drakemyre N Ayrs
188 D5 Drakes Broughton Worcs
213 G4 Drakes Cross Worcs
200 C5 Drakestone Green Suffk
17 F4 Drakewalls Cnwll
217 G2 Draughton Nhants
354 D4 Draughton N York
15 H5 Drawbridge Cnwll
345 F4 Drax N York
140 D3 Draycot Oxon
111 G4 Draycote Warwks
215 G6 Draycote Warwks
88 D2 Draycot Cerne Wilts
113 E4 Draycot Fitz Payne Wilts
113 G4 Draycot Foliat Swindn
275 G3 Draycott Derbys
135 H4 Draycott Gloucs
164 B2 Draycott Gloucs
236 B6 Draycott Shrops
67 E5 Draycott Somset
85 E4 Draycott Somset
188 C5 Draycott Worcs
274 B4 Draycott in the Clay Staffs
273 E1 Draycott in the Moors Staffs
41 F5 Drayford Devon
52 B3 Drayton C Port
218 A1 Drayton Leics
280 B2 Drayton Lincs
192 C2 Drayton Nhants
570 D3 Drayton Norfk
557 G2 Drayton Oxon
165 G1 Drayton Oxon
45 E4 Drayton Somset
66 C5 Drayton Somset
190 B3 Drayton Warwks
212 D4 Drayton Worcs
238 B4 Drayton Bassett Staffs
142 C2 Drayton Beauchamp Bucks
168 A4 Drayton Parslow Bucks
140 C5 Drayton St Leonard Oxon
355 E3 Drebley N York
322 h4 Dreemskerry IoM
151 H3 Dreenhill Pembks
128 D2 Drefach Carmth
129 G1 Drefach Carmth
153 F5 Drefach Carmth

153 H2 Drefach Carmth
153 H2 Drefelin Carmth
551 J4 Dreggie Highld
487 H6 Dreghorn C Edin
444 D2 Dreghorn N Ayrs
307 G6 Dre-gôch Denbgs
82 D2 Drellingore Kent
489 G4 Drem E Loth
272 D1 Dresden C Stke
593 D10 Dreumasdal W Isls
25 H4 Drewsteignton Devon
320 C5 Driby Lincs
360 C3 Driffield E R Yk
137 G5 Driffield Gloucs
2 D4 Drift Cnwll
376 D5 Drigg Cumb
342 D4 Drighlington Leeds
479 J5 Drimnagall Ag & B
518 E5 Drimnin Highld
29 H2 Drimpton Dorset
494 D4 Drimsynie Ag & B
361 E3 Dringhoe E R Yk
357 H5 Dringhouses York
595 K4 Drinisiadar W Isls
200 C2 Drinkstone Suffk
200 C2 Drinkstone Green Suffk
46 A3 Drive End Dorset
546 B5 Drochaid Lusa Highld
273 F4 Drointon Staffs
188 C2 Droitwich Worcs
584 C5 Droman Highld
500 B1 Dron P & K
314 D4 Dronfield Derbys
314 C4 Dronfield Woodhouse Derbys
445 F6 Drongan E Ayrs
514 A2 Dronley Angus
47 E3 Droop Dorset
106 B4 Drope V Glam
329 F6 Dropping Well Rothm
73 E6 Droxford Hants
326 C5 Droylsden Tamesd
342 C4 Drub Kirk
162 A2 Druggers End Worcs
287 E6 Druid Denbgs
125 E1 Druidston Pembks
520 F1 Druimarbin Highld
520 E7 Druimavuic Ag & B
479 J7 Druimdrishaig Ag & B
531 J6 Druimindarroch Highld
549 H2 Druimkinnerras Highld
488 C6 Drum C Edin
499 G4 Drum P & K
448 B2 Drumalbin S Lans
198 C3 Drumbeg Highld
558 D1 Drumblade Abers
569 L7 Drumblair Abers
408 B3 Drumbreddan D & G
421 F3 Drumbuie D & G
546 D3 Drumbuie Highld
399 H3 Drumburgh Cumb
483 H5 Drumchapel C Glas
565 K8 Drumchardine Highld
573 G6 Drumchork Highld
446 C2 Drumclog S Lans
558 D2 Drumdollo Abers
502 C4 Drumeldrie Fife
449 F3 Drumelzier Border
546 B6 Drumfearn Highld
468 B1 Drumgelloch N Lans
527 F4 Drumgley Angus
535 L3 Drumguish Highld
552 D2 Drumin Moray
433 H5 Drumjohn D & G
556 A3 Drumlasie Abers
456 D2 Drumlemble Ag & B
557 G1 Drumligair Abers
541 E3 Drumlithie Abers
323 G2 Drummersdale Lancs
410 C3 Drummodie D & G
565 K3 Drummond Highld
566 B8 Drummond Highld
411 E5 Drummoral D & G
408 C4 Drummore D & G
577 H4 Drummuie Highld
568 F7 Drummuir Moray
528 C6 Drummygar Angus
549 J4 Drumnadrochit Highld
569 J5 Drumnagorrach Moray
556 D5 Drumoak Abers
467 H1 Drumpellier N Lans
415 H4 Drumphail D & G
422 A5 Drumrash D & G
574 D2 Drumrunie Highld
483 H5 Drumry W Duns
561 E5 Drums Abers
532 D7 Drumsallie Highld
432 C2 Drumshang S Ayrs
423 F5 Drumsleet D & G
565 L7 Drumsmittal Highld
514 D2 Drumsturdy Angus
410 C3 Drumtroddan D & G
543 G7 Drumuie Highld
551 G5 Drumuillie Highld
497 G4 Drumvaich Stirlg
560 D2 Drumwhindle Abers
529 E5 Drunkendub Angus
288 C2 Drury Flints
248 B4 Drurylane Norfk
289 G6 Drury Lane Wrexhm
254 A4 Drury Square Norfk
380 B1 Drybeck Cumb
569 G3 Drybridge Moray
444 D2 Drybridge N Ayrs
135 K1 Drybrook Gloucs
452 A3 Dryburgh Border
450 B5 Dryden Border
487 H4 Dry Doddington Lincs
297 G5 Dry Doddington Lincs
197 E2 Dry Drayton Cambs
73 F2 Dry Hill Hants
96 C4 Dryhill Kent
450 B5 Dryhope Border
487 H4 Drylaw C Edin
4 B2 Drym Cnwll
483 G2 Drymen Stirlg
247 F3 Drymere Norfk
571 G6 Drymuir Abers
87 F3 Drynham Wilts
565 K6 Drynie Park Highld
545 J3 Drynoch Highld
139 H4 Dry Sandford Oxon
154 D5 Dryslwyn Carmth
121 H2 Dry Street Essex
234 D3 Dryton Shrops
579 G2 Duartmore Bridge Highld
24 A4 Dubbs Cross Devon
570 D3 Dubford Abers
557 G2 Dubford C Aber
565 L2 Dublin Highld
225 G6 Dublin Suffk
528 C4 Dubton Angus
389 E3 Dubwath Cumb
579 L6 Duchally Lodge Highld
202 D5 Duck Corner Suffk
194 D4 Duck End Beds
195 F6 Duck End Beds
167 G4 Duck End Bucks
196 B2 Duck End Cambs
171 H5 Duck End Essex
172 D3 Duck End Essex
172 D4 Duck End Essex
173 E5 Duckend Green Essex
110 A1 Duckhole S Glos
289 G5 Duckington Ches
140 A4 Ducklington Oxon

139 F3 Ducklington Oxon
315 E5 Duckmanton Derbys
195 G3 Duck's Cross Beds
144 B5 Ducks Island Gt Lon
162 B2 Duckswich Worcs
136 B4 Dudbridge Gloucs
119 E2 Dudden Hill Gt Lon
171 G2 Duddenhoe End Essex
488 B5 Duddingston C Edin
242 D4 Duddington Nhants
43 H3 Duddlestone Somset
78 B4 Duddleswell E Susx
211 F3 Duddlewick Shrops
474 D6 Duddo Nthumb
289 H1 Duddon Ches
362 D4 Duddon Bridge Cumb
289 H1 Duddon Common Ches
269 F2 Dudleston Shrops
269 G2 Dudleston Grove Shrops
269 G2 Dudleston Heath Shrops
212 D2 Dudley Dudley
431 E5 Dudley N Tyne
342 C3 Dudley Hill Brad
213 E1 Dudley Port Sandw
237 E4 Dudley's Fields Wsall
212 D2 Dudley Wood Dudley
310 C3 Dudlows Green Warrtn
48 D5 Dudsbury Dorset
142 D3 Dudswell Herts
151 E5 Dudwells Pembks
38 D4 Duerdon Devon
294 C6 Duffield Derbys
294 D6 Duffieldbank Derbys
130 C5 Duffryn Neath
107 E2 Duffryn Newpt
208 D3 Duffryn Shrops
557 G5 Duff's Hill Abers
568 E7 Dufftown Moray
568 B2 Duffus Moray
392 A4 Dufton Cumb
359 G1 Duggleby N York
546 D3 Duirinish Highld
546 B7 Duisdalebeg Highld
546 C7 Duisdalemore Highld
532 F7 Duisky Highld
214 C2 Duke End Warwks
403 G3 Dukesfield Nthumb
132 B2 Dukestown Blae G
326 D5 Dukinfield Tamesd
303 G3 Dulas IoA
85 G6 Dulcote Somset
27 H1 Dulford Devon
524 B6 Dull P & K
485 E4 Dullatur N Lans
198 C3 Dullingham Cambs
198 C3 Dullingham Ley Cambs
551 H5 Dulnain Bridge Highld
487 F2 Duloch Fife
195 H2 Duloe Beds
9 G2 Duloe Cnwll
551 G1 Dulsie Highld
42 B2 Dulverton Somset
119 G5 Dulwich Gt Lon
119 G5 Dulwich Village Gt Lon
483 F4 Dumbarton W Duns
163 F2 Dumbleton Gloucs
467 E2 Dumbreck C Glas
437 F4 Dumcrieff D & G
423 G4 Dumfries D & G
483 H3 Dumgoyne Stirlg
91 F5 Dummer Hants
74 C5 Dumpford W Susx
39 F6 Dumpinghill Devon
248 D2 Dumpling Green Norfk
325 H5 Dumplington Traffd
101 G2 Dumpton Kent
529 E3 Dun Angus
523 K4 Dunalastair P & K
480 A1 Dunamuck Ag & B
545 K4 Dunan Ag & B
552 E7 Dunandhu Abers
479 L3 Dunans Ag & B
481 E1 Dunans Ag & B
65 E3 Dunball Somset
490 C4 Dunbar E Loth
583 G3 Dunbeath Highld
506 E3 Dunbeg Ag & B
498 B4 Dunblane Stirlg
513 G6 Dunbog Fife
542 B6 Dùn Boreraig Highld
71 G4 Dunbridge Hants
605 G4 Duncansclett Shet
565 K5 Duncanston Highld
558 D4 Duncanstone Abers
598 D6 Dùn Chàrlabhaigh W Isls
26 D5 Dunchideock Devon
215 H5 Dunchurch Warwks
542 C7 Dùn Colbost Highld
338 C2 Duncombe Lancs
193 E4 Duncote Nhants
423 G3 Duncow D & G
500 B3 Duncrievie P & K
53 H1 Duncton W Susx
514 C3 Dundee C Dund
421 F2 Dundeugh D & G
66 D3 Dundon Somset
500 D6 Dundonald Fife
445 E3 Dundonald S Ayrs
444 D3 Dundonald Camp N Ayrs
66 D3 Dundon Hayes Somset
574 B6 Dundonnell Highld
399 G5 Dundraw Cumb
548 E7 Dundreggan Highld
412 D5 Dundrennan D & G
73 E6 Dundridge Hants
85 F1 Dundry N Som
498 C2 Dunduff P & K
467 H2 Dundyvan N Lans
556 D3 Dunecht Abers
487 F2 Dunfermline Fife
138 A5 Dunfield Gloucs
328 A4 Dunford Bridge Barns
592 D6 Dun Gainmhich W Isls
99 E3 Dungate Kent
87 F4 Dunge Wilts
81 G6 Dungeness Kent
314 B2 Dungworth Sheff
309 C5 Dunham-on-the-Hill Ches
317 F5 Dunham on Trent Notts
188 D2 Dunhampstead Worcs
188 B1 Dunhampton Worcs
311 E2 Dunham Town Traffd
311 E2 Dunham Woodhouses Traffd
318 C4 Dunholme Lincs
503 E2 Dunino Fife
485 G3 Dunipace Falk
510 C5 Dunira P & K
524 F7 Dunkeld P & K
527 E3 Dunkenny Angus
86 C3 Dunkerton BaNES
43 F6 Dunkeswell Devon
356 B5 Dunkeswick N York
221 H2 Dunkirk Cambs
309 H5 Dunkirk Ches
276 B2 Dunkirk C Nott
100 A4 Dunkirk Kent
255 C2 Dunkirk Norfk
110 D2 Dunkirk S Glos
291 G4 Dunkirk Staffs
88 A2 Dunkirk Wilts
97 F4 Dunk's Green Kent
540 A6 Dunlappie Angus

90 C4 Dunley Hants
212 A6 Dunley Worcs
466 B5 Dunlop E Ayrs
15 F5 Dunmere Cnwll
462 C2 Dunmore Ag & B
486 A2 Dunmore Falk
565 J7 Dunmore Highld
362 D6 Dunnerholme Cumb
589 G2 Dunnet Highld
528 B5 Dunnichen Angus
501 E6 Dunnikier Fife
499 G2 Dunning P & K
361 F4 Dunnington E R Yk
189 G4 Dunnington Warwks
358 C4 Dunnington York
362 D5 Dunningwell Cumb
340 C4 Dunnockshaw Lancs
37 F5 Dunnose IoW
234 B1 Dunnsheath Shrops
98 B2 Dunn Street Kent
99 F5 Dunn Street Kent
506 E3 Dunollie Ag & B
482 A4 Dunoon Ag & B
567 J7 Dunphail Moray
415 G5 Dunragit D & G
479 J5 Dunrostan Ag & B
314 A5 Dunsa Derbys
474 A4 Duns Border
36 B4 Dunsbury IoW
279 G4 Dunsby Lincs
325 G2 Dunscar Bolton
423 E3 Dunscore D & G
330 D3 Dunscroft Donc
397 F6 Dunsdale R & Cl
116 B4 Dunsden Green Oxon
38 D6 Dunsdon Devon
75 G2 Dunsfold Common Surrey
75 G2 Dunsfold Green Surrey
26 C5 Dunsford Devon
75 G2 Dunsford Surrey
501 E2 Dunshalt Fife
295 F2 Dunsill Notts
513 E3 Dunsinnan P & K
16 C4 Dunslea Cnwll
387 E2 Dunsley N York
212 C3 Dunsley Staffs
142 A3 Dunsmore Bucks
216 B4 Dunsmore Warwks
352 D4 Dunsop Bridge Lancs
169 E5 Dunstable Beds
273 G4 Dunstal Staffs
274 B5 Dunstall Staffs
188 C6 Dunstall Common Worcs
199 E2 Dunstall Green Suffk
236 D4 Dunstall Hill Wolves
455 G6 Dunstan Nthumb
63 F3 Dunster Somset
165 H4 Duns Tew Oxon
314 D5 Dunston Derbys
405 F2 Dunston Gatesd
298 D2 Dunston Lincs
249 H4 Dunston Norfk
272 D6 Dunston Staffs
11 G3 Dunstone Devon
12 D4 Dunstone Devon
272 D6 Dunston Heath Staffs
405 F2 Dunston Hill Gatesd
330 D3 Dunsville Donc
347 G2 Dunswell E R Yk
469 H5 Dunsyre S Lans
17 E3 Dunterton Devon
165 F4 Dunthrop Oxon
137 E3 Duntisbourne Abbots Gloucs
137 E3 Duntisbourne Leer Gloucs
137 E3 Duntisbourne Rouse Gloucs
46 C3 Duntish Dorset
483 G5 Duntocher W Duns
196 B6 Dunton Beds
167 H5 Dunton Bucks
260 A5 Dunton Norfk
216 B1 Dunton Bassett Leics
96 D3 Dunton Green Kent
260 A5 Dunton Patch Norfk
121 F1 Dunton Wayletts Essex
543 G2 Duntulm Highld
432 C1 Dunure S Ayrs
103 E3 Dunvant Swans
542 D7 Dunvegan Highld
14 D4 Dunveth Cnwll
65 F5 Dunwear Somset
227 F5 Dunwich Suffk
292 B3 Dunwood Staffs
8 C3 Duporth Cnwll
400 C4 Durdar Cumb
513 F5 Durdie P & K
5 E3 Durgan Cnwll
79 E3 Durgates E Susx
395 F1 Durham Dur
436 A4 Durisdeer D & G
435 H4 Durisdeermill D & G
329 E1 Durkar Wakefd
65 E4 Durleigh Somset
74 B5 Durleighmarsh W Susx
51 F1 Durley Hants
89 F2 Durley Wilts
72 D6 Durley Street Hants
101 E4 Durlock Kent
161 E2 Durlow Common Herefs
49 G6 Durns Town Hants
326 D1 Durn Rochdl
573 K5 Durnamuck Highld
585 H3 Durness Highld
66 D5 Durnfield Somset
559 G4 Durno Abers
50 A5 Durns Town Hants
520 D4 Duror Highld
588 F4 Durran Highld
80 C2 Durrant Green Kent
52 C3 Durrants Hants
88 D6 Durrington Wilts
54 D4 Durrington W Susx
54 D4 Durrington-on-Sea W Susx
602 D7 Durrisdale Ork
556 D5 Durris Ho Abers
135 G5 Dursley Gloucs
87 F4 Dursley Wilts
161 F5 Dursley Cross Gloucs
44 B2 Durston Somset
47 G3 Durweston Dorset
607 G5 Dury Shet
27 E4 Duryard Devon
193 F2 Duston Nhants
122 B3 Dutch Village Essex
551 G5 Duthil Highld
208 D4 Dutlas Powys
172 C4 Duton Hill Essex
23 G5 Dutson Cnwll
310 B4 Dutton Ches
197 G5 Duxford Cambs
139 F5 Duxford Oxon
210 A4 Duxmoor Shrops
305 F4 Dwygyfylchi Conwy
282 D2 Dwyran IoA
231 H4 Dwyrhiw Powys
557 F2 Dyce C Aber
64 C3 Dyche Somset
403 G3 Dye House Nthumb
109 F3 Dyer's Common S Glos
196 D5 Dyer's Green Cambs
130 C6 Dyffryn Brdgnd
153 G5 Dyffryn Carmth
179 F3 Dyffryn Cerdgn
151 F2 Dyffryn Pembks
106 A5 Dyffryn V Glam
264 D5 Dyffryn Ardudwy Gwynd
179 F3 Dyffryn-bern Cerdgn
155 G4 Dyffryn Ceidrych Carmth
130 C3 Dyffryn Cellwen Neath
279 G5 Dyke Lincs
567 H5 Dyke Moray
527 E2 Dykehead Angus
468 D3 Dykehead N Lans
497 E5 Dykehead Stirlg
526 B3 Dykend Angus
570 C7 Dykeside Abers
230 D6 Dylife Powys
81 H4 Dymchurch Kent
161 F3 Dymock Gloucs
110 C4 Dyrham S Glos
501 F6 Dysart Fife
307 E4 Dyserth Denbgs

E

544 E2 Eabost Highld
544 E1 Eabost West Highld
101 E4 Each End Kent
213 E4 Eachway Worcs
430 B5 Eachwick Nthumb
596 C1 Eadar Dha Fhadhail W Isls
351 F6 Eagland Hill Lancs
297 G1 Eagle Lincs
297 G1 Eagle Barnsdale Lincs
317 G6 Eagle Moor Lincs
384 C1 Eaglescliffe S on T
388 C4 Eaglesfield Cumb
425 E5 Eaglesfield D & G
467 E4 Eaglesham E Rens
168 B2 Eaglestone M Keyn
219 F1 Eaglethorpe Nhants
294 A2 Eagle Tor Derbys
325 G2 Eagley Bolton
322 d7 Eairy IoM
296 C2 Eakring Notts
331 G2 Ealand N Linc
118 D4 Ealing Gt Lon
402 B3 Eals Nthumb
391 E4 Eamont Bridge Cumb
354 A5 Earby Lancs
339 G5 Earcroft Bl w D
211 G1 Eardington Shrops
185 H3 Eardisland Herefs
185 F5 Eardisley Herefs
269 G5 Eardiston Shrops
211 F6 Eardiston Worcs
221 E4 Earith Cambs
454 B4 Earle Nthumb
324 D5 Earlestown St Hel
116 C5 Earley Wokham
249 G3 Earlham Norfk
542 F4 Earlish Highld
194 B2 Earls Barton Nhants
173 H4 Earls Colne Essex
189 E3 Earl's Common Worcs
162 C1 Earl's Croome Worcs
215 E4 Earlsdon Covtry
79 E6 Earl's Down E Susx
502 D5 Earlsferry Fife
119 F5 Earlsfield Gt Lon
278 B2 Earlsfield Lincs
560 B3 Earlsford Abers
200 D1 Earl's Green Suffk
239 H5 Earl Shilton Leics
202 A2 Earl Soham Suffk
293 E1 Earl Sterndale Derbys
452 A2 Earlston Border
445 F2 Earlston E Ayrs
90 D2 Earlstone Common Hants
201 F3 Earl Stonham Suffk
421 G3 Earlstoun D & G
134 A5 Earlswood Mons
95 F5 Earlswood Surrey
213 H5 Earlswood Warwks
53 E5 Earnley W Susx
467 G4 Earnock S Lans
338 D5 Earnshaw Bridge Lancs
591 D8 Earsairidh W Isls
431 F5 Earsdon N Tyne
436 D4 Earshaig D & G
226 C2 Earsham Norfk
226 A4 Earsham Street Suffk
358 B3 Earswick York
53 G3 Eartham W Susx
110 A2 Earthcott Green S Glos
385 F3 Easby N York
492 B1 Easdale Ag & B
74 D5 Easebourne W Susx
215 H4 Easenhall Warwks
93 F6 Eashing Surrey
141 E2 Easington Bucks
406 C6 Easington Dur
349 H6 Easington E R Yk
352 D4 Easington Lancs
455 E2 Easington Nthumb
141 E5 Easington Oxon
165 G2 Easington Oxon
397 H6 Easington R & Cl
406 C6 Easington Colliery Dur
406 B5 Easington Lane Sundld
371 G6 Easingwold N York
78 C6 Eason's Green E Susx
526 D5 Eassie Angus
105 G6 East Aberthaw V Glam
40 A2 Eastacombe Devon
40 B3 Eastacombe Devon
40 C3 Eastacott Devon
119 E3 East Acton Gt Lon
166 A2 East Adderbury Oxon
12 D3 East Allington Devon
41 H2 East Anstey Devon
90 B5 East Anton Hants
383 F5 East Appleton N York
343 E4 East Ardsley Leeds
53 E3 East Ashling W Susx
90 C5 East Aston Hants
557 E3 East Auchronie Abers
374 B2 East Ayton N York
515 F2 East Balmirmer Angus
132 D3 East Bank Blae G
319 F3 East Barkwith Lincs
97 H4 East Barming Kent
386 D2 East Barnby N York
144 C6 East Barnet Gt Lon
260 B5 East Barsham Norfk
200 B1 East Barton Suffk
53 F6 East Beach W Susx
261 G3 East Beckham Norfk
118 B5 East Bedfont Gt Lon
460 D5 East Bennan N Ayrs
175 E3 East Bergholt Suffk
254 B4 East Bilney Norfk
393 E2 East Blackdene Dur
56 D5 East Blatchington E Susx
47 G6 East Bloxworth Dorset
406 B2 East Boldon S Tyne
50 C4 East Boldre Hants
383 G2 Eastbourne Darltn
57 G5 Eastbourne E Susx
65 F4 East Bower Somset
84 B4 East Brent Somset
203 F1 Eastbridge Suffk
296 C6 East Bridgford Notts
393 G6 East Briscoe Dur
43 H3 Eastbrook Somset
106 C5 Eastbrook V Glam
577 J3 East Brora Highld
61 G5 East Buckland Devon
27 H6 East Budleigh Devon
360 B3 Eastburn E R Yk
117 F3 East Burnham Bucks
606 E6 East Burrafirth Shet
33 E2 East Burton Dorset
118 B1 Eastbury Herts
114 A4 Eastbury W Berk
404 D5 East Butsfield Dur
42 C6 East Butterleigh Devon
332 A3 East Butterwick N Linc
354 D4 Eastby N York
540 C4 East Cairnbeg Abers
487 E6 East Calder W Loth
249 G3 East Carleton Norfk
355 H6 East Carlton Leeds
217 H2 East Carlton Nhants
114 B2 East Challow Oxon
12 D4 East Charleton Devon
30 D1 East Chelborough Dorset
56 B2 East Chiltington E Susx
45 F5 East Chinnock Somset
88 D4 East Chisenbury Wilts
89 G5 East Cholderton Hants
123 F5 Eastchurch Kent
94 B4 East Clandon Surrey
167 F4 East Claydon Bucks
108 D5 East Clevedon N Som
577 J2 East Clyne Highld
45 G5 East Coker Somset
136 C4 Eastcombe Gloucs
64 C5 East Combe Somset
345 E3 East Common N York
69 E6 East Compton Dorset
67 G1 East Compton Somset
13 E1 East Cornworthy Devon
118 C2 Eastcote Gt Lon
193 E4 Eastcote Nhants
214 B4 Eastcote Solhll
118 C2 Eastcote Village Gt Lon
38 C4 Eastcott Cnwll
88 B3 Eastcott Wilts
345 G1 East Cottingwith E R Yk
195 F5 Eastcotts Beds
112 B6 Eastcourt Wilts
137 E6 Eastcourt Wilts
51 F5 East Cowes IoW
345 F5 East Cowick E R Yk
383 H4 East Cowton N York
431 E4 East Cramlington Nthumb
86 B6 East Cranmore Somset
33 G3 East Creech Dorset
550 B4 East Croachy Highld
551 G6 East Croftmore Highld
400 B5 East Curthwaite Cumb
555 E3 East Davoch Abers
57 F5 East Dean E Susx
161 F5 East Dean Gloucs
71 F4 East Dean Hants
53 G2 East Dean W Susx
329 G6 East Dene Rothm
514 D2 East Denside Angus
405 E1 East Denton N u Ty
311 G1 East Didsbury Manch
20 D2 Eastdon Devon
13 E3 Eastdown Devon
61 F3 East Down Devon
96 D2 Eastdown Kent
317 E4 East Drayton Notts
119 G5 East Dulwich Gt Lon
85 G1 East Dundry N Som
347 G4 East Ella C KuH
195 G3 East End Beds
167 H6 East End Bucks
48 B5 East End Dorset
348 C3 East End E R Yk
349 E4 East End E R Yk
361 F3 East End E R Yk
145 F2 Eastend Essex
148 D3 East End Essex
138 B4 East End Gloucs
50 C5 East End Hants
73 G5 East End Hants
90 C2 East End Hants
171 G4 East End Herts
80 B2 East End Kent
98 D6 East End Kent
123 F5 East End Kent
194 C6 East End M Keyn
194 D6 East End M Keyn
194 D6 East End M Keyn
109 E5 East End N Som
139 F2 East End Oxon
139 G1 East End Oxon
165 E5 Eastend Oxon
165 F3 East End Oxon
166 A2 East End Oxon
110 D5 East End S Glos
67 G4 East End Somset
85 G4 East End Somset
86 B5 East End Somset
175 F2 East End Suffk
201 G3 East End Suffk
549 K6 Easter Aberchalder Highld
565 L2 Easter Ardross Highld
500 C4 Easter Balgedie P & K
537 K4 Easter Balmoral Abers
525 H2 Easter Binzian P & K
549 J5 Easter Boleskine Highld
109 G3 Easter Compton S Glos
525 H7 Easter Essendy P & K
576 D6 Easter Fearn Highld
551 L5 Easter Fodderletter Moray
566 E7 Easter Galcantray Highld
53 G3 Eastergate W Susx
467 G1 Easterhouse C Glas
451 G2 Easter Housebyres Border
470 D2 Easter Howgate Mdloth
501 E2 Easter Kilwhiss Fife
565 K5 Easter Kinkell Highld
513 H6 Easter Kinsleith Fife
515 F2 Easter Knox Angus
451 G2 Easter Langlee Border
526 D2 Easter Lednathie Angus
527 G5 Easter Meathie Angus
214 D4 Eastern Green Covtry
557 E4 Easter Ord C Aber
601 J4 Easter Park Ork
605 H3 Easter Quarff Shet
384 D1 Easterside Middsb
604 F1 Easter Skeld Shet
452 D3 Easter Softlaw Border
88 B3 Easterton Wilts
88 B3 Easterton Sands Wilts
84 B4 Eastertown Somset
569 L2 Easter Whyntie Abers
89 E4 East Everleigh Wilts
95 E2 East Ewell Surrey
98 A4 East Farleigh Kent
217 F3 East Farndon Nhants
222 C5 East Fen Common Cambs
331 H5 East Ferry Lincs
451 G4 Eastfield Border
109 G4 Eastfield Bristl
244 A4 Eastfield C Pete
485 E5 Eastfield N Lans
431 E4 Eastfield Nthumb
374 C3 Eastfield N York
467 F2 Eastfield S Lans
468 D2 Eastfield S Lans
443 G3 Eastfield Hall Nthumb
90 D1 East Fields W Berk
501 E5 East Finglassie Fife
318 C2 East Firsby Lincs
32 A4 East Fleet Dorset
343 H3 East Garforth Leeds
114 B4 East Garston W Berk
244 A5 Eastgate C Pete
393 F2 Eastgate Dur
255 F3 Eastgate Norfk
405 G2 East Gateshead Gatesd
114 C2 East Ginge Oxon
174 A5 East Gores Essex
240 D2 East Goscote Leics
89 G2 East Grafton Wilts
92 C6 East Green Hants
198 D4 East Green Suffk
203 E1 East Green Suffk
71 E4 East Grimstead Wilts
77 G2 East Grinstead W Susx
59 F2 East Guldeford E Susx
217 E6 East Haddon Nhants
115 E2 East Hagbourne Oxon
170 A5 Easthall Herts
348 B6 East Halton N Linc
120 B3 East Ham Gt Lon
309 E3 Eastham Wirral
211 F6 Eastham Worcs
309 E3 Eastham Ferry Wirral
53 G3 East Hampnett W Susx
117 E6 Easthampstead Br For
185 H2 Easthampton Herefs
139 G6 East Hanney Oxon
147 F4 East Hanningfield Essex
344 B6 East Hardwick Wakefd
224 C2 East Harling Norfk
384 C5 East Harlsey N York
85 G3 East Harptree BaNES
431 E4 East Hartford Nthumb
74 B6 East Harting W Susx
69 F4 East Hatch Wilts
196 C4 East Hatley Cambs
255 E4 Easthaugh Norfk
383 E6 East Hauxwell N York
515 F2 East Haven Angus
92 C1 Eastheath Wokham
299 F6 East Heckington Lincs
394 C1 East Hedleyhope Dur
582 D6 East Helmsdale Highld
114 D2 East Hendred Oxon
329 H6 East Herringthorpe Rothm
406 B4 East Herrington Sundld
374 A4 East Heslerton N York
84 C2 East Hewish N Som
97 E2 East Hill Kent
528 B5 East Hills Angus
57 E1 East Hoathly E Susx
33 F2 East Holme Dorset
33 H1 East Holton Dorset
431 F5 East Holywell N Tyne
234 D5 Easthope Shrops
234 D5 Easthopewood Shrops
121 F2 East Horndon Essex
174 B5 Easthorpe Essex
277 H2 Easthorpe Leics
296 D4 Easthorpe Notts
85 G5 East Horrington Somset
94 B4 East Horsley Surrey
454 C3 East Horton Nthumb
605 G1 Easthouse Shet
471 F1 Easthouses Mdloth
48 D5 East Howe Bmouth
84 B5 East Huntspill Somset
169 G6 East Hyde Beds
61 H2 East Ilkerton Devon
114 D3 East Ilsley W Berk
603 M1 Easting Ork
41 E6 Eastington Devon
136 A3 Eastington Gloucs
138 A2 Eastington Gloucs
300 C2 East Keal Lincs
88 D1 East Kennett Wilts
356 D6 East Keswick Leeds
467 G4 East Kilbride S Lans
24 C3 East Kimber Devon
54 C4 East Kingston W Susx
300 B2 East Kirkby Lincs
373 G4 East Knapton N York
33 E2 East Knighton Dorset
41 G3 East Knowstone Devon
69 E3 East Knoyle Wilts
405 E4 East Kyo Dur
66 C6 East Lambrook Somset
576 F8 East Lamington Highld
52 B2 Eastland Gate Hants
83 F1 East Langdon Kent
217 F1 East Langton Leics
576 F2 East Langwell Highld
53 F3 East Lavant W Susx
53 G1 East Lavington W Susx
404 C4 East Law Dur
383 E2 East Layton N York
138 C3 Eastleach Martin Gloucs
138 B3 Eastleach Turville Gloucs
276 C4 East Leake Notts
453 G2 East Learmouth Nthumb
12 B2 East Leigh Devon
25 G1 East Leigh Devon
39 G2 Eastleigh Devon
72 C6 Eastleigh Hants
253 H4 East Lexham Norfk
454 C5 East Lilburn Nthumb
99 F3 Eastling Kent
490 A4 East Linton E Loth
74 B4 East Liss Hants
114 C2 East Lockinge Oxon
397 H6 East Loftus R & Cl
9 H3 East Looe Cnwll
331 G5 East Lound N Linc
19 G3 East Lounston Devon
33 F3 East Lulworth Dorset
374 A6 East Lutton N York
43 G2 East Lydeard Somset
67 F3 East Lydford Somset
44 C2 East Lyng Somset
556 B5 East Mains Abers
513 H2 East Mains Angus
472 D5 East Mains Border
467 F4 East Mains S Lans
528 B4 East Mains of Burnside Angus
97 H3 East Malling Kent
97 G3 East Malling Heath Kent
514 C2 East March Angus
53 E2 East Marden W Susx
316 D5 East Markham Notts
334 C2 East Marsh NE Lin
70 B6 East Martin Hants
354 B4 East Marton N York
69 E5 East Melbury Dorset
73 G5 East Meon Hants
42 C4 East Mere Devon
149 E2 East Mersea Essex
589 J2 East Mey Highld
118 C6 East Molesey Surrey
343 F5 East Moor Wakefd
106 D4 East Moors Cardif
47 H5 East Morden Dorset
355 E6 East Morton Brad
436 A4 East Morton D & G
56 A3 East Moulsecoomb Br & H
372 C4 East Ness N York
526 D6 East Nevay Angus
349 E2 East Newton E R Yk
372 B4 East Newton N York
52 B5 Eastney C Port
161 G2 Eastnor Herefs
241 G4 East Norton Leics
43 G3 East Nynehead Somset
91 F5 East Oakley Hants
331 H1 Eastoft N Linc
20 A3 East Ogwell Devon
52 C5 Eastoke Hants
109 H5 Easton Bristl
219 G5 Easton Cambs
399 H3 Easton Cumb
426 B5 Easton Cumb
12 B3 Easton Devon
25 H5 Easton Devon
32 B5 Easton Dorset
72 D3 Easton Hants
36 A3 Easton IoW
278 C4 Easton Lincs
249 F2 Easton Norfk
85 F5 Easton Somset
202 B3 Easton Suffk
114 C5 Easton W Berk
111 F5 Easton Wilts
111 F2 Easton Grey Wilts
109 F4 Easton-in-Gordano N Som
194 B3 Easton Maudit Nhants
243 E4 Easton on the Hill Nhants
89 F2 Easton Royal Wilts
67 G3 Easton Town Somset
111 F2 Easton Town Wilts
68 D6 East Orchard Dorset
475 E4 East Ord Nthumb
65 F4 Eastover Somset
23 H4 East Panson Devon
48 D5 East Parley Dorset
97 G5 East Peckham Kent
67 F2 East Pennard Somset
195 H1 East Perry Cambs
8 B5 East Portholland Cnwll
12 C5 East Portlemouth Devon
12 D5 East Prawle Devon
398 B3 East Preston D & G
54 C4 East Preston W Susx
46 D3 East Pulham Dorset
39 E4 East Putford Devon
64 B3 East Quantoxhead Somset
406 A5 East Rainton Sundld
334 B5 East Ravendale NE Lin
254 A2 East Raynham Norfk
244 C5 Eastrea Cambs
399 H1 Eastriggs D & G
356 D6 East Rigton Leeds
346 A3 Eastrington E R Yk
111 E5 Eastrip Wilts
84 C2 East Rolstone N Som
91 G4 Eastrop Hants
384 C4 East Rounton N York
25 G3 East Rowden Devon
253 G2 East Rudham Norfk
261 G3 East Runton Norfk
256 C4 East Ruston Norfk
101 F5 Eastry Kent
489 F6 East Saltoun E Loth
119 E4 East Sheen Gt Lon
605 G8 Eastshore Shet
601 H6 Eastside Ork
422 D2 East Skelston D & G
431 E3 East Sleekburn Nthumb
257 F5 East Somerton Norfk
405 F4 East Stanley Dur
331 G6 East Stockwith Lincs
33 F2 East Stoke Dorset
296 D5 East Stoke Notts
66 D6 East Stoke Somset
68 D5 East Stour Dorset
68 D5 East Stour Common Dorset
101 E3 East Stourmouth Kent
40 C2 East Stowford Devon
72 D2 East Stratton Hants
101 F4 East Street Kent
67 E2 East Street Somset
101 F6 East Studdal Kent
545 K3 East Suisnish Highld
16 A6 East Taphouse Cnwll
39 G2 East-the-Water Devon
452 B2 East Third Border
443 F5 East Thirston Nthumb
121 G4 East Tilbury Thurr
73 H3 East Tisted Hants
319 E3 East Torrington Lincs
64 B5 East Town Somset
67 G1 East Town Somset
87 F3 East Town Wilts
125 H5 East Trewent Pembks
249 E2 East Tuddenham Norfk
71 F4 East Tytherley Hants
111 H4 East Tytherton Wilts
26 C2 East Village Devon
105 F5 East Village V Glam
109 H4 Eastville Bristl
300 D3 Eastville Lincs
234 C6 East Wall Shrops
253 E4 East Walton Norfk
85 F4 East Water Somset
25 G4 East Week Devon
277 G4 Eastwell Leics
71 G5 East Wellow Hants
99 G5 Eastwell Park Kent
501 F5 East Wemyss Fife
469 F2 East Whitburn W Loth
513 E2 East Whitefield P & K
145 F2 Eastwick Herts
606 E2 Eastwick Shet
120 C4 East Wickham Gt Lon
126 C4 East Williamston Pembks
252 D4 East Winch Norfk
71 E3 East Winterslow Wilts
52 D5 East Wittering W Susx
369 F2 East Witton N York
341 F4 Eastwood Calder
161 E1 Eastwood Herefs
295 F5 Eastwood Notts
329 G6 Eastwood Rothm
122 C2 Eastwood Sthend
428 D2 East Woodburn Nthumb
245 F6 Eastwood End Cambs
295 F5 Eastwood Hall Notts
90 C2 East Woodhay Hants
86 D6 East Woodlands Somset
74 A2 East Worldham Hants
41 F5 East Worlington Devon
55 E4 East Worthing W Susx
224 B1 East Wretham Norfk
38 C4 East Youlstone Devon
215 F6 Eathorpe Warwks
290 B2 Eaton Ches
291 H1 Eaton Ches
186 C3 Eaton Herefs
277 G4 Eaton Leics
249 H3 Eaton Norfk
316 D4 Eaton Notts
139 G4 Eaton Oxon
209 G2 Eaton Shrops
210 C1 Eaton Shrops
160 A2 Eaton Bishop Herefs
168 D5 Eaton Bray Beds
234 D3 Eaton Constantine Shrops
195 H2 Eaton Ford Cambs
289 F2 Eaton Hall Ches
138 D5 Eaton Hastings Oxon
234 C3 Eaton Mascott Shrops
195 H3 Eaton Socon Cambs
271 F5 Eaton upon Tern Shrops
252 B4 Eau Brink Norfk
186 C6 Eau Withington Herefs
214 D3 Eaves Green Solhll

686 City, town and village index: Eavestone - Fallside

369 H6 Eavestone N York
40 B4 Ebberly Hill Devon
373 G3 Ebberston N York
69 G5 Ebbesbourne Wake Wilts
49 E3 Ebblake Dorset
132 C3 Ebbw Vale Blae G
404 D3 Ebchester Dur
84 C2 Ebdon N Som
75 F4 Ebernoe W Susx
27 F5 Ebford Devon
136 B4 Ebley Gloucs
289 G5 Ebnal Ches
186 B3 Ebnall Herefs
234 C1 Ebreywood Shrops
164 B1 Ebrington Gloucs
91 E2 Ecchinswell Hants
491 E6 Ecclaw Border
424 D5 Ecclefechan D & G
363 E4 Eccle Riggs Cumb
453 E1 Eccles Border
98 A2 Eccles Kent
325 H5 Eccles Salfd
314 C3 Ecclesall Sheff
329 E6 Ecclesfield Sheff
529 F1 Ecclesgreig Abers
272 B4 Eccleshall Staffs
342 C2 Eccleshill Brad
487 E5 Ecclesmachan W Loth
257 E4 Eccles on Sea Norfk
224 D1 Eccles Road Norfk
324 C1 Eccleston Lancs
289 F2 Eccleston St Hel
324 B5 Eccleston St Hel
324 B6 Eccleston Park St Hel
68 D4 Eccliffe Dorset
356 B6 Eccup Leeds
556 C3 Echt Abers
452 D4 Eckford Border
452 D4 Eckfordmoss Border
315 E4 Eckington Derbys
162 D1 Eckington Worcs
57 E2 Eckington Corner E Susx
328 C4 Ecklands Barns
39 F4 Eckworthy Devon
193 H2 Ecton Nhants
293 E3 Ecton Staffs
193 H2 Ecton Brook Nhants
313 F2 Edale Derbys
313 G2 Edale End Derbys
64 D3 Edbrook Somset
55 F2 Edburton W Susx
399 E5 Edderside Cumb
576 F6 Edderton Highld
100 C2 Eddington Kent
114 A6 Eddington W Berk
470 D5 Eddleston Border
467 H4 Eddlewood S Lans
96 B5 Edenbridge Kent
340 C6 Edenfield Lancs
391 F3 Edenhall Cumb
279 F5 Edenham Lincs
365 F4 Eden Mount Cumb
119 H6 Eden Park Gt Lon
314 A6 Edensor Derbys
495 G6 Edentaggart Ag & B
330 D3 Edenthorpe Donc
400 C3 Edentown Cumb
396 B2 Eden Vale Dur
87 F4 Eden Vale Wilts
493 E4 Ederline Ag & B
262 D3 Edern Gwynd
86 B5 Edford Somset
67 E2 Edgarley Somset
213 G3 Edgbaston Birm
192 B5 Edgcote Nhants
167 E5 Edgcott Bucks
62 C4 Edgcott Somset
4 D2 Edgcumbe Cnwll
136 B3 Edge Gloucs
233 G3 Edge Shrops
270 D5 Edgebolton Shrops
134 D2 Edge End Gloucs
339 H3 Edge End Lancs
261 E5 Edgefield Norfk
261 E5 Edgefield Street Norfk
325 F3 Edge Fold Bolton
339 H6 Edge Fold Bolton
289 G4 Edge Green Ches
224 D3 Edge Green Norfk
324 D5 Edge Green Wigan
309 E2 Edge Hill Lpool
191 F5 Edgehill Warwks
238 C5 Edge Hill Warwks
312 A2 Edgeley Stockp
328 D6 Edge Mount Sheff
269 F6 Edgerley Shrops
440 C2 Edgerston Border
342 B6 Edgerton Kirk
340 C5 Edgeside Lancs
136 D3 Edgeworth Gloucs
20 B4 Edginswell Torbay
189 F2 Edgiock Worcs
271 G6 Edgmond Wrekin
271 G5 Edgmond Marsh Wrekin
209 G2 Edgton Shrops
118 D1 Edgware Gt Lon
215 E3 Edgwick Covtry
325 G1 Edgworth Bl w D
237 G3 Edial Staffs
509 J5 Edinample Stirlg
542 E6 Edinbane Highld
488 B4 Edinburgh C Edin
238 C2 Edingale Staffs
296 C3 Edingley Notts
256 C3 Edingthorpe Norfk
256 C3 Edingthorpe Green Norfk
66 B2 Edington Somset
87 G4 Edington Wilts
84 C4 Edingworth Somset
38 B3 Edistone Devon
84 B5 Edithmead Somset
242 C3 Edith Weston Rutlnd
293 G6 Edlaston Derbys
168 D6 Edlesborough Bucks
443 E3 Edlingham Nthumb
319 G5 Edlington Lincs
48 C2 Edmondsham Dorset
405 F5 Edmondsley Dur
105 G1 Edmondstown Rhondd
242 B1 Edmondthorpe Leics
449 E1 Edmonston S Lans
603 G7 Edmonstone Ork
14 D4 Edmonton Cnwll
144 D6 Edmonton Gt Lon
404 B4 Edmundbyers Dur
452 D2 Ednam Border
274 C1 Ednaston Derbys
146 D4 Edney Common Essex
524 C5 Edradynate P & K
474 B3 Edrom Border
270 C3 Edstaston Shrops
190 B2 Edstone Warwks
187 F3 Edvin Loach Herefs
276 C2 Edwalton Notts
174 B1 Edwardstone Suffk
132 A5 Edwardsville Myr Td
155 F3 Edwinsford Carmth
296 B1 Edwinstowe Notts
170 B1 Edworth Beds
187 E3 Edwyn Ralph Herefs
540 B6 Edzell Angus
130 B5 Efail-fâch Neath
106 A3 Efail Isaf Rhondd
263 F3 Efailnewydd Gwynd
268 C4 Efail-rhyd Powys
152 C4 Efailwen Carmth
287 G3 Efenechtyd Denbgs
94 C4 Effingham Surrey
606 D7 Effirth Shet
439 G1 Effledge Border
238 B1 Efflinch Staffs
14 B4 Efflins Cnwll
11 E2 Efford C Plym
26 D2 Efford Devon
90 C4 Egbury Hants
188 D4 Egdon Worcs
325 G2 Egerton Bolton
99 E5 Egerton Kent
98 D5 Egerton Forstal Kent
289 H4 Egerton Green Ches
86 D5 Egford Somset
23 G5 Eggbeare Cnwll
344 C5 Eggborough N York
18 B6 Eggbuckland C Plym
40 D5 Eggesford Devon
168 C5 Eggington Beds
274 D4 Egginton Derbys
274 D4 Egginton Common Derbys
393 G5 Egglesburn Dur
384 C2 Egglescliffe S on T
393 H5 Eggleston Dur
117 G5 Egham Surrey
117 H5 Egham Hythe Surrey
117 G6 Egham Wick Surrey
242 B3 Egleton Rutlnd
455 E6 Eglingham Nthumb
15 E4 Egloshayle Cnwll
23 F5 Egloskerry Cnwll
305 H5 Eglwysbach Conwy
105 G6 Eglwys-Brewis V Glam
270 B1 Eglwys Cross Wrexhm
229 F5 Eglwys Fach Cerdgn
152 D2 Eglwyswen Pembks
152 C2 Eglwyswrw Pembks
316 D6 Egmanton Notts
260 A4 Egmere Norfk
376 B2 Egremont Cumb
308 D1 Egremont Wirral
386 D3 Egton N York
386 D3 Egton Bridge N York
342 A3 Egypt Brad
117 G2 Egypt Bucks
72 C1 Egypt Hants
114 C4 Egypt W Berk
174 B4 Eight Ash Green Essex
405 G3 Eighton Banks Gatesd
160 C2 Eign Hill Herefs
546 E6 Eilanreach Highld
451 H3 Eildon Border
507 H3 Eilean Duirinnis Ag & B
596 E2 Einacleit W Isls
597 J5 Eisgein W Isls
265 E3 Eisingrug Gwynd
430 C5 Eland Green Nthumb
183 E1 Elan Village Powys
109 H2 Elberton S Glos
84 C3 Elborough N Som
269 G5 Elbridge Shrops
53 G4 Elbridge W Susx
11 F3 Elburton C Plym
189 F2 Elcock's Brook Worcs
136 A5 Elcombe Gloucs
112 D3 Elcombe Swindn
114 B6 Elcot W Berk
113 E3 Eldene Swindn
244 D5 Eldernell Cambs
162 B3 Eldersfield Worcs
466 B2 Elderslie Rens
172 B3 Elder Street Essex
395 E4 Eldon Dur
395 E4 Eldon Lane Dur
353 F1 Eldroth N York
342 B1 Eldwick Brad
406 B5 Elemore Vale Sundld
455 F3 Elford Nthumb
238 B2 Elford Staffs
221 H5 Elford Closes Cambs
568 C3 Elgin Moray
545 J7 Elgol Highld
82 C2 Elham Kent
486 D6 Eliburn W Loth
502 D5 Elie Fife
303 E4 Elim IoA
50 C2 Eling Hants
115 E4 Eling W Berk
441 G5 Elishaw Nthumb
316 C4 Elkesley Notts
216 D4 Elkington Nhants
146 C4 Elkins Green Essex
137 E2 Elkstone Gloucs
20 C5 Ellacombe Torbay
550 F5 Ellan Highld
342 B5 Elland Calder
342 B5 Elland Lower Edge Calder
479 J6 Ellary Ag & B
293 F6 Ellastone Staffs
351 G3 Ellel Lancs
473 G2 Ellemford Border
506 B6 Ellenabeich Ag & B
388 B2 Ellenborough Cumb
7 E2 Ellenglaze Cnwll
272 B4 Ellenhall Staffs
76 A2 Ellen's Green Surrey
384 C5 Ellerbeck N York
373 F3 Ellerburn N York
386 D2 Ellerby N York
271 E5 Ellerdine Wrekin
271 E5 Ellerdine Heath Wrekin
27 F2 Ellerhayes Devon
520 E6 Elleric Ag & B
346 D4 Ellerker E R Yk
345 G2 Ellerton E R Yk
383 G5 Ellerton N York
271 G4 Ellerton Shrops
142 A3 Ellesborough Bucks
269 G3 Ellesmere Shrops
326 A5 Ellesmere Park Salfd
309 F4 Ellesmere Port Ches
63 F3 Ellicombe Somset
49 E3 Ellingham Hants
250 D6 Ellingham Norfk
455 F4 Ellingham Nthumb
369 G3 Ellingstring N York
219 H5 Ellington Cambs
431 E1 Ellington Nthumb
219 H5 Ellington Thorpe Cambs
515 G2 Elliot Angus
86 D5 Elliots Green Somset
132 C4 Elliot's Town Caerph
91 G5 Ellisfield Hants
543 J3 Ellishadder Highld
476 B6 Ellister Ag & B
451 H4 Elliston Border
239 G2 Ellistown Leics
561 E3 Ellon Abers
390 C2 Ellonby Cumb
227 E2 Ellough Suffk
346 D4 Elloughton E R Yk
134 D3 Ellwood Gloucs
245 G3 Elm Cambs
162 C6 Elmbridge Gloucs
212 D6 Elmbridge Worcs
94 B3 Elm Corner Surrey
112 D4 Elm Cross Wilts
171 G2 Elmdon Essex
214 B3 Elmdon Solhll
214 B3 Elmdon Heath Solhll
54 A4 Elmer W Susx
119 H6 Elmers End Gt Lon
324 B3 Elmers Green Lancs
74 D4 Elmers Marsh W Susx
239 H5 Elmesthorpe Leics
37 G2 Elmfield IoW
68 D4 Elm Hill Dorset
141 H1 Elmhurst Bucks
237 H2 Elmhurst Staffs
163 E1 Elmley Castle Worcs
212 C6 Elmley Lovett Worcs
136 A2 Elmore Gloucs
135 H1 Elmore Back Gloucs
120 D2 Elm Park Gt Lon
38 B3 Elmscott Devon
201 E5 Elmsett Suffk
186 C3 Elms Green Herefs
187 G1 Elms Green Worcs
365 G4 Elmslack Lancs
175 E4 Elmstead Essex
120 B5 Elmstead Gt Lon
175 E5 Elmstead Heath Essex
175 E4 Elmstead Market Essex
175 E5 Elmstead Market Essex
82 B1 Elmsted Kent
101 E3 Elmstone Kent
162 D4 Elmstone Hardwicke Gloucs
360 B3 Elmswell E R Yk
200 C2 Elmswell Suffk
315 G5 Elmton Derbys
579 H7 Elphin Highld
488 D5 Elphinstone E Loth
557 E3 Elrick Abers
409 G2 Elrig D & G
403 F2 Elrington Nthumb
185 F4 Elsdon Herefs
442 A6 Elsdon Nthumb
329 F4 Elsecar Barns
172 A4 Elsenham Essex
140 B2 Elsfield Oxon
333 E2 Elsham N Linc
255 E4 Elsing Norfk
354 B5 Elslack N York
51 H4 Elson Hants
269 G2 Elson Shrops
469 H6 Elsrickle S Lans
93 F6 Elstead Surrey
74 C6 Elsted W Susx
395 G5 Elstob Dur
26 B2 Elston Devon
297 E5 Elston Notts
88 C6 Elston Wilts
40 D4 Elstone Devon
195 F5 Elstow Beds
144 A5 Elstree Herts
348 D3 Elstronwick E R Yk
338 B2 Elswick Lancs
405 F2 Elswick N u Ty
338 B2 Elswick Leys Lancs
196 D2 Elsworth Cambs
378 B4 Elterwater Cumb
120 B5 Eltham Gt Lon
196 C3 Eltisley Cambs
326 A2 Elton Bury
243 F6 Elton Cambs
309 G4 Elton Ches
293 H2 Elton Derbys
135 F2 Elton Gloucs
210 B5 Elton Herefs
277 G2 Elton Notts
384 C1 Elton S on T
309 F4 Elton Green Ches
186 B6 Elton's Marsh Herefs
404 C2 Eltringham Nthumb
436 C1 Elvanfoot S Lans
275 G3 Elvaston Derbys
223 G4 Elveden Suffk
395 F1 Elvet Hill Dur
489 F5 Elvingston E Loth
101 E5 Elvington Kent
358 C5 Elvington York
61 G5 Elwell Devon
31 F6 Elwell Dorset
396 C3 Elwick Hartpl
455 E2 Elwick Nthumb
291 E2 Elworth Ches
63 H5 Elworthy Somset
222 B4 Ely Cambs
106 B4 Ely Cardif
194 B5 Emberton M Keyn
389 E3 Embleton Cumb
396 B4 Embleton Dur
455 G5 Embleton Nthumb
577 H5 Embo Highld
85 H4 Emborough Somset
577 G5 Embo Street Highld
354 D4 Embsay N York
120 D2 Emerson Park Gt Lon
110 B4 Emerson's Green S Glos
168 A3 Emerson Valley M Keyn
49 H3 Emery Down Hants
328 C2 Emley Kirk
116 C6 Emmbrook Wokham
116 B4 Emmer Green Readg
315 E4 Emmett Carr Derbys
141 F4 Emmington Oxon
245 G3 Emneth Norfk
245 H3 Emneth Hungate Norfk
252 A3 Emorsgate Norfk
242 D3 Empingham Rutlnd
74 A3 Empshott Hants
74 A3 Empshott Green Hants
190 D1 Emscote Warwks
234 C2 Emstrey Shrops
52 C3 Emsworth Hants
90 C1 Enborne W Berk
90 C2 Enborne Row W Berk
234 C5 Enchmarsh Shrops
240 B5 Enderby Leics
366 A3 Endmoor Cumb
292 B4 Endon Staffs
292 B4 Endon Bank Staffs
106 B2 Energlyn Caerph
144 D5 Enfield Gt Lon
213 F6 Enfield Worcs
145 E5 Enfield Highway Gt Lon
145 E5 Enfield Lock Gt Lon
144 D5 Enfield Town Gt Lon
145 E5 Enfield Wash Gt Lon
88 D4 Enford Wilts
606 C6 Engamoor Shet
303 E5 Engedi IoA
110 B3 Engine Common S Glos
115 G5 Englefield W Berk
117 G5 Englefield Green Surrey
291 E4 Englesea-brook Ches
134 D1 English Bicknor Gloucs
86 C2 Englishcombe BaNES
270 A4 English Frankton Shrops
14 B5 Engollan Cnwll
90 B5 Enham Alamein Hants
64 D5 Enmore Somset
186 B2 Enmore Field Herefs
69 E5 Enmore Green Dorset
376 D1 Ennerdale Bridge Cumb
8 B2 Enniscaven Cnwll
525 G3 Enochdhu P & K
517 K6 Ensay Ag & B
48 D5 Ensbury Bmouth
48 D6 Ensbury Park Bmouth
233 H1 Ensdon Shrops
40 B2 Ensis Devon
165 H6 Enslow Oxon
165 F5 Enstone Oxon
435 H4 Enterkinfoot D & G
384 D3 Enterpen N York
75 F1 Enton Green Surrey
212 B2 Enville Staffs
590 D6 Eòlaigearraidh W Isls
504 D6 Eorabus Ag & B
599 L2 Eòropaidh W Isls
135 H2 Epney Gloucs
296 C5 Epperstone Notts
145 G4 Epping Essex
145 F3 Epping Green Essex
144 C3 Epping Green Herts
145 F4 Epping Upland Essex
383 E2 Eppleby N York
347 F3 Eppleworth E R Yk
94 D2 Epsom Surrey
165 F1 Epwell Oxon
331 G4 Epworth N Linc
331 G4 Epworth Turbary N Linc
269 G1 Erbistock Wrexhm
546 D4 Erbusaig Highld
549 G1 Erchless Castle Highld
213 H1 Erdington Birm
493 G3 Eredine Ag & B
585 H5 Eriboll Highld
437 E2 Ericstane D & G
78 D2 Eridge Green E Susx
480 B4 Erines Ag & B
520 C7 Eriska Ag & B
223 E4 Eriswell Suffk
120 D4 Erith Gt Lon
87 H4 Erlestoke Wilts
318 B5 Ermine Lincs
12 A2 Ermington Devon
10 D2 Ernesettle C Plym
261 G5 Erpingham Norfk
99 E3 Erriottwood Kent
549 K5 Errogie Highld
513 G5 Errol P & K
483 G5 Erskine Rens
483 F5 Erskine Bridge Rens
414 C3 Ervie D & G
176 D3 Erwarton Suffk
184 A6 Erwood Powys
383 H3 Eryholme N York
288 B3 Eryrys Denbgs
394 D4 Escomb Dur
64 A4 Escott Somset
358 B6 Escrick N York
154 A4 Esgair Carmth
230 B3 Esgairgeiliog Powys
305 H4 Esgyryn Conwy
405 E6 Esh Dur
94 C2 Esher Surrey
450 B2 Eshiels Border
342 C1 Esholt Brad
443 G5 Eshott Nthumb
354 B3 Eshton N York
394 D1 Esh Winning Dur
549 H2 Eskadale Highld
471 F1 Eskbank Mdloth
377 E4 Eskdale Green Cumb
438 A5 Eskdalemuir D & G
335 E5 Eskham Lincs
345 E6 Eskholme Donc
476 F4 Esknish Ag & B
386 D4 Esk Valley N York
442 C2 Eslington Park Nthumb
394 C5 Esperley Lane Ends Dur
338 B2 Esprick Lancs
243 E2 Essendine Rutlnd
144 C3 Essendon Herts
549 L2 Essich Highld
237 E4 Essington Staffs
560 D3 Esslemont Abers
397 E6 Eston R & Cl
18 B6 Estover C Plym
25 E4 Estrayer Park Devon
607 G7 Eswick Shet
453 H2 Etal Nthumb
88 B2 Etchilhampton Wilts
79 F4 Etchingham E Susx
82 C3 Etchinghill Kent
273 F6 Etchinghill Staffs
78 C5 Etchingwood E Susx
394 D4 Etherley Dene Dur
529 E5 Ethie Mains Angus
254 D5 Etling Green Norfk
135 F3 Etloe Gloucs
117 G4 Eton W & M
117 G4 Eton Wick W & M
291 H5 Etruria C Stke
233 G4 Etsell Shrops
400 C3 Etterby Cumb
535 J4 Etteridge Highld
393 E4 Ettersgill Dur
291 E2 Ettiley Heath Ches
236 D5 Ettingshall Wolves
236 D6 Ettingshall Park Wolves
190 D5 Ettington Warwks
243 G3 Etton C Pete
360 B6 Etton E R Yk
438 B2 Ettrick Border
450 D5 Ettrickbridge Border
438 B2 Ettrickhill Border
274 D3 Etwall Derbys
274 D3 Etwall Common Derbys
211 F2 Eudon Burnell Shrops
211 F2 Eudon George Shrops
224 A4 Euston Suffk
339 E6 Euxton Lancs
105 F2 Evanstown Brdgnd
565 K3 Evanton Highld
298 D5 Evedon Lincs
212 D1 Eve Hill Dudley
577 G5 Evelix Highld
161 G1 Evendine Herefs
185 E2 Evenjobb Powys
166 C3 Evenley Nhants
164 C4 Evenlode Gloucs
160 D2 Even Pits Herefs
112 D3 Even Swindon Swindn
394 C5 Evenwood Dur
394 D5 Evenwood Gate Dur
603 K6 Everbay Ork
67 G2 Evercreech Somset
192 C3 Everdon Nhants
346 B1 Everingham E R Yk
89 E4 Everleigh Wilts
374 B2 Everley N York
168 D3 Eversholt Beds
30 D2 Evershot Dorset
122 A2 Eversley Essex
92 C2 Eversley Hants
92 C2 Eversley Centre Hants
92 C2 Eversley Cross Hants
346 D3 Everthorpe E R Yk
196 A4 Everton Beds
50 A6 Everton Hants
309 E1 Everton Lpool
316 C1 Everton Notts
425 H4 Evertown D & G
187 F5 Evesbatch Herefs
163 F1 Evesham Worcs
240 D4 Evington C Leic
82 B2 Evington Kent
388 B2 Ewanrigg Cumb
328 D5 Ewden Village Sheff
95 E2 Ewell Surrey
83 E2 Ewell Minnis Kent
115 G1 Ewelme Oxon
137 E5 Ewen Gloucs
105 E4 Ewenny V Glam
299 E5 Ewerby Lincs
299 E5 Ewerby Thorpe Lincs
425 H1 Ewes D & G
76 A1 Ewhurst Surrey
80 A5 Ewhurst Green E Susx
76 A2 Ewhurst Green Surrey
288 C1 Ewloe Flints
288 C1 Ewloe Green Flints
339 G4 Ewood Bl w D
340 B5 Ewood Bridge Lancs
24 B4 Eworthy Devon
92 D5 Ewshot Hants
159 G4 Ewyas Harold Herefs
25 F2 Exbourne Devon
50 D4 Exbury Hants
57 E5 Exceat E Susx
42 B3 Exebridge Somset
370 B2 Exelby N York
26 D4 Exeter Devon
62 C4 Exford Somset
234 A3 Exfords Green Shrops
189 H4 Exhall Warwks
215 F2 Exhall Warwks
115 H3 Exlade Street Oxon
342 A5 Exley Calder
341 G1 Exley Head Brad
27 E5 Exminster Devon
21 E2 Exmouth Devon
605 G8 Exnaboe Shet
198 C1 Exning Suffk
82 C2 Exted Kent
27 F5 Exton Devon
73 F5 Exton Hants
242 C2 Exton Rutlnd
63 E5 Exton Somset
26 D4 Exwick Devon
313 H4 Eyam Derbys
192 B4 Eydon Nhants
244 B4 Eye C Pete
186 B2 Eye Herefs
225 F5 Eye Suffk
244 B4 Eye Green C Pete
474 D2 Eyemouth Border
196 B5 Eyeworth Beds
98 C4 Eyhorne Street Kent
202 C4 Eyke Suffk
196 A3 Eynesbury Cambs
544 F4 Eynort Highld
96 D2 Eynsford Kent
139 G3 Eynsham Oxon
30 A4 Eype Dorset
30 A4 Eype's Mouth Dorset
543 G6 Eyre Highld
545 K3 Eyre Highld
240 C5 Eyres Monsell C Leic
101 E6 Eythorne Kent
186 B2 Eyton Herefs
209 G2 Eyton Shrops
233 G2 Eyton Shrops
288 D6 Eyton Wrexhm
234 D3 Eyton on Severn Shrops
235 E1 Eyton upon the Weald Moors Wrekin

F

89 G4 Faberstown Hants
90 B3 Faccombe Hants
384 D4 Faceby N York
283 F2 Fachell Gwynd
284 C2 Fachwen Gwynd
340 D6 Facit Lancs
295 F2 Fackley Notts
290 B4 Faddiley Ches
372 C2 Fadmoor N York
129 G4 Faerdre Swans
342 C3 Fagley Brad
129 G4 Fagwyr Swans
533 L2 Faichem Highld
483 H5 Faifley W Duns
109 F5 Failand N Som
445 G4 Failford S Ayrs
326 C4 Failsworth Oldham
229 E2 Fairbourne Gwynd
98 D4 Fairbourne Heath Kent
344 B4 Fairburn N York
120 C3 Fair Cross Gt Lon
326 B2 Fairfield Bury
498 D6 Fairfield Clacks
313 E5 Fairfield Derbys
81 E4 Fairfield Kent
309 E1 Fairfield Lpool
396 B6 Fairfield S on T
326 C5 Fairfield Tamesd
189 F6 Fairfield Worcs
212 B4 Fairfield Worcs
212 D4 Fairfield Worcs
86 C1 Fairfield Park BaNES
161 G3 Fairfields Gloucs
138 B4 Fairford Gloucs
252 D4 Fair Green Norfk
337 F4 Fairhaven Lancs
463 F5 Fairhaven N Ayrs
391 E3 Fair Hill Cumb
467 H4 Fairhill S Lans
93 G4 Fairlands Surrey
37 E2 Fairlee IoW
465 E3 Fairlie N Ayrs
59 E4 Fairlight E Susx
59 E4 Fairlight Cove E Susx
120 C1 Fairlop Gt Lon
49 E6 Fairmile Dorset
94 C2 Fairmile Surrey
488 A6 Fairmilehead C Edin
430 C2 Fair Moor Nthumb
132 C5 Fairoak Caerph
72 C6 Fair Oak Hants
91 E2 Fair Oak Hants
352 C5 Fair Oak Lancs
271 H3 Fairoak Staffs
91 H2 Fair Oak Green Hants
97 F2 Fairseat Kent
147 F1 Fairstead Essex
252 C4 Fairstead Norfk
163 E5 Fairview Gloucs
78 B4 Fairwarp E Susx
106 B4 Fairwater Cardif
133 E6 Fairwater Torfn
87 F4 Fairwood Wilts
39 F3 Fairy Cross Devon
260 B5 Fakenham Norfk
224 A4 Fakenham Magna Suffk
472 A2 Fala Mdloth
472 A2 Fala Dam Mdloth
471 G3 Falahill Border
160 D3 Falcon Herefs
238 A5 Falcon Lodge Birm
120 B4 Falconwood Gt Lon
192 C6 Falcutt Nhants
318 D3 Faldingworth Lincs
451 G3 Faldonside Border
35 J6 Faldouet Jersey
135 F6 Falfield S Glos
177 E2 Falkenham Suffk
177 E2 Falkenham Sink Suffk
485 H4 Falkirk Falk
501 E3 Falkland Fife
440 D2 Falla Border
294 C2 Fallgate Derbys
485 G1 Fallin Stirlg
294 B1 Fallinge Derbys
237 E5 Fallings Heath Wsall
326 B6 Fallowfield Manch
467 H2 Fallside N Lans

City, town and village index: Falmer - Ford Street 687

56 B3 Falmer E Susx
5 E2 Falmouth Cnwll
438 D3 Falnash Border
374 C2 Falsgrave N York
486 C6 Falside W Loth
428 A2 Falstone Nthumb
584 C7 Fanagmore Highld
169 E4 Fancott Beds
565 H8 Fanellan Highld
385 F6 Fangdale Beck N York
359 E4 Fangfoss E R Yk
485 F3 Fankerton Falk
517 L7 Fanmore Ag & B
146 D2 Fanner's Green Essex
452 B1 Fans Border
311 H5 Fanshowe Ches
98 A4 Fant Kent
365 F4 Far Arnside Cumb
330 D2 Far Bank Donc
338 B5 Far Banks Lancs
244 B6 Farcet Cambs
239 F4 Far Coton Leics
193 F3 Far Cotton Nhants
210 D4 Farden Shrops
51 G3 Fareham Hants
378 A5 Far End Cumb
237 G2 Farewell Staffs
211 G5 Far Forest Worcs
320 B4 Farforth Lincs
136 A4 Far Green Gloucs
294 D2 Farhill Derbys
274 A5 Far Hoarcross Staffs
138 D5 Faringdon Oxon
338 D5 Farington Lancs
338 D5 Farington Moss Lancs
401 G3 Farlam Cumb
313 E2 Farlands Booth Derbys
577 G2 Farlary Highld
294 D5 Far Laund Derbys
109 E6 Farleigh N Som
95 H2 Farleigh Surrey
95 H3 Farleigh Court Surrey
97 H4 Farleigh Green Kent
87 E3 Farleigh Hungerford Somset
91 G5 Farleigh Wallop Hants
87 E2 Farleigh Wick Wilts
321 E5 Farlesthorpe Lincs
366 A3 Farleton Cumb
352 B1 Farleton Lancs
294 B2 Farley Derbys
108 D5 Farley N Som
233 G3 Farley Shrops
235 E4 Farley Shrops
236 A5 Far Ley Staffs
293 E6 Farley Staffs
71 E4 Farley Wilts
199 E4 Farley Green Suffk
94 B5 Farley Green Surrey
92 C2 Farley Hill Wokham
135 H1 Farleys End Gloucs
52 B3 Farlington C Port
372 B6 Farlington N York
211 E3 Farlow Shrops
86 B2 Farmborough BaNES
146 C2 Farmbridge End Essex
163 G4 Farmcote Gloucs
212 A1 Farmcote Shrops
138 A1 Farmington Gloucs
139 G3 Farmoor Oxon
324 C4 Far Moor Wigan
4 C2 Farms Common Cnwll
239 F1 Farm Town Leics
569 J5 Farmtown Moray
294 C5 Farnah Green Derbys
96 B2 Farnborough Gt Lon
92 D4 Farnborough Hants
191 G5 Farnborough Warwks
114 C3 Farnborough W Berk
93 E3 Farnborough Green Hants
93 E3 Farnborough Park Hants
93 E3 Farnborough Street Hants
93 G5 Farncombe Surrey
194 C2 Farndish Beds
289 F4 Farndon Ches
297 E4 Farndon Notts
528 D3 Farnell Angus
48 B1 Farnham Dorset
171 G5 Farnham Essex
356 C2 Farnham N York
202 D3 Farnham Suffk
92 D5 Farnham Surrey
117 G2 Farnham Common Bucks
171 G4 Farnham Green Essex
117 G3 Farnham Park Bucks
117 G3 Farnham Royal Bucks
354 D5 Farnhill N York
96 D1 Farningham Kent
343 E3 Farnley Leeds
355 H5 Farnley N York
328 B2 Farnley Bank Kirk
328 B2 Farnley Tyas Kirk
296 C3 Farnsfield Notts
325 G3 Farnworth Bolton
309 G2 Farnworth Halton
136 D4 Far Oakridge Gloucs
536 B2 Farr Highld
550 B3 Farr Highld
586 F4 Farr Highld
549 K5 Farraline Highld
27 G4 Farringdon Devon
406 B4 Farringdon Sundld
47 F1 Farrington Dorset
85 H3 Farrington Gurney BaNES
343 E3 Far Royds Leeds
378 C5 Far Sawrey Cumb
342 D2 Farsley Leeds
147 G4 Farther Howegreen Essex
98 C2 Farthing Corner Medway
98 C5 Farthing Green Kent
166 B2 Farthinghoe Nhants
83 E2 Farthingloe Kent
192 D4 Farthingstone Nhants
136 C4 Far Thrupp Gloucs
28 C3 Farway Devon
29 F2 Farway Marsh Devon
542 B7 Fasach Highld
562 F5 Fasag Highld
518 C1 Fascadale Highld
524 D3 Faskally P & K
482 B2 Faslane Port Ag & B
520 E6 Fasnacloich Ag & B
540 B4 Fasque Abers
532 F7 Fassfern Highld
405 H4 Fatfield Sundld
569 L4 Fattahead Abers
487 E5 Fauchelдean W Loth
401 F4 Faugh Cumb
401 F5 Faugh Head Cumb
451 G3 Faughill Border
274 B4 Fauld Staffs
469 E2 Fauldhouse W Loth
451 E4 Fauldshope Border
147 F1 Faulkbourne Essex
86 C4 Faulkland Somset
270 D3 Fauls Shrops
383 G1 Faverdale Darltn
99 F2 Faversham Kent
552 F2 Favillar Moray
371 E5 Fawdington N York
442 C1 Fawdon Nthumb
430 D6 Fawdon N u Ty
293 E2 Fawfieldhead Staffs
97 E1 Fawkham Green Kent
113 H2 Fawler Oxon
139 F1 Fawler Oxon
116 C2 Fawley Bucks
51 E4 Fawley Hants
114 B3 Fawley W Berk
116 B2 Fawley Bottom Bucks
160 D4 Fawley Chapel Herefs
346 C5 Faxfleet E R Yk
76 D3 Faygate W Susx
323 G5 Fazakerley Lpool
238 C4 Fazeley Staffs
535 G4 Feagour Highld
369 G3 Fearby N York
566 E1 Fearn Highld
523 K7 Fearnan P & K
562 C5 Fearnbeg Highld
310 C1 Fearnhead Warrtn
562 C4 Fearnmore Highld
343 F2 Fearnville Leeds
236 D4 Featherstone Staffs
343 H5 Featherstone Wakefd
189 F2 Feckenham Worcs
304 C3 Fedw Fawr IoA
173 H5 Feering Essex
382 A5 Feetham N York
292 A4 Fegg Hayes C Stke
353 F1 Feizor N York
77 G2 Felbridge Surrey
261 H4 Felbrigg Norfk
77 G1 Felcourt Surrey
143 E3 Felden Herts
101 F4 Felderland Kent
310 D4 Feldy Ches
210 A2 Felhampton Shrops
156 D5 Felin-Crai Powys
128 C2 Felindre Carmth
153 G2 Felindre Carmth
154 D5 Felindre Carmth
155 G4 Felindre Carmth
158 C5 Felindre Powys
208 C3 Felindre Powys
232 C4 Felindre Powys
105 F3 Felindre Rhondd
129 F4 Felindre Swans
152 B2 Felindre Farchog Pembks
180 D3 Felinfach Cerdgn
158 A3 Felinfach Powys
128 D4 Felinfoel Carmth
154 D5 Felingwmisaf Carmth
154 D5 Felingwmuchaf Carmth
155 G2 Felin Newydd Carmth
158 B2 Felin-newydd Powys
268 D4 Felin Newydd Powys
288 D5 Felin Puleston Wrexhm
179 G4 Felin-Wnda Cerdgn
371 F3 Felixkirk N York
177 F3 Felixstowe Suffk
177 F2 Felixstowe Ferry Suffk
474 D6 Felkington Nthumb
329 F2 Felkirk Wakefd
388 C6 Felldyke Cumb
380 C5 Fell End Cumb
405 H2 Fellgate S Tyne
380 B2 Fell Head Cumb
405 G2 Felling Gatesd
405 G2 Felling Shore Gatesd
341 G1 Fell Lane Brad
389 H2 Fell Side Cumb
405 E3 Fellside Gatesd
194 D3 Felmersham Beds
256 A4 Felmingham Norfk
122 A2 Felmore Essex
53 H4 Felpham W Susx
200 B3 Felsham Suffk
172 D6 Felsted Essex
118 B5 Feltham Gt Lon
43 H4 Feltham Somset
118 B5 Felthamhill Surrey
255 G4 Felthorpe Norfk
186 D5 Felton Herefs
85 F1 Felton N Som
443 F4 Felton Nthumb
233 G1 Felton Butler Shrops
222 D1 Feltwell Norfk
328 B1 Fenay Bridge Kirk
340 C2 Fence Lancs
405 H4 Fence Houses Sundld
140 C1 Fencott Oxon
524 C2 Fenderbridge P & K
197 G2 Fen Ditton Cambs
220 D6 Fen Drayton Cambs
280 B5 Fen End Lincs
214 C5 Fen End Solhll
244 B5 Fengate C Pete
255 G3 Fengate Norfk
405 F1 Fenham N u Ty
280 B1 Fenhouses Lincs
339 F4 Feniscliffe Bl w D
339 F5 Feniscowles Bl w D
28 A3 Feniton Devon
195 F5 Fenlake Beds
211 H3 Fenn Green Shrops
43 G2 Fennington Somset
270 C2 Fenn's Bank Wrexhm
122 B4 Fenn Street Medway
293 G4 Fenny Bentley Derbys
28 B3 Fenny Bridges Devon
191 G4 Fenny Compton Warwks
239 F5 Fenny Drayton Leics
168 B3 Fenny Stratford M Keyn
430 C1 Fenrother Nthumb
300 B3 Fen Side Lincs
220 D6 Fenstanton Cambs
199 G4 Fenstead End Suffk
224 C4 Fen Street Suffk
225 E3 Fen Street Suffk
225 E4 Fen Street Suffk
220 D4 Fenton Cambs
292 A6 Fenton C Stke
401 E3 Fenton Cumb
297 G4 Fenton Lincs
317 F4 Fenton Lincs
454 B3 Fenton Nthumb
15 F3 Fentonadle Cnwll
489 G3 Fenton Barns E Loth
292 A5 Fenton Low C Stke
15 F6 Fenton Pits Cnwll
330 C1 Fenwick Donc
466 C6 Fenwick E Ayrs
429 G5 Fenwick Nthumb
454 D1 Fenwick Nthumb
457 F4 Feochaig Ag & B
7 F6 Feock Cnwll
478 C8 Feolin Ferry Ag & B
542 D8 Feorlig Highld
466 C2 Ferguslie Park Rens
531 H1 Ferindonald Highld
542 B6 Feriniquarrie Highld
35 d3 Fermain Bay Guern
527 G2 Fern Angus
117 E2 Fern Bucks
327 E5 Fern Bank Tamesd
78 D1 Ferndale Kent
131 F5 Ferndale Rhondd
48 D5 Ferndown Dorset
69 F5 Ferne Wilts
567 H8 Ferness Highld
378 D5 Ferney Green Cumb
113 G1 Fernham Oxon
326 B2 Fernhill Bury
131 G5 Fernhill Rhondd
199 G5 Fern Hill Suffk
77 E1 Fernhill W Susx
325 F3 Fernhill Gate Bolton
188 C3 Fernhill Heath Worcs
75 E4 Fernhurst W Susx
501 F1 Fernie Fife
468 A4 Ferniegair S Lans
451 E1 Ferniehirst Border
544 F3 Fernilea Highld
312 D4 Fernilee Derbys
7 E5 Fernsplatt Cnwll
356 D2 Ferrensby N York
347 E5 Ferriby Sluice N Linc
54 C4 Ferring W Susx
344 B5 Ferrybridge Wakefd
529 F3 Ferryden Angus
557 G3 Ferryhill C Aber
221 E3 Ferry Hill Cambs
395 F3 Ferryhill Dur
395 F3 Ferryhill Station Dur
127 H3 Ferryside Carmth
225 E3 Fersfield Norfk
534 C7 Fersit Highld
536 C2 Feshiebridge Highld
94 C3 Fetcham Surrey
571 H5 Fetterangus Abers
540 B5 Fettercairn Abers
565 K6 Fettes Highld
166 B4 Fewcott Oxon
355 G4 Fewston N York
355 G4 Fewston Bents N York
155 F5 Ffairfach Carmth
205 G6 Ffair-Rhos Cerdgn
181 F6 Ffaldybrenin Carmth
181 G6 Ffarmers Carmth
158 D6 Ffawyddog Powys
287 G2 Ffordd-las Denbgs
158 D2 Fforddlas Powys
104 D3 Ffordd-y-Gyfraith Brdgnd
129 E4 Fforest Carmth
103 F2 Fforest-fach Swans
130 A4 Fforest Gôch Neath
205 E6 Ffoshelyg Cerdgn
179 H4 Ffostrasol Cerdgn
131 H3 Ffos-y-frân Myr Td
288 D4 Ffos-y-go Wrexhm
232 C5 Ffridd Powys
284 C4 Ffridd Uchaf Gwynd
288 C3 Ffrith Flints
127 G1 Ffynnon Carmth
154 B5 Ffynnon-ddrain Carmth
151 F4 Ffynnon Gron Pembks
307 G3 Ffynnongroyw Flints
158 C1 Ffynnon Gynydd Powys
580 C5 Fiag Bridge Highld
96 A2 Fickleshole Surrey
504 C6 Fidden Ag & B
541 F3 Fiddes Abers
162 D3 Fiddington Gloucs
64 D3 Fiddington Somset
88 B4 Fiddington Sands Wilts
47 F2 Fiddleford Dorset
337 G5 Fiddler's Ferry Sefton
310 B2 Fiddler's Ferry Warrtn
571 K3 Fiddler's Green Abers
162 D5 Fiddler's Green Gloucs
160 D2 Fiddler's Green Herefs
248 D5 Fiddlers' Green Norfk
145 G4 Fiddlers Hamlet Essex
599 M7 Fidigeadh W Isls
185 F4 Field Herefs
85 H6 Field Somset
273 F3 Field Staffs
139 E2 Field Assarts Oxon
365 E3 Field Broughton Cumb
94 C1 Field Common Surrey
260 D4 Field Dalling Norfk
80 A3 Field Green Kent
240 A3 Field Head Leics
143 E3 Fields End Herts
185 H4 Field's Place Herefs
68 C5 Fifehead Magdalen Dorset
47 E2 Fifehead Neville Dorset
47 E2 Fifehead St Quintin Dorset
569 G5 Fife Keith Moray
164 C6 Fifield Oxon
117 F4 Fifield W & M
88 D4 Fifield Wilts
69 H4 Fifield Bavant Wilts
89 E5 Figheldean Wilts
111 G2 Filands Wilts
251 F2 Filby Norfk
251 F2 Filby Heath Norfk
139 H3 Filchampstead Oxon
57 F4 Filching E Susx
375 E3 Filey N York
30 A3 Filford Dorset
194 B5 Filgrave M Keyn
12 A1 Filham Devon
138 C4 Filkins Oxon
40 D2 Filleigh Devon
41 E5 Filleigh Devon
318 A2 Fillingham Lincs
214 D2 Fillongley Warwks
73 G4 Filmore Hill Hants
109 G4 Filton S Glos
109 G6 Filwood Park Bristl
359 G2 Fimber E R Yk
527 G3 Finavon Angus
493 F4 Finchairn Ag & B
309 F1 Fincham Lpool
246 D3 Fincham Norfk
92 C2 Finchampstead Wokham
52 C2 Finchdean Hants
172 D3 Finchingfield Essex
119 F1 Finchley Gt Lon
514 B5 Fincraigs Fife
275 E3 Findern Derbys
567 J4 Findhorn Moray
569 H2 Findochty Moray
512 B5 Findo Gask P & K
557 G5 Findon Abers
54 D3 Findon W Susx
565 L4 Findon Mains Highld
54 D3 Findon Valley W Susx
218 C5 Finedon Nhants
159 F2 Fine Street Herefs
225 H6 Fingal Street Suffk
559 H4 Fingask Abers
211 G5 Fingerpost Worcs
116 C1 Fingest Bucks
369 G2 Finghall N York
399 H3 Fingland Cumb
447 F6 Fingland D & G
101 F5 Finglesham Kent
174 D5 Fingringhoe Essex
215 E4 Finham Covtry
329 E5 Finkle Street Barns
509 J3 Finlarig Stirlg
166 D3 Finmere Bucks
522 F4 Finnart P & K
311 H3 Finney Green Ches
291 F5 Finney Green Staffs
225 E6 Finningham Suffk
331 E5 Finningley Donc
569 L5 Finnygaud Abers
595 H5 Finsbay W Isls
119 G3 Finsbury Gt Lon
119 G2 Finsbury Park Gt Lon
213 E6 Finstall Worcs
365 E2 Finsthwaite Cumb
139 F1 Finstock Oxon
600 E2 Finstown Ork
570 D5 Fintry Abers
514 C3 Fintry C Dund
484 C2 Fintry Stirlg
214 B6 Finwood Warwks
540 B1 Finzean Abers
504 C6 Fionnphort Ag & B
595 H5 Fionnsabhagh W Isls
379 H6 Firbank Cumb
315 H2 Firbeck Rothm
358 D1 Firby N York
370 B2 Firby N York
326 D2 Firgrove Rochdl
565 L3 Firhill Highld
56 D3 Firle E Susx
301 E2 Firsby Lincs
71 E3 Firsdown Wilts
325 E4 Firs Lane Wigan
573 H5 First Coast Highld
326 B6 Firswood Traffd
451 G5 Firth Border
600 F2 Firth Ork
606 F3 Firth Shet
383 H2 Firth Moor Darltn
528 C6 Firth Muir of Boysack Angus
314 D1 Firth Park Sheff
99 E6 Fir Toll Kent
394 C3 Fir Tree Dur
314 D1 Fir Vale Sheff
325 G2 Firwood Fold Bolton
51 G6 Fishbourne IoW
53 E4 Fishbourne W Susx
395 H3 Fishburn Dur
499 E5 Fishcross Clacks
559 F2 Fisherford Abers
168 B2 Fishermead M Keyn
488 C5 Fisherrow E Loth
55 G3 Fishersgate W Susx
72 C5 Fisher's Pond Hants
75 F3 Fisherstreet W Susx
566 C6 Fisherton Highld
432 C1 Fisherton S Ayrs
69 H2 Fisherton de la Mere Wilts
566 F5 Fisherton Highld
238 B3 Fisherwick Staffs
117 E3 Fishery W & M
151 G2 Fishguard Pembks
331 E2 Fishlake Donc
24 D1 Fishleigh Devon
25 E1 Fishleigh Castle Devon
251 E2 Fishley Norfk
237 E4 Fishley Wsall
280 C2 Fishmere End Lincs
29 G3 Fishpond Bottom Dorset
110 A4 Fishponds Bristl
326 B3 Fishpool Bury
161 F4 Fishpool Gloucs
356 A5 Fishpool N York
208 C6 Fishpools Powys
281 E1 Fishtoft Lincs
300 B5 Fishtoft Drove Lincs
474 D4 Fishwick Border
339 E4 Fishwick Lancs
544 E3 Fiskavaig Highld
318 C5 Fiskerton Lincs
296 D4 Fiskerton Notts
348 D3 Fitling E R Yk
88 D5 Fittleton Wilts
75 G6 Fittleworth W Susx
245 F2 Fitton End Cambs
326 D4 Fitton Hill Oldham
270 A6 Fitz Shrops
43 F2 Fitzhead Somset
329 G1 Fitzwilliam Wakefd
518 F6 Fiunary Highld
134 D2 Five Acres Gloucs
78 B5 Five Ash Down E Susx
78 D5 Five Ashes E Susx
63 H3 Five Bells Somset
187 E5 Five Bridges Herefs
310 A4 Fivecrosses Ches
44 D3 Fivehead Somset
36 C3 Five Houses IoW
351 H4 Five Lane Ends Lancs
16 B2 Fivelanes Cnwll
109 E1 Five Lanes Mons
97 F5 Five Oak Green Kent
35 i7 Five Oaks Jersey
76 A4 Five Oaks W Susx
128 C3 Five Roads Carmth
214 C6 Five Ways Warwks
98 C4 Five Wents Kent
342 B5 Fixby Kirk
80 C5 Flackley Ash E Susx
147 F1 Flack's Green Essex
117 E2 Flackwell Heath Bucks
189 E5 Fladbury Worcs
189 E5 Fladbury Cross Worcs
605 H4 Fladdabister Shet
313 F6 Flagg Derbys
187 E4 Flaggoners Green Herefs
375 G5 Flamborough E R Yk
143 F2 Flamstead Herts
144 D4 Flamstead End Herts
53 H4 Flansham W Susx
343 F5 Flanshaw Wakefd
341 H2 Flappit Spring Brad
354 B3 Flasby N York
292 D1 Flash Staffs
542 F6 Flashader Highld
75 F5 Flathurst W Susx
143 E4 Flaunden Herts
297 E6 Flawborough Notts
357 F1 Flawith N York
109 F6 Flax Bourton N Som
356 D3 Flaxby N York
275 E1 Flaxholme Derbys
249 F6 Flaxlands Norfk
135 F1 Flaxley Gloucs
340 B5 Flax Moss Lancs
64 B4 Flaxpool Somset
358 C2 Flaxton N York
240 D6 Fleckney Leics
192 B2 Flecknoe Warwks
317 F5 Fledborough Notts
32 A3 Fleet Dorset
52 C4 Fleet Hants
92 D4 Fleet Hants
281 E5 Fleet Lincs
121 E5 Fleet Downs Kent
51 F3 Fleetend Hants
281 E4 Fleet Hargate Lincs
51 G4 Fleetlands Hants
354 C2 Fleets N York
48 C6 Fleet's Corner Poole
350 D5 Fleetwood Lancs
251 E2 Fleggburgh Norfk
599 L7 Fleisirin W Isls
396 A1 Fleming Field Dur
101 E4 Flemings Kent
105 G5 Flemingston V Glam
467 F3 Flemington S Lans
467 H6 Flemington S Lans
223 G6 Flempton Suffk
595 H5 Fleoideabhagh W Isls
15 F5 Fletchersbridge Cnwll
96 D4 Fletcher's Green Kent
399 F6 Fletchertown Cumb
78 A5 Fletching E Susx
77 H5 Fletching Common E Susx
577 G5 Fleuchary Highld
132 C5 Fleur-de-lis Caerph
23 E1 Flexbury Cnwll
72 B5 Flexford Hants
93 F5 Flexford Surrey
388 B3 Flimby Cumb
79 G3 Flimwell E Susx
308 C5 Flint Flints
197 F6 Flint Cross Cambs
296 D5 Flintham Notts
405 E4 Flint Hill Dur
308 B5 Flint Mountain Flints
348 D2 Flinton E R Yk
214 D3 Flint's Green Solhll
185 F3 Flintsham Herefs
79 H2 Flishinghurst Kent
253 E2 Flitcham Norfk
380 D2 Flitholme Cumb
169 F2 Flitton Beds
169 E3 Flitwick Beds
332 B1 Flixborough N Linc
332 B2 Flixborough Stather N Linc
374 C4 Flixton N York
226 C2 Flixton Suffk
325 G6 Flixton Traffd
328 C2 Flockton Kirk
328 D1 Flockton Green Kirk
328 C2 Flockton Moor Kirk
592 E6 Flodaigh W Isls
453 H2 Flodden Nthumb
543 H2 Flodigarry Highld
185 E3 Floodgates Herefs
245 E6 Flood's Ferry Cambs
49 E1 Flood Street Hants
365 E4 Flookburgh Cumb
249 G5 Flordon Norfk
192 D3 Flore Nhants
272 D1 Florence C Stke
442 B4 Flotterton Nthumb
142 A5 Flowers Bottom Bucks
57 G2 Flowers Green E Susx
326 D5 Flowery Field Tamesd
201 E5 Flowton Suffk
484 B5 Fluchter E Duns
607 G5 Flugarth Shet
607 G2 Flukes Hole Shet
327 H3 Flush House Kirk
571 J6 Flushing Abers
5 F2 Flushing Cnwll
28 A4 Fluxton Devon
189 E4 Flyford Flavell Worcs
226 B5 Foals Green Suffk
121 H3 Fobbing Thurr
568 E4 Fochabers Moray
132 B3 Fochriw Caerph
346 B6 Fockerby N Linc
246 C3 Fodderstone Gap Norfk
565 J5 Fodderty Highld
67 F4 Foddington Somset
231 F2 Foel Powys
128 D2 Foel-gastell Carmth
527 F5 Foffarty Angus
345 H2 Foggathorpe E R Yk
312 B2 Foggbrook Stockp
473 H5 Fogo Border
606 B6 Fogrigarth Shet
568 C4 Fogwatt Moray
584 C7 Foindle Highld
526 A2 Folda Angus
340 D6 Fold Head Lancs
301 E4 Fold Hill Lincs
328 D6 Foldrings Sheff
273 F2 Fole Staffs
215 F3 Foleshill Covtry
212 B4 Foley Park Worcs
46 C2 Folke Dorset
82 D3 Folkestone Kent
279 F3 Folkingham Lincs
57 E4 Folkington E Susx
219 G1 Folksworth Cambs
374 C4 Folkton N York
559 G3 Folla Rule Abers
235 H5 Folley Shrops
356 C4 Follifoot N York
405 H2 Follingsby Gatesd
46 D4 Folly Dorset
151 F5 Folly Pembks
39 F6 Folly Cross Devon
25 E3 Folly Gate Devon
173 F4 Folly Green Essex
105 G6 Fonmon V Glam
23 E4 Fonston Cnwll
69 F3 Fonthill Bishop Wilts
69 F3 Fonthill Gifford Wilts
47 G1 Fontmell Magna Dorset
47 F2 Fontmell Parva Dorset
53 H3 Fontwell W Susx
105 G6 Font-y-gary V Glam
502 B1 Foodieash Fife
313 G4 Foolow Derbys
163 F4 Footbridge Gloucs
237 G4 Footherley Staffs
211 F5 Footrid Worcs
120 C5 Foots Cray Gt Lon
554 C2 Forbestown Abers
364 D1 Force Forge Cumb
96 B3 Force Green Kent
364 D1 Force Mills Cumb
383 E2 Forcett N York
24 D4 Forda Devon
60 C4 Forda Devon
493 E4 Ford Ag & B
141 G3 Ford Bucks
11 E2 Ford C Plym
315 E3 Ford Derbys
11 H3 Ford Devon
12 D4 Ford Devon
28 D2 Ford Devon
39 F3 Ford Devon
163 G4 Ford Gloucs
186 C3 Ford Herefs
100 D2 Ford Kent
454 A2 Ford Nthumb
151 G4 Ford Pembks
323 F5 Ford Sefton
233 H2 Ford Shrops
43 E2 Ford Somset
85 G4 Ford Somset
293 E4 Ford Staffs
70 D3 Ford Wilts
111 E5 Ford Wilts
54 B4 Ford W Susx
214 B2 Fordbridge Solhll
78 C1 Fordcombe Kent
500 B2 Fordel P & K
487 G2 Fordell Fife
232 D4 Forden Powys
146 D1 Ford End Essex
171 F3 Ford End Essex
10 D2 Forder Cnwll
19 G4 Forder Green Devon
65 F5 Fordgate Somset
292 A4 Ford Green C Stke
351 G5 Ford Green Lancs
222 C5 Fordham Cambs
174 B4 Fordham Essex
246 C5 Fordham Norfk
174 B4 Fordham Heath Essex
233 H2 Ford Heath Shrops
454 B2 Ford Hill Nthumb
236 D4 Fordhouses Wolves
510 D5 Fordie P & K
49 E1 Fordingbridge Hants
320 D5 Fordington Lincs
431 E5 Fordley N Tyne
374 D4 Fordon E R Yk
540 D4 Fordoun Abers
78 A4 Ford's Green E Susx
201 E1 Ford's Green Suffk
174 B4 Fordstreet Essex
43 G4 Ford Street Somset

26 C3 Fordton Devon
29 F2 Fordwater Devon
138 D2 Fordwells Oxon
100 C4 Fordwich Kent
569 K3 Fordyce Abers
272 D5 Forebridge Staffs
367 G6 Foredale N York
550 F4 Foregin Highld
444 D5 Forehill S Ayrs
37 G3 Foreland Fields IoW
275 K4 Foremark Derbys
34 C4 Forest Guern
353 F4 Forest Becks Lancs
442 D5 Forestburn Gate Nthumb
159 E5 Forest Coal Pit Mons
95 H2 Forestdale Gt Lon
120 B2 Forest Gate Gt Lon
52 A2 Forest Gate Hants
136 B4 Forest Green Gloucs
76 B1 Forest Green Surrey
431 E6 Forest Hall N Tyne
401 G3 Forest Head Cumb
119 H5 Forest Hill Gt Lon
140 C3 Forest Hill Oxon
113 F6 Forest Hill Oxon
340 C4 Forest Holme Lancs
393 E4 Forest-in-Teesdale Dur
356 C3 Forest Lane Head N York
499 E6 Forest Mill Clacks
356 C5 Forest Moor N York
39 E5 Forestreet Devon
78 A2 Forest Row E Susx
36 D3 Forest Side IoW
52 D2 Forestside W Susx
295 H2 Forest Town Notts
87 E2 Forewoods Common Wilts
527 G4 Forfar Angus
512 C6 Forgandenny P & K
6 C4 Forge Cnwll
230 B5 Forge Powys
133 E5 Forge Hammer Torfn
132 D3 Forge Side Torfn
468 A3 Forgewood N Lans
568 F5 Forgie Moray
569 L6 Forgue Abers
213 F4 Forhill Worcs
323 E3 Formby Sefton
249 F6 Forncett End Norfk
249 G6 Forncett St Mary Norfk
249 G6 Forncett St Peter Norfk
525 G6 Forneth P & K
199 G1 Fornham All Saints Suffk
223 H6 Fornham St Genevieve Suffk
199 G1 Fornham St Martin Suffk
22 B4 Forrabury Cnwll
567 J5 Forres Moray
468 D1 Forrestfield N Lans
173 F3 Forry's Green Essex
273 E1 Forsbrook Staffs
583 H3 Forse Highld
213 G5 Forshaw Heath Warwks
587 J8 Forsinard Highld
98 A3 Forstal Kent
31 F3 Forston Dorset
548 F8 Fort Augustus Highld
526 A2 Forter Angus
499 H1 Fortevoit P & K
566 D5 Fort George Highld
469 E4 Forth S Lans
162 C3 Forthampton Gloucs
135 G5 Forthay Gloucs
34 C2 Fort Hommet Guern
487 F4 Forth Road Bridge C Edin
523 K6 Fortingall P & K
119 F2 Fortis Green Gt Lon
35 e1 Fort le Marchant Guern
482 C4 Fort Matilda Inver
51 H4 Forton Hants
90 C6 Forton Hants
351 E4 Forton Lancs
234 A1 Forton Shrops
29 F1 Forton Somset
271 G5 Forton Staffs
234 A1 Forton Heath Shrops
561 E1 Fortrie Abers
570 B6 Fortrie Abers
566 C5 Fortrose Highld
32 B5 Fortuneswell Dorset
553 H8 Fort William Highld
117 F1 Forty Green Bucks
141 G4 Forty Green Bucks
144 D5 Forty Hill Gt Lon
201 E2 Forward Green Suffk
136 C4 Forwood Gloucs
89 H3 Fosbury Wilts
164 D5 Foscot Oxon
167 F2 Foscote Bucks
193 E5 Foscote Nhants
111 F4 Foscote Wilts
280 D3 Fosdyke Lincs
280 D3 Fosdyke Bridge Lincs
523 L4 Foss P & K
137 G3 Foss Cross Gloucs
137 G2 Fossebridge Gloucs
180 B2 Foss-y-ffin Cerdgn
99 H2 Fostall Kent
80 B2 Fosten Green Kent
331 E2 Fosterhouses Donc
193 E4 Foster's Booth Nhants
189 E1 Foster's Green Worcs
145 G3 Foster Street Essex
274 B3 Foston Derbys
240 B6 Foston Leics
297 G6 Foston Lincs
358 C1 Foston N York
361 E3 Foston on the Wolds E R Yk
320 B1 Fotherby Lincs
388 B3 Fothergill Cumb
243 F6 Fotheringhay Nhants
601 J4 Foubister Ork
245 G1 Foul Anchor Cambs
400 D3 Foulbridge Cumb
474 D3 Foulden Border
247 F5 Foulden Norfk
238 C5 Foul End Warwks
49 F3 Foulford Hants
57 G1 Foul Mile E Susx
57 F4 Foulride Green E Susx
340 D1 Foulridge Lancs
254 D3 Foulsham Norfk
3 G2 Foundry Cnwll
255 E2 Foundry Hill Norfk
104 D3 Fountain Brdgnd
471 H5 Fountainhall Border
142 B5 Four Ashes Bucks
214 A4 Four Ashes Solhll
212 B2 Four Ashes Staffs
236 D3 Four Ashes Staffs
224 D5 Four Ashes Suffk
34 C3 Four Cabots Guern
231 G3 Four Crosses Powys
269 E6 Four Crosses Powys
237 E3 Four Crosses Staffs
288 B4 Four Crosses Wrexhm
44 B6 Four Elms Devon
96 C5 Four Elms Kent
67 F3 Four Foot Somset
64 D4 Four Forks Somset
325 E3 Four Gates Bolton
245 F1 Four Gotes Cambs
91 G1 Four Houses Corner W Berk

328 D4 Four Lane End Barns
342 B3 Four Lane Ends Brad
325 H2 Four Lane Ends Bury
339 G4 Four Lane Ends Bury
6 C6 Four Lanes Cnwll
291 G3 Fourlanes End Ches
73 G2 Four Marks Hants
302 C5 Four Mile Bridge IoA
136 B2 Four Mile Elm Gloucs
214 C3 Four Oaks Birm
80 C5 Four Oaks E Susx
161 F4 Four Oaks Gloucs
99 F2 Four Oaks Kent
237 H5 Four Oaks Park Birm
577 H5 Fourpenny Highld
115 F4 Four Points W Berk
163 F1 Four Pools Worcs
128 C3 Four Roads Carmth
428 D6 Fourstones Nthumb
79 H4 Four Throws Kent
146 C2 Four Wantz Essex
79 H2 Four Wents Kent
79 H3 Four Wents Kent
69 H4 Fovant Wilts
561 E5 Foveran Abers
9 E3 Fowey Cnwll
65 F4 Fowler's Plot Somset
325 F5 Fowley Common Warrtn
513 H3 Fowlis Angus
511 G5 Fowlis Wester P & K
197 F5 Fowlmere Cambs
160 D3 Fownhope Herefs
175 E3 Foxash Estate Essex
466 C2 Foxbar Rens
120 B5 Foxbury Gt Lon
140 A4 Foxcombe Hill Oxon
168 C4 Fox Corner Beds
93 G4 Fox Corner Surrey
163 F6 Foxcote Gloucs
86 C3 Foxcote Somset
322 d7 Foxdale IoM
91 E4 Foxdown Hants
199 G6 Foxearth Essex
97 G1 Foxendown Kent
363 E4 Foxfield Cumb
215 E3 Foxford Covtry
111 H4 Foxham Wilts
146 B5 Fox Hatch Essex
86 D2 Fox Hill BaNES
187 F5 Fox Hill Herefs
50 B2 Foxhills Hants
8 B3 Foxhole Cnwll
23 F3 Foxhole Cnwll
249 H5 Foxhole Swans
103 E4 Fox Hole Swans
374 C5 Foxholes N York
69 E1 Fox Holes Wilts
78 C6 Foxhunt Green E Susx
93 E3 Fox Lane Hants
185 H5 Foxley Herefs
254 D3 Foxley Norfk
291 F4 Foxley Staffs
111 F2 Foxley Wilts
189 F1 Foxlydiate Worcs
342 D6 Fox Royd Kirk
174 D4 Fox Street Essex
292 D5 Foxt Staffs
197 F5 Foxton Cambs
395 H5 Foxton Dur
217 F2 Foxton Leics
384 C5 Foxton N York
367 H4 Foxup N York
310 C6 Foxwist Green Ches
211 E4 Foxwood Shrops
160 D4 Foy Herefs
549 H5 Foyers Highld
3 G3 Fraddam Cnwll
7 H2 Fraddon Cnwll
238 A2 Fradley Staffs
238 A2 Fradley Junction Staffs
238 B2 Fradley South Staffs
273 E3 Fradswell Staffs
361 F2 Fraisthorpe E R Yk
78 B5 Framfield E Susx
250 B4 Framingham Earl Norfk
250 B4 Framingham Pigot Norfk
202 B2 Framlingham Suffk
31 E3 Frampton Dorset
280 D2 Frampton Lincs
110 B3 Frampton Cotterell S Glos
163 F3 Frampton Court Gloucs
110 B3 Frampton End S Glos
136 D4 Frampton Mansell Gloucs
135 G3 Frampton on Severn Gloucs
280 C1 Frampton West End Lincs
201 G3 Framsden Suffk
405 G6 Framwellgate Moor Dur
136 D4 France Lynch Gloucs
212 B4 Franche Worcs
310 C4 Frandley Ches
308 B2 Frankby Wirral
256 B5 Frankfort Norfk
186 C5 Franklands Gate Herefs
213 E3 Frankley Worcs
213 E3 Frankley Green Worcs
213 E4 Frankley Hill Worcs
184 B3 Frank's Bridge Powys
215 G5 Frankton Warwks
234 B2 Frankwell Shrops
255 E5 Frans Green Norfk
78 D2 Frant E Susx
571 J2 Fraserburgh Abers
175 E5 Frating Essex
175 E5 Frating Green Essex
52 B4 Fratton C Port
238 C5 Freasley Warwks
10 C3 Freathy Cnwll
314 D3 Frecheville Sheff
222 D5 Freckenham Suffk
338 B4 Freckleton Lancs
94 D4 Fredley Surrey
314 C5 Freebirch Derbys
277 H6 Freeby Leics
90 D5 Freefolk Hants
273 F1 Freehay Staffs
139 G2 Freeland Oxon
483 G6 Freeland Rens
255 U4 Freeland Corner Norfk
50 C2 Freemantle C Sotn
469 G2 Freeport Village W Loth
606 F7 Freester Shet
251 E3 Freethorpe Norfk
326 B2 Free Town Bury
7 H4 Freewater Cnwll
145 E5 Freezy Water Gt Lon
300 C6 Freiston Lincs
300 C6 Freiston Shore Lincs
60 D5 Fremington Devon
382 B5 Fremington N York
110 A4 Frenchay S Glos
22 C4 Frenchbeer Devon
173 E5 Frenches Green Essex
71 F4 Frenchmoor Hants
96 C4 French Street Kent
338 D4 Frenchwood Lancs
74 C1 Frensham Surrey
225 F3 Frenze Norfk
587 K3 Fresgoe Highld
112 D3 Freshbrook Swindn
323 E3 Freshfield Sefton
86 D2 Freshford BaNES
36 A3 Freshwater IoW
36 A3 Freshwater Bay IoW
125 H3 Freshwater East Pembks

226 A4 Fressingfield Suffk
176 C2 Freston Suffk
589 K3 Freswick Highld
135 H3 Fretherne Gloucs
256 A6 Frettenham Norfk
501 E3 Freuchie Fife
526 B2 Freuchies Angus
125 F2 Freystrop Pembks
64 C4 Friarn Somset
237 F6 Friar Park Sandw
49 F6 Friars Cliff Dorset
78 B3 Friar's Gate E Susx
59 E4 Friar's Hill E Susx
512 D5 Friarton P & K
31 E5 Friar Waddon Dorset
245 G3 Friday Bridge Cambs
145 E6 Friday Hill Gt Lon
202 C4 Friday Street Suffk
202 D2 Friday Street Suffk
94 C5 Friday Street Surrey
359 G3 Fridaythorpe E R Yk
144 C6 Friern Barnet Gt Lon
516 F5 Friesland Ag & B
318 D4 Friesthorpe Lincs
318 B3 Frieston Lincs
298 A5 Friesthorpe Lincs
116 C2 Frieth Bucks
43 H2 Frieze Hill Somset
295 F4 Friezeland Notts
139 G5 Frilford Oxon
139 G5 Frilford Heath Oxon
115 E5 Frilsham W Berk
93 E3 Frimley Surrey
93 E3 Frimley Green Surrey
93 E3 Frimley Ridge Surrey
122 A6 Frindsbury Medway
259 E5 Fring Norfk
166 C4 Fringford Oxon
98 C3 Friningham Kent
173 E2 Frinkle Green Essex
98 D3 Frinsted Kent
176 D6 Frinton-on-Sea Essex
528 C5 Friockheim Angus
229 E2 Friog Gwynd
241 E4 Frisby Leics
277 E6 Frisby on the Wreake Leics
301 E3 Friskney Lincs
301 E3 Friskney Eaudyke Lincs
301 E4 Friskney Tofts Lincs
57 E5 Friston E Susx
203 E2 Friston Suffk
294 D4 Fritchley Derbys
99 E3 Frith Kent
49 G2 Fritham Hants
300 B5 Frith Bank Lincs
211 F6 Frith Common Worcs
39 G4 Frithelstock Devon
39 F4 Frithelstock Stone Devon
74 C2 Frithend Hants
142 C4 Frith-hill Bucks
93 G6 Frith Hill Surrey
143 E3 Frithsden Herts
300 B4 Frithville Lincs
80 B1 Frittenden Kent
13 E4 Frittiscombe Devon
250 A6 Fritton Norfk
251 F4 Fritton Norfk
257 E6 Fritton Norfk
166 B4 Fritwell Oxon
342 B2 Frizinghall Brad
376 C1 Frizington Cumb
199 F2 Frizzeler's Green Suffk
590 E2 Frobost W Isls
136 A4 Frocester Gloucs
233 E3 Frochas Powys
234 C4 Frodesley Shrops
332 B2 Frodingham N Linc
310 A4 Frodsham Ches
197 E4 Frog End Cambs
198 A3 Frog End Cambs
314 A4 Froggatt Derbys
292 D5 Froghall Staffs
49 F2 Frogham Hants
100 D5 Frogham Kent
96 B4 Froghole Kent
82 C3 Frogholt Kent
110 A3 Frogland Cross S Glos
102 C3 Frog Moor Swans
12 D4 Frogmore Devon
73 G5 Frogmore Hants
92 D2 Frogmore Hants
143 H4 Frogmore Herts
87 F4 Frogmore Wilts
444 D4 Frognal S Ayrs
243 H2 Frognall Lincs
7 E5 Frogpool Cnwll
188 B1 Frog Pool Worcs
172 B2 Frogs' Green Essex
256 A2 Frogshall Norfk
16 D5 Frogwell Cnwll
216 B1 Frolesworth Leics
86 D5 Frome Somset
135 H3 Fromebridge Gloucs
86 D5 Fromefield Somset
30 D2 Frome St Quintin Dorset
187 F5 Fromes Hill Herefs
186 C5 Fromington Herefs
287 F1 Fron Denbgs
263 F3 Fron Gwynd
283 F5 Fron Gwynd
184 A1 Fron Powys
231 E4 Fron Powys
232 C5 Fron Powys
232 D4 Fron Shrops
269 E2 Fron Shrops
268 D1 Fron-Bache Denbgs
269 E1 Froncysyllte Wrexhm
288 C5 Fron-deg Wrexhm
267 E2 Frongoch Gwynd
269 E1 Fron Isaf Wrexhm
26 B1 Frost Devon
227 F3 Frostenden Suffk
227 F3 Frostenden Corner Suffk
394 A2 Frosterley Dur
84 D2 Frost Hill N Som
50 D3 Frostlane Hants
248 D4 Frost Row Norfk
602 E6 Frotoft Ork
168 D3 Froxfield Beds
113 G6 Froxfield Wilts
73 H4 Froxfield Green Hants
72 B5 Fryern Hill Hants
146 C4 Fryerning Essex
121 H2 Fryerns Essex
372 C4 Fryton N York
70 C3 Fugglestone St Peter Wilts
298 A4 Fulbeck Lincs
430 C2 Fulbeck Nthumb
197 H3 Fulbourn Cambs
138 D2 Fulbrook Oxon
72 C4 Fulflood Hants
43 H2 Fulford Somset
273 E2 Fulford Staffs
358 B5 Fulford York
119 E4 Fulham Gt Lon
55 F2 Fulking W Susx
60 D3 Fullabrook Devon
467 F2 Fullarton C Glas
467 F2 Fullarton N Ayrs
343 E3 Fuller's End Essex
172 A4 Fuller's End Essex
289 G4 Fuller's Moor Ches
147 E1 Fuller Street Essex
71 H2 Fullerton Hants
320 A5 Fulletby Lincs
328 C4 Fullshaw Barns

358 D3 Full Sutton E R Yk
120 B1 Fullwell Cross Gt Lon
466 B4 Fullwood E Ayrs
326 D2 Fulmodeston Norfk
260 C5 Fulnetby Lincs
342 D3 Fulneck Leeds
318 D4 Fulnetby Lincs
280 C5 Fulney Lincs
190 D5 Fulready Warwks
311 G5 Fulshaw Park Ches
328 B3 Fulstone Kirk
334 D5 Fulstow Lincs
396 B5 Fulthorpe S on T
165 F5 Fulwell Oxon
406 B3 Fulwell Sundld
338 D3 Fulwood Lancs
314 C2 Fulwood Sheff
43 H3 Fulwood Somset
314 B2 Fulwood Hall Sheff
314 B2 Fulwood Head Sheff
249 G5 Fundenhall Norfk
52 D3 Funtington W Susx
51 G3 Funtley Hants
510 C4 Funtullich P & K
609 K6 Funzie Shet
30 B3 Furleigh Cross Dorset
87 F2 Furley Devon
493 H5 Furnace Ag & B
128 B4 Furnace Carmth
128 D4 Furnace Carmth
229 F5 Furnace Cerdgn
214 C1 Furnace End Warwks
77 F2 Furnace Green W Susx
77 F2 Furnace Wood W Susx
77 H4 Furner's Green E Susx
312 C3 Furness Vale Derbys
171 F4 Furneux Pelham Herts
44 C6 Furnham Somset
171 F3 Further Ford End Essex
80 C2 Further Quarter Kent
193 G6 Furtho Nhants
40 C2 Furze Devon
33 G3 Furzebrook Dorset
119 F5 Furzedown Gt Lon
71 H4 Furzedown Hants
62 A3 Furzehill Devon
48 C4 Furzehill Dorset
49 F2 Furze Hill Hants
52 A2 Furzeley Corner Hants
117 E3 Furze Platt W & M
50 C4 Furzey Lodge Hants
50 A1 Furzley Hants
168 A2 Furzton M Keyn
44 A5 Fyfett Somset
146 B3 Fyfield Essex
138 C4 Fyfield Gloucs
89 G5 Fyfield Hants
139 G5 Fyfield Oxon
112 D6 Fyfield Wilts
387 F4 Fylingthorpe N York
74 C5 Fyning W Susx
559 H2 Fyvie Abers

G

106 C4 Gabalfa Cardif
599 J3 Gabhsann bho Dheas W Isls
599 J3 Gabhsann bho Thuath W Isls
52 C5 Gable Head Hants
576 F5 Gablon Highld
466 C4 Gabroc Hill E Ayrs
95 E5 Gadbrook Surrey
241 E2 Gaddesby Leics
143 E3 Gadebridge Herts
303 G3 Gadfa IoA
162 A3 Gadfield Elm Worcs
445 F5 Gadgirth S Ayrs
269 G2 Gadlas Shrops
131 F4 Gadlys Rhondd
121 H5 Gadshill Kent
107 E2 Gaer Newpt
158 C5 Gaer Powys
134 A5 Gaer-fawr Mons
134 A5 Gaerllwyd Mons
285 E1 Gaerwen IoA
165 G5 Gagingwell Oxon
551 J4 Gaich Highld
236 D2 Gailey Staffs
236 D2 Gailey Wharf Staffs
139 E5 Gainfield Oxon
383 E1 Gainford Dur
97 G5 Gain Hill Kent
317 F2 Gainsborough Lincs
176 C1 Gainsborough Suffk
173 E2 Gainsford End Essex
562 D1 Gairloch Highld
533 J6 Gairlochy Highld
500 B5 Gairney Bank P & K
380 A3 Gaisgill Cumb
400 C5 Gaitsgill Cumb
472 D6 Galadean Border
451 F2 Galashiels Border
308 B5 Galdlys Flints
326 D1 Gale Rochdl
351 G3 Galgate Lancs
67 G4 Galhampton Somset
423 G3 Gallaberry D & G
506 D4 Gallanach Ag & B
517 G3 Gallanach Ag & B
289 H4 Gallantry Bank Ches
501 E6 Gallatown Fife
215 E1 Galley Common Warwks
147 E4 Galleyend Essex
298 D5 Galley Hill Lincs
320 D4 Galley Hill Lincs
147 E4 Galleywood Essex
402 C6 Galligill Cumb
522 F6 Gallin P & K
514 C1 Gallowfauld Angus
467 E3 Gallowhill C Glas
466 C1 Gallowhill Rens
571 K5 Gallowhills Abers
120 D1 Gallows Corner Gt Lon
174 B4 Gallows Green Essex
273 G1 Gallows Green Staffs
132 D3 Gallowsgreen Torfn
188 D2 Gallows Green Worcs
275 H1 Gallows Inn Derbys
115 H3 Gallowstree Common Oxon
546 E5 Galltair Highld
287 G3 Galltegfa Denbgs
284 C2 Gallt-y-foel Gwynd
78 B2 Gallypot Street E Susx
43 H3 Galmington Somset
12 B4 Galmisdale Highld
13 F1 Galmpton Devon
13 G4 Galmpton Torbay
131 G3 Galon Uchaf Myr Td
370 B5 Galphay N York
445 H2 Galston E Ayrs
542 B6 Galtrigill Highld
15 F3 Gam Cnwll
343 E3 Gamble Hill Leeds
391 G2 Gamblesby Cumb
147 F2 Gamble's Green Essex
273 H4 Gamelsby Cumb
313 G5 Gamesley Derbys
196 B4 Gamlingay Cambs
196 B4 Gamlingay Cinques Cambs

196 B4 Gamlingay Great Heath Cambs
39 G2 Gammaton Devon
39 G3 Gammaton Moor Devon
368 D3 Gammersgill N York
276 D2 Gamston Notts
316 D4 Gamston Notts
134 C1 Ganarew Herefs
506 E3 Ganavan Ag & B
161 G5 Ganders Green Gloucs
16 D5 Gang Cnwll
600 D3 Gangsti Pier Ork
265 G5 Ganllwyd Gwynd
68 C6 Gannetts Dorset
540 A5 Gannochy Angus
512 D5 Gannochy P & K
589 J8 Gansclet Highld
348 B3 Ganstead E R Yk
372 C5 Ganthorpe N York
374 B4 Ganton N York
120 B2 Gants Hill Gt Lon
144 C5 Ganwick Corner Herts
505 J3 Gaodhail Ag & B
20 B2 Gappah Devon
565 G3 Garbat Highld
493 H5 Garbhallt Ag & B
537 J4 Garbh Allt Shiel Abers
224 D3 Garboldisham Norfk
554 B3 Garchory Abers
132 C5 Garden City Blae G
308 D6 Garden City Flints
92 D1 Gardeners Green Wokham
570 E3 Gardenstown Abers
328 D5 Garden Village Sheff
129 E5 Garden Village Swans
288 D4 Garden Village Wrexhm
606 D8 Garderhouse Shet
347 E1 Gardham E R Yk
609 G6 Gardie Shet
609 J2 Gardie Shet
68 C1 Gare Hill Somset
482 B1 Garelochhead Ag & B
139 G5 Garford Oxon
343 H3 Garforth Leeds
354 B4 Gargrave N York
497 H6 Gargunnock Stirlg
479 K4 Gariob Ag & B
559 F1 Gariochsford Abers
305 E4 Garizim Conwy
8 C3 Garker Cnwll
43 G4 Garlandhayes Devon
400 D4 Garlands Cumb
418 C5 Garleffin S Ayrs
225 H3 Garlic Street Norfk
411 E3 Garlieston D & G
41 F2 Garliford Devon
101 F2 Garlinge Kent
100 B5 Garlinge Green Kent
556 D3 Garlogie Abers
272 A4 Garmelow Staffs
570 E5 Garmond Abers
395 G3 Garmondsway Dur
505 K2 Garmony Ag & B
568 E3 Garmouth Moray
235 E3 Garmston Shrops
262 D4 Garn Gwynd
208 B3 Garn Powys
129 G2 Garnant Carmth
132 D4 Garndiffaith Torfn
284 A6 Garndolbenmaen Gwynd
379 F5 Garnett Bridge Cumb
172 C6 Garnetts Essex
262 D4 Garnfadryn Gwynd
484 D6 Garnkirk N Lans
132 C2 Garnlydan Blae G
281 F5 Garnsgate Lincs
129 F3 Garn-swllt Swans
132 D3 Garn-yr-erw Torfn
599 L8 Garrabost W Isls
542 C7 Garrachan Highld
543 H3 Garrafad Highld
601 J4 Garralanga Ork
492 D3 Garraron Ag & B
4 D4 Garras Cnwll
307 G4 Garreg Flints
265 E1 Garreg Gwynd
233 E2 Garreg Bank Powys
214 A2 Garrets Green Birm
498 C2 Garrick P & K
392 B1 Garrigill Cumb
383 E6 Garriston N York
421 F3 Garroch D & G
408 C4 Garrochtrie D & G
543 H4 Garros Highld
511 E1 Garrow P & K
467 G2 Garrowhill C Glas
533 J2 Garrygualach Highld
434 A6 Garryhorn D & G
367 E2 Garsdale Cumb
367 F1 Garsdale Head Cumb
111 H2 Garsdon Wilts
273 E3 Garshall Green Staffs
140 C4 Garsington Oxon
351 G6 Garstang Lancs
143 G5 Garston Herts
309 F3 Garston Lpool
476 D5 Gartbreck Ag & B
484 D6 Gartcosh N Lans
104 D1 Garth Brdgnd
205 F3 Garth Cerdgn
307 G3 Garth Flints
304 C5 Garth Gwynd
133 F6 Garth Mons
107 E2 Garth Newpt
602 F2 Garth Ork
183 E5 Garth Powys
209 E5 Garth Powys
606 B6 Garth Shet
607 G7 Garth Shet
288 C6 Garth Wrexhm
288 C6 Garth Wrexhm
467 G1 Garthamlock C Glas
549 J6 Garthbeg Highld
157 G3 Garthbrengy Powys
557 G4 Garthdee C Aber
181 E3 Gartheli Cerdgn
232 C5 Garthmyl Powys
278 A5 Garthorpe Leics
346 C6 Garthorpe N Linc
208 A1 Garth Owen Powys
379 F5 Garth Row Cumb
288 C6 Garth Trevor Denbgs
468 B2 Gartlea N Lans
467 G1 Gartloch C Glas
558 C3 Gartly Abers
496 D5 Gartmore Stirlg
462 C3 Gartnagrenach Ag & B
468 B2 Gartness N Lans
483 G2 Gartness Stirlg
483 F2 Gartocharn W Duns
349 F2 Garton E R Yk
360 B3 Garton-on-the-Wolds E R Yk
467 H1 Gartsherrie N Lans
582 D7 Gartymore Highld
490 A5 Garvald E Loth
478 B3 Garvard Ag & B
564 F4 Garve Highld
248 D3 Garvestone Norfk
481 E1 Garvie Ag & B
540 C5 Garvock Abers
482 C5 Garvock Inver
487 F2 Garvock Hill Fife
160 B5 Garway Herefs
160 B5 Garway Common Herefs

160 A4 Garway Hill Herefs
597 K4 Garyvard W Isls
68 C3 Gasper Wilts
111 F6 Gastard Wilts
224 C3 Gasthorpe Norfk
145 G1 Gaston Green Essex
212 A2 Gatacre Park Shrops
36 D4 Gatcombe IoW
309 F2 Gateacre Lpool
366 A2 Gatebeck Cumb
317 F3 Gate Burton Lincs
315 H3 Gateford Notts
315 H3 Gateford Common Notts
344 D4 Gateforth N York
445 E2 Gatehead E Ayrs
358 A2 Gate Helmsley N York
428 B2 Gatehouse Nthumb
412 B3 Gatehouse of Fleet D & G
436 B5 Gatelawbridge D & G
254 C3 Gateley Norfk
370 C2 Gatenby N York
377 F1 Gatesgarth Cumb
405 F2 Gateshead Gatesd
289 G2 Gatesheath Ches
527 F6 Gateside Angus
437 F6 Gateside D & G
466 C3 Gateside E Rens
500 C3 Gateside Fife
465 H4 Gateside N Ayrs
436 A4 Gateslack D & G
288 D4 Gatewen Wrexhm
24 A6 Gatherley Devon
324 C3 Gathurst Wigan
133 F6 Gatlas Newpt
311 G2 Gatley Manch
170 C1 Gatley End Cambs
95 F4 Gatton Surrey
451 G3 Gattonside Border
135 G2 Gatwick Gloucs
207 G6 Gaufron Powys
241 E4 Gaulby Leics
514 B5 Gauldry Fife
512 C3 Gauls P & K
290 B5 Gauntons Bank Ches
48 C3 Gaunt's Common Dorset
110 A3 Gaunt's Earthcott S Glos
172 A4 Gaunt's End Essex
319 F5 Gautby Lincs
473 H4 Gavinton Border
329 E3 Gawber Barns
167 E3 Gawcott Bucks
312 A5 Gawsworth Ches
328 B1 Gawthorpe Wakefd
343 E5 Gawthorpe Wakefd
366 D2 Gawthrop Cumb
363 F5 Gawthwaite Cumb
147 F4 Gay Bowers Essex
191 F4 Gaydon Warwks
602 F1 Gayfield Ork
194 A5 Gayhurst M Keyn
367 H2 Gayle N York
382 D3 Gayles N York
76 A5 Gay Street W Susx
193 F4 Gayton Nhants
253 E4 Gayton Norfk
273 E4 Gayton Staffs
308 C3 Gayton Wirral
320 D2 Gayton Engine Lincs
320 D3 Gayton le Marsh Lincs
319 G2 Gayton le Wold Lincs
253 E4 Gayton Thorpe Norfk
252 C3 Gaywood Norfk
199 E2 Gazeley Suffk
590 E2 Gearraidh Bhailteas W Isls
597 K4 Gearraidh Bhaird W Isls
591 D8 Gearraidh Gadhal W Isls
590 E4 Gearraidh ma Mònadh W Isls
597 G1 Gearraidh na h-Aibhne W Isls
542 D4 Geary Highld
544 E1 Gearymore Highld
200 B3 Gedding Suffk
218 B3 Geddington Nhants
203 E5 Gedgrave Hall Suffk
545 J2 Gedintailor Highld
296 B6 Gedling Notts
281 F5 Gedney Lincs
281 E5 Gedney Broadgate Lincs
281 G4 Gedney Drove End Lincs
281 F4 Gedney Dyke Lincs
244 D2 Gedney Hill Lincs
326 D6 Gee Cross Tamesd
242 D4 Geeston Rutlnd
288 C4 Gegin Wrexhm
482 D4 Geilston Ag & B
307 F6 Geinas Denbgs
593 D9 Geirinis W Isls
588 E4 Geise Highld
596 E1 Geisiadar W Isls
226 D1 Geldeston Norfk
306 A6 Gell Conwy
152 B6 Gelli Pembks
131 F6 Gelli Rhondd
131 G3 Gellideg Myr Td
287 G2 Gellifor Denbgs
132 B5 Gelligaer Caerph
130 B6 Gelli-gaer Neath
132 C6 Gelligroes Caerph
132 C5 Gelli-hâf Caerph
265 F2 Gellilydan Gwynd
130 A4 Gellinud Neath
286 C6 Gellioedd Conwy
512 C2 Gellyburn P & K
129 H4 Gellygron Neath
153 F5 Gellywen Carmth
275 G6 Gelsmoor Leics
413 G3 Gelston D & G
297 H5 Gelston Lincs
361 G2 Gembling E R Yk
310 B1 Gemini Warrtn
103 F2 Gendros Swans
199 E3 Genesis Green Suffk
415 F5 Genoch Mains D & G
237 G2 Gentleshaw Staffs
595 J4 Geocrab W Isls
425 F1 Georgefield D & G
117 H3 George Green Bucks
60 C3 Georgeham Devon
41 E3 George Nympton Devon
132 B3 Georgetown Blae G
423 G5 Georgetown D & G
3 E2 Georgia Cnwll
602 D6 Georth Ork
129 F3 Gerdinen-isaf Swans
535 H4 Gergask Highld
284 D1 Gerlan Gwynd
24 B4 Germansweek Devon
467 F1 Germiston C Glas
3 G4 Germoe Cnwll
145 G4 Gernon Bushes Essex
5 G1 Gerrans Cnwll
271 H2 Gerrard's Bromley Staffs
117 G2 Gerrards Cross Bucks
609 J2 Gerratown Shet
386 B2 Gerrick R & Cl
207 E1 Geseilfa Powys
173 G2 Gestingthorpe Essex
232 D2 Geuffordd Powys
268 D1 Geufron Denbgs
206 D2 Geufron Powys
215 E5 Gibbet Hill Covtry
216 B3 Gibbet Hill Warwks
310 C4 Gibb Hill Ches

512 B2 Gibbieston P & K
213 F2 Gib Heath Birm
195 E5 Gibraltar Beds
141 F2 Gibraltar Bucks
82 D3 Gibraltar Kent
301 F3 Gibraltar Lincs
166 A6 Gibraltar Oxon
482 D5 Gibshill Inver
296 D5 Gibsmere Notts
111 F5 Giddeahall Wilts
33 E2 Giddy Green Dorset
120 D1 Gidea Park Gt Lon
120 D2 Gidea Park Gt Lon
25 G5 Gidleigh Devon
168 B1 Giffard Park M Keyn
467 E3 Giffnock E Rens
489 G6 Gifford E Loth
501 E2 Giffordtown Fife
326 B3 Gigg Bury
212 C1 Giggetty Staffs
353 F2 Giggleswick N York
94 D1 Giggshill Surrey
151 E5 Gignog Pembks
346 B4 Gilberdyke E R Yk
6 C5 Gilbert's Coombe Cnwll
188 B6 Gilbert's End Worcs
213 H5 Gilbert's Green Warwks
214 A3 Gilbertstone Birm
73 F3 Gilbert Street Hants
472 B1 Gilchriston E Loth
388 D2 Gilcrux Cumb
342 D4 Gildersome Leeds
342 D4 Gildersome Street Leeds
315 G2 Gildingwells Rothm
405 G6 Gilesgate Dur
405 G6 Gilesgate Moor Dur
105 G6 Gileston V Glam
132 B5 Gilfach Caerph
159 F3 Gilfach Herefs
105 F2 Gilfach Goch Rhondd
180 A3 Gilfachreda Cerdgn
388 B5 Gilgarran Cumb
354 C6 Gill N York
372 C2 Gillamoor N York
5 E4 Gillan Cnwll
606 D5 Gilarona Shet
378 C5 Gillbank Cumb
311 H3 Gillbent Stockp
542 D5 Gillen Highld
424 D1 Gillesbie D & G
372 B4 Gilling East N York
68 D4 Gillingham Dorset
98 B1 Gillingham Medway
227 E1 Gillingham Norfk
383 E3 Gilling West N York
323 G5 Gillmoss Lpool
601 H3 Gill of Garth Ork
291 H3 Gillow Heath Staffs
589 J2 Gills Highld
79 H3 Gill's Green Kent
238 C3 Gillway Staffs
450 C5 Gilmanscleuch Border
488 B6 Gilmerton C Edin
511 F5 Gilmerton P & K
382 A2 Gilmonby Dur
216 C2 Gilmorton Leics
446 D1 Gilmourton S Lans
325 G3 Gilnow Bolton
329 E4 Gilroyd Barns
402 A1 Gilsland Cumb
214 B2 Gilson Warwks
342 B2 Gilstead Brad
472 B2 Gilston Border
145 F2 Gilston Herts
145 F2 Gilston Park Herts
295 F5 Giltbrook Notts
162 B1 Gilver's Lane Worcs
145 E5 Gilwell Park Essex
132 D2 Gilwern Mons
256 B2 Gimingham Norfk
312 D2 Ginclough Ches
57 G2 Ginger's Green E Susx
596 E2 Giosla W Isls
201 E2 Gipping Suffk
299 H5 Gipsey Bridge Lincs
175 E2 Gipsy Row Suffk
347 G4 Gipsyville C KuH
343 F3 Gipton Leeds
444 D1 Girdle Toll N Ayrs
342 B3 Girlington Brad
606 F7 Girlsta Shet
319 G2 Girsby Lincs
384 B3 Girsby N York
67 G5 Girt Somset
412 B4 Girthon D & G
197 F2 Girton Cambs
297 F1 Girton Notts
419 E2 Girvan S Ayrs
353 G5 Gisburn Lancs
227 G2 Gisleham Suffk
225 E5 Gislingham Suffk
225 F2 Gissing Norfk
28 B3 Gittisham Devon
94 D4 Givons Grove Surrey
565 K6 Glackmore Highld
478 B3 Glac Mhòr Ag & B
184 D3 Gladestry Powys
489 F5 Gladsmuir E Loth
549 J2 Glaichbea Highld
546 D4 Glaick Highld
129 H4 Glais Swans
386 C3 Glaisdale N York
543 K8 Glame Highld
527 E5 Glamis Angus
304 C5 Glan Adda Gwynd
125 F1 Glanafon Pembks
129 G2 Glanaman Carmth
286 A4 Glan Conwy Conwy
181 E4 Glan Denys Cerdgn
260 D3 Glandford Norfk
132 D4 Glandwr Caerph
152 D4 Glandwr Pembks
284 A6 Glan Dwyfach Gwynd
152 C4 Glandy Cross Carmth
229 F5 Glandyfi Cerdgn
132 D1 Glangrwyney Powys
231 E5 Glanhanog Powys
208 C1 Glanmule Powys
205 E3 Glanrafon Cerdgn
152 C1 Glanrhyd Pembks
130 B3 Glan-rhyd Powys
443 H3 Glantlees Nthumb
442 D2 Glanton Nthumb
442 D2 Glanton Pyke Nthumb
205 E2 Glanvilles Wootton Dorset
305 H3 Glanwern Cerdgn
307 H4 Glanwydden Conwy
106 B3 Glan-y-llyn Rhondd
127 G2 Glan-y-mòr Carmth
132 B5 Glan-y-nant Caerph
207 E1 Glan-y-nant Powys
307 G3 Glan-yr-afon Gwynd
304 D3 Glan-yr-afon Gwynd
267 G1 Glan-yr-afon Shrops
268 D5 Glan-yr-afon Shrops
265 E3 Glan-y-wern Gwynd
219 E1 Glapthorn Nhants
295 F1 Glapwell Derbys
478 C5 Glas Aird Ag & B
538 B3 Glas-allt-Shiel Abers
158 C2 Glasbury Powys
306 D5 Glascoed Denbgs

133 F4 Glascoed Mons
208 A2 Glascoed Powys
232 B3 Glascoed Powys
288 B3 Glascoed Wrexhm
154 D6 Glascoed Isaf Carmth
554 C5 Glascorrie Abers
238 C4 Glascote Heath Staffs
184 C4 Glascwm Powys
307 G3 Glasdir Flints
520 E6 Glasdrum Ag & B
286 C5 Glasfryn Conwy
179 G4 Glasgoed Cerdgn
467 E2 Glasgow C Glas
543 H3 Glashvin Highld
304 C6 Glasinfryn Gwynd
107 E2 Glasllwch Newpt
531 J3 Glasnacardoch Highld
545 J7 Glasnakille Highld
542 B6 Glasphein Highld
229 G5 Glaspwll Powys
548 F3 Glassburn Highld
79 H2 Glassenbury Kent
410 D5 Glasserton D & G
468 A5 Glassford S Lans
344 A5 Glass Houghton Wakefd
161 F5 Glasshouse Gloucs
161 G5 Glasshouse Hill Gloucs
355 G2 Glasshouses N York
570 F4 Glaslaw Abers
500 D3 Glasslie Fife
388 B2 Glasson Cumb
399 G2 Glasson Cumb
351 F3 Glasson Lancs
391 F2 Glassonby Cumb
528 C4 Glasterlaw Angus
242 B4 Glaston Rutlnd
66 D2 Glastonbury Somset
219 H2 Glatton Cambs
310 D1 Glazebrook Warrtn
325 F5 Glazebury Warrtn
211 G2 Glazeley Shrops
314 D3 Gleadless Sheff
314 D3 Gleadless Valley Sheff
311 G6 Gleadsmoss Ches
591 D8 Gleann W Isls
590 F4 Gleann Dail bho Dheas W Isls
590 F4 Gleann dail bho Tuath W Isls
599 L6 Gleann Tholastaidh W Isls
364 C5 Gleaston Cumb
51 F1 Glebe Hants
549 J6 Glebe Highld
605 J2 Glebe Shet
405 H3 Glebe Sundld
343 F2 Gledhow Leeds
269 E2 Gledrid Shrops
207 F1 Gleiniant Powys
199 G5 Glemsford Suffk
417 G5 Glen D & G
568 D7 Glenallachie Moray
531 J4 Glenancross Highld
476 E8 Glenastle Ag & B
322 g4 Glen Auldyn IoM
458 D4 Glenbarr Ag & B
569 K5 Glenbeg Highld
518 E3 Glenbeg Highld
551 J4 Glenbeg Highld
542 F7 Glen Bernisdale Highld
541 E3 Glenbervie Abers
485 E6 Glenboig N Lans
518 F3 Glenborrodale Highld
494 C5 Glenbranter Ag & B
448 D5 Glenbreck Border
470 B1 Glenbrock C Edin
447 E4 Glenbuck E Ayrs
466 C2 Glenburn Rens
578 F5 Glencanisp Lodge Highld
423 G6 Glencaple D & G
513 E5 Glencarse D & G
521 G6 Glenceitlein Highld
520 F4 Glencoe Highld
500 C3 Glencraig Fife
422 C2 Glencrosh D & G
542 B7 Glendale Highld
451 G2 Glendearg Border
499 F4 Glenderby P & K
549 G8 Glendoebeg Highld
513 E5 Glendoick P & K
513 G6 Glenduckie Fife
499 E2 Gleneagles Hotel P & K
476 E6 Glenegedale Ag & B
546 E6 Glenelg Highld
500 B2 Glenfarg P & K
240 B3 Glenfield Leics
532 C6 Glenfinnan Highld
500 C1 Glenfoot P & K
465 G4 Glengarnock N Ayrs
518 B4 Glengorm Castle Ag & B
543 G8 Glengrasco Highld
542 D8 Glen Heysdal Highld
18 B5 Glenholt C Plym
421 G2 Glenhoul D & G
519 K2 Glenhurich Highld
438 B2 Glenkerry Border
554 B2 Glenkindie Abers
421 F3 Glenlea D & G
58 B5 Glenleigh Park E Susx
498 B2 Glenlichorn P & K
552 D3 Glenlivet Moray
412 D2 Glenlochar D & G
500 C4 Glenlomond P & K
415 G5 Glenluce D & G
526 B2 Glenmarkie Lodge Angus
485 E6 Glenmavis N Lans
486 C6 Glenmavis W Loth
322 c7 Glen Maye IoM
451 F3 Glenmayne Border
322 h5 Glen Mona IoM
492 D2 Glenmore Ag & B
545 G1 Glenmore Highld
527 E2 Glenmoy Angus
569 G5 Glen of Newmill Moray
527 F2 Glenogil Angus
125 F3 Glenowen Pembks
240 C5 Glen Parva Leics
568 F3 Glenprosen Village Angus
527 F2 Glenquiech Angus
449 H3 Glenreasdell Mains Ag & B
463 H3 Glenridding Cumb
378 C1 Glenridding Cumb
575 K3 Glen Rossal Highld
501 E4 Glenrothes Fife
519 K6 Glensanda Highld
540 C4 Glensaugh Abers
486 B3 Glensburgh Falk
494 B5 Glen Sluain Ag & B
414 B4 Glenstockadale D & G
481 F4 Glenstriven Ag & B
449 H2 Glenternie Border
318 C1 Glentham Lincs
497 G6 Glentirranmuir Stirlg
559 E5 Glenton Abers
450 B2 Glentress Border
420 B4 Glentrool Village D & G
318 A3 Glentworth Lincs
531 J7 Glenuig Highld
507 L4 Glenview Ag & B
486 A4 Glen Village Falk
322 e7 Glen Vine IoM
447 G4 Glespin S Lans
607 G7 Gletness Shet

160 C5 Glewstone Herefs
597 K3 Glib Cheòis W Isls
243 H3 Glinton C Pete
326 D4 Glodwick Oldham
153 E3 Glogue Pembks
241 G5 Glooston Leics
455 F3 Glororum Nthumb
327 F6 Glossop Derbys
443 H4 Gloster Hill Nthumb
162 A6 Gloucester Gloucs
609 G4 Gloup Shet
7 E5 Gloweth Cnwll
354 C6 Glusburn N York
606 D2 Gluss Shet
293 E1 Glutton Bridge Derbys
14 C6 Gluvian Cnwll
165 G5 Glympton Oxon
134 B5 Glyn Mons
207 E2 Glyn Powys
179 G4 Glynarthen Cerdgn
207 F3 Glynbrochan Powys
130 C4 Glyn Castle Neath
268 D2 Glyn Ceiriog Wrexhm
105 H1 Glyncoch Rhondd
132 C2 Glyncoed Blae G
130 D5 Glyncorrwg Neath
56 C3 Glynde E Susx
56 D2 Glyndebourne E Susx
268 B1 Glyndyfrdwy Denbgs
58 C5 Glyne Gap E Susx
132 C3 Glyn Etwy Blae G
206 D3 Glynhafren Powys
105 E2 Glynllan Brdgnd
269 F2 Glynmorlas Shrops
130 D3 Glyn-neath Neath
105 F2 Glynogwr Brdgnd
106 A2 Glyntaff Rhondd
130 C1 Glyntawe Powys
17 G6 Gnatham Devon
272 B5 Gnosall Staffs
272 B5 Gnosall Heath Staffs
241 G5 Goadby Leics
277 G4 Goadby Marwood Leics
112 B4 Goatacre Wilts
493 H4 Goatfield Ag & B
58 D3 Goatham Green E Susx
46 C1 Goathill Somset
386 D4 Goathland N York
65 E5 Goathurst Somset
96 C4 Goathurst Common Kent
596 C6 Gobhaig W Isls
91 G5 Gobley Hole Hants
269 F3 Gobowen Shrops
93 G6 Godalming Surrey
116 C1 Goddards Bucks
236 B6 Goddard's Corner Suffk
80 B3 Goddard's Green Kent
91 H1 Goddard's Green W Berk
77 E5 Goddards' Green W Susx
96 C1 Godden Green Kent
166 D4 Goddington Oxon
327 E5 Godley Tamesd
292 C6 Godleybrook Staffs
327 E6 Godley Hill Tamesd
77 G6 Godleys Green E Susx
220 C6 Godmanchester Cambs
31 F3 Godmanstone Dorset
99 G4 Godmersham Kent
66 D1 Godney Somset
3 G3 Godolphin Cross Cnwll
54 D4 Godre'r-graig Neath
48 C4 God's Blessing Green Dorset
49 F2 Godshill Hants
37 E4 Godshill IoW
95 G4 Godstone Surrey
49 F5 Godswinscroft Hants
12 A1 Godwell Devon
254 B3 Godwick Norfk
133 F3 Goetre Mons
302 B4 Goferydd IoA
144 D4 Goff's Oak Herts
487 G5 Gogar C Edin
305 G3 Gogarth Conwy
205 F3 Goginan Cerdgn
284 B6 Golan Gwynd
9 E3 Golant Cnwll
16 D4 Golberdon Cnwll
325 E5 Golborne Wigan
327 G1 Golcar Kirk
307 H4 Golch Flints
108 C3 Goldcliff Newpt
140 C5 Golden Balls Oxon
57 E2 Golden Cross E Susx
57 G2 Golden Cross E Susx
97 F5 Golden Green Kent
155 E6 Golden Grove Carmth
109 G4 Golden Hill Bristl
49 H5 Golden Hill Hants
125 G4 Golden Hill Pembks
151 G5 Golden Hill Pembks
38 B3 Golden Park Devon
92 B6 Golden Pot Hants
295 E4 Golden Valley Derbys
162 D5 Golden Valley Gloucs
187 F5 Golden Valley Herefs
186 D2 Golder Field Herefs
119 E2 Golders Green Gt Lon
91 E2 Goldfinch Bottom W Berk
148 B3 Goldhanger Essex
47 F2 Gold Hill Dorset
234 C4 Golding Shrops
195 F4 Goldington Beds
356 D3 Goldsborough N York
386 D2 Goldsborough N York
85 G2 Gold's Cross BaNES
237 E6 Golds Green Sandw
3 F3 Goldsithney Cnwll
271 G4 Goldstone Shrops
172 B1 Goldstones Essex
236 D5 Goldthorn Park Wolves
329 H4 Goldthorpe Barns
39 E3 Goldworthy Devon
80 A2 Golford Kent
308 C5 Golftyn Flints
101 E6 Golgotha Kent
568 F3 Gollachy Moray
566 E6 Gollanfield Highld
7 E3 Gollawater Cnwll
369 F3 Gollinglith Foot N York
288 D3 Golly Wrexhm
63 G4 Golsoncott Somset
577 H4 Golspie Highld
587 J4 Golval Highld
132 D4 Golynos Torfn
70 D2 Gomeldon Wilts
342 C4 Gomersal Kirk
94 B5 Gomshall Surrey
296 C5 Gonalston Notts
16 C4 Gonamena Cnwll
278 C2 Gonerby Hill Foot Lincs
606 E5 Gonfirth Shet
146 C2 Good Easter Essex
254 B3 Goodensdell Norfk
61 F5 Goodleigh Devon
96 B4 Goodley Stock Kent
359 G2 Goodmanham E R Yk
120 C2 Goodmayes Gt Lon
99 G2 Goodnestone Kent
101 E5 Goodnestone Kent
160 D6 Goodrich Herefs
20 B6 Goodrington Torbay

212 A3 Good's Green Worcs
340 C4 Goodshaw Lancs
340 C4 Goodshaw Chapel Lancs
340 C4 Goodshaw Fold Lancs
19 G3 Goodstone Devon
151 G2 Goodwick Pembks
71 G1 Goodworth Clatford Hants
215 E2 Goodyers End Warwks
398 D5 Goodyhills Cumb
345 G5 Goole E R Yk
189 F4 Goom's Hill Worcs
8 A3 Goonabarn Cnwll
6 D4 Goonbell Cnwll
6 D5 Goon Gumpas Cnwll
7 E5 Goonhavern Cnwll
4 C3 Goonhusband Cnwll
4 D1 Goonlaze Cnwll
6 D3 Goonown Cnwll
7 F6 Goon Piper Cnwll
7 E5 Goonvrea Cnwll
146 D6 Gooseberry Green Essex
341 G1 Goose Eye Brad
25 G1 Gooseford Devon
366 A3 Goose Green Cumb
175 F4 Goose Green Essex
50 B3 Goose Green Hants
145 E3 Goose Green Herts
80 B2 Goose Green Kent
97 F4 Goose Green Kent
338 C5 Goose Green Lancs
225 F2 Goose Green Norfk
110 C3 Goose Green S Glos
324 D4 Goose Green Wigan
74 B5 Goose Green W Susx
76 B6 Goose Green W Susx
38 B4 Gooseham Cnwll
38 B4 Gooseham Mill Cnwll
91 E2 Goose Hill Hants
343 G5 Goosehill Wakefd
188 D2 Goosehill Green Worcs
27 H5 Goosemoor Devon
272 B6 Goosemoor Staffs
237 G2 Goosemoor Green Staffs
44 A2 Goosenford Somset
160 B2 Goose Pool Herefs
60 D2 Goosewell Devon
114 B1 Goosey Oxon
338 D2 Goosnargh Lancs
311 F5 Goostrey Ches
467 E2 Gorbals C Glas
213 G6 Gorcott Hill Warwks
605 H5 Gord Shet
305 E5 Gorddinog Gwynd
473 E6 Gordon Border
577 H2 Gordonbush Highld
569 G2 Gordonsburgh Moray
559 G2 Gordonstoun Moray
569 K4 Gordonstown Abers
67 F6 Gore Dorset
101 E4 Gore Kent
471 F2 Gorebridge Mdloth
90 C2 Gore End Hants
245 F2 Gorefield Cambs
75 F5 Gorehill W Susx
173 H6 Gore Pit Essex
101 E2 Gore Street Kent
35 j7 Gorey Jersey
487 H5 Gorgie C Edin
143 G3 Gorhambury Herts
115 G3 Goring Oxon
54 D4 Goring-by-Sea W Susx
115 H4 Goring Heath Oxon
251 G4 Gorleston-on-Sea Norfk
212 D1 Gornalwood Dudley

570 C4 Gorrachie Abers
8 C5 Gorran Haven Cnwll
8 B5 Gorran High Lanes Cnwll
439 F5 Gorrenberry Border
180 B6 Gorrig Cerdgn
310 D1 Gorse Covert Warrtn
307 G4 Gorsedd Flints
113 E2 Gorse Hill Swindn
326 B5 Gorse Hill Traffd
129 E5 Gorseinon Swans
602 E8 Gorseness Ork
296 A1 Gorsethorpe Notts
294 B4 Gorseybank Derbys
180 C4 Gorsgoch Cerdgn
129 E2 Gorslas Carmth
161 F4 Gorsley Gloucs
161 F4 Gorsley Common Herefs
310 C5 Gorstage Ches
564 F4 Gorstan Highld
289 E2 Gorstella Ches
506 B3 Gorsten Ag & B
237 G3 Gorstey Ley Staffs
211 G5 Gorst Hill Worcs
291 E4 Gorstyhill Ches
273 H4 Gorsty Hill Staffs
476 E2 Gortantaoid Ag & B
518 F2 Gorteneorn Highld
518 E2 Gortenfern Highld
326 C5 Gorton Manch
461 E4 Gortonallister N Ayrs
480 C1 Gortonronach Ag & B
201 G3 Gosbeck Suffk
280 B3 Gosberton Lincs
280 B4 Gosberton Cheal Lincs
280 A3 Gosberton Clough Lincs
237 G2 Goscote Wsall
275 E5 Goseley Dale Derbys
173 F4 Gosfield Essex
28 A3 Gosford Devon
210 C6 Gosford Herefs
140 A2 Gosford Oxon
215 F4 Gosford Green Covtry
376 D4 Gosforth Cumb
430 D6 Gosforth N u Ty
314 C4 Gosforth Valley Derbys
199 F4 Gosland Green Suffk
174 C1 Gosling Green Suffk
99 G3 Gosmere Kent
170 A4 Gosmore Herts
212 B1 Gospel Ash Staffs
236 D6 Gospel End Village Staffs
75 E3 Gospel Green W Susx
119 F2 Gospel Oak Gt Lon
51 G5 Gosport Hants
72 A5 Gosport Hants
609 G8 Gossabrough Shet
194 D6 Gossard's Green Beds
135 G4 Gossington Gloucs
76 D2 Gossops Green W Susx
475 G6 Goswick Nthumb
48 D2 Gotham Dorset
58 A5 Gotham E Susx
276 B3 Gotham Notts
64 D4 Gotherington Gloucs
163 E4 Gotherington Gloucs
8 B2 Gothers Cnwll
516 C6 Gott Ag & B
605 H1 Gott Shet
44 A2 Gotton Somset
77 G2 Goudhurst Kent
319 G4 Goulceby Lincs
384 D4 Gouldon N York
559 H1 Gourdas Abers
514 A3 Gourdie C Dund
541 F5 Gourdon Abers
482 B4 Gourock Inver
466 D1 Govan C Glas
97 F4 Gover Hill Kent
296 C4 Goverton Notts

12 D3 Goveton Devon
133 E2 Govilon Mons
527 G4 Gowanbank Angus
571 J3 Gowanhill Abers
560 C1 Gowanwell Abers
345 E5 Gowdall E R Yk
103 E2 Gowerton Swans
312 D3 Gowhole Derbys
487 E2 Gowkhall Fife
468 B4 Gowkthrapple N Lans
359 E4 Gowthorpe E R Yk
361 F6 Goxhill E R Yk
348 B5 Goxhill N Linc
348 B4 Goxhill Haven N Linc
104 B2 Goytre Neath
139 H5 Gozzard's Ford Oxon
597 K4 Grabhair W Isls
279 F4 Graby Lincs
8 C2 Gracca Cnwll
488 B6 Gracemount C Edin
4 D6 Grade Cnwll
53 G1 Graffham W Susx
219 H6 Grafham Cambs
75 G1 Grafham Surrey
160 B2 Grafton Herefs
357 E2 Grafton N York
138 D4 Grafton Oxon
269 H6 Grafton Shrops
163 E2 Grafton Worcs
186 D2 Grafton Worcs
189 E3 Grafton Flyford Worcs
195 G5 Grafton Regis Nhants
218 C3 Grafton Underwood Nhants
98 D5 Grafty Green Kent
486 A3 Grahamston Falk
288 B3 Graianrhyd Denbgs
128 B4 Graig Carmth
305 H5 Graig Conwy
307 F5 Graig Denbgs
105 H2 Graig Rhondd
268 D2 Graig Wrexhm
129 F4 Graig-Fawr Swans
287 G4 Graig-fechan Denbgs
129 G4 Graig Felen Swans
105 F4 Graig Penllyn V Glam
103 G2 Graig Trewyddfa Swans
122 D4 Grain Medway
327 E3 Grains Bar Oldham
334 C5 Grainsby Lincs
393 E5 Grains o' th' Beck Dur
335 E5 Grainthorpe Lincs
335 E5 Grainthorpe Fen Lincs
331 G5 Graiselound N Linc
592 E6 Gramasdail W Isls
8 A4 Grampound Cnwll
7 H3 Grampound Road Cnwll
167 G4 Granborough Bucks
277 G2 Granby Notts
192 A1 Grandborough Warwks
35 I6 Grand Chemins Jersey
34 c2 Grandes Rocques Guern
140 B3 Grandpont Oxon
524 D5 Grandtully P & K
377 G1 Grange Cumb
48 C4 Grange Dorset
445 F2 Grange E Ayrs
309 H3 Grange Halton
36 C4 Grange IoW
339 E3 Grange Lancs
122 B6 Grange Medway
334 B3 Grange NE Lin
368 B1 Grange N York
513 G4 Grange P & K
310 C1 Grange Warrtn
308 B2 Grange Wirral
569 H5 Grange Crossroads Moray
49 E4 Grange Estate Dorset
395 E4 Grange Hill Dur
120 B1 Grange Hill Essex
294 A3 Grangemill Derbys
328 C1 Grange Moor Kirk
486 C3 Grangemouth Falk
500 D1 Grange of Lindores Fife
365 F4 Grange-over-Sands Cumb
486 D3 Grangepans Falk
144 D5 Grange Park Gt Lon
193 G4 Grange Park Nhants
324 B6 Grange Park St Hel
112 D3 Grange Park Swindn
106 C5 Grangetown Cardif
396 D5 Grangetown R & Cl
397 E5 Grangetown R & Cl
406 B4 Grangetown Sundld
405 F4 Grange Villa Dur
135 F2 Grange Village Gloucs
551 G7 Granish Highld
361 E3 Gransmoor E R Yk
172 D5 Gransmore Green Essex
151 E3 Granston Pembks
197 F3 Grantchester Cambs
278 C2 Grantham Lincs
370 A6 Grantley Hall N York
556 C1 Grantlodge Abers
487 H4 Granton C Edin
551 J4 Grantown-on-Spey Highld
186 C2 Grantsfield Herefs
474 A1 Grantshouse Border
310 C2 Grappenhall Warrtn
310 C2 Grappenhall Heys Warrtn
333 H4 Grasby Lincs
378 B3 Grasmere Cumb
327 E4 Grasscroft Oldham
309 E2 Grassendale Lpool
378 D5 Grassgarth Cumb
400 B6 Grassgarth Cumb
173 E2 Grass Green Essex
393 F5 Grassholme Dur
354 D2 Grassington N York
295 E1 Grassmoor Derbys
317 E6 Grassthorpe Notts
406 A4 Grasswell Sundld
71 F1 Grateley Hants
39 E5 Gratton Devon
273 F3 Gratwich Staffs
290 D1 Gravel Ches
100 D6 Gravel Castle Kent
196 C2 Graveley Cambs
170 B4 Graveley Herts
117 H1 Gravel Hill Bucks
234 B2 Gravelhill Shrops
326 D3 Gravel Hole Oldham
269 G2 Gravel Hole Oldham
213 G1 Gravelly Hill Birm
233 F5 Gravels Shrops
233 F4 Gravelsbank Shrops
606 F3 Graven Shet
99 G2 Graveney Kent
171 F4 Gravesend Herts
121 F5 Gravesend Kent
314 D3 Graves Park Sheff
597 K4 Gravir W Isls
332 C5 Grayingham Lincs
379 G5 Grayrigg Cumb
121 F4 Grays Thurr
74 D2 Grayshott Hants
388 A5 Grayson Green Cumb
75 E3 Grayswood Surrey
396 D4 Graythorp Hartpl
92 A1 Grazeley Wokham
92 A1 Grazeley Green W Berk
543 J4 Grealin Highld
329 G5 Greasbrough Rothm
308 B2 Greasby Wirral

295 F5 Greasley Notts
197 H5 Great Abington Cambs
218 D4 Great Addington Nhants
189 H3 Great Alne Warwks
323 F3 Great Altcar Lancs
380 B2 Great Asby Cumb
170 C4 Great Ashby Suffk
87 E2 Great Ashley Wilts
385 E2 Great Ayton N York
147 E3 Great Baddow Essex
172 D3 Great Bardfield Essex
195 G4 Great Barford Beds
237 F6 Great Barr Sandw
138 C2 Great Barrington Gloucs
309 G6 Great Barrow Ches
200 A1 Great Barton Suffk
372 D4 Great Barugh N York
429 F3 Great Bavington Nthumb
202 A5 Great Bealings Suffk
89 G2 Great Bedwyn Wilts
175 F5 Great Bentley Essex
121 G2 Great Berry Essex
193 H2 Great Billing Nhants
259 F5 Great Bircham Norfk
201 F4 Great Blakenham Suffk
390 D3 Great Blencow Cumb
271 E5 Great Bolas Wrekin
94 C4 Great Bookham Surrey
2 D3 Great Bosullow Cnwll
191 H5 Great Bourton Oxon
217 F2 Great Bowden Leics
99 G4 Great Bower Kent
198 D4 Great Bradley Suffk
147 H2 Great Braxted Essex
200 D4 Great Bricett Suffk
168 C3 Great Brickhill Bucks
237 E6 Great Bridge Sandw
272 C4 Great Bridgeford Staffs
193 E1 Great Brington Nhants
175 E4 Great Bromley Essex
388 C3 Great Broughton Cumb
385 F3 Great Broughton N York
97 G2 Great Buckland Kent
310 D4 Great Budworth Ches
383 H1 Great Burdon Darltn
121 G1 Great Burstead Essex
385 E3 Great Busby N York
172 B6 Great Canfield Essex
320 D2 Great Carlton Lincs
243 E3 Great Casterton Rutlnd
183 H2 Great Cellws Powys
87 F2 Great Chalfield Wilts
81 E1 Great Chart Kent
236 A2 Great Chatwell Staffs
291 H4 Great Chell C Stke
171 H1 Great Chesterford Essex
79 G1 Great Cheveney Kent
87 H4 Great Cheverell Wilts
395 F3 Great Chilton Dur
171 F2 Great Chishill Cambs
149 G1 Great Clacton Essex
147 F4 Great Claydons Essex
388 B4 Great Clifton Cumb
334 B2 Great Coates NE Lin
163 E1 Great Comberton Worcs
226 D2 Great Common Suffk
75 G4 Great Common W Susx
401 E4 Great Corby Cumb
174 A1 Great Cornard Suffk
361 G6 Great Cowden E R Yk
138 D6 Great Coxwell Oxon
370 A2 Great Crakehall N York
218 A4 Great Cransley Nhants
247 H4 Great Cressingham Norfk
323 F5 Great Crosby Sefton
389 G5 Great Crosthwaite Cumb
274 B2 Great Cubley Derbys
241 F2 Great Dalby Leics
194 B1 Great Doddington Nhants
134 C1 Great Doward Herefs
253 H5 Great Dunham Norfk
172 C5 Great Dunmow Essex
70 C2 Great Durnford Wilts
172 C4 Great Easton Essex
242 A6 Great Easton Leics
338 B1 Great Eccleston Lancs
372 D3 Great Edstone N York
248 D5 Great Ellingham Norfk
86 C5 Great Elm Somset
406 B5 Great Eppleton Sundld
197 E4 Great Eversden Cambs
383 G6 Great Fencote N York
112 C2 Greatfield Wilts
200 D3 Great Finborough Suffk
243 F2 Greatford Lincs
254 A5 Great Fransham Norfk
275 G3 Great Gaddesden Herts
142 C1 Greatgap Bucks
273 G1 Great Gate Staffs
219 G3 Great Gidding Cambs
359 F4 Great Givendale E R Yk
202 C2 Great Glemham Suffk
241 E5 Great Glen Leics
278 C2 Great Gonerby Lincs
196 C3 Great Gransden Cambs
196 C6 Great Green Cambs
200 B3 Great Green Suffk
225 E4 Great Green Suffk
225 E4 Great Green Suffk
373 E4 Great Habton N York
299 F6 Great Hale Lincs
171 H6 Great Hallingbury Essex
74 B3 Greatham Hants
396 C4 Greatham Hartpl
54 B1 Greatham W Susx
142 A4 Great Hampden Bucks
218 B5 Great Harrowden Nhants
340 A3 Great Harwood Lancs
140 D4 Great Haseley Oxon
361 F6 Great Hatfield E R Yk
256 B5 Great Hautbois Norfk
147 G5 Great Hayes Essex
273 F5 Great Haywood Staffs
215 E3 Great Heath Covtry
344 D5 Great Heck N York
173 H2 Great Henny Essex
87 G3 Great Hinton Wilts
142 D4 Great Hivings Bucks
248 C6 Great Hockham Norfk
140 D5 Great Holcombe Oxon
176 D6 Great Holland Essex
117 E6 Great Hollands Br For
167 H2 Great Holm M Keyn
174 C3 Great Horkesley Essex
171 F4 Great Hormead Herts
342 B3 Great Horton Brad
167 G3 Great Horwood Bucks
329 G3 Great Houghton Barns
193 G3 Great Houghton Nhants
326 D1 Great Howarth Rochdl
313 G4 Great Hucklow Derbys
80 B4 Great Job's Cross Kent
361 E3 Great Kelk E R Yk
360 C2 Great Kendale E R Yk
142 A3 Great Kimble Bucks
142 B5 Great Kingshill Bucks
383 G5 Great Langton N York
116 B6 Great Lea Common Wokham
147 E1 Great Leighs Essex
325 G3 Great Lever Bolton
333 G3 Great Limber Lincs
168 A1 Great Linford M Keyn

224 A5 Great Livermere Suffk
313 H5 Great Longstone Derbys
405 G5 Great Lumley Dur
234 B3 Great Lyth Shrops
121 G3 Great Malgraves Thurr
188 A5 Great Malvern Worcs
173 G3 Great Maplestead Essex
337 F2 Great Marton Bpool
337 F3 Great Marton Moss Lancs
253 G3 Great Massingham Norfk
140 D4 Great Milton Oxon
142 B4 Great Missenden Bucks
339 H2 Great Mitton Lancs
101 F5 Great Mongeham Kent
167 E5 Greatmoor Bucks
236 B5 Great Moor Staffs
312 B2 Great Moor Stockp
225 G1 Great Moulton Norfk
170 D5 Great Munden Herts
380 D2 Great Musgrave Cumb
96 D3 Greatness Kent
269 G6 Great Ness Shrops
173 E5 Great Notley Essex
133 G3 Great Oak Mons
176 C4 Great Oakley Essex
218 B2 Great Oakley Nhants
169 G4 Great Offley Herts
380 C1 Great Ormside Cumb
400 B4 Great Orton Cumb
357 F2 Great Ouseburn N York
217 F3 Great Oxendon Nhants
146 D3 Great Oxney Green Essex
247 G2 Great Palgrave Norfk
145 F3 Great Parndon Essex
98 A5 Great Pattenden Kent
196 B2 Great Paxton Cambs
337 G3 Great Plumpton Lancs
250 C2 Great Plumstead Norfk
278 C3 Great Ponton Lincs
343 H4 Great Preston Leeds
166 B2 Great Purston Nhants
220 C3 Great Raveley Cambs
164 B6 Great Rissington Gloucs
165 E3 Great Rollright Oxon
254 B2 Great Ryburgh Norfk
442 C2 Great Ryle Nthumb
234 B4 Great Ryton Shrops
172 D4 Great Saling Essex
391 E2 Great Salkeld Cumb
172 C2 Great Sampford Essex
310 B2 Great Sankey Warrtn
237 E3 Great Saredon Staffs
199 F2 Great Saxham Suffk
114 B4 Great Shefford W Berk
197 G4 Great Shelford Cambs
89 G5 Great Shoddesden Hants
384 A4 Great Smeaton N York
260 B5 Great Snoring Norfk
111 H3 Great Somerford Wilts
395 G5 Great Stainton Darltn
123 E1 Great Stambridge Essex
195 G1 Great Staughton Cambs
300 D2 Great Steeping Lincs
110 A3 Great Stoke S Glos
101 F4 Great Stonar Kent
81 G5 Greatstone-on-Sea Kent
241 E4 Great Stretton Leics
391 F5 Great Strickland Cumb
220 B5 Great Stukeley Cambs
319 G4 Great Sturton Lincs
309 E4 Great Sutton Ches
210 C3 Great Sutton Shrops
429 E4 Great Swinburne Nthumb
165 F4 Great Tew Oxon
174 A4 Great Tey Essex
371 F4 Great Thirkleby N York
36 D2 Great Thorness IoW
198 D4 Great Thurlow Suffk
39 H4 Great Torrington Devon
442 C4 Great Tosson Nthumb
147 H2 Great Totham Essex
319 G1 Great Tows Lincs
9 H2 Great Tree Cnwll
364 C5 Great Urswick Cumb
123 E2 Great Wakering Essex
200 A6 Great Waldingfield Suffk
260 B4 Great Walsingham Norfk
146 D2 Great Waltham Essex
121 E1 Great Warley Essex
163 E3 Great Washbourne Gloucs
25 H5 Great Weeke Devon
199 H3 Great Welnetham Suffk
175 E2 Great Wenham Suffk
429 G5 Great Whittington Nthumb
148 C1 Great Wigborough Essex
198 A3 Great Wilbraham Cambs
275 G3 Great Wilne Derbys
70 B2 Great Wishford Wilts
255 F3 Great Witchingham Norfk
136 D2 Great Witcombe Gloucs
187 H1 Great Witley Worcs
164 C3 Great Wolford Warwks
166 C1 Greatworth Nhants
198 D5 Great Wratting Suffk
170 B4 Great Wymondley Herts
237 E3 Great Wyrley Staffs
270 D6 Great Wytheford Shrops
251 G3 Great Yarmouth Norfk
173 F2 Great Yeldham Essex
340 D5 Greave Lancs
312 B1 Greave Stockp
320 D6 Grebby Lincs
322 e6 Greeba IoM
307 F6 Green Denbgs
386 C3 Green N York
125 G4 Green Pembks
233 E6 Green Powys
326 D3 Greenacres Oldham
310 C5 Greenbank Ches
365 E3 Green Bank Cumb
485 H4 Greenbank Falk
609 G4 Greenbank Shet
7 E5 Green Bottom Cnwll
135 F1 Green Bottom Gloucs
469 E2 Greenburn W Loth
367 E6 Green Close N York
160 C2 Green Crize Herefs
405 E4 Greencroft Dur
74 D2 Green Cross Surrey
312 A4 Greendale Ches
29 E2 Green Down Devon
85 G4 Greendown Somset
454 D4 Greendykes Nthumb
169 F2 Green End Beds
195 E5 Green End Beds
195 F2 Green End Beds
195 G4 Green End Beds
141 H5 Green End Bucks
168 C3 Green End Bucks
197 E3 Green End Cambs
220 B5 Green End Cambs
143 E3 Green End Herts
170 C3 Green End Herts
170 D3 Green End Herts
170 D5 Green End Herts
171 E4 Green End Herts
354 B5 Green End Lancs
468 A2 Greenend Oxon
386 D4 Green End N York
165 E5 Greenend Oxon
214 D2 Green End Warwks
570 D6 Greeness Abers
485 E5 Greenfaulds N Lans

169 F3 Greenfield Beds
467 K6 Greenfield C Glas
308 A4 Greenfield Flints
308 B4 Greenfield Flints
327 E4 Greenfield Oldham
116 B1 Greenfield Oxon
569 K6 Greenfold Moray
485 E6 Greenfoot N Lans
118 C3 Greenford Gt Lon
485 F5 Greengairs N Lans
376 D4 Greengarth Hall Cumb
42 D4 Green Gate Devon
254 D4 Greengate Norfk
326 D1 Greengate Rochdl
342 C2 Greengates Brad
388 C2 Greengill Cumb
142 A4 Green Hailey Bucks
337 G2 Greenhalgh Lancs
467 G3 Greenhall S Lans
29 H2 Greenham Somset
43 E3 Greenham Somset
90 D1 Greenham W Berk
357 F3 Green Hammerton N York
428 B2 Greenhaugh Nthumb
340 B4 Green Haworth Lancs
451 F4 Greenhead Border
400 C5 Green Head Cumb
468 C4 Greenhead N Lans
402 B1 Greenhead Nthumb
292 C5 Greenhead Staffs
237 E2 Green Heath Staffs
325 F4 Greenheys Salfd
424 C4 Greenhill D & G
406 B5 Greenhill Dur
485 G4 Greenhill Falk
118 D2 Greenhill Gt Lon
187 G5 Greenhill Herefs
98 B4 Green Hill Kent
100 C2 Greenhill Kent
344 A2 Green Hill Leeds
239 G2 Greenhill Leics
278 B2 Green Hill Sheff
314 C3 Greenhill Sheff
448 B3 Greenhill S Lans
112 C2 Green Hill Wilts
189 F5 Greenhill Worcs
212 B4 Greenhill Worcs
269 G2 Greenhill Bank Shrops
295 E5 Greenhillocks Derbys
467 F4 Greenhills S Lans
121 E4 Greenhithe Kent
446 A2 Greenholm E Ayrs
379 G3 Greenholme Cumb
451 H5 Greenhouse Border
601 G3 Greenhow N York
589 G3 Greenigoe Ork
314 D2 Greenland Sheff
589 G3 Greenland Mains Highld
116 C3 Greenlands Bucks
189 F1 Greenlands Worcs
19 G2 Green Lane Devon
187 E5 Green Lane Herefs
189 G2 Green Lane Worcs
215 E4 Green Lane Worcs
473 G5 Greenlaw Border
470 D2 Greenlaw Mains Mdloth
424 A4 Greenlea D & G
167 H1 Greenleys M Keyn
498 C3 Greenloaning P & K
289 G2 Greenlooms Ches
112 A3 Greenman's Lane Wilts
112 D2 Greenmeadow Swindn
133 E5 Greenmeadow Torfn
328 D5 Green Moor Barns
325 H2 Greenmount Bury
605 H5 Greenmow Shet
346 B4 Greenoak E R Yk
482 C4 Greenock Inver
482 C4 Greenock West Inver
364 D3 Greenodd Cumb
85 G4 Green Ore Somset
86 C4 Green Parlour Somset
379 E4 Green Quarter Cumb
469 E2 Greenrigg W Loth
399 E4 Greenrow Cumb
570 E6 Greens Abers
426 C2 Greens Border
212 B2 Greensforge Staffs
255 E4 Greensgate Norfk
469 G6 Greenshields S Lans
380 C4 Greenside Cumb
314 D4 Greenside Derbys
404 D2 Greenside Gatesd
328 B1 Greenside Kirk
328 B2 Green Side Kirk
343 E3 Green Side Leeds
326 C5 Greenside Tamesd
442 B1 Greensidehill Nthumb
193 E5 Greens Norton Nhants
568 D3 Greens of Coxton Moray
528 C4 Greens of Gardyne Angus
8 B2 Greenspot Cnwll
174 D4 Greenstead Suffk
173 G4 Greenstead Green Essex
146 A4 Greensted Essex
146 A4 Greensted Green Essex
146 C5 Green Street Essex
58 C4 Green Street E Susx
135 H4 Green Street Gloucs
136 C1 Green Street Gloucs
136 C2 Green Street Gloucs
144 A5 Green Street Herts
171 F5 Green Street Herts
162 C1 Green Street Worcs
162 C2 Green Street Worcs
188 C5 Green Street Worcs
76 B5 Green Street W Susx
141 H3 Green Street Green Gt Lon
121 E5 Green Street Green Kent
200 D5 Greenstreet Green Suffk
171 F6 Green Tye Herts
161 F3 Greenway Gloucs
152 B3 Greenway Pembks
43 G2 Greenway Somset
105 H5 Greenway V Glam
211 G5 Greenway Worcs
401 F3 Greenwell Dur
451 H3 Greenwells Border
120 A4 Greenwich Gt Lon
176 C1 Greenwich Suffk
69 F3 Greenwich Suffk
7 E5 Greenwith Common Cnwll
146 D5 Greenwoods Essex
602 B7 Greeny Ork
542 D8 Greep Highld
163 F3 Greet Gloucs
99 E3 Greet Kent
210 D3 Greete Shrops
320 B5 Greetham Lincs
242 C2 Greetham Rutlnd
342 A5 Greetland Calder
341 H5 Greetland Wall Nook Calder
332 C4 Greetwell N Linc
339 E4 Gregson Lane Lancs
232 A5 Gregynog Powys
591 D7 Grein W Isls
592 E2 Greinetobht W Isls
66 C2 Greinton Somset
605 J2 Gremista Shet
322 d8 Grenaby IoM
194 B2 Grendon Nhants

238 D5 Grendon Warwks
186 D3 Grendon Bishop Herefs
238 D5 Grendon Common Warwks
186 D3 Grendon Green Herefs
167 E5 Grendon Underwood Bucks
17 G4 Grenofen Devon
329 E6 Grenoside Sheff
595 K4 Greosabhagh W Isls
289 K4 Gresford Wrexhm
261 G4 Gresham Norfk
542 E6 Greshornish Highld
254 C4 Gressenhall Norfk
366 B6 Gressingham Lancs
382 C2 Greta Bridge Dur
400 B1 Greta Green Cumb
425 G6 Gretna D & G
425 G6 Gretna Green D & G
163 F3 Gretton Gloucs
242 C6 Gretton Nhants
234 C5 Gretton Shrops
163 F3 Gretton Fields Gloucs
370 A4 Grewelthorpe N York
86 A3 Greyfield BaNES
369 G5 Greygarth N York
331 G3 Grey Green N Linc
66 B3 Greylake Somset
66 C2 Greylake Fosse Somset
129 E3 Greynor Carmth
424 B2 Greyrigg D & G
116 B3 Greys Green Oxon
388 C4 Greysouthen Cumb
428 B2 Greystead Nthumb
390 C3 Greystoke Cumb
390 C4 Greystoke Gill Cumb
528 B6 Greystone Angus
365 H4 Greystone Cumb
366 D6 Greystonegill N York
314 C3 Greystones Sheff
189 G5 Greystones Warwks
160 D4 Greytree Herefs
92 B4 Greywell Hants
599 K6 Griais W Isls
599 J7 Grianan W Isls
29 G2 Gribb Dorset
345 H2 Gribthorpe E R Yk
504 E4 Gribun Ag & B
215 F2 Griff Warwks
213 F3 Griffins Hill Birm
133 E5 Griffithstown Torfn
275 G6 Griffydam Leics
98 D6 Grigg Kent
74 C3 Griggs Green Hants
6 C6 Grillis Cnwll
41 E3 Grilstone Devon
600 F2 Grimbister Ork
325 E2 Grimeford Village Lancs
213 G4 Grimes Hill Worcs
314 D2 Grimesthorpe Sheff
600 F2 Grimeston Ork
329 G3 Grimethorpe Barns
593 D7 Griminis W Isls
592 D2 Griminis W Isls
608 F6 Grimister Shet
188 B2 Grimley Worcs
601 H6 Grimness Ork
320 C2 Grimoldby Lincs
269 G4 Grimpo Shrops
339 E3 Grimsargh Lancs
165 H1 Grimsbury Oxon
334 C2 Grimsby NE Lin
192 D4 Grimscote Nhants
23 F1 Grimscott Cnwll
597 K2 Grimshader W Isls
339 H5 Grimshaw Bl w D
324 B2 Grimshaw Green Lancs
279 F5 Grimsthorpe Lincs
349 E2 Grimston E R Yk
277 E5 Grimston Leics
253 E3 Grimston Norfk
358 B4 Grimston York
31 E4 Grimstone Dorset
224 B6 Grimstone End Suffk
24 B4 Grinacombe Moor Devon
375 E5 Grindale E R Yk
605 J3 Grindiscol Shet
235 H4 Grindle Shrops
314 A4 Grindleford Derbys
353 E5 Grindleton Lancs
273 F4 Grindley Staffs
289 H6 Grindley Brook Shrops
313 G4 Grindlow Derbys
474 D6 Grindon Nthumb
396 A4 Grindon S on T
293 E4 Grindon Staffs
406 B3 Grindon Sundld
313 F2 Grindsbrook Booth Derbys
316 D1 Gringley on the Hill Notts
400 C3 Grinsdale Cumb
270 C5 Grinshill Shrops
201 E4 Grinstead Hill Suffk
382 B5 Grinton N York
597 K2 Griomsaigh W Isls
597 K2 Griomsidar W Isls
380 B6 Grisedale Cumb
516 F4 Grishipoll Ag & B
78 A5 Grisling Common E Susx
374 D3 Gristhorpe N York
248 B5 Griston Norfk
601 K4 Gritley Ork
112 B3 Grittenham Wilts
187 G5 Grittlesend Herefs
111 E3 Grittleton Wilts
363 E4 Grizebeck Cumb
378 B6 Grizedale Cumb
603 K7 Grobister Ork
606 C5 Grobsness Shet
240 B3 Groby Leics
287 E3 Groes Conwy
104 B2 Groes Neath
287 G1 Groes Efa Denbgs
105 H3 Groes-faen Rhondd
287 G1 Groes-fawr Denbgs
262 D3 Groesffordd Gwynd
158 A4 Groesffordd Powys
283 E4 Groeslon Gwynd
159 F5 Groes-lwyd Powys
232 D2 Groes-lwyd Powys
232 B3 Groespluan Powys
106 B2 Groes-wen Caerph
593 D10 Grogarry W Isls
462 D6 Grogport Ag & B
593 D10 Groigearraidh W Isls
202 D3 Gromford Suffk
307 F3 Gronant Flints
269 K4 Gronwen Shrops
78 C2 Groombridge E Susx
595 K4 Grosebay W Isls
159 G5 Grosmont Mons
386 D3 Grosmont N York
191 F3 Gross Green Warwks
174 C1 Groton Suffk
327 E4 Grotton Oldham
35 j7 Grouville Jersey
168 C5 Grove Bucks
32 B5 Grove Dorset
187 E6 Grove Herefs
100 D3 Grove Kent
316 D3 Grove Notts
114 C1 Grove Oxon
125 G4 Grove Pembks
238 B6 Grove End Birm
98 B3 Grove End Kent
164 D2 Grove End Warwks
98 B3 Grove Green Kent

347 G2 **Grovehill** E R Yk
57 F2 **Grove Hill** E Susx
143 F3 **Grovehill** Herts
100 D3 **Grove Hill** Kent
120 B5 **Grove Park** Gt Lon
101 E4 **Groves** Kent
129 E4 **Grovesend** Swans
344 B5 **Grove Town** Wakefd
237 F6 **Grove Vale** Sandw
121 E6 **Grubb Street** Kent
272 A4 **Grub Street** Staffs
564 E4 **Grudie** Highld
576 C3 **Gruids** Highld
544 F4 **Grula** Highld
505 G2 **Gruline** Ag & B
2 D4 **Grumbla** Cnwll
605 G4 **Grunasound** Shet
201 H4 **Grundisburgh** Suffk
353 F4 **Grunsagill** Lancs
606 C8 **Gruting** Shet
605 H8 **Grutness** Shet
282 D6 **Gryn Goch** Gwynd
521 G6 **Gualachulain** Highld
514 D6 **Guardbridge** Fife
341 G1 **Guard House** Brad
188 B5 **Guarlford** Worcs
524 F6 **Guay** P & K
173 E6 **Gubbion's Green** Essex
142 C2 **Gubblecote** Herts
59 E4 **Guestling Green** E Susx
59 E3 **Guestling Thorn** E Susx
255 E2 **Guestwick** Norfk
255 E2 **Guestwick Green** Norfk
339 C4 **Guide** Bl w D
326 D5 **Guide Bridge** Tamesd
431 E3 **Guide Post** Nthumb
196 C6 **Guilden Morden** Cambs
309 C6 **Guilden Sutton** Ches
93 H5 **Guildford** Surrey
93 G5 **Guildford Park** Surrey
469 F1 **Guildiehaugh** W Loth
512 D3 **Guildtown** P & K
515 E2 **Guildy** Angus
125 G3 **Guilford** Pembks
217 E5 **Guilsborough** Nhants
232 D2 **Guilsfield** Powys
315 E2 **Guilthwaite** Rothm
101 E4 **Guilton** Kent
60 D4 **Guineaford** Devon
385 G1 **Guisborough** R & Cl
342 C1 **Guiseley** Leeds
254 C2 **Guist** Norfk
603 G4 **Guith** Ork
163 G5 **Guiting Power** Gloucs
605 H3 **Gulberwick** Shet
489 F3 **Gullane** E Loth
162 C2 **Guller's End** Worcs
199 G3 **Gulling Green** Suffk
391 H4 **Gullom Holme** Cumb
3 E3 **Gulval** Cnwll
17 F4 **Gulworthy** Devon
126 B4 **Gumfreston** Pembks
217 E1 **Gumley** Leics
7 G2 **Gummow's Shop** Cnwll
345 G2 **Gunby** E R Yk
278 C5 **Gunby** Lincs
301 E1 **Gunby** Lincs
43 F3 **Gundenham** Somset
73 F3 **Gundleton** Hants
79 H3 **Gun Green** Kent
57 F2 **Gun Hill** E Susx
61 F5 **Gunn** Devon
381 G5 **Gunnerside** N York
429 E4 **Gunnerton** Nthumb
332 A2 **Gunness** N Linc
17 F4 **Gunnislake** Cnwll
605 J2 **Gunnista** Shet
236 C4 **Gunstone** Staffs
213 E1 **Guns Village** Sandw
75 F5 **Gunter's Bridge** W Susx
244 A4 **Gunthorpe** C Pete
331 G5 **Gunthorpe** N Linc
260 D5 **Gunthorpe** Norfk
296 C6 **Gunthorpe** Notts
242 B3 **Gunthorpe** Rutlnd
251 G5 **Gunton** Suffk
14 D3 **Gunvenna** Cnwll
36 D3 **Gunville** IoW
4 B4 **Gunwalloe** Cnwll
4 B4 **Gunwalloe Fishing Cove** Cnwll
63 F5 **Gupworthy** Somset
51 E5 **Gurnard** IoW
312 B5 **Gurnett** Ches
85 H5 **Gurney Slade** Somset
131 C3 **Gurnos** Myr Td
130 B3 **Gurnos** Neath
99 G3 **Gushmere** Kent
48 C2 **Gussage All Saints** Dorset
48 B2 **Gussage St Andrew** Dorset
48 B2 **Gussage St Michael** Dorset
83 F2 **Guston** Kent
609 G5 **Gutcher** Shet
280 A5 **Guthram Gowt** Lincs
528 C4 **Guthrie** Angus
14 D3 **Gutt Bridge** Cnwll
245 F4 **Guyhirn** Cambs
245 F4 **Guyhirn Gull** Cambs
190 D1 **Guy's Cliffe** Warwks
281 G4 **Guy's Head** Lincs
68 D5 **Guy's Marsh** Dorset
443 G4 **Guyzance** Nthumb
106 B3 **Gwaelod-y-garth** Cardif
307 F3 **Gwaenysgor** Flints
303 E5 **Gwalchmai** IoA
303 E5 **Gwalchmai Uchaf** IoA
3 F3 **Gwallon** Cnwll
154 C2 **Gwallt** Carmth
152 A5 **Gwastad** Pembks
228 D2 **Gwastadgoed** Gwynd
284 D3 **Gwastadnant** Gwynd
129 H2 **Gwaun-Cae-Gurwen** Neath
129 H2 **Gwaun-Leision** Neath
4 C3 **Gwavas** Cnwll
4 D6 **Gwavas** Cnwll
178 D4 **Gwbert** Cerdgn
4 B2 **Gwedna** Cnwll
4 C3 **Gweek** Cnwll
133 G4 **Gwehelog** Mons
304 B4 **Gweithdy** IoA
183 H6 **Gwenddwr** Powys
6 D5 **Gwennap** Cnwll
4 D5 **Gwenter** Cnwll
288 B2 **Gwernaffield-y-Waun** Flints
207 E1 **Gwernafon** Powys
207 G2 **Gwerneirin** Powys
208 C3 **Gwerneirin** Powys
133 H4 **Gwernesney** Mons
154 D3 **Gwernogle** Carmth
288 B4 **Gwernol** Denbgs
269 E4 **Gwern y brenin** Shrops
232 A4 **Gwernydd** Powys
288 B2 **Gwernymynydd** Flints
105 H4 **Gwern-y-Steeple** V Glam
288 D4 **Gwersyllt** Wrexhm
307 G3 **Gwespyr** Flints
7 F2 **Gwills** Cnwll
3 G2 **Gwinear** Cnwll
4 B1 **Gwinear Downs** Cnwll
3 G1 **Gwithian** Cnwll
154 C2 **Gwndwn** Carmth
303 E3 **Gwredog** IoA
132 C5 **Gwrhay** Caerph

287 F5 **Gwyddelwern** Denbgs
154 C2 **Gwyddgrug** Carmth
288 B4 **Gwynfryn** Wrexhm
183 H1 **Gwystre** Powys
286 B2 **Gwytherin** Conwy
288 D5 **Gyfelia** Wrexhm
305 G4 **Gyffin** Conwy
600 E4 **Gyre** Ork
287 H3 **Gyrn** Denbgs

H

609 G4 **Haa of Houlland** Shet
233 G4 **Habberley** Shrops
212 B4 **Habberley** Worcs
340 C3 **Habergham** Lancs
321 F6 **Habertoft** Lincs
74 C5 **Habin** W Susx
333 G2 **Habrough** NE Lin
20 B3 **Haccombe** Devon
279 E2 **Haceby** Lincs
202 B3 **Hacheston** Suffk
95 F1 **Hackbridge** Gt Lon
315 E3 **Hackenthorpe** Sheff
249 E4 **Hackford** Norfk
383 F6 **Hackforth** N York
290 C5 **Hack Green** Ches
602 D1 **Hackland** Ork
193 H3 **Hackleton** Nhants
101 F5 **Hacklinge** Kent
212 C4 **Hackman's Gate** Worcs
374 B1 **Hackness** N York
600 E6 **Hackness** Ork
84 B5 **Hackness** Somset
119 G3 **Hackney** Gt Lon
318 B3 **Hackthorn** Lincs
88 D5 **Hackthorpe** Cumb
391 E5 **Hackthorpe** Cumb
593 E8 **Haclait** W Isls
279 G4 **Haconby** Lincs
120 D3 **Hacton** Gt Lon
39 H3 **Haddacott** Devon
453 E2 **Hadden** Border
141 F3 **Haddenham** Bucks
221 G4 **Haddenham** Cambs
221 G4 **Haddenham End Field** Cambs
489 G5 **Haddington** E Loth
297 H2 **Haddington** Lincs
251 E5 **Haddiscoe** Norfk
219 G1 **Haddon** Cambs
328 A3 **Hade Edge** Kirk
238 B3 **Hademore** Staffs
213 E2 **Haden Cross** Sandw
327 F5 **Hadfield** Derbys
171 F6 **Hadham Cross** Herts
171 F5 **Hadham Ford** Herts
122 C2 **Hadleigh** Essex
200 D6 **Hadleigh** Suffk
144 B5 **Hadley** Gt Lon
188 C2 **Hadley** Worcs
235 F2 **Hadley** Wrekin
235 F2 **Hadley Castle** Wrekin
273 H5 **Hadley End** Staffs
144 C5 **Hadley Wood** Gt Lon
97 F5 **Hadlow** Kent
78 C5 **Hadlow Down** E Susx
97 F5 **Hadlow Stair** Kent
270 C5 **Hadnall** Shrops
67 H3 **Hadspen** Somset
198 B6 **Hadstock** Essex
443 H5 **Hadston** Nthumb
314 D5 **Hady** Derbys
188 D2 **Hadzor** Worcs
80 C1 **Haffenden Quarter** Kent
103 G3 **Hafod** Swans
286 B4 **Hafod-Dinbych** Conwy
178 C5 **Hafod Grove** Pembks
180 A4 **Hafodiwan** Cerdgn
307 E5 **Hafod-y-coedenn** Denbgs
132 D5 **Hafodyrynys** Caerph
325 F4 **Hag Fold** Wigan
326 D3 **Haggate** Oldham
340 D3 **Haggate** Oldham
426 C5 **Haggbeck** Cumb
606 E8 **Haggersta** Shet
119 G3 **Haggerston** Gt Lon
475 F6 **Haggerston** Nthumb
61 E2 **Hagginton Hill** Devon
606 D3 **Haggrister** Shet
485 F4 **Haggs** Falk
467 F1 **Haghill** C Glas
160 D1 **Hagley** Herefs
212 D3 **Hagley** Worcs
135 F3 **Hagloe** Gloucs
174 B2 **Hagmore Green** Suffk
300 B2 **Hagnaby** Lincs
321 E4 **Hagnaby** Lincs
300 B3 **Hagnaby Lock** Lincs
312 C2 **Hague Bar** Derbys
320 B6 **Hagworthingham** Lincs
328 D2 **Haigh** Barns
325 E3 **Haigh** Wigan
343 E5 **Haigh Moor** Leeds
339 E3 **Haighton Green** Lancs
339 E3 **Haighton Top** Lancs
376 C3 **Haile** Cumb
163 F3 **Hailes** Gloucs
145 E2 **Hailey** Herts
115 G2 **Hailey** Oxon
139 F2 **Hailey** Oxon
57 F3 **Hailsham** E Susx
137 G6 **Hailstone Hill** Wilts
195 H2 **Hail Weston** Cambs
233 F1 **Haimwood** Powys
120 C1 **Hainault** Gt Lon
101 G2 **Haine** Kent
255 H4 **Hainford** Norfk
68 C6 **Hains** Dorset
319 F3 **Hainton** Lincs
341 H2 **Hainworth Shaw** Brad
467 F4 **Hairmyres** S Lans
361 F2 **Haisthorpe** E R Yk
61 F4 **Hakeford** Devon
125 E3 **Hakin** Pembks
4 D2 **Halabezack** Cnwll
296 C4 **Halam** Notts
3 G3 **Halamanning** Cnwll
487 F2 **Halbeath** Fife
42 C5 **Halberton** Devon
44 A2 **Halcon** Somset
589 G4 **Halcro** Highld
144 B2 **Haldens** Herts
365 E4 **Hale** Cumb
309 G3 **Hale** Halton
70 D6 **Hale** Hants
101 E2 **Hale** Kent
98 B1 **Hale** Medway
68 C4 **Hale** Somset
92 D5 **Hale** Surrey
311 F2 **Hale** Traffd
309 G3 **Hale Bank** Halton
311 F2 **Hale Barns** Traffd
74 C5 **Halecommon** W Susx
84 D3 **Hale Coombe** N Som
120 A1 **Hale End** Gt Lon
57 F2 **Hale Green** E Susx
6 D5 **Hale Mills** Cnwll
351 E6 **Hale Nook** Lancs
250 D5 **Hales** Norfk
271 G3 **Hales** Staffs
187 E4 **Hales Bank** Herefs

235 G4 **Halesfield** Wrekin
280 D4 **Halesgate** Lincs
274 B1 **Hales Green** Derbys
250 D5 **Hales Green** Norfk
212 D3 **Halesowen** Dudley
211 H4 **Hales Park** Worcs
100 B4 **Hales Place** Kent
225 G2 **Hales Street** Norfk
97 G5 **Hale Street** Kent
160 D3 **Hales Wood** Herefs
226 D4 **Halesworth** Suffk
309 F2 **Halewood** Knows
26 D3 **Half Moon Village** Devon
210 A3 **Halford** Shrops
190 D5 **Halford** Warwks
366 A2 **Halfpenny** Cumb
127 F2 **Halfpenny Furze** Carmth
212 B1 **Halfpenny Green** Staffs
128 D4 **Halfway** Carmth
155 F3 **Halfway** Carmth
156 C3 **Halfway** Carmth
315 E3 **Halfway** Sheff
114 B6 **Halfway** W Berk
87 F5 **Halfway** Wilts
75 E5 **Halfway Bridge** W Susx
233 F2 **Halfway House** Shrops
335 H3 **Halfway Houses** Bury
123 E5 **Halfway Houses** Kent
83 E1 **Halfway Street** Kent
22 B5 **Halgabron** Cnwll
342 B5 **Halifax** Calder
542 C5 **Halistra** Highld
451 F1 **Halkburn** Border
466 B4 **Halket** E Ayrs
588 E5 **Halkirk** Highld
308 B5 **Halkyn** Flints
308 A5 **Halkyn Mountain** Flints
275 H2 **Hallam Fields** Derbys
57 E1 **Halland** E Susx
241 G5 **Hallaton** Leics
86 A3 **Hallatrow** BaNES
401 G3 **Hallbankgate** Cumb
328 A2 **Hall Bower** Kirk
314 B2 **Hall Broom** Sheff
338 B3 **Hall Cross** Lancs
377 G5 **Hall Dunnerdale** Cumb
109 F4 **Halen** S Glos
169 F2 **Hall End** Beds
195 E5 **Hall End** Beds
300 D4 **Hall End** Lincs
110 C2 **Hall End** S Glos
190 A1 **Hallend** Warwks
238 D4 **Hall End** Warwks
8 C2 **Hallew** Cnwll
294 D3 **Hallfield Gate** Derbys
213 E5 **Hall Flat** Worcs
406 A6 **Hallgarth** Dur
358 C4 **Hall Garth** N York
486 A4 **Hallglen** Falk
291 G3 **Hall Green** Ches
215 F3 **Hall Green** Covtry
173 F2 **Hall Green** Essex
324 C3 **Hall Green** Lancs
338 C4 **Hall Green** Lancs
213 H3 **Hall Green** Sandw
237 F6 **Hall Green** Sandw
329 E2 **Hall Green** Wakefd
270 B1 **Hall Green** Wrexhm
144 C2 **Hall Grove** Herts
451 F2 **Halliburton** Border
473 F5 **Halliburton** Border
542 D5 **Hallin** Highld
97 H2 **Halling** Medway
172 A6 **Hallingbury Street** Essex
320 A2 **Hallington** Lincs
429 F4 **Hallington** Nthumb
325 G2 **Hall i' th' Wood** Bolton
325 G2 **Halliwell** Bolton
571 L6 **Hallmoss** Abers
600 D3 **Hall of Clestrain** Ork
601 J3 **Hall of Tankerness** Ork
235 G5 **Hallon** Shrops
235 H5 **Hallonsford** Shrops
296 C4 **Halloughton** Notts
188 B3 **Hallow** Worcs
314 D4 **Hallowes** Derbys
188 B3 **Hallow Heath** Worcs
289 H1 **Hallowsgate** Ches
440 A2 **Hallrule** Border
490 C5 **Halls** E Loth
13 E5 **Hallsands** Devon
376 D4 **Hall Santon** Cumb
57 H3 **Hall's Close** E Susx
146 B4 **Hallsford Bridge** Essex
145 F3 **Halls Green** Essex
170 C4 **Hall's Green** Herts
96 D5 **Hall's Green** Kent
39 G3 **Hallspill** Devon
362 D4 **Hallthwaites** Cumb
377 E5 **Hall Waberthwaite** Cumb
161 F3 **Hallwood Green** Gloucs
22 D5 **Hallworthy** Cnwll
449 H2 **Hallyards** Border
449 G1 **Hallyne** Border
291 F5 **Halmer End** Staffs
187 F5 **Halmond's Frome** Herefs
135 F4 **Halmore** Gloucs
470 C3 **Halmyre Mains** Border
53 G3 **Halnaker** W Susx
323 G2 **Halsall** Lancs
166 C1 **Halse** Nhants
43 F2 **Halse** Somset
3 F2 **Halsetown** Cnwll
26 D4 **Halsfordwood** Devon
349 E4 **Halsham** E R Yk
60 D4 **Halsinger** Devon
173 G4 **Halstead** Essex
96 C2 **Halstead** Kent
241 F3 **Halstead** Leics
45 G6 **Halstock** Dorset
26 C4 **Halstow** Devon
64 B4 **Halsway** Somset
390 B2 **Haltcliff Bridge** Cumb
71 H5 **Halterworth** Hants
299 G2 **Haltham** Lincs
311 G3 **Haltoft End** Lincs
142 B2 **Halton** Bucks
310 A3 **Halton** Halton
351 H2 **Halton** Lancs
343 F3 **Halton** Leeds
429 H6 **Halton** Nthumb
269 F2 **Halton** Wrexhm
17 F5 **Halton Barton** Cnwll
309 H3 **Halton Brook** Halton
354 D4 **Halton East** N York
300 D2 **Halton Fenside** Lincs
368 A4 **Halton Gill** N York
351 H1 **Halton Green** Lancs
300 D1 **Halton Holegate** Lincs
402 A3 **Halton-Lea-Gate** Nthumb
343 F3 **Halton Moor** Leeds
429 G6 **Halton Shields** Nthumb
310 A2 **Halton View** Halton
353 G4 **Halton West** N York
402 C2 **Haltwhistle** Nthumb
251 E3 **Halvergate** Norfk
4 D2 **Halvosso** Cnwll
12 D2 **Halwell** Devon
24 B3 **Halwill** Devon
24 B3 **Halwill Junction** Devon
4 C2 **Halwin** Cnwll
11 E2 **Halwyn** Cnwll
28 D2 **Ham** Devon
135 F5 **Ham** Gloucs

163 E5 **Ham** Gloucs
118 D5 **Ham** Gt Lon
589 G2 **Ham** Highld
101 F5 **Ham** Kent
43 G3 **Ham** Somset
44 B3 **Ham** Somset
44 B5 **Ham** Somset
86 B5 **Ham** Somset
90 A2 **Ham** Wilts
606 D2 **Hamar** Shet
542 B7 **Hamaramore** Highld
542 B7 **Hamaraverin** Highld
603 H4 **Hamarhill** Ork
606 F5 **Hamars** Shet
116 C2 **Hambleden** Bucks
52 A2 **Hambledon** Hants
75 F2 **Hambledon** Surrey
51 E3 **Hamble-le-Rice** Hants
351 E6 **Hambleton** Lancs
344 C3 **Hambleton** N York
355 E4 **Hambleton** N York
337 G1 **Hambleton Moss Side** Lancs
66 B5 **Hambridge** Somset
110 A4 **Hambrook** S Glos
52 D3 **Hambrook** W Susx
68 D4 **Ham Common** Dorset
300 A1 **Hameringham** Lincs
219 G4 **Hamerton** Cambs
167 E6 **Ham Green** Bucks
72 B3 **Ham Green** Hants
187 G6 **Ham Green** Herefs
80 C4 **Ham Green** Kent
122 C6 **Ham Green** Kent
109 F4 **Ham Green** N Som
87 E2 **Ham Green** Wilts
189 F2 **Ham Green** Worcs
97 G2 **Ham Hill** Kent
240 D3 **Hamilton** C Leic
467 G3 **Hamilton** S Lans
607 H5 **Hamister** Shet
28 B3 **Hamlet** Devon
46 B3 **Hamlet** Dorset
74 D3 **Hammer** W Susx
74 D3 **Hammer Bottom** Hants
54 C3 **Hammerpot** W Susx
294 D4 **Hammersmith** Gt Lon
119 E4 **Hammersmith** Gt Lon
237 G3 **Hammerwich** Staffs
78 A2 **Hammerwood** E Susx
101 E4 **Hammill** Kent
144 D4 **Hammond Street** Herts
47 F2 **Hammoon** Dorset
605 G3 **Hamnavoe** Shet
606 B1 **Hamnavoe** Shet
607 G1 **Hamnavoe** Shet
607 G3 **Hamnavoe** Shet
186 C3 **Hamnish Clifford** Herefs
65 E4 **Hamp** Somset
57 G4 **Hampden Park** E Susx
163 F6 **Hampen** Gloucs
172 B3 **Hamperden End** Essex
209 H2 **Hamperley** Shrops
75 F5 **Hampers Green** W Susx
443 F3 **Hampeth** Nthumb
137 G1 **Hampnett** Gloucs
330 A2 **Hampole** Donc
48 C5 **Hampreston** Dorset
365 E3 **Hampsfield** Cumb
351 G4 **Hampson Green** Lancs
119 F2 **Hampstead** Gt Lon
119 E2 **Hampstead Garden Suburb** Gt Lon
115 E4 **Hampstead Norreys** W Berk
356 B3 **Hampsthwaite** N York
29 E3 **Hampton** Devon
118 C5 **Hampton** Gt Lon
100 C2 **Hampton** Kent
211 G2 **Hampton** Shrops
113 E1 **Hampton** Swindn
189 F6 **Hampton** Worcs
270 B3 **Hampton Bank** Shrops
233 F3 **Hampton Beech** Shrops
160 D2 **Hampton Bishop** Herefs
136 C5 **Hampton Fields** Gloucs
140 A1 **Hampton Gay** Oxon
289 H5 **Hampton Green** Ches
243 H6 **Hampton Hargate** C Pete
289 H5 **Hampton Heath** Ches
118 C5 **Hampton Hill** Gt Lon
214 C3 **Hampton in Arden** Solhll
211 G2 **Hampton Loade** Shrops
188 C1 **Hampton Lovett** Worcs
190 C3 **Hampton Lucy** Warwks
190 D1 **Hampton Magna** Warwks
190 D2 **Hampton on the Hill** Warwks
50 D1 **Hampton Park** C Sotn
160 C2 **Hampton Park** Herefs
140 A1 **Hampton Poyle** Oxon
97 F4 **Hamptons** Kent
118 D6 **Hampton Wick** Gt Lon
71 E6 **Hamptworth** Wilts
254 B3 **Hamrow** Norfk
56 C2 **Hamsey** E Susx
95 H3 **Hamsey Green** Surrey
135 H4 **Hamshill** Gloucs
273 H6 **Hamstall Ridware** Staffs
36 C2 **Hamstead** IoW
237 F6 **Hamstead** Sandw
90 C1 **Hamstead Marshall** W Berk
394 C3 **Hamsterley** Dur
404 D3 **Hamsterley** Dur
81 F3 **Hamstreet** Kent
67 F3 **Ham Street** Somset
34 A2 **Hamworthy** Poole
274 B4 **Hanbury** Staffs
189 E2 **Hanbury** Worcs
274 B4 **Hanbury Woodend** Staffs
279 E3 **Hanby** Lincs
198 C5 **Hanchett Village** Suffk
272 B1 **Hanchurch** Staffs
27 G3 **Hand and Pen** Devon
289 F7 **Handbridge** Ches
77 E4 **Handcross** W Susx
311 G3 **Handforth** Ches
290 A2 **Hand Green** Ches
209 G1 **Handless** Shrops
289 G3 **Handley** Ches
294 D3 **Handley** Derbys
237 G1 **Handley Green** Essex
237 G1 **Handsacre** Staffs
213 F1 **Handsworth** Birm
315 E2 **Handsworth** Sheff
213 F1 **Handsworth Wood** Birm
116 D1 **Handy Cross** Bucks
64 B5 **Handy Cross** Somset
272 C1 **Hanford** C Stke
47 F2 **Hanford** Dorset
49 F3 **Hangersley** Hants
96 C4 **Hanging Bank** Kent
239 E1 **Hanging Heaton** Kirk
217 F5 **Hanging Houghton** Nhants
70 A2 **Hanging Langford** Wilts
400 D3 **Hangingshaw** Border
424 B2 **Hangingshaw** D & G
55 G3 **Hangleton** Br & H
54 C4 **Hangleton** W Susx
331 E2 **Hangsman Hill** Donc
110 A5 **Hanham** S Glos
110 A5 **Hanham Green** S Glos
290 D5 **Hankelow** Ches
111 H1 **Hankerton** Wilts
57 G3 **Hankham** E Susx

292 A5 **Hanley** C Stke
188 B6 **Hanley Castle** Worcs
187 F1 **Hanley Child** Worcs
188 B6 **Hanley Swan** Worcs
187 F1 **Hanley William** Worcs
354 B2 **Hanlith** N York
270 B2 **Hanmer** Wrexhm
40 B2 **Hannaford** Devon
9 G3 **Hannafore** Cnwll
321 F4 **Hannah** Lincs
199 H4 **Hanningfields Green** Suffk
91 E3 **Hannington** Hants
217 H5 **Hannington** Nhants
138 B6 **Hannington** Swindn
138 B6 **Hannington Wick** Swindn
169 F3 **Hanscombe End** Beds
13 E3 **Hansel** S Ayrs
445 E3 **Hansel Village** S Ayrs
293 E6 **Hansley Cross** Staffs
193 H5 **Hanslope** M Keyn
118 D4 **Hanwell** Gt Lon
191 E6 **Hanwell** Oxon
234 A3 **Hanwood** Shrops
234 A3 **Hanwood Bank** Shrops
93 E1 **Hanworth** Br For
118 C5 **Hanworth** Gt Lon
261 G4 **Hanworth** Norfk
447 H3 **Happendon** S Lans
256 D4 **Happisburgh** Norfk
256 D4 **Happisburgh Common** Norfk
309 G5 **Hapsford** Ches
86 D5 **Hapsford** Somset
340 B3 **Hapton** Lancs
249 G6 **Hapton** Norfk
19 G6 **Harberton** Devon
12 D1 **Harbertonford** Devon
100 B4 **Harbledown** Kent
213 F3 **Harborne** Birm
216 A4 **Harborough Magna** Warwks
216 A4 **Harborough Parva** Warwks
442 A4 **Harbottle** Nthumb
56 C4 **Harbour Heights** E Susx
98 B3 **Harbourland** Kent
19 F5 **Harbourneford** Devon
189 E1 **Harbours Hill** Worcs
151 E2 **Harbour Village** Pembks
49 E3 **Harbridge** Hants
49 E3 **Harbridge Green** Hants
469 G2 **Harburn** W Loth
191 F3 **Harbury** Warwks
277 F3 **Harby** Leics
317 G5 **Harby** Notts
28 C4 **Harcombe** Devon
28 C4 **Harcombe** Devon
29 F3 **Harcombe Bottom** Devon
7 F6 **Harcourt** Cnwll
140 A4 **Harcourt Hill** Oxon
136 A2 **Hardeicke** Gloucs
328 A4 **Harden** Barns
342 A2 **Harden** Brad
237 F4 **Harden** Wsall
379 G2 **Hardendale** Cumb
311 G4 **Harden Park** Ches
556 D4 **Hardgate** Abers
413 F1 **Hardgate** D & G
356 B2 **Hardgate** N York
483 H5 **Hardgate** W Duns
313 H4 **Hardgatewall** Derbys
87 H4 **Hardham** W Susx
337 G2 **Hardhorn** Lancs
248 D4 **Hardingham** Norfk
293 E2 **Hardings Booth** Staffs
193 G3 **Hardingstone** Nhants
291 G4 **Hardings Wood** Staffs
86 C4 **Hardington** Somset
45 G5 **Hardington Mandeville** Somset
45 G5 **Hardington Marsh** Somset
45 G5 **Hardington Moor** Somset
38 B3 **Hardisworthy** Devon
50 D4 **Hardley** Hants
250 D4 **Hardley Street** Norfk
194 C5 **Hardmead** M Keyn
367 H1 **Hardraw** N York
294 C3 **Hardstoft** Derbys
295 E2 **Hardstoft Common** Derbys
51 G4 **Hardway** Hants
68 B3 **Hardway** Somset
167 H6 **Hardwick** Bucks
220 A6 **Hardwick** Cambs
218 A6 **Hardwick** Nhants
225 H2 **Hardwick** Norfk
139 F3 **Hardwick** Oxon
165 G1 **Hardwick** Oxon
166 C4 **Hardwick** Oxon
315 F2 **Hardwick** Rothm
209 G1 **Hardwick** Shrops
396 B5 **Hardwick** S on T
237 G5 **Hardwick** Wsall
136 A3 **Hardwicke** Gloucs
162 A6 **Hardwicke** Gloucs
185 E6 **Hardwicke** Herefs
162 B3 **Hardwick Green** Worcs
316 A3 **Hardwick Village** Notts
174 B3 **Hardy's Green** Essex
44 B4 **Hare** Somset
352 A3 **Hare Appletree** Lancs
300 B1 **Hareby** Lincs
342 A2 **Harecroft** Brad
352 C4 **Hareden** Lancs
314 C5 **Hare Edge** Derbys
51 E2 **Harefield** C Sotn
118 B1 **Harefield** Gt Lon
118 B1 **Harefield Grove** Gt Lon
292 C3 **Haregate** Staffs
175 E5 **Hare Green** Essex
116 D4 **Hare Hatch** Wokham
274 B2 **Harehill** Derbys
343 F3 **Harehills** Leeds
470 B3 **Harehope** Border
454 D5 **Harehope** Nthumb
405 H4 **Harelaw** Dur
468 B4 **Hareleeshill** S Lans
80 B2 **Hareplain** Kent
401 H6 **Haresceugh** Cumb
136 B3 **Harescombe** Gloucs
136 B3 **Haresfield** Gloucs
138 C6 **Haresfield** Swindn
324 C5 **Haresfinch** St Hel
468 C2 **Hareshaw** N Lans
484 D5 **Hareshaw** N Lans
72 C3 **Harestock** Hants
145 F3 **Hare Street** Essex
171 E4 **Hare Street** Herts
356 C5 **Harewood** Leeds
160 C4 **Harewood End** Herefs
18 D6 **Harford** Devon
61 E5 **Harford** Devon
225 F1 **Hargate** Norfk
327 F6 **Hargate Hill** Derbys
219 E5 **Hargrave** Ches
289 G2 **Hargrave** Nhants
199 F3 **Hargrave** Suffk
400 C2 **Harker** Cumb
388 C3 **Harker Marsh** Cumb
608 E7 **Harkland** Shet
145 F3 **Harknett's Gate** Essex
176 C3 **Harkstead** Suffk
238 C2 **Harlaston** Staffs
278 B3 **Harlaxton** Lincs

264 D3 Harlech Gwynd
277 E2 Harlequin Notts
234 C1 Harlescott Shrops
119 E3 Harlesden Gt Lon
315 F4 Harlesthorpe Derbys
12 D4 Harleston Devon
226 A3 Harleston Norfk
200 D2 Harleston Suffk
193 F2 Harlestone Nhants
340 D2 Harle Syke Lancs
329 F5 Harley Rothm
234 D4 Harley Shrops
58 C5 Harley Shute E Susx
136 B5 Harleywood Gloucs
224 C2 Harling Road Norfk
169 E3 Harlington Beds
330 A4 Harlington Donc
118 B4 Harlington Gt Lon
544 D1 Harlosh Highld
145 F3 Harlow Essex
145 G2 Harlowbury Essex
356 B4 Harlow Carr N York
405 G2 Harlow Green Gatesd
430 A6 Harlow Hill Nthumb
356 B4 Harlow Hill N York
345 G2 Harlthorpe E R Yk
197 E4 Harlton Cambs
14 B4 Harlyn Cnwll
98 D2 Harman's Corner Kent
33 H3 Harman's Cross Dorset
117 E6 Harmans Water Br For
369 F2 Harmby N York
144 C1 Harmer Green Herts
270 B5 Harmer Hill Shrops
118 B4 Harmondsworth Gt Lon
298 B2 Harmston Lincs
234 D4 Harnage Shrops
430 A3 Harnham Nthumb
70 C4 Harnham Wilts
137 G4 Harnhill Gloucs
120 D1 Harold Hill Gt Lon
121 E1 Harold Park Gt Lon
125 E1 Haroldston West Pembks
609 J2 Haroldswick Shet
120 D1 Harold Wood Gt Lon
372 B3 Harome N York
143 G2 Harpenden Herts
143 G2 Harpenden Common Herts
325 G3 Harper Green Bolton
405 E4 Harperley Dur
292 B3 Harper's Gate Staffs
254 B3 Harper's Green Norfk
28 A4 Harpford Devon
360 D2 Harpham E R Yk
253 F2 Harpley Norfk
187 F2 Harpley Worcs
193 E2 Harpole Nhants
588 E5 Harpsdale Highld
116 C3 Harpsden Oxon
116 B3 Harpsden Bottom Oxon
318 A2 Harpswell Lincs
184 D3 Harpton Powys
326 C4 Harpurhey Manch
313 E5 Harpur Hill Derbys
400 D4 Harraby Cumb
40 B2 Harracott Devon
546 B5 Harrapool Highld
388 A6 Harras Cumb
405 G4 Harraton Sundld
512 A4 Harrietfield P & K
98 D4 Harrietsham Kent
119 G2 Harringay Gt Lon
388 A4 Harrington Cumb
320 C5 Harrington Lincs
217 G4 Harrington Nhants
242 C5 Harringworth Nhants
530 B3 Harris Highld
291 H3 Harriseahead Staffs
389 E1 Harriston Cumb
356 B3 Harrogate N York
194 C3 Harrold Beds
327 F3 Harrop Dale Oldham
118 C2 Harrow Gt Lon
17 E4 Harrowbarrow Cnwll
18 B4 Harrowbeer Devon
278 C3 Harrowby Lincs
195 F5 Harrowden Beds
383 G1 Harrowgate Hill Darltn
395 F6 Harrowgate Village Darltn
199 H4 Harrow Green Suffk
135 F1 Harrow Hill Gloucs
118 D2 Harrow on the Hill Gt Lon
118 C1 Harrow Weald Gt Lon
110 A4 Harry Stoke S Glos
197 F4 Harston Cambs
278 A3 Harston Leics
346 B1 Harswell E R Yk
396 C3 Hart Hartpl
365 E1 Hartbarrow Cumb
430 A2 Hartburn Nthumb
396 B6 Hartburn S on T
109 G6 Hartcliffe Bristl
325 E4 Hart Common Bolton
199 G4 Hartest Suffk
199 G4 Hartest Hill Suffk
78 B2 Hartfield E Susx
220 B5 Hartford Cambs
310 C5 Hartford Ches
42 C2 Hartford Somset
310 C5 Hartfordbeach Ches
92 C3 Hartfordbridge Hants
172 D6 Hartford End Essex
383 E3 Harthill N York
68 D6 Hartgrove Dorset
144 D2 Hartham Herts
289 H3 Harthill Ches
169 G5 Hart Hill Luton
469 E2 Harthill N Lans
315 F3 Harthill Rothm
293 F2 Hartington Derbys
38 C3 Hartland Devon
38 B3 Hartland Quay Devon
212 D4 Hartle Worcs
235 G5 Hartlebury Shrops
212 B5 Hartlebury Worcs
212 B5 Hartlebury Common Worcs
396 D3 Hartlepool Hartpl
380 D3 Hartley Cumb
79 H3 Hartley Kent
121 F6 Hartley Kent
431 F4 Hartley Nthumb
121 E6 Hartley Green Kent
273 E4 Hartley Green Staffs
74 A2 Hartley Mauditt Hants
92 A3 Hartley Wespall Hants
92 C3 Hartley Wintney Hants
354 D2 Hartlington N York
98 C2 Hartlip Kent
68 C5 Hartmoor Dorset
577 G8 Hartmount Highld
386 C6 Hartoft End N York
358 B2 Harton N York
210 B2 Harton S Tyne
406 B2 Harton S Tyne
162 A5 Hartpury Gloucs
212 A3 Hartsgreen Shrops
199 H3 Hart's Green Suffk
342 C5 Hartshead Kirk
327 E4 Hartshead Green Tamesd
342 C4 Hartshead Moor Top Calder
327 E4 Hartshead Pike Tamesd
291 H5 Hartshill C Stke

212 D2 Hart's Hill Dudley
239 E6 Hartshill Warwks
239 E6 Hartshill Green Warwks
275 E5 Hartshorne Derbys
378 D2 Hartsop Cumb
396 C2 Hart Station Hartpl
43 E2 Hartswell Somset
193 G4 Hartwell Nhants
272 D2 Hartwell Staffs
355 H2 Hartwith N York
339 E6 Hartwood Lancs
468 C3 Hartwood N Lans
451 F4 Hartwoodburn Border
451 E5 Hartwoodmyres Border
97 F2 Harvel Kent
329 F2 Harvest Hill Covtry
214 D3 Harvil Hill Covtry
237 E6 Harvils Hawthorn Sandw
189 G5 Harvington Worcs
212 C5 Harvington Worcs
316 C1 Harwell Notts
114 D2 Harwell Oxon
177 E3 Harwich Essex
325 G2 Harwood Bolton
392 D3 Harwood Dur
429 G1 Harwood Nthumb
387 G5 Harwood Dale N York
325 G2 Harwood Lee Bolton
439 E3 Harwood on Teviot Border
316 B1 Harworth Notts
213 E3 Hasbury Dudley
75 F2 Hascombe Surrey
217 F4 Haselbech Nhants
45 F5 Haselbury Plucknett Somset
214 C6 Haseley Warwks
214 C6 Haseley Green Warwks
214 C5 Haseley Knob Warwks
189 H3 Haselor Warwks
162 B4 Hasfield Gloucs
124 D3 Hasguard Pembks
323 F3 Haskayne Lancs
202 A4 Hasketon Suffk
314 D6 Hasland Derbys
314 D6 Hasland Green Derbys
75 E3 Haslemere Surrey
75 F5 Haslingbourne W Susx
340 B5 Haslingden Lancs
340 B5 Haslingden Grane Lancs
197 F4 Haslingfield Cambs
291 E3 Haslington Ches
440 C2 Hass Border
291 F3 Hassall Ches
291 F3 Hassall Green Ches
82 A1 Hassell Street Kent
451 G5 Hassendean Border
559 F1 Hassiewells Abers
250 D3 Hassingham Norfk
55 G1 Hassocks W Susx
313 H5 Hassop Derbys
321 E6 Hasthorpe Lincs
589 G4 Hastigrow Highld
406 B4 Hasting Hill Sundld
82 A2 Hastingleigh Kent
58 D5 Hastings E Susx
44 C4 Hastings Somset
145 G3 Hastingwood Essex
142 C3 Hastoe Herts
270 C5 Haston Shrops
406 B6 Haswell Dur
396 A1 Haswell Moor Dur
395 H1 Haswell Plough Dur
449 G2 Haswellsykes Border
195 G5 Hatch Beds
12 C3 Hatch Devon
91 H4 Hatch Hants
44 C3 Hatch Beauchamp Somset
51 E2 Hatch Bottom Hants
195 F2 Hatch End Beds
118 C1 Hatch End Gt Lon
50 C4 Hatchet Gate Hants
70 D6 Hatchet Green Hants
74 D4 Hatch Farm Hill W Susx
44 C4 Hatch Green Somset
143 G2 Hatching Green Herts
310 B5 Hatchmere Ches
91 G5 Hatch Warren Hants
334 B4 Hatcliffe NE Lin
237 F6 Hateley Heath Sandw
331 E3 Hatfield Donc
186 D3 Hatfield Herefs
144 B3 Hatfield Herts
188 C4 Hatfield Worcs
146 A1 Hatfield Broad Oak Essex
331 F3 Hatfield Chase Donc
144 B2 Hatfield Garden Village Herts
146 A1 Hatfield Heath Essex
144 B2 Hatfield Hyde Herts
147 F2 Hatfield Peverel Essex
331 E3 Hatfield Woodhouse Donc
139 E6 Hatford Oxon
90 A4 Hatherden Hants
24 D2 Hatherleigh Devon
162 D5 Hatherley Gloucs
276 A5 Hathern Leics
138 B3 Hatherop Gloucs
314 A3 Hathersage Derbys
314 A3 Hathersage Booths Derbys
326 D4 Hathershaw Oldham
290 D5 Hatherton Ches
236 D2 Hatherton Staffs
196 C4 Hatley St George Cambs
601 G2 Hatson Ork
10 C1 Hatt Cnwll
327 E6 Hattersley Tamesd
71 G4 Hatt Hill Hants
73 F2 Hattingley Hants
561 G2 Hatton Abers
274 C3 Hatton Derbys
319 F4 Hatton Lincs
210 B1 Hatton Shrops
310 B3 Hatton Warrtn
190 C1 Hatton Warwks
570 D6 Hatton Castle Abers
560 B5 Hattoncrook Abers
235 H4 Hatton Grange Shrops
289 G2 Hatton Heath Ches
93 F2 Hatton Hill Surrey
470 D5 Hattonknowe Border
557 H1 Hatton of Fintray Abers
527 E6 Hatton of Ogilvie Angus
218 B6 Hatton Park Nhants
445 G4 Haugh E Ayrs
320 D4 Haugh Lincs
326 D2 Haugh Rochdl
320 B3 Haugham Lincs
450 C2 Haugh-head Border
454 C4 Haugh Head Nthumb
200 D2 Haughley Suffk
200 D2 Haughley Green Suffk
200 D2 Haughley New Street Suffk
569 G8 Haugh of Glass Moray
413 F1 Haugh of Urr D & G
290 B3 Haughton Ches
316 C5 Haughton Notts
269 F6 Haughton Powys
234 D1 Haughton Shrops
235 F5 Haughton Shrops
235 G3 Haughton Shrops
269 G4 Haughton Shrops
272 C5 Haughton Staffs
326 D6 Haughton Green Tamesd

383 H1 Haughton Le Skerne Darltn
91 F2 Haughurst Hill Hants
170 D5 Haultwick Herts
517 J6 Haunn Ag & B
590 F5 Haunn W Isls
238 C2 Haunton Staffs
35 H5 Hautes Croix Jersey
197 H4 Hauxton Cambs
291 H2 Havannah Ches
52 C3 Havant Hants
185 H4 Haven Herefs
186 D5 Haven Herefs
299 G4 Haven Bank Lincs
37 F3 Havenstreet IoW
329 F2 Havercroft Wakefd
125 F2 Haverfordwest Pembks
198 D5 Haverhill Suffk
362 D6 Haverigg Cumb
145 H6 Havering-atte-Bower Gt Lon
255 G4 Haveringland Norfk
193 H6 Haversham M Keyn
364 D3 Haverthwaite Cumb
396 C5 Haverton Hill S on T
97 H5 Haviker Street Kent
67 E2 Havyatt Somset
85 E2 Havyatt Green N Som
288 D1 Hawarden Flints
188 D5 Hawbridge Worcs
173 F5 Hawbush Green Essex
364 B5 Hawcoat Cumb
161 H3 Hawcross Gloucs
265 F6 Hawddamor Gwynd
179 G4 Hawen Cerdgn
367 H2 Hawes N York
250 A5 Hawes' Green Norfk
337 F3 Hawes Side Bpool
188 B2 Hawford Worcs
271 E4 Hawgreen Shrops
439 G2 Hawick Border
29 F2 Hawkchurch Devon
199 F4 Hawkedon Suffk
78 D2 Hawkenbury Kent
98 B6 Hawkenbury Kent
87 F4 Hawkeridge Wilts
27 H5 Hawkerland Devon
186 C5 Hawkersland Cross Herefs
110 D2 Hawkesbury S Glos
215 F3 Hawkesbury Warwks
110 D2 Hawkesbury Upton S Glos
214 D3 Hawkes End Covtry
213 F4 Hawkesley Birm
312 C2 Hawk Green Stockp
388 B4 Hawk Hill Cumb
443 G2 Hawkhill Nthumb
427 H2 Hawkhope Nthumb
79 G3 Hawkhurst Kent
78 C6 Hawkhurst Common E Susx
82 D3 Hawkinge Kent
172 D3 Hawkin's Hill Essex
74 A4 Hawkley Hants
324 D4 Hawkley Wigan
62 D5 Hawkridge Somset
400 C5 Hawksdale Cumb
237 E2 Hawks Green Staffs
325 H1 Hawkshaw Bury
378 B5 Hawkshead Cumb
378 B5 Hawkshead Hill Cumb
117 F2 Hawks Hill Bucks
94 D3 Hawk's Hill Surrey
447 G2 Hawksland S Lans
172 C3 Hawkspur Green Essex
341 E4 Hawks Stones Calder
368 C5 Hawkswick N York
342 C1 Hawksworth Leeds
297 E6 Hawksworth Notts
122 D1 Hawkwell Essex
92 D3 Hawley Hants
120 D5 Hawley Kent
28 D2 Hawley Bottom Devon
93 E3 Hawley Lane Hants
163 G5 Hawling Gloucs
371 G2 Hawnby N York
213 E3 Hawne Dudley
341 G2 Haworth Brad
378 B5 Haws Bank Cumb
199 H3 Hawstead Suffk
199 H3 Hawstead Green Suffk
406 C5 Hawthorn Dur
73 G3 Hawthorn Hants
106 A2 Hawthorn Rhondd
100 D2 Hawthorn Corner Kent
117 E5 Hawthorn Hill Br For
299 G3 Hawthorn Hill Lincs
279 E4 Hawthorpe Lincs
297 E4 Hawton Notts
358 A3 Haxby York
331 G5 Haxey N Linc
331 G4 Haxey Carr N Linc
96 B5 Haxted Surrey
89 E5 Haxton Wilts
14 D4 Hay Cnwll
211 E5 Haybridge Shrops
85 F5 Haybridge Somset
235 F2 Haybridge Wrekin
162 C5 Haydock St Hel
86 B4 Haydon BaNES
46 C1 Haydon Dorset
44 B3 Haydon Somset
85 G5 Haydon Somset
112 D2 Haydon Swindn
403 E2 Haydon Bridge Nthumb
112 D2 Haydon Wick Swindn
16 D4 Haye Cnwll
96 A1 Hayes Gt Lon
118 B3 Hayes Gt Lon
293 E2 Hayes Staffs
118 B3 Hayes End Gt Lon
112 D1 Hayes Knoll Wilts
312 D2 Hayfield Derbys
330 D5 Hay Field Donc
501 E6 Hayfield Fife
330 D5 Hayfield Green Donc
235 E2 Haygate Wrekin
44 A3 Haygrass Somset
146 B4 Hay Green Essex
170 D2 Hay Green Herts
252 A4 Hay Green Norfk
433 E4 Hayhill E Ayrs
515 E1 Hayhillock Angus
37 F2 Haylands IoW
3 G2 Hayle Cnwll
212 D3 Hayley Green Dudley
213 H3 Hay Mills Birm
44 C2 Haymoor End Somset
290 D4 Haymoor Green Ches
26 D1 Hayne Devon
169 G1 Haynes Beds
169 F1 Haynes Church End Beds
169 F1 Haynes West End Beds
158 D1 Hay-on-Wye Powys
151 E4 Hayscastle Pembks
151 F5 Hayscastle Cross Pembks
151 F5 Haysford Pembks
515 G1 Hayshead Angus
450 B2 Haystoun Border
171 E4 Hay Street Herts
48 C3 Haythorne Devon
557 D3 Hayton C Aber
388 D1 Hayton Cumb
401 F3 Hayton Cumb

359 F5 Hayton E R Yk
316 D3 Hayton Notts
210 C3 Hayton's Bent Shrops
19 G2 Haytor Vale Devon
39 E5 Haytown Devon
77 F5 Haywards Heath W Susx
330 C2 Haywood Donc
469 F4 Haywood S Lans
296 B3 Haywood Oaks Notts
58 A4 Hazelbank S Lans
468 C6 Hazelbank S Lans
125 F4 Hazelbeach Pembks
46 D3 Hazelbury Bryan Dorset
147 G4 Hazeleigh Essex
171 G5 Hazel End Essex
92 B3 Hazeley Hants
92 B3 Hazeley Bottom Hants
92 C3 Hazeley Heath Hants
92 B3 Hazeley Lea Hants
312 B2 Hazel Grove Stockp
325 H1 Hazelhurst Bury
92 B3 Hazelhurst Hants
325 H4 Hazelhurst Salfd
327 E4 Hazelhurst Tamesd
454 D3 Hazelrigg Nthumb
365 G4 Hazelslack Cumb
237 F2 Hazelslade Staffs
79 F2 Hazel Street Kent
98 D3 Hazel Street Kent
198 C5 Hazel Stub Suffk
513 H5 Hazelton Walls Fife
294 C5 Hazelwood Derbys
12 C2 Hazelwood Devon
96 B2 Hazelwood Gt Lon
328 B4 Hazlehead Barns
142 B5 Hazlemere Bucks
234 B6 Hazler Shrops
430 D5 Hazlerigg N Tyne
292 C5 Hazles Staffs
292 D5 Hazlescross Staffs
163 G6 Hazleton Gloucs
355 E4 Hazlewood N York
443 F4 Hazon Nthumb
258 D4 Heacham Norfk
72 C3 Headbourne Worthy Hants
185 F3 Headbrook Herefs
98 C6 Headcorn Kent
343 E2 Headingley Leeds
140 B3 Headington Oxon
140 B3 Headington Hill Oxon
394 D6 Headlam Dur
365 E4 Headless Cross Cumb
189 F1 Headless Cross Worcs
74 C2 Headley Hants
91 E2 Headley Hants
95 E4 Headley Surrey
74 C2 Headley Down Hants
213 G4 Headley Heath Worcs
109 G6 Headley Park Bristl
485 G3 Head of Muir Falk
23 H2 Headon Devon
316 D4 Headon Notts
467 H5 Heads S Lans
451 F5 Headshaw Border
401 E3 Heads Nook Cumb
118 C2 Headstone Gt Lon
487 E2 Headwell Fife
294 D4 Heage Derbys
382 B5 Healaugh N York
311 H2 Heald Green Stockp
326 C3 Healds Green Oldham
61 F2 Heale Devon
44 A4 Heale Somset
66 B4 Heale Somset
86 B6 Heale Somset
404 B3 Healey Nthumb
369 G3 Healey N York
326 C1 Healey Rochdl
343 E6 Healey Wakefd
443 E4 Healey Cote Nthumb
404 C5 Healeyfield Dur
404 B3 Healey Hall Nthumb
334 B2 Healing NE Lin
3 E3 Heamoor Cnwll
378 D5 Heaning Cumb
516 C7 Heanish Ag & B
295 E5 Heanor Derbys
295 E5 Heanor Gate Derbys
60 D4 Heanton Punchardon Devon
326 B2 Heap Bridge Rochdl
317 G2 Heapham Lincs
74 C2 Hearn Hants
98 D2 Hearnden Green Kent
449 F4 Hearthstane Border
294 C3 Hearthstone Derbys
98 D2 Hearts Delight Kent
62 A5 Heasley Mill Devon
545 L6 Heaste Highld
106 C4 Heath Cardif
295 E1 Heath Derbys
309 H3 Heath Halton
168 C4 Heath and Reach Beds
324 D2 Heath Charnock Lancs
54 D2 Heath Common W Susx
293 F2 Heathcote Derbys
271 F4 Heathcote Shrops
191 E4 Heathcote Warwks
25 H3 Heath Cross Devon
26 C4 Heath Cross Devon
142 D3 Heath End Bucks
90 C2 Heath End Hants
91 F2 Heath End Hants
142 B5 Heath End Hants
275 F5 Heath End S Glos
92 D5 Heath End Surrey
190 C2 Heath End Warwks
237 F4 Heath End W Susx
75 F6 Heath End W Susx
239 F2 Heather Leics
19 F1 Heathercombe Devon
545 H1 Heatherfield Highld
92 B4 Heather Row Hants
93 F3 Heatherside Surrey
197 F5 Heathfield Cambs
19 H2 Heathfield Devon
78 D5 Heathfield E Susx
135 G4 Heathfield Gloucs
51 G3 Heathfield Hants
433 G6 Heathfield Lincs
465 G4 Heathfield Rens
444 D5 Heathfield S Ayrs
43 G2 Heathfield Somset
140 B1 Heathfield Village Oxon
73 F2 Heath Green Hants
213 G5 Heath Green Worcs
237 F2 Heath Hayes Staffs
235 H2 Heath Hill Shrops
84 D5 Heath House Somset
92 D1 Heath Lanes Wrekin
271 E5 Heath Lanes Wrekin
120 D2 Heath Park Gt Lon
557 F5 Heathryfold C Aber
120 D5 Heath Side Kent
28 C2 Heathstock Devon
274 B1 Heathton Shrops
294 C3 Heathtop Derbys
236 D5 Heath Town Wolves
378 D5 Heathwaite Cumb
384 D4 Heathwaite N York
273 G4 Heatley Staffs
311 E2 Heatley Traffd
325 F3 Heaton Bolton

342 B2 Heaton Brad
351 F2 Heaton Lancs
405 G1 Heaton N u Ty
292 C2 Heaton Staffs
326 C6 Heaton Chapel Stockp
311 H1 Heaton Mersey Stockp
311 H1 Heaton Moor Stockp
312 A1 Heaton Norris Stockp
342 B2 Heaton Royds Brad
323 H2 Heaton's Bridge Lancs
67 G5 Heaven's Door Somset
97 E3 Heaverham Kent
312 B2 Heaviley Stockp
27 E4 Heavitree Devon
405 H2 Hebburn S Tyne
405 H1 Hebburn Colliery S Tyne
405 G2 Hebburn New Town S Tyne
354 D2 Hebden N York
341 F4 Hebden Bridge Calder
290 C2 Hebden Green Ches
170 D5 Hebing End Herts
152 D4 Hebron Carmth
303 G4 Hebron IoA
430 C2 Hebron Nthumb
424 B3 Heck D & G
331 G5 Heckdyke Notts
92 B2 Heckfield Hants
225 G4 Heckfield Green Suffk
174 B5 Heckfordbridge Essex
250 D5 Heckingham Norfk
299 E6 Heckington Lincs
342 D5 Heckmondwike Kirk
88 A1 Heddington Wilts
600 F2 Heddle Ork
40 D2 Heddon Devon
404 D1 Heddon-on-the-Wall Nthumb
250 C6 Hedenham Norfk
47 F3 Hedge End Dorset
51 F2 Hedge End Hants
299 H5 Hedgehog Bridge Lincs
117 G2 Hedgerley Bucks
117 G2 Hedgerley Green Bucks
117 G2 Hedgerley Hill Bucks
44 B2 Hedging Somset
394 C1 Hedley Hill Dur
404 C3 Hedley on the Hill Nthumb
237 F2 Hednesford Staffs
348 C4 Hedon E R Yk
117 F2 Hedsor Bucks
406 A2 Hedworth S Tyne
168 A2 Heelands M Keyn
314 D3 Heeley Sheff
186 D4 Hegdon Hill Herefs
381 E4 Heggerscales Cumb
390 B2 Heggle Lane Cumb
606 E7 Heglibister Shet
395 F5 Heighington Darltn
318 C6 Heighington Lincs
291 F5 Heighley Staffs
340 B5 Height End Lancs
211 H5 Heightington Worcs
327 E3 Heights Oldham
565 J4 Heights of Brae Highld
563 K4 Heights of Kinlochewe Highld
585 J5 Heilam Highld
452 D3 Heiton Border
380 D1 Helbeck Cumb
19 F3 Hele Devon
23 G4 Hele Devon
27 F2 Hele Devon
60 D2 Hele Devon
43 G3 Hele Somset
20 C4 Hele Torbay
23 E2 Helebridge Cnwll
482 D3 Helensburgh Ag & B
4 D3 Helford Cnwll
5 E3 Helford Passage Cnwll
145 E1 Helham Green Herts
253 H2 Helhoughton Norfk
172 C1 Helions Bumpstead Essex
315 C1 Hellaby Rothm
15 H4 Helland Cnwll
44 C3 Helland Somset
7 H4 Helland Barton Cnwll
15 H4 Hellandbridge Cnwll
90 B2 Hell Corner W Berk
249 H2 Hellesdon Norfk
5 F1 Hellesveor Cnwll
192 B3 Hellifield N York
353 H3 Hellifield N York
353 H3 Hellifield Green N York
57 F2 Hellingly E Susx
211 D2 Hellington Norfk
606 E8 Hellister Shet
172 B6 Hellman's Cross Essex
368 B1 Helm N York
450 D5 Helmburn Border
192 C6 Helmdon Nhants
327 G2 Helme Kirk
201 G3 Helmingham Suffk
394 D2 Helmington Row Dur
582 D7 Helmsdale Highld
340 B5 Helmshore Lancs
366 D2 Helmside Cumb
372 A3 Helmsley N York
371 E5 Helperby N York
374 B5 Helperthorpe N York
279 G1 Helpringham Lincs
243 G3 Helpston C Pete
309 G4 Helsby Ches
309 G4 Helsby Ches
23 E2 Helscott Cnwll
321 F5 Helsey Lincs
4 C3 Helston Cnwll
15 F2 Helstone Cnwll
7 E5 Helston Water Cnwll
391 E5 Helton Cumb
367 G6 Helwith Bridge N York
250 C2 Hemblington Norfk
250 C2 Hemblington Corner Norfk
67 F2 Hembridge Somset
143 F4 Hemel Hempstead Herts
11 G2 Hemerdon Devon
233 F4 Hemford Shrops
272 C1 Hem Heath C Stke
345 F3 Hemingbrough N York
319 G5 Hemingby Lincs
329 H3 Hemingfield Barns
220 C5 Hemingford Abbots Cambs
220 C5 Hemingford Grey Cambs
201 F4 Hemingstone Suffk
275 H4 Hemington Leics
219 F3 Hemington Nhants
86 C4 Hemington Somset
177 E1 Hemley Suffk
384 D2 Hemlington Middsb
226 D6 Hemp Green Suffk
360 D1 Hempholme E R Yk
250 A6 Hempnall Norfk
250 A6 Hempnall Green Norfk
567 L4 Hemprigg Moray
174 B4 Hemp's Green Essex
295 G6 Hempshill Vale C Nott
172 C2 Hempstead Essex
98 B2 Hempstead Medway
256 B3 Hempstead Norfk
261 E4 Hempstead Norfk
136 B1 Hempsted Gloucs
254 D2 Hempton Norfk
165 G3 Hempton Oxon
141 G4 Hempton Wainhill Oxon

251 F1 Hemsby Norfk
82 B2 Hemsted Kent
317 H1 Hemswell Lincs
318 B2 Hemswell Cliff Lincs
48 B3 Hemsworth Dorset
314 D3 Hemsworth Sheff
329 G2 Hemsworth Wakefd
43 F5 Hemyock Devon
38 B4 Henaford Devon
304 C5 Hen Bentref Llandegfan IoA
188 D1 Henbrook Worcs
109 G4 Henbury Bristl
312 A5 Henbury Ches
48 B5 Henbury Dorset
452 D2 Hendersyde Park Border
232 D5 Hendomen Powys
119 E2 Hendon Gt Lon
406 C3 Hendon Sundld
3 G4 Hendra Cnwll
4 C2 Hendra Cnwll
4 D1 Hendra Cnwll
4 D5 Hendra Cnwll
8 A2 Hendra Cnwll
8 B3 Hendra Cnwll
14 D6 Hendra Cnwll
22 B6 Hendra Cnwll
16 C5 Hendrabridge Cnwll
22 C5 Hendraburnick Cnwll
7 E2 Hendra Croft Cnwll
308 A6 Hendre Flints
228 D3 Hendre Gwynd
231 F5 Hendre Powys
286 B1 Hendre-ddu Conwy
106 B2 Hendredenny Park Caerph
105 F2 Hendreforgan Rhondd
287 G2 Hendrerwydd Denbgs
129 F3 Hendrewen Swans
129 E4 Hendy Carmth
105 G3 Hendy Rhondd
287 F2 Hên-efail Denbgs
303 F5 Heneglwys IoA
110 B4 Henfield S Glos
55 F1 Henfield W Susx
23 H4 Henford Devon
87 F6 Henfords Marsh Wilts
180 C2 Henfynyw Cerdgn
132 B5 Hengoed Caerph
287 F3 Hengoed Denbgs
184 D4 Hengoed Powys
269 E3 Hengoed Shrops
255 F4 Hengrave Norfk
223 G6 Hengrave Suffk
109 H6 Hengrove Bristl
109 G6 Hengrove Park Bristl
172 A4 Henham Essex
121 G6 Henhurst Kent
232 B3 Heniarth Powys
44 B3 Henlade Somset
109 G4 Henleaze Bristl
46 C4 Henley Dorset
136 D1 Henley Gloucs
210 B2 Henley Shrops
210 C4 Henley Shrops
66 C3 Henley Somset
201 F4 Henley Suffk
89 H3 Henley Wilts
111 E6 Henley Wilts
74 D4 Henley W Susx
74 D4 Henley Common W Susx
215 F3 Henley Green Covtry
190 A1 Henley-in-Arden Warwks
116 B3 Henley-on-Thames Oxon
93 F4 Henley Park Surrey
58 B4 Henley's Down E Susx
97 G1 Henley Street Kent
153 G1 Henllan Cerdgn
307 E6 Henllan Denbgs
152 D6 Henllan Amgoed Carmth
269 F3 Henlle Shrops
133 E6 Henllys Torfn
133 E6 Henllys Vale Torfn
170 A2 Henlow Beds
19 H1 Hennock Devon
173 H2 Henny Street Essex
305 G5 Henryd Conwy
152 A4 Henry's Moat Pembks
344 D5 Hensall N York
342 D1 Henshaw Leeds
402 D2 Henshaw Nthumb
376 B1 Hensingham Cumb
139 H1 Hensington Oxon
227 F2 Henstead Suffk
72 C5 Hensting Hants
61 E3 Henstridge Devon
68 B6 Henstridge Somset
68 B5 Henstridge Ash Somset
68 A5 Henstridge Bowden Somset
68 B5 Henstridge Marsh Somset
141 G4 Henton Oxon
85 E5 Henton Somset
16 C4 Henwood Cnwll
139 H4 Henwood Oxon
139 H4 Henwood and Lamborough Hill Oxon
79 E1 Henwood Green Kent
605 J2 Heogan Shet
128 C4 Heol-ddu Carmth
129 F5 Heol-ddu Swans
131 G3 Heolgerrig Myr Td
105 E3 Heol-laethog Brdgnd
105 E3 Heol-las Brdgnd
129 G5 Heol Las Swans
157 E5 Heol Senni Powys
105 E3 Heol-y-Cyw Brdgnd
158 C2 Heol-y-gaer Powys
104 D5 Heol-y-mynydd V Glam
454 D5 Hepburn Nthumb
442 B4 Hepple Nthumb
430 D3 Hepscott Nthumb
294 D2 Hepthorne Lane Derbys
341 F4 Heptonstall Calder
328 B3 Hepworth Kirk
224 C4 Hepworth Suffk
125 E3 Herbrandston Pembks
160 C2 Hereford Herefs
542 D7 Heribost Highld
543 G2 Heribusta Highld
471 G4 Heriot Border
487 G6 Hermiston C Edin
439 G5 Hermitage Border
31 E1 Hermitage Dorset
115 E5 Hermitage W Berk
52 D3 Hermitage W Susx
325 E6 Hermitage Green Warrtn
329 E4 Hermit Hill Barns
153 H3 Hermon Carmth
282 C2 Hermon IoA
153 E3 Hermon Pembks
12 D1 Hernaford Devon
100 C2 Herne Kent
100 C2 Herne Bay Kent
100 C3 Herne Common Kent
119 G5 Herne Hill Gt Lon
97 G4 Herne Pound Kent
40 B2 Herner Devon
99 H2 Hernhill Kent
4 D2 Herniss Cnwll
9 G1 Herodsfoot Cnwll
101 E5 Herolden Kent
121 F1 Herongate Essex
418 D5 Heronsford S Ayrs
143 E6 Heronsgate Herts

78 B4 Heron's Ghyll E Susx
85 F3 Herons Green BaNES
105 E4 Heronston V Glam
609 H6 Herra Shet
91 H5 Herriard Hants
251 F5 Herringfleet Suffk
195 F6 Herring's Green Beds
223 E6 Herringswell Suffk
315 E1 Herringthorpe Rothm
100 C3 Hersden Kent
38 B6 Hersham Cnwll
94 C2 Hersham Surrey
57 G2 Herstmonceux E Susx
34 B5 Herston Dorset
601 G6 Herston Ork
144 D2 Hertford Herts
145 E2 Hertford Heath Herts
144 D2 Hertingfordbury Herts
338 B5 Hesketh Bank Lancs
339 F1 Hesketh Lane Lancs
338 B5 Hesketh Moss Lancs
390 A2 Hesket Newmarket Cumb
324 C1 Heskin Green Lancs
396 B2 Hesleden Dur
428 C3 Hesleyside Nthumb
358 B4 Heslington York
357 G4 Hessay York
10 B2 Hessenford Cnwll
200 B2 Hessett Suffk
347 F4 Hessle E R Yk
344 A6 Hessle Wakefd
606 C7 Hestaford Shet
351 G1 Hest Bank Lancs
162 D5 Hester's Way Gloucs
605 G8 Hestingott Shet
604 E1 Hestinsetter Shet
118 C4 Heston Gt Lon
600 D1 Hestwall Ork
308 C3 Heswall Wirral
166 C4 Hethe Oxon
249 G4 Hethel Norfk
162 A4 Hethelpit Cross Gloucs
249 F4 Hethersett Norfk
401 E1 Hethersgill Cumb
400 D1 Hetherside Cumb
290 A5 Hetherson Green Ches
453 G4 Hethpool Nthumb
395 F2 Hett Dur
354 C3 Hetton N York
406 B5 Hetton Downs Sundld
406 B5 Hetton-le-Hill Sundld
406 B5 Hetton-le-Hole Sundld
430 A5 Heugh Nthumb
554 C2 Heugh-head Abers
226 C5 Heveningham Suffk
96 C6 Hever Kent
365 G3 Heversham Cumb
255 F2 Hevingham Norfk
8 B4 Hewas Water Cnwll
134 D4 Hewelsfield Gloucs
134 C4 Hewelsfield Common Gloucs
390 B2 Hewer Hill Cumb
356 A3 Hew Green N York
84 D2 Hewish N Som
45 E6 Hewish Somset
29 G2 Hewood Dorset
405 G2 Heworth Gatesd
358 B4 Heworth York
403 G2 Hexham Nthumb
120 D5 Hextable Kent
330 C4 Hexthorpe Donc
169 G3 Hexton Herts
18 D3 Hexworthy Devon
354 A6 Hey Lancs
146 C5 Heybridge Essex
147 H3 Heybridge Essex
147 H3 Heybridge Basin Essex
11 F4 Heybrook Bay Devon
171 F1 Heydon Cambs
255 F2 Heydon Norfk
279 E2 Heydour Lincs
327 F2 Hey Green Kirk
327 E4 Heyheads Tamesd
337 F4 Hey Houses Lancs
516 B7 Heylipol Ag & B
606 C1 Heylor Shet
208 D5 Heyop Powys
327 E5 Heyrod Tamesd
351 E2 Heysham Lancs
355 G2 Heyshaw N York
74 D6 Heyshott W Susx
74 D6 Heyshott Green W Susx
326 D3 Heyside Oldham
87 G6 Heytesbury Wilts
165 F4 Heythrop Oxon
326 B2 Heywood Rochdl
87 F4 Heywood Wilts
332 D4 Hibaldstow N Linc
199 H4 Hibb's Green Suffk
199 F6 Hickford Hill Essex
330 A4 Hickleton Donc
257 F5 Hickling Norfk
277 E4 Hickling Notts
257 F5 Hickling Green Norfk
257 E5 Hickling Heath Norfk
277 E4 Hickling Pastures Notts
99 H3 Hickmans Green Kent
100 C3 Hicks Forstal Kent
110 A6 Hicks Gate BaNES
7 E5 Hick's Mill Cnwll
77 E6 Hickstead W Susx
190 B6 Hidcote Bartrim Gloucs
164 B1 Hidcote Boyce Gloucs
235 G5 Hifnal Shrops
326 D3 Higginshaw Oldham
294 D3 Higham Derbys
121 H5 Higham Kent
340 C2 Higham Lancs
174 D2 Higham Suffk
199 E1 Higham Suffk
329 E3 Higham Common Barns
430 B4 Higham Dykes Nthumb
218 D6 Higham Ferrers Nhants
169 G3 Higham Gobion Beds
119 H1 Higham Hill Gt Lon
239 F5 Higham on the Hill Leics
24 C2 Highampton Devon
120 A1 Higham Park Gt Lon
97 F5 High Angerton Nthumb
430 A2 High Ardwell D & G
408 B2 High Bankhill Cumb
391 F1 High Bankhill Cumb
485 E4 High Banton N Lans
300 C2 High Barn Lincs
144 B5 High Barnet Gt Lon
145 F5 High Beach Essex
366 D6 High Bentham N York
40 C3 High Bickington Devon
366 B6 High Biggins Cumb
367 G4 High Birkwith N York
355 H3 High Birstwith N York
467 G3 High Blantyre S Lans
485 G6 High Bonnybridge Falk
328 D6 High Bradfield Sheff
354 D5 High Bradley N York
61 G5 High Bray Devon
400 C6 Highbridge Cumb
72 C5 Highbridge Hants
533 J6 Highbridge Highld
84 A5 Highbridge Somset
237 F4 Highbridge Wsall
77 G3 Highbrook W Susx

78 D1 High Brooms Kent
136 C2 High Brotheridge Gloucs
40 A3 High Bullen Devon
328 B2 Highburton Kent
52 B4 Highbury C Port
119 G2 Highbury Gt Lon
86 B5 Highbury Somset
295 G6 Highbury Vale C Nott
443 G3 High Buston Nthumb
430 C5 High Callerton Nthumb
365 E3 High Cark Cumb
366 C4 High Casterton Cumb
358 D4 High Catton E R Yk
430 C2 High Church Nthumb
90 C3 Highclere Hants
313 H4 Highcliffe Derbys
49 G6 Highcliffe Dorset
139 F3 High Cogges Oxon
248 C3 High Common Norfk
383 F1 High Coniscliffe Darltn
326 D2 High Crompton Oldham
197 F3 High Cross Cambs
4 D3 High Cross Cnwll
78 D4 High Cross E Susx
73 H4 High Cross Hants
143 G5 High Cross Herts
171 E6 High Cross Herts
107 E2 High Cross Newpt
190 B1 High Cross Warwks
76 D6 High Cross W Susx
467 F2 High Crosshill S Lans
378 C6 High Cunsey Cumb
460 B2 High Dougarie N Ayrs
405 H5 High Dubmire Sundld
393 G4 High Dyke Dur
146 C2 High Easter Essex
344 D5 High Eggborough N York
369 G3 High Ellington N York
435 H4 High Enoch D & G
68 A1 Higher Alham Somset
47 E4 Higher Ansty Dorset
26 D5 Higher Ashton Devon
339 G4 Higher Audley Bl w D
6 D3 Higher Bal Cnwll
337 G3 Higher Ballam Lancs
338 D3 Higher Bartle Lancs
308 D2 Higher Bebington Wirral
168 D3 Higher Berry End Beds
326 B4 Higher Blackley Manch
326 C3 Higher Boarshaw Rochdl
32 C1 Higher Bockhampton Dorset
2 C3 Higher Bojewyan Cnwll
2 C3 Higher Boscaswell Cnwll
13 G1 Higher Brixham Torbay
326 B4 Higher Broughton Salfd
66 C5 Higher Burrow Somset
27 G3 Higher Burrowtown Devon
289 H3 Higher Burwardsley Ches
270 D6 Higher Ercall Wrekin
30 D2 Higher Chalmington Dorset
28 B2 Higher Cheriton Devon
44 D5 Higher Chillington Somset
312 C1 Higher Chisworth Derbys
9 G2 Highercliff Cnwll
38 D3 Higher Clovelly Devon
6 C6 Higher Condurrow Cnwll
22 D3 Higher Crackington Cnwll
14 D5 Higher Cransworth Cnwll
339 G4 Higher Croft Bl w D
117 H2 Higher Denham Bucks
327 F5 Higher Dinting Derbys
312 C3 Higher Disley Ches
3 G3 Higher Downs Cnwll
19 F2 Higher Dunstone Devon
44 B2 Higher Durston Somset
324 C4 Higher End Wigan
30 A4 Higher Eype Dorset
325 F4 Higher Folds Wigan
340 D1 Higherford Lancs
20 C4 Higher Gabwell Devon
325 G4 Higher Green Wigan
45 G6 Higher Halstock Leigh Dorset
351 F2 Higher Heysham Lancs
340 D5 Higher Hogshead Lancs
68 A4 Higher Holton Somset
312 B4 Higher Hurdsfield Ches
30 C3 Higher Kingcombe Dorset
288 D2 Higher Kinnerton Flints
68 B5 Higher Marsh Somset
46 D4 Higher Melcombe Dorset
8 C2 Higher Menadew Cnwll
27 H4 Higher Metcombe Devon
61 H5 Higher Molland Devon
61 E4 Higher Muddiford Devon
68 B5 Higher Nyland Dorset
338 D4 Higher Penwortham Lancs
69 E2 Higher Pertwood Wilts
8 C3 Higher Porthpean Cnwll
312 B3 Higher Poynton Ches
24 A3 Higher Prestacott Devon
168 D3 Higher Rads End Beds
269 G3 Higher Ridge Shrops
20 B4 Higher Rocombe Barton Devon
48 C4 Higher Row Dorset
309 H3 Higher Runcorn Halton
67 G6 Higher Sandford Dorset
308 D6 Higher Shotton Flints
310 D5 Higher Shurlach Ches
19 G3 Higher Sigford Devon
60 D2 Higher Slade Devon
64 B3 Higher Street Somset
27 H2 Higher Tale Devon
14 B5 Higher Tolcarne Cnwll
46 B3 Higher Totnell Dorset
7 F5 Highertown Cnwll
8 C1 Highertown Cnwll
15 G2 Highertown Cnwll
3 d1 Higher Town IoS
63 F2 Higher Town Somset
16 B5 Higher Tremarcoombe Cnwll
64 B4 Higher Vexford Somset
17 G4 Higher Wairreddon Devon
339 E4 Higher Walton Lancs
310 B2 Higher Walton Warrtn
44 B6 Higher Wambrook Somset
60 C2 Higher Warcombe Devon
27 G1 Higher Weaver Devon
47 F4 Higher Whatcombe Dorset
339 F5 Higher Wheelton Lancs
310 C3 Higher Whitley Ches
310 D4 Higher Wincham Ches
32 D2 Higher Woodsford Dorset
30 D2 Higher Wraxall Dorset
289 G6 Higher Wych Ches
394 D4 High Etherley Dur
300 C5 High Ferry Lincs
325 G3 Highfield Bolton
50 D2 Highfield C Sotn
345 G2 Highfield E R Yk
404 D3 Highfield Gatesd
143 F3 Highfield Herts
228 B5 Highfield Kent
353 E4 High Field Lancs
376 B2 Highfield N Ayrs
166 C5 Highfield Oxon
314 C2 Highfield Sheff
324 C4 Highfield Wigan

197 E3 Highfields Cambs
240 C4 Highfields C Leic
295 E1 Highfields Derbys
330 B3 Highfields Donc
147 H1 Highfields Essex
135 H5 Highfields Gloucs
475 E4 Highfields Nthumb
272 D5 Highfields Staffs
405 F4 High Forge Dur
405 E3 High Friarside Dur
484 C5 High Gallowhill E Duns
173 H4 High Garrett Essex
213 G2 Highgate Birm
77 H3 Highgate E Susx
119 F2 Highgate Gt Lon
79 H3 Highgate Kent
232 B5 Highgate Powys
394 B5 High Grange Dur
370 A5 High Grantley N York
378 C4 High Green Cumb
248 B3 High Green Cumb
249 F3 High Green Norfk
254 B5 High Green Norfk
329 E5 High Green Sheff
211 G3 High Green Shrops
199 H2 High Green Suffk
188 C5 High Green Worcs
80 C2 High Halden Kent
122 B4 High Halstow Medway
66 C3 High Ham Somset
405 F4 High Handenhold Dur
388 B4 High Harrington Cumb
356 C3 High Harrogate N York
406 B6 High Haswell Dur
271 E5 High Hatton Shrops
443 H4 High Hauxley Nthumb
387 F3 High Hawsker N York
271 F4 High Heath Shrops
237 F4 High Heath Wsall
401 E6 High Hesket Cumb
396 C2 High Hesleden Dur
389 G5 High Hill Cumb
146 D2 High Houses Essex
367 G2 High Houses N York
328 D3 High Hoyland Barns
347 E2 High Hunsley E R Yk
78 B4 High Hurstwood E Susx
373 E6 High Hutton N York
389 F2 High Ireby Cumb
261 F3 High Kelling Norfk
371 G4 High Kilburn N York
566 F8 Highland Boath Highld
30 A4 Highlands Dorset
175 E3 Highlands Dorset
312 A6 Highlane Ches
312 B2 Highlane Derbys
187 F2 High Lane Herefs
312 B2 High Lane Stockp
3 G2 High Lanes Cnwll
146 A3 High Laver Essex
399 E5 Highlaws Cumb
161 H5 Highleadon Gloucs
311 E3 High Legh Ches
53 E5 Highleigh W Susx
384 D2 High Leven S on T
211 G3 Highley Shrops
86 A3 High Littleton BaNES
399 G5 High Longthwaite Cumb
389 E4 High Lorton Cumb
410 D5 High Mains D & G
373 F4 High Marishes N York
317 F5 High Marnham Notts
330 B4 High Melton Donc
404 C2 High Mickley Nthumb
399 H5 Highmoor Cumb
315 F4 High Moor Derbys
324 C2 High Moor Lancs
116 B2 Highmoor Oxon
315 F3 High Moor Rothm
116 A3 Highmoor Cross Oxon
109 E2 Highmoor Hill Mons
406 A5 High Moorsley Sundld
162 A6 Highnam Gloucs
162 A5 Highnam Green Gloucs
134 D2 High Nash Gloucs
365 F3 High Newton Cumb
455 G4 High Newton-by-the-Sea Nthumb
364 C2 High Nibthwaite Cumb
249 E4 Highoak Norfk
366 C1 High Oaks Cumb
272 A4 High Offley Staffs
146 B4 High Ongar Essex
236 B1 High Onn Staffs
236 B1 High Onn Wharf Staffs
366 A1 High Park N York
323 G1 High Park Sefton
85 G1 Highridge Bristl
109 G6 Highridge N Som
332 C2 High Risby N Linc
341 H4 Highroad Well Moor Calder
146 C1 High Roding Essex
200 B2 High Rougham Suffk
390 B2 High Row Cumb
390 B5 High Row Cumb
352 C2 High Salter Lancs
54 D3 High Salvington W Susx
399 F5 High Scales Cumb
367 H1 High Sellafield Cumb
356 B3 High Shaw N York
406 B1 High Shields S Tyne
395 F1 High Shincliffe Dur
389 F3 High Side Cumb
406 D3 High Southwick Sundld
404 D3 High Spen Gatesd
387 E2 High Stakesby N York
100 D2 Highstead Kent
98 D2 Highsted Kent
394 C1 High Stoop Dur
126 D1 High Street Carmth
8 B3 High Street Cnwll
79 G3 High Street Kent
100 A3 Highstreet Kent
126 D2 High Street Pembks
203 E3 High Street Suffk
226 D3 High Street Suffk
227 E5 High Street Suffk
173 F3 Highstreet Green Essex
200 D3 High Street Green Suffk
75 F2 Highstreet Green Surrey
451 F3 High Sunderland Border
424 B4 Hightae D & G
213 G4 Highter's Heath Birm
396 C3 High Throston Hartpl
291 H2 Hightown Ches
51 E2 Hightown Hants
49 F5 Hightown Hants
51 E2 Hightown C Sotn
169 F5 Hightown Sefton
323 F4 Hightown Sefton
235 G6 High Town Shrops
237 E2 High Town Staffs
288 D5 Hightown Wrexhm
200 C3 Hightown Green Suffk
442 A3 High Toynton Lincs
442 D5 High Trewhitt Nthumb
405 F4 High Urpeth Dur
486 D2 High Valleyfield Fife
376 B2 High Walton Cumb
403 G1 High Walton Nthumb
378 B5 High Warden Nthumb
6 D5 Highway Cnwll

186 B5 Highway Herefs
66 D5 Highway Somset
117 E3 Highway W & M
112 B5 Highway Wilts
20 A3 Highweek Devon
404 D3 High Westwood Dur
400 B4 High Whinnow Cumb
28 B1 Highwood Devon
33 F2 Highwood Dorset
49 F3 Highwood Hants
187 F1 Highwood Worcs
144 B6 Highwood Hill Gt Lon
134 D5 High Woolaston Gloucs
384 B3 High Worsall N York
138 C6 Highworth Swindn
39 F6 Highworthy Devon
378 C5 High Wray Cumb
145 G2 High Wych Herts
142 B6 High Wycombe Bucks
247 G4 Hilborough Norfk
137 E1 Hilcot Gloucs
295 F3 Hilcote Derbys
137 G4 Hilcot End Gloucs
88 D3 Hilcott Wilts
97 E5 Hildenborough Kent
97 E5 Hilden Park Kent
198 A5 Hildersham Cambs
161 E5 Hildersley Herefs
272 D3 Hilderstone Staffs
361 F1 Hilderthorpe E R Yk
31 E2 Hilfield Dorset
246 C5 Hilgay Norfk
237 H5 Hill Birm
135 E5 Hill S Glos
191 H1 Hill Warwks
344 C4 Hillam N York
125 H2 Hillblock Pembks
100 C3 Hillborough Kent
115 G4 Hill Bottom Oxon
48 C6 Hillbourne Poole
560 A5 Hillbrae Abers
569 K6 Hillbrae Abers
74 B4 Hill Brow W Susx
48 B4 Hillbutts Dorset
272 B2 Hill Chorlton Staffs
310 C3 Hillcliffe Warrtn
294 B5 Hillcliffelane Derbys
257 E5 Hill Common Norfk
43 F2 Hillcommon Somset
87 E5 Hill Corner Somset
162 C1 Hill Croome Worcs
275 E3 Hillcross C Derb
324 B2 Hill Dale Lancs
69 E1 Hill Deverill Wilts
300 B5 Hilldyke Lincs
527 G5 Hillend Angus
393 H2 Hill End Dur
487 F5 Hillend Fife
499 G5 Hill End Fife
162 C2 Hill End Gloucs
118 B1 Hill End Gt Lon
468 C1 Hillend N Lans
84 C3 Hillend N Som
355 E4 Hill End N York
236 B6 Hillend Shrops
45 G5 Hill End Somset
102 B3 Hillend Swans
188 D2 Hill End Worcs
161 F4 Hillend Green Gloucs
134 D2 Hillersland Gloucs
25 H3 Hillerton Devon
167 E3 Hillesden Bucks
167 E3 Hillesden Hamlet Bucks
110 D2 Hillesley Gloucs
43 G3 Hillfarrance Somset
13 E2 Hillfield Devon
214 A4 Hillfield Solhll
110 A5 Hillfields Bristl
215 E4 Hillfields Covtry
342 D3 Hillfoot Leeds
169 G3 Hillfoot End Beds
189 E5 Hill Furze Worcs
160 B4 Hill Gate Herefs
171 G3 Hill Green Essex
98 C2 Hill Green Kent
114 D4 Hillgreen W Berk
75 E4 Hillgrove W Susx
186 D5 Hillhampton Herefs
556 D2 Hillhead Abers
560 A5 Hillhead Abers
8 D1 Hillhead Cnwll
13 G2 Hillhead Devon
51 F4 Hill Head Hants
445 F2 Hillhead S Ayrs
445 F6 Hillhead S Ayrs
571 G4 Hillhead of Auchentumb Abers
571 K7 Hillhead of Cocklaw Abers
570 B5 Hillhead of Mountblairy Abers
96 C6 Hill Hoath Kent
237 G4 Hill Hook Birm
211 E4 Hill Houses Shrops
238 A2 Hilliard's Cross Staffs
588 F4 Hilliclay Highld
118 B3 Hillingdon Gt Lon
118 B3 Hillingdon Heath Gt Lon
466 D2 Hillington C Glas
253 E2 Hillington Norfk
216 B5 Hillis Corner IoW
43 F5 Hillmoor Devon
216 B5 Hillmorton Warwks
125 G3 Hill Mountain Pembks
554 C3 Hillockhead Abers
340 B4 Hillock Vale Lancs
487 F1 Hill of Beath Fife
498 D5 Hill of Drip Stirlg
577 H8 Hill of Fearn Highld
570 B5 Hill of Mountblairy Abers
51 F3 Hill Park Hants
96 B3 Hill Park Kent
212 C4 Hillpool Worcs
51 G1 Hillpound Hants
273 G6 Hill Ridware Staffs
314 C1 Hillsborough Sheff
529 E2 Hillside Angus
557 G5 Hillside Angus
328 C4 Hill Side Barns
19 E5 Hillside Devon
28 C1 Hill Side Hants
94 C4 Hillside Hants
328 B1 Hill Side Kirk
601 H5 Hillside Ork
602 C7 Hillside Ork
323 F2 Hillside Sefton
606 F5 Hillside Shet
210 D2 Hillside Shrops
112 C1 Hillside Wilts
187 H2 Hill Side Worcs
274 A3 Hill Somersal Derbys
315 F6 Hills Town Derbys
50 B1 Hillstreet Hants
82 B1 Hill Street Kent
606 C2 Hillswick Shet
328 D3 Hill Top Barns
132 C3 Hilltop Blae G
342 A3 Hill Top Brad
142 D4 Hilltop Bucks
294 C3 Hilltop Derbys
314 D4 Hill Top Derbys
330 A5 Hill Top Donc
393 G5 Hill Top Dur
405 F4 Hill Top Dur

405 F6 Hill Top Dur
50 D4 Hill Top Hants
327 G2 Hill Top Kirk
343 E3 Hill Top Leeds
295 F5 Hill Top Notts
355 G2 Hill Top N York
356 B2 Hill Top N York
314 D1 Hill Top Rothm
329 F6 Hill Top Rothm
325 G4 Hill Top Salfd
237 E6 Hill Top Sandw
314 B2 Hill Top Sheff
236 C3 Hill Top Staffs
214 D1 Hill Top Warwks
215 F1 Hill Top W Susx
74 D5 Hill Top W Susx
514 B3 Hilltown C Dund
48 B5 Hill View Dorset
406 B4 Hillview Sundld
37 G3 Hillway IoW
605 G8 Hillwell Shet
237 H4 Hill Wood Birm
215 E6 Hill Wootton Warwks
50 C1 Hillyfields Hants
512 C5 Hillyland P & K
112 B4 Hilmarton Wilts
87 F3 Hilperton Wilts
87 F2 Hilperton Marsh Wilts
52 B4 Hilsea C Port
349 E3 Hilston E R Yk
72 B5 Hiltingbury Hants
560 D3 Hilton Abers
474 C4 Hilton Border
557 G3 Hilton C Aber
196 C1 Hilton Cambs
392 B5 Hilton Cumb
274 C3 Hilton Derbys
47 E4 Hilton Dorset
566 B8 Hilton Highld
577 G7 Hilton Highld
577 K6 Hilton Highld
236 A5 Hilton Shrops
384 D2 Hilton S on T
394 D5 Hilton S on T
237 G4 Hilton Staffs
325 E3 Hilton House Bolton
566 F1 Hilton of Cadboll Highld
326 B4 Hilton Park Bury
188 D3 Himbleton Worcs
212 C1 Himley Staffs
365 H3 Hincaster Cumb
94 D2 Hinchley Wood Surrey
328 A3 Hinchliffe Mill Kirk
164 A3 Hinchwick Gloucs
239 G6 Hinckley Leics
30 B3 Hinckley Dorset
600 E2 Hindatown Ork
224 D4 Hinderclay Suffk
308 D4 Hinderton Ches
386 C1 Hinderwell N York
269 F3 Hindford Shrops
74 D2 Hindhead Surrey
340 A3 Hindle Fold Lancs
404 B3 Hindley Nthumb
325 E4 Hindley Wigan
325 E4 Hindley Green Wigan
188 C3 Hindlip Worcs
254 D2 Hindolveston Norfk
69 F3 Hindon Wilts
364 A6 Hindpool Cumb
260 C4 Hindringham Norfk
325 F4 Hindsford Wigan
248 D4 Hingham Norfk
271 F4 Hinstock Shrops
201 E6 Hintlesham Suffk
201 E6 Hintlesham Park Suffk
135 F4 Hinton Gloucs
49 G5 Hinton Hants
159 F2 Hinton Herefs
192 B4 Hinton Nhants
110 C4 Hinton S Glos
233 H3 Hinton Shrops
67 F5 Hinton Somset
73 F4 Hinton Ampner Hants
85 G3 Hinton Blewett BaNES
86 D3 Hinton Charterhouse BaNES
163 F1 Hinton Cross Worcs
166 C2 Hinton-in-the-Hedges Nhants
48 C3 Hinton Martell Dorset
163 F2 Hinton on the Green Worcs
48 B4 Hinton Parva Dorset
113 F3 Hinton Parva Swindn
45 E5 Hinton St George Somset
47 E1 Hinton St Mary Dorset
139 F5 Hinton Waldrist Oxon
211 E4 Hints Shrops
238 B4 Hints Staffs
194 C2 Hinwick Beds
233 G3 Hinwood Shrops
99 G6 Hinxhill Kent
197 G5 Hinxton Cambs
170 B1 Hinxworth Herts
342 B4 Hipperholme Calder
187 G3 Hipplecote Worcs
443 G2 Hipsburn Nthumb
383 E5 Hipswell N York
304 C5 Hiraeth Gwynd
152 D5 Hirael Carmth
556 C4 Hirn Abers
267 H5 Hirnant Powys
468 D2 Hirst N Lans
431 E2 Hirst Nthumb
345 E5 Hirst Courtney N York
287 G2 Hirwaen Denbgs
131 E3 Hirwaun Rhondd
105 E4 Hirwaun Common Brdgnd
40 A2 Hiscott Devon
438 D4 Hislop Border
87 F5 Hisomley Wilts
197 F2 Histon Cambs
200 C4 Hitcham Suffk
399 E1 Hitchill D & G
170 B4 Hitchin Herts
170 A4 Hitchin Hill Herts
68 D1 Hitcombe Bottom Wilts
120 A5 Hither Green Gt Lon
26 A3 Hittisleigh Devon
26 A3 Hittisleigh Barton Devon
346 B3 Hive E R Yk
273 F4 Hixon Staffs
101 E4 Hoaden Kent
159 G5 Hoaldalbert Mons
274 A5 Hoar Cross Staffs
160 C4 Hoarwithy Herefs
100 D3 Hoath Kent
96 C6 Hoath Corner Kent
209 F4 Hobarris Shrops
600 F3 Hobbister Ork
237 F3 Hobble End Staffs
199 E4 Hobbles Green Suffk
145 G5 Hobbs Cross Essex
145 G5 Hobbs Cross Essex
86 B3 Hobbs Wall BaNES
289 G4 Hob Hill Ches
440 A2 Hobkirk Border
327 F6 Hobroyd Derbys
405 E3 Hobson Dur
241 E1 Hoby Leics
43 F2 Hoccombe Somset
120 C6 Hockenden Gt Lon
171 G5 Hockerill Herts

255 E5 Hockering Norfk
255 E5 Hockering Heath Norfk
296 D3 Hockerton Notts
43 G3 Hockholler Somset
43 G3 Hockholler Green Somset
312 B3 Hockley Ches
214 D4 Hockley Covtry
147 G6 Hockley Essex
148 D3 Hockley Essex
99 F3 Hockley Kent
238 C4 Hockley Staffs
214 B5 Hockley Heath Solhll
168 D4 Hockliffe Beds
223 E2 Hockwold cum Wilton Norfk
42 D4 Hockworthy Devon
72 B5 Hocombe Hants
144 D3 Hoddesdon Herts
339 H5 Hoddlesden Bl w D
424 C5 Hoddom Mains D & G
189 G5 Hoden Worcs
292 B4 Hodgefield Staffs
213 H2 Hodgehill Birm
311 G6 Hodgehill Ches
126 A5 Hodgeston Pembks
528 D5 Hodgeton Angus
208 C1 Hodley Powys
271 E4 Hodnet Shrops
271 E4 Hodnetheath Shrops
316 B2 Hodsock Notts
97 F2 Hodsoll Street Kent
113 E3 Hodson Swindn
315 G4 Hodthorpe Derbys
73 E6 Hoe Hants
254 C4 Hoe Norfk
94 B5 Hoe Surrey
114 C6 Hoe Benham W Berk
51 H2 Hoe Gate Hants
392 A6 Hoff Cumb
280 B2 Hoffleet Stow Lincs
606 D2 Hogaland Shet
98 D3 Hogbarn Kent
99 G3 Hogben's Hill Kent
467 F1 Hogganfield C Glas
200 A3 Hoggard's Green Suffk
167 H4 Hoggeston Bucks
87 E3 Hoggington Wilts
214 C1 Hoggrill's End Warwks
592 B3 Hogha Gearraidh W Isls
92 D5 Hog Hatch Surrey
390 D4 Hoghouse Hill Cumb
339 F4 Hoghton Lancs
339 F4 Hoghton Bottoms Lancs
327 H3 Hogley Green Kirk
293 H4 Hognaston Derbys
321 F5 Hogsthorpe Lincs
48 A3 Hogstock Dorset
281 E4 Holbeach Lincs
281 E4 Holbeach Bank Lincs
280 D4 Holbeach Clough Lincs
244 D2 Holbeach Drove Lincs
212 A4 Holbeache Worcs
281 E4 Holbeach Hurn Lincs
280 D6 Holbeach St Johns Lincs
281 E3 Holbeach St Marks Lincs
281 E3 Holbeach St Matthew Lincs
343 E3 Holbeck Leeds
315 G5 Holbeck Notts
315 G5 Holbeck Woodhouse Notts
189 F3 Holberrow Green Worcs
11 H3 Holbeton Devon
97 G2 Holborough Kent
294 D6 Holbrook Derbys
315 E3 Holbrook Sheff
176 C2 Holbrook Suffk
110 B5 Holbrook Common S Glos
294 D5 Holbrook Moor Derbys
215 E3 Holbrooks Covtry
454 C2 Holburn Nthumb
50 D4 Holbury Hants
325 H1 Holcombe Bury
20 D3 Holcombe Devon
86 B5 Holcombe Somset
325 H2 Holcombe Brook Bury
43 E4 Holcombe Rogus Devon
217 G6 Holcot Nhants
145 E5 Holdbrook Gt Lon
353 F5 Holden Lancs
217 E6 Holdenby Nhants
326 D3 Holden Fold Oldham
48 D5 Holdenhurst Dorset
172 C4 Holder's Green Essex
119 E1 Holders Hill Gt Lon
162 C2 Holdfast Worcs
210 D2 Holdgate Shrops
298 D5 Holdingham Lincs
29 F2 Holditch Dorset
342 A4 Holdsworth Calder
314 B1 Holdworth Sheff
341 G2 Hole Brad
38 D4 Hole Devon
341 E4 Hole Bottom Calder
453 F3 Holefield Border
468 B1 Holehills N Lans
312 D1 Holehouse Derbys
161 E4 Hole in the Wall Herefs
527 G6 Holemill Angus
24 B1 Holemoor Devon
17 F5 Hole's Hole Devon
435 H1 Holestane D & G
294 C2 Holestone Derbys
54 D2 Hole Street W Susx
61 H4 Holewater Devon
64 C3 Holford Somset
358 A4 Holgate York
365 E4 Holker Cumb
260 A3 Holkham Norfk
24 A2 Hollacombe Devon
26 C2 Hollacombe Devon
11 F3 Hollacombe Hill Devon
602 F1 Holland Ork
603 K7 Holland Ork
96 A4 Holland Surrey
299 G5 Holland Fen Lincs
324 C3 Holland Lees Lancs
149 H1 Holland-on-Sea Essex
45 G4 Hollands Somset
603 L1 Hollandstoun Ork
425 F6 Hollee D & G
202 C6 Hollesley Suffk
20 B5 Hollicombe Torbay
272 B5 Hollies Common Staffs
310 D1 Hollinfare Warrtn
98 C3 Hollingbourne Kent
55 H3 Hollingbury Br & H
55 H3 Hollingdean Br & H
168 B4 Hollingdon Bucks
58 A2 Hollingrove E Susx
274 C2 Hollington Derbys
58 C4 Hollington E Susx
90 C3 Hollington Hants
273 G2 Hollington Staffs
90 C3 Hollington Cross Hants
274 C2 Hollington Grove Derbys
315 E5 Hollingwood Derbys
327 E5 Hollingworth Tamesd
341 E2 Hollin Hall Lancs
343 F2 Hollin Park Leeds
325 G3 Hollins Bolton
326 B3 Hollins Bury
366 D1 Hollins Cumb
314 C5 Hollins Derbys
291 G4 Hollins Staffs

292 B3 Hollins Staffs
292 C5 Hollins Staffs
293 E1 Hollinsclough Staffs
314 D3 Hollins End Sheff
291 E2 Hollinsgreen Ches
310 D1 Hollins Green Warrtn
351 G4 Hollins Lane Lancs
235 G3 Hollinswood Wrekin
326 D4 Hollinwood Oldham
270 C2 Hollinwood Shrops
43 E6 Hollis Green Devon
27 F2 Hollis Head Devon
40 C5 Hollocombe Devon
40 C5 Hollocombe Town Devon
294 C3 Holloway Derbys
116 D3 Holloway W & M
69 E3 Holloway Wilts
93 G6 Holloway Hill Surrey
85 G2 Hollow Brook BaNES
217 E5 Hollowell Nhants
314 A2 Hollow Meadows Sheff
309 G6 Hollowmoor Heath Ches
47 F6 Hollow Oak Dorset
425 H4 Hollows D & G
100 D3 Hollow Street Kent
237 H4 Holly Bank Wsall
214 D3 Hollyberry End Solhll
85 F5 Holly Brook Somset
132 C4 Hollybush Caerph
292 A6 Hollybush C Stke
433 E2 Hollybush E Ayrs
133 E6 Hollybush Torfn
161 H2 Hollybush Worcs
289 F6 Holly Bush Wrexhm
117 G2 Hollybush Corner Bucks
200 B3 Hollybush Corner Suffk
99 E3 Hollybushes Kent
117 G3 Hollybush Hill Bucks
175 F6 Hollybush Hill Essex
239 G6 Hollycroft Leics
116 D3 Holly Cross Wokham
245 H3 Holly End Norfk
141 G4 Holly Green Bucks
162 C1 Holly Green Worcs
383 E4 Holly Hill N York
234 B5 Hollyhurst Shrops
215 F2 Hollyhurst Warwks
349 H4 Hollym E R Yk
211 H4 Hollywaste Shrops
74 C3 Hollywater Hants
213 G4 Hollywood Worcs
39 H2 Holmacott Devon
43 H4 Holman Clavel Somset
327 H3 Holmbridge Kirk
94 C6 Holmbury St Mary Surrey
8 C3 Holmbush Cnwll
29 G2 Holmbush Dorset
272 D4 Holmcroft Staffs
196 A6 Holme Beds
342 C3 Holme Brad
220 A2 Holme Cambs
365 H4 Holme Cumb
327 H3 Holme Kirk
332 C3 Holme N Linc
297 F3 Holme Notts
370 D3 Holme N York
33 F2 Holmebridge Dorset
340 D4 Holme Chapel Lancs
196 A6 Holme Green Beds
344 C1 Holme Green N York
92 D1 Holme Green Wokham
248 A3 Holme Hale Norfk
390 D3 Holme Head Cumb
334 C3 Holme Hill NE Lin
160 D2 Holme Lacy Herefs
276 D2 Holme Lane Notts
185 F4 Holme Marsh Herefs
365 H4 Holme Mills Cumb
346 A2 Holme-on-Spalding-Moor E R Yk
360 B5 Holme on the Wolds E R Yk
276 D2 Holme Pierrepont Notts
160 C1 Holmer Herefs
142 C5 Holmer Green Bucks
338 B6 Holmes Lancs
398 D5 Holme St Cuthbert Cumb
291 F1 Holmes Chapel Ches
314 D4 Holmesdale Derbys
314 C4 Holmesfield Derbys
339 E3 Holme Slack Lancs
57 E2 Holmes's Hill E Susx
324 A1 Holmeswood Lancs
95 F4 Holmethorpe Surrey
342 C3 Holme Wood Brad
295 E1 Holmewood Derbys
341 H4 Holmfield Calder
327 H3 Holmfirth Kirk
341 H4 Holmfield Calder
542 B7 Holmisdale Highld
314 D4 Holmley Common Derbys
349 G5 Holmpton E R Yk
376 D5 Holmrook Cumb
605 J2 Holmsgarth Shet
405 F5 Holmside Dur
28 D2 Holmsleigh Green Devon
445 E5 Holmston S Ayrs
94 D6 Holmwood Corner Surrey
401 F5 Holmwrangle Cumb
19 F4 Holne Devon
46 C3 Holnest Dorset
63 E2 Holnicote Somset
23 G2 Holsworthy Devon
39 E6 Holsworthy Beacon Devon
48 C4 Holt Dorset
92 B4 Holt Hants
261 E4 Holt Norfk
309 G1 Holt St Hel
87 F2 Holt Wilts
188 B2 Holt Worcs
289 F4 Holt Wrexhm
358 C4 Holtby York
73 G2 Holt End Hants
213 G6 Holt End Worcs
188 B2 Holt Fleet Worcs
323 G4 Holt Green Lancs
327 G2 Holt Head Kirk
48 D4 Holt Heath Dorset
188 B2 Holt Heath Worcs
97 H3 Holt Hill Kent
274 A4 Holton Oxon
68 A4 Holton Somset
227 E4 Holton Suffk
319 C4 Holton cum Beckering Lincs
334 C1 Holton le Clay Lincs
333 F5 Holton le Moor Lincs
175 E2 Holton St Mary Suffk
343 E1 Holt Park Leeds
92 D6 Holt Pound Hants
326 D4 Holts Oldham
117 F1 Holtspur Bucks
48 C3 Holt Wood Dorset
78 B2 Holtye E Susx
29 G1 Holway Dorset
67 G5 Holway Flints
308 A4 Holway Flints
44 A3 Holway Somset
46 C2 Holwell Dorset
169 H3 Holwell Herts
277 F5 Holwell Leics
138 C3 Holwell Oxon
86 C6 Holwell Somset

169 H3 Holwellbury Beds
393 F4 Holwick Dur
32 D3 Holworth Dorset
73 H1 Holybourne Hants
29 E2 Holy City Devon
431 F6 Holy Cross N Tyne
212 D4 Holy Cross Worcs
145 E4 Holyfield Essex
28 A4 Holyford Devon
302 C4 Holyhead IoA
450 D2 Holylee Border
314 C6 Holymoorside Derbys
117 F4 Holyport W & M
442 B4 Holystone Nthumb
468 B2 Holytown N Lans
3 d2 Holy Vale IoS
143 E1 Holywell Beds
220 D5 Holywell Cambs
7 E2 Holywell Cnwll
30 D2 Holywell Dorset
308 A4 Holywell Flints
135 H6 Holywell Gloucs
159 G1 Holywell Herefs
143 F5 Holywell Herts
431 F5 Holywell Nthumb
45 G5 Holywell Somset
190 B1 Holywell Warwks
342 A6 Holywell Green Calder
43 E3 Holywell Lake Somset
223 E4 Holywell Row Suffk
423 F3 Holywood D & G
162 D3 Homedowns Gloucs
235 E4 Homer Shrops
323 F4 Homer Green Sefton
226 B2 Homersfield Suffk
119 H2 Homerton Gt Lon
160 D5 Hom Green Herefs
70 C4 Homington Wilts
35 G2 Hommet Guern
189 G6 Honeybourne Worcs
25 F2 Honeychurch Devon
195 G3 Honeydon Beds
84 D2 Honey Hall N Som
100 B3 Honey Hill Kent
92 D1 Honeyhill Wokham
88 D2 Honeystreet Wilts
174 C2 Honey Tye Suffk
168 D5 Honeywick Beds
11 E2 Honicknowle C Plym
214 C5 Honiley Warwks
256 C4 Honing Norfk
249 F2 Honingham Norfk
298 A6 Honington Lincs
224 A5 Honington Suffk
164 D1 Honington Warwks
28 C2 Honiton Devon
288 D3 Honkley Wrexhm
328 A2 Honley Kirk
328 A2 Honley Moor Kirk
235 G1 Honnington Wrekin
119 G5 Honor Oak Gt Lon
119 G5 Honor Oak Park Gt Lon
326 D1 Honresfeld Rochdl
101 E3 Hoo Kent
202 B3 Hoo Suffk
329 G5 Hoober Rothm
212 B5 Hoobrook Worcs
329 E4 Hood Green Barns
329 F5 Hood Hill Rothm
310 B2 Hood Manor Warrtn
11 F3 Hooe C Plym
58 A5 Hooe E Susx
58 A4 Hooe Common E Susx
170 A6 Hoo End Herts
289 H2 Hoofield Ches
311 E3 Hoo Green Ches
341 G4 Hoo Hole Calder
245 F6 Hook Cambs
29 F1 Hook Devon
345 H4 Hook E R Yk
94 D2 Hook Gt Lon
51 F3 Hook Hants
92 B4 Hook Hants
125 G2 Hook Pembks
112 C3 Hook Wilts
234 B3 Hook-a-gate Shrops
162 B1 Hook Bank Worcs
30 C3 Hooke Dorset
146 B5 Hook End Essex
115 H3 Hook End Oxon
214 C3 Hook End Solhll
404 D3 Hooker Gate Gatesd
271 E2 Hookgate Staffs
79 F2 Hook Green Kent
97 F1 Hook Green Kent
120 D5 Hook Green Kent
121 F5 Hook Green Kent
93 G3 Hook Heath Surrey
165 E3 Hook Norton Oxon
51 E4 Hook Park Hants
170 C5 Hook's Cross Herts
135 F5 Hook Street Gloucs
112 C3 Hook Street Wilts
53 E1 Hooksway W Susx
26 D3 Hookway Devon
95 F6 Hookwood Surrey
289 F1 Hoole Ches
309 F6 Hoole Bank Ches
95 F3 Hooley Surrey
326 B2 Hooley Bridge Rochdl
326 C2 Hooley Brow Rochdl
326 D5 Hooley Hill Tamesd
18 B4 Hoo Meavy Devon
134 C3 Hoop Mons
49 H6 Hooper's Hill Hants
87 E4 Hoopers Pool Wilts
39 E3 Hoops Devon
122 B5 Hoo St Werburgh Medway
309 E4 Hooton Ches
315 G1 Hooton Levitt Rothm
330 A3 Hooton Pagnell Donc
330 A5 Hooton Roberts Rothm
605 G1 Hoove Shet
165 H5 Hopcroft's Holt Oxon
313 G3 Hope Derbys
288 D3 Hope Flints
585 J5 Hope Highld
233 E3 Hope Powys
233 E3 Hope Shrops
293 F3 Hope Staffs
210 B1 Hope Bagot Shrops
389 E5 Hopebeck Cumb
210 B1 Hope Bowdler Shrops
293 F4 Hopedale Staffs
172 B5 Hope End Green Essex
312 B3 Hope Green Ches
568 B2 Hopeman Moray
161 E6 Hope Mansell Herefs
233 F4 Hope Park Shrops
209 G3 Hopesay Shrops
233 F4 Hopesgate Shrops
122 B2 Hope's Green Essex
187 E5 Hope's Rough Herefs
186 C4 Hope under Dinmore Herefs
115 E6 Hopgoods Green W Berk
505 G1 Hopkinstown Rhondd
185 H2 Hopley's Green Herefs
357 E3 Hopperton N York
244 C2 Hop Pole Lincs
215 G3 Hopsford Warwks
233 A6 Hopstone Shrops
294 B4 Hopton Derbys
269 G5 Hopton Shrops

272 D4 Hopton Staffs
224 C4 Hopton Suffk
211 E4 Hoptonbank Shrops
210 C3 Hopton Cangeford Shrops
209 G4 Hopton Castle Shrops
210 C3 Hoptongate Shrops
273 E4 Hopton Heath Staffs
251 G5 Hopton on Sea Norfk
211 E4 Hopton Wafers Shrops
238 B3 Hopwas Staffs
326 C3 Hopwood Rochdl
213 F5 Hopwood Worcs
23 G2 Hopworthy Devon
78 D6 Horam E Susx
279 G2 Horbling Lincs
343 E6 Horbury Wakefd
138 A4 Horcott Gloucs
396 B1 Horden Dur
209 G2 Horderley Shrops
49 H5 Hordle Hants
269 G3 Hordley Shrops
128 C3 Horeb Carmth
154 D4 Horeb Carmth
180 A6 Horeb Cerdgn
288 C3 Horeb Flints
109 H3 Horfield Bristl
595 G3 Horgabost W Isls
225 H5 Horham Suffk
347 E6 Horkstow N Linc
347 E6 Horkstow Wolds N Linc
191 G6 Horley Oxon
95 F6 Horley Surrey
29 G2 Horn Ash Dorset
67 F3 Hornblotton Somset
67 F3 Hornblotton Green Somset
366 B6 Hornby Lancs
383 F6 Hornby N York
384 B3 Hornby N York
319 H6 Horncastle Lincs
115 H5 Horncastle Readg
120 D2 Hornchurch Gt Lon
474 D5 Horncliffe Nthumb
474 C5 Horndean Border
452 B2 Horndean Hants
18 B1 Horndon Devon
121 G3 Horndon on the Hill Thurr
95 G6 Horne Surrey
62 D2 Horner Somset
147 F4 Horne Row Essex
174 C1 Horner's Green Suffk
174 D3 Hornestreet Essex
542 D7 Horneval Highld
78 B4 Horney Common E Susx
143 E6 Horn Hill Bucks
64 D3 Horn Hill Somset
8 B3 Hornick Cnwll
527 F2 Horniehaugh Angus
250 C1 Horning Norfk
241 E5 Horninghold Leics
274 C4 Horninglow Staffs
197 G2 Horningsea Cambs
68 D1 Horningsham Wilts
254 B3 Horningtoft Norfk
9 H1 Horningtops Cnwll
44 C5 Hornsbury Somset
401 F4 Hornsby Cumb
39 E3 Horns Cross Devon
58 D2 Horns Cross E Susx
361 G5 Hornsea E R Yk
361 G5 Hornsea Burton E R Yk
119 G2 Hornsey Gt Lon
119 G2 Hornsey Vale Gt Lon
96 C3 Horns Green Gt Lon
82 C3 Horn Street Kent
97 G2 Horn Street Kent
191 F6 Hornton Oxon
113 F3 Horpit Swindn
18 B3 Horrabridge Devon
199 G2 Horringer Suffk
325 F2 Horrocks Fold Bolton
353 E6 Horrocksford Lancs
98 D4 Horsalls Kent
17 F4 Horsebridge Devon
71 G3 Horsebridge Hants
233 G3 Horsebridge Shrops
292 C4 Horse Bridge Staffs
19 F6 Horsebrook Devon
236 C2 Horsebrook Staffs
84 D1 Horsecastle N Som
111 E4 Horsedown Wilts
4 B2 Horsedowns Cnwll
235 F3 Horsehay Wrekin
198 B5 Horseheath Cambs
368 D3 Horsehouse N York
237 E6 Horseley Heath Sandw
93 G3 Horsell Surrey
93 G3 Horsell Birch Surrey
270 A1 Horseman's Green Wrexhm
146 A5 Horseman Side Essex
54 A4 Horsemere Green W Susx
141 G4 Horsenden Bucks
136 B2 Horsepools Gloucs
221 F2 Horseway Cambs
185 F2 Horseway Head Herefs
257 F5 Horsey Norfk
65 F4 Horsey Somset
257 F5 Horsey Corner Norfk
137 G6 Horsey Down Wilts
255 G4 Horsford Norfk
187 G3 Horsham Worcs
76 C3 Horsham W Susx
255 H5 Horsham St Faith Norfk
78 B1 Horshoe Green Kent
319 F6 Horsington Lincs
68 B5 Horsington Somset
294 D6 Horsley Derbys
136 B5 Horsley Gloucs
404 C1 Horsley Nthumb
441 F5 Horsley Nthumb
175 F4 Horsley Cross Essex
175 F4 Horsleycross Street Essex
451 G6 Horsleyhill Border
406 B1 Horsley Hill S Tyne
404 C5 Horsleyhope Dur
141 G3 Horsleys Green Bucks
294 D5 Horsley Woodhouse Derbys
79 G1 Horsmonden Kent
140 C4 Horspath Oxon
256 B6 Horstead Norfk
78 B6 Horsted Green E Susx
77 G4 Horsted Keynes W Susx
168 C6 Horton Bucks
48 C3 Horton Dorset
100 B4 Horton Kent
353 H4 Horton Lancs
193 H4 Horton Nhants
110 D3 Horton S Glos
270 B3 Horton Shrops
44 C5 Horton Somset
292 B3 Horton Staffs
102 C4 Horton Swans
117 H4 Horton W & M
88 B2 Horton Wilts
235 G2 Horton Wrekin
48 D3 Horton Common Dorset
44 C5 Horton Cross Somset
140 D2 Horton-cum-Studley Oxon
289 G5 Horton Green Ches
310 B1 Horton Heath Devon
51 E1 Horton Heath Hants
367 G5 Horton in Ribblesdale N York

121 E6 **Horton Kirby** Kent
234 A2 **Hortonlane** Shrops
168 C6 **Horton Wharf** Bucks
235 F2 **Hortonwood** Wrekin
325 E2 **Horwich** Bolton
312 E3 **Horwich End** Derbys
39 H2 **Horwood** Devon
110 C3 **Horwood Riding** S Glos
324 B2 **Hoscar** Lancs
277 F4 **Hose** Leics
453 E3 **Hoselaw** Border
96 C4 **Hosey Hill** Kent
511 E5 **Hosh** P & K
592 B3 **Hosta** W Isls
605 H6 **Hoswick** Shet
346 C2 **Hotham** E R Yk
99 F6 **Hothfield** Kent
142 B4 **Hotley Bottom** Bucks
276 C5 **Hoton** Leics
109 G5 **Hotwells** Bristl
609 J6 **Houbie** Shet
516 A6 **Hough** Ag & B
291 E4 **Hough** Ches
311 H4 **Hough** Ches
297 G6 **Hougham** Lincs
309 G2 **Hough Green** Halton
297 H5 **Hough-on-the-Hill** Lincs
220 C5 **Houghton** Cambs
400 C3 **Houghton** Cumb
71 G3 **Houghton** Hants
404 D1 **Houghton** Nthumb
125 G3 **Houghton** Pembks
54 B2 **Houghton** W Susx
395 E5 **Houghton Bank** Darltn
169 E1 **Houghton Conquest** Beds
80 D5 **Houghton Green** E Susx
310 C1 **Houghton Green** Warrtn
395 E5 **Houghton-le-Side** Darltn
406 A5 **Houghton-le-Spring** Sundld
241 E4 **Houghton on the Hill** Leics
168 D5 **Houghton Regis** Beds
260 B4 **Houghton St Giles** Norfk
324 C4 **Houghwood** St Hel
605 G2 **Houlland** Shet
605 H6 **Houlland** Shet
606 D7 **Houlland** Shet
607 G1 **Houlland** Shet
386 B3 **Houlsyke** N York
51 E3 **Hound** Hants
92 B3 **Hound Green** Hants
48 B4 **Hound Hill** Dorset
91 G4 **Houndmills** Hants
136 B4 **Houndscroft** Gloucs
473 E5 **Houndslow** Border
43 F2 **Houndsmoor** Somset
45 G4 **Houndstone** Somset
474 B2 **Houndwood** Border
50 C2 **Hounsdown** Hants
85 F2 **Hounsley Batch** N Som
118 C4 **Hounslow** Gt Lon
172 C6 **Hounslow Green** Essex
118 C4 **Hounslow West** Gt Lon
602 B8 **Hourston** Ork
607 G6 **Housabister** Shet
471 H1 **House o' Muir** E Loth
328 C1 **Houses Hill** Kirk
608 D8 **Housetter** Shet
145 H2 **Housham Tye** Essex
605 G4 **Houss** Shet
466 B1 **Houston** Rens
582 F2 **Houstry** Highld
600 E4 **Houton** Ork
55 G4 **Hove** Br & H
342 B5 **Hove Edge** Calder
296 C5 **Hoveringham** Notts
256 C6 **Hoveton** Norfk
373 H5 **Hovingham** N York
401 E3 **How** Cumb
290 D5 **Howbeck Bank** Ches
329 E3 **Howbrook** Barns
161 E3 **How Caple** Herefs
345 G4 **Howden** E R Yk
487 E6 **Howden** W Loth
342 D4 **Howden Clough** Kirk
394 C3 **Howden-le-Wear** Dur
405 H1 **Howdon** N Tyne
406 A1 **Howdon Pans** N Tyne
589 J4 **Howe** Highld
322 b9 **Howe** IoM
250 B4 **Howe** Norfk
370 C3 **Howe** N York
325 F4 **Howe Bridge** Wigan
147 E4 **Howe Green** Essex
147 G4 **Howegreen** Essex
171 H6 **Howe Green** Essex
215 E2 **Howe Green** Warwks
299 E5 **Howell** Lincs
169 E1 **How End** Beds
570 D6 **Howe of Teuchar** Abers
146 D2 **Howe Street** Essex
172 D3 **Howe Street** Essex
183 H3 **Howey** Powys
450 E2 **Howford** Border
450 D5 **Howford** Border
453 E4 **Howgate** Border
388 A5 **Howgate** Cumb
470 D3 **Howgate** Mdloth
380 A5 **Howgill** Cumb
353 G5 **Howgill** Lancs
355 E3 **Howgill** N York
96 C5 **How Green** Kent
256 D6 **How Hill** Norfk
134 C5 **Howick** Mons
455 H6 **Howick** Nthumb
338 C4 **Howick Cross** Lancs
271 F5 **Howle** Shrops
43 G4 **Howleigh** Somset
172 B3 **Howlett End** Essex
135 G6 **Howley** Gloucs
44 B6 **Howley** Somset
310 C2 **Howley** Warrtn
593 D10 **Howmore** W Isls
453 E6 **Hownam** Border
438 C3 **Howpasley** Border
188 A4 **Howsen** Worcs
333 E4 **Howsham** N Linc
358 D2 **Howsham** N York
453 G3 **Howtel** Nthumb
98 D1 **Howt Green** Kent
159 H4 **Howton** Herefs
390 C6 **Howtown** Cumb
143 G4 **How Wood** Herts
466 A3 **Howwood** Rens
601 G6 **Hoxa** Ork
225 G4 **Hoxne** Suffk
600 C4 **Hoy** Ork
308 B2 **Hoylake** Wirral
329 F4 **Hoyland Common** Barns
328 D3 **Hoylandswaine** Barns
75 E6 **Hoyle** W Susx
329 F3 **Hoyle Mill** Barns
96 D4 **Hubbard's Hill** Kent
368 B4 **Hubberholme** N York
125 E3 **Hubberston** Pembks
365 F1 **Hubbersty Head** Cumb
299 H6 **Hubbert's Bridge** Lincs
356 B5 **Huby** N York
357 H1 **Huby** N York
162 C6 **Hucclecote** Gloucs
98 C3 **Hucking** Kent
295 G5 **Hucknall** Notts
327 H1 **Huddersfield** Kirk
188 D3 **Huddington** Worcs

38 D4 **Huddisford** Devon
238 B2 **Huddlesford** Staffs
340 B5 **Hud Hey** Lancs
143 E2 **Hudnall** Herts
134 C4 **Hudnalls** Gloucs
382 D4 **Hudswell** N York
111 F6 **Hudswell** Wilts
359 H3 **Huggate** E R Yk
38 C3 **Hugglepit** Devon
239 G2 **Hugglescote** Leics
142 B5 **Hughenden Valley** Bucks
234 B5 **Hughley** Shrops
340 C5 **Hugh Mill** Lancs
313 E3 **Hugh Town** IoS
326 B5 **Hulme** Manch
292 B5 **Hulme** Staffs
310 C1 **Hulme** Warrtn
293 E3 **Hulme End** Staffs
291 G1 **Hulme Walfield** Ches
311 E3 **Hulseheath** Ches
36 B4 **Hulverstone** IoW
227 F2 **Hulver Street** Suffk
20 B2 **Humber** Devon
186 C3 **Humber** Herefs
334 D3 **Humberston** NE Lin
240 D3 **Humberstone** C Leic
334 D3 **Humberston Fitties** NE Lin
472 B2 **Humbie** E Loth
406 B4 **Humbledon** Sundld
200 B5 **Humble Green** Suffk
348 D3 **Humbleton** E R Yk
454 B4 **Humbleton** Nthumb
279 E3 **Humby** Lincs
452 D1 **Hume** Border
383 G2 **Hummersknott** Darltn
429 E5 **Humshaugh** Nthumb
589 K2 **Huna** Highld
340 B3 **Huncoat** Lancs
240 B5 **Huncote** Leics
452 B6 **Hundalee** Border
314 D4 **Hundall** Derbys
393 G5 **Hunderthwaite** Dur
160 B2 **Hunderton** Herefs
300 C1 **Hundleby** Lincs
299 G4 **Hundle Houses** Lincs
450 A2 **Hundleshope** Border
125 G4 **Hundleton** Pembks
199 E5 **Hundon** Suffk
51 G2 **Hundred Acres** Hants
338 B5 **Hundred End** Lancs
184 B4 **Hundred House** Powys
241 E3 **Hungarton** Leics
343 G4 **Hungate** Leeds
210 C2 **Hungerford** Shrops
63 G3 **Hungerford** Somset
116 D5 **Hungerford** W & M
113 H6 **Hungerford** W Berk
115 F4 **Hungerford Green** W Berk
114 B5 **Hungerford Newtown** W Berk
324 C2 **Hunger Hill** Lancs
325 F3 **Hunger Hill** Lancs
78 D2 **Hungershall Park** Kent
160 A2 **Hungerstone** Herefs
278 B3 **Hungerton** Lincs
542 F2 **Hungladder** Highld
271 F4 **Hungreyhatton** Shrops
374 D4 **Hunmanby** N York
375 E4 **Hunmanby Moor** N York
215 F6 **Hunningham** Warwks
191 F1 **Hunningham Hill** Warwks
213 E3 **Hunnington** Worcs
36 D3 **Hunny Hill** IoW
145 F2 **Hunsdon** Herts
145 F2 **Hunsdonbury** Herts
357 E4 **Hunsingore** N York
343 F3 **Hunslet** Leeds
391 F2 **Hunsonby** Cumb
589 F2 **Hunspow** Highld
258 D3 **Hunstanton** Norfk
403 G5 **Hunstanworth** Dur
290 D5 **Hunsterson** Ches
224 C6 **Hunston** Suffk
53 F4 **Hunston** W Susx
200 C1 **Hunston Green** Suffk
86 A2 **Hunstrete** BaNES
342 C4 **Hunsworth** Kirk
189 F2 **Hunt End** Worcs
87 E5 **Huntenhull Green** Wilts
116 A2 **Huntercombe End** Oxon
100 C2 **Hunters Forstal** Kent
482 A4 **Hunter's Quay** Ag & B
44 C2 **Huntham** Somset
220 B5 **Huntingdon** Cambs
226 C3 **Huntingfield** Suffk
68 D4 **Huntingford** Dorset
135 G6 **Huntingford** Gloucs
289 F2 **Huntington** Ches
471 E4 **Huntington** E Loth
160 B1 **Huntington** Herefs
185 E4 **Huntington** Herefs
237 E2 **Huntington** Staffs
235 E3 **Huntington** Wrekin
358 B4 **Huntington** N York
512 C5 **Huntingtower** P & K
512 C4 **Huntingtower Haugh** P & K
161 G6 **Huntley** Gloucs
273 E1 **Huntley** Staffs
558 C1 **Huntly** Abers
72 C2 **Hunton** Hants
97 H5 **Hunton** Kent
369 G1 **Hunton** N York
603 J6 **Hunton** Ork
224 D2 **Hunt's Corner** Norfk
63 E3 **Huntscott** Somset
309 H3 **Hunt's Cross** Lpool
142 B4 **Hunt's Green** Bucks
238 B5 **Hunts Green** Warwks
114 C6 **Hunt's Green** W Berk
42 C3 **Huntsham** Devon
39 H3 **Huntshaw** Devon
39 H3 **Huntshaw Water** Devon
142 A5 **Hunt's Hill** Bucks
239 H4 **Hunt's Lane** Leics
195 H5 **Huntspill** Somset
65 E5 **Huntstile** Somset
65 F5 **Huntworth** Somset
394 D3 **Hunwick** Dur
261 E4 **Hunworth** Norfk
44 D4 **Hurcott** Somset
67 E4 **Hurcott** Somset
212 C4 **Hurcott** Worcs
70 D3 **Hurdcott** Wilts
233 E6 **Hurdley** Powys

312 B5 **Hurdsfield** Ches
383 E4 **Hurgill** N York
466 D2 **Hurlet** C Glas
116 D3 **Hurley** W & M
238 C5 **Hurley** Warwks
116 D3 **Hurley Bottom** W & M
238 C5 **Hurley Common** Warwks
445 G2 **Hurlford** E Ayrs
600 D7 **Hurliness** Ork
323 G2 **Hurlston** Lancs
323 G2 **Hurlston Green** Lancs
49 E5 **Hurn** Dorset
347 F1 **Hurn** E R Yk
29 H2 **Hursey** Dorset
72 B5 **Hursley** Hants
390 C1 **Hurst** Cumb
32 D1 **Hurst** Dorset
382 B4 **Hurst** N York
66 B6 **Hurst** Somset
326 D4 **Hurst** Tamesd
116 C5 **Hurst** Wokham
90 C5 **Hurstbourne Priors** Hants
90 B4 **Hurstbourne Tarrant** Hants
326 D1 **Hurstead** Rochdl
213 E2 **Hurst Green** Dudley
149 E1 **Hurst Green** Essex
79 G4 **Hurst Green** E Susx
339 G2 **Hurst Green** Lancs
96 A4 **Hurst Green** Surrey
236 D6 **Hurst Hill** Dudley
185 F5 **Hurstley** Herefs
118 C6 **Hurst Park** Surrey
55 G1 **Hurstpierpoint** W Susx
55 G1 **Hurst Wickham** W Susx
340 D3 **Hurstwood** Lancs
601 J4 **Hurtiso** Ork
93 G5 **Hurtmore** Surrey
383 H2 **Hurworth-on-Tees** Darltn
383 G2 **Hurworth Place** Darltn
393 G6 **Hury** Dur
216 D2 **Husbands Bosworth** Leics
168 D2 **Husborne Crawley** Beds
371 G4 **Husthwaite** N York
12 D1 **Hutcherleigh** Devon
467 E2 **Hutchesontown** C Glas
344 D5 **Hut Green** N York
295 F3 **Huthwaite** Notts
451 E5 **Hutlerburn** Border
340 D5 **Huttock Top** Lancs
321 F4 **Huttoft** Lincs
474 D4 **Hutton** Border
390 C4 **Hutton** Cumb
360 C4 **Hutton** E R Yk
146 C4 **Hutton** Essex
84 B3 **Hutton** N Som
384 A4 **Hutton Bonville** N York
374 B3 **Hutton Buscel** N York
370 C5 **Hutton Conyers** N York
360 C4 **Hutton Cranswick** E R Yk
390 C4 **Hutton End** Cumb
385 F1 **Hutton Gate** R & Cl
369 F4 **Hutton Hang** N York
396 B2 **Hutton Henry** Dur
372 D2 **Hutton-le-Hole** N York
382 D2 **Hutton Magna** Dur
146 C6 **Hutton Mount** Essex
366 B4 **Hutton Roof** Cumb
390 B4 **Hutton Roof** Cumb
384 D3 **Hutton Rudby** N York
373 E6 **Huttons Ambo** N York
371 F4 **Hutton Sessay** N York
385 E2 **Hutton Village** R & Cl
357 G4 **Hutton Wandesley** N York
27 E3 **Huxham** Devon
67 F2 **Huxham Green** Somset
289 G2 **Huxley** Ches
606 A6 **Huxter** Shet
606 E7 **Huxter** Shet
607 J5 **Huxter** Shet
309 G1 **Huyton** Knows
309 F1 **Huyton Park** Knows
309 G1 **Huyton Quarry** Knows
309 F1 **Huyton-with-Roby** Knows
362 B4 **Hycemoor** Cumb
30 B4 **Hyde** Dorset
136 C4 **Hyde** Gloucs
163 G4 **Hyde** Gloucs
49 F2 **Hyde** Hants
72 C3 **Hyde** Hants
186 B4 **Hyde** Herefs
327 E6 **Hyde** Tamesd
147 F4 **Hyde Chase** Essex
91 F2 **Hyde End** W Berk
142 C4 **Hyde Heath** Bucks
272 C3 **Hyde Lea** Staffs
330 C4 **Hyde Park** Donc
75 F1 **Hydestile** Surrey
406 B3 **Hylton Castle** Sundld
406 B3 **Hylton Red House** Sundld
256 A4 **Hyltons Crossways** Norfk
340 A3 **Hyndburn Bridge** Lancs
448 B1 **Hyndford Bridge** S Lans
450 B2 **Hyndhope** Border
516 B8 **Hynish** Ag & B
586 C6 **Hysbackie** Highld
233 F6 **Hyssington** Powys
135 F5 **Hystfield** Gloucs
50 D3 **Hythe** Hants
82 C4 **Hythe** Kent
84 D4 **Hythe** Kent
117 H5 **Hythe End** W & M
571 J5 **Hythie** Abers
362 B4 **Hyton** Cumb

569 G2 **Ianstown** Moray
598 D8 **Iarsiadar** W Isls
47 E3 **Ibberton** Dorset
294 A3 **Ible** Derbys
467 E2 **Ibrox** C Glas
49 F3 **Ibsley** Hants
239 G2 **Ibstock** Leics
141 G6 **Ibstone** Bucks
90 B4 **Ibthorpe** Hants
387 F4 **Iburndale** N York
91 F4 **Ibworth** Hants
84 C1 **Icelton** N Som
507 H3 **Ichrachan** Ag & B
247 G6 **Ickburgh** Norfk
118 B2 **Ickenham** Gt Lon
364 D2 **Ickenthwaite** Cumb
140 D3 **Ickford** Bucks
84 B3 **Ickham** Kent
170 A3 **Ickleford** Herts
59 E3 **Icklesham** E Susx
197 G6 **Ickleton** Cambs
223 F5 **Icklingham** Suffk
354 C6 **Ickornshaw** N York
195 H5 **Ickwell** Beds
195 H5 **Ickwell Green** Beds
164 C5 **Icomb** Gloucs
12 B3 **Icy Park** Devon
164 C6 **Idbury** Oxon
40 B6 **Iddesleigh** Devon
26 D4 **Ide** Devon
20 B2 **Ideford** Devon
96 C4 **Ide Hill** Kent
80 D5 **Iden** E Susx
79 G2 **Iden Green** Kent
80 A3 **Iden Green** Kent

342 C2 **Idle** Brad
342 C2 **Idle Moor** Brad
7 F4 **Idless** Cnwll
190 D6 **Idlicote** Warwks
70 D2 **Idmiston** Wilts
128 B1 **Idole** Carmth
294 B5 **Idridgehay** Derbys
294 B5 **Idridgehay Green** Derbys
542 F4 **Idrigill** Highld
113 G3 **Idstone** Oxon
528 B5 **Idvies** Angus
140 B4 **Iffley** Oxon
76 D2 **Ifield** W Susx
77 E2 **Ifield Green** W Susx
76 D2 **Ifieldwood** W Susx
75 G3 **Ifold** W Susx
49 E6 **Iford** Bmouth
56 C3 **Iford** E Susx
269 F2 **Ifton Heath** Shrops
270 D2 **Ightfield** Shrops
270 D2 **Ightfield Heath** Shrops
97 E3 **Ightham** Kent
97 E3 **Igtham Common** Kent
203 E3 **Iken** Suffk
293 F4 **Ilam** Staffs
67 E5 **Ilchester** Somset
67 E5 **Ilchester Mead** Somset
454 C5 **Ilderton** Nthumb
100 D5 **Ileden** Kent
120 B2 **Ilford** Gt Lon
44 D4 **Ilford** Somset
60 D2 **Ilfracombe** Devon
275 G1 **Ilkeston** Derbys
226 D2 **Ilketshall St Andrew** Suffk
226 D3 **Ilketshall St Lawrence** Suffk
226 C2 **Ilketshall St Margaret** Suffk
355 F5 **Ilkley** Brad
16 C3 **Illand** Cnwll
213 E3 **Illey** Dudley
291 F2 **Illidge Green** Ches
224 B2 **Illington** Norfk
341 H4 **Illingworth** Calder
6 C5 **Illogan** Cnwll
6 C5 **Illogan Highway** Cnwll
214 A5 **Illshaw Heath** Solhll
241 F5 **Illston on the Hill** Leics
141 G3 **Ilmer** Bucks
190 B6 **Ilmington** Warwks
44 D5 **Ilminster** Somset
19 G2 **Ilsington** Devon
103 E3 **Ilston** Swans
369 G4 **Ilton** N York
44 C4 **Ilton** Somset
460 B1 **Imachar** N Ayrs
87 H5 **Imber** Wilts
476 E7 **Imeraval** Ag & B
334 A2 **Immingham** NE Lin
334 A1 **Immingham Dock** NE Lin
197 G2 **Impington** Cambs
309 G4 **Ince** Ches
323 F4 **Ince Blundell** Sefton
324 D4 **Ince-in-Makerfield** Wigan
528 D1 **Inchbare** Angus
568 E4 **Inchberry** Moray
529 E3 **Inchbraoch** Angus
136 B4 **Inchbrook** Gloucs
563 J4 **Incheril** Highld
539 E4 **Inchgrundle** Angus
573 J5 **Inchina** Highld
470 D1 **Inchinnan** C Edin
483 G6 **Inchinnan** Rens
533 J2 **Inchlaggan** Highld
554 D5 **Inchmarnoch** Abers
548 F1 **Inchmore** Highld
565 K7 **Inchmore** Highld
579 J5 **Inchnadamph** Highld
520 E3 **Inchree** Highld
14 D6 **Inchs** Cnwll
513 E5 **Inchture** P & K
513 E5 **Inchyra** P & K
7 H2 **Indian Queens** Cnwll
476 E8 **Ineraval** Ag & B
146 D5 **Ingatestone** Essex
328 C3 **Ingbirchworth** Barns
356 B1 **Ingerthorpe** N York
273 E5 **Ingestre** Staffs
318 A3 **Ingham** Lincs
256 D4 **Ingham** Norfk
223 G5 **Ingham** Suffk
256 D4 **Ingham Corner** Norfk
245 G2 **Ingleborough** Norfk
275 E4 **Ingleby** Derbys
384 C4 **Ingleby Arncliffe** N York
384 D4 **Ingleby Cross** N York
385 F3 **Ingleby Greenhow** N York
25 F1 **Ingleigh Green** Devon
347 G3 **Inglemire** C KuH
86 B2 **Inglesbatch** BaNES
138 B5 **Inglesham** Swindn
394 D5 **Ingleton** Dur
366 D5 **Ingleton** N York
338 D2 **Inglewhite** Lancs
527 F5 **Ingliston** Angus
487 F5 **Ingliston** C Edin
357 E4 **Ingmanthorpe** N York
429 G4 **Ingoe** Nthumb
338 D3 **Ingol** Lancs
258 D5 **Ingoldisthorpe** Norfk
321 G6 **Ingoldmells** Lincs
279 E3 **Ingoldsby** Lincs
190 C3 **Ingon** Warwks
442 C1 **Ingram** Nthumb
74 C5 **Ingrams Green** W Susx
121 F1 **Ingrave** Essex
341 G2 **Ingrow** Brad
378 D5 **Ings** Cumb
109 J2 **Ingst** S Glos
242 D3 **Ingthorpe** Rutlnd
255 G2 **Ingworth** Norfk
91 F2 **Inhurst** Hants
189 F3 **Inkberrow** Worcs
394 B2 **Inkerman** Dur
315 E5 **Inkersall** Derbys
315 E5 **Inkersall Green** Derbys
213 G5 **Inkford** Worcs
560 D2 **Inkhorn** Abers
90 B2 **Inkpen** W Berk
90 B2 **Inkpen Common** W Berk
589 H2 **Inkstack** Highld
52 D3 **Inlands** W Susx
87 G2 **Inmarsh** Wilts
481 H5 **Innellan** Ag & B
523 J4 **Innerhadden** P & K
12 B5 **Inner Hope** Devon
450 C2 **Innerleithen** Border
514 D6 **Innerleven** Fife
415 E4 **Innermessan** D & G
600 C3 **Innerton** Worcs
490 D5 **Innerwick** E Loth
523 G6 **Innerwick** P & K
507 K4 **Innis Chonain** Ag & B
575 K3 **Innis nan Damh** Highld
86 D5 **Innox Hill** Somset
139 G4 **Innsworth** Gloucs
559 E4 **Insch** Abers
556 B2 **Insh** Highld
584 D5 **Inshegra** Highld
584 F3 **Inshore** Highld
534 D5 **Inskip** Lancs
338 C2 **Inskip Moss Side** Lancs
60 C5 **Instow** Devon
235 E2 **Insworke** Cnwll

339 H4 **Intack** Bl w D
330 C4 **Intake** Donc
314 D3 **Intake** Sheff
188 A5 **Interfield** Worcs
249 G4 **Intwood** Norfk
537 K4 **Inver** Abers
577 J7 **Inver** Highld
512 B1 **Inver** P & K
531 L6 **Inverailort** Highld
545 H1 **Inveralligin** Highld
562 E5 **Inveralligin** Highld
571 J2 **Inverallochy** Abers
559 G5 **Inveramsay** Abers
576 C4 **Inveran** Highld
494 B3 **Inveraray** Ag & B
545 K2 **Inverarish** Highld
527 G6 **Inverarity** Angus
508 D6 **Inverarnan** Stirlg
495 G5 **Inverbeg** Ag & B
541 F5 **Inverbervie** Abers
570 B3 **Inverboyndie** Abers
550 E3 **Inverbrough** Highld
575 K3 **Invercassley** Highld
481 F4 **Invercharnain** Ag & B
521 G6 **Invercharnan** Highld
564 C6 **Inverchoran** Highld
520 E6 **Invercreran** Ag & B
551 G7 **Inverdruie** Highld
560 D3 **Inverebrie** Abers
525 H2 **Invereddrie** P & K
488 C5 **Inveresk** E Loth
507 G2 **Inveresragan** Ag & B
537 G5 **Inverey** Abers
549 J5 **Inverfarigaig** Highld
520 C7 **Inverfolla** Ag & B
534 B2 **Invergarry** Highld
537 K4 **Invergelder** Abers
510 C4 **Invergeldie** P & K
566 C3 **Invergordon** Highld
514 A3 **Invergowrie** P & K
546 C8 **Inverguseran** Highld
553 H2 **Inverharroch** Moray
531 L3 **Inverie** Highld
507 G6 **Inverinan** Ag & B
547 G5 **Inverinate** Highld
529 E5 **Inverkeilor** Angus
487 F3 **Inverkeithing** Fife
569 L6 **Inverkeithny** Abers
482 A5 **Inverkip** Inver
578 E6 **Inverkirkaig** Highld
574 D6 **Inverlael** Highld
534 B7 **Inverlair** Highld
488 A4 **Inverleith** C Edin
508 F6 **Inverlochlarig** Stirlg
533 H8 **Inverlochy** Highld
479 G4 **Inverlussa** Ag & B
531 J8 **Invermoidart** Highld
549 G6 **Invermoriston** Highld
586 E4 **Invernaver** Highld
480 A3 **Inverneill** Ag & B
566 B8 **Inverness** Highld
571 L7 **Invernettie** Abers
494 C3 **Invernoaden** Ag & B
527 E3 **Inverquharity** Angus
571 J6 **Inverquhomery** Abers
533 L6 **Inverroy** Highld
520 C4 **Inversanda** Highld
547 G6 **Invershiel** Highld
576 C4 **Invershin** Highld
583 H3 **Invershore** Highld
495 G3 **Inversnaid** Stirlg
571 K6 **Inverugie** Abers
495 G5 **Inveruglas** Ag & B
536 B2 **Inveruglass** Highld
578 F5 **Inveruplan** Highld
559 G5 **Inverurie** Abers
523 J6 **Invervar** P & K
559 G1 **Inverythan** Abers
24 D3 **Inwardleigh** Devon
234 B5 **Inwood** Shrops
173 H6 **Inworth** Essex
593 D8 **Iochdar** W Isls
592 D5 **Iolaraigh** W Isls
74 D5 **Iping** W Susx
20 A4 **Ipplepen** Devon
115 G2 **Ipsden** Oxon
189 G1 **Ipsley** Worcs
292 D5 **Ipstones** Staffs
176 C1 **Ipswich** Suffk
308 C3 **Irby** Wirral
301 E2 **Irby in the Marsh** Lincs
334 A4 **Irby Upon Humber** NE Lin
194 C1 **Irchester** Nhants
389 F2 **Ireby** Cumb
366 D4 **Ireby** Lancs
169 G1 **Ireland** Beds
600 E3 **Ireland** Ork
605 G6 **Ireland** Shet
87 E4 **Ireland** Wilts
271 G1 **Ireland's Cross** Shrops
343 E2 **Ireland Wood** Leeds
363 E6 **Ireleth** Cumb
393 E2 **Ireshopeburn** Dur
294 B5 **Ireton Wood** Derbys
325 G6 **Irlam** Salfd
279 E4 **Irnham** Lincs
110 B3 **Iron Acton** S Glos
245 G5 **Iron Bridge** Cambs
235 F4 **Ironbridge** Wrekin
189 F4 **Iron Cross** Warwks
423 F4 **Irongray** D & G
421 H4 **Ironmacannie** D & G
95 F5 **Irons Bottom** Surrey
295 E4 **Ironville** Derbys
256 D5 **Irstead** Norfk
256 D6 **Irstead Street** Norfk
401 F2 **Irthington** Cumb
218 C5 **Irthlingborough** Nhants
374 C3 **Irton** N York
444 D2 **Irvine** N Ayrs
340 B5 **Irwell Vale** Lancs
431 E3 **Isabella Pit** Nthumb
302 B5 **Isallt Bach** IoA
588 B3 **Isauld** Highld
602 B7 **Isbister** Ork
602 D8 **Isbister** Ork
607 J5 **Isbister** Shet
608 D6 **Isbister** Shet
389 E3 **Isel** Cumb
56 C1 **Isfield** E Susx
218 B5 **Isham** Nhants
92 C6 **Isington** Hants
332 D3 **Island Carr** N Linc
196 A2 **Islands Common** Cambs
44 D3 **Isle Abbotts** Somset
44 D3 **Isle Brewers** Somset
222 C5 **Isleham** Cambs
331 G5 **Isle of Axholme** N Linc
423 H4 **Isle of Man** D & G
411 E5 **Isle of Whithorn** D & G
546 B7 **Isleornsay or Eilean Iarmain** Highld
606 D4 **Islesburgh** Shet
423 C5 **Islesteps** D & G
35 d2 **Islet Village** Guern
118 C4 **Isleworth** Gt Lon
275 C5 **Isley Walton** Leics
596 B2 **Islibhig** W Isls
119 G2 **Islington** Gt Lon
218 D4 **Islip** Nhants
140 B2 **Islip** Oxon
596 B2 **Isliving** W Isls
235 E2 **Isombridge** Wrekin
121 F6 **Istead Rise** Kent

696 City, town and village index: Isycoed - Kings Ripton

289 F4 Isycoed Wrexhm
50 D2 Itchen C Soth
72 D3 Itchen Abbas Hants
73 E3 Itchen Stoke Hants
76 B4 Itchingfield W Susx
110 B2 Itchington S Glos
281 F5 Itteringham Norfk
255 G2 Itteringham Common Norfk
25 G3 Itton Devon
134 B5 Itton Mons
134 B5 Itton Common Mons
400 D6 Ivegill Cumb
381 G5 Ivelet N York
118 A3 Iver Bucks
118 A3 Iver Heath Bucks
212 C3 Iverley Staffs
404 D4 Iveston Dur
236 B2 Ivetsey Bank Staffs
142 C1 Ivinghoe Bucks
168 C6 Ivinghoe Aston Bucks
186 B3 Ivington Herefs
186 B3 Ivington Green Herefs
12 A1 Ivybridge Devon
145 G4 Ivy Chimneys Essex
81 F4 Ivychurch Kent
69 E5 Ivy Cross Dorset
97 E4 Ivy Hatch Kent
248 A3 Ivy Todd Norfk
123 E6 Iwade Kent
47 F2 Iwerne Courtney or Shroton Dorset
47 G2 Iwerne Minster Dorset
84 D2 Iwood N Som
224 B5 Ixworth Suffk
224 B5 Ixworth Thorpe Suffk

J

399 E4 Jack Green Lancs
355 G4 Jack Hill N York
27 G3 Jack-in-the-Green Devon
295 E4 Jacksdale Notts
172 B5 Jack's Green Essex
136 C2 Jack's Green Gloucs
328 B3 Jackson Bridge Kirk
559 G3 Jackstown Abers
467 E4 Jackton S Lans
22 D3 Jacobstow Cnwll
25 E2 Jacobstowe Devon
93 G4 Jacobs Well Surrey
342 A6 Jagger Green Calder
126 B5 Jameston Pembks
438 B5 Jamestown D & G
565 H5 Jamestown Highld
483 E3 Jamestown W Duns
500 C5 Jamphlars Fife
588 D3 Janetstown Highld
589 J6 Janetstown Highld
174 B4 Janke's Green Essex
406 A1 Jarrow S Tyne
78 C3 Jarvis Brook E Susx
173 E4 Jasper's Green Essex
505 L3 Java Ag & B
485 G5 Jawcraig Falk
343 E5 Jaw Hill Leeds
149 F2 Jaywick Essex
117 E5 Jealott's Hill Br For
472 C6 Jeaniefield Border
452 B5 Jedburgh Border
126 B3 Jeffreyston Pembks
566 C3 Jemimaville Highld
115 F5 Jennetts Hill W Berk
356 B3 Jennyfield N York
35 d4 Jerbourg Guern
326 B2 Jericho Bury
103 H3 Jersey Marine Neath
468 D5 Jerviswood S Lans
405 G1 Jesmond N u Ty
57 F4 Jevington E Susx
23 F2 Jewell's Cross Devon
134 B2 Jingle Street Mons
143 E2 Jockey End Herts
311 F5 Jodrell Bank Ches
390 C3 Johnby Cumb
241 F3 John O'Gaunt Leics
589 K2 John o' Groats Highld
58 B2 John's Cross E Susx
529 G1 Johnshaven Abers
325 F2 Johnson Fold Bolton
339 E5 Johnson's Hillock Lancs
256 D6 Johnson Street Norfk
125 F2 Johnston Pembks
466 B2 Johnstone Rens
424 B1 Johnstonebridge D & G
154 A6 Johnstown Carmth
288 D5 Johnstown Wrexhm
6 D4 Jolly's Bottom Cnwll
488 C5 Joppa C Edin
3 G2 Joppa Cnwll
445 F6 Joppa S Ayrs
255 E3 Jordan Green Norfk
117 G1 Jordans Bucks
151 F3 Jordanston Pembks
314 D3 Jordanthorpe Sheff
329 G6 Jordon Rothm
484 A6 Jordonhill C Glas
120 D5 Joyden's Wood Kent
134 D2 Joyford Gloucs
135 E1 Joy's Green Gloucs
326 D2 Jubilee Oldham
271 H2 Jugbank Staffs
329 F4 Jump Barns
49 E6 Jumpers Common Dorset
78 B3 Jumper's Town E Susx
403 G3 Juniper Nthumb
487 G6 Juniper Green C Edin
322 f3 Jurby IoM
25 G6 Jurston Devon
59 G3 Jury's Gap E Susx

K

380 D2 Kaber Cumb
469 F5 Kaimend S Lans
488 B6 Kaimes C Edin
557 G4 Kaimhill C Aber
449 E1 Kaimrig End Border
606 E8 Kalliness Shet
480 D5 Kames Ag & B
446 D4 Kames E Ayrs
213 E1 Kates Hill Dudley
7 F5 Kea Cnwll
332 A2 Keadby N Linc
300 C2 Keal Cotes Lincs
356 C5 Kearby Town End N York
356 C5 Kearby with Netherby N York
83 E2 Kearnsey Kent
325 H4 Kearsley Bolton
366 B4 Kearstwick Cumb
382 A5 Kearton N York
584 E2 Kearvaig Highld
353 E1 Keasden N York
341 G5 Kebroyd Calder
310 B3 Keckwick Halton
320 B2 Keddington Lincs
320 C2 Keddington Corner Lincs
199 E5 Kedington Suffk
275 E1 Kedleston Derbys
514 B6 Kedlock Fife
514 B5 Kedlock Feus Fife
451 G1 Kedslie Border
376 B1 Keekle Cumb
174 D5 Keelars Tye Essex
333 H2 Keelby Lincs
291 G6 Keele Staffs
195 E5 Keeley Green Beds
342 A3 Keelham Brad
402 D3 Keenley Nthumb
64 D4 Keenthorne Somset
146 B2 Keeres Green Essex
151 F6 Keeston Pembks
87 G3 Keevil Wilts
276 A4 Kegworth Leics
6 B5 Kehelland Cnwll
559 E6 Keig Abers
341 H1 Keighley Brad
498 D6 Keilarsbrae Clacks
570 C4 Keilhill Abers
479 H5 Keillbeg Ag & B
479 H5 Keillmore Ag & B
513 G1 Keillor P & K
511 H4 Keillour P & K
478 C8 Keills Ag & B
478 E8 Keils Ag & B
67 F3 Keinton Mandeville Somset
435 H6 Keir Mill D & G
279 E4 Keisby Lincs
589 J4 Keiss Highld
543 G6 Keistle Highld
569 G5 Keith Moray
571 L6 Keith Inch Abers
528 C2 Keithock Angus
354 B6 Kelbrook Lancs
465 E3 Kelburn N Ayrs
279 E1 Kelby Lincs
355 G6 Kelcliffe Leeds
379 F2 Keld Cumb
381 F4 Keld N York
372 D2 Keldholme N York
355 F2 Keld Houses N York
331 H4 Kelfield N Linc
344 D2 Kelfield N York
297 E3 Kelham Notts
424 C6 Kelhead D & G
24 A5 Kellacott Devon
338 B4 Kellamergh Lancs
505 G2 Kellan Ag & B
505 G2 Kellan Mill Ag & B
514 C2 Kellas Angus
568 B5 Kellas Moray
12 D5 Kellaton Devon
111 H4 Kellaways Wilts
380 B3 Kelleth Cumb
360 C3 Kelleythorpe E R Yk
261 E3 Kelling Norfk
344 C5 Kellingley N York
344 D5 Kellington N York
609 G4 Kellister Shet
395 G2 Kelloe Dur
435 E2 Kelloholm D & G
376 B1 Kells Cumb
15 E4 Kelly Cnwll
17 E2 Kelly Devon
17 E4 Kelly Bray Cnwll
217 F4 Kelmarsh Nhants
138 D5 Kelmscott Oxon
202 D1 Kelsale Suffk
309 H6 Kelsall Ches
170 D2 Kelshall Herts
399 F4 Kelsick Cumb
452 D3 Kelso Border
294 C2 Kelstedge Derbys
319 G1 Kelstern Lincs
308 C5 Kelsterton Flints
86 C1 Kelston BaNES
523 L6 Keltneyburn P & K
423 G5 Kelton D & G
393 F5 Kelton Dur
500 B6 Kelty Fife
500 B5 Keltybridge P & K
173 G6 Kelvedon Essex
146 B5 Kelvedon Hatch Essex
467 F4 Kelvin S Lans
484 B6 Kelvindale C Glas
484 B6 Kelvinside C Glas
2 C4 Kelynack Cnwll
61 G2 Kemacott Devon
502 C1 Kemback Fife
235 G4 Kemberton Shrops
137 E5 Kemble Gloucs
137 E5 Kemble Wick Gloucs
162 D2 Kemerton Worcs
133 F4 Kemeys Commander Mons
311 G6 Kemincham Ches
556 C1 Kemnay Abers
99 G5 Kempe's Corner Kent
161 F4 Kempley Gloucs
161 F4 Kempley Green Gloucs
188 C5 Kempsey Worcs
138 B5 Kempsford Gloucs
214 A5 Kemps Green Warwks
91 G4 Kempshott Hants
195 E5 Kempston Beds
195 E5 Kempston Church End Beds
195 E6 Kempston Hardwick Beds
194 D5 Kempston West End Beds
23 G3 Kempthorne Devon
209 G3 Kempton Shrops
55 H4 Kemp Town Br & H
97 E3 Kemsing Kent
99 E1 Kemsley Kent
98 C2 Kemsley Street Kent
81 E3 Kenardington Kent
186 A6 Kenchester Herefs
138 D4 Kencot Oxon
379 F6 Kendal Cumb
213 E5 Kendal End Worcs
159 H4 Kenderchurch Herefs
110 B4 Kendleshire S Glos
132 C5 Kendon Caerph
421 G2 Kendoon D & G
543 G2 Kendram Highld
329 F4 Kendray Barns
104 B3 Kenfig Brdgnd
104 C3 Kenfig Hill Brdgnd
214 D5 Kenilworth Warwks
509 G2 Kenknock Stirlg
234 D4 Kenley Shrops
95 G3 Kenley Surrey
562 D5 Kenmore Highld
523 L6 Kenmore P & K
27 E5 Kenn Devon
108 D6 Kenn N Som
462 D2 Kennacraig Ag & B
23 F6 Kennards House Cnwll
3 G4 Kenneggy Cnwll
3 G4 Kenneggy Downs Cnwll
26 C1 Kennerleigh Devon
486 B1 Kennet Clacks
198 D1 Kennet End Cambs
558 C4 Kennethmont Abers
222 D6 Kennett Cambs
27 E5 Kennford Devon
224 D2 Kenninghall Norfk
119 G4 Kennington Gt Lon
99 G6 Kennington Kent
140 B4 Kennington Oxon
121 E3 Kennington Park Gt Lon
466 D2 Kennishead C Glas
108 D6 Kenn Moor Gate N Som
501 G4 Kennoway Fife
44 C4 Kenny Somset
222 D4 Kenny Hill Suffk
359 E1 Kennythorpe N York
516 B6 Kenovay Ag & B
543 G6 Kensaleyre Highld
119 E3 Kensal Green Gt Lon
119 F4 Kensington Gt Lon
309 E1 Kensington Lpool
169 E6 Kensworth Beds
520 E4 Kentallen Highld
159 H4 Kentchurch Herefs
199 E1 Kentford Suffk
43 E6 Kentisbeare Devon
61 F3 Kentisbury Devon
61 F3 Kentisbury Ford Devon
378 D4 Kentmere Cumb
27 E6 Kenton Devon
118 D2 Kenton Gt Lon
405 F1 Kenton N u Ty
201 G1 Kenton Suffk
430 D6 Kenton Bankfoot N u Ty
430 D6 Kenton Bar N u Ty
201 H1 Kenton Corner Suffk
136 A2 Kenton Green Gloucs
518 F2 Kentra Highld
379 F6 Kentrigg Cumb
22 D3 Kents Cnwll
365 E4 Kents Bank Cumb
161 G5 Kent's Green Gloucs
168 B2 Kents Hill M Keyn
71 G5 Kent's Oak Hants
97 G4 Kent Street Kent
76 D5 Kent Street W Susx
269 H3 Kenwick Shrops
269 H4 Kenwick Park Shrops
7 F4 Kenwyn Cnwll
325 E5 Kenyon Warrtn
585 G3 Keoldale Highld
497 E6 Kepdowrie Stirlg
89 E3 Kepnal Wilts
520 E3 Keppanach Highld
547 G5 Keppoch Highld
371 F1 Kepwick N York
255 E3 Kerdiston Norfk
215 E3 Keresley Covtry
215 E2 Keresley Newlands Warwks
450 B2 Kerfield Border
7 E5 Kerley Downs Cnwll
12 D4 Kernborough Devon
160 D6 Kerne Bridge Herefs
312 B4 Kerridge Ches
312 B5 Kerridge-end Ches
2 D4 Kerris Cnwll
548 E3 Kerrow Highld
208 B2 Kerry Powys
464 B2 Kerrycroy Ag & B
292 B5 Kerry Hill Staffs
562 E2 Kerrysdale Highld
159 G3 Kerry's Gate Herefs
326 B4 Kersal Salfd
296 D2 Kersall Notts
27 H6 Kersbrook Devon
16 D3 Kersbrook Cross Cnwll
40 C2 Kerscott Devon
200 D6 Kersey Suffk
200 C6 Kersey Tye Suffk
200 C6 Kersey Upland Suffk
597 J4 Kershader W Isls
426 C3 Kershopefoot Cumb
163 E2 Kersoe Worcs
28 A1 Kerswell Devon
188 C5 Kerswell Green Worcs
3 G3 Kerthen Wood Cnwll
201 H6 Kesgrave Suffk
227 G2 Kessingland Suffk
227 G2 Kessingland Beach Suffk
8 B4 Kestle Cnwll
7 F2 Kestle Mill Cnwll
96 B2 Keston Gt Lon
96 B1 Keston Mark Gt Lon
389 G5 Keswick Cumb
249 H4 Keswick Norfk
256 D3 Keswick Norfk
124 D4 Kete Pembks
161 G3 Ketford Gloucs
235 F2 Ketley Wrekin
235 F2 Ketley Bank Wrekin
320 C4 Ketsby Lincs
218 B4 Kettering Nhants
249 G4 Ketteringham Norfk
513 F2 Kettins P & K
200 C4 Kettlebaston Suffk
501 F3 Kettlebridge Fife
238 C4 Kettlebrook Staffs
202 B2 Kettleburgh Suffk
97 H4 Kettle Corner Kent
171 F6 Kettle Green Herts
501 F3 Kettlehill Fife
424 C4 Kettleholm D & G
386 D1 Kettleness N York
312 C4 Kettleshulme Ches
355 H3 Kettlesing N York
356 A3 Kettlesing Bottom N York
607 H2 Kettlester Shet
260 C5 Kettlestone Norfk
317 F4 Kettlethorpe Lincs
329 E1 Kettlethorpe Wakefd
603 K4 Kettletoft Ork
368 C5 Kettlewell N York
242 D4 Ketton Rutlnd
120 C6 Kevingtown Gt Lon
118 D4 Kew Gt Lon
85 F6 Keward Somset
84 B2 Kewstoke N Som
328 D3 Kexbrough Barns
317 G2 Kexby Lincs
358 C4 Kexby York
15 F4 Keybridge Cnwll
98 D2 Keycol Kent
86 D5 Keyford Somset
292 A2 Key Green Ches
386 C4 Key Green N York
241 E3 Keyham Leics
35 H2 Keyhaven Hants
571 K4 Keyhead Abers
348 D4 Keyingham E R Yk
55 H1 Keymer W Susx
86 A1 Keynsham BaNES
145 E3 Keysers Estate Essex
79 F2 Key's Green Kent
195 F2 Keysoe Beds
195 F2 Keysoe Row Beds
219 E4 Keyston Cambs
98 D2 Key Street Kent
276 C3 Keyworth Notts
405 F3 Kibblesworth Gatesd
241 E6 Kibworth Beauchamp Leics
241 E6 Kibworth Harcourt Leics
120 B4 Kidbrooke Gt Lon
388 C5 Kidburngill Cumb
343 H2 Kiddal Lane End Leeds
236 B3 Kiddemore Green Staffs
212 B4 Kidderminster Worcs
165 G5 Kiddington Oxon
571 G7 Kiddshill Abers
249 F4 Kidd's Moor Norfk
140 A1 Kidlington Oxon
116 A4 Kidmore End Oxon
289 G5 Kidnal Ches
410 D5 Kidsdale D & G
291 G4 Kidsgrove Staffs
368 B3 Kidstones N York
128 B3 Kidwelly Carmth
506 F2 Kiel Crofts Ag & B
440 B6 Kielder Nthumb
115 F6 Kiff Green W Berk
466 B2 Kilbarchan Rens
531 H1 Kilbeg Highld
462 B2 Kilberry Ag & B
465 G4 Kilbirnie N Ayrs
483 G5 Kilbowie W Duns
492 C1 Kilbride Ag & B
506 E4 Kilbride Ag & B
545 K5 Kilbride Highld
481 E1 Kilbridemore Ag & B
294 D5 Kilburn Derbys
119 E3 Kilburn Gt Lon
371 G4 Kilburn N York
240 D5 Kilby Leics
240 D5 Kilby Bridge Leics
462 D2 Kilchamaig Ag & B
464 C3 Kilchattan Bay Ag & B
456 D2 Kilchenzie Ag & B
506 D2 Kilcheran Ag & B
476 B4 Kilchiaran Ag & B
518 C3 Kilchoan Highld
476 C4 Kilchoman Ag & B
507 H5 Kilchrenan Ag & B
502 D4 Kilconquhar Fife
161 F4 Kilcot Gloucs
565 K6 Kilcoy Highld
482 B3 Kilcreggan Ag & B
385 F3 Kildale N York
457 F3 Kildalloig Ag & B
566 D1 Kildary Highld
463 H1 Kildavanan Ag & B
542 E5 Kildonan Highld
461 E5 Kildonan N Ayrs
530 E5 Kildonnan Highld
485 F5 Kildrum N Lans
555 E1 Kildrummy Abers
503 F2 Kilduncan Fife
354 D5 Kildwick N York
480 C4 Kilfinan Ag & B
533 L3 Kilfinnan Highld
126 C3 Kilgetty Pembks
432 B4 Kilgrammie S Ayrs
134 B5 Kilgwrrwg Common Mons
8 D2 Kilhallon Cnwll
360 D2 Kilham E R Yk
453 G3 Kilham Nthumb
516 A7 Kilkenneth Ag & B
163 E6 Kilkenny Gloucs
457 E3 Kilkerran Ag & B
432 D4 Kilkerran S Ayrs
38 C5 Kilkhampton Cnwll
315 E3 Killamarsh Derbys
410 B3 Killantrae D & G
7 G1 Killaworgey Cnwll
103 F3 Killay Swans
462 A6 Killean Ag & B
483 H2 Killearn Stirlg
456 D3 Killellan Park Ag & B
566 B5 Killen Highld
394 D6 Killerby Darltn
522 F4 Killichonan P & K
533 K6 Killiechonate Highld
505 G2 Killiechronan Ag & B
524 D3 Killiecrankie P & K
504 F3 Killiemor Ag & B
547 G3 Killilan Highld
589 J5 Killimster Highld
509 J3 Killin Stirlg
476 E2 Killinallan Ag & B
356 B3 Killinghall N York
366 C2 Killington Cumb
61 G2 Killington Devon
431 E5 Killingworth N Tyne
431 E5 Killingworth Moor N Tyne
431 E5 Killingworth Village N Tyne
492 D5 Killinochonoch Ag & B
6 B6 Killivose Cnwll
472 B5 Killochyett Border
458 D5 Killocraw Ag & B
518 E6 Killundine Highld
483 E6 Kilmacolm Inver
497 F3 Kilmahog Stirlg
520 B4 Kilmahumaig Ag & B
543 G2 Kilmalieu Highld
543 G2 Kilmaluag Highld
514 B5 Kilmany Fife
545 J6 Kilmarie Highld
445 F2 Kilmarnock E Ayrs
492 D5 Kilmartin Ag & B
445 E1 Kilmaurs E Ayrs
492 D2 Kilmelford Ag & B
476 F3 Kilmeny Ag & B
86 B4 Kilmersdon Somset
73 E4 Kilmeston Hants
493 G6 Kilmichael Beg Ag & B
493 E6 Kilmichael Glassary Ag & B
479 K4 Kilmichael of Inverlussa Ag & B
29 E3 Kilmington Devon
68 C2 Kilmington Wilts
68 C2 Kilmington Common Wilts
516 B6 Kilmoluaig Ag & B
533 J6 Kilmonivaig Highld
565 H8 Kilmorack Highld
506 E4 Kilmore Ag & B
531 H1 Kilmore Highld
479 J6 Kilmory Ag & B
518 D1 Kilmory Highld
530 C2 Kilmory Highld
460 D5 Kilmory N Ayrs
542 D7 Kilmuir Highld
542 F2 Kilmuir Highld
566 B7 Kilmuir Highld
566 D2 Kilmuir Highld
481 H3 Kilmun Ag & B
476 D2 Kilnave Ag & B
468 D5 Kilncadzow S Lans
79 G2 Kilndown Kent
161 E6 Kiln Green Herefs
116 D4 Kiln Green Wokham
389 F3 Kilnhill Cumb
329 H5 Kilnhurst Rothm
517 K6 Kilninian Ag & B
506 D5 Kilninver Ag & B
404 B4 Kiln Pit Hill Nthumb
335 F1 Kilnsea E R Yk
368 C6 Kilnsey N York
359 F4 Kilnwick Percy E R Yk
478 B2 Kiloran Ag & B
460 C4 Kilpatrick N Ayrs
160 A3 Kilpeck Herefs
582 C6 Kilphedir Highld
345 H4 Kilpin E R Yk
345 H4 Kilpin Pike E R Yk
503 F4 Kilrenny Fife
216 C5 Kilsby Nhants
513 F4 Kilspindie P & K
485 E4 Kilsyth N Lans
549 J1 Kiltarlity Highld
316 A4 Kilton Notts
397 H6 Kilton R & Cl
64 C3 Kilton Somset
397 G6 Kilton Thorpe R & Cl
542 F3 Kilvaxter Highld
64 C3 Kilve Somset
297 F6 Kilvington Notts
465 G6 Kilwinning N Ayrs
249 E4 Kimberley Norfk
295 F6 Kimberley Notts
329 F6 Kimberworth Rothm
329 G6 Kimberworth Park Rothm
405 F5 Kimblesworth Dur
141 G3 Kimble Wick Bucks
219 G6 Kimbolton Cambs
186 C2 Kimbolton Herefs
71 G4 Kimbridge Hants
216 C2 Kimcote Leics
33 G4 Kimmeridge Dorset
454 A2 Kimmerston Nthumb
89 G5 Kimpton Hants
170 A6 Kimpton Herts
38 D5 Kimworthy Devon
565 L4 Kinbeachie Highld
581 L3 Kinbrace Highld
498 B4 Kinbuck Stirlg
444 D6 Kincaidston S Ayrs
514 D6 Kincaple Fife
486 B2 Kincardine Fife
576 D6 Kincardine Highld
486 B2 Kincardine Br Fife
82 C3 Kincardine Br Kent
555 G5 Kincardine O'Neil Abers
513 E2 Kinclaven P & K
557 E5 Kincluny Abers
557 G4 Kincorth C Aber
536 B1 Kincraig Highld
524 E6 Kincraigie P & K
524 E5 Kindallachan P & K
328 D4 Kine Moor Barns
163 G4 Kineton Gloucs
191 E4 Kineton Warwks
214 A3 Kineton Green Solhll
513 E5 Kinfauns P & K
519 K5 Kingairloch Highld
464 B3 Kingarth Ag & B
37 E5 Kingates IoW
16 C4 Kingbeare Cnwll
134 A3 Kingcoed Mons
85 F2 Kingdown BaNES
570 C4 King Edward Abers
333 E6 Kingerby Lincs
93 G3 Kingfield Surrey
23 F1 Kingford Devon
40 C4 Kingford Devon
164 D5 Kingham Oxon
69 E4 Kinghay Wilts
423 G5 Kingholm Quay D & G
488 B2 Kinghorn Fife
500 D5 Kinglassie Fife
449 E4 Kingledores Border
514 A4 Kingoodie P & K
160 B1 King's Acre Herefs
10 D3 Kingsand Cnwll
142 B3 Kingsash Bucks
503 F2 Kingsbarns Fife
12 C4 Kingsbridge Devon
63 F4 Kingsbridge Somset
12 D3 Kingsbridgefork Cross Devon
238 A1 King's Bromley Staffs
542 F5 Kingsburgh Highld
118 D2 Kingsbury Gt Lon
238 C5 Kingsbury Warwks
66 C5 Kingsbury Episcopi Somset
67 H6 Kingsbury Regis Somset
160 D4 King's Caple Herefs
486 D4 Kingscavil W Loth
91 E3 Kingsclere Hants
91 E2 Kingsclere Woodlands Hants
243 E5 King's Cliffe Nhants
136 B5 Kingscote Gloucs
40 A4 Kingscott Devon
189 G3 King's Coughton Warwks
136 B4 Kingscourt Gloucs
461 E4 Kingscross N Ayrs
600 F2 King's Dale Ork
162 D5 Kingsditch Gloucs
29 E4 Kingsdon Devon
67 E4 Kingsdon Somset
99 E3 Kingsdown Kent
101 G6 Kingsdown Kent
113 E2 Kingsdown Swindn
87 E1 Kingsdown Wilts
244 B5 King's Dyke Cambs
487 F1 Kingseat Fife
487 E2 Kingseathill Fife
166 C5 King's End Oxon
188 B4 King's End Worcs
18 B1 Kingsett Devon
141 F3 Kingsey Bucks
186 C5 Kingsfield Herefs
338 D4 Kingsfold Lancs
76 C2 Kingsfold W Susx
466 B5 Kingsford E Ayrs
212 B3 Kingsford Worcs
347 F6 Kingsforth N Linc
91 G4 King's Furlong Hants
101 G1 Kingsgate Kent
161 H3 King's Green Gloucs
187 H2 King's Green Worcs
200 B2 Kingshall Green Suffk
200 B2 Kingshall Street Suffk
61 E4 Kingsheanton Devon
213 G3 King's Heath Birm
193 F2 King's Heath Nhants
197 F2 Kings Hedges Cambs
135 G5 Kingshill Gloucs
137 F4 Kings Hill Gloucs
97 G3 King's Hill Kent
112 D3 Kingshill Swindn
237 E5 King's Hill Wsall
162 B5 Kingsholm Gloucs
509 J5 Kingshouse Stirlg
214 B2 Kingshurst Solhll
399 E4 Kingside Hill Cumb
20 B4 Kingskerswell Devon
501 E3 Kingskettle Fife
487 G5 Kingsknowe C Edin
30 A3 Kingsland Dorset
186 A2 Kingsland Herefs
302 B4 Kingsland IoA
234 B2 Kingsland Shrops
143 F4 Kings Langley Herts
310 B5 Kingsley Ches
74 B2 Kingsley Hants
292 D5 Kingsley Staffs
74 D3 Kingsley Green W Susx
292 D5 Kingsley Holt Staffs
292 C5 Kingsley Moor Staffs
193 G2 Kingsley Park Nhants
236 A5 Kingslow Shrops
252 C3 King's Lynn Norfk
391 G5 King's Meaburn Cumb
51 G2 Kingsmead Hants
34 c3 King's Mills Guern
275 G4 King's Mills Leics
288 D5 King's Mills Wrexhm
145 F3 Kingsmoor Essex
324 C4 Kings Moss St Hel
527 G5 Kingsmuir Angus
450 A2 Kings Muir Border
215 H4 King's Newnham Warwks
275 F4 King's Newton Derbys
211 H2 Kingsnordley Shrops
81 F2 Kingsnorth Kent
122 C5 Kingsnorth Medway
213 G4 King's Norton Birm
241 E4 King's Norton Leics
40 D4 King's Nympton Devon
34 D2 King's Park Bmouth
49 E6 King's Park Bmouth
467 F2 Kings Park C Glas
186 A4 Kings Pyon Herefs
220 C4 Kings Ripton Cambs

City, town and village index: King's Somborne - Lana 697

71 G3 King's Somborne Hants
46 D2 King's Stag Dorset
136 B4 King's Stanley Gloucs
166 A2 Kings Sutton Nhants
11 E2 King's Tamerton C Plym
237 G6 Kingstanding Birm
20 B3 Kingsteignton Devon
567 G5 Kingsteps Highld
313 E5 King Sterndale Derbys
160 B3 King's Thorn Herefs
193 G2 Kingsthorpe Nhants
193 G2 Kingsthorpe Hollow Nhants
196 D3 Kingston Cambs
52 B4 Kingston C Port
12 A3 Kingston Devon
13 F2 Kingston Devon
27 H5 Kingston Devon
33 H4 Kingston Dorset
47 E3 Kingston Dorset
489 G3 Kingston E Loth
49 E4 Kingston Hants
36 D4 Kingston IoW
100 C5 Kingston Kent
168 B2 Kingston M Keyn
568 E2 Kingston Moray
202 B5 Kingston Suffk
326 D5 Kingston Tamesd
139 G5 Kingston Bagpuize Oxon
141 F5 Kingston Blount Oxon
55 F3 Kingston by Sea W Susx
68 D2 Kingston Deverill Wilts
159 H2 Kingstone Herefs
161 E5 Kingstone Herefs
44 D5 Kingstone Somset
273 G4 Kingstone Staffs
113 G2 Kingstone Winslow Oxon
54 C4 Kingston Gorse W Susx
113 H2 Kingston Lisle Oxon
32 C1 Kingston Maurward Dorset
56 B3 Kingston near Lewes E Susx
276 B4 Kingston on Soar Notts
430 D6 Kingston Park N u Ty
30 D4 Kingston Russell Dorset
43 H2 Kingston St Mary Somset
84 C1 Kingston Seymour N Som
141 F4 Kingston Stert Oxon
348 B4 Kingston upon Hull C KuH
118 D6 Kingston upon Thames Gt Lon
119 E5 Kingston Vale Gt Lon
400 C3 Kingstown Cumb
146 B4 King Street Essex
169 H5 King's Walden Herts
86 C2 Kingsway BaNES
309 H2 Kingsway Halton
13 F2 Kingswear Devon
557 F3 Kingswells C Aber
212 C2 Kingswinford Dudley
167 E6 Kingswood Bucks
121 H2 Kingswood Essex
185 E4 Kingswood Herefs
143 G4 Kingswood Herts
98 C4 Kingswood Kent
232 D4 Kingswood Powys
110 B5 Kingswood S Glos
110 C1 Kingswood S Glos
64 B4 Kingswood Somset
95 E3 Kingswood Surrey
310 B1 Kingswood Warrtn
214 B5 Kingswood Warwks
214 B5 Kingswood Brook Warwks
236 B4 Kingswood Common Staffs
187 G1 Kingswood Common Worcs
72 C3 Kings Worthy Hants
185 F3 Kington Herefs
109 H1 Kington S Glos
189 E3 Kington Worcs
111 G4 Kington Langley Wilts
68 C5 Kington Magna Dorset
111 F4 Kington St Michael Wilts
535 K2 Kingussie Highld
67 E3 Kingweston Somset
560 D3 Kinharrachie Abers
540 D4 Kinkell Abers
499 E1 Kinkell Bridge P & K
561 F1 Kinknockie Abers
426 D4 Kinkry Hill Cumb
211 G3 Kinlet Shrops
501 E2 Kinloch Fife
530 D3 Kinloch Highld
546 B6 Kinloch Highld
579 K3 Kinloch Highld
525 H7 Kinloch P & K
526 C6 Kinloch P & K
496 C4 Kinlochard Stirlg
584 D5 Kinlochbervie Highld
532 E7 Kinlocheil Highld
563 J4 Kinlochewe Highld
532 E1 Kinloch Hourn Highld
534 F5 Kinloch Laggan Highld
521 H3 Kinlochleven Highld
531 K8 Kinlochmoidart Highld
521 H3 Kinlochmore Highld
523 J4 Kinloch Rannoch P & K
505 J5 Kinlochspelve Ag & B
531 J5 Kinloid Highld
567 K4 Kinloss Moray
306 D3 Kinmel Bay Conwy
560 B6 Kinmuck Abers
560 C6 Kinmundy Abers
565 L8 Kinmylies Highld
571 H7 Kinnadie Abers
513 F4 Kinnaird P & K
524 E4 Kinnaird P & K
576 F3 Kinnauld Highld
541 G5 Kinneff Abers
486 C3 Kinneil Falk
436 D4 Kinnelhead D & G
528 D4 Kinnell Angus
269 F5 Kinnerley Shrops
185 F5 Kinnersley Herefs
188 C6 Kinnersley Worcs
184 D2 Kinnerton Powys
288 D2 Kinnerton Green Flints
500 C4 Kinnesswood P & K
394 B5 Kinninvie Dur
527 E4 Kinnordy Angus
277 E3 Kinoulton Notts
500 B4 Kinross P & K
513 E3 Kinrossie P & K
271 F1 Kinsey Heath Ches
185 G2 Kinsham Herefs
162 D2 Kinsham Worcs
329 G2 Kinsley Wakefd
48 D5 Kinson Bmouth
479 J4 Kintallan Ag & B
90 B1 Kintbury W Berk
567 H4 Kintessack Moray
500 B1 Kintillo P & K
555 G3 Kintocher Abers
209 H5 Kinton Herefs
269 G6 Kinton Shrops
556 D1 Kintore Abers
477 G6 Kintour Ag & B
476 E7 Kintra Ag & B
504 C5 Kintra Ag & B
492 D3 Kintraw Ag & B
551 G6 Kinveachy Highld
212 B3 Kinver Staffs
214 D2 Kinwalsey Warwks
405 F4 Kip Hill Dur
383 G5 Kiplin N York
343 H3 Kippax Leeds
497 G6 Kippen Stirlg
413 F4 Kippford or Scaur D & G
451 G4 Kippilaw Border
451 G4 Kippilaw Mains Border
79 E2 Kipping's Cross Kent
96 D4 Kippington Kent
600 C2 Kirbister Ork
600 F3 Kirbister Ork
602 B6 Kirbuster Ork
603 K7 Kirbuster Ork
250 B3 Kirby Bedon Norfk
277 F6 Kirby Bellars Leics
250 D6 Kirby Cane Norfk
214 D4 Kirby Corner Covtry
176 D5 Kirby Cross Essex
240 B4 Kirby Fields Leics
250 D6 Kirby Green Norfk
359 H1 Kirby Grindalythe N York
370 D6 Kirby Hill N York
382 D3 Kirby Hill N York
371 F2 Kirby Knowle N York
176 D5 Kirby-le-Soken Essex
373 E4 Kirby Misperton N York
240 B4 Kirby Muxloe Leics
250 D6 Kirby Row Norfk
384 C6 Kirby Sigston N York
359 E3 Kirby Underdale E R Yk
370 D3 Kirby Wiske N York
75 G4 Kirdford W Susx
589 H5 Kirk Highld
605 J3 Kirkabister Shet
607 G4 Kirkabister Shet
607 G6 Kirkabister Shet
412 B5 Kirkandrews D & G
400 C3 Kirkandrews-on-Eden Cumb
516 C6 Kirkapol Ag & B
609 J2 Kirkaton Shet
400 A3 Kirkbampton Cumb
398 B3 Kirkbean D & G
388 B2 Kirkborough Cumb
330 D2 Kirk Bramwith Donc
399 G3 Kirkbride Cumb
370 B1 Kirkbridge N York
528 B6 Kirkbuddo Angus
450 B2 Kirkburn Border
360 B3 Kirkburn E R Yk
328 B2 Kirkburton Kirk
323 H5 Kirkby Knows
333 F6 Kirkby Lincs
385 E3 Kirkby N York
300 B2 Kirkby Fenside Lincs
383 G6 Kirkby Fleetham N York
298 D3 Kirkby Green Lincs
295 F3 Kirkby in Ashfield Notts
363 E5 Kirkby-in-Furness Cumb
299 E5 Kirkby la Thorpe Lincs
366 C4 Kirkby Lonsdale Cumb
354 A2 Kirkby Malham N York
239 H4 Kirkby Mallory Leics
370 A5 Kirkby Malzeard N York
372 D2 Kirkby Mills N York
372 C2 Kirkbymoorside N York
299 G2 Kirkby on Bain Lincs
356 C5 Kirkby Overblow N York
380 D3 Kirkby Stephen Cumb
391 G4 Kirkby Thore Cumb
279 F4 Kirkby Underwood Lincs
344 C1 Kirkby Wharfe N York
295 F4 Kirkby Woodhouse Notts
488 B1 Kirkcaldy Fife
426 D6 Kirkcambeck Cumb
413 E5 Kirkcarswell D & G
414 D3 Kirkcolm D & G
435 E2 Kirkconnel D & G
412 C2 Kirkconnell D & G
423 G6 Kirkconnell D & G
416 C4 Kirkcowan D & G
412 C4 Kirkcudbright D & G
323 F6 Kirkdale Lpool
356 D4 Kirk Deighton N York
347 F4 Kirk Ella E R Yk
468 D6 Kirkfieldbank S Lans
501 E4 Kirkforthar Feus Fife
413 G1 Kirkgunzeon D & G
275 G2 Kirk Hallam Derbys
338 B3 Kirkham Lancs
358 D1 Kirkham N York
343 E5 Kirkhamgate Wakefd
357 F3 Kirk Hammerton N York
326 B4 Kirkhams Bury
429 G3 Kirkharle Nthumb
342 C6 Kirkheaton Kirk
429 G4 Kirkheaton Nthumb
529 E2 Kirkhill Angus
467 E3 Kirkhill E Rens
565 K7 Kirkhill Highld
470 D2 Kirkhill Mdloth
487 E5 Kirkhill W Loth
326 C2 Kirkholt Rochdl
450 D5 Kirkhope Border
436 C3 Kirkhope S Lans
450 C3 Kirkhouse Border
401 G3 Kirkhouse Cumb
545 J6 Kirkibost Highld
606 B7 Kirkidale Shet
526 D6 Kirkinch Angus
410 D2 Kirkinner D & G
484 D5 Kirkintilloch E Duns
294 B4 Kirk Ireton Derbys
388 C6 Kirkland Cumb
391 G3 Kirkland Cumb
399 H5 Kirkland Cumb
422 D1 Kirkland D & G
435 E2 Kirkland D & G
501 E3 Kirkland Fife
501 G4 Kirkland Dam Fife
389 E1 Kirkland Guards Cumb
274 D2 Kirk Langley Derbys
397 E5 Kirkleatham R & Cl
326 A2 Kirklees Bury
384 C3 Kirklevington S on T
227 G1 Kirkley Suffk
296 C3 Kirklington Notts
370 C3 Kirklington N York
400 D1 Kirklinton Cumb
487 F5 Kirkliston C Edin
408 B2 Kirkmabreck D & G
408 C4 Kirkmaiden D & G
395 F3 Kirk Merrington Dur
322 e4 Kirk Michael IoM
525 G3 Kirkmichael P & K
432 D3 Kirkmichael S Ayrs
423 H2 Kirkmichael Mains D & G
468 B6 Kirkmuirhill S Lans
453 H3 Kirknewton Nthumb
470 A1 Kirknewton W Loth
558 C3 Kirkney Abers
468 C2 Kirk of Shotts N Lans
391 F1 Kirkoswald Cumb
432 B3 Kirkoswald S Ayrs
423 F1 Kirkpatrick D & G
422 C5 Kirkpatrick Durham D & G
425 F5 Kirkpatrick-Fleming D & G
330 D3 Kirk Sandall Donc
362 C5 Kirksanton Cumb
467 H2 Kirkshaw N Lans
330 B1 Kirk Smeaton N York
450 B5 Kirkstead Border
299 F2 Kirkstead Lincs
558 C2 Kirkstile Abers
589 J2 Kirkstyle Highld
559 E4 Kirkton Abers
570 B5 Kirkton Abers
571 L5 Kirkton Abers
514 C2 Kirkton Angus
515 G1 Kirkton Angus
527 F5 Kirkton Angus
439 G2 Kirkton Border
423 G3 Kirkton D & G
488 A2 Kirkton Fife
514 B4 Kirkton Fife
546 E4 Kirkton Highld
547 G1 Kirkton Highld
577 G4 Kirkton Highld
511 H6 Kirkton P & K
496 D4 Kirkton Stirlg
469 G1 Kirkton W Loth
483 E5 Kirktonhill W Duns
449 H2 Kirkton Manor Border
526 D4 Kirkton of Airlie Angus
514 A2 Kirkton of Auchterhouse Angus
559 G1 Kirkton of Auchterless Abers
566 E7 Kirkton of Barevan Highld
560 B5 Kirkton of Bourtie Abers
513 E3 Kirkton of Collace P & K
529 E3 Kirkton of Craig Angus
559 E3 Kirkton of Culsalmond Abers
501 F3 Kirkton of Cults Fife
556 D5 Kirkton of Durris Abers
554 C1 Kirkton of Glenbuchat Abers
526 B2 Kirkton of Glenisla Angus
526 D4 Kirkton of Kingoldrum Angus
512 D1 Kirkton of Lethendy P & K
561 E4 Kirkton of Logie Buchan Abers
524 D2 Kirkton of Lude P & K
557 F5 Kirkton of Maryculter Abers
528 B2 Kirkton of Menmuir Angus
515 E2 Kirkton of Monikie Angus
559 F4 Kirkton of Oyne Abers
559 F3 Kirkton of Rayne Abers
557 E3 Kirkton of Skene Abers
555 H2 Kirkton of Tough Abers
445 F1 Kirktoun E Ayrs
571 K5 Kirktown Abers
570 B3 Kirktown of Alvah Abers
569 H3 Kirktown of Deskford Moray
541 F2 Kirktown of Fetteresso Abers
568 E8 Kirktown of Mortlach Moray
470 B6 Kirkurd Border
601 H2 Kirkwall Ork
429 F3 Kirkwhelpington Nthumb
424 C4 Kirkwood D & G
467 H2 Kirkwood N Lans
453 F4 Kirk Yetholm Border
333 G2 Kirmington N Linc
333 H6 Kirmond le Mire Lincs
482 A4 Kirn Ag & B
527 E4 Kirriemuir Angus
250 B5 Kirstead Green Norfk
425 E5 Kirtlebridge D & G
425 F3 Kirtleton D & G
198 D3 Kirtling Cambs
198 D3 Kirtling Green Cambs
166 A6 Kirtlington Oxon
586 F4 Kirtomy Highld
280 D2 Kirton Lincs
316 C6 Kirton Notts
177 E2 Kirton Suffk
469 G1 Kirton Campus W Loth
280 C2 Kirton End Lincs
280 C1 Kirton Holme Lincs
332 C5 Kirton in Lindsey N Linc
502 C4 Kirton of Largo or Upper Largo Fife
362 B4 Kiskin Cumb
193 E3 Kislingbury Nhants
29 F2 Kitbridge Devon
328 C3 Kitchenroyd Kirk
164 C3 Kitebrook Warwks
190 B1 Kite Green Warwks
37 F2 Kite Hill IoW
215 H6 Kites Hardwick Warwks
68 D6 Kit Hill Dorset
136 C4 Kitlye Gloucs
98 A2 Kit's Coty Kent
324 D3 Kitt Green Wigan
43 E3 Kittisford Somset
103 E4 Kittle Swans
144 B5 Kitts End Herts
214 A2 Kitt's Green Birm
312 A3 Kitt's Moss Stockp
29 G2 Kittwhistle Dorset
557 G3 Kittybrewster C Aber
213 E3 Kitwell Birm
73 G3 Kitwood Hants
160 B3 Kivernoll Herefs
315 F3 Kiveton Park Rothm
317 F3 Knaith Lincs
317 F2 Knaith Park Lincs
93 G3 Knaphill Surrey
12 C3 Knap Mill Devon
72 B5 Knapp Hants
513 G3 Knapp P & K
44 B2 Knapp Somset
70 A4 Knapp Wilts
69 E4 Knapp Hill Dorset
296 D3 Knapthorpe Notts
216 D2 Knaptoft Leics
256 C3 Knapton Norfk
357 H4 Knapton York
186 A4 Knapton Green Herefs
196 D2 Knapwell Cambs
356 D3 Knaresborough N York
402 B4 Knarsdale Nthumb
602 C7 Knarston Ork
97 E2 Knatts Valley Kent
570 F7 Knaven Abers
100 C3 Knave's Ash Kent
201 F1 Knaves Green Suffk
358 A5 Knavesmire York
371 E2 Knayton N York
170 C6 Knebworth Herts
345 G4 Knedlington E R Yk
296 D2 Kneesall Notts
196 D6 Kneesworth Cambs
296 C5 Kneeton Notts
102 C4 Knelston Swans
272 D2 Knenhall Staffs
224 C3 Knettishall Suffk
61 F4 Knightacott Devon
191 F4 Knightcote Warwks
84 C3 Knightcott N Som
272 B4 Knightley Staffs
272 B5 Knightley Dale Staffs
240 C4 Knighton C Leic
11 F4 Knighton Devon
46 B2 Knighton Dorset
113 G2 Knighton Oxon
48 D5 Knighton Poole
209 E5 Knighton Powys
64 C3 Knighton Somset
271 G1 Knighton Staffs
271 G4 Knighton Staffs
113 G5 Knighton Wilts
189 F3 Knighton Worcs
240 C4 Knighton Fields C Leic
211 E5 Knighton on Teme Worcs
8 C2 Knightor Cnwll
162 C4 Knightsbridge Gloucs
119 F4 Knightsbridge Gt Lon
245 F6 Knight's End Cambs
90 B5 Knights Enham Hants
15 F2 Knightsmill Cnwll
486 D6 Knightsridge W Loth
483 H6 Knightswood C Glas
187 G3 Knightwick Worcs
185 E2 Knill Herefs
378 B5 Knipe Fold Cumb
506 D5 Knipoch Ag & B
278 A3 Knipton Leics
404 D5 Knitsley Dur
293 H4 Kniveton Derbys
505 G3 Knock Ag & B
392 A4 Knock Cumb
569 J5 Knock Moray
582 F4 Knockally Highld
537 K4 Knockan Abers
504 E6 Knockan Ag & B
579 H7 Knockan Highld
552 E4 Knockandhu Moray
568 B7 Knockando Moray
576 F2 Knockarthur Highld
565 K8 Knockbain Highld
565 L5 Knockbain Highld
569 J5 Knockbog Moray
542 D4 Knockbreck Highld
412 A5 Knockbrex D & G
588 F4 Knockdee Highld
418 D4 Knockdolian S Ayrs
481 G5 Knockdow Ag & B
111 E2 Knockdown Wilts
559 E4 Knockenbaird Abers
461 E4 Knockenkelly N Ayrs
445 E2 Knockentiber E Ayrs
294 A4 Knockerdown Derbys
565 J5 Knockfarrel Highld
414 D5 Knockglass D & G
588 C4 Knockglass Highld
121 E5 Knockhall Kent
96 C3 Knockholt Kent
96 C3 Knockholt Pound Kent
269 F5 Knockin Shrops
269 F5 Knockin Heath Shrops
442 D4 Knocklaw Nthumb
97 E2 Knockmill Kent
456 D3 Knocknaha Ag & B
414 C4 Knocknain D & G
478 F7 Knockrome Ag & B
456 D4 Knockstapple Ag & B
422 B5 Knockvennie D & G
203 E2 Knodishall Suffk
203 E2 Knodishall Common Suffk
66 D5 Knole Somset
108 D2 Knollbury Mons
64 D4 Knoll Green Somset
311 G4 Knolls Green Ches
355 G1 Knoll Top N York
269 G2 Knolton Shrops
269 G2 Knolton Bryn Wrexhm
69 F1 Knook Wilts
241 H3 Knossington Leics
312 D6 Knotbury Staffs
542 F6 Knott Highld
351 E5 Knott End-on-Sea Lancs
195 E2 Knotting Beds
195 E2 Knotting Green Beds
344 B5 Knottingley Wakefd
326 D4 Knott Lanes Oldham
44 D5 Knott Oak Somset
353 F4 Knotts Lancs
309 F1 Knotty Ash Lpool
39 F2 Knotty Corner Devon
142 C6 Knotty Green Bucks
210 D5 Knowbury Shrops
416 C2 Knowe D & G
609 G8 Knowe Shet
400 C3 Knowefield Cumb
421 G1 Knowehead D & G
490 B4 Knowes E Loth
429 F2 Knowesgate Nthumb
432 C2 Knoweside S Ayrs
569 K5 Knowes of Elrick Abers
468 A3 Knowetop N Lans
451 G6 Knowetownhead Border
291 F5 Knowl Bank Staffs
109 H5 Knowle Bristl
21 E1 Knowle Devon
26 B2 Knowle Devon
27 G1 Knowle Devon
60 C4 Knowle Devon
210 D5 Knowle Shrops
214 B4 Knowle Solhll
65 F4 Knowle Somset
89 E2 Knowle Wilts
189 F3 Knowle Fields Worcs
210 D5 Knowlegate Shrops
339 F2 Knowle Green Lancs
118 A5 Knowle Green Surrey
214 B5 Knowle Grove Solhll
93 G1 Knowle Hill Surrey
341 H1 Knowle Park Brad
44 C5 Knowle St Giles Somset
211 G1 Knowlesands Shrops
20 B3 Knowles Hill Devon
51 G3 Knowle Village Hants
173 F1 Knowl Green Essex
116 D4 Knowl Hill Wokham
48 C3 Knowlton Dorset
101 E5 Knowlton Kent
272 B2 Knowl Wall Staffs
341 E5 Knowl Wood Calder
323 H5 Knowsley Knows
41 G3 Knowstone Devon
80 A1 Knox Bridge Kent
209 E5 Knucklas Powys
194 C1 Knuston Nhants
311 F4 Knutsford Ches
291 G5 Knutton Staffs
339 H4 Knuzden Brook Lancs
292 A3 Knypersley Staffs
341 H6 Krumlin Calder
4 D5 Kuggar Cnwll
546 D4 Kyleakin Highld
546 C4 Kyle of Lochalsh Highld
467 G2 Kylepark S Lans
546 D5 Kylerhea Highld
579 H3 Kylesku Highld
579 H3 Kylestrome Highld
134 C2 Kymin Mons
186 D6 Kymin Mons
160 C4 Kynaston Herefs
269 G5 Kynaston Shrops
235 F1 Kynnersley Wrekin
187 E2 Kyre Worcs
187 E2 Kyre Green Worcs
187 E2 Kyre Park Worcs
211 E6 Kyrewood Worcs

L

35 d3 La Bellieuse Guern
598 F5 Labost W Isls
597 J3 Lacasaidh W Isls
599 J8 Lacasdail W Isls
334 B3 Laceby NE Lin
334 B3 Laceby Acres NE Lin
142 A4 Lacey Green Bucks
311 G3 Lacey Green Ches
311 E5 Lach Dennis Ches
289 E2 Lache Ches
397 E6 Lackenby R & Cl
223 F5 Lackford Suffk
111 G6 Lacock Wilts
191 G3 Ladbroke Warwks
5 E4 Laddenvean Cnwll
97 G5 Laddingford Kent
81 G5 Lade Kent
300 C4 Lade Bank Lincs
355 F1 Ladies Riggs N York
312 D5 Ladmanlow Derbys
7 G3 Ladock Cnwll
72 B5 Ladwell Hants
603 K3 Lady Ork
501 F3 Ladybank Fife
432 B4 Ladybank S Ayrs
295 G2 Ladybrook Notts
482 D4 Ladyburn Inver
23 G5 Ladycross Cnwll
214 D5 Ladyes Hills Warwks
448 B4 Ladygill S Lans
323 F4 Lady Green Sefton
362 D4 Lady Hall Cumb
210 B4 Lady Halton Shrops
326 D2 Lady House Rochdl
474 C5 Ladykirk Border
233 G4 Ladyoak Shrops
405 F3 Lady Park Gatesd
160 D3 Ladyridge Herefs
570 F3 Ladysford Abers
199 F3 Lady's Green Suffk
119 H5 Ladywell Gt Lon
270 B3 Ladywell Shrops
486 D6 Ladywell W Loth
213 F2 Ladywood Birm
343 F2 Lady Wood Leeds
188 C2 Ladywood Worcs
324 C5 Laffak St Hel
35 d4 La Fosse Guern
518 F3 Laga Highld
507 L4 Laganbuidhe Ag & B
476 F7 Lagavulin Ag & B
478 F6 Lagg Ag & B
460 C5 Lagg N Ayrs
476 D5 Laggan Ag & B
533 L3 Laggan Highld
535 H4 Laggan Highld
419 G5 Laggan S Ayrs
536 C2 Lagganlia Highld
504 F2 Lagganulva Ag & B
34 b3 La Girouette Guern
53 F4 Lagness W Susx
35 d1 La Greve Guern
35 g5 La Greve de Lecq Jersey
35 i7 La Hougue Bie Jersey
34 b3 La Houguette Guern
573 G5 Laide Highld
467 G5 Laigh Carnduff S Lans
466 C6 Laigh Fenwick E Ayrs
444 D6 Laigh Glengall S Ayrs
446 C5 Laigh Glenmuir E Ayrs
467 H4 Laighstonehall S Lans
121 G2 Laindon Essex
11 F2 Laira C Plym
563 J7 Lair Highld
576 C2 Lairg Highld
549 K2 Lairgmore Highld
576 C2 Lairg Muir Highld
390 D3 Laithes Cumb
393 F5 Laithkirk Dur
6 C4 Laity Moor Cnwll
24 D5 Lake Devon
39 F6 Lake Devon
61 E5 Lake Devon
37 F4 Lake IoW
34 A2 Lake Poole
70 C2 Lake Wilts
117 F4 Lake End Bucks
250 A3 Lakenham Norfk
223 E3 Lakenheath Suffk
75 G2 Laker's Green Surrey
245 H5 Lakes End Norfk
365 E2 Lakeside Cumb
121 E4 Lakeside Thurr
189 G1 Lakeside Worcs
35 e1 La Lande Guern
118 B6 Laleham Surrey
104 D3 Laleston Brdgnd
470 C4 Lamancha Border
5 E2 Lamanva Cnwll
174 A2 Lamarsh Essex
256 A5 Lamas Norfk
174 D3 Lamb Corner Essex
473 G6 Lambden Border
80 B4 Lamberden Kent
324 C4 Lamberhead Green Wigan
79 F2 Lamberhurst Kent
79 F2 Lamberhurst Quarter Kent
475 E3 Lamberton Border
213 E1 Lambert's End Sandw
119 G4 Lambeth Gt Lon
199 E4 Lambfair Green Suffk
389 E3 Lambfoot Cumb
484 B6 Lambhill C Glas
296 B5 Lambley Notts
402 B3 Lambley Nthumb
114 A4 Lambourn W Berk
7 E3 Lambourne Cnwll
145 G5 Lambourne Essex
145 G6 Lambourne End Essex
113 H4 Lambourn Woodlands W Berk
86 D1 Lambridge BaNES
30 B3 Lambrook Dorset
98 B5 Lamb's Cross Kent
48 B5 Lambs Green Dorset
76 D2 Lambs Green W Susx
125 E1 Lambston Pembks
405 G3 Lambton Sundld
16 B6 Lamellion Cnwll
17 G3 Lamerton Devon
25 E3 Lamerton Cross Devon
405 F3 Lamesley Gatesd
603 J4 Laminess Ork
566 C1 Lamington Highld
448 C3 Lamington S Lans
461 E3 Lamlash N Ayrs
8 C5 Lamledra Cnwll
339 G4 Lammack Bl w D
390 C2 Lamonby Cumb
15 E6 Lamorick Cnwll
2 D4 Lamorna Cnwll
7 G5 Lamorran Cnwll
202 B2 Lampardbrook Suffk
181 E5 Lampeter Cerdgn
126 D2 Lampeter Velfrey Pembks
388 C5 Lamplugh Cumb
217 F5 Lamport Nhants
118 C4 Lampton Gt Lon
67 H2 Lamyatt Somset
23 G1 Lana Devon
23 G3 Lana Devon

698 City, town and village index: Lanark - Liddaton

469 E6 Lanark S Lans
351 G2 Lancaster Lancs
405 E5 Lanchester Dur
55 E4 Lancing W Susx
35 d1 L'Ancresse Guern
197 G2 Landbeach Cambs
39 G3 Landcross Devon
556 C4 Landerberry Abers
71 F6 Landford Wilts
71 F5 Landfordwood Wilts
324 D4 Land Gate Wigan
37 F4 Landguard Manor IoW
24 B3 Landhill Devon
308 C2 Landican Wirral
102 C3 Landimore Swans
61 E5 Landkey Devon
61 E5 Landkey Newland Devon
103 G2 Landore Swans
52 A4 Landport C Port
56 C2 Landport E Susx
10 C1 Landrake Cnwll
19 G4 Landscove Devon
125 H2 Landshipping Pembks
125 H2 Landshipping Quay Pembks
327 E5 Landslow Green Tamesd
10 D1 Landulph Cnwll
222 C6 Landwade Suffk
237 E3 Landywood Staffs
7 F1 Lane Cnwll
23 E6 Laneast Cnwll
341 H3 Lane Bottom Brad
340 D2 Lane Bottom Lancs
341 G2 Lane End Brad
116 D1 Lane End Bucks
15 E5 Lane-end Cnwll
376 D6 Lane End Cumb
295 E2 Lane End Derbys
24 B2 Lane End Devon
33 F1 Lane End Dorset
288 C2 Lane End Flints
73 E4 Lane End Hants
73 G4 Lane End Hants
161 E6 Lane End Herefs
37 H3 Lane End IoW
121 E5 Lane End Kent
353 H5 Lane End Lancs
329 F5 Lane End Sheff
74 C1 Lane End Surrey
87 E5 Lane End Wilts
291 E3 Lane Ends Ches
312 C3 Lane Ends Ches
291 H4 Lane Ends C Stke
364 D3 Lane Ends Cumb
274 C3 Lane Ends Derbys
325 E1 Lane Ends Lancs
340 B3 Lane Ends Lancs
353 E4 Lane Ends Lancs
342 D2 Lane Ends Leeds
354 C6 Lane Ends N York
312 C1 Lane Ends Stockp
236 C4 Lane Green Staffs
317 F4 Laneham Notts
313 G4 Lane Head Derbys
392 D1 Lanehead Dur
328 B3 Lane Head Kirk
428 B2 Lanehead Nthumb
125 H4 Lane Head Pembks
325 E5 Lane Head Wigan
237 E4 Lane Head Wsall
338 B2 Lane Heads Lancs
32 B4 Lanehouse Dorset
401 G2 Lanercost Cumb
8 D2 Lanescot Cnwll
142 C3 Lanes End Bucks
126 B3 Lanesend Pembks
211 E3 Lane's End Shrops
236 D5 Lanesfield Wolves
341 E1 Laneshaw Bridge Lancs
340 B5 Lane Side Lancs
237 E3 Laney Green Staffs
24 B3 Langaford Devon
11 G2 Langage Devon
519 H1 Langal Highld
44 B2 Langaller Somset
277 F3 Langar Notts
483 E5 Langbank Rens
355 E4 Langbar N York
385 E2 Langbaurgh N York
353 G2 Langcliffe N York
374 A1 Langdale End N York
393 E3 Langdon Beck Dur
23 G5 Langdon Cross Cnwll
121 G2 Langdon Hills Essex
50 D3 Langdown Hants
501 F4 Langdyke Fife
174 D6 Langenhoe Essex
170 A1 Langford Beds
27 E3 Langford Devon
27 G2 Langford Devon
147 G3 Langford Essex
297 F3 Langford Notts
138 C4 Langford Oxon
43 H2 Langford Somset
43 F3 Langford Budville Somset
27 G2 Langford Green Devon
85 E3 Langford Green N Som
68 C4 Langham Dorset
174 D3 Langham Essex
260 D3 Langham Norfk
242 A2 Langham Rutlnd
44 C5 Langham Somset
224 C6 Langham Suffk
449 H3 Langhaugh Border
339 H3 Langho Lancs
425 H3 Langholm D & G
331 G5 Langholme N Linc
451 E5 Langhope Border
103 E4 Langland Swans
451 G2 Langlee Border
454 A5 Langleeford Nthumb
451 G2 Langlee Mains Border
486 A3 Langlees Falk
312 B5 Langley Ches
295 E5 Langley Derbys
171 F3 Langley Essex
163 F4 Langley Gloucs
50 D4 Langley Hants
170 B5 Langley Herts
98 C4 Langley Kent
403 E2 Langley Nthumb
139 E1 Langley Oxon
326 C3 Langley Rochdl
213 E2 Langley Sandw
117 H4 Langley Slough
43 E2 Langley Somset
190 B2 Langley Warwks
74 C4 Langley W Susx
111 G4 Langley Burrell Wilts
274 D2 Langley Common Derbys
92 C1 Langley Common Wokham
117 H3 Langley Corner Bucks
274 D2 Langley Green Derbys
174 A5 Langley Green Essex
213 E2 Langley Green Sandw
190 B2 Langley Green Warwks
77 E2 Langley Green W Susx
98 C4 Langley Heath Kent
43 E2 Langley Marsh Somset
295 E5 Langley Mill Derbys
395 F1 Langley Moor Dur
405 F6 Langley Park Dur
250 D4 Langley Street Norfk
95 E3 Langley Vale Surrey
467 H2 Langloan N Lans
57 G4 Langney E Susx
316 A2 Langold Notts
23 F5 Langore Cnwll
66 C4 Langport Somset
299 H5 Langrick Lincs
299 H5 Langrick Bridge Lincs
110 C6 Langridge BaNES
40 B3 Langridgeford Devon
380 D2 Langrigg Cumb
399 F5 Langrigg Cumb
73 H5 Langrish Hants
328 C4 Langsett Barns
451 G2 Langshaw Border
467 E2 Langside C Glas
602 E3 Langskaill Ork
19 F1 Langstone Devon
52 C3 Langstone Hants
108 C1 Langstone Newpt
370 A1 Langthorne N York
356 D1 Langthorpe N York
382 B4 Langthwaite N York
360 C1 Langtoft E R Yk
243 G2 Langtoft Lincs
394 D6 Langton Dur
319 G6 Langton Lincs
320 C5 Langton Lincs
359 E1 Langton N York
319 E4 Langton by Wragby Lincs
78 C2 Langton Green Kent
225 F5 Langton Green Suffk
31 E6 Langton Herring Dorset
47 G3 Langton Long Blandford Dorset
34 B5 Langton Matravers Dorset
39 F4 Langtree Devon
39 G4 Langtree Week Devon
391 F3 Langwathby Cumb
574 D3 Langwell Lodge Highld
315 G6 Langwith Derbys
315 G6 Langwith Junction Derbys
318 D4 Langworth Lincs
173 F5 Lanham Green Essex
15 E6 Lanivet Cnwll
8 B3 Lanjeth Cnwll
14 D6 Lanjew Cnwll
15 F3 Lank Cnwll
8 D2 Lanlivery Cnwll
6 D6 Lanner Cnwll
9 F2 Lanreath Cnwll
497 G4 Lanrick Stirlg
9 F3 Lansallos Cnwll
106 C2 Lansbury Park Caerph
110 C6 Lansdown BaNES
162 D5 Lansdown Gloucs
15 F2 Lanteglos Cnwll
9 E3 Lanteglos Highway Cnwll
452 B5 Lanton Border
454 A3 Lanton Nthumb
14 D5 Lantuel Cnwll
9 E2 Lantyan Cnwll
213 E3 Lapal Dudley
41 E6 Lapford Devon
41 E6 Lapford Cross Devon
476 F7 Laphroaig Ag & B
236 C2 Lapley Staffs
35 f7 La Pulente Jersey
214 B5 Lapworth Warwks
519 G6 Larachbeg Highld
485 G3 Larbert Falk
337 G1 Larbreck Lancs
338 C3 Larches Lancs
290 B4 Larden Green Ches
559 E3 Largie Abers
480 C2 Largiemore Ag & B
502 D3 Largoward Fife
464 D2 Largs N Ayrs
559 E1 Largue Abers
461 E5 Largybeg N Ayrs
461 E5 Largymeanoch N Ayrs
461 F5 Largymore N Ayrs
27 H3 Larkbeare Devon
482 B4 Larkfield Inver
97 H3 Larkfield Kent
342 D2 Larkfield Leeds
86 D1 Larkhall BaNES
468 B4 Larkhall S Lans
325 F4 Lark Hill Wigan
88 D6 Larkhill Wilts
275 H1 Larklands Derbys
201 G5 Larks' Hill Suffk
224 C2 Larling Norfk
35 j8 La Rocque Jersey
35 d2 La Roussaillerie Guern
160 D2 Larport Herefs
16 D3 Larrick Cnwll
439 G6 Larriston Border
410 C4 Larrock D & G
382 B1 Lartington Dur
554 B4 Lary Abers
136 B6 Lasborough Gloucs
73 G1 Lasham Hants
80 B1 Lashenden Kent
292 B3 Lask Edge Staffs
500 B6 Lassodie Fife
471 F1 Lasswade Mdloth
372 D1 Lastingham N York
84 D5 Latcham Somset
10 C2 Latchbrook Cnwll
171 E5 Latchford Herts
141 E4 Latchford Oxon
310 C2 Latchford Warrtn
148 A4 Latchingdon Essex
17 F4 Latchley Cnwll
91 G2 Latchmere Green Hants
325 F5 Lately Common Wigan
194 B5 Lathbury M Keyn
583 G3 Latheron Highld
583 G3 Latheronwheel Highld
324 B2 Lathom Lancs
502 D3 Lathones Fife
142 D5 Latimer Bucks
110 B3 Latteridge S Glos
68 A4 Lattiford Somset
175 E2 Lattinford Hill Suffk
137 G5 Latton Wilts
145 G3 Latton Bush Essex
556 C2 Lauchintilly Abers
472 C5 Lauder Border
472 C5 Lauder Barns Border
127 F2 Laugharne Carmth
187 H3 Laughern Hill Worcs
317 F4 Laughterton Lincs
57 E2 Laughton E Susx
217 E2 Laughton Leics
279 F3 Laughton Lincs
332 A5 Laughton Lincs
56 D2 Laughton Common E Susx
315 G2 Laughton Common Rothm
315 G2 Laughton en le Morthen Rothm
23 F1 Launcells Cross Cnwll
23 G6 Launceston Cnwll
85 F6 Launcherley Somset
340 C5 Laund Lancs
241 G4 Launde Abbey Leics
166 D5 Launton Oxon
540 D5 Laurencekirk Abers
412 C1 Laurieston D & G
486 B3 Laurieston Falk
194 C4 Lavendon M Keyn
200 B5 Lavenham Suffk
437 F5 Laverhay D & G
450 B2 Laverlaw Border
67 F2 Laverley Somset
106 C6 Lavernock V Glam
401 E2 Laversdale Cumb
70 D3 Laverstock Wilts
90 D5 Laverstoke Hants
163 G2 Laverton Gloucs
370 A5 Laverton N York
86 D4 Laverton Somset
35 d3 La Villette Guern
88 B3 Lavington Sands Wilts
289 E3 Lavister Wrexhm
8 C2 Lavrean Cnwll
468 C4 Law S Lans
510 B2 Lawers P & K
510 D5 Lawers P & K
175 E3 Lawford Essex
64 B4 Lawford Somset
215 H5 Lawford Heath Warwks
468 C4 Law Hill S Lans
17 E2 Lawhitton Cnwll
353 F1 Lawkland N York
353 F1 Lawkland Green N York
234 C5 Lawley Shrops
235 F3 Lawley Wrekin
113 E3 Lawn Swindn
272 B4 Lawnhead Staffs
343 F5 Lawns Wakefd
287 E1 Lawnt Denbgs
107 F2 Lawrence Hill Newpt
109 F4 Lawrence Weston Bristl
125 H3 Lawrenny Pembks
125 H3 Lawrenny Quay Pembks
199 H4 Lawshall Suffk
200 A4 Lawshall Green Suffk
186 A3 Lawton Herefs
210 C3 Lawton Shrops
291 G3 Lawton-gate Ches
291 F3 Lawton Heath End Ches
597 J3 Laxay W Isls
599 J8 Laxdale W Isls
322 g6 Laxey IoM
226 B5 Laxfield Suffk
605 H1 Laxfirth Shet
607 G6 Laxfirth Shet
584 D7 Laxford Bridge Highld
606 F5 Laxo Shet
606 F3 Laxobigging Shet
346 A4 Laxton E R Yk
242 D5 Laxton Nhants
296 D1 Laxton Notts
341 G1 Laycock Brad
174 B6 Layer Breton Essex
174 C6 Layer de la Haye Essex
174 B6 Layer Marney Essex
358 B4 Layerthorpe York
29 G2 Laymore Dorset
117 G1 Layters Green Bucks
345 H2 Laytham E R Yk
337 F2 Layton Bpool
397 E6 Lazenby R & Cl
391 F2 Lazonby Cumb
294 C3 Lea Derbys
28 D3 Lea Devon
161 F5 Lea Herefs
338 C3 Lea Lancs
317 F2 Lea Lincs
209 G2 Lea Shrops
233 H3 Lea Shrops
111 H2 Lea Wilts
119 H2 Lea Bridge Gt Lon
295 E4 Leabrooks Derbys
309 E5 Lea by Backford Ches
596 E7 Leacainn W Isls
595 J4 Leac a' Li W Isls
546 E2 Leacanashie Highld
565 L8 Leachkin Highld
591 D8 Leadaig W Isls
470 D3 Leadburn Mdloth
272 D2 Leadendale Staffs
298 A4 Leadenham Lincs
146 B2 Leaden Roding Essex
402 C6 Leadgate Cumb
404 D4 Leadgate Dur
435 H1 Leadhills S Lans
98 D4 Leadingcross Green Kent
313 H3 Leadmill Derbys
288 B2 Leadmill Flints
213 F5 Lea End Worcs
139 E1 Leafield Oxon
111 F6 Leafield Wilts
291 E5 Lea Forge Ches
169 F5 Leagrave Luton
49 H6 Leagreen Hants
309 H1 Lea Green St Hel
214 A2 Lea Hall Birm
273 F4 Lea Heath Staffs
371 E1 Leake N York
300 C4 Leake Commonside Lincs
300 D4 Leake Fold Hill Lincs
300 D5 Leake Hurn's End Lincs
386 C3 Lealholm N York
386 C3 Lealholm Side N York
161 F5 Lea Line Herefs
479 H3 Lealt Ag & B
543 J4 Lealt Highld
314 A4 Leam Derbys
238 C6 Lea Marston Warwks
215 G6 Leamington Hastings Warwks
191 E2 Leamington Spa Warwks
237 G3 Leamonsley Staffs
209 H2 Leamoor Common Shrops
237 E4 Leamore Wsall
405 H5 Leamside Dur
566 D8 Leanach Highld
212 B5 Leapgate Worcs
478 E7 Leargybreck Ag & B
386 D4 Lease Rigg N York
143 H2 Leasey Bridge Herts
365 G3 Leasgill Cumb
298 D5 Leasingham Lincs
395 F4 Leasingthorne Dur
102 C3 Leason Swans
308 C1 Leasowe Wirral
94 D3 Leatherhead Surrey
94 D3 Leatherhead Common Surrey
135 G4 Leathern Bottle Gloucs
356 A5 Leathley N York
270 B6 Leaton Shrops
235 E2 Leaton Wrekin
270 B6 Leaton Heath Shrops
338 C3 Lea Town Lancs
99 F4 Leaveland Kent
174 C2 Leavenheath Suffk
359 E2 Leavening N York
96 B2 Leaves Green Gt Lon
367 F2 Lea Yeat Cumb
374 D3 Lebberston N York
34 c4 Le Bigard Guern
34 c4 Le Bourg Guern
35 j8 Le Bourg Jersey
16 D2 Leburnick Cnwll
138 C5 Lechlade on Thames Gloucs
366 C4 Leck Lancs
72 A2 Leckford Hants
586 F5 Leckfurin Highld
167 F2 Leckhampstead Bucks
114 C4 Leckhampstead W Berk
114 C4 Leckhampstead Thicket W Berk
162 D6 Leckhampton Gloucs
574 D5 Leckmelm Highld
106 B5 Leckwith V Glam
360 C6 Leconfield E R Yk
506 F2 Ledaig Ag & B
518 C4 Ledaig Ag & B
168 B5 Ledburn Bucks
161 F2 Ledbury Herefs
509 H4 Ledcharrie Stirlg
161 F3 Leddington Gloucs
185 H4 Ledgemoor Herefs
185 H2 Ledicot Herefs
579 H7 Ledmore Highld
577 G5 Lednabirichen Highld
587 G4 Lednagullin Highld
309 E5 Ledsham Ches
344 A4 Ledsham Leeds
344 A4 Ledston Leeds
344 A3 Ledston Luck Leeds
165 G4 Ledwell Oxon
504 E6 Lee Ag & B
60 C2 Lee Devon
61 E2 Lee Devon
120 A5 Lee Gt Lon
71 H6 Lee Hants
352 B3 Lee Lancs
403 G3 Lee Nthumb
269 H3 Lee Shrops
606 D8 Leeans Shet
213 G2 Lee Bank Birm
605 H5 Leebotten Shet
234 B5 Leebotwood Shrops
270 C4 Lee Brockhurst Shrops
364 B6 Leece Cumb
121 G2 Lee Chapel Essex
109 E2 Leechpool Mons
142 C4 Lee Clump Bucks
142 C4 Lee Common Bucks
98 C4 Leeds Kent
343 F3 Leeds Leeds
3 G3 Leedstown Cnwll
62 B2 Leeford Devon
142 B3 Lee Gate Bucks
354 B2 Lee Gate N York
235 F2 Leegomery Wrekin
51 F3 Lee Ground Hants
327 F6 Lee Head Derbys
395 E3 Leeholme Dur
292 C3 Leek Staffs
292 C4 Leekbrook Staffs
214 D6 Leek Wootton Warwks
11 G2 Lee Mill Devon
341 G3 Leeming Brad
370 B2 Leeming N York
370 B1 Leeming Bar N York
353 E5 Leemings Lancs
18 C5 Lee Moor Devon
343 F4 Lee Moor Wakefd
51 F4 Lee-on-the-Solent Hants
149 F2 Lee-over-Sands Essex
274 D2 Lees Derbys
327 E4 Lees Oldham
241 G2 Leesthorpe Leics
288 C1 Leeswood Flints
513 F5 Leetown P & K
310 D5 Leftwich Ches
158 D6 Legar Powys
320 C3 Legbourne Lincs
389 H6 Legburthwaite Cumb
472 D6 Legerwood Border
75 E5 Leggatt Hill W Susx
34 c3 Le Gron Guern
319 E2 Legsby Lincs
35 i8 Le Haguais Jersey
35 i8 Le Hocq Jersey
240 B3 Leicester Leics
240 B4 Leicester Forest East Leics
215 G1 Leicester Grange Warwks
41 E5 Leigh Devon
46 B3 Leigh Dorset
47 E3 Leigh Dorset
48 C5 Leigh Dorset
97 E5 Leigh Kent
233 F4 Leigh Shrops
95 E5 Leigh Surrey
325 F4 Leigh Wigan
112 C1 Leigh Wilts
188 A4 Leigh Worcs
18 B6 Leigham C Plym
122 C3 Leigh Beck Essex
68 B3 Leigh Common Somset
111 F4 Leigh Delamere Wilts
80 D3 Leigh Green Kent
63 G4 Leighland Chapel Somset
122 C2 Leigh-on-Sea Sthend
52 C3 Leigh Park Hants
187 H4 Leigh Sinton Worcs
237 G4 Leighswood Wsall
111 E1 Leighterton Gloucs
369 G4 Leighton N York
232 D3 Leighton Powys
235 E3 Leighton Shrops
86 C6 Leighton Somset
219 G4 Leighton Bromswold Cambs
168 C4 Leighton Buzzard Beds
528 D2 Leightonhill Angus
86 B5 Leigh upon Mendip Somset
109 F5 Leigh Woods N Som
458 C2 Leim Ag & B
210 A6 Leinthall Earls Herefs
210 A6 Leinthall Starkes Herefs
209 G5 Leintwardine Herefs
216 B1 Leire Leics
585 H3 Leirinmore Highld
203 F2 Leiston Suffk
526 C5 Leitfie P & K
488 B4 Leith C Edin
474 A6 Leitholm Border
3 F2 Lelant Cnwll
3 F2 Lelant Downs Cnwll
348 D3 Lelley E R Yk
211 G5 Lem Hill Worcs
405 E1 Lemington Gatesd
453 E3 Lempitlaw Border
597 K5 Lemreway W Isls
144 B2 Lemsford Herts
366 D2 Lenacre Cumb
167 E3 Lenborough Bucks
189 F5 Lenchwick Worcs
418 D4 Lendalfoot S Ayrs
98 D4 Lenham Kent
99 E4 Lenham Forstal Kent
99 E5 Lenham Heath Kent
549 J4 Lenie Highld
453 F1 Lennel Border
484 C4 Lennoxtown E Duns
117 F3 Lent Bucks
287 E1 Lenten Pool Denbgs
276 C2 Lenton C Nott
279 E3 Lenton Lincs
276 B2 Lenton Abbey C Nott
565 K7 Lentran Highld
117 F3 Lent Rise Bucks
255 E4 Lenwade Norfk
484 D5 Lenzie E Duns
485 F5 Lenziemill N Lans
514 B2 Leoch Angus
555 F2 Leochel Cushnie Abers
186 B3 Leominster Herefs
136 A4 Leonard Stanley Gloucs
125 F3 Leonardston Pembks
476 F7 Leorin Ag & B
35 g6 Leoville Jersey
50 D5 Lepe Hants
542 B7 Lephin Highld
480 D1 Lephinchapel Ag & B
480 D1 Lephinmore Ag & B
359 E2 Leppington N York
328 C2 Lepton Kirk
34 b3 L'Eree Guern
9 E2 Lerryn Cnwll
605 J2 Lerwick Shet
34 b3 Les Arquets Guern
443 G2 Lesbury Nthumb
35 d3 Les Hubits Guern
558 D5 Leslie Abers
500 D4 Leslie Fife
34 c3 Les Lohiers Guern
447 F2 Lesmahagow S Lans
34 c4 Les Murchez Guern
22 C4 Lesnewth Cnwll
34 c4 Les Nicolles Guern
35 d2 Les Quartiers Guern
35 g7 Les Quennevais Jersey
34 b3 Les Sages Guern
558 D1 Lessendrum Abers
256 D4 Lessingham Norfk
120 C4 Lessness Heath Gt Lon
399 G4 Lessonhall Cumb
34 c4 Les Villets Guern
414 D4 Leswalt D & G
35 f6 L'Etacq Jersey
143 H5 Letchmore Heath Herts
170 A3 Letchworth Garden City Beds
114 B2 Letcombe Bassett Oxon
114 B2 Letcombe Regis Oxon
528 B5 Letham Angus
486 A2 Letham Falk
501 F2 Letham Fife
512 C5 Letham P & K
528 D5 Letham Grange Angus
440 C3 Lethem Border
560 B1 Lethenty Abers
202 B3 Letheringham Suffk
260 D4 Letheringsett Norfk
25 G6 Lettaford Devon
603 M2 Lettan Ork
556 D2 Letter Abers
563 H2 Letterewe Highld
546 F5 Letterfearn Highld
533 K4 Letterfinlay Highld
531 K5 Lettermorar Highld
518 C6 Lettermore Ag & B
574 D6 Letters Highld
151 F4 Letterston Pembks
551 J6 Lettoch Highld
551 K3 Lettoch Highld
185 F5 Letton Herefs
209 G5 Letton Herefs
248 C3 Letton Green Norfk
104 D2 Letty Brongu Brdgnd
144 C2 Letty Green Herts
315 H2 Letwell Rothm
152 D4 Let-y-bwlch Pembks
514 D5 Leuchars Fife
597 K5 Leumrabhagh W Isls
597 K2 Leurbost W Isls
8 C4 Levalsa Meor Cnwll
482 B4 Levan Inver
607 G5 Levaneap Shet
236 C1 Levedale Staffs
107 E2 Level of Mendalgief Newpt
171 G5 Level's Green Essex
361 E5 Leven E R Yk
502 B4 Leven Fife
460 D5 Levencorroch N Ayrs
488 D5 Levenhall E Loth
502 B4 Leven Links Fife
365 G2 Levens Cumb
469 E3 Leven Seat W Loth
171 E5 Levens Green Herts
326 C6 Levenshulme Manch
342 B3 Leventhorpe Brad
605 H6 Levenwick Shet
595 G5 Leverburgh W Isls
325 G3 Lever Edge Bolton
245 F2 Leverington Cambs
245 F3 Leverington Common Cambs
143 F3 Leverstock Green Herts
300 C5 Leverton Lincs
114 A5 Leverton W Berk
300 D5 Leverton Highgate Lincs
300 D5 Leverton Lucasgate Lincs
300 D5 Leverton Outgate Lincs
34 c2 Le Villocq Guern
176 D2 Levington Suffk
373 F1 Levisham N York
549 G6 Levishie Highld
139 E3 Lew Oxon
16 C2 Lewannick Cnwll
30 D1 Lewcombe Dorset
24 B5 Lewdown Devon
56 B2 Lewes E Susx
151 F5 Leweston Pembks
120 A5 Lewisham Gt Lon
549 J4 Lewiston Highld
105 E2 Lewistown Brdgnd
141 F5 Lewknor Oxon
61 G4 Leworthy Devon
99 F2 Lewson Street Kent
338 C2 Lewth Lancs
19 G2 Lewthorn Cross Devon
24 B5 Lewtrenchard Devon
174 C4 Lexden Essex
555 F2 Ley Abers
16 A5 Ley Cnwll
62 C4 Ley Somset
97 G3 Leybourne Kent
369 F1 Leyburn N York
291 F5 Leycett Staffs
238 B3 Leyfields Staffs
169 H5 Ley Green Herts
312 C2 Ley Hey Park Stockp
237 H5 Ley Hill Birm
142 D4 Ley Hill Bucks
110 B1 Leyhill S Glos
339 E5 Leyland Lancs
556 D2 Leylodge Abers
327 H1 Leymoor Kirk
571 J5 Leys Abers
388 C6 Leys Cumb
513 F2 Leys P & K
292 D5 Leys Staffs
123 G5 Leysdown-on-Sea Kent
160 D6 Leys Hill Herefs
528 D5 Leysmill Angus
527 E5 Leys of Cossans Angus
186 D2 Leysters Herefs
120 A2 Leyton Midland Road Gt Lon
16 D3 Lezant Cnwll
322 g4 Lezayre IoM
4 C2 Lezerea Cnwll
252 D4 Leziate Norfk
568 D3 Lhanbryde Moray
157 F4 Libanus Powys
469 F6 Libberton S Lans
188 D3 Libbery Worcs
488 B6 Liberton C Edin
595 J4 Liceasto W Isls
238 A2 Lichfield Staffs
213 E4 Lickey Worcs
213 E5 Lickey End Worcs
75 E4 Lickfold W Susx
212 A5 Lickhill Worcs
17 F2 Liddaton Devon

601 H8 Liddel Ork
519 J4 Liddesdale Highld
125 E3 Liddeston Pembks
113 F3 Liddington Swindn
113 E3 Liden Swindn
314 C4 Lidgate Derbys
199 E3 Lidgate Suffk
331 E4 Lidget Donc
296 B1 Lidgett Notts
343 F2 Lidgett Park Leeds
58 D3 Lidham Hill E Susx
168 D2 Lidlington Beds
53 G4 Lidsey W Susx
98 B2 Lidsing Kent
165 F5 Lidstone Oxon
588 D4 Lieurary Highld
514 A3 Liff Angus
213 G4 Lifford Birm
24 A5 Lifton Devon
23 H5 Liftondown Devon
342 B4 Lightcliffe Calder
270 C3 Lighteach Shrops
338 D3 Lightfoot Green Lancs
191 E3 Lighthorne Warwks
191 E3 Lighthorne Heath Warwks
191 E3 Lighthorne Rough Warwks
235 F3 Lightmoor Wrekin
292 B4 Light Oaks Staffs
136 B4 Lightpill Gloucs
93 F2 Lightwater Surrey
271 F4 Lightwood C Stke
314 D3 Lightwood Derbys
211 E1 Lightwood Shrops
292 D6 Lightwood Staffs
290 C6 Lightwood Green Ches
269 G1 Lightwood Green Wrexhm
216 C4 Lilbourne Nhants
325 F4 Liford Wigan
44 C3 Lillesdon Somset
235 C1 Lilleshall Wrekin
169 G4 Lilley Herts
114 C4 Lilley W Berk
451 G5 Lilliesleaf Border
167 F2 Lillingstone Dayrell Bucks
167 F1 Lillingstone Lovell Bucks
46 B2 Lillington Dorset
191 E1 Lillington Warwks
34 B3 Lilliput Poole
121 E2 Lillyputts Gt Lon
64 C3 Lilstock Somset
482 D5 Lilybank Inver
235 G2 Lilyhurst Shrops
81 G2 Lilyvale Kent
324 D1 Limbrick Lancs
169 F5 Limbury Luton
185 G1 Limebrook Herefs
326 B2 Limefield Bury
569 J5 Limehillock Moray
326 D4 Limehurst Tamesd
467 H4 Limekilnburn S Lans
315 F5 Limekiln Field Derbys
487 E3 Limekilns Fife
485 G5 Limerigg Falk
36 C4 Limerstone IoW
326 D4 Lime Side Oldham
402 D4 Limestone Brae Nthumb
162 B3 Lime Street Worcs
214 D4 Lime Tree Park Covtry
67 E5 Limington Somset
446 C4 Limmerhaugh Muir E Ayrs
250 D4 Limpenhoe Norfk
251 E4 Limpenhoe Hill Norfk
68 D3 Limpers Hill Wilts
86 D2 Limpley Stoke Wilts
96 A4 Limpsfield Surrey
96 B4 Limpsfield Common Surrey
441 G3 Linbriggs Nthumb
487 F6 Linburn W Loth
295 G4 Linby Notts
74 D3 Linchmere W Susx
423 G4 Lincluden D & G
318 B5 Lincoln Lincs
212 B6 Lincomb Worcs
12 C4 Lincombe Devon
19 F6 Lincombe Devon
365 F3 Lindale Cumb
364 C4 Lindal in Furness Cumb
451 F3 Lindean Border
136 B1 Linden Gloucs
77 F4 Lindfield W Susx
74 C2 Lindford Hants
342 B6 Lindley Kirk
356 A5 Lindley N York
501 E1 Lindores Fife
311 G4 Lindow End Ches
211 F6 Lindridge Worcs
172 C4 Lindsell Essex
200 C6 Lindsey Suffk
200 C6 Lindsey Tye Suffk
342 A5 Lindwell Calder
188 B1 Lineholt Worcs
188 B1 Lineholt Common Worcs
65 G4 Liney Somset
327 E3 Linfitts Oldham
49 F3 Linford Hants
121 G4 Linford Thurr
342 A2 Lingbob Brad
385 H1 Lingdale R & Cl
185 G1 Lingen Herefs
383 H2 Lingfield Darltn
96 A6 Lingfield Surrey
96 A6 Lingfield Common Surrey
310 B2 Lingley Green Warrtn
310 B1 Lingley Mere Warrtn
595 H6 Lingreabhagh W Isls
250 D3 Lingwood Norfk
439 E4 Linhope Border
442 B1 Linhope Nthumb
542 F3 Linicro Highld
85 E3 Link N Som
603 H4 Linkataing Ork
162 B3 Linkend Worcs
90 B3 Linkenholt Hants
80 B4 Linkhill Kent
16 D4 Linkinhorne Cnwll
601 H7 Linklater Ork
603 M1 Linklet Ork
602 E2 Links Ork
600 C4 Linksness Ork
601 J2 Linksness Ork
488 B1 Linktown Fife
233 G6 Linley Shrops
235 F5 Linley Shrops
235 F5 Linley Brook Shrops
187 F4 Linley Green Herefs
235 F5 Linleygreen Shrops
486 D3 Linlithgow W Loth
486 C4 Linlithgow Bridge W Loth
574 C2 Linnerineach Highld
565 K6 Linnie Highld
525 J1 Linns Angus
325 G4 Linnyshaw Salfd
26 A5 Linscott Devon
441 G3 Linshiels Nthumb
597 G1 Linsiadar W Isls
576 B4 Linsidemore Highld
168 C5 Linslade Beds
226 C4 Linstead Parva Suffk
400 D3 Linstock Cumb
396 C6 Linthorpe Middsb
235 E5 Linthurst Worcs
327 H2 Linthwaite Kirk
474 B3 Lintlaw Border
569 J2 Lintmill Moray

453 E4 Linton Border
198 B5 Linton Cambs
238 D1 Linton Derbys
161 F4 Linton Herefs
98 A5 Linton Kent
356 D5 Linton Leeds
431 E1 Linton Nthumb
354 C2 Linton N York
238 D1 Linton Heath Derbys
161 F5 Linton Hill Herefs
357 F2 Linton-on-Ouse N York
161 G3 Lintridge Gloucs
405 E3 Lintz Dur
404 D3 Lintzford Gatesd
403 G6 Lintzgarth Dur
49 F3 Linwood Hants
318 D2 Linwood Lincs
466 C2 Linwood Rens
593 D8 Lionacleit W Isls
593 D8 Lionacuidhe W Isls
599 L2 Lional W Isls
78 D6 Lions Green E Susx
74 C3 Liphook Hants
271 G3 Lipley Shrops
145 E5 Lippitts Hill Essex
86 B4 Lipyeate Somset
308 C1 Liscard Wirral
62 D5 Liscombe Somset
16 C6 Liskeard Cnwll
74 B4 Liss Hants
361 E3 Lissett E R Yk
74 B4 Liss Forest Hants
319 E3 Lissington Lincs
315 F1 Listerdale Rothm
44 C3 Listock Somset
321 F5 Listoft Lincs
199 H6 Liston Essex
199 G5 Liston Garden Essex
106 C3 Lisvane Cardif
107 F2 Liswerry Newpt
253 H4 Litcham Norfk
105 E3 Litchard Brdgnd
192 D4 Litchborough Nhants
90 C4 Litchfield Hants
275 F3 Litchurch C Derb
323 F5 Litherland Sefton
196 D6 Litlington Cambs
57 E4 Litlington E Susx
186 C5 Litmarsh Herefs
198 A5 Little Abington Cambs
218 D3 Little Addington Nhants
345 G4 Little Airmyn E R Yk
170 A4 Little Almshoe Herts
190 A2 Little Alne Warwks
323 F3 Little Altcar Sefton
90 A6 Little Amwell Herts
270 B1 Little Arowry Wrexhm
380 B3 Little Asby Cumb
87 E2 Little Ashley Wilts
237 G4 Little Aston Staffs
36 D4 Little Atherfield IoW
600 E6 Little Ayre Ork
606 D5 Little-ayre Shet
385 F2 Little Ayton N York
147 F3 Little Baddow Essex
111 E3 Little Badminton S Glos
524 D5 Little Ballinluig P & K
399 H3 Little Bampton Cumb
172 C3 Little Bardfield Essex
196 A3 Little Barford Beds
261 F5 Little Barningham Norfk
138 B2 Little Barrington Gloucs
309 G5 Little Barrow Ches
373 E4 Little Barugh N York
429 F4 Little Bavington Nthumb
79 E2 Little Bayham E Susx
202 A5 Little Bealings Suffk
163 E3 Little Beckford Worcs
89 G1 Little Bedwyn Wilts
175 F4 Little Bentley Essex
144 C3 Little Berkhamsted Herts
193 H2 Little Billing Nhants
168 C5 Little Billington Beds
160 C3 Little Birch Herefs
337 F1 Little Bispham Bpool
201 F5 Little Blakenham Suffk
390 C4 Little Blencow Cumb
237 F4 Little Bloxwich Wsall
75 G5 Little Bognor W Susx
294 B4 Little Bolehill Derbys
311 E2 Little Bollington Ches
326 A5 Little Bolton Salfd
94 C4 Little Bookham Surrey
41 G5 Littleborough Devon
191 H6 Littleborough Notts
217 F2 Littleborough Rochdl
142 C5 Little Bosullow Cnwll
100 C4 Littlebourne Kent
191 H6 Little Bourton Oxon
217 F2 Little Bowden Leics
142 C5 Little Boys Heath Bucks
198 D4 Little Bradley Suffk
174 C4 Little Braiswick Essex
389 F5 Little Braithwaite Cumb
209 G3 Little Brampton Shrops
147 G2 Little Braxted Essex
61 G4 Little Bray Devon
528 C2 Little Brechin Angus
30 D5 Littlebredy Dorset
168 C3 Little Brickhill M Keyn
193 E2 Little Brington Nhants
110 C1 Little Bristol S Glos
189 H4 Little Britain Warwks
175 E4 Little Bromley Essex
213 H2 Little Bromwich Birm
167 G3 Little Broughton Cumb
388 C3 Little Broughton Cumb
290 C1 Little Budworth Ches
121 G1 Little Burstead Essex
171 H2 Littlebury Essex
171 G2 Littlebury Green Essex
279 E6 Little Bytham Lincs
7 E3 Little Callestock Cnwll
172 C4 Little Cambridge Essex
172 B5 Little Canfield Essex
48 C5 Little Canford Dorset
337 F2 Little Carleton Bpool
320 C2 Little Carlton Lincs
297 E3 Little Carlton Notts
243 E3 Little Casterton Rutlnd
361 E6 Little Catwick E R Yk
219 F5 Little Catworth Cambs
320 C3 Little Cawthorpe Lincs
87 F2 Little Chalfield Wilts
142 D5 Little Chalfont Bucks
99 E5 Little Chart Kent
99 F5 Little Chart Forstal Kent
291 H4 Little Chell C Stke
275 F2 Little Chester C Derb
171 H1 Little Chesterford Essex
166 C5 Little Chesterton Oxon
88 A4 Little Cheverell Wilts
171 F2 Little Chishill Cambs
176 C6 Little Clacton Essex
138 D4 Little Clanfield Oxon
326 D2 Little Clegg Rochdl
388 C4 Little Clifton Cumb
334 B3 Little Coates NE Lin
189 E6 Little Comberton Worcs
16 D2 Little Comfort Cnwll
58 B5 Little Common E Susx
280 D4 Little Common Lincs
209 G4 Little Common Shrops
75 E5 Little Common W Susx
164 D3 Little Compton Warwks

401 E3 Little Corby Cumb
174 B2 Little Cornard Suffk
168 A5 Little Cowarne Herefs
88 D4 Littlecott Wilts
187 E4 Little Coxwell Oxon
138 D6 Little Crakehall N York
370 A1 Little Cransley Nhants
218 A4 Little Crawley M Keyn
194 C5 Little Creaton Nhants
217 F5 Little Cressingham Norfk
247 H5 Little Crosby Sefton
323 F4 Little Cubley Derbys
274 B2 Little Dalby Leics
241 G2 Little Dartmouth Devon
13 F3 Little Dawley Wrekin
235 F3 Littledean Gloucs
135 F2 Littledean Hill Gloucs
135 F2 Little Dens Hants
571 K7 Little Dewchurch Herefs
160 C3 Little Ditton Cambs
198 D3 Little Doward Herefs
134 C1 Littledown Bmouth
49 E6 Littledown Hants
90 A3 Little Downham Cambs
221 H3 Little Drayton Shrops
271 H3 Little Driffield E R Yk
360 C3 Little Drybrook Gloucs
134 C3 Little Dunham Norfk
247 H2 Little Dunkeld P & K
512 B1 Little Dunmow Essex
172 C5 Little Durnford Wilts
70 C3 Little Eastbury Worcs
188 B3 Little Easton Essex
172 C5 Little Eaton Derbys
275 F1 Little Eccleston Lancs
338 B1 Little Ellingham Norfk
248 D5 Little End Cambs
195 H3 Little End E R Yk
346 B2 Little End Essex
146 A4 Little Everdon Nhants
192 C3 Little Everleigh Wilts
197 E4 Little Eversden Cambs
138 C4 Little Faringdon Oxon
383 G6 Little Fencote N York
344 C2 Little Fenton N York
577 H4 Littleferry Highld
334 C3 Littlefield NE Lin
93 F4 Littlefield Common Surrey
116 D4 Littlefield Green W & M
200 D4 Little Finborough Suffk
248 A2 Little Fransham Norfk
99 E3 Little Frith Kent
142 D2 Little Gaddesden Herts
236 A5 Littlegain Shrops
219 G3 Little Gidding Cambs
266 H6 Little Glemham Suffk
512 A3 Little Glenshee P & K
161 F4 Little Gorsley Herefs
196 C4 Little Gransden Cambs
196 C5 Little Green Cambs
296 D6 Little Green Notts
86 C5 Little Green Somset
225 E5 Little Green Suffk
270 B1 Little Green Wrexhm
236 B1 Little Grimsby Lincs
320 B1 Little Gringley Notts
316 D3 Little Gruinard Highld
372 D4 Little Habton N York
171 F5 Little Hadham Herts
279 G1 Little Hale Lincs
248 B3 Little Hale Norfk
275 H1 Little Hallam Derbys
171 H6 Little Hallingbury Essex
21 E1 Little Hamgen Bucks
39 F3 Littleham Devon
609 J3 Littlehamar Shet
142 B4 Little Hampden Bucks
54 B4 Littlehampton W Susx
136 B3 Little Haresfield Gloucs
218 B5 Little Harrowden Nhants
339 G4 Little Harwood Bl w D
140 D4 Little Haseley Oxon
361 F6 Little Hatfield E R Yk
256 B5 Little Hautbois Norfk
124 D2 Little Haven Pembks
76 C3 Little Haven W Susx
237 H4 Little Hay Staffs
312 D2 Little Hayfield Derbys
273 F5 Little Haywood Staffs
289 F1 Little Heath Ches
215 E3 Little Heath Covtry
120 C2 Little Heath Gt Lon
143 E3 Little Heath Herts
272 C6 Little Heath Staffs
94 C2 Little Heath Surrey
115 H5 Little Heath W Berk
344 D5 Little Heck N York
19 H5 Littlehempston Devon
172 A4 Little Henham Essex
173 H2 Little Henny Essex
163 E6 Little Hereford Herefs
210 C6 Little Hereford Herefs
160 B4 Little Hill Somset
44 B5 Little Hill Somset
50 D4 Little Holbury Hants
125 F3 Little Honeyborough Pembks
338 C5 Little Hoole Moss Houses Lancs
174 C3 Little Horkesley Essex
171 F4 Little Hormead Herts
78 B6 Little Horsted E Susx
342 B3 Little Horton Brad
88 B2 Little Horton Wilts
167 G3 Little Horwood Bucks
329 G3 Little Houghton Barns
193 H3 Little Houghton Nhants
443 G1 Littlehoughton Nthumb
313 G4 Little Hucklow Derbys
325 G4 Little Hulton Salfd
115 E5 Little Hungerford W Berk
141 E3 Little Ickford Bucks
120 B2 Little Ilford Gt Lon
273 E5 Little Ingestre Staffs
189 F3 Little Inkberrow Worcs
194 C1 Little Irchester Nhants
86 D5 Little Keyford Somset
141 H3 Little Kimble Bucks
191 E4 Little Kineton Warwks
142 B5 Little Kingshill Bucks
21 F1 Little Knowle Devon
199 F3 Little Knowles Green Suffk
378 B4 Little Langdale Cumb
70 B2 Little Langford Wilts
146 A3 Little Laver Essex
215 H4 Little Lawford Warwks
337 F2 Little Layton Bpool
310 C4 Little Leigh Ches
147 E1 Little Leighs Essex
328 C2 Little Lepton Kirk
360 D5 Little Lever N York
325 G3 Little Linford M Keyn
333 G2 Little Limber Lincs
194 A6 Little Linford M Keyn
198 B5 Little Linton Cambs
66 D5 Little Load Somset
342 C2 Little London Brad
140 D2 Little London Bucks
142 B3 Little London Bucks
245 F5 Little London Cambs
280 D4 Little London E Susx
209 G4 Little London Lincs
172 D2 Little London Essex
78 D6 Little London E Susx
161 F6 Little London Gloucs

90 B5 Little London Hants
91 G3 Little London Hants
280 B5 Little London Lincs
281 F5 Little London Lincs
319 E2 Little London Lincs
320 B5 Little London Lincs
247 F5 Little London Norfk
255 G3 Little London Norfk
256 B3 Little London Norfk
261 F5 Little London Norfk
140 B4 Little London Oxon
207 G3 Little London Powys
26 A5 Little London Somset
201 E3 Little London Suffk
210 C2 Little London Worcs
211 E5 Little London Worcs
135 G2 Little Longstone Derbys
555 G5 Little Lynturk Abers
234 B3 Little Lyth Shrops
291 F5 Little Madeley Staffs
161 H1 Little Malvern Worcs
288 D1 Little Mancot Flints
173 G3 Little Maplestead Essex
161 F2 Little Marcle Herefs
117 E2 Little Marlow Bucks
340 D2 Little Marsden Lancs
167 E5 Little Marsh Bucks
260 D4 Little Marsh Norfk
87 F3 Little Marsh Wilts
337 G3 Little Marton Bpool
147 E4 Little Massingham Norfk
253 F3 Little Massingham Norfk
249 G3 Little Melton Norfk
185 E5 Little Merthyr Herefs
125 G2 Little Milford Pembks
433 G1 Littlemill E Ayrs
567 G6 Littlemill Highld
97 G5 Little Mill Kent
133 F4 Little Mill Mons
140 D4 Little Mill E R Yk
139 E2 Little Minster Oxon
142 C5 Little Missenden Bucks
101 F5 Little Mongeham Kent
294 D2 Littlemoor Derbys
32 B3 Littlemoor Dorset
340 A1 Little Moor Lancs
312 B2 Little Moor Stockp
340 A4 Little Moor End Lancs
140 B4 Littlemore Oxon
191 E3 Little Morrell Warwks
326 D5 Littlemoss Tamesd
288 C2 Little Mountain Flints
380 D2 Little Musgrave Cumb
269 H6 Little Ness Shrops
308 C4 Little Neston Ches
151 G4 Little Newcastle Pembks
394 C6 Little Newsham Dur
56 C2 Little Norlington E Susx
45 F4 Little Norton Somset
176 D4 Little Oakley Essex
218 B2 Little Oakley Nhants
194 D3 Little Odell Beds
169 G4 Little Offley Herts
236 B1 Little Onn Shrops
380 C1 Little Ormside Cumb
400 C3 Little Orton Cumb
239 E3 Little Orton Leics
222 C2 Little Ouse Cambs
357 E2 Little Ouseburn N York
275 E3 Littleover C Derb
269 G1 Little Overton Wrexhm
146 D3 Little Oxney Green Essex
214 C3 Little Packington Warwks
196 A2 Little Paxton Cambs
14 C4 Little Petherick Cnwll
569 G6 Little Pitlurg Moray
337 G3 Little Plumpton Lancs
250 C2 Little Plumstead Norfk
278 C3 Little Ponton Lincs
222 B2 Littleport Cambs
51 F4 Little Posbrook Hants
337 G2 Little Preston Kent
98 A3 Little Preston Leeds
343 G3 Little Preston Leeds
290 C1 Littler Ches
482 B2 Little Rahane Ag & B
220 B3 Little Raveley Cambs
346 B5 Little Reedness E R Yk
102 C4 Little Reynoldston Swans
356 B3 Little Ribston N York
164 B6 Little Rissington Gloucs
576 F3 Little Rogart Highld
164 D3 Little Rollright Oxon
254 C2 Little Ryburgh Norfk
442 C2 Little Ryle Nthumb
234 B4 Little Ryton Shrops
89 E2 Little Salisbury Wilts
391 F2 Little Salkeld Cumb
172 D3 Little Sampford Essex
92 D3 Little Sandhurst Br For
236 D3 Little Saredon Staffs
199 G2 Little Saxham Suffk
564 F5 Little Scatwell Highld
324 D2 Little Scotland Wigan
197 H4 Little Shelford Cambs
89 G5 Little Shoddesden Hants
190 C1 Little Shrewley Warwks
136 D1 Little Shurdington Gloucs
42 B6 Little Silver Devon
60 D3 Little Silver Devon
337 G2 Little Singleton Lancs
345 F2 Little Skipwith N York
330 B1 Little Smeaton N York
384 A4 Little Smeaton N York
260 B5 Little Snoring Norfk
110 C3 Little Sodbury S Glos
110 C3 Little Sodbury End S Glos
72 A3 Little Somborne Hants
111 H3 Little Somerford Wilts
271 G4 Little Soudley Shrops
353 G1 Little Stainforth N York
395 G5 Little Stainton Darltn
118 D1 Little Stanney Ches
309 F5 Little Stanney Ches
195 G2 Little Staughton Beds
116 B4 Littlestead Green Oxon
300 D2 Little Steeping Lincs
607 H1 Littlester Shet
199 H3 Little Stoke S Glos
272 D3 Little Stoke Staffs
81 G5 Littlestone-on-Sea Kent
261 E4 Little Stonham Suffk
241 E4 Little Stonham Suffk
391 G5 Little Strickland Cumb
370 F1 Little Stretton Leics
210 A1 Little Stretton Shrops
391 F5 Little Strickland Cumb
220 B4 Little Studley N York
272 B3 Little Stukeley Cambs
309 E4 Little Sugnall Staffs
281 G5 Little Sutton Ches
210 C3 Little Sutton Lincs
429 F4 Little Sutton E R Yk
161 E1 Little Swinburne Nthumb
165 F4 Little Tarrington Herefs
174 A5 Little Tew Oxon
221 H4 Little Tey Essex
198 B5 Little Thetford Cambs
261 E4 Little Thornage Norfk
337 G1 Little Thornton Lancs
406 C6 Little Thorpe Dur
342 C6 Little Thorpe Kirk
370 D5 Littlethorpe Leics
198 A5 Little Thurlow Suffk
198 D4 Little Thurlow Green Suffk

121 F3 Little Thurrock Thurr
85 F2 Littleton BaNES
289 F1 Littleton Ches
47 G4 Littleton Dorset
72 C3 Littleton Hants
513 G3 Littleton P & K
66 C3 Littleton Somset
93 G5 Littleton Surrey
118 B6 Littleton Surrey
87 G2 Littleton Wilts
118 B5 Littleton Common Surrey
111 E3 Littleton Drew Wilts
88 A4 Littleton Panell Wilts
109 G2 Littleton-upon-Severn S Glos
576 F4 Little Torboll Highld
39 G4 Little Torrington Devon
148 A2 Little Totham Essex
389 F6 Little Town Cumb
28 C3 Littletown Devon
406 A6 Littletown Dur
577 H6 Littletown Highld
37 E2 Littletown IoW
342 C5 Littletown Kirk
339 G2 Little Town Lancs
325 E6 Little Town Warrtn
142 C2 Little Tring Herts
239 E3 Little Twycross Leics
364 C5 Little Urswick Cumb
470 B2 Little Vantage W Loth
123 E2 Little Wakering Essex
172 A1 Little Walden Essex
200 B5 Little Waldingfield Suffk
260 B4 Little Walsingham Norfk
147 E2 Little Waltham Essex
216 A3 Little Walton Warwks
121 E1 Little Warley Essex
238 D4 Little Warton Warwks
163 E3 Little Washbourne Gloucs
347 E3 Little Weighton E R Yk
162 B2 Little Welland Worcs
200 A2 Little Welnetham Suffk
320 A2 Little Welton Lincs
175 E2 Little Wenham Suffk
235 E3 Little Wenlock Wrekin
67 G4 Little Weston Somset
36 D2 Little Whitehouse IoW
226 B4 Little Whittingham Green Suffk
116 D4 Littlewick Green W & M
148 C1 Little Wigborough Essex
198 A3 Little Wilbraham Cambs
30 A2 Littlewindsor Dorset
279 G3 Little Wisbeach Lincs
136 D1 Little Witcombe Gloucs
187 H2 Little Witley Worcs
140 C4 Little Wittenham Oxon
164 D2 Little Wolford Warwks
237 F2 Littlewood Staffs
142 C4 Little Wood Corner Bucks
189 G3 Littlewood Green Warwks
33 H3 Little Woolgarston Dorset
195 F6 Littleworth Beds
330 D5 Littleworth Donc
136 C4 Littleworth Gloucs
146 A2 Littleworth Gloucs
115 G1 Littleworth Oxon
139 E5 Littleworth Oxon
140 C3 Littleworth Oxon
237 F2 Littleworth Staffs
272 F5 Littleworth Staffs
190 C2 Littleworth Warwks
89 E2 Littleworth Wilts
188 C5 Littleworth Worcs
189 E2 Littleworth Worcs
76 C5 Littleworth W Susx
117 F2 Littleworth Common Bucks
233 F3 Little Worthen Shrops
238 B5 Littleworth End Staffs
198 D5 Little Wratting Suffk
194 C1 Little Wymington Beds
170 B4 Little Wymondley Herts
237 F3 Little Wyrley Staffs
270 D6 Little Wytheford Shrops
173 F2 Little Yeldham Essex
146 D1 Littley Green Essex
313 G5 Litton Derbys
353 H2 Litton N York
85 G4 Litton Somset
30 D4 Litton Cheney Dorset
313 G5 Litton Mill Derbys
597 K2 Liurbost W Isls
20 C5 Livermead Torbay
308 D2 Liverpool Lpool
342 C5 Liversedge Kirk
19 H2 Liverton Devon
386 F1 Liverton R & Cl
397 H6 Liverton Mines R & Cl
98 D4 Liverton Street Kent
97 H4 Livesey Street Kent
27 F2 Livingshayes Devon
487 E6 Livingston W Loth
469 G1 Livingston Village W Loth
307 H5 Lixwm Flints
4 D6 Lizard Cnwll
180 B3 Llaingarreglwyd Cerdgn
302 B4 Llaingoch IoA
207 H3 Llaithddu Powys
105 E4 Llampha V Glam
265 E6 Llanaber Gwynd
263 E2 Llanaelhaearn Gwynd
205 F5 Llanafan Cerdgn
183 F3 Llanafan-fawr Powys
303 G4 Llanallgo IoA
304 B2 Llanallgo IoA
208 A5 Llananno Powys
263 G3 Llanarmon Gwynd
268 B3 Llanarmon Dyffryn Ceiriog Wrexhm
268 B4 Llanarmon Mynydd-mawr Powys
288 A3 Llanarmon-yn-Ial Denbgs
180 B3 Llanarth Cerdgn
133 G2 Llanarth Mons
154 D5 Llanarthne Carmth
307 F3 Llanasa Flints
303 E3 Llanbabo IoA
205 E3 Llanbad Rhondd
205 E3 Llanbadarn Fawr Cerdgn
207 H2 Llanbadarn Fynydd Powys
184 B5 Llanbadarn-y-garreg Powys
133 G4 Llanbadoc Mons
302 D3 Llanbadrig IoA
108 C1 Llanbeder Newpt
264 D4 Llanbedr Gwynd
158 D5 Llanbedr Powys
184 B5 Llanbedr Powys
287 G3 Llanbedr-Dyffryn-Clwyd Denbgs
303 G4 Llanbedrgoch IoA
263 E4 Llanbedrog Gwynd
305 F6 Llanbedr-y-cennin Conwy
284 C3 Llanberis Gwynd
105 G5 Llanbethery V Glam
205 E3 Llanbister Powys
105 F5 Llanblethian V Glam
205 G6 Llanboidy Carmth
106 B1 Llanbradach Caerph
230 C4 Llanbrynmair Powys
105 G4 Llancadle V Glam
105 G4 Llancaiach Caerph
105 H5 Llancarfan V Glam

133 G4 Llancayo Mons
160 B5 Llancloudy Herefs
208 C1 Llancowrid Powys
205 E1 Llancynfelyn Cerdgn
132 C4 Llan-dafal Blae G
106 C4 Llandaff Cardif
106 B4 Llandaff North Cardif
264 D4 Llandanwg Gwynd
103 H3 Llandarcy Neath
127 F2 Llandawke Carmth
283 E1 Llanddaniel Fab IoA
128 D1 Llanddarog Carmth
204 D5 Llanddeiniol Cerdgn
283 F2 Llanddeiniolen Gwynd
267 F2 Llandderfel Gwynd
156 B5 Llanddeusant Carmth
302 D3 Llanddeusant IoA
157 H3 Llanddew Powys
102 B4 Llanddewi Swans
181 G3 Llanddewi-Brefi Cerdgn
133 F5 Llanddewi Rhos Mons
183 G5 Llanddewi'r Cwm Powys
133 F2 Llanddewi Rhydderch Mons
133 F1 Llanddewi Skirrid Mons
126 C1 Llanddewi Velfrey Pembks
208 B6 Llanddewi Ystradenni Powys
285 H2 Llanddoged Conwy
304 C4 Llanddona IoA
127 F2 Llanddowror Carmth
306 C4 Llanddulas Conwy
264 D5 Llanddwywe Gwynd
304 B4 Llanddyfnan IoA
265 E2 Llandecwyn Gwynd
157 G3 Llandefaelog Powys
158 B3 Llandefaelog-tre'r-graig Powys
158 A2 Llandefalle Powys
304 C5 Llandegai Gwynd
304 C5 Llandegfan IoA
288 A4 Llandegla Denbgs
184 B2 Llandegley Powys
133 F5 Llandegveth Mons
155 F5 Llandeilo Carmth
184 A6 Llandeilo Graban Powys
156 D3 Llandeilo'r-Fan Powys
151 E4 Llandeloy Pembks
133 H4 Llandenny Mons
133 H4 Llandenny Walks Mons
108 D1 Llandevaud Newpt
108 C2 Llandevenny Mons
152 C4 Llandilo Pembks
154 C5 Llandilo-yr-ynys Carmth
160 C4 Llandinabo Herefs
207 G2 Llandinam Powys
152 C5 Llandissilio Pembks
134 C4 Llandogo Mons
105 F5 Llandough V Glam
106 C4 Llandough V Glam
156 B3 Llandovery Carmth
105 E5 Llandow V Glam
155 G1 Llandre Carmth
205 E2 Llandre Cerdgn
267 G2 Llandrillo Denbgs
306 A3 Llandrillo-yn-Rhos Conwy
183 G2 Llandrindod Wells Powys
269 E6 Llandrinio Powys
150 C5 Llandruidion Pembks
305 G3 Llandudno Conwy
305 G4 Llandudno Junction Conwy
262 D3 Llandudwen Gwynd
282 D4 Llandwrog Gwynd
129 F1 Llandybie Carmth
128 B2 Llandyfaelog Carmth
129 F1 Llandyfan Carmth
153 G1 Llandyfriog Cerdgn
303 F3 Llandyfrydog IoA
179 E5 Llandygwydd Cerdgn
288 A6 Llandynan Denbgs
287 F1 Llandyrnog Denbgs
269 E6 Llandysilio Powys
232 C5 Llandyssil Powys
154 B1 Llandysul Cerdgn
106 C4 Llanedeyrn Cardif
106 D3 Llanedeyrn Cardif
283 F2 Llanedwen IoA
157 H2 Llaneglwys Powys
229 E3 Llanegryn Gwynd
154 D5 Llanegwad Carmth
303 G2 Llaneilian IoA
306 B4 Llaneilian-yn-Rhos Conwy
287 G4 Llanelidan Denbgs
158 C3 Llanelieu Powys
133 E2 Llanellen Mons
128 D4 Llanelli Carmth
265 G6 Llanelltyd Gwynd
132 D2 Llanelly Mons
132 D2 Llanelly Hill Mons
183 G4 Llanelwedd Powys
264 D5 Llanenddwyn Gwynd
262 D5 Llanengan Gwynd
233 F6 Llanerch Powys
306 C5 Llanerchemrys Powys
305 F4 Llanerchymedd IoA
231 G3 Llanerfyl Powys
303 G3 Llaneuddog IoA
132 B6 Llanfabon Caerph
132 D6 Llanfach Caerph
302 D4 Llanfachraeth IoA
266 B5 Llanfachreth Gwynd
302 D6 Llanfaelog IoA
304 D4 Llanfaes IoA
157 G4 Llanfaes Powys
302 D3 Llanfaethlu IoA
283 E3 Llanfaglan Gwynd
264 D4 Llanfair Gwynd
232 B3 Llanfair Caereinion Powys
181 F4 Llanfair Clydogau Cerdgn
287 G3 Llanfair Dyffryn Clwyd Denbgs
305 E4 Llanfairfechan Gwynd
133 F3 Llanfair Kilgeddin Mons
152 D2 Llanfair-Nant-Gwyn Pembks
304 B5 Llanfair P G IoA
306 C5 Llanfair Talhaiarn Conwy
208 D4 Llanfair Waterdine Shrops
302 C5 Llanfairynghornwy IoA
302 D2 Llanfairyneubwll IoA
152 D6 Llanfallteg Carmth
152 C6 Llanfallteg West Carmth
183 H4 Llanfaredd Powys
204 D4 Llanfarian Cerdgn
268 C5 Llanfechain Powys
183 F4 Llanfechan Powys
303 E2 Llanfechell IoA
228 D3 Llanfendigaid Gwynd
288 A2 Llanferres Denbgs
265 G1 Llan Ffestiniog Gwynd
302 D3 Llanfflewyn IoA
302 D4 Llanfigael IoA
154 B2 Llanfihangel-ar-arth Carmth
286 D5 Llanfihangel Glyn Myfyr Conwy
183 G2 Llanfihangel-helygen Powys
157 E3 Llanfihangel Nant Bran Powys
184 C3 Llanfihangel-Nant-Melan Powys

184 C1 Llanfihangel Rhydithon Powys
108 D2 Llanfihangel Rogiet Mons
158 B4 Llanfihangel Tal-y-llyn Powys
134 A4 Llanfihangel Tor y Mynydd Mons
154 C5 Llanfihangel uwch-Gwili Carmth
205 F4 Llanfihangel-y-Creuddyn Cerdgn
232 A1 Llanfihangel-yng-Ngwynfa Powys
302 D5 Llanfihangel yn Nhowyn IoA
229 F3 Llanfihangel-y-pennant Gwynd
284 B6 Llanfihangel-y-pennant Gwynd
158 B3 Llanfilo Powys
133 E2 Llanfoist Mons
267 E2 Llanfor Gwynd
133 F6 Llanfrechfa Torfn
265 E1 Llanfrothen Gwynd
158 A4 Llanfrynach Powys
287 G3 Llanfwrog Denbgs
302 D4 Llanfwrog IoA
268 B6 Llanfyllin Powys
155 F4 Llanfynydd Carmth
288 C3 Llanfynydd Flints
153 E3 Llanfyrnach Pembks
231 F2 Llangadfan Powys
128 B3 Llangadog Carmth
155 H4 Llangadog Carmth
282 C2 Llangadwaladr IoA
268 C3 Llangadwaladr Powys
282 D2 Llangaffo IoA
128 A1 Llangain Carmth
183 E5 Llangammarch Wells Powys
105 E4 Llangan V Glam
160 C5 Llangarron Herefs
158 B4 Llangasty-Talyllyn Powys
155 E5 Llangathen Carmth
158 C6 Llangattock Powys
159 F5 Llangattock Lingoed Mons
134 A1 Llangattock-Vibon-Avel Mons
268 C5 Llangedwyn Powys
303 G5 Llangefni IoA
105 E2 Llangeinor Brdgnd
181 F3 Llangeitho Cerdgn
153 H2 Llangeler Carmth
228 D3 Llangelynnin Gwynd
128 D4 Llangennech Carmth
102 B3 Llangennith Swans
158 D6 Llangenny Powys
306 B6 Llangernyw Conwy
133 G4 Llangeview Mons
262 D5 Llangian Gwynd
129 H3 Llangiwg Neath
151 F3 Llangloffan Pembks
152 D4 Llanglydwen Carmth
304 D4 Llangoed IoA
178 D4 Llangoedmor Cerdgn
268 C1 Llangollen Denbgs
152 C4 Llangolman Pembks
158 B4 Llangors Powys
205 E3 Llangorwen Cerdgn
134 B3 Llangovan Mons
267 E3 Llangower Gwynd
179 G3 Llangranog Cerdgn
303 F6 Llangristiolus IoA
160 C6 Llangrove Herefs
159 G4 Llangua Mons
208 C5 Llangunllo Powys
154 B5 Llangunnor Carmth
207 E4 Llangurig Powys
286 D6 Llangwm Conwy
133 H4 Llangwm Mons
125 G3 Llangwm Pembks
262 B4 Llangwnnadl Gwynd
287 G1 Llangwyfan Denbgs
303 F5 Llangwyllog IoA
205 E5 Llangwyryfon Cerdgn
181 E4 Llangybi Cerdgn
263 G2 Llangybi Gwynd
133 G5 Llangybi Mons
129 F5 Llangyfelach Swans
128 C2 Llangynderyn Carmth
287 G2 Llangynhafal Denbgs
158 B6 Llangynidr Powys
232 B3 Llangyniew Powys
153 E6 Llangynin Carmth
127 G1 Llangynog Carmth
267 G4 Llangynog Powys
104 D2 Llangynwyd Brdgnd
158 A4 Llanhamlach Powys
105 G3 Llanharan Rhondd
105 G3 Llanharry Rhondd
107 F1 Llanhennock Mons
132 D4 Llanhilleth Blae G
150 D4 Llanhowel Pembks
207 F3 Llanidloes Powys
262 D4 Llaniestyn Gwynd
206 D3 Llanigon Powys
158 D1 Llanilar Cerdgn
205 E5 Llanilar Cerdgn
105 F3 Llanilid Rhondd
181 F3 Llanio Cerdgn
125 G4 Llanion Pembks
106 C3 Llanishen Cardif
134 B4 Llanishen Mons
154 C4 Llanllawddog Carmth
304 D6 Llanllechid Gwynd
133 G5 Llanllowell Mons
231 G4 Llanllugan Powys
154 A6 Llanllwch Carmth
232 B6 Llanllwchaiarn Powys
154 C2 Llanllwni Carmth
208 C3 Llanllyfni Shrops
283 E5 Llanllyfni Gwynd
102 B3 Llanmadoc Swans
106 B4 Llanmaes Cardif
105 F6 Llanmaes V Glam
108 C2 Llanmartin Newpt
232 B6 Llanmerewig Powys
105 F5 Llanmihangel V Glam
126 C2 Llan-mill Pembks
127 F3 Llanmiloe Carmth
102 D3 Llanmorlais Swans
306 D5 Llannefydd Conwy
308 A4 Llannerch-y-môr Flints
128 A3 Llannon Carmth
263 F3 Llannor Gwynd
180 D1 Llanon Cerdgn
150 D3 Llanon Pembks
133 G3 Llanover Mons
154 B4 Llanpumsaint Carmth
125 G4 Llanreath Pembks
287 F2 Llanrhaeadr Denbgs
268 B4 Llanrhaeadr-ym-Mochnant Powys
150 D3 Llanrhian Pembks
102 C3 Llanrhidian Swans
305 G3 Llanrhos Conwy
302 D3 Llanrhyddlad IoA
204 C6 Llanrhystud Cerdgn
160 B6 Llanrothal Herefs
283 F3 Llanrug Gwynd
285 H2 Llanrwst Conwy
127 F2 Llansadurnen Carmth
155 G3 Llansadwrn Carmth

304 C4 Llansadwrn IoA
128 A3 Llansaint Carmth
129 G5 Llansamlet Swans
305 G4 Llansanffraid Glan Conwy Conwy
286 C1 Llansannan Conwy
105 F4 Llansannor V Glam
204 C6 Llansantffraed Cerdgn
158 B5 Llansantffraed Powys
207 E6 Llansantffraed-Cwmdeuddwr Powys
184 A3 Llansantffraed-in-Elwel Powys
268 D5 Llansantffraid-ym-Mechain Powys
155 F2 Llansawel Carmth
130 A6 Llansawel Neath
268 D4 Llansilin Powys
134 A4 Llansoy Mons
157 G4 Llanspyddid Powys
125 F3 Llanstadwell Pembks
127 G2 Llansteffan Carmth
158 B1 Llanstephan Powys
133 E6 Llantarnam Torfn
159 F5 Llanteems Mons
126 D2 Llanteg Pembks
159 E4 Llanthony Mons
133 G1 Llantilio Crossenny Mons
133 F1 Llantilio Pertholey Mons
303 E4 Llantrisant IoA
133 G5 Llantrisant Mons
105 H3 Llantrisant Rhondd
105 G5 Llantrithyd V Glam
130 B5 Llantwit Neath
106 A2 Llantwit Fardre Rhondd
105 E6 Llantwit Major V Glam
266 D3 Llanuwchllyn Gwynd
108 D1 Llanvaches Newpt
134 A6 Llanvair Discoed Mons
133 G2 Llanvapley Mons
133 G1 Llanvetherine Mons
159 E3 Llanveynoe Herefs
159 F5 Llanvihangel Crucorney Mons
133 F3 Llanvihangel Gobion Mons
134 A2 Llanvihangel-Ystern-Llewern Mons
160 B4 Llanwarne Herefs
267 G6 Llanwddyn Powys
133 E2 Llanwenarth Mons
180 C5 Llanwenog Cerdgn
108 C2 Llanwern Newpt
153 F4 Llanwinio Carmth
283 E4 Llanwnda Gwynd
151 F2 Llanwnda Pembks
180 D5 Llanwnnen Cerdgn
231 G6 Llanwnog Powys
155 H3 Llanwrda Carmth
230 B4 Llanwrin Powys
182 F2 Llanwrthwl Powys
88 D1 Llanwrtyd Powys
182 D5 Llanwrtyd Wells Powys
231 H4 Llanwyddelan Powys
268 D5 Llanyblodwel Shrops
127 G2 Llanybri Carmth
180 D6 Llanybydder Carmth
152 B5 Llanycefn Pembks
151 G2 Llanychaer Pembks
267 E3 Llanycil Gwynd
181 F5 Llanycrwys Carmth
267 E6 Llanymawddwy Gwynd
269 E5 Llanymynech Powys
302 C4 Llanynghenedl IoA
287 G2 Llanynys Denbgs
289 E4 Llan-y-pwll Wrexhm
241 G4 Llanyrafon Torfn
133 E5 Llanyre Powys
183 G2 Llanyre Powys
263 H3 Llanystumdwy Gwynd
158 A4 Llanywern Powys
126 B1 Llawhaden Pembks
268 D3 Llawnt Shrops
262 D5 Llawr Dref Gwynd
207 E1 Llawr-y-glyn Powys
288 D3 Llay Wrexhm
303 E4 Llechcynfarwy IoA
263 H2 Llecheiddior Gwynd
158 A4 Llechfaen Powys
265 F6 Llechfraith Gwynd
132 B3 Llechrhyd Caerph
179 E5 Llechryd Cerdgn
268 D3 Llechrydau Wrexhm
305 F4 Llechwedd Conwy
205 E5 Lledrod Cerdgn
128 C4 Llettyrychen Carmth
103 G2 Llewelyn Park Swans
154 D2 Llidiad-Nenog Carmth
266 D2 Llidiardau Gwynd
287 G6 Llidiart-y-Parc Denbgs
263 E2 Lithfaen Gwynd
307 G4 Lloc Flints
288 C2 Llong Flints
158 C1 Llowes Powys
208 D4 Lloyney Powys
229 G5 Llugwy Gwynd
180 D3 Llundain-fach Cerdgn
179 G5 Llwch-yr-hâl Cerdgn
104 C1 Llwydarth Brdgnd
131 F4 Llwydcoed Rhondd
287 F2 Llwyn Denbgs
209 E3 Llwyn Shrops
180 B3 Llwyncelyn Cerdgn
179 H2 Llwyndafydd Cerdgn
207 E2 Llwyn-derw Powys
232 C4 Llwynderw Powys
133 E1 Llwyn-du Mons
179 E5 Llwynduris Cerdgn
263 F2 Llwyndyrys Gwynd
94 C5 Llwyneinion Wrexhm
197 E2 Llwyneinion Wrexhm
228 D3 Llwyngwril Gwynd
128 D5 Llwynhendy Carmth
266 D2 Llwyn-mawr Wrexhm
131 G2 Llwyn-on Village Myr Td
126 D1 Llwynpinner Pembks
129 E3 Llwyn-têg Carmth
126 D1 Llwyn-y-brain Carmth
269 F5 Llwyn-y-go Shrops
206 D1 Llwynypia Rhondd
181 E3 Llwyn-y-groes Cerdgn
131 F6 Llwynypia Rhondd
153 E3 Llwyn-yr-hwrdd Pembks
269 E5 Llynclys Shrops
303 F5 Llynfaes IoA
304 C5 Llyny Gors IoA
306 B4 Llysfaen Conwy
158 B2 Llyswen Powys
105 E5 Llysworney V Glam
152 A5 Llys-y-frân Pembks
156 D3 Llywel Powys
205 G3 Llywernog Cerdgn
314 B2 Load Brook Sheff
486 C4 Loan Falk
577 H8 Loandhu Highld
474 A6 Loanend Nthumb
471 E1 Loanhead Mdloth
444 D3 Loans S Ayrs
430 D3 Loansdean Nthumb
566 F1 Loans of Tullich Highld
60 C4 Lobb Devon
8 C4 Lobb's Shop Cnwll
24 C5 Lobhillcross Devon
192 D1 Lobley Hill Gatesd
278 C2 Lobthorpe Lincs
593 E9 Loch a' Charnain W Isls
597 J2 Loch a' Ghainmhich W Isls

531 L6 Lochailort Highld
519 G7 Lochaline Highld
551 G5 Lochanhully Highld
415 E5 Lochans D & G
423 G3 Locharbriggs D & G
566 B8 Lochardil Highld
579 G4 Lochassynt Lodge Highld
493 F1 Lochavich Ag & B
507 K4 Lochawe Ag & B
590 F3 Loch Baghasdail W Isls
590 F3 Lochboisdale W Isls
505 J6 Lochbuie Ag & B
546 F2 Lochcarron Highld
505 L4 Lochdon Ag & B
479 K6 Lochead Ag & B
509 J5 Lochearnhead Stirlg
514 B3 Lochee C Dund
488 B5 Lochend C Edin
549 K2 Lochend Highld
589 H3 Lochend Highld
436 C5 Locherben D & G
592 F5 Loch Euphort W Isls
423 E5 Lochfoot D & G
480 C1 Lochgair Ag & B
549 J6 Lochgarthside Highld
500 C6 Lochgelly Fife
480 B2 Lochgilphead Ag & B
495 E4 Lochgoilhead Ag & B
410 B3 Loch Head D & G
568 D3 Lochhill Moray
578 E5 Lochinver Highld
511 E5 Lochlane P & K
564 E4 Lochluichart Highld
424 B3 Lochmaben D & G
592 G4 Lochmaddy W Isls
579 J2 Lochmore Lodge Highld
592 G4 Loch nam Madadh W Isls
500 C5 Lochore Fife
592 G3 Lochportain W Isls
463 F4 Lochranza N Ayrs
593 E10 Loch Sgioport W Isls
529 F2 Lochside Abers
423 F4 Lochside D & G
566 E6 Lochside Highld
581 L2 Lochside Highld
585 J5 Lochside Highld
444 D5 Lochside S Ayrs
577 H7 Lochslin Highld
584 E8 Lochstack Lodge Highld
541 E1 Lochton Abers
556 C5 Lochton of Leys Abers
512 C4 Lochty P & K
519 J4 Lochuisge Highld
465 H3 Lochwinnoch Rens
467 G1 Lochwood C Glas
437 E5 Lochwood D & G
533 H7 Lochyside Highld
8 C1 Lockengate Cnwll
424 C3 Lockerbie D & G
112 D6 Lockeridge Wilts
88 D1 Lockeridge Dene Wilts
71 F4 Lockerley Hants
401 F5 Lockhills Cumb
84 C3 Locking N Som
120 B5 Locking Stumps Warrtn
274 C2 Lockington E R Yk
115 E5 Lockington Leics
109 H4 Lockleaze Bristl
96 B1 Locksbottom Gt Lon
86 C2 Locksbrook BaNES
36 C2 Locksgreen IoW
51 E3 Locks Heath Hants
373 F2 Lockton N York
328 A1 Lockwood Kirk
241 G4 Loddington Leics
217 H4 Loddington Nhants
12 C3 Loddiswell Devon
250 D5 Loddon Norfk
250 D5 Loddon Ingloss Norfk
198 A2 Lode Cambs
214 B3 Lode Heath Solhll
30 B4 Loders Dorset
270 D2 Lodgebank Shrops
381 H5 Lodge Green N York
214 D3 Lodge Green Solhll
213 F3 Lodge Hill Birm
16 B6 Lodge Hill Cnwll
48 C5 Lodge Hill Poole
343 E5 Lodge Hill Wakefd
100 D6 Lodge Lees Kent
314 B2 Lodge Moor Sheff
189 F1 Lodge Park Worcs
75 E3 Lodsworth W Susx
75 E5 Lodsworth Common W Susx
109 F4 Lodway N Som
343 H4 Lofthouse Leeds
369 F5 Lofthouse N York
343 H4 Lofthouse Gate Wakefd
397 H6 Loftus R & Cl
408 B3 Logan D & G
446 B5 Logan E Ayrs
469 F2 Loganlea W Loth
408 B3 Logan Mains D & G
288 A2 Loggerheads Denbgs
271 G2 Loggerheads Staffs
574 C5 Loggie Highld
529 E2 Logie Angus
514 C3 Logie Fife
567 J6 Logie Moray
554 D4 Logie Coldstone Abers
566 D1 Logie Hill Highld
559 F2 Logie Newton Abers
529 E2 Logie Pert Angus
524 E5 Logierait P & K
152 D5 Login Carmth
94 C5 Logmore Green Surrey
197 E2 Lolworth Cambs
340 C2 Lomeshaye Lancs
266 D2 Lôn Gwynd
562 B6 Lonbain Highld
359 G5 Londesborough E R Yk
119 F3 London Gt Lon
8 C1 London Apprentice Cnwll
80 C2 London Beach Kent
144 A4 London Colney Herts
370 C2 Londonderry N York
213 F2 Londonderry Sandw
212 D1 London Fields Dudley
50 A2 London Minstead Hants
278 C2 Londonthorpe Lincs
573 G7 Londubh Highld
572 E8 Lonemore Highld
577 G6 Lonemore Highld
211 H5 Long Ashton N Som
211 H5 Long Bank Worcs
465 G4 Longbar N Ayrs
310 G4 Longbarn Warrtn
297 F6 Long Bennington Lincs
431 E6 Longbenton N Tyne
164 B4 Longborough Gloucs
30 D4 Long Bredy Dorset
213 F4 Longbridge C Plym
190 D2 Longbridge Birm
69 E1 Longbridge Warwks
110 A5 Longbridge Deverill Wilts
291 G4 Longbridge Hayes Staffs
192 D1 Long Buckby Nhants
192 D1 Long Buckby Wharf Nhants
400 B3 Longburgh Cumb
30 D4 Longburton Dorset
15 G5 Longcause Devon
277 F4 Long Clawson Leics

294 A3 Longcliffe Derbys
51 F1 Long Common Hants
272 C5 Long Compton Staffs
164 D3 Long Compton Warwks
113 G6 Longcot Oxon
141 E3 Long Crendon Bucks
48 B2 Long Crichel Dorset
399 G3 Longcroft Cumb
485 F4 Longcroft Falk
17 F3 Longcross Devon
93 G1 Longcross Surrey
68 C3 Long Cross Wilts
380 A4 Longdale Cumb
401 F6 Longdales Cumb
111 F4 Long Dean Wilts
234 A3 Longden Shrops
234 A4 Longden Common Shrops
94 D1 Long Ditton Surrey
237 G2 Longdon Staffs
162 B2 Longdon Worcs
237 G2 Longdon Green Staffs
162 B2 Longdon Heath Worcs
162 B2 Longdon Hill End Worcs
235 E1 Longdon on Tern Wrekin
26 D4 Longdowns Devon
4 D2 Longdowns Cnwll
345 F4 Long Drax N York
315 E5 Long Duckmanton Derbys
276 A3 Long Eaton Derbys
121 F6 Longfield Kent
605 G7 Longfield Shet
87 F3 Longfield Wilts
121 F6 Longfield Hill Kent
34 B2 Longfleet Poole
215 E3 Longford Covtry
274 C2 Longford Derbys
162 B5 Longford Gloucs
118 A4 Longford Gt Lon
96 D3 Longford Kent
271 E3 Longford Shrops
310 C1 Longford Warrtn
271 G6 Longford Wrekin
274 C2 Longfordlane Derbys
513 H4 Longforgan P & K
473 F3 Longformacus Border
443 E4 Longframlington Nthumb
173 G2 Long Gardens Essex
353 F3 Long Gill N York
309 G5 Long Green Ches
225 E4 Long Green Suffk
162 B3 Long Green Worcs
48 D5 Longham Dorset
254 B4 Longham Norfk
139 G2 Long Hanborough Oxon
561 G2 Longhaven Abers
87 E6 Longhedge Wilts
430 D2 Longhirst Nthumb
161 F6 Longhope Gloucs
600 D6 Longhope Ork
443 F6 Longhorsley Nthumb
443 G1 Longhoughton Nthumb
86 B2 Longhouse BaNES
191 G1 Long Itchington Warwks
389 G2 Longlands Cumb
120 B5 Longlands Gt Lon
274 C2 Longlane Derbys
115 E5 Longlane W Berk
235 E1 Long Lane Wrekin
215 H4 Long Lawford Warwks
342 A1 Long Lee Brad
162 B6 Longlevens Gloucs
341 H5 Longley Calder
328 A3 Longley Kirk
314 C1 Longley Estate Sheff
187 G4 Longley Green Worcs
66 D5 Long Load Somset
570 C3 Longmanhill Abers
142 C1 Long Marston Herts
357 F4 Long Marston N York
190 B5 Long Marston Warwks
391 H5 Long Marton Cumb
198 A2 Long Meadow Cambs
209 G3 Long Meadowend Shrops
199 H5 Long Melford Suffk
74 B3 Longmoor Camp Hants
568 C4 Longmorn Moray
312 A5 Longmoss Ches
111 G1 Long Newnton Gloucs
452 A4 Longnewton Border
384 B1 Longnewton S on T
135 H2 Longney Gloucs
489 E4 Longniddry E Loth
234 B4 Longnor Shrops
236 C2 Longnor Staffs
293 E2 Longnor Staffs
234 B4 Longnor Park Shrops
269 G5 Long Oak Shrops
90 C6 Longparish Hants
400 D2 Longpark Cumb
72 B3 Long Park Hants
353 F3 Long Preston N York
136 C3 Longridge Gloucs
339 F2 Longridge Lancs
236 D1 Longridge Staffs
469 E2 Longridge W Loth
162 B5 Longridge End Gloucs
485 G5 Longriggend N Lans
485 G5 Longriggend N Lans
348 B1 Long Riston E R Yk
3 E1 Longrock Cnwll
330 D3 Long Sandall Donc
355 H3 Longscales N York
292 B4 Longsdon Staffs
293 E5 Longshaw Wigan
334 C4 Longshaw Wigan
571 J6 Longside Abers
526 C5 Longslow Shrops
271 F2 Longslow Shrops
400 C4 Longsowerby Cumb
197 E1 Longstanton Cambs
71 G2 Longstock Hants
487 H5 Longstone C Edin
3 F2 Longstone Cnwll
15 F4 Longstone Cnwll
66 B4 Longstone Somset
196 C3 Longstowe Cambs
249 G6 Long Stratton Norfk
193 G5 Long Street M Keyn
88 D4 Longstreet Wilts
92 B5 Long Sutton Hants
281 F5 Long Sutton Lincs
66 D4 Long Sutton Somset
243 H5 Longthorpe C Pete
224 D6 Long Thurlow Suffk
390 C5 Longthwaite Cumb
292 A6 Longton C Stke
338 C4 Longton Lancs
426 A6 Longtown Cumb
159 F4 Longtown Herefs
35 i7 Longueville Jersey
224 C6 Longville in the Dale Shrops
294 C4 Longway Bank Derbys
605 H5 Longwell Shet
110 A5 Longwell Green S Glos
276 A5 Long Whatton Leics
141 G4 Longwick Bucks
140 B6 Long Wittenham Oxon
430 C2 Longwitton Nthumb
412 C6 Longwood D & G
139 F5 Longworth Oxon
472 C1 Longyester E Loth
155 G3 Lon-las Swans

571 J4 Lonmay Abers
542 D7 Lonmore Highld
9 H3 Looe Cnwll
16 B6 Looe Mills Cnwll
98 B4 Loose Kent
25 H1 Loosebeare Devon
280 D4 Loosegate Lincs
98 B4 Loose Hill Kent
141 H4 Loosley Row Bucks
71 E2 Lopcombe Corner Wilts
45 E5 Lopen Somset
45 E5 Lopen Head Somset
364 B4 Loppergarth Cumb
270 B4 Loppington Shrops
17 G6 Lopwell Devon
442 C3 Lorbottle Nthumb
246 B2 Lordsbridge Norfk
50 C1 Lord's Hill C Sotn
93 H6 Lordshill Common Surrey
50 D1 Lordswood C Sotn
98 B2 Lords Wood Medway
525 J6 Lornty P & K
295 E5 Loscoe Derbys
343 H5 Loscoe Wakefd
30 C3 Loscombe Dorset
595 H3 Losgaintir W Isls
568 C1 Lossiemouth Moray
476 B5 Lossit Ag & B
271 E3 Lostford Shrops
325 F3 Lostock Bolton
310 D4 Lostock Gralam Ches
310 D5 Lostock Green Ches
338 D4 Lostock Hall Lancs
325 F3 Lostock Junction Bolton
9 E2 Lostwithiel Cnwll
582 B7 Lothbeg Highld
354 C5 Lothersdale N York
471 F2 Lothianbridge Mdloth
582 C7 Lothmore Highld
67 F3 Lottisham Somset
117 F1 Loudwater Bucks
143 E5 Loudwater Herts
276 B6 Loughborough Leics
129 E5 Loughor Swans
168 A2 Loughton M Keyn
211 E3 Loughton Shrops
279 F6 Lound Lincs
316 C2 Lound Notts
251 G5 Lound Suffk
314 D5 Loundsley Green Derbys
275 F6 Lount Leics
320 B2 Louth Lincs
18 B4 Lovaton Devon
340 C4 Love Clough Lancs
52 B2 Lovedean Hants
118 A3 Lower Green Bucks
71 E5 Lover Wilts
330 C5 Loversall Donc
146 C4 Loves Green Essex
126 B3 Loveston Pembks
67 F3 Lovington Somset
329 H1 Low Ackworth Wakefd
441 G6 Low Alwinton Nthumb
430 A3 Low Angerton Nthumb
161 H3 Lowbands Gloucs
318 D5 Low Barlings Lincs
366 D6 Low Bentham N York
366 C4 Low Biggins Cumb
467 G3 Low Blantyre S Lans
379 H4 Low Borrowbridge Cumb
314 B1 Low Bradfield Sheff
354 D5 Low Bradley N York
390 C1 Low Braithwaite Cumb
112 A5 Low Bridge Wilts
429 E5 Low Brunton Nthumb
331 G4 Low Burnham N Linc
388 A5 Lowca Cumb
358 D4 Low Catton E R Yk
225 F1 Low Common Norfk
326 D3 Low Compton Oldham
383 F2 Low Coniscliffe Darltn
401 E4 Low Cotehill Cumb
445 F6 Low Coylton S Ayrs
289 G4 Lowcross Hill Ches
373 G2 Low Dalby N York
296 C5 Lowdham Notts
384 A2 Low Dinsdale Darltn
380 C5 Low Dovengill Cumb
410 B4 Low Drumskeog D & G
270 B3 Lowe Shrops
314 C3 Lowedges Sheff
292 C3 Lowe Hill Staffs
405 G3 Low Eighton Gatesd
369 H3 Low Ellington N York
64 D4 Lower Aisholt Somset
235 G5 Lower Allscot Shrops
14 D4 Lower Amble Cnwll
47 E4 Lower Ansty Dorset
577 J7 Lower Arboll Highld
504 D6 Lower Ardtun Ag & B
166 D6 Lower Arncott Oxon
94 D3 Lower Ashtead Surrey
26 C6 Lower Ashton Devon
116 B3 Lower Assendon Oxon
568 F3 Lower Auchenreath Moray
579 G1 Lower Badcall Highld
337 G3 Lower Ballam Lancs
338 C3 Lower Bartle Lancs
115 G4 Lower Basildon W Berk
278 D4 Lower Bassingthorpe Lincs
185 G3 Lower Bearwood Herefs
308 D3 Lower Bebington Wirral
76 D4 Lower Beeding W Susx
218 D2 Lower Benefield Nhants
189 E1 Lower Bentley Worcs
212 A1 Lower Beobridge Shrops
134 D2 Lower Berry Hill Gloucs
190 B4 Lower Binton Warwks
295 E4 Lower Birchwood Derbys
97 E4 Lower Bitchet Kent
47 G3 Lower Blandford St Mary Dorset
112 D1 Lower Blunsdon Swindn
145 H3 Lower Bobbingworth Green Essex
32 C1 Lower Bockhampton Dorset
192 A4 Lower Boddington Nhants
261 F4 Lower Bodham Norfk
2 D3 Lower Bodinnar Cnwll
142 D4 Lower Bois Bucks
73 G5 Lower Bordean Hants
2 C2 Lower Boscaswell Cnwll
92 D6 Lower Bourne Surrey
237 E5 Lower Bradley Wolves
165 E2 Lower Brailes Warwks
546 B5 Lower Breakish Highld
312 B1 Lower Bredbury Stockp
160 B2 Lower Breinton Herefs
188 B3 Lower Broadheath Worcs
71 G4 Lower Brook Hants
326 B5 Lower Broughton Salfd
185 G4 Lower Broxwood Herefs
129 H2 Lower Brynamman Neath
14 D6 Lower Brynn Cnwll
161 E3 Lower Buckenhill Herefs
50 B5 Lower Buckland Hants
160 C2 Lower Bullingham Herefs
72 B1 Lower Bullington Hants
290 B3 Lower Bunbury Ches
49 F1 Lower Burgate Hants
66 C5 Lower Burrow Somset
185 H3 Lower Burton Herefs
121 G6 Lower Bush Medway

141 H4 Lower Cadsden Bucks
195 H5 Lower Caldecote Beds
135 G4 Lower Cam Gloucs
84 C3 Lower Canada N Som
289 G4 Lower Carden Ches
192 B3 Lower Catesby Nhants
19 E2 Lower Cator Devon
116 B5 Lower Caversham Readg
157 G2 Lower Chapel Powys
137 F2 Lower Chedworth Gloucs
28 B2 Lower Cheriton Devon
69 G3 Lower Chicksgrove Wilts
89 H4 Lower Chute Wilts
119 H2 Lower Clapton Gt Lon
212 D3 Lower Clent Worcs
10 A1 Lower Clicker Cnwll
190 B3 Lower Clopton Warwks
91 G6 Lower Common Hants
92 C2 Lower Common Hants
132 D1 Lower Common Mons
133 F4 Lower Common Mons
234 A3 Lower Common Shrops
339 E5 Lower Copthurst Lancs
79 F3 Lower Cousley Wood E Susx
98 C2 Lower Cox Street Kent
26 C2 Lower Creedy Devon
15 E4 Lower Croan Cnwll
312 D3 Lower Crossings Derbys
328 C3 Lower Cumberworth Kirk
48 D2 Lower Daggons Hants
339 G5 Lower Darwen Bl w D
219 F6 Lower Dean Beds
19 F5 Lower Dean Devon
328 C3 Lower Denby Kirk
14 B5 Lower Denzell Cnwll
562 D4 Lower Diabaig Highld
57 E2 Lower Dicker E Susx
210 B3 Lower Dinchope Shrops
588 B3 Lower Dounreay Highld
163 F5 Lower Dowdeswell Gloucs
209 F3 Lower Down Shrops
550 B1 Lower Drummond Highld
357 E2 Lower Dunsforth N York
44 B2 Lower Durston Somset
116 B5 Lower Earley Wokham
249 G4 Lower East Carleton Norfk
214 D4 Lower Eastern Green Covtry
187 E5 Lower Egleton Herefs
293 E5 Lower Elkstone Staffs
293 F6 Lower Ellastone Staffs
141 E3 Lower End Bucks
167 F3 Lower End Bucks
137 E4 Lower End Gloucs
168 C2 Lower End M Keyn
168 D5 Lower End M Keyn
193 G4 Lower End Nhants
193 G5 Lower End Nhants
193 H3 Lower End Nhants
194 B2 Lower End Nhants
139 E1 Lower End Oxon
89 E4 Lower Everleigh Wilts
30 A4 Lower Eype Dorset
101 E6 Lower Eythorne Kent
109 F5 Lower Failand N Som
211 F2 Lower Faintree Shrops
177 E2 Lower Falkenham Suffk
73 G2 Lower Farringdon Hants
118 B5 Lower Feltham Gt Lon
75 G6 Lower Fittleworth W Susx
340 C2 Lowerford Lancs
211 G2 Lower Forge Shrops
322 d7 Lower Foxdale IoM
269 G3 Lower Frankton Shrops
125 G2 Lower Freystrop Pembks
92 C6 Lower Froyle Hants
20 C4 Lower Gabwell Devon
576 C5 Lower Gledfield Highld
85 E6 Lower Godney Somset
101 E3 Lower Goldstone Kent
212 D1 Lower Gornal Dudley
342 B3 Lower Grange Brad
169 G2 Lower Gravenhurst Beds
147 E4 Lower Green Essex
147 E4 Lower Green Essex
170 A3 Lower Green Essex
173 E3 Lower Green Essex
171 F3 Lower Green Herts
78 D1 Lower Green Kent
79 E1 Lower Green Kent
260 C4 Lower Green Norfk
236 D3 Lower Green Staffs
199 E1 Lower Green Suffk
94 C1 Lower Green Surrey
216 B6 Lower Green Warwks
90 B2 Lower Green W Berk
325 G5 Lower Green Wigan
160 C4 Lower Grove Common Herefs
202 C3 Lower Hacheston Suffk
542 C5 Lower Halistra Highld
45 G6 Lower Halstock Leigh Dorset
98 D1 Lower Halstow Kent
110 C5 Lower Hamswell S Glos
34 A3 Lower Hamworthy Poole
100 B5 Lower Hardres Kent
185 H3 Lower Hardwick Herefs
185 E2 Lower Harpton Herefs
98 C2 Lower Hartlip Kent
294 D4 Lower Hartshay Derbys
141 G2 Lower Hartwell Bucks
272 B2 Lower Hatton Staffs
363 E4 Lower Hawthwaite Cumb
97 E5 Lower Haysden Kent
210 B3 Lower Hayton Shrops
109 H2 Lower Hazel S Glos
291 H2 Lower Heath Ches
100 B5 Lower Heppington Kent
185 E3 Lower Hergest Herefs
100 C2 Lower Herne Kent
166 A5 Lower Heyford Oxon
351 E2 Lower Heysham Lancs
121 H5 Lower Higham Kent
116 B3 Lower Highmoor Oxon
176 C2 Lower Holbrook Suffk
29 F2 Lower Holditch Dorset
48 D2 Lower Holwell Dorset
162 B1 Lower Hook Worcs
19 F1 Lower Hookner Devon
342 C6 Lower Hopton Kirk
269 G5 Lower Hopton Shrops
269 G4 Lower Hordley Shrops
75 G6 Lower Horncroft W Susx
57 F2 Lower Horsebridge E Susx
312 B4 Lower House Ches
309 G3 Lower House Halton
340 B3 Lower House Lancs
328 B1 Lower Houses Kirk
188 A5 Lower Howsell Worcs
213 E3 Lower Illey Dudley
100 B2 Lower Island Kent
84 D4 Lower Kersal Salfd
294 D5 Lower Kilburn Derbys
478 B3 Lower Kilchattan Ag & B
110 D2 Lower Kilcott Gloucs
476 D8 Lower Killeyan Ag & B
30 D3 Lower Kingcombe Dorset
95 E4 Lower Kingswood Surrey
288 D2 Lower Kinnerton Ches
185 F2 Lower Kinsham Herefs
44 C2 Lower Knapp Somset
109 G5 Lower Knowle Bristl

85 E3 Lower Langford N Som
502 C4 Lower Largo Fife
174 D1 Lower Layham Suffk
210 C5 Lower Ledwyche Shrops
273 F2 Lower Leigh Staffs
164 C3 Lower Lemington Gloucs
162 C3 Lower Lode Gloucs
39 H2 Lower Lovacott Devon
61 F4 Lower Loxhore Devon
134 D1 Lower Lydbrook Gloucs
185 H1 Lower Lye Herefs
106 D2 Lower Machen Newpt
159 F3 Lower Maes-coed Herefs
48 D3 Lower Mannington Dorset
86 D6 Lower Marsh Somset
134 C4 Lower Meend Gloucs
8 C2 Lower Menadue Cnwll
64 C5 Lower Merridge Somset
166 B1 Lower Middleton Cheney Nhants
275 E5 Lower Midway Derbys
7 G6 Lower Mill Cnwll
542 A6 Lower Milovaig Highld
85 F5 Lower Milton Somset
112 B1 Lower Moor Wilts
189 E5 Lower Moor Worcs
110 A1 Lower Morton S Glos
288 D3 Lower Mountain Flints
145 E3 Lower Nazeing Essex
211 E1 Lower Netchwood Shrops
133 F5 Lower New Inn Torfn
3 E3 Lower Ninnes Cnwll
273 F3 Lower Nobut Staffs
142 B5 Lower North Dean Bucks
190 C2 Lower Norton Warwks
68 B5 Lower Nyland Dorset
106 D2 Lower Ochrwyth Caerph
45 G4 Lower Odcombe Somset
136 B6 Lower Oddington Gloucs
545 J2 Lower Ollach Highld
115 F6 Lower Padworth W Berk
106 C5 Lower Penarth V Glam
236 C5 Lower Penn Staffs
50 B6 Lower Pennington Hants
338 D4 Lower Penwortham Lancs
311 E5 Lower Peover Ches
312 A5 Lower Pexhill Ches
295 E2 Lower Pilsley Derbys
577 J7 Lower Pitkerrie Highld
326 D2 Lower Place Rochdl
141 F2 Lower Pollicot Bucks
105 H6 Lower Porthkerry V Glam
8 C3 Lower Porthpean Cnwll
190 B5 Lower Quinton Warwks
184 D4 Lower Rabber Powys
133 E4 Lower Race Torfn
140 B5 Lower Radley Oxon
98 C1 Lower Rainham Medway
71 G5 Lower Ratley Hants
174 D2 Lower Raydon Suffk
136 B1 Lower Rea Gloucs
28 D2 Lower Ridge Devon
269 F3 Lower Ridge Shrops
63 G4 Lower Roadwater Somset
7 E3 Lower Rose Cnwll
48 C4 Lower Row Dorset
352 C2 Lower Salter Lancs
187 F2 Lower Sapey Worcs
111 H3 Lower Seagry Wilts
145 G2 Lower Sheering Essex
194 D6 Lower Shelton Beds
116 C4 Lower Shiplake Oxon
192 A2 Lower Shuckburgh Warwks
103 F3 Lower Sketty Swans
72 A4 Lower Slackstead Hants
164 B5 Lower Slaughter Gloucs
150 D5 Lower Solva Pembks
343 E5 Lower Soothill Kirk
135 F2 Lower Soudley Gloucs
161 G1 Lower Southfield Herefs
111 G3 Lower Stanton St Quintin Wilts
215 E5 Lower Stoke Covtry
122 C4 Lower Stoke Medway
169 H2 Lower Stondon Beds
135 F6 Lower Stone Gloucs
237 G4 Lower Stonnall Staffs
248 C6 Lower Stow Bedon Norfk
45 E5 Lower Stratton Somset
113 E2 Lower Stratton Swindn
58 A4 Lower Street E Susx
256 B2 Lower Street Norfk
261 G5 Lower Street Norfk
176 C3 Lower Street Suffk
199 F4 Lower Street Suffk
162 D1 Lower Strensham Worcs
310 C3 Lower Stretton Warrtn
30 B3 Lower Strode Dorset
87 F3 Lower Studley Wilts
118 B6 Lower Sundon Beds
169 F4 Lower Sundon Beds
110 C6 Lower Swainswick BaNES
51 E3 Lower Swanwick Hants
164 B4 Lower Swell Gloucs
119 H5 Lower Sydenham Gt Lon
165 F2 Lower Tadmarton Oxon
27 H2 Lower Tale Devon
249 G5 Lower Tasburgh Norfk
273 F2 Lower Tean Staffs
192 B5 Lower Thorpe Nhants
289 F6 Lower Threapwood Ches
251 E5 Lower Thurlton Norfk
351 F3 Lower Thurnham Lancs
274 C2 Lower Thurvaston Derbys
209 H4 Lower Todding Herefs
543 J4 Lower Tote Highld
4 C3 Lowertown Cnwll
8 D1 Lowertown Cnwll
24 C6 Lowertown Devon
42 D5 Lower Town Devon
187 E6 Lower Town Herefs
3 d1 Lower Town IoS
151 G2 Lower Town Pembks
188 C3 Lower Town Pembks
16 D3 Lower Trebullett Cnwll
136 B2 Lower Tuffley Gloucs
49 E3 Lower Turmer Hants
39 E4 Lower Twitchen Devon
122 C6 Lower Twydall Medway
191 E5 Lower Tysoe Warwks
72 D6 Lower Upham Hants
122 B5 Lower Upnor Medway
64 B4 Lower Vexford Somset
141 G4 Lower Wainhill Oxon
310 C2 Lower Walton Warrtn
113 F3 Lower Wanborough Swindn
64 B3 Lower Weacombe Somset
167 G2 Lower Weald M Keyn
27 E5 Lower Wear Devon
84 D4 Lower Weare Somset
192 D3 Lower Weedon Nhants
185 E5 Lower Welson Herefs
332 A1 Lower Westholme Somset
190 B4 Lower Weston
366 D5 Lower Westhouse N York
162 D2 Lower Westmancote Worcs
86 C1 Lower Weston BaNES
47 F4 Lower Whatcombe Dorset
86 C5 Lower Whatley Somset
603 K6 Lower Whitehall Ork

310 C4 Lower Whitley Ches
135 G5 Lower Wick Gloucs
188 B4 Lower Wick Worcs
73 F1 Lower Wield Hants
57 F4 Lower Willingdon E Susx
311 G5 Lower Withington Ches
188 D4 Lower Wolverton Worcs
559 F6 Lower Woodend Abers
116 C2 Lower Woodend Bucks
70 C2 Lower Woodford Wilts
45 G4 Lower Woodley Cnwll
144 B3 Lower Woodside Herts
67 H4 Lower Woolston Somset
15 E6 Lower Woon Cnwll
30 D2 Lower Wraxall Dorset
67 G2 Lower Wraxall Somset
87 E2 Lower Wraxall Wilts
289 G6 Lower Wych Ches
187 H6 Lower Wyche Worcs
342 C4 Lower Wyke Brad
60 C5 Lower Yelland Devon
68 C3 Lower Zeals Wilts
395 F1 Lowes Barn Dur
241 F3 Lowesby Leics
227 G1 Lowestoft Suffk
388 D5 Loweswater Cumb
394 D4 Low Etherley Dur
405 G3 Low Fell Gatesd
314 D2 Lowfield Sheff
77 E1 Lowfield Heath W Susx
342 D2 Low Fold Leeds
51 E2 Lowford Hants
280 C5 Low Fulney Lincs
386 B3 Low Garth N York
403 F7 Low Gate Nthumb
370 B6 Low Gate N York
339 H5 Lowgill Cumb
352 D2 Lowgill Lancs
370 A5 Low Grantley N York
355 H3 Low Green N York
199 H2 Low Green Suffk
404 D2 Low Greenside Gatesd
212 B4 Low Habberley Worcs
66 C4 Low Ham Somset
443 H4 Low Hauxley Nthumb
387 F3 Low Hawsker N York
401 E5 Low Hesket Cumb
236 D4 Low Hill Wolves
359 E1 Low Hutton N York
364 C2 Lowick Cumb
218 D3 Lowick Nhants
454 C2 Lowick Nthumb
364 C2 Lowick Bridge Cumb
364 C2 Lowick Green Cumb
391 E6 Low Knipe Cumb
355 G2 Low Laithe N York
329 F4 Low Laithes Barns
133 E5 Lowlands Torfn
312 D2 Low Leighton Derbys
389 E4 Low Lorton Cumb
410 D5 Low Mains D & G
373 F4 Low Marishes N York
317 F6 Low Marnham Notts
386 A5 Low Mill N York
342 C4 Low Moor Brad
340 A1 Low Moor Lancs
406 A5 Low Moorsley Sundld
388 A5 Low Moresby Cumb
372 C1 Lowna N York
365 F3 Low Newton Cumb
455 G5 Low Newton-by-the-Sea Nthumb
527 G5 Lownie Moor Angus
451 G2 Lowood Border
404 C2 Low Prudhoe Nthumb
332 C1 Low Risby N Linc
399 F6 Low Row Cumb
401 G2 Low Row Cumb
382 A5 Low Row N York
354 C3 Low Snaygill N York
214 B6 Lowsonford Warwks
248 D3 Low Street Norfk
121 G4 Low Street Thurr
249 G5 Low Tharston Norfk
391 E5 Lowther Cumb
399 G1 Lowthertown D & G
37 F5 Lowtherville IoW
405 E2 Low Thornley Gatesd
360 D2 Lowthorpe E R Yk
43 G4 Lowton Somset
325 E5 Lowton Wigan
325 E5 Lowton Common Wigan
325 E5 Lowton Heath Wigan
325 E5 Lowton St Mary's Wigan
486 D2 Low Torry Fife
235 G6 Low Town Shrops
320 A5 Low Toynton Lincs
329 G4 Low Valley Barns
486 C2 Low Valleyfield Fife
376 B2 Low Waters S Lans
467 H4 Low Waters S Lans
404 C3 Low Westwood Dur
400 B4 Low Whinnow Cumb
382 B5 Low Whita N York
384 B2 Low Worsall N York
42 B4 Loxbeare Devon
120 B2 Loxford Gt Lon
75 G2 Loxhill Surrey
61 F4 Loxhore Devon
61 F4 Loxhore Cott Devon
314 C2 Loxley Sheff
190 D4 Loxley Warwks
273 G3 Loxley Green Staffs
161 G1 Loxter Herefs
84 C3 Loxton N Som
75 G3 Loxwood W Susx
145 H2 Loyter's Green Essex
99 F2 Loyterton Kent
213 G2 Lozells Birm
211 E4 Lubberland Shrops
575 H3 Lubcroy Highld
217 E2 Lubenham Leics
586 C4 Lubinvullin Highld
144 D4 Lucas End Herts
339 E5 Lucas Green Surrey
93 F3 Lucas Green Surrey
39 E4 Luccombe Somset
455 F3 Luccombe Village IoW
17 E4 Luckett Cnwll
173 G3 Luckington Wilts
111 E3 Luckington Wilts
514 C5 Lucklawhill Fife
62 D4 Luckwell Bridge Somset
186 A2 Lucton Herefs
590 F5 Ludag W Isls
334 C5 Ludborough Lincs
12 B2 Ludbrook Devon
126 C2 Ludchurch Pembks
341 G4 Luddenden Calder
341 G5 Luddenden Foot Calder
365 F1 Ludderburn Cumb
97 G1 Luddesdown Kent
332 A1 Luddington N Linc
190 B4 Luddington Warwks
219 G3 Luddington in the Brook Nhants
319 F2 Ludford Lincs
210 C5 Ludford Shrops
141 E3 Ludgershall Bucks
89 G4 Ludgershall Wilts
3 F3 Ludgvan Cnwll

256 D6 Ludham Norfk
210 B5 Ludlow Shrops
335 E5 Ludney Lincs
44 D5 Ludney Somset
161 F2 Ludstock Herefs
236 B6 Ludstone Shrops
69 F5 Ludwell Wilts
395 F1 Ludworth Dur
170 C4 Luffenhall Herts
23 G4 Luffincott Devon
45 G4 Lufton Somset
446 B5 Lugar E Ayrs
472 A6 Lugate Border
490 A5 Luggate Burn E Loth
186 A2 Lugg Green Herefs
485 F5 Luggiebank N Lans
309 H3 Lugsdale Halton
466 B4 Lugton E Ayrs
160 D1 Lugwardine Herefs
545 K4 Luib Highld
509 G4 Luib Stirlg
159 H1 Lulham Herefs
238 D2 Lullington Derbys
86 D4 Lullington Somset
85 F1 Lulsgate Bottom N Som
187 G3 Lulsley Worcs
33 E3 Lulworth Camp Dorset
328 B2 Lumb Kirk
340 B6 Lumb Lancs
340 C5 Lumb Lancs
17 G4 Lumburn Devon
341 E5 Lumbutts Calder
344 B3 Lumby N York
52 D3 Lumley W Susx
405 G4 Lumley Thicks Dur
484 C5 Lumloch E Duns
555 G4 Lumphanan Abers
487 G1 Lumphinnans Fife
491 G6 Lumsdaine Border
558 B5 Lumsden Abers
529 E4 Lunan Angus
527 G4 Lunanhead Angus
512 C4 Luncarty P & K
360 B5 Lund E R Yk
345 F3 Lund N York
609 H4 Lund Shet
513 G2 Lundie Angus
502 C4 Lundin Links Fife
329 F3 Lundwood Barns
226 A1 Lundy Green Norfk
492 C3 Lunga Ag & B
607 G4 Lunna Shet
607 G4 Lunning Shet
606 E3 Lunnister Shet
102 D4 Lunnon Swans
97 G3 Lunsford Kent
58 B4 Lunsford's Cross E Susx
323 F4 Lunt Sefton
185 G3 Luntley Herefs
309 H2 Lunts Heath Halton
238 A1 Lupin Staffs
28 C1 Luppitt Devon
12 C2 Lupridge Devon
343 F6 Lupset Wakefd
366 B3 Lupton Cumb
75 E4 Lurgashall W Susx
383 E5 Lurley Devon
320 B6 Lusby Lincs
234 C5 Lushcott Shrops
11 G3 Luson Devon
479 G2 Lussagiven Ag & B
495 H6 Luss Ag & B
542 D5 Lusta Highld
19 G1 Lustleigh Devon
19 G1 Lustleigh Cleave Devon
186 B2 Luston Herefs
68 A3 Lusty Somset
540 C6 Luthermuir Abers
514 A6 Luthrie Fife
212 D3 Lutley Dudley
20 C2 Luton Devon
28 A2 Luton Devon
169 G5 Luton Luton
98 B1 Luton Medway
38 B4 Lutsford Devon
216 B2 Lutterworth Leics
18 C6 Lutton Devon
19 E5 Lutton Devon
281 F4 Lutton Lincs
219 G2 Lutton Nhants
281 F5 Lutton Gowts Lincs
41 F4 Lutworthy Devon
63 F4 Luxborough Somset
161 F5 Luxley Gloucs
96 B2 Luxted Gt Lon
43 H5 Luxton Devon
8 D2 Luxulyan Cnwll
327 E4 Luzley Tamesd
326 D3 Luzley Brook Oldham
45 G5 Lyatts Somset
583 H2 Lybster Highld
134 D1 Lydbrook Gloucs
209 G2 Lydbury North Shrops
61 G4 Lydcott Devon
81 F5 Lydd Kent
83 E1 Lydden Kent
101 F2 Lydden Kent
242 B5 Lyddington Rutlnd
81 G6 Lydd-on-Sea Kent
233 F4 Lyde Shrops
64 B5 Lydeard St Lawrence Somset
186 C6 Lyde Cross Herefs
92 B3 Lyde Green Hants
110 B4 Lyde Green S Glos
24 D5 Lydford Devon
67 F3 Lydford Fair Place Somset
67 F3 Lydford-on-Fosse Somset
327 E4 Lydgate Oldham
341 E4 Lydgate Oldham
209 F1 Lydham Shrops
112 C2 Lydiard Green Wilts
112 C2 Lydiard Millicent Wilts
112 C2 Lydiard Plain Wilts
112 D3 Lydiard Tregoze Swindn
323 G4 Lydiate Sefton
213 G4 Lydiate Ash Worcs
46 D2 Lydlinch Dorset
44 D6 Lydmarsh Somset
135 G2 Lydney Gloucs
126 B5 Lydstep Pembks
212 D3 Lye Dudley
85 E2 Lye Cross N Som
142 D4 Lye Green Bucks
78 C3 Lye Green E Susx
190 B1 Lye Green Warwks
87 E3 Lye Green Wilts
211 H5 Lye Head Worcs
85 F2 Lye Hole N Som
78 C2 Lyewood Common E Susx
139 F6 Lyford Oxon
82 B2 Lymbridge Green Kent
312 B5 Lyme Green Ches
29 F4 Lyme Regis Dorset
438 D4 Lymiecleuch Border
82 C2 Lyminge Kent
50 B6 Lymington Hants
54 B4 Lyminster W Susx
310 C2 Lymm Warrtn
50 A6 Lymore Hants
81 H2 Lympne Kent
84 B4 Lympsham Somset
27 F6 Lympstone Devon

61 H2 Lynbridge Devon
90 D5 Lynch Hants
63 E2 Lynch Somset
535 L2 Lynchat Highld
209 G2 Lynchgate Shrops
90 D5 Lynch Hill Hants
117 F3 Lynch Hill Slough
50 B3 Lyndhurst Hants
242 B4 Lyndon Rutlnd
214 A2 Lyndon Green Birm
449 H1 Lyne Border
579 J7 Lyne Highld
93 H1 Lyne Surrey
270 A3 Lyneal Shrops
270 B3 Lyneal Mill Shrops
270 A3 Lyneal Wood Shrops
161 E3 Lyne Down Herefs
164 D5 Lyneham Oxon
112 B4 Lyneham Wilts
431 F1 Lynemouth Nthumb
549 J5 Lyne of Gorthleck Highld
556 D2 Lyne of Skene Abers
600 E6 Lyness Ork
449 H2 Lyne Station Border
223 G1 Lynford Norfk
255 E4 Lyng Norfk
44 C2 Lyng Somset
256 B3 Lyngate Norfk
256 C4 Lyngate Norfk
44 A2 Lyngford Somset
61 H2 Lynmouth Devon
237 G4 Lynn Staffs
236 A1 Lynn Wrekin
465 F5 Lynn Glen N Ayrs
439 F2 Lynnwood Border
100 C6 Lynsore Bottom Kent
99 E2 Lynsted Kent
23 E1 Lynstone Cnwll
61 H2 Lynton Devon
550 F7 Lynwilg Highld
163 E5 Lynworth Gloucs
406 B5 Lyons Sundld
31 F1 Lyon's Gate Dorset
248 B2 Lyon's Green Norfk
147 E1 Lyons Hall Essex
185 F3 Lyonshall Herefs
136 D3 Lypiatt Gloucs
188 C3 Lyppard Grange Worcs
48 A5 Lytchett Matravers Dorset
48 A6 Lytchett Minster Dorset
589 H4 Lyth Highld
337 G4 Lytham Lancs
337 F3 Lytham Moss Lancs
337 F4 Lytham St Anne's Lancs
224 B3 Lythbank Shrops
386 D2 Lythe N York
601 H7 Lythes Ork

M

5 E2 Mabe Burnthouse Cnwll
97 E6 Mabledon Kent
321 F3 Mablethorpe Lincs
312 A5 Macclesfield Ches
312 C5 Macclesfield Forest Ches
570 C2 Macduff Abers
501 E4 Macedonia Fife
175 E1 Mace Green Suffk
468 B4 Machan S Lans
457 E5 Macharioch Ag & B
106 D2 Machen Caerph
460 B3 Machrie N Ayrs
456 C2 Machrihanish Ag & B
263 E5 Machroes Gwynd
259 G2 Machynlleth Powys
128 D5 Machynys Carmth
75 G4 Mackerel's Common W Susx
143 H1 Mackerye End Herts
43 G6 Mackham Devon
115 F2 Mackney Oxon
440 B2 Mackside Border
275 E2 Mackworth Derbys
475 B4 Macmerry E Loth
511 G5 Madderty P & K
88 C3 Maddington Wilts
486 B4 Maddiston Falk
125 G2 Maddox Moor Pembks
54 A2 Madehurst W Susx
291 F6 Madeley Staffs
235 F4 Madeley Wrekin
291 F5 Madeley Heath Staffs
213 E4 Madeley Heath Worcs
271 H1 Madeley Park Wood Staffs
16 D4 Maders Cnwll
43 F5 Madford Devon
197 E2 Madingley Cambs
68 C5 Madjeston Dorset
159 H2 Madley Herefs
188 B5 Madresfield Worcs
2 D3 Madron Cnwll
24 C3 Madworthy Devon
303 G4 Maenaddwyn IoA
152 B4 Maenclochog Pembks
105 G4 Maendy V Glam
5 E3 Maenporth Cnwll
265 F1 Maentwrog Gwynd
180 A3 Maen-y-groes Cerdgn
38 B6 Maer Cnwll
272 A2 Maer Staffs
155 F5 Maerdy Carmth
287 E6 Maerdy Conwy
131 F5 Maerdy Rhondd
205 F3 Maes-bangor Cerdgn
269 E5 Maesbrook Shrops
269 F4 Maesbury Shrops
269 F4 Maesbury Marsh Shrops
304 C5 Maesgeirchen Gwynd
107 E2 Maes-glas Newpt
152 D5 Maesgwynne Carmth
288 A2 Maeshafn Denbgs
179 H5 Maes llyn Cerdgn
183 F5 Maesmynis Powys
307 H4 Maes Pennant Flints
104 C1 Maesteg Brdgnd
129 E1 Maesybont Carmth
105 H2 Maesycoed Rhondd
154 C1 Maesycrugiau Carmth
132 C5 Maesycwmmer Caerph
288 B2 Maes-y-dre Flints
132 D2 Maesygwartha Mons
231 F5 Maesypandy Powys
208 A1 Maesyrhandir Powys
145 H3 Magdalen Laver Essex
568 E6 Maggieknockater Moray
171 G4 Maggots End Essex
57 G2 Magham Down E Susx
323 G4 Maghull Sefton
216 B3 Magna Park Leics
108 D2 Magor Mons
225 E4 Magpie Green Suffk
119 F3 Maida Vale Gt Lon
77 E2 Maidenbower W Susx
68 D2 Maiden Bradley Wilts
20 C4 Maidencombe Torbay
201 F6 Maidenhall Suffk
29 E3 Maidenhayne Devon
85 G1 Maiden Head N Som
117 E3 Maidenhead W & M
117 F3 Maidenhead Court W & M
405 E5 Maiden Law Dur
31 E3 Maiden Newton Dorset
486 C3 Maidenpark Falk
432 B3 Maidens S Ayrs
202 B5 Maidensgrave Suffk
117 E5 Maiden's Green Br For
116 B2 Maidensgrove Oxon
443 G5 Maiden's Hall Nthumb
15 G4 Maidenwell Cnwll
320 B4 Maidenwell Lincs
125 G5 Maiden Wells Pembks
192 C4 Maidford Nhants
167 E2 Maids Moreton Bucks
98 B3 Maidstone Kent
217 F4 Maidwell Nhants
605 H5 Mail Shet
609 J4 Mailand Shet
470 D6 Mailingsland Border
107 F2 Maindee Newpt
106 C4 Maindy Cardif
445 E5 Mainholm S Ayrs
388 C5 Mains Cumb
395 G3 Mainsforth Dur
515 E3 Mains of Ardestie Angus
528 B4 Mains of Balgavies Angus
528 B2 Mains of Balhall Angus
527 E4 Mains of Ballindarg Angus
566 F7 Mains of Clunas Highld
551 L3 Mains of Dalvey Highld
540 D3 Mains of Dellavaird Abers
556 D5 Mains of Drum Abers
570 F5 mains of Fedderate Abers
557 F2 Mains of Grandhome C Aber
514 A3 Mains of Gray C Dund
571 J6 Mains of Kinmundy Abers
528 B3 Mains of Melgund Angus
524 D3 Mains of Orchil P & K
540 C5 Mains of Thornton Abers
529 F3 Mains of Usan Angus
398 A3 Mainsriddle D & G
209 E2 Mainstone Shrops
162 B5 Maisemore Gloucs
213 G4 Major's Green Worcs
294 D6 Makeney Derbys
452 C3 Makerstoun Border
592 D3 Malacleit W Isls
12 B5 Malborough Devon
313 E3 Malcoff Derbys
94 D2 Malden Rushett Gt Lon
147 H3 Maldon Essex
233 G3 Malehurst Shrops
354 B2 Malham N York
543 H4 Maligar Highld
314 C2 Malinbridge Sheff
235 F3 Malinslee Wrekin
291 F3 Malkin's Bank Ches
531 J3 Mallaig Highld
531 J3 Mallaig Bheag Highld
531 J3 Mallaigmore Highld
470 C1 Malleny Mills C Edin
171 G4 Mallows Green Essex
282 D2 Malltraeth IoA
230 D2 Mallwyd Gwynd
111 G2 Malmesbury Wilts
62 B2 Malmsmead Somset
289 G5 Malpas Ches
7 F5 Malpas Cnwll
107 E1 Malpas Newpt
115 G5 Malpas W Berk
161 G4 Malswick Gloucs
320 B3 Maltby Lincs
330 B6 Maltby Rothm
384 D2 Maltby S on T
321 E3 Maltby le Marsh Lincs
199 E4 Malting End Suffk
99 E6 Maltman's Hill Kent
373 E5 Malton N York
188 A6 Malvern Common Worcs
188 A5 Malvern Link Worcs
161 H1 Malvern Wells Worcs
482 B2 Mambeg Ag & B
211 F5 Mamble Worcs
133 F4 Mamhilad Mons
5 E3 Manaccan Cnwll
11 E2 Manadon C Plym
232 B4 Manafon Powys
595 J5 Manais W Isls
19 G1 Manaton Devon
320 C2 Manby Lincs
239 E5 Mancetter Warwks
326 B5 Manchester Manch
288 D1 Mancot Flints
288 D1 Mancot Royal Flints
533 L2 Mandally Highld
221 G2 Manea Cambs
237 H5 Maney Birm
383 F2 Manfield N York
606 D3 Mangaster Shet
30 B3 Mangerton Dorset
110 B4 Mangotsfield S Glos
169 G5 Mangrove Green Herts
596 C1 Mangurstadh W Isls
4 C2 Manhay Cnwll
178 D4 Manian-fawr Cerdgn
595 J5 Manish W Isls
341 F5 Mankinholes Calder
309 H5 Manley Ches
42 C5 Manley Devon
309 H5 Manley Common Ches
132 C4 Manmoel Caerph
516 B7 Mannal Ag & B
11 E2 Mannamead C Plym
486 D4 Mannerston Falk
88 D3 Manningford Abbots Wilts
88 D3 Manningford Bohune Wilts
88 D3 Manningford Bruce Wilts
76 D4 Mannings Heath W Susx
48 C3 Mannington Dorset
175 E3 Manningtree Essex
557 G4 Mannofield C Aber
126 B5 Manorbier Pembks
126 A5 Manorbier Newton Pembks
11 E4 Manor Bourne Devon
155 G4 Manordeilo Carmth
314 D2 Manor Estate Sheff
452 C3 Manorhill Border
281 F6 Manor Hill Corner Lincs
215 F3 Manor House Covtry
151 F2 Manorowen Pembks
355 G5 Manor Park Brad
141 H2 Manor Park Bucks
291 E1 Manor Park Ches
78 B5 Manor Park E Susx
120 B2 Manor Park Gt Lon
310 A3 Manor Park Halton
276 C3 Manor Park Notts
314 D2 Manor Park Sheff
117 G3 Manor Park Slough
6 C4 Manor Parsley Cnwll
77 E2 Manor Royal W Susx
173 E2 Man's Cross Essex
423 E3 Mansegate D & G
103 E4 Manselfield Swans
185 G6 Mansell Gamage Herefs
185 H5 Mansell Lacy Herefs
103 F2 Manselton Swans
366 B3 Mansergh Cumb
467 E2 Mansewood C Glas
434 C2 Mansfield E Ayrs
295 G2 Mansfield Notts
295 H2 Mansfield Woodhouse Notts
248 D4 Manson Green Norfk
364 C3 Mansriggs Cumb
47 F1 Manston Dorset
101 F2 Manston Kent
343 G3 Manston Leeds
48 B3 Manswood Dorset
243 F1 Manthorpe Lincs
278 C2 Manthorpe Lincs
142 C5 Mantles Green Bucks
332 C4 Manton N Linc
316 A4 Manton Notts
242 B4 Manton Rutlnd
113 E6 Manton Wilts
332 C3 Manton Warren N Linc
171 G4 Manuden Essex
146 A2 Manwood Green Essex
341 H2 Manywells Height Brad
67 H4 Maperton Somset
296 C2 Maplebeck Notts
143 E6 Maple Cross Herts
115 H4 Mapledurham Oxon
92 A4 Mapledurwell Hants
172 B2 Maple End Essex
76 C5 Maplehurst W Susx
293 G5 Mapleton Derbys
296 A6 Mapperley C Nott
295 E6 Mapperley Derbys
276 C1 Mapperley Park C Nott
30 C3 Mapperton Dorset
47 G5 Mapperton Dorset
189 G1 Mappleborough Green Warwks
361 G6 Mappleton E R Yk
329 E3 Mapplewell Barns
46 D3 Mappowder Dorset
596 F6 Màraig W Isls
7 F3 Marazanvose Cnwll
3 F3 Marazion Cnwll
597 L4 Marbhig W Isls
290 B5 Marbury Ches
245 F5 March Cambs
436 C2 March S Lans
139 H5 Marcham Oxon
270 D4 Marchamley Shrops
270 D3 Marchamley Wood Shrops
274 A3 Marchington Staffs
273 H4 Marchington Woodlands Staffs
289 E5 Marchwiel Wrexhm
50 C2 Marchwood Hants
105 E6 Marcross V Glam
528 B3 Marcus Angus
186 C5 Marden Herefs
98 A6 Marden Kent
431 F5 Marden N Tyne
88 C3 Marden Wilts
146 B4 Marden Ash Essex
98 A6 Marden Beech Kent
78 B3 Marden's Hill E Susx
98 B6 Marden Thorn Kent
170 C6 Mardleybury Herts
209 E3 Mardu Shrops
133 F1 Mardy Mons
269 E3 Mardy Shrops
241 F3 Marefield Leics
300 A2 Mareham le Fen Lincs
320 A6 Mareham on the Hill Lincs
294 D5 Marehay Derbys
75 H6 Marehill W Susx
78 B5 Maresfield E Susx
78 B5 Maresfield Park E Susx
348 B4 Marfleet C KuH
289 E3 Marford Wrexhm
104 B2 Margam Neath
68 D6 Margaret Marsh Dorset
146 B2 Margaret Roding Essex
146 D4 Margaretting Essex
146 D4 Margaretting Tye Essex
101 F1 Margate Kent
95 E4 Margery Surrey
461 E3 Margnaheglish N Ayrs
385 H1 Margrove Park R & Cl
247 E3 Marham Norfk
23 E2 Marhamchurch Cnwll
243 G4 Marholm C Pete
307 F4 Marian Flints
307 F4 Marian Cwm Denbgs
304 C3 Mariandyrys IoA
304 B3 Marian-glas IoA
41 E3 Mariansleigh Devon
123 E5 Marine Town Kent
556 C3 Marionburgh Abers
543 H4 Marishader Highld
424 B3 Marjoriebanks D & G
84 C5 Mark Somset
96 C6 Markbeech Kent
321 E4 Markby Lincs
84 C5 Mark Causeway Somset
78 D3 Mark Cross E Susx
275 E2 Markeaton C Derb
239 G4 Market Bosworth Leics
243 G2 Market Deeping Lincs
271 F3 Market Drayton Shrops
217 F2 Market Harborough Nhants
88 B4 Market Lavington Wilts
242 B1 Market Overton Rutlnd
319 E2 Market Rasen Lincs
319 G4 Market Stainton Lincs
315 H6 Market Warsop Notts
359 G6 Market Weighton E R Yk
224 C4 Market Weston Suffk
240 A2 Markfield Leics
145 G2 Mark Hall North Essex
145 G2 Mark Hall South Essex
132 C4 Markham Caerph
316 D5 Markham Moor Notts
501 F4 Markinch Fife
356 B1 Markington N York
325 F3 Markland Hill Bolton
489 H4 Markle E Loth
86 B2 Marksbury BaNES
36 D2 Mark's Corner IoW
120 C1 Marks Gate Gt Lon
173 G4 Markshall Essex
174 B5 Marks Tey Essex
10 C2 Markwell Cnwll
143 F1 Markyate Herts
326 C2 Marland Rochdl
160 A4 Marlas Herefs
162 A1 Marl Bank Worcs
113 E6 Marlborough Wilts
186 C4 Marlbrook Herefs
213 E5 Marlbrook Worcs
189 G4 Marlcliff Warwks
20 B5 Marldon Devon
57 F1 Marle Green E Susx
162 D5 Marle Hill Gloucs
202 C3 Marlesford Suffk
100 C5 Marley Kent
101 F5 Marley Kent
290 B5 Marley Green Ches
74 D3 Marley Heights W Susx
405 F3 Marley Hill Gatesd
406 B3 Marley Pots Sundld
249 F3 Marlingford Norfk
124 C3 Marloes Pembks
116 D2 Marlow Bucks
209 G4 Marlow Herefs
116 D2 Marlow Bottom Bucks
116 D2 Marlow Common Bucks
96 B5 Marlpit Hill Kent
58 B4 Marlpits E Susx
295 E6 Marlpool Derbys
68 C6 Marnhull Dorset
569 K5 Marnoch Abers
485 E6 Marnock N Lans
312 B2 Marple Stockp
312 C2 Marple Bridge Stockp
312 C2 Marpleridge Stockp
330 B3 Marr Donc
582 D6 Marrel Highld
89 F2 Marr Green Wilts
382 C5 Marrick N York
607 H5 Marrister Shet
127 E3 Marros Carmth
327 F2 Marsden Kirk
406 B2 Marsden S Tyne
340 D2 Marsden Height Lancs
368 A2 Marsett N York
341 G2 Marsh Brad
141 H3 Marsh Bucks
44 A5 Marsh Devon
327 H1 Marsh Kirk
475 E3 Marshall Meadows Nthumb
309 H1 Marshall's Cross St Hel
66 D3 Marshall's Elm Somset
143 H1 Marshalls Heath Herts
29 G2 Marshalsea Dorset
143 H3 Marshalswick Herts
255 G3 Marsham Norfk
352 B4 Marshaw Lancs
140 C5 Marsh Baldon Oxon
90 C1 Marsh Benham W Berk
101 F4 Marshborough Kent
210 A2 Marshbrook Shrops
335 E5 Marshchapel Lincs
109 G3 Marsh Common S Glos
162 B2 Marsh End Worcs
107 E3 Marshfield Newpt
110 D5 Marshfield S Glos
290 D3 Marshfield Bank Ches
22 C4 Marshgate Cnwll
114 A6 Marsh Gate W Berk
166 D5 Marsh Gibbon Bucks
27 G4 Marsh Green Devon
96 B6 Marsh Green Kent
291 H3 Marsh Green Staffs
309 H4 Marsh Green Staffs
324 C3 Marsh Green Wigan
235 E2 Marsh Green Wrekin
351 G4 Marsh Houses Lancs
245 H3 Marshland St James Norfk
315 E4 Marsh Lane Derbys
134 D3 Marsh Lane Gloucs
64 C4 Marsh Mills Somset
144 B3 Marshmoor Herts
100 D2 Marshside Kent
259 F3 Marsh Side Norfk
337 G6 Marshside Sefton
63 F3 Marsh Street Somset
29 G3 Marshwood Dorset
382 D4 Marske N York
397 F5 Marske-by-the-sea R & Cl
310 D4 Marston Ches
185 G3 Marston Herefs
297 G6 Marston Lincs
140 B3 Marston Oxon
236 B2 Marston Staffs
272 D4 Marston Staffs
215 G4 Marston Warwks
238 B6 Marston Warwks
87 H3 Marston Wilts
86 D6 Marston Bigot Somset
191 H3 Marston Doles Warwks
86 D5 Marston Gate Somset
214 B2 Marston Green Solhll
137 H5 Marston Hill Wilts
215 F2 Marston Jabbett Warwks
67 F5 Marston Magna Somset
138 A5 Marston Meysey Wilts
274 A2 Marston Montgomery Derbys
168 D1 Marston Moretaine Beds
274 C4 Marston on Dove Derbys
192 B6 Marston St Lawrence Nhants
186 D3 Marston Stannett Herefs
217 E2 Marston Trussell Nhants
160 D6 Marstow Herefs
142 C2 Marsworth Bucks
89 G2 Marten Wilts
311 G4 Marthall Ches
257 E6 Martham Norfk
366 C1 Marthwaite Cumb
70 B6 Martin Hants
83 F1 Martin Kent
299 E2 Martin Lincs
299 G1 Martin Lincs
390 C6 Martindale Cumb
299 F2 Martin Dales Lincs
70 B5 Martin Drove End Hants
61 G2 Martinhoe Devon
61 G2 Martinhoe Cross Devon
188 C3 Martin Hussingtree Worcs
83 F1 Martin Mill Kent
299 G2 Martin Moor Lincs
310 C2 Martinscroft Warrtn
291 G2 Martin's Moss Ches
31 E5 Martinstown or Winterborne St Martin Dorset
202 B5 Martlesham Suffk
202 A5 Martlesham Heath Suffk
126 A2 Martletwy Pembks
187 H3 Martley Worcs
66 C6 Martock Somset
311 H6 Marton Ches
364 B4 Marton Cumb
348 C2 Marton E R Yk
317 F3 Marton Lincs
385 E1 Marton Middsb
357 E2 Marton N York
372 D3 Marton N York
233 E4 Marton Shrops
270 A5 Marton Shrops
215 G6 Marton Warwks
372 A6 Marton Abbey N York
310 C6 Marton Green Ches
396 C6 Marton Grove Middsb
372 A6 Marton-in-the-Forest N York
370 D5 Marton-le-Moor N York
215 G6 Marton Moor Warwks
337 F3 Marton Moss Side Bpool
94 B3 Martyr's Green Surrey
72 D3 Martyr Worthy Hants
602 A7 Marwick Ork
60 D4 Marwood Devon
565 H6 Marybank Highld
566 C1 Marybank Highld
565 J5 Maryburgh Highld
10 D2 Maryfield Cnwll
474 B2 Marygold Border
484 B6 Maryhill C Glas
529 E1 Marykirk Abers
134 C3 Maryland Mons
324 D3 Marylebone Wigan
568 B8 Marypark Moray
388 B2 Maryport Cumb
408 C5 Maryport D & G
24 B6 Marystow Devon
18 B2 Mary Tavy Devon
527 E4 Maryton Angus
529 E3 Maryton Angus
555 G5 Marywell Abers
557 G5 Marywell Abers
528 D6 Marywell Angus
329 G6 Masbrough Rothm
125 G3 Mascle Bridge Pembks
369 H3 Masham N York
146 C2 Mashbury Essex
366 D4 Masongill N York
445 E5 Masonhill S Ayrs
315 F4 Mastin Moor Derbys
557 F3 Mastrick C Aber
189 G1 Matchborough Worcs
145 H2 Matching Essex
146 A2 Matching Green Essex
145 H2 Matching Tye Essex
429 G5 Matfen Nthumb
79 F1 Matfield Kent
109 F1 Mathern Mons
187 G5 Mathon Herefs
151 E3 Mathry Pembks
261 G5 Matlaske Norfk
327 E5 Matley Tamesd
294 C3 Matlock Derbys
294 C2 Matlock Bank Derbys
294 B3 Matlock Bath Derbys
294 B3 Matlock Bridge Derbys
294 C3 Matlock Cliff Derbys
294 B3 Matlock Dale Derbys
30 C4 Matravers Dorset
338 D1 Matshead Lancs
136 C2 Matson Gloucs
390 B5 Matterdale End Cumb
316 C2 Mattersey Notts
316 C1 Mattersey Thorpe Notts
316 C2 Mattersey Thorpe Notts
116 D6 Matthewsgreen Wokham
92 B3 Mattingley Hants
249 E2 Mattishall Norfk
249 E2 Mattishall Burgh Norfk
445 G4 Mauchline E Ayrs
571 G6 Maud Abers
8 D1 Maudlin Cnwll
29 G1 Maudlin Dorset
53 F3 Maudlin W Susx
29 G1 Maudlin Cross Dorset
35 i6 Maufant Jersey
164 C5 Maugersbury Gloucs
322 h4 Maughold IoM
169 F2 Maulden Beds
380 A1 Maulds Meaburn Cumb
370 C2 Maunby N York
186 D4 Maund Bryan Herefs
43 E2 Maundown Somset
470 D2 Mauricewood Mdloth
251 F2 Mautby Norfk
237 G1 Mavesyn Ridware Staffs
300 C1 Mavis Enderby Lincs
398 D5 Mawbray Cumb
324 B2 Mawdesley Lancs
104 B3 Mawdlam Brdgnd
4 D4 Mawgan Cnwll
14 A5 Mawgan Porth Cnwll
291 E3 Maw Green Ches
6 D4 Mawla Cnwll
5 E3 Mawnan Cnwll
5 E3 Mawnan Smith Cnwll
330 D1 Mawson Green Donc
321 E5 Mawthorpe Lincs
243 G3 Maxey C Pete
214 C2 Maxstoke Warwks
82 B2 Maxted Street Kent
452 B3 Maxton Border
83 E2 Maxton Kent
423 G4 Maxwelltown D & G
432 C4 Maxwelston S Ayrs
23 F4 Maxworthy Cnwll
103 E3 Mayals Swans
291 H5 May Bank Staffs
432 D3 Maybole S Ayrs
93 H3 Maybury Surrey
50 C2 Maybush C Sotn
569 K6 Mayen Moray
213 F1 Mayer's Green Sandw
76 B2 Mayes Green Surrey
125 H4 Mayeston Pembks
119 F3 Mayfair Gt Lon
78 D4 Mayfield E Susx
588 E3 Mayfield Highld
471 G2 Mayfield Mdloth
431 E4 Mayfield Nthumb
293 F5 Mayfield Staffs
486 B6 Mayfield W Loth
93 G3 Mayford Surrey
161 F5 May Hill Gloucs
134 C2 May Hill Mons
103 F3 Mayhill Swans
148 B4 Mayland Essex
148 A4 Maylandsea Essex
78 D6 Maynard's Green E Susx
2 C4 Mayon Cnwll
96 C2 Maypole Gt Lon
3 d2 Maypole IoS
100 C2 Maypole Kent
120 D5 Maypole Kent
134 B1 Maypole Mons
174 C5 Maypole Green Essex
251 E5 Maypole Green Norfk
200 B3 Maypole Green Suffk
226 B6 Maypole Green Suffk
84 C2 May's Green N Som
116 B4 Mays Green Oxon
94 B3 May's Green Surrey
110 B3 Mayshill S Glos
328 B3 Maythorn Barns
296 C3 Maythorne Notts
605 G6 Maywick Shet
19 G3 Mead Devon
38 B4 Mead Devon
49 H5 Mead End Hants
52 B2 Mead End Hants
69 H5 Mead End Wilts
86 B3 Meadgate BaNES
141 H3 Meadle Bucks
488 B5 Meadowbank C Edin
310 C6 Meadowbank Ches
173 E1 Meadowend Essex
395 E2 Meadowfield Dur
465 E5 Meadowfoot N Ayrs
187 G3 Meadow Green Herefs
314 C3 Meadow Head Sheff
211 F1 Meadowley Shrops
489 E5 Meadowmill E Loth
276 C2 Meadows C Nott
233 F4 Meadowtown Shrops
57 G5 Meads E Susx
140 C6 Meadside Oxon
95 F5 Mead Vale Surrey
17 F2 Meadwell Devon
272 C2 Meaford Staffs
355 G3 Meagill N York
599 K8 Mealabost W Isls
599 J3 Mealabost Bhuirgh W Isls
596 B3 Mealasta W Isls
379 F5 Meal Bank Cumb
328 B3 Meal Hill Kirk
399 E5 Mealrigg Cumb
389 F1 Mealsgate Cumb
343 E2 Meanwood Leeds
353 G2 Mearbeck N York
66 D1 Meare Somset
44 B3 Meare Green Somset
44 C2 Meare Green Somset
86 B3 Mearns BaNES
466 D3 Mearns E Rens
194 A1 Mears Ashby Nhants
329 F3 Measborough Dike Barns
239 E2 Measham Leics
95 F6 Meath Green Surrey
365 F3 Meathop Cumb

347 G2 **Meaux** E R Yk
4 C5 **Meaver** Cnwll
18 B4 **Meavy** Devon
241 G6 **Medbourne** Leics
167 H2 **Medbourne** M Keyn
430 B5 **Medburn** Nthumb
38 C4 **Meddon** Devon
315 H6 **Meden Vale** Notts
96 C5 **Medhurst Row** Kent
300 B3 **Medlam** Lincs
338 B2 **Medlar** Lancs
233 H6 **Medlicott** Shrops
4 D2 **Medlyn** Cnwll
116 C3 **Medmenham** Bucks
404 D4 **Medomsley** Dur
73 F2 **Medstead** Hants
292 C2 **Meerbrook** Staffs
185 G4 **Meer Common** Herefs
214 C5 **Meer End** Solhll
30 B2 **Meerhay** Dorset
314 C3 **Meersbrook** Sheff
171 F3 **Meesden** Herts
271 F5 **Meeson** Wrekin
271 E5 **Meeson Heath** Wrekin
40 A6 **Meeth** Devon
40 D3 **Meethe** Devon
571 L6 **Meethill** Aber
199 E3 **Meeting Green** Suffk
256 C4 **Meeting House Hill** Norfk
449 G5 **Meggethead** Border
153 F5 **Meidrim** Carmth
232 C2 **Meifod** Powys
464 D1 **Meigle** N Ayrs
526 C6 **Meigle** P & K
467 H4 **Meikle Earnock** S Lans
464 B3 **Meikle Kilchattan Butts** Ag & B
410 B3 **Meikle Killantrae** D & G
513 E2 **Meikleour** P & K
540 B5 **Meikle Strath** Abers
561 E4 **Meikle Tarty** Abers
569 J4 **Meikle Toux** Abers
559 G3 **Meikle Wartle** Abers
513 E3 **Meikle Whitefield** P & K
128 C2 **Meinciau** Carmth
272 D1 **Meir** C Stke
272 D1 **Meir Heath** Staffs
197 E6 **Melbourne** Cambs
275 F4 **Melbourne** Derbys
358 D6 **Melbourne** E R Yk
470 A6 **Melbourne** S Lans
69 E5 **Melbury Abbas** Dorset
30 D1 **Melbury Bubb** Dorset
45 H6 **Melbury Osmond** Dorset
30 D1 **Melbury Sampford** Dorset
606 A6 **Melby** Shet
195 E1 **Melchbourne** Beds
65 E5 **Melcombe** Somset
47 E4 **Melcombe Bingham** Dorset
32 B3 **Melcombe Regis** Dorset
25 E4 **Meldon** Devon
430 B3 **Meldon** Nthumb
197 E5 **Meldreth** Cambs
492 D2 **Meldrum** Ag & B
534 E3 **Melfort** Ag & B
307 F3 **Melgarve** Highld
230 C5 **Meliden** Denbgs
230 C5 **Melinbyrhedyn** Powys
132 B5 **Melin Caiach** Myr Td
130 C4 **Melincourt** Neath
130 A5 **Melincryddan** Neath
7 H6 **Melinsey** Cnwll
285 H2 **Melin-y-coed** Conwy
232 A3 **Melin-y-ddôl** Powys
287 E5 **Melin-y-Wig** Denbgs
453 G1 **Melkington** Nthumb
391 F4 **Melkinthorpe** Cumb
402 C2 **Melkridge** Nthumb
87 F2 **Melksham** Wilts
87 G2 **Melksham Forest** Wilts
4 C3 **Mellangoose** Cnwll
480 C5 **Melldalloch** Ag & B
114 D4 **Mell Green** W Berk
400 D5 **Mellguards** Cumb
366 B5 **Melling** Lancs
323 G4 **Melling** Sefton
14 C4 **Mellingey** Cnwll
323 H4 **Melling Mount** Sefton
225 F5 **Mellis** Suffk
225 E5 **Mellis Green** Suffk
573 G5 **Mellon Charles** Highld
573 G4 **Mellon Udrigle** Highld
339 G3 **Mellor** Lancs
312 C2 **Mellor** Stockp
339 F3 **Mellor Brook** Lancs
86 C5 **Mells** Somset
226 D4 **Mells** Suffk
86 C5 **Mells Green** Somset
391 G2 **Melmerby** Cumb
369 E2 **Melmerby** N York
370 C4 **Melmerby** N York
199 G3 **Melon Green** Suffk
30 B3 **Melplash** Dorset
451 G3 **Melrose** Border
600 D7 **Melsetter** Ork
383 E3 **Melsonby** N York
327 G2 **Meltham** Kirk
327 H2 **Meltham Mills** Kirk
347 E4 **Melton** E R Yk
202 B4 **Melton** Suffk
359 E4 **Meltonby** E R Yk
260 D5 **Melton Constable** Norfk
277 G6 **Melton Mowbray** Leics
333 F2 **Melton Ross** N Linc
572 D6 **Melvaig** Highld
233 F1 **Melverley** Shrops
269 F6 **Melverley Green** Shrops
587 J4 **Melvich** Highld
11 G4 **Membland** Devon
29 E2 **Membury** Devon
571 H3 **Memsie** Abers
527 F3 **Memus** Angus
8 C1 **Mena** Cnwll
8 D3 **Menabilly** Cnwll
6 B5 **Menadarva** Cnwll
6 D4 **Menagissey** Cnwll
304 B5 **Menai Bridge** IoA
226 B3 **Mendham** Suffk
201 F1 **Mendlesham** Suffk
201 E2 **Mendlesham Green** Suffk
373 E6 **Menethorpe** N York
52 C5 **Mengham** Hants
16 C6 **Menheniot** Cnwll
4 C1 **Menherion** Cnwll
211 G6 **Menithwood** Worcs
7 H3 **Menna** Cnwll
435 G3 **Mennock** D & G
355 G6 **Menston** Brad
498 C5 **Menstrie** Clacks
345 F3 **Menthorpe** N York
168 C6 **Mentmore** Bucks
449 E5 **Menzion** Border
531 L5 **Meoble** Highld
234 B2 **Meole Brace** Shrops
308 B2 **Meols** Wirral
51 F4 **Meon** Hants
73 F6 **Meonstoke** Hants
97 F1 **Meopham** Kent
97 F1 **Meopham Green** Kent
97 F1 **Meopham Station** Kent
221 F3 **Mepal** Cambs
169 G2 **Meppershall** Beds
185 F5 **Merbach** Herefs
294 B6 **Mercaton** Derbys

342 C4 **Merchant Fields** Kirk
488 A5 **Merchiston** C Edin
311 E3 **Mere** Ches
68 C3 **Mere** Wilts
338 B6 **Mere Brow** Lancs
340 D3 **Mereclough** Lancs
237 H5 **Mere Green** Birm
188 C3 **Mere Green** Worcs
270 A2 **Merehead** Wrexhm
310 D5 **Mere Heath** Ches
98 C2 **Meresborough** Medway
337 F3 **Mereside** Bpool
271 H5 **Meretown** Staffs
97 G4 **Mereworth** Kent
541 E2 **Mergie** Abers
143 G5 **Meriden** Herts
214 C3 **Meriden** Solhll
544 F3 **Merkadale** Highld
566 B7 **Merkinch** Highld
461 E2 **Merkland** N Ayrs
419 F3 **Merkland** S Ayrs
580 B4 **Merkland Lodge** Highld
96 A5 **Merle Common** Surrey
48 C5 **Merley** Poole
125 F2 **Merlin's Bridge** Pembks
125 G4 **Merlin's Cross** Pembks
236 C5 **Merridale** Wolves
64 D5 **Merridge** Somset
37 F4 **Merrie Gardens** IoW
13 E3 **Merrifield** Devon
23 F2 **Merrifield** Devon
270 B5 **Merrington** Shrops
125 F5 **Merrion** Pembks
30 C3 **Merriott** Dorset
45 E5 **Merriott** Somset
45 E5 **Merriottsford** Somset
49 E5 **Merritown** Dorset
18 B2 **Merrivale** Devon
161 E5 **Merrivale** Herefs
93 H4 **Merrow** Surrey
383 F2 **Merrybent** Darltn
48 C4 **Merry Field Hill** Dorset
143 G6 **Merry Hill** Herts
236 C5 **Merry Hill** Wolves
116 C5 **Merryhill Green** Wokham
467 E3 **Merrylee** E Rens
239 H3 **Merry Lees** Leics
16 C5 **Merrymeet** Cnwll
15 F4 **Merry Meeting** Cnwll
50 D2 **Merry Oak** C Sotn
81 F2 **Mersham** Kent
95 F4 **Merstham** Surrey
53 F4 **Merston** W Susx
37 E4 **Merstone** IoW
7 G5 **Merther** Cnwll
7 G5 **Merther Lane** Cnwll
153 H5 **Merthyr** Carmth
157 F2 **Merthyr Cynog** Powys
106 B5 **Merthyr Dyfan** V Glam
104 D4 **Merthyr Mawr** Brdgnd
131 G3 **Merthyr Tydfil** Myr Td
132 A5 **Merthyr Vale** Myr Td
40 A5 **Merton** Devon
119 F6 **Merton** Gt Lon
248 B5 **Merton** Norfk
166 C6 **Merton** Oxon
119 E6 **Merton Park** Gt Lon
440 C2 **Mervinslaw** Border
41 F4 **Meshaw** Devon
174 A6 **Messing** Essex
332 B4 **Messingham** N Linc
237 E5 **Mesty Croft** Sandw
150 D3 **Mesur-y-dorth** Pembks
395 F2 **Metal Bridge** Dur
28 A4 **Metcombe** Devon
226 B3 **Metfield** Suffk
226 B4 **Metfield Common** Suffk
17 F5 **Metherell** Cnwll
298 D2 **Metheringham** Lincs
202 B5 **Methersgate** Suffk
502 B5 **Methil** Fife
501 G4 **Methilhill** Fife
343 G4 **Methley** Leeds
343 G4 **Methley Junction** Leeds
343 G4 **Methley Lanes** Wakefd
560 C2 **Methlick** Abers
512 B4 **Methven** P & K
247 E6 **Methwold** Norfk
247 E5 **Methwold Hythe** Norfk
226 D2 **Mettingham** Suffk
261 H4 **Metton** Norfk
8 C5 **Mevagissey** Cnwll
353 E1 **Mewith Head** N York
329 H4 **Mexborough** Donc
589 H2 **Mey** Highld
34 C2 **Meyrick Park** Bmouth
137 H4 **Meysey Hampton** Gloucs
595 J3 **Miabhaig** W Isls
596 D6 **Miabhaig** W Isls
598 B8 **Miabhaig** W Isls
572 F8 **Mial** Highld
598 B8 **Miavaig** W Isls
160 C4 **Michaelchurch** Herefs
159 F3 **Michaelchurch Escley** Herefs
184 D4 **Michaelchurch-on-Arrow** Powys
106 B5 **Michaelston-le-Pit** V Glam
106 B4 **Michaelston-super-Ely** Cardif
106 D3 **Michaelston-y-Fedw** Newpt
15 F3 **Michaelstow** Cnwll
19 E4 **Michelcombe** Devon
72 D2 **Micheldever** Hants
71 H4 **Michelmersh** Hants
201 F2 **Mickfield** Suffk
330 B6 **Micklebring** Donc
386 C2 **Mickleby** N York
117 E1 **Micklefield** Bucks
344 A3 **Micklefield** Leeds
143 E5 **Micklefield Green** Herts
94 D4 **Mickleham** Surrey
327 E4 **Micklehurst** Tamesd
275 E2 **Mickleover** C Derb
342 B1 **Micklethwaite** Brad
400 A4 **Micklethwaite** Cumb
393 G5 **Mickleton** Dur
190 B6 **Mickleton** Gloucs
343 G4 **Mickletown** Leeds
309 F6 **Mickle Trafford** Ches
314 C4 **Mickley** Derbys
370 B4 **Mickley** N York
271 E3 **Mickley** Shrops
199 G3 **Mickley Green** Suffk
404 C2 **Mickley Square** Nthumb
50 D2 **Midanbury** C Sotn
571 G3 **Mid Ardlaw** Abers
482 D5 **Mid Auchinleck** Inver
602 E3 **Midbea** Ork
555 H4 **Mid Beltie** Abers
609 G4 **Midbrake** Shet
469 H1 **Mid Calder** W Loth
583 J2 **Mid Clyth** Highld
116 B2 **Middle Assendon** Oxon
166 A4 **Middle Aston** Oxon
513 F4 **Middlebank** P & K
165 G4 **Middle Barton** Oxon
214 C3 **Middle Bickenhill** Solhll
425 E4 **Middlebie** D & G
49 F5 **Middle Bockhampton** Dorset
92 D5 **Middle Bourne** Surrey
109 E4 **Middle Bridge** N Som

524 C2 **Middlebridge** P & K
514 C2 **Middle Brighty** Angus
84 B5 **Middle Burnham** Somset
373 E5 **Middlecave** N York
45 F5 **Middle Chinnock** Somset
167 F4 **Middle Claydon** Bucks
292 C4 **Middle Cliff** Staffs
329 G4 **Middlecliffe** Barns
24 B1 **Middlecott** Devon
25 H5 **Middlecott** Devon
26 A1 **Middlecott** Devon
22 C3 **Middle Crackington** Cnwll
315 E5 **Middlecroft** Derbys
528 C3 **Middle Drums** Angus
137 E3 **Middle Duntisbourne** Gloucs
557 G3 **Middlefield** C Aber
486 A3 **Middlefield** Falk
338 D4 **Middleforth Green** Lancs
571 L6 **Middle Grange** Abers
117 H3 **Middle Green** Bucks
43 F4 **Middle Green** Somset
199 E1 **Middle Green** Suffk
369 F2 **Middleham** N York
315 E4 **Middle Handley** Derbys
224 C2 **Middle Harling** Norfk
406 B4 **Middle Herrington** Sundld
16 C5 **Middlehill** Cnwll
125 F2 **Middle Hill** Pembks
111 E6 **Middlehill** Wilts
211 E6 **Middlehope** Shrops
480 C2 **Middle Kames** Ag & B
189 G5 **Middle Littleton** Worcs
43 H5 **Middle Luxton** Devon
159 F3 **Middle Maes-coed** Herefs
31 F1 **Middlemarsh** Dorset
60 D4 **Middle Marwood** Devon
293 F6 **Middle Mayfield** Staffs
150 D4 **Middle Mill** Pembks
560 D5 **Middlemuir** Abers
570 F4 **Middlemuir** Abers
570 F7 **Middlemuir** Abers
291 H5 **Middleport** C Stke
80 C2 **Middle Quarter** Kent
406 A5 **Middle Rainton** Sundld
318 D2 **Middle Rasen** Lincs
486 B4 **Middlerig** Falk
20 C4 **Middle Rocombe** Devon
352 C2 **Middle Salter** Lancs
396 D6 **Middlesbrough** Middsb
390 B1 **Middlesceugh** Cumb
366 B2 **Middleshaw** Cumb
424 C4 **Middleshaw** D & G
393 F4 **Middle Side** Dur
369 E5 **Middlesmoor** N York
43 G3 **Middle Stoford** Somset
215 F4 **Middle Stoke** Covtry
19 E3 **Middle Stoke** Devon
122 C4 **Middle Stoke** Medway
395 F3 **Middlestone** Dur
395 E3 **Middlestone Moor** Dur
84 D5 **Middle Stoughton** Somset
328 D1 **Middlestown** Wakefd
486 B5 **Middle Strath** W Loth
135 H4 **Middle Street** Gloucs
15 H6 **Middle Taphouse** Cnwll
358 A5 **Middlethorpe** York
560 B6 **Middleton** Abers
516 A7 **Middleton** Ag & B
528 C5 **Middleton** Angus
366 C2 **Middleton** Cumb
293 G2 **Middleton** Derbys
294 B3 **Middleton** Derbys
173 H2 **Middleton** Essex
90 C6 **Middleton** Hants
396 D3 **Middleton** Hartpl
210 C6 **Middleton** Herefs
35 H3 **Middleton** IoW
351 F3 **Middleton** Lancs
471 G3 **Middleton** Mdloth
466 A4 **Middleton** N Ayrs
218 A1 **Middleton** Nhants
252 D4 **Middleton** Norfk
429 H2 **Middleton** Nthumb
454 D2 **Middleton** Nthumb
343 E4 **Middleton** N York
354 C6 **Middleton** N York
355 F5 **Middleton** N York
373 E2 **Middleton** N York
500 B3 **Middleton** P & K
525 H6 **Middleton** P & K
326 B3 **Middleton** Rochdl
210 C4 **Middleton** Shrops
233 E5 **Middleton** Shrops
269 F4 **Middleton** Shrops
227 E6 **Middleton** Suffk
102 B3 **Middleton** Swans
238 B5 **Middleton** Warwks
211 E1 **Middleton Baggot** Shrops
166 A1 **Middleton Cheney** Nhants
273 E2 **Middleton Green** Staffs
454 B4 **Middleton Hall** Nthumb
393 G4 **Middleton-in-Teesdale** Dur
326 C4 **Middleton Junction** Oldham
227 E6 **Middleton Moor** Suffk
525 H4 **Middleton of Dalrulzian** P & K
384 B2 **Middleton One Row** Darltn
384 D3 **Middleton-on-Leven** N York
53 H5 **Middleton-on-Sea** W Susx
186 C2 **Middleton on the Hill** Herefs
360 A5 **Middleton-on-the-Wolds** E R Yk
557 G2 **Middleton Park** C Aber
362 B3 **Middleton Place** Cumb
211 E1 **Middleton Priors** Shrops
370 C4 **Middleton Quernhow** N York
384 A2 **Middleton St George** Darltn
211 F2 **Middleton Scriven** Shrops
166 B5 **Middleton Stoney** Oxon
383 F3 **Middleton Tyas** N York
376 B3 **Millerston** C Glas
3 d1 **Middle Town** IoS
108 C5 **Middletown** N Som
233 E2 **Middletown** Powys
189 G2 **Middletown** Warwks
191 E6 **Middle Tysoe** Warwks
71 F2 **Middle Wallop** Hants
167 G2 **Middle Weald** M Keyn
291 E1 **Middlewich** Ches
135 G5 **Middle Wick** Gloucs
111 F5 **Middlewick** Wilts
71 E3 **Middle Winterslow** Wilts
312 B3 **Middlewood** Ches
16 C3 **Middlewood** Cnwll
184 D5 **Middlewood** Herefs
185 E6 **Middlewood** Herefs
314 C1 **Middlewood** Sheff
70 C2 **Middle Woodford** Wilts
201 E2 **Middlewood Green** Suffk
136 B4 **Middleyard** Gloucs
65 G5 **Middlezoy** Somset
395 F4 **Middridge** Dur
66 C3 **Midelney** Somset
586 C3 **Midfield** Highld
86 D2 **Midford** BaNES
439 H1 **Midgard** Border
338 D1 **Midge Hall** Lancs
341 F4 **Midgehole** Calder

402 A3 **Midgeholme** Cumb
115 F6 **Midgham** W Berk
115 F6 **Midgham Green** W Berk
328 D2 **Midgley** Wakefd
341 G4 **Midgley** Wakefd
609 G5 **Mid Ho** Shet
94 D5 **Mid Holmwood** Surrey
328 C5 **Midhopestones** Sheff
74 D5 **Midhurst** W Susx
600 E4 **Midland** Ork
53 E3 **Mid Lavant** W Susx
451 E4 **Midlem** Border
448 C5 **Midlock** S Lans
549 G2 **Mid Main** Highld
437 E5 **Mid Murthat** D & G
408 B2 **Mid Ringuinea** D & G
86 A4 **Midsomer Norton** BaNES
546 F2 **Mid Strome** Highld
482 B4 **Midton** Inver
572 F6 **Midtown** Highld
586 C4 **Midtown** Highld
566 F7 **Midtown** Highld
300 C3 **Midville** Lincs
606 B7 **Mid Walls** Shet
312 B3 **Midway** Ches
86 A5 **Midway** Somset
609 G6 **Mid Yell** Shet
576 D5 **Migdale** Highld
554 D3 **Migvie** Abers
20 B3 **Milber** Devon
68 A6 **Milborne Port** Somset
47 A6 **Milborne St Andrew** Dorset
67 H5 **Milborne Wick** Somset
430 B5 **Milbourne** Nthumb
111 G2 **Milbourne** Wilts
391 H4 **Milburn** Cumb
110 B1 **Milbury Heath** S Glos
371 E6 **Milby** N York
173 E5 **Milch Hill** Essex
9 G2 **Milcombe** Abers
165 G3 **Milcombe** Oxon
200 C5 **Milden** Suffk
222 D4 **Mildenhall** Suffk
113 F5 **Mildenhall** Wilts
209 F5 **Milebrook** Powys
98 B5 **Milebush** Kent
249 H2 **Mile Cross** Norfk
112 A6 **Mile Elm** Wilts
222 B3 **Mile End** Cambs
20 A3 **Mile End** Devon
174 C4 **Mile End** Essex
134 D2 **Mile End** Gloucs
119 H3 **Mile End** Gt Lon
199 G4 **Mile End** Suffk
254 B4 **Mileham** Norfk
55 F3 **Mile Oak** Br & H
97 G6 **Mile Oak** Kent
269 F4 **Mile Oak** Staffs
238 B4 **Mile Oak** Staffs
30 A4 **Miles Cross** Dorset
291 G5 **Miles Green** Staffs
93 F3 **Miles Green** Surrey
343 E2 **Miles Hill** Leeds
487 E2 **Milesmark** Fife
326 C4 **Miles Platting** Manch
115 E6 **Miles's Green** W Berk
123 E5 **Mile Town** Kent
454 A3 **Milfield** Nthumb
294 D5 **Milford** Derbys
38 B3 **Milford** Devon
208 A1 **Milford** Powys
269 H5 **Milford** Shrops
273 E5 **Milford** Staffs
93 F6 **Milford** Surrey
70 D4 **Milford** Wilts
125 F3 **Milford Haven** Pembks
35 G2 **Milford on Sea** Hants
89 E2 **Milkhouse Water** Wilts
470 D5 **Milkieston** Border
134 D3 **Milkwall** Gloucs
69 F5 **Milkwell** Wilts
f5 **Millais** Jersey
74 C4 **Milland** W Susx
466 C2 **Millarston** Rens
557 E5 **Millbank** Abers
341 G5 **Mill Bank** Calder
588 E3 **Millbank** Highld
100 C2 **Millbank** Kent
389 G4 **Millbeck** Cumb
603 H4 **Millbounds** Ork
571 J6 **Millbreck** Abers
570 E7 **Millbrex** Abers
74 D1 **Millbridge** Surrey
169 E2 **Millbrook** Beds
10 D3 **Millbrook** Cnwll
50 C2 **Millbrook** C Sotn
29 F3 **Millbrook** Devon
62 B5 **Millbrook** Devon
35 h7 **Millbrook** Staffs
327 E5 **Millbrook** Tamesd
312 C2 **Millbrook** Stockp
445 F4 **Millburn** S Ayrs
250 C4 **Mill Common** Norfk
80 B5 **Mill Corner** E Susx
566 B2 **Millcraig** Highld
293 F4 **Milldale** Staffs
366 D6 **Mill Dam** N York
406 B1 **Mill Dam** S Tyne
557 H1 **Millden** Abers
528 B4 **Mildens** Angus
116 C2 **Mill End** Bucks
198 D3 **Mill End** Cambs
135 H5 **Millend** Gloucs
136 A3 **Millend** Gloucs
137 H2 **Mill End** Gloucs
143 E6 **Mill End** Herts
170 D3 **Mill End** Herts
172 C4 **Mill End Green** Essex
9 H3 **Millendreath** Cnwll
488 C6 **Millerhill** Mdloth
313 F5 **Miller's Dale** Derbys
294 B4 **Millers Green** Derbys
146 B3 **Miller's Green** Essex
484 D5 **Millersneuk** E Duns
484 C6 **Millerston** C Glas
555 E5 **Millfield** Abers
244 A4 **Millfield** C Pete
406 B3 **Millfield** Sundld
340 D6 **Millgate** Lancs
255 G2 **Millgillhead** Cumb
198 C5 **Mill Green** Cambs
146 C4 **Mill Green** Essex
91 E2 **Mill Green** Hants
144 B2 **Mill Green** Herts
225 F3 **Mill Green** Norfk
271 F4 **Mill Green** Shrops
237 G4 **Mill Green** Staffs
200 B6 **Mill Green** Suffk
200 C3 **Mill Green** Suffk
201 F2 **Mill Green** Suffk
185 E5 **Millhalf** Herefs
97 H3 **Millhall** Kent
28 D2 **Millhayes** Devon
43 F5 **Millhayes** Devon
365 G5 **Millholme** Cumb
468 A4 **Millheugh** S Lans
339 G4 **Mill Hill** Bl w D
325 G3 **Mill Hill** Bolton
17 G4 **Millhill** Devon
147 G6 **Mill Hill** Essex
57 G4 **Mill Hill** E Susx

134 D3 **Mill Hill** Gloucs
119 E1 **Mill Hill** Gt Lon
101 G5 **Mill Hill** Kent
301 F1 **Mill Hill** Lincs
199 H4 **Mill Hill** Suffk
202 B5 **Mill Hill** Suffk
355 G2 **Mill Hirst** N York
366 B1 **Millholme** Cumb
480 D5 **Millhouse** Ag & B
390 B2 **Millhouse** Cumb
424 C2 **Millhousebridge** D & G
314 C3 **Millhouses** Sheff
466 B2 **Millikenpark** Rens
125 G2 **Millin Cross** Pembks
359 F4 **Millington** E R Yk
294 B5 **Millington Green** Derbys
411 E3 **Millisle** D & G
457 E2 **Mill Knowe** Ag & B
92 C4 **Mill Lane** Hants
272 B3 **Millmeece** Staffs
43 F5 **Millmoor** Devon
565 J5 **Millnain** Highld
366 A3 **Millness** Cumb
514 C2 **Mill of Brighty** Angus
556 C4 **Mill of Echt** Abers
483 F3 **Mill of Haldane** W Duns
540 C4 **Mill of Kincardine** Abers
560 B4 **Mill of Kingoodie** Abers
528 B3 **Mill of Marcus** Angus
557 F5 **Mill of Monquich** Abers
559 G4 **Mill of Pitcaple** Abers
602 B8 **Mill of Rango** Ork
362 D5 **Millom** Cumb
22 D3 **Millook** Cnwll
196 B6 **Millow** Beds
457 E5 **Mill Park** Ag & B
3 G3 **Millpool** Cnwll
15 G4 **Millpool** Cnwll
464 D3 **Millport** N Ayrs
501 F2 **Mills** Fife
343 E3 **Mill Shaw** Leeds
365 F3 **Mill Side** Cumb
561 F3 **Mills of Leask** Abers
97 G3 **Mill Street** Kent
255 E4 **Mill Street** Norfk
174 C2 **Mill Street** Suffk
314 C4 **Millthorpe** Derbys
279 G3 **Millthorpe** Lincs
366 D1 **Millthrop** Cumb
557 F4 **Milltimber** C Aber
552 F7 **Milltown** Abers
8 D2 **Milltown** Cnwll
15 G5 **Milltown** Cnwll
425 G4 **Milltown** D & G
294 C2 **Milltown** Derbys
61 E4 **Milltown** Devon
512 C5 **Milltown of Aberdalgie** P & K
568 F7 **Milltown of Auchindoun** Moray
570 D4 **Milltown of Craigston** Abers
568 D7 **Milltown of Edinvillie** Moray
555 E1 **Milltown of Kildrummy** Abers
569 J6 **Milltown of Rothiemay** Moray
554 D2 **Milltown of Towie** Abers
119 H4 **Millwall** Gt Lon
29 F3 **Millway Rise** Devon
566 B3 **Milnafua** Highld
500 B4 **Milnathort** P & K
289 G2 **Milners Heath** Ches
483 H5 **Milngavie** E Duns
485 G4 **Milnquarter** Falk
326 D2 **Milnrow** Rochdl
340 A4 **Milnshaw** Lancs
365 G3 **Milnthorpe** Cumb
329 E1 **Milnthorpe** Wakefd
468 A3 **Milnwood** N Lans
155 E6 **Milo** Carmth
542 B7 **Milovaig** Highld
211 E5 **Milson** Shrops
99 E3 **Milstead** Kent
89 E5 **Milston** Wilts
192 C5 **Milthorpe** Nhants
527 E5 **Milton** Angus
329 F4 **Milton** Barns
197 G2 **Milton** Cambs
484 B6 **Milton** C Glas
52 B5 **Milton** C Port
292 B4 **Milton** C Stke
366 A3 **Milton** Cumb
401 G2 **Milton** Cumb
415 H6 **Milton** D & G
422 D5 **Milton** D & G
275 G4 **Milton** Derbys
549 H3 **Milton** Highld
550 F7 **Milton** Highld
562 C8 **Milton** Highld
564 E5 **Milton** Highld
565 K7 **Milton** Highld
566 D2 **Milton** Highld
567 H6 **Milton** Highld
589 J6 **Milton** Highld
121 G5 **Milton** Kent
552 D5 **Milton** Moray
569 J3 **Milton** Moray
108 C2 **Milton** Newpt
316 D5 **Milton** Notts
84 B2 **Milton** N Som
114 D1 **Milton** Oxon
165 G2 **Milton** Oxon
499 F2 **Milton** P & K
511 G2 **Milton** P & K
126 A4 **Milton** Pembks
184 D4 **Milton** Powys
66 D5 **Milton** Somset
496 D4 **Milton** Stirlg
483 F5 **Milton** W Duns
69 E3 **Milton** Wilts
47 H4 **Milton Abbas** Dorset
17 F3 **Milton Abbot** Devon
471 E2 **Milton Bridge** Mdloth
168 D3 **Milton Bryan** Beds
67 H2 **Milton Clevedon** Somset
561 E2 **Milton Coldwells** Abers
17 G5 **Milton Combe** Devon
141 E4 **Milton Common** Oxon
39 E5 **Milton Damerel** Devon
568 B3 **Miltonduff** Moray
135 G2 **Milton End** Gloucs
138 A4 **Milton End** Gloucs
195 E3 **Milton Ernest** Beds
289 F3 **Milton Green** Ches
17 F3 **Milton Green** Devon
114 D1 **Milton Heights** Oxon
20 C2 **Milton Hill** Devon
114 D1 **Milton Hill** Oxon
167 G2 **Milton Keynes** M Keyn
168 B2 **Milton Keynes Village** M Keyn
89 E2 **Milton Lilbourne** Wilts
193 H3 **Milton Malsor** Nhants
509 K2 **Milton Morenish** P & K
555 H3 **Milton of Auchinhove** Abers
501 F4 **Milton of Balgonie** Fife
483 F1 **Milton of Buchanan** Stirlg
556 A4 **Milton of Campfield** Abers
484 C4 **Milton of Campsie** E Duns
556 B3 **Milton of Corsindae** Abers

511 F5 Milton of Cultoquhey P & K
555 F2 Milton of Cushnie Abers
524 E5 Milton of Dalcapon P & K
540 D3 Milton of Dellavaird Abers
524 E4 Milton of Edradour P & K
527 G3 Milton of Finavon Angus
566 D6 Milton of Gollanfield Highld
558 B4 Milton of Lesmore Abers
550 B1 Milton of Leys Highld
557 F4 Milton of Murtle C Aber
558 B4 Milton of Noth Abers
527 E6 Milton of Ogilvie Angus
554 C5 Milton of Tullich Abers
68 D4 Milton on Stour Dorset
114 D1 Milton Park Oxon
98 D1 Milton Regis Kent
57 E4 Milton Street E Susx
164 C6 Milton under Wychwood Oxon
43 F2 Milverton Somset
191 E1 Milverton Warwks
273 E3 Milwich Staffs
308 A5 Milwr Flints
93 G2 Mimbridge Surrey
493 G5 Minard Ag & B
493 G6 Minard Castle Ag & B
48 B2 Minchington Dorset
136 C4 Minchinhampton Gloucs
453 F3 Mindrum Nthumb
63 F2 Minehead Somset
288 C4 Minera Wrexhm
22 D3 Mineshope Cnwll
112 B1 Minety Wilts
229 G2 Minffordd Gwynd
265 E2 Minffordd Gwynd
304 C5 Minffordd Gwynd
519 G2 Mingarrypark Highld
590 E2 Mingearraidh W Isls
6 D4 Mingoose Cnwll
300 B2 Miningsby Lincs
16 C4 Minions Cnwll
432 D2 Minishant S Ayrs
92 D3 Minley Manor Hants
230 C2 Minllyn Gwynd
560 D5 Minnes Abers
417 E3 Minnigaff D & G
570 D3 Minnonie Abers
174 E2 Minnow End Essex
290 D2 Minshull Vernon Ches
356 D2 Minskip N York
49 H2 Minstead Hants
74 D5 Minsted W Susx
101 E3 Minster Kent
123 E5 Minster Kent
404 B3 Minsteracres Nthumb
233 G4 Minsterley Shrops
139 E2 Minster Lovell Oxon
135 H1 Minsterworth Gloucs
31 E2 Minterne Magna Dorset
31 F2 Minterne Parva Dorset
319 F5 Minting Lincs
571 J6 Mintlaw Abers
571 H6 Mintlaw Station Abers
451 H5 Minto Border
451 G5 Minto Kames Border
209 H1 Minton Shrops
379 F6 Mintsfeet Cumb
126 A2 Minwear Pembks
214 B1 Minworth Birm
602 C8 Mirbister Ork
376 B1 Mirehouse Cumb
589 J4 Mireland Highld
342 C6 Mirfield Kirk
136 D3 Miserden Gloucs
226 B2 Misery Corner Norfk
105 G3 Miskin Rhondd
131 G5 Miskin Rhondd
69 H5 Misselfore Wilts
331 E6 Misson Notts
216 C3 Misterton Leics
331 G6 Misterton Notts
45 E6 Misterton Somset
331 G5 Misterton Soss Notts
175 F3 Mistley Essex
175 F3 Mistley Heath Essex
119 F6 Mitcham Gt Lon
161 F6 Mitcheldean Gloucs
7 G3 Mitchell Cnwll
449 E3 Mitchell Hill Border
436 C5 Mitchellslacks D & G
472 B5 Mitchelston Border
134 B2 Mitchel Troy Mons
376 D5 Mite Houses Cumb
430 C2 Mitford Nthumb
6 D3 Mithian Cnwll
6 D4 Mithian Downs Cnwll
162 D3 Mitton Gloucs
236 C1 Mitton Staffs
166 D3 Mixbury Oxon
341 H4 Mixenden Calder
292 D3 Mixon Staffs
9 E3 Mixtow Cnwll
609 G4 Moarfield Shet
426 B5 Moat Cumb
514 C2 Moatmill Angus
200 D3 Moats Tye Suffk
311 F4 Mobberley Ches
273 F1 Mobberley Staffs
290 D6 Moblake Ches
142 B4 Mobwell Bucks
185 F6 Moccas Herefs
305 H4 Mochdre Conwy
207 H2 Mochdre Powys
410 B3 Mochrum D & G
49 F3 Mockbeggar Hants
82 B2 Mockbeggar Kent
122 A5 Mockbeggar Medway
388 C5 Mockerkin Cumb
12 B2 Modbury Devon
272 D2 Moddershall Staffs
315 G5 Model Village Derbys
191 G2 Model Village Warwks
97 E6 Modest Corner Kent
10 D1 Moditonham Quay Cnwll
586 E4 Modsarie Highld
306 D5 Moelfre Conwy
304 B2 Moelfre IoA
268 C4 Moelfre Powys
283 F4 Moel Tryfan Gwynd
308 A6 Moel-y-crio Flints
437 E3 Moffat D & G
468 B2 Moffat Mills N Lans
95 E4 Mogador Surrey
195 G5 Moggerhanger Beds
41 H4 Mogworthy Devon
239 E1 Moira Leics
158 C1 Moity Powys
99 G4 Molash Kent
545 G7 Mol-chlach Highld
288 B2 Mold Flints
172 B5 Molehill Green Essex
173 E6 Molehill Green Essex
347 F1 Molescroft E R Yk
430 B3 Molesden Nthumb
219 F4 Molesworth Cambs
8 C2 Molinnis Cnwll
545 K3 Moll Highld
41 G2 Molland Devon
309 E6 Mollington Ches
191 G5 Mollington Oxon
485 E5 Mollinsburn N Lans
303 F6 Mona IoA

180 D2 Monachty Cerdgn
509 G6 Monachyle Stirlg
208 D6 Monaughty Powys
540 D4 Monboddo Abers
512 D6 Moncreiffe P & K
233 F3 Mondaytown Shrops
541 E4 Mondynes Abers
509 J3 Monemore Stirlg
202 A3 Monewden Suffk
466 B4 Moneyacres E Ayrs
512 C4 Moneydie P & K
143 E6 Moneyhill Herts
275 F6 Money Hill Leics
117 E4 Moneyrow Green W & M
292 D5 Moneystone Staffs
5 E2 Mongleath Cnwll
422 C1 Moniaive D & G
515 E3 Monifieth Angus
514 D2 Monikie Angus
501 E2 Monimail Fife
178 C5 Monington Pembks
329 F3 Monk Bretton Barns
383 G2 Monk End N York
144 B5 Monken Hadley Gt Lon
344 C4 Monk Fryston N York
396 B2 Monk Hesleden Dur
187 E6 Monkhide Herefs
400 B3 Monkhill Cumb
344 B5 Monkhill Wakefd
235 E6 Monkhopton Shrops
186 B3 Monkland Herefs
39 G3 Monkleigh Devon
234 C2 Monkmoor Shrops
105 E5 Monknash V Glam
25 E1 Monkokehampton Devon
17 E4 Monkscross Cnwll
431 F5 Monkseaton N Tyne
200 C5 Monks Eleigh Suffk
200 C5 Monks Eleigh Tye Suffk
76 D4 Monk's Gate W Susx
311 G5 Monk's Heath Ches
91 G3 Monk Sherborne Hants
560 A1 Monkshill Abers
80 C1 Monks Hill Kent
63 H4 Monksilver Somset
215 H3 Monks Kirby Warwks
173 G2 Monks Lodge Essex
201 H1 Monk Soham Suffk
95 H1 Monks Orchard Gt Lon
111 F6 Monk's Park Wilts
214 A4 Monkspath Solhll
141 G4 Monks Risborough Bucks
300 D1 Monksthorpe Lincs
168 B2 Monkston Park M Keyn
501 E3 Monkston Fife
172 C4 Monk Street Essex
343 F2 Monkswood Leeds
471 F2 Monkswood Mdloth
133 F4 Monkswood Mons
28 C2 Monkton Devon
101 E2 Monkton Kent
125 G4 Monkton Pembks
445 E4 Monkton S Ayrs
405 H2 Monkton S Tyne
105 E5 Monkton V Glam
86 D2 Monkton Combe BaNES
69 E2 Monkton Deverill Wilts
87 E1 Monkton Farleigh Wilts
488 C5 Monkton Heath E Loth
44 B2 Monkton Heathfield Somset
48 C2 Monkton Up Wimborne Dorset
29 F3 Monkton Wyld Dorset
406 B3 Monkwearmouth Sundld
30 A3 Monkwood Dorset
73 G3 Monkwood Hants
188 B3 Monkwood Green Worcs
186 C5 Monmarsh Herefs
236 D5 Monmore Green Wolves
134 B2 Monmouth Mons
159 G4 Monmouth Cap Mons
185 G6 Monnington on Wye Herefs
410 C4 Monreith D & G
410 C4 Monreith Mains D & G
45 F4 Montacute Somset
325 F2 Montcliffe Bolton
464 C2 Montford Ag & B
233 H2 Montford Shrops
234 A1 Montford Bridge Shrops
555 G1 Montgarrie Abers
445 H4 Montgarswood E Ayrs
232 D3 Montgomery Powys
93 E4 Montgomery Lines Hants
465 G6 Montgreenan N Ayrs
325 H5 Monton Salfd
109 G3 Montpelier Bristl
501 G3 Montrave Fife
529 F3 Montrose Angus
148 D5 Montsale Essex
214 D1 Monwode Lea Warwks
89 H6 Monxton Hants
293 G1 Monyash Derbys
556 B1 Monymusk Abers
511 F5 Monzie P & K
484 D5 Moodiesburn N Lans
44 D5 Moolham Somset
80 C4 Moon's Green Kent
213 G6 Moon's Moat Worcs
501 F1 Moonzie Fife
45 E4 Moor Somset
69 G3 Mooray Wilts
30 A3 Moorbath Dorset
300 A2 Moorby Lincs
388 A4 Moorclose Cumb
326 C3 Moorclose Rochdl
116 D1 Moor Common Bucks
185 G3 Moorcot Herefs
48 B3 Moor Crichel Dorset
18 D6 Moor Cross Devon
48 D6 Moordown Bmouth
310 B3 Moore Halton
342 A2 Moor Edge Brad
328 D4 Moor End Barns
328 D4 Moor End Beds
116 D1 Moor End Bucks
341 G4 Moor End Calder
197 E5 Moor End Devon
400 B4 Moor End Cumb
425 E5 Moorend D & G
293 H5 Moorend Derbys
40 D6 Moorend Devon
405 G6 Moorend Dur
346 B2 Moor End E R Yk
135 G4 Moorend Gloucs
136 C2 Moorend Gloucs
163 E5 Moor End Gloucs
351 E6 Moor End Lancs
357 E5 Moor End Leeds
344 D2 Moor End N York
356 D2 Moor End N York
110 A4 Moor End S Glos
312 C2 Moor End Stockp
188 D3 Moor End Worcs
358 C3 Moor End York
187 G5 Moorend Cross Herefs
371 E6 Moor End Field N York
331 E1 Moorends Donc
327 F6 Moorfield Derbys
255 G2 Moorgate Norfk
315 E1 Moorgate Rothm
213 G3 Moor Green Birm
51 E1 Moorgreen Hants

170 D4 Moor Green Herts
295 F5 Moorgreen Notts
273 E1 Moor Green Staffs
111 F6 Moor Green Wilts
295 G2 Moorhaigh Notts
237 H5 Moor Hall Birm
314 C5 Moorhall Derbys
185 G5 Moorhampton Herefs
12 B1 Moorhaven Village Devon
44 A6 Moorhayne Devon
342 B2 Moorhead Brad
328 C2 Moor Head Kirk
342 D4 Moor Head Leeds
326 D4 Moorhey Oldham
315 E3 Moorhole Sheff
399 H4 Moorhouse Cnwll
400 B3 Moorhouse Cumb
330 A2 Moorhouse Donc
297 E1 Moorhouse Notts
96 B4 Moorhouse Bank Surrey
299 H3 Moorhouses Lincs
26 C3 Moorlake Devon
85 G2 Moorledge BaNES
66 C2 Moorlinch Somset
357 G3 Moor Monkton N York
357 G3 Moor Monkton Moor N York
556 B2 Moor of Balvack Abers
567 K5 Moor of Granary Moray
388 C2 Moor Park Cumb
160 B1 Moor Park Herefs
143 F6 Moor Park Herts
93 E5 Moor Park Surrey
376 C2 Moor Row Cumb
399 G5 Moor Row Cumb
386 A2 Moorsholm R & Cl
342 C4 Moor Side Brad
308 C4 Moorside Ches
68 C6 Moorside Dorset
404 C5 Moor Side Dur
338 B3 Moor Side Lancs
338 C2 Moor Side Lancs
342 D2 Moorside Leeds
299 G3 Moor Side Lincs
327 E3 Moorside Oldham
325 H4 Moorside Salfd
81 H2 Moorstock Kent
98 C1 Moor Street Medway
16 B6 Moorswater Cnwll
329 H2 Moorthorpe Wakefd
342 C5 Moor Top Kirk
18 B3 Moortown Devon
23 G3 Moortown Devon
39 H4 Moortown Devon
49 F4 Moortown Hants
36 C4 Moortown IoW
333 F5 Moortown Lincs
271 E6 Moortown Wrekin
577 G7 Morangie Highld
531 J4 Morar Highld
275 G2 Moravian Settlement Derbys
302 C4 Morawelon IoA
219 C1 Morborne Cambs
41 F6 Morchard Bishop Devon
26 B2 Morchard Road Devon
29 G4 Morcombelake Dorset
242 C4 Morcott Rutlnd
269 E4 Morda Shrops
47 H5 Morden Dorset
119 F6 Morden Gt Lon
170 C1 Morden Cambs
95 E1 Morden Park Gt Lon
160 D2 Mordiford Herefs
474 D3 Mordington Holdings Border
395 G4 Mordon Dur
209 F1 More Shrops
42 B2 Morebath Devon
453 E5 Morebattle Border
351 F2 Morecambe Lancs
112 D2 Moredon Swindn
488 B6 Moredun C Edin
574 C4 Morefield Highld
82 D3 Morehall Kent
12 D2 Moreleigh Devon
509 J2 Morenish P & K
388 B6 Moresby Parks Cumb
72 D4 Morestead Hants
32 D2 Moreton Dorset
145 H3 Moreton Essex
186 B2 Moreton Herefs
139 G4 Moreton Oxon
141 E4 Moreton Oxon
236 A1 Moreton Staffs
274 A4 Moreton Staffs
308 C1 Moreton Wirral
270 C5 Moreton Corbet Shrops
26 A5 Moretonhampstead Devon
164 C3 Moreton-in-Marsh Gloucs
186 D5 Moreton Jeffries Herefs
191 E3 Moreton Morrell Warwks
186 C5 Moreton on Lugg Herefs
191 E4 Moreton Paddox Warwks
192 C5 Moreton Pinkney Nhants
271 E3 Moreton Say Shrops
135 H3 Moreton Valence Gloucs
271 E2 Moretonwood Shrops
128 D5 Morfa Carmth
129 E2 Morfa Carmth
179 G3 Morfa Cerdgn
262 B4 Morfa Gwynd
128 D5 Morfa Bacas Carmth
127 H2 Morfa Bach Carmth
264 C2 Morfa Bychan Gwynd
282 D4 Morfa Dinlle Gwynd
130 D3 Morfa Glas Neath
262 D2 Morfa Nefyn Gwynd
287 G2 Morfydd Denbgs
106 B3 Morganstown Cardif
70 D5 Morgan's Vale Wilts
205 E4 Moriah Cerdgn
134 D3 Mork Gloucs
391 F5 Morland Cumb
311 G3 Morley Ches
275 F1 Morley Derbys
394 C4 Morley Dur
343 E4 Morley Leeds
311 G3 Morley Green Ches
294 D5 Morleymoor Derbys
294 D5 Morley Park Derbys
249 E5 Morley St Botolph Norfk
275 F1 Morley Smithy Derbys
16 D4 Mornick Cnwll
488 A5 Morningside C Edin
468 C3 Morningside N Lans
225 H1 Morningthorpe Norfk
430 D2 Morpeth Nthumb
529 F2 Morphie Abers
274 A6 Morrey Staffs
292 D4 Morridge Side Staffs
273 E2 Morrilow Heath Staffs
129 G5 Morriston Swans
106 C5 Morristown V Glam
260 D3 Morston Norfk
60 C2 Mortehoe Devon
315 F2 Morthen Rothm
91 G2 Mortimer W Berk
185 H2 Mortimer's Cross Herefs
91 G2 Mortimer West End Hants
119 E4 Mortlake Gt Lon
329 E5 Mortomley Sheff
390 C2 Morton Cumb

400 C4 Morton Cumb
294 D2 Morton Derbys
37 G3 Morton IoW
279 G5 Morton Lincs
297 G2 Morton Lincs
317 F1 Morton Lincs
255 F4 Morton Norfk
296 D4 Morton Notts
110 A1 Morton S Glos
269 E5 Morton Shrops
189 H2 Morton Bagot Warwks
269 E5 Morton Common Shrops
436 A5 Morton Mains D & G
270 D5 Morton Mill Shrops
370 C1 Morton-on-Swale N York
189 F4 Morton Spirt Worcs
394 D5 Morton Tinmouth Dur
189 F3 Morton Underhill Worcs
2 C2 Morvah Cnwll
9 H2 Morval Cnwll
547 H5 Morvich Highld
577 G3 Morvich Highld
235 F6 Morville Shrops
235 F6 Morville Heath Shrops
17 F5 Morwellham Quay Devon
38 B4 Morwenstow Cnwll
315 E3 Mosborough Sheff
445 G1 Moscow E Ayrs
211 H1 Mose Shrops
390 B3 Mosedale Cumb
213 G3 Moseley Birm
236 D5 Moseley Wolves
188 B3 Moseley Worcs
325 G3 Moses Gate Bolton
325 F3 Mosley Common Wigan
516 B7 Moss Ag & B
330 C2 Moss Donc
519 G2 Moss Highld
288 D4 Moss Wrexhm
558 B6 Mossat Abers
310 A2 Moss Bank Halton
606 F2 Mossbank Shet
324 C5 Moss Bank St Hel
388 A4 Mossbay Cumb
445 F5 Mossblown S Ayrs
311 E2 Mossbrow Traffd
440 C1 Mossburnford Border
421 G5 Mossdale D & G
426 C6 Mossdale Cumb
351 F5 Moss Edge Lancs
351 F6 Moss Edge Lancs
117 E5 Moss End Br For
310 D4 Moss End Ches
468 B2 Mossend N Lans
388 D5 Mosser Cumb
388 D4 Mosser Mains Cumb
272 C5 Mossgate Staffs
445 G4 Mossgiel E Ayrs
451 G2 Mosshouses Border
324 A5 Moss Houses Ches
527 F4 Mosside Angus
312 B5 Moss Lane Ches
291 H2 Mossley Ches
327 E4 Mossley Tamesd
309 E4 Mossley Hill Lpool
311 G2 Moss Nook St Hel
324 C6 Moss Nook St Hel
568 C3 Moss of Barmuckity Moray
466 D3 Mosspark C Glas
272 D5 Moss Pit Staffs
399 F4 Moss Side Cumb
566 F6 Moss-side Highld
324 A5 Moss Side Knows
351 G5 Moss Side Lancs
326 B5 Moss Side Manch
569 J5 Moss-side Moray
323 G4 Moss Side Sefton
337 G3 Moss Side Sefton
559 E2 Moss-side of Monellie Abers
568 E3 Mosstodloch Moray
528 B6 Mosston Angus
324 C2 Mossy Lea Lancs
30 A1 Mosterton Dorset
309 E5 Moston Ches
326 C4 Moston Manch
270 D4 Moston Shrops
291 E2 Moston Green Ches
307 G3 Mostyn Flints
68 D4 Motcombe Dorset
11 G4 Mothecombe Devon
390 C4 Motherby Cumb
468 B3 Motherwell N Lans
95 E1 Motspur Park Gt Lon
120 B5 Mottingham Gt Lon
71 G4 Mottisfont Hants
36 B4 Mottistone IoW
327 E5 Mottram in Longdendale Tamesd
327 E5 Mottram Rise Tamesd
311 H4 Mottram St Andrew Ches
145 H1 Mott's Green Essex
78 C2 Mott's Mill E Susx
34 C3 Mouilpied Guern
309 H5 Mouldsworth Ches
524 D4 Moulin P & K
56 A3 Moulsecoomb Br & H
115 F3 Moulsford Oxon
147 E3 Moulsham Essex
168 C1 Moulsoe M Keyn
310 D6 Moulton Ches
280 C5 Moulton Lincs
193 G1 Moulton Nhants
383 F4 Moulton N York
198 D2 Moulton Suffk
105 H5 Moulton V Glam
280 C6 Moulton Chapel Lincs
244 D1 Moulton Eaugate Lincs
193 G2 Moulton Park Nhants
250 D3 Moulton St Mary Norfk
280 D4 Moulton Seas End Lincs
538 B4 Moulzie Angus
7 E2 Mount Cnwll
15 G5 Mount Cnwll
302 B4 Mountain Brdgnd
132 B3 Mountain Air Blae G
131 H5 Mountain Ash Rhondd
111 E4 Mountain Bower Wilts
470 B5 Mountain Cross Border
99 H4 Mountain Street Kent
6 D5 Mount Ambrose Cnwll
109 E2 Mount Ballan Mons
450 B4 Mountbenger Border
450 B4 Mountbengerburn Border
483 G5 Mountblow W Duns
122 C1 Mount Bovers Essex
174 A3 Mount Bures Essex
8 C3 Mount Charles Cnwll
15 E5 Mount Charles Cnwll
89 G4 Mount Cowdown Wilts
145 G4 Mount End Essex
78 B6 Mount Ephraim E Susx
68 C6 Mounters Dorset
58 B2 Mountfield E Susx
565 K4 Mountgerald Highld
11 E3 Mount Gould C Plym
6 D4 Mount Hawke Cnwll
4 D5 Mount Hermon Cnwll
93 G3 Mount Hermon Surrey
56 B4 Mount High Highld
110 B5 Mount Hill S Glos
7 G1 Mountjoy Cnwll
23 H3 Mount Lane Devon
146 C5 Mountnessing Essex

134 C6 Mounton Mons
167 E3 Mount Pleasant Bucks
291 G3 Mount Pleasant Ches
8 C1 Mount Pleasant Cnwll
292 A6 Mount Pleasant C Stke
238 D1 Mount Pleasant Derbys
275 E4 Mount Pleasant Derbys
294 C5 Mount Pleasant Derbys
28 C2 Mount Pleasant Dur
392 D1 Mount Pleasant Dur
395 F3 Mount Pleasant Dur
56 C1 Mount Pleasant E Susx
56 D4 Mount Pleasant E Susx
308 B5 Mount Pleasant Flints
405 G2 Mount Pleasant Gatesd
118 A1 Mount Pleasant Gt Lon
588 E3 Mountpleasant Highld
101 E2 Mount Pleasant Kent
385 E2 Mount Pleasant Middsb
132 A5 Mount Pleasant Myr Td
130 B5 Mount Pleasant Neath
248 C6 Mount Pleasant Norfk
125 H3 Mount Pleasant Pembks
234 B2 Mount Pleasant Shrops
396 B5 Mount Pleasant S on T
199 E5 Mount Pleasant Suffk
215 F2 Mount Pleasant Warwks
163 F2 Mount Pleasant Worcs
189 E2 Mount Pleasant Worcs
12 D3 Mounts Devon
288 C4 Mount Sion Wrexhm
139 F1 Mount Skippett Oxon
571 G4 Mountsolie Abers
240 C2 Mountsorrel Leics
70 A5 Mount Sorrel Wilts
341 H4 Mount Tabor Calder
467 G2 Mount Vernon C Glas
10 D3 Mount Wise C Plym
75 E1 Mousehill Surrey
3 E4 Mousehole Cnwll
455 E3 Mousen Nthumb
214 C6 Mousley End Warwks
424 B5 Mouswald D & G
38 C2 Mouth Mill Devon
338 C5 Mowbreck Lancs
291 H3 Mow Cop Staffs
383 G1 Mowden Darltn
147 F2 Mowden Essex
453 F2 Mowhaugh Border
240 C3 Mowmacre Hill C Leic
96 C5 Mowshurst Kent
216 D2 Mowsley Leics
358 A1 Moxby N York
237 E5 Moxley Wsall
534 D6 Moy Highld
550 D3 Moy Highld
568 C3 Moycroft Moray
550 D2 Moy Hall Highld
178 C3 Moylgrove Pembks
467 E2 Mt Florida C Glas
458 D3 Muasdale Ag & B
541 H1 Muchalls Abers
160 C3 Much Birch Herefs
187 E5 Much Cowarne Herefs
160 B3 Much Dewchurch Herefs
66 C5 Muchelney Somset
66 C5 Muchelney Ham Somset
171 F6 Much Hadham Herts
338 C5 Much Hoole Lancs
338 C5 Much Hoole Moss Houses Lancs
338 C5 Much Hoole Town Lancs
9 G2 Muchlarnick Cnwll
161 F3 Much Marcle Herefs
548 B5 Muchrachd Highld
235 E4 Much Wenlock Shrops
121 G3 Mucking Thurr
31 E4 Muckleford Dorset
271 E4 Muckleton Staffs
259 G4 Muckleton Norfk
270 D5 Muckleton Shrops
558 D5 Muckletown Abers
235 E5 Muckley Shrops
237 G3 Muckley Corner Staffs
235 E5 Muckley Cross Shrops
320 C3 Muckton Lincs
280 D2 Muckton Bottom Lincs
580 D2 Mudale Highld
327 E6 Mudd Tamesd
61 E4 Muddiford Devon
60 D5 Muddlebridge Devon
57 E2 Muddles Green E Susx
35 E2 Mudeford Dorset
67 F6 Mudford Somset
67 F6 Mudford Sock Somset
84 D5 Mudgley Somset
509 G4 Mugdock Stirlg
545 G2 Mugeary Highld
294 B6 Mugginton Derbys
294 B6 Muggintonlane End Derbys
95 F4 Mugswell Surrey
576 E3 Muie Highld
537 G5 Muir Abers
472 C5 Muircleugh Border
515 F2 Muirden Abers
515 F2 Muirdrum Angus
501 E3 Muiredge Fife
467 E3 Muirend C Glas
514 A3 Muirhead Angus
501 E3 Muirhead Fife
484 D6 Muirhead N Lans
444 D3 Muirhead S Ayrs
487 H4 Muirhouse C Edin
468 B4 Muirhouse N Lans
527 E3 Muirhouses Angus
486 D3 Muirhouses Falk
513 G5 Muirhouses P & K
446 D4 Muirkirk E Ayrs
555 F1 Muir of Alford Abers
555 H6 Muir of Fairburn Highld
555 G2 Muir of Fowlis Abers
568 E3 Muir of Lochs Moray
565 J6 Muir of Ord Highld
514 C2 Muir of Pert Angus
565 J6 Muir of Tarradale Highld
533 H6 Muirshearlich Highld
557 F5 Muirskie Abers
561 E2 Muirtack Abers
570 E6 Muirtack Abers
566 C4 Muirton Highld
499 E2 Muirton P & K
512 D4 Muirton P & K
565 H6 Muirton Mains Highld
525 J7 Muirton of Ardblair P & K
529 E2 Muirton of Ballochy Angus
570 D5 Muiryfold Abers
381 G5 Muker N York
249 G4 Mulbarton Norfk
568 F5 Mulben Moray
15 E5 Mulberry Cnwll
3 E3 Mulfra Cnwll
476 F5 Mulindry Ag & B
598 E6 Mullach Charlabhaigh W Isls
60 D3 Mullacott Cross Devon
89 G5 Mullenspond Hants
4 C5 Mullion Cnwll
4 C5 Mullion Cove Cnwll
130 B5 Mumbles Hill Swans
321 F5 Mumby Lincs
326 D3 Mumps Oldham
187 F4 Munderfield Row Herefs
187 F4 Munderfield Stocks Herefs

City, town and village index: Mundesley - Newlands 705

256 C2 **Mundesley** Norfk
247 G6 **Mundford** Norfk
250 C5 **Mundham** Norfk
147 H4 **Mundon** Essex
557 G2 **Mundurno** C Aber
99 E5 **Mundy Bois** Kent
533 L2 **Munerigie** Highld
609 J4 **Muness** Shet
573 J5 **Mungasdale** Highld
390 B3 **Mungrisdale** Cumb
565 L6 **Munlochy** Highld
161 F1 **Munsley** Herefs
210 C2 **Munslow** Shrops
186 C6 **Munstone** Herefs
106 C5 **Murch** V Glam
25 G5 **Murchington** Devon
163 G1 **Murcot** Worcs
140 C1 **Murcott** Oxon
111 H1 **Murcott** Wilts
497 G5 **Murdieston** Stirlg
310 B3 **Murdishaw** Halton
469 H2 **Murieston** W Loth
588 F3 **Murkle** Highld
532 F4 **Murlaggan** Highld
534 B6 **Murlaggan** Highld
600 C4 **Murra** Ork
487 H5 **Murrayfield** C Edin
424 C5 **Murraythwaite** D & G
92 B3 **Murrell Green** Hants
161 G3 **Murrell's End** Gloucs
161 G4 **Murrell's End** Gloucs
162 A5 **Murrell's End** Gloucs
514 D2 **Murroes** Angus
245 E3 **Murrow** Cambs
167 H4 **Mursley** Bucks
99 E2 **Murston** Kent
527 G3 **Murthill** Angus
512 C2 **Murthly** P & K
392 B5 **Murton** Cumb
406 B5 **Murton** Dur
475 E5 **Murton** Nthumb
431 F5 **Murton** N Tyne
103 E4 **Murton** Swans
358 C4 **Murton** York
371 G2 **Murton Grange** N York
12 C1 **Murtwell** Devon
29 E4 **Musbury** Devon
48 D5 **Muscliff** Bmouth
372 C3 **Muscoates** N York
192 D2 **Muscott** Nhants
506 F5 **Musdale** Ag & B
212 D2 **Mushroom Green** Dudley
488 C5 **Musselburgh** E Loth
124 D3 **Musselwick** Pembks
257 E6 **Mustard Hyrn** Norfk
278 A2 **Muston** Leics
374 D4 **Muston** N York
212 C5 **Mustow Green** Worcs
119 F1 **Muswell Hill** Gt Lon
412 C5 **Mutehill** D & G
227 F2 **Mutford** Suffk
498 D1 **Muthill** P & K
27 G2 **Mutterton** Devon
78 D5 **Mutton Hall** E Susx
235 G2 **Muxton** Wrekin
307 H4 **Mwdwl-eithin** Flints
288 A1 **Mwynbwll** Flints
588 F6 **Mybster** Highld
156 B3 **Myddfai** Carmth
270 B5 **Myddle** Shrops
270 B5 **Myddlewood** Shrops
129 F2 **Myddyn-fych** Carmth
180 C3 **Mydroilyn** Cerdgn
338 C2 **Myerscough** Lancs
339 F3 **Myerscough Smithy** Lancs
5 F1 **Mylor Bridge** Cnwll
5 F2 **Mylor Churchtown** Cnwll
106 C4 **Mynachdy** Cardif
131 G5 **Mynachdy** Rhondd
152 C3 **Mynachlog-ddu** Pembks
209 G5 **Mynd** Shrops
209 G2 **Myndtown** Shrops
205 G4 **Mynydd Bach** Cerdgn
134 B6 **Mynydd-bach** Mons
103 F2 **Mynydd-Bach** Swans
103 F2 **Mynydd-bach-y-glo** Swans
303 G3 **Mynydd Bodafon** IoA
262 D6 **Mynydd Gilan** Gwynd
288 B2 **Mynydd Isa** Flints
132 C6 **Mynyddislwyn** Caerph
307 G5 **Mynydd-llan** Flints
284 D1 **Mynydd Llandegai** Gwynd
306 B4 **Mynydd Marian** Conwy
303 E3 **Mynydd Mechell** IoA
303 F4 **Mynydd-Mwyn** IoA
303 F4 **Mynydd Mwyn Mawr** IoA
302 D4 **Mynydd-y-gôf** IoA
302 D4 **Mynydd-yr-eithin** IoA
263 E4 **Mynytho** Gwynd
556 C5 **Myrebird** Abers
589 H5 **Myrelandhorn** Highld
156 B3 **Myrtle Hill** Carmth
93 E3 **Mytchett** Surrey
93 E3 **Mytchett Place** Surrey
341 F4 **Mytholm** Calder
341 G4 **Mytholmroyd** Calder
337 G3 **Mythop** Lancs
190 D2 **Myton** Warwks
357 E1 **Myton Hall** N York
357 E1 **Myton-on-Swale** N York
234 A1 **Mytton** Shrops

N

572 F7 **Naast** Highld
342 C6 **Nab Hill** Kirk
339 F4 **Nab's Head** Lancs
595 G4 **Na Buirgh** W Isls
358 A5 **Naburn** York
342 B2 **Nab Wood** Brad
99 G6 **Naccolt** Kent
100 C5 **Nackington** Kent
176 D1 **Nacton** Suffk
26 D4 **Nadderwater** Devon
360 B3 **Nafferton** E R Yk
598 D6 **Na Gearrannan** W Isls
136 C5 **Nag's Head** Gloucs
307 H4 **Naid-y-march** Flints
135 E1 **Nailbridge** Gloucs
43 H2 **Nailsbourne** Somset
109 E6 **Nailsea** N Som
239 G3 **Nailstone** Leics
86 C2 **Nailwell** BaNES
566 F5 **Nairn** Highld
95 E5 **Nalderswood** Surrey
3 F3 **Nanceddan** Cnwll
4 B2 **Nancegollan** Cnwll
3 G1 **Nancemellin** Cnwll
4 D3 **Nancenoy** Cnwll
3 E2 **Nancledra** Cnwll
326 B1 **Nangreaves** Bury
262 D4 **Nanhoron** Gwynd
265 G5 **Nannau** Gwynd
307 H6 **Nannerch** Flints
240 B1 **Nanpantan** Leics
8 B2 **Nanpean** Cnwll
2 C4 **Nanquidno** Cnwll
15 E5 **Nanstallon** Cnwll
154 B6 **Nant** Carmth
288 A3 **Nant** Denbgs
269 E3 **Nant** Shrops
288 A1 **Nant Alyn** Flints
131 G2 **Nant-ddu** Powys
179 H2 **Nanternis** Cerdgn
154 C5 **Nantgaredig** Carmth
106 B2 **Nantgarw** Rhondd
154 A3 **Nantgerdinen** Carmth
183 F2 **Nant Glas** Powys
287 E2 **Nantglyn** Denbgs
207 F4 **Nantgwyn** Powys
4 C4 **Nantithet** Cnwll
283 F5 **Nantlle** Gwynd
288 C2 **Nant Mawr** Flints
268 D5 **Nantmawr** Shrops
183 G1 **Nantmel** Powys
284 D5 **Nantmor** Gwynd
284 C3 **Nant Peris** Gwynd
207 F5 **Nantserth** Powys
290 C4 **Nantwich** Ches
182 B6 **Nant-y-Bai** Carmth
132 B2 **Nant-y-Bwch** Blae G
130 C3 **Nant-y-cafn** Neath
154 C6 **Nantycaws** Carmth
269 E4 **Nant y Caws** Shrops
106 D2 **Nant-y-ceisiad** Caerph
133 F3 **Nant-y-derry** Mons
305 E5 **Nant-y-felin** Conwy
155 E3 **Nant-y-ffin** Carmth
130 D6 **Nantyffyllon** Brdgnd
132 C2 **Nantyglo** Blae G
268 D4 **Nant-y-gollen** Shrops
131 E6 **Nant-y-moel** Brdgnd
305 E6 **Nant-y-pandy** Conwy
285 H3 **Nant-y-Rhiw** Conwy
590 F5 **Na Pairceanan** W Isls
83 F1 **Napchester** Kent
142 B5 **Naphill** Bucks
188 C5 **Napleton** Worcs
271 G2 **Napley** Staffs
271 G2 **Napley Heath** Staffs
353 G4 **Nappa** N York
368 C1 **Nappa Scar** N York
191 H2 **Napton on the Hill** Warwks
126 B2 **Narberth** Pembks
126 B2 **Narberth Bridge** Pembks
240 B5 **Narborough** Leics
253 E5 **Narborough** Norfk
29 E1 **Narfords** Devon
10 B2 **Narkurs** Cnwll
493 F2 **Narrachan** Ag & B
39 E4 **Narracott** Devon
251 E2 **Narrowgate Corner** Norfk
283 E6 **Nasareth** Gwynd
217 E4 **Naseby** Nhants
591 C8 **Nasg** W Isls
167 G3 **Nash** Bucks
96 B2 **Nash** Gt Lon
185 F2 **Nash** Herefs
101 E4 **Nash** Kent
107 F3 **Nash** Newpt
211 E5 **Nash** Shrops
45 G5 **Nash** Somset
136 C3 **Nashend** Gloucs
211 H3 **Nash End** Worcs
91 H5 **Nashes Green** Hants
142 A3 **Nash Lee** Bucks
57 F2 **Nash Street** E Susx
121 F6 **Nash Street** Kent
243 E5 **Nassington** Nhants
136 A3 **Nastend** Gloucs
171 E5 **Nasty** Herts
38 C3 **Natcott** Devon
380 D3 **Nateby** Cumb
351 G6 **Nateby** Lancs
92 B4 **Nately Scures** Hants
365 H2 **Natland** Cumb
162 D3 **Natton** Gloucs
200 D5 **Naughton** Suffk
163 H5 **Naunton** Gloucs
162 C2 **Naunton** Worcs
189 E4 **Naunton Beauchamp** Worcs
75 E4 **Navant Hill** W Susx
298 B3 **Navenby** Lincs
146 A5 **Navestock Heath** Essex
146 B5 **Navestock Side** Essex
582 D6 **Navidale** Highld
372 C3 **Nawton** N York
174 C3 **Nayland** Suffk
145 F3 **Nazeing** Essex
145 F3 **Nazeing Gate** Essex
145 F4 **Nazeing Long Green** Essex
145 E3 **Nazeing Mead** Essex
49 F5 **Neacroft** Hants
400 B4 **Nealhouse** Cumb
215 E3 **Neal's Green** Warwks
99 G3 **Neames Forstal** Kent
607 G6 **Neap** Shet
355 F1 **Near Hardcastle** N York
378 C5 **Near Sawrey** Cumb
167 H4 **Nearton End** Bucks
119 E2 **Neasden** Gt Lon
384 A2 **Neasham** Darltn
165 F5 **Neat Enstone** Oxon
130 B5 **Neath** Neath
130 A5 **Neath Abbey** Neath
74 A1 **Neatham** Hants
168 B1 **Neath Hill** M Keyn
256 C5 **Neatishead** Norfk
348 C3 **Neat Marsh** E R Yk
248 B4 **Neaton** Norfk
180 D1 **Nebo** Cerdgn
286 A3 **Nebo** Conwy
283 E5 **Nebo** Gwynd
303 G2 **Nebo** IoA
190 B6 **Nebsworth** Warwks
213 G2 **Nechells** Birm
247 H3 **Necton** Norfk
578 F3 **Nedd** Highld
430 D3 **Nedderton** Nthumb
85 G4 **Nedge Hill** Somset
200 C5 **Nedging** Suffk
200 D5 **Nedging Tye** Suffk
226 A3 **Needham** Norfk
146 A1 **Needham Green** Essex
201 E3 **Needham Market** Suffk
199 E1 **Needham Street** Suffk
220 D5 **Needingworth** Cambs
274 B5 **Needwood** Staffs
7 F2 **Neeham** Cnwll
211 F4 **Neen Savage** Shrops
211 F5 **Neen Sollars** Shrops
211 E2 **Neenton** Shrops
269 F2 **Nefod** Shrops
263 E2 **Nefyn** Gwynd
86 A5 **Neighbourne** Somset
188 D3 **Neight Hill** Worcs
466 C3 **Neilston** E Rens
165 G1 **Neithrop** Oxon
132 B5 **Nelson** Caerph
340 D2 **Nelson** Lancs
431 E4 **Nelson Village** Nthumb
468 C6 **Nemphlar** S Lans
85 F2 **Nempnett Thrubwell** N Som
244 C3 **Nene Terrace** Lincs
402 B5 **Nenthall** Cumb
402 D6 **Nenthead** Cumb
452 C2 **Nenthorn** Border
26 B3 **Neopardy** Devon
54 D3 **Nepcote** W Susx
388 C4 **Nepgill** Cumb
55 F1 **Nep Town** W Susx
476 C5 **Nerabus** Ag & B
288 B2 **Nercwys** Flints
467 F3 **Nerston** S Lans
454 B3 **Nesbit** Nthumb
308 D4 **Ness** Ches
269 G6 **Nesscliffe** Shrops
308 D4 **Nessholt** Ches
603 M1 **Nesstoun** Ork
308 C4 **Neston** Ches
111 F6 **Neston** Wilts
213 G2 **Netchells Green** Birm
109 H5 **Netham** Bristl
468 C5 **Nethanfoot** S Lans
311 G4 **Nether Alderley** Ches
88 D5 **Netheravon** Wilts
472 C6 **Nether Blainslie** Border
313 F2 **Nether Booth** Derbys
570 D4 **Netherbrae** Abers
600 D1 **Netherbrough** Ork
277 E4 **Nether Broughton** Leics
468 C5 **Netherburn** S Lans
366 C4 **Nether Burrow** Lancs
274 D2 **Nether Burrows** Derbys
30 B3 **Netherbury** Dorset
426 A5 **Netherby** Cumb
356 C5 **Netherby** N York
438 A4 **Nether Cassock** D & G
31 F3 **Nether Cerne** Dorset
314 C5 **Nether Chanderhill** Derbys
44 A3 **Netherclay** Somset
413 H3 **Nether Clifton** D & G
67 F6 **Nether Compton** Dorset
165 H1 **Nethercote** Oxon
192 B2 **Nethercote** Warwks
23 H3 **Nethercott** Devon
60 C4 **Nethercott** Devon
166 A5 **Nethercott** Oxon
64 B5 **Nethercott** Somset
560 B5 **Nether Crimond** Abers
568 F3 **Nether Dallachy** Moray
529 E4 **Nether Dysart** Angus
314 C3 **Nether Edge** Sheff
314 B5 **Nether End** Derbys
134 D5 **Netherend** Gloucs
328 C3 **Nether End** Kirk
241 F2 **Nether End** Leics
27 E3 **Nether Exe** Devon
58 B3 **Netherfield** E Susx
168 B2 **Netherfield** M Keyn
276 D1 **Netherfield** Notts
436 B2 **Nether Fingland** S Lans
255 E2 **Nethergate** Norfk
240 D3 **Nether Hall** C Leic
70 C4 **Netherhampton** Wilts
315 E4 **Nether Handley** Derbys
514 B1 **Nether Handwick** Angus
329 G5 **Nether Haugh** Rothm
316 D4 **Nether Headon** Notts
294 D4 **Nether Heage** Derbys
193 E3 **Nether Heyford** Nhants
450 C2 **Nether Horsburgh** Border
600 E1 **Netherhouse** Ork
436 D2 **Nether Howecleuch** D & G
365 H6 **Nether Kellet** Lancs
470 D6 **Nether Kidston** Border
571 J7 **Nether Kinmundy** Abers
466 C3 **Nether Kirkton** E Rens
273 H3 **Netherland Green** Staffs
315 G5 **Nether Langwith** Notts
412 D5 **Netherlaw** D & G
29 H1 **Netherlay** Dorset
561 F3 **Nether Leask** Abers
467 E3 **Netherlee** E Rens
557 F6 **Netherley** Abers
327 F2 **Netherley** Kirk
309 F2 **Netherley** Lpool
314 C6 **Nether Loads** Derbys
424 A2 **Nethermill** D & G
569 J5 **Nethermills** Moray
294 D1 **Nether Moor** Derbys
570 F7 **Nethermuir** Abers
95 F3 **Netherne-on-the-Hill** Surrey
314 B4 **Nether Padley** Derbys
466 D3 **Netherplace** E Rens
357 H3 **Nether Poppleton** York
451 G5 **Netherraw** Border
568 C6 **Nether Ringorm** Moray
389 H2 **Nether Row** Cumb
238 D2 **Netherseal** Derbys
471 H5 **Nether Shiels** Border
384 D6 **Nether Silton** N York
209 E5 **Nether Skyborry** Shrops
200 B2 **Nether St** Suffk
45 G6 **Netherstoke** Dorset
237 H2 **Nether Stowe** Staffs
64 C4 **Nether Stowey** Somset
146 B2 **Nether Street** Essex
145 F1 **Nether Street** Herts
446 B6 **Netherthird** E Ayrs
328 A3 **Netherthong** Kirk
315 E5 **Netherthorpe** Derbys
528 B3 **Netherton** Angus
309 H4 **Netherton** Ches
16 C4 **Netherton** Cnwll
388 B2 **Netherton** Cumb
20 B3 **Netherton** Devon
212 D2 **Netherton** Dudley
138 B4 **Netherton** Gloucs
90 B3 **Netherton** Hants
160 C4 **Netherton** Herefs
327 H2 **Netherton** Kirk
468 B4 **Netherton** N Lans
442 B3 **Netherton** Nthumb
139 G5 **Netherton** Oxon
525 H5 **Netherton** P & K
323 G4 **Netherton** Sefton
211 G3 **Netherton** Shrops
484 B4 **Netherton** Stirlg
328 D1 **Netherton** Wakefd
163 E1 **Netherton** Worcs
376 B3 **Nethertown** Cumb
589 J1 **Nethertown** Highld
339 H2 **Nethertown** Lancs
273 H6 **Nethertown** Staffs
500 C3 **Nether Urquhart** Fife
71 G2 **Nether Wallop** Hants
403 G1 **Nether Warden** Nthumb
377 E4 **Nether Wasdale** Cumb
400 C5 **Nether Welton** Cumb
164 C5 **Nether Westcote** Gloucs
192 A5 **Nether Whitacre** Warwks
141 F2 **Nether Winchendon or Lower Winchendon** Bucks
430 B1 **Netherwitton** Nthumb
446 C4 **Netherwood** E Ayrs
165 G3 **Nether Worton** Oxon
551 J5 **Nethy Bridge** Highld
50 D3 **Netley** Hants
51 E2 **Netley Hill** Hants
50 B2 **Netley Marsh** Hants
27 E3 **Nettacott** Devon
145 F2 **Netteswell** Essex
116 A2 **Nettlebed** Oxon
86 B5 **Nettlebridge** Somset
30 C3 **Nettlecombe** Dorset
37 E5 **Nettlecombe** IoW
143 E2 **Nettleden** Herts
318 C4 **Nettleham** Lincs
97 G4 **Nettlestead** Kent
201 E5 **Nettlestead** Suffk
97 G4 **Nettlestead Green** Kent
37 G2 **Nettlestone** IoW
405 F5 **Nettlesworth** Dur
136 D2 **Nettleton** Gloucs
333 F4 **Nettleton** Lincs
111 E4 **Nettleton** Wilts
111 E4 **Nettleton Green** Wilts
111 E4 **Nettleton Shrub** Wilts
333 G5 **Nettleton Top** Lincs
70 C2 **Netton** Wilts
155 G5 **Neuadd** Carmth
122 A1 **Nevendon** Essex
152 B1 **Nevern** Pembks
395 F1 **Nevilles Cross** Dur
241 H6 **Nevill Holt** Leics
398 B1 **New Abbey** D & G
570 F3 **New Aberdour** Abers
96 A2 **New Addington** Gt Lon
355 H5 **Newall** Leeds
311 G2 **Newall Green** Manch
73 E3 **New Alresford** Hants
526 B5 **New Alyth** P & K
244 B4 **Newark** C Pete
603 L3 **Newark** Ork
297 F4 **Newark-on-Trent** Notts
214 D2 **New Arley** Warwks
360 C6 **New Arram** E R Yk
468 B3 **Newarthill** N Lans
97 F1 **New Ash Green** Kent
297 F4 **New Balderton** Notts
318 D4 **Newball** Lincs
82 C3 **Newbarn** Kent
121 F6 **New Barn** Kent
144 C5 **New Barnet** Gt Lon
333 F2 **New Barnetby** N Linc
364 B5 **Newbarns** Cumb
194 B2 **New Barton** Nhants
276 C1 **New Basford** C Nott
471 F1 **Newbattle** Mdloth
105 G5 **New Beaupre** V Glam
119 H5 **New Beckenham** Gt Lon
454 D5 **New Bewick** Nthumb
399 F1 **Newbie** D & G
364 C6 **Newbiggin** Cumb
366 B4 **Newbiggin** Cumb
376 D6 **Newbiggin** Cumb
390 D4 **Newbiggin** Cumb
401 G5 **Newbiggin** Cumb
393 F4 **Newbiggin** Dur
404 D5 **Newbiggin** Dur
391 G4 **Newbiggin** Nthumb
403 G5 **Newbiggin** Nthumb
368 C1 **Newbiggin** N York
368 C2 **Newbiggin** N York
431 F2 **Newbiggin-by-the-sea** Nthumb
513 G1 **Newbigging** Angus
514 C2 **Newbigging** Angus
514 D2 **Newbigging** Angus
440 D1 **Newbigging** Border
487 F4 **Newbigging** C Edin
469 G5 **Newbigging** S Lans
603 K3 **Newbiggings** Ork
430 C6 **Newbiggin Hall Estate** N u Ty
380 C3 **Newbiggin-on-Lune** Cumb
216 A4 **New Bilton** Warwks
314 D5 **Newbold** Derbys
241 G3 **Newbold** Leics
275 G6 **Newbold** Leics
326 D2 **Newbold** Rochdl
239 G4 **Newbold Heath** Leics
216 A4 **Newbold on Avon** Warwks
190 C5 **Newbold-on-Stour** Warwks
190 D3 **Newbold Pacey** Warwks
236 D4 **Newbolds** Wolves
239 G4 **Newbold Verdon** Leics
300 A3 **New Bolingbroke** Lincs
315 F5 **New Bolsover** Derbys
244 B3 **Newborough** C Pete
273 H4 **Newborough** Staffs
324 D5 **New Boston** St Hel
140 A3 **New Botley** Oxon
166 B2 **Newbottle** Nhants
406 A4 **Newbottle** Sundld
318 B5 **New Boultham** Lincs
202 B6 **Newbourne** Suffk
167 H1 **New Bradwell** M Keyn
395 E1 **New Brancepeth** Dur
86 C1 **Newbridge** BaNES
132 D5 **Newbridge** Caerph
487 F5 **Newbridge** C Edin
2 D3 **Newbridge** Cnwll
7 E5 **Newbridge** Cnwll
16 D5 **Newbridge** Cnwll
423 G4 **Newbridge** D & G
78 A3 **Newbridge** E Susx
50 A1 **Newbridge** Hants
36 C3 **Newbridge** IoW
340 C2 **Newbridge** Lancs
373 F2 **Newbridge** N York
139 F4 **Newbridge** Oxon
269 E4 **Newbridge** Shrops
236 C5 **Newbridge** Wolves
269 E1 **Newbridge** Wrexhm
162 B2 **Newbridge Green** Worcs
133 G6 **Newbridge on Usk** Mons
183 G3 **Newbridge-on-Wye** Powys
342 B2 **New Brighton** Brad
288 B1 **New Brighton** Flints
52 D3 **New Brighton** Hants
323 E6 **New Brighton** Wirral
288 C4 **New Brighton** Wrexhm
314 D5 **New Brimington** Derbys
295 F4 **New Brinsley** Notts
397 G5 **New Brotton** R & Cl
428 D6 **Newbrough** Nthumb
288 D4 **New Broughton** Wrexhm
225 E1 **New Buckenham** Norfk
86 B3 **New Buildings** BaNES
26 B2 **Newbuildings** Devon
34 A4 **New Buildings** Dorset
561 E5 **Newburgh** Abers
513 F6 **Newburgh** Fife
324 B2 **Newburgh** Lancs
405 E1 **Newburn** N u Ty
325 G3 **New Bury** Bolton
99 E2 **Newbury** Kent
86 B4 **Newbury** Somset
114 D6 **Newbury** W Berk
68 D1 **Newbury** Wilts
391 F5 **Newby** Cumb
353 G5 **Newby** Lancs
356 B5 **Newby** N York
367 E5 **Newby** N York
370 D6 **Newby** N York
374 C1 **Newby** N York
385 E2 **Newby** N York
365 E2 **Newby Bridge** Cumb
367 E5 **Newby Cote** N York
401 E3 **Newby East** Cumb
391 F5 **Newby Head** Cumb
570 E5 **New Byth** Abers
400 C4 **Newby West** Cumb
370 D2 **Newby Wiske** N York
104 D3 **Newcastle** Brdgnd
134 A1 **Newcastle** Mons
208 D3 **Newcastle** Shrops
153 F1 **Newcastle Emlyn** Carmth
426 C2 **Newcastleton or Copshaw Holm** Border
291 G5 **Newcastle-under-Lyme** Staffs
405 F2 **Newcastle upon Tyne** N u Ty
250 A2 **New Catton** Norfk
153 E2 **Newchapel** Pembks
207 F3 **Newchapel** Powys
291 H4 **Newchapel** Staffs
77 G1 **Newchapel** Surrey
110 A5 **New Cheltenham** S Glos
73 E4 **New Cheriton** Hants
132 C2 **Newchurch** Blae G
154 A5 **Newchurch** Carmth
37 E3 **Newchurch** IoW
81 G3 **Newchurch** Kent
340 C5 **Newchurch** Lancs
134 A5 **Newchurch** Mons
184 D4 **Newchurch** Powys
185 G4 **Newchurch** Powys
274 A5 **Newchurch** Staffs
340 C2 **Newchurch in Pendle** Lancs
249 G2 **New Costessey** Norfk
44 A6 **Newcott** Devon
395 E3 **New Coundon** Dur
399 E5 **New Cowper** Cumb
488 C5 **Newcraighall** C Edin
329 F1 **New Crofton** Wakefd
205 E4 **New Cross** Cerdgn
119 H4 **New Cross** Gt Lon
116 C4 **New Cross** Oxon
66 C6 **New Cross** Somset
434 C2 **New Cumnock** E Ayrs
479 H6 **New Danna** Ag & B
570 F6 **New Deer** Abers
431 E4 **New Delaval** Nthumb
327 E3 **New Delph** Oldham
118 A3 **New Denham** Bucks
76 C1 **Newdigate** Surrey
2 C3 **New Downs** Cnwll
6 D3 **New Downs** Cnwll
193 F2 **New Duston** Nhants
358 B3 **New Earswick** York
295 F5 **New Eastwood** Notts
330 B5 **New Edlington** Donc
568 C3 **New Elgin** Moray
348 C2 **New Ellerby** E R Yk
117 E5 **Newell Green** Br For
120 B5 **New Eltham** Gt Lon
319 G5 **New End** Lincs
189 G3 **New End** Worcs
80 B4 **Newenden** Kent
244 A4 **New England** C Pete
198 D6 **New England** Essex
301 F3 **New England** Lincs
161 G4 **Newent** Gloucs
135 E4 **Newerne** Gloucs
342 D3 **New Farnley** Leeds
308 D2 **New Ferry** Wirral
291 H4 **Newfield** C Stke
395 E3 **Newfield** Dur
405 F4 **Newfield** Dur
566 D1 **Newfield** Highld
244 A5 **New Fletton** C Pete
91 F4 **Newfound** Hants
150 D5 **Newgale** Pembks
421 G4 **New Galloway** D & G
602 B8 **Newgarth** Ork
324 C3 **Newgate** Lancs
261 E3 **Newgate** Norfk
251 E2 **Newgate Corner** Norfk
144 C3 **Newgate Street** Herts
502 C3 **New Gilston** Fife
609 H3 **Newgord** Shet
143 G3 **New Greens** Herts
3 C1 **New Grimsby** IoS
142 D2 **New Ground** Herts
49 F2 **Newgrounds** Hants
277 F6 **New Guadaloupe** Leics
488 C5 **Newhailes** E Loth
255 H4 **New Hainford** Norfk
290 B5 **Newhall** Ches
274 D5 **Newhall** Derbys
470 C3 **Newhall** Mdloth
310 B2 **New Hall** Warrtn
214 D2 **Newhall Green** Warwks
340 C5 **New Hall Hey** Lancs
300 A4 **Newham** Lincs
455 F4 **Newham** Nthumb
431 F4 **New Hartley** Nthumb
488 B4 **Newhaven** C Edin
293 G3 **Newhaven** Derbys
39 E3 **Newhaven** Devon
56 D4 **Newhaven** E Susx
602 E1 **New Haven** Ork
94 B2 **New Haw** Surrey
345 F3 **Newhay** N York
140 B3 **New Headington** Oxon
453 G1 **New Heaton** Nthumb
126 C4 **New Hedges** Pembks
406 A4 **New Herrington** Sundld
326 D2 **Newhey** Rochdl
329 G5 **Newhill** Rothm
557 F3 **Newhills** C Aber
140 B4 **New Hinksey** Oxon
393 E2 **New Ho** Dur
259 H4 **New Holkham** Norfk
342 A2 **New Holland** Brad
347 G5 **New Holland** N Linc
387 E2 **Newholm** N York
312 D3 **New Horwich** Derbys
295 G1 **New Houghton** Derbys
253 F2 **New Houghton** Norfk
451 G5 **Newhouse** Border
121 F5 **New House** Kent
468 B2 **Newhouse** N Lans
472 C6 **Newhouses** Border
367 G5 **New Houses** N York
324 C4 **New Houses** Wigan
394 D3 **New Hunwick** Dur
366 B1 **New Hutton** Cumb
97 H3 **New Hythe** Kent
77 H5 **Newick** E Susx
81 H2 **Newingreen** Kent
488 B5 **Newington** C Edin
119 G4 **Newington** Gt Lon
82 C3 **Newington** Kent
98 C1 **Newington** Kent
101 G2 **Newington** Kent
331 E6 **Newington** Notts
140 D5 **Newington** Oxon
209 H3 **Newington** Shrops
136 B6 **Newington Bagpath** Gloucs
154 C2 **New Inn** Carmth
39 F6 **New Inn** Devon
133 F4 **New Inn** Mons
134 B4 **New Inn** Mons
209 E4 **New Invention** Shrops
563 G8 **New Kelso** Highld
276 B4 **New Kingston** Notts
405 E4 **New Kyo** Dur
474 C5 **New Ladykirk** Border
468 D6 **New Lanark** S Lans
347 G3 **Newland** C KuH
364 C4 **Newland** Cumb
134 C3 **Newland** Gloucs
345 F5 **Newland** N York
346 B4 **Newland** N York
139 F2 **Newland** Oxon
188 A5 **Newland** Worcs
364 C3 **Newland Bottom** Cumb
188 C2 **Newland Common** Worcs
99 E5 **Newland Green** Kent
514 D1 **Newlandhead** Angus
471 G2 **Newlandrig** Mdloth
439 G6 **Newlands** Border
451 G5 **Newlands** Border
467 E2 **Newlands** C Glas
389 F5 **Newlands** Cumb
390 A2 **Newlands** Cumb
423 G2 **Newlands** D & G
295 E5 **Newlands** Derbys
566 D7 **Newlands** Highld

568 D5	Newlands Moray	452 A5	Newton Border
295 H2	Newlands Notts	104 C4	Newton Brdgnd
404 C3	Newlands Nthumb	197 H5	Newton Cambs
273 G5	Newlands Staffs	245 F2	Newton Cambs
94 A5	Newlands Corner Surrey	106 D4	Newton Cardif
467 F4	Newlandsmuir S Lans	289 H3	Newton Ches
588 D3	Newlands of Geise Highld	309 F6	Newton Ches
568 F3	Newlands of Tynet Moray	309 H4	Newton Ches
302 C4	Newlands Park IoA	15 F6	Newton Cnwll
324 A2	New Lane Lancs	364 B5	Newton Cumb
325 E5	New Lane End Warrtn	425 F5	Newton D & G
425 G2	New Langholm D & G	437 F6	Newton D & G
300 C3	New Leake Lincs	295 E3	Newton Derbys
571 H5	New Leeds Abers	330 C4	Newton Donc
487 F5	Newliston C Edin	47 E2	Newton Dorset
500 D6	Newliston Fife	159 G3	Newton Herefs
329 E3	New Lodge Barns	185 E6	Newton Herefs
338 C4	New Longton Lancs	186 C4	Newton Herefs
601 J1	Newlot Ork	209 G6	Newton Herefs
415 G4	New Luce D & G	566 C7	Newton Highld
3 E4	Newlyn Cnwll	566 D3	Newton Highld
560 C6	Newmachar Abers	579 H3	Newton Highld
468 C3	Newmains N Lans	589 K7	Newton Highld
119 E6	New Malden Gt Lon	337 F2	Newton Lancs
145 H2	Newman's End Essex	352 D4	Newton Lancs
200 A6	Newman's Green Suffk	366 B5	Newton Lancs
185 E5	Newman's Place Herefs	279 E2	Newton Lincs
135 B5	Newmarket Gloucs	568 B3	Newton Moray
198 C2	Newmarket Suffk	463 F4	Newton N Ayrs
599 J7	Newmarket W Isls	253 G4	Newton Norfk
397 F5	New Marske R & Cl	277 E1	Newton Notts
140 B3	New Marston Oxon	404 B2	Newton Nthumb
269 F2	New Marton Shrops	237 F6	Newton Sandw
344 A3	New Micklefield Leeds	110 A1	Newton S Glos
439 E2	Newmill Border	235 G5	Newton Shrops
3 E5	New Mill Cnwll	269 H3	Newton Shrops
7 F4	New Mill Cnwll	448 B3	Newton S Lans
376 D4	New Mill Cumb	467 G2	Newton S Lans
142 C2	New Mill Herts	64 B4	Newton Somset
328 B3	New Mill Kirk	273 F4	Newton Staffs
569 G5	Newmill Moray	174 B1	Newton Suffk
89 E2	New Mill Wilts	103 E4	Newton Swans
169 G6	New Mill End Beds	327 E5	Newton Tamesd
527 F2	Newmill of Inshewan Angus	216 B4	Newton Warwks
472 C5	New Mills Border	218 B3	Newton Warwks
487 G6	Newmills C Edin	71 E5	Newton Wilts
7 H3	New Mills Cnwll	308 B2	Newton Wirral
23 F5	New Mills Cnwll	487 E4	Newton W Loth
311 F3	New Mills Derbys	20 B3	Newton Abbot Devon
312 C2	New Mills Derbys	399 G3	Newton Arlosh Cumb
486 D2	Newmills Fife	395 F5	Newton Aycliffe Dur
135 E4	New Mills Gloucs	396 C4	Newton Bewley Hartpl
161 G2	New Mills Herefs	194 C4	Newton Blossomville M Keyn
566 B4	New Mills Highld	194 D1	Newton Bromswold Nhants
232 B4	New Mills Powys	239 F3	Newton Burgoland Leics
512 D3	Newmiln P & K	318 C2	Newton by Toft Lincs
445 H2	Newmilns E Ayrs	151 E4	Newton Cross Pembks
49 G5	New Milton Hants	11 F4	Newton Ferrers Devon
175 F3	New Mistley Essex	594 D7	Newton Ferry W Isls
152 B4	New Moat Pembks	249 H5	Newton Flotman Norfk
565 J6	Newmore Highld	471 F2	Newtongrange Mdloth
326 C4	New Moston Manch	109 F1	Newton Green Mons
269 G3	Newnes Shrops	405 G5	Newton Hall Dur
146 D3	Newney Green Essex	404 B3	Newton Hall Nthumb
197 F3	Newnham Cambs	240 D5	Newton Harcourt Leics
135 F2	Newnham Gloucs	326 C4	Newton Heath Manch
92 A4	Newnham Hants	557 G6	Newtonhill Abers
170 B2	Newnham Herts	565 K8	Newtonhill Highld
99 F3	Newnham Kent	343 F5	Newton Hill Wakefd
192 C3	Newnham Nhants	273 G4	Newton Hurst Staffs
190 B2	Newnham Warwks	290 D1	Newtonia Ches
211 E6	Newnham Worcs	395 G5	Newton Ketton Darltn
211 E6	Newnham Bridge Worcs	357 F5	Newton Kyme N York
316 C6	New Ollerton Notts	369 H2	Newton-le-Willows N York
237 G6	New Oscott Birm	324 D5	Newton-le-Willows St Hel
309 H5	New Pale Ches	240 B3	Newton Linford Leics
19 H2	New Park Cnwll	168 A3	Newton Longville Bucks
356 B3	New Park N York	466 D3	Newton Mearns E Rens
240 C3	New Parks C Leic	528 D2	Newtonmill Angus
109 F2	New Passage S Glos	535 J3	Newtonmore Highld
570 F4	New Pitsligo Abers	383 F3	Newton Morrell N York
14 C3	New Polzeath Cnwll	166 D4	Newton Morrell Oxon
291 H3	Newpool Staffs	386 C1	Newton Mulgrave N York
23 G5	Newport Cnwll	518 F1	Newton of Ardtoe Highld
61 E5	Newport Devon	500 C2	Newton of Balcanquhal P & K
47 G6	Newport Dorset	503 E4	Newton of Balcormo Fife
346 C4	Newport E R Yk	528 D5	Newton of Boysack Angus
171 H3	Newport Essex	501 E3	Newton of Falkland Fife
135 F5	Newport Gloucs	499 G2	Newton of Pitcairns P & K
552 F5	Newport Highld	444 D5	Newton on Ayr S Ayrs
37 E3	Newport IoW	357 G3	Newton-on-Ouse N York
107 F2	Newport Newpt	373 F1	Newton-on-Rawcliffe N York
251 G1	Newport Norfk	270 B5	Newton on the Hill Shrops
152 B2	Newport Pembks	443 F3	Newton on the Moor Nthumb
44 C3	Newport Somset	317 F5	Newton on Trent Lincs
271 G6	Newport Wrekin	481 G6	Newton Park Ag & B
514 C4	Newport-on-tay Fife	324 D6	Newton Park St Hel
194 B6	Newport Pagnell M Keyn	48 A5	Newton Peveril Dorset
75 G4	Newpound Common W Susx	28 A5	Newton Poppleford Devon
180 A2	New Quay Cerdgn	166 D3	Newton Purcell Oxon
7 E1	Newquay Cnwll	238 D3	Newton Regis Warwks
250 B2	New Rackheath Norfk	390 D3	Newton Reigny Cumb
184 D2	New Radnor Powys	390 D3	Newton Rigg Cumb
404 C3	New Ridley Nthumb	26 D3	Newton St Cyres Devon
354 C6	New Road Side N York	250 A1	Newton St Faith Norfk
81 G5	New Romney Kent	86 B2	Newton St Loe BaNES
330 D5	New Rossington Donc	39 F5	Newton St Petrock Devon
205 G6	New Row Cerdgn	274 D4	Newton Solney Derbys
339 F2	New Row Lancs	72 B1	Newton Stacey Hants
275 H3	New Sawley Derbys	417 E4	Newton Stewart D & G
291 G1	Newsbank Ches	71 E1	Newton Tony Wilts
559 F3	Newseat Abers	40 A2	Newton Tracey Devon
571 K6	Newseat Abers	385 F2	Newton under Roseberry R & Cl
171 G2	Newsells Herts	430 B2	Newton Underwood Nthumb
338 D2	Newsham Lancs	358 D5	Newton upon Derwent E R Yk
431 E3	Newsham Nthumb	73 H3	Newton Valence Hants
370 D3	Newsham N York	338 B3	Newton-with-Scales Lancs
382 D3	Newsham N York	326 D5	Newton Wood Tamesd
341 G2	Newsholme Brad	314 C4	New Totley Sheff
345 G4	Newsholme E R Yk	494 B3	New Town Ag & B
353 G4	Newsholme Lancs	85 G2	New Town BaNES
406 B4	New Silksworth Sundld	86 D3	New Town BaNES
397 G6	New Skelton R & Cl	213 G2	Newtown Birm
313 E3	New Smithy Derbys	132 C3	Newtown Blae G
328 A2	Newsome Kirk	142 D4	Newtown Bucks
144 C6	New Southgate Gt Lon	219 G6	Newtown Cambs
325 E3	New Springs Wigan	488 B5	New Town C Edin
250 A2	New Sprowston Norfk	312 C2	Newtown Ches
275 H2	New Stanton Derbys	3 G4	Newtown Cnwll
451 H3	Newstead Border	16 C3	Newtown Cnwll
272 C1	Newstead C Stke	50 D2	New Town C Sotn
295 G4	Newstead Notts	398 D5	Newtown Cumb
455 E4	Newstead Nthumb	400 C3	Newtown Cumb
329 F2	Newstead Wakefd	401 E2	Newtown Cumb
468 B2	New Stevenston N Lans	310 A4	Newtown Derbys
97 F2	New Street Kent	27 H3	Newtown Devon
293 E4	New Street Staffs	41 F3	Newtown Devon
271 E2	Newstreet Lane Shrops	48 B1	New Town Dorset
34 B4	New Swanage Dorset	48 B3	New Town Dorset
239 G1	New Swannington Leics	68 C5	New Town Dorset
569 G6	Newtack Moray	69 G6	New Town Dorset
20 B3	Newtake Devon	489 E5	New Town E Loth
371 E3	New Thirsk N York	78 B5	New Town E Susx
295 F5	Newthorpe Notts	72 D4	Newtown Falk
344 B3	Newthorpe N York	135 F4	Newtown Gloucs
295 F5	Newthorpe Common Notts	136 A3	Newtown Gloucs
122 B2	New Thundersley Essex		
318 C2	Newtoft Lincs		
494 A5	Newton Ag & B		
196 B6	Newton Beds		
451 G6	Newton Border		

162 D3	Newtown Gloucs	566 B2	Nonikiln Highld
49 H2	Newtown Hants	101 E5	Nonington Kent
51 E3	Newtown Hants	366 A3	Nook Cumb
51 F1	Newtown Hants	426 C4	Nook Cumb
51 H2	Newtown Hants	606 C6	Noonsbrough Shet
51 H5	Newtown Hants	311 G4	Noonsun Ches
71 F5	Newtown Hants	3 G3	Noonvares Cnwll
73 H2	Newtown Hants	527 G2	Noranside Angus
74 C3	Newtown Hants	118 D6	Norbiton Gt Lon
90 D2	Newtown Hants	337 E1	Norbreck Bpool
160 C3	Newtown Herefs	187 G5	Norbridge Herefs
187 E6	Newtown Herefs	290 B5	Norbury Ches
534 B2	Newtown Highld	273 H1	Norbury Derbys
36 C2	Newtown IoW	119 G6	Norbury Gt Lon
120 D5	New Town Kent	233 G6	Norbury Shrops
339 E2	New Town Lancs	272 A5	Norbury Staffs
169 F5	New Town Luton	290 B5	Norbury Common Ches
97 G3	New Town Medway	272 A5	Norbury Junction Staffs
97 H2	New Town Medway	312 B2	Norbury Moor Stockp
251 E2	Newtown Norfk	371 E3	Norby N York
442 C4	Newtown Nthumb	606 A6	Norby Shet
454 C4	Newtown Nthumb	212 B6	Norchard Worcs
116 C3	Newtown Oxon	137 F4	Norcote Gloucs
163 F3	New Town Oxon	310 C3	Norcott Brook Ches
164 C3	New Town Oxon	337 F1	Norcross Lancs
164 C4	New Town Oxon	246 B4	Nordelph Norfk
48 C6	Newtown Poole	248 D2	Nordelph Corner Norfk
208 B1	Newtown Powys	33 G3	Norden Dorset
106 D1	Newtown Rhondd	326 C2	Norden Rochdl
131 H5	Newtown Rhondd	235 F5	Nordley Shrops
325 H4	Newtown Salfd	474 D5	Norham Nthumb
338 D6	Newtown Salfd	474 D5	Norham West Mains Nthumb
213 E1	New Town Sandw	95 E3	Nork Surrey
269 H5	Newtown Shrops	341 H5	Norland Town Calder
270 B3	Newtown Shrops	87 F4	Norleaze Wilts
30 B2	Newtown Somset	310 B5	Norley Ches
44 B5	Newtown Somset	24 D2	Norley Devon
45 H4	Newtown Somset	93 H6	Norley Common Surrey
65 E4	Newtown Somset	50 C5	Norleywood Hants
67 H6	Newtown Somset	56 C2	Norlington E Susx
85 E5	New Town Somset	332 B1	Normanby N Linc
235 E4	Newtown Staffs	372 D3	Normanby N York
237 E4	Newtown Staffs	396 D6	Normanby R & Cl
292 B2	Newtown Staffs	318 C2	Normanby-by-Spital Lincs
293 E2	Newtown Staffs	317 G3	Normanby by Stow Lincs
324 B5	Newtown St Hel	333 G5	Normanby le Wold Lincs
406 A2	New Town S Tyne	219 H1	Norman Cross Cambs
406 B5	New Town Sundld	93 F4	Normandy Surrey
113 E3	New Town Swindn	135 G5	Norman Hill Gloucs
344 B6	New Town Wakefd	58 A5	Norman's Bay E Susx
115 G4	New Town W Berk	27 H2	Norman's Green Devon
324 D3	Newtown Wigan	251 G6	Normanston Suffk
69 F4	Newtown Wilts	275 E3	Normanton C Derb
88 D4	New Town Wilts	277 G1	Normanton Leics
89 G2	New Town Wilts	298 B5	Normanton Lincs
113 G5	New Town Wilts	296 D4	Normanton Notts
187 H3	Newtown Worcs	242 C3	Normanton Rutlnd
188 C2	Newtown Worcs	343 G5	Normanton Wakefd
237 G3	New Town Wsall	70 C1	Normanton Wilts
76 C4	New Town W Susx	239 F2	Normanton le Heath Leics
4 D4	Newtown-in-St Martin Cnwll	276 B5	Normanton on Soar Notts
452 A3	Newtown St Boswells Border	276 D3	Normanton-on-the-Wolds Notts
240 A4	Newtown Unthank Leics	317 E6	Normanton on Trent Notts
132 B4	New Tredegar Caerph	314 D3	Normanton Spring Sheff
447 G2	New Trows S Lans	240 A5	Normanton Turville Leics
513 H1	Newtyle Angus	93 F6	Norney Surrey
479 J5	New Ulva Ag & B	342 A2	Norr Brad
330 C3	New Village Donc	87 F2	Norrington Common Wilts
347 G3	New Village E R Yk	17 F5	Norris Green Cnwll
334 C4	New Waltham NE Lin	323 G6	Norris Green Lpool
207 H4	New Well Powys	239 E1	Norris Hill Leics
232 F3	New Wells Powys	602 D8	Norseman Ork
314 D4	New Whittington Derbys	248 C5	Northacre Norfk
489 E5	New Winton E Loth	119 E3	North Acton Gt Lon
270 D1	New Woodhouses Shrops	168 C5	Northall Bucks
235 F3	New Works Wrekin	384 B6	Northallerton N York
139 F2	New Yatt Oxon	254 C5	Northall Green Norfk
118 B2	Newyears Green Gt Lon	50 D2	Northam C Sotn
299 G3	New York Lincs	39 F2	Northam Devon
431 F5	New York N Tyne	193 G3	Northampton Nhants
355 G2	New York N York	315 G3	North Anston Rothm
112 B4	New Zealand Wilts	117 F5	North Ascot Br For
185 F3	Nextend Herefs	166 A4	North Aston Oxon
125 G3	Neyland Pembks	144 C4	Northaw Herts
322 C7	Niarbyl IoM	29 G2	Northay Devon
269 H6	Nib Heath Shrops	44 B5	Northay Somset
135 F3	Nibley Gloucs	603 G4	North Ayre Shet
110 B3	Nibley S Glos	609 G7	North Aywick Shet
135 G5	Nibley Green Gloucs	72 A6	North Baddesley Hants
606 D3	Nibon Shet	520 F3	North Ballachulish Highld
43 E4	Nicholashayne Devon	67 G4	North Barrow Somset
102 D4	Nicholaston Swans	260 B4	North Barsham Norfk
356 C2	Nidd N York	279 F1	Northbeck Lincs
488 B5	Niddrie C Edin	23 G4	North Beer Cnwll
557 G4	Nigg C Aber	122 B2	North Benfleet Essex
566 F2	Nigg Highld	53 G4	North Bersted W Susx
566 D3	Nigg Ferry Highld	489 G3	North Berwick E Loth
287 E3	Nilig Denbgs	394 D3	North Bitchburn Dur
326 D4	Nimble Nook Oldham	431 F3	North Blyth Nthumb
110 C5	Nimlet S Glos	51 H2	North Boarhunt Hants
44 C5	Nimmer Somset	49 F5	North Bockhampton Dorset
146 B4	Nine Ashes Essex	243 H3	Northborough C Pete
402 D4	Ninebanks Nthumb	48 D5	Northbourne Bmouth
119 F4	Nine Elms Gt Lon	101 F5	Northbourne Kent
112 D2	Nine Elms Swindn	26 A6	North Bovey Devon
4 C1	Nine Maidens Downs Cnwll	30 A3	North Bowood Dorset
27 G4	Nine Oaks Devon	87 F3	North Bradley Wilts
187 E2	Nineveh Worcs	17 G2	North Brentor Devon
211 F5	Nineveh Worcs	68 B2	North Brewham Somset
514 B3	Ninewells C Dund	79 G5	Northbridge Street E Susx
134 D2	Ninewells Gloucs	46 D5	Northbrook Dorset
150 C5	Nine Wells Pembks	72 D6	Northbrook Hants
58 B4	Ninfield E Susx	166 A5	Northbrook Oxon
36 B3	Ningwood IoW	88 B4	Northbrook Wilts
36 B3	Ningwood Common IoW	196 C6	North Brook End Cambs
3 F2	Ninnes Bridge Cnwll	485 H3	North Broomage Falk
452 C4	Nisbet Border	60 C3	North Buckland Devon
607 J5	Nisthouse Shet	250 D2	North Burlingham Norfk
435 H5	Nithbank D & G	67 G4	North Cadbury Somset
423 G4	Nithside D & G	414 C2	North Cairn D & G
37 E5	Niton IoW	93 E4	North Camp Hants
466 D2	Nitshill C Glas	318 A4	North Carlton Lincs
282 D2	Niwbwrch IoA	316 A3	North Carlton Notts
97 E3	Noah's Arks Kent	456 D4	North Carrine Ag & B
189 E2	Noah's Green Worcs	346 C2	North Cave E R Yk
121 G1	Noak Bridge Essex	137 G5	North Cerney Gloucs
121 G1	Noak Hill Gt Lon	77 G5	North Chailey E Susx
146 A6	Noak Hill Gt Lon	75 F4	Northchapel W Susx
325 G3	Nob End Bolton	70 D6	North Charford Hants
171 F6	Nobland Green Herts	455 F5	North Charlton Nthumb
234 B2	Nobold Shrops	95 E1	North Cheam Gt Lon
193 E2	Nobottle Nhants	68 A4	North Cheriton Somset
72 C5	Nob's Crook Hants	29 H4	North Chideock Dorset
298 D2	Nocton Lincs	142 D3	Northchurch Herts
308 C2	Noctorum Wirral	346 C2	North Cliffe E R Yk
114 C4	Nodmore W Berk	317 F5	North Clifton Notts
119 G1	Noel Park Gt Lon	395 F3	North Close Dur
250 D4	Nogdam End Norfk	320 C1	North Cockerington Lincs
338 C2	Nog Tow Lancs	45 G5	North Coker Somset
140 B2	Noke Oxon	608 C8	North Collafirth Shet
122 A5	Noke Street Medway	110 B3	North Common S Glos
151 E6	Nolton Pembks	253 F4	North Common Suffk
151 E6	Nolton Haven Pembks	506 F3	North Connel Ag & B
289 H5	No Man's Heath Ches	104 C3	North Cornelly Brdgnd
238 D3	No Man's Heath Warwks	5 E5	North Corner Cnwll
10 A2	No Man's Land Cnwll	110 B3	North Corner S Glos
41 G5	Nomansland Devon	461 E2	North Corriegills N Ayrs
49 G1	Nomansland Hants	28 C2	Northcote Devon
72 D4	No Man's Land Hants	40 C4	Northcote Manor Devon
143 H2	Nomansland Herts		
270 B4	Noneley Shrops		

334 D4	North Cotes Lincs	94 D5	North Holmwood Surrey
38 B6	Northcott Cnwll	71 G3	North Houghton Hants
23 G4	Northcott Devon	345 H3	North Howden E R Yk
43 E5	Northcott Devon	12 C1	North Huish Devon
43 F6	Northcott Devon	118 C4	North Hyde Gt Lon
6 C5	North Country Cnwll	298 A1	North Hykeham Lincs
140 B5	Northcourt Oxon	406 A3	North Hylton Sundld
227 F2	North Cove Suffk	80 B5	Northiam E Susx
383 G4	North Cowton N York	195 H5	Northill Beds
529 E2	North Craigo Angus	512 H1	North Inch P & K
569 L5	North Cranna Abers	135 G3	Northington Gloucs
194 C6	North Crawley M Keyn	73 E2	Northington Hants
120 C5	North Cray Gt Lon	333 E4	North Kelsey Lincs
259 H4	North Creake Norfk	333 E4	North Kelsey Moor Lincs
44 C2	North Curry Somset	566 B7	North Kessock Highld
609 J2	Northdale Shet	333 G1	North Killingholme N Linc
359 H4	North Dalton E R Yk	371 E2	North Kilvington N York
16 C4	North Darley Cnwll	216 D3	North Kilworth Leics
601 H4	North Dawn Ork	49 F4	North Kingston Hants
356 D4	North Deighton N York	461 E4	North Kiscadale N Ayrs
251 G2	North Denes Norfk	299 E4	North Kyme Lincs
101 G1	Northdown Kent	55 E3	North Lancing W Susx
514 A2	North Dronley Angus	375 G5	North Landing E R Yk
345 F2	North Duffield N York	300 B4	Northlands Lincs
602 A7	Northdyke Ork	406 C4	Northlea Dur
391 E5	North Dykes Cumb	137 H2	Northleach Gloucs
99 F3	North Eastling Kent	142 A3	North Lee Bucks
294 D2	Northedge Derbys	370 C5	North Lees N York
82 C2	North Elham Kent	28 C3	Northleigh Devon
320 A1	North Elkington Lincs	61 F5	Northleigh Devon
254 C3	North Elmham Norfk		
330 A2	North Elmsall Wakefd		
488 D5	North Elphinestone E Loth		
85 H2	North End BaNES		
110 D6	North End BaNES		
194 D5	North End Beds		
195 E3	North End Beds		
116 B1	North End Bucks		
167 E4	North End Bucks		
168 A4	North End Bucks		
52 B4	North End C Port		
400 B3	North End Cumb		
43 E4	North End Devon		
68 D4	North End Dorset		
405 G6	North End Dur		
348 B5	North End E R Yk		
349 E3	North End E R Yk		
361 F4	North End E R Yk		
148 C4	Northend Essex		
171 H2	North End Essex		
172 D6	North End Essex		
173 F2	North End Essex		
119 F2	North End Gt Lon		
120 D4	North End Gt Lon		
49 E1	North End Hants		
73 E4	North End Hants		
240 C1	North End Leics		
280 B1	North End Lincs		
320 C1	North End Lincs		
320 D2	North End Lincs		
321 E4	North End Lincs		
333 E5	North End Lincs		
334 D4	North End Lincs		
348 B5	North End N Linc		
224 D1	North End Norfk		
84 D1	North End N Som		
443 E4	North End Nthumb		
44 B2	North End Somset		
191 F4	Northend Warwks		
90 C2	North End Wilts		
137 F6	North End Wilts		
54 A4	North End W Susx		
54 D2	North End W Susx		
77 G2	North End W Susx		
311 G1	Northenden Manch		
311 G1	Northern Moor Manch		
572 D7	North Erradale Highld		
240 D4	North Evington C Leic		
332 A4	North Ewster N Linc		
147 H5	North Fambridge Essex		
545 K2	North Fearns Highld		
344 A5	North Featherstone Wakefd		
118 C5	North Feltham Gt Lon		
460 C4	North Feorline N Ayrs		
347 E4	North Ferriby E R Yk		
213 F4	Northfield Birm		
451 H4	Northfield Border		
474 D1	Northfield Border		
557 F3	Northfield C Aber		
488 B5	Northfield C Edin		
347 F4	Northfield E R Yk		
168 B1	Northfield M Keyn		
65 E4	Northfield Somset		
72 C4	Northfields Hants		
119 F1	North Finchley Gt Lon		
121 F5	Northfleet Kent		
121 F5	Northfleet Green Kent		
560 A3	North Flobbets Abers		
101 H2	North Foreland Kent		
361 E4	North Frodingham E R Yk		
465 G6	North Furgushill N Ayrs		
280 A4	Northgate Lincs		
43 E2	Northgate Somset		
77 E2	Northgate W Susx		
606 D2	North Gluss Shet		
49 F2	North Gorley Hants		
225 H2	North Green Norfk		
248 D3	North Green Norfk		
202 C3	North Green Suffk		
202 D1	North Green Suffk		
226 C4	North Green Suffk		
318 C5	North Greetwell Lincs		
373 F6	North Grimston N York		
97 G1	North Halling Medway		
118 C2	North Harrow Gt Lon		
52 C4	North Hayling Hants		
62 A5	North Heasley Devon		
114 D5	North Heath W Berk		
75 H5	North Heath W Susx		
16 C3	North Hill Cnwll		
118 B3	North Hillingdon Gt Lon		
140 B3	North Hinksey Village Oxon		

City, town and village index: North Leigh - Oreton 707

82 B1 **North Leigh** Kent
139 F2 **North Leigh** Oxon
317 E3 **North Leverton with Habblesthorpe** Notts
24 D3 **Northlew** Devon
189 G5 **North Littleton** Worcs
95 E2 **North Looe** Surrey
224 D3 **North Lopham** Norfk
242 C4 **North Luffenham** Rutlnd
52 D1 **North Marden** W Susx
167 G5 **North Marston** Bucks
471 G3 **North Middleton** Mdloth
454 B5 **North Middleton** Nthumb
415 E6 **North Milmain** D & G
41 E2 **North Molton** Devon
38 C4 **Northmoor** Devon
139 G4 **Northmoor** Oxon
65 F5 **Northmoor Corner** Somset
65 F5 **Northmoor Green or Moorland** Somset
115 F2 **North Moreton** Oxon
28 A5 **Northmostown** Devon
468 A3 **North Motherwell** N Lans
56 A3 **North Moulsecoomb** Br & H
527 E3 **Northmuir** Angus
53 F4 **North Mundham** W Susx
297 E3 **North Muskham** Notts
600 E6 **North Ness** Ork
526 D6 **North Nevay** Angus
346 D2 **North Newbald** E R Yk
165 G2 **North Newington** Oxon
88 D3 **North Newnton** Wilts
65 F5 **North Newton** Somset
52 C4 **Northney** Hants
135 G5 **North Nibley** Gloucs
91 E4 **North Oakley** Hants
121 E3 **North Ockendon** Gt Lon
118 C3 **Northolt** Gt Lon
308 B6 **Northop** Flints
308 C6 **Northop Hall** Flints
396 D6 **North Ormesby** Middsb
334 C6 **North Ormsby** Lincs
342 D5 **Northorpe** Kirk
243 F1 **Northorpe** Lincs
280 A2 **Northorpe** Lincs
332 B5 **Northorpe** Lincs
370 D2 **North Otterington** N York
66 D2 **Northover** Somset
67 E5 **Northover** Somset
333 F6 **North Owersby** Lincs
342 B4 **Northowram** Calder
45 F6 **North Perrott** Somset
65 E5 **North Petherton** Somset
23 F5 **North Petherwin** Cnwll
247 H3 **North Pickenham** Norfk
189 E4 **North Piddle** Worcs
30 C3 **North Poorton** Dorset
33 G2 **Northport** Dorset
49 F3 **North Poulner** Hants
605 G6 **Northpunds** Shet
487 F3 **North Queensferry** Fife
62 A5 **North Radworthy** Devon
298 C5 **North Rauceby** Lincs
559 F3 **North Rayne** Abers
326 C6 **North Reddish** Stockp
256 A2 **Northrepps** Norfk
320 C3 **North Reston** Lincs
356 B5 **North Rigton** N York
49 F5 **North Ripley** Hants
292 A1 **North Rode** Ches
608 D7 **North Roe** Shet
389 F3 **North Row** Cumb
252 C4 **North Runcton** Norfk
24 D4 **North Russell** Devon
364 A6 **North Scale** Cumb
297 G1 **North Scarle** Lincs
431 E2 **North Seaton** Nthumb
431 E2 **North Seaton Colliery** Nthumb
520 C7 **North Shian** Ag & B
431 F6 **North Shields** N Tyne
123 E2 **North Shoebury** Sthend
337 F2 **North Shore** Bpool
244 C5 **North Side** C Pete
388 B4 **North Side** Cumb
602 B6 **Northside** Ork
397 G6 **North Skelton** R & Cl
335 F5 **North Somercotes** Lincs
370 B4 **North Stainley** N York
381 E1 **North Stainmore** Cumb
28 A5 **North Star** Devon
121 E3 **North Stifford** Thurr
110 C6 **North Stoke** BaNES
115 G2 **North Stoke** Oxon
52 B2 **North Stoke** W Susx
50 D1 **North Stoneham** Hants
70 D6 **North Street** Hants
73 F3 **North Street** Hants
99 G3 **North Street** Kent
122 C5 **North Street** Medway
115 G5 **North Street** W Berk
455 G3 **North Sunderland** Nthumb
451 F5 **North Synton** Border
23 G3 **North Tamerton** Cnwll
25 G2 **North Tawton** Devon
334 C5 **North Thoresby** Lincs
67 F3 **North Tidworth** Wilts
443 G4 **North Togston** Nthumb
594 F5 **Northton** W Isls
39 G6 **North Town** Devon
93 E4 **North Town** Hants
601 H5 **Northtown** Ork
605 G8 **North Town** Shet
67 F1 **North Town** Somset
67 E2 **North Town** Somset
117 E3 **North Town** W & M
254 D5 **North Tuddenham** Norfk
120 C4 **Northumberland Heath** Gt Lon
133 E5 **Northville** Torfn
430 C6 **North Walbottle** N u Ty
603 L3 **Northwall** Ork
364 A6 **North Walney** Cumb
256 A3 **North Walsham** Norfk
91 F5 **North Waltham** Hants
92 B4 **North Warnborough** Hants
529 E1 **North Water Bridge** Angus
44 B6 **North Waterhayne** Devon
143 G5 **North Watford** Herts
589 G5 **North Watten** Highld
39 E3 **Northway** Devon
162 D3 **Northway** Gloucs
43 F2 **Northway** Somset
103 E4 **Northway** Swans
145 G4 **North Weald Bassett** Essex
50 A4 **North Weirs** Hants
118 D2 **North Wembley** Gt Lon
609 G7 **North Westerhouse** Shet
109 E5 **North Weston** N Som
141 E3 **North Weston** Oxon
317 E2 **North Wheatley** Notts
20 B4 **North Whilborough** Devon
173 E6 **North Whitehouse** Essex
310 C5 **Northwich** Ches
85 G1 **North Wick** BaNES
109 G2 **Northwick** S Glos
84 C5 **Northwick** Somset
188 B3 **Northwick** Worcs
85 G3 **North Widcombe** BaNES
319 F2 **North Willingham** Lincs
295 E2 **North Wingfield** Derbys
278 C5 **North Witham** Lincs
247 F5 **Northwold** Norfk
294 B2 **Northwood** Derbys
118 B1 **Northwood** Gt Lon
51 E6 **Northwood** IoW
101 G2 **Northwood** Kent
323 H5 **Northwood** Knows
291 H6 **Northwood** Staffs
292 A5 **Northwood** Staffs
270 B3 **Northwood** Wrexhm
135 G1 **Northwood Green** Gloucs
118 B1 **Northwood Hills** Gt Lon
46 C2 **North Wootton** Dorset
252 C3 **North Wootton** Norfk
67 F1 **North Wootton** Somset
111 E4 **North Wraxall** Wilts
112 D3 **North Wroughton** Swindn
314 D3 **Norton** Derbys
13 F2 **Norton** Devon
38 C2 **Norton** Devon
330 B2 **Norton** Donc
212 C3 **Norton** Dudley
56 D4 **Norton** E Susx
162 C5 **Norton** Gloucs
310 A3 **Norton** Halton
170 B3 **Norton** Herts
36 A3 **Norton** IoW
160 A5 **Norton** Mons
192 D2 **Norton** Nhants
315 H5 **Norton** Notts
84 B2 **Norton** N Som
185 F1 **Norton** Powys
210 B3 **Norton** Shrops
234 D3 **Norton** Shrops
235 G4 **Norton** Shrops
396 B5 **Norton** S on T
200 C1 **Norton** Suffk
102 C4 **Norton** Swans
103 F4 **Norton** Swans
111 F3 **Norton** Wilts
188 C4 **Norton** Worcs
189 F5 **Norton** Worcs
53 F5 **Norton** W Susx
53 G3 **Norton** W Susx
99 F2 **Norton Ash** Kent
87 G6 **Norton Bavant** Wilts
272 C3 **Norton Bridge** Staffs
237 F3 **Norton Canes** Staffs
185 G5 **Norton Canon** Herefs
255 E2 **Norton Corner** Norfk
297 G3 **Norton Disney** Lincs
237 F3 **Norton East** Staffs
68 C2 **Norton Ferris** Wilts
43 G2 **Norton Fitzwarren** Somset
292 A4 **Norton Green** C Stke
170 B5 **Norton Green** Herts
36 A3 **Norton Green** IoW
214 B5 **Norton Green** Solhll
85 G2 **Norton Hawkfield** BaNES
146 C4 **Norton Heath** Essex
86 B4 **Norton Hill** BaNES
271 G2 **Norton in Hales** Shrops
292 A4 **Norton-in-the-Moors** C Stke
239 E3 **Norton-Juxta-Twycross** Leics
371 E5 **Norton-le-Clay** N York
190 C2 **Norton Lindsey** Warwks
200 C1 **Norton Little Green** Suffk
85 H1 **Norton Malreward** BaNES
146 B4 **Norton Mandeville** Essex
373 F5 **Norton-on-Derwent** N York
86 D3 **Norton St Philip** Somset
250 D5 **Norton Subcourse** Norfk
45 F4 **Norton sub Hamdon** Somset
108 D5 **Norton's Wood** N Som
314 D3 **Norton Woodseats** Sheff
297 E2 **Norwell** Notts
296 D2 **Norwell Woodhouse** Notts
250 A3 **Norwich** Norfk
609 K2 **Norwick** Shet
315 F3 **Norwood** Derbys
30 C1 **Norwood** Dorset
146 B3 **Norwood End** Essex
118 C4 **Norwood Green** Gt Lon
95 E6 **Norwood Hill** Surrey
119 G5 **Norwood New Town** Gt Lon
245 F5 **Norwoodside** Cambs
241 F5 **Noseley** Leics
589 K6 **Noss** Highld
605 G7 **Noss** Shet
11 G4 **Noss Mayo** Devon
370 B3 **Nosterfield** N York
198 C6 **Nosterfield End** Cambs
546 F4 **Nostie** Highld
163 H5 **Notgrove** Gloucs
175 E2 **Notley Enterprise Park** Suffk
104 C4 **Nottage** Brdgnd
10 C1 **Notter** Cnwll
276 C2 **Nottingham** C Nott
119 E3 **Notting Hill** Gt Lon
31 E6 **Nottington** Dorset
329 E2 **Notton** Wakefd
111 G6 **Notton** Wilts
147 F2 **Nounsley** Essex
188 A1 **Noutard's Green** Worcs
310 C6 **Nova Scotia** Ches
109 G6 **Novers Park** Bristl
163 E5 **Noverton** Gloucs
199 H2 **Nowton** Suffk
233 H2 **Nox** Shrops
179 E4 **Noyadd Trefawr** Cerdgn
179 E4 **Noyadd Wilym** Cerdgn
115 H2 **Nuffield** Oxon
344 C1 **Nun Appleton** N York
359 F5 **Nunburnholme** E R Yk
295 G4 **Nuncargate** Notts
406 E3 **Nunclose** Cumb
215 F1 **Nuneaton** Warwks
140 B5 **Nuneham Courtenay** Oxon
115 H4 **Nuney Green** Oxon
119 H4 **Nunhead** Gt Lon
340 D5 **Nun Hills** Lancs
423 G4 **Nunholm** D & G
357 G3 **Nun Monkton** N York
86 C5 **Nunney** Somset
86 C5 **Nunney Catch** Somset
372 B4 **Nunnington** N York
442 D6 **Nunnykirk** Nthumb
395 G4 **Nunstainton East** Dur
334 B3 **Nunsthorpe** NE Lin
385 E2 **Nunthorpe** Middsb
70 D4 **Nunton** Wilts
428 D5 **Nunwick** Nthumb
370 C5 **Nunwick** N York
423 F4 **Nunwood** D & G
135 E5 **Nupdown** S Glos
168 B6 **Nup End** Bucks
136 A3 **Nupend** Gloucs
136 B5 **Nupend** Gloucs
145 H6 **Nuper's Hatch** Essex
134 D4 **Nuppend** Gloucs
117 E5 **Nuptown** Br For
50 C1 **Nursling** Hants
74 B5 **Nursted** Hants
88 B2 **Nursteed** Wilts
105 H6 **Nurston** V Glam
236 B5 **Nurton** Staffs
236 B5 **Nurton Hill** Staffs
52 D3 **Nutbourne** W Susx
76 A6 **Nutbourne** W Susx
76 A6 **Nutbourne Common** W Susx
72 A5 **Nutburn** Hants
74 D3 **Nutcombe** Surrey
95 G4 **Nutfield** Surrey
324 B6 **Nut Grove** St Hel
295 G6 **Nuthall** Notts
171 E3 **Nuthampstead** Herts
214 A5 **Nuthurst** Warwks
76 C4 **Nuthurst** W Susx
78 A4 **Nutley** E Susx
91 G6 **Nutley** Hants
326 A1 **Nuttall** Bury
330 D4 **Nutwell** Donc
589 K4 **Nybster** Highld
84 D2 **Nye** N Som
53 F5 **Nyetimber** W Susx
74 C5 **Nyewood** W Susx
84 D4 **Nyland** Somset
41 E6 **Nymet Rowland** Devon
26 A2 **Nymet Tracey** Devon
136 B4 **Nympsfield** Gloucs
43 F3 **Nynehead** Somset
66 C3 **Nythe** Somset
113 E2 **Nythe** Swindn
53 G3 **Nyton** W Susx

O

240 D4 **Oadby** Leics
98 D2 **Oad Street** Kent
188 B2 **Oakall Green** Worcs
292 D6 **Oakamoor** Staffs
326 B3 **Oak Bank** Bury
470 A1 **Oakbank** W Loth
24 D3 **Oak Cross** Devon
132 C5 **Oakdale** Caerph
356 B3 **Oakdale** N York
48 C6 **Oakdale** Poole
43 G2 **Oake** Somset
43 G2 **Oake Green** Somset
236 C4 **Oaken** Staffs
352 A5 **Oakenclough** Lancs
235 G2 **Oakengates** Wrekin
308 B5 **Oakenholt** Flints
395 E2 **Oakenshaw** Dur
342 C4 **Oakenshaw** Kirk
340 A3 **Oakenshaw** Lancs
294 D4 **Oakerthorpe** Derbys
327 H1 **Oakes** Kirk
170 A4 **Oakfield** Herts
37 F2 **Oakfield** IoW
133 E6 **Oakfield** Torfn
180 C3 **Oakford** Cerdgn
42 B3 **Oakford** Devon
42 B3 **Oakfordbridge** Devon
312 B6 **Oakgrove** Ches
168 B2 **Oakgrove** M Keyn
242 A3 **Oakham** Rutlnd
213 E2 **Oakham** Sandw
291 F4 **Oakhanger** Ches
74 B2 **Oakhanger** Hants
291 H6 **Oak Hill** C Stke
86 A5 **Oakhill** Somset
202 D5 **Oak Hill** Suffk
76 C3 **Oakhill** W Susx
97 E4 **Oakhurst** Kent
197 E2 **Oakington** Cambs
128 B1 **Oaklands** Carmth
285 H3 **Oaklands** Conwy
144 B1 **Oaklands** Herts
144 C6 **Oakleigh Park** Gt Lon
161 H6 **Oakle Street** Gloucs
195 E4 **Oakley** Beds
140 D2 **Oakley** Bucks
486 D2 **Oakley** Fife
163 E5 **Oakley** Gloucs
91 F4 **Oakley** Hants
141 F4 **Oakley** Oxon
48 C5 **Oakley** Poole
271 G2 **Oakley** Staffs
225 G4 **Oakley** Suffk
115 G2 **Oakley Court** Oxon
117 F4 **Oakley Green** W & M
225 G4 **Oakley Park** Suffk
115 G2 **Oakley Wood** Oxon
310 B6 **Oakmere** Ches
91 G4 **Oakridge** Hants
136 D4 **Oakridge Lynch** Gloucs
233 H4 **Oaks** Shrops
137 E6 **Oaksey** Wilts
274 B3 **Oaks Green** Derbys
426 D4 **Oakshaw Ford** Cumb
74 A4 **Oakshott** Hants
240 A1 **Oaks in Charnwood** Leics
239 E2 **Oakthorpe** Leics
384 B2 **Oak Tree** Darltn
342 D4 **Oakwell** Kirk
275 F2 **Oakwood** C Derb
144 C5 **Oakwood** Gt Lon
343 F2 **Oakwood** Leeds
403 G1 **Oakwood** Nthumb
310 D1 **Oakwood** Warrtn
341 G2 **Oakworth** Brad
575 J3 **Oape** Highld
99 F2 **Oare** Kent
62 B2 **Oare** Somset
115 E5 **Oare** W Berk
89 E2 **Oare** Wilts
62 C2 **Oareford** Somset
279 E2 **Oasby** Lincs
66 B4 **Oath** Somset
29 H1 **Oathill** Dorset
527 G3 **Oathlaw** Angus
467 E2 **Oatlands** C Glas
356 C4 **Oatlands** N York
94 B2 **Oatlands Park** Surrey
506 E3 **Oban** Ag & B
596 F7 **Oban** W Isls
506 C6 **Oban Seil** Ag & B
209 F4 **Obley** Shrops
67 G6 **Oborne** Dorset
566 B3 **Obsdale Park** Highld
290 D2 **Occlestone Green** Ches
225 G5 **Occold** Suffk
50 D2 **Ocean Village** C Sotn
445 H5 **Ochiltree** E Ayrs
307 F4 **Ochr-y-foel** Denbgs
498 C1 **Ochtermuthill** P & K
511 E5 **Ochtertyre** P & K
275 G2 **Ockbrook** Derbys
237 E6 **Ocker Hill** Sandw
187 H2 **Ockeridge** Worcs
93 G6 **Ockford Ridge** Surrey
94 B3 **Ockham** Surrey
518 E1 **Ockle** Highld
76 B1 **Ockley** Surrey
186 D5 **Ocle Pychard** Herefs
605 H4 **Ocraquoy** Shet
41 E4 **Odam Barton** Devon
45 G4 **Odcombe** Somset
86 C2 **Odd Down** BaNES
379 G2 **Oddendale** Cumb
188 D3 **Oddingley** Worcs
140 C2 **Oddington** Oxon
194 D3 **Odell** Beds
24 C2 **Odham** Devon
603 J6 **Odie** Ork
92 B4 **Odiham** Hants
170 C2 **Odsey** Cambs
70 C4 **Odstock** Wilts
239 F3 **Odstone** Leics
191 F1 **Offchurch** Warwks
189 G5 **Offenham** Worcs
189 G5 **Offenham Cross** Worcs
312 B2 **Offerton** Stockp
406 A3 **Offerton** Sundld
312 B2 **Offerton Green** Stockp
56 B2 **Offham** E Susx
97 F3 **Offham** Kent
54 B3 **Offham** W Susx
272 A4 **Offleyhay** Staffs
272 A4 **Offleymarsh** Staffs
272 A4 **Offleyrock** Staffs
196 B1 **Offord Cluny** Cambs
196 B1 **Offord D'Arcy** Cambs
201 E5 **Offton** Suffk
28 C3 **Offwell** Devon
113 E5 **Ogbourne Maizey** Wilts
113 E5 **Ogbourne St Andrew** Wilts
113 F5 **Ogbourne St George** Wilts
341 H3 **Ogden** Calder
49 F2 **Ogdens** Hants
527 F2 **Ogil** Angus
430 B4 **Ogle** Nthumb
104 D4 **Ogmore** V Glam
104 C5 **Ogmore-by-Sea** V Glam
105 E1 **Ogmore Vale** Brdgnd
47 F2 **Okeford Fitzpaine** Dorset
25 E3 **Okehampton** Devon
25 E4 **Okehampton Camp** Devon
294 B2 **Oker** Derbys
76 B2 **Okewood Hill** Surrey
161 H4 **Okle Green** Gloucs
112 D3 **Okus** Swindn
99 H5 **Olantigh** Kent
20 B2 **Olchard** Devon
217 G5 **Old** Nhants
557 G3 **Old Aberdeen** C Aber
73 E3 **Old Alresford** Hants
578 E3 **Oldany** Highld
214 D1 **Old Arley** Warwks
514 B2 **Old Balkello** Angus
484 C6 **Old Balornock** C Glas
295 H6 **Old Basford** C Nott
91 H4 **Old Basing** Hants
254 C4 **Old Beetley** Norfk
451 H5 **Old Belses** Border
189 H1 **Oldberrow** Warwks
454 D5 **Old Bewick** Nthumb
120 C5 **Old Bexley** Gt Lon
524 C2 **Old Blair** P & K
300 C1 **Old Bolingbroke** Lincs
26 B1 **Oldborough** Devon
324 D5 **Old Boston** St Hel
356 A6 **Old Bramhope** Leeds
314 C5 **Old Brampton** Derbys
524 C2 **Old Bridge of Tilt** P & K
413 E1 **Old Bridge of Urr** D & G
422 C6 **Old Bridge of Urr** D & G
168 B2 **Oldbrook** M Keyn
225 E1 **Old Buckenham** Norfk
406 B4 **Old Burdon** Sundld
90 D3 **Old Burghclere** Hants
97 E3 **Oldbury** Kent
213 E2 **Oldbury** Sandw
211 G1 **Oldbury** Shrops
239 E6 **Oldbury** Warwks
135 E6 **Oldbury Naite** S Glos
135 E6 **Oldbury-on-Severn** S Glos
111 E2 **Oldbury on the Hill** Gloucs
371 G2 **Old Byland** N York
491 F6 **Old Cambus** Border
15 G5 **Old Cardinham Castle** Cnwll
399 H5 **Old Carlisle** Cumb
395 G2 **Old Cassop** Dur
159 F5 **Oldcastle** Mons
289 G5 **Oldcastle Heath** Ches
426 D1 **Old Castleton** Border
250 A2 **Old Catton** Norfk
165 E4 **Old Chalford** Oxon
233 E6 **Old Churchstoke** Powys
334 C3 **Old Clee** NE Lin
63 G3 **Old Cleeve** Somset
296 A2 **Old Clipstone** Notts
306 B4 **Old Colwyn** Conwy
234 B3 **Old Coppice** Shrops
569 K4 **Old Cornhill** Abers
316 A2 **Oldcotes** Notts
95 G3 **Old Coulsdon** Gt Lon
187 G6 **Old Country** Herefs
135 E3 **Oldcroft** Gloucs
79 F1 **Old Cryals** Kent
432 B5 **Old Dailly** S Ayrs
277 E5 **Old Dalby** Leics
313 F3 **Old Dam** Derbys
571 H6 **Old Deer** Abers
329 H5 **Old Denaby** Donc
85 F5 **Old Ditch** Somset
342 B3 **Old Dolphin** Brad
85 H4 **Old Down** Somset
330 B5 **Old Edlington** Donc
395 E4 **Old Eldon** Dur
348 C2 **Old Ellerby** E R Yk
136 A3 **Oldends** Gloucs
236 D4 **Old Fallings** Wolves
237 E2 **Oldfallow** Staffs
168 C2 **Old Farm Park** M Keyn
177 F2 **Old Felixstowe** Suffk
341 G2 **Oldfield** Brad
388 C4 **Oldfield** Cumb
328 A2 **Oldfield** Kirk
210 B4 **Old Field** Shrops
211 F2 **Oldfield** Shrops
188 B2 **Oldfield** Worcs
311 F2 **Oldfield Brow** Traffd
86 C2 **Oldfield Park** BaNES
244 A5 **Old Fletton** C Pete
405 G2 **Old Fold** Gatesd
119 H3 **Old Ford** Gt Lon
86 D5 **Oldford** Somset
160 D6 **Old Forge** Herefs
292 D6 **Oldfurnace** Staffs
133 E4 **Old Furnace** Torfn
281 F5 **Old Gate** Lincs
327 F6 **Old Glossop** Derbys
205 F3 **Old Goginan** Cerdgn
345 G5 **Old Goole** E R Yk
161 E4 **Old Gore** Herefs
400 B1 **Old Graitney** D & G
3 c1 **Old Grimsby** IoS
207 E3 **Old Hall** Powys
466 D2 **Oldhall** Rens
171 E5 **Old Hall Green** Herts
200 A3 **Oldhall Green** Suffk
256 C3 **Old Hall Street** Norfk
326 D4 **Oldham** Oldham
326 D3 **Oldham Edge** Oldham
490 D5 **Oldhamstocks** E Loth
145 G2 **Old Harlow** Essex
174 D5 **Old Heath** Essex
79 E5 **Old Heathfield** E Susx
213 E2 **Old Hill** Sandw
188 B5 **Old Hills** Worcs
258 D3 **Old Hunstanton** Norfk
220 C4 **Oldhurst** Cambs
366 B2 **Old Hutton** Cumb
235 G5 **Oldington** Shrops
438 A5 **Old Johnstone** D & G
7 F5 **Old Kea** Cnwll
483 F5 **Old Kilpatrick** W Duns
556 C3 **Old Kinnernie** Abers
110 B5 **Oldland** S Glos
110 B5 **Oldland Common** S Glos
339 H2 **Old Langho** Lancs
322 g6 **Old Laxey** IoM
300 C4 **Old Leake** Lincs
168 C4 **Old Linslade** Beds
95 E1 **Old Malden** Gt Lon
373 E5 **Old Malton** N York
269 F3 **Old Marton** Shrops
172 A4 **Old Mead** Essex
560 A4 **Oldmeldrum** Abers
17 E4 **Old Mill** Cnwll
49 G6 **Old Milton** Hants
191 E1 **Old Milverton** Warwks
84 B3 **Oldmixon** N Som
467 H2 **Old Monkland** N Lans
529 E3 **Old Montrose** Angus
452 C2 **Old Nenthorn** Border
51 E2 **Old Netley** Hants
207 H2 **Old Neuadd** Powys
201 E2 **Old Newton** Suffk
16 B5 **Old Park** Cnwll
47 H5 **Old Park** Dorset
235 F3 **Old Park** Wrekin
275 F6 **Old Parks** Leics
109 G2 **Old Passage** S Glos
236 C5 **Old Perton** Staffs
486 D4 **Old Philpstoun** W Loth
486 B4 **Old Polmont** Falk
52 A5 **Old Portsmouth** C Port
395 G2 **Old Quarrington** Dur
184 D3 **Old Radnor** Powys
559 F4 **Old Rayne** Abers
26 C3 **Oldridge** Devon
81 F4 **Old Romney** Kent
512 D4 **Old Scone** P & K
50 C2 **Old Shirley** C Sotn
584 C5 **Oldshore Beg** Highld
55 F3 **Old Shoreham** W Susx
584 D5 **Oldshoremore** Highld
343 H5 **Old Snydale** Wakefd
110 D3 **Old Sodbury** S Glos
278 C3 **Old Somerby** Lincs
371 G4 **Oldstead** N York
395 H5 **Old Stillington** S on T
187 G4 **Old Storridge Common** Worcs
167 G1 **Old Stratford** Nhants
524 B2 **Old Struan** P & K
309 E1 **Old Swan** Lpool
443 F4 **Old Swarland** Nthumb
212 C3 **Old Swinford** Dudley
327 E3 **Old Tame** Oldham
379 H3 **Old Tebay** Cumb
371 E3 **Old Thirsk** N York
450 D4 **Old Tinnis** Border
445 E5 **Old Toll** S Ayrs
341 F4 **Old Town** Calder
488 A5 **Old Town** C Edin
366 B3 **Old Town** Cumb
401 E6 **Old Town** Cumb
375 F6 **Old Town** E R Yk
57 F5 **Old Town** E Susx
58 B5 **Old Town** E Susx
58 D5 **Old Town** E Susx
170 B4 **Old Town** Herts
576 C6 **Oldtown** Highld
3 d2 **Old Town** IoS
113 E3 **Old Town** Swindn
569 L4 **Oldtown of Ord** Abers
326 B5 **Old Trafford** Traffd
100 D3 **Old Tree** Kent
294 D1 **Old Tupton** Derbys
102 C3 **Oldwalls** Swans
195 G6 **Old Warden** Beds
288 D2 **Old Warren** Flints
44 D4 **Old Way** Somset
103 E4 **Oldway** Swans
20 B5 **Oldway** Torbay
41 H2 **Oldways End** Somset
559 F4 **Old Westhall** Abers
219 G4 **Old Weston** Cambs
161 F2 **Old Wharf** Herefs
570 F5 **Oldwhat** Abers
314 D5 **Old Whittington** Derbys
214 C5 **Oldwich Lane** Solhll
196 D4 **Old Wimpole** Cambs
117 G5 **Old Windsor** W & M
396 A2 **Old Wingate** Dur
99 H3 **Old Wives Lees** Kent
93 H3 **Old Woking** Surrey
167 H1 **Old Wolverton** M Keyn
186 D1 **Oldwood** Worcs
319 G6 **Old Woodhall** Lincs
290 B6 **Old Woodhouses** Shrops
165 G6 **Old Woodstock** Oxon
588 D5 **Olgrinmore** Highld
273 H6 **Olive Green** Staffs
72 C4 **Oliver's Battery** Hants
606 E1 **Ollaberry** Shet
593 D9 **Ollag** W Isls
313 F2 **Ollerbrook Booth** Derbys
311 F4 **Ollerton** Ches
296 C1 **Ollerton** Notts
271 F4 **Ollerton** Shrops
339 F5 **Ollerton Fold** Lancs
271 F4 **Ollerton Lane** Shrops
172 C1 **Olmstead Green** Cambs
194 B4 **Olney** M Keyn
214 A3 **Olton** Solhll
109 H2 **Olveston** S Glos
188 B2 **Ombersley** Worcs
296 C1 **Ompton** Notts
606 E8 **Omunsgarth** Shet
322 f7 **Onchan** IoM
292 D3 **Onecote** Staffs
200 D3 **Onehouse** Suffk
134 A2 **Onen** Mons
328 D6 **Onesacre** Sheff
252 B3 **Ongar Hill** Norfk
209 G6 **Ongar Street** Herefs
210 B4 **Onibury** Shrops
520 E3 **Onich** Highld
130 C2 **Onllwyn** Neath
291 F6 **Onneley** Staffs
93 G5 **Onslow Village** Surrey
445 F2 **Onthank** E Ayrs
326 C5 **Openshaw** Manch
294 D5 **Openwoodgate** Derbys
562 C2 **Opinan** Highld
573 G4 **Opinan** Highld
569 G3 **Oran** Moray
252 A3 **Orange Row** Norfk
597 K5 **Orasaigh** W Isls
590 F3 **Oratobht** W Isls
468 A3 **Orbiston** N Lans
542 C8 **Orbost** Highld
301 E1 **Orby** Lincs
39 G2 **Orchard Hill** Devon
142 D4 **Orchard Leigh** Bucks
44 A3 **Orchard Portman** Somset
88 B5 **Orcheston** Wilts
160 B4 **Orcop** Herefs
160 B4 **Orcop Hill** Herefs
545 L7 **Ord** Highld
566 C2 **Ord** Highld
609 J3 **Ordale** Shet
556 B2 **Ordhead** Abers
555 E4 **Ordie** Abers
569 K4 **Ordiquhill** Abers
568 E4 **Ordiquish** Moray
403 G3 **Ordley** Nthumb
559 F6 **Ord Mill** Abers
316 C3 **Ordsall** Notts
326 B5 **Ordsall** Salfd
58 D4 **Ore** E Susx
11 F3 **Oreston** C Plym
211 F3 **Oreton** Shrops

203 E5 Orford Suffk
310 C1 Orford Warrtn
33 G1 Organford Dorset
315 E2 Orgreave Sheff
238 A1 Orgreave Staffs
162 A4 Oridge Street Gloucs
124 D3 Orlandon Pembks
81 E3 Orleston Kent
186 B1 Orleton Herefs
187 F1 Orleton Worcs
210 B6 Orleton Common Herefs
218 B5 Orlingbury Nhants
593 C11 Ormacleit W Isls
389 G4 Ormathwaite Cumb
385 E1 Ormesby R & Cl
251 F1 Ormesby St Margaret Norfk
251 F2 Ormesby St Michael Norfk
480 D3 Ormidale Ag & B
573 G5 Ormiscaig Highld
439 G2 Ormiston Border
489 E6 Ormiston E Loth
518 C3 Ormsaigbeg Highld
518 C3 Ormsaigmore Highld
479 J7 Ormsary Ag & B
364 A5 Ormsgill Cumb
323 G3 Ormskirk Lancs
405 E5 Ornsby Hill Dur
96 B1 Orpington Gt Lon
323 F5 Orrell Sefton
324 C3 Orrell Wigan
324 C4 Orrell Post Wigan
322 e4 Orrisdale IoM
487 H2 Orrock Fife
413 E5 Orroland D & G
121 F3 Orsett Thurr
121 F4 Orsett Heath Thurr
236 B1 Orslow Staffs
277 G1 Orston Notts
389 F3 Orthwaite Cumb
352 A4 Ortner Lancs
379 H3 Orton Cumb
568 E5 Orton Moray
217 G4 Orton Nhants
236 C5 Orton Staffs
243 G5 Orton Brimbles C Pete
243 H5 Orton Goldhay C Pete
243 H5 Orton Longueville C Pete
243 H5 Orton Malbourne C Pete
239 E4 Orton-on-the-Hill Leics
400 B4 Orton Rigg Cumb
243 G6 Orton Southgate C Pete
243 H5 Orton Waterville C Pete
243 G5 Orton Wistow C Pete
197 E4 Orwell Cambs
339 F3 Osbaldeston Lancs
339 F3 Osbaldeston Green Lancs
358 B4 Osbaldwick York
239 G4 Osbaston Leics
269 F5 Osbaston Shrops
270 D6 Osbaston Wrekin
239 G3 Osbaston Hollow Leics
279 F2 Osbournby Lincs
289 G1 Oscroft Ches
544 E1 Ose Highld
46 C3 Osehill Green Dorset
275 G6 Osgathorpe Leics
318 D1 Osgodby Lincs
345 E3 Osgodby N York
374 C3 Osgodby N York
345 E2 Osgodby Common N York
144 C6 Osidge Gt Lon
545 J2 Oskaig Highld
504 F2 Oskamull Ag & B
274 C2 Osleston Derbys
275 F3 Osmaston C Derb
293 G6 Osmaston Derbys
32 C3 Osmington Dorset
32 C3 Osmington Mills Dorset
384 D5 Osmotherley N York
140 A3 Osney Oxon
576 F6 Ospisdale Highld
99 F2 Ospringe Kent
60 C3 Ossaborough Devon
49 G5 Ossemsley Hants
343 E6 Osset Spa Wakefd
343 E5 Ossett Wakefd
296 D2 Ossington Notts
148 B5 Ostend Essex
256 D3 Ostend Norfk
118 C4 Osterley Gt Lon
372 B4 Oswaldkirk N York
339 H4 Oswaldtwistle Lancs
269 F4 Oswestry Shrops
594 E7 Otairnis W Isls
333 G6 Otby Lincs
269 H3 Oteley Shrops
96 D3 Otford Kent
98 B4 Otham Kent
98 C4 Otham Hole Kent
236 D2 Otherton Staffs
66 B3 Othery Somset
355 H5 Otley Leeds
201 H3 Otley Suffk
72 C5 Otterbourne Hants
441 G6 Otterburn Nthumb
353 H3 Otterburn N York
441 G5 Otterburn Camp Nthumb
99 E4 Otterden Place Kent
480 C3 Otter Ferry Ag & B
43 H5 Otterford Somset
22 D4 Otterham Cnwll
64 D3 Otterhampton Somset
98 C1 Otterham Quay Kent
22 D5 Otterham Station Cnwll
594 E7 Otternish W Isls
93 H2 Ottershaw Surrey
309 E2 Otterspool Lpool
609 G7 Otterswick Shet
28 A6 Otterton Devon
50 D4 Otterwood Hants
17 F3 Ottery Devon
28 B3 Ottery St Mary Devon
82 C2 Ottinge Kent
349 E5 Ottringham E R Yk
400 A3 Oughterby Cumb
367 H3 Oughtershaw N York
388 D1 Oughterside Cumb
328 D6 Oughtibridge Sheff
310 D2 Oughtrington Warrtn
371 G5 Oulston N York
399 G4 Oulton Cumb
343 G4 Oulton Leeds
255 F2 Oulton Norfk
272 A5 Oulton Staffs
272 D2 Oulton Staffs
251 G6 Oulton Suffk
251 G6 Oulton Broad Suffk
272 D3 Oultoncross Staffs
272 D2 Oulton Grange Staffs
255 G2 Oulton Street Norfk
219 E2 Oundle Nhants
236 C6 Ounsdale Staffs
391 G3 Ousby Cumb
582 E6 Ousdale Highld
199 E3 Ousden Suffk
346 B5 Ousefleet E R Yk
355 F6 Ousel Hole Brad
405 F4 Ouston Dur
402 D4 Ouston Nthumb
429 H5 Ouston Nthumb
364 C4 Out Cumb
100 C5 Out Elmstead Kent
12 B4 Outer Hope Devon
600 C2 Outertown Ork
378 C5 Outgate Cumb
380 D4 Outhgill Cumb
189 H1 Outhill Warwks
271 H3 Outlands Staffs
342 A6 Outlane Kirk
309 F4 Outlet Village Ches
87 F2 Outmarsh Wilts
349 G5 Out Newton E R Yk
338 B1 Out Rawcliffe Lancs
245 H4 Outwell Norfk
70 C6 Outwick Hants
325 H3 Outwood Bury
44 B2 Outwood Somset
95 G5 Outwood Surrey
343 F5 Outwood Wakefd
275 F6 Outwoods Leics
272 A6 Outwoods Staffs
274 C5 Outwoods Staffs
214 C3 Outwoods Warwks
343 F4 Ouzlewell Green Leeds
342 A4 Ovenden Calder
221 E5 Over Cambs
290 C1 Over Ches
162 B6 Over Gloucs
109 G3 Over S Glos
603 K3 Overbister Ork
366 C4 Over Burrow Lancs
274 D2 Over Burrows Derbys
163 E2 Overbury Worcs
32 B3 Overcombe Dorset
46 A1 Over Compton Dorset
243 F6 Over End Cambs
314 B5 Over End Derbys
213 E3 Overend Sandw
514 C1 Over Finlarg Angus
238 B6 Over Green Birm
570 F5 Overhill Abers
325 F3 Over Haddon Derbys
365 H6 Over Kellet Lancs
165 G5 Over Kiddington Oxon
311 F4 Over Knutsford Ches
451 G1 Over Langshaw Border
66 D2 Overleigh Somset
238 B1 Overley Staffs
134 C2 Over Monnow Mons
292 C5 Overmoor Staffs
165 E4 Over Norton Oxon
311 F5 Over Peover Ches
309 E4 Overpool Ches
233 G5 Overs Shrops
238 D1 Overseal Derbys
384 D6 Over Silton N York
216 A5 Oversland Warwks
99 H3 Oversland Kent
189 G3 Oversley Green Warwks
193 H1 Overstone Nhants
64 C4 Over Stowey Somset
256 B1 Overstrand Norfk
45 E4 Over Stratton Somset
311 E3 Over Tabley Ches
342 D6 Overthorpe Kirk
166 A1 Overthorpe Nhants
557 F2 Overton C Aber
309 H4 Overton Ches
398 B2 Overton D & G
135 G2 Overton Gloucs
91 E5 Overton Hants
482 C5 Overton Inver
351 F3 Overton Lancs
357 H3 Overton N York
210 C5 Overton Shrops
273 F2 Overton Staffs
102 C4 Overton Swans
328 D1 Overton Wakefd
269 G1 Overton Wrexhm
289 E6 Overton Bridge Wrexhm
340 D4 Over Town Lancs
366 C4 Overtown Lancs
468 C4 Overtown N Lans
113 E4 Overtown Swindn
329 F1 Overtown Wakefd
71 F2 Over Wallop Hants
214 C1 Over Whitacre Warwks
165 G4 Over Worton Oxon
167 G5 Oving Bucks
53 G3 Oving W Susx
56 A4 Ovingdean Br & H
404 C2 Ovingham Nthumb
382 D2 Ovington Dur
173 F1 Ovington Essex
73 E3 Ovington Hants
248 B4 Ovington Norfk
404 C2 Ovington Nthumb
274 C4 Owen's Bank Staffs
50 B1 Ower Hants
32 D2 Owermoigne Dorset
315 E6 Owlcotes Derbys
220 B4 Owl End Cambs
314 B4 Owler Bar Derbys
314 C2 Owlerton Sheff
342 C2 Owlet Brad
136 A5 Owlpen Gloucs
93 E2 Owlsmoor Br For
141 G3 Owlswick Bucks
315 E3 Owlthorpe Sheff
333 F4 Owmby Lincs
318 C2 Owmby-by-Spital Lincs
114 C5 Ownham W Berk
72 D5 Owslebury Hants
330 B2 Owston Donc
241 G3 Owston Leics
331 H4 Owston Ferry N Linc
349 E3 Owstwick E R Yk
349 H4 Owthorne E R Yk
277 E3 Owthorpe Notts
396 C4 Owton Manor Hartpl
247 E4 Oxborough Norfk
30 B3 Oxbridge Dorset
315 E3 Oxclose Sheff
405 G3 Oxclose Sundld
320 B4 Oxcombe Lincs
315 F5 Oxcroft Derbys
315 F5 Oxcroft Estate Derbys
172 D4 Oxen End Essex
161 G4 Oxenhall Gloucs
366 A2 Oxenholme Cumb
341 G3 Oxenhope Brad
364 D2 Oxen Park Cumb
66 C1 Oxenpill Somset
163 E3 Oxenton Gloucs
89 G3 Oxenwood Wilts
291 H4 Oxford C Stke
140 B3 Oxford Oxon
484 C5 Oxgang E Duns
488 A6 Oxgangs C Edin
143 G5 Oxhey Herts
405 E4 Oxhill Dur
191 E5 Oxhill Warwks
236 D4 Oxley Wolves
148 B2 Oxley Green Essex
58 A2 Oxley's Green E Susx
221 G2 Oxlode Cambs
452 D6 Oxnam Border
256 A5 Oxnead Norfk
94 C2 Oxshott Surrey
96 A4 Oxted Surrey
472 B4 Oxton Border
296 B4 Oxton Notts
357 G6 Oxton N York
308 C2 Oxton Wirral
314 C5 Oxton Rakes Derbys
102 C4 Oxwich Swans
102 C4 Oxwich Green Swans
254 B3 Oxwick Norfk
575 H3 Oykel Bridge Highld
559 F4 Oyne Abers
103 F4 Oystermouth Swans
136 A6 Ozleworth Gloucs

P

599 L8 Pabail Iarach W Isls
599 L8 Pabail Uarach W Isls
305 H4 Pabo Conwy
94 D3 Pachesham Park Surrey
46 D2 Packers Hill Dorset
239 F2 Packington Leics
291 H4 Packmoor C Stke
190 D1 Packmores Warwks
214 B5 Packwood Solhll
214 B5 Packwood Gullet Solhll
527 F4 Padanaram Angus
167 F3 Padbury Bucks
310 C2 Paddington Warrtn
82 C2 Paddlesworth Kent
97 G2 Paddlesworth Kent
99 F4 Paddock Kent
327 H1 Paddock Kirk
568 C4 Paddockhaugh Moray
311 G4 Paddockhill Ches
97 G6 Paddock Wood Kent
270 B3 Paddolgreen Shrops
288 C2 Padeswood Flints
327 F5 Padfield Derbys
310 C1 Padgate Warrtn
146 C5 Padham's Green Essex
340 C3 Padiham Lancs
222 A5 Padney Cambs
286 A4 Padog Conwy
355 G3 Padside N York
355 G3 Padside Green N York
25 E3 Padson Devon
14 C4 Padstow Cnwll
91 G1 Padworth W Berk
91 G2 Padworth Common W Berk
136 B3 Paganhill Gloucs
395 E2 Page Bank Dur
309 F1 Page Moss Knows
201 F1 Page's Green Suffk
53 F5 Pagham W Susx
148 B6 Paglesham Churchend Essex
123 L1 Paglesham Eastend Essex
592 C4 Paibeil W Isls
20 B5 Paignton Torbay
215 H3 Pailton Warwks
273 F3 Painleyhill Staffs
184 C5 Painscastle Powys
404 C2 Painshawfield Nthumb
96 B4 Pains Hill Surrey
359 F3 Painsthorpe E R Yk
136 C3 Painswick Gloucs
99 F3 Painter's Forstal Kent
170 C6 Painter's Green Herts
270 C1 Painters Green Wrexhm
329 E1 Painthorpe Wakefd
44 C6 Paintmoor Somset
598 F5 Pairc Shiaboist W Isls
466 C2 Paisley Rens
227 G1 Pakefield Suffk
200 B1 Pakenham Suffk
267 F2 Pale Gwynd
172 D1 Pale Green Essex
78 B6 Palehouse Common E Susx
71 F1 Palestine Hants
117 E4 Paley Street W & M
237 F5 Palfrey Wsall
420 B3 Palgowan D & G
225 F4 Palgrave Suffk
376 B2 Pallaflat Cumb
32 D1 Pallington Dorset
406 B3 Pallion Sundld
396 D6 Pallister Middsb
82 B4 Palmarsh Kent
274 A3 Palmer Moor Derbys
16 A3 Palmersbridge Cnwll
75 G1 Palmers Cross Surrey
236 C4 Palmers Cross Wolves
134 D3 Palmer's Flat Gloucs
144 D6 Palmers Green Gt Lon
79 F1 Palmer's Green Kent
106 B6 Palmerstown V Glam
431 E5 Palmersville N Tyne
100 C6 Palmstead Kent
413 F3 Palnackie D & G
417 E4 Palnure D & G
315 F6 Palterton Derbys
91 G3 Pamber End Hants
91 F3 Pamber Green Hants
91 G2 Pamber Heath Hants
162 D3 Pamington Gloucs
48 B4 Pamphill Dorset
197 H5 Pampisford Cambs
37 E3 Pan IoW
85 E5 Panborough Somset
515 F2 Panbride Angus
137 G2 Pancakehill Gloucs
23 F1 Pancrasweek Devon
105 G6 Pancross V Glam
229 E4 Pandy Gwynd
229 G1 Pandy Gwynd
266 D4 Pandy Gwynd
159 F5 Pandy Mons
231 E4 Pandy Powys
268 C2 Pandy Shrops
289 F6 Pandy Wrexhm
287 F2 Pandy'r Capel Denbgs
286 B2 Pandy Tudur Conwy
173 E4 Panfield Essex
115 G4 Pangbourne Oxon
187 E5 Panks Bridge Herefs
356 C1 Pannal N York
356 B4 Pannal Ash N York
199 F6 Pannel's Ash Essex
209 E5 Panpunton Powys
288 B4 Pant Denbgs
307 G5 Pant Flints
262 C4 Pant Gwynd
131 H3 Pant Myr Td
231 G4 Pant Shrops
269 E5 Pant Shrops
288 C5 Pant Wrexhm
289 E3 Pant Wrexhm
307 G4 Pantasaph Flints
104 B1 Pantdu Neath
180 C2 Panteg Pembks
151 F2 Panteg Pembks
133 F5 Panteg Torfn
15 H5 Pantersbridge Cnwll
263 H1 Pant Glâs Gwynd
230 B5 Pant-glas Powys
269 E3 Pant-glas Shrops
179 E4 Pantgwyn Cerdgn
129 G4 Pant-lasau Swans
106 B3 Pantmawr Cardif
206 D3 Pant Mawr Powys
319 F4 Panton Lincs
287 E2 Pant-pastynog Denbgs
229 G4 Pantperthog Gwynd
132 D5 Pantside Caerph
152 C4 Pant-y-Caws Carmth
205 E4 Pant-y-crûg Cerdgn
207 F5 Pant-y-dwr Powys
232 C4 Pant-y-ffridd Powys
129 F2 Pantyffynnon Carmth
154 C6 Pantyffynnon Carmth
133 G4 Pantygasseg Torfn
288 A2 Pantymwyn Flints
105 E3 Pant-y-pyllau Brdgnd
105 E2 Pant-yr-awel Brdgnd
307 F2 Pant y Wacco Flints
250 C2 Panxworth Norfk
388 C2 Papcastle Cumb
270 D4 Papermill Bank Shrops
589 K6 Papigoe Highld
605 G4 Papil Shet
219 G2 Papley Nhants
490 A5 Papple E Loth
295 G4 Papplewick Notts
196 C2 Papworth Everard Cambs
196 C2 Papworth St Agnes Cambs
8 D3 Par Cnwll
136 C2 Paradise Gloucs
186 C5 Paradise Green Herefs
8 B4 Paramoor Cnwll
101 E3 Paramour Street Kent
324 B2 Parbold Lancs
513 H6 Parbroath Fife
67 F2 Parbrook Somset
76 A5 Parbrook W Susx
266 D3 Parc Gwynd
6 C5 Parc Erissey Cnwll
103 C3 Parc-hendy Swans
154 D5 Parc-Henri Carmth
65 F4 Parchey Somset
303 G4 Parciau IoA
179 E3 Parcllyn Cerdgn
106 B1 Parc Mawr Caerph
108 D1 Parc Seymour Newpt
91 F5 Pardown Hants
388 C2 Pardshaw Cumb
388 D4 Pardshaw Hall Cumb
202 C2 Parham Suffk
15 E4 Park Cnwll
423 F1 Park D & G
26 C3 Park Devon
113 E3 Park Swindn
93 G4 Park Barn Surrey
543 G6 Park Bernisdale Highld
6 C5 Park Bottom Cnwll
326 D4 Park Bridge Tamesd
400 D3 Park Broom Cumb
354 A6 Park Close Lancs
57 E2 Park Corner BaNES
78 C2 Park Corner E Susx
116 A2 Park Corner Oxon
194 D4 Park End Beds
198 B2 Park End Cambs
135 E3 Parkend Gloucs
136 A2 Parkend Gloucs
396 D6 Park End Middsb
428 D4 Park End Nthumb
418 C5 Park End S Ayrs
64 C5 Park End Somset
291 F4 Park End Staffs
211 H5 Park End Worcs
7 G4 Parkengear Cnwll
115 G5 Parkfield S Glos
236 D5 Parkfield Wolves
485 G4 Parkfoot Falk
308 C4 Parkgate Ches
311 F5 Parkgate Ches
399 G5 Parkgate Cumb
423 H2 Parkgate D & G
46 D3 Park Gate Dorset
172 D6 Parkgate Essex
51 F3 Park Gate Hants
80 B3 Parkgate Kent
82 C1 Park Gate Kent
328 C2 Parkgate Kirk
329 G5 Parkgate Rothm
199 E3 Parkgate Suffk
95 E6 Parkgate Surrey
171 G4 Park Gate Worcs
269 F3 Park Hall Shrops
483 G5 Parkhall W Duns
39 E3 Parkham Devon
39 E3 Parkham Ash Devon
557 F5 Parkhead Abers
467 F2 Parkhead C Glas
390 A1 Parkhead Cumb
391 F1 Park Head Cumb
294 D4 Park Head Derbys
328 B3 Park Head Kirk
314 C3 Parkhead Sheff
590 A1 Parkhill Inver
81 E3 Park Hill Kent
314 D2 Park Hill Sheff
324 B4 Park Hill St Hel
134 C4 Parkhouse Mons
295 E2 Parkhouse Green Derbys
36 D2 Parkhurst IoW
343 F2 Parklands Leeds
236 C3 Park Lane Staffs
269 H2 Park Lane Wrexhm
120 A6 Park Langley Gt Lon
483 G5 Park Mains Rens
102 D4 Parkmill Swans
402 D2 Parkneuk Fife
118 D3 Park Royal Gt Lon
169 E5 Parkside Beds
376 C1 Parkside Cumb
406 C5 Parkside Dur
468 B3 Parkside N Lans
272 C4 Parkside Staffs
289 E4 Parkside Wrexhm
34 B2 Parkstone Poole
76 B3 Park Street W Susx
169 F5 Park Town Luton
140 B3 Park Town Oxon
402 B2 Park Village Nthumb
236 D4 Park Village Wolves
161 G2 Parkway Herefs
67 F5 Parkway Somset
98 B4 Park Wood Medway
98 C2 Park Wood Medway
314 C2 Parkwood Springs Sheff
48 D5 Parley Cross Dorset
48 C5 Parley Green Dorset
200 C6 Parliament Heath Suffk
343 H2 Parlington Leeds
116 C2 Parmoor Bucks
23 G1 Parnacott Devon
174 D3 Parney Heath Essex
324 C2 Parr St Hel
61 G3 Parracombe Devon
325 G4 Parr Brow Wigan
152 A2 Parrog Pembks
106 B3 Parslow's Hillock Bucks
142 D3 Parsonage Green Essex
146 D2 Parsonage Green Essex
388 D2 Parsonby Cumb
314 C1 Parson Cross Sheff
245 E3 Parson Drove Cambs
119 E4 Parsons Green Gt Lon
174 C4 Parson's Heath Essex
466 D1 Partick C Glas
311 E1 Partington Traffd
320 D6 Partney Lincs
388 A5 Parton Cumb
400 A4 Parton Cumb
422 E4 Parton D & G
185 F5 Parton Herefs
146 F2 Partridgegreen Essex
76 C6 Partridge Green W Susx
159 E5 Partrishow Powys
293 G4 Parwich Derbys
236 B5 Pasford Staffs
167 G2 Passenham Nhants
74 C3 Passfield Hants
145 H5 Passingford Bridge Essex
145 F3 Passmores Essex
244 A4 Paston C Pete
256 C5 Paston Norfk
256 C3 Paston Green Norfk
273 E5 Pasturefields Staffs
24 C3 Patchacott Devon
55 H3 Patcham Br & H
143 G5 Patchetts Green Herts
54 C3 Patching W Susx
61 F3 Patchole Devon
109 H3 Patchway S Glos
355 F4 Pateley Bridge N York
391 E4 Pategill Cumb
65 G5 Pathe Somset
468 B4 Pather N Lans
26 C4 Pathfinder Village Devon
434 C2 Pathhead E Ayrs
501 E6 Pathhead Fife
405 E2 Path Head Gatesd
471 G4 Pathhead Mdloth
190 B3 Pathlow Warwks
499 E6 Path of Condie P & K
500 A2 Pathstruie P & K
171 F4 Patient End Herts
171 F4 Patmore Heath Herts
433 F2 Patna E Ayrs
88 C3 Patney Wilts
322 c6 Patrick IoM
369 H1 Patrick Brompton N York
325 H5 Patricroft Salfd
349 F5 Patrington E R Yk
349 F5 Patrington Haven E R Yk
100 C4 Patrixbourne Kent
60 D4 Patsford Devon
378 C1 Patterdale Cumb
487 E3 Pattiesmuir Fife
236 B5 Pattingham Staffs
193 E4 Pattishall Nhants
173 C5 Pattiswick Essex
234 D5 Patton Shrops
379 F5 Patton Bridge Cumb
3 E4 Paul Cnwll
193 F5 Paulerspury Nhants
348 C4 Paull E R Yk
4 B2 Paul's Green Cnwll
52 A3 Paulsgrove C Port
86 B3 Paulton BaNES
486 C6 Paulville W Loth
442 D6 Pauperhaugh Nthumb
235 H1 Pave Lane Wrekin
194 D3 Pavenham Beds
84 B6 Pawlett Somset
84 B6 Pawlett Hill Somset
453 F3 Pawston Nthumb
164 B2 Paxford Gloucs
474 D4 Paxton Border
99 E4 Payden Street Kent
313 E4 Peak Dale Derbys
313 F4 Peak Forest Derbys
244 C1 Peak Hill Lincs
243 F3 Peakirk C Pete
100 B3 Pean Hill Kent
68 C4 Pear Ash Somset
527 E3 Pearsie Angus
97 G6 Pearson's Green Kent
275 F3 Pear Tree C Derb
146 B5 Peartree Green Essex
160 D3 Peartree Green Herefs
75 F2 Peartree Green Surrey
140 A2 Peartree Hill Oxon
342 A1 Peas Acre Brad
86 C3 Peasedown St John BaNES
295 E5 Peasehill Derbys
254 D4 Peaseland Green Norfk
114 C4 Peasemore W Berk
226 C6 Peasenhall Suffk
77 E3 Pease Pottage W Susx
245 F5 Peas Hill Cambs
94 B6 Peaslake Surrey
324 C5 Peasley Cross St Hel
80 C5 Peasmarsh E Susx
44 C5 Peasmarsh Somset
93 G5 Peasmarsh Surrey
471 H1 Peaston E Loth
472 A1 Peastonbank E Loth
571 G2 Peathill Abers
502 D3 Peat Inn Fife
240 C6 Peatling Magna Leics
216 C2 Peatling Parva Leics
210 C2 Peaton Shrops
210 C3 Peatonstrand Shrops
173 H3 Pebmarsh Essex
58 C5 Pebsham E Susx
190 A5 Pebworth Worcs
341 F4 Pecket Well Calder
290 A3 Peckforton Ches
119 G4 Peckham Gt Lon
97 G5 Peckham Bush Kent
115 G5 Peckingell Wilts
67 G2 Pecking Mill Somset
239 F4 Peckleton Leics
209 F5 Pedair-ffordd Powys
146 A3 Pediars End Essex
210 B3 Pedlar's Rest Shrops
82 B3 Pedlinge Kent
212 D3 Pedmore Dudley
142 C4 Pednor Bottom Bucks
142 C4 Pednormead End Bucks
66 C2 Pedwell Somset
450 B1 Peebles Border
451 E2 Peel Border
322 c6 Peel IoM
337 G3 Peel Lancs
51 G4 Peel Common Hants
325 G4 Peel Green Salfd
337 H3 Peel Hall Manch
337 G3 Peel Hill Lancs
467 F4 Peel Park S Lans
82 C3 Peene Kent
80 C6 Peening Quarter Kent
275 G6 Peggs Green Leics
169 H2 Pegsdon Beds
430 D2 Pegswood Nthumb

City, town and village index: Pegwell - Pitcur 709

101 G3 Pegwell Kent
543 G5 Peinaha Highld
545 J3 Peinchorran Highld
543 G7 Peiness Highld
543 G5 Peinlich Highld
543 G7 Peinmore Highld
545 H1 Peinmore Highld
405 G2 Pelaw Gatesd
151 F6 Pelcomb Pembks
125 F1 Pelcomb Bridge Pembks
151 F6 Pelcomb Cross Pembks
148 C1 Peldon Essex
51 G6 Pelhamfield IoW
79 E3 Pell Green E Susx
341 H4 Pellon Calder
237 F4 Pelsall Wsall
237 F4 Pelsall Wood Wsall
405 G4 Pelton Dur
405 G4 Pelton Fell Dur
399 E5 Pelutho Cumb
9 G3 Pelynt Cnwll
128 D4 Pemberton Carmth
98 D5 Pembles Cross Kent
128 B4 Pembrey Carmth
185 G3 Pembridge Herefs
125 G4 Pembroke Pembks
125 F4 Pembroke Dock Pembks
125 G4 Pembroke Ferry Pembks
79 E1 Pembury Kent
17 E3 Pempwell Cnwll
160 D4 Pen-allt Herefs
134 C2 Penallt Mons
126 C5 Penally Pembks
8 C5 Penare Cnwll
208 B2 Penarron Powys
106 C5 Penarth V Glam
106 C5 Penarth Moors Cardif
3 F2 Penbeagle Cnwll
307 H6 Penbedw Flints
153 E2 Pen-bedw Pembks
2 D5 Penberth Cnwll
159 F5 Penbidwal Mons
126 C1 Penblewin Pembks
262 D4 Penbodlas Gwynd
205 F3 Pen-bont Rhydybeddau Cerdgn
153 H2 Penboyr Carmth
179 F3 Penbryn Cerdgn
153 F2 Pencader Carmth
263 G2 Pencaenewydd Gwynd
130 B5 Pencaerau Neath
102 D2 Pen-caer-fenny Swans
489 E6 Pencaitland E Loth
303 E6 Pencarnisiog IoA
180 F2 Pencarreg Carmth
22 C6 Pencarrow Cnwll
128 D2 Penceiliogi Carmth
158 A4 Pencelli Powys
102 D2 Pen-clawdd Swans
105 F3 Pencoed Brdgnd
160 D4 Pencombe Herefs
131 E3 Pen-common Powys
160 C4 Pencoyd Herefs
6 C6 Pencoys Cnwll
160 D5 Pencraig Herefs
303 G5 Pencraig IoA
267 G4 Pencraig Powys
133 F3 Pencroesoped Mons
22 D4 Pencuke Cnwll
343 G2 Pendas Fields Leeds
2 C3 Pendeen Cnwll
131 F3 Penderyn Rhondd
127 E3 Pendine Carmth
326 A4 Pendlebury Salfd
340 B2 Pendleton Lancs
326 B5 Pendleton Salfd
162 A3 Pendock Gloucs
15 E3 Pendoggett Cnwll
45 G5 Pendomer Somset
105 H4 Pendoylan V Glam
105 E3 Pendre Brdgnd
228 D4 Pendre Gwynd
157 G4 Pendre Powys
15 F4 Pendrift Cnwll
230 B4 Penegoes Powys
7 F5 Penelewey Cnwll
98 B3 Penenden Heath Kent
152 B5 Penffordd Pembks
132 C5 Pengam Caerph
119 G5 Penge Gt Lon
6 C6 Pengegon Cnwll
22 B6 Pengelly Cnwll
158 C3 Pengenffordd Powys
3 G2 Pengersick Cnwll
284 C2 Pen-gilfach Gwynd
22 C4 Pengold Cnwll
303 G2 Pengorffwysfa IoA
16 C5 Pengover Green Cnwll
160 C5 Penguithal Herefs
307 E4 Pengwern Denbgs
4 C5 Penhale Cnwll
7 G2 Penhale Cnwll
4 B3 Penhale Jakes Cnwll
5 E5 Penhallick Cnwll
6 C5 Penhallick Cnwll
7 E3 Penhallow Cnwll
6 C6 Penhalurick Cnwll
6 C6 Penhalvean Cnwll
229 E5 Penhelig Gwynd
60 D5 Penhill Devon
112 D2 Penhill Swindn
108 D1 Penhow Newpt
58 A3 Penhurst E Susx
470 D2 Penicuik Mdloth
154 B5 Peniel Carmth
287 E2 Peniel Denbgs
545 H1 Penifiler Highld
457 E1 Peninver Ag & B
284 C2 Penisa'r Waun Gwynd
328 C4 Penistone Barns
5 E2 Penjerrick Cnwll
310 A2 Penketh Warrtn
291 H6 Penkhull C Stke
432 B5 Penkill S Ayrs
411 E3 Penkiln D & G
87 F5 Penknap Wilts
236 D2 Penkridge Staffs
103 F2 Pen-lan Swans
151 E3 Pen-Lan-mabws Pembks
269 H2 Penley Wrexhm
262 C4 Penllech Gwynd
129 F5 Penllergaer Swans
132 C5 Penllwyn Caerph
205 E3 Penllwyn Cerdgn
303 E4 Pen-llyn IoA
105 F4 Penllyn V Glam
282 D3 Pen-lôn IoA
285 G4 Penmachno Conwy
132 C5 Penmaen Caerph
102 D4 Penmaen Swans
305 F4 Penmaenan Conwy
305 E4 Penmaenmawr Conwy
265 F6 Penmaenpool Gwynd
105 H6 Penmark V Glam
6 D1 Penmarth Cnwll
14 C3 Penmayne Cnwll
304 D3 Penmon IoA
179 G3 Penmorfa Cerdgn
264 C1 Penmorfa Gwynd
303 G6 Penmynydd IoA
142 C6 Penn Bucks
29 F3 Penn Dorset
236 C5 Penn Wolves
229 G4 Pennal Gwynd
570 E2 Pennan Abers
6 D5 Pennance Cnwll
180 D2 Pennant Cerdgn
286 B3 Pennant Conwy
230 D5 Pennant Powys
267 G4 Pennant Melangell Powys
125 G4 Pennar Pembks
103 E4 Pennard Swans
125 F4 Pennar Park Pembks
142 C6 Penn Bottom Bucks
233 F5 Pennerley Shrops
364 C4 Pennington Cumb
50 B6 Pennington Hants
325 F5 Pennington Wigan
325 E3 Pennington Green Wigan
158 B4 Pennorth Powys
142 C5 Penn Street Bucks
27 E4 Pennsylvania Devon
110 C5 Pennsylvania S Glos
364 D3 Penny Bridge Cumb
505 G5 Pennycross Ag & B
17 E2 Pennycross C Plym
256 C5 Pennygate Norfk
505 G5 Pennyghael Ag & B
518 F7 Pennygown Ag & B
315 G4 Penny Green Derbys
341 H6 Penny Hill Calder
281 E4 Penny Hill Lincs
324 B3 Pennylands Lancs
41 H5 Pennymoor Devon
142 B2 Pennypot Kent
249 F5 Penny's Green Norfk
15 E3 Pennytinney Cnwll
406 B3 Pennywell Sundld
105 H6 Pen-onn V Glam
179 E4 Penparc Cerdgn
150 D3 Penparc Pembks
204 D4 Penparcau Cerdgn
132 B5 Penpedairheol Caerph
133 F4 Penpedairheol Mons
133 F2 Penpergym Mons
133 F4 Penperlleni Mons
22 B5 Penpethy Cnwll
8 D2 Penpillick Cnwll
153 H6 Penplas Carmth
7 F6 Penpol Cnwll
9 E3 Penpoll Cnwll
6 B6 Penponds Cnwll
15 F4 Penpont Cnwll
435 G6 Penpont D & G
105 F3 Penprysg Brdgnd
12 A2 Penquit Devon
263 F3 Penrallt Gwynd
207 E2 Penrallt Powys
153 F2 Penrherber Carmth
106 D1 Penrhiw Caerph
131 G5 Penrhiwceiber Rhondd
130 A2 Pen-Rhiw-fawr Neath
132 D4 Penrhiwgarreg Blae G
155 E6 Penrhiwgoch Carmth
153 H1 Penrhiw-llan Cerdgn
179 G4 Penrhiw-pal Cerdgn
130 A5 Penrhiwtyn Neath
263 E4 Penrhos Gwynd
185 F3 Penrhos Herefs
302 C4 Penrhos IoA
133 H2 Penrhos Mons
130 B2 Penrhos Powys
288 C4 Pen-rhos Wrexhm
302 B4 Penrhosfeilw IoA
263 E4 Penrhos Garnedd Gwynd
303 F2 Penrhyd Lastra IoA
306 A3 Penrhyn Bay Conwy
178 C4 Penrhyn Castle Pembks
205 E3 Penrhyn-coch Cerdgn
264 D2 Penrhyndeudraeth Gwynd
305 H3 Penrhyn-side Conwy
131 F5 Penrhys Rhondd
102 C4 Penrice Swans
391 E3 Penrith Cumb
14 B4 Penrose Cnwll
15 F3 Penrose Cnwll
4 B3 Penrose Hill Cnwll
390 C4 Penruddock Cumb
5 E2 Penryn Cnwll
154 B6 Pensarn Carmth
306 D4 Pensarn Conwy
263 G2 Pen-sarn Gwynd
264 D4 Pen-sarn Gwynd
211 G6 Pensax Worcs
308 C3 Pensby Wirral
68 C3 Penselwood Somset
85 H2 Pensford BaNES
188 D6 Pensham Worcs
406 A4 Penshaw Sundld
96 D6 Penshurst Kent
16 C5 Pensilva Cnwll
212 D2 Pensnett Dudley
489 E5 Penston E Loth
26 B2 Penstone Devon
6 D4 Penstraze Cnwll
129 E2 Pen-t?wyn Carmth
8 C4 Pentewan Cnwll
208 D3 Pentiken Shrops
284 C1 Pentir Gwynd
7 E1 Pentire Cnwll
233 F4 Pentirvin Shrops
126 C3 Pentlepoir Pembks
199 G6 Pentlow Essex
199 G5 Pentlow Street Essex
253 E5 Pentney Norfk
89 H5 Penton Corner Hants
89 H5 Penton Grafton Hants
118 A6 Penton Hook Surrey
90 A5 Penton Mewsey Hants
119 G3 Pentonville Gt Lon
153 F6 Pentowin Carmth
304 B4 Pentraeth IoA
132 C4 Pentrapeod Caerph
128 D2 Pentre Carmth
287 G3 Pentre Denbgs
287 H2 Pentre Flints
288 B2 Pentre Flints
288 B3 Pentre Flints
308 D6 Pentre Flints
207 H2 Pentre Powys
209 E1 Pentre Powys
232 D3 Pentre Powys
131 F5 Pentre Rhondd
232 B2 Pentre Shrops
233 G1 Pentre Shrops
268 D4 Pentre Shrops
268 B3 Pentre Wrexhm
269 E1 Pentre Wrexhm
181 E5 Pentre-bâch Cerdgn
131 H4 Pentrebach Myr Td
157 E3 Pentre-bach Powys
106 A2 Pentrebach Rhondd
129 F3 Pentrebach Swans
156 C3 Pentrebach Swans
106 B4 Pentrebane Cardif
283 E1 Pentre Berw IoA
285 F4 Pentre-bont Conwy
288 D4 Pentre Broughton Wrexhm
288 C5 Pentre Bychan Wrexhm
153 G1 Pentrecagal Carmth
268 D4 Pentre-cefn Shrops
287 H4 Pentre-celyn Denbgs
230 D3 Pentre-celyn Powys
103 G3 Pentre-chwyth Swans
268 D2 Pentre Cilgwyn Wrexhm
269 E3 Pentre-clawdd Shrops
130 C3 Pentreclwydau Neath
269 G2 Pentre-coed Shrops
154 A2 Pentre-cwrt Carmth
183 F6 Pentre Dolau Honddu Powys
288 A5 Pentredwr Denbgs
103 G2 Pentre-dwr Swans
155 E5 Pentrefelin Carmth
181 F5 Pentrefelin Cerdgn
305 H5 Pentrefelin Conwy
288 B6 Pentrefelin Denbgs
264 C2 Pentrefelin Gwynd
303 F2 Pentrefelin IoA
308 C5 Pentre-Ffwrndan Flints
286 B4 Pentrefoelas Conwy
132 C5 Pentref-y-groes Caerph
152 D3 Pentre Galar Pembks
179 H3 Pentregat Cerdgn
129 F1 Pentre-Gwenlais Carmth
264 D4 Pentre Gwynfryn Gwynd
308 A5 Pentre Halkyn Flints
232 D6 Pentreheyling Shrops
209 F4 Pentre Hodre Shrops
306 B6 Pentre Isaf Conwy
287 F2 Pentre-Llanrhaeadr Denbgs
232 B5 Pentre Llifior Powys
154 B1 Pentrellwyn Cerdgn
304 C3 Pentrellwyn IoA
183 E4 Pentre-llwyn-llwyd Powys
205 E4 Pentre-llyn Cerdgn
286 D4 Pentre-llyn-cymmer Conwy
289 E5 Pentre Maelor Wrexhm
105 F4 Pentre Meyrick V Glam
154 B4 Pentre-Morgan Carmth
269 E2 Pentre-newydd Shrops
128 D4 Pentre-Poeth Carmth
107 E2 Pentre-poeth Newpt
133 E4 Pentre-Poid Torfn
232 C2 Pentre'r beirdd Powys
305 H6 Pentre'r Felin Conwy
287 G1 Pentre'r-felin Denbgs
157 E3 Pentre'r-felin Powys
285 H2 Pentre-tafarn-y-fedw Conwy
156 C2 Pentre-ty-gwyn Carmth
306 B4 Pentre-uchaf Conwy
263 F3 Pentreuchaf Gwynd
294 D4 Pentrich Derbys
70 A6 Pentridge Dorset
152 B3 Pentrisil Pembks
132 B4 Pentwyn Caerph
132 D4 Pen-twyn Caerph
106 A3 Pentwyn Cardif
106 D3 Pentwyn Cardif
133 E4 Pen-twyn Torfn
132 A5 Pentwyn Berthlwyd Myr Td
132 C5 Pentwyn-mawr Caerph
106 B3 Pentyrch Cardif
308 A5 Pen-Uchar Plwyf Flints
181 E2 Penuwch Cerdgn
7 E3 Penwartha Cnwll
7 E3 Penwartha Coombe Cnwll
7 E5 Penweathers Cnwll
8 C2 Penwithick Cnwll
90 C2 Penwood Hants
338 D4 Penwortham Lane Lancs
130 D1 Penwyllt Powys
307 H4 Pen-y-Ball Top Flints
129 F2 Penybanc Carmth
154 B5 Pen-y-banc Carmth
155 F5 Pen-y-banc Carmth
132 A4 Pen-y-bank Myr Td
128 B4 Penybedd Carmth
132 D3 Pen-y-Bont Blae G
153 G4 Pen-y-bont Carmth
205 E2 Penybont Cerdgn
265 E4 Pen-y-bont Gwynd
184 B2 Penybont Powys
268 A5 Penybontfawr Powys
268 D5 Pen-y-bont Llanerch Emrys Powys
132 B5 Penybryn Caerph
264 B2 Pen-y-Bryn Gwynd
265 F6 Pen-y-bryn Gwynd
178 D5 Pen-y-bryn Pembks
232 C4 Pen-y-bryn Powys
269 F2 Pen-y-Bryn Shrops
288 C6 Pen-y-bryn Wrexhm
105 E3 Pen-y-cae Brdgnd
104 B2 Pen-y-cae Neath
130 C2 Pen-y-cae Powys
288 C5 Penycae Wrexhm
133 G5 Pen-y-cae-mawr Mons
262 C5 Penycaerau Gwynd
307 G4 Pen-y-cefn Flints
134 B3 Pen-y-clawdd Mons
269 E5 Pen-y-coed Shrops
105 H2 Pen-y-coedcae Rhondd
151 E5 Penycwm Pembks
131 H3 Pen-y-Darren Myr Td
129 G4 Penydre Swans
104 D3 Pen-y-fai Brdgnd
128 C4 Pen-y-fai Carmth
128 D5 Pen-y-fan Carmth
134 C3 Pen-y-fan Mons
151 E4 Penyfeidr Pembks
307 G6 Pen-y-felin Flints
307 E4 Pen-y-ffordd Denbgs
288 D2 Penyffordd Flints
307 G3 Pen-y-ffordd Flints
283 F4 Penyffrid Gwynd
269 E5 Pen y Foel Powys
155 E3 Pen-y-garn Carmth
205 E2 Pen-y-garn Cerdgn
133 E4 Penygarn Torfn
304 B4 Pen-y-garnedd IoA
268 B5 Penygarnedd Powys
208 B1 Penygelli Powys
262 B4 Pen-y-graig Gwynd
105 F1 Penygraig Rhondd
303 F3 Penygraigwen IoA
129 E2 Pen-y-groes Carmth
283 E5 Penygroes Gwynd
152 D2 Penygroes Pembks
262 C4 Pen-y-groeslon Gwynd
106 C4 Pen-y-lan Cardif
107 E3 Pen-y-lan Newpt
105 F4 Pen-y-lan V Glam
308 A4 Pen-y-maes Flints
288 D2 Penymynydd Flints
185 E6 Pen-y-Park Herefs
151 G2 Penyraber Pembks
131 E5 Pen-yr-englyn Rhondd
105 E3 Pen-yr-heol Brdgnd
106 B2 Penyrheol Caerph
134 A2 Pen-yr-heol Mons
129 E5 Penyrheol Swans
133 E5 Penyrheol Torfn
105 H2 Pen-y-rhiw Rhondd
303 F2 Penysarn IoA
288 A4 Pen-y-stryt Denbgs
131 F4 Penywaun Rhondd
209 F4 Pen-y-wern Shrops
3 E4 Penzance Cnwll
188 D4 Peopleton Worcs
311 F5 Peover Heath Ches
93 F6 Peper Harow Surrey
271 E5 Peplow Shrops
39 E3 Peppercombe Devon
342 B4 Pepper Hill Calder
443 G1 Peppermoor Nthumb
146 C2 Pepper's Green Essex
444 D1 Perceton N Ayrs
540 A1 Percie Abers
5 G2 Percuil Cnwll
571 H2 Percyhorner Abers
406 A1 Percy Main N Tyne
34 D3 Perelle Guern
307 G4 Per-ffordd-llan Flints
89 G5 Perham Down Wilts
63 F2 Periton Somset
118 D3 Perivale Gt Lon
555 G3 Perkhill Abers
27 G4 Perkin's Village Devon
405 F4 Perkinsville Dur
316 B5 Perlethorpe Notts
7 E6 Perranarworthal Cnwll
7 E3 Perrancoombe Cnwll
3 F3 Perran Downs Cnwll
6 D3 Perranporth Cnwll
3 F4 Perranuthnoe Cnwll
7 E3 Perranwell Cnwll
7 E6 Perranwell Cnwll
7 E6 Perranwell Station Cnwll
7 E6 Perran Wharf Cnwll
7 E3 Perranzabuloe Cnwll
137 F3 Perrott's Brook Gloucs
237 G6 Perry Birm
26 D1 Perry Devon
101 E4 Perry Kent
213 G1 Perry Barr Birm
237 G6 Perry Beeches Birm
237 G6 Perry Common Birm
238 C4 Perry Crofts Staffs
212 D5 Perryfields Worcs
313 F3 Perryfoot Derbys
173 G5 Perry Green Essex
145 F1 Perry Green Herts
65 E4 Perry Green Somset
111 H2 Perry Green Wilts
86 C2 Perrymead BaNES
161 E4 Perrystone Hill Herefs
121 F5 Perry Street Kent
29 F1 Perry Street Somset
99 G3 Perrywood Kent
272 B4 Pershall Staffs
188 D5 Pershore Worcs
528 D1 Pert Angus
195 F1 Pertenhall Beds
512 C5 Perth P & K
131 G5 Perthcelyn Rhondd
269 G3 Perthy Shrops
160 D1 Perton Herefs
236 C5 Perton Staffs
58 C3 Pestalozzi Children's Village E Susx
99 G4 Pested Kent
244 B4 Peterborough C Pete
572 D7 Peterburn Highld
159 G2 Peterchurch Herefs
557 E4 Peterculter C Aber
571 L6 Peterhead Abers
396 B1 Peterlee Dur
468 B2 Petersburn N Lans
73 H5 Petersfield Hants
23 H5 Peter's Finger Devon
169 G6 Peter's Green Herts
39 G5 Peters Marland Devon
107 E3 Peterstone Wentlooge Newpt
106 A4 Peterston-super-Ely V Glam
160 D5 Peterstow Herefs
18 B2 Peter Tavy Devon
600 D4 Petertown Ork
6 D3 Peterville Cnwll
100 B5 Petham Kent
23 F5 Petherwin Gate Cnwll
39 H6 Petrockstowe Devon
194 B5 Petsoe End M Keyn
59 E4 Pett E Susx
201 G3 Pettaugh Suffk
82 B2 Pett Bottom Kent
100 C5 Pett Bottom Kent
79 F1 Petteridge Kent
469 F6 Pettinain S Lans
97 F2 Pettings Kent
202 B4 Pettistree Suffk
59 E4 Pett Level E Susx
42 D3 Petton Devon
270 A4 Petton Shrops
96 B1 Petts Wood Gt Lon
559 H2 Petty Abers
110 D2 Petty France S Glos
560 D5 Pettymuick Abers
255 E3 Pettywell Norfk
75 F5 Petworth W Susx
57 H4 Pevensey E Susx
57 G4 Pevensey Bay E Susx
11 E2 Peverell C Plym
89 E2 Pewsey Wilts
89 E2 Pewsey Wharf Wilts
310 C3 Pewterspear Warrtn
490 A4 Phantassie E Loth
602 E2 Pharays Park Ork
172 C5 Pharisee Green Essex
116 C2 Pheasants Bucks
116 C2 Pheasant's Hill Bucks
237 G5 Pheasey Wsall
188 D3 Phepson Worcs
406 A4 Philadelphia Sundld
38 C3 Philham Devon
451 E4 Philiphaugh Border
3 G2 Phillack Cnwll
7 G6 Philleigh Cnwll
132 B4 Phillip's Town Caerph
172 C6 Philpot End Essex
486 D4 Philpstoun W Loth
161 E4 Phocle Green Herefs
92 B3 Phoenix Green Hants
394 D4 Phoenix Row Dur
66 C4 Pibsbury Somset
154 B6 Pibwrlwyd Carmth
388 B5 Pica Cumb
329 G5 Piccadilly Rothm
238 C5 Piccadilly Warwks
226 B2 Piccadilly Corner Norfk
143 F3 Piccotts End Herts
330 B3 Pickburn Donc
188 B6 Picken End Worcs
373 E3 Pickering N York
405 E3 Pickering Nook Dur
528 C4 Pickerton Angus
49 F3 Picket Hill Hants
90 B5 Picket Piece Hants
49 F3 Picket Post Hants
214 D3 Pickford Covtry
214 D3 Pickford Green Covtry
370 C3 Pickhill N York
161 G4 Picklenash Gloucs
234 A5 Picklescott Shrops
341 G2 Pickles Hill Brad
325 F4 Pickley Green Wigan
310 D4 Pickmere Ches
43 G2 Pickney Somset
271 G5 Pickstock Wrekin
340 A5 Pickup Bank Bl w D
60 C3 Pickwell Devon
241 G2 Pickwell Leics
111 F5 Pickwick Wilts
341 H5 Pickwood Scar Calder
279 E3 Pickworth Lincs
242 D2 Pickworth Rutlnd
309 F5 Picton Ches
307 G3 Picton Flints
384 C3 Picton N York
66 C4 Pict's Hill Somset
56 C4 Piddinghoe E Susx
141 G6 Piddington Bucks
193 H4 Piddington Nhants
140 D1 Piddington Oxon
46 D5 Piddlehinton Dorset
220 D4 Pidley Cambs
46 D3 Pidney Dorset
6 C6 Piece Cnwll
187 E2 Pie Corner Herefs
383 E1 Piercebridge Darltn
145 G5 Piercing Hill Essex
602 E2 Pierowall Ork
162 D4 Piff's Elm Gloucs
430 C2 Pigdon Nthumb
64 D4 Pightley Somset
48 C4 Pig Oak Dorset
146 C3 Pigstye Green Essex
341 G6 Pike End Calder
293 G3 Pikehall Derbys
340 D3 Pike Hill Lancs
327 F1 Pike Law Calder
50 A3 Pikeshill Hants
186 C5 Pikestye Herefs
48 C4 Pilford Dorset
146 B5 Pilgrims Hatch Essex
332 B6 Pilham Lincs
294 A1 Pilhough Derbys
109 F4 Pill N Som
125 F3 Pill Pembks
17 E6 Pillaton Cnwll
236 D2 Pillaton Staffs
191 E5 Pillerton Hersey Warwks
190 D5 Pillerton Priors Warwks
209 E6 Pilleth Powys
329 E4 Pilley Barns
163 E6 Pilley Gloucs
50 B5 Pilley Hants
50 B5 Pilley Bailey Hants
107 F2 Pillgwenlly Newpt
351 F5 Pilling Lancs
351 E5 Pilling Lane Lancs
39 G3 Pillmouth Devon
135 E3 Pillowell Gloucs
162 A4 Pillows Green Gloucs
68 C6 Pillwell Dorset
439 F2 Pilmuir Border
567 J5 Pilmuir Moray
109 G2 Pilning S Glos
488 B4 Pilrig C Edin
293 F2 Pilsbury Derbys
29 H3 Pilsdon Dorset
243 F3 Pilsgate C Pete
295 E2 Pilsley Derbys
314 A5 Pilsley Derbys
295 E2 Pilsley Green Derbys
250 D2 Pilson Green Norfk
78 A5 Piltdown E Susx
488 A4 Pilton C Edin
60 D5 Pilton Devon
219 E3 Pilton Nhants
242 C4 Pilton Rutlnd
67 F1 Pilton Somset
102 B4 Pilton Green Swans
67 F2 Piltown Somset
326 B2 Pimhole Bury
119 F4 Pimlico Gt Lon
143 F3 Pimlico Herts
353 F6 Pimlico Lancs
45 H6 Pimperne Dorset
47 G3 Pimperne Dorset
280 B4 Pinchbeck Lincs
280 B5 Pinchbeck West Lincs
331 E1 Pincheon Green Donc
385 F2 Pinchinthorpe R & Cl
87 E2 Pinckney Green Wilts
338 D6 Pincock Lancs
83 F1 Pineham Kent
168 B1 Pineham M Keyn
112 D2 Pinehurst Swindn
136 B4 Pinfarthings Gloucs
323 G2 Pinfold Lancs
328 D4 Pinfold Hill Barns
168 C3 Pinfoldpond Beds
199 H3 Pinford End Suffk
128 B4 Pinged Carmth
116 A6 Pingewood W Berk
170 B4 Pin Green Herts
27 F4 Pinhoe Devon
214 D3 Pinkett's Booth Covtry
213 G6 Pink Green Worcs
488 D5 Pinkie Braes E Loth
111 F2 Pinkney Wilts
116 D3 Pinkneys Green W & M
43 F4 Pinksmoor Somset
190 C1 Pinley Green Warwks
419 F4 Pinmore S Ayrs
145 F3 Pinnacles Essex
118 C2 Pinner Gt Lon
118 C1 Pinner Green Gt Lon
118 C1 Pinnerwood Park Gt Lon
188 B5 Pin's Green Worcs
290 B5 Pinsley Green Ches
210 B2 Pinstones Shrops
188 D5 Pinvin Worcs
239 E4 Pinwall Leics
419 E4 Pinwherry S Ayrs
295 E4 Pinxton Derbys
186 C6 Pipe and Lyde Herefs
210 B5 Pipe Aston Herefs
271 G1 Pipe Gate Shrops
237 G3 Pipehill Staffs
86 D3 Pipehouse BaNES
566 F6 Piperhill Highld
273 G6 Pipe Ridware Staffs
309 F6 Piper's Ash Ches
162 B3 Piper's End Worcs
189 E2 Piper's Hill Worcs
23 F6 Pipers Pool Cnwll
218 A2 Pipewell Nhants
60 D4 Pippacott Devon
339 E5 Pippin Street Lancs
121 G2 Pipps Hill Essex
79 H3 Pipsden Kent
93 F3 Pirbright Surrey
93 F3 Pirbright Camp Surrey
463 E6 Pirnmill N Ayrs
169 H3 Pirton Herts
188 C5 Pirton Worcs
205 F4 Pisgah Cerdgn
498 B4 Pisgah Stirlg
116 B2 Pishill Oxon
116 B1 Pishill Bank Oxon
314 D1 Pismire Hill Sheff
263 E2 Pistyll Gwynd
133 G3 Pit Mons
524 B2 Pitagowan P & K
571 H2 Pitblae Abers
512 C4 Pitcairngreen P & K
566 E2 Pitcalnie Highld
559 G4 Pitcaple Abers
136 B3 Pitchcombe Gloucs
167 G5 Pitchcott Bucks
200 B3 Pitcher's Green Suffk
234 C4 Pitchford Shrops
141 G4 Pitch Green Bucks
74 D2 Pitch Place Surrey
93 G4 Pitch Place Surrey
68 A3 Pitcombe Somset
487 F2 Pitcorthie Fife
86 B5 Pitcot Somset
104 D5 Pitcot V Glam
490 B4 Pitcox E Loth
513 F2 Pitcur P & K

514 B3 **Pitempton** C Dund
556 B1 **Pitfichie** Abers
541 F4 **Pitforthie** Abers
577 G5 **Pitgrudy** Highld
528 B4 **Pitkennedy** Angus
501 F3 **Pitlessie** Fife
524 D4 **Pitlochry** P & K
566 D1 **Pitmaduthy** Highld
560 C4 **Pitmedden** Abers
43 H4 **Pitminster** Somset
528 C5 **Pitmuies** Angus
556 B1 **Pitmunie** Abers
66 D4 **Pitney** Somset
514 B2 **Pitpointie** Angus
527 G5 **Pitreuchie** Angus
502 C2 **Pitscottie** Fife
122 A2 **Pitsea** Essex
326 D4 **Pitses** Oldham
217 G6 **Pitsford** Nhants
64 B5 **Pitsford Hill** Somset
314 D2 **Pitsmoor** Sheff
142 C1 **Pitstone** Bucks
142 C2 **Pitstone Hill** Bucks
72 C4 **Pitt** Hants
135 H5 **Pitt Court** Gloucs
568 B3 **Pittendreich** Moray
576 F3 **Pittentrail** Highld
503 F4 **Pittenweem** Fife
501 E5 **Pitteuchar** Fife
406 A6 **Pittington** Dur
102 B4 **Pitton** Swans
71 E3 **Pitton** Wilts
291 H4 **Pitts Hill** C Stke
571 H2 **Pittulie** Abers
162 D5 **Pittville** Gloucs
14 C3 **Pityme** Cnwll
405 G5 **Pity Me** Dur
226 A4 **Pixey Green** Suffk
188 B5 **Pixham** Worcs
161 F2 **Pixley** Herefs
271 F4 **Pixley** Herefs
97 G4 **Pizien Well** Kent
373 G5 **Place Newton** N York
570 C5 **Plaidy** Abers
9 H3 **Plaidy** Cnwll
3 F3 **Plain-an-Gwarry** Cnwll
6 C5 **Plain-an-Gwarry** Cnwll
152 B6 **Plain Dealings** Pembks
468 B1 **Plains** N Lans
64 C4 **Plainsfield** Somset
295 H4 **Plain Spot** Notts
14 D3 **Plain Street** Cnwll
234 C5 **Plaish** Shrops
120 A3 **Plaistow** Gt Lon
120 A5 **Plaistow** Gt Lon
75 G3 **Plaistow** W Susx
173 G4 **Plaistow Green** Essex
71 F6 **Plaitford** Wilts
71 F5 **Plaitford Green** Hants
325 E4 **Plank Lane** Wigan
379 E5 **Plantation Bridge** Cumb
437 F6 **Plantationfoot** D & G
272 B5 **Plardiwick** Staffs
269 G5 **Plasau** Shrops
288 A6 **Plâs Berwyn** Denbgs
288 D4 **Plas Coch** Wrexhm
207 G2 **Plas Dinam** Powys
154 C4 **Plas Fawr** Carmth
205 E3 **Plas Gogerddan** Cerdgn
284 D4 **Plas Gwynant** Gwynd
128 B3 **Plashet** Gt Lon
127 F3 **Plashett** Carmth
232 A4 **Plasiolyn** Powys
230 B4 **Plas Llwyngwern** Powys
231 E5 **Plas Llysyn** Powys
232 C5 **Plas Meredydd** Powys
268 C2 **Plas Nantyr** Wrexhm
231 F5 **Plasnewydd** Powys
303 G5 **Plas Penmynydd** IoA
85 F2 **Plaster's Green** BaNES
91 E2 **Plastow Green** Hants
97 F3 **Platt** Kent
325 E4 **Platt Bridge** Wigan
270 C2 **Platt Lane** Shrops
329 F4 **Platts Common** Barns
98 D4 **Platt's Heath** Kent
405 G5 **Plawsworth** Dur
97 F4 **Plaxtol** Kent
59 F2 **Playden** E Susx
201 H5 **Playford** Suffk
116 B4 **Play Hatch** Oxon
7 F5 **Playing Place** Cnwll
161 H3 **Playley Green** Gloucs
234 A3 **Plealey** Shrops
43 F4 **Pleamore Cross** Somset
485 G2 **Plean** Stirlg
126 C3 **Pleasant Valley** Pembks
339 F4 **Pleasington** Bl w D
295 H3 **Pleasley** Derbys
295 G2 **Pleasleyhill** Notts
46 D2 **Pleck** Dorset
68 C6 **Pleck** Dorset
237 E5 **Pleck** Wsall
339 G3 **Pleckgate** Bl w D
47 E4 **Pleck or Little Ansty** Dorset
172 B4 **Pledgdon Green** Essex
329 E1 **Pledwick** Wakefd
35 d2 **Pleinheaume** Guern
35 f5 **Plemont** Jersey
309 G5 **Plemstall** Ches
440 D2 **Plenderleith** Border
402 C2 **Plenmeller** Nthumb
146 D2 **Pleshey** Essex
546 E3 **Plockton** Highld
595 K4 **Plocrapol** W Isls
67 E3 **Plot Gate** Somset
67 E2 **Plot Street** Somset
239 E6 **Plough Hill** Warwks
209 G2 **Plowden** Shrops
233 G4 **Ploxgreen** Shrops
99 E5 **Pluckley** Kent
99 E6 **Pluckley Thorne** Kent
101 E3 **Plucks Gutter** Kent
389 E2 **Plumbland** Cumb
315 E3 **Plumbley** Sheff
99 F3 **Plumford** Kent
311 E4 **Plumley** Ches
135 F1 **Plump Hill** Gloucs
390 D2 **Plumpton** Cumb
56 B2 **Plumpton** E Susx
337 G3 **Plumpton** Lancs
193 F5 **Plumpton** Nhants
390 D2 **Plumpton End** Nhants
56 B1 **Plumpton Foot** Cumb
391 E2 **Plumpton Green** E Susx
120 B4 **Plumpton Head** Cumb
261 F5 **Plumstead** Gt Lon
120 B4 **Plumstead** Norfk
261 F5 **Plumstead Common** Gt Lon
261 F5 **Plumstead Green** Norfk
276 D3 **Plumtree** Notts
98 C5 **Plumtree Green** Kent
276 D3 **Plumtree Park** Notts
277 G3 **Plungar** Leics
16 C3 **Plusha** Cnwll
16 D4 **Plush** Dorset
16 D4 **Plush** Dorset
4 D5 **Plushabridge** Cnwll
9 H3 **Plwmp** Cerdgn
1 E2 **Plymouth** C Plym
1 F2 **Plympton** C Plym
1 F3 **Plymstock** C Plym

27 G2 **Plymtree** Devon
327 F3 **Pobgreen** Oldham
132 C3 **Pochin Houses** Blae G
325 E5 **Pocket Nook** Wigan
372 B2 **Pockley** N York
359 F5 **Pocklington** E R Yk
248 B5 **Pockthorpe** Norfk
253 G2 **Pockthorpe** Norfk
254 D3 **Pockthorpe** Norfk
255 E4 **Pockthorpe** Norfk
280 B5 **Pode Hole** Lincs
67 E5 **Podimore** Somset
194 C2 **Podington** Beds
212 C5 **Podmoor** Worcs
254 C5 **Podmore** Norfk
272 A2 **Podmore** Staffs
136 B1 **Poffley End** Oxon
139 F2 **Pogmoor** Barns
329 E3 **Point Clear** Essex
149 E1 **Point Clear** Essex
279 C3 **Pointon** Lincs
34 D2 **Pokesdown** Bmouth
590 E5 **Pol a' Charra** W Isls
416 B2 **Polbae** D & G
10 B2 **Polbathic** Cnwll
469 G2 **Polbeth** W Loth
17 E6 **Polbrock** Cnwll
15 E5 **Polborder** Cnwll
437 E4 **Polbrook** Cnwll
219 F2 **Polebrook** Nhants
188 B5 **Pole Elm** Worcs
57 F4 **Polegate** E Susx
327 G1 **Pole Moor** Kirk
577 G5 **Poles** Highld
43 E3 **Poleshill** Somset
87 E4 **Pole's Hole** Wilts
238 D4 **Polesworth** Warwks
4 C1 **Polgear** Cnwll
2 C5 **Polgigga** Cnwll
573 K2 **Polglass** Highld
8 B3 **Polgooth** Cnwll
54 B4 **Poling** W Susx
54 B3 **Poling Corner** W Susx
8 D3 **Polkerris** Cnwll
585 G6 **Polla** Highld
4 B2 **Polladras** Cnwll
172 C2 **Pollards Cross** Essex
256 C3 **Pollard Street** Norfk
98 D4 **Pollhill** Kent
308 C3 **Poll Hill** Wirral
345 E6 **Pollington** E R Yk
519 J2 **Polloch** Highld
466 D2 **Pollok** C Glas
467 E2 **Pollokshaws** C Glas
467 E2 **Pollokshields** C Glas
542 B7 **Pollosgan** Highld
467 E2 **Polmadie** C Glas
549 H3 **Polmaily** Highld
4 D1 **Polmarth** Cnwll
8 D3 **Polmassick** Cnwll
486 B4 **Polmont** Falk
14 D4 **Polmorla** Cnwll
433 F2 **Polnessan** E Ayrs
531 K6 **Polnish** Highld
219 E4 **Polopit** Nhants
4 D3 **Polpenwith** Cnwll
9 G3 **Polperro** Cnwll
9 E3 **Polruan** Cnwll
85 F6 **Polsham** Somset
434 D4 **Polskeoch** D & G
27 E4 **Polsloe** Devon
174 C2 **Polstead** Suffk
174 C1 **Polstead Heath** Suffk
492 D5 **Poltalloch** Ag & B
4 D5 **Poltesco** Cnwll
27 F3 **Poltimore** Devon
471 E1 **Polton** Mdloth
473 G4 **Polwarth** Border
4 D3 **Polwheveral** Cnwll
16 C2 **Polyphant** Cnwll
14 C3 **Polzeath** Cnwll
470 D3 **Pomathorn** Mdloth
313 F6 **Pomeroy** Derbys
11 F3 **Pomphlett** C Plym
288 C5 **Ponciau** Wrexhm
43 F2 **Pond Close** Somset
158 B2 **Ponde** Powys
220 B1 **Pondersbridge** Cambs
145 E5 **Ponders End** Gt Lon
142 D4 **Pond Park** Bucks
171 G2 **Pond Street** Essex
37 G2 **Pondwell** IoW
2 D2 **Poniou** Cnwll
4 D3 **Ponjeravah** Cnwll
4 D1 **Ponsanooth** Cnwll
42 C6 **Ponsford** Devon
376 C3 **Ponsonby** Cumb
5 E5 **Ponsongath** Cnwll
19 F3 **Ponsworthy** Devon
9 E3 **Pont** Cnwll
35 j8 **Pontac** Jersey
129 F2 **Pontamman** Carmth
128 B2 **Pontantwn** Carmth
129 G4 **Pontardawe** Swans
129 E4 **Pontarddulais** Swans
154 D5 **Pont-ar-gothi** Carmth
156 D3 **Pont ar Hydfer** Powys
156 A5 **Pont-ar-llechau** Carmth
154 B4 **Pontarsais** Carmth
288 C2 **Pontblyddyn** Flints
155 G5 **Pontbren Araeth** Carmth
106 C4 **Pontcanna** Cardif
180 D4 **Pont Creuddyn** Cerdgn
230 D5 **Pont Crugnant** Powys
285 F3 **Pont Cyfyng** Conwy
269 E1 **Pont Cysyllte** Denbgs
231 G6 **Pontdolgoch** Powys
344 B5 **Pontefract** Wakefd
430 C5 **Ponteland** Nthumb
205 G3 **Ponterwyd** Cerdgn
233 H3 **Pontesbury** Shrops
233 G3 **Pontesbury Hill** Shrops
233 H3 **Pontesford** Shrops
268 D2 **Pontfadog** Wrexhm
151 H3 **Pontfaen** Pembks
157 F3 **Pont-faen** Powys
269 E2 **Pont-Faen** Shrops
179 G3 **Pontgarreg** Cerdgn
233 F1 **Ponthen** Shrops
128 C3 **Pont Henri** Carmth
133 F6 **Ponthir** Torfn
179 H4 **Ponthirwaun** Cerdgn
302 B4 **Pont Hwfa** IoA
151 F2 **Pontiago** Pembks
158 C2 **Pontithel** Powys
129 F4 **Pontlianfraith** Caerph
231 C1 **Pontliw** Swans
282 D5 **Pontllyfni** Gwynd
132 B3 **Pontlottyn** Caerph
131 E3 **Pontneddfechan** Powys
128 B3 **Pont-newydd** Carmth
288 A1 **Pont-newydd** Flints
133 E5 **Pontnewydd** Torfn
133 E6 **Pontnewynydd** Torfn
284 D2 **Pont Pen-y-benglog** Conwy
182 A1 **Pontrhydfendigaid** Cerdgn
206 C3 **Pont Rhydgaled** Powys
157 F2 **Pont Rhyd-y-berry** Powys
104 D2 **Pont Rhyd-y-cyff** Brdgnd

130 B6 **Pontrhydyfen** Neath
205 G5 **Pont-rhyd-y-groes** Cerdgn
133 E5 **Pontrhydyrun** Torfn
283 F3 **Pont-Rhythallt** Gwynd
159 H4 **Pontrilas** Herefs
232 A2 **Pontrobert** Powys
283 F3 **Pont-rug** Gwynd
57 H1 **Ponts Green** E Susx
161 E5 **Pontshill** Herefs
180 B5 **Pont-Siân** Cerdgn
106 A1 **Pont Siôn Norton** Rhondd
131 G2 **Pontsticill** Myr Td
130 D3 **Pont-Walby** Neath
128 C3 **Pontyates** Carmth
128 C3 **Pontyberem** Carmth
105 G3 **Pontybodkin** Flints
288 C3 **Pont-y-blew** Flints
104 D1 **Pontyclun** Rhondd
152 C2 **Pontycymer** Brdgnd
131 G6 **Pontyglasier** Pembks
106 D1 **Pontygwaith** Rhondd
133 E4 **Pontymister** Caerph
285 F4 **Pontymoel** Torfn
133 E4 **Pont-y-pant** Conwy
105 G2 **Pontypool** Torfn
151 F4 **Pontypridd** Rhondd
105 G3 **Pont-yr-hafod** Pembks
287 F2 **Pont-y-rhyl** Brdgnd
158 B2 **Pont-Ystrad** Denbgs
132 D6 **Pont-y-wal** Powys
50 C2 **Pontywaun** Caerph
6 C5 **Pool** Cnwll
3 c2 **Pool** IoS
356 A6 **Pool** Leeds
188 A6 **Poolbrook** Worcs
573 G7 **Pool Crofts** Highld
344 B4 **Poole** N York
34 B3 **Poole** Poole
43 F3 **Poole** Somset
292 C3 **Poolend** Staffs
46 D1 **Poolestown** Dorset
572 F7 **Poolewe** Highld
390 D5 **Pooley Bridge** Cumb
225 E3 **Pooley Street** Norfk
292 A3 **Poolfold** Staffs
186 C4 **Pool Head** Herefs
270 B3 **Poolhead** Shrops
323 G1 **Pool Hey** Lancs
161 G4 **Poolhill** Gloucs
160 D5 **Poolmill** Herefs
499 F4 **Pool of Muckhart** Clacks
233 E2 **Pool Quay** Powys
315 E5 **Poolsbrook** Derbys
324 D4 **Poolstock** Wigan
63 F4 **Pooltown** Somset
96 C5 **Pootings** Kent
125 F2 **Pope Hill** Pembks
135 F2 **Pope's Hill** Gloucs
116 D6 **Popeswood** Br For
61 H5 **Popham** Devon
91 F6 **Popham** Hants
119 H3 **Poplar** Gt Lon
335 F5 **Poplar Grove** Lincs
170 C5 **Poplars** Herts
91 G4 **Popley** Hants
66 C4 **Porchester** Notts
66 D2 **Porchfield** IoW
213 G5 **Poringland** Norfk
162 A3 **Porkellis** Cnwll
476 B6 **Porlock** Somset
409 G3 **Porlockford** Somset
312 B1 **Porlock Weir** Somset
10 C3 **Portachoillan** Ag & B
546 D3 **Port-an-eorna** Highld
480 C2 **Port Ann** Ag & B
520 C6 **Port Appin** Ag & B
605 G4 **Port Arthur** Shet
69 G3 **Portash** Wilts
478 C8 **Port Askaig** Ag & B
480 C6 **Portavadie** Ag & B
481 F6 **Port Bannatyne** Ag & B
488 B1 **Port Brae** Cnwll
20 B6 **Port Bridge** Devon
109 F5 **Portbury** N Som
399 G2 **Port Carlisle** Cumb
476 D5 **Port Charlotte** Ag & B
51 G3 **Portchester** Hants
549 G7 **Portclair** Highld
396 C5 **Port Clarence** S on T
480 D5 **Port Driseach** Ag & B
467 E1 **Port Dundas** C Glas
14 D3 **Porteath** Cnwll
487 F4 **Port Edgar** C Edin
476 F7 **Port Ellen** Ag & B
559 H6 **Port Elphinstone** Abers
414 D2 **Portencalzie** D & G
464 D5 **Portencross** N Ayrs
466 C1 **Porterfield** Rens
322 b9 **Port Erin** IoM
561 G2 **Porter's End** Herts
143 H1 **Porter's End** Herts
30 D5 **Portesham** Dorset
569 G2 **Portessie** Moray
322 h4 **Port e Vullen** IoM
102 C4 **Port-Eynon** Swans
66 C4 **Portfield** Somset
53 F4 **Portfield** W Susx
125 F1 **Portfield Gate** Pembks
24 B5 **Portgate** Devon
15 E2 **Port Gaverne** Cnwll
482 D4 **Port Glasgow** Inver
568 F3 **Portgordon** Moray
582 C7 **Portgower** Highld
14 A6 **Porth** Cnwll
105 G1 **Porth** Rhondd
5 E4 **Porthallow** Cnwll
9 G3 **Porthallow** Cnwll
104 B4 **Porthcawl** Brdgnd
262 B4 **Porth Colmon** Gwynd
14 A4 **Porthcothan** Cnwll
2 C5 **Porthcurno** Cnwll
150 D3 **Portheiddy** Pembks
562 C2 **Port Henderson** Highld
150 D3 **Porthgain** Pembks
2 C5 **Porthgwarra** Cnwll
116 A2 **Port Hill** Oxon
234 B2 **Port Hill** Shrops
14 C3 **Porthilly** Cnwll
7 F5 **Porth Kea** Cnwll
106 A6 **Porthkerry** V Glam
4 B3 **Porthleven** Cnwll
303 F2 **Porthllechog** IoA
3 c2 **Portholoo** IoS
264 C2 **Porthmadog** Gwynd
2 D2 **Porthmeor** Cnwll
4 D3 **Porth Navas** Cnwll
5 F4 **Porthoustock** Cnwll
6 C4 **Porthtowan** Cnwll
302 B4 **Porth-y-felin** IoA
128 D1 **Porthyrhyd** Carmth
155 H2 **Porthyrhyd** Carmth
268 D5 **Porth-y-waen** Shrops
324 B6 **Portico** St Hel
495 E6 **Portincaple** Ag & B
35 f5 **Portinfer** Jersey
17 F3 **Portington** Jersey
346 A3 **Portington** E R Yk
493 G2 **Portinnisherrich** Ag & B
389 F5 **Portinscale** Cumb
14 D2 **Port Isaac** Cnwll
108 D4 **Portishead** N Som
482 C3 **Portkil** Ag & B
569 H2 **Portknockie** Moray

90 D2 **Pound Street** Hants
78 C5 **Pounsley** E Susx
411 E3 **Pouton** D & G
120 C6 **Poverest** Gt Lon
77 E1 **Povey Cross** Surrey
442 D1 **Powburn** Nthumb
27 F6 **Powderham** Devon
97 E5 **Powder Mills** Kent
147 F1 **Powers Hall End** Essex
30 C3 **Powerstock** Dorset
399 E3 **Powfoot** D & G
187 F6 **Pow Green** Herefs
399 G3 **Powhill** Cumb
188 B4 **Powick** Worcs
39 E4 **Powler's Piece** Devon
499 G5 **Powmill** P & K
311 G3 **Pownall Park** Ches
32 C3 **Powntley Copse** Hants
32 C3 **Poxwell** Dorset
117 H4 **Poyle** Slough
75 J4 **Poynings** W Susx
67 G6 **Poyntington** Dorset
312 B3 **Poynton** Ches
270 D6 **Poynton** Wrekin
270 D6 **Poynton Green** Wrekin
151 E6 **Poyston** Pembks
151 G6 **Poyston Cross** Pembks
200 C3 **Poystreet Green** Suffk
3 G4 **Praa Sands** Cnwll
543 G7 **Prabost** Highld
98 A3 **Pratling Street** Kent
96 C2 **Pratt's Bottom** Gt Lon
4 B1 **Praze-an-Beeble** Cnwll
270 D3 **Prees** Shrops
351 E5 **Preesall** Lancs
351 E5 **Preesall Park** Lancs
270 D3 **Prees Green** Shrops
269 E2 **Preesgweene** Shrops
270 D2 **Prees Heath** Shrops
269 F3 **Preeshenlle** Shrops
270 D2 **Prees Higher Heath** Shrops
270 D3 **Prees Lower Heath** Shrops
270 D3 **Prees Wood** Shrops
288 C2 **Prenbrigog** Flints
125 G1 **Prendergast** Pembks
150 C5 **Prendergast** Pembks
474 D3 **Prenderguest** Border
442 C2 **Prendwick** Nthumb
180 B6 **Pren-gwyn** Cerdgn
264 D1 **Prenteg** Gwynd
308 D2 **Prenton** Wirral
309 G1 **Prescot** St Hel
43 E5 **Prescott** Devon
163 E4 **Prescott** Gloucs
211 F3 **Prescott** Shrops
270 A5 **Prescott** Shrops
569 G3 **Preshome** Moray
526 A1 **Presnerb** Angus
294 D1 **Press** Derbys
453 F2 **Pressen** Nthumb
307 F3 **Prestatyn** Denbgs
312 A4 **Prestbury** Ches
163 E4 **Prestbury** Gloucs
185 F2 **Presteigne** Powys
234 C5 **Presthope** Shrops
67 G1 **Prestleigh** Somset
325 F1 **Prestolee** Bolton
474 A3 **Preston** Border
55 H3 **Preston** Br & H
32 B3 **Preston** Dorset
488 D5 **Preston** E Loth
490 A4 **Preston** E Loth
348 C3 **Preston** E R Yk
137 F4 **Preston** Gloucs
161 F3 **Preston** Gloucs
118 D2 **Preston** Gt Lon
169 H5 **Preston** Herts
99 G2 **Preston** Kent
101 E3 **Preston** Kent
339 E4 **Preston** Lancs
455 F4 **Preston** Nthumb
431 F6 **Preston** N Tyne
242 B4 **Preston** Rutlnd
20 B3 **Preston** Torbay
20 B5 **Preston** Torbay
112 B4 **Preston** Wilts
113 G5 **Preston** Wilts
190 B1 **Preston Bagot** Warwks
167 E4 **Preston Bissett** Bucks
43 F2 **Preston Bowyer** Somset
270 C5 **Preston Brockhurst** Shrops
310 B3 **Preston Brook** Halton
73 F1 **Preston Candover** Hants
192 C4 **Preston Capes** Nhants
115 G1 **Preston Crowmarsh** Oxon
193 G3 **Preston Deanery** Nhants
488 B5 **Prestonfield** C Edin
190 B1 **Preston Fields** Warwks
431 F5 **Preston Grange** N Tyne
190 B1 **Preston Green** Warwks
270 B6 **Preston Gubbals** Shrops
395 G5 **Preston-le-Skerne** Dur
186 C5 **Preston Marsh** Herefs
398 B3 **Prestonmill** D & G
233 H2 **Preston Montford** Shrops
190 B5 **Preston on Stour** Warwks
384 C1 **Preston-on-Tees** S on T
310 B3 **Preston on the Hill** Halton
159 G1 **Preston on Wye** Herefs
488 D5 **Prestonpans** E Loth
45 G4 **Preston Plucknett** Somset
200 B4 **Preston St Mary** Suffk
369 E1 **Preston-under-Scar** N York
235 F1 **Preston upon the Weald Moors** Wrekin
186 D5 **Preston Wynne** Herefs
326 A3 **Prestwich** Bury
430 C5 **Prestwick** Nthumb
444 D4 **Prestwick** S Ayrs
276 C5 **Prestwold** Leics
142 C5 **Prestwood** Bucks
212 C2 **Prestwood** Staffs
273 H1 **Prestwood** Staffs
93 G3 **Prey Heath** Surrey
105 F3 **Price Town** Brdgnd
222 B3 **Prickwillow** Cambs
85 F3 **Priddy** Somset
24 B1 **Priestacott** Devon
313 G5 **Priestcliffe** Derbys
313 G5 **Priestcliffe Ditch** Derbys
85 H2 **Priest Down** BaNES
236 D5 **Priestfield** Wolves
188 B6 **Priestfield** Worcs
439 F4 **Priesthaugh** Border
466 C2 **Priesthill** C Glas
366 A5 **Priest Hutton** Lancs
446 B2 **Priestland** E Ayrs
384 B4 **Priestley Green** Calder
72 B3 **Prieston** Border
399 E1 **Priestside** D & G
233 E5 **Priest Weston** Shrops
117 E6 **Priestwood** Br For
97 F2 **Priestwood** Kent
240 B6 **Priestwood Green** Kent
240 A3 **Primethorpe** Leics
105 E4 **Primrose** Cumbr
250 C2 **Primrose Corner** Norfk
255 E4 **Primrose Green** Norfk
85 C1 **Primrose Hill** BaNES
212 D2 **Primrose Hill** Dudley
119 F3 **Primrose Hill** Gt Lon

City, town and village index: Primrose Valley - Rhewl 711

375 E4 Primrose Valley N York
188 C2 Primsland Worcs
291 E6 Prince Hill Ches
513 F1 Princeland P & K
342 B6 Prince Royd Kirk
237 E6 Princes End Sandw
126 C2 Princes Gate Pembks
74 B4 Prince's Marsh Hants
309 E2 Princes Park Lpool
141 H4 Princes Risborough Bucks
215 G5 Princethorpe Warwks
193 E3 Princetown Caerph
18 C3 Princetown Devon
52 D3 Prinsted W Susx
96 D6 Printstile Kent
287 F2 Prion Denbgs
503 E2 Prior Muir Fife
475 E4 Prior Park Nthumb
426 C6 Prior Rigg Cumb
160 D2 Prior's Frome Herefs
210 B4 Priors Halton Shrops
191 H3 Priors Hardwick Warwks
235 G2 Priorslee Wrekin
192 A3 Priors Marston Warwks
162 C5 Prior's Norton Gloucs
162 C3 Priors Park Gloucs
44 A2 Priorswood Somset
125 E3 Priory Pembks
200 B6 Priory Green Suffk
201 G6 Priory Heath Suffk
185 E5 Priory Wood Herefs
105 G4 Prisk V Glam
40 A2 Pristacott Devon
86 B2 Priston BaNES
225 F2 Pristow Green Norfk
122 D2 Prittlewell Sthend
51 G5 Privett Hants
73 G4 Privett Hants
60 D4 Prixford Devon
7 G4 Probus Cnwll
577 G5 Proncy Highld
388 D1 Prospect Cumb
237 F2 Prospect Village Staffs
4 B2 Prospidnick Cnwll
467 F1 Provanmill C Glas
8 A1 Providence Cnwll
26 C1 Prowse Devon
404 C2 Prudhoe Nthumb
3 G4 Prussia Cove Cnwll
86 A2 Publow BaNES
171 E6 Puckeridge Herts
66 B6 Puckington Somset
110 B4 Pucklechurch S Glos
72 A5 Pucknall Hants
162 C2 Puckrup Gloucs
136 B3 Puckshole Gloucs
19 G5 Puddaven Devon
311 E6 Puddinglake Ches
338 D2 Pudding Pie Nook Lancs
308 D5 Puddington Ches
41 G5 Puddington Devon
8 D2 Puddle Cnwll
44 C5 Puddlebridge Somset
96 C4 Puddledock Kent
120 D5 Puddledock Kent
225 E1 Puddledock Norfk
46 D6 Puddletown Dorset
44 C5 Pudleigh Somset
186 D3 Pudleston Herefs
341 E4 Pudsey Calder
342 D3 Pudsey Leeds
75 G6 Pulborough W Susx
342 A4 Pule Hill Calder
271 G5 Puleston Wrekin
289 E3 Pulford Ches
46 C3 Pulham Dorset
225 G2 Pulham Market Norfk
225 H2 Pulham St Mary Norfk
109 H1 Pullens Green S Glos
234 B3 Pulley Shrops
80 B3 Pullington Kent
169 F3 Pulloxhill Beds
506 E4 Pulpit Hill Ag & B
234 A4 Pulverbatch Shrops
487 E6 Pumpherston W Loth
155 G1 Pumsaint Carmth
151 H4 Puncheston Pembks
30 C5 Puncknowle Dorset
79 E5 Punnett's Town E Susx
52 B3 Purbrook Hants
49 F6 Purewell Dorset
121 E4 Purfleet Thurr
65 F3 Puriton Somset
147 G4 Purleigh Essex
95 G2 Purley Gt Lon
115 G4 Purley on Thames W Berk
549 K2 Purlie Lodge Highld
209 E4 Purlogue Shrops
87 F1 Purlpit Wilts
221 G2 Purls Bridge Cambs
84 B3 Purn N Som
68 A6 Purse Caundle Dorset
209 G3 Purslow Shrops
344 A6 Purston Jaglin Wakefd
44 D6 Purtington Somset
135 F4 Purton Gloucs
114 D4 Purton W Berk
112 C2 Purton Wilts
112 C2 Purton Common Wilts
112 C1 Purton Stoke Wilts
170 B4 Purwell Herts
193 F5 Pury End Nhants
139 F5 Pusey Oxon
161 E2 Putley Herefs
161 E2 Putley Common Herefs
161 F2 Putley Green Herefs
136 A3 Putloe Gloucs
119 E5 Putney Gt Lon
195 F4 Putnoe Beds
60 B3 Putsborough Devon
160 C2 Putson Herefs
142 B2 Puttenham Herts
93 F5 Puttenham Surrey
173 F1 Puttock End Essex
172 B5 Puttock's End Essex
32 A3 Putton Dorset
47 E2 Puxey Dorset
167 G1 Puxley Nhants
84 D2 Puxton N Som
128 C4 Pwll Carmth
232 C4 Pwll Powys
308 A5 Pwll-clai Flints
125 F4 Pwllcrochan Pembks
287 G4 Pwll-glâs Denbgs
157 G3 Pwllgloyw Powys
263 F4 Pwllheli Gwynd
106 D4 Pwll-Mawr Cardif
308 A5 Pwll-melyn Flints
109 F1 Pwllmeyric Mons
127 F1 Pwll-trap Carmth
130 B6 Pwll-y-glaw Neath
106 C2 Pwllypant Caerph
295 E4 Pye Bridge Derbys
55 G2 Pyecombe W Susx
27 E3 Pye Corner Devon
98 D5 Pye Corner Kent
107 F2 Pye Corner Newpt
110 A4 Pye Corner S Glos
212 E2 Pye Green Staffs
295 E4 Pye Hill Notts
334 B2 Pyewipe NE Lin
104 C3 Pyle Brdgnd
36 D5 Pyle IoW
103 E4 Pyle Swans
72 C6 Pylehill Hants
93 G3 Pyle Hill Surrey
64 B5 Pyleigh Somset
67 G2 Pylle Somset
221 G2 Pymoor Cambs
30 B4 Pymore Dorset
213 H1 Pype Hayes Birm
93 H3 Pyrford Surrey
94 A3 Pyrford Green Surrey
94 A3 Pyrford Village Surrey
44 A2 Pyrland Somset
141 E5 Pyrton Oxon
218 B5 Pytchley Nhants
23 G2 Pyworthy Devon

Q

208 D3 Quabbs Shrops
78 A3 Quabrook E Susx
280 B3 Quadring Lincs
280 B3 Quadring Eaudike Lincs
74 D5 Quags Corner W Susx
167 F6 Quainton Bucks
132 A5 Quaker's Yard Myr Td
405 E4 Quaking Houses Dur
388 A6 Quality Corner Cumb
136 C4 Quarhouse Gloucs
89 G6 Quarley Hants
327 H1 Quarmby Kirk
275 E1 Quarndon Derbys
275 E1 Quarndon Common Derbys
466 B2 Quarrelton Rens
141 H1 Quarrendon Bucks
37 F2 Quarr Hill IoW
465 H1 Quarriers Village Inver
298 C6 Quarrington Lincs
395 G2 Quarrington Hill Dur
290 A1 Quarrybank Ches
212 D2 Quarry Bank Dudley
576 F7 Quarryhill Highld
238 C4 Quarry Hill Staffs
512 D4 Quarrymill P & K
568 B3 Quarrywood Moray
467 H4 Quarter S Lans
511 G5 Quarterbank P & K
211 G1 Quatford Shrops
600 F1 Quatquoy Ork
211 H2 Quatt Shrops
405 E6 Quebec Dur
74 B5 Quebec W Susx
136 B2 Quedgeley Gloucs
602 B6 Queena Ork
222 B3 Queen Adelaide Cambs
122 D5 Queenborough Kent
67 F5 Queen Camel Somset
86 A1 Queen Charlton BaNES
44 G4 Queen Dart Devon
162 B2 Queenhill Worcs
68 C3 Queen Oak Wilts
37 F4 Queen's Bower IoW
342 A3 Queensbury Brad
118 D2 Queensbury Gt Lon
74 C4 Queen's Corner W Susx
308 C6 Queensferry Flints
487 F4 Queensferry W Loth
269 F4 Queen's Head Shrops
467 G1 Queenslie C Glas
195 E5 Queen's Park Beds
339 G4 Queen's Park Bl w D
289 F1 Queen's Park Ches
146 D5 Queen's Park Essex
193 G2 Queen's Park Nhants
337 F2 Queenstown Bpool
97 G5 Queen Street Kent
501 E4 Queensway Fife
484 D4 Queenzieburn N Lans
112 B6 Quemerford Wilts
605 G8 Quendale Shet
171 H3 Quendon Essex
240 D2 Queniborough Leics
138 A4 Quenington Gloucs
351 H2 Quernmore Lancs
237 G6 Queslett Birm
16 D6 Quethiock Cnwll
606 F4 Quhamm Shet
600 C2 Quholm Ork
327 E4 Quick Edge Tamesd
115 F4 Quick's Green W Berk
224 D2 Quidenham Norfk
91 E4 Quidhampton Hants
70 C3 Quidhampton Wilts
560 C2 Quilquox Abers
270 C3 Quina Brook Shrops
192 D4 Quinbury End Nhants
601 G6 Quindry Ork
213 E3 Quinton Dudley
193 G4 Quinton Nhants
7 G1 Quintrell Downs Cnwll
273 H1 Quixhill Staffs
24 B3 Quoditch Devon
511 E5 Quoig P & K
290 A5 Quoisley Ches
7 H1 Quoit Cnwll
240 C1 Quorn (Quorndon) Leics
448 C2 Quothquan S Lans
602 A7 Quoyloo Ork
600 D4 Quoyness Ork
606 E8 Quoyness Shet
607 G5 Quoys Shet
609 J2 Quoys Shet
606 F7 Quoys of Catfirth Shet

R

98 B5 Rabbit's Cross Kent
115 G1 Rabbits Hill Oxon
170 B6 Rableyheath Herts
399 F4 Raby Cumb
308 D4 Raby Wirral
201 G6 Racecourse Suffk
89 G6 Racedown Hants
449 F3 Rachan Mill Border
304 D6 Rachub Gwynd
139 G4 Rack End Oxon
41 G4 Rackenford Devon
54 C2 Rackham W Susx
250 B2 Rackheath Norfk
84 C4 Rackley Somset
424 A5 Racks D & G
600 C5 Rackwick Ork
602 E2 Rackwick Ork
274 D2 Radbourne Derbys
325 H3 Radcliffe Bury
443 H4 Radcliffe Nthumb
276 D1 Radcliffe on Trent Notts
167 E3 Radclive Bucks
138 D5 Radcot Oxon
566 C5 Raddery Highld
42 D2 Raddington Somset
27 E2 Raddon Devon
502 D3 Radernie Fife
100 B3 Radfall Kent
99 E2 Radfield Kent
86 B3 Radford BaNES
276 C1 Radford C Nott
215 E3 Radford Covtry
165 G5 Radford Oxon
189 F3 Radford Worcs
165 F5 Radfordbridge Oxon
191 E2 Radford Semele Warwks
32 B3 Radipole Dorset
64 D4 Radlet Somset
143 G5 Radlett Herts
140 B5 Radley Oxon
146 C3 Radley Green Essex
140 B5 Radley Park Oxon
233 H3 Radlith Shrops
295 G2 Radmanthwaite Notts
271 E5 Radmoor Shrops
290 B3 Radmore Green Ches
273 G4 Radmore Wood Staffs
141 G5 Radnage Bucks
6 D5 Radnor Cnwll
483 G5 Radnor Park W Duns
86 B3 Radstock BaNES
166 C1 Radstone Nhants
191 F5 Radway Warwks
291 F3 Radway Green Ches
194 D3 Radwell Beds
170 B2 Radwell Herts
172 C2 Radwinter Essex
172 C2 Radwinter End Essex
106 B3 Radyr Cardif
437 E6 Raehills D & G
506 D5 Raera Ag & B
93 E3 Rafborough Hants
256 B5 RAF Coltishall Norfk
567 K5 Rafford Moray
608 F6 Raga Shet
277 E5 Ragdale Leics
210 B1 Ragdon Shrops
342 A3 Raggalds Brad
89 H5 Ragged Appleshaw Hants
589 J8 Raggra Highld
3 E4 Raginnis Cnwll
133 H3 Raglan Mons
225 E1 Ragmere Norfk
113 H5 Ragnal W Berk
317 F5 Ragnall Notts
482 B2 Rahane Ag & B
314 B2 Rails Sheff
607 G7 Railsbrough Shet
188 B3 Rainbow Hill Worcs
324 B4 Rainford St Hel
324 B4 Rainford Junction St Hel
98 C1 Rainham Medway
120 D3 Rainham Medway
309 G1 Rainhill St Hel
309 G1 Rainhill Stoops St Hel
312 C4 Rainow Ches
312 B4 Rainowlow Ches
326 B1 Rain Shore Rochdl
326 B4 Rainsough Bury
370 D4 Rainton N York
406 A5 Rainton Bridge Sundld
405 H5 Rainton Gate Dur
296 A3 Rainworth Notts
380 A3 Raisbeck Cumb
402 C5 Raise Cumb
513 F4 Rait P & K
320 A3 Raithby Lincs
300 C1 Raithby by Spilsby Lincs
74 B4 Rake W Susx
74 B4 Rake Common Hants
273 G6 Rake End Staffs
340 C5 Rake Head Lancs
273 G1 Rakes Dale Staffs
273 F1 Rakeway Staffs
326 D2 Rakewood Rochdl
61 E5 Raleigh Devon
102 D3 Rallt Swans
181 E5 Ram Carmth
606 E2 Ramah Shet
89 F2 Ram Alley Wilts
542 B8 Ramasaig Highld
4 D2 Rame Cnwll
10 D4 Rame Cnwll
110 B3 Ram Hill S Glos
99 F5 Ram Lane Kent
609 J4 Ramnageo Shet
30 D2 Rampisham Dorset
350 B1 Rampside Cumb
221 F6 Rampton Cambs
317 E4 Rampton Notts
325 H1 Ramsbottom Bury
569 K5 Ramsburn Moray
113 G5 Ramsbury Wilts
582 F4 Ramscraigs Highld
73 H5 Ramsdean Hants
91 F3 Ramsdell Hants
96 C1 Ramsden Gt Lon
139 E1 Ramsden Oxon
188 D5 Ramsden Worcs
147 E6 Ramsden Bellhouse Essex
147 E5 Ramsden Heath Essex
341 E5 Ramsden Wood Calder
220 C2 Ramsey Cambs
176 D3 Ramsey Essex
322 h4 Ramsey IoM
438 B2 Ramseycleuch Border
220 D2 Ramsey Forty Foot Cambs
220 C3 Ramsey Heights Cambs
148 B3 Ramsey Island Essex
220 C2 Ramsey Mereside Cambs
220 C2 Ramsey St Mary's Cambs
101 G3 Ramsgate Kent
369 F5 Ramsgill N York
394 C4 Ramshaw Dur
403 H5 Ramshaw Dur
177 F1 Ramsholt Suffk
293 E5 Ramshorn Staffs
25 F4 Ramsley Devon
78 D2 Ramslye Kent
75 F3 Ramsnest Common Surrey
597 K2 Ranais W Isls
319 G4 Ranby Lincs
316 C3 Ranby Notts
318 D4 Rand Lincs
136 B3 Randwick Gloucs
466 A2 Ranfurly Rens
274 B5 Rangemore Staffs
110 B2 Rangeworthy S Glos
433 G2 Rankinston E Ayrs
173 F6 Rank's Green Essex
314 C2 Ranmoor Sheff
94 C4 Ranmore Common Surrey
532 B6 Ranochan Highld
316 B2 Ranskill Notts
272 C5 Ranton Staffs
272 B5 Ranton Green Staffs
250 D2 Ranworth Norfk
599 J8 Raon na Cruadha W Isls
76 B3 Rapkyns W Susx
498 B6 Raploch Stirlg
603 G3 Rapness Ork
44 C4 Rapps Somset
346 B2 Rascal Moor E R Yk
413 E5 Rascarrel D & G
481 G3 Rashfield Ag & B
483 G5 Rashielee Rens
188 D1 Rashwood Worcs
371 F5 Raskelf N York
132 C2 Rassau Blae G
342 B5 Rastrick Calder
547 G6 Ratagan Highld
240 B3 Ratby Leics
239 E5 Ratcliffe Culey Leics
276 A4 Ratcliffe on Soar Notts
240 D2 Ratcliffe on the Wreake Leics
111 H5 Ratford Wilts
125 E2 Ratford Bridge Pembks
70 D1 Ratfyn Wilts
571 J3 Rathen Abers
514 B5 Rathillet Fife
353 G3 Rathmell N York
487 F5 Ratho C Edin
487 F5 Ratho Station C Edin
569 G2 Rathven Moray
72 B5 Ratlake Hants
191 F5 Ratley Warwks
100 D5 Ratling Kent
233 H5 Ratlinghope Shrops
27 F3 Ratsloe Devon
589 H2 Rattar Highld
389 H1 Ratten Row Cumb
389 H2 Ratten Row Cumb
400 C5 Ratten Row Cumb
338 B1 Ratten Row Lancs
19 F5 Rattery Devon
200 C3 Rattlesden Suffk
526 A5 Rattray P & K
400 C5 Raughton Cumb
400 C5 Raughton Head Cumb
218 D5 Raunds Nhants
487 H5 Ravelston C Edin
330 A5 Ravenfield Rothm
376 D5 Ravenglass Cumb
324 B6 Ravenhead St Hel
187 G4 Ravenhills Green Worcs
250 D5 Raveningham Norfk
387 G4 Ravenscar N York
342 C2 Ravenscliffe Brad
291 G4 Ravenscliffe C Stke
482 B4 Ravenscraig Inver
322 f4 Ravensdale IoM
195 F4 Ravensden Beds
381 F4 Ravenseat N York
175 F5 Raven's Green Essex
291 E5 Ravenshall Staffs
295 H4 Ravenshead Notts
290 C4 Ravensmoor Ches
243 H4 Ravensthorpe C Pete
342 D5 Ravensthorpe Kirk
217 E5 Ravensthorpe Nhants
239 F2 Ravenstone Leics
194 A4 Ravenstone M Keyn
380 C4 Ravenstonedale Cumb
365 E4 Ravenstown Cumb
469 E5 Ravenstruther S Lans
92 D1 Ravenswood Village Settlement Wokham
382 D3 Ravensworth N York
387 F3 Raw N York
345 F5 Rawcliffe E R Yk
358 A4 Rawcliffe York
345 G5 Rawcliffe Bridge E R Yk
342 D2 Rawdon Leeds
342 D2 Rawdon Carrs Leeds
342 C5 Rawfolds Kirk
328 D3 Raw Green Barns
403 G3 Rawgreen Nthumb
329 G5 Rawmarsh Rothm
237 F2 Rawnsley Staffs
147 F6 Rawreth Essex
147 F6 Rawreth Shot Essex
28 C1 Rawridge Devon
294 D5 Rawson Green Derbys
340 C5 Rawtenstall Lancs
342 C6 Rawthorpe Kirk
468 B1 Rawyards N Lans
175 E2 Raydon Suffk
354 B5 Raygill N York
429 E1 Raylees Nthumb
122 C1 Rayleigh Essex
29 F3 Raymond's Hill Devon
173 E5 Rayne Essex
118 C2 Rayners Lane Gt Lon
119 E6 Raynes Park Gt Lon
233 G4 Reabrook Shrops
198 B1 Reach Cambs
340 B3 Read Lancs
147 E4 Reader's Corner Essex
116 B5 Reading Readg
135 E1 Readings Gloucs
80 D3 Reading Street Kent
101 G2 Reading Street Kent
9 E3 Readymoney Cnwll
137 H4 Ready Token Gloucs
391 G6 Reagill Cumb
576 F5 Rearquhar Highld
241 E2 Rearsby Leics
318 D4 Reasby Lincs
290 C4 Rease Heath Ches
589 H3 Reaster Highld
604 F2 Reawick Shet
4 B1 Reawla Cnwll
587 L4 Reay Highld
562 F5 Rechullin Highld
100 D2 Reculver Kent
604 F1 Redayre Shet
43 E4 Red Ball Devon
126 B4 Redberth Pembks
143 G2 Redbourn Herts
143 G2 Redbournbury Herts
332 D4 Redbourne N Linc
50 C2 Redbridge C Sotn
32 D2 Redbridge Dorset
120 B2 Redbridge Gt Lon
365 G4 Red Bridge Lancs
134 C2 Redbrook Gloucs
270 C1 Redbrook Wrexhm
291 G3 Red Bull Ches
271 G2 Red Bull Staffs
565 K3 Redburn Highld
567 G7 Redburn Highld
402 D2 Redburn Nthumb
397 F5 Redcar R & Cl
529 E4 Redcastle Angus
565 K7 Redcastle Highld
108 D4 Redcliff Bay Bristl
212 C5 Redcross Worcs
399 G5 Red Dial Cumb
238 A5 Reddicap Heath Birm
486 B4 Redding Falk
486 B4 Reddingmuirhead Falk
310 D2 Reddish Warrtn
326 C6 Reddish Warrtn
213 G6 Redditch Worcs
199 F3 Rede Suffk
226 B3 Redenhall Norfk
89 H5 Redenham Hants
441 F5 Redesdale Camp Nthumb
428 D3 Redesmouth Nthumb
528 C6 Redford Angus
30 D1 Redford Dorset
394 B3 Redford Dur
74 D4 Redford W Susx
438 D1 Redfordgreen Border
512 C4 Redgorton P & K
224 D4 Redgrave Suffk
527 F2 Redheugh Angus
556 D4 Redhill Abers
559 F2 Redhill Abers
48 D5 Red Hill Bmouth
52 C2 Red Hill Hants
160 C2 Red Hill Herefs
170 D3 Redhill Herts
97 G4 Red Hill Kent
240 B5 Red Hill Leics
295 H5 Redhill Notts
85 F2 Redhill N Som
151 F6 Red Hill Pembks
234 B3 Redhill Shrops
235 G2 Redhill Shrops
272 B4 Redhill Staffs
95 F4 Redhill Surrey
344 A4 Red Hill Wakefd
190 A3 Red Hill Warwks
188 C4 Red Hill Worcs
235 G2 Redhill Wrekin
390 D4 Redhills Cumb
26 D4 Redhills Devon
77 G5 Red House Common E Susx
476 F4 Redhouses Ag & B
226 D3 Redisham Suffk
109 G4 Redland Bristl
602 D6 Redland Ork
142 A4 Redland End Bucks
31 F6 Redlands Dorset
66 D3 Redlands Somset
113 E1 Redlands Swindn
43 H5 Redlane Somset
225 G5 Redlingfield Suffk
222 D5 Red Lodge Suffk
326 B1 Red Lumb Rochdl
68 A3 Redlynch Somset
71 E5 Redlynch Wilts
388 D3 Redmain Cumb
161 H3 Redmarley D'Abitot Gloucs
396 A5 Redmarshall S on T
277 G2 Redmile Leics
368 D1 Redmire N York
38 C4 Redmonsford Devon
8 D1 Redmoor Cnwll
560 B3 Redmoss Abers
213 E4 Rednal Birm
269 G4 Rednal Shrops
452 A2 Redpath Border
255 E2 Red Pits Norfk
562 C3 Redpoint Highld
23 F1 Red Post Cnwll
160 C4 Red Rail Herefs
71 G1 Red Rice Hants
324 D3 Red Rock Wigan
127 E2 Red Roses Carmth
443 G5 Red Row Nthumb
6 C5 Redruth Cnwll
339 E3 Red Scar Lancs
470 D6 Redscarhead Border
87 G2 Redstocks Wilts
126 C1 Redstone Cross Pembks
291 G4 Red Street Staffs
15 E6 Redtye Cnwll
326 A3 Redvales Bury
304 B3 Red Wharf Bay IoA
108 D3 Redwick Newpt
109 F2 Redwick S Glos
269 F5 Redwith Shrops
395 E5 Redworth Darltn
171 E2 Reed Herts
170 D2 Reed End Herts
299 G3 Reedham Lincs
251 E4 Reedham Norfk
340 C2 Reedley Lancs
346 A5 Reedness E R Yk
299 G4 Reed Point Lincs
453 G3 Reedsford Nthumb
340 C5 Reeds Holme Lancs
26 C5 Reedy Devon
7 E3 Reen Manor Cnwll
318 C5 Reepham Lincs
255 F3 Reepham Norfk
382 B5 Reeth N York
214 D4 Reeves Green Solhll
232 C4 Refail Powys
322 g3 Regaby IoM
119 F3 Regent's Park Gt Lon
85 F2 Regil N Som
566 F6 Regoul Highld
578 C7 Reiff Highld
95 F5 Reigate Surrey
95 E4 Reigate Heath Surrey
372 D5 Reighton N York
597 G7 Reinigeadal W Isls
589 J6 Reiss Highld
7 F2 Rejerrah Cnwll
4 C2 Releath Cnwll
3 G3 Relubbus Cnwll
567 H7 Relugas Moray
116 C3 Remenham Wokham
116 C3 Remenham Hill Wokham
523 L7 Remony P & K
276 C5 Rempstone Notts
576 F3 Remusaig Highld
137 F3 Rendcomb Gloucs
202 D2 Rendham Suffk
202 C4 Rendlesham Suffk
466 C1 Renfrew Rens
195 F4 Renhold Beds
315 E4 Renishaw Derbys
600 F2 Rennibister Ork
455 F6 Rennington Nthumb
236 B3 Renshaw Wood Shrops
483 E4 Renton W Duns
401 G6 Renwick Cumb
251 E1 Repps Norfk
275 E4 Repton Derbys
546 E4 Reraig Highld
605 G7 Rerwick Shet
566 B7 Resaurie Highld
8 B5 Rescassa Cnwll
528 B4 Rescobie Angus
8 C2 Rescorla Cnwll
519 H5 Resipole Highld
6 B5 Reskadinnick Cnwll
566 B3 Resolis Highld
130 C4 Resolven Neath
488 B5 Restalrig C Edin
495 E3 Rest and be thankful Ag & B
474 C2 Reston Border
379 E5 Reston Cumb
5 F1 Restronguet Passage Cnwll
112 C2 Restrop Wilts
8 C2 Resugga Green Cnwll
528 B4 Reswallie Angus
14 C5 Retallack Cnwll
316 D3 Retford Notts
15 E6 Retire Cnwll
147 F5 Rettendon Essex
147 F5 Rettendon Place Essex
300 A2 Revesby Lincs
300 B2 Revesby Bridge Lincs
339 G4 Revidge Bl w D
12 C5 Rew Devon
19 G3 Rew Devon
46 D3 Rew Dorset
27 E3 Rewe Devon
51 E6 Rew Street IoW
24 B5 Rexon Devon
24 B5 Rexon Cross Devon
111 G6 Reybridge Wilts
227 F4 Reydon Suffk
227 F4 Reydon Smear Suffk
248 D3 Reymerston Norfk
126 B3 Reynalton Pembks
102 C4 Reynoldston Swans
17 E3 Rezare Cnwll
133 G4 Rhadyr Mons
306 A5 Rhandir Conwy
182 B6 Rhandirmwyn Carmth
207 F6 Rhayader Powys
262 D4 Rhedyn Gwynd
578 E6 Rhegreanoch Highld
565 J7 Rheindown Highld
518 E5 Rhemore Highld
543 G6 Rhenetra Highld
308 A5 Rhes-y-cae Flints
287 G2 Rhewl Denbgs
269 F3 Rhewl Shrops

269 G2 Rhewl Wrexhm
288 A6 Rhewl Wrexhm
307 G3 Rhewl-fawr Flints
307 G3 Rhewl-Mostyn Flints
580 E4 Rhian Highld
578 E4 Rhicarn Highld
584 D6 Rhiconich Highld
566 B2 Rhicullen Highld
271 E2 Rhiews Shrops
586 F7 Rhifail Highld
131 E3 Rhigos Rhondd
576 F2 Rhilochan Highld
179 F5 Rhippinllwyd Cerdgn
179 G5 Rhippinllwyd Cerdgn
574 C6 Rhiroy Highld
586 C5 Rhitongue Highld
566 C2 Rhives Highld
584 D6 Rhivichie Highld
262 C5 Rhiw Gwynd
287 G1 Rhiwbebyll Denbgs
106 C3 Rhiwbina Cardif
285 E5 Rhiwbryfdir Gwynd
105 F3 Rhiwceiliog Brdgnd
107 E2 Rhiwderin Newpt
284 C2 Rhiwen Gwynd
105 G2 Rhiwinder Rhondd
267 E2 Rhiwlas Gwynd
284 C1 Rhiwlas Gwynd
268 C3 Rhiwlas Powys
65 E5 Rhode Somset
99 H3 Rhode Common Kent
326 B3 Rhodes Bury
315 H3 Rhodesia Notts
82 B2 Rhodes Minnis Kent
204 D5 Rhodmad Cerdgn
131 F5 Rhondda Rhondd
412 D3 Rhonehouse or Kelton Hill D & G
105 H6 Rhoose V Glam
154 A2 Rhos Carmth
287 G2 Rhôs Denbgs
130 A4 Rhos Neath
233 E1 Rhos Powys
130 A2 Rhosaman Carmth
304 B4 Rhoscefnhir IoA
302 C5 Rhoscolyn IoA
269 E6 Rhôs Common Powys
125 F4 Rhoscrowther Pembks
262 C3 Rhos-ddu Gwynd
288 D4 Rhosddu Wrexhm
266 D4 Rhosdylluan Gwynd
308 B6 Rhosesmor Flints
152 C4 Rhosfach Pembks
263 F3 Rhos-fawr Gwynd
283 F4 Rhosgadfan Gwynd
303 F3 Rhosgoch IoA
184 C5 Rhos-goch Powys
263 H2 Rhosgyll Gwynd
180 D2 Rhos Haminiog Cerdgn
152 D1 Rhos-Hill Pembks
262 B5 Rhoshirwaun Gwynd
283 E4 Rhos Isaf Gwynd
264 B1 Rhoslan Gwynd
228 D3 Rhoslefain Gwynd
288 D5 Rhosllanerchrugog Wrexhm
303 G3 Rhôs Lligwy IoA
155 F5 Rhosmaen Carmth
303 G5 Rhosmeirch IoA
302 D6 Rhosneigr IoA
288 D4 Rhosnesni Wrexhm
306 A3 Rhôs-on-Sea Conwy
288 D4 Rhosrobin Wrexhm
102 B4 Rhossili Swans
150 B4 Rhosson Pembks
303 F6 Rhostrehwfa IoA
283 E4 Rhostryfan Gwynd
288 D5 Rhostyllen Wrexhm
269 E2 Rhoswiel Shrops
303 F3 Rhosybol IoA
268 B5 Rhos-y-brithdir Powys
151 F2 Rhosycaerau Pembks
179 E4 Rhosygadair Newydd Cerdgn
269 F3 Rhosygadfa Shrops
205 E5 Rhos-y-garth Cerdgn
153 E1 Rhosygilwen Pembks
267 E3 Rhos-y-gwaliau Gwynd
262 C3 Rhos-y-llan Gwynd
269 F1 Rhos y madoc Wrexhm
286 B1 Rhos-y-mawn Conwy
288 C6 Rhosymedre Wrexhm
209 E6 Rhos-y-meirch Powys
153 F5 Rhosyn-coch Carmth
462 D2 Rhu Ag & B
482 C3 Rhu Ag & B
307 F4 Rhualt Denbgs
290 B2 Rhuddall Heath Ches
307 E4 Rhuddlan Denbgs
574 C4 Rhue Highld
506 F1 Rhugarbh Ag & B
184 B5 Rhulen Powys
462 B5 Rhunahaorine Ag & B
584 D6 Rhunahaorine Highld
179 F5 Rhyd Cerdgn
265 E1 Rhyd Gwynd
231 F4 Rhyd Powys
154 B4 Rhydargaeau Carmth
155 E2 Rhydcymerau Carmth
188 B5 Rhydd Worcs
284 C4 Rhyd-Ddu Gwynd
188 B6 Rhydd Green Worcs
130 A5 Rhydding Neath
286 D2 Rhydgaled Conwy
179 G4 Rhydlewis Cerdgn
262 B5 Rhydlios Gwynd
286 B4 Rhydlydan Conwy
231 G6 Rhydlydan Powys
180 B5 Rhydowen Carmth
152 D4 Rhydowen Pembks
204 D6 Rhyd-Rosser Cerdgn
184 D5 Rhydspence Herefs
288 B4 Rhydtalog Flints
267 E2 Rhyd-uchaf Gwynd
302 D3 Rhydwyn IoA
152 B5 Rhyd-y-Brown Pembks
263 E4 Rhyd-y-clafdy Gwynd
268 D3 Rhydcroesau Shrops
208 C3 Rhyd-y-cwm Shrops
153 F2 Rhydyfelin Carmth
204 D4 Rhydyfelin Cerdgn
232 A6 Rhydyfelin Powys
106 A2 Rhydyfelin Rhondd
306 C2 Rhyd-y-foel Conwy
129 H3 Rhyd-y-fro Neath
151 E5 Rhydgele Pembks
129 G4 Rhyd-y-gwin Swans
263 G3 Rhyd-y-gwystl Gwynd
266 B5 Rhydymain Gwynd
133 F4 Rhyd-y-meirch Mons
287 G4 Rhyd-y-meudwy Denbgs
288 B1 Rhydmwyn Flints
229 E4 Rhyd-yr-onen Gwynd
265 F1 Rhyd-y-sarn Gwynd
152 D6 Rhydywrach Carmth
307 E3 Rhyl Denbgs
132 B3 Rhymney Caerph
269 F2 Rhyn Shrops
3 E5 Rhynd P & K
8 B4 Rhynie Abers
577 H8 Rhynie Highld
212 A5 Ribbesford Worcs
295 F4 Ribblehead N York
120 D3 Ribbleton Lancs

338 B3 Ribby Lancs
339 F2 Ribchester Lancs
294 C3 Riber Derbys
586 C6 Ribigill Highld
334 A3 Riby Lincs
345 E2 Riccall N York
445 F2 Riccarton E Ayrs
210 B6 Richards Castle Herefs
101 F3 Richborough Port Kent
118 A4 Richings Park Bucks
118 D5 Richmond Gt Lon
383 E4 Richmond N York
315 E2 Richmond Sheff
34 b2 Richmond Fort Guern
172 C4 Richmond's Green Essex
64 B5 Rich's Holford Somset
39 F2 Rickard's Down Devon
541 F2 Rickarton Abers
400 D3 Rickerby Cumb
272 D5 Rickerscote Staffs
85 E3 Rickford N Som
224 D4 Rickinghall Suffk
405 G4 Rickleton Sundld
171 G3 Rickling Essex
171 H4 Rickling Green Essex
57 G3 Rickmansworth Herts
451 G5 Riddell Border
295 E4 Riddings Derbys
40 C5 Riddlecombe Devon
355 E6 Riddlesden Brad
467 F1 Riddrie C Glas
213 F3 Ridgacre Birm
85 G3 Ridge BaNES
29 E1 Ridge Devon
33 G2 Ridge Dorset
71 G6 Ridge Hants
351 G2 Ridge Lancs
69 G3 Ridge Wilts
73 H5 Ridge Common Hants
95 F5 Ridge Green Surrey
327 E5 Ridge Hill Tamesd
238 D5 Ridge Lane Warwks
142 D6 Ridgemarsh Bucks
82 D2 Ridge Row Kent
109 H4 Ridgeway Bristl
294 D3 Ridgeway Derbys
315 E3 Ridgeway Derbys
81 G2 Ridgeway Kent
107 E2 Ridgeway Newpt
126 C3 Ridgeway Pembks
86 C6 Ridgeway Somset
292 A4 Ridgeway Staffs
187 G5 Ridgeway Cross Herefs
315 E3 Ridgeway Moor Derbys
173 E1 Ridgewell Essex
33 G2 Ridge Wharf Dorset
78 B6 Ridgewood E Susx
168 D2 Ridgmont Beds
209 G2 Ridgway Shrops
94 A3 Ridgway Surrey
68 B4 Riding Gate Somset
404 B2 Riding Mill Nthumb
97 F2 Ridley Kent
402 D2 Ridley Nthumb
428 A2 Ridley Stokoe Nthumb
289 E4 Ridleywood Wrexhm
256 C3 Ridlington Norfk
242 A4 Ridlington Rutlnd
256 C3 Ridlington Street Norfk
429 E3 Ridsdale Nthumb
525 G6 Riechip P & K
578 B4 Rienachait Highld
371 H3 Rievaulx N York
133 E4 Rifle Green Torfn
396 C3 Rift House Hartpl
400 A1 Rigg D & G
485 F5 Riggend N Lans
320 D4 Rigsby Lincs
448 A3 Rigside S Lans
339 F4 Riley Green Lancs
237 H2 Rileyhill Staffs
16 C4 Rilla Mill Cnwll
16 C4 Rillaton Cnwll
373 F5 Rillington N York
321 E1 Rimac Lincs
501 E4 Rimbleton Fife
353 G5 Rimington Lancs
67 G5 Rimpton Somset
349 F4 Rimswell E R Yk
349 F4 Rimswell Valley E R Yk
151 G4 Rinaston Pembks
235 G4 Rindleford Shrops
605 G8 Ringasta Shet
412 C3 Ringford D & G
275 H6 Ringing Hill Leics
314 B3 Ringinglow Sheff
108 C2 Ringland Newpt
255 F5 Ringland Norfk
78 B5 Ringles Cross E Susx
98 A3 Ringlestone Kent
98 D3 Ringlestone Kent
325 H4 Ringley Bolton
56 C2 Ringmer E Susx
12 A3 Ringmore Devon
20 C3 Ringmore Devon
324 D2 Ring o' Bells Lancs
568 D7 Ringorm Moray
245 F4 Ring's End Cambs
226 D2 Ringsfield Suffk
226 D2 Ringsfield Corner Suffk
142 D2 Ringshall Bucks
200 D4 Ringshall Suffk
201 E4 Ringshall Stocks Suffk
218 D4 Ringstead Nhants
259 E3 Ringstead Norfk
146 D1 Ringtail Green Essex
49 E3 Ringwood Hants
101 G6 Ringwould Kent
554 D1 Rinmore Abers
600 E6 Rinnigill Ork
3 G4 Rinsey Cnwll
3 G4 Rinsey Croft Cnwll
598 C8 Riof W Isls
57 E2 Ripe E Susx
295 E4 Ripley Derbys
49 F5 Ripley Hants
356 B2 Ripley N York
94 A3 Ripley Surrey
347 E3 Riplingham E R Yk
370 C5 Ripon N York
99 F6 Ripper's Cross Kent
279 F4 Rippingale Lincs
101 G6 Ripple Kent
162 C2 Ripple Worcs
341 G6 Ripponden Calder
573 K4 Rireavach Highld
476 E8 Risabus Ag & B
186 D3 Risbury Herefs
347 F3 Risby E R Yk
319 E1 Risby Lincs
199 G1 Risby Suffk
106 D1 Risca Caerph
348 B1 Rise E R Yk
135 G2 Rise Carr Darltn
383 G1 Riseden Kent
79 G2 Riseden Kent
294 B3 Rise End Derbys
280 B4 Risegate Lincs
318 B5 Riseholme Lincs
388 B3 Risehow Cumb
195 E2 Riseley Beds
92 B2 Riseley Hants
295 H5 Rise Park C Nott
120 D1 Rise Park Gt Lon

225 G6 Rishangles Suffk
339 H3 Rishton Lancs
341 G6 Rishworth Calder
340 B4 Rising Bridge Lancs
272 D5 Risingbrook Staffs
140 C3 Risinghurst Oxon
17 E4 Rising Sun Cnwll
275 H2 Risley Derbys
325 F6 Risley Warrtn
370 A6 Risplith N York
585 H3 Rispond Highld
89 H2 Rivar Wilts
173 G6 Rivenhall Essex
147 G1 Rivenhall End Essex
83 E2 River Kent
75 E5 River W Susx
222 A6 River Bank Cambs
96 D3 Riverhead Kent
47 E2 Rivers' Corner Dorset
106 C4 Riverside Cardif
10 D2 Riverside Devon
498 B6 Riverside Stirlg
213 F6 Riverside Worcs
338 D4 Riverside Docklands Lancs
61 F5 Riverton Devon
121 G5 Riverview Park Kent
325 E2 Rivington Lancs
47 E2 Rixon Dorset
310 D1 Rixton Warrtn
339 F4 Roach Bridge Lancs
327 E4 Roaches Tamesd
41 G3 Roachill Devon
193 G4 Roade Nhants
28 D4 Road Green Devon
250 B6 Road Green Norfk
426 D5 Roadhead Cumb
468 D5 Roadmeetings S Lans
588 F4 Roadside Highld
541 G4 Roadside of Catterline Abers
541 F4 Roadside of Kinneff Abers
63 G4 Roadwater Somset
192 D3 Road Weedon Nhants
542 D8 Roag Highld
571 L6 Roanheads Abers
171 G3 Roast Green Essex
106 C4 Roath Cardif
106 C4 Roath Park Cardif
439 E2 Roberton Border
448 B4 Roberton S Lans
79 G5 Robertsbridge E Susx
568 C7 Robertstown Moray
131 G4 Robertstown Rhondd
126 B2 Robeston Back Pembks
125 E3 Robeston Cross Pembks
126 B1 Robeston Wathen Pembks
125 E3 Robeston West Pembks
80 D3 Robhurst Kent
292 B3 Robin Hill Staffs
314 B5 Robin Hood Derbys
324 C2 Robin Hood Lancs
343 F4 Robin Hood Leeds
172 D2 Robinhood End Essex
387 G3 Robin Hood's Bay N York
74 C4 Robins W Susx
215 E1 Robinson's End Warwks
18 B5 Roborough Devon
40 B4 Roborough Devon
484 C6 Robroyston C Glas
309 F1 Roby Knows
324 C3 Roby Mill Lancs
273 H2 Rocester Staffs
151 E5 Roch Pembks
326 B2 Rochdale Rochdl
8 B1 Roche Cnwll
292 C2 Roche Grange Staffs
121 H6 Rochester Medway
441 F5 Rochester Nthumb
122 D1 Rochford Essex
211 E6 Rochford Worcs
151 E5 Roch Gate Pembks
132 C5 Roch Caerph
14 C3 Rock Cnwll
29 E2 Rock Devon
130 B6 Rock Neath
455 G5 Rock Nthumb
44 C3 Rock Somset
211 G5 Rock Worcs
54 D2 Rock W Susx
27 G4 Rockbeare Devon
70 C6 Rockbourne Hants
400 C2 Rockcliffe Cumb
413 F4 Rockcliffe D & G
340 D5 Rockcliffe Lancs
400 B2 Rockcliffe Cross Cumb
292 A3 Rock End Staffs
308 D2 Rock Ferry Wirral
577 K7 Rockfield Highld
134 B2 Rockfield Mons
62 A2 Rockford Devon
49 F3 Rockford Hants
210 C4 Rockgreen Shrops
135 F6 Rockhampton S Glos
22 B6 Rockhead Cnwll
209 E4 Rockhill Shrops
218 B1 Rockingham Nhants
248 C5 Rockland All Saints Norfk
250 C4 Rockland St Mary Norfk
248 C5 Rockland St Peter Norfk
316 D5 Rockley Notts
113 E5 Rockley Wilts
86 C4 Rockley Ford Somset
136 B5 Rockness Gloucs
79 E3 Rockrobin E Susx
309 H3 Rocksavage Halton
78 B5 Rocks Park E Susx
135 H5 Rockstowes Gloucs
482 B1 Rockville Ag & B
116 C2 Rockwell End Bucks
43 F3 Rockwell Green Somset
5 d2 Rocky Hill IoS
236 D2 Rodbaston Staffs
136 B4 Rodborough Gloucs
112 D2 Rodbourne Swindn
111 G3 Rodbourne Wilts
111 G3 Rodbourne Bottom Wilts
199 H6 Rodbridge Corner Suffk
185 F2 Rodd Herefs
454 C5 Roddam Nthumb
31 E6 Rodden Dorset
185 F2 Rodd Hurst Herefs
394 C2 Roddymoor Dur
87 E4 Rode Somset
291 G3 Rode Heath Ches
292 A1 Rodeheath Ches
87 E4 Rode Hill Somset
595 G6 Rodel W Isls
234 D1 Roden Wrekin
110 B3 Rodford S Glos
68 B5 Rodgrove Somset
63 G4 Rodhuish Somset
234 D2 Rodington Wrekin
234 D2 Rodington Heath Wrekin
135 H2 Rodley Gloucs
342 D2 Rodley Leeds
136 D5 Rodmarton Gloucs
56 C3 Rodmell E Susx
341 E4 Rodmer Clough Calder
99 E2 Rodmersham Kent
99 E2 Rodmersham Green Kent
85 E4 Rodney Stoke Somset
274 C1 Rodsley Derbys
65 E3 Rodway Somset
271 F6 Rodway Wrekin

32 B4 Rodwell Dorset
327 E3 Roebuck Low Oldham
356 D1 Roecliffe N York
327 E5 Roe Cross Tamesd
56 A4 Roedean Br & H
143 E1 Roe End Herts
144 B3 Roe Green Herts
170 D3 Roe Green Herts
119 E5 Roehampton Gt Lon
339 G3 Roe Lee Bl w D
606 D4 Roesound Shet
144 B3 Roestock Herts
76 C3 Roffey W Susx
74 C5 Rogart Highld
83 E2 Rogate W Susx
378 C5 Roger Ground Cumb
107 E2 Rogerstone Newpt
467 F3 Rogerton S Lans
595 G6 Roghadal W Isls
109 E2 Roglet Mons
245 E3 Rogues Alley Cambs
140 D6 Roke Oxon
140 D6 Rokemarsh Oxon
406 C3 Roker Sundld
251 E1 Rollesby Norfk
241 F4 Rolleston Leics
296 D4 Rolleston Notts
314 D3 Rollestone Sheff
88 C6 Rollestone Wilts
88 C6 Rolleston Camp Wilts
274 C4 Rolleston on Dove Staffs
47 E2 Rolls Mill Dorset
361 G5 Rolston E R Yk
80 B3 Rolstone N Som
80 C3 Rolvenden Kent
80 C3 Rolvenden Layne Kent
393 G5 Romaldkirk Dur
384 B6 Romanby N York
251 G6 Roman Hill Suffk
470 C2 Romannobridge Border
41 E3 Romansleigh Devon
543 G6 Romesdal Highld
120 D2 Romford Dorset
79 E1 Romford Gt Lon
79 E1 Romford Kent
312 C1 Romiley Stockp
96 D2 Romney Street Kent
71 G5 Romsey Hants
197 G3 Romsey Town Cambs
212 A3 Romsley Shrops
213 E4 Romsley Worcs
213 E4 Romsley Hill Worcs
601 G6 Ronaldsvoe Ork
235 G3 Rondlay Wrekin
188 C4 Ronkswood Worcs
213 F2 Rood End Sandw
381 E2 Rookby Cumb
172 A3 Rook End Essex
403 G6 Rookhope Dur
378 D1 Roking Cumb
37 E4 Rookley IoW
37 E4 Rookley Green IoW
84 C4 Rooks Bridge Somset
200 B4 Rooksey Green Suffk
97 E4 Rooks Hill Kent
136 B4 Rooksmoor Gloucs
64 A5 Rook's Nest Somset
68 D3 Rook Street Wilts
369 H2 Rookwith N York
52 D5 Rookwood W Susx
349 E3 Roos E R Yk
364 B6 Roosebeck Cumb
364 B6 Roosecote Cumb
198 D6 Roost End Essex
565 K6 Rootfield Highld
195 G3 Rootham's Green Beds
99 E5 Rooting Street Kent
469 F4 Rootpark S Lans
73 F3 Ropley Hants
73 F3 Ropley Dean Hants
73 G3 Ropley Soke Hants
278 C4 Ropsley Lincs
571 K5 Rora Abers
559 F6 Rorandle Abers
233 F4 Rorrington Shrops
6 B5 Roscroggan Cnwll
7 E3 Rose Cnwll
98 B3 Roseacre Kent
338 B2 Roseacre Lancs
3 F2 Rose-an-Grouse Cnwll
41 F3 Rose Ash Devon
484 D5 Rosebank E Duns
468 C5 Rosebank S Lans
471 F4 Rosebery Mdloth
152 B4 Rosebush Pembks
22 D3 Rosecare Cnwll
144 D4 Rosedale Herts
386 B5 Rosedale Abbey N York
454 C5 Roseden Nthumb
14 C5 Rosedinnick Cnwll
38 C3 Rosedown Devon
566 F6 Rosefield Highld
174 B4 Rose Green Essex
174 B4 Rose Green Suffk
200 C6 Rose Green Suffk
53 G5 Rose Green W Susx
340 C3 Rose Grove Lancs
575 K3 Rosehall Highld
468 A2 Rosehall N Lans
571 G4 Rosehearty Abers
339 H5 Rosehill Bl w D
325 C3 Rose Hill Bolton
117 F3 Rose Hill Bucks
557 F3 Rosehill C Aber
275 E3 Rose Hill C Derb
7 E3 Rosehill Cnwll
15 E6 Rosehill Cnwll
56 D1 Rose Hill E Susx
95 F1 Rosehill Gt Lon
340 C3 Rose Hill Lancs
405 H1 Rosehill N Tyne
140 B4 Rose Hill Oxon
125 E1 Rosehill Pembks
271 F3 Rosehill Shrops
201 G6 Rose Hill Suffk
94 D5 Rosehill Surrey
311 F2 Rosehill Traffd
567 L3 Roseisle Moray
16 C6 Roseland Cnwll
57 G4 Roselands E Susx
125 G3 Rosemarket Pembks
566 C5 Rosemarkie Highld
43 G5 Rosemary Lane Devon
8 C2 Rosemelling Cnwll
2 D1 Rosemergy Cnwll
557 C2 Rosemount P & K
526 A6 Rosemount P & K
445 E4 Rosemount S Ayrs
14 D5 Rosenannon Cnwll
5 E4 Rosenithon Cnwll
78 D5 Roser's Cross E Susx
8 C2 Rosevean Cnwll
4 C4 Rosevear Cnwll
236 D6 Roseville Dudley
5 G1 Rosevine Cnwll
4 B1 Rosewarne Cnwll
6 B5 Rosewarne Cnwll
471 E2 Rosewell Mdloth
396 B5 Roseworth S on T
6 B6 Roseworthy Cnwll
7 E4 Roseworthy Cnwll
6 B6 Roseworthy Barton Cnwll
379 F1 Rosgill Cumb

121 F5 Rosherville Kent
531 K7 Roshven Highld
6 B5 Roskear Croft Cnwll
542 D7 Roskhill Highld
5 E4 Roskorwell Cnwll
400 B5 Rosley Cumb
471 E2 Roslin Mdloth
238 C1 Rosliston Derbys
482 B3 Rosneath Ag & B
475 E2 Ross Border
412 B6 Ross D & G
455 E2 Ross Nthumb
510 D5 Ross P & K
289 E3 Rossett Wrexhm
356 C4 Rossett Green N York
187 H2 Ross Green Worcs
529 E3 Rossie Island Angus
500 A2 Rossie Ochill P & K
330 D5 Rossington Donc
566 B3 Rosskeen Highld
48 D6 Rossmore Poole
161 E5 Ross-on-Wye Herefs
583 J2 Roster Highld
311 E3 Rostherne Ches
330 C3 Rostholme Donc
363 E3 Rosthwaite Cumb
377 H2 Rosthwaite Cumb
274 A1 Roston Derbys
3 G4 Rosudgeon Cnwll
487 F3 Rosyth Fife
174 B3 Rotchfords Essex
86 A3 Rotcombe BaNES
442 D4 Rothbury Nthumb
75 F5 Rotherbridge W Susx
241 E1 Rotherby Leics
78 D4 Rotherfield E Susx
116 B3 Rotherfield Greys Oxon
116 B3 Rotherfield Peppard Oxon
315 E1 Rotherham Rothm
119 H3 Rotherhithe Gt Lon
193 F3 Rothersthorpe Nhants
160 C2 Rotherwas Herefs
92 B3 Rotherwick Hants
568 D6 Rothes Moray
464 B2 Rothesay Ag & B
559 G2 Rothiebrisbane Abers
559 G2 Rothienorman Abers
603 J7 Rothiesholm Ork
240 C2 Rothley Leics
240 C2 Rothley Plain Leics
559 E4 Rothmaise Abers
559 E4 Rothney Abers
343 H3 Rothwell Leeds
333 H5 Rothwell Lincs
217 H3 Rothwell Nhants
360 D4 Rotsea E R Yk
538 D6 Rottal Angus
173 E4 Rotten End Essex
92 C3 Rotten Green Hants
214 B4 Rotten Row Solhll
115 F5 Rotten Row W Berk
56 B4 Rottingdean Br & H
376 B2 Rottington Cumb
213 F2 Rotton Park Birm
424 A4 Roucan D & G
37 E4 Roud IoW
253 G3 Rougham Norfk
200 B2 Rougham Suffk
200 A2 Rougham Green Suffk
326 D2 Rough Bank Rochdl
534 C6 Roughburn Highld
272 D2 Rough Close Staffs
100 B4 Rough Common Kent
292 B6 Roughcote Staffs
586 F7 Rough Haugh Highld
274 C5 Rough Hay Staffs
340 C1 Roughlee Lancs
237 H5 Roughley Birm
43 G2 Roughmoor Somset
112 D2 Roughmoor Swindn
554 B2 Roughrigg Abers
485 G5 Roughrigg N Lans
426 D4 Roughsike Cumb
299 G2 Roughton Lincs
261 H4 Roughton Norfk
235 H6 Roughton Shrops
299 G2 Roughton Moor Lincs
97 F4 Roughway Kent
147 G4 Roundbush Essex
143 G5 Round Bush Herts
146 B2 Roundbush Green Essex
45 E6 Roundham Somset
343 F2 Roundhay Leeds
96 C2 Round Hill Kent
200 C6 Round Maple Suffk
212 D2 Round Oak Dudley
209 G3 Round Oak Shrops
213 G3 Round's Green Sandw
95 F2 Roundshaw Gt Lon
193 G1 Round Spinney Nhants
121 G6 Round Street Kent
75 H4 Roundstreet Common W Susx
60 D5 Roundswell Devon
311 G2 Roundthorn Manch
379 G4 Roundthwaite Cumb
88 B2 Roundway Wilts
527 E4 Roundyhill Angus
29 E4 Rousdon Devon
165 H5 Rousham Oxon
189 F4 Rous Lench Worcs
464 B2 Routenburn N Ayrs
360 D6 Routh E R Yk
141 G5 Rout's Green Bucks
15 F3 Row Cnwll
365 F2 Row Cumb
391 G3 Row Cumb
426 B4 Rowanburn D & G
162 D5 Rowanfield Gloucs
495 H5 Rowardennan Stirlg
312 D2 Rowarth Derbys
51 F2 Row Ash Hants
43 H2 Rowbarton Somset
85 E3 Rowberrow Somset
88 A2 Rowde Wilts
25 F3 Rowden Devon
356 B3 Rowden N York
364 C4 Rowe Head Cumb
305 F5 Rowen Conwy
402 B2 Rowfoot Nthumb
173 E5 Row Green Essex
175 F6 Row Heath Essex
174 D5 Rowhedge Essex
94 A2 Rowhill Surrey
76 B3 Rowhook W Susx
214 C6 Rowington Warwks
214 C6 Rowington Green Warwks
313 H5 Rowland Derbys
52 C2 Rowland's Castle Hants
405 E3 Rowland's Gill Gatesd
161 F2 Rowland's Green Herefs
92 D6 Rowledge Surrey
159 G4 Rowlestone Herefs
233 F3 Rowley Shrops
144 B3 Rowley Green Gt Lon
332 B2 Rowley Hill Kirk
272 D5 Rowley Park Staffs
213 E2 Rowley Regis Sandw
215 E3 Rowley's Green Covtry
101 E5 Rowling Kent
94 C3 Rowly Surrey

City, town and village index: Rownall - Sandybank 713

292 C5 Rownall Staffs
51 G4 Rowner Hants
213 F5 Rowney Green Worcs
50 C1 Rownhams Hants
311 G4 Row-of-trees Ches
388 C6 Rowrah Cumb
168 B6 Rowsham Bucks
294 A1 Rowsley Derbys
114 D2 Rowstock Oxon
298 D3 Rowston Lincs
295 F2 Rowthorne Derbys
289 F2 Rowton Ches
233 G2 Rowton Shrops
271 E5 Rowton Wrekin
289 F2 Rowton Moor Ches
94 A2 Row Town Surrey
452 C3 Roxburgh Border
452 C4 Roxburgh Mains Border
332 C1 Roxby N Linc
386 C1 Roxby N York
118 C2 Roxeth Gt Lon
195 H4 Roxton Beds
146 C3 Roxwell Essex
97 H3 Royal British Legion Village Kent
395 E5 Royal Oak Dur
323 H4 Royal Oak Lancs
375 E4 Royal Oak N York
290 C6 Royal's Green Ches
78 D2 Royal Tunbridge Wells Kent
533 L6 Roybridge Highld
328 C4 Royd Barns
328 C2 Roydhouse Kirk
329 G2 Royd Moor Wakefd
145 F2 Roydon Essex
225 E3 Roydon Norfk
253 E3 Roydon Norfk
145 F3 Roydon Hamlet Essex
343 F4 Royds Green Leeds
329 E2 Royston Barns
467 F1 Royston C Glas
171 E1 Royston Herts
44 A5 Royston Water Somset
326 D3 Royton Oldham
35 j6 Rozel Jersey
288 D6 Ruabon Wrexhm
516 D6 Ruaig Ag & B
7 H6 Ruan High Lanes Cnwll
7 G5 Ruan Lanihorne Cnwll
4 D5 Ruan Major Cnwll
4 D5 Ruan Minor Cnwll
161 E6 Ruardean Gloucs
135 E1 Ruardean Hill Gloucs
135 E1 Ruardean Woodside Gloucs
213 E4 Rubery Birm
593 E9 Rubha Ghaisinis W Isls
467 F1 Ruchazie C Glas
484 B6 Ruchill C Glas
401 F6 Ruckcroft Cumb
160 A2 Ruckhall Herefs
81 F3 Rucking Kent
320 B4 Ruckland Lincs
234 C4 Ruckley Shrops
151 G5 Rudbaxton Pembks
384 D3 Rudby N York
276 C3 Ruddington Notts
135 F2 Ruddle Gloucs
162 A5 Rudford Gloucs
236 B5 Rudge Shrops
87 E4 Rudge Wilts
236 A5 Rudge Heath Shrops
110 A2 Rudgeway S Glos
75 H3 Rudgwick W Susx
161 E4 Rudhall Herefs
311 F4 Rudheath Ches
311 E5 Rudheath Woods Ches
147 G4 Rudley Green Essex
111 E6 Rudloe Wilts
106 C2 Rudry Caerph
360 D1 Rudston E R Yk
292 B3 Rudyard Staffs
270 B4 Ruewood Shrops
324 A1 Rufford Lancs
357 G4 Rufforth York
295 G5 Ruffs Notts
216 B4 Rugby Warwks
273 F6 Rugeley Staffs
43 G4 Ruggin Somset
432 C4 Ruglen S Ayrs
443 F2 Rugley Nthumb
565 J7 Ruilick Highld
565 J7 Ruisaurie Highld
44 B3 Ruishton Somset
594 E6 Ruisigearraidh W Isls
118 B2 Ruislip Gt Lon
118 B2 Ruislip Common Gt Lon
118 B2 Ruislip Gardens Gt Lon
118 C2 Ruislip Manor Gt Lon
212 D1 Ruiton Dudley
310 B5 Ruloe Ches
499 G5 Rumbling Bridge P & K
212 D4 Rumbow Cottages Worcs
226 C3 Rumburgh Suffk
213 H5 Rumbush Solhll
237 E3 Rumer Hill Staffs
7 F1 Rumford Cnwll
486 B4 Rumford Falk
106 D4 Rumney Cardif
61 E5 Rumsam Devon
43 G3 Rumwell Somset
309 H3 Runcorn Halton
53 F4 Runcton W Susx
246 C3 Runcton Holme Norfk
93 E5 Runfold Surrey
248 D3 Runhall Norfk
251 F2 Runham Norfk
251 G3 Runham Vauxhall Norfk
327 F3 Running Hill Head Oldham
43 F3 Runnington Somset
395 G1 Running Waters Dur
147 F3 Runsell Green Essex
338 D5 Runshaw Moor Lancs
386 D1 Runswick Bay N York
538 B6 Runtaleave Angus
147 F6 Runwell Essex
136 B3 Ruscombe Gloucs
116 C4 Ruscombe Wokham
161 G5 Ruscote Oxon
161 E3 Rushall Herefs
225 G3 Rushall Norfk
88 D3 Rushall Wilts
237 F4 Rushall Wsall
200 A2 Rushbrooke Suffk
210 C1 Rushbury Shrops
48 B5 Rushcombe Bottom Dorset
170 D3 Rushden Herts
194 D1 Rushden Nhants
123 E5 Rushenden Kent
78 D4 Rusher's Cross E Susx
240 D3 Rushey Mead C Leic
17 F3 Rushford Devon
224 D3 Rushford Suffk
149 G2 Rush Green Essex
120 D2 Rush Green Gt Lon
170 B5 Rush Green Herts
249 E3 Rush Green Norfk
310 D2 Rushgreen Warrtn
86 C2 Rush Hill BaNES
50 B2 Rushington Hants
79 E6 Rushlake Green E Susx
173 F2 Rushley Green Essex
168 C4 Rushmere Beds
227 F2 Rushmere Suffk
201 H5 Rushmere St Andrew Suffk
201 H5 Rushmere Street Suffk
74 D1 Rushmoor Surrey
235 E2 Rushmoor Wrekin
52 B2 Rushmore Hants
96 C2 Rushmore Hill Gt Lon
185 E3 Rushock Herefs
212 C5 Rushock Worcs
326 C6 Rusholme Manch
290 B2 Rushton Ches
33 F2 Rushton Dorset
218 A3 Rushton Nhants
374 A3 Rushton N York
235 E3 Rushton Shrops
292 B2 Rushton Spencer Staffs
188 B4 Rushwick Worcs
395 F4 Rushyford Dur
56 D2 Rushy Green E Susx
497 F4 Ruskie Stirlg
298 D4 Ruskington Lincs
364 D2 Rusland Cumb
364 D2 Rusland Cross Cumb
170 A5 Rusling End Herts
76 C2 Rusper W Susx
135 F2 Ruspidge Gloucs
95 G2 Russell Hill Gt Lon
58 B4 Russell's Green E Susx
212 D1 Russell's Hall Dudley
116 B2 Russell's Water Oxon
226 B5 Russel's Green Suffk
76 D1 Russ Hill Surrey
602 B8 Russland Ork
78 D2 Rusthall Kent
54 B4 Rustington W Susx
360 D2 Ruston Parva E R Yk
387 E3 Ruswarp N York
210 D2 Ruthall Shrops
452 B3 Rutherford Border
467 E2 Rutherglen C Glas
15 E5 Ruthernbridge Cnwll
287 G3 Ruthin Denbgs
105 F4 Ruthin V Glam
557 G4 Ruthrieston C Aber
569 J6 Ruthven Abers
526 C5 Ruthven Angus
535 L3 Ruthven Highld
550 E3 Ruthven Highld
7 H1 Ruthvoes Cnwll
389 F2 Ruthwaite Cumb
399 E1 Ruthwell D & G
120 C5 Ruxley Gt Lon
160 D4 Ruxton Herefs
160 C6 Ruxton Green Herefs
269 G5 Ruyton-XI-Towns Shrops
429 G5 Ryal Nthumb
339 G5 Ryal Fold Bl w D
29 H4 Ryall Dorset
162 C1 Ryall Worcs
97 G3 Ryarsh Kent
549 H3 Rychraggan Highld
378 C3 Rydal Cumb
51 H6 Ryde IoW
94 C1 Rydens Surrey
93 G4 Rydeshill Surrey
20 B3 Rydon Devon
59 F2 Rye E Susx
270 C3 Ryebank Shrops
92 C4 Rye Common Hants
341 H2 Ryecroft Brad
329 G5 Ryecroft Rothm
292 B2 Ryecroft Gate Staffs
136 B4 Ryeford Gloucs
59 E2 Rye Foreign E Susx
59 F3 Rye Harbour E Susx
559 F4 Ryehill Abers
348 D4 Ryehill E R Yk
116 B6 Ryeish Green Wokham
186 B3 Ryelands Herefs
145 E3 Rye Park Herts
162 A2 Rye Street Worcs
163 E5 Ryeworth Gloucs
243 E2 Ryhall Rutlnd
329 F2 Ryhill Wakefd
406 C4 Ryhope Sundld
315 F6 Rylah Derbys
276 B2 Rylands Notts
354 C3 Rylstone N York
46 A2 Ryme Intrinseca Dorset
344 D2 Ryther N York
405 E2 Ryton Gatesd
161 G3 Ryton Gloucs
373 E4 Ryton N York
235 H4 Ryton Shrops
215 F2 Ryton Warwks
215 F5 Ryton-on-Dunsmore Warwks
404 D2 Ryton Woodside Gatesd

S

546 B8 Saasaig Highld
340 B2 Sabden Lancs
146 A5 Sabine's Green Essex
602 B7 Sabiston Ork
174 B2 Sackers Green Suffk
170 D6 Sacombe Herts
170 D6 Sacombe Green Herts
405 F5 Sacriston Dur
384 A1 Sadberge Darltn
459 F5 Saddell Ag & B
216 D1 Saddington Leics
252 C4 Saddle Bow Norfk
55 G2 Saddlescombe W Susx
29 G2 Saddle Street Dorset
379 E3 Sadgill Cumb
186 C4 Saffron's Cross Herefs
172 A2 Saffron Walden Essex
126 B4 Sageston Pembks
248 B4 Saham Hills Norfk
248 B4 Saham Toney Norfk
245 H2 Saighdinis W Isls
289 F2 Saighton Ches
474 D1 St Abbs Border
567 L3 St Aethans Moray
6 D3 St Agnes Cnwll
143 H3 St Albans Herts
7 F3 St Allen Cnwll
34 c3 St Andrew Guern
503 E1 St Andrews Fife
106 B5 St Andrews' Major V Glam
30 B4 St Andrew's Well Dorset
27 H1 St Andrew's Wood Devon
337 F4 St Annes Lancs
109 H5 St Anne's Park Bristl
276 C1 St Ann's C Nott
437 E6 St Ann's D & G
17 F4 St Ann's Chapel Cnwll
12 B3 St Ann's Chapel Devon
5 F2 St Anthony Cnwll
5 E3 St Anthony-in-Meneage Cnwll
405 G2 St Anthony's N u Ty
134 C5 St Arvans Mons
307 E5 St Asaph Denbgs
105 G6 St Athan V Glam
35 g7 St Aubin Jersey
100 B5 St Augustine's Kent
8 C3 St Austell Cnwll
50 B5 St Austins Hants
376 B2 St Bees Cumb
8 D2 St Blazey Cnwll
8 D3 St Blazey Gate Cnwll
452 A3 St Boswells Border
35 g7 St Brelade Jersey
35 g7 St Brelade's Bay Jersey
14 D4 St Breock Cnwll
15 F3 St Breward Cnwll
134 D4 St Briavels Gloucs
134 C4 St Briavels Common Gloucs
124 C2 St Brides Pembks
104 D5 St Bride's Major V Glam
106 A4 St Bride's-super-Ely V Glam
107 E3 St Brides Wentlooge Newpt
136 C1 Saintbridge Gloucs
10 D2 St Budeaux C Plym
163 H2 Saintbury Gloucs
2 C4 St Buryan Cnwll
110 D5 St Catherine BaNES
494 C3 St Catherines Ag & B
49 E5 St Catherine's Hill Dorset
136 B4 St Chloe Gloucs
127 F1 St Clears Carmth
16 B5 St Cleer Cnwll
7 F5 St Clement Cnwll
35 j8 St Clement Jersey
23 E6 St Clether Cnwll
464 A1 St Colmac Ag & B
14 C6 St Columb Major Cnwll
14 A6 St Columb Minor Cnwll
7 G2 St Columb Road Cnwll
571 K3 St Combs Abers
72 C4 St Cross Hants
226 C3 St Cross South Elmham Suffk
529 F2 St Cyrus Abers
511 H5 St David's P & K
150 C4 St David's Pembks
6 D5 St Day Cnwll
63 H3 St Decumans Somset
8 B2 St Dennis Cnwll
50 D2 St Denys C Sotn
133 E6 St Dials Torfn
178 C4 St Dogmaels Pembks
17 F5 St Dominick Cnwll
105 E6 St Donat's V Glam
28 D4 St Dympna's Devon
14 D3 St Endellion Cnwll
7 G2 St Enoder Cnwll
10 C2 St Erney Cnwll
3 G2 St Erth Cnwll
3 G2 St Erth Praze Cnwll
14 B4 St Ervan Cnwll
14 B5 St Eval Cnwll
8 B4 St Ewe Cnwll
106 B4 St Fagans Cardif
571 K5 St Fergus Abers
510 B5 St Fillans P & K
126 B4 St Florence Pembks
22 D3 St Gennys Cnwll
109 H5 St George Bristl
306 D4 St George Conwy
84 C2 St Georges N Som
326 B5 St George's Traffd
106 B4 St George's V Glam
235 G2 St George's Wrekin
94 B2 St George's Hill Surrey
42 D6 St George's Well Devon
10 C2 St Germans Cnwll
119 F3 St Giles Gt Lon
318 B5 St Giles Lincs
40 A4 St Giles in the Wood Devon
23 G4 St Giles on the Heath Devon
72 C4 St Giles's Hill Hants
5 E2 St Gluvias Cnwll
213 E6 St Godwalds Worcs
207 F5 St Harmon Powys
238 D4 St Helena Warwks
394 D4 St Helen Auckland Dur
329 F3 St Helen's Barns
388 B3 St Helens Cumb
58 D4 St Helen's E Susx
37 G3 St Helens IoW
324 C5 St Helens St Hel
58 D4 St Helen's Wood E Susx
95 F1 St Helier Gt Lon
35 h7 St Helier Jersey
3 F3 St Hilary Cnwll
105 G5 St Hilary V Glam
43 E6 Saint Hill Devon
77 G2 Saint Hill W Susx
170 A4 St Ibbs Herts
132 D4 St Illtyd Blae G
170 A4 St Ippollytts Herts
127 H3 St Ishmael Carmth
124 D3 St Ishmael's Pembks
14 C4 St Issey Cnwll
16 D5 St Ive Cnwll
16 D5 St Ive Cross Cnwll
220 D5 St Ives Cambs
3 F1 St Ives Cnwll
49 E4 St Ives Dorset
69 E5 St James Dorset
119 F3 St James Gt Lon
256 B5 St James Norfk
193 F2 St James's End Nhants
226 C3 St James South Elmham Suffk
14 C5 St Jidgey Cnwll
10 D3 St John Cnwll
35 h5 St John Jersey
78 C3 St John's E Susx
119 H4 St Johns Gt Lon
322 d6 St John's IoM
78 D1 St John's Kent
96 D3 St John's Kent
344 A2 St John's Leeds
93 G3 St Johns Surrey
214 D5 St Johns Warwks
188 B4 St Johns Worcs
39 H2 St John's Chapel Devon
393 E2 St John's Chapel Dur
246 A2 St John's Fen End Norfk
245 H2 St John's Highway Norfk
37 F2 St John's Park IoW
421 G3 St John's Town of Dalry D & G
119 F3 St John's Wood Gt Lon
322 f3 St Jude's IoM
143 G3 St Julians Herts
107 F2 St Julians Newpt
2 C3 St Just Cnwll
5 G1 St Just in Roseland Cnwll
89 F2 St Katharines Wilts
560 A3 St Katherines Abers
5 E4 St Keverne Cnwll
15 E3 St Kew Cnwll
15 E3 St Kew Highway Cnwll
9 G1 St Keyne Cnwll
15 E5 St Lawrence Cnwll
148 C4 St Lawrence Essex
37 E5 St Lawrence IoW
35 h6 St Lawrence Jersey
101 G2 St Lawrence Kent
142 C3 St Leonards Bucks
49 E4 St Leonards Dorset
58 C5 St Leonards E Susx
467 F4 Saint Leonards S Lans
97 G3 St Leonard's Street Kent
2 C5 St Levan Cnwll
275 E2 St Luke's C Derb
106 B5 St Lythans V Glam
15 E4 St Mabyn Cnwll
513 E5 St Madoes P & K
159 G3 St Margarets Herefs
83 G2 St Margaret's at Cliffe Kent
601 G6 St Margaret's Hope Ork
226 C3 St Margaret South Elmham Suffk
162 D5 St Mark's Gloucs
322 d8 St Marks IoM
4 D4 St Martin Cnwll
9 H2 St Martin Cnwll
35 d3 St Martin Guern
35 j6 St Martin Jersey
512 D3 St Martins P & K
269 F2 St Martin's Shrops
269 F2 St Martin's Moor Shrops
35 g6 St Mary Jersey
90 C4 St Mary Bourne Hants
20 C4 St Marychurch Torbay
96 C1 St Mary Cray Gt Lon
105 F4 St Mary Hill V Glam
122 C4 St Mary Hoo Medway
81 G4 St Mary in the Marsh Kent
3 d2 St Mary's IoS
601 H4 St Mary's Ork
81 G4 St Mary's Bay Kent
134 B1 St Maughans Mons
134 B1 St Maughans Green Mons
5 F2 St Mawes Cnwll
14 B5 St Mawgan Cnwll
17 E5 St Mellion Cnwll
106 D3 St Mellons Cardif
14 B4 St Merryn Cnwll
8 B3 St Mewan Cnwll
8 B5 St Michael Caerhays Cnwll
7 G5 St Michael Penkevil Cnwll
514 C5 St Michaels Fife
80 C2 St Michaels Kent
20 B6 St Michaels Torbay
186 D1 St Michaels Worcs
309 E2 St Michael's Hamlet Lpool
338 C1 St Michael's on Wyre Lancs
226 C3 St Michael South Elmham Suffk
14 D3 St Minver Cnwll
503 E4 St Monans Fife
16 A5 St Neot Cnwll
196 A3 St Neots Cambs
7 F2 St Newlyn East Cnwll
170 B4 St Nicholas Herts
151 E2 St Nicholas Pembks
106 A5 St Nicholas V Glam
101 E2 St Nicholas at Wade Kent
244 B1 St Nicholas House Lincs
226 C3 St Nicholas South Elmham Suffk
239 F6 St Nicolas Park Warwks
485 G1 St Ninians Stirlg
251 F5 St Olaves Norfk
149 F1 St Osyth Essex
175 F6 St Osyth Heath Essex
35 g6 St Ouen Jersey
160 C5 St Owen's Cross Herefs
162 B6 St Paul's Gloucs
120 C6 St Paul's Cray Gt Lon
170 A5 St Paul's Walden Herts
35 g6 St Peter Jersey
35 d2 St Peter Port Guern
162 D5 St Peter's Gloucs
101 G2 St Peter's Kent
405 G2 St Peter's N u Ty
226 C3 St Peter South Elmham Suffk
188 C4 St Peter The Great Worcs
125 G5 St Petrox Pembks
34 b3 St Pierre du Bois Guern
16 B6 St Pinnock Cnwll
445 E5 St Quivox S Ayrs
4 D6 St Ruan Cnwll
35 d2 St Sampson Guern
34 c3 St Saviour Guern
35 i7 St Saviour Jersey
78 C1 Saint's Hill Kent
8 A3 St Stephen Cnwll
10 D2 St Stephens Cnwll
23 G5 St Stephens Cnwll
143 G3 St Stephens Herts
15 F2 St Teath Cnwll
27 E4 St Thomas Devon
103 G3 St Thomas Swans
15 F3 St Tudy Cnwll
125 F5 St Twynnells Pembks
9 E2 St Veep Cnwll
528 D6 St Vigeans Angus
146 B6 St Vincent's Hamlet Essex
14 D6 St Wenn Cnwll
160 B5 St Weonards Herefs
9 E2 St Winnow Cnwll
106 A4 St y-Nyll V Glam
307 G4 Saith ffynnon Flints
12 C5 Salcombe Devon
28 B5 Salcombe Regis Devon
148 B2 Salcott-cum-Virley Essex
167 H4 Salden Bucks
311 G1 Sale Manch
321 E4 Saleby Lincs
188 D3 Sale Green Worcs
79 G5 Salehurst E Susx
155 F4 Salem Carmth
205 F3 Salem Cerdgn
6 D5 Salem Cnwll
518 E7 Salen Ag & B
519 G3 Salen Highld
327 H1 Salendine Nook Kirk
451 F5 Salenside Border
339 G3 Salesbury Lancs
188 D3 Saleway Worcs
168 C2 Salford Beds
164 D4 Salford Oxon
326 B5 Salford Salfd
168 C2 Salford Ford Beds
189 G4 Salford Priors Warwks
95 F5 Salfords Surrey
250 B2 Salhouse Norfk
499 G6 Saline Fife
70 D3 Salisbury Wilts
391 E2 Salkeld Dykes Cumb
547 G3 Sallachy Highld
576 B2 Sallachy Highld
255 F3 Salle Norfk
96 D6 Salmans Kent
320 B5 Salmonby Lincs
515 F2 Salmond's Muir Angus
26 C3 Salmonhutch Devon
163 G5 Salperton Gloucs
163 G6 Salperton Park Gloucs
195 F4 Salph End Beds
468 C2 Salsburgh N Lans
398 D5 Salta Cumb
273 E4 Salt Staffs
10 C2 Saltash Cnwll
566 C3 Saltburn Highld
397 G5 Saltburn-by-the-Sea R & Cl
278 B4 Saltby Leics
399 F4 Salt Coates Cumb
376 D5 Saltcoats Cumb
489 F3 Saltcoats E Loth
444 B1 Saltcoats N Ayrs
337 G4 Saltcotes Lancs
56 B4 Saltdean E Susx
348 C4 Salt End E R Yk
388 A4 Salterbeck Cumb
354 A5 Salterforth Lancs
91 G3 Salters Heath Hants
271 E4 Saltershill Shrops
246 B4 Salters Lode Norfk
213 H5 Salter Street Solhll
290 C1 Salterswall Ches
70 C2 Salterton Wilts
335 G6 Saltfleet Lincs
321 E1 Saltfleetby All Saints Lincs
320 D1 Saltfleetby St Clement Lincs
320 D2 Saltfleetby St Peter Lincs
86 B1 Saltford BaNES
117 G3 Salt Hill Slough
364 B6 Salthouse Cumb
261 E3 Salthouse Norfk
213 G2 Saltley Birm
107 F3 Saltmarsh Newpt
346 A5 Saltmarshe E R Yk
600 D6 Saltness Ork
289 E2 Saltney Flints
372 D4 Salton N York
39 G3 Saltrens Devon
405 F2 Saltwell Gatesd
430 C3 Saltwick Nthumb
82 C3 Saltwood Kent
516 D6 Salum Ag & B
54 D3 Salvington W Susx
188 C2 Salwarpe Worcs
30 A3 Salwayash Dorset
189 F2 Sambourne Warwks
87 F6 Sambourne Wilts
271 G5 Sambrook Wrekin
592 D5 Samhla W Isls
339 E3 Samlesbury Lancs
339 F4 Samlesbury Bottoms Lancs
43 F4 Sampford Arundel Somset
63 H3 Sampford Brett Somset
25 F2 Sampford Chapple Devon
25 F2 Sampford Courtenay Devon
43 F4 Sampford Moor Somset
42 D5 Sampford Peverell Devon
18 B3 Sampford Spiney Devon
603 K6 Samsonslane Ork
123 F2 Samuel's Corner Essex
489 F5 Samuelston E Loth
546 E1 Sanachan Highld
476 C2 Sanaigmore Ag & B
2 D4 Sancreed Cnwll
346 D2 Sancton E R Yk
573 H5 Sand Highld
606 D8 Sand Shet
84 D5 Sand Somset
516 A7 Sandaig Ag & B
531 K2 Sandaig Highld
389 F1 Sandale Cumb
343 F6 Sandal Magna Wakefd
530 E6 Sandavore Highld
291 E2 Sandbach Ches
291 F2 Sandbach Heath Ches
481 H3 Sandbank Ag & B
34 B3 Sandbanks Poole
148 D3 Sandbeach Essex
273 H6 Sandborough Staffs
333 G4 Sandbraes Lincs
569 J2 Sandend Abers
95 G2 Sanderstead Gt Lon
104 A1 Sandfields Neath
237 H3 Sandfields Staffs
380 C1 Sandford Cumb
26 C2 Sandford Devon
33 G2 Sandford Dorset
49 F4 Sandford Hants
37 E4 Sandford IoW
84 D3 Sandford N Som
269 F5 Sandford Shrops
270 D3 Sandford Shrops
467 H6 Sandford S Lans
188 C5 Sandford Worcs
84 D3 Sandford Batch N Som
561 H1 Sandfordhill Abers
140 B4 Sandford-on-Thames Oxon
67 G5 Sandford Orcas Dorset
165 G4 Sandford St Martin Oxon
365 E4 Sand Gate Cumb
82 D4 Sandgate Kent
412 A4 Sandgreen D & G
571 H2 Sandhaven Abers
408 C1 Sandhead D & G
329 G3 Sandhill Barns
167 F4 Sandhill Bucks
222 B2 Sandhill Cambs
30 D2 Sandhills Dorset
46 C2 Sandhills Dorset
343 G2 Sandhills Leeds
323 F6 Sandhills Lpool
140 C3 Sandhills Oxon
75 E2 Sandhills Surrey
403 H1 Sandhoe Nthumb
493 H5 Sandhole Ag & B
346 A2 Sand Hole E R Yk
346 B3 Sandholme E R Yk
280 D2 Sandholme Lincs
93 E2 Sandhurst Br For
162 B5 Sandhurst Gloucs
80 A4 Sandhurst Kent
80 A4 Sandhurst Cross Kent
358 D3 Sand Hutton N York
370 D3 Sandhutton N York
275 H2 Sandiacre Derbys
321 F3 Sandilands Lincs
448 A2 Sandilands S Lans
310 C5 Sandiway Ches
49 E2 Sandleheath Hants
98 B3 Sandling Kent
291 F1 Sandlow Green Ches
606 A6 Sandness Shet
147 E4 Sandon Essex
170 D3 Sandon Herts
272 D4 Sandon Staffs
272 D4 Sandonbank Staffs
37 G4 Sandown IoW
79 E1 Sandown Park Kent
30 A2 Sandpit Dorset
162 B4 Sandpits Gloucs
143 H2 Sandridge Herts
252 D2 Sandringham Norfk
142 A6 Sands Bucks
119 F4 Sands End Gt Lon
387 E2 Sandsend N York
363 E5 Sand Side Cumb
364 C4 Sandside Cumb
365 G3 Sandside Cumb
412 C5 Sand Side D & G
351 F4 Sand Side Lancs
606 E8 Sandsound Shet
331 F3 Sandtoft N Linc
608 D6 Sandvoe Shet
98 D4 Sandway Kent
213 F2 Sandwell Sandw
101 F4 Sandwich Kent
101 G4 Sandwich Bay Estate Kent
390 C6 Sandwick Cumb
601 G7 Sandwick Ork
605 H6 Sandwick Shet
607 H5 Sandwick Shet
597 L1 Sandwick W Isls
376 B2 Sandwith Cumb
376 B2 Sandwith Newtown Cumb
195 H5 Sandy Beds
128 C4 Sandy Carmth
299 H3 Sandy Bank Lincs
603 G5 Sandybank Ork

396 A1 Sandy Carrs Dur
288 D1 Sandycroft Flints
78 D6 Sandy Cross E Susx
93 E5 Sandy Cross Surrey
50 B5 Sandy Down Hants
291 H4 Sandygate C Stke
437 G6 Sandyford D & G
20 B3 Sandygate Devon
27 F4 Sandy Gate Devon
322 f3 Sandygate IoM
314 C2 Sandygate Sheff
124 D3 Sandy Haven Pembks
413 G3 Sandyhills D & G
9 E1 Sandylake Cnwll
351 F2 Sandylands Lancs
43 F3 Sandylands Somset
342 B2 Sandy Lane Brad
102 D4 Sandylane Swans
111 H6 Sandy Lane Wilts
269 H1 Sandy Lane Wrexhm
24 A3 Sandymoor Cross Devon
400 C1 Sandysike Cumb
36 D4 Sandy Way IoW
237 H3 Sandyway Staffs
585 H3 Sangobeg Highld
585 G3 Sangomore Highld
90 A1 Sanham Green W Berk
310 B2 Sankey Bridges Warrtn
188 A1 Sankyns Green Worcs
518 B2 Sanna Highld
593 E9 Sanndabhaig W Isls
597 L1 Sanndabhaig W Isls
463 H5 Sannox N Ayrs
435 F3 Sanquhar D & G
270 C5 Sansaw Heath Shrops
376 D4 Santon Cumb
322 e8 Santon IoM
332 C2 Santon N Linc
377 E4 Santon Bridge Cumb
223 G2 Santon Downham Suffk
240 A6 Sapcote Leics
187 G3 Sapey Bridge Herefs
187 G3 Sapey Common Herefs
224 B4 Sapiston Suffk
220 B5 Sapley Cambs
274 B3 Sapperton Derbys
136 D4 Sapperton Gloucs
279 E3 Sapperton Lincs
280 D4 Saracen's Head Lincs
589 J8 Sarclet Highld
129 E3 Sardis Carmth
126 C3 Sardis Pembks
51 F3 Sarisbury Hants
105 E3 Sarn Brdgnd
307 G4 Sarn Flints
208 D1 Sarn Powys
153 G6 Sarnau Carmth
179 G3 Sarnau Cerdgn
267 F2 Sarnau Gwynd
157 G3 Sarnau Gwynd
232 D1 Sarnau Powys
263 E5 Sarn Bach Gwynd
185 G4 Sarnesfield Herefs
262 C4 Sarn Meyllteyrn Gwynd
129 E2 Saron Carmth
153 H2 Saron Carmth
287 E2 Saron Denbgs
283 E4 Saron Gwynd
283 F2 Saron Gwynd
143 E5 Sarratt Herts
143 E5 Sarratt Bottom Herts
101 E2 Sarre Kent
164 D5 Sarsden Oxon
164 D5 Sarsden Halt Oxon
585 G4 Sarsgrum Highld
234 A2 Sascott Shrops
404 D6 Satley Dur
83 E3 Satmar Kent
545 G3 Satran Highld
381 G5 Satron N York
40 D3 Satterleigh Devon
378 B6 Satterthwaite Cumb
116 A3 Satwell Oxon
556 B2 Sauchen Abers
513 E3 Saucher P & K
499 E6 Sauchie Clacks
540 C6 Sauchieburn Abers
432 D2 Sauchrie S Ayrs
309 E5 Saughall Ches
308 B2 Saughall Massie Wirral
487 G5 Saughton C Edin
439 H5 Saughtree Border
135 G3 Saul Gloucs
317 E2 Saundby Notts
126 C4 Saundersfoot Pembks
141 G4 Saunderton Bucks
141 G5 Saunderton Lee Bucks
60 B4 Saunton Devon
320 C6 Sausthorpe Lincs
576 C2 Saval Highld
518 F6 Savary Highld
7 E5 Saveock Cnwll
273 E2 Saverley Green Staffs
342 A5 Savile Park Calder
342 D5 Savile Town Kirk
192 B1 Sawbridge Warwks
145 G1 Sawbridgeworth Herts
374 A3 Sawdon N York
275 H3 Sawley Derbys
353 F5 Sawley Lancs
370 A6 Sawley N York
341 G3 Sawood Brad
197 G5 Sawston Cambs
219 H3 Sawtry Cambs
43 G3 Sawyer's Hill Somset
112 B1 Sawyers Hill Wilts
277 H6 Saxby Leics
318 C2 Saxby Lincs
53 H4 Saxby W Susx
332 D1 Saxby All Saints N Linc
277 F5 Saxelbye Leics
201 E2 Saxham Street Suffk
317 H4 Saxilby Lincs
260 D4 Saxlingham Norfk
250 A5 Saxlingham Green Norfk
250 A5 Saxlingham Nethergate Norfk
202 D2 Saxmundham Suffk
277 E2 Saxondale Notts
198 D3 Saxon Street Cambs
202 B1 Saxtead Suffk
202 B2 Saxtead Green Suffk
202 B1 Saxtead Little Green Suffk
261 F5 Saxthorpe Norfk
344 B2 Saxton N York
77 E6 Sayers Common W Susx
372 B5 Scackleton N York
595 K4 Scadabhagh W Isls
316 C1 Scaftworth Notts
373 F5 Scagglethorpe N York
340 B4 Scaitcliffe Lancs
478 B3 Scalasaig Ag & B
346 B4 Scalby E R Yk
374 B2 Scalby N York
374 C1 Scalby Mills N York
195 F3 Scald End Beds
217 G5 Scaldwell Nhants
400 D2 Scaleby Cumb
400 D2 Scaleby Hill Cumb
351 G2 Scale Hall Lancs
347 G3 Scale Houses Cumb
364 C5 Scales Cumb
402 A4 Scales Cumb
388 G6 Scales Cumb

277 G5 Scalford Leics
386 B2 Scaling R & Cl
386 B2 Scaling Dam N York
505 K3 Scallastle Ag & B
605 G3 Scalloway Shet
320 A4 Scamblesby Lincs
359 E6 Scamland E R Yk
532 B8 Scamodale Highld
373 G4 Scampston N York
318 B4 Scampton Lincs
601 G3 Scapa Ork
327 G1 Scapegoat Hill Kirk
603 K2 Scar Ork
374 D2 Scarborough N York
7 H3 Scarcewater Cnwll
315 F6 Scarcliffe Derbys
343 G1 Scarcroft Leeds
564 C6 Scardroy Highld
606 B1 Scarff Shet
589 H2 Scarfskerry Highld
382 B2 Scargill Dur
378 A6 Scar Head Cumb
516 C7 Scarinish Ag & B
323 G2 Scarisbrick Lancs
389 F3 Scarness Cumb
248 B2 Scarning Norfk
277 F1 Scarrington Notts
324 A3 Scarth Hill Lancs
344 B2 Scarthingwell N York
334 C3 Scartho NE Lin
604 E2 Scarvister Shet
602 A7 Scarwell Ork
605 G8 Scatness Shet
606 E3 Scatsta Shet
332 D3 Scawby N Linc
330 B4 Scawsby Donc
330 C3 Scawthorpe Donc
371 H3 Scawton N York
77 G5 Scayne's Hill W Susx
158 B4 Scethrog Powys
291 G3 Scholar Green Ches
342 B3 Scholemoor Brad
328 B3 Scholes Kirk
341 G2 Scholes Kirk
342 C4 Scholes Kirk
343 G2 Scholes Leeds
329 F5 Scholes Rothm
395 E5 School Aycliffe Dur
290 C2 School Green Ches
173 E3 School Green Essex
36 A3 School Green IoW
92 B1 Schoolgreen Wokham
556 D4 Schoolhill Abers
557 G5 Schoolhill Abers
29 G2 School House Dorset
388 A6 Scilly Bank Cumb
328 D2 Scissett Kirk
151 F3 Scleddau Pembks
12 A3 Scobbiscombe Devon
316 B3 Scofton Notts
225 G4 Scole Norfk
225 F3 Scole Common Norfk
592 C2 Scolpaig W Isls
512 D4 Scone P & K
545 J3 Sconser Highld
502 B4 Scoonie Fife
512 D5 Scoonieburn P & K
504 E7 Scoor Ag & B
298 D3 Scopwick Lincs
573 K4 Scoraig Highld
360 C5 Scorborough E R Yk
6 D5 Scorrier Cnwll
19 E4 Scorriton Devon
351 H5 Scorton Lancs
383 G4 Scorton N York
256 B5 Sco Ruston Norfk
592 E6 Scotbheinn W Isls
400 D4 Scotby Cumb
383 E3 Scotch Corner N York
294 C5 Scotches Derbys
351 G3 Scotforth Lancs
327 H2 Scotgate Kirk
291 G5 Scot Hay Staffs
318 C4 Scothern Lincs
241 E5 Scotland Leics
275 F5 Scotland Lincs
279 E4 Scotland Lincs
115 F6 Scotland W Berk
165 E3 Scotland End Oxon
431 E3 Scotland Gate Nthumb
236 D4 Scotlands Wolves
174 C2 Scotland Street Suffk
500 C4 Scotlandwell P & K
325 E3 Scot Lane End Bolton
325 E3 Scot Lane End Wigan
566 C1 Scotsburn Highld
514 C4 Scotscraig Fife
429 G2 Scots' Gap Nthumb
540 D5 Scotston Abers
524 D7 Scotston P & K
483 H6 Scotstoun C Glas
519 K3 Scotstown Highld
405 F2 Scotswood N u Ty
93 F1 Scotswood W & M
531 K2 Scottas Highld
332 B4 Scotter Lincs
332 B4 Scotterthorpe Lincs
332 B5 Scotton Lincs
356 C3 Scotton N York
383 E5 Scotton N York
256 B5 Scottow Norfk
279 F2 Scott Willoughby Lincs
490 B3 Scoughall E Loth
464 C3 Scoulag Ag & B
248 C4 Scoulton Norfk
273 G4 Scounslow Green Staffs
584 C8 Scourie Highld
584 B8 Scourie More Highld
605 G7 Scousburgh Shet
328 C3 Scout Dike Barns
379 G3 Scout Green Cumb
327 E3 Scouthead Oldham
134 D2 Scowles Gloucs
588 E2 Scrabster Highld
452 C6 Scraesburgh Border
320 B6 Scrafield Lincs
98 C2 Scragged Oak Kent
442 B3 Scrainwood Nthumb
281 E1 Scrane End Lincs
123 E5 Scrapsgate Kent
241 E3 Scraptoft Leics
251 G1 Scratby Norfk
358 D2 Scrayingham N York
8 C3 Scredda Cnwll
279 F1 Scredington Lincs
43 E2 Screedy Somset
320 D6 Scremby Lincs
475 F5 Scremerston Nthumb
296 D6 Screveton Notts
299 H1 Scrivelsby Lincs
356 C3 Scriven N York
351 F5 Scronkey Lancs
316 B1 Scrooby Notts
274 B3 Scropton Derbys
299 G3 Scrub Hill Lincs
370 C1 Scruton N York
268 C5 Scrwgan Powys
426 B6 Scuggate Cumb
347 G3 Sculcoates C KuH
260 A5 Sculthorpe Norfk
332 C2 Scunthorpe N Linc
102 C4 Scurlage Swans
44 C5 Sea Somset

30 B2 Seaborough Dorset
291 G6 Seabridge Staffs
82 C4 Seabrook Kent
406 B3 Seaburn Sundld
308 D1 Seacombe Wirral
79 G3 Seacox Heath E Susx
343 F2 Seacroft Leeds
301 G2 Seacroft Lincs
280 D2 Seadyke Lincs
485 F5 Seafar N Lans
557 G4 Seafield C Aber
470 D2 Seafield Mdloth
444 D5 Seafield S Ayrs
609 G6 Seafield Shet
469 G1 Seafield W Loth
56 D5 Seaford E Susx
323 F5 Seaforth Sefton
276 D6 Seagrave Leics
111 H3 Seagry Heath Wilts
406 C5 Seaham Dur
455 G3 Seahouses Nthumb
97 E3 Seal Kent
308 D6 Sealand Flints
93 E5 Seale Surrey
374 C3 Seamer N York
384 D2 Seamer N York
364 C6 Sea Mill Cumb
464 D5 Seamill N Ayrs
109 F4 Sea Mills Bristl
14 C4 Sea Mills Cnwll
257 E4 Sea Palling Norfk
333 F3 Searby Lincs
100 A2 Seasalter Kent
376 C4 Seascale Cumb
513 G5 Seaside P & K
301 G1 Seathorne Lincs
377 G2 Seathwaite Cumb
377 G5 Seathwaite Cumb
365 E3 Seatle Cumb
377 E3 Seatoller Cumb
515 H1 Seaton Angus
557 G3 Seaton C Aber
10 B3 Seaton Cnwll
388 B3 Seaton Cumb
28 D4 Seaton Devon
431 F4 Seaton Dur
361 F5 Seaton E R Yk
100 D1 Seaton Kent
242 B5 Seaton Rutlnd
406 B4 Seaton Sundld
430 D5 Seaton Burn N Tyne
396 D4 Seaton Carew Hartpl
431 F4 Seaton Delaval Nthumb
28 D3 Seaton Junction Devon
345 H1 Seaton Ross E R Yk
431 F4 Seaton Sluice Nthumb
29 H4 Seatown Dorset
568 C1 Seatown Moray
569 G2 Seatown Moray
6 D6 Seureaugh Moor Cnwll
385 F4 Seave Green N York
37 G2 Seaview IoW
399 F4 Seaville Cumb
44 D5 Seavington St Mary Somset
45 E4 Seavington St Michael Somset
149 F2 Seawick Essex
133 E5 Sebastopol Torfn
390 A1 Sebergham Cumb
238 D3 Seckington Warwks
573 H5 Second Coast Highld
29 F3 Sector Devon
366 C1 Sedbergh Cumb
134 C6 Sedbury Gloucs
368 A1 Sedbusk N York
195 H5 Seddington Beds
163 F2 Sedgeberrow Worcs
278 B2 Sedgebrook Lincs
395 H4 Sedgefield Dur
259 E4 Sedgeford Norfk
69 E4 Sedgehill Wilts
214 C4 Sedgemere Solhll
236 D6 Sedgley Dudley
326 B4 Sedgley Park Bury
365 H2 Sedgwick Cumb
58 C3 Sedlescombe E Susx
141 G2 Sedrup Bucks
99 E3 Seed Kent
339 E4 Seed Lee Lancs
326 A5 Seedley Salfd
87 G2 Seend Wilts
87 G2 Seend Cleeve Wilts
87 G2 Seend Head Wilts
117 G1 Seer Green Bucks
250 C5 Seething Norfk
94 D1 Seething Wells Gt Lon
606 D7 Sefster Shet
323 G4 Sefton Sefton
309 E2 Sefton Park Lpool
51 F3 Segensworth Hants
431 E5 Seghill Nthumb
210 B3 Seifton Shrops
272 C5 Seighford Staffs
595 H3 Seilebost W Isls
283 F2 Seion Gwynd
236 B6 Seisdon Staffs
599 L8 Seisiadar W Isls
269 E3 Selattyn Shrops
74 A3 Selborne Hants
345 E3 Selby N York
99 G3 Selgrove Kent
75 E5 Selham W Susx
95 G1 Selhurst Gt Lon
451 F4 Selkirk Border
160 D4 Sellack Herefs
160 D4 Sellack Boat Herefs
609 G5 Sellafirth Shet
2 D3 Sellan Cnwll
603 L3 Sellibister Ork
43 H4 Sellick's Green Somset
81 H2 Sellindge Kent
99 G3 Selling Kent
87 G2 Sells Green Wilts
387 E3 Selly Hill N York
213 F3 Selly Oak Birm
213 F3 Selly Park Birm
57 E3 Selmeston E Susx
95 H2 Selsdon Gt Lon
212 A3 Selsey W Susx
101 H4 Selson Kent
82 D2 Selsted Kent
295 F4 Selston Notts
295 E4 Selston Common Notts
295 E4 Selston Green Notts
63 G2 Selworthy Somset
200 D5 Semer Suffk
69 E4 Sem Hill Wilts
87 F2 Semington Wilts
69 E4 Semley Wilts
279 G3 Sempringham Lincs
94 A3 Send Surrey
93 H2 Send Grove Surrey
94 A3 Send Marsh Surrey
106 D1 Senghenydd Caerph
2 C4 Sennen Cnwll
2 C4 Sennen Cove Cnwll
157 E4 Sennybridge Powys
316 B2 Serlby Notts

70 B2 Serrington Wilts
371 E4 Sessay N York
252 C5 Setchey Norfk
50 B4 Setley Hants
489 E5 Seton E Loth
489 E6 Seton Mains E Loth
605 K2 Setter Shet
606 F7 Setter Shet
607 G1 Setter Shet
602 D8 Settiscarth Ork
353 G2 Settle N York
64 C5 Seven Ash Somset
163 F5 Sevenhampton Gloucs
113 E1 Sevenhampton Swindn
120 C2 Seven Kings Gt Lon
96 D4 Sevenoaks Kent
96 D4 Sevenoaks Common Kent
96 D4 Sevenoaks Weald Kent
130 C3 Seven Sisters Neath
137 E1 Seven Springs Gloucs
174 B4 Seven Star Green Essex
12 B3 Seven Stones Cross Devon
109 F3 Severn Beach S Glos
188 B6 Severn Stoke Worcs
195 F4 Sevick End Beds
81 F1 Sevington Kent
172 B2 Sewards End Essex
145 E5 Sewardstone Essex
145 E5 Sewardstonebury Essex
168 D5 Sewell Beds
375 F6 Sewerby E R Yk
4 D2 Seworgan Cnwll
278 B5 Sewstern Leics
384 D3 Sexhow N York
164 B3 Sezincote Gloucs
591 D8 Sgallairidh W Isls
595 G4 Sgarasta Bheag W Isls
595 G4 Sgarasta Mhor W Isls
584 C6 Sgeir Iosal Highld
599 L2 Sgiogarstaigh W Isls
542 C4 Sgoir Beag Highld
478 B2 Sgreadan Ag & B
141 E3 Shabbington Bucks
136 D1 Shab Hill Gloucs
236 D1 Shackerley Shrops
239 F3 Shackerstone Leics
275 G3 Shacklecross Derbys
93 F5 Shackleford Surrey
341 F4 Shackleton Calder
119 G2 Shacklewell Gt Lon
341 E5 Shade Calder
395 G1 Shadforth Dur
227 E3 Shadingfield Suffk
81 E2 Shadoxhurst Kent
339 H4 Shadsworth Bl w D
136 A5 Shadwell Gloucs
119 H3 Shadwell Gt Lon
343 F2 Shadwell Leeds
224 B3 Shadwell Norfk
292 C4 Shaffalong Staffs
171 F2 Shaftenhoe End Herts
69 E5 Shaftesbury Dorset
329 F2 Shafton Barns
329 F2 Shafton Two Gates Barns
33 E3 Shaggs Dorset
271 F4 Shakeford Shrops
325 F4 Shakerley Wigan
161 F3 Shakesfield Gloucs
89 H2 Shalbourne Wilts
36 B3 Shalcombe IoW
73 G1 Shalden Hants
92 A6 Shalden Green Hants
20 C3 Shaldon Devon
36 C3 Shalfleet IoW
173 E4 Shalford Essex
93 H5 Shalford Surrey
173 E4 Shalford Green Essex
40 D2 Shallowford Devon
61 H3 Shallowford Devon
272 C4 Shallowford Staffs
100 A5 Shalmsford Street Kent
166 D2 Shalstone Bucks
94 A6 Shamley Green Surrey
482 C2 Shandon Ag & B
566 F2 Shandwick Highld
241 F5 Shangton Leics
431 E4 Shankhouse Nthumb
37 F4 Shanklin IoW
557 H4 Shannaburn Abers
460 D5 Shannochie N Ayrs
496 D5 Shannochill Stirlg
558 C2 Shanquhar Abers
379 G2 Shap Cumb
135 F1 Shapridge Gloucs
48 A4 Shapwick Dorset
66 D2 Shapwick Somset
88 C3 Sharcott Wilts
214 A2 Shard End Birm
275 G3 Shardlow Derbys
236 D3 Shareshill Staffs
343 G6 Sharlston Wakefd
343 G6 Sharlston Common Wakefd
213 F3 Sharmans Cross Solhll
122 B5 Sharnal Street Medway
194 D3 Sharnbrook Beds
340 D5 Sharneyford Lancs
216 A1 Sharnford Leics
46 D3 Sharnhill Green Dorset
338 D3 Sharoe Green Lancs
370 C2 Sharow N York
169 F3 Sharpenhoe Beds
442 B4 Sharperton Nthumb
325 G2 Sharples Bolton
273 G2 Sharpley Heath Staffs
135 F4 Sharpness Gloucs
78 D6 Sharpsbridge E Susx
78 D6 Sharp's Corner E Susx
86 D3 Sharpstone BaNES
256 D5 Sharp Street Norfk
77 G3 Sharpthorne W Susx
16 C4 Sharptor Cnwll
188 D1 Sharpway Gate Worcs
260 D4 Sharrington Norfk
314 C2 Sharrow Sheff
311 G2 Sharston Manch
212 A3 Shatterford Worcs
101 E4 Shatterling Kent
313 G3 Shatton Derbys
18 B5 Shaugh Prior Devon
291 E4 Shavington Ches
341 G2 Shaw Brad
326 D3 Shaw Oldham
112 D2 Shaw Swindn
114 D6 Shaw W Berk
87 F1 Shaw Wilts
210 B3 Shawbank Shrops
210 B3 Shawbirch Wrekin
598 E5 Shawbost W Isls
270 C4 Shawbury Shrops
326 C2 Shawclough Rochdl
161 F4 Shaw Common Gloucs
442 D2 Shawdon Hall Nthumb
216 B3 Shawell Leics
78 C3 Shawfield Rochdl
273 H3 Shawfield Staffs
356 B4 Shawfield Head N York
72 C5 Shawford Hants
86 D4 Shawford Somset
340 C5 Shawforth Lancs
170 C3 Shaw Green Herts
338 D6 Shaw Green Lancs

356 B4 Shaw Green N York
423 E4 Shawhead D & G
468 A2 Shawhead N Lans
311 F4 Shaw Heath Ches
312 A2 Shaw Heath Stockp
467 E2 Shawlands C Glas
356 A2 Shaw Mills N York
468 B4 Shawsburn S Lans
326 D3 Shaw Side Oldham
467 G5 Shawton S Lans
467 G5 Shawtonhill S Lans
398 C1 Shearington D & G
216 D1 Shearsby Leics
65 E5 Shearston Somset
39 F6 Shebbear Devon
271 H4 Shebdon Staffs
588 C4 Shebster Highld
467 E3 Sheddens E Rens
411 E5 Sheddock D & G
557 F5 Sheddocksley C Aber
51 F2 Shedfield Hants
293 F2 Sheen Staffs
314 D5 Sheepbridge Derbys
114 A4 Sheepdrove W Berk
602 F2 Sheepheight Ork
405 E3 Sheep Hill Dur
168 C3 Sheeplane Beds
117 E2 Sheepridge Bucks
342 C6 Sheepridge Kirk
136 C2 Sheepscombe Gloucs
18 C4 Sheepstor Devon
24 C1 Sheepwash Devon
430 D2 Sheepwash Nthumb
109 E4 Sheepway N Som
239 E4 Sheepy Magna Leics
239 E4 Sheepy Parva Leics
145 H2 Sheering Essex
123 E4 Sheerness Kent
93 H2 Sheerwater Surrey
74 B5 Sheet Hants
210 C5 Sheet Shrops
93 F3 Sheets Heath Surrey
3 E4 Sheffield Cnwll
314 D5 Sheffield Sheff
115 G5 Sheffield Bottom W Berk
77 H4 Sheffield Green E Susx
314 D2 Sheffield Park Sheff
169 G2 Shefford Beds
114 B5 Shefford Woodlands W Berk
584 C4 Sheigra Highld
468 A2 Sheildmuir N Lans
235 E4 Sheinton Shrops
209 H4 Shelderton Shrops
214 B3 Sheldon Birm
313 G6 Sheldon Derbys
43 F6 Sheldon Devon
99 G3 Sheldwich Kent
99 G3 Sheldwich Lees Kent
105 E3 Shelf Brdgnd
342 B4 Shelf Calder
225 F3 Shelfanger Norfk
189 H2 Shelfield Wsall
237 F4 Shelfield Warwks
189 H2 Shelfield Green Warwks
193 F3 Shelfleys Nhants
277 E1 Shelford Notts
215 G2 Shelford Warwks
189 E3 Shelland Suffk
200 D3 Shellbrook Leics
239 E1 Shellbrook Leics
146 A3 Shelley Essex
328 C2 Shelley Kirk
174 D2 Shelley Suffk
328 C2 Shelley Woodhouse Kirk
341 G1 Shell Green Halton
139 E6 Shellingford Oxon
146 C3 Shellow Bowells Essex
94 D5 Shellwood Cross Surrey
187 G2 Shelsley Beauchamp Worcs
187 G2 Shelsley Walsh Worcs
276 B6 Shelthorpe Leics
219 E6 Shelton Beds
292 E5 Shelton C Stke
225 H1 Shelton Norfk
297 E6 Shelton Notts
234 B2 Shelton Shrops
226 A1 Shelton Green Norfk
275 F3 Shelton Lock C Derb
272 B2 Shelton under Harley Staffs
233 F5 Shelve Shrops
28 C2 Shelvin Devon
100 D2 Shelvingford Kent
186 C6 Shelwick Herefs
186 C6 Shelwick Green Herefs
146 B6 Shenfield Essex
191 F6 Shenington Oxon
144 A4 Shenley Herts
168 A2 Shenley Brook End M Keyn
143 H4 Shenleybury Herts
168 A2 Shenley Church End M Keyn
213 F3 Shenley Fields Birm
168 A2 Shenley Lodge M Keyn
167 H2 Shenley Wood M Keyn
159 G2 Shenmore Herefs
416 C2 Shennanton D & G
237 H4 Shenstone Staffs
212 D4 Shenstone Worcs
237 H4 Shenstone Woodend Staffs
239 F4 Shenton Leics
548 B2 Shenval Highld
552 E3 Shenval Moray
244 D2 Shepeau Stow Lincs
170 C5 Shephall Herts
119 C3 Shepherd's Bush Gt Lon
252 B4 Shepherd's Gate Norfk
116 B3 Shepherd's Green Oxon
75 E3 Shepherd's Hill Surrey
135 G4 Shepherd's Patch Gloucs
277 F7 Shepherd's Port Norfk
101 E6 Shepherdswell or Sibertswold Kent
328 B3 Shepley Kirk
135 E5 Shepperdine S Glos
94 B1 Shepperton Surrey
197 E5 Shepreth Cambs
275 H6 Shepshed Leics
44 B5 Shepton Beauchamp Somset
85 H6 Shepton Mallet Somset
68 A3 Shepton Montague Somset
98 B4 Shepway Kent
396 B3 Sheraton Dur
18 D3 Sherberton Devon
46 B1 Sherborne Dorset
138 B2 Sherborne Gloucs
85 G3 Sherborne Somset
91 G3 Sherborne St John Hants
190 D2 Sherbourne Warwks
174 B1 Sherbourne Street Suffk
395 G1 Sherburn Dur
374 A4 Sherburn N York
405 H6 Sherburn Grange Dur
395 G1 Sherburn Hill Dur
344 B3 Sherburn in Elmet N York
94 B5 Shere Surrey
254 C2 Shereford Norfk
71 F5 Sherfield English Hants
91 G3 Sherfield on Loddon Hants

340 B4 Sherfin Lancs
12 D4 Sherford Devon
47 H6 Sherford Dorset
43 H3 Sherford Somset
235 H2 Sheriffhales Shrops
405 G2 Sheriff Hill Gatesd
358 C1 Sheriff Hutton N York
189 F5 Sheriff's Lench Worcs
261 G3 Sheringham Norfk
194 B5 Sherington M Keyn
261 G3 Sheringwood Norfk
76 D6 Shermanbury W Susx
188 D2 Shernal Green Worcs
259 E5 Shernborne Norfk
188 A5 Sherrard's Green Worcs
144 B2 Sherrardspark Herts
69 G2 Sherrington Wilts
111 F2 Sherston Wilts
295 H6 Sherwood C Nott
40 B3 Sherwood Green Devon
79 E1 Sherwood Park Kent
467 F2 Shettleston C Glas
324 C3 Shevington Wigan
324 C2 Shevington Moor Wigan
324 C3 Shevington Vale Wigan
10 C2 Sheviock Cnwll
444 D2 Shewalton N Ayrs
342 A4 Shibden Head Brad
37 E3 Shide IoW
547 G6 Shiel Bridge Highld
562 D2 Shieldaig Highld
562 E6 Shieldaig Highld
466 D1 Shieldhall C Glas
424 A3 Shieldhill D & G
486 A4 Shieldhill Falk
448 D1 Shieldhill S Lans
405 F4 Shield Row Dur
519 G1 Shielfoot Highld
527 F3 Shielhill Angus
524 C3 Shierglas P & K
235 H3 Shifnal Shrops
443 F3 Shilbottle Nthumb
443 G3 Shilbottle Grange Nthumb
395 E4 Shildon Dur
466 B3 Shillford E Rens
593 C10 Shilligarry W Isls
42 C3 Shillingford Devon
140 C6 Shillingford Oxon
27 E5 Shillingford Abbot Devon
26 D5 Shillingford St George Devon
47 F2 Shillingstone Dorset
169 G3 Shillington Beds
441 G3 Shillmoor Nthumb
138 D3 Shilton Oxon
215 G3 Shilton Warwks
31 E6 Shilvinghampton Dorset
430 C3 Shilvington Nthumb
225 G3 Shimpling Norfk
199 H4 Shimpling Suffk
199 H4 Shimpling Street Suffk
395 F1 Shincliffe Dur
405 H4 Shiney Row Sundld
116 B6 Shinfield Wokham
196 D5 Shingay Cambs
247 F3 Shingham Norfk
202 D6 Shingle Street Suffk
19 G5 Shinner's Bridge Devon
97 E4 Shipbourne Kent
248 B3 Shipdham Norfk
84 D3 Shipham Somset
20 B4 Shiphay Torbay
116 C4 Shiplake Oxon
116 A3 Shiplake Bottom Oxon
116 B4 Shiplake Row Oxon
84 C3 Shiplate N Som
470 D5 Shiplaw Border
342 C2 Shipley Brad
295 E5 Shipley Derbys
236 B5 Shipley Shrops
76 B5 Shipley W Susx
77 F1 Shipley Bridge Surrey
295 E6 Shipley Common Derbys
472 B5 Shipley Gate Border
226 D1 Shipmeadow Suffk
126 C3 Shipping Pembks
139 H5 Shippon Oxon
164 D1 Shipston-on-Stour Warwks
167 G4 Shipton Bucks
163 F6 Shipton Gloucs
357 H3 Shipton N York
210 D1 Shipton Shrops
89 F5 Shipton Bellinger Hants
30 B4 Shipton Gorge Dorset
53 E5 Shipton Green W Susx
167 F5 Shipton Lee Bucks
111 F2 Shipton Moyne Gloucs
163 F6 Shipton Oliffe Gloucs
140 A1 Shipton-on-Cherwell Oxon
163 F6 Shipton Solers Gloucs
359 G6 Shiptonthorpe E R Yk
164 D6 Shipton under Wychwood Oxon
141 E5 Shirburn Oxon
323 G2 Shirdley Hill Lancs
315 F5 Shirebrook Derbys
314 C1 Shirecliffe Sheff
314 F6 Shiregreen Sheff
109 F4 Shirehampton Bristl
431 F5 Shiremoor N Tyne
134 B6 Shirenewton Mons
237 F4 Shire Oak Wsall
313 E3 Shireoaks Derbys
315 G3 Shireoaks Notts
486 D2 Shires Mill Fife
80 D2 Shirkoak Kent
294 D3 Shirland Derbys
235 F5 Shirlett Shrops
50 D2 Shirley C Sotn
274 C1 Shirley Derbys
95 H1 Shirley Gt Lon
49 F5 Shirley Hants
213 H4 Shirley Solhll
213 H4 Shirley Heath Solhll
50 A5 Shirley holms Hants
50 C2 Shirley Warren C Sotn
186 A3 Shirl Heath Herefs
51 G2 Shirrell Heath Hants
61 E4 Shirwell Devon
460 C4 Shiskine N Ayrs
47 F6 Shitterton Dorset
185 G2 Shobdon Herefs
49 F3 Shobley Hants
274 C5 Shobnall Staffs
26 D2 Shobrooke Devon
277 E5 Shoby Leics
289 F5 Shocklach Ches
289 F5 Shocklach Green Ches
123 E3 Shoeburyness Sthend
101 G5 Sholden Kent
51 E2 Sholing C Sotn
51 E2 Sholing Common C Sotn
326 D3 Sholver Oldham
71 G5 Shootash Hants
142 D3 Shootersway Herts
233 H2 Shoot Hill Shrops
14 B4 Shop Cnwll
38 B5 Shop Cnwll
39 E5 Shop Devon
176 D3 Shop Corner Suffk
427 E5 Shopford Cumb
64 C5 Shopnoller Somset
75 E4 Shopp Hill W Susx
53 F4 Shopwyke W Susx
341 E4 Shore Calder
326 D1 Shore Rochdl
28 D2 Shore Bottom Devon
119 G3 Shoreditch Gt Lon
44 A3 Shoreditch Somset
380 D4 Shoregill Cumb
96 D2 Shoreham Kent
55 F4 Shoreham Beach W Susx
55 F4 Shoreham-by-Sea W Susx
475 E5 Shoresdean Nthumb
139 F2 Shores Green Oxon
474 D5 Shoreswood Nthumb
565 L4 Shoreton Highld
73 E4 Shorley Hants
82 C3 Shorncliffe Camp Kent
137 F5 Shorncote Gloucs
121 G5 Shorne Kent
121 G5 Shorne Ridgeway Kent
121 G5 Shorne West Kent
24 D5 Shortacombe Devon
10 A2 Shortacross Cnwll
78 A5 Shortbridge E Susx
213 E3 Short Cross Dudley
92 D6 Shortfield Common Surrey
56 D1 Shortgate E Susx
225 E2 Short Green Norfk
165 E6 Shorthampton Oxon
237 G6 Short Heath Birm
239 E2 Short Heath Derbys
74 B2 Shortheath Hants
92 D6 Shortheath Surrey
237 E4 Short Heath Wsall
233 H3 Shorthill Shrops
120 A6 Shortlands Gt Lon
7 F4 Shortlanesend Cnwll
445 F2 Shortlees E Ayrs
28 D2 Shortmoor Devon
30 B2 Shortmoor Dorset
20 B5 Shorton Torbay
466 C1 Shortroods Rens
134 D2 Shortstanding Gloucs
195 F5 Shortstown Beds
87 E5 Short Street Wilts
136 B5 Shortwood Gloucs
110 B4 Shortwood S Glos
36 D4 Shorwell IoW
86 B3 Shoscombe BaNES
86 B3 Shoscombe Vale BaNES
269 G5 Shotatton Shrops
250 B5 Shotesham Norfk
147 F6 Shotgate Essex
242 C5 Shotley Nhants
176 D2 Shotley Suffk
404 C4 Shotley Bridge Dur
404 C4 Shotleyfield Nthumb
176 D3 Shotley Gate Suffk
99 G4 Shottenden Kent
74 D3 Shottermill Surrey
190 B4 Shottery Warwks
191 G5 Shotteswell Warwks
202 C6 Shottisham Suffk
294 C5 Shottle Derbys
294 C5 Shottlegate Derbys
395 H4 Shotton Dur
396 B2 Shotton Dur
308 C6 Shotton Flints
430 D4 Shotton Nthumb
453 F3 Shotton Nthumb
396 B1 Shotton Colliery Dur
468 D2 Shotts N Lans
308 D5 Shotwick Ches
246 D3 Shouldham Norfk
246 D3 Shouldham Thorpe Norfk
188 B3 Shoulton Worcs
79 E3 Shover's Green E Susx
291 F5 Shraleybrook Staffs
233 H1 Shrawardine Shrops
188 A2 Shrawley Worcs
117 H3 Shreding Green Bucks
214 C6 Shrewley Warwks
234 C2 Shrewsbury Shrops
88 C6 Shrewton Wilts
53 G4 Shripney W Susx
113 F2 Shrivenham Oxon
248 C6 Shropham Norfk
174 C5 Shrub End Essex
93 G1 Shrubs Hill Surrey
186 D6 Shucknall Herefs
198 C6 Shudy Camps Cambs
543 H8 Shulishadermor Highld
543 G2 Shulista Highld
162 D6 Shurdington Gloucs
116 D5 Shurlock Row W & M
189 F2 Shurnock Worcs
588 C5 Shurrery Highld
64 D3 Shurton Somset
214 C1 Shustoke Warwks
26 D2 Shute Devon
28 D3 Shute Devon
70 D4 Shute End Wilts
165 F1 Shutford Oxon
272 C5 Shut Heath Staffs
162 C2 Shuthonger Gloucs
193 F5 Shutlanger Nhants
9 H3 Shutta Cnwll
236 C3 Shutt Green Staffs
238 D3 Shuttington Warwks
82 C2 Shuttlesfield Kent
315 F5 Shuttlewood Derbys
340 C6 Shuttleworth Bury
161 E4 Shutton Herefs
104 D2 Shwt Brdgnd
598 E5 Siabost W Isls
598 F5 Siabost bho Dheas W Isls
598 F5 Siabost bho Thuath W Isls
599 H4 Siadar W Isls
599 H4 Siadar Iarach W Isls
599 H4 Siadar Uarach W Isls
424 C2 Sibbaldbie D & G
217 E3 Sibbertoft Nhants
209 H3 Sibdon Carwood Shrops
165 F2 Sibford Ferris Oxon
165 F2 Sibford Gower Oxon
173 F3 Sible Hedingham Essex
172 C4 Sibley's Green Essex
300 C4 Sibsey Lincs
300 B4 Sibsey Fen Side Lincs
243 F5 Sibson Cambs
239 F4 Sibson Leics
297 E5 Sibthorpe Notts
316 D5 Sibthorpe Notts
226 D6 Sibton Suffk
199 H2 Sicklesmere Suffk
356 D5 Sicklinghall N York
28 B5 Sid Devon
44 B2 Sidbrook Somset
28 B4 Sidbury Devon
211 F2 Sidbury Shrops
84 D3 Sidcot N Som
120 C5 Sidcup Gt Lon
342 B5 Siddal Calder
388 B3 Siddick Cumb
311 G5 Siddington Ches
137 F5 Siddington Gloucs
311 G5 Siddington Heath Ches
213 E5 Sidemoor Worcs
325 G2 Side of the Moor Bolton
256 B2 Sidestrand Norfk
292 A6 Sideway C Stke
28 B4 Sidford Devon
53 F5 Sidlesham W Susx
53 F4 Sidlesham Common W Susx
58 B5 Sidley E Susx
95 F5 Sidlow Surrey
28 B5 Sidmouth Devon
271 H2 Sidway Staffs
19 G3 Sigford Devon
361 F5 Sigglesthorne E R Yk
487 G5 Sighthill C Edin
467 E1 Sighthill C Glas
105 F5 Sigingstone V Glam
138 C2 Signet Oxon
67 G5 Sigwells Somset
91 G2 Silchester Hants
597 H4 Sildinis W Isls
240 D1 Sileby Leics
362 C5 Silecroft Cumb
249 F5 Silfield Norfk
39 F2 Silford Devon
181 E4 Silian Cerdgn
72 B5 Silkstead Hants
328 D3 Silkstone Barns
328 D4 Silkstone Common Barns
298 D6 Silk Willoughby Lincs
502 B4 Sillerhole Fife
399 E4 Silloth Cumb
569 J5 Sillyearn Moray
156 A2 Siloh Carmth
374 B1 Silpho N York
354 D5 Silsden Brad
169 F2 Silsoe Beds
68 C4 Silton Dorset
556 C5 Silverbank Abers
470 D2 Silverburn Mdloth
365 G4 Silverdale Lancs
291 G5 Silverdale Staffs
365 G5 Silverdale Green Lancs
212 D2 Silver End Dudley
173 G6 Silver End Essex
570 D3 Silverford Abers
255 G2 Silvergate Norfk
250 B6 Silver Green Norfk
58 C4 Silverhill E Susx
79 G4 Silver Hill E Susx
58 C4 Silverhill Park E Susx
67 H5 Silver Knap Somset
487 G4 Silverknowes C Edin
226 B4 Silverley's Green Suffk
469 E5 Silvermuir S Lans
193 E6 Silverstone Nhants
136 A4 Silver Street Gloucs
98 D2 Silver Street Kent
67 E3 Silver Street Somset
213 G4 Silver Street Worcs
27 F2 Silverton Devon
483 F4 Silverton W Duns
467 H4 Silvertonhill S Lans
120 B4 Silvertown Gt Lon
6 D4 Silverwell Cnwll
211 E4 Silvington Shrops
604 E2 Silwick Shet
328 D4 Sim Hill Barns
326 B3 Simister Bury
327 F6 Simmondley Derbys
309 H2 Simm's Cross Halton
324 C4 Simm's Lane End St Hel
428 D5 Simonburn Nthumb
62 B4 Simonsbath Somset
43 F4 Simonsburrow Devon
406 A2 Simonside S Tyne
340 B3 Simonstone Lancs
367 H1 Simonstone N York
474 C5 Simprim Border
168 B2 Simpson M Keyn
151 E6 Simpson Pembks
151 E6 Simpson Cross Pembks
474 B4 Sinclair's Hill Border
433 G1 Sinclairston E Ayrs
501 E6 Sinclairtown Fife
370 C3 Sinderby N York
403 E4 Sinderhope Nthumb
311 E1 Sinderland Green Traffd
116 C6 Sindlesham Wokham
275 E3 Sinfin C Derb
275 F3 Sinfin Moor C Derb
167 G3 Singleborough Bucks
86 C3 Single Hill Somset
337 G2 Singleton Lancs
53 F2 Singleton W Susx
121 F5 Singlewell Kent
288 D3 Singret Wrexhm
80 B1 Sinkhurst Green Kent
555 E2 Sinnahard Abers
372 D2 Sinnington N York
188 B2 Sinton Worcs
188 B2 Sinton Green Worcs
86 C1 Sion Hill BaNES
118 B4 Sipson Gt Lon
132 B2 Sirhowy Blae G
250 C5 Sisland Norfk
80 A2 Sissinghurst Kent
110 B4 Siston S Glos
110 B5 Siston Common S Glos
4 B3 Sithney Cnwll
4 B3 Sithney Common Cnwll
4 B3 Sithney Green Cnwll
98 D2 Sittingbourne Kent
560 B5 Sittyton Abers
212 A2 Six Ashes Staffs
132 D4 Six Bells Blae G
276 D5 Six Hills Leics
319 F2 Sixhills Lincs
82 B2 Sixmile Kent
198 B3 Six Mile Bottom Cambs
48 B1 Sixpenny Handley Dorset
35 h6 Six Rues Jersey
203 F2 Sizewell Suffk
25 F4 Skaigh Devon
586 F7 Skail Highld
601 K3 Skaill Ork
602 A8 Skaill Ork
602 F5 Skaill Ork
433 H1 Skares E Ayrs
490 D4 Skateraw E Loth
607 J4 Skaw Shet
543 G7 Skeabost Highld
602 B7 Skeabrae Ork
383 F4 Skeeby N York
82 B2 Skeete Kent
241 F4 Skeffington Leics
349 G6 Skeffling E R Yk
295 F2 Skegby Notts
317 E5 Skegby Notts
609 J2 Skeggie Shet
301 G2 Skegness Lincs
605 G7 Skelberry Shet
608 D7 Skelberry Shet
577 G4 Skelbo Highld
577 G5 Skelbo Muir Highld
330 B2 Skelbrooke Donc
280 D2 Skeldyke Lincs
439 E4 Skelfhill Border
317 H5 Skellingthorpe Lincs
607 G7 Skellister Shet
312 B3 Skellorn Green Ches
330 B2 Skellow Donc
328 C2 Skelmanthorpe Kirk
324 B3 Skelmersdale Lancs
560 C2 Skelmonae Abers
482 A6 Skelmorlie N Ayrs
571 H7 Skelmuir Abers
586 F5 Skelpick Highld
390 C2 Skelton Cumb
345 H4 Skelton E R Yk
382 C4 Skelton N York
397 F6 Skelton R & Cl
357 H3 Skelton York
370 D6 Skelton on Ure N York
602 F3 Skelwick Ork
378 B4 Skelwith Bridge Cumb
320 D6 Skendleby Lincs
320 D5 Skendleby Psalter Lincs
160 A5 Skenfrith Mons
360 C3 Skerne E R Yk
383 G2 Skerne Park Darltn
456 D1 Skeroblingarry Ag & B
586 E4 Skerray Highld
584 D6 Skerricha Highld
446 B6 Skerrington E Ayrs
125 F2 Skerryford Pembks
351 G2 Skerton Lancs
215 G1 Sketchley Leics
103 F3 Sketty Swans
103 H2 Skewen Neath
14 D5 Skewes Cnwll
372 B5 Skewsby N York
256 A4 Skeyton Norfk
256 B4 Skeyton Corner Norfk
515 E1 Skichen Muir Angus
320 D1 Skidbrooke Lincs
335 F6 Skidbrooke North End Lincs
347 F3 Skidby E R Yk
42 C2 Skilgate Somset
30 B4 Skilling Dorset
278 B4 Skillington Lincs
399 E3 Skinburness Cumb
486 B3 Skinflats Falk
542 C7 Skinidin Highld
6 D4 Skinner's Bottom Cnwll
90 C1 Skinners Green W Berk
577 J7 Skinnerton Highld
586 C4 Skinnet Highld
397 H6 Skinningrove R & Cl
463 E3 Skipness Ag & B
337 G1 Skippool Lancs
400 C5 Skiprigg Cumb
361 F3 Skipsea E R Yk
361 F4 Skipsea Brough E R Yk
354 C4 Skipton N York
370 D4 Skipton-on-Swale N York
345 F2 Skipwith N York
300 B6 Skirbeck Lincs
300 B6 Skirbeck Quarter Lincs
354 C2 Skirethorns N York
348 B2 Skirlaugh E R Yk
449 E2 Skirling Border
116 C2 Skirmett Bucks
358 D3 Skirpenbeck E R Yk
391 G3 Skirwith Cumb
589 K3 Skirza Highld
400 D1 Skitby Cumb
351 F6 Skitham Lancs
141 G4 Skittle Green Bucks
546 B5 Skulamus Highld
586 D4 Skullomie Highld
209 E5 Skyborry Green Shrops
173 H5 Skye Green Essex
551 H5 Skye of Curr Highld
150 D4 Skyfog Pembks
417 H5 Skyreburn D & G
355 E2 Skyreholme N York
341 F4 Slack Calder
294 C2 Slack Derbys
327 G1 Slack Kirk
327 E3 Slackcote Oldham
313 E3 Slackhall Derbys
365 G4 Slack Head Cumb
568 F3 Slackhead Moray
321 F5 Slackholme End Lincs
570 F6 Slacks of Cairnbanno Abers
136 C3 Slad Gloucs
161 H4 Sladbrook Gloucs
176 C6 Sladbury's Old House Essex
43 F6 Slade Devon
60 D2 Slade Devon
99 E4 Slade Kent
125 F1 Slade Pembks
115 F1 Slade End Oxon
120 D4 Slade Green Gt Lon
236 D3 Slade Heath Staffs
315 G2 Slade Hooton Rothm
90 C4 Sladen Green Hants
15 E4 Sladesbridge Cnwll
162 C3 Slades Green Worcs
402 B4 Slaggyford Nthumb
353 E4 Slaidburn Lancs
327 G2 Slaithwaite Kirk
294 B3 Slaley Derbys
404 A3 Slaley Nthumb
485 H5 Slamannan Falk
65 F4 Slape Cross Somset
385 G1 Slapewath R & Cl
168 C5 Slapton Bucks
13 E4 Slapton Devon
192 D5 Slapton Nhants
487 H5 Slateford C Edin
314 C6 Slatepit Dale Derbys
326 C3 Slattocks Rochdl
77 E4 Slaugham W Susx
22 C5 Slaughterbridge Cnwll
111 E5 Slaughterford Wilts
291 E3 Slaughter Hill Ches
241 G6 Slawston Leics
74 C2 Sleaford Hants
298 D6 Sleaford Lincs
391 F6 Sleagill Cumb
270 B4 Sleap Shrops
235 E1 Sleapford Wrekin
144 B3 Sleapshyde Herts
125 H1 Slebech Pembks
162 B3 Sledge Green Worcs
360 A2 Sledmere E R Yk
78 D3 Sleeches Cross E Susx
72 C4 Sleepers Hill Hants
426 C4 Sleetbeck Cumb
295 E4 Sleet Moor Derbys
48 B5 Sleight Dorset
381 H2 Sleightholme Dur
387 E3 Sleights N York
47 H6 Slepe Dorset
593 D7 Sliabh na h-Airde W Isls
589 H3 Slickly Highld
460 C5 Sliddery N Ayrs
213 E5 Slideslow Worcs
551 J5 Sliemore Highld
545 H4 Sligachan Highld
135 G4 Slimbridge Gloucs
272 B3 Slindon Staffs
53 H3 Slindon W Susx
76 B3 Slinfold W Susx
134 D3 Sling Gloucs
372 C4 Slingsby N York
558 D2 Slioch Abers
169 F6 Slip End Beds
170 C2 Slip End Herts
341 G1 Slippery Ford Brad
218 C4 Slipton Nhants
237 F1 Slitting Mill Staffs
550 E5 Slochd Highld
525 H2 Slochnacraig P & K
492 D5 Slockavullin Ag & B
408 B5 Slockmill D & G
256 B5 Sloley Norfk
26 A5 Sloncombe Devon
321 E5 Sloothby Lincs
185 F2 Slough Powys
117 G4 Slough Slough
44 B3 Slough Green Somset
77 E4 Slough Green W Susx
199 H4 Slough Hill Suffk
550 F5 Sluggan Highld
543 H8 Sluggans Highld
81 E3 Sly Corner Kent
93 G4 Slyfield Surrey
351 G1 Slyne Lancs
452 C2 Smailholm Border
326 D2 Smallbridge Rochdl
26 D3 Smallbrook Devon
134 D4 Smallbrook Gloucs
256 C5 Smallburgh Norfk
561 F1 Smallburn Abers
446 D4 Smallburn E Ayrs
313 E4 Smalldale Derbys
313 G3 Smalldale Derbys
55 F2 Small Dole W Susx
300 D3 Small End Lincs
295 E6 Smalley Derbys
275 G1 Smalley Common Derbys
295 E6 Smalley Green Derbys
95 G6 Smallfield Surrey
144 A3 Smallford Herts
213 G2 Small Heath Birm
424 B4 Smallholm D & G
80 C3 Small Hythe Kent
40 B3 Smallmarsh Devon
273 E3 Smallrice Staffs
29 E2 Smallridge Devon
326 D4 Smallshaw Tamesd
292 A4 Smallthorne C Stke
67 G3 Small Way Somset
291 G2 Smallwood Ches
189 F1 Smallwood Worcs
200 B3 Smallwood Green Suffk
351 E5 Smallwood Hey Lancs
224 D3 Smallworth Norfk
90 B5 Smannell Hants
380 C3 Smardale Cumb
80 C1 Smarden Kent
98 D6 Smarden Bell Kent
78 C1 Smart's Hill Kent
43 G5 Smeatharpe Devon
501 E6 Smeaton Fife
81 G2 Smeeth Kent
241 E6 Smeeton Westerby Leics
590 E4 Smeircleit W Isls
355 G2 Smelthouses N York
583 G3 Smerral Highld
212 B1 Smestow Staffs
234 A5 Smethcott Shrops
213 F2 Smethwick Sandw
291 G2 Smethwick Green Ches
528 B6 Smiddy Hill Angus
63 G5 Sminhays Corner Somset
531 H7 Smirisary Highld
275 E6 Smisby Derbys
188 C3 Smite Hill Worcs
11 G2 Smithaleigh Devon
75 E5 Smithbrook W Susx
187 H4 Smith End Green Worcs
400 D1 Smithfield Cumb
351 G4 Smith Green Lancs
329 F3 Smithies Barns
43 E5 Smithincott Devon
329 F4 Smithley Barns
171 E2 Smith's End Herts
291 F4 Smith's Green Ches
311 G5 Smiths Green Ches
172 B5 Smith's Green Essex
172 D1 Smith's Green Essex
572 E8 Smithstown Highld
566 C7 Smithton Highld
200 B4 Smithwood Green Suffk
326 D1 Smithy Bridge Rochdl
308 A4 Smithy Gate Flints
311 E5 Smithy Green Stockp
311 H2 Smithy Green Stockp
311 H3 Smithy Green Stockp
294 D5 Smithy Houses Derbys
323 G2 Smithy Lane Ends Lancs
602 F2 Smittaldy Ork
54 C1 Smock Alley W Susx
215 H2 Smockington Leics
141 H3 Smoky Row Bucks
585 H3 Smoo Highld
600 F3 Smoogro Ork
585 H3 Smoo Lodge Highld
174 B6 Smythe's Green Essex
80 A5 Snagshall E Susx
233 G4 Snailbeach Shrops
45 F5 Snails Hill Somset
169 H3 Snailswell Herts
222 C6 Snailwell Cambs
373 H3 Snainton N York
393 G4 Snaisgill Dur
345 E5 Snaith E R Yk
370 B3 Snape N York
202 D3 Snape Suffk
323 G2 Snape Green Lancs
329 G4 Snape Hill Barns
314 D4 Snape Hill Derbys
61 E5 Snapper Devon
120 A2 Snaresbrook Gt Lon
239 E3 Snarestone Leics
318 C3 Snarford Lincs
81 E4 Snargate Kent
133 E4 Snatchwood Torfn
81 F4 Snave Kent
188 C4 Sneachill Worcs
209 F1 Snead Powys
211 G6 Snead Common Worcs
212 C6 Sneads Green Worcs
225 F2 Sneath Common Norfk
387 E3 Sneaton N York
387 E3 Sneatonthorpe N York
276 C2 Sneinton C Nott
318 D3 Snelland Lincs
168 A3 Snelshall East M Keyn
167 H3 Snelshall West M Keyn
293 G6 Snelston Derbys
224 C1 Snetterton Norfk
258 D5 Snettisham Norfk
609 G5 Snevlabreck Shet
292 A5 Sneyd Green C Stke
109 G4 Sneyd Park Bristl
239 G2 Snibston Leics
162 A4 Snig's End Gloucs
99 E2 Snipeshill Kent
593 D11 Sniseabhal W Isls
442 C4 Snitter Nthumb
332 D6 Snitterby Lincs
190 C3 Snitterfield Warwks
294 B2 Snitterton Derbys
210 D4 Snitton Shrops
210 D5 Snittongate Shrops
159 F1 Snodhill Herefs
97 G2 Snodland Kent
404 C4 Snods Edge Nthumb
328 D4 Snowden Hill Barns
100 D5 Snowdown Kent
171 F3 Snow End Herts
290 C4 Snow Hill Ches
343 F5 Snow Hill Wakefd
342 A6 Snow Lea Kirk
163 G3 Snowshill Gloucs
225 E3 Snow Street Norfk
343 H5 Snydale Wakefd
52 B2 Soake Hants
12 C5 Soar Devon
265 E2 Soar Gwynd
282 C1 Soar IoA
157 F3 Soar Powys
51 H1 Soberton Hants

51 H2 Soberton Heath Hants
390 D4 Sockbridge Cumb
384 A3 Sockburn Darltn
30 B1 Sockety Dorset
307 F5 Sodom Denbgs
112 B3 Sodom Wilts
269 F2 Sodylt Bank Shrops
222 B5 Soham Cambs
222 B4 Soham Cotes Cambs
119 F3 Soho Gt Lon
213 F2 Soho Sandw
86 B5 Soho Somset
592 E3 Solas W Isls
38 D5 Soldon Cross Devon
73 G3 Soldridge Hants
100 A6 Sole Street Kent
121 G6 Sole Street Kent
214 B4 Solihull Solhll
213 G4 Solihull Lodge Solhll
543 G2 Solitote Highld
185 H3 Sollers Dilwyn Herefs
161 E3 Sollers Hope Herefs
338 B6 Sollom Lancs
150 D5 Solva Pembks
425 F4 Solwaybank D & G
241 G2 Somerby Leics
333 F3 Somerby Lincs
295 E4 Somercotes Derbys
110 B6 Somerdale BaNES
291 G1 Somerford Ches
49 F6 Somerford Dorset
236 C3 Somerford Staffs
137 F5 Somerford Keynes Gloucs
53 E5 Somerley W Susx
251 F5 Somerleyton Suffk
274 A3 Somersal Herbert Derbys
320 B5 Somersby Lincs
220 D4 Somersham Cambs
201 E5 Somersham Suffk
52 A5 Somers Town C Port
107 F2 Somerton Newpt
166 A4 Somerton Oxon
66 C4 Somerton Somset
199 G4 Somerton Suffk
66 D4 Somerton Hill Somset
234 D2 Somerwood Shrops
55 E4 Sompting W Susx
55 E3 Sompting Abbotts W Susx
116 C4 Sonning Wokham
116 B3 Sonning Common Oxon
116 C4 Sonning Eye Oxon
288 D5 Sontley Wrexhm
295 G1 Sookholme Notts
49 F5 Sopley Hants
143 H3 Sopwell Herts
111 E2 Sopworth Wilts
410 D3 Sorbie D & G
588 E4 Sordale Highld
517 H3 Sorisdale Ag & B
12 C3 Sorley Devon
446 B4 Sorn E Ayrs
445 H3 Sornhill E Ayrs
492 C4 Soroba Ag & B
506 E4 Soroba Ag & B
589 H4 Sortat Highld
319 F4 Sotby Lincs
315 E3 Sothall Sheff
227 E4 Sotherton Corner Suffk
299 E2 Sots Hole Lincs
227 E3 Sotterley Suffk
210 B1 Soudley Shrops
271 G4 Soudley Shrops
328 B4 Soughley Barns
288 B1 Soughton Flints
168 B4 Soulbury Bucks
380 C2 Soulby Cumb
390 D4 Soulby Cumb
166 B3 Souldern Oxon
194 D2 Souldrop Beds
290 C5 Sound Ches
605 J2 Sound Shet
606 E7 Sound Shet
608 E8 Sound Shet
290 C5 Sound Heath Ches
110 A4 Soundwell S Glos
453 F5 Sourhope Border
602 E5 Sourin Ork
444 B1 Sourlie N Ayrs
390 B1 Sour Nook Cumb
24 D4 Sourton Devon
363 E5 Soutergate Cumb
253 G5 South Acre Norfk
118 D4 South Acton Gt Lon
82 D2 South Alkham Kent
118 C3 Southall Gt Lon
12 D5 South Allington Devon
486 A1 South Alloa Falk
376 B2 Southam Cumb
163 E4 Southam Gloucs
191 G2 Southam Warwks
75 E5 South Ambersham W Susx
50 C2 Southampton C Sotn
315 G3 South Anston Rothm
117 F6 South Ascot W & M
81 F1 South Ashford Kent
66 C6 Southay Somset
609 G7 South Aywick Shet
50 C5 South Baddesley Hants
520 E4 South Ballachulish Highld
396 D5 South Bank R & Cl
358 A4 South Bank York
67 F4 South Barrow Somset
263 F4 South Beach Gwynd
431 F4 South Beach Nthumb
95 F2 South Beddington Gt Lon
122 B2 South Benfleet Essex
406 C2 South Bents Sundld
53 G4 South Bersted W Susx
472 C6 South Blainslie Border
49 F5 South Bockhampton Dorset
96 B1 Southborough Gt Lon
78 D1 Southborough Kent
94 D1 Southborough Surrey
34 D2 Southbourne Bmouth
52 D3 Southbourne W Susx
30 A3 South Bowood Dorset
557 E6 South Brachmont Abers
330 D2 South Bramwith Donc
19 E5 South Brent Devon
68 B2 South Brewham Somset
120 A3 South Bromley Gt Lon
68 D3 Southbrook Dorset
485 H3 South Broomage Falk
443 G4 South Broomhill Nthumb
248 C4 Southburgh Norfk
250 D3 South Burlingham Norfk
360 B4 Southburn E R Yk
67 G4 South Cadbury Somset
414 C3 South Cairn D & G
318 A4 South Carlton Lincs
316 A3 South Carlton Notts
16 A2 South Carne Cnwll
346 D3 South Cave E R Yk
137 G5 South Cerney Gloucs
77 G6 South Chailey E Susx
29 F1 South Chard Somset
B5 South Charlton Nthumb
E4 South Cheriton Somset
C2 South Church Dur
C2 South Cliffe E R Yk
D2 South Clifton Notts
K1 South Clunes Highld

320 C2 South Cockerington Lincs
557 F6 South Cookney Abers
165 E4 Southcoombe Oxon
104 C3 South Cornelly Brdgnd
461 E3 South Corriegills N Ayrs
424 D3 South Corrielaw D & G
116 A5 Southcote Readg
22 D3 Southcott Cnwll
39 F4 Southcott Devon
89 E3 Southcott Wilts
141 H2 Southcourt Bucks
227 G3 South Cove Suffk
259 H4 South Creake Norfk
189 F1 Southcrest Worcs
327 H2 South Crosland Kirk
241 E2 South Croxton Leics
95 G2 South Croydon Gt Lon
542 F4 South Cuil Highld
360 B5 South Dalton E R Yk
121 E6 South Darenth Kent
440 B3 Southdean Border
323 H5 Southdene Knows
251 G4 South Denes Norfk
86 C2 Southdown BaNES
10 D3 Southdown Cnwll
72 C5 South Down Hants
43 H5 South Down Somset
345 F3 South Duffield N York
95 F5 South Earlswood Surrey
56 C3 Southease E Susx
320 A2 South Elkington Lincs
329 H2 South Elmsall Wakefd
488 D5 South Elphinstone E Loth
456 D5 Southend Ag & B
116 C2 Southend Bucks
168 B4 South End Bucks
350 B2 South End Cumb
348 C1 South End E R Yk
135 G5 Southend Gloucs
120 A5 Southend Gt Lon
49 E1 South End Hants
145 F1 South-end Herts
348 B5 South End N Linc
224 C1 South End Norfk
140 C4 Southend Oxon
114 C4 Southend W Berk
115 F5 Southend W Berk
122 D3 Southend-on-Sea Sthend
24 D5 Southerly Devon
390 B2 Southernby Cumb
55 G3 Southern Cross W Susx
104 D5 Southerndown V Glam
398 B4 Southerness D & G
170 D3 Southern Green Herts
602 A8 Southerquoy Ork
562 C2 South Erradale Highld
28 A4 Southerton Devon
246 C6 Southery Norfk
173 F3 Southey Green Essex
147 H5 South Fambridge Essex
93 E4 South Farnborough Hants
114 B3 South Fawley W Berk
460 C4 South Feorline N Ayrs
347 E5 South Ferriby N Linc
347 F4 South Field E R Yk
500 D5 Southfield Fife
431 E4 Southfield Nthumb
117 G4 South Field W & M
121 G2 Southfields Essex
119 E5 Southfields Gt Lon
121 G3 Southfields Thurr
121 F5 Southfleet Kent
560 A3 South Flobbets Abers
37 E5 Southford IoW
532 E7 South Garvan Highld
204 D4 Southgate Cerdgn
144 D6 Southgate Gt Lon
255 F3 Southgate Norfk
259 H5 Southgate Norfk
103 E4 Southgate Swans
77 E2 Southgate W Susx
199 H2 Southgate Bridge Suffk
606 D2 South Gluss Shet
95 H5 South Godstone Surrey
49 F2 South Gorley Hants
431 E6 South Gosforth N u Ty
146 D6 South Green Essex
174 D6 South Green Essex
98 C2 South Green Kent
252 A3 South Green Norfk
225 G5 South Green Norfk
487 G5 South Green Suffk
608 D7 South-haa Shet
119 H3 South Hackney Gt Lon
91 G4 South Ham Hants
147 E5 South Hanningfield Essex
118 B2 South Harefield Gt Lon
118 C2 South Harrow Gt Lon
74 B6 South Harting W Susx
144 B3 South Hatfield Herts
52 C5 South Hayling Hants
142 C4 South Heath Bucks
175 F6 South Heath Essex
56 D4 South Heighton E Susx
406 B6 South Hetton Dur
329 F2 South Hiendley Wakefd
16 D4 South Hill Cnwll
84 B3 South Hill N Som
124 D2 South Hill Pembks
140 B4 South Hinksey Oxon
38 B3 South Hole Devon
372 C4 South Holme N York
94 D5 South Holmwood Surrey
120 D3 South Hornchurch Gt Lon
85 G5 South Horrington Somset
12 B4 South Huish Devon
298 A2 South Hykeham Lincs
406 B3 South Hylton Sundld
169 G1 Southill Beds
32 B3 Southill Dorset
90 D5 Southington Hants
333 E5 South Kelsey Lincs
565 L7 South Kessock Highld
333 G1 South Killingholme N Linc
371 E3 South Kilvington N York
216 D3 South Kilworth Leics
514 D3 South Kingennie Angus
329 H2 South Kirkby Wakefd
556 D3 South Kirkton Abers
461 E4 South Kiscadale N Ayrs
240 D4 South Knighton C Leic
19 H3 South Knighton Devon
299 F5 South Kyme Lincs
119 F4 South Lambeth Gt Lon
55 E4 South Lancing W Susx
32 B4 Southlands Dorset
328 D3 South Lane Barns
28 D4 Southleigh Devon
139 F3 South Leigh Oxon
317 E3 South Leverton Notts
189 G5 South Littleton Worcs
397 H6 South Loftus R & Cl
224 D4 South Lopham Norfk
242 C4 South Luffenham Rutlnd
56 C2 South Malling E Susx
68 B3 Southmarsh Somset
113 E2 South Marston Swindn
109 G4 Southmead Bristl
95 F4 South Merstham Surrey
454 B5 South Middleton Nthumb
344 B3 South Milford N York
12 C4 South Milton Devon
144 B4 South Mimms Herts

148 C5 Southminster Essex
41 E3 South Molton Devon
405 E4 South Moor Dur
139 F5 Southmoor Oxon
115 F2 South Moreton Oxon
527 E4 Southmuir Angus
53 F4 South Mundham W Susx
297 E3 South Muskham Notts
346 D2 South Newbald E R Yk
364 B6 South Newbarns Cumb
165 G3 South Newington Oxon
431 F4 South Newsham Nthumb
70 B3 South Newton Wilts
295 E3 South Normanton Derbys
119 G6 South Norwood Gt Lon
95 G5 South Nutfield Surrey
121 E3 South Ockendon Thurr
195 H2 Southoe Cambs
225 G6 South Ormsby Lincs
320 C4 Southorpe C Pete
243 F4 Southorpe C Pete
370 D2 South Otterington N York
30 B5 Southover Dorset
31 E4 Southover Dorset
56 C3 Southover E Susx
79 F4 Southover E Susx
333 F6 South Owersby Lincs
342 B5 Southowram Calder
143 G6 South Oxhey Herts
95 E5 South Park Surrey
501 E4 South Parks Fife
405 G4 South Pelaw Dur
30 B1 South Perrott Dorset
45 E4 South Petherton Somset
16 D2 South Petherwin Cnwll
247 G4 South Pickenham Norfk
10 D2 South Pill Cnwll
12 D4 South Pool Devon
30 C3 South Poorton Dorset
323 E1 Southport Sefton
514 C3 South Powrie C Dund
605 H7 Southpunds Shet
487 H4 South Queensferry C Edin
560 C2 South Quilquox Abers
62 B5 South Radworthy Devon
298 C5 South Rauceby Lincs
253 H3 South Raynham Norfk
312 A1 South Reddish Stockp
256 B2 South Reston Lincs
320 D3 Southrepps Norfk
299 E1 Southrey Lincs
138 C4 Southrop Gloucs
165 F3 Southrop Oxon
91 H6 Southrope Hants
118 C2 South Ruislip Gt Lon
246 C3 South Runcton Norfk
297 F2 South Scarle Notts
605 G7 South Scousburgh Shet
52 A5 Southsea C Port
288 C4 Southsea Wrexhm
506 F1 South Shian Ag & B
406 B1 South Shields S Tyne
337 E3 South Shore Bpool
394 C4 South Side Dur
603 H6 Southside Ork
335 F6 South Somercotes Lincs
356 C2 South Stainley N York
381 E2 South Stainmore Cumb
405 E4 South Stanley Dur
121 F4 South Stifford Thurr
86 C2 Southstoke BaNES
115 F3 South Stoke Oxon
54 B3 South Stoke W Susx
81 F2 South Stour Kent
514 C5 South Straiton Fife
77 G6 South Street E Susx
96 B3 South Street Gt Lon
97 F2 South Street Kent
98 C2 South Street Kent
99 H3 South Street Kent
100 B2 South Street Kent
25 G4 South Tawton Devon
6 B5 South Tehidy Cnwll
320 D4 South Thoresby Lincs
89 F5 South Tidworth Wilts
27 F6 South Town Devon
73 G2 South Town Hants
251 G3 Southtown Norfk
601 H5 Southtown Ork
44 C4 Southtown Somset
67 F2 Southtown Somset
86 C2 South Twerton BaNES
364 D4 South Ulverston Cumb
91 G4 South View Hants
12 C4 Southville Devon
133 E5 Southville Torfn
400 D6 Southwaite Cumb
250 D2 South Walsham Norfk
92 B5 South Warnborough Hants
76 C4 Southwater W Susx
76 C4 Southwater Street W Susx
11 E1 Southway C Plym
67 E1 Southway Somset
146 B6 South Weald Essex
32 B5 South Weirs Hants
296 C4 Southwell Notts
141 E5 South Weston Oxon
23 E4 South Wheatley Cnwll
317 E2 South Wheatley Notts
605 G2 South Whiteness Shet
51 H3 Southwick Hants
219 E1 Southwick Nhants
84 C5 Southwick Somset
406 B3 Southwick Sundld
87 E3 Southwick Wilts
55 F4 Southwick W Susx
85 G3 South Widcombe BaNES
240 C5 South Wigston Leics
81 F1 South Willesborough Kent
319 F3 South Willingham Lincs
119 F5 South Wimbledon Gt Lon
396 B2 South Wingate Dur
294 D3 South Wingfield Derbys
278 C6 South Witham Lincs
227 G4 Southwold Suffk
39 E6 South Wonford Devon
72 C2 South Wonston Hants
275 E5 Southwood Derbys
92 D3 Southwood Hants
250 D3 Southwood Norfk
67 F3 Southwood Somset
187 G2 Southwood Worcs
320 A1 South Woodford Gt Lon
147 G5 South Woodham Ferrers Essex
252 D3 South Wootton Norfk
87 E2 South Wraxall Wilts
213 H3 South Yardley Birm
24 D2 South Yeo Devon
25 G4 South Zeal Devon
341 G5 Sowerby Calder
371 E3 Sowerby N York
341 H5 Sowerby Bridge Calder
390 B3 Sowerby Row Cumb
351 E6 Sower Carr Lancs
42 A3 Sowerhill Somset
199 E4 Sowley Green Suffk
342 A6 Sowood Calder
342 A6 Sowood Green Calder
27 F4 Sowton Devon
26 C1 Sowton Barton Devon
576 C6 Soyal Highld
341 G5 Soyland Town Calder

356 C4 Spacey Houses N York
256 C3 Spa Common Norfk
280 B5 Spalding Lincs
345 H3 Spaldington E R Yk
219 G5 Spaldwick Cambs
317 F6 Spalford Notts
279 F2 Spanby Lincs
482 B5 Spango Inver
92 A3 Spanish Green Hants
255 E4 Sparham Norfk
255 E4 Sparhamhill Norfk
364 D3 Spark Bridge Cumb
67 G4 Sparkford Somset
213 G3 Sparkhill Birm
18 C6 Sparkwell Devon
2 C5 Sparnon Cnwll
6 C5 Sparnon Gate Cnwll
254 B5 Sparrow Green Norfk
84 D2 Sparrow Hill Somset
313 E3 Sparrowpit Derbys
79 E3 Sparrow's Green E Susx
72 B3 Sparsholt Hants
114 B2 Sparsholt Oxon
403 F5 Spartylea Nthumb
273 G3 Spath Staffs
372 D2 Spaunton N York
64 D2 Spaxton Somset
533 K6 Spean Bridge Highld
71 G4 Spearywell Hants
67 F5 Speckington Somset
97 E1 Speed Gate Kent
110 A5 Speedwell Bristl
142 A4 Speen Bucks
114 D6 Speen W Berk
375 F5 Speeton N York
309 F3 Speke Ches
78 C1 Speldhurst Kent
171 G6 Spellbrook Herts
165 F5 Spelsbury Oxon
130 D6 Spelter Brdgnd
342 C4 Spen Kirk
92 B1 Spencers Wood Wokham
291 G2 Spen Green Ches
212 B5 Spennells Worcs
369 F2 Spennithorne N York
395 E3 Spennymoor Dur
189 G2 Spernall Warwks
188 C4 Spetchley Worcs
47 H4 Spetisbury Dorset
226 D3 Spexhall Suffk
536 B1 Speybank Highld
568 F3 Spey Bay Moray
551 J4 Speybridge Highld
300 D1 Spilsby Lincs
455 E3 Spindlestone Nthumb
315 F4 Spinkhill Derbys
193 G2 Spinney Hill Nhants
240 C4 Spinney Hills C Leic
576 E6 Spinningdale Highld
295 H1 Spion Kop Notts
112 A4 Spirthill Wilts
117 G4 Spital W & M
308 D3 Spital Wirral
145 E3 Spitalbrook Herts
293 G5 Spitalhill Derbys
330 D6 Spital Hill Donc
318 B1 Spital in the Street Lincs
405 F1 Spital Tongues N u Ty
294 C1 Spitewinter Derbys
56 C1 Spithurst E Susx
25 G3 Spitler Cross Devon
416 D5 Spittal D & G
497 F4 Spittal E Loth
359 E4 Spittal E R Yk
588 F6 Spittal Highld
475 F4 Spittal Nthumb
151 G5 Spittal Pembks
483 G2 Spittal Stirlg
512 D1 Spittalfield P & K
538 B3 Spittal of Glenmuick Abers
525 H2 Spittal of Glenshee P & K
278 C3 Spittlegate Lincs
250 A2 Spixworth Norfk
14 C3 Splatt Cnwll
23 E5 Splatt Cnwll
25 E1 Splatt Devon
64 D4 Splatt Somset
78 A5 Splayne's Green E Susx
106 C4 Splott Cardif
356 D4 Spofforth N York
275 G2 Spondon C Derb
215 E4 Spon End Covtry
288 C2 Spon Green Flints
249 F5 Spooner Row Norfk
236 B5 Spoonleygate Shrops
247 H2 Sporle Norfk
326 C2 Spotland Bridge Rochdl
490 C4 Spott E Loth
217 F6 Spratton Nhants
74 C1 Spreakley Surrey
25 G3 Spreyton Devon
11 F3 Spriddlestone Devon
318 C3 Spridlington Lincs
141 G5 Sprig's Alley Oxon
389 F5 Spring Bank Cumb
162 D5 Springbank Gloucs
467 F2 Springboig C Glas
239 E1 Spring Cottage Leics
147 F3 Spring Elms Essex
381 H5 Spring End N York
213 G3 Springfield Birm
132 C5 Springfield Caerph
425 G6 Springfield D & G
147 E3 Springfield Essex
501 F2 Springfield Fife
566 B4 Springfield Highld
168 B2 Springfield M Keyn
567 J5 Springfield Moray
213 E2 Springfield Sandw
324 D3 Springfield Wigan
236 D5 Springfield Wolves
86 D5 Spring Gardens Somset
354 B6 Spring Green Lancs
118 C4 Spring Grove Gt Lon
121 F5 Spring Head Kent
327 E4 Springhead Oldham
466 C3 Springhill E Rens
51 F5 Spring Hill IoW
340 A4 Spring Hill Lancs
468 D3 Springhill N Lans
326 D3 Spring Hill Oldham
237 E4 Springhill Staffs
237 G3 Springhill Staffs
236 C5 Spring Hill Wolves
422 D6 Springholm D & G
425 F5 Springkell D & G
95 H1 Spring Park Gt Lon
445 E2 Springside N Ayrs
317 G2 Springthorpe Lincs
187 F4 Spring Vale Barns
171 H1 Springwell Essex
405 G3 Springwell Sundld
406 B3 Springwell Sundld
348 C3 Sproatley E R Yk
291 E1 Sproston Green Ches
330 B4 Sprotbrough Donc
201 F6 Sproughton Suffk
453 G2 Sprouston Border
250 A2 Sprowston Norfk
278 B5 Sproxton Leics

372 B3 Sproxton N York
400 C5 Sprunston Cumb
269 H3 Spunhill Shrops
142 B5 Spurlands End Bucks
290 A3 Spurstow Ches
210 D6 Spurtree Shrops
30 C4 Spyway Dorset
150 D3 Square and Compass Pembks
337 F3 Squires Gate Bpool
516 B6 Sraid Ruadh Ag & B
595 G6 Srannda W Isls
235 G5 Stableford Shrops
272 B2 Stableford Staffs
314 B1 Stacey Bank Sheff
353 G1 Stackhouse N York
125 G5 Stackpole Pembks
224 D1 Stacksford Norfk
340 C5 Stacksteads Lancs
200 C5 Stackyard Green Suffk
11 F3 Staddiscombe C Plym
346 B4 Staddlethorpe E R Yk
23 H2 Staddon Devon
38 C3 Staddon Devon
313 E5 Staden Derbys
140 D5 Stadhampton Oxon
593 C10 Stadhlaigearraidh W Isls
291 H3 Stadmorslow Staffs
401 F6 Staffield Cumb
543 H3 Staffin Highld
272 D5 Stafford Staffs
235 G3 Stafford Park Wrekin
148 C1 Stafford's Corner Essex
67 G5 Stafford's Green Dorset
186 B3 Stagbatch Herefs
146 C1 Stagden Cross Essex
472 A6 Stagehall Border
194 D5 Stagsden Beds
194 D5 Stagsden West End Beds
40 D2 Stag's Head Devon
388 B4 Stainburn Cumb
356 B5 Stainburn N York
278 C5 Stainby Lincs
342 D5 Staincliffe Kirk
329 E2 Staincross Barns
394 C5 Staindrop Dur
118 A5 Staines Surrey
144 C2 Staines Green Herts
279 F4 Stainfield Lincs
319 E5 Stainfield Lincs
330 D2 Stainforth Donc
353 G1 Stainforth N York
337 G2 Staining Lancs
342 A6 Stainland Calder
387 F3 Stainsacre N York
295 E1 Stainsby Derbys
320 B5 Stainsby Lincs
365 H2 Stainton Cumb
390 D4 Stainton Cumb
400 C3 Stainton Cumb
330 C6 Stainton Donc
384 D2 Stainton Middsb
394 B6 Stainton Middsb
382 C5 Stainton N York
318 D4 Stainton by Langworth Lincs
387 G5 Staintondale N York
394 B6 Stainton Grove Dur
334 A6 Stainton le Vale Lincs
364 B5 Stainton with Adgarley Cumb
389 F5 Stair Cumb
445 F5 Stair S Ayrs
329 F3 Stairfoot Barns
415 H6 Stairhaven D & G
386 C1 Staithes N York
431 E2 Stakeford Nthumb
326 C3 Stake Hill Rochdl
212 C4 Stakenbridge Worcs
351 F5 Stake Pool Lancs
68 B6 Stalbridge Dorset
46 D1 Stalbridge Weston Dorset
256 D4 Stalham Norfk
256 D4 Stalham Green Norfk
99 F4 Stalisfield Green Kent
46 B1 Stallen Dorset
334 B2 Stallingborough NE Lin
368 B2 Stalling Busk N York
272 D2 Stallington Staffs
351 E5 Stalmine Lancs
351 E5 Stalmine Moss Side Lancs
327 E5 Stalybridge Tamesd
212 D3 Stambermill Dudley
63 G4 Stamborough Somset
173 G4 Stambourne Essex
173 G4 Stambourne Green Essex
243 E3 Stamford Lincs
309 G6 Stamford Bridge Ches
358 B3 Stamford Bridge E R Yk
430 A5 Stamfordham Nthumb
119 G2 Stamford Hill Gt Lon
467 E3 Stamperland E Rens
52 A4 Stamshaw C Port
351 E6 Stanah Lancs
144 B2 Stanborough Herts
168 D5 Stanbridge Beds
48 C4 Stanbridge Dorset
168 D5 Stanbridgeford Beds
172 C4 Stanbrook Essex
188 B5 Stanbrook Worcs
341 G4 Stanbury Brad
342 B4 Stand Bury
485 F6 Stand N Lans
486 B5 Standburn Falk
236 D3 Standeford Staffs
80 C1 Standen Kent
340 A1 Standen Hall Lancs
80 A3 Standen Street Kent
87 E4 Standerwick Somset
74 C3 Standford Hants
271 C5 Standford Bridge Wrekin
399 H5 Standingstone Cumb
136 B3 Standish Gloucs
324 D2 Standish Wigan
324 D2 Standish Lower Ground Wigan
139 F4 Standlake Oxon
72 B4 Standon Hants
171 E5 Standon Herts
272 B3 Standon Staffs
171 E6 Standon Green End Herts
468 D3 Stane N Lans
444 D2 Stanecastle N Ayrs
291 H4 Stanfield C Stke
254 B3 Stanfield Norfk
169 H1 Stanford Beds
82 B3 Stanford Kent
247 G6 Stanford Norfk
233 F2 Stanford Shrops
187 F4 Stanford Bishop Herefs
187 G1 Stanford Bridge Worcs
115 F3 Stanford Dingley W Berk
92 B2 Stanford End Wokham
276 B5 Stanford Hills Notts
139 G3 Stanford in the Vale Oxon
121 G3 Stanford-le-Hope Thurr
216 C4 Stanford on Avon Nhants
276 B5 Stanford on Soar Notts
187 F1 Stanford on Teme Worcs
146 A4 Stanford Rivers Essex
315 F5 Stanfree Derbys
386 A1 Stanghow R & Cl
244 B5 Stanground C Pete
340 A5 Stanhill Lancs

City, town and village index: Stanhoe - Stratton Audley 717

259 G4 Stanhoe Norfk
449 F4 Stanhope Border
393 G2 Stanhope Dur
81 E1 Stanhope Kent
218 C2 Stanion Nhants
364 B5 Stank Cumb
212 C5 Stanklyn Worcs
343 G2 Stanks Leeds
275 G1 Stanley Derbys
405 F4 Stanley Dur
324 B3 Stanley Lancs
295 F2 Stanley Notts
512 D3 Stanley P & K
211 F3 Stanley Shrops
211 G3 Stanley Shrops
292 B4 Stanley Staffs
343 F5 Stanley Wakefd
111 H5 Stanley Wilts
295 E6 Stanley Common Derbys
394 D2 Stanley Crook Dur
136 B4 Stanley Downton Gloucs
343 G5 Stanley Ferry Wakefd
324 A3 Stanley Gate Lancs
48 C6 Stanley Green Poole
270 C2 Stanley Green Shrops
311 H3 Stanley Green Stockp
187 F6 Stanley Hill Herefs
292 B4 Stanley Moor Staffs
163 E3 Stanley Pontlarge Gloucs
131 G6 Stanleytown Rhondd
309 F4 Stanlow Ches
236 A5 Stanlow Shrops
56 A3 Stanmer Br & H
118 D1 Stanmore Gt Lon
72 C4 Stanmore Hants
211 G1 Stanmore Shrops
114 D4 Stanmore W Berk
185 E3 Stanner Powys
514 C3 Stannergate C Dund
427 H2 Stannersburn Nthumb
93 G2 Stanners Hill Surrey
199 H3 Stanningfield Suffk
430 D4 Stannington Nthumb
314 C2 Stannington Sheff
430 D3 Stannington Station Nthumb
35 E2 Stanpit Dorset
185 F2 Stansbatch Herefs
199 F4 Stansfield Suffk
293 F4 Stanshope Staffs
199 G5 Stanstead Suffk
145 E2 Stanstead Abbots Herts
97 F2 Stansted Kent
171 G4 Stansted Mountfitchet Essex
290 D1 Stanthorne Lodge Ches
274 D6 Stanton Derbys
163 G3 Stanton Gloucs
159 F5 Stanton Mons
430 B2 Stanton Nthumb
293 F5 Stanton Staffs
224 C5 Stanton Suffk
168 A1 Stantonbury M Keyn
275 F4 Stanton by Bridge Derbys
275 H2 Stanton-by-Dale Derbys
224 C5 Stanton Chare Suffk
85 G2 Stanton Drew BaNES
113 E1 Stanton Fitzwarren Swindn
276 A2 Stanton Gate Derbys
139 G3 Stanton Harcourt Oxon
295 F2 Stanton Hill Notts
294 A2 Stanton in Peak Derbys
210 B4 Stanton Lacy Shrops
294 B2 Stanton Lees Derbys
210 D1 Stanton Long Shrops
276 D3 Stanton-on-the-Wolds Notts
86 B2 Stanton Prior BaNES
88 C2 Stanton St Bernard Wilts
140 C3 Stanton St John Oxon
111 G3 Stanton St Quintin Wilts
200 C1 Stanton Street Suffk
239 H2 Stanton under Bardon Leics
270 D5 Stanton upon Hine Heath Shrops
85 H2 Stanton Wick BaNES
135 G2 Stantway Gloucs
269 H5 Stanwardine in the Fields Shrops
269 H4 Stanwardine in the Wood Shrops
174 B5 Stanway Essex
163 G3 Stanway Gloucs
174 C5 Stanway Green Essex
226 A6 Stanway Green Suffk
118 A5 Stanwell Surrey
118 A5 Stanwell Moor Surrey
218 D5 Stanwick Nhants
383 E2 Stanwick-St-John N York
400 C3 Stanwix Cumb
326 C3 Stanycliffe Rochdl
606 C7 Stanydale Shet
593 C11 Staoinebrig W Isls
386 C6 Stape N York
48 C4 Stapehill Dorset
290 D5 Stapeley Ches
274 D5 Stapenhill Staffs
101 E4 Staple Kent
42 D4 Staple Cross Devon
79 H5 Staplecross E Susx
77 E4 Staplefield W Susx
44 B4 Staple Fitzpaine Somset
197 G4 Stapleford Cambs
144 D1 Stapleford Herts
277 G6 Stapleford Leics
297 G3 Stapleford Lincs
276 A2 Stapleford Notts
70 B2 Stapleford Wilts
145 H5 Stapleford Abbotts Essex
145 H5 Stapleford Tawney Essex
43 H2 Staplegrove Somset
43 H3 Staplehay Somset
110 A4 Staple Hill S Glos
213 E5 Staple Hill Worcs
98 B6 Staplehurst Kent
44 A4 Staple Lawns Somset
37 E3 Staplers IoW
75 G4 Staples Hill W Susx
99 G2 Staplestreet Kent
109 H4 Stapleton Bristl
23 E3 Stapleton Cnwll
426 D5 Stapleton Cumb
185 F1 Stapleton Herefs
239 G5 Stapleton Leics
344 C6 Stapleton N York
383 G2 Stapleton N York
234 B4 Stapleton Shrops
66 D5 Stapleton Somset
43 G5 Stapley Somset
195 G2 Staploe Beds
161 F1 Staplow Herefs
501 F4 Star Fife
153 E3 Star Pembks
84 D3 Star Somset
356 C3 Starbeck N York
368 C5 Starbotton N York
20 D1 Starcross Devon
215 E5 Stareton Warwks
405 E2 Stargate Gatesd
134 B4 Star Hill Mons
294 C3 Starkholmes Derbys
325 H2 Starling Bury
171 G3 Starlings Green Essex
58 C4 Starr's Green E Susx
225 H3 Starston Norfk
13 E4 Start Devon
382 B1 Startforth Dur
171 H5 Start Hill Essex
111 G3 Startley Wilts
142 C2 Startop's End Bucks
110 D2 Starveall S Glos
97 F5 Starvecrow Kent
101 E4 Statenborough Kent
310 D2 Statham Warrtn
66 B4 Stathe Somset
277 G3 Stathern Leics
399 G5 Station Hill Cumb
396 B2 Station Town Dur
248 D5 Statland Common Norfk
195 G1 Staughton Green Cambs
195 G2 Staughton Highway Cambs
195 G2 Staughton Moor Beds
134 D2 Staunton Gloucs
162 A4 Staunton Gloucs
297 F6 Staunton in the Vale Notts
185 G2 Staunton on Arrow Herefs
185 G5 Staunton on Wye Herefs
355 H3 Staupes N York
379 E5 Staveley Cumb
315 E5 Staveley Derbys
356 D2 Staveley N York
365 E2 Staveley-in-Cartmel Cumb
19 G5 Staverton Devon
162 C5 Staverton Gloucs
192 B2 Staverton Nhants
87 F2 Staverton Wilts
65 G4 Stawell Somset
43 E3 Stawley Somset
589 K6 Staxigoe Highld
374 C4 Staxton N York
205 E2 Staylittle Cerdgn
206 D1 Staylittle Powys
351 E6 Staynall Lancs
296 D4 Staythorpe Notts
355 F5 Stead Brad
135 E1 Steam Mills Gloucs
369 E5 Stean N York
67 F2 Steanbow Somset
372 B5 Stearsby N York
65 E2 Steart Somset
67 F4 Steart Somset
172 D5 Stebbing Essex
172 D5 Stebbing Green Essex
214 A2 Stechford Birm
80 C2 Stede Quarter Kent
74 D5 Stedham W Susx
403 G2 Steel Nthumb
428 D3 Steel Nthumb
314 C2 Steel Bank Sheff
78 C3 Steel Cross E Susx
486 D1 Steelend Fife
439 G6 Steele Road Border
439 G6 Steeleroad-end Border
362 D6 Steel Green Cumb
270 C2 Steel Heath Shrops
186 C3 Steen's Bridge Herefs
74 A4 Steep Hants
37 E5 Steephill IoW
341 G5 Steep Lane Calder
33 G3 Steeple Dorset
148 B4 Steeple Essex
87 G3 Steeple Ashton Wilts
166 A4 Steeple Aston Oxon
165 G4 Steeple Barton Oxon
172 D1 Steeple Bumpstead Essex
199 E5 Steeplechase Suffk
167 E4 Steeple Claydon Bucks
219 G3 Steeple Gidding Cambs
70 A2 Steeple Langford Wilts
196 C6 Steeple Morden Cambs
74 A4 Steep Marsh Hants
235 F3 Steeraway Wrekin
354 D6 Steeton Brad
542 D5 Stein Highld
599 J8 Steinis W Isls
559 H1 Steinmanhill Abers
405 E2 Stella Gatesd
82 B1 Stelling Minnis Kent
107 E2 Stelvio Newpt
66 C5 Stembridge Somset
102 C3 Stembridge Swans
588 F4 Stemster Highld
8 C2 Stenalees Cnwll
43 E5 Stenhill Devon
487 H5 Stenhouse C Edin
435 F6 Stenhouse D & G
485 H3 Stenhousemuir Falk
319 H3 Stenigot Lincs
4 C1 Stennack Cnwll
600 D2 Stenness Ork
606 B2 Stenness Shet
543 H3 Stenscholl Highld
602 D6 Stenso Ork
275 E4 Stenson Derbys
606 E7 Stenswall Shet
490 B5 Stenton E Loth
501 E5 Stenton Fife
43 F6 Stentwood Devon
278 A2 Stenwith Lincs
599 H8 Steòrnabhagh W Isls
126 C3 Stepaside Pembks
207 H2 Stepaside Powys
119 H3 Stepney Gt Lon
312 B2 Stepping Hill Stockp
169 E2 Steppingley Beds
484 D6 Stepps N Lans
313 F6 Sterndale Moor Derbys
202 D2 Sternfield Suffk
88 B3 Stert Wilts
34 B2 Sterte Poole
198 C3 Stetchworth Cambs
170 B5 Stevenage Herts
58 A3 Steven's Crouch E Susx
444 C1 Stevenston N Ayrs
40 A4 Stevenstone Devon
91 E5 Steventon Hants
114 D1 Steventon Oxon
210 C5 Steventon Shrops
198 C6 Steventon End Essex
194 D4 Stevington Beds
145 F3 Stewards Essex
169 E1 Stewartby Beds
456 D3 Stewarton Ag & B
410 D3 Stewarton D & G
466 B5 Stewarton E Ayrs
168 B4 Stewkley Bucks
168 A4 Stewkley Dean Bucks
44 C4 Stewley Somset
320 C2 Stewton Lincs
37 G3 Steyne Cross IoW
55 E2 Steyning W Susx
125 F3 Steynton Pembks
38 B5 Stibb Cnwll
254 C2 Stibbard Norfk
39 F5 Stibb Cross Devon
89 F2 Stibb Green Wilts
243 F5 Stibbington Cambs
452 D2 Stichill Border
8 B3 Sticker Cnwll
300 C3 Stickford Lincs
96 C6 Stick Hill Kent
25 F4 Sticklepath Devon
60 D5 Sticklepath Devon
44 C5 Sticklepath Somset
63 G4 Sticklepath Somset
67 F2 Sticklinch Somset
171 G3 Stickling Green Essex
300 B3 Stickney Lincs
260 C3 Stiffkey Norfk
187 G5 Stifford's Bridge Herefs
98 D2 Stiff Street Kent
66 D1 Stileway Somset
344 D1 Stillingfleet N York
372 A6 Stillington N York
395 H5 Stillington S on T
219 H2 Stilton Cambs
135 G5 Stinchcombe Gloucs
32 C1 Stinsford Dorset
233 F4 Stiperstones Shrops
213 G3 Stirchley Birm
235 G3 Stirchley Wrekin
561 H1 Stirling Abers
498 C6 Stirling Stirlg
196 A1 Stirtloe Cambs
354 C4 Stirton N York
173 G5 Stisted Essex
113 F6 Stitchcombe Wilts
187 H4 Stitchin's Hill Worcs
4 D1 Stithians Cnwll
566 B2 Stittenham Highld
215 E4 Stivichall Covtry
299 F1 Stixwould Lincs
309 F5 Stoak Ches
430 C3 Stobhill Nthumb
430 D2 Stobhillgate Nthumb
446 C2 Stobieside S Lans
449 G2 Stobo Border
449 G2 Stobo Castle Border
33 G2 Stoborough Dorset
33 G2 Stoborough Green Dorset
439 G3 Stobs Castle Border
443 G6 Stobswood Nthumb
146 D5 Stock Essex
353 H5 Stock Lancs
85 E2 Stock N Som
330 C3 Stockbridge Donc
71 H2 Stockbridge Hants
53 F4 Stockbridge W Susx
323 H6 Stockbridge Village Knows
447 F2 Stockbriggs S Lans
98 C2 Stockbury Kent
114 C6 Stockcross W Berk
400 C6 Stockdalewath Cumb
136 B3 Stockend Gloucs
99 F4 Stocker's Head Kent
241 H5 Stockerston Leics
557 G3 Stockethill C Aber
214 A2 Stockfield Birm
189 E3 Stock Green Worcs
52 C3 Stockheath Hants
224 C6 Stock Hill Suffk
331 G3 Stockholes Turbary N Linc
161 E3 Stocking Herefs
215 E1 Stockingford Warwks
172 B2 Stocking Green Essex
171 F4 Stocking Pelham Herts
28 D2 Stockland Devon
64 D3 Stockland Bristol Somset
213 G1 Stockland Green Birm
97 E6 Stockland Green Kent
26 C1 Stockleigh English Devon
26 D2 Stockleigh Pomeroy Devon
112 B6 Stockley Wilts
44 D4 Stocklinch Somset
312 B1 Stockport Stockp
328 D5 Stocksbridge Sheff
404 C2 Stocksfield Nthumb
97 E5 Stocks Green Kent
173 G5 Stockstreet Essex
186 C2 Stockton Herefs
250 D6 Stockton Norfk
233 E4 Stockton Shrops
235 G5 Stockton Shrops
191 G2 Stockton Warwks
69 G2 Stockton Wilts
235 H1 Stockton Wrekin
292 B4 Stockton Brook Staffs
310 C2 Stockton Heath Warrtn
396 A6 Stockton-on-Tees S on T
187 G1 Stockton on Teme Worcs
358 C3 Stockton on the Forest York
233 E4 Stocktonwood Shrops
27 F2 Stockwell Devon
136 D2 Stockwell Gloucs
119 G4 Stockwell Gt Lon
236 C4 Stockwell End Wolves
273 G5 Stockwell Heath Staffs
67 F5 Stockwitch Cross Somset
110 A6 Stockwood Bristl
30 D1 Stockwood Dorset
189 F3 Stock Wood Worcs
110 A6 Stockwood Vale BaNES
351 G3 Stodday Lancs
100 D3 Stodmarsh Kent
261 E4 Stody Norfk
578 D4 Stoer Highld
45 H5 Stoford Dorset
70 B2 Stoford Wilts
43 E6 Stoford Water Devon
64 A4 Stogumber Somset
64 D3 Stogursey Somset
215 F4 Stoke Covtry
11 E2 Stoke C Plym
38 B3 Stoke Devon
52 C4 Stoke Hants
90 C4 Stoke Hants
122 C4 Stoke Medway
201 G6 Stoke Suffk
30 B2 Stoke Abbott Dorset
217 G2 Stoke Albany Nhants
215 F4 Stoke Aldermoor Covtry
225 F5 Stoke Ash Suffk
276 D1 Stoke Bardolph Notts
187 F2 Stoke Bliss Worcs
193 F4 Stoke Bruerne Nhants
199 E6 Stoke by Clare Suffk
174 C2 Stoke-by-Nayland Suffk
27 E3 Stoke Canon Devon
72 C2 Stoke Charity Hants
17 E4 Stoke Climsland Cnwll
72 C5 Stoke Common Hants
187 E4 Stoke Cross Herefs
94 C3 Stoke D'Abernon Surrey
219 E2 Stoke Doyle Nhants
242 B5 Stoke Dry Rutlnd
161 E1 Stoke Edith Herefs
238 B5 Stoke End Warwks
70 A4 Stoke Farthing Wilts
246 D4 Stoke Ferry Norfk
13 F3 Stoke Fleming Devon
33 F2 Stokeford Dorset
13 F1 Stoke Gabriel Devon
109 H3 Stoke Gifford S Glos
239 G5 Stoke Golding Leics
194 A5 Stoke Goldington M Keyn
210 D3 Stokegorse Shrops
117 G3 Stoke Green Bucks
317 E4 Stokeham Notts
168 B4 Stoke Hammond Bucks
215 F3 Stoke Heath Covtry
271 E4 Stoke Heath Shrops
212 D6 Stoke Heath Worcs
27 E4 Stoke Hill Devon
187 E5 Stoke Hill Herefs
250 A4 Stoke Holy Cross Norfk
20 C3 Stokeinteignhead Devon
187 E5 Stoke Lacy Herefs
187 E4 Stoke Lane Herefs
166 C4 Stoke Lyne Oxon
142 A2 Stoke Mandeville Bucks
141 G5 Stokenchurch Bucks
119 G2 Stoke Newington Gt Lon
13 E4 Stokenham Devon
271 E4 Stoke on Tern Shrops
292 B5 Stoke-on-trent C Stke
162 D4 Stoke Orchard Gloucs
175 F1 Stoke Park Suffk
117 G3 Stoke Poges Bucks
213 E6 Stoke Pound Worcs
186 C3 Stoke Prior Herefs
188 D1 Stoke Prior Worcs
61 F4 Stoke Rivers Devon
278 C4 Stoke Rochford Lincs
115 H3 Stoke Row Oxon
44 C2 Stoke St Gregory Somset
44 B3 Stoke St Mary Somset
86 B5 Stoke St Michael Somset
210 D3 Stoke St Milborough Shrops
209 H3 Stokesay Shrops
251 E2 Stokesby Norfk
385 E3 Stokesley N York
66 D6 Stoke sub Hamdon Somset
141 E5 Stoke Talmage Oxon
68 B4 Stoke Trister Somset
47 E3 Stoke Wake Dorset
30 B2 Stoke Water Dorset
189 E1 Stoke Wharf Worcs
428 A2 Stokoe Nthumb
64 D2 Stolford Somset
146 B4 Stondon Massey Essex
245 G6 Stonea Cambs
141 G2 Stone Bucks
135 F5 Stone Gloucs
121 E5 Stone Kent
315 H2 Stone Rothm
67 F3 Stone Somset
272 D3 Stone Staffs
212 C5 Stone Worcs
234 B6 Stoneacton Shrops
84 D4 Stone Allerton Somset
85 H4 Ston Easton Somset
188 D5 Stonebow Worcs
123 E2 Stonebridge Essex
119 E3 Stonebridge Gt Lon
224 B1 Stonebridge Norfk
84 C3 Stonebridge N Som
214 C3 Stonebridge Solhll
94 D5 Stonebridge Surrey
99 E5 Stonebridge Green Kent
295 E3 Stonebroom Derbys
468 C6 Stonebyres Holdings S Lans
342 B4 Stone Chair Calder
325 H3 Stoneclough Bolton
61 E3 Stonecombe Devon
78 C4 Stone Cross E Susx
79 E3 Stone Cross E Susx
57 G4 Stone Cross Kent
78 C2 Stone Cross Kent
81 F2 Stone Cross Kent
101 F4 Stone Cross Kent
237 F6 Stone Cross Sandw
79 F3 Stonecrouch Kent
439 H3 Stonedge Border
109 E5 Stone-edge Batch N Som
348 B3 Stoneferry C KuH
467 G3 Stonefield S Lans
272 C3 Stonefield Staffs
79 F4 Stonegate E Susx
386 C3 Stonegate N York
372 B4 Stonegrave N York
314 D5 Stonegravels Derbys
83 E1 Stonehall Kent
188 C5 Stonehall Worcs
428 B4 Stonehaugh Nthumb
541 G2 Stonehaven Abers
354 B6 Stone Head N York
273 E2 Stone Heath Staffs
331 E3 Stone Hill Donc
81 G2 Stone Hill Kent
99 E5 Stone Hill Kent
110 A5 Stone Hill S Glos
93 H2 Stonehill Surrey
51 E4 Stonehills Hants
11 E3 Stonehouse C Plym
367 F2 Stone House Cumb
136 B3 Stonehouse Gloucs
402 B3 Stonehouse Nthumb
468 B5 Stonehouse S Lans
273 E1 Stonehouses Staffs
80 D4 Stone in Oxney Kent
95 E2 Stoneleigh Surrey
215 E5 Stoneleigh Warwks
290 C4 Stoneley Green Ches
195 G1 Stonely Cambs
189 E3 Stonepits Worcs
77 G2 Stonequarry W Susx
400 D5 Stone Raise Cumb
73 H4 Stoner Hill Hants
277 H5 Stonesby Leics
139 F1 Stonesfield Oxon
176 C4 Stones Green Essex
97 E4 Stone Street Kent
174 C2 Stone Street Suffk
226 D3 Stone Street Suffk
81 F2 Stonestreet Green Kent
377 H2 Stonethwaite Cumb
191 H4 Stoneton Warwks
121 E5 Stonewood Kent
187 G6 Stoneyard Green Herefs
488 C5 Stoneybank E Loth
593 C11 Stoneybridge W Isls
469 F2 Stoneyburn W Loth
20 B4 Stoneycombe Devon
309 E1 Stoneycroft Lpool
49 H2 Stoney Cross Hants
326 C2 Stoneyfield Rochdl
295 E5 Stoneyford Derbys
42 D6 Stoneyford Devon
561 F2 Stoneygate Abers
240 D4 Stoneygate C Leic
213 E5 Stoney Hill Worcs
148 B5 Stoneyhills Essex
340 C3 Stoneyholme Lancs
415 E6 Stoneykirk D & G
210 D4 Stoneylane Shrops
313 H4 Stoney Middleton Derbys
342 A5 Stoney Royd Calder
240 A6 Stoney Stanton Leics
68 B3 Stoney Stoke Somset
67 H2 Stoney Stratton Somset
233 G3 Stoney Stretton Shrops
557 F2 Stoneywood C Aber
485 F3 Stoneywood Falk
609 G4 Stonganess Shet
201 F3 Stonham Aspal Suffk
237 G4 Stonnall Staffs
116 B2 Stonor Oxon
241 F5 Stonton Wyville Leics
71 F4 Stony Batter Hants
604 D3 Stonybreck Shet
39 H2 Stony Cross Devon
186 C1 Stony Cross Herefs
187 G5 Stony Cross Herefs
296 D6 Stony Dale Notts
566 B2 Stonyfield Highld
50 B1 Stonyford Hants
406 A4 Stony Gate Sundld
142 B5 Stony Green Bucks
404 D4 Stony Heap Dur
91 F3 Stony Heath Hants
295 F1 Stony Houghton Derbys
29 G2 Stony Knaps Dorset
40 A2 Stonyland Devon
86 C3 Stony Littleton BaNES
71 G4 Stonymarsh Hants
167 G1 Stony Stratford M Keyn
42 B4 Stoodleigh Devon
151 F2 Stop-and-Call Pembks
314 B2 Stopes Sheff
44 A6 Stopgate Devon
75 G6 Stopham W Susx
353 G5 Stopper Lane Lancs
169 G5 Stopsley Luton
14 C3 Stoptide Cnwll
308 D3 Storeton Wirral
355 E4 Storiths N York
512 D4 Stormontfield P & K
87 E5 Stormore Wilts
599 H8 Stornoway W Isls
187 G5 Storridge Herefs
54 C2 Storrington W Susx
378 C6 Storrs Cumb
314 B2 Storrs Sheff
171 G5 Stortford Park Herts
365 G4 Storth Cumb
358 D6 Storwood E R Yk
568 C1 Stotfield Moray
170 B2 Stotfold Beds
211 F3 Stottesdon Shrops
240 D4 Stoughton Leics
93 G4 Stoughton Surrey
53 E2 Stoughton W Susx
84 D5 Stoughton Cross Somset
188 D5 Stoulton Worcs
212 C3 Stourbridge Staffs
47 G3 Stourpaine Dorset
212 A5 Stourport-on-Severn Worcs
68 C5 Stour Provost Dorset
68 D5 Stour Row Dorset
343 F3 Stourton Leeds
212 C2 Stourton Staffs
164 D2 Stourton Warwks
68 C3 Stourton Wilts
46 D1 Stourton Caundle Dorset
165 E2 Stourton Hill Warwks
66 C3 Stout Somset
603 J4 Stove Ork
605 H6 Stove Shet
609 J2 Stove Shet
227 E3 Stoven Suffk
472 B6 Stow Border
317 G3 Stow Lincs
246 C3 Stow Bardolph Norfk
248 C5 Stow Bedon Norfk
246 B3 Stowbridge Norfk
197 H2 Stow cum Quy Cambs
134 D3 Stowe Gloucs
185 E5 Stowe Herefs
243 G2 Stowe Lincs
209 F5 Stowe Shrops
237 H3 Stowe Staffs
273 F4 Stowe-by-Chartley Staffs
134 D3 Stowe Green Gloucs
137 G2 Stowell Gloucs
68 A5 Stowell Somset
167 E2 Stowe Park Bucks
85 G3 Stowey BaNES
134 D1 Stowfield Gloucs
24 B3 Stowford Devon
24 B5 Stowford Devon
28 B5 Stowford Devon
38 C5 Stowford Devon
40 C2 Stowford Devon
61 F3 Stowford Devon
244 A2 Stowgate Lincs
224 C6 Stowlangtoft Suffk
236 D5 Stow Lawn Wolves
219 G5 Stow Longa Cambs
147 G5 Stow Maries Essex
200 D3 Stowmarket Suffk
164 B4 Stow-on-the-Wold Gloucs
107 E2 Stow Park Newpt
81 H1 Stowting Kent
82 B2 Stowting Common Kent
81 H1 Stowting Court Kent
201 E3 Stowupland Suffk
464 A2 Straad Ag & B
585 G6 Strabeg Highld
540 C1 Strachan Abers
494 B4 Strachur Ag & B
226 A5 Stradbroke Suffk
199 E4 Stradishall Suffk
246 D4 Stradsett Norfk
297 G4 Stragglethorpe Lincs
113 H5 Straight Soley Wilts
471 E1 Straiton Mdloth
433 E4 Straiton S Ayrs
560 C5 Straloch Abers
524 F3 Straloch P & K
273 G2 Stramshall Staffs
135 G2 Strand Gloucs
119 F3 Strand Gt Lon
362 D5 Strands Cumb
322 f7 Strang IoM
326 B5 Strangeways Manch
160 D4 Strangford Herefs
88 D6 Strangways Wilts
557 F5 Stranog Abers
415 E4 Stranraer D & G
182 B1 Strata Florida Cerdgn
91 H2 Stratfield Mortimer W Berk
92 A2 Stratfield Saye Hants
92 A3 Stratfield Turgis Hants
196 A5 Stratford Beds
120 A3 Stratford Gt Lon
162 C2 Stratford Worcs
120 A3 Stratford New Town Gt Lon
202 C2 Stratford St Andrew Suffk
174 D3 Stratford St Mary Suffk
70 C3 Stratford Sub Castle Wilts
70 B4 Stratford Tony Wilts
190 C4 Stratford-upon-Avon Warwks
572 F8 Strath Highld
499 E1 Strathallan Castle P & K
532 E4 Strathan Highld
547 G2 Strathan Highld
578 E5 Strathan Highld
586 C4 Strathan Highld
586 D4 Strathan Skerray Highld
467 H6 Strathaven S Lans
484 B4 Strathblane Stirlg
467 E2 Strathbungo C Glas
574 C3 Strathcanaird Highld
547 G1 Strathcarron Highld
505 K4 Strathcoil Ag & B
588 E5 Strathcoul Highld
554 B2 Strathdon Abers
502 D1 Strathkinness Fife
500 D3 Strathmiglo Fife
565 H5 Strathpeffer Highld
564 F2 Strathrannoch Highld
524 C5 Strathtay P & K
461 E2 Strathwhillan N Ayrs
587 H3 Strathy Highld
496 D1 Strathyre Stirlg
23 E1 Stratton Cnwll
31 E4 Stratton Dorset
137 F4 Stratton Gloucs
166 D4 Stratton Audley Oxon

86 B4 Stratton-on-the-Fosse Somset
113 E2 Stratton St Margaret Swindn
249 H6 Stratton St Michael Norfk
255 H3 Stratton Strawless Norfk
503 E2 Stravithie Fife
365 E2 Strawberry Bank Cumb
78 D2 Strawberry Hill E Susx
118 D5 Strawberry Hill Gt Lon
344 A5 Strawberry Hill Wakefd
56 B1 Streat E Susx
119 G5 Streatham Gt Lon
119 G5 Streatham Hill Gt Lon
119 F5 Streatham Park Gt Lon
119 F5 Streatham Vale Gt Lon
169 F4 Streatley Beds
115 F3 Streatley W Berk
380 A3 Street Cumb
28 C5 Street Devon
351 H4 Street Lancs
386 B4 Street N York
29 G1 Street Somset
66 D2 Street Somset
44 B5 Street Ash Somset
215 G3 Street Ashton Warwks
269 F2 Street Dinas Shrops
73 E5 Street End Hants
100 B5 Street End Kent
53 F5 Street End W Susx
405 F2 Street Gate Gatesd
238 A2 Streethay Staffs
343 G5 Streethouse Wakefd
357 G5 Street Houses N York
383 H5 Streetlam N York
294 D5 Street Lane Derbys
237 G5 Streetly Birm
270 A2 Street Lydan Wrexhm
198 C5 Streetly End Cambs
67 G2 Street on the Fosse Somset
210 A2 Strefford Shrops
276 C3 Strelley Notts
358 B3 Strensall York
162 D1 Strensham Worcs
41 G5 Stretch Down Devon
84 A6 Stretcholt Somset
13 E3 Strete Devon
27 G3 Strete Raleigh Devon
186 A3 Stretford Herefs
186 A3 Stretford Herefs
326 A6 Stretford Traffd
171 G2 Strethall Essex
221 H5 Stretham Cambs
53 F3 Strettington W Susx
289 F4 Stretton Ches
294 D3 Stretton Derbys
242 D1 Stretton Rutlnd
236 C2 Stretton Staffs
274 C3 Stretton Staffs
310 C3 Stretton Warrtn
239 E2 Stretton en le Field Leics
187 E6 Stretton Grandison Herefs
233 G2 Stretton Heath Shrops
215 G5 Stretton-on-Dunsmore Warwks
164 C2 Stretton-on-Fosse Warwks
186 B6 Stretton Sugwas Herefs
215 G3 Stretton under Fosse Warwks
234 D5 Stretton Westwood Shrops
571 G4 Strichen Abers
312 C2 Strines Stockp
64 C3 Stringston Somset
194 B2 Strixton Nhants
134 B3 Stroat Gloucs
85 F2 Strode N Som
546 F3 Stromeferry Highld
546 E2 Stromemore Highld
600 C3 Stromness Ork
533 K6 Stronaba Highld
499 H3 Stronachie P & K
496 A2 Stronachlachar Stirlg
520 F1 Stronchreggan Highld
579 H6 Stronchrubie Highld
482 A3 Strone Ag & B
533 H6 Strone Highld
535 K2 Strone Highld
549 J4 Strone Highld
482 C5 Strone Inver
518 D4 Strongarbh Ag & B
507 L4 Stronmilchan Ag & B
417 E4 Stronord D & G
519 K3 Strontian Highld
481 H7 Stronvochlan Ag & B
80 C3 Strood Kent
121 H6 Strood Medway
95 E5 Strood Green Surrey
75 G5 Strood Green W Susx
76 B3 Strood Green W Susx
403 F2 Strothers Dale Nthumb
136 C3 Stroud Gloucs
73 H5 Stroud Hants
75 E3 Stroud Surrey
49 E6 Strouden Bmouth
122 D1 Stroud Green Essex
136 B3 Stroud Green Gloucs
482 B3 Stroul Ag & B
278 C3 Stroxton Lincs
38 D4 Stroxworthy Devon
544 E1 Struan Highld
524 B2 Struan P & K
544 E2 Struanmore Highld
321 E3 Strubby Lincs
187 H1 Structon's Heath Worcs
280 C2 Strugg's Hill Lincs
250 D1 Strumpshaw Norfk
468 B5 Strutherhill S Lans
592 F4 Struth Mòr W Isls
548 F1 Struy Highld
302 B4 Stryd IoA
302 D4 Stryd y Facsen IoA
288 C5 Stryt-issa Wrexhm
571 H6 Stuartfield Abers
257 E5 Stubb Norfk
52 C3 Stubbermere W Susx
237 F4 Stubber's Green Wsall
116 D3 Stubbings W & M
225 E5 Stubbing's Green Suffk
51 F4 Stubbington Hants
338 D1 Stubbins Lancs
340 B6 Stubbins Lancs
376 D3 Stubble Green Cumb
115 H4 Stubbles W Berk
81 E2 Stubb's Cross Kent
250 D5 Stubbs Green Norfk
340 D5 Stubbylee Park Lancs
47 H2 Stubhampton Dorset
324 D4 Stubshaw Cross Wigan
297 G5 Stubton Lincs
273 G5 Stubwood Staffs
495 G4 Stuckgowan Ag & B
49 F2 Stuckton Hants
101 F6 Studdal Kent
100 C2 Studd Hill Kent
295 G5 Studfold Notts
G5 Studfold N York
E2 Stud Green Ches
E4 Stud Green W & M
E1 Studham Beds
B4 Studland Dorset
D2 Studley Warwks
45 Studley Wilts

189 G2 Studley Common Warwks
141 G5 Studley Green Bucks
87 E3 Studley Green Wilts
370 B5 Studley Roger N York
370 B5 Studley Royal N York
163 G5 Stumps Cross Gloucs
222 A4 Stuntney Cambs
57 G2 Stunts Green E Susx
272 B3 Sturbridge Staffs
87 E6 Sturford Wilts
317 G2 Sturgate Lincs
198 D6 Sturmer Essex
47 E2 Sturminster Common Dorset
48 B5 Sturminster Marshall Dorset
47 E2 Sturminster Newton Dorset
100 C3 Sturry Kent
38 B5 Stursdon Cnwll
332 D4 Sturton N Linc
317 G3 Sturton by Stow Lincs
317 E3 Sturton le Steeple Notts
225 F4 Stuston Suffk
344 B1 Stutton N York
175 F3 Stutton Suffk
311 G3 Styal Ches
97 E3 Styants Bottom Kent
271 E2 Styche Hall Shrops
339 G2 Stydd Lancs
316 B1 Styrrup Notts
599 L2 Suainebost W Isls
599 K8 Suardail W Isls
553 J1 Succoth Abers
495 F3 Succoth Ag & B
187 G4 Suckley Worcs
187 G4 Suckley Green Worcs
187 G4 Suckley Knowl Worcs
172 B4 Sucksted Green Essex
218 D3 Sudborough Nhants
203 E4 Sudbourne Suffk
298 B6 Sudbrook Lincs
109 F2 Sudbrook Mons
318 C4 Sudbrooke Lincs
274 B3 Sudbury Derbys
118 D2 Sudbury Gt Lon
173 H1 Sudbury Suffk
326 C2 Sudden Rochdl
136 D3 Sudgrove Gloucs
256 A3 Suffield Norfk
374 B1 Suffield N York
272 A3 Sugnall Staffs
160 A1 Sugwas Pool Herefs
545 K2 Suisnish Highld
545 K6 Suisnish Highld
542 F6 Suladale Highld
599 L7 Sulaisiadar W Isls
322 F4 Sulby IoM
192 C5 Sulgrave Nhants
405 H3 Sulgrave Sundld
115 G5 Sulham W Berk
115 G6 Sulhampstead Abbots W Berk
115 G6 Sulhampstead Bannister Upper End W Berk
115 G6 Sulhamstead W Berk
54 C2 Sullington W Susx
54 C2 Sullington Warren W Susx
606 D3 Sullom Shet
106 C6 Sully V Glam
605 H9 Sumburgh Shet
355 G2 Summerbridge N York
7 G2 Summercourt Cnwll
101 E4 Summerfield Kent
259 E4 Summerfield Norfk
212 B5 Summerfield Worcs
213 F2 Summerfield Park Birm
348 B3 Summergangs C KuH
116 B1 Summer Heath Bucks
315 E6 Summerhill C Aber
72 C2 Summerhill C Aber
202 C6 Summer Hill E Susx
165 E2 Summerhill Newpt
371 F3 Summerhill Pembks
237 E6 Summer Hill Sandw
237 G3 Summerhill Staffs
212 B4 Summerhill Worcs
271 G6 Summerhill Wrekin
288 D4 Summerhill Wrexhm
394 D6 Summerhouse Darltn
365 H2 Summerlands Cumb
45 G4 Summerlands Somset
108 D3 Summerleaze Mons
294 D5 Summerley Derbys
355 F4 Summerscales N York
53 F3 Summersdale W Susx
326 A2 Summerseat Bury
484 B5 Summerston C Glas
167 E5 Summerstown Bucks
140 B3 Summertown Oxon
326 B2 Summit Oldham
326 D3 Summit Rochdl
341 E6 Summit Rochdl
380 A3 Sunbiggin Cumb
364 C5 Sunbrick Cumb
118 B6 Sunbury Surrey
118 B5 Sunbury Common Surrey
135 F6 Sundayshill S Glos
389 E2 Sunderland Cumb
351 F3 Sunderland Lancs
406 C3 Sunderland Sundld
395 F2 Sunderland Bridge Dur
450 C4 Sundhope Border
169 F4 Sundon Park Luton
120 B5 Sundridge Gt Lon
96 C3 Sundridge Kent
327 E5 Sun Green Tamesd
137 H4 Sunhill Gloucs
122 C3 Sunken Marsh Essex
349 E6 Sunk Island E R Yk
117 G6 Sunningdale W & M
117 F6 Sunninghill W & M
140 A4 Sunningwell Oxon
394 C2 Sunniside Dur
405 E3 Sunniside Gatesd
406 A4 Sunniside Sundld
326 B3 Sunny Bank Bury
601 G2 Sunnybank Ork
339 H3 Sunny Bower Bl w D
394 D3 Sunnybrow Dur
330 B3 Sunnyfields Donc
275 E3 Sunny Hill C Derb
339 G5 Sunnyhurst Bl w D
498 B5 Sunnylaw Stirlg
140 B3 Sunnymead Oxon
117 H4 Sunnymeads W & M
146 D6 Sunnyside Essex
330 A6 Sunnyside Rothm
77 G2 Sunnyside W Susx
185 F3 Sunset Herefs
89 F4 Sunton Wilts
94 D1 Surbiton Gt Lon
280 C4 Surfleet Lincs
280 C4 Surfleet Seas End Lincs
250 C3 Surlingham Norfk
173 H5 Surrex Essex
246 A6 Suspension Bridge Norfk
261 G4 Sustead Norfk
332 A4 Susworth Lincs
38 D5 Sutcombe Devon
38 D5 Sutcombemill Devon
507 G1 Sutherlands Grove Ag & B
249 E5 Suton Norfk
566 E3 Sutors of Cromarty Highld
320 C5 Sutterby Lincs
280 C2 Sutterton Lincs

280 C3 Sutterton Dowdyke Lincs
527 G4 Suttieside Angus
196 B5 Sutton Beds
117 H4 Sutton Bucks
221 F4 Sutton C Pete
243 F5 Sutton C Pete
12 C4 Sutton Devon
330 C2 Sutton Donc
56 D5 Sutton E Susx
95 F2 Sutton Gt Lon
101 F6 Sutton Kent
297 G4 Sutton Lincs
256 D5 Sutton Norfk
277 G2 Sutton Notts
344 B4 Sutton N York
139 G3 Sutton Oxon
125 F1 Sutton Pembks
211 G2 Sutton Shrops
269 G4 Sutton Shrops
271 F3 Sutton Shrops
67 G3 Sutton Somset
234 B2 Sutton Staffs
271 H5 Sutton Staffs
324 C6 Sutton St Hel
202 C5 Sutton Suffk
53 H1 Sutton W Susx
94 C5 Sutton Abinger Surrey
120 D5 Sutton at Hone Kent
217 G1 Sutton Bassett Nhants
111 G4 Sutton Benger Wilts
45 G5 Sutton Bingham Somset
276 B4 Sutton Bonington Notts
281 G5 Sutton Bridge Lincs
239 G4 Sutton Cheney Leics
237 G5 Sutton Coldfield Birm
281 F4 Sutton Corner Lincs
140 B6 Sutton Courtenay Oxon
281 F5 Sutton Crosses Lincs
316 C3 Sutton cum Lound Notts
54 A1 Sutton End W Susx
212 B4 Sutton Farm Worcs
295 G3 Sutton Forest Side Notts
221 F4 Sutton Gault Cambs
370 B5 Sutton Grange N York
309 E4 Sutton Green Ches
93 G4 Sutton Green Surrey
289 F5 Sutton Green Wrexhm
235 G4 Sutton Hall Shrops
324 B6 Sutton Heath St Hel
48 C3 Sutton Holms Dorset
370 C4 Sutton Howgrave N York
295 F3 Sutton in Ashfield Notts
354 D6 Sutton-in-Craven N York
348 B3 Sutton Ings C KuH
240 B6 Sutton in the Elms Leics
186 C5 Sutton Lakes Herefs
312 B5 Sutton Lane Ends Ches
310 A1 Sutton Leach St Hel
235 H4 Sutton Maddock Shrops
65 G4 Sutton Mallet Somset
69 G4 Sutton Mandeville Wilts
309 H1 Sutton Manor St Hel
186 C6 Sutton Marsh Herefs
354 D6 Sutton Mill N York
67 G5 Sutton Montis Somset
348 B3 Sutton-on-Hull C KuH
321 F3 Sutton on Sea Lincs
357 H2 Sutton-on-the-Forest N York
274 C3 Sutton on the Hill Derbys
297 E1 Sutton on Trent Notts
32 C3 Sutton Poyntz Dorset
69 G4 Sutton Row Wilts
245 E2 Sutton St Edmund Lincs
281 E6 Sutton St James Lincs
186 C5 Sutton St Michael Herefs
186 C5 Sutton St Nicholas Herefs
315 E6 Sutton Scarsdale Derbys
72 C2 Sutton Scotney Hants
202 C6 Sutton Street Suffk
165 E2 Sutton-under-Brailes Warwks
371 F3 Sutton-under-Whitestonecliffe N York
358 D5 Sutton upon Derwent E R Yk
98 C5 Sutton Valence Kent
69 E1 Sutton Veny Wilts
47 G1 Sutton Waldron Dorset
310 A4 Sutton Weaver Ches
85 G3 Sutton Wick BaNES
140 A6 Sutton Wick Oxon
320 C4 Swaby Lincs
274 D6 Swadlincote Derbys
247 F3 Swaffham Norfk
198 B2 Swaffham Bulbeck Cambs
198 B2 Swaffham Prior Cambs
256 B3 Swafield Norfk
58 C2 Swaile's Green E Susx
384 D4 Swainby N York
342 C2 Swain House Brad
160 B1 Swainshill Herefs
249 H4 Swainsthorpe Norfk
329 F4 Swaithe Barns
165 F2 Swalcliffe Oxon
100 B2 Swalecliffe Kent
362 C3 Swalehurst Cumb
333 H4 Swallow Lincs
318 B6 Swallow Beck Lincs
69 G4 Swallowcliffe Wilts
92 B2 Swallowfield Wokham
19 H5 Swallowfields Devon
315 E3 Swallownest Rothm
146 C5 Swallows Cross Essex
405 F2 Swalwell Gatesd
90 C4 Swampton Hants
34 B5 Swanage Dorset
271 F1 Swanbach Ches
600 E3 Swanbister Ork
113 E1 Swanborough Swindn
142 C3 Swan Bottom Bucks
167 H4 Swanbourne Bucks
106 C6 Swanbridge V Glam
311 E5 Swan Green Ches
226 B5 Swan Green Suffk
347 E4 Swanland E R Yk
135 G5 Swanley Gloucs
120 D6 Swanley Kent
120 D6 Swanley Village Kent
51 G1 Swanmore Hants
37 F2 Swanmore IoW
239 G1 Swannington Leics
255 F4 Swannington Norfk
318 A5 Swanpool Lincs
121 F4 Swanscombe Kent
103 G3 Swansea Swans
309 F1 Swanside Knows
470 D1 Swanston C Edin
488 A6 Swanston C Edin
12 C4 Swan Street Essex
256 B4 Swanton Abbot Norfk
256 B4 Swanton Hill Norfk
254 D4 Swanton Morley Norfk
260 D5 Swanton Novers Norfk
98 D3 Swanton Street Norfk
213 E1 Swan Village Sandw
295 E4 Swanwick Derbys
51 F3 Swanwick Hants
279 E1 Swarby Lincs
343 G2 Swarcliffe Leeds
249 G4 Swardeston Norfk
609 G8 Swarister Shet
275 F4 Swarkestone Derbys
443 F4 Swarland Nthumb

73 E2 Swarraton Hants
355 E5 Swartha Brad
364 C4 Swarthmoor Cumb
314 D6 Swathwick Derbys
279 G2 Swaton Lincs
220 D6 Swavesey Cambs
49 H5 Sway Hants
278 D5 Swayfield Lincs
50 D1 Swaythling C Sotn
187 F2 Sweet Green Worcs
26 D3 Sweetham Devon
78 C4 Sweethaws E Susx
43 G3 Sweethay Somset
391 E6 Sweetholme Cumb
22 C3 Sweets Cnwll
8 D1 Sweetshouse Cnwll
202 C2 Sweffling Suffk
44 D3 Swell Somset
557 F5 Swellhead Abers
73 G1 Swelling Hill Hants
239 F2 Swepstone Leics
165 F3 Swerford Oxon
291 G1 Swettenham Ches
369 G5 Swetton N York
132 D5 Swffryd Blae G
98 D6 Swift's Green Kent
201 G4 Swilland Suffk
338 C3 Swillbrook Lancs
343 G3 Swillington Leeds
40 C2 Swimbridge Devon
61 F5 Swimbridge Newland Devon
138 D2 Swinbrook Oxon
342 D4 Swincliffe Kirk
356 A3 Swincliffe N York
61 G3 Swincombe Devon
353 H4 Swinden N York
297 G2 Swinderby Lincs
212 C1 Swindon Gloucs
112 D2 Swindon Staffs
348 B2 Swindon Swindn
345 H5 Swine E R Yk
110 B6 Swinefleet E R Yk
195 E1 Swineford S Glos
280 B1 Swineshead Beds
299 G6 Swineshead Lincs
369 E3 Swineside N York
317 G6 Swinethorpe Lincs
583 H2 Swiney Highld
216 C4 Swinford Leics
139 G3 Swinford Oxon
295 F6 Swingate Notts
221 E2 Swingbrow Cambs
82 D2 Swingfield Minnis Kent
82 D2 Swingfield Street Kent
200 C5 Swingleton Green Suffk
468 B5 Swinhill S Lans
455 G4 Swinhoe Nthumb
334 B5 Swinhope Lincs
607 G4 Swining Shet
606 D1 Swinister Shet
368 D2 Swinithwaite N York
161 F1 Swinmore Common Herefs
440 B1 Swinnie Border
342 D3 Swinnow Moor Leeds
293 F5 Swinscoe Staffs
389 F5 Swinside Cumb
440 D1 Swinside Hall Border
440 D1 Swinside Townfoot Border
279 E5 Swinstead Lincs
474 B5 Swinton Border
369 H4 Swinton N York
373 E5 Swinton N York
329 G5 Swinton Rothm
325 H4 Swinton Salfd
329 H5 Swinton Bridge Rothm
474 B5 Swinton Hill Border
474 B5 Swintonmill Border
326 A4 Swinton Park Salfd
128 D4 Swiss Valley Carmth
240 C2 Swithland Leics
565 K3 Swordale Highld
576 D5 Swordale Highld
531 L4 Swordland Highld
586 F4 Swordly Highld
310 D3 Sworton Heath Ches
181 G1 Swyddffynnon Cerdgn
272 B2 Swynnerton Staffs
30 C5 Swyre Dorset
29 E1 Sycamore Devon
152 B2 Sychpant Pembks
288 D3 Sydallt Wrexhm
136 D2 Syde Gloucs
141 F4 Sydenham Oxon
65 F4 Sydenham Somset
17 F3 Sydenham Damerel Devon
259 G5 Syderstone Norfk
31 E3 Sydling St Nicholas Dorset
90 D3 Sydmonton Hants
291 E3 Sydney Ches
296 D5 Syerston Notts
326 C1 Syke Rochdl
330 D1 Sykehouse Donc
352 C4 Sykes Lancs
225 H4 Syleham Suffk
128 D3 Sylen Carmth
607 H5 Symbister Shet
471 H5 Symington Border
445 E3 Symington S Ayrs
448 D2 Symington S Lans
30 A4 Symondsbury Dorset
134 C1 Symonds Yat Herefs
29 G2 Synderford Dorset
180 B4 Synod Inn Cerdgn
451 F5 Synton Border
451 F5 Synton Mains Border
135 H6 Synwell Gloucs
586 E8 Syre Highld
163 F5 Syreford Gloucs
166 D1 Syresham Nhants
240 D2 Syston Leics
278 C1 Syston Lincs
188 B1 Sytchampton Worcs
212 A1 Sytch Ho Green Shrops
271 E5 Sytch Lane Wrekin
193 H1 Sywell Nhants

T

311 E4 Tabley Hill Ches
230 B1 Tabor Gwynd
597 J4 Tabost W Isls
599 L2 Tabost W Isls
191 E2 Tachbrook Mallory Warwks
63 G4 Tacker Street Somset
12 C4 Tacket Wood Devon
165 H5 Tackley Oxon
598 C8 Tacleit W Isls
249 F6 Tacolneston Norfk
357 F6 Tadcaster N York
48 B4 Tadden Dorset
313 F5 Taddington Derbys
163 G3 Taddington Gloucs
39 G4 Taddiport Devon
86 B5 Tadhill Somset
91 G2 Tadley Hants
115 E2 Tadlow Cambs
196 C5 Tadmarton Oxon
165 F2 Tadmarton Oxon
32 D2 Tadnoll Dorset

110 C5 Tadwick BaNES
95 E3 Tadworth Surrey
132 B2 Tafarnaubach Blae G
152 B3 Tafarn-y-bwlch Pembks
288 A2 Tafarn-y-Gelyn Denbgs
132 B5 Taff Merthyr Garden Village Myr Td
106 B3 Taff's Well Rhondd
230 D4 Tafolwern Powys
173 E2 Tagley Essex
104 B2 Taibach Neath
268 B4 Tai-bach Powys
262 D5 Tai-morfa Gwynd
577 G7 Tain Highld
589 G3 Tain Highld
288 C5 Tai-nant Wrexhm
596 F7 Tairbeart W Isls
157 F4 Tai'r Bull Powys
129 H2 Tairgwaith Neath
132 B6 Tai'r-heol Caerph
129 G5 Tai'r-ysgol Swans
172 B5 Takeley Essex
172 A5 Takeley Street Essex
157 H3 Talachddu Powys
307 G3 Talacre Flints
266 D4 Talardd Gwynd
27 H3 Talaton Devon
124 D2 Talbenny Pembks
105 G3 Talbot Green Rhondd
48 D6 Talbot Heath Poole
110 B1 Talbot's End S Glos
48 D6 Talbot Village Bmouth
48 D6 Talbot Woods Bmouth
28 A3 Taleford Devon
231 E4 Talerddig Powys
27 H3 Talewater Devon
180 B4 Talgarreg Cerdgn
158 C3 Talgarth Powys
102 B4 Talgarth's Well Swans
544 E3 Talisker Highld
291 G4 Talke Staffs
291 G4 Talke Pits Staffs
401 F3 Talkin Cumb
563 G2 Talladale Highld
449 F5 Talla Linnfoots Border
9 G3 Talland Cnwll
289 F6 Tallarn Green Ches
388 D2 Tallentire Cumb
155 F3 Talley Carmth
243 F3 Tallington Lincs
586 C4 Talmine Highld
153 G4 Talog Carmth
180 B3 Talsarn Cerdgn
265 E2 Talsarnau Gwynd
14 C5 Talskiddy Cnwll
303 G5 Talwrn IoA
288 C4 Talwrn Wrexhm
288 C5 Talwrn Wrexhm
205 F2 Tal-y-bont Cerdgn
305 G6 Tal-y-Bont Conwy
264 D5 Tal-y-bont Gwynd
304 D5 Tal-y-bont Gwynd
303 F3 Tal -y-bontan IoA
158 B5 Talybont-on-Usk Powys
305 G5 Tal-y-cafn Conwy
133 H1 Tal-y-coed Mons
229 G3 Tal-y-llyn Gwynd
158 A4 Talyllyn Powys
283 E5 Talysarn Gwynd
285 E5 Tal-y-waenydd Gwynd
133 E4 Talywain Torfn
230 C4 Tal-y-Wern Gwynd
385 E3 Tame Bridge N York
325 E4 Tamer Lane End Wigan
11 E1 Tamerton Foliot C Plym
327 E3 Tame Water Oldham
485 H4 Tamfourhill Falk
238 C4 Tamworth Staffs
281 E1 Tamworth Green Lincs
357 F3 Tancred N York
80 D2 Tanden Kent
466 A2 Tandlehill Rens
95 H4 Tandridge Surrey
154 B5 Tanerdy Carmth
405 E3 Tanfield Dur
405 E4 Tanfield Lea Dur
356 A3 Tang N York
591 D7 Tangasdal W Isls
358 B4 Tang Hall York
151 G6 Tangiers Pembks
90 A4 Tangley Hants
153 G3 Tanglwst Carmth
53 F3 Tangmere W Susx
606 B2 Tangwick Shet
405 G5 Tan Hills Dur
206 D2 Tan Hinon Powys
324 B3 Tanhouse Lancs
88 A2 Tanis Wilts
601 J3 Tankerness Ork
329 F5 Tankersley Barns
100 B2 Tankerton Kent
285 G2 Tan-lan Conwy
307 G3 Tanlan Flints
284 D6 Tan-lan Gwynd
307 G3 Tanlan Banks Flints
589 J7 Tannach Highld
527 G3 Tannadice Angus
226 A6 Tanner's Green Worcs
226 A6 Tannington Suffk
226 A6 Tannington Place Suffk
467 H2 Tannochside N Lans
201 F2 Tan Office Pembks
199 F3 Tan Office Green Suffk
501 E4 Tanshall Fife
294 C3 Tansley Derbys
213 E2 Tansley Hill Dudley
294 C2 Tansley Knoll Derbys
219 F1 Tansor Nhants
338 D3 Tanterton Lancs
405 E4 Tantobie Dur
385 E2 Tanton N York
299 E2 Tanvats Lincs
212 C5 Tanwood Worcs
213 H5 Tanworth-in-Arden Warwks
265 F1 Tan-y-bwlch Gwynd
286 D2 Tan-y-fron Conwy
288 C4 Tanyfron Wrexhm
285 E5 Tanygrisiau Gwynd
179 F4 Tan-y-groes Cerdgn
263 F3 Tan-y-mynydd Gwynd
307 F3 Tan-yr-allt Denbgs
284 D1 Tanysgafel Gwynd
590 F5 Taobh a' Chaolais W Isls
590 F2 Taobh a Deas Loch Aineort W Isls
597 K4 Taobh a' Ghlinne W Isls
590 F2 Taobh a Tuath Loch Aineort W Isls
596 E7 Taobh Siar W Isls
594 F5 Taobh Tuath W Isls
117 F3 Taplow Bucks
51 F2 Tapnage Hants
314 C2 Tapton Derbys
314 C2 Tapton Hill Sheff
458 C1 Tarbert Ag & B
479 C5 Tarbert Ag & B
480 B6 Tarbert Ag & B
596 F7 Tarbert W Isls
495 G4 Tarbet Ag & B
531 L4 Tarbet Highld
584 C7 Tarbet Highld
309 G2 Tarbock Green Knows
445 F4 Tarbolton S Ayrs

469 G3 Tarbrax S Lans
213 E6 Tardebigge Worcs
338 D4 Tardy Gate Lancs
539 F4 Tarfside Angus
555 E4 Tarland Abers
338 B5 Tarleton Lancs
338 B5 Tarleton Moss Lancs
577 G7 Tarlogie Highld
324 A2 Tarlscough Lancs
137 E5 Tarlton Gloucs
342 C2 Tarn Brad
352 B3 Tarnbrook Lancs
84 C4 Tarnock Somset
399 E5 Tarns Cumb
365 F1 Tarnside Cumb
290 A2 Tarporley Ches
122 B2 Tarpots Essex
64 B5 Tarr Somset
400 D3 Tarraby Cumb
47 H4 Tarrant Crawford Dorset
48 A2 Tarrant Gunville Dorset
48 A2 Tarrant Hinton Dorset
47 H4 Tarrant Keyneston Dorset
48 A3 Tarrant Launceston Dorset
48 B3 Tarrant Monkton Dorset
48 A3 Tarrant Rawston Dorset
48 A3 Tarrant Rushton Dorset
577 J7 Tarrel Highld
56 C4 Tarring Neville E Susx
161 E1 Tarrington Herefs
161 E2 Tarrington Common Herefs
512 D5 Tarsappie P & K
545 K8 Tarskavaig Highld
270 A2 Tarts Hill Shrops
560 C3 Tarves Abers
565 G5 Tarvie Highld
524 F3 Tarvie P & K
289 G1 Tarvin Ches
309 G6 Tarvin Sands Ches
249 G5 Tasburgh Norfk
235 F6 Tasley Shrops
165 F5 Taston Oxon
213 E2 Tat Bank Sandw
274 C5 Tatenhill Staffs
274 B5 Tatenhill Common Staffs
193 H5 Tathall End M Keyn
366 C6 Tatham Lancs
320 B3 Tathwell Lincs
117 H2 Tatling End Bucks
96 B3 Tatsfield Surrey
289 G3 Tattenhall Ches
168 A3 Tattenhoe M Keyn
253 H2 Tatterford Norfk
253 G2 Tattersett Norfk
299 G3 Tattershall Lincs
299 G3 Tattershall Bridge Lincs
299 G3 Tattershall Thorpe Lincs
175 F2 Tattingstone Suffk
175 F2 Tattingstone White Horse Suffk
190 B2 Tattle Bank Warwks
311 E3 Tatton Dale Ches
29 F1 Tatworth Somset
44 A3 Taunton Somset
326 D4 Taunton Tamesd
255 G5 Taverham Norfk
172 B6 Taverners Green Essex
126 D2 Tavernspite Pembks
17 G4 Tavistock Devon
25 G3 Taw Green Devon
40 B2 Tawstock Devon
312 D4 Taxal Derbys
462 A5 Tayinloan Ag & B
523 L6 Taymouth Castle P & K
479 J5 Taynish Ag & B
161 G5 Taynton Gloucs
138 C2 Taynton Oxon
507 H3 Taynuilt Ag & B
514 D4 Tayport Fife
479 J4 Tayvallich Ag & B
479 J4 Tayvullin Ag & B
169 G5 Tea Green Herts
319 E1 Tealby Lincs
514 C2 Tealing Angus
405 F2 Teams Gatesd
405 F2 Team Valley Gatesd
273 E1 Teanford Staffs
546 B8 Teangue Highld
592 D5 Teanna Mhachair W Isls
78 C2 Teasley Mead E Susx
379 H4 Tebay Cumb
168 D4 Tebworth Beds
26 C4 Tedburn St Mary Devon
163 E3 Teddington Gloucs
118 D5 Teddington Gt Lon
163 E3 Teddington Hands Gloucs
269 G4 Tedsmore Shrops
187 F3 Tedstone Delamere Herefs
187 F3 Tedstone Wafer Herefs
396 C6 Teesside Park S on T
396 D6 Teesville R & C
217 E5 Teeton Nhants
69 G3 Teffont Evias Wilts
69 G3 Teffont Magna Wilts
153 E3 Tegryn Pembks
242 B1 Teigh Rutlnd
20 B3 Teigngrace Devon
20 C3 Teignmouth Devon
20 A1 Teign Village Devon
235 G3 Telford Wrekin
58 C4 Telham E Susx
87 E3 Tellisford Somset
56 C4 Telscombe E Susx
56 B4 Telscombe Cliffs E Susx
424 B2 Templand D & G
484 A6 Temple C Glas
15 G4 Temple Cnwll
471 F3 Temple Mdloth
116 D3 Temple W & M
87 E6 Temple Wilts
214 C4 Temple Balsall Solhll
155 E6 Temple Bar Carmth
180 D4 Temple Bar Cerdgn
53 F3 Temple Bar W Susx
314 D1 Templeborough Sheff
85 H3 Temple Cloud BaNES
68 B5 Templecombe Somset
140 B3 Temple Cowley Oxon
199 G6 Temple End Essex
198 D4 Temple End Suffk
83 E2 Temple Ewell Kent
189 H3 Temple Grafton Warwks
163 G4 Temple Guiting Gloucs
514 D2 Templehall Angus
501 E6 Templehall Fife
513 H4 Templehall P & K
191 F4 Temple Herdewyke Warwks
120 D4 Temple Hill Kent
345 E5 Temple Hirst N York
29 H2 Templeman's Ash Dorset
119 H2 Temple Mills Gt Lon
315 E6 Temple Normanton Derbys
391 G4 Temple Sowerby Cumb
528 D5 Templeton Angus
42 A5 Templeton Devon
126 C2 Templeton Pembks
90 B1 Templeton W Berk
42 A5 Templeton Bridge Devon
404 D4 Templetown Dur
195 H4 Tempsford Beds
213 G3 Ten Acres Birm
524 F3 Tenandry P & K

210 D6 Tenbury Wells Worcs
126 C4 Tenby Pembks
9 G3 Tencreek Cnwll
175 F5 Tendring Essex
175 F4 Tendring Green Essex
175 F4 Tendring Heath Essex
246 B5 Ten Mile Bank Norfk
600 D1 Tenston Ork
80 C3 Tenterden Kent
306 C4 Terfyn Conwy
284 C2 Terfyn Gwynd
64 C5 Terhill Somset
147 F1 Terling Essex
271 E3 Ternhill Shrops
8 A3 Terras Cnwll
423 F4 Terregles D & G
56 D1 Terrible Down E Susx
142 A3 Terrick Bucks
142 B6 Terriers Bucks
372 C5 Terrington N York
252 B4 Terrington St Clement Norfk
252 A5 Terrington St John Norfk
425 H2 Terrona D & G
213 H5 Terry's Green Warwks
74 C5 Terwick Common W Susx
97 G4 Teston Kent
50 C2 Testwood Hants
23 G3 Tetcott Devon
320 B5 Tetford Lincs
331 G2 Tetley N Linc
334 D4 Tetney Lincs
334 D4 Tetney Lock Lincs
141 E4 Tetsworth Oxon
236 C4 Tettenhall Wolves
236 C5 Tettenhall Wood Wolves
196 B4 Tetworth Cambs
561 G2 Teuchan Abers
570 D6 Teuchar Abers
295 F2 Teversal Notts
197 G3 Teversham Cambs
439 E3 Teviothead Border
144 C2 Tewin Herts
144 C1 Tewin Wood Herts
365 H5 Tewitfield Lancs
162 C3 Tewkesbury Gloucs
99 F2 Teynham Kent
99 F2 Teynham Street Kent
342 C2 Thackley Brad
342 C2 Thackley End Brad
388 D5 Thackthwaite Cumb
54 D1 Thakeham W Susx
141 F3 Thame Oxon
94 D1 Thames Ditton Surrey
122 A3 Thames Haven Thurr
137 E5 Thames Head Oxon
120 C3 Thamesmead Gt Lon
100 B4 Thanington Kent
448 C2 Thankerton S Lans
249 G6 Tharston Norfk
90 D1 Thatcham W Berk
324 B6 Thatto Heath St Hel
172 C3 Thaxted Essex
543 G6 The Aird Highld
370 C2 Theakston N York
346 C6 Thealby N Linc
238 B4 The Alders Staffs
85 E5 Theale Somset
115 G5 Theale W Berk
248 A5 The Arms Norfk
347 G5 Thearne E R Yk
185 E6 The Bage Herefs
511 E6 The Balloch P & K
291 G3 The Bank Ches
312 C2 The Banks Stockp
112 B4 The Banks Wilts
290 D4 The Barony Ches
602 B6 The Barony Ork
112 C4 The Barton Wilts
110 B5 The Batch S Glos
137 F4 The Beeches Gloucs
324 C3 The Bell Wigan
273 F3 The Bents Staffs
203 E1 Theberton Suffk
273 F4 The Blythe Staffs
233 G5 The Bog Shrops
119 G4 The Borough Gt Lon
92 D6 The Bourne Surrey
189 E3 The Bourne Worcs
545 J3 The Braes Highld
291 G5 The Brampton Staffs
240 B2 The Brand Leics
236 C6 The Bratch Staffs
600 E4 The Breck Ork
99 G2 The Brents Kent
47 E2 The Bridge Dorset
186 B2 The Broad Herefs
225 E4 The Brook Suffk
314 D4 The Brushes Derbys
133 F3 The Bryn Mons
322 f5 The Bungalow IoM
212 B6 The Burf Worcs
540 B5 The Burn Abers
73 H2 The Butts Hants
136 D3 The Camp Gloucs
143 H3 The Camp Herts
190 D1 The Cape Warwks
96 C4 The Chart Kent
270 B1 The Chequer Wrexhm
237 F5 The Chuckery Wsall
141 G5 The City Bucks
160 C4 The Cleaver Herefs
53 F4 The Close W Susx
165 E2 The Colony Oxon
85 H2 The Common BaNES
167 G3 The Common Bucks
47 E2 The Common Dorset
271 F4 The Common Shrops
102 D3 The Common Swans
71 E3 The Common Wilts
87 F2 The Common Wilts
112 B3 The Common Wilts
76 C3 The Common W Susx
79 F1 The Corner Kent
210 A2 The Corner Shrops
134 C5 The Cot Mons
575 K5 The Craigs Highld
375 G5 The Crofts E R Yk
322 e3 The Cronk IoM
239 E4 The Cross Hands Leics
134 B6 The Cwm Mons
73 G2 Thedden Grange Hants
216 D2 Theddingworth Leics
321 E2 Theddlethorpe All Saints Lincs
321 E2 Theddlethorpe St Helen Lincs
237 F5 The Delves Wsall
465 G4 The Den N Ayrs
404 D4 The Dene Dur
90 B4 The Dene Hants
79 F2 The Down Kent
211 F1 The Down Shrops
75 E2 The Downs Surrey
288 D4 The Dunks Wrexhm
428 B2 The Eals Nthumb
135 E3 The Eaves Gloucs
343 F4 The Fall Leeds
134 C3 The Fence Gloucs
135 G1 The Flat Gloucs

427 E4 The Flatt Cumb
275 G2 The Flourish Derbys
143 H2 The Folly Herts
110 D5 The Folly S Glos
161 E4 The Fording Herefs
185 F3 The Forge Herefs
81 F2 The Forstal Kent
275 E6 The Forties Derbys
271 F3 The Four Alls Shrops
112 C2 The Fox Wilts
211 E3 The Foxholes Shrops
71 F3 The Frenches Hants
144 B2 The Frythe Herts
111 E4 The Gibb Wilts
449 H2 The Glack Border
582 C2 The Glutt Highld
210 D3 The Gore Shrops
255 F3 The Grange Norfk
385 F5 The Grange N York
328 C4 The Green Barns
196 C6 The Green Beds
365 G4 The Green Cumb
365 G4 The Green Cumb
173 F6 The Green Essex
71 F4 The Green Hants
193 G6 The Green Nhants
194 B6 The Green Nhants
249 E4 The Green Norfk
261 E4 The Green Norfk
261 E5 The Green Norfk
165 H4 The Green Oxon
209 F3 The Green Shrops
190 B3 The Green Warwks
69 E3 The Green Wilts
404 C4 The Grove Dur
143 F5 The Grove Herts
210 A3 The Grove Shrops
233 G3 The Grove Shrops
162 C1 The Grove Worcs
294 C5 The Gutter Derbys
213 E4 The Gutter Worcs
110 B1 The Hacket S Glos
327 F6 The Hague Tamesd
609 J5 The Hall Shet
347 G5 The Hallands N Linc
87 F4 The Ham Wilts
272 C5 The Handfords Staffs
98 C5 The Harbour Kent
76 A3 The Haven W Susx
396 D3 The Headland Hartpl
254 B2 The Heath Norfk
255 G3 The Heath Norfk
273 G3 The Heath Staffs
175 F2 The Heath Suffk
235 G3 The Hem Shrops
134 B2 The Hendre Mons
221 F5 The Hermitage Cambs
95 E4 The Hermitage Surrey
58 B5 The Highlands E Susx
362 D5 The Hill Cumb
235 G6 The Hobbins Shrops
292 B3 The Hollands Staffs
297 F4 The Hollies Staffs
116 C4 The Holt Wokham
162 B1 The Hook Worcs
210 D4 The Hope Shrops
142 B4 The Lee Bucks
99 G4 The Lees Kent
162 C4 The Leigh Gloucs
238 B4 The Leys Staffs
322 f2 The Lhen IoM
250 C5 The Ling Norfk
331 E3 The Lings Donc
248 D3 The Lings Norfk
111 F6 The Linleys Wilts
224 D4 Thelnetham Suffk
237 E5 The Lunt Wolves
225 G3 Thelveton Norfk
310 C2 Thelwall Warrtn
53 E4 The Manor W Susx
291 G2 The Marsh Ches
186 B3 The Marsh Powys
233 F5 The Marsh Shrops
271 F4 The Marsh Shrops
272 B4 The Marsh Staffs
225 E4 The Marsh Suffk
225 F4 The Marsh Suffk
254 D3 Themelthorpe Norfk
405 F4 The Middles Dur
74 B4 The Mint Hants
288 D1 The Moor Flints
79 H4 The Moor Kent
160 C3 The Moors Herefs
30 B3 The Mount Dorset
116 B5 The Mount Readg
103 H4 The Mumbles Swans
467 F4 The Murray S Lans
162 C3 The Mythe Gloucs
288 C4 The Nant Wrexhm
134 C3 The Narth Mons
556 C5 The Neuk Abers
166 B1 Thenford Nhants
170 B5 The Node Herts
270 D3 The Nook Shrops
271 F5 The Nook Shrops
112 B6 Theobald's Green Wilts
86 C2 The Oval BaNES
162 D5 The Park Gloucs
330 D3 The Parks Donc
70 B4 The Pitts Wilts
140 C4 The Platt Oxon
135 E1 The Pludds Gloucs
20 D1 The Point Devon
550 F8 The Polchar Highld
570 B4 The Pole of Itlaw Abers
177 E3 The Port of Felixstowe Suffk
161 G3 The Pound Gloucs
135 G5 The Quarry Gloucs
234 B2 The Quarry Shrops
80 C3 The Quarter Kent
98 D6 The Quarter Kent
162 B3 The Rampings Worcs
162 D5 The Reddings Gloucs
170 D2 The Rhos Pembks
125 H2 The Rhos Pembks
160 B3 The Rhydd Herefs
186 B2 The Riddle Herefs
111 F6 The Ridge Wilts
92 D2 The Ridges Wokham
403 G1 The Riding Nthumb
450 C1 The Riggs Border
451 F3 The Rink Border
117 F6 The Rise W & M

235 F3 The Rock Wrekin
97 H3 The Rocks Kent
110 C3 The Rocks S Glos
307 E5 The Roe Denbgs
143 G6 The Rookery Herts
291 H3 The Rookery Staffs
365 G4 The Row Lancs
272 B2 The Rowe Staffs
238 B2 The Sale Staffs
95 E5 The Sands Surrey
161 G4 The Scarr Gloucs
111 E5 The Shoe Wilts
272 D3 The Shruggs Staffs
394 C4 The Slack Dur
115 E5 The Slade W Berk
246 A2 The Smeeth Norfk
235 F5 The Smithies Shrops
87 G2 The Spa Wilts
214 D5 The Spring Warwks
133 E5 The Square Torfn
80 D4 The Stocks Kent
87 G2 The Stocks Wilts
212 D1 The Straits Dudley
74 B2 The Straits Hants
87 G3 The Strand Wilts
143 E5 The Swillett Herts
271 F3 The Sydnall Shrops
243 G2 Thetford Lincs
224 A3 Thetford Norfk
170 D2 The Thrift Herts
92 D1 The Throat Wokham
272 D6 The Toft Staffs
3 G2 The Towans Cnwll
3 C1 The Town IoS
162 C2 The Twittocks Gloucs
162 D6 The Tynings Gloucs
213 F3 The Vale Birm
290 D3 The Valley Ches
99 F4 The Valley Kent
126 C3 The Valley Pembks
186 C5 The Vauld Herefs
212 C2 The Village Dudley
107 F1 The Village Newpt
117 G5 The Village W & M
212 B5 The Walshes Worcs
99 F6 The Warren Kent
89 F1 The Warren Wilts
233 G4 The Waterwheel Shrops
160 C3 The Weaven Herefs
94 D2 The Wells Surrey
288 C4 The Wern Wrexhm
334 B3 The Willows NE Lin
269 F5 The Wood Shrops
270 B4 The Wood Shrops
240 D5 The Woodlands Leics
175 E1 The Woodlands Suffk
175 F2 The Woodlands Suffk
237 E5 The Woods Sandw
58 B5 The Wrangle BaNES
95 F1 The Wrythe Gt Lon
235 G3 The Wyke Shrops
186 C5 The Wymm Herefs
172 B6 Theydon Bois Essex
145 G5 Theydon Mount Essex
210 D3 The Yeld Shrops
86 B3 Thicket Mead BaNES
111 E5 Thickwood Wilts
319 G6 Thimbleby Lincs
384 D5 Thimbleby N York
238 A6 Thimble End Birm
395 F3 Thinford Dur
111 F5 Thingley Wilts
308 C3 Thingwall Wirral
464 D5 Thirdpart N Ayrs
371 F3 Thirlby N York
472 D5 Thirlestane Border
369 H2 Thirn N York
371 E3 Thirsk N York
348 C3 Thirtleby E R Yk
338 B2 Thistleton Lancs
242 C1 Thistleton Rutlnd
172 D6 Thistley Green Essex
222 D4 Thistley Green Suffk
359 F2 Thixendale N York
429 E4 Thockrington Nthumb
245 F3 Tholomas Drove Cambs
357 F1 Tholthorpe N York
126 C3 Thomas Chapel Pembks
390 C1 Thomas Close Cumb
558 D2 Thomastown Abers
105 F2 Thomastown Rhondd
248 B5 Thompson Norfk
568 C4 Thomshill Moray
121 G5 Thong Kent
328 B3 Thongsbridge Kirk
368 D2 Thoralby N York
316 B5 Thoresby Notts
321 E4 Thoresthorpe Lincs
333 H5 Thoresway Lincs
334 B5 Thorganby Lincs
345 H2 Thorganby N York
388 B5 Thorgill N York
227 E5 Thorington Suffk
174 D2 Thorington Street Suffk
354 C4 Thorlby N York
171 G6 Thorley Herts
36 B3 Thorley IoW
171 G5 Thorley Houses Herts
36 B3 Thorley Street IoW
371 F5 Thormanby N York
25 G3 Thorn Devon
185 E2 Thorn Powys
384 D1 Thornaby-on-Tees S on T
261 E4 Thornage Norfk
167 F3 Thornborough Bucks
370 B4 Thornborough N York
342 C3 Thornbury Brad
39 F6 Thornbury Devon
187 E3 Thornbury Herefs
109 H2 Thornbury S Glos
400 A4 Thornby Cumb
217 E4 Thornby Nhants
328 C2 Thorncliff Kirk
292 D3 Thorncliffe Staffs
29 G2 Thorncombe Dorset
36 C4 Thorncross IoW
225 F6 Thorndon Suffk
24 D4 Thorndon Cross Devon
23 E2 Thorne Cnwll
331 E2 Thorne Donc
67 E6 Thorne Coffin Somset
39 F4 Thornehillhead Devon
24 A5 Thorne Moor Devon
111 H4 Thornend Wilts
343 G1 Thorner Leeds
237 G4 Thornes Staffs
43 E3 Thorne St Margaret Somset
118 A4 Thorney Bucks
244 C4 Thorney C Pete
317 G5 Thorney Notts
66 C5 Thorney Somset
406 B4 Thorney Close Sundld
201 E2 Thorney Green Suffk
49 F5 Thorney Hill Hants
244 D4 Thorney Toll Cambs
276 C1 Thorneywood Notts
44 B3 Thornfalcon Somset
46 B2 Thornford Dorset
402 D1 Thorngrafton Nthumb
65 G5 Thorngrove Somset
348 D4 Thorngumbald E R Yk
259 E3 Thornham Norfk

326 C3 Thornham Fold Rochdl
225 E5 Thornham Magna Suffk
225 F5 Thornham Parva Suffk
243 F4 Thornhaugh C Pete
106 B3 Thornhill Caerph
51 E2 Thornhill C Sotn
376 C3 Thornhill D & G
436 A5 Thornhill D & G
313 G3 Thornhill Derbys
343 E6 Thornhill Kirk
329 G6 Thornhill Rothm
497 G5 Thornhill Stirlg
133 E5 Thornhill Torfn
112 C4 Thornhill Wilts
342 D6 Thornhill Edge Kirk
51 E2 Thornhill Park C Sotn
361 E2 Thornholme E R Yk
47 G4 Thornicombe Dorset
451 E2 Thornielee Border
394 C2 Thornley Dur
395 H2 Thornley Dur
466 D3 Thornliebank E Rens
466 C2 Thornly Park Rens
560 C3 Thornroan Abers
381 F4 Thorns N York
199 E3 Thorns N York
314 A1 Thornseat Sheff
312 D2 Thornsett Derbys
311 F3 Thorns Green Ches
389 F4 Thornthwaite Cumb
355 G3 Thornthwaite N York
527 E5 Thornton Angus
342 A3 Thornton Brad
167 F2 Thornton Bucks
359 E5 Thornton E R Yk
501 E5 Thornton Fife
337 F1 Thornton Lancs
239 H3 Thornton Leics
319 G6 Thornton Lincs
384 D2 Thornton Middsb
474 D5 Thornton Nthumb
125 E3 Thornton Pembks
323 F4 Thornton Sefton
347 G6 Thornton Curtis N Linc
467 E3 Thorntonhall S Lans
119 G6 Thornton Heath Gt Lon
308 D3 Thornton Hough Wirral
354 A5 Thornton-in-Craven N York
366 D5 Thornton in Lonsdale N York
370 D1 Thornton-le-Beans N York
358 C1 Thornton-le-Clay N York
373 F4 Thornton-le-Dale N York
333 E5 Thornton le Moor Lincs
370 D2 Thornton-le-Moor N York
309 F5 Thornton-le-Moors Ches
371 G2 Thornton-le-Street N York
491 E5 Thorntonloch E Loth
368 C2 Thornton Rust N York
369 G2 Thornton Steward N York
370 A2 Thornton Watlass N York
145 G3 Thornwood Common Essex
540 B5 Thornyhill Abers
277 G1 Thoroton Notts
326 D3 Thorp Oldham
357 E5 Thorp Arch Leeds
390 D4 Thorpe Cumb
293 F4 Thorpe Derbys
360 B5 Thorpe E R Yk
321 E3 Thorpe Lincs
251 E5 Thorpe Norfk
297 E5 Thorpe Notts
354 D2 Thorpe N York
117 H6 Thorpe Surrey
225 G4 Thorpe Abbotts Norfk
276 B5 Thorpe Acre Leics
277 G5 Thorpe Arnold Leics
329 H1 Thorpe Audlin Wakefd
373 G5 Thorpe Bassett N York
123 E2 Thorpe Bay Sthend
242 B5 Thorpe by Water Rutlnd
177 E2 Thorpe Common Suffk
238 D3 Thorpe Constantine Staffs
301 E2 Thorpe Culvert Lincs
342 C2 Thorpe Edge Brad
250 B2 Thorpe End Norfk
301 E2 Thorpe Fendykes Lincs
176 C5 Thorpe Green Essex
339 E5 Thorpe Green Lancs
200 B4 Thorpe Green Suffk
117 H6 Thorpe Green Surrey
329 F5 Thorpe Hesley Rothm
330 C2 Thorpe in Balne Donc
217 F1 Thorpe Langton Leics
396 A4 Thorpe Larches Dur
279 G1 Thorpe Latimer Lincs
117 H5 Thorpe Lea Surrey
317 H3 Thorpe le Fallows Lincs
176 C5 Thorpe-le-Soken Essex
361 F6 Thorpe le Street E R Yk
319 F1 Thorpe le Vale Lincs
218 A4 Thorpe Malsor Nhants
192 B5 Thorpe Mandeville Nhants
256 A2 Thorpe Market Norfk
255 G5 Thorpe Marriott Norfk
200 B4 Thorpe Morieux Suffk
203 F3 Thorpeness Suffk
343 F4 Thorpe on The Hill Leeds
297 G1 Thorpe on the Hill Lincs
248 C3 Thorpe Row Norfk
250 B3 Thorpe St Andrew Norfk
301 E2 Thorpe St Peter Lincs
315 G3 Thorpe Salvin Rothm
241 F2 Thorpe Satchville Leics
224 D4 Thorpe Street Suffk
396 A5 Thorpe Thewles S on T
299 E3 Thorpe Tilney Lincs
217 G3 Thorpe Underwood Nhants

357 E3 Thorpe Underwood N York
219 E3 Thorpe Waterville Nhants
344 D3 Thorpe Willoughby N York
344 D3 Thorpe Wood N York
246 C3 Thorpland Norfk
175 E5 Thorrington Essex
27 E2 Thorverton Devon
87 E5 Thoulstone Wilts
225 F4 Thrandeston Suffk
218 A4 Thrapston Nhants
468 B1 Thrashbush N Lans
389 E2 Threapland Cumb
354 C2 Threapland N York
289 F5 Threapwood Ches
292 D6 Threapwood Staffs
432 D3 Threave S Ayrs
91 G2 Three Ashes Hants
160 C5 Three Ashes Herefs
209 G4 Three Ashes Shrops
86 A5 Three Ashes Somset
320 D2 Three Bridges Lincs
77 E2 Three Bridges W Susx
6 D4 Three Burrows Cnwll
80 B2 Three Chimneys Kent
251 E6 Three Cocked Hat Norfk
158 C2 Three Cocks Powys
423 E3 Three Crofts D & G
103 E3 Three Crosses Swans
79 E5 Three Cups Corner E Susx
270 B1 Three Fingers Wrexhm
46 B3 Three Gates Dorset
256 C6 Threehammer Common Norfk
23 E5 Three Hammers Cnwll

245 H4 Three Holes Norfk
15 E4 Three Holes Cross Cnwll
279 F2 Threekingham Lincs
79 F3 Three Leg Cross E Susx
48 D3 Three Legged Cross Dorset
293 E5 Threelows Staffs
213 H4 Three Maypoles Solhll
116 A6 Three Mile Cross Wokham
7 E5 Threemilestone Cnwll
486 D4 Threemiletown W Loth
58 D4 Three Oaks E Susx
472 C6 Threepwood Border
287 F2 Three Sisters Denbgs
15 E5 Threewaters Cnwll
389 H4 Threlkeld Cumb
145 G3 Threshers Bush Essex
354 C2 Threshfield N York
251 F2 Thrigby Norfk
393 F5 Thringarth Dur
275 G6 Thringstone Leics
383 H6 Thrintoft N York
197 F5 Thriplow Cambs
315 G2 Throapham Rothm
244 D3 Throckenholt Lincs
170 D3 Throcking Herts
405 E1 Throckley N u Ty
189 E5 Throckmorton Worcs
49 E5 Throop Bmouth
47 F6 Throop Dorset
430 B2 Throphill Nthumb
442 C4 Thropton Nthumb
485 G1 Throsk Stirlg
136 D3 Througham Gloucs
423 E3 Throughgate D & G
25 G4 Throwleigh Devon
99 F3 Throwley Kent
99 F4 Throwley Forstal Kent
374 C2 Throxenby N York
276 B3 Thrumpton Notts
316 D3 Thrumpton Notts
589 J7 Thrumster Highld
442 D2 Thrunton Nthumb
85 H5 Thrupe Somset
136 C4 Thrupp Gloucs
138 D5 Thrupp Oxon
140 A1 Thrupp Oxon
355 F3 Thruscross N York
24 B5 Thrushelton Devon
352 C2 Thrushgill Lancs
241 E1 Thrussington Leics
89 G5 Thruxton Hants
160 A3 Thruxton Herefs
329 H5 Thrybergh Rothm
275 G3 Thulston Derbys
329 F6 Thundercliffe Grange Sheff
463 E5 Thundergay N Ayrs
57 E2 Thunder's Hill E Susx
122 B2 Thundersley Essex
144 D1 Thundridge Herts
240 C2 Thurcaston Leics
315 F2 Thurcroft Rothm
38 C5 Thurdon Cnwll
261 G5 Thurgarton Norfk
296 C5 Thurgarton Notts
328 D4 Thurgoland Barns
240 B5 Thurlaston Leics
215 H5 Thurlaston Warwks
44 B3 Thurlbear Somset
243 F1 Thurlby Lincs
297 G2 Thurlby Lincs
321 E4 Thurlby Lincs
195 E3 Thurleigh Beds
12 B4 Thurlestone Devon
65 E5 Thurloxton Somset
328 C4 Thurlstone Barns
251 E5 Thurlton Norfk
251 E5 Thurlton Links Norfk
291 F3 Thurlwood Ches
240 D3 Thurmaston Leics
240 D4 Thurnby Leics
251 E1 Thurne Norfk
98 C3 Thurnham Kent
219 F3 Thurning Nhants
255 E2 Thurning Norfk
329 G3 Thurnscoe Barns
329 H3 Thurnscoe East Barns
400 B4 Thursby Cumb
260 C5 Thursford Norfk
260 C5 Thursford Green Norfk
74 D2 Thursley Surrey
588 D3 Thurso Highld
588 E3 Thurso East Highld
308 B3 Thurstaston Wirral
200 B1 Thurston Suffk
327 E3 Thurston Clough Oldham
199 F4 Thurston End Suffk
400 B3 Thurstonfield Cumb
328 B2 Thurstonland Kirk
250 C4 Thurton Norfk
274 A2 Thurvaston Derbys
274 C2 Thurvaston Derbys
248 D3 Thuxton Norfk
381 F5 Thwaite N York
225 F6 Thwaite Suffk
364 B5 Thwaite Flat Cumb
364 D1 Thwaite Head Cumb
342 A1 Thwaites Brad
250 C6 Thwaite St Mary Norfk
374 D5 Thwing E R Yk
512 C5 Tibbermore P & K
161 H5 Tibberton Gloucs
188 C3 Tibberton Worcs
271 F5 Tibberton Wrekin
225 F2 Tibenham Norfk
295 E2 Tibshelf Derbys
295 F2 Tibshelf Wharf Notts
360 B3 Tibthorpe E R Yk
79 F3 Ticehurst E Susx
73 E3 Tichborne Hants
242 D3 Tickencote Rutlnd
108 D5 Tickenham N Som
194 B6 Tickford End M Keyn
330 C6 Tickhill Donc
117 E5 Tickleback Row Br For
210 B1 Ticklerton Shrops
136 B5 Tickmorend Gloucs
275 F5 Ticknall Derbys
347 E1 Tickton E R Yk
213 H4 Tidbury Green Solhll
89 G3 Tidcombe Wilts
140 D4 Tiddington Oxon
190 C3 Tiddington Warwks
79 E4 Tidebrook E Susx
10 B2 Tideford Cnwll
10 B1 Tideford Cross Cnwll
134 D5 Tidenham Gloucs
134 C5 Tidenham Chase Gloucs
313 G4 Tideswell Derbys
115 G5 Tidmarsh W Berk
190 D2 Tidmington Warwks
160 D2 Tidnor Herefs
70 B6 Tidpit Hants
89 F5 Tidworth Wilts
125 F2 Tiers Cross Pembks
193 H2 Tiffield Nhants
560 A1 Tifty Abers
527 B2 Tigerton Angus
593 B3 Tigh a' Ghearraidh W Isls
593 C3 Tigh a' Ghearraidh W Isls
593 C3 Tigharry W Isls
511 B1 Tigh-na-Blair P & K
481 B2 Tighnabruaich Ag & B
573 G6 Tighnafiline Highld

495 F4 Tighness Ag & B
19 G5 Tigley Devon
219 F6 Tilbrook Cambs
121 F4 Tilbury Thurr
173 E1 Tilbury Green Essex
173 F1 Tilbury Juxta Clare Essex
214 B2 Tile Cross Birm
145 H3 Tilegate Green Essex
214 D4 Tile Hill Covtry
214 B4 Tilehouse Green Solhll
146 D5 Tilehurst Readg
115 H5 Tilehurst Readg
171 H5 Tilekiln Green Essex
46 C3 Tiley Dorset
93 E6 Tilford Surrey
93 E6 Tilford Common Surrey
93 E6 Tilford Reeds Surrey
77 E2 Tilgate W Susx
77 E3 Tilgate Forest Row W Susx
173 G5 Tiikey Essex
10 B1 Tilland Cnwll
558 B2 Tillathrowie Abers
161 F3 Tillers' Green Gloucs
270 C4 Tilley Shrops
270 C4 Tilley Green Shrops
499 E5 Tillicoultry Clacks
468 C5 Tillietudlem S Lans
148 C4 Tillingham Essex
186 B5 Tillington Herefs
272 D5 Tillington Staffs
75 F5 Tillington W Susx
186 B5 Tillington Common Herefs
24 A4 Tillislow Devon
29 F2 Tilworth Devon
528 B1 Tillyarblet Angus
560 D5 Tillycorthie Abers
89 H5 Tilly Down Hants
555 H5 Tillydrine Abers
557 G3 Tillydrone C Aber
556 A2 Tillyfourie Abers
555 H6 Tillygarmond Abers
560 C5 Tillygreig Abers
560 B5 Tillykerrie Abers
527 E4 Tillyloss Angus
101 F5 Tilmanstone Kent
252 B4 Tilney All Saints Norfk
252 B5 Tilney cum Islington Norfk
246 A2 Tilney Fen End Norfk
252 B4 Tilney High End Norfk
252 A5 Tilney St Lawrence Norfk
135 G5 Tilsdown Gloucs
88 B5 Tilshead Wilts
78 D5 Tilsmore E Susx
211 E5 Tilsop Shrops
270 C2 Tilstock Shrops
289 G4 Tilston Ches
290 B3 Tilstone Bank Ches
290 B2 Tilstone Fearnall Ches
168 D5 Tilsworth Beds
241 F3 Tilton on the Hill Leics
330 C3 Tilts Donc
136 B5 Tiltups End Gloucs
172 B4 Tilty Essex
96 D2 Timberden Bottom Kent
212 D5 Timberhonger Worcs
299 E3 Timberland Lincs
292 A2 Timbersbrook Ches
63 F3 Timberscombe Somset
355 G4 Timble N York
98 D3 Timbold Hill Kent
17 E3 Timbrelham Cnwll
311 F2 Timperley Traffd
86 B3 Timsbury BaNES
71 G5 Timsbury Hants
598 A8 Timsgarry W Isls
598 A8 Timsgearraidh W Isls
223 H6 Timworth Suffk
223 H6 Timworth Green Suffk
32 D1 Tincleton Dorset
401 H3 Tindale Cumb
394 D4 Tindale Crescent Dur
172 C3 Tindon End Essex
166 D3 Tingewick Bucks
343 E4 Tingley Leeds
169 E3 Tingrith Beds
602 E7 Tingwall Ork
24 A5 Tinhay Devon
167 G4 Tinkers End Bucks
314 D1 Tinsley Sheff
77 E2 Tinsley Green W Susx
22 A5 Tintagel Cnwll
134 C4 Tintern Mons
134 C4 Tintern Parva Mons
67 E6 Tintinhull Somset
327 F5 Tintwistle Derbys
423 H3 Tinwald D & G
243 E3 Tinwell Rutlnd
52 A4 Tipner C Port
62 B2 Tippacott Devon
214 D2 Tipper's Hill Warwks
561 E4 Tipperty Abers
23 G5 Tipple Cross Devon
245 H5 Tipps End Cambs
146 B4 Tip's Cross Essex
49 H5 Tiptoe Hants
213 E1 Tipton Sandw
213 E1 Tipton Green Sandw
28 A4 Tipton St John Devon
148 A1 Tiptree Essex
148 A2 Tiptree Heath Essex
156 D1 Tirabad Powys
129 G5 Tircanol Swans
103 F2 Tirdeunaw Swans
524 C2 Tirinie P & K
162 B4 Tirley Gloucs
162 B4 Tirley Knowle Gloucs
132 B4 Tirphil Caerph
391 E4 Tirril Cumb
580 E2 Tirryside Highld
606 E2 Tirvister Shet
132 B5 Tir-y-berth Caerph
129 F2 Tir-y-dail Carmth
69 F4 Tisbury Wilts
75 H3 Tisman's Common W Susx
293 G4 Tissington Derbys
38 B2 Titchberry Devon
51 F3 Titchfield Hants
51 F3 Titchfield Common Hants
51 F3 Titchfield Park Hants
219 E4 Titchmarsh Nhants
259 F3 Titchwell Norfk
90 B1 Titcomb W Berk
277 F2 Tithby Notts
273 G1 Tithebarn Staffs
324 D5 Tithe Barn Hillock St Hel
185 F2 Titley Herefs
443 E1 Titlington Nthumb
96 B4 Titsey Surrey
23 E2 Titson Cnwll
272 C2 Tittensor Staffs
210 C3 Titterhill Shrops
117 E3 Tittle Row W & M
254 A3 Tittleshall Norfk
212 B6 Titton Worcs
74 D4 Titty Hill W Susx
290 B2 Tiverton Ches
42 C5 Tiverton Devon
225 G2 Tivetshall St Margaret Norfk
225 G2 Tivetshall St Mary Norfk
213 E1 Tividale Sandw
63 E2 Tivington Somset
63 E3 Tivington Knowle Somset

388 A5 Tivoli Cumb
328 D3 Tivy Dale Barns
273 E5 Tixall Staffs
242 D4 Tixover Rutlnd
601 J3 Toab Ork
605 G8 Toab Shet
294 C4 Toadmoor Derbys
227 G2 Toad Row Suffk
518 C4 Tobermory Ag & B
492 B3 Toberonochy Ag & B
593 D10 Tobha Beag W Isls
593 D10 Tobha Mòr W Isls
598 D8 Tobhtaral W Isls
598 C7 Tobson W Isls
335 G6 Toby's Hill Lincs
559 F3 Tocher Abers
112 B4 Tockenham Wilts
112 B3 Tockenham Wick Wilts
339 C5 Tockholes Bl w D
109 H2 Tockington S Glos
357 F4 Tockwith N York
68 C6 Todber Dorset
169 E4 Toddington Beds
163 F3 Toddington Gloucs
54 B4 Toddington W Susx
571 K6 Toddlehills Abers
164 C2 Todenham Gloucs
514 C2 Todhills Angus
400 C2 Todhills Cumb
395 E3 Todhills Dur
341 E5 Todmorden Calder
315 F3 Todpool Cnwll
197 E3 Todwick Rothm
243 F1 Toft Cambs
215 H5 Toft Warwks
394 D4 Toft Hill Dur
299 G2 Toft Hill Lincs
251 E6 Toft Monks Norfk
318 C2 Toft next Newton Lincs
254 A2 Toftrees Norfk
396 D4 Tofts Hartpl
342 C4 Toftshaw Brad
248 C2 Toftwood Norfk
443 G4 Togston Nthumb
545 L7 Tokavaig Highld
116 B4 Tokers Green Oxon
598 D7 Tolastadh a' Chaolais W Isls
15 H3 Tolborough Cnwll
3 E4 Tolcarne Cnwll
4 C2 Tolcarne Cnwll
6 C6 Tolcarne Cnwll
4 C1 Tolcarne Wartha Cnwll
7 H1 Toldish Cnwll
6 C5 Tolgus Mount Cnwll
79 F3 Tolhurst E Susx
188 C3 Tolladine Worcs
64 B5 Tolland Somset
48 A1 Tollard Farnham Dorset
69 F6 Tollard Royal Wilts
330 C3 Toll Bar Donc
243 E3 Toll Bar Rutlnd
324 B6 Toll Bar St Hel
215 F4 Tollbar End Covtry
237 E6 Toll End Sandw
30 D3 Tollerford Dorset
30 D3 Toller Fratrum Dorset
30 D3 Toller Porcorum Dorset
276 D3 Tollerton Notts
357 G2 Tollerton N York
30 C2 Toller Whelme Dorset
148 C2 Tollesbury Essex
385 E1 Tollesby Middsb
148 B2 Tolleshunt D'Arcy Essex
148 B2 Tolleshunt Knights Essex
148 B2 Tolleshunt Major Essex
561 F3 Toll of Birness Abers
599 K8 Tolm W Isls
144 C4 Tolmers Herts
47 E6 Tolpuddle Dorset
6 C5 Tolskithy Cnwll
599 L5 Tolstadh bho Thuath W Isls
6 C5 Tolvaddon Downs Cnwll
536 B3 Tolvah Highld
94 D1 Tolworth Gt Lon
511 F5 Tomaknock P & K
597 K5 Tom an Fhuadain W Isls
550 D4 Tomatin Highld
550 B3 Tombreck Highld
548 C7 Tomchrasky Highld
533 J2 Tomdoun Highld
548 E4 Tomich Highld
566 C2 Tomich Highld
537 H4 Tomich Highld
552 D5 Tomintoul Abers
191 G2 Tomlow Warwks
553 J2 Tomnacross Highld
552 E3 Tomnavoulin Moray
7 E5 Tomperrow Cnwll
292 B4 Tompkin Staffs
77 H3 Tompset's Bank E Susx
505 J3 Tomsluaibhe Ag & B
313 E4 Tomthorn Derbys
133 G5 Ton Mons
105 F4 Ton Breigam V Glam
97 E5 Tonbridge Kent
410 D5 Tonderghie D & G
104 D3 Tondu Brdgnd
43 F3 Tone Somset
43 F3 Tonedale Somset
43 G3 Tone Green Somset
228 D4 Tonfanau Gwynd
342 D3 Tong Brad
98 C5 Tong Kent
236 A3 Tong Shrops
275 G5 Tonge Leics
99 E1 Tonge Corner Kent
325 G3 Tonge Fold Bolton
325 G2 Tonge Moor Bolton
236 A3 Tong Forge Shrops
99 F4 Tong Green Kent
93 E5 Tongham Surrey
412 C4 Tongland D & G
236 A3 Tong Norton Shrops
342 C3 Tong Street Brad
586 C5 Tongue Highld
279 H6 Tongue End Lincs
168 B1 Tongwell M Keyn
106 B3 Tongwynlais Cardif
130 B5 Tonmawr Neath
130 B5 Tonna Neath
131 F6 Ton Pentre Rhondd
106 A2 Ton-teg Rhondd
144 D1 Tonwell Herts
105 F1 Tonypandy Rhondd
132 C5 Ton-y-pistyll Caerph
105 G2 Tonyrefail Rhondd
605 G4 Toogs Shet
140 C4 Toot Baldon Oxon
342 B5 Toothill Calder
312 B4 Toothill Ches
145 H4 Toot Hill Essex
72 A6 Toothill Hants
273 G1 Toot Hill Staffs
112 D3 Toothill Swindn
119 F5 Tooting Graveney Gt Lon
343 E4 Topcliffe Leeds
370 D4 Topcliffe N York
250 B6 Topcroft Norfk
226 B1 Topcroft Street Norfk
195 E2 Top End Beds
297 G6 Top End Notts
330 D1 Topham Donc

75 E6 Topleigh W Susx
325 E3 Top Lock Wigan
326 C3 Top of Hebers Rochdl
339 E5 Top o'th' Lane Lancs
327 E3 Top o' th' Meadows Oldham
173 E2 Toppesfield Essex
325 G2 Toppings Bolton
249 G5 Toprow Norfk
27 F5 Topsham Devon
295 H5 Top Valley C Nott
460 B4 Torbeg N Ayrs
468 D3 Torbothie N Lans
549 L1 Torbreck Highld
485 F1 Torbrex Stirlg
19 H4 Torbryan Devon
468 C3 Torbush N Lans
533 H7 Torcastle Highld
13 E4 Torcross Devon
565 L6 Tore Highld
9 E3 Torfrey Cnwll
534 D6 Torgulbin Highld
462 D2 Torinturk Ag & B
312 B2 Torkington Stockp
317 F4 Torksey Lincs
593 D7 Torlum W Isls
533 H7 Torlundy Highld
110 D4 Tormarton S Glos
476 B5 Tormisdale Ag & B
419 F3 Tormore Highld
531 H2 Tormore Highld
552 D1 Tormore Highld
460 B3 Tormore N Ayrs
566 D7 Tornagrain Highld
554 A3 Tornahaish Abers
555 H3 Tornaveen Abers
549 K4 Torness Highld
394 D3 Toronto Dur
389 F2 Torpenhow Cumb
486 C5 Torphichen W Loth
487 C6 Torphin C Edin
555 H4 Torphins Abers
10 D3 Torpoint Cnwll
20 C5 Torquay Torbay
472 A5 Torquhan Border
11 G3 Torr Devon
18 D5 Torr Devon
493 E4 Torran Ag & B
543 K7 Torran Highld
484 C5 Torrance E Duns
504 F5 Torrans Ag & B
465 G6 Torranyard N Ayrs
63 G3 Torre Somset
20 C5 Torre Torbay
562 F5 Torridon Highld
555 H2 Torries Abers
568 B4 Torrieston Moray
545 K5 Torrin Highld
586 E4 Torrisdale Highld
586 E4 Torrisdale Ag & B
576 B4 Torrisholme Lancs
558 B4 Torroble Highld
576 B4 Torroy Highld
558 A1 Torry Abers
557 H3 Torry C Aber
486 D2 Torryburn Fife
460 D5 Torrylinn N Ayrs
472 B6 Torsonce Border
571 K6 Torsonce Mains Border
34 b4 Torteval Guern
423 H4 Torthorwald D & G
54 B3 Tortington W Susx
212 B5 Torton Worcs
109 F3 Tortworth S Glos
543 H8 Torvaig Highld
378 A6 Torver Cumb
485 G3 Torwood Falk
451 F2 Torwoodlee Mains Border
316 B2 Torworth Notts
38 C3 Tosberry Devon
546 C2 Toscaig Highld
196 B2 Toseland Cambs
353 F3 Tosside N York
517 K6 Tostary Ag & B
200 B2 Tostock Suffk
542 B6 Totaig Highld
544 F2 Totardor Highld
543 G7 Tote Highld
587 H3 Totegan Highld
71 F5 Tote Hill Hants
74 D5 Tote Hill W Susx
73 E2 Totford Hants
147 H2 Totham Hill Essex
148 A2 Totham Plains Essex
90 D2 Tot Hill Hants
320 D3 Tothill Lincs
35 H3 Totland IoW
314 B3 Totley Sheff
314 C5 Totley Brook Sheff
314 C5 Totley Rise Sheff
273 E2 Totmonslow Staffs
46 B3 Totnell Dorset
19 H5 Totnes Devon
160 D3 Totnor Herefs
276 A2 Toton Notts
276 B3 Toton Notts
516 F4 Totronald Ag & B
542 F3 Totscore Highld
119 G1 Tottenham Gt Lon
119 G2 Tottenham Hale Gt Lon
246 C2 Tottenhill Norfk
246 C2 Tottenhill Row Norfk
142 B6 Totteridge Bucks
144 B6 Totteridge Gt Lon
168 D5 Totternhoe Beds
110 C3 Totteroak S Glos
209 G2 Totterton Shrops
328 B3 Tottington Bolton
248 A5 Tottington Norfk
364 D3 Tottlebank Cumb
340 A3 Tottleworth Lancs
50 C2 Totton Hants
117 E4 Touchen-end W & M
357 E6 Toulston N York
64 C5 Toulton Somset
577 J7 Toulvaddie Highld
573 G7 Tournaig Highld
571 H5 Toux Abers
98 A4 Tovil Kent
14 A4 Towan Cnwll
6 D4 Towan Cross Cnwll
481 G6 Toward Ag & B
22 A5 Toward Quay Ag & B
193 H5 Towcester Nhants
3 E2 Towednack Cnwll
141 H6 Towerage Bucks
252 D4 Tower End Norfk
83 F2 Tower Hamlets Kent
84 D3 Towerhead N Som
237 G6 Tower Hill Birm
312 B4 Tower Hill Ches
23 H4 Tower Hill Devon
177 E3 Tower Hill Essex
143 E4 Tower Hill Herts
323 H4 Tower Hill Knows
94 D5 Tower Hill Surrey
76 C4 Tower Hill W Susx
141 F3 Towersey Oxon
402 D2 Tow House Nthumb
554 D2 Towie Abers
568 B4 Towiemore Moray
394 C2 Tow Law Dur
26 B4 Town Barton Devon

235 F3 Town Centre Wrekin
141 G5 Town End Bucks
245 F5 Town End Cambs
365 E2 Town End Cumb
365 F3 Town End Cumb
366 C3 Town End Cumb
378 B3 Town End Cumb
378 C4 Town End Cumb
378 C5 Town End Cumb
391 G4 Town End Cumb
313 E3 Townend Derbys
313 G4 Town End Derbys
358 C4 Town End E R Yk
327 G1 Town End Kirk
309 G2 Town End Knows
273 E2 Townend Staffs
483 F4 Townend W Duns
403 G5 Townfield Dur
290 C2 Town Fields Ches
401 F5 Towngate Cumb
243 G2 Towngate Lincs
323 H3 Town Green Lancs
250 D2 Town Green Norfk
324 D5 Town Green Wigan
464 B2 Townhead Ag & B
328 B4 Townhead Barns
467 E1 Townhead C Glas
378 B2 Town Head Cumb
378 D4 Town Head Cumb
379 H2 Town Head Cumb
380 B2 Town Head Cumb
388 C2 Townhead Cumb
391 E2 Townhead Cumb
391 G4 Townhead Cumb
391 G5 Town Head Cumb
392 A5 Town Head Cumb
412 C5 Townhead D & G
313 G4 Town Head Derbys
467 H1 Townhead N Lans
441 G6 Townhead Nthumb
353 G3 Town Head N York
367 F6 Town Head N York
432 B4 Townhead S Ayrs
314 B3 Townhead Sheff
292 D5 Town Head Staffs
412 D1 Townhead of Greenlaw D & G
487 F2 Townhill Fife
103 F3 Townhill Swans
50 D1 Townhill Park C Sotn
395 H2 Town Kelloe Dur
17 F4 Townlake Devon
80 D3 Townland Green Kent
325 F4 Town Lane Wigan
77 H6 Town Littleworth E Susx
324 D5 Town of Lowton Wigan
310 A3 Town Park Halton
78 D4 Town Row E Susx
85 G3 Townsend BaNES
141 F3 Townsend Bucks
166 D5 Town's End Bucks
40 C2 Townsend Devon
30 D1 Town's End Dorset
33 H3 Town's End Dorset
47 G5 Town's End Dorset
68 B6 Towns End Dorset
91 F3 Towns End Hants
143 G3 Townsend Herts
114 B2 Townsend Oxon
124 C3 Townsend Pembks
85 F4 Townsend Somset
86 B5 Town's End Somset
87 H3 Townsend Wilts
88 B3 Townsend Wilts
340 C5 Townsend Fold Lancs
3 G3 Townshend Cnwll
162 B4 Town Street Gloucs
110 B1 Townwell S Glos
453 F4 Town Yetholm Border
359 H2 Towthorpe E R Yk
358 B3 Towthorpe York
344 B2 Towton N York
306 D4 Towyn Conwy
309 E2 Toxteth Lpool
300 C2 Toynton All Saints Lincs
300 C2 Toynton Fen Side Lincs
300 C2 Toynton St Peter Lincs
96 C4 Toy's Hill Kent
445 F5 Trabboch E Ayrs
445 G5 Trabbochburn E Ayrs
4 D4 Traboe Cnwll
472 C5 Trabrown Border
43 E3 Tracebridge Somset
566 F5 Tradespark Highld
601 H3 Tradespark Ork
326 A5 Trafford Park Traffd
157 F4 Trallong Powys
105 H1 Trallwn Rhondd
103 F2 Trallwn Swans
15 F2 Tramagenna Cnwll
160 B3 Tram Inn Herefs
133 E4 Tranch Torfn
489 E5 Tranent E Loth
308 D2 Tranmere Wirral
587 J6 Trantlebeg Highld
587 J6 Trantlemore Highld
430 C3 Tranwell Nthumb
155 F6 Trapp Carmth
490 A4 Traprain E Loth
213 G6 Trap's Green Warwks
90 B2 Trapshill W Berk
450 C3 Traquair Border
115 H6 Trash Green W Berk
341 E2 Trawden Lancs
157 H3 Trawscoed Powys
265 G2 Trawsfynydd Gwynd
181 E1 Trawsnant Cerdgn
133 G1 Treadam Mons
160 C5 Treaddow Herefs
4 D5 Treal Cnwll
105 H1 Trealaw Rhondd
338 B3 Treales Lancs
302 C5 Trearddur IoA
542 F6 Treaslane Highld
5 E3 Treath Cnwll
14 B3 Treator Cnwll
105 G1 Tre-Aubrey V Glam
105 G1 Trebanog Rhondd
129 H4 Trebanos Neath
15 G3 Trebartha Cnwll
16 C3 Trebarwith Cnwll
22 B5 Trebarwith Strand Cnwll
23 F5 Trebeath Cnwll
153 H1 Trebedw Cerdgn
105 F6 Tre-Beferad V Glam
8 D1 Trebell Green Cnwll
158 B4 Treberfydd Powys
14 B3 Trebetherick Cnwll
8 B1 Trebilcock Cnwll
64 B5 Treble's Holford Somset
63 G4 Treborough Somset
7 G1 Trebudannon Cnwll
16 D3 Trebullett Cnwll
15 F3 Treburgett Cnwll
16 B6 Treburley Cnwll
16 D3 Treburrick Cnwll
14 B4 Trebyan Cnwll
156 D4 Trecastle Powys
106 B2 Trecenydd Caerph
25 F2 Trecott Devon

151 G3 Trecwn Pembks
131 F4 Trecynon Rhondd
15 E4 Tredannick Cnwll
16 B2 Tredaule Cnwll
2 D4 Tredavoe Cnwll
132 B3 Tredegar Blae G
233 E1 Trederwen Powys
268 D5 Tre-derwen Powys
15 F4 Tredethy Cnwll
162 D4 Tredington Gloucs
190 C6 Tredington Warwks
2 D3 Tredinnick Cnwll
8 C2 Tredinnick Cnwll
9 G2 Tredinnick Cnwll
14 C4 Tredinnick Cnwll
15 H5 Tredinnick Cnwll
105 H6 Tredogan V Glam
132 B6 Tredomen Caerph
158 B3 Tredomen Powys
38 B4 Tredown Devon
14 D3 Tredrizzick Cnwll
133 G6 Tredunnock Mons
158 B3 Tredustan Powys
136 B1 Tredworth Gloucs
2 C5 Treen Cnwll
2 D2 Treen Cnwll
8 D2 Treesmill Cnwll
315 E2 Treeton Rothm
262 D4 Trefasser Gwynd
9 G2 Trefanny Hill Cnwll
151 E2 Trefasser IoA
282 D1 Trefdraeth IoA
158 B3 Trefeca Powys
204 D3 Trefechan Cerdgn
131 G3 Trefechan Myr Td
288 C5 Trefechan Wrexhm
207 F1 Trefeglwys Powys
158 B3 Trefeitha Powys
205 E6 Trefenter Cerdgn
151 F5 Treffgarne Pembks
150 D4 Treffynnon Pembks
151 E4 Trefgarn Owen Pembks
132 B2 Trefil Blae G
180 D3 Trefilan Cerdgn
150 D3 Trefin Pembks
269 E4 Treflach Shrops
232 C1 Trefnanney Powys
307 E5 Trefnant Denbgs
269 E4 Trefonen Shrops
263 F1 Trefor Gwynd
303 F1 Trefor IoA
15 F2 Treforda Cnwll
105 H2 Treforest Rhondd
179 E4 Treforgan Cerdgn
130 B3 Tre-Forgan Neath
285 G2 Trefriw Conwy
16 D3 Trefrize Cnwll
16 D2 Trefrize Cnwll
2 D4 Tregadgwith Cnwll
23 F6 Tregadillett Cnwll
134 C3 Tre-gagle Mons
303 F5 Tregaian IoA
6 C5 Tregajorran Cnwll
14 C6 Tregamere Cnwll
22 A6 Tregardock Cnwll
133 H2 Tregare Mons
9 G2 Tregarland Cnwll
9 G2 Tregarlandbridge Cnwll
5 E4 Tregarne Cnwll
181 G3 Tregaron Cerdgn
9 G2 Tregarrick Mill Cnwll
304 D6 Tregarth Gwynd
14 D5 Tregaswith Cnwll
14 C6 Tregatillian Cnwll
22 B5 Tregatta Cnwll
2 D4 Tregavarah Cnwll
4 C4 Tregear Cnwll
7 G3 Tregear Cnwll
23 E5 Tregeare Cnwll
268 C3 Tregeiriog Wrexhm
303 E2 Tregele IoA
15 E3 Tregellist Cnwll
2 C3 Tregeseal Cnwll
5 F2 Tregeseal Cnwll
131 F3 Tre-Gibbon Rhondd
5 E4 Tregidden Cnwll
150 B5 Treginnis Pembks
150 D4 Treglemais Pembks
22 D3 Tregole Cnwll
4 D1 Tregolls Cnwll
14 B5 Tregona Cnwll
14 C4 Tregonce Cnwll
14 D6 Tregonetha Cnwll
14 C4 Tregonna Cnwll
7 G2 Tregonning Cnwll
7 H4 Tregony Cnwll
22 C6 Tregoodwell Cnwll
15 E4 Tregorden Cnwll
8 C3 Tregorrick Cnwll
8 B1 Tregoss Cnwll
158 C2 Tregoyd Powys
158 C2 Tregoyd Mill Powys
15 F2 Tregreenwell Cnwll
8 C3 Tregrehan Mills Cnwll
180 B6 Tregroes Cerdgn
15 F6 Tregullon Cnwll
14 B5 Tregurrian Cnwll
3 F3 Tregurtha Downs Cnwll
7 G1 Tregustick Cnwll
151 E2 Tregydgulan Pembks
232 A5 Tregynon Powys
154 B6 Tre-gynwr Carmth
105 G1 Trehafod Rhondd
208 A1 Trehafren Powys
10 C2 Trehan Cnwll
16 C6 Trehane Cnwll
132 A5 Treharris Caerph
14 B4 Trehemborne Cnwll
131 E5 Treherbert Rhondd
106 A5 Tre-hill V Glam
16 D6 Trehunist Cnwll
131 F3 Tre-Ifor Rhondd
16 B5 Trekeivesteps Cnwll
16 D3 Trekenner Cnwll
14 B6 Trekenning Cnwll
22 B5 Treknow Cnwll
4 D5 Trelan Cnwll
287 H1 Tre-lan Flints
22 D4 Trelash Cnwll
307 F4 Trelawnyd Flints
153 F3 Trelech Carmth
150 B4 Treleddyd-fawr Pembks
6 D5 Treleigh Cnwll
5 F1 Trelew Cnwll
132 B5 Trelewis Myr Td
22 B6 Treligga Cnwll
14 D3 Trelights Cnwll
15 E3 Trelill Cnwll
7 H3 Trelion Cnwll
7 F4 Trelissick Cnwll
7 F6 Trelissick Cnwll
14 D5 Treliver Cnwll
134 C3 Trellech Mons
134 B4 Trellech Grange Mons
307 G4 Treloggan Flints
10 A2 Trelowia Cnwll
8 B3 Trelowth Cnwll
233 E4 Trelystan Powys
264 D2 Tremadog Gwynd
22 D5 Tremail Cnwll
179 E4 Tremain Cerdgn
23 E5 Tremaine Cnwll

105 E4 Tremains Brdgnd
16 C5 Tremar Cnwll
10 C2 Trematon Cnwll
10 D2 Trematon Castle Cnwll
4 B1 Tremayne Cnwll
16 C5 Trembraze Cnwll
3 E2 Tremedda Cnwll
307 F5 Tremeirchion Denbgs
2 D3 Tremethick Cross Cnwll
154 B3 Tremle Carmth
15 E6 Tremore Cnwll
15 E6 Tremorebridge Cnwll
106 D4 Tremorfa Cardif
307 G4 Tre-Mostyn Flints
22 B5 Trenale Cnwll
14 B5 Trenance Cnwll
14 D6 Trenance Cnwll
14 D4 Trenant Cnwll
16 B5 Trenant Cnwll
8 C4 Trenarren Cnwll
15 H5 Trenay Cnwll
235 F3 Trench Wrekin
116 A4 Trench Green Oxon
97 E5 Trench Wood Kent
7 F1 Trencreek Cnwll
22 D3 Trencreek Cnwll
3 F2 Trencrom Cnwll
7 G3 Trendeal Cnwll
4 C2 Trendear Cnwll
22 D5 Treneglos Cnwll
3 G2 Trenerth Cnwll
9 F3 Trenewan Cnwll
16 B5 Trengale Cnwll
22 D4 Trengune Cnwll
16 C3 Trenhorne Cnwll
15 E6 Treningle Cnwll
7 F1 Treninnick Cnwll
4 D5 Trenoon Cnwll
4 D2 Trenoweth Cnwll
67 F6 Trent Dorset
272 C1 Trentham C Stke
61 F2 Trentishoe Devon
276 A3 Trentlock Derbys
4 B2 Trenwheal Cnwll
105 E4 Treoes V Glam
131 F5 Treorchy Rhondd
132 B5 Treowen Caerph
208 B1 Treowen Powys
105 E5 Tre-pit V Glam
15 E3 Trequite Cnwll
205 F1 Tre'r-ddôl Cerdgn
105 G4 Trerhyngyll V Glam
4 D5 Trerise Cnwll
5 E3 Trerose Cnwll
10 B2 Trerulefoot Cnwll
179 F3 Tresaith Cerdgn
6 D6 Tresamble Cnwll
15 F4 Tresarrett Cnwll
6 D6 Tresavean Cnwll
7 G4 Tresawle Cnwll
7 E4 Tresawsen Cnwll
8 C1 Trescoll Cnwll
236 B5 Trescott Staffs
3 G3 Trescowe Cnwll
7 E2 Tresean Cnwll
4 D1 Tresevern Croft Cnwll
110 D1 Tresham Gloucs
7 G4 Tresillian Cnwll
15 G2 Tresinney Cnwll
151 F1 Tresinwen Pembks
6 D5 Treskerby Cnwll
6 C6 Treskillard Cnwll
8 C2 Treskilling Cnwll
23 E3 Treskinnick Cross Cnwll
6 B6 Treslothan Cnwll
23 E5 Tresmeer Cnwll
3 G4 Tresowes Green Cnwll
4 B3 Tresoweshill Cnwll
22 C4 Tresparrett Cnwll
22 C4 Tresparrett Posts Cnwll
576 E3 Tressady Highld
524 B3 Tressait P & K
606 E7 Tresta Shet
609 J6 Tresta Shet
317 E4 Treswell Notts
6 B5 Treswithian Cnwll
6 B5 Treswithian Downs Cnwll
205 F1 Tre Taliesin Cerdgn
6 D6 Trethellan Water Cnwll
5 G1 Trethem Cnwll
22 B5 Trethevy Cnwll
5 G1 Trethewell Cnwll
2 C5 Trethewey Cnwll
14 B3 Trethillick Cnwll
106 C2 Trethomas Caerph
8 A3 Trethosa Cnwll
8 C3 Trethowel Cnwll
8 C2 Trethurgy Cnwll
150 C4 Tretio Pembks
160 C5 Tretire Herefs
158 C5 Tretower Powys
288 B3 Treuddyn Flints
16 C3 Trevadlock Cnwll
7 E2 Trevail Cnwll
22 B4 Trevalga Cnwll
3 E1 Trevalgan Cnwll
289 E3 Trevalyn Wrexhm
14 C4 Trevance Cnwll
14 C3 Trevanger Cnwll
14 D4 Trevanson Cnwll
3 E3 Trevarrack Cnwll
7 H1 Trevarren Cnwll
14 B5 Trevarrian Cnwll
8 B5 Trevarrick Cnwll
6 D5 Trevarth Cnwll
127 E1 Trevaughan Carmth
154 A5 Trevaughan Carmth
3 E1 Treveal Cnwll
2 C4 Trevegean Cnwll
15 F3 Treveighan Cnwll
6 D3 Trevellas Cnwll
16 B6 Trevelmond Cnwll
14 C4 Trevelver Cnwll
7 F2 Trevemper Cnwll
4 B3 Trevena Cnwll
22 B5 Treven Cnwll
4 C3 Trevena Cnwll
4 C3 Trevenen Bal Cnwll
15 F3 Trevenning Cnwll
8 B5 Treveor Cnwll
8 C2 Treverbyn Cnwll
8 C2 Treverbyn Cnwll
16 A5 Treverva Cnwll
5 E2 Treverva Cnwll
2 C5 Trevescan Cnwll
133 E4 Trevethin Torfn
22 B6 Trevia Cnwll
16 D5 Trevigro Cnwll
15 E4 Trevilder Cnwll
7 F6 Trevilla Cnwll
22 D4 Trevillick Cnwll
7 F2 Trevilson Cnwll
14 D3 Trevine Cnwll
8 A2 Treviscoe Cnwll
6 D6 Treviskey Cnwll
3 E4 Trevithal Cnwll
7 F2 Trevoll Cnwll
14 B3 Trevone Cnwll
288 C6 Trevor Denbgs
14 C4 Trevorrick Cnwll
288 B6 Trevor Uchaf Denbgs
7 E2 Trevowah Cnwll
2 D2 Trevowhan Cnwll

4 B3 Trew Cnwll
15 F2 Trewalder Cnwll
22 B5 Trewarmett Cnwll
3 F2 Trewartha Cnwll
7 H6 Trewartha Cnwll
22 C5 Trewarthenick Cnwll
16 B2 Trewassa Cnwll
2 C3 Treween Cnwll
22 B6 Trewellard Cnwll
109 E1 Trewen Mons
4 C3 Trewen Cnwll
15 F2 Trewen Cnwll
233 E2 Trewennack Cnwll
15 E2 Trewennan Cnwll
15 E2 Trewern Powys
15 E3 Trewetha Cnwll
14 D3 Trewethen Cnwll
2 D2 Trewethern Cnwll
9 H2 Trewey Cnwll
16 B2 Trewidland Cnwll
16 C6 Trewindle Cnwll
22 D3 Trewint Cnwll
5 G1 Trewint Cnwll
23 F5 Trewint Cnwll
8 C5 Trewithian Cnwll
16 A4 Trewithick Cnwll
4 C5 Trewoodloe Cnwll
8 B3 Trewoon Cnwll
7 G5 Trewoon Cnwll
134 A3 Treworga Cnwll
7 G6 Treworgan Common Mons
22 C4 Treworlas Cnwll
14 D4 Treworld Cnwll
16 B5 Treworrick Cnwll
7 G6 Treworthal Cnwll
23 G2 Trewyn Devon
159 F5 Tre-wyn Mons
14 B4 Treyarnon Cnwll
74 B4 Treyford W Susx
8 B2 Trezaise Cnwll
3 E3 Trezelah Cnwll
341 G5 Triangle Calder
134 C4 Triangle Gloucs
237 G3 Triangle Staffs
48 C3 Trickett's Cross Dorset
28 D3 Tricombe Devon
151 G5 Triffleton Pembks
29 E3 Trill Devon
23 F5 Trillacott Cnwll
395 H3 Trimdon Dur
396 A3 Trimdon Colliery Dur
395 H2 Trimdon Grange Dur
256 D2 Trimingham Norfk
177 E2 Trimley Lower Street Suffk
177 E2 Trimley St Martin Suffk
177 E2 Trimley St Mary Suffk
212 A4 Trimpley Worcs
128 C4 Trimsaran Carmth
171 G6 Trims Green Herts
523 K3 Trinafour P & K
132 C4 Trinant Caerph
142 C2 Tring Herts
142 C2 Tringford Herts
142 C2 Tring Wharf Herts
528 D2 Trinity Angus
488 A4 Trinity C Edin
27 F1 Trinity Devon
35 i6 Trinity Jersey
511 H6 Trinity Gask P & K
205 G4 Trisant Cerdgn
64 B4 Triscombe Somset
533 G8 Trislaig Highld
7 F3 Trispen Cnwll
430 D1 Tritlington Nthumb
7 G2 Troan Cnwll
512 A2 Trochry P & K
132 C3 Troearhiwgwair Blae G
183 F4 Troedrhiwdalar Powys
154 B1 Troedrhiwffenyd Cerdgn
132 B4 Troedrhiwfuwch Caerph
179 G4 Troedyraur Cerdgn
131 H4 Troedyrhiw Myr Td
306 B5 Trofarth Conwy
35 h6 Trois Bois Jersey
57 G2 Trolliloes E Susx
606 E3 Trondavoe Shet
602 B7 Tronston Ork
6 C6 Troon Cnwll
444 D3 Troon S Ayrs
125 C2 Trooper's Inn Pembks
423 G4 Troqueer D & G
224 B5 Troston Suffk
128 D5 Trostre Carmth
133 G4 Trostrey Common Mons
23 E4 Troswell Cnwll
605 H7 Troswickness Shet
188 C3 Trotshill Worcs
74 C4 Trotten Marsh W Susx
123 E2 Trotters Essex
514 C3 Trottick C Dund
97 F2 Trottiscliffe Kent
74 C5 Trotton W Susx
340 D5 Trough Gate Lancs
378 D5 Troutbeck Cumb
390 B4 Troutbeck Cumb
378 D4 Troutbeck Bridge Cumb
28 C5 Trow Devon
314 D4 Troway Derbys
106 D3 Trowbridge Cardif
87 E3 Trowbridge Wilts
276 A2 Trowell Notts
134 D3 Trow Green Gloucs
87 E3 Trowle Common Wilts
143 H2 Trowley Bottom Herts
452 C3 Trows Border
250 B3 Trowse Newton Norfk
342 D3 Troydale Leeds
96 B5 Troy Town Kent
99 H6 Troy Town Kent
98 A1 Troy Town Medway
22 B5 Truas Cnwll
326 C3 Trub Rochdl
86 C6 Trudoxhill Somset
213 G4 Trueman's Heath Worcs
19 H5 True Street Devon
43 H3 Trull Somset
592 F7 Trumaisgearraidh W Isls
330 D2 Trumfleet Donc
542 C4 Trumpan Highld
161 F2 Trumpet Herefs
197 G4 Trumpington Cambs
93 G1 Trumps Green Surrey
256 B3 Trunch Norfk
350 D6 Trunnah Lancs
7 F4 Truro Cnwll
23 G5 Truscott Cnwll
20 B1 Trusham Devon
274 D2 Trusley Derbys
4 C3 Trussall Cnwll
321 F3 Trusthorpe Lincs
7 F3 Truthan Cnwll
3 F3 Truthwall Cnwll
252 C5 Trwstllewelyn Powys
303 F4 Tryfil IoA
236 C6 Trysull Staffs
3 E3 Trythogga Cnwll
8 B5 Tubbs Mill Cnwll
139 G5 Tubney Oxon

79 H3 Tubslake Kent
13 E1 Tuckenhay Devon
17 F5 Tuckermarsh Devon
44 B2 Tuckerton Somset
212 A2 Tuckhill Shrops
86 D2 Tucking Mill BaNES
6 C5 Tuckingmill Cnwll
15 F3 Tuckingmill Cnwll
23 E4 Tuckingmill Cnwll
69 F4 Tuckingmill Wilts
34 D2 Tuckton Bmouth
223 E5 Tuddenham Suffk
201 G5 Tuddenham St Martin Suffk
97 F5 Tudeley Kent
97 F5 Tudeley Hale Kent
29 F2 Tudhay Devon
395 F3 Tudhoe Dur
395 F3 Tudhoe Grange Dur
237 H5 Tudor Hill Birm
160 D5 Tudorville Herefs
262 C3 Tudweiliog Gwynd
323 G6 Tuebrook Lpool
16 B5 Tuelmenna Cnwll
75 F1 Tuesley Surrey
80 D1 Tuesnoad Kent
136 B1 Tuffley Gloucs
119 F2 Tufnell Park Gt Lon
90 D5 Tufton Hants
152 A4 Tufton Pembks
241 G4 Tugby Leics
210 C2 Tugford Shrops
455 G4 Tughall Nthumb
568 E2 Tugnet Moray
606 D8 Tulkie Shet
74 C4 Tullecombe W Susx
499 E2 Tullibardine P & K
498 D6 Tullibody Clacks
494 B1 Tullich Ag & B
566 C2 Tullich Highld
524 E5 Tulliemet P & K
541 E5 Tulloch Abers
551 H6 Tulloch Highld
576 D5 Tulloch Highld
512 C4 Tulloch P & K
493 G5 Tullochgorm Ag & B
528 B5 Tulloes Angus
557 G4 Tullos C Aber
510 C5 Tullybannocher P & K
483 G2 Tullycross Stirlg
526 A4 Tullymurdoch P & K
558 D6 Tullynessle Abers
119 G5 Tulse Hill Gt Lon
128 D2 Tumble Carmth
173 G4 Tumbler's Green Essex
299 H3 Tumby Woodside Lincs
523 L4 Tummel Bridge P & K
135 G4 Tumpy Green Gloucs
186 D5 Tumpy Lakes Herefs
122 B5 Tunbridge Wells Kent
424 D3 Tundergarth Mains D & G
599 J7 Tunga W Isls
256 B4 Tungate Norfk
86 B3 Tunley BaNES
136 D4 Tunley Gloucs
162 B1 Tunnel Hill Worcs
331 F4 Tunnel Pits N Linc
326 D2 Tunshill Rochdl
291 H4 Tunstall E R Yk
98 D2 Tunstall Kent
366 C5 Tunstall Lancs
251 E3 Tunstall Norfk
383 F5 Tunstall N York
271 H4 Tunstall Staffs
202 D3 Tunstall Suffk
406 B4 Tunstall Sundld
313 F5 Tunstead Derbys
256 B5 Tunstead Norfk
327 F4 Tunstead Oldham
91 H5 Tunworth Hants
160 C1 Tupsley Herefs
294 D1 Tupton Derbys
48 C6 Turbary Common Poole
15 F5 Turfdown Cnwll
570 F6 Turfhill Abers
326 D2 Turf Hill Rochdl
447 G2 Turfholm S Lans
29 E2 Turfmoor Devon
269 G6 Turfmoor Shrops
92 A3 Turgis Green Hants
528 B4 Turin Angus
163 H6 Turkdean Gloucs
51 G2 Turkey Island Hants
74 B6 Turkey Island W Susx
160 C4 Turkey Tump Herefs
241 F5 Tur Langton Leics
87 E2 Turleigh Wilts
211 H2 Turleygreen Shrops
34 A2 Turlin Moor Poole
49 E3 Turmer Hants
340 C6 Turn Lancs
159 F2 Turnastone Herefs
432 A3 Turnberry S Ayrs
11 E3 Turnchapel C Plym
294 B5 Turnditch Derbys
339 F3 Turner Green Lancs
79 E3 Turner's Green E Susx
79 E6 Turner's Green E Susx
214 B6 Turner's Green Warwks
116 E6 Turner's Green W Berk
77 F2 Turners Hill W Susx
47 F6 Turners Puddle Dorset
487 G5 Turnhouse C Edin
291 H4 Turnhurst C Stke
312 D4 Turnstead Milton Derbys
47 F3 Turnworth Dorset
570 C6 Turriff Abers
395 G2 Tursdale Dur
325 G1 Turton Bottoms Bl w D
244 C5 Turves Cambs
213 F4 Turves Green Birm
194 C4 Turvey Beds
116 C1 Turville Bucks
116 B1 Turville Heath Bucks
166 D2 Turweston Bucks
450 C6 Tushielaw Border
274 C4 Tutbury Staffs
213 E5 Tutnall Worcs
135 E4 Tutnalls Gloucs
134 C6 Tutshill Gloucs
99 F5 Tutt Hill Kent
256 A4 Tuttington Norfk
115 F5 Tutts Clump W Berk
17 E3 Tutwell Cnwll
316 D3 Tuxford Notts
602 B7 Twatt Ork
606 D7 Twatt Shet
485 E4 Twechar E Duns
471 E4 Tweedale Wrekin
475 E4 Tweedmouth Nthumb
449 E5 Tweedsmuir Border
7 E5 Twelveheads Cnwll
58 A2 Twelve Oaks E Susx
16 A5 Twelvewoods Cnwll
311 F6 Twemlow Green Ches
101 F2 Twenties Kent
279 H5 Twenty Lincs
86 C2 Twerton BaNES
118 C5 Twickenham Gt Lon

162 B5 Twigworth Gloucs
77 E6 Twineham W Susx
77 E5 Twineham Green W Susx
86 C3 Twinhoe BaNES
173 H2 Twinstead Essex
173 H2 Twinstead Green Essex
325 F5 Twiss Green Warrtn
29 E2 Twist Devon
353 G6 Twiston Lancs
62 B5 Twitchen Devon
209 G4 Twitchen Shrops
62 B5 Twitchen Mill Devon
101 E4 Twitham Kent
96 D3 Twitton Kent
18 D3 Two Bridges Devon
135 F3 Two Bridges Gloucs
6 D4 Two Burrows Cnwll
294 B2 Two Dales Derbys
238 C4 Two Gates Staffs
167 H2 Two Mile Ash M Keyn
76 B4 Two Mile Ash W Susx
110 A5 Two Mile Hill Bristl
20 A4 Two Mile Oak Cross Devon
308 D5 Two Mills Ches
60 D3 Two Pots Devon
302 B4 Twr IoA
239 E4 Twycross Leics
98 B1 Twydall Medway
167 E4 Twyford Bucks
275 E4 Twyford Derbys
69 E6 Twyford Dorset
72 C4 Twyford Hants
241 F2 Twyford Leics
254 D3 Twyford Norfk
165 H2 Twyford Oxon
269 F4 Twyford Shrops
116 C4 Twyford Wokham
189 F5 Twyford Worcs
160 C3 Twyford Common Herefs
132 D2 Twyn-Allws Mons
412 C4 Twynholm D & G
162 C2 Twyning Gloucs
162 D2 Twyning Green Gloucs
156 A5 Twynllanan Carmth
129 G2 Twynmynydd Carmth
132 C6 Twyn Shôn-Ifan Caerph
131 H3 Twynyrodyn Myr Td
106 B5 Twyn-yr-odyn V Glam
133 H3 Twyn-y-Sheriff Mons
218 D4 Twywell Nhants
159 G2 Tyberton Herefs
214 A1 Tyburn Birm
255 E2 Tyby Norfk
103 F3 Ty-coch Swans
129 E2 Tycroes Carmth
282 B1 Ty Croes IoA
268 B6 Tycrwyn Powys
281 G6 Tydd Gote Lincs
245 F1 Tydd St Giles Cambs
281 F6 Tydd St Mary Lincs
207 F2 Tyddyn Powys
287 F5 Tyddyn Angharad Denbgs
303 F2 Tyddyn Dai IoA
103 G3 Ty-draw Swans
52 C4 Tye Hants
146 D6 Tye Common Essex
145 F3 Tye Green Essex
146 C2 Tye Green Essex
146 D5 Tye Green Essex
172 A5 Tye Green Essex
172 B2 Tye Green Essex
173 F5 Tye Green Essex
342 C3 Tyersal Brad
134 A5 Ty-fry Mons
105 G5 Tyganol V Glam
262 B4 Ty-hen Gwynd
128 D5 Ty-isaf Carmth
132 D2 Tyla Mons
105 E2 Tylagwyn Brdgnd
325 F4 Tyldesley Wigan
155 G4 Tyle Carmth
105 G3 Tyle-garw Rhondd
100 B3 Tyler Hill Kent
144 C3 Tylers Causeway Herts
142 B6 Tylers Green Bucks
145 H3 Tyler's Green Essex
95 G4 Tyler's Green Surrey
142 D4 Tyler's Hill Bucks
132 C3 Ty Llwyn Blae G
131 G5 Tylorstown Rhondd
207 F3 Tylwch Powys
306 D4 Ty-mawr Conwy
286 B5 Ty Mawr Cwm Conwy
180 D3 Ty-nant Cerdgn
286 D6 Ty-nant Conwy
267 E4 Ty-nant Gwynd
105 H3 Tynant Rhondd
508 D3 Tyndrum Stirlg
406 A1 Tyne Dock S Tyne
33 F3 Tyneham Dorset
471 G3 Tynehead Mdloth
431 G6 Tynemouth N Tyne
406 A1 Tyne Tunnel S Tyne
179 E4 Tynewydd Cerdgn
204 C6 Ty-Newydd Cerdgn
130 C3 Tynewydd Neath
131 E5 Tynewydd Rhondd
86 B3 Tyning BaNES
490 A4 Tyninghame E Loth
283 E4 Tyn-lon Gwynd
435 G6 Tynron D & G
109 F5 Tyntesfield N Som
131 H5 Tyntetown Rhondd
105 F2 Ty'n-y-bryn Rhondd
269 E4 Tyn-y-coed Shrops
106 C2 Tyn-y-coedcae Caerph
129 F4 Tyn-y-cwm Swans
286 D1 Tynyfedw Conwy
307 E5 Ty'n-y-ffordd Denbgs
268 B3 Tyn-y-ffridd Powys
104 D3 Ty'n-y-garn Brdgnd
304 B3 Tynygongl IoA
205 F6 Tynygraig Cerdgn
183 G5 Tyn-y-graig Powys
305 G5 Tyn-y-groes Conwy
206 D2 Tynyrwtra Powys
168 D3 Tyrells End Beds
94 D3 Tyrrell's Wood Surrey
286 B2 Ty'r-felin-isaf Conwy
106 B3 Ty Rhiw Rhondd
152 D1 Tyrhos Pembks
571 G3 Tyrie Abers
194 B5 Tyringham M Keyn
213 H3 Tyseley Birm
107 E1 Ty-Sign Caerph
39 F4 Tythecott Devon
104 D4 Tythegston Brdgnd
312 B4 Tytherington Ches
110 B2 Tytherington S Glos
86 D5 Tytherington Somset
69 F1 Tytherington Wilts
111 H5 Tytherton Lucas Wilts
143 H3 Tyttenhanger Herts
8 D2 Tywardreath Cnwll
8 D2 Tywardreath Highway Cnwll
305 G4 Tywyn Conwy
228 D4 Tywyn Gwynd

722 City, town and village index: Uachdar - Walcot

U

592 D6 Uachdar W Isls
226 C5 Ubbeston Suffk
226 C5 Ubbeston Green Suffk
85 F3 Ubley BaNES
383 F4 Uckerby N York
78 B5 Uckfield E Susx
162 C2 Uckinghall Worcs
162 D5 Uckington Gloucs
234 D3 Uckington Shrops
467 G2 Uddingston S Lans
447 H3 Uddington S Lans
59 E3 Udimore E Susx
85 E2 Udley N Som
560 C4 Udny Green Abers
560 D5 Udny Station Abers
467 G3 Udston S Lans
467 H5 Udstonhead S Lans
112 D4 Uffcott Wilts
43 E5 Uffculme Devon
243 F3 Uffington Lincs
113 H2 Uffington Oxon
234 C2 Uffington Shrops
243 F4 Ufford C Pete
202 B4 Ufford Suffk
191 F2 Ufton Warwks
115 G6 Ufton Green W Berk
91 G1 Ufton Nervet W Berk
459 F6 Ugadale Ag & B
12 B1 Ugborough Devon
70 B3 Ugford Wilts
227 E3 Uggeshall Suffk
387 E3 Ugglebarnby N York
314 B1 Ughill Sheff
171 H4 Ugley Essex
171 H4 Ugley Green Essex
386 C2 Ugthorpe N York
591 C8 Uidh W Isls
516 F5 Uig Ag & B
542 B6 Uig Highld
542 F4 Uig Highld
598 B8 Uigen W Isls
543 G7 Uigshader Highld
504 D7 Uisken Ag & B
583 K1 Ulbster Highld
390 C5 Ulcat Row Cumb
320 D5 Ulceby Lincs
333 G2 Ulceby N Linc
333 G1 Ulceby Skitter N Linc
98 C5 Ulcombe Kent
389 G2 Uldale Cumb
136 A5 Uley Gloucs
430 D1 Ulgham Nthumb
574 C5 Ullapool Highld
43 H6 Ullcombe Devon
189 H1 Ullenhall Warwks
136 D1 Ullenwood Gloucs
344 C2 Ulleskelf N York
216 A2 Ullesthorpe Leics
315 F2 Ulley Rothm
186 D5 Ullingswick Herefs
189 H5 Ullington Worcs
544 E2 Ullinish Highld
388 C5 Ullock Cumb
389 F5 Ullock Cumb
377 F6 Ulpha Cumb
361 F3 Ulrome E R Yk
369 F2 Ulshaw N York
607 G1 Ulsta Shet
214 A3 Ulverley Green Solhll
363 F6 Ulverston Cumb
34 B4 Ulwell Dorset
435 F3 Ulzieside D & G
40 B3 Umberleigh Devon
28 D3 Umborne Devon
579 H3 Unapool Highld
328 A3 Under Bank Kirk
365 G1 Underbarrow Cumb
342 C3 Undercliffe Brad
26 D5 Underdown Devon
69 E3 Underhill Wilts
609 H4 Underhoull Shet
98 B5 Underlining Green Kent
96 D4 Underriver Kent
97 E4 Underriver Ho Kent
100 D2 Under the Wood Kent
314 B2 Under Tofts Sheff
211 F1 Underton Shrops
11 F2 Underwood C Plym
108 C2 Underwood Newpt
295 F4 Underwood Notts
125 G2 Underwood Pembks
222 D3 Undley Suffk
108 D2 Undy Mons
606 C6 Unifirth Shet
322 f7 Union Mills IoM
79 G3 Union Street E Susx
6 D5 United Downs Cnwll
314 D4 Unstone Derbys
314 D4 Unstone Green Derbys
326 B3 Unsworth Bury
390 C2 Unthank Cumb
391 G1 Unthank Cumb
400 C5 Unthank Cumb
314 C4 Unthank Derbys
88 D3 Upavon Wilts
31 E2 Up Cerne Dorset
122 C6 Upchurch Kent
38 B4 Upcott Devon
40 B6 Upcott Devon
40 D6 Upcott Devon
60 C4 Upcott Devon
185 F4 Upcott Herefs
43 G3 Upcott Somset
198 D3 Upend Cambs
194 C5 Up End M Keyn
27 E2 Up Exe Devon
255 F4 Upgate Norfk
225 E1 Upgate Street Norfk
226 B1 Upgate Street Norfk
92 C2 Up Green Hants
30 D2 Uphall Dorset
487 E5 Uphall W Loth
41 H6 Upham Devon
72 D5 Upham Hants
185 G2 Uphampton Herefs
188 B2 Uphampton Worcs
162 D5 Up Hatherley Gloucs
19 H5 Uphempston Devon
84 B3 Uphill N Som
84 B3 Uphill Manor N Som
324 C4 Up Holland Lancs
136 C3 Uplands Gloucs
103 F3 Uplands Swans
466 B3 Uplawmoor E Rens
161 H4 Upleadon Gloucs
161 H4 Upleadon Court Gloucs
397 F6 Upleatham R & Cl
99 F2 Uplees Kent
30 C4 Uploders Dorset
42 D4 Uplowman Devon
29 F4 Uplyme Devon
52 D2 Up Marden W Susx
121 E2 Upminster Gt Lon
57 F6 Up Mudford Somset
2 B4 Up Nately Hants
3 H6 Upottery Devon
A2 Uppacott Devon
J3 Uppat Highld
G4 Uppend Essex
A2 Upper Affcot Shrops
D6 Upper Ardchronie Highld
211 H3 Upper Arley Worcs
140 D1 Upper Arncott Oxon
270 C6 Upper Astley Shrops
236 B6 Upper Aston Shrops
166 B2 Upper Astrop Nhants
578 F1 Upper Badcall Highld
304 C5 Upper Bangor Gwynd
115 F4 Upper Basildon W Berk
270 C6 Upper Battlefield Shrops
55 E2 Upper Beeding W Susx
218 D2 Upper Benefield Nhants
189 E1 Upper Bentley Worcs
587 J5 Upper Bighouse Highld
295 E3 Upper Birchwood Derbys
472 C6 Upper Blainslie Border
106 B2 Upper Boat Rhondd
559 E3 Upper Boddam Abers
192 A4 Upper Boddington Nhants
37 F5 Upper Bonchurch IoW
313 F2 Upper Booth Derbys
204 D2 Upper Borth Cerdgn
571 G3 Upper Boyndlie Abers
164 D2 Upper Brailes Warwks
248 D3 Upper Brandon Parva Norfk
546 B5 Upper Breakish Highld
160 B1 Upper Breinton Herefs
341 H4 Upper Brockholes Calder
277 E4 Upper Broughton Notts
185 G4 Upper Broxwood Herefs
216 D2 Upper Bruntingthorpe Leics
129 H2 Upper Brynamman Carmth
160 D3 Upper Buckenhill Herefs
115 E6 Upper Bucklebury W Berk
72 C1 Upper Bullington Hants
49 E1 Upper Burgate Hants
557 E5 Upper Burnhaugh Abers
97 G1 Upper Bush Medway
400 D4 Upperby Cumb
195 H5 Upper Caldecote Beds
135 H5 Upper Cam Gloucs
583 J1 Upper Camster Highld
84 C3 Upper Canada N Som
49 H2 Upper Canterton Hants
192 B3 Upper Catesby Nhants
213 E5 Upper Catshill Worcs
157 G1 Upper Chapel Powys
44 A2 Upper Cheddon Somset
69 G3 Upper Chicksgrove Wilts
105 H2 Upper Church Village Rhondd
89 G4 Upper Chute Wilts
90 A6 Upper Clatford Hants
137 E1 Upper Coberley Gloucs
270 D3 Upper College Shrops
187 H6 Upper Colwall Herefs
91 G5 Upper Common Hants
293 E5 Upper Cotton Staffs
234 D3 Upper Cound Shrops
85 F6 Upper Croxley Somset
329 F3 Upper Cudworth Barns
328 C3 Upper Cumberworth Kirk
133 E5 Upper Cwmbran Torfn
133 E6 Upper Cwmbran Torfn
313 G5 Upperdale Derbys
606 A7 Upperdale Shet
568 F3 Upper Dallachy Moray
436 A3 Upper Dalveen D & G
101 G5 Upper Deal Kent
219 E6 Upper Dean Beds
19 F5 Upper Dean Devon
328 C1 Upper Denby Barns
328 C3 Upper Denby Kirk
401 H1 Upper Denton Cumb
551 J3 Upper Derraid Highld
562 E4 Upper Diabaig Highld
57 F2 Upper Dicker E Susx
210 A3 Upper Dinchope Shrops
160 D2 Upper Dormington Herefs
588 C3 Upper Dounreay Highld
176 D3 Upper Dovercourt Essex
163 F6 Upper Dowdeswell Gloucs
550 B1 Upper Drummond Highld
357 E2 Upper Dunsforth N York
142 C2 Upper Dunsley Herts
93 G6 Upper Eashing Surrey
214 D3 Upper Eastern Green Covtry
566 D4 Upper Eathie Highld
187 E5 Upper Egleton Herefs
293 E3 Upper Elkstone Staffs
293 F6 Upper Ellastone Staffs
95 H1 Upper Elmers End Gt Lon
313 E4 Upper End Derbys
137 F3 Upper End Gloucs
137 H2 Upper End Gloucs
241 F2 Upper End Leics
90 B4 Upper Enham Hants
211 H1 Upper Farmcote Shrops
73 H2 Upper Farringdon Hants
542 D8 Upper Feorlig Highld
44 C3 Upper Fivehead Somset
211 G2 Upper Forge Shrops
135 H2 Upper Framilode Gloucs
92 C6 Upper Froyle Hants
213 E6 Upper Gambolds Worcs
589 J2 Upper Gills Highld
533 L5 Upper Glenfintaig Highld
85 E6 Upper Godney Somset
101 E3 Upper Goldstone Kent
236 D6 Upper Gornal Dudley
169 G2 Upper Gravenhurst Beds
171 F3 Upper Green Essex
343 E4 Upper Green Leeds
159 G6 Upper Green Mons
199 E2 Upper Green Suffk
90 B2 Upper Green W Berk
160 C4 Upper Grove Common Herefs
254 D2 Upper Guist Norfk
294 B2 Upper Hackney Derbys
92 D5 Upper Hale Surrey
542 C5 Upper Halistra Highld
118 B6 Upper Halliford Surrey
97 G2 Upper Halling Medway
162 C2 Upper Ham Worcs
242 C3 Upper Hambleton Rutlnd
186 C3 Upper Hamnish Herefs
527 E6 Upper Handwick Angus
100 B4 Upper Harbledown Kent
100 B5 Upper Hardres Court Kent
185 H3 Upper Hardwick Herefs
78 B3 Upper Hartfield E Susx
294 D4 Upper Hartshay Derbys
163 F1 Upper Haselor Worcs
272 B2 Upper Hatton Staffs
329 G5 Upper Haugh Rothm
97 E6 Upper Hayesden Kent
210 C3 Upper Hayton Shrops
342 C6 Upper Heaton Kirk
249 H2 Upper Hellesdon Norfk
358 C3 Upper Helmsley N York
269 E3 Upper Hengoed Shrops
185 E4 Upper Hergest Herefs
193 E3 Upper Heyford Nhants
166 A4 Upper Heyford Oxon
186 B4 Upper Hill Herefs
135 F5 Upper Hill S Glos
441 E3 Upper Hindhope Border
119 F2 Upper Holloway Gt Lon
226 D4 Upper Holton Suffk
342 D6 Upper Hopton Kirk
57 F2 Upper Horsebridge E Susx
188 A5 Upper Howsell Worcs
292 D2 Upper Hulme Staffs
37 F4 Upper Hyde IoW
75 G3 Upper Ifold Surrey
138 C5 Upper Inglesham Swindn
570 F5 Upper Ironside Abers
503 F2 Upper Kenley Fife
606 F6 Upper Kergord Shet
470 D6 Upper Kidston Border
478 B2 Upper Kilchattan Ag & B
110 D2 Upper Kilcott Gloucs
103 E3 Upper Killay Swans
185 G1 Upper Kinsham Herefs
568 B7 Upper Knockando Moray
113 H3 Upper Lambourn W Berk
237 E3 Upper Landywood Staffs
85 E3 Upper Langford N Som
315 G5 Upper Langwith Derbys
174 D1 Upper Layham Suffk
273 F2 Upper Leigh Staffs
85 G2 Upper Littleton N Som
314 C6 Upper Loads Derbys
556 B5 Upper Lochton Abers
162 C3 Upper Lode Worcs
237 G2 Upper Longdon Staffs
236 B5 Upper Ludstone Shrops
583 J2 Upper Lybster Highld
135 E1 Upper Lydbrook Gloucs
186 B6 Upper Lyde Herefs
185 G1 Upper Lye Herefs
159 F2 Upper Maes-coed Herefs
341 G2 Upper Marsh Brad
185 G3 Upper Marston Herefs
328 C5 Upper Midhope Sheff
274 D5 Upper Midway Derbys
327 E3 Uppermill Oldham
542 A7 Upper Milovaig Highld
138 D1 Upper Milton Oxon
85 F5 Upper Milton Somset
112 B1 Upper Minety Wilts
189 E5 Upper Moor Worcs
342 D3 Upper Moor Side Leeds
110 B1 Upper Morton S Glos
125 H4 Upper Nash Pembks
607 H1 Upper Neepaback Shet
211 E1 Upper Netchwood Shrops
314 D5 Upper Newbold Derbys
273 F2 Upper Nobut Staffs
142 A5 Upper North Dean Bucks
119 G6 Upper Norwood Gt Lon
75 E6 Upper Norwood W Susx
106 D2 Upper Ochrwyth Caerph
164 C4 Upper Oddington Gloucs
545 J2 Upper Ollach Highld
314 A4 Upper Padley Derbys
557 F2 Upper Persley C Aber
111 E5 Upper Pickwick Wilts
141 F2 Upper Pollicott Bucks
357 H4 Upper Poppleton York
97 F5 Upper Postern Kent
190 B5 Upper Quinton Warwks
133 E5 Upper Race Torfn
71 G5 Upper Ratley Hants
164 C5 Upper Rissington Gloucs
211 E6 Upper Rochford Worcs
99 E2 Upper Rodmersham Kent
601 J4 Upper Sanday Ork
187 F2 Upper Sapey Herefs
277 E2 Upper Saxondale Notts
111 G3 Upper Seagry Wilts
194 D6 Upper Shelton Beds
261 F3 Upper Sheringham Norfk
50 D2 Upper Shirley C Sotn
137 F5 Upper Siddington Gloucs
482 B6 Upper Skelmorlie N Ayrs
72 A4 Upper Slackstead Hants
164 A5 Upper Slaughter Gloucs
150 C5 Upper Solva Pembks
135 F2 Upper Soudley Gloucs
605 H2 Uppersound Shet
85 H2 Upper Stanton Drew BaNES
195 G2 Upper Staploe Beds
215 F3 Upper Stoke Covtry
250 A4 Upper Stoke Norfk
169 G2 Upper Stondon Beds
192 D3 Upper Stowe Nhants
113 E2 Upper Stratton Swindn
70 D6 Upper Street Hants
225 G4 Upper Street Norfk
250 D1 Upper Street Norfk
256 A2 Upper Street Norfk
256 C5 Upper Street Norfk
175 F3 Upper Street Suffk
199 F4 Upper Street Suffk
201 F4 Upper Street Suffk
162 C2 Upper Strensham Worcs
87 E3 Upper Studley Wilts
169 E4 Upper Sundon Beds
110 C6 Upper Swainswick BaNES
51 G1 Upper Swanmore Hants
164 B4 Upper Swell Gloucs
329 E5 Upper Tankersley Barns
273 F2 Upper Tean Staffs
328 A3 Upperthong Kirk
315 F3 Upperthorpe Derbys
331 G4 Upperthorpe N Linc
289 F5 Upper Threapwood Ches
351 G4 Upper Thurnham Lancs
500 B3 Upper Tillyrie P & K
57 F4 Upperton E Susx
141 E6 Upperton Oxon
75 F5 Upperton W Susx
119 F5 Upper Tooting Gt Lon
543 J5 Upper Tote Highld
294 A4 Upper Town Derbys
294 B3 Upper Town Derbys
294 C2 Uppertown Derbys
394 B2 Upper Town Dur
186 D5 Upper Town Herefs
589 J1 Uppertown Highld
85 F1 Upper Town N Som
428 D5 Uppertown Nthumb
224 B6 Upper Town Suffk
111 H4 Upper Town Wilts
209 E4 Upper Treverward Shrops
566 C2 Upper Tullich Highld
191 E6 Upper Tysoe Warwks
137 F5 Upper Up Wilts
113 F4 Upper Upham Wilts
122 A5 Upper Upnor Medway
606 D2 Upper Urafirth Shet
86 B5 Upper Vobster Somset
120 A2 Upper Walthamstow Gt Lon
192 A5 Upper Wardington Oxon
74 C4 Upper Wardley W Susx
167 G2 Upper Weald M Keyn
192 D3 Upper Weedon Nhants
162 A1 Upper Welland Worcs
56 C2 Upper Wellingham E Susx
185 E4 Upper Welson Herefs
67 F1 Upper Westholme Somset
86 C1 Upper Weston BaNES
226 A4 Upper Weybread Suffk
315 F2 Upper Whiston Rothm
135 G5 Upper Wick Gloucs
188 B4 Upper Wick Worcs
73 F2 Upper Wield Hants
269 F2 Upper Wigginton Shrops
141 F2 Upper Winchendon Bucks
213 G1 Upper Witton Birm
140 A3 Upper Wolvercote Oxon
188 D4 Upper Wolverton Worcs
294 C3 Upperwood Derbys
559 F6 Upper Woodend Abers
70 C2 Upper Woodford Wilts
115 F6 Upper Woolhampton W Berk
91 F4 Upper Wootton Hants
111 E5 Upper Wraxall Wilts
187 H6 Upper Wyche Worcs
26 D2 Uppincott Devon
242 A5 Uppingham Rutlnd
48 C3 Uppington Dorset
235 E3 Uppington Shrops
235 E3 Uppper Longwood Shrops
371 E2 Upsall N York
200 B6 Upsher Green Suffk
145 F4 Upshire Essex
72 A3 Up Somborne Hants
100 D3 Upstreet Kent
609 J3 Upswall Shet
31 E2 Up Sydling Dorset
135 H4 Upthorpe Gloucs
224 C5 Upthorpe Suffk
141 G2 Upton Bucks
219 H4 Upton Cambs
16 C4 Upton Cnwll
23 E2 Upton Cnwll
243 G4 Upton C Pete
389 H2 Upton Cumb
12 C4 Upton Devon
28 A2 Upton Devon
48 B6 Upton Dorset
361 E4 Upton E R Yk
120 B3 Upton Gt Lon
309 F6 Upton Halton
309 G2 Upton Halton
50 C1 Upton Hants
90 B3 Upton Hants
37 F2 Upton IoW
101 G2 Upton Kent
239 F5 Upton Leics
317 G2 Upton Lincs
193 F2 Upton Nhants
250 D2 Upton Norfk
296 D4 Upton Notts
316 D4 Upton Notts
138 C2 Upton Oxon
115 E2 Upton Slough
117 G4 Upton Slough
42 C2 Upton Somset
66 D4 Upton Somset
330 A2 Upton Wakefd
189 H3 Upton Warwks
69 E3 Upton Wilts
308 C2 Upton Wirral
161 F4 Upton Bishop Herefs
110 B6 Upton Cheyney S Glos
235 E6 Upton Cressett Shrops
161 E4 Upton Crews Herefs
16 C4 Upton Cross Cnwll
169 G3 Upton End Beds
296 D4 Upton Field Notts
250 D2 Upton Green Norfk
92 A5 Upton Grey Hants
309 F6 Upton Heath Ches
26 C2 Upton Hellions Devon
117 G3 Upton Lea Slough
69 F1 Upton Lovell Wilts
234 C2 Upton Magna Shrops
68 B2 Upton Noble Somset
120 B3 Upton Park Gt Lon
27 E3 Upton Pyne Devon
309 H2 Upton Rocks Halton
136 C2 Upton St Leonards Gloucs
87 F5 Upton Scudamore Wilts
188 D4 Upton Snodsbury Worcs
162 C1 Upton upon Severn Worcs
212 D6 Upton Warren Worcs
53 G2 Upwaltham W Susx
222 A6 Upware Cambs
245 G4 Upwell Norfk
245 H4 Upwell Norfk
31 F6 Upwey Dorset
171 F5 Upwick Green Herts
220 C3 Upwood Cambs
605 H3 Uradale Shet
606 D2 Urafirth Shet
478 B2 Uragaig Ag & B
89 E3 Urchfont Wilts
186 C5 Urdimarsh Herefs
606 B1 Ure Shet
370 C5 Ure Bank N York
67 F5 Urgashay Somset
596 F8 Urgha W Isls
596 F7 Urgha Beag W Isls
384 B2 Urlay Nook S on T
325 H6 Urmston Traffd
405 F4 Urpeth Dur
568 D3 Urquhart Moray
385 F4 Urra N York
565 J6 Urray Highld
529 F4 Usan Angus
395 E1 Ushaw Moor Dur
133 G4 Usk Mons
333 F6 Usselby Lincs
405 G3 Usworth Sundld
290 A1 Utkinton Ches
355 E6 Utley Brad
26 C3 Uton Devon
334 D6 Utterby Lincs
273 G3 Uttoxeter Staffs
262 B5 Uwchmynydd Gwynd
118 B3 Uxbridge Gt Lon
118 A3 Uxbridge Moor Gt Lon
609 H4 Uyeasound Shet
125 G2 Uzmaston Pembks

V

604 b3 Vaasetter Shet
150 C4 Vachelich Pembks
67 E6 Vagg Somset
604 D1 Vaila Hall Shet
341 E4 Vale Calder
35 d2 Vale Guern
24 D5 Vale Down Devon
269 G5 Valeswood Shrops
302 C5 Valley IoA
486 D2 Valleyfield Fife
72 B5 Valley Park Hants
22 B6 Valley Truckle Cnwll
609 J2 Valsgarth Shet
543 J4 Valtos Highld
598 B7 Valtos W Isls
106 C2 Van Caerph
207 E2 Van Powys
121 H2 Vange Essex
605 G7 Vanlop Shet
232 D2 Varchoel Powys
3 F3 Varfell Cnwll
133 E3 Varteg Torfn
607 G7 Vassa Shet
112 B3 Vastern Wilts
605 G6 Vatsetter Shet
609 G7 Vatsetter Shet
542 D8 Vatten Highld
516 C6 Vaul Ag & B
213 G2 Vauxhall Birm
119 G4 Vauxhall Gt Lon
308 D1 Vauxhall Lpool
283 F2 Vaynol Hall Gwynd
131 G2 Vaynor Myr Td
605 H2 Veensgarth Shet
60 C4 Velator Devon
186 D6 Veldo Herefs
158 C2 Velindre Powys
3 F3 Vellanoweth Cnwll
64 A4 Vellow Somset
38 C3 Velly Devon
601 J3 Veltigar Ork
19 G5 Velwell Devon
606 D6 Vementry Shet
603 H6 Veness Ork
12 C3 Venn Devon
39 E5 Venngreen Devon
233 F3 Vennington Shrops
28 A4 Venn Ottery Devon
186 C5 Venn's Green Herefs
26 C3 Venny Tedburn Devon
16 D4 Venterdon Cnwll
60 C3 Vention Devon
37 F5 Ventnor IoW
11 G2 Venton Devon
25 G4 Venton Devon
7 E3 Ventongimps Cnwll
3 G2 Ventonleague Cnwll
143 E4 Venus Hill Herts
41 F2 Veraby Devon
167 F4 Verney Junction Bucks
90 A3 Vernham Bank Hants
90 A3 Vernham Dean Hants
90 A3 Vernham Row Hants
90 B3 Vernham Street Hants
210 B3 Vernolds Common Shrops
48 D3 Verwood Dorset
7 H6 Veryan Cnwll
7 H5 Veryan Green Cnwll
28 D5 Vicarage Devon
289 F1 Vicarscross Ches
364 A6 Vickerstown Cumb
328 B3 Victoria Barns
8 B1 Victoria Cnwll
348 B4 Victoria Dock Village C KuH
142 A2 Victoria Park Bucks
466 D1 Victory Gardens Rens
607 G4 Vidlin Shet
467 H2 Viewpark N Lans
237 F4 Vigo Wsall
97 G2 Vigo Village Kent
35 d3 Village de Putron Guern
35 f5 Ville la Bas Jersey
34 c3 Villiaze Guern
108 D2 Vinegar Hill Mons
58 C2 Vinehall Street E Susx
97 E4 Vines Kent
78 D6 Vines Cross E Susx
135 F3 Viney Hill Gloucs
30 C4 Vinney Cross Dorset
110 B4 Vinney Green S Glos
117 G6 Virginia Water Surrey
24 A4 Virginstow Devon
86 C5 Vobster Somset
606 D1 Voe Shet
606 F5 Voe Shet
609 J3 Voesgarth Shet
6 D5 Vogue Cnwll
84 C5 Vole Somset
24 C4 Voulsdon Cross Devon
159 G2 Vowchurch Herefs
159 G2 Vowchurch Common Herefs
43 F4 Voxmoor Somset
606 E3 Voxter Shet
600 D1 Voy Ork
233 F3 Vron Gate Shrops
324 D6 Vulcan Village St Hel

W

377 E6 Waberthwaite Cumb
394 D5 Wackerfield Dur
187 E3 Wacton Herefs
225 G1 Wacton Norfk
225 G2 Wacton Common Norfk
606 F8 Wadbister Shet
188 C5 Wadborough Worcs
29 F2 Wadbrook Devon
141 F1 Waddesdon Bucks
13 F1 Waddeton Devon
323 G5 Waddicar Sefton
41 H2 Waddicombe Devon
332 D5 Waddingham Lincs
353 E6 Waddington Lancs
298 B2 Waddington Lincs
319 F5 Waddingworth Lincs
20 B2 Waddon Devon
31 E5 Waddon Dorset
95 G2 Waddon Gt Lon
14 D4 Wadebridge Cnwll
44 B5 Wadeford Somset
338 D5 Wade Hall Lancs
218 D3 Wadenhoe Nhants
290 D2 Wades Green Ches
170 D6 Wadesmill Herts
79 E3 Wadhurst E Susx
314 C5 Wadshelf Derbys
314 C1 Wadsley Sheff
314 C1 Wadsley Bridge Sheff
111 E6 Wadswick Wilts
90 C4 Wadwick Hants
330 C5 Wadworth Donc
286 D2 Waen Denbgs
287 G1 Waen Denbgs
307 H5 Waen Flints
207 F1 Waen Powys
268 D6 Waen Powys
307 F6 Waen Aberwheeler Denbgs
232 D1 Waen-fâch Powys
284 C1 Waen-pentir Gwynd
304 C6 Waen-wen Gwynd
582 D4 Wag Highld
233 G4 Wagbeach Shrops
66 C4 Wagg Somset
272 C2 Waggersley Staffs
29 F2 Waggs Plot Devon
133 E4 Wainfelin Torfn
301 E3 Wainfleet All Saints Lincs
301 E3 Wainfleet Bank Lincs
301 F3 Wainfleet St Mary Lincs
301 E3 Wainfleet Tofts Lincs
226 C1 Wainford Norfk
295 E5 Waingroves Derbys
22 D3 Wainhouse Corner Cnwll
291 H3 Wain Lee Staffs
122 A5 Wainscott Medway
341 G4 Wainstalls Calder
380 D3 Waitby Cumb
334 C4 Waithe Lincs
343 F5 Wakefield Wakefd
213 G3 Wake Green Birm
369 G5 Wake Hill N York
170 D4 Wakeley Herts
242 D5 Wakerley Nhants
174 A4 Wakes Colne Essex
174 A3 Wakes Colne Green Essex
227 F5 Walberswick Suffk
53 H3 Walberton W Susx
405 E1 Walbottle N u Ty
400 D2 Walby Cumb
85 F5 Walcombe Somset
86 C1 Walcot BaNES
279 F2 Walcot Lincs
346 C5 Walcot N Linc
165 E6 Walcot Oxon
209 F3 Walcot Shrops

113 E3 Walcot Swindn
188 D5 Walcot Worcs
234 D2 Walcot Wrekin
216 C3 Walcote Leics
189 H3 Walcote Warwks
225 F3 Walcot Green Norfk
299 E3 Walcott Lincs
256 D2 Walcott Norfk
368 D3 Walden N York
368 C3 Walden Head N York
330 C1 Walden Stubbs N York
328 C2 Waldershaigh Sheff
98 B2 Walderslade Medway
52 D2 Walderton W Susx
30 B4 Walditch Dorset
273 H2 Waldley Derbys
405 G4 Waldridge Dur
202 B6 Waldringfield Suffk
202 B6 Waldringfield Heath Suffk
78 D6 Waldron E Susx
78 C5 Waldron Down E Susx
315 F3 Wales Rothm
67 F5 Wales Somset
315 F3 Wales Bar Rothm
319 E1 Walesby Lincs
316 C5 Walesby Notts
319 E1 Walesby Grange Lincs
199 F5 Wales End Suffk
315 F3 Waleswood Rothm
160 D5 Walford Herefs
209 G5 Walford Herefs
270 A5 Walford Shrops
44 B2 Walford Somset
272 B3 Walford Staffs
270 B6 Walford Heath Shrops
290 D5 Walgherton Ches
217 H5 Walgrave Nhants
162 B5 Walham Gloucs
50 B5 Walhampton Hants
325 G4 Walkden Salfd
405 G2 Walker N u Ty
312 C5 Walker Barn Ches
450 D2 Walkerburn Border
339 G1 Walker Fold Lancs
317 E1 Walkeringham Notts
331 G6 Walkerith Lincs
170 C4 Walkern Herts
186 C5 Walker's Green Herefs
213 G4 Walker's Heath Birm
383 F5 Walkerville N York
407 G6 Walkford Dorset
18 B4 Walkhampton Devon
347 E2 Walkington E R Yk
314 C2 Walkley Sheff
340 D3 Walk Mill Lancs
233 G6 Walkmill Shrops
234 B5 Walkmills Shrops
4 B1 Wall Cnwll
429 E6 Wall Nthumb
237 H3 Wall Staffs
486 A4 Wallacestone Falk
422 D2 Wallaceton D & G
432 C4 Wallacetown S Ayrs
444 D5 Wallacetown S Ayrs
56 C2 Wallands Park E Susx
323 E6 Wallasey Wirral
12 B3 Wallaton Cross Devon
326 C1 Wallbank Lancs
234 C6 Wall Bank Shrops
236 D6 Wallbrook Dudley
79 F3 Wallcrouch E Susx
363 E5 Wall End Cumb
120 B3 Wallend Gt Lon
100 D3 Wall End Kent
161 F2 Waller's Green Herefs
290 D2 Walley's Green Ches
212 C1 Wall Heath Dudley
327 E3 Wall Hill Oldham
115 G2 Wallingford Oxon
95 F2 Wallington Gt Lon
51 G3 Wallington Hants
170 C3 Wallington Herts
315 H3 Wallingwells Notts
151 H4 Wallis Pembks
48 B2 Wallisdown Poole
76 B2 Walliswood Surrey
86 B3 Wall Mead BaNES
405 F5 Wall Nook Dur
136 B5 Wallow Green Gloucs
429 G4 Wallridge Nthumb
606 B8 Walls Shet
405 G1 Wallsend N u Ty
106 B3 Wallston V Glam
325 F2 Wallsuches Bolton
162 B5 Wallsworth Gloucs
210 C1 Wall under Heywood Shrops
488 D5 Wallyford E Loth
101 G5 Walmer Kent
338 C5 Walmer Bridge Lancs
326 A2 Walmersley Bury
358 B4 Walmgate Stray York
238 A6 Walmley Birm
320 C4 Walmsgate Lincs
512 D6 Walnut Grove P & K
168 B2 Walnut Tree M Keyn
171 G5 Walnuttree Green Herts
65 E3 Walpole Somset
226 D5 Walpole Suffk
281 H5 Walpole Cross Keys Norfk
245 H2 Walpole Highway Norfk
281 G6 Walpole Marsh Norfk
281 H6 Walpole St Andrew Norfk
245 H1 Walpole St Peter Norfk
84 B5 Walrow Somset
214 B4 Walsal End Solhll
237 F5 Walsall Wsall
237 F5 Walsall Wood Wsall
341 E5 Walsden Calder
215 F3 Walsgrave on Sowe Covtry
224 D5 Walsham Le Willows Suffk
325 H2 Walshaw Bury
357 E4 Walshford N York
245 G2 Walsoken Cambs
160 A5 Walson Mons
469 G5 Walston S Lans
170 A3 Walsworth Herts
142 A5 Walter's Ash Bucks
78 C1 Walter's Green Kent
105 H5 Walterston V Glam
159 F4 Walterstone Herefs
100 B6 Waltham Kent
334 C4 Waltham NE Lin
145 E4 Waltham Abbey Essex
51 G2 Waltham Chase Hants
145 E4 Waltham Cross Herts
277 H4 Waltham on the Wolds Leics
116 D4 Waltham St Lawrence W & M
172 D3 Waltham's Cross Essex
119 H2 Walthamstow Gt Lon
142 A3 Walton Bucks
244 A4 Walton C Pete
401 F2 Walton Cumb
314 D6 Walton Derbys
357 E5 Walton Leeds
216 C2 Walton Leics
323 G6 Walton Lpool
168 B2 Walton M Keyn
184 D3 Walton Powys
210 B4 Walton Shrops
66 D2 Walton Somset
272 C4 Walton Staffs

177 E2 Walton Suffk
329 F1 Walton Wakefd
190 D4 Walton Warwks
270 D6 Walton Wrekin
272 C3 Walton Wrekin
162 D3 Walton Cardiff Gloucs
141 H2 Walton Court Bucks
151 H5 Walton East Pembks
68 C6 Walton Elm Dorset
166 B3 Walton Grounds Nhants
51 H3 Walton Heath Hants
245 G2 Walton Highway Norfk
108 D5 Walton in Gordano N Som
339 E4 Walton-le-Dale Lancs
140 B3 Walton Manor Oxon
94 C1 Walton-on-Thames Surrey
273 E5 Walton-on-the-Hill Staffs
95 E3 Walton on the Hill Surrey
177 E5 Walton on the Naze Essex
276 C6 Walton on the Wolds Leics
274 C6 Walton-on-Trent Derbys
212 D4 Walton Pool Worcs
198 B6 Waltons Essex
108 D5 Walton St Mary N Som
339 E4 Walton Summit Lancs
253 E4 Walton Warren Norfk
125 E2 Walton West Pembks
307 G4 Walwen Flints
307 H5 Walwen Flints
308 B4 Walwen Flints
429 E5 Walwick Nthumb
395 E6 Walworth Darltn
119 G4 Walworth Gt Lon
395 E5 Walworth Gate Darltn
125 E2 Walwyn's Castle Pembks
44 B6 Wambrook Somset
399 G4 Wampool Cumb
93 F5 Wanborough Surrey
113 F3 Wanborough Swindn
448 B4 Wandel S Lans
448 C4 Wandel Dyke S Lans
95 G1 Wandle Park Gt Lon
169 G5 Wandon End Herts
119 F5 Wandsworth Gt Lon
227 F4 Wangford Suffk
240 D2 Wanlip Leics
435 H2 Wanlockhead D & G
57 F4 Wannock E Susx
243 F5 Wansford C Pete
360 D3 Wansford E R Yk
90 C2 Wanshurst Green Kent
22 D2 Wanson Cnwll
120 B2 Wanstead Gt Lon
68 B1 Wanstrow Somset
135 F4 Wanswell Gloucs
114 C2 Wantage Oxon
187 G3 Wants Green Worcs
110 C4 Wapley S Glos
215 F6 Wappenbury Warwks
192 D5 Wappenham Nhants
119 G3 Wapping Gt Lon
79 E6 Warbleton E Susx
52 C3 Warblington Hants
140 C6 Warborough Oxon
220 D3 Warboys Cambs
337 F2 Warbreck Bpool
23 E4 Warbstow Cnwll
23 E4 Warbstow Cross Cnwll
310 D2 Warburton Traffd
311 F3 Warburton Green Traffd
380 C1 Warcop Cumb
123 G5 Warden Kent
403 G1 Warden Nthumb
185 E2 Warden Powys
213 H2 Ward End Birm
162 D5 Warden Hill Gloucs
35 H3 Warden Point IoW
195 G6 Warden Street Beds
329 E4 Ward Green Barns
200 D2 Ward Green Suffk
339 F2 Ward Green Cross Lancs
169 F2 Wardhedges Beds
603 J6 Wardhill Ork
192 A5 Wardington Oxon
438 B1 Wardlaw Border
290 C3 Wardle Ches
326 D1 Wardle Rochdl
290 C3 Wardle Bank Ches
405 G2 Wardley Gatesd
242 A5 Wardley Rutlnd
325 H4 Wardley Salfd
74 C4 Wardley W Susx
313 G5 Wardlow Derbys
69 F4 Wardour Wilts
485 F4 Wardpark N Lans
141 H4 Wardrobes Bucks
312 B3 Wardsend Ches
221 G3 Wardy Hill Cambs
29 F4 Ware Devon
145 E2 Ware Herts
101 E3 Ware Kent
33 G2 Wareham Dorset
81 E3 Warehorne Kent
455 H4 Warenford Nthumb
455 H3 Waren Mill Nthumb
454 D3 Warenton Nthumb
145 E1 Wareside Herts
196 C4 Waresley Cambs
212 B6 Waresley Worcs
98 C3 Ware Street Kent
117 E5 Warfield Br For
13 F2 Warfleet Devon
280 B3 Wargate Lincs
324 D6 Wargate St Hel
116 C4 Wargrave Wokham
160 B2 Warham Herefs
260 B3 Warham Norfk
327 E5 Warhill Tamesd
213 H5 Waring's Green Solhll
428 D4 Wark Nthumb
453 F2 Wark Nthumb
453 F2 Wark Common Nthumb
40 C3 Warkleigh Devon
218 B3 Warkton Nhants
166 A1 Warkworth Nhants
443 H3 Warkworth Nthumb
370 C1 Warlaby N York
341 E5 Warland Calder
15 H5 Warleggan Cnwll
86 D2 Warleigh BaNES
146 B6 Warley Essex
341 G4 Warley Town Calder
213 F2 Warley Woods Sandw
95 G3 Warlingham Surrey
294 B4 Warmbrook Derbys
343 G5 Warmfield Wakefd
290 D2 Warmingham Ches
54 D2 Warmington Nhants
219 F1 Warmington Warwks
191 H3 Warminster Wilts
87 F5 Warminster Common Wilts
98 C5 Warmlake Kent
110 B5 Warmley S Glos
110 A5 Warmley Hill S Glos
110 B5 Warmley Tower S Glos
330 B4 Warmonds Hill Nhants
330 B4 Warmsworth Donc
32 D2 Warmwell Dorset
92 B4 Warnborough Green Hants
188 C3 Warndon Worcs
143 E3 Warners End Herts
73 F5 Warnford Hants
76 C3 Warnham W Susx

54 B3 Warningcamp W Susx
77 E4 Warninglid W Susx
140 D5 Warpsgrove Oxon
312 A5 Warren Ches
33 F1 Warren Dorset
125 F5 Warren Pembks
329 F5 Warren Sheff
397 E5 Warrenby R & Cl
74 A4 Warren Corner Hants
92 D5 Warren Corner Hants
201 H6 Warren Heath Suffk
116 D3 Warren Row W & M
170 C4 Warren's Green Herts
99 E4 Warren Street Kent
194 B4 Warrington M Keyn
310 C2 Warrington Warrtn
488 B4 Warriston C Edin
51 E3 Warsash Hants
589 J2 Warse Highld
355 H1 Warsill N York
293 E3 Warslow Staffs
315 H6 Warsop Vale Notts
213 G4 Warstock Birm
237 E3 Warstone Staffs
359 G4 Warter E R Yk
369 G4 Warthermarske N York
358 C3 Warthill N York
57 H3 Wartling E Susx
277 E5 Wartnaby Leics
338 B4 Warton Lancs
365 H5 Warton Lancs
442 B4 Warton Nthumb
238 D4 Warton Warwks
337 G4 Warton Bank Lancs
190 D1 Warwick Warwks
401 E3 Warwick Bridge Cumb
401 E3 Warwick-on-Eden Cumb
426 B4 Warwicksland Cumb
95 G4 Warwick Wold Surrey
602 D5 Wasbister Ork
377 F3 Wasdale Head Cumb
313 E3 Wash Derbys
171 F3 Washall Green Herts
15 E5 Washaway Cnwll
12 D2 Washbourne Devon
84 D4 Washbrook Somset
175 F1 Washbrook Suffk
201 F6 Washbrook Street Suffk
90 C2 Wash Common W Berk
245 H1 Wash Dyke Norfk
292 B5 Washerwall Staffs
42 B4 Washfield Devon
382 C4 Washfold N York
63 H3 Washford Somset
189 G1 Washford Worcs
41 G5 Washford Pyne Devon
318 C5 Washingborough Lincs
219 G2 Washingley Cambs
405 H3 Washington Sundld
54 D2 Washington W Susx
405 H3 Washington Village Sundld
200 B5 Washmere Green Suffk
328 A3 Washpit Kirk
90 C2 Wash Water W Berk
213 G2 Washwood Heath Birm
91 F2 Wasing W Berk
404 C5 Waskerley Dur
190 D3 Wasperton Warwks
95 G5 Wasp Green Surrey
298 D2 Wasps Nest Lincs
371 G4 Wass N York
214 C6 Waste Green Warwks
12 A3 Wastor Devon
28 D3 Watchcombe Devon
63 H3 Watchet Somset
113 F1 Watchfield Oxon
84 B5 Watchfield Somset
379 F5 Watchgate Cumb
399 F6 Watchhill Cumb
172 D5 Watch House Green Essex
399 G1 Watchill D & G
20 C4 Watcombe Torbay
378 A1 Watendlath Cumb
19 G1 Water Devon
340 C4 Water Lancs
197 G2 Waterbeach Cambs
53 F3 Waterbeach W Susx
425 E4 Waterbeck D & G
143 G4 Waterdale Herts
260 A4 Waterden Norfk
49 F5 Waterditch Hants
168 B3 Water Eaton M Keyn
140 B2 Water Eaton Oxon
169 F2 Water End Beds
195 G5 Water End Beds
196 B5 Water End Beds
141 G5 Waterend Bucks
388 D5 Waterend Cumb
346 A2 Water End E R Yk
172 B1 Water End Essex
135 H2 Waterend Gloucs
92 A4 Water End Hants
143 E2 Water End Herts
144 A2 Water End Herts
144 B4 Water End Herts
293 E4 Waterfall Staffs
459 G4 Waterfoot Ag & B
390 D5 Waterfoot Cumb
340 C5 Waterfoot S Lans
467 E4 Waterfoot S Lans
50 B6 Waterford Hants
144 D2 Waterford Herts
344 B4 Water Fryston Wakefd
364 A6 Water Garth Nook Cumb
9 G3 Watergate Cnwll
15 G2 Watergate Cnwll
45 E4 Watergore Somset
146 H5 Waterhales Essex
99 H2 Waterham Kent
137 G6 Waterhay Wilts
378 C4 Waterhead Cumb
12 B3 Waterhead Devon
434 A2 Waterhead E Ayrs
470 D4 Waterheads Border
251 E6 Waterheath Norfk
394 D1 Waterhouses Dur
293 E4 Waterhouses Staffs
97 G4 Wateringbury Kent
136 C1 Waterlane Gloucs
86 B6 Waterloo BaNES
106 C2 Waterloo Caerph
15 G4 Waterloo Cnwll
295 E2 Waterloo Derbys
185 F5 Waterloo Herefs
546 B5 Waterloo Highld
468 C4 Waterloo N Lans
225 F4 Waterloo Norfk
251 E6 Waterloo Norfk
255 H4 Waterloo Norfk
512 C2 Waterloo P & K
125 G4 Waterloo Pembks
48 C6 Waterloo Poole
72 C3 Waterloo Sefton
270 C3 Waterloo Shrops
326 D4 Waterloo Tamesd
339 G4 Waterloo Tamesd
323 F5 Waterloo Park Sefton
283 E3 Waterloo Port Gwynd
52 B3 Waterlooville Hants
136 C1 Waterman Quarter Kent
176 C5 Watermead Gloucs
436 C2 Watermeetings S Lans
58 B4 Watermill E Susx

390 C5 Watermillock Cumb
137 F4 Watermoor Gloucs
243 G5 Water Newton Cambs
214 B1 Water Orton Warwks
140 D3 Waterperry Oxon
42 D2 Waterrow Somset
54 B1 Watersfield W Susx
326 D3 Watersheddings Oldham
339 H5 Waterside Bl w D
142 D4 Waterside Bucks
399 G5 Waterside Cumb
312 D3 Waterside Derbys
331 E2 Waterside Donc
433 F3 Waterside E Ayrs
466 C6 Waterside E Ayrs
466 C6 Waterside E Ayrs
484 D5 Waterside E Duns
96 A5 Waterside E Rens
484 D5 Waterside E Rens
365 G4 Waterslack Lancs
325 F3 Water's Nook Bolton
542 A7 Waterstein Highld
140 D3 Waterstock Oxon
125 F3 Waterston Pembks
167 E3 Water Stratford Bucks
271 E6 Waters Upton Wrekin
315 E3 Waterthorpe Sheff
561 E3 Waterton Abers
105 E4 Waterton V Glam
364 C2 Water Yeat Cumb
143 F5 Watford Herts
216 C6 Watford Nhants
237 H4 Watford Gap Birm
143 G6 Watford Heath Herts
106 B2 Watford Park Caerph
380 B3 Wath N York
369 F6 Wath N York
370 C4 Wath N York
372 C4 Wath N York
376 C2 Wath Brow Cumb
472 A5 Watherston Border
329 G4 Wath Upon Dearne Rothm
136 B4 Watledge Gloucs
110 B3 Watley's End S Glos
246 C2 Watlington Norfk
141 E6 Watlington Oxon
295 G5 Watnall Notts
376 B2 Watson Hill Cumb
589 G6 Watten Highld
224 D5 Wattisfield Suffk
200 D4 Wattisham Suffk
200 C4 Wattisham Stone Suffk
249 F5 Wattlefield Norfk
233 F2 Wattlesborough Heath Shrops
30 B4 Watton Dorset
360 C4 Watton E R Yk
248 B4 Watton Norfk
170 D6 Watton at Stone Herts
145 H5 Watton's Green Essex
485 F6 Wattston N Lans
131 G6 Wattstown Rhondd
106 D1 Wattsville Caerph
528 D5 Waulkmill Angus
410 D3 Waulkmill D & G
512 D4 Waulkmill P & K
528 D6 Waulkmills Angus
284 C2 Waun Gwynd
103 E3 Waunarlwydd Swans
150 C4 Waun Beddau Pembks
205 E3 Waun Fawr Cerdgn
283 F4 Waunfawr Gwynd
153 G2 Waungilwen Carmth
129 E4 Waungron Swans
132 C3 Waun-Lwyd Blae G
128 B4 Waun y Clyn Carmth
104 C2 Waun y Gilfach Brdgnd
168 C2 Wavendon M Keyn
168 C2 Wavendon Gate M Keyn
399 G5 Waverbridge Cumb
289 G2 Waverton Ches
399 G5 Waverton Cumb
309 E2 Wavertree Lpool
114 B6 Wawcott W Berk
347 G2 Wawne E R Yk
257 E4 Waxham Norfk
349 F4 Waxholme E R Yk
101 F2 Way Kent
19 G3 Waye Devon
161 G2 Wayend Street Herefs
98 B2 Wayfield Medway
29 G1 Wayford Somset
270 D1 Waymills Shrops
159 H6 Wayne Green Mons
290 C1 Way's Green Ches
39 E3 Waytown Devon
61 E5 Waytown Devon
30 B3 Waytown Dorset
42 A5 Way Village Devon
84 C2 Way Wick N Som
569 L4 Weachyburn Abers
64 B3 Weacombe Somset
139 E4 Weald Oxon
118 D2 Wealdstone Gt Lon
10 D2 Wearde Cnwll
356 B6 Weardley Leeds
84 D4 Weare Somset
39 G3 Weare Giffard Devon
393 E2 Wearhead Dur
66 C4 Wearne Somset
380 B4 Weasdale Cumb
253 G3 Weasenham All Saints Norfk
253 H3 Weasenham St Peter Norfk
326 A5 Weaste Salfd
95 G6 Weatherhill Surrey
213 G5 Weatheroak Hill Worcs
310 C5 Weaverham Ches
98 B3 Weavering Street Kent
274 A6 Weaverslake Staffs
374 B5 Weaverthorpe N York
84 C3 Webbington Somset
189 F1 Webheath Worcs
270 B5 Webscott Shrops
52 B2 Wecock Hants
560 C3 Wedderlairs Abers
101 E4 Weddington Kent
239 F6 Weddington Warwks
88 D5 Wedhampton Wilts
84 D5 Wedmore Somset
237 E5 Wednesbury Sandw
237 E6 Wednesbury Oak Sandw
236 D4 Wednesfield Wolves
297 F1 Weecar Notts
167 H6 Weedon Bucks
192 D3 Weedon Bec Nhants
192 D5 Weedon Lois Nhants
238 A4 Weeford Staffs
17 G2 Week Devon
19 G5 Week Devon
40 B2 Week Devon
41 E4 Week Devon
26 B1 Week Devon
72 C3 Week Hants
23 E3 Week Green Cnwll
218 B3 Weekley Nhants
185 H4 Weekmoor Somset
37 F2 Weeks IoW
23 E3 Week St Mary Cnwll
347 G2 Weel E R Yk
175 F5 Weeley Essex
176 C5 Weeley Heath Essex
334 C3 Weelsby NE Lin
524 C1 Weem P & K

272 D5 Weeping Cross Staffs
189 G3 Weethley Warwks
189 F4 Weethley Bank Warwks
189 G4 Weethley Bank Warwks
189 F4 Weethley Gate Warwks
223 F2 Weeting Norfk
349 G5 Weeton E R Yk
337 G3 Weeton Lancs
356 B5 Weeton N York
343 E2 Weetwood Leeds
289 H1 Weetwood Common Ches
122 B2 Weir Essex
340 D4 Weir Lancs
269 F5 Weirbrook Shrops
17 F6 Weir Quay Cnwll
606 E7 Weisdale Shet
315 H5 Welbeck Abbey Notts
249 E3 Welborne Norfk
298 B4 Welbourn Lincs
249 E3 Welbourne Common Norfk
372 C3 Welburn N York
372 D6 Welburn N York
384 B4 Welbury N York
278 D2 Welby Lincs
221 G2 Welches Dam Cambs
38 B4 Welcombe Devon
324 D1 Weld Bank Lancs
218 C2 Weldon Nhants
443 E5 Weldon Nthumb
216 D3 Welford Nhants
114 B5 Welford W Berk
190 A4 Welford-on-Avon Warwks
217 G1 Welham Leics
316 D3 Welham Notts
67 H3 Welham Somset
346 A3 Welhambridge E R Yk
144 B3 Welham Green Herts
92 C5 Well Hants
320 D5 Well Lincs
370 B3 Well N York
162 A2 Welland Worcs
162 B2 Welland Stone Worcs
514 D2 Wellbank Angus
340 B5 Well Bank Lancs
47 H1 Well Bottom Dorset
78 D4 Wellbrook E Susx
399 F1 Welldale D & G
117 E2 Well End Bucks
144 A5 Well End Herts
96 D6 Weller's Town Kent
190 D3 Wellesbourne Warwks
311 F2 Well Green Traffd
169 H4 Well Head Herts
342 A3 Well Heads Brad
96 C2 Well Hill Kent
115 E5 Wellhouse W Berk
120 C4 Welling Gt Lon
194 B1 Wellingborough Nhants
253 H5 Wellingham Norfk
298 B3 Wellingore Lincs
376 D4 Wellington Cumb
186 B5 Wellington Herefs
43 F3 Wellington Somset
235 E2 Wellington Wrekin
161 F1 Wellington Heath Herefs
343 G2 Wellington Hill Leeds
43 E3 Wellisford Somset
86 C3 Wellow BaNES
36 B3 Wellow IoW
334 C3 Wellow NE Lin
296 C1 Wellow Notts
71 F5 Wellow Wood Hants
115 G2 Well Place Oxon
171 F5 Wellpond Green Herts
342 D2 Wellroyd Leeds
85 G5 Wells Somset
239 F4 Wellsborough Leics
290 D4 Wells Green Ches
260 B3 Wells-next-the-sea Norfk
43 H2 Wellsprings Somset
97 G3 Well Street Kent
172 C6 Wellstye Green Essex
20 C5 Wellswood Torbay
15 G5 Welltown Cnwll
42 B6 Well Town Devon
487 E2 Wellwood Fife
245 H6 Welney Norfk
38 C3 Welsford Devon
270 A3 Welshampton Shrops
160 D6 Welsh Bicknor Gloucs
270 C2 Welsh End Shrops
269 G3 Welsh Frankton Shrops
119 E2 Welsh Harp Gt Lon
151 F4 Welsh Hook Pembks
160 B6 Welsh Newton Herefs
160 C6 Welsh Newton Common Herefs
232 D3 Welshpool Powys
105 H4 Welsh St Donats V Glam
174 D4 Welshwood Park Essex
19 F3 Welstor Devon
86 B4 Welton BaNES
400 C6 Welton Cumb
445 H4 Welton E Ayrs
347 E4 Welton E R Yk
318 C4 Welton Lincs
192 C1 Welton Nhants
318 C3 Welton Hill Lincs
321 E6 Welton le Marsh Lincs
319 H2 Welton le Wold Lincs
349 F5 Welwick E R Yk
144 B1 Welwyn Herts
144 C2 Welwyn Garden City Herts
270 C4 Wem Shrops
65 E4 Wembdon Somset
118 D3 Wembley Gt Lon
11 F4 Wembury Devon
40 D6 Wemworthy Devon
482 A6 Wemyss Bay Inver
205 F5 Wenallt Cerdgn
229 G1 Wenallt Gwynd
267 F1 Wenallt Gwynd
171 H2 Wendens Ambo Essex
166 C6 Wendlebury Oxon
254 B5 Wendling Norfk
142 B3 Wendover Bucks
142 B3 Wendover Dean Bucks
4 C2 Wendron Cnwll
196 D5 Wendy Cambs
15 F4 Wenfordbridge Cnwll
227 E4 Wenhaston Suffk
227 E4 Wenhaston Black Heath Suffk
220 B4 Wennington Cambs
120 D3 Wennington Gt Lon
366 C5 Wennington Lancs
294 B2 Wensley Derbys
369 F1 Wensley N York
330 A1 Wentbridge Wakefd
209 G1 Wentnor Shrops
221 G4 Wentworth Cambs
329 F5 Wentworth Rothm
106 B5 Wenvoe V Glam
185 G4 Weobley Herefs
185 H4 Weobley Marsh Herefs
213 F3 Weoley Castle Birm
54 B3 Wepham W Susx
308 C6 Wepre Flints
246 D4 Wereham Norfk
246 D4 Wereham Row Norfk
291 F4 Wereton Staffs
236 C4 Wergs Wolves
264 C2 Wern Gwynd

132 B1 Wern Powys
233 E2 Wern Powys
269 E5 Wern Powys
269 E3 Wern Shrops
102 D3 Wern Swans
268 D4 Wern ddu Shrops
326 D4 Werneth Oldham
312 C1 Werneth Low Tamesd
102 D3 Wernffrwd Swans
159 F5 Wern-Gifford Mons
269 F5 Wernlas Shrops
103 E3 Wern-olau Swans
133 G2 Wernrheolydd Mons
105 F3 Wern Tarw Brdgnd
133 G3 Wern-y-cwrt Mons
308 B6 Wern-y-gaer Flints
23 G5 Werrington Cnwll
243 H4 Werrington C Pete
292 B5 Werrington Staffs
309 H5 Wervin Ches
356 B5 Wescoe Hill N York
338 B3 Wesham Lancs
294 D3 Wessington Derbys
294 D3 Wessington Green Derbys
105 G6 West Aberthaw V Glam
61 E5 Westacott Devon
253 F4 West Acre Norfk
118 D3 West Acton Gt Lon
165 H2 West Adderbury Oxon
475 E5 West Allerdean Nthumb
431 F5 West Allotment N Tyne
12 C4 West Alvington Devon
70 C1 West Amesbury Wilts
41 G2 West Anstey Devon
383 F6 West Appleton N York
343 E4 West Ardsley Leeds
466 C3 West Arthurlie E Rens
319 H5 West Ashby Lincs
60 D4 West Ashford Devon
53 E3 West Ashling W Susx
87 F3 West Ashton Wilts
394 D4 West Auckland Dur
374 B3 West Ayton N York
64 C5 West Bagborough Somset
515 F2 West Balmirmer Angus
132 D3 West Bank Blae G
309 H3 West Bank Halton
319 F3 West Barkwith Lincs
386 D2 West Barnby N York
119 E6 West Barnes Gt Lon
490 B4 West Barns E Loth
260 A5 West Barsham Norfk
30 B4 West Bay Dorset
261 F4 West Beckham Norfk
118 B5 West Bedfont Surrey
468 D2 West Benhar N Lans
460 D5 West Bennan N Ayrs
100 C3 Westbere Kent
174 C4 West Bergholt Essex
30 C5 West Bexington Dorset
253 E4 West Bilney Norfk
393 E2 West Blackdene Dur
17 G2 West Blackdown Devon
55 G3 West Blatchington Br & H
450 D2 West Bold Border
406 B2 West Boldon S Tyne
297 G6 Westborough Lincs
34 C2 Westbourne Bmouth
201 F5 Westbourne Suffk
52 D3 Westbourne W Susx
119 F3 Westbourne Green Gt Lon
68 C4 West Bourton Dorset
342 C3 West Bowling Brad
353 E6 West Bradford Lancs
67 F2 West Bradley Somset
328 D2 West Bretton Wakefd
276 C2 West Bridgford Notts
119 F4 West Brompton Gt Lon
213 F1 West Bromwich Sandw
185 E6 Westbrook Herefs
101 F1 Westbrook Kent
93 G6 Westbrook Surrey
310 B2 Westbrook Warrtn
114 C5 Westbrook W Berk
87 H1 Westbrook Wilts
225 F3 Westbrook Green Norfk
143 E3 Westbrook Hay Herts
274 A3 West Broughton Derbys
61 G5 West Buckland Devon
43 G3 West Buckland Somset
467 G2 Westburn S Lans
540 C5 West Burnside Abers
606 C6 West Burrafirth Shet
368 D2 West Burton N York
54 A2 West Burton W Susx
166 D2 Westbury Bucks
233 G3 Westbury Shrops
87 F4 Westbury Wilts
87 F4 Westbury Leigh Wilts
135 G2 Westbury-on-Severn Gloucs
109 G4 Westbury on Trym Bristl
85 F5 Westbury-sub-Mendip Somset
404 D6 West Butsfield Dur
332 A3 West Butterwick N Linc
337 G3 Westby Lancs
278 D4 Westby Lincs
94 A2 West Byfleet Surrey
251 G2 West Caister Norfk
469 G2 West Calder W Loth
67 F5 West Camel Somset
355 H6 West Carlton Leeds
347 G3 West Carr C KuH
331 F3 West Carr N Linc
114 B2 West Challow Oxon
12 D4 West Charleton Devon
30 C1 West Chelborough Dorset
443 G5 West Chevington Nthumb
76 A6 West Chiltington W Susx
54 C1 West Chiltington Common W Susx
45 F5 West Chinnock Somset
431 F6 West Chirton N Tyne
88 D4 West Chisenbury Wilts
94 A4 West Clandon Surrey
34 C2 West Cliff Bmouth
387 E2 West Cliff N York
83 F2 West Cliffe Kent
122 D3 Westcliff-on-Sea Sthend
577 J2 West Clyne Highld
45 G5 West Coker Somset
19 G5 Westcombe Devon
66 D4 Westcombe Somset
67 H2 Westcombe Somset
50 D4 West Common Hants
30 D4 West Compton Dorset
67 F1 West Compton Somset
395 G3 West Cornforth Dur
114 A2 Westcot Oxon
240 C4 Westcotes C Leic
141 F1 Westcott Bucks
27 G2 Westcott Devon
233 G4 Westcott Shrops
94 C5 Westcott Surrey
165 G2 Westcott Barton Oxon
99 F2 Westcourt Wilts
5 E5 West Cowick E R Yk
179 H3 Westcroft M Keyn
213 D4 Westcroft Wolves
98 B3 West Cross Kent
103 G4 West Cross Swans
111 F3 West Crudwell Wilts
22 D6 West Curry Cnwll

400 B5 West Curthwaite Cumb
57 E5 Westdean E Susx
71 E4 West Dean Hants
53 F2 West Dean W Susx
243 G3 West Deeping Lincs
125 F2 West Denant Pembks
55 G3 Westdene Br & H
514 D2 West Denside Angus
405 E1 West Denton N u Ty
323 G6 West Derby Lpool
246 D4 West Dereham Norfk
311 G1 West Didsbury Manch
455 E5 West Ditchburn Nthumb
60 D3 West Down Devon
72 A2 West Down Hants
88 B5 Westdown Camp Wilts
15 E6 West Downs Cnwll
22 A6 Westdowns Cnwll
118 B4 West Drayton Gt Lon
316 D3 West Drayton Notts
589 G2 West Dunnet Highld
118 D3 West Ealing Gt Lon
294 C2 West Edge Derbys
347 F4 West Ella E R Yk
194 D4 West End Beds
195 F2 West End Beds
132 D5 West End Caerph
400 B3 West End Cumb
331 E3 West End Donc
47 G4 West End Dorset
346 D3 West End E R Yk
348 C3 West End E R Yk
349 E4 West End E R Yk
360 C2 West End E R Yk
361 F3 West End E R Yk
263 F4 West End Gwynd
51 E2 West End Hants
73 F2 West End Hants
144 C3 West End Herts
99 E3 West End Kent
100 C2 West End Kent
342 C4 West End Kirk
339 H4 West End Lancs
351 F2 West End Lancs
342 D2 West End Leeds
275 G6 West End Leics
300 C5 West End Lincs
335 E5 West End Lincs
134 A5 West End Mons
248 B3 West End Norfk
251 G2 West End Norfk
109 E6 West End N Som
344 C1 West End N York
344 D2 West End N York
355 F3 West End N York
115 F2 West End Oxon
165 E5 Westend Oxon
110 C2 West End S Glos
134 D6 Westend S Glos
136 C5 West End S Glos
469 F5 West End S Lans
68 A3 West End Somset
85 G4 West End Somset
227 F3 West End Suffk
51 G3 West End Surrey
74 C1 West End Surrey
92 D6 West End Surrey
93 F2 West End Surrey
94 C2 West End Surrey
116 D5 West End W & M
117 E5 West End W & M
69 F5 West End Wilts
69 G5 West End Wilts
111 H4 West End Wilts
139 G4 West End Worcs
163 G2 West End Worcs
55 E1 West End W Susx
91 H2 West End Green Hants
402 D1 Westend Town Nthumb
105 E6 West-end Town V Glam
82 B3 Westenhanger Kent
549 J6 Wester Aberchalder Highld
577 J7 Wester Arboll Highld
484 C5 Wester Auchinloch N Lans
500 C1 Wester Balgedie P & K
490 C4 Wester Broomhouse E Loth
569 L3 Wester Culbeuchly Abers
588 E6 Westerdale Highld
385 H3 Westerdale N York
486 D5 Wester Dechmont W Loth
450 C5 Wester Deloraine Border
526 D6 Wester Denoon Angus
538 C5 Wester Eggie Angus
525 H7 Wester Essendy P & K
451 E5 Wester Essenside Border
606 E7 Westerfield Shet
201 G5 Westerfield Suffk
557 E1 Wester Fintray Abers
557 L5 Wester Fodderletter Moray
527 F5 Wester Foffarty Angus
53 G3 Westergate W Susx
570 D3 Wester Greenskares Abers
575 L5 Wester Gruinards Highld
487 H6 Wester Hailes C Edin
96 B4 Westerham Kent
405 E1 Westerhope N u Ty
451 G2 Wester Housebyres Border
450 D4 Wester Kershope Border
565 L2 Wester Lealty Highld
110 B4 Westerleigh S Glos
110 C4 Westerleigh Hill S Glos
399 G5 Western Bank Cumb
502 C3 Western Newburn Fife
83 F2 Western Heights Kent
405 G6 Western Hill Dur
240 C3 Western Park C Leic
423 H2 Western Parkgate D & G
605 H3 Wester Quarff Shet
604 E2 Wester Skeld Shet
529 E4 Westerton Angus
395 E3 Westerton Dur
53 F3 Westerton W Susx
525 H2 Westerton of Runavey P & K
604 E2 Westerwick Shet
95 E2 West Ewell Surrey
97 H4 West Farleigh Kent
192 B4 West Farndon Nhants
269 F4 West Felton Shrops
514 C3 West Ferry C Dund
83 F1 Westfield Angus
576 E2 Westfield Highld
88 A4 Westfield BaNES
388 A4 Westfield Cumb
58 D3 Westfield E Susx
52 C5 Westfield Highld
187 G5 Westfield Herefs
588 D4 Westfield Highld
342 D3 Westfield Kirk
342 C1 Westfield Leeds
348 B6 West Field N Linc
248 C3 Westfield Norfk
397 E5 Westfield R & Cl
315 E3 Westfield Sheff
93 H3 Westfield Surrey
485 E5 Westfield W Loth
486 B5 Westfield W Loth
357 H4 West Field York
46 D3 Westfield Dorset
160 B1 Westfields Herefs
90 D1 West Fields W Berk

526 A5 Westfields of Rattray P & K
98 B2 Westfield Sole Kent
56 D3 West Firle E Susx
455 F4 West Fleetham Nthumb
453 H3 West Flodden Nthumb
565 L3 Westford Highld
43 F3 Westford Somset
343 G3 West Garforth Leeds
401 G6 Westgarth Hill Cumb
393 F2 Westgate Dur
331 E3 Westgate N Linc
260 C3 Westgate Norfk
342 D4 Westgate Hill Brad
101 F1 Westgate on Sea Kent
255 G3 Westgate Street Norfk
114 C2 West Ginge Oxon
326 C5 West Gorton Manch
89 F2 West Grafton Wilts
329 F3 West Green Barns
119 G2 West Green Gt Lon
92 B3 West Green Hants
77 E2 West Green W Susx
71 E4 West Grimstead Wilts
76 C5 West Grinstead W Susx
344 D4 West Haddlesey N York
216 D5 West Haddon Nhants
115 E2 West Hagbourne Oxon
212 D4 West Hagley Worcs
559 F4 Westhall Abers
227 E3 Westhall Suffk
275 G1 West Hallam Derbys
138 C2 Westhall Hill Oxon
346 D5 West Halton N Linc
32 B4 Westham Dorset
57 G4 West Ham E Susx
120 A3 West Ham Gt Lon
91 G4 West Ham Hants
84 D5 Westham Somset
53 F3 Westhampnett W Susx
119 E2 West Hampstead Gt Lon
314 D4 West Handley Derbys
139 F6 West Hanney Oxon
147 E5 West Hanningfield Essex
343 H6 West Hardwick Wakefd
224 C2 West Harling Norfk
384 C5 West Harlsey N York
85 G3 West Harptree BaNES
118 C2 West Harrow Gt Lon
74 B5 West Harting W Susx
406 B2 West Harton S Tyne
44 B3 West Hatch Somset
69 F4 West Hatch Wilts
66 C1 Westhay Somset
324 A3 Westhead Lancs
246 B3 West Head Norfk
213 F4 West Heath Birm
291 G2 West Heath Ches
120 C4 West Heath Gt Lon
91 F3 West Heath Hants
93 E3 West Heath Hants
582 D6 West Helmsdale Highld
119 E2 West Hendon Gt Lon
114 C2 West Hendred Oxon
606 B2 West Heogaland Shet
406 A4 West Herrington Sundld
373 H4 West Heslerton N York
84 C2 West Hewish N Som
186 D6 Westhide Herefs
557 E3 Westhill Abers
28 A4 West Hill Devon
348 D2 Westhill E R Yk
361 F1 West Hill E R Yk
58 D4 West Hill E Susx
119 E5 West Hill Gt Lon
566 C8 Westhill Highld
109 E4 West Hill N Som
68 B4 West Hill Somset
87 F1 West Hill Wilts
77 F3 West Hill W Susx
528 B6 West Hills Angus
77 G3 West Hoathly W Susx
33 F2 West Holme Dorset
431 F5 West Holywell N Tyne
382 B3 West Hope Dur
186 B4 Westhope Herefs
210 B2 Westhope Shrops
121 F2 West Horndon Essex
192 B4 Westhorpe Nhants
280 B3 Westhorpe Notts
296 C4 Westhorpe Suffk
224 D6 West Horrington Somset
85 G5 West Horsley Surrey
94 B4 West Horton Nthumb
454 C3 West Hougham Kent
83 E2 Westhoughton Bolton
325 E3 West Houlland Shet
606 C7 West Houses Derbys
295 E3 Westhouses Derbys
300 B4 West Houses Lincs
48 C5 West Howe Bmouth
63 E4 West Howetown Somset
94 D1 Westhumble Surrey
236 A2 West Huntspill Somset
280 C5 West Hurn Dorset
49 E5 West Hyde Herts
516 B8 West Hynish Ag & B
82 B4 West Hythe Kent
61 H2 West Ilkerton Devon
114 D3 West Ilsley W Berk
609 H3 West Ing Shet
164 A2 Westington Gloucs
52 D4 West Itchenor W Susx
405 F1 West Jesmond N u Ty
300 C2 West Keal Lincs
112 D6 West Kennett Wilts
119 E4 West Kensington Gt Lon
465 K5 West Kilbride N Ayrs
97 E2 West Kingsdown Kent
54 C4 West Kingston W Susx
111 E4 West Kington Wilts
111 E4 West Kington Wick Wilts
308 B2 West Kirby Wirral
373 G4 West Knapton N York
32 C2 West Knighton Dorset
69 E3 West Knoyle Wilts
405 E4 West Kyo Dur
11 H3 Westlake Devon
66 C6 West Lambrook Somset
171 F5 Westland Green Herts
291 G6 Westlands Staffs
188 C2 Westlands Worcs
83 F1 West Langdon Kent
576 E2 West Langwell Highld
88 A4 West Lavington Wilts
74 D5 West Lavington W Susx
382 D3 West Layton N York
406 C5 West Lea Dur
47 F1 Westlea Nthumb
112 D6 Westlea Wilts
276 B4 West Leake Notts
453 F2 West Learmouth Nthumb
25 G1 West Leigh Devon
39 G2 Westleigh Devon
43 E4 Westleigh Devon
52 C3 West Leigh Hants
64 B5 West Leigh Somset
325 E4 Westleigh Wigan
227 E6 Westleton Suffk
253 G4 West Lexham Norfk
233 G3 Westley Shrops
199 G2 Westley Suffk
121 G2 Westley Heights Essex

198 C2 Westley Waterless Cambs
358 B1 West Lilling N York
141 G2 Westlington Bucks
470 C4 West Linton Border
400 C2 Westlinton Cumb
74 B4 West Liss Hants
110 D4 West Littleton S Glos
114 C2 West Lockinge Oxon
9 G3 West Looe Cnwll
63 F2 West Luccombe Somset
33 E3 West Lulworth Dorset
374 A6 West Lutton N York
67 F3 West Lydford Somset
186 D6 West Lydiatt Herefs
62 A2 West Lyn Devon
44 C2 West Lyng Somset
252 C3 West Lynn Norfk
187 H5 West Malvern Worcs
162 D2 Westmancote Worcs
52 D2 West Marden W Susx
316 D5 West Markham Notts
101 E3 Westmarsh Kent
334 C2 West Marsh NE Lin
354 A4 West Marton N York
69 E5 West Melbury Dorset
329 G4 West Melton Rothm
73 F5 West Meon Hants
73 F4 West Meon Woodlands Hants
148 D2 West Mersea Essex
56 A2 Westmeston E Susx
169 H3 Westmill Herts
171 E4 Westmill Herts
30 C3 West Milton Dorset
119 F4 Westminster Gt Lon
123 E5 West Minster Kent
118 C6 West Molesey Surrey
431 F5 West Monkseaton N Tyne
44 B2 West Monkton Somset
431 E5 West Moor N Tyne
388 D2 Westmoor End Cumb
48 D4 West Moors Dorset
47 H5 West Morden Dorset
355 E6 West Morton Brad
67 F5 West Mudford Somset
527 E4 Westmuir Angus
528 C2 West Muir Angus
372 C4 West Ness N York
602 D6 Westness Ork
399 E6 Westnewton Cumb
348 C2 West Newton E R Yk
252 D2 West Newton Norfk
453 H3 Westnewton Nthumb
44 B2 West Newton Somset
119 G5 West Norwood Gt Lon
25 G3 West Nymph Devon
406 B1 Westoe S Tyne
19 H3 West Ogwell Devon
86 C1 Weston BaNES
312 A5 Weston Ches
50 D3 Weston C Sotn
28 B2 Weston Devon
28 C5 Weston Devon
30 C1 Weston Dorset
32 B5 Weston Dorset
291 E4 Weston Halton
309 H3 Weston Halton
73 H5 Weston Hants
170 C3 Weston Herts
280 C5 Weston Lincs
192 C5 Weston Nhants
297 E1 Weston Notts
355 G5 Weston N York
355 H3 Weston N York
126 A2 Weston Pembks
185 G3 Weston Shrops
209 F5 Weston Shrops
234 D6 Weston Shrops
269 E4 Weston Shrops
270 D4 Weston Shrops
469 G5 Weston S Lans
273 E4 Weston Staffs
227 E2 Weston Suffk
114 B5 Weston W Berk
67 G4 Weston Bampfylde Somset
160 D1 Weston Beggard Herefs
111 F2 Westonbirt Gloucs
217 G1 Weston by Welland Nhants
72 D2 Weston Colley Hants
198 C4 Weston Colville Cambs
51 E2 Weston Common C Sotn
270 A4 Westoncommon Shrops
92 A5 Weston Corbett Hants
222 D4 Weston Ditch Suffk
193 G2 Weston Favell Nhants
198 C4 Weston Green Cambs
255 F5 Weston Green Norfk
94 D1 Weston Green Surrey
236 A2 Weston Heath Shrops
280 C5 Weston Hills Lincs
215 F2 Weston in Arden Warwks
169 E3 Westoning Beds
109 E5 Weston in Gordano N Som
271 H5 Weston Jones Staffs
255 F4 Weston Longville Norfk
269 H4 Weston Lullingfields Shrops
35 H3 Weston Manor IoW
11 E2 Weston Mill C Plym
190 B4 Weston-on-Avon Warwks
166 B6 Weston-on-the-Green Oxon
275 F4 Weston-on-Trent Derbys
92 A5 Weston Patrick Hants
309 G3 Weston Point Ches
269 E2 Weston Rhyn Shrops
190 B4 Weston Sands Warwks
164 A1 Weston-Sub-Edge Gloucs
84 A2 Weston-super-Mare Somset
68 B1 Weston Town Somset
142 A2 Weston Turville Bucks
236 B2 Weston-under-Lizard Staffs
161 E5 Weston under Penyard Herefs
215 F6 Weston under Wetherley Warwks
294 B6 Weston Underwood Derbys
194 B4 Weston Underwood M Keyn
269 H4 Westonwharf Shrops
65 G4 Westonzoyland Somset
47 F1 West Orchard Dorset
112 D6 West Overton Wilts
359 E1 Westow N York
64 B5 Westowe Somset
43 F5 Westown Devon
513 F4 Westown P & K
23 G4 West Panson Devon
347 G4 West Park C KuH
396 C3 West Park Hartpl
343 E2 West Park Leeds
324 C5 West Park St Hel
406 B1 West Park S Tyne
48 D5 West Parley Dorset
393 F5 West Pasture Dur
97 F4 West Peckham Kent

405 F4 West Pelton Dur
67 E2 West Pennard Somset
7 E1 West Pentire Cnwll
195 G1 West Perry Cambs
133 E5 West Pontnewydd Torfn
250 B4 West Poringland Norfk
62 D2 West Porlock Somset
66 B6 Westport Somset
8 A5 West Portholland Cnwll
483 F5 West Porton Rens
46 D3 West Pulham Dorset
39 E4 West Putford Devon
64 B3 West Quantoxhead Somset
486 B4 Westquarter Falk
106 B5 Westra V Glam
405 H5 West Rainton Dur
318 C2 West Rasen Lincs
334 B5 West Ravendale NE Lin
253 H2 West Raynham Norfk
316 C3 West Retford Notts
115 F3 Westridge Green W Berk
469 E1 Westrigg W Loth
408 B2 West Ringuinea D & G
136 B3 Westrip Gloucs
111 F5 Westrop Wilts
115 E5 Westrop Green W Berk
384 C4 West Rounton N York
222 D4 West Row Suffk
253 G2 West Rudham Norfk
118 B2 West Ruislip Gt Lon
333 E3 Westrum Lincs
261 G3 West Runton Norfk
473 E5 Westruther Border
245 F5 Westry Cambs
472 B1 West Saltoun E Loth
26 C2 West Sandford Devon
608 E7 West Sandwick Shet
342 A3 West Scholes Brad
369 E3 West Scrafton N York
85 H6 West Shepton Somset
557 F5 Westside Abers
132 C3 West Side Blae G
603 G5 West Side Ork
422 D2 West Skelston D & G
431 E2 West Sleekburn Nthumb
257 F6 West Somerton Norfk
34 D2 West Southbourne Bmouth
32 C2 West Stafford Dorset
331 G6 West Stockwith Notts
19 E3 West Stoke Devon
66 D6 West Stoke Somset
53 E3 West Stoke W Susx
381 F4 West Stonesdale N York
84 D5 West Stoughton Somset
68 C5 West Stour Dorset
100 D3 West Stourmouth Kent
223 G5 West Stow Suffk
88 D2 West Stowell Wilts
586 C4 West Strathan Highld
72 D1 West Stratton Hants
98 D4 West Street Kent
101 F5 West Street Kent
121 H4 West Street Medway
224 C5 West Street Suffk
370 B4 West Tanfield N York
15 H6 West Taphouse Cnwll
462 D1 West Tarbert Ag & B
54 D4 West Tarring W Susx
452 B2 West Third Border
443 F4 West Thirston Nthumb
52 D4 West Thorney W Susx
315 E4 Westthorpe Derbys
121 E4 West Thurrock Thurr
121 G4 West Tilbury Thurr
73 G4 West Tisted Hants
247 G6 West Tofts Norfk
512 D3 West Tofts P & K
6 C5 West Tolgus Cnwll
319 E3 West Torrington Lincs
26 D3 West Town Devon
38 D3 West Town Devon
52 C5 West Town Hants
186 A2 West Town Herefs
109 E6 West Town N Som
67 E2 West Town Somset
85 F2 West Town Somset
55 G1 West Town W Susx
71 F3 West Tytherley Hants
342 A5 West Vale Calder
323 G5 Westvale Knows
396 C2 West View Hartpl
105 F5 West Village V Glam
12 C4 Westville Devon
295 G5 Westville Notts
245 G2 West Walton Norfk
399 H6 Westward Cumb
39 F2 Westward Ho! Devon
9 F3 West Watergate Cnwll
143 G5 West Watford Herts
24 B4 Westweekmoor Devon
99 F5 Westwell Kent
138 C2 Westwell Oxon
99 F5 Westwell Leacon Kent
71 F6 West Wellow Hants
111 F6 Westwells Wilts
501 F6 West Wemyss Fife
513 E3 West Whitefield P & K
197 F1 Westwick Cambs
382 C1 Westwick Dur
256 B4 Westwick Norfk
84 C2 West Wick N Som
198 C5 West Wickham Cambs
98 A1 West Wickham Gt Lon
126 A3 West Williamston Pembks
298 B6 West Willoughby Lincs
252 C4 West Winch Norfk
71 E3 West Winterslow Wilts
52 D5 West Wittering W Susx
369 E2 West Witton N York
243 H5 West Woodburn Nthumb
90 B2 West Woodhay W Berk
214 D4 Westwood Heath Covtry
86 D6 West Woodlands Somset
174 C3 Westwood Park Essex
325 H5 Westwood Park Salfd
331 F5 Westwoodside N Linc
74 A2 West Worldham Hants
41 F5 West Worlington Devon
54 D4 West Worthing W Susx
198 B4 West Wratting Cambs
141 H6 West Wycombe Bucks
404 D2 West Wylam Nthumb
310 C2 Westy Warrtn
111 E4 West Yatton Wilts
608 F8 West Yell Shet
65 F5 West Yeo Somset
97 E2 West Yoke Kent
38 C4 West Youlstone Cnwll
122 C6 Wetham Green Kent
400 D4 Wetheral Cumb
401 E3 Wetheral Plain Cumb
357 E5 Wetherby Leeds

200 D2 **Wetherden** Suffk
200 D1 **Wetherden Upper Town** Suffk
201 F1 **Wetheringsett** Suffk
173 E3 **Wethersfield** Essex
606 E4 **Wethersta** Shet
201 F2 **Wetherup Street** Suffk
292 C5 **Wetley Rocks** Staffs
274 D5 **Wetmore** Staffs
290 C2 **Wettenhall** Ches
290 C2 **Wettenhall Green** Ches
210 A2 **Wettles** Shrops
293 F3 **Wetton** Staffs
360 A3 **Wetwang** E R Yk
271 H3 **Wetwood** Staffs
89 G3 **Wexcombe** Wilts
117 G3 **Wexham Street** Bucks
261 F3 **Weybourne** Norfk
93 E5 **Weybourne** Surrey
226 A3 **Weybread** Suffk
94 B1 **Weybridge** Surrey
29 F2 **Weycroft** Devon
588 E3 **Weydale** Highld
89 H5 **Weyhill** Hants
32 B4 **Weymouth** Dorset
184 D3 **Weythel** Powys
167 H3 **Whaddon** Bucks
197 E5 **Whaddon** Cambs
136 B2 **Whaddon** Gloucs
163 E5 **Whaddon** Gloucs
70 D4 **Whaddon** Wilts
87 F2 **Whaddon** Wilts
196 D5 **Whaddon Gap** Cambs
391 E5 **Whale** Cumb
315 G5 **Whaley** Derbys
312 D3 **Whaley Bridge** Derbys
315 G5 **Whaley Thorns** Notts
583 K1 **Whaligoe** Highld
340 A2 **Whalley** Lancs
340 A2 **Whalley Banks** Lancs
326 B6 **Whalley Range** Manch
324 B3 **Whalleys** Lancs
430 B3 **Whalton** Nthumb
353 F2 **Wham** N York
280 D5 **Whaplode** Lincs
244 D2 **Whaplode Drove** Lincs
280 D5 **Whaplode St Catherine** Lincs
191 G4 **Wharf** Warwks
367 F6 **Wharfe** N York
338 B2 **Wharles** Lancs
194 C6 **Wharley End** Beds
403 F1 **Wharmley** Nthumb
328 D6 **Wharncliffe Side** Sheff
359 G1 **Wharram le Street** N York
310 D6 **Wharton** Ches
186 B3 **Wharton** Herefs
332 A6 **Wharton** Lincs
310 D6 **Wharton Green** Ches
383 E3 **Whashton** N York
365 G3 **Whasset** Cumb
47 F4 **Whatcombe** Dorset
191 E6 **Whatcote** Warwks
238 C5 **Whateley** Warwks
200 D5 **Whatfield** Suffk
29 G1 **Whatley** Somset
86 C5 **Whatley** Somset
58 C3 **Whatlington** E Susx
211 E5 **Whatmore** Shrops
82 B2 **Whatsole Street** Kent
294 C4 **Whatstandwell** Derbys
277 F2 **Whatton** Notts
410 D3 **Whauphill** D & G
382 A4 **Whaw** N York
3 G2 **Wheal Alfred** Cnwll
7 E5 **Wheal Baddon** Cnwll
6 D5 **Wheal Busy** Cnwll
7 E3 **Wheal Frances** Cnwll
6 D3 **Wheal Kitty** Cnwll
6 D5 **Wheal Rose** Cnwll
4 B2 **Wheal Vor** Cnwll
251 F6 **Wheatacre** Norfk
294 D3 **Wheatcroft** Derbys
135 H3 **Wheatenhurst** Gloucs
234 B4 **Wheathall** Shrops
143 H2 **Wheathampstead** Herts
211 E3 **Wheathill** Shrops
67 F3 **Wheathill** Somset
91 E2 **Wheat Hold** Hants
341 H4 **Wheatley** Calder
330 C4 **Wheatley** Donc
74 B1 **Wheatley** Hants
140 C2 **Wheatley** Oxon
396 A2 **Wheatley Hill** Dur
330 C4 **Wheatley Hills** Donc
340 C2 **Wheatley Lane** Lancs
330 C3 **Wheatley Park** Donc
236 B2 **Wheaton Aston** Staffs
63 E4 **Wheddon Cross** Somset
558 B4 **Wheedlemont** Abers
82 C1 **Wheeelbarrow Town** Kent
12 C2 **Wheeldon** Devon
141 H6 **Wheeler End** Bucks
75 E1 **Wheelerstreet** Surrey
291 E3 **Wheelock** Ches
291 E3 **Wheelock Heath** Ches
339 F5 **Wheelton** Lancs
538 D5 **Wheen** Angus
344 B4 **Wheldale** Wakefd
358 C5 **Wheldrake** York
138 B5 **Whelford** Gloucs
324 D3 **Whelley** Wigan
142 D4 **Whelpley Hill** Bucks
389 H2 **Whelpo** Cumb
200 B5 **Whelp Street** Suffk
308 B4 **Whelston** Flints
170 D5 **Whempstead** Herts
372 B6 **Whenby** N York
199 G3 **Whepstead** Suffk
3 E4 **Wherry Town** Cnwll
176 C1 **Wherstead** Suffk
72 A1 **Wherwell** Hants
313 F4 **Wheston** Derbys
30 C3 **Whetley** Dorset
30 B2 **Whetley Cross** Dorset
97 G5 **Whetsted** Kent
240 B5 **Whetstone** Leics
210 A3 **Whettleton** Shrops
362 C5 **Whicham** Cumb
165 E3 **Whichford** Warwks
405 E2 **Whickham** Gatesd
60 D4 **Whiddon** Devon
25 G4 **Whiddon Down** Devon
468 A2 **Whifflet** N Lans
527 G6 **Whigstreet** Angus
192 D3 **Whilton** Nhants
192 D2 **Whilton Locks** Nhants
23 H2 **Whimble** Devon
27 G3 **Whimple** Devon
256 D4 **Whimpwell Green** Norfk
248 C3 **Whinburgh** Norfk
383 H1 **Whinfield** Darltn
468 A1 **Whinhall** N Lans
337 H2 **Whin Lane End** Lancs
295 H2 **Whinney Hill** Notts
329 H6 **Whinney Hill** Rothm
412 D4 **Whinnieliegate** D & G
561 G3 **Whinnyfold** Abers
339 G4 **Whinny Heights** Bl w D
396 A6 **Whinny Hill** S on T
485 F1 **Whins of Milton** Stirlg
341 H2 **Whins Wood** Brad
43 E4 **Whipcott** Devon
51 F6 **Whippingham** IoW

14 A6 **Whipsiderry** Cnwll
169 E6 **Whipsnade** Beds
27 E4 **Whipton** Devon
312 A4 **Whirley Grove** Ches
314 C3 **Whirlow** Sheff
314 C3 **Whirlow Brook** Sheff
297 H1 **Whisby** Lincs
241 H2 **Whissendine** Rutlnd
254 B3 **Whissonsett** Norfk
311 G5 **Whisterfield** Ches
495 E6 **Whistlefield** Ag & B
116 C3 **Whistley Green** Wokham
165 H4 **Whistlow** Oxon
194 A2 **Whiston** Nhants
315 F2 **Whiston** Rothm
236 C2 **Whiston** Staffs
292 D5 **Whiston** Staffs
324 B5 **Whiston** St Hel
309 G1 **Whiston Cross** Knows
236 A4 **Whiston Cross** Shrops
238 C6 **Whitacre Heath** Warwks
390 C4 **Whitbarrow Village** Cumb
362 C5 **Whitbeck** Cumb
187 G3 **Whitbourne** Herefs
87 E5 **Whitbourne Moor** Wilts
406 C2 **Whitburn** S Tyne
469 E2 **Whitburn** W Loth
309 E4 **Whitby** Ches
387 E2 **Whitby** N York
309 E5 **Whitbyheath** Ches
109 H6 **Whitchurch** BaNES
167 H5 **Whitchurch** Bucks
106 B4 **Whitchurch** Cardif
17 G4 **Whitchurch** Devon
90 D5 **Whitchurch** Hants
160 C6 **Whitchurch** Herefs
150 C4 **Whitchurch** Pembks
270 C1 **Whitchurch** Shrops
68 B5 **Whitchurch** Somset
29 G4 **Whitchurch Canonicorum** Dorset
115 G4 **Whitchurch Hill** Oxon
115 G4 **Whitchurch-on-Thames** Oxon
32 C2 **Whitcombe** Dorset
67 G5 **Whitcombe** Somset
209 G1 **Whitcot** Shrops
209 E3 **Whitcott Keysett** Shrops
568 D6 **Whiteacen** Moray
100 B6 **Whiteacre** Kent
173 F3 **Whiteash Green** Essex
43 E4 **White Ball** Somset
339 G4 **Whitebirk** Bl w D
549 H6 **Whitebridge** Highld
134 C3 **Whitebrook** Mons
95 F5 **Whitebushes** Surrey
560 D6 **Whitecairns** Abers
339 E1 **Whitechapel** Lancs
186 D5 **Whitechurch Maund** Herefs
134 D2 **Whitecliff** Gloucs
400 D3 **Whiteclosegate** Cumb
173 H4 **White Colne** Essex
339 F6 **White Coppice** Lancs
342 D2 **Whitecote** Leeds
488 C5 **Whitecraig** E Loth
466 D3 **Whitecraigs** E Rens
135 E3 **Whitecroft** Gloucs
483 H5 **Whitecrook** W Duns
85 G3 **White Cross** BaNES
85 H3 **White Cross** BaNES
3 F3 **Whitecross** Cnwll
4 C4 **White Cross** Cnwll
7 G2 **White Cross** Cnwll
9 E3 **Whitecross** Cnwll
14 D4 **Whitecross** Cnwll
30 B3 **Whitecross** Dorset
486 C4 **Whitecross** Falk
160 B1 **White Cross** Herefs
66 C5 **Whitecross** Somset
84 B5 **White Cross** Somset
272 C5 **Whitecross** Staffs
68 C3 **White Cross** Wilts
221 G4 **White Cross Hill** Cambs
162 A3 **White End** Worcs
576 E6 **Whiteface** Highld
460 B1 **Whitefarland** N Ayrs
432 C3 **Whitefaulds** S Ayrs
326 B3 **Whitefield** Bury
47 G6 **Whitefield** Devon
43 E2 **Whitefield** Somset
309 G2 **Whitefield Lane End** Knows
445 H4 **Whiteflat** E Ayrs
559 G4 **Whiteford** Abers
310 C6 **Whitegate** Ches
326 C4 **White Gate** Oldham
29 F1 **White Gate** Somset
233 F5 **White Grit** Powys
339 G5 **Whitehall** Bl w D
109 H5 **Whitehall** Bristl
43 F5 **Whitehall** Devon
60 D4 **Whitehall** Devon
92 B4 **Whitehall** Herts
170 C5 **White Hall** Herts
170 D3 **Whitehall** Herts
76 B5 **Whitehall** W Susx
605 J6 **Whitehall Village** Ork
439 F1 **Whitehaugh** Border
388 A6 **Whitehaven** Cumb
269 E5 **Whitehouse** Shrops
56 A4 **Whitehawk** Br & H
213 E2 **Whiteheath Gate** Sandw
74 C2 **Whitehill & Bordon** Hants
86 C3 **White Hill** BaNES
341 G1 **White Hill** Brad
78 C4 **Whitehill** E Susx
500 D5 **Whitehill** Fife
99 G3 **Whitehill** Kent
471 G1 **Whitehill** Mdloth
569 J5 **Whitehill** Moray
126 B4 **Whitehill** Pembks
467 H3 **Whitehill** S Lans
291 H4 **Whitehill** Staffs
68 D3 **White Hill** Wilts
570 B2 **Whitehills** Abers
527 G4 **Whitehills** Angus
405 G2 **Whitehills** Gatesd
193 F2 **White Hills** Nhants
467 F2 **Whitehills** S Lans
337 F1 **Whiteholme** Bpool
312 D3 **Whitehough** Derbys
555 H2 **Whitehouse** Abers
462 D2 **Whitehouse** Ag & B
201 F5 **White House** Suffk
238 A5 **Whitehouse Common** Birm
115 G6 **Whitehouse Green** W Berk
316 D4 **White Houses** Notts
466 D1 **Whiteinch** C Glas
490 A3 **Whitekirk** E Loth
394 A2 **White Kirkley** Dur
116 B5 **Whiteknights** Readg
46 D5 **White Lackington** Dorset
44 D1 **Whitelackington** Somset
188 D4 **White Ladies Aston** Worcs
141 H4 **Whiteleaf** Bucks
406 B2 **Whiteleas** S Tyne
161 H2 **Whiteleaved Oak** Worcs
440 D4 **Whitelee** Nthumb
451 H3 **Whitelees** Nthumb
445 E3 **Whitelees** S Ayrs
405 E4 **White-le-Head** Dur
37 F4 **Whiteley Bank** IoW

312 B4 **Whiteley Green** Ches
94 B2 **Whiteley Village** Surrey
314 C3 **Whiteley Wood** Sheff
351 F2 **White Lund** Lancs
134 C4 **Whitelye** Mons
77 E4 **Whitemans Green** W Susx
154 C5 **White Mill** Carmth
567 H6 **Whitemire** Moray
276 B1 **Whitemoor** C Nott
8 B2 **Whitemoor** Cnwll
294 D5 **White Moor** Derbys
214 D5 **Whitemoor** Warwks
292 A2 **Whitemoor** Staffs
559 G3 **Whitemyres** Abers
71 H5 **Whitenap** Hants
605 G2 **White Ness** Shet
173 F6 **White Notley** Essex
120 D6 **White Oak** Kent
139 E2 **Whiteoak Green** Oxon
86 C3 **White Ox Mead** BaNES
71 E5 **Whiteparish** Wilts
320 C4 **White Pit** Lincs
68 D2 **Whitepits** Wilts
78 C1 **White Post** Kent
296 B3 **White Post** Notts
560 B5 **Whiterashes** Abers
451 H3 **Whiterigg** Border
104 D4 **Whiterock** Brdgnd
160 A5 **White Rocks** Herefs
146 A2 **White Roothing or White Roding** Essex
589 K7 **Whiterow** Highld
75 E4 **White's Green** W Susx
136 B3 **Whiteshill** Gloucs
110 A4 **Whiteshill** S Glos
427 G6 **Whiteside** Nthumb
469 F1 **Whiteside** W Loth
57 E2 **Whitesmith** E Susx
423 F2 **Whitespots** D & G
338 D4 **White Stake** Lancs
44 B5 **Whitestaunton** Somset
26 D4 **Whitestone** Devon
186 D6 **White Stone** Herefs
215 F1 **Whitestone** Warwks
174 C2 **Whitestreet Green** Suffk
108 D2 **Whitewall Common** Mons
373 E6 **Whitewall Corner** N York
117 E4 **White Waltham** W & M
86 C3 **Whiteway** BaNES
33 F3 **Whiteway** Dorset
136 B5 **Whiteway** Gloucs
136 D2 **Whiteway** Gloucs
15 F2 **Whitewell** Cnwll
352 C5 **Whitewell** Lancs
270 B1 **Whitewell** Wrexhm
340 C5 **Whitewell Bottom** Lancs
18 D3 **Whiteworks** Devon
568 C4 **Whitewreath** Moray
83 F2 **Whitfield** Kent
166 D2 **Whitfield** Nhants
402 D3 **Whitfield** Nthumb
110 B1 **Whitfield** S Glos
93 G3 **Whitfield Court** Surrey
402 D3 **Whitfield Hall** Nthumb
28 D3 **Whitford** Devon
307 G4 **Whitford** Flints
346 B5 **Whitgift** E R Yk
272 C4 **Whitgreave** Staffs
426 C2 **Whithaugh** Border
603 H5 **Whithebeir** Ork
410 D4 **Whithorn** D & G
461 E4 **Whiting Bay** N Ayrs
126 D1 **Whitland** Carmth
472 B5 **Whitlaw** Border
11 E1 **Whitleigh** C Plym
445 E5 **Whitletts** S Ayrs
310 C4 **Whitley** Ches
215 E4 **Whitley** Covtry
344 D5 **Whitley** N York
116 B5 **Whitley** Readg
329 E6 **Whitley** Sheff
324 D3 **Whitley** Wigan
87 F1 **Whitley** Wilts
431 G5 **Whitley Bay** N Tyne
344 D5 **Whitley Bridge** N York
403 G3 **Whitley Chapel** Nthumb
354 D6 **Whitley Head** Brad
272 B4 **Whitley Heath** Staffs
342 D6 **Whitley Lower** Kirk
310 C3 **Whitley Reed** Ches
431 G5 **Whitley Sands** N Tyne
344 D5 **Whitley Thorpe** N York
116 B6 **Whitley Wood** Readg
213 H4 **Whitlock's End** Solhll
135 H3 **Whitminster** Gloucs
43 E5 **Whitmoor** Devon
48 D3 **Whitmore** Dorset
272 B1 **Whitmore** Staffs
215 E3 **Whitmore Park** Covtry
42 D4 **Whitnage** Devon
191 E2 **Whitnash** Warwks
64 D4 **Whitnell** Somset
44 C5 **Whitney Bottom** Somset
185 E5 **Whitney-on-Wye** Herefs
389 F2 **Whitrigg** Cumb
399 G3 **Whitrigg** Cumb
399 G3 **Whitrigglees** Cumb
439 H1 **Whitriggs** Border
70 C6 **Whitsbury** Hants
472 C4 **Whitslaid** Border
474 C4 **Whitsome** Border
474 C5 **Whitsomehill** Border
108 C3 **Whitson** Newpt
100 B2 **Whitstable** Kent
23 F3 **Whitstone** Cnwll
23 F3 **Whitstone Head** Cnwll
442 D2 **Whittingham** Nthumb
210 A2 **Whittingslow** Shrops
314 D5 **Whittington** Derbys
163 F5 **Whittington** Gloucs
366 C4 **Whittington** Lancs
247 E5 **Whittington** Norfk
269 F3 **Whittington** Shrops
238 B3 **Whittington** Staffs
212 C3 **Whittington** Staffs
288 B3 **Whittington** Staffs
272 A3 **Whittington** Staffs
238 D5 **Whittington** Warwks
188 C4 **Whittington** Worcs
314 C5 **Whittington Moor** Derbys
193 E6 **Whittlebury** Nhants
244 D3 **Whittlesey** Cambs
197 G5 **Whittlesford** Cambs
339 H6 **Whittlestone Head** Bl w D
453 E5 **Whitton** Border
118 C5 **Whitton** Gt Lon
209 H5 **Whitton** Herefs
346 C5 **Whitton** N Linc
442 D4 **Whitton** Nthumb
185 E1 **Whitton** Powys
210 D5 **Whitton** Shrops
395 H5 **Whitton** S on T
201 F5 **Whitton** Suffk
113 G6 **Whittonditch** Wilts
404 C3 **Whittonstall** Nthumb
210 A4 **Whittytree** Shrops
90 D3 **Whitway** Hants
315 G4 **Whitwell** Derbys
169 H5 **Whitwell** Herts
37 E5 **Whitwell** IoW
383 G5 **Whitwell** N York
242 D3 **Whitwell** Rutlnd
358 D1 **Whitwell-on-the-Hill** N York

255 F3 **Whitwell Street** Norfk
239 G1 **Whitwick** Leics
343 H5 **Whitwood** Wakefd
340 D6 **Whitworth** Lancs
270 C3 **Whixall** Shrops
357 E3 **Whixley** N York
215 E4 **Whoberley** Covtry
486 B3 **Wholeflats** Falk
382 D2 **Whorlton** Dur
384 D4 **Whorlton** N York
58 B5 **Whydown** E Susx
428 B4 **Whygate** Nthumb
380 B2 **Whygill Head** Cumb
53 F4 **Whyke** W Susx
186 D2 **Whyle** Herefs
95 G3 **Whyteleafe** Surrey
134 D5 **Wibdon** Gloucs
342 B3 **Wibsey** Brad
215 H2 **Wibtoft** Leics
3 E2 **Wicca** Cnwll
188 A2 **Wichenford** Worcs
99 E3 **Wichling** Kent
35 E2 **Wick** Bmouth
28 C2 **Wick** Devon
589 K6 **Wick** Highld
110 C5 **Wick** S Glos
605 H3 **Wick** Shet
64 D3 **Wick** Somset
189 E5 **Wick** Somset
54 B4 **Wick** Somset
222 B5 **Wick** V Glam
70 D5 **Wick** Wilts
189 E5 **Wick** Worcs
54 B4 **Wick** W Susx
222 B5 **Wicken** Cambs
167 F2 **Wicken** Nhants
171 G3 **Wicken Bonhunt** Essex
318 D3 **Wickenby** Lincs
188 B4 **Wick Episcopi** Worcs
315 F1 **Wickersley** Rothm
174 C1 **Wicker Street Green** Suffk
296 B6 **Wicketwood Hill** Notts
147 E6 **Wickford** Essex
51 G2 **Wickham** Hants
114 B5 **Wickham** W Berk
147 G2 **Wickham Bishops** Essex
100 D4 **Wickhambreaux** Kent
199 E4 **Wickhambrook** Suffk
405 F3 **Wickham Fell** Gatesd
163 G1 **Wickhamford** Worcs
225 E6 **Wickham Green** Suffk
114 B5 **Wickham Green** W Berk
114 C6 **Wickham Heath** W Berk
202 B3 **Wickham Market** Suffk
251 E3 **Wickhampton** Norfk
173 G2 **Wickham St Paul** Essex
67 E3 **Wickham's Cross** Somset
225 E6 **Wickham Skeith** Suffk
199 F4 **Wickham Street** Suffk
225 E6 **Wickham Street** Suffk
117 E5 **Wick Hill** Br For
80 B1 **Wick Hill** Kent
92 C2 **Wick Hill** Wokham
96 D5 **Wickhurst** Kent
86 B3 **Wicklane** BaNES
249 E4 **Wicklewood** Norfk
261 G5 **Wickmere** Norfk
162 B4 **Wickridge Street** Gloucs
110 C5 **Wick Rocks** S Glos
84 C1 **Wick St Lawrence** N Som
57 E3 **Wickstreet** E Susx
136 C3 **Wick Street** Gloucs
110 C2 **Wickwar** S Glos
87 E3 **Widbrook** Wilts
86 D2 **Widcombe** BaNES
172 A3 **Widdington** Essex
443 G5 **Widdrington** Nthumb
443 G6 **Widdrington Station** Nthumb
19 F2 **Widecombe in the Moor** Devon
601 H3 **Wideford** Ork
10 A2 **Widegates** Cnwll
160 C1 **Widemarsh** Herefs
23 E2 **Widemouth Bay** Cnwll
430 D5 **Wideopen** N Tyne
601 G6 **Widewall** Ork
11 E1 **Widewell** C Plym
146 D3 **Widford** Essex
145 F1 **Widford** Herts
198 D3 **Widgham Green** Cambs
112 C2 **Widham** Wilts
52 B3 **Widley** C Port
142 B5 **Widmer End** Bucks
276 D4 **Widmerpool** Notts
117 F2 **Widmoor** Bucks
309 H2 **Widnes** Halton
28 D3 **Widworthy** Devon
98 B5 **Wierton** Kent
208 B2 **Wig** Powys
324 C3 **Wigan** Wigan
372 C5 **Wiganthorpe** N York
48 C3 **Wigbeth** Dorset
45 E4 **Wigborough** Somset
104 C4 **Wig Fach** Brdgnd
28 B4 **Wiggaton** Devon
252 B5 **Wiggenhall St Germans** Norfk
246 B2 **Wiggenhall St Mary Magdalen** Norfk
252 B5 **Wiggenhall St Mary The Virgin** Norfk
252 C5 **Wiggenhall St Peter** Norfk
172 D1 **Wiggens Green** Essex
293 E2 **Wigginstall** Staffs
142 C2 **Wigginton** Herts
165 F3 **Wigginton** Oxon
269 F2 **Wigginton** Shrops
238 B3 **Wigginton** Staffs
358 A3 **Wigginton** York
142 C3 **Wigginton Bottom** Herts
165 F2 **Wigginton Heath** Oxon
353 G3 **Wigglesworth** N York
400 A4 **Wiggonby** Cumb
54 B1 **Wiggonholt** W Susx
357 F5 **Wighill** N York
260 B4 **Wighton** Norfk
236 C5 **Wightwick** Staffs
314 C5 **Wigley** Derbys
50 B1 **Wigley** Hants
269 G4 **Wigmarsh** Shrops
209 H6 **Wigmore** Herefs
98 B2 **Wigmore** Medway
317 G5 **Wigsley** Notts
219 E3 **Wigsthorpe** Nhants
240 D5 **Wigston** Leics
240 D5 **Wigston Harcourt** Leics
240 D5 **Wigston Magna** Leics
215 H2 **Wigston Parva** Leics
316 A3 **Wigthorpe** Notts
280 C2 **Wigtoft** Lincs
399 H5 **Wigton** Cumb
417 E5 **Wigtown** D & G
328 C5 **Wigtwizzle** Sheff
356 C6 **Wike** Leeds
331 E2 **Wike Well End** Donc
221 G5 **Wilbarston** Nhants
358 D4 **Wilberfoss** E R Yk
327 G2 **Wilberlee** Kirk
221 G5 **Wilburton** Cambs
194 B1 **Wilby** Nhants
224 D2 **Wilby** Norfk
226 A5 **Wilby** Suffk
88 D2 **Wilcot** Wilts

269 G6 **Wilcott** Shrops
269 G6 **Wilcott Marsh** Shrops
10 D2 **Wilcove** Cnwll
108 C2 **Wilcrick** Newpt
314 C5 **Wildboarclough** Ches
312 C6 **Wildboarclough** Ches
195 F3 **Wilden** Beds
212 B5 **Wilden** Worcs
51 E2 **Wildern** Hants
96 D3 **Wildernesse** Kent
310 C2 **Wilderspool** Warrtn
325 E2 **Wilderswood** Bolton
222 D4 **Wilde Street** Suffk
90 B4 **Wildhern** Hants
144 C3 **Wildhill** Herts
468 C4 **Wildmanbridge** S Lans
104 D3 **Wild Mill** Brdgnd
92 A3 **Wildmoor** Hants
140 A5 **Wildmoor** Oxon
212 D4 **Wildmoor** Worcs
117 E6 **Wildridings** Br For
331 H5 **Wildsworth** Lincs
272 D5 **Wildwood** Staffs
276 C2 **Wilford** C Nott
276 C2 **Wilford Hill** Notts
99 F3 **Wilgate Green** Kent
271 F1 **Wilkesley** Ches
577 K6 **Wilkhaven** Highld
487 F6 **Wilkieston** W Loth
67 H5 **Wilkinthroop** Somset
300 A2 **Wilksby** Lincs
338 C2 **Willacy Lane End** Lancs
42 D5 **Willand** Devon
43 G5 **Willand** Somset
42 D5 **Willand Moor** Devon
79 G5 **Willard's Hill** E Susx
290 D4 **Willaston** Ches
308 D4 **Willaston** Ches
270 D2 **Willaston** Shrops
168 B1 **Willen** M Keyn
215 F4 **Willenhall** Covtry
237 E5 **Willenhall** Wsall
347 F3 **Willerby** E R Yk
374 B4 **Willerby** N York
163 H2 **Willersey** Gloucs
185 F5 **Willersley** Herefs
81 F1 **Willesborough** Kent
99 G6 **Willesborough Lees** Kent
119 E3 **Willesden** Gt Lon
119 E3 **Willesden Green** Gt Lon
239 E2 **Willesley** Leics
111 F2 **Willesley** Wilts
64 B5 **Willett** Somset
235 F5 **Willey** Shrops
216 A3 **Willey** Warwks
93 F4 **Willey Green** Surrey
451 E3 **Williamhope** Border
191 H5 **Williamscot** Oxon
605 G6 **Williamsetter** Shet
174 C1 **William's Green** Suffk
471 F6 **Williamslee** Border
105 G1 **Williamstown** Rhondd
295 E1 **Williamthorpe** Derbys
467 E3 **Williamwood** E Rens
170 B3 **Willian** Herts
402 D2 **Willimontswick** Nthumb
146 B3 **Willingale** Essex
60 C3 **Willingcott** Devon
57 F4 **Willingdon** E Susx
221 F5 **Willingham** Cambs
227 E3 **Willingham** Suffk
317 G3 **Willingham by Stow** Lincs
198 C4 **Willingham Green** Cambs
195 G5 **Willington** Beds
275 E4 **Willington** Derbys
394 D3 **Willington** Dur
98 B4 **Willington** Kent
405 H1 **Willington** N Tyne
164 D2 **Willington** Warwks
290 A1 **Willington Corner** Ches
405 H1 **Willington Quay** N Tyne
201 E4 **Willisham** Suffk
225 F4 **Willisham Tye** Suffk
345 G3 **Willitoft** E R Yk
63 H3 **Williton** Somset
321 E5 **Willoughby** Lincs
192 B1 **Willoughby** Warwks
300 C5 **Willoughby Hills** Lincs
276 D4 **Willoughby-on-the-Wolds** Notts
240 C6 **Willoughby Waterleys** Leics
332 C6 **Willoughton** Lincs
118 A2 **Willowbank** Bucks
310 C4 **Willow Green** Ches
187 H3 **Willow Green** Worcs
400 C3 **Willow Holme** Cumb
325 F3 **Willows** Bolton
173 E6 **Willows Green** Essex
132 C2 **Willowtown** Blae G
321 E2 **Will Row** Lincs
110 B5 **Willsbridge** S Glos
273 G3 **Willslock** Staffs
234 B5 **Willstone** Shrops
190 B3 **Wilmcote** Warwks
36 B3 **Wilmington** BaNES
86 B2 **Wilmington** BaNES
28 D3 **Wilmington** Devon
57 H4 **Wilmington** E Susx
120 D5 **Wilmington** Kent
57 E3 **Wilmington Green** E Susx
17 G3 **Wilminstone** Devon
311 G3 **Wilmslow** Ches
311 H3 **Wilmslow Park** Ches
238 C4 **Wilnecote** Staffs
225 E3 **Wilney Green** Norfk
342 A2 **Wilsden** Brad
298 C6 **Wilsford** Lincs
70 C2 **Wilsford** Wilts
88 C3 **Wilsford** Wilts
62 B2 **Wilsham** Devon
327 H2 **Wilshaw** Kirk
330 C5 **Wilsic** Donc
355 G2 **Wilsill** N York
79 H2 **Wilsley Green** Kent
80 A2 **Wilsley Pound** Kent
73 H2 **Wilsom** Hants
160 D5 **Wilson** Herefs
275 G5 **Wilson** Leics
515 E2 **Wilsonhall** Angus
469 E3 **Wilsontown** S Lans
195 F6 **Wilstead** Beds
276 A3 **Wilsthorpe** Derbys
243 F2 **Wilsthorpe** Lincs
142 B2 **Wilstone** Herts
142 C2 **Wilstone Green** Herts
329 E3 **Wilthorpe** Barns
459 F1 **Wilton** Border
376 C2 **Wilton** Cumb
160 D5 **Wilton** Herefs
373 G3 **Wilton** N York
397 E6 **Wilton** R & Cl
43 H3 **Wilton** Somset
70 B3 **Wilton** Wilts
89 C2 **Wilton** Wilts
390 B4 **Wilton Hill** Cumb
117 G1 **Wilton Park** Bucks
41 G4 **Wiltown** Devon
66 B5 **Wiltown** Somset
172 B2 **Wimbish** Essex
172 C3 **Wimbish Green** Essex
237 F2 **Wimblebury** Staffs
119 E5 **Wimbledon** Gt Lon

92 D5 **Wimble Hill** Hants
221 F1 **Wimblington** Cambs
309 F5 **Wimbolds Trafford** Ches
48 C4 **Wimborne Minster** Dorset
48 C2 **Wimborne St Giles** Dorset
246 C3 **Wimbotsham** Norfk
196 D5 **Wimpole** Cambs
50 C2 **Wimpson** C Sotn
190 C5 **Wimpstone** Warwks
68 A4 **Wincanton** Somset
320 B6 **Winceby** Lincs
310 D4 **Wincham** Ches
487 E5 **Winchburgh** W Loth
163 F4 **Winchcombe** Gloucs
59 E3 **Winchelsea** E Susx
59 F3 **Winchelsea Beach** E Susx
72 B3 **Winchester** Hants
132 C2 **Winchestown** Blae G
79 G1 **Winchet Hill** Kent
92 C4 **Winchfield** Hants
92 C4 **Winchfield Hurst** Hants
142 C5 **Winchmore Hill** Bucks
144 D6 **Winchmore Hill** Gt Lon
292 C1 **Wincle** Ches
314 D1 **Wincobank** Sheff
388 B6 **Winder** Cumb
378 C5 **Windermere** Cumb
165 E1 **Winderton** Warwks
364 C5 **Wind Hill** Cumb
330 A4 **Windhill** Donc
565 J7 **Windhill** Highld
126 B5 **Wind Hill** Pembks
608 F6 **Windhouse** Shet
114 B5 **Winding Wood** W Berk
308 D4 **Windle Hill** Ches
312 C2 **Windlehurst** Stockp
93 F2 **Windlesham** Surrey
294 C6 **Windley** Derbys
14 B4 **Windmill** Cnwll
109 G5 **Windmill Hill** Bristl
315 E3 **Windmill Hill** Derbys
57 G2 **Windmill Hill** E Susx
310 B3 **Windmill Hill** Halton
98 C1 **Windmill Hill** Kent
44 C4 **Windmill Hill** Somset
188 D5 **Windmill Hill** Worcs
138 B2 **Windrush** Gloucs
331 G2 **Windsor** N Linc
117 G4 **Windsor** W & M
136 B4 **Windsoredge** Gloucs
200 A4 **Windsor Green** Suffk
44 D6 **Windwhistle** Somset
309 G1 **Windy Arbor** Knows
214 D5 **Windy Arbour** Warwks
451 E2 **Windydoors** Border
557 F6 **Windyedge** Abers
501 F4 **Windygates** Fife
311 G5 **Windyharbour** Ches
288 D4 **Windy Hill** Wrexhm
486 C6 **Windyknowe** W Loth
405 G2 **Windy Nook** Gatesd
568 C2 **Windyridge** Moray
276 C4 **Windyridge** Notts
466 C4 **Windy-Yett** E Ayrs
76 D6 **Wineham** W Susx
349 F5 **Winestead** E R Yk
341 E2 **Winewall** Lancs
225 E2 **Winfarthing** Norfk
37 F4 **Winford** IoW
85 F1 **Winford** N Som
185 E5 **Winforton** Herefs
33 E3 **Winfrith Newburgh** Dorset
168 B5 **Wing** Bucks
242 B4 **Wing** Rutlnd
396 B2 **Wingate** Dur
325 E3 **Wingates** Bolton
443 E5 **Wingates** Nthumb
314 D6 **Wingerworth** Derbys
168 D4 **Wingfield** Beds
329 G5 **Wingfield** Rothm
225 H4 **Wingfield** Suffk
87 E3 **Wingfield** Wilts
225 H4 **Wingfield Green** Suffk
294 D4 **Wingfield Park** Derbys
100 D4 **Wingham** Kent
100 D4 **Wingham Green** Kent
100 D4 **Wingham Well** Kent
82 C1 **Wingmore** Kent
168 B6 **Wingrave** Bucks
296 D3 **Winkburn** Notts
117 F5 **Winkfield** Br For
117 F5 **Winkfield Place** Br For
117 E5 **Winkfield Row** Br For
293 E4 **Winkhill** Staffs
96 C5 **Winkhurst Green** Kent
91 G4 **Winklebury** Hants
40 C6 **Winkleigh** Devon
370 B5 **Winksley** N York
49 F5 **Winkton** Dorset
405 E2 **Winlaton** Gatesd
405 E2 **Winlaton Mill** Gatesd
589 J6 **Winless** Highld
268 D5 **Winllan** Powys
351 G5 **Winmarleigh** Lancs
160 A3 **Winnal** Herefs
160 A2 **Winnal Common** Herefs
72 C3 **Winnall** Hants
188 B1 **Winnall** Worcs
14 C5 **Winnard's Perch** Cnwll
116 C5 **Winnersh** Wokham
310 C5 **Winnington** Ches
271 G2 **Winnington** Staffs
233 F2 **Winnington Green** Shrops
273 F1 **Winnothdale** Staffs
388 B4 **Winscales** Cumb
84 D1 **Winscombe** N Som
26 D3 **Winscott Barton** Devon
290 C2 **Winsford** Ches
62 D5 **Winsford** Somset
60 C4 **Winsham** Devon
29 G1 **Winsham** Somset
274 B1 **Winshill** Staffs
103 G2 **Winsh-wen** Swans
314 D6 **Winsick** Derbys
391 F3 **Winskill** Cumb
37 E4 **Winslade** Devon
91 H5 **Winslade** Hants
356 A2 **Winsley** N York
87 E2 **Winsley** Wilts
167 G4 **Winslow** Bucks
161 E2 **Winslow Mill** Herefs
137 G3 **Winson** Gloucs
213 F2 **Winson Green** Birm
50 B2 **Winsor** Hants
324 C4 **Winstanley** Wigan
324 D3 **Winstanleys** Wigan
378 D6 **Winster** Cumb
294 A2 **Winster** Derbys
382 D1 **Winston** Dur
201 G2 **Winston** Suffk
137 E3 **Winstone** Gloucs
201 G2 **Winston Green** Suffk
39 G5 **Winswell** Devon
32 C2 **Winterborne Came** Dorset
47 F4 **Winterborne Clenston** Dorset
B2 **Winterborne Herrington** Dorset
F4 **Winterborne Houghton** Dorset
G5 **Winterborne Kingston** Dorset

31 F5 **Winterborne Monkton** Dorset
47 G5 **Winterborne Muston** Dorset
77 F5 **Winterborne Stickland** Dorset
47 F4 **Winterborne Tomson** Dorset
47 G5 **Winterborne Whitechurch** Dorset
47 G5 **Winterborne Zelston** Dorset
99 H3 **Winterbourne** Kent
110 A3 **Winterbourne** S Glos
114 C5 **Winterbourne** W Berk
31 E4 **Winterbourne Abbas** Dorset
112 C5 **Winterbourne Bassett** Wilts
70 D3 **Winterbourne Dauntsey** Wilts
110 B3 **Winterbourne Down** S Glos
70 D3 **Winterbourne Earls** Wilts
70 D2 **Winterbourne Gunner** Wilts
112 D5 **Winterbourne Monkton** Wilts
31 E5 **Winterbourne Steepleton** Dorset
70 B1 **Winterbourne Stoke** Wilts
115 G2 **Winterbrook** Oxon
354 B3 **Winterburn** N York
86 A3 **Winterfield** BaNES
122 B3 **Winter Gardens** Essex
44 C4 **Winterhay Green** Somset
84 D3 **Winterhead** Somset
346 D5 **Winteringham** N Linc
291 E3 **Winterley** Ches
329 F1 **Wintersett** Wakefd
72 D6 **Wintershill** Hants
346 D6 **Winterton** N Linc
257 F6 **Winterton-on-Sea** Norfk
44 B3 **Winter Well** Somset
301 G1 **Winthorpe** Lincs
297 F3 **Winthorpe** Notts
48 D6 **Winton** Bmouth
380 D2 **Winton** Cumb
57 F2 **Winton** E Susx
384 C5 **Winton** N York
325 H5 **Winton** Salfd
373 G5 **Wintringham** N York
219 G3 **Winwick** Cambs
216 D5 **Winwick** Nhants
325 E6 **Winwick** Warrtn
310 B1 **Winwick Quay** Warrtn
30 B1 **Winyard's Gap** Dorset
189 G1 **Winyates** Worcs
213 G6 **Winyates Green** Worcs
294 B4 **Wirksworth** Derbys
294 B4 **Wirksworth Moor** Derbys
290 A6 **Wirswall** Ches
245 G2 **Wisbech** Cambs
245 F3 **Wisbech St Mary** Cambs
75 G4 **Wisborough Green** W Susx
316 D2 **Wiseton** Notts
136 D3 **Wishanger** Gloucs
468 B3 **Wishaw** N Lans
238 B6 **Wishaw** Warwks
94 B3 **Wisley** Surrey
319 G5 **Wispington** Lincs
80 C1 **Wissenden** Kent
226 D4 **Wissett** Suffk
209 H2 **Wistanstow** Shrops
271 F4 **Wistanswick** Shrops
290 D4 **Wistaston** Ches
290 D4 **Wistaston Green** Ches
151 H6 **Wiston** Pembks
448 C3 **Wiston** S Lans
54 D2 **Wiston** W Susx
448 B3 **Wiston Mains** S Lans
220 C3 **Wistow** Cambs
240 D5 **Wistow** Leics
344 D2 **Wistow** N York
340 A2 **Wiswell** Lancs
221 G4 **Witcham** Cambs
48 B3 **Witchampton** Dorset
221 G4 **Witchford** Cambs
66 D5 **Witcombe** Somset
39 F4 **Witcott** Devon
147 F2 **Witham** Essex
68 B1 **Witham Friary** Somset
243 E1 **Witham on the Hill** Lincs
297 G2 **Witham St Hughs** Lincs
319 H3 **Withcall** Lincs
55 H3 **Withdean** Br & H
79 E4 **Witherenden Hill** E Susx
256 B4 **Withergate** Norfk
41 G5 **Witheridge** Devon
116 A3 **Witheridge Hill** Oxon
239 G5 **Witherley** Leics
174 D2 **Withermarsh Green** Suffk
320 D3 **Withern** Lincs
349 F4 **Withernsea** E R Yk
348 C1 **Withernwick** E R Yk
226 B3 **Withersdale Street** Suffk
99 H5 **Withersdane** Suffk
198 D5 **Withersfield** Suffk
365 F3 **Witherslack** Cumb
406 B3 **Witherwack** Sundld
67 F2 **Withial** Somset
14 D5 **Withiel** Cnwll
63 F5 **Withiel Florey** Somset
15 E5 **Withielgoose** Cnwll
15 E5 **Withielgoose Mills** Cnwll
137 F1 **Withington** Gloucs
186 D6 **Withington** Herefs
326 B6 **Withington** Manch
234 D2 **Withington** Shrops
273 F3 **Withington** Staffs
311 G5 **Withington Green** Ches
186 D6 **Withington Marsh** Herefs
42 B5 **Withleigh** Devon
339 F5 **Withnell** Lancs
339 F5 **Withnell Fold** Lancs
213 F5 **Withybed Green** Worcs
198 D3 **Withybrook** Somset
215 G3 **Withybrook** Warwks
125 G1 **Withybush** Pembks
63 G3 **Withycombe** Somset
21 E1 **Withycombe Raleigh** Devon
86 B3 **Withyditch** BaNES
78 B2 **Withyham** E Susx
86 B3 **Withy Mills** BaNES
212 D2 **Withymoor Village** Dudley
215 F3 **Withypool** Somset
292 B5 **Withystakes** Staffs
109 G6 **Withywood** Bristl
75 E2 **Witley** Surrey
212 A3 **Witnells End** Worcs
201 G4 **Witnesham** Suffk
139 E2 **Witney** Oxon
50 A2 **Wittensford** Hants
243 F4 **Wittering** C Pete
80 C4 **Wittersham** Kent
213 G1 **Witton** Birm
250 C3 **Witton** Norfk
188 C2 **Witton** Worcs
256 C3 **Witton Bridge** Norfk
405 F5 **Witton Gilbert** Dur
187 H2 **Witton Hill** Worcs
394 C3 **Witton-le-Wear** Dur
394 D3 **Witton Park** Dur

43 E2 **Wiveliscombe** Somset
73 G2 **Wivelrod** Hants
77 F5 **Wivelsfield** E Susx
299 H2 **Wivelsfield Green** E Susx
172 B4 **Wivenhoe** Essex
260 D3 **Wiveton** Norfk
176 C4 **Wix** Essex
189 G4 **Wixford** Warwks
270 D4 **Wixhill** Shrops
199 E6 **Wixoe** Essex
168 C3 **Woburn** Beds
168 C3 **Woburn Sands** M Keyn
187 F4 **Wofferwood Common** Herefs
93 H3 **Woking** Surrey
116 C6 **Wokingham** Wokham
20 B3 **Wolborough** Devon
53 F4 **Woldhurst** W Susx
96 A3 **Woldingham** Surrey
95 H3 **Woldingham Garden Village** Surrey
374 C5 **Wold Newton** E R Yk
334 B5 **Wold Newton** NE Lin
250 B5 **Wolferd Green** Norfk
187 F2 **Wolferlow** Herefs
252 C2 **Wolferton** Norfk
192 B1 **Wolfhampcote** Warwks
513 E3 **Wolfhill** P & K
151 E3 **Wolf's Castle** Pembks
151 F5 **Wolfsdale** Pembks
151 F5 **Wolfsdale Hill** Pembks
451 F5 **Woll** Border
212 C3 **Wollaston** Dudley
194 C2 **Wollaston** Nhants
233 F2 **Wollaston** Shrops
276 B2 **Wollaton** C Nott
271 E3 **Wollerton** Shrops
271 E3 **Wollerton Wood** Shrops
212 D3 **Wollescote** Dudley
451 F5 **Wollrig** Border
394 B2 **Wolsingham** Dur
291 H5 **Wolstanton** Staffs
326 B1 **Wolstenholme** Rochdl
215 G4 **Wolston** Warwks
398 D4 **Wolsty** Cumb
261 G5 **Wolterton** Norfk
140 A3 **Wolvercote** Oxon
309 F4 **Wolverham** Ches
236 D5 **Wolverhampton** Wolves
270 B3 **Wolverley** Shrops
212 B4 **Wolverley** Worcs
28 B2 **Wolverstone** Devon
91 F3 **Wolverton** Hants
83 E2 **Wolverton** Kent
167 H1 **Wolverton** M Keyn
210 B2 **Wolverton** Shrops
190 C2 **Wolverton** Warwks
68 C3 **Wolverton** Wilts
91 E2 **Wolverton Common** Hants
167 H1 **Wolverton Mill** M Keyn
134 A5 **Wolvesnewton** Mons
215 G2 **Wolvey** Warwks
215 G2 **Wolvey Heath** Warwks
396 B4 **Wolviston** S on T
185 E2 **Womaston** Powys
372 C3 **Wombleton** N York
236 C6 **Wombourne** Staffs
235 F2 **Wombridge** Wrekin
329 F4 **Wombwell** Barns
100 D5 **Womenswold** Kent
344 C6 **Womersley** N York
134 B2 **Wonastow** Mons
93 H5 **Wonersh** Surrey
27 E4 **Wonford** Devon
25 G5 **Wonson** Devon
46 D3 **Wonston** Dorset
72 C2 **Wonston** Hants
117 F2 **Wooburn** Bucks
117 F2 **Wooburn Green** Bucks
151 E5 **Wood** Pembks
44 C4 **Wood** Somset
39 E6 **Woodacott** Devon
39 E6 **Woodacott Cross** Devon
368 D4 **Woodale** N York
309 E5 **Woodbank** Ches
210 D2 **Woodbank** Shrops
250 C1 **Woodbastwick** Norfk
317 E4 **Woodbeck** Notts
189 G4 **Wood Bevington** Warwks
296 B5 **Woodborough** Notts
88 C3 **Woodborough** Wilts
28 C3 **Woodbridge** Devon
68 D6 **Woodbridge** Dorset
137 F2 **Woodbridge** Gloucs
431 E2 **Woodbridge** Nthumb
454 B3 **Woodbridge** Nthumb
202 B5 **Woodbridge** Suffk
93 G4 **Woodbridge Hill** Surrey
202 D5 **Woodbridge Walk** Suffk
193 E5 **Wood Burcote** Nhants
117 F2 **Woodburn Common** Bucks
117 F1 **Woodburn Moor** Bucks
27 G5 **Woodbury** Devon
27 G5 **Woodbury Salterton** Devon
136 B4 **Woodchester** Gloucs
80 D3 **Woodchurch** Kent
308 C2 **Woodchurch** Wirral
87 F6 **Woodcock** Wilts
273 F4 **Woodcock Heath** Staffs
213 F3 **Woodcock Hill** Birm
118 A1 **Woodcock Hill** Herts
63 E2 **Woodcombe** Somset
51 G4 **Woodcot** Hants
95 F2 **Woodcote** Gt Lon
115 G3 **Woodcote** Oxon
95 E3 **Woodcote** Surrey
235 H1 **Woodcote** Wrekin
95 F2 **Woodcote Green** Gt Lon
212 D5 **Woodcote Green** Worcs
90 C4 **Woodcott** Hants
134 C5 **Woodcroft** Gloucs
48 B1 **Woodcutts** Dorset
255 E2 **Wood Dalling** Norfk
198 D3 **Woodditton** Cambs
140 B2 **Woodeaton** Oxon
272 B6 **Wood Eaton** Staffs
295 F3 **Wooden** Pembks
190 D1 **Wood End** Beds
195 E5 **Wood End** Beds
195 F1 **Wood End** Beds
167 G3 **Wood End** Bucks
312 C2 **Wood End** Ches
215 F3 **Wood End** Covtry
376 C2 **Wood End** Cumb
377 F5 **Wood End** Cumb
388 C5 **Wood End** Cumb
389 F4 **Wood End** Cumb
146 B2 **Wood End** Essex
161 E1 **Wood End** Herefs
170 D4 **Wood End** Herts
192 D5 **Wood End** Herts
295 F3 **Wood End** Nhants
326 D3 **Wood End** Oldham
274 B4 **Wood End** Staffs
326 D2 **Wood End** Tamesd
117 F5 **Wood End** W & M
213 H5 **Wood End** Warwks
214 D2 **Wood End** Warwks
238 C5 **Wood End** Warwks
487 E4 **Wood End** W Loth
500 C5 **Wood End** W Loth

236 D4 **Wood End** Wolves
53 E3 **Woodend** W Susx
299 H2 **Wood Enderby** Lincs
172 B4 **Woodend Green** Essex
118 B3 **Wood End Green** Gt Lon
70 D5 **Woodfalls** Wilts
135 G5 **Woodfield** Gloucs
166 C5 **Woodfield** Oxon
444 D5 **Woodfield** S Ayrs
38 B5 **Woodford** Cnwll
11 F2 **Woodford** C Plym
28 B3 **Woodford** Devon
135 F5 **Woodford** Gloucs
120 B1 **Woodford** Gt Lon
218 D4 **Woodford** Nhants
63 H4 **Woodford** Somset
85 F6 **Woodford** Somset
312 A3 **Woodford** Stockp
120 B1 **Woodford Bridge** Gt Lon
192 B4 **Woodford Halse** Nhants
145 E6 **Woodford Wells** Gt Lon
213 E3 **Woodgate** Birm
43 E4 **Woodgate** Devon
254 D4 **Woodgate** Norfk
274 A4 **Woodgate** Staffs
189 E1 **Woodgate** W Susx
188 B1 **Woodgate** Worcs
326 B2 **Woodgate Hill** Bury
172 B4 **Woodgates End** Essex
211 E5 **Woodgates Green** Worcs
213 E3 **Woodgate Valley** Birm
145 F4 **Wood Green** Essex
119 G1 **Wood Green** Gt Lon
70 D6 **Wood Green** Hants
139 F2 **Wood Green** Oxon
237 E5 **Wood Green** Sandw
188 B1 **Wood Green** Worcs
171 G3 **Wood Hall** Essex
144 B2 **Woodhall** Herts
482 D5 **Woodhall** Inver
345 F3 **Woodhall** N York
368 C1 **Woodhall** N York
299 F2 **Woodhall Spa** Lincs
167 E6 **Woodham** Bucks
395 F4 **Woodham** Dur
94 A2 **Woodham** Surrey
147 F5 **Woodham Ferrers** Essex
147 G4 **Woodham Mortimer** Essex
147 G3 **Woodham Walter** Essex
95 F5 **Woodhatch** Surrey
514 C4 **Woodhaven** Fife
236 D4 **Wood Hayes** Wolves
560 A2 **Woodhead** Abers
570 F3 **Woodhead** Abers
423 F5 **Woodhead** D & G
472 C5 **Woodheads** Border
326 A1 **Woodhey** Bury
290 B4 **Woodhey** Wirral
290 B4 **Woodhey Green** Ches
147 F4 **Woodhill** Essex
109 E4 **Woodhill** N Som
211 G3 **Woodhill** Shrops
44 D2 **Woodhill** Somset
431 F2 **Woodhorn** Nthumb
342 B5 **Woodhouse** Calder
365 H3 **Woodhouse** Cumb
376 B1 **Woodhouse** Cumb
90 B5 **Woodhouse** Hants
353 E4 **Woodhouse** Leeds
240 B1 **Woodhouse** Leics
331 G3 **Woodhouse** N Linc
315 E2 **Woodhouse** Sheff
343 G5 **Woodhouse** Wakefd
109 H2 **Woodhouse Down** S Glos
240 B2 **Woodhouse Eaves** Leics
292 B2 **Woodhouse Green** Staffs
470 D2 **Woodhouselee** Mdloth
311 G2 **Woodhouse Park** Manch
309 G4 **Woodhouses** Ches
400 B4 **Woodhouses** Cumb
326 D4 **Woodhouses** Oldham
237 G3 **Woodhouses** Staffs
274 A6 **Woodhouses** Staffs
311 F1 **Woodhouses** Traffd
220 D4 **Woodhurst** Cambs
56 B3 **Woodingdean** Br & H
71 F5 **Woodington** Hants
343 E5 **Woodkirk** Kirk
47 G6 **Woodlake** Dorset
363 E4 **Woodland** Cumb
11 H2 **Woodland** Devon
19 G4 **Woodland** Devon
394 B4 **Woodland** Dur
82 B2 **Woodland** Kent
198 D6 **Woodland Green** Essex
26 B3 **Woodland Head** Devon
556 D5 **Woodlands** Abers
342 A4 **Woodlands** Calder
424 B4 **Woodlands** D & G
330 B3 **Woodlands** Donc
48 C3 **Woodlands** Dorset
118 C4 **Woodlands** Gt Lon
50 B2 **Woodlands** Hants
97 E2 **Woodlands** Kent
356 C4 **Woodlands** N York
67 E2 **Woodlands** Somset
327 E5 **Woodlands** Tamesd
116 C3 **Woodlands** Worcs
48 D3 **Woodlands Common** Dorset
116 D4 **Woodlands Park** W & M
114 A4 **Woodlands St Mary** W Berk
269 H3 **Wood Lane** Shrops
274 A5 **Wood Lane** Staffs
291 G4 **Wood Lane** Staffs
312 B3 **Wood Lanes** Ches
12 C3 **Woodleigh** Devon
343 G4 **Woodlesford** Leeds
71 H5 **Woodley** Hants
326 D6 **Woodley** Stockp
116 C5 **Woodley** Wokham
116 C5 **Woodley Green** Wokham
165 G6 **Woodleys** Oxon
295 E5 **Woodlinkin** Derbys
190 D1 **Woodloes Park** Warwks
137 F3 **Woodmancote** Gloucs
163 E4 **Woodmancote** Gloucs
188 C6 **Woodmancote** Worcs
52 D1 **Woodmancote** W Susx
55 F2 **Woodmancote** W Susx
73 E1 **Woodmancott** Hants
347 F2 **Woodmansey** E R Yk
58 C3 **Woodmansgreen** W Susx
74 D4 **Woodmansterne** Surrey
95 F3 **Woodmanton** Devon
274 A5 **Woodmill** Staffs
69 G5 **Woodminton** Wilts
101 F4 **Woodnesborough** Kent
243 E6 **Woodnewton** Nhants
314 C5 **Woodnook** Derbys
340 B4 **Woodnook** Lancs
278 C3 **Woodnook** Lincs
254 D4 **Wood Norton** Norfk
189 F5 **Wood Norton** Worcs
338 D3 **Woodplumpton** Lancs
43 H4 **Woodram** Somset
248 C4 **Woodrising** Norfk

326 A2 **Wood Road** Bury
142 C5 **Woodrow** Bucks
399 G5 **Woodrow** Cumb
46 D2 **Woodrow** Dorset
343 G4 **Wood Row** Leeds
189 G1 **Woodrow** Worcs
212 C4 **Woodrow** Worcs
237 E5 **Woods Bank** Wsall
79 F6 **Wood's Corner** E Susx
79 H3 **Woodsden** Kent
327 E6 **Woodseats** Derbys
329 E5 **Wood Seats** Sheff
185 E5 **Woods Eaves** Herefs
271 F3 **Woodseaves** Shrops
272 A4 **Woodseaves** Staffs
125 E2 **Woodsend** Pembks
325 G5 **Woods End** Traffd
113 F4 **Woodsend** Wilts
236 D6 **Woodsetton** Dudley
315 H3 **Woodsetts** Rothm
188 B5 **Woodsfold** Lancs
338 C2 **Woodsford** Dorset
32 D1 **Woodsford** Dorset
79 E3 **Wood's Green** E Susx
145 G4 **Woodside** Beds
195 F4 **Woodside** Beds
342 B4 **Woodside** Brad
117 F5 **Woodside** Br For
557 G3 **Woodside** C Aber
290 C2 **Woodside** Ches
309 H5 **Woodside** Ches
424 A5 **Woodside** D & G
294 D6 **Woodside** Derbys
315 F5 **Woodside** Derbys
212 D2 **Woodside** Dudley
394 D4 **Woodside** Dur
501 E4 **Woodside** Fife
502 C3 **Woodside** Fife
95 G1 **Woodside** Gt Lon
50 B6 **Woodside** Hants
143 G4 **Woodside** Herts
144 C3 **Woodside** Herts
51 F6 **Woodside** IoW
567 K5 **Woodside** Moray
331 F4 **Woodside** N Linc
513 F2 **Woodside** P & K
126 C3 **Woodside** Pembks
209 E3 **Woodside** Shrops
235 F4 **Woodside** Wrekin
171 H6 **Woodside Green** Essex
99 E3 **Woodside Green** Kent
556 C5 **Woodside of Arbeadie** Abers
144 B6 **Woodside Park** Gt Lon
312 B2 **Woods Moor** Stockp
114 C6 **Woodspeen** W Berk
84 B1 **Woodspring Priory** N Som
163 G3 **Wood Stanway** Gloucs
98 D2 **Woodstock** Kent
139 H1 **Woodstock** Oxon
152 A4 **Woodstock** Pembks
244 A5 **Woodston** C Pete
172 B2 **Woodstone** Essex
256 D5 **Wood Street** Norfk
93 F4 **Wood Street Village** Surrey
315 E5 **Woodthorpe** Derbys
320 D3 **Woodthorpe** Lincs
240 B1 **Woodthorpe** Notts
296 A6 **Woodthorpe** Notts
357 H5 **Woodthorpe** York
250 B6 **Woodton** Norfk
39 G2 **Woodtown** Devon
323 F2 **Woodvale** Sefton
528 D6 **Woodville** Angus
275 E6 **Woodville** Derbys
68 D5 **Woodville** Derbys
528 C6 **Woodville Feus** Angus
272 A3 **Woodwall Green** Staffs
220 B3 **Wood Walton** Cambs
115 E3 **Woodway** Oxon
215 F3 **Woodway Park** Covtry
218 D4 **Woodwell** Nhants
602 D7 **Woodwick** Ork
290 B3 **Woodworth Green** Ches
69 H6 **Woodyates** Dorset
61 G2 **Woody Bay** Devon
210 C6 **Woofferton** Shrops
85 F5 **Wookey** Somset
85 F5 **Wookey Hole** Somset
33 E2 **Wool** Dorset
60 B3 **Woolacombe** Devon
100 D6 **Woolage Green** Kent
100 D5 **Woolage Village** Kent
134 D5 **Woolaston** Gloucs
134 D4 **Woolaston Common** Gloucs
134 D4 **Woolaston Slade** Gloucs
134 D4 **Woolaston Woodside** Gloucs
65 G3 **Woolavington** Somset
74 D5 **Woolbeding** W Susx
328 B3 **Wooldale** Kirk
454 B4 **Wooler** Nthumb
309 F1 **Woolfall Heath** Knows
41 G6 **Woolfardisworthy** Devon
38 D3 **Woolfardisworthy or Woolsery** Devon
326 A2 **Woolfold** Bury
469 F3 **Woolfords Cottages** S Lans
46 C3 **Woolford's Water** Dorset
34 A4 **Woolgarston** Dorset
91 F1 **Woolhampton** W Berk
161 E2 **Woolhope** Herefs
161 E2 **Woolhope Cockshoot** Herefs
47 E3 **Woolland** Dorset
86 A2 **Woollard** BaNES
236 C1 **Woollaston** Staffs
39 G5 **Woollaton** Devon
144 D2 **Woollensbrook** Herts
110 C6 **Woolley** BaNES
219 H5 **Woolley** Cambs
38 C4 **Woolley** Cnwll
294 C2 **Woolley** Derbys
329 E2 **Woolley** Wakefd
87 E2 **Woolley** Wilts
327 F5 **Woolley Bridge** Tamesd
117 F3 **Woolley Green** W & M
87 E2 **Woolley Green** Wilts
189 E2 **Woolmere Green** Worcs
170 C6 **Woolmer Green** Herts
74 D3 **Woolmer Hill** Surrey
65 E5 **Woolmersdon** Somset
44 D6 **Woolminstone** Somset
80 C2 **Woolpack Corner** Kent
200 C2 **Woolpit** Suffk
200 C2 **Woolpit Green** Suffk
200 C2 **Woolpit Heath** Suffk
162 B5 **Woolridge** Gloucs
48 D3 **Woolsbridge** Dorset
216 A6 **Woolscott** Warwks
26 B2 **Woolsgrove** Devon
430 C6 **Woolsington** N u Ty
290 D3 **Woolstanwood** Ches
234 B5 **Woolstaston** Shrops
277 H3 **Woolsthorpe by Belvoir** Lincs
278 C5 **Woolsthorpe-by-Colsterworth** Lincs
16 C5 **Woolston** Cnwll
50 D2 **Woolston** C Sotn
12 C4 **Woolston** Devon
209 H2 **Woolston** Shrops
269 F5 **Woolston** Shrops

64 A4 **Woolston** Somset
67 G4 **Woolston** Somset
310 C2 **Woolston** Warrtn
163 E3 **Woolstone** Gloucs
168 B2 **Woolstone** M Keyn
113 C2 **Woolstone** Oxon
19 G4 **Woolston Green** Devon
309 F2 **Woolton** Lpool
90 C2 **Woolton Hill** Hants
84 C2 **Woolverstone** Suffk
176 C2 **Woolverton** Somset
86 D4 **Woolwell** Devon
18 B5 **Woolwich** Gt Lon
120 B4 **Woolwich** Gt Lon
120 B4 **Woolwich Ferry** Gt Lon
8 C2 **Woon** Cnwll
185 F4 **Woonton** Herefs
186 F2 **Woonton** Herefs
454 C5 **Wooperton** Nthumb
451 F1 **Wooplaw** Border
291 E6 **Woore** Shrops
116 C6 **Woose Hill** Wokham
30 B3 **Wooth** Dorset
210 D5 **Wooton** Shrops
211 H2 **Wooton** Shrops
226 A5 **Wootten Green** Suffk
195 E5 **Wootton** Beds
49 G5 **Wootton** Hants
160 D2 **Wootton** Herefs
185 F4 **Wootton** Herefs
51 F6 **Wootton** IoW
82 D1 **Wootton** Kent
193 G3 **Wootton** Nhants
333 F1 **Wootton** N Linc
140 A4 **Wootton** Oxon
165 G5 **Wootton** Oxon
210 A4 **Wootton** Shrops
269 F4 **Wootton** Shrops
272 B4 **Wootton** Staffs
293 F5 **Wootton** Staffs
112 C3 **Wootton Bassett** Wilts
194 D5 **Wootton Bourne End** Beds
37 E2 **Wootton Bridge** IoW
195 E6 **Wootton Broadmead** Beds
37 E2 **Wootton Common** IoW
63 E3 **Wootton Courtenay** Somset
29 G3 **Wootton Fitzpaine** Dorset
194 D6 **Wootton Green** Beds
214 C4 **Wootton Green** Solhll
89 E2 **Wootton Rivers** Wilts
273 G2 **Woottons** Staffs
91 F4 **Wootton St Lawrence** Hants
190 A2 **Wootton Wawen** Warwks
33 F4 **Worbarrow** Dorset
188 B3 **Worcester** Worcs
95 E1 **Worcester Park** Gt Lon
212 C2 **Wordsley** Dudley
223 G5 **Wordwell** Suffk
235 H5 **Worfield** Shrops
33 G2 **Worgret** Dorset
601 H2 **Work** Ork
256 C5 **Workhouse Common** Norfk
195 G4 **Workhouse End** Beds
174 B2 **Workhouse Green** Suffk
174 C3 **Workhouse Hill** Essex
388 A4 **Workington** Cumb
315 H4 **Worksop** Notts
320 B4 **Worlaby** Lincs
333 E2 **Worlaby** N Linc
142 A3 **World's End** Bucks
144 D5 **World's End** Gt Lon
52 A2 **Worlds End** Hants
214 A3 **Worlds End** Solhll
200 C3 **World's End** Suffk
114 D4 **World's End** W Berk
77 F6 **World's End** W Susx
84 B2 **Worle** N Som
84 B2 **Worlebury** N Som
290 D3 **Worleston** Ches
136 B5 **Worley** Gloucs
227 E2 **Worlingham** Suffk
60 C5 **Worlington** Devon
222 D5 **Worlington** Suffk
225 H6 **Worlingworth** Suffk
159 H3 **Wormbridge** Herefs
159 H3 **Wormbridge Common** Herefs
246 D2 **Wormegay** Norfk
160 B3 **Wormelow Tump** Herefs
313 F5 **Wormhill** Derbys
174 B3 **Wormingford** Essex
140 D3 **Worminghall** Bucks
163 F2 **Wormington** Gloucs
85 G6 **Worminster** Somset
514 B4 **Wormit** Fife

191 G4 **Wormleighton** Warwks
145 E3 **Wormley** Herts
75 E2 **Wormley** Surrey
144 D3 **Wormleybury** Herts
212 D5 **Worms Ash** Worcs
79 G2 **Worms Hill** Kent
98 D3 **Wormshill** Kent
185 H5 **Wormsley** Herefs
291 G1 **Wornish Nook** Ches
93 G4 **Worplesdon** Surrey
314 B1 **Worrall** Sheff
135 E2 **Worrall Hill** Gloucs
329 F4 **Worsbrough** Barns
329 E4 **Worsbrough Common** Barns
329 F4 **Worsbrough Dale** Barns
138 D2 **Worsham** Oxon
325 G4 **Worsley** Salfd
324 D4 **Worsley Hall** Wigan
324 D4 **Worsley Mesnes** Wigan
256 C4 **Worstead** Norfk
340 D3 **Worsthorne** Lancs
11 G3 **Worston** Devon
353 F6 **Worston** Lancs
99 F6 **Worth** Kent
101 F4 **Worth** Kent
85 F5 **Worth** Somset
77 E2 **Worth** W Susx
77 F3 **Worth Abbey** W Susx
225 E4 **Wortham** Suffk
233 F4 **Worthen** Shrops
289 F5 **Worthenbury** Wrexhm
254 D4 **Worthing** Norfk
55 E4 **Worthing** W Susx
275 F5 **Worthington** Leics
34 A5 **Worth Matravers** Dorset
62 D2 **Worthy** Somset
134 B2 **Worthybrook** Mons
91 F4 **Worting** Hants
328 D5 **Wortley** Barns
110 D1 **Wortley** Gloucs
343 E3 **Wortley** Leeds
368 C1 **Worton** N York
139 H2 **Worton** Oxon
87 H3 **Worton** Wilts
226 B2 **Wortwell** Norfk
233 E4 **Wotherton** Shrops
243 E3 **Wothorpe** C Pete
18 C5 **Wotter** Devon
162 B6 **Wotton** Gloucs
94 C5 **Wotton** Surrey
19 G4 **Wotton Cross** Devon
135 H6 **Wotton-under-Edge** Gloucs
141 E1 **Wotton Underwood** Bucks
168 B2 **Woughton on the Green** M Keyn
97 H2 **Wouldham** Kent
235 H6 **Woundale** Shrops
176 C3 **Wrabness** Essex
60 C4 **Wrafton** Devon
319 E4 **Wragby** Lincs
335 E5 **Wragholme** Lincs
249 F3 **Wramplingham** Norfk
19 E6 **Wrangaton** Devon
330 A2 **Wrangbrook** Wakefd
559 E3 **Wrangham** Abers
300 D4 **Wrangle** Lincs
300 D4 **Wrangle Bank** Lincs
300 D4 **Wrangle Lowgate** Lincs
300 D4 **Wrangle Low Ground** Lincs
43 F4 **Wrangway** Somset
44 C3 **Wrantage** Somset
333 E3 **Wrawby** N Linc
30 D2 **Wraxall** Dorset
109 E5 **Wraxall** N Som
67 G2 **Wraxall** Somset
366 C6 **Wray** Lancs
95 F4 **Wray Common** Surrey
117 H5 **Wraysbury** W & M
366 C5 **Wrayton** Lancs
338 B3 **Wrea Green** Lancs
363 E4 **Wreaks End** Cumb
44 C6 **Wreath** Somset
527 F6 **Wreaths** Angus
390 C5 **Wreay** Cumb
400 D5 **Wreay** Cumb
92 D5 **Wrecclesham** Surrey
405 G3 **Wrekenton** Gatesd
373 E2 **Wrelton** N York
290 B5 **Wrenbury** Ches
249 G5 **Wreningham** Norfk
227 F3 **Wrentham** Suffk
343 F5 **Wrenthorpe** Wakefd
233 H4 **Wrentnall** Shrops
224 D6 **Wressle** E R Yk
345 G3 **Wressle** N Linc
332 D3 **Wressle** N Linc
196 C5 **Wrestlingworth** Beds
224 B2 **Wretham** Norfk
246 D5 **Wretton** Norfk

289 E4 **Wrexham** Wrexhm
19 G1 **Wreyland** Devon
212 A4 **Wribbenhall** Worcs
211 E2 **Wrickton** Shrops
324 C2 **Wrightington Bar** Lancs
145 H1 **Wright's Green** Essex
310 C3 **Wrights Green** Warrtn
291 F5 **Wrinehill** Staffs
23 G5 **Wringsdown** Cnwll
85 E2 **Wrington** N Som
38 D3 **Wrinkleberry** Devon
86 C4 **Writhlington** Somset
146 D3 **Writtle** Essex
235 E2 **Wrockwardine** Wrekin
331 H1 **Wroot** N Linc
97 E3 **Wrotham** Kent
97 F3 **Wrotham Heath** Kent
144 B5 **Wrotham Park** Herts
113 E3 **Wroughton** Swindn
168 B2 **Wroughton Park** M Keyn
37 F5 **Wroxall** IoW
214 C5 **Wroxall** Warwks
234 D3 **Wroxeter** Shrops
250 C1 **Wroxham** Norfk
165 G1 **Wroxton** Oxon
293 G6 **Wyaston** Derbys
146 C5 **Wyatt's Green** Essex
334 B3 **Wybers Wood** NE Lin
280 D1 **Wyberton** Lincs
195 H3 **Wyboston** Beds
290 D4 **Wybunbury** Ches
188 D1 **Wychbold** Worcs
77 H3 **Wych Cross** E Susx
187 H6 **Wyche** Herefs
238 B1 **Wychnor** Staffs
238 B1 **Wychnor Bridges** Staffs
74 B2 **Wyck** Hants
164 B5 **Wyck Hill** Gloucs
164 B5 **Wyck Rissington** Gloucs
382 D2 **Wycliffe** Dur
341 E2 **Wycoller** Lancs
277 G5 **Wycomb** Leics
117 E1 **Wycombe Marsh** Bucks
171 E3 **Wyddial** Herts
355 H4 **Wydra** N York
99 H5 **Wye** Kent
99 E4 **Wyebanks** Kent
134 D3 **Wyegate Green** Gloucs
134 C2 **Wyesham** Mons
277 G6 **Wyfordby** Leics
68 C4 **Wyke** Dorset
342 C4 **Wyke** Kirk
235 E4 **Wyke** Shrops
93 F4 **Wyke** Surrey
67 H3 **Wyke Champflower** Somset
29 E3 **Wyke Green** Devon
280 C4 **Wykeham** Lincs
373 F4 **Wykeham** N York
374 B3 **Wykeham** N York
215 F3 **Wyken** Covtry
235 H6 **Wyken** Shrops
32 B4 **Wyke Regis** Dorset
269 G4 **Wykey** Shrops
239 F5 **Wykin** Leics
404 D1 **Wylam** Nthumb
210 B6 **Wylde** Herefs
237 H6 **Wylde Green** Birm
132 C6 **Wyllie** Caerph
69 H2 **Wylye** Wilts
162 D5 **Wymans Brook** Gloucs
167 H2 **Wymbush** M Keyn
52 A3 **Wymering** C Port
276 D5 **Wymeswold** Leics
194 D2 **Wymington** Beds
278 B6 **Wymondham** Leics
249 F4 **Wymondham** Norfk
170 B4 **Wymondley Bury** Herts
338 D5 **Wymott** Lancs
105 E1 **Wyndham** Brdgnd
106 A4 **Wyndham Park** V Glam
161 G1 **Wynds Point** Herefs
30 D3 **Wynford Eagle** Dorset
600 E6 **Wyng** Ork
187 E5 **Wynn's Green** Herefs
396 B4 **Wynyard Village** S on T
189 E5 **Wyre Piddle** Worcs
276 D4 **Wysall** Notts
186 C1 **Wyson** Herefs
213 G5 **Wythall** Worcs
159 H3 **Wytham** Oxon
311 G2 **Wythenshawe** Manch
389 E4 **Wythop Mill** Cumb
348 C3 **Wyton** E R Yk
224 D6 **Wyverstone** Suffk
200 D1 **Wyverstone Green** Suffk
224 D6 **Wyverstone Street** Suffk
278 B4 **Wyville** Lincs

Y

332 B3 **Yaddlethorpe** N Linc
36 C4 **Yafford** IoW
384 A6 **Yafforth** N York
451 F3 **Yair** Border
20 B6 **Yalberton** Torbay
97 H4 **Yalding** Kent
109 F6 **Yanley** N Som
391 E4 **Yanwath** Cumb
137 G2 **Yanworth** Gloucs
359 E4 **Yapham** E R Yk
54 A4 **Yapton** W Susx
84 C3 **Yarberry** N Som
334 B3 **Yarborough** NE Lin
37 G3 **Yarbridge** IoW
335 E6 **Yarburgh** Lincs
44 A6 **Yarcombe** Devon
63 H4 **Yarde** Somset
80 D1 **Yardhurst** Kent
213 H2 **Yardley** Birm
193 G6 **Yardley Gobion** Nhants
194 B3 **Yardley Hastings** Nhants
213 H4 **Yardley Wood** Birm
184 D3 **Yardro** Powys
43 H2 **Yarford** Somset
188 A1 **Yarhampton** Worcs
187 H1 **Yarhampton Cross** Worcs
187 E6 **Yarkhill** Herefs
272 C4 **Yarlet** Staffs
85 E5 **Yarley** Somset
67 H4 **Yarlington** Somset
364 B6 **Yarlside** Cumb
384 C2 **Yarm** S on T
36 B3 **Yarmouth** IoW
61 F5 **Yarnacott** Devon
87 F4 **Yarnbrook** Wilts
272 C3 **Yarnfield** Staffs
190 B1 **Yarningale Common** Warwks
40 B3 **Yarnscombe** Devon
140 A2 **Yarnton** Oxon
186 B2 **Yarpole** Herefs
450 B2 **Yarrow** Border
427 H2 **Yarrow** Nthumb
84 C5 **Yarrow** Somset
450 C4 **Yarrow Feus** Border
451 E2 **Yarrowford** Border
185 H5 **Yarsop** Herefs
243 F5 **Yarwell** Nhants
110 C3 **Yate** S Glos
92 D2 **Yateley** Hants
110 C3 **Yate Rocks** S Glos
112 C5 **Yatesbury** Wilts
115 E5 **Yattendon** W Berk
186 A1 **Yatton** Herefs
84 D1 **Yatton** N Som
111 F4 **Yatton Keynell** Wilts
37 G3 **Yaverland** IoW
29 F4 **Yawl** Devon
317 G1 **Yawthorpe** Lincs
248 D2 **Yaxham** Norfk
220 A1 **Yaxley** Cambs
225 F5 **Yaxley** Suffk
185 H5 **Yazor** Herefs
45 E4 **Yeabridge** Somset
118 C3 **Yeading** Gt Lon
342 D1 **Yeadon** Leeds
365 H5 **Yealand Conyers** Lancs
365 G4 **Yealand Redmayne** Lancs
365 G4 **Yealand Storrs** Lancs
11 G3 **Yealmbridge** Devon
11 G3 **Yealmpton** Devon
397 E5 **Yearby** R & Cl
399 E6 **Yearngill** Cumb
372 A5 **Yearsley** N York
270 A6 **Yeaton** Shrops
274 B1 **Yeaveley** Derbys
373 G4 **Yedingham** N York
195 E1 **Yelden** Beds
294 A6 **Yeldersley Hollies** Derbys
139 F4 **Yelford** Oxon
60 C5 **Yelland** Devon
196 C2 **Yelling** Cambs
98 C2 **Yelsted** Kent
216 D4 **Yelvertoft** Nhants
18 B4 **Yelverton** Devon
250 B4 **Yelverton** Norfk
68 B5 **Yenston** Somset
26 B3 **Yeoford** Devon
23 G5 **Yeolmbridge** Cnwll
41 G2 **Yeo Mill** Devon
39 F3 **Yeo Vale** Devon
45 G4 **Yeovil** Somset
67 E6 **Yeovil Marsh** Somset
67 E5 **Yeovilton** Somset
126 B3 **Yerbeston** Pembks
600 C1 **Yesnaby** Ork
442 C3 **Yetlington** Nthumb
46 A2 **Yetminster** Dorset
468 B3 **Yett** N Lans
27 G5 **Yettington** Devon

499 G4 **Yetts o' Muckhart** Clacks
190 C1 **Yew Green** Warwks
99 F3 **Yewhedges** Kent
237 F5 **Yew Tree** Sandw
327 E5 **Yew Tree** Tamesd
82 C2 **Yewtree Cross** Kent
207 E2 **Y Fan** Powys
283 F2 **Y Felinheli** Gwynd
178 D4 **Y Ferwig** Cerdgn
263 F3 **Y Ffôr** Gwynd
307 E3 **y-Ffrith** Denbgs
205 E4 **Y Gors** Cerdgn
207 E1 **Y Gribyn** Powys
468 D4 **Yieldshields** S Lans
118 B3 **Yiewsley** Gt Lon
601 J2 **Yinstay** Ork
129 F3 **Ynus-tawelog** Swans
264 D2 **Ynys** Gwynd
131 H5 **Ynysboeth** Rhondd
131 G5 **Ynysddu** Caerph
129 G5 **Ynysforgan** Swans
131 G6 **Ynyshir** Rhondd
130 B3 **Ynys-isaf** Powys
229 E6 **Ynyslas** Cerdgn
130 A5 **Ynysmaerdy** Neath
105 G3 **Ynysmaerdy** Rhondd
129 H3 **Ynysmeudwy** Neath
228 D6 **Ynys Tachwedd** Cerdgn
129 G4 **Ynystawe** Swans
130 C2 **Ynyswen** Powys
131 F5 **Ynyswen** Rhondd
131 G6 **Ynysybwl** Rhondd
104 B1 **Ynysygwas** Neath
368 B4 **Yockenthwaite** N York
233 H3 **Yockleton** Shrops
43 E5 **Yodercott** Devon
346 B5 **Yokefleet** E R Yk
483 H6 **Yoker** C Glas
569 K6 **Yonder Bognie** Abers
18 C6 **Yondertown** Devon
30 B4 **Yondover** Dorset
97 E4 **Yopps Green** Kent
339 H3 **York** Lancs
358 A4 **York** York
467 E1 **Yorkhill** C Glas
100 A3 **Yorkletts** Kent
135 E3 **Yorkley** Gloucs
135 E3 **Yorkley Slade** Gloucs
471 F3 **Yorkston** Mdloth
93 E3 **York Town** Surrey
270 B5 **Yorton** Shrops
270 B5 **Yorton Heath** Shrops
376 C4 **Yottenfews** Cumb
293 G2 **Youlgreave** Derbys
359 E3 **Youlthorpe** E R Yk
357 F2 **Youlton** N York
171 E6 **Youngsbury** Herts
173 E6 **Young's End** Essex
319 E5 **Young Wood** Lincs
274 A6 **Yoxall** Staffs
226 D6 **Yoxford** Suffk
205 G4 **Ysbyty Cynfyn** Cerdgn
286 A5 **Ysbyty Ifan** Conwy
205 G5 **Ysbyty Ystwyth** Cerdgn
307 H5 **Ysceifiog** Flints
287 F3 **Ysgeibion** Denbgs
129 E5 **Yspitty** Carmth
130 A3 **Ystalyfera** Neath
131 F5 **Ystrad** Rhondd
180 D3 **Ystrad Aeron** Cerdgn
131 E2 **Ystradfelite** Powys
182 B5 **Ystradffin** Carmth
130 B2 **Ystradgynlais** Powys
205 G6 **Ystradmeurig** Cerdgn
132 C6 **Ystrad Mynach** Caerph
130 B2 **Ystradowen** Carmth
105 G4 **Ystradowen** V Glam
232 A4 **Ystrad Uchaf** Powys
205 G4 **Ystumtuen** Cerdgn
560 D3 **Ythanbank** Abers
559 E2 **Ythanwells** Abers
560 C3 **Ythsie** Abers

Z

25 H2 **Zeal Monachorum** Devon
68 C3 **Zeals** Wilts
7 F3 **Zelah** Cnwll
3 E2 **Zennor** Cnwll
5 E5 **Zoar** Cnwll
276 B5 **Zouch** Notts

Distances and journey times

The mileage chart shows distances in miles between two towns along AA-recommended routes. Using motorways and other main roads this is normally the fastest route, though not necessarily the shortest.

The journey times, shown in hours and minutes, are average off-peak driving times along AA-recommended routes. These times should be used as a guide only and do not allow for unforeseen traffic delays, rest breaks or fuel stops.

For example, the 378 miles (608 km) journey between Glasgow and Norwich should take approximately 7 hours 28 minutes.

journey times

The chart is a triangular distance/journey-time matrix with the following place names listed along the diagonal:

Aberdeen, Aberystwyth, Barnstaple, Birmingham, Brighton, Bristol, Cambridge, Cardiff, Carlisle, Carmarthen, Dorchester, Dover, Edinburgh, Exeter, Fort William, Glasgow, Gloucester, Guildford, Hereford, Holyhead, Hull, Inverness, Kendal, Leeds, Lincoln, Liverpool, Maidstone, Manchester, Middlesbrough, Newcastle, Northampton, Norwich, Nottingham, Oxford, Penzance, Perth, Peterborough, Plymouth, Portsmouth, Preston, Salisbury, Sheffield, Shrewsbury, Southampton, Stoke-on-Trent, Stranraer, Taunton, Wick, York, LONDON

Distances in miles (one mile equals 1.6093 km)